1978
BRITANNICA
BOOK OF THE YEAR

ROBERT MAYNARD HUTCHINS
January 17, 1899—May 14, 1977

Those who were privileged to know Robert Hutchins give testimony to the influence he exerted upon their lives and the affection he aroused in all who had the good fortune to be touched intimately by the elegance of his style; by the integrity of his character; by the beauty and grace of his person; by the keenness and wit of his mind; and by his gentleness, kindness, and compassion.

The measured judgment which will be formed retrospectively, with the passage of time, cannot exaggerate his contribution to the improvement of the University of Chicago and of education generally, here and abroad; to the realization of the highest ideals of a democratic society; to world peace and the establishment of a world community, founded, with justice, on liberty and equality for all the peoples of the earth; to the furtherance of the moral, intellectual, and spiritual revolution that was always the controlling objective of his thought and action; and last, but not least, to the advancement of knowledge itself, knowledge illuminated by the light that is cast upon what we know by the understanding of basic ideas, and is directed toward the wisdom derived from a consideration of first principles and final ends.

His intellectual virtues are best exemplified by his scholarship in the field of law and jurisprudence; by his understanding of the great ideas in the tradition of Western thought through the study of its great books; and by the philosophical cast of his mind that made him pursue wisdom by grappling with fundamental issues in every sphere of thought, always patiently submitting his mind to the controversies they engendered.

These virtues characterized his service to Encyclopaedia Britannica as a member of its board of directors from 1943, and as chairman of its board of editors from 1948, until his retirement from both posts. During all those years, he was not only the moral conscience of the publishing company, but its persistent mentor as well. His leadership provided the guidance and the inspiration that led to the publication of Great Books of the Western World, and to the production of the radically reconstructed and greatly improved Fifteenth Edition of the encyclopaedia.

MORTIMER J. ADLER

1978
BRITANNICA
BOOK OF THE YEAR

ENCYCLOPÆDIA BRITANNICA, INC.

CHICAGO, TORONTO, LONDON, GENEVA, SYDNEY, TOKYO, MANILA, SEOUL

THE UNIVERSITY OF CHICAGO

*The Britannica Book of the Year is published with the editorial advice
of the faculties of the University of Chicago.*

FOREWORD

The 1978 edition of the Britannica Book of the Year *retains much that is familiar and customary in this authoritative publication. The detailed information, the tables, the charts, the maps, the statistics, and the careful recording of significant events that readers have come to expect from this reliable reference source are here. There is also much that is new, because the passage of time and the push and pull of events compel change.*

The primary change is the addition of certain content items to make even broader the scope and coverage of the book. For example, new in this edition is a special section, beginning on page 54, titled "Unusual But Noteworthy Events of 1977." It describes unusual events that occurred during the year but that would not ordinarily be reported in any of the regular departments in this book or in any other permanent reference source.

More important, we have expanded the number of Feature articles and Special Reports, which are helpful in understanding complex and interrelated developments in the world today. In considering the events and happenings of the past year, the editors found that certain topics kept suggesting themselves in one form or another for Features and Reports. Three themes in particular kept recurring: human rights, energy, and the environment.

The cause of human rights has been given high priority by the administration of President Jimmy Carter. The Coordinator for Human Rights and Humanitarian Affairs for the Department of State, Patricia M. Derian, has written a significant article entitled "Human Rights–The U.S. Initiative," in which she articulates the Carter administration's position on this issue of world-wide significance. The struggle of less developed nations to achieve their economic rights is described by British economist Barbara Ward in a lucid article titled "Toward a New International Economic Order." The belated recognition of the legal rights of two American Indian tribes that have claimed a large portion of the State of Maine is discussed in a Special Report, "Give It Back to the Indians," by the Indians' lawyer, Thomas N. Tureen.

In addition to the Book of the Year's extensive regular coverage of energy, an important Feature article, "A New Alternative in the Energy Crisis," by J. Dicken Kirschten, energy writer for the National Journal, discusses what its advocates call a "soft path" solution of the world's energy problems. The need for energy also looms large in "The Australian Uranium Debate," by A. R. G. Griffiths, a Special Report reviewing the controversy that raged during the year over proposed uranium mining in Australia. What happens to life-styles when previously poor Mid-Eastern nations are suddenly inundated by oil wealth is described in the Feature "Petrodollars and Social Change," by Peter Mansfield.

Concern for a very special part of the environment is expressed in "Managing the World's Oceans," by Elisabeth Mann Borgese. This Feature article presents much vital information about an enormous resource that belongs not to any one nation but to the world. "Nor Any Drop to Drink" by Jon Tinker is a provocative Feature about another important resource–fresh water, telling how little of it there is, and what happens when there is not enough or it is used unwisely.

What society can do about potential environmental hazards from DNA research is examined in the Special Report "DNA Research and the Law" by Chicago Daily News *science editor Arthur J. Snider.*

Feature articles and Special Reports are the two areas in the Book of the Year *where personal opinions of authors may be expressed. A personal, and rather sardonic, opinion of the metric system ("The Coming of Metricated Man" by Herbert Greenberg) appeared in the 1977* Book of the Year, *and prompted some protest mail. Among the protesters was Louis F. Sokol, president of the U.S. Metric Association, Inc., who wrote us a cogent and thoughtful letter. We accordingly invited Mr. Sokol to prepare an article stating the case in favour of the metric system, and he did. His article begins on page 739.*

A major purpose of the Book of the Year *is to provide* Britannica *subscribers with the facts and information that help to keep their sets up to date. The* Encyclopædia *itself is being constantly revised and updated, and a large amount of significant new information is generated in that process. We are including in this edition of the* Book of the Year *important new material on two subjects. The* Britannica *article "South Africa, History of" has been heavily revised to take into account recent developments in that strife-torn area. A reprint of a portion (dealing with the period from 1900 to the present) of this revised article begins on page 148. The article "Novosibirsk," on the principal city of Siberia, was entirely rewritten for the 1978 printing of the* Encyclopædia *because of the enormous changes that have taken place in this major city within the last few years. The new article is printed in its entirety, beginning on page 158.*

Last but not least, the appearance of the book has also changed. Since its establishment 40 years ago the Book of the Year *has been set in hot metal, one of the oldest and most traditional methods of typesetting. During the last decade, however, electronic technicians working with experienced metal typecasters have developed computerized typesetting that is able to combine computer speed with traditional typographic craftsmanship. This edition of your yearbook is the first that Britannica has ever set using computer technology.*

The change to computer typesetting necessitated a change in typefaces, and for this new edition we have selected Palatino, a contemporary typeface that is more readable than Binney Old Style, the hot-metal face used in previous editions. To complement the Palatino, we have selected Optima, another modern typeface that combines grace with clarity, for Features and Special Reports. There are other minor design changes, too. Together they add up to what we think is a better-looking as well as a more useful book. We hope you like it.

The Editors

CONTENTS

SPECIAL REPORTS

HUBERT HORATIO HUMPHREY
May 27, 1911—January 13, 1978

Hubert Humphrey, although born in South Dakota, claimed Minnesota as his home for most of his life. He held many jobs, including those of pharmacist and teacher, but the real business of his life began in 1944 when he became President Roosevelt's Minnesota campaign manager. Thereafter Humphrey was first, last, and always a politician. And he was one of the best.

Elected mayor of Minneapolis in 1945, he plunged into national politics three years later when he shocked the Democratic National Convention and the nation with an impassioned plea for minority rights. Southern state delegations stormed from the convention hall and formed their own party. It appeared certain that Harry S. Truman and the Democrats were headed for defeat in the 1948 elections. But Truman won the White House, and Hubert Humphrey captured the seat in the U.S. Senate that he was to hold for 23 years, with time off to be Vice President of the United States.

His proudest achievement in the Senate, where he built a reputation as one of the most vibrant and steadfastly committed members that body has ever known, was his successful support of the Civil Rights Act of 1964. He led it to final enactment through months of legislative difficulties, including filibuster, parliamentary maneuvering, and enormous public pressure.

He never won the presidency, which was always his ultimate goal. He tried hard many times and came very close once, in 1968, when he inherited the mantle of the Democrats from the retiring President Lyndon Johnson—and with it the terrible burden of the war in Vietnam. He was torn between his abhorrence of the war and his loyalty to Johnson, but, if he ever fully resolved the conflict in his own thoughts, he did not make it known soon enough. He lost the White House to Richard Nixon by a scant half a million votes.

He was a long-time friend of Britannica, recognizing in this company a devotion to education in the best sense that in some respects is unique. After his defeat in 1968 he joined the Britannica Board of Directors and served with distinction for two years, until his reelection to the Senate in 1970.

During Hubert Humphrey's last months his struggle with terminal cancer became a public event, and the greatest battle of his life. His cheerfulness and courage in the face of an unbeatable foe made everybody realize, at this time, how much they had always loved and trusted him. Nor did they hold back from telling him, both in public and in private. "You can cut back on the funeral," he told an aide a few days before his death, "because all the eulogies have already been delivered."

We at Britannica want to add one more, a simple eulogy for a good man and a valiant friend: We are all somehow better because we knew him.

HUMAN RIGHTS–THE U.S. INITIATIVE

by Patricia M. Derian

Because we are free we can never be indifferent to the fate of freedom elsewhere. Our moral sense dictates a clear-cut preference for those societies which share with us an abiding respect for individual human rights. We do not seek to intimidate, but it is clear that a world which others can dominate with impunity would be inhospitable to decency and a threat to the well-being of all people.—U.S. Pres. Jimmy Carter's Inaugural Address

President Carter made it clear in this inaugural statement that he was not enunciating a new or innovative policy, but rather reaffirming a commitment to the principles and ideals upon which the United States was founded. "I have no new dream to set forth today, but rather urge a fresh faith in the old dream," he said.

The president was stating his intention to reaffirm and reestablish unequivocally the identification of the U.S. with the ideals that shaped its birth. Perhaps more important, he was signaling that the considerations of human dignity—in all their political, civil, economic, and social ramifications—would be reinstalled as the guiding philosophy of both domestic and foreign policy.

The roots of what is today called our human rights policy are found in the philosophical beliefs that underpinned the creation of our constitutional system. Leaders of the American Revolution, whether "conservatives" associated with mercantile and agrarian interests like John Adams, George Washington, Payton Randolph, or John Hancock, or "radical" ideologues like Patrick Henry, Sam Adams, or Tom Paine, were united in a passionate belief in and a fierce determination to secure "natural rights" for each individual.

A statement of the principle of natural rights was

Patricia M. Derian is Coordinator for Human Rights and Humanitarian Affairs in the U.S. Department of State.

enunciated by Thomas Jefferson in the Declaration of Independence:

We hold these truths to be self-evident, that all men are created equal, that they are endowed by their Creator with certain unalienable Rights, that among these are Life, Liberty and the pursuit of Happiness.

"Unalienable" to our forefathers meant that these were birthrights at the very core of the dignity of every human being and, as such, could not be sold, transferred, or taken away. The insistence for recognition of these natural rights by our ancestors runs through most of the great documents of our Revolutionary period and was made explicit in the first ten amendments to the U.S. Constitution, commonly called the Bill of Rights. Thomas Jefferson and others were so determined that these rights be interpreted expansively that they had the following language incorporated into the Constitution as the Ninth Amendment:

The enumeration in the Constitution, of certain rights, shall not be construed to deny or disparage others retained by the people.

From time to time in our 200-year history we have strayed from the ideals which motivated the men who presided over our founding. Indeed, as black Americans are profoundly aware, it would be nearly another century before slavery was ended and still another century more before society was to begin to redress meaningfully the social and economic discrimination suffered by nonwhites in the United States. Distracted as we became by certain events within and outside our borders, we sometimes ignored the signposts that were set up to direct our destiny, and we ventured into murky areas. Segregation, the hysteria of the McCarthy era, and the loss of historical perspective that led us into the Vietnam war are but more recent examples.

By the measure of history, our nation's 200 years

"I have no new dream to set forth today, but rather urge a fresh faith in the old dream," Pres. Jimmy Carter's inaugural address of Jan, 20, 1977.

are very brief, and our rise to world eminence is briefer still. It dates from 1945 when Europe and the old international order lay in ruins. Before that time the U.S. was largely on the periphery of world affairs, but since then it has inescapably been at the centre of world affairs.

U.S. policy during this latter period was almost exclusively focused on the containment of Soviet expansion—to the neglect of a positive focus on the human values that give the industrial democracies their essential vitality. That policy could not last forever unchanged. Time and the changes it brings have weakened its foundation. The unifying threat of conflict with the Soviet Union has become less intensive, even though the competition has become more extensive.

We are now free of that inordinate fear of communism that once led us to embrace any dictator who joined us in that fear. We are now confident once again of our own future.

But for too many years, we were willing to adopt the principles and tactics of our adversaries, sometimes abandoning our own values for theirs. We fought fire with fire, never thinking that perhaps there was a better way to put out fire. This approach failed, with Vietnam the most distressing example of its intellectual and moral poverty. But by recognizing failure, we have found our way back to our own principles and values, and we have regained our lost confidence.

In less than a generation, we have seen the world change dramatically. The daily lives and aspirations of most human beings have been transformed. Colonialism is nearly gone. A new sense of national identity now exists in almost 100 new countries that have been formed in the last generation. Knowledge has become more widespread; rapid communication reaches almost everywhere. As more people have been freed from traditional constraints, more have been determined to achieve for the first time

12

The framers of the Declaration of Independence (left to right) Robert Livingston, Roger Sherman, John Adams (standing), Thomas Jefferson, and Ben Franklin.

in their lives social justice. Most look to the United States for guidance in that endeavour.

The world is still divided by ideological disputes, dominated by regional conflicts, and threatened by the danger that we will not resolve the differences of race and wealth without wars that would inevitably threaten to involve the major military powers. We can no longer separate the traditional issues of war and peace from the new global questions of justice, equity, and human rights.

In the early years of our civil rights movement, many Americans believed the issue was a "Southern" problem. They were wrong. It was and is a problem for all of us. Now, as a nation, we must not make a comparable mistake when we see injustices anywhere. Protection of human rights is a challenge for all countries, not for just a few. In meeting that challenge, our country has a deep obligation to its past and to what we should have learned about human values from our forebears.

We have no illusion that changes in repressive regimes will come easily or soon. But it would be a mistake to undervalue the power of words and of the ideas that words embody. In our own history, that power has been demonstrated many times, from Thomas Paine's *Common Sense* to Martin Luther King, Jr.'s "I Have a Dream."

In the life of the human spirit, words are action, much more so than many may realize who live in countries where freedom of expression is easily and casually taken for granted. The leaders of totalitarian nations understand this very well. The proof is that words are precisely the action for which dissi-

dents in those countries are being persecuted. People are killed, jailed, expelled, or ostracized for simply speaking or writing.

Nonetheless, we can already see dramatic worldwide advances in the protection of the individual from the arbitrary power of the state. For us to ignore this trend would be to lose influence and moral authority in the world. To lead it will be to regain the moral stature that we once had.

The great democracies are not free because we are strong and prosperous. We are strong and influential and prosperous because we are free.

Throughout the world today, in free nations and in totalitarian countries as well, there is a preoccupation with the subject of human freedom, human rights, and I believe it is incumbent on us in this country to keep that discussion, that debate, that contention alive. No other country is as well qualified as ours to set an example.

After too long a time, we have reaffirmed America's commitment to human rights as a fundamental tenet of our foreign policy. In ancestry, religion, colour, place of origin, and cultural background, we Americans are as diverse a nation as the world has ever seen. However, all Americans are drawn together by a belief in and a passionate insistence upon human freedom. We realize that our merit and worth as a society extend far beyond our material and technological accomplishments.

This does not mean that we can conduct our foreign policy by rigid moral maxims or impose specifically American values on a diverse world. Yet, significantly, the UN has since its founding devel-

A civil rights march (above), organized by Martin Luther King, Jr. (right), advanced from Selma to Montgomery, Alabama, in 1965. A few months later Congress passed important voting rights legislation.

oped in declarations, covenants, and other instruments a body of human rights principles that have acquired international recognition.

President Carter stressed human rights in his first major address to the United Nations and in particular signaled that the criteria we are using are those established by the UN. He stated that:

> All the signatories of the UN Charter have pledged themselves to observe and to respect basic human rights. Thus, no member of the United Nations can claim that mistreatment of its citizens is solely its own business. Equally, no member can avoid its responsibilities to review and to speak when torture or unwarranted deprivation occurs in any part of the world.

We have drawn from the internationally recognized rights contained in UN instruments—principally the Universal Declaration of Human Rights and the International Covenants on Civil and Political Rights and on Economic, Social and Cultural Rights. We have developed from these documents three basic areas or categories of human rights which we consider in assessing a country's performance in respecting the human dignity of its citizens. These are: (1) respect for the integrity of the person, which includes freedom from torture, arbitrary arrest and detention, and all forms of cruel and inhuman punishment; freedom from denial of fair trial; and freedom from invasion of the home; (2) economic and social rights, and whether a government's policies genuinely seek to meet its citizens' basic human needs for food, shelter, health care, and education; (3) political and civil liberties, including freedom of the press, of assembly, and of religion; freedom to move within and outside one's own country; and, in general, provision for participation in government by the governed.

The focal point in the U.S. Department of State for translating our human rights philosophy into applied foreign policy is the Bureau for Human Rights and Humanitarian Affairs, which I head as an assistant secretary of state, in the Department of State. Working under Secretary of State Cyrus Vance and closely with the bureaus in the State Department—and these include those for the different geographic regions and those with specialized functions (international organizations, economic policy, consular services, etc.)—we seek to promote respect for human rights as a central objective of our foreign policy. As a specific example, we implement the body of our congressional legislation, which, in essence, seeks to ensure that U.S. military and economic aid, as well as U.S. voting on other countries' loan applications in several international development assistance institutions, will be designed to deny that assistance to governments that consistently engage in "gross violations" of their citizens' human rights. We, of course, generally monitor allegations of human rights violations in any of the more than 130 countries with which we have diplomatic relations. Additionally, we seek to promote increased multilateral action to advance human rights through international organizations, primarily in the UN system. We are also particularly involved with more narrowly regional efforts such as the Inter-American Commission on Human Rights of the Organization of American States and with implementation of the human rights provisions of the Final Act of the Conference on Security and Cooperation in Europe signed in Helsinki, Finland, in 1975.

Our practical policy approach has been to communicate clearly and constructively our concern to the government involved when human rights violations occur in a country. We seek positive change in a government's actions, rather than a diplomatic confrontation. Only if there is no response do we resort to using what is termed the "leverage" of our bilateral aid.

The year since the Carter administration took office is of course a very short time span by which to gauge either the integrity or results of a policy, particularly one which by its very nature must deal with the reality of proudly, and properly, held principles of national sovereignty. Moreover, since the basic goal of the policy is largely intangible—to promote respect for human dignity—there are no easy statistical yardsticks.

However, I believe we can point to having conveyed convincingly in all of our bilateral relationships that a country's record regarding the human

Protesting in Washington against tyrannies abroad. Demonstrators protest against the regime in Chile (right) and against the military dictatorship of Argentina (below).

"In the life of the human spirit words are action . . . . " British women protesting in London against Russian treatment of Soviet Jews.

rights of its citizens is as important a determinant of our relations as are the more traditional factors of military security, political interests, or economic and commercial ties.

In concrete terms we have undertaken diplomatic initiatives in innumerable countries to urge the release of prisoners, the end of suspensions of constitutional due process safeguards, and an end to torture. In several instances where there has been either no response or an inadequate one we have halted or reduced security assistance programs and withheld commercial licenses for straight sales of military or security force equipment. We have closely examined our development assistance programs with a view to ensuring that these go to help the neediest levels of the recipient country's populations. I would like to note here, however, that we have tried to be careful not to penalize the poor and needy in a country for the human rights violations of its government. In accordance with the law and the intentions of Congress we have continued aid programs in some of these countries when our help is programmed directly and demonstrably to meet basic human needs of the most disadvantaged part of the populace.

We have opposed or expressed official objec-

tions to nearly half a billion dollars of loans by various international financial institutions to several countries in various parts of the world on the grounds of human rights considerations.

In the UN system we have begun an unprecedented effort to increase its capability and improve its existing machinery for promoting human rights. We are seeking an apolitical treatment of human rights complaints and an extension of official UN action and concern beyond those few countries that have become "safe" political targets.

We are, however, only at the beginning of a policy. Our achievements must be viewed as much in terms of policy processes seriously and honestly undertaken as in terms of goals attained. In a word, the effort is in itself an achievement.

Moreover, much of our success depends on the strength—or weakness—of our own example in advancing the rights and dignity of all our citizens. So in this important and fundamental sense our human rights policy cannot be for export only. It is as much or more of a challenge to ourselves as a people to realize our unparalleled potential for achieving a more equitable domestic order here at home. It is a challenge that the world expects us to meet if they are to accept the values we have advocated to them.

TOWARD A NEW INTERNATIONAL ECONOMIC ORDER

by Barbara Ward

There are a number of ways of thinking about a "new international economic order." For instance, it would be quite rational to decide that no issue is so new or so important in the world economy as our sudden perception, in the 1970s, that there may be limits to the world's supplies of raw materials, thresholds to the amount of pollution the world's ecosystems can bear, and wholly unforeseen physical interdependence—of soil, of water, of winds and climates—which, unsuspected even a decade ago, could do permanent planetary damage affecting rich and poor nations alike. But in fact the phrase a "new international economic order" today means something much more political, specific, and precise. Its roots lie in the less developed nations' fundamental aspiration to follow the political ending of colonization by a comparable economic and social emancipation.

The idea is clear. But given the interweaving of world economic interests, the complexity of the thousands upon thousands of transactions in planetary commerce, and, above all, the degree of economic dependence that grew up during the colonial years, the task is proving more complicated than the political terminations of empire. With a few tragic exceptions, the whole process—celebrating the first formal Independence Day, running down the flag, signing up the new constitution, and taking one's seat in the United Nations—proved straightforward enough compared with trying to unweave and reweave the patterns created in several centuries of deepening trade relations in a world market.

President of the International Institute for Environment and Development, Barbara Ward (Baroness Jackson of Lodsworth, DBE) is an internationally renowned economist with a special interest in the problems of the third world. Her many publications include The International Share-Out (1938), Interplay of East and West (1957), The Rich Nations and the Poor Nations (1962), Spaceship Earth (1966), Only One Earth (with René Dubos; 1972), and The Home of Man (1976).

In formal terms, the idea can be said to have come to birth in May 1974 at the sixth special session of the UN General Assembly. A long resolution, carried by consensus—but, significantly, with strong reservations on the part of the U.S., Britain, Japan, and West Germany—laid down a number of basic principles: (1) that nations should enjoy sovereignty over their own resources, including the right to nationalize them; (2) that these resources should be developed by processes of industrialization and adaption or invention of appropriate technologies under local control; (3) that the conduct of world trade should neither set special obstacles in the way of nations' access to other national markets nor work against a more equitable balance between the higher export earnings derived from manufactured goods on the one hand and the lower prices for most raw materials and semimanufactures on the other; (4) that more concessionary funds should be made available to the poorer nations by the already industrialized and hence wealthy states.

It is perhaps significant that nothing was said about the need for institutional change *within* less developed states in order to make them more able to benefit from changes at the international level. Clearly no amount of aid or trade will transform a feudal economy with 90% of the land owned by 10% of the people or achieve the modernization of a military dictatorship bent on spending every available cent on arms or prestige. But the General Assembly is an *international* forum, and to insist on internal reform is not its specific function.

Where the assembled nations did go into greater detail was in the reordering required in international trade. There was reference to the need for some kind of special fund to underpin the financing of buffer stocks in order to achieve greater price stability for a range of vulnerable commodities—coffee, sugar, tea, sisal, and a number of minerals. Compensatory finance to offset sudden falls in export incomes was also brought up. The issue was raised whether primary exports supplied by poor

17

"In places like Bengal, new Lancashire textiles wiped out the spinners and weavers and they had nowhere to go."

nations might not in some way be "indexed" so that their prices would automatically rise if the manufactures imported from industrialized countries continued to reflect an upward movement of inflation. Such, in broad outline, was the first statement of the new economic order. But naturally it has a very long history behind it and some very vivid consequences flowing from it. Both must be examined if its full meaning is to be understood.

The Historic Background. The starting point is the very end of the 15th century and the fleet of little cockleshell boats of the merchant adventurers going out from Western Europe to trade for all the goods and luxuries of the East. Between the 16th and the 19th century, these men and their successors established a world market. They were not particularly interested in founding empires. They simply wanted to trade. They obeyed all the restrictive ground rules for commerce laid down by the great Mughal emperor Akbar and his successors in India until the dynasty collapsed into local rivalries and wars. As late as the 1820s, British trade with China was confined to Canton, and British merchants were not even allowed to take boat trips on the river. The experience was clear. Wherever strong local rule prevailed, the Europeans had no choice— or even perhaps desire—but to remain traders. Some of their governments at home were not sure

that they even wanted trade. It is ironic to remember that in mid-18th-century Britain, when fears for the balance of payments were disturbing the government, a semiofficial outcry occurred against the new middle classes' habit of buying foreign textiles (damasks from Damascus, calico from Calicut, muslins from Muslim Bengal) and thus putting Britain into debt to foreign governments.

But wherever local authority was weak, disorganized, or tribal, the traders moved in. Their reasons were various enough to demonstrate how little the takeovers were acts of institutional imperialism. Some wanted to protect their trade against local disorder, some simply went in for loot. Sometimes the genuinely imperial ambitions of a local proconsul, a Clive or a Wellesley, played a key role. But, above all, the British, the French, the Dutch, the Spaniards, and the Portuguese were usually conspiring, supporting local rivals and finally moving in largely to keep the others out. The outcome of four centuries of confused local resistances, collapses, revivals, and interventions was a world system controlled from Europe, either by settlement as in the Americas or by colonial rule almost everywhere else. All in all, the system was still broadly intact as late as 1945. And one of the fundamental purposes of its rulers was to trade and invest in a worldwide market with the least possible interference.

At this point it is necessary to look at one or two of the basic characteristics of a market, not simply a world market but any market. In spite of its vast advantage as a decentralized, objective, unregimented means of providing the infinite variety and number of goods and services people usually desire, it has certain characteristics that affect its usefulness and acceptability at both the local and the planetary level. Any market is determined to a considerable degree by power. The early theorists of the market—Adam Smith, David Ricardo—on the whole assume a rough equality in the bargain between buyers and sellers. In this case, the market is indeed an indispensable tool. But suppose the power is totally unequal? In the early 19th century the mass of the workers had nothing to offer but their labour. They could not bargain at all, and by what was called "the iron law of wages" their reward for factory work would fall to equal the bare basic cost of keeping them alive. This level of "reward," as Engels and Marx pointed out, would hardly provide purchasing power to match the increasing productivity and output of the new machines. So, they said, the system would collapse under crises of "overproduction" that were really ones of underconsumption.

However, by the end of the 19th century, the scarcity of workers in North America, the increase in workers' skills and education in Western Europe, the action of reformers, the beginnings of trade unionism with collective bargaining, and, above all, adult suffrage started a change in the *power* relationships of industrialized markets. Then, after

World War II, the Keynesian idea that the maintenance of effective demand—in other words, consumption—would be the key to economic growth helped to produce a 25-year boom. True, in the 1970s the question whether this power of ever rising consumption, intensified by high corporate rewards and by union strength, may not be surpassing the economy's capacity to satisfy it without inflation is a critical factor in the developed world's reaction to the workings of the market, at home or abroad. But the important point here is to underline the element of power in determining the general functioning of any market system.

A man who can corner or control the market in a certain essential resource has virtually absolute power, at least for a time. The Arab nations with vast oil reserves and small populations are in this position. North America's monopoly of surplus grain is as great. Australia, North America, and South Africa are not far short of a monopoly in uranium. Then again, nations with obviously superior military power can monopolize the market. It is often said, for instance, that the root of the weakness of less developed nations in trade is their enforced concentration on raw materials. But the Soviet Union can fix the prices for its exports of raw materials to Eastern Europe and buy back their industrial goods at an advantage. And, in the light of history, we have to realize that one of the most effective means of securing very great and even monopoly power is quite simply by colonial control. Throughout its four centuries of existence, the world market has been, broadly speaking, subject to the power

"The colonial rulers . . . were in control of a system whereby raw materials flowed out of the 'South'—Latin America, black Africa, and Asia—to the North . . ."

and regulation of the peoples of Europe and latterly of their settler descendants in the United States.

Milch Cow Economy. This colonial control was, in part, both caused and reinforced by another factor—the Industrial Revolution. After about 1750, first Britain, then Western Europe and America's northeastern seaboard moved into wholly new types of mass production of goods for people's daily needs and of the production of machines to make those goods. Local handicraft producers were all but wiped out and moved into the factories along with the dispossessed, landless workers. But in places like Bengal, new Lancashire textiles wiped out the spinners and weavers and they had nowhere to go. The muslins came from Manchester now, not Dacca. As the 19th century developed, the old trading patterns were simply reversed. Europeans no longer sought Asian manufactures. They opened up mines and plantations to provide their own factories with basic materials. Africa, partly by direct investment, partly by way of the detestable export of slaves, had long been drawn into the system since slave labour helped to produce the cotton and sugar and tobacco in much of the New World. The small elites of feudal rulers in Latin America also joined in the trade, selling sugar, coffee, grain, and meat in return for Western industrial goods. Without anyone in particular planning it, a world market was set up in which the power of the newly industrialized nations was the determining factor—although it was called "comparative advantage." The colonial rulers, the developed industrial firms, the traditional local leaders were in control of a system whereby raw materials flowed out of the "South"—Latin America, black Africa, and Asia—to the North Atlantic core, there to be transformed into manufactured goods and sold in local markets and back to the primary producers.

In the process, all the services—shipping, banking, insurance, research for new products—remained with the Atlantic powers. All the "value added" which comes from, say, turning a cocoa bean into dessert chocolate was equally engrossed by the industrialized states. As late as the 1970s, the export of the 12 major raw materials (if we exclude oil) from the poorer nations earned $30 billion a year for the producers. But they cost purchasers $200 billion before they reached the final consumer. The $170 billion balance represents the whole "value added" of the industrial process, almost entirely absorbed by the industrialized nations.

The distinguished Dominican economist Père Lebret had a word for this basic world exchange. He called it *l'économie de traite* (the "milch cow economy"), in which everything is sucked out of the "South" and sent North with just enough re-

turned to keep the system functioning. All the local services, all the means of communication, all the developed sectors of the "South" served this pattern. The roads and railways led to the coast. Virtually all the big cities—from Shanghai to Valparaiso—were ports and acted as entrepôt centres for an essentially external system. Latin America's coastal cities gave the continent a higher degree of urbanization in the early 20th century—with not even 5% of the people in industry—than was the case in Western Europe with at least 20% in manufacturing jobs. Thus there grew up a subservient urbanism, attached not to the local hinterland but to the external Atlantic system. This, incidentally, is a basic root of the huge, unbalanced metropolises of the less developed world today.

Colonization's Aftermath. Such, broadly speaking, was the economic background, in part still hidden and misunderstood, of the world that emerged in 1945. The industrialized nations, made up of mixed and planned economies, contained about 35% of the world's peoples, enjoyed 75 to 80% of the world's wealth, 85% of its trade, 90% of its services, well over 90% of its industry, and nearly 100% of its research—percentages that have since remained virtually unchanged (save that the percentage of world population living in the rich nations has fallen still further). The 70% of the world's peoples living in the less developed world, or the "South," as it has come to be called, suffered—and still suffer—the corresponding opposite percentages and hence lack of power. A world market exists but is wholly biased toward the needs of the industrialized giants. The question after 1945 has been not so much whether such a system could endure as how soon its inequities and instabilities would begin to emerge into the political arena.

The 1950s and '60s marked a number of vital preliminary changes. The first was the ending of direct colonial control by Western market economies and the establishment, through the UN and its agencies, of at least the concept of a worldwide system of cooperation which transcended both power relations and purely economic interests. The second was a modest acceptance by the developed market societies (the socialist bloc states played only a very small part here) of the fact that ordinary commercial methods were not enough to secure world growth. Aid-giving and concessionary lending—the equivalent of 19th-century philanthropy—would be needed to give the new nations an extra shove toward evolving their own productive base and then, by following traditional "stages of growth," reaching at last the felicity of the industrialized consumer society. The third change was the phenomenal growth of large multinational corpora-

"The industrialized nations, made up of mixed and planned economies, contained about 35% of the world's peoples, enjoyed 75 to 80% of the world's wealth, 85% of its trade, 90% of its services, well over 90% of its industry . . ."

tions, based in the main in North America (with a few in Europe). Their leaders felt quite able to conduct world trade without the backing of colonial control and indeed saw themselves—however inappropriate their highly capital-intensive technology in labour-rich economies—as main tools of modernization in "Southern" markets. They were often encouraged by every kind of concession to enter these markets, usually to hasten by all possible means local industrialization, the Cinderella of colonial times.

The fourth development was the uneasy sense, which began as early as the mid-1950s, that this combination of a formal ending of political colonization, together with the rapid expansion of Western-based (and usually Western-owned) local industrialization, might in fact be leaving the old relations of dependence intact. Nominally the world was free. Actually, the pattern of its economy was still colonial. This was the fundamental uneasiness which began to express itself in a series of third world conferences. The Afro-Asian conference at Bandung, Indon., in 1955 was the first. Then came the series of "nonaligned nations" conferences—Belgrade in 1961, Cairo in 1964, Lusaka, Zambia, in 1970, Algiers in 1973, and Colombo, Sri Lanka, in 1976. At the same time, the less developed nations began to wonder whether their

fundamental inherited role as suppliers of raw materials would be much changed by such new international agencies as the General Agreement on Tariffs and Trade (GATT) or the International Monetary Fund (IMF). They noted that over 80% of their trade was still in primary produce. They had barely 7% of the world's industry, and although the 1950s and '60s were years of rapid and even unprecedented growth—the average annual growth rate was of the order of 5%—they seemed to remain on the lower steps of a moving staircase for, as they went up, the rich went up ahead. The old dependence remained. Indeed, it was becoming reinforced by the new debts incurred for modernization. With these preoccupations, they persuaded the "North" to join with them in establishing a new trade organization, the UN Conference on Trade and Development (UNCTAD), to give more weight to both their decisions and their difficulties. Then, at UNCTAD's 1964 session, they set up the third world Group of 77 (which by 1977 had grown to 114 members) to be an instrument of greater influence—in other words, of power—in world trade negotiations.

The Oil Weapon. Such was the position in 1973. The Northern states felt they had behaved with reasonable openness and generosity, abandoning colonial control, transferring about $12 billion a year in aid, giving some openings to third world trade

through a careful list of General Preferences, and joining in endless discussions with their Southern partners, all designed to disentangle difficulties and grievances. But these seemed relatively small advantages compared with the massively unchanged relationships of power and wealth. Only a few developing states—South Korea, Taiwan, Brazil—had lessened their dependence on primary exports. It was in this scene of deep felt disadvantage that the decision of the Organization of Petroleum Exporting Countries (OPEC) to raise oil prices as much as fivefold in 1973 had its revolutionary effect.

It was not a simple or uniform effect. Indeed, for non-oil producers such as the Indian subcontinent, the increased costs in fuel and fertilizer were catastrophic. Some others—highly populated oil-producing states like Nigeria or Indonesia, for instance—felt the increase mainly as a partial relief from insurmountable economic difficulties. The chief shock was in the North. France, West Germany, and Japan had become largely dependent on imported oil. America's reserves were declining. Above all, after a 25-year "binge" in growing use of oil at under $2 a barrel (up to 15% a year in Japan, for instance), the developed market economies suddenly found themselves sharing something of the traditional position of the Southerners—to be no longer in control of one of their most crucial economic decisions. "The new economic order" came to be generally seen—as, in the eyes of the South, it always had been—as a question of change in the balance of power in the market, the power without which economic bargains are invariably biased toward the heavyweights.

The new strength of OPEC was enough at least to open in very short order new and more serious negotiations between North and South on the best means of regulating their economic relations with each other. Once again, the planned economies

played virtually no part. The two chief forums of negotiation have been UNCTAD and the Conference on International Economic Cooperation (the so-called North-South conference) in Paris, an ad hoc body of 27 nations—8 from the North and 19 (including 8 OPEC members) from the South. On the agenda of both groups have been the main points of the UN General Assembly's sixth special session resolution.

It must be admitted at once that, after two years of discussion, there is not too much progress to report. The reason lies in the very disturbance and disarray of the world economy. The OPEC price rise coincided with an almost universal boom in the industrialized nations and with a harvest failure in the Soviet Union so great that the U.S.S.R. quietly bought up virtually the entire North American grain reserve in 1972–73. The result was a tripling of world food prices, and all three together—boom, fuel (with fertilizer), and food—set in motion an inflationary spiral that even tough recessionary measures did not check. The phenomenon of "stagflation," of falling jobs and rising prices, dragged on in the North, and there could hardly have been a less favourable background for consideration of the South's main demands.

To transfer more concessional aid to the South when internal unemployment was above 6–7% (and among young workers up to 25%) was felt in domestic terms to be politically impossible in the North. To give greater access to third world manufactures—say, of shirts and shoes—would knock out yet more labour-intensive industries in the unemployed sectors. To link raw material prices to the cost of manufactures by a form of indexing could be seen as a method of institutionalizing inflation. Even the concept of greater stability of prices achieved through a common fund purchasing a variety of buffer stocks in times of high supply or low demand and releasing them to offset incipient scarcities seemed too much like concessionary aid for easy acceptance. In any case, the North could not be sure that the one commodity whose price they would wish to see stabilized—oil—would ever figure in the program. The result of these direct and biting conflicts of interest has at least not been breakdown. But so far a constant postponement of decisions until the next meeting has proved the chief means of evading deadlock.

The Outlook. Yet there are four reasons for modest optimism. The first is simply based upon moral experience. The rich have learned, especially under pressure, to be more just and understanding toward the poor. The modern world economy has its reformers, just as had Victorian Britain. The pattern has not been lost.

The proof lies in the second reason. The wealthy industrialized powers have not, in fact, shown themselves entirely obdurate or lacking in all readiness to abandon their relative positions of power. For instance, in 1974 the IMF set up a "special facility" of $3 billion to help the poorest nations meet new fuel costs and raised it to $10 billion in 1977. In February 1975, at Lomé, Togo, the members of the European Economic Community met with a wide range of associated states from Africa, the Pacific, and the Caribbean. Some important—and possibly exemplary—agreements were reached on the issues most close to the less developed nations' concerns. Duty-free access to the EEC market without any reciprocity of concessions was arranged for most of the poor countries' industrial products and—with certain restrictions—for their agricultural exports. A fund of $450 million was established to be used (over five years) to offset price fluctuations in important primary products—the so-called Stabex scheme. In addition, a general aid figure of $3,550,000,000 was negotiated, also for the next five years.

This sense of rather greater responsiveness was apparent again at the seventh special session of the UN General Assembly later in 1975 where, although without specific agreements, there emerged a certain readiness to recognize the fact of the South's long-standing grievances of trade discrimination and to express some signs of a new understanding that there could be a genuine interdependence of interests between North and South.

And this is the third reason for moderate optimism. Although the negotiations since 1976 in UNCTAD have been adjourned and the Paris talks have virtually ended, there has been some progress. A new body, the Brandt Commission, will now take up the joint interests of both North and South, and there is greater readiness to look at world order

together precisely because changed power relationships are bringing firmer *Northern* interests into play, and here it is possible to discern common ground. "Stagflation" in the North cannot be broken without an end to the pressure on prices. Equally, in the short run, as they build up their economies the Southern states need a reasonably prosperous North to provide capital and markets. The combination of pressure from the "underprivileged" and enlightened self-interest on the part of the fortunate may, as in Victorian Britain, be beginning to work.

The fourth reason for moderate optimism lies not in the present specific stage of the negotiations for the new economic order but in the wider experience of the world economy in the 20th century. It was the collapse, between 1927 and 1929, of purchasing power among primary producers, ending with the U.S. farmers, that started the crisis of 1929. Then the increased protectionism of the industrialized nations turned it into the universal crash of 1931. Nothing was done and the drift to war began. In 1947, once again purchasing power was totally enfeebled, this time in Europe and throughout its colonies by six years of battle. This time, however, the challenge met a remarkable response. The U.S., with half its present standards of prosperity, gave away with the Marshall Plan some 2.5% of its gross national product—ten times the present percentage of its aid—for four or five years to restore Europe and revive the trade of the whole world. It is surely not Pollyanna optimism to hope that it will occur to the statesmen of the North that the place where purchasing power today is nonexistent but resources are waiting to be developed is in the quarter of the world that subsists on an average per capita income of little more than $150 a year. A ten-year "Marshall Plan," financed by the North and OPEC, to build up the South's agriculture and industry, to enfranchise the mass of poor consumers, make them productive and give them steady work and just rewards, would create new resources and new markets for both North and South and allow the rhetoric of interdependence to be turned into a genuine alliance of productive interest.

In the 20th century, we have contrived both to fail and to succeed. It is hard to believe that, with such immediate historical experience of the way up and the way down, we shall choose the path of disaster. By the next meeting—in Paris or in UNCTAD—perhaps the genuine "global compact" of the 1980s will begin to take shape. Perhaps the world can move from the hope and the dream to the substance of reality. To use, not inappropriately, a Muslim metaphor, we can pass from "the Gates of Ivory to the Gates of Horn."

Basque flags decorating balconies in Bilbao, Spain.

THE NEW NATIONALISM: CONFLICTS AND HOPES

by Elie Kedourie

In the last decade or so numerous nationalist movements, with varying success, have challenged the authority of existing states in various parts of the world. It has not seemed to matter whether the states so challenged were old and stable or newly established. In Western Europe, the Irish Republican Army has attempted since 1969 to overthrow British rule in Northern Ireland, thus calling into question the territorial integrity of the United Kingdom. In Great Britain itself, Scots and Welsh nationalists advocate, if not separatism, a large measure of autonomy for Scotland and Wales—an autonomy that, if it were realized, might sensibly diminish the power of the U.K. government and deal a severe blow to the principle of the legal sovereignty of Parliament. In France, a state quite as old as the United Kingdom, Breton, Provencal, and Corsican movements clamour for autonomy, claiming that the Paris government devours their cultural substance and damages their economic interests by a rigorous, overweening, and insensitive centralization. In Spain, another state with roots that go deep into the past, Basque and Catalan nationalists have violently challenged both the Franco regime and its successor, again demanding an autonomy sanctioned by differences of language and culture.

In North America, where political attitudes and traditions form a continuum with those of Western Europe, Canadian federalism has been attacked by the Parti Québécois, which is now in power in Quebec. This party, appealing to the French-speaking majority in the province, strives to defend the

Professor of politics at the London School of Economics and Political Science and fellow of the British Academy, Elie Kedourie has held visiting professorships at Princeton, Harvard, Monash (Melbourne), and Tel Aviv. His publications include Nationalism (1960), Nationalism in Asia and Africa (1968), Arabic Political Memoirs (1974), *and* In the Anglo-Arab Labyrinth (1976).

French language, French culture, and provincial economic interests by imposing severe restrictions on the use of English in the schools and in public and commercial life. It has also promised to put to the test of a referendum the issue of withdrawal from the federation and the creation, if need be, of a new independent French state in North America.

Nationalism Versus Communism. Eastern Europe, with its vastly different political traditions and regimes, has also been experiencing a growth of nationalism. None of the political structures there is as old as those of Western Europe or North America. The Soviet Union was set up at the end of World War I, and the states of Central and Eastern Europe live under Communist regimes that came to power following World War II. Nationalist agitations have been in evidence in these countries, despite strict governmental control over publications and public speech and assembly. In the Soviet Union, Ukrainians, Georgians, Balts, and the Muslims of Central Asia have shown signs of discontent with a state which, federal in form, is unitary and centralized in practice and dominated by the Great Russian element. Sometimes, as in the Ukraine, this has led to the arrest and trial of persons suspected of spreading subversive ideas.

A Communist regime that is not now under Soviet control or influence, namely Yugoslavia, has also suffered in recent years from severe strains ascribable to nationalist discontents. Yugoslavia was established as part of the peace settlement that followed the war of 1914–18. It was put together on the theory that its populations all belonged to one nation, that of the South Slavs or Yugoslavs. Indeed, it was belief in this very theory and the consequent anti-Habsburg irredentism prevalent in Serbia that sparked World War I. But Yugoslavia between the wars was itself the scene of nationalist strife, as some of the groups that had been joined together to form the new state (particularly the Roman Catholic Croats) complained bitterly of the dominance which the (Orthodox) Serbs exercised in the new kingdom. For a time the Communist regime that came to power in 1945 seemed to have stilled these discontents, but the last decade has witnessed their revival—a revival that has led the authorities to control and repress the activities of Croat intellectuals.

Another phenomenon in Central and Eastern Europe may be noticed in this connection. It has been said that the states in this area are Communistic only because the Soviet Union, since 1945, has been able to extend its domination over the area. One can go so far as to say that the presence of the Soviet Army facilitated and made possible the seizure of power by small groups of local Communists with little popular following. The peoples of these states, then, see the Communist regimes under which they live as the outcome and visible expression of Soviet military might. There is little doubt that the Polish, Czech, and Hungarian uprisings have expressed nationalist dislike of foreign—that is Russian—domination as much as discontent with the heavy-handed regimentation associated with the Soviet style of government.

Colonialism's Heritage. When the European powers controlled large areas of Asia and Africa, nationalism in these territories was directed against the colonial rulers. But although "decolonization" is now complete or very nearly so, nationalist griev-

Russian army vehicles were set afire by Budapest citizens during the 1956 Hungarian uprising.

ances have not ceased to be aired. By and large, these grievances have taken two forms. In the first place, it has been claimed that European rule has not really disappeared; it has only assumed a new form, that of "neocolonialism." The idea of neocolonialism rests on the assumption that imperialism is the natural outgrowth of capitalism and serves merely to ensure economic exploitation of the colonies for the benefit of the colonizers. Since capitalism remains, and since capitalist enterprises engage in trade and other economic activities in the former colonies, it is argued that the same old exploitation still exists in a disguised form.

This view of the character and basis of colonial rule is clearly a variant of Marxism. The idea was propagated at the beginning of the 20th century by the English economist J. A. Hobson. It was subsequently taken up by Lenin, who gave expression to it in his tract *Imperialism, the Highest Stage of Capitalism,* first published in 1917. Since the Soviet Union is now a superpower conducting a worldwide foreign policy, Marxism-Leninism—the official ideology of the regime—has been spread with zeal and pertinacity and has attracted large numbers of adherents; hence the worldwide popularity of these notions of "neocolonialism."

But more striking than the accusations of neocolonialism aimed at erstwhile European rulers is the rise of nationalist movements in Asia and Africa directed against indigenous regimes, more often than not the heirs of the European rulers. Thus nationalist leaders in East Pakistan, all Muslims themselves, successfully challenged the government of Pakistan, a state formed in 1947 to unite and protect the Muslims of the Indian subcontinent, and (with Indian help) proclaimed the new state of Bangladesh. Less fortunate in their endeavours, Muslims in the Philippines, formed into the Moro National Liberation Front, have been fighting to secure autonomy within the Philippine state, itself a U.S. possession until 1946. Another such movement is that of the South Moluccans, who are striving to obtain independence from Indonesia. In this case, however, the struggle is taking place not in Indonesia but in The Netherlands, the former colonial power. Settled in The Netherlands following Indonesian independence in 1949, the South Moluccans have recently staged spectacular hijackings and kidnappings to dramatize their demands.

The Middle East. In the Middle East, the Kurds have intermittently rebelled against Iraq ever since the British conferred independence on that state in 1932. The beneficiaries of independence were largely Arabs, especially the Sunni Muslims, and the Kurds have objected to being governed by them. In the 1960s Kurdish discontent flared into large-scale

rebellion, which thwarted the Iraqi Army as long as the Kurds were helped by, and found sanctuary in, neighbouring Iran. When, in 1975, Iran decided that supporting the Kurds no longer served its interests and closed its frontiers to them, the Iraqi Army at last was able to overrun the Kurdish mountain strongholds. This put an end, for the time being at any rate, to a guerrilla war that for more than a decade had proved beyond Iraq's ability to master.

Perhaps the most publicized nationalist movement of the last decade also belongs to the Middle East. This is the Palestine Liberation Organization (PLO), which was formed in 1964 but came into prominence only after the Arab-Israeli war of June 1967. The movement is dedicated to the creation of a "democratic and secular" Palestinian state. This aim, if it were to be realized, would necessarily mean the disappearance of the state of Israel, which came into being in 1948 in the teeth of Arab opposition. In the Palestine war of 1948 and in the subsequent hostilities, the Arab states took the lead in the fight against Zionism and Israel while their Palestinian fellow Arabs played a more or less passive role. For reasons mainly having to do with inter-Arab politics, this situation changed somewhat in the 1960s. The PLO—which was in fact set up chiefly through Egyptian initiative—came to be recognized as the spokesman of the Palestinians and the promoter of a distinctively Palestinian ideology.

Africa: Tribal and Religious Divisions. Africa presents similar phenomena. Angola, after the end of Portuguese rule in 1975, became prey to a struggle between an African government in the capital, Luanda, claiming countrywide authority, and two resistance movements: the National Union for the Total Independence of Angola and the National Front for the Liberation of Angola. Each of the three is supported by different tribes, and those supporting the resistance movements claim that the central government would suppress their individuality and keep them in continual subjection.

A similar state of affairs exists in the former Spanish Sahara, divided between Morocco and Mauritania by agreement with Spain following the latter's withdrawal from the territory in 1976. This partition was resisted by some of the inhabitants and, with Algerian support, they formed the Polisario Front, which opposes Moroccan and Mauritanian rule as tending to suppress the "Saharawi nation." A similar movement has existed for some years in the Tibesti region in northern Chad, where Muslim dissidents challenge the legitimacy of the government that took over from the French in 1960.

Yet another African state, Ethiopia, is subject to nationalist challenges in important and extensive areas of its territory. In the southeast a West Soma-

In Ethiopia, Eritrean insurgents train for battle.

lia Liberation Front (supported by Somalia) claims that the Addis Ababa government has no right to rule over Somalis, who ought to join their fellows in the independent Somali republic; in the northeast Eritrean secessionist groups also reject Ethiopian rule as alien and (with the support of some Arab states) aspire to an independent Eritrea. The Sudan has been the scene of a separatist movement drawing its strength from the Christian and pagan south, which feared oppression by the Muslim north after the proclamation of the Sudanese republic in 1956. Over the last two decades disturbances have flared sporadically in the south, while the Khartoum government alternated between suppression and conciliation. Since 1972 the regime of Pres. Gaafar Nimeiry has established a modus vivendi with the southerners that, for the moment at least, has preserved the unity of Sudan and quieted the southerners' sense of grievance.

Nationalism's Roots. Can any common features be discerned among the nationalist movements of the last decade or so, scattered as they are over several continents and making their appearance in areas that differ greatly in politics, culture, and economic development? For one thing, there is no doubt that these movements reflect, and give expression to, the diversity that exists in the states where they manifest themselves. These states are not homogeneous in population. In the United Kingdom, English, Scots, Irish, and Welsh are, by and large, distinguished from one another and reside in more or less well-defined areas. Again, the French Republic, *une et indivisible* as it aspires to

be, is in reality a mosaic of various groups that, through accidents of dynastic marriage and war, came together to form a unitary state. The same is true of Spain. It is because these three states are well established and comparatively ancient that nationalist challenges there come as something of a shock. What they reveal to us are "geologic faults" in the structures of the states, which for a long time have been hidden or forgotten. Such "faults" are much more visible and thus less surprising in the newer states of Central and Eastern Europe and the still newer ones of Asia and Africa.

Another feature common to all these nationalist movements is precisely the doctrine that serves to justify their claims and their activities. The nationalist doctrine to which all these movements refer is one and the same, with its emphasis on diversity, its belief that humanity is naturally divided into nations, and its insistence that the only legitimate government is one in which nationals exercise authority over fellow nationals in a homogeneous state. Invented in Europe around the end of the 18th century, it was elaborated upon by such writers as Johann Gottfried von Herder, Johann Gottlieb Fichte, Giuseppe Mazzini, and a host of others and became prodigiously popular in Europe in the 19th century. From there it was transmitted to the Ottoman Empire, to India, the Far East, and Africa. The new nationalists of the last decade or two have not, on the whole, made any fundamental innovations in this theory, although some have tried to amalgamate with it other, later theories that have also become popular and widespread.

A Radical Doctrine. There is yet another feature that is common to all these nationalist movements simply because it is, and has to be, implicit in all nationalism. These movements may be described as radical in the sense that they call into question, and aim to subvert, an existing state of affairs. This is not merely a matter of seeking change because a new state of affairs would be more profitable to those who seek the change. Rather, what is involved is the belief that an existing state of affairs is unnatural and thus fundamentally wrong. If it could somehow be eliminated, a new state of affairs might be inaugurated that would be right, just, stable, and hence conducive to universal welfare.

Furthermore, the state of affairs in question is political, the change that is sought is political change, and the new, beneficent state of affairs is based on political arrangements. This belief in the efficacy of political action, which arose in modern Europe, underlies all radical and activist doctrines such as nationalism. It has proved extremely seductive, and its effects have been powerful and incalculable. It has moved people to engage in desperate struggles and seemingly foolhardy enterprises, to sacrifice themselves, and to inflict the cruelest sufferings on others, all in order that a new day may dawn that will inaugurate perpetual joy and happiness for everyone. Without it a doctrine like nationalism would be inert and feeble. It is the secret of modern Europe, which has now been communicated to the rest of the world.

Ideology of Discontent. The question, of course, arises as to why this doctrine attracts followers in one area or in one period rather than in another. More specifically, why have nationalist movements of the kind described above spread to so many parts of the world during the last decade or so? To this question there can be no simple answer. Take, for instance, the United Kingdom. It has always contained English, Scots, Welsh, and Irish. Leaving aside the Irish (whose modern nationalist struggle began in earnest in the aftermath of the Easter Rising of 1916), there have always been Scots and Welsh in Great Britain, recognizing themselves, and recognized by others, as such. For nearly three centuries the question of Scottish and Welsh autonomy or separation was never seriously raised. That it is now an issue actively agitated in British politics is perhaps attributable to the fact that, in spite of greatly improved communications, the ordinary citizen today feels remote and cut off from the centres of power. The official bureaucracy that was created to provide for the citizen's welfare and happiness has paradoxically ended by becoming distant and impersonal, seen by the citizen as alien and "alienating." What is more natural than to

Symbolizing Scottish pride, Scottish leader William Wolfe raises the banner of Scotland beneath a statue of Robert the Bruce.

think that government on a smaller scale, dealing with a smaller area, carried on by people of the same nationality as those whom they govern, dedicated to preserving the identity of the group and its cultural values, would be more satisfactory and more conducive to happiness?

A similar explanation may serve to account for Breton, Provençal, and Corsican separatism. France has a long history as a strictly centralized state, but there, as in the United Kingdom, centralization has increased with the extension of social services and of government intervention in the economy. There, too, ideas of popular participation, the virtues of small-scale government, and the preservation of one's cultural traditions, easily spread through modern means of communication, lead people to invest their communal identity with a political significance which, in turn, must be backed by organized political action. In other words, discontent has found an ideology to explain and justify it.

In Spain other circumstances and other issues were to the fore. The Basques and Catalans supported the Republican government in the long and bitter civil war from which Franco, in 1939, emerged the victor. As a result, these two groups were treated with suspicion and severity by the new regime. But with the tranquillity and prosperity that Spain has enjoyed in recent decades have come the stirrings of political life. The rancours and animosities of the Civil War have been revived, augmented now by the resentments accumulated under Franco's long and repressive reign. Hence the feeling of a distinct identity requiring a political expression is all the keener and more intransigent.

Eastern Europe and the Soviet Union introduce other considerations. In contrast to the open societies of Western Europe, where citizens enjoy freedom of movement and access to a variety of political opinions, the inhabitants of these areas live under governments that recognize only one legitimate doctrine, their version of Marxism-Leninism, and ban any publication or discussion likely to call it into question. Since most aspects of life in these societies—which are heterogeneous in the extreme—are tightly controlled, it is not surprising that a great deal of resentment and discontent has been created.

Those who harbour such feelings will not pause to distinguish between the Communist domination from which they suffer and the Russians, who ultimately control both the Soviet Union and its Eastern European appendages. Furthermore, since Marxism-Leninism is an ideology, it is natural that opposition to it should adopt an ideological guise. For the non-Russians the ideology of nationalism offers itself as the most likely and most familiar alternative. And in one respect, at least, nationalism and Marxism-Leninism are identical: they both put their trust in the political and look to political action to transform life and lead man to abiding happiness. What is true of the Soviets is, mutatis mutandis, true of Yugoslavia, where Communism and the Serbian element which dominates the regime are associated with one another.

Unstable Regimes. When we examine conditions in Asia and Africa, still other points suggest themselves. Most of the regimes established there are the heirs of European empires, and even those that are not are imbued with European values. Belief in the sovereign virtue of politics marks the rulers of these states. But these westernized rulers govern large masses of men who, for their part, have retained a traditional outlook and therefore inhabit a universe of discourse quite distinct from that of their rulers. The westernized regimes thus find themselves narrowly based, unable to take for granted civic loyalty and a language of politics common to rulers and ruled. Hence they are given to doubts about their legitimacy and are driven to rely on centralization and on a high-handed style of government which, paradoxically, elicits the very instability it was designed to avoid.

In particular, the heterogeneity of the population (in these states the rule rather than the exception),

which did not constitute a threat to the imperial powers, becomes a formidable one to their native successors. We see these new rulers exerting great efforts to "mobilize" the ruled and instill in them a "national" outlook and ideology. But since the arguments and methods they use are also available to their rivals and competitors, tribal, linguistic, and cultural differences come to be invested with ideological significance and may lead to claims for secession. Kurds become utterly convinced of the supreme value of Kurdishness, Somalis find rule by Ethiopians intolerable, Saharawis die in order to assert the value of Saharawi culture, and to South Moluccans what differentiates them from Sumatrans and Javanese becomes the most important fact in the world.

Yet another element serves to exacerbate these nationalist conflicts in Asia and Africa. This very large area is industrially and militarily weak. For the superpowers it constitutes a coveted prize to acquire, or at any rate to deny to a rival. Thus international instability is added to internal instability—or, rather, the internal instability tempts rival superpowers to acquire friends and clients by encouraging nationalist dissidence, something that is not (or not yet) feasible in Europe or in Canada.

Nationalism and Marxism Conjoined. Finally, a notable characteristic of Asian and African nationalist doctrine is that it has been further radicalized by being amalgamated, so to speak, with Marxism. The best-known exponent of this "third world" version of nationalism is Frantz Fanon, the ideologue of the anti-French Algerian rebellion. Fanon's version (in which he was anticipated by some Chinese, Japanese, Indonesian, and Soviet Muslim thinkers) is that the "nations" of the third world constitute the true proletarian class in history, not (as orthodox Marxism has it) the working class produced by the Industrial Revolution in Europe. Thus, to the classic nationalist contention that a nation is ipso facto entitled to enjoy self-rule is added the further claim that a third world nation, in struggling to assert itself, is simultaneously engaged in expropriating the expropriators. In so doing, it is helping to secure for the whole world that classless society which is the fulfillment of history and the inauguration of the reign of perfect justice.

This amalgam of nationalism and Marxism is powerful and explosive. Its corollary is the inevitable confrontation between a rich "North" and a poor "South." But since poverty is relative, there is no reason to suppose that this doctrine will not be used to justify the many conflicts between groups all claiming to belong to the "South"—conflicts that will no doubt continue to erupt in the coming years and decades.

JANUARY

1 *Episcopal Church ordains a woman priest*

Having officially sanctioned the ordination of women in 1976, the Episcopal Church conferred priestly ordination on a woman from Indianapolis, Ind. Some 40 other women were scheduled to enter the priesthood in the months ahead. None of the 15 women who had previously been irregularly ordained was required to repeat the ceremony.

3 *Britain given international loan*

The International Monetary Fund approved a loan to Great Britain of U.S. $3.9 billion, the largest single loan in IMF history. The credit, good for two years, was designed to bolster the declining value of the pound and help Britain overcome pressing economic problems. To secure the loan, the British government agreed to reduce its budget deficit by raising taxes and cutting expenditures.

4 *U.S. Senate chooses new leaders*

Democrats in the U.S. Senate chose Robert C. Byrd of West Virginia as majority leader, succeeding Sen. Mike Mansfield of Montana, who retired. Senate Republicans elected Howard H. Baker, Jr., of Tennessee, as minority leader to succeed retired Sen. Hugh Scott of Pennsylvania.

Gary Mark Gilmore was executed by firing squad on January 17.

Egyptians rioted in Cairo to protest increased food prices.

Carter announces ethics code for his administration

President-elect Jimmy Carter announced guidelines designed to prevent conflicts of interest during his administration. The code, which affects Cabinet members and all political appointees and career civil servants holding executive policy-making positions, requires full disclosure of financial net worth.

6 *Czechoslovak intellectuals issue manifesto on human rights*

A manifesto signed by 240 prominent intellectuals in Czechoslovakia proclaimed the formation of Charter 77, a group demanding implementation of human rights as spelled out in the Helsinki agreement of 1975. Though police began rounding up the signatories, their number rapidly swelled to over 600.

7 *Argentine inflation runs wild*

The Argentine government reported that the cost of living rose by 347.5% during 1976, the highest rate of inflation in Argentina's history.

9 *Oakland wins Super Bowl XI*

The Oakland Raiders trounced the Minnesota Vikings 32–14 in Super Bowl XI at Pasadena, Calif., to win the U.S. professional football championship.

11 *France releases Palestinian terrorist*

Abu Daoud, a member of the Palestinian Revolutionary Council and the suspected leader of terrorists who murdered 11 Israeli athletes during the 1972 Olympic Games in Munich, West Germany, was released by a French court just four days after he was apprehended in Paris.

12 *President Ford delivers final state of the union message*

In his third and final state of the union message to the U.S. Congress, Pres. Gerald Ford cited the "constant buildup" of military power by the Soviet Union and warned that a decline in U.S. military spending could be dangerous.

17 *Capital punishment resumes in the U.S.*

Convicted murderer Gary Mark Gilmore, who repeatedly requested that his death sentence be carried out, was executed by a firing squad at the Utah State Prison. It was the first execution in the U.S. in nearly ten years and partially calmed an intense national debate over the resumption of the death penalty. In an important decision in July 1976, the Supreme Court ruled that such punishment did not violate the U.S. Constitution.

Egyptian price increases spark riots

The Egyptian government announced substantial price increases on food and other items, to take effect the following day. Thousands of students and workers rioted for two days in Cairo and other cities; at least 79 persons died before the government rescinded its order.

Sorensen withdraws as nominee for director of the CIA

Theodore C. Sorensen, nominated by President-elect Carter to be director of the Central Intelligence Agency, withdrew his name in the face of growing opposition within the Senate Select Committee on Intelligence. Carter expressed regret that the government "lost the services of an extremely talented and dedicated man."

Catholic schools defy South Africa's colour bar

Roman Catholic schools in South Africa began admitting black and Coloured (mixed-race) students into formerly all-white schools, thereby breaching the government's policy of racial segregation.

18 *Prime Minister Gandhi calls for national elections*

India's Prime Minister Indira Gandhi announced a relaxation of the 19-month-old state of emergency as a prelude to parliamentary elections in March. She also issued orders that freed some of her imprisoned political opponents.

Cause of "Legionnaire's disease" identified

The director of the Center for Disease Control in Atlanta, Ga., announced that a hitherto unknown bacterium was "quite definitely associated" with the mysterious "Legionnaire's disease" that claimed 29 lives after an American Legion convention in Philadelphia in July 1976. Medical scientists hoped to gain further knowledge of the bacterium through continued research.

19 *"Tokyo Rose" pardoned*

In one of his last official acts as president, Gerald Ford pardoned Iva Toguri D'Aquino, known as "Tokyo Rose" to U.S. servicemen on duty in the Pacific area during World War II. Many who urged the pardon argued that D'Aquino's conviction on charges of treason was a miscarriage of justice brought about by postwar anti-Japanese sentiment.

Scientists detect water outside Earth's galaxy

Radio astronomers at the Max Planck Institute in Bonn, West Germany, reported finding water molecules in a nebula about 2.2 million light-years away. They interpreted this as an indication that extragalactic solar systems may exist with physical conditions resembling those of our solar system.

Pres. and Mrs. Jimmy Carter walked to the White House after his inauguration ceremony.

20 *Carter becomes U.S. president*

Jimmy Carter was sworn in as the 39th president of the United States by Chief Justice Warren E. Burger. After the ceremony on Capitol Hill the new president delighted the crowd of onlookers by walking the mile and a half to his new home in the White House.

21 *Draft evaders receive pardon*

President Carter issued a pardon to some 10,000 men who illegally evaded the country's military draft between Aug. 4, 1964, and March 28, 1973. Though the pardon did not extend to some 100,000 military deserters and to the nearly 500,000 servicemen who received less than honourable discharges, spokesmen for veterans' organizations denounced the action in strong terms. Those favouring total amnesty bitterly complained that the pardon was too restrictive.

24 *Negotiations over Rhodesia falter*

Britain's attempt to achieve a settlement between Rhodesia's ruling white minority and its black majority was stalemated when Prime Minister Ian D. Smith rejected the British proposals for a transition to black rule in 14 months. Though Smith planned to seek an agreement with the blacks through direct negotiations, a spokesman for the black nationalist movement concluded that the government had in effect opted for war.

26 *Spain beset by political unrest*

The Spanish government banned public demonstrations after five Communists were killed in a flare-up of violence as strikes paralyzed the country.

U.S. rebukes Czechoslovakia on human rights

In a statement approved by Secretary of State Cyrus R. Vance, the U.S. State Department publicly deplored Czechoslovakia's violation of the 1975 Helsinki agreement. At issue were the arrest and harassment of Czechoslovak citizens agitating for human rights.

27 *Carter proposes plan to stimulate the economy*

To stimulate the U.S. economy, President Carter proposed to Congress that it authorize $21.9 billion in tax cuts and $9.3 billion for public service jobs for the years 1977 and 1978.

U.S. cautions Soviets on human rights

The U.S. State Department warned the Soviet Union that efforts to silence Andrey D. Sakharov, winner of the 1975 Nobel Peace Prize and an outspoken champion of human rights, would "conflict with accepted international standards of human rights." President Carter approved the statement as reflecting his own attitude and also reasserted his intention to press the issue of human rights without seeking to aggravate relations between the U.S. and the Soviet Union.

FEBRUARY

1 *NBC to broadcast Moscow Olympics*

The National Broadcasting Co. announced that after prolonged negotiations it had signed contracts to exclusive U.S. rights to televise the 1980 Summer Olympic Games from Moscow. Though the cost to NBC was not immediately publicized, a spokesman later acknowledged that the agreement involved more than $100 million. Other U.S. television networks withdrew from negotiations earlier because the cost was so extravagant.

2 *Ram resigns from India Cabinet post*

Declaring that "citizens of the country have been deprived of all their freedoms," Jagjivan Ram resigned as India's minister of agriculture and joined those opposing Prime Minister Indira Gandhi in the upcoming March elections.

3 *Ethiopian chief of state is killed*

Brig. Gen. Teferi Benti, Ethiopia's chief of state and chairman of the Provisional

Military Administrative Council, was shot and killed when fighting broke out among the council members. Unconfirmed reports indicated that six others also lost their lives as a result of the incident. Lieut. Col. Mengistu Haile Mariam, first vice-chairman of the council, became the new government leader.

4 *U.S. Senate consolidates committees*

In a move toward greater efficiency, the U.S. Senate voted 89–1 to function with

25 rather than 31 committees. A more drastic reduction to just 15 committees was proposed earlier but did not survive for a formal Senate vote.

6 Queen Elizabeth marks 25 years as monarch

Queen Elizabeth II observed the 25th anniversary of her accession to the throne of Great Britain. She spent the day with her family in Windsor Castle after attending a morning service in the Royal Chapel. The anniversary of her coronation falls on June 2.

Missionaries killed in Rhodesia

Black Rhodesian guerrillas killed seven white Roman Catholic missionaries at St. Paul's Mission, some 35 mi from Salisbury. The two priests, four nuns, and one lay brother came from Britain, Ireland, Kenya, and West Germany.

7 West Berlin sends aid to U.S.

Citizens of West Berlin, responding to a campaign initiated by the president of the city council, contributed $225,000 in three days to help alleviate the effects of a severe winter in the U.S. The gift was meant to be an expression of solidarity between West Berliners and the people of the U.S., who had aided West Berlin during times of need.

8 Larry Flynt convicted in Ohio

Larry C. Flynt, publisher of *Hustler* magazine, was convicted by a court in Cincinnati, Ohio, for pandering obscenity and engaging in organized crime. His

sentence included 7 to 25 years in prison and a fine of $11,000. Flynt was later released on a $55,000 bond, pending appeal. The case was regarded as a test of the extent to which local standards of obscenity can dictate the content of national publications. Some lawyers contended that if the conviction stands, all national publications would be placed in jeopardy.

9 Madrid resumes ties with Communist nations

Spain reestablished diplomatic relations with the Soviet Union, Hungary, and Czechoslovakia after a rift dating back to the end of the Spanish Civil War in 1939. Relations with Romania, Bulgaria, Poland, and Yugoslavia were resumed in January.

"Roots" breaks records as television drama

The A. C. Nielsen Co. reported that the televised dramatization of Alex Haley's best-selling book *Roots* had set new records. The program, presented on eight consecutive nights (January 23–30) during prime time, was viewed by some 130 million persons—more Americans than had watched any other program in television history. An average of about 35% of all U.S. households were tuned in to the program. The final episode attracted an estimated 80 million viewers.

10 Catholic bishops criticize apartheid

Roman Catholic bishops in southern Africa denounced South Africa for its policy of apartheid (racial separation). Urging full civil and human rights for all inhabi-

Indira Gandhi's aunt joined the opposition in India's elections.

tants of South Africa, the prelates called attention to "the common humanity of all men, taught by our Lord Jesus Christ."

Another Soviet dissident is arrested

Yuri Orlov, a physicist active in the human rights movement in the Soviet Union, became the fourth dissident in ten days to be taken into custody. The Communist Party newspaper *Pravda* said the dissidents were "just a handful of individuals who do not represent anyone or anything and . . . exist only because they are supported, paid, and praised by the West."

13 Indira Gandhi's aunt joins opposition

Vijaya Lakshmi Pandit, former ambassador to the U.S. and sometime president of the United Nations General Assembly, publicly joined political opponents of Indian Prime Minister Indira Gandhi. Pandit vowed to work strenuously for the defeat of her niece in the parliamentary elections.

14 Israeli Labour Party shaken by scandal

Israel's governing Labour Party was badly shaken when Asher Yadlin admitted in a Tel Aviv district court that he had taken real estate kickbacks and had bowed to political pressure by turning over the equivalent of about U.S. $9,000 to the Labour Party for its 1973 election campaign. Yadlin, whose nomination as head of the Bank of Israel was pending at the time of his arrest in October 1976, was convicted on four counts of bribery and one count of tax evasion. On February 22 he was sentenced to five years in prison and fined approximately $28,000.

Nuns carry the coffin of a slain sister who was murdered by terrorists in Rhodesia.

17 *Three Ugandan leaders reported killed*

The government of Uganda announced that the Anglican archbishop of Uganda and two Cabinet ministers died in an auto accident the previous day. The three, accused of plotting to overthrow Pres. Idi Amin, were reportedly being taken to an interrogation centre. Many, however, believed they were murdered.

Carter sends letter to Soviet dissident

President Carter sent a letter to Soviet dissident Andrey D. Sakharov in which he declared human rights to be "a central concern of my administration." He continued: ". . . the American people and our government will continue our firm commitment to promote respect for human rights not only in our country but also abroad." The Soviet government expressed displeasure at attempts to interfere in its "internal affairs."

19 *Churchill's widow hard pressed for cash*

Lady Spencer-Churchill, the 91-year-old widow of Britain's wartime leader Sir Winston Churchill, was reported to be selling some of her husband's paintings and other items of great sentimental value to make ends meet. Inflation, taxation, a weak stock market, and the need for medical care had aggravated her financial situation. Her government pension amounts to £15.30 (about $26) per week, the same amount given to all single pensioners by the British Treasury.

21 *New British foreign secretary chosen*

David Owen, a 38-year-old physician, was named foreign secretary of Great Britain, replacing the late Anthony Crosland. Owen, who previously served as minister of state in the Foreign Office, became the youngest British foreign secretary since Anthony Eden was named to that post in 1935.

23 *Carter denounces Idi Amin, who replies with veiled threats*

After President Carter denounced Idi Amin for "horrible murders" of his political opponents, the Ugandan president forbade some 200 Americans to leave his country until they met with him in Kampala, the nation's capital. After twice postponing the meeting, Amin finally lifted the travel ban on March 1.

24 *British scientists explore gene*

British scientists reported in *Nature* magazine that they had discovered the complete genetic structure of a living organism, a virus. They said their research disproved the common belief that each gene carries a code for reproduction of only one type of protein molecule.

MARCH

2 *Communist leaders meet in Spain*

Santiago Carrillo, secretary-general of the Spanish Communist Party, met privately in Madrid with Georges Marchais and Enrico Berlinguer, respective leaders of the French and Italian Communist parties. The Supreme Court in Spain had not yet ruled for or against the legalization of a Communist party in Spain.

House approves ethics code for its members

The U.S. House of Representatives voted 402–22 to adopt a stringent code of ethics for itself, including an $8,625 yearly limit on outside earned income.

4 *Earthquake kills hundreds in Romania*

The most disastrous earthquake in Romanian history destroyed a large part of Bucharest, the nation's capital, and claimed well over 1,500 lives. Tremors were felt all across eastern and southern Europe.

5 *Carter accepts phone calls from U.S. citizens*

In an unprecedented two-hour radio-broadcast, President Carter spoke over the telephone with 42 callers from 26 states, answering questions, explaining policies, and responding to complaints from ordinary citizens. The program was in keeping with the president's promise to keep in close touch with the American people who elected him to office.

7 *Saudi Arabia offers aid to Africa*

At an international meeting in Cairo, the Saudi Arabian foreign minister told representatives of 59 African and Arab coun-

TONY BOSCO—GAMMA/LIAISON AGENCY

Much of Bucharest lay in ruins after an earthquake on March 4.

tries that Saudi Arabia was prepared to give black African nations U.S. $1 billion in aid. In his opening speech to the conference, Pres. Anwar as-Sadat of Egypt urged Arab and black leaders to manifest solidarity by mutually supporting each other's causes.

Bhutto's party wins Pakistan election in landslide

In Pakistan's first general election since 1970, and the first under civilian rule since Pakistan gained independence in 1947, Prime Minister Zulfikar Ali Bhutto's Pakistan People's Party won 155 of 200 seats in the National Assembly and even greater victories in each of four provincial assemblies. Political opponents of Bhutto angrily protested the vote count.

8 *Hussein and Arafat confer in Cairo*

King Hussein of Jordan and Yasir Arafat, head of the Palestine Liberation Organization, held their first face-to-face meeting since 1970, when a virtual civil war erupted over the activities of Palestinian commandos operating out of Jordan. The two leaders exchanged views about the proposed establishment of an independent Palestinian state.

MARCH

9 *Gunmen seize three buildings in Washington, D.C.*

Members of the Hanafi Muslim sect seized control of three buildings in the nation's capital. One person was killed and nearly a score injured before the terrorists secured the Islamic Center and Mosque, the headquarters of B'nai B'rith, and the city hall. To meet a demand of the gunmen, the premiere showing of the motion picture *Mohammad, Messenger of God* was canceled, but none of the hostages was released.

FDA bans saccharin

The U.S. Food and Drug Administration announced a ban on saccharin, an artificial sweetener used in foods and beverages. The agency's action was prompted by findings of a Canadian research team that attributed cancer in rats to heavy consumption of saccharin. Though the ban was not immediately effective, it was strenuously opposed by diabetics, weight watchers, and many others.

10 *Zaire reports invasion from Angola*

The government of Zaire announced that three days earlier invaders from neighbouring Angola had seized control of three important cities in Zaire's southern province of Shaba. Zaire, rich in copper and other resources and one of Africa's largest countries, helped arm and train the National Front for the Liberation of Angola. That group was defeated in the Angolan civil war by Soviet-backed forces reinforced by Cuban soldiers.

Carter welcomes British prime minister

James Callaghan, prime minister of Great Britain, arrived in Washington, D.C., on a two-day visit to discuss economic problems with President Carter. In welcoming Callaghan, Carter reaffirmed that a "special relationship" exists between the U.S. and "America's mother country."

11 *Hanafi Muslims surrender in Washington, D.C.*

Twelve Hanafi Muslim gunmen surrendered to police in Washington, D.C., after holding 134 hostages for two days. Ambassadors from three Muslim countries persuaded the leader of the group, Hamaas Abdul Khaalis, to forgo further violence. A former Black Muslim himself, Khaalis had demanded, among other things, custody of the Black Muslims convicted of murdering several of his children, a grandson, and a close friend in 1973.

Brazil cancels U.S. military aid treaty

The Brazilian government, angered by what it described as intolerable interference in its domestic affairs, rejected further military aid from the U.S. by abruptly canceling a 25-year-old treaty. The U.S. State Department earlier criticized Brazil's violations of human rights.

12 *Chile cracks down on dissent*

Pres. Augusto Pinochet Ugarte's military junta, which has ruled Chile since September 1973, outlawed all forms of activity related to non-Marxist political parties. The government also reaffirmed its right to arrest dissenters and hold them without court order and without being charged. In addition, new restrictions were placed on the press and censorship of mail was intensified.

14 *Student riots rock Italy*

Both the Italian Communists and the ruling Christian Democrats were badly frightened by violent student riots that erupted in Rome, Bologna, Florence, Milan, Naples, and Turin. Though most students marched only to protest the death of a student shot by police, those responsible for the burning of cars and the smashing of windows seemed to be left-wing extremists disenchanted with the Italian Communist Party for cooperating with the government.

15 *New premier appointed in Yugoslavia*

Veselin Djuranovic was confirmed by Yugoslavia's Federal Assembly as the nation's premier, replacing the late Dzemal Bijedic. His official title was president of the Federal Executive Council.

16 *Drama ends in Zürich after 10,000-mi hijacking*

An Italian mechanic, seeking custody of two young daughters, commandeered a Boeing 727 after it took off from Barcelona, Spain. In west Africa he collected a ransom of $140,000 and picked up his three-year-old daughter living with her mother in Ivory Coast. The plane then returned to Europe but the mother of the second child, in Turin, Italy, would not release her daughter. The 44-hour ordeal ended when Swiss police overpowered the gunman at the Zürich airport. None of the 36 persons aboard the plane was injured.

17 *Carter addresses United Nations*

In his first address before the General Assembly of the United Nations, President Carter called upon all nations to dedicate themselves to persistent efforts to maintain peace and reduce the arms race, to build a better and more cooperative international economic system, and to work with friends and potential foes to advance the cause of human rights.

18 *Vietnam returns remains of American pilots*

The Vietnamese government turned over 12 caskets to a special commission of U.S. officials visiting Hanoi and promised to do what it could to determine the fate of other American military personnel still unaccounted for since the Vietnam war. U.S. medical examiners in Hawaii later discovered that one of the deceased had been misidentified as an American and returned the body to Vietnam.

President of Congo is assassinated

Maj. Marien Ngouabi, the 38-year-old president of the Congo, was shot and killed at his official residence in Brazzaville. An 11-man military committee temporarily assumed control of the government.

20 *Indira Gandhi defeated in Indian election*

In a stunning defeat, Prime Minister Indira Gandhi lost her parliamentary seat, and the Congress Party, which had ruled India since it gained independence in 1947, lost control of the government. The prime minister's son, Sanjay Gandhi, who was running for Parliament, was also defeated. Of the 542 seats in the lower house, the Janata Party captured 270 and had the support of the Democracy Party, which won 28 seats. The Congress Party won 153 seats.

France holds municipal elections

In municipal elections throughout France, the leftists extended their control to more than 75% of the nation's largest cities. In Paris, where the office of mayor was reinstituted after an interval of more than 100 years, former premier Jacques Chirac, a neo-Gaullist, was assured of

Zaire troops protected their border with Angola after clashes erupted in March.

the post after a sufficient number of his supporters won seats in the 109-member city council.

21 Japan's Prime Minister Fukuda visits the U.S.

Prime Minister Takeo Fukuda of Japan, on a visit to the U.S., urged President Carter to maintain U.S. military forces in the western Pacific to preserve stability in the area. Carter responded to the request by promising to consult both the South Korean and Japanese governments before withdrawing ground troops from the Korean Peninsula.

24 Desai replaces Gandhi as prime minister of India

Morarji R. Desai was sworn in as India's fourth prime minister, replacing Indira Gandhi, who two months before had released her political opponent from jail. The 81-year-old leader of the Janata Party pledged to eliminate the mood of fear that had settled over the country during the 21-month "national emergency." During that period nearly 29,000 persons were imprisoned for political activities and strict press censorship was imposed.

26 Coup fails in Thailand

A Thai general, reportedly angry over his dismissal as deputy commander in chief of the Army, failed in a bid to oust the military junta that rules the country under a civilian prime minister. The general and four other officers reportedly left the country after the abortive revolt, which took one life.

DENNIS BRACK—BLACK STAR

Hanafi Muslim terrorists seized 134 hostages in three Washington, D.C., buildings on March 9.

Philippine president grants autonomy to southern rebels

Pres. Ferdinand E. Marcos of the Philippines, seeking to alleviate long-festering problems with Muslim rebels living in the Sulu Archipelago and on the islands of Mindanao and Palawan, granted autonomy to the region after a broad agreement was worked out with Col. Muammar al-Qaddafi, the Muslim leader of Libya, who served as mediator. Final ratification of the arrangement would depend on regional voters, who were awaiting details of the new formula.

27 Two jumbo jets collide in Canary Islands

In a bizarre accident involving two Boeing 747 jumbo jets, a Dutch-owned KLM plane taking off without proper clearance from Tenerife, largest of the Canary Islands, struck a Pan American jet that was slowly taxiing along the airport's only runway. All 248 persons aboard the KLM and 334 of the 396 aboard the Pan American plane perished. The crash was the worst air disaster in history.

30 Soviet Union rejects U.S. plans for limiting arms

Leonid I. Brezhnev, general secretary of the Soviet Communist Party, rejected as "inequitable" two alternative proposals made in Moscow by U.S. Secretary of State Cyrus R. Vance to limit nuclear arms. President Carter expressed disappointment, but promised to continue the complicated negotiations in the hope that a satisfactory accord could be reached before the current five-year limited agreement on missiles expired in October.

APRIL

1 Brazilian leader moves to strengthen military government

Rightist Pres. Ernesto Geisel suspended Brazil's Congress indefinitely after the centre-left opposition blocked passage of a government-sponsored judicial reform bill. Opponents of the bill claimed it did not restore the right of habeas corpus to political prisoners or protect judges from government pressure. Later in the month, in another blow at the growing strength of the minority party, Geisel decreed indirect future elections for the president, state governors, and one-third of the senators.

Chad reports unsuccessful coup in capital

The Chad government announced that an attempted coup was crushed overnight during an exchange of gunfire near the palace of Pres. Félix Malloum in the capital city of N'Djamena. Members of the Army's Nomad Guard had attacked the presidential palace.

U.S. Senate adopts rigorous ethics code

In a move to bolster public confidence in Congress, the U.S. Senate approved a strict code of conduct by a vote of 86–9. Similar to but more stringent than one adopted by the House in March, the Senate code included provisions for extensive financial disclosure and for periodic audits by the General Accounting Office. It also provided for an $8,625 yearly limit on outside earned income of Senate members, including fees for speeches.

3 Soviet interests in Africa underscored by Podgorny tour

Soviet Pres. Nikolay V. Podgorny returned to Moscow following a two-week African tour highlighted by visits to Tanzania, Zambia, and Somalia and by the signing of a treaty of friendship with Mozambique. The trip was seen by some political analysts as an attempt to reaffirm close ties with black African nationalists in the wake of the anticolonialist diplomacy wielded by former U.S. secretary of state Henry Kissinger.

6 Carter signs bill to permit government reorganization

President Carter signed legislation that restored to the White House wide authority to undertake changes in the structure of the executive branch of the U.S. government, subject to veto from either house of Congress. Carter's new powers did not extend to Cabinet-level departments, but they gave him great latitude in abolishing, transferring, merging, or modifying existing bodies within departments and agencies, including the Executive Office of the President.

7 Britain receives apology from U.S. diplomat

Andrew Young, U.S. ambassador to the United Nations, offered an apology to the British government for having referred to the U.K. as "a little chicken" on racial matters during a television inter-

SVEN SIMON/KATHERINE YOUNG

Spain legalized the Communist Party in April after a 38-year ban.

view two days previously. Also presenting his regrets personally to Britain's chief UN delegate, Ivor Richard, Young said that he had not intended to single out one country in a world rife with racial tension.

West German prosecutor slain

West Germany's chief prosecutor, Siegfried Buback, was assassinated in Karlsruhe by two motorcyclists who sprayed his limousine with submachine-gun fire. Buback, who had been pressing charges against leaders of the anarchist Baader-Meinhof gang accused in the bombing deaths of four U.S. servicemen, was the second legal figure killed since the arrest of the gang leaders in 1972.

8 Israeli prime minister plunges country into political turmoil

Prime Minister Yitzhak Rabin, head of Israel's caretaker government, withdrew as Labour Party candidate for prime minister in the May elections following revelations that he had violated Israeli currency laws by maintaining illegal U.S. bank accounts. Rabin, who with his wife received fines for the admitted violations, later handed over the reins of government to Defense Minister Shimon Peres, the Labour Party's new candidate in the elections.

9 Madrid legalizes Communist Party

Amid some sharp dissension, especially from the military, the Spanish government legalized the Communist Party after a 38-year ban imposed by the late, long-reigning chief of state, Francisco

Franco. The Communists had fought hard for legalization in time to enter candidates in parliamentary elections scheduled for later in the spring.

U.S. seizes Soviet trawler for fishing violations

Under fire from American fishermen and congressional backers of the recently imposed 200-mi fishing limit, President Carter authorized seizure of a Soviet fishing trawler and part of the cargo from its mother ship for exceeding the take allowed for certain species of fish. After several weeks of detention under Coast Guard custody in Boston Harbor, the trawler and crew were released upon agreement to a $240,000 settlement from the ship's owners and a $10,000 fine from its captain.

10 Zaire receives military aid in battling rebels

Responding to requests from Zaire and Morocco, France announced it had agreed to a loan of military aircraft to be used in transporting recently committed Moroccan forces to Zaire, which was under invasion from neighbouring Angola by rebel exiles. Two days later the U.S. announced that it was assisting the Zairian government with $13 million in "nonlethal" military equipment, primarily a C-130 transport plane.

12 Carter commutes Liddy's jail term

"In the interest of equity and fairness, based on a comparison of Mr. Liddy's sentence with those of all others convicted in Watergate-related prosecutions," President Carter announced he had reduced from 20 to 8 years the prison term of G. Gordon Liddy, the only one of the original Watergate-burglary defendants still serving a sentence. The action made Liddy eligible for parole in July.

15 China unveils new Mao work

China published the long-awaited fifth volume of Mao Tse-tung's *Selected Works*, which seemed to portray the late Chinese leader as a moderate socialist concerned with economic growth. Accompanied by an editor's note explaining "some necessary technical editing," the book's publication was seen by some as a tool of the new Chinese regime to subtly "de-Maoify" the country while maintaining Mao's legacy.

17 Philippine Muslims reject referendum on regional autonomy

Citing violations of "the letter and spirit" of an agreement with the Philippine government in March, Muslim Moro insurgents of 13 southern provinces boycotted a referendum to permit residents of the newly proclaimed autonomous region to decide on questions of self-administration. Almost 98% of those who voted cast

ballots against rebel control of the region. Hope for an end to Muslim-Christian strife dimmed further later in the month when a panel of Islamic negotiators from the Middle East abandoned talks with the Philippine government over the Moro demands.

Women vote in Liechtenstein

Choosing among candidates for justice of the peace in the capital of Vaduz, Liechtensteiner women voted for the first time in the history of their principality. For several years woman suffrage in national elections had been rejected consistently by the male electorate, but in 1976 a law passed by Parliament empowered the individual assemblies of Liechtenstein's communes to permit their women to vote on local issues.

20 Carter unveils new energy plan for U.S.

After preparing U.S. citizens on April 18 with admittedly "unpleasant talk" of a possible "national catastrophe," President Carter presented Congress with a national energy program designed to raise fuel costs, penalize energy overuse, and reward those who work toward conservation goals with tax credits, rebates, and other incentives. While most lawmakers praised Carter for his courage in facing a major problem, heavy criticism of specific elements in his plan signaled a tough fight ahead between the White House and Capitol Hill.

21 Martial law ordered for three Pakistani cities

The newly reelected government of Pakistani Prime Minister Zulfikar Ali Bhutto imposed martial law on three major cities following six weeks of strikes, riots, and demonstrations that had taken more than 230 lives. The military crackdown was intended to cool agitation mounted by the country's nine-party opposition coalition, which had charged massive rigging in the March 7 voting and was demanding new parliamentary elections.

23 Ethiopia closes U.S. offices

Citing a recent U.S. decision to reduce military aid to Ethiopia because of reputed human rights violations, the Ethiopian government ordered the closing of five American offices, including the U.S. consulate in the provincial capital of Asmara in Eritrea.

27 U.S., West Germany at odds over nuclear proliferation

West Germany approved a $2.7 billion program of energy research that emphasized plutonium-based reactors as a major export industry. The announcement followed reaffirmation of the Bonn government's determination to sell Brazil a nuclear industry having a weapons-fabrication potential. Both decisions were opposed by U.S. President Carter, who was seeking power from Congress to control the export of nuclear technology and material to countries from which more stringent nuclear nonproliferation guarantees were desired.

28 *U.S. moves to ease discrimination against handicapped*

Joseph A. Califano, Jr., U.S. secretary of health, education, and welfare, signed regulations, effective June 1, prohibiting discrimination against the nation's disabled, rehabilitated alcoholics and drug addicts, and other handicapped persons in schools, hospitals, and other institutions that receive federal support.

Washington and Havana reach fishing agreement

Seen as a step toward the normalization of relations between Cuba and the U.S., an accord on fishing rights was announced by the two countries following a month of negotiations. Need for the pact arose March 1 when each country, only 90 mi from the other, extended its fishing-rights jurisdiction to 200 mi from shore.

Nine-year mystery of missing uranium reported

That a 200-ton shipload of uranium ore vanished at sea between Belgium and Italy in 1968 was revealed in stories appearing in two U.S. newspapers and a day

ARTHUR GRACE—SYGMA

A Soviet fishing trawler (right) in Boston Harbor after it was seized for illegal fishing.

later in a speech by former U.S. Senate aide Paul Leventhal. The news stories reported that some American and European intelligence officials believed the uranium had gone to Israel for use in nuclear weapons. On May 5 the European Economic Community officially confirmed the disappearance of the uranium.

30 *North Sea oil-well blowout plugged*

An offshore Norwegian oil well gushing out of control for eight days into the

North Sea was capped after four unsuccessful attempts by a U.S. and Norwegian team headed by U.S. oil-field-disaster expert Paul "Red" Adair. A blowout protection device on the well, erroneously installed upside down by the drilling crew, presented a major problem during the capping tries. While an estimated 20,000 metric tons of oil spilled from the Ekofisk platform during the blowout, the slick almost completely disappeared by May 2 and serious biological damage was not expected.

MAY

1 *May Day rally in Turkey disrupted by gun battle*

A huge rally, organized by the Confederation of Progressive Labour Unions, was shattered by violence when rooftop snipers fired into a crowd of over 100,000 gathered in Istanbul's Taksim Square. Leftist extremists were blamed for the deaths of at least 30 persons and for injuries to some 200 others. Police using teargas, water cannons, and armoured cars made 400 arrests before the two-hour riot was quelled.

2 *General strike called in Northern Ireland*

A general strike called by militant Protestants in Northern Ireland coincided with the bombing of several stores in Belfast and of railway tracks on the outskirts of the city. It was not clear whether the violence was caused by the Protestants to intimidate workers or by the Irish Republican Army. Though trouble did not subside for several days, the strike was essentially ineffective because most people failed to support it.

Soviet Union said to have new military potential

Aviation Week and Space Technology, a respected U.S. journal, reported that the Soviet Union has achieved a major technological breakthrough that could lead to the development of a charged particle beam weapon capable of neutralizing U.S. strategic missiles. After consultation with various advisers, however, President Carter announced: "We do not see any likelihood at all, based on our constant monitoring of the Soviet Union as best we can, that they have any prospective breakthrough in the new weapons systems that would endanger the security of our country."

3 *U.S. and Vietnam open talks in Paris*

U.S. and Vietnam officials met in Paris to discuss normalization of relations. Though the U.S. delegation described the first session as "frank, friendly, and useful," sensitive issues were not expected to be quickly resolved. There was hope, however, that some basic principles could be established.

4 *Richard Nixon interviewed on television*

Former U.S. president Richard M. Nixon, during the first of a series of televised interviews with David Frost, conceded that he had "let the American people down" by lying and abetting the Watergate cover-up. He insisted, however, that because he was motivated by political interests and by a humanitarian desire to help his aides, his actions as president could not be termed criminal, or impeachable, or obstructive of justice.

5 *Vietnam to receive no aid from U.S.*

The U.S. State Department, following a 266–131 vote in the House of Representatives against any form of financial aid to Vietnam, confirmed that no such assistance would be offered in negotiations with Vietnamese government officials.

6 *U.S. unemployment drops to 29-month low*

The U.S. Labor Department announced that unemployment dropped to 7% dur-

MAY

ing April, the lowest figure in nearly two and one-half years. Though 6,737,000 people were still unemployed, a record 90,023,000 were holding jobs.

Ethiopia and Soviet Union sign accords

Lieut. Col. Mengistu Haile Mariam, visiting Moscow for the first time since seizing power in Ethiopia in February, signed a series of accords that drew Ethiopia and the Soviet Union closer economically and politically.

9 Leaders of industrialized countries end London meeting

National leaders from Canada, France, Great Britain, Italy, Japan, the United States, and West Germany concluded a two-day meeting in London during which they underscored the seriousness of unemployment, especially among young workers, and the need for close cooperation in solving such problems as trade deficits.

11 Spray-can chlorofluorocarbons to be banned

Three U.S. government agencies announced that in two years chlorofluorocarbons would be outlawed as propellants in spray cans. The joint decision of the Food and Drug Administration, the Environmental Protection Agency, and the Consumer Product Safety Commission was prompted by studies that indicate a growing risk of cancer when the ozone layer surrounding the Earth is depleted by increased amounts of chlorofluorocarbons.

13 Carter signs bills to create new jobs

President Carter signed a bill authorizing works projects worth $4 billion. He also signed a $20 billion appropriations bill to finance this bill and other public service employment programs that were expected to provide more than one million jobs, mainly for construction workers and young people.

Bhutto agrees to new election

In an effort to defuse political violence that had plagued Pakistan since early March, Prime Minister Zulfikar Ali Bhutto suggested to the National Assembly that his recent election, widely denounced as dishonest, be subjected to confirmation by a public referendum. Such a procedure would require an amendment to the constitution.

17 Labour Party defeated in Israeli national election

In an upset victory that surprised even its supporters, Israel's Likud Party, led by Menahem Begin, won 43 seats in the 120-seat Knesset (parliament). The Labour Party, which had ruled Israel since its independence in 1948, lost 19 of its 51

seats for a new total of 32. Begin, who viewed the West Bank and the Gaza Strip (captured in the 1967 Arab-Israeli war) as part of the historical Jewish homeland, hoped to form a workable coalition government. His election, however, cast a heavy shadow over the protracted negotiations for a permanent peace settlement in the Middle East.

19 Kenya bans big-game hunting

The government of Kenya issued an immediate ban on big-game hunting in an effort to preserve the country's diminishing wildlife. With safaris limited to photographic tours, the country's profitable tourist industry was sure to suffer. Licensed hunters blamed poachers for the devastating decrease in wild animal life.

21 UN concludes African conference

The United Nations concluded a six-day meeting in Maputo, capital of Mozambique, during which representatives of 87 nations and organizations heard UN Secretary-General Kurt Waldheim warn that unless peaceful solutions to problems in southern Africa were found, Africa and the world would be confronted with "a disaster of grave dimensions." Rhodesia, South Africa, and Namibia (South West Africa) were the main topics of discussion. Andrew Young, U.S. ambassador to the UN, attended the meeting during the course of an African tour.

Major General Singlaub disciplined for public statements

President Carter held a 30-minute meeting in the White House with Maj. Gen. John K. Singlaub, U.S. army chief of staff in South Korea. The general had publicly declared that most Americans in Korea believed as he did that Carter's plan to withdraw American troops from the Ko-

rean Peninsula would lead to war. On May 27 Singlaub, a highly respected professional, was reassigned to Ft. McPherson, Georgia, as chief of staff of the Army's largest command. The transfer was interpreted as a severe reprimand even though Singlaub was reassigned to a task described as being "of equivalent responsibility and stature."

22 "Orient Express" makes last run across Europe

After 94 years of service, the famed "Orient Express" completed its last 1,900-mi run between Paris and Istanbul, Turkey. During the 60-hour trip many train passengers turned the event into an uninterrupted celebration even though they had to supply all their own food and drink, including water.

23 Carter signs bill reducing taxes

President Carter signed into law a tax bill that would reduce federal income taxes by $34.2 billion over the next 28 months. Low- and middle-income taxpayers benefited immediately from the $5 billion reduction applicable to 1977. The legislation, which also simplified tax filing procedures and provided tax credits to businesses as an economic stimulant, slightly increased the taxes of those who earn more than $13,750 annually and use the standard deduction method for computing their federal taxes.

South Moluccans seize hostages in The Netherlands

Two groups of South Moluccan extremists, whose homeland was a longtime Dutch colony before becoming part of Indonesia after World War II, seized 165 hostages in northern Netherlands in an apparent effort to dramatize their demand for Moluccan independence. The

Corpses lay on the streets of Istanbul after snipers fired into crowds at a rally on May 1.

hostages, held near Groningen in an elementary school and aboard a hijacked train, included more than 100 elementary school children. The following day the 13 terrorists demanded a Boeing 747 and the release of 21 South Moluccans jailed in The Netherlands for previous terrorist acts. Tensions remained high because the Dutch government had no effective way to influence Indonesian domestic policy and because authorities refused to consider any demands until the children were released.

24 Podgorny ousted from the Politburo

In a move that took Western observers by surprise, Nikolay V. Podgorny was removed from the Politburo of the Soviet Communist Party without explanation. Many political analysts believed his political career was over and he would soon lose his post as chairman of the Presidium of the Supreme Soviet.

WIDE WORLD

Richard Nixon was interrogated on television by David Frost in a series beginning May 4.

30 U.S. and Cuba to exchange diplomats

The U.S. and Cuba agreed to set up "interest sections" of eight to ten diplomats and consular officials in each other's national capital as an important procedural step toward establishment of full diplomatic relations.

31 Supreme Court upholds seniority system

In a 7–2 ruling, the U.S. Supreme Court held that the Civil Rights Act of 1964 (effective July 2, 1965) did not invalidate bona fide seniority systems that de facto perpetuate the effects of earlier racial discrimination, provided there is no intent to discriminate. As a consequence, labour unions and employers may continue to use established seniority systems, even if they place minority groups at a disadvantage in competing for better jobs and other benefits.

JUNE

3 International talks on economic reform end inconclusively

The Conference on International Economic Cooperation, a Paris-based dialogue between 8 industrialized nations and 19 less developed countries, including oil exporters, concluded after 18 months of limited progress toward a "new world economic order." While conceding to some third-world demands, the industrial world failed to achieve its principal aims, among them the creation of an international body for continuing discussions with oil producers on oil supplies and prices.

4 Soviets unveil new constitution

The Soviet Union released for publication the draft of its most recent constitution, the fourth since the Russian Revolution of 1917. Study of the document by Western analysts revealed its similarity to the existing Stalinist constitution, particularly with regard to the status of human rights, which are granted by the state only "in conformity with the interests of the working people and for the purpose of strengthening the socialist system." The new constitution also stated for the first time the dominant role of the Communist Party in ruling the U.S.S.R.

5 Former South Korean CIA head describes illegal lobbying in U.S.

A government scandal involving alleged South Korean influence peddling in the U.S., which had been a target of three federal probes during the year, was fueled by a press account of statements made by Kim Hyung Wook, a former director of the South Korean Central Intelligence Agency (KCIA). Kim identified

Korean businessman Park Tong Sun as a KCIA agent who since the early 1970s had illegally spent millions of dollars to influence American policy toward South Korea. He also named several other Koreans living in the U.S. as KCIA operatives.

Ecevit's party gains in Turkey's elections

Voters in Turkey's general election gave former prime minister Bulent Ecevit's leftist Republican People's Party 213 seats, or 12 short of a majority, in the 450-seat National Assembly. In second place with 189 seats, for a gain of about 40, was Prime Minister Suleyman Demirel's Justice Party, which had been governing in a four-party conservative coalition. Ecevit's failure to achieve a majority in the legislature signaled a possibly difficult struggle ahead for the vote of confidence his government needed to retain power.

Elizabeth II celebrates Silver Jubilee

Touching off a 30-ft bonfire near Windsor Castle, Queen Elizabeth II inaugurated a week of pageants, processions, fairs, and other festivities honouring her 25-year reign as British monarch. On June 7 an estimated one million well-wishers crowded the streets for Elizabeth's coach ride to St. Paul's Cathedral, where she led a thanksgiving service on behalf of the British people.

6 U.S. high court rules on death penalty use

In a 5–4 decision, the U.S. Supreme Court declared that states cannot make punishment by death a mandatory, automatic sentence for persons convicted of

killing a police officer, without regard to mitigating circumstances. Later in the month, with two dissensions, the court also ruled that imposing the death penalty for rape of adults is unconstitutional, being cruel and unusual punishment.

7 Italian abortion bill defeated

A bill that virtually would have allowed abortion on demand was unexpectedly killed in the Italian Senate by a two-vote margin. Opposed by the Vatican and the governing Christian Democrats, liberalization of the Roman Catholic country's rigorous antiabortion laws had been a source of political and social strife for several years.

10 Rules-of-war conference ends

Negotiators from 109 nations concluded a conference in Geneva that represented a four-year effort to update the 1949 Geneva conventions on the rules of war. Final approval was given to two protocols dealing with civil and international conflicts. One provision granted guerrillas fighting against "colonial or racist regimes" the same rights as soldiers engaged in international wars.

11 Marines free Dutch hostages

In synchronized assaults involving armoured vehicles and jet fighters, Royal Dutch Marines overcame South Moluccan terrorists who were holding 51 hostages on a hijacked train and 4 in a school in northern Netherlands. Nearly three weeks of negotiations with the Dutch government had failed to end the ordeal, which began on May 23. Six terrorists and two hostages were killed in the attack on the train. More than 100 children had been held hostage at the school until a flu-like viral epidemic among them prompted their release on May 27.

12 *Swiss reject tax boost*

A financial reform measure aimed at stemming a growing federal deficit was soundly rejected by Swiss voters, despite its support by all major trade unions and political parties excluding the Socialists. The plan included the largest tax increase ever requested of the Swiss citizenry and would have raised the country's cost-of-living index by 2.5–3%.

First Lady ends Latin-American visit

Rosalynn Carter, wife of U.S. President Carter, concluded a two-week tour of seven Latin-American and Caribbean nations: Jamaica, Costa Rica, Ecuador, Peru, Brazil, Colombia, and Venezuela. Mixing goodwill and policy in what American officials considered to be highly successful diplomacy, Mrs. Carter reportedly impressed several national leaders with her preparedness and the authoritative confidence with which she engaged in political and economic discussions on behalf of her husband.

14 *Pakistani prime minister, opposition agree to new vote*

The government of Prime Minister Zulfikar Ali Bhutto and an alliance of opposition parties announced their agreement to hold new parliamentary elections in Pakistan before the end of the year. Negotiations had been under way since June 3 following two months of nationwide riots and bloodshed touched off by charges of rigging in the March 7 general elections that had enabled Bhutto's party to remain in power.

India's ruling party takes eight state elections

Expanding its political power after its solid victory in the March national elections over former prime minister Indira Gandhi's Congress Party, India's Janata Party captured majorities in eight of ten elections for state assemblies that began June 10. A Marxist coalition took West Bengal State, which upon installation of its assembly on June 21 became the only Communist-dominated state in the country.

15 *Spain chooses new leaders for first time in 41 years*

Prime Minister Adolfo Suárez led his centre-right Democratic Centre coalition to victory in the first free parliamentary elections in Spain since 1936, capturing 106 of 207 elected Senate seats and 165 seats in the newly created 350-member Chamber of Deputies. The Socialist Workers Party, which took 60 seats in the Senate and 118 Chamber seats, was expected to lead the leftist opposition in the new government. The Communist

KEYSTONE

Queen Elizabeth II began celebration of her Silver Jubilee in June.

Party and the right-wing Popular Alliance each won a small minority of seats.

Preparations for Helsinki accords review conference begin

Representatives of 35 European and North American countries met in Belgrade, Yugos., to prepare for a session later in the year that would review implementation of the 1975 Helsinki accords on European security and cooperation. Soviet nonobservance of the accords was criticized in a report issued June 6 by the Carter administration.

16 *Brezhnev named Soviet chief of state*

Soviet Communist Party general secretary Leonid I. Brezhnev was elected chief of state by the Supreme Soviet, thus becoming the first leader in the U.S.S.R. to occupy both posts concurrently. Such a move had been expected following the ouster in May of Pres. Nikolay V. Podgorny from the Politburo of the Soviet Communist Party.

17 *Bonn yields on nuclear proliferation*

In what was regarded by some as a major concession to President Carter, West German Chancellor Helmut Schmidt revealed that his country would halt the export of nuclear technology that could be diverted to the production of atomic weapons. He stressed that this did not alter a previous commitment to supply Brazil with a nuclear industry that would include reprocessing plants, nor did it limit future deals to export uranium-enrichment technology.

20 *Trans-Alaska pipeline opens*

The first oil from Alaska's frozen North Slope began flowing into the trans-Alaska pipeline on its 800-mi journey from Prudhoe Bay to the ice-free port of Valdez on the state's southern coast. The pipe was expected to fill completely with oil in 30–40 days.

21 *Israel's Begin takes office*

Following a lively 8½-hour debate, 63 members of the 120-seat Israeli Knesset (parliament) gave Likud Party leader Menahem Begin the vote of confidence he needed to assume duties as the country's sixth prime minister since it emerged as a nation in 1948. Begin later introduced 12 appointees to his 15-member Cabinet, leaving three posts open as an invitation for another party to enter his coalition government.

Workers listened for the sound of oil flow as the trans-Alaska pipeline went into operation.

UPI COMPIX

24 *Industrial nations set economic growth goal*

The annual ministerial meeting of the Organization for Economic Cooperation and Development ended in Paris with a commitment by the major non-Communist industrial nations to take measures to achieve a higher average rate of economic growth as a means to stem rising European unemployment. The goal was set at 5% for 1978, or 1% higher than the 24 members were expected to achieve as a group in 1977.

26 *Crowds demonstrate for gay freedom in U.S.*

Thousands of men and women in New York, Miami, San Francisco, Los Angeles, Chicago, and several other major cities throughout the U.S. marched in coordinated demonstrations to end discrimination against homosexuals. Much of the demonstrators' enthusiasm was attributed to resentment over the outcome of a June 7 referendum in the Miami area, where residents voted overwhelmingly to repeal a local ordinance that gave homosexuals broad legal protection with respect to housing, employment, and public accommodation.

27 *Republic of Djibouti proclaimed*

Pres. Hassan Gouled Aptidon hoisted the new flag of Djibouti over the presidential palace as the tiny country became Africa's 49th independent state. Known variously as the Territory of Afars and Issas and French Somaliland during its 115 years of French rule, the former colony had voted nearly unanimously for independence in a referendum held May 8.

30 *SEATO dissolved after 23 years*

The Southeast Asia Treaty Organization (SEATO), a regional defense league founded in 1954 in response to Communist expansion in the area, dissolved itself with the general understanding that it had outlived its usefulness as a cold-war weapon. Its member countries—Thailand, the Philippines, Pakistan (withdrew 1973), Australia, and New Zealand, with the U.S., the U.K., and France (partially withdrew 1974) as guarantors—contributed no standing forces to SEATO but participated in combined military exercises and in cultural and economic activities peripherally related to defense.

UN Security Council calls for aid to Mozambique

Responding to an appeal from Mozambique made two days earlier, the UN Security Council voted unanimously to ask member nations to provide "material" assistance to that African country in its defense against continuing heavy attacks by forces of neighbouring Rhodesia. The Rhodesian white-minority government admitted that it had been conducting border raids against black nationalist guerrillas based in Mozambique.

JULY

3 *Prime Minister Ecevit of Turkey resigns*

Bulent Ecevit, whose centre-left Republican People's Party won a plurality of 214 seats in the 450-seat National Assembly in the June 5 election, submitted his resignation after just a few days in office. Suleyman Demirel, whose Justice Party was supported by two right-wing allies in the 229–217 no-confidence vote against Ecevit, was expected to revive the coalition that had been unable to curb violence or solve the explosive Cyprus issue during its two-year rule.

5 *Black African leaders meet in Gabon*

Leaders of 48 African nations, all members of the Organization of African Unity, concluded a four-day meeting in Gabon during which they failed to resolve fundamental differences that ranged from territorial disputes to acceptance of development aid from Western countries. Several of the more radical African leaders declined to attend the conference and sent lower-ranking envoys. Before adjourning the conference, the members endorsed the efforts of the Patriotic Front, which was fighting for black rule in Rhodesia, but it did not disavow other factions fighting for the same cause.

European nations agree to develop breeder reactors

Representatives from Belgium, France, Italy, The Netherlands, and West Germany signed agreements in Paris that guaranteed further research and development of nuclear breeder reactors. Such reactors are designed to produce additional nuclear fuel in the form of plutonium as a direct by-product of reactor operation. The fact that plutonium can also be used as a nuclear explosive had prompted President Carter earlier in the year to call for a temporary moratorium on breeder reactors in favour of conventional reactors, from which plutonium cannot be recovered without special equipment.

7 *Chinese pilot defects to Taiwan*

During a routine patrol over Fukien Province, a 41-year-old Chinese Air

Inmates who seized a prison in Madrid were finally subdued by police on July 21.

CUEVAS—KAPPA PRESS/KATHERINE YOUNG

Force squadron pilot suddenly broke formation, swept across the Taiwan Strait, and defected to Taiwan. After landing his MiG-19 at the Tainan air base, he described life in mainland China as "miserable" and said he could no longer bear to live there. His wife and three children were left behind. The pilot qualified for about $600,000 in gold, the Nationalist government's standard offer to any Chinese pilot who defects to Taiwan with his plane.

Neutron weapons planned for NATO

The U.S. Defense Department expressed hope that within 18 months neutron weapons would be deployed in West Germany as part of NATO's tactical defense system. The production and deployment of such weapons, already approved by NATO officials, would need approval of President Carter and the U.S. Congress. Neutron weapons, also known as enhanced radiation warheads, which produce very high concentrations of short-lived radiation, are designed to kill enemy troops in a relatively circumscribed area without extensively damaging property.

8 *Pump station on trans-Alaska pipeline explodes*

A double explosion and fire at Pump Station No. 8 on the trans-Alaska pipeline killed one technician, injured five workers, and necessitated an immediate shutdown of valves that were controlling the first movement of Alaskan North Slope oil to the southern port of Valdez. Burning oil ran from the pumphouse near Fairbanks for 45 minutes. Investigators later announced that human error was responsible for the accident.

10 Japan holds elections for upper house of Diet

In an election involving one-half of the members of the House of Councillors (upper house of the Diet), Japanese voters failed to give the ruling Liberal-Democratic Party (LDP) under Prime Minister Takeo Fukuda an absolute majority. With the support of three independents, however, the LDP gained control of 128 of the 252 seats. The election followed the pattern established in December 1976 when the LDP emerged with a total of only 249 of 511 seats in the House of Representatives but maintained control in the lower house with the support of several independents.

11 Local London strike becomes national issue

An 11-month-old dispute over a union's right to act as arbitrator for 137 of some 500 workers at the Grunwick photo-processing plant in London reached national proportions when 4,000 policemen clashed with 11,000 pickets, many of whom came from other parts of the country. The pickets were also actively supported by 19 Labour Party members of Parliament.

13 Disastrous blackout hits New York

Several bolts of lightning triggered a series of massive power failures that finally plunged Westchester County and New York City into total darkness at 9:34 PM. When word spread that power could not be restored until the following day, the sweltering evening turned into a night of near-total chaos. Though volunteers quickly appeared to direct traffic with flashlights and help keep order in other ways, fires were set and thousands of stores were looted of food, clothing, furniture, and new cars. Police arrested some 3,200 looters, but they could not effectively contain the rampaging mobs.

British labour unions end voluntary wage restraints

The ruling Labour Party in Great Britain was told by labour leaders that the "social contract," voluntarily agreed to by workers in 1975 to help stem inflation, was no longer acceptable. In reply, Prime Minister Callaghan reportedly told union representatives that the government was still determined to limit wage increases to 10% during the next 12 months to protect Britain's uncertain economy and prevent another upsurge of inflation.

15 Carter approves admission of Indochinese refugees

Acceding to a request of the U.S. State Department, President Carter approved

The skyline of New York City at dawn during the blackout on July 13–14.

the admission to the U.S. of some 15,000 Laotian, Cambodian, and Vietnamese refugees, about half of whom were living on boats because they could not gain admission to other countries. The U.S. had previously accepted more than 150,000 Indochinese who had fled their homelands following Communist takeovers in 1975. Several other Western countries had also agreed to take in some refugees, including Australia, Canada, and New Zealand.

16 North Korea releases three bodies, surviving crewman from downed helicopter

Following a day of calm but intense negotiation with the U.S., North Korea returned the bodies of three American servicemen whose CH-47 helicopter was shot down on July 14 when it inadvertently strayed into North Korean airspace. A fourth crewman, who survived the crash with apparently only minor injury, was released at the same time. Although President Carter welcomed North Korea's prompt return of the crew, he condemned what he felt was an unwarranted loss of life.

17 Israel announces anti-inflation steps

Israel's newly formed government acted to check the country's soaring inflation rate with the announcement of a major austerity policy, to include an "unprecedented cut" in government spending. An immediate rise in the price of most basic goods and services was expected.

South Korea frees 14 government foes

In an apparent goodwill gesture to President Carter, South Korean Pres. Park Chung Hee released 14 of an estimated

260 of his political opponents under detention in government prisons, a move that came on the 29th anniversary of the country's first republican constitution. Among those freed were four Christian clergymen arrested in 1976 on charges of plotting to overthrow the government. President Park cited the repentance and good behaviour of the 14 and indicated that other prisoners who behaved as well would also be released.

18 Rhodesia's Smith calls for voter mandate on black rule

Rhodesian Prime Minister Ian Smith announced the immediate dissolution of Parliament and called for new general elections to be held August 31. He attributed his decision to the unsuitability of recent British proposals for settlement of the issue of black majority rule. The elections would test voter approval of an internal political settlement with certain black nationalist leaders that would include a new constitution and a broad-based government incorporating black Rhodesians.

20 CIA experiments in behaviour control revealed

According to U.S. Central Intelligence Agency documents obtained for public use under the 1966 Freedom of Information Act, the CIA conducted secret medical experiments from 1949 through the mid-1960s to develop methods of controlling human behaviour through the use of chemical, biological, and radiological agents. Public access to other agency documents later revealed the involvement of private medical research foundations and nongovernment scientists in the program, which encouraged and funded the testing of drugs and other materials and techniques on human subjects, including prisoners and mental patients.

21 Thais and Cambodians engage in major border clash

A battle between heavily armed Cambodian and Thai troops, in which 17 Thai soldiers and an estimated 50 Cambodians were killed, erupted along the Thai-Cambodian frontier in the vicinity of Aranyaprathet, the main regional Thai town. The clash, which involved Thai tanks and air support, was described by the Thai military command as a sharp escalation of the border skirmishes that had been almost daily occurrences since the Communist takeover of Cambodia in 1975.

Egypt and Libya intensify border war

Climaxing a series of border clashes in recent weeks, Egypt and Libya mounted bloody forays into each other's territory, with both sides employing armoured vehicles and air strikes against military targets along the Mediterranean seacoast. After four days of conflict during which Egyptian jets attacked deep inside Libya, Egyptian Pres. Anwar as-Sadat on July 24 unilaterally called for a cease-fire, which was also observed by Libya. Mediation efforts by Arab leaders including Algerian Pres. Houari Boumédienne and Yasir Arafat, head of the Palestine Liberation Organization, met with success in maintaining the truce.

Prison riot crushed in Spain

Spanish riot police used tear gas, rubber bullets, and dynamite to end a four-day mutiny at Madrid's Carabanchel prison. The rebellion had been at the centre of countrywide riots and demonstrations by more than 2,000 prisoners, who were demanding that the amnesty program of King Juan Carlos be extended to include all common criminals. Since commencement of the program in August 1976 about 600 political prisoners and 6,000

inmates held for nonpolitical offenses had been released.

Prime Minister Bandaranaike defeated in Sri Lanka vote

The United National Party of Junius Richard Jayawardene swept to an overwhelming victory over supporters of Prime Minister Sirimavo Bandaranaike in parliamentary elections. The United Nationals took 139 seats, up from 19, in the 168-member National State Assembly, whereas Mrs. Bandaranaike's ruling Freedom Party kept only 8 of the 91 seats it had held in the previous Assembly. As the new prime minister, Jayawardene announced his intentions to replace Sri Lanka's parliamentary system of government with a presidential system modeled after that of France.

22 Purged Chinese leader returns to power

In an official communiqué the Chinese government announced the rehabilitation of purged leader Teng Hsiao-p'ing, who had fallen into disgrace in April 1976 during the struggle for power that followed the death of Premier Chou En-lai. Teng was reinstated as deputy premier, a post that gave him third ranking among Chinese leaders. The same announcement described the political expulsion of the "gang of four," a group of Teng's ultraradical opponents that included Chiang Ch'ing, the widow of Mao Tse-tung.

23 Three Hanafi Muslims convicted of second-degree murder

After deliberating for more than 19 hours, an all-black jury found Hanafi Muslim leader Hamaas Abdul Khaalis and two followers guilty of kidnapping, conspiracy, and second-degree murder during the seizure in March of three buildings in Washington, D.C. Nine other co-defendants were convicted of conspiracy and kidnapping. On September 6

a Superior Court judge imposed heavy sentences, tantamount to life imprisonment, on the principal defendants. He then ordered the defendants' court-appointed attorney to file an appeal.

26 U.S. agrees to slow Korean pullout

Responding to South Korean requests for a strong deterrent force to remain as long as possible, the U.S. announced its agreement to retain the bulk of its Korean-based ground troops in that country until the final year of its planned combat-troop withdrawal sometime in the early 1980s. In June, Carter administration officials had announced a timetable for the pullout, which included plans for the phased departure of all 33,000 ground troops within 4–5 years. Implementation of the new agreement would keep two brigades in South Korea until the last months of the pullout.

28 Alaskan oil finally reaches Valdez

The first oil from Alaska's Prudhoe Bay oil fields, originally scheduled to reach the southern port of Valdez in 7½ days, finally reached its terminus after more than 38½ days. Accidents, faulty welds, and sabotage required several shutdowns during the transit of the oil.

31 Demonstrators clash with police at French nuclear complex

A massive protest march, supported by thousands of West Germans, Swiss, Scandinavians, Belgians, and Italians, erupted into violence when 5,000 riot policemen tried to prevent helmeted youths, armed with clubs, from invading the construction site of a fast breeder nuclear reactor complex at Creys-Malville in eastern France. The protesters were especially incensed that the reactor was designed to be fueled by plutonium, which can be diverted to military use. A policeman lost a hand when a tear-gas grenade exploded before it could be thrown and one demonstrator was trampled to death.

AUGUST

1 North Korea establishes "military sea boundary"

North Korea announced the creation of a "military sea boundary" extending up to 50 mi along both its western and eastern borders. All foreign ships and planes would need permission to enter. South Korea, Japan, the U.S., and the UN Command all said that they would not recognize such boundaries.

Pakistan election slated for mid-October

Four days after freeing former Prime Minister Zulfikar Ali Bhutto from prison,

the military government of Pakistan announced that national and provincial elections would be held October 18. Gen. Mohammad Zia-ul-Haq, chief martial law administrator, who led the overthrow of Bhutto on July 5, urged Bhutto to be a candidate even though his election on March 7, which was denounced as fraudulent, had led to prolonged nationwide riots.

4 Carter approves new Department of Energy

President Carter signed legislation creating a Department of Energy, the director of which would become a member of the

Cabinet. Two days earlier the measure was approved in the U.S. Senate by a vote of 76–14 and in the House of Representatives by 353–57.

Carter urges action on the status of illegal aliens

As a step toward solving numerous problems stemming from the presence of between 4 million and 12 million illegal aliens in the U.S., President Carter presented Congress with a series of proposals that included the issuance of permanent resident alien status to illegal aliens who had entered the U.S. before the end of 1969 and had resided continuously in

An illegal alien trapped at the
U.S.–Mexican border.

the U.S. since that time. A five-year temporary resident alien status was suggested for those who arrived between 1970 and the end of 1976. Civil fines of up to $1,000 were suggested for those who knowingly hire an illegal alien, and criminal penalties for those who act as brokers in such hirings.

5 Nyerere and Carter agree on African policy

After two days of talks with Pres. Julius Nyerere of Tanzania, President Carter said the two had reached "almost complete agreement" on a diplomatic policy that would promote a peaceful transition to black majority rule in both Rhodesia and South West Africa (Namibia).

Vorster denounces U.S. African policy

Describing U.S. policy for southern Africa as "strangulation with finesse," Prime Minister B.J. Vorster of South Africa bitterly characterized President Carter's recent statements as an effort to placate U.S. blacks who helped elect him to the presidency. Vorster's remarks raised doubts about his continued willingness to help end white minority rule in Rhodesia, which was dependent on South Africa for oil, arms, and access to the sea.

6 IMF loans arranged for financially pressed nations

At a meeting in Paris, 14 nations agreed to contribute a total of some $10 billion to a loan fund, which the International Monetary Fund would make available to countries suffering financial difficulties provided they adopted recommended fiscal policies. The two largest contributions

came from Saudi Arabia, which promised $2.5 billion, and from the U.S., which pledged $1.7 billion.

New welfare program proposed by Carter

The outline of an entirely new welfare system was explained by President Carter, who expressed hope that Congress would begin legislative action in 1978. The program, calling for the creation of up to 1.4 million government-provided jobs, would strengthen work requirements for welfare recipients and provide financial incentives for workers to leave public service jobs for private industry.

7 New prime minister named in Iran

Jamshid Amouzegar, a 54-year-old engineer who served as his country's minister of oil, was named prime minister of Iran. Emir Abbas Hoveida, who resigned the prime ministership after more than 12 years in office, became a key adviser to the shah as minister of the imperial court.

10 Queen Elizabeth visits Northern Ireland

As part of her Silver Jubilee celebration, Queen Elizabeth II began a two-day visit to Northern Ireland under heavy security. Roman Catholics, protesting English rule in Northern Ireland, set off bombs and clashed with police when the protesters attempted to reach Hillsborough Castle where the queen received her guests. The violence, which began before the queen arrived, continued after her departure for Scotland.

Panama and the U.S. reach agreement on Panama Canal's future

Panamanian and U.S. negotiators announced they had reached "agreement in principle" on "the basic elements" of a new accord that would give Panama complete control over the Panama Canal and the Panama Canal Zone by the year 2000. Though President Carter affirmed that the two new treaties and the economic agreement would "help to usher in a new day in hemispheric relations," a fierce political battle was certain to erupt in the U.S. Senate, where a two-thirds majority is needed for ratification. Former governor Ronald Reagan of California was also expected to organize strong and vocal opposition to the proposal.

Argentina's cost of living still rising, but more slowly

Argentina's military government announced that the cost of living rose 7.6% during the month of July, for a total increase of 64.1% during the first seven months of the year. The predicted inflation rate of 140% for the entire year would, however, be a dramatic improvement over the 347.5% reported for 1976.

11 Casualties mount in Somali-Ethiopian conflict

During an intense month-long battle in southeastern Ethiopia, Somali and Ethiopian casualties were unofficially estimated to be in the tens of thousands. The Ethiopian government accused the neighbouring Somali Democratic Republic of actively aiding the West Somalia Liberation Front, arguing that the ethnic Somalis in Ethiopia could not conduct air strikes and other effective military operations without such support. Somalia denied the charges.

13 Demonstrators clash in London

Members of the right-wing National Front and hundreds of supporters moved into Lewisham, a multiracial neighbourhood of London, to protest widespread muggings in the city. A bloody street fight followed when the marchers were confronted by angry counterdemonstrators in the area. Riot police arrested about 214 persons. Some 100 persons, including many police officers, were injured during the disturbance.

14 Northern Territory assured of Australian statehood

Voters in Australia's Northern Territory renewed the Liberal-Country Party's control of the legislative assembly after being assured during the campaign that the territory would become Australia's seventh state.

17 Egypt suspends trade with the Soviet Union

The Egyptian government suspended trade with the Soviet Union and Czechoslovakia after claiming that recent trade agreements had been deliberately violated. Egyptian officials stated that the delivery of tanks, already paid for, tools, spare parts, and many other items had been so long overdue that Egyptian cotton and other products earmarked for the U.S.S.R. would now be offered to such countries as China, Japan, West Germany, and Switzerland.

18 Bermuda premier announces resignation

After two years in office, Premier John Sharpe, under pressure from his own strife-ridden United Bermuda Party, agreed to resign on August 26. Earlier in the year most of the Cabinet ministers denounced Sharpe as incompetent and resigned their posts.

China concludes 11th party congress

The 11th congress of the Chinese Communist Party ended in Peking after the selection of a new 23-member Politburo, the publication of a new party constitution, and the announcement that the arrest in 1976 of Mao Tse-tung's widow and three of her close associates marked the "triumphant conclusion" of the Cultural Revolution, which created a great upheaval during the late 1960s. Sinologists, working with meagre information, generally agreed that China was now clearly moving away from many basic policies established by Chairman Mao. The three pivotal leaders—Hua Kuo-feng, Yeh Chien-ying, and Teng Hsiao-p'ing—were expected to place great emphasis on modern technology, productivity, and education. No reconciliation between China and the Soviet Union was expected in the foreseeable future.

19 *Government workers in Australia forbidden to strike*

After a week-long strike by some 3,000 postal workers in Sydney, the Australian Parliament passed legislation that outlawed strikes by government employees. The move increased the possibility that Prime Minister Malcolm Fraser would call for an early national election to challenge the power of the labour unions.

22 *South Africa denies planning nuclear tests*

In a direct reply to an inquiry from President Carter, South Africa informed the U.S. that, contrary to reports circulated by the Soviet news agency Tass and reinforced by statements of the foreign minister of France, South Africa had no intention of conducting nuclear tests "now or in the future."

25 *March for human rights dispersed in Manila*

During the World Peace Through Law Conference held in Manila, some 2,000 persons defied a 1972 martial law decree by holding a three-hour rally followed by a protest march to denounce alleged violations of human rights in the Philippines. The police used water cannons and nightsticks to disperse the marchers, some 100 of whom were injured in the melee.

Australia lifts ban on mining and export of uranium

Prime Minister Malcolm Fraser announced that the Australian government had rescinded its ban on the mining and export of uranium. The decision to increase sources of energy for an energy-deficient world, Fraser said, was taken with due regard for the environment and the need to restrict the proliferation of nuclear weapons.

Vance ends visit to China

U.S. Secretary of State Cyrus R. Vance concluded four days of talks with Chinese leaders in Peking on the normalization of Sino-American relations. In guarded statements Vance described the discussions as "candid and serious," add-

ing that they had "enhanced our mutual understanding." Reporters concluded that China was still demanding that the U.S. abrogate its 1954 mutual security treaty with Taiwan and completely sever all other ties with the Nationalist government.

26 *Quebec passes new language bill*

The government of Quebec passed a new law making French the official language of the province. One of the major sections of the bill concerned access to English-language schools. Bill 101 permits children to attend such schools if either parent received an English-language elementary school education in Quebec; or if either parent, domiciled in Quebec at the time the law was passed, received an elementary school education in English outside Quebec. A child (as well as younger brothers and sisters) may also continue his or her education in an English-language secondary or lower-level

Demonstrators protested Queen Elizabeth II's visit to Belfast in August.

PETER MARLOW—SYGMA

school provided the original enrollment was in accord with government regulations. Such restrictions were designed to prevent English-speaking Canadians from other parts of Canada and the children of immigrants from entering English-language schools in Quebec. Camille Laurin, the sponsor of the bill, made it clear that the provincial government intended to make Quebec as French as Ontario is English.

27 *Philippines releases 500 prisoners*

Military authorities announced the release of 500 prisoners, all imprisoned since the imposition of martial law on Sept. 23, 1972. Though most were ordinary criminals, 89 had been accused of sedition. Of the 4,700 martial law prisoners reported to be under detention two months earlier, 1,500 had since been released.

29 *Violence subsides in Sri Lanka*

The *Daily News* of Colombo reported that most of the violence directed against the Tamil minority in Sri Lanka had ended after two weeks of nationwide turmoil. More than 100 persons lost their lives as arsonists and looters attacked thousands of stores and homes. The trouble began in northern Sri Lanka, where most of the new Tamil immigrants from India had settled. The long smoldering antagonism that the Sinhalese and Tamils had harboured toward each other was rekindled during the national election in July when the Tamil United Liberation Front campaigned for an independent Tamil state in the north and won the second-largest party representation in the National State Assembly (parliament).

30 *Tito given warm welcome in Peking*

Marshal Tito, president of Yugoslavia, received an enthusiastic welcome on his first visit to China. He was met at the airport by Chairman Hua Kuo-feng and other leading officials, who arranged the largest reception in years for a visiting head of state. Tito, whose journey first took him to the Soviet Union and North Korea, was not expected to discuss substantive issues during his stay.

31 *Ian Smith wins crucial Rhodesian vote*

Prime Minister Ian Smith's Rhodesian Front Party won a resounding victory in national elections by capturing all 50 seats available to whites in the 66-seat Parliament. The newly formed Rhodesian Action Party, a vocal right-wing group of whites, won only 9% of the popular vote, compared with 83% for the Rhodesian Front. Smith viewed his victory as a mandate to negotiate a direct political settlement with the black majority, which was demanding an end to white minority rule. Proposals submitted by British and U.S. goodwill negotiators were, at least temporarily, in abeyance.

SEPTEMBER

1 Cuba and the U.S. exchange low-level missions

Cuba and the U.S. took a modest step toward gradual restoration of full diplomatic recognition by opening "interest sections" in each other's capital. The agreement to do so had been reached on May 30.

6 Park Tong Sun indicted on felony charges

The U.S. Department of Justice formally charged Korean businessman Park Tong Sun with 36 felonies. U.S. Attorney General Griffin B. Bell told reporters he wanted Park returned to the U.S. from South Korea to face charges of conspiracy, bribery, mail fraud, and racketeering; Park was also accused of making illegal campaign contributions and failing to register as a foreign agent working for the benefit of the South Korean government. Named as unindicted co-conspirators were two former heads of the South Korean Central Intelligence Agency and Richard T. Hanna, a former U.S. Democratic congressman from California.

7 Panama Canal accords signed in Washington, D.C.

U.S. President Carter and Panamanian leader Brig. Gen. Omar Torrijos Herrera signed accords that, after ratification by both countries, would give Panama eventual control over the Panama Canal and the Panama Canal Zone. Representatives from 26 other Western Hemisphere countries supported the measure by attending the ceremony at the invitation of President Carter. The U.S. Senate was not expected to vote on ratification until sometime next year.

British unions agree to one yearly raise

The 11.5 million members of British labour unions, voting through some 1,000 delegates at the Trades Union Congress in Blackpool, England, substantially endorsed (62%) a return to free collective bargaining after two years of controls. In a significant gesture, however, the unions agreed to just one raise each year to avoid upsetting the nation's economy.

Wisconsin judge ousted by irate voters

In the first judicial recall election in Wisconsin history, Dane County Judge Archie E. Simonson was voted out of office by outraged citizens who refused to accept his contention that rape is a "normal" male reaction to provocative female dress and modern society's permissive attitude toward sex. Simonson's comments were meant to explain why he had sentenced a 15-year-old boy to just one year of probation in the custody of his parents for the rape of a modestly dressed 16-year-old girl.

8 Trudeau and Carter agree on gas pipeline from Alaska

Prime Minister Pierre Elliott Trudeau of Canada and President Carter announced an agreement on the construction of a pipeline to carry Alaskan natural gas across Canada to the lower 48 states. After final details were worked out, the project would require approval of both the Canadian Parliament and the U.S. Congress.

12 Norwegians retain Prime Minister Nordli

Norwegian voters gave the ruling Labour Party of Prime Minister Odvar Nordli 76 seats in the 155-seat Storting (parliament), an increase of 14 but still 2 short of a majority. Nordli's Socialist Left supporters lost heavily, but the two seats they won gave the Labour Party a 78–77 working majority over the three-party nonsocialist opposition.

15 South Africa arrests 1,200 students mourning death of Biko

South African police arrested 1,200 black students who had gathered at the University of Fort Hare in Alice to commemorate the death of Steven Biko, the country's best known young black leader. Even though no violence had occurred, the government cited violations of the Riotous Assemblies Act to justify its action. Officials reported that Biko, taken into police custody a month earlier, was on a hunger strike for eight days before he died in Pretoria. Though an autopsy report was promised, some newspaper editors and politicians also demanded a judicial inquiry.

Pakistan ends state of emergency

Gen. Mohammad Zia-ul-Haq declared an end to Pakistan's state of emergency, which had been in effect since November 1971. The announcement preceded by three days the start of political campaigns leading up to national elections on October 18. General Zia also cut two months from all prison terms, thereby permitting six leaders of former prime minister Zulfikar Ali Bhutto's Pakistan People's Party to begin immediate preparations for the campaign.

16 Dissidents reject Episcopal Church

At the end of a three-day meeting in St. Louis, Mo., some 1,700 Episcopalians enthusiastically supported a charter calling for the establishment of an independent body to be named the Anglican Church in North America. The decision was prompted mainly by the Episcopal Church's endorsement in September 1976 of priestly ordination of women. A substantial revision of The Book of Common Prayer and liberal attitudes toward abortion and divorce also disturbed the dis-

The body of Steven Biko being carried on an oxcart in a funeral procession in South Africa.

SELWYN TAIT—SYGMA

senters, who characterized their stand as simple fidelity to traditional church teachings. The successionist charter provides for a constitutional assembly, to be convoked by bishops and entrusted with the task of working out a permanent church structure.

17 *China explodes nuclear device*

The Chinese news agency Hsinhua announced in Peking that China had exploded its 22nd nuclear device. Specific details about the nature and size of the blast were not disclosed. The last such test in China occurred on Nov. 17, 1976.

20 *Vietnam and Djibouti admitted to UN membership*

At the opening of the 32nd annual session of the UN General Assembly, Vietnam was admitted to membership together with Djibouti, a former French colony in eastern Africa. The assembly also elected Lazar Mojsov, deputy foreign minister of Yugoslavia, president. The UN was expected to devote most of its time to critical problems in southern Africa and the Middle East.

Amin bans most Christian churches in Uganda

Pres. Idi Amin categorized 27 religious organizations in Uganda as security risks and banned them from the country. Among those affected were Baha'i, the Salvation Army, the Seventh-day Adventists, and the Uganda Baptists. The only religious groups exempted were Muslims, Anglicans, Roman Catholics, and Orthodox Christians.

South African elections set for late November

Faced with a mounting political crisis, Prime Minister B. J. Vorster of South Africa dissolved the nation's all-white Parliament and the provincial councils, then called for general elections on November 30. Besides seeking local endorsement of South Africa's right to determine its own domestic policies without foreign interference, Vorster hoped for approval of a new constitution that would sanction three separate parliaments: one for whites, one for Coloureds (citizens of mixed blood), and one for Indians. All three bodies would function under a president and his Cabinet. South Africa's 18 million Bantu would continue to be classified as citizens of black tribal homelands still existing within the country.

21 *Bert Lance resigns post under pressure*

President Carter announced he had accepted with "regret and sorrow" the resignation of Bert Lance as director of the Office of Management and Budget. On September 15 the Senate Governmental Affairs Committee began to question

WIDE WORLD

Nguyen Duy Trinh (right), Vietnam foreign minister, and Hassan Gouled Aptidon (left), president of newly independent Djibouti, were welcomed at the United Nations by General Assembly President Lazar Mojsov of Yugoslavia.

Lance about alleged improprieties connected with his personal financial dealings while chief executive officer of the Calhoun (Ga.) First National Bank and later as president of the National Bank of Georgia in Atlanta. Attention focused on Lance's huge personal bank overdrafts, alleged use of the same collateral for two bank loans, and the use of a business airplane for trips that reportedly also involved politics. Though Lance contended that he had done nothing illegal, he was apparently convinced that only resignation would quell the storm and minimize the adverse effect it could have on the Carter administration.

23 *Concorde landings across the U.S. get qualified support*

U.S. Secretary of Transportation Brock Adams proposed that the current fleet of 16 Concorde supersonic planes, developed at great cost by Great Britain and France, be allowed to land at 13 U.S. cities unless local authorities banned them as a result of "reasonable, nondiscriminatory noise rules." The planes, however, would not be allowed to travel over land at supersonic speeds nor could they move in and out of airports between 10 PM and 7 AM. If more Concordes were built, they would have to meet all U.S. federal noise standards before being granted landing rights.

25 *Swiss reject more liberal abortion law*

In a national referendum in Switzerland, a bill seeking to extend abortion to any

woman during the first 12 weeks of her pregnancy failed to win either of the two majorities it needed for passage. The measure was rejected by 17 of the 25 cantons and by an overall majority of voters. The current law on abortion requires a statement from two doctors that a pregnancy endangers a woman's life or at least seriously threatens her health.

Biko funeral in South Africa emotional but nonviolent

Steven Biko, a 30-year-old black leader who died in police custody on September 12, was buried in a simple grave outside King William's Town. In an unprecedented demonstration of support for South African blacks, 13 Western nations sent official representatives. Before the funeral, emotions ran high during a three-and-one-half-hour ceremony at a local rugby field, but no major violence occurred. Later, however, two black policemen were reportedly stoned to death by mourners returning to the black township of Mdantsane.

26 *Laker Airways begins cheap London– New York flights*

Laker Airways completed its first daily transatlantic low-fare flight from London to New York with 270 passengers aboard its 345-seat DC-10 Skytrain. Each paid approximately $102 for the no-frills flight, which was booked on a first-come, first-served basis on the day of departure. Tickets for the New York to London flight were about $30 more expensive. Other British and U.S. airlines quickly announced that they would inaugurate competitive services.

Cease-fire declared in Israeli-Lebanon border area

After ten days of intense fighting between Palestinian guerrillas and Israeli-supported Lebanese Christians, a cease-fire went into effect. Israeli troops then returned to positions south of the Lebanese border. Although details of the cease-fire were not published, the Palestinians were expected to move away from Israel's northern border and its nearby settlements.

28 *Cambodian leader arrives in China*

In his first publicized visit outside Cambodia since the end of the Indochina war, Pol Pot was warmly received in Peking by top Chinese leaders. For the first time Pol Pot—whose true identity remained a matter of conjecture—was publicly identified as secretary of the Central Committee of the Cambodian Communist Party. No previous mention of a Communist Party in Cambodia had ever been made. A Phnom Penh radio station simultaneously announced that the Cambodian Communist Party would celebrate the 17th anniversary of its founding on September 29.

OCTOBER

1 U.S. and Soviet Union issue joint statement on Middle East

In an effort to encourage Arabs and Israelis to reconvene the Geneva conference before the end of the year, U.S. and Soviet diplomats issued a joint statement urging "all the parties in the conflict to understand the necessity for careful consideration of each other's legitimate rights and interests and to demonstrate mutual readiness to act accordingly." Although the statement included no specific recommendations for a peace settlement and made no mention of an independent homeland for the Palestinians, an Israeli official said his government rejected the declaration "with both hands."

Pakistan national elections canceled

Gen. Mohammad Zia-ul-Haq, head of Pakistan's military government since the overthrow of former prime minister Zulfikar Ali Bhutto on July 5, canceled national elections slated for October 18 on the grounds that elections that soon would be "an invitation to a new crisis." Zia announced no new date for the elections but said that criminal charges against Bhutto and some of his aides, should be settled first.

3 Indira Gandhi arrested in India

Former prime minister Indira Gandhi of India was arrested on two charges of corruption while in office, but she was released within 24 hours when a court magistrate ruled there was insufficient evidence to support the accusations. Since her defeat in the March elections, Gandhi had been holding political rallies around the country.

Japanese hijackers surrender in Algeria

Eleven members of the Japanese Red Army, a left-wing terrorist group, surrendered to authorities in Algiers, ending a five-day ordeal that began on September 28 with the hijacking of a Japan Air Lines DC-8 over India. The plane first landed at Dacca, Bangladesh, where 115 of the 151 hostages were set free after the Japanese government paid $6 million in ransom and flew six members of the Red Army to Dacca after their release from prison. Seven additional hostages were let go in Kuwait, 10 in Damascus, Syria, and the last 19 in Algiers.

Supreme Court refuses to hear cases on homosexual rights

The U.S. Supreme Court refused to hear two cases involving homosexuals who contended their constitutional rights had been violated when they were no longer

HENRI BUREAU—SYGMA

The body of the slain pilot of a West German airliner is carried away from the plane at Mogadishu, Somalia.

permitted to teach. The Supreme Court thus let stand decisions of lower courts in the states of Washington and New Jersey.

7 Soviet Union adopts new constitution

With only minor changes, the Soviet Union adopted the new constitution first publicized in draft form on June 4. As with the old Stalinist constitution of 1936, no assumption was made that Soviet citizens have any rights other than those granted by the state.

8 Wages of Chinese workers to be increased

In an attempt to spur the nation's economy through greater worker productivity, the Central Committee of China's Communist Party approved wage increases. The move was interpreted as a departure from the policies of the late Mao Tse-tung and was expected to benefit most those at the lowest levels of the wage scale.

10 Soviet cosmonauts abort space mission

After less than 50 hours in space, two Soviet cosmonauts returned to Earth after failing to link their Soyuz 25 spacecraft to the orbiting Salyut 6 scientific research space station. No official explanation was given for abandoning the mission.

Moro insurgents kill Filipino general and aides

A brigadier general of the Philippine Army and 33 other military personnel were killed without warning when they arrived at a market on Jolo Island to discuss amnesty with a leader of the Moro National Liberation Front. Though thou-

sands of Moros had reportedly been won over by government offers during the past few years, others were still demanding political and economic autonomy for their region.

11 President of Yemen assassinated

Col. Ibrahim al-Hamdi, president of the Yemen Arab Republic, was machine-gunned to death in the capital city of San'a' by unidentified assassins. His brother, Col. Abdullah Mohammed al-Hamdi, also died in the attack.

13 Carter attacks U.S. oil industry

With his energy program being dismantled in the U.S. congress, Carter accused petroleum lobbyists of being the chief opponents of his program. The president then noted that a veto, gasoline rationing, and a tax on imported oil were options available to him if Congress failed to pass acceptable legislation.

14 Former U.S. congressman indicted for part in Korean scandal

A federal grand jury indicted former U.S. representative Richard T. Hanna of California on 40 felony charges, which included conspiracy to manipulate the policies of the U.S. government and Congress in favour of the Republic of Korea and attempts to secure bribes for his illegal activities.

17 U.S. Supreme Court permits Concorde landing in New York

After 19 months of legal battles, a ruling by the U.S. Supreme Court finally cleared the way for the supersonic Concorde to begin test flights into New York City's Kennedy International Airport. If noise standards were met, the Anglo-French plane was expected to start commercial flights on November 22.

18 West German troops storm hijacked plane in Somalia

A specially trained West German commando unit, flown to Mogadishu, Somalia, attacked a hijacked Lufthansa 737 with explosives, "blinding" grenades, and automatic firearms in the early hours of the morning. Three of the four hijackers were killed in the assault but all 86 hostages were freed. The pilot, however, had been shot in Yemen, reportedly for refusing to take off for Somalia. The plane, which was hijacked by Palestinian terrorists shortly after it took off from Majorca, made successive stops in Italy, Cyprus, Bahrain, Dubai, and the Yemen Arab Republic before finally landing in Somalia. The hijackers had demanded the release of 11 terrorists jailed in West Germany and two Palestinians imprisoned in Turkey.

Queen Elizabeth II visits Canada

During a six-day Silver Jubilee visit to Canada, Queen Elizabeth II opened a new session of Parliament with a speech from the throne which, as always, expressed the official views and goals of the ruling party. Speaking alternately in English and French, the queen referred to the current crisis of unity in the country and acknowledged that at present French Canadians were not provided with "the opportunity to fulfill their reasonable aspirations."

Three German terrorists die in prison

West German officials announced that three members of the Baader-Meinhof terrorist group had committed suicide in a maximum-security prison in Stuttgart. One died by hanging, the others from gunshot wounds. Prison officials could not explain how the guns were acquired and concealed. Leftists insisted that the prisoners had been murdered and vowed vengeance.

Yankees win World Series

The New York Yankees, representing the American League, won the World Series of professional baseball by defeating the Los Angeles Dodgers of the National League four games to two. Yankee outfielder Reggie Jackson set several records, including three consecutive home runs, all on the first pitch, during the final game.

19 South Africa intensifies control over blacks

In one of the most drastic curtailments of political freedom in years, the South African government banned numerous or-

ganizations, rounded up dozens of political activists, suppressed the principal black newspaper, the *World*, arrested its editor, Percy Qoboza, and suspended the civil rights of some whites who opposed apartheid. Many of those affected by the government's action were publicly committed to peaceful change. On October 13 a government official announced that the ban on proscribed organizations would be permanent.

20 Thailand's civilian government ousted by military

The civilian government of Prime Minister Thanin Kraivichien was ousted by the same military officers who installed it one year earlier. The junta, which charged that the government had created disunity and was responsible for the nation's economic decline, promised elections during the coming year and said that in the interim it would rule through a panel of civilians.

21 Tito completes overseas trip

President Tito of Yugoslavia returned home to Belgrade after a ten-day tour that took him to France, Portugal, and Algeria. During August the 85-year-old ruler spent 24 days visiting the Soviet Union, North Korea, and China. Observers believed that the energetic but aging leader, who had not yet designated a successor, was seeking to solidify Yugoslavia's international relations and reaffirm the nation's nonalignment policy while he was still vigorous enough to travel.

Pope Paul VI being greeted by crowds at Pescara, Italy.

HENRI BUREAU—SYGMA

22 United Nations urged to debate airline security

After pilots on international flights threatened a two-day strike to protest inadequate security measures at some airports and the harbouring of hijackers by certain countries, representatives of 42 nations urged the United Nations to debate the issue of airline safety in the General Assembly. The initiative was not endorsed by Arab nations, the Soviet Union, other Communist countries and African nations.

23 Panama Canal treaties ratified in plebiscite

In the highest voter turnout in Panama's history, voters ratified the Panama Canal treaties by a 2–1 margin. Though the government hoped for a 90% majority, it expressed satisfaction with the result. Those who voted against ratification generally objected that Panama was not getting complete and unqualified control over the canal.

29 Pope Paul VI concludes synod in Rome

Pope Paul VI concluded the four-week-long fifth synod of Roman Catholic bishops with an appeal to government leaders to protect and promote the human rights of individuals and to grant them true freedom of religion. The synod, which discussed ways to make religious instruction of adults and children more effective, concurred with Asian and especially African prelates that religious instruction should be adapted to specific cultures.

30 Israel moves toward a freer economy

After living for 29 years under socialist policies espoused by successive Labour Party governments, Israelis were unprepared for the sudden price increases that followed a government announcement that new economic policies would include an end to export incentives and to subsidies for basic commodities. In addition, the value-added tax on all goods and services would go from 8 to 12%. Various groups of workers staged short protest strikes and the Histadrut labour federation demanded a 10% increase in salaries by January.

31 UN move to impose economic sanctions against South Africa vetoed

An African-sponsored resolution calling for severe economic sanctions against South Africa was vetoed in the UN Security Council by Britain, France, and the U.S. Canada and West Germany also voted against the measure. The other ten members voted for sanctions. There was, however, unanimous agreement in condemning South Africa for recent "massive violence and repression" directed against the country's blacks.

NOVEMBER

1 U.S. quits International Labour Organization

With the approval of President Carter, the U.S. announced that it was formally canceling its membership in the International Labour Organization. The U.S. had given the required two-year notice earlier, and stated at the time that it would dissociate itself from the ILO unless the organization shed its political bias and applied a single standard in evaluating labour conditions in all parts of the world. The U.S. also ceased its $20 million annual contribution, which covered about 25% of the ILO's budget.

New law increases U.S. minimum wage

President Carter signed into law legislation that would increase the minimum wage from $2.30 an hour to $2.65 on Jan. 1, 1978. In successive years it would increase, respectively, to $2.90, $3.10, and finally to $3.35 on Jan. 1, 1981. The overall increase would amount to 45%. The first minimum wage bill was signed by Pres. Franklin D. Roosevelt in June 1938 and went into effect the following October. It "put a floor under wages and a ceiling over hours" by making it illegal to pay wage workers less than 25 cents an hour or work them more than 44 hours a week without compensation for overtime.

4 Former head of CIA sentenced

Richard Helms, former director of the U.S. Central Intelligence Agency, was fined $2,000 and given a suspended two-year sentence by U.S. District Court Judge Barrington Parker. On October 31 Helms pleaded no contest when charged with two counts of failing to testify "fully, completely, and accurately" before a Senate committee investigating CIA activities in Chile. Helms's lawyer contended that his client had been "impaled on the horns of a moral and legal dilemma" because the oath of secrecy he was required to take as director of the agency was in direct conflict with the oath required before giving testimony to the Senate.

UN orders arms embargo against South Africa

All 15 member nations of the UN Security Council approved a resolution calling for an immediate mandatory ban on military aid to South Africa. The action was directly linked to the government's repressive social policies and marked the first time in UN history that such punitive measures were applied against a member nation. The UN resolution could affect current as well as future contracts having military significance. However,

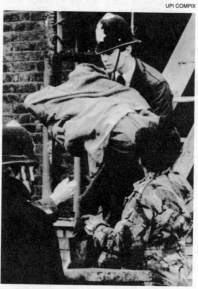

UPI COMPIX

The body of a child is removed from a burned building in London by police during a national strike by firemen.

South Africa was capable of satisfying most of its own military needs.

9 Egypt and Israel move toward peace

Anwar as-Sadat, president of Egypt, declared in an unexpected statement that he was "ready to go to the Israeli parliament itself" in order to overcome obstacles that had so long stood in the way of permanent peace in the Middle East. In an emotional reply on November 11, Prime Minister Menahem Begin of Israel welcomed Sadat's proposal and urged Egyptians and Israelis to join in "a silent oath" that there would be "no more wars, no more bloodshed, and no more threats." These dramatic developments created worldwide excitement and raised hopes that, despite formidable differences of opinion, a lasting peace might finally take hold in that troubled area.

Israeli jets raid Lebanon

Following the shelling of the northern Israeli town of Nahariyya on November 6 and 8 by forces of the Palestine Liberation Organization, Israeli jets attacked areas in southern Lebanon, the first such Israeli raids in nearly two years. Government officials in Lebanon reported widespread damage and more than 100 fatalities, most of them Lebanese civilians.

13 Somalia expels Soviets and Cubans

In an abrupt announcement, the government of Somalia ordered several thousand Soviet advisers to leave the country within a week and Cuban personnel to

depart within 48 hours. The Somali government also broke diplomatic relations with Cuba and terminated its 1974 treaty of friendship and cooperation with the U.S.S.R., one consequence of which was to deny the Soviets further use of several strategically important military bases. Somalia charged that the U.S.S.R. and Cuba had brazenly supported the central government of Ethiopia in its war against ethnic Somalis in the Ogaden region of the country. The Somalis were seeking to separate the Ogaden from Ethiopia.

14 British firemen strike

Some 30,000 British firemen began a national strike to back up their demand for a 30% increase in pay; the government had rejected the demand because it was three times greater than the maximum allowed under current guidelines. Army troops assigned to fire-fighting duty were forced to use outdated trucks because the strikers would not release equipment under their control.

15 Sadat receives formal invitation to visit Israel

Prime Minister Menahem Begin of Israel used the services of the U.S. ambassadors to Israel and Egypt to transmit a formal invitation to President Sadat of Egypt to visit Israel. The U.S. praised Sadat as "very courageous," but the Soviet Union criticized the visit as an Israeli device to disrupt Arab unity. The Libyan government described the planned visit as a "regrettable and dramatic collapse of Arab confrontation against the Zionist enemy." Iraq and radical Palestinians also denounced the visit, but leaders of other Arab states were content to wait for further developments. The following day Sadat flew to Damascus but failed to win the backing of Hafez al-Assad, president of Syria.

Carter welcomes shah as demonstrators clash

Shah Mohammad Reza Pahlavi of Iran was welcomed to the White House by President Carter as demonstrators for and against the shah clashed nearby. During the outdoor ceremony, tear gas released by riot police floated across the White House grounds and caused many officials to wipe their smarting eyes. During their two-day meeting, the leaders discussed Iran's domestic human rights policy, its request for fighter planes and nuclear power plants, and the future price of oil.

19 Rioting mars Taiwan election

In provincial elections on Taiwan, the ruling Kuomintang (KMT) captured 85% of the 1,318 contested posts, but for the first time independents won four mayoral and magistrates' seats and non-KMT candidates captured 21 of 77 seats available in the Provincial Assembly. Violence occurred in the city of Chungli in T'ao-yuan county when a KMT election official reportedly smudged ballots to render them invalid. Fire was set to cars, trucks, and to the police and fire stations before police restored order.

20 *Sadat addresses Knesset*

Pres. Anwar as-Sadat of Egypt arrived in Jerusalem on November 19 and was accorded full honours as a visiting head of state, even though Egypt and Israel had no diplomatic relations. The next day, after visiting al-Aqsa Mosque and other religious sites, Sadat addressed the Knesset (parliament). In his speech, and in the reply delivered by Prime Minister Begin of Israel, there was a note of restraint, even though both leaders firmly reiterated their previous conditions for peace. Sadat demanded withdrawal of all Israeli troops from Arab lands occupied since the 1967 war and insisted that "there can be no peace without the Palestinians." Begin warned that Israel "will not be put within range of its annihilation," a clear refusal to accept an independent Palestinian state on the West Bank of the Jordan River. No resolution of significant differences was expected or achieved before Sadat departed on November 21, but psychological barriers to peace had been removed and further negotiations were planned.

Karamanlis wins reelection in Greece

In a national election for the 300-seat Greek Parliament, the New Democracy Party of Prime Minister Konstantinos Karamanlis won 173 seats, a net loss of 42. The Panhellenic Socialist Movement (PASOK) headed by Andreas Papandreou increased its representation by 77 seats and emerged as the new opposition with a total of 92 seats. Georgios Mavros' Democratic Centre Union won only 15 seats,

Pres. Anwar as-Sadat of Egypt
urges the Israeli Knesset to seek peace.

WILLIAM KAREL—SYGMA

©SAM C. PIERSON, JR.—PHOTO RESEARCHERS

Three first ladies attended the National Women's Conference in Houston, Texas. Listening to Rep. Barbara Jordan are (right to left) Lady Bird Johnson, Betty Ford, Rosalynn Carter, and former representative Bella Abzug.

42 less than its previous total of 57. Smaller parties won the remaining 20 seats. Karamanlis called the election to gain support for negotiations with Turkey over Cyprus and the Aegean and to win backing for his efforts to have Greece join the European Economic Community (EEC). Papandreou opposed, on economic grounds, union with the EEC and rejected membership in NATO and close ties with Western countries, notably the U.S.

21 *National Women's Conference held in Houston*

More than 1,400 voting delegates to the first National Women's Conference ended a three-day meeting in Houston, Texas, after approving 24 proposals that were intended to serve as guidelines for federal legislation. About 20% of the delegates, who described themselves as "pro-life" and "pro-family," were most vehement in their opposition to abortion, lesbian rights, and the Equal Rights Amendment—all of which were endorsed by the conference. About 15,000 persons held a counter "pro-family rally" across town on November 19 to "reject the antifamily goal of the Equal Rights Amendment and the International Women's Year."

24 *Smith offers equal suffrage to blacks*

Prime Minister Ian D. Smith of Rhodesia said he was willing to concede one-man, one-vote suffrage to blacks as a starting point for negotiations with black leaders living within the country. While agreeing in principle to black majority rule as a step toward settling Rhodesia's domestic problems, Smith added that minority rights would also have to be safeguarded in a new constitution. Joshua Nkomo and Robert Mugabe of the Patriotic Front,

based outside Rhodesia, both declared they would continue their guerrilla war against the Rhodesian government.

27 *Sadat calls for Cairo conference on Middle East*

In an effort to resolve procedural difficulties standing in the way of a Geneva peace conference, President Sadat of Egypt issued invitations for a preparatory conference in Cairo. Israel, the U.S., and the United Nations said they would send representatives, but the Soviet Union said it would not. Syria announced its intention to go to Tripoli, Libya, to attend a meeting of opponents of Sadat's initiatives with Israel. Kurt Waldheim, secretary-general of the UN, suggested a UN-sponsored conference after the meeting in Cairo.

29 *U.S. dockworkers end long strike*

U.S. dockworkers from Maine to Texas ended a 60-day selective strike that began over demands that longshoremen loading and unloading container vessels be given job security. The settlement guaranteed New York dockworkers 2,080 hours of pay a year, even if there was not that much work available. Workers in other ports agreed to a lower guaranteed income. The master contract would raise the employers' cost to $14.15 an hour by the start of the third year.

30 *Vorster's party wins election in South Africa*

The National Party of Prime Minister John Vorster scored an overwhelming victory in national elections, winning 134 seats in the 165-seat South African Parliament, for a gain of 18 seats. Only whites were allowed to vote.

DECEMBER

2 *South African police absolved of guilt in Biko's death*

After a three-week inquest, the chief magistrate of Pretoria, South Africa, declared that no one was to blame for the death of Steven Biko, a black leader who died in police custody on September 12 after sustaining brain injuries. The U.S. State Department, declaring itself "shocked" by the ruling, stated: "It seems inconceivable on the basis of the evidence presented that the inquiry could render a judgment that no one was responsible. Even if individual responsibility was not established, Mr. Biko's death clearly resulted from a system that permits gross mistreatment in violation of the most basic human rights."

British troops summoned to Bermuda

Rioting and arson intensified in Bermuda after two convicted black political activists were hanged for murder. Peter Ramsbotham, governor of the British colony, declared a national emergency and ordered a dusk to dawn curfew in an attempt to control the situation. On December 4 British troops, requested by the governor, arrived from Belize and Britain to reinforce the local police and one of the island's militia units.

4 *Bokassa crowns himself emperor in Africa*

Just one year after declaring the Central African Republic to be an empire, the former Jean-Bédel Bokassa rode in splendour to a sports stadium in the capital city of Bangui and crowned himself emperor. His Imperial Majesty Bokassa I then crowned his wife Empress Catherine. The extravaganza was witnessed by 3,500 guests from more than 40 nations and cost an estimated $20 million. Bokassa's pearl-studded coronation robe and the empress' gold lamé gown alone were worth more than $200,000. It was expected that much of the cost would be covered by French aid. Though the country is one of the world's poorest, it is believed to have great undeveloped mineral deposits.

5 *Hard-line Arabs meet in Tripoli*

Arab critics of Egyptian Pres. Anwar as-Sadat concluded a stormy four-day meeting in Tripoli, Libya, after Iraq walked out in protest because Syrian Pres. Hafez al-Assad "showed he still believes in a policy of peaceful surrender and negotiation." The Palestine Liberation Organization joined the four Arab states of Algeria, Libya, Syria, and Yemen (Aden) in issuing the Tripoli Declaration which, among other things, "froze" diplomatic relations with Egypt.

Sadat reacts to Tripoli Declaration

In retaliation for action taken by hard-line Arabs at their meeting in Tripoli, President Sadat of Egypt broke off diplomatic relations with Algeria, Iraq, Libya, Yemen (Aden), and Syria. On December 7 Sadat also ordered the closing of all cultural centres and some consulates belonging to the U.S.S.R., Czechoslovakia, East Germany, Hungary, and Poland because of Communist support for the Arab bloc opposed to Sadat's peace overtures to Israel.

6 *U.S. coal miners go on strike*

After two months of negotiations, some 160,000 members of the United Mine Workers went on strike following expiration of their contracts with the Bituminous Coal Operators Association, an organization representing 130 of the largest coal companies in the Midwest and Appalachian regions of the country. The main points of disagreement involved medical and pension funds and wildcat strikes. Anticipating a long strike, utility companies and other heavy users of coal had stockpiled large supplies of fuel before the strike began.

South Africa grants Bophuthatswana independence

The South African government officially granted independence to Bophuthatswana, a black homeland consisting of six separate districts. In a similar move in October 1976, Transkei had become an independent nation, but no member of the UN recognized either of the two homelands as a legitimate country. More than half of the 2.5 million Tswanas work outside the new homeland areas and many feared they would automatically lose their South African citizenship and with it the few rights they possess under the system of apartheid.

10 *U.S. farmers demonstrate across nation*

Thousands of farmers drove tractors and trucks into Washington, D.C., and into some 30 state capitals to focus national attention on the financial difficulties they were encountering because of low prices for their commodities. Though there was widespread sympathy for their cause, it did not appear likely that very much would be done. Many protesting farmers said they would not join a strike that entailed withholding farm products from the market. The orderly columns of vehicles were escorted by police who tried to minimize problems created by snarled traffic. The largest tractor motorcade moved into Atlanta, Ga., capital of President Carter's home state.

NBC PHOTO

Bokassa I was crowned emperor of the Central African Empire in a $20 million ceremony.

Australian coalition government wins federal election

The Liberal-Country Party coalition government of Prime Minister Malcolm Fraser won an overwhelming victory in a national election that mainly focused on domestic economic issues. Former prime minister Gough Whitlam announced after the election that he would resign as leader of the opposition Labor Party.

14 *Conference on Middle East opens in Cairo*

Representatives of Egypt and Israel and U.S. and UN observers met in Cairo to discuss procedural problems connected with a future peace conference on the Middle East. Though Syria, Lebanon, Jordan, the U.S.S.R., and the Palestine Liberation Organization refused to attend, their seats were left vacant in the hope that they would reconsider. Kurt Waldheim, secretary-general of the United Nations, said it would be inappropriate for a UN representative to act as chairman of the meeting because UN participation at the conference had not been formally authorized by member nations.

18 *Indira Gandhi resigns from party post*

Former prime minister Indira Gandhi of India formally resigned from the executive committee of the Congress Party, but not from the party itself, because she felt it was dealing ineffectually with the nation's major problems. The Congress Party had ruled India uninterruptedly from its independence in 1947 to the March 1977 elections.

19 New government formed in The Netherlands

Prime Minister Andreas van Agt was sworn in as head of a new centre-right coalition in The Netherlands, thereby ending a seven-month crisis during which the country functioned with only a caretaker administration. After van Agt's Christian Democrats (CDA) won the support of the conservative Liberal Party (VVD), the coalition had a slim majority of 77 seats in the 150-seat lower house of Parliament. There was, however, discontent among some members of the CDA, who threatened not to vote with the government because of policy concessions made to the VVD.

20 Carter signs new Social Security tax bill

President Carter signed into law a new Social Security tax bill that would exact progressively larger contributions from both employers and employees and extend the taxable wage base from $16,500 in 1977 to $29,700 in 1981. It was hoped that the new law would put the program on a sound financial basis for about 50 years. The current 5.85% paid on gross income up to $16,500 would rise on Jan. 1, 1978, to 6.05% on $17,700. The tax would be 6.65% in 1981 and 7.65% in 1990. The mandatory 7.9% applied to the self-employed in 1977 would increase to 9.3% by 1981 and to 10.75% by 1990.

Indonesia claims 10,000 prisoners are freed

The Indonesian government announced the release of 10,000 political prisoners who had been arrested in 1965 and held since that time without trial. Amnesty International, which had called worldwide attention to the situation, said in London that there was "no basis for believing at face value" the government announcement because no data were provided on names, dates, and prisons. It further claimed that Indonesia could still be holding as many as 100,000 additional political prisoners.

21 OPEC defers increase in price of crude oil

At the end of a two-day meeting in Caracas, Venezuela, ministers of the 13 nations constituting the Organization of Petroleum Exporting Countries (OPEC) agreed not to raise the price of crude oil until another meeting was held sometime in the future. The decision reflected a desire to prevent the kind of split that occurred a year earlier when two different prices were announced after the various ministers could not reconcile their differing views. Both Saudi Arabia and Iran favoured a temporary freeze because of the current surplus of oil and because a price increase would endanger the economic recovery of oil-importing nations. Other members of OPEC argued for increases ranging from 5 to 23%.

26 Sadat and Begin meet in Egypt

Prime Minister Menahem Begin returned to Israel after discussing Middle East peace for two days with Egyptian Pres. Anwar as-Sadat in Ismailia. The two leaders agreed to continue negotiations through representatives and declared that the meeting had been a success, even though they issued no joint statement setting forth principles upon which a settlement would be based.

28 Burns replaced as head of Federal Reserve Board

President Carter appointed G. William Miller chairman of the Board of Governors of the Federal Reserve System which, among other things, sets interest rates and controls the nation's money supply. The former chairman of Textron Inc. replaced Arthur F. Burns, who had headed the Federal Reserve System since February 1970 and had the option of remaining one of its seven governors until his term expired on Jan. 31, 1984.

29 Carter begins second overseas trip

President Carter left the U.S. on a nine-day, 18,500-mi trip that was scheduled to take him first to Poland, then to Iran, India, Saudi Arabia, France, and Belgium. Carter was expected to hold an open news conference in Warsaw, the first given by a U.S. president in Eastern Europe. He was also slated to deliver major speeches in New Delhi and Paris. The trip, scheduled for November, was postponed when the debate on the energy bill reached a crucial stage.

31 Cambodia severs relations with Vietnam

In a brief radio statement from the capital city of Phnom Penh, the Foreign Ministry of Cambodia broke off diplomatic relations with its Communist neighbour Vietnam. Each had accused the other of armed incursions across territorial borders during several weeks of sometimes intense fighting. The conflict had international overtones inasmuch as Cambodia was largely backed by China and Vietnam by the Soviet Union.

Spain approves limited autonomy for Basque provinces

Faced with the threat of potentially violent demonstrations on January 4, Premier Adolfo Suárez of Spain approved the draft of a statute granting limited home rule to the three Basque provinces of Guipúzcoa, Vizcaya, and Alava on the northern coast of Spain. Navarre was also included in the proposal, but its representatives in Parliament reacted negatively to the proposal that Navarre also join a general council for the region. Voters in all four provinces would eventually have an opportunity to express their views on a final version of the statute. Similar limited autonomy was granted to Catalonia on September 29.

Turkish government falls

The five-month-old right-wing coalition government of Prime Minister Suleyman Demirel resigned after it lost a vote of confidence in the lower house of the Turkish National Assembly by a margin of 228 to 218. The country had been plagued by such economic problems as a high balance of payments deficit and by political violence that had taken more than 200 lives during the year. Former prime minister Bulent Ecevit was expected to return to power after being asked by Pres. Fahri Koruturk to form a new government.

Tractors clogged the streets of Washington, D.C., as farmers carried their protests to the capital.

GRACE—SYGMA

UNUSUAL BUT NOTEWORTHY EVENTS OF 1977

Not all the news events of 1977 made prominent headlines. Among items reported less breathlessly in the worldwide press were the following:

Fund-raisers for the St. Paul, Minn., Chamber of Commerce and Arts Council were presumably embarrassed when they turned over only $1,900 after taking in $84,725 during the "Greatest Garage Sale on Earth." A spokesman explained that in addition to predicted expenses for advertising, utilities, and salaries, other unexpected expenses were incurred. These included paying for a pair of crutches that were sold when a woman momentarily left them outside a washroom and replacing a forklift truck that was accidentally sold for $35. The promoter next plans to put on the "Greatest Bingo Game in the U.S."

Dr. George E. Moore and a colleague at the Denver, Colo., General Hospital implanted sterilized dimes in the peritoneal cavities of a group of rats. The doctors later published their findings in a medical journal and summarized the results of the experiments in a headline that read: "Money causes Cancer: Ban it." Other scientists, and presumably the rats, were not amused.

The new fourth edition of the *Dictionary of Occupational Titles* put out by the U.S. Department of Labor weighs more than five pounds and took a dozen years to complete. The staff faced the formidable task of formulating some 20,000 job titles and job descriptions without making any reference to sex or age. For just $12 readers can see for themselves that batboys and governesses no longer exist. They have been replaced by bat handlers and children's tutors. And even though busboys have become dining room attendants and TV repairmen have become TV repairers, a dog bather is still a dog bather.

Canadian residents of Petit Rocher, possibly unaware of the roles that Hollywood has traditionally assigned to town folks in such encounters, wrote their own scenario of events when a motorcycle gang rode into town. They set fire to the motorcycles, terrorized the drivers' girl friends, then chased them all out of town.

U.S. congressmen were presumably surprised to learn that 15 months of instruction are required to turn out a bandmaster at the Pentagon's School of Music, but only 13 months are needed to train a jet pilot.

Luigi Mario Valsania of Italy observed the 30th anniversary of his last awakening on April 14, 1977. After returning home from a party in 1947 he went to bed, but sleep did not come. He has not been able to sleep since that time. Physicians say he is in good health except for his aggressive insomnia. While everyone else sleeps, Valsania reads travel books. He can't afford to visit the places he reads about, but he shrugs and remarks philosophically, "Even though I can't sleep, I can dream, can't I?"

The Iowa Conservation Commission is compiling a list of the state's endangered plants and animals, but the list will not be publicized. Officials explained that there are just too many people who like to go around collecting anything that is considered rare.

Sen. William Proxmire (Dem., Wis.), who has gained a reputation for a no-nonsense approach to federal funding of scientific projects, was particularly outraged when he learned of a $50,000 grant to Roland Hutchinson of Kalamazoo, Mich. The money was authorized to help determine why rats, monkeys, and humans clench their jaws. After clenching his own jaw, Proxmire made a speech on the Senate floor that included the remark: "Dr. Hutchinson's studies should make the taxpayers, as well as the monkeys, grind their teeth. In fact, the good doctor has made a fortune from his monkeys and, in the process, made a monkey of the American taxpayer." Hutchinson filed an $8 million libel suit, but a federal judge ruled that Proxmire and his colleagues can say anything they want on the floor of the Senate—with or without clenching their jaws.

Sally Rand, still spry at age 73, danced at a Detroit suburban supper club and showed she still knows how to keep the customers cool by fluttering her fans.

Farrah Fawcett-Majors complained through her lawyers that a novelty company had infringed on her rights by bringing out a poster that featured a faucet labeled Farrah Faucet. Lawyers warned poster creator Dale Dahlgren that he was exploiting the actress and that if the practice did not cease "our client will take appropriate remedies." The poster showed a faucet with a handle that had four chromed knobs. Said Dahlgren: "I don't see the likeness."

Michael Styles of Springfield, Ohio, scared his flight instructor half to death when he roared down the runway in a Mooney M-20F. He remembered to retract the landing gear, but he forgot that this is normally done after the plane leaves the ground.

Luftwaffe Master Sgt. Siegfried Schmidt depleted West Germany's military ranks by 5,000 men with just one deep breath. He confessed that he had created that number of imaginary soldiers so he could collect their pay. Apparently he spent all of the estimated $500,000 before beginning a prison sentence for embezzlement.

C. K. Johnson of Lancaster, Calif., is president of the International Flat Earth Research Society, which reportedly has a membership of 1,400. Johnson explains that "the upper classes are more receptive to our issues because they are less set in their ways." The organization, founded in Britain in 1800, contends that the Earth neither

This Muscovy duck presumably set a new world record when she gave birth to 25 ducklings (count them) in Wrangle Common, Lincolnshire, England. As she listened to the patter of 50 little feet behind her, she had three reasons to feel superior to her sister, who last year became the mother of only 22 offspring.

spins nor orbits the Sun. The U.S. and Soviet space programs are dismissed as "multimillion-dollar hoaxes." But what about those trips to the Moon made by U.S. astronauts? Simple; just another of Hollywood's many science fiction adventures.

Sen. John Melcher, a Montana Democrat who represents cattle country voters, moved to correct a magazine article that identified him not as a veterinarian, which he is, but as a vegetarian, which he isn't.

Bowing to pressure, U.S. postal officials rescinded an order and permitted scores of small American towns to retain their identities by remaining on the postal map, even if economy measures eventually force a closure of their post offices. By way of illustration, the Postal Service noted that the post office in Berrys Lick, Ky., costs $4,000 a year to operate, but it took in only $37.67 during an entire year. Like the three families in Berrys Lick, the residents of Zap, N.D., are delighted that they continue to get mail addressed to their hometown. Incidentally, the zip for Zap is 58580.

A crane operator in Lewes, England, was so irritated when $17 was deducted from his paycheck for repayment of a loan that he climbed aboard the crane and demolished the company's construction office. In addition to momentary personal satisfaction, he got a two-year jail sentence. And after he pays off the loan, he'll start paying for the company's new office.

The U.S. Congress is sometimes accused of political myopia, but sometimes its view of the future is exceptionally realistic. Such was the case when members of Congress began consideration of a bill to establish a cemetery for themselves.

Ros Howard, displeased at what he had been reading in newspapers about the county clerk of Boulder, Colo., granting marriage licenses to homosexuals, rode into town to lodge a protest. The 65-year-old cowboy strode into the clerk's office and asked for a marriage license so he could marry Dolly—his horse. The clerk, who reportedly later returned to more traditional views of marriage, refused to comply on the grounds that Colorado law forbids the issuance of a license when one of the applicants is only eight years old.

Judge Richard Bone of Hutchinson, Kan., awarded Marcia Borders permanent custody of the family cat, but he gave Mrs. Borders' ex-husband visitation rights.

The governor of Wisconsin, Martin Schreiber, began wondering about a desk telephone that never rang. Finally he picked it up and heard a voice say, "Who's this?" It was Milwaukee Mayor Henry Maier. The hot-line telephone was installed during the civil unrest of the 1960s and was never disconnected.

Some people collect stamps. Others collect butterflies or coins. But apparently Caio D'Aurelio likes to collect books, especially from New York City libraries. When he failed to pay the rent on his street-level apartment for three consecutive months

Erwin Kreuz, a brewery worker in West Germany, speaks no English, but that didn't bother him when he booked a flight to San Francisco. When the plane landed he disembarked and spent three days vacationing in Bangor, Maine, before he realized why he hadn't yet seen the Golden Gate Bridge. Kreuz eventually saw the bridge and a whole lot more before heading back to Frankfurt with a large tag around his neck.

and was not seen by any of his neighbours, the building superintendent opened the door. The apartment contained some 7,000 books ranging in subject matter from flowers to archaeology. Librarians estimated that the collection would fill more than 300 three-foot shelves. Even if D'Aurelio read an average of four or five books a week, it would have taken him 30 years to read them all, provided he stayed out of public libraries and acquired nothing new.

Federal statisticians in the U.S., after rechecking their figures, softly announced that not only is the aggregate imported stock of down up but the price of down is also up.

Employees of the Arthur D. Little Co. in Cambridge, Mass., were quite convinced that, contrary to popular belief, lead balloons can indeed fly. Accordingly, they constructed an 8 ft by 14 ft balloon of lead foil that was just one-quarter the thickness of a human hair. The balloon was then filled with helium and sent aloft. When last sighted, the lead balloon was floating near Boston's Logan Airport at an altitude of 4,000 ft.

Police in Passaic, N.J., got a report that Mike Maryn had been mugged. Because the name sounded familiar, the police checked and rechecked their files and discovered that Maryn had been mugged 83 times in five years. On 20 occasions he was hospitalized for broken bones, knife wounds, or other injuries. The police described Maryn as the perfect target because he is slightly

built and uses a cane. Maryn himself adds that muggers think he has money because "I always dress up."

President Carter received a 12-generation genealogical history. After studying his "roots" he announced that some of his ancestors were horse thieves. And he also confessed, "One of my relatives was even in the newspaper business."

The Soviet Institute of Gerontology, trying to find out why some U.S.S.R. citizens live to a ripe old age, began a scientific study of some 40,000 senior citizens. It later reported that about 80% of those being studied were "very loquacious."

Alice Huyler-Ramsey of Covina, Calif., became one of the U.S.'s first female transcontinental motorists when she crossed the country in 1909 driving a 30-hp Maxwell. The trip took nearly two months. She now drives a 1968 Mercedes and still makes the trip each year. The 90-year-old woman says she understands why the state requires her to take a road test every three years: "They're just trying to keep some of the old fogies off the road."

Saudi Arabia's foreign minister, Saud al-Faisal, wanted to purchase an 18-room apartment in a cooperative located on New York City's Park Avenue. Even though he had the required $600,000, other tenants voted to keep him out because they feared he might attract kidnappers to the neighbourhood.

Beating the odds has become almost routine for Walter Maycenic, a 49-year-old Yugoslav-born butcher, who migrated to Canada 25 years ago. He doesn't consider himself a gambler but admits that more often than not he comes out ahead when he plays poker or bingo. And, he might add, when he buys lottery tickets. In a period of less than 14 months, he won five free lottery tickets, ten $25 prizes, one $100 prize, and $2,500 at a drawing on Halloween. In mid-December he held ticket 51858, which entitled him to $100,000. Maycenic now more or less expects that one of these days he'll win the $1 million Loto Canada. He explained that when you hold a winning ticket at least every few weeks, you begin to take winning for granted. It's like having a second job, except that you don't have to work. The reason most other people don't win is simple; they keep buying lottery tickets with the wrong numbers.

Maine legislators ended several weeks of debate by ordaining that on each December 21 the state would honour Chester Greenwood, the man who reportedly invented earmuffs.

A $500 mannequin adorned with $1,700 worth of fashion attire was set up in the Denver zoo so that advertising photos could be taken. A male lion that was let in sniffed, turned, and walked away. A lioness was then allowed to enter. She studied the mannequin for a few moments, then dismembered it and tore the clothing to shreds. There is an important lesson here for couturiers, zoologists, or sociologists—if anyone can figure out what the lesson is.

Jane Wingert, proprietor of a store in Thiensville, Wis., unpacked a shipment of newly published books and discovered that the covers were *Roots* and the insides were *Gone with the Wind.* She promptly decided that the printer's goof made the unlikely combination a rare edition and slapped a $1,600 price on each copy.

Store burglars operating in Reading, Mich., carted off, among other things, a $600 burglar alarm that didn't go off when they invaded the premises of Baker's Acres.

British postal officials met stiff resistance when they tried to change the name of a Welsh village called Llanfairpwllgwyngyllgogerychwyrndrobwllllantysiliogogogoch. Residents pleaded for understanding, protesting that the village name was their only tourist attraction. They may be right because an estimated 100,000 tourists visit the town annually, mostly to buy T-shirts and other souvenirs emblazoned with the village's name. Postmaster Jim Evans, who explains that the name means, approximately, "St. Mary's Church in a hollow by the white hazel near the fierce whirlpool by the red cave of St. Tysilio," swears he can pronounce the name in a single breath. He confesses, however, that most of the other 3,000 residents shorten it to the first 20 letters—a little bit more than halfway to the only legitimate hyphen.

Dan Knopf, employed as a whiskey taster by a distillery in Louisville, Ky., provided a tip for those who might want to become experts in his profession. He advises against drinking coffee while on the job because "coffee will trick you—everything you taste becomes delicious."

Melchor and Victoria Javier requested the transfer of $1,000 from their account in a West Virginia bank to a bank in Manila. It took the West Virginia bank several days to discover that three extra zeros had been added to the amount and then send an urgent request for the immediate return of $999,000. The Javiers replied that most of the money was gone. They promised, however, to return what remained—but not if the bank kept bothering them.

Rear Admiral David Haslam of the Royal Navy plans to relocate the British Isles. It's fairly easy for him to do so because he heads a staff of 950 people whose job it is to map the exact position of the British coastline. Though English seamen have been told for generations to put their faith in God and in the charts drawn by the Admiralty, Haslam insists current maps are 100 yards off the mark. And he has evidence from six U.S. satellites to prove it. If future tourists to London take their bearings from outdated maps, one can't help but wonder if they'll find themselves neck-deep in the River Thames when they expected to be strolling down the corridors of the Houses of Parliament.

Traffic superintendent Hurley Johnson of Huron, S.D., disclosed that someone had stolen two signs marking the city's Easy St. He conceded, however, that it didn't make a great deal of difference because in Huron nobody lives on Easy St.

Two English lads from Winchester went treasure hunting, but they had no success before a sudden shower sent them scurrying for protection beneath the limbs of a large tree. When their metal detectors began buzzing, the boys began digging, and up came 97 gold coins, dated 1773 to 1822. A special jury ruled that the coins had been hidden for more than 100 years and, therefore, belonged to the crown.

American treasure hunters fared somewhat better. On a visit to Crater of Diamonds State Park near Murfreesboro, Ark., George Stepp filled a bucket with soil and carried it back to his Arkansas home in Carthage where he discovered a four-carat diamond. Kim Jones of Scotland, Pa., paid 25 cents for a bucket of souvenir rocks from a South Carolina ruby mine. As he examined his collection he spotted a ruby that was estimated to be worth between $20,000 and $100,000.

A judge in Rockville, Md., had to come up with a legal definition of a horse before making a ruling on a case that was pending in his court. Opposing attorneys differed in their definitions. After careful consideration the judge solemnly announced: "A horse is a four-legged animal produced by two other horses."

What do you do when you want to see the midnight sun and you happen to be a thousand miles away? If you are Sheikh Abdul Mutalip al-Kasemi, oil minister of Kuwait, you round up some of the others attending a convention in Stockholm and fly off to Kiruna, a town in Lapland, above the Arctic Circle. Then you watch the midnight sun for an hour and return to Stockholm where officials of the Organization of Petroleum Exporting Countries are discussing energy supply and demand.

A mountain of ice 25 mi long and 20 mi wide—half the size of Rhode Island—broke away from Antarctica and began floating north. Scientists, who predicted the iceberg would melt as it neared the Equator, speculated it contained enough water to meet most of the needs of parched California for many years, if only it could get there. A few weeks later, 119 scientists met at landlocked Iowa State University to discuss the general subject of icebergs. The conference was principally sponsored by Prince Muhammed Faisal of Saudi Arabia, who figures that icebergs could provide fresh water for desert regions at about half the cost of desalinized water. Faisal indicated that the estimated $100 million needed for research and engineering to get the icebergs moving was available. A 4,785-lb chip of ice from Antarctica was flown to the meeting, was carefully inspected, then used to cool the drinks.

Officials in Evanston, a suburb of Chicago, pondered what to do about the complaint of a policeman who accused another member of the force of putting a voodoo hex on him.

U.S. Social Security officials happily reported a decline in the use of number 078-05-1120. Forty years ago a wallet manufacturer used that number (his secretary's) on a specimen card to show how it fit into the company's product. Tens of thousands of Social Security deductions were credited to that number because purchasers of the wallets thought the number on the card had been assigned to them. Although the card was clearly marked "specimen," some wallet owners apparently thought the number belonged to their families, for it was handed down to sons and daughters. After about 20 years the mess began to get straight-

Overruling family objections, a Los Angeles probate judge ordered Sandra West to be buried exactly as she had instructed, dressed in a lace nightgown and seated in her 1964 Ferrari—both gifts from her departed husband. The judge ruled that whereas the request was unusual, it was not illegal. And so the car was enclosed in concrete and lowered into a grave beside that of oil millionaire Ike West, in San Antonio, Texas.

UPI COMPIX

George Willig, a 26-year-old mountain climber, set out one bright May morning to scale the only sheer mountain he could find in New York City—the 110-story, 1,350-ft south tower of Manhattan's World Trade Center. Using specially designed T-shaped metal blocks that fitted into tracks used to guide window washers' scaffolds, Willig moved steadily upward as a gawking crowd gathered on the street below. Two policemen followed Willig in a motorized scaffold and arrested him when he reached the top 3-1/2 hours later. City officials briefly considered a $250,000 lawsuit, but decided it didn't make political sense to hassle a local hero. They settled on a $1.10 fine, one penny for each story.

A school board in La Crosse, Wis., fired Myron McKee, a junior high school principal who was accused of cuffing unruly pupils. That blow to school discipline so stunned voters that, in the biggest recall election in Wisconsin history, they struck back by firing the school board.

A New York judge took a few sips of coffee during a coffee break and didn't like what he was drinking. He thereupon ordered the vendor to be brought before him, "in handcuffs, if necessary." When coffee vendor Thomas Zarcone was brought handcuffed into court, he got a ten-minute public tongue-lashing. But that wasn't all he got. A federal court in Brooklyn ruled that Suffolk County Judge William Perry had violated Zarcone's rights and ordered Perry to pay Zarcone $140,000.

Tommie Overstreet, serving time for murder at the Missouri State Prison, complained that officials had no right to remove a bullet from his buttocks and use it to convict him. The Supreme Court of Missouri agreed and ordered a new trial on the grounds that removal of the bullet constituted illegal search and seizure.

Nurse Marsha Maitland passed the time by reading Agatha Christie's *A Pale Horse* as she sat at the bedside of a gravely ill 19-month-old girl from Qatar. The semiconscious child, who had been flown to London's Hammersmith Hospital, was suffering from a mysterious illness and was near death. As Maitland continued to read, she suddenly realized that the child's symptoms were being accurately described on the pages of the novel. She then notified the physicians that their young patient might have been poisoned by a compound of thallium, a substance so rare in Britain that the hospital had no readily available means to verify the fact. Laboratory technicians from Scotland Yard were called in, tests were made, and the presence of the compound was confirmed. After treatment was begun, the little girl gradually recovered.

Gov. Ella T. Grasso of Connecticut hoped she wouldn't be considered a foe of higher education when she asked University of Connecticut trustees why one of the school's librarians was scheduled to receive a salary of $46,000, another $44,000, while she as governor was drawing a salary of only $42,000.

Prasanta Mukherjee set out for India from southern England in a 25-ft boat loaded down with food and water. A mile offshore he asked coast guardsmen on a patrol launch, "Which way is Calcutta?" Although they pointed in the right direction, Prasanta somehow lost his way and finally gave up the journey with just 7,500 mi still to go.

The "Cantiki," a seagoing craft built of 15,000 resealed empty beer cans, set out for Singapore from Sydney, Australia, on September 4. Shortly after leaving port the new crew debated whether they should return to Sydney. Caught up in the hustle and bustle of packing away gear and bidding farewells, no one remembered to bring along the beer.

ened out, but Social Security officials predict there will be a residue of confusion for many more years. The secretary eventually was given a new number—before millions of dollars in retirement benefits could be credited to her account.

An Ontario physician began resuscitating a Guelph woman found frozen in an unheated house trailer, even though there was "every sign of death and no sign of life." After 35 days in a hospital, the woman returned home and four months later had resumed a normal life with no memory of the incident.

In Rhyl, Wales, a group of women and children entered a jewelry store, then opened a box and released a fluttering pigeon. With the assistance of flustered clerks who ran about the store trying to shoo the bird back to its box, the visitors finally captured the pigeon and left the store—carrying with them an assortment of rings valued at $1,200.

Voters in Gimco City, Ind., turned out in force to decide whether or not their city should be annexed to neighbouring Alexandria. The balloting, witnessed by 12 reporters, was completed long before the polls officially closed at 7 PM, but the ballots could not be counted until that time. As predicted, annexation was overwhelmingly approved, with all four votes favouring the proposition. The seven residents of Gimco City then set to work notifying their friends of a change of address.

57

DISASTERS OF 1977

The loss of life and property from disasters in 1977 included the following.

AVIATION

January 13, Alma-Ata, U.S.S.R. A Soviet Tu-104 airliner exploded at an altitude of 3,200 ft and crashed into an open field when the aircraft attempted to land at Alma-Ata; at least 90 passengers and crewmen were reported dead.

January 14, Terrace, B.C. A Twin Otter passenger airplane crashed into a hillside known as Little Herman Mountain during a flight from Prince George to Prince Rupert; nine passengers and three crewmen were killed.

January 19, Near Valencia, Spain. A Spanish Air Force transport plane crashed in a mountainous area southwest of Valencia; all 11 occupants of the aircraft were killed.

March 3, Near Pisa, Italy. An Italian Air Force Hercules C-130 transport plane slammed into the side of a mountain ten miles east of Pisa during a training flight; 38 cadets, 1 naval officer, and the crew of 5 air force officers lost their lives in the crash.

March 27, Tenerife, Canary Islands. A KLM-Royal Dutch Airlines Boeing 747 that had begun its takeoff without proper clearance from the control tower ripped off the roof over the right wing of a Pan American World Airways Boeing 747 taxiing off the runway to an access ramp; all 248 persons on the KLM were killed, and of the 396 aboard the Pan American airplane only 62 survived the worst air disaster to date.

April 4, New Hope, Ga. A Southern Airways DC-9 twin-engine jet flying from Huntsville, Ala., to Atlanta, Ga., crashed onto a roadway and crushed automobiles and buildings in its path when heavy hail apparently knocked out both engines; 25 persons were injured and more than 70 others were killed.

May 10, Near Jericho, Jordan. A U.S.-built CH-53 Sikorsky helicopter crashed and burst into flames minutes after takeoff during a military training exercise; none of the 54 Israelis aboard survived the crash, attributed to pilot negligence.

May 16, New York City. An S-61 Sikorsky helicopter idling on a heliport atop the Pan American Building in New York City tipped over on a broken landing gear and snapped off a huge rotor blade; four persons on the rooftop were slashed to death by the blade, one pedestrian was killed when the blade plunged 59 stories to the ground, and six others were injured, five seriously, by shattered glass and flying debris.

May 27, Havana. An Aeroflot Il-62 airliner en route from Moscow to Cuba slammed into a row of trees shortly before its final approach and crashed at José Martí Airport; of the 68 persons aboard, only 2 survived.

June 21, Near Wake Island. A C-130 four-engine navy reconnaissance plane crashed into the Pacific Ocean shortly after takeoff from Wake Island, where it had refueled for its return to Guam; all 16 persons aboard were believed dead.

July 24, Puerto Montt, Chile. A Chilean DC-6 military transport plane crashed in southern Chile; 38 persons survived the crash that killed 38 others, including a general.

July 25, Yoro, Honduras. A Honduran Air Force DC-3 transport plane carrying civil servants from the Justice and Interior ministries to Tegucigalpa, the Honduran capital, crashed on takeoff; 12 persons were injured and 22 were killed.

September 4, Near Cuenca, Ecuador. A Viscount airliner flying from Guayaquil to Cuenca crashed into a peak in the Cajas Mountains; all 33 persons aboard were killed.

September 15, Near Albuquerque, N.M. An Air Force EC-135 communications aircraft struck a mountainside and exploded three minutes after takeoff from Kirtland Air Force Base; the 20 military personnel aboard were killed.

September 22, Near Urziceni, Rom. A Hungarian Tu-134 jet traveling from Istanbul to Budapest crashed and burned 40 mi east of Bucharest when the pilot attempted an emergency landing; 24 passengers jumped to safety when nearby farmers rushed to the scene and helped them escape the burning wreckage, but 29 persons including the 8-member Hungarian crew were killed.

September 27, Near Kuala Lumpur, Malaysia. A Japan Air Lines DC-8 jet flying from Tokyo to Singapore via Hong Kong and Kuala Lumpur crashed in a rubber plantation north of Kuala Lumpur during a thunderstorm; of the 79 persons aboard, 45 were seriously injured and 34 were killed.

October 21, Mindoro Island, Phil. A U.S. Marine Corps CH-53 helicopter carrying 39 servicemen crashed and burned while taking part in an amphibious exercise; serious injuries and at least ten deaths were reported.

November 19, Near Funchal, Madeira Islands. A Portuguese Boeing 727 airliner attempting to land during a rainstorm crashed and burned at the Madeira airport; 130 of the 164 passengers and crew members aboard were killed.

November 21, Near Bariloche, Arg. A twin-engine BAC-111 jet traveling from Buenos Aires to the resort of Bariloche crashed after making several attempts to position its landing gear; 45 of the 79 persons aboard were killed.

December 2, Northeastern Libya. A chartered Bulgarian jetliner carrying Muslims home from a pilgrimage to Mecca crashed while attempting to make an emergency landing; at least 56 of the 159 passengers were believed dead.

December 8, Off the coast of Louisiana. A helicopter attempting to land on the deck of an offshore oil rig during high winds crashed into the rig and dropped some 130 ft into rough seas; two oil workers were injured and the 17 others aboard were killed.

December 11, Hierro, Canary Islands. A U.S. military plane flying at 1,200 ft in clouds and rain crashed into a 4,200-ft mountain peak and exploded; all 12 servicemen aboard were killed.

December 13, Evansville, Ind. A chartered DC-3 transporting the University of Evansville basketball team to Nashville, Tenn., crashed and burned within two minutes of takeoff; 29 persons were killed, including all 14 members of the Evansville basketball team and its coach.

December 18, Near Funchal, Madeira Islands. A chartered Swiss airliner plunged into the sea on its approach landing at the Madeira airport; 19 of the 57 persons aboard were killed and another 17 were missing and believed dead.

The ravaged wreckage of two 747's lies on the airstrip at Tenerife in the Canary Islands; 582 persons were killed in March in the worst disaster in aviation history.

Fire destroyed the overcrowded Beverly Hills Supper Club in Southgate, Kentucky, in May, killing 164 persons.

FIRES AND EXPLOSIONS

January 2, Shamokin, Pa. An intense early morning fire that burned out of control for more than five hours at a four-story motel injured two and took the lives of nine, including the owner.

January 28, Breckenridge, Minn. A predawn fire that swept a four-story brick hotel in blizzard-like conditions, with a wind chill factor of $-85°$ F $(-65°C)$ prevailing, claimed the lives of 22 persons.

Mid-February, Southern Australia. Brushfires occurring in the states of Victoria, South Australia, and Tasmania destroyed nearly 500,000 ac of valuable grazing land, killed three million sheep, and took the lives of five persons.

February 25, Moscow. A major fire caused by a technical fault in an elevator motor shot upward through an elevator shaft from the 5th floor to the 12th floor of the Rossiya, the world's largest hotel; a Soviet medical source reported at least 45 fatalities.

April 19, Galveston, Texas. A fire that leveled a three-story hotel claimed the lives of 8 persons; 18 others were reported missing.

May 9, Amsterdam. After a fire gutted the Polen Hotel 5 guests were still missing in the debris and 28 others were killed.

May 22, Brussels. A raging fire broke out in the first floor snack bar at the Duc de Brabant Hotel where 150 guests were registered; 40 persons were injured, 15 were killed, and another 12 were missing and presumed dead.

May 25, New York City. A fire reduced a homosexual bathhouse to rubble when a mattress fire, presumably extinguished, reignited; ten persons were injured and nine were killed when flames consumed the building.

May 28, Southgate, Ky. A fast-burning fire poured heavy smoke throughout the Beverly Hills Supper Club where some 3,500 persons awaited the arrival of singer John Davidson. A private investigating team linked a short circuit to the cause of the blaze that injured more than 130 persons and killed 164.

June 9, Abidjan, Ivory Coast. A fire trapped patrons of a nightclub when flames destroyed an electrical system operating an automatic exit; 4 persons were listed in critical condition and 41 others perished in the blaze, presumably from asphyxiation.

June 21, Saint John, N.B. An intense fire that apparently started in padding ripped from the walls of a jail cell fused the locks on several cell doors; several policemen were hospitalized and 20 prisoners were killed.

June 26, Columbia, Tenn. A fire started by a prisoner in his cell at Maury County Jail burned vinyl-covered plastic foam padding, sending noxious cyanide and carbon monoxide fumes through the jail's ventilation system; 34 inmates and 8 visitors succumbed in the smoke-laden prison.

November 11, Iri, South Korea. An explosion aboard a freight train loaded with 33 tons of dynamite leveled some 400 buildings, left a crater nearly 50 ft deep, injured more than 1,300, and killed more than 50 persons in the city of Iri; the cause of the blast was attributed to a security guard who had fallen asleep with candles burning.

November 14, Manila. An early morning blaze aggravated by ferocious typhoon winds swept through a hotel, injured 9, and killed at least 47 persons; some 150 guests were forced to grope for possible means of escape because the raging storm had plunged the hotel into total darkness.

November 27, Rio de Janeiro, Brazil. A fire that broke out in a convention centre adjoining a luxury hotel killed at least 11 persons in Rio de Janeiro.

December 9–10, Cartagena, Colombia. A series of explosions at a petrochemical plant seriously injured 30 workers and claimed the lives of at least 25 others.

December 16, Manila. A fire in an overcrowded mental hospital destroyed the interior of a building that housed some 1,200 patients although it was only designed for 400; rescue workers said the 32 persons who were killed would have been saved had they cooperated with the rescue team.

December 22, Near New Orleans, La. A chain-reaction explosion that apparently started in the weighing office of a 73-silo grain elevator completely leveled the structure of reinforced steel and concrete to a 120-ft pile of rubble; 10 persons were injured, 6 seriously, and rescue workers reported that 36 persons were killed in the worst grain industry disaster in the U.S. to date.

MARINE

January 17, Barcelona harbour, Spain. A 56-ft U.S. Navy launch, rounding a pier in early morning darkness, collided with the 380-ton "Urela," a Spanish coastal freighter; of the more than 100 sailors and marines being ferried back to the helicopter carrier "Guam" and the landing ship "Trenton," at least 46 were killed and 18 of 84 survivors were seriously injured.

January 19, Gulf of Mexico. The Panamanian freighter "Ukola" snapped in two and sank about 200 mi off the coast of Florida after being buffeted by a gale and 20-ft-high waves; of the 23 crew members aboard only 3 survived in the turbulent waters.

March 20, Southeast of Wilmington, N.C. The "Claude Conway," a 43,000-ton Panamanian oil tanker carrying 536,000 gal of oil, exploded and split in two when sparks from a welding torch ignited gas fumes deep within the tanker's hold; the captain and nine crewmen lost their lives.

April 21, Mediterranean Sea. An excursion boat capsized while carrying 50 passengers on a Mediterranean cruise around the Crusader battlements at Acre, Israel; at least eight persons drowned.

June 11, North of Sabah, Malaysia. A boat carrying Vietnamese refugees en route to the Philippines capsized when it struck a cluster of rocks off the northern coast of Borneo; only 4 of the more than 30 aboard were rescued.

August 17, South Pacific. A South Korean fishing vessel sank in the South Pacific; rescue teams were unable to locate the 17 crewmen reported to be afloat on a life raft.

October 31, Bay of Biscay. The Greek freighter "Tina" sank in the Bay of Biscay north of Spain; 10 of the 21 crew members aboard the vessel were killed and 6 others were missing and believed drowned.

MINING

March 1, Tower City, Pa. A flood at the Kocher Coal Co. anthracite mine swept away timber supports and choked the tunnel with fallen rock and debris; 9 workers were killed and 3 seriously injured; 94 other miners escaped unharmed.

May 11, Hokkaido, Japan. A gas explosion at the colliery of Mitsui Mining Co. on the northern island of Hokkaido killed 25 miners and injured 8 others.

May 20, Randfontein, South Africa. A rush of mud that slammed into the bottom of a gold mine shaft at Randfontein Estates claimed the lives of at least six workers and injured four others.

July 15, Amaga, Colombia. A gas explosion at a mine in the northwestern department of Antioquia in Colombia was reportedly the worst in the country's history; 135 persons were killed in the blast.

August 2, Moatize, Mozambique. An explosion that ripped through a coal mine in northern Mozambique trapped 150 miners and killed 70; rioting ensued following the explosion and claimed the lives of 9 additional persons.

September 3, South Africa. An earth tremor caused cave-ins at Blyvooruitzicht and Hartebeestfontein gold mines, trapping miners beneath tons of rock and earth; at least 21 miners were killed and 16 others were missing and believed dead.

MISCELLANEOUS

January 3, Bantayan Island, Phil. In the central island of Bantayan, 25 of 37 persons suffering from poliomyelitis succumbed to the disease.

Early January, Sumbawa, Indon. A cholera outbreak claimed the lives of 49 persons in Sumbawa, one of the Lesser Sunda Islands of Indonesia.

March 7, Dar es Salaam, Tanzania. A pack of at least 300 stray dogs rampaging throughout Tanzania were shot after fatally infecting 50 persons with rabies.

March 31, Dera Ghazi Khan, Pak. A bus carrying 30 persons plummeted into the Indus River in Punjab Province when a drawbridge collapsed; 22 persons lost their lives, 4 were rescued, and 4 others were missing.

Mid-April, Northwest Haiti. A severe drought ravaged cattle herds and crops in northwestern Haiti, causing some 300 people to die of starvation and others to strip their homes of doors and windows to raise money for food.

May 14, Peru. A yellow fever epidemic, the first reported in the last decade, claimed the lives of 26 persons.

Early August, Jakarta, Indon. An outbreak of cholera attributed to unclean food and water claimed the lives of nearly 40 persons, most of whom were children.

August 17, Pushkino, U.S.S.R. A crowded footbridge over a main rail line collapsed under the weight of more than 100 persons who had arrived at Pushkino station about 20 mi northeast of Moscow; dozens were injured and at least ten persons were crushed to death by the wreckage of the bridge and other victims who fell some 30 ft to the tracks.

August–September, Middle East. An epidemic of cholera that spread throughout the neighbouring countries of Syria, Jordan, Lebanon, Kuwait, Iraq, and Saudi Arabia claimed the lives of at least 98 persons, 90 of them in Syria.

September 7, Near Jaipur, India. The roof of a village classroom collapsed under the weight of a troop of baboons; 15 schoolgirls were killed instantly.

September, Bangladesh. An outbreak of cholera killed at least 350 persons in Bangladesh.

October, Near Cairo. An outbreak of dengue fever, caused by a mosquito-borne virus, afflicted some 10,000 people in a farming area 50 mi northeast of Cairo and claimed the lives of 60 persons.

November–December, Tanzania. An outbreak of cholera claimed the lives of more than 100 persons in Tanzania within a two-month period.

NATURAL

January 10, Goma, Zaire. The Nyiragongo volcano, Africa's second highest active volcano at 11,000 ft, erupted and spewed lava on the town of Goma eight miles away; early reports said 2,000 persons were killed.

January 19, Brazil. Heavy rains that caused two rivers to overflow their banks caused extensive damage in the southwest region of Brazil; 60 persons died in the floodwaters and some 3,500 others were left homeless.

Early February, Madagascar. A cyclone accompanied by heavy rains swept through the island of Madagascar and destroyed 30,000 homes and 150,000 ha of rice fields; 5 persons were injured and 31 were killed.

February 15, Gaza District, Mozambique. The provincial capital of Xai-Xai was flooded under five feet of water from the Limpopo River after a safety dike burst; at least 300 persons were killed.

March 4, Svishtov, Veliko Turnovo Province, Bulg. An earthquake in the port city of Svishtov injured 164 persons and killed 130.

March 4, Romania. An earthquake measuring 7.1 on the Richter scale devastated the Romanian capital of Bucharest and several major industrial centres; more than 11,000 people were injured, 80,000 were left homeless, and more than 1,500 were killed.

Mid-March, Central U.S. A late winter blizzard swept through South Dakota, blocking 100 mi of interstate highway and killing nine persons in Colorado, four in Nebraska, and two in Kansas.

March 22, Southern Iran. A major earthquake measuring approximately 7 on the Richter scale struck near Bandar Abbas where several buildings were severely damaged; at least 60 persons were killed in the adjoining villages of Khvorgu and Qaleh Qazi.

March 25, Eastern Turkey. The fourth major earthquake in four months along the geologic fault running from southern Iran to northern Italy damaged 400 buildings in the town of Palu; rescuers reported 30 fatalities.

April 1, Bangladesh. A tornado that struck the two widely separated areas of Madaripur 80 mi southwest of Dacca, and Kishorganj in northern Bangladesh devastated at least three villages, injured 1,500 persons, and claimed the lives of more than 600.

April 4, Southern U.S. Tornadoes, heavy rain, and flooding ravaged the southern states of West Virginia, Virginia, Alabama, Mississippi, Georgia, Tennessee, and Kentucky, where the Cumberland River crested 18 ft above its flood stage; property damage was estimated at $275 million and the death toll was at 40.

April 6, Central and southwestern Iran. Earth tremors measuring 6.5 on the open-ended Richter scale left the villages of Ardal, Borujen, Dow Polan, and Gandoman in ruins; an estimated 500 persons lost their lives.

Mid-April, Fagarasului Mountains, Rom. An avalanche that occurred in Romania's Fagarasului Mountains claimed the lives of 19 high school students and 4 teachers during a skiing trip.

April 24, Northern Bangladesh. A cyclone accompanied by 100-mph winds ripped through northern Bangladesh, killing 13 persons and injuring nearly 100.

May 20, Moundou, Logone Prefecture, Chad. A tornado that swept through southeastern Chad injured 100 persons and killed 13 others.

May 23, Khorramabad, Iran. A flood following heavy rains in Khorramabad claimed the lives of 13 persons, many of whom were children.

June 4, Northwestern Iran. Heavy rains that caused rivers to overflow their banks killed at least ten persons near the towns of Zanjan and Takestan.

Mid-June, Oman. A tropical cyclone leveled 98% of the buildings, injured more than 40, and claimed the lives of 2 persons on the island of Masirah; three days later torrential rains hit Dhofar Province, which suffered even greater destruction when an estimated 15,000 animals were swept away in the floodwaters, large quantities of crops were destroyed, and more than 100 persons were killed.

June 24, Kyushu, Japan. A mud and rock slide estimated at 70,000 tons crashed down a rain-soaked mountain on the Japanese island of Kyushu; 15 homes were demolished and 11 persons were believed dead.

Early July, Southwestern France. Severe flooding following days of torrential rain destroyed nearly 90% of the region's cereal and tobacco crops, killed livestock, and contributed to millions of dollars in property damage; 26 persons lost their lives in the worst flooding to engulf southwestern France in the 20th century.

Early July, Seoul, South Korea. Torrential rains followed by flooding and landslides in Seoul and surrounding areas left 80,000 people homeless, more than 480 injured, and at least 200 dead.

July 20, Johnstown, Pa. An overnight nine-inch rainfall caused massive flooding in Johnstown and surrounding areas and left the town accessible only by helicopter; property damage was estimated at $200 million, 30 persons were missing, and some 70 lost their lives in the rampaging waters.

July 25, Kao-hsiung, Taiwan. A typhoon packing winds of up to 120 mph destroyed nearly 20,000 homes in Kao-hsiung, Taiwan's major seaport and industrial centre; 31 persons lost their lives in the storm nicknamed Typhoon Thelma.

July 31, Northern Taiwan. The second typhoon to lash Taiwan in a week struck the towns of Taipei, T'ao-yuan, and Nan-t'ou; at least 38 persons were killed.

August 19, Eastern Indonesia. A major earthquake that struck eastern Indonesia measured between 7.7 and 8.7 in various locations on the open-ended Richter scale and was one of the strongest ever recorded; 98 persons were injured, 76 were reported missing, and at least 187 were killed.

September 13, Kansas City, Mo. Flash floods in rivers, creeks, and drainage ditches following 12 in of torrential rain ravaged Kansas City; the flood damage was estimated at more than $100 million and at least 26 persons lost their lives in the raging waters.

September 18, Near Kathmandu, Nepal. A landslide destroyed part of a village north of Kathmandu and buried 18 persons alive.

Late September, Taipei, Taiwan. Following 16 consecutive hours of torrential rainfall in Taipei, at least 14 persons were known dead in Taiwan's worst flooding in seven years.

Mid-October, Northwestern Italy. Severe flooding following steady rainfall caused $350 million in damage in Genoa and regions of Piedmont, Liguria, and Lombardy and claimed the lives of 15 persons.

October 22, Gampola, Sri Lanka. A landslide that swept over workers' quarters on a tea plantation flattened rooms that housed nine families; at least 27 persons were believed dead.

Four crowded elevated cars tumbled from the tracks in Chicago's Loop in February, killing 11 persons.

November 2–3, Athens and Piraeus, Greece. Heavy flooding following 15 hours and 2.7 in of rain caused the normally shallow Kifissos and Ilissos rivers to rise 6.5 ft and overflow their banks; 26 persons, all residents of Piraeus, were killed, and the damage caused by the river waters was estimated at millions of dollars.

November 6, Toccoa, Ga. A 35-year-old earthen dam, weakened by several days of heavy rain, collapsed and loosed a 30-ft wall of water that injured 45 and killed at least 39 persons housed on the campus of Toccoa Falls Bible College.

November 8, Palghat, Kerala, India. Flash floods and landslides injured 3 and claimed the lives of at least 24 persons.

November 10, Northern Italy. Floods and landslides following five days of torrential rain left thousands of people homeless and killed at least 15 persons; the cities of Genoa and Venice were both inundated.

November 12, Southern India. A tropical cyclone that whipped through the southern state of Tamil Nadu claimed the lives of more than 400 persons.

November 14, Northern Philippines. A typhoon that swept through the northern Philippines left nearly 50,000 people homeless and killed at least 30 persons, most of whom were drowned in swollen rivers or struck by falling trees and flying debris.

November 19, Southern India. A cyclone and tidal wave that devastated the coastal state of Andhra Pradesh left more than 2 million people homeless and claimed the lives of an estimated 20,000; 21 villages were totally washed away and 44 others were severely battered in India's worst cyclone disaster of the century.

November 23, Western Argentina. A major earthquake measuring 7 on the Richter scale destroyed thousands of homes, injured hundreds, and killed at least 75 persons; although tremors were felt in Chile, Peru, and Brazil, the greatest damage was reported in San Juan Province, Argentina.

December 20, Kerman Province, Iran. A major earthquake that struck a series of villages in south central Iran in freezing temperatures hit the villages of Babtangal, Gisk, and Sarasiab the hardest; although the official death toll was reported at 521, the final figure was expected to rise much higher.

RAILROADS

January 18, Near Sydney, Australia. A commuter train derailed and rammed into a steel bridge pier causing 500-ton concrete deck slabs from the overhead roading to collapse onto the third and fourth cars of the train, flattening them like matchboxes; 82 were killed and nearly 90 were injured, some critically, in Australia's worst railroad disaster to date.

February 4, Chicago. A Dan Ryan route elevated train, rounding a curve during the early-evening rush hour, smashed into a halted Ravenswood route train in Chicago's Loop; two cars of the Dan Ryan train crashed 30 ft onto the street below and two others dangled precariously from the metal structure; 11 persons were killed and 189 were treated for injuries, in some cases after waiting several hours to be freed from the wreckage.

February 28, Near Barcelona, Spain. Two suburban commuter trains filled to capacity crashed head-on near San Andrés de la Barca some 20 mi west of Barcelona in a collision so intense that the engine and first passenger car of one train bounced atop the two cars of the other train; the casualty list included 2 engineers and 22 passengers killed and 85 commuters injured.

May 2, Belorussia, U.S.S.R. A collision involving two passenger trains at Krizhovka Junction, 400 mi southwest of Moscow, claimed the lives of 19 persons.

May 30, Assam State, India. An express train plunged into a flood-swollen river in northeastern India as a result of a rain-weakened rail line; there were 44 fatalities.

June 27, Near Lebus, East Germany. A passenger express train traveling from Zittau in the southeast to Stralsund on the Baltic burst into flames as it smashed into the rear of a freight train after inadvertently being switched from a main line onto a minor track; 29 were killed and 7 others injured.

July 9, Near Wroclaw, Poland. A train traveling from Prague to Moscow by way of Warsaw slammed into a diesel locomotive near the suburban station of Wroclaw Psie Poli; 11 were killed and 40 others injured.

July 24, Pusan, South Korea. Two passenger trains crashed when an express train carrying vacationers from Seoul to Pusan rammed into the rear of another train standing at the station; 53 persons were injured and at least 12 were killed on the express train.

September 8, Near Assiut, Egypt. A passenger train carrying 700 persons and traveling at 80 mph derailed near Assiut, 220 mi south of Cairo, after the locomotive crew ignored the restricted speed zone; hundreds of passengers were trapped under overturned cars, 150 were injured, and 40 were killed.

September 18, Tukh, Egypt. Two trains, so overloaded that passengers were clinging to the outsides, roared past each other in northern Egypt; 15 persons were crushed to death after being hurled to the ground.

October 10, Near Allahabad, India. A passenger express train traveling to Delhi rammed into the rear of a stationary freight train in northern India; 150 persons were injured and more than 60 were killed, including the engineer of the passenger train.

November 23, Near Rewari, India. The derailment of the locomotive and ten cars of a mail train 50 mi from its Delhi destination claimed the lives of more than 20 persons, including a member of India's Parliament; evidence at the site indicated possible sabotage.

December 3, Near Vereeniging, South Africa. Two locomotives, four passenger coaches, and two freight cars derailed when a freight train slammed into the rear of a standing passenger train at Kleigrond Station; some 200 persons were injured and at least 14 others were killed.

TRAFFIC

January 23, Near Kumanovo, Yugos. A bus traveling from Turkey to Yugoslavia crashed through an overpass guard barrier as it was overtaking a truck; 24 passengers were killed and 19 injured, some critically.

April 3, Cairo. A bus carrying some 100 persons plunged into an irrigation canal after swerving to avoid hitting a child; 19 died and 15 were injured.

June 28, Near São Paulo, Brazil. Two trucks crashing into one another on the fog-shrouded highway linking São Paulo to the coastal city of Santos created a chain reaction of collisions involving 46 buses, 12 trucks, and 14 automobiles; at least 15 persons were killed and 229 injured in the mishap.

August 21, Near Hermosillo, Mexico. A bus traveling on a highway between Hermosillo and Nogales toppled into a water-filled ditch after rain washed out the roadway; 20 persons were killed and 27 were injured.

September 24, Near Dera Ismail Khan, Pak. A bus veered off a road while making a sharp turn and plunged into a ravine; 14 persons were killed in the crash.

October 2, Near Tampa, Fla. A St. Petersburg-bound Amtrak passenger train collided with a pickup truck about 15 mi west of Tampa; all ten persons riding in the truck were killed.

November 9, Near Pietermaritzburg, South Africa. A tractor-trailer traveling along the highway to Pietermaritzburg killed 11 persons crowded where an accident had occurred moments earlier.

December 25, Azuay Province, Ecuador. A bus traveling on a mountain road in the southern province of Azuay plunged over the side of the road; 26 persons were killed and 30 others were injured.

MANAGING THE WORLD'S OCEANS

by Elisabeth Mann Borgese

That the oceans, covering almost three-fourths of the globe, are our "last frontier" has become a cliche of the '70s. It is, nevertheless, true. Mankind has mismanaged the Earth. The decline of land-based resources, the pressure of rising and irrationally distributed populations, large-scale industrialization, and advancing technologies have brought the Industrial Revolution to the oceans. This has both its blessings and its curses.

The wealth of the oceans is enormous. Food from the sea could be multiplied and diversified so as to make a substantial contribution to mankind's struggle against hunger. The oceans are the world's greatest repository of metals and minerals. There is far more oil and gas under the seas than on land and, what is more, the oceans offer new, unconventional energy resources that could solve the world's energy crisis several times over. And, in spite of the development of air traffic, the oceans are still the world's most economical medium of transportation: "God's Road," as Tsar Ivan the Terrible of Russia called them.

Nor is this all. Marine scientific research has assumed unprecedented importance in today's world. The links between oceans and atmosphere and the effect of the oceans on the world's climate—indeed on all life on Earth—have become matters of prime interest and concern. At the same time, recent discoveries in marine geology and geophysics have led to a radical reconception of the physical makeup of our globe and to a new understanding of the evolution not only of the ocean system but of the planet as a whole. And if the oceans have had considerable "geopolitical" and strategic importance throughout history, they have now become crucial. In the deep seas the great powers are hiding their arsenals of first- and second-strike nuclear power—weapons systems that would be too vulnerable on land, exposed to detection by satellites and high-flying spy planes.

The opaqueness of the deep and the mobility it affords make of the oceans the pivot of the balance of terror. Finally, if on the seventh day man is supposed to rest, the oceans offer the greatest environment for recreation, generating one more multibillion-dollar, high-profit industry.

Father Ocean, however—primordial, untamed, and all motion—is less patient than Mother Earth. Of course, the onslaught of the marine revolution is more ruthless and more sophisticated than that of the Industrial Revolution on land. We are living in a later and more advanced phase of this Industrial Revolution, and the effects of technologies on the environment—which used to be locally circumscribed—have become far wider, often transcending national boundaries. The oceans, furthermore, carry them around the globe. What they are asked to absorb, finally, is not only the waste of the marine revolution—offshore oil, navigational debris, the drillings and spillings of deep-sea mining. It is land-based pollution as well: industrial runoffs, domestic sewage, atmospheric particulate matter, organic and inorganic wastes, solid, fluid and gaseous—all exudations of our civilization's sick metabolism. We are destroying our "last frontier" faster than we are learning to develop it, and by destroying the oceans we are destroying ourselves.

The management of ocean space and resources thus is assuming unprecedented importance in the economy and ecology of every nation, from the most developed to the most "primitive," and in the balance of the global household as well. Schools of marine and coastal management, of interdisciplinary and international ocean affairs, are much in demand. That the management of ocean space and resources has a strong international component goes without saying, for waves and currents move, fish migrate without regard to political boundaries, and even geophysical structures displace themselves on the ocean floor. The oceans are one ecological whole, and their problems must be solved with a view to the whole or they cannot be solved at all. What complicates the problem further is that there is, at present, no legal basis for the management of ocean space and resources. With the revo-

Elisabeth Mann Borgese is a leading figure in the International Ocean Institute and a member of the Permanent Austrian Mission to the United Nations. She is currently engaged in the ongoing UN Conference on the Law of the Sea.

lutionary transformation of traditional uses and the introduction of so many novel uses of the oceans, the traditional law of the sea, based on the freedom of the high seas and national sovereignty over a narrow strip of coastal waters, has been rendered totally obsolete and dysfunctional.

This whole complex of issues was joined dramatically in the historic intervention by Ambassador Arvid Pardo of Malta before the United Nations General Assembly on Nov. 1, 1967. His initiative led to ten years of intense activity, culminating in the third United Nations Conference on the Law of the Sea. That conference, which still continued its deliberations in 1977, was given the awesome mandate to create a new order for the oceans, part and forerunner of a new order for the world.

Rational decisions on questions of ocean management must be grounded on a data base of many interrelated and interacting components. Such a data base is hard to come by in an era of departmentalization, specialized and fragmented knowledge, and in an area where serious research is comparatively recent. The International Ocean Institute in Malta has just begun publication of an *Ocean Yearbook* with the object of contributing to the establishment of such an integrated data base. The data used in the following discussion are drawn from Vol. I of the *Ocean Yearbook* (University of Chicago Press, 1978), to which the reader is referred for more complete information.

Living Resources. Optimism with regard to the oceans' living resources cannot be based on recent fishing statistics, nor can it take refuge in science fiction. It can, and must, rely on rather long-term changes, natural and man-made, taking place in the fishing industry.

THE CRISIS IN FISHING. Unquestionably, commercial fisheries are passing through a period of decline. In the hundred years from 1850 to 1950, the world fish catch increased tenfold, at an average rate of about 25% per decade. It doubled between 1950 and 1960 and almost doubled again between 1960 and 1970. In 1970 development began to slow down, and shortly thereafter decline set in. The most dramatic examples are the collapse of the Peruvian anchoveta fishery in the early '70s, which lowered the world fish catch by about 10%, and the collapse of the whaling industry which, in the '30s, still yielded 16% of the world's total marine catch and now provides barely 2%. Similar examples of declining fisheries have mounted in recent years. The herring, the most popular and populous fish in the North Sea, is disappearing, and the European Commission has recommended the complete closure of this fishery.

The reasons for this stagnation and decline are

Three dead whales lie in the water off South Africa as a factory ship approaches.

overfishing, pollution, waste, and mismanagement, all interacting with natural changes in ocean currents and temperatures.

TOWARD NEW RESOURCES. This, however, is not the end of the story. The decline of the commercial fisheries is part of a radical transformation. Declining natural stocks, rising fuel prices, legal and political restrictions arising from the new law of the sea are beginning to cause a displacement toward so-called unconventional resources such as squid, lantern fish, and Antarctic krill. Krill are planktonic animals, like tiny shrimp. They live in prodigious quantities in the Southern Ocean where the great whales, now sadly depleted, feed on them. Annual catches could rise to about 50 million metric tons, and Soviet experts estimate a sustainable yield ten times higher—about 500 million tons. Technologies to harvest krill in bulk have been developed in recent years, as have technologies to process them into palatable food for human consumption. Krill paste, as the Russians make it, is delicious. The Japanese freeze the little creatures whole and use them for cooking.

Squid and lantern fish, which inhabit the middle and deeper layers of the oceans, above the continental shelves and beyond, now can also be trawled and processed. This, again, could triple or quadruple the world fish catch.

AQUACULTURE. Advancing science and technology, furthermore, have given a tremendous impulse to the development of aquaculture in recent years. Aquaculture is becoming an increasingly important part of agriculture and, at the same time, a major component of the fishing industry. Depleted stocks—e.g., of salmon or tuna—can be replenished by land-based hatcheries where seed fish are produced artificially and reared to fingerling size. The fish are then released, and survival rates are ten- to a hundredfold higher than the survival rates of fish hatched naturally and growing in the wild. Bait fish can be produced artificially. Some fishes, such as seabass or yellowtail, can be grown in cages in the sea. Others, such as milkfish, can be raised in lagoons and enclosed bays. Whole seas, like the Baltic, the Mediterranean, or the Caspian, could be turned into fish farms or "ranches." One Soviet expert has suggested that the Antarctic sea might become a colossal whale farm—one way of saving the whale from extinction. What is more, through human intervention species can be transplanted, hybridized, genetically improved.

In 1975 the products of aquaculture throughout the world totaled an estimated 6 million tons. Of this, 66% consisted of freshwater, brackish-water, and marine fish, about 16.2% of mollusks, 17.5% of seaweeds, and 0.3% of crustaceans. Some 85% of the total came from the countries of the Far East and Southeast Asia, where aquaculture has a very long tradition and is deeply imbedded in the whole social and economic structure. China alone accounts for 45% of world production of finfish and seaweeds, and the production of seaweeds in China has increased a hundredfold over the past 30 years. The potential for aquaculture production is limitless. The area presently under aquaculture is estimated to be between three and four million hectares. A tenfold expansion of this area is considered feasible if the necessary investment is forthcoming. Production per hectare could be increased from a few hundred kilograms to over 20 tons a year. Even with existing technologies and without dramatic expansion, a doubling of world production is anticipated during the next ten years.

Thus the present "crisis" in the exploitation of the living resources of the sea—like the "energy crisis"—is not primarily a crisis of resources. It is a crisis of management and politics, complicated by the lack of legal infrastructure. The Conference on the Law of the Sea is barely beginning to supply this lack. It will be up to the continuing mechanisms established by the conference to restructure and strengthen regional and global fisheries organizations so they can cope with the new circumstances and requirements.

Wealth from the Deep. OIL AND GAS. While the total monetary value of the world fish catch was estimated at U.S. $15 billion in 1974, the value of offshore oil resources in 1976 can be estimated at $1,610 billion. To this must be added another $335 billion for offshore gas. (See Table I.) Thus petroleum is still the economically most important resource of the oceans, and its value may rise further. Offshore reserves, constituting an increasingly large percentage of world hydrocarbon reserves, are being located farther and farther out—beyond the edge of the continental margin, in the deep seabed, and, conceivably, on the mid-ocean ridges. Studies

A large percentage of the world's production of edible seaweed is consumed in the Far East and in Southeast Asia.

Table I. Offshore Oil and Gas Production

Country	1975	1974	1973	1972
Oil production (In 000 bbl per day)				
Venezuela [1]	1,737.10	2,071.23	2,700.00	2,500.00
Saudi Arabia [1]	1,385.81	2,024.59	1,990.40	1,490.70
United States	909.59	1,427.54	1,697.46	1,664.58
Iran	481.19	455.19	452.41	467.80
Abu Dhabi	462.71	512.97	454.43	345.20
Nigeria	431.33	648.92	518.04	409.00
Australia	412.52	217.28	348.20	303.00
Neutral Zone	315.07	333.90 [1]	394.04	409.80
Brunei/Malaysia	141.22-B 84.49-M	287.10	264.16	218.00
Dubai	249.32	132.89	221.49	129.50
Indonesia	246.45	247.36	174.22	69.90
U.S.S.R.	230.00	231.00	236.00	236.00
Norway	189.57	35.62	32.30	32.30
Gabon	179.88	59.45	57.20	43.60
Trinidad and Tobago	174.04	135.10	110.97	155.00
Egypt	165.00	147.15	130.75	157.00
Angola/Cabinda	141.20	140.44	144.23	137.40
United Kingdom	83.00	....	....	....
Mexico	45.00	11.90	20.80	38.00
Tunisia	43.00	24.85	0	0
Sharjah	38.36	....	....	....
Congo	37.25	45.97	34.80	7.90
Spain	32.88	34.08	20.00	....
Peru	28.86	34.42	31.35	23.80
Brazil	18.95	20.37	17.21	8.20
Italy	10.41	10.23	12.74	10.90
Denmark	3.30	1.91	2.68	....
Japan	.86	1.91	1.00	1.19
Total	8,264.36	9,293.46	10,067.28	8,858.68
Gas production (In 000,000 cu ft per day)				
United States	5,506.85	6,504.10 [2]	7,130.81	9,119.62
Saudi Arabia	3,825.39 [3]	711.40	721.74	690.17
United Kingdom	3,600.00	3,600.00	3,000.00	2,560.36
U.S.S.R.	764.00	725.00	670.00	....
Nigeria	314.00	....	....	....
Australia	203.00	217.28	173.60	121.77
The Netherlands	186.00	....	....	....
Indonesia	158.80	155.05	108.00	0
Trinidad and Tobago	123.00	18.00	16.79	10.69
Egypt	120.00	....	....	....
Peru	77.00	69.85	60.79	61.17
Brazil	25.00	21.50	....	....
Norway	16.50	....	....	....
Ghana	3.70	....	....	....
Total	14,923.24	12,022.18	11,881.73	12,563.78

[1] Many fields in these countries lie both on and offshore. Since production is reported as a single total, it is impossible to precisely separate the exact amount flowing from offshore.

[2] Estimated.

[3] Almost all the natural gas produced in Saudi Arabia is associated with oil production and none of the gas is marketed. The jump in figures is due to reporting changes by the government.

Source: *Offshore* (June 20, 1976).

of the geology of the deep ocean areas extending from the Voring Plateau off Norway to the waters north of Iceland have given some promising results. The United States Deep Sea Drilling Project has revealed the presence of hydrocarbons in very deep waters and of organic-rich sediments in deep ocean areas formerly assumed to be barren.

As oil discoveries and exploitation expand from the traditional areas of the Middle East and the Gulf of Mexico to the North Sea, eastern Asia, eastern Africa, northwestern Africa, South America, the Arctic, and Antarctica, the energy "balance of power" is shifting. This creates a host of new problems. The effects of the expanding oil industry and the building of superports and pipelines spells doom for many so-called primitive peoples, such as the natives of Palau and Tonga and the Eskimos of Greenland and the Faroe Islands. Increasing tanker traffic is bound to multiply environmental problems. Even more serious, political and legal conflicts loom over

ownership of the oil-rich ocean floor in the Aegean Sea, the Barents Sea, around the Falkland Islands, in the South China Sea (Nansha Archipelago), the Central Mediterranean, and the Gulf of Suez—to name only the most hotly contested areas.

The Composite Negotiating Text now before the Law of the Sea Conference contains a provision that would enable the projected International Sea-Bed Authority to regulate production of all minerals in the international area of the oceans. Sooner or later, this may include petroleum—a fact, or fear, that will no doubt induce the oil companies to press claims for the extension of national jurisdictions still further. Carried to the extreme, this would leave the seabed of the world oceans divided among coastal states, just as the seabeds of the North Sea and other enclosed seas have already been divided. Needless to say, such a development would create many more problems than it could solve and would not be to the best advantage of the majority of the world's people.

WAVES AND TIDES. While oil still is the lifeblood of the world economy, there have been alarming symptoms of circulatory disease, threatening paralysis of the system. But here too, as the old disappears, the new takes over. An "energy revolution" is, in fact, in progress, and the oceans are playing a role of unprecedented importance in it. For the oceans are a source of unlimited and eternally renewable energy, and new technologies are on hand that will harness this energy in its multiple forms.

Ocean currents and tides release annually the fabulous amount of 10^{10} watts of energy. Obviously not all of this can be harnessed. But the French have built a large tidal plant in the estuary of the Rance River which produces up to 350 megawatts (Mw) of electricity annually. The Soviets have an experimental tidal plant at Kislaya Bay and are constructing a second at Mezen Bay to keep up with industrial expansion in the Soviet European Arctic. Canada plans to build, during the 1980s, a tidal power plant in the upper Bay of Fundy with an annual output of 6,500 gigawatt-hours (Gw-hr). India included in its fifth five-year plan the study of a facility in the Rann of Kutch. According to the geologist and geographer Roger Charlier, the northwest coast of Australia could produce as much as 300,000 Mw. An Argentine facility now under study, to be placed either in the Golfo San Matías or in the Golfo Nuevo (Valdes Peninsula), would have a capacity of 600 Mw. A U.S.-Canadian plant in Maine—under consideration for several decades—would have a 1,800-Mw capacity and produce 44 Gw-hr daily throughout the year.

The oceans are traversed by an enormous system of "rivers." Meandering without riverbeds or fixed boundaries, they carry their water masses around the globe. The Gulf Stream carries about 30 million cu m of water per second past Miami. The kinetic energy available from the Florida segment of the Gulf Stream alone is equal to the power produced by 25 conventional 1,000-Mw power plants. Of this, 2,000 Mw can be produced with existing technologies. The electricity generated in this manner could be priced competitively by 1980, according to current predictions.

Great Britain has one of the world's most favoured coastlines for the tapping of wave power. Energy contained in the waves there is variously estimated at from 40 to 70 kw per m, depending on the location. It has been estimated that 50% of Britain's electrical power needs could be produced by harnessing waves along a 1,000-km stretch of coast. Various technologies for wave-energy transformation are under study, funded by the British government. By summing an average of surf conditions over all the world's coastlines, scientists from the Scripps Institution of Oceanography at La Jolla, Calif., have calculated that 2.5×10^{12} w of power could be produced!

OTHER ENERGY FORMS. There is ocean energy in yet another form: that of thermal energy. Seawater is always colder at the bottom. The difference between deep-sea water and surface water may amount to something between 15° and 25° C. The conversion of this heat differential into electrical energy would yield a continuous supply much greater than mankind can now use. In the United States, the Department of Energy is sponsoring a variety of research projects on ocean thermal technologies. If capital costs can be reduced to $1,000 per kilowatt—a figure considered quite attainable by most experts—the Department of Energy will test an experimental 1,000-kw plant in 1979 and plans systems of 5,000, 25,000 and 100,000 kw for 1980, 1981, and 1984, respectively. The largest of these plants could provide electricity for a city of 75,000 inhabitants. Commercial-size plants of 400,000 kw and more could be built by the end of next decade.

There are other, even more sophisticated and still experimental technologies to utilize the boundless, eternally renewable energy of the oceans. Huge amounts of energy could be derived from the contact of salt and fresh water, especially at the mouths of big rivers. Should mankind move—at least partially—toward a hydrogen-fueled economy, this fuel could be extracted from the oceans by physical, chemical, or biological processes; e.g., through systems involving specialized bacteria produced through biological engineering. To increase the profitability of energy production, systems are be-

A giant impounding dam at the mouth of the Rance River in France generates up to 350 Mw of electricity annually.

ing designed that will combine energy production with the production of fresh water, of minerals, and of cultured seafood.

MINING THE SEABED. Once we get used to thinking in terms of the oceans' renewable, nonpolluting, and inexhaustible energy resources, we begin to reason as well in terms of inexhaustible mineral resources, for the production of the latter depends on the availability of the former. The oceans, in fact, are a universal liquid mine containing all the minerals and metals that exist on Earth. (See Table II.) Even with presently available technologies and energy resources, ocean mining is becoming an important part of the world economy. The total value of mineral production from the oceans (excluding hydrocarbons) in 1976 was about $700 million, and it is likely to double over the next ten years. Some experts, like John Mero of Ocean Resources Inc., La Jolla, have predicted that ocean mining will gradually displace land-based mining. The consequences, in world economic and political terms, would be profound.

The most dramatic development in this direction is the production of nickel, copper, cobalt, and manganese from the polymetallic nodules that peb-

Table II. Recoverable Minerals from the Marine Environment

Mineral	Geographic location	Water depth (feet)	Mining status
Sand and gravel	Atlantic and Pacific coasts—U.S.	<100	mineable
Glass and foundry sand	Atlantic and Pacific coasts—U.S.	<200	mineable
Magnetite	Australia, India, Japan, Pacific Coast—U.S.	100–400	mineable
Glauconite	Pacific Coast—U.S.	30–6,000	mineable
Rutile	Australia, Atlantic Coast—U.S.	<100	mineable
Zircon	Australia	<100	mineable
Tin	Malaysia, Indonesia, Thailand, Alaska, United Kingdom	<400	mineable
Silver	Pacific and Alaskan coasts—U.S.	<400	mineable
Gold	Pacific and Alaskan coasts—U.S.	<400	mineable
Platinum	Pacific and Alaskan coasts—U.S.	<400	mineable
Diamonds	Southwest Africa	<200	mineable
Manganese	Atlantic and Pacific oceans, Mediterranean Sea	4,000–18,000	mineable; 5 to 20 years
Phosphorite	Atlantic and Pacific coasts—U.S., Australia, Africa	100–4,000	mineable
Coal	Canada, United Kingdom, Japan	<400	mineable
Monazite	Southern India, Ceylon	0–200	mineable
Shell	Gulf and Pacific coasts—U.S., Iceland	<100	mineable
Sulfur	Gulf Coast—U.S.	<100	mineable

Source: J. L. Goodier, "How to Mine Marine Minerals," *World Mining* (July 1967).

ble the deep ocean floor in the middle of the Pacific, Atlantic, and Indian oceans. According to the current plans of the major consortia involved, as many as 10 million–12 million tons of nodules may be extracted and processed by 1985. Investments and profits are in the billion-dollar range. This explains the toughness and slowness of the negotiations at the Law of the Sea Conference, which is attempting to create a new type of international organization to mine this common heritage of mankind for the benefit of all peoples.

The Politics of the Ocean. The technological and economic imperatives of the oceans are irresistible forces. In meeting these forces, the existing international order may seem to be an immovable object. In fact it is not. A new international order is even now being created under the impact of these imperatives. In this sense, the oceans are not our last frontier; they are wide open toward the future. A number of events that have advanced this new international order took place in 1976–77. We can mention only a few.

SAFETY AT SEA. On July 15, 1977, at 12:00 Greenwich Time, the Convention on the International Regulations for Preventing Collisions at Sea (1972) came into force. For the first time in modern history, the "rules of the road" or the "common law of the sea" had been embodied in an enforceable treaty. Routing schemes for various parts of the world will become institutionalized, and obligations will be imposed on vessels navigating in or near such routing schemes. This regulation of the "freedom of navigation" is an inevitable consequence of the development of maritime traffic and its interaction with other uses of the sea.

Between 1972 and 1976 more than one million

tons of shipping were lost each year. One million tons of shipping represents more ships than are in the individual fleets of nearly a hundred nations. In the first quarter of 1976, 317,738 tons of shipping were lost, and in the second quarter 177,833, mainly (according to the intelligence department of Lloyds) due to fire, explosion, and collision. Considering the loss of life, the damage to the environment, and the monetary losses involved, the new convention is indeed timely. Serious consideration should now be given to the question of whether special-purpose carriers and deep-draft ships should be made subject to compulsory routing and forced to travel to schedule throughout their voyages, just as large aircraft are.

The international organization responsible for navigational safety is IMCO, the Intergovernmental Maritime Consultative Organization. The inevitable enlargement of its scope and its regulatory and planning powers in response to technological imperatives is paralleled by the equally inevitable enlargement of the scope and powers of coastal states. The interweaving of national and international jurisdiction in different areas of ocean space is one of the great challenges before the Law of the Sea Conference.

POLLUTION. Within the last two years a series of important regional developments have taken place, mostly under the auspices of the UN Environment Program (UNEP), dealing with the problem of pollution of the oceans. The most important of these is the adoption of the Convention of Barcelona in 1976 by 15 out of 18 states with Mediterranean coastlines. The convention sets up a general framework for cooperation between governments and for the development of additional legal protocols, institutional arrangements, and procedures for the settlement of disputes. By August 1977 it had been signed by Cyprus, Egypt, France, Greece, Israel, Italy, Lebanon, Libya, Malta, Monaco, Morocco, Spain, Tunisia, Turkey, Yugoslavia, and the European Economic Community (EEC).

A regional centre to combat oil pollution has been established in Malta to serve as a central information service and to advise those concerned of the occurrence of oil spills, the availability of clean-up assistance, the dangers of environmental damage, and similar matters. The centre, under the auspices of UNEP and IMCO, was inaugurated in December 1976. In February 1977, UNEP convened an intergovernmental meeting in Athens to discuss principles for a Draft Protocol for the Protection of the Mediterranean from Land-Based Sources of Pollution. This is the principal cause of pollution of the seas and the most difficult to cope with, since the required action implies a rather profound rethink-

More than seven million gallons of crude oil were dumped into the Atlantic Ocean when this tanker, the "Argo Merchant," ran aground near Nantucket Island in 1976.

ing of the concept of national sovereignty and eventual modification of national production systems. The adoption of the Barcelona Convention is being followed by a host of activities involving regional economic and social planning. Other important regional developments are in progress with regard to East Asian Waters, the Caribbean, the Persian Gulf, the Gulf of Guinea, the Red Sea, the Baltic, the North Sea, and the South Pacific.

TOWARD AN INTERNATIONAL REGIME. Policies of environmental conservation interact with all the uses of ocean space and resources (as well as with land uses). Regional organization interacts with global organization, which it must articulate and which it sometimes precedes. Hence all these activities and developments bear on the proceedings of the third UN Conference on the Law of the Sea. This huge conference of over 150 sovereign states and 3,000 participants completed its sixth session in the summer of 1977 with the release of a voluminous document, the Informal Composite Negotiating Text, consisting of 303 articles in 16 parts plus 7 annexes.

The Composite Text is in fact a nascent world constitution, a document radically different from and far more advanced than the United Nations Charter. Its provisions move from national ocean space—which has been redefined and expanded to include internal waters, the territorial sea, the contiguous zone, the exclusive economic zone, and the legal continental shelf—to international ocean space, which consists of the high seas and the international seabed area. Needless to say, the problems of delimitations and jurisdictions are as numerous as the provisions. The Text moves from

noninstitutional provisions—the codification and updating of the traditional law of the sea—to institutional provisions—the creation of entirely new types of international organization. These include an International Sea-Bed Authority, which would manage the common heritage for the benefit of mankind as a whole, and a dispute-settlement machinery tying together the whole system of organizations dealing with the uses of ocean space and resources.

In one way or another, the text deals with all peaceful uses of the oceans: mining, fishing, navigation, and scientific research. In a wider sense it is faced with problems of food, minerals and metals, energy, trade and communication, science policy, the transfer of technology, multinational corporations, the arms race, arms reduction and arms control, environmental conservation, economic development, the necessity of accommodating in one system socialist and market-economy countries, less developed and industrialized states—in other words, the whole range of basic issues that are now facing the international community. It is in this sense that the new Law of the Sea is not only an essential part but conceivably a model and forerunner of a new world order.

Ten brief years have passed since Ambassador Pardo's prophetic and revolutionary call for a new order for the oceans, based on the principle of the common heritage of mankind. One should marvel that, by 1977, the international community has moved as far as it has in the direction he indicated in 1967, rather than muttering and grumbling because it has not moved further!

NOR ANY DROP TO DRINK

by Jon Tinker

During 1977, as part of a series of meetings that began with the human environment conference in Stockholm, Sweden, in 1972, the United Nations concentrated on water. The first of the 1977 conclaves, the world water conference held in Mar del Plata, Argentina, in March, achieved little beyond a stack of pious, multilingual resolutions; but the second, the UN Conference on Desertification (UNCOD), held in Nairobi, Kenya, in September, marked a major shift in the determination of the nascent international community to grapple with the hydra-headed crisis of food, population, pollution, resources, and the inequitable North-South division of global wealth. For the first time, the UN showed itself capable of the synthesis of science and politics which is the prerequisite for tackling these interconnected crises; and the endorsement

Environment consultant Jon Tinker is director of Earthscan, the UN-funded but editorially independent information service of the International Institute for Environment and Development, London.

at Nairobi of the principle of international taxation to pay for the antidesertification program marked a significant step toward the creation of the "new international economic order" to which the UN General Assembly pledged itself in 1974.

The Blue Planet. U.S. astronaut Neil Armstrong dubbed Earth the blue planet—"a beautiful jewel in space." The colour blue testifies to the Earth's superabundance of water just as Mars, the red planet, derives its name from its arid, stony deserts. Earth carries with it through space some 1,400,000,000 cu km of water, a fixed quantity that man can neither increase nor diminish. Since this works out to no less than 350 million cu m per head of population, there ought to be enough to go round. Yet hydrologists today echo Coleridge's Ancient Mariner when they grumble: "Water, water, everywhere, Nor any drop to drink."

Our planet's watery cornucopia is largely salt, and until the technologists discover a cheap and effective means of desalination it is useless for most human purposes. Of the 2.7% of the global water supply that is sweet, over three-quarters is locked away in glaciers and the polar ice caps. More than one-fifth is held as groundwater and soil moisture, leaving barely a third of 1% of Earth's fresh water readily available to man.

The natural hydrologic cycle is a gigantic solar-powered desalination process, which evaporates water from the salt seas into the atmosphere and precipitates it onto the land as fresh rain and snow; from there, it returns to the oceans once again, either directly via the rivers, indirectly via plant transpiration, or after a more or less lengthy period of storage in ice or underground aquifers. It is only during that comparatively brief part of the hydrologic cycle when water is on the surface of the land that it may be considered a usable resource—and then only as long as it remains reasonably pure. This resource is not very equitably divided among the regions of the world. The key figure in water resources is runoff: the annual precipitation less the loss from evaporation. North America has an annual runoff to the sea that is equivalent to 242 mm (9.5 in) of rainfall over the whole continent. And while Europe, Asia, and Australia have figures that are roughly similar, Africa has only half North America's runoff, and South America has more than two and a half times more.

Of course, the populations that must share this runoff vary considerably. Australians have over ten times as much runoff water per head as North Americans, and South Americans have three and a half times as much. Europeans, on the other hand, have only three-quarters as much runoff as North Americans; Africans have less than half; and Asians have only one-sixth. Even these figures are somewhat misleading, for they imply that all the waters of the continents are equally accessible. Much of Asia's water, for example, runs off northward into the Arctic Ocean, while the people live mainly on the southern and eastern fringes of the continent. In South America the overwhelming proportion of the runoff goes down the Amazon, whose basin is hardly colonized. And, unlike such resources as food, uranium, copper, or oil, it is not practicable to shift water very far. The world's water problems must be resolved locally and regionally.

An International Problem. If this is so, in what sense can a world water problem be said to exist? And why should international institutions be asked to consider it? There are two answers to this question. On the regional level, many states may depend on the same river system for their water, and as their common water resource is more and more fully exploited, disputes arise and may be expected to increase. Some such disagreements are being re-

solved reasonably amicably, but this does not apply everywhere. India, according to its downstream neighbours Pakistan and Bangladesh, is taking more than its fair share of the irrigation and hydroelectric potential of both the Indus and the Ganges. And the future may well see wars or rumours of war over the failure of Brazil and Argentina, for example, to agree on how to share the resources of the Paraná.

Water as a threat to peace, though, is perhaps not the main reason why the UN was addressing this problem in 1977. During the '70s' the international community has begun to confront the realities of planetary life. A whole series of international gatherings, beginning with the Stockholm environment conference, has painted a picture of hunger, disease, inadequate shelter, cold, and human misery that ignores national frontiers. The fact that women in scores of countries throughout the less developed world must walk mile after weary mile carrying pitchers and tin cans of polluted water so their families may drink and wash is increasingly seen as a world scandal. Slowly and painfully, a sense of global commonality has begun to transcend the jealously guarded sovereignties of the 150-odd United Nations.

The dimensions of deprivation which comprise the world water crisis may perhaps be best understood in terms of human health. At the very least, well over one billion people today must drink contaminated water. Among them, diarrhea is the primary cause of infant mortality. According to one study by the World Health Organization (WHO), a staggering 80% of all the world's sickness and disease may be traced to inadequate water supplies.

The statistics themselves are hard to comprehend: 400 million cases of gastroenteritis a year, 250 million of elephantiasis, 200 million of bilharzia, 160 million of malaria, 30 million of river blindness. Abstract figures mean little. How much more they would mean—and how much more notice rich nations, which control the UN purse strings, would take of them—if these miserable millions were concentrated into a few countries instead of being spread throughout the third world.

What would happen if the entire population of Western Europe suffered at once from the loose, bleeding bowels of gastroenteritis? Or if every citizen of the Soviet Union tottered on the flabby, grotesquely swollen legs of elephantiasis? That, repeated year after dreary year, is the reality of inadequate and polluted water in the shantytowns and remote villages of our blue and water-rich planet.

Making It Flow Uphill. Habitat, the UN Conference on Human Settlements held in Vancouver, B.C., in June 1976, set a target date of 1990 for supplying clean water to city and village alike. A year later, the World Water Conference failed to take any realistic steps toward translating this objective into reality. "Water ordinarily flows downhill," commented a UN conference official with uncharacteristic candour, "except when it flows uphill toward money."

Just how far uphill must the world's water be made to flow? In local terms, the price tag is often remarkably low. An unpleasant parasite called the guinea worm, for example, is widespread in tropical Africa, Asia, and the Middle East. The mature female worm, up to a yard long, lives beneath the skin of the human leg, its genital pore lying underneath a blister near the ankle. This blister bursts when wet, releasing a swarm of tiny larvae. If these larvae are eaten by the microscopic aquatic crustacean *Cyclops*, they develop in their new host, to reinfect man when he drinks the contaminated water. Removing a guinea worm from one's leg is laborious and painful, but interrupting the life cycle of the guinea worm is relatively simple. One merely has to stop the well from being reinfected by water splashing off the legs of women drawing water. In Nigeria, when wells were surrounded by outward-sloping concrete rims costing a mere $1.40 apiece, the local incidence of guinea worm fell from over 50% to zero.

Not all water problems can be resolved as cheaply, however. In 1975, according to WHO, 23% of the world's urban population and 78% of rural people had no adequate access to clean water—figures that are themselves suspect in that many countries conveniently exclude from official urban statistics the millions who live in unofficial squatter settlements. WHO estimates that by 1990, given 1975 rates of investment, 22% of urban dwellers and 62% of rural dwellers will still be drinking contaminated water—far behind the Habitat target. If clear water for all is to be a political reality by 1990, the world needs to find roughly $9 billion every year—approximately $3 per head for every man, woman, and child in the less developed world. The distinguished delegates gathered in Mar del Plata declared that this was far too expensive.

Technological Roadblocks. The question of how to supply adequate water for man, his crops, and his animals is, however, still unresolved in technological and political as well as financial terms.

The condition of Israel perhaps best typifies the technological dilemma. An arid land surrounded by hostile neighbours, Israel has learned to conserve and exploit every precious drop of rainfall. A complex network of canals, pipelines, and aqueducts, called the National Water Carrier, links Lake Kinneret (the Sea of Galilee) in the north with the greenhouses and orchards of the once-barren deserts in

the southern Negev. Throughout the country, wells and boreholes are regularly checked and measured, so that the undergound aquifers as well as the surface streams are fully exploited.

Slowly, though, as the groundwater is pumped to the surface, the water table is falling. The aquifer is becoming increasingly saline, as salts are leached down from the soil, as seawater seeps in near the coast, and as a result of pollution. Israel's hydrologists now treat their aquifer as a huge underground reservoir, pumping treated sewage into the soil to force back the invading seawater and to replenish the falling water levels. Israel is already utilizing 95% of its annual runoff. By the end of the century, half of its irrigation water may be treated sewage, and the continuously recycled groundwater may have become so saline that bottled drinking water will have to be sold in the shops. Special aquifer pumping stations will function like environmental kidneys—extracting the groundwater, purifying it, and putting it back underground.

At one level, this projection of Israeli hydrology reveals a triumph of the technologist's art. At another, it is a horrifying picture of the end point of much of present-day water engineering: the inevitable, insidious pollution of the whole water cycle.

The mixed blessings brought by water technology were a recurrent theme of the 1977 conferences. Agriculture, for instance, is estimated to account for 80% of global water demand. The Green Revolution of the 1960s was based on high-yielding varieties of rice, wheat, and other staple grains, but among the disadvantages of these improved strains is their remarkable thirst. Irrigation has become a key component of conventional agricultural development. And while building the dams and watering the fields is relatively easy, comparatively little attention has been given to making sure that the agriculture that follows is truly sustainable.

Desertification. *Delenda est Carthago*—"Carthage must be destroyed"—declared the Roman statesman Cato 200 years before Christ. The city was duly pulled down stone by stone, and the fields that fed it were sown with salt. Today, the same process is usually supervised by the UN Food and Agriculture Organization, funded by the World Bank, and called irrigation.

The Nairobi desertification conference revealed that throughout the world as much irrigated land is lost to waterlogging and salinization each year as is gained by new irrigation schemes. Such schemes often lack two components essential to their success: an adequate drainage system and an extension service to advise farmers. Typically, when a new dam brings water to an arid area, a network of feeder canals and ditches is built to flood the fields

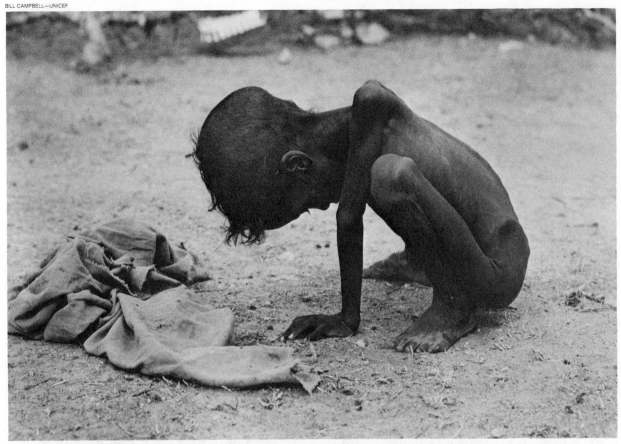

Around the world there are 400 million cases of gastroenteritis a year among people who have to drink polluted water.

with water. Over the next five to ten years rich crops are grown, but then the yields begin to drop off. The soil becomes waterlogged, and the rising water table lifts salt from the subsoil toward the surface. Eventually, as can be seen in Rajasthan only an hour's drive out of Delhi, a white, shimmering scum of salt lies on the surface, and the soil reverts to barren desert. Once waterlogging and salinization have occurred, drainage systems will have to be installed if agriculture is to continue. But the recovery of salinized irrigated land is neither quick nor cheap, and examples of fully successful schemes are few.

In the Tigris-Euphrates Valley, for example, irrigation has been practiced for over 4,000 years. The traditional farming system is known as *nirin*—the land is flood-irrigated until the salinity rises too high and then abandoned to fallow, so the rain can wash the salt down out of the soil. Even so, over the millennia the land has become progressively more and more saline, until today the once-fertile crescent is mainly desert.

The 640-sq km Greater Mussayeb irrigation project was started by Iraq in the Euphrates Valley in 1953. Few drains were laid; canals were badly surveyed and poorly maintained; and the settlers were given no training. Worst of all, the scheme went

ahead with no pilot project, so not even its architects had much idea of what crops could be grown. By 1969 waterlogging was common, and two-thirds of the soil was saline. Waterlogged fields and stagnant canals caused widespread tuberculosis and bilharzia. Wheat was grown less and less, being replaced first by the more salt-tolerant barley and then by the traditional 50% fallow of the *nirin* system. From 1970 UN aid subsidized a rehabilitation scheme, and by 1974 one-third of the saline land had been drained and reclaimed. But with a largely illiterate population and virtually no extension services, the new drains are still inadequately maintained, and the fertile life of the reclaimed land is rarely more than five years.

In India, Syria, Egypt, Tunisia, Mexico, the western U.S., and many other arid parts of the world, a similar picture is emerging. Irrigation without adequate drainage can indeed make the desert blossom like the rose. But it can equally well return the soil to desert within a generation or two.

The Lesson of the Sahel. The paradox that water can itself be the cause of desertification emerged several times at the Nairobi conference, nowhere more dramatically than in the analysis of the Sahel tragedy. In the years 1968 to 1973, rainfall in the Sudano-Sahel, a belt of steppe and savanna along

73

the southern margins of the Sahara from the Atlantic to the Red Sea, was markedly below normal. By the time the rains came again in the mid-1970s, perhaps a quarter of a million people were dead, and millions more had been reduced to penury by the loss of their animals and crops.

As emergency aid was flown in from a conscience-stricken world, scientists of many disciplines tried to discover what had gone wrong. And by the time the Nairobi conference took place, the answer had become clear. The drought itself was not primarily caused by man, but its ecological and human effects most certainly were.

The 1968–73 drought was by no means exceptional. In 1910–14, for example, the Sahel had an even more severe drought, when the level of Lake Chad and the flows of the Senegal, Upper Niger, and Nile rivers fell lower than in 1968–73. Why then were the effects of the recent drought so much more intense? The answers lie in the three great causes of desertification: overcultivation, overcutting for firewood, and overgrazing.

Regular agriculture is unwise in areas with less than 400 mm of rainfall a year. If cultivation does

take place, the soil gradually becomes more desiccated, the humus content falls, and nutrient levels drop. Then, if rainfall is unusually low, the soil becomes useless dust and blows away in the wind. Throughout the Sahel, the decades prior to the 1968–73 drought had seen the northward spread of cultivation, with land that should have been retained as pasture plowed up and planted.

The second cause of desertification is woodcutting, for timber, fuelwood, and charcoal. The camel caravans have gradually denuded the Sahel of trees, bushes, and even stumps and roots for a hundred kilometres and more around the main cities. Without trees, the steeper slopes of the subdesert lands are subject to erosion. Heavy rain rushes down the wadis as flash floods, instead of soaking into the soil to replenish the groundwater.

The third cause of desertification is overgrazing, an increase in the nomadic herds of camels, cattle, sheep, and goats beyond the carrying capacity of the land. Thus, over the 15 years from 1955 to 1970, livestock in Mali increased by 62%, in Senegal by 89%, and in Mauritania by 125%. One reason for the increase was improved animal husband-

Open wells, like the one on the left, are a link in infestation by guinea worms, a painful parasite. Building a concrete rim around a well (right), sometimes at a cost of only $1.40, prevents the spread of the worms.

ry, but the main trigger was, undoubtedly, the sinking of hundreds and hundreds of new water holes. Around most watering points in the Sahel there is a circle of totally denuded ground, up to three or four kilometres across, where the trampling and grazing of thousands of animals has removed every blade of grass. Beyond that is a badly degraded zone, and along the nomadic migration routes this degraded region may stretch 50 or 100 km from the watering point. Even in times of drought, however, most water holes do not run dry. In 1968–73 the Sahelian livestock did not die of thirst but of starvation. The rangelands had become badly overgrazed, and there was not enough vegetation on the desert pastures to support so many animals.

The People of the Dry Lands. The spread of desert conditions is rarely the advance of giant sand dunes onto farmland, although this process does take place—on the irrigated strip alongside the Nile, for example, or in some of the desert oases in the Sudan. More often, desertification is like a skin disease. Unwise land use causes a few spots and pustules to erupt through the soil's protective layer of vegetation. Too much grazing, too many trees felled, too much land under the plow, and the skin dries and flakes off—the soil blows away in the wind. In times of normal rainfall, the process may be hard to recognize. In times of drought, the desert will race over the land. Like a cat stalking its prey, the desert creeps stealthily forward. When the drought comes, it pounces.

This process threatens the very existence of the 600 million–700 million people living in the arid zones of the world. At the current rate, humanity will lose one-third of its agricultural lands to the desert by the end of the century, yet by the same date the increase in world population will require one-third more food merely to maintain present nutrition standards. Desertification is no local problem: it is central to planetary survival.

The preparation for the Nairobi meeting was unusually thorough for a UN conference, and the scientists' prescriptions against desertification were precise and practicable. Unfortunately, there was less understanding of the economic, sociological, and political means of implementing the solutions.

Consider, for example, the Sahelian region itself. The scientists were unanimous that in areas receiving less than 400 mm of rainfall, nomadic pastoralism was the most satisfactory form of land use. The nomads, by their ability to migrate between dry- and wet-season grazing areas and to react to

drought in one area by shifting their herds to another, can harvest the limited and irregular productivity of the region in a way no other society can. So, said the scientists, let nomadism be encouraged. Let the boreholes be turned on and off to keep the herds at a realistic level and to prevent overgrazing in any one area. Let improved facilities for buying, slaughtering, and transporting livestock be established to allow an increased offtake from the subdesert herds.

The Sahelian governments were less than enthusiastic. Representing the political interests of the settled farmers and the city dwellers, they inherited from their colonial predecessors a deep distrust of nomads, regarding them as folk of doubtful political loyalties, disinclined to pay taxes, too fond of crossing frontiers without paying customs dues, and with an anarchic and anachronistic tendency to carry arms.

Some governments—those of Tunisia and Sudan, for example—have begun to change their traditional policies toward nomads, but the shift from outright opposition to firm support for nomadic pastoralism will take time. And how are the nomads

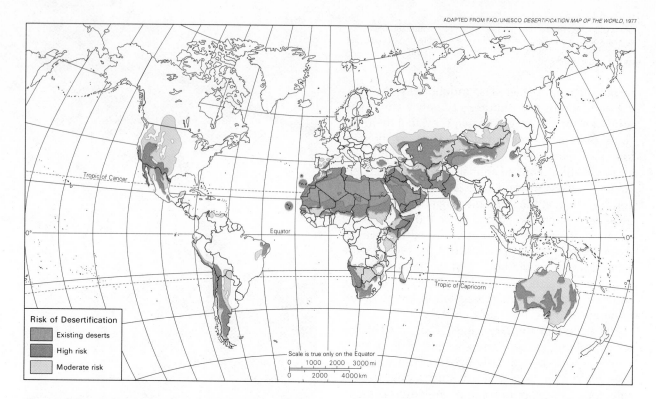

ADAPTED FROM FAO/UNESCO *DESERTIFICATION MAP OF THE WORLD,* 1977

Risk of Desertification

▦ Existing deserts

▦ High risk

▦ Moderate risk

Scale is true only on the Equator
0   1000   2000   3000 mi
0   2000   4000 km

themselves to be persuaded to limit their herds? How are they to shift from a subsistence basis in which livestock are an insurance against drought to a cash economy in which they rear animals for market? How can watering points or grazing areas be opened and closed to tribal leaders whose opposition is backed by guns and knives? How are educa-

Starving cattle wander aimlessly on overgrazed ranchlands in Kenya. More cattle in the area die from starvation than from thirst.

HOLTON—UNICEF

tion and health services to be provided to a nomadic population that is rarely near schools or clinics? These questions have barely yet been asked. There is certainly no international consensus on how to answer them.

This inability to resolve the sociological and economic implications of the new ecological imperatives reappears in many other aspects of the world water crisis. It is now widely accepted that Western systems and standards are both inappropriate and extravagant for the villages of the rural third world. Instead of large reservoirs, the latest chlorination plants, massive pumping stations, and miles of water mains, national and international development funds are beginning to go to simpler, more appropriate technologies. Even the World Bank is shifting its emphasis from funding multibillion-dollar dams to financing village wells. But even the most appropriate and indigenously based technologies are not always sociologically acceptable. And in many instances they cannot work without a degree of administrative and political autonomy at the local, village level—something that centralized and hierarchical governments are not anxious to encourage.

A Short Step Forward. In spite of an inability to follow its scientific recommendations through to their economic, sociological, and political conclusions, the UN deserts conference—in marked contrast to the Mar del Plata meeting on water—must be considered a success. Like all UN meetings, it did not decide anything. The UN is not an executive organization, and it takes decisions only for its

An encroaching desert is moving resolutely onto once fertile land in the Nile Valley south of Cairo (above).
Map at left shows the worldwide spread of desertification.

own, limited staff. The role of the UN is to create and then fuel an international consensus, and on that basis Nairobi was highly successful. But there was another way in which it was important—indeed, which may have made it one of the most important gatherings in UN history.

This aspect arose indirectly from the conservatism of the Western powers and directly from an initiative by Mostafa K. Tolba, an Egyptian microbiologist who is executive director of the UN Environment Program and was secretary-general of UNCOD. The U.S. and the other industrialized states, which still largely finance the UN although they no longer dominate it politically, went to Nairobi determined upon one thing: that no new UN fund was to be established to finance the antidesertification program. As the delegates debated ways of finding new sources of funding without creating any new funds, Tolba proposed something no one had expected: international taxation.

His suggestion was simple enough in concept if not in implementation: a 0.1% value-added tax on all sales in industrialized countries of desert minerals (notably oil and phosphates), and a similar tax on all exports from industrialized states of equipment and machinery going to desert areas—oil rigs, heavy trucks, road-building machinery, and the like. Such a tax, Tolba suggested, would raise the useful annual sum of $450 million.

The outcome was not, of course, any formal endorsement of his value-added tax; the UN does not move that fast. But the conference did appoint a committee of financial experts to advise the UN on how to finance action against the deserts, and this committee was instructed to consider favourably international taxation or some other system of automatic financing.

The principle of automaticity has been around in UN circles for several years now. In the long term it is clear that if the UN is to evolve into any sort of world community, the present system of financing the development of the poorer nations by charity will have to come to an end. Justice and equity will sooner or later demand some form of automatic financing on a global scale. The committee of financial experts set up after UNCOD may never be heard of again, but Nairobi will surely be recalled as the first time an intergovernmental meeting endorsed the international taxation principle.

Barbara Ward, Margaret Mead, Maurice Strong, and a score of other distinguished world citizens issued a warning to the UN at its Habitat conference in 1976. History, they said, suggested that rich elites, entrenched in their wealth and unwilling to create institutions of wider sharing, would be swept away by the growing revolt of the oppressed. In 19th-century Europe, the Hungry Forties led to the Year of Revolutions in 1848. "Can we be sure that the Hungry Eighties will not confront the world with comparable disruption?" they asked.

Their question will not be answered for some years yet, but the ways in which the world community tackled the problems of water in 1977 give some grounds for cautious optimism.

PEOPLE OF THE YEAR

BIOGRAPHIES

The following is a selected list of men and women who influenced events significantly in 1977.

Adair, Paul Neal ("Red")

On April 22, 1977, Well 14 of the Bravo platform in the North Sea's Ekofisk oil field blew out of control. A stream of hot crude oil shot 200 ft into the air. Executives of Phillips Petroleum Co., which operated the well, called at once on "Red" Adair. He sent two of his associates. When they failed to kill the well, Adair himself flew to Bravo platform. Using a new piece of equipment that could generate greater hydraulic pressure than previous devices, he stopped the blowout on April 30. Later in the year he capped a blowout in California.

Oil beneath the ground is often under great pressure. When a well is drilled, the crude petroleum may gush to the surface and shoot into the air. For this reason, oil wells have safety valves and devices called blowout preventers that contain hydraulic rams to stop the oil flow. At Bravo platform, a gauge that had been lowered into the well stuck and partially blocked the

GARY BISHOP—CAMERA 5

flow of oil. Roustabouts pumped drilling mud into the well in order to reduce the pressure of the oil from below and thereby stop its flow so that they could recover the gauge. They apparently succeeded in this effort and, because the well was presumably killed, they removed the protective valves from the wellhead. As a precaution, they installed a blowout preventer. Somehow, this device was put on upside down, rendering it useless. For reasons unknown, mud began to seep from the wellhead. The crew realized that a blowout was imminent and fled to safety.

During the next eight days, an estimated 20,000 metric tons of oil spewed into the North Sea, creating a slick that covered roughly 1,000 sq mi. Ecologists feared that the slick would damage marine life or float to shore and foul the coastline of Norway. Fortunately this did not happen. Some of the oil evaporated, some was recovered by skimmer boats, and some was rendered harmless by wave action.

Paul ("Red") Adair, the man who finally killed Well 14, was 61 years old in 1977. With three associates, Asgar Hansen, Richard Hatteberg, and Edward Matthews, he operated the only firm in the world that specializes in controlling oil-well blowouts and fighting oil-well fires. He began to do this work in 1939 when Myron Kinley, the first such oil-well tamer, hired him. Kinley had just seen Adair thrown 50 ft into the air by a blowout, after which Adair had risen and gone straight back to work.   (VICTOR M. CASSIDY)

Amouzegar, Jamshid

Sworn in as Iran's prime minister on Aug. 7, 1977, Jamshid Amouzegar, as minister of finance and, more recently, of the interior, had upheld his country's interests within the Organization of Petroleum Exporting Countries (OPEC) and had showed himself to be a skilled negotiator in dealings with international petroleum companies. In December 1975 he was among those kidnapped by terrorists who attacked the OPEC Vienna conference. With the other hostages he was taken to Algiers, then to Tripoli, Libya, and back to Algiers

DANIEL VITTET—GAMMA/LIAISON

and released there. On his return to Teheran he received a hero's welcome.

In May 1974 Prime Minister Emir Abbas Hoveida made Amouzegar minister of the interior. He was also entrusted with supervision of the State Organization for Civil Service and Administrative Affairs, with the task of decentralizing the civil service and preparing for the first general elections under the new national party, the Rastakhiz ("National Resurgence"), held in June 1975. In September 1976 Amouzegar, a member of the party's progressive wing, was unanimously elected general secretary of Rastakhiz by the party congress. Thus, when the shah relieved Hoveida of his premiership, his choice of Amouzegar to succeed him was welcomed as a sound one. On assuming office, Amouzegar gave up the party secretaryship.

The son of Habib Amouzegar, a noted Persian scholar, Jamshid was born in Teheran in 1922. He attended the university there and gained degrees in both law and engineering. He then went to Cornell University in the U.S. and there took a degree in health and environmental sanitation, going on to take a doctorate and to lecture at Cornell. In the early 1950s he returned to Teheran and entered the Ministry of Health, rising to be an undersecretary.

In 1958 he became the youngest member of Manuchehr Ikbal's government as a progressive minister of labour. He also served as minister of agriculture and in 1964 was made minister of health in Hassan Ali Mansur's government. In 1965, in Hoveida's Cabinet, he became minister of finance and held the post for nine years, acquitting himself brilliantly in oil negotiations.   (R. M. GOODWIN)

Arledge, Roone Pinckney, Jr.

Early in May 1977, Roone Arledge, Jr., was named president of ABC News, the news department of the American Broadcasting Co. Arledge had previously made a reputation as the innovative and highly successful president of ABC Sports. Network executives doubtless hoped that he would employ his inventive and organizational gifts to revitalize their news programming.

Arledge had spent his entire professional career in the competitive field of U.S. television broadcasting. Three television networks—ABC, the National Broadcasting Co. (NBC), and the Columbia Broadcasting System (CBS)—contend for the attention of the U.S. television audience and for millions of dollars in advertising revenues. For many years ABC had finished third in this competition. Under Arledge's direction, ABC Sports forged ahead of its rivals.

Arledge was born on July 8, 1931, in Forest Hills, N.Y., and graduated 21 years later from Columbia University. After two years of service in the U.S. Army, he joined NBC, where he rose to a position of producer-director of children's and public affairs programming. Arledge came to ABC Sports in 1960.

At ABC, Arledge invented the "instant replay," a telecasting technique that improves the viewer's understanding of a sports event. When an important action (such as a scoring play) occurs, it can be rebroadcast in slow motion moments after it happens. Arledge also initiated the use of isolated cameras to record the action from several angles. The engineer in the broadcast booth would look at many pictures of the same play and would select the best one. During his years with ABC Sports Arledge won more than 125 of television's Emmy Awards, for such programs as "Monday Night Football" and "ABC's Wide World of Sports" and for coverage of the Olympic Games.

Not every Arledge project was a success. In the spring of 1977, ABC Sports committed $1.5 million to produce and televise a professional U.S. boxing championship. In May the network canceled the tournament after seven programs. Subsequent investigations showed that the records of some fighters had been falsified and that some boxers had paid bribes or kickbacks to appear in the tournament. It appeared that ABC Sports had been misled by some dishonest fight promoters.
                          (VICTOR M. CASSIDY)

Bauer, Charita

A kind of birthday was celebrated for Charita Bauer on June 30, 1977, when "The Guiding Light" marked its 25th anniversary as a television serial. The drama was actually 40 years old, beginning on radio in 1937. Bauer, who continued in her original role as Bertha Bauer—a surname that is reportedly coincidental—joined the radio cast in 1950. When the serial was carried on two media simultaneously for a while, she played Bertha on both. And with the silver anniversary past, she showed no signs of abandoning the show. (Her representatives declined to reveal her vital statistics, but it seemed safe to say that she was approximately as old as the show.)

"The Guiding Light" is not the oldest soap opera on television, "Search for Tomorrow" and "Love of Life" having both begun a year earlier. But it is one of the most successful and in 1977 held its audience of about six million regular viewers at a time when the daytime soap-opera ratings were down slightly.

It seemed possible that nighttime dramas may have contributed to the slight audience decline. Producers noted that "miniseries," series of about five nighttime episodes, had become new competitors for the dramatic performer's talents.

Critics and other aesthetes might carp at the dramatic standards of soap opera. But for young actors and actresses the daytime soaps represent fertile fields of opportunity. Since the demise of vaudeville and the eclipse of resident summer stock by "packaged" traveling shows, soap opera has been one of the best places for a young thespian to gain experience. From the actors' viewpoint, these serials offer five hour-long dramas a week. "The Guiding Light" alone counts among its alumni such celebrated performers as Chris Sarandon, Sandy Dennis, Jan Sterling, Cicely Tyson, James Earl Jones, Billy Dee Williams, Ruby Dee, and Blythe Danner.
                          (PHILIP KOPPER)

Begin, Menahem

With its victory at Israel's general election of May 17, 1977, the Likud Party displaced the Labour Alignment as the largest party in the Knesset (parliament), and its leader, Menahem Begin, began to form his government as prime minister on June 7. With Moshe Dayan as foreign minister, he conducted bold diplomacy, from his meeting with U.S. Pres. Jimmy Carter in Washington, D.C., in July to the heady days of his invitation and welcome of Pres. Anwar as-Sadat (q.v.) of Egypt to Israel on November 19–21, his second visit to Carter on December 14–19, visits to London, December 2–7 and 20, and dispatch of Israel's envoys to the Middle East preliminary peace conference, which opened in Cairo on December 14. On December 25 Begin himself visited Egypt briefly to confer with Sadat.

In the negotiations Begin proposed self-rule for the Israeli-occupied territories on the West Bank of the Jordan River and the Gaza Strip with Israeli troops maintained in those areas for security purposes. After an 11½-hour debate on December 28, the Knesset approved the plan.

Begin was born in Brest-Litovsk, Poland (now Soviet Union), on Aug. 16, 1913. In 1935 he obtained his law degree at Warsaw University, where he had become an active organizer for the nationalist Betar Youth Movement opposed to the more

BRIAN ALPERT—KEYSTONE

moderate Zionist establishment. After the Soviet entry into Poland in 1939 in World War II, he was deported to Siberia but was later released to join the Polish Army in exile and was sent to Palestine. There, in 1943, he took command of the underground Irgun Zvai Leumi extremist organization. Because of his unsubstantiated claim that the Irgun was the principal instrument that compelled Britain to abandon its Palestine mandate, Begin clashed with David Ben-Gurion and the Israeli armed forces during the 1948 war of independence. Later, when the Irgun was transformed into a parliamentary opposition party, Begin mellowed in his political style, conveying a quiet English-gentleman image.

Begin joined the National Unity government on the eve of the June 1967 Arab-Israeli war as minister without portfolio. He served until August 1970 without having left a noticeable imprint. But as prime minister he was very much the master of his administration, refusing to allow ministers to talk to the press about matters discussed by the Cabinet. He began replacing officials and senior civil servants by new men, almost invariably old colleagues from the heyday of the Irgun.   (JON KIMCHE)

Bell, Griffin Boyette

Campaigning for U.S. president in the wake of the Watergate scandals, candidate Jimmy Carter had promised that he would take the United States Department of Justice out of politics. But after a fruitless search among other candidates, president-elect Carter designated an old political ally and friend, Griffin Bell, as U.S. attorney general. A native of Americus, Ga., and a graduate of Mercer University law school, Bell had been a federal appeals court judge for 14 years before returning to the law firm that also housed Carter political adviser Charles Kirbo and Jack H. Watson, Jr., of the White House staff.

Bell's nomination provoked an immedi-

TOM SHINE—BLACK STAR

ALAIN NOGUES—SYGMA

ate protest from black groups, who objected both to his spotty civil-rights record as a
judge and to his membership in private,
white-only clubs in Atlanta, Ga. Bell had
also endorsed Pres. Richard Nixon's nomination of G. Harrold Carswell to the U.S.
Supreme Court, despite the latter's record
of meagre judicial achievement and questionable racial attitudes.

Bell faced vigorous opposition from the
Senate Judiciary Committee, undergoing
the most probing confirmation process of
any Carter nominee. Before being confirmed he quit the private clubs and agreed
to an arrangement proposed by Senate majority leader Robert Byrd that would guarantee FBI Director Clarence Kelley his job
until the end of 1977 and thus a full federal
pension.

As attorney general, Bell himself led a
search for Kelley's replacement. A special
committee had selected five possible nomi-
nees, but none suited Bell or Carter. It was
Bell who finally persuaded U.S. District
Court Judge Frank M. Johnson, Jr., to take
over the FBI, but Johnson later had to withdraw because of ill health, leaving the
problem of FBI leadership still unsolved.

The wisdom of Carter's campaign promise about keeping the attorney general
clear of politics was borne out several times
during the year. Bell's closeness to Carter
and his Georgia staffers raised suspicions
during the Bert Lance case as to whether
Bell's Department of Justice could fairly investigate Lance's affairs. Bell also was at
some pains to persuade skeptics that his
department was vigorously pursuing the
investigation of alleged Korean influence-
buying among Democrats on Capitol Hill.
The department did finally bring some indictments against former congressmen.

(JOHN F. STACKS)

Bokassa I

In a spectacular ceremony on Dec. 4, 1977,
Bokassa I was crowned emperor of the new

Central African Empire, an impoverished
country with just over two million inhabitants, known until December 1976 as the
Central African Republic. Emulating his
hero, Napoleon I, he crowned himself. The
splendid coronation ceremony and festivities, featuring cavalry and 100,000 marchers, a banquet for 2,000 guests, and a
French-made eagle throne, crowns, and
coronation robes, were estimated to cost
about U.S. $20 million, more than 20% of
the national income, although French aid
was expected to foot most of the bill.

Emperor Bokassa, formerly Field Marshal Pres. Eddine Ahmed (christened Jean-
Bédel) Bokassa, was by training and character a capable, if flamboyant, soldier.
Born at Bobangui on Feb. 22, 1921, he received Christian missionary education,
joined the French Army in 1939, and rose
through the ranks to become a captain. He
fought with the French colonial forces in
Indochina, was made a member of the
French Legion of Honour, and was awarded the Croix de Guerre. When his country
became independent in 1960, he was invited to set up a small army and became its
first military director general. He was
made commander in chief of the Central
African Army in 1963. He held various
ministerial posts while retaining his military command. On Jan. 1, 1966, he led a
military coup which brought him to the
presidency. In the coup he overthrew his
cousin, Pres. David Dacko.

Bokassa ruled his country in a toughly
autocratic fashion. On several occasions he
gained notoriety for his cruelty. Once he
personally led troops into a prison and ordered them to beat up the prisoners merci-
lessly as an example to other criminals.
When a British journalist who had written
unflatteringly about the emperor was
brought before him, Bokassa struck him to
the ground. In a typical reversal of character he kissed the same journalist warmly
on both cheeks after granting him permission to leave the country.   (COLIN LEGUM)

Bongo, Omar

Pres. Omar Bongo of Gabon served as
chairman of the Organization of African
Unity (OAU) in 1977 and presided over the

organization's summit conference of heads
of state at Libreville, capital of Gabon, on
July 2–5. His chairmanship gave rise to
some discord within the OAU, for Gabon
was accused by the government of Benin of
involvement in an abortive attack upon its
capital, Cotonou, in January; Benin was
not represented at the July conference.
During 1977, in advance of the OAU summit meeting, Bongo bought space in foreign newspapers to deny that his country
had economic links with South Africa or
that it connived at breaking sanctions imposed against Rhodesia. He tightened
bonds with France and visited French
Pres. Valéry Giscard d'Estaing in Paris
three times during the year.

Born on Dec. 30, 1935, in the Franceville
region of what was then French Equatorial
Africa, Albert Bernard Bongo belonged to
a Gabonese ethnic minority group, the Ba-
teko. After receiving a diploma in commerce from the Brazzaville Technical College, he entered the public service in 1958.
He was conscripted into the French armed
forces and served with the Air Force from
1958 to 1960. On leaving the armed services he entered Gabon's Ministry of Foreign Affairs in 1960, the year that the
country gained its independence, was appointed assistant director of the ministry
in the same year, and then became director
of the presidential office, with responsibility for organizing security, defense, and
information. He was appointed the republic's deputy prime minister in November
1966 and was elected vice-president in
March 1967.

After the death of the ailing president,
Léon M'ba, on Nov. 28, 1967, Bongo succeeded to the presidency of Gabon on December 2, not quite aged 32. He established a single-party state by forming the
new ruling Democratic Party of Gabon in
1968. In 1973 he became a Muslim convert,
adopting the name Omar.

During his regime Bongo remained a
firm believer in state-directed private enterprise and in foreign investment. He
strongly upheld his country's links with
France and the French-speaking African
community. In his first decade in office he
proved himself to be a consummate politician who completely dominated his country, guiding it to considerable economic
achievements.   (COLIN LEGUM)

Brearley, John Michael

The schoolboy batsman of unusual promise made good with a vengeance in 1977, at
the age of 35, when Mike Brearley brilliantly captained England against Australia in the home cricket test series. England
won by three matches to none, with two
drawn, thereby recovering "the Ashes."
Also during the season Brearley captained
Middlesex to a first-place tie in the county
championship and to victory in the Gillette
Cup. In 1976 Middlesex under his captaincy won the county championship outright,
and in 1975 it had reached the finals of the
Gillette Cup and of the Benson & Hedges
competition. Ever since he had given up an
academic career to return to full-time cricket in 1971, to lead Middlesex after a captaincy crisis, Brearley had concentrated on
the problems of captaincy and of making
himself a top-class batsman. Under his
calm and thoughtful leadership, Middlesex

steadily advanced, and in 1977 England did too, when he replaced A. W. Greig as its captain.

Brearley was born at Harrow, Middlesex (now Greater London), on April 20, 1942, the son of a Yorkshire father who had played first-class cricket. A brilliant schoolboy batsman, he played for Cambridge University. As a freshman he scored a century against Richie Benaud's Australian side, and as captain for his last two years scored his second century against Oxford University. In 1964 he was named "Young Cricketer of the Year" and visited South Africa with the Marylebone Cricket Club (MCC) but did not make the team for the international matches.

After playing for Middlesex in 1965, Brearley gave up first-class cricket to concentrate on academic work. He took top honours at Cambridge in classics and just missed a double first in a degree in moral sciences. Thus equipped, he taught at the universities of California and Newcastle upon Tyne, but the cricket authorities had not forgotten him, and in 1967 he was invited to lead an MCC under-25 team to Pakistan. There, in a phenomenal burst of scoring, he made one triple and one double century. He played for Middlesex again in 1968–70, but only during the Newcastle vacation.　　　　　　(REX ALSTON)

Brezhnev, Leonid Ilich

In 1977—the 60th anniversary of the Bolshevik Revolution—Leonid I. Brezhnev's political career reached its summit. He was already general secretary of the Central Committee of the Communist Party of the Soviet Union (CPSU), as well as marshal of the Soviet Union since May 8, 1976. On June 16, 1977, the 70-year-old Soviet Communist leader was unanimously elected by the 1,517-member-strong Supreme Soviet of the U.S.S.R. as president of its Presidium (and, effectively, of the Soviet Union, the first man to hold the posts of party leader and chief of state at the same time).

Brezhnev's road to power had been laborious. Born of Russian parents on Dec. 19, 1906, at Kamenskoye (now Dneprodzerzhinsk) in the Ukraine, he joined the Communist Party in 1931. During World War II, as a political commissar, he attained the rank of major general. After the war he assisted Nikita S. Khrushchev in the restoration of the economy and the suppression of nationalist opposition in the Ukraine. In 1952 he was elected a member of the Central Committee of the CPSU, but after Stalin's death his career suffered a setback. Then, in 1957, he became a full member of the Politburo, and on May 7, 1960, chairman of the Presidium of the Supreme Soviet (titular head of state), a post he held until July 1964. After the fall of Khrushchev in October 1964, Brezhnev was elected first secretary (general secretary after April 1966) of the CPSU in his place, and with Aleksey N. Kosygin as premier and Nikolay V. Podgorny as chairman of the Presidium was to reestablish collective leadership. After the Soviet invasion of Czechoslovakia in 1968, he formulated the so-called Brezhnev Doctrine, upholding the right of the socialist countries to interfere in the affairs of a deviant member. But he sought détente in dealings with the West, particularly with the U.S.

On May 24, 1977, Podgorny was suddenly dismissed from the Politburo, and three weeks later Brezhnev took on the presidency, ending the collective leadership. Also on May 24 Brezhnev had submitted a new draft constitution to the Central Committee and in his speech (not fully published until June 5) spoke of the repression of the 1930s which "must never be repeated." The final text of the constitution was approved on October 7, but it showed no basic differences from the Stalin constitution of 1936. On November 2 Brezhnev acclaimed the 60th anniversary (November 7) of the "first victorious socialist revolution in world history . . . that opened the road along which the whole of mankind is destined to move." On the same day he offered the West a suspension of all nuclear explosions, peaceful as well as warlike.　　(K. M. SMOGORZEWSKI)

Brown, Arnold

Elected general—in other words international leader—of the Salvation Army by the organization's High Council in May 1977, Arnold Brown, like his predecessor, Gen. Clarence Wiseman, was a Canadian. Brown was born in London in 1913, emigrated as a boy to Canada, and entered the Army's officer-training college in Toronto from Belleville, Ont. Commissioned an officer in 1935, he served as corps officer at Bowmanville, Ont., before spending ten years in the Army's editorial department as assistant editor of the Canadian edition of the *War Cry* newspaper.

Brown assisted in establishing Salvation Army summer music camps in Canada and in 1942 directed the first music camp in Newfoundland. He also became music director of the first all-Ohio State Music Camp. In 1947 he was appointed territorial publicity officer for Canada, and as such originated the Salvation Army's radio series, "This Is My Story," and "The Living Word" television series, which continued to be used in the U.S., Canada, Australasia, and several other countries. His keen interest in the welfare of youth was given full rein in 1962 when he was appointed territorial youth secretary for Canada and Bermuda.

In 1964 Brown was transferred to England as head of the Public Relations Department at international headquarters in London. Immediately, he became involved in preparations for the movement's massive international centenary celebrations, and he shared in launching a drive to update and expand the Army's social services in Britain, including the building of 26 new social projects in 15 major population centres at a cost of £3 million.

In 1969, as commissioner, he was appointed chief of staff, and as second in command of the international Salvation Army he was directly responsible for the world-encircling "thin red line" of about 25,000 officers directing the Army's work in 82 countries. In 1974 he became territorial commander for Canada and Bermuda. Following his election as the Army's 11th general, he succeeded General Wiseman when the latter retired in July 1977. General Brown was the author of *"What Hath God Wrought?"* (1952), the official history of the Salvation Army in Canada.

(JOHN M. BATE)

Bryant, Anita

"The 'normal majority' have said, 'Enough! Enough! Enough!' " So spoke Anita Bryant before a cheering audience of her supporters in Miami Beach, Fla., on the evening of June 7, 1977. Bryant had just led a successful campaign to repeal a Dade County, Fla., ordinance that outlawed discrimination against homosexuals in housing, employment, and public accommodations. Bryant, a popular singer, was best known for several hit recordings and for television commercials promoting Florida orange juice. Prior to 1977, she had never participated publicly in political affairs.

In January 1977 the Dade County Metro Commission was considering enactment of an ordinance that would outlaw discrimination on the basis of sexual preference. Bryant, who lived in the county, opposed passage of this legislation on religious grounds. A devout Baptist, she believed that homosexuality contravenes divine law. She quoted from Leviticus in the Old Testament: "If a man also lie with mankind, as he lieth with a woman, both of them have committed an abomination." After considerable hesitation Bryant decided to testify against the proposed ordinance.

When the commission passed the ordinance, Bryant joined with some friends to form Save Our Children, Inc. This organization circulated petitions and forced a public referendum. She was opposed by an organization that came to be called the Coalition for Human Rights.

The referendum campaign attracted national attention and provoked a debate on homosexual rights. In the end, the people of Dade County voted 2–1 to repeal the ordinance. Bryant then vowed to carry her campaign to other parts of the U.S. A rumour that she had become too controversial to advertise orange juice was scratched when the Florida Citrus Commission extended her contract through August 1979.

FLIP SCHULKE—BLACK STAR

Anita Bryant was born on March 25, 1940, to a poor couple in Barnsdall, Okla. As a girl, she dreamed of becoming an entertainer. At the age of eight she was "born again" and asked to be baptized as a Southern Baptist. Bryant began her singing career with an appearance on "Arthur Godfrey's Talent Scouts," a popular radio and television program. Soon afterward, she won a beauty contest in Oklahoma and placed high in the Miss America competition. Numerous appearances on television and radio followed. Her first million-selling hit record was "Till There Was You." Bryant was married in 1960 and the first of her four children was born in 1963.

(VICTOR M. CASSIDY)

Brzezinski, Zbigniew

When Jimmy Carter, newly elected to the U.S. presidency, named Zbigniew Brzezinski to be his assistant for national security affairs, the major questions in Washington did not concern Brzezinski's views on foreign policy. Instead, attention focused on how his personal style would compare with that of his predecessor, the flamboyant Henry Kissinger, and whether he would become involved in a power struggle with Secretary of State Cyrus Vance.

In his first year at the helm of the National Security Council, Brzezinski surprised everyone by keeping a low profile, and he appeared to have avoided friction with Vance. He envisioned a far different role for the NSC than it played during the early Kissinger years. Instead of making and executing foreign policy, the NSC under Brzezinski attempted to be a "think tank," to serve as a catalyst for others, and to "synthesize" the options available to the president. It might be that Brzezinski's major diplomatic achievement in his first year was getting along with other agencies and personalities involved in shaping U.S. foreign policy.

Yet in crucial areas of foreign policy, the Carter administration's initiatives bore Brzezinski's imprint. Thus the controversial tactic of inviting the Soviet Union into early, cooperative efforts to reconvene the Geneva Middle East peace conference re-

DENNIS BRACK—BLACK STAR

flected Brzezinski's view that the Soviet Union eventually had to be a part of any meaningful Mideast negotiations. Despite Soviet rejection of fresh U.S. proposals for the strategic arms limitation talks in the spring, Brzezinski was convinced that the two superpowers could cooperate in specific areas of mutual interest even while they competed in others.

This thinking represented a change from the hard-line, anti-Communist views Brzezinski often expressed when he was building his reputation as an expert on Eastern Europe. The son of a Polish diplomat, he was born March 28, 1928, in Warsaw but was raised and educated in Canada, where until 1945 his father served as Polish consul in Montreal. He graduated from McGill University, earned his doctorate at Harvard, and taught there before moving on to Columbia, where he became director of the Research Institute on Communist Affairs.

(HAL BRUNO)

Bukovsky, Vladimir Konstantinovich

A remarkable exchange—arranged between the Soviet Union and Chile, with the U.S. government as intermediary—took place at the Zürich (Switz.) airport on Dec. 18, 1976. Vladimir K. Bukovsky, a 33-year-old Soviet dissident, stepped out of a plane from Moscow to freedom in the West, while Luis Corvalán, general secretary of the Communist Party of Chile, released from Santiago, was to be transferred to Moscow. The freeing of Bukovsky was the price the Soviet Union had to pay for Chile's release of Corvalán. On March 1, 1977, Bukovsky met with U.S. Pres. Jimmy Carter at the White House and urged commitment to human rights. Later, he was attacked by the Soviet media for damaging U.S.-Soviet relations.

Bukovsky was born in Moscow on Dec. 30, 1942. The son of a writer, he attended a Moscow high school. After Stalin died (1953), young Bukovsky, disillusioned by the subsequent revelations, published a school magazine in which the Soviet authorities were satirized. He was expelled as a result, and later he was expelled from Moscow University for his unorthodox opinions. He became involved in literary protest meetings and *samizdat* (self-publishing) and was arrested on June 1, 1963, for possessing a copy of Yugoslav Milovan Djilas' *The New Class*, published in Paris. Taken to the Serbsky Institute of Forensic Psychiatry, he was declared unaccountable for his actions and was admitted to the Leningrad Psychiatric Prison Hospital, where he endured "15 months of hell." Released in 1965, he helped to plan a demonstration against the arrest of dissident writers and was promptly arrested again and taken away for eight more months of psychiatric treatment. Bukovsky was arrested again in 1967 on similar charges and sentenced to three years in a labour camp.

In January 1970 Bukovsky returned to Moscow and began collecting material on the Soviet misuse of psychiatry. Arrested for a fourth time in 1971 for transmitting this information to the West, he was sentenced to two years in jail plus five years in a strict labour camp and five years' exile. After serving the first part of his sentence, he was interrogated about the *samizdat*

journal *Chronicle of Current Events*. Sent to the Perm labour camp, he collaborated there with psychiatrist Semyon Gluzman on one of the most daring documents to appear in such conditions—*A Manual on Psychiatry for Dissidents*. On his sudden release, Bukovsky was told that he, his mother, sister, and a nephew had been deprived of Soviet citizenship and banished. In December 1977, during a tour of U.S. cities arranged by the AFL-CIO, Bukovsky criticized the West for its diffidence at the Belgrade conference in exposing Soviet abuses of human rights.

(K.M. SMOGORZEWSKI)

Byrd, Robert Carlyle

Some politicians think of a seat in the U.S. Senate as a stepping-stone to the presidency; others consider the Senate an end in itself. Sen. Robert C. Byrd of West Virginia is in the latter group. Despite a halfhearted favourite-son bid for the presidency in 1976, Byrd is, as he himself said, "the Senate's man." In 1977 his loyalty to "the world's most exclusive club" was rewarded when his Democratic colleagues elected him majority leader.

For Byrd, this was the culmination of a long and methodical effort that began in 1967, when he was chosen as secretary to the Senate Democratic Caucus. With the diligence that characterized his entire career, Byrd used his new position to round up votes and monitor action on the Senate floor for the then majority whip, Sen. Edward M. Kennedy of Massachusetts. In 1971 Byrd was encouraged to make a run for the whip's position himself—and stunned many political observers by defeating Kennedy on a 31–24 vote. When longtime majority leader Mike Mansfield of Montana retired in 1976, his loyal lieutenant, Byrd, was the overwhelming choice to replace him.

Byrd had overcome many obstacles in his climb up the political ladder. His mother died when he was ten months old. Rejected by his father, he was raised by im-

TOM SHINE—BLACK STAR

poverished relatives in a small West Virginia mining town. After graduation from high school, he worked as a meat cutter and a shipyard welder. In 1946 he launched his political career and, despite his membership in the Ku Klux Klan during the 1940s (a fact he later dismissed as a "youthful mistake"), was elected to three terms in the West Virginia state legislature. In 1952 he ran successfully for the U.S. House of Representatives, moving to the Senate in 1958.

As a senator, Byrd gradually shifted from bedrock to what he termed "moderate conservatism." In 1975 he voted for an extension of the Voting Rights Act, which he had opposed in 1965. During his first year as majority leader, he established himself as a shrewd, at times high-handed, tactician, maintaining a delicate balance between support for the legislative program of Pres. Jimmy Carter and support for the Democratic members of the Senate, who seemed increasingly resistant to presidential leadership.

Byrd was born Cornelius Calvin Sale, Jr., on Nov. 20, 1917, in North Wilkesboro, N.C. His name was changed by his foster parents. While he was a member of Congress, Byrd earned a law degree at American University.   (STANLEY W. CLOUD)

Califano, Joseph Anthony, Jr.

In 1961 Joseph A. Califano, Jr., first arrived in Washington, D.C., to serve as an assistant to Cyrus Vance, then the general counsel for the U.S. Department of Defense. Califano's talent and energy quickly moved him into a job as special assistant to U.S. Secretary of Defense Robert McNamara. Shortly afterward, he moved to the White House as an assistant for domestic affairs to Pres. Lyndon Johnson.

In the Johnson White House Califano became the architect for many of Johnson's "Great Society" programs, such as Model Cities and the Office of Economic Opportunity. He became known as a sort of deputy president for the Great Society.

Since those days of rapidly expanding federal initiatives to solve the problems of the poor, a wave of skepticism and eight years of Republican government seemed to have brought the idea of such programs into some disrepute. It was thus a bit ironic when Califano was appointed by U.S. Pres. Jimmy Carter to the office of secretary of health, education, and welfare and charged with weeding out the Great Society programs that had failed and reforming those that were not working.

Califano, the grandson of a fruit vendor, was born in Brooklyn, N.Y., on May 15, 1931. A graduate of Harvard University law school, he left a $500,000-a-year law practice in Washington to take over the 149,000-employee department that annually spends $140 billion and is charged with executing nearly every important social welfare program operated by the federal government. The department's sheer size has made it nearly unmanageable for a succession of secretaries, and its programs have long been a focus of sharp political debate.

At the top of the long list of problems Califano faced was the necessity of reforming the nation's costly and inefficient welfare system. Despite failures of past presidents to rework the system, Califano proposed in August a major overhaul that would replace three of the largest welfare programs with single cash grants, add some 2 million people to the 30 million receiving some sort of welfare assistance, increase federal costs from about $28 billion to $32 billion a year, and reduce state welfare costs by about $2 billion. The program also promised creation of 1.4 million public service jobs for welfare recipients unable to find work in the private sector.

(JOHN F. STACKS)

Carew, Rod

When a scout for the Minnesota Twins first saw him, Rod Carew was playing baseball at a New York City park across the street from Yankee Stadium. He was ushered across the street for a tryout, but it lasted only five minutes. At the end of that time Minnesota manager Sam Mele said, "Get him out of here and sign him before the Yankees see him."

It was a good move for Minnesota. Carew spent the first ten years of his major league career making heads turn as he batted over .300 eight straight times, and then in 1977 he made heads shake with amazement. On July 1 he was batting .411, and it looked as if he might become the first .400 hitter in the major leagues since Ted Williams batted .406 in 1941.

Carew did not make .400, finishing the season with a .388 average, but it was baseball's best since Williams' .388 in 1957, and his season total of 239 hits had not been matched since 1930. He also set or equaled career highs in every other important offensive statistic, scoring 128 runs and driving in 100, and hitting 38 doubles, 16 triples, and 14 home runs. He led the American League in runs scored, batting average, hits, and triples and tied for third in doubles. He was voted the league's most valuable player. His 11-year career average

WIDE WORLD

of .335 was by far the best among active players.

Unlike the patient Williams, Carew says, "I like to swing the bat, and if a pitch is close enough to handle I'll go for it. The most important thing is making contact." Nor is he the power hitter Williams was, spraying the ball instead to whichever parts of the field are least inhabited and basing his batting success more on science and speed.

But his batting style cost him money after the 1974 season, when he had his previous high average of .364. An arbitrator denied his salary request because he had averaged only three home runs in the previous five years. Carew responded by giving them what they wanted, hitting 14 homers in 1975 and still batting .359. "If he'd been in the National League, with all their artificial surfaces, he'd already have hit .400," said his manager, Gene Mauch.

Rodney Cline Carew was born Oct. 1, 1945, on a train in Panama and grew up using sticks for bats and balls of foam rubber covered by tape. His family moved to New York City when he was 16, but he could not play high school baseball because he had to work two jobs.

(KEVIN M. LAMB)

Carrillo, Santiago

The general secretary of the 100,000-member Spanish Communist Party (PCE), Santiago Carrillo, received wide publicity in 1977 from the publication of his book *Eurocommunism and the State* and from his outspoken views on the need for increased freedom and independence within and for the party. He favoured working for "a plurality of political parties and for democratic alternation between the majority and the minority," and he supported the Basque and Catalan sections of the PCE in their desire to take an independent stance based on the needs of their own regions.

Born in 1915, Carrillo joined the Communist Party at the time of the Popular Front's electorial victory in Spain in 1936. He was in charge of public order in Madrid, and some held him responsible for the massacre of prisoners at Paracuellos in November of that year. After the Civil War he went to the Americas, and later spent many years in Paris. He participated in the founding, in July 1974, of the Junta Democrática Española, which partially united the opposition to the Franco regime, and in March 1977 he helped found the Coordinación Democrática, which incorporated the opposition parties and Spain's regional autonomy movements. In December 1976 he entered Spain clandestinely and held a press conference; he was arrested for illegal membership in a political party but was released on bail and later set free.

After its legalization in 1977, the PCE maintained a low profile up to the elections on June 15. It obtained 9% of the vote and 20 seats in the lower house of the Cortes (the third largest bloc), but Carrillo's call for a coalition government was denied. The PCE, however, cooperated in the drafting of Spain's new constitution and supported the government in its attempts to cope with Spain's economic difficulties and its efforts to overcome terrorism.

PCE relations with the Kremlin worsened considerably in November, when Carrillo visited the U.S.S.R. for the celebration of the 60th anniversary of the Bolshevik Revolution. Although he had been invited to deliver a speech, he was informed that he would not be invited to the platform to deliver it. Yet in talks with Yugoslav Communist leaders in Belgrade a week later he denied that there were differences between him and the Soviet party. Later in November he visited the U.S. to lecture on Eurocommunism at Harvard and Yale universities.   (MICHAEL WOOLLER)

Carter, Billy

Many U.S. presidents have had brothers, but there had never been one quite like Pres. Jimmy Carter's younger brother, Billy. A self-proclaimed Georgia "redneck," Billy was gregarious where Jimmy was taciturn, iconoclastic where the president was pious. Jimmy, 13 years older than his brother, finished second in his Plains, Ga., high school class; Billy finished 25th among 26 graduating seniors. If Jimmy did not smoke and drank only rarely, Billy worked his way through seven packs of cigarettes and an average of 12 beers a day.

A close bond appeared to exist between the two brothers. Indeed, for all their differences, there were also many similarities between them. Both were avid readers and strong family men, fierce competitors, and, when they were partners in the family's peanut warehouse operation, serious and successful businessmen. Billy might sometimes poke fun at Jimmy's political career, but he had worked hard to get his brother elected president. Billy himself ran twice for mayor of Plains—and lost.

Yet Billy Carter seemed to delight in emphasizing the differences. The higher Jimmy moved in the political world, the more Billy insisted on living "his own life," hanging out with the "good ol' boys" at "Billy Carter's filling station" in Plains. After the 1976 presidential election, Billy hired an agent and took his performance on the road. At $5,000 a throw, he appeared on TV shows and at county fairs, auto races, and amusement parks. He even sold his name to a brewing company that brought out a beer called, simply, "Billy."

Some observers feared that Billy might be damaging the president's reputation, but neither he nor Jimmy seemed very concerned. Nevertheless, Billy, who owned 16% of the Carter warehouse business, was turned down when he tried to buy his brother's two-thirds share, which had been placed in a blind trust after the election. Billy thereupon resigned as manager of the business and, with his wife, Sybil, and their six children, moved to a new house some distance from Plains. The town, he indicated, was becoming a tourist trap.

Born William Alton Carter III on March 29, 1937, in Plains, the youngest of four children, Billy joined the Marine Corps after graduation from high school. Following service in the Marines, he attended Emory University in Atlanta for nearly two years, then held several jobs around the state. He moved back to Plains in 1964.
                    (STANLEY W. CLOUD)

Carter, Jimmy

For Jimmy Carter, the 39th president of the United States, 1977 was a year of both triumph and considerable difficulty. In his long-shot bid for the presidency, Carter, a Democrat and a former governor of Georgia, had campaigned as an "outsider" bent on reforming the federal government. He converted an appealing campaign style and a good sense of the national mood into victory over the Republican incumbent, Gerald Ford. Carter was inaugurated on January 20. By the end of the year, however, he was slipping in the popular opinion polls.

Carter had hardly taken the oath of office before he set out to reinforce his image as a populist citizen-president. He ordered that the use of limousines by government officials be strictly limited and discouraged the playing of "Hail to the Chief" in his own honour. Some critics charged that he was emphasizing "style over substance," but his efforts to reduce the pomp of the presidency were generally well received.

The difficulties began when Carter set forth his ambitious programs. Domestically, he proposed legislation that addressed itself to, among other things, the energy crisis, potential deficits in the Social Security system, government reorganization, economic recovery, and welfare reform. He ordered a tax-reform study and seriously considered a major cut in income taxes, although, for technical and political reasons, he proposed no legislation on either matter in 1977.

In international affairs, the president, to the irritation of the Soviet Union and other countries, stressed his administration's commitment to human rights and an "open" foreign policy. In March Carter sent to the Soviet government a far-reaching proposal for strategic arms reductions, which was later set aside in the hope of achieving a more limited—and realistic—treaty. His administration signed treaties with Panama that would, if ratified by the Senate, end U.S. sovereignty over the Panama Canal by the year 2000.

Conservatives found Carter too liberal, and liberals thought him too conservative, especially on economic policy. He was sometimes criticized for what was seen as a lack of commitment to his own programs and for failing to convert concepts into effective action. Although the Congress, controlled by Carter's party, passed many of his legislative proposals, the fate of others (including the Panama Canal treaties and the energy program) was in serious doubt. Possibly the worst period for Carter was when he was accused of "cronyism" in his defense of an old friend, Bert Lance (q.v.), the director of management and budget, who was ultimately forced to resign because of questionable business dealings prior to his appointment.

Jimmy Carter was born James Earl Carter, Jr., on Oct. 1, 1924, in Archery, Ga., near the town of Plains to which the family later moved. He was graduated from the U.S. Naval Academy in 1946 and resigned his commission in 1953 to return to civilian life at Plains, where he managed the fami-

ly's farming and warehousing business. He served as governor of Georgia from 1971 to 1974.   (STANLEY W. CLOUD)

Cartland, Barbara

After her father died for king and country in World War I and left the family destitute, Barbara Cartland remembers, "Mummy said to me, 'You must get a job. I think you should be a receptionist or a secretary to a doctor.' She chose that because she thought doctors had no interest in sex—something, I can tell you, that's *quite* unrelated to fact. Anyway, I had no intention of being a secretary to anybody." Instead, she became a reporter and, at 21, a successful novelist. *Jigsaw*, her first book, "wasn't very good, but it was a huge success, simply because I was a debutante—a girl who was supposed to be a lady and had soiled her lily-white hands with work." She went on to become an aviatrix of note and to write some 200 books.

Credentials like those might have made the twice-married grandmother a hero of the women's movement today. Not so, however, because her more than 170 novels are unmitigated romances, and she became the champion of virginity. In an article in *The Times* (London), Cartland contradicted some tenets of feminist dogma: "However much 'Women's Lib' may talk of equality of the sexes, it is, as it happens, medically impossible for men and women to be equal when it comes to sex. . . . Personally I want to be loved, adored, worshipped, cosseted, and protected. . . . It is women who inspired the great masterpieces in every known culture. . . . [The male is only] at his greatest when his spiritual capabilities are accentuated by the pure, mystical perfection of his ideal—The Virgin Woman."

"About fifteen years ago, publishers told their romantic authors that they should 'go modern' and write about divorce and unsanctified love—I refused. . . . With the result that when the Romantic boom burst I had more than 150 virgins in print." Indeed, the romantic market seemed to be booming; several recent series of such novels proved surprisingly popular. Cartland, who was born in England in 1904, noted that her own sales "have leaped into astronomical figures" in the past two years. Copies of her books now number some 70 million worldwide. (PHILIP KOPPER)

Cauthen, Steve

The day that 17-year-old Steve Cauthen became the first jockey ever to win $5 million in purses in one year, he said, "$5 million is all right, but I made 45 bucks in a card game today. That's even better." At 17, it seems, a guy has to put his priorities in order.

Cauthen had earned more than $6 million by the end of 1977, breaking the one-year-old single-season record of $4,709,500 in purse winnings by veteran Angel Cordero, Jr. But his victory total was short of Chris McCarron's record 547, largely because McCarron rides in Maryland and Cauthen faced the nation's best jockeys nearly all year in New York.

The 5-ft 1-in, 95-lb sensation attracted national attention during the second week of 1977, when he won 23 of his 51 races and had a remarkable 76.5% of his finishes in the money (third or better). It took him only 43 days to break the Aqueduct Race Track record of 104 victories that Ron Turcotte had set in 91 days. But there was skepticism from the older jockeys who knew Cauthen's biggest test was yet to come because he had never been seriously injured.

That happened on May 23, when his horse, Bay Streak, broke its right foreleg and Cauthen went down in a three-horse pile. He broke his right arm, two fingers, and a rib, suffered a concussion, and required 25 stitches on his hand and face. He was expected to miss six to eight weeks of racing, but his next mount was June 23. Cauthen had only 275 victories and about $3 million in winnings at that point.

Cauthen also did not slow down after losing the five-pound advantage he was given as an apprentice through June 26. No apprentice ever had approached his first-year figure of 524 victories.

Cauthen was born May 1, 1960, in Covington, Ky., and grew up in nearby Walton. His father, Ronald ("Tex") Cauthen, was a blacksmith at the Latonia and River Downs tracks near Cincinnati and his mother, Myra, was a licensed owner-trainer of horses. Cauthen started riding at 2, was breaking yearlings at 12, and decided to become a jockey when he was 14. "Racing is part of life," he said, planning to finish high school by correspondence.

Cauthen wasn't allowed to become an apprentice until his 16th birthday, and his first ride was a 136–1 long shot on May 12, 1976. After his first winner five days later, he finished the 1976 season at River Downs with 240 victories and $1,240,000 million in purse winnings. (KEVIN M. LAMB)

Cheever, John

The publication of John Cheever's much acclaimed novel *Falconer* (1977), a book described by critic John Gardner as "an extraordinary work of art," solidified the author's reputation as a major American novelist as well as one of the foremost contemporary short-story writers.

Falconer is the name of the prison in which Cheever's hero is confined for an unusual crime—fratricide. But Cheever describes Falconer as a metaphor for a broader confinement, a metaphor continued from his earlier works. In *The Wapshot Chronicle* (1957) and *The Wapshot Scandal* (1964), the symbol of confinement is the small, traditional New England village of St. Botolphs; in many of his short stories and in *Bullet Park* (1969), the symbol is the affluent world of suburbia. The recurring theme is the struggle for freedom, not only from prisons but from confining emotional bonds as well. Cheever's voice is often ironic or nostalgic, but he reveals in his

world "the inestimable richness of human nature."

Cheever was born in Quincy, Mass., on May 27, 1912, and was educated at Thayer Academy, whence he was expelled at the age of 16. That expulsion gave him the subject for his first publication, a story that appeared in *The New Republic* in 1930. During most of the 1930s he lived in New York City and published stories in various national magazines, especially *The New Yorker*. In 1943 he published his first collection of short stories, *The Way Some People Live*.

After serving in the U.S. Army in World War II, Cheever worked for a time as a television scriptwriter, but short stories remained his primary interest. *The Enormous Radio, and Other Stories* in 1953 strengthened his reputation, its title story becoming one of his most frequently anthologized works. His other short-story collections include *The Housebreaker of Shady Hill* (1958), *Some People, Places, and Things that Will Not Appear in My Next Novel* (1961), *The Brigadier and the Golf Widow* (1964), and *The World of Apples* (1973). Cheever's novels, in general, have inspired less unanimous critical praise than his stories, although *The Wapshot Chronicle* won the National Book Award for fiction in 1958. (JOAN NATALIE REIBSTEIN)

Chirac, Jacques René

As the general election scheduled for March 1978 drew closer, Jacques Chirac had become a key figure and at the same time the mystery man in French political life. A protégé of former president Georges Pompidou, he had become premier following Valéry Giscard d'Estaing's election to the presidency after Pompidou's death in 1974. Chirac had played a major part in securing Giscard's election, but after two years they disagreed. Following his resignation in August 1976, Chirac was replaced as premier by Raymond Barre and thereafter figured increasingly as a potential rival to the president and as a critic of government policies—especially the "Plan Barre" counterinflationary program.

Chirac's election as mayor of Paris in March 1977 against the president's candidate greatly increased his influence. Leader of the Rassemblement pour la République—the new name adopted by the Gaullists in December 1976—he hoped to emerge from the 1978 election as the leader of a victorious majority in order to "re-Gaullize" France. On his side he had a boxer's energy, a will to win, and the claim to represent "order with progress." Against him were the hostility of the president and his premier, both of whom had every intention of carrying on with "de-Gaullizing" the country, and the disquiet he aroused among moderates to whom he seemed both too dynamic and in too much of a hurry.

Chirac was playing a risky game. Defeat for his new-look Gaullist party would mean the liquidation of the post-de Gaulle movement as well as the end of his own ambitions. But if he won, he would gain a double victory, first for the parliamentary majority over the left, and second within

Steve Cauthen

UPI COMPIX

HENRI BUREAU—SYGMA

the majority since, as head of the dominant party, he would remain its leader. Then he would have to establish himself as a credible successor to Giscard in the 1981 presidential election and again defeat the left in that election.

Born in Paris on Nov. 29, 1932, the son of a company director, Chirac was a graduate of the École Nationale d'Administration. He was a member of Pompidou's personal staff from 1962 until 1967, when he was elected to the National Assembly as deputy for Corrèze. He subsequently served as minister for parliamentary relations (1971–72), for agriculture and rural development (1972–74), and of the interior (March–May 1974) during Pompidou's presidency. (PIERRE VIANSSON-PONTÉ)

Coffin, William Sloane, Jr.

A noted civil-rights activist and antiwar leader of the 1960s, William Sloane Coffin, Jr., in the 1970s became a prominent figure in another movement. This one was theological, a shift away from the secularization that characterized many liberal churches during a decade of social activism and toward an increased spiritualism. Coffin, who retired in 1975 from his position as chaplain of Yale University after 17 years, in 1977 was named senior minister of New York City's interdenominational Riverside Church.

Coffin's new interest came to public attention on Jan. 26, 1975, when he and 17 other prominent leaders of nine Christian denominations issued a statement entitled the "Hartford Appeal for Theological Affirmation." The controversial document deplored what the signers viewed as the worldliness of recent liberal religion. Coffin denied charges from some church activists who regarded the Hartford statement as a retreat from the struggle for social and political justice. He viewed it not as a withdrawal from action but rather as a call for basing such action in deeper spiritual conviction.

Still, Coffin was not entirely satisfied with the Hartford statement. "This paper doesn't begin to be scandalous or passionate enough. Genuine prophesies are always scandalous, theology has to be passionate, all great theological statements of the Bible came out of very passionate confrontations with evil," he said in an interview reported in the New York Times Magazine in 1976.

Coffin was born in New York City on June 1, 1924. A graduate of the Yale University School of Music and the Union Theological Seminary, he served as a paratrooper during World War II and from 1950 to 1953 worked for the U.S. Central Intelligence Agency. He was ordained to the ministry of the Presbyterian Church in 1956, afterward becoming acting chaplain at Phillips Academy and then chaplain at Williams College. He was appointed university chaplain at Yale in 1958.

Coffin's activism in the civil rights movement was marked by several arrests (in 1961, 1963, and 1964) for participating in various protest demonstrations against racial segregation. In 1965 Coffin became a leader in the growing opposition to U.S. participation in the war in Vietnam. His actions led to his conviction on charges of joining a conspiracy to violate federal draft laws. Coffin nonetheless continued his work against the war, in the belief that it was "stupid politically, inept militarily, and morally unjust."

(JOAN NATALIE REIBSTEIN)

Cowen, Sir Zelman

Installed as governor-general of Australia on Dec. 8, 1977, Sir Zelman Cowen replaced Sir John Kerr, the most controversial viceroy in Australian history, who decided to step down before reaching the end of his allotted period of office. Immediately after Cowen's appointment was announced, he was asked whether he thought a governor-general could possibly be justified in sacking a prime minister—as his predecessor had done in 1975. Cowen, a leading academic and constitutional lawyer, stoutly adopted a viceregal pose of diplomatic impartiality and refused to be drawn into the controversy.

Although he remained silent on that occasion, Cowen's views were well known, having been set out in a contribution to a book published in August 1977, Republican Australia. The invocation of the prerogative power by the governor-general in November 1975 to dismiss a prime minister—Gough Whitlam, the Labor Party leader—and his government was, Cowen believed, "breathtaking" and exposed in the most striking way the scope and potentialities of royal authority. He further pointed out, through a lengthy discussion of precedents and relevant issues, that Sir John's action was part of a tradition in which the governor-general was no "nodding automaton."

There was, Cowen stressed, no charge of illegality from Prime Minister Whitlam when Kerr dismissed him. Cowen recalled that Whitlam had a majority in the lower house but could not obtain supply because the Liberal-Country Party majority in the Senate deferred budget appropriation bills. However, Whitlam refused to resign, and it was on this basis that Kerr withdrew his commission. Most significantly, Cowen observed that a subsequent general elec-

tion supported the party that the governor-general commissioned, thereby implying that Sir John's action, having been ratified by the electorate, could be taken as a precedent.

Zelman Cowen was born on Oct. 7, 1919, and educated at the universities of Melbourne and Oxford. During a distinguished academic and public career he was a fellow of Oriel College, Oxford, professor of law at the University of Melbourne, and vice-chancellor of the universities of New England (New South Wales) and Queensland. He was knighted in 1976.

(A. R. G. GRIFFITHS)

Daoud, Abu

Arrested in Paris by French security police on Jan. 7, 1977, Muhammad Daoud Auda, known as Abu Daoud, became the central figure in an international cause célèbre. Traveling on an Iraqi passport under an assumed name, he had arrived in Paris on January 5 as part of a Palestine Liberation Organization (PLO) delegation to the funeral of Mahmoud Saleh, a Palestinian who had been assassinated two days earlier. As part of the PLO delegation he had held talks with French Foreign Ministry officials. The arrest was made under an order issued by Interpol at the request of the West German government because Abu Daoud was alleged to have masterminded the murder of the Israeli athletes at the 1972 Munich Olympic Games.

In accordance with a 1971 Franco-Israeli extradition agreement, Israel requested France to extend Abu Daoud's detention for 60 days to enable Israeli legal authorities to prepare evidence for a request for extradition. On January 11, however, at a magistrates' hearing in the Paris Court of Appeal, he was released on the grounds that neither Israel nor West Germany had satisfied the conditions necessary for extradition. He flew at once to Algiers. Israel protested strongly, while the Arab states commended France's action. In a press interview Abu Daoud denied involvement in the Munich massacre and declared his willingness to go to West Germany to stand trial.

Muhammad Daoud Auda was born in the Jordanian West Bank village of Selwa near Jerusalem in 1937. After completing his secondary education he worked as a teacher in Jordan and Saudi Arabia and then served in the Kuwait Ministry of Justice. While in Kuwait he broke away from the Jordanian Communist Party and joined al-Fatah, the main organization within the PLO. He returned to Jordan in 1968 and was thought to have headed al-Fatah intelligence operations there. In February 1973 he was arrested in Amman on charges of plotting acts of sabotage and was sentenced to death. The following month his release was demanded by guerrillas holding diplomats hostage in the Saudi embassy in Khartoum. King Hussein later commuted his death sentence to life imprisonment, and in September 1973 he was released under a general amnesty for Palestinian guerrillas.

(PETER MANSFIELD)

d'Aquino, Iva Toguri ("Tokyo Rose")

Shortly before he left the White House in 1977, U.S. Pres. Gerald Ford granted a pardon to Mrs. Iva Toguri d'Aquino, a woman of 60 who operated a gift shop in Chicago. Ford and many others were convinced that Mrs. d'Aquino, a convicted traitor who had served several years in a federal penitentiary, was in fact a loyal American who had been unfairly accused and tried.

During World War II, the Japanese government directed radiobroadcasts of popular music at U.S. servicemen in the Pacific. These programs, which included misleading news reports and commentary in the English language, were intended to demoralize the U.S. troops. There were 13 announcers, all women, who worked at different times. A U.S. serviceman invented the name "Tokyo Rose" and applied it to the female voices he heard over the radio.

One of those announcers was Iva d'Aquino. She was a Japanese-American who had been born on July 4, 1916, in Los Angeles, Calif. In June 1941 she graduated from college and soon thereafter sailed to Japan to visit an ailing relative. Then World War II began, and she could not leave.

Iva d'Aquino was outspoken in her loyalty to the U.S. and refused to become a Japanese citizen. Eventually, she found a job at Radio Tokyo. There she met an Australian and an American who were prisoners of war. These men had been ordered to write English-language broadcast material to demoralize Allied servicemen. Secretly, they were attempting to subvert the entire operation. Iva d'Aquino was recruited to announce for them and made her first broadcast in November 1943.

When the war ended, Mrs. d'Aquino was detained by U.S. authorities, questioned at great length, and declared innocent of aiding the enemy. She decided to remain in Japan, but in 1947 changed her mind and declared her intention of returning to the U.S. (She was still a U.S. citizen.)

When "Tokyo Rose's" plans became known, many in the U.S. said that she should be tried for treason. She became an issue in the 1948 presidential election campaign. As she entered the U.S., she was seized, charged with treason, and on Oct. 7, 1949, sentenced to ten years in prison and fined $10,000. She was released from jail in 1956 with time off for good behaviour. A campaign began in 1976 for her pardon.　　　　　　　(VICTOR M. CASSIDY)

De Niro, Robert

Newsweek magazine called him "a star for the '70s," describing Robert De Niro as "the heir apparent to the post of American Cultural Symbol once occupied by Marlon Brando and the late James Dean." But, unlike Brando and Dean, De Niro does not project a strong, independent, rebellious personality on the screen. Instead, he symbolizes the self-searching that has characterized the decade. Total immersion in a role distinguishes De Niro's approach to acting. He denies that he has a personal style. "What I try to do is to make things as clear and authentic as possible," he says.

In his quest for authenticity and clarity, De Niro goes to great lengths to research the parts he plays. In 1973 he portrayed a dull-witted baseball catcher from Georgia who was dying of Hodgkin's disease (*Bang the Drum Slowly*). Before filming began, De Niro traveled to Georgia, talked to people

LÉONARD DE RAEMY—SYGMA

there, and learned to reproduce their speech patterns. He spent hours catching and batting baseballs and watching major league players at work. In 1977 De Niro starred as a saxophone player in *New York, New York*, a musical film set in the 1940s. He studied the tenor saxophone with George Auld, who had performed with many big bands during the swing era. De Niro practiced the saxophone day and night until he could play every tune in the score, even though the actual music for the sound track was dubbed. A role for which he received considerable acclaim was as a paranoid cabby in *Taxi Driver*.

De Niro occasionally baffles his colleagues by his methods of arriving at a characterization. Those who know him well say that he must never be judged during early rehearsals. At that time he is searching, often in an eccentric way, for the key to his role. Bernardo Bertolucci, who directed De Niro in *1900*, said that "the first few days were a nightmare." De Niro did everything wrong, it seemed. But Bertolucci had faith in his star, worked patiently with him, and, as he put it, "slowly a fantastic actor emerged."

De Niro was born in 1943 and raised in the "Little Italy" section of New York City. His father and mother, both artists, separated when he was two years old. Never fond of the classroom, young De Niro spent much time in the streets. He drifted from one high school to the next and attended several acting schools for brief periods.　　　　　(VICTOR M. CASSIDY)

Desai, Morarji

India's octogenarian prime minister, Morarji Desai, who spent 19 months in jail during the emergency rule of his predecessor, Indira Gandhi, was a staunch believer in the teachings of Mahatma Gandhi. A puritan and health faddist, he was a strict vegetarian and teetotaler, living almost entirely on dry fruits and cow's milk. After becoming prime minister on March 24, 1977, he vowed to impose prohibition throughout the country even if it meant the downfall of his government.

Desai was born in Bulsar District of Gu-

jarat State, on the west coast of India, on Feb. 29, 1896. After his education in Bombay he joined the Civil Service in 1918. He first came into prominence in 1930, when, after resigning from the service, he joined the Civil Disobedience Movement, launched by Mahatma Gandhi against the British. He served as secretary of the Gujarat Provincial Congress Committee during 1931–37 and 1939–46. During the period of home rule in India in 1946, he was taken into the Bombay Provincial Cabinet as minister for home and revenue and remained in that post until 1952, when he became chief minister of Bombay.

The then prime minister, Jawaharlal Nehru, called Desai to the central government in 1956 as minister of commerce and industry and later made him finance minister. He was given the additional portfolio of deputy prime minister by Indira Gandhi in 1967, but the two soon fell out over financial policies, and Desai resigned in 1969. A major split in the ruling Congress Party soon developed, and Desai became a leader of the smaller faction called Organization, or Opposition, Congress. Though the strength of his group declined steadily, he kept himself in politics by getting elected to Parliament regularly from his home state.

FRANÇOIS LOCHON—GAMMA/LIAISON

On his release from jail two months before the March 1977 elections, Desai quickly rallied the opposition against Indira Gandhi and trounced her at the polls. His selection by the victorious Janata Party coalition to head the government enabled him to achieve his lifelong ambition of becoming the prime minister of India.

(GOVINDAN UNNY)

Didion, Joan

"Had I been blessed with even limited access to my own mind there would have been no reason to write. I write entirely to find out what I'm thinking, what I'm looking at, what I see and what it means. What I want and what I fear." Thus wrote Joan

Didion in an article entitled "Why I Write" in the *New York Times Book Review*, which appeared shortly before the publication of her latest novel, *A Book of Common Prayer* (1977). The statement helps to explain in part the heroine of the novel, Charlotte Douglas, a woman without "even limited access" to her own mind. Charlotte is a sleepwalker in a bad dream, ignorant of history and politics yet moving through revolutionary times.

Though Charlotte's life and her senseless death are played out in an imaginary Central American republic, she is, in a roundabout fashion, a fugitive from California. And despairing California women are the focus of Didion's other novels, *Play It as It Lays* (1970) and *Run River* (1963). The former describes the disintegrating life of a Hollywood movie star, the latter, another tragic California marriage. *Slouching Towards Bethlehem* (1968), a collection of highly personal magazine articles, again concentrates on the California scene. The title essay deals with the dropouts and drug addicts of the Haight-Ashbury district of San Francisco, which in the 1960s became the mecca of the "flower children." Didion employs a spare, laconic prose to define people who, as she says of herself, suffer from a "pervasive sense of loss."

Joan Didion sets her work in an area she knows well, for she is a fifth-generation Californian, born in Sacramento on Dec. 5, 1934. She attended the University of California at Berkeley, graduating in 1956. After winning *Vogue* magazine's Prix de Paris, she moved to New York City, working as an associate feature editor at *Vogue* until 1963. She married writer John Gregory Dunne in 1964, and the couple returned to California. The marriage, as well as a contemplated divorce that never occurred, served as a subject for both husband and wife.

Didion has written free-lance articles for such diverse magazines as *Life, Esquire, Mademoiselle,* the *American Scholar,* and *Holiday.* With her husband she has also written Hollywood screenplays, including *The Panic in Needle Park, Play It as It Lays,* and *A Star Is Born.*   (JOAN NATALIE REIBSTEIN)

Elizabeth II

During 1977 Queen Elizabeth II celebrated the Silver Jubilee of her accession (Feb. 6, 1952), receiving loyal addresses from Parliament (May 4), innumerable congratulatory letters from the public, and the enthusiastic plaudits of the vast crowds that gathered, often in fitful rain, to watch her many official progresses. She lit a beacon at Windsor (June 6), triggering similar conflagrations throughout Britain and Australia; and on June 7, a special public holiday, drove to St. Paul's Cathedral for a service of thanksgiving. Two days later she attended a London fireworks display, and again hundreds lined her route and gathered around Buckingham Palace. In the tradition of her ancestors, she also made progresses throughout her realm. On all these trips, except in Northern Ireland, she spent some time on foot among the crowds, talking to people and accepting an

ever increasing and bizarre assortment of gifts.

Elizabeth II was queen of 11 countries and head of the 36-member Commonwealth of Nations. An important feature in the celebrations, therefore, was the banquet she gave to Commonwealth leaders in London (June 8). She also made Jubilee tours in the Pacific and Australasia, in Canada, and in the Caribbean.

The queen seemed to have chosen as the theme of her jubilee the celebration and promotion of unity in diversity. She reminded the British that she had been "crowned queen of the United Kingdom" and later in the year called for a united Canada. Her dedicated interest in Commonwealth affairs had far outstripped that of most British politicians. She also admitted to finding that a Silver Jubilee was not "exactly a period of rest;" but perhaps the spontaneous manifestations of goodwill made it all seem worthwhile.

Elizabeth, the elder daughter of the duke of York, who became King George VI in 1936, was born in London on April 21, 1926. She married Prince Philip, duke of Edinburgh (formerly Prince Philip of Greece), on Nov. 20, 1947; of their four children, Prince Charles was born Nov. 14, 1948; Princess Anne, Aug. 15, 1950; Prince Andrew, Feb. 19, 1960; and Prince Edward, March 10, 1964. Her first grandchild (Princess Anne's son) was born on Nov. 15, 1977.   (STEPHANIE MULLINS)

Enoki, Misako

Japan's most militant feminist, Misako Enoki, bemused, startled, and sometimes enraged her compatriots during her five-year battle for women's rights. In 1972 she organized Chupiren ("abortion-pill-federation") to demand abolition of anti-abortion laws and free access to birth-control pills. On matters affecting sexual equality, she preferred confrontation when others opted for negotiations or debate. Accordingly, she and her followers donned pink helmets on at least 2,500 occasions and stormed into the offices of errant husbands to demand an end to illicit affairs or payment of overdue alimony. Such startling tactics often produced dramatic re-

UPI COMPIX

sults and forced some men to quit their jobs.

In 1976 Enoki, a graduate pharmacist and the wife of a doctor, launched a new religion for women only. She promised that *Josei fukko* ("women's revival") would be entirely free of the discrimination against females that characterizes such established religions as Buddhism, Islam, and Christianity. Her religion, in fact, would produce a society without male privilege. A temporary "female dictatorship" might be necessary, during which time all government ministers and corporation managers would be female. In time "male rights would be partially restored, if men behaved themselves." A man might even be appointed to a Cabinet post to oversee male affairs. Enoki reported that some 5,000 women showed interest, but only time would tell whether the male-dominated government bureau that registers new religions would give its approval.

After slating ten members of her Japan Women's Party as candidates for the upper house of the Diet, Enoki told them that if they hoped to confront male members of the Diet on equal terms they should learn karate. Though women comprise more than half of the Japanese electorate, none of Enoki's candidates was elected in July. After her defeat, she announced the dissolution of Chupiren and vowed to give up politics. Few who knew her well believed that the 32-year-old firebrand from Tokushima Prefecture would retire for long. As Enoki resumed her role of simple housewife she had to figure out a way to repay a 10 million yen loan (about $38,000) that her husband had given her for the campaign.   (JOHN RODERICK)

Fabre, Robert Charles Victor

Nothing had seemed to destine Robert Fabre for the important role in French national politics that he assumed in 1977. A peaceful main-square druggist in his native Villefranche-de-Rouergue, a charming little medieval town in Aveyron, he had been mayor there since 1953. He was a radical but seemingly in the mold of many local leaders of southwestern France, who tend to dress up somewhat conservative ideas in republican and progressive-sounding language.

Fabre's dedication and serious approach earned him election as a deputy to the National Assembly in 1962. He did not shine in parliamentary debate but quickly came to carry weight on the left of the Radical Party. In 1972 the Radicals split when the Socialist Party under François Mitterrand concluded a pact for a "joint program of government" with the Communists. Fabre became leader of the faction that signed this joint program and, consequently, of the "third component" of the united left. With scarcely a dozen deputies, it was a small component but a useful one since it represented an opening to the centre that was essential to the success of the leftist coalition. The parliamentary majority and the opposition being of roughly equal strength, the 3% of centre-left electors would decide the issue in the March 1978 election. The other faction of the Radicals, led by Jean-Jacques Servan-Schreiber, remained loyal to the majority and to Pres. Valéry Giscard d'Estaing.

Fabre intended to ask a high price for his essential 3%. No collectivist, still less a Marxist, he had often disagreed with his two powerful allies. For example, when he was asked in September to approve an increase in the number of nationalizations of business and industry proposed in their joint program, he walked out of the meeting in protest against the Communist demands. His departure seemed to presage a breakdown of the union of the left, although discussions among the three parties were later resumed. Torn between the reunification of the Radical movement, appeals from the majority, and promises from his Socialist allies, Fabre was faced with a choice of direction that would play a significant and perhaps decisive part in the outcome of the 1978 election.

Born on Dec. 21, 1915, Fabre went to school in Villefranche-de-Rouergue and qualified as a pharmacist at Toulouse. From 1955 he was president of the Aveyron pharmacists' association.

(PIERRE VIANSSON-PONTÉ)

Flynt, Larry

Larry Flynt set out to publish a pornographic magazine that would "talk about sex the way we talked about it . . . in the Navy." He succeeded, faced criminal charges as a result, and—in the civil liberties debate that followed—was defended by some of the most sedate journals in the U.S.

The facts of the case seemed simple enough. Flynt, born in Kentucky in 1943, founded *Hustler* in 1974 in Columbus, Ohio, after serving in the Army and the Navy and operating bars in Columbus. A national magazine that prided itself on being "tasteless," it was sold in Cincinnati where a county prosecutor brought criminal charges against Flynt as its editor and publisher. In the trial that followed, a jury decided the magazine violated local sensibilities. Hence, by virtue of a controversial U.S. Supreme Court ruling, it was deemed legally obscene. The jury also decided that since Flynt produced the magazine with other individuals (*i.e.*, a professional staff), a state "organized crime" statute applied to the case. In February 1977 Flynt received a sentence of 7 to 25 years in prison and an \$11,000 fine.

The debate that followed was not concerned with his magazine's merits but, rather, with the power of the government to effectively censor it. Civil libertarians said that the case was part of an odious pattern that threatened the right of free speech. They charged that the U.S. Department of Justice in, effect, railroading defendants in carefully chosen jurisdictions, places where the conservative moral attitudes of jurors virtually guaranteed guilty verdicts.

However objectionable a magazine might be, many journalists defended the publisher's right to produce it without fear of government censorship in the form of criminal charges. Writing in *Nation's Business* James Kilpatrick summed up *Hustler* as "tasteless, crude, vulgar, patently offensive . . . pitched at the literary level of an Army latrine . . . It is as crummy a publication as one can find on a newsstand anywhere—sleazy, morbid, dirty, contemptible. But the question is: should Larry Flynt be sent to prison for publishing it? Reluctantly, glumly, I have to say no."

At the end of the year, Flynt made headlines again by announcing that he had undergone a religious awakening under the tutelage of evangelist Ruth Carter Stapleton, U.S. Pres. Jimmy Carter's sister, and claiming to be a "born again" Christian. Whether this change of heart would affect *Hustler's* editorial or graphic content remained to be seen. In December Flynt resigned as publisher, and Paul Krassner, appointed to replace him, said that from now on the magazine would be "erotic rather than raunchy."

(PHILIP KOPPER)

Frampton, Peter

His work had generated little enthusiasm among music critics, but English rock star Peter Frampton probably did not mind. Critical indifference had not diminished his popularity among millions of rock fans. By mid-1977 his album "Frampton Comes Alive!" was reported to have sold some 12 million copies, more than any other long-playing recording in history. His June 11, 1977, concert at John F. Kennedy Stadium in Philadelphia, his first appearance in seven months and the opening of a four-month U.S. tour, attracted about 91,000 listeners. Frampton's schedule for the coming year also included the filming of a movie entitled *Sgt. Pepper's Lonely Hearts Club Band*, in which Frampton was to sing the Beatles' songs.

Frampton explained his success this way: "I do what Jolson, Sinatra, Tony Bennett, and the Beatles did—what all the greats do. I communicate." Obviously, many people agreed. In 1976 he was elected "Artist of the Year" in a *Rolling Stone* poll. Some of Frampton's appeal undoubtedly rested in his easy baritone voice and his skill on a guitar, as well as in his long golden curls and his wide-set hazel eyes—in the general impression he seemed to give of being "nice."

Some critics called his melodic and romantic music pop rather than true rock. John Rockwell of the *New York Times* described Frampton's style as rock "stripped of its darker connotations." John Milward, reviewing Frampton's 1977 album, "I'm in You," for *Rolling Stone*, said, "Frampton's

UPI COMPIX

primary virtue is that he's consistently pleasant . . . the listener is neither challenged nor surprised, but left to drift in Frampton's sugary romanticism. His execution . . . is professionally smooth, but devoid of any truly creative fire."

Born in 1950, Frampton was scarcely a newcomer to rock music. After attending school in Bromley, Kent, he became the lead singer of a band called the Herd, and by the age of 16 he was a national celebrity in Britain. After the Herd broke up in 1969, Frampton joined with Steve Marriott to form a band called Humble Pie. Although the group was successful, Frampton soon left to become a studio musician for well-known stars. Frampton's first three albums did not sell particularly well, but "Frampton Comes Alive!", recorded live from his onstage performances, brought not only superstar status but also more than \$6 million in income.

(JOAN NATALIE REIBSTEIN)

Fraser, Douglas Andrew

Douglas A. Fraser's election as president of the United Auto Workers in May 1977 continued a line of succession that had begun more than 30 years earlier with the late Walter Reuther, who molded the UAW in his own liberal image. The UAW was still a powerful and vital labour organization, heavily involved with the liberal-progressive wing of the Democratic Party. But the 61-year-old Fraser could be the last president in the Reuther line. Like Reuther, he took part in the bitter struggle for union recognition by the auto industry and was personally committed to working for social change.

The son of a Scottish immigrant and auto worker, Fraser was born Dec. 28, 1916, in Glasgow, raised in Detroit, and began work on the De Soto assembly line, where he became a UAW organizer and Reuther disciple. He served as Reuther's chief assistant for eight years and was groomed to be his successor, but when Reuther was killed in a plane crash in 1970 the union's executive board narrowly voted to give the presidency to Leonard Woodcock. Despite his personal disappointment, Fraser served under Woodcock as a vice-president. When Woodcock retired and was named U.S. envoy to China, the UAW board unanimously chose Fraser to succeed him, and the 3,000-delegate convention approved that choice by acclamation.

In contrast to the aesthetic Reuther and the intellectual Woodcock, Fraser was described as a "down-to-earth working guy" who was at ease with the rank and file. Despite his personal popularity, it seemed unlikely that he would soon realize his hope of bringing the UAW back into the AFL-CIO, which it left in 1968. Many UAW members feared a loss of independence or felt the larger organization was too conservative. A more immediate problem was the energy crisis and government pressure on Detroit to produce smaller, more efficient cars—which could mean fewer jobs for the UAW's 1.4 million members. Other issues facing the union included the ongoing drive for a four-day workweek and the

ANDREW SACKS—BLACK STAR

need for more successful organizing in plants that had moved to the South and Southwest. But the long-range challenge facing Fraser before his mandatory retirement in 1983 was to develop new and younger leaders from a rank-and-file membership that had become more affluent and, lacking personal identification with the battles of the past, cared less for the social and political causes Reuther had championed and his successors had carried on.   (HAL BRUNO)

Frost, David Paradine

Once unkindly called the man who "rose without a trace," David Frost in 1977 reached new heights in his personal television career. His million-dollar deal to film a series of interviews with former U.S. president Richard Nixon, announced the year before, had been greeted with skepticism and even ridicule. As a television interviewer he had seemed soft-centred, and his ability to master the detail needed to quiz Nixon on Watergate, and then to put the tough question, was in doubt. So was the expensive project's success, since the major U.S. networks rejected it.

In the event, even Frost's critics had to grant him success on both levels. His own organization syndicated the interviews to independent stations across the U.S. and sold them round the world, and it could not be denied that the ex-president was made to face his problems. By the time the series was made and screened, Frost had crossed the Atlantic to make a series with another former political leader, Sir Harold Wilson. Then, in December, came the announcement that he was to join NBC—struggling to improve its ratings—for a series of current affairs programs featuring live interviews.

Born April 7, 1939, at Tenterden, Kent, the son of a Methodist minister, Frost won a scholarship to Cambridge, where he took a second-class honours degree in history and also became involved in theatrical ac-

tivities. He taught for a time, then became a trainee researcher with a regional independent television (ITV) company. His swift rise came when he was hired, on the strength of his cabaret performances, to be anchorman in the pioneering BBC satirical television program "That Was the Week that Was." Although it was very much a team show, Frost became its best-known performer. He moved on to the successor series ("Not So Much a Programme, More a Way of Life") and then switched to ITV, becoming, by 1967, a major figure in London Weekend Television. He next set his sights on the U.S. networks, and during the early 1970s he was commuting across the Atlantic between his own U.S. and British shows. In recent years he had shifted increasingly into the roles of producer, impresario, and businessman.

(PETER FIDDICK)

Fukuda, Takeo

When Takeo Fukuda became prime minister of Japan in December 1976, Japan's chief problems were economic. Fukuda's promise to revitalize the economy was backed up by impressive credentials: expertise in finance, long experience in government, and support from big business. But one year later the economy was still floundering, unemployment was high, and Japan's trading partners were unhappy over Japan's $18 billion balance of payments surplus. In October the prime minister announced that the economy had entered a phase of moderate expansion but conceded that recovery in the private sector was progressing more slowly. Critics accused Fukuda of timidity and indecision and blamed the situation on his failure to take bold steps to alleviate the crisis. In one area, Fukuda spoke with greater confidence. He felt sure that Japan's economy would achieve a 6.7% growth rate in real terms for the fiscal year, a figure the U.S. said would contribute substantially to international economic recovery. But by November even this goal seemed in jeopardy because the yen, after a considerable period of stability at around 280 to U.S. $1, suddenly rose in October to a high of 247–1. This was good news for countries exporting to Japan, but it was bad news for export-oriented Japanese firms whose products became more expensive on foreign markets. Any additional rise would further damage Japan's economy and could not but hurt Fukuda politically.

Fukuda was born into a wealthy farming family of Gumma Prefecture on Jan. 14,

1905. He attended the finest schools and entered politics while still in his 20s. In 1947, when he was about to become vice-minister of finance, he was indicted on bribery charges but won acquittal. Thereafter he held various important posts in the Liberal-Democratic Party (LDP) and in the government. When he successfully challenged Takeo Miki for the party presidency, he was also guaranteed the post of prime minister. The LDP had been taking a battering in recent elections because, among other things, some of its members were implicated in the Lockheed bribery scandal. An October 1977 poll taken by Kyoto News Service showed that only 37.5% of those interviewed approved of the government's performance, as compared with 50.4% who disapproved. If Fukuda hoped to win reelection toward the end of 1978 he would have to restore confidence in his leadership and contend with Masayoshi Ohira, an LDP veteran with political ambitions of his own.

(JOHN RODERICK)

Garozzo, Benito

Widely hailed as the outstanding contract bridge player of all time, Benito Garozzo was introduced to the game as a teenager. In the late 1940s he went to Egypt, where he had spent some of his early childhood (he was born in Naples, Italy, in 1927) and where he received encouragement from the country's top players. Returning to Naples about 1950, he began to interest himself in tournament bridge, joining the famous Italian Blue Team, the reigning world champions since 1957, for the 1961 Bermuda Bowl (world championship) contest. The partnership of Garozzo and Pietro Forquet was an instant success. For the next ten years they were the world's most effective pair, undefeated in major competitions. From 1961 up to and including 1975, Garozzo won every world and European championship in which he competed. He missed only the 1970 and 1971 championships, which the Blue Team did not enter.

Meanwhile, Garozzo accepted the sponsorship of a New York-based Taiwanese shipbuilder, C. C. Wei, who had invented a new bidding system, the Precision Club. Garozzo revived the Blue Team and trained them in this method. Reappearing in December 1971 in Las Vegas, Nev., they won a $15,000 match against the Dallas Aces, a commercially sponsored U.S. team that had won the 1970 and 1971 world championships. The Blue Team—now the Precision Club team—went on to win the

Takeo Fukuda

PETER TATINER—LIAISON

1972 Olympiad and the Bermuda Bowl contests of 1973, 1974, and 1975.

Garozzo now had the Italian automobile company Lancia as sponsor. On the eve of the 1976 Bermuda Bowl and Olympic contests, allegations of malpractice unsettled the Italians, who lost both titles and, one year later, the European title as well. In late 1977 their contract with Lancia ended.

Garozzo's reputation as a player was almost equaled by his fame as an innovator. He was largely responsible for a worldwide swing to One Club approach-bidding systems, building a sophisticated method extending the uses of the 46-word vocabulary that includes all bids from "no bid" to "seven no trumps" to make it possible to describe distributions and high-card holdings accurately. The method was published in *The Blue Team Club* and *Super Precision*. (HAROLD FRANKLIN)

Gouled Aptidon, Hassan

Hassan Gouled Aptidon, who became the first president of Djibouti when the former French-ruled Territory of the Afars and Issas became independent on June 27, 1977, was an Issa. For many years the Issas, a Somali clan, had contested with the Afars for political ascendancy in the small Red Sea territory. The new president's power rested on the mainly Issa-supported Popular African League for Independence (LPAI), which had strong links with Somalia.

On assuming power, Hassan Gouled pledged to maintain the sovereign independence of Djibouti and to develop close relations between the Issas and Afars. Nevertheless, tribal rivalry continued, and in December Premier Ahmed Dini Ahmed and four other ministers, all Afars, resigned to protest repressive measures against their tribe following a bombing incident. Gouled accused Ethiopia of arming terrorist elements among the Afars.

Born in Djibouti in 1916, Hassan Gouled was a venerable-looking figure with gray hair and a bushy mustache. A former trucking contractor, he was greatly respected by Djiboutians and by the French. Since entering politics in 1950 he had always been regarded as a moderate, and initially he was a firm supporter of continued French rule, as well as a convinced Gaullist. A member first of the Gaullist Rassemblement du Peuple Français and then of its successor, the Union pour la Nouvelle République (UNR), he represented Djibouti (then French Somaliland) in the French National Assembly as a senator from 1952 to 1958. Having voted, with his supporters, in favour of de Gaulle's proposals for a French Community, he was appointed head of the Djibouti territorial government in December 1958. He returned to France in April 1969 to represent the territory as a deputy.

Meanwhile, Gouled's political activities in Djibouti continued. After heading the UNR-affiliated Party for the Defense of Economic and Social Interests of the Territory, in 1963 he formed the Issa Democratic Union. In January 1967 he became political secretary of the Party of the Popular Movement, which was proscribed six months later. Then, in March 1972, he founded the African People's League, which in February 1975 merged with other groups to form the LPAI. (COLIN LEGUM)

Greene, Robert

Nine months after Phoenix newspaperman Don Bolles was murdered, a special report on organized crime in Arizona was published throughout the nation as a unique tribute to Bolles and as a warning to others that killing a reporter will not stop his investigative work. At the time of his death, Bolles, a prizewinning reporter for the *Arizona Republic*, was investigating alleged fraudulent land deals involving organized crime and state politicians. He was fatally injured on June 2, 1976, by a bomb that had been planted in his car. Before he died, Bolles gasped the word "Mafia" and the name of a minor Phoenix crime figure.

A few months after his murder, journalists from throughout the U.S. gathered in Phoenix to form a special team sponsored by "Investigative Reporters and Editors." Their purpose was to take up where Bolles had left off when he was killed. The group was headed by Robert Greene, an investigative reporter and senior editor of *Newsday* (Long Island, N.Y.), who had been instrumental in winning two Pulitzer Prizes for his paper.

The reporters on the special team worked for six months to investigate and write a 23-part series of articles that revealed links between organized crime and Arizona business and political leaders. The series, which began appearing on March 5, 1977, described how a network of Eastern and Midwestern gangsters had established themselves in Arizona and taken over organized crime operations and legitimate businesses. Among those named in the stories as having been friendly with underworld figures were U.S. Sen. Barry Goldwater, his brother, Robert, and Harry Rosenzweig, a former Republican state chairman and Goldwater political ally. Senator Goldwater denied the charges and threatened to file a libel suit.

In the Bolles case itself, authorities brought conspiracy and first-degree murder charges against Max Dunlap, a contractor, and James Robison, a plumber, both of whom were found guilty by a jury in Phoenix on Nov. 6, 1977. John Harvey Adamson, whose name Bolles had gasped before he died, pleaded guilty to second-degree murder and testified in court that Robison had hired him and detonated the bomb he planted in Bolles's car and that Dunlap had paid him $6,000 for the job.

Greene was born July 12, 1929, in New York, N.Y. After attending Fordham University he worked from 1950 to 1955 as an investigator for the New York City Anti-Crime Commission. He joined the staff of *Newsday* as a reporter in 1955 and was named senior editor in 1970. With other *Newsday* staffers he wrote the spoof *Naked Came the Stranger* (1969) and also authored *The Heroin Trail* (1973). (HAL BRUNO)

Haley, Alex

As a boy Alex Haley spent much time in Henning, Tenn., where his grandmother entranced him with family stories that had been passed down through the generations. The tales involved the family's forebears all the way back to "the African," who had been kidnapped by slave traders from his native village while searching the forest for wood to make a drum.

Though his parents were teachers, Haley was an indifferent student. Born in Ithaca, N.Y., on Aug. 11, 1921, he joined the U.S. Coast Guard and spent World War II in the galley of a supply ship plying the Pacific. To kill time he began to read and then to write narrative accounts of events taken from official records. The Coast Guard created a new rating for him, that of journalist. When he left the Coast Guard in 1959, he became a free-lance writer.

Some lean years followed; once Haley was down to 18 cents and two cans of sardines. But he interviewed jazz musician Miles Davis, and the transcript became the first of *Playboy* magazine's celebrated monthly interviews. Later, he was ghost writer for the widely read *Autobiography of Malcolm X*.

Visiting the National Archives in Washington, D.C., Haley checked some century-old census records and found the names of people his grandmother had mentioned. A monumental search began—to connect those names with Henning, Tenn., and 18th-century Africa. Working with a linguist, Haley deduced that some of the words his grandmother attributed to "the African" might be of the Mandinka language. In Senegal, where aged "griots" still recite the oral history of their people, he listened to one tell, in passing, of a young warrior who went off searching for wood to make a drum and never returned. Dovetailing chronological clues in the narrative with British Museum records, Haley deduced that "the African," Kunta Kinte, sailed in the "Lord Ligonier" to Annapolis in 1767. Two hundred years later to the day Haley stood near the spot where Kunta Kinte had been captured. From there he traced American records to put together the rest of his family's history.

The search took him 500,000 mi in 12 years and resulted in *Roots: The Saga of an American Family*. A best-seller, it earned Haley a special citation from the National Book Award judges in 1977 and a Pulitzer

Prize and was dramatized in a television series that achieved high ratings in prime time. It also sparked a wave of interest in genealogy in general and created something of a tourist boom in West Africa as other American blacks sought to duplicate Haley's quest.

Some investigators later questioned the griot's veracity. But Haley maintained that he had created a work of "faction," historical material made readable by fictional embellishment. It was "a symbolic history of a people." (PHILIP KOPPER)

Hall, Sir Peter

The year in which Queen Elizabeth II dubbed the son of a Suffolk railway stationmaster a knight was a jubilee year not only for the queen but also for Peter Hall. After four years as director of London's National Theatre, succeeding Lord Olivier in that post in 1973, Sir Peter weathered the violent storm of criticism directed at his stewardship, justified his management, successfully explained that the year's deficit was largely the result of building delays outside his control, and generally received a clean bill of health in the annual report of the Arts Council of Great Britain. (See THEATRE.)

Peter Reginald Frederick Hall was born on Nov. 22 1930, at Bury St. Edmunds, Suffolk, and was educated at Perse School and St. Catharine's College, Cambridge, of which he became an honorary fellow in 1964. Originally bent on a musical career, he became a student director of plays at Cambridge and thus laid the foundation for his theatrical career. After a year at the Oxford Playhouse and three at the London Arts Theatre, he joined the Royal Shakespeare Company (RSC) in 1958 and became its managing director (1960–68). During his time there he opened the RSC's London home at the Aldwych Theatre, and presented some 15 productions a year of classical and modern plays.

His productions for the commercial theatre, the RSC, the National Theatre, and in New York numbered over 100; he staged opera in London and at Glyndebourne; made eight films; and was associate professor of drama at the University of Warwick. His "firsts" included the English premiere of *Waiting for Godot* (1955); *The Wars of the Roses* and the historical plays, staged in cycle with John Barton, in Shakespeare's quatercentenary year (1964); several plays by Harold Pinter (including the Austrian premiere of *Old Times* at the Vienna Burgtheater), Tennessee Williams, and Edward Albee; and the inaugural productions for the opening of the new National Theatre of *Hamlet* and *Tamburlaine the Great*. During 1977 he staged the highly popular *Bedroom Farce* by Alan Ayckbourn, *Volpone* by Ben Jonson, and *The Country Wife* by William Wycherley. His production at Glyndebourne of Mozart's *Don Giovanni* was transferred to the National Theatre and won the Society of West End Theatre award for the year's outstanding achievement in opera. (OSSIA TRILLING)

Havel, Vaclav

One of the original spokesmen for the Charter 77 human rights initiative launched in Czechoslovakia in January 1977, playwright Vaclav Havel was in October sentenced to 14 months in prison on charges of having attempted to "harm the interests of the republic abroad." Havel differed from many other members of the Czechoslovak opposition in that his career had been predominantly nonpolitical, at least until 1968. He first made his name in the 1960s as a dramatist of great originality and imagination, and several of his plays—notably *The Memorandum*—were performed in the West. His themes were the nature of totalitarianism and the dehumanization of much of technological civilization; his approach and method drew both on absurdity and on the legacy of Franz Kafka.

Born into an upper-middle-class family on Oct. 5, 1936, Havel was largely excluded from the country's educational system after the Communist takeover on the grounds of class origins. He worked as a technician in a chemical laboratory from the age of 15, performed military service, and in 1959 became a stagehand at Prague's ABC Theatre. His education was completed at evening classes.

At the time of the "Prague spring" movement toward liberalization in 1968, Havel began to play a more overtly political role, although he remained a committed non-Communist throughout. He published a much-discussed article on the need for pluralism in society and was also active in founding the Circle of Independent Writers, an autonomous group within the official Union of Writers, which stood for coexistence between non-Communist and Communist writers and pluralism in literature and the arts. His activities in 1968 subsequently earned him the disapproval of the post-Soviet-invasion leadership, so that after 1969 he was entirely excluded from the country's intellectual life.

This exclusion was evidently one of the factors that drew him into the political opposition. In April 1975 he allowed the text of a lengthy open letter to Gustav Husak, the party leader, to be released; in it Havel was strongly critical of the stagnation that existed in Czechoslovakia and the denial of human rights. He was arrested soon after the launching of Charter 77 and detained on unspecified charges until May 20.

(GEORGE SCHÖPFLIN)

Hawkesworth, John

John Hawkesworth's name first became familiar to television viewers in Britain and America as one of the leading credits to the highly successful London Weekend Television (LWT) drama series "Upstairs, Downstairs." The program won several Emmy awards among many other distinctions. In 1975, when it was finished, Hawkesworth moved from independent (commercial) television (ITV) to the British Broadcasting Corporation (BBC) to develop another drama series set in England during the Edwardian period, "The Duchess of Duke Street." This also attracted large audiences on both sides of the Atlantic. In 1977 he returned to ITV to produce for Thames Television a series about a bomb-disposal unit in London during World War II.

Before working on the creation of "Upstairs, Downstairs" with actresses Jean Marsh and Eileen Atkins and then producing it for five years and writing many of the scripts, Hawkesworth had a long and varied career in British films and television. Born in London on Dec. 7, 1920, the son of an army officer, he was educated at Rugby School and then read history at Oxford and at the Sorbonne in Paris, where he also studied painting. During World War II he served as an officer in the Grenadier Guards. Faced with the "threat" of having to enter business life after the war, he joined the art department of London Films as personal assistant to Vincent Korda. He was art director of such celebrated films as *The Third Man* and *The Sound Barrier* before going free-lance to work on, among others, *The Man Who Never Was* and *Father Brown*.

Hawkesworth's own first film production, *Rowlandson's England*, was shown at a Royal Command Performance and won

Sir Peter Hall

several prizes. He later worked as a producer with the Rank Organisation and produced *Wyndham's Way* and *Tiger Bay*, for which he wrote his first original screenplay. He then turned to writing full time and, moving to television, won a Screenwriters' Guild award in 1969 for a 13-part series of Sir Arthur Conan Doyle stories for the BBC.

In 1967 Hawkesworth and John Whitney formed Sagitta Productions Ltd., which later sold "The Gold Robbers," a successful series which Hawkesworth produced and largely wrote, to LWT. Sagitta's second project for LWT was "Upstairs, Downstairs"; from the first episode, its success was assured.　　　　(PETER FIDDICK)

Higuchi, Hisako

Like millions of other Japanese, Hisako ("Chako") Higuchi loves to play golf. She shot her first round at 16 and was about as exciting to watch as a sand trap. If she stuck with the game, the odds were heavy that one day she would reach her peak as a weekend duffer. But that was before she began taking lessons from Torakichi Nakamura, the man who started Japan's golf craze when he teamed up with Koichi Ono in 1957 to give Japan its first Canada Cup (now called the World Cup).

Golf aficionados who followed Higuchi's progress were in near unanimous agreement on one point: her swing was atrocious. But on June 12, 1977, she was among those who teed off for the final round of the Ladies' Professional Golfers' Association (LPGA) tournament at North Myrtle Beach, S.C. She got five birdies and two bogeys for a 69 round and wound up with a five-under-par total of 279, three strokes better than her three closest rivals. When Higuchi was handed a $22,500 check for her first victory in the U.S., she exclaimed in Japanese, "It's going to be a great thing in Japan." And indeed it was. The Fuji Xerox Co., her sponsor, threw a $40,000 party at the Imperial Hotel in Tokyo and hoped it could hold similar affairs again, and again, and again.

Higuchi was born in Tokyo on Oct. 13, 1945, and is married to a professional golfer, Isao Matsui. After gaining experience and confidence in Japan, where she won several major tournaments, she decided to test the greens in the U.S. In 1970 she joined the LPGA tour and found that life could be exciting—especially inside boutiques that featured women's golf wear. She bought impulsively, and even felt impelled to copy every new technique she spotted on the golf course. Gradually she realized that she had to settle down and develop her own style of play. Her first major victory outside Japan came in 1976 when she won the European Colgate in Sunningdale, England. Higuchi won both the U.S. and Japan LPGA tournaments in 1977, in addition to the Japan Open and Tokai Classic.

Before the U.S. LPGA there were many nonbelievers, even after Higuchi led the TALK tournament at Wykagyl in New York with a 69. Few believed she could survive such competition—not with a swing like that. But soft-spoken Higuchi remained calm and unconcerned in the face of criticism. She continued to sway as she swung and she kept her balls on the fairways, as onlookers shook their heads in disbelief. During the LPGA that followed, Higuchi showed the same control. While others struggled with the greens and saw their balls roll awry, she feathered in her shots with remarkable consistency. In the process she became the darling of the galleries. In the eyes of the purists, Higuchi may violate fundamental canons of sound golf, but the purpose in playing pro golf is to win. And Higuchi has done just that.

(TAKEAKI KANEDA)

Holyoake, Sir Keith Jacka

The first practicing politician to be named governor-general of New Zealand had previously had some experience with the kind of controversy that developed as a result of his appointment. Keith Holyoake was prime minister when he was knighted in 1970, the first New Zealand prime minister to be so honoured while still in power, and it was with aplomb that he had dealt with inquiries over his retirement plans until he stepped down in early 1972. A much sharper controversy was sparked by Queen Elizabeth's announcement, at the end of her jubilee tour early in 1977, that she had offered Sir Keith, still in Parliament and minister of state in the Muldoon administration, the post of governor-general.

The fierce debate that ensued revolved around the question of whether a partisan from Parliament, now resigned from that arena but still only months away from his allegiances, could possibly act impartially in refereeing a political impasse. But the debaters never cast reflections on Holyoake's personal capacity to do the job, his personal suitability, or how appropriate the appointment was as climax of an outstanding career. Indeed, by the time he was sworn in on October 26, the personal triumph was beginning to mellow reactions to the political precedent.

During his 11½ years as prime minister Holyoake practiced a refined form of consensus politics that defused issues as inflammatory as that of participation in the war in Vietnam. This contrasted markedly with the more pugnacious styles of S. G. Holland, National Party leader-prime minister before him, or Robert Muldoon who succeeded him in the leadership.

Great-grandson of a settler of 1842 from Warwickshire, England, Holyoake was born Feb. 11, 1904, in the sheep farming hills of Mangamutu, near the country town of Pahiatua. His parents ran a general store there, but with their family of seven they later went back to farming, eventually to the original Holyoake settlement at Riwaka. The younger members of the family went on to college, but Keith, after primary schooling, was required to assist with the fruit, hop, and tobacco growing to boost the family income. While representing the district at rugby and tennis, he began to interest himself in local farm affairs and in 1932 began his long parliamentary career.　　(JOHN A. KELLEHER)

Hooks, Benjamin

As the audience at the 1977 Freedom Fund Dinner of the National Association for the Advancement of Colored People shouted, "We want Hooks!," the former federal communications commissioner and newly

elected executive director of the nation's oldest civil rights organization set the tone for his forthcoming administration. "We are tired of celebrating partial victories and seeing them snatched away. We are tired of eating the crumbs off the table of democracy. We are tired of being America's stepchildren."

Delegates to the organization's July convention in St. Louis, Mo., roared their approval. Just months before, however, it had seemed as though Hooks's election would tear the NAACP apart. Many members felt that he was not the right person for the job which 75-year-old Roy Wilkins had occupied for so many years, and even some of those who expressed admiration for him questioned the legality of his election.

The agenda for the NAACP's Nov. 6, 1976, board of directors meeting had called for consideration of candidates for executive director suggested by the search and screening committee. Only a preliminary discussion was expected to take place, and several members failed to attend. But the committee came in with just one name—Benjamin Hooks—and the vote of the board members in attendance was unanimous. Several of the absentee members were furious, and even a repeat polling of the full board in January—which produced the same result—failed to curb the growing dissension. In April the clerical and professional staffs of the NAACP's Manhattan branch walked off their jobs in a dispute that, at least in part, grew out of the crisis at the top.

Thus Hooks knew what he was up against months before he took office. In addition to the internal dissension, NAACP membership had been declining as liberal whites and alienated blacks left the fold. But at a press conference he promised to "shake up this country," and his speech at the Freedom Fund Dinner was designed to convey his activist spirit to the faithful. At Hooks's inauguration on July 28, 1977, Wilkins, voicing the new optimism, predicted that "Ben will be a strong and able leader."

Born in Memphis, Tenn., on Jan. 31, 1925, Hooks received his law degree from DePaul University of Chicago in 1948. He returned to Memphis and assumed the position of pastor at the Middle Baptist Church; later he served as a judge for the Shelby County criminal court. At the time of his appointment to the FCC, Hooks held the position of financial secretary for the Southern Christian Leadership Conference. He resigned from the FCC shortly before assuming his new responsibilities with the NAACP.   (JEROLD L. KELLMAN)

Jackson, Reggie

It almost wrecked the New York Yankees when Reggie Jackson said he was "the straw that stirs the drink," but Jackson had lived up to his words by the time the World Series ended. He had provided the bat that served the Yankees champagne, becoming the only player besides Babe Ruth to hit three home runs in a World Series game. He did it in the deciding sixth game, when the Yankees gained their Series victory over the Los Angeles Dodgers. It was New York's 21st baseball championship and its first since 1962.

Jackson had been the most coveted of baseball's free agents after the 1976 season, and Yankee owner George Steinbrenner signed him for an estimated $2.9 million over five years. But the Yankees had won the American League pennant without Jackson the year before, and the size of his wallet left bruises on some egos.

In mid-June, with the Yankees surprisingly in third place, manager Billy Martin benched Jackson in the middle of an inning for what he considered loafing in right field. Martin was nearly fired two days later, but Jackson persuaded Steinbrenner to reconsider; however, Jackson's relationship with Martin was never better than cool. The lowest point for Jackson was the night of the July 19 All-Star game at Yankee Stadium, when he was accused of roughing up a youth who cursed him in the parking lot.

The Yankees were five games out of first place on August 10 when Martin made Jackson the cleanup hitter, a move Steinbrenner had suggested all season. After that, they won 24 of their next 27 games and 40 of their next 50. Jackson finished the season with 32 home runs, 93 runs scored, a .286 batting average, and 110 runs batted in, all figures above his career averages. His five home runs, eight runs batted in, ten runs, and .450 batting average made him a clear choice as the World Series' most valuable player.

The spotlight was never far from Reginald Martinez Jackson during his major league career. Born May 18, 1946, in Philadelphia, Jackson in his second full season, 1969, challenged Roger Maris' record of 61 homers before slumping and finishing with 47. He led the league with 32 homers in 1973 and tied for the lead with 36 in 1975. He was most valuable player in the American League and in the World Series in 1973, the middle year of the five pennants and three World Series he helped win for the Oakland A's.   (KEVIN M. LAMB)

Jayawardene, Junius Richard

Following the overwhelming electoral victory of his United National Party (UNP) in July 1977, J. R. Jayawardene became prime minister of Sri Lanka in succession to Mrs. Sirimavo Bandaranaike of the defeated Sri Lanka Freedom Party. One of his country's leading politicians for more than three decades, he had helped form the UNP in 1946 and had been successively its treasurer, secretary, vice-president, and, from 1973, president.

As leader of the opposition during Mrs. Bandaranaike's regime, Jayawardene, popularly known as "J. R.," had fought hard to force the government to hold the election, which his predecessor had twice postponed. During the preelection campaign he attempted to give a socialist orientation to the UNP, which previously had the image of a capitalist party. His first serious test as prime minister came within weeks of his election, when violence between the Tamil-speaking and Sinhalese-speaking sectors of the population erupted in various parts of the country, causing more than 100 deaths and leaving many thousands homeless. His scheme for introducing the French-style presidential system of government received parliamentary approval in September, and he was expected to become Sri Lanka's first president in early 1978.

Born in Colombo on Sept. 17, 1906, the son of a Supreme Court judge, Jayawardene, a Buddhist by religion, took a law degree at the University of Ceylon and practiced as a barrister until 1943. He entered politics early in life, joining the Ceylon National Congress formed in 1918 to agitate for political reforms and freedom from British rule. In 1943 he was elected to the State Council as a National Congress member. After independence in 1948 he became finance minister in Stephen Senanayake's UNP government and in 1950 initiated the Commonwealth aid and development scheme known as the Colombo Plan. He remained finance minister under Dudley Senanayake (who became prime minister on his father's death in 1952) and was then minister of food and agriculture in Sir John Kotelawala's Cabinet (1953–56). After the UNP's four years in opposition he became finance minister once more in Dudley Senanayake's brief administration in 1960. When the UNP returned to power in 1965 he became minister of state and government chief whip (1965–70). On Senanayake's death in 1973 Jayawardene succeeded him as party leader.   (GOVINDAN UNNY)

Jordan, (William) Hamilton

He seemed almost allergic to neckties. He wore work boots and tan safari trousers in the White House. He had never eaten in Washington's fashionable Sans Souci restaurant and vowed he never would. In 1977 he was only 33 years old, and although he was one of the two or three closest political advisers to the president of the United States, he affected an easygoing, down-home manner and never publicly admitted to being worried about anything. But White House newsmen noted that Jordan bit his fingernails to the quick.

Completely devoted to his boss, U.S. Pres. Jimmy Carter, Jordan had worked with Carter longer than any other member of the White House staff. As a student at the University of Georgia, he laboured in Carter's unsuccessful 1966 gubernatorial campaign. The two teamed up for a second try in 1970, and this time, with Jordan as campaign manager, Carter won. He rewarded Jordan by making him his executive secretary. In 1973, when Carter was named chairman of the Democratic Party's national campaign for the 1974 off-year elections, he dispatched Jordan to Washington as liaison to the Democratic National Committee. What Carter and Jordan—but few others—knew at the time was that Carter was planning to run for president in 1976. Part of their plan was to use contacts made in the 1974 campaign as a base for Carter's presidential bid.

The plan worked, and when Carter won the presidential election, Jordan was named assistant to the president. Many assumed he would function as chief of staff, but Jordan did not want the job, and Carter preferred a less structured staff organization. Thus, Jordan and Press Secretary Jody Powell, along with one or two others, functioned primarily as political advisers and troubleshooters. The loose-knit system and the inexperience of Carter's personal staff led to considerable criticism during 1977. Some adjustments were rumoured, but no major changes seemed likely.

Jordan was born in Charlotte, N.C., on Sept 21, 1944, and raised in Albany, Ga. He recalled that as a youth he was offended by civil rights demonstrations, but eventually came to respect the efforts of Martin Luther King, Jr., and other civil rights leaders. Jordan was graduated from the University of Georgia and during the late 1960s spent ten months in Vietnam as a social worker with the International Voluntary Service.   (STANLEY W. CLOUD)

Kermit the Frog

Kermit the Frog appeared in his first Macy's Thanksgiving Day parade in 1977, having celebrated his 21st birthday the year before on Dinah Shore's television show. Kermit is a celebrity with Ping-Pong balls for eyes and Jim Henson's sleeve where his legs ought to be. He is a Muppet, and one of the originals at that.

For the unaware, Muppets are hybrids of puppets and marionettes. Worn on the puppeteer's hand, they have their mouths and expressions controlled by hidden fingers, while arms, legs, tails, etc., move in response to another offstage operator who pulls strings, pushes sticks, and the like. Making them properly animated is no mean trick, since "five degrees of tilt can convey a different emotion," according to their master manipulator.

Kermit and his kind were invented by Henson, then a University of Maryland theatre-arts student. They first appeared regularly on a five-minute television show on a Washington, D.C., station as a local curtain raiser for the "Tonight Show." By 1957 Kermit had grown up enough to appear on that program himself. Wearing a blond wig, he sang "I've Grown Accustomed to Your Face" to a small purple monster operated by Jane Nebel, Henson's assistant.

The purple monster has not been seen often since. But Kermit survived, Henson

A.T.V., LONDON

Kermit the Frog

married Nebel, and they all became famous. In 1969 the Henson Muppets sparkplugged "Sesame Street," the extraordinarily successful educational program for preschoolers. Within a few years it was estimated that approximately half of the three–five-year-olds in the U.S. watched it.

In 1976 these foam rubber and fabric humorous humanoid animals struck out on their own in television with "The Muppet Show." Because the U.S. networks were at first uninterested, the show was produced by Britain's Associated Television company. By its second year it was broadcast in 100 countries and was being seen each week by perhaps 250 million people—of all ages. It won many awards, including the prestigious Golden Rose of the Montreux Festival.

Besides Kermit, the only Muppet to appear regularly on both "Sesame Street" and "The Muppet Show," the company includes such veterans as Big Bird, Oscar the Grouch, the Cookie Monster, and, off-camera of course, Henson, who was born in Greenville, Miss., on Sept. 24, 1936. New characters appear regularly. A favourite was Miss Piggy, a lovestruck sow who danced with Rudolf Nureyev in "The Muppet Show" ballet *Swine Lake*.

(PHILIP KOPPER)

Khaalis, Hamaas Abdul

For 38 hours in March 1977, Hamaas Abdul Khaalis and 11 accomplices held 134 persons hostage in three buildings in Washington, D.C. Though eventually all the hostages were released, this act of terrorism left one person dead and more than a dozen others injured.

Khaalis was the leader of the Hanafi Muslims, a small religious sect whose members are black Americans. Born 56 years earlier in Indiana as Ernest McGhee, he had a history of mental illness. He was discharged from the U.S. Army during World War II as a psychiatric misfit. Later,

he joined the Black Muslims, an all-black religious group that practiced a form of Islam and denounced white people as "devils." Khaalis rose to an important position with the Black Muslims, but in 1958 he broke with them. Several years later he formed his own rival sect, which he called the Hanafi. In late 1972 he attacked the Black Muslims in an open letter sent to ministers across the country. In January 1973 seven Black Muslims broke into Khaalis' Washington, D.C., home and killed several of his children, his infant grandson, and a follower. The murderers were caught, tried, and sent to prison, but Khaalis was not satisfied. He wanted revenge and vowed to fight a jihad, or holy war.

On the morning of March 9, 1977, Khaalis and several heavily armed followers took over by force the Washington, D.C., headquarters of B'nai B'rith, a Jewish service organization, gathering numerous hostages into a conference room. Later that day three Hanafis seized the Islamic Center, and two gunmen invaded Washington's District Building, killing a radio reporter in the process.

The police and FBI soon surrounded all three buildings and began to negotiate with Khaalis, who was threatening to behead the hostages. Khaalis made many demands, some of which were granted. A motion picture called *Mohammad, Messenger of God*, which the Hanafis found sacrilegious, was temporarily withdrawn from circulation. But the police would not bring the killers of Khaalis' children to him nor would they ask two prominent Black Muslims to come to the B'nai B'rith building for a meeting.

The situation was worsening when three Muslim diplomats—Ambassadors Zahedi of Iran, Ghorbal of Egypt, and Yaqub-Khan of Pakistan—volunteered to negotiate with Khaalis. Accompanied by FBI agents and local police, the three entered

the B'nai B'rith headquarters, calmed Khaalis with quotations from the Koran, and persuaded him to surrender peacefully. The police agreed to release Khaalis without bail if he would give up. They honoured this promise but jailed eight of the other Hanafis. In July Khaalis and 11 followers were convicted of conspiracy, second-degree murder, and kidnapping; in September they were sentenced to prison terms ranging from 24 to 78 years.

(VICTOR M. CASSIDY)

Kim Hyung Wook

In the tangled investigation of the relationship between some U.S. congressmen and a South Korean businessman who allegedly bought their influence with cash, both Department of Justice and congressional investigators were hampered by the absence from the U.S. of the chief suspect, the businessman Park Tong Sun. But Kim Hyung Wook, the former chief of the Korean Central Intelligence Agency, was in Washington, D.C., and he provided some detailed testimony.

Kim testified before congressional committees that during his tenure as chief of the South Korean spy agency he had met with Park and a U.S. congressman, Richard T. Hanna of California, to plan the influence-buying scheme. The plan centred on Park's desire to become the chief broker for lucrative rice sales from the United States to South Korea. Kim told the House Ethics Committee that former congressman Hanna had agreed to the scheme, which allegedly earned Park some $9 million in commissions and allegedly helped finance his efforts to buy influence in Washington. Hanna was indicted for accepting thousands of dollars as his part in the payoff arrangements.

The KCIA, which Kim ran from 1963 to 1969, also funded some of Park's operations in Washington, including the purchase of Washington's exclusive George Town Club, where Park entertained many of Washington's power elite. Kim himself was named an unindicted co-conspirator when the Department of Justice charged Park with illegally trying to influence Congress.

Kim, a Korean native now in his early 50s, was a close ally of South Korean Pres. Park Chung Hee and supported the coup that brought Park to power in 1961. Park made Kim head of his intelligence operation, but in 1973 Kim fled South Korea as a political exile when he became a bitter foe of President Park.

The two remained enemies, and part of Kim's reason for testifying appeared to be a desire to undermine the Park regime. Kim told newspaper reporters in July that President Park had sent a South Korean Cabinet minister to the U.S. in June to try to dissuade him from disclosing what he knew about the bribery operation. In October Kim testified that by 1969 Park Tong Sun reported to him that he was having great success with his payoff operations, passing out bundles of "$1,000, $2,000, $5,000 and $10,000 to prominent officials."

(JOHN F. STACKS)

King, Don

After standing the boxing world on its cauliflower ear for nearly three years with his exotic heavyweight championship fights, promoter Don King found himself down for the count during much of 1977. The United States Championships boxing tournament, which King had promoted and the American Broadcasting Co. had televised, was suspended April 16 after charges that boxers' records had been falsified, that King controlled most of the tournament's boxers and officials, and that fighters had to pay kickbacks to participate. The outcome of the scandal was still in doubt when the year closed, but King was back on his feet when ABC televised the bout he promoted November 5 between the top two heavyweight challengers, Jimmy Young and Ken Norton.

King made a name for himself as a boxing promoter in the fall of 1974, when he arranged the "Rumble in the Jungle" in which Muhammad Ali regained the heavyweight title with a knockout of George Foreman. Both fighters were guaranteed an unprecedented $5 million for that bout in Kinshasa, Zaire, and King's penchant for expensive spectaculars took him the next year to Kuala Lumpur, Malaysia, for Ali's successful title defense against Joe Bugner and to the Philippines for Ali's "Thrilla in Manila" victory over Joe Frazier.

"My magic lies in my ghetto ties. As long as I recognize who I am and where I came from, I'll survive," says King, who was born Aug. 20, 1931, in Cleveland, Ohio, and became a kingpin in the numbers game there in the 1950s. He was shot at in 1957 after implicating an underworld figure in a kickback scheme; his house was dynamited by rival mobsters, and a tavern he managed was firebombed.

In 1967 he began a four-year prison term for beating a numbers runner to death, but in jail he became self-educated. By 1977 he was working out of a $7,000-a-month office in Manhattan's Rockefeller Center and riding in a $25,000 custom-made limousine.

ABC promised King $1.5 million and 23 hours of air time for his U.S. Boxing Championships, scheduled to run from January to June. He denied knowing that *The Ring* magazine, often called the "Bible of boxing," had falsified records to make boxers in his tournament look better, and also denied knowing that fighters had to give kickbacks to Paddy Flood and Al Braverman, who had helped provide the contestants. He denied that his associates had stolen fighters from other managers.

(KEVIN M. LAMB)

Koch, Edward

Hardly anyone took him seriously in March 1977, when Edward Koch, a balding, 52-year-old congressman, began his campaign to be mayor of New York City. But eight months and two primaries later, Koch was overwhelmingly elected mayor of the largest city in the U.S.

To gain the office, Koch first had to beat six other Democratic candidates, including

Edward Koch

the incumbent mayor, Abraham Beame. Other Democrats in the crowded field were former congresswoman Bella Abzug, Manhattan borough president Percy Sutton, U.S. Congressman Herman Badillo, New York Secretary of State Mario Cuomo, and Joel Harnett, a businessman. With the exception of Harnett, all the candidates were better known throughout the city than Koch, and some had the backing of powerful elements in the party.

Koch, however, had a valuable asset in David Garth, the media expert who 12 years earlier had helped elect John Lindsay mayor from the same East Side "silk stocking" district in Manhattan that Koch represented during his five terms in the U.S. Congress. Garth designed a media campaign in which Koch came out as a strong law-and-order candidate, in favour of a tight budget, fiscal responsibility to restore the city's ruined finances, and a tough posture in dealing with New York's labour unions.

It was a neat bit of political magic in view of Koch's liberal, pro-labour voting record in Congress. With crime, welfare, and the city's fiscal crisis as the main issues, some of the Democratic candidates — including Koch — campaigned as if they were in a contest to see who could sound the most conservative.

Thanks partly to the splintered field, Koch narrowly finished first in the September 8 primary, getting 20% of the vote to Cuomo's 19%. Mayor Beame was third with 18%, followed by Abzug with 17%, Sutton with 14%, and Badillo with 11%. Beame then supported Koch in the runoff against Cuomo. Cuomo attempted to link Koch to the unpopular Lindsay, but Koch held the city's Jewish vote in all boroughs and cut into Cuomo's strength among the city's ethnic minorities and Roman Catholics. Koch carried 55% of the total vote in the September 19 runoff to win the Democratic nomination. In the November 8 general election, Koch again defeated Cuomo, who ran as the Liberal Party candidate, plus Republican Roy Goodman and radio

commentator Barry Farber, the Conservative Party candidate.

Koch was born Dec. 12, 1924, in New York City, and received a law degree from New York University. He first gained political notice by beating the once-powerful Carmine De Sapio to become his district's Democratic Party leader in 1963. He was elected to the city council in 1966 and two years later won the congressional seat vacated by Lindsay.

(HAL BRUNO)

Kulikov, Viktor Georgyevich

The new commander in chief of the joint armed forces of the Warsaw Treaty Organization from Jan. 8, 1977, 56-year-old Gen. Viktor G. Kulikov (promoted marshal of the Soviet Union on January 14), was one of the younger generation of Soviet military leaders. An ambitious battle commander during World War II, he had had an almost meteoric career in the postwar years. From May 1971, when he was appointed chief of the General Staff of the So-

viet armed forces and first deputy minister of defense, he gained a reputation as a first-rate strategist and as an innovator, intent on promoting to responsible posts younger generals with technological backgrounds. In 1971 the 24th congress of the Communist Party elected him a member of the Central Committee, and he was reelected in 1976. He was also a deputy to the Supreme Soviet of the U.S.S.R.

Kulikov was born on July 5, 1921, at Verkhnyaya Lyubovsha, Orel Province, into a peasant family. He served in the Red (later Soviet) Army from 1939. Graduating from an officers' infantry school in 1941, he joined the Communist Party in 1942. In World War II he fought against Germany as a junior commander of armoured units in several sectors, serving from February 1943 to May 1945 as deputy chief of staff and later as chief of staff of an armoured brigade attached to Gen. K. K. Rokossovsky's 1st Belorussian Army Group. In the final campaign Kulikov's brigade helped to liberate northern Poland. After the war he graduated from higher military academies, in 1959 from that of the General Staff. He then held a series of commands, of a regiment, a mechanized division, an army, the forces of the Kiev military district, and, from November 1969, the Soviet forces in East Germany.

Kulikov's latest appointment followed the death of his predecessor, Marshal Ivan I. Yakubovsky, on Nov. 30, 1976. In May 1977 he presided over a meeting of the Military Council of the Warsaw Pact forces, held in Prague, Czechoslovakia.

(K.M. SMOGORZEWSKI)

Laker, Frederick Alfred

It took Freddie Laker six years to beat the monopolistic aviation bureaucracies and win a license to operate cut-rate walk-on flights across the Atlantic by Laker Airways Skytrain. With 272 passengers, most of whom stood in line for the £59 seats, the first Skytrain took off for New York on Sept. 26, 1977. Laker first applied for a license in 1971. In his fight with the civil aviation authorities, government departments, and the big airlines he had more staying power than they did. But he had to go to the Court of Appeal to get a decision in his favour. And at that point the big airlines introduced economy flights that were within a few dollars of Skytrain.

Laker, a big, bluff, outspoken tycoon in shirt sleeves, was informal to the point of giving his office telephone number in Who's Who. He admitted to being obsessed with airplanes. "It isn't really the money," he told a reporter. "I love aeroplanes. I don't really think of anything else." Born in Canterbury, England, on Aug. 6, 1922, an only son in a poor family, he got his first job in Short Brothers' aircraft factory—as floor sweeper and tea-boy. He later became an aeroengineering apprentice and during World War II served in air ferrying with the Air Transport Auxiliary.

After the war, Laker's entrepreneurial flair quickly began to show. With the help of a loan from a friend, he bought a dozen converted bombers, sold six, and operated the others on the Berlin airlift. With the profits, he bought and sold vast quantities of aircraft scrap and launched the first cross-Channel air ferry. He then moved to

British United Airways, where the successful BAC 111 short-haul transport was designed to his specifications. In 1966 he set up his own airline. Laker Airways expanded quickly through deals with tour operators. Ten years later it was carrying one million passengers a year, and Laker was reckoned to be worth £20 million. But it managed to operate with a fleet of only 11 planes, few enough for Laker to keep in mind where all of them were. Naturally enough, Freddie Laker was there on the first Skytrain trip, the life and soul of the party. In December he announced plans to apply for permission to begin service between London and Los Angeles.

(HARFORD THOMAS)

Lance, Thomas Bertram

When Bert Lance arrived in Washington, D.C., in January 1977, to take up his post as director of Pres. Jimmy Carter's Office of Management and Budget, he was excited by the prospect of being the president's closest adviser. "This is the biggest thrill of my life," he said. He rented a limousine for the inaugural ceremonies, complete with license plates saying "BERT" in the front and "LANCE" in the back. He and his wife LaBelle rented an elegant Georgetown house that quickly became a focal point for social and political Washington. But by September, Bert and LaBelle were home in Georgia, the casualties of Lance's past financial dealings and the symbols of Carter's first presidential crisis.

Lance, born June 3, 1931, in Gainesville, Ga., was one of Carter's first major appointments after his election. The two had been close personal, political, and financial friends for years, with Lance serving in the Cabinet when Carter was governor of Georgia. Carter urged Lance to run for governor to succeed him in 1974, and that campaign was the reason for a series of large overdrafts on Lance's Calhoun (Ga.) First National Bank that contributed to his problems in Washington.

Although Lance was easily confirmed by the Senate early in 1977, questions about his past financial dealings began to emerge in the spring when stories detailing his huge debts and questioning his ability to pay them off appeared in the press. When Carter asked the Senate to grant Lance an extension of an agreement to sell his bank stock, investigations of Lance's past began in earnest. The U.S. Senate first treated Lance tenderly, but later, as more allegations about his overdrafts and borrowing practices emerged, it launched its own investigation.

Carter and his intimates in the White House tended to believe that Lance was being treated unfairly, and they rallied around their Georgia friend. By Labor Day, however, it seemed clear that Lance was headed toward resignation, and on September 21 a saddened president announced Lance's departure. Investigations into Lance's activities continued, however, in both the Department of Justice and the Securities and Exchange Commission.

Lance did find a buyer for his bank stock. Late in the year he agreed to sell 60% of his stock in the National Bank of Georgia to a Saudi Arabian businessman at $3 more a share than he had paid.

(JOHN F. STACKS)

Land, Edwin H.

"A new art has been born." With those words, in the introduction to Polaroid Corp.'s annual report, Edwin H. Land—company founder, chairman, and director of research—made public the creation of instant motion-picture equipment and film. Called Polavision, the new system consists of a lightweight, battery-powered camera, recording-type cassettes containing the film and processing fluid, and a TV-like viewer with a 12-in screen.

The camera itself closely resembles the ordinary Super-8 motion-picture cameras. The innovations reside mainly inside the cassettes and to a lesser extent in the viewer. Polavision film runs at 400 ft a minute past a tiny plastic slit from which a processing fluid is exuded; the fluid contacts the film and dries in less than a minute. Processing takes place once the photographer removes the cassette, with the exposed film inside, from the camera and pushes it into a slot in the top of the viewer. After processing, the film is then rewound and projected automatically on the viewer screen, which 10 to 12 people can watch comfortably at one time. The viewer even has a fast rewind feature to permit instant replays. Each cassette has a running time of 2 min 40 sec.

Displaying Polavision to shareholders at the company's annual meeting, Land revealed that it had taken more than nine years and $100 million to develop and that many further refinements lay ahead. He was a good deal less precise about when Polavision would be available and at what cost. He indicated that limited quantities would reach stores by the end of 1977. Polaroid pegged the price at $699.

The creator of Polavision was born on May 7, 1909, in Bridgeport, Conn. Although he attended Harvard University, he was never graduated, withdrawing instead to devote all his energy to creating a light-polarizing substance which he later applied to sunglasses, camera filters, and other optical devices. During the early 1940s Land developed a process used in three-dimensional motion-picture cameras, but it was his introduction of the Polaroid Land Camera and instantaneous (60-sec) developing film later in the decade that made his name a household word. In July 1977 he was granted his 501st patent, for an improvement in the reproduction of silver photographic images.

(JEROLD L. KELLMAN)

Lucas, George

The film comprised "flotsam and jetsam from the period when I was 12 years old. All the books and films and comics that I liked when I was a child. The plot is simple: good against evil—and the film is designed to be all the fun things and fantasy things I remember. The word for this movie is fun." So director George Lucas described the film Star Wars, and apparently audiences agreed. By the end of 1977 it had exceeded the all-time gross set by Jaws, and the American Film Institute included it among the ten best films of all time, along with *Casablanca* and *Gone with the Wind*.

Theoretically science fiction, *Star Wars* was, in the words of a *Time* reporter, "A combination of Flash Gordon, the Wizard of Oz, the Errol Flynn swashbucklers . . . almost every western ever screened . . . the Hardy Boys, Sir Gawain and the Green Knight and the Faerie Queene" (not to mention the World War II movies, whose aerial dogfights provided the pattern for *Star Wars'* stunning space battles). Its characters were nearly as diverse and unreal: the chaste but spunky Princess Leia, the earnest innocent Luke Skywalker, the gruff but noble Han Solo, and the unspeakably villainous Darth Vader (who got away, raising the possibility of a sequel). Sharing billing with the humans were two captivating robots—the prissy C3PO and R2D2, best described by one reviewer as an animated sparkplug—and Chewbacca the Wookie, behind whose apelike exterior lurked the sidekick of a thousand Westerns.

But perhaps the true stars of the film were the special effects, which some viewers found more startling than those in Stanley Kubrick's *2001: A Space Odyssey* of ten years before. Lucas was able to use computers in the cutting room that Kubrick never had, and *Star Wars* may have been the most visually and aurally complex movie ever made.

Lucas planned *Star Wars* as a change of pace from his earlier hit, *American Graffiti*, which documented the growing pains of the high school class of '62 in Lucas' hometown of Modesto, Calif. *Film Quarterly* described *Graffiti* as "probably as close to an autobiographical film as a studio-financed Hollywood production will ever be," and Lucas admitted as much. Its denouement involved a drag race wreck; Lucas himself was nearly killed in a crash.

Abandoning the drivers' seats of hot rods, Lucas took up sports car still photography and through it met cinematographer Haskell Wexler, who encouraged him to attend the University of Southern California film school. There he made a short, *THX 1138*, later expanded into a science fiction feature that was rereleased in 1977 in an effort to cash in on *Star Wars'* popularity. (PHILIP KOPPER)

Mandel, Marvin

For Maryland Gov. Marvin Mandel the end of a long political road came on Aug. 23, 1977, when a federal court jury in Baltimore found him guilty of corruption charges. He was sentenced to four years in prison. Though he was free while the case was being appealed, it seemed certain that, whatever the outcome, Mandel's once-brilliant political career had ended.

Ironically, Mandel had succeeded Spiro Agnew as governor when Agnew was elected vice-president of the U.S. on the ticket with Richard Nixon. Agnew later was forced to resign after pleading no contest to federal tax evasion charges. Mandel's conviction was the latest in a series of trials involving state, county, and local officials that had made Maryland notorious for corrupt politics.

Mandel was born in Baltimore on April 19, 1920, and began his political career as a justice of the peace, after serving in the Army during World War II and practicing law. He was elected to the Maryland House of Delegates in 1952 and became a powerful Democratic leader during the 17 years he served in the legislature. The General Assembly chose him to succeed Agnew in 1969, and Maryland voters elected him to a term of his own in 1970.

Among the nation's governors, Mandel quickly earned respect as one of the best minds in state government. He was chairman of the National Governors' Conference in 1972–73. Personally popular with the voters, he was easily reelected to another term in 1974, despite a highly publicized divorce from his wife of 32 years and remarriage to a younger woman. Testimony at his trial subsequently revealed that $150,000 in illegal gifts had been used for his divorce settlement.

At the trial Mandel was charged with receiving $350,000 in gifts and services from friends who owned secret interests in the Marlboro Race Track. He was accused of using his influence as governor to obtain favourable racing dates for the track. The jury deliberated 12 days before returning a verdict that found Mandel and his co-defendants guilty on 15 counts of mail fraud and one of racketeering. (HAL BRUNO)

Matthews, Victor Collin

It was said that life began at 40 for Victor Matthews. Born on Dec. 5, 1919, it was not until 1960 that he went into business on his own in the construction industry, having learned the trade in one of Britain's biggest construction firms, Trollope and Colls. He started out with capital of a few thousand pounds. Seventeen years later he became boss of Beaverbrook Newspapers, one of Britain's dynastic newspaper empires, including the *Daily Express*, the *Sunday Express*, and the London *Evening Standard*.

His was a classic rags-to-riches story. A north London Cockney boy growing up through the hard times of the 1930s, Matthews started out as a schoolboy delivering newspapers. At 14 he got his first full-time job, as an office boy, and then served through World War II in the Navy as an able seaman. It was only in the 1960s that he discovered his talent for business. After five years he had made such a success of his construction company that he was able to sell out to the prestigious conglomerate Trafalgar House Investments Ltd., where by 1973 he had become deputy chairman and also chairman of the world-famous shipping line Cunard, which Trafalgar House had taken over.

In June 1977 Trafalgar House bought the ailing Beaverbrook empire for £13.7 million, thus acquiring Fleet Street property said to be worth £20 million. Matthews moved in as chairman, his primary task being to rescue the *Daily Express*, which was losing £2 million a year. He confessed to knowing nothing about newspapers but he knew what he wanted—"a family newspaper which cares for Britain." The slogan he adopted might have been taken direct from the founder, Lord Beaverbrook: "Believe in Britain and look for the good things."

Within weeks Matthews brought in a new editor, Derek Jameson, from the *Daily Mirror*. Previously he had said that his editors would enjoy editorial freedom "as long as they agree with the policy I have laid down." Within a couple of months he was in his first confrontation with the unions. In an industry notorious for wobbling and wavering, Matthews stood firm. The *Daily Express* in London did not appear for six days but continued to print in Manchester. At the end of a week the London printers were back at work. Matthews called it "a historic turning point."

(HARFORD THOMAS)

Mengistu Haile Mariam

Lieut. Col. Mengistu Haile Mariam emerged in 1977 as Ethiopia's strong man with no rivals within the ruling Provisional Military Administrative Council (known as the Dirgue, an Amharic word for committee), whose chairman he became on February 11. He established his position through a series of bloody purges within the revolutionary leadership. Some nine members of the Dirgue, including the previous chairman, Brig. Gen. Teferi Benti, perished in February, and Mengistu's rival, Vice-Chairman Lieut. Col. Atnafu Abate, was executed in November. Shootings and executions of lesser functionaries took place at various times.

Mengistu succeeded in steering Ethiopia toward becoming an authoritarian-Marxist state. Even before breaking in April with the U.S. (Ethiopia's traditional arms supplier), he had turned to the U.S.S.R. for military aid and ideological inspiration. He received a congratulatory visit from Cuban Pres. Fidel Castro in March. But even with Soviet backing, Mengistu's regime showed deep malaise, especially in its conflict with Somali rebels.

The 39-year-old Mengistu was born to humble Christian parents of the Galla (Oromo) people, who for centuries had been dominated by the lighter-skinned Amharas. His low status and impoverished

PATRICK FRILET—SIPA PRESS/BLACK STAR

parents prevented him from going to school, but he was helped by a wealthy Amhara nobleman in whose household his mother was a servant. As a youngster Mengistu developed a deep antipathy for Ethiopian royalty and Amhara domination. His inadequate education prevented him from going to the elitist Harar Military Academy, another source of grievance. Instead, he enrolled as a cadet at the less prestigious college at Guennete. As an ordnance officer, he spent two brief periods in the U.S. for further military training.

Mengistu was one of the 120 men who originally comprised the Dirgue when it led the soldiers' rebellion that overthrew Emperor Haile Selassie in 1974. He personally directed the final humiliation of the emperor when he was dethroned on Sept. 12, 1974, and also the squad of men who shot the former chairman of the Dirgue, Gen. Aman Andom, when he resisted arrest on Nov. 23, 1974.   (COLIN LEGUM)

Mobutu Sese Seko

Zaire's president, Gen. Mobutu Sese Seko, survived two major crises in 1977—one economic, the other an attempt to overthrow him through a military invasion staged by political opponents based in neighbouring Angola. Throughout his presidency Mobutu had faced internal rebellions and attempted coups, but his position was threatened from a new source after Angola achieved its independence in 1975. Mobutu had worked hard to prevent Agostinho Neto's Marxist movement from taking power there, and this led to considerable enmity between the two. The Angolan regime openly connived in the March 1977 invasion of Zaire by Angola-based Katangese, which was intended to overthrow Mobutu but which he defeated by enlisting the support of Morocco and France. However, the poor showing of the Zairian Army and the country's economic difficulties left Mobutu's political authority severely shaken. Nevertheless, in December he was reelected for an additional seven-year term by over 98% of the electorate.

Mobutu was born in Lisala, Équateur Province, Belgian Congo (now Zaire), on

WIDE WORLD

Oct. 14, 1930. After primary and secondary schooling in Christian mission institutions, he received higher education at the Institute of Social Studies in Brussels. He joined the Belgian Force Publique in the Congo as an accountant in 1949 and rose to the rank of sergeant major. Seven years later he left the force to become a journalist and joined Patrice Lumumba's Mouvement National Congolais in 1958. After independence in 1960 he quickly rose to the command of the Congolese Army, a position he continued to hold thereafter. In the power struggle between Lumumba and Pres. Joseph Kasavubu in 1960–61, Mobutu backed Kasavubu, only to oust him in turn in a November 1965 coup, when he assumed the presidency himself.

Mobutu launched a black authenticity movement, in connection with which the country was renamed Zaire in October 1971, and he called on all Zairians to de-europeanize their names. He abandoned his own baptismal name, Joseph Désiré, to assume his "warrior" names, Sese Seko Kuku Ngbendu Wa Za Banga.
                                    (COLIN LEGUM)

Mondale, Walter Frederick

On Jan. 20, 1977, Walter Mondale became the 42nd vice-president of the United States—and something more. He became, quite possibly, the first U.S. vice-president to play an important role in the daily business of running the government. Pres. Jimmy Carter, who had selected Mondale as his running mate on the Democratic ticket in 1976, had said he would give a prominent role to his vice-president. Skeptics noted that presidents always say such things before they take office, but by the end of the year it seemed clear that Carter had kept his promise.

On the surface, the president and vice-president were quite different personalities. Mondale, a former U.S. senator, was an "insider" in Washington and in Democratic politics, while Carter was a self-proclaimed "outsider." Mondale was a conventional liberal, a protégé of liberal elder statesman and fellow Minnesotan Hubert H. Humphrey; Carter preferred the middle of the political road. Still, the two men had become political and personal friends. During their first year in office, Mondale, one of Carter's handful of close advisers, probably saw and talked with Carter more than any other person except the First Lady. He also attended to more conventional vice-presidential duties, including a number of overseas and domestic trips to sell the administration's policies.

Mondale brought to his new position experience, political judgment, and an easy ability to deal with people—whether recalcitrant senators or leaders of new African nations. And while the president and vice-president might sometimes disagree on matters of policy, once a decision was made by the president, the vice-president acted as a loyal team member.

Mondale was born Jan. 5, 1928, in Ceylon, Minn., of Norwegian immigrant stock. In 1948 he worked in Humphrey's first campaign for the U.S. Senate. Later, because of financial problems, he dropped out of college and moved to Washington, D.C., as head of the student wing of Americans for Democratic Action, then chaired

DENNIS BRACK—BLACK STAR

by Humphrey. Returning to college a year later, Mondale was graduated from the University of Minnesota in 1951 and received his LL.B. from that institution in 1956. In 1964, while serving as attorney general in Minnesota, he was appointed to fill Humphrey's vacant Senate seat when Humphrey became vice-president under Lyndon B. Johnson. Mondale was reelected in 1966 and 1972.   (STANLEY W. CLOUD)

Mori, Hanae

Hanae Mori was already an institution in her native Japan and had won acclaim in the U.S. and Europe before she made her debut in the rarefied atmosphere of Paris fashions in 1977. Other Japanese designers had preceded her to the French capital, but their field was ready-to-wear. Mori's boutique on Avenue Montaigne was the first to offer Japanese creations in the highly competitive area of haute couture. "The Japanese sun rose on Paris haute couture Thursday," observed one critic, who noted that Mori had "provided an Oriental touch to clothes so light they looked airborne."

For Mori, success did not come easily. She wanted to be a painter, but when her family frowned on the idea she studied designing instead. In 1951 she opened her first shop over a Chinese noodle restaurant in the Shinjuku district of Tokyo and, with the help of two young friends, turned out her first dresses on secondhand sewing machines. As Japan's reigning queen of fashions, Mori now rules over a glittering empire that produces highly marketable items worth roughly $80 million a year. She has 48 boutiques in Japan that employ 1,500 workers, and others in the U.S., England, Australia, West Germany, and other parts of Europe. Japanese flight attendants and bank employees are among those who wear her label. She eventually branched out into sheets, towels, neckties, handkerchiefs, swim suits, aprons, umbrellas, and even perfumes. Her 1965 de-

but in the ballroom of the old Hotel Delmonico in New York City featured Japanese fabrics and motifs. Four years later she created a sensation with a collection that fluttered with patterns of large and small butterflies.

The petite and attractive Mori was born on Jan. 8, 1926, in Shimane Prefecture. She still works 12 hours a day, six days a week, personally checking designs for her six annual collections, three for haute couture and three for ready-to-wear. Her husband is the firm's general manager. One son is in charge of a Tokyo boutique, while another works as a designer. Repelled by the drabness of postwar Japan, Mori set out to show Japanese women how to be elegant in clothes other than traditional kimonos. And she succeeded beyond her wildest dreams. (JOHN RODERICK)

Morrice, Norman

That muse of British ballet, Dame Marie Rambert, inspired not only succeeding generations of British choreography but also, it seemed, of artistic direction. Those choreographers emerging from her Ballet Club of the 1930s—such as Frederick Ashton, Antony Tudor, Frank Staff, and Walter Gore—later became involved in direction of various kinds. Norman Morrice, who in 1977 succeeded Kenneth MacMillan as artistic director of the Royal Ballet, was also a former pupil, and later a close associate, of Dame Marie.

It was doubtful whether Morrice, who was born in Mexico in 1931, had aspirations of one day directing one of the greatest dance companies in Western Europe. He intended to become a dancer and, in England, studied locally in Mansfield and later at the Rambert School. He joined the Rambert company in 1952, rising to become a principal dancer. From the outset his main interest was choreography, and his first creation was *Two Brothers* (Dohnanyi) in 1958. Its success led to a succession of works, the most important being *Hazaña* (Surinach) in 1959.

In 1961 Morrice spent a year in the U.S. studying contemporary techniques with Martha Graham; this changed his attitude toward dance and greatly influenced his future choreography. After that he went on to write works such as *The Travellers* (Salzedo; 1963), *Them and Us* (Xenakis; 1968), *Blind-Sight* (Bob Downes; 1969), *That Is the Show* (Berio; 1971), and many others for Ballet Rambert and other companies, mainly in West Germany and Israel.

In 1966 Morrice became joint director, with Dame Marie, of Ballet Rambert and was mainly responsible for changing the orientation of the company from classical to contemporary dance, with the performers trained in both techniques. In 1974 he resigned so that he could work free-lance throughout the world, but he returned to Ballet Rambert for *Smiling Immortal* (Jonathan Harvey), the company's contribution to the 1977 celebrations of the royal Silver Jubilee year.

Morrice's first association with the Royal Ballet was in 1965 when he created *The Tribute* for its touring company. With his great experience—as dancer, choreographer, and director—he seemed ideally fitted for his new post as its artistic director.
(PETER WILLIAMS)

Morton, Craig

The first time the Denver Broncos' new quarterback met the Denver Broncos' new coach before the 1977 season, coach Red Miller told quarterback Craig Morton, "We were 9–5 last year and with people like you, we can really go places this year."

With people like Morton, the Broncos went all the way to the Super Bowl, further than any previous National Football League team that had never before made the play-offs. In 17 years the Broncos had tried 25 quarterbacks and never qualified for post-season competition. So before the 1977 season they acquired Morton from the New York Giants for Steve Ramsey, a quarterback who did not even make the last-place Giants' roster. That's how expendable the Giants considered Morton after his 12 NFL seasons. Even though he had passed for 16,013 yd and had started five play-off games, Morton was never thought of as anything more than an adequate workman.

But after 1977, Morton had a new reputation. He was selected the American Conference's most valuable player, completing 131 of 254 passes (51.6%) for 1,929 yd and 14 touchdowns, throwing a conference-low eight interceptions, and ranking second among conference quarterbacks with 82.1 rating points. The Super Bowl was an anticlimax. Denver lost to the Dallas Cowboys and Morton—plagued by a hip injury—gave a lacklustre performance. But even that could not dim the record of an outstanding season and the comeback story of the year.

Born Feb. 5, 1943, Morton turned down a baseball bonus offer, choosing instead to attend the University of California, where he became an All-American quarterback. The Dallas Cowboys drafted him in the first round in 1965 and paid him $200,000 to sign. But during his ten-year Dallas career Morton bounced in and out of the line-up. Don Meredith was the starting quarterback during Morton's first four pro sea-

sons, and when Morton finally made the first string in 1969 he hurt his shoulder in the fourth game after leading the league with a 71% completion record and no interceptions. The next year, he guided the Cowboys to their first Super Bowl, which they lost, but after the Chicago game in 1971, Morton was back on the bench.

Except for half of the 1972 season when Roger Staubach was hurt, he stayed there, frequently asking to be traded. The Giants traded for him midway through the 1974 season, but their record was 9–27 during his 2½ seasons in New York and when the Giants opened their new stadium in 1976, their fans booed when Morton was introduced and cheered when he was sacked.
(KEVIN M. LAMB)

Mugabe, Robert

One of the most influential black nationalist leaders involved throughout 1977 in moves toward a resolution of the Rhodesian constitutional impasse, Robert Mugabe was joint leader with Joshua Nkomo (*q.v.*) of the Patriotic Front of Zimbabwe (Rhodesia) and president general of the Zimbabwe African National Union (ZANU). A militant radical, although he disavowed any Marxist label, Mugabe had been in exile since 1975 and was the political spokesman for a major Mozambique-based guerrilla section of the Zimbabwe People's Army.

Born the son of a village carpenter in Kutama in 1925, Mugabe was trained as a teacher in a Roman Catholic mission school. Introduced to nationalist politics while a student at the University College of Fort Hare, South Africa, he had his first brush with authority when he threatened to "box the ears" of the then Rhodesian prime minister, R. S. Garfield Todd, over a government deduction from the meagre salaries paid to teachers. He spent some years in the late 1950s in Kwame Nkrumah's Ghana, where he married a Ghanaian and sharpened his radical politics.

Mugabe returned home in 1960, and in 1963 helped the Rev. Ndabaningi Sithole (*q.v.*) to form ZANU as a breakaway from Nkomo's Zimbabwe African People's Union (ZAPU). In 1964 he was arrested for "subversive speech" and spent the next ten years in prison. During that period he ac-

quired three law degrees by correspondence courses. While still in prison he led a coup in 1974 deposing Sithole as ZANU's leader.

Mugabe envisaged an independent Zimbabwe as a nonracial and nonaligned state guided by socialist principles. He described his partnership with his old political rival, Nkomo, as a tactical alliance during the struggle for independence.

(COLIN LEGUM)

Muhammad, Wallace

"The movement has abandoned virtually all its peculiar views." Those words, in *Time* magazine, summed up the changes that Wallace Muhammad had brought to the U.S. religious sect commonly known as the Black Muslims. Beginning in 1975, Muhammad changed the movement's official name, opened its membership to people of all races, made its finances public, and redirected its religious practices toward what he called "pure Islam."

Until 1975 the Black Muslims were led by Elijah Muhammad, the father of Wallace. During the 1930s, the elder Muhammad met W. D. Fard, an itinerant silk peddler who claimed to be the personal embodiment of the Prophet Muhammad. Fard preached that white people were "devils" and that Allah would soon destroy their corrupt civilization. He urged black Americans to form a separate nation of their own in the United States. Fard disappeared in 1934, and Elijah Muhammad began to preach and elaborate his doctrine. He urged black Americans to take pride in themselves and to lead moral lives.

Elijah Muhammad died on Feb. 25, 1975. By that time his movement, called the Nation of Islam, had roughly 40,000 members and assets exceeding $20 million. Wallace Muhammad succeeded his father as leader of the movement. Though the press had speculated that a bloody power struggle might follow Elijah Muhammad's death, nothing of the sort happened. Wallace took charge at once and began to make changes. Repudiating racism, he said, "We have caught hell from the white man for 400 years, but we have grown to where if the white man respects us, we will respect him." Wallace also appointed the movement's first woman minister.

A year later, Wallace Muhammad revealed that the Nation of Islam was in debt because of bad management of some of its holdings. He called for austerity. He also reorganized the movement to make its leaders more accountable to the membership. In March 1977 he announced that membership had risen by 75% to 70,000 during his two years of leadership.

Wallace Muhammad was born in Detroit, Mich., on Oct. 30, 1933. He was educated by several of his father's followers and in a Muslim school but did not always obey his father or accept his teachings. Twice he was expelled from the movement for heresy but then was taken back.

(VICTOR M. CASSIDY)

Murdoch, Rupert

In the course of 1977, international press tycoon Rupert Murdoch was likened to Lord Beaverbrook, Citizen Kane, and "the Burger King of Journalism." Late in the previous year he had purchased the *New*

York Post, the city's only surviving afternoon paper, and soon thereafter he bought *New York* magazine from under the nose of its editor.

Acquisition of *New York* (along with its parent company, the venerable *Village Voice* weekly, and the fledgling *New West* magazine) occurred in a flurry of financial prestidigitation. New Yorkers were startled by the astonishing resources at Murdoch's command—he spent on the order of $45 million in two months. What concerned them even more was the chance that he would do to his new possessions what he had done to papers in Australia, Texas, and London.

Murdoch's usual—and highly successful—approach was to replace hard news with soft porn and sports. He had turned *The Sun* (London) from a stodgy political sheet into a scandal rag that daily featured a bare-breasted pinup on page 3. In New York, however, he moved slowly, perhaps because he understood that *New York*'s readers liked the way it catered to suppertime intellectuals and that the *Post*, founded in 1801 by Alexander Hamilton and owned by Dorothy Schiff for nearly 40 years, had a loyal constituency among the city's liberals. About all he did to the paper was to brighten the makeup, add some features, and increase circulation slightly.

Murdoch was born in Melbourne, Australia, March 11, 1931. His father, Sir Keith Murdoch, was a celebrated World War I correspondent and newspaper editor. After studying at Oxford, he returned home after his father's death to take over the family's small holdings, which included the *Adelaide News*. Two years later he bought a Sunday paper in Perth for $400,000, and four years after that a major Sydney journal for $4 million. By 1977, through a complicated stock arrangement, he controlled 50 Australian papers (including a serious national journal he established himself) and five television stations, plus some book companies, an airline, and other holdings. He had broadcasting and publishing interests in England (*The News of the World* weekly and a piece of London Weekend Television) as well as the *National Star*, and an occult/self-help weekly circulated across the U.S.

(PHILIP KOPPER)

Muzorewa, Abel Tendekayi

President of the United African National Council (UANC), Bishop Abel Muzorewa was generally considered to be one of the more moderate Rhodesian black nationalist leaders. In December 1977, with the Rev. Ndabaningi Sithole (*q.v.*) and others, he began talks with Prime Minister Ian Smith in the hope of reaching an agreement on Rhodesia's future constitution.

The UANC was formed in Lusaka (Zambia) at the end of 1975 as an umbrella organization intended to unify the divided black Rhodesian leaders and rival movements, the Zimbabwe African People's Union (ZAPU) and Zimbabwe African National Union (ZANU). When this unification effort failed, Bishop Muzorewa continued to operate as an independent political leader in rivalry with Sithole, Joshua Nkomo, and Robert Mugabe (*qq.v.*).

Muzorewa first emerged as a political figure in the 1970s during the time when most major black politicians were in prison or detention, leaving a political vacuum in Rhodesia. He founded the African National Council in 1971, and the following year successfully mobilized black opinion against proposals for a settlement tentatively agreed upon between the British government and Ian Smith's regime.

Muzorewa was born on April 14, 1925, in Umtali. He received his education mainly at Methodist institutions in Rhodesia, rounded off by five years (1958–63) in the U.S. at the Central Methodist College, Fayette, Mo., and Scarritt College, Nashville, Tenn. After working for five years as a teacher, lay preacher, youth work organizer, and pastor, he became a bishop of the United Methodist Church in 1968.

Although reckoned a moderate, Muzorewa was militantly committed to independence and majority rule for Zimbabwe (the name chosen for an independent Rhodesia). He began to think actively about politics when he was 32 as a result of hearing a white Rhodesian leader say on a political

platform that he did not believe black men
went to heaven when they died.

(COLIN LEGUM)

Nkomo, Joshua Mqabuko Nyongolo

Although Joshua Nkomo took no part in
talks proceeding in Rhodesia at the end of
1977 between his more moderate rivals,
Bishop Abel Muzorewa and the Rev. Ndabaningi Sithole (*qq. v.*), and Prime Minister Ian Smith, his eventual involvement in
any viable agreement on the future constitution of the country seemed inevitable.
Nkomo was the doyen of black Rhodesian
nationalist politicians, having been elected
to the presidency of the African National
Congress (ANC) in 1957 and of the Zimbabwe African People's Union (ZAPU) in
1961. In 1976 he joined with another old
political rival, Robert Mugabe (*q.v.*), in
setting up the Patriotic Front of Zimbabwe
(Rhodesia). Despite this alliance he maintained ZAPU as an independent political
force and had built up a large and reportedly well trained and equipped guerrilla
force based in Zambia.

Nkomo was born on June 19, 1917, in
the Semokwe Reserve, Matabeleland, the
son of a cattle-owning teacher and lay
preacher. Although often regarded as a
Ndebele (Matabele), the dominant community in the southern part of Rhodesia,
he was in fact a Karanga. After primary
schooling in Rhodesia he went to South
Africa to complete his education, first at
Adams College, Natal, and later at the Jan
Hofmeyer School of Social Work in Johannesburg. Returning home in 1945, he
worked for a time as a social welfare officer
with Rhodesian Railways, but soon became general secretary of the Rhodesian
Railways African Employees' Association.
Meanwhile, he continued to study and in
1951 obtained an external B.A. degree from
the University of South Africa.

When the ANC was banned early in
1959, Nkomo went to England to escape
imprisonment. He returned in 1960 and
founded the National Democratic Party
(NDP); in 1961, when the NDP was banned
in turn, he founded ZAPU. After two prior
periods of detention during 1962–64, he
was confined from April 1964 until December 1974 in the remote Gonakudzingwa detention camp. After release he traveled
widely in Africa and Europe to promote
the nationalist cause.

A burly, genial man given to addressing
people as "my dear," Nkomo, beneath his
affable manner, possessed considerable
toughness and resolution. His skill as a political tactician enabled him to win support
from both the U.S.S.R. and important
Western interests, as well as from moderate and radical African leaders such as
Zambia's Pres. Kenneth Kaunda. He also
had the support of some white Rhodesians,
including the former prime minister, R. S.
Garfield Todd. Nkomo was essentially a
middle-of-the-road nationalist who aspired
to the presidency of an independent Zimbabwe, in which he insisted there would
be a place for the white minority.

(COLIN LEGUM)

Nujoma, Sam

As president of the South West Africa People's Organization (SWAPO), Sam Nujoma
figured prominently during 1977 in the
diplomatic initiative taken by the major
Western nations to mediate between his
liberation movement and the South African government to ensure a peaceful transition to independence for Namibia (South
West Africa). The burly, bearded, and be-
spectacled Namibian guerrilla leader was
born at Ongandjera on May 12, 1929, the
eldest son of a farm worker's family. He
received a Christian mission education,
first from the Finnish Protestants in his
home region, Ovamboland, and later from
the St. Barnabas Anglicans in the trust territory's capital, Windhoek. He began work
as a railway sweeper when he was 18 and
made his way up to the post of clerk. When
Ghana achieved its independence in 1957,
Nujoma became an avid reader of Ghanaian political pamphlets and helped found
the Ovambo People's Organization. In
1960 this group was transformed into
SWAPO.

Nujoma left his country illegally in 1960
for a hazardous journey on foot and horse-
back, and by bus, across West Africa in
order to appear before the UN as a peti-
tioner to protest South African rule of the
trust territory. He then established his organization's exile headquarters in Dar es
Salaam, Tanzania, where in 1961 a start
was made toward building up a guerrilla
liberation force. SWAPO operated for some
years from Tanzania and neighbouring
Zambia, but moved its main activities to
Angola after the latter gained independence in 1975.

Nujoma managed better than most liberation leaders to preserve the nonaligned
character of his movement. He spent as
much time in Western capitals as in those
of Communist countries, and he avoided
getting embroiled in the Sino-Soviet conflict. SWAPO published a constitution for an
independent Namibia that envisioned a
nonracial, democratic state; at the same
time, Nujoma insisted on his organization's exclusive right to act as spokesman
for black Namibians, an attitude rejected
by other political parties in the territory as
well as by the South African government.

(COLIN LEGUM)

O Fiaich, Monsignor Tomas

The pope's appointment, on Aug. 22,
1977, of Msgr Tomas O Fiaich as Roman
Catholic archbishop of Armagh and primate of All Ireland, in succession to William Cardinal Conway (see OBITUARIES),
caused some controversy in both Northern
Ireland and the republic. Msgr O Fiaich
(he preferred the Irish form of his name to
the anglicized Thomas Fee) was of a strong
nationalist disposition and came from the
most staunchly republican area in Northern Ireland, near Crossmaglen, County
Armagh. A fierce Irish language enthusiast, he was a churchman with a well-de-
veloped sense of secular politics. He had
urged the prime minister of the republic to
take a new look at church-state relations,
and he made no secret of his hope for eventual Irish unity. But he expressed abhorrence for violence, whether committed by
paramilitary organizations or by "what are

normally referred to as the forces of law
and order."

Tomas O Fiaich was born at Anamar,
near Crossmaglen, County Armagh, on
Nov. 3, 1923. He was educated at Creggan-
duff School and St. Patrick's College in
Armagh, going from there to St. Patrick's
College, Maynooth, County Kildare, in
1940. He followed the normal seminary
course, but also took a bachelor's degree in
Celtic studies, with first class honours. His
education, which was interrupted by serious ill health, was completed at St. Peter's
College, Wexford, and he was ordained in
1948 for the Armagh diocese. Subsequently
he took a master's degree in early and
medieval Irish history at University College, Dublin, and then went on to Louvain
University in Belgium. He was appointed
lecturer in modern history at Maynooth in
1953. In 1959 he was made professor, in
1970 vice-president, and in 1975 president
of the college—the largest Roman Catholic
seminary in the British Isles.

Msgr O Fiaich was the author of several
works on historical subjects and served on
a number of organizations connected with
Irish education and the Irish language. His
consecration as archbishop of Armagh took
place in St. Patrick's Cathedral, Armagh,
on Oct. 2, 1977, and it was expected that
he would also be created a cardinal.

(BRUCE ARNOLD)

Owen, David Anthony Llewellyn

At the age of 38, Dr. David Owen became
the youngest British foreign secretary since
Anthony Eden in the 1930s. He was minister of state at the Foreign Office when
Anthony Crosland (see OBITUARIES), then
foreign secretary, died in February 1977.
Owen stepped into the vacancy. He had
made a reputation for himself as one of the
youngest and most able of the middle-
ranking ministers in the government, but
it was a surprise appointment of a man
who was hardly known to the public. "Dr.
Who?" was the headline comment.

Owen quickly became known to the
world by his tireless traveling abroad, notably and most persistently by his frequent
visits to the capitals of Africa in pursuit of
a Rhodesian settlement. His declared commitment to the third world helped him to
win confidence in black Africa. While his
youthful good looks and his bland bedside
manner were not always an asset (*The
Guardian* newspaper called him "the bland
bombshell"), there was toughness and determination in his stands on principle,
particularly on human rights. In his first
speech in the Commons as foreign secretary he said that British foreign policy
must project the values that lay at the core
of British society. He had shown that he
was ready to act on principle when he resigned from the Labour "shadow cabinet"
in 1972 because he objected to the equivocal attitude toward the European Economic
Community being taken by the party at
that time.

Born on July 2, 1938, Owen came from a
middle-class professional background with
Welsh forebears ("I am a deeply romantic
Welshman"). He was educated as a physician and seemed headed for a distinguished career in medicine as a neurologist
until he won a seat in Parliament in 1966.
After that victory there was no question

about his political ambition. He was said to stand on the right wing of the Labour Party, although he himself disputed this. His lack of labour union roots was a disadvantage, but he chose to test his strength in the party by campaigning for election to the Labour national executive committee in October 1977. He got 176,000 votes, not enough to win a place on the committee but reckoned to be more than promising for a first try. (HARFORD THOMAS)

Packer, Kerry (Francis Bullmore)

In 1977 Kerry Packer, director of an Australian commercial television network, obtained exclusive rights to televise live the summer series of cricket test matches between England and Australia. Packer then signed contracts with the top players in all cricket-playing countries, contracts that bound the athletes to perform in a series of so-called "Super Tests" sponsored by Packer's company, World Series Cricket Pty Ltd. (WSC). These matches would be played for the Packer television network and would take precedence over any commitments to national or other teams.

The International Cricket Conference (ICC), cricket's world governing body, and the Test and County Cricket Board (TCCB) in England decided in return to ban any players who played for the Packer "cricket circus." Tony Greig was sacked as captain of the English team, and in Australia players who signed with Packer were warned that they would be banned from playing for their district, state, or country. In Australia, too, Packer was forbidden to describe his series as "tests," and in his players' litigation, similar to that in England, against the Australian Cricket Control Board, both sides agreed to accept the English High Court's decision. The ICC and TCCB were also taken to court in Britain by

Packer's WSC company. After a six-week hearing before the High Court in London, Mr. Justice Slade held that the ban by the ICC and TCCB on players who had signed with Packer constituted an unreasonable restraint of trade, and duly found for the WSC.

Packer was born on Dec. 17, 1937, the son of newspaper magnate Sir Frank Packer. As a trainee executive for his father's enterprises, he specialized in advertising and printing problems. In 1974, following his father's death, he became chairman and managing director of his father's Consolidated Press Holdings Ltd., Television Corporation Ltd., and Australian Consolidated Press Ltd. These companies controlled Sydney's TCN9 television station with its Channel 9 network, the Australian *Women's Weekly*, sales leader in its field, and *The Bulletin* news weekly. With such subsidiary interests as ski resorts, directories, and other magazines, the Packer empire was now launching into sports television as a multi-million-dollar investment, aiming to spend A$12 million over three years on Super Test cricket alone. A sportsman like his father, Packer had been a cricket enthusiast since his days at Geelong Grammar School. (A. R. G. GRIFFITHS)

Park Tong Sun

The central figure in an allegedly widespread attempt to buy influence in the U.S. Congress, Park Tong Sun was indicted in September by a federal grand jury on 36 felony counts, including conspiracy to bribe a public official, operating a corrupt enterprise, failing to register as a foreign government's agent, illegal campaign contributions, and mail fraud. Park, born in Korea in 1935, was charged with operating his payoff scheme in Washington, D.C., as an agent for the South Korean government. He allegedly agreed with officials of the Korean Central Intelligence Agency in 1967 to obtain military aid for South Korea in exchange for exclusive rights as a broker on sales of U.S. rice to that country.

The so-called Koreagate scandal simmered for months in Washington, casting suspicion on the ethics of Congress. There were demands for a special prosecutor to relieve the Justice Department of the investigatory work in the case, leading the House of Representatives to call in former Watergate special prosecutor Leon Jaworski to head an investigation of the affair. Park, however, had fled the U.S. a year before the indictments were handed down. His absence slowed both congressional and Justice Department investigations, and except for former California congressman Richard Hanna no U.S. legislators were formally charged with accepting payoffs from him. A number of past and present members of Congress were named in the indictments as having been recipients of contributions from Park, but without direct testimony from the Korean it appeared that there would be great difficulty in proving that they had done anything illegal in return.

For months, investigators sought ways to return Park to Washington, first from London and then from Seoul. Park's refusal to be questioned, and the South Korean government's refusal to extradite him to face the U.S. charges, undermined the investigations, and so Attorney General Griffin Bell and Pres. Jimmy Carter directly urged the South Korean government to make Park available.

The Koreans at first refused. But congressional irritation at the unfinished investigation led to a threatened reduction in U.S. aid to the South Korean government. In response to this threat the Koreans began to soften their refusals. In December it was agreed that the Justice Department could question Park in Seoul and that he would testify in U.S. criminal cases stemming from the affair. In return for "truthful" testimony, he would be granted immunity. No provision was made, however, for his questioning by congressional committees. (JOHN F. STACKS)

Piggott, Lester

At 5 ft 7 in he was tall for his job, and he was nicknamed "the long fellow," but Britain's star jockey Lester Piggott developed a style of riding with short leathers, standing balanced in the stirrups until the time came to get down and ride the horse out. Rapport with his mount and horsemanship, judgment of pace and opportunity, and incomparable strength in a driving finish were among his assets.

His range was displayed in 1977. He rode Irish-trained The Minstrel in his own record-breaking eighth Derby victory and to win the Irish Sweeps Derby and the King George VI and Queen Elizabeth Diamond Stakes at Ascot. He steered the French stayer Sagaro to win the Ascot Gold cup—a record third successive victory for both horse and rider. He rode Irish-trained Artaius to victory in Sandown Park's Eclipse Stakes and in Goodwood's Sussex Stakes. Longchamp, Paris, set the seal on the season, when he rode a dream race on Irish-trained Alleged to take Europe's richest prize, the Prix de l'Arc de Triomphe. All were prestige races, against fancied opponents. Piggott was British champion jockey nine times between 1960 and 1971, and he had won all the English classic races, the St. Leger seven times as well as the Derby eight times.

Piggott was born on Nov. 5, 1935, the son of Keith Piggott, a well-known National Hunt jockey and trainer, to whom Lester was apprenticed for five years. Lester rode his first winner in 1948. He was a natural horseman who, until dissuaded, rode over hurdles in winter National Hunt racing. In 1954 he rode his first Derby winner, Never Say Die. In the same season youthful recklessness and determination led to a three-month suspension for dangerous riding.

He became stable jockey to Britain's leading trainer, Noel Murless, and then, in 1967, elected to ride free-lance. He began to ride on the Continent more often—a choice that eventually cost him his chance of remaining champion jockey—and later became associated with Vincent O'Brien's powerful stable in Tipperary, Ireland. The key factor in Piggott's success was sheer ability. In a tight finish, it was often felt he would have won on the second horse had he chosen to ride it. (R. M. GOODWIN)

Qaddafi, Muammar al-

In 1977 Libya's head of state, Col. Muammar al-Qaddafi, continued to pursue a lonely path as apostle of his own brand of Arab nationalism derived from former Egyptian president Gamal Abdel Nasser. At home he practiced a brand of populist government that he claimed was a model for all other nations. His vigorous pursuit of his own revolutionary objectives had brought him into conflict with nearly every Arab country except Algeria. After he was kept out of the planning of the 1973 Arab-Israeli war by Egypt and Syria his relations with both countries deteriorated. His hostility toward the Egyptian regime and personal antagonism toward Pres. Anwar as-Sadat were especially bitter. Charges and countercharges of sabotage and subversion deteriorated into open warfare in July 1977, and the border situation remained tense. Qaddafi denounced Sadat as a "traitor and apostate" after the latter's peace initiative toward Israel in November, and on December 2–5 held in Tripoli a meeting of "rejectionist" Arab leaders as a counterblast to Sadat's Cairo meeting with Israel.

While maintaining his puritan Islamic principles, Qaddafi moved closer to the Soviet Union, on which he became dependent for military supplies, and he was the only Arab leader to support the Ethiopian Marxist regime against Somali and Eritrean Muslim insurgents. His search for a "third way" between Western parliamentary democracy and the Communist system, as outlined in his *Green Book* (1976–77), led in March 1977 to his establishment of a form of "direct popular power" expressed through people's congresses, labour unions, and professional organizations. National defense became the responsibility of every citizen rather than of the regular Army, and the Cabinet was replaced by a General People's Committee in which former ministers were called secretaries. Libya's official name became the People's Socialist Libyan Arab Jamahiriyah (democracy).

Born in a Bedouin tent in the desert south of Tripoli in September 1942, Qaddafi was almost unknown until 1969 when he led a coup that deposed King Idris. Thereafter he became chairman of the Revolutionary Command Council (RCC), commander in chief of Libya's armed forces, and (from January 1970) prime minister and defense minister. In July 1972 he relinquished the premiership to Abdul Salam Jalloud but as chairman of the RCC continued to dominate the regime.

(PETER MANSFIELD)

Rahman, Ziaur

Forty-two-year-old Maj. Gen. Ziaur Rahman rose to power in Bangladesh in the confusion of coups and countercoups that followed the assassination of the country's first prime minister and second president, Sheikh Mujibur Rahman, in August 1975. As chief of staff of the armed forces, he became the de facto leader of Bangladesh under Pres. Abu Sadat Mohammed Sayem in November 1975, a position that was consolidated a year later when Sayem appointed him chief martial-law administrator. Then, on April 21, 1977, Zia became president following Sayem's resignation for health reasons. Zia announced that he would hold a referendum in May 1977 and general elections some time at the end of 1978. In the May referendum he obtained popular approval for his continued rule.

Born in 1935 in the Sylhet district of former East Bengal, Zia enrolled in the Pakistan Army after finishing school and rose to the rank of lieutenant colonel just before the 1971 war that liberated Bangladesh from Pakistan. He was in command of a regiment in Chittagong when he decided to defect and join the freedom movement, and he was one of the first to proclaim Bangladesh's independence after seizing the Chittagong radio station. Hailed as a hero of the liberation struggle, he became one of the top officers in the newly established Bangladesh armed forces under Sheikh Mujibur.

After the assassination of Mujib, Khandakar Mushtaque Ahmed, who succeeded him as president, selected Zia for the post of chief of staff. Zia was briefly removed from the scene in a coup by young army officers in early November 1975, but later the same month a countercoup reestablished his position. President Ahmed was then forced to resign and was succeeded by Sayem. In November 1976 Ahmed and other political leaders who opposed the postponement of elections were arrested and jailed. In early October Zia crushed a short-lived rebellion by low-ranking dissident soldiers.

General Zia paid a state visit to China on January 2–5, in the course of which agreements on economic and technical cooperation and trade and payments were signed. In December he visited Pakistan.

(GOVINDAN UNNY)

Reddy, Neelam Sanjiva

Sworn in on July 25, 1977, as India's sixth president, Neelam Sanjiva Reddy had once given up aspiring to that high post and retired to his farm in Anantapur district in southern India. He had lost his first contest for the presidency in 1969, when, as a candidate of the opposition Congress wing, he was defeated by V. V. Giri, a nominee of the then prime minister, Indira Gandhi. Having lost a subsequent parliamentary election, he kept away from the political scene until he decided to respond to a call from his old colleague Morarji Desai (*q.v.*) to contest the general election in March 1977. Reddy made history by becoming the lone non-Congress candidate to win the parliamentary poll from his state of Andhra Pradesh.

Born into a peasant family in southern India in May 1913, Reddy obtained his early education at the Theosophical High School in Madras. He pursued his studies at the Government Arts College of the University of Madras but gave them up to join the freedom movement in 1931. In 1936 he became secretary of the Andhra Pradesh Congress Committee and remained in that office for ten years. He was imprisoned by the British authorities during a major part of World War II.

In independent India Reddy quickly rose to become an important Congress politician, first in Madras and then in the newly created Andhra Pradesh state where he led the government as chief minister during 1956–59 and again during 1962–64. He also held the post of president of the Congress Party for a term. He was brought into the central government by the then prime minister Lal Bahadur Shastri in 1964, holding first the portfolio of steel and mines and later that of transport and aviation. In 1967, a year after Indira Gandhi became prime minister, Reddy was given the post of speaker of the Lok Sabha (lower house of Parliament). He resigned from this post to make his abortive bid for the presidency in 1969, but resumed it after returning to Parliament in March 1977.

Soon after taking office, President Reddy announced that he would not live in the presidential palace and also that he would only take 30% of his monthly salary of Rs 10,000.

(GOVINDAN UNNY)

Rippon, Angela

Even in the jubilee year, Angela Rippon ranked as one of the most celebrated women in Britain. Her road to fame: reading the television news. She joined the British Broadcasting Corporation's BBC 1 news team as a reporter in August 1973 and 18 months later took over as one of the two presenters of the late-night "News Extra" program on the minority channel, BBC 2. By the following year she was so well established that, when the main BBC 1 evening newscast reverted to single-handed presentation, she was first to do it. She was also the only woman news reader on any of the national television channels.

It was at Christmas 1976 that Rippon was finally established as a media celebrity, via a guest appearance on "The Morecambe and Wise Show," regularly one of the top-rated variety shows of the year, in which she danced in a spoof Fred Astaire-Ginger Rogers routine. The press's fight to snatch exclusive pictures of her legs during the secret rehearsals lost one BBC newsman his job. Afterward, offers for cabaret engagements came streaming in, including

SVEN SIMON/KATHERINE YOUNG

one from Liberace asking her to appear in his Las Vegas show.

Angela Rippon was born Oct. 12, 1944, in Plymouth, Devon, left school at 17, and joined the local daily newspaper. In 1966 she joined the BBC in Plymouth as reporter and presenter of the nightly regional news magazine, and two and a half years later she switched to the West Country's commercial station, Westward TV, as editor of women's programs. Her four-and-a-half-year spell there saw her reporting, presenting, emceeing a quiz show, and editing a weekly current affairs program. Her first documentary film, a piece on a Cornish mining area, *Silent Valley*, which she researched and wrote, won a silver medal at the New York Film Festival.

Rippon resisted the label of "the British Barbara Walters," not least because she earned a great deal less. She still lived in Devon, where her husband was in business, and refused nearly all personal appearances in order to spend her free time there. She continued to practice her craft as a television journalist through a series of documentaries, shown only in the West Country, called "Rippon Reports," a set of interviews, and film reports for a regional motoring program.   (PETER FIDDICK)

Romero, Carlos Humberto

As all too frequently occurs in Latin American elections, the February 1977 contest in El Salvador between Gen. Carlos Humberto Romero and Col. Ernesto Claramount spilled into the streets and turned into a bloody confrontation. From Romero's election victory to his inauguration on July 1, the Army in El Salvador killed at least 40 people protesting against apparent fraud in the balloting.

General Romero, 52 years old at the time of his election, was the candidate of the National Conciliation Party, a group dominated by ultraconservatives and the long-standing political powers in the country. He had been war minister during the years preceding his election, and before that had received training in counterinsurgency in the U.S. Claramount was the candidate of the left-of-centre/centre National Opposition Union.

By February 24 the final results had been computed, showing Romero defeating Claramount by 812,281 votes to 394,661. Although the National Opposition Union declared these figures fraudulent, many protesters resigned themselves and lifted the roadblocks they had set up in the suburbs surrounding the capital city of San Salvador. Many others, though, refused to accept Romero's election as legitimate. In March the antigovernment forces called for a nationwide general strike, and soon lame-duck president Arturo Armando Molina ordered the Army to silence the Claramount supporters, some of whom were burning vehicles and breaking shop windows. The soldiers fired on unarmed demonstrators, and uneasy tranquillity was restored.

The testimony of many independent observers corroborated the charges of election fraud, but the Salvadoran Legislative Assembly refused to investigate and instead declared a state of siege for 30 days. Although the Assembly also prohibited any citizen from entering or leaving the country, Colonel Claramount escaped and went into exile in Costa Rica.

Sworn in on July 1, Romero pledged to eliminate terrorism, saying, "My government desires no violent confrontations with anyone. But it will exercise its rights of legitimate defense to preserve, protect, and maintain peace and harmony." While the new president was speaking at the ceremonies inside the National Gymnasium, some 2,000 troops were on patrol outside, and all of El Salvador's security forces were on alert following the explosion of two bombs in the ruling party's offices.

(JEROLD L. KELLMAN)

Romero Barceló, Carlos Antonio

The surprise election of Carlos Antonio Romero Barceló as governor of the U.S. Commonwealth of Puerto Rico could very possibly lead to statehood for that Caribbean island. At the very least, the issue would be debated in the months to come.

Romero took office on Jan. 2, 1977, after narrowly defeating Rafael Hernández Colon, Puerto Rico's incumbent governor. The condition of Puerto Rico's economy—stagnation and a 20% rate of unemployment—was a major issue in the campaign. Romero had proposed an eight-point program to revive the island.

But statehood, supported by Romero and his New Progressive Party, was the issue that could have the greatest effect on Puerto Rico. At present, the island is a U.S. commonwealth. Puerto Ricans are U.S. citizens but are not represented in Congress and cannot vote for president. On the other hand, Puerto Ricans pay no federal income taxes. The island's tax structure is attractive to industry and has played an important part in Puerto Rico's economic development over the years.

Romero maintained that Puerto Ricans are "politically disenfranchised" and that the island has a "semicolonial political status." He hoped to hold a plebiscite on the statehood question and then, if the vote was favourable, to petition the U.S. Congress for admission to the Union. With its comparatively large population, Puerto Rico as a state would be entitled to two senators and seven representatives. This would make the island more powerful in Congress than many of the present states.

Romero was born on Sept. 4, 1932, in Santurce, Puerto Rico. His father, an engineer, lawyer, and Supreme Court justice, sent Carlos to Phillips Exeter Academy, a private preparatory school in the U.S., and then to Yale University. Romero graduated from Yale in 1953 with a degree in economics and political science. He then returned home, earned a law degree at the University of Puerto Rico, and practiced law in San Juan. In 1968 Romero was elected for the first of two terms as the mayor of San Juan.

(VICTOR M. CASSIDY)

Sadat, Anwar as-

In November 1977 Egypt's Pres. Anwar as-Sadat, despairing of the slow progress toward a Middle East settlement, made the daring and spectacular gesture of offering to explain his views directly to the Israeli government and Knesset (parliament). At the invitation of Israeli Prime Minister Menahem Begin (*q.v.*) he visited Jerusalem November 19–21 and affirmed that Egypt and Israel would never again go to war and that Egypt welcomed Israel to the region. But he also said that the "price of peace" must be a full Israeli withdrawal from all the occupied territories, including "Arab Jerusalem," and the acceptance of Palestinian rights.

The warmth of Sadat's reception by the Israelis was matched by that of the Egyptian public on his return, but his action jeopardized Egypt's relations with the rest of the Arab world. Only Sudan and Morocco fully endorsed it, and Jordan expressed cautious approval. Egypt's principal ally, Saudi Arabia, voiced dismay that Sadat should have broken the Arab front, while Syria, the leadership of the Palestine Liberation Organization (PLO), Iraq, and Libya denounced his action as treachery. However, President Sadat invited all parties to the Middle East conflict to attend a meeting in Cairo to prepare for a full-scale peace conference in Geneva. Only Israel and the U.S. accepted the invitation to the talks, which began in Cairo on December 14 with UN and U.S. observers looking on.

On December 25–26 Sadat met with Prime Minister Begin at Ismailia in Egypt. Begin proposed a phased return of the Sinai to Egypt and limited self-rule for Israeli-held territory on the West Bank of the Jordan River and in the Gaza Strip, with an Israeli armed presence maintained in those areas for security purposes. Sadat rejected the proposal and continued to press for total Israeli withdrawal from all occupied territories and a fully independent Palestinian state.

Born Dec. 25, 1918, in the al-Minufiyah Governorate of the Nile Delta, Sadat graduated from the Cairo Military Academy in 1938. During World War II he plotted to evict the British from Egypt and was captured in 1942, but later escaped into hiding. In 1950 he joined Gamal Abdel Nasser's Free Officers, and after the 1952 revolution held various high offices culmi-

G. CHAUVEL—SYGMA

nating in the vice-presidency (1964). He became acting president on Nasser's death and was elected president in a national plebiscite on Oct. 15, 1970.

(PETER MANSFIELD)

Sa-ngad Chaloryu

After student riots in 1973 ended the long reign of field marshals Thanom Kittika-chorn and Praphas Charusathiara, Thailand's armed forces were generally bereft of flamboyant personalities. In 1976 the relatively unknown Adm. Sa-ngad Chaloryu headed a team of officers who overthrew Seni Pramoj's civilian government. But they quickly installed a new civilian administration and withdrew to the sidelines. Just as that government was about to mark its first anniversary in October 1977, however, the military group was on centre stage again. This time Admiral Sa-ngad became nominal head of a new military regime, assuming the office of chairman of the National Policy Council in November.

For the admiral, it all happened after he formally left the service. Born March 3, 1915, in Suphan Buri Province northwest of Bangkok, Sa-ngad went from elementary school to Thailand's Royal Navy Cadet Academy. After commanding the Thai fleet that participated in the Korean War, he rose to become deputy chief of staff of the Navy. In 1971 he became deputy chief of staff of the armed forces, and in October 1975 he was appointed supreme commander.

During that seemingly steady career, there was an uncertain interlude when Sa-ngad burned his fingers in the political fire. The Navy was involved in an abortive coup attempt in 1951, and Sa-ngad was detained and interrogated for three months. Thereafter it was plain sailing for the burly, golf-loving admiral until he retired in September 1976.

Then his career took a hectic turn. Immediately on retirement he was invited by Seni Pramoj to become defense minister. Within days of that appointment, he ousted the riot-battered Seni government. Un-

der Thanin Kraivichien, Sa-ngad continued as defense minister as well as head of the Administration Reform Council that sought to guide the government. When Thanin was ousted, he assumed chairmanship of the military's newly formed Revolutionary Party.

Military insiders in Thailand indicated that Sa-ngad was only titular head of the new government and that the real power behind him was the suave and experienced Supreme Commander Kriangsak Chamanand, who on Nov. 12, 1977, became prime minister. (T. J. S. GEORGE)

Schlafly, Phyllis

If the proposed Equal Rights Amendment (ERA) to the U.S. Constitution should fail to be ratified, Phyllis Schlafly would undoubtedly deserve much of the blame, or credit. Schlafly, chairman since 1972 of a national organization called Stop ERA, had spent much of her time traveling around the U.S. to address state legislatures, appear on national and local television programs, and give radio and newspaper interviews attacking the amendment.

The ERA says: "Equality of rights under the law shall not be denied or abridged by the United States or by any State on account of sex." Schlafly claims: "The Equal Rights Amendment pretends to be an advance for women, but actually it will do nothing at all for women. It will not give women . . . any new employment advantages, rights or benefits. . . . What ERA will do is to require us to 'neuterize' all Federal and state laws. . . . Every change this requires will deprive women of a right, benefit or exemption that they now enjoy."

While few constitutional experts agreed with Schlafly's interpretation (and some proponents of the amendment charged her with making deliberate distortions), her campaign seemed to be influencing public opinion. By the end of 1977 the ERA needed ratification by three more states, and the prospects of its succeeding were in serious doubt.

Long active in conservative political affairs, Schlafly served as a delegate to the Republican national conventions in 1956, 1964, and 1968 and as an alternate in 1960. She was president of the Illinois Federation of Republican Women from 1960 to 1964 and first vice-president of the National Federation of Republican Women from 1965 to 1967. She ran unsuccessfully for Congress in 1952 and 1970.

Schlafly's eight books, all presenting conservative political positions, included *A Choice Not an Echo* (1964), *Safe—Not Sorry* (1967), and *The Power of the Positive Woman* (1977), a tract against the women's liberation movement. From 1967 she published a monthly newsletter entitled the *Phyllis Schlafly Report*. Born Aug. 15, 1924, in St. Louis, Mo., she received a B.A. from Washington University in that city in 1944 and an M.A. from Radcliffe College, Cambridge, Mass., in 1945; she was scheduled to complete work for her law degree from Washington University in 1978.

(JOAN NATALIE REIBSTEIN)

Schlesinger, James

It was a case of matching the toughest job in Washington with the toughest man in town when U.S. Pres. Jimmy Carter named

James Schlesinger to be his secretary of energy. As head of the newly created Department of Energy, Schlesinger became directly responsible for solving what many believed to be the country's major crisis. In less than a year, he had to analyze the problem, draft the president's comprehensive program, battle for it in Congress, and organize the department, while at the same time attempting to convince the U.S. public that a genuine crisis existed.

Polls indicated that most people in the U.S. refused to believe that there was a problem and were against efforts to deprive them of their big "gas guzzling" cars. Schlesinger was heavily engaged on all fronts of the energy "war," trying to persuade Congress, business, labour, environmentalists, and a doubting public of the need for the strong measures in the administration's energy bill. By year's end, however, when Congress adjourned with the bill still in conference committee, some sections had been compromised to the point where they bore little resemblance to what the White House originally had proposed.

Undaunted, Schlesinger fought to keep the program on the course that he and his staff had charted. Their long-range objective was to cut down drastically on waste while making greater use of coal to conserve oil and gas supplies until practical alternate sources of energy could be developed.

There was wide agreement on the goals, but there was wide disagreement over how they could best be achieved. Schlesinger had to play the role of lobbyist, a difficult one for a man who spoke bluntly and, in the past, had not easily compromised on anything. As Pres. Gerald Ford's secretary of defense, Schlesinger had clashed head-on with Secretary of State Henry Kissinger and the president himself over cuts in the Defense Department budget, and it had cost him his job.

Schlesinger was born in New York City on Feb. 15, 1929. After receiving a Ph.D. in economics from Harvard University, he taught at the University of Virginia and then worked at the Rand Corporation. He came to Washington in 1969 to be Pres. Richard Nixon's assistant director of the budget. In 1971 he was named chairman of the Atomic Energy Commission and then

PICTORIAL PARADE

was asked to straighten out inefficiency at the Central Intelligence Agency. In nine months as CIA director, Schlesinger earned a fearsome reputation by ruthlessly firing 1,500 employees. He became Nixon's secretary of defense in 1973, but two years later was fired by Ford.　　　　(HAL BRUNO)

Serban, Andrei

"I never prepare the scenes at home. I must work with the actors. When I am in contact with their energy, in five minutes I can stage a scene. But if you ask me a day before what I am going to do at the rehearsal, I will tell you, 'I have no idea.'" Thus Andrei Serban explained the process of theatrical direction that had placed him in the forefront of contemporary dramatic circles. By utilizing techniques that placed a premium on emotion rather than intellect, Serban scored a series of spectacular triumphs, the most prominent being his productions of Greek tragedies by Euripides and Sophocles and his version of Chekhov's *The Cherry Orchard.*

Born in Romania in 1944, Serban staged plays at his Bucharest home while still a child. He enrolled in the Film and Theatre Institute after graduating from high school and quickly turned to directing. Though controversial from the start—he once staged Shakespeare's *Julius Caesar* as a Kabuki play—by the time he was 23 he was recognized as the directing prodigy of Romanian theatre. With the aid of Ellen Stewart's La Mama complex in New York, he migrated to the U.S. in 1969.

Put off by what he deemed to be cheap and sloppy elements in the U.S. approach to the avant-garde, Serban insisted on total—almost religious—dedication to theatrical excellence. He gathered about him his own company of actors, whom he taught to express the emotion of the text—in gestures as well as words—rather than trying to play the scene in a traditional manner. Telling the actors to improvise, he studied them intensely, seeking to find in their spontaneous gestures the central emotive concepts around which he could build his production. To these movements he added coordinated sounds—singing, wailing, chanting—in an effort to give primal human forces physical expression. In Aeschylus' *Agamemnon,* for example, Serban incorporated ancient Greek to jolt the audience into understanding the drama's mythical and emotional content.

During 1977 Serban was recognized as a leading artist of the contemporary theatre. Following his production of *The Cherry Orchard* at New York's Lincoln Center, he received the award of the Outer Critics Circle for "virtuoso direction." In July he was named an associate director of the Yale Repertory Theater.　　(JEROLD L. KELLMAN)

Sithole, the Rev. Ndabaningi

Detained for many years as one of the most extreme Rhodesian black nationalist leaders, and afterward an exile in Zambia, the Rev. Ndabaningi Sithole returned to Rhodesia in July 1977. By the year's end he was participating in talks initiated by Prime Minister Ian Smith with the object of achieving an "internal settlement" of the country's constitutional future. Also participating was Bishop Abel Muzorewa (*q.v.*), but the Patriotic Front of Joshua

Nkomo and Robert Mugabe (*qq.v.*), controlling the externally based nationalist guerrilla forces, was not represented.

Sithole was the leader of a "dissident" wing of the Zimbabwe African National Union (ZANU), whose main body was led by his former lieutenant, Mugabe. They had together formed the movement in 1963 as a breakaway from the Zimbabwe African People's Union (ZAPU) led by Nkomo.

Born in Matabeleland on July 21, 1920, of illiterate peasant parents, Sithole gained a bachelor's degree by correspondence with the University of South Africa. After spending 14 years as a teacher in Rhodesia (1941–55), he attended the Andover Newton Theological School, Newton, Mass., and on his return in 1958 was ordained as a minister of the Congregationalist Church. In 1960 he entered politics, at first as a member of Nkomo's new National Democratic Party. He became party treasurer, but the organization was banned soon afterward.

Sithole established a reputation as the leading intellectual among black nationalists with the publication in 1959 of his *African Nationalism.* He subsequently wrote other books, of which the most recent, *Roots of a Revolution,* appeared in October 1977. He was first sentenced to 12 months in prison in 1963 and subsequently was detained as a political prisoner following the Smith regime's unilateral declaration of independence in 1965. In February 1969 he was sentenced to six years of hard labour on a charge of having planned the murder of Smith and two of his ministers while he was still in prison. Released at the end of 1974, he went into exile.　　(COLIN LEGUM)

Smeal, Eleanor Cutri

Eleanor Cutri Smeal identifies herself as a housewife. But she is a housewife who, on April 24, 1977, took office as president of the National Organization for Women (NOW). She was elected to a two-and-a-half-year term by an overwhelming majority of the 675 delegates attending the organization's seventh national conference.

Smeal came to her position at a critical time in the history of NOW. The organization, ten years old and 55,000 members strong, was facing a major battle over the fate of the proposed Equal Rights Amendment (ERA) to the U.S. Constitution. As president, Smeal also became head of a national "strike force," with broad authority to work for ratification of the amendment, NOW's top-priority project.

The controversial ERA states that "Equality of rights under the law shall not be denied or abridged by the United States or by any State on account of sex." In order to become part of the Constitution, the ERA, already passed by the U.S. House of Representatives and the Senate, would have to be ratified by 38 states by March 22, 1979, unless Congress extended the time limit. By the end of 1977, 35 states had ratified (3 subsequently voted to rescind, although the legal status of such recision was in dispute). Gathering the remaining three promised to be an uphill struggle; Smeal took office just after the amendment had been rejected by several states.

Smeal cited as her second major goal closing the income gap between men and women over the next ten years. Perhaps

connected with that goal was the fact that Smeal was not only the first housewife to become president of NOW, she was also the first person in that office to receive a salary ($17,500). The economic security of housewives and homemakers was of particular concern to her. "That's what most women are," she said. "It's important work."

Smeal was born on Jan. 30, 1939, in Ashtabula, Ohio, and received a master's degree in political science from the University of Florida at Gainesville. Research for her doctoral dissertation—a survey to determine women's attitudes toward women political candidates—led to her involvement with NOW. She joined the organization in 1970, becoming the first president of the Pennsylvania organization in 1971 and chairperson of the national board in 1975.　　(JOAN NATALIE REIBSTEIN)

Söder, Karin Anne-Marie

Europe's first woman foreign minister in 25 years, Karin Söder held that post in the government that took office in Sweden after the September 1976 general election. A member of the Riksdag (parliament) for the Centre Party from 1971, she had quickly moved to the top of the party hierarchy as adviser to its leader, Thorbjörn Fälldin, who became prime minister of the centre-right coalition government formed after the election—Sweden's first nonsocialist regime since 1932.

Mrs. Söder reportedly was considered for several posts, and when offered the Foreign Ministry she did not immediately accept. "I . . . knew that there would be much publicity because I am a woman. . . . In the end I accepted because my colleagues made it clear that they thought I was capable." Under her direction Sweden's traditional foreign policy of neutrality, supported by all of the nation's political parties, remained unchanged. The one possible variation, she said, was the greater weight placed on Nordic and European cooperation.

It was noticeable, however, that the out-

SVEN SIMON/KATHERINE YOUNG

spoken foreign policy utterances of Mrs. Söder's Social Democratic predecessors, and especially of former prime minister Olof Palme, which on occasion had annoyed the superpowers, were being softened in tone. Thus she was taken to task in 1977 by the Social Democrats for not adopting a more critical stance toward the neutron bomb proposed by U.S. Pres. Jimmy Carter. Generally approved by Swedes of all parties was her initiative in calling for the UN to impose a ban on investments in South Africa. She also believed that Sweden should continue to campaign, in the UN and elsewhere, for disarmament, human rights, and East-West détente.

Karin Bergenfur was born in Frykerud, Värmland County, western Sweden, in 1928. She qualified as a teacher in Farlund in 1950, then in 1954 moved to the Stockholm area and studied political science and economics. From the age of 20 she was a member of the Agrarian Party, which in 1957 changed its name to Centre Party in order to attract more urban voters. Her husband, Gunnar Söder, a paper and pulp industry executive and also an active Centre Party member, was currently an undersecretary of state in the Department of Industry.   (ROGER NYE CHOATE)

Stallone, Sylvester

In the motion picture *Rocky*, Sylvester Stallone shuffled, hustled, and bluffed his way into film-cult fame as the oddball outsider for whom nothing really goes right, the dauntless drudge who always loses—except once. The man behind and in front of *Rocky*, Stallone shared with Orson Welles and Charlie Chaplin the distinction of being nominated for Academy Awards as both star and writer of the same film. Though he got neither, *Rocky* was named best picture in the 1977 award presentations.

Stallone was born July 6, 1946, in the violent, squalid Hell's Kitchen section of New York City. His father, a Sicilian immigrant, was studying to be a hairdresser; his mother was a part-time chorus girl at Billy Rose's Diamond Horseshoe nightclub. For a while the boy was shunted among foster homes until the family reunited in a suburb of Washington, D.C.

"I was not an attractive child," Stallone remembers. "My personality was abhorrent to other children." He had a lisp and a slack face from a birth injury. A chronic runaway, he was expelled from numerous schools. He recalls his father saying, "You weren't born with much of a brain so you'd better develop your body." He turned to weight lifting, and at 16 his biceps measured nearly 17 inches.

Athletics offered a way out of nowhere. Stallone briefly worked as coach at the American School of Switzerland. While there, he played Biff in the drama *Death of a Salesman*. He then went to the University of Miami (Fla.), where he studied drama, and from there to New York City. Between roles in off-off-Broadway flops he tossed salads in a deli, cleaned fish in a market, and swept out the lions' cage at the Central Park Zoo. Finally he landed a role in the

motion picture *The Lords of Flatbush*. Few people saw the film, but Stallone got a credit for writing additional dialogue and received good notices for his acting.

Watching Muhammad Ali beat a nobody on closed-circuit television one night, Stallone got the idea for *Rocky*. The film involved a Philadelphia pug who gets a crack at fighting the champion and manages to stay in the ring 15 rounds; he does not win, he survives. Before the fight he trains with superb dedication and becomes a hero to the neighbourhood and himself.
          (PHILIP KOPPER)

Teng Hsiao-p'ing

Teng Hsiao-p'ing, the twice-purged Chinese leader, came back to power again in 1977. He was officially rehabilitated in July by the Central Committee of the Chinese Communist Party, which restored his former positions as vice-chairman of the Central Committee, vice-premier, and chief of the general staff of the Army. His posts were reconfirmed during the 11th party congress in August. Though nominally the third-ranking member of the Chinese hierarchy after Chairman Hua Kuo-feng and Defense Minister Yeh Chien-ying, Teng seemed to be China's real administrator. He had organizational talents, extensive government experience, proven administrative ability, and the support of senior party and army leaders.

Born into a family of landlords in southwestern Szechwan Province in 1904, Teng was 16 when he left China to study in France. In Paris he worked closely with Chou En-lai in Communist activities. After a brief stay in the Soviet Union, he returned to China in 1926 to play an active part in the Communist movement. He participated in the historic Long March (1934–35), when the Communist forces, pursued by Chiang Kai-shek's Nationalist Army, moved from their mountain base in southeast China to Yenan in the northwest. Years later Teng played a decisive role in the final elimination of the Nationalist forces from the mainland. After the establishment of the People's Republic in 1949, Teng was appointed general secretary of the party and in 1956 became vice-premier. During the Cultural Revolution of 1966–69, however, he was purged for his "revisionist" policies. In 1973 he made a dramatic return to power, having apparently

ALAIN VOLOCH—GAMMA/LIAISON

been chosen to succeed Premier Chou En-lai, whose health was failing. But shortly after Chou's death in January 1976, Teng became the target of Chiang Ch'ing (Mao's wife) and her radical faction, later called the "gang of four." Denounced as a "capitalist roader," Teng was dismissed from all his party, army, and government posts in April 1976, when Hua Kuo-feng was officially chosen to succeed Chou and groomed to succeed Mao. It was only after Mao's death in September 1976 and the purge of the "gang of four" that Teng reemerged as a powerful leader.

In sharp contrast to Mao, Teng was known for pragmatism rather than ideology. Since the 1950s he had stressed stability and economic modernization and growth. His realistic approach to China's economic problems, his emphasis on the need for higher wages and other benefits for workers, his stance on law and order, and his support for higher living standards all won wide support. A tough negotiator, he favoured a strong anti-Soviet line and moved toward normalization of relations with the U.S. Teng, a durable figure with a forceful personality, played increasingly important roles in China's economic, political, and foreign affairs after his return from his second political exile.   (WINSTON L. Y. YANG)

Tharp, Twyla

By creating a unique, witty synthesis of the whole range of human movement—from elegant classical ballet steps to the comic pratfall—dancer and choreographer Twyla Tharp became one of the shapers of modern American dance. During the 1970s her appeal broadened to include among her audiences not just aficionados of avant-garde dance but also the larger public, as evidenced by appearances on both commercial and public television. Her dance company also completed a successful season at the Brooklyn Academy of Music.

Tharp's work has been well received by critics as well as by the populace at large. *New York Times* reviewer Clive Barnes said of Tharp early on in her career, "She is certainly not yet a good choreographer; yet she is bad in a rather interesting way." Since then she has become "good." Arlene Croce, writing in *The New Yorker* in 1977, stated, "Her dances have reconditioned our values and swept away the ideological dividing lines between 'classical' and 'modern' and 'bop.'"

Tharp's early work is generally characterized as severe and austere, often designed to be performed on a bare stage (or just an open space), with simple costumes and lighting, no scenery, and no music. Some of her best-known pieces of this period are *Re-Moves* (1966) and *Generation* (1967).

About 1970 Tharp decided to incorporate music into her work and to consciously accept the role of performer. *Eight Jelly Rolls* and *The Bix Pieces* (both 1971), set to the music of jazz musicians Jelly Roll Morton and Bix Beiderbecke, show this new concern. What Tharp calls the "good humor, spunk, and verve" of the music are represented in her dances. Her success led to an invitation to choreograph three works for the Joffrey Ballet, *Deuce Coupe* (1973), *As Time Goes By* (1973), and *Cacklin' Hen* (1976). *Push Comes to Shove* (1976) was cre-

UPI COMPIX

STANLEY TRETICK—SYGMA

ated for the American Ballet Theatre.

Tharp was born on July 1, 1941, in Portland, Ind. (and was named Twyla after the princess of a Midwestern pig-calling contest), and began musical training at an early age. While majoring in art history at Barnard College in New York City, she also studied dance, and after working under Merce Cunningham for several years, joined the Paul Taylor Dance Company. She left that group in 1965 and began choreographing for her own company.

(JOAN NATALIE REIBSTEIN)

Torrijos Herrera, Omar

"What people can bear the humiliation of seeing a foreign flag planted in the very heart of its nation?" That question—posed in 1971 by Panama's virtual dictator, Brig. Gen. Omar Torrijos Herrera—has been the basis of Panamanian domestic and foreign policy ever since Torrijos seized power in 1968. With the signing of new Panama Canal treaties in Washington, D.C., on Sept. 7, 1977, however, the era of humiliation to which Torrijos had referred appeared to be drawing to a close.

The new treaties, signed by Torrijos and U.S. Pres. Jimmy Carter, required ratification by both countries before they could take effect. On October 23 Panamanians voted their approval of the treaties by a two-to-one margin in a national referendum. In the U.S., though, where ratification required two-thirds approval of the U.S. Senate, prospects for passage were highly questionable. Many in the U.S. were troubled by the main document, which called for U.S. surrender of the Panama Canal by the year 2000.

Almost as disturbing to those opposing the treaty was the idea of negotiating with General and Chief of Government (the latter a title he took in 1972) Torrijos. Even treaty advocates could not deny that Torrijos exercised dictatorial powers in Panama and that he had delivered several left-wing speeches; in addition, he was one of the few Latin-American leaders who had visit-

ed and expressed admiration for Cuba's Fidel Castro. On the other hand, he had cracked down on leftist labour agitators and students in Panama.

This political enigma was born on Feb. 13, 1929, in Santiago, Panama, the son of lower-middle-class teachers from rural Panama. Educated at a military school in El Salvador, Torrijos also studied various war-related subjects in the U.S. and Venezuela. In 1952 he was commissioned second lieutenant in the Panama National Guard and moved up the ranks to lieutenant colonel (1966), colonel (1968), and brigadier general (1969). The support of the 8,000-man National Guard was—and in 1977 remained—the bulwark of his power in Panamanian affairs.

As commander of the National Guard he led a coup d'etat in October 1968, overthrowing Pres. Arnulfo Arias. Claiming that he had a revolutionary program to help the poor, Torrijos won the support of Panama's peasants and leftward-leaning students. (JEROLD L. KELLMAN)

Turner, Stansfield

U.S. Pres. Jimmy Carter's original choice to be director of the Central Intelligence Agency was Theodore Sorensen, a former adviser and speechwriter to Pres. John F. Kennedy. But Sorensen was less than popular with some key members of Congress. His admission, during Senate confirmation hearings, that he had taken official documents with him when he left the White House raised a storm of protest, and shortly before the new administration took office, Sorensen asked that his name be withdrawn. Less than a month later, Carter chose a replacement: Adm. Stansfield Turner, then commander of NATO forces in southern Europe.

Turner and Carter had been classmates at the U.S. Naval Academy during World War II. After receiving his commission, Turner, a standout at Annapolis, had earned a master's degree in foreign affairs at Oxford as a Rhodes scholar. At sea, he specialized in service aboard destroyers. Promoted to rear admiral in 1970, he commanded a 6th Fleet carrier task group, later serving as director of systems analysis at the Pentagon, president of the Naval War College from 1972 to 1974, and commander of the 2nd Fleet. Unlike Sorensen, Turner breezed through the Senate confirmation process. Conservatives liked the fact that he was a military man (he retained his commission when he moved to the CIA), and liberals were impressed with his reputation as an intellectual and his belief that the CIA should be reformed.

Indeed, Turner had hardly settled into his new job before he began a process of reorganization and reform. He recommended to the president that he be given operational and budgetary control not only over the CIA but also over the Defense Department's intelligence agencies. The Pentagon balked, but a compromise was worked out whereby Turner was given charge of the budgets for all agencies engaged in overseas intelligence gathering while his operational control was limited to the CIA. Turner was, however, made chairman of two new intelligence policy committees. At the CIA he initiated a major reduction in the number of people as-

signed to the agency's operational division.

Born in Chicago on Dec. 1, 1923, Turner attended Amherst (Mass.) College before shifting to the Naval Academy, where he was commissioned an ensign in 1946. He was promoted to full admiral in 1975.

(STANLEY W. CLOUD)

Turner, Ted

Though he is an iconoclast who goes around leaving cigar butts in the finger bowls of yachting's high society, Ted Turner earned salutes from above even the bluest of noses when he won the America's Cup yacht races in September 1977. Turner skippered "Courageous" to four straight victories over the Australian challenger, "Australia," to keep the world's oldest sporting trophy in the hands of the New York Yacht Club.

Turner was a millionaire the masses could identify with. When he was not complaining about the sails he was prevented from buying, he was making himself an underdog in the national pastime by challenging baseball commissioner Bowie Kuhn in court and making himself manager-for-a-day of the Atlanta Braves, the team he owns. At Braves games, he was a shirtsleeved, tobacco-chomping back-slapper who led the crowd in cheers. In January, he also bought into professional basketball's Atlanta Hawks.

Turner was not as successful with his baseball team as with his 12-m yacht, finishing last in both of his seasons with them, and so he sought to attract fans with promotional gimmickry and to woo top stars with old-fashioned money. On January 25 Kuhn suspended him for a year after fining the Braves $10,000 and their first-round draft choice. Turner's faux pas had occurred at the 1976 World Series, when he told San Francisco Giants co-owner Bob Lurie that he would top any offer Lurie made to Giant outfielder Gary Matthews, whose contract had not yet officially expired.

Turner delayed his suspension by taking the matter to court, and so when the Braves lost their 16th straight game on May 12 he was able to take a drastic measure. He gave manager Dave Bristol an unheard-of ten-day leave of absence and replaced Bristol with himself. His managerial term was limited to one game, however, as Kuhn invoked a rule prohibiting owners from managing. The next week Turner's suspension was upheld in court, ending his baseball season.

Yachting had always been a favourite pastime for Turner, who was born Robert Edward Turner III on Nov. 19, 1938, in Cincinnati, Ohio, with a silver sail on his bassinet. At Brown University, he was commodore of the school yachting club and vice-president of its debating union. He was named general manager of Turner Advertising in 1960, and his company became Turner Communications in the 1970s with its acquisition of television and radio stations.   (KEVIN M. LAMB)

Usui, Yoshimi

When Yasunari Kawabata committed suicide in 1972, four years after becoming Japan's first Nobel laureate in literature, he left no clue as to his motive. In mid-1977 Yoshimi Usui, a distinguished literary critic, suggested a motive in his novel *Jiko no tenmatsu* ("The Circumstances of the Incident") and thereby created a whirlwind. In his novel, first serialized in the monthly magazine *Tenbo* ("Perspectives") and later published as a book by its parent company, Chikuma Shobo, Usui asserted that 72-year-old Kawabata had become despondent when a young housemaid in his Kamakura home had rejected his love. When the story was published, a libel suit was filed in a Tokyo district court by Kawabata's widow and adopted daughter, who asked damages of 50 million yen (about U.S. $190,000), a public apology in Tokyo's three leading newspapers, the publication in *Tenbo* of a rebuttal by the Kawabata family, and an injunction against further distribution of the book. The Kawabatas argued that the honour of the author should be protected for 50 years after his death or until all members of his immediate family had died.

These demands gave rise to a legal complication involving the interpretation of Japanese law. Civil law does not recognize allegations as libelous if they are directed at the dead. The same is true of the penal code, except in cases where the allegations are proved to be false. Though the courts did not resolve the legal dilemma, the matter was put to rest in an out-of-court settlement. The Kawabatas withdrew their demand for damages and accepted apologies made to themselves and to the maid by Chikuma Shobo, which also agreed to halt publication of the book. Usui also publicly apologized for his inconsiderateness. The settlement was hastened by widespread discussion of Usui's suggestion that Kawabata was attracted to the girl because both may have been Burakumin. In ancient Japan, Burakumin were butchers, leather workers, executioners, and slaughterhouse workers, and as such were considered pariahs of society. Though their existence was officially recognized in 1868, the beginning of Japan's modern era, discrimination remains.

Usui was born in Nagano Prefecture on June 17, 1905, and joined Chikuma Shobo in 1933 as editor in chief of *Tenbo*. His column "Observation Deck" established his literary reputation and helped call attention to the talents of young writers who later gained renown.   (JOHN RODERICK)

Vance, Cyrus Roberts

In an arena filled with shrill voices and strong personalities seeking the limelight, U.S. Secretary of State Cyrus Vance was an island of calm and quiet as he went about the world methodically doing his job with a minimum of fanfare and attention. While there were no spectacular triumphs during his first year as Pres. Jimmy Carter's secretary of state, Vance successfully maintained the relationships initiated by his predecessor, Henry Kissinger, and opened up some new territory of his own, especially among the third world nations.

In total contrast to Kissinger's personalized and flamboyant style, Vance often slipped in and out of Washington almost unnoticed as he journeyed to Europe, Asia, Africa, and the Middle East. Aside from the signing of the Panama Canal treaty, which faced serious ratification problems in the U.S. Senate, he shunned the ceremonial aspects of his job and concentrated on diplomatic talks that might be more productive in the long run.

The hazards of highly publicized diplomacy were encountered early in Moscow, where Vance and the Carter administration began with an embarrassing setback as the Soviet Union rejected their proposals for the second stage of strategic arms limitation talks (SALT II). But by the end of the year behind-the-scenes diplomacy seemed to be producing some results, and the prospects looked somewhat brighter for an eventual Soviet-U.S. agreement on further reductions in nuclear weapons.

The Middle East continued to be the most dangerous area, and Vance traveled between Washington, Israel, and the Arab capitals, trying to implement President Carter's plans for reconvening the Geneva Middle East peace conference. After the peace initiative of Egyptian Pres. Anwar as-Sadat, Vance traveled to the Middle East in early December in an effort to persuade other Arab nations to join Egypt in direct negotiations with Israel.

His low-key performance as secretary of state was in keeping with Vance's style throughout his public career. Always known as a "team player," he spent many years serving as a deputy in a variety of government posts. Born in Clarksburg, W.Va., on March 27, 1917, Vance was educated at Yale University, served in the Navy during World War II, and was a corporate lawyer in New York before going to Washington in 1961. Pres. John Kennedy named him general counsel to the U.S. Department of Defense, where he later served as secretary of the army and then as deputy secretary of defense for Pres. Lyndon Johnson.   (HAL BRUNO)

Veeck, William Louis

A Chicago sports fan, a writer for the old *Holiday* magazine once said, is a person who sits in the stands and waits for his heart to be broken. And no followers of the city's also-ran and almost-ran athletic teams have had more broken hearts than the fans of the White Sox, the venerable American League baseball franchise on the South Side. But 1977 brought signs of rejuvenation—for the Sox and for the no-longer-young, frequently ailing, peglegged eccentric who owned them.

This was Bill Veeck's second time around as owner of the Sox. The first time—in 1959–61—he had brought them a pennant and their first moment of glory since the "Black Sox" gambling scandal of 1919. Veeck left baseball after '61 and later became president of Suffolk Downs racetrack in Massachusetts. Meanwhile, the Sox resumed their losing ways, and by late 1975 it was rumoured that the league would move the franchise to Seattle. At the last minute, Veeck appeared with an offer.

The owners were not eager to welcome back the man who gave baseball the exploding scoreboard and who once put a midget in the lineup (to reduce the strike zone). They imposed far more stringent financial standards on him than are usual in such cases, but he finally won out. The 1976 season, however, was dismal. By fall the Sox were in last place, and Veeck was nearly broke. Some said he had lost his touch.

Then came the turning point. Over the winter, while other owners were paying huge sums for free agents, Veeck put together an agglomeration of retreads and unknowns that led the league's West Division into July and finally finished third. And the fans came back, 1,657,135 of them, 742,190 more than in the 1976 season.

The team would not be the same in 1978. Two of the brightest stars, outfielders Oscar Gamble (31 homers) and Richie Zisk (101 RBI's), left for higher salaries elsewhere. But Veeck was wheeling and dealing again, and he forecast an even better team next year.

DENNIS BRACK—BLACK STAR

Veeck was born in Chicago on Feb. 9, 1914, the son of a former sportswriter who was president of the Chicago Cubs for 24 years, and he learned baseball in the Cubs organization. In 1941 he became owner and president of the Milwaukee Brewers (then in the American Association). He was president and owner of the Cleveland Indians from 1946 to 1949 and of the St. Louis Browns from 1951 to 1953. He served with the Marine Corps during World War II, receiving the wound that eventually cost him a leg.   (DAPHNE DAUME)

Wade, (Sarah) Virginia

Patriotic fervour knew no bounds at the Wimbledon tennis championships on July 1, 1977, when in the presence of Queen Elizabeth II in her Silver Jubilee year, and in the centenary year of the tournament, a British player won the women's singles. Virginia Wade, the first home winner of the event since 1969 and only the fifth since 1914, inspired the singing of "Land of Hope and Glory" and "For She's a Jolly Good Fellow" by spectators more noted for calm than frenzy. She had first competed in 1962, but year after year the patriotic hopes she raised had been dashed—until, on that royal occasion, imperious and effective, she crowned her career.

Born July 10, 1945, at Bournemouth, England, Virginia Wade was raised in South Africa where her father was archdeacon of Durban. She returned with her family to England at 15 and won recognition as a junior tennis player of promise, with a bold, aggressive approach to the game. This characteristic of her play deviated little throughout her career. She made her debut as a British Wightman Cup player in 1965, and the next year, when that contest was held at Wimbledon, fitted it in with her final examinations for an honours degree in mathematics and general science at the University of Sussex. She gained her first Wightman Cup success and got her degree as well.

In 1968 Wade achieved a triple success: she became the first woman open champion by winning the singles in the British Hard Court Championships at Bournemouth when that event initiated a new era in the game; won the first U.S. Open women's singles in New York; and was the main instrument of Britain's winning the Wightman Cup that year. In 1971 she won the singles championship of Italy and in 1972 that of Australia.

Wade's career coincided with an increase of prize money earnings for women. Her earnings during 1972–76 were estimated at more than $491,000. With the most lucrative tournaments being staged in the U.S. and with a contract to play for the New York team in the World Team Tennis league, her role became increasingly American. At the same time her British loyalties remained: she played continuously for Great Britain in the Wightman and Federation Cup contests from 1965 and 1967, respectively.   (LANCE TINGAY)

Walton, Bill

The big man who stands up for little guys found himself surrounded by 250,000 of them. Bill Walton had just led the Portland Trail Blazers to the National Basketball Association championship, and in the huge celebration that followed he became separated from his bicycle. No matter. The bike was returned a few days later. Walton had said all along that the real crooks were running the country, not running in the streets.

The problem was, he had said things like that too bluntly for those who were not accustomed to a 6-ft 11-in vegetarian basketball centre who wore flannel shirts, a red beard, and his hair in a pony tail. Sports fans who were used to hearing their heroes talk only about putting it all together and playing 110% were suddenly confronted with a superstar who called the FBI an enemy, listened passionately to the Grateful Dead, and greeted telephone callers in 1974 by saying "Impeach Nixon" instead of "hello." It made many of them happy when Walton's professional career hardly got off to a slam-dunk of a start.

William Theodore Walton III, born in La Mesa, Calif., on Nov. 5, 1952, was the first player chosen in the 1974 NBA draft after he finished his college career at UCLA with a .651 field-goal percentage and 1,370 career rebounds, a school record at the college of Kareem Abdul-Jabbar. His UCLA teams had won 88 straight games and two national collegiate championships. But with a five-year professional contract worth an estimated $2 million, Walton was victimized by injuries in his first two seasons. He missed 78 of his team's 164 games as Portland failed twice to make the play-offs.

Before the 1976–77 season, though, the Trail Blazers rid themselves of several players that Walton had often complained about as being selfish. Missing only 17 games, Walton had per-game averages of 14.4 rebounds, 18.6 points, and 3.2 blocked shots, and his field-goal percentage improved from .471 to .528. More important, he blended into a strong unit that finished second in its division behind Los Angeles, which it eliminated in four straight play-off games as Walton played Abdul-Jabbar head-to-head.

Participating in all 19 play-off games, Walton was the tournament's most valuable player with 15.2 rebounds, 18.2 points, and 3.4 blocked shots per game. The Blazers won all but five games, including all ten at home.   (KEVIN M. LAMB)

Ward, (Henry Reginald) George

At the centre of one of Britain's most bitter and longest running industrial disputes was a 44-year-old Anglo-Indian, George Ward. Born in New Delhi in 1933, he first visited England with his family as a child before World War II and then settled there in 1948. Trained as a chartered accountant, he set up a small film-processing laboratory in north London in 1965. Ten years later it was one of the most thriving film-processing businesses in the country, with an annual turnover of £4 million. Its name was Grunwick, and George Ward was its owner and managing director.

A personal dispute in Grunwick's Willesden plant during August 1976 led to the firing of one man. This led 137 fellow employees to strike in sympathy. They were dismissed. The Association of Professional, Executive, Clerical and Computer Staff (APEX) sought trade union recognition in the factory and reinstatement of the men.

Ward refused, and Grunwick became a headline name.

Ward turned out to be a man of inflexible purpose. He would not take the strikers back, and he would not have the union in his plant. By the summer of 1977 the dispute had escalated into mass picketing of the plant and violent clashes between police and demonstrators. For some weeks, post office workers refused to handle Grunwick mail. The dispute was taken through the whole hierarchy of the British law, to the lord chief justice in the High Court, to the Appeal Court, to the House of Lords, and to a special court of inquiry headed by Lord Justice Scarman. Despite the broadly pro-APEX findings of the special court, Ward continued to say no and kept the plant operating, manned mainly by Asian immigrants. In December the House of Lords ruled against the special court's findings and at year's end no resolution of the dispute was in sight.

Ward based his stand on an appeal to high principle, which he repeated week after week and month after month. "This is not a wage dispute," he told the secretary of state for employment. "This is a fight for individual liberty and the rights of workers not to be coerced into joining a union which is not of their choice." He insisted that he had done nothing against the law. And he said he would close down the plant rather than give in.   (HARFORD THOMAS)

Watson, Tom

Jack Nicklaus, golf's sun-bronzed legend, was putting on a show with final rounds of 65 and 66 on the hallowed fairways of the British Open, the oldest of all the major tournaments. Tom Watson had to be impressed. But eventually the most impressed was Nicklaus, because Watson finished with rounds of 65 and 65 and overcame a two-stroke deficit in the last six rounds to win. His score of 268 broke the tournament record by eight strokes.

The British Open was the third major win of Watson's career, his others being the 1977 Masters (also a head-to-head finish against Nicklaus) and the 1975 British Open. There had been a suspicion that Watson might someday displace Nicklaus as the top U.S. golfer ever since he beat Nicklaus by two strokes in the 1975 World Series of Golf. Any doubt was removed in 1977, when Watson was the Professional Golfers Association leading money winner with $310,653, the third highest total in history. He won four tour tournaments, plus the national events in Britain and Spain. The big year was a sudden upturn for Watson, who in 1976 brought his five-year professional winnings past $500,000 but failed to win a tournament.

Thomas Sturges Watson, born Sept. 4, 1949, in Kansas City, Mo., and educated at Stanford University, won four Missouri amateur titles as a teenager but found first place more elusive after turning professional in 1972. His first victory was at the 1974 Western Open in Chicago, when Tom Weiskopf double bogeyed on the last two holes. Just before that Watson had blown a one-shot lead at the U.S. Open, and even in 1977 he lost final-day leads twice before winning the Masters.

Watson's reddish-brown hair and freckles gave him the look of a Huckleberry Finn in doubleknits. His boy-next-door image persisted with his fondness for singing country-western music while accompanying himself on the guitar and his insistence on saying "yes, sir" and "no, sir." At the 1976 U.S. Open when John Mahaffey blew a lead in the last three holes, Watson waited two hours in the locker room in case Mahaffey might need some comforting. He explained that Mahaffey had done the same for him after the 1974 Open.

(KEVIN M. LAMB)

Weir, Peter

The Last Wave, Peter Weir's third feature film, which had its world premiere at the 1977 Paris film festival, established him as Australia's best-known director at a time when the national film industry was enjoying a remarkable upsurge. In the catastrophe genre of *Earthquake* and *Jaws*, *The Last Wave*, linking Aboriginal tribal myth with impending disaster (a tidal wave), confirmed Weir's skill in evoking atmosphere and his strong vein of mysticism.

Weir's first film, *The Cars that Ate Paris*, was widely acclaimed at the 1974 Cannes festival. But because the techniques of Australian film makers were ahead of those of their distributors, it was erroneously promoted as a horror movie and remained almost unknown in its native land. Weir conceived the idea of *Cars* in a period of black humour. An anarchic fantasy, it describes a small outback town whose inhabitants, in the manner of the Cornish shipwreckers, live by luring cars into disaster situations. The remains of the wrecked cars are then pirated and sold. By the simple expedient of a few misleading signs, the small community supports itself—until the horrifying denouement when the cars gobble up the town.

Picnic at Hanging Rock, Weir's second feature film, on the other hand, is memorable for its limpid beauty. Subtitled *A Recollection of Evil*, it describes a picnic outing in the early 1900s by a group of schoolgirls, in a mountain area where supernatural forces presumably devour two of the girls. *Picnic* received the 1977 British Academy award for best cinematography, and its dreamy evocation of *fin de siècle* Australia recalled the techniques of the great Swedish directors Jan Troell and Bo Widerberg. It also won the Australian Film Institute's award for the best film of 1975 and was shown in Italy, France, and other European countries, but it failed to break into the North American market.

Weir was born on Aug. 21, 1944, and briefly attended Sydney University before dropping out and entering his father's real estate business. In 1965 he went abroad and spent 18 months doing odd jobs before returning to Australia to become engrossed in the making of films. (A.R.G. GRIFFITHS)

Whitehouse, (Constance) Mary

In July 1977, in a prosecution initiated by Mary Whitehouse, the British magazine *Gay News* was convicted of blasphemous libel for publishing a poem describing a Roman centurion's homosexual love for Christ. The case was merely the most recent and dramatic of Whitehouse's attacks on "sexual permissiveness" since she launched her 1963 "Clean up TV" campaign. That effort had resulted in the formation (1965) of the 31,000-strong National Viewers' and Listeners' Association. As its full-time honorary secretary-general, she traveled ceaselessly, addressing meetings and lobbying controllers of radio and television, often attracting virulent personal abuse. Although in 1974 she lost, on a legal point, a private prosecution of London's Curzon cinema for showing the film *Blow Out*, the resultant publicity ensured the exclusion from Britain of *Deep Throat*. She successfully opposed (January 1975) an attempt to abolish film censorship in London, and claimed credit for the rejection of Danish producer Jens J. Thorsen's request to make in Britain a film about the sex life of Christ.

Mention of Mary Whitehouse's name usually produced groans or laughter; although she also castigated violence on television, she had become Britain's major symbol of repressive and guilt-ridden attitudes toward sex. Her fundamentalist Christianity and her association with Moral Rearmament were responsible for some of her anti-intellectualism and proneness to equate personal unconscious wishes with the will of God; and her career in teaching (1932–65), with gaps for the early years of her three sons) confirmed a latent schoolmarm image. In the public mind these characteristics obscured much that was praiseworthy. Actually, her first public initiative (1945) had been in organizing aid for starving German civilians.

Born at Shrewsbury, England, on June 13, 1910, she married an industrial coppersmith (also a fundamentalist) in 1940. She published her autobiography, *Who Does She Think She Is?*, in 1971; a second book, *Whatever Happened to Sex?*, giving details of all her campaigns, appeared in 1977, with co-editions in Australia, Canada, the U.S., and South Africa. (STEPHANIE MULLINS)

Wyeth, Andrew

On May 4, 1977, Andrew Wyeth was inducted as a member of the prestigious French Academy of Fine Arts, the second American in the history of the 182-year-old academy to be so honoured. The event marked a significant recognition of an artist whose career had run a course independent of the main currents of contemporary art. Wyeth's realistic, emotionally evocative paintings nevertheless place him among the best-known and most beloved of American artists.

Wyeth's subjects have been drawn from two primary locations—his winter home at Chadds Ford, Pa., and his summer home at Cushing, Me. Wyeth described the farms belonging to his neighbours (the Kuerners in Pennsylvania and the Olsons in Maine) as the most important environments in his life. The landscapes and the people of these places appear as solitary, austere, silent in Wyeth's art; their colours are subtle earth colours.

Andrew Wyeth was born on July 12, 1917, in Chadds Ford, the son of the noted artist and illustrator N. C. Wyeth, under whom Andrew studied. His earliest works include pen-and-ink drawings made at the age of 12 and published in a book done by his father. The young man soon turned to watercolour, which, along with tempera (the use of which he learned from artist Peter Hurd), comprise his preferred mediums. At 19 he had his first exhibition at the Art Alliance in Philadelphia; this was followed by a highly successful one-man exhibit of watercolours at the Macbeth Gallery in New York City in 1937.

The death of his father in 1945 was a turning point in the artist's career, marked by increasing emotional involvement. "Winter 1946," his first tempera done after the elder Wyeth's death, evokes the son's sense of loss. His most famous painting, "Christina's World" (1948), shows his neighbour Christina Olson, a woman partially crippled by poliomyelitis, looking back at her home while out in a field picking berries. Of the painting Wyeth has said, " 'Christina's World' is more than just her portrait. It really was her whole life and that is what she liked in it."

Wyeth's works are represented in most major museums. He had a large retrospective at the Pennsylvania Academy of the Fine Arts in 1966 and a one-man exhibit at the White House in 1970, the first such ever held there.

(JOAN NATALIE REIBSTEIN)

Yadin, Yigael

After returning to political life in 1976 as head of the new Democratic Movement for Change (DMC), Yigael Yadin became Israel's deputy prime minister in October 1977. The DMC, whose program emphasized domestic reform rather than international diplomacy, had won 15 seats in the Knesset (parliament) in the May election and in October entered into a coalition with the Likud under Menahem Begin.

Yadin was born in Jerusalem on March 21, 1917, nine months before the British captured the city from the Turks. His father, Eleazar Sukenik, was a noted archaeologist. Yadin joined the Haganah, the "official" Jewish underground, and in 1947

was appointed its chief of operations and planning—a central role during the war of independence of 1948. With Prime Minister David Ben-Gurion, he established the Israel Defense Forces (IDF) and planned the Negev campaign against Egypt.

As chief of staff (i.e., military commander in chief, 1949–52) after the war, he introduced order and discipline in the armed forces. With Ben-Gurion's support, he insisted that there could be no parallel military forces; the left-wing Palmach and the right-wing Irgun Zvai Leumi were absorbed, and officers were screened before being commissioned in the IDF. During Yadin's three years as chief of staff the IDF was transformed into a powerful striking force with a standing army as its hard core, compulsory military service, and a system of reserve duty that became its backbone.

In 1952 Yadin returned to academic life (he had taken his degree in archaeology at the Hebrew University in 1945 and was to become professor there in 1963). He concentrated on his major excavation projects at Hazor, Masada, and in the Judaean desert, enlisting the help of volunteers from Israel and abroad. His name was linked with the acquisition of the Dead Sea Scrolls by Israel, and he saw them housed in the Shrine of the Book at the Israel Museum in Jerusalem.

Yadin served as one of two surveyors of the security and intelligence services. Prime Minister Levi Eshkol appointed him as his military adviser during the June 1967 Arab-Israeli war. After the October 1973 Arab-Israeli war he was a member of the Agranat committee of inquiry into the war's conduct. Meanwhile, he had turned down all political offers, including one to become prime minister in 1966.

(JON KIMCHE)

Yhombi-Opango, Joachim

On April 4, 1977, two weeks after the assassination of Pres. Marien Ngouabi (see OBITUARIES) in an attempted coup, his close colleague Col. Joachim Yhombi-Opango was named head of state of the Congo People's Republic, and three days later he was sworn in. Formerly acting minister of defense and security, Yhombi-Opango also became president of the Congolese Labour Party's 11-man Military Committee, which had run the country since Ngouabi's death. On April 5 he issued a decree abrogating the 1973 constitution.

Born in Owando, northern Congo, in 1940, Yhombi-Opango began his military career as a noncommissioned officer in the French Army. After graduating as a second lieutenant at the Saint-Cyr military academy, he returned to the Congo in 1962 and in 1965 became military aide to Pres. Alphonse Massamba-Débat (see OBITUARIES). After the National Council of the Revolution brought the Army to power in 1968, he became chief of staff (1969–73), inspector general of the armed forces (1973–74), secretary-general of the Council of State (1974–75), and acting minister of defense from June 1975.

There was a break in Yhombi-Opango's career in 1970 when he was suspended during investigations into charges of "embourgeoisement and corruption" against the Army, but he was acquitted of any im-

proper behaviour. Later, he twice came under a cloud in connection with coup attempts. Nevertheless, he retained Ngouabi's confidence to the end and became the most powerful man in the country.

The Congo's new leader was respected for his efforts to mediate the regional disputes that lay at the heart of the country's political problems. Although he strongly favoured maintaining the Congo's close military and other links with the U.S.S.R. and Cuba, he was also concerned with improving relations with France. In June 1977 he paid a private visit to Paris for talks with the French president and premier, and later in the year agreements providing for CFA Fr. 415 million (U.S. $1.7 million) in French aid for transport, housing, and health were announced.   (COLIN LEGUM)

Young, Andrew Jackson, Jr.

In 1976, just before he won the Democratic Party's presidential nomination, Jimmy Carter was asked to list the people to whom he owed political debts. He gave only one name: "Andy Young." That may have been an exaggeration, but there was no doubt that Andrew Young, civil rights leader and former member of Congress, played a crucial role in Carter's 1976 victories. Young's support and endorsement were the keys that gained Carter an overwhelming percentage of the black vote in state after state, often with decisive results. Carter rewarded Young's efforts by giving him the job of U.S. ambassador to the UN.

Young's first months on the job were marked by controversy, often stemming from his undiplomatic use of language. He suggested that Cuban troops brought "a certain stability" to Angola and, referring to racial tensions in Rhodesia, said that the British "almost invented racism." Asked if he considered the government of South Africa illegitimate, he offhandedly replied, "Yeah." In the resulting furor Carter stood by his ambassador, though without necessarily endorsing everything Young said.

As the year wore on, Carter's judgment seemed to be confirmed. Young moderated his language, while his efforts—especially in black Africa—helped lead to significantly improved relations with a number of less developed countries. Moreover, with Carter, Young committed the U.S. to black majority rule in southern Africa. When a permanent embargo on arms shipments to

DENNIS BRACK—BLACK STAR

South Africa was proposed in the UN, Young cast his vote in the Security Council in favour of the measure. By the end of the year it was obvious that Andy Young was one of the two or three most influential advisers to the president on foreign policy.

Young was born in New Orleans, La., on March 12, 1932, graduated from Howard University in 1951, and was ordained a Congregationalist minister after study at the Hartford Theological Seminary (now Foundation) in Connecticut. He served in a number of small-town churches in Georgia and Alabama, eventually moving to Atlanta, where he became Martin Luther King's chief tactician during the civil rights movement of the '60s. In 1972 he was elected to Congress from Georgia's 5th district, the first black to represent that state in Congress since 1871.   (STANLEY W. CLOUD)

Zia-ul-Haq, Mohammad

Pakistan's fourth military dictatorship since the nation was founded in 1947 was established on July 5, 1977, when Gen. Mohammad Zia-ul-Haq seized power from Prime Minister Zulfikar Ali Bhutto in a bloodless coup. Like the previous Army chiefs, General Zia said he was taking over temporarily to check the "drift toward political chaos," and he promised democratic elections in three months. But he reneged on his word—as had been generally predicted—and a new election was not expected to take place in Pakistan until some time in 1978.

Born in Jullundur, in undivided Punjab, in 1924, Zia was commissioned in 1945 from the Royal Indian Military Academy at Dehra Dun. His group was among the last to be commissioned from the academy before Britain gave independence to India and Pakistan in 1947, and he served in Burma, Malaya, and Indonesia at the end of World War II. After 19 years in various staff and command appointments, General Zia, then a lieutenant colonel, was made instructor at the Command and Staff College in Quetta. During 1966–68 he commanded a cavalry regiment and, on promotion to colonel in 1968, was attached to an armoured division. He was made a brigadier a year later and commanded, successively, an armoured brigade, a division, and a corps. A major general from 1972, he was president of the military courts that tried several army and air force officers alleged to have plotted against the Bhutto government in 1972.

Between 1972 and 1975 Zia attended advanced command courses in the U.S. and the U.K., and in April 1975 he was promoted to the rank of lieutenant general. In March 1976 Bhutto, who had become prime minister in 1973 after stepping down as president and who had followed Zia's career closely, made him chief of staff of the Army. He retained that position, combining it with that of chief martial-law administrator, after the military takeover. A devout Muslim, General Zia made a pilgrimage to Mecca in 1976. As head of Pakistan's new military government, he visited Iran in September 1977 and China in December.   (GOVINDAN UNNY)

In 1977 the Nobel Prizes were selected with more dispatch and greeted with less dissent than has been the case in many years. Only the 1976 peace prize, awarded a year late, was criticized, and that for being either dilatory or premature.

Continuing what has become almost a tradition, U.S. scientists monopolized the physics and medicine prizes, receiving five of the six awards. In addition, two Englishmen were honoured, one for work in physics and the other for economics, an award also shared by a Swede, and two Irish women won a peace prize. A Belgian won the chemistry award and a Spaniard the prize for literature. In all, the seven prizes were shared by 12 laureates and one organization. The 1977 awards each carried an honorarium of $145,000.

As in the past, the selection committees cited scientific work that had been performed by deceased collaborators of the Nobel laureates. This led to the suggestion that such persons, who are ineligible for Nobel prizes, be honoured by a plaque or special citation.

Prize for Peace

The 1977 Prize for Peace was awarded to Amnesty International, an organization that works on behalf of political prisoners around the world. The Nobel committee also announced that the 1976 Prize for Peace would be conferred a year behind schedule, on two Belfast women who organized the Community of Peace People in Northern Ireland.

Though sectarian hate and bloodshed in Ulster have deep historical roots, it was a 1969 student-led civil rights movement that sparked the current troubles. Demonstrations were followed by more violent acts until bombings, kidnappings, and murders became commonplace. Eventually the radical wing of the Irish Republican Army (IRA), an old Catholic group, and the Ulster Defense Association (UDA), a Protestant guerrilla movement, became implacable enemies. In desperation the British government imposed martial law,

Mairead Corrigan and
Betty Williams

which was enforced by occupation troops. Some 1,700 people were killed in seven years.

In August 1976 a British soldier shot the driver of an IRA getaway car that went out of control and killed three small children. Their aunt, Mairead Corrigan, a 32-year-old secretary, publicly condemned the IRA for triggering the death of these innocents. Betty Williams, a 34-year-old mother who lived near the scene, went door-to-door asking neighbours to demonstrate against violence. The two women later met when 200 others decided to "declare war on war" and staged a peaceful march. One week later 10,000 Protestants and Catholics joined a second march despite cries of treason by sectarian firebrands. Under the auspices of the informal group, Catholics and Protestants met to discuss their common goals and declared: "We condemn all violence whether it is from the UDA, the IRA, or the British Army." The response from outside the group was enormous.

When the Nobel committee announced there would be no 1976 peace prize (apparently because this movement was still taking shape when the nominations were considered), 22 Norwegian newspapers raised $324,000 as a "People's Peace Prize" for the two Catholic women. The "Peace People" used the money to build community centres, to send former terrorists into voluntary exile, and to support peaceful reconstruction. Though the women realized they had not brought lasting peace to Northern Ireland, violent deaths decreased dramatically.

Amnesty International (AI) was founded in 1961 by Peter Benenson, a London lawyer. Sean MacBride, a recipient of the 1974 Nobel Prize for Peace, was chairman of AI from 1961 to 1975. The organization, which now has 170,000 members in 107 nations, works for the release of any prisoner who has been jailed for political or religious reasons. By one account, AI has been involved in the cases of some 16,000 individuals, more than 10,000 of whom have been released. The organization,

however, never takes public credit for a specific case. The resources of the AI include a relatively modest budget, a staff that works in 21 languages, and international public opinion. When a victimized person is identified and "adopted," AI members around the world initiate an avalanche of mail that, according to MacBride, is intended to annoy the governments involved. "Soon the issue is being raised at Cabinet level, and everyone is wondering whether the guy is worth all the trouble. The answer is frequently no."

Prize for Literature

Vicente Aleixandre, winner of the literature prize, is a Spanish poet whose life has been deeply affected by chronic illness and political repression. Born in Seville on April 26, 1898, raised in Málaga, and educated in Madrid, he belonged to the "Generation of 1927," a school of young writers who found their artistic inspiration in Spain's 16th- and 17th-century Golden Age of literature. When the Spanish Civil War erupted, Aleixandre, an invalid, could neither fight nor flee. So he remained in Republican territory and was ostracized when Francisco Franco came to power. He was then forbidden to publish his works for five years, even though he had won the nation's highest literary award three years before the Civil War began.

"The Civil War came and from his bed he listened to the bombs exploding," the Swedish Academy recalled. "When it was over and his friends and fellow writers went into exile, they had to leave the invalid behind. But mentally, too, he survived the Franco regime, never submitting and thus becoming a rallying point and key figure in what remained of Spain's spiritual life." A Harvard University professor calls him "a father figure for most of the young poets in Spain today," albeit an elusive one. A sick and timid bachelor who lives with his sister in a Madrid villa, Aleixandre avoids admirers and devotes his limited strength to writing.

"In my work I have gathered the lyric traditions of the Spanish people and, above all, of the Andalusian people, and blended them into the modern stream," he said. "I wanted to spend my life seeking to communicate with all human beings; I will continue." Poetry, he believes, "is the deepest and most precise means of expression."

His work, which has been described as surreal and as free verse that evolves into prose poetry, has been translated into French, German, and English. Among his best-known collections are *Espadas como labios* (1932; "Swords as Lips"); *Sombra del paraíso* (1944; "Shadow of Paradise"); *Historia del corazón* (1954; "Story of the Heart"); and most recently *Diálogos del conocimiento* (1974; "Dialogues of Insight"). One of Aleixandre's translators remarked: "He is a poet of intellectual vigor, spiritual depth and tenacity. He did the work. He went far down into the soul and brought back pieces of life as a gift for the rest of us."

(PHILIP KOPPER)

TERENCE SPENCER—CAMERA PRESS

Prize for Chemistry

Ilya Prigogine won the Nobel Prize for Chemistry for widening the scope of one of the fundamental branches of the natural sciences: thermodynamics, the part of physics that deals with the relationships between heat and work. Since thermodynamics was formulated during the 19th century, it has been relevant mainly to fields—physics, chemistry, and, to some extent, biology and engineering—that are amenable to laboratory study under reproducible conditions. Prigogine's work has made thermodynamic principles applicable to many disciplines, including sociology, ecology, and demography, that are denied the luxury of classic, controlled experimental techniques. The kind of reasoning that in 1824 explained the amount of work that a steam engine, under ideal conditions, could extract from a given quantity of fuel has been broadened, by Prigogine's efforts, into a form appropriate to such puzzles as how life originated, how world resource policies should be formulated, and how traffic jams might be prevented.

The laws of thermodynamics govern a host of phenomena and accurately account for the qualities of physical systems under conditions of equilibrium, the state in which the properties and composition of a specified assemblage of matter have no tendency to change. They rationalize the fact that a collection of hydrogen atoms will pair off as molecules of a colourless gas, and so will a collection of oxygen atoms, but that if the two gases are mixed, the different kinds of particles will seize the first opportunity to combine into molecules of water, an entirely distinct substance. Moreover, during the process, part of the energy inherent in the original particles is set free and can be used—say, by a steam engine—to perform work. Reversal of the process (decomposition of water into the elements hydrogen and oxygen) is possible, but only if energy in some form is supplied from an external source.

Observations of numerous physical systems led to recognition of their general tendency to assume the states marked by the most disorder by undergoing processes that dissipate energy and can, in principle, produce work. This universal law, however, stated nothing about how it could be possible for a more orderly system—such as a living creature—to arise spontaneously from a less orderly one and maintain itself in defiance of the dissipative tendency. Order can be created and preserved only by processes that flow "uphill" in the thermodynamic sense and that are compensated by "downhill" events elsewhere in the universe. Such coupled occurrences, resulting in ordered entities that owe their existence to absorption of energy from their surroundings, are entirely consistent with the classical laws of thermodynamics, but their spontaneity had remained an enigma.

Soon after World War II Prigogine developed mathematical models of what he called "dissipative" systems of just this kind. The models showed how matter and energy could interact creatively, forming organisms that can sustain themselves and grow in opposition to the drift toward universal chaos. Summarizing his work and its importance, the Royal Swedish Academy of Sciences asserted that ". . . it is possible in principle to distinguish between two types of structures: equilibrium structures, which can exist as isolated systems . . ., and dissipative systems, which can only exist in symbiosis with their surroundings. Dissipative structures display two types of behavior: close to equilibrium their order tends to be destroyed; but far from equilibrium order can be maintained and new structures formed. The probability for order to arise out of disorder is infinitesimal according to the laws of chance. The formation of ordered, dissipative systems demonstrates, however, that it is possible to create order from disorder." Prigogine was born in Moscow in 1917; as a child he was taken by his family to western Europe in 1921. Settling in Belgium in 1929, Prigogine has risen to his present post as professor of physical chemistry and theoretical physics at the Free University of Brussels. He simultaneously holds the directorship of the Center for Statistical Mechanics and Thermodynamics at the University of Texas in Austin.

Prize for Physics

The Nobel Prize for Physics was shared equally by John H. Van Vleck of Harvard, Sir Nevill F. Mott of Cambridge, and Philip W. Anderson, who is associated with the Bell Telephone Laboratories and Princeton University. The three were honoured for their independent but closely related contributions to the understanding of the behaviour of electrons in magnetic, noncrystalline solid materials. Their researches underlie many of the electronic devices that have become the hallmarks of the late 20th century—tape recorders, office copying machines, high-speed computers, lasers, and solar energy converters.

Van Vleck, a native of Middletown, Conn., spent most of his career at Harvard, where from 1951 until his formal retirement in 1969 he held the Hollis professorship of mathematics and natural philosophy, the oldest endowed chair in the U.S. He has earned informal recognition as "the father of modern magnetism" by dedication of his scientific career to the study of the sources of that phenomenon in the structure of atoms. One of his first major achievements, in the early years of quantum mechanics, was the refinement of that technique to give an accurate explanation of the magnetic properties of individual atoms of whole series of chemical elements. During the 1930s he formulated the ligand field theory, which accounts for the magnetic, electrical, and optical properties of many elements and compounds by considering the influences exerted on the electrons in particular atoms by the other atoms in the neighbourhood; the theory remains one of the chemist's most useful tools in understanding the patterns of chemical bonds present in complex compounds.

Mott was born in Leeds in 1905; as did Van Vleck, he played a part in the wholesale reformulation of physics that attended the burgeoning of wave mechanics in the late 1920s. The productiveness of his long career has been ascribed to the "extraordinary powers of intuition that enabled him rapidly to transfer intricate abstract theories to the real world." He worked with

WIDE WORLD

Sir Nevill F. Mott

Niels Bohr and Lord Rutherford but in 1933, when he took charge of the theoretical physics department at the University of Bristol, his attention shifted from nuclear physics to the study of metals, semiconductors, and photographic emulsions and then to electrical conduction in noncrystalline solids. His name is connected with formulas that describe the scattering of a beam of particles by atomic nuclei and with transitions—explored during his tenure at the Cavendish Laboratory at Cambridge (1954–71)—of certain substances between electrically conductive (metallic) states and insulating (nonmetallic) states.

Anderson, born in Indianapolis in 1923, was a student of Van Vleck at Harvard and later, as a visiting professor at the Cavendish Laboratory, a colleague of Mott. His diverse contributions to physics include methods of deducing details of molecular interactions from the shapes of spectral peaks; extension of the Bardeen-Cooper-Schrieffer theory to account for the effects of impurities on the properties of superconductors and to establish correlations between superconductivity, superfluidity, and laser action (all involve coherent waves of matter or energy); and the interatomic effects that underlie the magnetic properties of individual metals and alloys. With Mott, he dealt with the semiconducting properties of disordered solid materials; their results indicate that it should be possible to develop electronic switching devices, computer memory elements, and solar energy converters based on inexpensive glassy solids rather than the costly crystalline materials that have been used up to now.

Prize for Physiology or Medicine

The Nobel Prize for Physiology or Medicine was shared unequally by three Americans, Rosalyn Sussman Yalow, who is affiliated with the Bronx Veterans Administration Hospital and the Mount Sinai School of Medicine in New York City; Roger Guillemin of the Salk Institute for Biological Studies, San Diego, Calif.; and Andrew Schally, who is on the staffs of the New Orleans (La.) VA Hospital and Tulane University.

Andrew Schally, Rosalyn
Sussman Yalow, and
Roger Guillemin

Yalow received half of the Nobel hono-rarium in recognition of her role in the de-velopment of the radioimmunoassay, a uniquely sensitive and specific technique now widely used for measuring the con-centrations of hundreds of biologically ac-tive substances, many of which are pres-ent in the body in such small quantities that they are practically undetectable by any other method. For 22 years her partner in research was Solomon Berson, who died in 1972. In the early 1950s Yalow and Ber-son undertook a study of the resistance that certain diabetics developed to the ac-tion of insulin, a protein hormone that is commercially obtained from cattle, sheep, and pigs and that for more than 50 years has been used by diabetics to control blood sugar. They found that in the resistant dia-betics, the immune system was producing an antibody that neutralized the foreign protein. This effect was already well known in the case of other proteins—it is the basis of the blood-group classifications, for example—but skepticism greeted their report that insulin, a fairly small and sim-ple substance as proteins go, was capable of producing it. Berson and Yalow persist-ed in the research and found that the anti-body does not differentiate between a mol-ecule of ordinary insulin and one contain-ing an atom of radioactive iodine—a label that made it possible to measure, by using a radiation counter, the proportion of ra-dioactive insulin bound by a limited amount of antibody in the presence of ordi-nary insulin. By comparing the proportion bound in the presence of known amounts of ordinary insulin with the proportion bound under the same conditions in the presence of the unknown amount of insu-lin in a sample of a body fluid, they could now determine the amount of insulin in the sample. Since antibodies specific for practically any biologically active material can be obtained by inoculating rabbits or guinea pigs with the materials, the tech-nique can be extended to the analysis of any of them.

Guillemin, who was born in 1924 in Di-jon, France, joined the staff of the Baylor College of Medicine in Houston, Texas, in 1953 and undertook the task of verifying the proposal, made by the late English anatomist Geoffrey W. Harris, that the se-cretion of hormones by the pituitary gland is itself regulated by other hormones re-leased by the hypothalamus, a portion of the brain joined to the pituitary by a trunk of blood vessels and nerve fibres.

Schally was born in 1926 in Wilno, Po-land (now Vilnius, the capital of the Lithu-anian S.S.R.), and fled with his family to Britain in 1939. He accepted a position at the Baylor College of Medicine in 1957 and joined Guillemin in the laborious separa-tion of fragments of the brains of about seven million sheep and pigs.

Their initial efforts were directed toward isolating the substance that controls the re-lease of ACTH, the pituitary hormone that stimulates the adrenal cortex to secrete its steroid hormones. The search for that ma-terial proved beyond the power of the methods available, and the two scientists turned their attention to TRH, the hormone that causes the pituitary to produce its hor-mone TSH, which then stimulates the thy-roid to produce still other hormones that in turn influence the metabolic rate through-out the body.

After Schally departed for New Orleans in 1962, he carried on the work there while Guillemin continued it at Houston, where he stayed until 1970. In 1968 and 1969, both succeeded in isolating and identifying TRH. The single milligram of pure TRH they obtained represented about two-trillionths of the amount of tissue they started with; it turned out to be a fairly simple compound that can be synthesized without difficulty for clinical evaluation. It is already in use for treating several conditions related to deficiencies in pituitary hormone secre-tion. Continuation of the parallel efforts of the two investigators resulted in the dis-covery of LHRH (the hormone that controls the luteinizing hormone, which is vital to ovulation in women) in 1971 by Schally and somatostatin (another hormone that is being investigated for use in treating dia-betes and peptic ulcers) in 1973 by Guille-min.   (JOHN V. KILLHEFFER; PHILIP KOPPER)

Prize for Economics

Nobel prizes have often been awarded for work performed a generation earlier. The economics prize, which followed this pat-tern, was given to a Swede and a Briton for decades-old discoveries that did not be-come current or widely applicable for years. The laureates were Bertil Ohlin and James Meade, whose major treatises on in-ternational trade were published, respec-tively, in the 1930s and 1950s. The Swed-ish Academy of Sciences noted: "The breadth and importance of Ohlin's and Meade's contributions have . . . not become obvious until the '60s and '70s in conjunc-tion with the growing internationalization of the economic system. . . . It has become increasingly clear that problems related to the allocation of resources, business cycles and the distribution of income are very much international problems. This means that foreign trade, international price fluc-tuations, the international allocation of economic activities and the transfer of re-sources, as well as the international pay-ments systems have become dominant fac-tors in economic analysis and economic policy."

Ohlin noted that the production of dif-ferent commodities generally involves var-iable mixes of such factors of production as available labour, land, and capital. Na-tions, therefore, tend to produce goods that best utilize their special advantages over others. Whereas labour-intensive markets tend to concentrate on manufac-turing, nations with abundant land tend to emphasize such things as agriculture and cattle raising. As each nation's inter-national trade expands, the special advan-tages it holds also take on greater impor-tance. But it is the growing importance of this advantage that will eventually make it more costly because of increased demand. Ohlin thus contends that international trade gradually equalizes the initial rela-tive advantages that each nation has over its trading partners.

Building on Ohlin's foundations, Meade "demonstrated the effect of domestic eco-nomic policy on foreign trade and pene-trated the problems of stabilization policies in 'open' economies," according to the award committee. He showed how tax cuts adversely affect the balance of payments and how monetary policy and exchange rates affect economic stabilization.

Ohlin was born in Klippan, Sweden, on April 23, 1899, entered college at 15, and was a Copenhagen University professor at 25. In the 1930s he gained prominence by contradicting John Maynard Keynes who contended that Germany could not afford to pay World War I reparations. By 1944 Ohlin was chairman of the Swedish Liber-al Party, a post he held for 23 years. He served as minister of commerce in a coali-tion government in 1944–45, but never at-tained his goal of becoming prime minis-ter. For many years, he was a professor at the Stockholm School of Economics. Be-cause he belongs to the Nobel committee that selects the winner of the economics prize, he was politely asked not to attend meetings during deliberations regarding the 1977 award.

Meade was born in 1907, and edited the League of Nations' *World Economic Surveys* until the outbreak of World War II, when he returned home to serve as Britain's chief war economist. During 1946–47 he was the Labour government's top economist. After teaching at the London School of Econom-ics, he became a professor at Cambridge and was a senior research fellow at Christ's College from 1969 to 1974. A modest man who makes few public appearances, he has been called "the last of the utilitarians who trace from Jeremy Bentham." Meade has "a burning interest in promoting welfare," wrote Nobel laureate Paul A. Samuelson. "[He would] give his cloak to a shivering beggar, not only because he feels it is right and fair to do so, but also for the reason that the beggar would receive more plea-sure from it than a well-off professor of po-litical economy."   (PHILIP KOPPER)

OBITUARIES

The following is a selected list of prominent men and women who died during 1977.

Abelin, Pierre, French parliamentarian (b. Poitiers, France, May 16, 1909—d. Poitiers, May 23, 1977), was a champion for centrist principles in French parliamentary social democracy. Abelin sat in the two Constituent Assemblies of 1945 and was twice a member for the Vienne département in the National Assembly, (1946–58, 1962–75). A member of the Mouvement Républicain Populaire, he held various government secretaryships in the late 1940s and 1950s but was an opponent of Gen. Charles de Gaulle's regime. Abelin assisted Jean Lecanuet in the formation of the Centre Démocratie et Progrès in 1965 and promoted the Mouvement Réformateur with the Radicals and other moderates in 1971 in the hope of achieving the victory of centrism as a "third way" in French politics in the elections of 1973. Under the presidency of Valéry Giscard d'Estaing the opposition centrists rejoined the government and Abelin served as minister of overseas cooperation (1974–76). In 1976 he helped to create the Centre des Démocrates Sociaux and was one of the party's vice-presidents.

Adrian, Edgar Douglas Adrian, 1st Baron, of Cambridge, British physiologist (b. London, England, Nov. 30, 1889—d. London, Aug. 4, 1977), shared the Nobel Prize for Physiology or Medicine (1932) with Sir Charles Sherrington for discoveries relating to the nerve cell and its processes. Adrian graduated from Trinity College, Cambridge, where he spent a major portion of his professional career conducting research on nerve impulses that led to a better understanding of the physical basis of sensation and the mechanism of muscular control. His studies (1934) on the electrical activity of the brain opened new fields of investigation in epilepsy and in the location of cerebral lesions. Adrian was awarded the Order of Merit in 1942. He subsequently served as president of the Royal Society (1950–55) and was created a baron in 1955. His writings include *The Basis of Sensation* (1928), *The Mechanism of Nervous Action* (1932), and *The Physical Background of Perception* (1947).

Ahmed, Fakhruddin Ali, Indian politician (b. Delhi, India, May 13, 1905—d. New Delhi, India, Feb. 11, 1977), succeeded V. V. Giri as president of India from Aug. 24, 1974. Ahmed graduated

from St. Catharine's College, Cambridge, in 1927 and was called to the bar by the Inner Temple in 1928. After joining the Congress Party in 1931 he was elected to the Assam state legislature in 1935 and became its minister of finance and revenue (1938–39). After World War II and Indian independence in 1947, he held various ministerial posts in Assam and, from 1966, served in Indira Gandhi's national government. When the Congress Party split into two parliamentary factions in 1969, he stood firmly by Mrs. Gandhi. Ahmed was the fifth person and the second Muslim to hold the office of president of India.

Alia, Queen of Jordan (ALIA BAHA EDDIN TOUKAN), Jordanian consort (b. Cairo, Egypt, Dec. 25, 1948—d. near at-Tafilah, Jordan, Feb. 9, 1977), was the third wife of King Hussein and the first he proclaimed queen of the Hashemite Kingdom of Jordan. Inspired by her father, Alia disregarded traditional restrictions placed on women and aspired to a career in the foreign service. A spirit

GENEVIEVE CHAUVEL—SYGMA

of independence also characterized her days at Hunter College in New York City, where she developed a liking for fast cars, water skiing, and blue jeans. She was killed in a helicopter crash after inspecting a hospital in at-Tafilah.

Amaury, Émilien, French newspaper owner (b. Étampes, France, March 5, 1909—d. Vineuil-Saint-Firmin, France, Jan. 2, 1977), founded (1944) *Parisien Libéré,* a daily newspaper that by 1974 had the largest circulation (785,000) in France. In January 1975 Amaury became involved in a bitter dispute with the Communist-affiliated printers' union, which he accused of conspiring to ruin the newspaper industry. In March 1975 Amaury stopped publication, laying off 52 journalists and more than 200 printers. A tabloid was produced with nonunion help, but in May union members occupied Amaury's two printing plants. When the union and the newspaper owners reached an agreement in mid-1976, Amaury refused to accept it. During World War II he collaborated with the Vichy government in a nonpolitical capacity while organizing a resistance network. After the liberation of France Amaury was among the founders of the Mouvement Républicain Populaire but in April 1947 he

joined Gen. Charles de Gaulle's Rassemblement du Peuple Français. He also founded the right-wing weekly *Carrefour* and the daily sports paper *L'Équipe.*

Anderson, Eddie ("ROCHESTER"), U.S. comedian (b. Oakland, Calif., Sept. 18, 1905—d. Los Angeles, Calif., Feb. 28, 1977), became a national radio, television, and movie favourite as comedian Jack Benny's valet, Rochester. Anderson's raspy delivery of the one-liner "What's that, boss?" became a classical put-down of Benny's pompous penny pinching. Anderson's one-shot radio appearance as a Pullman porter on a 1937 "Jack Benny Program" generated such enthusiastic audience response that he was signed to a contract and remained with the show through its last episode in 1965.

Avon, (Robert) Anthony Eden, 1st Earl, British politician (b. Windlestone, England, June 12, 1897—d. Alvediston, England, Jan. 14, 1977), was Britain's foreign secretary (1935–38, 1940–45, and 1951–55) and prime minister (April 1955–January 1957). Eden, who believed that international aggression should be opposed, resigned as foreign secretary when Prime Minister Neville Chamberlain's 1938 Munich pact allowed Hitler to dismember Czechoslovakia. When World War II broke out, Eden reentered Chamberlain's government as dominions secretary, and when Winston Churchill became prime minister (1940), Eden again served as foreign secretary. He handled the formidable problems of the wartime alliance, was instrumental in ending the French war in Indochina (1950s), and helped establish NATO as an adequate Western European defense system. In 1952 Eden married a niece of Churchill. The next year he became seriously ill, and, despite a number of operations, never fully regained his health. Nevertheless, he succeeded Churchill as prime minister (1955) and devoted much of his effort to an attempt to relax international tensions. Eden's political downfall began when Col. Gamal Abdel Nasser, head of the Egyptian state, nationalized the Suez Canal Co. (July 26, 1956). This action led to an Israeli invasion (October 29), which was supported one week later by Anglo-French troops. Eden was accused of flouting the UN, alienating the U.S., offending the Commonwealth nations, and risking a third world war. Under world pressure the Anglo-French troops were withdrawn and replaced by UN emergency units. Eden resigned his post the following month, citing ill health as the reason. He was educated at Eton College in Berkshire and Christ Church, Oxford. Eden pub-

BOOK OF THE YEAR

lished his memoirs in three volumes: *Full Circle* (1960), *Facing the Dictators* (1962), and *The Reckoning* (1965). He was made a knight of the Garter in 1954 and was created earl of Avon in 1961.

Baader, Andreas, German terrorist (b. 1943?—d. Stuttgart, West Germany, Oct. 18, 1977), became an urban guerrilla under the influence of Ulrike Meinhof and was co-leader of the Baader-Meinhof gang, a part of the Red Army Faction revolutionary organization that believed only active violence would overthrow West Germany's "bourgeois-imperialist" government. Baader failed to obtain a university degree, unsuccessfully attempted journalism, and cultivated university political extremism before he set fire to two Frankfurt am Main department stores with Gudrun Ensslin and two others in 1968. Both he and she were arrested in 1969 but were helped by Meinhof to escape in 1970. Together with Meinhof, they turned to political bank robbery and murder, were arrested in 1972, and after a protracted trial were sentenced to life imprisonment in 1977. Both Baader and Ensslin committed suicide in their cells on the same day after learning that an attempt to secure their release by hijacking a Lufthansa airliner had failed in Somalia.

Baden-Powell, Olave St. Clair, Lady, British youth leader (b. Derbyshire, England, Feb. 22, 1889—d. Bramley, England, June 26, 1977), was largely responsible for the global success of the World Association of Girl Guides and Girl Scouts. After her marriage (1912) to Gen. Robert Baden-Powell, she and her husband channeled their energies into work for children. Lady Baden-Powell became Britain's chief guide in 1918 and was unanimously elected world chief guide in 1930 by delegates from 28 countries constituting the newly formed world association. During the next 40 years, she traveled some 500,000 mi to promote Scouting for both girls and boys.

Balcon, Sir Michael Elias, British film producer (b. Birmingham, England, May 19, 1896—d. Hartfield, Sussex, England, Oct. 17, 1977), was a pioneer of the British film industry who gained renown for the "Ealing Comedies" series, which included *Kind Hearts and Coronets* (1949), *Whisky Galore!* (1949), and *The Lavender Hill Mob* (1951). Balcon shared a film partnership after World War I and later founded Gainsborough Pictures Ltd. (1928), which produced *Journey's End* (1930). He joined Gaumont-British Picture Corp. Ltd. (1931) and produced *Rome Express* (1932), an important success for the British film industry. In 1937 he became associated with MGM British Studios Ltd. and produced *A Yank at Oxford* (1938), which starred Robert Taylor. He began work with Ealing Studios in 1938 and turned out such World War II adventures as *San Demetrio-London* (1943) and *The Overlanders* (1946). A governor of the British Film Institute, he was knighted in 1948.

Beel, Louis Joseph Maria, Dutch politician (b. Roermond, Neth., April 12, 1902—d. Utrecht, Neth., Feb. 11, 1977), practiced law after graduating from the Catholic University of Nijmegen, and in the 1940s accepted a role in government administration. Beel twice held the post of prime minister (1946–48, 1958–59), was vice-president (1959–72) of the Council of State, and served as high commissioner (1948–49) in the Dutch East Indies, during which time The Netherlands agreed to relinquish all claims to Indonesia.

Beresford, Jack, British oarsman (b. Chiswick, Middlesex, England, Jan. 1, 1899—d. December 1977), represented Great Britain in the five successive Olympic Games from 1920 through 1936, in which he won three gold and two silver medals in the single sculls, double sculls, coxless fours, and eight-oared events. At his last Olympic appearance, in Berlin, he carried Britain's team flag, and in 1949 the International Olympic Committee awarded him the rare Olympic Diploma of Merit. In 1960 Beresford was made Commander of the Order of the British Empire.

Bhaktivedanta, A. C., Swami Prabhupāda, (ABHAY CHARAN DE), Indian religious leader (b. Calcutta, India, Sept. 1, 1896—d. Vrindāvan, India, Nov. 14, 1977), founded (1966) the International Society for Krishna Consciousness, commonly known as the Hare Krishna movement. Bhaktivedanta abandoned his profession as a Calcutta drug manufacturer, broke family ties, and sailed (1965) for Boston, Mass., with only 50 rupees to spread the teachings of the Vedic culture. He maintained that his teachings would profoundly affect the consciousness of a world afflicted with rampant materialism. In 1968 his organization purchased a farm in West Virginia that became a monastic community (ashram). A total of 108 temples were established on five continents.

Biggs, E(dward George) Power, British-born musician (b. Westcliff, England, March 29, 1906—d. Boston, Mass., March 10, 1977), dedicated a major part of his career to reviving in the U.S. the classic organ and the classical style through concert tours and weekly radio broadcasts. Because Biggs was a classicist noted for his reserve, he was inevitably criticized by those who preferred the style of the romanticists. For 25 years Biggs traveled to Europe and played on the classic organs used by such masters as Bach, Handel, and

Bijedic, Dzemal, Yugoslav politician (b. Mostar, Hercegovina, April 12, 1917—d. near Sarajevo, Yugos., Jan. 18, 1977), attempted to curb inflation and strengthen the economy as president of the Federal Executive Council (premier) of Yugoslavia from 1971. After graduating in law from the University of Belgrade, Bijedic, a Muslim, joined the Communist Party in 1939 and fought with Marshal Tito's partisans during World War II. Later, Bijedic held party posts in the republic of Bosnia and Hercegovina and in 1974, during the congress of the League of Communists, was elected to the 39-member Presidium, the most powerful political body in Yugoslavia. He and his wife were killed when their government plane crashed in a snowstorm.

Biko, Steven Bantu, South African black leader (b. King William's Town, near Durban, South Africa, 1947—d. Pretoria, South Africa, Sept. 12, 1977), founded the Black Consciousness movement, the South African Students' Organization, the Black People's Convention, and the Zimele Trust, a fund to aid the families of political prisoners in South Africa. Biko, who sought peaceful reconciliation rather than violent confrontation with white South Africans, was forced by a ban to give up his medical studies at the University of Natal in 1973. He was placed in detention four times and was prosecuted for breaking apartheid regulations. Biko apparently died of unexplained head wounds sustained while he was in police custody. After a three-week inquest, the security police and all others who had dealt with Biko were absolved of all responsibility for his death. Representatives of a number of Western countries attended his funeral, as well as some 20,000 blacks. (*See* SOUTH AFRICA.)

Bolan, Marc (MARK FELD), British rock star (b. London, England, Sept. 30, 1947—d. London, Sept. 16, 1977), was a teenybopper idol who launched a rock music career in the early 1970s with a hit album "Beard of Stars" and a single "Hot Love." Bolan made a solo record in 1965 and with Steve Peregrine Took formed the folk duo Tyrannosaurus Rex (1967), for which he wrote words and music and played the acoustic guitar. Bolan turned to electric "glitter" rock in 1969 with Mickey Finn, and the duo scored major successes for some three years. Bolan was making a comeback on television, with projected tours and recordings to follow, when he was killed in a road accident.

E. Power Biggs

Mozart. He viewed the use of electronic organs (such as the one installed in Carnegie Hall in 1974) as intolerable. Biggs, who studied at the Royal Academy of Music in London, was afflicted with arthritis in his final years and spent more and more time editing organ music.

Braun, Wernher von, German-born space scientist (b. Wirsitz, Germany [now Poland], March 23, 1912—d. Alexandria, Va., June 16, 1977), was already fascinated with space travel when he began building rockets at age 12, and by age 18 was one of a dedicated group of amateurs and engineers experimenting with rockets. After Braun received a Ph.D. in engineering physics (1934) from the University of Berlin, he was employed by the German Army and directed a research team that produced a series of liquid-propellent rockets, notably the V-2 that devastated London in 1944–45. Following World War II, Braun and his team of scientists and engineers surrendered to the U.S. and accepted positions with the U.S. Army Ordnance Department to do research at Ft. Bliss, Texas, and later at Huntsville, Ala. In 1960 Braun and his team were transferred from the U.S. Army Ballistic Missile Agency to the newly formed National Aeronautics and Space Administration (NASA) Marshall Space Flight Center, with Braun serving as its director. The Braun NASA team launched the first U.S. satellite, Explorer 1, on Jan. 31, 1958, and on July 16, 1969, the Apollo 11, which carried the first astronauts to land on the Moon. He retired from NASA in 1972 to become vice-president of Fairchild Indus-

BACHARACH—NASA

tries, Inc., in Germantown, Md. Braun wrote hundreds of articles and several books, including *Across the Space Frontier* (1952), *History of Rocketry and Space Travel* (1966), and *The Rockets' Red Glare* (1976).

Bruce, David Kirkpatrick Este, U.S. diplomat (b. Baltimore, Md., Feb. 12, 1898 – d. Washington, D.C., Dec. 5, 1977), was a skilled and gifted diplomat who served under six successive U.S. presidents, beginning in 1949 when Harry Truman appointed him ambassador to France. Bruce returned to the U.S. in 1952 to become undersecretary of state and in the following year was named special U.S. observer at negotiations aimed at setting up the abortive European Defense Community. After serving with the European High Authority for Coal and Steel, in 1957 he was appointed ambassador to West Germany and in 1961 to Great Britain, where he remained for eight years. Bruce was called out of retirement in 1970 to head the U.S. delegation at the Vietnam peace talks in Paris and in 1973 to become chief delegate of the U.S. liaison office in Peking. His final commission was as chief U.S. representative to NATO from 1974 to 1976. Bruce, who attended law schools at the universities of Virginia and Maryland, also played an important role in the organization of the Office of Strategic Services (forerunner of the Central Intelligence Agency), which he commanded (1943–45) in the European Theatre of Operations.

Budker, Gersh Itskovich, Soviet physicist (b. Murasa, Vinnitsa Province, Ukraine, May 1, 1918 – d. Novosibirsk, U.S.S.R., July 1977), was director (1957–77) of the Nuclear Physics Institute of the Siberian branch of the Soviet Academy of Sciences where he conducted important research on atomic reactors, charged-particle accelerators, and plasma physics. His views on the creation of thermonuclear installations with magnetic traps were known throughout the world. His many publications include *A Stabilized Relativistic Electron Beam* (1956) and *En Route to Anti-Matter* (1963).

Bush, Jack, Canadian artist (b. Toronto, Ont., 1909 – d. Toronto, Jan. 24, 1977), was a founder of Painters Eleven, a Toronto group of artists, who in the 1950s became the first Canadians to devote themselves seriously to abstract colour art. Bush was best known for figure-and-ground abstraction of pure colour and forms inspired by Canadian landscapes. Largely self-taught, he had many shows at home and abroad and was being featured in a touring retrospective exhibition at the time of his death.

Bustamante, Sir William Alexander (WILLIAM ALEXANDER CLARKE), Jamaican politician (b. Blenheim, Jamaica, Feb. 24, 1884 – d. Irish Town, Jamaica, Aug. 6, 1977), was Jamaica's dynamic

first prime minister (1962–67), who helped draft the constitution that made Jamaica an independent nation within the Commonwealth of Nations. An imposing figure, dubbed "the Lion of the Caribbean" because of his fearless attitude toward Fidel Castro, Bustamante inaugurated programs for new schools, housing, roads, and land reforms. The son of a poor Irish planter and a Jamaican mother, Bustamante assumed the surname of the Spanish officer who adopted him. He went to New York in the 1920s, working as a dietician and amassing a small fortune through shrewd investments during the stock market crash. Returning to Jamaica in 1932 an independently wealthy man, Bustamante crusaded for the people, organized the Bustamante Industrial Trade Union, and formed the Jamaica Labour Party. He stepped down as prime minister in 1967 because of poor health.

Cabot, Sebastian, British-born actor (b. London, England, July 6, 1918 – d. Victoria, B.C., Aug. 23, 1977), in the 1966–69 television series "Family Affair" portrayed the portly, bearded "French," who sustained his dignity despite his role as valet-nanny to a bachelor and three children. Cabot, who appeared as a detective in the television series "Checkmate," also played Porthos in a 26-episode version of "The Three Musketeers" on European television. In addition to his many film credits, which include *Ivanhoe, Romeo and Juliet,* and *The Time Machine,* Cabot appeared on Broadway (1947) in *Love for Love.* He was a regular panelist on the television game show "Stump the Stars."

Cain, James Mallahan, U.S. novelist (b. Annapolis, Md., July 1, 1892 – d. University Park, Md., Oct. 27, 1977), was a "tough guy writer of the 1930s" whose violent sexual melodramas shocked and scandalized his readers. His first novel, *The Postman Always Rings Twice,* was tried on obscenity charges in Boston but was revived by Hollywood and adapted to the screen in 1946 after the box office successes of *Double Indemnity* (1944) and *Mildred Pierce* (1945). Although Cain wrote 18 books after graduating (1910) from Washington College in Maryland, his writing reputation rested on *The Postman Always Rings Twice* (1934), *Double Indemnity* (1936), *Serenade* (1937), and *Mildred Pierce* (1941). In his final years Cain studied Shakespeare's sonnets and was working on a contemporary interpretation of Shakespeare's marriage to Anne Hathaway.

Callas, Maria (MARIA KALOGEROPOULOS), U.S. opera singer (b. New York, N.Y., Dec. 2, 1923 – d. Paris, France, Sept. 16, 1977), was a tempestuous soprano whose emotional and dramatic performances led to the revival of the 19th-century bel canto operas. It was not so much her voice as her extraordinary dramatic presence and acting that made Callas one of the great figures of modern opera. Callas made her debut with the Athens

KEYSTONE

Opera in 1945, sang the title role of *La Gioconda* in Verona, Italy, in 1947, and thereafter accepted only leading roles in major operas, primarily at La Scala in Milan. A temperamental artist who regularly canceled engagements, broke contracts, and walked out on performances, Callas elicited international headlines wherever she traveled. In 1952 she refused a contract with the Metropolitan Opera in New York because her husband, Giovanni Battista Meneghini, was unable to obtain a visa, but in 1959 the couple separated after Callas became emotionally involved with shipping magnate Aristotle Onassis. In 1974 an electrified audience witnessed Callas' last public performance in New York's Carnegie Hall.

Carpentier, Marcel Maurice, French general (b. Preuilly-sur-Claise, Indre-et-Loire, France, March 2, 1895 – d. Tours, France, Sept. 14, 1977), commanded the North Atlantic Treaty Organization (NATO) ground forces in Central Europe from 1953 to 1956. In World War I he was wounded ten times and became France's youngest captain at age 20. In World War II he served in North Africa (1940–43) under Gen. Alphonse Juin, as chief of staff with the French Expeditionary Corps in Italy (1943–44), and later under Gen. Jean de Lattre de Tassigny with the French 1st Army. After senior command in Indochina, he became deputy chief of staff to Gen. Dwight D. Eisenhower, NATO supreme commander in Europe, in 1951. After serving as inspector general of the infantry from 1952 to 1953, he returned to NATO until he retired in 1956.

Carr, Sir William Emsley, British newspaper proprietor (b. May 30, 1912 – d. Halland, Sussex, Nov. 14, 1977), was graduated from Clifton and Trinity colleges, Cambridge, before joining his father's *News of the World* organization in 1937. He became chairman of *News of the World* in 1952 and chairman of the parent organization in 1960. Before his tenure in both positions ended in 1969, the companies (known as News International Ltd.) had expanded into British and French television. In 1969 Carr lost control of the family enterprises to Rupert Murdoch, an ambitious Australian, who provided the money needed to prevent Robert Maxwell of Pergamon Press from taking over *News of the World,* the largest English-language Sunday newspaper in the world. Carr, who also served (1960–67) as a director of Reuters, was knighted in 1957.

Casalegno, Carlo, Italian journalist (b. Turin, Italy, Feb. 15, 1916 – d. Turin, Nov. 29, 1977), was deputy editor of *La Stampa,* a Turin daily newspaper with a national circulation of more than 400,000. After studying literature at the University of Turin, Casalegno became a teacher and during World War II joined the Italian resistance movement. He started his journalistic career on the staff of *Il Popolo* in Milan but left to join *Stampa Sera* and later *La Stampa.* Casalegno was shot by extremist Red Brigade terrorists near his home and died 13 days later.

Castle, William, U.S. film producer (b. New York, N.Y., April 24, 1914 – d. Los Angeles, Calif., May 31, 1977), shocked and horrified millions with the production of such spine tinglers as *Rosemary's Baby, Bug,* and *Let's Kill Uncle.* Despite frequent criticism, Castle grossed millions of dollars by using such extravagant promotions as offering ticket holders to *Macabre* an insurance policy promising $1,000 to anyone dying of fright. Castle, who maintained that audiences thrive on surprise, shock, and gimmickry, wired theatre seats to produce mild electric shocks for *The Tingler* and discharged a suspended skeleton into the audience during *The House on Haunted Hill.* He produced and directed over 100 films, one of his most memorable being *Strait-Jacket* (1964), starring Joan Crawford in a gripping dramatic performance.

Chaplin, Charlie (CHARLES SPENCER CHAPLIN), British actor (b. London, England, April 16, 1889 – d. Vevey, Switz., Dec. 25, 1977), captivated audiences around the world as a pathetic but endearing "little tramp" who somehow managed to survive life's hardships with humour and resignation. The caricature that he created included baggy pants, derby hat, tight frock coat, outsized shoes, mustache, and cane. After seven years (1906–13) with the Fred Karno vaudeville troupe, Chaplin made his film debut in *Making a Living* (1914). His first motion picture classic, *The Tramp* (1915), introduced the immortal character

WIDE WORLD

who reappeared in such films as *Shoulder Arms* (1918), *The Kid* (1921), *The Gold Rush* (1925), and *City Lights* (1931). Chaplin's one-reel comedies became so popular that his salary soared from $1,250 a week with Essanay (1915) to $10,000 a week, plus a $150,000 bonus the following year for signing with Mutual Film Corp. When he contracted to make eight pictures with First National (1917) he received $1 million and became his own producer. In 1919 he founded United Artists Corp. together with D. W. Griffith, Mary Pickford, and Douglas Fairbanks and thereafter produced all his own films with the exception of *A Countess from Hong Kong* (1966). Later feature films that achieved critical acclaim included *The Great Dictator* (1940), his first talkie, and the autobiographical *Limelight* (1952). In the 1940s Chaplin was pressured by the U.S. government for payment of back taxes and after the appearance of *Monsieur Verdoux* (1947) he was labeled a subversive, as were many others during the McCarthy era of rampant anti-communism. When Chaplin left the U.S. in 1952 and was informed that his reentry rights would be questioned (he never became a U.S. citizen), he surrendered his reentry permit in Switzerland, where he took up permanent residence. Chaplin, who weathered stormy periods in his life, including three divorces and a paternity suit, was generally recognized as the greatest single personality to emerge in the film industry during its first three-quarters of a century. In 1973 he returned to the U.S. to receive a special award from the Academy of Motion Picture Arts and Sciences, and in 1975 was knighted by Queen Elizabeth II.

Chiang Yee, Chinese scholar (b. Chiu-chiang, Kiangsi Province, China, June 14, 1903 – d. Peking, China, Oct. 17, 1977), was a professor of painting, sculpture, calligraphy, and East Asian languages at Columbia University where he taught for 16 years (1955–71). Chiang, who studied chemistry in Nanking, was noted for his volume *Chinese Calligraphy* (1938) and a series of 11 illustrated travel books which highlighted famous cities of the world. Over a span of 40 years, Chiang wrote and illustrated more than 25 books. Before he left China in 1933, Chiang served as governor of four districts in Kiangsi and Anhwei provinces (1927–32). He was a lecturer in Chinese at London University and a curator at Wellcome Historical Medical Museum in London before joining the faculty at Columbia University.

Chick, Dame Harriette, British nutritionist (b. London, England, Jan. 6, 1875 – d. Cambridge, England, July 9, 1977), carried forward the study of nutrition for over 50 years. After graduating from University College in London, she worked at the Hygienic Institutes of Vienna and Munich under Max Gruber. In 1904 she was made a doctor of science for her work on the function of green algae in polluted waters, and in 1905 she went to the Lister Institute, where she examined disinfectants, blood proteins, and antitoxins. In 1914 she turned from bacteriology to nutrition and recommended that allied soldiers serving in Egypt and Palestine during World War I supplement their diets with dried eggs and dried yeast to combat a nutritional disorder resembling beriberi. In 1919 she jointly led a team to study nutrition and rickets in postwar Vienna and proved that rickets could be treated, cured, and prevented with cod liver oil and exposure to ultraviolet light. Returning to London in 1922, Chick continued her research on proteins and vitamins, particularly vitamin B and cereal protein (which produced Britain's World War II "national loaf" in 1940). Chick retired in 1946, but at the age of 100 attended the annual general meeting of the Lister Institute. She was made a dame of the British Empire in 1949.

Churchill, Lady: *see* SPENCER-CHURCHILL, BARONESS.

Clark, Gregory, Canadian journalist (b. Toronto, Ont., Sept. 25, 1892 – d. Toronto, Feb. 3, 1977), was well known for humorous features that appeared in the *Toronto Star* and the *Toronto Globe and Mail*'s *Weekend* magazine. His talent as a raconteur was often called into play when he spoke of his long friendships with Ernest Hemingway, Morley Callaghan, and Gordon Sinclair. Clark's humorous view of life has been preserved in *Greg's Choice* (1968), *May Your First Love Be Your Last* (1969), and *The Bird of Promise* (1973).

Clark, Tom Campbell, U.S. Supreme Court justice (b. Dallas, Texas, Sept. 23, 1899 – d. New York, N.Y., June 13, 1977), initiated the investigation and prosecution of U.S. Communist leaders for conspiracy while serving (1945–49) as attorney general in the Truman administration. Clark, who was appointed a justice of the Supreme Court in 1949, shifted from conservative to more moderate opinion during the successive tenures of Fred Vinson and Earl Warren as chief justice. Clark's constitutional philosophy was expressed in his support of federal rules excluding illegally obtained evidence, the one-man, one-vote principle in legislative apportionment, and the banning of daily Bible reading in public schools. Clark retired from the Supreme Court in 1967 when his son Ramsey was named U.S. attorney general by Pres. Lyndon B. Johnson. Thereafter he served as a judge in the U.S. Court of Appeals.

Clouzot, Henri-Georges, French film director (b. Niort, France, Nov. 20, 1907 – d. Paris, France, Jan. 12, 1977), was best known internationally for his psychological thrillers *Le Salaire de la peur* (1952; *The Wages of Fear*) and *Les Diaboliques* (1954; *The Fiends*). Clouzot entered the film industry in 1931 as a scriptwriter but turned to directing during World War II, making his mark with *Le Corbeau* (1943; *The Crow*), an acid portrayal of French provincial life that was produced by the German-controlled Continental Films. Clouzot was boycotted for a period after the war, but in 1947 he reestablished himself with *Quai des Orfèvres*, an atmospheric police thriller that won him the director's prize at the Venice Biennale. Subsequent films included *Manon* (1948), *Le Mystère Picasso* (1956; *The Picasso Mystery*), and *La Vérité* (1960; *The Truth*), starring Brigitte Bardot. His last film, *La Prisonnière* (*Woman in Chains*), was released in 1968.

Cobham, Charles John Lyttelton, 10th Viscount, British sportsman and company director (b. Aug. 8, 1909 – d. March 20, 1977), succeeded a long line of service officers as one of the most popular governors-general of New Zealand (1957–62). After returning to England he became lord lieutenant of Worcestershire (1964–74) and lord steward to the queen's household (1967–72). A keen cricketer who captained the Worcestershire County team (1935–39), he was president of the Marylebone Cricket Club (MCC) in 1954. Lord Cobham, who was made a knight of the Garter in 1964, was made a privy councillor in 1967 and became chancellor of the order in 1972.

Cochrane, Sir Ralph (Alexander), British air chief marshal (b. Feb. 24, 1895 – d. Burford, Oxfordshire, England, Dec. 17, 1977), organized the World War II bombing operation that in October 1943 breached the Mohne and Eder dams in Germany. Cochrane began his career in the Royal Naval Air Service, then transferred to the Royal Air Force (RAF) in 1919. After service in the Middle East he became an adviser on air defense in New Zealand and in 1939 was appointed deputy director of intelligence. He returned to Bomber Command as air vice-marshal and organized the Number 5 Group that carried out the spectacular "dambusting" mission on the Ruhr River. He also planned Operation Window, the dropping of metallic strips that confused German radar. Cochrane was made a knight of the British Empire in 1945 and took charge of Transport Command in preparation for operations against Japan. He was made air officer commanding in chief of RAF Flying Training Command in 1947 and air chief marshal in 1950.

Cohen of Birkenhead, Henry Cohen, 1st Baron, British physician (b. Birkenhead, England, Feb. 21, 1900 – d. Bath, England, Aug. 7, 1977), was highly regarded both for his expertise in clinical medicine and for his administrative ability within the British National Health Service (NHS). After graduating with honours in medicine from Liverpool (1924), Cohen was appointed an assistant physician to the Royal Infirmary, Liverpool. In 1934 he became professor of medicine at the University of Liverpool, where he spent the greater part (1934–65) of his professional career. His acute memory and speaking ability served him well when he was called upon to assist in establishing the NHS. He was named first vice-chairman of the Central Health Services Council in 1949 and chairman in 1957. Cohen also served as president of both the British Medical Association (1951) and the General Medical Council (1961). He was knighted in 1949 and raised to the peerage in 1956.

Cole, Edward N., U.S. corporate executive (b. Marne, Mich., Sept. 17, 1909 – d. Kalamazoo, Mich., May 2, 1977), was a mechanical engineer whose automotive innovations and ingenuity earned him the presidency (1967) of General Motors Corp. (GM). The Cole-designed Corvair, introduced in 1969, became a target for consumer advocate Ralph Nader in his book *Unsafe at Any Speed*. Although subsequent government regulations regarding safety and pollution displeased Cole, he ordered GM engineers to meet the new standards. Intent on building a more efficient taxicab, Cole purchased control of Checker Motors following his retirement from GM in 1974.

Cone, Fairfax Mastick, U.S. advertising executive (b. San Francisco, Calif., Feb. 21, 1903 – d. Carmel, Calif., June 20, 1977), was the co-founder

(1942), chairman of the board (1948–51), president (1951–57), and director emeritus of the Foote, Cone & Belding advertising agency, whose prestigious clientele included major marketers of soaps, facial tissue, greeting cards, and other consumer items. Cone's straightforward and direct approach to advertising was in marked contrast to the so-called creative revolution in the 1960s that flooded the media with ads based on sex appeal. His pungent office memorandums, called "Blue Streaks," criticized this innovation and were later circulated throughout the industry.

Conway, William Cardinal, Irish prelate (b. Belfast, Ireland [now Northern Ireland], Jan. 22, 1913—d. Armagh, Northern Ireland, April 17, 1977), was archbishop of Armagh and primate of All Ireland. As leader of the island's Roman Catholics he made countless pleas for an end to bloodshed. Conway, who condemned the civil turmoil in Northern Ireland, referred to both Protestant and Catholic terrorists as "monsters." A theological scholar whose counsel was sought by several popes, Conway was placed on several papal commissions and gave advice on modernizing the church. Educated at Queen's University, Belfast, and at St. Patrick's College, Maynooth, he was ordained in 1937 and awarded a doctorate of divinity in 1938. In 1958 he was made auxiliary bishop to John Cardinal D'Alton, archbishop of Armagh, and in 1962 accompanied him to the Second Vatican Council in Rome. Conway succeeded D'Alton in 1963 and was made a cardinal in 1965.

Corcoran, Fred, U.S. golf executive (b. Cambridge, Mass., April 4, 1905—d. New York, N.Y., June 23, 1977), was the tournament manager (1936–47) of the Professional Golfers' Association (PGA) whose ingenuity prompted widespread enthusiasm for golf as both a participant and a spectator sport. Corcoran, who helped initiate the Ladies' Professional Golf Association in 1950, overcame numerous problems to establish the professional golf tour as a prosperous business. A promotional director (1952–55) of the PGA, Corcoran was rebuffed by sports directors when he suggested television coverage of golf, later a million-dollar enterprise. Corcoran, who almost single-handedly organized and managed the World Cup, an annual championship consisting of two-man teams from over 45 countries, also improvised the modern scoreboard with a fistful of crayons at a U.S. Open tournament.

Cortez, Ricardo (JACK KRANTZ), U.S. actor (b. Vienna, Austria, Sept. 19, 1889—d. New York, N.Y., April 28, 1977), was a silent screen idol of the 1920s who played opposite such glamour queens as Greta Garbo, Gloria Swanson, Joan Crawford, Irene Dunne, and Claudette Colbert. Cortez, cast in the role of a dark, handsome Latin lover in such films as *The Torrent, Thirteen Women,* and *Torch Singer,* had no Spanish blood. After his final screen role, *The Last Hurrah* (1958), Cortez joined a brokerage firm in New York.

Cotzias, George C., Greek-born neurologist (b. Canea, Crete, June 16, 1918—d. New York, N.Y., June 13, 1977), was a research scientist whose systematic and persistent investigations into the metabolism of the brain proved that Levo-dihydroxyphenylalanine (L-dopa) could reverse most or all major manifestations of Parkinson's disease, a chronic malady affecting the central nervous system. His revolutionary therapeutic agent remedied the deficiency of dopamine in the brain, thereby eliminating the need for brain surgery. L-dopa, which was introduced into the practice of medicine in the 1970s, proved effective against brain damage from manganese poisoning and remained the preferred treatment for patients afflicted with Parkinson's disease, despite its sometimes toxic side effects.

Cox, Warren Earle, U.S. antique dealer (b. Oak Park, Ill., Aug. 27, 1895—d. New York, N.Y., May 22, 1977), was a specialist in Oriental art whose first financial success came from converting rare antiques into lamps and selling them to wealthy buyers. This aspect of his life was detailed in *Lighting and Lamp Design* (1952). Although Cox was disinherited by his father, a one-time part-owner of Encyclopædia Britannica, he gradually accumulated a sizable fortune in ceramics and Chinese porcelain. As art director of the 14th edition (1929) of the *Encyclopædia Britannica,* Cox had a rare opportunity to utilize the vast storehouse of knowledge he had amassed through years of study. *The Book of Pottery and Porcelain* (1944) has long been a standard reference for connoisseurs and art historians.

Crathorne, Thomas Lionel Dugdale, 1st Baron, British politician (b. London, England, July 20, 1897—d. Crathorne, Cleveland, England, March 26, 1977), was a Conservative member of Parliament from 1929 to 1959 who held appointments as deputy chief government whip (1941–42) and vice-chairman of the Conservative Party Organization (1942–44). Having been created a baronet in 1945, Dugdale became his party's spokesman on agricultural matters during the first post-World War II Labour government, and on the Conservatives' return to power in 1951 he was made minister of agriculture and fisheries. In 1954 he resigned as a result of the so-called Crichel Down affair, when a public inquiry strongly criticized ministry officials for the way they disposed of compulsorily acquired farmland. On retiring from Parliament in 1959 he was raised to the peerage, and chaired various public committees.

Crawford, Joan (LUCILLE LESUEUR), U.S. actress (b. San Antonio, Texas, March 23, 1908—d. New York, N.Y., May 10, 1977), was a multifaceted screen star whose dramatic performances as a waitress, blackmailer, prostitute, and schizophrenic enshrined her as one of Hollywood's perennial stars. After a stint in nightclubs as Billie Cassin, she changed her name to Joan Crawford and danced her way to film stardom in *Our Dancing Daughters* (1928), *Dance Fools, Dance* (1931), and *Dancing Lady* (1933). Crawford, who competed with Greta Garbo, Norma Shearer, and Greer Garson for challenging roles, broke with Metro-

KEYSTONE

Goldwyn-Mayer and in 1943 joined Warner Brothers, where she manipulated directors and producers to gain better scripts. A major turning point in her career came when she won an Academy Award as best actress in *Mildred Pierce* (1945). Thereafter, the dynamic Crawford played in a multitude of films, and in 1962 starred in

What Ever Happened to Baby Jane?, the first of many suspense thrillers. Crawford, who married four times and adopted four children, remained grande dame of the screen world until her death. From 1959 she was a director of the Pepsi-Cola Co.

Crosby, Bing (HARRY LILLIS CROSBY), U.S. entertainer (b. Tacoma, Wash., May 2, 1904—d. near Madrid, Spain, Oct. 14, 1977), was possibly the most universally admired entertainer in all of show business and certainly one of its most enduring stars. Though he could not read music, he had an unfailing sense of rhythm that, coupled with a nonchalant style that belied the care with which he prepared his numbers, gave modern music a uniquely smooth and carefree air. Crosby began his career in 1927 as one of the Rhythm Boys with Paul Whiteman's orchestra and four years later appeared in the early talkie *King of Jazz.* During the dismal days of the Depression his popularity soared as more and more people came to know him through his upbeat songs. In the 1940s Crosby starred on radio and showed a flair for comedy in a series of "Road" films with Bob Hope and Dorothy Lamour. He made "White Christmas" a sentimental favourite dur-

LONDON DAILY EXPRESS/PICTORIAL PARADE

ing and after World War II; it was surpassed in sales only by his rendition of "Silent Night." In 1944 Crosby won an Academy Award for his performance in *Going My Way,* but he gained equal critical acclaim as an alcoholic in *The Country Girl* (1954). His personal favourite, however, was *High Society* (1956), during which he crooned "True Love" to Grace Kelly. Crosby had four sons by his first wife, Dixie Lee, who died in 1952. Five years later he married Kathryn Grant, who bore him two sons and a daughter. Shortly before Crosby collapsed and died after a round of golf on a course outside Madrid, he had completed arrangements with Hope and Lamour for a final "Road" film to be called *The Road to the Fountain of Youth.*

Crosland, (Charles) Anthony Raven, British politician (b. London, England, Aug. 29, 1918—d. Oxford, England, Feb. 19, 1977), was appointed secretary of state for foreign and Commonwealth affairs in April 1976. He also served as minister of state for economic affairs (1964–65), secretary of state for education and science (1965–67), president of the Board of Trade (1967–69), secretary of state for local government and regional planning (1969–70), and minister for environment (1974–76). His studies at Trinity College, Oxford, were interrupted by active service during World War

Obituaries

II. Crosland lectured in economics there from 1947 until 1950, when he became a Labour member of Parliament. He established his reputation as a political philosopher and concluded in *The Future of Socialism* (1956) and other writings that a mixed economy is essential to democracy and state collectivism is incompatible with liberty. In his bid for the party leadership after Sir Harold Wilson resigned (March 1976), Crosland finished last among six candidates.

Dery, Tibor, Hungarian author (b. Budapest, Austria-Hungary, Oct. 18, 1894—d. Budapest, Hungary, Aug. 18, 1977), was a gifted writer of novels, short stories, and plays whose support for the 1956 Hungarian uprising brought him a nine-year prison sentence. Dery joined the March 1919 revolution that briefly brought Bela Kun to power; after its collapse, Dery went into exile in Western Europe. He returned to Hungary on the eve of World War II and was imprisoned by the Horthy regime. In 1945 he again joined the pro-Soviet revolutionary movement, but after a decade he became disillusioned with Matyas Rakosi's regime and joined other intellectuals who favoured an uprising against Stalinist tyranny. Though the insurrection failed, Dery continued to insist that the revolt expressed "the will of the people." He was imprisoned, but was paroled in 1960 and pardoned a year later. In 1973 he was awarded the Kossuth Prize for literature. His best works available in English include *The Giant* (1964) and *The Portuguese Princess* (1966), a collection of short stories.

Devine, Andy (ANDREW DEVINE), U.S. actor (b. Flagstaff, Ariz., Oct. 7, 1905—d. Orange, Calif., Feb. 18, 1977), reached the height of his popularity in the role of Jingles, a merry, crackly voiced deputy sheriff in the television series "Wild Bill Hickok," which starred Guy Madison in the 1950s. Devine's vocal cords were permanently damaged in childhood when he fell with a stick in his mouth. His successful transition from si-

PHOTO TRENDS

lent films to talkies was assured when he turned his affliction into a comic asset. During his long career, Devine appeared in over 300 films, usually as a bumbling sidekick of fast-shooting cowboys.

Dorfman, Nat N., U.S. press agent (b. New York, N.Y., Nov. 18, 1895—d. New York, July 3, 1977), was a newspaper reporter for the *American* whose assignments brought him into contact with such personalities as George M. Cohan, David Warfield, and the Barrymores and sparked his interest in becoming a press agent for the the-

atre. Dorfman, who promoted more than 300 Broadway plays and musicals, also spent several years in Hollywood writing for Metro-Goldwyn-Mayer, 20th Century, and Columbia Pictures. A part-time playwright, Dorfman wrote *Take My Tip* (1934), *Errant Lady* (1934), and several sketches for the musicals *Blackbirds* and *Rhapsody in Black*. Taking his leave of Broadway in 1960, Dorfman served as public-information director of the New York City Opera, where he handled the press for more than 2,500 performances until his retirement in 1977.

DuBois, Shirley Graham, U.S. writer (b. Evansville, Ind., Nov. 11, 1907—d. Peking, China, March 27, 1977), was a longtime sympathizer and supporter of leftist causes and organizations as was her husband, William DuBois, co-founder of the National Association for the Advancement of Colored People (NAACP) and self-proclaimed Communist. In 1961 the couple relinquished their U.S. citizenship, moved to Ghana at the invitation of Pres. Kwame Nkrumah, and became associated with the Communist Party. Before her marriage to DuBois, Shirley Graham studied musical composition at the Sorbonne in Paris and wrote two operas and eight books, most of which are biographies. Following the death of her husband (1963) and the overthrow of Nkrumah (1967), DuBois fled to Cairo, where she lived for several years. DuBois, who made five visits to China, died of cancer while under the care of Peking physicians.

Duhamel, Jacques, French parliamentarian (b. Paris, France, Sept. 24, 1924—d. Paris, July 8, 1977), was a lawyer by profession who began an administrative career in the Departments of Finance and Justice but entered active politics as a centrist deputy for Dole in 1962; he was reelected in 1967 and 1968. In 1969 he was a founder of the Centre Démocratie et Progrès, a liberal, reformist party. After Gen. Charles de Gaulle's resignation and Georges Pompidou's election as president in 1969, Duhamel served as minister of agriculture (1969–71) and then as minister of culture until illness forced him to retire in 1973.

Eccles, Marriner Stoddard, U.S. business executive (b. Logan, Utah, Sept. 9, 1890—d. Salt Lake City, Utah, Dec. 18, 1977), was a prominent banker and industrialist whose business interests included mining, shipping, construction, sugar, and lumber, but who was better known in public circles as chairman (1936–48) of the Board of Governors of the Federal Reserve System during the administration of Pres. Franklin D. Roosevelt. Eccles helped shape the New Deal, expanded credit for U.S. European allies and for domestic arms industries during World War II, and restored the independence of the Federal Reserve System after the war. Although Eccles was not reappointed chairman in 1948 by Pres. Harry S. Truman, he served on the Board of Governors until 1951.

Eda, Saburo, Japanese politician (b. Okayama Prefecture, Japan, July 29, 1907—d. Tokyo, Japan, May 22, 1977), was a leader and co-founder after World War II of the Japan Socialist Party (JSP), the major political opposition to the ruling Liberal-Democrats. In 1962, at odds with Peking over its attempts to "force its ideology" on the JSP, he publicly voiced his disagreement and lost his position as secretary-general. Eda summed up his ideal of Japanese socialism as a marriage of American material progress, Soviet social security, the British parliamentary system, and Japan's constitution that outlawed war. In 1975 Eda visited the U.S. as leader of six Japanese socialists who were seeking an exchange of views with American officials and political leaders. After losing his seat in the lower house of the Diet in December 1976, he left the JSP in March 1977 intending to run in the July parliamentary election as the head of a new, more moderate Socialist Citizens' League.

Eden, (Robert) Anthony: see AVON, (ROBERT), ANTHONY EDEN, 1ST EARL.

Eglevsky, André, Russian-born dancer (b. Moscow, U.S.S.R., Dec. 21, 1917—d. Elmira, N.Y., Dec. 4, 1977), was a leading classical ballet dancer noted for his skillful techniques, spectacular control, and the smoothness and ease with which he performed pirouettes. Eglevsky, who emigrated to France with his mother during the Bolshevik Revolution, was trained in the traditional style and technique of the Imperial Russian Ballet by such dancers as Lubov Egorova, Mathilde Kschessinskaya, and Alexandre Volinine in Paris and by Nicholas Legat in London. His first performance at age 14 with Col. W. de Basil's Ballet Russe de Monte Carlo marked the beginning of an illustrious career in Europe and the U.S. Eglevsky danced with René Blum-Michel Fokine Ballets de Monte Carlo, American Ballet, and Ballet Theatre (now American Ballet Theatre) before joining the New York City Ballet, where he had leading roles in *Scotch Symphony* (1952) and *Caracole* (1952; now called Divertimento No. 15) during his seven years with the company (1951–58). He also gave life to the characters of Albrecht in *Giselle*, Siegfried in *Swan Lake*, Paris in *Helen of Troy*, and Tristan in *Mad Tristan*. In 1961, following his retirement as a performer, he formed the Eglevsky Ballet and continued to instruct aspiring dancers.

Eiseley, Loren Corey, U.S. anthropologist (b. Lincoln, Neb., Sept. 3, 1907—d. Philadelphia, Pa., July 9, 1977), eloquently expounded his theories on the mysteries of man and nature in a poetic style that bridged the gap between art and science. Eiseley perhaps best expressed the motiva-

WIDE WORLD

tion for his career as writer, scientist, and educator in the essay "The Enchanted Glass," which concerns the role of the contemplative naturalist in a technological world. He recalled in his autobiography, *All the Strange Hours* (1975), that his interest in anthropology had been kindled under the influence of William Duncan Strong. Eiseley's national reputation was established through such books as *The Immense Journey* (1957), *The Mind as Nature* (1962), *The Invisible Pyramid* (1970), and *The Night Country* (1971).

Elder, Ruth, U.S. aviatrix (b. Anniston, Ala., 1904—d. San Francisco, Calif., Oct. 9, 1977), made a daring but unsuccessful attempt (Oct. 11, 1927) to become the first woman to fly across the Atlantic Ocean. Thirty-six hours after Elder and her co-pilot, George Haldeman, took off from Roosevelt Field in New York, their airplane, "The American Girl," began losing oil pressure and was forced to land at sea. The pair were rescued and taken aboard a Dutch tanker moments before the aircraft exploded in the water. When Elder returned to New York, she was greeted with a $250,000 contract for a nationwide vaudeville tour and later starred in two Hollywood silent films.

Embry, Sir Basil Edward, British air chief marshal (b. Barnwood, Gloucestershire, England, Feb. 28, 1902 – d. Boyup Brook, Western Australia, Dec. 8, 1977), was a formidable and often-decorated fighter and bomber pilot before becoming a commander in chief with NATO after World War II. He joined the Royal Air Force (RAF) in 1921 and was assigned to Iraq until 1927. After a course at the RAF Staff College, he was posted to the North-West Frontier, India. Embry was stationed at the RAF's Indian headquarters when he was given command (1937) of an army cooperation squadron. He was with the Air Ministry in London at the outbreak of World War II and assigned to a bomber squadron. After being shot down near Dunkirk and escaping to Spain, he returned to England and accepted the lower rank of wing commander in order to command a night-fighter wing on the coast. In May 1943, having been promoted to air vice-marshal, he commanded Number 2 Group, which supported the Allied invasion of Normandy by pinpoint bombings of targets from Denmark to northern France. In 1949 he was appointed air officer commanding in chief, Fighter Command. His last appointment (1953–56) was as commander in chief, Allied Air Forces Central Europe, NATO.

Erhard, Ludwig, German statesman (b. Fürth, Bavaria, Germany, Feb. 4, 1897 – d. Bonn, West Germany, May 5, 1977), became the second chancellor of the Federal Republic of Germany (1963–66) after serving as its economics minister (1949–63); he was credited with formulating and implementing programs that led to West Germany's extraordinary economic recovery after World War II. Erhard studied at Frankfurt University and in 1928 joined the Institute of Industrial Research at Nürnberg, where he later served as chairman until the Nazis dismissed him in 1942. After the war he was appointed economics minister in the Bavarian administration (1946), and when the U.S. and Britain merged their two occupied zones of Germany into one, he became director of economics at Frankfurt am Main. In the first federal German elections in 1949 he won the Ulm constituency for the Christian Democrats and joined Konrad Adenauer's first government as economics minister. He remained in that post until 1963, when he succeeded Adenauer as chancellor. He stimulated trade and industry through free competition, introduced currency reform, and, with U.S. aid, rapidly transformed West Germany's economy into the most prosperous in Europe. After the 1957 victory of the Christian Democrats, Adenauer made Erhard his vice-chancellor but bitterly contested his natural succession to the chancellorship until Erhard was nominated by his party in 1963 and duly elected chancellor on October 16. Erhard's laissez-faire policy had nurtured his country's "economic miracle," but he was ineffectual in dealing with major problems of foreign policy. Relations with both the U.S. and France

SVEN SIMON/KATHERINE YOUNG

ran into difficulties, although full diplomatic relations were established with Israel. Finally, in 1966, faced with the prospect of tax increases to meet a budget deficit, the Free Democrats left the coalition formed with the Christian Democrats and Chancellor Erhard resigned on November 30.

Faulkner of Downpatrick, (Arthur) Brian (Deane) Faulkner, Baron, British politician (b. Northern Ireland, Feb. 18, 1921 – d. near Saintfield, Northern Ireland, March 3, 1977), succeeded James Chichester-Clark as prime minister (1971–72) of Northern Ireland at a time when violence had reached such proportions that Great Britain, heeding the demands of the Unionists for more forceful action, suspended the Stormont (Northern Ireland parliament) and assumed direct control over the territory. In a further attempt to restore law and order, Faulkner persuaded the British government to back the internment of suspected terrorists. After the Sunningdale conference of December 1973, he became (1974) chief executive member of the short-lived Northern Ireland Executive. Faulkner first entered Stormont as a Unionist member in 1949 and held the office of chief whip from 1956 to 1959. He later served as minister of commerce (1963–69) and development (1969–71). After the suspension of Stormont he was a Unionist member of the subsequent Assembly (1973–75) and then of the constitutional convention (1975–76). In August 1976 he withdrew from politics and in the new year honours was made a life peer. Faulkner, a keen horseman and fox hunter, was killed in a riding accident.

Fedin, Konstantin Aleksandrovich, Soviet writer (b. Saratov, Russia, Nov. 24, 1892 – d. U.S.S.R., July 15, 1977), gained official approval for his writings when he moved from pre-Revolutionary romantic lyricism and nostalgia to the approved school of Socialist Realism. Fedin's first novels, including *Cities and Years* (1924) and *The Brothers* (1928), described intellectuals who became disillusioned with the Bolshevik Revolution, but when *The Rape of Europe* (1933), *First Joys* (1945; Eng. trans., 1950), and *An Unusual Summer* (1948; Eng. trans., 1950) emerged it was clear that Fedin had become a conformist. He was awarded the Order of Lenin several times, was made a deputy to the Supreme Soviet of the U.S.S.R. and a member of the editorial board of the magazine *Novy Mir*, and in 1959 was appointed first secretary of the Union of U.S.S.R. Writers.

Ferris, Daniel J., U.S. sports executive (b. Pauling, N.Y., July 7, 1889 – d. Amityville, Long Island, N.Y., May 2, 1977), was an official of the U.S. Amateur Athletic Union (AAU) for seven decades and a U.S. sports representative to some 40 countries. He joined the AAU in 1907 as secretary to the president and became secretary-treasurer of the organization in 1927, a post he held until his retirement in 1957. For the next 20 years he continued to report daily to the AAU office. Ferris was extremely strict in his interpretation of what constituted amateur status. As a consequence of his decisions, Jim Thorpe was deprived of his 1912 Olympic gold medals for having briefly played professional baseball, Lee Calhoun was suspended from track events for one year for getting married on a national television show, and Eleanor Holm was dropped from the 1936 Olympic swimming team for drinking champagne. Ferris is also remembered for welcoming black participants to major competitions. In 1926, about two decades before Jackie Robinson became the first black athlete to play professional baseball, the AAU switched its national championships to Lincoln, Neb., because a black athlete was not acceptable to authorities in New Orleans, La.

Finch, Peter (WILLIAM MITCHELL), British actor (b. London, England, Sept. 28, 1916 – d. Los Angeles, Calif., Jan. 14, 1977), won the Academy Award (1977) for best actor for his portrayal in

Network of Howard Beale, a television anchorman who becomes demented when his job is threatened because of falling ratings. Finch was the first person to be awarded an Oscar posthumously. After working as a waiter, reporter, magazine salesman, and small-time actor in both Australia and England, he was discovered by Laurence Olivier. Having been signed to a personal contract by Olivier, Finch performed at the Old Vic in London and completed some 35 films during his acting career.

Flickenschildt, Elisabeth, German actress (b. Hamburg, Germany, ' March 16, 1905 – d. Stade, West Germany, Oct. 26, 1977), was a leading personality in the German theatre before and after World War II, known especially for her highly mannered style and eccentricities. Flickenschildt established her reputation with the great actor and director Gustaf Gründgens in Berlin, Düsseldorf, and Hamburg and played such roles as Brecht's Mother Courage and Shakespeare's Lady Macbeth. She also starred as Volumnia in Shakespeare's *Coriolanus* and acted in plays by Schiller, Goethe, and T. S. Eliot.

Frend, Charles, British film director (b. Pulborough, England, Nov. 21, 1909 – d. London, England, Jan. 8, 1977), was associated with some of the best action films produced by Ealing Studios; his own most notable success was *The Cruel Sea* (1953). Working at British International Pictures, Elstree, and then for Gaumont-British Picture Corp. Ltd., he edited MGM's *A Yank at Oxford* and *Goodbye, Mr. Chips* in the 1930s. His own films, made at Ealing, included *San Demetrio-London* (1943), *Johnny Frenchman* (1944), *Scott of the Antarctic* (1948), *The Long Arm* (1955), and the comedy *A Run for Your Money* (1949). He later directed various television series, including "Interpol" and "Danger Man."

Gabo, Naum (NAUM NEEMIA PEVSNER), Russian-born artist (b. Briansk, Russia, Aug. 5, 1890 – d. Waterbury, Conn., Aug. 23, 1977), was a leader in the Constructivist movement in art which rejected the use of traditional materials in favour of glass, metal, and plastic. Gabo studied medicine, natural science, and engineering at the University of Munich, and following his return to Russia formulated and issued (1920) the Realistic Manifesto, a document that affirmed the value of space and motion as sculptural elements, over mass and immobility. Two years later Gabo traveled to the All-Russian Exhibition in Berlin, where he lived for ten years, and later he settled in France (1932), England (mid-1930s), and finally the U.S. (1946), where he taught (1953–54) at the Harvard University Graduate School of Design. His works include paintings, drawings, and such sculptures as "Spiral Theme," "Translucent Variation on Spheric Theme," and an 80-ft vertical composition in metal and plastic erected in the plaza of the Bijenkorf Building in Rotterdam.

Gilroy, Norman Thomas Cardinal, Australian Roman Catholic prelate (b. Sydney, Australia, Jan. 22, 1896–d. Sydney, Oct. 21, 1977), was archbishop of Sydney (1940–71) when he became the first Australian to be made a cardinal (1946). A graduate of the Marist Brothers' School, he trained and was ordained in Rome and was appointed secretary to the apostolic delegate to Australasia. After serving as chancellor of the diocese of Lismore, New South Wales, he was made bishop of Port Augusta, South Australia, in 1935. Two years later he was appointed coadjutor to the archbishop of Sydney, whom he succeeded.

Goldmark, Peter Carl, U.S. engineer (b. Budapest, Hungary, Dec. 2, 1906–d. Westchester County, N.Y., Dec. 7, 1977), developed the first colour television system used in commercial broadcasts (1940) and the 33⅓-rpm long-playing (LP) phonograph record (1948), both while working for the Columbia Broadcasting System (CBS) Laboratories from 1936 to 1971. The LP, which permitted the equivalent of six 78-rpm records to be compressed into one 33⅓-rpm record, was a major innovation in the recording industry. Goldmark, who became a vice-president of CBS in 1950 and president of CBS Laboratories in 1954, was also credited with the development of an electronic video recording (EVR) system and a scanning system that allowed spacecraft to relay photographs 238,000 mi from the Moon to Earth.

LISI STEINER—KEYSTONE

Two weeks before his death, Goldmark was awarded the National Medal of Science by Pres. Jimmy Carter for his contributions to communications, education, and culture.

Gollan, John, British Communist (b. Edinburgh, Scotland, April 2, 1911–d. London, England, Sept. 5, 1977), was general secretary of the Communist Party of Great Britain from 1956 to 1975. Gollan joined the Communist Party at age 16 and served a six-month prison sentence at 20 for distributing antimilitarist literature to soldiers. He also edited the *Young Worker* newspaper and became secretary of the Young Communist League. After serving as party secretary for Scotland during World War II, he went to London and became assistant editor of the party's national newspaper, the *Daily Worker* (later *Morning Star*), before succeeding Harry Pollitt as party general secretary.

Goscinny, René, French cartoon author (b. Paris, France, Aug. 14, 1926–d. Paris, Nov. 5, 1977), created the comic strip character Astérix the Gaul and his friend Obélix. Throughout a series of 23 adventures, the indomitable Gaul steadfastly refused to yield his native homestead to the Roman legions. The strip, illustrated by Albert Uderzo, was translated into 15 languages, and after its appearance in book form (1959) sold 18 million copies worldwide. Goscinny, who was educated in Buenos Aires, Arg., worked with children's books in New York before returning to Paris (1951) to direct a press agency. He also created the cowboy Lucky Luke, another immensely popular cartoon character.

Gouin, Félix, French politician (b. Peypin, Bouches-du-Rhône, France, Oct. 4, 1884–d. Nice, France, Oct. 25, 1977), was president of the provisional government of France from January to June 1946. A lawyer, he joined the Socialist Party and was elected a parliamentary deputy for Bouches-du-Rhône in 1924. Gouin was one of the 80 deputies who voted against according plenary power to Marshal Philippe Pétain during the occupation of France in 1940. In 1942 he joined Gen. Charles de Gaulle's Free French administration, and after the Allied landings in North Africa he was elected president of the Consultative Assembly in Algiers, which later moved to liberated Paris. In October 1945 he was elected to the Constituent Assembly that confirmed de Gaulle as head of the provisional government, and in November he became the Assembly president. When de Gaulle suddenly resigned in January 1946, Gouin held the office until June, afterward became deputy prime minister to Georges Bidault and then minister of state under Paul Ramadier. He retired from politics in 1958.

Grauer, Benjamin Franklin, U.S. radio announcer (b. New York, N.Y., June 2, 1908–d. New York, May 31, 1977), joined NBC in 1930, fresh out of college, and during the next 43 years became one of the network's most reliable radio and television reporters and a master of improvisation. NBC assigned him to cover the 1932 Olympic Games in Los Angeles, the national political conventions of 1948—the first ever televised—and the U.S. visit of Pope Paul VI in 1965. Most Americans, however, identified Grauer as the man who stood in Times Square on New Year's Eve counting down the final seconds before midnight.

Green, George Kenneth, U.S. physicist (b. St. David, Ill., Nov. 3, 1911–d. Brownsville, Texas, Aug. 15, 1977), designed and supervised the construction of atomic particle accelerators, notably the cosmotron and the alternating gradient synchrotron at Brookhaven National Laboratory in New York. Green, who graduated from the University of Illinois, where he earned a Ph.D. in physics, entered the Army Signal Corps (1942), where he helped invent the proximity fuse, a triggering mechanism for firing artillery and rockets. He joined Brookhaven in 1947 as a senior scientist and established himself as one of the world's finest particle accelerator designers.

Gribov, Aleksey Nikolayevich, Soviet actor (b. Moscow, Russia, Jan. 31, 1902–d. Moscow, U.S.S.R., Dec. 4, 1977), was celebrated for his wry and comic caricature of the Russian national character on stage, film, and television. Gribov, who joined the Moscow Art Theatre in 1924 after graduating from its Third Studio, made his debut as Mr. Craggs in Charles Dickens' *The Battle of Life.* His most successful roles included Dostigayev in Gorky's *Yegor Bulychev,* Yepikhodov in Chekhov's *The Cherry Orchard,* and Sobakevich in Gogol's *Dead Souls.*

Haagen-Smit, Arie Jan, Dutch-born biochemist (b. Utrecht, Neth., Dec. 22, 1900–d. Pasadena, Calif., March 17, 1977), conducted ozone experiments that dramatically demonstrated the then little-understood dangers of air pollution. As a result of Haagen-Smit's work, pollution of the air was viewed for the first time as a serious and urgent problem. Almost single-handedly Haagen-Smit battled oil and auto industries, who were blamed for the chemical pollutants emanating from petroleum facilities and auto exhausts. An outstanding teacher and research scientist at the California Institute of Technology (1937–1971), Haagen-Smit received such honours as the Hodgkins Medal of the Smithsonian Institution and the $150,000 John and Alice Tyler Ecology Award.

Hafez, Abdel Halim (ABDEL HALIM SHABANA), Egyptian singer (b. Halawat, Egypt, 1930–d. London, England, March 30, 1977), was crowned "the Tan Nightingale" by the Arab world for his emotional renditions of romantic and nationalistic songs. No one was considered his equal in singing such songs as *Safini Marra* and *Ala Kad el Shouk.* Despite Hafez' love of native Egyptian music, he felt that the Moog synthesizer (akin to an electronic organ) and other Western instruments could enrich the music that he sang. After his first film, *Lahn El Wafaa* (1954), Hafez began yearly treatments in London for bilharzia, an infectious parasitic disease that eventually took his life. Over 100,000 grief-stricken mourners thronged the streets of Cairo as the funeral procession made its way through the city.

Hambro, Edvard, Norwegian jurist and diplomat (b. Oslo, Norway, Aug. 22, 1911–d. France, Feb. 1, 1977), was Norway's permanent representative to the UN from 1966 to 1971 and president of the 25th UN General Assembly (1970–71). Hambro was a member of the Norwegian government in exile in London during World War II and in 1946 became first registrar of the International Court of Justice at The Hague. In 1959 he was appointed professor of law at the Norwegian School of Economics and Business Administration in Bergen and from 1961 to 1966 represented Bergen as Conservative member of the Storting (parliament). In 1976 he was named Norwegian ambassador to France. He also served on the International Law Commission and with the Institute of International Law.

Haston, Dougal, Scottish mountaineer (b. Currie, near Edinburgh, Scotland, April 19, 1940–d. Leysin, Switz., Jan. 17, 1977), reached the summit of Mt. Everest by the southwest face with Doug Scott in Chris Bonnington's expedition in September 1975. Haston's notable climbs included his direct winter ascents of the Eiger (1966) and the Matterhorn (1967), the ascent of Annapurna via the south face (1970), and a difficult route up Mt. McKinley in Alaska (1976). Haston, who wrote *The Eiger* (1974) and an autobiography, *In High Places* (1972), took part in several documentary films about climbing and was understudy for Clint Eastwood in the film *The Eiger Sanction.* He was killed by an avalanche while skiing at Leysin, where he had become director of John Harlin's International School of Mountaineering after Harlin's death in 1966.

Hawks, Howard, U.S. film director (b. Goshen, Ind., May 30, 1896–d. Palm Springs, Calif., Dec. 26, 1977), was a leading motion-picture director whose films reflected a consistent personal style within the framework of their respective genres. His first important film, *A Girl in Every Port* (1928), was followed by international favourites that included such adventures as *The Dawn Patrol* (1930), *Only Angels Have Wings* (1939), and *Hatari!* (1962); such gangster films as *Scarface* (1932) and *To Have and Have Not* (1944); and a series of westerns including *Rio Bravo* (1959) and *El Dorado* (1967). Hawks, who was generally regarded as one of Hollywood's top four motion-picture directors, received an honorary Academy Award in 1975.

Heezen, Bruce Charles, U.S. oceanographer (b. Vinton, Iowa, April 11, 1924–d. near

Reykjanes, Iceland, June 21, 1977), confirmed through his maps and expeditions with Maurice Ewing that the several great sections of the known active oceanic ridges and rifts form a continuous 45,000-mi network. Heezen, whose findings constituted a landmark in geology and lent credence to the theory of plate tectonics, also discovered the role of underwater flows of suspended sediments, called turbidity currents, in shaping the contours of the sea floor. Heezen used deep-diving submarines to explore sea-floor features, and at the time of his death was aboard the navy research submarine NR-1 en route to submerged mid-Atlantic mountains off the coast of Iceland.

Helpern, Milton, U.S. forensic pathologist (b. East Harlem, N.Y., April 17, 1902—d. San Diego, Calif., April 22, 1977), was a key witness in numerous murder trials during the more than 40 years he spent as a medical examiner for New York City. His uncanny ability to uncover and interpret evidence was often a decisive factor in convicting the guilty and freeing the innocent. Colleagues called Helpern "Sherlock Holmes with a microscope," and police officers were of-

ten awed by his seemingly limitless knowledge of his field. Helpern contributed to *Legal Medicine: Pathology and Toxicology,* a 1,350-page work that became a classic in its field and a favourite source book for writers of mystery stories.

Hershey, Lewis Blaine, U.S. general (b. Steuben County, Ind., Sept. 12, 1893—d. Angola, Ind., May 20, 1977), spent four years (1936–40) with the War Department General Staff and with the joint Army and Navy Selective Service Committee before being named deputy director (1940) and director (1941) of the Selective Service Sys-

tem. During the war in Vietnam Hershey became a prime target for those who opposed the military draft and U.S. involvement in Indochina. His proposal to punish antiwar demonstrators by speeding their induction into the armed forces was frustrated by a court ruling. Hershey, who retired in 1973 as a four-star general, wrote several books dealing with selective service during times of peace and war.

Hill, Archibald Vivian, British scientist (b. Bristol, England, Sept. 26, 1886—d. Cambridge, England, June 3, 1977), shared the Nobel Prize for Physiology or Medicine in 1922 for discoveries relating to heat production in muscles. Hill, who began his physiological studies at Cambridge University in 1911, shared the Nobel Prize with German biochemist Otto Meyerhof. After World War I Hill was professor of physiology at Manchester University (1920–23) and at University College in London (1923–25). A member of the Royal Society from 1918, he was its Foulerton research professor (1926–51) and its secretary (1935–45). From 1940 until 1945 Hill was an Independent Conservative member of Parliament for Cambridge University, and he was a member of the War Cabinet Scientific Advisory Committee (1940–46). After World War II he reestablished his laboratory at University College as a centre for biophysical research. His writings include *Muscular Activity* (1926), *Living Machinery* (1927), and *Muscular Movement in Man* (1927).

Hobbs, Leonard Sinclair, U.S. engineer (b. Carbon, Wyo., Dec. 20, 1896—d. Hartford, Conn., Nov. 1, 1977), developed the engines that powered the first U.S. jetliners and B-52 intercontinental bombers as chief engineer (1927–58) of Pratt & Whitney Aircraft (now United Technologies Corp.). Hobbs's J-57 engine, commercially adapted to power the Boeing 707, served as a model for succeeding engines, including those for Boeing 747 jumbo jets, and initiated the airline industry's transition from propeller to jet planes. He retired in 1958 and served on United's board of directors until 1968.

Holden, David, British journalist (b. Sunderland, England, Nov. 20, 1924—d. Nasser City, Egypt, Dec. 7, 1977), was a chief foreign correspondent of *The Sunday Times* of London who specialized in the Middle East. After serving as Middle East correspondent for *The Times* (1956–60), Holden became a roving correspondent for *The Guardian* and joined *The Sunday Times* in 1965. A frequent broadcaster on radio and television, he also wrote *Farewell to Arabia* (1966) and *Greece Without Columns* (1972). Holden was found shot to death near the Cairo airport the day after he arrived to cover developments in connection with Pres. Anwar as-Sadat's peace initiative.

Hollis, (Maurice) Christopher, British author (b. Axford, Somerset, England, March 29, 1902—d. Mells, Somerset, May 5, 1977), was a prolific writer whose articles in newspapers and periodicals covered a wide range of interests. He was educated at Eton College in Berkshire and at Balliol College at Oxford, where he was president of the Oxford Union in 1923. After World War II, Hollis sat in Parliament as member for Devizes, Wiltshire (1945–55), and was a Conservative spokesman on education. His first book, *The American Heresy* (1927), was a study of some of the U.S. presidents. He then turned to economics with *The Breakdown of Money* (1934), which resulted in a lectureship at the University of Notre Dame in Indiana (1935–39), and followed that with *Death of a Gentleman* (1943), which summed up his Conservative viewpoint. Hollis, a convert to Roman Catholicism, also wrote biographies of Ignatius Loyola and Sir Thomas More.

Howe, Quincy, U.S. newscaster (b. Boston, Mass., Aug. 17, 1900—d. New York, N.Y., Feb. 17, 1977), was a familiar voice to millions of CBS radio listeners during World War II and a pioneer in providing an analysis of major news events. Howe was later in constant demand on television

because of his low-keyed style and fair reporting. His opposition to U.S. involvement in a European war was expostulated in the controversial book *England Expects Every American to Do His Duty* (1937), but after the fall of France he gave full support to the Allied cause. As director (1932–40) of the American Civil Liberties Union and president (1940s) of the National Board of Review of Motion Pictures, he led a battle against censorship. He was also a founder (1961) and editor of *Atlas* magazine.

Hubbard, (Robert) Cal(vin), U.S. athlete and baseball umpire (b. Keytesville, Mo., Oct. 31, 1900—d. St. Petersburg, Fla., Oct. 17, 1977), was the only man in the history of sports who was inducted into both the Football Hall of Fame (1963) and the National Baseball Hall of Fame (1976). He had also been elected to the National (collegiate) Football Hall of Fame (1962) for his play at Centenary College in Louisiana and at Geneva College in Pennsylvania. Hubbard, who retired after nearly ten seasons as an outstanding tackle with the Green Bay Packers, was recruited by the New York Giants and played for them in six games. He later served as a baseball umpire in the American League for 16 years, becoming league supervisor, a position he held for 18 years, after a hunting accident impaired his eyesight in 1951.

Hulman, Anton ("Tony"), Jr., U.S. sports executive (b. Terre Haute, Ind., Feb. 11, 1901—d. Indianapolis, Ind., Oct. 27, 1977), purchased the Indianapolis Motor Speedway (1945), renovated the decrepit grandstands and racetrack, and promoted the Indy 500, which became one of the world's most prestigious auto races, with a purse exceeding $1 million. Hulman's command at the beginning of the race, "Gentlemen, start your engines!" became a racing tradition. But when Janet Guthrie became the first woman driver to qualify for the event (May 1977), Hulman modified his command to: "In company with the first lady ever to qualify at Indianapolis, gentlemen, start your engines!" Hulman spent nearly $1 million on safety improvements following the 1973 race, during which numerous spectators were injured and four lives were lost. His financial interests included the Coca-Cola franchise for Indiana and a wholesale grocery business in Terre Haute.

Hutchins, Robert M(aynard), U.S. educator (b. Brooklyn, N.Y., Jan. 17, 1899—d. Santa Barbara, Calif., May 14, 1977), was an educator and administrator whose views on what constitutes a good society and how one might be established had far-reaching effects on public affairs and higher education. Hutchins graduated from Yale Law School in 1925 and was named dean in 1927. At age 30 he became president of the University of Chicago, where he remained until 1951; he served as chancellor the last six years. He was active in forming the Committee to Frame a World Constitution (1945), led the Commission on Freedom of the Press (1946), and vigorously defended academic freedom, leading opposition to faculty loyalty oaths in the 1950s. Hutchins, who was a controversial but effective administrator, reorganized the departments for undergraduate and graduate study at Chicago. His undergraduate plan provided for liberal education at earlier ages and introduced study of the Great Books at various stages in the curriculum. After serving as associate director of the Ford Foundation for three years, he became president of the Fund for the Republic (1954) and, as part of the Fund's main objective, founded (1959) the Center for the Study of Democratic Institutions in Santa Barbara, Calif. Hutchins was a member of the board of directors of Encyclopædia Britannica, Inc. (1943–72; honorary director 1972–77), and chairman of the board of editors of *Encyclopædia Britannica* (1948–74). He was editor in chief of the 54-volume *Great Books of the Western*

BOOK OF THE YEAR

World (1952) and in 1961 became co-editor of *The Great Ideas Today*. His views on society and education appear in *No Friendly Voice* (1936), *The Higher Learning in America* (1936), *The University of Utopia* (1953), and *The Learning Society* (1968). (See *Memorial*, page 2.)

Ilyushin, Sergey Vladimirovich, Soviet aircraft designer (b. Didyalevo, Vologda Province, Russia, March 30, [March 18, old style], 1894—d. Moscow, U.S.S.R., Feb. 9, 1977), whose contributions to aviation included the Il-18 Moskva four-engine turboprop transport (1957), widely used throughout Eastern Europe and China. Among his other notable accomplishments were the Il-2 Stormovik, the Soviet Union's World War II armoured attack aircraft, the Il-62 turbojet transport (1962), and the Il-86 four-engine, 350-seat airbus, which made its first flight in 1976. Before qualifying as a pilot in 1917, Ilyushin served as a mechanic in the Russian Imperial Army's air arm. He subsequently entered the Zhukovsky Air Force Engineering Academy, Moscow, grad-

WIDE WORLD

uating in 1926. He became a lieutenant general in the Engineering and Technical Service and professor at the Zhukovsky Academy. Ilyushin was awarded the Order of Lenin several times.

Jain, Shanti Prasad, Indian industrialist (b. Najibabad, United Provinces [now Uttar Pradesh], India, Jan. 3, 1912—d. New Delhi, India, Oct. 27, 1977), was highly influential in Indian affairs as chairman of Bennett, Coleman & Co. Ltd., India's largest newspaper and magazine publisher. Several publications including the *Times of India*, a daily English newspaper, and the *Illustrated Weekly of India*, a prominent magazine, were produced under his supervision. Jain, who was educated in his native state at the Banaras Hindu and Agra universities, also served as president of the Federation of Indian Chambers of Commerce and Industry.

Johnson, Harry Gordon, Canadian economist (b. Toronto, Ont., May 26, 1923—d. Geneva, Switz., May 8, 1977), was an expert on international finance whose principal target was the monetarist school of economics. Johnson, who lectured and traveled widely, also wrote extensively for professional journals. He believed that unemployment was a greater social problem than inflation and advocated devaluation of the dollar and a guaranteed minimum income. A graduate of Harvard University, where he earned his doctoral degree in 1958, Johnson became professor of economics at the University of Chicago in 1959 and from 1966 to 1974 was also a professor at the London School of Economics and Political Sci-

ence. His writings on monetary economics, the theory of tariffs, and income distribution analysis include *International Trade and Economic Growth* (1958) and *Essays in Monetary Economics* (1967).

Johnson, Nunnally, U.S. screenwriter (b. Columbus, Ga., Dec. 5, 1897—d. Los Angeles, Calif., March 25, 1977), was one of Hollywood's most respected and highly paid script writers. Also a part-time producer and director, Johnson had a rare gift for matching words and situations. His long list of credits, covering a span of some 35 years, includes such favourites as *The Grapes of Wrath*, *Tobacco Road*, *The Three Faces of Eve*, and *The Man in the Gray Flannel Suit*.

Jones, James, U.S. writer (b. Robinson, Ill., Nov. 6, 1921—d. Southampton, Long Island, N.Y., May 9, 1977), was a World War II veteran whose army experiences of five years provided the background for *From Here to Eternity* (1951), a novel filled with brawling misfits and adventurers who represented the devil-may-care types found

WIDE WORLD

in the enlisted ranks at the end of the Depression years. Jones, who received his first and only National Book Award for *Eternity*, was never able to recapture his first success in later novels. *Some Came Running* (1957), followed by *The Pistol* (1959) and *The Thin Red Line* (1962), failed to arouse critical acclaim.

Jullian, Philippe, French author and painter (b. Bordeaux, France, 1920—d. Paris, France, Sept. 28, 1977), was an authority on the fin-de-siècle art and literature centred in Paris. He was the author of an important study of Symbolist painters, *Esthètes et Magiciens* (1969; Eng. trans., *Dreamers of Decadence*). He also wrote *The Symbolists* (1973) and biographies of Robert de Montesquiou (1967) and Oscar Wilde (1968). Jullian was also known for such novels as *Gilberte Regained* (1957) and *Chateau Bonheur* (1962) and for his Art Nouveau-like paintings and stylish book illustrations.

Jumblatt, Kamal, Lebanese politician (b. Moukhtara, Lebanon, Dec. 6, 1917—d. near Baaklin, Lebanon, March 16, 1977), was head of one of the two leading Druze clans of Lebanon and an influential political leader of left-wing forces allied with the Palestinians in the civil war that erupted in 1975. He studied sociology and law in Beirut and Paris, entered the Lebanese Parliament in 1947, and in 1949 founded the Progressive Socialist Party, advocating social reform and secularization of communal politics. Jumblatt, who in the course of his career held several Cabinet posts, used his influence to bring about the

downfall of presidents whom he initially had supported. After Syrian troops intervened in the civil war and Elias Sarkis was elected president in 1976, Jumblatt's influence waned. He was killed by unidentified gunmen who ambushed his car on a mountain road.

Kantor, MacKinlay, U.S. writer (b. Webster City, Iowa, Feb. 4, 1904—d. Sarasota, Fla., Oct. 11, 1977), won a Pulitzer Prize (1956) for *Andersonville*, a stark portrayal of the brutalities in a Confederate prisoner-of-war camp during the Civil War. Although Kantor produced over 40 books, his only other major success was scored when his novel *Glory for Me* (1945) was adapted for the screen and became *The Best Years of Our Lives* (1946), an Academy Award-winning film underscoring the trauma of war veterans returning home.

Keita, Modibo, Mali politician (b. Bamako, French Sudan, June 4, 1915—d. Bamako, Mali, May 16, 1977), crusaded for the short-lived Federation of Mali (including Mali and Senegal) before becoming the first president of the Republic of Mali in 1960. Keita, who was deposed in a 1968 military

WIDE WORLD

coup, thereafter lived under house arrest. A Muslim and graduate of what is now the University of Dakar, Senegal, he became an uncompromising African nationalist and socialist and was a founder in 1945 of the Union Soudanaise, a militant West African anticolonial movement that in 1946 merged with the Rassemblement Démocratique Africain. A member of the government of the French Sudan in 1948, Keita also sat as a deputy and vice-president in the French National Assembly in Paris from 1956 to 1958. He was appointed state secretary for overseas territories in 1957.

Keller, the Rev. James Gregory, U.S. Catholic priest (b. Oakland, Calif., June 27, 1900—d. New York, N.Y., Feb. 7, 1977), founded (1945) the Christophers, a Roman Catholic movement based on the belief that one person can change the world. A member of the Maryknoll Fathers, a missionary group, Keller used syndicated television and radio programs as well as newspaper columns to promote the notion that individuals can transform society simply by living Christian lives. The movement has no organizational structures, formal membership, dues, or meetings.

Kennedy, (James) Walter, U.S. sports executive (b. Stamford, Conn., June 8, 1913—d. Stamford, June 26, 1977), was the energetic commissioner of the National Basketball Association (NBA) from 1963 to 1975 whose experience in business, public relations, and sports enabled him to promote basketball successfully. Kennedy, who demanded unquestioned authority from the board of governors, enforced the league's bylaws and rules without favouritism and organized the televising of NBA games (1963). Following the emergence of the rival American Basketball Association (1967), Kennedy was involved in a bidding war for players that escalated salaries into the million-dollar range. A former mayor of Stamford (1959–62), he retired there and became chairman of the board of the First Stamford Bank and Trust Co., chairman of the board of the Special Olympics for the Mentally Retarded, and president of the Naismith Basketball Hall of Fame in Springfield, Mass.

Kido, Koicho (MARQUIS KOICHO KIDO), Japanese politician (b. Tokyo, Japan, July 18, 1889–d. Tokyo, April 6, 1977), acted as chief adviser to Emperor Hirohito during World War II and became lord keeper of the privy seal (1940–45). Arrested by Allied occupation forces and charged with war crimes, Kido was tried by the International Military Tribunal and sentenced (1948) to life imprisonment. His parole in 1955 came three years after the U.S. occupation had ended and Japan had returned to full sovereignty. Kido's extensive diary (1930–45) was cited by both prosecution and defense attorneys in the postwar trials of Japanese leaders.

Knorr, Nathan Homer, U.S. religious leader (b. Bethlehem, Pa., April 23, 1905–d. Wallkill, N.Y., June 8, 1977), was an accomplished preacher and longtime president (1942–77) of the Watch Tower Bible and Tract Society, the legal corporation of Jehovah's Witnesses. Knorr, who warned and believed that the biblical Armageddon was near at hand, was the third president of the fundamentalist denomination and helped build its membership from 113,000 members to two million in 216 lands during his 35-year leadership. Following his high school graduation, Knorr worked in the shipping department at the Witnesses' international headquarters and printing plant, was quickly promoted to coordinator of all printing operations, and in 1932 was named general manager of the publishing office and plant. In 1935 he became vice-president and seven years later president, a position he held until his death.

Langlois, Henri, French cineast (b. Izmir, Turkey, Nov. 13, 1914–d. Paris, France, Jan 12, 1977), founded with Georges Franju the Cinémathèque française to house and show his film library, which grew to over 50,000 films. A journalist, Langlois formed (1935) the Cercle du Cinéma to screen his unique collection of silent films. The Cinémathèque later received state support, but

BOIFFIN-VIVIER NORMA/KATHERINE YOUNG

Langlois's proprietary attitude aroused some opposition. He was summarily dismissed (February 1968) from the directorship, but protests were so intense and widespread that he was reinstated, although the state subsidy was not renewed. In 1972 Langlois established the Musée du Cinéma in the Palais de Chaillot, Paris. He received a special award from the U.S. Academy of Motion Picture Arts and Sciences in 1974.

Laurence, William Leonard (WILLIAM L. SIEW), Lithuanian-born news reporter (b. Salantai, Lithuania, March 7, 1888–d. Majorca, Spain, March 19, 1977), was one of the first specialized science reporters for the *New York Times*. His ability to present complex scientific concepts in nontechnical language attracted a wide readership. Laurence's talents were given special recognition when U.S. officials selected him to write an eyewitness report on the atomic bombing (1945) of Nagasaki, Japan. His series on the development, production, and explosion of the bomb brought Laurence his second Pulitzer Prize (1946). His first Pulitzer was shared with four other science writers for their coverage (1936) of the Harvard Tercentenary Conference of Arts and Sciences held in Cambridge, Mass.

Lilje, Johannes Ernst Richard, German Lutheran churchman (b. Hanover, Germany, Aug. 20, 1899–d. Hanover, West Germany, Jan. 6, 1977), was a pioneer official of the World Council of Churches who was bishop of Hanover from 1947 to 1971. Ordained in 1926, he opposed the Nazi regime and suffered a year's imprisonment. He was president of the Lutheran World Federation (1952–57) and presiding bishop of the United Evangelical Lutheran Church of Germany (1955–69). His books include *The Valley of the Shadow* (1947), an account of his opposition to Nazism, and several studies of Luther's life and philosophy.

Lilly, Eli, U.S. pharmaceutical chemist (b. Indianapolis, Ind., April 1, 1885–d. Indianapolis, Jan. 24, 1977), played a leading role in shaping modern pharmacology while serving as president (1932–48) and chairman (1948–61, 1966–69) of the company founded by his grandfather. Eli Lilly & Co. developed such drugs as insulin for diabetes and liver extract for pernicious anemia (1920s), barbiturates (1930s), penicillins and polio vaccines (1940–50s), and new agricultural compounds used for weed control and animal health (1960–70s). He received his degree as a pharmaceutical chemist in 1907 from the Philadelphia College of Pharmacy and Science.

Littlewood, John Edensor, British mathematician (b. Rochester, England, June 9, 1885–d. Cambridge, England, Sept. 6, 1977), was a theoretician whose work, particularly during a 35-year collaboration with Godfrey H. Hardy, led to impressive discoveries in the theory of series, the Riemann zeta function, inequalities, and theory of functions. Their series of papers entitled "Partitio numerorum" utilized the new Hardy-Ramanujan-Littlewood analytical method. Littlewood was a scholar of Trinity College, Cambridge, where he became a life fellow, and Rouse Ball professor of mathematics. At 30 he was elected a fellow of the Royal Society and later received its Royal (1929), Sylvester (1943), and Copley (1958) medals.

Lombardo, Guy (Albert), Canadian-born bandleader (b. London, Ont., June 19, 1902–d. Houston, Texas, Nov. 5, 1977), revolutionized popular dance music as the innovative bandleader for the Royal Canadians whose velvet orchestrations purveyed the "sweetest music this side of heaven" during the late 1920s and early 1930s. Lombardo's band introduced more than 300 songs, including "Gimme a Little Kiss, Will ya Huh?," "Little White Lies," and "Easter Parade." Its first network radio broadcast was made in Chicago in 1927. His theme song, "Auld Lang Syne," was a reminder of the 48 years he and his band engaged in the traditional New Year's Eve festivi-

WIDE WORLD

ties at the Roosevelt Grill and later at the Waldorf-Astoria Grand Ballroom in New York City. His mellow music survived the Swing Era of the mid-1930s and continued to attract huge audiences in concert halls throughout the 1970s. His film credits include *Many Happy Returns* (1934), *Stage Door Canteen* (1943), and *No Leave, No Love* (1946).

Lowell, Robert (Traill Spence), Jr., U.S. poet (b. Boston, Mass., March 1, 1917–d. New York, N.Y., Sept. 12, 1977), was a master of the English language whose haunting poetry and controlled metrics won him (1947) the Pulitzer Prize for poetry for his second volume of poems, *Lord Weary's Castle*. His poems expressed the major tensions of the times and paralleled his rejection of the Puritan tradition (which he equated with money), his conversion to Catholicism (which he later renounced), and the five months of a prison sentence he served during World War II as a conscientious objector. Although Lowell suffered from manic-depressive symptoms, as documented in his National Book Award winner, *Life Studies* (1959), he survived sporadic visits to mental institutions, and he bared his tortuous struggles, including three marriages, in such volumes as *Life Studies, Imitations* (1961), and *For the Union Dead* (1964). The great-grandnephew of author James Russell Lowell and the cousin of poet and critic Amy Lowell, Robert Lowell sustained the family literary tradition and at the time of his death was enjoying the success of his last book, *Day by Day*.

Lunt, Alfred, U.S. actor (b. Milwaukee, Wis., Aug. 19, 1893–d. Chicago, Ill., Aug. 3, 1977), was a longtime star on Broadway who together with his wife, Lynn Fontanne, held critics and audiences alike spellbound for nearly four decades during which they appeared as co-stars in 27 plays. The couple, who were married in 1922, starred in classics by Shakespeare and Shaw, but many of their hit roles were comedies focusing on marital infidelity. The Lunts, who avoided Hollywood, appeared jointly in only a few films. Although the Lunts favoured comic roles, they appeared in two dramas, *There Shall Be No Night* (1940), a Pulitzer Prize-winning play by Robert Sherwood, and *The Visit* (1960), their last contribution to the stage. In a final tribute, Broadway's marquees were darkened for one minute for one of the stage's brightest lights, Alfred Lunt.

Lupescu, Magda (PRINCESS ELENA), Romanian princess-consort (b. Issi, Romania, 1902 – d. Estoril, Port., June 29, 1977), was the longtime mistress (1925–47) of King Carol II of Romania before the couple's marriage in 1947. Lupescu was ordered out of the country in 1925, and Carol, heir apparent to the throne, left his wife, renounced his claim to the throne, and took Lupescu to the French Riviera. Carol's son Michael became king (1927) following the death of King Ferdinand, but after two years of political turmoil, the government asked Carol to return as king. Lupescu, who was regarded as the power behind the throne, exerted a wide-ranging influence on Romanian public affairs during the 1930s. She encouraged Carol to set up a dictatorial constitution (1938), but in 1940, under pressure from the Nazis, he abdicated. The couple fled to Latin America and were married in 1947 when Lupescu was critically ill. At this time, Carol created for her the title Princess Elena. They finally settled in Estoril, Port.

McClellan, John Little, U.S. politician (b. near Sheridan, Ark., Feb. 25, 1896 – d. Little Rock, Ark., Nov. 27, 1977), was a longtime (1942–77) Democratic senator from Arkansas who became chairman of the Appropriations Committee and second senior member of the Senate (outranked only by James O. Eastland of Mississippi). McClellan, who entered politics in the 1920s as city attorney for Malvern, Ark., defended military appropriations, opposed civil rights legislation, and advocated severe penalties for criminals. After serving two terms (1935–39) in the House of Representatives, he made an unsuccessful bid for the Senate, but won his second race in 1942. In 1953 he led a Democratic boycott of the Permanent Investigations Subcommittee headed by Republican Sen. Joseph R. McCarthy, then at the height of his anti-Communist crusade. Two years later McClellan became chairman of the same subcommittee and conducted a dramatic three-year investigation into the activities of organized labour, which resulted in the imprisonment of Dave Beck and James Hoffa of the International Brotherhood of Teamsters. McClellan also persuaded syndicate figure Joseph Valachi to testify during the 1963 hearings on organized crime. Thereafter, McClellan devoted much of his effort to revising the U.S. Criminal Code.

McMillan, William, British sculptor (b. Aberdeen, Scotland, Aug. 31, 1887 – d. Richmond, Surrey, England, Sept. 25, 1977), was an academic classical realist who created a number of London's familiar public monuments. McMillan was noted for the sensitivity of his work and for care in the choice of appropriate materials. Besides figures for the Beatty Memorial Fountain in Trafalgar Square and the statue of King George VI in Carlton Gardens, both in London, he produced the statues of King George V for Calcutta and of Earl Haig for Clifton College in Bristol, charming garden sculpture, and much architectural work. McMillan studied at Gray's School of Art in Aberdeen and the Royal Academy Schools before he became a Royal Academician in 1933.

Makarios III (MIKHAIL KHRISTODOLOU MOUSKOS), Cypriot churchman and statesman (b. Pano Panayia, Paphos, Cyprus, Aug. 13, 1913 – d. Nicosia, Cyprus, Aug. 3, 1977), was archbishop of the autocephalous Orthodox Church of Cyprus and, from 1960, the first president of the Republic of Cyprus. A novice monk at age 13, Makarios took his divinity degree at the University of Athens (1942) and became a priest in 1946. While studying theology and sociology at Boston University (1947–48), he was elected bishop of Kition. After the death of Makarios II he was elected archbishop and assumed the role of ethnarch, or national leader, in 1950. In 1955 the underground guerrilla organization EOKA (National Organization of Cypriot Struggle), led by Georg-

ios Grivas, opened a violent campaign for Cyprus' independence from British rule and union with Greece (*enosis*). Makarios was suspected of collaboration and was exiled to the Seychelles for one year. After his release he resided in Athens, and after prolonged negotiations Makarios dropped his demands for a union with Greece and signed the 1959 London agreement that granted Cyprus independence. Makarios, who for nearly 30 years sought solutions to the troubles that beset Cyprus, preserved his nation's independence despite EOKA's persistent terrorism, tension between the Greek and Turkish Cypriot communities that at times flared into armed conflict, and an attempted 1974 coup by the Greek Cypriot National Guard, which attacked the presidential palace. After Makarios was rescued by a British helicopter and taken to Akrotiri base, Turkey invaded Cyprus and proclaimed a separate state for Turkish Cypriots in the north. When the Greek military junta fell, Makarios returned to Nicosia and vowed to resist partition. The Greek and Turkish conflict over Cyprus was still unresolved when Makarios died.

Malcuzynski, Witold, Polish pianist (b. Warsaw, Poland, Aug. 10, 1914 – d. Palma, Majorca, Spain, July 17, 1977), was an interpreter of Frederic Chopin's pianoforte music. He studied at the Warsaw Conservatory and later under Ignacy Paderewski in Switzerland. During World War II he toured the Americas, making his U.S. debut in 1942 at Carnegie Hall in New York City. In 1945 he appeared in London with the London Philharmonic Orchestra and thereafter made two world tours (1949 and 1956) and 14 tours of the U.S. Malcuzynski, a member of international competition juries, was an honorary member of the Chopin Society of Warsaw.

Marx, Julius Henry (GROUCHO MARX), U.S. actor (b. New York, N.Y., Oct. 2, 1890 – d. Los Angeles, Calif., Aug. 19, 1977), was the zany ringleader of the Marx Brothers comedy team, who plunged audiences into helpless laughter with irreverent insults, spontaneous ad-libs, and eccentric antics. Groucho entered show business at the age of ten, and when he was in his teens his mother, Minnie, formed the "Six Musical Mascots," which later evolved into the Marx Brothers. At the height of his career Groucho, armed with his painted-on mustache and cigar, starred with his brothers Harpo (Arthur), Chico (Leonard), and Zeppo (Herbert) in such farcical films as *Animal Crackers, Duck Soup,* and *A Night at the Opera.* After the Marx Brothers disbanded he became the host (1947) of the radio and television quiz show "You Bet Your Life." Groucho's letters

and manuscripts, including *Groucho and Me* and *Memoirs of a Mangy Lover,* were housed in the Library of Congress.

Marx, Milton (GUMMO MARX), U.S. comedian (b. New York, N.Y., 1894 – d. Palm Springs, Calif., April 21, 1977), turned his back on the glamour of Hollywood and what was to become the legendary Marx Brothers comedy team to follow a career in the garment industry. In early vaudeville appearances, Gummo formed a comedy quartet with his brothers Groucho (Julius), Harpo (Arthur), and Chico (Leonard). When Gummo later became manager of the group, Zeppo (Herbert) replaced him on the stage.

Massamba-Débat, Alphonse, Congolese politician (b. Nkolo, Middle Congo, French Equatorial Africa, 1921 – d. Brazzaville, Congo, March 25, 1977), was president of the Congo from 1963 to 1968. A teacher by profession, he joined the Democratic Union for the Defense of African Interests, headed by Abbé Fulbert Youlou, who later became first president of the Congo. Three years after Congo gained independence (1960), Massamba-Débat became provisional head of the government when Youlou was forced to resign; later that year he was elected president. In 1968 Massamba-Débat was forced out of office following a coup led by Marien Ngouabi, who on Jan. 1, 1969, succeeded to the presidency. More than eight years later, Massamba-Débat was accused of plotting the assassination of President Ngouabi and was summarily executed.

Mast, Charles, French army officer (b. Paris, France, Jan. 7, 1889 – d. Paris, October 1977), was a stormy petrel in French military politics and a specialist on East Asian affairs. During World War II he was captured by the Germans but was soon released. He joined the Vichy government in France, but later switched allegiance and joined Gen. Henry Giraud in Algeria, where he helped prepare for the Allied landings. When Gen. Charles de Gaulle arrived in North Africa in August 1943, Mast was made French resident-general in Tunisia. In 1947 he was named director of the Institut des hautes Études de Défense Nationale in Paris. Mast's public career came to an end in 1949 when he was accused of helping to inform the Vietminh of France's deteriorating position in Vietnam. He emerged from obscurity in 1969 with the publication of *Histoire d'une rébellion.*

Masterman, Sir John Cecil, British intelligence agent (b. Kingston upon Thames, England, Jan. 12, 1891 – d. Oxford, England, June 6, 1977), was director of the British counter-intelligence unit during World War II (1941–45) who infiltrated and controlled the German espionage system by feeding his double agents false information. His greatest accomplishment, as recounted in his book *The Double Cross System* (1972), was to lead the Germans into thinking that the 1944 Allied invasion would take place near Calais rather than in Normandy. Masterman had served in the British Navy and studied at Worcester College, Oxford, and in Germany, where he was interned during World War I. Following World War II he returned to Oxford and served as provost of Worcester College (1946–61). Masterman was knighted in 1959 and published his autobiography, *On the Chariot Wheel*, in 1975.

Moran, Charles McMoran Wilson, 1st Baron, British physician (b. Skipton, Yorkshire, England, Nov. 10, 1882–d. near Alton, Hampshire, England, April 12, 1977), was personal physician and confidant to Winston Churchill for 25 years (1940–65). Moran graduated (1908) from St. Mary's Hospital Medical School in London, where he later was dean (1920–45). His own accomplishments were often overlooked during his years as Churchill's physician, but he was one of the nation's most respected medical advisers and was president of the Royal College of Physicians (1941–50). His publication (1966) of *Winston Churchill: The Struggle For Survival, 1940–1965* was resented by the Churchill family and denounced by the British Medical Association because the 877-page volume described in clinical detail Churchill's pathetic decline in his final years.

Morgenstern, Oskar, German-born economist (b. Görlitz, Germany, Jan. 24, 1902–d. Princeton, N.J., July 26, 1977), formulated the game theory, a method of applying mathematics to a game, a business situation, or a military problem in order to maximize gain or minimize loss. Morgenstern, who was one of the first to combine mathematics and economics, was often disturbed when an economic theory was unable to match the rigours of mathematics. His preoccupation with perfection, and collaboration with the mathematician John von Neumann, led to the introduction of convex sets and point set topology, a form of mathematics appearing only recently in economic journals. His Princeton-based company, Mathematics, Inc., completed numerous studies for government and corporate clients including such subjects as the space shuttle, energy, state lotteries, and national defense strategy.

Mostel, Zero (SAMUEL JOEL MOSTEL), U.S. actor (b. Brooklyn, N.Y., Feb. 28, 1915–d. Philadelphia, Pa., Sept. 8, 1977), the elephantine star of the 1964 Broadway musical *Fiddler on the Roof*, whose memorable interpretation of the character of Tev-

PICTORIAL PARADE

ye, a Russian-Jewish dairyman, served as a prototype for the many actors who succeeded him in the part. Mostel appeared in several films after making his professional acting debut in a Manhattan cafe at age 27, but received little critical notice. In the 1950s his career was interrupted when his name appeared on a blacklist of supposedly pro-Communist entertainers, but in 1958 he returned triumphantly to the stage in *Ulysses in Nighttown*. Mostel, who was also a smash hit in the plays *Rhinoceros* (1961) and *A Funny Thing Happened on the Way to the Forum* (1962), received three Tony Awards. In his last motion picture, *The Front*, he portrayed a blacklisted entertainer trying to make a comeback. He was rehearsing the role of Shylock in *The Merchant*, based on Shakespeare's *The Merchant of Venice*, at the time of his death.

Mowrer, Edgar Ansel, U.S. foreign correspondent (b. Bloomington, Ill., March 8, 1892–d. Madeira Islands, Port., March 2, 1977), was a student in Paris, still undecided about his future, when Paul Scott (his brother) persuaded him to cover World War I for the *Chicago Daily News*. Thus began a 55-year career that included expulsion from Germany, Italy, and the Soviet Union. In his syndicated news column Mowrer excoriated totalitarian regimes and won a Pulitzer Prize (1933) for *Germany Puts the Clock Back*, his eyewitness accounts of the rise of Hitler. His autobiography, *Triumph and Turmoil—a Personal History of Our Time* (1968), is as much a history of the times as a correspondent's view of himself. Joseph Goebbels, Hitler's minister of propaganda, was so incensed over *Germany Puts the Clock Back* that he was reportedly willing to dispatch an entire army division to capture the author.

Mueller, Erwin Wilhelm, German-born physicist (b. Berlin, Germany, June 13, 1911–d. Washington, D.C., May 17, 1977), devised the field ion microscope (1956), which has a magnification of one million times. Using this instrument, Mueller became the first person to visually observe the images of single atoms located on a metal surface and the atomic structures and atomic processes that occur on such a surface. Mueller, who also invented the field emission microscope and the atom probe, graduated from the University of Berlin, where he studied under Nobel laureate Gustav Hertz. Before migrating to the U.S. in 1952, Mueller taught physics at the Kaiser–Wilhelm Institute for Physical Chemistry (1947–52). He joined the faculty of Pennsylvania State University in 1952, where he remained until his retirement in 1976.

Muschenheim, Carl, U.S. physician (b. New York, N.Y., Feb. 4, 1905–d. New York, April 27, 1977), revolutionized the treatment of tuberculosis by introducing the use of isonicotinic hydrazide, a drug that reduced the death rate in the U.S. from tuberculosis by some 70%. Having been afflicted with tuberculosis as a resident physician in the early 1930s, Muschenheim turned to research and became one of the country's leading authorities on diseases of the lung and an ardent advocate of better health care, especially for the Eskimos and American Indians. In 1955 his contributions to medical science were given special recognition when he received an Albert Lasker medical research award.

Nabokov, Vladimir, Russian-born U.S. novelist and lepidopterist (b. St. Petersburg, Russia, April 23, 1899–d. Montreux, Switz., July 2, 1977), attained sudden, late fame and fortune with a major novel, *Lolita* (Paris, 1955; New York, 1958), the story of a middle-aged man's passion for a 12-year-old nymphet (Nabokov's own coinage). The son of an anglophile intellectual who was a political liberal leader, he knew English and French as written languages before Russian. In 1919 his family quit Russia for exile in London, and Vladimir went to Trinity College, Cambridge. After his father had been mistakenly shot dead by Russian reactionaries in Berlin, the family moved there and later to Paris,

UPI COMPIX

where Vladimir tutored. During this period he wrote, in Russian, under the pseudonym "V. Sirin," but had changed to English by the time he left for the U.S. in 1940. In 1945 Nabokov became a U.S. citizen. He pursued an academic career, first at Stanford, next at Wellesley College and simultaneously at Harvard, where he studied butterflies (he discovered several species), and finally as professor of Russian and European literature at Cornell University (1948–59). Meanwhile, he continued writing, notably two novels, *The Real Life of Sebastian Knight* (1941) and *Bend Sinister* (1947). *Lolita*, with film rights (1962), made him rich. He returned to Europe, settling at Montreux in 1959. *Pale Fire* (1962), *Ada* (1969), and *Look at the Harlequins!* (1974) were among his later novels. At the same time he translated his earlier Russian novels into English, among them *Mary* (1926; 1970), *The Defense* (1932; 1964), and *The Gift* (1937; 1963). He was accepted as a writer of genius with an intellectualized sense of humour, whose passion for literature and the word was comparable with that of James Joyce and Samuel Beckett. His revised autobiographical work *Speak, Memory!* appeared in 1967, *Poems* and *Poems and Problems* in 1959 and 1971, respectively. Besides collections of short stories and a biography, *Nikolai Gogol* (1944), he translated Russian works, including Aleksandr Pushkin's *Eugene Onegin*, with a commentary (4 vol., 1964).

Neilson-Terry, Phyllis, British actress (b. London, England, Oct. 15, 1892–d. Appledore, England, Sept. 25, 1977), the niece of Ellen Terry and the daughter of Fred Terry and Julia Neilson, had the beauty, the voice, and the presence that made her an ideal Shakespearean heroine in the roles of Viola, Rosalind, Portia, and Desdemona. She toured the U.S. (1914–19) and between World Wars I and II acted at the Apollo Theatre and the Open Air Theatre in London and at Stratford-on-Avon. She later appeared in television and film roles and in Terence Rattigan's *Separate Tables* when it was staged in London and New York during the 1950s.

Ngouabi, Marien, Congolese head of state (b. French Equatorial Africa, 1938–d. Brazzaville, Congo, March 18, 1977), transformed the Congo into a Marxist state during his more than eight years as president. He graduated from the Saint-Cyr military academy in France in 1962 and under Pres. Alphonse Massamba-Débat served on the central committee of the Congo's sole political party, the National Movement for the Revolution (MNR). In August 1968 Ngouabi led a military coup against the president and on Jan. 1, 1969, officially assumed leadership of the nation. One year later he changed the country's name to

BOOK OF THE YEAR

the People's Republic of the Congo. As Ngouabi strengthened ties with Communist countries, relations with neighbouring Zaire perceptibly deteriorated. Ngouabi was killed in an abortive coup allegedly planned by Massamba-Débat.

Nin, Anaïs, French-born author (b. Neuilly, France, Feb. 21, 1903–d. Los Angeles, Calif., Jan. 14, 1977), launched her literary career with the publication of *D. H. Lawrence: An Unprofessional Study* (1932). The book led to lifelong friendships with Henry Miller and other significant authors. Though Nin continued to publish a wide variety of prose, she did not receive popular acclaim until the first volume of her diary appeared in 1966. While setting forth her observa-

EVA SERENY—SYGMA

tions and impressions of friends, Nin analyzed her own thoughts and emotions in ways that reflected her earlier studies of psychoanalysis under Otto Rank. Though she wrote such noteworthy novels as *The House of Incest* (1936), *Under a Glass Bell* (1944), *Ladders to Fire* (1946), and *Collages* (1964), the six published volumes of her uncompleted diary were considered her most important work.

Nossack, Hans Erich, German novelist (b. Hamburg, Germany, Jan. 30, 1901–d. Hamburg, Nov. 2, 1977), was a major writer in West Germany whose work was banned by the Nazis before World War II and destroyed in the Allied air raids on Hamburg in 1943. His reminiscences of the raids, *Der Untergang,* and *Gedichte* ("Poems," 1947) were followed by the nihilistic and self-questioning novels *Nekyia* (1947), *Spätestens in November* (1955), and *Der Fall d'Arthez* (1968). In his later works Nossack was critical of the West German "economic miracle" and its materialism.

O'Donnell, Kenneth Patrick, U.S. politician (b. Worcester, Mass., March 4, 1924–d. Boston, Mass., Sept. 9, 1977), served as appointments secretary to Pres. John F. Kennedy from 1961 to 1963. Following Kennedy's assassination, O'Donnell worked under Lyndon B. Johnson in the same capacity, planning the president's White House schedule, arranging his trips, and controlling the access of visitors to the president. In 1965 he resigned his post and returned to private business. Although he was a close confidant of President Kennedy, he was not well known as a public figure, and his 1966 and 1970 bids for the Massachusetts governorship were unsuccessful. In 1970 he collaborated with White House special assistant David Powers on *Johnny, We Hardly Knew Ye,* a biography highlighting the career of President Kennedy.

Packer, Joy, South African writer (b. Cape Town, South Africa, Feb. 11, 1905–d. Cape Province, South Africa, Sept. 6, 1977), was a free-lance journalist and novelist who wrote extensively about her native country. Her ten novels, including *Valley of the Vines* (1955) and *The Dark Curtain* (1977), were translated into nine languages. Packer, who traveled over three continents with her husband, Adm. Sir Herbert Packer, also wrote five autobiographical travel books and a biography of her husband, *Deep as the Sea* (1976).

Parma, Prince Xavier of Bourbon, duke of, Spanish nobleman (b. Camaiore, Lucca, Italy, May 25, 1889–d. Chur, Switz., May 7, 1977), was Carlist pretender to the throne of Spain but delegated his leadership of the Carlist movement to his elder son, Carlos Hugo, on April 8, 1975. Educated in Paris, Prince Xavier was named regent in January 1936 by his dying uncle Alfonso Carlos. Though Xavier supported General Franco in the Spanish Civil War, he and his family were exiled from Spain by Franco in 1937. His support of the French Resistance in World War II nearly cost him his life at the hands of the Gestapo. After returning to Spain in 1952 he was again expelled by Franco after his supporters proclaimed him "king" in Barcelona.

Patocka, Jan, Czech political dissident (b. 1908?–d. Prague, Czechoslovakia, March 13, 1977), was one of the three prominent spokesmen for Charter 77, a manifesto first circulated in late 1976 and eventually signed by more than 600 dissident intellectuals, who charged Czechoslovak authorities with violating the human-rights guarantees of the 1975 Helsinki agreements. Patocka, a retired professor of philosophy respected by Communists and non-Communists alike, was considered an ideal mediator who could plead the cause of human rights without inflaming political animosities. Summoned to the Interior Ministry after a meeting with Dutch Foreign Minister Max van der Stoel, Patocka was released after two days of intensive questioning and appeared to be in a state of exhaustion. He died approximately one week later of a cerebral hemorrhage.

Paul, Alice, U.S. suffragette (b. Moorestown, N.J., Jan. 11, 1885–d. Moorestown, July 9, 1977), vigorously crusaded for passage of the 19th Amendment to the U.S. Constitution, granting women the right to vote, and after its ratification drafted a prototype of the proposed Equal Rights Amendment. During her more than 50-year suffrage fight Paul was arrested and jailed several times, and on one occasion was force-fed by na-

UPI COMPIX

sal tubes for four weeks after refusing to eat. While a graduate student in England she joined the British Suffragists and organized the World Woman's Party. When she returned to the U.S., Paul founded and became chairman of the then 50,000-member-strong National Woman's Party.

Paz, Alberto Gainza, Argentine newspaper proprietor (b. Buenos Aires, Argentina, March 16, 1899–d. Buenos Aires, Dec. 26, 1977), became a hero in the eyes of journalists all over the world when he continued to publish his newspaper, *La Prensa,* after the government of Pres. Juan Perón instigated labour troubles, rationed his newsprint, and created a whole series of other difficulties. Paz continued to criticize the government until he was forced into exile in Uruguay. Five months after Perón was overthrown (September 1955), Paz was again publishing *La Prensa* in Buenos Aires.

Peer, Lyndon Arthur, U.S. physician (b. Asbury Park, N.J., Dec. 12, 1898–d. Boca Raton, Fla., Oct. 8, 1977), developed methods for reconstructive surgery, especially for accident victims or persons born without ears (1940s), years before plastic surgery was established as a specialty. Peer's metal ear mold was filled with small pieces of cartilage taken from the chest and implanted in the patient's abdomen for several months. When the natural healing ability of the body knitted the cartilage together, he removed the mold and attached the ear to the skull under the skin. Peer, who was affiliated with St. Barnabas Hospital in New Jersey, was one of the first to suggest that maternal stress or drug use during early pregnancy could adversely affect the fetus. He also helped establish the American Society of Plastic and Reconstructive Surgery and wrote and edited some of the first books on tissue transplants.

Pellicer, Camara Carlos, Mexican poet (b. Tabasco, Mexico, Jan. 16, 1897–d. Mexico City, Mexico, Feb. 16, 1977), was a poet of considerable merit whose literary talents were apparent with the publication of his first two books: *Colores en el Mar* ("Colours in the Sea"; 1921) and *Piedra de Sacrificios* ("Sacrificial Stone"; 1924). During the 1950s Pellicer helped calm troubled waters by persuading his close friend and fellow Communist Diego Rivera to yield to government objections by removing the words "God does not exist" from one of his public works of art. Pellicer was representing his native state of Tabasco in the Senate at the time of his death.

Poincelet, Roger, French jockey (b. France, 1921?–d. Paris, France, Nov. 1, 1977), became one of France's greatest jockeys in the process of riding more than 3,000 horses into the winner's circle. Since his first winner, for Prince Aly Khan, in 1937, his triumphs included three Prix de l'Arc de Triomphe, three Grands Prix de Paris, and five English classics. Poincelet, who rode such mounts to victory as Dankaro, Vimy, Right Royal V, Never Too Late II, and Hula Dancer, also captured the Epsom Derby in 1961 riding Psidium.

Powers, Francis Gary, U.S. pilot (b. Jenkins, Ky., Aug. 17, 1929–d. Encino, Calif., Aug. 1, 1977), made international headlines as a U-2 spy plane pilot when he was shot down during a CIA photo-to-reconnaissance mission (May 1, 1960) over the Soviet Union. His photographic and electronic surveillance equipment was seized, and Powers himself was captured and sentenced to ten years in prison, but he was released (1962) in exchange for Soviet spy Rudolf Abel. Powers' capture precipitated a diplomatic incident when Soviet Premier Nikita Khrushchev canceled a major international conference with U.S. Pres. Dwight Eisenhower, who had initially tried to conceal the purpose of Powers' mission.

Powers, John Robert, U.S. business executive (b. Easton, Pa., Sept. 14, 1896–d. Glendale, Calif., July 19, 1977), created a billion-dollar industry with the founding (1923) of the world's first modeling agency. Powers, who boasted that his 100 models were the most beautiful and poised women in the world, employed such glamorous future motion-picture stars as Lauren Bacall and Barbara Stanwyck. His agency offered ten weeks of instruction in voice, posture, and poise, and eventually served as a stepping-stone to stardom for many aspiring actors including Henry Fonda, Tyrone Power, and Frederick March, all of whom became Hollywood box-office idols. Powers' instant success was attributed to a catalog of pictures that he compiled and distributed to advertising agencies interested in models for magazines.

Presley, Elvis Aron, U.S. singer (b. Tupelo, Miss., Jan. 8, 1935—d. Memphis, Tenn., Aug. 16, 1977), was the pulsating "king of rock 'n' roll" whose curled lip, gyrating hips, country rock guitar, and emotion-charged singing made him the focus of a new era of music. Presley, who was idolized by teenagers throughout the world although he never performed outside the U.S., cultivated his own style by blending black rhythm and blues with white rockabilly (pop music with rock and country overtones). After signing with RCA Victor in 1956, Presley recorded "Heartbreak Hotel," the first of 45 records that sold more than one million copies each, appeared in *Love Me Tender*, the first of 33 motion pictures, and was a smash hit on the televised "Ed Sullivan Show," where viewers saw "Elvis the Pelvis" only from the waist up. Presley, who dominated rock 'n' roll with the release of 80 singles and nearly as many albums, sold 600 million records during his 20 years of concert touring, and

WIDE WORLD

grossed an estimated $4.3 billion. His early hits "All Shook Up," "Don't Be Cruel," and "Hound Dog" were followed by such favourites as "It's Now or Never," "Are You Lonesome Tonight?," and "Burning Love." A former truck driver, Presley was drafted into the Army in 1958. He married Priscilla Beaulieu in 1967, and the couple had one daughter before being divorced in 1973. Presley gave gifts, especially Cadillacs, to friends and even strangers but was often confined to his Graceland mansion in Memphis, his only refuge from the mobs that besieged him. His death was attributed to a heart attack.

Prévert, Jacques, French author (b. Neuilly-sur-Seine, France, Feb. 4, 1900—d. Omonville-la-Petite, Normandy, France, April 11, 1977), initially worked in films with his brother Pierre, Jean Grémillon, and Jean Renoir before collaborating (1937–50) with Marcel Carné in the scenarios for eight films, including *Quai des brumes* (1938), *Le Jour se lève* (1939), and *Les Enfants du paradis* (1943–44). Prévert, who wrote the plays *Le Dîner de têtes* and *En Famille*, also was involved in docu-

G. BOTTI—SYGMA

mentary films, radio, and television. After World War II he began publishing poetry. His first volume, *Paroles* (1945), *Histoires* (with André Verdet, 1946), *Spectacle* (1951), *La Pluie et le beau temps* (1955), and *Imaginaires* (1970) all received wide recognition in France and sold hundreds of thousands of copies. His verse was later put to music and sung by such stars as Juliette Greco, Yves Montand, and Charles Trenet.

Printemps, Yvonne (YVONNE WIGNIOLLE), French singer (b. Ermont, France, July 25, 1894—d. Paris, France, Jan. 18, 1977), performed in operettas, films, and musical comedies written and produced by her husband, Sacha Guitry, including *L'Amour Masqué* (1923), *Mozart* (1925), and *Chagrin d'amour* (1931). Printemps, who made her singing debut at age 13, was given an important part in Louis Verneuil's revue *1915* at the Palais-Royal and later that year worked for Guitry, whom she married in 1917. After their marriage ended in 1934, she appeared in London (1934) in Noel Coward's *Conversation Piece*. She later married the actor Pierre Fresnay.

Prinze, Freddie, U.S. actor (b. New York, N.Y., June 22, 1954—d. Los Angeles, Calif., Jan. 29, 1977), was the co-star with Jack Albertson of the television series "Chico and the Man," a comedy based on the ethnic and generation gap between a young Chicano and an older white. Prinze, who had launched his career at age 19, was starring in the third season of his only professional role when he took his life; he was apparently deeply despondent over the breakup of his 15-month-old marriage.

Prío, Carlos Socarrás, Cuban politician (b. Bahía Honda, Cuba, July 14, 1903—d. Miami Beach, Fla., April 6, 1977), launched a campaign to rid Cuba of Communist influence during his term as the country's last constitutionally elected president (1948–52). Overthrown in a coup d'etat and charged with corruption by Gen. Fulgencio Batista, Prío formed a temporary alliance with Fidel Castro, who successfully deposed Batista in 1959. In 1961, however, Prío attacked Castro's Communist tyranny and fled to Miami, Fla., where he remained in exile. Shortly before his death he met with U.S. Secretary of State Cyrus Vance to voice opposition to U.S. détente with Cuba.

Railton, Reid Antony, British engineer (b. June 25, 1895—d. Berkeley, Calif., Sept. 1, 1977), designed automobiles that held world land speed records for nearly 30 years (until 1960). After studying at Manchester University he served under the experimental engineer J. G. Parry Thomas at Leyland Motors. Railton began designing his own two-litre, four-cylinder, overhead camshaft-engine automobile, the Arab, but abandoned the project when Thomas was killed during a speed attempt in 1927. Railton joined Kenneth Thomson and G. H. Kenneth Taylor and fit-

ted a 1,400-brake horsepower Napier Lion engine into Malcolm Campbell's "Bluebird," which raised the land speed record five times between 1931 and 1935; the last attempt exceeded 300 mph. He also helped to design speedboats for Campbell, whose "Bluebird II" achieved a record 141.74 mph. Railton was closely associated with John Cobb, who drove the Napier-Railton car to a new record of 394 mph in 1947.

Rattigan, Sir Terence Mervyn, British playwright (b. London, England, June 10, 1911—d. Hamilton, Bermuda, Nov. 30, 1977), was a leading exponent of sentimental comedy who wrote for his imaginary middlebrow "Aunt Edna" sitting in the audience. His themes often centred on difficulties Britons encountered in coming to terms with life and sex. Among his light-comedy successes were *French Without Tears* (1936), *Love in Idleness* (1944), *The Sleeping Prince* (1953), and *Variation on a Theme* (1958). Rattigan was educated at Harrow School and Trinity College, Oxford. After his World War II experiences he produced *Flare Path* (1942) and *While the Sun Shines* (1943). Among his more serious plays were *The Winslow Boy* (1946), *The Browning Version* (1948), *The Deep Blue Sea* (1952), *Separate Tables* (1954), *Ross* (1960), and *Cause Célèbre* (1977), about a celebrated British murder trial. Rattigan also wrote many film scripts, including those for *The Yellow Rolls-Royce* (1965) and *Goodbye, Mr. Chips* (1969). He was knighted in 1971.

Ray, Ted (CHARLIE OLDEN), British comedian (b. Wigan, Lancashire, England, Nov. 21, 1906?—d. Nov. 8, 1977), was known for his radio comedy series that began in 1949, "Ray's A Laugh," for his work as host of the British Broadcasting Corporation's "Calling All Forces" (1950), and, on television, for "The Ted Ray Show" (1955). He also made six films and wrote the comically autobiographical *Raising the Laughs* (1952), *My Turn Next* (1963), and *Golf—My Slice of Life* (1972).

Rivett, Rohan Deakin, Australian journalist (b. Melbourne, Australia, Jan. 16, 1917—d. Melbourne, Oct. 6, 1977), was a war correspondent in Singapore (1941–42) when he was captured by the Japanese and put to work in their railroad camps. After the war he became a correspondent for the Melbourne *Herald* in China (1947) and in Britain (1949–51) and was named (1951) editor in chief and director of News Ltd. in Adelaide, South Australia, before becoming director of the International Press Institute in Zürich, Switz. (1962). Rivett, who was educated at the University of Melbourne and Balliol College, Oxford, also wrote weekly columns for the *Canberra Times*. He was the author of several books, mainly about Australia, and received the Commonwealth Literary Award in 1967.

Roberts, Clifford, U. S. golf executive (b. Morning Sun, Iowa, 1893—d. Augusta, Ga., Sept. 19, 1977), was a co-founder and longtime chairman (1934–76) of the Masters golf tournament held each spring at Augusta National Golf Club. Roberts, who drew up stringent rules for qualification in the invitational Masters tournament, one of four tournaments in the sport's "grand slam," made the event one of the most elite in golf. He took pride in the fact that the tournament champion prized the symbolic green jacket as much as the cash award. Roberts had suffered a stroke early in the year and was in ill health when he took his life.

Rosen, Count Carl Gustaf von, Swedish pilot and international relief worker (b. Helgesta, Södermanland, Sweden, Aug. 19, 1909—d. Gode, Eth., July 13, 1977), devoted over 40 years of his life to flying air relief missions for the victims of African conflicts. Rosen earned his pilot's license in 1929 and his commercial license in 1934. He flew Swedish ambulance planes in Ethi-

opia during the Italian invasion of 1935 and later volunteered to fight for Finland in its 1939–40 war with the U.S.S.R. After World War II he rebuilt the depleted Ethiopian Air Force. Rosen also flew relief missions for the UN in the Congo in the early 1960s and for the Joint Church Aid mission to Biafra in 1968–69. In May 1969 he became the centre of an international controversy when he reportedly used his relief planes to attack Nigerian forces fighting the Biafrans. In 1974 he undertook air relief and nomad resettlement in Ethiopia and was killed during an attack by guerrillas while visiting Gode to discuss a resettlement project.

Ross, Nellie Tayloe, U.S. politician (b. St. Joseph, Mo., Nov. 29, 1876–d. Washington, D.C., Dec. 19, 1977), was the first woman in the U.S. to be elected governor of a state. Ross, who served as governor of Wyoming (1925–27), was later appointed by Alfred E. Smith to the vice-chairmanship of the Democratic National Committee, a position she held for six years (1928–34). In 1933 she was named director of the U.S. Mint by Pres. Franklin D. Roosevelt, one of the first women to hold a federal post of that importance.

Rossellini, Roberto, Italian film director (b. Rome, Italy, May 8, 1906–d. Rome, June 3, 1977), helped create the Neorealist school of motion pictures with his film *Roma, Città Aperta (Rome, Open City)* in 1945. Though he had made his first feature film, *La Nave Bianca,* four years earlier, it was the documentary, almost newsreel quality of *Roma, Città Aperta* that brought Rossellini to the attention of critics worldwide. His next two films, *Paisan* (1946) and *Germania, Anno Zero* (1947), were also regarded as Neorealist classics. In 1950, after leaving Anna Magnani, his principal actress, Rossellini married Swedish film actress Ingrid Bergman, who had moved to Italy to act in his films. Their highly publicized relation-

ship ended in legal separation in 1957. After a series of unremarkable films, *Viaggio in Italia* (1953) revived his reputation. Rossellini also directed *India* (1958), for the Indian government, *Il Generale della Rovere,* which won the Grand Prix at the 1959 Venice Film Festival, and *Viva L'Italia* (1960), on the rise of Garibaldi. In later years he directed several Italian and French television films, including *Socrates* (1970) and *Le Messie (The Messiah,* 1975). He was chairman of the awards jury at the 1977 Cannes Film Festival.

Rostand, Jean, French biologist (b. Paris, France, Oct. 30, 1894–d. Saint-Cloud, Paris, Sept. 3, 1977), became as well known for his satirical and

moral writings, which protested France's Pacific Ocean nuclear tests (1970), as for his genetic experiments in parthenogenesis. Rostand served at the military hospital of Val-de-Grâce in Paris during World War I. He later conducted independent biological research into genes and chromosomes, established a reputation as a moralist and satirist, and became a member of the French Academy in 1959. His works include *La Loi des riches* (1920), *Julien: ou Une Conscience* (1928), and *Inquiétudes d'un biologiste* (1967).

Rupp, Adolph F., U.S. sports coach (b. Halstead, Kan., Sept. 2, 1901–d. Lexington, Ky., Dec. 10, 1977), whose teams won a record 879 games during his 42-year career (1930–72) as head coach of the University of Kentucky's Wildcats. Rupp, who never experienced a losing season, won four national titles and 27 Southeastern Conference championships, usurping the title previously held by Forrest ("Phog") Allen of the University of Kansas as college basketball's foremost winning coach.

Russell, Sir Guy Herbrand Edward, British naval officer (b. April 14, 1898–d. Wisborough Green, Sussex, England, Sept. 25, 1977), was commander of the battleship "Duke of York," which ended Germany's last serious maritime threat of World War II when it sank the battle cruiser "Scharnhorst" on Dec. 26, 1943. Russell served at sea throughout World War I, was promoted to captain in 1936, and in 1938 became assistant director of plans to the Cabinet Office. He served as chief of staff at Gibraltar and Malta (1942) and was promoted to rear admiral in 1945. After being made admiral (1952), Russell was commander in chief, Far East Station during the Korean War (1951–53), second sea lord and chief of naval personnel (1953–55), and commandant of the Imperial Defence College (1956–58). He was made a knight Commander of the Bath in 1951 and a knight Grand Cross of the British Empire in 1953.

Sabah as-Salim as-Sabah, Kuwaiti head of state (b. Kuwait, 1913–d. Kuwait, Dec. 31, 1977), became the second ruler of the oil-rich Persian Gulf state of Kuwait on Nov. 24, 1965, when he succeeded his brother Sheikh Abdullah as-Salim as-Sabah. Sabah, who served as minister of foreign affairs from 1961 to 1963, became prime minister in 1964.

Sakomizu, Hisatsune, Japanese politician (b. Kagoshima City, Japan, Aug. 5, 1902–d. Tokyo, Japan, July 25, 1977), drafted (1945) Emperor Hirohito's World War II surrender message to the Japanese people announcing Japan's unconditional surrender to the Allied forces. As

private secretary to Prime Minister Keisuke Okada in 1936, he had narrowly escaped when army officers attacked them in an attempted coup. He was banned from politics by the U.S. occupation authorities until 1952, but afterward Sakomizu, a member of the Liberal-Democrat Party, was twice elected to the House of Representatives, served as director general of the Economic Planning Agency in 1960 and 1961, and was minister of telecommunications (1961–62). He was serving his fourth term as a member of the upper house of the Diet at the time of his death.

Saypol, Irving Howard, U.S. lawyer (b. New York, N.Y., Sept. 3, 1903–d. New York, June 30, 1977), was the strong-willed prosecutor in the 1951 espionage and conspiracy trial of Julius and Ethel Rosenberg, the first U.S. civilians to be put to death for espionage. Saypol, while serving as the U.S. attorney for the Southern District of New York (1949–51), supervised the government's cases against several alleged subversives, including Alger Hiss, a State Department official convicted of perjury for denying that he had given government secrets to Whittaker Chambers, an acknowledged Communist spy. In 1952 Saypol was appointed justice of the New York Supreme Court, where he was known as a stickler for decorum. He held Adam Clayton Powell in criminal contempt of court in 1966 when the congressman, who was vacationing in the Bahamas, refused to return to New York for a court appearance.

Schermerhorn, Willem, Dutch politician (b. Akersloot, Neth., Dec. 17, 1894–d. Haarlem, Neth., March 10, 1977), headed an interim coalition government from June 1945 until the general election of 1946 as The Netherlands' first post-World War II prime minister. Schermerhorn was commissioner general for the Dutch East Indies from September 1946 to November 1947 and sought to reach an agreement on independence with nationalist leaders. After entering Parliament he served as a Labour Party member in the lower house (1948–51) and in the Senate (1951–63). A noted land surveyor, he founded the Dutch Institute of Geodesy, which he headed until 1931. He accepted commissions from the Dutch government (1936) to survey New Guinea and from Chiang Kai-shek (1937) to act as cartographical adviser to the Chinese government.

Schippers, Thomas, U.S. conductor (b. Kalamazoo, Mich., March 9, 1930–d. New York, N.Y., Dec. 16, 1977), was named music director (1970) of the Cincinnati (Ohio) Symphony Orchestra after proving his talents with such internationally renowned opera houses as La Scala in Italy and Bayreuth in West Germany. Schippers first conducted at La Scala in 1954 and was conducting with the New York Philharmonic Orchestra and the New York City Opera Company when he was still in his 20s. His reputation was established to a great extent through neglected works and a romantic repertory. Schippers gave his first performance at the Metropolitan Opera House in 1955. He not only became the first American to conduct an opening night there but ultimately conducted more opening nights than anyone else in 40 years.

Schleyer, Hanns-Martin, German industrialist (b. Offenburg, Baden, Germany, May 1, 1915–d. October 1977), was president of West Germany's employers' association and also of its federation of industry. After World War II Schleyer was imprisoned by the Allies for his role in the Nazi Party organization. In 1951 he joined the Daimler-Benz motor company and rose to the managing board in 1959, with responsibility for personnel. Schleyer was kidnapped by terrorists in Cologne on Sept. 5, 1977, and was found dead in eastern France on October 19.

Schumacher, Ernst Friedrich, German-born economist (b. Bonn, Germany, Aug. 16, 1911–d. Switzerland, Sept. 4, 1977), was a zealous conservationist whose best-seller *Small Is Beautiful* (1973) challenged Western assumptions as to the best means of securing progress in the less developed world. Schumacher's theory maintained that continuous growth is not necessarily desirable and called for a nonenergy-, noncapital-intensive society. Schumacher founded the Intermediate Technology Development Group in Britain (1965), and his views, pointing toward a true "alternative society," prompted the U.S. government to set up a $20 million fund for research in alternative technologies. In 1937 Schumacher left Nazi Germany for England, where he had studied as a Rhodes scholar at New College, Oxford University. He was economic adviser to the British Control Commission in West Germany (1945–50), then to Britain's National Coal Board (1950–70), and became president of the Soil Association in 1970. His last book, *A Guide for the Perplexed* (1977), was published posthumously.

Schuschnigg, Kurt von, Austrian politician (b. Riva, South Tirol, Austria [now Italy], Dec. 14, 1897–d. Tirol, Austria, Nov. 18, 1977), was Austria's last chancellor before the Nazi takeover in 1938. After joining the Christian-Social Party, he was elected to the Nationalrat (chamber of deputies) in 1927 and 1930. He served as minister of justice and education at the time of the abortive Nazi rising (July 1934) when Chancellor Engelbert Dollfuss was assassinated. After Schuschnigg formed the new Christian-Social government, Franz von Papen arrived in Vienna as Hitler's new ambassador. The two signed an agreement in July 1936 that identified Austria as a German state and guaranteed that the Third Reich would respect Austrian sovereignty. Schuschnigg also agreed to appoint two Nazi sympathizers to his Cabinet. In 1938 Hitler made further demands that included amnesty for all Nazis accused in the assassination of Dollfuss and the appointment of a Nazi as head of the Austrian police. After Schuschnigg announced a March 13 plebiscite on the question of Austrian independence, Hitler ordered his army to invade Austria. Schuschnigg was imprisoned for seven years. After his release in 1945, he taught politics in Missouri, then returned to Austria in 1967 where he published his autobiography, *Im Kampf gegen Hitler* (1969; *The Brutal Takeover*, 1971).

Semmler, Alexander, German-born composer (b. Dortmund, Germany, Nov. 12, 1900–d. Kingston, N.Y., April 24, 1977), was a multitalented musician whose versatility extended to composing, conducting, and piano concertizing for the Columbia Broadcasting System (CBS). Educated in Europe and influenced by the works and philosophy of Paul Hindemith, Semmler performed in concert at age 15 in Europe and the U.S. After a score of years with CBS, Semmler traveled (1951) to West Berlin, where he became administrator of the music department at Radio in American Sector. He later organized (1953) the Centro de Compositores Mexicanos in Mexico City, and became (1954–69) the program director of the Maverick Summer Concerts in Woodstock, N.Y. Among his hundreds of musical scores, *The Eagle's Brood* and *Suite* (Opus 19) for violin are considered two of the most outstanding.

Shankar, Uday, Indian dancer and choreographer (b. Udaipur, India, 1900?–d. Calcutta, India, Sept. 26, 1977), was a dancer of striking grace and strength celebrated for his presentation of Indian dance to the West. He studied painting at the Royal College of Art in London in 1919 but began a professional dancing career in 1923 as the partner of Russian ballerina Anna Pavlova, for whom he composed two Indian-style ballets. The couple toured North America extensively, but when Shankar returned to India he formed his own company of Indian dancers and musicians and returned to New York a decade later with his own troupe. In 1938 he founded his India Culture Centre at Almora, Uttar Pradesh, to study and develop Indian dance and music. His younger brother Ravi, the notable sitarist, was trained there.

Shipton, Eric Earle, British mountaineer and explorer (b. Ceylon [now Sri Lanka], Aug. 1, 1907–d. Ansty Manor, near Salisbury, England, March 28, 1977), made numerous ascents in the Alps and Africa before he attempted to reach the 29,028-ft peak of Mt. Everest in the Himalayas. Shipton, who made three assaults on the world's highest mountain (1933, 1936, and 1938), also led Everest reconnaissance expeditions in 1935 and 1951. But it was not until 1953 that Sir Edmund Hillary and Tenzing Norgay reached the peak. During and after World War II Shipton was British consul general at Kashgar (1940–42, 1946–48) and at Kunming, China (1949–51). Beginning in 1958 he undertook a number of exploratory journeys to the Galápagos Islands and Patagonia. In 1964 he acted as geographic adviser to the Chilean government in a boundary dispute with Argentina. Shipton's several books include *Mountains of Tartary* (1951), *That Untravelled World* (1969; autobiography), and *Tierra del Fuego* (1973).

Shor, Toots (BERNARD SHOR), U.S. self-styled saloonkeeper (b. Philadelphia, Pa., May 6, 1903–d. New York, N.Y., Jan. 23, 1977), became a legendary restaurateur by dispensing strong drinks and affectionate insults to a clientele that includ-

WIDE WORLD

ed many celebrities. Though some were taken aback by Shor's heavy-handed humour and never returned, actor Pat O'Brien expressed the sentiments of countless others when he said, "If he doesn't insult you, he doesn't love you." Shor's,

KEYSTONE

which was relocated several times in central Manhattan, was padlocked in 1971 by the Internal Revenue Service for nonpayment of taxes.

Spencer-Churchill, Clementine Ogilvy Spencer-Churchill, Baroness, British aristocrat (b. April 1, 1885–d. London, England, Dec. 12, 1977), was the wife of Sir Winston Churchill and a public figure in her own right. She was a noted society beauty when she married (1908) Churchill, then president of the Board of Trade. Throughout their more than 50 years of reciprocal devotion, she supported her husband in his life of politics and statecraft and listened to his great speeches in the House of Commons. She actively supported such causes as welfare of the young, for which she was awarded the Order of the Red Banner of Labour, and Red Cross Aid to Russia in World War II. After being made a life peeress in 1965 she attended sittings in the House of Lords, voting "on the liberal side of the question." She had four daughters and a son who became his father's biographer.

Stakhanov, Aleksey Gregoriyevich, Soviet coal miner (b. Ukraine, 1905–d. U.S.S.R., Nov. 5, 1977), was proclaimed a national hero after hewing 102 tons of coal on the night of Aug. 30–31, 1935, in 5 hr 45 min in a Donbass coal mine, some 14 times a miner's normal production in a shift. In December 1935 he extracted 227 tons of coal in a shift. The government then established higher worker output quotas through a "Stakhanovite" movement of emulation.

Stokowski, Leopold (Antony), British-born conductor (b. London, England, April 18, 1882–d. Nether Wallop, England, Sept. 13, 1977), was the flamboyant and innovative musical director of the Philadelphia Orchestra (1912–36) whose imaginative interpretations and experimentation elicited a rich, sonorous orchestral sound. Stokowski, who received his training at the Royal College of Music in London and Queen's College, Oxford University, made his conducting debut in Paris (1908) and with very little experience became the conductor of the Cincinnati (Ohio) Orchestra one year later. He later conducted the NBC Symphony (1941–44), directed the New York Philharmonic (1946–50) and the Houston (Texas) Symphony (1955–60), and formed (1962) the American Symphony Orchestra in New York City. Stokowski made three films with the Philadelphia Orchestra, including Walt Disney's *Fantasia,* a cartoon that was innovative in its electronic sound techniques. Under Stokowski's guiding hands (he abandoned the baton early in his career), the Philadelphia Orchestra was transformed into one of the world's finest musical ensembles.

Leopold Stokowski

BOOK OF THE YEAR

Tcherepnin, Aleksander Nikolayevich, Russian-born pianist and composer (b. St. Petersburg, Russia, Jan. 21, 1899–d. Paris, France, Sept. 30, 1977), was professor of piano and composition at De Paul University in Chicago (1949–64) and was associated with the Chicago Symphony Orchestra, for which he was composing his fourth symphony at the time of his death. After leaving Russia in 1921 with his father, the prominent composer Nikolay Nikolayevich Tcherepnin, he continued his studies at the Paris Conservatoire and was influenced by the music of Sergey Prokofiev, who had been taught by Tcherepnin's fa-

UPI COMPIX

ther. Tcherepnin's works included cantatas, orchestral suites, and pieces for unusual combinations of instruments, such as a concerto for harmonica and orchestra. He composed his first ballet, *Ajantas Frescoes* (1923), for Anna Pavlova. Other ballets, the scoring of Modest Mussorgsky's unfinished opera, *The Marriage* (1937), choral works *Pan Kéou* and *Jeu de la Nativité* (both 1945), and three symphonies (1927, 1945–51, 1955) followed. He was also interested in the folk music of many countries and established a firm in Tokyo for the publication of works by Japanese and Chinese composers.

Thomson, Sir (Arthur) Landsborough, British ornithologist (b. Edinburgh, Scotland, Oct. 8, 1890–d. June 9, 1977), was an authority on bird migration whose system for banding (ringing) birds became universally adopted. Thomson, who graduated from Aberdeen University in Scotland, held administrative posts in medical research, notably on the Medical Research Committee and Council (1919–57), after World War I. Thomson's greatest achievement as an ornithologist was the editing of *New Dictionary of Birds* (1964), containing definitions and authoritative accounts of topics related to birds. His *Bird Migration, a Short Account* (1936) and other books on migration became standard works. He was appointed chairman of the Ringing Committee of the British Trust for Ornithology in 1937 and was the trust's chairman from 1941 to 1947. Thomson was president of the British Ornithologists' Union (1948–55) and of the Zoological Society of London (1954–60).

Traglia, Luigi Cardinal, Italian Roman Catholic prelate (b. Albano Laziale, near Rome, Italy, April 3, 1895–d. Rome, Nov. 22, 1977), was the dean and senior member of the Sacred College of Cardinals, known in Vatican circles as the "living archive." Traglia was ordained in 1917 and became titular archbishop of Cesarea in Palestine (1936). In 1960 Pope John XXIII made Traglia a cardinal and from 1965 to 1968 he was Pope Paul VI's pro-vicar general of Rome, responsible for

ANSA/PHOTO TRENDS

the seal of ecclesiastical approval bestowed on all books published in Rome.

Untermeyer, Louis, U.S. author (b. New York, N.Y., Oct. 1, 1885–d. Newtown, Conn., Dec. 18, 1977), produced some 90 books, primarily anthologies that were widely used in schools and colleges as standard textbooks and helped to establish the reputations of such literary figures as Robert Frost and Amy Lowell. A minor poet in his own right, Untermeyer wrote over 1,000 poems and was also a leader of American literature's revolt against Victorian social and industrial codes.

Vasilevsky, Aleksandr Mikhailovich, Soviet marshal (b. Novopokrovskoe, Ivanovo Province, Russia, Sept. 30, 1895–d. Moscow, U.S.S.R., Dec. 5, 1977), played an important part in planning the World War II battles of Moscow (1941), Stalingrad (1942), and Kursk (1943). After graduating (1915) from the Alekseyev Military School in Moscow, he commanded an infantry battalion and later a regiment. After Germany attacked the U.S.S.R. in 1941 he was named chief of the General Staff (1942). After being promoted to marshal of the Soviet Union in 1943, he was appointed commander in chief (1945) of the three Soviet Army groups in the Far East. In 1946 he was reappointed chief of the General Staff and first deputy minister of defense, later becoming minister. In 1953, after Stalin's death, he was demoted to deputy minister of defense and retired in 1957. Vasilevsky's memoirs, *Delo vsei zhizni* ("The Whole Life's Work"), appeared in 1974.

Velasco Alvarado, Juan, Peruvian politician (b. Castilla, Peru, June 16, 1910–d. Lima, Peru, Dec. 24, 1977), led a coup against Pres. Fernando Belaúnde Terry (1968) and served as president of Peru until 1975. He nationalized transportation, communications, and electric power and transformed millions of acres of privately owned farms into worker-run cooperatives. General Velasco, plagued with a variety of illnesses in his final years, was brought down in a military coup in 1975.

Wand, the Right Rev. (John) William Charles, British Anglican prelate (b. Grantham, England, Jan. 25, 1885–d. Lingfield, Surrey, England, Aug. 16, 1977), was a respected churchman, preacher, and administrator as bishop of London (1945–55). Wand also served as canon and treasurer of St. Paul's Cathedral (1956–69). A theological scholar at Oxford University, he became dean of Oriel College, Oxford (1925–34). From 1934 to 1943 Wand was archbishop of Brisbane, Australia, and then was bishop of Bath and

Wells, England (1943–45). In 1955 he was made a knight commander of the Royal Victorian Order and a member of the Privy Council. Included in his writings are *The Latin Doctors* (1948), *The Life of Christ* (1954), and *Letters on Preaching* (1974).

Waters, Ethel, U.S. entertainer (b. Chester, Pa., Oct. 31, 1896–d. Chatsworth, Calif., Sept. 1, 1977), was a versatile blues-based singer who recorded with jazz musicians Duke Ellington and Benny Goodman. Although Waters claimed that she derived little pleasure from singing and preferred acting, she popularized such songs as "Dinah," "St. Louis Blues," and "Stormy Weather."

UPI COMPIX

She performed on Broadway (1927–59) in over a dozen productions, including *Africana, The Blackbirds,* and *Heat Wave,* but her most notable role was as Berenice Sadie Brown in *A Member of the Wedding.* Waters also appeared in nine motion pictures and received an Academy Award nomination for her performance in *Pinky* (1949). In the 1960s she regularly participated at evangelist Billy Graham's crusades and often sang the hymn "His Eye Is on the Sparrow," which was also the title of her 1951 autobiography.

Wheatley, Dennis Yeats, British novelist (b. London, England, Jan. 8, 1897–d. London, Nov. 11, 1977), was a prolific writer of thrillers and adventure fiction whose more than 60 books were translated into 29 languages and sold more than 45 million copies. After serving in World War I, Wheatley sold his father's wine business (1931) and attained instant success with his first novel, *The Forbidden Territory* (1933). He later delved into the occult in such books as *The Devil Rides Out* (1935) and *The Devil and All His Works* (1971), a modern textbook on satanism. When World War II broke out, he turned to spy stories with *The Scarlet Imposter* (1940). *The Young Man Said,* the first book of a completed five-volume autobiography, was published in 1977.

White, Katharine (KATHARINE SERGEANT), U.S. editor (b. Winchester, Mass., Sept. 17, 1892–d. North Brooklin, Maine, July 20, 1977), was *The New Yorker*'s first fiction editor (1925) and transformed that magazine from a satirical weekly to a prestigious literary showcase for struggling young authors. As a sponsor of such writers as John Cheever, John Updike, Irwin Shaw, and Ogden Nash, she procured, printed, and paid a liberal rate for short stories of superior calibre and aided young authors in getting their work published. White, who represented a dedication to elegance and precision in language, had a reputation for literary expertise. She retired in 1959. Together with her husband, the writer E. B. White, she edited *A Subtreasury of American Humor* (1941).

Wilcox, Herbert, British film director (b. London, England, April 19, 1890–d. London, May 15, 1977), was one of the creators of the British film industry. He formed a film company in 1919; among his early credits were *The Dawn of the World* and *Chu Chin Chow.* Wilcox built the first sound-film studio in Britain in 1929 and in 1932 directed *Good Night Vienna,* starring Anna Neagle, whom he later married. Wilcox reserved leading roles for his wife in musical, historical, and comedy films including *Victoria the Great, Spring in Park Lane,* and *Sixty Glorious Years.* His company declined in the 1960s after a series of earlier successes that included *Odette, The Lady with a Lamp,* and *King's Rhapsody;* later, the musical play *Charlie Girl* somewhat restored his fortunes.

Williams, Sir William Emrys, British educator and publisher (b. Capel Isaac, Carmarthen, Wales, Oct. 5, 1896–d. Stoke Mandeville, England, March 30, 1977), influenced and promoted the spread of adult education in Britain as chief editor and director of Penguin Books (1935–65) and secretary of the British Institute of Adult Education (1934–40). He was also director of the Army Bureau of Current Affairs (1941–45), trustee of the National Gallery (1949–56), and secretary-general of the Arts Council (1951–63). Williams received the American Medal of Freedom and was knighted in 1955 for his work at the Arts Council.

Wilson, Edward Meryon, British Hispanicist (b. Kendal, Westmorland [now Cumbria], England, 1906–d. Cambridge, England, Nov. 21, 1977), fostered an appreciation of Spain's Golden Age as professor of Spanish at Cambridge University (1953–73). After specializing in 17th-century Spanish literature, he translated the *Solitudes* of Góngora into English verse (1931). He was Cervantes professor of Spanish at the University of London (1945–53) and also served as president of the Cambridge Bibliographical Society in 1976.

Wolfe, Bertram David, U.S. writer (b. Brooklyn, N.Y., Jan 19, 1896–d. San Jose, Calif., Feb. 21, 1977), founded the U.S. Communist Party in 1919 but later denounced Stalin because of his purges during the 1930s. An expert on Marxism and the Soviet Union, he remained active in socialist and labour politics despite his contempt for Stalin and wrote such books as *Six Keys to the Soviet System, Khrushchev and Stalin's Ghost,* and *Marxism: 100 Years in the Life of a Doctrine.* His *Three Who Made a Revolution,* a classic study of Lenin, Trotsky, and Stalin, was translated into 28 languages.

Woodham-Smith, Cecil Blanche, British writer (b. Tenby, Wales, April 1896–d. London, England, March 16, 1977), established a reputation as a biographer and historian of the Victorian era with four works of meticulous scholarship and great narrative power. Her first volume, *Florence Nightingale* (1950), received widespread critical acclaim and was followed by *The Reason Why* (1953), which analyzed the Crimean War episode of the charge of the Light Brigade. Woodham-Smith also wrote *The Great Hunger* (1962), a study of Ireland during the famine years, and at the time of her death was working on the second volume of *Queen Victoria: Her Life and Times* (1972), the first volume of which shed new light on the queen's childhood and marriage.

Woodworth, Laurence Neal, U.S. tax specialist (b. Loudonville, Ohio, March 22, 1918–d. Newport News, Va., Dec. 7, 1977), was a distinguished member and chief of staff of the Joint Congressional Committee on Internal Revenue Taxation for some 30 years (1944–74) before joining the Carter administration as assistant secretary of the trea-

sury for tax policy. Woodworth, who was the chief draftsman of the tax reduction and revision bill that Pres. Jimmy Carter planned to submit to Congress in January 1978, was also the chief spokesman for and proponent of the tax portions of the administration's energy proposals. Although Woodworth was widely sought after by private firms because of his unequaled knowledge of tax laws, he preferred to work for the government, where he felt he could influence tax-reform legislation.

Wrigley, Philip Knight, U.S. corporate executive (b. Chicago, Ill., Dec. 5, 1894–d. Elkhorn, Wis., April 12, 1977), was the multimillionaire chairman of the William Wrigley Jr. Co., the world's largest manufacturer of chewing gum, and the owner of the Chicago Cubs baseball team, both previously operated by his father. Though Wrigley was essentially a businessman, he was most often in the news as the nonconformist owner of the Cubs, a team that had not won a league championship in 32 years and whose owner had not attended a home game in 20 seasons. Despite such aloofness, Wrigley followed the game closely and at one time ordered coaches, working in rotation, to carry out the functions of a manager.

WIDE WORLD

He was also the only owner of a major league team who refused to install lights in his ball park because, he said, "they would disturb the neighbors."

Yang Sen, Chinese general (b. Kuang-an, Szechwan Province, China, March 13, 1887–d. Taipei, Taiwan, May 15, 1977), was a hero in China whose early victories over Communist forces and whose battles with the Japanese during World War II helped stabilize Chiang Kai-shek's position as head of government. Yang, who served as governor of Kweichow Province (1945–47) and mayor of Chungking (1948–49), retreated to Taiwan (1949) under orders from Chiang when Communist forces again challenged the Chinese government and seized power. His later years were spent as a national strategy adviser to Chiang.

Yim, Young Shin (LOUISE YIM), Korean politician (b. Kumsan, Korea, Nov. 20, 1899–d. Seoul, South Korea, Feb. 17, 1977), was the organizer (1945) and the first president of the Women's Nationalist Democratic Party. As the first Korean delegate to the United Nations, she assisted in drafting the resolution that granted Korea independence from Japan in 1948. Subsequently appointed minister of commerce and industry by Pres. Syngman Rhee, she became the first woman to hold a Cabinet post in South Korea. One of

her lifelong interests was Chungang University in Seoul, of which she became president in 1953.

Yoshida, Kenichi, Japanese writer (b. Tokyo, Japan, March 27, 1912–d. Tokyo, Aug. 3, 1977), translated D. H. Lawrence's novel *Sons and Lovers,* specialized in the study of William Shakespeare, and was twice awarded the coveted Yomiuri Literary Prize. Yoshida, who taught at Seisen Women's College in Tokyo, became proficient in the English language while studying French and English literature at Cambridge University. He was the eldest son of Shigeru Yoshida, Japanese prime minister after World War II.

Zambrowski, Roman, Polish Communist leader (b. Warsaw, Poland, Aug. 15, 1909–d. Warsaw, Aug. 19, 1977), joined the Communist Union of Polish Youth in 1925, the Communist Party of Poland in 1936, and was a member of the Sejm (parliament) from 1947 to 1965. During World War II Zambrowski was a political commissar with the Polish forces under Soviet command and became a member of the Politburo of the Polish Workers' Party formed in 1942 (which merged into the Polish United Workers' Party in 1948). During 1956, when Poland was struggling to formulate new policies following Stalin's death (1953), Zambrowski supported a measure of liberalization. In 1963, under pressure from the "Partisans" (Communists active within Poland during the German occupation), he resigned from the Politburo and Secretariat. In 1976 *Zeszyty Historyczne,* a Polish-language historical journal appearing in Paris, published an article by Zambrowski which revealed that the Red Army's march on Warsaw (1920) was ordered by Lenin to create a Soviet republic from the newly reborn independent Poland.

Zuckmayer, Carl, German-born playwright (b. Nackenheim, Germany, Dec. 27, 1896–d. Visp, Switz., Jan 18, 1977), was a socially committed writer whose early works depicted Germany during the rise of the Nazis. Internationally, he was best known for *The Captain of Köpenick* (1931; Eng. trans., 1932), and *The Devil's General* (1946; Eng. trans., 1962). The first of these, a brilliant satire on militarism, marked him as an anti-Nazi, and in 1933 his plays were banned in Germany. Previously, he had been associated with Bertolt Brecht under Max Reinhardt at the Deutsches Theater. He also wrote the screenplays for such films as *The Blue Angel* and *Rembrandt.* During World War II he lived in the U.S. His autobiography, *A Part of Myself* (1966; Eng. trans., 1970), illuminates the personalities of Brecht, Reinhardt, and Ernest Hemingway.

SVEN SIMON/KATHERINE YOUNG

PETRODOLLARS AND SOCIAL CHANGE

by Peter Mansfield

> The mode of human life . . . is tribal and nomadic, a life economically precarious, politically unstable, but socially fixed and unalterable . . . . The prosperity of the tribe is measured by the number and condition of its camels. The sources of wealth are good pastures and the manly prowess of its members . . . . For a man and woman to live together [outside marriage] is unknown, and would be impossible in a tribal society in which the liberty of the individual is subordinated to the interests of the clan and its posterity, and whose rigorous moral code is rooted in age-long experience, secure from the philosophical speculations of . . . professors . . . . Man treats woman as an inferior, a chattel. This is perhaps natural in the desert environment, where . . . physical fitness, brute strength, and an aggressive character are the qualities which Nature demands and rewards.
> —Bertram Thomas, *Arabia Felix*

In the early 1930s a British official traveling in the Arabian desert could still describe the society he encountered in these terms. This austere, puritanical culture has not yet entirely disappeared, but in the years since Thomas made his journeys the countries of Arabia and the surrounding areas of the Middle East have become rich beyond the wildest fantasies of Scheherazade. What changes has the petrodollar genie brought to a civilization Arnold Toynbee once thought the modern world had passed by?

All the Arab states of the Middle East and North Africa and also Iran have been affected to some extent by the increasing income from oil exports. The process began in Iran and Iraq before World War II, accelerated with the introduction of the principle of 50–50 profit sharing between governments and oil companies in the early 1950s, and made a quantum leap with the remarkable increase in world oil prices in 1973–74. Those states that are major oil exporters have naturally been most affected, but even those with small oil resources or none, such as Lebanon, Jordan, and Egypt, have been influenced substantially. A major part of Lebanon's commercial prosperity before its disastrous civil war could be ascribed to the provision of services to the Arab oil states, while the current economic

Formerly Middle East correspondent of the London Sunday Times, *Peter Mansfield has written widely on the Arab world. He is the author of* The Ottoman Empire and Its Successors *(1973),* The Middle East: A Political and Economic Survey *(1973), and* The Arab World: A Comprehensive History *(1976).*

boom in the Yemen Arab Republic is largely due to the injection of aid from Saudi Arabia. Even the Marxist People's Democratic Republic of Yemen, which isolated its economy from that of the Arab oil states, accepted some aid from Saudi Arabia in 1976. Kuwait was the pioneer among the leading Arab oil exporters in establishing a development fund to help poorer Arab states, and others have since followed its example.

Many Dollars, Few People. The major oil producers of the Middle East may also be divided into two categories. For some, such as Algeria, Iran, and Iraq, oil revenues are vital to social and economic development, but they have other resources as well. Also, because they have substantial populations in relation to the size of their revenues, they are not accumulating huge financial reserves. In countries of the other category, which includes Kuwait, Qatar, the United Arab Emirates, and Libya, the populations are so small in relation to oil revenues that the living standards of the people have been transformed, or are being transformed, in the period of a single generation. Saudi Arabia must also be included in this category because, although it has a population of about seven million, its oil output and revenues are vastly greater than those of the other major producers.

It is to be expected that the social changes derived from petrodollars should be most profound in the countries of this second category. It so happens that these states were the poorest and most deprived before the oil boom began. The total income of the Saudi kingdom during World War II was a few million dollars a year. Today it is about $2 million an *hour*.

Certain general observations may be made about the effect of oil wealth on all these societies. In the initial stages, when the new income began to flow in the 1950s, much was wasted by the profligate spending of the ruling families on luxuries—palaces, private jet aircraft and yachts, and French perfume imported by the barrel. The record was not uniformly bad. In some states, such as Kuwait, money was diverted into social services from an early stage. But it was essentially the attacks on the

The two-way flow of contact between Arabs and non-Arabs has acted as a modernizing and westernizing influence on these highly conservative societies.

"oil sheikhs" by the Nasser regime in Egypt, which were broadcast over Cairo radio to all corners of the Arab world, that obliged the more spendthrift ruling families of Arabia to mend their ways out of a sense of self-preservation. This was the main reason for the removal of King Saud from power in Saudi Arabia in 1958 and his replacement by his more financially provident brother Faisal. Similarly, the popularity of Col. Muammar al-Qaddafi inside Libya rests on the feeling that more of Libya's oil wealth is being spent on the mass of the people than was the case under the monarchy which he replaced in 1969. In all these states, therefore, a high and generally increasing proportion of oil revenues has been spent on health, education, and other social services. Since in every case these services were either nonexistent or rudimentary before the increase in oil revenues, the social effects have been profound.

In education the effect has been most striking for the girls. A generation ago only a tiny minority of females in the Arab oil states had access to education, but in every case the rulers have now accepted the principle that girls should be educated. Often this was attained only with a struggle, as in Saudi Arabia where the late King Faisal had to use all his authority against the conservative religious leadership to achieve the opening of girls' schools. It still cannot be said that girls have equal opportunity; the full effect of this revolutionary change will be seen only in the next generation.

Western Influences. The rise and spread of wealth has meant increased contacts between these states and their populations and the rest of the world. (The most extreme case is Oman, which was almost inaccessible to foreigners before the present sultan overthrew his father in 1970 and opened up the country. Under the former sultan nearly every Omani who left went into exile.) Physical communication has improved with the building of modern airports and hotels and the inauguration of frequent air services. Because facilities for higher education were extremely limited in the area (and, though increasing, are still inadequate for the rising numbers who receive secondary education), many of the younger generation go abroad to universities—either in the Arab world (especially Cairo and Beirut) or in Europe and North America. In addition, it has become the habit among the people of the Arab oil states to leave during the hottest summer months. It is not only the millionaire oil sheikhs but members of the rapidly growing Arabian middle class who can be seen in Western capitals (especially London) during July and August.

Inevitably, the two-way flow of contact created by non-Arabs (mostly Westerners and Japanese) entering the oil states as business representatives or on contract work and by the local inhabitants traveling abroad has acted as a modernizing and westernizing influence on these highly conservative societies. Many young Arabs are attracted to various aspects of Western culture and way of life, to a relatively permissive society, and to sexual liberty and equality. The readjustment they have to make on their return—especially the women—is difficult, and in some cases they will choose quasi-permanent exile if this is possible. At the same time, it is remarkable that such a high proportion of those who leave are prepared to return and to conform to the totally different norms of a conservative Muslim society. Conformity is not of course total. The ban on alcohol, for example, can be evaded at a very high cost through the black market. But in most matters of importance there can be no avoidance.

Along with the westernizing influence, a totally different trend is also discernible. Islam is a civilization as well as a religion, and the Arabs hold a special place in this civilization. In a very real sense, every Arab is to some extent a Muslim, even if he is a Christian—or a religious skeptic. Therefore, the renaissance of the Arab nation and its acquisition of a share of world power through oil wealth after centuries of domination by the Christian West have led to a certain reassertion of Arab self-confidence and hence of traditional Islamic values.

This can be seen most clearly in Saudi Arabia, which happens to be both the wealthiest and most influential of the oil states of the Arabian Peninsula and also the one in which a puritan Islamic tradition is strongest, as a result of the alliance between the House of Saud and the Wahhabi reformers of the 18th century. Saudi ascendancy throughout Arabia and growing Saudi influence in the rest of the Arab world have already had some visible effects—in the growth of Islamic revival movements, as in Egypt, and in the reassertion of the Islamic Shariʿah law in all aspects of life, as in the United Arab Emirates. The rulers of Saudi Arabia see no virtue in moving toward a Western form of liberal government with representative institutions, and they have influenced both Kuwait and Bahrain to retreat from their tentative steps in that direction.

These Omani women are obeying the strict Muslim law that women may be heard but not seen.

At the same time, neither the Saudi regime nor the rulers of the other Arab oil states have retreated from their desire to catch up with the West in terms of material strength and technical knowledge. Increasing resources have been poured into educational programs in all these countries. A conflict between Islamic traditionalism and Western science would appear inevitable (the president of one Saudi university still maintains that the Earth is flat), but it has so far been avoided to a remarkable degree.

Immigrant Labour. Another, more direct threat to the social fabric of these countries derives from the flow of oil wealth and the drive for rapid development. From the beginning of the oil boom much of the work has had to be done by imported labour. Because the local populations lacked both numbers and the necessary skills, Palestinians, Egyptians, Lebanese, Syrians, Indians, Pakistanis, Omanis, Yemenis, and, more recently, Koreans and Taiwanese have been brought in. Since local nationality has been granted to only a very few of these immigrants, in Kuwait, Abu Dhabi, and Qatar the local population is now in a minority. This has not happened in Saudi Arabia, which has a much larger indigenous population, but the proportion of immigrants, estimated at between one-quarter and one-third, is growing because the Saudi government has acknowledged that its immensely ambitious second development plan (1975–80) can be achieved only through the import of foreign labour.

The potentially disruptive political consequences of this trend are obvious, but it also has powerful social effects. Unskilled manual labour and most unpleasant jobs are performed by immigrants. The highly skilled elite of the oil states—increasing but still very small—works hard for immense rewards. Aramco's oil drillers, for example, are now almost exclusively Saudi. But for most of the nationals of the oil states the incentives to work hard are clearly diminished. Vocational and technical colleges have difficulty finding enough pupils. High school students prefer either to go straight to university or to enter the private commercial sector with its virtually guaranteed easy profits.

This tends to erode all the institutions of the state, which cannot attract the manpower they need. In Saudi Arabia the Ministry of the Interior has been forced to impose severe penalties on soldiers and policemen who were found to be driving taxis in their spare time. Army pay has been doubled, but there is still no prospect that Saudi Arabia can increase its regular armed forces to the size needed to make it a military power of consequence without recruiting non-Saudis. The Riyadh post office has half as many sorters for the 150,000 letters a day it now handles as it had for 75,000 letters a day in 1974. Jidda has 35 postmen and needs 300.

Meanwhile, the flow of easy money destroys all sense of value among the local nationals. It has been observed that cars, the essential status symbols of every national of the oil states, have a life span of about two years. The fringes of the cities are littered with abandoned vehicles that, with a little repair, would provide 20 years' livelihood for an Egyptian taxi driver.

National Variations. While similar social trends exist to some degree in all the Arab oil states, there are certain differences in the quality of the changes that are attributable to variations in natural circumstances and political regimes. These differences are summarized below.

KUWAIT. By the early 1950s—some 20 years before any of the other major oil producers of the Arabian Peninsula—Kuwait had begun to receive more oil revenues than it could spend. Although initially the revenues were regarded as accruing to the ruling family, a decision was taken to spread the wealth throughout the population and also to provide free social services to the immigrants. Thus, although Kuwait is not the richest oil state in the world and its per capita income is less than that of Abu Dhabi, its citizens have more money to spend and invest at home and abroad than those of other states. It can be said that poverty has been eliminated among Kuwaitis; the entire younger generation is at school (about 225,000 out of 900,000), and health standards are high (except for ailments associated with affluence, such as heart disease).

Kuwait has a long tradition as a trading community; it has now acquired considerable expertise in such contemporary aspects of the capitalist system as banking and investment and has become a developed capital market. Because education has been provided for both sexes over the past generation, Kuwaiti women are more emancipated than elsewhere in Arabia. A handful even hold senior administrative posts. Kuwait has had cinemas (still banned in Saudi Arabia) for some 20 years, and until the government restrictions of 1976 it had the freest press in the Arab world after Lebanon. Yet in some respects Kuwaiti society remains highly conservative. Soon after its creation in 1963, the National Assembly imposed a total ban on alcohol, even for non-Muslims, against the wishes of the ruler. More recently there have been moves to tighten the application of traditional Islamic law.

Modern high rises shoot up from the desert sands of Kuwait alongside ancient nomadic trading routes.

QATAR. The smallest of the major Arab oil producers, Qatar had a population of about 40,000 at the time oil was discovered in the 1940s. This means that its per capita income is comparable to that of Kuwait, and poverty has been eliminated among Qataris. However, unlike Kuwait, it is too small to play any significant independent political role and its indigenous population (about 80,000 out of 180,000) too few in numbers to develop a distinctive social and cultural life.

BAHRAIN. Although Bahrain is not and never has been a major oil producer, the discovery of some small fields in the early 1930s brought the beginnings of socioeconomic change well before World War II. For centuries Bahrain had been associated with entrepôt trade and pearling. The pearling has been largely discontinued, but Bahrain has developed as the commercial and communications centre of the Gulf area. Its recent encouragement of offshore banking has accelerated its development as a capital market, and it has even assumed some of the role formerly played by Beirut. While change and development in Bahrain have been greatly accelerated by the flow of petrodollars into the region, its own population of around 250,000 is large enough to avoid the need for any large-scale immigration of labour. Bahrainis have enjoyed educational opportunities much longer than their neighbours. The island has relatively few multimillionaires, but it has a large educated middle class.

UNITED ARAB EMIRATES (U.A.E.). Among the U.A.E., Abu Dhabi is the supreme example of the "rags to riches" oil state. As recently as the early 1960s it consisted of a few thousand undernourished tribesmen living in tents and mud shacks. Within a decade it became a major city with eight-lane highways, an ultramodern airport, schools, hospitals, and a 4,000-man army with a jet fighter squadron. Immigrants heavily outnumber the local population. The fact that Abu Dhabi has been established as the capital of the U.A.E. and is in a position to make large loans to other Arab and Islamic states has given the country a political role out of proportion to its size.

Dubai differs from Abu Dhabi in that it was an important commercial centre before the discovery of oil in the 1960s. The ruler of Dubai, a tribal sheikh who is also a businessman of proven ability, has concentrated on economic affairs while leaving political matters to Abu Dhabi. He has adopted a liberal policy toward immigrants, and Dubai is probably the most rapidly expanding business centre in the Middle East. The other, smaller members of the U.A.E. are all being transformed rapidly. The old mud houses are being replaced by modern high-rise apartment buildings and hotels. With the spread of education women are emerging into public life, but only very gradually. In the summer of 1977 the government of the U.A.E. imposed stricter Islamic law.

OMAN. It is in Oman that social change promoted by petrodollars has been most rapid, because it began there most recently. The late sultan, who ruled until he was overthrown by his son in 1970, kept the country in medieval isolation—virtually without schools, medical services, or modern transport of any kind. Under the present sultan many self-exiled Omanis have returned home to accelerate the social change that is taking place at breakneck speed, especially in the coastal area around the capital. The limiting factor is that oil resources are much smaller than in Kuwait, Qatar, or Abu Dhabi, and production will soon decline if no new discoveries are made. Omani women have long been relatively emancipated, so the change in their status can proceed more rapidly. On the other hand, there are areas of the mountainous interior that only gradually will be affected by developments on the coast.

SAUDI ARABIA. Because of the unmatched scale of its wealth (the second-largest financial reserves in the world, after West Germany) and the extremely puritanical traditionalism of its society, which is conscious of its special role at the heart of Islam, Saudi Arabia suffers or enjoys all the effects of the flow of petrodollars but to a greater extent. The paradoxes and contrasts are extreme. By 1980 virtually all Saudi boys and about half the girls will be receiving primary and intermediate education, and enrollment in higher education is increasing proportionately. Yet social mores have changed very little. Cinemas are still forbidden, television services are rudimentary, and alcohol is strictly illegal throughout the kingdom. The sexes are not mixed in education. Women (including non-Saudis) may not drive a car or even hire a taxi on their own. The law forbidding Saudi women to travel abroad without a male guardian was tightened in 1977. It is possible that change will accelerate as a new generation of the Saudi royal family and the technocrats who share in administering the country take over power, but there were few signs of this happening in 1977.

LIBYA. With its socialist and highly egalitarian regime, Libya differs from the other Arab states with a surplus of petrodollars. Salaries and wages have been raised substantially and the social services expanded, but there is much less accumulation of private wealth than in the Arabian oil states. In general, the social laws of Islam are enforced as strictly as in Arabia, with the principal exception that Libyan girls are being encouraged to play a role in the country's new style of popular democracy and even to undergo paramilitary training.

A NEW ALTERNATIVE IN THE ENERGY CRISIS

by J. Dicken Kirschten

The huge Cariba Dam in Zambia produces vast amounts of electrical power for that nation's copper mining and smelting operations.

Modern industrial society has an addiction problem, warns English economist Barbara Ward. It is "hooked" on ever increasing supplies of energy. And, as typically befalls the addict, once a habit is established, the cost of maintaining it rises sharply. "Then," as Ward points out, "comes the crisis."

For the United States and other energy-dependent, industrial nations, the crisis, indeed, has arrived. Since 1973 world petroleum suppliers have raised their prices fourfold. Even at present high prices, consumption of oil and natural gas contin-

ues so high that these fuels will run out altogether within 50 years. If the analogy to addiction is valid, however, there is a far more serious issue at stake than the current thrust of the U.S. energy debate might suggest. This debate swirls around incentives for conservation, for searching out and developing new oil and gas sources, and over developing abundant and expensive substitute fuels (including large amounts of coal) and new nuclear plants. But the behaviour of an addict is fundamentally irrational and ultimately self-destructive, says Ward; what we should be discussing is whether society can break itself of a habit—"the Great Energy Jag"—that imperils its very survival.

J. Dicken Kirschten is a staff correspondent for the National Journal.

To an increasing number of critics, conventional energy strategies—massive increases in coal combustion; stepped-up production of remaining petroleum resources; development of expensive fuel synthetics from oil shale, coal, and tar sands; and accelerated reliance on nuclear power—seem to be designed only to feed the dangerous habit. Such approaches, according to Ward, represent "a desperate search for means of continuing the old abundance." Out of such desperation, she says, society's leaders "wave aside the risks" and succumb to "the temptations of the nuclear economy," behind which "stands the appalling possibility of nuclear war—possibly the 'final solution' itself."

The thinking of those who seek an alternative approach to the energy problem has been crystallized in the work of a remarkably influential and articulate young physicist named Amory B. Lovins.

Lovins, 30, has flashed like a comet across the energy horizon since his provocative article, "Energy Strategy: The Road Not Taken?" appeared in the October 1976 edition of the prestigious quarterly *Foreign Affairs*.

It is Lovins' contention that if we want to preserve the freedoms and social values that we now enjoy, we must turn away from the huge, centralized, and terribly expensive energy schemes that he characterizes as the "hard" energy technologies.

First and foremost, he argues that we still can—and, indeed, must—put the nuclear genie back into the bottle before it has worked cataclysmic mischief. Already we are beginning to fear one of its disastrous side effects—what to do with vast quantities of dangerous waste. The Lovins agenda calls for a concerted effort to phase out all nuclear armaments and all nuclear power plants as well.

Beyond the risk of atomic warfare, Lovins sees the nuclear enterprise as symbolic of the whole trend toward increasingly centralized energy facilities, which tie up astronomical amounts of capital while creating vulnerability to the massive disruption that results from region-wide power failures. This trend must lead, according to Lovins, toward a more brittle and authoritarian society.

By contrast, there is a different course—dubbed by Lovins the "soft energy path"—upon which society can embark that will lead to a much more satisfactory resolution of the current fuels dilemma. By following the soft path, a smooth transition would be made from the era of oil and gas to an era of renewable energy sources—sun, wind, tides, streams, and liquid fuels derived from vegetation. Not only are such sources sustainable, according to Lovins, but they are economically and environmentally more attractive.

Reaction to Lovins' article—since expanded into

The unusual design of this building in Odeillo, France, enables it to harness solar power for heating and lighting.

a book—has been widespread. The Edison Electric Institute, chief trade association of U.S. privately owned electric utility companies, circulated a collection of ten critical essays purporting to explain why Lovins' soft path "was not taken." Among the essayists taking issue with Lovins are solar researchers Aden and Marjorie Meinel, energy consultant and author Ralph Lapp, former U.S. labour secretary Peter J. Brennan, and Bruce Adkins of the Organization for Economic Cooperation and Development. Cornell University physics professor Hans Bethe also engaged in a critical exchange of letters with Lovins which appeared in *Foreign Affairs*.

But Lovins also drew a large following of enthusiastic backers. He was chosen to write the chapter on energy for *The Unfinished Agenda*, a report on environmental issues published in February 1977 under the sponsorship of the Rockefeller Brothers Fund. The task force of environmental leaders who prepared the report supported Lovins' contention that "nuclear fission is rapidly dying as an energy option because of its high capital, environmental, social and energy costs."

Lovins appeared before committees of the U.S. Congress and in public debates with his critics, and met with Pres. Jimmy Carter and his top energy advisers in the White House. He also was named a member of the governing board of New Directions, an organization of prominent U.S. leaders concerned with global issues, led by anthropologist Margaret Mead, former White House adviser Russell W. Peterson, and Jack T. Conway of United Way of America.

Lovins has displayed immense skill in defending the premises upon which he bases his "soft path" strategy. The bulk of the criticism he has received has been addressed toward his insistence that the hard and soft energy paths are mutually exclusive.

To complete the transition to total reliance upon "benign, resilient and sustainable" energy sources may take 50 years, Lovins says. But to ensure that society survives long enough to make the shift, he insists that a firm commitment must be made now to turn away from the hard path of big-coal, synthetic petroleum, and nuclear technologies.

The hard path, Lovins contends, not only exposes the world to the potentially catastrophic risks of nuclear weapons proliferation but also, because of its inherent waste and inefficiency, will become unaffordable. With a memorable turn of phrase, he suggests that using a nuclear temperature of millions of degrees to generate electricity ultimately used to heat a home to 70° F (21° C) is "like cutting butter with a chainsaw."

Such energy mismatches, he says, are characteristic of the highly centralized, increasingly electrified, power systems that are being fostered by present-day national energy policies. They are the result, Lovins insists, of a failure to tailor energy supply systems to fit the purposes for which the power ultimately is to be used. It must be kept in mind, he says, that "people do not want electricity or oil, nor such economic abstractions as 'residential services,' but rather comfortable rooms, light, vehicular motion, food, tables, and other real things."

The nation's growing commitment to electrification is perhaps the best example of Lovins' contention that the energy system is so preoccupied by the forest—supply—that it loses sight of the trees—end uses. According to his analysis the U.S. needs electricity for only 8% of its present energy needs, for such purposes as lighting, electronics, telecommunications, home appliances, subways and railways, and various industrial processes. With improved conservation measures, he says, this figure might in time be lowered to 5%.

The other 92% of our energy requirements, by Lovins' estimates, are for heating—58%, divided equally among high- and low-temperature needs—and for transportation—34%. (Frank von Hippel and Robert H. Williams, physicists at Princeton University's Center for Environmental Studies, have performed work that closely parallels and supports Lovins' studies. However, in an article in the October 1977 *Bulletin of the Atomic Scientists*, von

Hippel and Williams express less optimism about reducing U.S. end-use consumption of electricity. They estimate that "about 20 per cent [of U.S. energy goes] for end uses which are currently and probably will continue to be electric.")

As of 1977, however, electricity was being used to meet 13% of the nation's end-use needs, and 29% of its fossil fuels were being consumed to generate it, according to Lovins. With a commitment to the hard path of expanded reliance upon coal and uranium, both best suited for use in huge electric-generating plants, as much as 20–40% of end-use energy consumption may be in the form of electricity, most of it unnecessary, says Lovins.

Limiting reliance upon electricity is central to the success of the soft-path energy strategy. Stated quite simply, the production of large amounts of electricity requires more raw energy than the "soft" technologies preferred by Lovins can be expected to produce in the foreseeable future.

As Lovins explains it, "the laws of physics require, broadly speaking, that a power station change three units of fuel into two units of almost useless waste heat plus one unit of electricity. This electricity can do more difficult kinds of work than can the original fuel, but unless this extra quality and versatility are used to advantage, the costly process of upgrading the fuel—and losing two-thirds of it—is all for naught."

Excessive preoccupation with electrification also could delay the introduction of renewable energy sources, particularly power from the Sun. Lovins declares that "not all solar technologies are soft." He scoffs at esoteric solar-electric research efforts—"huge collectors in the desert . . . or . . . Brooklyn Bridge-like satellites in outer space"—that hope to capture the Sun's energy in a form that can be fed into the high-powered electrical grid.

While Lovins concedes that the U.S. needs electricity for 5–8% of its end-use needs, he points out that the nation uses 29% of its consumed energy for low-temperature heating. This use is well matched to the capabilities of smaller and simpler solar technologies, such as rooftop collectors that can heat water for individual buildings or perhaps whole neighbourhoods.

An additional 29% of end-use energy needs are for high-temperature (above the boiling point of water) heating. Lovins would meet those needs by using "fossil fuels intelligently to buy the time we need" to further develop soft technologies, such as solar furnaces for industrial purposes and a large-scale vegetation-based liquid-fuel supply.

The transportation system, with its requirements for liquid fuels, accounts for the final 34% of end-use energy consumption in Lovins' calculations. In

(Top) A giant windmill at Mikonos, Greece. (Bottom) The control room of a nuclear power plant at Zion, Illinois.

this area, the soft path leads toward a variety of renewable biological resources. According to Lovins, "exciting developments in the conversion of agricultural, forestry and urban wastes to methanol and other liquid and gaseous fuels now offer practical, economically interesting technologies sufficient to run an efficient U.S. transport sector."

Improvements in Efficiency. Besides carefully matching energy sources with end uses, Lovins' soft-path strategy is predicated on numerous improvements in efficiency that will permit the U.S. economy to survive on considerably less energy than more conventional planners expect. Instead of a growth in consumption from 74.2 quadrillion British thermal units, or quads, in 1976 to a hard-path level of 160 quads by the year 2000, Lovins maintains that the soft path will lead to a consumption level of roughly 95 quads by 2000 followed by a gradual decline in total energy demand thereafter.

His strategy calls for both "social changes," such as greater use of public transportation and smaller cars, and "technical fixes," ranging from improvements in insulation to "cogeneration"—the process of using the formerly wasted, leftover steam from industrial activities to generate small but significant amounts of electricity. Such waste heat, in some cases, can be utilized to help heat nearby buildings, a concept Lovins refers to as "district heating."

In addition, the soft path emphasizes decentralization to cut down on the amount of energy required simply to deliver power to the location where it will be used. The crux of Lovins' argument is that the hard path, which he says will consume some 225 quads a year by 2025, will actually deliver less, if any, additional energy for actual end uses than will the soft path.

Dam No. 26 at Alton, Illinois.

Wasted Energy

Examples of usable energy sources close to home are many. Some of these sources, like the following, are potentially large.

Lock and Dam No. 11 are located on the Mississippi River at Dubuque, Iowa. That far upriver the volume of water is not nearly so high as it is downstream, but even so, an average of 40,000 cubic feet of water comes churning, roiling, and roaring through the sluice gates over a fall of 11 feet at Dam No. 11 every second. No generating turbines harvest this tremendous free-flowing power. No power lines are strung from the dam into Dubuque, which sits right on the riverbank by the dam.

Electrical engineers at Commonwealth Edison, the largest electrical utility in the Midwest, calculate that the volume of water at the Dubuque dam would be sufficient to generate 30,000 kilowatts of electricity, or enough to meet about half the total electricity needs of the city of Dubuque.

Dam No. 11 is but one of 27 such dams between the headwaters of the Mississippi and the city of St. Louis, yet electrical power is generated at only four of these dams, and at these by private power companies.

Electrical engineers estimate that if all of these dams were turned into power-producing stations they would do much to light up the entire Mississippi Valley with continuously available, nonpolluting energy. At Dam No. 26 at Alton, Ill., for example, the water volume averages 98,570 cubic feet per second and the lift is 24 feet, giving a potential power yield of 167,000 kilowatts.

A July 1977 report by the U.S. Army Corps of Engineers states, "The development of all of the hydropower potential at existing hydropower and non-hydropower dams could generate almost 160 billion kilowatt hours of electricity and save 727,000 barrels of oil per day."

"Roughly half, perhaps more, of the gross primary energy being produced in the hard path in 2025," Lovins says, "is lost in conversions. A further appreciable fraction is lost in distribution. Delivered end-use energy is thus not vastly greater than in the soft path, where conversion and distribution losses have been all but eliminated. (What is lost can often be used locally for heating, and is renewable, not depletable.)"

Transitional Technologies. To build a bridge to the nonnuclear, totally renewable energy economy that he envisions by 2025, Lovins calls for transitional technologies to fill in on an interim basis for the dwindling supplies of oil and natural gas.

Assuming that there is a rapid development of alcohol fuels from biomass (vegetation) sources and that such conservation measures as cogenerating electricity from existing industrial steam and using existing waste heat for district heating become widespread, Lovins sees the principal near- and middle-term problems as being a shortage of "clean sources of heat." This shortage he proposes to fill through "the sophisticated use of coal, chiefly at modest scale." While conceding that such coal-burning technologies are in need of development, he nonetheless suggests that at least one such method is at hand.

"Perhaps the most exciting current development," says Lovins, "is the so-called fluidized-bed system for burning coal (or virtually any other combustible material). Fluidized beds are simple, versatile devices that add the fuel a little at a time to a much larger mass of small, inert, red-hot particles—sand or ceramic pellets—kept suspended as an agitated fluid by a stream of air continuously blown up through it from below."

The merits of the fluidized-bed system, according to Lovins, are its high efficiencies of combustion and heat transfer and its potential for reducing air-pollution problems by removing sulfur from the stack gases that are emitted. Lovins says that small-sized fluidized-bed units, suitable for the sorts of decentralized uses that he advocates, are currently marketed in Europe.

Criticism of the Soft Path. Not surprisingly, much of the criticism of Lovins' soft-path energy strategy centres on the rapidity with which such new technologies as fluidized-bed combusters, biomass alcohol fuels, and solar- and wind-power systems can be brought into widespread commercial use. Lovins' optimism about the ready or near-ready availability of these soft technologies is by no means universally shared.

For example, the U.S. Congress' Office of Technology Assessment, in its June 1977 analysis of the Carter administration's national energy plan, expressed concern about proposals that would force industries "to shift to coal before advanced coal technologies are commercially available." The report urged flexibility in the timing of such conversions in order "to not lock out technologies" that would be especially suitable for cogeneration once they have been "perfected and commercialized."

Lovins also has been attacked for his bias against any of the nuclear technologies, particularly fusion, which—though still far down the line—is seen by its proponents as a clean, safe, and inexhaustible energy source. To this contention, Lovins responds:

"Fusion is a clever way to do something we don't really want to do, namely to find *yet another* complex, costly, large-scale, centralized, high-technology way to make electricity—all of which goes in the wrong direction." He further adds that "fast neutrons" produced by the fusion process probably could be used to make "bomb materials," and even if not, there is the danger that fusion would be so overused that "the resulting heat release will alter global climate."

Critics also accuse Lovins of vastly overstating the likely net energy demand that will result from the pursuit of present policies, which include attention to many of the conservation measures of the soft-path strategy. The prediction that the hard path will require 160 quads by 2000 is vigorously disputed, for instance, by Ian A. Forbes, technical director of Energy Research Group, Inc., and a former member of the Union of Concerned Scientists, a group highly critical of the nuclear industry.

Forbes, in congressional testimony, charged that Lovins' soft-path strategy "taken as a whole . . . is infeasible in scale, structure and economic cost." He said that Lovins' use of the 160 quads figure for the hard path "is a 'straw man' that shows future growth well in excess of what most thoughtful projections see as being likely or necessary." Forbes suggested that 115 to 125 quads would more realistically describe the hard path.

Quibbling over details aside, there is no denying the appeal of the simple and bold philosophical thrust of Lovins' central argument—that it is warmth and security and mobility, not complex systems that society desires.

And, as Barbara Ward so sensibly states, it would seem to make immense good sense to place our reliance on "a single nuclear reactor, meticulously engineered, carefully tested, and thoughtfully sited a safe 150 million kilometres away—in fact, the sun itself. . . ."

Amory B. Lovins and his many supporters, including Barbara Ward, believe that if we use our ingenuity the Sun will prove to be "quite enough" to meet our energy needs.

The subcontinent of southern Africa is a vast region that, only a century ago, was still largely "dark." Today, the former colonies of Great Britain, Portugal, and Germany have become the independent states of Angola, Botswana, Lesotho, Malawi, Mozambique, Rhodesia, South Africa, Swaziland, Transkei, and Zambia, plus the United Nations Trust Territory of South West Africa (Namibia).

Southern Africa is no longer dark, but it is still rather mystifying to large numbers of readers of the Book of the Year. *We therefore reprint here a portion of the Britannica article on the region—dealing with events in southern Africa since 1900—because of the great importance of the subcontinent to our current world, and because of the many and rapid changes that have taken place there in the last few years.*

Three separate (although connected) historical narratives are intertwined in these pages: the story of South Africa and its immediate neighbours; the story of Northern and Southern Rhodesia (now called Zambia and Rhodesia); and the story of the former Portuguese colonies, notably Mozambique and Angola. Lying behind these stories is a background of unending exploitation of man by man, of expropriation under the cover of law, of desperate poverty contrasted to vast wealth, and of constant, bitter racial strife.

Events may conspire in the near future to make our decision to reprint these pages seem prophetic. At any rate, some insight into the recent past will serve to make tomorrow's headlines more intelligible—and headlines from southern Africa are a sure bet for some time to come.

SOUTHERN AFRICA, HISTORY OF

III. Southern Africa, 1900–45

For black and white southern Africa, the 20th century has wrought vast changes, though north of the Zambezi and in the Portuguese territories, where colonial development was hampered by the two world wars and a depression, they were initially less dramatic. Nevertheless, by 1945 in most areas Western administrative, medical, and educational practices, however inadequate, were established, roads and railways built, minerals exploited, and Africans drawn into the world economy more intensively than ever before. New frontiers had been created, which have become the boundaries of modern states; and everywhere the demands of new rulers were undermining traditional authority and small-scale precolonial societies and creating new class and political alignments.

Farther south, where this process had first begun, whites increased their political, economic, and military hold through the unification of the South African colonies, creating, by 1945, the most highly industrialized state in Africa. The Union (later Republic) of South Africa has dominated its neighbours throughout the 20th century. Capital expansion northward was initiated by the south and was paralleled by a vast labour migration to the mines and farms of South Africa. At the same time, class and colour relations shaped by the early days on the diamond and gold fields and given characteristic form by the first decades of the century in South Africa were repeated both in the development of second-

ary industries in the union and in the mines and the industries of the Rhodesias.

In all the territories, the economic exploitation of blacks was facilitated by the development of a racist ideology. Africans were seen essentially as a source of cheap unskilled labour, not, as elsewhere in colonial Africa, as cash-crop producers. Discriminatory policies, whether described as segregation or parallel development, were prompted by settlers' fears of African political and economic competition and lent respectability by anthropologists and paternalist administrators anxious to preserve African societies from rapid social change. Though in the Portuguese colonies "native policy" was theoretically to assimilate Africans to a Portuguese way of life, obstacles to the *assimilado* progress were in practice greater in the 20th century than they had been in the 19th; and the *indigenato* policy, in force from 1926 to 1961, while granting equal rights to a very small handful of assimilated Africans, established separate administration, lawcourts, institutions, and status for the vast majority.

WHITE SETTLERS SOUTH OF THE LIMPOPO

If the South African War was the high-water mark of direct British intervention in South Africa, the tide rapidly receded in the next five years. In 1906–07 the British granted self-government to the defeated republics, and by 1910 the four self-governing colonies had been uni-

The unification of South Africa

fied. This unification was dictated largely by the demands of the industrial revolution consequent on the mineral discoveries. With the South Africa Act, the 1,250,000 enfranchised whites achieved complete political control over approximately 4,250,000 unrepresented Africans, 500,000 Coloureds, and 165,000 Indians.

Though there was talk of incorporating the landlocked British protectorates, or High Commission Territories, of Basutoland (now Lesotho), Bechuanaland (now Botswana), and Swaziland, the opposition of the Africans of the protectorates, as well as that of the radical lobby in Britain, led to their exclusion from the union. Until the mid-20th century, however, it was thought in Britain that the protectorates would ultimately be incorporated, and on a number of occasions—especially during the 1930s—South African politicians demanded this. Strong African opposition, the effective lobbying of radical groups in Britain, and, finally, the outbreak of World War II prevented this from happening; nevertheless, the assumption meant that the territories were fully locked into South Africa's migrant labour system and became increasingly impoverished. Administrators were often South African; and local chiefs, subject to a virtually unassailable paramount chief, were left to run their tribes as they saw fit. Though this dual administration, as well as the stagnant economy of the territories, was severely castigated by the so-called Pim Commission of 1934–35, and moderate reforms were instituted, the High Commission Territories remained backward and neglected.

Though South Africa failed to incorporate the High Commission Territories, after World War I it acquired the vast German colony of South West Africa. Despite a League of Nations mandate that the territory be administered as a "sacred trust," white settlement was encouraged and subsidized from the outset. Though almost half of the German population was repatriated at the end of the war and the rest were naturalized in 1924, Nazi demands in the 1930s for the return of German colonial possessions had a counterpart in South West Africa; by that time there were about 30,000 whites in the territory, largely from South Africa, and considerable vested interests had grown up, especially in diamond mining and fishing. There were almost annual criticisms from the Permanent Mandates Commission of the League about the lack of economic and educational development for Africans, and the League was much disquieted by the violent confrontations between the South African government and the Bondelswarts (1922), the Rehoboth community (1924–25), and the Ovambo (1932). Nonetheless, the major preoccupation of the mandatory power continued to be to foster white prosperity, generally at the expense of African tribesmen.

White politics in the union

Within the union, between 1910 and 1948, whites were divided by class and ethnicity. Until 1924 the South African Party (SAP) was in power under the leadership of two successive prime ministers, Louis Botha (1910–19) and Jan Smuts (q.v.; 1919–24), representative of the more successful Afrikaner farmers and in close alliance from 1914 with the Unionists, the party of mining capital, which the SAP absorbed in 1920. The SAP's essential aims were to reconcile the English- and Afrikaans-speaking communities, to maintain the imperial connection, and to promote commercial farming and mining interests. This led to an increasingly bitter conflict with the white working class on the Rand as well as with the Afrikaner nationalists, who broke away from the SAP in 1913–14 under the leadership of Gen. J.B.M. Hertzog.

In 1924 a coalition of Hertzog's Nationalists and the predominantly British Labour Party removed Smuts from power. Between 1924 and 1929 legislation protected white workers from African competition, while the state sponsorship of industrial and agricultural development was accelerated in an attempt to help solve the "poor white" problem. Largely through Hertzog's efforts, the nature of the British Commonwealth connection was redefined in 1929–30, and the concept of dominion independence was fully enunciated.

In 1933, in the face of South Africa's worsening economic position during the Great Depression and the crisis of confidence surrounding its abandonment of the gold standard, the Afrikaner generals Smuts and Hertzog formed a coalition government, and in 1934 their parties fused as the United Party. The outbreak of World War II destroyed their somewhat precarious consensus. As in World War I, when fierce civil war erupted between the Afrikaners on the issue of South Africa's participation on the British side, Afrikaners again were divided over the country's contribution to the Allied forces. When South Africa voted by a narrow margin to fight the Germans, Hertzog resigned.

Even before this, in 1934, a group of nationalists—largely members of the extreme Broederbond, a secret society that aimed at Afrikaner economic advance and ultimately Afrikaner dominance in a republic—had left the United Party to form the Purified Nationalist Party. Though their electoral support remained relatively small in the '30s, the Purified Nationalists built up their power through the establishment of extensive welfare and economic subsidiary organizations, directed on the one hand at promoting the interests of Afrikaner petty bourgeoisie and on the other to gaining the support of the Afrikaner rural poor and workers in the towns through the provision of cultural, social, and trade union organizations outside the predominantly English-speaking Labour and Communist parties.

Purified Nationalist Party

Though Hertzog now rejoined the Purified Nationalist Party, the alliance was uneasy; the history of the Nationalists during the war is a complicated series of manoeuvres by disunited factions. Through the war years, General Smuts, by this time a prominent world statesman and for the second time a member of the British War Cabinet, headed the government and the United Party, which was now supported by virtually all English-speaking whites and contained within its ranks both extreme right-wingers and liberals. The Afrikaner divisions, however, masked the fact that Smuts had lost the support of the group that by this time made up the clear majority of the South African white population.

WHITE SETTLERS NORTH OF THE LIMPOPO

Though the Union of South Africa had by far the most powerful and complex settler polity, in the first half of the 20th century settlers acquired firm control over Southern Rhodesia (now Rhodesia), too, while even in Nyasaland and Northern Rhodesia (now Malawi and Zambia), which came under the jurisdiction of the British Colonial Office in 1892 and in 1924, respectively, it was accepted that white settlers would provide the necessary economic development. Until 1923, Rhodesia was administered by the British South Africa Company. In 1898 a Legislative Council was established, and by World War I the 25,000 settlers had an elective majority in it. The colour-blind franchise qualifications, modelled on those of the Cape, were sufficiently high to exclude all but a handful of Africans. In 1922, when the company handed over formal responsibility for the territory to the British crown, the settlers rejected a proposal to join the Union of South Africa in favour of self-government. Again there was no attempt to include Africans in government; though the constitution provided for an imperial veto over discriminatory legislation, the veto was never exercised, and complete control of the police and armed forces was handed over to the minority government.

Though a number of white political parties flourished under a variety of names between the 1920s and 1950s, there were basically two parties of importance: (1) the "government" party, closely allied to big business interests, and (2) the "opposition" party, more eager to secure the position of white farmers and workers in the face of African competition. Outside formal politics, farmers, mining companies, and trade unions formed crucial pressure groups. Apart from socio-economic issues, the major issue in the late 1920s and '30s, as indeed later on, was over relations with Northern Rhodesia, where the wealth of the Copperbelt proved a considerable attraction.

Across the Zambezi the handful of white settlers were in

a far weaker position than those farther south. In Northern Rhodesia, white traders and farmers, largely from South Africa, were granted an advisory council in 1918, but it had very little real power. When, in 1924, the company withdrew from its administration, the territory came under crown colony rule. Settler numbers jumped to 11,000 by 1930, with the discovery and exploitation of the rich deposits of copper by British, South African, and American capital. Various attempts by the whites of Northern Rhodesia in the 1920s and '30s to amalgamate with Southern Rhodesia in order to bolster their political position and to secure independence from imperial control were defeated by the Colonial Office, which enunciated a doctrine of trusteeship. Nevertheless, in crucial areas, such as the stabilization of African labour, equal pay for white and black, and the job colour bar, the Colonial Office was not prepared to counter the opposition of either the copper companies or white workers.

In Nyasaland, also, though the principle of African "paramountcy" was frequently proclaimed, it has been shown that British imperial interests generally prevailed and led to the territory's depressed economy. The Shire Highlands were considered highly suited to white settlement, and the demands of the planters there for labour and communications were acceded to. Moreover, in railway construction more attention was paid to the needs of British capitalist strategy than to those of the territory, which was saddled with huge public indebtedness.

Though the number of settlers in the Portuguese colonies was roughly comparable with those in Southern Rhodesia, they never achieved comparable political power. Despite the transfer to civilian government in the colonies during the republican period in Portugal (1910–26) and supposedly greater local autonomy, real power was in the hands of the governor general, or, as he became in 1921, the high commissioner, the highest colonial representative of the Portuguese government.

The republican period saw a flurry of activity among settler political groups, some of them in alliance with African *assimilados* and *mestiços* angry at Portuguese neglect and maladministration. This culminated in Angola in 1930 when the governor was forced temporarily to withdraw from Luanda. With the consolidation of António Salazar's regime in Portugal, however, strict government vigilance was exerted over all economic and political activity in the interests of stability, though in 1942 municipal politics were revived among the settlers. Though the greater control in the hands of the administration could, and at times did, restrain the exploitation of Africans by foreign interests, the final conquest of Africans, the greater power in the hands of the government, and increased demands for African labour and crop production led to their everyday lives being ever more strictly controlled.

LAND, LABOUR, AND COLOUR BARS

At the root of relationships between black and white in the 20th century in southern Africa are the closely connected issues of land and labour.

Alienation of land. At the beginning of the century, the vast majority of Africans in the subcontinent lived on the land, which in many areas is now claimed by white settlers. South of the Limpopo, the century-long battle over land and water was largely won by whites, though increasingly crowded pockets of land were reserved for Africans in the Transkei, Zululand, and the three High Commission Territories. In the latter, further land alienation to whites could not take place without the express agreement of the high commissioner, although in Swaziland land concessions granted to whites by chiefs in the 19th century had already alienated one-third of the land resources of the kingdom and constituted a continuing source of unrest and friction.

In the reserves and protectorates of southern Africa, governments retained African tribal organization and governed through sufficiently compliant chiefs and headmen. Economically, these areas were largely based on subsistence agriculture.

In the union about 40 percent of the African population lived on reserves, and about the same number lived on white-owned farms either as labour- or rent-paying tenants or sharecrop farmers (squatters). The poorly paid labourers were immobilized by master-and-servant laws and Pass Laws, which made strikes and desertion criminal offenses. Small numbers of Africans, from the second half of the 19th century, were successfully producing cash crops for the new markets; increasingly, however, because of government subsidizing of white farmers and preventing further land purchase by Africans, and because of African population pressure and soil erosion, these initiatives were crushed.

Probably the crucial blow to the Africans in South Africa was the Natives Land Act of 1913, a complex measure aimed at securing a supply of cheap labour by limiting African land ownership to the already existing reserves and by transforming African sharecroppers and tenants into wage labourers. Under this act and the complementary Native Land and Trust Act of 1936, about 12–13 percent of the land was scheduled for more than 4,000,000 Africans, while 87 percent of the land was reserved for 1,250,000 whites. Though the 1913 act prevented the total dispossession of Africans and ensured a rural base for migrant labourers where their welfare costs could be borne, it also led to the dislocation of thousands of Africans, who were to swell the numbers already working for whites.

In South West Africa, the white farming population increased at the expense of both the Herero and Nama. In 1921 the administration set aside apparently large reserves for the two indigenous groups, pursuing the policy of segregation established by the South African Natives Land Act, but these were generally in the dry hinterland of the Kalahari or on sandveld unsuited to man or beast. By the 1930s settlers were in control of more than a third of the land.

In Southern Rhodesia the pattern was not dissimilar, though Africans retained a higher proportion of land. After the Shona and Ndebele rebellions, the administration sold large tracts of land to settlers and speculators, with little concern for African rights. As hopes of vast mineral wealth were disappointed, the British South Africa Company turned to the development of white commercial agriculture—maize (corn), cattle ranching, and tobacco. By the 1920s, of 96,200,000 acres of land in Southern Rhodesia, 31,000,000 were in the hands of about 11,000 whites; 21,100,000 had been reserved for the 676,000 Africans; and 44,100,000 acres remained open to purchase and occupation by people of any race. In 1930 the Land Apportionment Act, modelled in part on South African legislation, attempted to define areas of ownership by barring African land purchase outside the reserves and by a special native purchase area of 8,000,000 acres, which soon proved inadequate.

As in South Africa, a considerable number of Africans "squatted" on white-owned and crown lands in Southern Rhodesia. By the 1920s, with the increased utilization of land by commercial farmers and their demands for labour, there was little room for such practices, while the initiatives of the Shona at cash-crop production were also crushed by the artificially created land shortage, discriminatory marketing practices, and the distance of the reserves from roads and railways. The rapid growth of the African population and its stock in the limited reserves, combined with its lack of security in urban areas, made the land question increasingly acute through the 1930s and '40s. Though in 1951 the Native Land Husbandry Act was adopted, allegedly to grapple with the problems of overstocking and erosion in the reserves and to implement the necessary agrarian reform, for a variety of reasons it remained unimplemented.

In Northern Rhodesia, land never became as crucial an issue, except along the railway line in Tonga country and at Fort Jameson, where white settlers, mainly from South Africa, established themselves; in the reserves drawn up in 1928–29, however, there were problems of overcrowding and overstocking.

[margin notes:]

Colonial rule in British Central Africa

Republican Portugal

Natives Land Act of 1913

The Native Land Husbandry Act of 1951

In Nyasaland, despite Johnston's attempts to control land alienation after 1896, about 15 percent had passed to whites by the turn of the century, particularly in the Shire Highlands, where tobacco, cotton, coffee, and tea plantations were established. On their lands, planters charged rent or demanded labour of Africans who wished to remain. Though by the end of World War II the amount of land in settler hands had been reduced to 5 percent, about 10 percent of the African population lived on white-owned plantations as tenants-at-will, squatters, or labourers. In the first three decades of the century, the administration favoured white plantation agriculture over African cash-crop production, though this gradually changed. In 1936 the bulk of the land was vested in a Native Trust. By the end of the war there was serious overcrowding in the southern provinces of Nyasaland, especially in Cholo and Mlanje districts, where, in 1953, the population density was estimated at 250 to the square mile. This congestion led to very serious rural discontent, which erupted in riots in Blantyre in 1943, in Cholo in 1945, and in Cholo and Mlanje in 1953.

In Angola and Mozambique at the beginning of the century, despite the then sparse settler population, a land policy was initiated by which all land not privately owned was in the hands of the state. Though Africans were to be left on their communally owned lands, the way was open to their expropriation in response to the demands of the concession companies and, later, of white settlers. In the Portuguese territories, however, land alienation never became the key method of forcing out African labour, which was more directly provided for in the labour codes of 1878, 1899, and 1928. The codes institutionalized a variety of forced labour practices.

In addition, from the 1930s until 1961, with economic development directed solely to Portugal's benefit, Africans in certain areas had to pick stipulated cotton or coffee quotas, which had to be sold to the companies or government at a fixed price below the world market level.

African labour. In the British-controlled territories, as in South Africa in the 19th century, before Africans felt the effects of land shortage, the most important method of forcing out labour was taxation, which had the double advantage of producing revenue for administration. In Nyasaland, tax collection started in 1892 and extended over the entire territory by 1904. In Southern Rhodesia, the British South Africa Company imposed a hut tax in 1898, which was doubled in 1904, while in Northern Rhodesia the whole country became subject to tax in the first decade of the 20th century. Taxation increased steadily in all of the territories until World War II, though in many areas Africans working for whites received rebates.

Taxation At the beginning of the century by far the most dramatic demand for labour resulted from the mineral discoveries in South Africa, and it was here that much of the subsequent pattern of southern Africa's industrialization was established. Initially, Africans went to the diamond fields and later to the gold mines for short periods, leaving their families behind on the reserves. The mineowners soon realized the advantages of employing unorganized migrant workers, who could be paid low wages on the grounds that they were single men who worked only for specific targets. On the diamond fields, Africans were housed in closed compounds to maximize control and prevent desertion. Both the compound system and migrant labour became features of the gold mines of South Africa and Southern Rhodesia, as well as of the copper mines of Northern Rhodesia in the 1920s and '30s.

With the opening up of the gold mines, demands for African labour expanded far beyond the frontiers of the Union of South Africa. In 1889 the Chamber of Mines was formed and soon came to control African wages by monopolizing the labour supply. By the early years of the century the chamber's recruiting agents had spread as far afield as Barotseland and Nyasaland.

From the first decade of the 20th century, by far the largest number of workers for the gold mines came from Mozambique. Under conventions signed between Portugal and the South African government in 1903, 1909, and 1928, Mozambique received a grant for every worker sent to the mines, while the bulk of the Africans' wages was handed over to Portuguese officials for repayment in the territory. The grant constituted a major source of the colony's income. In Angola this system had its counterpart in the contract labour sent to the cocoa plantations of São Tomé. In South Africa, where the effect of this ready supply of powerless labour enabled the Chamber of Mines to prevent any rise in real wages for Africans between 1911 and 1971, the system was relatively unremarked. In 1911 African wages in the mines were lower than they had been in 1897.

Part of the justification for the very low wages paid to black migrants in the white economy was, and still is, the assumption that their families were able to subsist on agriculture in the reserves. Nevertheless, the continual absence of the majority of adult men broke up families and contributed to the impoverishment, underdevelopment, and demoralization of the rural areas, while hampering the growth of working class consciousness in the towns and thus the improvement of urban wages and living conditions. The justification for low wages

The job colour bar. While it was possible for the mining industry to acquire cheap unskilled labour through a variety of administrative techniques, skilled labour had to be attracted from overseas to the interior of South Africa by the promise of extremely high wages. Though by the turn of the century many Africans had acquired the requisite skills, and it was in the economic interests of the mineowners to substitute Africans for the increasingly expensive white labour, the political power of white workers and, later, trade union organization, together with the powerlessness of the Africans, enabled white workers to establish a job colour bar, which was legally entrenched in South Africa in the Mines and Works acts of 1911 and 1926.

In 1922 the Chamber of Mines in South Africa attempted to relax the job colour bar and cut white wages, but this led to a wave of strikes on the Witwatersrand that culminated in a five-day battle between white workers and troops and resulted in the firmer entrenchment of the job colour bar.

Though the job and wage colour bars had their counterparts in the Rhodesias and the Portuguese territories, on the Copperbelt of Northern Rhodesia white unionists were ultimately too weak to protect their privileged position. The major copper companies were the Anglo American Corporation of South Africa and the Rhodesian (later Roan) Selection Trust, with mainly American capital.

Though production slumped during the Great Depression, by 1935 the copper mines were already recovering. Ten years later Northern Rhodesia was one of the world's greatest copper producers, and the job colour bar, the enormous differential between black and white wages, and discriminatory practices had become essential features of the Copperbelt. By the mid-century, however, the growth of trade unionism and skills among Africans and the political weakness of the white working class enabled the mining magnates to replace white miners with trained Africans. Today the well-organized African miners on the Copperbelt constitute a highly paid elite.

Urbanization of white and black Africans. Although the first major battleground over the colour bar appeared in the mining industry, the presence of an increasing number of Africans in the urban areas outside the mining compounds brought new problems for government in southern Africa from the 1920s onward. By the turn of the 20th century, indeed, there was already a substantial number of Africans in the four major cities of South Africa, and by 1921 there were more than 500,000 Africans in towns. These numbers increased sharply to 1,250,000 in the late 1930s, as South Africa's economy recovered from the world depression and the growth of secondary industry led to greatly increased demands for

African labour. By the end of World War II there were probably 2,000,000 Africans in the towns and by 1970 more than 3,500,000.

From the beginning of the 20th century the stream of black migrants making their way to the towns was paralleled by a stream of Afrikaners displaced from the land. By the early 1930s the drift had become a flood, and one in five of the white population was classified as "poor white." Poor, unskilled, semi-literate, they were in direct competition with the equally poor and semi-literate Africans, some of whom had more industrial skills.

Although commission after commission attributed the plight of the "poor whites" to their refusal to do what was designated Kaffir work (i.e., manual labour, Kaffir having been a derogatory name for the Xhosa), the Afrikaners were at a double disadvantage in the towns. Whereas the black Africans left their families to subsist, at however low a level, with their kin in the reserves, the Afrikaner was totally dependent on his urban wage. At the same time, at the high wages demanded by organized labour, he was unemployable. Not surprisingly, therefore, Afrikaner nationalism in the first half of the 20th century had a distinct anti-capitalist edge.

In the territories of Central Africa, also, by the third decade of the 20th century, Africans were increasingly making their way to the urban centres, pushed out of the rural areas by economic necessity and attracted by the higher wages and wider experience of the towns. Until the end of World War II, however, white administrators, capitalists, and settlers alike were determined that the towns should be the white man's preserve. Nowhere were authorities prepared to see the establishment of a permanent African urban population. The results were low wages, appalling living conditions, poverty, and broken family life. It was only after World War II, when change was speeded up all over the continent, that more serious consideration was given to the problems of African urbanization, although even then, administrations, whether colonial or later independent African, could never keep pace with the move to the towns.

THE AFRICAN RESPONSES

The reactions of the African peoples who had been drawn painfully into the settler-dominated capitalist society of southern Africa and subjected to ever-increasing administrative, economic, and political control were varied. Once their traditional economic and social structures had been defeated and undermined, it became necessary to find new ways of expressing their opposition to white rule. In certain areas, dreams of resistance organized along traditional lines continued well into the 20th century, especially in the Portuguese territories but also in Mashonaland in the 1930s and in the High Commission Territories in the 1950s and '60s. Indeed, in isolated rural regions, there may still be small groups of traditionalists who have been relatively unaffected by the 20th-century nationalist struggles against colonialism.

In some regions—pre-eminently those in which large centralized states had existed at the time of the colonial takeover—royal family politics continued to be of greatest significance. In Barotseland, Swaziland, and Basutoland, where the paramount chiefs were given special recognition by colonial regimes, the traditional aristocracy combined with the educated to protect their position and to demand redress of their grievances. In Matabeleland, the first decades of the 20th century were marked by an attempt to see a restoration of the kingship, while in Nyasaland in the 1930s the elite combined with traditionalists to seek a Tonga paramountcy and to restore the Ngoni king. In general, these attempts were most successful during the 1930s, when theories of indirect rule generally prevailed, and in areas where the settlers were weakest. In all territories, tribal and regional divisions and rivalries, despite African attempts to overcome them, continued to shape African responses to colonial rule and have remained easily exploitable in some areas.

The experience of white rule for Africans has been longest and most intense south of the Limpopo and in the Portuguese territories, although the existence of a substantial but unprivileged Coloured and Indian minority in the former and of assimilados and mestiços and settlers lacking political rights in the latter gave an extra dimension to anti-colonialism.

In South Africa, between 1906 and 1913, Gandhi led the first large-scale nonwhite, nonviolent resistance campaigns against anti-Indian legislation and gained very limited successes, though restrictions on Indian movement and immigration to South Africa remained in force. After his departure (1914), however (despite the formation of the South African Indian Congress in 1919), the initial militancy of Indian opposition was lost until after World War II, when younger, more radical groups won power from their moderate middle-class precursors who had dominated the party.

Compared to the Indians, the Coloureds of the Cape and Transvaal were never as successfully mobilized, though the African Political (later People's) Organization, founded as a South Africa-wide body in 1902, was the first large nonwhite political organization. It was, however, soon eclipsed by more vigorous African nationalist movements, and for most of the century the marginal Coloured population has been divided and relatively voiceless, though the predominantly Coloured Non-European Unity Movement, founded in the 1940s, has influenced African political thought.

The African response to settler rule in South Africa has in many ways been paralleled in the territories farther north. As early as the time of the unification of South Africa, educated Africans—teachers, preachers, clerks, small traders, and more prosperous farmers, as well as a sprinkling of professional men—had begun to feel the need for some organization larger in scale than the local vigilance and welfare associations that had grown up in the Cape in the last decades of the 19th century.

These were paralleled elsewhere in South Africa immediately after the South African War and in the Central African territories in the second and third decades of the 20th century. In 1912 the South African Native National Congress, which became the African National Congress (ANC) in 1917, was founded to represent African grievances, to overcome African tribal divisions, and to attempt to gain acceptance within the white polity through self-help, education, and the accumulation of property. Though demands for industrial education, individual land tenure, and some form of representation in Parliament later broadened to include attacks on the Pass Laws, the industrial colour bar, and the Natives Land Act of 1913, their methods remained strictly constitutional and they appealed mainly to the black middle class. Again, the territory-wide ANC has had its counterparts in Central Africa: in Southern Rhodesia in 1934, Nyasaland in 1944, and Northern Rhodesia in 1949–51. Though there have been local differences, the methods were similar, at least until after World War II, with South Africa leading the way.

Despite the increased numbers of Africans in industry in South Africa by the end of World War I, African trade unions were hampered by the Pass Laws, nonrecognition, and police harassment; spontaneously organized strikes were regarded as criminal offenses and often suppressed with violence. Nevertheless, in 1920 the Industrial and Commercial Workers' Union (ICU) was founded in Cape Town by the fiery Clements Kadalie, a migrant worker from Nyasaland. Based initially on Coloured workers in Cape Town, the ICU spread rapidly among Africans, both in towns and on the reserves and white farms of the countryside, claiming at its height some 100,000 members and establishing branches in Rhodesia and South West Africa by the mid-1920s. ICU, however, like the ANC, soon divided between those who wished to proceed constitutionally and those who demanded greater militancy and mass participation; by 1929 it had virtually disintegrated.

From the early 1920s in South Africa and from the 1930s in Central Africa, governments attempted to provide channels for the expression of African grievances through a variety of local consultative councils, often

*Assimi-
lado
goals*

with a strong component of chiefs. Despite their power-lessness, educated Africans participated in them in the hope of gaining greater concessions, though by the end of World War II they were increasingly disillusioned with the prospects for reform.

In Angola and Mozambique during the republican period in Portugal (1910–26) the Congress movements and ICU had their counterpart in *assimilado* political organizations, trade unions, and a local press. For a brief period in Angola it seemed as if the *assimilados* and Europeans would fight for common reformist goals; but the Africans soon broke away from the less radical European organizations to form their own Liga Angolana and Centro (later Grêmio) Africano, which had their equivalents in the Grêmio (later Associação) Africano in Mozambique. These associations engaged in petitions to demand limited educational and welfare benefits and to make African grievances more widely known. In this they were partly inspired by the formation of political associations among colonial Africans in Lisbon from 1910 onward; these, by the 1920s, were influenced by broader Pan-African diaspora movements. In general, however, they were dominated by middle-class moderates and had little influence beyond the urban areas. Even before the advent of the Salazar regime, these nationalist stirrings were crushed by the autocratic governor of Angola Norton de Matos (1921–26). Though the associations revived as ostensibly social and educational organizations, officially recognized by the government in the 1930s and '40s, it was not until the 1950s that they returned to militantly political expression.

Political participation and organized political movements, even at the height of their popularity, never reached more than a fraction of the African population. For the aspirations of many, however, independent churches, which broke away from the orthodox white-controlled missions, provided another outlet. In South Africa the first independent church was founded in the 1880s; by the turn of the century European administrators noted with alarm the growth of Ethiopianism, as it was called, with the existence of some 15 to 20 independent sects; by the 1960s there were well over 2,000, ranging in size and organization from little more than a family group to vast churches with thousands of members and links with the overseas world.

In the early years of the century, Europeans in South Africa interpreted the separatist church movement as politically dangerous and in some areas sought to crush it administratively. By and large, however, the independent churches in South Africa probably diffused African energies. The only violent episode involving the separatists in South Africa took place in 1921, when nearly 200 members of a sect known as the Israelites were killed by police gunfire when they refused to move from an African location near Queenstown in the eastern Cape, where they were living peacefully, if illegally, awaiting the millennium.

In northern Nyasaland in the first decades of colonial rule and in Northern Rhodesia in the 1930s, the millennial doctrines of the Watch Tower movement (Jehovah's Witnesses) were far more politically explosive. Within a year of its establishment in northern Nyasaland in 1909, Watch Tower had more than 10,000 adherents, who were partly attracted by its prophecies that British rule would end in 1914. In 1915 John Chilembwe, greatly influenced by its millenarianism as well as by his own colonial experiences, led an unsuccessful rebellion against British rule.

For the rural Shona, also faced by severe economic crises in the late 1920s, the millennial dreams of Watch Tower provided the most adequate substitute for traditional religious and political supports. As in Nyasaland, however, the outburst of Watch Tower was replaced relatively quickly by more subdued Christian independency, which, by the mid-century, had tens of thousands of followers and offered solutions to contemporary problems by drawing on fundamental ideas of Shona religion as well as by providing form and discipline in times of social upheaval.

In Angola, too, and especially among the Kongo (living in northern Angola and the Belgian and French Congos), prophet movements, influenced by the Protestant missionaries and Watch Tower, drew on traditional religious and cultural beliefs, imparting as well a specifically anti-European message, which partly prepared the ground for the anti-colonial war of the 1960s.

*Prophet
move-
ments*

Though the initial break with the mission church betokened a desire for independence from the white man, there were many motives, including the religious, for separatism. The prophet movements and independent churches expressed the millennial dreams of an insecure and poverty-stricken population torn from its traditional moorings.

By 1945, despite the fact that Africans had not established mass nationalist movements anywhere in the subcontinent, a remarkable range of protest movements existed, which became merged in many areas in the next decade to produce modern nationalist parties and give them their characteristic shape.

IV. Southern Africa since 1945

If, in the first half of the 20th century, policies in the southern African territories were remarkably similar, after World War II their political destinies diverged. During World War II, politics all over southern Africa appeared to stand still. Nevertheless, when the colonizers turned their attention once again to the African colonies, it was in the context of a very different world. The colonizing nations emerged from the war as secondary powers, under attack from the United States and the Soviet Union, which, for their own reasons, demanded rapid decolonization. The Bandung Conference of Asian and African nations (1955), the founding of the United Nations, and the liberation of South Asia were significant milestones also for the colonized peoples of Africa. There was increased awareness in Britain that the African territories, too, had to be prepared for independence, and the tentative beginnings of colonial development were accelerated. The indirect rule policies of the 1930s were abandoned, and in all territories steps were taken toward granting representative institutions.

The economic effects of the war had been profound. In South Africa and Southern Rhodesia it had brought about a tremendous increase in urbanization and secondary industry. The boom on the Copperbelt shifted the economic focus in Central Africa northward and further radicalized African politics; and in the Portuguese territories, greatly accelerated white immigration and the coffee boom in Angola had a similar effect in the 1950s.

In the south these developments led to the victory of the (Afrikaner) National Party, determined that whites should maintain total social, political, and economic control in both South and South West Africa. In the British Central African territories, after a short-lived experiment in multiracial federation, they resulted in 1964 in the emergence of independent African states in Malawi (formerly Nyasaland) and Zambia (Northern Rhodesia) and in 1965 in the unilateral and unconstitutional declaration of independence by white settlers in Rhodesia.

*Inde-
pendent
states in
the 1960s
and '70s*

For the High Commission Territories, the "winds of change" in Africa also brought political independence: Lesotho (formerly Basutoland) and Botswana (formerly Bechuanaland) in 1966 and Swaziland in 1968. In Angola and Mozambique violent anti-colonial struggles that lasted more than a decade led to the downfall of the Salazar regime in Portugal and to the ultimate independence (1975) of the territories themselves.

Despite the political differences, in socio-economic terms the subcontinent has been welded together into areas of high capital development, supported by rural areas of increasing impoverishment that provide a large reservoir of cheap labour. Most striking has been the very rapid industrial growth in South Africa, which accounts for 74 percent of production in the area.

As in the first half of the century, white South Africa, with its immense wealth, dominates its neighbours,

153

black and white. The Portuguese withdrawal, however, together with increasingly explosive internal pressures, has opened a new era of uncertainty for white rule in the subcontinent.

SOUTH AND SOUTH WEST AFRICA

In 1948 the tentative and ambiguous moves in South Africa toward less rigid social policies were swept aside by the electoral victory of the National Party, which had reunited after the dissensions of the war years under the leadership of Daniel F. Malan (prime minister 1948–54). Though the Nationalists fought the election on the "race issue" under the new slogan of apartheid, the essence of the change was over which group of whites was to control the South African economy. Whereas up to 1948 every Cabinet had drawn its members from both language groups, the Nationalists were able, unlike any previous Afrikaner party, to unite the majority of their people behind them and to consolidate the victory in the following 20 years. Initially, the Nationalists secured only 40 percent of the vote, but by 1966 this had increased to 60 percent. By this time an increasing number of English-speaking voters had accepted the government claim that it alone was capable of securing white dominance—this despite the fact that in 1960–61 South Africa was forced out of the British Commonwealth and declared a republic.

Behind the Nationalists' electoral success lay South Africa's accelerated industrialization. Although this process was already under way by the end of World War II, South Africa's economic growth between 1948 and 1970 was surpassed only by that of Japan, undoubtedly partly the result of government intervention in the control of labour, the direction of investment into industry, and the provision of essential infrastructure through the increased number of para-state corporations designed to increase the Afrikaner hold on the economy. Apart from 1948 and 1960–61, when there was a flight of foreign capital from South Africa in response to the regime's apparent political instability, capital investment from the United Kingdom, the United States, and western Europe, attracted by the high rate of profit, contributed greatly to South Africa's economic growth. Since 1945 secondary industry has replaced mining and agriculture as the major economic sector.

Thus, by the 1960s, if not before, white South Africans enjoyed one of the highest standards of living in the world. It was achieved very largely at the expense of Africans, through the rigorous control of their labour power. The reverse of the high per capita income of the small white population is the extremely low per capita income of the blacks. Thus, in 1969, the average monthly wage of a white man was $133, that of a black man $10. Despite wage increases, in real terms wages were little different in the mid-1970s, while the absolute white–black wage gap had widened.

Extending the philosophy that only those Africans who were of service to the whites were to be allowed in towns, remaining African rights in the urban areas were removed, and thousands of Africans returned to their so-called tribal homelands. The basis of the black work force, both in the towns and on white-owned farms, reverted to the system of migrant labour, which had been breaking down since the 1930s. As a result, in the mid-1970s some 2,500,000 Africans were arrested each year for statutory offenses—750,000 for infringing the Pass Laws alone.

In the 1950s Hendrik Verwoerd, the minister for native affairs and from 1958 to 1966 prime minister, developed the second aspect of the National Party's apartheid policies. Verwoerd argued that the only solution to racial antagonisms in South Africa was to balance African rightlessness in the white areas with the establishment of ethnically defined "Bantu Homelands," where Africans could develop semi-autonomous states, or "Bantustans." The territorial bases for the Bantustans were the African reserves set aside in 1913 and 1936. In 1954–55, the government-appointed Tomlinson Commission, which pro-

Industrialization in South Africa

duced a plan for territorial segregation, admitted that the reserves were incapable of carrying their current population, let alone the increase necessary if Africans were to be removed from the white areas. Nor was it ever intended that this should happen; though more than 3,000,-000 Africans have been forcibly moved out of white rural areas and so-called surplus Africans have been moved from towns under a variety of apartheid laws to the poverty-stricken reserves, the number of rightless Africans returning regularly to so-called white areas has nonetheless steadily increased to keep pace with labour demands.

Legislation in 1951 and 1959 attempted to resurrect the authority of the chiefs in the reserves and establish tribal, regional, and territorial advisory councils. While many hereditary chiefs still retained some popular support, the new policy created profound discontent in the rural areas as chiefs walked a tightrope between popular hostility if they implemented government policy and government anger if they failed to do so. In several rural areas there was violent resistance and apartheid chiefs were assassinated, while in the Transkei, which held its first Bantustan elections in 1963, a state of emergency had to be declared and was still in force in the 1970s. Under the constitution granted to the Transkei and later to the other Bantustans, the South African government still controls crucial aspects of internal and external affairs. "Full independence" was demanded by the Transkei. This was opposed by other African leaders, who feared the fragmentation of their cause, but the Republic of Transkei was nonetheless proclaimed on October 26, 1976. Despite the militant tone of some Bantustan leaders, notably Chief Gatsha Buthelezi, whose Zulu constituency in KwaZulu is the largest of any "homeland," their room for manoeuvre is limited by their total economic dependence on South Africa. In the 1960s the Bantustan policies were also extended to South West Africa.

The Coloured and Indian minorities, who cannot be repatriated to "tribal homelands," have also suffered from such segregatory legislation as the Group Areas Act and the Population Registration Act, which led to widespread removals of people.

During the 1950s the practices and policies of apartheid in South Africa were under heavy fire both internally and abroad. India's complaints in the United Nations in 1946 about South Africa's treatment of the Indian population initiated a series of UN resolutions condemning South Africa. Its treatment of Africans in South West Africa became a serious point of contention at the United Nations from the 1950s. The issue was taken to the International Court of Justice at The Hague, which finally gave judgment against South Africa in 1970. With the admission of new African nations to the UN and the formation of the Organization of African Unity in 1963, the international attitude became increasingly hostile.

Internally, too, the 1950s was a decade of unprecedented opposition to government policies. The growth of African and Indian militancy after the war may have contributed to the National Party victory. The measures of the Nationalist government gave the deliberations of the African National Congress new urgency. With the suppression of the Communist Party in 1951, many white radicals joined the liberation struggle, while the increasing awareness of the need for a united opposition among Indian, African, and Coloured leaders found expression in a passive resistance campaign in 1952 and in the founding of the Congress Alliance by African, Indian, and white opponents of the government in 1955. Despite the arrest in 1956 of more than 150 Congress leaders on charges of treason (all of them were subsequently released), the later 1950s saw increased militancy among the African nationalists. In 1958 the Pan-Africanist Congress (PAC) was formed, and in 1960 it launched a campaign against the Pass Laws. It was during this campaign that police fired on a peaceful crowd of unarmed demonstrators at Sharpeville, killing about 70 persons and wounding hundreds of others; this led to an even greater outcry overseas against South Africa's racial policies and

Authority of the chiefs

Growth of Indian and African militancy

to the South African government's banning of both the ANC and the PAC.

Though underground sabotage movements were founded in 1961–64, the wide use of spies and informers —a regular feature of the regime—and draconian security legislation led to their swift collapse. Many Africans fled to Zambia and Tanzania, where guerrilla training was undertaken and outside support sought.

Since 1945 a liberal tradition has continued in South Africa, with the emergence of a Liberal and later a Progressive Party, and there have been constant protests against government policies from students at English-language universities, from prominent church leaders, and from such organizations as the Springbok Legion, the War Veterans' Torch Commando (which faded away after the election of 1953) and the Women's Defence of the Constitution League (called the Black Sash). Essentially, however, the opposition movements were weak and divided. White liberals were never wholeheartedly behind the destruction of white law and order, while the ANC, though increasingly militant, was easily overwhelmed by a government with vast military and security resources.

After 1973, however, black opposition again began to mount within the country. Initially, most serious for the government was the industrial unrest, particularly in Durban and in the gold mines, where much violence occurred, at a time when the future of the external migrant labour supply on which the mines are dependent was diminishing. A variety of black worker organizations was formed, while black students, partly influenced by the black power movement in the United States, formed the militant South African Students Organization, with African, Indian, and Coloured members; this had its counterpart in the Black Peoples' Convention. All these groups were encouraged to more militant aspirations by the Frelimo victory in Mozambique (see below).

Nevertheless, despite a number of ambiguous statements by the prime minister, B.J. Vorster, and at the United Nations, there was no lessening in the essentials of apartheid. From 1975, increasing inflation and black unemployment (officially estimated at more than 17 percent in 1976) exacerbated tensions in the African townships. By April 1976, Chief Buthelezi was warning of serious trouble ahead if the government did not change its course, and this erupted in June, ostensibly over the enforced use of Afrikaans as the medium of instruction in black schools. Although the government retracted this policy, it was only after police had fired on thousands of demonstrating schoolchildren and the disturbances had spread over most of the republic, especially to the black townships around Cape Town. Unrest continued through the second half of the year, with thousands dead, injured, and imprisoned. Key symbols of apartheid were destroyed—beer halls (the proceeds of which are used to finance "Bantu" administration) and administrative buildings and schools—and the protest extended far beyond the original language issue. Thus increasing internal strains within South African society were paralleling the changing external pressures, and the widely held assumption that economic growth would improve the lot of Africans had been proved false both by events since June 1976 and by the increasing evidence of black unemployment and rural impoverishment.

The weak and divided black African states—despite their protests of the early 1960s—posed little threat to South Africa, which until the Portuguese coup seemed a corner of stability in the continent. In improving its diplomatic and economic relations with its black African neighbours, South Africa established close trade and diplomatic relations with Malawi and improved its customs agreements with the former High Commission Territories. The Cabora Bassa hydroelectric scheme aimed at uniting South Africa even more closely with the territories of Central Africa, while roads and railways connected South Africa with South West Africa and Angola. With the growth of secondary industry, South Africa found it increasingly essential to establish markets in Africa. The Anglo American Corporation of South Africa, with its vast interests in the subcontinent, played an important role in fostering the policy of "détente" and in maintaining overseas confidence in the regime.

With the withdrawal of the Portuguese from the region, détente became more urgent for security reasons. Realizing Rhodesia's vulnerability once Mozambique and Angola achieved independence, South Africa joined with black African leaders to try to achieve a negotiated settlement of this issue.

In August 1976 a constitutional committee (the Turnhalle Committee) in South West Africa (Namibia), with the tacit approval of the South African government, announced plans for a form of political independence in the territory by the end of 1978. The South West Africa People's Organisation, however, which the UN recognizes as representing the territory's inhabitants, was excluded from the committee's discussions, and the guerrilla struggle intensified on the northern frontier.

THE HIGH COMMISSION TERRITORIES

Their proximity to the economically dominant South Africa has been most acutely felt by the three High Commission Territories. Despite British abandonment of the idea of their political incorporation into South Africa after 1948, the absence of a large proportion of the working population as migrant labour in South Africa—as high as 43 percent in Basutoland and 28 percent in Swaziland in the 1960s—stultified economic and constitutional advance. From the mid-1930s, British aid, though inadequate, was made available, agricultural improvement schemes were instituted, and a Native Treasuries Finance Committee and advisory councils were established; attempts were also made to reform the courts and, most importantly, the system of chieftainship, a necessity in Basutoland in particular, where petty chiefs had proliferated. Most of these reforms became more effective after World War II, and by 1960–61 legislative councils had been established in all three territories. Basutoland and Bechuanaland became the independent states of Lesotho and Botswana in 1966; Swaziland, where the existence of a number of white settlers and considerable South African economic interest complicated the transfer of power, became independent in 1968.

In all three territories, but especially in Swaziland, where traditional chiefs have remained extremely powerful, modern nationalist movements emerged relatively late. In all three, conservative governments anxious to avoid provoking their powerful neighbour emerged in the first elections after independence, though Swaziland, with greater economic potential and a shrewd, if autocratic, king, and Botswana, with its outlet to the north and sophisticated leadership, have had greater scope for manoeuvre than small Lesotho, which is entirely surrounded by South Africa.

BRITISH CENTRAL AFRICA

In the colonies of British Central Africa—Northern and Southern Rhodesia and Nyasaland—the immediate postwar years also brought significant economic and political changes. In Southern Rhodesia as in South Africa, secondary industry overtook mining and agriculture as the main sector of the economy; and from 1946 the influx of emigrants from Britain averaged 10,000 a year, increasing the white population to 125,000 by 1953. At the same time, in Northern Rhodesia the copper boom set off new conflicts as the colour bar intensified, while as early as 1935 and 1940 widespread strikes by African miners showed the potential of the African working class. Settlers, led by the white labour leader and former railway worker Roy Welensky, began agitating for some form of amalgamation with Southern Rhodesia.

Powerful economic arguments were used; and big business, especially the powerful Anglo American Corporation of South Africa, with its interests in both territories, gave the movement its backing. The National Party victory in South Africa in 1948 gave it further impetus. The British Colonial Office, anxious to strengthen Nyasaland's weak economy, insisted on its inclusion in any

(marginal notes:)

Opposition movements

South Africa and its black neighbours

form of closer union. In 1953 the Federation of Rhodesia and Nyasaland (Central African Federation) was formed.

In all three territories, where economic developments and the general trend of world opinion had strengthened the African political organizations of the interwar period, politically articulate Africans were almost unanimously opposed to federation. As talk of closer union mounted among whites between 1949 and 1953, the Congress movements became more widespread and representative. In all three, Africans feared that federation would lead to further land alienation, undermine the position of chiefs, prevent political advance, and extend farther north the colour bar and discrimination of Southern Rhodesia.

With the establishment of the federation, however, the Africans, especially in Southern Rhodesia, were initially cooperative. But by the mid-1950s, the economic advantages of federation seemed so exclusively to benefit the whites of Southern Rhodesia that African hostility was re-aroused. Though federal leaders preached racial partnership, and in Southern Rhodesia urban African housing was improved and a multiracial university built, greatly increased white immigration from South Africa and Britain intensified black–white conflict. The continued demands by federal leaders for dominion independence status confirmed the Africans' worst fears.

In Nyasaland by 1955 a group of young radicals had emerged to demand universal suffrage and self-government and for the first time turned to the masses to achieve their ends. By 1957 they claimed 60,000 members and were developing a modern mass nationalist party. Feeling the need for a leader of standing they invited Hastings (later H. Kamuzu) Banda, at that time practicing medicine in Ghana, to return and take over the leadership of the Congress movement. Banda returned in 1958 and vigorously denounced federation.

In Northern Rhodesia, African political opposition revived in 1957 after a period of quiescence, when the Congress organization had been eclipsed by the rise of the millenarian Lumpa Church of Alice Lenshina. In 1958–59 the removal of the more conservative president of Congress and the influx of new militants under the leadership of Kenneth Kaunda transformed the organization. Like its counterpart in Nyasaland, it became far more radical and created branches all over the country.

Southern Rhodesian opposition became more radical in the later 1950s also, as urban and rural discontents were united for the first time, and a group of young leaders formed the Southern Rhodesian African National Congress under Joshua Nkomo in 1957. This was later to become the Zimbabwe African People's Union (ZAPU).

The rise of mass nationalist movements brought direct confrontation between the Africans and the colonial and federal authorities. In 1959, after sporadic disturbances in Nyasaland, a state of emergency was declared, nationalist leaders were arrested and their parties banned, to be replaced in all the territories by new parties under new names by 1960. The banning of the nationalist parties was followed by disturbances and disorders all over the federation, but particularly in Southern Rhodesia, where the worst rioting occurred in the impoverished African townships. While in Nyasaland and in Northern Rhodesia the rioting was sufficient to persuade a distant Colonial Office to grant majority rule, in Southern Rhodesia it increased white determination to hold more tightly onto their position. In 1961 Nyasaland and Northern Rhodesian leaders were released, and new constitutions were granted to the territories; and in 1963, after further disorder in Northern Rhodesia, the federation was finally dissolved. In the following year Northern Rhodesia and Nyasaland became the independent states of Zambia and Malawi, governed by the nationalist leaders who had fought for independence.

Despite independence, however, many problems remained in both territories. In Malawi the unity of the nationalists was short-lived, and after an abortive uprising in 1965 Banda stifled all internal opposition. Regional differences—the result of Malawi's uneven economic

and educational development—continued, while Banda's policy of close ties with settler regimes was resented by many black Africans, large numbers of whom were still dependent on the white south for wage employment.

When, in 1964, Zambia achieved its independence, it was still a poverty-stricken and backward country, despite the potential of the Copperbelt. Indeed it was not until 1964 that the British South Africa Company ceded its concession rights to copper royalties, which had, over the years, gone to enrich the company and the British treasury rather than the territory itself. The result was that very little capital had been made available for investment in the increasingly impoverished rural areas or for welfare and educational services. Despite attempts, since independence, at reform, the countryside continues to be drained of manpower as thousands of hopeful young people make their way to the towns. In the towns, however, neither housing nor welfare is adequate, and unemployment grows. Fluctuations in the world price of copper and the oil crisis in the 1970s greatly aggravated Zambia's weakness; regional, ethnic, and rural–urban divisions persisted also. During the period of the transference of power, Lozi separatism was a serious problem, while the Lumpa Church became increasingly opposed to the government. In 1964 open warfare broke out between the church and the state; more than 700 people were killed and the church was banned.

In both Malawi and Zambia, but especially in the latter, the problems were compounded by developments in Southern Rhodesia. There, the violence in the early 1960s as well as events in the rest of Africa roused white fears and led to an increasing number of emergency laws against political opponents. Though limited concessions were made to Africans by the government in 1961, these were rejected both by the African nationalists, who refused to participate in the new elections, and by white farmers and artisans, whose support for the new right-wing Rhodesian Front Party led to its electoral victory in 1962.

With the end of federation, the Rhodesian Front, after crushing African opposition and increasing its internal support, renewed its demands for independence. Britain was unwilling to concede to these demands without evidence of progress toward majority rule and of the end of racial discrimination. In 1965, in a highly emotional atmosphere, the Rhodesian Front, under the leadership of Ian Smith, unilaterally declared Rhodesian independence. Total opposition to the prospect of black rule became policy.

Despite international pressure, Britain refused to use force against the illegal regime, though it did support the economic sanctions imposed by the UN. These, however, were never fully effective, largely because of continued support of Rhodesia by South Africa and Portugal. Sanctions did, however, put considerable strain on Zambia, whose main routes of communication with the outside world lay through Rhodesia and which was dependent on Rhodesia for coal and for manufactured goods. Nevertheless, attempts were made by President Kaunda to carry out sanctions and, more important, to find alternative outlets by constructing roads and a railway to Tanzania; the latter, the Tan-Zam Railway, was completed in 1974.

With Rhodesia's declaration of independence, many African nationalists fled across the Zambezi to mount guerrilla resistance. Crippled, however, by internal rivalries, this proved ineffective until Mozambique's independence transformed the situation. Until then, Britain's attempts to achieve a negotiated settlement had failed. With the realignment of forces after the Portuguese withdrawal, however, Ian Smith came under unrelenting pressure from South Africa to release and negotiate with imprisoned black nationalist leaders. They in turn were under pressure from Zambia and Tanzania to engage in talks with Smith, in an attempt to avoid war. At the end of 1975, despite divisions within African nationalist ranks, the veteran leader Joshua Nkomo and Ian Smith undertook to try to establish a basis for talks.

In the spring of 1976, after South Africa's invasion force had to withdraw from Angola (see below), the pressures were intensified. Mozambique opened its frontiers to training and base camps for Rhodesian guerrilla fighters, who intensified their war in Rhodesia (now being called Zimbabwe). Fears of open war and Communist intervention led the Western powers to the view that it was necessary to get rid of minority rule, at least in its extreme form as represented by the Smith regime, before the last chance of a gradualist compromise vanished. The U.S. secretary of state, Henry Kissinger, had two meetings in Europe with the South African prime minister, B.J. Vorster, who realized that he might have to sacrifice the Smith regime in the interests of his own. After meeting Kissinger in Pretoria on September 19, 1976, Smith told his electorate, though in somewhat ambiguous terms, that majority rule would have to come in two years' time. A conference under the chairmanship of a British diplomat assembled in Geneva at the end of October to plan the transfer of power; whether the conflicting demands of the nationalists and of the Smith regime were capable of peaceful resolution was doubtful.

ANGOLA AND MOZAMBIQUE

In the Portuguese territories, developments since World War II have in some ways been more dramatic than elsewhere in the subcontinent, with more than a decade of warfare leading to an army coup in Portugal itself and the ultimate transfer of power in the African territories. In both Angola and Mozambique, economic progress and development lagged behind the rest of the subcontinent. The Portuguese dictator António de Oliveira Salazar blocked economic development in the colonies for years in the interests of "stability" and Portuguese advantage, and it was not until 1961 that the territories were opened to overseas investment. Nevertheless the coffee boom in Angola in the 1950s and the discovery there of minerals and petroleum largely stimulated immigration and outside interest in the territory. White immigration increased Angola's settler population by 400 percent between 1940 and 1960 and doubled that in Mozambique between 1950 and 1960. Though this immigration was mainly to the towns, the government also instituted large agricultural settlements for whites, especially in the coffee-growing areas of Angola and in the fertile river valleys of Mozambique. Despite Portuguese claims that their policies were based on racial harmony, the increase in white settlement led to greater demands for African land and labour, while economic development brought little benefit to the African population.

The general movement toward colonial independence also affected the Portuguese territories. With the Indian attack on Goa in 1961, world attention was drawn to Portuguese colonial policies. Salazar responded by making the territories overseas provinces of Portugal and by granting limited local autonomy and increased participation in elections to the Portuguese National Assembly to whites and the handful of *assimilados*.

In the face of these new developments, African nationalist movements revived among *assimilados*, secondary school students, and trade union members in the towns. In neither of the territories, however, were the nationalists equipped for a political or military struggle. The divisions between the *assimilado* and *mestiço* elite in the towns and the rural masses, especially in Angola, were probably greater than elsewhere in southern Africa, while the meagre industrial and urban development and educational facilities before the 1950s militated against any broad national consciousness. Apart from a few areas where Protestant missionaries provided the organizational example, there were few nationalist leaders outside the towns.

In Luanda, however, from the early 1950s political associations proliferated. From among these the Movimento Popular de Libertação de Angola (MPLA), with a strong Marxist strain, emerged as the most important group by 1956, though an abortive uprising in Luanda in 1961 led to its temporary suppression by the Portuguese secret police. From the mid-1960s, the fortunes of the MPLA revived under its poet–president Agostinho Neto; moving its headquarters from Brazzaville (in the Congo) to Lusaka (in Zambia), it extended guerrilla operations in eastern Angola and resuscitated urban political activity. Although it failed to build up its base in eastern Angola, where it was supplanted by Jonas Savimbi's União Nacional pela Independência Total de Angola (UNITA) in the late 1960s and early '70s, the MPLA retained its hold on the capital and among Mbundu speakers.

In March 1961 the Kongo people of northern Angola—an area suffering most acutely from land alienation and forced labour practices, and with a long anti-colonial tradition—revolted. With their favourable terrain and the support of their newly independent kinsmen in Zaire, the most militant of the Kongo political organizations, the União das Populacões de Angola (UPA), later the Frente Nacional de Libertação de Angola (FNLA), threatened the Portuguese hold in the north. Hampered by ethnic, ideological, religious, and personal rivalries, and the constant proliferation of Kongo exile political organizations in Zaire and the Central African Republic, the movement failed to spread beyond the Kongo area. Despite Portuguese military reprisals, however, a war of attrition continued, with neither side able to press home its advantage for more than a dozen years.

In Mozambique the nationalist organizations, though also initially plagued by divisions, were more successful in overcoming their disunity. In 1962 three exiled organizations based in Tanzania came together to form the Frente de Libertação de Moçambique (Frelimo) and began organizing a political and military underground movement. By building on pre-existing political networks, such as the cooperative movement in northern Mozambique, and by educating selected leaders, Frelimo carefully prepared the ground before moving its guerrilla fighters into the northern provinces of Mozambique in 1964. Within three years they claimed to have an army 8,000 strong and to have established their own administrative, educational, and marketing networks in Cabo Delgado and Niassa districts.

Though Portugal's initial response to the outbreak of revolt was savage military repression, and some 70,000 to 100,000 Portuguese troops were kept in each territory, the uprisings produced a number of reforms. It was, however, always a case of too little and too late, and ultimately the sheer cost of the wars led to the revolt of Portuguese army officers and the downfall of the regime in Europe. After a short transitional period, Mozambique became independent in June 1975 under a Frelimo government headed by Samora Machel. It faced a number of urgent political and economic problems, largely connected with the poverty of its resources, the need to create a new state, and the nature of its relationship with Rhodesia and especially with South Africa. During this difficult period, it found it necessary, at least in the short term, to establish a relationship with neighbouring South Africa.

In Angola, unlike Mozambique, the transitional period found the three main liberation movements—MPLA in the centre, FNLA in the north, and UNITA in the south—vying for control of any future government. Their rivalries were greatly exacerbated by the involvement of the great powers, Portuguese settlers, Zaire, and South Africa in their struggles. When on November 11, 1975, the governor general withdrew from Luanda, the country was in the throes of a civil war, which threatened to expand far wider as the Soviet Union flew in arms in support of MPLA and the U.S. indirectly aided the FNLA–UNITA alliance through Zaire. Meanwhile South Africa, equally anxious to avoid an MPLA government, played a hazardous interventionist role which drew its troops from the Angola–Namibia frontier almost to the outskirts of Luanda in support of UNITA. Although the South Africans were forced to withdraw by MPLA, now assisted by Cuban troops, and eventually MPLA under the leadership of Agostinho Neto established its control, sporadic fighting, especially in the UNITA-dominated region in the south, continued.

(SHULA E. MARKS)

Margin notes:

Rhodesian guerrilla pressures

The MPLA in Angola

Independent Mozambique

If Siberia were independent it would be the largest country on Earth; instead, it helps to give the Soviet Union, of which it is the largest part, that distinction. Siberia is not only enormous, it is also in a sense the last great frontier in the world, and as such bears comparison to the American West of a century past. The differences are obvious enough: Siberia, and its capital Novosibirsk, are Russian, Communist, and aggressively modern. Some of the exciting frontier character is nevertheless revealed in the article reprinted here.

NOVOSIBIRSK

One of the most important cities of the Soviet Union, Novosibirsk is the administrative centre of Novosibirsk *oblast* (province) of the Russian Soviet Federated Socialist Republic and in many respects the capital of all Siberia. Its nodal position on the Trans-Siberian Railroad has caused the town to expand very greatly and rapidly, in step with the economic development of Siberia as a whole. With a population of 1,286,000 in 1976, Novosibirsk is the eighth largest city of the Soviet Union and outstanding both for industrial production and for its educational and scientific research facilities. The town stands on the Ob River, here about half a mile wide, where it is bridged by the Trans-Siberian Railroad just below the confluence of the Inya River. The relatively flat plateau on which Novosibirsk is built is deeply cut by ravines, the continued growth of which presents the city with a major problem; already ravines occupy nearly 15,000 acres (6,000 hectares) of the city territory. Novosibirsk *oblast* covers 68,800 square miles (178,200 square kilometres) and in 1975 had a population of 2,543,000; apart from Novosibirsk itself, it is mainly an agricultural area, with small local urban centres.

Climate

Novosibirsk has an extreme continental climate with a very severe winter. The mean temperature in January is 3.2° F (−16° C), in July 65.8° F (18.8° C). The highest summer temperatures reach 98.6° F (37° C), and in winter the temperature has been known to drop to −58° F (−50° C). In early winter, strong and bitterly cold winds are common. Annual precipitation averages 19.5 inches (495 millimetres), but it is extremely variable from year to year; more than half the total falls in summer, frequently in the form of torrential thunderstorms and hailstorms.

HISTORY

Novosibirsk might well be described as an offspring of the railway. In 1891 the engineer N.G. Garin-Mikhaylovsky, surveying the route for the Trans-Siberian Railroad, chose the small village of Krivoshchekovo on the Ob as the site for the bridging of the river. In 1893 work on the bridge was begun, and beside it a small settlement grew up. By 1897 the bridge was completed, and the settlement had developed into a township of 7,832 people. A landing was built on the Ob, and transshipment and river trade developed briskly. The new settlement was known variously as Gusevka or Aleksandrovsky, but in 1895 it was renamed Novonikolayevsk in honour of the accession of Tsar Nicholas II.

The next two decades saw steady growth, based chiefly on movement of freight by rail and river and on the locomotive depot. A number of small industrial enterprises were established, using local products and including two saw mills, seven flour mills, a tannery, a distillery, a soap works, and two iron-casting works—the beginnings of what was to become a major metallurgical and engineering industry. Shops, warehouses, a small hospital, and a cathedral were built, and in 1903 formal town status was

conferred. By the time of the Revolution of 1917 the population had reached 69,000 within the old city boundaries. During the subsequent civil war, Novonikolayevsk was occupied in turn by the independent Czech brigade, the White Army of Adm. A.V. Kolchak and finally, at the end of 1919, by the Red Army. In 1925 the town was renamed Novosibirsk (meaning New Siberia).

Kuzbass

The opening up of the mineral and timber wealth of Siberia in the Soviet period, especially after the beginning of the five-year plans in 1928, brought about a remarkably rapid growth of the city. In particular the development of the Kuznetsk (Kuzbass) Basin coalfield about a hundred miles to the east of the town, where mining had begun in the late 19th century, and the establishment there of a large-scale metallurgical industry, fostered the importance of Novosibirsk as a transit point. In 1934 a railway was completed directly linking the town to Novokuznetsk (then called Stalinsk), the principal town on the coalfield. A second factor in the growth of Novosibirsk was the completion in the early 1930s of the Turkistan-Siberian (Turksib) Railway, providing a direct link with Tashkent and Central Asia. Large new factories were established, and the town grew to 120,100 population in 1926 and to 405,600 in 1939, an average annual increment of almost 22,000, mostly by in-migration from other parts of the country.

World War II, with its eastward evacuation of people and industrial plant from the war zone, still further stimulated growth. By 1959 the population was 886,000, and in 1963 the city passed the million mark. Although growth in the postwar years has been continuous, its rate has slackened; average growth between 1959 and 1970 was 3 percent per year, compared with 6 percent between 1939 and 1959 and 18 percent between 1926 and 1939. In terms of absolute increment there has been relatively little change, 24,000 annually between 1939 and 1959 and 25,000 between 1959 and 1970. To some extent Novosibirsk is affected by the high rate of labour turnover and out-migration that has been characteristic of most of Siberia since about 1960, although less acutely so than elsewhere; many migrants to the city are young and unskilled and leave after only a short stay, giving rise to problems of establishing a stable and skilled labour force.

THE CONTEMPORARY CITY

Administration and setting. Novosibirsk is designated an *oblast* town; that is, its town council is subordinated to the Novosibirsk *oblast* council, although both administrations are located in the town itself. The city limits enclose an area of 184 square miles (477 square kilometres), the third largest city territory in the Soviet Union, although this includes considerable areas of farmland and forest beyond the built-up area. Originally only on the right bank of the Ob, the town now extends to either side of the river and comprises nine administrative wards. Central Ward, on the right bank, is the oldest part of Novosibirsk and contains most of the principal public buildings, many constructed in the ponderous architectural style of the Stalin era, with much use of locally quarried gray granite. These include the offices of the city council and the local Communist Party organization and various branches of all-union and republican ministries, concerned with the economic development of West Siberia as a whole. In this central area some buildings of the pre-Revolutionary period survive, but, because of its relative youth, the city lacks buildings of historic interest. Most of the theatres and cultural establishments and the largest shops are in the centre. Krasny Prospekt (Red Avenue), the principal street, bisects the centre, running north from the Ob to the local airport and linking the town's three largest squares, Kalinin and Lenin squares and Square of the Soviets. As in most Soviet cities, multistory apartment buildings with two- and three-room flats account for high population densities even in the most central parts.

Although industry is found in all parts of the city, the principal industrial sectors are in the east along the Trans-Siberian line, and on the opposite, left bank of the Ob, where are located the largest engineering and metallurgical factories. An imposing road bridge over the Ob links Kirov Ward to the rest of the city. North of the centre is found a large range of light industrial and food-processing plants. Housing everywhere is in very large apartment buildings. Those in central areas are usually five to seven stories high and generally constructed of stone or brick; those in outer parts of the built-up area, prefabricated buildings constructed in the later 1960s and '70s, are frequently 12 to 20 stories high, giving population densities as great as in the centre. The apartment buildings are grouped in "micro-regions," or neighbourhood units, each of which is provided with basic services such as shops, schools, a polyclinic, and a cinema.

Economy. Novosibirsk is one of the most important manufacturing centres in the Soviet Union. Although there is a wide range of industries, metallurgy and engineering predominate, employing two-thirds of all industrial workers in Novosibirsk. The old, pre-Revolutionary iron industry has been transformed into the modern Kuzmin steelworks, producing hot and cold rolled steel, cold rolled sheet steel, and steel tubes. The tin smelter is the largest in the country, utilizing tin concentrates from distant sources in northern Yakutiya, Transbaikalia, the Far East, and Kirgiziya. A highly specialized metalworking plant is the gold refinery, which refines all gold mined in the Soviet Union. In the range of engineering works, pride of place is taken by the Yefremov heavy machinery and hydraulic press factory and by the large electrical generator plant. Other plants manufacture electrothermal equipment in the form of steel furnaces of 180 tons' capacity, ore concentrating and mining machinery, and agricultural machinery (including disk harrows, seeding and husking machines, and tractor spares). Precision and light engineering plants make machine tools, instruments, radios, and automatic looms. Also part of this vast engineering complex are the big locomotive repair and servicing shops and the ship repair yards on the Ob.

During the 1960s and '70s the chemical industry developed rapidly, producing synthetic resin, plastics, and pharmaceutical goods. Other industries are primarily concerned with supplying the city and surrounding area with construction materials and with consumer goods—furniture, pianos, shoes, textiles, knitwear, and foodstuffs. The early-established flour-milling industry continues.

Power for the industries is supplied by a 220-kilovolt line from the Kuzbass coalfield and by the Novosibirsk hydroelectric station, constructed between 1951 and 1959 on the Ob some 15 miles (24 kilometres) upstream from the city. The barrage is three miles long and impounds a reservoir that has flooded more than 400 square miles (1,000 square kilometres) and that extends 110 miles upstream. The station has seven generators with a total capacity of 400,400 kilowatts. There are also two thermal power stations in the city itself. Novosibirsk is on the trunk petroleum pipeline that crosses Siberia from the Urals to Angarsk.

Industries

Electricity

Communications and transport. In addition to the trunk railway services via the Trans-Siberian, Kuzbass, and Turksib lines, which have played such a major part in the city's growth, local electric commuter trains link the suburbs to the city centre. Up to 70,000 passengers daily use Novosibirsk Main station alone. In First of May Ward, in the southeast sector of the town, is one of the largest marshalling yards in the country. There are two airports, a smaller one serving local air connections and a large main airport with direct flights to Moscow and other major cities of the Soviet Union. The river port has been enlarged and modernized with electric gantry cranes, and in the ice-free season it handles bulk freight moving on the Ob; this is made up chiefly of timber and building materials, with lesser quantities of coal, cement, fuel oil, and grain. There are also passenger services along the Ob, and small craft, including hydrofoils, link the parts of the town along the river. Transportation within the city is by bus, streetcar, and trolleybus.

Culture and education. Novosibirsk is the principal cultural and educational centre in Siberia. Its six theatres include an imposing opera and ballet theatre, begun in 1931 and opened in 1945, seating 2,000 persons, the Red Torch Drama Theatre, a children's theatre, and a circus. There are botanical gardens, an art gallery, and four museums, as well as a symphony orchestra. The city has a television and radio centre, linked to Moscow (1,752 miles away) by communications satellite. It is an important publishing centre, with the Siberian branch of the Nauka (Science) Publishing House and the West Siberian Publishing House. Several local newspapers and journals are published. The State Public Scientific and Technical Library of the Academy of Sciences of the U.S.S.R. is one of the copyright libraries of the Soviet Union, with a collection of more than 5,000,000 books and reading rooms that can seat 1,000 persons.

Novosibirsk has some 220 general schools and 37 specialist schools—music, ballet, languages, science, and technology. There are 14 higher educational institutions, headed by the Novosibirsk State University, founded in 1959; other higher educational establishments include railway engineering, electrotechnical, medical, agricultural, and teacher-training institutes. The university and a number of these institutes are located in one of the most remarkable developments of Novosibirsk. This is the satellite town of Akademgorodok (Academic Town), which lies 15 miles south of the city centre on the shores of the Novosibirsk reservoir but within the city limits in Soviet Ward. Construction of this suburb was begun in the 1950s to house the Siberian Department of the Academy of Sciences of the U.S.S.R., established in 1957, initially under the energetic directorship of M.A. Lavrentyev. Since then a very large concentration of research and educational institutions has grown up in Akademgorodok. Among these are most of the 22 specialist research institutes that the Academy of Sciences maintains in Novosibirsk, with staffs totalling about 11,500 persons, of whom more than 3,000 are research workers. In Akademgorodok also are the Siberian branches of the All-Union Agricultural Academy, constructed in the early 1970s, and the Academy of Medical Sciences. This concentration of scientific research workers and higher educational teachers has attracted a great deal of attention, both within the Soviet Union and internationally. A feature of the town is the special scientific boarding school for specially gifted children. Akademgorodok is regarded as a prototype for further academic settlements planned for Leningrad, Vladivostok, and other Soviet cities.

Health and recreation. Each micro-region of the town has a polyclinic, providing day to day medical, dental, and public health services. The city is adequately supplied with hospitals, including a large unit of 1,500 beds, built in the 1970s. There are several parks, the principal one of which lies along the right bank of the Ob in the north of the city. In the outer rural fringe are children's holiday camps, while the reservoir and its shores are much used for recreation.   (RICHARD A. FRENCH)

Akademgorodok

BOOK OF THE YEAR
1977

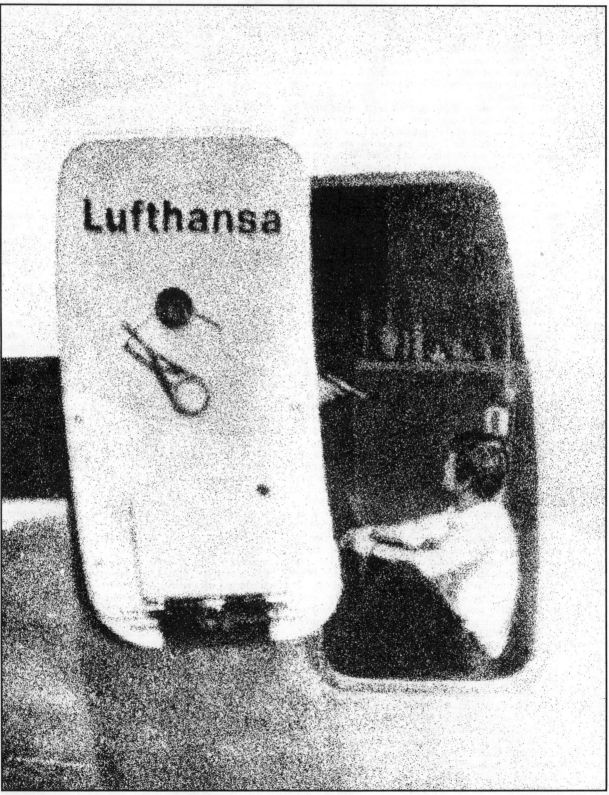

Aerial Sports

There was no superabundance of new world records in aerial sports during 1977, but some events were quite remarkable.

Gliding. Paul MacCready, an aeronautical engineer and former international soaring champion from Pasadena, Calif., was awarded the £50,000 ($86,000) Kremer Prize for creating the world's first successful man-powered aircraft. The prize, administered by the Royal Aeronautical Society in London, was awarded for a pedal-powered aircraft, the 77-lb Gossamer Condor, which had a wingspan of 96 ft and was made of corrugated cardboard, balsa wood, rope, paper-thin aluminum, piano wire, Styrofoam, Scotch tape, and Mylar film. Piloted by Bryan Allen, the Gossamer Condor completed the required three-mile course, which involved clearing a ten-foot-high start-finish line, making a figure eight around two pylons set one-half mile apart, and returning over the start-finish mark. The flight was made in California on August 23.

In May 1977 Karl Striedieck of the U.S. flew a 1,015-mi round trip from Lock Haven, Pa., to Oak Ridge, Tenn., in his AS-W 17 to become the first pilot ever to exceed 1,000 mi in a cross-country flight. Ingo Renner of Australia, the reigning world standard class soaring champion, won the 1977 Smirnoff Sailplane Derby across the U.S. from Los Angeles to Frederick, Md. Former world

Pilot Bryan Allen pedals the first successful man-powered aircraft, the Gossamer Condor. Designed by Paul Mac-Cready, the plane won a £50,000 prize.

champion George Moffat of the U.S. won the 1977 European championship at Angers, France, nosing out 72 other contestants from ten countries. Hans Werner Grosse of West Germany, flying an AS-W 17 at Waikerie, Australia, set a world single-place glider record of 661 mi for distance over a triangular course. A world altitude gain record of 11,247 ft for Class DM–2 motor gliders was set by Dieter Mayr and Frank Adler of West Germany in an AS-K 16. A 95-mi flight by George Worthington of the U.S. in a Mitchell Wing hang glider set a record for ultralight sailplanes.

Ballooning. Charting a course similar to that flown by Charles Lindbergh in 1927, U.S. balloonists Ben Abruzzo and Maxie Anderson of Albuquerque, N.M., went aloft at Marshfield, Mass., in September. Their "Double Eagle" balloon, however, was forced to ditch off the Icelandic coast. One month later another balloon bound for Europe, launched from Bar Harbor, Maine, by Dewey Reinhard and Steve Stephenson of Colorado Springs, Colo., splashed down off the Nova Scotia coast after two days aloft. These were the 15th and 16th unsuccessful attempts to complete the 3,000-mi transatlantic crossing since 1873.

Karl Thomas, who hoped to establish distance and duration records in February with an overland balloon flight from Los Angeles to Florida, was blown off course and into Mexico. Ed Yost's 2,475-mi distance record and 107-hour duration record, set during his attempted crossing of the Atlantic in 1976, were officially recognized. Kingswood Sprott, Jr., of the U.S. broke his own world class hot-air balloon altitude record in March by attaining 41,000 ft over Lakeland, Fla.

The U.S. swept the world hot-air balloon championships in Castle Howard, England, with Paul M. Woessner, Jr., Bruce Comstock, and Michael Scudder taking first, second, and third places, respectively.

Parachuting. A 40-man free-fall box formation was achieved by a U.S. free-fall parachuting team during competitions at Tahlequah, Okla. Alloys

A host of balloons takes to the air in the world hot-air balloon championships in Castle Howard, England. In all, about 48 balloons went aloft.

Hang glider Marcel La-
chat of Geneva pilots his
Delta-glider from the
peak of the Matterhorn
to the valley below.

Riesendeck of West Germany claimed a world
record for individual precision jumps for men with
50 consecutive dead-centre landings, surpassing
the 1976 record of 33. Milian Sinic, a Yugoslav
skydiver with 586 previous jumps, almost lost his
life while making a jump in Yugoslavia. When he
became caught in ropes attached to the airplane,
he was left helplessly dangling 2,400 ft in the air.
When observers on the ground saw Sinic's
predicament, another plane took off and the pilot
was able to throw a knife to the upside-down Sinic, who then cut himself free.

(MICHAEL D. KILIAN)

Afghanistan

A republic in central Asia, Afghanistan is bordered by the U.S.S.R., China, Pakistan, and Iran.
Area: 653,000 sq km (252,100 sq mi). Pop. (1977
est.): 20,330,000, including (1963 est.) Pashtoon
59%; Tadzhik 29%; Uzbek 5%; Hazara 3%. Cap.
and largest city: Kabul (pop., 1976 est., 749,000).
Language: Dari Persian and Pashto. Religion: Muslim. President in 1977, Sardar Mohammad Daud
Khan.

After the failure of the retired army officers' plot
in November 1976, Pres. Mohammad Daud Khan's
position was further strengthened by the proceedings of the Grand National Assembly in January
and February 1977. This body of notables nominated by the provincial governors had last met in 1973
to ratify the abolition of the monarchy and the
birth of the republic. Its task in 1977 was to approve a new constitution, the main features of
which were the vesting of wide powers in the
president as head of state, henceforward to be
elected by the Grand Assembly every six years,
and the reaffirmation of Islamic institutions as the
core of national life. After this the Assembly was
dissolved.

The Assembly had endorsed the president's
policy of nonalignment in foreign affairs and the

Afghanistan

AFGHANISTAN

Education. Primary (1975), pupils 694,240, teachers 19,-
158; secondary, pupils (1974) 166,361, teachers (1973) 7,-
376; vocational (1973), pupils 4,729, teachers 445; teacher
training (1973), students 5,332, teachers 426; higher
(1973), students 9,399, teaching staff 1,264.

Finance. Monetary unit: afghani, with (Sept. 19, 1977)
a free rate of 45 afghanis to U.S. $1 (78 afghanis = £1
sterling). Gold, SDR's, and foreign exchange (Feb. 1977)
U.S. $164,640,000. Budget (1974–75 rev. est.): revenue
10,934,000,000 afghanis; expenditure 9,721,000,000 afghanis. Money supply (Jan. 1977) 16,303,000,000 afghanis.

Foreign Trade. (1975–76) Imports U.S. $293 million;
exports c. U.S. $235 million. Import sources (1973–74):
U.S.S.R. 21%; Japan 17%; U.S. 12%; India 10%; West Germany 6%. Export destinations (1972–73): U.S.S.R. 29%;
India 24%; U.K. 16%; West Germany 6%. Main exports:
fruits and nuts 29%; natural gas 20%; cotton 13%; carpets
7%; karakul (persian lamb) skins 5%.

Transport and Communications. Roads (1973) 17,973
km. Motor vehicles in use (1971): passenger 38,400; commercial (including buses) 26,100. Air traffic (1975): 256
million passenger-km; freight 11 million net ton-km. Telephones (Dec. 1974) 23,000. Radio receivers (Dec. 1976)
c. 900,000.

Agriculture. Production (in 000; metric tons; 1976):
corn c. 790; wheat c. 2,950; rice c. 450; barley c. 400;
cotton, lint c. 50; wool, clean c. 15. Livestock (in 000;
1975): cattle c. 3,610; sheep c. 17,300; karakul sheep
(1971) c. 6,800; horses c. 422; asses c. 1,240; goats c. 2,350;
camels c. 300.

Industry. Production (in 000; metric tons; 1974–75):
coal 187; natural gas (cu m) 2,946,000; cotton fabrics (m)
68,100; rayon fabrics (m) 20,685; cement 144; electricity
(kw-hr) 527,200.

cultivation of friendship with other Islamic countries. Relations with Pakistan continued to improve; agreement on the resumption of air
communications was reached at the beginning of
March. The idea of a "Pakhtun" state was not
abandoned, but support for it was less strident. A
trade treaty was concluded with the Soviet Union
after a visit by the president to Moscow in April.

(L. F. RUSHBROOK WILLIAMS)

African Affairs

The number of independent African states rose to
49 on June 27, 1977, when the French Territory of
the Afars and Issas became the Republic of Djibouti. With its independence, only two territories on
the continent—Rhodesia (which had declared its
independence from the U.K. unilaterally in 1965)
and Namibia (South West Africa)—remained as
foreign dependencies. The increasing violence produced by the struggle for independence in both
those territories brought greater involvement by
the Western governments.

South Africa granted independence to another
homeland, Bophuthatswana, in December 1977
but, as with Transkei in 1976, Bophuthatswana
was denied international recognition. The Saharan
Arab Democratic Republic pressed its claim to sovereignty over the former Spanish Sahara territories, absorbed by Morocco and Mauritania in 1976.
Two active liberation movements in Ethiopia—the
Eritreans and the Somalis of Ogaden Province—
produced conflicts and international involvement.

The Organization of African Unity (OAU).
The organization of 49 African member states
grappled ineffectively with major conflicts among

Dancers entertained a huge audience during the second World Black and African Festival of Arts and Culture in Lagos, Nigeria.

its members. At its 14th annual summit conference in Libreville, Gabon, in July a conciliation commission was appointed to resolve the conflicts between Ethiopia and Somalia over the latter's support for the West Somalia Liberation Front; between Morocco, Mauritania, and Algeria over the former Spanish Sahara; and Chad's complaints of territorial annexation against Libya. The commission had no success in ending any of the conflicts. In the Zimbabwe (black Rhodesia) leadership dispute the OAU recognized the Patriotic Front representing the Zimbabwe People's Army.

Southern Africa. A warlike atmosphere continued to build up in southern Africa after the failure in 1976 of African and Western initiatives to negotiate settlements in Rhodesia and Namibia and because of the growth of black opposition in South Africa.

In Rhodesia the fighting threatened to engulf neighbouring Mozambique, Zambia, and Botswana. After the failure of the 1976 Geneva talks, a fresh Anglo-U.S. initiative was launched. The new proposals were supported by the "front-line" presidents (of Tanzania, Zambia, Mozambique, Botswana, and Angola) but were rejected by Rhodesian Prime Minister Ian Smith on January 24. Then the new British foreign secretary, David Owen (*see* BIOGRAPHY), with support from U.S. Pres. Jimmy Carter's administration, undertook personal diplomacy. The South African prime minister, B. J. Vorster, and the African front-line presidents backed this initiative, but objections by Smith and conflicts among Zimbabwe factions blocked negotiations. In September the UN Security Council voted general support of the Anglo-U.S. plan, under which a UN peacekeeping force would maintain a cease-fire to be arranged by the designated British resident commissioner, Field Marshal Lord Carver. On November 24 Smith unexpectedly endorsed the principle of one man, one vote as a starting point for negotiations with three black organizations based within Rhodesia,

but shortly thereafter Rhodesian forces launched their biggest strike thus far against guerrilla bases in Mozambique. Talks between Smith and the black leaders began in early December but accomplished little before adjourning December 23.

In Namibia a collective initiative by the five Western members of the Security Council (Britain, France, Canada, West Germany, and the U.S.) induced South Africa to negotiate further for an internationally acceptable basis for Namibia's independence. The Council members sought to

Coffin containing the body of Steven Biko is taken from a stadium to its burial site. Biko, a black South African leader, died in Johannesburg while in police custody.

have South Africa accept participation in the talks by the South West Africa People's Organization (SWAPO). Although differences between South Africa and SWAPO had narrowed by the year's end, the last two hurdles (removal of South Africa's armed forces from the territory and the future of Walvis Bay) held up a final agreement. Militant black opposition increased in South Africa. Violence, which had begun in 1976, continued in the black city of Soweto, a satellite of Johannesburg, and the troubles spread to other parts of the country. South Africa also came under external pressures because of its internal policies. President Carter sent Vice-Pres. Walter Mondale to meet Vorster in Vienna in May to communicate U.S. intentions to adopt a tougher attitude unless South Africa took positive steps to introduce representative government. The European Economic Community (EEC) also took a more critical stance, establishing a Code of Employment Practice for European firms operating in South Africa. When the South African government banned all the Black Consciousness movements in October, the Western countries supported a Security Council mandatory arms embargo against the nation.

The Horn of Africa. The conflicts in the northeast corner of Africa bounded by the Red Sea flared into serious warfare during 1977. The U.S.S.R., having supplied arms to Somalia since 1968, replaced the U.S. as supplier to Ethiopia. This support of Ethiopia by the U.S.S.R. and also by Cuba angered Somalia. Since gaining independence in 1960, Somalia had disputed its borders with Ethiopia, claiming the Ogaden Province because of the Somalis living there. On November 12, Somalia broke its Soviet friendship treaty and ordered the evacuation of Soviet advisers. The Soviet Navy lost the right to use the port of Berbera and its telecommunications centre there. Somalia then joined the anti-Soviet alliance of Arab states led by Sudan, Egypt, and Saudi Arabia. This alliance sought Western military assistance for Somalia to replace Soviet aid, but, although the U.S. and Great Britain promised in August to supply a limited amount of "defensive weapons," these

Weapon-carrying guards of the West Somalia Liberation Front patrol the streets of Mustahil, in the Ogaden region of Ethiopia, after the town was captured from Ethiopian forces.

were not in fact delivered because of Somalia's role in the fighting in the Ogaden.

All the Arab states, except for Libya and the People's Democratic Republic of Yemen (Aden; South Yemen), also supported the Eritrean liberation movement against Ethiopia. The Sudan, especially, also gave support to the Ethiopian Democratic Union, another movement opposed to the Addis Ababa regime. On the other side, the Marxist regime in Ethiopia won support from Libya, South Yemen, and Kenya. Kenya also expressed concern about Somalia's claim to a northern strip of its territory.

Coups and Inter-African Relations. In an attempted coup in the Congo People's Republic, Pres. Marien Ngouabi was assassinated on March 18, but the regime's policies were continued by his successor, Col. Joachim Yhombi-Opango (*see* BIOGRAPHY). At least four attempts were made on the life of Pres. Idi Amin of Uganda. An attempt was made by a dissident Marxist group to overthrow Pres. Agostinho Neto of Angola. A plot to assassinate Togo's president, Gen. Gnassingbe Eyadema, was thwarted by British intelligence, which discovered it in October. Ethiopia's principal Marxist theoretician, Haile Frida, was secretly executed, and revolutionary council Vice-Chairman Lieut. Col. Atnafu Abate was executed in November. After revolutionary killings in February, Lieut. Col. Mengistu Haile Mariam (*see* BIOGRAPHY) emerged as chairman of the Provisional Military Administrative Council.

Disputes between neighbour states continued to produce continental instability. Several serious military and other conflicts occurred in addition to

A Libyan soldier walks through the remains of a home in Tobruk demolished in a border clash with Egyptians in July.

those already mentioned in southern Africa and the Horn of Africa. Morocco threatened to go to war with Algeria over its support for Polisario, the Saharan nationalist organization that was challenging King Hassan and his ally Mauritania for sovereignty over the former Spanish Sahara. Libya and Egypt engaged in open warfare in July as the Egyptians struck back against Libya following hostile border movements. Sudan entered into a formal joint defense agreement with Egypt after the Libyans and Ethiopians threatened Pres. Gaafar Nimeiry's regime.

An invasion by Zairian rebels from Angolan territory was made into Zaire in March. The Angolan justification for permitting this attack was that Zaire's Pres. Mobutu Sese Seko (see BIOGRAPHY) was allegedly involved in Operation Cobra, a plan for the invasion of Angola's oil-rich Cabinda by Neto's opponents. The threat to the Zaire regime was so serious that President Mobutu sought external help to assist his hard-pressed Army. France provided aircraft for Moroccan troops to be flown in, and Egypt and Sudan offered military support. The border tension between Ghana and Togo worsened as a result of attempts by political elements of the Ewe tribe (which straddled the border) to establish their own separate state.

Political Systems. The 16-nation Economic Community of West African States (ECOWAS), launched at the end of 1976, began to function actively in 1977. Led by Nigeria and Ivory Coast, ECOWAS linked English-speaking and French-speaking nations economically and sought to improve trade and communications and to coordinate common services. A treaty between ECOWAS and the EEC provided for technical and other types of cooperation.

There were signs of healthier democratic institutions in some nations. Nigeria elected a constituent assembly, a move toward restoration of civilian parliamentary rule, to be introduced in 1979. Senegal and Egypt institutionalized a multiparty parliamentary system; both countries legalized three political parties, representing the left, the centre, and the right. Morocco also revived a multiparty system, though it was heavily dependent on the king. Both Ghana and Upper Volta submitted to popular pressures to abandon military rule in favour of elected civilian governments in the near future. The Gambia, a model democracy, held a successful parliamentary election. In October President Nimeiry was reconciled with his National Front opposition leader, Sadik al-Mahdi, with agreement to give the Sudan a democratic constitution.

External Relations. The most dramatic development was the military involvement by the Soviet Union and Cuba in the Red Sea area conflicts. It led to an active anti-Soviet alliance headed by Sudan, Egypt, and Somalia, which had all previously enjoyed close relations with Moscow. Other African governments, notably Ivory Coast and Morocco, took a strong stand against Moscow's Africa policies. Conversely, Angola, Mozambique, Libya, Ethiopia, and Algeria developed closer relations with the U.S.S.R.

African relations with the West, especially with

Soviet Pres. Nikolay V. Podgorny (left) walks with Tanzanian Pres. Julius Nyerere after arriving at the airport at Dar es Salaam.

the new U.S. administration, improved. Egypt and Sudan adopted more openly pro-Western attitudes as their quarrels with Moscow deepened, and the state visit of Nigeria's head of state, Lieut. Gen. Olusegun Obasanjo, to the U.S. in October marked the end of a long period of friction between those two countries. France was only mildly criticized in Africa for allowing its air force to be used to assist Zaire against invasion. African relations with China remained friendly, but few governments showed any willingness to become involved in the Sino-Soviet dispute.

Economic Performance. The continent's social and economic conditions declined in 1977 despite improved world prices for some commodities. Except in major oil-producing countries (Nigeria, Gabon, Libya, Algeria, and Angola), African economies had not yet recovered from the quintupling of oil prices since 1973 and the subsequent heavy increase in the cost of imports. Most African countries resorted to deficit financing, which further aggravated inflationary pressures. The debt burden, which quadrupled from $7 billion in 1965 to $28 billion in 1974, rose further in 1977. Some countries spent 30% of their export earnings on interest and amortization charges on debts, as compared with the 10% ceiling proposed by the World Bank. This dismal economic picture was compounded by the continued failure of agriculture in almost every African country.

The gloomy survey for 1977 of the Economic Commission for Africa concluded, "Africa more than any other region in the Third World, is faced with a development crisis of great portent." Since the early 1960s only nine African countries had achieved a growth rate capable of producing relatively substantial increases in real per capita income. (COLIN LEGUM)

See also Dependent States; articles on the various political units.

Agriculture and Food Supplies

World food production probably nearly matched growth in population in 1977, although per capita output was down slightly in the less developed countries, most notably in parts of Africa and West and East Asia. However, heavily populated South Asia, the focus of famine concerns a few years earlier, managed to equal 1976 per capita output. This and the maintenance of large grain stocks into 1978, heavily concentrated in exporting countries, created fairly optimistic expectations about short-term world food security and led the United States to introduce production restraints. Stocks were maintained despite an expected 2% decline in world grain production for the 1977–78 crop year. Once again, the Soviet Union provided the largest source of fluctuation, this time downward, but at the same time increased its food consumption.

Ample grain reserves simplified the achievement of food aid targets and stimulated some movement toward creation of an international system of grain reserves. U.S. food aid legislation was revamped, along with domestic farm programs, and a domestic grain reserve was created. The commitment of external resources for agricultural development in the less developed countries slackened but was expected to regain momentum.

Late in the year a loosely knit organization of U.S. farmers, the American Agriculture Movement, began calling for a nationwide farm strike. U.S. farmers had suffered a decline in their net income of about 33% from the all-time high in 1973, and many were angry that the new U.S. farm bill had not provided them with higher levels of government crop-support payments. The discontent spread from American Agriculture's home base in Colorado to many parts of the U.S. and manifested itself in "tractorcades" through Washington, D.C., and many state capitals. The strikers did not, however, have the support of the major farm organizations, and U.S. Pres. Jimmy Carter indicated that he would probably resist their demands for sharply higher support payments.

AGRICULTURE AND FOOD PRODUCTION

Production Indexes. World agricultural output (excluding China) may have increased a little more than 1% in 1977, according to preliminary estimates (in December) contained in indexes prepared by the Economics, Statistics, and Cooperatives Service (ESCS) of the U.S. Department of Agriculture (USDA). China may only have equaled its 1976 level of output because of a disappointing grain harvest.

Agricultural production in the developed countries rose about 1%, held back mainly by large shortfalls in Soviet grain crops and also by declines occurring in Canada and Oceania. The most notable gains were Western Europe's recovery from the 1976 drought and a substantial increase in U.S. output.

A sharp increase in Latin-American agricultural production and moderate gains in South and East Asia more than offset reduced production in Africa —especially in Ethiopia and parts of the Sahel— and in the West Asian countries of the Mediterranean Basin. Therefore, agricultural output in the less developed countries increased about 2% in 1977.

Total world food production (excluding China) also increased perhaps a little better than 1%, slower than the estimated 1.8% annual increase in world population (excluding China). Thus, per capita world food production did not increase and may well have declined slightly in 1977. Food output in the developed countries increased at about the same rate as their annual 0.8% increase in population. Although the less developed countries increased food production about 2%, their estimated 2.4% growth in population resulted in a

Table I. Indexes of World Agricultural and Food Production (excluding China)
1961–65 = 100

Region or country	Total agricultural production						Total food production						Per capita food production					
	1972	1973	1974	1975	1976	1977[1]	1972	1973	1974	1975	1976	1977[1]	1972	1973	1974	1975	1976	1977[1]
Developed countries	123	131	129	128	134	136	125	133	131	130	137	138	115	121	118	116	121	121
United States	120	122	117	126	129	132	126	128	122	134	136	139	114	115	109	119	120	121
Canada	120	123	112	127	140	134	122	123	112	128	143	135	106	106	95	106	117	110
Western Europe	121	123	128	125	123	129	121	123	128	125	123	129	113	115	119	115	113	118
EEC	119	122	125	121	119	126	119	122	125	121	118	126	112	114	116	112	109	116
Eastern Europe	132	135	140	137	143	143	132	135	140	137	143	144	124	127	130	127	131	131
U.S.S.R.	129	155	145	130	153	149	128	155	144	128	152	148	117	140	129	113	133	129
Japan	110	110	110	115	110	115	110	110	111	115	109	115	100	98	97	100	94	98
Oceania	115	117	120	125	124	122	123	127	127	136	136	134	104	107	105	111	110	107
South Africa	143	119	148	139	140	147	150	125	157	146	148	156	118	95	117	107	105	108
Less developed countries	125	131	134	141	145	148	126	132	135	145	149	151	100	103	103	108	108	107
East Asia	133	146	149	155	165	167	130	142	147	156	166	167	104	111	112	116	121	119
Indonesia	120	132	139	141	146	148	119	134	142	143	148	150	96	106	109	108	109	108
Philippines	133	143	146	163	173	175	134	145	147	165	175	177	103	108	107	117	121	120
South Asia	120	129	124	138	135	139	119	130	123	141	137	141	98	104	97	108	103	103
Bangladesh	103	117	109	123	117	118	102	119	114	129	120	122	82	93	87	96	87	86
India	119	129	122	139	136	139	119	130	121	141	136	140	98	104	96	109	103	104
Pakistan	156	157	162	155	163	173	152	159	163	161	175	180	117	119	118	114	119	120
West Asia	139	129	144	152	169	168	137	127	141	152	169	167	107	96	104	109	118	113
Africa	123	119	126	126	130	127	122	119	126	129	132	128	97	92	95	95	95	89
Egypt	119	120	118	119	122	126	122	124	125	131	135	137	97	97	95	98	98	98
Ethiopia	114	111	114	103	106	100	113	111	112	101	105	98	91	87	86	76	76	70
Nigeria	119	112	120	122	124	126	119	113	120	122	124	126	95	87	90	89	88	87
Latin America	125	130	138	141	145	153	130	138	144	151	159	164	102	105	107	109	112	112
Mexico	132	141	142	151	150	157	141	152	150	169	167	172	104	108	102	112	107	106
Argentina	104	115	122	123	133	135	108	120	126	127	138	139	95	105	109	108	115	115
Brazil	134	137	150	152	157	167	142	152	162	166	184	190	111	115	120	119	129	129
World	124	131	131	132	138	140	125	133	132	135	141	143	110	115	113	113	117	117

[1] Preliminary.
Source: U.S. Department of Agriculture, Economic Research Service.

A healthy bollworm who fed on normal soybean leaves is contrasted with a stunted companion who was given only insect-resistant leaves.

small decline in per capita output. Heavily populated South Asia maintained per capita production at the 1976 level as did Latin America, but output per person fell sharply in less developed Africa and West Asia and was moderately lower in East Asia.

Grains. Based on December estimates of crops already harvested in the Northern Hemisphere and preharvest reports for the Southern Hemisphere, world grain supplies in 1978 were again expected to be ample despite a 2% decline in output. Carry-over grain stocks were also expected to be maintained near the relatively high levels of 1976–77. The resulting lower grain prices influenced the introduction of production restraints in the U.S., where stocks were heavily concentrated.

World grain production in the 1977–78 crop year (wheat, coarse grains, and milled rice) was estimated at 1,308,000,000 metric tons, a decline of about 32 million tons from 1976–77, largely because of an unexpectedly poor Soviet grain crop. This totaled 195 million tons, almost 20 million below the Soviet target and almost 30 million below the record 1976 crop.

World wheat output was expected to total 380 million tons, down 33 million from a year earlier. Harvested area was estimated to have dropped nearly 5 million hectares (2.5%) from 1976–77, with the largest reductions in the U.S., Canada, the European Economic Community (EEC), and Argentina. The major reason for the reduced output, however, was the 6% decline in global yields caused by bad weather in Europe, the Mediterranean Basin, Australia, Argentina, and Brazil.

Coarse grain production at 684 million tons was forecast to be down only 8 million tons from 1976–77, as a 25 million-ton decline in the Soviet harvest (to 90 million tons) and small reductions in Australian, Argentine, South African, Thai, and Bra-

zilian crops more than offset an 8 million-ton increase in the U.S. harvest (to a record 202 million) and the 14 million-ton rebound in Western European output (to 87 million).

World milled rice production was expected to exceed the previous record, reaching 244 million tons. India's crop was expected to be 6 million tons larger despite the effects of a typhoon, and that for China could be 2 million tons larger. Other Asian rice crop prospects were favourable, except in drought-stricken Laos, Cambodia, Vietnam, Thailand, and Indonesia.

Total world grain utilization could climb 25 million tons in 1977–78, reaching 1,311,000,000 for the second consecutive year of record use. The increase was largely the result of feeding 495 million tons of grain, 4% more, to animals.

Per capita world grain utilization was expected to be little changed in 1977–78 at 315 kg. Per capita usage of wheat rose a little, but that of coarse grains and milled rice was down. Per capita grain use in the less developed countries might fall a little despite record production because of more rapid population growth. If the animal feed component is subtracted—a much smaller amount in the less developed countries as compared with the developed nations—per capita grain consumption in the less developed countries could total 168 kg, compared with the world average of 209 kg.

World trade in grains for 1977–78 was expected to reach nearly 175 million tons, up almost 5% from 1976–77, largely because of an 8 million-ton increase in wheat trade to a record 70 million tons. Wheat imports by Western Europe, the U.S.S.R., and China increased substantially, while the greatest export gains were made by the U.S. and Canada. Trade in coarse grains was expected to decline less than 2 million tons to about 81 million, as a sharp increase in expected Soviet imports was

Table II. World Production and Trade of Principal Grains (in 000 metric tons)

	Wheat Production 1961–65 average	Wheat Production 1976	Wheat Imports−/Exports+ 1973–76 average	Barley Production 1961–65 average	Barley Production 1976	Barley Imports−/Exports+ 1973–76 average	Oats Production 1961–65 average	Oats Production 1976	Oats Imports−/Exports+ 1973–76 average	Rye Production 1961–65 average	Rye Production 1976	Rye Imports−/Exports+ 1973–76 average	Corn(Maize) Production 1961–65 average	Corn(Maize) Production 1976	Corn(Maize) Imports−/Exports+ 1973–76 average	Rice Production 1961–65 average	Rice Production 1976	Rice Imports−/Exports+ 1973–76 average
World total	254426	417478	−66448[1] +69319[1]	99716	189654	−12211[1] +12182[1]	47811	50373	−1338[1] +1399[1]	33816	27660	−1230[1] +1257[1]	216069	334014	−49132[1] +49786[1]	253234	345386	−9051[1] +9022[1]
Algeria	1254	c2200	−c1660[1]	476	c600	−c50[1] +22[1]	28	c90	+2[1]	—	—	—	4	c5[3]	−c40[1]	7	c3[3]	−9[1]
Argentina	7541	11200	−141[1] +2399	679	c760	+78	676	530	+128	422	330	+52	4984	5855	+4126	193	309	+49
Australia	8222	c12000	+7604	978	c2840	+1473	1172	c1190	+264	11	c15	−2[1]	176	129	−1[1] +4[1]	136	417	+202
Austria	704	1234	−21[1]	563	1287	−58[1] +2[1]	322	c283	−12[1]	393	410	—	197	936	−60[1] +1[1]	—	—	−33[1]
Bangladesh	37	117[3]	−2000[1]	15	16[3]								4	3[3]		15048	c18500	−292
Belgium	826	932	−1335[1][2] +594[1][2]	485	641	−1136[2] +241[1][2]	389	c145	−52[1][2] +6[1][2]	120	c47	−10[1][2] +4[1][2]	2	c40	−1475[2] +201[1][2]	—	—	−92[1] +27[1][2]
Brazil	574	c3200	−2804	26	18[3]	−26[1]	20	39	−24[1]	17	14	—	10112	17929	−4[1] +918	6123	9560	−32[1] +42
Bulgaria	2213	c3100	−62[1] +158[1]	694	c1800	−178[1] +5[1]	141	c60	—	58	c20	−20[1]	1601	c2900	−217[1] +75[1]	37	c61[3]	−5[1]
Burma	38	64[3]	−13[4]	—	—	—	—	—	−5[1]	—	—	—	58	c75[3]	+4[1]	7786	c9400	+c310
Canada	15364	23523	+11024	3860	10303	+3310	6075	4961	−1[1] +206	319	561	−1[1] +177	1073	3675	−912 +7[1]	—	—	−73[1]
Chile	1082	c850	−893	74	78	−6[1] +13[1]	89	77	−1[1]	7	11	−7[1]	204	273	−118[1] +3[1]	85	76[3]	−33[1]
China	22200	c43000	−c5570[1]	c15000	c21500	−c260[1]	c1690	c3000	—	—	—	—	c22600	c34000	−c2300[1] +c70[1]	c83000	c114000	−c50[1] +c2000
Colombia	118	c85[3]	−c314	106	c71	−50[4]	—	—	−11[1]	—	—	—	826	c884	−59[1]	576	1560	+62[1]
Czechoslovakia	1779	4640	−711	1556	c3100	−104[1] +42[1]	792	c580	+12[1]	897	c530	−2[1] +54[1]	474	c500	−591	—	—	−70[1]
Denmark	535	578	−17 +184[1]	3506	4767	−134 +437	713	267	−32 +7	380	c236	−2[1] +15[1]	—	—	−231	—	—	−12[1] +2[1]
Egypt	1459	1960	−2365	137	123	—	—	—	—	—	—	—	1913	c2710	−c390	1845	c2530	+157
Ethiopia	663	694	−4[1] +3[1]	1323	c800	−c2[1]	5	c5	—	—	—	—	743	c1200	+1[1]	—	—	
Finland	448	654	−13[1] +64[1]	400	1553	−10[1] +3[1]	828	1573	−2[1] +6[1]	141	178	−20[1]	—	—	−99	—	—	−15[1] +1[1]
France	12495	16089	−303 +7006	6594	8280	−48 +3500	2583	1424	−1[1] +129	367	283	−2[1] +61	2760	5477	−516 +2963	120	37	−166 +3
Germany, East	1357	c2600	−1371[1]	1291	c3300	−c200[1]	850	c600	—	1741	c1400	−8[1]	3	c32[3]	−c1300[1]	—	—	−51[1]
Germany, West	4607	6702	−1852 +733	3462	6487	−1576 +382	2185	2497	−391 +43	3031	2100	−78 +146	55	480	−3383 +267	—	—	−161 +31[1]
Greece	1765	c2351	−83[1] +102	248	955	−57[1] +7[1]	143	c104	−1[1]	19	c6	—	239	c551	−c763	88	c84	−4[1] +5[1]
Hungary	2020	5138	−12[1] +890	970	746	−211[1] +34[1]	108	86	−32[1]	271	156	−22[1] +20[1]	3350	c5200	−3[1] +635[1]	36	c40	−14[1] +3[1]
India	11191	28336	−c4717 +137[1]	2590	3196	−1[1]	—	—	—	—	—	—	4593	c6500	−3[1]	52733	c70500	−155 +23[1]
Indonesia	—	—	−684[1]	—	—	—	—	—	—	—	—	−2[1]	2804	c2532	+143[1]	12396	22950	−1243
Iran	2873	c6000	−c1240[1]	792	1487	−c175[1]	—	—	—	—	—	—	24	c60[3]	−c138[1]	851	c1500	−177[1] +3[1]
Iraq	849	c1312	−446[1] +51[1]	851	579	−c8[1]	—	—	—	—	—	—	6	c14[3]	—	142	163	−111[1]
Ireland	343	216	−187 +19	575	c973	−75 +44	357	c123	−11	1	c1[3]	—	—	—	−253	—	—	−3[1]
Italy	8857	9528	−2045 +22[1]	276	c760	−c1050	545	440	−147 +2[1]	87	35	−10[1]	3633	5082	−4690 +3[1]	612	976	−10[1] +c370
Japan	1332	222	−5561	1380	c210	−1525	145	22	−142	2	c1[3]	−68	1	—	−7741	16444	15292	−36 +287[1]
Kenya	122	c158	−57[1] +13[1]	15	31	−1[1] +1[1]	2	c4	—	—	—	—	1110	c1360	+136[1]	14	c32[3]	+2[1]
Korea, South	169	82	−1546[1]	1150	c1759	−506[1]	—	—	—	18	6	—	—	—	−508[1]	4809	7250	−398[1] +9[1]
Malaysia	—	—	−409[1]	—	—	—	—	—	−5[1]	—	—	—	8	c12[3]	−247[1] +1[1]	1140	c1880	−291[1] +18[1]
Mexico	1672	3354	−446 +18	175	c460	−110[1]	76	c79	−6[1]	—	—	—	7369	8945	−1486 +10[1]	314	c450	−36[1] +5[1]
Morocco	1336	2190	−1049	1316	2862	−c50[1]	18	36	—	2	c2	—	361	c430	−31[1]	20	29[3]	—
Netherlands, The	606	710	−1892[1] +813[1]	390	263	−324 +203	421	103	−40[1] +73[1]	312	65	−35[1] +28[1]	—	c7[3]	−c4790 +1933	—	—	−124 +43[1]
New Zealand	248	427	−91 +10[1]	98	344	−5[1] +30[1]	34	41	—	—	c1[3]	—	16	205[3]	+3[1]	—	—	−6[1]
Nigeria	16	c6[3]	−386[1]	—	—	—	—	—	—	—	—	—	754	c1050	−2[1]	212	c405	−2[1]
Norway	19	48[3]	−307	440	486	−106	126	287	−1[1] +27[1]	3	7	−81	—	—	−93 +1[1]	—	—	−6[1]
Pakistan	4153	8636	−1302[1]	118	130	+38[1]	—	—	—	—	—	—	514	c711	−2[1]	1824	3942	+c680
Peru	150	c148	−732	185	c165	−26	4	c1	−12[1]	1	c1	−1[1]	490	c670	−274[1] +1[1]	324	570	−26[1] +20[1]
Philippines	—	—	−551	—	—	—	—	—	−3[1]	—	—	—	1305	c2710	−104[1]	3957	c6439	−212[1] +1[1]
Poland	2988	c5741	−1790	1368	c3608	−c1080[1] +47[1]	2641	c2696	−c88[1] +5[1]	7466	c6914	−c66[1] +205[1]	20	c50[3]	−754[4]	—	—	−78
Portugal	562	c680	−292	61	104	−16[1]	87	133	—	177	147	−2[1][2]	617	357	−995 +2[1]	167	89	−40[1] +1[1]
Romania	4321	c6730	−141[1] +605[1]	415	c1400	−c40[4]	154	c48	—	95	c49	−38[1]	5853	c11700	−c340[1] +c270[1]	40	c32	−55[4]
South Africa	834	2060	−6[1] +235[1]	37	64[3]	−8[1]	107	88	+4[1]	10	4	−2[1]	5248	7312	−3[1] +2476	2	3[3]	−85 +4[1]
Spain	4365	4176	−31 +68[1]	1959	5163	−34 +88	447	505	+5[1]	385	209	—	1101	1543	−3636 +1[1]	386	c392	+38
Sweden	909	1788	−12 +661	1167	1831	−39[1] +167[1]	1304	1281	−29[1] +101	142	418	−2[1] +112	—	—	−73	—	—	−17[1]
Switzerland	355	c405	−364	102	c193	−538	40	c55	−159	52	c32	−32	14	c120[3]	−270	—	—	−24[1]
Syria	1093	1790	−103[1] +41[1]	649	c1059	−11[1] +2[1]	2	2	—	—	—	—	7	32[3]	−2[1] +2[1]	1	3[3]	−65
Thailand	—	—	−c87[1]	—	—	—	—	—	—	—	—	—	816	c2700	+2265	11267	14900	+1186
Turkey	8585	c16500	−540[1] +104[1]	3447	5100	−34[1] +30[1]	495	c400	—	734	c900	—	950	c1230	—	222	262[3]	−43[1]
U.S.S.R.	64207	c96900	−4841 +3780	20318	c69500	−1060[1] +671[1]	6052	c17000	−70[1] +30[1]	15093	c12000	−660[1]	13122	c10300	−5970 +415[1]	390	c2100	−209[1] +81[1]
United Kingdom	3520	4773	−3517 +79	6670	7793	−563 +425	1541	806	−29 +19[1]	21	20	−32[1] +1[1]	—	—	−3359 +38	—	—	−144 +1[1]
United States	33040	58444	−32 +31644[5]	8676	8215	−253 +1233	13848	8164	−7 +368	828	423	−9 +263	95561	157893	−38 +35224[5]	3084	5308	−6[1] +1787
Uruguay	465	505	−c97[1] +57	28	47	−1[1] +8[1]	66	48	—	—	—	—	148	c210	−3[1] +4[1]	67	215	+66[1]
Venezuela	1	1[3]	−568[1]	—	—	—	—	—	−10[1]	—	—	—	477	c532	−c260[1]	136	277	+30
Yugoslavia	3599	c5980	−486 +2[1]	557	653	−10[1] +49[1]	343	320	−4[1] +1[1]	169	105	—	5618	c9112	−42[1] +270	23	37[3]	−19[1]

Note: (—) indicates quantity nil or negligible. (c) indicates provisional or estimated. [1]1973–75 average. [2]Belgium-Luxembourg economic union. [3]1975. [4]1973–74 average. [5]Including foreign aid shipments.

Sources: *FAO Monthly Bulletin of Agricultural Economics and Statistics; FAO Production Yearbook 1975; FAO Trade Yearbook 1975.*

(M. C. MacDONALD)

more than offset by a large drop in Western European import needs because of recovery from the 1976 drought. Rice exports increased by about 1 million tons in calendar 1977 over 1976, reaching about 9.3 million tons mostly because of record Thai and U.S. exports. In 1978, however, exports were projected to decline about a million tons because of generally good rice crops.

A 55 million-ton buildup in world grain stocks during 1976–77 raised carrying stocks for 1977–78 to about 187 million tons (52% wheat, 40% coarse grains, and 8% rice). The expected 14 million-ton drawdown in wheat stocks during 1977–78 was expected to occur mostly in the U.S.S.R., Canada, Australia, and Argentina. U.S. wheat stocks were expected to increase 2 million tons, resulting in the U.S. holding about 60% of world stocks, Canada 14%, and the EEC 9%. Coarse grain stocks were expected to increase about 6 million tons despite a sharp reduction in the U.S.S.R., because U.S. stocks were forecast to reach about 42 million tons (nearly 50% of world coarse grain stocks), up about 12 million tons. A substantial buildup in rice stocks was forecast during 1977–78, but rice prices were little affected because the larger stocks are mostly held by countries that usually are not exporters.

Thus, carry-over stocks for 1977–78 were forecast to total about 185 million tons (45% wheat, 45% coarse grains, and 10% rice). This would comprise about 14% of the forecast total world grain utilization in 1977–78, compared with almost 15% in 1976–77 and the lows of under 11% in the recent years of scarcity, 1973–74 and 1974–75.

Starchy Roots. The UN Food and Agriculture Organization (FAO) suggested that cassava production might not achieve the 3.3% trend rate of annual increase in 1977 because of drought in Togo and parts of the Central African Empire, Tan-

zania, and Zaire. Thailand's output, which is mostly for export, was expected to increase substantially.

Protein Meal and Vegetable Oils. Calendar 1977 (roughly corresponding to the U.S. 1976–77 oilseed marketing year) was one of tight supplies for both oilseed meals and oils, largely because of substantial shortfalls in 1976 U.S., Canadian, and Soviet oilseed harvests. Production of oil meal (including fish meal) in 1977 declined about 9% to 66 million tons (44% soybean meal equivalent), while consumption remained stable at nearly 70 million tons. This resulted in a decline in stocks, particularly in the U.S. and the EEC.

Production of edible vegetable oils declined 6% to about 31 million tons (soybean oil equivalent), but oil consumption increased about 3% to almost 33 million tons, resulting in a drawdown in stocks in 1977. Although high prices led to a decline in consumption in developed countries, this was more than offset by increases in the less developed countries.

World output of oil meal was forecast (in December) to rise about 19% to 79 million tons in 1978 as a result of a sharp recovery in 1977 oilseed production in most major producing regions. U.S. 1977 soybean output jumped 33% to almost 46 million tons, and substantial increases were forecast for spring-harvested Brazilian (to 12.8 million tons) and Argentine (to 1.7 million tons) soybean crops. Canadian rapeseed output was estimated to recover to 1.8 million tons; Argentine flaxseed production was expected to be higher; and EEC oilseed output returned to historical levels after the 1976 drought. The Soviet sunflower seed crop was estimated to have recovered to between 6 and 6.5 million tons. Preliminary estimates indicated no rise in Indian peanut production, but Nigerian and Senegalese prospects were less favourable. Pe-

Chinese farmers use newly acquired farm machinery to plant rice. The mechanization of Chinese agriculture was ordered by the late Chairman Mao.

GARY SETTLE—THE NEW YORK TIMES

Rancher Robert Fear surveys his hungry herd on drought-stricken ranch near Sutherland, Nebraska.

ruvian fish meal production was expected to remain at about 440,000 tons in 1978.

The predicted increase in meal production helped push down meal prices below year-earlier levels. Low meal prices relative to meal grain were expected to lead to increased meal use in feed rations, and world meal consumption was forecast to rise 6% in 1978 to almost 74 million tons. Most of the expansion was expected to occur in the U.S., the EEC, and Japan.

The ample oilseed supplies in 1977 were largely responsible for the predicted rise in world production of edible vegetable oils in 1978 of 15% to about 36 million tons, although palm oil was also forecast to increase. Consumption was forecast to increase 8% to about 35 million tons as prices retreated from the high levels of 1977, with the developed nations expanding use a little more rapidly than the centrally planned and less developed countries. Stocks of both meals and oils, held mostly in the form of seeds, were expected to increase significantly in 1978 because production of both was forecast to exceed consumption.

Meat. Production, consumption, and trade of meat in 1977 in the world's two largest meat-consuming regions, the U.S. and the EEC, were estimated in December to remain near 1976 levels. Total U.S. red meat and poultry production reached a new record in 1977, as increases in pork and broilers overcame a 2–3% decline from 1976 in beef production because of a drop in nonfed beef output. U.S. beef production was forecast to decline another 3–5% in 1978. Fed beef output could rise 4–5% above 1977 (reaching perhaps 75% of total beef production) as nonfed beef dropped perhaps one-fifth, reflecting a winding down of

the liquidation phase of the cattle cycle. U.S. pork output could increase 10–12%, and poultry 4–6%, over 1977.

Beef production in the EEC was estimated to have declined about 5% in 1977, but the drop was offset by a rise in pork output. The decline in beef production was expected to continue into 1978, and pork also was expected to begin dropping. The EEC had narrowly balanced net beef trade, at about 300,000 tons (carcass weight), with production, at about 6 million tons, since imposing tight import restrictions in 1974. Thus, 1978 EEC beef imports might again approximate 450,000 tons, with offsetting exports of about 150,000 tons.

The tight Japanese system of quantitative restrictions probably held beef imports to about 140,000 tons, lamb and mutton to 290,000 tons, pork to 145,000 tons, and horsemeat to 77,000 tons in 1977. Australia was faced with severe pressures to find outlets for its beef. The herd was very large and sensitive to drought; prices were low; and herd liquidation was into its second year, with cattle numbers declining from 33 million at the beginning of 1976 to about 30 million by the end of 1977. Beef production rose about 5% to 2 million tons in 1977 and was expected to about equal that amount in 1978.

Argentine cattle numbers were also large—expected to remain stable at the 1976 level of 85 million through 1978—and sensitive to drought. Production was also high, and the country sought to keep 1978 beef exports at the 530,000-ton level through market diversification.

Soviet cattle herds were brought through the poor weather of recent years in reasonably good condition with balanced age distribution. Meat imports in 1977 probably totaled between 350,000 and 400,000 tons, compared with 362,000 in 1976. Eastern European meat production and supplies were normal in 1977, and exports were directed to the U.S.S.R. because of tight markets in Western Europe.

Dairy. Milk production in 36 major producing countries was estimated (in December) to be up 2% over the 387 million tons of 1976, with the largest gains in the U.S.S.R., the EEC, and the U.S. Dairy price supports in those countries had risen in the past few years, and output was generally outrunning commercial sales. As a result, nonfat dry milk stocks continued near the same 2 million-ton level (about one-half of annual production) reached at the end of 1976, and butter stocks were increasing significantly despite larger governmental donations to food aid programs and mandated purchases (as in the EEC) for domestic feed programs. Casein output and trade was growing as some producing countries found it an attractive alternative to nonfat dry milk.

Considerable pressure existed for continued growth in milk output in 1978 and, therefore, of nonfat dry milk and butter stocks, although cheese markets were expected to be in better balance. Although Australia and Canada were successful in curbing milk output, EEC marketing penalties and conversion programs were not expected to restrict milk output significantly because the cows being culled were mostly inefficient producers. Consequently, the EEC continued to hold—despite large disposals of products at highly subsidized prices—better than half of world nonfat dry milk and butter stocks.

The bulk of dairy output in the major producing countries covered by USDA data was from devel-

Ewes and their lambs are isolated for several days following lambing to enable ewes to claim their own lambs. In open pastures ewes sometimes fail to claim their lambs, resulting in lamb mortality.

A young chicken being tested for airsacculitis, a disease caused by mycoplasma bacteria, which attack during cold weather.

oped or centrally planned economies. Milk production in the less developed countries probably accounted for as little as one-fifth of the world total. The dairy economy in most of those countries was one of deficit production, with low output more often the result of low yields than of low animal numbers. The seasonality of crops often made it difficult to ensure adequate forage year round. Marketing inefficiencies and the perishability of milk have also limited the consumer market. Government pricing policies also often favoured consumers over producers.

In some of the less developed countries, especially in the oil-rich ones, investments were being made in milk-processing plants to supply milk throughout the year by supplementing domestic production with processed dry milk during periods of shortage. Some countries were also investing in the purchase of high-yielding dairy stock, particularly in Latin America but increasingly in the Middle East.

Sugar. The world price of sugar continued at exceptionally low levels, falling to 7 cents per pound (stowed at Greater Caribbean ports and Brazil) in October. Prospects for short-term recovery apparently were largely dependent upon implementation of the new International Sugar Agreement (ISA).

World sugar production in 1977–78 was expected to reach almost 91 million tons, 4% above 1976–77. Consumption was forecast to rise only 3.5% to nearly 86 million tons, creating the prospect that stocks could rise 5 million tons—the fourth consecutive year of stock accumulation—to reach 27 million tons by the end of 1977–78. This would total nearly 30% of annual consumption, compared with the low of 18% in 1973–74.

Beet sugar output was expected to rise 6.5% to almost 36 million tons, largely because of increased Soviet and Eastern European crops. U.S. output fell because of water shortages in the western states. World cane sugar production was forecast to rise about 2% to 55 million tons. Brazil's expected record outturn of 8.6 million tons suggested that its 1980 goal of 10 million tons could be attained a year early. Asian production was likely to be down, largely because of drought in Thailand and tight credit that reduced harvested area and yields.

World sugar imports in 1977 were expected to rise above those in 1976, with importers attracted by low prices and exporters unloading stocks before the ISA became operational. The new ISA would come into force provisionally on Jan. 1, 1978. Final ratification was to be completed by the end of 1978, but signers agreed to accept the ISA's obligations during the interim. The ISA's primary objectives were to achieve conditions in the international trade in sugar that would avoid excessive price fluctuations and provide prices that were both remunerative to producers and equitable to consumers, and to increase world sugar trade, particularly by less developed country exporters.

The five-year agreement aimed at stabilizing the world free market price between 11 cents and 21 cents per pound by means of export quotas and stocks; earlier ISA's had no stock provisions. Export quotas did not, however, apply to certain special arrangements outside the world free market, such as exports by 46 African, Caribbean, and Pacific countries to the EEC under the Lomé Convention, nor by Cuba to the U.S.S.R. or Eastern Europe.

Basic export tonnages were established for each country to determine its share of the global export quota for the first two years of the agreement and would be subject to renegotiation thereafter. The global export quota would be progressively reduced in 5% steps as prices dropped below 13, 12, and 11.5 cents per pound and cut an additional 2.5% if the price remained under 11 cents for 75 days. These reductions would be restored as prices rose and exceeded 13, 14, and 14.5 cents a pound. Quotas would be suspended above 15 cents but restored when prices fell below 14 cents.

To help boost prices to within the target range, members were to accumulate "special stocks,"

Freezing weather in Florida's citrus belt during the 1976–77 winter destroyed about 30% of the citrus crop.

UPI COMPIX

generally in proportion to their export quotas. These were to total 1 million tons in each of the first two years and 500,000 in the third. Holders of special stocks would be able to obtain interest-free loans financed by a fee assessed on all sugar trade under the ISA. One-third of these stocks would have to be released should prices exceed 19 cents per pound, another third above 20 cents, and the remainder above 21 cents.

Because the market in 1978 could not absorb the 17 million tons of potential exports by ISA members and also raise prices to the desired level, the ISA limited 1978 shipments to 13.5 million tons. An additional 400,000-ton reduction might be imposed if prices remained below 11 cents.

Coffee. World coffee production in 1977–78 recovered about 14% to an estimated (in October) 69.9 million bags (60 kg each), permitting an increase of almost 20% in exportable production to nearly 53 million bags. A nearly 80% jump in Brazilian output, reflecting the results of increased plantings in the early 1970s, more than offset a decline of about 25% in output by the world's usual second largest producer, the Ivory Coast, because of dry weather. Brazil was not expected to return to its customary output level of about 25 million bags until 1979.

The International Coffee Organization (ICO) composite price for green coffee peaked at $3.34 per pound in April, compared with $1.51 a year earlier. It then declined steadily to about $2.22 in October, when ten Latin-American producers announced they were holding off exports to bolster prices. The decline in green coffee prices largely reflected the withdrawal of some major importers from the market, declines in roastings, and relatively favourable inventories in all trade positions.

Mexico proposed in August the establishment of a fund for the stabilization of coffee prices within the framework of the International Coffee Agreement. The proposal was endorsed by ten other Latin-American countries for presentation to the Executive Board of the ICO. The board then authorized its executive director to draw up terms of reference for a study of the feasibility of an international stock arrangement for approval by the ICO. The ICO in September established a working group on coffee price stabilization that was scheduled to meet in London in January.

Tea. Most tea-producing countries increased output in 1977 in response to sharply higher prices. World tea production (excluding China) was forecast (in October) at 1,390,000 tons, about 7% above the 1976 crop, largely because of record Indian and Kenyan harvests and the recovery in Sri Lanka's output. Tea consumption was given a boost by high coffee prices, and tea importers were increasing their orders in anticipation of greater demand. This sudden upsurge in consumption resulted in a tightening of tea supplies and a sharp increase in tea prices. The London auction price for all teas reached a record high of $1.87 per pound in April—compared with an average of 70 cents in 1976—but it eased somewhat as supplies from the large 1977 crop began to reach the market.

Efforts continued under UNCTAD (UN Conference on Trade and Development) auspices to establish an International Tea Agreement (ITA). However, the Intergovernmental Group on Tea, which met in London in February 1977, could not reach an agreement, although it was decided to discuss the matter in future meetings. A Working Party of Tea Exporting Countries met in Rome in September. It recommended an intensive promotional campaign for tea consumption; the gradual elimination of all tariff and nontariff barriers to trade in tea; and regular consultations among exporting countries to coordinate the timing and volume of shipments to the London auction. It also asked the FAO secretariat, in cooperation with the UNCTAD secretariat, to analyze the possible implications of stocking arrangements for tea, and recommended that compensatory financing in relation to export earnings from tea should be included in the ITA.

Cocoa. A buildup in cocoa stocks was expected in calendar 1978 following two consecutive years of inventory reductions. The 1977–78 world cocoa crop was forecast to increase about 9% over the disappointing 1976–77 harvest of 1,360,000 tons. Tight supplies and record-high cocoa prices contributed to a 10% decline in grindings in 1977 to about 1,370,000 tons, and to the increased use of substitutes and extenders.

Cocoa prices had begun to recede from the peak of $2.60 per pound in September (New York spot for Accra beans), about double the year-earlier levels and well above the 1976 average level of $1.10. Prices were expected to moderate further as 1977–78 supplies began to come on the market.

In October the price range of the International Cocoa Agreement (ICA) was increased from 39–55 cents per pound to 65–81 cents. The new range had no influence on the world cocoa market because market prices were greatly in excess of the range. ICA revenues from collection of the 1 cent-per-pound levy on cocoa exports from member producers to finance the plan to purchase buffer stocks were in excess of $100 million, but at the year's end no stocks had been purchased.

Cotton. A 6% increase in planted area and record yields because of excellent growing conditions resulted in a prediction of a record cotton crop, 13% larger than the 58 million bales (480 lb) of 1976–77. The U.S. was expected to account for more than half of the increase, with lesser gains by Mexico, India, Pakistan, Turkey, and the U.S.S.R.

The sluggish performance of the world economy was expected to dampen textile demand and to keep 1977–78 cotton consumption near the 61.2 million bales of 1976–77. Consumption prospects were best in cotton-producing countries that exported yarn and cloth, but domestic textile industries in importing countries, particularly in Europe, were pressing to restrict the expansion of textile imports. Such a move could affect cotton use in several Asian countries.

High world prices for cotton in 1976–77 encouraged the substitution of man-made fibres for cotton in many countries, but the decline in prices after March 1977, by one-third in some cases, made cotton more competitive. Time would be required, however, for mills to switch over to cotton production. Meanwhile, world capacity to produce synthetic fibres continued to expand.

World cotton exports could expand nearly 1 million bales over the 18.1 million of 1976–77, with substantial increases by Turkey, Mexico, and Central America, but a small U.S. decline. Cotton stocks were forecast to increase—after two years of drawdowns that took them to the lowest level since 1962—to about 23.3 million bales by the end of 1977–78, 3.3 million higher than in 1976–77. Almost all of the increase was expected to go into U.S. stocks.

Wool. World wool production in 1976 (including the 1976–77 season in the Southern Hemisphere) declined an estimated 1% from the 2,480,000 tons (greasy basis) produced in 1975 because of smaller clips in Australia and the U.S.S.R., where bad weather reduced the number shorn. These declines more than offset small increases in Argentina, South Africa, and New Zealand.

Consumption was thought to have increased approximately 8% over the 1.3 million tons of 1975 (clean basis) because of an upsurge in mill usage associated both with general economic recovery and with fashion trends favouring natural fibres. Production may have declined in 1977, and a slowdown in the use of virgin wool may have resulted in the rebuilding of stocks in countries producing coarse and medium grades and a further buildup in those producing fine wools.

Tobacco. World tobacco output was estimated (in December) to have declined about 3% to 5.4 million tons (farm-sales weight) after a record 1976 production, influenced by a 10% reduction in U.S. output because of drought and lower production quotas. The world flue-cured crop was expected to decline 1% to 2,258,000 tons, burley to rise slight-

Horticulturist Paul Soderholm examines berries on an experimental coffee plant. Work on developing a hardy cold-resistant coffee plant was being carried on by the U.S. Department of Agriculture at a research centre in Florida.

WIDE WORLD

UPI COMPIX

Farmers protesting falling farm prices lined up their tractors in a show of solidarity at Pueblo, Colorado.

ly to 585,000 tons, and oriental to decline 20% to 611,000 tons.

Tobacco use was expected to rise only a little, but stocks were likely to be drawn down in 1978 for the third consecutive year. Higher prices, excise taxes, and intensified antismoking publicity might again limit the growth of cigarette production to about 2%.

FOOD SECURITY ISSUES

Grain Reserves. Negotiations toward establishing an international system of nationally held grain reserves moved forward in June with the introduction of a new U.S. proposal at a meeting of the International Wheat Council (IWC). In September 1975 the U.S. had called for world grain reserves totaling 25 million tons of wheat and 5 million tons of rice beyond working stock levels; these were to be used to meet production shortfalls but not to stabilize prices. The new U.S. formula, proposed within the framework of a draft International Wheat Agreement (IWA), stressed the need for a reserve stock mechanism designed to reduce wide fluctuations around the long-term trend in market prices and indicated a willingness to consider price indicators as a trigger for certain reserve actions.

The U.S. position did not place sole reliance upon the acceptance by all major exporters and importers of meaningful obligations for reserve

stocks with common guidelines for acquisition and release. It also stressed the importance of agreed-upon measures to facilitate adjustments of consumption and production in response to changing supply conditions, including the reduction of trade barriers that had in the past severely inhibited such adjustments. The U.S. also called for a sharing of the cost of reserve stocks among both exporting and importing nations, and included special provisions to assist poor nations in meeting their share.

Preparatory groups considered two IWC secretariat draft agreements in the fall, but the IWC announced in early December that it would schedule a meeting Jan. 10, 1978, to decide whether or not to convene a full negotiating conference on a new IWA, with such a conference probably held in late February. A new Food Aid Convention would likely be considered at the same time.

Some of the remaining unresolved issues appeared to include the following: the degree of rigidity of the price triggers for reserve actions; the extent to which countries with protected agricultural sectors should ease trade barriers or modify domestic agricultural policies in order to facilitate adjustments in consumption or production, particularly those involving the feeding of grain to livestock; and the treatment of countries that might choose not to join the IWA. There was little public comment about specific reserve or price levels, or whether or not coarse grains might also be included.

In August the U.S. announced proposals for a comprehensive plan to place 30 to 35 million tons of grain in a domestic reserve no later than October 1978. The Carter administration announced that it would seek congressional approval to create, as part of this reserve, a special six-million-ton International Emergency Food Reserve that could be released only for noncommercial food aid for nutrition assistance and to meet U.S. obligations consistent with its international reserve proposals in the IWC.

Under the plan, the farmer-owned wheat and rice reserve program announced in April would be expanded to include 17 to 19 million tons of feed grain. The minimum release price was expected to equal 125% of the loan rate ($2.50 for corn) established in the U.S. farm bill signed on September 29, with the loan expected to be called when the price reached 140% of the loan rate ($2.80). At least 8,160,000 tons of wheat and 600,000 tons of rice would be held until the price exceeded 140% of the loan rate, with loans called when prices exceeded 175% of the loan rate. In addition, some 1975-crop rice and 1976-crop wheat had been or was to be turned over to the government and become part of the overall grain reserve when CCC (Commodity Credit Corporation) price-support loans began maturing in late 1977.

These proposals were related to provisions of the Food and Agriculture Act of 1977, which continued for four years the dual target price and loan rate system to provide price and income support protection to U.S. farmers. Under the act, target prices are the basis for providing deficiency payments—in an amount equal to that by which market prices are below the target—to producers who participate in wheat, feed grain, cotton, and rice programs. Payments, however, cannot exceed the difference between the target price and the price support loan level. The latter is the rate at which farmers can obtain nonrecourse loans from the CCC using their crop as collateral. Farmers may choose to give title to the CCC in full payment of their loan and interest if they decide it is not to their advantage to market the crop themselves.

The act also authorized the secretary of agriculture to introduce production restraints in the form of "set-asides" that induce a farmer to remove a specified percentage of his land from production in order to make himself eligible for participation in support programs. A 20% acreage set-aside was announced for the 1978 U.S. wheat crop and a 10% set-aside for corn, the latter subject to possible change later in 1978. Production of those crops would not be expected to decline proportionately because farmers would be expected to remove less-fertile land from production first.

Food Aid. Total commitments of food aid in cereal grains for 1977–78 were estimated by the FAO (in November) at 9.6 million tons, compared with the 1974 World Food Conference target of 10 million tons and the estimated 8.8 million shipped in 1976–77. The U.S., with its commitment of 6.7 million tons, was largely responsible for the increase. Canada committed 1 million tons; the EEC Council

was expected to approve a 1.3 million-ton commitment; and other countries promised a total of 600,000 tons. Australia announced plans to increase its grain aid to 400,000 tons by 1979–80.

Commitments of nonfat dry milk as food aid for 1977–78 were estimated by the FAO at well over 200,000 tons, one-third more than 1976–77 shipments, with the EEC, the U.S., and Canada the major donors. Contributions from Canada, Australia, and New Zealand may have declined from the previous year because of reduced nonfat dry milk surpluses there. Food aid in the form of butter-oil was expected to rise 25% in 1977–78 to about 50,000 tons, almost exclusively from the EEC. Food aid supplies of vegetable oils were also expected to be higher, reaching about 250,000 tons, largely because of increased U.S. shipments.

The World Food Program's (WFP) Committee on Food Aid Policies and Programs in November adopted a $950 million pledging target for the WFP in 1979–80. It also raised the emergency relief allocation for 1977 and 1978 by $5 million to a total of $45 million for each year. The WFP's new Emergency Food Reserve had reached 360,000 tons of cereal grains for 1977–78 by November—the Seventh Special Session of the UN General Assembly had recommended 500,000 tons—compared with 115,000 tons in 1976–77, largely because of increased contributions by the U.S., Australia, Canada, The Netherlands, India, and Japan.

A new global target for cereals food aid was discussed in several international meetings because 1977–78 was the last year of the 1974 World Food Conference three-year target of 10 million tons annually. The new figure seemed likely to emerge from negotiations of a new Food Aid Convention as part of a new International Grain Agreement. A target of at least 10 million tons appeared likely.

The new U.S. farm bill also extended the life of PL 480, the basic U.S. food aid legislation, for another four years. It and the International Development and Food Assistance Act of 1977 contained several provisions affecting U.S. food aid programs.

By the terms of the new bill at least 75% of Title I food aid commodities (concessional sales that are the principal component of PL 480) must go to countries at the poverty level determined by the International Development Association (less than $550 per capita, compared with $300 under the old law) that are unable to obtain sufficient food from their own production or commercial imports. No Title I agreement is to be made with countries engaging in a consistent pattern of gross violations of internationally recognized human rights, unless it is determined that the aid commodities or proceeds from their sales would be used for programs that would directly benefit the needy people of that country.

The minimum authorization for commodities under Title II (grants) was increased from 1.3 million to 1.6 million tons for fiscal years 1978–80; not less than 1.3 million tons were to be distributed through voluntary agencies and the WFP. The maximum authorization for Title II was increased from $600 million to $750 million. Only the export market price of price-supported commodities was to be

**Agriculture and
Food Supplies**

A land imprinter for use in semiarid
regions is tested near Tombstone,
Arizona. The device reduces water
runoff and evaporation and directs
moisture to spots where needed.

charged to the Title II program, not the cost to the
CCC; the difference would be charged to the CCC
program.

A new Title III aimed to encourage countries to
use the foreign currency proceeds from the sale of
commodities authorized under Title I to increase
food supplies, improve the access of the poor to
food, and improve the well-being of the rural poor.
Foreign currency accruing from the sale of Title I
commodities used to finance specified programs—
for rural and agricultural development, nutrition,
health services, and population planning (with
emphasis on activities to assist small farmers,
sharecroppers, and landless farm labourers)—was
to be credited as if it had been used in repayment
for concessional sales.

Agreements under Title III could extend as long
as five years. The value of such agreements authorized was at least 5% of the value of Title I agreements in fiscal 1978, a minimum of 10% in 1979,
and at least 15% in each succeeding fiscal year.
This requirement may be waived if it is determined that insufficient projects qualify or if the
humanitarian purposes of PL 480 would be better
served under other provisions. A similar provision
was in force during the last year of the old legislation, but no projects were ever approved.

AGRICULTURAL DEVELOPMENT

Foreign Assistance. Official commitments of external assistance to agriculture in the less developed countries—excluding that from centrally

planned economies and broadly defined to include
rural infrastructure, agro-industries, fertilizer
production, and regional river basin projects—declined perhaps 6% in 1976 to about $5.4 billion
according to preliminary data from the FAO and
the Consultative Group on Food Production and
Investment. The decline, which followed two
years of unusually large increases, partly reflected
a sharp reduction of assistance provided by OPEC
(Organization of Petroleum Exporting Countries),
although the effect may have been less than suggested to the extent that resources may have been
shifted to the OPEC Special Fund, not covered by
these data.

The other major reduction was that of commitments by multilateral agencies, especially by the
World Bank but also by the Asian and African
development banks. These reductions were only
partly offset by increases by the Inter-American
Development Bank and the EEC. The exhaustion of
IDA (International Development Association)
funds for lending on easy terms, as well as the
smaller proportion of such funds being used for
agriculture, was a major factor in the decline. The
fifth replenishment of the IDA was approved by 26
countries in March; it amounted to $7.6 billion for
the period July 1977 to June 1980, although the
agreement did not become fully effective July 1
because legislative approval was still needed in
some countries. The U.S. was pledged to contribute $800 million. If the IDA continued to disburse
about 30% of its funds for food and agricultural

"AGRICULTURAL RESEARCH"

Experimental jack-gate in Arizona is
inspected by agricultural engineer
Allen R. Dedrick. The jack-gates
"pulse" water through ditches for
dead-level irrigation.

projects in less developed countries, there could be
about $750 million in commitments for such pur-
poses in 1977–78, about $300 million more than in
1976–77.

The $1,020,000,000 International Fund for
Agricultural Development (IFAD) – proposed by
the OPEC countries at the 1974 World Food Conference – finally became operational in December
1977 with the announcement that the $750 million
ratification target had been exceeded (by some
$150 million) and the convening of the first session
of the Governing Council. It was estimated that
IFAD would fully commit its present resources in
two to three years, in support of agricultural projects in the less developed countries, with special
priority given to small farmers and landless
agricultural labourers. Voting power in the IFAD
was to be equally divided between the developed
countries belonging to the OECD (Organization for
Economic Cooperation and Development), the
members of OPEC, and the less developed countries. Large contributors, such as the United States
with $200 million, had greater than average influ-
ence in their respective groups because of a formula for voting partially weighted by the size of
the amount contributed.

Another important new source of agricultural
lending was the so-called third window of the
World Bank, designed to provide development assistance on terms easier than the Bank's regular
loans but harder than those for IDA's concessional
lending. Between January 1976 and March 1977,

$350 million, or 55%, of such loans went to agri-
culture.

Significant efforts were under way to direct a
greater proportion of investment resources to
agricultural production in the poorest countries.
Nevertheless, the FAO estimated that during 1974–
75, $1.30 per person in external capital commit-
ments was made for agricultural development in
the 29 nations comprising the 45% of the population of the less developed countries that have a
gross national product (GNP) of less than $150 per
capita. This compared with $2.50 for those coun-
tries with $150–$300 per capita, and $2.75 for those
with over $300.

The most significant increases, according to the
FAO, in the proportion of development assistance
going to the poorest countries were the commitments of the OECD countries (bilateral), the Asian
Development Bank, and, to a lesser extent, OPEC.
The reduced availability of IDA funds caused a
sharp percentage reduction in such commitments
by the World Bank, but the replenishment of the
IDA and the start-up of IFAD should increase the
share of multilateral aid going to the poorest countries. Lending terms for the poorer countries eased
in 1974–75 because of the heavy concentration of
IDA loans (70%) going to countries with per capita
GNP under $150. This occurred despite a general
hardening of terms for agriculture in the less developed countries in 1973–75 because of steadily
rising interest rates in private capital markets and
the smaller volume of IDA funds available.

**Table III. Estimates of World Fertilizer Production Capacity [1]
1976–77 to 1981–82**

In million metric tons of nutrient

Regions	1976–77	1977–78	1978–79	1979–80	1980–81	1981–82
			Nitrogen			
Developed market economies	37.31	39.28	41.42	42.25	42.61	42.94
Less developed market economies	11.32	14.50	16.47	18.98	21.28	21.53
Centrally planned economies	28.77	33.09	35.22	38.18	39.80	43.50
Total world	77.40	86.87	93.11	99.41	103.69	107.97
			Phosphate			
Developed market economies	16.77	17.10	17.29	17.68	17.91	17.91
Less developed market economies	4.59	4.67	5.08	6.20	8.67	9.00
Centrally planned economies	4.60	4.80	4.91	5.20	6.19	6.52
Total world	25.96	26.57	27.28	29.08	32.77	33.43
			Potash			
Developed market economies	17.60	17.88	18.25	18.52	18.61	18.75
Less developed market economies	.33	.33	.33	.33	.33	.38
Centrally planned economies	12.42	13.34	14.46	15.38	16.40	17.05
Total world	30.35	31.55	33.04	34.23	35.34	36.18

[1] Based upon rated nameplate capacity of existing facilities and those under construction or firmly committed by May 1977. Nitrogen capacity is for anhydrous ammonia only. Phosphate is for wet process phosphoric acid only, and potash capacity is based on marketable production of potash minerals.
Source: FAO. *Current Situation and Outlook*, FERT/77/3—August 1977, Commission on Fertilizers, Fourth Session, Rome, September 27–30, 1977. Based upon estimates by the FAO/UNIDO/World Bank Working Group on Fertilizers, June 1977.

Table IV. Estimates of World Fertilizer Supply Capability [1], Demand [2], and Balance, 1976–77 to 1981–82

In 000,000 metric tons of nutrient

	Estimated 1976–77	1977–78	1978–79	Forecast 1979–80	1980–81	1981–82
Nitrogen						
Supply	46.01	51.01	55.36	59.51	63.74	67.45
Demand	45.85	49.57	52.54	55.88	59.53	63.09
Balance	0.16	1.44	2.82	3.63	4.21	4.36
Phosphate						
Supply	30.53	31.95	32.69	33.65	35.52	37.03
Demand	26.28	28.19	29.96	31.89	33.48	35.13
Balance	4.25	3.76	2.73	1.76	2.04	1.90
Potash						
Supply	26.37	27.49	28.87	29.98	31.01	32.50
Demand	23.76	24.95	25.95	27.14	28.32	29.64
Balance	2.61	2.54	2.92	2.84	2.69	2.86

[1] Supply figures are derived by reducing estimated production potential to reflect nonfertilizer uses and losses in processing, storage, handling, and transportation. [2] Demand figures reflect absorptive capacities of the nations of the world, taking foreign exchange availabilities into account and assuming that prices will remain between the low levels of 1971–72 and the peaks of 1973–74.
Source: FAO. *Current Situation and Outlook*, FERT/77/3—August 1977, Commission on Fertilizers, Fourth Session, Rome, September 27–30, 1977. Based upon estimates by the FAO/UNIDO/World Bank Working Group on Fertilizers, June 1977.

Fertilizer Production. World fertilizer use reached nearly 96 million tons (nutrient basis) in 1976–77, about 11 million more than in 1975–76, according to preliminary FAO estimates. Consumpton in 1975–76 was 10% above that of the previous year, so that the rate of increased fertilizer use in the last two years was back in line with the average of the past decade following the decline of 1974–75. All regions participated in the increase in 1976–77, with growth highest in the less developed countries. An additional increase of 8% in world demand for fertilizer was projected by the FAO for 1977–78. The most notable 1976–77 gains in the less developed countries were in India, where demand increased by almost 18%, and in Brazil, where it rose about 13%.

The trend of increasing world fertilizer supplies continued in 1976–77 and into 1977–78. International prices for most fertilizers reached the bottom of their downward plunge in early 1976–77, moved moderately upward until late 1977, and then softened, largely because of a cutback in fertilizer use in the U.S. World nitrogen supplies were expected to rise more than 10% in 1977–78, with phosphate up 4% and potash 5%.

China, Pakistan, India, Brazil, and Iran were all expected to reduce their fertilizer imports in 1977–78 because of increased nitrogen production, and Libya, Mexico, the U.S.S.R., and Canada were all expected to increase their capacities to both produce and export ammonia. The U.S., which was importing large amounts of urea following curtailment of U.S. natural gas production, was expected to import large quantities of urea and ammonia from Canada in 1977–78. South Korea and Indonesia became new export suppliers of nitrogen to East Asia in 1976–77, while Japan's urea exports fell below one million tons for the first time in ten years.

An unsuccessful attempt was made in 1977 to form an Afro-Arab consortium, including Morocco, Tunisia, Jordan, and Senegal, to export phosphate rock.

FAO projections of world supply and demand for fertilizers indicated that world supplies should be more than adequate to meet demand through 1981–82. Surpluses for nitrogen were expected to increase, while those for phosphate would decrease and those for potash would remain unchanged. With output somewhat exceeding demand, fertilizer prices were expected to be relatively free from upward price pressure.

The less developed market economies as a group were expected to increase substantially the portion of domestic use of fertilizers met from their own production. Although net imports by these countries were expected to decrease substantially, some less developed countries were expected to increase their imports from other less developed countries.

For nitrogen fertilizers, less developed countries were expected to be 92% self-sufficient by 1981–82, compared with 69% in 1975–76, and to cut their 2.3 million tons of imports in half. Mexico, Trinidad and Tobago, Venezuela, South Korea, Indonesia, and Middle Eastern nations were expected to increase output substantially and were largely responsible for the fact that the less developed countries accounted for one-third of the projected increase in world nitrogen output.

For phosphates, import demand in the less developed countries—1.2 million tons in 1975–76—was expected nearly to disappear by 1981–82; this compared with 66% self-sufficiency in 1975–76. Substantial phosphate production increases were expected in the Middle East, North Africa, West Africa, and Brazil. Potash self-sufficiency in the less developed countries, however, was not expected to keep pace, especially with the closing of a mine in the Congo in 1977 because of flooding and delays in opening a Jordanian production facility.

Outside the less developed countries, the most notable production increases expected by 1981–82 included those for nitrogen by the centrally planned economies; this was especially true for the U.S.S.R., which was expanding export capacity, and for China, which was moving toward self-sufficiency. Other increases were registered for phosphate by South Africa, the U.S., and the U.S.S.R.; and for potash by Canada and the U.S.S.R.

The less developed countries were also expected to increase substantially their share of world consumption—of nitrogen from 19 to 23% in 1981–82, of phosphate from 15 to 20%, and of potash from

KEYSTONE

Researchers at the Institute of
Agricultural Research in Czechoslovakia study ways of improving
wheat yields by varying the light
and temperature.

9 to 12%. The centrally planned economies were expected to increase their share of nitrogen consumption from 37 to 45% and of phosphate from 15 to 36% as the developed market countries' share dropped.

FAO analysts, however, questioned whether the currently projected rate of increased fertilizer demand in the less developed market economies, nearly 10% per year, was sufficient to support the 4% annual growth target for these countries. These analysts claimed that, based on the ratio between the rate of growth of agricultural production and fertilizer use, which had remained stable during the last 20 years, the projected rate might only support a 2.3% increase in agricultural output. If this is the case, it would make necessary a substantial increase in fertilizer assistance to the less developed countries, particularly those with balance of payments problems.

Nevertheless, the increased use of fertilizers by the less developed countries, including the poorest, was a promising sign of progress in the important task of deploying improved technology to meet future world food needs. The International Food Policy Research Institute estimated that 58% of the increased cereal output in the less developed market economies from 1960 to 1966 resulted from expansion in area and 42% from greater yields, but that increased yields accounted for 70% of the in-

creased output in 1967–75. The institute found the increased yields of the latter period to be associated largely with the spread of new wheat and rice varieties that responded well to fertilizer, especially in Asia.

The FAO reported that growth in the use of such high-yielding cereal varieties appeared to have picked up again following a slowdown because of high prices and short supplies of fertilizer during 1974–75. The primary obstacles to greater fertilizer use in the less developed countries appeared to be agricultural practices, agricultural policies that did not give farmers incentives for the use of fertilizers, and the scarcity of foreign exchange for their importation.

(RICHARD M. KENNEDY)

See also Environment; Fisheries; Food Processing; Gardening; Industrial Review: *Alcoholic Beverages; Textiles; Tobacco.*

Albania

A people's republic in the western Balkan Peninsula, Albania is on the Adriatic Sea, bordered by Greece and Yugoslavia. Area: 28,748 sq km (11,100 sq mi). Pop. (1977 est.): 2,618,000. Cap. and largest city: Tirana (pop., 1975 est., 192,000). Language: Albanian. Religion: officially atheist; historically

Albania

ALBANIA

Education. (1971–72) Primary, pupils 518,002, teachers 20,555; secondary, pupils 23,229, teachers 1,318; vocational and teacher training, pupils 62,212, teachers 1,712; higher (including Tirana University), students 28,668, teaching staff 1,153.

Finance. Monetary unit: lek, with (Sept. 17, 1977) a commercial exchange rate of 5.80 leks to U.S. $1 (10.10 leks = £1 sterling). Budget (1976 est.): revenue 7.3 billion leks; expenditure 6.3 billion leks.

Foreign Trade. (1964; latest available) Imports 490.6 million leks; exports 299,620,000 leks. Import sources: China 63%; Czechoslovakia 10%; Poland 8%. Export destinations: China 40%; Czechoslovakia 19%; East Germany 10%; Poland 10%. Main exports: fuels, minerals, and metals (including bitumen, crude oil, chrome ore, iron ore, and copper) 54%; foodstuffs (including vegetables, wine, and fruit) 23%; raw materials (including tobacco and wool) 17%.

Transport and Communications. Roads (1969) 4,827 km. Motor vehicles in use (1970): passenger c. 3,500; commercial (including buses) c. 11,200. Railways: (1974) c. 300 km; traffic (1971) 291.4 million passenger-km, freight 187.6 million net ton-km. Shipping (1976): merchant vessels 100 gross tons and over 20; gross tonnage 57,368. Shipping traffic (1973): goods loaded c. 2.6 million metric tons, unloaded c. 720,000 metric tons. Telephones (Dec. 1963) 10,150. Radio receivers (Dec. 1974) 174,000. Television receivers (Dec. 1974) 4,000.

Agriculture. Production (in 000; metric tons; 1975): corn c. 245; wheat c. 330; oats c. 28; potatoes c. 104; sugar, raw value c. 20; sunflower seed c. 20; olives c. 47; grapes c. 66; tobacco c. 14; cotton, lint c. 7. Livestock (in 000; Dec. 1975): sheep c. 1,165; cattle c. 397; pigs c. 117; goats c. 674; poultry c. 2,310.

Industry. Production (in 000; metric tons; 1974): crude oil c. 2,200; lignite c. 850; petroleum products c. 1,655; chrome ore (oxide content) 286; copper ore (metal content) c. 7; nickel ore (metal content) c. 6; cement c. 360; electricity (kw-hr) c. 1,700,000.

Muslim, Orthodox, and Roman Catholic communities. First secretary of the Albanian (Communist) Party of Labour in 1977, Enver Hoxha; president of the Presidium of the People's Assembly, Haxhi Leshi; chairman of the Council of Ministers (premier), Mehmet Shehu.

Albania, at odds with the U.S.S.R. since 1960, made news during 1977 when its press attacked China, its powerful but distant friend, and Yugoslavia, its most important neighbour. Peking and Belgrade took the attacks calmly and maintained diplomatic relations with Tirana.

After 16 years of "unbreakable friendship" with China, *Zeri i Popullit* ("Voice of the People"), the Albanian party organ, published on July 7 an 8,500-word article—probably written by Enver Hoxha himself—castigating the "three-worlds" theory lately invoked by Chinese leaders to justify better relations with the U.S. and the West. Hoxha was clearly dissatisfied with the shrinking aid Albania was receiving from China. Chinese credits, granted under the agreement of October 1970, were drying up, and of the 3,000 Chinese technicians who had been helping in the construction of 30 major industrial plants less than half remained in the country. An additional motive for Hoxha's ill humour was the invitation to Peking extended to his personal enemy, President Tito of Yugoslavia. On September 2 *Zeri i Popullit* published another article—this time signed by Hoxha—stating bluntly that "embracing Tito leads to embracing U.S. imperialism."

On July 18 Albania and Greece concluded an agreement for air service between Tirana and Athens. (K. M. SMOGORZEWSKI)

Algeria

A republic on the north coast of Africa, Algeria is bounded by Morocco, Western (Spanish) Sahara, Mauritania, Mali, Niger, Libya, and Tunisia. Area: 2,322,164 sq km (896,592 sq mi). Pop. (1976 est.): 17,304,000. Cap. and largest city: Algiers (pop., 1975 UN est., 1,179,000). Language: Arabic, Berber, French. Religion: Muslim. President in 1977, Col. Houari Boumédienne.

Elections were held on Feb. 25, 1977, for the new 261-member National Assembly, and among those elected were six government ministers. Since the new constitution did not require the president to choose his ministers from the Assembly, their democratic election was seen as an additional attempt to legitimize the regime. In April, in a major reshuffle, 10 ministers were dropped and 14 new appointments made, enlarging the Cabinet to 25 members. The administration was modified at the same time, mainly to promote efficiency but also to remove any possible threats to Pres. Houari

Algerian Pres. Houari Boumédienne and his wife cast ballots in the legislative election on February 25. The election was the first held in Algeria since Boumédienne came to power in 1965.

Boumédienne's position (as head of state, government, defense, and the armed forces since his re-election as president on Dec. 10, 1976). A new Ministry for the Environment was created, and the dominant Ministry of Energy and Industry was broken up into three ministries—for energy and petrochemicals, light industry, and heavy industry.

Government and administrative reform only partly solved the nation's economic and social problems. Algeria continued to sustain a trade deficit in 1977 because of low oil sales and prices. The resulting severe controls on imports affected development planning, and unemployment increased. The 1974–77 development plan would not generate the 450,000 new jobs needed, nor had the gross domestic product grown at the projected figure of 10% annually. The 1976 agreement with the European Economic Community (EEC) enabled Algeria to reduce its commercial dependence on France and turn toward other EEC member states. Algeria also improved commercial relationships with the U.S., when the U.S. Federal Power Commission in April approved a major liquid gas deal. It obtained an additional $170 million in development credits from the World Bank.

Algeria supported the struggle of the Front for the Liberation of Saguia el Hamra and Rio de Oro (Polisario Front) to liberate the Western Sahara but did not give direct military aid as in 1976. Algeria did provide aid to 22 refugee camps around Tindouf, receiving $1 million from the World Food Program for that purpose in June. Algerian dip-

lomatic support for the Polisario Front was less successful, the Organization of African Unity (OAU) refusing to admit the Front as a liberation organization. Despite its presence at the Lomé, Togo, meeting of the OAU in February, which caused a walkout by Morocco and Mauritania, Polisario was barred from the Libreville, Gabon, meeting in July. Algeria took part in the December meeting in Tripoli, Libya, of hard-line Arab states opposing Egyptian Pres. Anwar as-Sadat's approaches to Israel, and Egypt severed diplomatic relations with Algeria on December 5.

Social conditions inside Algeria suffered as a consequence of the deteriorating economic circumstances. Supply problems in the cities, particularly the well-established black market; unemployment was exacerbated by the continual migration from the countryside into the towns; and tensions persisted between the Kabyles and the Arab majority.   (EMIL G. H. JOFFÉ)

Algeria

Andorra

Andorra

An independent co-principality of Europe, Andorra is in the Pyrenees Mountains between Spain and France. Area: 464 sq km (179 sq mi). Pop. (1975 est.): 26,600. Cap.: Andorra la Vella (commune pop., 1975 est., 10,900). Language: Catalan (official), French, Spanish. Religion: predominantly Roman Catholic. Co-princes: the president of the French Republic and the bishop of Urgel, Spain, represented by their *veguers* (provosts) and *batlles* (prosecutors). An elected Council General of 24 members elects the first syndic; in 1977, Julià Reig-Ribó.

At the beginning of 1977 Andorra was in the grip of a political crisis. On February 15, for the first time, the Council General of the Valleys was forced to suspend its meeting because of a boycott by 12 councillors from Andorra la Vella. Ten of the 12 protesters belonged to the Andorran Democratic Association, formed in November 1976 as the first political party in the principality.

Also, in November 1976, the Council General had proposed to include in the 1977 budget an increase of indirect taxation as well as—for the first time in the country's history—a personal income tax. As the two co-princes—Pres. Valéry Giscard d'Estaing of France and Msgr. Joan Martí Alanis, bishop of Urgel—appeared to be unwilling to agree to these changes in Andorran finances, the Council General threatened to resign unless the co-

---

ALGERIA

Education. (1976–77) Primary, pupils 2,785,264, teachers 70,498; secondary, pupils 592,265, teachers 20,861; vocational, pupils 11,806, teachers 843; teacher training, students 8,230, teachers 901; higher (including 4 universities; 1975–76), students 41,847, teaching staff 4,670.

Finance. Monetary unit: dinar, with (Sept. 19, 1977) a free rate of 4.10 dinars to U.S. $1 (7.10 dinars = £1 sterling). Gold, SDR's, and foreign exchange (June 1977) U.S. $1,933,000,000. Budget (1976 est.) balanced at 14.6 billion dinars. Money supply (Dec. 1976) 39,587,000,000 dinars.

Foreign Trade. (1976) Imports 22,123,000,000 dinars; exports 21,499,000,000 dinars. Import sources (1975): France 34%; West Germany 12%; U.S. 11%; Italy 8%. Export destinations (1975): U.S. 27%; West Germany 19%; France 15%; Italy 11%. Main exports: crude oil 86%; petroleum products 5%.

Transport and Communications. Roads (1974) 78,408 km. Motor vehicles in use (1974): passenger 204,137; commercial (including buses) 103,147. Railways: (1976) 3,837 km; traffic (1974) 1,058,000,000 passenger-km, freight 1,901,000,000 net ton-km. Air traffic (1975): 1,039,000,000 passenger-km; freight 6.5 million net ton-km. Shipping (1976): merchant vessels 100 gross tons and over 86; gross tonnage 463,094. Shipping traffic (1974): goods loaded 44,824,000 metric tons, unloaded 9,447,000 metric tons. Telephones (Jan. 1976) 250,000. Radio receivers (Dec. 1974) 3,220,000. Television receivers (Dec. 1974) 410,000.

Agriculture. Production (in 000; metric tons; 1976): wheat c. 2,200; barley c. 600; oats c. 90; potatoes c. 592; tomatoes c. 139; onions c. 107; dates c. 185; figs (1975) c. 61; oranges c. 340; mandarin oranges and tangerines c. 150; watermelons c. 170; olives c. 197; wine c. 500; tobacco c. 3. Livestock (in 000; Nov. 1974): sheep c. 8,600; goats c. 2,300; cattle c. 1,245; asses c. 400; horses c. 145; camels c. 180.

Industry. Production (in 000; metric tons; 1975): iron ore (53–55% metal content) 3,200; phosphate rock (1974) 802; crude oil (1976) 50,094; natural gas (cu m) c. 9,530,000; electricity (excluding most industrial production; kw-hr) 3,120,000.

ANDORRA

Education. (1974–75) Primary, pupils 3,779, teachers 146; secondary, pupils 1,626, teachers 120.

Finance and Trade. Monetary units: French franc and Spanish peseta. Foreign trade (1976): imports from France Fr 472,661,000 (U.S. $98.9 million), from Spain 3,835,415,000 pesetas (U.S. $57.3 million); exports to France Fr 18,330,000 (U.S. $3.8 million), to Spain 133,568,000 pesetas (U.S. $2 million). Tourism (1976) c. 4 million visitors.

Communications. Telephones (Jan. 1976) 3,860. Radio receivers (Dec. 1974) 6,500. Television receivers (Dec. 1969) 1,700.

Agriculture. Production: cereals, potatoes, tobacco, wool. Livestock (in 000; 1976): sheep c. 25; cattle c. 3; horses c. 1.

Alcoholic Beverages:
see Industrial Review

American Literature:
see Literature

princes held a meeting with Andorra's first syndic, Julià Reig-Ribó. A review of the principality's financial situation took place during the summer, with the two *veguers* representing their respective co-princes. (K. M. SMOGORZEWSKI)

Angola

Angola

Located on the west coast of southern Africa, Angola is bounded by Zaire, Zambia, South West Africa (Namibia), and the Atlantic Ocean. The small exclave of Cabinda, a district of Angola, is bounded by the Congo and Zaire. Area: 1,246,700 sq km (481,353 sq mi). Pop. (1976 est.): 6,761,000. Cap. and largest city: Luanda (pop., 1970, 480,600). Language: Bantu languages (predominant), Portuguese (official), and some Khoisan dialects. Religion: traditional beliefs about 50%; Roman Catholicism about 38%; Protestantism 12%. President in 1977, Agostinho Neto; premier, Lopo do Nascimento.

Estimates as to the extent of support for Agostinho Neto's government among the population of Angola in 1977 were conflicting. In January a Cuban news agency published extracts from a report setting out the degree of Cuban involvement in the pacification of Angola and the establishment of the Popular Movement for the Liberation of Angola (MPLA) government. It was difficult to assess how far the government continued to rely on the presence of an estimated 15,000 Cuban troops but, despite Pres. Fidel Castro's previous assurances, they were not withdrawn.

Jonas Savimbi's National Union for the Total Independence of Angola (UNITA) guerrillas, with their firm base in the Ovimbundu tribe in southeastern Angola, became increasingly active as the year progressed, harassing the Benguela railway and menacing the port of Lobito. In the north, Holden Roberto's National Front for the Liberation

New recruits begin their training at a UNITA camp in Angola near the Zambia border. The UNITA forces are attempting to overthrow the ruling Cuban-backed MPLA movement in Angola.

KEYSTONE

ANGOLA

Education. (1972–73) Primary, pupils 536,599, teachers 13,230; secondary, pupils 59,209, teachers 3,060; vocational, pupils 15,511, teachers 1,107; teacher training, students 334, teachers 47; higher, students 2,942, teaching staff 274.

Finance and Trade. Monetary unit: kwanza, with a free rate (Sept. 19, 1977) of 40.50 kwanzas to U.S. $1 (70.50 kwanzas = £1 sterling). Budget (1974 est.) balanced at 19,475,000,000 kwanzas. Foreign trade (1974): imports 15,853,000,000 kwanzas; exports 31,215,000 kwanzas. Import sources (1973): Portugal 26%; West Germany 13%; U.S. 10%; U.K. 8%; France 7%; South Africa 6%; Japan 6%. Export destinations (1973): U.S. 28%; Portugal 25%; Canada 10%; Japan 9%; West Germany 5%. Main exports (1973): crude oil 30%; coffee 27%; diamonds 10%; iron ore 6%.

Transport and Communications. Roads (1974) 72,323 km. Motor vehicles in use (1974): passenger 133,512; commercial (including buses) 26,943. Railways: (1975) c. 3,000 km; traffic (1974) c. 403 million passenger-km, freight c. 5,460,000,000 net ton-km. Shipping traffic (1974): goods loaded 10,040,000 metric tons, unloaded 3,980,000 metric tons. Telephones (Jan. 1974) 38,000. Radio licenses (Dec. 1974) 116,000.

Agriculture. Production (in 000; metric tons; 1976): corn c. 450; millet c. 80; cassava (1975) c. 1,600; sweet potatoes (1975) c. 160; dry beans c. 70; sugar, raw value (1975) c. 40; bananas c. 300; palm kernels c. 12; palm oil c. 40; coffee c. 72; cotton, lint c. 17; sisal c. 65; timber (cu m; 1975) 7,836; fish catch (1975) c. 184. Livestock (in 000; Dec. 1974): cattle c. 2,950; sheep c. 200; goats c. 900 ; pigs c. 355.

Industry. Production (in 000; metric tons; 1974): cement 760; iron ore (60–65% metal content; 1975) 5,600; diamonds (metric carats) c. 2,100; crude oil (1976) 6,281; petroleum products c. 750; fish meal 63; electricity (81% hydroelectric; kw-hr) c. 1,050,000.

of Angola (FNLA) forces were much less active, but relations with Zaire, across the northern border, were exacerbated by the presence in Angola of refugee Katangese gendarmes. These refugees were involved in an attack on Zaire in March that was repulsed only with the assistance of Morocco and France. (*See* ZAIRE.) Zaire accused Angola of being involved in the attack, but the Angolan government denied the charge.

On the southern border UNITA forces threatened the Angolan town of Cuangar, which they occupied briefly in mid-June and then in greater strength a fortnight later. The government of Angola claimed that this was the work of South African troops bent on revenge for the assistance given by Angola to the South West Africa People's Organization (SWAPO). It also accused South African forces of having shot down an Angolan passenger plane in July.

On May 27 there was a rising among dissident troops in Luanda. It was quickly suppressed, but Neto acknowledged that five members of the Revolutionary Council had been killed, together with five other leaders of the government. Initially the president claimed that the rising was the work of extreme left-wing elements inside the MPLA. Subsequently, however, there were claims that the rising had been supported by right-wing powers outside Angola, and Neto himself thought it advisable to reaffirm his alliance with the U.S.S.R. and Cuba (he visited Havana in August).

The leaders of the rising were recognized as being Nito Alves, who had lost his post as interior minister when the office was abolished in October 1976 and who, only a few days before the rising, had been expelled from the party, and José van Dunem, formerly political commissar of the armed forces, who was captured shortly afterward. Several close associates of the president were also believed to have been involved, and many were imprisoned. In Cabinda the Front for the Liberation of the Enclave of Cabinda (FLEC) announced in a Paris communiqué on May 2 that a provisional government of the Republic of Cabinda had been installed at Sanda-Massala in Cabinda.

Although continuing to receive advisers and generous arms supplies from the U.S.S.R., the government tried to widen its friendly contacts with other powers. After raising its diplomatic link with France to ambassadorial level on January 31, the government attempted in March to arrange a large-scale armaments purchase from France. In April, President Neto paid official visits to Yugoslavia and Poland. After prolonged negotiations, a three-year aid agreement was signed with Italy in August, and a preliminary trade agreement was made with Zambia whereby Angola would secure corn and tobacco in return for fish meal, coarse salt, and cottonseed cake.   (KENNETH INGHAM)

Antarctica

The 1976–77 Antarctic field season was marked by increased attention to living resources, notably the harvesting of krill, by the return of an independent Norwegian expedition for the first time since 1960, and by the discovery of large new fractures in the floor of the South Atlantic. Active scientific programs were conducted by the 11 nations operating permanent bases on the continent, and new bases were built by Argentina, Poland, and the U.K. In July 1977 Poland gained Antarctic Treaty consultative status, the first nation to do so since

the treaty went into effect in 1961. The other nations that acceded to the treaty do not participate in consultative meetings.

International Research Projects. The international cooperation that has marked Antarctic exploration since the 1950s continued, with exchanges of scientists among the various national expeditions. A U.S. government-funded study on the feasibility of extracting mineral resources concluded that not enough is known about potential mineral deposits. The Taiwanese research ship "Hoi Kung" harvested 100 metric tons of krill in Antarctic waters. Poland, Japan, the U.S.S.R., and West Germany also harvested krill during the 1976–77 season. The U.S. National Science Foundation launched an intensive study of krill, centred at Palmer Station.

The ninth Antarctic Treaty Consultative Meeting was held in September in London. At special preparatory meetings in London in March, the primary topic was the exploration and exploitation of mineral resources of Antarctica and the adjacent continental shelf. At the September meeting the delegates made substantial progress on an agreed measure on living resources and recommended further study of the environmental implications of mineral resource activities prior to the tenth consultative meeting scheduled for 1979 in Washington, D.C. Some 150 scientific papers were presented at the third Symposium on Antarctic Geology and Geophysics, held in Madison, Wis., in August.

Scientific Programs. ARGENTINA. Research continued at nine Argentine bases and camps, despite the loss of three aircraft and 17 men. American scientists aboard the oceanographic ship "Islas Orcadas," a U.S. ship operated by Argentina, discovered a huge V-shaped submarine canyon some 700 km (435 mi) long in the South Atlantic Ocean,

The U.S. National Science Foundation's Palmer Station in Antarctica, where a new laboratory was planned for studying krill.

COURTESY, NATIONAL SCIENCE FOUNDATION

Anglican Communion:
see Religion

one of four new fractures discovered between South America, Antarctica, and Africa. A new base, Primavera, was built on the west side of the Antarctic Peninsula.

AUSTRALIA. Three permanent bases were manned. Nine men from Mawson traveled 2,000 km (1,240 mi) to Mt. King for a summer research program.

CHILE. The ice-strengthened ship "Piloto Pardo" was used to survey Peter I Island prior to building Chile's fourth permanent Antarctic base there. Pres. Augusto Pinochet and an official party visited Chilean stations in the Antarctic Peninsula.

FRANCE. A planned summer ice-core drilling program to 1,000 m (3,280 ft) depth was canceled when the resupply ship "Thala Dan" arrived at Dumont d'Urville Base one month late after encountering two-metre-thick pack ice and striking an uncharted rock.

JAPAN. Forty winter-over scientists conducted a multidisciplinary program at Syowa Station and at Mizuho Camp. An unmanned geophysical station was established at 69° 35′ S, 42° E.

NEW ZEALAND. A full scientific program was conducted at Scott Base and in the McMurdo Sound-Dry Valleys area. Construction of a new Scott Base began. A Hovercraft was tested near Scott Base with satisfactory results and would be returned next season after minor modifications.

NORWAY. An independent expedition was sent to Antarctica for the first time in 16 years. Geologists, meteorologists, and glaciologists worked from Camp Norway 3 and Camp Norway 4 in Queen Maud Land, and oceanographers and marine biologists worked off the ship "Polarsirkel" along the Queen Maud Land coast and in the Weddell Sea.

POLAND. In February the Polish Antarctic Expedition established a year-round station, Arctow-

ski, on King George Island. Eight scientists planned to winter over and conduct research in geomorphology, hydrography, meteorology, marine biology, ichthyology, and medicine.

SOUTH AFRICA. At SANAE (South African National Antarctic Expedition) Base the programs to observe the atmosphere and ionosphere continued, but the geology and glaciology programs were delayed until 1978 when helicopter support was expected to be available.

UNITED KINGDOM. The British Antarctic Survey closed 16-year-old Adelaide Station in March 1977, replacing it with a new station at Rothera Point, 64 km (40 mi) to the northeast. Seventy-nine scientists and support personnel remained through the 1977 winter. Three men from Argentine Islands (later renamed Faraday) Station died after climbing the 1,800-m (5,900 ft) Mt. Peary.

U.S.S.R. More than 450 members of the 22nd Soviet Antarctic Expedition were joined by scientists from East Germany and the U.S. in a multidisciplinary research program at the seven Soviet bases in Antarctica and on board seven ships. Glaciologists traversing between Mirnyy and Vostok stations initiated the "Geophysical Polygon in Antarctica" project, part of the International Antarctic Glaciological Program.

UNITED STATES. More than 85 projects were under way at the four permanent U.S. stations and at field camps in the dry valleys around McMurdo Sound, in the Pensacola Mountains, and along the Antarctic Peninsula. After two years' delay the Ross Ice Shelf Project began drilling through the ice shelf and reached 330 m (1.080 ft) depth before the drill became stuck. It was expected that the remaining 90 m (295 ft) would be drilled during the 1977–78 season, enabling scientific instruments to be lowered into the water below the ice shelf. (*See* EARTH SCIENCES.)

Scientists on the U.S. research ship "Islas Orcadas" (formerly "Eltanin"), operated by Argentina, discovered a huge submarine canyon, 700 kilometres long, off the coast of Antarctica.

The U.S. Arms Control and Disarmament Agency inspected five stations of four nations under the provisions of Art. VII of the Antarctic Treaty. All observed activities and facilities were in compliance.　　　　　　　　　　(PETER J. ANDERSON)

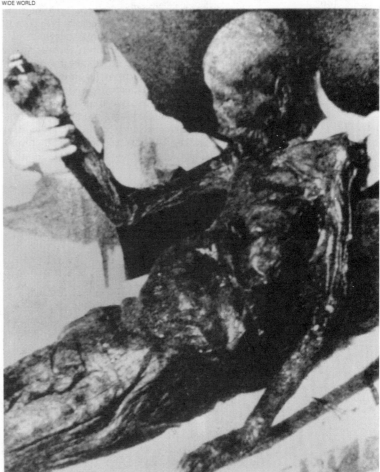

Anthropology

The past few years have seen important advances in the field of paleoanthropology, or the study of early human evolution and lifeways, which involves not only anthropology but also the allied areas of paleontology, geology, zoology, ecology, and, of course, archaeology. In 1977 such advances included the discovery and (re-)interpretation of new fossils and the continued development of systematic philosophy.

Until recently, species were often grouped in terms of the number of common anatomical (including biochemical) features they shared, sometimes with different types of characteristics weighted more or less heavily. During the past decade, the cladistic approach, building on the work of the late German entomologist Willi Hennig, has argued that this method is imprecise and that phyletic linkages should be based only on shared "derived" features inherited relatively recently from a common ancestor, discounting shared "ancestral" characters or conservative retentions. The application of this approach, discussed in 1977 for paleoanthropology by Frederick Szalay, Eric Delson, Niles Eldredge, and Ian Tattersall (*Journal of Human Evolution* and *American Scientist*), permits several new fossil discoveries to be interpreted more clearly.

Formerly, it had been generally agreed that early, forest-dwelling "apes" called *Dryopithecus* were widespread over Eurasia and Africa from 16 million to 10 million years ago. Alongside them in a few areas were found less complete fossil remains of *Ramapithecus*, which appeared to have several derived features in common with later humans, including perhaps thick enamel on the rear or molar teeth (to delay wear from tough food) and small canines. By comparison, modern apes (and, it was thought, all *Dryopithecus*) have thin-enameled, faster-wearing, and relatively small molars with large canines and incisors.

New finds of both *Ramapithecus* and *Dryopithecus* have recently been made in eastern Europe, while specimens from Turkey, western China, and Pakistan were announced in 1977. Based on these finds and reinterpretation of known specimens, three workers semi-independently suggested a new view. According to Peter Andrews, David Pilbeam, and Elwyn Simons, the species of "*Dryopithecus*" from eastern Europe and Asia all share with *Ramapithecus* such derived, human-like features as thick molar enamel, large molars for body size, and jaws buttressed to withstand heavy chewing stresses.

It thus appears that early African *Dryopithecus* (c. 24 million–16 million years ago) were forest dwellers with thin enamel and may have been at the source of both men and apes, as long thought. But by 17 million years ago at least one group of these entered Eurasia over a forest "corridor," where they adapted to life in more open environments, requiring feeding on harsher plant foods which caused faster tooth wear. These early "ground apes," to use Simons' term, developed thicker enamel and larger molars but retained large front teeth; they are known as *Sivapithecus*, are found from Hungary to China, and may be ancestral to two other forms.

Over the same range and also in East Africa occurs *Ramapithecus*, which differs from *Sivapithecus* in having low-crowned canines that function almost like the small incisors—both derived features shared with later humans. Finally, the very large *Gigantopithecus* (long known from later deposits in China and now Vietnam) has been found in place with fossils of *Sivapithecus* and *Ramapithecus* in Pakistan by Pilbeam. It is like *Ramapithecus*, but differs in its huge jaws and in canines which, though low, act like grinding premolars, not cutting incisors. *Ramapithecus*, whose earliest fossils date to over 16 million years ago, is thus still the closest known form to later humans and suggests that our ancestry diverged from that of modern apes still earlier. This runs counter to the idea of a long common history of African apes and humans developed on the basis of biochemistry. The fossils show that major derived conditions were present in a whole group of "ground apes," one of which probably led to modern humans.

The 700-year-old body of a man was discovered in the Chinese province of Kiangsu. According to Chinese newspapers, the body was so well preserved that its joints were still movable.

The youngest known *Ramapithecus* is some nine million years old, and over the next five million years the fossil record of the human lineage is nearly empty. From about four million to nearly one million years ago, however, there are many fossils from southern and eastern Africa, mostly of the early human genus *Australopithecus*. This has long been known to occur in two major forms which share the thick-enameled large molars now recognized for *Ramapithecus* and its allies, as well as upright posture, bipedality, and larger brains than living apes (although much smaller than in modern humans).

(Right) An artist's depiction of human sacrifice practiced by the Aztecs in the 15th century in ancient Mexico. (Below) The royal city of Tenochtitlán, showing sacrificial pyramids.

The older, "gracile" form, *A. africanus*, is most common in South Africa, but may also occur in eastern Africa between three million and two million years ago—a nearly complete skeleton was found recently by Donald Johanson in Ethiopia in an area dated rather precisely at just under three million years by a combination of the potassium-argon, fission-track, and paleomagnetic methods (James Aronson and colleagues, *Nature*). After two million years, a change to more open environments is accompanied by rapid spread of a larger *Australopithecus*, *A. robustus*. This form is derived in ways unlike later humans, with jaws and teeth indicative of feeding on tough vegetable matter (*see*, for example, E. Lloyd Du Brul in *American Journal of Physical Anthropology*). By comparison, *A. africanus* is morphologically conservative and probably was omnivorous. Although such workers as Milford Wolpoff continued to argue that the two kinds of *Australopithecus* were merely variants of one species, most researchers have thought that *A. africanus* was close to the ancestor of later humans, while *A. robustus* represented a "dead end."

More recently, Mary Leakey and Johanson have found specimens dating between three million and four million years ago which suggest a *Homo* older than known *A. africanus*. Some have taken this to mean that *Australopithecus* evolved from *Homo*, but a more likely explanation is that not all the fossils have been found. Thus, the two genera probably diverged earlier than previously thought, and the as yet unknown early (five million years ago?) common ancestor in fact resembled the conservative forms we know as *A. africanus*.

Alternative views are found in *Early African Hominids*, edited by Clifford Jolly. For example, Kay Behrensmeyer, considering taphonomy (how and where the fossils were incorporated into rocks), has suggested that *A. robustus* may have more commonly frequented gallery forests fringing rivers, as well as coexisting with early true *Homo* species in more open environments. The ear-

liest evidence of tool making is now at 2.5 million–3 million years ago, presumably produced by *Homo habilis* for hunting small game, while later *Homo erectus* made larger "hand axes" after 1.5 million years ago as part of a gathering and large-game-hunting culture. As Karl Butzer notes in *American Scientist,* evidence is mounting that humans of fully modern type lived in southern Africa as early as 115,000 years ago and slightly later in the Near East, contemporaneous with the Neanderthals of glaciated Europe.

There was continued reaction in 1977 to sociobiology, a new biological synthesis which attempts to explain many aspects of behaviour in terms of genetics. While many students of animal behaviour tried to test the hypotheses propounded by E. O. Wilson, Robert Trivers, and others, cultural anthropologists tended to reject their suggestions that much of human behaviour is under genetic control, including altruistic and intersexual behaviour. Marshall Sahlins published *The Use and Abuse of Biology: An Anthropological Critique of Sociobiology* as an attempt to refute these views, and they were discussed at several major meetings.

Another controversial hypothesis proposed in 1977 drew upon archaeology and ethnology for support. Michael Harner (in *American Ethnologist* and, less formally, in *Natural History*) proposed that the Aztec sacrifice of up to 100,000 humans yearly in pre-Conquest Mexico was more than religious ritual or authoritarian oppression. He suggested that, because of local environmental conditions, sources of animal protein were rare in central Mexico and that the Aztec nobles consumed some of their victims cannibalistically.

(ERIC DELSON)

See also Archaeology.
[411–413; 10/36.B]

Small, geometrically shaped clay tokens (top) discovered at various Mesopotamian sites indicate that the origin of writing can be traced twice as far back into the past as had previously been believed. Early writing, according to this theory, evolved directly from the shapes of the tokens. Diagram (A) compares several tokens with their corresponding pictographs—the earliest known form of writing. Diagram (B) traces the word "food" from token through pictograph to cuneiform.

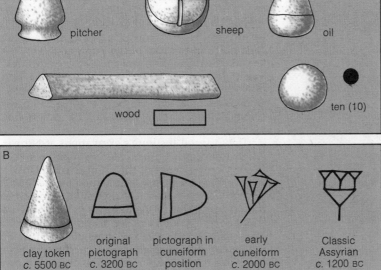

A

pitcher   sheep   oil

wood   ten (10)

B

clay token
c. 5500 BC

original
pictograph
c. 3200 BC

pictograph in
cuneiform
position

early
cuneiform
c. 2000 BC

Classic
Assyrian
c. 1200 BC

Archaeology

Eastern Hemisphere. It was estimated that, before it returned to Egypt, the great loan exhibition of treasures from the tomb of Tutankhamen would have been seen by some five million people in six U.S. cities. Never before had there been so tangible a sign of the U.S. public's fascination with archaeology. In what was perhaps an attempt to capitalize on this fascination, the year witnessed an abnormal increase in the number of pseudo-scientific books, movies, and television programs on quasi-archaeological subjects. Naturally, also, a rash of "King Tut" T-shirts and cheap costume jewelry accompanied the exhibition.

No spectacular archaeological discoveries were reported for the 1976–77 field year itself. The broader implications of the great cache of cuneiform tablets discovered in 1975 in northern Syria were becoming more clear. Written in a hitherto unknown west Semitic dialect of *c.* 2500 BC, the tablets give a wealth of detailed information about a city-state, Ebla (now Tell Mardikh), which was contemporary with the later aspects of both Sumerian and Akkadian Mesopotamia.

Archaeologists inspecting a 4,000-year-old tomb uncovered in the Chinese province of Chinghai. In addition to bones, the tomb contained numerous funerary pots.

KEYSTONE

The mummy of the pharaoh Ramses II, sent to Paris in 1976 to be cured of infections of fungi and bacteria, was returned to Cairo "cured of all infection and immunized for the future." Denise Schmandt-Besserat of the University of Texas at Austin proposed that geometric clay objects—balls, cones, triangles, disks, etc.—were used as tallies in the Near East as early as 7000 BC and may well have been the direct antecedents of Sumerian writing. Two further physical methods for establishing chronology by means of the analysis of mineral materials, radioisotope dating with a cyclotron and fission-track dating, were described in the journal *Science.* A new archaeological salvage program announced by the Turkish government called for excavations before the pools behind new dams on the Euphrates River in southern Turkey flooded a number of sites.

PLEISTOCENE PREHISTORY. Reports of archaeological finds in the Paleolithic and earlier time ranges appeared to be delayed in 1977. In the case of Africa, this may have reflected the political unrest in much of that continent. For South Africa, *Science* (July 8, 1977) contained a useful summary by Richard G. Klein. Much excavation apparently went on in western Europe, but reported results seemed mainly to elaborate existing knowledge.

THE NEAR EAST. A joint Canadian, British, and U.S. team, clearing through later debris in East Karnak, Egypt, began the exposure of a temple of the pharaoh Akhenaton. The Franco-Egyptian work of recording and preservation of the Amon temple at Karnak proceeded, as did the University of Chicago Oriental Institute's similar work on the Luxor temples.

In Israel the American Schools of Oriental Research worked on the great Roman-Byzantine port city of Caesarea and at several mounds with earlier materials. The Israeli work at some sites had something of the hurried nature of salvage archaeology; at Hasorea, for example, the kibbutz that owned the mound urgently wanted to build modern houses on top of the ancient site. At least two U.S. and French, British, Dutch, and Italian expeditions were known to have been at work in Syria but, understandably, there was no archaeological news from Lebanon and little from Jordan. Surface survey work proceeded or was being planned in Saudi Arabia and Yemen. In Syria, in the region just north of the pool of the Euphrates dam, two riverside mounds, Ashara and Tell Hadidi, yielded middle to late 2nd millennium BC materials. Earlier strata in either of the mounds could—if found—complement the new chapter in ancient Near Eastern history based on the tablets from nearby Tell Mardikh.

The Oriental Institute's excavations at Nippur, in Iraq, proceeded, under McGuire Gibson's direction. More evidence of the original city plan was recovered, as was new information on the Kassite levels. Gibson hoped to supplement information on certain historical periods not yet recovered at Nippur by work on smaller nearby mounds with clear surface indications of these missing periods. In Iran a joint Canadian-Danish surface survey for sites in Luristan was reported to have had great success, especially in locating late prehistoric sites.

Heads of statues on Notre Dame Cathedral, chopped off during the French Revolution and believed lost, were discovered in the courtyard of an old mansion in Paris.

Near her main excavations at Chogha Mish, Helene Kantor made preliminary clearances on an important early village site, Chogha Banu. A joint University of Pennsylvania Museum-Italian expedition returned to Tepe Hissar on the Iranian plateau, where the University Museum excavated a key archaeological sequence in the mid-1930s.

For Pakistan, Rafique Mughal reported that a concentrated series of surface surveys throughout the vast lower basin of the Indus River had resulted in the location of over 300 new Harappan or earlier sites. The year's archaeological results in Turkey were detailed by Machteld Mellink in the *American Journal of Archaeology*. The new work on the Bronze Age horizons at Demirci Huyuk was continued by Manfred Korfmann of the German Archaeological Institute, with a rich yield from some burned buildings. Important new information on the growth of the Hittite capital city at Bogazkoy was recovered by Peter Neve, also of the German Archaeological Institute. At Masat, Tahsin Ozguc continued to recover cuneiform tablets and Mycenaean pottery in the Hittite levels.

THE GRECO-ROMAN REGIONS. Based on a stela with a trilingual inscription in Aramaic, Greek, and Lycian, found by a French expedition at Xanthus, Turkey, in 1973, understanding of the long-forgotten Lycian language was well advanced. In Greece itself, British excavators at Sparta cleared houses of the 15th century BC. In his second season at Kommos, an extensive Minoan port town in southern Crete, Joseph Shaw of the Royal Ontario Museum, endeavouring to broaden his exposures over the earlier restricted test trenches, encountered post-Minoan materials and much drifted sand. The Greek government's exposures at Macedonian Pella, Alexander the Great's birthplace, encountered many tombs, a cache of coins, and a marble statue. Late in 1977 a dispute arose over whether a rich tomb found in the village of Vergina was actually—as claimed by the discoverer—that of Alexander's father, Philip II. A spectacular mosaic was found at Kiras Vrisi, west of Athens; it had been the floor of a commodious bathhouse, destroyed about AD 410.

Near Rome a sanctuary or temple, said to be one

Eros, Greek god of love, rides a dolphin in a mosaic found in Kiras Vrisi, Greece. The well-preserved mosaic, 65 feet by 25 feet, is believed to be about 2,000 years old.

of the city's oldest (about 700 BC), was found. It yielded about 1,000 bronze plates with male and female figures and some 50 small, stylized statuettes. Vatican labourers discovered elaborate decorations in catacombs that had been the burial places of rich Roman Jews. An important international salvage effort was organized for clearances in the harbour area of ancient Carthage, now in danger of being overrun by the urban sprawl of modern Tunis. Lawrence Stager described this work in the journal *Archaeology* (May 1977). Farther west, near Moroccan Ceuta on the Strait of Gibraltar, Charles Redman concluded a third season's work on a medieval port fortress.

POST-CLASSICAL EUROPE. One of the year's more remarkable finds was the recovery of 21 sculptured heads, together with many fragments, which had been lopped off the sculpture on Notre Dame Cathedral in Paris during the French Revolution. The heads were those of the kings of Judea, sculpted between AD 1200 and 1240. Excavations were undertaken in Yorkshire, England, on the remains of a deserted medieval village. The archaeological results attested to the decline in the rural population during the late Middle Ages. Much had been learned of Kiev's past by salvage teams of the Institute of Archaeology of the Soviet Academy of Sciences. Already a settlement in Roman times, Kiev was settled by Slavic tribes in the 6th century AD, and by the 13th century the population may have numbered 50,000 people.

FURTHER ASIA. Over a hundred tombs, said to be about 5,000 years old, were found in Kwangtung Province, China. Some 3,000 objects were said to have been recovered. An important summary article on the later prehistory and earliest historical periods of Japan and Korea, by Richard Pearson, appeared in *Science* (Sept. 23, 1977). Pearson relates evidence for a succession of settlement patterns and the development of different fishing and collecting techniques to the traces of changing post-glacial environments in the two regions.

(ROBERT J. BRAIDWOOD)

Western Hemisphere. The year 1977 appeared likely to mark a turning point for U.S. policy concerning the preservation of cultural resources,

both at home and abroad. At issue was the continued failure of congress to confirm a UNESCO agreement on cultural properties. Legislation introduced in 1976 received no action, and a revised and potentially weaker version faced strong opposition from the American Association of Dealers in Ancient, Oriental, and Primitive Art. Congressional reluctance to write decisive legislation could jeopardize research activities by North Americans in Latin America for many years to come.

The first court test of a 1971 Mexican-U.S. treaty providing for "the recovery and return of stolen archaeological, historical, and cultural properties" occurred in 1977. The defendants in the case were convicted of conspiracy and theft of Mexican artifacts, but the ruling was overturned by a higher court. The U.S. Justice Department was anxious to retry the case, however, and if the government was successful in its second attempt, the law would consider every pre-Columbian artifact exported after 1897 without specific consent of the Mexican government to be stolen property.

SOUTH AMERICA. An important gap was narrowed in the understanding of the earliest pre-Inca centre of Andean cultural influence. Previous research based on excavations at the Early Horizon site of Chavín de Huántar (c. 1200–700 BC) had focused on elaborate ceremonial architecture, stone sculpture, and ritual offerings of fancy, elite pottery. Richard Berger, University of California at Berkeley, concentrating on the less elaborate zone of habitation surrounding the site, demonstrated that Chavín de Huántar was not exclusively a ceremonial centre but also a centre of urban activity extending over 40 ha. It was now clear that this elaborate temple complex did not represent the culmination of a long developmental sequence, as previously believed, but was built following the relatively sudden influx of Chavín settlers from outside the Andean valley.

Archaeologists have long debated the origins and age of agriculture in the tropical lowlands. Recent research in the Parmana region of the Middle Orinoco River of Venezuela by Anna Roosevelt, Museum of the American Indian (Heye Foundation), defined a 3,000-year sequence of pre-

Three to five centuries ago, a Makah Indian village, near Pullman, Washington, was buried in a mud slide. Archaeologists discovered the site and unearthed a past civilization.

WIDE WORLD

historic cultural changes. From 2100 to 800 BC, small, permanent settlements subsisted primarily on manioc cultivation, augmented by hunting and gathering. Between 900 and 400 BC, a major shift in agricultural orientation, coupled with a fourfold increase in population, is indicated by the appearance of carbonized corn and domesticated legumes. After AD 500 further increases in the quantity of maize, domesticated legumes, and seed-grinding tools attest to the establishment of intensive crop cultivation, supporting settlements with a population 20 times larger than during the initial period of occupation.

On the Ecuadorian coast, Donald W. Lathrap, Jorge G. Marcos, and James A. Zeidler, University of Illinois, and Carlos Zevallos Mendendez, University of Guayaquil, reported on their recent excavations at the "Valdivia style" site of Real Alto, previously thought to be based on a hunting and gathering economy. Their research revealed that the early Valdivia culture was agriculturally oriented. Even more significant, remains of ceremonial platform mounds and raised multiple dwelling platforms suggest the first evidence in the New World of centralized planning, community-wide work projects, and the potential for a class society. This predates comparable evidence of stratified society in Mesoamerica and the Andes by at least 500 years.

MESOAMERICA. Working in Guatemala, Ruth Gruhn and Alan L. Bryan, University of Alberta, discovered the first known Early Man habitation site in the highlands of Central America. Radiocarbon dating from the lowest cultural levels yielded dates of 9220 BC and 8060 BC. The campsite and hunting station, known as Los Tapiales, occurs at an elevation of 10,000 ft. This discovery caused archaeologists generally to reorient their research from the valley bottoms to high mountain passes in their search for evidence of Early Man sites in this and other regions.

The year saw the publication of major new insights into the origins and antiquity of Classic Maya (c. AD 300–900) civilization. Until now, the earliest known antecedents of lowland Maya culture could be dated no earlier than 900 BC, leading

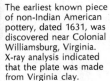

The earliest known piece of non-Indian American pottery, dated 1631, was discovered near Colonial Williamsburg, Virginia. X-ray analysis indicated that the plate was made from Virginia clay.

many scholars to see the Olmec culture of eastern Veracruz as the stimulus for cultural development in the Maya lowland and elsewhere in Mexico. However, this view has recently been set aside by the discovery of an entirely new and very early culture in the Belize valley (dating to between 2400 and 1700 BC). Norman Hammond (currently at Rutgers University) excavated the site of Cuello and discovered previously identified house platforms that can be associated with a new regional pottery style, predating all known lowland ceram-

The handle of a ceremonial club and a canoe paddle were among the 40,000 objects recovered at the Pullman, Washington, site.

RUTH AND LOUIS KIRK

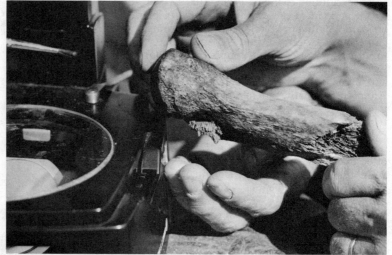

A broken spear point protrudes from the rib of an 11,000-year-old mastodon found near Sequim, Washington. This discovery was interpreted as proof that early North American man lived in the same area with the ancient elephants.

ics by 1,500 years. It now appears that the Maya originated in the lowlands and that the Classic Maya culture was based on a very long sequence of social, economic, and technological change within the lowland area.

The second major discovery pertains to the origins of the Mayan hieroglyphic system, which in the Maya heartland appears fully developed after AD 250. Until recently, the stelae and stone carvings found at the Pacific coastal site of Izapa were considered the earliest antecedents of Classic Mayan glyphs. However, during 1976 and 1977, John A. Graham, University of California at Berkeley, identified a new and different style of early glyphs and monumental sculpture at the site of Abaj Takalik, in the Pacific coast province of Retalhuleu, Guatemala, which predates all known examples, thus reopening the debate on the origins of Mesoamerican writing systems.

Ginger Steen-McIntyre of the U.S. Geological Survey provided geologic evidence supporting Payson D. Sheets's (University of Colorado) suggestion that devastating volcanic activity in the Guatemalan highlands caused entire populations to move into the Mayan lowlands during the first few centuries AD. It was found that the Guatemalan highlands were subject to at least two massive volcanic upheavals which rendered over 3,000 km of the eastern mountain slopes an uninhabitable wasteland for at least 200 years.

In the Valley of Mexico, research increasingly focused on the economic networks upon which the large urban centre of Teotihuacán (c. AD 100–600) based its strength and control over surrounding provinces. A survey directed by Thomas H. Charlton, University of Iowa, identified the location and nature of several key trade routes to and from the capital. This study documents an increase in the influx of raw materials into the capital city and in the production of craft products for export during the Classic Period.

NORTH AMERICA. Within the U.S., a major portion of archaeological research activities continued to take place under the auspices of federally funded cultural resource management programs, mandated by recent environmental protection legisla-

tion. In Arizona the local Highway Salvage Program facilitated the excavation of 18 prehistoric irrigation canals associated with the agriculturally based Hohokam society. Controlled excavations by W. Bruce Masse, Arizona State Museum, revealed that the prehistoric Hohokam peoples were building canal systems between AD 600 and 1400, with the majority dating in the time span AD 900–1150.

In New Mexico high prices in the art market, combined with weak state and federal antiquities legislation, had led to extensive looting of the beautifully made Mimbres pottery. A frantic research effort directed by Steven A. LeBlanc, UCLA, was under way to salvage the heavily battered remnants—vestiges of the famous, but almost completely undocumented, Mimbres culture. This controlled survey and excavation program provided the first prehistoric chronology of the area. An unexpectedly early tree-ring date of AD 1107 was recorded for the classic phase of the Mimbres sequence.

Several projects threw new light on the activities of Early Man during the post-Pleistocene era. In the central Plains area, George C. Frison, University of Wyoming, excavated a large Folsom campsite, as well as a mammoth kill site. The 11,000-year-old mammoth kill site revealed the bones of at least six animals stacked in two piles, with a single mammoth skull on top of each. Along the Mid-Atlantic region of the eastern U.S., excavations by John Covallo, Monmouth (N.J.) College, overturned some long-held assumptions. While over 200 sporadic surface finds of early fluted points are known for the region, the lack of actual habitation sites dating to the Paleo-Indian period had led many scholars to conclude that such sites were situated along the prehistoric coastline and had been covered by the rising sea between 15,000 and 6,000 years ago. Covallo's work revealed the first known Paleo-Indian habitation site within the coastal plain—seven miles inland from the current shoreline—suggesting that similar localities could be presumed to exist along interior river systems.   (JOEL W. GROSSMAN)

See also Anthropology.
[723.G.8.c; 10/41.B.2.a.ii]

Architecture

Worldwide, 1977 began with indications that the recession that had badly affected the building industry in the previous few years was abating and that architects could look forward to an increase in new work and a more favourable economic climate. In the U.S. the Department of Commerce forecast that there would be an 11% increase in construction activity in 1977 over the previous year. The forecast for total construction spending was estimated to be $157.5 billion. An upsurge in work was certainly hoped for in Britain, where it was reported that one-quarter of the country's architects were unemployed.

As social and economic problems loomed slightly less large, a new concern for the quality of design was discernible. No one trend emerged, as designers continued to build in a multitude of different ways using materials that varied from traditional masonry and timber to space frames and geodesic domes. In February the U.S. magazine *Architectural Record* expressed in an editorial the new concern for design quality. Pointing out that for the past few years the architectural profession had been of necessity preoccupied by environmental and economic considerations, the magazine said that the time had come to place emphasis on design, which was, after all, what architecture was about. In recent years the American Institute of Architects (AIA) had lobbied strongly for building awareness, a meaningful and workable energy policy, laws to protect the natural and built environment, and effective urban and housing policies. Now it too was asked to look again at ways in which the quality of design could be improved. The unifying theme of the AIA's convention in San Diego, Calif., in June was an attempt to depict tomorrow—to show how the built environment would look in the future.

Other trends of the year were evidenced by the giving over of the March issue of the U.S. magazine *Progressive Architecture* to examining the role of women in architecture (this coincided with an exhibition on the same subject that opened at the Brooklyn Museum, New York), and by the devoting of an issue of the British periodical *Architectural Review* to the United Arab Emirates. The magazine examined the cultural and economic heritage of the emirates as well as their traditional building styles in order that architects concerned with new projects there could form an understanding of the characteristics of this still unfamiliar area.

The Middle East continued to provide a fruitful source of new commissions for Western firms. William Wesley Peters, architect of the Frank Lloyd Wright Foundation, designed two palaces in Iran for Princess Shams Pahlavi, the sister of the shah of Iran. The first was a new residence 30 mi outside Teheran, described by one writer as "a contemporary interpretation of the essence of Persian culture." It featured two large translucent domes, which created a kind of "cosmic tent" of space. The other palace was an L-shaped complex at Mehrafarin overlooking the Caspian Sea. It included four

The gleaming 73-story Detroit Plaza Hotel rises out of the midst of Detroit's new Renaissance Center. Portman & Associates designed the hotel.

guest houses and a tea pavilion and was inspired by native Persian structures. The complex had steeply pitched roofs that were covered with serrated blue-glazed ceramic tiles, and the roofs and walls were of steel-frame construction, heavily insulated to conserve energy.

Awards. AIA medalists of 1977 "for artistic achievement related to architecture" included sculptors Louise Nevelson and Claes Oldenburg, the latter best known for his mammoth pop-art sculptures of hamburgers. Arthur Drexler, director of the Department of Architecture and Design at the Museum of Modern Art, New York, and also of the Historic American Buildings Survey, received a medal for "significant achievement in recording architectural accomplishments." Other medalists were G. Holmes Perkins, former dean of the Graduate School of Fine Arts, University of Pennsylvania, and British economist Barbara Ward, the moving force behind the 1976 UN Habitat conference.

Among 17 AIA Honor Awards for 1977, architects Shepley Bulfinch Richardson & Abbott won a prize for the new wing of Main Hall at Vassar College, Poughkeepsie, N.Y. Designed by Jean Paul Carlhian, the new wing juxtaposed old and new, adding two high skylit atriums to the

(Top) The Centre National d'Art et de Culture Georges Pompidou aroused great controversy in Paris. What appears to be scaffolding is actually part of the structure. (Right) View of the galleries in the centre. The exposed ceiling is an architectural feature of the building.

Second Empire-style building of 1865 that was the original Vassar College. Main Hall was expanded by this addition into a college centre, but the original building, including the famous facade, was left intact. The brick chosen for the new extension perfectly matched the old brick. Other 1977 AIA awards included the Gold Medal, which was awarded posthumously to the California architect Richard J. Neutra who died in 1970. The AIA Architectural Firm Award for 1977 went to Sert Jackson & Associates of Cambridge, Mass.

In Britain, the Royal Institute of British Architects (RIBA) awarded its Gold Medal for 1977 to Sir Denys Lasdun, architect of the new National Theatre in London and of many other outstanding buildings. The RIBA said, "At a time when we are right to encourage the virtues of preservation and gentle renewal, we are right too to recognize that we need artists who give us new things to enjoy. Of such artists, Lasdun is one of the distinguished few."

Museums and Educational Buildings. Among the most notable individual buildings of the year were a number of new museums and galleries. Of these the most controversial was surely the Centre

National d'Art et de Culture Georges Pompidou in Paris, designed by architects Renzo Piano of Italy and Richard Rogers of Britain. Writing in the *Architectural Review*, British critic Reyner Banham described this large multicoloured structure as a "facility," not a "building." He further called it "blue, green, and orange tubage." Nevertheless, the structure raised interesting discussions about its place in the context of modern architecture; it came close to being the ultimate expression of one branch of the profession, which had steadily moved toward a machinelike appearance. The centre's unusual design was emphasized by its being sited on the fringe of the historic and protected Marais area of Paris. Opened in January, the cultural centre housed four separate activities: a museum of modern art, a public library, a centre for industrial design, and a centre for musical and acoustical research. In addition, there were the usual support facilities, including parking spaces, a restaurant, and offices. The total area was about one million square feet, and about half the site was left as open space.

In the U.S. the Yale Center for British Art at New Haven, Conn., was opened. This was the last building designed by Louis I. Kahn (d. 1974) and was one-third completed at the time of his death. Architects Pellecchia & Meyers of Philadelphia, Pa., supervised its completion. The structure comprised four stories, incorporating shops at the street level of its factorylike exterior of glass and stainless steel. Given by Paul Mellon, it housed his collection of British art and rare books, the largest such collection outside the U.K. The interior was organized around two skylit courts and included a library, research facilities, and a lecture hall, as well as gallery space and offices. Natural light served the galleries wherever possible.

Architects Roche & Dinkeloo completed the Robert Lehman Wing at the Metropolitan Museum of Art, New York City, the first of their current group of additions to the museum. The new structure housed the Lehman collection in a diamond-shaped wing that incorporated a skylit courtyard. The same architects also redesigned the popular Egyptian installation in the museum.

José L. Sert was the architect for the Museo de Arte Contemporáneo Fundación Joan Miró, a new museum in Barcelona, Spain, dedicated to the work of the Spanish painter and sculptor Joan Miró. The museum was inspired by Sert's Fondation Maeght of 1964 at Saint-Paul-de-Vence in France and was composed of carefully varied shapes and spaces; the exterior was of reinforced concrete with a board-marked texture. Work and research spaces were differentiated from gallery space by their inclusion in a distinct three-story octagon. The white vaulted gallery was lit by clerestory windows and was strongly influenced by traditional Mediterranean building styles. In London the Museum of London by Powell Moya & Partners opened in the Barbican redevelopment area. It consolidated two museums formerly housed in Kensington Palace and in the Guildhall. One critic complained that the building was so reticent that it was impossible to find.

At the campus of the University of California at

CENTRAL PRESS/PICTORIAL PARADE

Santa Barbara the Clerk Kerr Learning Resources Hall, which opened in 1975, was designed to accommodate existing electronic equipment and also to provide for that which might be developed in the future. The keynote of the building, designed by Marquis & Stoller, was flexibility of spaces. The hall was a kind of library for visual and audio material and was divided into two sections separated by a skylit arcade. One section housed video production facilities such as studios, and the other contained such support facilities as offices and set storage. The skylit arcade was a particularly attractive feature.

Commercial Buildings and Offices. In Los Angeles, Calif., the Bonaventure Hotel by architects John Portman & Associates opened in March. Situ-

Gifts from Arab governments helped finance the new Central Mosque in London's Regent's Park. The mosque was designed by Sir Frederick Gibberd & Partners.

COURTESY, RICHARD MEIER & ASSOCIATES, ARCHITECTS

Winner of the Bard Award for Excellence in Architecture and Urban Design was the Bronx Development Center, completed in June. A facility for mentally retarded children, the structure has an outer sheath of gray aluminum siding.

ated in the downtown Bunker Hill redevelopment area, the $100 million complex incorporated five levels of retail stores and consisted of five tall silvery cylindrical shapes, the tallest of which reached 35 stories. The complex was linked by aerial walkways to nearby buildings, including the ARCO Plaza and the World Trade Center. Portman & Associates were also the architects for the new 73-story Detroit Plaza Hotel in Detroit, Mich. This hotel was part of a 33-ac development project bordering the Detroit River and was hailed as yet another example of the "megacentre" concept of the 1970s.

A new complex of offices in Canberra, Australia, was designed by Harry Seidler to house three federal government departments. The buildings provided flexible column-free interior space, a tribute to the constructional expertise of the designers and engineers. The Mutual Life and Citizens Assurance Company's MLC Centre in Sydney, also by Seidler, was under construction and would ultimately consist of a 68-story office tower, two shopping levels, an underground parking garage, a club, open landscaped piazzas, restaurants, a 1,100-seat theatre, and a "water wall" fountain, providing Australia with a complex similar to the megacentres of the U.S.

The new U.S. embassy office building in Tokyo,

Japan, was designed by Cesar Pelli, dean of the school of architecture at Yale University. The building was meticulously detailed and appeared almost two-dimensional with silvery horizontal bands of mirror glass alternating with anodized aluminum cladding.

In Denver, Colo., construction began on a 29-story office building by Urban Investment and Development Co. This was part of a large development project for the financial district of Denver. The tower was constructed of a concrete core with a steel frame, all of which was wrapped with bronze-tinted glass and beige-coloured precast concrete.

Public Buildings. Architects P. I. Nwamu & Associates of Nigeria, together with the U.S. firm of Litchfield Grosfeld Associates of New York, were commissioned to develop designs for a network of six regional appellate court centres in Nigeria as part of the establishment of a new federal judicial system. The six buildings would each contain approximately 33,000 sq ft of space and would be almost identical except for slight variations in external appearance intended to make each blend with the indigenous building style of its locale. Each building would face a landscaped entrance courtyard with fountains. The same architects were also commissioned to design a group of six hostels for the Nigerian Law School in Lagos.

Building plans by Middle Eastern and Arab governments continued to provide important new jobs for European and U.S. firms. The Iranian government announced an international design competition for the Pahlavi National Library, which was intended to be built in Shahestan Pahlavi, the future city centre of Teheran. The winning designer would receive a prize of $50,000, together with the commission to build the library. Another of Iran's modern buildings was the Queen Farah Stadium, designed by Djahanguir Darvich as part of the Farahabad Sports Centre. The stadium featured a hyperbolic paraboloid roof suspended from two tall pylons over a reinforced-concrete structure, and provided seating for 30,000 spectators.

In East Germany the government restored the Bauhaus workshop building at Dessau, a pioneering work of Walter Gropius. Restoration of this crucial monument of International Style architecture was undertaken in celebration of the 50th anniversary of its dedication, and the workshop was made a protected landmark.

In Minneapolis, Minn., the Hennepin County Government Center was the focal point of a new civic centre designed by John Carl Warnecke & Associates, who also prepared the master plan for the whole complex. The design was ideally suited to the severe Minnesota winters with a 350-ft-high atrium created between two tall towers and bordered with exposed steel diagonal bracing. The glass end walls and large skylight provided plenty of daylight in the atrium. The carnelian-red granite facing on the solid exterior walls complemented the nearby municipal buildings, which dated from 1906. The total cost of the centre was $49.3 million.

Religious Architecture. Surely the most remarkable church being built in 1977 was the gigantic Crystal Cathedral for California designed

Temple Beth El in West Palm Beach, Florida, was named "Spiraloid" by its architect, Alfred Browning Parker. The structure was patterned after the shape of a mollusk.

BO PARKER, NEW YORK CITY

by architects Johnson/Burgee for the Rev. Robert Schuller of Garden Grove.The star-shaped cathedral was supported by a steel pipe space truss, and the entire building was to be sheathed in glass, posing considerable technical complications for the designers. When completed, the sanctuary was to hold 4,000 worshippers.

"Spiraloid" was the name given to the structure of Temple Beth El in West Palm Beach, Fla., by its architect, Alfred Browning Parker. The temple swirled upward like a shell and, according to Parker, was in fact inspired by the shell of a marine mollusk. Lighting was by means of a large clerestory window, and 24 exposed laminated wooden arches defined the main space ascending like a spiral staircase to an apex of almost 52 ft. The walls were of cedar, and there was seating for 800. The design united the existing social hall, chapel, classrooms, and administrative offices, and its total cost was $1.3 million.

In Little Rock, Ark., Christ the King Roman Catholic Church was designed as a centrepiece for a collection of still-to-be-built structures, including a rectory, parish hall, school, and convent. The church, by architects and engineers Wittenberg, Delony & Davidson, Inc., followed the ancient basilica form with a three-aisled plan. The structural frame was of concrete with infill, and the whole was reminiscent of the church built at Le Raincy near Paris by Auguste Perret more than 50 years earlier. Another unusual structure could be seen at the Chapel of the Assumption, Medellín, Colombia, designed by architects Laureano Forero and Rodrigo Arboleda. Built in a cemetery, the church was composed of two triangular frames that rose over 90 ft and supported 52 white concrete ribs, which sprang up to reach an apex. The spaces between the ribs were filled with gray glass. In London the Central Mosque in Regent's Park, designed for the Muslim community in Britain by Sir Frederick Gibberd & Partners, was completed at a cost of £4 million, mostly donated by Arab governments. (SANDRA MILLIKIN)

See also Engineering Projects; Historic Preservation; Industrial Review: *Building and Construction.*
[626.A.1–5; 626.C]

Arctic Regions

The last official weld of the more than 100,000 that joined the 1,300-km (800-mi) Alaska pipeline was made on May 30, 1977. Almost immediately, security of the pipeline against sabotage became an issue. It was estimated that at least 50 bullets had been fired at the pipeline, necessitating the replacement of some sections. Full-time protection was not thought practical, however; it was estimated that the cost of employing guards along the entire system would exceed $1 billion per year.

After an expenditure of nearly $8 billion, oil finally began to flow through the pipeline on June 20, the culmination of nearly a decade of planning and construction. Pipeline operations were soon suspended, however, because of a series of accidents and operational problems; oil eventually reached the terminal port of Valdez on July 28.

With tanker disasters making almost weekly news during early 1977, the U.S. government announced plans for a $100 million oil-spill liability fund for tankers carrying crude oil from Alaska to the lower 48 states. The U.S. Coast Guard also was advising tankers to stay 160 km (100 mi) off the California and Canadian coasts.

In Canada a dramatic chronology of events took place surrounding the question of pipelines. The U.S. and Canada signed a transit pipeline treaty in January to confirm a policy of noninterference with, and nondiscrimination for, pipelines carrying petroleum products across one another's territory. In February the U.S. Federal Power Commission issued an initial decision recommending approval of the Arctic Gas Project proposal to bring Alaskan gas across the northern Yukon and down the Mackenzie River Valley to markets in the continental United States. The Alaska Highway Pipeline Inquiry, headed by Kenneth M. Lysyk, was established in April to examine the social and economic aspects of the Alcan Pipeline Project, a pipeline system to transport Alaskan gas to U.S. markets via an overland route across Canada. This proposal called for a 120-cm-diameter (48-in) pipeline running from Prudhoe Bay south to Fairbanks, Alaska, and then southwest along the Alaska Highway through the southern Yukon, northern British Columbia, and Alberta to latitude 49° N.

After several years of study and public hearings, a report on the proposed Mackenzie Valley pipeline was presented on May 9 to the Canadian House of Commons. It recommended a ten-year moratorium on the building of any pipeline in the Mackenzie Valley and a permanent moratorium on all pipelines across the northern Yukon, and suggested that there would be fewer environmental difficulties associated with the Alcan Project. On July 4 the Canadian National Energy Board recommended approval of the Alcan Project. After a two-day debate in the House of Commons, Prime Minister Pierre Trudeau of Canada announced in early August that a northern pipeline through the southern Yukon would be in Canada's national interest. Later in the month the Arctic Gas Project was abandoned by its sponsors after an expenditure of nearly $140 million on research and planning. On September 8 the Alcan Pipeline Project, described as the largest single private energy project in history, was approved in principle by Trudeau and U.S. Pres. Jimmy Carter.

Because of the uncertainty caused by the government's decision to choose a Yukon instead of a Mackenzie Valley pipeline, the modern economic base of the western Canadian Arctic was jeopardized, and there were indications of sharply reduced employment of northerners in petroleum exploration and related activities. Toward the end of the year there was growing agreement that the Canadian North might require an alternative development strategy looking toward an economy based on a combination of renewable and nonrenewable resources.

As various native groups in Canada formulated their land claims and as various economic development proposals were considered, constitutional issues assumed an increasing importance in the Northwest Territories and the Yukon. The three major factors involved were that territorial governments were generally demanding a greater degree of self-government, native people were determined to achieve greater recognition of their rights and political power, and there was an urgent need for direction and pacing of the northern economy, which had long been subject to the vagaries and fluctuations of nonrenewable resource activities. In August Prime Minister Trudeau announced a special commission on constitutional matters headed by Charles M. Drury to advise on measures to extend and improve representative and responsive government in the Northwest Territories.

Canada and Denmark signed an interim marine pollution contingency plan applicable to the Arctic waters that separate Canada and Greenland. The plan was intended to provide a coordinated response to oil pollution caused by offshore drilling accidents. In September it was reported that drilling operations were being conducted by three separate groups off the coast of Greenland.

On August 17 the 75,000-hp Soviet nuclear icebreaker "Arktika" became the first ship ever to break its way through the polar ice to the North

The first surface ship ever to ram its way through the icepack to the North Pole reached its destination in August. The ship was the Soviet icebreaker "Arktika."

POPPERFOTO

Pole. Also during the year two vessels became the first pleasure sailing craft ever to conquer the perilous Northwest Passage. The 43-ft "Williwaw," captained by Willy de Roos of The Netherlands, completed the voyage on September 8; the 35-ft "J. E. Bernier II," captained by Réal Bouvier of Canada, arrived at Tuktoyaktuk just four days later.

(KENNETH DE LA BARRE)

Argentina

The federal republic of Argentina occupies the southeastern section of South America and is bounded by Bolivia, Paraguay, Brazil, Uruguay, Chile, and the Atlantic Ocean. It is the second-largest Latin-American country, after Brazil, with an area of 2,776,900 sq km (1,072,200 sq mi). Pop. (1977 est.): 26,056,000. Cap. and largest city: Buenos Aires (pop., 1977 est., 2,980,000). Language: Spanish. Religion: mainly Roman Catholic. President in 1977, Lieut. Gen. Jorge Rafaél Videla.

Despite some signs of political relaxation early in 1977, Pres. Jorge Rafaél Videla stated on April 1 that there would not be a prompt return to civilian rule. Later in the year the military revealed that it might not relinquish power until the 1990s; a "national reconstruction" plan, to be issued in consultation with various economic and intellectual sectors of society, would be developed by the newly established Ministry of Planning to strengthen future democratic institutions.

Violence continued to be part of political life in 1977, with the third unsuccessful attempt on the life of President Videla taking place on February 18: a bomb went off next to the runway at Newbery Airport (Buenos Aires) as his aircraft took off. Labour union activity, on the other hand, was subdued after talks with the authorities at the beginning of the year, when leaders of some 70 unions warned the government that a further decline in the standard of living and in the rate of employment could lead to internal strife. The only protest action was taken by the electrical light and power workers when the regime decided to increase the latter's workweek from 35 to 42 hours; their protest took the form of power cuts and work slowdowns.

Complaints were also made about the lack of information provided by the security forces on the fate of political prisoners, both at home and abroad. The United States decided to reduce military aid to Argentina from $36 million to $15 million because of the human rights issue, but the government rejected even this amount, accusing the U.S. of interfering in Argentina's internal affairs. Amnesty International published a report claiming that some 5,000 political prisoners were being held by the authorities. At Geneva in February the Argentine Commission for Human Rights claimed that in the 11 months since Videla seized power his regime had killed 2,300 persons, held as many as 10,000 in prison for political reasons, and had caused between 20,000 and 30,000 to "disappear."

A sensation was caused by the revelation of the so-called Graiver affair at the end of April. It ap-

ARGENTINA

Education. (1975) Primary, pupils 3,579,304, teachers 195,997; secondary, pupils 454,194, teachers 62,334; vocational, pupils 788,864, teachers 99,525; higher, students 596,736, teaching staff 45,204.

Finance. Monetary unit: peso, with (Sept. 19, 1977) a free rate of 456 pesos to U.S. $1 (free rate of 794 pesos = £1 sterling). Gold, SDR's, and foreign exchange (March 1977) U.S. $1,705,000,000. Budget (1976 actual): revenue 421,390,000,000 pesos; expenditure 1,029,970,000,000 pesos. Gross national product (1975) 1,341,200,000,000 pesos. Money supply (March 1977) 1,541,000,000,000 pesos. Cost of living (Buenos Aires; 1970 = 100; March 1977) 13,274.

Foreign Trade. (1976) Imports 454,006,000,000 pesos; exports 741,954,000,000 pesos. Import sources (1975): U.S. 16%; Japan 13%; West Germany 11%; Brazil 9%; Italy 5%. Export destinations (1975): Italy 10%; U.S.S.R. 10%; The Netherlands 8%; Brazil 7%; U.S. 7%; Mexico 6%; Spain 5%; Cuba 5%; Japan 5%. Main exports: meat 13%; corn 9%; wheat 9%.

Transport and Communications. Roads (1975) 311,893 km. Motor vehicles in use (1975): passenger 2,446,000; commercial (including buses) 1,050,000. Railways: (1976) 39,780 km; traffic (1975) 14,390,000,000 passenger-km, freight 10,680,000,000 net ton-km. Air traffic (1976): 4,161,000,000 passenger-km, freight 103 million net ton-km. Shipping (1976): merchant vessels 100 gross tons and over 379; gross tonnage 1,469,754. Shipping traffic (1975): goods loaded 15,283,000 metric tons, unloaded 9,160,000 metric tons. Telephones (Jan. 1976) 2,469,000. Radio receivers (Dec. 1973) 21 million. Television receivers (Dec. 1974) 4.5 million.

Agriculture. Production (in 000; metric tons; 1976): wheat 11,200; corn 5,855; sorghum 5,200; barley c. 760; oats 530; rice 309; potatoes 1,528; sugar, raw value c. 1,592; linseed c. 630; soybeans 695; sunflower seed 1,085; tomatoes c. 505; oranges 691; lemons 224; apples 577; wine c. 2,445; tobacco 93; cotton, lint 133; beef and veal c. 2,792; cheese c. 226; wool 86; quebracho extract (1974) 86. Livestock (in 000; June 1976): cattle c. 60,500; sheep c. 36,500; pigs c. 5,000; goats c. 5,600; horses (1975) c. 3,500; chickens c. 34,700.

Industry. Fuel and power (in 000; metric tons; 1976): crude oil 20,920; natural gas (cu m; 1975) 7,690,000; coal 615; electricity (kw-hr) c. 30,800,000. Production (in 000; metric tons; 1976): cement 5,603; crude steel 2,410; cotton yarn 85; nylon, etc., yarn and fibres 41; passenger cars (including assembly; units) 141; commercial vehicles (including assembly; units) 36. Merchant vessels launched (100 gross tons and over; 1976) 39,000 gross tons.

---

peared that David Graiver, a financier who had served as the undersecretary of social welfare under Gen. Alejandro Lanusse in 1971–73 and who was presumed to have been killed in an air crash in Mexico in August 1976, had invested some $17 million (much of it alleged to be booty from kidnappings and holdups) for the left-wing Montoneros, paying them some $130,000 interest a month. Many of Graiver's relatives were thereupon arrested, as were Jacobo Timerman and Enrique Jara, publisher and editor, respectively, of the daily *La Opinión*, for their suspected connection with the Graiver case. In December eight of Graiver's relatives and former employees were court-martialed and sentenced to up to 15 years in prison. Robert Cox, the editor of the *Buenos Aires Herald*, was briefly arrested for the publication of news about a press conference held on April 20 by the secretary-general of the Montoneros, Mario Firmenich, in Rome. Firmenich told reporters that the Montoneros and the Authentic Peronist Party had established an alliance and then announced an eight-point program for return to civilian rule through elections, the renewal of labour union activities, and the release of political prisoners, if need be with the use of violence. Cox was acquitted in September.

María Estela Perón, the former president deposed in March 1976, continued to be held in detention. Reports in July of her poor health and attempted suicide were discounted. On July 1 she was charged with the misappropriation of $1 million intended for the relief of flood victims. This was the sixth fraud charge brought against her.

At an international level, Argentina continued to negotiate on the future of the Falkland Islands with Great Britain, with which it shared a long-disputed claim to sovereignty. A brief stir was caused by reports in March 1977 that a group of Argentine businessmen intended to purchase the Falkland Islands Co., which owned some 46% of the islands' land; the possibility of any sale was later denied by Charringtons Industrial Holdings of the U.K., the company's owners. Argentina also lost claim to sovereignty over three Beagle Channel islands, Nueva, Picton, and Lennox, after an international court of arbitration adjudicated them to Chile in May. Argentina stated at the time, however, that it would, as permitted, consider the

ruling over the next nine months before coming to a decision. Throughout the year Argentina attempted to improve its relations with its Latin-American neighbours; President Videla visited several countries during the period, including Bolivia, Venezuela, Peru, Chile, and Uruguay.

The gross domestic product fell in real terms by 2.9% in 1976. Declines occurred mainly in construction (14.1%), commerce (6.3%), and transport and communications (3.4%), but increases were registered in agriculture (4.4%) and a variety of services. Industry fell by 4.7%, with declines especially in textiles, timber products, and beverages and foodstuffs; in the second quarter of 1976, however, manufacturing registered an increase of 1.6%, the first sign of growth in two years.

A trade surplus of $800 million was recorded in 1976, with exports at $3.9 billion and imports at $3 billion. The overall balance of payments surplus of $1 billion reflected loans contracted at midyear totaling some $1.3 billion and also the much-improved trade balance due to large grain sales after the production of a bumper crop. At mid-1977 the overall surplus was $700 million, showing continued good performance by the export sector.

Argentina's main problem continued to be inflation and the expansion of the budget deficit in 1976 and 1977. The annual rate of inflation in 1976 was 347.5% and, in spite of a four-month price truce to July 7, 108.8% in the first nine months of 1977. It was forecast that the annual 1977 rate would be kept to 150%. (BARBARA WIJNGAARD)

Argentina

Art Exhibitions

When, in the summer of 1977, the Arts Council of Great Britain held the Hayward Annual second exhibition devoted to the work of modern British artists, it came under heavy criticism for the choice of works displayed. In response to the criticism, the council organized a well-attended discussion session during which members of the general public had an opportunity to question the organizers and selectors about the works included. One conclusion to emerge was that, although the public was willing to look at modern art, it still found much of what it saw incomprehensible and meaningless, if not laughable. The discussion en-

Henry Moore's huge sheep sculpture was exhibited in Battersea Park, London, as part of a major exhibit of British sculptors during Britain's Silver Jubilee celebration.

abled devotees and artists as well as critics to air their views.

In general, the taste for exhibitions that explored wide-ranging social and historical themes continued to increase and, although the year had its share of large single-artist retrospectives, many more popular exhibitions took almost didactic themes. Perhaps this indicated that art exhibitions were attracting a wider segment of the public and often were becoming popular occasions for family outings.

"Trends of the Twenties" was the theme of a major art exhibition in West Berlin.

"Pompeii AD 79" was an example of such a show. Mounted at the Royal Academy, Burlington House, London, it was designed to show everyday life in Pompeii, and in no way could it have been thought to be of purely archaeological interest. The theme chosen by the selector was "art and craftsmanship as seen in the context of the way of life of ordinary Pompeiians just before the eruption of August AD 79." Thus the show, which was very popular, had an immediacy that, combined with the high quality of objects on display, made it irresistible. Many of the objects exhibited had caused a sensation when they were discovered in the 18th century. Among the main attractions were a model of the House of the Menander and a replica of the initiation room at the Villa of the Mysteries. This was the largest exhibition devoted to Pompeiian art ever held and included such diverse objects as portrait busts, jewelry, and cooking pots.

The Bicentennial exhibition touring the U.S. under the auspices of the International Exhibition Foundation, Washington, D.C., was also historical in theme. Entitled "American Naval Prints: The Beverley R. Robinson Collection, United States Naval Academy Museum," it consisted of 65 works from the Robinson collection of naval battle prints and formed the largest group of works ever to circulate from this important collection. The show reflected the naval histories of both Europe and America and included prints ranging in date from the 16th through the 19th century. Most of the battle scenes were recorded by contemporary artists from eyewitness accounts. One notable work was a lithograph of 1862 by Nathaniel Currier and James Merritt Ives showing the clash between the "Monitor" and the "Merrimack."

The Smithsonian Institution in Washington, D.C., held one of the largest Bicentennial exhibitions of all in its National Museum of History and Technology. Entitled "A Nation of Nations," it was to remain on view until 1981. The show relived U.S. history through national treasures such as the desk upon which Thomas Jefferson wrote the Declaration of Independence. The exhibition had four major themes: the way in which people from every part of the world came to the U.S. ("People for a New Nation"), the diversity of their cultures ("Old Ways in a New Nation"), the experiences that bonded them into a nation ("Shared Experiences"), and the ways by which improved technologies extended the country's interactions with the rest of the world ("A Nation Among Nations"). Exhibits included a working "ham" radio station and a World War II barracks.

In Britain the Silver Jubilee of Queen Elizabeth II was marked by many art exhibitions. Chief among these was the Jubilee Exhibition at the Queen's Gallery, Buckingham Palace, London, where the organizers had selected 146 paintings, drawings, and miniatures from the priceless Royal Collection designed "to demonstrate, in microcosm, the tastes and collecting achievements of our monarchs from Tudor times until the present day." Many of the pictures chosen had seldom been seen by the public and had been newly cleaned for the occasion. A Jubilee exhibition at the

British Museum was held in the King's Library, a splendid room designed by Sir Robert Smirke. It illustrated such royal occasions as investitures, coronations, and progresses, as well as specific royal associations with the British Museum and Library.

"This Brilliant Year" was the title of a Jubilee exhibition held at the Royal Academy. The year was 1887, and the jubilee was the 50th anniversary of the coronation of Queen Victoria. This retrospective of Victoria's life was composed of portraits, genre paintings showing royal occasions, and memorabilia. Many items on show were lent by the Royal Collection, and among these were eight paintings by Franz Xaver Winterhalter that had not been exhibited in public before. From July to October an exhibition "London and the Thames" was held in Somerset House, London. It included works by Canaletto, Gainsborough, Turner, Constable, Monet, Camille Pissarro, André Derain, and Oskar Kokoschka and was a record of both the passage of time over a historic waterway and its interpretation by a series of painters of different European schools.

Oriental art was again a popular theme for exhibitions. The Los Angeles County Museum of Art showed 62 fine Chinese jade carvings, all lent by southern California collections and spanning four millennia from Neolithic times to the 20th century. A highlight of the show was a "mountain" carved of white nephrite which exploited the natural colour of the stone to reproduce the russet brown slopes and gray pines of an actual mountain. The Royal Ontario Museum, Toronto, showed an exhibition of spectacular Chinese costumes in the summer. It was the first major Chinese costume exhibition since 1946, and over 250 pieces selected from the museum's famous costume collection were specially prepared for display. The show surveyed costume development from 1644, the date the Manchu conquerors took power in China, to 1911, when their dynasty came to an end. Highlights of the show included priceless dragon coats and recreated scenes showing a Chinese wedding and the interior of a Chinese shop.

"Islam in National Collections" was the theme of an exhibition at the Grand Palais, Paris, planned as a sequel to the show of Islamic art held at the Orangerie in Paris in 1971. While not comparable with the exhibition held in London in 1976 to mark the World of Islam Festival, it was still remarkable for its range and quality and displayed about 700 objects, all lent by national collections in the Paris area. The three main sections of the show illustrated sources of Islamic art: Islam as a civilization (including themes such as religion, the ruler, luxury and pleasure, hunting and war, and intellectual life) and four great Islamic cultures (Maghrib in North Africa, the Ottoman Empire, Iran, and Mughal India).

The Grand Palais was also the site for the largest retrospective ever devoted to the growth of Buddhism. Covering more than a thousand years from the 8th century to the end of the 19th century, it included some 400 paintings, bronzes, textiles, and ritual and liturgical objects lent from the great museums of the world. The exhibition, which was also seen in Munich, illustrated the style of Buddhist art and the various external influences that shaped it. An exhibition in Brussels and Amsterdam was devoted to bas-reliefs, statues, and jewels from the massive Buddhist temple of Borobudur, Java, Indonesia. The temple was being restored with the help of funds raised in an international appeal launched by UNESCO. (*See* HISTORIC PRESERVATION.) Shown during the winter season in Paris, an exhibition of prints and illustrated books by the Japanese artist Kitagawa Utamaro (1753–1806), also known as Utamaro, was held at the Wildenstein Gallery in London in the spring. More than 100 works from public and private collections were shown.

The Field Museum in Chicago, in joint sponsorship with the University of Chicago, showed the largest exhibition of Tutankhamen treasures ever to be sent abroad by Egypt. Included were 18 pieces never before seen outside Egypt. Altogether, there were 55 jeweled, alabaster, and gold items, including the inlaid solid-gold funeral mask of the young pharaoh. The Field was the second stop of a tour that had begun in Washington, D.C., in 1976 and would include New Orleans, La., Los Angeles, Seattle, Wash., and New York City.

Dazzling gold objects were also on display at the Montreal Museum of Fine Art, where the largest exhibition of pre-Columbian gold artifacts ever to visit Canada was shown. The 365 pre-Inca and Inca gold objects and other artifacts came from the Museo Oro del Perú and constituted the largest number of such pieces ever shown together outside Peru. The displays ranged in date from 400 BC to AD 1532. The exhibition was made possible by arrangement with the Mujica Gallo Foundation and the government of Peru. Canadian Eskimo art, a subject unfamiliar to most Europeans, was shown at the Maison de la Culture, Liège, Belgium, and included masks carved in ivory and bone.

"Women Artists 1550–1950" was the title of an exhibition held at the Los Angeles County Museum of Art. There were items by little-known female artists as well as works by such well-known women as Berthe Morisot, Käthe Kollwitz, Mary

Rubens' drawings are admired by a young student during an exhibition of Rubens' work held at the British Museum.

KEYSTONE

An exhibition, "Cézanne: The Late Work," opened at New York's Museum of Modern Art in October. The works shown are "Still Life with Plaster Cupid" and "Pines and Rocks."

Cassatt, and Gwen John. The exhibition, which was financed by grants from the National Endowment for the Arts and the Alcoa Foundation, was also seen at the University of Texas Art Museum in Austin, the Carnegie Institute in Pittsburgh, Pa., and the Brooklyn (N.Y.) Museum. "Women in American Architecture" opened in February at the Brooklyn Museum and later traveled to the Hayden Gallery of the Massachusetts Institute of Technology and the Colorado Springs Fine Arts Center. The show examined the work of academically trained women architects such as Julia Morgan, who practiced in California, and also looked at other contributions made by women to the built environment as designers, theorists, and critics. The exhibits included about 100 drawings as well as models and sketches ranging in date from the 17th century to the present.

Exhibitions devoted to the work of 19th-century French artists continued to prove popular. Among the most interesting of these was a retrospective of work by the underrated painter Gustave Caillebotte, who was usually remembered as a friend, patron, and collector of the Impressionists. This show, organized by the Houston (Texas) Museum of Fine Arts and also shown at the Brooklyn Museum, numbered over 100 paintings, drawings, and oil sketches, including Caillebotte's most important works. It was the largest such showing of his work since 1894 and allowed visitors to reevaluate this artist. Pierre Puvis de Chavannes (1824–98), a French painter known primarily for his highly decorative murals, was the subject of a retrospective at the Grand Palais, Paris. Many of his drawings were included in the more than 200 exhibits, and a complementary selection of drawings by him was on view at the same time at the Petit Palais. A retrospective devoted to the work of Georges Rouault was organized by the Fondation Prouvost at Marcq-en-Baroeul near Lille, France.

The display of about 100 paintings and engravings included his most famous subjects: Christ, judges, and prostitutes.

A retrospective exhibition of the works of Britain's foremost living sculptor, Henry Moore, was held at the Orangerie in Paris during the summer and was the city's first major showing of this artist. On view were 116 sculptures and 107 drawings. A comprehensive exhibition of some 200 British paintings from three centuries, "British Paintings from Gainsborough to Bacon," was held at the Galerie des Beaux-Arts, Bordeaux, France.

In January the Louvre in Paris showed 82 French drawings lent by the Art Institute of Chicago, including works by Watteau, Fragonard, David, Géricault, Cézanne, Degas, Seurat, and Picasso. The collections of Armand Hammer, a wealthy U.S. businessman and collector, were shown in Paris at the Musée Jacquemart-André and the Cabinet de Dessins at the Louvre. The collection, which had been amassed only since 1970 and would ultimately be divided between the Los Angeles County Museum of Art and the National Gallery in Washington, D.C., consisted of old masters and of 19th- and 20th-century works of art. One of the most notable of the old masters was Rembrandt's "Juno" of about 1665. The show attracted more than 1,000 visitors a day, a new attendance record at the museum.

"Paris-New York" was the title of the first exhibition to be held at the Centre National d'Art et de Culture Georges Pompidou (see ARCHITECTURE) in Paris. It illustrated the exchange of ideas between the U.S. and France in the development of modern art since 1905 and was presented chronologically, with a large selection devoted to the Armory show of 1913 in New York. Also included was a reconstruction of Gertrude Stein's studio in Paris with some of her canvases by Cézanne, Picasso, and Matisse.

In West Berlin in the autumn one of the year's most important exhibitions was held, "Trends of the Twenties." Set up by the Council of Europe and housed in Ludwig Mies van der Rohe's New National Gallery and other locations, it comprised some 3,000 paintings, drawings, architects' drawings, sculptures, photographs, models, posters, documents, and artifacts and offered a unique overview of the avant-garde abstract and constructivist movements of the decade, with works by such exponents as Piet Mondrian, Theo van Doesburg, El Lissitzky, Vladimir Tatlin, and Aleksandr Rodchenko on view. An important exhibition of German art of the period 1910 to 1939, "Apocalypse and Utopia," was mounted at Fischer Fine Art in London. It gave English viewers a conspectus of the major German painters and draftsmen of the period, notably Wassily Kandinsky, Franz Marc, Max Beckmann, Otto Dix, Karl Schmidt-Rottluff, George Grosz, Kurt Schwitters, Paul Klee, and Laszlo Moholy-Nagy.

The 400th anniversary of the birth of the great Flemish painter Peter Paul Rubens was celebrated in 1977 with large exhibitions in Antwerp and elsewhere. The British Museum exhibited more than 200 oil sketches and drawings, including 62 items lent by public and private collections in Britain and the U.S. Preliminary drawings for many of Rubens' well-known paintings gave viewers insight into how the artist worked.

Decorative objects were on view in many museums' special exhibitions. A popular example of such shows was that devoted to Peter Carl Fabergé at the Victoria and Albert Museum, London. Fabergé's work had been almost entirely neglected by museums since his death in 1920, and this show included exquisite objects of gold and precious gems. Included were a number of his famous jeweled Easter eggs, the creation of which was a custom established by Tsar Alexander III in 1884. The Brooklyn Museum showed 120 examples of lace ranging in date from the 17th to the 20th century, all of which were selected from the museum's permanent collection.

The Museum of Fine Arts at St. Petersburg, Fla., mounted an exhibition devoted to the "Art of European Glass 1600–1800." The theme was the changes in style that occurred as a result of changing techniques and changing decoration. The 67 pieces on show were lent by museums and private collectors along the eastern seaboard of the U.S. and the Gulf of Mexico. Many strikingly ornamental examples of decorative art could be enjoyed at an exhibition at the Petit Palais, Paris. It was devoted to Hungarian works of art of the period around 1900 and included over 500 items.

An exhibition at the Yale University Art Gallery in New Haven, Conn., was designed to teach viewers how to recognize fakes, misattributions, alterations, restorations, revivals, and reproductions. Entitled "The Eye of the Beholder," it comprised 130 examples of American furniture and decorative arts, paintings, and prints, shown in pairs to facilitate comparison.

(SANDRA MILLIKIN)

See also Art Sales; Museums; Photography.
[613.D.1.b]

Art Sales

Market Trends. If it had not been plain already, 1976–77 underlined the fact that the art market was now big business. In June 1977 Sotheby Parke Bernet went public, and in July the auctioneers announced the highest annual turnover ever achieved by any auction house, £122.5 million. Christie's, their nearest rival, had a turnover of £66.4 million. In the autumn it was announced that Artemis, the first and most high powered of art investment groups, was also to go public. It had turned in a net profit of £850,000 for its last trading year. This development emphasized the growing investment orientation of the art market as a whole. Artemis was a heavily capitalized art-dealing operation, but managed money from investment trusts and pension and insurance funds was now being used by many other major dealers. And the British Rail pensions fund was said to have invested some £12 million in works of art on Sotheby's advice, which it intended merely to hold for 20 years or so as an inflation hedge.

Sotheby's and Christie's, the London firms, had now cornered a very large proportion of art auctioneering business worldwide. Their strategy of distributing this business among various centres was underlined during the year: Sotheby's held sales in New York, Amsterdam, Zürich, Monte Carlo, Florence, Hong Kong, and Johannesburg; Christie's held sales in Australia, Geneva, Amsterdam, and Rome. It also became clear that a battle was to be waged for the U.S. market. Sotheby Parke Bernet had dominated it since the early 1960s, but in May 1977 Christie's opened for business in New York with a prestige sale of Impressionist and modern pictures worth $7 million. Only $4.1 million's worth sold, including a Van Gogh oil, "La fin de la journée," at $880,000. Phillips, London's third-largest auction house, also opened for business in New York in the autumn of 1977, handling chiefly routine art works.

Works of Art. Most sensational was Sotheby's sale in England in May of the contents of Mentmore Towers in Buckinghamshire, a Mannerist castle built in the 19th century by Baron Meyer de Rothschild. The sale took ten days and realized £6.4 million, despite the fact that the British government had negotiated the acquisition of the prime treasures before the sale. These included a desk made for Augustus III of Poland, on which there was an open market valuation of around £500,000, and a portrait of Mme de Pompadour in old age by Drouais, valued at £600,000. Top prices in the auction proper included £90,000 for a Louis XV automaton of a singing bird in an orange tree, £70,000 for an Augsburg altar clock, and £60,000 for a Sèvres porcelain imitation of a milk pail made for Marie-Antoinette's dairy at Rambouillet. After the auction, David Caritt of Artemis, who had spent £8,800 with premium on a painting catalogued as "The Toilet of Venus" by Carle van Loo, demonstrated that it was in fact a lost work by Fragonard, "Psyche Showing Cupid's Presents to Her Sisters," probably worth £1 million.

KEYSTONE

Five paintings from the collection of Sir Winston Churchill were sold at Christie's for a total of £86,300 ($146,700). Churchill's painting "Mimizan" (right) brought £48,000 ($81,600). The works were put up for sale by Churchill's widow a few months before her death to supplement her tiny government pension.

Christie's retained a much lower profile with the dispersal of the library and collection of John Evelyn, the 17th-century diarist. A table given to Evelyn by Grinling Gibbons made £25,000 in March, while a cabinet constructed from *pietra dura* panels he had purchased in Florence (recorded in his diary) made £26,000 in April. A pair of silver-gilt flagons that had been in the Mostyn family since they were made in 1601 were sold by Lord Mostyn at Christie's in June for £62,000, while a Bronze Age gold torque that had been in his family since it was dug up in the garden in Harlech Castle in 1692 sold for £30,000 in July.

In the general run of sales, two major influences were discernible; decorative appeal was preferred

to scholarly significance, and exceptionally high prices were paid for rarities in every field. The preference for "decorative" works was particularly noticeable in Old Master paintings. Eight new auction records were set in the Wetzlar collection sale in Amsterdam in June, including a Jan Brueghel flower piece at 800,000 guilders. In the modern picture field there was a notable swing away from abstract paintings in favour of the figurative.

Middle East money ran some ornate 19th-century pieces to remarkable levels. A silver table in Louis XVI style, made in St. Petersburg in 1884, brought SFr 160,000 in Geneva in November 1976, and a pair of rifles embellished with Qajar enamels of about 1820 made £75,000 in London. A Michelangelo drawing made £162,000 and a drawing by his friend Sebastiano del Piombo, £104,000. A pair of large 19th-century jadeite carved screens made HK$1.4 million; a 19th-century gold and enamel Chinese market watch by Dupont, SFr 500,000; an ancient Egyptian granite statue of Ser, the priest of Amun in Karnak, £110,000; an elaborately inlaid Stradivarius violin of 1709, $170,000; a Fabergé Easter egg of 1913, SFr 550,000; a Daumier oil, "Don Quichotte et Sancho Pança," Fr 1.29 million; and a Hawaiian parrot-feather cloak, £140,000. The London National Gallery bought an oil "Portrait of a Collector" by the Italian Mannerist Parmigianino for £650,000, the highest auction price of the year.

Books. Interest in illustrated topographical books was almost universal, but the top prices were paid for works treating the U.S., the Middle East, and German-speaking Europe. Christie's sold a copy of J. J. Audubon's *Birds of America* in New York in May for $352,000; the last copy on the market made £90,000 in 1969. There were also two opportunities to purchase Edward S. Curtis' 40-vol. photographic documentary, *The North American Indian* (1907–30); the sets made $60,000 in January and $60,500 in May. The most favoured works on Middle East topography were the early 19th-

Bidding was disappointing at Christie's first New York sale in May with sales below one-half of the presale estimate. Renoir's "Baigneuse Couchée" brought $600,000.

MARILYNN K. YEE—THE NEW YORK TIMES

century prints of Thomas and William Dabiell and David Roberts. The set of 150 aquatints for their *Oriental Scenery* sold for £9,000 at Christie's in October, while the two sets of coloured lithographs by Roberts, *The Holy Land* and *Egypt and Nubia,* made £18,000 in February. Early 19th-century German views by the Batty family had been creeping up in price, and in the Mentmore sale the original drawings by Lieut. Col. Robert Batty for his *Hanoverian, Saxon and Danish Scenery* made £40,000.

The unpredictable market in material of Middle Eastern interest saw a strong rise in prices for calligraphy and a collapse in the value of Qajar paintings and lacquer. Here the sensation of the year was the sale of seven pages from the Houghton *Shahnameh,* a superb illuminated manuscript commissioned by Shah Isma'il (1487–1524), for £785,-000; a single miniature was sold for £280,000. The French Bibliothèque Nationale acquired the complete autograph manuscript of Charles Gounod's *Faust* in a Paris sale in June for Fr 680,000 and a manuscript of 13 songs by Claude Debussy for Fr 380,000.

Prices paid for important autograph material continued to advance. A vast archive of William Beckford's manuscripts, correspondence, and personal papers was sold for £120,000 in July. Two volumes of Jane Austen's early writings appeared on the market; Volume the Third made £30,000 in December and Volume the Second £40,000 in July. William Bligh's diary, kept on the 3,000-mi voyage following the mutiny of the "Bounty," made £55,000 in November, and a group of 30 letters from Ernest Hemingway to his parents made $65,-000 in March.

A sale of books from the Sion College library, London, founded in 1624, made £455,365 at Sotheby's in June. A late-13th-century illuminated *Bestiary* made £88,000 and the first book printed in English, Caxton's *Historyes of Troye* of 1474–75, £40,000. The first two sales of books from the library of John Evelyn at Christie's in June made £252,811. The most important group of Western manuscripts and miniatures ever assembled by Sotheby's into a single sale met some price resistance in July; a 13th-century illuminated school of Paris Psalter made £135,000, and the *Roman de la Rose* with 101 miniatures by the Bedford Master of around 1405 made £91,000.

(GERALDINE NORMAN)

Astronomy

Probably the most startling and refreshing discovery in astronomy during 1977 occurred March 10 when several groups of astronomers almost simultaneously detected the presence of rings around the planet Uranus. First identified as such by James L. Elliot, Edward Dunham, and Douglas Mink of Cornell University, Ithaca, N.Y., they were also observed by Robert Millis and Lawrence Wasserman (Lowell Observatory, Flagstaff, Ariz.) and Peter Birch (Perth Observatory, Bickley, Western Australia), and confirmed by groups in India and South Africa.

The discovery was made during observations of the predicted occultation of the relatively bright (9th magnitude) star SAO 158687 by Uranus. By watching the variation in the light intensity of the star as it disappeared behind the planet, the groups headed by Elliot and Millis had expected to learn more about the density, composition, and temperature of the atmosphere of Uranus and to refine estimates of the planet's size and shape.

Elliot, who was observing aboard an airborne observatory above the Indian Ocean southwest of Australia, and Millis on the ground at Perth detected brief disappearances of the star before its major disappearance behind the planet. Elliot observed similar disappearances after the planetary occultation. Taken together, the phenomena implied the existence of at least five narrow rings, each less than 100 km (60 mi) in width, encircling the planet at distances of approximately 42,200–54,300 km (26,200–33,700 mi) from the centre.

Two intriguing footnotes to this discovery should be added. Though these rings were totally impossible to see even with the help of the largest modern ground-based telescope, William Herschel, who discovered Uranus on March 13, 1781, thought he saw two rings around the planet in 1787 and 1789. By 1798 he became convinced that no such rings existed. Nearly two centuries later, in 1970, photographs of the planet's surface were taken from a telescope carried above much of the Earth's atmosphere by balloons. Recent reexaminations of the photographs by two scientists from the Harvard-Smithsonian Center for Astrophysics in Massachusetts, Giuseppe Colombo and Fred Franklin, uncovered what was possibly an image of the shadow of one of the rings, with just the intensity and position angle predicted from the occultation observations.

The solar system yielded yet another of its secrets in November when Charles Kowal of the Hale Observatories, Pasadena, Calif., announced discovery of a "miniplanet" circling the Sun between the orbits of Saturn and Uranus. Calculations based on images of the faint object, which were captured on photographic plates a month earlier as part of a sky survey, assigned it a tentative diameter between 160 and 640 km (100 and 400 mi), about the size of a fairly large asteroid and much too small to be considered a true planet. Its estimated solar distance of 2,400,000,000 km (1,500,000,000 mi) made it significantly the smallest astronomical body ever found in solar orbit so far from the Sun. Whereas there was no indication that the object is related to the known asteroids, which are all much closer to the Sun, there was speculation that it was one of an undiscovered belt of similar bodies distributed between Saturn and Uranus.

Supernovas. In the half century since Walter Baade and Fritz Zwicky of the California Institute of Technology suggested that supernovas represent the catastrophic finale to the evolution of some stars, studies of supernovas centred chiefly on what they are and how they come about. During the past year, interest shifted to how these violent explosions can trigger formation of new stars in our Galaxy. Though such a theory had been

Earth Perihelion and Aphelion, 1978

January 1	Perihelion, 147,104,000 km (91,406,000 mi) from the Sun
July 5	Aphelion, 152,099,000 km (94,510,000 mi) from the Sun

Equinoxes and Solstices, 1978

March 20	Vernal equinox, 23:34 [1]
June 21	Summer solstice, 18:10 [1]
Sept. 23	Autumnal equinox, 9:26 [1]
Dec. 22	Winter solstice, 5:21 [1]

Eclipses, 1978

March 24	Moon, total (begins 13:29 [2]), visible extreme NW part of N. America, most of Pacific O., New Zealand, Australia, part of Antarctica, Asia, Indian O., Africa except the extreme W part, and Europe except the W part.
April 7	Sun, partial (begins 13:03 [2]), visible extreme S part of Africa, extreme SW part of Indian O., S part of Atlantic O., part of Antarctica, extreme S part of S. America, and extreme SE part of Pacific O.
Sept. 16	Moon, total (begins 16:22 [2]), visible New Zealand, Australia, part of Antarctica, W half of Pacific O., Asia, Indian O., Africa, Europe, E part of Atlantic O., and extreme NE part of S. America.
Oct. 2	Sun, partial (begins 4:32 [2]), visible NW part of Pacific O., NE part of Asia N of the Himalayas except for extreme NE part, extreme N part of Europe including Scandinavian peninsula except for SW part of Norway, extreme N part of Atlantic O., and parts of Arctic region.

[1] Universal time.
[2] Ephemeris time.
Source: *The American Ephemeris and Nautical Almanac for the Year 1978* (Washington, D.C.; 1976).

proposed by scientists more than 20 years earlier, optical astronomer William Herbst and radio astronomer George Assousa (Carnegie Institution, Washington, D.C.) presented the first reasonably strong evidence for a cause and effect relationship. They studied a cloud of gas in the constellation Canis Major that appeared at both visible and radio wavelengths to be a 600,000-year-old supernova remnant, the oldest known to date. Within the region are many young stars that were thought to be about the same age as the supernova remnant. Their abundance, age, and location seemed to confirm the existence of supernova-induced star formation.

If supernovas can induce star formation elsewhere, could one have led to the formation of our solar system? In two independent studies of isotope anomalies in meteorites, groups headed by Gerald Wasserburg (Caltech) and Robert N. Clayton (University of Chicago) found excess amounts of magnesium-26 and oxygen-16 in several samples relative to the mean values for the solar system. Whereas some U.S. scientists interpreted this as evidence for the injection of new material into the protostar destined to become the solar system, others went one step further to conclude that a nearby supernova triggered the formation of the solar system and provided the rare isotopes found in present-day meteorites.

Pulsars and Neutron Stars. For a decade since the discovery of radio-emitting pulsars, only one of the approximately 200 known objects had been observed as well at optical wavelengths, the pulsar in the Crab Nebula. Finally, in 1977, astronomers from the Royal Greenwich (England) Observatory and the Anglo-Australian Telescope (AAT) group used the new 153-in AAT at Siding Spring, New South Wales, Australia, and extremely sensitive

light-gathering instruments to detect optical emission from the Vela pulsar in the Gum Nebula. Flashing about 11 times per second, the pulsar was estimated to be about 24th–25th magnitude, the dimmest object ever detected photoelectrically and about 100 million times too faint to be seen by the naked eye.

In 1977, X-ray observations of a binary X-ray source provided what might be the first direct evidence for the enormous magnetic fields assumed to exist in neutron stars. Both radio pulsars and pulsating binary X-ray sources were thought to contain rapidly rotating magnetized neutron stars. However, whereas pulsars are powered by their own rotation, slowing down as they lose energy, neutron stars in binary systems were believed to accrete matter from their companions, radiate the energy liberated from infall of this matter, and spin faster. Following recent observations of the binary X-ray source Hercules X-1, Joachim Trümper and colleagues of the Max Planck Institute for Radio Astronomy and the University of Tübingen in West Germany reported detection of an X-ray line in the spectrum of this object with an energy of about 53 keV (thousand electron volts). They interpreted this line as radiation arising from the spiraling motion of accreted electrons in the magnetic field of the neutron star and derived a field strength of more than a million million gauss, 10^{12} times the magnetic field of the Earth.

Other observations of binary X-ray sources provided the most sensitive and direct confirmation of the special theory of relativity to date. By analyzing the orbital parameters derived from the time between pulses from the pulsating binary X-ray sources Hercules X-1, Centaurus X-3, and SMC X-1, Kenneth Brecher of the Massachusetts Institute of Technology showed that the velocity of

Part of the most sensitive array of radio telescopes in the world, several component antennas of the "Very Large Array" (VLA) went into use in New Mexico. Full operation was scheduled for 1981.

light is independent of the velocity of its source to an accuracy of better than one part in a billion.

New Astronomies. For millennia, astronomical observations were carried out only by the human eye. Less than a half century ago, radio astronomy was developed. Infrared, ultraviolet, and X-ray astronomy were born during succeeding decades with the advent of balloon, rocket, and satellite technologies. The past year might be said to have witnessed, if not the birth, then surely the coming of age of two new astronomies. The first, called extreme-ultraviolet (EUV) astronomy, sought to detect radiation lying near X-ray energies, as much as a hundred times more energetic than visible light. The second, gamma-ray astronomy, studied radiation at least a million times as energetic as visible light. Though quite different in capability, both astronomies required observations to be made above the absorbing layer of the Earth's atmosphere.

Most astronomers had expected that absorption by interstellar gas would further obstruct EUV observations. It came as a surprise, therefore, when a group from the University of California at Berkeley, headed by Stuart Bowyer, reported detection of several objects with an EUV telescope carried aboard the U.S.-Soviet Apollo/Soyuz spaceflight mission in July 1975. Two are white dwarfs, collapsed stars that have undergone evolution as normal stars. Called HZ 43 and Feige 24, they were found to be nearly 20 times as hot as the Sun.

Though initiated in 1961 with the Explorer 11 satellite, gamma-ray astronomy finally achieved a measure of sophistication with the launch of the American SAS-2 satellite in 1972 and the European COS-B satellite in 1975. In addition to the detection of a flux of gamma rays whose intensity varies with the 33-millisecond period of the pulsar in the Crab Nebula, a dozen other sources were revealed in data analyzed as of mid-1977, including the Vela pulsar in the Gum Nebula. A diffuse gamma-ray flux from the galactic plane was also detected, perhaps because of a superposition of unresolved discrete sources.

Galaxies and Cosmology. Patrick Osmer (Cerro Tololo Inter-American Observatory, Chile) and Malcolm Smith (Anglo-Australian Observatory) reported the discovery of four new distant quasars, bringing to more than 600 the number of such objects known. If estimates of its tremendous distance (10,400,000,000 light-years) from the Earth are correct, one of the quasars, called Q0420-388, is the most luminous object ever seen, more than a hundred times as bright as the entire Milky Way Galaxy.

In new observations made with the West German 100-m radio telescope, W. Reich of the Max Planck Institute for Radio Astronomy and P. Kalberla and J. Neidhofer of the Rhenish Friedrich Wilhelm University of Bonn in West Germany found several faint radio sources around the bright radio galaxy 3C 123. If physically associated with the galaxy, the radio lobes extend over a distance of more than a hundred million light-years, making it the largest known object in the universe.

Finally, and perhaps most surprisingly, three astronomers using the new Kitt Peak 4-m optical

telescope in Arizona reported for the first time the discovery of optical emission from the centres of radio lobes surrounding the radio galaxies 3C 285, 3C 390.3, and 3C 265. Totally unexpected, these observations were thought by some to offer new insight into the causes and nature of nonthermal explosive phenomena in galaxies.

(KENNETH BRECHER)

See also Earth Sciences; Space Exploration.
[131.A.3.d–f; 131.E.2; 132.A–C; 133.A–C; 723.E.1.b]

An artist's conception of the rings around the planet Uranus. Discovery of the existence of the rings was made by James Elliot of Cornell University and others.

Australia

A federal parliamentary state and a member of the Commonwealth of Nations, Australia occupies the smallest continent and, with the island state of Tasmania, is the sixth largest country in the world. Area 7,682,300 sq km (2,966,200 sq mi). Pop. (1977 est.): 14,035,900. Cap.: Canberra (metro. pop., 1976, 214,700). Largest city: Sydney (metro. pop., 1976, 3,021,300). Language: English. Religion (1971): Church of England 31%; Roman Catholic 27%; Uniting Church 17%. Queen, Elizabeth II; governors-general in 1977, Sir John Kerr and, from December 8, Sir Zelman Cowen; prime minister, Malcolm Fraser.

Domestic Affairs. Queen Elizabeth II visited Australia in March 1977, in her Silver Jubilee year. Her visit was welcomed enthusiastically and was the brightest spot in a grim period, characterized by record unemployment, especially among the young, the ethnic minorities, and unskilled workers. It was announced on July 14 that the resignation of the governor-general, Sir John Kerr, had been accepted by the queen and would take effect in December, 18 months short of his five-year term. He was succeeded by Sir Zelman Cowen (*see* BIOGRAPHY) on December 8. Ever since he had dismissed Gough Whitlam's Labor government in 1975, Sir John had been the target of many Labor partisans and left-wing demonstrators.

For the fourth time in five years, Australians went to the polls on December 10, and the result was a resounding victory for Prime Minister Malcolm Fraser's Liberal-Country Party (LCP) govern-

Australia

Athletics:
see articles on the various sports

ment. Fraser had called the election 14 months before his term of office ended so that it would coincide with a scheduled election for half the Senate and also, presumably, to strengthen his hand in dealing with the country's economic problems. With a few seats still in doubt, the LCP had won at least 83 seats in the 124-seat House of Representatives, as against at least 33 for the Australian Labor Party (ALP), and appeared certain to gain control of the Senate. Shortly after the election Whitlam resigned as ALP leader. He was replaced, on December 22, by former treasurer William Hayden, whom he had narrowly defeated in the Labor caucus election at the end of May.

A minor surprise was the emergence of Don Chipp as leader of a new party, the Australian Democrats, which won one seat in the election. Chipp had resigned from the LCP in March after 16 years' membership. The Australian Democrats, a centre party more progressive than the LCP, had attracted 8 to 12% support in national opinion polls in the fall, suggesting that it might come to hold the balance of power between the LCP and the ALP in the future.

Treasurer Phillip Lynch resigned on November 18 over questioned land deals but, cleared of any impropriety, rejoined the Cabinet as minister of trade and industry on December 19.

The major political dispute during the year concerned the government's decision to go ahead with uranium mining. (*See* Special Report.) While Fraser assured the electorate that the LCP was merely bringing to fruition policy begun under the ALP, there was general disquiet over the adequacy of the safeguard provisions and the effects on the environment and on the culture of the Aboriginals living in the area to be mined.

The major social problem was unemployment. Over a third of a million workers were registered with the Commonwealth Employment Service, and it was feared that many young people had left school to become a lost generation, psychologically unfit to work because of their early habituation to a life on social service benefits. The debate over

unemployment was bitter. One group stigmatized the unemployed as "dole bludgers," another called for even more "structured unemployment" to reduce inflation, and the ALP demanded stimulation of the economy through well-chosen public works and a reduction in interest rates.

There seemed to be some chance of a breakthrough in the cycle of inflation when, on April 13, all the state premiers and the federal government unanimously called for a three-month wage and price freeze. R. J. Hamer, the premier of Victoria, steered the proposal through the premiers' conference in Canberra. Hoping for a breathing space brought about through voluntary cooperation, Hamer proposed a national conference of governments, trade unions, and employer organizations. He expected that this group would express a common determination to break inflation by cooperative action, which would involve the deferment for three months of applications for wage increases, a freeze of all price increases, and a freeze of all increases in state government charges. The experiment failed, however, because the ALP premiers opposed any element of compulsion in the price and wage freeze.

Fraser was more successful with referendum proposals to change the constitution. On May 21 four proposals were presented to the people of Australia. Three of the referenda—for the retirement of judges at age 70, filling Senate vacancies caused by death or resignation by members of the same party, and permitting residents of the Northern Territory and the Capital Territory to vote in referenda—were carried, but the fourth, enabling simultaneous elections for both the upper and lower houses of the federal Parliament, was defeated. The ALP supported the LCP's policy on the referenda, but groups in Fraser's party opposed some aspects of the proposals on the ground that they would erode the rights of the states. Fraser scored a noteworthy success in view of the Australian voters' traditional practice of voting "no" in referenda to change the constitution.

Concern about narcotics grew during 1977, and both the state and federal governments set up inquiries into the abuse of drugs. The federal government, for its part, took evidence designed to help stamp out the importation of heroin. The members of the Narcotics Bureau charged that they were hampered by cutbacks in government funds and that only a tiny percentage of the heroin smuggled in was ever detected. The disappearance on July 15 and suspected murder by a Mafia-type organization of a celebrated antidrug crusader, Donald Mackay, led to an immediate, if belated, inquiry from the state government of New South Wales, and the South Australian government also set up an inquiry into the drug traffic. Some concern was expressed over revelations that members of the U.S. Central Intelligence Agency had been officials in the U.S. embassy in Canberra, but on May 24 Fraser told Parliament he was satisfied that the U.S. government was not engaging in improper activities in Australia.

The deputy leader of the Country Party and minister for primary industry, Ian Sinclair, was the object of protests following his attack on Au-

Part of the area threatened by proposed uranium mining in Australia. Mount Brockman, in the Alligator Rivers area, is regarded as holy by the Aboriginals.

MICHAEL JENSEN—AUSTRALIAN INFORMATION SERVICE

gust 5 on some British-born trade-union leaders in Australia. Sinclair claimed that the British-born trade-union leaders had imported "the British disease" into Australia, meaning that British-born shop stewards had been noticeably active in industrial disputes and that Australia's economic life was threatened by industrial guerrilla warfare tactics learned in the U.K. In response, the British high commissioner, Sir Donald Tebbit, pointed out the high place in world trade occupied by the U.K. and made some stinging comparisons between industrial unrest, inflation, unemployment, and interest rates in the two countries. Unrepentant, Sinclair stuck to his guns and was supported by his parliamentary leader, Deputy Prime Minister Douglas Anthony, who said that the disruptive tactics of British-born trade-union leaders in Australia would not be tolerated in the drab and colourless iron-curtain countries they so much admired.

Foreign Affairs. Andrew Peacock, the minister for foreign affairs, indicated in March the main aspects of Australian foreign policy during the 15 months the LCP had been in office. Building a sound relationship with Japan was the key to Australian foreign policy strategy. Australia's concern was to consolidate important and substantial economic relationships by recognizing mutual interests. This intention was frustrated, however, by trading difficulties between the two nations. The most abrasive issue was that of the long-term sugar contract, which Japan had signed in 1975 at a time of high world prices and was endeavouring to back out of when world prices were low. The Colonial Sugar Refinery (CSR) refused to lower the agreed contract price for sugar unless the Japanese entered into further contracts for future years at the 1977 market price. Japan, however, remained obdurate.

Relations with Japan were also strained over Australia's delay in deciding the uranium question. In March the Japanese ambassador in Australia, Yoshio Okawara, broke normal diplomatic protocol and said that for some time he had had the impression that the commonwealth favoured the development and export of Australian uranium. He had had no formal or informal notification of the government's attitude, but he noted that the Australian foreign minister's statements, which dwelt on safeguards rather than bans, indicated

SYNDICATION INTERNATIONAL/PHOTO TRENDS

that Australia favoured going ahead. In any event, warned the ambassador, Japanese power companies would go to South Africa for uranium supplies if the federal government banned the mining and export of uranium.

Australia's second foreign policy objective was to strengthen ties with Pres. Jimmy Carter's administration in the United States. Fraser visited Washington in June and came away convinced that Australia had a key role in assisting the U.S. in the crucial areas of energy policy and nuclear power. By exporting its uranium, he believed, Australia could prevent the spread of fast breeder nuclear reactors.

As part of a June tour of Europe held in conjunction with his visit to London for the Silver Jubilee celebrations and the meeting of Commonwealth heads of government, Fraser called on the heads of government of the European Economic Community (EEC). Fraser stressed that Australia was prepared to insist on reciprocal treatment for its exports of primary products in return for sales of uranium. On returning to Australia, Fraser painted a grim picture of a future Europe without Australian uranium, bereft of power, its factories

Queen Elizabeth's Silver Jubilee tour reached Australia in March. The queen and Prince Philip inspect the guard of honour.

AUSTRALIA

Education. (1976) Primary, pupils 1,842,101, teachers 81,747; secondary, vocational, and teacher training, pupils 1,118,149, teachers 77,638; higher, students 184,343, teaching staff 20,848.

Finance. Monetary unit: Australian dollar, with (Sept. 19, 1977) a free rate of A$0.91 to U.S. $1 (A$1.58 = £1 sterling). Gold, SDR's, and foreign exchange (June 1977) U.S. $2,751,000,000. Budget (1976–77 est.) balanced at A$24,321,000,000. Gross national product (1975–76) A$69.4 billion. Money supply (March 1977) A$10,826,000,000. Cost of living (1970 = 100; Jan.–March 1977) 201.

Foreign Trade. (1976) Imports A$9,140,000,000; exports A$10,647,000,000. Import sources: Japan 21%; U.S. 20%; U.K. 12%; West Germany 7%. Export destinations: Japan 33%; U.S. 9%; New Zealand 5%; U.K. 5%. Main exports: wool 12%; coal 10%; wheat 9%; iron ore 8%.

Transport and Communications. Roads (1973) 864,000 km. Motor vehicles in use (1975): passenger 4,899,700; commercial 1,138,000. Railways: (government; 1974) 40,604 km; freight traffic (1974–75) 29,-800,000,000 net ton-km. Air traffic (1975): 18,084,-000,000 passenger-km; freight 361.3 million net ton-km. Shipping (1976): merchant vessels 100 gross tons and over 424; gross tonnage 1,247,172. Shipping traffic (1976): goods loaded 165,483,000 metric tons, unloaded 23,116,000 metric tons. Telephones (June 1975) 5,267,000. Radio licenses (June 1974) 2,851,000. Television licenses (June 1974) 3,022,000.

Agriculture. Production (in 000; metric tons; 1976): wheat c. 12,000; barley c. 2,840; oats c. 1,190; corn 129; rice 417; potatoes c. 700; sugar, raw value c. 3,400; tomatoes c. 170; apples c. 331; oranges 384; wine c. 377; wool, clean 449; milk 6,471; butter 148; beef and veal 1,783; mutton and lamb c. 584.

Livestock (in 000; March 1976): sheep c. 149,140; cattle c. 33,412; pigs c. 2,178; horses (1975) c. 446; chickens c. 44,944.

Industry. Fuel and power (in 000; metric tons; 1976): coal 74,854; lignite 31,240; crude oil 20,515; natural gas (cu m) 5,900,000; manufactured gas (cu m; 1975) c. 7,100,000; electricity (kw-hr) 80,281,000. Production (in 000; metric tons; 1976): iron ore (64% metal content) 93,120; bauxite 23,541; pig iron 7,417; crude steel 7,758; aluminum 232; copper 161; lead 182; tin 5.6; zinc 242; nickel concentrates (metal content; 1974–75) 49; sulfuric acid 1,582; cement 5,039; newsprint 207; cotton yarn 23; wool yarn 21; gold (troy oz; 1975–76) 558; silver (troy oz; 1975–76) 25,186; passenger cars (units) 386; commercial vehicles (units) 89. Dwelling units completed (1976) 142,000.

and homes in darkness. The EEC governments were not readily responsive to Fraser's arguments, however, and it proved necessary to appoint a Cabinet minister with special responsibility for gaining access to EEC markets for Australian primary products.

The members of the Association of Southeast Asian Nations (ASEAN), the Philippines, Singapore, Thailand, Malaysia, and Indonesia, consolidated and developed their ties with Australia, although there were difficulties over the balance of trade between Australia and ASEAN, which was heavily in Australia's favour. Australia's protectionist policies were criticized when the ASEAN heads of government met in Kuala Lumpur, Malaysia, early in August. Fraser met the demand for liberalization of trade barriers with an offer to establish special consultative machinery to oversee changes in market access for ASEAN. At the same time, he sternly pointed out that Australia offered entry to ASEAN goods on more favourable terms than they received elsewhere, despite the high local unemployment in areas where ASEAN products were competing.

Relations with Indonesia continued to be smooth, despite the existence in Australia of a vocal group that opposed the annexation of East Timor by Indonesia, and the determination of the Australian Journalists' Association to keep before the public eye the unexplained deaths of Australian journalists covering the fighting in East Timor.

The Economy. Pressure on the Australian dollar caused its value to fluctuate more widely than the government had hoped after the record 17½% devaluation on Nov. 28, 1976. The currency was revalued upward by 5%, only to slip back 1½% on Aug. 3, 1977, in response to the falling value of the U.S. dollar on world markets. At that point Australia had sufficient overseas reserves to cover the cost of only three months' imports, so the Treasury attempted to shore up the vulnerable Australian dollar by revaluing its gold reserves.

The government increasingly attributed the problem of unemployment to two sources: the Conciliation and Arbitration Commission and the Industries Assistance Commission (IAC). Fraser vigorously attacked the IAC, claiming that it had injured rather than assisted private enterprise, and in August he ordered an inquiry into it. Most industries that were investigated by the IAC were fearful rather than hopeful, because the IAC showed little sympathy for the cost problems that confronted Australian industries facing low-cost imports from cheap-labour countries. Typical of IAC procedure was its call for an end to excessive tariff protection for the textile industry. There was considerable public sympathy for opponents of the IAC report, since the textile and clothing industry had suffered high unemployment after cheaper imported clothing entered Australia.

Unemployment was laid at the door of the Conciliation and Arbitration Commission by Treasurer Phillip Lynch. Lynch argued that the grave imbalance between wages and productivity resulting from the 1974 wage explosion was Australia's major economic problem. The Arbitration Com-

mission, according to Lynch, had failed to award small enough increases in the quarterly national wage cases which followed the cost of living increases. The Arbitration Commission denied this, however, and Sir John Moore, president of the commission, stated that Australians had suffered a decline in real wages. The consumer price index had increased by 13.4% in the year to June 1977, while wages had risen by between 10.8 and 11.8%. Remarking that it was "highly contentious" whether employment recovery would have been greater or less if the commission had awarded smaller wage increases during 1976–77, Sir John made it clear that henceforth the Arbitration Commission would look hard at submissions from the government.

The main lever of government economic policy was the annual budget, introduced in the House of Representatives on August 16 by Lynch. Lower personal taxes and a rise in the rate of company tax and in the price of gasoline (petrol) were the main features of the budget. No tax was to be paid on annual incomes of less than A$3,750. Above that amount, individuals paid 32% tax, with a first surcharge of 14% on incomes above A$16,000 and a second surcharge of 28% on incomes above A$32,000. About 90% of Australians paid personal income tax at the 32% rate. Company tax, however, rose by 3.5%, bringing the general rate to 46%.

The largest loss to the consumer was in gasoline prices, which were set to rise 2.5 cents a litre in 1977–79. While the world price of crude oil had risen dramatically in latter years, only very minor adjustments had been made in the price of crude at Australian wells. Thus Australian crude oil was very substantially underpriced, and without significant new discoveries in the next few years, indigenous crude oil, which currently met about 70% of Australian total demand, would fall to about 30% by 1985. Lynch explained that Australia could not afford a pricing policy that flew in the face of energy conservation principles by condoning excessive consumption of the country's known supplies of crude oil. Rather, what Australia needed was a pricing policy that would encourage new exploration. In addition, the government accepted the IAC's suggestion that the price of Australian crude oil should be brought up to world parity by increases of 20, 35, and 50% over the next three years.

There was less industrial unrest than had been the case for a decade. The consistent award of wage increases in line with cost-of-living increases led to substantial compliance with the directions of the Arbitration Court. The only cloud on the industrial relations horizon was legislation passed in the Parliament on August 19, enabling the government to lay off public servants in the event of industrial disputes in the commonwealth public service. This legislation was drafted during a week-long air traffic controllers' strike (which showed how a handful of key workers could disrupt the life of the nation) and introduced into Parliament during a strike by postal workers.

(A. R. G. GRIFFITHS)

See also Dependent States.

THE AUSTRALIAN URANIUM DEBATE

by A.R.G. Griffiths

"Uranium mining may now proceed," announced Australia's Prime Minister Malcolm Fraser on Aug. 25, 1977, "but only in ways which will not destroy or spoil the national heritage." Although the uranium debate could not be ended by Fraser's announcement, the government considered that the time had come for action. Development of the first mine, on the Ranger deposits in the Northern Territory, was expected by the end of 1977, and the mine was scheduled to be in production by 1981. Although the actual sales prospects could not be known until Australia actively sought long-term contracts in the market, gross revenue by the year 2000 was expected to exceed A$20 billion in current money values. But Fraser claimed that neither financial considerations nor the prospects of increased employment were his primary motive for giving the green light. Australia had acted because of the world energy crisis and in order to strengthen the nuclear nonproliferation treaty and so help to make a safer world.

The government's decision followed a commission of inquiry recommendation in November 1976 that there be a reasonable time for democratic public and parliamentary debate. Whether ten months was enough time to allow for public debate of such a momentous issue was a moot point. But to some extent the debate on uranium had been in existence below the surface since the late 1960s, and it had gradually replaced the Vietnam war as potentially the most divisive issue in Australian society.

Tony Grey, one of the chief public spokesmen for the Uranium Producers' Forum (UPF), pointed out that the mines in Australia had been left at a point of readiness for almost a decade. On the eve of the government's decision, the UPF commissioned a public opinion poll which found that 59% of Australians favoured the developing and export of Australia's uranium for peaceful purposes. Grey and the UPF were loud in demanding action. Those who

A. R. G. Griffiths is a senior lecturer in the School of Social Sciences, The Flinders University of South Australia. His works include Contemporary Australia *(1977).*

urged caution, on the other hand, pointed out that there were growing signs of a swing in public opinion on the uranium question and that these changes were bound to accelerate when opinion polarized after the government's decision.

Labor's Policy. Nowhere was the change in public opinion more evident than in the ranks of the Australian Labor Party (ALP). In 1973 the ALP minister for minerals and energy, Reginald Connor, promised that Labor would stimulate the growth of nuclear technology and establish power stations using enriched uranium. By 1977 the ALP, at its annual conference, passed resolutions that would in effect ban all future mining of uranium in Australia.

Australian parliamentary democracy had operated on a two-party basis since 1949, with the ALP briefly in power between December 1972 and November 1975. Because of the apparent mismanagement of the economy by the conservative Liberal-Country Party (LCP) since the ALP left office, Labor felt it was highly likely that it would again be in power by 1978. With this in mind, the ALP conference at Perth in July 1977 set out to map the party program for the coming elections, and the conference decided to

Aboriginal cave paintings in the Obiri Rock section in the Northern Territory of Australia, a part of the area affected by proposed uranium mining.

MICHAEL JENSEN—AUSTRALIAN INFORMATION SERVICE

211

make a stand against uranium mining. In adopting this line, the rank and file trade-union delegates ranged themselves against the party leaders, ALP president Bob Hawke (also president of the Australian Council of Trade Unions) and parliamentary party leader Gough Whitlam. When he was prime minister, Whitlam spent considerable resources trying to sell uranium to the Japanese and Western Europeans, and he believed that Australian public opinion was less concerned with uranium mining as an election issue than with unemployment, inflation, and the alleged extreme radicalism of some trade unions. While the ALP conference at Perth decided that there ought to be an indefinite moratorium on uranium mining, it agreed that existing contracts, for 9,200 metric tons, ought to be honoured.

Nevertheless, the ALP conference decision was a body blow to the uranium producers. Under the heading "No to ALP Policy on Uranium," the UPF published two short tables, from a public opinion poll it had commissioned, in all Australian daily newspapers.

Recently the ALP Conference made a decision to ban all future uranium mining in Australia indefinitely. Do you agree or disagree with that suggestion?	The ALP Conference also decided that if the ALP became the government, they would break and cancel all uranium contracts made by the existing government. Do you agree or disagree with that decision?
Disagree 59.5%	Disagree 58.1%
Agree 28.2%	Agree 26.6%
Undecided 12.3%	Undecided 15.2%

The Fox Report. The main sources of ammunition in the war of words being waged over uranium were two reports presented by the Ranger Uranium Environmental Inquiry, a commission set up by the Labor government in 1975 under the presidency of Justice R. W. Fox. The first report was issued on Oct. 28, 1976, the second on May 25, 1977.

The initial Fox report began from the standpoint that uranium was a very special metal: it contained fissile atoms. It was used in nuclear reactors to produce heat which converted water into steam which in turn drove turbines to generate electricity. There were substantial deposits of uranium ore at the Ranger site in the Northern Territory. The Australian Atomic Energy Commission and the Ranger Uranium Mines Pty. Ltd. had made a proposal to mine and mill uranium. The Fox commission was established to inquire into the environmental aspects of the proposal.

The uranium oxide that came from Australian mills was not to be used in Australia but was to be exported to countries that produced electricity from nuclear reactors. It was submitted to the commission that there were serious risks and disadvantages associated with the various operations of the nuclear power industry. There could be accidental releases of radioactivity. Wastes had a high level of radioactivity. Terrorists could use the plutonium produced by reactors. The extension of the nuclear power industry involved increased risks of nuclear war, flowing from the availability of plutonium, or enriched uranium, which could be used in the manufacture of nuclear weapons.

Following the release of the first report, in which all these issues were examined in exhaustive detail, Prime Minister Fraser announced that the government fully supported the inquiry's main finding—that there should be full and effective safeguards for uranium exports. But an added air of urgency entered the debate following U.S. Pres. Jimmy Carter's April 1977 statement on nuclear energy, in which he emphasized the need to restrain the spread of nuclear weapons without forgoing the tangible benefits of nuclear power. In a statement to Parliament on May 24, Fraser observed that President Carter's concern with establishing a framework of control within which the benefits of nuclear energy could be realized was of added significance to Australia because of the country's potential as a uranium supplier. Although known Australian reserves were not great, the cost of extracting ore was such that it possessed 15-20% of the Western world's most economically accessible reserves. Fraser added that, should it decide to allow exports, the government would be selective about the countries to which uranium would be sold. Australia would not be prepared to export uranium to countries where the International Atomic Energy Agency could not inspect safeguards applied under the nuclear nonproliferation treaty.

Decision Reached. Fraser's announcement on August 25 of the historic decision to go ahead with uranium mining was followed by lengthy statements by other ministers which took almost three hours to deliver. The deputy prime minister, Douglas Anthony, said that the government had decided that the Ranger project would go ahead on the basis of the existing memorandum of understanding between the former Whitlam government and Peko-EZ Ltd., the owners. Under this agreement, the commonwealth was to provide 75% of the capital needed to develop the Ranger mine in return for 50% of the net profits. The direct financial participation of the commonwealth in a mining project was, Anthony admitted, contrary to the LCP's political philosophy. But the government was prepared to honour the agreement, which it had inherited from the Whitlam government.

The acting minister for foreign affairs, Ian Sinclair, told Parliament that, far from hindering the cause of nonproliferation, uranium export, subject to the

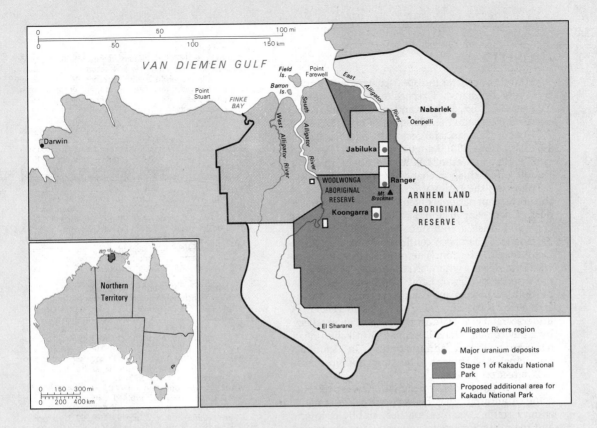

Alligator Rivers region

● Major uranium deposits

Stage 1 of Kakadu National Park

Proposed additional area for Kakadu National Park

fullest and most effective possible safeguards, would actually place Australia in a position to assist in the development of an increasingly effective nonproliferation regime.

The minister for the environment, Kevin Newman, announced that, in accord with recommendations in the second Fox report, Northern Territory uranium mining would go hand in hand with the development of a new national park, the Kakadu National Park, and that Aboriginals would have a special relationship with the park and would be trained as rangers. Since the question of the treatment of Aboriginals was a key issue in the uranium debate, Robert I. Viner, the minister for Aboriginal affairs, elaborated on their share in the project. Hitherto exploited, neglected, and almost universally unemployed, Australia's Aboriginals were to be among the financial beneficiaries of the project. Arnhem Land Aboriginals were to share in royalties from uranium mining totaling an estimated A$400 million. Royalties of at least 2.5% would be payable to the Aboriginals benefit trust account for mining within the Ranger area, and 30% of these payments would go to the local Aboriginal communities affected by mining development in the region. A further 30% would be available for advancing the well-being of Aboriginals throughout the Northern Territory on the advice of an all-Aboriginal advisory committee. Viner also stressed that attention would be given to programs suggested in the Fox report to

reduce dependence on alcohol among the Aboriginals and to establish special control measures.

The Debate Continues. The decision to mine uranium and export the ore dismayed conservationists, who pointed to events in France where thousands of demonstrators marched on a nuclear power station. Fraser's opponents urged the government to consider the possibility that world opinion might be turning against nuclear power and that the Australian government was therefore heading for economic disaster in trying to develop nuclear technology.

Overseas reaction to Fraser's announcement was mixed. In Moscow *Pravda* accused Fraser of being hypocritical in disclaiming financial motives for the decision to go ahead with uranium export. In Washington, London, and Tokyo the decision was applauded, and Australia's concern for safeguards was singled out for special praise. But in the streets of the capital cities of Australia, the antinuclear lobby began to close ranks. The New South Wales Police Association asked to be equipped with new riot gear in order to protect themselves while keeping the pro- and antiuranium groups apart. Demonstrations grew, trade unions threatened not to handle the ore, and it became clear that the August 1977 announcement, far from being an anticlimax and the end of the debate, signaled a new phase in the campaign for acceptance of the nuclear power industry by Australians. Nor did the results of the December general election resolve the issue.

Austria

Austria

A republic of central Europe, Austria is bounded by West Germany, Czechoslovakia, Hungary, Yugoslavia, Italy, Switzerland, and Liechtenstein. Area: 83,860 sq km (32,380 sq mi). Pop. (1976 est.): 7,513,000. Cap. and largest city: Vienna (pop., 1976 est., 1,592,800). Language: German. Religion (1977): Roman Catholic 90%. President in 1977, Rudolf Kirchschläger; chancellor, Bruno Kreisky.

Following the resignation on May 30, 1977, of the minister of national defense, Gen. Karl Lütgendorf, Chancellor Bruno Kreisky made the first changes in his Cabinet since the Socialist Party of Austria (SPÖ) had been confirmed in power by the October 1975 election. The new defense minister was Otto Rösch, who was replaced as minister of the interior by Erwin Lanc. The latter's previous portfolio, transport and communications, was taken over by Karl Lausecker, who was succeeded as undersecretary of state in the federal chancellery by a newcomer, Franz Löschnak, until then head of personnel and administration in Vienna's municipal government. The new appointments took effect on June 8.

General Lütgendorf's resignation was the outcome of an affair that had occupied Parliament, administration, political parties, public opinion, and the media for several months. This concerned the export of arms (rifles and ammunition) to a belligerent state—Syria—in possible contravention of Austria's status of permanent neutrality. A parliamentary commission of inquiry severely criticized General Lütgendorf's conduct in the matter, and subsequently regulations affecting the import, export, and transit of munitions—and controls on their observance—were tightened.

The November 1976 minority language census, which had been partially boycotted by the Slovene community, was followed by further acts of violence during 1977 in mixed-language areas of Carinthia. Nevertheless, in accordance with legislation designed to implement the state treaty's provision for minority rights, the setting up of

A new feature on the Viennese landscape was the UN's International Headquarters and Conference Centre, called the Danube Park Centre, which neared completion at year's end. The building will provide offices and numerous public facilities.

bilingual signposts began in June and proceeded without incident.

During 1976–77, in Austria as elsewhere, there was much controversy over the use of nuclear energy for power production, and with the approaching inauguration of Austria's first nuclear power station in Zwentendorf, near Vienna, protests and demonstrations increased. Opinion for and against seemed to be divided more or less equally among the population, regardless of political allegiance. Foremost among the supporters were, naturally, the utilities, which had already invested 7 billion schillings in the Zwentendorf project and feared that there would be power shortages if it did not come into use. Also in favour were many economists and industrialists concerned with future economic growth, full employment, and the possible effects of increased oil imports on the country's currency reserves. In July 1977 the SPÖ's executive made known its own decision: up to 1980 the Austrian economy was expected to expand at the rate of 3–4% a year, with the creation of 300,000 additional jobs, so that expansion of existing energy potential and the introduction of new energy sources, including utilization of nuclear energy, would be essential—provided

UNITED NATIONS

that a politically and scientifically acceptable solution to the problem of nuclear-waste disposal could be found.

Austria continued to pursue its policy of active neutrality. The Danube Park Centre in Vienna, designed to house 4,700 UN officials and to serve as a venue for large international conferences, neared completion. In May Kreisky visited the Middle East and spoke in favour of reopening the Geneva Middle East conference. In Syria an officer of the Austrian UN contingent was killed.

Austria weathered the general recession relatively well, and the schilling maintained its hard-currency parity. Real growth in the gross national product was somewhat above the European average, while inflation was below it and unemployment considerably below it. Nevertheless, significant budgetary and balance of payments deficits arose. On October 3 Kreisky announced an austerity program that included increases in the value-added tax on certain items (mainly luxury goods) from 18 to 30%, effective Jan. 1, 1978, and a reduction in state subsidies to employees' social security payments.　　　(ELFRIEDE DIRNBACHER)

Bahamas, The

A member of the Commonwealth of Nations, The Bahamas comprise an archipelago of about 700 islands in the North Atlantic Ocean just southeast of the United States. Area: 13,864 sq km (5,353 sq mi). Pop. (1977 est.): 218,000. Cap. and largest city: Nassau (urban area pop., 1976 est., 125,400). Language: English (official). Religion (1970): Baptist 28.8%; Anglican 22.7%; Roman Catholic 22.5%; Methodist 7.3%; Saints of God and Church of God 6%; others and no religion 12.7%. Queen, Elizabeth II; governor-general in 1977, Sir Milo B. Butler; prime minister, Lynden O. Pindling.

In 1977 Prime Minister Lynden Pindling's Progressive Liberal Party (PLP), ending its third term of office, held fast to its commitment to self-reliance and a mixed economy, with increased state participation in the private sector. It incurred charges of economic mismanagement and corruption from the Bahamian Democratic Party and the

Free National Movement, both dedicated to private ownership and a greater level of foreign investment. The two opposition parties' chances of defeating the incumbent PLP in the parliamentary elections, which were held on July 19, were diminished by their failure to unite on a joint ticket, and the PLP won 30 seats out of 38. The government, while admitting mistakes, stood on its record of continuous political stability and social advancement for Bahamian blacks.

Unemployment stood at 20%; job growth in tourism had stopped; foreign investment was at a standstill; and the nation had incurred its first balance of payments deficit in 1976. Other news included the growth of insurance into The Bahamas' third largest industry, and reports that the government might introduce an income tax and that West Germany might be considering a Bahamian location instead of Jamaica for its Caribbean diplomatic headquarters.　　　(SHEILA PATTERSON)

The Bahamas

Bahrain

An independent monarchy (emirate), Bahrain consists of a group of islands in the Persian Gulf, lying between the Qatar Peninsula and Saudi Arabia. Total area: 662 sq km (256 sq mi). Pop. (1976 est.): 256,600. Cap.: Manama (pop., 1976 est., 105,400). Language: Arabic (official), Persian. Religion (1971): Muslim 95.7%; Christian 3%; others 1.3%. Emir in 1977, Isa ibn Sulman al-Khalifah; prime minister, Khalifah ibn Sulman al-Khalifah.

In 1977 Bahrain continued to develop as a financial centre and to benefit from the increasing commercial prosperity of the whole Gulf area. Total assets of foreign banks taking advantage of new offshore banking facilities were estimated early in the year at $6,250,000,000, of which $2.5 billion were Arab assets and funds. Bahrain's crude oil production continued its slow decline from about 58,000 bbl a day in 1976, but natural gas production increased. In the record 1977 budget, revenues were estimated at $588 million, a 20% increase over 1976, while expenditure, at $623,750,000, was up 27%. About half of government capital spending was allocated to housing. Inflation was unofficially estimated at 40%, and in June the government for the first time issued development bonds to mop up excess liquidity.

Bahrain

BAHAMAS, THE

Education. Primary (1975–76), pupils 34,941, teachers (state only) 549; secondary (1975–76), pupils 25,069, teachers (state only) 565; vocational (1971–72), pupils 427, teachers 60; teacher training (1971–72), students 534, teachers 32; higher (at universities overseas; 1974–75), students c. 400.

Finance and Trade. Monetary unit: Bahamian dollar, with (Sept. 19, 1977) an official rate of B$1 to U.S. $1 (B$1.74 = £1 sterling). Budget (1976 est.): revenue B$148 million; expenditure B$147.9 million. Cost of living (1970 = 100; May 1977) 157. Foreign trade (1976): imports B$2,892,600,000; exports B$2,601,600,000. Import sources (1975): Saudi Arabia 38%; Nigeria 18%; Libya 14%; Indonesia 7%; U.S. 7%; Iran 5%. Export destinations: U.S. 76%; Liberia 5%. Main exports (1975): crude oil 56%; petroleum products 40%. Tourism: visitors (1975) 1,381,000; gross receipts (1974) U.S. $328 million.

Transport and Communications. Shipping (1976): merchant vessels 100 gross tons and over 119; gross tonnage 147,817. Telephones (Jan. 1976) 57,000. Radio receivers (Dec. 1974) 90,000. Television receivers (Dec. 1964) c. 4,500.

BAHRAIN

Education. (1975–76) Primary, pupils 44,790, teachers 2,253; secondary, pupils 16,936, teachers 755; vocational, pupils 1,665, teachers 79; higher, students 595, teaching staff 79.

Finance and Trade. Monetary unit: Bahrain dinar, with (Sept. 19, 1977) an official rate of 0.396 dinar to U.S. $1 (free rate of 0.687 dinar = £1 sterling). Gold, SDR's, and foreign exchange (June 1977) U.S. $466.6 million. Budget (1976–77 est.): revenue 181 million dinars; expenditure 191 million dinars. Foreign trade (1976): imports 658.3 million dinars; exports 532.5 million dinars. Import sources: Saudi Arabia 42%; U.K. 10%; Japan 8%; U.S. 8%. Export destinations (1975): U.S. 23%; Japan 15%; Australia 9%; Saudi Arabia 7%; Singapore 7%; United Arab Emirates 5%. Main exports: petroleum products 74%; aluminum 8%.

Industry. Production (in 000; metric tons): crude oil (1976) 2,916; petroleum products (1975) c. 10,500.

The U.S. lease of the Jufair naval base was terminated as of June 30, although U.S. vessels could continue to take on supplies there. The Bahraini foreign minister had said in February that both U.S. and Soviet influence in the Gulf area must end, and the action was seen as removing any grounds for the U.S.S.R. to try establishing bases in the region.   (PETER MANSFIELD)

Bangladesh

Bangladesh

An independent republic and member of the Commonwealth of Nations, Bangladesh is bordered by India on the west, north, and east, by Burma in the southeast, and by the Bay of Bengal in the south. Area: 143,998 sq km (55,598 sq mi). Pop. (1976 est.): 78,664,200. Cap. and largest city: Dacca (pop., 1974, 1,679,600). Language: Bengali. Religion: Muslim 85%, with Hindu, Christian, and Buddhist minorities. Presidents in 1977, Abu Sadat Mohammed Sayem and, from April 21, Maj. Gen. Ziaur Rahman.

Maj. Gen. Ziaur Rahman (*see* BIOGRAPHY), who had been appointed chief martial-law administrator on Nov. 29, 1976, was made president of Bangladesh on April 21, 1977, after Pres. Abu Sadat Sayem resigned on grounds of ill health. The first part of President Zia's program was carried out on May 30, when a referendum was held on his martial-law rule. The referendum was called for by the president on April 22 to endorse his 19-point program, and it confirmed him as president and martial-law administrator. The remarkable feature of the referendum was the unprecedented voter turnout and unanimity; more than 88% of the country's 38 million voters took part, 99.89% of them voting "aye."

The president's program was based on a fundamental commitment to Islam; restoration of democracy, nationalism, and socialism; and assurance of economic and social justice. General Zia amended, through proclamation (also on April 22 when the referendum was sought), some clauses of the constitution framed in December 1972 during Sheikh Mujibur Rahman's rule. The amendments were fundamental. Secularism, which had been one of the four basic principles of the state, was replaced by the words "complete trust and faith in the Almighty Allah." Socialism, another state principle, was redefined to keep it in line with Islamic ideas of social justice and economic equality. In foreign affairs, it was made a constitutional responsibility to seek closer relations with Muslim countries.

The referendum was followed in August by elections to the municipal councils. According to Zia, these elections were steps toward establishing representative government; he said that he would follow the time schedule for the restoration of democracy, implying the probability of civilian government by December 1978. Of more than a score of parties that chose to campaign in the municipal elections, only nine secured seats. The Awami League headed the list, winning 27 posts of head of local bodies, followed by its traditional rival, the Muslim League, which gained 24. The

remaining dozen seats were shared by the other parties.

To build up support for his policies, Zia launched a heavily village-oriented development program. Of the 20 million people engaged in agriculture in the country, estimates of those unemployed ranged from 6.9 million to 9.7 million. The rural self-help program was based on a food-for-work project. In return for such labour as moving earth for minor irrigation works and road building, the otherwise unemployed were given three seers (a seer = 2 lb) of wheat for 70 cu ft of earthwork. The wheat stocks came from supplies provided by affluent nations.

The budget for 1977–78 also reflected the determination of the government to pursue planned development. The government proposed to spend approximately 11.5 billion taka on development in 1977, more than 50% of its overall estimated spending of 20,560,000,000 taka.

In foreign relations, the Indo-Bangladesh dialogue over the division of the waters of the Ganges, following the construction of a barrage at Farakka in India, had an uneven course and to an extent soured relations between the two countries. Eventually, on September 29 in New Delhi, they reached agreement on the sharing of the waters, and a treaty was signed in Dacca on November 5.

On October 2, during negotiations with the

Japanese hijackers of a Japan Air Lines plane that had landed at the Dacca airport on September 28, a group of Bangladesh soldiers attempted a coup. The attempt was put down at once, but at the cost of some 200 lives.

On the domestic scene, Zia and his deputy martial-law administrators, Rear Adm. M. H. Khan and Air Vice-Marshal A. G. Mahmood, provided the country with a degree of stability that Bangladesh had lacked previously. As a result of a relaxation of the Emergency Powers Act, certain legal cases within the purview of the special tribunals could now be taken up by ordinary courts. Similarly, detainees under certain provisions would now be informed as to why they had been taken into custody.　(GOVINDAN UNNY)

Barbados

The parliamentary state of Barbados is a member of the Commonwealth of Nations and occupies the most easterly island in the southern Caribbean Sea. Area: 430 sq km (166 sq mi). Pop. (1977 est.): 258,500; 91% Negro, 4% white, 4% mixed. Cap. and largest city: Bridgetown (pop., 1970, 8,900). Language: English. Religion: Anglican 53%; Methodist 9%; Roman Catholic 4%; Moravian 2%; others 32%. Queen, Elizabeth II; governor-general in 1977, Sir Deighton Lisle Ward; prime minister, J. M. G. Adams.

Prime Minister J. M. G. Adams stated firmly in 1977 that he had no intention of indulging in Marxist-Leninist experiments. The opposition Democratic Labour Party's position was less clear, with the former prime minister, Errol Barrow, continuing a pragmatic, moderate line while Rameses Caddle, his challenger for the party leadership, held more radical views.

Barbados enjoyed a higher standard of living than most Caribbean islands, achieved by diversifying the fragile single-crop economy, based on sugar, into tourism, light industry, agricultural development other than sugar, and fishing. The sugar industry also looked into the development of by-products, including petrochemicals. In June 1977 the government announced its intention of establishing tax haven facilities for outside banking and financial institutions. The main worry continued to be unemployment, variously estimated at between 13 and 27%, including 32% of the 16–25-year age-group. The renewed campaign to bring industry to Barbados was intended to create new jobs, and outside investors were attracted by the fact that there was little unrest.

(SHEILA PATTERSON)

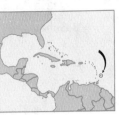

Barbados

Baseball

Baseball, once thought to be slipping in popularity, enjoyed another highly successful year in 1977. Major-league attendance reached a record level of 38.7 million spectators, more than 7 million above the 1976 total. Only 6 of the 26 franchises failed to show an increase in attendance, and the Los Angeles Dodgers established a major-league mark by attracting 2,955,087 customers to 79 games for an average of 37,406.

World Series. The New York Yankees, who had not captured a World Series championship since 1962, won their 21st title by beating the Los Angeles Dodgers, 4 games to 2. Reggie Jackson (see BIOGRAPHY), the talented right fielder whom the Yankees signed as a free agent to a reported five-year, $2.9 million contract, hit three home runs as the Yankees clinched the Series triumph with an 8–4 victory over the Dodgers in Yankee Stadium on October 18. "I guess this proves that we are the best team that money can buy," laughed Jackson, whose stormy season culminated with most valuable player honours for the Series. He hit a record five home runs.

"I am happy, more than anything, for the city of New York. It is a city of champions that has taken a lot of bad raps, but now it has another champion," said George Steinbrenner, the team owner, who had spent large quantities of money to attract such available talent as Jackson, Catfish Hunter, and Don Gullett.

Mid-season battles forgotten, Reggie Jackson is hugged by New York Yankee manager Billy Martin and teammates after his third home run in the final game of the World Series.

UPI COMPIX

Lou Brock triumphantly waves second base over his head after sliding safely into second for his 893rd stolen base. The St. Louis outfielder beat the previous record held by Ty Cobb.

The New Yorkers, slight underdogs in the Series, won the opener 4–3 in 12 innings on October 11 at Yankee Stadium. Paul Blair, nominally a defensive replacement, batted in the winning run as Yankee pitcher Sparky Lyle won the game with 3⅔ innings of strong relief.

In the second game Burt Hooton allowed just five hits and struck out eight as the Dodgers evened the Series with a 6–1 victory at New York. Hunter, a star in former Series who had not pitched in a month because of an injury, started for the Yankees but was hit hard.

Mike Torrez, a strong right-hander, struck out nine and pitched a seven-hitter as the Yankees beat the Dodgers 5–3 to take a 2–1 lead in games at Los Angeles October 14. Then the Yankees received another strong pitching performance to capture

the fourth game 4–2. Ron Guidry, a slim left-hander who almost failed to make the team in spring training, threw a four-hitter.

The Dodgers routed New York 10–4 the next day, October 16, to avoid losing the Series before their home fans. Los Angeles buffeted Yankee starter Gullett for an early lead, and Don Sutton cruised to the victory.

But when the Series shifted back to New York, the Yankees revived to win the final game, moving Jackson to remark, "Billy Martin should win the Nobel Peace Prize for winning with this season." Martin, the fiery Yankee manager, had been part of the ongoing turmoil that surrounded the team throughout the season. It reached from the owner's office to the clubhouse, and sometimes beyond. For instance, in a nationally televised game at Boston on June 18, Martin pulled Jackson off the field in the middle of an inning for what the manager considered lack of hustle. With cameras zooming in on the Yankee dugout, Martin and Jackson almost came to blows.

"That was the turning point of our season . . . it showed everybody that I was boss, not Jackson," said Martin. Though Martin seemed close to losing his job several times during the summer, he finished the Series with a vote of confidence from Steinbrenner, a big bonus for a "job well done," and even a bear hug of affection from Jackson.

Play-offs. The Yankees captured their 31st American League pennant by winning the East Division and then beating the Kansas City Royals, first-place team in the West Division, in the best-of-five championship play-off. Kansas City won the opener in New York 7–2, and the Yankees evened the series at home 6–2. Then the Royals triumphed in Kansas City 6–2 to assume a 2–1 lead in games. But in the fourth game Lyle hurled 5⅓ splendid innings to ice a 6–4 New York triumph, and finally on October 9 the Yankees scored three runs in the top of the ninth inning to beat the Royals 5–3 and take the pennant before a stunned Kansas City audience.

The Dodgers, champions of the National League West, also gained their pennant in dramatic fashion. The Philadelphia Phillies, easy winners in the National League East, took the first game of the play-off 7–5 in Los Angeles. The Dodgers won the next night 7–1, but appeared doomed in game three at Philadelphia on October 7. They trailed 5–3 with two out in the ninth inning, but rallied to win 6–5. The shocked Phillies then succumbed in the rain 4–1 on October 8, and the Dodgers won the play-off in four games. It was the Dodgers' sixth pennant since their move to Los Angeles from Brooklyn two decades earlier, and a triumph for Tom Lasorda in his first season as Dodger manager.

Regular Season. The Yankees, despite their considerable payroll, won the American League East by only 2½ games over the Boston Red Sox and Baltimore Orioles. In the West the surprising Chicago White Sox led the division through July, only to be left in the wake of a strong finish by the Royals, who won 16 straight games, 35 of their last 39, and wound up with 102 victories—most in the major leagues.

Final Major League Standings, 1977

American League
East Division

Club	W.	L.	Pct.	G.B.	N.Y.	Bos.	Balt.	Det.	Clev.	Mil.	Tor.	Cal.	Chi.	K.C.	Min.	Oak.	Sea.	Tex.
New York .	100	62	.617	...	...	7	7	9	12	7	9	7	7	5	8	9	6	7
Boston	97	64	.602	2½	8	...	9	8	9	12	7	3	5	4	8	10	6
Baltimore .	97	64	.602	2½	8	6	...	12	11	11	10	5	5	4	6	8	7	4
Detroit ...	74	88	.457	26	6	6	3	...	7	10	10	6	6	3	5	5	5	2
Cleveland .	71	90	.441	28½	3	7	4	8	...	11	9	4	4	3	2	7	7	2
Milwaukee .	67	95	.414	33	8	6	4	5	4	...	8	5	5	2	3	5	7	5
Toronto ..	54	107	.335	45½	6	3	5	5	5	7	...	4	3	2	1	3	6	4

West Division

Club	W.	L.	Pct.	G.B.	K.C.	Tex.	Chi.	Min.	Cal.	Sea.	Oak.	Balt.	Bos.	Clev.	Det.	Mil.	N.Y.	Tor.
Kansas City	102	60	.630	...	...	8	7	10	9	11	9	7	5	7	8	8	5	8
Texas.....	94	68	.580	8	7	...	9	7	10	6	13	6	4	9	8	5	3	7
Chicago...	90	72	.556	12	8	6	...	10	7	10	10	5	7	6	4	6	3	8
Minnesota .	84	77	.522	17½	6	8	5	...	8	7	8	4	6	9	5	8	2	9
California .	74	88	.457	28	6	5	8	7	...	9	5	6	3	6	4	5	4	4
Seattle....	64	98	.395	38	4	9	5	8	6	...	8	3	1	3	6	3	4	4
Oakland ..	63	98	.391	38½	6	2	5	6	10	7	...	2	3	5	5	2	1	7

National League
East Division

Club	W.	L.	Pct.	G.B.	Phil.	Pitt.	St.L.	Chi.	Mon.	N.Y.	Atl.	Cin.	Hou.	L.A.	S.D.	S.F.
Philadelphia.	101	61	.623	...	...	3	11	12	11	13	10	4	8	6	9	9
Pittsburgh ..	96	66	.593	5	10	...	9	11	11	14	9	9	8	3	10	2
St. Louis ..	83	79	.512	18	7	9	...	11	6	10	11	7	7	6	4	5
Chicago....	81	81	.500	20	6	7	7	...	10	9	7	7	6	6	7	9
Montreal ...	75	87	.463	26	7	7	12	8	...	10	6	5	4	5	5	6
New York ..	64	98	.395	37	5	4	8	9	9	...	5	2	6	4	6	7

West Division

Club	W.	L.	Pct.	G.B.	L.A.	Cin.	Hou.	S.F.	S.D.	Atl.	Chi.	Mon.	N.Y.	Phil.	Pitt.	St.L.
Los Angeles .	98	64	.605	...	...	8	9	14	12	13	6	7	8	6	9	6
Cincinnati ...	88	74	.543	10	10	...	5	10	11	14	5	7	10	8	3	5
Houston	81	81	.500	17	9	13	...	9	8	9	6	8	6	4	4	5
San Francisco	75	87	.463	23	4	8	9	...	10	10	3	6	5	3	10	7
San Diego ...	69	93	.426	29	6	7	10	8	...	7	5	7	6	3	2	8
Atlanta	61	101	.377	37	5	4	9	8	11	...	5	6	7	2	3	1

The Philadelphia Phillies, who trailed the up-start Chicago Cubs at the All-Star break, also closed with a rush and finished five games ahead of the Pittsburgh Pirates. The Dodgers started strongly and were never caught, dislodging incumbent division champion Cincinnati by ten games in the National League West.

Rod Carew (see BIOGRAPHY), perhaps the finest modern-day hitter, batted .388 for the Minnesota Twins and won the American League title for a sixth time. Jim Rice of the Boston Red Sox led the league with 39 home runs, while Minnesota's Larry Hisle had 119 runs batted in to top that department. Three pitchers won 20 games: Jim Palmer of the Baltimore Orioles, Dennis Leonard of Kansas City, and Dave Goltz of Minnesota.

Dave Parker of the Pittsburgh Pirates batted .338 to nudge teammate Rennie Stennett (.336) for the National League crown. George Foster, the soft-spoken outfielder for the Cincinnati Reds, had a spectacular season for power; his 52 home runs and 149 runs batted in led the league in each category. Steve Carlton of the Phillies won 23 games to top the pitchers. Tom Seaver, traded from the New York Mets to Cincinnati in a noteworthy midseason transaction, hurled 21 wins. Pittsburgh's John Candelaria, Chicago's Rick Reuschel, Los Angeles' Tommy John, and St. Louis Cardinal Bob Forsch each won 20 games.

Carew was voted the most valuable player in the American League, while Foster of the Reds won the honours in the National League. Sparky Lyle of the Yankees became the first relief pitcher to win the Cy Young award in the American League; the National League prize went to the Phillies' Carlton for the second time in his career. Rookies of the year were Andre Dawson of Montreal in the National League and Eddie Murray of Baltimore in the American. Earl Weaver of Baltimore and LaSorda of Los Angeles were, respectively, American and National League managers of the year.

In 1977 two expansion teams made their debuts. The Seattle Mariners finished ½ game ahead of the last-place Oakland A's in the American League West; the Toronto Blue Jays could not avoid the basement in the American East, but Canada's second major-league franchise enjoyed an excellent season at the gate, drawing more than 1.7 million customers. Baseball lost one of its most colourful figures in December when Charles Finley announced that he was selling the Oakland A's franchise to a Denver oilman.

The National League captured the annual All-Star Game in Yankee Stadium. Pitcher Don Sutton of the Los Angeles Dodgers was named most valuable player.

Latin America. Every winter, major-league players join teams in Venezuela, Puerto Rico, the Dominican Republic, and Mexico to participate in the winter league season of about 60 games. This is particularly helpful to players who, because of injury or other reasons, were not able to participate frequently with their major-league clubs. Championship teams during the past season were Magallanes in Venezuela, Caguas in Puerto Rico, Licey in the Dominican Republic, and Mazatlán in Mexico. (ROBERT WILLIAM VERDI)

Japan. The Pacific League champion Hankyu Braves of Nishinomiya beat the highly favoured Central League champion Yomiuri Giants of Tokyo four games to one in the best-of-seven Japan Series. The triumph was Hankyu's third straight in Series competition. Among those who contributed to the victory were pitcher Hisashi Yamada and outfielder Yutaka Fukumoto. Yamada was chosen as the most valuable player of the Series.

Partly helped by the lack of power of rival teams, the Yomiuri Giants had rather easily won the Central League pennant in 1977 for the second consecutive season. Batting power and good pitching were, of course, driving forces for the team's victory, but much credit was also given to manager Shigeo Nagashima.

The Hankyu Braves had beaten the Lotte Orions 3–2 in a best-of-five play-off series, capturing the Pacific League pennant for the third consecutive season. As in the last season, the Braves victory was achieved by the well-balanced combination of pitching by 16-game winner Yamada and 17-game winner Mitsuo Inaba and the batting of Kinji Shimatani, Hideji Kato, and Fukumoto.

Attracting the most attention during the season was Japan's superstar, Sadaharu Oh of the Giants, who slammed his 756th home run on September 3 to surpass Hank Aaron's U.S. major-league record of 755. Winner of both the home-run championship with 50 and the runs-batted-in crown with 124, Oh was named as the Central League's most valuable player; he also received the newly created People's Honour Award, personally conferred on him by the Japanese prime minister, Takeo Fukuda. For the second time Tsutomu Wakamatsu of the Yakult Swallows of Tokyo was the league's leading hitter with .358.

In the Pacific League, Leron Lee of the Lotte Orions of Sendai swept both the home-run title with 34 and the runs-batted-in crown with 109. His teammate Michiyo Arito won the batting title with .329. Most valuable player awards went to Yamada in the first half-season and to Choji Murata of the Orions in the second half-season. Yamada was also chosen as the most valuable player for the entire season. (RYUSAKU HASEGAWA)

Taiwan's third baseman Hung Chih-hsiung is safe at home in the championship game of the Little League World Series in Williamsport, Pennsylvania. Taiwan won 7–2 over El Cajon, California.

UPI COMPIX

THE FIRST YEAR OF THE FREE AGENTS

by Dave Anderson

When the 1977 major league season began, baseball's most controversial question was: "Can any of the expensive free agents possibly be worth the big money some club owners have invested?" By the time the World Series had ended, Reggie Jackson (*see* BIOGRAPHY), who had been the most expensive free agent of all, had answered that question with his bat. He hit three home runs, tying a record held by Babe Ruth, in the New York Yankees' 8–4 victory in the final game, and his total of five home runs had established a Series record as the Yankees conquered the Los Angeles Dodgers, four games to two, to win their first world championship in 15 years.

Jackson, an outfielder whose 31st birthday occurred early in the season, had signed a five-year Yankee contract for a total of $2.9 million. It was the most lucrative of the deals involving the 24 players who elected to become free agents in the first year since the demise of baseball's venerable reserve clause, which bound a player to the team that first signed him or to which he was traded. In 1975 a federal arbitration panel ruled that Andy Messersmith and Dave McNally had become free agents after playing a year without signing a contract. With some modifications, the ruling was incorporated into a 1976 collective bargaining contract between the owners and the Players Association.

The Best Team Money Can Buy. "As soon as I signed the contract," Jackson said, "everybody wanted to know how I could be worth that much. But to me, that was never the point. I never said I was worth that much. But when the Yankees offered me that . . . , I don't see how anybody can blame me for taking it."

The Yankees also signed free agent Don Gullett, a left-handed pitcher formerly with the Cincinnati Reds, for nearly $2 million over six years. Three years earlier, when right-hander Jim ("Catfish") Hunter of the Oakland A's became available because of a contract dispute with owner Charles O. Finley, the Yankees had signed him for $3.5 million over five years.

Dave Anderson is a sportswriter and columnist for the New York Times.

Such acquisitions by George Steinbrenner, the free-spending principal owner, earned the Yankees the sobriquet of "the best team money can buy." The label annoyed Yankee executives. "Whether it's trading, buying or developing," said Yankee president Gabe Paul, "you get ballplayers any way you can get them as long as it's within the rules."

Thirteen other teams took advantage of the new rules to sign free agents, but the Yankees made the most successful investments. Even before his World Series heroics overshadowed his reputation for clubhouse controversy, Jackson had dominated the Yankees' late-season drive to the American League East divisional title. Over the year he hit 32 homers and drove in 110 runs, ending the season with a .286 average. Gullett, despite a variety of arm ailments, compiled a 14–4 won-lost record. Dollar for dollar, however, the most valuable of the free agents was probably Bill Campbell, a right-handed relief pitcher signed by the Boston Red Sox to a $1 million, four-year contract. Campbell was credited with 31 saves, and his 13–9 record was tops on the staff.

The most disappointed team was the California Angels, thought to be a contender until injuries deprived them of outfielder Joe Rudi ($2 million over five years) and shortstop Bobby Grich ($1.5 million over five years). Another free agent, outfielder Don Baylor ($1.6 million over six years), racked up 25 home runs, 75 RBI's, and a .251 average, but without Rudi and Grich, the Angels slipped to fifth place in the AL West.

The Poor Little Rich Boys. The expensive contracts created a new kind of pressure for the free agents. In a sense, they were like rookies who had to prove themselves to their new club owners, their new managers, their new teammates, and, perhaps most of all, their new fans.

Jackson probably felt that pressure more than any of the others, especially early in the season when the team was losing and he was quarreling with Billy Martin, the Yankee manager, and Thurman Munson, the team's captain and catcher. In 1976 the Yankees had lost the World Series in four games to the Reds; nothing less than a Series victory in 1977 would justify Jackson's presence.

But comparable pressure surrounded Wayne Garland, a right-handed pitcher who was guaranteed $2.3 million over ten years by the Cleveland Indians. A surprise 20-game winner for the Baltimore Orioles in 1976, Garland was almost a 20-game loser a year later. Bothered by an ailing shoulder in spring training, he lost his first four starts and ended the season with a 13–19 record. "I guess I wasn't prepared for all this pressure," he acknowledged. "I thought I was, but I guess I wasn't."

By obtaining shortstop Bert Campaneris for

$1 million over five years and right-hander Doyle Alexander for nearly $1 million over six years, the Texas Rangers believed they had produced a contender in the AL West. Campaneris, however, hit .253 and drove in only 47 runs. Alexander had a respectable 17–11 record, but the Rangers finished far behind the Kansas City Royals, who had not signed any free agents at all.

Bargains and Boo-Boos. Among the other free agents, the record was also mixed. Bill Veeck (*see* BIOGRAPHY), the flamboyant president of the Chicago White Sox, acquired the best bargains—third baseman Eric Soderholm (.280, 25 homers, 68 RBI's) and right-handed pitcher Steve Stone (15–12). "I didn't sign anybody to a million-dollar contract," Veeck explained. "Some of the figures I offered, I suppose I should have been embarrassed about." Another bargain, second baseman Billy Smith, helped keep the Orioles in the AL East race until the final weekend. Smith's statistics were unspectacular, but he was a dependable fielder. Paul Dade of the Indians—a much less expensive free agent than Garland—batted .291. Tito Fuentes, an aging second baseman, appeared rejuvenated by Detroit's Tiger Stadium and batted .309. Third baseman Sal Bando,

Reggie Jackson chuckles in the dugout beneath a taunting banner.

signed to a five-year, $1.4 million contract, drove in 83 runs, hit 17 homers, and compiled a .251 average with the hapless Milwaukee Brewers.

In the National League, where only five teams signed a total of six free agents, the most dramatic development was supplied by 39-year-old Willie McCovey, who rejoined the San Francisco Giants, the team of his glory years. To the surprise of many baseball people, he hit 28 home runs (for a career total of 493), drove in 86 runs, and batted .282. Of the NL teams, the Padres made the biggest investment in the free-agent market, signing relief pitcher Rollie Fingers and catcher Gene Tenace for $1.6 million and $1.5 million, respectively. Fingers maintained his reputation as a bullpen ace with 35 saves— best in either league—but Tenace hit only .233. The Padres skidded to fifth in the NL West.

Richie Hebner, a first baseman and pinch hitter with 18 homers and 62 RBI's, helped the Philadelphia Phillies win the NL East. They did it despite the departure of star second baseman Dave Cash, who batted .289 after joining the Montreal Expos for $1.5 million over five years. Atlanta Braves outfielder Gary Matthews ($1.7 million over five years) hit .283 with 17 homers and 64 RBI's.

Nate Colbert, a 31-year-old first baseman, was the only free agent to be ignored. He tried out with the Toronto Blue Jays but was not signed and spent the season selling cars in San Diego.

Baseball's Expensive New Look. Rather than risk the possible departure of their best players, some teams signed them to lucrative long-term contracts. Mike Schmidt and Greg Luzinski of the Phillies agreed to reported $3 million deals. Other highly paid performers included Steve Garvey of the Dodgers and Joe Morgan, Johnny Bench, and Pete Rose of the Reds.

Some teams balked at signing free agents, notably the New York Mets, who traded Tom Seaver, known for a decade as their "Franchise," to the Reds after he publicly quarreled with board chairman M. Donald Grant. The Mets also disposed of slugger Dave Kingman after a contract dispute and finished a poor last in the NL East.

Either by inclination or because of insufficient funds, several other clubowners remained adamant against the signing of free agents. They pointed out that the Dodgers had won the NL pennant without any. But the Royals, who lost the AL championship series to the Yankees for the second consecutive year, vowed to improve their team with free agents. So did the Rangers—and so did the Yankees.

"We're going to keep spending," said George Steinbrenner, "to keep the team winning."

"There is no substitute for talent," said Gabe Paul. "And the talent is available."

Basketball

United States. PROFESSIONAL. After eight seasons in the National Basketball Association (NBA), the Portland Trail Blazers finally made it to the play-offs in 1977. And when they got there, they knew exactly what to do. They won the championship.

As they raced past talent-rich Philadelphia, the Trail Blazers seemed intent on publicizing the reasons why they should wear the robes of kings. The biggest reason of all was 6-ft 11-in centre Bill Walton (*see* BIOGRAPHY). Although he averaged 18.5 points per game, Walton was more interested in passing, rebounding, and defense, and his unselfishness set the tone for the Trail Blazers. Muscular, menacing Maurice Lucas, a tireless worker under the boards, and gaunt, clever Bob Gross, a deft jumpshooter, complemented each other perfectly at forward. In the backcourt, veterans Dave Twardzik and Lionel Hollins and rookie Johnny Davis turned games into track meets with a full-court press that piled up points.

The conductor of Portland's basketball symphony was Jack Ramsay, a physical fitness devotee and holder of a Ph.D. in education. After years of either middling or no success in Philadelphia and Buffalo, he found himself coaching a team that responded eagerly to his preachments about pattern offense and aggressive defense. If ever the Trail Blazers' commitment to Ramsay was tested, it was after they began the best-of-seven final round in Philadelphia by losing two games filled with mistakes and fights. They repented by winning the next two games, in Portland, by a total of 54 points.

This was no ragtag Philadelphia team they were humiliating. Indeed, the 76ers were considered to

It was a meeting of the Titans when Lakers' Kareem Abdul-Jabbar (holding the ball) squared off against Trail Blazers' Bill Walton (centre) in the Western Conference playoff series.

UPI COMPIX

have more raw talent than anybody in the league. Forward George McGinnis and guard Doug Collins were almost without equal, and 20-year-old Darryl Dawkins was on the verge of becoming one of the NBA's dominant centres. The player who was supposed to have guaranteed Philadelphia the championship, however, was Julius Erving, a smooth-operating forward better known as Dr. J. The 76ers paid $6.5 million to buy him from the New York Nets. The spectacular 6-ft 7-in Erving proved his worth in the finals by averaging 30 points a game. But his teammates were hamstrung by differences among themselves as well as by Portland's speed and teamwork. So the Trail Blazers concentrated on them, let Erving go, and captured the crown with 110–104 and 109–107 victories.

The league over which Portland found itself reigning was bigger than ever. Before the season began it grew to 22 teams when the American Basketball Association (ABA) disbanded and Denver, Indiana, San Antonio, and the New York Nets joined the NBA. Of all the newly arrived players, the most closely watched was Erving, who had almost single-handedly kept the ABA in business for four seasons. He lived up to his sensational reputation, but somehow the sportswriters failed to vote him onto their post-season all-star team.

Selected ahead of him were forwards Elvin Hayes of Washington and David Thompson of Denver, centre Kareem Abdul-Jabbar of Los Angeles, and guards Pete Maravich of New Orleans and Paul Westphal of Phoenix. Abdul-Jabbar was voted most valuable player for the fifth time. The acrobatic Maravich led in scoring with a 31.1 average. Adrian Dantley, a thickset Buffalo forward, performed well enough to become rookie of the year, and then was traded to Indiana after the season. The other major post-season move was made by the New York Nets, who shifted their franchise to New Jersey.

COLLEGE. Al McGuire ended his 13-year career as Marquette University's basketball coach by leaving the Milwaukee school with a gift it would never forget, its first National Collegiate Athletic Association (NCAA) championship. The grand finale for McGuire was a title-clinching 67–59 victory over the University of North Carolina that was a study in what made his Warriors winners. There was the board play of Bo Ellis, a stringbean forward, and the steadying influence of guard Butch Lee, the outstanding player in the NCAA finals. Perhaps most important, there were also the good breaks fate handed Marquette.

For one thing, North Carolina was without its gifted centre, 6-ft 10-in Tom LaGarde, who was out with a knee injury. For another, in the biggest game of the year, Dean Smith, the Tar Heels' astute coach, made what may have been his only major mistake of the season. He ordered his team into a slowdown as soon as it got a 45–43 lead on Marquette in the second half. Unfortunately, the Tar Heels succeeded only in slowing themselves down, scoring just four points in the last 12 minutes. The Warriors, meanwhile, connected on 16 of their last 17 foul shots. By the time there was a minute left, the 48-year-old McGuire, who retired to become an executive in private industry, was crying joyfully and unashamedly on the sidelines.

It was a dramatic ending to a season rife with drama. In the NCAA semifinals, for example, Marquette edged the University of North Carolina at Charlotte, 51–49, on a last-second basket by Jerome Whitehead, and North Carolina squeaked past the University of Nevada at Las Vegas, 84–83, on five consecutive free throws by senior guard John Kuester.

The University of San Francisco, loaded with young talent, knocked off 29 straight opponents before Notre Dame ended its streak. The nation's three top-ranked teams—Michigan, UCLA, and Kentucky—were all eliminated from the NCAA tournament in regional competition. St. Bonaventure, a powerhouse from years past, tasted glory once again by stinging Houston, 94–91, to win the National Invitational Tournament championship. Thanks to Lucy Harris, a 6-ft 3-in centre, and Debbie Brock, a 4-ft 11-in guard, Delta State of Cleveland, Miss., walked off with the title in the Association of Intercollegiate Athletics for Women. After the season, UCLA coach Gene Bartow, unable to live with the intense pressure of succeeding the legendary John Wooden, announced his resignation.

Selected as the Associated Press player of the year was Marques Johnson, a forward at UCLA. He was joined on the AP's All-American team by forward Bernard King of Tennessee, centre Kent Benson of Indiana, and guards Rickey Green of Michigan and Phil Ford of North Carolina.

(JOHN SCHULIAN)

World Amateur. The 27th South American championships for men were played in Valdivia, Chile, during February and March 1977. The superiority of the Brazilians quickly became evident when they scored devastating victories over Bolivia 124–50 and Colombia 132–55; the only team that could really challenge them was Argentina, which they beat 71–60. Second and third in the standings were determined when Uruguay defeated Argentina 95–81. The final placings in order were: Brazil, Uruguay, Argentina, Venezuela, Peru, Chile, Colombia, Paraguay, and Bolivia.

In the men's European Champions' Cup, Mobilgirgi of Varese (Italy) looked set to retain its title when it met Maccabi of Tel Aviv (Israel) in Belgrade, Yugos., for the final game. The Italian club had scored convincing wins over Real Madrid (Spain) and TSKA Moscow, which put it in first place while the Israeli club had been helped into second by forfeits by the Soviet and Czechoslovak clubs, which had withdrawn for political reasons. The two finalists had met in the final pool, both games resulting in wins for the Italian club. But a dramatic change took place in the final, as the Israeli club played its best match of the season to win the game and title from the Italians 78–77.

In the Men's Cup-Winners' Cup Birra Forst of Cantù (Italy) retained the trophy by beating BC Radnicki of Belgrade in the final, which took place in Majorca, Spain. In the Women's Cup TTT Daugawa of Riga (U.S.S.R.) won the prize for the 16th time, 79–53, from Clermont Université Club of Clermont-Ferrand (France), which took second

The first basketball game in many years between U.S. and Cuban teams was played in Havana in April. Senator George McGovern of South Dakota accompanied the U.S. team.

place for the fifth time in the past seven years. Spartak of Moscow won the Ronchetti Cup, triumphing easily over Mineur of Pernik (Bulg.) in the final game, 97–54.

Belgium was host for the 20th European championships for men, which took place during September at Ostend and Liège. The 12 teams taking part, after the elimination process had been completed in April, were divided into two groups; one played in Liège and one in Ostend, with the finals being played in Liège. In the games at Ostend, Czechoslovakia finished first, having surprisingly edged the Yugoslavs into second position. Meanwhile, in Liège, Italy played magnificently to defeat the powerful Soviet team and take first place with the U.S.S.R. second. In the semifinals at Liège, Yugoslavia, which had improved with every game, had little trouble beating Italy, which was well below form, and Czechoslovakia was defeated by the U.S.S.R. In the final game the Yugoslavs were unstoppable; at the half they led by 41–27 and at the final whistle by 74–61, to repeat their victory over U.S.S.R. at the previous European championships. Final placings in order were as follows: Yugoslavia, U.S.S.R., Czechoslovakia, Italy, Israel, Bulgaria, The Netherlands, Belgium, Spain, Finland, France, and Austria.

(K. K. MITCHELL)

Belgium

A constitutional monarchy on the North Sea coast of Europe, Belgium is bordered by The Netherlands, West Germany, Luxembourg, and France. Area: 30,514 sq km (11,782 sq mi). Pop. (1977 est.): 9,823,300. Cap. and largest urban area: Brussels (pop., 1977 est., commune 152,800, urban agglomeration 1,042,000). Language: Dutch, French, and

Belgium

German. Religion: predominantly Roman Catholic. King, Baudouin I; prime minister in 1977, Léo Tindemans.

February 1977 proved to be a crucial month for the Tindemans government, in office since 1974. Discussions among a group of 36 parliamentarians to determine future relations between the language communities, which had been running smoothly since their inception in November 1976, were jolted by a series of ultimatums from P.-H. Gendebien, leader of the Rassemblement Wallon (RW), one of the coalition partners. In December 1976 Léo Tindemans had had to reshuffle his government when three RW members rallied to the Walloon Liberals after Gendebien published a left-leaning manifesto.

Meanwhile, the government had been preparing its "Egmont Plan" to cope with the deteriorating economic and financial situation. Its proposals, especially a 0.4% "solidarity levy" on all incomes to meet the rising cost of the unemployment benefits, stirred up strong trade-union reaction, and the Socialist and Social Christian trade unions decided on strike action. When the RW refused to vote for the economic affairs budget, Tindemans first dismissed the two remaining RW ministers and then announced the dissolution of Parliament on March 9.

Elections on April 17 gave the following results: Social Christians 80 (+8); Socialists 62 (+3); Liberals 33 (unchanged); Walloon and Brussels Federalists (RW and Front Démocratique des Francophones [FDF]) 15 (−7); Flemish Federalists (Volksunie) 20 (−2); Communists 2 (−2).

After prolonged negotiations, a four-party coalition government (Social Christian, Socialist, Volksunie, and FDF) with Tindemans as prime minister was sworn in on June 3. Tindemans had been reluctant to lead a new government unless some kind of general agreement between Belgium's language communities could be worked out by the leaders of the coalition parties. Talks started in the Egmont Palace at Brussels on May 24 and, after the new government had received a huge vote of confidence in Parliament on June 9, the so-called Egmont Pact was signed.

According to the pact, matters relating to persons would be dealt with by the so-called community councils. Each of the regions (Flanders, Wallonia, and Brussels) would also have its own elected council and executive. On the other hand, the Senate's powers would be considerably reduced, and most legislative work at the national level would be entrusted to the House of Representatives. "Enrollment rights" would be granted to French-speaking inhabitants now residing in a number of Flemish communes in the Brussels periphery, allowing them to vote in the bilingual urban agglomeration. These new "facilities" drew strong protests from Flemish cultural organizations and lobbies, and this opposition spread. A steering committee was set up to put the agreement into legal texts.

The continuing economic crisis forced the new Tindemans government to examine ways to reduce unemployment and the budget deficit. The Socialist minister of employment, Guy Spitaels, submitted a plan intended to lower the number of jobless by 80,000 without, however, really creating new employment. Older workers would be retired prematurely, and jobless people would be put to work at odd jobs in the public sector.

The steel and textile industries were especially hard hit by foreign competition. Cockerill, a steel giant in Liège, requested government financial aid amounting to BFr 5 million, and many small plants, most of them located in Wallonia, closed down. Friction between the Belgian and Luxembourg governments developed following a decision by Luxembourg owners of a steel plant at Athus, in Luxembourg Province, southeastern Belgium, to reduce production there considerably before a novel "unemployment unit" could be created to take on laid-off workers until new jobs were found. A large number of textile workers in Flanders also lost their jobs.

A major cultural event which drew great crowds was the Rubens quatercentenary exhibition at Antwerp. (*See* ART EXHIBITIONS.)

(JAN R. ENGELS)

BELGIUM

Education. (1975–76) Primary, pupils 955,929, teachers (1967–68) 47,902; secondary, pupils 288,567, teachers (1967–68) 40,074; vocational, pupils 315,510, teachers (1967–68) 47,956; higher, pupils 159,652, teaching staff (universities only; 1973–74) *c.* 5,300.

Finance. Monetary unit: Belgian franc, with (Sept. 19, 1977) a free rate of BFr 35.90 to U.S. $1 (BFr 62.50 = £1 sterling). Gold, SDR's, and foreign exchange (June 1977) U.S. $4,676,000,000. Budget (1976 actual): revenue BFr 665.3 billion; expenditure BFr 798.4 billion. Gross national product (1975) BFr 2,320,000,000,000. Money supply (March 1977) BFr 687.3 billion. Cost of living (1970 = 100; June 1977) 175.

Foreign Trade. (Belgium-Luxembourg economic union; 1976) Imports BFr 1,366,000,000,000; exports BFr 1,265,-000,000,000. Import sources: EEC 68% (West Germany 23%, The Netherlands 17%, France 16%, U.K. 7%); U.S. 6%. Export destinations: EEC 74% (West Germany 23%, France 21%, The Netherlands 17%, U.K. 6%, Italy 5%). Main exports: chemicals 12%; machinery 12%; iron and steel 12%; motor vehicles 11%; food 8%; textile yarns and fabrics 7%; petroleum products 5%. Tourism (1975) gross receipts (Belgium-Luxembourg) U.S. $880 million.

Transport and Communications. Roads (1975) 93,596 km (including 1,018 km expressways). Motor vehicles in use (1975): passenger 2,577,000; commercial 235,000. Railways: (1975) 3,998 km; traffic (1976) 8,203,000,000 passenger-km, freight 6,638,000,000 net ton-km. Air traffic (1976): 3,893,000,000 passenger-km; freight 325,810,000 net ton-km. Navigable inland waterways in regular use (1975) 1,534 km. Shipping (1976): merchant vessels 100 gross tons and over 258; gross tonnage 1,499,431. Shipping traffic (1976): goods loaded 32,863,000 metric tons, unloaded 57,534,000 metric tons. Telephones (Jan. 1976) 2,777,000. Radio licenses (Dec. 1974) 3,769,000. Television licenses (Dec. 1974) 2,464,000.

Agriculture. Production (in 000; metric tons; 1976): wheat 932; barley 641; oats *c.* 145; potatoes *c.* 1,306; tomatoes *c.* 135; apples 227; sugar, raw value *c.* 772; pork *c.* 616; beef and veal *c.* 292; milk *c.* 3,100; fish catch (1975) 49. Livestock (in 000; May 1976): cattle 3,011; pigs 4,765; sheep 86; horses (1975) 53; chickens *c.* 32,000.

Industry. Fuel and power (in 000; 1976): coal (metric tons) 7,237; manufactured gas (cu m; 1975) 2,514,000; electricity (kw-hr) 47,350,000. Production (in 000; metric tons; 1976): pig iron 9,868; crude steel 12,149; copper 456; lead 108; tin 6.1; zinc 240; sulfuric acid 1,890; fertilizers (nutrient content; 1975–76) nitrogenous 610, phosphate 516; cement 7,506; newsprint 85; cotton yarn 54; cotton fabrics (1975) 55; wool yarn 84; woolen fabrics (1975) 30; rayon and acetate yarn and fibres (1975) 13. Merchant vessels launched (100 gross tons and over; 1976) 211,000 gross tons.

Benin

A republic of West Africa, Benin is located north of the Gulf of Guinea and is bounded by Togo, Upper Volta, Niger, and Nigeria. Area: 112,600 sq km (43,475 sq mi). Pop. (1977 est.): 3,249,000, mainly Dahomean and allied tribes. Cap.: Porto-Novo (pop., 1973 est., 97,000). Largest city: Cotonou (pop., 1972 est., 175,000). Language: French and local dialects. Religion: mainly animist, with Christian and Muslim minorities. President in 1977, Lieut. Col. Mathieu Kerekou.

On Jan. 16, 1977, Benin announced the defeat of a group of some 80–100 mercenaries said to have landed at Cotonou airport. It was later claimed that the allegedly European-led soldiers had been recruited in Senegal and the Ivory Coast on behalf of opponents of Pres. Mathieu Kerekou's military regime, including former president Émile Zinsou, who had been overthrown in 1969. Guinea sent a small military contingent to Benin to help restore order. A commission set up by the Benin government and including Guinean and Nigerian representatives reported on February 18 that the mercenaries had been trained in Morocco and transported to Libreville, Gabon, on the eve of the raid. Benin also accused Togo of complicity and on March 14 closed their common frontier, which, however, was reopened a week later after mediation by Nigeria. After considering a complaint by Benin implicating France, Gabon, Ivory Coast, Morocco, and Senegal, the UN Security Council adopted on April 14 a resolution condemning "armed aggression" against Benin but without naming any aggressor. Benin unsuccessfully opposed the choice of Gabon as host in July of the 1977 summit conference of the Organization of African Unity, which it did not attend.

On May 22 President Kerekou outlined plans for a new constitution in accordance with "the socialist option based on Marxism-Leninism." Under this constitution the National Revolutionary Council would be replaced by a National Assembly. (PHILIPPE DECRAENE)

BENIN
Education. (1973–74) Primary, pupils 244,032, teachers 4,708; secondary, pupils 39,744, teachers 1,112; vocational, pupils 854, teachers (1968–69) 102; teacher training, students 170, teachers 5; higher, students 1,911, teaching staff 119.
Finance. Monetary unit: CFA franc, with (Sept. 19, 1977) a parity of CFA Fr 50 to the French franc and a free rate of CFA Fr 246.50 to U.S. $1 (CFA Fr 429.50 = £1 sterling). Budget (1976 est.) balanced at CFA Fr 16,080,000,000.
Foreign Trade. (1974) Imports CFA Fr 35,170,000,000; exports CFA Fr 8,190,000,000. Import sources (1973): France 36%; West Germany 7%; China 7%; U.K. 5%; The Netherlands 5%; U.S. 5%. Export destinations (1973): France 36%; West Germany 12%; The Netherlands 10%; Italy 6%; Japan 5%. Main exports (1972): cotton 28%; cocoa 19%; palm products 17%; cottonseed 5%; coffee 5%.
Agriculture. Production (in 000; metric tons; 1976): sorghum 57; corn (1975) c. 310; cassava (1975) c. 750; yams (1975) c. 610; dry beans 15; peanuts 46; palm kernels c. 85; palm oil c. 35; coffee (1975) c. 2.7; cotton, lint c. 15; fish catch (1975) c. 29. Livestock (in 000; 1975): sheep c. 820; cattle c. 760; goats c. 820; pigs c. 358.

Bhutan

A monarchy situated in the eastern Himalayas, Bhutan is bounded by China and India. Area: 46,100 sq km (17,800 sq mi). Pop. (1977 est.): 1,232,000. Official cap.: Thimphu (pop., approximately 10,000). Administrative cap.: Paro (population unavailable). Language: Dzongkha (official). Religion: approximately 75% Buddhist, 25% Hindu. Druk gyalpo (king) in 1977, Jigme Singye Wangchuk.

A World Bank economic atlas published in January 1977 estimated the per capita gross national product of Bhutan in 1975 as the lowest in the world. During 1976–77 the government continued its struggle to better the nation's standard of living; among other measures it set up the Food Corporation of Bhutan to channel essential foodstuffs to the public through government-controlled retail stores and the granting of loans on easy terms to farmers.

India's aid contribution of Rs 120 million for the period was being utilized to improve irrigation facilities and boost Bhutan's power supply. The National Assembly decided to levy minimum taxes on farmers, civil servants, and businessmen to recover at least part (an estimated 15%) of the 10.9 million ngultrum spent yearly on health services.

In April King Jigme Singye Wangchuk visited New Delhi, where the leaders of the new Janata government reassured him that India's generous help would continue. The king said his visit had reaffirmed the "unique links of friendship and brotherhood" between the two countries.

The strategic northern borders with China remained calm, with no troop movements on either side. (GOVINDAN UNNY)

Benin

Bhutan

BHUTAN
Education. (1976–77) Primary, pupils 16,671, teachers 382; secondary, pupils 981, teachers 300; vocational, pupils 463, teachers 28; teacher training, pupils 79, teachers 20; higher, pupils 275, teaching staff 25.
Finance and Trade. Monetary unit: ngultrum, at par with the Indian rupee (which is also in use), with (Sept. 19, 1977) a free rate of 8.69 ngultrum to U.S. $1 (15.13 ngultrum = £1 sterling). Budget (1974–75): revenue 25 million ngultrum; expenditure 48 million ngultrum. Virtually all external trade is with India. Main exports: timber, coal, fruit and fruit products, alcoholic spirits.

Billiard Games

Billiards. The American Billiard Association (ABA) held its Classic Three-Cushion Championship during February in Oak Park, Mich. All who participated first qualified through ABA competitions during the preceding 12 months. Allen Gilbert of North Hollywood, Calif., who had five wins and no losses on the first day, clinched the title the following day when he dropped just one match to George Ashly, who finished second. The highlight of the Classic was a run of 19 clean billiards by Bill Hawkins, who surpassed the ABA

Bermuda:
see Dependent States

Bicycling:
see Cycling

Tom Jennings successfully defended his U.S. Open billiards title with a come-from-behind victory in the finals during which he won seven straight matches.

tournament record of 17 set by Luis Campos in 1970.

Pocket Billiards. The 12th U.S. Open pocket billiards championships, sponsored by the Billiard Congress of America (BCA), were held in Dayton, Ohio, in September 1977. More than half of the 16 men and 8 women finalists had learned the game in high school or college. Tom Jennings from Edison, N.J., had an indifferent year and seemed a poor bet to retain his title. After losing the first game of the finals 135–150 to Tom Kollins, he needed six victories without a loss to reach the title match. After outscoring Tom Reid 150–38, he defeated former champion Dallas West 150–78, Scott Kitto 150–62, and Bill Stigall 150–120. Jennings got two more vital victories by twice outshooting former champion Joe Balsis, 150–54 and 150–43. In the 200-point championship match against Dick Lane from Dallas, Texas, Jennings was tired and lost his touch. When the score stood at 197–42, Lane lined up a break shot and prepared to sink the last four balls as fans moved toward the exits. But Lane missed and Jennings was still alive. In a 2½-hour string of spectacular shots, runs, and near perfect safeties, Jennings sank 158 balls and won the title 200–196 in 35 innings. He collected $5,000 and was given the table used in the championship.

In the women's competition, Jean Balukas from Brooklyn, N.Y., had no such problems in breaking former champion Dorothy Wise's record of five consecutive titles. Balukas, who recently graduated from high school, won her sixth straight championship by vanquishing Belinda Campos, Vicki Frechen, and Gloria Walker in straight matches. In the process she set a dozen women's records, including a new high run of 51, a best-game record of three innings, and a balls-per-inning average of 4.71. For her victory she received $1,000 and a billiard table. The Open was followed by the first national Eight-Ball Tournament, which featured 71 finalists chosen from almost 3,000 who attempted to qualify throughout the U.S. and Canada. In the final match, "a race to seven," Tom Kilburn from South Bend, Ind., defeated Dick Spitzer from Rapid City, S.D., by a score of 7–5 and was given a billiard table of his choice.

The Professional Pool Players Association held its second annual World Open tournament in August in Asbury Park, N.J. The men played in two divisions, each of which produced a winner after double-elimination competitions. In the final match, Allen Hopkins from Cranford, N.J., defeated Pete Margo from Staten Island, N.Y., 200–55 in 14 innings to win the championship and laid claim to the $15,000 first-place prize. Women also played in Convention Hall for the first women's World Open title. Jean Balukas continued to dominate her competition by defeating Gloria Walker 100–57. Larry Lisciotti, the 1976 World Open winner, and Tom Jennings, the BCA champion, met in Green Brook, N.J., in a $10,000 Challenge of Champions.

Jean Balukas, a recent high school graduate, won her sixth straight U.S. Open championship, breaking the record set by Dorothy Wise.

The rules called for play to end on the first day when one player reached 200 points. The next day each player started with his previous total and played until one of them reached 400. This 200-point catch-up system was followed throughout the five-day tournament. On the last night Lisciotti ran his total to 999 with a run of 125 before he missed. Jennings' score stood at 713 when he moved to the table, but the best he could do was 57 balls. Lisciotti then dropped the seven ball into a side pocket and won the duel 1,000 to 770.

Snooker. The world professional snooker championship was held in England during May. Eight of the 25 players who participated were seeded, with all others competing for a place in the final field of 16. Cliff Thorburn, the unseeded Canadian champion, quickly served notice that he was a serious contender when he narrowly defeated Australian champion Eddie Charlton 13–12. He advanced through the next round by upsetting world champion Ray Readon of England 13–6. After victories over English amateur champion Chris Ross and Dennis Taylor, also of England, Thorburn became the first Canadian ever to reach the final of the world snooker championship. His opponent was two-time winner John Spencer of England. Thorburn took a 15–13 lead before he began to falter. After the match was tied, he rallied briefly, but finally lost 21–25. Spencer won $11,000 along with another world title. Though snooker is growing in popularity in the U.S., Canada is producing world class players of superior quality in far greater abundance. Bill Werbeniuk, the North American champion, for example, defeated Thor-

burn earlier in the year but was unable to attend the three-week-long world championship in May.

(ROBERT E. GOODWIN)

[452.B.4.h.v]

Bolivia

Bolivia

A landlocked republic in central South America, Bolivia is bordered by Brazil, Paraguay, Argentina, Chile, and Peru. Area: 1,098,581 sq km (424,165 sq mi). Pop. (1976): 4,687,700, of whom more than 50% were Indian. Language: Spanish, Quechua, Aymara. Religion (1975 est.): Roman Catholic 94.2%. Judicial cap.: Sucre (pop., 1976 est., 90,000). Administrative cap. and largest city: La Paz (pop., 1976 est., 800,000). President in 1977, Col. Hugo Banzer Suárez.

In August 1977 Pres. Hugo Banzer Suárez' military regime completed six years in office, giving Bolivia an appearance of stability and implying a great deal of political expertise on the part of the president, in view of the country's turbulent history of coups d'etat. During 1977 the authorities suppressed political, industrial, and student unrest, as well as disquiet generated among the armed forces as a result of the stalemate in negotiations on access to the sea. In December the government announced that there had been a coup attempt by unidentified civilians and military officers but that it had been put down without difficulty. The regime remained publicly committed to a return to some sort of democratic political system. On November 9 Banzer announced that Bolivia would return to constitutional democracy in 1978, and on December 1 he set July 9, 1978, as the date for election of a president, vice-president, and members of a constituent assembly. Banzer said he would not be a candidate for the presidency and that this decision was "irrevocable."

In foreign affairs the government's priority continued to be the attainment of access to the sea. Banzer had accepted Chile's offer made at the end of 1975 of an exchange of territory, but both Bolivia and Chile rejected the Peruvian counterproposal for a tripartite sovereignty over the port of Arica and Bolivia's corridor to the sea. Banzer and nationalist segments of the armed forces were becoming restive over the long delays in negotiations; in January 1976 the three heads of the armed services had been replaced by men more faithful to Banzer. After Banzer's visit to Brazil in August, he won tacit Brazilian support for his sea access aspirations. Bolivia was to export 240 million cu ft of gas a day to Brazil in exchange for aid in developing an iron and steel industry and building railways and roads.

After the March 1976 coup in Argentina, relations improved between that country and Bolivia. Argentina planned to expand its natural-gas imports to 220 million cu ft by 1979 under the 20-year contract of 1972. Argentina was also to participate in a joint venture with Bolivia and Colombia to produce pesticides from 1979 in Bolivia.

Bolivia's popularity among international lending agencies and banks remained high. In July the World Bank agreed to arrange up to 90% of the

BOLIVIA

Education. (1975) Primary, pupils 912,998, teachers 39,835; secondary, pupils 124,092, teachers 8,044; vocational, pupils 37,498, teachers 718; teacher training (1973), students 5,896, teachers 314; higher (at 9 universities only; 1974), students 34,030, teaching staff 2,270.

Finance. Monetary unit: peso boliviano, with (Sept. 19, 1977) an official rate of 20 pesos to U.S. $1 (free rate of 34.84 pesos = £1 sterling). Gold, SDR's, and foreign exchange (April 1977) U.S. $179.5 million. Budget (1975 est.): revenue 5,689,000,000 pesos; expenditure 6,293,000,000 pesos. Gross national product (1975) 42,451,000,000 pesos. Money supply (April 1977) 6,610,000,000 pesos. Cost of living (La Paz; 1970 = 100; May 1977) 277.

Foreign Trade. Imports (1975) U.S. $558 million; exports (1976) U.S. $513 million. Import sources: U.S. 25%; Japan 16%; Argentina 14%; Brazil 14%; West Germany 8%. Export destinations (1975): U.S. 31%; Argentina 25%; U.K. 11%. Main exports: tin 44%; crude oil 22%; natural gas 11%; zinc 8%; tungsten 7%; antimony 6%; silver 5%.

Transport and Communications. Roads (1974) 37,313 km. Motor vehicles in use (1974): passenger 29,600; commercial (including buses) 33,000. Railways: (1975) 3,676 km; traffic (1973) 270 million passenger-km, freight 365 million net ton-km. Air traffic (1976): 444 million passenger-km; freight 4.3 million net ton-km. Telephones (Jan. 1974) 49,000. Radio receivers (Dec. 1974) 425,000. Television receivers (Dec. 1975) c. 45,000.

Agriculture. Production (in 000; metric tons; 1976): barley c. 80; rice (1975) 119; corn (1975) c. 330; wheat (1975) c. 65; cassava (1975) c. 286; potatoes c. 876; bananas c. 282; sugar, raw value (1975) 225; coffee c. 16; cotton, lint 15; rubber c. 3. Livestock (in 000; Oct. 1974): cattle 2,420; sheep 7,694; goats 2,804; pigs 1,158; horses c. 345; asses c. 707.

Industry. Production (in 000; metric tons; 1975): cement 226; crude oil (1976) 1,964; electricity (kw-hr; 1974) 967,000; gold (troy oz; 1974) 42; tin 30; lead 16; antimony 14; tungsten (oxide content) c. 2; zinc 46; copper 5.9; silver 0.2.

financing for investments of $2,260,000,000 under the 1976–80 national development plan. The country's overall balance of payments surplus of $9 million in 1976 compared favourably with the deficit of $50 million in 1975. As a result of the increase in exports, the curtailment of imports, and foreign investors' confidence, reserves rose from $115 million at the end of 1975 to $171 million at the end of 1976. Internal investment in 1976 totaled $1.2 billion, 80% of which was raised locally.

The growth of the economy owed much to the government's foreign-exchange and fiscal policies. The hardening of prices in 1977 for major export items, the increased internal investment, and the full program up to 1980 implied a continuing growth cycle; the consequent confidence of investors was expected to enable the government to finance its program. Newly discovered reserves of gas and hydrocarbons and minerals provided additional economic stimulation.

(MICHAEL WOOLLER)

Botswana

Botswana

A landlocked republic of southern Africa and a member of the Commonwealth of Nations, Botswana is bounded by South Africa, South West Africa, Zambia, and Rhodesia. Area: 576,000 sq km (222,000 sq mi). Pop. (1976 est.): 718,000, almost 99% African. Cap. and largest city: Gaborone (pop., 1976 est., 36,900). Language: English (official) and Setswana. Religion: Christian 60%; animist. President in 1977, Sir Seretse Khama.

Botswana's entanglement in Rhodesian affairs increased in 1977 when Joshua Nkomo's Zimbabwe African People's Union forces in southwest Rhodesia spilled over the border. In January 400 black Rhodesian children from the Manama Swedish Evangelical mission school crossed the border into Botswana. The Rhodesian government claimed that the children had been abducted by insurgents, but Botswana maintained that they had crossed the border voluntarily. Botswana later let the children be transferred to insurgent camps in Zambia. In March Botswana called for $56.6 million in international aid to expand its police force in order to form a paramilitary border patrol, to support refugee camps, and to develop a standard

> **BOTSWANA**
> **Education.** (1976) Primary, pupils 125,588, teachers 3,-921; secondary, pupils 13,991, teachers 599; vocational, pupils 1,722, teachers 207; teacher training, students 562, teachers 51; higher, students 465, teaching staff 56.
> **Finance and Trade.** Monetary unit: pula, with (Sept. 19, 1977) an official rate of 0.83 pula to U.S. $1 (free rate of 1.44 pula = £1 sterling). Budget (1975–76 est.): revenue 79,315,000 pula; expenditure 73,274,000 pula. Foreign trade (1975): imports 153.3 million pula (65% from South Africa in 1966); exports 98.5 million pula (18% to South Africa in 1966). Main exports: mineral products (mainly diamonds) 49%; meat and products 36%.
> **Agriculture.** Production (in 000; metric tons; 1975): sorghum c. 30; corn c. 10; millet c. 4; peanuts c. 6. Livestock (in 000; 1975): cattle c. 2,300; sheep c. 420; goats c. 1,000; chickens c. 530.
> **Industry.** Production (in 000; 1974): diamonds 2,718 metric carats; coal (1975) 69 metric tons; electricity 237,-000 kw-hr.

rail link in order to relieve Botswana's dependence upon the Rhodesian railway for exporting its beef, nickel, and diamonds. In May the UN Security Council approved a loan of $53 million. The first road link with Zambia, 300 km (190 mi) roughly parallel with the Rhodesian border, was opened in January.

The 1977 budget estimated expenditures at 73.3 million pula and revenue at 94.2 million pula, an increase of 26 million pula over 1976. The currency was devalued by 5% against the U.S. dollar on April 30 to counteract inflation and an unfavourable balance of trade. During the past five years mining investment for diamonds, nickel, copper, and coal deposits had increased the gross national product by an average of 10% annually and, because the annual population growth was only 2–3%, had thereby raised the standard of living.

(MOLLY MORTIMER)

Bowling

Tenpin Bowling. WORLD. The Fédération Internationale des Quilleurs (FIQ), governing body of pin bowling sports, held its Silver Jubilee Congress in 1977, in Helsinki, Fin. Frank K. Baker of Milwaukee, Wis., was elected president to succeed Kauko Ahlström of Helsinki. Delegates adopted the Eligibility Code of the International Olympic Committee and decided to continue pressing for recognition of tenpin bowling as an Olympic sport.

The fifth European tenpin bowling championships were held in Helsinki in June. The men's division was made up of 143 bowlers from 17 countries and the women's division of 84 women from

One of the year's biggest bowling money winners was Tommy Hudson of Akron, Ohio, who emerged as a contender for Bowler of the Year honours.

13 countries. On the newly resurfaced lanes of the superb Tali Bowling Arena, 19 of 26 records were bettered. Juan Guisasola (Spain) and Ove Jonasson (Sweden) each rolled a one-game men's record of 278; Göran Bergendorff (Sweden) rolled the high three-game series with 694; Bernard Pujol (France) bowled the six-game mark with 1,292 and the 28-game of all-events with 5,766. Among women, Pieternella Tel (Neth.) scored a game of 270; Lea Hilokoski (Fin.) bowled 1,251 for her six games and 4,755 for her 24 games all-events. Other results: in men's teams of eight, Sweden scored 12,-769, followed by West Germany with 12,651; in men's doubles, Norway tallied 2,490, followed by Norway's second and third doubles with 2,444 and 2,435; in men's teams of five, France bowled 5,950, followed by Sweden with 5,949; in men's individual all-events, Pujol scored 5,766, followed by Norbert Griesert (West Germany) with 5,732 and Mats Karlsson (Sweden) with 5,700; in women's teams of six, West Germany tallied 6,688, followed by Belgium with 6,514; in women's doubles, Finland's 2,398 topped West Germany's 2,298; in women's teams of five, West Germany scored 5,708, followed by Sweden with 5,559; in women's individual all-events, Hilokoski bowled 4,755, followed by Pauline Bowry (Great Britain) with 4,676.

Ten countries were represented at the fourth Asian tenpin bowling championships held in Jakarta, Indon., in August 1976. In the men's teams of eight, Japan bowled 12,116, followed by Thailand with 12,077; in men's doubles, the Philippines tallied 2,344, followed by Japan with 2,338; in men's teams of five, Thailand scored 5,812, followed by Japan with 5,669; in men's individual all-events, R. Nepomuceno (Phil.) bowled 5,764, followed by K. Saitoh (Japan) with 5,561; in women's teams of six, the Philippines scored 6,755, followed by Singapore with 6,396; in women's doubles, the Philippines garnered 2,270, followed by Australia with 2,231; in women's teams of five, Japan tallied 5,572, followed by Australia with 5,485; in women's individual all-events, N. Castillo (Phil.) bowled 4,518, followed by Bong Coo (Phil.) with 4,513.

(YRJÖ SARAHETE)

UNITED STATES. The growing worldwide interest in tenpins was reflected in the annual Women's International Bowling Congress (WIBC) tournament held in Milwaukee, Wis., when Akiko Yamaga of Tokyo became the first foreign entrant to win a championship. Yamaga bowled 714 to win the Open Division singles title and captured the all-events honours by adding 594 in doubles and 587 in team scoring for a total of 1,895. During the year WIBC membership reached 4 million for the first time. In the WIBC Open Division competition, the team title went to Allgauer's Fireside Restaurant of Chicago with 2,818 and the doubles crown to Ozella Houston and Dorothy Jackson of Detroit with 1,234. The Division I team championship was won by the Sunbeam Girls of Birmingham, Ala., with 2,670; the doubles title was won by Viola Coombs and Jackie Headrick of Tempe, Ariz., with 1,175. Edna Ruth of Belpre, Ohio, won the singles championship with 644. Marlene Willett of

COURTESY, WOMEN'S INTERNATIONAL BOWLING CONGRESS

The first bowler from outside the U.S. to win a championship in the Women's International Bowling Congress tournament was Akiko Yamaga of Tokyo who was the winner in the Open Division singles competition.

Marietta, Ga., and Pat Booth of Memphis, Tenn., shared the all-events title with 1,739.

In men's professional bowling, the three-year reign of Earl Anthony from Tacoma, Wash., appeared to have ended as Mark Roth of New York City and Tommy Hudson of Akron, Ohio, emerged as chief contenders for the 1977 Bowler of the Year title. With only a few regional Professional Bowlers Association (PBA) tournaments remaining, Roth shared the PBA national doubles crown with Marshall Holman of Medford, Ore., and had three California tournament victories to his credit. Roth also led the PBA in total earnings with $105,-583. Hudson finished first in the PBA national at Seattle, Wash., and was first in Windsor Locks, Conn., and in Springfield, Va. Hudson's prize money amounted to $89,393. Anthony, who won $72,690, took PBA titles in Torrance, Calif., and Waukegan, Ill. In the 74th annual American Bowling Congress tournament held in Reno, Nev., the winners in the Classic Division were: team, Columbia Bowling Balls of San Antonio, Texas, with 3,122; doubles, Frank Werman and Randy Neal of Los Angeles, who tied with Kevin Gannon of Long Beach, Calif., and Don Bell of Santa María, Calif., each team scoring 1,337; singles, Mickey Higham of Kansas City, Mo., with 801; all-events, Dick Ritger of River Falls, Wis., with 1,964. In Regular Division play the winners were: team, Rendel's GMC of Joliet, Ill., with 3,075; doubles, Bob and Walt Roy of Glenwood Spring, Colo., with 1,318; singles, Frank Gadaleto of Lansing, Mich., with 738; all-events, Charles (Bud) Debenham of Los Angeles with 2,117.

Duckpins. In the 1977 national duckpin tournament, the winners in the men's competition were: team, Lambis 5 of Silver Spring, Md., 2,330; doubles, John Garrison and Al Hauser of Hamden,

Conn., 1,042; singles, Dick Najarian of Cheshire, Conn., 604. In women's events, the results were: team, Craan T.V. of Baltimore, Md., 2,080; doubles, Denise Przybyz and JoAnn Russell of Baltimore, 882; and singles, Linda Rosen of Salisbury, Md., 526. The mixed team title was won by Sea Cove No. 2 of Kannapolis, N.C., with 2,205.

(JOHN J. ARCHIBALD)

Lawn Bowls. The women's world championships in 1977 were staged at Worthing, England, by the English Women's Bowling Association (EWBA). After the EWBA yielded to pressure and withdrew its invitation to South Africa, the International Women's Bowling Board (IWBB) passed a new rule requiring host countries for world championships to invite all member countries of the IWBB, irrespective of their governments' policies. Dorothy Ellis (England) became president of the IWBB. In play, Elsie Wilkie (New Zealand), after losing three of her first five singles, retained the title she won in 1973; Helen Wong and Elvie Chok (Hong Kong) won the pairs; Joan Osborn, Margot Pomeroy, and Enid Morgan (Wales), the triples; and Lorna Lucas, Connie Hicks, Merl Richardson, and Dot Jenkinson (Australia) the fours. The overall winning country was Australia.

Teams from Australia, England, Rhodesia, Scotland, South Africa, and Wales took part in the first-ever Blind Bowlers Games, held in Johannesburg, South Africa. The gold medal for singles went to Bob Farmer (Australia).   (C. M. JONES)

Elsie Wilkie of New Zealand retained her world lawn bowls championship at Worthing, England.

Brazil

A federal republic in eastern South America, Brazil is bounded by the Atlantic Ocean and all the countries of South America except Ecuador and Chile. Area: 8,512,000 sq km (3,286,500 sq mi). Pop. (1976 est.): 109,181,000. Principal cities (pop., 1975 est.): Brasília (cap.; federal district) 763,300; São Paulo 7,198,600; Rio de Janeiro 4,857,700. Language: Portuguese. Religion: Roman Catholic 89%. President in 1977, Gen. Ernesto Geisel.

Domestic Affairs. The political situation continued uncertain under the regime imposed by the military leaders of the 1964 revolution. Pres. Ernesto Geisel repeatedly expressed his intention of returning the country to some sort of democracy, inviting the leaders of both legally recognized parties to assist him in what he called the "perfecting" of the national political institutions. However, the leaders of the opposition party, the Brazilian Democratic Movement (MDB), insisted that so long as the Institutional Act number 5 (AI-5) and other emergency measures remained in force there could be no real democracy. The AI-5 authorizes the president to cancel the mandate of any elected or appointed government official and to annul his political rights for ten years. Since the enactment of Institutional Act number 5 in December 1968 more than 260 federal and state officials, and three former presidents of the republic, were said to have lost their political rights.

Both parties had considered the municipal elections of Nov. 15, 1976, of crucial importance and engaged in active political propaganda. President

Brazil

Boxing:
see Combat Sports

BRAZIL

Education. (1974) Primary, pupils 15,837,283, teachers (1972) 525,628; secondary, pupils 4,077,506, teachers (1972) 266,328; vocational, students 782,827, teachers (1972) 67,468; teacher training, students 270,723, teachers (1972) 37,468; higher, students (1973) 668,857, teaching staff 64,479.

Finance. Monetary unit: cruzeiro, with a free rate (Sept. 19, 1977) of 14.98 cruzeiros to U.S. $1 (26.09 cruzeiros = £1 sterling). Gold, SDR's, and foreign exchange (Feb. 1977) U.S. $5,690,000,000. Budget (1976 actual): revenue 166,220,000,000 cruzeiros; expenditure 165,795,-000,000 cruzeiros. Gross domestic product (1975) 895.9 billion cruzeiros. Money supply (March 1977) 235,-340,000,000 cruzeiros. *Cost of living (São Paulo; 1970 = 100; May 1977) 348.

Foreign Trade. (1976) Imports U.S. $13,623,000,000; exports U.S. $10,130,000,000. Import sources: U.S. 23%; Saudi Arabia 9%; Iraq 9%; West Germany 8%; Japan 7%. Export destinations: U.S. 18%; West Germany 9%; The Netherlands 7%; Japan 6%. Main exports (1975): sugar 13%; coffee 11%; iron ore 11%; soybeans 8%; machinery 7%; animal fodder 6%.

Transport and Communications. Roads (1975) 1,397,-386 km. Motor vehicles in use (1975): passenger 5,118,000; commercial 635,000. Railways: (1975) 33,000 km; traffic (1973) 10,603,000,000 passenger-km, freight 42,698,-000,000 net ton-km. Air traffic (1976): 10,364,000,000 passenger-km; freight 478 million net ton-km. Shipping (1976): merchant vessels 100 gross tons and over 520; gross tonnage 3,096,293. Shipping traffic (1976): goods loaded 89,687,000 metric tons, unloaded 61,312,000 metric tons. Telephones (Jan. 1976) 3,371,000. Radio receivers (Dec. 1974) 6,275,000. Television receivers (Dec. 1974) 8,650,000.

Agriculture. Production (in 000; metric tons; 1976): wheat c. 3,200; corn 17,929; rice 9,560; cassava (1975) 27,207; potatoes c. 1,811; sweet potatoes (1975) c. 1,700; peanuts 514; sugar, raw value c. 7,200; dry beans 2,085; soybeans 11,227; coffee c. 400; cocoa c. 233; bananas c. 7,526; oranges 7,286; cotton, lint 403; sisal c. 190; tobacco c. 304; rubber c. 20; timber (cu m; 1975) 164,000; beef and veal 2,220; pork c. 765; fish catch (1975) c. 674. Livestock (in 000; Dec. 1975): cattle c. 94,802; pigs c. 35,636; sheep c. 27,137; goats c. 16,200; horses (1974) c. 9,500; chickens c. 280,445.

Industry. Fuel and power (in 000; metric tons; 1976): crude oil 8,470; coal (1975) 2,710; natural gas (cu m) c. 1,600,000; electricity (kw-hr; 1975) 78,070,000 (95% hydroelectric in 1974). Production (in 000; metric tons; 1976): pig iron 8,170; crude steel 9,090; iron ore (68% metal content; 1976) 66,645; bauxite (1975) 1,280; manganese ore (1975) 2,828; gold (troy oz) 300; cement 17,-873; asbestos (1973) 819; wood pulp (1974) 1,311; paper (1974) 1,854; passenger cars (including assembly; units) 556; commercial vehicles (including assembly; units) 416. Merchant vessels launched (100 gross tons and over; 1976) 407,000 gross tons.

Geisel himself joined the leaders of the government-sponsored party, the National Renewal Alliance (ARENA), in intensive campaigning throughout the country. Encouraged by its unexpected victory in the congressional and state assembly elections of 1974, the MDB declared that the 1976 elections would be considered as a plebiscite regarding the merits of the regime established by the revolution. The results of the elections appeared to have been mostly favourable to the government party, which won a majority in 70% of the municipalities. The MDB, however, increased the number of its members who were elected mayors and aldermen, mostly in the large cities.

After the municipal elections both parties renewed their political activity in preparation for the congressional and gubernatorial elections scheduled for Nov. 15, 1978. The MDB hoped to win a substantial majority in both houses of Congress, which would permit it to abrogate the emer-

UPI COMPIX

Slum dwellers had to be evacuated from their homes in Rio de Janeiro when a 10,000-ton boulder threatened to tumble down a mountain.

gency measures, amend the 1967 constitution, and even to elect the next president and vice-president. Under the current system, the president and the vice-president were elected by an electoral college composed of all the members of the Congress and a number of delegates selected by the state assemblies.

At the end of 1976 and early in 1977 a new source of political friction arose. A project was submitted by the president to the Congress for reforming the judiciary system. The proposal included 53 constitutional amendments, but because it did not restore habeas corpus or abrogate the AI-5, the MDB refused to cooperate in passing it. A constitutional amendment had to be approved by a two-thirds majority in two successive sessions of Congress to become law.

As a consequence of the failure to pass the law, President Geisel dismissed Congress on April 1, declaring it in recess. During the following days, under the authority granted him by article 182 of the constitution, the president decreed laws that amended the constitution to include the proposed reform of the judiciary. The decrees also provided for the indirect election of state governors and one-third of the federal senators; extended the presidential term of office to six years; kept in force the

so-called *Lei Falcão*, which restricts political propaganda over radio and television; provided that the number of members of the Chamber of Deputies would henceforth be based on the total population of the states instead of the number of their registered voters; stipulated that an absolute majority of the members of the Congress would be sufficient to approve any constitutional amendment; and scheduled the next presidential election for Oct. 15, 1978, instead of Jan. 15, 1979.

Congress reopened on April 15. As a result of attacks in Congress against the administration, two deputies lost their mandates when the government invoked AI-5. There were strikes in several cities in protest against the new government policies.

The Economy. Brazil's economy remained in critical condition, in large measure because of the worldwide crisis precipitated by the increase in oil prices. The country's imports of oil reached $4 billion a year. As a result, the trade deficit rose to an unprecedented level ($6 billion at the end of 1976), as did the foreign debt (estimated at $27 billion). Inflation, which had been considered under control by 1974, reached an annual rate of 30% in 1975 and was up to 45% at the end of 1976.

Concern was expressed in international financial

UPI COMPIX

The bust of former U.S. president John F. Kennedy was blindfolded and gagged by students in Rio de Janeiro who were protesting repressive policies of the Brazilian government.

circles over Brazil's rapidly increasing foreign debt. As a consequence, President Geisel decided to scrap a number of important internal development programs; to cut imports; to reduce foreign travel by Brazilian citizens; and to increase exports. By the middle of 1977 the value of imports and exports seemed to be even, and the government turned its attention to the struggle against inflation. The prices of certain commodities were frozen, and government expenditures were greatly reduced.

Foreign Affairs. Relations with the United States remained strained because of the repression of the political opposition and the determination of Brazil to go ahead with its nuclear development program. The visit by the wife of U.S. Pres. Jimmy Carter to Brazil (June 6–8) and the assurance by the U.S. that the 1975 memorandum of understanding between the two countries was considered in force helped to dispel, to some extent, the antagonism of Brazilians toward the U.S. In November the Carter administration announced that it had approved the export of 54 tons of low-enriched uranium for use in the new nuclear power station at Agra dos Reis. Later in the month, however, U.S. Secretary of State Cyrus Vance, during a visit to Brazil, warned that future transfers of nuclear fuel and technology from the U.S. might be endangered if Brazil pursued its plans to recover plutonium by reprocessing spent fuel.　　　　(RAUL D'EÇA)

Bulgaria

A people's republic of Europe, Bulgaria is situated on the eastern Balkan Peninsula along the Black Sea, bordered by Romania, Yugoslavia, Greece, and Turkey. Area: 110,912 sq km (42,823 sq mi). Pop. (1975) 8,729,700. Cap. and largest city: Sofia (pop., 1975, 965,700). Language: chiefly Bulgarian. First secretary of the Bulgarian Communist Party and chairman of the State Council in 1977, Todor Zhivkov; chairman of the Council of Ministers (premier), Stanko Todorov.

Bulgaria

Brazilian Literature:
see Literature

Bridge:
see Contract Bridge

An exchange of views on Soviet-Bulgarian cooperation had been held in Moscow on Dec. 2, 1976, between the Soviet leader Leonid I. Brezhnev and Todor Zhivkov. Another meeting between the two leaders took place in the Crimea on Aug. 9, 1977, when they expressed confidence that "despite . . . certain imperialist circles which are counting on an intensified arms race, the process of relaxation of international tensions will continue. . . ."

On April 13 Stanko Todorov presented to the National Assembly a report on the status of the current five-year plan (1976–80). In 1976 industrial production rose by 7.9% over the previous year; agriculture accounted for 20% of gross national product and 35% of exports. In the same year Bulgaria's imports from the Soviet Union amounted to 2,227,000,000 rubles (about 54% of the total) and its exports to that country to 2,189,000,000 rubles. By the end of 1976 Bulgaria's outstanding international hard currency debt stood at about $2 billion. Todorov said that the earthquake of March 4, 1977, in the Danubian area, which caused the deaths of an estimated 130 people, had resulted in material losses totaling 200 million leva.

On May 12 Boris Velchev was relieved of his membership in the Politburo and in the Central

BULGARIA

Education. (1975–76) Primary and secondary, pupils 1,098,889, teachers 56,082; vocational, pupils 286,995, teachers 19,408; teacher training, students 19,779, teachers 982; higher (including 3 universities), students 106,055, teaching staff 11,248.

Finance. Monetary unit: lev, with a commercial exchange rate of 0.97 lev to U.S. $1 (free rate of 1.63 lev = £1 sterling). Budget (1975 est.): revenue 9,157,000,000 leva; expenditure 9,139,000,000 leva.

Foreign Trade. (1976) Imports 5,436,000,000 leva; exports 5.2 billion leva. Main import sources (1975): U.S.S.R. 51%; West Germany 8%; East Germany 7%; Poland 5%. Main export destinations (1975): U.S.S.R. 55%; East Germany 7%; Czechoslovakia 5%. Main exports (1974): machinery 30%; tobacco and cigarettes 11%; transport equipment 9%; fruit and vegetables 8%; nonferrous metals 6%; chemicals 6%; iron and steel 6%; wines and spirits 5%. Tourism: visitors (1975) 4,049,000; gross receipts (1974) U.S. $198 million.

Transport and Communications. Roads (1975) 36,161 km. Motor vehicles in use (1975): passenger c. 198,000; commercial (including buses) c. 43,000. Railways: (1975) 4,290 km; traffic (1976) 7,500,000,000 passenger-km, freight 17,055,000,000 net ton-km. Air traffic (1975): 398 million passenger-km; freight 7 million net ton-km. Navigable inland waterways (1973) 471 km. Shipping (1976): merchant vessels 100 gross tons and over 176; gross tonnage 933,361. Telephones (Jan. 1976) 777,000. Radio licenses (Dec. 1974) 2,273,000. Television licenses (Dec. 1974) 1,457,000.

Agriculture. Production (in 000; metric tons; 1976): wheat c. 3,100; corn c. 2,900; barley c. 1,800; potatoes c. 319; sunflower seed c. 451; tomatoes c. 768; grapes c. 1,120; apples c. 369; tobacco c. 162; meat c. 568. Livestock (in 000; Jan. 1976): sheep 10,014; cattle 1,656; goats 321; pigs 3,889; horses (1975) 137; asses (1975) 317; chickens 35,891.

Industry. Fuel and power (in 000; metric tons; 1976): lignite 25,173; coal 288; crude oil 120; natural gas (cu m; 1974) 180,000; electricity (kw-hr) 27,741,000. Production (in 000; metric tons; 1976): iron ore (33% metal content) 2,320; manganese ore (metal content; 1974) 9.6; copper ore (metal content; 1975) 55; lead ore (metal content; 1975) 110; zinc ore (1974) 80; pig iron 1,581; crude steel 2,459; cement 4,362; sulfuric acid 852; soda ash (1975) 1,009; cotton yarn 78; cotton fabrics (m) 361,000; wool yarn 33; woolen fabrics (m) 34,000. Merchant vessels launched (100 gross tons and over; 1976) 133,000 gross tons.

Committee, including his post as secretary of the latter body, which he had held since 1959; he had been a member of the Politburo since 1962.

On September 14 in Sofia, during his state visit, Erich Honecker, East German head of state, signed with Zhivkov a treaty of alliance between the German Democratic Republic and Bulgaria.

(K. M. SMOGORZEWSKI)

Burma

A republic of Southeast Asia, Burma is bordered by Bangladesh, India, China, Laos, Thailand, the Bay of Bengal, and the Andaman Sea. Area: 676,577 sq km (261,288 sq mi). Pop. (1977 est.): 32,762,000. Cap. and largest city: Rangoon (pop., 1973, 2.1 million). Language: Burmese. Religion (1977): Buddhist 80%. Chairman of the State Council in 1977, U Ne Win; prime ministers, U Sein Win and, from March 29, U Maung Maung Kha.

In February 1977 the third congress of the ruling Burma Socialist Program Party set the broad agenda for the next Parliament, to be elected in January 1978. Devoting itself to the problem of resurrecting the national economy, the congress tempered its socialist ideology with a limited turn toward liberalization.

An outspoken report to the congress by U San Yu, the party general secretary, called for a halt to the deterioration in the country's political, economic, and social conditions, of which the 195% rise in the inflation rate between 1972 and 1976

BURMA

Education. (1974–75) Primary, pupils 3,449,552, teachers 73,653; secondary, pupils 945,719, teachers 26,761; vocational (1972–73), pupils 6,777, teachers 570; teacher training, students 4,428, teachers 301; higher, students 57,965, teaching staff 3,404.

Finance. Monetary unit: kyat, with (Sept. 19, 1977) a free rate of 7.26 kyats to U.S. $1 (12.65 kyats = £1 sterling). Gold, SDR's, and foreign exchange (June 1977) U.S. $125.2 million. Budget (1975–76 est.): revenue 14,472,000,000 kyats; expenditure 15,521,000,000 kyats.

Foreign Trade. (1976) Imports 789.1 million kyats; exports 1,260,300,000 kyats. Import sources (1975): Japan 33%; China 9%; U.K. 8%; U.S. 7%; West Germany 7%; South Korea 5%. Export destinations (1975): Indonesia 14%; Singapore 13%; Sri Lanka 11%; Japan 10%; The Netherlands 6%; Mauritius 6%. Main exports: rice 58%; teak 23%.

Transport and Communications. Roads (1974) 21,745 km. Motor vehicles in use (1974): passenger 36,300; commercial (including buses) 39,300. Railways: (1974) 4,328 km; traffic (1976) 2,847,000,000 passenger-km, freight 421 million net ton-km. Air traffic (1975): 187 million passenger-km; freight 2.5 million net ton-km. Shipping (1976): merchant vessels 100 gross tons and over 39; gross tonnage 68,867. Telephones (Dec. 1974) 30,000. Radio licenses (Dec. 1974) 659,000.

Agriculture. Production (in 000; metric tons; 1976): rice c. 9,400; dry beans c. 160; onions 108; sugar, raw value c. 70; bananas c. 220; sesame seed 137; peanuts c. 520; cotton, lint c. 16; jute c. 41; tobacco c. 75; rubber c. 16; timber (cu m; 1975) 21,655. Livestock (in 000; March 1976): cattle c. 7,300; buffalo c. 1,700; pigs 1,500; goats c. 550; sheep c. 180; chickens c. 16,000.

Industry. Production (in 000; metric tons; 1976): crude oil 1,160; electricity (excluding most industrial production; kw-hr) 845,000; cement 238; lead concentrates (metal content; 1974) 9.8; zinc concentrates (metal content) 4.1; tin concentrates (metal content) 0.4; tungsten concentrates (oxide content; 1974) 0.4.

KEYSTONE

was symptomatic. Prime Minister U Sein Win and his colleagues tried to blame the problems on floods and cyclones and pleaded that the country still had been able to achieve increased growth— 2.6% in 1974, 4.8% in 1975, and an estimated 6% in 1976. The statistical claims were of no avail, however; on March 29 U Sein Win and two of his colleagues resigned, and 57-year-old U Maung Maung Kha was named prime minister. Further shake-ups were reported in the fall, and in November, following a special party congress, U Ne Win announced that the party had been purged of "opportunists."

In July the start of a five-year program to substitute the cultivation of food for that of opium in Burma was announced by the UN Fund for Drug Abuse Control in Geneva. Clashes between army units and Communist insurgents continued during the year. (GOVINDAN UNNY)

Burundi

A republic of eastern Africa, Burundi is bordered by Zaire, Rwanda, and Tanzania. Area: 27,834 sq km (10,747 sq mi). Pop. (1977 est.): 3,964,000, mainly Hutu, Tutsi, and Twa. Cap. and largest city: Bujumbura (pop., 1970 est., 110,000). Language: Kirundi and French. Religion: Roman Catholic 61%; most of the remainder are animist; there is a small Protestant minority. President in 1977, Lieut. Col. Jean-Baptiste Bagaza; prime minister, Lieut. Col. Edouard Nzambimana.

On Jan. 7, 1977, the Supreme Revolutionary Council fixed Pres. Jean-Baptiste Bagaza's mandate for five years (renewable) and announced its own demise, once the Unity and National Progress Party had been reorganized. Bagaza, bent on quick reform, arrested over 70 officials for misappropriation of public funds and issued a decree forbidding investment in other countries (existing investments were given six months for disposal). Himself a Tutsi, he included four Hutu in his

Construction crews work to restore centuries-old buildings in Burma following the severe earthquake in 1975.

Burma

Burundi

Bridges:
see Engineering Projects

British Commonwealth:
see Commonwealth of Nations; *articles on the various member states*

Brunei:
see Dependent States

Buddhism:
see Religion

Building and Construction Industry:
see Engineering Projects; Industrial Review

BURUNDI

Education. (1974–75) Primary, pupils 130,048, teachers (1971–72) 4,980; secondary, pupils 6,309, teachers (1971–72) 343; vocational, pupils 905, teachers (1971–72) 290; teacher training, students 5,078, teachers (1971–72) 243; higher, students 482, teaching staff (1971–72) 108.

Finance. Monetary unit: Burundi franc, with (Sept. 19, 1977) an official rate of BurFr 90 to U.S. $1 (free rate of BurFr 156.98 = £1 sterling). Gold, SDR's, and foreign exchange (June 1977) U.S. $39,920,000. Budget (1975 actual): revenue BurFr 2,224,600,000; expenditure BurFr 3,283,300,000.

Foreign Trade. (1976) Imports BurFr 5,027,000,000; exports BurFr 4,937,000,000. Import sources: Belgium-Luxembourg 18%; France 13%; West Germany 11%; Iran 8%; The Netherlands 6%; Italy 6%; Kenya 5%; U.S. 5%. Export destinations: U.S. 43%; West Germany 17%; Belgium-Luxembourg 5%; U.K. 5%. Main export coffee 89%.

Agriculture. Production (in 000; metric tons; 1976): corn c. 160; cassava (1975) c. 4,100; potatoes (1975) c. 240; sweet potatoes (1975) c. 1,257; millet c. 27; sorghum c. 125; dry beans c. 148; bananas (1975) c. 1,563; coffee c. 21; cotton, lint (1975) c. 2. Livestock (in 000; Dec. 1974): cattle 784; sheep 313; goats 655; pigs 32.

CAMBODIA

Education. (1973–74) Primary, pupils 429,110, teachers 18,794; secondary, pupils 98,888, teachers 2,226; vocational, pupils 4,856, teachers 202; teacher training, students 553, teachers 18; higher, students 11,570, teaching staff 276.

Finance. Monetary unit: riel, with (Sept. 19, 1977) a free rate of 1,200 riels to U.S. $1 (2,090 riels = £1 sterling). Budget (1974 est.): revenue 22.8 billion riels; expenditure 71 billion riels.

Foreign Trade. (1973) Imports 14.2 billion riels; exports 2,732,000,000 riels. Import sources: U.S. c. 69%; Thailand c. 11%; Singapore c. 5%; Japan c. 5%. Export destinations: Hong Kong c. 23%; Japan c. 22%; Malaysia c. 18%; France c. 12%; Spain c. 10%. Main export rubber 93%.

Transport and Communications. Roads (1975) c. 11,000 km. Motor vehicles in use: passenger (1972) 27,200; commercial (including buses; 1973) 11,000. Railways (including sections not in operation; 1973): 649 km; traffic 54,070,000 passenger-km, freight 9,780,000 net ton-km. Air traffic (1975): 42 million passenger-km; freight 400,000 net ton-km. Inland waterways (including Mekong River; 1975) c. 1,400 km. Telephones (Dec. 1972) 9,200. Radio receivers (Dec. 1974), 1,112,000. Television receivers (Dec. 1974) 26,000.

Agriculture. Production (in 000; metric tons; 1976): rice c. 1,800; corn (1974) c. 70; bananas c. 90; oranges (1975) c. 33; dry beans c. 20; rubber (1975) c. 8; jute (1975) c. 3. Livestock (in 000; 1976): cattle c. 1,940; buffalo c. 868; pigs c. 900.

government, somewhat reducing the imbalance of representation.

In March Prime Minister Edouard Nzambimana, also planning minister, announced an investment budget of BurFr 3 billion (far outstripping 1976's BurFr 993 million); internal self-help was to take precedence over external aid. Nevertheless, Burundi relied on foreign aid, which at about $45 million nearly equaled the budget revenue. During the year coffee produced 88% of the nation's revenue, with prices and production both soaring. But there remained a fast-growing, mostly illiterate population with only 20% of children at school. In response, the International Development Association mounted a $10 million education program. (MOLLY MORTIMER)

Cambodia

A republic of Southeast Asia, Cambodia (officially Democratic Kampuchea) is the southwest part of the Indochinese Peninsula, on the Gulf of Thailand, bordered by Vietnam, Laos, and Thailand. Area: 181,035 sq km (69,898 sq mi). Pop. (1976

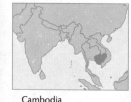

Cambodia

Premier Pol Pot (left), secretary of the Central Committee of the Cambodian Communist Party, was greeted by Chairman Hua Kuo-feng of the People's Republic of China when a Cambodian delegation visited Peking in September.

UPI COMPIX

est.): 7,735,300 according to official figures, although foreign observers estimated that figure to be overstated by as much as one million persons. It is estimated to comprise: Khmer 93%; Vietnamese 4%; Chinese 3%. Cap.: Phnom Penh (pop., 1976 est., between 40,000 and 100,000). Language: Khmer (official) and French. Religion: Buddhist. Head of state in 1977, Khieu Samphan; premier, Pol Pot.

The veil of secrecy covering Democratic Kampuchea (Cambodia) lifted marginally during 1977 to reveal something of the country's power centre. For two years Phnom Penh had told the world that it was ruled by the Angkar Loeu (Organization on High), which was differentiated from anything Communist. Indeed, the government's most visible representative, Foreign Minister Ieng Sary, said in Singapore: "We are not Communists. We are revolutionaries."

In September, however, Premier Pol Pot announced that the 17-year-old Communist Party of Cambodia was in fact the directing force in the country. It was the first public admission of the existence of a Communist party. Two days after the announcement, Pol Pot, who was also the party secretary, went on an official visit to China and North Korea. The timing suggested that Cambodia's formal entry into the ranks of the world's Communist states was intended to appease China, its main supplier of material aid and technical expertise. Some observers thought it was also a move to give Cambodia a new face untainted by the Angkar Loeu's two-year reign of terror.

Although Pol Pot emerged as the real strong man of Cambodia, there were no apparent changes in the rest of the leadership structure. Khieu Samphan remained head of state, while Nuon Chea continued as the permanent chairman of the People's Representative Assembly; in September Chea was also identified as deputy secretary of the Central Committee of the Communist Party. The man previously described as the Communist boss, Saloth Sar, had disappeared, giving rise to speculation that he and Pol Pot were one and the same. Former head of state Prince Norodom Sihanouk was believed to be a prisoner in Phnom Penh.

Pol Pot's China visit seemed to mark a new period of consolidation for the Khmer rulers. It was accompanied by a slowdown in the border clashes between Cambodia and Thailand and in the raids on Thai villages in which scores of people had been killed. There was also a slowdown in the border clashes between Cambodia and Vietnam, but fighting on this front flared up late in the fall and appeared to reach a new level of intensity by year's end. On December 31 Cambodia broke diplomatic relations with Vietnam and accused the Vietnamese of having attacked deep into Cambodian territory. Details were unclear, but major military engagements were known to have taken place. Differences between the two countries were ideological as well as territorial, Cambodia being close to China and Vietnam suspicious of Peking.

Throughout the year Cambodian news media claimed major strides in the economy, although diplomatic and refugee reports pointed to the contrary. Most of the war-damaged factories and plantations were said to be functioning again with Chinese assistance. Diplomats reported that thousands of Chinese technicians were in the country.

(T. J. S. GEORGE)

Cameroon

A republic of west Africa on the Gulf of Guinea, Cameroon borders on Nigeria, Chad, the Central African Empire, the Congo, Gabon, and Equatorial Guinea. Area: 465,054 sq km (179,558 sq mi). Pop. (1976 census): 7,663,200. Cap.: Yaoundé (pop., 1975 est., 274,400). Largest city: Douala

CAMEROON
Education. (1974–75) Primary, pupils 1,074,021, teachers 20,803; secondary, pupils 93,934, teachers 3,699; vocational, pupils 27,524, teachers 1,240; teacher training, students 1,115, teachers 130; higher, students 6,171, teaching staff (1972–73) 328.
Finance. Monetary unit: CFA franc, with (Sept. 19, 1977) a parity of CFA Fr 50 to the French franc and a free rate of CFA Fr 246.50 to U.S. $1 (CFA Fr 429.50 = £1 sterling). Federal budget (1976–77 est.) balanced at CFA Fr 128 billion.
Foreign Trade. (1976) Imports CFA Fr 146 billion; exports CFA Fr 122 billion. Import sources (1975): France 46%; West Germany 8%; U.S. 7%; Italy 6%; Gabon 5%. Export destinations (1975): France 27%; The Netherlands 22%; U.S.S.R. 10%; West Germany 7%; Gabon 5%. Main exports (1975): cocoa 25%; coffee 24%; timber 7%.
Transport and Communications. Roads (1973) 43,508 km (including 2,913 km with improved surface). Motor vehicles in use (1975): passenger 51,949; commercial 28,953. Railways (1976): 1,173 km; traffic 264 million passenger-km, freight 534 million net ton-km. Telephones (June 1973) 22,000. Radio receivers (Dec. 1974) 603,000.
Agriculture. Production (in 000; metric tons; 1976): corn c. 355; millet c. 390; sweet potatoes (1975) c. 550; cassava (1975) c. 853; bananas c. 96; peanuts c. 179; coffee c. 93; cocoa c. 102; palm kernels c. 40; palm oil c. 60; rubber c. 16; cotton, lint c. 22. Livestock (in 000; Dec. 1974): cattle c. 2,600; pigs c. 400; sheep c. 2,050; goats c. 1,550; chickens c. 8,650.
Industry. Production: aluminum (1974) 49,000 metric tons; electricity (1975) 1,440,000,000 kw-hr.

(pop., 1975 est., 485,800). Language: English and French (official), Bantu, Sudanic. Religion: mainly animist, with Roman Catholic (24%), Protestant, independent Christian, and Muslim minorities. President in 1977, Ahmadou Ahidjo; prime minister, Paul Biya.

Cameroon

The government maintained its basic policy of caution and nonalignment in foreign affairs in 1977. At the same time, Cameroon strengthened its ties with France. Robert Galley, the French minister of cooperation, visited Yaoundé in June and was followed a few weeks later by Louis de Guiringaud, the French foreign minister. France agreed to provide CFA Fr 750 million to double the capacity of the port at Douala to 5 million tons annually. The total cost of the project was estimated at CFA Fr 25 billion. In March the European Economic Community (EEC) agreed to release just over $3 million from the European Development Fund to the Dibombari palm oil complex. Cameroon expected to receive $92 million in aid from the EEC.

In August Pres. Ahmadou Ahidjo paid a four-day "working and friendly" visit to Algeria, where he was welcomed by Pres. Houari Boumédienne. During the same month the minister for youth and sport, Félix Topye Mbog, inaugurated the planting of one million trees to launch Operation Green Sahel, an international effort to check the southward advance of the Sahara.

(PHILIPPE DECRAENE)

Canada

Canada is a federal parliamentary state and member of the Commonwealth of Nations covering North America north of conterminous United States and east of Alaska. Area: 9,976,139 sq km (3,851,809 sq mi). Pop. (1977 est.): 23.2 million, including (1971) British 44.6%; French 28.7%; other European 23%; Indian and Eskimo 1.4%. Cap.: Ottawa (metro. pop., 1976 census, 693,300). Largest cities: Toronto (metro. pop., 1976 census, 2,803,100); Montreal (metro. pop., 1976 census, 2,802,500). Language (mother tongue; 1976 prelim. census): English 61%; French 25%; others 14%. Religion (1971): Roman Catholic 46%; Protestant 42%. Queen, Elizabeth II; governor-general in 1977, Jules Léger; prime minister, Pierre Elliott Trudeau.

Canada

Domestic Affairs. The consequences of Quebec's election of the separatist Parti Québécois (PQ) to office on Nov. 15, 1976, dominated Canadian affairs in 1977. Calling the PQ victory "the greatest challenge to Canada's nationhood since Confederation" (in 1867), Prime Minister Pierre Elliott Trudeau sought to meet the danger by proposing constitutional changes to ensure access to French-language education throughout the country. While the federal government stressed language equality, however, the new PQ administration, led by René Lévesque, passed a sweeping measure designed to make Quebec a unilingual (French) society.

Also worrying was the depressed state of Canada's economy in 1977. With only marginal growth in real gross national product (GNP), the country endured a high rate of unemployment (8.3% of the labour force over the year) coupled with a renewed bout of inflation (a 12-month increase in the cost of living of over 8%). Trudeau and the federal Liberal Party, in power since 1968, found themselves in a difficult position. They won fresh popular support for their efforts on behalf of unity, but their failure to cope with economic problems brought them unpopularity in many quarters.

The PQ government's language policy, unveiled in April, symbolized the force of cultural nationalism behind Quebec separatism. (*See* Special Report.) It also presented a brutal challenge to Prime Minister Trudeau's cherished aim of establishing official bilingualism as a reality across Canada. "For the first time in Quebec," announced the PQ government, "a law proclaims that every Quebecer has the right to work, be educated and served in French . . . ." The law limited access to English schools to children who had at least one parent educated in English at a Quebec primary school or at least one parent, domiciled in Quebec when the law was passed, who had received an elementary education in English outside the province. Exemptions would be provided for temporary residents. The result of the new policy was unmistakable: the proportion of children educated in English in Quebec would decline. The restrictions would be especially severe for the children of immigrants, who would not be allowed to attend English-language schools as many had preferred in the past. French would also be imposed as a language of work by requiring companies to obtain certificates of "francization" by 1983. The only official versions of court judgments, laws, and government regulations would be the French ones. Public institutions would have to be francized, and even English place-names in the province changed to French.

Trudeau attacked the measure as marking a regression "towards the Dark Ages" and insisted that such an approach would actually work against the survival of the French community in Quebec. A better way to protect the 2% of North Americans who were French-speakers, he said, was through the official bilingualism policy, which upheld the

position of French in Quebec and other parts of Canada but did not take away the freedoms of other ethnic communities.

The Quebec language bill, after a painfully slow progress through the legislature during which the government introduced some modifications, was adopted by the National Assembly on August 26 by a vote of 54–32. In spite of the turmoil it had created by its language law, the PQ had registered a major victory in winning its adoption. Lévesque and his colleagues were now free to direct their attention to economic and social projects. Most importantly, they turned to preparing the ground for the promised plebiscite that would test support for Quebec independence. This meant a campaign to promote the goal of sovereignty for Quebec, with the expectation that the new state would have an economic association with the rest of Canada.

The response to the charter of the French language in Quebec came during the summer from both Ottawa and the other provinces. The federal government, recognizing that there was "considerable insecurity" in Quebec regarding the preservation of French, announced that it would "reluctantly" go along with the Quebec government's restrictions on freedom of language choice in education "in the short term." It would also work energetically with the provinces to extend the rights of French minorities across Canada, particularly in the establishment of schools in their language. Ottawa announced the formation of a seven-member national unity task force to advise it on the question and to cooperate with nonofficial organizations working for a united Canada. Two co-chairmen were appointed to the task force: Jean-Luc Pepin, a former Liberal Cabinet minister who had recently served as head of the Anti-Inflation Board, and John Robarts, Conservative premier of Ontario from 1961 to 1971.

At the end of August the annual premiers' conference was held at the Bay of Fundy resort of St. Andrews, N.B. Premier Lévesque attended the meeting, where he advanced the proposal that Quebec would permit access to English schools for children moving there from other provinces if those provinces would sign "reciprocal agreements" guaranteeing educational rights for French-speaking minorities. This plan received only lukewarm support from most of the premiers, who promised, however, to devote their "best efforts to provide education in English and French wherever numbers warrant," regardless of what Quebec might do.

The federal government developed this approach in early September when Trudeau wrote to each of the premiers, stating his willingness to negotiate a constitutional amendment recognizing the right of parents to have their children educated in the language of their choice wherever a sufficient number of persons speaking either French or English warranted it. Quebec would be allowed to restrict freedom of choice for English-speaking Quebecers and for non-English-speaking immigrants. There would have to be complete freedom of choice, however, for Canadians moving from other provinces into Quebec. Lévesque bluntly rejected Trudeau's proposed amendment, and it was

A federal bill that gave Canadian immigration officials authority to reject undesirable immigrants caused demonstrations in Ottawa.

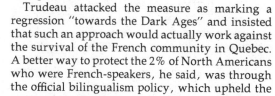

clear that the search for a new constitutional arrangement governing language rights would have to continue.

The PQ figured prominently in the revelations of misconduct on the part of the Royal Canadian Mounted Police that captured public attention throughout the last half of the year. On October 28 Solicitor General Francis Fox told Parliament that in 1973 a security unit of the RCMP had broken into PQ offices in Montreal and removed and copied records, which were then surreptitiously returned. The Mounties were accused of a number of alleged illegal acts, including other break-ins, tampering with private mail, infiltrating political and other organizations, and obtaining confidential medical and tax records. Investigations into the charges were begun in Ottawa and Quebec.

Public opinion polls revealed a dramatic increase in popular support for the Liberals in 1977. The trend was attributable to the widespread belief that Prime Minister Trudeau was best qualified, among national leaders, to deal with the language issue and the larger question of national unity. The party made a determined effort to pick up support in the West, where it was weak—an effort that culminated in the defection of Jack Horner, a prominent Alberta Conservative, to the Liberal ranks. Horner's move brought a major spokesman for the West into the Cabinet, since he was appointed minister of industry, trade, and commerce when Trudeau rearranged his Cabinet on September 16. The Liberals also rejoiced in winning five out of six federal by-elections on May 24. Five of the contests were in Quebec, where the Liberals regained four seats lost through resignations and a death. A Liberal gain also occurred in a traditionally Conservative seat in Prince Edward Island. The elections left the standing in the House of Commons as follows: Liberals 141; Progressive Conservatives 95; New Democratic Party 16; Social Credit 11; independent 1, for a total of 264.

The Cabinet reshuffle of September 16 was caused by the resignation ten days earlier of Trudeau's closest associate from Ontario, Donald Macdonald, who had held the difficult finance portfolio for two years. Macdonald resigned for "personal

Under the gaze of a medicine man, Britain's Prince Charles, a nonsmoker, took a puff on a peace pipe to commemorate a 100-year-old treaty between the British and the Blackfoot Indians in Calgary, Alberta.

and family reasons," denying that there had been any differences with his colleagues. There were 12 changes of portfolio in the new Cabinet. The most significant was the appointment of the first French-Canadian minister of finance in Canada's 110-year history, Jean Chrétien, a lawyer from Shawinigan, Que., who had served as minister of industry, trade, and commerce. Allan MacEachen, the president of the Privy Council, was named deputy prime minister to indicate his seniority in the Cabinet. The new Cabinet totaled 33 persons, making it the largest in Canadian history.

Trudeau's personal life was clouded by his separation from his wife, Margaret, whom he had married in 1971. At the time he had been 51, she 22.

The second session of Canada's 30th Parliament ran from Oct. 12, 1976, to July 25, 1977. A third session began on October 18, with the traditional speech from the throne being read by Queen Elizabeth II during her five-day Jubilee visit to Canada. Although the pace of legislation moved slowly, the government managed to secure approval for 42

CANADA

Education. (1976–77) Primary, pupils 2,753,553, teachers (including preprimary; 1972–73) 142,900; secondary, vocational, and teacher training, pupils 2,577,190, teachers (1970–71) 101,844; higher (including 45 main universities), students 613,120, teaching staff 50,003.

Finance. Monetary unit: Canadian dollar, with a free rate (Sept. 19, 1977) of Can$1.07 to U.S. $1 (Can$1.87 = £1 sterling). Gold, SDR's, and foreign exchange (June 1977) U.S. $4,138,000,000. Budget (1975–76 actual): revenue Can$36,120,000,000; expenditure Can$37,470,000,000. Gross national product (1976) Can$184,490,000,000. Money supply (April 1977) Can$24,660,000,000. Cost of living (1970 = 100; June 1977) 165.

Foreign Trade. (1976) Imports Can$40,071,000,000; exports Can$39,672,000,000. Import sources: U.S. 69%; EEC 9%. Export destinations: U.S. 68%; EEC 12% (U.K. 5%); Japan 6%. Main exports: motor vehicles 22%; metal ores 7%; crude oil 6%; wood pulp 6%; aluminum 6%; newsprint 5%; wheat 5%. Tourism (1975): visitors 36,218,000; gross receipts U.S. $1,534,000,000.

Transport and Communications. Roads (publicly administered; 1971) 834,152 km (including 2,765 km expressways). Motor vehicles in use (1974): passenger 8,472,000; commercial 2,161,000. Railways: (1975) 70,714 km; traffic (main railways only; 1976) 2,650,000,000 passenger-km, freight 193,526,000,000 net ton-km. Air traffic (1976): 24,000,000,000 passenger-km; freight 630 million net ton-km. Shipping (1976): merchant vessels 100 gross tons and over 1,269; gross tonnage 2,638,692. Shipping traffic (includes Great Lakes and St. Lawrence traffic; 1976): goods loaded 113,942,000 metric tons, unloaded 56,325,000 metric tons. Telephones (Jan. 1976) 13,142,000. Radio receivers (Dec. 1974) 20,252,000. Television receivers (Dec. 1974) 8,232,000.

Agriculture. Production (in 000; metric tons; 1976): wheat 23,523; barley 10,303; oats 4,961; rye 561; corn 3,675; potatoes 2,651; tomatoes c. 393; apples 398; rapeseed 937; linseed 297; soybeans 252; tobacco c. 95; beef and veal 1,080; pork c. 475; timber (cu m; 1975) 121,206; fish catch (1975) 1,024. Livestock (in 000; Dec. 1975): cattle 13,704;

sheep 523; pigs 5,481; horses (1974) c. 345; chickens c. 82,683.

Industry. Labour force (Dec. 1976) 10,230,000. Unemployment (June 1976) 7.5%. Index of industrial production (1970 = 100; 1976) 127. Fuel and power (in 000; metric tons; 1976): coal 20,798; lignite 4,678; crude oil 63,790; natural gas (cu m) 74,500,000; electricity (kw-hr) 293,400,000. Metal and mineral production (in 000; metric tons; 1976): iron ore (shipments; 61% metal content) 56,012; crude steel 13,135; copper ore (metal content) 723; nickel ore (metal content) 245; zinc ore (metal content) 1,157; lead ore (metal content) 247; aluminum (1975) 878; uranium ore (metal content; 1975) 5.5; asbestos (1975) 1,037; gold (troy oz) 1,700; silver (troy oz) 41,000. Other production (in 000; metric tons; 1976): cement 9,898; wood pulp (1974) 19,132; newsprint 8,070; other paper and paperboard (1974) 4,379; sulfuric acid (1975) 2,720; synthetic rubber 210; passenger cars (units) 1,137; commercial vehicles (units) 503. Dwelling units completed (1976) 236,000. Merchant vessels launched (100 gross tons and over; 1976) 244,000 gross tons.

measures, including 4 substantial ones. Changes in the Unemployment Insurance Act were designed to lengthen the period a claimant must work before he could draw benefits but provided longer benefit periods for regions of high unemployment, such as the Maritime Provinces and Quebec. The Immigration Act was overhauled in order to set down, for the first time, specific objectives; immigration officials were given new powers to reject undesirable immigrants. An important tax-sharing bill, transferring a larger proportion of federal income tax receipts to the provinces, was passed; in return, the provinces assumed sole (rather than shared) financial responsibility for hospital insurance, medical care, and postsecondary education. A new gun-control law imposed tighter regulations on the holders of firearms.

After adjournment on July 25, Parliament was called back into session to deal with two pressing matters. Following a two-day debate (August 4–5) approval was given to the Alaska-Yukon gas pipeline route, and a short session on August 9 passed legislation sending striking air traffic controllers back to work.

Two provinces held elections in 1977. In Ontario the Conservative government of Premier William Davis, in a minority position since 1975, sought to strengthen its standing, but the election of June 9 was a setback to its hopes. Although the Conservatives elected 58 members rather than the 51 they had had in the legislature before, they still found themselves in a minority. Thirty-four Liberals were elected, together with 33 from the New Democratic Party, which thus lost its second-place position.

In Manitoba, governed by the New Democratic Party under Premier Ed Schreyer for eight years, an election was held on October 11. To the surprise of most observers, the Manitoba voters swung to the right and brought the Conservative Party to power. Sterling Lyon, a Winnipeg lawyer, campaigned on a platform of tax cuts, less government intervention in the economy, and more efficient administration in the public sector. The Conservatives won 33 seats, a gain of 10, and the New Democratic Party dropped from 31 to 23. The Liberals elected only one member, compared with three in the previous House.

Foreign Affairs. Canada and the United States agreed to embark on an $8 billion pipeline to carry Alaskan natural gas through Canada to the U.S. The decision represented the choice of an overland route rather than the tanker route down the west coast of North America suggested by the El Paso Alaska Co. It also meant the rejection of another suggested route along the Mackenzie River Valley from the Arctic coast in favour of one following the existing Alaska Highway. (*See* ARCTIC REGIONS.) The agreement was signed on September 20 by Allan MacEachen, the Canadian minister responsible for negotiations, and U.S. Secretary of Energy James Schlesinger.

The controversial Garrison diversion irrigation project, intended to help bring under cultivation 250,000 ac of arid land in North Dakota, received a setback on September 19 when the International Joint Commission, a Canadian-U.S. body set up to regulate boundary waters, pronounced that the scheme would have adverse environmental effects in Canada. Changes to discharge surplus waters into the Missouri River system rather than to the north were recommended.

The Canadian Cabinet blocked a regulatory agency order that had required the deletion of commercials from television programs being beamed into Canada by U.S. stations along the border. The suspension would remain in effect while changes in Canadian taxation that would eliminate deductions for advertising placed with U.S. broadcasting stations were being studied.

Following major purchases of long-range patrol aircraft and tanks in 1976, the Trudeau government continued to work toward improvement in Canada's defense preparedness. In March Defense Minister Barnett Danson announced that six aircraft companies in the U.S. and Europe were being invited to bid for a contract to supply Canada with 130–150 supersonic fighter planes. At over $2 billion, this would be the largest single defense purchase in Canadian history. By 1981 the planes would replace aircraft currently in use by Canada in North American air defense and with NATO forces in Europe.

Relations with France were somewhat strained in early November when the French government awarded the Legion of Honour to visiting Premier Lévesque and agreed to annual meetings between French and Quebec leaders.

The Economy. Canada suffered an economic slump in 1977. Over the year real GNP was expected to grow by only 2%, an increase too small to prevent unemployment rates from rising. While the pace of inflation slowed somewhat early in the year, over the 12 months it was still higher than the figure desired by the government when it introduced wage and price controls in October 1975. Higher food prices and depreciation in the value of the Canadian dollar resulted in a cost-of-living rate about 2% above the government's objective for 1977. In October the Canadian dollar fell to 91 U.S. cents, its lowest value since World War II. One positive factor could be cited in a disappointing economic picture: Canadian wage settlements were moderating, a trend that would help to make the country's products more competitive.

Finance Minister Macdonald introduced his second budget on March 31. It provided tax concessions to companies in an effort to get them to create more jobs. The expenditure of $100 million in federal job-creating programs was also announced. There were no significant changes in personal taxation. On a national accounts basis, Ottawa expected to take in $38.4 billion in the fiscal year ending in March 1978, while spending $44.1 billion. Although the rate of increase in government spending was lower than in 1976, the deficit for 1977–78 would be much higher than in the previous year. By October it was estimated it might total as much as $8 billion. On October 20 Finance Minister Chrétien announced new measures to stimulate the economy, including a $700 million cut in personal income tax, a new program to create jobs, and an end to wage and price controls in 1978.

(D. M. L. FARR)

THE CASE FOR QUEBEC

by Rodrigue Biron

As a federal state made up of ten provincial governments and a central government seated in Ottawa, Canada has been seen by much of the world as a vast and diversified country, blessed with an enormous wealth of natural resources, devoted to the cause of peace and democracy and having few inner tensions; in short, a land of plenty and opportunity for all. But the election of a Parti Québécois government in the province of Quebec on Nov. 15, 1976, with its political platform favouring independence for Quebec and economic association with the rest of Canada, has shattered this stereotyped image. It has brought into the open a previously hidden and largely unknown reality that is now threatening the future cohesion of the Canadian federation.

To say the least, Canada is presently in a crisis

Rodrigue Biron is the leader of the Union Nationale party in the Quebec National Assembly.

situation. What can account for a development that would have seemed unthinkable to most Canadians —and most non-Canadians as well—only a few short years ago? Why did the people of Quebec democratically elect a separatist government with a strong majority of 71 seats out of 110 in the Quebec National Assembly? It is impossible to answer these questions without first explaining what Canada and Quebec are all about and what they represent to Canadians and Quebecers alike.

Two Communities. In order to understand the present crisis, one must realize at the outset that Canada is not merely a federation of ten provinces. It is also the home of two major linguistic and cultural groups, an English-speaking community and a French-speaking community, each with its own distinct ways and philosophies of life. This fundamental reality is at the basis of the inner tensions that are rocking the political structure of the country. Nevertheless, it was not officially recognized by the federal government until 1968, when the Trudeau government passed the controversial Official Languages Act legally establishing bilingualism in all federal institutions throughout Canada. The only province to follow suit has been New Brunswick, which has a French-speaking minority numbering approximately 32.9% of its population.

Of Canada's two major linguistic groups, the English-speaking community is by far the larger, and it

A sign of the times is this billboard erected by the Mohawk Indians near Quebec.

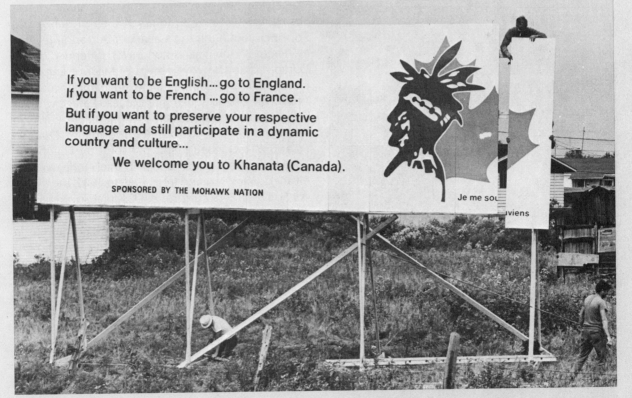

MONTREAL STAR

controls the political institutions in all the provinces except Quebec. The latest figures released by Statistics Canada (Aug. 29, 1977), based on preliminary results of the June 1, 1976, census, reveal that, of a total population of 22,992,605, (1) 14,043,250 (61.1%) declared English to be their mother tongue; (2) 5,865,365 (25.5%) declared French to be their mother tongue; and (3) 4,972,090 (79.8%) of those who declared French to be their mother tongue were living in the province of Quebec on the day the census was taken. Better than any words, these figures demonstrate that, among all the provinces, Quebec stands out as the heartland and mainstay of French Canada and the only province where French-speaking Canadians have the political strength that comes from numerical superiority (4,972,090 out of a total of 6,234,445) and hence the possibility of controlling their own destiny.

Since the first days of confederation—in 1867, when Canada was born—the Quebec government has been the only one in Canada that has spoken and acted consistently and instinctively on behalf of a French-speaking majority. It has been the only one to provide French-speaking Canadians with institutions, a life pattern, and an environment tailored to

Leader of the separatist movement in Quebec is René Lévesque, whose Parti Québécois won a stunning upset victory in 1976.

PHILIPPE LEDRU—SYGMA

their everyday needs and unique culture. This very special situation, which has existed for more than 110 years, has created in the minds and hearts of French-speaking Quebecers an attachment to their government and their province that transcends the ties normally uniting all Canadians. It has also evoked inside Quebec a vibrant form of nationalism which, through the years and together with the socioeconomic transformation of Quebec from a predominantly rural society to a well-organized industrial society, has forged a cultural identity peculiar to Quebec and its people. Regardless of the complexion of the government of the day, the fact of this cultural identity has considerably influenced, if not dominated, political life in the province for the past 30 to 40 years.

The Politics of Identity. Since the end of World War II, regardless of what political party was in power, Quebec governments have personified this unique cultural reality. With astonishing regularity, they have taken strong nationalistic stands against the federal government's efforts to preempt, wholly or in part, responsibilities that were assigned to the provinces under the 1867 constitution (the British North America Act).

The slogans adopted by the various political parties that held power in Quebec during this period of rapid economic and social change reflect the concerns of the community. Increasingly, a majority of Quebecers became aware that their collective existence was in peril and that its survival depended largely on their own efforts. And with this awareness came a determination to assert their presence as a distinct community in Canada. *L'Autonomie Provinciale* ("Provincial Autonomy"), defended by the Union Nationale government of Maurice Duplessis from 1944 to 1959; the "Quiet Revolution" instigated by the Liberal government of Jean Lesage with his slogan of *Maître chez-nous* ("Master in our own House") from 1960 to 1966; the call of *Québec d'abord* ("Quebec first") put forth by Union Nationale governments under Daniel Johnson and Jean-Jacques Bertrand from 1966 to 1970; the theory of *Souveraineté culturelle* ("Cultural Sovereignty") developed by the Liberal government of Robert Bourassa from 1970 to 1976—all were unanimous in condemning the status quo in the relationship between the provincial governments and the central government in Ottawa and in demanding a revision of the constitution. All insisted on a division of responsibilities, a sharing of powers between governments, that would give Quebec the vital instruments needed to preserve its cultural identity.

It was Daniel Johnson, in his opening address at the Confederation of Tomorrow Conference in Toronto in November 1967, who explained most

clearly and concisely the basic demands of the Quebec people:

> Specifically, what does Quebec want? As the mainstay of a nation (in the sociological sense of the word), it wants free rein to make its own decisions affecting the growth of its citizens as human beings (*i.e.*, education, social security and health in all respects), their economic development (*i.e.*, the forging of any economic and financial tool deemed necessary), their cultural fulfillment (which takes in not only art and literature but the French language as well) and the presence abroad of the Quebec community (*i.e.*, relations with certain countries and international organizations).

The following year, at the Canadian Intergovernmental Conference convened to discuss the constitutional problem as a whole, he stated in a few words the viewpoint of the vast majority of French Canadians in Quebec. His words remain as true today as they were in 1968:

> If there is a lesson to be learned from our history, it is this: French Canadians in Quebec cannot be expected to entrust the direction of their social and cultural life to a government in which their representatives are in the minority and which is also subject to the workings of cabinet responsibility and party discipline. Of course, they want a central government to handle problems common to both communities or questions which have no bearing on distinctive cultural or sociological traits; but Quebec is where they spontaneously wish to turn for decisions pertaining to the establishment of the conditions necessary for development of their own personality and dynamism.
>
> In other words, if in a ten-partner Canada Quebec is a province like the others, the situation is different in a two-partner Canada. As the homeland and mainstay of French Canada, Quebec must assume responsibilities which are peculiar to her; and it goes without saying that her powers must be proportionate to her responsibilities.

A Personal View. The ability of Canadians as a whole to comprehend the full meaning of this basic reality, together with the administrative blunders and constitutional hanky-panky of the Bourassa regime, opened wide the doors of power to the Parti Québécois. Yet this reality constitutes a vital part of Canada and its history.

I cannot help but believe that the English-speaking Canadians themselves are largely responsible for the Parti Québécois's victory. I remain convinced that the polarization of opinion it has created will be successfully resolved only if all Canadians join together to build a new Canada. Most Quebecers do not support separation. What they want is a new form of federalism based on a greater decentralization of powers and the formal recognition of our cultural duality.

Up to Nov. 15, 1976, Quebec's aspirations were not aimed at destroying Canada. Had they been met in good time, with reason and openness of spirit, they would have ensured our country much greater stability and harmony than it has now.

Is Quebec separation likely or possible? I am tempted to answer this question, which is in the minds of all Canadians, by another question. What has Canada to offer to Quebecers as an alternative to separatism? That question will have to be answered sooner or later, and the answer will determine the likelihood or the possibility of an eventual Quebec separation.

Canadians' Views on Separation

A survey of Canadians' attitudes about federation and the possibility of Quebec's separation was conducted for the *Toronto Star* and Southam Press Ltd. during the summer of 1977. About 2,000 Canadians coast to coast were interviewed in depth in sessions that lasted up to two hours. The tabulation of the results showed that 84% of Canadians opposed Quebec's separation, including 71% of Quebecers themselves. Furthermore, indications were that sentiment for separation was diminishing even among Quebecers. In February 1977, 33% of Quebecers favoured separation, but in July that number had fallen to 25%.

Similarly, Quebecers themselves opposed the controversial Bill 101 which mandates a French-only Quebec in terms of government language usage. Fifty-six percent of Quebecers stated opposition to the bill, and nationwide opposition came to 77%.

A report from the survey published on September 29 in the *Toronto Star* stated that more than one million Quebecers, both French- and English-speaking, would leave Quebec should the province separate from the federation. In addition, according to sociologist Martin Goldfarb, who conducted the survey, approximately 750,000 Canadians outside Quebec would probably leave Canada if the federation was broken up.

Reproduced with permission: The Toronto Star and Southam Newspapers.

Cape Verde

Cape Verde

An independent African republic, Cape Verde is located in the Atlantic Ocean about 620 km (385 mi) off the west coast of Africa. Area: 4,033 sq km (1,557 sq mi). Pop. (1976 est.): 303,000. Cap.: Praia (pop., 1970, 21,500). Largest city: Mindelo (pop., 1970, 28,800). Language: Portuguese. Religion: mainly Roman Catholic. President in 1977, Aristide Pereira; premier, Maj. Pedro Pires.

Talks in Luanda, Angola, between delegates from Cape Verde and Angola resulted in the signing of an agreement on cooperation on Dec. 15, 1976. On Jan. 19, 1977, it was announced that Cape Verde would accede to the Lomé agreement for trade and cooperation with the European Economic Community. Also on January 19, the premier, Maj. Pedro Pires, arrived in Lisbon on a three-day official visit, and a bomb believed to have been planted by former Portuguese colonists exploded at the airport.

In June some 40 people were arrested after a report of a plot to kill some of the leaders of the ruling African Party for the Independence of Guinea-Bissau and Cape Verde and to sabotage key installations in preparation for foreign intervention aimed at overthrowing the government. About half the captives, some of whom were Portuguese, were subsequently released.   (KENNETH INGHAM)

CAPE VERDE
  Education. (1975–76) Primary, pupils 61,000, teachers 1,350; secondary, pupils 5,600, teachers 205; vocational, pupils 680, teachers 80; teacher training, pupils 370, teachers 32.
  Finance and Trade. Monetary unit: escudo Caboverdiano, at par with the Portuguese escudo and with a free rate (Sept. 19, 1977) of 40.50 escudos to U.S. $1 (70.50 escudos = £1 sterling). Budget (1974 est.) balanced at 265,120,000 escudos. Foreign trade (1975): imports 1,010,-853,000 escudos; exports 61,277,000 escudos (excluding transit trade). Import sources: Portugal 63%; Angola 11%. Export destination Portugal 89%. Main exports: fish 18% (including shellfish 7%); fish products 6%.
  Transport. Ships entered (1972): vessels totaling 5,977,-000 net registered tons; goods loaded (1975) 20,000 metric tons, unloaded 145,000 metric tons.

Central African Empire

Central African Empire

The landlocked Central African Empire is bounded by Chad, the Sudan, the Congo, Zaire, and Cameroon. Area: 624,977 sq km (241,305 sq mi). Pop. (1977 est.): 1,870,000 according to estimates by external analysts; recent official estimates range up to 750,000 persons higher. Cap. and largest city: Bangui (pop., 1968, 298,600). Language: French (official); local dialects. Religion: animist 60%; Christian 35%; Muslim 5%. Emperor, Bokassa I; premier in 1977, Ange Patassé.

A year after he had restyled the Central African Republic as the Central African Empire, Emperor Bokassa I (see BIOGRAPHY) crowned himself at Bangui on Dec. 4, 1977. The elaborate ceremony, patterned after the coronation of Napoleon I, was estimated to have cost approximately $20 million.

CENTRAL AFRICAN EMPIRE
  Education. (1973–74) Primary, pupils 200,445, teachers 3,083; secondary (1972–73), pupils 14,710, teachers 396; vocational (1972–73), pupils 1,397, teachers 141; teacher training (1972–73), students 451, teachers 48; higher, students 380, teaching staff (1971–72) 6.
  Finance. Monetary unit: CFA franc, with (Sept. 19, 1977) a parity of CFA Fr 50 to the French franc and a free rate of CFA Fr 246.50 to U.S. $1 (CFA Fr 429.50 = £1 sterling). Budget (1974 est.): revenue CFA Fr 15,706,000,000; expenditure CFA Fr 17.2 billion.
  Foreign Trade. (1975) Imports CFA Fr 14,614,000,000; exports CFA Fr 10,112,000,000. Import sources: France 58%; Yugoslavia 9%; West Germany 7%. Export destinations: France 42%; Belgium-Luxembourg 9%; U.S. 8%; Italy 8%; Chad 5%; South Africa 5%; Israel 5%. Main exports: coffee 23%; diamonds 20%; cotton 18%.
  Agriculture. Production (in 000; metric tons; 1976): millet c. 43; cassava (1975) c. 1,100; corn (1975) 46; sweet potatoes (1975) c. 54; peanuts c. 36; bananas c. 71; coffee c. 10; cotton, lint c. 11. Livestock (in 000; 1975): cattle c. 463; pigs c. 61; sheep c. 74; goats c. 556; chickens c. 1,236.
  Industry. Production (in 000; 1974): diamonds (metric carats) 435; cotton fabrics (m) 6,000; electricity (kw-hr) 53,000.

Bokassa's 32-ft ermine and velvet coronation robe alone cost $145,000, and the royal crown, made by Paris jewelers, cost $2 million. From January 1977, by Bokassa's decision, every citizen had to become a member of the Movement for the Social Evolution of Black Africa (MESAN), a single party of which the emperor was life president and "renewer" and the "arbiter and controller of the efficient functioning of its institutions."

In July two journalists, Michael Goldsmith of the Associated Press and Jonathan Randal of the *Washington Post*, were arrested and accused of spying and insulting the emperor. After several weeks in detention they were set free. Goldsmith, a British citizen, subsequently related how he was

Emperor Bokassa I of the Central African Empire declared himself life president of the ruling Movement for the Social Evolution of Black Africa.

CAMERAPIX/KEYSTONE

brought before Bokassa, who struck him unconscious with his staff of office.

The country's economy was hampered by its poor internal communications. In May plans were announced for a four-year, internationally financed CFA Fr 500 million road improvement scheme.   (PHILIPPE DECRAENE)

Chad

A landlocked republic of central Africa, Chad is bounded by Libya, the Sudan, the Central African Empire, Cameroon, Nigeria, and Niger. Area: 1,-284,000 sq km (495,755 sq mi). Pop. (1977 est.): 4,195,000, including Saras, other Africans, and Arabs. Cap. and largest city: N'Djamena (pop., 1975 est., 224,000). Language: French (official). Religion: Muslim 52%; animist 43%; Roman Catholic 5%. President and premier in 1977, Brig. Gen. Félix Malloum.

Gen. Félix Malloum's government faced domestic and international difficulties in 1977. Following an army mutiny on April 1, nine soldiers were executed on April 6. The French ethnologist Françoise Claustre, seized by Toubou rebels in 1974, was released by them on January 30 after Libyan leader Col. Muammar al-Qaddafi's intervention. A recurrence of drought and starvation in the north had to be met with foreign assistance.

The Libyan government cited an agreement made in 1935 between France and Italy, but disavowed in 1938, to justify its occupation of a strip of Chadian territory. Libya appeared to consider the new frontier as fixed and also gave military aid to the Toubou rebels, in spite of its official denials. This made it possible for the Toubous to launch an offensive in July in the Tibesti region, where they took the town of Bardai. France supplied weapons to the official forces.   (PHILIPPE DECRAENE)

CHAD

Education. Primary, pupils (1974–75) 208,071, teachers (1973–74) 2,540; secondary (1973–74), pupils 11,255, teachers 528; vocational, pupils (1973–74) 1,114, teachers (1965–66) 30; teacher training (1973–74), students 199, teachers 26; higher (1973–74), students 605, teaching staff 85.

Finance. Monetary unit: CFA franc, with (Sept. 19, 1977) a parity of CFA Fr 50 to the French franc and a free rate of CFA Fr 246.50 to U.S. $1 (CFA Fr 429.50 = £1 sterling). Budget (1976 est.) balanced at CFA Fr 15,785,000,000. Cost of living (N'Djamena; 1970 = 100; May 1977) 166.

Foreign Trade. (1974) Imports CFA Fr 20,859,000,000; exports CFA Fr 9,053,000,000. Import sources: France 37%; Nigeria 12%; U.S. 10%. Export destinations: not separately distinguished 74%; Zaire 5%. Main exports: cotton 67%; beef and veal (1973) 7%; cattle (1973) 5%.

Chemistry

Physical and Inorganic Chemistry. In the 1970s the cornerstone of solid-state electronics was crystalline, ultrapure silicon. It and its many counterparts—germanium, gallium arsenide, gallium phosphide, cadmium sulfide, zinc sulfide, etc.—generally owed their development not to inorganic chemists but to physicists, electrical engineers,

COURTESY, MOBIL TYCO SOLAR ENERGY CORPORATION, WALTHAM, MASSACHUSETTS; PHOTO, CAROL LEE

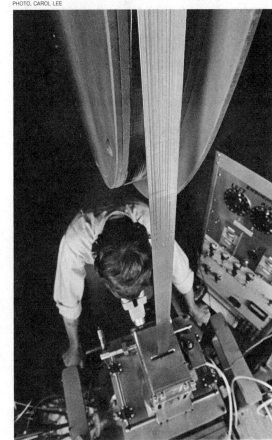

Chad

A ribbon of silicon crystal emerges from a machine at the Mobil Tyco Solar Energy Corp. in Waltham, Mass. Solar cells made from the crystal promise to reduce the cost of solar energy production.

and metallurgists. Crystallinity and ultrahigh purity were found to be essential properties, and preparation and processing of suitable material were consequently very expensive.

One of the main technological objectives of the late 1970s was the direct conversion of solar energy into electricity. Although crystalline silicon solar cells could perform this task with an efficiency of 22%, they were too expensive to produce on the large scale necessary to make the process economical. In recent months a series of technological breakthroughs was made that promised economic realization of solar energy conversion and questioned the requirement of crystallinity in inorganic semiconductors. Walter Spear and Peter Le Comber at the University of Dundee, Scotland, prepared thin films of amorphous silicon by subjecting silane gas (SiH_4) to an electric discharge. The electrical conductivity of this film could be varied by a factor of 600–1,000 by addition of small amounts of the two most common doping agents, phosphorus and boron. It was also established that the presence of hydrogen in the amorphous film was essential for semiconductor behaviour.

These workers, together with Stewart Kinmond of the University of Dundee and Marc Brodsky of IBM, fabricated from amorphous silicon the p-n junction used in solar cells. This was followed by report of an operating solar cell by David Carlson and Christopher Wronski of RCA Laboratories, Princeton, N.J. The conversion efficiency of the RCA cell was only 2.4%, an order of magnitude lower than that of the best crystalline silicon cell.

However, the amorphous silicon cell could be made inexpensively for large-scale use. Work was being carried out in many research centres to understand the unusual behaviour of amorphous films and to increase the efficiency of the amorphous silicon cell.

Materials of high molecular weight (polymers, proteins, nucleoproteins, etc.) occupied the interest of a large number of chemists and biochemists. The properties of these materials were highly dependent not only on their size but also on the distribution of sizes. Conventional methods of physical chemistry (*e.g.*, ultracentrifugation, electrophoresis, osmosis, and electron microscopy) required expensive apparatus and were time consuming. A simple and inexpensive method for characterizing materials of high molecular weight, called size-exclusion chromatography, was recently made possible by the availability of materials with uniform pore size in the range of 30–1,000 Å (angstrom; 1 Å = 10^{-8} cm). The principle of the method is illustrated by the following experiment: A column is filled with a special powder having a uniform pore diameter of 60 Å. A solution of dextran (a substance of high molecular weight) and benzyl alcohol is passed through. Unable to enter the pores, dextran passes out of the column before benzyl alcohol, which becomes entrapped and thus temporarily retained in the pores. By a proper choice of column material, not only a separation but also a size distribution of the retarded material could be obtained.

(JOHN TURKEVICH)

[122.A.6.a; 125.B; 125.E. and F]

Organic Chemistry. The past year saw major advances in the structural determination and synthesis of complex molecules and in new ways to carry out separations and transformations of organic substances.

A highly significant achievement was the elucidation of the structure of the genome, or genetic endowment, of the bacterial virus phiX174 by Frederick Sanger and co-workers of the MRC Laboratory of Molecular Biology, Cambridge, England. This genome is a single-stranded circular DNA of approximately 5,400 nucleotides, coding for nine known proteins. Sequencing of its nucleotides provided for the first time a viral genome of known structure and offered the possibility of understanding all functions of this molecule in terms of its structure. (*See* LIFE SCIENCES: *Molecular Biology.*) Also of interest was the determination of the structure of Q* nucleoside in transfer-RNA's, which are substances important in the synthesis of proteins in living systems. In contrast to these enormously complex nucleic-acid structures, one of the simplest naturally occurring substances identified this past year was the malodorous component associated with the mink and polecat, a four-membered ring (1) containing a sulfur atom.

Important progress occurred in the synthesis of complex molecules, primarily ones of biochemical interest. The molecular family of the prostaglandins, a group of naturally occurring substances of marked physiological activity and of great therapeutic interest, was shown to include the important thromboxanes and prostacyclins. Total laboratory syntheses of prostaglandins PGE_1 and A_2 from simple carbohydrates and of thromboxane B_2 were reported recently. Synthesis of prostaglandins within living organisms was shown to involve molecular oxygen and the unsaturated fatty acid arachidonic acid, leading to an endoperoxide, and two groups reported laboratory syntheses of the basic endoperoxide unit. Advances also took place in the synthesis of compounds of use in the treatment of cancer. Some of the most powerful anticancer drugs available in the late 1970s were complex, naturally occurring materials. Syntheses of adriamycin, daunomycin, vindoline, vinblastine, and vernolepin were reported, as well as several promising attempts to create derivatives of these drugs that were more active yet less toxic to healthy cells. Special mention also should be made of the total syntheses of two other naturally occurring substances—the antibiotic gliotoxin (2), which possesses an unusual sulfur-containing bicyclic component, and saxitoxin (3), a powerful, nonprotein nerve poison isolated from Alaska butter clams, which feed on toxin-forming species of dinoflagellates.

The year also witnessed improved methods of effecting specific changes in bonding. Of particular interest were applications of zirconium, selenium, and silicon derivatives in organic synthesis. An example of the last type is the reaction of fluoride ion with β-halo-organosilicon species to create molecules containing remarkably strained carbon-carbon double bonds. A significant contribution to the synthesis of ring systems and to an understanding of these reactions appeared, in which the relative ease of formation of three- to seven-mem-

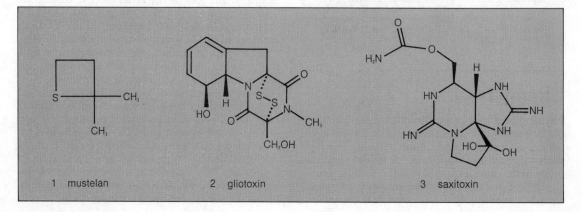

1 mustelan 2 gliotoxin 3 saxitoxin

bered rings was explained in terms of the preferred angle for nucleophilic attack on pi and sigma bonds.

Strong interest was developing in the use of tunable lasers as specific energy sources for inducing chemical reactions. Recent studies of infrared laser radiation of organic systems comprised a major advance in chemistry. Contrary to original expectations, it was found that many photons could be pumped into a specific vibrational state of a molecule before redistribution of the additional energy took place. This phenomenon permitted a new method for selective activation of molecular species and was likely to see much future use.

Novel techniques for chemical transformations and separations were developed in recent studies concerned with solvation. Many-atom ring systems (crown ethers and cryptates) containing oxygen, nitrogen, or sulfur were shown to have high affinity for inorganic cations, and an anion-complexing cryptate also was reported. The concept was extended to the synthesis of cyclic, oxygen-containing systems (called hosts) capable of complexing selectively with organic substrates (or guests). In one case, use of an optically active host permitted the separation of racemic amino acids (the guests) into their optically active forms. These notions of specific solvation also led to greatly improved ways of effecting desired reactions in heterogeneous systems, through a process called phase transfer catalysis. Addition of catalytic amounts of certain species, generalized Q^+X^- (usually quaternary ammonium or phosphonium salts), resulted in the transfer of a water-soluble reactant, $e.g.$, a nucleophile, N^-, across the aqueous-organic interface into the organic phase as Q^+N^-, where a homogeneous reaction could take place rapidly. The versatility, simplicity, and speed of phase transfer catalysis made it suitable in many alkylation, elimination, addition, condensation, oxidation, and reduction reactions.

(FREDERICK D. GREENE)

[122.B; 122.E.q and r; 123.D. and H]

Applied Chemistry. Chemical investigators were particularly active in the development of materials with unique properties and practical applications. Several companies developed metal powders that acted as "sponges" to hold twice the volume of hydrogen that could be contained in an identical volume of the liquefied gas. The powders, usually composed of nickel, lanthanum, and certain rare-earth elements, reacted reversibly with hydrogen to form an easily manageable solid hydride. In addition to storage, the concept was expected to find application in waste-gas purification and energy systems.

Two types of synthetic fibres that outperformed natural ones were developed by European firms. Courtaulds, Ltd., of London created a tubular viscose fibre that provided less weight and a more luxurious feel than the solid version. It could absorb 120% of its weight of water, and allowed about 13.5% moisture uptake before wearers perceived any dampness—about the same as wool. A lightweight, moisture-absorbing acrylic fibre produced by Bayer Aktiengesellschaft of West Germany was 25% lighter than conventional acrylics,

A technician examines a cloth sample treated with a conventional permanent-press formulation and an experimental catalyst. Catalytic bisulfate salts of the light metals were under study as nonpolluting alternatives to currently used zinc and halide salts.

did not swell appreciably during water uptake, and could absorb almost 19% by weight of water before dampness became perceptible.

A family of materials that froze and thawed at room temperatures found new application at Michigan Technological University. Called clathrates, the substances were lattice-like molecules that enclosed another molecule, in this case water. With a melting point of 50°–85° F, the materials took up or released heat equal to that of water when it changes phase from liquid to ice. Sealed in exterior walls of homes or in similar boundaries, clathrates might help moderate interior temperature by solidifying to release heat when the weather was cold and by melting to absorb heat when the weather was warm.

Scientists at Los Alamos Scientific Laboratory in New Mexico developed a process for making an extremely hard, nonbrittle composite of tantalum carbide and graphite. The substance had a melting point of 6,760° F and was expected to find applications in space vehicles and in high-speed tools, dies, and other industrial equipment.

Hybrid-material parts to lighten trucks and autos and improve gas mileage were under intensive investigation by industry, especially in the U.S. where increasingly strict fuel economy standards for auto manufacturers were in force. Ford Motor Co. was testing springs made of a carbon-glass-epoxy composite that weighed as little as one-sixth of steel equivalents. In addition, carbon-reinforced plastics required only a fraction of the energy needed to make steel or aluminum.

Enrichment of uranium by liquid-phase techniques was announced by the French Atomic Energy Commission. Although the method was shrouded in traditional nuclear secrecy, it was said to compare favourably with present gaseous-diffusion and centrifugal enrichment processes. Although it made reactor-grade fuel, the method was extremely slow and impractical for preparing weapons-grade uranium, a major advantage given international efforts to stem proliferation of nuclear-weapons technology. (FREDERICK C. PRICE)

See also Materials Sciences; Nobel Prizes.

Chess

Though the year 1977 was lively and full of incident, perhaps its most important aspect was something that did not happen. Former world champion Bobby Fischer remained obstinately in retirement, and though he was, it seemed, still keenly interested in chess, he refused all offers of either match or tournament. He did, however, send a letter of congratulation to Viktor Korchnoi on his defection in 1976 from the Soviet Union.

Korchnoi was one of the chief actors in the Candidates series of matches held to find a challenger for world champion Anatoly Karpov in 1978. He surmounted what was potentially his highest hurdle when he met and narrowly beat former world champion Tigran Petrosian (U.S.S.R.) by 6½ points to 5½ points in the quarterfinals in February and March. In the same period Boris Spassky (U.S.S.R.) won an even harder victory against Vlastimil Hort (Czech.), 8½–7½. The other quarterfinals were won by Lajos Portisch (Hung.) over Bent Larsen (Den.), 6½–3½, and by Lev Polugayevsky (U.S.S.R.) over Henrique Mecking (Brazil), 6½–5½. The semifinals were played in July and August 1977. Korchnoi crushed Polugayevsky, 8½–4½, and Spassky won, though with more difficulty, against Portisch, 8½–6½. In the 20-game final match in the Candidates, Korchnoi led Spassky 7½–5½ at the end of 1977.

Meanwhile, Karpov had been demonstrating in a number of strong events that, with Fischer out of action, he was undoubtedly the world's leading player. He won the 44th Soviet championship in December 1976 (his first win of the title), won a strong international tournament at Bad Lauterberg, West Germany, in March 1977, and, playing on top board for the U.S.S.R. at the European team championship finals in Moscow in April, scored 5 out of 5. The Soviet team had little difficulty in retaining the championship at that event, finishing 10½ points ahead of the second team, Hungary.

Twelve-year-old Nigel Short, from Lancashire, England, was the youngest player ever to compete in the British Chess Federation championships.

RUSH/KATHERINE YOUNG

QGD Half-Slav Defense, Meran Variation (seventh game of the match at Evian, France, 1977)

White V. Korchnoi	Black L. Polugayevsky	White V. Korchnoi	Black L. Polugayevsky
1 P—QB4	Kt—KB3	23 P—Kt5	PxP
2 Kt—QB3	P—K3	24 QxKKtP	Q—K2
3 Kt—B3	P—Q4	25 Q—R5	P—Kt3
4 P—Q4	P—B3	26 Q—R6	Q—B3
5 P—K3	QKt—Q2	27 B—B4	P—Q6
6 B—Q3	PxP	28 P—K5	Q—B4
7 BxBP	P—QKt4	29 RxP	B—K5
8 B—Q3	B—Kt2	30 R—Q6	Q—Kt5
9 0—0	P—Kt5	31 R—KB6	B—B4
10 Kt—K4	B—K2	32 P—QKt3	B—Q5
11 KtxKt ch	KtxKt	33 KtxB	QxKt
12 P—K4	0—0	34 RxP ch	BxR
13 Q—B2	P—KR3	35 QxB ch	K—R1
14 B—K3	R—B1	36 Q—R6 ch	K—Kt1
15 KR—Q1	P—B4	37 P—K6	Q—K5
16 PxP	Kt—Kt5	38 PxP ch	RxP
17 B—Q4	P—K4	39 Q—KB6	Q—Kt8 ch
18 P—KR3	PxB	40 K—R2	Q—R2 ch
19 PxKt	RxP	41 K—Kt3	Q—Q6 ch
20 Q—Q2	P—QR4	42 P—B3	QxB
21 QR—B1	Q—Q2	43 Q—Q8 ch	resigns
22 RxR	BxR		

English Opening (played in the international tournament at Las Palmas, Grand Canary, Spain, 1977)

White S. Tatai	Black A. Karpov	White S. Tatai	Black A. Karpov
1 Kt—KB3	P—QB4	17 P—Q3	P—QKt4
2 P—B4	Kt—KB3	18 B—K3	P—Kt5
3 Kt—B3	P—Q4	19 Kt—Q1	R—K1
4 PxP	KtxP	20 PxP	PxP
5 P—KKt3	P—KKt3	21 BxKt	QxB
6 B—Kt2	B—Kt2	22 P—QR3	B—Kt5
7 Q—R4 ch	Kt—B3	23 Q—B2	Q—Q6
8 Kt—KKt5	P—K3	24 PxQ	PxP dis ch
9 Kt(Kt5)—K4	Kt—Kt3	25 K—Q2	R—K7 ch
10 Q—Kt5	P—B5	26 KxP	R—Q1 ch
11 Kt—R4	0—0	27 K—B4	RxQ ch
12 KtxKt	PxKt	28 KxP	R(B7)—Q7
13 QxBP	P—K4	29 P—B3	B—B1 ch
14 Q—B2	Kt—Q5	30 K—R5	B—Q2
15 Q—Kt1	P—B4	resigns	
16 Kt—B3	P—K5		

In May, Karpov came first at Las Palmas in the Grand Canary, no less than 2½ points ahead of Larsen. His one comparative failure occurred when he tied for fourth/fifth place with R. Vaganian (U.S.S.R.) with 10 points, below O. Romanishin and M. Tal (both U.S.S.R.), 11½, and V. Smyslov (U.S.S.R.), 10½. But in the strongest tournament of the year, at Tilburg, Neth., in September, he was the only player to remain unbeaten and was an easy first, a full point ahead of Tony Miles (Great Britain).

The women's world champion, Nona Gaprindashvili (U.S.S.R.), accomplished what was probably the best performance of all time by a woman player when she shared first place with grand masters Y. Balashov (U.S.S.R.) and O. Panno (Arg.) at the exceedingly strong Swiss system tournament at Lone Pine, Calif., in March. The women's Candidates matches, to determine who should challenge Gaprindashvili for her title in 1978, went at a slower tempo than the men's events. Soviet players dominated the quarterfinals with the following results: M. Chiburdanidze 5½, N. Alexandria 4½; E. Fatalibekova 6, V. Kozlovskaya 2; E. Akhmilovskaya 6½, T. Lematchko (Bulg.) 5½; A. Kushnir (Israel) 6, I. Levitina 3. Except for the two players designated, all were from the U.S.S.R.

The Soviet team easily retained its championship in the 1976 Students' Olympiad at Caracas, Venezuela, and in the 1977 event in Mexico City, but at the 1976 World Junior championship it was the U.S. player Mark Diesen who won the title. The Soviets came back at the 1977 event at Innsbruck, Austria, where Yusupov came first with 10½ out of 13. A non-Soviet grand master who notably increased his reputation was the 22-year-old British player Tony Miles; two first prizes in strong tournaments were at Biel, Switz., and the IBM tournament in Amsterdam were followed by an impressive second place in the great tournament at Tilburg, a point below Karpov but also a point ahead of four grand masters, Hort, F. Hübner (West Germany), L. Kavalek (U.S.), and J. Timman (Neth.). Another young grand master who did very well was Romanishin, who won first prize at Hastings, England, and followed this with his first at Leningrad.

Other good results in strong tournaments were the tie for first place at Wijk-aan-Zee, Neth., between E. Geller (U.S.S.R.) and G. Sosonko (Neth.) and Larsen's first prize at Geneva, even though he started two days late in this tournament immediately after losing his match to Portisch. A strong Open championship at Fairfax, Va., in 1976 ended in a tie between two grand masters, A. Lein and L. Shamkovich. The 1977 British championship was won by George Botterill at Brighton.

Politics again bedeviled international chess. An Extraordinary General Assembly of the World Chess Federation (FIDE), convoked at Lucerne, Switz., reversed (by 28 to 23 votes) the decision of the 1976 FIDE meeting, which had restored the South African Chess Federation to full participation in FIDE events. FIDE's president, Max Euwe, subsequently issued a report deploring renewed political activities on the part of many member federations. (HARRY GOLOMBEK)

[452.C.3.c.i]

Chile

A republic extending along the southern Pacific coast of South America, Chile has an area of 756,-626 sq km (292,135 sq mi), not including its Antarctic claim. It is bounded by Argentina, Bolivia, and Peru. Pop. (1977 est.): 10,655,800. Cap. and largest city: Santiago (metro. pop., 1975 est., 3,263,000). Language: Spanish. Religion: predominantly Roman Catholic. President in 1977, Gen. Augusto Pinochet Ugarte.

In September 1977 the Chilean junta celebrated its fourth year of existence. It retained full control of the country, and there was little apparent prospect of major changes in the near future. The state of siege continued in force, and a curfew was maintained. In March the junta dissolved the remaining political parties and in July announced long-term plans for a return to civilian rule, which the authorities clearly wished to be on the basis of non-Marxist parties untainted by what they considered to be vices of the old political factions. Whether the junta was capable of establishing a new political tradition which it termed an "authoritarian democracy" (involving an appointed legislature in 1981 and direct voting for two-thirds of the legislature in 1985 and the presidency in 1991) remained to be seen.

The various political groups in exile, covering a wide political spectrum from the far-left parties of the Unidad Popular (UP) coalition of Communists and Socialists to the Christian Democrats, appeared to be incapable of forming a united opposition to the junta. Christian Democrats, in particular party members still in Chile, felt that too close an association with UP parties would alienate potential supporters. Indeed, a number of Christian Democrats were working within the government.

By 1977 the junta had released virtually all political prisoners, but critics of its human rights policy had not received satisfactory official explanations of the large number of mysterious disappearances. On August 6 the secret police, the infamous DINA, was disbanded and replaced by the Central Nacional de Informaciones, which like the DINA reported directly to the president. To critics this appeared to be merely a cosmetic change. During the year criticism of official policies became more public and more vocal.

On September 8, at the ceremonies marking the signature of two new Panama Canal treaties, Pres. Augusto Pinochet Ugarte and U.S. Pres. Jimmy Carter had a personal meeting that marked the end of the near state of ostracism imposed on Chile by the U.S. But U.S. policy, combining both pragmatic and idealistic tendencies, continued to exert strong pressure on Chile and other Latin-American countries concerning human rights.

Despite the easing in official relations with the U.S., Chile continued to suffer from a poor image in the rest of the world; indeed, at the same time as the September meeting in Washington, D.C., U.S. authorities made known to the press their belief that the DINA had been responsible for organizing the murder, by Cuban exiles, of Orlando Letelier, the former Socialist minister, in Washington on Sept. 21, 1976.

The Panama Canal treaty ceremonies in Washington also provided the opportunity for a meeting between the presidents of Chile, Bolivia, and Peru, the first for 100 years, to discuss the problem of Bolivian access to the Pacific Ocean. The only result of the meeting was apparently a decision that the countries' foreign ministers would attack

Chile

Copper mining in Chile was given a boost by the construction of a large hydroelectric plant at Coya to supply power to the huge El Teniente copper mining complex.

CAMERA PRESS/PHOTO TRENDS

the problem with renewed vigour. Because of this issue Chile's relations with Peru continued to oscillate, and rumours of the possibility of armed conflict came to the surface several times. Points of conflict also arose with Chile's powerful neighbour Argentina. The latter appeared to be unwilling to accept the award to Chile in May, by an international court of arbitration, of three islands in the Beagle Channel—Nueva, Picton, and Lennox. Both countries had nine months in which to study the court's decision. Soon protests were made by both governments concerning alleged incursions into territorial waters and air space. Behind the question of the islands themselves lay the issues of territorial waters and the potential of offshore oil. Virtually all of Chile's remaining links with the Andean common market were severed in August when Chile withdrew from the Andean Development Corporation.

The slow recovery of the economy continued. The government's orthodox policies reduced the overall budget deficit to nearly 10% of expenditure, while the deficit as expressed in terms of gross domestic product (GDP) fell from 23.5% in 1973 to 2.7% in 1976. The rate of inflation was expected to fall to 60–65% in 1977, and there were official hopes for a reduction to 20–25% in 1978. The GDP was expected to grow at 8–9% in 1977, double the rate of the previous year. Agricultural production in 1977 was expected to record one of the largest increases ever.

Despite these improvements, problem areas remained, such as the high (though decreasing) rate of unemployment and the need to increase the rate of investment. The latter was the cause of the favourable conditions granted by Chile to foreign investment and announced on March 18. One of the sectors where such investment was encouraged was mining; unfortunately, this tended to be capital rather than labour intensive. Some experts did not expect an upturn in the world copper market until 1979 and, in spite of diversification, copper still accounted for over 50% of Chilean exports. The 1977 budget and balance of payments projections were based on a world price of copper of 60 U.S. cents per pound; by September the average world price for 1977 to date had fallen to a little above that level. The overall balance of payments was expected to result in a deficit of $150 million for 1977, but Chile was not expected to have difficulty in meeting its debt repayments.

(JOHN HALE)

China

The most populous country in the world and the third largest in area, China is bounded by the U.S.S.R., Mongolia, North Korea, Vietnam, Laos, Burma, India, Bhutan, Nepal, Pakistan, and Afghanistan and also by the Sea of Japan, the Yellow Sea, and the East and South China seas. From 1949 the country has been divided into the People's Republic of China (Communist) on the mainland and on Hainan and other islands, and the Republic of China (Nationalist) on Taiwan. (*See* TAIWAN.) Area: 9,561,000 sq km (3,691,521 sq mi), including Tibet but excluding Taiwan. Population of the People's Republic: most recent official figures total 866 million; other unofficial estimates ranged upward to 986 million in 1977. Capital: Peking (metro. pop., 1975 est., 8,487,000). Largest city: Shanghai (metro. pop., 1975 est., 10,888,000). Language: Chinese (varieties of the Peking dialect predominate). Chairman of the Communist Party and premier in 1977, Hua Kuo-feng.

In 1977 crucial questions arose over who was to lead the nation, what ideology was to be followed, and what compromises could best resolve personal differences in the post-Mao era. The sometimes bitter disputes were rather conclusively settled by reinstating Teng Hsiao-p'ing and by convening the 11th national congress of the Chinese Communist Party. These steps were taken against a backdrop of events that in 1976 included the following: the death in January of Premier Chou En-lai, a stabilizing factor in times of political crisis; the T'ien An Men riots in April, during which crowds gathered to honour Chou's memory and to protest the dogmatic measures of Chairman Mao and his wife, Chiang Ch'ing; an antirightist campaign in April, instigated by Chiang and her close associates, which sought to purge Teng Hsiao-p'ing as heir apparent to the premiership; and, in July, the death of veteran leader Gen. Chu Teh, founder of the Red Army and chairman of the Standing Committee of the People's Congress. Finally, on September 9, China suffered its greatest loss with the death of Chairman Mao Tse-tung, founder of the People's Republic.

About one month after the death of Mao, Hua Kuo-feng, who became the first vice-chairman of the party and premier of the State Council in April 1976, was proclaimed Mao's successor as chairman of the party and its Military Commission. With the support and cooperation of Defense Minister Yeh Chien-ying and other military commanders in the capital region, Hua apparently outmaneuvered Mao's unpopular widow, who was arrested together with three of her close associates (Chang Ch'un-ch'iao, Wang Hung-wen, and Yao Wen-yuan). All were accused of attempting to seize power. Though they had been known as ultraleftists during Mao's Cultural Revolution, they were condemned as "ultrarightists and counterrevolutionary revisionists" and were officially branded the "gang of four" by the new leadership. The new

CAMERA PRESS

leadership under Hua first sought to consolidate its power by campaigning against the gang of four and reshuffling Cabinet ministers and leaders of some provincial organizations.

In order to clear the way for a plenary meeting of the Central Committee and later of a party congress, the rectification campaign was intensified in about half of China's 29 provincial units during the first half of the year. In July the third plenum of the tenth party congress met and approved retroactively the appointment of Hua as chairman of the party. It also reinstated Teng in his high posts for the second time, and decided to convene the 11th party congress before the end of the year. The congress apparently formulated clear domestic and foreign policies before adjourning just four days before U.S. Secretary of State Cyrus Vance arrived in Peking on August 22.

Internal Politics. Because Chairman Mao had left no clear instruction concerning his successor, a power struggle was inevitable between the moderate faction led by Hua and the leftist group headed by Chiang Ch'ing. The strength of the gang of four stemmed from their positions on the Politburo, from their prominence during the Cultural Revolution, and from their control over the mass media, cultural institutions, the city of Shanghai, and the militia. Their weaknesses were a lack of real power within the party, the Army, and the state bureaucracy.

The death of Mao so weakened the hand of the leftists that Hua and his Politburo supporters were able to control events. An article in the *People's Daily* of Dec. 18, 1976, accused the gang of four of conniving against the party and the state immediately after Mao's death by appropriating the name of the General Office of the party and by instructing local branches of the party to report to them instead of to the Central Committee headed by Hua. To bolster their authority, the leftists cited Mao's purported last words: "Act according to the principles laid down," which was interpreted to include criticism of Teng and his ideas. Hua struck back on October 2, charging that the gang had fabricated Mao's last words. Hua claimed that Mao's final written words to him were: "Act in line with the past principles," and "With you in charge, I am at ease." Millions of copies of this

At the 11th national party congress at Peking in August, Chairman Hua Kuo-feng (extreme left) lines up with the four vice-chairmen (left to right): Yeh Chien-ying, Teng Hsiao-p'ing, Li Hsien-nien, and Wang Tung-hsing.

China

CHINA

Education. Primary, pupils (1959–60) 90 million, teachers (1964) c. 2.6 million; secondary (1958–59), pupils 8,520,000; vocational (1958–59), pupils 850,000; teacher training, students (1958–59) 620,000; higher (1962–63), students 820,000.

Finance. Monetary unit: yuan, with (Sept. 17, 1977) a free rate of 1.85 yuan to U.S. $1 (3.21 yuan = £1 sterling). Gold reserves (1973 est.) U.S. $2 billion. Budget (1960 est.; latest published) balanced at 70,020,000 yuan. Gross national product (1975 est.) U.S. $286 billion.

Foreign Trade. (1975) Imports c. U.S. $7.3 billion; exports c. U.S. $6.9 billion. Import sources: Japan c. 34%; West Germany c. 8%; France c. 6%; Canada c. 6%; Australia c. 5%; U.S. c. 5%. Export destinations: Japan c. 20%; Hong Kong c. 18%. Main exports: foodstuffs (meat and products, cereals, fruits and vegetables) c. 30%; textiles and clothing c. 20%; crude oil c. 12%.

Transport and Communications. Roads (1975) c. 750,000 km. Motor vehicles in use (1975): passenger c. 37,000; commercial (including buses) c. 675,000. Railways: (1976) c. 48,000 km; traffic (1959) 45,670,000,000 passenger-km, freight (1971) 301,000,000,000 net ton-km. Air traffic (1960): 63,882,000 passenger-km; freight 1,967,000 net ton-km. Inland waterways (including Yangtze River; 1975) c. 160,000 km. Shipping (1976): merchant vessels 100 gross tons and over 551; gross tonnage 3,588,726. Telephones (1951) 255,000. Radio receivers (Dec. 1970) c. 12 million. Television receivers (Dec. 1973) 500,000.

Agriculture. Production (in 000; metric tons; 1976): rice c. 114,000; corn c. 34,000; wheat c. 43,000; barley c. 21,500; millet c. 24,500; potatoes c. 40,700; dry peas c. 4,800; soybeans c. 12,000; peanuts c. 2,800; rapeseed c. 1,300; sugar, raw value c. 4,000; pears c. 1,000; tobacco c. 950; tea c. 320; cotton, lint c. 2,400; jute c. 500; cow's milk c. 3,700; beef and buffalo meat (1975) c. 1,900; pork (1975) c. 9,700; timber (cu m; 1975) c. 190,000; fish catch (1975) c. 6,800. Livestock (in 000; 1976): horses c. 7,000; asses c. 11,800; cattle c. 64,000; buffalo c. 30,000; sheep c. 74,000; pigs c. 233,000; goats c. 60,500.

Industry. Fuel and power (in 000; metric tons; 1976): coal (including lignite) c. 500,000; coke (1974) c. 28,000; crude oil c. 90,000; electricity (kw-hr; 1975) c. 120,000,000. Production (in 000; metric tons; 1975): iron ore (metal content) c. 40,000; pig iron c. 36,000; crude steel c. 27,000; lead c. 100; copper c. 100; zinc c. 100; bauxite c. 600; aluminum c. 150; magnesite c. 1,000; manganese ore c. 300; tungsten concentrates (oxide content) c. 11; cement c. 20,000; sulfuric acid (1966) c. 2,500; fertilizers (nutrient content; 1975–76) nitrogenous c. 3,300; phosphate c. 1,200; potash c. 300; cotton yarn (1969) c. 1,450; cotton fabrics (1973) c. 8,000; man-made fibres c. 85; paper c. 4,700.

The first anniversary of the death of Mao Tsetung was observed in Peking by a ceremonial dedication of a white marble mausoleum honouring the former chairman.

statement were circulated to legitimize the position of Hua as chairman prior to the meeting of the 11th party congress. Hua and Yeh Chien-ying used that forum to reiterate Mao's personal choice of Hua as his successor. They also cited Hua's appointment to the new post of first vice-chairman of the party and to the premiership in April 1976, "a major strategic decision of Chairman Mao" to ensure that "the party and state leadership would not fall into the hands of the gang of four."

Hua tightened his hold on power by invoking Mao's Thought and creed. Mao's 1956 circular "The Ten Major Relations," directed to party leaders, was published and circulated in January. It was a middle-of-the-road statement rejecting extremes and factionalism, and five of its ten points dealt with the economy. In April the long-delayed fifth volume of Mao's *Selected Works*, edited by Hua, was published. It contained Mao's speeches and papers covering the period of 1949–57 before the turmoil of the Great Leap Forward. The publication was obviously intended to enhance the position of the new leadership by presenting the late chairman as a moderate socialist devoted to economic growth.

When the Politburo named Hua as Mao's successor in October 1976, it was still divided on the question of Teng's reinstatement. After the purge of the gang of four, public pressure intensified and southern military leaders pressed their demands that Teng be returned to power. On January 8, the first anniversary of Chou En-lai's death, tens of thousands of people gathered in Peking and other cities to pay tribute to him and call for the rehabilitation of Teng. By that time the role that Teng and his political and military supporters could play in solving the twin problems of establishing Hua's authority and of revitalizing the economy had become obvious. In March a central working conference of Chinese leaders, apparently including Teng, was held in Peking to discuss Teng's future. Since Teng's dismissal in 1976 had been sanctioned by Mao and had the unanimous support of the Politburo members (including Hua), delicacy was called for. At the working conference Hua concluded that "all slanders and unfounded charges" made by the gang of four against Teng should be repudiated, and that the restoration of Teng to all his posts embodied "the wishes of party members and the people." In return, Teng presumably agreed to support Hua and Vice-Chairman Yeh, and all agreed to accept Mao's Thought as the main source of authority. To implement the agreement the third plenary session of the Central Committee was held from July 16 to 21. The plenum first unanimously confirmed the appointment of Hua as chairman of the party and its Military Commission. It also unanimously supported the restoration of Teng to all his former posts and expelled the gang of four from the party. In addition, it decided to convene the 11th party congress to discuss the political report of the Central Committee, a revision of the party constitution, and elections to the Central Committee.

The 11th national party congress, which was held from August 12 to 18 and attended by 1,510 delegates representing over 35 million party members, was officially described as the congress to resolve the 11th struggle between "the proletariat and the bourgeoisie." Following the tenth congress third plenum of "unity and victory" in smashing the gang of four, the 11th party congress announced the conclusion of the Great Proletarian Cultural Revolution. But the official communiqué of the congress also stated that this did not mean the end of the continued revolution under the dictatorship of the proletariat. The reports on political development and on the constitutional revision stressed the need and importance of modernizing China's agriculture, industry, defense, and technology in order to reach Chou's goal of making China a strong socialist country by the end of the century. In his lengthy political report to the congress on August 12, Hua called on the delegates to carry out Mao's behests and endorsed the new emphasis on the economy, science, and education. Praising Hua's able and wise leadership, Yeh reported on the revision of the party constitution, which was largely based on that of 1973 but contained important new provisions on the probation-ary period for membership and intraparty discipline. At its plenary session on August 18, the congress elected the Central Committee of 333 members and unanimously adopted both Hua's political report and the new constitution. It decided to convene the fifth People's Congress "at an appropriate time" to restructure the State Council. In the closing address, Teng said that a new period in China's socialist revolution and construction had begun. Though the Congress underscored modernization and practical goals rather than ideology, the Thought of Mao was still viewed as the foundation of China's Communist system. Teng also emerged as a powerful force in the new leadership.

The 11th Central Committee, consisting of 201 full and 132 alternate members, held its first plenary session on August 19. About one-third of the members were new, with more specialists and fewer representatives of the masses appearing on the roster. The plenum elected Hua as chairman and named four vice-chairmen: Yeh Chien-ying, Teng Hsiao-p'ing, Li Hsien-nien, and Wang Tung-hsing. Together they formed the Standing Committee of the Politburo, which consisted of 23 regulars and three alternates. Some observers called Hua, Yeh, and Teng the triumvirate of China's new leadership. Li was valued for his broad experience in economic and foreign affairs. Wang, who commanded Mao's bodyguards and played a crucial role in the arrest of the gang of four, rose to new prominence in the 11th congress. Twelve of the 23 regular Politburo members had military backgrounds and six new members had been purged in the Cultural Revolution and later rehabilitated. The makeup of the new Politburo was thus clearly different from the one that presided over the Cultural Revolution.

The Economy. China's economy suffered a setback in 1976. U.S. analysts estimated that China's grain production decreased from nearly 290 million tons in 1975 to about 275 million tons in 1976, while 1976 industrial output rose by only 3–5%, compared with 10% in 1975. Official statements proclaimed a notable increase in overall production for the first six months of 1977, but hard statistics were lacking. China contracted to purchase some five million tons of wheat in 1977 from Argentina, Australia, and Canada. In an attempt to revitalize the economy, China's new leaders approved material incentives outlawed by the Cultural Revolution, upgraded science and technology, and sanctioned the purchase of advanced foreign technology and equipment. One of the most striking changes directly affected university education. The Ministry of Education published a series of major reforms that reintroduced unified competitive entrance examinations and permitted senior middle school (high school) graduates to continue their studies without first spending two years as ordinary labourers. The overall goal was "to bring up a mighty contingent of working-class intellectuals as fast as possible."

Foreign Affairs. The new leadership, stressing continuity, chose to follow Chairman Mao's revolutionary policy guidelines by opposing the hegemonism of the two superpowers, "the source

of a new world war," by strengthening friendship with nations of the second world as a counterbalance to Soviet expansion and U.S. dominance, and by enhancing unity and solidarity with nonaligned nations of the third world.

Sino-Soviet relations remained strained. After the death of Mao, Deputy Foreign Minister Leonid F. Ilyichev returned to Peking to resume border talks after an interval of 18 months, but negotiations remained deadlocked. *Pravda* charged on May 14, just before the resumption of U.S.-Soviet talks on strategic arms limitation in Geneva, that China was preparing for war and accused Peking of obstructing disarmament and détente. In a speech at a June state banquet for visiting Sudanese Pres. Gaafar Nimeiry, Vice-Premier Li accused Moscow of pretending to improve relations while hurling malicious slander at China. Li lauded the Sudan for expelling Soviet military experts and accused the U.S.S.R. of trying to dominate southern Africa and the Red Sea region. When Li criticized Moscow's African policies at an official dinner for Vice-Pres. Ismail Ali Aboker of Somalia on June 20, Soviet bloc diplomats walked out in protest. On September 24, Teng Hsiao-p'ing announced that China's 1950 treaty of friendship with the Soviet Union was "no longer valid." President Tito of Yugoslavia, once branded by Maoists as a Communist traitor, arrived in Peking on August 30 and was given an enthusiastic reception.

Sino-U.S. relations continued to revolve around the Shanghai Communiqué of February 1972, but establishment of full diplomatic relations between China and the U.S. was hampered by three pre-

A Chinese hydrogen bomb blast created this spectacular atomic cloud. The photograph was released by China in July, but the date of the test was not disclosed.

UPI COMPIX

conditions laid down by Peking: derecognition of the Republic of China (Taiwan), abrogation of the 1954 U.S.-Taiwan mutual defense treaty, and withdrawal of U.S. forces, now numbering only about 1,200, from the island. U.S. Pres. Jimmy Carter remained committed to his campaign promise of seeking normalization of relations with Peking without, however, sacrificing the security of Taiwan. Toward the end of 1976 a congressional fact-finding mission visited five Asian countries, including China and Taiwan. In its report to Congress in January the group stated that strategic, economic, and other reasons should restrain the U.S. from recognizing Peking on its own terms. Peking showed signs of growing impatience over the slow pace of U.S. withdrawal from Taiwan. On February 8, when President Carter told Huang Chen of the Chinese liaison office in Washington, D.C., of his desire to strengthen Sino-U.S. relations, Huang asked Carter and Vance if they were aware that the Nixon and Ford administrations had virtually pledged to end diplomatic ties with the Republic of China. In a show of good will, Vance briefed Huang on his unsuccessful mission to Moscow. In addition, President Carter's son Chip, accompanying a bipartisan congressional delegation that visited China in late April, carried a presidential message to the new Chinese leaders. In announcing Vance's mission to Peking, Carter expressed hope that full diplomatic relations could be established with Peking while ensuring peace for Taiwan. Shortly before Vance arrived in Peking on August 22, Hua reiterated the three preconditions for normalization of relations and warned that China's determination to liberate Taiwan was entirely a question of internal affairs, "which brooks no foreign interference whatsoever." At the conclusion of four days of talks with top Chinese leaders, Vance gave no hint that the U.S. was ready to abandon Taiwan. On September 6, Teng revealed that Vance's offer to set up an official liaison in Taiwan and an embassy in Peking was a step backward from Pres. Gerald Ford's offer in December 1975 to break diplomatic relations with the Nationalist regime. Vance's proposal was thus deemed unacceptable, and the Taiwan issue remained unresolved. (HUNG-TI CHU)

Colombia

A republic in northwestern South America, Colombia is bordered by Panama, Venezuela, Brazil, Peru, and Ecuador and has coasts on both the Caribbean Sea and the Pacific Ocean. Area: 1,138,914 sq km (439,737 sq mi). Pop. (1977 est.): 24,893,800. Cap. and largest city: Bogotá (pop., 1977 est., 3,618,800). Language: Spanish. Religion: Roman Catholic (96%). President in 1977, Alfonso López Michelsen.

In April 1977 Pres. Alfonso López Michelsen threatened to resign over the alleged financial misdealings of his sons, but an investigation ordered by the president himself cleared them. Kidnappings and violence continued, and on July 6 a senior air force officer, Col. Osiris Maldonado, was assassinated by a Maoist guerrilla organization.

Colombia

COLOMBIA

Education. (1975) Primary, pupils 3,953,242, teachers 131,211; secondary, pupils 977,648, teachers 51,232; vocational, pupils 260,963, teachers 14,894; teacher training, students 67,664, teachers 3,995; higher, students 192,887, teaching staff 21,163.

Finance. Monetary unit: peso, with (Sept. 19, 1977) an official rate of 36.23 pesos to U.S. $1 (free rate of 64.50 pesos = £1 sterling). Gold, SDR's, and foreign exchange (June 1977) U.S. $1,566,000,000. Budget (1976 actual): revenue 48,816,000,000 pesos; expenditure 44,086,000,000 pesos. Gross national product (1975) 411,570,000,000 pesos. Money supply (Oct. 1976) 68,251,000,000 pesos. Cost of living (Bogotá; 1970 = 100; May 1977) 377.

Foreign Trade. (1976) Imports 59,795,000,000 pesos; exports 55,575,000,000 pesos. Import sources (1975): U.S. 43%; West Germany 9%; Japan 9%. Export destinations (1975): U.S. 32%; West Germany 15%; The Netherlands 6%; Venezuela 6%. Main exports: coffee 53%; textile yarns and fabric 7%. Tourism (1974): visitors 363,000; gross receipts U.S. $102 million.

Transport and Communications. Roads (1975) 49,248 km. Motor vehicles in use (1975): passenger 305,000; commercial 56,000. Railways: (1974) 3,424 km; traffic (1976) 511 million passenger-km, freight 1,247,000,000 net ton-km. Air traffic (1975): 2,778,000,000 passenger-km; freight 126.3 million net ton-km. Shipping (1976): merchant vessels 100 gross tons and over 53; gross tonnage 211,691. Telephones (Jan. 1976) 1,286,000. Radio receivers (Dec. 1974) 2,805,000. Television receivers (Dec. 1975) c. 1.8 million.

Agriculture. Production (in 000; metric tons; 1976): corn c. 884; rice 1,560; potatoes c. 1,000; cassava (1975) c. 1,320; sorghum c. 428; soybeans c. 75; bananas c. 1,100; cane sugar, raw value 959; palm oil c. 50; coffee c. 522; tobacco c. 54; sisal c. 41; cotton, lint 133; beef and veal c. 542. Livestock (in 000; Dec. 1975): cattle c. 24,724; sheep c. 2,036; pigs c. 2,001; goats c. 657; horses (1974) c. 860; chickens c. 40,944.

Industry. Production (in 000; metric tons; 1976): crude oil 7,547; natural gas (cu m; 1974) c. 1,700,000; coal (1974) c. 3,150; electricity (kw-hr) c. 14,500,000; crude steel 255; gold (troy oz; 1975) 309; emeralds (carats; 1972) 1,750; salt (1974) 1,545; cement c. 3,640.

At the end of 1976 in a Cabinet reshuffle Abdón Espinosa Valderrama was appointed minister of finance following the resignation of Rodrigo Botero Montoya. The new minister attempted to counteract spiraling inflation and the rapid growth of the money supply, intensified by high income from coffee exports. The government adopted fiscal and monetary policies aimed at encouraging imports, limiting public and private indebtedness, avoiding a budget deficit, and restricting credit. These policies, however, limited industrial expansion, and investment by the private sector reached an all-time low. The money supply expanded because of foreign exchange revenues from coffee exports and contraband trade in coffee, marijuana, and cocaine, while the worker's cost-of-living index continued upward following a rise of 26% for 1976.

The steep rise in the cost of living produced violent clashes, demonstrations, and strike action. At the beginning of September the government reactivated its emergency powers, which had been in force (although rarely used) since the state of siege was reimposed in October 1976. Under these powers strikes were illegal. Negotiations between the unions and the government for higher wages broke down, and the government issued a decree making strike leaders liable to dismissal and imprisonment for up to 180 days. Nevertheless, the nation's four major unions called for a 24-hour general strike on September 14, the country's first in over 20 years. The strike resulted in violence in Bogotá, where 18 people were killed, many injured, and almost 4,000 arrested in two days of looting and riots. Eleven Cabinet ministers resigned on September 29, most in protest of the handling of the strike.

Foreign trade showed a healthy growth at the end of the first half of 1977, with exports increasing to $1,249,000,000 ($807 million in January–June 1976). Of this, coffee accounted for $892 million ($456 million) and nontraditional exports for $358 million ($351 million). At the annual meeting of the Council of the International Coffee Organization, Colombia called on fellow producing nations to lower prices of coffee because of the decline in world consumption. (SARAH CAMERON)

Combat Sports

Boxing. Muhammad Ali remained undefeated as world heavyweight champion in 1977 after twice defending his title. He won 15-round decisions over Alfredo Evangelista, an Uruguayan living in Spain, and Earnie Shavers (U.S.). The heavyweight upset of the year was the defeat of former world champion George Foreman (U.S.) by Jimmy Young (U.S.). Foreman was expected to win and then meet Ali in a return match. The World Boxing Council (WBC) agreed that Ken Norton (U.S.) and Jimmy Young should meet for the right to challenge Ali. The contest went the limit with Norton the victor on points. Among the light-heavyweights, Víctor Galíndez (Arg.) retained the World Boxing Association (WBA) title by outpointing Richie Kates (U.S.), Álvaro López (U.S.), and Eddie Gregory (U.S.). John Conteh (England) stopped Len Hutchins (U.S.) in a WBC title bout, but was stripped of his title when he declined to fight Miguel Cuello (Arg.). The WBC then decided that Cuello would meet Jesse Burnett (U.S.) for the vacant championship. Cuello knocked out Burnett and was recognized as champion. The WBC later sanctioned a title fight between Cuello and Conteh.

Middleweight Carlos Monzón (Arg.), the only undisputed champion besides Ali, ended an era at age 35 when he retired after outpointing Rodrigo Valdés (Colombia). Monzón lost only 3 of 102 bouts, was never knocked out, and did not lose a fight in 13 years. Both world bodies agreed that Valdés and Bennie Briscoe (U.S.) would meet for the vacant title. When they came together in Italy, Valdés won on points.

Two new champions took over at junior middleweight. Eddie Gazo (Nicaragua) won the WBA title with a decision over Miguel Ángel Castellini (Arg.), then successfully defended his crown by beating Koichi Wajima (Japan) and Kenji Shibata (Japan). After Eckhard Dagge (West Germany) retained his WBC title with a draw against Maurice Hope (England), he was knocked out by Rocky Mattioli (Italy). Carlos Palomino (U.S.), WBC welterweight champion, defeated Armando Muñiz (U.S.), Dave Green (England), Everaldo Costa Azevedo (Arg. and Italy), and José Palacios (Mexico). José "Pipino" Cuevas (Mexico) kept

UPI COMPIX

Muhammad Ali feigns stunned surprise while battling Earnie Shavers during their bout in Madison Square Garden in September. Ali won the 15-round decision.

the WBA crown by knocking out Miguel Campanino (Arg.) and Clyde Gray (Canada), both in two rounds, and stopping Ángel Espada (P.R.) in 11 rounds. Saensak Muangsurin (Thailand) made successful defenses of the WBC junior welterweight title with victories over Monroe Brooks (U.S.), "Guts" Ishimatsu (Japan), Perico Fernández (Spain), Mike Everett (U.S.), and Saoul Mamby (U.S.). Antonio Cervantes (Colombia) regained the WBA crown when he stopped Carlos María Giminez (Arg.).

Roberto Durán (Panama) continued to reign as WBA lightweight champion for the fifth year; he defeated Vilomar Fernández (Dominican Republic) in 13 rounds. Esteban de Jesús (P.R.) remained WBC champion after beating Shinji "Buzzsaw" Yamabe (Japan) and Vicente "Mijares" Saldívar (Mexico). Both junior lightweight champions retained their titles: in WBA matches Samuel Serrano (P.R.) beat Alberto Herrera (Ecuador), Leonel Hernández (Venezuela), and Tao Ho Kim (South Korea); and Alfredo Escalera (P.R.) had WBC wins over Tyrone Everett (U.S.), Ronnie McGarvey (U.S.), Carlos Becerril (Mexico), and Sigfredo Rodríguez (Mexico). Rafael Ortega (Panama) won the vacant WBA featherweight title by outpointing Francisco Coronado (Nicaragua), then lost the crown to Celio Lastra (Spain). Danny López (U.S.) kept his WBC title in a fight against José Torres (Mexico). The junior featherweight (or super bantamweight) title, recognized only by the WBC, was held by Wilfredo Gómez (P.R.), who stopped Yum Dong-Kyun (South Korea) in 12 rounds and later knocked out Raúl Tirado (Mexico). Among the bantams, Carlos Zárate (Mexico) retained the WBC crown (and was also named WBC fighter of the year) with victories over Fernando Cabanela (Phil.), Wariunge Nakayama (Japan), Danilo Batista (Brazil), and Juan Rodríguez (Spain). WBA champion Alfonso Zamora lost his title to Jorge Luján (Panama) in November.

Competitors from Japan and West Germany reached the finals of the International Amateur Karate Federation second World Championship held in Tokyo in July. Japan came away the winner.

technical knockout of José Urtain (Spain). Coopman then lost the title to Lucien Rodríguez (France), who in turn lost it to Alfredo Evangelista. Mate Parlov (Yugos.) successfully defended his light-heavyweight title against François Fiol (Spain) and Harald Skog (Norway), but gave it up to challenge for the world title. Alan Minter (England) won the middleweight championship from Germano Valsecchi (Italy) but lost it to Gratien Tonna (France). Jorgen Hansen (Denmark) won the welterweight crown by beating Marco Scano (Italy), but lost to Jörg Eipel (West Germany) on a 13th-round disqualification. The British heavyweight title remained vacant after the retirement of Bugner. Flyweight John McCluskey (Scotland) relinquished the title he had held for ten years because he could no longer find suitable opponents.

In the U.S. the integrity of a tournament promoted by Don King (see BIOGRAPHY) to establish national champions was called into question and a federal grand jury was ordered to investigate.

(FRANK BUTLER)

Wrestling. In each of the two 1977 world championships, the U.S.S.R. team finished ahead of Bulgaria. During the freestyle tournament held at Lausanne, Switz., the Soviet wrestlers amassed 46 points to 23 by the Bulgarians. Four other teams were almost evenly matched: East Germany 19, U.S. 18, Iran 17, and Japan 17. The point totals were not so lopsided at the world Greco-Roman championships held at Göteborg, Sweden. The U.S.S.R. scored 39, Bulgaria 29, Romania 26, Hungary 14, Poland 14, and Sweden 14. During the Pan-American Games in Mexico City, the U.S. finished ahead of second-place Cuba and third-place Canada in both the freestyle (42, 40, 24) and Greco-Roman (35, 29, 19) events. The National Collegiate Athletic Association team title was won by Iowa State University.   (MARVIN G. HESS)

Fencing. Despite the absence of two Olympic stars, Viktor Sidyak and Viktor Krovopouskov, Soviet fencers won four of eight titles at the 12-day world championships held in Buenos Aires, Arg. In the only women's events, the foil team title went to the U.S.S.R. and the individual title to

Guty Espadas (Mexico) retained the WBA flyweight championship by stopping Jiro Takada (Japan), Alfonso López (Panama), and Alex Santana (Nicaragua). Miguel Canto (Mexico) outpointed Reyes Arnal (Venezuela), Kimio Furesawa (Japan), and Martín Vargas (Chile) to remain WBC champion. Yoko Gushiken retained his WBA junior flyweight championship in bouts against Jaime Ríos (Panama), Rigoberto Marcano (Venezuela), and Montsayarm Mahachai (Thailand). Luis Lumumba Estaba (Venezuela) successfully defended his WBC title, beating Rafael Pedroza (Panama), Ricardo Estupiñan (Colombia), Juanito Álvarez (Mexico), Orlando Hernández (Costa Rica), and Netornoi Vorasingh (Thailand).

In Europe junior middleweight Maurice Hope (England), junior lightweight Natale Vezzoli (Italy), and flyweight Franco Udella (Italy) remained champions. After heavyweight Joe Bugner (England) retired, the vacant title was taken by Jean-Pierre Coopman (Belgium) with a fourth-round

Table I. Boxing Champions
As of Dec. 31, 1977

Division	World	Europe	Commonwealth	Britain
Heavyweight	Muhammad Ali, U.S.	Alfredo Evangelista, Spain & Uruguay	vacant	vacant
Light heavyweight	Miguel Cuello, Arg.* Victor Galindez, Arg.†	vacant	Tony Mundine, Australia	Bunny Johnson, England
Middleweight	Rodrigo Valdes, Colombia	Gratien Tonna, France	Monty Betham, N.Z.	Alan Minter, England
Junior middleweight	Rocky Mattioli, Italy* Eddie Gazo, Nicaragua†	Maurice Hope, England	Maurice Hope, England	Jimmy Batten, England
Welterweight	Carlos Palomino, U.S.* José Cuevas, Mexico†	Jörg Eipel, Germany	Clyde Gray, Canada	Henry Rhiney, England
Junior welterweight	Saensak Muangsurin, Thailand* Antonio Cervantes, Colombia†	Jean-Baptiste Piedvache, France	Baby Cassius Austin, Australia	Colin Powers, England
Lightweight	Esteban de Jesús, Puerto Rico* Roberto Durán, Panama†	Jim Watt, Scotland	Lennox Blackmore, Guyana	vacant
Junior lightweight	Alfredo Escalera, Puerto Rico* Sam Serrano, Puerto Rico†	Natale Vezzoli, Italy	Billy Moeller, Australia	. . .
Featherweight	Danny López, U.S.* Celio Lastra, Spain†	Manuel Masson, Spain	Eddie Ndukwu, Nigeria	Alan Richardson, England
Junior featherweight	Wilfredo Gomez, Puerto Rico	. . .	. . .	. . .
Bantamweight	Carlos Zárate, Mexico* Jorge Lujan, Panama†	Franco Zurlo, Italy	Sulley Shittu, Ghana	Johnny Owen, Wales
Flyweight	Miguel Canto, Mexico* Guty Espadas, Mexico†	Franco Udella, Italy	Patrick Mambwe, Zambia	Charlie Magri
Junior flyweight	Luis Lumumba Estaba, Venez.* Yoko Gushiken, Japan†	. . .	. . .	. . .

*World Boxing Council champion.   †World Boxing Association champion.

Valentina Sidorova (U.S.S.R.). The individual men's foil championship was taken by Aleksandr Romankov (U.S.S.R.). The most exciting event on the schedule turned out to be a contest between Italy and West Germany for the team foil championship. A capacity crowd of 3,000 watched Italy take a 7–1 lead before the West German fencers began to rally. The German athletes then took the next eight points for one of the most stunning come-from-behind performances in years. In the épée competition, Sweden captured the team championship and produced the individual medalist in the person of Johan Harmenberg. Before the competition got under way the West Germans were heavily favoured because Alexander Pusch and Jurgen Hehn had won the gold and silver medals at the 1976 Olympics. The event concluded with a four-man fence-off, won by Harmenberg. Rolf Edling (Sweden) was second, followed by Patrice Gaille (Switz.) and Daniel Giger (Switz.). The U.S.S.R. won its second team title in the sabre event, but lost the individual title, which went to Pal Gerevich (Hung.). The U.S. failed to win any medals; its best showing was given by the foil team, which finished seventh for its finest performance since 1950. Many were surprised at the enthusiasm of the spectators in Argentina, especially since there are fewer than two dozen fencing clubs in all of South America. Kuwait sent representatives for the first time, mainly to gain experience and to learn by watching others. Though China sent a team to the Olympic Games, it did not compete in Argentina. It did, however, send fencers to the junior world championships held in Vienna. The most impressive performances were given by fencers from the U.S.S.R., Hungary, and France. Fencing in the U.S. continued to attract ever larger numbers, with women comprising about half of those considered active fencers. The National Collegiate Athletic Association championships were held in South Bend, Ind. The University of Notre Dame completed its second straight season undefeated after tying New York University at the end of the regular tournament.

(MICHAEL STRAUSS)

Judo. Yasuhiro Yamashita at 19 became the youngest national judo champion in Japanese history when he captured first place in the 1977 All-Japan Judo Championships on April 29 in Tokyo, the world's only major judo tournament without weight classes. The 5-ft 11-in, 282-lb heavyweight edged the 1976 champion, 26-year-old Sumio Endo, in a split decision. Although the canceling of the world championships scheduled for September in Spain was a disappointment, Japanese judoka won five of the seven titles contested at the Paris International Tournament in January. In the first part of a three-nation Friendship Tournament in Tokyo, Japan defeated France 9–0 with two draws and topped the Soviet Union 5–0 with three draws; France edged the U.S.S.R. 4–3. In the second half of the tourney in Fukuoka, Japan downed the U.S.S.R. 4–2 and France 8–2, while the U.S.S.R. defeated France 5–1.

The annual All-Japan Weight Class Championships were held July 5 in Fukuoka, with Yamashita repeating his victory over Sumio Endo in the open-weights class. Kazuhiro Ninomiya, light-heavyweight gold medalist at the Montreal Olympics, solidified his hold on the title by pinning Takafumi Ueguchi; another Olympic gold medalist, Isamu Sonoda, captured the middleweight title. Three-time world middleweight champion Shozo Fujii won the light-middleweight class; Kazuhiro Yoshimura took the welterweight category and Yoshiaki Minami the lightweight title. Japan also won three of the five titles at the World Junior Championships in Madrid.

Karate. The 1977 karate scene in Japan was highlighted by the Japan Karate Association's (JKA —Shotokan style) second World Championships in July and by the fourth All-Styles World Championships in December. The July tourney was marred by the last-minute banning of the Israeli team. Masahiko Tanaka, 37-year-old JKA instructor, retained the title he won in the 1975 JKA world meet in Los Angeles by decisioning Willie Willrodt of West Germany on points in the kumite competition. Japanese also won the men's team kumite final as well as the individual and team titles in the *kata* (prescribed forms) for both men and women. At the fourth World Karate-do Championships in December, The Netherlands took both the team and individual championships, Otti Roethof triumphing over Eugene Codrington (U.K.) 1–0 with a punch to the kidney.

The All-Japan Rembu-kai Championship in June was won by 27-year-old Yukio Tottori, who also finished first in the 1975 tourney. Mas Oyama's Kyokushin-kai held its seventh national championships in November with Takashi Azuma, the runner-up in 1974, finally capturing his first title. In the All-Japan Shotokan (JKA) Tournament, held one day prior to the JKA World Championships in Tokyo, the kumite title went to Takashi Miki. There were no meets for the other major styles, Wado-kai, Goju-kai, and Shito-kai. The Japan Self-Defense Forces held their first national championships during March.

Sumo. Although 29-year-old *yokozuna* (grand champion) Wajima won three of the six annual 15-day *basho* (tournaments), it was 24-year-old Kitanoumi who, for the third time, was named wrestler of the year. Kitanoumi finished first in two *basho*, was runner-up in the other four, and had 80 victories to Wajima's 70 during the annual 90-bout schedule. Kitanoumi was one victory short of tying the all-time one-year record set in 1963 by the great *yokozuna* Taiho. Kitanoumi's growing dominance of the sport was strikingly evident when he won both the March and September *basho* with perfect 15–0 records. Wajima won the opening Hatsu *basho* in January (12–3) and the Nagoya

---

Table II. World Wrestling Champions

Weight class	Freestyle	Greco-Roman
48 kg (105.5 lb)	A. Beloglazov, U.S.S.R.	A. Shumakov, U.S.S.R.
52 kg (114.5 lb)	Y. Takada, Japan	N. Ginga, Romania
57 kg (125.5 lb)	T. Sasaki, Japan	P. Ukkola, Finland
62 kg (136.5 lb)	V. Uymin, U.S.S.R.	L. Reczi, Hungary
68 kg (149.5 lb)	P. Pinigin, U.S.S.R.	H. Wehling, E. Germany
74 kg (163 lb)	S. Dziedzic, U.S.	V. Macha, Czech.
82 kg (180.5 lb)	A. Seger, W. Germany	V. Sarov, U.S.S.R.
90 kg (198 lb)	A. Prokopchuk, U.S.S.R.	F. Andersson, Sweden
100 kg (220 lb)	A. Bisultanov, U.S.S.R.	N. Balboshin, U.S.S.R.
100+ kg	S. Andyev, U.S.S.R.	N. Dinev, Bulgaria

basho handily in July (15–0), and then overpowered the 5-ft 11-in, 353-lb Kitanoumi in the Kyushu *basho* in November to win that *yusho* (championship) in impressive style (14–1). The November victory also gave 6-ft ¼-in, 278-lb Wajima his 12th career title and tied him for second place with the legendary *yokozuna* Futabayama. Taiho holds the all-time record with 32 *yusho*. The year's other tourney, the Natsu *basho* in May, was won by Wakamisugi (13–2), one of the four *sumotori* holding the second-highest rank of *ozeki*. Kaiketsu regained *ozeki* rank for the second time in March, but lost it in September after his second straight losing record. Hawaiian-American Takamiyama set a new record by winning his sixth Outstanding Performance Award. The 6-ft 3-in, 400-lb *sumotori* also tied the all-time record with 10 *kinboshi* (gold medals), awarded to Makuuchi division wrestlers when they defeat a *yokozuna*. Veteran Tochiazuma retired and became a sumo stable coach.

Kendo. During 1977 Japan was the scene of several domestic competitions. On May 3 in Osaka, men's teams battled for the national championship and the women for individual titles. The Metropolitan Osaka team narrowly defeated Kanagawa Prefecture 3–2 for the men's crown and C. Nemoto of Osaka defeated Y. Horibe 1–0 with a *kote* strike on her opponent's forearm guard to become the new All-Japan women's champion. In the men's individual All-Japan championships held in December, Isao Ogawa of Osaka defeated Eiji Sueno of Kagoshima Prefecture 2–1 with two *men* strikes to his opponent's helmet.

Yuki Ono of the Tokyo Metropolitan Police Department won the national police championship in May for the third straight year. West Japan downed East Japan for the fifth consecutive year. Other national championships involved high schools, night and correspondence schools, universities, teachers, and industrial companies. Four Japanese instructors also attended the European championships in April, afterwards providing instruction to 54 kendo students from ten European countries at Arnhem, Neth.

(ANDREW M. ADAMS)

Commonwealth of Nations

In 1977, her Silver Jubilee year, Queen Elizabeth II (*see* BIOGRAPHY) celebrated 25 years as head of the Commonwealth. She proved herself to be the organization's most constant and stabilizing factor, offering warm support to visiting officials and organizations and, accompanied by her husband, Prince Philip, visiting every part of the Commonwealth.

The 21st meeting of Commonwealth heads of government was held in London on June 8–15. Of the 35 independent Commonwealth countries entitled to attend (the number excludes Nauru on account of its "special" membership), only two were unrepresented: Seychelles, where a coup took place on June 5, and Uganda, whose "massive violation of basic human rights" was condemned by fellow members in the meeting's final com-

muniqué. The communiqué also included militant statements on the struggle in southern Africa, which dominated conference politics. The Commonwealth Games were saved by a smoothing over of New Zealand's sporting contacts with South Africa.

The Soviet shadow lengthened over Commonwealth Africa, exemplified by Soviet-armed guerrillas in southern Africa, Soviet aid to Uganda, and Pres. Nikolay V. Podgorny's flamboyant visit to Tanzania and Zambia. In Asia, Malaysia signed a new border agreement with Thailand in March for combined operations against Communist terrorists. In the Indian subcontinent, too, elections in India and Sri Lanka and a military coup in Pakistan showed some awareness of the Communist danger but still more of a desire to be rid of oppressively entrenched governments open to corruption. In Sri Lanka the election also pinpointed a race problem involving the Tamil minority.

The conflict in Cyprus between Greeks and Turks continued during the year and was no less dangerous after the death of the president, Archbishop Makarios III (*see* OBITUARIES), in August. Cyprus remained critical for the Commonwealth's and NATO's strategic position in the eastern Mediterranean. Canada had its race problems with American Indian self-awareness and with French separatism in Quebec; the nation also experienced less cordial relations with its Caribbean Community and Common Market partners, Jamaica turning to Cuba and Guyana to the Soviet bloc's Council for Mutual Economic Assistance.

For the North-South (rich-poor) dialogue about the world economy, at the Conference on International Economic Cooperation in Paris, April 26–June 3, the Group of Experts, set up at the Commonwealth conference at Kingston, Jamaica, in 1975, had provided guidelines to both the UN and the UN Conference on Trade and Development. This work represented the only package of measures and approaches agreed upon by any group designated from both sides. The final report of the Group of Experts to the 1977 Commonwealth conference emphasized debt recycling, land reform, and International Monetary Fund support for balance of payment fluctuations and commodity stabilization.

The Commonwealth Fund for Technical Cooperation was budgeted for £11 million in 1977 (Britain, Canada, and Nigeria contributed most financially), but in 1976, out of 275 experts needed, 45% came from poor countries. For example, Sierra Leone learned rubber processing in Malaysia, Nigeria advised Lesotho on aviation, and students went to the agricultural centre organized by the Commonwealth Development Corporation in Swaziland. British overseas aid for 1977 was £515 million, mostly to Commonwealth countries. India with £112 million was the largest single recipient. A new experiment under the aegis of the Commonwealth Foundation was the grant of £50,000 for a two-year program of economic cooperation with French-speaking nations in Africa.

(MOLLY MORTIMER)

See also articles on the various political units.
[972.A.1.a]

Comoro Islands

An island state lying in the Indian Ocean off the east coast of Africa between Mozambique and Madagascar, the Comoros in 1977 administratively comprised three main islands, Grande Comore, Moheli, and Anjouan; the fourth island of the archipelago, Mayotte, continued to be a de facto dependency of France (its current administrative status, "special collectivity," was designated as of Sept. 17, 1976). Area: 1,792 sq km (692 sq mi). Pop. (1976 est.): 344,300. Cap. and largest city: Moroni (pop., 1976 est., 18,300), on Grande Comore. Mayotte: area 373 sq km (144 sq mi); pop. (1976 est.) 46,500. Language: French. Religion: mainly Muslim. President in 1977, Ali Soilih; premier, Abdallah Mohammed.

In January 1977 several hundred Comorans who had been victims of racial conflicts in Madagascar in December returned to their islands; hundreds of others, natives of Mayotte, sought the protection of the French consular authorities and demanded repatriation to Mayotte, which was still under French tutelage. In February some 200 occupied the French consulate at Antananarivo when the Malagasy authorities refused to risk a confrontation with the Comoran government over such a step. In March the Comoran government claimed to have uncovered a counterrevolutionary plot for an invasion of Grande Comore with the aid of European mercenaries. In June Radio Moroni announced another foiled coup, this time on Anjouan.

In April Pres. Ali Soilih announced the investing of control of local administration in the National People's Council, assisted by the Army and militia; preparation of a constitution to be submitted to a referendum; and the lowering of the voting age to 14 years. On April 23 the National People's Council promulgated a "fundamental law" regulating the exercise of power. At the conference of Islamic foreign ministers held in Tripoli, Libya, in May and the Libreville, Gabon, summit meeting of the Organization of African Unity in June, the Comoran government received support for its denunciation of France's encouragement of Mayotte's secession. However, the rejection of the Comoros' application to join the Arab League, allegedly because Arabic was not their official language, was a diplomatic setback.

(PHILIPPE DECRAENE)

COMORO ISLANDS
   Education. (Including Mayotte; 1976–77) Primary, pupils 34,181, teachers 849; secondary, pupils 2,541, teachers 115; teacher training, students 45, teachers 3.
   Finance and Trade. Monetary unit: CFA franc, with (Sept. 19, 1977) a parity of CFA Fr 50 to the French franc and a free rate of CFA Fr 246.50 to U.S. $1 (CFA Fr 429.50 = £1 sterling). Budget (including Mayotte; 1975 rev. est.) balanced at CFA Fr 2,949,000,000. Foreign trade (including Mayotte; 1974): imports CFA Fr 6,203,000,000; exports CFA Fr 2,138,000,000. Import sources: France c. 50%; Madagascar c. 15%; Kenya c. 5%. Export destinations: France c. 75%; Madagascar c. 9%; Italy c. 7%. Main exports (1972): vanilla 41%; essential oils 33%; cloves 11%; copra 6%.

Computers

Estimated revenues for the computer manufacturing and services industries more than doubled in the five-year period ended in 1976. World revenues were $14.4 billion in 1971 and $31.9 billion in 1976.

A dramatic trend in computer hardware usage became apparent when one compared the number of mini- and special-application computer systems with the number of general-purpose computer systems. (In this context, "systems" may include more than one computer; for example, mini- and special-application computer systems may include minicomputers as well as larger computers.) The number of U.S.-built mini- and special-application computer systems rose from 253,500 in 1976 to 325,100 in 1977. By contrast, the increase in the number of general-purpose computer systems was less than half as great, rising from 149,900 in 1976 to 182,400 in 1977.

Another significant trend affecting the computer industry was the shift from batch services to remote access services. ("Batch services" are those involving serial or sequential execution of computer programs, while "remote access services" are those in which communications to data-processing facilities are accomplished through one or more terminals located at a distance from the main computer facility.) This shift caused a decline in the number of keypunch, key/tape, and key/cassette stations and an offsetting increase in the

Comoro Islands

IRA WYMAN—THE NEW YORK TIMES

Thousands of visitors attended Boston's "Computermania," an exhibit of microcomputers designed for home use.

Desk-top computers that perform more functions than giant computers of the 1950s featured tiny solid-state integrated circuits which do the work of thousands of vacuum tubes.

number of general-purpose computer terminals. International Data Corp. informally estimated that 600,000 general-purpose terminals were in use in the U.S. in 1976. This is considered a conservative figure because it excludes an equal number of auto-transaction and special-purpose terminals. (Auto-transaction terminals are terminal equipment units designed for a single application, such as point-of-sale cash registers and automated teller machines.)

Other highlights of the year included the direct intervention by U.S. Pres. Jimmy Carter and the Congress in the decision not to allow the Control Data Corp. (CDC) Cyber #76 system to be exported to the Soviet Union because of the strategic value to the Soviets of such computer power, and slashes by IBM of 30 to 35% in the purchase, lease, and rental prices for some of its System/370 models. The IBM price cuts were seen by some as the beginning of a price war among the manufacturers of mainframes for large computers.

Home Computers and Computer Hobby Shops. Two major developments in 1977 included an increase in the number of home computers and the proliferation of computer hobby shops. Estimates showed that in 1977 there were more than 20,000 general-purpose computers in U.S. homes, with a projected increase of 40% per year. Costs of home computers in 1977 ranged from $500 to $2,500, with the average about $1,500. Prices, however, were decreasing rapidly. A microcomputer introduced in mid-1977 with a price tag of $599.95 included a 12-in cathode-ray tube (CRT) display, keyboard, a cassette-tape recorder, and 4,096 bytes. (A byte is a unit of eight bits, a convenient information size to represent an alphanumeric character.) The hobby computer market was aimed at the do-it-yourself computer enthusiast. The initial investment of computer hobbyists was about $2,000, primarily in computer kits, microprocessor chip sets, and individual system compo-

nents. The first entry into this market was the Altair 8800 computer kit, offered by MITS Inc. in January 1975. By March 1977 there were at least 50 other companies in the business.

Hardware Technology. Computer hardware technology continued its rapid advance during 1977. By late in the year a single large-scale integrated (LSI) circuit could contain more active elements than the most complex electronic equipment of 25 years earlier. Reduction in size by a factor of two had been achieved every five years since 1960. As an example of hardware progress, one could compare the ENIAC, the first electronic digital computer (late 1940s), and the Fairchild F8 microcomputer (1977). The latter is 20 times faster, 10,000 times more reliable, and requires 56,000 times less power than the ENIAC; it also weighs less than one pound compared with 30 tons for its predecessor. The F8 can be fabricated for about $100, while the ENIAC cost from $5 million to $10 million to build.

After years in the laboratory, magnetic bubble memories entered the computer market. On March 9 Texas Instruments Inc. announced the availability of a $200, 92,000-bit magnetic bubble memory chip in a 14-pin packet about one inch square. On April 15 the firm announced the use of these bubble memory chips in its portable computer terminals. The average cost was just over two-tenths of a cent per bit, which meant that the first marketed bubble memory chips did not yet compete economically with other secondary storage devices such as small disks. A magnetic bubble is a cylindrical magnetic domain with its poles in the opposite direction of the polarity of the magnetic material that contains it. The magnetic bubble memory is constructed in such a way that the bubble positions are uniformly spaced. The presence of a bubble signifies a binary "one," while the absence of a bubble equates to a binary "zero." Bubbles are most common in noncrystalline films of gadolinium-cobalt and gadolinium-iron or in garnet crystals.

Charge-coupled devices (CCD's) were also being marketed as memory chips in 1977. The largest commercial CCD memory chips available during the year offered a 65,000-bit memory on one chip. CCD's are arrays of metal-oxide semiconductors along which a charge is transferred.

Another feature of the 1977 scene was the increasing popularity of "smart" terminals and peripheral devices that were more logically sophisticated than the microcomputers with which they were connected. As one example, Intel's most advanced central processor of 1977 (the 8085) contained the equivalent of 6,500 to 7,000 transistors; however, some of the chips in one of the firm's series of keyboard/display controllers contained more than 22,000 transistor-equivalent devices.

Microprocessors. In 1977 many applications were found for microprocessors. General Motors, Ford, and Chrysler used them to control fuel injection and other carburetor functions in their new cars. Microwave ovens incorporated microprocessors for timing and sequencing controls. Microprocessors in radio navigation systems enabled business aircraft to fly directly to distant points instead of following the traditional zigzag navigation paths, reducing operating costs by about 20%.

Microprocessors pervaded the instrument and office automation fields. Their use radically changed terminal guidance systems for missiles, making possible a missile that could home in on its target autonomously. They also made possible the marketing for $4,000 of the first home robot, which opens the door, announces guests, and performs simple household chores.

Programming for microprocessors thus became a major concern in 1977. Unfortunately, the state of the microprocessor programming art was primitive. A recent survey in the U.S. showed that more than 36% of microprocessor programs were being written in the cumbersome hexadecimal numerical notation, while 85% of the programs contained more than 1,000 bytes. "Programmed chips" remained expensive.

Software and System Reliability. Software, the programs and routines used to extend the capabilities of computers, was the most expensive component of computer systems in 1977, ranging from 60 to 90% of total computer system costs. As of 1977 there was still no mathematically rigorous way to prove programs correct except for those containing on the order of 100 statements. Therefore, engineering and statistical techniques were being developed as substitutes for mathematical rigour. An example was computer auditing. The first book devoted entirely to this subject, *Computer Control and Audit*, was published in 1976. Also during 1977 a two-year research project on computer auditing, the first of its kind, was completed. The study, conducted by Stanford Research Institute and sponsored by IBM, produced reports aimed at reducing the potential for loss associated with the use of computer systems.

(RUTH M. DAVIS)

[735.D; 10/23.A.6–7]

Congo

Congo

A people's republic of equatorial Africa, the Congo is bounded by Gabon, Cameroon, the Central African Empire, Zaire, Angola, and the Atlantic Ocean. Area: 342,000 sq km (132,047 sq mi). Pop. (1977 est.): 1,416,000, mainly Bantu. Cap. and largest city: Brazzaville (pop., 1974 prelim., 299,-000). Language: French (official) and Bantu dialects. Religion: Roman Catholic 38%; most of the remainder are animist. Presidents in 1977, Maj. Marien Ngouabi until March 18 and, from April 4, Col. Joachim Yhombi-Opango; premier, Maj. Louis Sylvain Ngoma.

On March 18, 1977, Pres. Marien Ngouabi (*see* OBITUARIES) was assassinated, and an 11-member military committee took over the government of the country. For his suspected complicity in the assassination, Alphonse Massamba-Débat (*see* OBITUARIES), president of the country from 1963 to 1968, was arrested and executed on March 25. Meanwhile, members of Ngouabi's family had murdered the archbishop of Brazzaville, Émile Cardinal Biayenda, on the night of March 22–23. Six more executions followed, and Pascal Lissouba, a former premier, and others were condemned to life imprisonment.

The way was now clear for those who had liquidated their rivals after charging them with responsibility for eliminating Ngouabi. On April 4 Col. Joachim Yhombi-Opango (*see* BIOGRAPHY) became head of state, while Maj. Louis Sylvain Ngoma and Maj. Denis Sassou Nguesso remained, respectively, premier and defense minister and were named vice-presidents. There were no civilians in the government. Thus, a handful of officers, on the pretext of defending Marxism-Leninism, set

---

CONGO

Education. (1974–75) Primary, pupils 307,194, teachers 5,053; secondary, pupils 81,541, teachers 1,703; vocational, pupils 5,526, teachers 390; teacher training, students 901, teachers 50; higher (1973–74), students 2,570, teaching staff 166.

Finance. Monetary unit: CFA franc, with (Sept. 1977) a parity of CFA Fr 50 to the French franc and a free rate of CFA Fr 246.50 to U.S. $1 (CFA Fr 429.50 = £1 sterling). Budget (1976 est.) balanced at CFA Fr 52,042,000,000.

Foreign Trade. (1975) Imports CFA Fr 33,890,000,000; exports CFA Fr 52,070,000,000. Import sources (1973): France 56%; West Germany 7%; U.S. 6%; The Netherlands 6%. Export destinations (1973): France 29%; Italy 14%; West Germany 10%; South Africa 9%; The Netherlands 7%. Main exports: crude oil 54%; timber (1974) 19%.

Transport and Communications. Roads (1975) c. 11,-000 km. Motor vehicles in use (1974): passenger 19,000; commercial (including buses) 10,500. Railways: (1974) 801 km; traffic (1976) 246 million passenger-km, freight 508 million net ton-km. Air traffic (including apportionment of Air Afrique; 1975): 118 million passenger-km; freight 12.4 million net ton-km. Telephones (Dec. 1974) 10,000. Radio receivers (Dec. 1974) 80,000. Television receivers (Dec. 1973) 3,800.

Agriculture. Production (in 000; metric tons; 1975): cassava c. 609; sweet potatoes c. 94; peanuts c. 28; sugar, raw value c. 32; bananas c. 36; coffee c. 2; palm oil c. 2. Livestock (in 000; 1975): cattle c. 45; sheep c. 33; goats c. 45; pigs c. 15; chickens c. 729.

Industry. Production (in 000; metric tons): crude oil (1976) 2,002; potash (oxide content; 1974) 475; electricity (kw-hr; 1975) 110,000.

Premier Louis Sylvain Ngoma, one of the 11-member military committee which took control of the Congo on April 4, later visited Chairman Hua Kuo-feng in China.

up what amounted to a neocolonial regime, in which northerners had the upper hand and from which civilians were excluded.

(PHILIPPE DECRAENE)

Consumerism

Consumer groups gained a number of victories in 1977, including the U.S. Supreme Court ruling that overturned the Arizona law forbidding attorneys to advertise. In 1976 the Supreme Court, in a similar decision on drug advertising, ruled that advertising was protected by the free-speech guarantees of the U.S. Constitution. Consumer groups claimed in both cases that rules against advertising by professional organizations restricted competitive pricing, making it difficult for consumers to obtain information to make purchasing decisions. The Federal Trade Commission introduced lawsuits against the American Medical Association and the American Dental Association in 1977, charging that they fixed prices by not allowing physicians and dentists to advertise.

During the first half of 1977 the price of coffee doubled. New York City Consumer Affairs Commissioner Elinor Guggenheimer called for a one-week boycott throughout the U.S., and other consumer boycotts took place in California, Texas, Washington, the Virgin Islands, and Canada. Coffee consumption fell significantly during the year, and by the end of 1977 the price of coffee was on the decline. The restrictions on cigarette use moved to hotels in addition to airplanes, elevators, restaurants, and other public places. The Hyatt International Corp. introduced a pilot program in which its hotels designated a group of rooms or an entire floor as off limits to smokers.

A number of private organizations and governmental agencies introduced new consumer-affairs

programs in 1977. In Pennsylvania the state instituted a toll-free telephone line to gather consumer complaints on anticompetitive practices. Shell Oil Co. distributed 225 million booklets on driving and car care. Polaroid Corp. established a consumer services department to review advertisements that might mislead consumers. Despite these efforts a market research study issued in September 1977, based on responses of more than 11,000 people, reported that buyers had little confidence in the consumerism activities of industry, government, and labour unions. Only the airline industry received favourable marks.

New provisions of the Equal Credit Opportunity Act went into effect in June 1977 to open the way for married women to establish credit ratings in their own names. The provisions stipulated that all lender's reports to credit bureaus include the names of both spouses if both use the account and if either requests the dual reporting.

Government Action. In March 1977 the U.S. Food and Drug Administration banned saccharin from the market as a result of a Canadian study that indicated saccharin produced cancer in test animals. The Delaney clause of 1958 forces the FDA to ban any food additives that produce cancer in humans or laboratory animals no matter what the dosage. A public outcry against the saccharin action prompted congressmen to introduce legislation to change the Delaney clause. Legislation was introduced to allow manufacturers using saccharin in their products 18 more months to determine whether or not the product was safe.

In 1977 the FDA began a five-year safety study of 2,100 additives. The results of the study were expected to identify chemicals that are unsafe to consumers. In April the Consumer Product Safety Commission banned the use of the substance Tris, a flame retardant used in children's sleepwear, because of probable cancer risks.

The U.S. Department of Commerce introduced a program under which manufacturers would put performance labels on consumer products. The department developed methods for measuring product performance. Participation by individual companies was voluntary, the household appliance industry becoming the first group of manufacturers to adopt the program. At the same time, the Environmental Protection Agency proposed that manufacturers of household appliances such as dishwashers and blenders be required to label them to show how much noise they emit.

In November 1977 label warnings appeared on dozens of aerosol products containing chlorofluorocarbon propellants. By 1979 aerosols containing the chemical were to be banned from the marketplace by the FDA because the spray product contains a chemical that may harm the public health and the environment by reducing the ozone in the upper atmosphere. Chlorofluorocarbon propellants are used for such products as deodorants, antiperspirants, and fragrances. Some drug products were exempted because use of the chemical in them was necessary.

In Australia the control and investigation of consumer contracts and complaints was extended to include contracts for the performance of work, the provision of facilities for recreation or instruction, and the conferring of rights or privileges for which remuneration is payable in the form of a royalty or levy. New legislation enacted in Canada expanded the civil review process to encompass a number of fields involving the structure of the economy, such as mergers and some monopolistic practices; it reinforced provisions prohibiting certain market practices, obliged federal agencies to take competition factors into account, and set up a Competition Board with the primary responsibility of undertaking new civil review functions. The board was to determine whether major corporate mergers, specialization agreements, and monopolistic practices were justified.

Legislation that came into force in Finland in March prohibited all advertising of tobacco and alcohol in newspapers. The smoking of tobacco in public buildings was also prohibited. In Luxembourg a draft bill concerning the legal protection of consumers laid down the principle that contract clauses which unduly upset the fair balance between the interests of the two parties to a contract must be made null and void. It contained a number of examples of improper clauses, such as the ones restricting guarantees, providing for a fixed increase in price in the event of dispute, or prohibiting the consumer from withholding payment if the other party does not fulfill his obligations.

Consumer Organizations. A symposium for consumer organizations, held in Brussels at the end of 1976 under the auspices of the European Commission, revealed that the many and varied bodies looking after the interests of Europe's consumers were adopting a new approach to their mission and attempting to give consumerism a wider and more positive content. The concept of "consumer protection" was being replaced by the broader one of "promotion of consumer interests"

Consumer resistance, abetted by food store campaigns, significantly reduced coffee consumption in the U.S. during 1977.

Automobile manufacturers were ordered to install air bags on all standard-size and luxury cars beginning with 1982 models and on all other cars by model year 1984. Ralph Nader, consumer advocate, observed a demonstration of one such device.

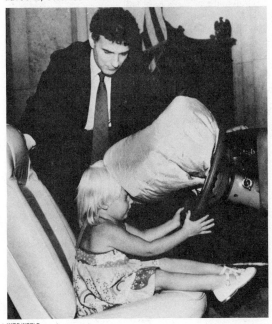

or, as one of the consumer leaders said at the Mediterranean Consumer Conference, ". . . a movement, a way of thinking, a way of behaving, that is not political in the party political sense but which will lead us to prepare a better world for ourselves and our children. A world that avoids the waste and the squander of a producer-oriented society, that avoids the monotony and choicelessness of a worker-oriented society, but which we believe will give us the best of all worlds . . . a consumers' society."

International organizations active in the consumer field during the year included the council of the Organization for Economic Cooperation and Development, which adopted a recommendation in April that called on member countries to strengthen consumer protection in the field of consumer credit. In the European Community, the Council of Ministers adopted directives relating to the labeling, presentation, and advertising of foodstuffs for sale to the final consumer, all measures aimed at giving consumers more information to enable them to make fairer comparisons when shopping. Another council directive of consumer concern laid down limits on noise emitted by motor vehicles; the present maximum of 91 decibels was to be reduced by 1980 to limits varying between 80 and 88, according to the type of vehicle.

Consumer protection in the field of business was the subject of draft regulations produced by the European Commission covering transactions concluded away from business premises. The propos-

Sales of smoke detectors for residences boomed during the year with about eight million such units sold in the U.S.

als stated that with limited exceptions (if the transaction is specifically initiated by the customer, is negotiated solely in writing, is under about $20, is concerned with immovable property) certain conditions must be complied with by the trader or the contract becomes void.

(ISOLA VAN DEN HOVEN; EDWARD MARK MAZZE)

See also Economy, World; Industrial Review: *Advertising.*

[532.B.3; 534.H.5; 534.K]

Contract Bridge

In 1976 a leading Italian bridge player, Leandro Burgay, released a "tape" of an alleged telephone conversation between himself and Benito Bianchi, sometime member of the Italian world and European championship teams, in which Bianchi admitted that he had employed an illicit method of signaling in partnership with Pietro Forquet, with whom he had been paired on two winning world championship teams. In May 1976, at emergency meetings of the Executive Committee of the World Bridge Federation (WBF), the president of the Italian Bridge Federation (IBF), Luigi Firpo, undertook, on behalf of the IBF, "to continue energetically the inquiry into the Burgay-Bianchi affair and to report in detail its findings and decisions together with full documentation including a certified copy of the tape to the European Bridge League and to the World Bridge Federation." Should the inquiry determine that the tape was authentic and that the declaration by Bianchi of his cheating with Forquet was confirmed, then the Italian Bridge Federation would renounce all European world titles won with either Bianchi or Forquet on the team. By a year later, IBF findings

Cosmetics:
see Fashion and Dress

appeared neither to invalidate the tape nor to find anybody guilty of irregular practices at the table. The WBF under its new president, Jaime Ortiz-Patino, was determined that disciplinary matters should be dealt with promptly. In pursuance of this policy, a letter from the WBF's management committee on June 2, 1977, gave the IBF three months in which to investigate. The WBF Executive Council met in Manila on October 26. It was not satisfied with the steps taken by the IBF and by unanimous vote determined to suspend it from the WBF, the suspension to become effective on March 15, 1978. This gave the IBF a grace period in which to meet the WBF's requirements.

Meanwhile, Italy fielded a top-strength team, headed by Benito Garozzo (*see* BIOGRAPHY) and Giorgio Belladonna, in the European championships at Elsinore, Den., but finished second to Sweden. Italy won the ladies' series, with Britain second and Sweden third. Teams from the U.S., Argentina, Australia, and Taiwan joined Sweden in the Bermuda Bowl (the official world championship) in Manila to challenge the defending champions, Erik Paulsen, Hugh Ross, Ira Rubin, Fred Hamilton, Ron Von der Porten, and Mike Passell of the U.S.; a second U.S. team also qualified. The two North American teams met in the final. The defending champions raced into a commanding lead and were 42½ points ahead when the final sessions of 32 boards began. But after 16 boards they were 17½ points behind, and the final score was 245–215 in favour of the challengers. Thus, Billy Eisenberg became a fourth-time winner of the Bermuda Bowl; Bob Hammon and Bobby Wolff scored their third success; Paul Soloway his second; and Eddie Kantar, John Swanson, and nonplaying captain Roger Stern their first. A subsequent decision of the WBF precluded the possibility of two teams from the same zone competing in future Bermuda Bowls.

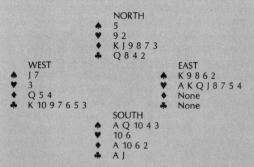

Bridge players often complain that the computer deals a high proportion of "freaks." The hand that follows was dealt in the Bermuda Bowl final:

```
                    NORTH
                    ♠ 5
                    ♥ 9 2
                    ♦ K J 9 8 7 3
                    ♣ Q 8 4 2
  WEST                              EAST
  ♠ J 7                             ♠ K 9 8 6 2
  ♥ 3                               ♥ A·K Q J 8 7 5 4
  ♦ Q 5 4                           ♦ None
  ♣ K 10 9 7 6 5 3                  ♣ None
                    SOUTH
                    ♠ A Q 10 4 3
                    ♥ 10 6
                    ♦ A 10 6 2
                    ♣ A J
```

Dealer, South. North-South Game.

At both tables South opened one spade, West made a weak jump overcall of three clubs, and East bid four hearts. For the challengers Billy Eisenberg, at South, made the neutral lead of a trump, and declarer gave up three spade tricks to score 420 for the defending champions.

At the other table North, Ira Rubin, doubled the final contract of four hearts, which persuaded his partner to lead an ace. Unfortunately, he chose the wrong ace—diamonds. Had he opened with the ace of spades and a second spade, North would have ruffed and returned a trump and South would have made two more spade tricks. As it was, the challengers scored 590.

In another scandal, Roger Stern's championship team had played the final North American trial against a team captained by George Rosenkrantz of Mexico. With only 32 boards to play Rosenkrantz led by 43 points. At that point, two of his players, Richard Katz and Larry Cohen, both from California, emerged from a conference with American Contract Bridge League (ACBL) officials. It was announced that they had withdrawn from the trials and resigned from membership of the American Contract Bridge League. The match was then conceded to their opponents. Subsequently, Katz and Cohen filed suit against the ACBL and some of its officers for damages of $44 million.

(HAROLD FRANKLIN)

[452.C.3.a.i]

Costa Rica

A Central American republic, Costa Rica lies between Nicaragua and Panama and has coastlines on the Caribbean Sea and the Pacific Ocean. Area: 50,898 sq km (19,652 sq mi). Pop. (1977 est.): 2,044,200, including white and mestizo 98%. Cap. and largest city: San José (metro. pop., 1977 est., 547,200). Language: Spanish. Religion: predominantly Roman Catholic. President in 1977, Daniel Oduber Quirós.

In February 1977 Costa Rica and Cuba reestablished diplomatic relations which had been severed in 1961. Later a new economic treaty between Peru and Costa Rica and a three-year technological exchange agreement with Romania were signed.

In 1977 Costa Rica experienced an economic

UPI COMPIX

growth rate estimated at 6% (5% in 1976), thanks mostly to the good performance of its two main sources of export earnings, coffee and bananas, valued at $300 million and $150 million, respectively. The trade balance deficit was expected to decrease to about $80 million, as compared with $185 million in 1976. Industrial production rose by 6.1% in 1976 (4.8% in 1975), and many industrial projects were initiated. The cost-of-living index was expected to rise by 8% in 1977, as compared with 5% in 1976 and 20.5% in 1975. Per capita income rose to $1,000 in 1976, the highest in Central America and the fourth highest in Latin America.

The government, to compensate for low private investment, increased public investment by 1 billion colones to 3 billion colones to finance, in particular, the construction of roads between the Central Valley and the Atlantic coast, the expansion of the port of Limón, and the Arenal hydroelectric project. (FRANÇOISE LOTERY)

Mario Charpentier, Costa Rican minister of security, together with an army major and newsmen, huddled under bushes along the Frio River after Nicaraguan helicopters strafed a boat in which Charpentier was riding.

Costa Rica

COSTA RICA

Education. (1974) Primary, pupils 377,111, teachers 14,-808; secondary, pupils 114,816; vocational, pupils 17,558; secondary and vocational, teachers 5,229; higher, students 27,625, teaching staff c. 3,500

Finance. Monetary unit: colón, with (Sept. 19, 1977) an official rate of 8.57 colones to U.S. $1 (free rate of 14.98 colones = £1 sterling). Gold, SDR's, and foreign exchange (June 1977) U.S. $213,370,000. Budget (1976 actual): revenue 2,692,000,000 colones; expenditure 3,666,000,000 colones. Gross national product (1976) 19,447,000,000 colones. Money supply (Feb. 1977) 4,043,000,000 colones. Cost of living (San José; 1970 = 100; June 1977) 207.

Foreign Trade. (1976) Imports 6,629,000,000 colones; exports 5,045,000,000 colones. Import sources (1975): U.S. 37%; Japan 10%; Guatemala 6%; West Germany 6%; Nicaragua 6%; El Salvador 5%. Export destinations (1975): U.S. 40%; West Germany 11%; Nicaragua 8%; Guatemala 7%; El Salvador 6%. Main exports: coffee 26%; bananas 25%; sugar (1975) 10%; meat (1975) 8%. Tourism: visitors (1974) 282,000; gross receipts U.S. $46 million.

Transport and Communications. Roads (1972) 21,667 km (including 665 km of Pan-American Highway). Motor vehicles in use (1974): passenger 55,145; commercial 34,-401. Railways: (1975) 1,389 km (including 310 km plantation); traffic (1973) c. 97 million passenger-km, freight c. 20 million net ton-km. Air traffic (1976): 326 million passenger-km; freight 13.5 million net ton-km. Telephones (Jan. 1976) 112,000. Radio receivers (Dec. 1974) 142,000. Television receivers (Dec. 1974) 150,000.

Agriculture. Production (in 000; metric tons; 1976): sorghum c. 36; corn (1975) 57; rice (1975) 132; potatoes (1975) c. 22; dry beans c. 18; bananas c. 1,350; oranges c. 70; sugar, raw value (1975) c. 178; cocoa c. 4; coffee c. 88; palm oil c. 24. Livestock (in 000; 1975): cattle c. 1,816; horses c. 100; pigs c. 225; chickens c. 4,800.

Industry. Electricity production (1975) 1,536,000,000 kw-hr (85% hydroelectric in 1974); petroleum products (1974) 397,000 metric tons.

Court Games

Handball. Naty Alvarado of Juárez, Mexico, capped the finest season a professional handball player had ever enjoyed when he won the National Open handball tournament at St. Louis, Mo. In the final he defeated defending champion Fred Lewis of Miami, Fla., 21–5, 21–16. It was Alvarado's sixth win in eight tournaments on the $100,000 Spalding Pro Tour and made him, at 21, the youngest player ever to win a national singles title. His earlier victories were won at San Diego, Seattle, Denver, Austin (Texas), and Tucson.

In the United States Handball Association (USHA) open doubles competition, Matt Kelly and Skip McDowell of Long Beach, Calif., defeated Jeff and Jay Capell of San Jose 21–14, 21–9. In masters play for men 40 and over, Jim Faulk of Dallas defeated Dick Miller of Vienna, Va., 21–19, 21–18 for the singles title, while Burt Dinkin and Jack Steb-

Cost of Living:
see Economy, World

Council for Mutual Economic Assistance:
see Economy World

Naty Alvarado of Juárez, Mexico (right), defeated defending champion Fred Lewis of Miami, Fla. (left), in the National Open handball tournament at St. Louis, Mo.

bins of Milwaukee topped Gil Singerman and Dick Argen of Cleveland 21–10, 21–9 for the doubles championship. A hometown St. Louis player, Jack Briscoe, won the golden masters singles (50 years and over), defeating Fred DeNuccio of Norfolk, Va., 21–18, 21–5. Julie Rothman and Phil Harlahan of New York dethroned Rudy Stadlberger and Tom Kelly of San Francisco 21–15, 21–14 in the golden masters doubles. In super masters doubles for veterans 60 and over, Joe Ardito and Ben Costello of Chicago defeated fellow Chicagoans Al Marchi and Lloyd Leinweber 17–21, 21–9, 11–2, the only final match that had to be decided by the newly adopted 11-point tie breaker.

Memphis State University captured its first USHA intercollegiate title by winning two of the three events in A singles and doubles. Sophomore Mike Lloyd won the singles by defeating Steve Stanisvich of Montana Tech 21–6, 21–6, and Rod Pagello and Jeff Miller teamed to win the doubles. Dave Dohman of second-place Lake Forest (Ill.) College won the B singles. In junior competition for players 19 and under, Jack Roberts of Cincinnati won his second straight singles crown, defeating Lou Crilla of Miami 21–14, 21–4. His younger brother Chris Roberts won the 15-and-under championship, and Oscar Calzada of Juárez, Mexico, won the 17-and-under title.

(TERRY CHARLES MUCK)

[452.B.4.h.xv]

Jai Alai. France won the 1976 world amateur jai alai championship held in Miami, Fla., in December 1976. Mexico was second, the U.S. third, and Spain fourth. The tournament, attended by more than 10,000 spectators and sanctioned by the Federación Internacional de Pelota Vasca, called for 35-point matches with each of the four teams playing the others twice. The French frontcourt team of Remy Duperou and Francis Abeberry was supported in the backcourt by Francis Etcheverry and Charles Iratzoqui. Against Mexico, France won one match 35–34, but lost another 32–35 for its only defeat. Abeberry and Iratzoqui later signed professional contracts with World Jai-Alai Inc. of the U.S. The next world championship was slated for the fall of 1978 in Biarritz, France.

Professional jai alai continued to grow rapidly in the U.S. as new frontons opened in Las Vegas, Nev.; Milford, Conn.; and Fort Walton Beach, Fla. A new fronton was also planned for Reno, Nev. The Milford fronton, which seats some 9,500 spectators and was built at a cost of $12 million, had a 43-player roster. Its mutuel handled more than $70 million during its first May through November season. Delaware became the latest entry into the jai alai pari-mutuel betting game, with such states as Illinois, California, Ohio, and Michigan also considering its possibilities.

(ROBERT H. GROSSBERG)

Volleyball. The year 1977 was mainly a time for reevaluating national teams and experimenting with new players. However, the first world junior volleyball championships, open to players under 21 years of age, were played in Brazil in September. In men's competition, the U.S.S.R. finished first, followed by China and Brazil. South Korea won the women's title, with China second and Japan third. The World University Games, a biennial competition in ten different sports, was held during August in Sofia, Bulg. In the women's division the U.S.S.R. won the volleyball championship, as Cuba finished second and Bulgaria third. Bulgaria won the men's division by finishing ahead of Czechoslovakia and Korea. The World Cup of volleyball for men and women was played in Japan in November. The eight male and female teams that automatically qualified for the tournament were: the defending world champion, the defending Olympic champion, the defending World Cup champion, the host nation, and the current zonal champions from North America, South America, Europe, and Asia. The Soviet Union won the men's championship and Japan, the women's. Looking ahead to the 1980 Olympics, the Japanese women were favourites to repeat as gold medalists and the Soviet men were expected to dethrone the Polish men. Cuba and China were also strong. All these teams would be watched with great interest during the 1978 world championships, scheduled for the Soviet Union (women) and Italy (men). (ALBERT M. MONACO, JR.)

Cricket

Highlights in cricket competition during 1976–77 included the defeat of India in India by England for the first time in 42 years, the Australia v. England Centenary Match, the surprisingly good form of Pakistan in Australia, the recovery of "the Ashes" by England from Australia, and the controversial bombshell delivered by Kerry Packer (see BIOGRAPHY) with his projected World Series.

At the beginning of the English season, Packer, an Australian television and magazine proprietor, startled cricket sportsmen with his preparations for a sponsored World Series of test matches to be played in Australia between an Australian team and the rest of the world and televised by his company. Most of the Australian team, along with A. W. Greig and celebrities from England and other countries, were among the players under contract to Packer for high remuneration.

The prime objections to the series were its denial

of contracted players to national test teams while it is under way and the likelihood of its diverting public interest and money away from test cricket played under the International Cricket Conference (ICC). After a fruitless meeting with Packer in June, the ICC and the English Test and County Cricket Board countered by banning Packer's players, for which they were taken to the High Court in England in September by Packer and three of his cricketers for restraint of trade and inducing breach of contract.

During the season's play, Pakistan outclassed New Zealand, 2–0, with 20-year-old Javed Miandad making 504 runs in five innings, including scores of 206 and 163; the captain, Mushtaq Mohammad, made 101 and 107, Majid Khan scored 112 and 98, and Asif Iqbal and Sadiq Mohammad also made centuries. For New Zealand, M. G. Burgess and W. K. Lees made centuries, Lees being the first New Zealand wicketkeeper to do so, and opening bowler R. J. Hadlee took five wickets in an innings once.

India won its test series against New Zealand with two victories and a draw. In the drawn game, every batsman made double figures, six men making over 50 each. New Zealand tied the second test because of a century by its captain, G. M. Turner, and a not out 84 by A. D. G. Roberts. The leading Indian batsmen were S. M. Gavaskar, G. R. Viswanath, B. P. Patel, wicketkeeper S. M. H. Kirmani, and A. D. Gaekwad, and as usual most of the wickets were taken by B. S. Bedi and B. S. Chandrasekhar. For New Zealand, J. M. Parker and Burgess were Turner's main batting supporters, while Hadlee and B. L. Cairns were most successful in a weak bowling side.

In India, after England had won the first three matches, the Indian spin bowlers came into their own to win the fourth. Then, in a tense finish, England tied the fifth. England's leading batsmen were D. L. Amiss and the captain, A. W. Greig; leading bowlers were J. K. Lever, R. G. D. Willis,

Geoff Boycott of England became the 18th cricketer in history to reach a career total of 100 centuries. He attained the goal in a test match against Australia.

and D. L. Underwood. The best Indian batsman was Gavaskar, while slow bowlers E. A. S. Prasanna, Bedi (the captain), and Chandrasekhar shared most of the wickets.

Against Australia, Pakistan, after drawing the first test and losing the second, squared the series by winning the third by eight wickets. This was the Pakistanis' first test win ever in Australia. They owed most to the batting of Zaheer Abbas (85, 101, and 90), Asif (152 not out and 120), and Sadiq (105) and to the bowling of fast medium Imran Khan, who took 5 wickets in the second test

Test Series Results, October 1976–August 1977				
Test	Host country and its scores		Visiting country and its scores	Result
1st	Pakistan	417 and 105 for 4 wkt	New Zealand 157 and 360	Pakistan won by 6 wkt
2nd	Pakistan	478 for 3 wkt dec and 2 for 0 wkt	New Zealand 219 and 254	Pakistan won by 10 wkt
3rd	Pakistan	565 for 9 wkt dec and 290 for 5 wkt dec	New Zealand 468 and 262 for 7 wkt	Match drawn
1st	India	399 and 202 for 4 wkt dec	New Zealand 298 and 141	India won by 162 runs
2nd	India	524 for 9 wkt dec and 208 for 2 wkt dec	New Zealand 350 and 193 for 7 wkt	Match drawn
3rd	India	298 and 201 for 5 wkt dec	New Zealand 140 and 143	India won by 216 runs
1st	India	122 and 234	England 381	England won by an innings and 25 runs
2nd	India	155 and 181	England 321 and 16 for 0 wkt	England won by 10 wkt
3rd	India	164 and 83	England 262 and 185 for 9 dec	England won by 200 runs
4th	India	253 and 259 for 9 dec	England 195 and 177	India won by 140 runs
5th	India	338 and 192	England 317 and 152 for 7 wkt	Match drawn
1st	Australia	454 and 261 for 6 wkt	Pakistan 272 and 466	Match drawn
2nd	Australia	517 for 8 wkt dec and 315 for 8 wkt dec	Pakistan 333 and 151	Australia won by 348 runs
3rd	Australia	211 and 180	Pakistan 360 and 32 for 2 wkt	Pakistan won by 8 wkt
1st	New Zealand	357 and 293 for 8 wkt	Australia 552 and 154 for 4 wkt dec	Match drawn
2nd	New Zealand	229 and 175	Australia 377 and 28 for 0 wkt	Australia won by 10 wkt
1st	West Indies	421 and 251 for 9 wkt	Pakistan 435 and 291	Match drawn
2nd	West Indies	316 and 206 for 4 wkt	Pakistan 180 and 340	West Indies won by 6 wkt
3rd	West Indies	448 and 154 for 1 wkt	Pakistan 194 and 540	Match drawn
4th	West Indies	154 and 222	Pakistan 341 and 301 for 9 wkt dec	Pakistan won by 266 runs
5th	West Indies	280 and 359	Pakistan 198 and 301	West Indies won by 140 runs
1st	England	216 and 305	Australia 296 and 114 for 6 wkt	Match drawn
2nd	England	437 and 82 for 1 wkt	Australia 297 and 218	England won by 9 wkt
3rd	England	364 and 189 for 3 wkt	Australia 243 and 309	England won by 7 wkt
4th	England	436	Australia 103 and 248	England won by an innings and 85 runs
5th	England	214 and 57 for 2 wkt	Australia 385	Match drawn

and 12 in the third. For Australia, K. D. Walters, I. C. Davis, R. B. McCosker, G. J. Cosier, and G. S. Chappell all made centuries, while D. K. Lillee took five wickets in the first test and ten in the second.

Against Australia, New Zealand drew at Christchurch, thanks to a defiant 107 not out by B. E. Congdon and sound batting by Burgess and H. J. Howarth, but Australia won overwhelmingly at Auckland, where a dominant Lillee took 11 wickets. For Australia, Walters made his highest score (250), G. J. Gilmour made 101, and McCosker 84, and the leg spin of K. J. O'Keefe complemented Lillee's speed.

In the West Indies, the first test match should have been won by Pakistan, but a 90-minute last-wicket stand saved the host team. C. G. Greenidge and R. C. Fredericks batted well, and fast bowler C. Croft took 8 for 29 in the second test. The third match was tied. For Pakistan, Wasim Raja and Majid were outstanding batsmen; Mushtaq won the fourth test by making 121 and 56 and taking 8 wickets; and Imran (6 for 90) and Asif (135) excelled in the fifth test.

The Australia v. England Centenary Match at Melbourne, Victoria, was a memorable occasion. In the last innings, England, needing 463 to win, went down in a blaze of glory by making 417 to lose by 45 runs — the exact result in the 1877 match. The particular heroes were wicketkeeper R. W. Marsh (110 not out) and fast bowler Lillee (11 wickets) for Australia, and D. W. Randall (174) for England.

England's success at home against Australia in recovering "the Ashes" owed much to the return to test cricket of G. Boycott after three years of self-imposed exile. His first three innings were 107, 80 not out, and 191, which was his 100th first-class century, after R. A. Woolmer had made centuries in the first two tests (the first at Lord's, London, was named the Jubilee Test). Greig was removed from the captaincy for his involvement with the Kerry Packer affair, though allowed to be chosen to play on merit. His successor, J. M. Brearley (see BIOGRAPHY), made an admirable opening partner, first with Amiss and later with Boycott.

In English county cricket, the championship was shared by Kent and Middlesex, with Gloucestershire third. Winners of the one-day competitions were Middlesex, which beat Glamorgan by five wickets in the Gillette Cup final; Gloucestershire, which beat Kent by 64 runs in the Benson and Hedges final; and Leicestershire, which won the John Player League, with Essex second.

In Australia, Western Australia won the Sheffield Shield, while in New Zealand, Otago won the Shell Shield. Natal retained the Currie Cup in South Africa, and in the West Indies, Barbados won the Shell Shield. In India, Bombay retained the Ranji Trophy and the Irani Trophy. West Zone won the Duleep Trophy and Sri Lanka retained the Topalan Trophy. In Pakistan, Pakistan International Airlines won the Pentangular, United Bank won the Qaid-i-Azam Trophy and the S. A. Bhutto Memorial Cup, and Habib Bank won the Patron's Trophy.   (REX ALSTON)

[452.B.4.h.ix]

Crime and Law Enforcement

Violent Crime. TERRORISM. Throughout 1977 the disturbing frequency and increasing magnitude of politically motivated acts of terrorist violence represented a problem of worldwide significance. While the UN and other international organizations continued their seemingly endless debate about the problem, individual governments were forced to deal with the immediate realities of killings, hijackings, kidnappings, and bombings. Nowhere were these realities more apparent than in West Germany. In April, Chief Federal Prosecutor Siegfried Buback, who had led the government's case against the Baader-Meinhof terrorist gang, was machine-gunned to death in an ambush. Shortly afterward three members of the gang, including its co-leader Andreas Baader, were sentenced to life imprisonment for the slaying of four U.S. soldiers in 1972. Ulrike Meinhof, the other accused co-leader, had been found hanged in her jail cell in May 1976.

Both before and after their conviction and sentencing, the members of the Baader-Meinhof gang had been kept under supposedly maximum security conditions in a fortress-like prison in Stuttgart. Nevertheless, some of their defense lawyers were strongly suspected of conspiring with their clients and acting as couriers, enabling the prisoners not only to maintain contact with each other but also to help their comrades outside organize fresh terrorist actions. Thus, on September 5, in a hail of gunfire that killed several bodyguards and a chauffeur, terrorists kidnapped 62-year-old industrialist Hanns-Martin Schleyer. As part of the ransom for his safe return, Schleyer's captors demanded release of the imprisoned Baader-Meinhof gang members. The government refused, invoking instead a tough law that sought to cut off alleged and convicted terrorists from contact with the outside world, including their defense counsel.

On October 13 the terrorists responded by hijacking a Lufthansa jetliner en route from Palma de Majorca in Spain to Frankfurt am Main and demanding a massive ransom as well as the release of the Baader-Meinhof gang and terrorists imprisoned in other countries. Tense negotiations ensued as the jet hopped from one airfield to another throughout the Mediterranean and Middle East, eventually landing at Aden, where the terrorists executed the captain of the aircraft, and, on October 17, at Mogadishu, Somalia. Finally, during the early morning hours of October 18, German commandos launched a rescue operation, freeing all the hostages and killing or capturing the hijackers. Within hours Baader and two colleagues allegedly committed suicide in their prison cells, and the next day Schleyer's body was found in Mulhouse in northeastern France.

This bizarre series of episodes provoked an international outcry for more stringent efforts to control terrorism. The Japanese government, which earlier in October submitted to the demands of a

Red Army terrorist group that had hijacked a Japan Air Lines jet to Dacca, Bangladesh, came under particular attack for its "soft policy" toward guerrilla attacks. The tough response seemed to attract increasing support following the success of the Mogadishu rescue and a similar operation mounted by the Dutch government in June to free hostages held by South Moluccan train hijackers. Even so, a UN committee, set up in December 1976 to draft an international treaty outlawing the taking of hostages, failed to meet its first deadline. The major problem, as one observer put it, was that "one man's hostage taker is another man's freedom fighter."

A more promising development was the signing of an antiterrorist treaty in January by 17 of 19 members of the Council of Europe. Each signatory agreed that it would extradite or try any individual accused of committing an act of terrorism in any one of the other countries. Only days before one of the signatories, France, had come under sustained criticism for releasing Abu Daoud (*see* BIOGRAPHY), suspected mastermind of the attack on Israeli athletes at the 1972 Munich Olympics.

North America did not remain unscathed, as was demonstrated by the dramatic March seizure of hostages at three locations in Washington, D.C., by members of the small Hanafi Muslim sect led by Hamaas Abdul Khaalis (*see* BIOGRAPHY). When the assault came to a conclusion after 38 hours, one man had been shot dead and 19 others had been shot, stabbed, or beaten. Assisted by the ambassadors to the U.S. of Iran, Pakistan, and Egypt, a highly trained police hostage negotiation team finally brought an end to the drama without having to use force.

The fear that new technologies would put even more powerful and intimidating weapons into the hands of terrorists was emphasized in a report issued during the year by the U.S. government-sponsored National Advisory Committee on Criminal Justice Standards and Goals. The committee concluded that the threat of attack by terrorists possessing nuclear, biological, or chemical weapons was "very real and ought to be realistically and urgently faced."

OTHER VIOLENT CRIME. As a U.S. House of Representatives subcommittee pursued its troubled investigation of the assassinations of Pres. John F. Kennedy and Martin Luther King, Jr., an organized crime figure, Charles Nicoletti, who had been sought for questioning by the committee, was found slain in Chicago in classic gangland style. Nicoletti was the third such figure to meet his death following contacts with congressional committees investigating the Kennedy assassination. Suspicions of a possible syndicate role in the King assassination also surfaced when James Earl Ray, serving a 99-year sentence for the crime, escaped from a Tennessee penitentiary in June. However, when Ray was recaptured following a massive manhunt, it appeared that his escape had been accomplished without outside assistance.

The growing power of the "Cuban Mafia" in syndicate ranks gave law-enforcement officers increasing cause for concern. Since the late 1960s some Cuban refugees, many of them with CIA

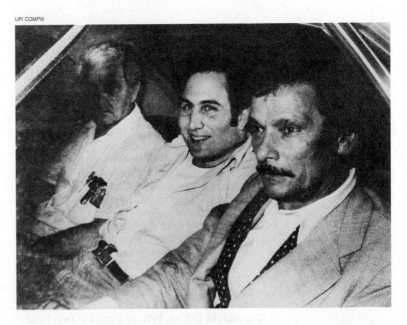

training, were believed to have been operating one of the world's largest smuggling rings, shipping narcotics, guns, and prostitutes through Miami to syndicate outlets in New Orleans, Chicago, Las Vegas, and various East Coast cities. It was also believed that certain Cubans had established themselves as professional killers, and they were thought to be responsible for at least 20 murders in which .22 calibre guns had been used. The FBI began a special investigation of the ".22 murders," the victims of which were mostly syndicate "turncoats" cooperating with federal prosecutors.

On January 17 convicted murderer Gary Gilmore was shot to death by a firing squad in accordance with the law in the state of Utah, the first prisoner to be legally executed in the U.S. in almost a decade. The American Civil Liberties Union and other organizations fighting capital punishment had expected his death to open the door to a flood of executions, but no more had taken place in the U.S. by year's end. Nevertheless, there were signs that the public's attitude toward the treatment of criminals was hardening. (*See* PRISONS AND PENOLOGY: *Special Report.*)

Calls for more severe punishment were frequently heard in political campaigns, especially that for mayor of New York City, where for months residents had lived in fear of a killer who—in notes to the police and media—identified himself as "Son of Sam." Over the course of a year, "Son of Sam" murdered at least six persons and wounded seven others with a .44 calibre revolver. His victims were young people, gunned down at night in lonely streets or parking places. One of the largest and most publicized manhunts in history finally resulted in the capture, in August, of 24-year-old David Berkowitz. After psychological examination, Berkowitz was declared fit to stand trial, but the massive and sensational media attention given to the case, which even reached the front pages of the Vatican's *L'Osservatore Romano* and the Soviet Union's *Izvestia*, raised serious questions as to whether it would be possible for him to receive a fair hearing.

A smiling David Berkowitz (centre), charged with the "Son of Sam" killings, was arrested August 10 outside his Yonkers, N.Y., apartment.

Crowds gathered at the funeral of slain diamond broker Pinchos Jaroslawicz, murdered in Manhattan, N.Y., in September. A series of crimes had plagued New York City's diamond district.

Women's groups, continuing to agitate for stronger measures against the crime of rape, applauded a damages award of $1,475,000 made to singer Connie Francis. Francis had been staying at a Howard Johnson Motel in Long Island, N.Y., in 1974 when an intruder entered her room and raped her. She subsequently brought suit against the restaurant and motel chain for $6 million, alleging that the company had failed to provide her with a safe and secure room. The suit was ultimately settled out of court, but the decision prompted hotel operators to strengthen security guard forces and to consider new security techniques.

Another group of crime victims who were gaining increased attention were the elderly. Although experts disagreed as to whether crimes against the elderly were, in reality, statistically more frequent than those against other population groups, such crimes clearly represented a serious social problem. Many elderly persons, fearing to venture onto the streets, became virtual prisoners in their own homes.

Nonviolent Crime. WHITE-COLLAR AND POLITICAL CRIME. The reverberations of the 1976 Lockheed bribery scandal continued to be felt in high government and business circles in 1977. The heaviest political fallout was in Japan, where 14 persons were indicted for Lockheed-related offenses, mainly bribery, foreign currency violations, tax offenses, and perjury. The trial of former prime minister Kakuei Tanaka, the most impor-

tant person implicated in the affair, began in January. Expected to last several years, it involved charges of accepting $1.6 million in bribes to encourage the purchase of Lockheed jets in Japan.

In the aftermath of Lockheed, the world's political and business leaders could reach little consensus on methods of preventing a recurrence. In the fiercely competitive international export trade, it was far from clear when a commission paid to an agent became improper, nor was it certain whether multinational companies like Lockheed should be bound in their dealings by the standards of law or morality pertaining in their own countries. At a summit meeting of seven major industrialized countries in London in May, U.S. Pres. Jimmy Carter and other leaders urged that "irregular practices and improper conduct should be eliminated from international trade, banking and commerce." But despite such brave assertions, no new legislation or treaty emerged to create standards for national or international commercial behaviour. Instead, it was believed to be business as usual in most countries. The current bribe rate for most arms sales in Paris, for instance, was reported to be 15%.

Alleged widespread buying of political favours and other influence in Washington, D.C., by agents of the South Korean government—dubbed Koreagate by some cynics—led to a series of congressional and Justice Department investigations in the U.S. One result was the indictment, by a federal grand jury, of a South Korean businessman, Park Tong Sun (*see* BIOGRAPHY), on 36 felony violations involving influence peddling. Named as unindicted co-conspirators were a former congressman and two former heads of the South Korean Central Intelligence Agency. Efforts were being made to extradite Park from South Korea, where he had gone when the investigations began. Meanwhile, the House Ethics Committee appointed Leon Jaworski, former Watergate special prosecutor, as a special counsel to assist it in the investigation of possible improper and illegal congressional conduct.

Other notable names appeared on the list of those accused of misconduct. Ex-prime minister Zulfikar Ali Bhutto, deposed as the ruler of Pakistan in a military coup, went on trial before a military court in October on a charge of having conspired to murder a political opponent in 1974. (*See* PAKISTAN.) In India the government of former prime minister Indira Gandhi was the subject of an investigation, and Mrs. Gandhi herself was arrested briefly on charges involving alleged corrupt practices. (*See* INDIA.) In the United States Gov. Marvin Mandel (*see* BIOGRAPHY) of Maryland, sentenced to serve four years in prison for mail fraud and racketeering, became the first sitting governor to be convicted of a federal crime in more than 40 years.

THEFT. At a time when pilferage from docks in the U.S. was declining, due largely to the introduction of prepackaged cargo containers, thefts from other freight depots were mushrooming. The problem was particularly acute in the New York and New Jersey areas, where the giant Conrail Freight Yard, the nation's largest piggyback rail

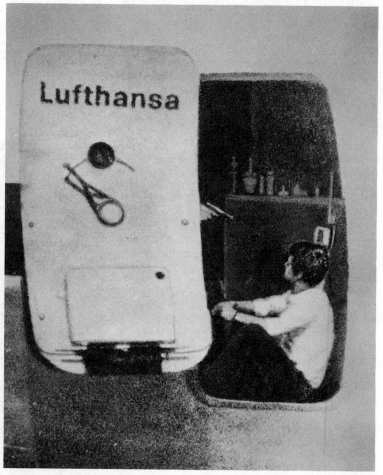

Jürgen Schumann, pilot of a hijacked Lufthansa airliner, sat at gunpoint in the doorway of the plane at Dubai, United Arab Emirates. Schumann was later killed and his body thrown from the plane.

WIDE WORLD

facility, was a prime target. The volume of merchandise passing through the facility, or sitting in row after row of trailers, presented an almost insoluble security problem.

The theft of art treasures continued to be a serious problem in many countries. In France, where a special police branch was created to deal with this type of theft, more than 7,000 art objects were stolen in 1976. At least 50% of these stolen objects were believed to have been smuggled abroad, particularly to the U.S. and Japan. In the U.S. an ingenious method of "fingerprinting" paintings was being used. Minute X-ray details of an artwork, such as brush patterns and wood, paint, and canvas typologies, were stored, making it far easier to trace the objects if they were stolen.

Law Enforcement. Cheered somewhat by FBI figures indicating that serious reported crime in the U.S. had not increased in 1976, the Carter administration moved cautiously to effect promised changes in the federal government's law enforcement structure. After a six-month search for a new FBI director, the president nominated federal judge Frank M. Johnson, Jr., of Alabama for the position, but in late November he withdrew his name from nomination because of ill health. All this came at a time of low employee morale at the FBI as the new attorney general, Griffin Bell, pursued an investigation into "bag jobs"—the bureau's euphemism for illegal break-ins—and other past illicit activities by bureau personnel. The investigation raised difficult issues, foremost among them being whether the government could order or encourage its agents to commit illegal acts and whether, if they did so, it should prosecute them. In April, for the first time in history, an FBI agent was indicted on a felony count for his alleged involvement in wiretapping and opening of mail without warrants.

A U.S. General Accounting Office report released in March was highly critical of past federal law enforcement efforts to combat organized crime. Not only was organized crime "flourishing," the report stated, but "there is no agreement on what organized crime is and, consequently, against precisely whom or what the government is fighting." Reacting to the report, Attorney General Bell said that he was concerned about some of its conclusions, but that one of his top priorities would be investigations of fraud against the government, which he termed one of the more widespread forms of criminal activity. Supporting this view, a computer analysis by the newly established Office of the Inspector General indicated that of 250 million Medicaid billings submitted by physicians and pharmacists in 1976, an estimated 47,000 contained "abnormalities"; of these, 2,000 were selected for detailed investigation and possible prosecution.

A Police Foundation study of shootings by law enforcement officers in seven U.S. cities showed widely varying local policies on the use of deadly force. Noting that police are seldom punished when they shoot someone, the foundation called for the development of more carefully defined standards for police use of firearms and for stronger management to enforce such guidelines. Subsequently, the Los Angeles Police Department announced the implementation of its first written policy on use of firearms by police. The department had come under criticism following the shooting deaths of 29 persons during one year.

In several countries where the police were themselves the targets of extremist violence, there was a disturbing tendency to respond in kind. In India, for instance, the preliminary findings of an official inquiry confirmed allegations that police officers had systematically tortured and killed members of a revolutionary terrorist group known as Naxalites. The policemen responsible were put on trial for homicide.

In Italy, racked throughout the year by urban terrorism, the government sought parliamentary sanction to allow police to question suspects without the presence of their lawyers and to make preventive arrests under which suspects could be held incommunicado for 48 hours. Critics of the proposals feared they were a serious threat to civil rights. A march by fascists in London in August, which resulted in 214 arrests and injuries to 55 police and 56 civilians, led to a review of existing U.K. legislation designed to control demonstrations.

In his final report as commissioner of the Metropolitan Police in London, Sir Robert Mark noted that elimination of corruption had been one of his main objectives during his five years in office. As a result of the work of the A10 unit, set up in 1972 to investigate serious charges against police, more than 450 officers had left the force voluntarily or had been fired, including senior officers in charge of the antipornography squad. These officers were convicted in May of what the trial judge described as "an evil conspiracy which turned the obscene publication squad into a vast protection racket."

(DUNCAN CHAPPELL)

See also Prisons and Penology.
[522.C.6; 543.A.5; 552.C and F; 737.B; 10/36.C.5.a]

Cuba

Cuba

The socialist republic of Cuba occupies the largest island in the Greater Antilles of the West Indies. Area: 110,922 sq km (42,827 sq mi), including several thousand small islands and cays. Pop. (1976 est.): 9,404,900, including (1953) white 72.8%; mestizo 14.5%; Negro 12.4%. Cap. and largest city: Havana (pop., 1976 est., 1,861,000). Language: Spanish. Religion: Roman Catholic (52%). President of the Council of State in 1977, Fidel Castro Ruz.

Cuba experienced political stability during 1977, but made no economic headway. Progress continued to be made toward the formation of permanent official institutions that would bring the administrative system more into line with those of the Eastern European countries. On July 13 the 479-member National Assembly held its first ordinary sessions to discuss and approve laws with this in view. Pres. Fidel Castro consolidated his personal position: on Dec. 3, 1976, he had assumed the post of president of the Council of State, which combined the offices of president and prime minister, and in January 1977 he took the rank of major

Crops:
see Agriculture and
Food Supplies

general as part of a restoration of officers' ranks in the armed forces.

Much attention was focused on moves by Havana and Washington to improve relations. (*See* Special Report.) Throughout the year the U.S. suspended reconnaissance flights over Cuba and, after the U.S. lifted its ban on travel to Cuba in March, U.S. tourists visited Havana and other Cuban cities, via Canada. In April a 52-man mission from the Greater Minneapolis Chamber of Commerce visited Havana, and its members had a lengthy meeting with Castro. On April 27 the two countries completed negotiations for a fishing agreement which granted Cuba a quota in waters within 200 mi of U.S. coastlines; a separate agreement set a "preliminary boundary" between the overlapping 200-mi economic zones in waters between the two countries. Cuba announced that it would not formally renew the anti-air piracy treaty, which expired on April 15, but would continue to act within the spirit of the accord, particularly as regards the reciprocal return of hijackers.

An official Cuban delegation was allowed to take part in the International Citrus Congress held in Florida in June; a passenger shipping service between New Orleans and Havana was authorized; and the first commercial air service between the U.S. and Cuba since 1960 began on June 15. On May 10 the U.S. Senate Foreign Relations Committee voted to ease the U.S. trade embargo against Cuba by permitting the latter to buy medicine and certain agricultural supplies in the U.S. market. In August, following a visit to Havana by Sen. Frank Church (Dem., Idaho), it was announced that 84 U.S. citizens and their Cuban dependents would be allowed to leave Cuba.

On September 1 the two countries took steps to reestablish partial diplomatic relations following a break of 16 years. "Interest sections" were opened for the U.S. at the Swiss embassy in Havana and for Cuba at the Czechoslovak embassy in Washington. The U.S. administration indicated that a full resumption of diplomatic ties was unlikely until there had been a settlement of U.S. claims for nationalized property (estimated at $1.8 billion), release of U.S. citizens held in Cuban jails, and reduction or cessation of the Cuban presence in Africa.

Castro paid unscheduled visits to Algeria (where his African tour began and ended), Libya, Yemen (Aden), Ethiopia, Somalia, Tanzania, Mozambique, and Angola in March, and it was reported that he offered advisers and military assistance to some of the countries. On April 4 he arrived in Moscow, by way of East Berlin, and on April 8 Cuba and the U.S.S.R. pledged further support for guerrilla movements abroad. It was privately estimated in May that Cuba maintained 20,000–25,000 military personnel and advisers in Africa, including 15,000–20,000 in Angola. In July Castro announced that Cuban aid to less developed countries would be increased, and in November it was reported that a further 2,600 Cuban civilian advisers were to be sent to Angola.

Soviet aid to Cuba was estimated at $820 million in 1976 and was reportedly running at $4 million a day in the first nine months of 1977. In April,

Curling:
see Winter Sports

Moscow agreed to help build a nuclear power plant with an initial output of 400,000 kw, to be expanded to 1.7 million kw. In November 1976, following a visit to Moscow by the Venezuelan president, Carlos Andres Pérez, an agreement had been made by the U.S.S.R. and Venezuela providing for the supply and transport of Venezuelan oil to Cuba.

The Cuban economy was in a state of crisis, mainly as a result of a sharp decrease in foreign exchange revenue from sugar due to very low international prices; sugar had accounted for 80–85% of Cuban exports in recent years. Heavy rains in the western and central growing regions and a drought in the eastern areas badly affected the 1977 sugar crop. No official data had been released by mid-September as to the size of the crop, but it was expected to be considerably less than 6 million tons, the average annual production for 1974–76. The austerity program announced by Castro in September 1976 was intensified during the year; rations for sugar, rice, and coffee were drastically reduced in February, and in March charges for telephone calls and entertainments were made for the first time. Because of the shortage of foreign exchange, the Cubans requested suppliers from Western countries to delay shipment of orders for capital goods or to accept postponements in payments for those already delivered. At the end of June 1977, the total Cuban debt to non-Communist countries was estimated at $1.2 billion, with annual service payments amounting to $400 million, or about half of Cuban exports in the boom years of 1975 and 1976, when sugar prices were at record levels.   (ROBIN CHAPMAN)

CUBA

Education. (1974–75) Primary, pupils 1,923,290, teachers 78,451; secondary, pupils 337,524, teachers 26,504; vocational, pupils 82,038, teachers 6,289; teacher training, students 35,498, teachers 2,719; higher (university only; 1975–76), students 76,900, teaching staff 5,725.

Finance. Monetary unit: peso, with (Sept. 19, 1977) a free rate of 0.79 peso to U.S. $1 (1.38 peso = £1 sterling). Budget (1966; latest published) balanced at 2,718,000,000 pesos. Gross national product (1975 est.) U.S. $7,430,000,000.

Foreign Trade. (1975) Imports 3,207,000,000 pesos; exports 2,948,000,000 pesos. Import sources (1974): U.S.S.R. 47%; Japan 8%; United Kingdom 5%. Export destinations (1974): U.S.S.R. 36%; Japan 17%; Spain 7%; East Germany 5%. Main exports (1974): sugar 86%; nickel and copper ores 6%.

Transport and Communications. Roads (1974) 27,074 km (including 1,220 km of the Central Highway). Motor vehicles in use (1973): passenger c. 70,000; commercial (including buses) c. 33,000. Railways: (1974) 5,243 km (excluding c. 9,500 km plantation); traffic (1972) 946 million passenger-km, freight (1973) 1,617,000,000 net ton-km. Air traffic (1975): 517 million passenger-km; freight 15.5 million net ton-km. Shipping (1976): merchant vessels 100 gross tons and over 294; gross tonnage 603,750. Telephones (Dec. 1973) 281,000. Radio receivers (Dec. 1974) 1,805,000. Television receivers (Dec. 1974) 595,000.

Agriculture. Production (in 000; metric tons; 1976): rice c. 420; corn (1975) c. 125; cassava (1975) c. 239; sweet potatoes (1975) c. 245; tomatoes c. 184; sugar, raw value c. 5,700; oranges c. 125; coffee c. 25; tobacco c. 53; jute c. 3; fish catch (1975) c. 165. Livestock (in 000; 1976): cattle c. 5,500; pigs c. 1,450; sheep c. 340; goats c. 92; horses (1975) c. 854.

Industry. Production (in 000; metric tons; 1974): crude oil c. 140; petroleum products c. 5,330; electricity (kw-hr) 6,016,000; copper ore (metal content) 5.9; chrome ore (oxide content; 1973) 13; nickel ore (metal content) c. 32.

CUBA: SIXTEEN YEARS LATER

by Brian Pollitt

In 1977, almost 20 years after the overthrow of Fulgencio Batista and the institution of a revolutionary, Marxist government in Cuba, the U.S. State Department lifted its restrictions on travel to the island by U.S. nationals. In the intervening years, the American picture of Cuba had been compounded of memories of exotic nightclubs and gambling dens, the enthusiasms of young radicals who thought they recognized the wave of the future, and rumours of a drab, regimented society beset by shortages. What would returning tourists actually find?

Recent years have seen the limited revival in Cuba of a tourist industry that was a source of both fame and shame prior to the 1959 revolution. As Canadians—currently the most important North American source of tourist dollars—have been able to see, Havana is much changed. Its major buildings are much the same, if somewhat dilapidated in part, but the familiar Latin-American juxtaposition of extreme wealth and poverty has gone. The stores are no longer filled with U.S. consumer goods, and revo-lutionary slogans and portraits have replaced the street adornments that once advertised them. The latest-model Cadillacs do not glide by carrying white-suited gentlemen and their ladies, and the U.S. dollar, once interchangeable in street or market with the Cuban peso, must now be formally exchanged (and at a less favourable rate). But gone too are the beggars and the prostitutes. If conspicuous affluence seems to have disappeared, so too has much of the squalor.

The beaches and the climate remain as attractive as always, and in the hotels and restaurants tourists are insulated from the more general austerity. Havana's once-famous nightclubs—closed in the late 1960s in a temporary burst of puritanical fervour—may still be visited, and the showgirls are as flamboyantly, if scantily, clad as ever. Even discretely isolated gambling facilities have been reopened for tourists who are so inclined. Free movement around the capital has been made easier by the recent modernization and expansion of Havana's taxi fleet—with Chevrolets acquired from General Motors' subsidiary in Argentina.

But tourists confining themselves to such a world would be closing themselves off in a somewhat anemic relic of Cuba's past. If they wish to see what is new, they will tour the countryside where, together with much natural beauty, they can observe a host of new schools, hospitals, dams, and agricultural research stations, and a rural population relieved of the abysmal poverty and unemployment seen before the revolution by those rare visitors interested enough to look. Whatever final impressions the

The first U.S. cruise ship to visit Cuba since 1961 was the "Daphne," which sailed from New Orleans to Havana in May.

LAFFONT—SYGMA

new tourists may take away, they will be unlikely to fit the more extreme caricatures of life in Fidel Castro's Cuba that derive from so many years of mutual isolation and hostility.

The Closed Door Comes Ajar. In January 1961 the U.S. government, then headed by Pres. Dwight Eisenhower, severed diplomatic relations with the Republic of Cuba, and the policy of nonrecognition was maintained under four succeeding presidents. Faced with the embarrassing fact of a self-proclaimed Communist government "90 miles from shore," the United States tried to turn Castro's Cuba into a noncountry. Trade and tourism were strictly off limits. Such contacts as existed were carried on at arm's length, through the Swiss and Czechoslovak diplomatic missions in Havana and Washington.

Such was the situation until 1977, when the Carter administration, formed amid expectations of new departures in both domestic and foreign policy, initiated an exchange of notes with the Cuban government. As a result, on May 30, 1977, the two countries agreed to establish ten-member "interest sections" in each others' capitals. The heads of these "interest sections" formally occupied their posts on September 1.

While it lacked the fanfare that accompanied Nixon's opening to China, the step was in some ways analogous. Even the sporting preamble was there. Prior to more formal exchanges, a U.S. table-tennis team had visited China, initiating a period of what became popularly known as "Ping-Pong diplomacy." Similarly, a basketball team representing two universities in South Dakota—the home state of Sen. George McGovern, who had visited Havana previously—toured Cuba in the spring of 1977. The Cuban national team then followed with a tour of eight U.S. cities in November.

Like the China initiative, these limited steps toward restoring normal relations seemed long overdue. A number of prominent U.S. politicians had visited Cuba in recent years and, during 1976 and 1977, more than 200 U.S. businessmen went to the island to explore commercial possibilities in the event of an end to the U.S. trade embargo. In October 1977 the Cuban minister for foreign trade announced an intended visit to Washington for informal talks with businessmen and politicians. However, the U.S. State Department let it be known that there was "no early prospect" of ending the embargo, and the visit was abandoned. Evidently progress along the road to full normalization would be a delicate and protracted process.

Stumbling Blocks. It appeared that a number of issues would have to be resolved before fully normal relations could be established. On the U.S. side, one was the question of compensation for nationalized U.S. property. Claims filed by affected companies and individuals amounted to $1.8 billion—a formidable sum, approximately equal to the value of Cuban exports of raw and refined sugar, tobacco, and minerals for three years in the decade before the 1959 revolution. The ubiquitous question of "human rights" in Cuba would also be subject to negotiations, according to U.S. spokesmen, as would the release of U.S. citizens—reportedly fewer than ten—currently imprisoned on the island. In the sphere of foreign policy, Cuba would apparently be required to restrict—if not entirely cease—its military involvement in Africa.

The Cuban government was less assertive. Stressing that the limited links currently being established stemmed from U.S. and not Cuban initiatives, it—probably wisely—formulated no comparable list of preconditions. Instead, it requested the minimal attributes of "normality" itself. "Normal" commercial relations—by which Cuba meant most-favoured-nation status—could follow the ending of the trade embargo. More "normal" intergovernmental political relations would attend continued curbing of the more violent activities of Cuban exile groups and the U.S. Central Intelligence Agency (activities given credence by the interim report of the U.S. Senate Intelligence Committee, which documented several plots against Castro's life—some exceedingly exotic in character—for the period 1960–65). This comparatively modest degree of "normality" was viewed by the Cuban government as a necessary first stage, to be reached before more thorny issues could be negotiated. Of these issues, the future of the U.S.-leased naval base at Guantanamo Bay was an obvious example.

Ninety Miles from Shore. It has proved difficult for the U.S. to divest itself of the notion that it can and should be the ultimate arbiter of affairs in the nations south of its borders. This was apparent in the opposition to the proposed treaty that would give Panama sovereignty over the Panama Canal by the end of the century. But if a hysterical note was detectable in the opposition to the Panama treaty, its locus was outside the U.S. government. This contrasted sharply with the period immediately following the Cuban revolution. "We were hysterical about Castro at the time of the Bay of Pigs and thereafter," testified former U.S. defense secretary Robert McNamara before the Senate Intelligence Committee in 1975. That hysteria appeared to originate partly in the sheer implausibility of Castro's survival in the face of U.S. efforts to bring him down.

In the early years of the revolution, the U.S. trade embargo was an immensely damaging weapon. It resulted in the premature obsolescence of a major proportion of Cuba's capital stock as spare parts and maintenance know-how became unobtainable or nearly so. It led to cannibalization of plant and equipment, while all the energies of Cuba's then diminishing supply of engineers, mechanics, and administrators were needed merely to maintain existing industrial and transportation capacity—to the detriment of the island's early efforts toward industrialization. Also, it imposed enormous strains on port and storage facilities as virtually all trade was perforce shifted to geographically distant countries.

On the military front, the Bay of Pigs invasion of April 1961—mounted by Cuban exiles with CIA backing—was essentially a maritime reprise of the operation that had successfully removed Pres. Jacobo Arbenz of Guatemala in 1954. It was predicated on a belief that the Cuban populace shared Washington's view of Castro and his works, and the defeat and capture, within 72 hours, of the well-armed expeditionary force shocked those who had trained and unleashed it.

If the opening period of the Cuban revolution was associated with U.S. frustration, the picture in subsequent years was more mixed. The missile crisis of October 1962 was resolved by direct transactions between Washington and Moscow (to the fury of Havana). The defeat and death of Che Guevara in Bolivia in October 1967 marked an end to the phase of Cuban-supported guerrilla struggles in Latin America. Those very efforts assisted U.S. policy which, given its failure to overthrow Castro's regime, sought to isolate it. By the mid–1960s, Mexico and Canada were the only Western Hemisphere nations to maintain diplomatic relations with the island. Domestically, economic difficulties attending the rupture of Cuban-U.S. relations were compounded by overambitious development plans, most notably the costly—and unsuccessful—effort to raise sugar production to ten million tons in 1970. But a traditional Cuban nickname for the country is Cork Island—storms may batter it, but it will not sink. In a continent wracked by political and social upheavals, Castro's regime not only survived but emerged as an example of conspicuous stability.

Emerging from Isolation. That Cuba should receive aid and succour from the Soviet bloc was to be expected, but in the course of the 1960s a number of U.S. allies in Western Europe concluded that the Cuban revolution was not going to be undone and that it might as well be lived with and traded with. Spain established a swift, if ideologically implausible, modus vivendi with Cuba in the early post-revolutionary years and gave signs of taking quiet pleasure from U.S. discomfiture in an area that was once part of the old Spanish empire. Britain came to terms with Cuba's nationalization policies—most notably, of Anglo-Dutch oil-refining interests—and

became an important supplier of public transportation facilities and agricultural equipment. France and Italy expanded their trade with Cuba in the later 1960s, becoming, with Japan, Spain, the U.K., and Canada, among Cuba's most important trading partners in the 1970s.

Of greater political importance, perhaps, has been the crumbling of Cuba's political and economic isolation within the Western Hemisphere. Although right-wing military coups in the Southern Cone of Latin America set the process back at times, an increasing number of members of the Organization of American States, from which Cuba was expelled in 1962, ceased to oppose its readmission. The U.S. itself, in an act of "followership" rather than leadership, passed from active opposition on the question to a position of abstention.

Even more significantly, long-standing nationalist sensibilities in the region began to express themselves in forms that made Cuba's ideological isolation less extreme. Cuba's expropriation of foreign capital had been the most significant act of economic nationalism in Latin America since the Mexican nationalization of foreign oil interests in 1938. By 1977, however, governments in Peru, Venezuela, Guyana, and Jamaica had assumed control of major productive sectors previously in foreign hands. Venezuela's nationalization of its oil fields paved the way for a resumption in 1976—albeit on a limited scale—of oil shipments to Cuba, severed by foreign oil companies in 1960. The radicalization of political and economic policies in Guyana and Jamaica brought a growing rapport between the three Caribbean neighbours.

In such a context, the case for U.S. "normalization" of relations with Cuba was no more than simple recognition of the fact that the politics of "abnormality" had failed to achieve the desired results. Politically, economically, and militarily, Cuba was stronger, more stable, and more influential in 1977 than it had been a decade earlier. That Cuba would effect major policy changes at the behest of the U.S. seemed vastly implausible, although conciliatory gestures were another matter. Given this, plus the long history of political antagonism (especially in the U.S. Congress), swift progress toward political and commercial normality appeared unlikely. Yet maintenance of the status quo had come to seem, not an instrument of creative diplomacy, but part of a sterile vendetta that might be ended with mutual benefit.

The author of numerous articles on pre- and post-revolutionary Cuba, Brian Pollitt, a lecturer at Glasgow University's Institute of Latin-American Studies, was visiting professor at the University of Massachusetts in 1977.

Cycling

Only two years after seriously entering international track competition Japanese riders gained their first major victory, in the 1977 professional sprint at the world championships in San Cristóbal, Venezuela. K. Nakano outrode defending champion John Nicholson (Australia) in a semifinal and then took the gold medal by beating Y. Sugata in an all-Japanese final. The men's amateur track championships were dominated by East German riders and, after a year's absence from the world series, Soviet women were supreme. The U.S. provided the chief opposition in the sprint, while Canadian girls finished third and fourth in the pursuit; Karen Strong's bronze was her country's first world cycling medal since 1899. Contested at 3,000 ft above sea level, the championships attained speeds that approached those achieved at very high altitude in the 1968 Olympic Games at Mexico City.

Italian riders scored a notable "double" in the individual road championships, 1976 runner-up Francesco Moser winning the professional title and Claudio Corti the amateur. Moser's success atoned for a lean season in European one-day and multistage races. Even more conspicuous by his absence from the winners' list was Eddy Merckx. After seven years of supremacy the Belgian could only pick up an occasional placing, and the mantle of superchampion was assumed by his compatriot Freddy Maertens, most frequent winner of the year. After a rigorous early season Maertens did not ride the 2,500-mi Tour de France, which started quietly and ended with an intense struggle between Bernard Thévenet (France) and Hennie Kuiper (The Netherlands). Thévenet won the race by 48 sec.

The U.S.S.R. provided both the individual winner and the leading team in the two most important mid-season amateur stage races. Aavo Pikkuss was best in the Warsaw–Berlin–Prague "Peace Race" and Said Gusseinov won an unusually close

A jubilant Constant Tourne of Belgium waves his arms after crossing the finish line a winner in the 50-kilometre points race at the World Cycling Championships, San Cristóbal, Venezuela.

Milk Race Tour of Britain in which only 31 sec separated the first eight riders. Britain's top home-based professional, Sid Barras, was too good for the amateurs in the Tour of Scotland Milk Race, which was open to professionals for the first time.

(J. B. WADLEY)

Nearing the end of a three-week bicycle race, Bernard Thévenet pedals along the Champs Élysées in Paris. Thévenet won the classic Tour de France with an elapsed time of 115 hours, 38 minutes, and 30 seconds.

1977 Cycling Champions

Event	Winner	Country
WORLD AMATEUR CHAMPIONS—TRACK		
Men		
1,000-m time trial	L. Thoms	East Germany
Sprint	H.-J. Geschke	East Germany
Tandem sprint	V. Vackar and M. Vymazal	Czechoslovakia
Individual pursuit	N. Durpisch	East Germany
Team pursuit		East Germany
50-km points	C. Tourne	Belgium
50-km motor-paced	G. Minneboo	The Netherlands
Women		
Sprint	G. Tsareva	U.S.S.R.
Individual pursuit	V. Kuznetsova	U.S.S.R.
WORLD PROFESSIONAL CHAMPIONS—TRACK		
Sprint	K. Nakano	Japan
Individual pursuit	G. Braun	West Germany
One-hour motor-paced	C. Stam	The Netherlands
WORLD AMATEUR CHAMPIONS—ROAD		
Men		
100-km team time trial		U.S.S.R.
Individual race	C. Corti	Italy
Women		
Individual road race	J. Bost	France
WORLD PROFESSIONAL CHAMPION—ROAD		
Individual road race	F. Moser	Italy
WORLD CHAMPIONS—CYCLO CROSS		
Amateur	R. Vermeire	Belgium
Professional	A. Zweifel	Switzerland
MAJOR PROFESSIONAL ROAD-RACE WINNERS		
Het Volk	F. Maertens	Belgium
Milan–San Remo	J. Raas	The Netherlands
Tour of Flanders	R. de Vlaeminck	Belgium
Paris–Roubaix	R. de Vlaeminck	Belgium
Amstel Gold Race	J. Raäs	The Netherlands
Ghent–Wevelghem	B. Hinault	France
Flèche Wallonne	F. Maertens	Belgium
Liège–Bastogne–Liège	B. Hinault	France
Grand Prix of Frankfurt	G. Knetemann	The Netherlands
Bordeaux–Paris	H. Van Springel	Belgium
Paris–Brussels	L. Peeters	Belgium
Tours–Versailles	J. Zoetemelk	The Netherlands
Tour of Lombardy	G. Baronchelli	Italy
Grand Prix des Nations time-trial	B. Hinault	France
Tour de France	B. Thévenet	France
Tour of Italy	M. Pollentier	Belgium
Tour of Spain	F. Maertens	Belgium
Tour of Switzerland	M. Pollentier	Belgium
Tour of Luxembourg	B. Pronk	The Netherlands
Tour of Sardinia	F. Maertens	Belgium
Semana Catalana	F. Maertens	Belgium
Four Days of Dunkirk	G. Knetemann	The Netherlands
Dauphiné Libéré	B. Hinault	France
Paris–Nice	F. Maertens	Belgium
Midi-Libre	V. Panizza	Italy

Cyprus

An island republic and a member of the Commonwealth of Nations, Cyprus is in the eastern Mediterranean. Area: 9,251 sq km (3,572 sq mi). Pop. (1976 est.): 639,000, including Greeks 82%; Turks 18%. Cap. and largest city: Nicosia (pop., 1976 est., 146,000). All these population figures should be considered unreliable, as they do not take into account the extensive internal migration or the recent and reportedly extensive Turkish immigration and Greek emigration, for which authoritative data are not available. Language: Greek and Turkish. Religion: Greek Orthodox 77%; Muslim 18%. Presidents in 1977, Archbishop Makarios III until August 3 and, from August 31, Spyros Kyprianou.

Archbishop Makarios III (*see* OBITUARIES), who had led his country since independence in 1960, died on Aug. 3, 1977. He was succeeded by Spyros Kyprianou, president of the Parliament, who became acting president upon Makarios' death and was proclaimed president on August 31. Kypri-

Cyprus

CYPRUS

Education. (Greek schools; 1976–77) Primary, pupils 55,366, teachers 2,159; secondary, pupils 44,059, teachers 2,136; vocational, pupils 6,574, teachers 442; teacher training, students 97, teachers 15; higher, students 685, teaching staff 63. (Turkish schools; 1972–73) Primary, pupils 16,014; secondary, pupils 7,190; vocational, pupils 753; teacher training, students 13.

Finance. Monetary unit: Cyprus pound, with (Sept. 19, 1977) a free rate of C£0.41 to U.S. $1 (C£0.71 = £1 sterling). The Turkish lira is also in use in North Cyprus (Turkish Federated State). Gold, SDR's, and foreign exchange (May 1977) U.S. $279.7 million. Budget (1976 est.): revenue C£56,026,000; expenditure C£67,745,000 (excludes expenditure of Turkish Federated State).

Foreign Trade. (1976) Imports C£177.8 million; exports C£104.5 million. Import sources: U.K. 20%; Greece 10%; Italy 9%; West Germany 7%; Turkey c. 6%; U.S. 6%; France 5%. Export destinations: U.K. 28%; Lebanon 17%; Syria 6%; Saudi Arabia 6%; Libya 6%; U.S.S.R. 5%. Main exports: potatoes 17%; cement 9%; clothing 8%; cigarettes 6%; wine 5%; citrus fruit 5%. Tourism: visitors (1975) 47,000; gross receipts (1974) U.S. $38 million.

Transport and Communications. Roads (1974) 9,494 km. Motor vehicles in use (1975): passenger 68,700; commercial 14,300. Air traffic (1976): 304 million passenger-km; freight 6.6 million net ton-km. Shipping (1976): merchant vessels 100 gross tons and over 765; gross tonnage 3,114,263. Telephones (Jan. 1976) 71,000. Radio licenses (Dec. 1974) 206,000. Television licenses (Dec. 1974) 85,000.

Agriculture. Production (in 000; metric tons; 1976): barley 86; wheat (1975) 40; grapes c. 175; potatoes (1975) c. 164; oranges c. 60; grapefruit (1975) c. 55; olives c. 8. Livestock (in 000; Dec. 1974): sheep 275; cattle 17; pigs 114; goats 220.

Industry. Production (in 000; metric tons; 1975): asbestos 28; iron pyrites (exports) 408; copper ore (exports; metal content; 1974) 13; chromium ore (oxide content) 19; cement (1976) 1,026; electricity (kw-hr; 1976) 802,000.

anou's term of office would run only until February 1978.

Early in December 1976 the UN had reported that fewer than 4,000 Greek Cypriots remained in the northern zone of Cyprus, the so-called Turkish Federated State of Cyprus dominated by "President" Rauf Denktash and maintained by Turkish troops. Peace between the two communities was enforced by a UN contingent whose mandate the Security Council was obliged to renew on June 15, 1977, and again on Dec. 15.

The only intercommunal talks held in 1977 took

In an attempt to achieve peace in Cyprus, UN Secretary-General Kurt Waldheim (centre) brought together Archbishop Makarios III, then president of Cyprus (left), and Rauf Denktash, president of the self-proclaimed Turkish Federated State of Cyprus (right), for a discussion on the future of the island.

CAMERA PRESS/PHOTO TRENDS

place in Vienna and Nicosia between March 31 and May 26, after intense diplomatic activity on the part of the UN, leaders of the European Economic Community, and U.S. Pres. Jimmy Carter's special representative Clark Clifford, who visited Cyprus in February. Neither side offered the "concessions" deemed necessary by the other. The Turkish Cypriot interlocutor, Umit Onan, required, inter alia, a central government with limited powers and a council of ministers in which his people would be represented on equal terms with the Greeks. His opposite number, Tassos Papadopoulos, offered a plan for a strong central government in which the Turkish Cypriots would be represented according to their numbers. Onan refused to discuss territorial concessions.

The death of Makarios introduced the prospect of interparty strife among the Greek Cypriots and lent weight to Denktash's threats to declare his "state" independent. Denktash, however, depended on the Turkish government, and Turkey, for its part, realized that progress toward a solution of the Cyprus problem would quicken the delivery of U.S. military and economic assistance promised in March 1976. On October 2 the foreign ministers of Greece and Turkey agreed, in New York City, to press for a new round of intercommunal talks at which the Turkish Cypriots should make clear proposals on the territorial question.

In December Greek Cypriot extremists kidnapped President Kyprianou's 21-year-old son, Achilleas, and threatened to kill him unless political prisoners were released. The president refused the demands, stating that he would sacrifice his son "but never my country." He did, however, promise that the kidnappers would not be punished, and shortly thereafter Achilleas was released unharmed.

The Greek Cypriots had made remarkable economic progress since the 1974 Turkish invasion. Despite the loss of the chief tourist attractions, prime agricultural land, and the sources of industrial raw materials, production was now running at about four-fifths of the pre-1974 level.

In the north, which before 1974 provided 70% of the island's wealth, the economy was depressed. The tourist industry was barely operating, and trade was chiefly with the Turkish mainland.

(L. J. D. COLLINS)

Czechoslovakia

Dams:
see Engineering Projects

Czechoslovakia

A federal socialist republic of central Europe, Czechoslovakia lies between Poland, the U.S.S.R., Hungary, Austria, and East and West Germany. Area: 127,877 sq km (49,374 sq mi). Pop. (1977 est.): 15,030,600, including (1976 est.) Czech 68%; Slovak 32%. Cap. and largest city: Prague (pop., 1977 est., 1,179,600). Language: Czech and Slovak (official). General secretary of the Communist Party of Czechoslovakia and president in 1977, Gustav Husak; federal premier, Lubomir Strougal.

The Czechoslovak leadership in 1977 found itself no nearer to a solution of its single most pressing political problem, that of establishing some kind of communication with the population and strength-

ening its own popular legitimacy. If anything, the situation deteriorated markedly with the emergence in January of the Charter 77 manifesto. The leadership itself remained divided, and from time to time this division between the conservatives around the party leader, Gustav Husak, and the ultra-hard-liners associated with Vasil Bilak came into the open. A case in point was the sacking of Jiri Hajek, editor of the weekly journal *Tvorba*, who had cautiously promoted a policy of reconciliation with the supporters of the 1968 reforms. On the other hand, on Dec. 10, 1976, the last four dissidents who had been imprisoned in 1972 were released, partly as a result of Western European Communist pressure.

Shortly after this, on Jan. 7, 1977, the Charter 77 initiative was made public. This initiative was first and foremost a legal rather than a political challenge to the authorities, although its political implications were far-reaching. In essence, the charter called on the Czechoslovak government to abide by its own legislation in the field of human rights, political rights, and social rights. It explicitly denied that it had a political program, but in a society where the government arrogated the right of initiative to itself, any such challenge was by definition political in the broader sense.

CZECHOSLOVAKIA

Education. (1975–76) Primary, pupils 1,935,361, teachers 101,183; secondary, pupils 128,917, teachers 8,511; vocational and teacher training, pupils 634,974, teachers 27,050; higher (including 9 main universities), students 151,282, teaching staff 17,009.

Finance. Monetary unit: koruna, with (Sept. 17, 1977) a commercial rate of 5.70 koruny to U.S. $1 (9.90 koruny = £1 sterling) and a tourist rate of 9.70 koruny to U.S. $1 (16.90 koruny = £1 sterling). Budget (1975 est.): revenue 278,113,000,000 koruny; expenditure 273,774,000,000 koruny.

Foreign Trade. (1976) Imports 55,996,000,000 koruny; exports 52,137,000,000 koruny. Import sources (1975): U.S.S.R. 32%; East Germany 12%; Poland 10%; West Germany 6%; Hungary 5%. Export destinations (1975): U.S.S.R. 33%; East Germany 12%; Poland 9%; Hungary 6%; West Germany 6%. Main exports (1975): machinery 36%; iron and steel 11%; motor vehicles 8%; chemicals 5%.

Transport and Communications. Roads (1974) 145,455 km (including 79 km expressways). Motor vehicles in use (1975): passenger 1,401,000; commercial 261,000. Railways (1975): 13,215 km (including 2,707 km electrified); traffic 18,470,000,000 passenger-km, freight (1976) 70,747,000,000 net ton-km. Air traffic (1976): 1,325,200,000 passenger-km; freight 17,164,000 net ton-km. Navigable inland waterways (1974) *c.* 480 km. Shipping (1976): merchant vessels 100 gross tons and over 14; gross tonnage 148,689. Telephones (Jan. 1976) 2,615,000. Radio licenses (Dec. 1974) 3,910,000. Television licenses (Dec. 1974) 3,602,000.

Agriculture. Production (in 000; metric tons; 1976): wheat 4,640; barley *c.* 3,100; oats *c.* 580; rye *c.* 530; corn *c.* 500; potatoes *c.* 4,500; sugar, raw value *c.* 685; beef and veal *c.* 447; pork *c.* 738. Livestock (in 000; Jan. 1976): cattle 4,555; pigs 6,683; sheep 805; chickens 38,720.

Industry. Index of industrial production (1970 = 100; 1976) 146. Fuel and power (in 000; metric tons; 1976): coal 28,266; brown coal 89,467; crude oil 131; manufactured gas (cu m) 7,940,000; electricity (kw-hr) 62,629,000. Production (in 000; metric tons; 1976): iron ore 1,906; pig iron 9,610; crude steel 14,698; cement 9,551; sulfuric acid 1,241; fertilizers (nutrient content; 1975–76) nitrogenous *c.* 525, phosphate 425; cotton yarn 125; cotton fabrics (m) 563,000; woolen fabrics (m) 65,000; rayon and acetate yarn and fibres 72; nylon, etc., yarn and fibres 75; passenger cars (units) 179; commercial vehicles (units) 74. Dwelling units completed (1976) 132,000.

During the first nine months of 1977, the spokesmen for Charter 77 issued 13 documents dealing with various shortcomings in different areas of Czechoslovak life. Some were concerned with immediate issues, like lists of signatories (in excess of 700 by the middle of the year) and details of repressive measures taken by the authorities against charter activists. Others were analyses of violations of human rights in specific areas.

The reaction of the authorities took various and at times contradictory forms, oscillating between very hard-line repression and milder, more conciliatory attempts to defuse the situation. This oscillation evidently reflected the division within the leadership and the weakness of its political base. Speaking privately to a meeting of party activists, the minister of the interior, Jaromir Obzina, practically admitted that the authorities were uncertain how the challenge should be handled. He explained that the security police had been aware of the preparations for the charter but did not proceed against its organizers at that stage because the government did not know what it was dealing with.

Concrete measures taken by the authorities included arrests of Charter 77 activists on unspecified charges, the launching of "counter-charter" declarations of loyalty and ritualistic demonstrations, virulent propaganda in the media, expatriation, and constant harassment of activists. This last included firings, house searches, repeated police interrogations (it was this that led to the death of Jan Patocka in March; see OBITUARIES), and the expulsion of individuals from their homes. As of September, eight of those arrested were being held in prison without charge, and there were a number of trials outside Prague. Vilem Sacher, a signatory of the original charter, was demoted from his rank of lieutenant general to private and was forbidden to wear his World War II decorations; his retirement pension dropped correspondingly. The dramatist Vaclav Havel (see BIOGRAPHY) was released after four months in prison. Another charter spokesman, Jiri Hajek, namesake of the *Tvorba* editor and foreign minister in 1968, was placed under virtual house arrest.

It was evident, however, that the authorities had failed in their attempt to stifle the emergent opposition. Indeed, they might even have helped to strengthen it by their rather crude attacks. A large number of people came to hear of the charter only through the denunciations. By mobilizing public opinion against the charter, the authorities forced people to take a political stance, something which they had not had to do in the depoliticized post-1968 atmosphere.

Charter 77 overshadowed other developments and, indeed, influenced some of them, notably the country's international position. Whatever Czechoslovakia might have gained by its 1976 foreign policy offensive was largely lost through unfavourable world reaction. Western European Communists were also quick to attack the Prague government for its repressive measures. This mounting isolation led to increased contacts with other Eastern European states. Pres. Gustav Husak met with the Communist leaders of Poland, Hungary, and Romania and also with Leonid Brezhnev, the Soviet leader, during the regular annual "holiday" taken by Eastern European party chiefs in the Crimea in August. Czechoslovakia also held negotiations with the Vatican, in which the filling of bishoprics was the most important subject. Only 2 out of 14 sees had residential bishops, and many parishes were without priests.

The performance of the economy, a key issue for the authorities who could not afford to allow the standard of living to deteriorate, was spotty. Production cost per unit remained relatively high, and labour productivity did not show any substantial improvement. Labour morale was likewise poor, and there were complaints of inadequate use of machinery. Nor was the situation helped by the continuing problems of the country's foreign trade position. In July 1977 the Czechoslovak government introduced price increases of up to 50% for certain foodstuffs (notably coffee) and of up to 40% for some consumer durables.

(GEORGE SCHÖPFLIN)

Dance

The economic recession caught up with the world of dance in 1977. The New York City Ballet, staggered by a musicians' strike that curtailed its winter season in New York City, was rescued by a $1 million grant from the National Endowment for the Arts. American Ballet Theatre, with a near-$1 million deficit, engaged Herman Krawitz, formerly of the Metropolitan Opera, as executive producer to oversee a major reorganization. The Martha Graham Dance Company, following a New York season, became inactive as it too embarked on fund-raising activities.

Christine Sarry and Mikhail Baryshnikov blended humour and agility as they performed "Variations on 'America'" with music by Charles Ives at the New York City Center.

MARTHA SWOPE

Regional ballet groups also suffered curtailment of support and increased deficits. The Dance Collection of the New York Public Library, the largest dance archives in the world, was forced to cut both personnel and services. A symptom of financial need was the recurring pattern of resorting to dance "galas" as fund-raisers. The Louis Falco Dance Company enlisted the box-office appeal of television personalities such as Dick Cavett.

For her fund-raising gala on Broadway, Graham obtained the services of Dame Margot Fonteyn and Rudolf Nureyev, but her engagement also featured new productions and revivals of major Graham works. The new pieces included *Shadows*, with a score by Gian Carlo Menotti, and *O Thou Desire Who Art About to Sing*, a tribute to the late Alexander Calder (music by Meyer Kupferman). *Plain of Prayer*, a comparatively recent Graham piece, was presented with major revisions, and the major revival was the historic *Primitive Mysteries* (1931), with a score by Louis Horst and with Pearl Lang dancing Graham's original role.

Novelty and nostalgia went side by side, along with a fund-raising gala, for the José Limón Dance Company in celebration of the 30th anniversary of its founding. Dances by Limón and his artistic director, Doris Humphrey, were featured, along with representations by Pauline Koner, an alumna of the troupe, and two later choreographers, Murray Louis and Daniel Lewis. Also in the modern dance field were engagements by Merce Cunningham and his company and by the Paul Taylor Dance Company, which featured Taylor's new *Images* (set to Debussy piano pieces) and a collaboration with Charles Ludlam, director of the

Ridiculous Theatre Company, called *Aphrodisiamania*. The multimedia programs of the world-circling Alwin Nikolais Dance Theatre featured a new work, *Guignol*, as well as the institutionally related (with a common school) Murray Louis Dance Company in the premieres of *Ceremony* and *Déja Vu*.

The Dance Theatre of Harlem performed in repertory, and the Alvin Ailey American Dance Theater, with its extensive touring and regular New York engagements, featured revivals and new creations, among them Donald McKayle's *Blood Memories*, a black heritage journey focusing on three rivers, the Nile, the Mississippi, and the Harlem. There were performances by Lee Theodore's American Dance Machine, a company dedicated to preserving and performing dances and production numbers from Broadway musicals. Pilobolus—four men and two women who combined virtuosic gymnastics with dance—made its Broadway debut in a season sponsored by Pierre Cardin. Dennis Wayne's company called simply Dancers, partly funded by actress Joanne Woodward, made its New York debut in a two-week engagement with a repertory extending from classical to pure modern dance.

The New York City Ballet featured a major new work by its artistic director, George Balanchine, *Vienna Waltzes*, set to the works of Johann Strauss, Franz Lehár, and Richard Strauss, with settings by Rouben Ter-Arutunian and costumes by Karinska. Stanley Williams, a product of the Royal Danish Ballet and a principal teacher at the NYCB's school, staged *Bournonville Divertissements*, composed of excerpts from ballets by the great 19th-century Danish ballet master. Peter Martins, also of the Royal Danish Ballet and a premier danseur with the NYCB, choreographed *Calcium Light Night*, to music by Charles Ives, first for his own touring ensemble and then for the NYCB.

The American Ballet Theatre mounted a new production of Michel Fokine's *Firebird* (Stravinsky) especially for Natalia Makarova. Its repertory season also included a Fokine festival, featuring such classics as *Les Sylphides*, *Le Spectre de la Rose* (danced by Mikhail Baryshnikov), and *Petrouchka*. Cynthia Gregory returned to the company following a brief retirement and then left late in the year to do free-lance appearances with international troupes.

The Joffrey Ballet, skipping its spring season because of financial difficulties, returned to the New York City Center in the fall for a repertory period featuring *Cacklin' Hen* by Twyla Tharp (see BIOGRAPHY), *Touch Me* (a new solo for Christian Holder choreographed by Gerald Arpino), new productions of Sir Frederick Ashton's *Jazz Calendar* and *Les Patineurs*, Balanchine's *Tarantella*, the first North American production of a full-length *Romeo and Juliet* (Prokofiev) by the Argentine choreographer Oscar Araiz, and a re-creation of Arthur Saint-Léon's 19th-century *Vivandière* pas de six, reconstructed from the choreographer's script by the dance notation expert Ann Hutchinson. The Eliot Feld Ballet, also playing at the City Center, featured Feld's *Variations on "America,"* to music of Charles Ives and starring Baryshnikov, and *A*

George Balanchine presented a grand spectacle with his "Vienna Waltzes" for the New York City Ballet at the Lincoln Center in New York City.

MARTHA SWOPE

Footstep of Air, set to a collection of British and Irish folk songs orchestrated by Beethoven.

Among ballet companies based outside New York, the San Francisco Ballet recovered from a financial crisis that had nearly closed the company two seasons earlier and was able to extend its repertory and engagements. The Pittsburgh (Pa.) Ballet Theatre replaced Nicolas Petrov with John Gilpin as artistic director, but illness caused the English dancer-teacher to withdraw, and selection of his successor was scheduled for early 1978. The Pennsylvania Ballet featured among its new works *Equinox*, choreographed by Lynne Taylor to music of Victor Bond. The Houston (Texas) Ballet mounted a full-length *Swan Lake* (staged by the director, Ben Stevenson) on the occasion of the 100th anniversary of the first (Moscow version) performance of the classic. The Chicago Ballet was host to the First North American International Dance Festival, featuring Baryshnikov and an array of international guest stars.

Canada's National Ballet performed at New York's Metropolitan Opera House with Peter Schaufuss as guest artist (he later became a regular member of the troupe). The repertory featured *Collective Symphony* (by the three principal choreographers of the Dutch National Ballet, Rudi van Dantzig, Hans van Manen, and Toer van Schayk), Ashton's *La Fille Mal Gardée*, and *Mad Shadows*, an all-Canadian ballet choreographed by Ann Dichtburn to a score by André Gagnon.

The great Cuban ballerina Alicia Alonso, granted permission by the U.S. State Department to perform in the U.S., appeared at the Spoleto U.S.A. festival in Charleston, S.C. (an American extension of Menotti's celebrated festival in Spoleto, Italy), and also in New York, where she danced her renowned interpretation of *Giselle* with her alma mater, the American Ballet Theatre, for the first time in nearly 20 years. Later it was announced that Alonso and the Ballet Nacional de Cuba would visit the U.S. in 1978.

Two major dance movies were released during the year: *Valentino*, starring Rudolf Nureyev as the silent screen star, and *The Turning Point*, starring Shirley MacLaine and Anne Bancroft and featuring Alexandra Danilova, Baryshnikov, Antoinette Sibley, and other dancers of the American Ballet Theatre.

Among television dance events were the series "Dance in America," produced by Public Broadcasting Service, and a television production of Baryshnikov's version of *The Nutcracker*. Announcement was made of a project to prepare and publish an eight-volume dance encyclopaedia, with dance historian Selma Jeanne Cohen as chairman of the 15-member editorial board. Clive Barnes, dance and drama critic of the *New York Times*, was relieved of his drama duties at midyear and left in November to join the *New York Post*. The Harkness Theatre on Broadway, bought and redesigned by Rebekah Harkness for her ballet company in 1974, was sold and demolished.

(WALTER TERRY)

Britain's two large-scale classical companies produced little that was new during the 1976–77 season. The Covent Garden Royal Ballet (retitled to

With the help of 20-foot wings and strong cables, Icarus settles to earth in Maurice Béjart's "Notre Faust" in the Uris Theatre, New York City. Béjart himself played both Faust and Mephistopheles in the ballet.

distinguish it from its smaller section, the Sadler's Wells Royal Ballet) added three works that had been created by foreign companies: Glen Tetley's *Voluntaries* (Poulenc), van Manen's *Adagio Hammerklavier* (Beethoven), and John Cranko's *The Taming of the Shrew* (Kurt-Heinz Stolze after Scarlatti). The only work created for the company was John Neumeier's *The Fourth Symphony* (Mahler). All these works gave ample opportunity to the dancers in a company missing its principal male star, Anthony Dowell, off for a year because of injury. Norman Morrice (*see* BIOGRAPHY), formerly Ballet Rambert's co-director, took over the artistic directorship of the Royal Ballet from Kenneth MacMillan, who then became the company's resident choreographer.

The main creative focus in the Royal Ballet organization was on its smaller group, now based at the Sadler's Wells Theatre. For this company, Peter Wright created *Summertide* (Mendelssohn). Lynn Seymour, in her first creation for the Royal Ballet, wrote *Rashomon* (Bob Downes) and, later, as the company's contribution to the Silver Jubilee, *The Court of Love* (Howard Blake). From David Morse there was *Birdscape* (Martinu). New to the repertory were revivals of Tetley's *Gemini* (Henze) and Balanchine's *The Four Temperaments* (Hindemith), *Concerto Barocco* (Bach), and *Apollo* (Stravinsky). André Prokovsky revived a shortened version of his *Soft Blue Shadows* (Fauré).

In addition to three London seasons—two at Festival Hall, one at the London Coliseum—Britain's other large-scale classical company, London Festival Ballet, toured extensively in the provinces and overseas with Nureyev. The full-length *The Nutcracker*, the company's most staple classic in its 27 years, was entirely rethought in a new production by Ronald Hynd and Peter Docherty. The other major production was Nureyev's full-length *Romeo and Juliet*, created principally for the company's second Australian tour. Alicia Markova revived Fokine's *Les Sylphides* (Chopin) in the manner originally taught to her by the great choreographer himself.

The more contemporary companies provided greater stimulation, and a feature of the year was the proliferation of small experimental groups in London and the regions. Ballet Rambert, in its 51st year, showed that its pioneering spirit remained strong as ever. The company's co-artistic director, Christopher Bruce, created *Promenade* (Bach) and *Echoes of a Night Sky* (George Crumb) and, together with the mime artist Lindsay Kemp, devised a full-evening spectacle inspired by the life and work of García Lorca, *Cruel Garden* (Carlos Miranda). Morrice returned to create *Smiling Immortal* (Jonathan Harvey), and one of the company's principal dancers, Zoltan Imre, created *Musical Offering* (Bach). An interesting experiment was *Frames, Pulses and Interruptions*, created by choreographer Jaap Flier and composer Harrison Birtwistle in collaboration.

For the London Contemporary Dance Theatre 1977 was a year of great expansion, with two highly successful Paris seasons and a U.S. tour in addition to its London seasons and provincial touring. The company's artistic director, Robert Cohan, created *Nymphéas* (Debussy), *Khamsin* (Downes), and *Forest* (Brian Hodgson); Cohan also collaborated with Micha Bergese, Siobhan Davies, and Robert North in *Night Watch* (Downes), which was the company's contribution to the Silver Jubilee celebrations. Independently, Davies created *Step at a Time* (Geoffrey Burgon); Bergese, *Nema* (Eberhard Schoener); and North, *Just a Moment* (Downes/Kool and the Gang) and *Meeting and Parting* (Howard Blake).

Among the regional companies, the Scottish Bal-

Rudolf Nureyev performed as Romeo and Patricia Ruanne as Juliet in Nureyev's new production of ''Romeo and Juliet'' at the London Coliseum.

KEYSTONE

let added the full-length *Swan Lake* to its classical repertory. Its director, Peter Darrell, produced the work using the score as it was originally written for the first Moscow production. In Manchester, Northern Ballet Theatre (retitled by its new director, Robert de Warren) enlarged its repertory with a revival of Kurt Jooss's *The Big City* (Tansman) and Charles Czarny's *Concerto Grosso* (Handel).

A new addition to the regional scene was the formation, by the East Midlands Regional Arts Association, of the EMMA Dance Company. Directed by former Rambert dancer Gideon Avrahami, the group worked mainly in its own region but with occasional tours to other areas. Two companies succumbed to financial difficulties. New London Ballet, formed by Prokovsky and Galina Samsova, had brought fine classical dancing to the middle-scale touring theatres for the past three years. The other casualty was the South African-financed but London-based Ballet International.

An interesting new development was the John Curry Theatre of Skating. The Olympic gold medalist devised programs in which skaters, who also had dance training, appeared in works by distinguished choreographers.

In France the Paris Opéra Ballet's principal productions were Alonso's revival of Petipa's *The Sleeping Beauty* and Yury Grigorovich's revival of his two-act *Ivan the Terrible* (Prokofiev). Shorter works concentrated on 20th-century composers: George Skibine's *La Péri* (Dukas), Jerome Robbins' *En Sol* (Ravel), Maurice Béjart's *Rite of Spring* (Stravinsky), and two works to Mahler by Araiz—*Mahlers Lieder* and *Adagietto*. The company also gave seasons at the Opéra Comique; one was devoted to romantic 19th-century revivals, the most interesting being Pierre Lacotte's reconstruction of dances from *La Vivandière*. Lacotte later staged Rameau's opera ballet *Platée* in the same theatre. For the Opéra's experimental theatre group, Carolyn Carlson choreographed *This, That and the Other* (Igor Wakhevitch), in which the three parts, created at different times, were finally combined in a full-evening piece.

The Roland Petit Ballets de Marseille, France's foremost regional company, concentrated mainly on full-length works. In addition to his now famous new-look *Coppélia* (Delibes), Petit also brought a fresh approach to *The Nutcracker*. His *Nôtre-Dame de Paris* (Jarre), originally created for the Opéra, also went into the Marseille repertory. Béjart's most important creation for his Brussels-based Ballet of the Twentieth Century, *Le Molière Imaginaire* (Nino Rota), was first given at Molière's theatre, the Comédie Française.

In West Germany the Stuttgart Ballet's most successful creation was Kenneth MacMillan's *Requiem* (Fauré); Rosella Hightower mounted *The Sleeping Beauty*. The Hamburg State Opera Ballet gave an all-Stravinsky program, the creations being Neumeier's *Petrushka Variations* and Fred Howald's *Orpheus*; later, Neumeier's *A Midsummer Night's Dream* (Mendelssohn/Ligeti/Klaus Arp) had great success. The West Berlin Opera Ballet had a new production by Valery Panov of *Cinderella* (Prokofiev); an all-Ravel program included Balanchine's *La Valse*, Jooss's *Pavane*, van Manen's *Daphnis and*

KEYSTONE

The Korean National Dance Company, one of the world's most famous dance companies, performed in September at the Sadler's Wells Theatre in London.

Chloë, and Béjart's *Bolero.* In Cologne, Tanz-Forum's most important production was Jochen Ulrich's *Walzerträume* (Kurt Schwertsik). Pina Bausch's main creation for the Wuppertal Dance Theatre was the full-evening *Bluebeard* (Bartok).

The Dutch National Ballet's principal creations were van Dantzig's *Ginastera* (Ginastera), van Manen's *Octet Opus 20* (Mendelssohn), and van Schayk's *Jeux* (Debussy). The Netherlands Dance Theatre's director, Jiri Kylian, created *Verklärte Nacht* (Nordheim); other creations included Eric Hampton's *Overcast* (Debussy), Nils Christe's *Miniatures* (Stravinsky), van Manen's *Lieder Ohne Worte* (Mendelssohn), Louis Falco's *Lobster Quadrille* (Tredici), and Jennifer Muller's *Beach* (Alcantara). In Austria the Vienna State Opera's principal creation was Neumeier's *Legend of Joseph* (Richard Strauss). The Royal Danish Ballet offered Murray Louis's *Cleopatra* (Joe Clark).

(PETER WILLIAMS)

See also Music; Theatre.
[652]

Defense

The use of force rose sharply in 1977, notably in Africa, as the Soviet Union demonstrated its willingness to intervene in local conflicts with military aid, including Cuban troops. International terrorism by political extremists also increased, as did the use of violence in domestic politics, particularly in Italy and West Germany. Even the possibility of a settlement in the Middle East was based on the relative balance of military forces. Egypt's armed forces had been greatly weakened by Pres. Anwar as-Sadat's break with his Soviet arms suppliers, while Israel had stockpiled enough U.S. equipment to fight for a month without U.S. aid. Military spending by both nations was far higher than their economies could afford (37% of gross national product [GNP] for Egypt and 35% for Israel).

The Soviet Union's willingness to intervene in local disputes, turning potential into actual conflict and supporting almost any group calling itself pro-Soviet and anti-Western, reflected its leaders' view that the U.S.S.R. was the ascending, and the U.S. the descending, superpower. The Soviet leaders saw their nation as having military power and the political will to use it, in sharp contrast to a lack of both in the U.S. The acceptance by the Carter administration of the widespread, if questionable, Western idea that force was no longer usable as an instrument of foreign policy accentuated this perceived difference between the two powers (*see* Special Report). The allies of the U.S. felt less certain that it could or would protect them, while the U.S.S.R. appeared to be more able, and more likely, to aid its friends.

On the 60th anniversary of the Bolshevik Revolution, the Soviet Union in some ways seemed more czarist than Communist. Internally, the Communist Party retained power by the force of its secret police. Mass terror on the scale used by Joseph Stalin was unnecessary; the threat of arrest and the impossibility of changing the political system reduced the number of dissidents. Major figures, such as author Aleksandr I. Solzhenitsyn, were exiled rather than executed, though lesser figures received harsh treatment. Within Eastern Europe the U.S.S.R. used its army to retain the last true colonial empire. The greater independence allowed to local Communist parties there could not obscure their ultimately enforced obedience to Moscow.

Soviet forces in Eastern Europe and those of the Warsaw Treaty Organization had undergone major improvements at all levels. Soviet technology continued to lag behind that of the West but much less so than in previous years, and it was deployed in such quantities as to give the Warsaw Pact major advantages over the North Atlantic Treaty Organization (NATO). These changes had been gradual, but their cumulative effect was consider-

Danish Literature:
see Literature

Deaths:
see Demography; *see also biographies of prominent persons who died in 1977, listed under* People of the Year

"What really gets me is having to plan mass destruction on a tight budget."

MAHOOD–PUNCH/ROTHCO

able. Thus, since 1970, Warsaw Pact personnel had increased from 1,190,000 to 1,216,000 (versus NATO's decline from 1,099,300 to 1,045,200); in medium tanks the Pact had gone from 14,500 to 16,000, while NATO figures increased only from 6,535 to 6,615; in tactical aircraft the Pact had maintained about 2,500 and NATO about 1,800, but the capabilities of the Pact's aircraft had vastly increased. The overall breadth and depth of the drive by the Soviet Union to increase its forces, together with its consistent allocation of a high percentage (11–13%) of GNP to defense, caused increasing concern, especially in Western Europe.

What was particularly threatening to international security was that its increased capabilities made the U.S.S.R. a global superpower, able to intervene anywhere in the world. This had its roots in the defeat of Soviet leader Nikita Khrushchev by U.S. Pres. John F. Kennedy in the 1962 Cuban missile crisis, a setback that occurred because the U.S.S.R. then lacked such capabilities. But the Soviet threat to intervene in Egypt's favour in the 1973 Middle East war and in Africa since 1975 made it increasingly likely that the U.S.S.R. intended to use its new capabilities to expand its influence. The Soviet view seemed to be that if the U.S. and the U.S.S.R. were both global superpowers, then both could play at the game of global intervention. If the U.S., after the Vietnam war, believed that this game would benefit neither itself nor its allies, then this made it easier for the U.S.S.R. to try to see if it could gain some advantages.

AFRICA SOUTH OF THE SAHARA

Opportunities for Soviet intervention were plentiful in southern Africa, where the targets were the white governments of Rhodesia and South Africa, and also in central and eastern Africa, where local conflicts were endemic and participants were increasingly tempted to ask for Soviet aid. In southern Africa, the West was at a fundamental disadvantage: no foreseeable Western pressures could persuade the Rhodesian and South African governments to transfer power to their black populations. Only guerrilla warfare could do this, and only the U.S.S.R. or, to a much lesser extent, China, could provide the military aid the guerrillas needed. This had been given, but it was limited

in scale and effectiveness until 1975. Then, the abrupt withdrawal of Portugal from its colonies presented the U.S.S.R. with the choice of sending major reinforcements to their MPLA (Popular Movement for the Liberation of Angola) allies or seeing them defeated by rival guerrilla movements aided by South Africa, China, and the U.S. The Soviets, correctly estimating that the U.S. would not oppose them, therefore sent in equipment and regular Cuban forces, who quickly secured victory for the MPLA in 1976. The success of the intervention, plus the need to protect the MPLA from its guerrilla rivals, who remained strong in southern Angola, led the Soviet Union to increase Cuban personnel there to 19,000 military and 4,000 civilians. Those not tied down in fighting opposition guerrilla groups served as advisers to many African countries.

The Cubans supported the pro-Soviet factions in guerrilla forces raiding South West Africa (Namibia) and Rhodesia. In both areas fighting escalated sharply, with South African and Rhodesian troops launching strikes against guerrilla bases in adjacent countries and conducting hot pursuit regardless of national boundaries. Rhodesia with its tiny (and declining) white population of 270,000 (out of a total of 6,740,000) clearly could not maintain internal and external security against these increased pressures. The acceptance by Rhodesian Prime Minister Ian Smith late in 1977 of the principle of black majority rule was an attempt to ensure that any black government would be led by Bishop Abel Muzorewa (*see* BIOGRAPHY), leader of the African National Council (ANC), the most moderate black group. Whether the other groups, notably the Zimbabwe People's Army of Robert Mugabe (*see* BIOGRAPHY), would accept such a deal was doubtful, as were Smith's intentions of implementing it. The key element would be the policy of the South African government. It had supported Smith militarily and economically as a forward defense against guerrillas, but drastically reduced this support in 1976 when the former Portuguese colonies came under black governments. But Cuban pressure against South West Africa and U.S. pressure on South Africa for internal reforms restored South African support for Smith provided that he would negotiate with moderate Africans to form a government that could be kept in power with South African aid.

South Africa's rejection of any basic change in its apartheid system and its determination to fight to the finish was understandable only in light of the history and position of the whites. During the settlement of South Africa in the 1800s, the ancestors of the Dutch-speaking whites had fought the African tribes as the U.S. settlers had fought the Indians, often using their wagon trains to form defensive laagers. Eventually these Dutch-speaking Afrikaners gained control of South Africa, a nation in which by 1977 roughly 4.5 million whites controlled 18.5 million nonwhites.

Because most of the whites had no colonial homeland to return to, their response to Soviet-supported guerrilla attacks and to U.S. demands for political reform, publicized by Pres. Jimmy Carter and his UN ambassador, Andrew Young (*see* BIOGRAPHY), was to revert to the laager mentality, fortifying South Africa and knowing that most other whites had no alternative but to join them. Militarily, South Africa was strong enough to make this option viable in the short run. The nation had built up an indigenous arms manufacturing industry that supplied most of its needs, in anticipation of arms embargoes such as that approved by the UN in the fall. Qualitatively, South Africa's forces were far superior to any that their African opponents could bring against them. Although the African armies looked formidable on paper, they basically resembled World War I infantry, having only light arms and little transport,

artillery, armour, or air cover. Their nominal totals were far greater than the actual numbers available, and their fighting value was often negligible. In contrast, South Africa had a fully operational, modern air force, a small but effective navy, and an army that was training substantial reserves of white manpower. Nominally, army reserves were 130,000 plus 90,000 paramilitary commandos and 35,500 South African Police, but much larger numbers could be tapped.

South Africa's comparative strength could be reduced if the U.S.S.R. supplied the guerrillas with sophisticated technology and Cuban operators, by increased white casualties (especially to urban guerrilla warfare and unrest, which was increasing), and by economic pressures. But South Africa's will to resist was strong, and its technological base could give it a nuclear capability and, less publicized but potentially more useful in combat, the ability to manufacture chemical weapons, including sophisticated nerve gases. And, ultimately, there was the question always posed by Prime Minister B. J. Vorster: could the West afford to let a Soviet-dominated black government control South Africa's vast mineral wealth?

The Soviet Union's certainty that it could only gain by intervention in southern Africa encouraged intervention farther north, with less success. In March and April an invasion of Shaba (formerly Katanga) Province of Zaire was launched from Angola, nominally by 6,000 ex-Katangese "gendarmerie" (actually light infantry). In reality, the insurgents were clearly acting

Flying in salute to the U.S. Air Force's 30th anniversary on September 18, the famed Thunderbird flight demonstration team formed a brilliant arrow in the sky.

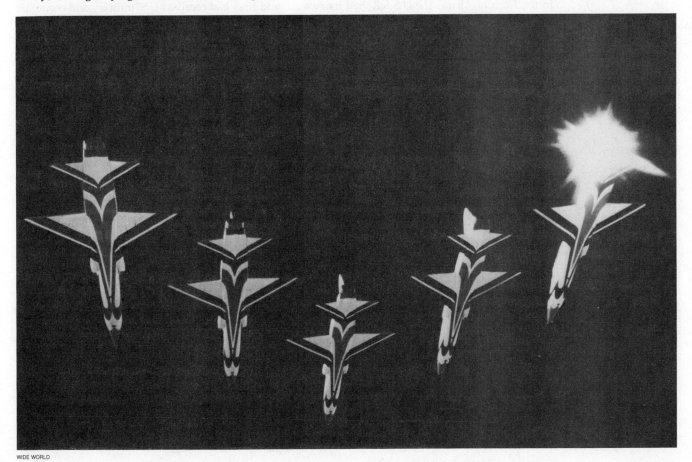

The U.S. Army/NASA XV-15, an air-cushion vehicle, is able to fly either like a helicopter or like a conventional aircraft.

under Soviet orders and with Cuban support in their attempt to seize the mineral-rich province. On paper, the 30,000-man Army of Zaire Pres. Mobutu Sese Seko (*see* BIOGRAPHY) should have defeated this attack easily, but in the end it could do so only with the aid of French military equipment and some 2,000–4,000 Moroccan troops. The U.S. refusal to provide comparable aid to Mobutu, although he was a U.S. ally, was criticized by some as strengthening doubts about its willingness to check Soviet aggression.

In the Horn of Africa, the U.S.S.R. had made a major investment in supporting Somalia, supplying military aid and more than 3,000 advisers and in return gaining air and naval facilities at Berbera and Kismayu that could control the entrances to the Persian Gulf and the Red Sea. Somali Pres. Muhammad Siyad Barrah seemed to be a firm Soviet ally, but in November he broke with the U.S.S.R., expelling its personnel and taking over its base facilities.

This abrupt politico-military defeat for the U.S.S.R. resulted from the local conflicts that had

One of the last super-carriers to be built, the "USS Dwight D. Eisenhower" took to water for commissioning in Norfolk, Va., in October. The giant vessel weighs more than 91,000 tons.

previously enabled it to make such gains in Africa. These conflicts often resulted from the fact that new nations had been created within colonial boundaries, ignoring local conditions and tribal ambitions. Somalia itself had been created in 1960 by merging the former British and Italian Somalilands, the boundaries of which had reflected Ethiopian expansion in the 1870s. Ethiopia thus had gained the Ogaden region, claimed by Somalia on grounds of tradition. Ethiopian Emperor Haile Selassie, deposed in 1974, had been pro-Western and thus had received U.S. military and economic aid. This had forced Somalia to turn to the U.S.S.R. But the new military regime in Ethiopia was anti-Western, thereby cutting itself off from U.S. aid. It was, however, so unstable that the U.S.S.R., which also wanted to preserve its investment in Somalia, gave it only limited assistance. Somalia, however, seeing the Ethiopian Army gravely weakened by revolutionary purges and lack of supplies, decided the time had come to regain the Ogaden. Guerrilla raids by the West Somalia Liberation Front were stepped up, increasingly supported by regular Somali forces.

By the summer of 1977, Gen. Siyad Barrah had fully committed his forces on the understanding that the U.S. had guaranteed him support. President Carter's denial of such a guarantee reinforced the image of U.S. weakness; the U.S. failed to replace the Soviet Union as Somalia's backer, instead maintaining an arms embargo against Somalia. In contrast, Saudi Arabia and Iran offered military and economic aid, and West Germany was secretly adding to this aid in return for Somalia's having allowed its crack antiterrorist squad to land at the Mogadishu airport to free hostages held by terrorists in a Lufthansa jet.

Meanwhile, the U.S.S.R. was trying to recover lost ground by similar means. Having failed to stop Somalia's offensive by threatening to withhold aid and giving Ethiopia limited aid, the Soviets swung their support behind Ethiopia, airlifting equipment and Cuban advisers. It seemed unlikely that Ethiopian troops could hold, or regain, the Ogaden region; mass mobilization had produced a

Approximate Strengths of Regular Armed Forces of the World

Country	Military personnel in 000s			Warships			Total major surface combat vessels	Jet aircraft[3]		Tanks[4]	Defense expenditure as % of GNP
	Army	Navy	Air Force	Aircraft carriers/cruisers[1]	Submarines[2]	Destroyers/frigates		Bombers	Fighters/recon-naissance		
I. NATO											
Belgium	62.0	4.2	19.4	—		2	2	90 FB	36, 18 R	408	3.0
Canada	28.5	13.4	36.6	—	3	23	23	—	120	255	1.9
Denmark	21.8	5.8	7.1	—	6 C	2	2	60 FB	40, 16 R	368	2.8
France[5]	330.0	68.5	103.6	2 CV, 2 CA	21, 4 SSBN	42	46	32 SB, 318 FB	120, 58 R	1,060	3.7
Germany, West	341.0	38.0	110.0	—	24 C	22	22	384 FB	60, 113 R	3,837	3.6
Greece	160.0	17.5	22.5	—	6	15	15	112 FB	95, 20 R	962	5.5
Italy	218.0	42.0	70.0	1 CA	8	18	19	162 FB	72	1,500	2.6
Luxembourg	0.6	—	—	—	—	—	—			—	1.2
Netherlands, The	75.0	17.0	17.7	—	6	17	17	108 FB	36	810	3.4
Norway	20.0	9.0	10.0	—	15 C	5	5	97 FB	16, 13 R	116	3.1
Portugal	36.0	12.8	10.0	—	3	7	7	18 FB	20	100	3.9
Turkey	375.0	43.0	47.0	—	14	14	14	258 FB	25, 36 R	2,800	5.6
United Kingdom	175.2	76.7[6]	87.2	1 CV, 2 CVH, 2 CA	18, 9 N, 4 SSBN	68	73	106 B, 120 FB	108, 58 R	910	5.1
United States	981.0[6]	536.0	571.0	2 CVN, 11 CV, 8 CVH, 5 CAN, 21 CA	10, 68 N, 41 SSBN	136	188	1,400 FB, 373 SB, 68 B	1,240, 100 R	10,000	6.0
II. WARSAW PACT											
Bulgaria	115.0	8.5	25.0	—	4	—	—	72 FB	127	1,900	2.6
Czechoslovakia	135.0	—	46.0	—	—	—	—	158 FB	250	3,400	3.5
Germany, East	105.0	16.0	36.0	—	—	2	2	35 FB	270, 16 R	2,400	6.0
Hungary	83.0	—	20.0	—	—	—	—	—	176	1,000	2.6
Poland	220.0	25.0	62.0	—	4	1	1	218 FB, 6 B	440, 81 R	3,500	3.6
Romania	140.0	10.0	30.0	—	—	—	—	75 FB	237, 15 R	1,500	1.8
U.S.S.R.	1,825.0	450.0[6]	1,025.0	1 CV, 2 CVH, 32 CA	128, 39 N, 55 SSBN, 7 SSBN-S, 20 SSB-D-S, 43 N/CMS, 24 CMS	194	229	135 SB, 1,044 B, 4,000 FB	4,000	43,000	11–13
III. OTHER EUROPEAN											
Albania	34.0	3.0	8.0	—	4	—	—	—	113	100	...
Austria	33.0	—	4.3	—	—	—	—	30 FB	—	270	1.1
Finland	30.3	3.0	3.0	—	—	3	3	—	47	—	1.1
Ireland	13.3	0.5	0.7	—	—	—	—	6 FB	—	—	1.6
Spain	220.0	48.0[6]	41.0	1 CVH	10	27	28	120 FB	—	675	1.7
Sweden	46.0	12.0	10.5	—	17	12	12	126 FB	306	750	3.7
Switzerland[7]	10.5/580.0	—	8.0/45.0	—	—	—	—	290 FB	39, 16 R	540	2.3
Yugoslavia	193.0	27.0	40.0	—	5	1	1	130 FB	110, 21 R	2,150	5.0
IV. MIDDLE EAST AND MEDITERRANEAN; SUB-SAHARAN AFRICA; LATIN AMERICA[8]											
Algeria	67.0	3.8	5.0	—	—	—	—	90 FB, 24 B	35	400	...
Egypt	300.0	20.0	25.0	—	12	5	5	311 FB, 30 B	132	1,850	37.0
Iran	220.0	22.0	100.0	—	—	7	7	285 FB	40, 16 R	1,620	12.0
Iraq	160.0	3.0	25.0	—	—	—	—	200 FB, 14 B	135	1,400	...
Israel[7]	138.0/375	5.0/6.0	21.0/25.0	—	1	—	—	535 FB	14	3,000	35.3
Jordan	61.0	—	6.6	—	—	—	—	60 FB	18	520	11.7
Lebanon[9]	17.0	—	1.0	—	—	—	—	12 FB	9	—	...
Libya	22.0	2.7	4.5	—	—	1	1	50 FB, 12 B	62, 10 R	1,200	3.2
Morocco	75.0	4.0	5.6	—	—	—	—	24 FB	21	100	...
Saudi Arabia	45.0	1.5	15.0	—	—	—	—	70 FB	37	475	...
Sudan	50.0	0.6	1.5	—	—	—	—	17 FB	10	130	...
Syria	200.0	2.5	25.0	—	—	—	—	175 FB	220	2,500	...
Ethiopia[10]	50/125.0[7]	1.5	2.0	—	—	—	—	27 FB, 2 B	—	70	...
Nigeria	221.0	3.5	6.0	—	—	1	1	32 FB, 4 B	—	—	...
South Africa	41.0	5.5	8.5	—	3	4	4	32 FB, 15 B	43	170	4.7
Zaire	30.0	—	3.0	—	—	—	—	—	17	—	...
Somalia[10]	30.0	0.5	1.0	—	—	—	—	40 FB, 3 B	12	—	...
Argentina	80.0	32.9[6]	17.0	1 CVH, 2 CA	4	10	17	100 FB, 9 B	14	120	2.8
Brazil	180.0	49.0[6]	42.8	1 CVH	8	14	15	33 FB	15	60	1.3
Chile	50.0	24.0	11.0	2 CA	3	8	10	—	50	76	0.9
Colombia	42.0	8.0	6.5	—	2	4	4	—	16	—	0.9
Cuba	160.0	9.0	20.0	—	—	—	—	75 FB	120	600	0.8
Mexico	220.0	17.5	6.0	—	—	3	3	—	—	—	...
Peru	46.0	14.0	10.0	4 CL	8	6	10	34 B	70	310	...
V. FAR EAST AND OCEANIA[8]											
Australia	31.8	16.2	21.6	1 CV	4	11	12	84 FB, 13 RB	—	163	2.8
Bangladesh	65.0	0.3	3.0	—	—	—	—	—	11	30	...
Burma	153.0	9.0	7.5	—	—	2	2	—	—	—	...
China	3,250.0	300.0[6]	400.0	—	66	22	22	1,180 FB, 710 B	4,500	10,000	...
India	950.0	46.0	100.0	1 CV, 2 CL	8	28	31	240 FB, 50 B	400, 6 R	1,780	...
Indonesia	180.0	39.0[6]	28.0	—	3	11	11	16 FB	—	—	...
Japan	155.0	40.0	43.0	—	15	45	45	100 FB	250, 14 R	610	0.9
Korea, North	430.0	25.0	45.0	—	10	7	7	320 FB, 80 B	230	1,750	...
Korea, South	580.0[6]	25.0	30.0	—	—	7	7	303 FB	12 R	1,000	...
Laos[11]	46.0	—	2.0	—	—	—	—	—	—	—	...
Malaysia	52.5	5.5	6.0	—	—	2	2	14 FB	—	—	1.7
New Zealand	5.5	2.7	4.3	—	—	4	4	13 FB	—	—	1.7
Pakistan	400.0	11.0	17.0	—	3	5	5	160 FB, 11 B	58, 13 R	1,000	6.2
Philippines	63.0	20.0[6]	16.0	—	—	7	7	20 FB	20	—	2.4
Singapore	30.0	3.0	3.0	—	—	—	—	72 FB	—	—	...
Taiwan	355.0[6]	35.0	70.0	—	2	18	18	263 FB	8 R	150	...
Thailand	141.0	28.0[6]	42.0	—	—	7	7	14 FB	—	—	...
Vietnam[12]	600.0	3.0	12.0	—	—	—	—	170 FB, 10 B	150	900	...

Note: Data exclude paramilitary, security, and irregular forces. Naval data exclude vessels of less than 100 tons standard displacement. Figures are for July 1977.

[1] Aircraft carriers (CV); helicopter carriers (CVH); heavy cruisers (CA); light cruisers (CL); N denotes nuclear.

[2] Nuclear hunter-killers (N); ballistic missile submarines, nuclear (SSBN); ballistic missile submarines, nuclear, short-range (SSBN-S); ballistic missile submarines, diesel, short-range (SSB-D-S); long-range cruise missile submarines, nuclear (CMS, N/CMS); coastal (C).

[3] Medium and heavy bombers (B), fighter-bombers (FB), strategic bombers (SB), reconnaissance planes (R).

[4] Medium and heavy tanks (31 tons and over).

[5] French forces were withdrawn from NATO in 1966, but France remains a member of NATO.

[6] Includes marines.

[7] Second figure is fully mobilized strength.

[8] Sections IV and V list only those states with significant military forces.

[9] Figures before Lebanon's civil war and division.

[10] Before Ethiopian-Somali war.

[11] Lao People's Liberation Army.

[12] Equipment of former South Vietnamese forces not included.

Sources: International Institute for Strategic Studies, 18 Adam Street, London, *The Military Balance 1977–78, Strategic Survey 1976.*

People's Militia 75,000 strong, but the men lacked basic training, let alone the ability to operate sophisticated Soviet equipment. The U.S.S.R. would have to decide whether to commit Cuban troops to battle and might well do so, having learned that influence in Africa could be relatively easily won but equally easily lost.

THE MIDDLE EAST

Though the Middle East continued to represent a great threat to international security, in late 1977, for the first time since Israel was founded in 1948, it seemed possible that Egypt and perhaps Jordan would accept its existence. The possibility arose from President Sadat's peace initiative. (*See* MIDDLE EASTERN AFFAIRS.) Sadat's move was denounced by the Soviet Union because it meant that, 21 years after taking a first step toward becoming a global superpower by aiding Egypt in 1956, it had lost its influence there. At the height of that influence, in 1971, the U.S.S.R. had signed a treaty of alliance with Egypt and had supplied 20,000 advisers. In 1972 the treaty was terminated and the advisers were expelled by Sadat because he believed Soviet influence had become excessive.

Egypt moved toward the U.S. because Secretary of State Henry A. Kissinger's negotiation of the cease-fire in 1973 and of the Sinai disengagement agreement in 1975 convinced Sadat that only the U.S. could make Israel give Egypt back the territories it had lost in the 1967 war. This the U.S. tried to do, using the threat of withholding arms and other aid to Israel as a lever, but without success.

By 1977, when hard-liner Menahem Begin became Israel's prime minister, that nation's strategy was to prepare for a war that would destroy the Egyptian, Syrian, and Jordanian capacity to attack it for a decade. Israel had gained nothing from its restraint in 1973, when, at U.S. insistence, it had not struck first, and it was skeptical that Carter's proposed Middle East peace conference could guarantee its security. If the conference failed, Israel seemed to believe it could protect itself best by attacking. The Egyptian Army was too short of spare parts to advance in the Sinai, and Jordan was too weak to cross the Jordan River. Israel could, therefore, concentrate its forces against Syria, destroy its army, and then turn against Egypt.

The raw military data for the region were misleading; quantitatively, these three Arab states had an overwhelming advantage over Israel in equipment, and they had demonstrated in 1973 that they could use it. But the 1973 war had underlined the importance of Israel's qualitative edge; initially surprised, Israel had in ten days advanced to within 20 mi of Damascus and was poised to take Cairo. The war did not demonstrate the obsolescence of tactical air power and armour in the face of modern antiaircraft and antitank missiles, as was at first argued. The missiles had decimated overconfident Israeli air and tank attacks, but once the Israelis learned to launch coordinated attacks, using all arms, they had defeated the Arabs. After 1973 the Israelis intensively analyzed and applied the lessons of the war, producing new tactics and equipment in an effort to regain their advantage.

Soviet 122-mm self-propelled howitzers were displayed publicly for the first time in Red Square, Moscow, during the parade celebrating the Bolshevik Revolution.

WIDE WORLD

A strange looking air-cushion vehicle was developed for the West German Ministry of Defense by VFW-Fokker. The craft can fly freely if necessary and can leap over obstacles.

The resulting incentives for an Israeli preemptive attack in 1978 made the Middle East even more of a powder keg than usual, with the Palestinian liberation movements trying to ignite it. Paradoxically, this instability could provide the basis for a settlement by underlining its urgency. Egypt and Jordan could not long afford the state of no war–no peace, and neither could easily survive another conflict. Nor did they see why they should fight one for the benefit of the Palestinian extremists (whom they had both expelled) and the Arab oil producers. On the other hand, Israel could return the Egyptian territory conquered in 1967 and establish an area for Palestinian settlement controlled by itself and Jordan, where they could suppress any extremists—as Jordan had done with brutal efficiency in 1970. Moreover, if Israel were willing to negotiate at all, the negotiations could best be conducted by Begin, Sadat, and Jordan's King Hussein directly, excluding the Arab extremists and the superpowers. The former would demand too much from Israel to make a settlement possible, and the latter would try to impose their ideas of a settlement on the three countries that would have to live with it.

President Sadat's initiative and its acceptance by Prime Minister Begin drew vigorous responses from the Arab world. The various Palestinian liberation movements denounced Sadat's Jerusalem visit, correctly from their viewpoint, as a sellout. So did some of the Arab oil producers, notably Libya's Col. Muammar al-Qaddafi, who had been stopped from attacking Sadat and other moderates in northeast Africa only by a four-day Egyptian attack on Libya in August. Similar Syrian denunciations posed that nation's Soviet supporters with an awkward choice: if they did not support their major Arab allies, Syria, Libya, and the Palestinians, they could alienate them despite the leverage provided by arms supplies and clandestine intelligence operations. But not participating in negotiations would expose the U.S.S.R. as opposing a Middle East settlement because continued conflict between Israelis and Arabs forced the U.S. to support Israel, making the Arabs the natural allies of the Soviets. U.S. critics of the U.S.S.R. would also be strengthened, further weakening what little was left of détente. Initially, the U.S.S.R. chose not to participate in negotiations; its eventual posi-

tion remained uncertain at the year's end. President Carter's administration agreed to participate but had clearly been cut out of the major action, proving its argument that the U.S. ability to impose its will on the rest of the world was much less than previously thought.

Whether the three principals could negotiate a Middle East peace settlement remained questionable. The alternative was almost certainly a war of considerable duration, death, and destruction, in which the U.S.S.R. might intervene and thereby drag in the U.S. To these prospects had to be added the threat posed by Israel's growing nuclear stockpile, (officially nonexistent), which could be delivered against the southern U.S.S.R. or its Mediterranean fleet.

THE FAR EAST

President Carter's moves to implement his campaign promise to withdraw U.S. ground forces from South Korea over the next five years emphasized the difference between the views of regional security balances held by his administration and by the governments affected. The U.S. was optimistic that its policies would contribute to greater stability at less cost to all, while local powers were pessimistic about the chances of preserving stability and certain that it would cost them more. The actual U.S. forces involved in the pullout, the 30,-000-man U.S. 2nd Division, were small when compared with South Korea's 580,000-man Army, with 1,000 tanks, and North Korea's 430,000-man Army and 1,750 tanks. U.S. air support, essential for delivery of tactical nuclear weapons, would remain, though those weapons would no longer be stored in South Korea. The U.S. would retain its treaty commitments to defend South Korea, and the means to implement these with reinforcements from its Pacific bases.

The immediate questions concerned the role of U.S. forces in South Korea. The Carter administration argued that they made little difference to South Korea's ability to defend itself against a North Korean attack. Critics, including Maj. Gen. John Singlaub, before his removal the third-ranking U.S. officer in South Korea, argued that the key role of U.S. ground troops, one for which there was no substitute, was deterrence. Verbal or written U.S. promises of aid were, the critics maintained, much less effective. Moreover, the Carter administration's broader Pacific strategy cast doubt on whether the U.S. could provide adequate reinforcements.

Essentially, the U.S. government assumed that U.S. military resources should be concentrated against the Soviet-Warsaw Pact threat to NATO. Given the U.S. need to hold down defense spending, this meant that forces and bases in the Pacific would have to be drastically reduced while forces in the continental U.S. were trained and assigned as Pacific reinforcements. Carter's South Korean and Pacific strategies combined could thus create an incentive for North Korea, still bent on Korean unification, to persuade the U.S.S.R. that this time an attack on the South could succeed. In addition, in this view, President Carter's South Korean and Pacific policies seemed likely to conflict with his opposition to nuclear proliferation; South Korea, Taiwan, and Japan were all potential nuclear powers whose incentive to acquire nuclear weapons would be vastly increased by doubts concerning the U.S. guarantees. Both South Korea and Taiwan were acquiring nuclear power plants and Taiwan had reportedly built facilities for extracting weapons-grade plutonium, reports the Taiwanese government strongly denied.

On balance, Carter's strategy of U.S. withdrawal from major military involvements in the Pacific

A new French armoured car was designed to attack both ground installations and low-flying aircraft.

area seemed correct. The North Vietnamese defeat and absorption of South Vietnam had brought Communist governments to power in Cambodia and Laos, leaving as U.S. allies on the Indochina peninsula only Thailand and Malaysia, with Singapore a few miles offshore. All other U.S. allies could be protected from direct Communist attack by U.S. seapower and local forces. The U.S. would not directly intervene in operations against Communist guerrillas. But this strategy left South Korea conspicuously vulnerable to direct attack. Withdrawing all U.S. ground forces rather than reducing them (as was the current plan) seemed to be taking an excessive risk with the nation's security for marginal cost savings.

A chilling footnote to the Vietnam war was the increasing evidence that the Khmer Rouge Communists had killed more than one million Cambodians since taking power in 1975. There was also growing evidence that Cambodia and Vietnam had turned against each other, both using weapons left behind by the U.S. Meanwhile, China flatly contradicted President Carter by insisting that the U.S.S.R. would attack both China and NATO within a very few years and could be deterred or defeated only by increasing military strength. The Chinese Army, stressing the need for greater professionalism and modern equipment, was exploring the possibilities of buying sophisticated military technology abroad. The reappointment of Teng Hsiao-p'ing as chief of the People's Liberation Army emphasized the rejection of the Maoist view that men were more important than equipment. China's nuclear weapons testing continued, as did the growth of its nuclear weapons stockpile. Its long-range delivery systems remained limited to 30–40 CSS-2 intermediate-range ballistic missiles (IRBM's) and 30–40 CSS-1 medium-range ballistic missiles (MRBM's) plus 80 Tu-16 medium bombers.

Although not large, China's strategic forces underlined the Soviet Union's problem in facing four nuclear powers: the U.S., China, the U.K., and France. The U.K. retained four nuclear-powered ballistic missile submarines (SSBN's), each with 16 Polaris A-3 missiles, plus tactical weapons systems. France continued to build up its nuclear force, deploying 16 of the new M-20 missiles (3,000-mi range, 1-megaton warhead) in one SSBN, 16 M-2s (1,900-mi range, 500-kiloton warhead) in another SSBN, and 32 M-1s (1,550-mi range, 500-kiloton warhead) in two more SSBN's. A fifth SSBN was under construction, and a new IRBM, the S-3 (1,865-mi range, 1-megaton warhead), was tested.

The effectiveness of the nuclear weapons of China, the U.K., and France would be greatly increased if they obtained U.S. long-range cruise missile (LRCM) technology because it could provide strategic delivery systems at a fraction of existing costs and could be deployed so widely that Soviet chances of wiping out these nuclear forces in a first strike would disappear. Thus, the U.S.S.R. was attempting to limit LRCM's in SALT II.

(ROBIN RANGER)

See also Space Exploration.
[535.B.5.c,ii; 544.B.5–6; 736]

KEYSTONE

THE POLITICS OF SALT II

by Robin Ranger

During his campaign for the presidency of the U.S., Jimmy Carter had advocated much stronger U.S. policies to limit and reduce strategic arms, prevent nuclear proliferation, and curb conventional arms sales. His personal commitment to these ideals was greater than that of any of his predecessors and with characteristic vigour, he quickly initiated policies to implement them. The results, however, fell far short of expectations. The U.S. secured an outline agreement concerning the second round of the strategic arms limitation talks (SALT II) but only by means of unilateral concessions to the U.S.S.R., dropping all proposed limits on the latter's forces. The U.S.S.R. also seemed likely to agree to a comprehensive test ban covering only the superpowers and the U.K., a significant arms-control step but one that increased the already strong criticism of the nuclear test limitation package the Carter administration wanted ratified by the U.S. Senate.

On nuclear proliferation, Carter reduced planned U.S. nuclear electric power and established much stricter controls over U.S. export of nuclear power plants and fuel, establishing more stringent safeguards to prevent their being used to develop nuclear weapons, as India had done with Canadian and U.S. supplies. But he failed to persuade the other major nuclear exporting countries to do likewise, notably West Germany, which refused to cancel its 1975 agreement to sell Brazil a complete nuclear fuel cycle. Moreover, Carter's opposition to nuclear power and the resulting uncertainties over U.S. ability to meet fuel supply commitments increased Western European and Japanese determination to become self-sufficient in those fields, since they lacked the alternative fuel sources open to the U.S. Potential new nuclear weapons powers became more interested in such arms as security guarantees when Carter reduced U.S. overseas forces.

Carter's conventional arms sales policy was officially still being developed, suggesting that it was unlikely to be effective or coherent. Meanwhile, some cuts in arms exports were made but not to

Robin Ranger is assistant professor of political science at St. Francis Xavier University, Antigonish, Nova Scotia, and the author of Arms and Politics.

such major U.S. allies as Iran or Saudi Arabia. The consequent uncertainty about the availability of U.S. arms over the long run was, however, sufficient to increase interest in self-sufficiency and alternate sources of supply in buying countries, while U.S. rivals in the international arms trade (notably the Western European nations) were quick to take advantage of the situation.

The basic problem with Carter's policy on arms control was his fondness for simplistic solutions to complex problems, his overcommitment to his chosen solutions, his resultant inability to listen to alternative arguments, and his difficulty in cooperating with other political powers, within or outside the U.S. Since arms control problems are complex, and can only be solved by close cooperation between the U.S. and its allies, Carter's approach was often counterproductive. This was especially true because of the exceptionally high degree of ideological conformity to one version of arms control thinking in his administration. All Carter's appointees in the national security field (notably special adviser on national security affairs Zbigniew Brzezinski, Secretary of Defense Harold Brown, and Paul Warnke, head of the SALT negotiating team) believed in the liberal theory of arms control. This held that the superpowers had accepted the strategic doctrine of mutual assured destruction (MAD), whereby each could deter an attack by being able to guarantee to inflict unacceptable damage on an attacker, even after absorbing a first strike on its own deterrent forces. In the real world, according to this view, very low levels of damage would deter any rational government from even risking the use of nuclear weapons, which were therefore politically useless. U.S. strategic forces were thus more than adequate for deterrence for the foreseeable future no matter what forces the U.S.S.R. developed, enabling the U.S. to hold down its military spending (hence Carter's cancellation of the B-1 bomber) and accept Soviet advantages in SALT II (*see* TABLE). While the superpowers sought to contain the strategic arms race, they should also work along with other countries to contain the proliferation of nuclear and conventional weapons on the principle that security was better served by arms control than arms.

This view of arms control had become the dominant one in the U.S. But there were many critics of this concept, who argued that it was incorrect and disproved by experience. They pointed especially to Soviet pursuit of strategic advantage vis-à-vis the U.S. under SALT and in unstable regions of the world. Also, to these critics, those holding the dominant view were ethnocentric, assuming that decisionmakers in other nations, especially the U.S.S.R., either did or should think as they did and would

Changes in Nuclear-Strike Forces Under SALT I: 1972–77

Weapons systems	Maximum range (mi)	Missile warheads		Throw weight (000 lb)		Speed (Mach)	Aircraft Weapons load (000 lb)		Deployment	Number 1972 (July)	1977 (July)	Total equivalent megatonnage [2]	Maximum number of strategic targets [3]	Nuclear submarine launch vehicles	
		Number	Yield (each) [1]	Range	Total		Each	Total	First					1972	1977
UNITED STATES															
Intercontinental ballistic missiles (ICBM) [4]															
Titan II	7,000	1	5–10 mt	7.5		—	—	—	1962	54	54			—	—
Minuteman I	7,500	1	1 mt	...		—	—	—	1962	300	0			—	—
Minuteman II	7,000	1	1–2 mt	1–1.5		—	—	—	1966	500	450			—	—
Minuteman III	7,500	3 [5]	170 kt	1.5–2		—	—	—	1970	200	550			—	—
Total					2,200					1,054	1,054	1,460	2,154		
(SALT I allowance)										(1,054)					
Submarine-launched ballistic missiles (SLBM) [4]															
Polaris A-2	1,750	1	800 kt	...		—	—	—	1962	128	0			8	0
Polaris A-3	2,880	3 [6]	200 kt	1		—	—	—	1964	368	160			23	10
Poseidon C-3	2,880	10 [5]–14 [6]	50 kt	2		—	—	—	1971	160	496			10	31
Total					1,100					656	656	830	5,120	41	41
(SALT I allowance)										(656 or 710 [7])				(41 or 44 [7])	
Short-range ballistic missiles (SRBM)															
Pershing	450	1	kt range	...		—	—	—	1962	250	108 [8]			—	—
Lance	70	1	kt range	...		—	—	—	1972	—	36 [8]			—	—
Total					...					250	144	...			
Strategic bombers															
B-52 D–F	11,500	—	—	—		0.95	60		1956	172	373			—	—
B-52 G/H	12,500	—	—	—		0.95	70		1959	283	373			—	—
Total								22,800		455	373	4,400	4,056		
Other nuclear-strike aircraft															
F-B-111A	3,800	—	—	—		2.5	37.5		1969	76	68			—	—
F-111A/E	3,800	—	—	—		2.5	25		1967					—	—
F-105D	2,100	—	—	—		2.25	16.5		1960	550	550 [8]			—	—
F-4	2,300	—	—	—		2.4	16		1962					—	—
A-7A/B/D/E [9]	3,400	—	—	—		0.9	15		1966					—	—
Total								...		626	618	...			
SOVIET UNION															
Intercontinental ballistic missiles (ICBM) [4]															
SS-7 Saddler	6,900	1	5 mt	3–4		—	—	—	1961	210	109			—	—
SS-8 Sasin	6,900	1	5 mt	3–4		—	—	—	1963					—	—
SS-9 Scarp	7,500	1 or 3 [6]	18 or 25 mt / 4–5 mt	12–15		—	—	—	1965	290	238			—	—
SS-11 Sego	6,500	1 or 3 [6]	1–2 mt / kt range	1.5–2		—	—	—	1966	970	840			—	—
SS-13 Savage	5,000	1	1 mt	1		—	—	—	1968	60	60			—	—
SS-17	6,500	4 [5] or 1	kt range / 5 mt	6		—	—	—	1975	—	40			—	—
SS-18	7,500	1 or 8 [5]	15–25 mt / 2 mt	15–18		—	—	—	1975	—	50			—	—
SS-19	6,500	6 [5] or 1	kt range / 5 mt	7		—	—	—	1975	—	140			—	—
Total					7,800					1,530	1,477	2,950	2,647		
(SALT I allowance)										(1,618)					
Submarine-launched ballistic missiles (SLBM) [4]															
SS-N-5 Serb	750	1	1–2 mt	...		—	—	—	1964	30	21			10	7
SS-N-6 Sawfly	1,750	1 or 3 [6]	1–2 mt / kt range	1.5		—	—	—	1969	464	544			29	34
SS-N-8	4,800	1	1–2 mt	1.5		—	—	—	1972	—	284			21	
Total					1,300					494	849	860 [10]	909 [10]	39	62
(SALT I allowance)										(950)				(62)	
Medium/intermediate-range ballistic missiles (M/IRBM)															
SS-4 Sandal	1,200	1	1 mt	...		—	—	—	1959	500	500			—	—
SS-5 Skean	2,300	1	1 mt	...		—	—	—	1961	100	100			—	—
SS-20	3,000	3 [6]	kt range	1.2		—	—	—	1977	—	20			—	—
Total					...					600	620	...			
Long-range cruise missiles (LRCM)															
SS-N-3 Shaddock	450	1	kt range	...		—	—	—	1962	433	424 [11]	...			
Short-range ballistic missiles (SRBM)															
SS-1b Scud A	50	1	kt range	...		—	—	—	1957					—	—
SS-1c Scud B	185	1	kt range	...		—	—	—	1965	300	750			—	—
SS-12 Scaleboard	500	1	kt range	...		—	—	—	1969					—	—
Total					...					300	750				
Strategic bombers															
Tu-95 Bear	7,800	—	—	—		0.78	40		1956	100	100			—	—
Mya-4 Bison	6,000	—	—	—		0.87	20		1956	40	35			—	—
Total								4,700		140	135	780	270		
Other nuclear-strike aircraft															
Tu-16 Badger	4,000	—	—	—		0.8	20		1955	800	740			—	—
Tu-? Backfire B	5,500	—	—	—		2.5	20		1974	—	65			—	—
Su-7 Fitter A	900	—	—	—		1.7	4.5		1959					—	—
Tu-22 Blinder	1,400	—	—	—		1.5	12		1962					—	—
MiG-21 Fishbed J/K/L	1,150	—	—	—		2.2	2		1970	750	1,000 [8]			—	—
MiG-27 Flogger D	1,800	—	—	—		2.5	2.8		1971					—	—
Su-17–20 Fitter C	1,100	—	—	—		1.6	5		1974					—	—
Su-19 Fencer A	1,800	—	—	—		2.3	8		1974					—	—
Total								...		1,550	1,805	...			

[1] Kiloton (kt) range means less than one megaton (mt).
[2] Equivalent megatonnage measures damage to unprotected area targets and is expressed as the two-thirds power of a weapon's explosive yield.
[3] Only separately-targetable delivery vehicles (warheads) are included in missile totals; bomber totals assume both stand-off and gravity-bomb deployment.
[4] Covered by SALT I agreements.
[5] Multiple independently-targetable reentry vehicles (MIRV).
[6] Multiple reentry vehicle.
[7] If the Titan missiles were to be replaced by SLBM's.
[8] Figures for systems deployed in Europe only.
[9] A-7A/B/E are carrier-based aircraft.
[10] Includes capabilities of 60 missiles carried by diesel-powered submarines.
[11] 100 land-based, about 300 in 43 nuclear and 24 diesel-powered submarines, and the remainder carried by surface ships.

Sources: International Institute for Strategic Studies, 18 Adam Street, London, *The Military Balance 1977–1978, Strategic Survey 1976.*

To cut down on U.S. defense spending, Pres. Jimmy Carter canceled plans to build the B-1 bomber, which he said was not needed.

therefore follow any arms control policies proposed by the U.S. But, as President Carter quickly discovered, neither the U.S.S.R. nor many U.S. allies thought as did his arms control advisers. Instead of accepting his proposals, they countered with their own, based on their perceptions of their strategic and nuclear energy requirements.

Carter's negotiations with the U.S.S.R. produced his first substantive agreements, SALT II and a comprehensive test ban, but these underlined his failure to achieve effective rather than just cosmetic arms control. The SALT negotiations had been deadlocked since then secretary of state Henry Kissinger's January 1976 Moscow visit because the U.S.S.R. insisted that its Backfire bomber should not be counted as a strategic delivery vehicle under the Vladivostok force limits but that the U.S. long-range cruise missile (LRCM) be severely restricted in range and numbers. The Soviets also rejected any restrictions on their strategic force buildup. U.S. Secretary of State Cyrus Vance (see BIOGRAPHY) therefore carried two proposals to Moscow in March 1977. The deferral plan sidestepped the Backfire/LRCM problem and was therefore rejected by the U.S.S.R. The U.S. comprehensive plan aimed at real strategic arms control, limiting intercontinental ballistic missiles (ICBM's) equipped with multiple independently targetable reentry vehicles (MIRV's), heavy Soviet ICBM's, and missile flight-testing. These, and the rest of the package, would lessen the imminent danger of either side acquiring an effective counterforce capability by means of rapid increases in missile accuracy. The U.S.S.R.'s increasing superiority in throw-weight (payload) gave it a greater counterforce capability, which the U.S. wanted restrained. In exchange the U.S. offered modest limits on the range of air-launched cruise missiles (ALCM's).

The Soviet Union rejected, as it had always done,

any limits on its forces, calculating that Carter's personal and political requirements for a SALT II would force U.S. acceptance of its terms, as in the previous negotiations with Kissinger and Presidents Richard Nixon and Gerald Ford. The Soviet leadership bitterly opposed Carter's campaign for human rights in the U.S.S.R. but were sure he would drop this for a SALT II. They were right on both counts and secured an outline SALT II by October, in which Carter dropped all significant limitations on Soviet but not on U.S. forces. The U.S. ALCM force would be half that required to substitute for the canceled B-1 bomber, and very low range limits would be imposed on ground- and submarine-launched cruise missiles, (G/SLCM's), claimed by Carter to his NATO allies to offset the massive buildup by the U.S.S.R. of its conventional ground forces, SS-20 IRBM's, and long-range strike aircraft. Moreover, despite Carter administration claims that the U.S. Minuteman force would be safe from a Soviet attack well into the 1980s, such an attack could be sure of destroying two to four times the number of existing U.S. ICBM silos by 1980. The new, mobile ICBM would be less vulnerable to such an attack because it would move back and forth along trenches 12 mi long, breaking out of these to fire. But this weapon, procurement of which was approved in September, had been so delayed that it could not enter service before 1983. Until then, the only new U.S. strategic forces being deployed would be the Trident I missile and submarine and the ALCM launcher aircraft. In contrast, the U.S.S.R. was deploying its fourth generation of strategic missiles, replacing the SS-7 through SS-13 series. They were also testing fifth-generation strategic missiles.

Carter's SALT II was thus open to the same criticisms as Kissinger's SALT I agreements and proposals. It imposed unilateral restraint on U.S. strategic

Major U.S.-U.S.S.R. Strategic Arms Control Agreements, 1969–77

1. Agreement to start Strategic Arms Limitation Talks (SALT) (1969)
2. SALT I agreements (1972)
   a. Anti-Ballistic Missile (ABM) Treaty
      Signed May 26, 1972. As a treaty, it required the consent of the U.S. Senate (by a two-thirds majority) for ratification, given on August 3; entered into force Oct. 3, 1972, for indefinite period but subject to review every five years. Limited each side to 2 ABM deployment areas (each with up to 100 ABM launchers and radars), one defending their capital city and one defending their ICBM's. Banned the testing of surface-to-air missiles (SAM's) "in an ABM mode."
   b. Interim Agreement and Protocol on the Limitations of Strategic Offensive Arms (Interim Agreement).
      Signed May 26, 1972. As an executive agreement by the U.S. president this did not legally require U.S. Senate consent for ratification, but Section 33 of the 1961 act creating the U.S. Arms Control and Disarmament Agency (ACDA) bars action to reduce or limit U.S. arms except by Treaty or "unless authorized by further affirmative legislation by Congress." The Interim Agreement was, therefore, submitted to the U.S. Senate and House of Representatives for approval by a joint resolution. This was given on Sept. 30, 1972, only *after* the inclusion of Sen. Henry Jackson's (Dem., Wash.) amendment, which required U.S. equality with the U.S.S.R. in future SALT agreements. The Interim Agreement entered into force Oct. 3, 1972, for five years. It limited ICBM's and SLBM's to maximum totals for the U.S. and U.S.S.R.
   c. Agreed Interpretations, Common Understandings, and Unilateral U.S. Statements on SALT I
      These claimed to define the key terms of SALT I but essentially represented U.S. interpretations that did not legally restrain the U.S.S.R. from subsequently deploying new strategic forces, especially ICBM's with vastly increased throw-weight. The U.S.S.R.'s only violation of the *letter* of SALT I would have been the testing and/or deployment of SAM's and radars "in an ABM mode."
   d. Standing Consultative Commission (SCC) on Arms Limitations
      Established on Dec. 21, 1972. The SCC was supposed to "promote the objectives and implementation" of SALT I. It did so only at a formal, legal level, avoiding substantive issues.
3. Basic Principles of U.S.-U.S.S.R. Relations (May 29, 1972)
   This formalized détente on paper. The superpowers agreed to "avoid military confrontations and to prevent the outbreak of nuclear war," each refraining from seeking "unilateral advantage at the expense of the other" and basing their relations on the "principle of equality and the renunciation of the use or threat of force".
4. Threshold Test Ban Treaty (TTBT) (July 3, 1974) and Peaceful Nuclear Explosions Treaty (PNET) (May 28, 1976)
   The TTBT limited underground nuclear weapons tests to a maximum yield of 150-kt provided an equivalent limit could be set on peaceful nuclear explosions (PNE's) to prevent their use as weapons tests, since the U.S.S.R. insisted on the right to conduct such. The PNET limited any one PNE to 150-kt yield, though a group explosion could exceed that total. These provisions may be verified by instrumentation and observers provided by the other party to the treaties. President Carter sought Senate ratification while trying to negotiate a comprehensive test ban treaty with the U.K. and U.S.S.R. that would ban all nuclear weapons tests.
5. Protocol to the ABM Treaty (July 3, 1974)
   Reduced permitted ABM deployments to one from two sites each. Formalized the status quo of U.S. deployment of one at Grand Forks, N.D., protecting ICBM's (closed down in 1975) and Soviet deployment of one site defending Moscow (and some ICBM's).
6. Vladivostok Accord (Nov. 24, 1974)
   Set framework for negotiations for a SALT II agreement to be in force from October 1977 to Dec. 31, 1985. Each side would be limited to a total of 2,400 strategic delivery vehicles, including bombers, of which only 1,320 could carry multiple independently-targetable reentry vehicles. The key aide-mémoire (official record of conversation) interpreting these terms was still secret in 1977.
7. Extension of the Interim Agreement (September 1977)
   The U.S. and U.S.S.R. issued statements that each would behave as if the Interim Agreement was still in force after it expired on Oct. 3, 1977, pending its replacement by SALT II.

forces without establishing any reciprocal restraint on Soviet troops or on the increasing Soviet counterforce capabilities vis-à-vis the U.S. These defects meant that even if SALT II could be completed it would have difficulty in securing the required U.S. Senate approval.

Carter's negotiation, in principle, of a comprehensive test ban with the U.S.S.R. appeared his one real success, provided the details could be worked out. For 20 years, such a ban had been regarded as a major restraint on nuclear-weapons development and testing. It could also lessen the chances of counterforce attacks, because, as with missiles, large numbers of tests are required before the necessary high confidence in the weapons can be developed.

The major obstacle to a test ban, initially, had been verification. Could the U.S. unilaterally verify Soviet compliance, using seismic detectors to monitor earthquakes and distinguish these from clandestine nuclear testing? By the late 1960s U.S. verification systems had been able to do this. The later and more significant obstacle was the military

The cruise missile, which can be launched from land, from aircraft, or from surface ships and submarines, has been called an inexpensive alternative to the high-technology B-1 bomber.

requirement for testing in order to develop new weapons and evaluate the performance of existing ones. This need caused the U.S.S.R.'s acceptance of a test ban to be puzzling; even if the Soviets were satisfied with their existing nuclear weapons, pressures would eventually build up for the development of new ones.

Doubts about Carter's ability to live up to his promises were reinforced by the failure to produce effective new policies limiting nuclear proliferation and conventional arms sales. Whether these could be devised and imposed solely by the U.S. was doubtful. The most the U.S. could hope to do was to coordinate its own extremely uncoordinated policies on these issues and try to persuade its allies to do likewise. Even then, success would be modest: the rate of proliferation of nuclear power plants, weapons, and of conventional arms could be slowed but not halted.

By the end of 1977 the Carter administration had made some progress on nuclear proliferation. Internally, the bureaucratic maze dealing with the export of nuclear power and the prevention of weapons proliferation (two conflicting aims) was being sorted out so that it could implement antiproliferation policies. Externally, France was persuaded to join the group of nuclear exporters formed in 1975 to try to formulate common policies on nuclear exports and safeguards. The problem of proliferation was dramatized in August, when the Soviet Union alleged that South Africa was about to conduct a nuclear test and secured U.S. and French cooperation in preventing them from doing so; however, France did not cancel its contract to supply South Africa with nuclear reactors. Moreover, this modest success was not matched by any progress in limiting the transfers of conventional but highly sophisticated weapons to the nations of the third world.

In conclusion, Carter appeared correct in his campaign claims that U.S. arms control policies had been far less successful than their Republican Party architects, notably Kissinger, had claimed. Carter also rightly stressed the reemergence of nuclear proliferation as a major problem, also recognized by the Ford administration. But Carter's acceptance of liberal arms control thinking and his assumptions of U.S. omnipotence and righteousness in this field created expectations that could not be fulfilled and impeded such progress as could have been made, except in the case of the U.S.S.R. There he secured agreements by repeating Kissinger's practice of excessively one-sided U.S. concessions to the U.S.S.R. SALT II and the comprehensive test ban would not remove the U.S.S.R.'s counterforce capability vis-à-vis the U.S. and seemed unlikely to produce political gains worth their cost.

Demography

With the world population exceeding 4,000,000,-000 persons, according to 1976 estimates, the UN and other international agencies encouraged and supported activities related to improving population estimates. Governments were urged to take censuses, improve civil registration systems, and plan surveys aimed at obtaining estimates of births and deaths. Particular attention was directed toward the study of fertility, the principal determinant of population change.

The less developed countries maintained high rates of growth because of lowered death rates and relatively high birthrates, despite the lowering of fertility in some areas. In Latin America several countries had in excess of 3% annual growth, which might double their populations in as little as 20 years. The developed countries were generally characterized by declining birthrates and aging populations; growth rates in Europe averaged less than 1% per year. International migration continued to have an important effect on population change in Africa, Asia, and the Americas. Internal migration in almost all countries consisted mainly of a continued and frequently increased flow from rural to urban areas. (See MIGRATION, INTERNATIONAL.)

Birth Statistics. In 1976 there were an estimated 3,165,000 live births in the U.S., less than 1% over 1975. Reports by the National Center for Health Statistics attributed the increase to the growth in the number of women in the childbearing ages (15–44) rather than to a change in the rate at which women were bearing children. The birthrate moved from 14.8 per 1,000 population in 1975 to 14.7 in 1976, the lowest ever recorded in the U.S. The fertility rate (live births per 1,000 women 15–44 years of age) also fell to a new low, from the final 1975 figure of 66.7 to 65.6 in 1976. The total fertility rate (the current rate of childbearing) dropped from 2 children per woman in 1972 to 1.8 children in 1975 and was estimated to be at this latter level in 1976. Monthly provisional data for the first half of 1977 indicated that the birthrate was tending upward. There were 7% more births than for the same period of 1976; the birthrate was 6% higher; and the fertility rate 5% higher.

According to final statistics for 1975, the white population experienced a decline of 1.4% in the birthrate between 1974 and 1975; the "other than white" category, a decline of 0.9%; and the black population, one of 0.5%. The birthrate for the white group (13.8) was substantially lower than for all others (21.2). While a gap in rates between white and other populations remained, the pattern of decline in all these groups after 1959 was quite similar.

The decline in fertility was also indicated in lower rates for all age-of-mother groups from 15–19 years through 40–44 years, and for all birth orders. The only increase was for girls 10–14 years old, but these accounted for only 0.4% of the total. In a special study of teenage children in the period 1966–75, the National Center for Health Statistics found that births to teenagers had risen from 17 to 19% of all births. In 1975 over half of children born to mothers 15–17 years of age and a third born to mothers 18–19 were illegitimate. There were an estimated 447,900 illegitimate births in 1975, an increase of 7% over the previous year.

The rate of natural increase (excess of births over deaths per 1,000 population) continued to decline in industrialized countries, and in some there was a shift to natural decrease. Austria joined East Germany, West Germany, and Luxembourg as a country with more deaths than births. Belgium experienced a near balance of births and deaths, and England and Wales, Scotland, The Netherlands, and Sweden were only a few points away. In the U.S. the rate fell from 5.9 persons per 1,000 population in 1975 to an estimated 5.8 in 1976. Preliminary figures for the first half of 1977 showed a rise in the rate over the same period of 1976, due primarily to the increase in births.

Death Statistics. There were 1,912,000 deaths in the U.S. in 1976, and the death rate was 8.9 per 1,000 population, according to provisional statistics released by the National Center for Health Statistics. This represented a slight increase over the final figure for 1975, but the mortality rate remained the same. High death rates, related to a serious outbreak of influenza, were reported for February, March, and April. The death rate for the first half of 1977 was slightly below that for the same period of 1976 and, for the 12-month period ended July 1977, was 8.8 per 1,000 population.

Provisional death rates by age, colour, and sex for 1976 showed declines for all groups except for white females; the rate for this group was affected by a sharp rise in mortality among women 85 years

Table I. Birthrates and Death Rates per 1,000 Population and Infant Mortality per 1,000 Live Births in Selected Countries, 1976[1]

Country	Birth-rate	Death rate	Infant mortality	Country	Birth-rate	Death rate	Infant mortality
Africa				Norway	13.3	9.9	11.1[4]
Egypt[2]	35.4	12.6	101.3	Poland	19.5	8.8	23.8
Mauritius	26.0	7.8	40.2	Portugal[4]	19.0	10.4	38.9
Nigeria[3]	49.3	22.7	...	Romania[4]	19.7	9.3	34.7
South Africa[3]	42.9	15.5	...	Spain	18.2	8.0	10.7
Tunisia[4]	36.6	7.3	62.6[5]	Sweden	11.9	11.0	8.7
Asia				Switzerland	11.7	9.0	10.5
Cyprus	19.8	9.7	26.9	United Kingdom	12.1	12.2	14.3
Hong Kong[4]	18.2	4.9	15.0	Yugoslavia	18.1	8.4	36.4
Israel	28.1	6.9	22.9	North America			
Japan	16.4	6.3	9.3	Antigua[4]	19.3	6.6	38.2
Kuwait[4]	43.4	4.8	39.3	Bahamas, The[4]	19.8	5.4	34.7
Lebanon[5]	24.5	4.3	13.6[6]	Barbados	18.6	9.2	37.7[5]
Malaysia[7]	33.2	6.5	36.4	Canada[4]	15.7	7.3	15.0[2]
Philippines[4]	26.7	6.3	58.9[2]	Costa Rica[4]	29.3	4.9	38.2
Singapore	18.8	5.1	11.6	Cuba[4]	20.7	5.4	27.3
Thailand[4]	27.1	5.7	26.3	El Salvador[4]	40.1	8.0	58.3
Europe				Guatemala[2]	42.8	11.8	75.4
Austria	11.6	12.6	18.3	Jamaica	30.0	7.1	20.4
Belgium	12.3	12.1	13.9	Mexico[4]	37.5	6.7	49.7
Bulgaria	16.5	10.1	23.2	Panama	32.2	5.2	35.6
Czechoslovakia	19.2	11.4	20.8	Puerto Rico[4]	22.3	6.1	20.9
Denmark	12.9	10.7	10.3	United States	14.7	8.9	15.1
Finland	14.1	9.4	10.5	Oceania			
France	13.6	10.5	12.5	American Samoa	36.5	4.4	18.8
Germany, East	11.6	14.0	14.1	Australia	16.7	8.3	14.3[4]
Germany, West	9.8	11.9	17.4	Fiji[4]	29.0	6.9	40.9
Greece	15.7	8.2	22.6	Guam[4]	30.4	4.2	20.3
Hungary	17.6	12.5	29.7	New Zealand[4]	18.5	8.2	16.0
Iceland	19.4	6.2	11.7	Pacific Islands,			
Ireland	21.6	10.5	14.6	Trust Terr. of	28.7	3.0	18.1
Italy	14.0	9.7	19.1	Western Samoa	36.9	6.7	40.0
Netherlands, The	12.9	8.3	10.5	U.S.S.R.	18.5	9.5	27.7[2]

[1] Registered births and deaths only.   [5] 1973.
[2] 1974.   [6] 1960.
[3] 1970–75 UN estimate.   [7] 1972.
[4] 1975.

Sources: United Nations, *Population and Vital Statistics Report*; various national publications.

continued on page 298

Table II. World Populations and Areas[1]

	AREA AND POPULATION: MIDYEAR 1976			POPULATION AT MOST RECENT CENSUS					Age distribution (%)[2]					
Country	Area in sq km	Total population	Persons per sq km	Date of census	Total population	% Male	% Female	% Urban	0–14	15–29	30–44	45–59	60–74	75+
AFRICA														
Algeria	2,322,164	17,304,000	7.5	1966	11,833,126	50.2	49.8	38.8	47.1	22.4	14.9	8.7	5.0	1.8
Angola	1,246,700	6,761,000	5.4	1970	5,646,166	52.1	47.9	14.2	...	...	...	...	...	...
Benin	112,600	3,197,000	28.4	1961	2,082,511	49.0	51.0	9.3	46.0	22.7	16.4	9.3	—5.6—	
Botswana	576,000	718,000	1.2	1971	574,094	45.7	54.3	8.4	46.1	21.7	12.8	9.0	5.0	5.4
British Indian Ocean Territory	60	—	—	1971	110	...	...	...	...	...	...	...	...	...
Burundi	27,834	3,864,000	138.8	1970–71	3,350,000	...	...	3.5	...	...	...	...	...	...
Cameroon	465,054	7,663,000	16.5	1976	7,663,246	49.0	51.0	...	...	...	...	...	...	...
Cape Verde Islands	4,033	303,000	75.1	1970	272,071	48.2	51.8	19.7	47.0	20.8	14.2	8.7	6.2	3.0
Central African Empire	624,977	1,829,000	2.9	1959–60	1,177,000	47.8	52.2	6.8	40.0	21.9	25.7	10.4	—2.0—	
Chad	1,284,000	4,116,000	3.2	1964	3,254,000	48.2	51.8	7.8	45.6	22.2	19.3	9.3	—3.6—	
Comoros[3]	1,792	344,000	192.0	1966	244,905	49.2	50.8	13.5	44.1	23.6	15.7	8.7	4.2	3.8
Congo	342,000	1,390,000	4.1	1974	1,300,120	48.7	51.3	39.8	...	...	...	...	...	...
Djibouti	23,000	226,000	9.8	1960–61	81,200	...	...	57.4	...	...	...	...	...	...
Egypt	1,002,000	38,067,000	38.0	1976	36,656,180	51.0	49.0	44.0	...	...	...	...	...	...
Equatorial Guinea	28,051	316,000	11.3	1965	277,240	52.8	47.2	...	35.1	—48.5—		—16.4—		
Ethiopia	1,221,900	28,668,000	23.5	1970	24,068,800	50.7	49.3	9.7	43.5	27.0	16.3	8.8	3.7	0.7
French Southern and Antarctic Lands	7,366	—												
Gabon	267,667	1,156,000	4.3	1970	950,009	47.9	52.1	26.9	35.4	19.2	22.2	16.3	6.3	0.6
Gambia, The	10,689	538,000	50.3	1973	493,499	51.0	49.0	15.0	41.3	—44.1—		—14.6—		
Ghana	238,533	10,309,000	43.2	1970	8,559,313	49.6	50.4	28.9	46.9	24.4	15.8	7.5	3.8	1.6
Guinea	245,857	4,529,000	18.4	1972	5,143,284				43.1	—56.9—				
Guinea-Bissau	36,125	912,000	25.2	1970	487,448	48.7	51.3	11.1	...	...	...	...	...	...
Ivory Coast	322,463	6,703,000	20.8	1975	6,702,866	52.0	48.0	32.4	44.6	—55.4—				
Kenya	582,646	13,847,000	23.8	1969	10,942,705	50.1	49.9	9.9	48.4	25.1	13.6	7.5	3.9	1.5
Lesotho	30,355	1,214,000	40.0	1976	1,213,960	...	...	...	...	...	...	...	...	...
Liberia	111,400	1,751,000	15.7	1974	1,503,368	51.0	49.0	...	41.0	—59.0—				
Libya	1,749,000	2,444,000	1.4	1973	2,249,222	53.0	47.0	...	48.8	22.2	15.3	8.2	4.0	1.6
Madagascar	587,041	8,266,000	14.1	1966	6,200,000	49.2	50.8	...	46.5	22.3	15.2	10.1	—5.9—	
Malawi	118,573	5,175,000	43.6	1966	4,039,583	47.4	52.6	5.0	43.9	25.3	15.5	9.7	—5.7—	
Mali	1,240,142	6,035,000	4.9	1976	6,035,272	49.0	51.0	...	...	...	...	...	...	...
Mauritania	1,030,700	1,481,000	1.4	1976	1,481,000	...	...	...	...	...	...	...	...	...
Mauritius	2,040	895,000	438.7	1972	851,334	50.0	50.0	42.9	40.3	28.6	14.5	11.0	4.9	0.7
Mayotte	378	46,500	123.0	1966	32,494	50.3	49.7	...	48.9	—51.1—				
Morocco	458,730	17,828,000	38.9	1971	15,379,259	50.1	49.9	35.4	46.2	22.4	16.0	8.3	5.3	1.8
Mozambique	799,380	9,444,000	11.8	1970	8,168,933	49.4	50.6	...	45.3	22.5	19.1	9.1	3.8	0.3
Niger	1,186,408	4,727,000	4.0	1959–60	2,611,473	49.7	50.3	...	...	...	...	...	...	...
Nigeria	923,800	76,600,000	82.9	1973	79,760,000	...	...	...	...	...	...	...	...	...
Réunion	2,512	510,000	203.0	1974	476,675	...	...	...	...	...	...	...	...	...
Rhodesia	390,245	6,530,000	16.7	1969	5,099,350	50.3	49.7	16.8	47.2	25.4	15.7	8.4	—3.3—	
Rwanda	26,338	4,289,000	162.8	1970	3,735,585	47.8	52.2	3.2	43.8	24.2	15.2	11.6	—5.2—	
St. Helena	412	6,000	14.6	1976	5,147	...	...	29.4	35.3	24.6	15.8	11.7	9.5	3.0
São Tomé & Príncipe	964	81,000	84.0	1970	73,811	50.8	49.2	...	...	...	...	...	...	...
Senegal	196,722	5,115,000	26.0	1976	5,085,388	49.2	50.8	...	...	...	...	...	...	...
Seychelles	443	59,000	131.2	1977	61,950	...	...	...	...	...	...	...	...	...
Sierra Leone	71,740	3,111,000	43.4	1974	2,729,479	39.6	60.4	...	36.7	27.2	19.4	9.0	—7.6—	
Somalia	638,000	3,261,000	5.1	—	—	—	—	—	—	—	—	—	—	—
South Africa	1,222,375	26,156,000	21.4	1970	21,794,328	49.2	50.8	47.9	40.8	26.1	16.7	10.0	5.0	1.3
Bophuthatswana[4]	40,430	1,039,000	25.7	1970	880,312	46.9	53.1	14.2	44.7	26.4	12.5	—13.5—		1.3
Transkei[4]	41,002	2,061,000	50.3	1970	1,745,992	41.2	58.8	3.2	46.4	22.8	14.1	—15.3—		1.2
South West Africa	824,268	883,000	1.1	1970	763,630	50.8	49.2	24.9	...	...	...	...	...	...
Sudan	2,505,813	16,126,000	6.4	1973	14,171,732[5]	...	...	...	...	...	...	...	...	...
Swaziland	17,364	499,000	28.7	1976	499,046	...	...	...	...	...	...	...	...	...
Tanzania	945,087	15,607,000	16.5	1967	12,313,469	48.8	51.2	5.5	43.9	24.7	15.4	8.6	4.1	3.3
Togo	56,785	2,283,000	40.2	1970	1,953,778	48.1	51.9	...	49.8	21.5	15.1	8.0	3.6	2.0
Tunisia	164,150	5,737,000	34.9	1975	5,588,209	50.8	49.2	49.0	...	...	...	...	...	...
Uganda	241,139	11,943,000	49.5	1969	9,548,847	50.5	49.5	7.7	46.2	24.0	15.7	8.3	4.2	1.6
Upper Volta	274,200	6,174,000	22.5	1975	6,144,013	...	...	...	...	...	...	...	...	...
Western Sahara	266,769	128,000	.5	1970	76,425	57.5	42.5	45.3	42.9	27.2	16.3	7.4	4.4	1.8
Zaire	2,344,885	25,629,000	10.9	—	—	—	—	—	—	—	—	—	—	—
Zambia	752,614	5,138,000	6.8	1969	4,056,995	49.0	51.0	29.6	46.3	24.0	16.6	9.4	3.0	0.7
Total AFRICA	30,174,283	427,931,500	14.2											
ANTARCTICA total	14,244,900	[6]	—	—	—	—	—	—	—	—	—	—	—	—
ASIA														
Afghanistan	653,000	19,803,000	30.3	—	—	—	—	—	—	—	—	—	—	—
Bahrain	662	257,000	388.2	1971	216,078	53.8	46.2	78.1	44.3	25.3	16.9	9.0	3.7	0.8
Bangladesh	143,998	78,664,000	546.3	1974	71,479,071	51.9	48.1	8.8	48.1	22.0	15.6	8.7	4.6	1.1
Bhutan	46,100	1,202,000	26.1	1969	1,034,774	...	...	...	...	...	...	...	...	...
Brunei	5,765	177,000	30.7	1971	136,256	53.4	46.4	63.6	43.4	28.0	15.7	8.1	3.9	0.9
Burma	676,577	30,834,000	45.6	1973	28,885,867	49.7	50.3	...	40.5	—53.4—		—6.0—		
Cambodia	181,035	7,735,000	42.7	1962	5,728,771	50.0	50.0	10.3	43.8	24.9	16.8	9.8	4.1	0.6
China	9,561,000	852,133,000	89.1	1953	574,205,940	51.8	48.2	13.3	35.9	25.1	18.8	12.9	6.3	1.0
Cyprus	9,251	639,000	69.1	1973	631,778	49.5	50.5	42.2	28.8	27.3	17.0	13.3	10.4	3.2
Hong Kong	1,050	4,420,000	4,209.5	1976	4,402,990	51.1	48.9	...	30.1	30.3	15.5	15.0	7.4	1.7
India	3,287,782	610,077,000	185.6	1971	547,949,809	51.8	48.2	19.9	41.9	24.1	17.8	10.2	4.9	1.1
Indonesia	1,919,494	136,044,000	70.9	1971	118,367,850	49.3	50.7	17.5	44.0	23.9	18.6	9.1	3.8	0.7
Iran	1,648,000	33,592,000	20.4	1976	33,591,875	...	...	...	...	...	...	...	...	...
Iraq	437,522	11,505,000	26.3	1965	8,047,415	51.0	49.0	44.1	47.9	21.0	15.3	8.7	4.9	2.2
Israel	20,700	3,465,000	167.4	1972	3,147,683	50.3	49.7	85.3	32.6	26.9	15.6	13.6	9.2	2.0
Japan	377,582	112,768,000	298.7	1975	111,939,643	49.7	50.3	75.9	24.3	24.9	23.1	15.9	9.2	2.5
Jordan	95,396	2,779,000	29.1	1961	1,706,226	50.9	49.1	43.9	45.4	26.1	13.7	7.5	5.1	1.8
Korea, North	121,200	16,246,000	134.0	—	—	—	—	—	—	—	—	—	—	—
Korea, South	98,799	35,860,000	363.0	1975	34,680,644	50.3	49.7	48.4	38.3	27.8	17.9	10.3	4.6	1.0

Table II. World Populations and Areas[1] (Continued)

Country	AREA AND POPULATION: MIDYEAR 1976 Area in sq km	Total population	Persons per sq km	POPULATION AT MOST RECENT CENSUS Date of census	Total population	% Male	% Female	% Urban	Age distribution (%)[2] 0–14	15–29	30–44	45–59	60–74	75+
Kuwait	16,918	1,031,000	60.9	1975	994,837	54.7	45.3	85.9	44.3	26.7	19.3	7.0	2.1	0.5
Laos	236,800	3,383,000	14.3	—	—	—	—	—	—	—	—	—	—	—
Lebanon	10,230	2,961,000	289.4	1970	2,126,325	50.8	49.2	60.1	42.6	23.8	16.7	9.1	—7.7—	
Macau	16	275,000	17,187.5	1970	248,636	51.4	48.6	100.0	37.6	28.9	15.0	11.3	5.9	1.1
Malaysia	329,747	12,300,000	37.3	1970	10,434,034[7]	50.4	49.6	26.1	44.9	25.5	15.2	9.2	—5.2—	
Maldives	298	132,000	443.0	1974	128,697	53.1	46.9		44.9	22.8	19.0	9.4	3.4	0.4
Mongolia	1,565,000	1,488,000	1.0	1969	1,197,600	49.9	50.1	44.0	...	...	...	...	...	...
Nepal	145,391	13,289,000	91.5	1971	11,555,983	49.7	50.3	13.8	40.5	25.5	18.7	9.7	—5.6—	
Oman	300,000	791,000	2.6	—	—	—	—	—	—	—	—	—	—	—
Pakistan	796,095	72,368,000	90.9	1972	64,892,000	53.0	47.0	25.5	...	...	...	...	...	...
Philippines	300,000	43,751,000	145.8	1975	41,831,045	...	...	...	...	...	...	...	...	...
Qatar	11,400	180,000	15.8	—	—	—	—	—	—	—	—	—	—	—
Saudi Arabia	2,240,000	7,188,000	3.2	1974	7,012,642	...	...	...	...	...	...	...	...	...
Singapore	602	2,278,000	3,784.4	1970	2,074,507	51.2	48.8	100.0	38.8	28.1	16.9	10.5	4.9	0.8
Sri Lanka	65,610	14,270,000	217.5	1971	12,689,897	51.3	48.7	22.4	39.3	27.8	15.9	10.5	5.2	1.3
Syria	185,180	7,595,000	41.0	1970	6,304,685	51.3	48.7	43.5	49.3	22.4	14.3	7.5	4.8	1.7
Taiwan	35,982	16,330,000	453.8	1975	16,206,183	51.8	48.2	...	36.7	29.8	16.4	11.7	4.6	0.8
Thailand	542,373	42,960,000	72.2	1970	34,397,374	49.6	50.4	13.4	45.5	24.9	16.1	8.6	—4.9—	
Turkey	779,452	40,198,000	51.6	1975	40,197,669	...	...	...	...	...	...	...	...	...
United Arab Emirates	83,600	670,000	8.0	1975	655,973	...	...	...	...	...	...	...	...	...
Vietnam	338,392	47,840,000	141.4	—	—	—	—	—	—	—	—	—	—	—
Yemen (Aden)	287,680	1,749,000	6.1	1973	1,590,275	49.5	50.5	33.3	47.3	20.8	15.8	8.6	—6.6—	
Yemen (San'a')	200,000	5,238,000	26.2	1975	5,237,893	47.6	52.4	8.2	46.7	—53.3—				
Total ASIA[8,9]	44,586,717	2,360,865,000	52.9											
EUROPE														
Albania	28,748	2,548,000	88.6	1960	1,626,315	51.4	48.6	30.9	42.7	—57.3—				
Andorra	464	29,000	62.5	1975	26,558	...	...	...	...	...	...	...	...	...
Austria	83,860	7,513,000	89.6	1971	7,456,403	47.0	53.0	51.9	24.4	20.5	18.3	16.5	15.5	4.8
Belgium	30,514	9,889,000	324.1	1970	9,650,944	48.9	51.1	...	23.5	21.0	19.4	17.1	14.4	4.6
Bulgaria	110,912	8,761,000	79.0	1975	8,729,720	49.9	50.1	58.0	...	...	...	...	...	...
Channel Islands	194	129,000	664.9	1971	126,363	48.5	51.5	...	21.8	21.4	18.4	18.1	14.9	5.3
Czechoslovakia	127,877	14,918,000	116.7	1970	14,344,987	48.7	51.3	55.5	23.1	24.8	18.4	16.7	13.6	3.4
Denmark	43,075	5,079,000	117.9	1970	4,937,579	49.6	50.4	79.9	23.2	23.8	17.7	17.8	13.4	4.1
Faeroe Islands	1,399	40,000	28.6	1970	38,612	52.2	47.8	...	31.8	23.0	16.5	16.0	9.4	3.3
Finland	337,032	4,727,000	14.0	1970	4,598,336	48.3	51.7	50.9	24.3	26.0	18.6	16.6	11.6	2.9
France	544,000	52,915,000	97.3	1975	52,599,430	48.9	51.1	70.0	22.6	24.4	17.8	16.2	13.3	5.6
Germany, East	108,328	16,786,000	155.0	1971	17,068,318	46.1	53.9	73.8	23.3	19.9	20.1	14.7	16.9	5.1
Germany, West	248,620	61,498,000	247.4	1970	60,650,599	47.6	52.4	...	23.2	21.3	19.7	16.6	15.0	4.2
Gibraltar	6	30,000	500.0	1970	26,833	48.1	51.9	91.9	22.9	22.7	21.1	18.7	11.2	3.4
Greece	131,990	9,165,000	69.4	1971	8,768,640	49.8	50.2	53.2	24.9	20.4	21.9	16.5	12.5	3.8
Hungary	93,032	10,596,000	113.9	1970	10,322,099	48.5	51.5	45.2	21.1	23.6	20.5	17.7	13.6	3.5
Iceland	103,000	220,000	2.1	1970	204,930	50.6	49.4	...	32.3	25.1	16.4	13.7	9.0	3.5
Ireland	70,283	3,162,000	44.9	1971	2,978,248	50.2	49.8	52.2	31.3	22.0	15.2	15.9	11.6	4.0
Isle of Man	572	62,000	108.4	1976	61,723	47.5	52.5	...	20.5	19.1	15.6	17.3	20.2	7.3
Italy	301,245	56,189,000	186.6	1971	54,136,547	48.9	51.1	...	24.4	21.2	20.7	17.0	12.8	3.9
Jan Mayen	373	—	—	1973	37	...	...	—	...	...	...	...	...	...
Liechtenstein	160	24,000	137.5	1970	21,350	49.7	50.3	...	27.9	27.1	18.6	14.5	9.3	2.6
Luxembourg	2,586	358,000	138.4	1970	339,841	49.0	51.0	68.4	22.1	20.5	21.4	17.5	14.6	3.9
Malta	316	322,000	1,019.0	1967	314,216	47.9	52.1	94.3	29.8	25.9	17.6	13.8	10.2	2.7
Monaco	1.89	25,000	13,227.5	1968	23,035	45.2	54.8	100.0	12.9	17.5	18.4	20.9	21.2	9.1
Netherlands, The	41,160	13,710,000	333.1	1971	13,045,785	50.0	50.0	...	...	...	...	...	...	...
Norway	323,886	4,027,000	12.4	1970	3,874,133	49.7	50.3	42.4	24.4	22.5	16.0	18.8	13.5	4.8
Poland	312,677	34,362,000	103.1	1970	32,642,270	48.6	51.4	52.3	26.4	25.5	20.4	14.6	10.6	2.5
Portugal	91,632	9,694,100	105.8	1970	8,663,252	47.4	52.6	...	28.4	21.9	19.0	16.2	11.2	3.3
Romania	237,500	21,446,000	90.3	1966	19,103,163	48.9	51.1	38.2	26.3	23.1	23.3	15.3	9.9	2.1
San Marino	61	20,000	327.9	1947	12,100	49.3	50.7	...	28.4	—71.6—				
Spain	504,750	35,971,000	71.3	1970	33,956,376	48.9	51.1	54.7	27.8	22.0	19.9	16.1	10.8	3.4
Svalbard	62,050	—	—	1974	3,472	...	...	—	...	...	...	...	...	...
Sweden	449,964	8,222,000	18.3	1975	8,208,442	49.7	50.3	82.7	20.7	21.3	18.8	18.1	15.4	5.7
Switzerland	41,293	6,346,000	153.7	1970	6,269,783	49.0	51.0	52.0	23.4	23.7	20.2	16.3	12.5	3.9
United Kingdom	244,035	55,928,000	229.2	1971	55,515,602	48.5	51.5	...	24.1	21.0	17.6	18.3	14.3	4.7
Vatican City	.44	1,000	2,272.7	—	—	—	—	—	—	—	—	—	—	—
Yugoslavia	255,804	21,560,000	84.3	1971	20,522,972	49.1	50.9	38.6	27.2	24.6	22.7	13.5	9.8	2.2
Total EUROPE[9]	10,504,464	668,572,000	63.6											
NORTH AMERICA														
Anguilla	91	7,000	76.9	1960	5,810	44.5	55.5	...	45.7	18.8	11.8	12.9	7.3	3.5
Antigua	440	71,000	161.4	1970	64,794	47.2	52.8	33.7	44.0	24.2	12.0	11.7	—8.0—	
Bahamas, The	13,864	211,000	15.2	1970	168,812	50.0	50.0	71.4	43.6	24.3	16.8	9.8	4.4	1.1
Barbados	430	247,000	574.4	1970	235,229	48.0	52.0	3.7	35.9	27.2	12.9	12.8	8.7	2.5
Belize	22,965	144,000	6.3	1970	119,934	50.6	49.4	54.4	49.3	22.5	13.0	8.7	5.0	1.5
Bermuda	46	57,000	1,239.1	1970	52,976	50.2	49.8	6.9	30.0	25.8	20.5	14.4	7.7	2.0
British Virgin Islands	153	12,000	78.4	1970	10,298	53.0	47.0	21.9	39.2	29.1	14.7	10.0	5.1	1.9
Canada	9,976,139	23,143,000	2.3	1976	22,992,604	...	...	...	...	...	...	...	...	...
Canal Zone	1,432	44,000	30.7	1970	44,198	53.9	46.1	5.8	31.8	31.3	19.8	14.1	2.2	0.8
Cayman Islands	288	14,000	48.6	1970	10,249	46.8	53.2	61.1	37.1	21.7	16.0	11.1	7.4	2.9
Costa Rica	50,898	2,012,000	39.5	1973	1,871,780	50.1	49.9	40.6	43.3	27.0	14.2	8.4	4.4	2.7
Cuba	110,922	9,405,000	84.8	1970	8,569,121	51.3	48.7	60.3	27.0	25.0	16.9	12.1	6.8	2.2
Dominica	772	76,000	98.4	1970	70,302	47.4	52.6	46.2	49.1	21.2	11.2	10.0	6.3	2.2
Dominican Republic	48,442	4,835,000	99.8	1970	4,006,405	49.4	50.6	40.0	47.2	24.8	15.2	7.8	3.8	1.2
El Salvador	21,041	4,123,000	196.0	1971	3,541,010	49.6	50.4	39.4	46.2	25.1	15.2	8.2	4.3	1.0
Greenland	2,175,600	50,000	0.02	1970	46,531	52.5	47.5	...	43.4	24.8	18.8	8.5	3.9	0.6
Grenada	344	106,000	308.1	1970	96,542	46.2	53.8	...	47.1	23.0	11.6	9.4	6.6	2.2
Guadeloupe	1,705	360,000	211.1	1974	324,500	...	...	41.9	41.2	22.8	14.3	10.4	5.3	1.7
Guatemala	108,889	6,451,000	59.2	1973	5,211,929	50.0	50.0	33.6	45.1	26.7	15.1	8.3	—4.8—	
Haiti	27,700	4,668,000	168.5	1971	4,314,628	48.2	51.8	20.4	41.5	25.8	16.5	9.5	5.0	1.7

Table II. World Populations and Areas[1] (Continued)

Country	AREA AND POPULATION: MIDYEAR 1976			POPULATION AT MOST RECENT CENSUS						Age distribution (%)[2]					
	Area in sq km	Total population	Persons per sq km	Date of census	Total population	% Male	% Female	% Urban	0–14	15–29	30–44	45–59	60–74	75+
Honduras	112,088	2,831,000	25.3	1974	2,653,857	49.5	50.5	37.5	48.1	25.8	13.9	7.8	3.6	0.9
Jamaica	10,991	2,057,000	187.1	1970	1,813,594	49.8	50.2	41.4	37.5	25.1	15.2	12.4	7.5	2.3
Martinique	1,079	369,000	335.5	1974	324,800	...	...	...	39.5	25.0	14.2	11.8	7.3	2.2
Mexico	1,972,546	62,329,000	31.6	1970	48,225,238	49.9	50.1	58.7	46.2	25.6	14.6	8.0	4.4	1.2
Montserrat	102	13,000	127.5	1970	11,458	46.9	53.1	31.7	37.9	20.6	9.8	12.1	10.7	8.9
Netherlands Antilles	993	241,000	242.7	1972	223,196	48.8	51.2	...	38.0	26.7	167.3	10.3	6.4	1.8
Nicaragua	128,875	2,233,000	17.3	1971	1,877,972	48.3	51.7	48.0	48.1			51.9		
Panama	75,650	1,719,000	22.7	1970	1,428,082	50.7	49.3	47.6	43.4	26.1	15.2	9.6	4.3	1.4
Puerto Rico	8,897	3,213,000	361.1	1970	2,712,033	49.0	51.0	58.1	36.5	26.1	15.9	11.9	7.1	2.5
St. Christopher-Nevis (-Anguilla)[10]	269	47,000		1970	44,884	46.9	53.1	31.7	48.4	18.9	9.5	12.1	8.7	2.4
St. Lucia	623	110,000	176.6	1970	99,806	47.2	52.8	36.9	49.6	21.3	11.6	9.8	5.5	2.2
St. Pierre & Miquelon	242	6,000	24.8	1974	5,840	49.4	50.6	...	33.8	24.7	18.0	12.9	10.5	
St. Vincent	389	94,000	241.6	1970	89,129	47.4	52.6	...	51.2	21.7	11.0	8.8	7.2	
Trinidad and Tobago	5,128	1,149,000	224.0	1970	931,071	49.4	50.6	...	42.1	40.4			17.5	
Turks and Caicos Islands	500	6,000	12.0	1970	5,558	47.4	52.6	—	47.1	20.4	12.0	11.1	7.0	2.5
United States	9,363,123	215,118,000	23.0	1970	203,211,926	48.7	51.3	73.5	28.6	24.0	17.0	16.3	10.4	3.7
Virgin Islands (U.S.)	345	96,000	279.1	1970	62,468	49.9	50.1	24.4	35.7	28.3	19.4	10.8	4.4	1.4
Total NORTH AMERICA	24,244,001	347,667,000	14.3											
OCEANIA														
American Samoa	197	31,000	157.4	1974	29,200	...	...	...	...	...	...	...	...	...
Australia	7,682,300	13,916,000	1.8	1976	13,915,500	50.0	50.0	86.0	27.2	25.5	18.3	15.7	9.8	3.2
Canton and Enderbury Islands	70	—	—	1970	0	—	—	—						
Christmas Island	135	3,000	22.2	1971	2,691	64.4	35.6	0	30.8	34.6	22.0	10.8	1.4	0.4
Cocos Islands	14	1,000	71.4	1971	618	49.0	51.0	0	27.3	38.6	21.8	8.9	3.3	0.2
Cook Islands	241	18,000	74.7	1976	18,112	51.3	48.7	...	...	...	...	...	...	...
Fiji	18,272	580,000	31.7	1976	588,068	)			...	...	...	...	...	...
French Polynesia	3,265	132,000	40.4	1971	117,664	53.1	46.9	19.0	45.5	23.7	16.6	9.0	3.7	1.5
Gilbert Islands	272	53,000	194.8	1973	51,926	49.3	50.7	...	44.1	24.8	15.3	9.7	5.1	1.1
Guam	549	102,000	185.8	1970	84,996	55.7	44.3	25.5	39.7	29.1	19.3	8.9	2.5	0.5
Johnston Island	3	1,000	333.3	1970	1,007	...	...	0	...	...	...	...	...	...
Midway Islands	5	2,000	400.0	1970	2,220	...	...	0	...	...	...	...	...	...
Nauru	21	8,000	381.0	1966	6,055	53.3	46.7	0	40.0	24.7	23.9	9.2	2.1	0.1
New Caledonia	19,079	133,000	8.0	1976	133,233	52.0	48.0	38.6	26.3	18.6	10.4	4.9	1.1	...
New Hebrides	11,870	97,000	8.2	1967	77,988	52.1	47.9	12.0	45.6	26.0	15.5	8.5	4.4	
New Zealand	268,704	3,095,000	11.5	1976	3,129,383				46.2	23.8	13.6	7.9	5.8	2.6
Niue Island	259	4,000	15.4	1976	3,843	50.1	49.9	0	25.2	20.7	19.7	18.9	12.5	2.9
Norfolk Island	35	2,000	57.1	1971	1,683	49.0	51.0	0	46.2	25.8	12.7	9.1	5.9	
Pacific Islands, Trust Territory of the	1,880	123,000	65.2	1973	114,973	51.7	48.3	...	45.2	24.5	17.4	9.9	1.4	1.6
Papua New Guinea	462,840	2,829,000	6.1	1973	2,489,935	52.0	48.0	11.1						
Pitcairn Island	4	74	18.5	1976	74	...	...	0	...	...	...	...	...	...
Solomon Islands	28,446	200,000	7.0	1976	196,823	52.2	47.8	...	47.8	24.1	14.5	8.4	3.6	1.3
Tokelau	10	2,000	200.0	1974	1,574	46.1	53.9	...	48.2	18.3	14.3	9.4	9.6	
Tonga	748	90,000	120.3	1976	90,128	51.1	48.9	...	...	...	...	...	...	...
Tuvalu	26	6,000	230.8	1973	5,887	46.3	53.7	...	40.8	23.3	14.5	13.4	6.4	1.6
Wake Island	8	2,000	250.0	1970	1,647	...	...	...	95.7				4.2	
Wallis and Futuna	255	9,000	35.4	1969	8,546	48.9	51.1	...	...	...	...	...	...	...
Western Samoa	2,784	151,000	54.2	1976	151,515	...	...	21.2	...	...	...	...	...	...
Total OCEANIA	8,502,242	21,590,000	2.5											
SOUTH AMERICA														
Argentina	2,776,900	25,719,000	9.3	1970	23,390,050	49.7	50.3	80.4	29.3	24.6	19.9	15.4	8.6	2.2
Bolivia	1,098,581	4,688,000	4.3	1976	4,687,718				42.2	26.7	16.3	9.4	5.1	
Brazil	8,512,000	109,181,000	12.9	1970	93,139,037	49.7	50.3	55.9	39.0	25.5	16.6	10.4	5.6	2.9
Chile	756,626	10,454,000	13.8	1970	8,884,768	48.8	51.2	75.1	44.1	27.3	14.9	8.5	4.1	1.0
Colombia	1,138,914	24,372,000	21.4	1973	20,575,657	48.6	51.4	63.6						
Ecuador	281,334	7,305,000	26.0	1974	6,521,710	50.1	49.9	41.3	44.6	26.5	14.7	8.4	4.6	1.3
Falkland Islands	16,265	2,000	0.1	1972	1,957	55.2	44.8	44.7	26.7	22.4	51.9			
French Guiana	90,000	62,000	0.7	1974	55,125	...	...	...	...	...	...	...	...	...
Guyana	215,000	783,000	3.6	1970	699,848	49.7	50.3	33.3	47.1	25.1	13.4	9.0	4.4	1.0
Paraguay	406,752	2,724,000	6.7	1972	2,357,955	49.6	50.4	37.4	44.9	25.4	14.5	9.2	4.5	1.5
Peru	1,285,216	16,090,000	12.5	1972	13,538,208	50.0	50.0	59.6	43.9	25.8	15.6	8.7	5.9	
Surinam	181,455	435,000	2.4	1971	384,903	50.0	50.0	...	48.0	52.0				
Uruguay	176,215	3,101,000	17.6	1975	2,763,964	49.1	50.9	...	...	...	...	...	...	...
Venezuela	899,180	12,361,000	13.7	1971	10,721,522	50.0	50.0	75.0	35.1	31.7	17.5	10.0	4.4	1.3
Total SOUTH AMERICA	17,834,438	217,277,000	12.2											
U.S.S.R.[9]	22,402,100	256,700,000	11.5	1970	241,720,134	46.0	54.0	56.3	30.9	19.9	23.5	13.8	11.8	
in Asia[9]	16,831,038	64,400,000	3.8											
in Europe[9]	5,571,064	192,300,000	34.5											
TOTAL WORLD[11]	150,091,095	4,043,902,500	29.8											

[1] Any presentation of population data must include data of varying reliability. This table provides published and unpublished data about the latest census (or comparable demographic survey) and the most recent or reliable midyear 1976 population estimates for the countries of the world. Census figures are only a body of estimates and samples of varying reliability whose quality depends on the completeness of the enumeration. Some countries tabulate only persons actually present, while others include those legally resident, but actually outside the country, on census day. Population estimates are subject to continual correction and revision; their reliability depends on: number of years elapsed since a census control was established, completeness of birth and death registration, international migration data, etc.
[2] Data for persons of unknown age excluded, so percentages may not add to 100.0.
[3] Excludes Mayotte, shown separately.

[4] Transkei received its independence from South Africa on Oct 26, 1976; Bophuthatswana received its independence from South Africa on Dec. 6, 1977. Both are Bantu homeland states whose independence is not internationally recognized.
[5] Sudan census excludes three southern autonomous provinces.
[6] May reach a total of 2,000 persons of all nationalities during the summer.
[7] West Malaysia only.
[8] Includes 7,000 sq mi of Iraq-Saudi Arabia neutral zone.
[9] Asia and Europe continent totals include corresponding portions of U.S.S.R.
[10] Excludes Anguilla, shown separately.
[11] Area of Antarctica excluded in calculating world density.

continued from page 294

and over. All the age-specific death rates for both sexes were lower in 1976 than in 1975 except for the age groups 1–4 years and 85 years and over, which increased by 2.1 and 3%, respectively. Detailed final data for 1975 indicated that there was a drop in all rates by sex and colour from 1974. As in the two previous years, the 1975 age-adjusted death rate for the male population was 1.8 times that for the female population and the rate for persons other than white was 1.4 times the rate for the white group.

The ten leading causes of death in the U.S. in 1976, shown below, accounted for 83.6% of all deaths in that year. The provisional death rates for 1976 showed a decline from 1975 for all causes except diseases of the heart, malignant neoplasms, and influenza and pneumonia.

Cause of death	Estimated rate per 100,000 population
Diseases of the heart	338.6
Malignant neoplasms	174.6
Cerebrovascular diseases	88.1
Accidents	46.8
Influenza and pneumonia	29.3
Diabetes mellitus	16.3
Cirrhosis of the liver	14.5
Arteriosclerosis	13.4
Suicide	11.7
Certain diseases of early infancy	11.6

For the period 1965–75 the UN estimated the world death rate at 13 per 1,000 population. Regional death rates ranged from 8 for the U.S.S.R. to 20 for Africa. Data for 1976 indicated that the range of rates within regions was quite extensive; for Asia the estimated death rates ranged from about 7 to 30 per 1,000 population. Data were incomplete for most of the less developed world.

Expectation of Life. The expectation of life at birth, according to provisional statistics, was 72.8 years for the total population of the U.S. In the ten-year period 1967–76, life expectancy increased by 2.3 years. Final 1975 data by sex and colour showed that life expectancy values rose for all segments of the population as compared with 1974. Life expectancy at birth for males was 68.7 years and for females, 76.5 years. It was 73.2 years for white persons and 67.9 years for all others. The highest lifetime estimate for males was reported for Sweden (72.1 years, averaged over 1970–74), followed by Norway, The Netherlands, Japan, and Denmark, while the highest for women was reported for Norway (77.6 years in 1972–73), followed by Sweden, The Netherlands, France, and Canada.

Recent regional estimates of life expectancy were: Africa 45, Asia 56, northern America 71, Latin America 62, Europe 71, U.S.S.R. 70, and Oceania 65.

Infant and Maternal Mortality. In the U.S. in 1976 there were an estimated 47,800 deaths of infants under one year of age. The infant mortality rate was 15.1 per 1,000 live births, representing a decline of 6% from the final rate of 1975. The rates for white and nonwhite infants dropped to 13.5 and 27, respectively. Both the neonatal (under 28 days) and the postneonatal (28 days to 11 months) rates fell in 1976, and the overall decline continued

through the first half of 1977. The provisional rate for the 12-month period ended July 1977 was 14.5, compared with 15.5 in the same period of 1976.

The low infant mortality rate narrowed the gap between the U.S. and other countries with traditionally lower rates. In 1976 the rate was 8.7 for Sweden, 10.3 for Denmark, and 10.5 for Finland, The Netherlands, and Switzerland. For Japan in 1976 it was 9.3. There had been a general decline in infant mortality in developed countries, but reliable data for the less developed countries were sparse. Data from a few countries where reasonable measures exist indicated that rates in less developed countries were at relatively high levels, as in Chile (55.6), Guatemala (75.4), and Liberia (159.2).

There were an estimated 460 deaths of mothers due to complications of pregnancy, childbirth, and the period immediately following childbirth

Table III. Life Expectancy at Birth, in Years, for Selected Countries

Country	Period	Male	Female
Africa			
Burundi	1975[1]	41.4	44.6
Egypt	1966	48.5	51.2
Liberia	1971	45.8	44.0
Madagascar	1966	37.5	38.3
Nigeria	1965–66	37.2	36.7
Upper Volta	1975[1]	37.5	40.6
Asia			
Hong Kong	1976[1]	68.0	75.5
India	1971–76[1]	51.3	49.6
Indonesia	1975[1]	48.7	51.3
Israel[2]	1975	70.3	73.8
Japan	1976	72.2	77.4
Korea, South	1975	66.0	70.0
Pakistan	1975[1]	52.4	52.1
Taiwan	1975	68.4	73.3
Thailand	1964–67	53.9	58.6
Europe			
Albania	1969–70	66.5	69.0
Austria	1974	67.4	74.7
Belgium	1968–72	67.8	74.2
Bulgaria	1969–71	68.6	73.9
Czechoslovakia	1975	66.9	73.7
Denmark	1973–74	70.8	76.6
Finland	1974	66.9	75.4
France	1973	68.9	76.5
Germany, East	1974	68.9	74.4
Germany, West	1973–75	68.0	74.5
Greece	1970	70.1	73.6
Hungary	1974	66.5	72.4
Iceland	1966–70	70.7	76.3
Ireland	1965–67	68.6	72.8
Italy	1970–72	69.0	74.9
Netherlands, The	1974	71.6	77.6
Norway	1973–74	71.5	77.8
Poland	1975	67.1	74.3
Portugal	1974	65.3	72.0
Romania	1973–75	67.3	71.8
Spain	1970	69.7	75.0
Sweden	1971–75	72.1	77.6
Switzerland	1968–73	70.3	76.2
United Kingdom	1971–73	68.8	75.1
Yugoslavia	1970–72	65.4	70.2
North America			
Barbados	1975[1]	68.0	73.0
Canada	1970–72	69.3	76.4
Costa Rica	1973	66.0	69.0
Guatemala	1973	61.7	63.2
Mexico	1965–70	61.0	63.7
Panama	1970	64.3	67.5
Puerto Rico	1971–73	68.9	76.0
United States	1975	68.7	76.5
Oceania			
Australia	1970–72	67.8	74.5
New Zealand	1970–72	68.6	74.6
South America			
Argentina	1976	65.2	71.4
Brazil	1960–70	57.6	61.1
Chile	1969–70	60.5	66.0
Peru	1960–65	52.6	55.5
Surinam	1963	62.5	66.7
Uruguay	1963–64	65.5	71.6
Venezuela	1975[1]	64.6	68.3
U.S.S.R.	1971–72	64.0	74.0

[1] Projection.
[2] Jewish population only.
Sources: United Nations, *Demographic Yearbook* (1975); *Statistical Yearbook* (1976); official country sources.

in the U.S. in 1976. The provisional maternal mortality rate was 14.5 deaths per 1,000 live births, an increase over 1975 but consistent with the trend prevailing prior to that year. Maternal mortality continued to be a severe public health problem in many parts of the world. Conservative estimates placed the number of deaths directly related to maternal causes in excess of 50,000 per year.

Marriage and Divorce Statistics. A 15-year rise in the number of marriages in the U.S. ended in 1973, and the decline continued through 1976. There were an estimated 2,133,000 marriages in 1976, a decrease of 0.9% from the final 1975 total of 2,152,662. The provisional marriage rate was 9.9 marriages per 1,000 population, 2% lower than the final rate for 1975. Provisional data for the first half of 1977 indicated a slight increase in number and rate over the first six months of 1976; the marriage rate for the 12-month period ended July 1977 was 10.1, compared with 10 in 1976. The median age at marriage, after remaining relatively constant from the mid-'60s to 1974, increased for both brides and grooms in 1975, to 20.8 years and 22.7 years, respectively. The median age at remarriage continued its downward trend; it was 32 years for brides and 35.5 for grooms. The proportion of marriages that were first marriages was also declining. In 1968 about 77% of brides and grooms were previously single; by 1975 this had fallen to 70% for brides and 68% for grooms.

Reliable data on marriages were available from only a few countries, and national variations in statistical definitions and social customs make it difficult to compare rates, even in countries with almost complete coverage. Abnormally low marriage rates for parts of Latin America and Africa result from the high incidence of consensual unions. The low rate for the Dominican Republic in 1975, 4.1 marriages per 1,000 population, has a different meaning from the lowest European rate of the same year, that of Sweden at 5.3, because of varying social circumstances.

Numbers and rates of divorce in the U.S. had increased annually after 1962. According to provisional statistics, there were an estimated 1,077,000 divorces in 1976, representing a 3.8% increase over the final figure of 1,036,000 in 1975. The divorce rate was 5 per 1,000 population, the highest on record. Provisional data for the first half of 1977 indicated that the number of divorces rose, but the rate of divorce was the same as for 1976.

A more specific divorce measure, the rate per 1,000 married women, was available for 1975. This rate, at 20.3, was a record high. For the third consecutive year the rates exceeded the previous high point of 17.9 established in 1946. The median duration of marriage prior to divorce or annulment was 6.5 years, the same as in 1974. There were an estimated 1,123,000 children involved in these actions. International variations in the meaning of the term divorce and other limitations make it virtually impossible to compare rates among countries. Relatively high rates were recorded for some countries in Europe and for the U.S.S.R., but for the most part they were less than half the U.S. rate.

(ANDERS S. LUNDE)

[338.F.5.b; 525.A:10/36.C.5.d]

Denmark

Denmark

A constitutional monarchy of north central Europe lying between the North and Baltic seas, Denmark includes the Jutland Peninsula and 100 inhabited islands in the Kattegat and Skagerrak straits. Area (excluding Faeroe Islands and Greenland): 43,075 sq km (16,631 sq mi). Pop. (1976 est.): 5,079,000. Cap. and largest city: Copenhagen (pop., 1976 est., 709,300). Language: Danish. Religion: predominantly Lutheran. Queen, Margrethe II; prime minister in 1977, Anker Jørgensen.

A general election on Feb. 15, 1977, left Anker Jørgensen's minority Social Democrat government in power, with a total of 65 seats out of 179 in the Folketing (parliament; 53 in the 1975 election). The Liberal Democrat (Venstre) representation fell catastrophically, from 42 to 21, as did that of the Radical Liberals (Radikale Venstre), from 13 to 6. Mogens Glistrup's Progress Party won 26 seats (24 previously) to become the second largest of the 11 parties in the Folketing. There were only minor changes among the more extreme left-wing parties. A new party, inspired by the theories of the 19th-century U.S. land reformer and economist Henry George, the Retsforbund (Justice Party), won six seats. Party divisions were too great to permit formation of a coalition government, and the Social Democrat administration continued, receiving endorsement from the Folketing on a day-to-day basis.

The Danes continued to be worried by their country's balance of payments position, by the numbers still out of work, and by the constant threat of inflation. The balance of payments had been in deficit every year from 1960 onward, under a succession of precarious governments. At the beginning of the year, Denmark's balance of payments deficit amounted to 11.5 billion kroner, while unemployment stood at 150,000. Foreign indebtedness by the end of the year had risen, by 10 billion kroner, to 50 billion kroner. The krone was devalued twice in 1977, in April by 3%, influenced by Sweden's 6% devaluation, and in August by 5% for a similar reason; Denmark,

Prime Minister Anker Jørgensen applauds as election results showed his governing party, the Social Democrats, gained 12 seats in Parliament in the February general election.

Denmark

A British helicopter hovers overhead while a boarding party from the British frigate "Plymouth" (background) approaches a Danish trawler in the North Sea to check on the fish catch. The British were strictly enforcing their ban on herring fishing.

however, remained in the "snake" of certain European currencies.

None of the so-called bourgeois parties could attempt a renegotiation of the unpopular labour-

DENMARK

Education. (1974–75) Primary, pupils 559,745; secondary, pupils 223,134; primary and secondary, teachers 58,-405; vocational, pupils 89,169, teachers (1973–74) c. 4,200; higher (including 5 main universities), students 112,457, teaching staff 7,865.

Finance. Monetary unit: Danish krone, with (Sept. 19, 1977) a free rate of 6.18 kroner to U.S. $1 (10.76 kroner = £1 sterling). Gold, SDR's, and foreign exchange (June 1977) U.S. $2,009,600,000. Budget (1975–76 est.): revenue 62,055,000,000 kroner; expenditure 64,710,000,000 kroner. Gross national product (1975) 201,780,000,000 kroner. Money supply (April 1977) 52,930,000,000 kroner. Cost of living (1970 = 100; June 1977) 187.

Foreign Trade. (1976) Imports 75,011,000,000 kroner; exports 55,034,000,000 kroner. Import sources: EEC 47% (West Germany 21%, U.K. 10%, The Netherlands 5%); Sweden 14%; U.S. 5%; Norway 5%. Export destinations: EEC 45% (U.K. 17%, West Germany 14%, Italy 5%); Sweden 16%; Norway 7%; U.S. 6%. Main exports: machinery 21%; meat 14%; chemicals 7%; dairy products 6%; ships and boats 5%.

Transport and Communications. Roads (1975) 66,137 km (including 367 km expressways). Motor vehicles in use (1975): passenger 1,297,000; commercial 225,000. Railways: (1975) state 1,999 km, private 494 km; traffic (state only; 1975–76) 3,250,000,000 passenger-km, freight 1,860,000,000 net ton-km. Air traffic (including apportionment of international operations of Scandinavian Airlines System; 1976): 2,413,000,000 passenger-km; freight 111,-107,000 net ton-km. Shipping (1976): merchant vessels 100 gross tons and over 1,413; gross tonnage 5,143,022. Shipping traffic (1975): goods loaded 7,540,000 metric tons, unloaded 29,650,000 metric tons. Telephones (including Faeroe Islands and Greenland; Jan. 1976) 2,316,-000. Radio receivers (Dec. 1975) 1,693,000. Television licenses (Dec. 1975) 1,556,000.

Agriculture. Production (in 000; metric tons; 1976): wheat 578; barley 4,767; oats 267; rye c. 236; potatoes c. 630; sugar, raw value c. 440; apples c. 111; rapeseed 90; butter c. 139; cheese 157; pork c. 727; beef and veal c. 233; fish catch (1975) 1,767. Livestock (in 000; July 1976): cattle c. 2,060; pigs c. 7,585; sheep c. 59; horses (1975) 56; chickens c. 15,417.

Industry. Production (in 000; metric tons; 1976): crude steel 722; cement 2,355; fertilizers (nutrient content; 1975-76) nitrogenous 80, phosphate 78; manufactured gas (cu m) 330,000; electricity (net; excluding most industrial production; kw-hr) 19,248,000. Merchant vessels launched (100 gross tons and over; 1976) 1,034,000 gross tons.

market and incomes-policy agreements, and a proposed settlement by an official arbitrator was made law; this gave the Folketing breathing space to seek fresh compromise solutions. The "four old parties" (Social Democrats, Liberals, Conservatives, and Radical Liberals) agreed, after hard bargaining among themselves, on a second "August compromise," on the 1976 model, whereby a series of traditional taxes were increased—*e.g.*, on gasoline, oil, and cigarettes—and the value-added tax was raised from 15 to 18% as of the beginning of October. The taxes were aimed at controlling consumption and thus improving Denmark's balance of payments position. The sum of 10 billion kroner was to be invested in an employment scheme, with an increase in public-sector employment to improve such services as, for example, police, old-age care, and road building.

Publication of the newspaper *Berlingske Tidende* was stopped by a strike on January 31 that did not end until June 21. In the latter part of the year new and more optimistic forecasts suggested that North Sea oil might cover 25% of Denmark's consumption (currently 15 million tons a year), though a dispute between the government and the holder of the Danish concession might delay developments.

Disagreements with neighbouring countries over fisheries policy and fishing rights were a cause of anxiety and aggravation in the Danish fishing industry, a major sector of the economy employing some 15,000 fishermen with 10,000 craft, most of them small. Greenland and the Faeroe Islands were directly dependent on fishing. Among other issues, Denmark was concerned over Sweden's extension of its territorial fishing zone to the middle of the Baltic Sea and Great Britain's proposal, made at the end of 1976, to ban herring fishing for the time being. (The EEC had already agreed to a ban until the end of September.) A ban on herring fishing would shut down ten processing plants in north Jutland; the Danish Fisheries Ministry agreed that herring stocks should be built up but maintained that a complete ban must be avoided. (STENER AARSDAL)

See also Dependent States.

Dentistry:
see Health and Disease

Dependent States

In 1977 one dependent state, Djibouti, in the Horn of Africa, achieved independence with international recognition. It had formerly been the French Territory of the Afars and Issas (*see* DJIBOUTI).

Europe and the Atlantic. In the North Atlantic an economic zone was extended for 200 mi from the coasts of the French islands of Saint Pierre and Miquelon by a decree of Feb. 27, 1977, but little progress was made in France toward the islands' becoming an overseas *département*. Also in the Western Hemisphere, Great Britain was concerned with the Falkland Islands and Belize (*see Caribbean* below). The visit by Edward Rowlands, the British minister of state at the Foreign and Commonwealth Office, to the Falkland Islands and Argentina in February 1977 aroused fear among the islanders that the U.K. planned to hand the islands over to Argentina, and Rowlands' statement that he had their agreement to a future discussion of sovereignty was denied by them. Argentine businessmen were reported to have offered to purchase the Falkland Islands Co., which controlled the territory economically. The British government, moreover, refused to extend the airstrip to take long-distance planes and free the islands from air dependence on Argentine airports. High-level negotiations between the U.K. and Argentina on the future of the Falklands opened in New York City in mid-December. The islands' economic potential was linked with the exploitation of Antarctic resources.

In the Azores an independence party, the Front for the Liberation of the Azores, waged a campaign of demonstrations and violence against the Portuguese government for having granted only regional autonomy in 1976. A similar movement was exerting pressure in Madeira.

In Europe, oil, as well as Scottish home rule, was responsible for demands by the British Shetland Islands and Orkney Islands for self-government. The Shetland Council (to report in March 1978) appeared to favour evolution on the model of the Danish Faeroe Islands as a self-governing state under the crown. Denmark's other territory, Greenland, established an independence commission, due to report in February 1978 for proposed independence in May 1979, with control of oil resources as the only disputed issue. These island communities, together with Norway's Svalbard (Spitsbergen), possessed strategic value for the North Atlantic Treaty Organization (the U.S. had five tracking bases on Greenland). Norway set up a department to administer Svalbard after discovering uranium there and demarcating an exclusive fishing zone, disputed by the U.S.S.R., in 1977.

Caribbean. St. Lucia and Dominica pressed their demands for independence during the year. Representatives of Prime Minister John Compton's government in St. Lucia, along with members of the opposition St. Lucia Labour Party, went to London in October 1977 to try again to fix a date. Bananas provided 80% of St. Lucia's export earnings, and the pegging of the East Caribbean dollar to the U.S. dollar in July 1976 had caused losses in earnings. An industrialization program was being pursued. Dominica also looked toward independence in 1978 with Prime Minister Patrick John outlining a policy of moderate socialism. Guyana and Jamaica were providing economic and technical assistance to diversify the banana-based economy. Dominica's black power movement was relatively quiescent.

Similar Cuban initiatives were reported in St. Vincent, which was not moving so urgently toward independence and where a national bank was set up in June 1977 and an $11 million flour mill was to start operating in late 1977 with Canadian participation. In Antigua, the only associated state in the Caribbean resisting full independence, Prime Minister Vere Bird's government gave priority to the strengthening of regional links. Chief Minister Austin Bramble of Montserrat was also concerned less with independence than with getting a better deal from the Caribbean Community and Common Market. Antigua and Montserrat received loans from the Caribbean Investment Corp. fund of risk capital for industrial development. Antigua's agriculture was adversely

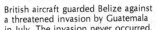
British aircraft guarded Belize against a threatened invasion by Guatemala in July. The invasion never occurred.

The Statue of Liberty briefly wore a Puerto Rican flag on her brow when Puerto Rican terrorists seized the statue for nine hours in October.

affected by drought, and unemployment was reported up to 49%. Prime Minister Robert Bradshaw of St. Kitts-Nevis demanded independence, despite the ten-year de facto secession of Anguilla and the continued support for separatism on Nevis. In Anguilla itself, Chief Minister Ronald Webster was defeated on a no-confidence vote and was replaced by Emile Gumbs, a former sea captain. A British frigate went to the island after disturbances by Webster supporters during the swearing-in of Gumbs.

Among the smaller dependencies, the British Virgin Islands sent a delegation to London in early 1977 to plead for additional aid. Some was received, but it was regarded as inadequate. In the Turks and Caicos the general election of September 1976 was won by "Jags" McCartney's People's Democratic Party, dubbed "black power boys" by the former government. In 1976 there had been street violence and a doubling of the police force.

The U.S. Virgin Islands reached agreement with the U.S. government on a draft constitution granting control over local affairs. Puerto Rican secessionist terrorists disrupted life in the U.S. from

time to time; in August they planted bombs in two New York City office buildings and, with telephone threats of other bombs, caused more than 100,000 workers to leave buildings in the city. Carlos Romero Barceló (*see* BIOGRAPHY) of the pro-statehood New Progressive Party was inaugurated as the fifth elected governor of Puerto Rico.

In Belize independence demands and the Guatemala border dispute continued. Mexico, Cuba, and Panama favoured the territory's independence. Guatemala feared Cuban interference, claimed a corridor to the Caribbean, and was reportedly interested in possible oil deposits there. After troop movements in July, Britain and Guatemala agreed to negotiate a settlement.

There was movement toward independence in Bermuda, but a Green Paper put before the British Parliament in July pointed out that independence could damage tourism and international finance. A power struggle in the ruling United Bermuda Party ended with Prime Minister Sir John Sharpe's resignation in August and his replacement by John David Gibbons, a millionaire businessman. The

continued on page 307

ANTARCTIC

Claims on the continent of Antarctica and all islands south of 60° S remain in status quo according to the Antarctic Treaty, to which 19 nations are signatory. Formal claims within the treaty area include the following: Australian Antarctic Territory, the mainland portion of French Southern and Antarctic Lands (Terre Adélie), Ross Dependency claimed by New Zealand, Queen Maud Land and Peter I Island claimed by Norway, and British Antarctic Territory, of which some parts are claimed by Argentina and Chile. No claims have been recognized as final under international law.

AUSTRALIA

CHRISTMAS ISLAND

Christmas Island, an external territory, is situated in the Indian Ocean 1,410 km NW of Australia. Area: 135 sq km (52 sq mi). Pop. (1977 est.): 3,-300. Cap.: The Settlement (pop., 1971, 1,300).

COCOS (KEELING) ISLANDS

Cocos (Keeling) Islands is an external territory located in the Indian Ocean 3,685 km W of Darwin, Australia. Area: 14 sq km (5.5 sq mi). Pop. (1977 est.): 447.

NORFOLK ISLAND

Norfolk Island, an external territory, is located in the Pacific Ocean 1,720 km NE of Sydney, Australia. Area 35 sq km (13 sq mi). Pop. (1977 est.): 1,600. Cap. (de facto): Kingston.

DENMARK

FAEROE ISLANDS

The Faeroes, an integral part of the Danish realm, are a self-governing group of islands in the North Atlantic about 580 km W of Norway. Area: 1,399 sq km (540 sq mi). Pop. (1976 est.): 40,000. Cap.: Thorshavn (pop., 1975 est., 11,300).

Education. (1975–76) Primary, pupils 6,097; secondary, pupils 2,332; primary and secondary, teachers 441; vocational, pupils 846, teachers (1966–67) 88; teacher training, students 89, teachers (1966–67) 12; higher, students 34.

Finance and Trade. Monetary unit: Faeroese krone, at par with the Danish krone, with (Sept. 19, 1977) a free rate of 6.18 kroner to U.S. $1 (10.76 kroner = £1 sterling). Budget (1975–76 est.): revenue 270,443,000 kroner; expenditure 269,887,000 kroner. Foreign trade (1975): imports 651 million kroner; exports 464 million kroner. Import sources: Denmark 66%; Norway 19%. Export destinations: Denmark 19%; U.S. 15%; U.K. 13%; Portugal 11%; Spain 10%; Italy 9%; West Germany 5%; France 5%. Main exports: fish and products 80% (including fish meal 16%).

Transport. Shipping (1976): merchant vessels 100 gross tons and over 162; gross tonnage 54,552.

Agriculture and Industry. Fish catch (1975) 286,000 metric tons. Livestock (in 000; Dec. 1973): sheep 68; cattle 2.2. Electricity production (1974–75) c. 90 million kw-hr (c 61% hydroelectric).

GREENLAND

An integral part of the Danish realm, Greenland, the largest island in the world, lies mostly within the Arctic Circle. Area: 2,175,600 sq km (840,000 sq mi), 84% of which is covered by ice cap. Pop. (1976 est.): 50,000. Cap.: Godthaab (pop., 1975 est., 8,300).

Education. (1975–76) Primary, pupils 10,205; secondary and vocational, pupils 2,498; primary, secondary, and vocational, teachers 1,021; teacher training, students (1970–71) 58, teachers (1967 –68) 3.

Finance and Trade. Monetary unit: Danish krone. Budget (1974 est.): revenue 59,904,000 kroner; expenditure 69,613,000 kroner. Foreign trade (1975): imports 742 million kroner (89%

from Denmark, 7% from U.K.); exports 509 million kroner (38% to Denmark, 18% to Finland, 14% to Spain, 11% to France, 6% to West Germany). Main exports: zinc ores 47%; fish and products 40%; lead ores 7%.

Agriculture. Fish catch (1975) 47,000 metric tons. Livestock (in 000; Nov. 1974): sheep 20; reindeer 2.2.

Industry. Production (in 000; metric tons; 1974): lead ore 37; zinc ore 168; cryolite 38; electricity (kw-hr) c. 125,000.

FRANCE

FRENCH GUIANA

French Guiana is an overseas département situated between Brazil and Surinam on the northeast coast of South America. Area: 90,000 sq km (34,-750 sq mi). Pop. (1976 est.): 62,000. Cap.: Cayenne (pop., 1974, 30,500).

Education. (1973–74) Primary, pupils 6,830, teachers 298; secondary (1972–73), pupils 3,063, teachers (1972–73) 229; vocational, pupils 1,348, teachers (1972–73) 79.

Finance and Trade. Monetary unit: French (metropolitan) franc, with (Sept. 19, 1977) a free rate of Fr 4.93 to U.S. $1 (Fr 8.59 = £1 sterling). Budget (1976 est.) balanced at Fr 190,578,000. Foreign trade (1976): imports Fr 412,360,000; exports Fr 19 million. Import sources (1975): France 71%; Trinidad and Tobago 6%. Export destinations (1975): U.S. 46%; France 25%; Guadeloupe 8%; Martinique 8%; Brazil 8%. Main exports (1975): shrimp 44%; timber 14%; transport equipment 9%; hides and skins 5%.

FRENCH POLYNESIA

An overseas territory, the islands of French Polynesia are scattered over a large area of the south central Pacific Ocean. Area of inhabited islands: 3,265 sq km (1,261 sq mi). Pop. (1976 est.): 132,000. Cap.: Papeete, Tahiti (pop., 1971, 25,600).

Education. (1973–74) Primary, pupils 34,348, teachers 1,213; secondary, pupils 6,585, teachers 405; vocational, pupils 1,693, teachers 135; teacher training, students 144, teachers 18.

Finance and Trade. Monetary unit: CFP franc, with (Sept. 19, 1977) a parity of CFP Fr 18.18 to the French franc and a free rate of CFP Fr 89.66 to U.S. $1 (CFP Fr 156.18 = £1 sterling). Budget (1976) balanced at CFP Fr 14 billion. Foreign trade (1975): imports CFP Fr 22,317,000,000 (54% from France, 17% from U.S.); exports CFP Fr 1,-969,000,000 (84% to France). Main exports: copra, vanilla, mother of pearl, coffee. Tourism (1974) 84,000 visitors.

GUADELOUPE

The overseas département of Guadeloupe, together with its dependencies, is in the eastern Caribbean between Antigua to the north and Dominica to the south. Area: 1,705 sq km (658 sq mi). Pop. (1974 census): 324,500. Cap.: Basse-Terre (pop., 1974, 15,500).

Education. (1974–75) Primary, pupils 75,036, teachers 2,473; secondary, pupils 35,624, teachers 840; vocational, pupils 7,516, teachers 381; teacher training (1972–73), students 304, teachers 22; higher, students 1,614, teaching staff 33.

Finance and Trade. Monetary unit: French (metropolitan) franc. Budget (1972 est.) balanced at Fr 583 million. Cost of living (Basse-Terre; 1970 = 100; June 1977) 197. Foreign trade (1976): imports Fr 1,514,690,000 (74% from France, 5% from Martinique, 5% from U.S. and Puerto Rico in 1975); exports Fr 429,350,000 (73% to France, 12% to U.K., 10% to Martinique in 1975). Main exports (1975): sugar 41%; bananas 37%; rum 7%; wheat meal and flour 6%.

MARTINIQUE

The Caribbean island of Martinique, an overseas département, lies 39 km N of St. Lucia and about 50 km SE of Dominica. Area: 1,079 sq km (417 sq mi). Pop. (1974 census): 324,800. Cap.: Fort-de-France (pop., 1974 census, 98,800).

Education. (1973–74) Primary, pupils 61,428, teachers 2,457; secondary, pupils 38,505, teachers (1972–73) 1,978; vocational, pupils 4,819, teachers (1972–73) 245; teacher training (1972–73), students 219, teachers 20.

Finance and Trade. Monetary unit: French (metropolitan) franc. Budget (1972 est.) balanced at Fr 392 million. Cost of living (Fort-de-France; 1970 = 100; April 1977) 200. Foreign trade (1976): imports Fr 1,826,810,000 (65% from France, 6% from Venezuela, 5% from Algeria in 1975); exports Fr 594,040,000 (69% to France, 23% to Guadeloupe in 1975). Main exports (1975): bananas 48%; petroleum products 20%; rum 13%; fruit preserves 7%.

MAYOTTE

An African island dependency of France that was formerly a part of the Comoro Islands, Mayotte lies in the Indian Ocean off the east coast of Africa. Mayotte voted to remain a part of France in February 1976. Its current administrative status of "special collectivity" was designated on Sept. 17, 1976. Area: 378 sq km (146 sq mi). Pop. (1976 est.): 46,500. Cap.: Dzaoudzi (pop., about 3,200).

Education. (1976) Primary, pupils c. 3,000.

Finance and Trade. Monetary unit: French (metropolitan) franc. Main exports: vanilla, essential oils, copra.

NEW CALEDONIA

The overseas territory of New Caledonia, together with its dependencies, is in the South Pacific 1,-210 km E of Australia. Area: 19,079 sq km (7,366 sq mi). Pop. (1976 census): 133,200. Cap.: Nouméa (pop., 1976 census, 56,100).

Education. (1977) Primary, pupils 32,766, teachers 1,489; secondary, pupils 7,268, teachers 467; vocational, pupils 2,461, teachers 252; teacher training, students 150, teachers 25; higher, students 411, teaching staff 30.

Finance and Trade. Monetary unit: CFP franc. Budget (1975 est.): revenue CFP Fr 9,990,000,000; expenditure CFP Fr 9,699,000,000. Foreign trade: imports (1976) CFP Fr 24,179,000,000; exports (1975) CFP Fr 22,380,000,000. Import sources (1975): France 41%; Australia 9%; Singapore 5%. Export destinations: France 59%; Japan 23%; U.S. 12%. Main exports: ferronickel 53%; nickel 22%; nickel castings 20%.

Industry. Production (in 000; 1974): nickel ore (metal content; metric tons) 137; electricity (kw-hr) 1,790,000.

RÉUNION

The overseas département of Réunion is located in the Indian Ocean about 720 km E of Madagascar and 180 km SW of Mauritius. Area: 2,512 sq km (970 sq mi). Pop. (1974 census): 476,700. Cap.: Saint-Denis (pop., 1974 census, 104,600).

Education. (1974–75) Primary, pupils 126,827, teachers 4,148; secondary and vocational, pupils 46,389, teachers 2,224; teacher training, students 500, teachers (1973–74) 21; higher, students 1,764, teaching staff (1966–67) 26.

Finance and Trade. Monetary unit: French (metropolitan) franc. Budget (1975 est.) balanced at Fr 2,471,000,000. Cost of living (Saint-Denis; 1970 = 100; May 1977) 198. Foreign trade (1976): imports Fr 2,152,210,000 (63% from France, 8% from Madagascar, 6% from Italy, 5% from South Africa in 1975); exports Fr 450,280,000 (94% to France in 1975). Main exports (1975): sugar 82%; rum 7%; essential oils 5%.

SAINT PIERRE AND MIQUELON

The self-governing overseas département of Saint Pierre and Miquelon is located about 20 km off the south coast of Newfoundland. Area: 242 sq km (93 sq mi). Pop. (1974 census): 5,800. Cap.: Saint Pierre, Saint Pierre.

Dependent States

Education. (1974–75) Primary, pupils 1,287, teachers 53; secondary, pupils 377, teachers 32; vocational, pupils 107, teachers 12.

Finance and Trade. Monetary unit: French (metropolitan) franc. Budget (1973 est.) balanced at Fr 3.4 million. Foreign trade (1974): imports Fr 125,553,000; exports Fr 59,352,000. Import sources: Canada 54%; France 38%. Export destinations (excluding ship's stores): Canada 70%; U.S. 25%; France 5%. Main exports: petroleum products (as ship's stores) 53%; cattle 30%; fish 12%.

WALLIS AND FUTUNA

Wallis and Futuna, an overseas territory, lies in the South Pacific west of Western Samoa. Area: 255 sq km (98 sq mi). Pop. (1977 est.): 9,000. Cap.: Mata Utu, Uvea (pop., 1969, 600).

NETHERLANDS, THE

NETHERLANDS ANTILLES

The Netherlands Antilles, a self-governing integral part of the Netherlands realm, consists of an island group near the Venezuelan coast and another group to the north near St. Kitts-Nevis. Area: 993 sq km (383 sq mi). Pop. (1976 est.): 241,000. Cap.: Willemstad, Curaçao (pop., 1970 est., 50,000).

Education. (1973–74) Primary, pupils 38,170, teachers 1,492; secondary and vocational, pupils 12,104, teachers 631; higher (university only; 1972–73), students 215, teaching staff 17.

Finance. Monetary unit: Netherlands Antilles guilder or florin, with (Sept. 19, 1977) a par value of 1.80 Netherlands Antilles guilders to U.S. $1 (free rate of 3.12 Netherlands Antilles guilders = £1 sterling). Budget (1972 rev. est.): revenue 116 million Netherlands Antilles guilders; expenditure 126 million Netherlands Antilles guilders. Cost of living (Curaçao; 1970 = 100; Dec. 1976) 167.

Foreign Trade. Imports (1975) 5,088,000,000 Netherlands Antilles guilders; exports (1976) 4,395,000,000 Netherlands Antilles guilders. Import sources (1975): Venezuela 57%; Saudi Arabia 17%; Nigeria 6%; U.S. 6%. Export destinations (1975): U.S. 62%; The Netherlands 5%. Main exports (1974): petroleum products 80%; crude oil 16%. Tourism: visitors (1975) 241,000; gross receipts (1973) U.S. $145 million.

Transport and Communications. Roads (1972) 1,150 km. Motor vehicles in use (1975): passenger 50,136; commercial 5,650. Shipping traffic (1973): goods loaded 42,960,000 metric tons, unloaded c. 46,878,000 metric tons. Telephones (Jan. 1976) 47,000. Radio receivers (Dec. 1974) 131,000. Television receivers (Dec. 1974) 34,000.

Industry. Production (in 000; metric tons; 1974): petroleum products c. 36,030; phosphate rock c. 107; electricity (kw-hr) c. 1,600,000.

NEW ZEALAND

COOK ISLANDS

The self-governing territory of the Cook Islands consists of several islands in the southern Pacific Ocean scattered over an area of about 2.2 million sq km. Area: 241 sq km (93 sq mi). Pop. (1976 census): 18,100. Seat of government: Rarotonga Island (pop., 1976, 9,800).

Education. (1975) Primary, pupils 5,339; secondary, pupils 1,276; primary and secondary, teachers 360; teacher training (1971), students 75, teachers 10.

Finance and Trade. Monetary unit: New Zealand dollar, with (Sept. 19, 1977) a free rate of NZ$1.03 to U.S. $1 (NZ$1.80 = £1 sterling). Budget (1975–76; 15 months ended March 31): revenue NZ$7,724,000 (excluding New Zealand aid of NZ$4,333,000); expenditure NZ$12,056,000. Foreign trade (1973): imports NZ$4,947,000 (83% from New Zealand, 5% from Japan); exports NZ$2,877,000 (98% to New Zealand in 1970). Main exports: citrus juice 41%; bananas 6%; canned fruit 6%; pineapple juice 5%.

NIUE ISLAND

The self-governing territory of Niue Island is situated in the Pacific Ocean about 2,400 km NE of New Zealand. Area: 259 sq km (100 sq mi). Pop. (1976 census): 3,800. Capital: Alofi (pop., 1976 census, 953).

Education. (1976) Primary, pupils 906, teachers 56; secondary, pupils 447, teachers 29; vocational, students 22, teachers 2; teacher training, students 10, teachers 1.

Finance and Trade. Monetary unit: New Zealand dollar. Budget (1975–76): revenue NZ$579,000 (excluding New Zealand subsidy of NZ$2,516,000); expenditure NZ$3.7 million. Foreign trade (1975): imports NZ$2,095,000 (79% from New Zealand); exports NZ$197,000 (73% to New Zealand). Main exports (1973): passion fruit 23%; copra 15%; plaited ware 10%; honey 8%.

TOKELAU ISLANDS

The territory of Tokelau Islands lies in the South Pacific about 1,130 km N of Niue Island and 3,380 km NE of New Zealand. Area: 10 sq km (4 sq mi). Pop. (1976 est.) 2,000.

NORWAY

JAN MAYEN

The island of Jan Mayen, a Norwegian dependency, lies within the Arctic Circle between Greenland and northern Norway. Area: 373 sq km (144 sq mi). Pop. (1973 est.): 37.

SVALBARD

A group of islands and a Norwegian dependency, Svalbard is located within the Arctic Circle to the north of Norway. Area: 62,050 sq km (23,957 sq mi). Pop. (1975 est.): 3,500.

PORTUGAL

MACAU

The overseas territory of Macau is situated on the mainland coast of China 60 km W of Hong Kong. Area 16 sq km (6 sq mi). Pop. (1977 est.): 266,-500.

Education. (1975–76) Primary, pupils 25,499, teachers 838; secondary, pupils 8,198, teachers 427; vocational, pupils 3,884, teachers 184; teacher training, students 61, teachers 6; higher, students 113, teachers 9.

Finance and Trade. Monetary unit: patacá, with (Sept. 19, 1977) a free rate of 5.01 patacás to U.S. $1 (8.73 patacás = £1 sterling). Budget (1976 est.) balanced at 132.7 million patacás. Foreign trade (1976): imports 1,097,443,000 patacás; exports 1,266,629,000 patacás. Import sources (1975): Hong Kong 71%; China 19%. Export destinations (1975): France 21%; West Germany 14%; U.S. 11%; Hong Kong 10%; Portugal 6%; The Netherlands 6%; U.K. 6%. Main exports (1975): clothing 48%; textile yarns and fabrics 36%.

Transport. Shipping traffic (1974): goods loaded 147,000 metric tons, unloaded 299,000 metric tons.

SOUTH WEST AFRICA (NAMIBIA)

South West Africa has been a UN territory since 1966, when the General Assembly terminated South Africa's mandate over the country, renamed Namibia by the UN. South Africa considers the UN resolution illegal. Area: 824,268 sq km (318,251 sq mi). Pop. (1976 est.): 883,000. National cap.: Windhoek (pop., 1975 est., 77,400). Summer cap.: Swakopmund (pop., 1975 est., 13,-700).

Education. (1973) Primary and secondary: Bantu, pupils 116,320, teachers 2,662; Coloured, pupils 15,941, teachers 797; white, pupils 22,775, teachers 1,232.

Finance and Trade. Monetary unit: South African rand, with (Sept. 19, 1977) an official rate of R 0.87 to U.S. $1 (free rate of R 1.52 = £1 ster-ling). Budget (1975–76) balanced at R 104 million. Foreign trade (included in the South African customs union; 1972 est.): imports c. R 170 million (c. 80% from South Africa); exports c. R 240 million (c. 50% to South Africa). Main exports: diamonds c. 40%; fish and products 20%; livestock c. 15%; karakul pelts c. 14%.

Agriculture. Production (in 000; metric tons; 1975): corn c. 15; millet c. 19; beef and veal c. 131; mutton and goat meat c. 24; fish catch c. 87. Livestock (in 000; 1975): cattle c. 2,740; sheep c. 4,473; goats c. 1,923; horses c. 41; asses c. 62.

Industry. Production (in 000; metric tons; 1975): lead ore (metal content) 52; zinc ore (metal content) 46; copper ore (metal content) 25; tin concentrates (metal content) 0.7; vanadium ore (metal content; 1974) 0.8; diamonds (metric carats) 1,750; salt (1973) 147; asbestos (1969) 90; electricity (kw-hr; 1963) 188,000.

UNITED KINGDOM

ANGUILLA

Formally a part of the associated state of St. Kitts-Nevis-Anguilla, the island of Anguilla comprises a separate administrative entity, having received a constitution separating its government from that of St. Kitts-Nevis in 1976. Area: 91 sq km (35 sq mi). Pop. (1976 est.): 7,000.

Education. (1976) Number of schools, primary 5, secondary 1.

Finance and Trade. Monetary unit: East Caribbean dollar, with (Sept. 19, 1977) an official rate of ECar$2.70 to U.S. $1 (free rate of ECar$4.70 = £1 sterling). Foreign trade included with St. Kitts–Nevis.

ANTIGUA

The associated state of Antigua, with its dependencies Barbuda and Redonda, lies in the eastern Caribbean approximately 60 km N of Guadeloupe. Area: 440 sq km (170 sq mi). Pop. (1976 est.): 71,400. Cap.: Saint John's (pop., 1974 est., 23,500).

Education. (1975–76) Primary, pupils 12,875, teachers 469; secondary, pupils 5,082, teachers 231; vocational, pupils 134, teachers 20; teacher training, students 96, teachers 13.

Finance and Trade. Monetary unit: East Caribbean dollar. Budget (1976 est.): revenue ECar$27 million; expenditure ECar$36 million. Foreign trade (1974): imports ECar$143,750,000; exports ECar$66,468,000. Import sources (1973): Venezuela 31%; U.K. 22%; U.S. 16%; Canada 6%. Export destinations (1973): bunkers 37%; U.S. 21%; Switzerland 11%; Canada 9%; Bermuda 5%. Main exports (1973): petroleum products 84%; aircraft and engines (reexports) 6%. Tourism (1976) 62,970 visitors.

BELIZE

Belize, a self-governing colony, is situated on the Caribbean coast of Central America, bounded on the north and northwest by Mexico and by Guatemala on the remainder of the west and south. Area: 22,965 sq km (8,867 sq mi). Pop. (1976 est.): 144,000. Cap.: Belmopan (pop., 1975 est., 320).

Education. (1975–76) Primary, pupils 32,567, teachers 1,207; secondary, pupils 5,135, teachers 439; vocational, pupils 280, teachers (1973–74) 10; teacher training, students 120, teaching staff (1973–74) 22; higher (overseas), students 224.

Finance and Trade. Monetary unit: Belize dollar, with (Sept. 19, 1977) an official rate of Bel$2 = U.S. $1 (free rate of Bel$3.48 = £1 sterling). Budget (1976 est.) balanced at Bel$68.9 million. Foreign trade (1975): imports Bel$185.5 million; exports Bel$129.6 million. Import sources (1970): U.S. 34%; U.K. 25%; Jamaica 7%; The Netherlands 7%. Export destinations (1970): U.S. 30%; U.K. 24%; Mexico 22%; Canada 13%. Main exports (1970): sugar 48%; timber 8%; orange juice 7%; clothing c. 6%; grapefruit segments 5%; lobster 5%.

BERMUDA

The colony of Bermuda lies in the western Atlantic about 920 km E of Cape Hatteras, North Carolina. Area: 46 sq km (18 sq mi). Pop. (1977 est.): 58,000. Cap.: Hamilton, Great Bermuda (pop., 1970 census, 2,100).

Education. (1974–75) Primary, pupils 6,919, teachers 397; secondary, pupils 4,700, teachers 325; vocational, pupils 510, teachers 49.

Finance and Trade. Monetary unit: Bermuda dollar, at par with the U.S. dollar (free rate, at Sept. 19, 1977, of Ber$1.74 = £1 sterling). Budget (1975–76 est.): revenue Ber$65.4 million; expenditure Ber$62.9 million. Foreign trade (1975): imports Ber$162,369,000; exports Ber$36,154,000. Import sources: U.S. 43%; U.K. 24%; Canada 7%; Netherlands Antilles 5%. Export destinations: bunkers 31%; U.S. 19%; U.K. 8%; The Netherlands 6%. Main exports: drugs and medicines 39%; bunkers 31%. Tourism: visitors (1975) 511,000; gross receipts (1971) U.S. $97 million.

Transport and Communications. Roads (1975) 212 km. Motor vehicles in use (1974): passenger 12,200; commercial (including buses) 2,200. Shipping (1976): merchant vessels 100 gross tons and over 69; gross tonnage 1,562,483. Telephones (Jan. 1976) 37,000. Radio receivers (Dec. 1974) 50,000. Television receivers (Dec. 1974) 20,000.

BRITISH INDIAN OCEAN TERRITORY

Located in the western Indian Ocean, this colony consists of the islands of the Chagos Archipelago. Area: 60 sq km (23 sq mi). No permanent civilian population remains. Administrative headquarters: Victoria, Seychelles.

BRITISH VIRGIN ISLANDS

The colony of the British Virgin Islands is located in the Caribbean to the east of the U.S. Virgin Islands. Area: 153 sq km (59 sq mi). Pop. (1977 est.): 12,000. Cap.: Road Town, Tortola (pop., 1973 est., 3,500).

Education. (1975–76) Primary, pupils 1,856; secondary and vocational, pupils 830; primary and secondary, teachers 145.

Finance and Trade. Monetary unit: U.S. dollar (free rate, at Sept. 19, 1977, of U.S. $1.74 = £1 sterling). Budget (1976 est.): revenue U.S. $5,927,000; expenditure U.S. $6,661,000. Foreign trade (1974): imports U.S. $11,606,000; exports U.S. $52,900. Import sources (1973): U.S. 24%; Puerto Rico 19%; U.K. 16%; U.S. Virgin Islands 15%; Trinidad and Tobago 8%. Export destinations (1973): U.S. Virgin Islands 59%; Netherlands Antilles 12%; St. Martin (Guadeloupe) 8%; U.K. 7%. Main exports (1973): motor vehicles (reexports) 15%; nonelectric machines (reexports) 14%; sand 10%; fish 9%; timber (reexports) 6%; beverages (reexports) 5%.

BRUNEI

Brunei, a protected sultanate, is located on the north coast of the island of Borneo, surrounded on its landward side by the Malaysian state of Sarawak. Area: 5,765 sq km (2,226 sq mi). Pop. (1976 est.): 177,000. Cap.: Bandar Seri Begawan (pop., 1976 est., 48,000).

Education. (1975) Primary, pupils 31,605, teachers 1,621; secondary, pupils 13,687, teachers 876; vocational, pupils 314, teachers 61; teacher training, students 613, teachers 48.

Finance and Trade. Monetary unit: Brunei dollar, with (Sept. 19, 1977) a free rate of Br$2.44 to U.S. $1 (Br$4.26 = £1 sterling). Budget (1976 est.): revenue Br$1.6 billion; expenditure Br$495 million. Foreign trade (1975): imports Br$648,-860,000; exports Br$2,465,420,000. Import sources: U.S. 23%; Japan 22%; Singapore 17%; U.K. 12%; The Netherlands 5%; Malaysia 5%. Export destinations: Japan 78%; South Africa 7%; U.S. 7%; Malaysia 5%. Main exports: crude oil 78%; natural gas 17%.

Agriculture. Production (in 000; metric tons; 1975): rice c. 4; cassava c. 2; bananas c. 2; rubber c. 0.5. Livestock (in 000; Dec. 1974): cattle c. 3; buffaloes c. 18; pigs c. 15; chickens c. 856.

Industry. Production (in 000; 1974): crude oil (metric tons) 9,284; natural gas (cu m) c. 5,-000,000.

CAYMAN ISLANDS

The colony of the Cayman Islands lies in the Caribbean about 270 km NW of Jamaica. Area: 288 sq km (111 sq mi). Pop. (1976 est.): 14,000. Cap.: George Town, Grand Cayman (pop., 1970 census, 3,800).

Education. (1975–76) Primary, pupils 1,964, teachers 72; secondary, pupils 1,355, teachers 93.

Finance and Trade. Monetary unit: Cayman Islands dollar, with (Sept. 19, 1977) a free rate of CayI$0.83 to U.S. $1 (CayI$1.45 = £1 sterling). Budget (1976 est.): revenue CayI$11,611,000; expenditure CayI$9,834,000. Foreign trade (1975): imports CayI$22,519,000; exports CayI$204,000. Most trade is with the U.S. (about two-thirds) and Jamaica. Main export (1974) turtle products 93%. Tourism (1975) 54,100 visitors.

Shipping. (1976) Merchant vessels 100 gross tons and over 84; gross tonnage 78,251.

DOMINICA

The associated state of Dominica lies in the Caribbean between Guadeloupe to the north and Martinique to the south. Area: 772 sq km (300 sq mi). Pop. (1977 est.): 77,000. Cap.: Roseau (pop., 1974 est., 10,200).

Education. (1975–76) Primary, pupils 20,827, teachers 560; secondary, pupils 2,415, teachers 114; vocational, pupils 86, teachers 43; teacher training, students 11, teachers 6.

Finance and Trade. Monetary unit: East Caribbean dollar. Budget (1974–75 est.): revenue ECar$12,611,000 (excluding U.K. government aid); expenditure ECar$15,916,000. Foreign trade (1975): imports ECar$45.1 million; exports ECar$23.8 million. Import sources: U.K. 30%; U.S. 10%; Canada 10%. Export destination U.K. 78%. Main exports: bananas 58%; grapefruit 11%.

FALKLAND ISLANDS

The colony of the Falkland Islands and dependencies is situated in the South Atlantic about 800 km NE of Cape Horn. Area: 16,265 sq km (6,-280 sq mi). Pop. (1976 est.): 1,900. Cap.: Stanley (pop., 1976 est., 1,100).

Education. (1976) Primary, pupils 203, teachers 17; secondary, pupils 109, teachers 8.

Finance and Trade. Monetary unit: Falkland Island pound, at par with the pound sterling (U.S.1.74 = £1 sterling). Budget (excluding dependencies; 1976–77 est.): revenue FI£1,051,-000; expenditure FI£1,111,000. Foreign trade (1975): imports FI£1,525,800 (83% from U.K. in 1971); exports FI£1,172,700 (93% to U.K. in 1971). Main export wool.

GIBRALTAR

Gibraltar, a self-governing colony, is a small peninsula that juts into the Mediterranean from southwestern Spain. Area: 5.80 sq km (2.25 sq mi). Pop. (1976 est.): 30,000.

Education. (1974–75) Primary, pupils 2,759, teachers 145; secondary, pupils 1,561, teachers 120; vocational, pupils 52, teachers 22.

Finance and Trade. Monetary unit: Gibraltar pound, at par with the pound sterling. Budget (1975–76 est.): revenue Gib£11,807,000; expenditure Gib£10,323,000. Foreign trade (1974): imports Gib£25,089,000 (71% from U.K.); reexports Gib£10,484,000 (31% to EEC, 16% to U.K. in 1971). Main reexports: petroleum products 89%; tobacco 9%. Tourism (1974) 140,000 visitors.

Transport. Shipping (1976): merchant vessels 100 gross tons and over 10; gross tonnage 21,526. Ships entered (1974) vessels totaling 13,973,000 net registered tons; goods loaded 5,000 metric tons, unloaded 411,000 metric tons.

GILBERT ISLANDS

The Gilbert Islands comprise 16 main islands, together with associated islets and reefs, straddling the Equator just west of the International Date Line in the western Pacific Ocean. Area: 272 sq km (105 sq mi). Pop. (1976 est.): 53,300. Seat of government: Bairiki, on Tarawa Atoll (pop., 1974 est., 17,100).

Education. (1977) Primary, pupils 13,679, teachers 435; secondary, pupils 1,000, teachers

71; vocational, pupils 183, teachers 28; teacher training, students 73, teachers 12.

Finance and Trade. Monetary unit: Australian dollar, with (Sept. 19, 1977) a free rate of A$0.91 to U.S. $1 (A$1.58 = £1 sterling). Budget (including Tuvalu; 1974 est.): revenue A$15,426,000; expenditure A$12,701,000. Foreign trade (including Tuvalu; 1974): imports A$7,247,000 (54% from Australia, 14% from U.K., 5% from New Zealand in 1973); exports A$23,736,000 (62% to New Zealand, 30% to Australia, 5% to U.K. in 1972). Main exports: phosphates 86%; copra 14%.

Industry. Production (in 000; 1974): phosphate rock (metric tons) 562; electricity (kw-hr) c. 3,000.

GUERNSEY

Located 50 km W of Normandy, France, Guernsey, together with its small island dependencies, is a crown dependency. Area: 78 sq km (30 sq mi). Pop. (1976 est.): 53,700. Cap.: St. Peter Port (pop., 1971, 16,300).

Education. (1975–76) Primary and secondary, pupils 9,763.

Finance and Trade. Monetary unit: Guernsey pound, at par with the pound sterling. Budget (1975): revenue £19,330,000; expenditure £16,014,000. Foreign trade included with the United Kingdom. Main exports (1974): tomatoes c. 50%; flowers c. 20%. Tourism (1975) 304,000 visitors.

HONG KONG

The colony of Hong Kong lies on the southeastern coast of China about 60 km E of Macau and 130 km SE of Canton. Area: 1,050 sq km (405 sq mi). Pop. (1976 census): 4,420,400. Cap.: Victoria (pop., 1976, 501,700).

Education. (1976–77) Primary, pupils 606,860, teachers 19,695; secondary, pupils 384,656; vocational, pupils 12,494; secondary and vocational, teachers 13,077; higher, students 19,690, teaching staff 2,328.

Finance. Monetary unit: Hong Kong dollar, with (Sept. 19, 1977) a free rate of HK$4.67 to U.S. $1 (HK$8.14 = £1 sterling). Budget (1976–77 est.): revenue HK$6,857,000,000; expenditure HK$7,212,000,000.

Foreign Trade. (1976) Imports HK$34,020,-000,000; exports HK$31,455,000,000. Import sources: Japan 22%; China 18%; U.S. 12%; Taiwan 7%; Singapore 6%. Export destinations: U.S. 29%; West Germany 10%; U.K. 8%; Japan 7%. Main exports: clothing 35%; instruments 13%; electrical machinery 12%; textile yarns and fabrics 10%; toys 5%. Tourism: visitors (1975) 1,301,000; gross receipts (1974) U.S. $476 million.

Transport and Communications. Roads (1975) 1,073 km. Motor vehicles in use (1975): passenger 122,000; commercial 34,000. Railways: (1975) 33 km; traffic (1976) 251.2 million passenger-km, freight 46.1 million net ton-km. Shipping (1976): merchant vessels 100 gross tons and over 98; gross tonnage 423,218. Shipping traffic (1976): goods loaded 5,968,000 metric tons, unloaded 17,370,000 metric tons. Telephones (Jan. 1976) 1,034,000. Radio receivers (Dec. 1974) c. 1 million. Television licenses (Dec. 1974) 785,000.

ISLE OF MAN

The Isle of Man, a crown dependency, lies in the Irish Sea approximately 55 km from both Northern Ireland and the coast of northwestern England. Area: 572 sq km (221 sq mi). Pop. (1976 census): 61,700. Cap.: Douglas (pop., 1976, 20,300).

Education. (1975–76) Primary, pupils 5,527; secondary, pupils 3,532; vocational, pupils 3,000.

Finance and Trade. Monetary unit: Isle of Man pound, at par with the pound sterling. Budget (1976–77 est.): revenue £36.9 million; expenditure £35.6 million. Foreign trade includ-

Dependent States

ed with the United Kingdom. Main exports: beef and lamb, fish, livestock. Tourism (1976) 496,850 visitors.

JERSEY

The island of Jersey, a crown dependency, is located about 30 km W of Normandy, France. Area: 117 sq km (45 sq mi). Pop. (1971): 72,600. Cap.: St. Helier (pop., 1971, 28,100).

Education. (1975–76) Primary, pupils 5,393; secondary, pupils 4,312.

Finance. Monetary unit: Jersey pound, at par with the pound sterling. Budget (1975): revenue £46,984,000; expenditure £33,780,000.

Foreign Trade. (1976) Imports £122,562,000 (80% from U.K.); exports £49,015,000 (70% to U.K.). Main exports: potatoes 12%; motor vehicles 11%; knitted fabrics 10%; machinery 8%; musical instruments 7%; jewelry 7%; tomatoes 7%; chocolate preparations 6%. Tourism: visitors (1975) c. 1,140,000; gross expenditure (1974) U.S. $110 million.

MONTSERRAT

The colony of Montserrat is located in the Caribbean between Antigua, 43 km NE, and Guadeloupe, 60 km SE. Area: 102 sq km (40 sq mi). Pop. (1976 est.): 12,200. Cap.: Plymouth (pop., 1974 est., 3,000).

Education. (1976) Primary, pupils 2,635, teachers 106; secondary, pupils 482, teachers 35; vocational, pupils 53, teachers 8.

Finance and Trade. Monetary unit: East Caribbean dollar. Budget (1976 est.) balanced at ECar$8,475,000 (including U.K. aid of ECar$2,- 647,000). Foreign trade (1975): imports ECar$16,- 544,000; exports ECar$1,019,000. Import sources: U.K. 29%; Trinidad and Tobago 18%; U.S. 18%; Canada 10%. Export destinations: Guadeloupe 22%; U.K. 18%; St. Kitts-Nevis 17%; Antigua 14%; Trinidad and Tobago 7%; Dominica 6%. Main exports (domestic only): cattle 25%; potatoes 24%; cotton, lint 18%; recapped tires 10%; mangoes 7%; tomatoes 5%.

PITCAIRN ISLAND

The colony of Pitcairn Island is in the central South Pacific, 5,150 km NE of New Zealand and 2,170 km SE of Tahiti. Area: 4.53 sq km (1.75 sq mi). Pop. (1976 census): 74, all of whom live in the de facto capital, Adamstown.

ST. HELENA

The colony of St. Helena, including its dependencies of Ascension Island and the Tristan da Cunha island group, is spread over a wide area of the Atlantic off the southwestern coast of Africa. Area: 412 sq km (159 sq mi). Pop. (1976 census): 5,100. Cap.: Jamestown (pop., 1976 census, 1,500).

Education. (1975–76) Primary, pupils 774; secondary, pupils 509; primary and secondary, teachers 70; teacher training, students 5, teachers 2.

Finance and Trade. Monetary unit: pound sterling. Budget (1975–76 est.): revenue £1,482,- 000; expenditure £1,544,000. Foreign trade (1974–75): imports £1,115,000 (61% from U.K., 28% from South Africa in 1968); exports nil.

ST. KITTS-NEVIS

This associated state consists of the islands of St. Kitts and Nevis (Anguilla received a separate constitution in 1976). Area: 269 sq km (104 sq mi). Pop. (1976 est.): 47,000. Cap.: Basseterre, St. Kitts (pop., 1976 est., 15,900).

Education. (1975–76) Primary, pupils 9,629, teachers 344; secondary, pupils 4,966, teachers 253; vocational, pupils 183, teachers 22; higher, students 35, teaching staff 11.

Finance and Trade. Monetary unit: East Caribbean dollar. Budget (1977 est.) balanced at ECar$54 million. Foreign trade (including An-

guilla; 1973) imports ECar$35.9 million; exports ECar$15.8 million. Import sources (1971): U.K. 35%; Puerto Rico 14%; U.S. 10%; Trinidad and Tobago 9%; Canada 8%. Export destinations (1971): U.K. 61%; Puerto Rico 22%. Main exports (1971): sugar 65%; electrical equipment 24%.

ST. LUCIA

The Caribbean island of St. Lucia, an associated state, lies 39 km S of Martinique and 34 km NE of St. Vincent. Area: 623 sq km (241 sq mi). Pop. (1975 est.): 111,800. Cap.: Castries (pop., 1970, 3,600).

Education. (1975–76) Primary pupils 30,577, teachers 930; secondary, pupils 4,105, teachers 232; vocational, pupils 237, teachers 32; teacher training, students 156, teachers 15.

Finance and Trade. Monetary unit: East Caribbean dollar. Budget (1974 est.): revenue ECar$29,390,000; expenditure ECar$49,504,000. Foreign trade (1975): imports ECar$100,425,000; exports ECar$34,453,000. Import sources (1973): U.K. 30%; U.S. 16%; Trinidad and Tobago 13%; Canada 5%. Export destinations (1973): U.K. 60%; Jamaica 10%; Barbados 8%; U.S. 6%. Main exports (1974): bananas 64%; cardboard boxes 10%; coconut oil 10%. Tourism (1974) 51,800 visitors.

ST. VINCENT

St. Vincent, including the northern Grenadines, is an associated state in the eastern Caribbean about 160 km W of Barbados. Area: 389 sq km (150 sq mi). Pop. (1975 est.): 93,000. Cap.: Kingstown (pop., 1973 est., 22,000).

Education. (1974–75) Primary, pupils 27,862, teachers (1971–72) 1,765; secondary, pupils 4,586, teachers (1968–69) 92; teacher training (1971–72), students 362, teachers 11.

Finance and Trade. Monetary unit: East Caribbean dollar. Budget (1976–77 est.): revenue ECar$23.1 million; expenditure ECar$26.8 million. Foreign trade (1974): imports ECar$52,204,000; exports ECar$14,687,000. Import sources (1972): U.K. 28%; Trinidad and Tobago 17%; Canada 9%; U.S. 9%. Export destinations (1972): U.K. 61%; Barbados 15%; Trinidad and Tobago 11%; U.S. 6%. Main exports (1972): bananas 49%; animal and vegetable oils 14%; arrowroot 11%.

SOLOMON ISLANDS

The Solomon Islands is a self-governing protectorate in the southwestern Pacific east of the island of New Guinea. Area: 28,446 sq km (10,983 sq mi). Pop. (1976 census): 196,800. Cap.: Honiara, Guadalcanal (pop., 1976, 14,900).

Education. (1973) Primary, pupils 25,952, teachers 1,088; secondary, pupils 1,303, teachers 99; vocational, pupils 696, teachers 61; teacher training, students 88, teachers 18.

Finance and Trade. Monetary unit: Australian dollar. Budget (1976 est.) balanced at A$10.3 million (excluding capital expenditure of A$8.1 million). Foreign trade (1975): imports A$21,803,000; exports A$11,861,000. Import sources: Australia 35%; U.K. 14%; Japan 13%; Singapore 10%. Export destinations: Japan 29%; U.K. 11%; France 8%; Denmark 8%; West Germany 7%; The Netherlands 6%; Norway 6%; Sweden 5%. Main exports: copra 39%; timber 27%; fish 11%; canned fish 10%.

TURKS AND CAICOS ISLANDS

The colony of the Turks and Caicos Islands is situated in the Atlantic southeast of The Bahamas. Area: 500 sq km (193 sq mi). Pop. (1976 est.): 6,- 000. Seat of government: Grand Turk Island (pop., 1970, 2,300).

Education. (1976–77) Primary, pupils 1,802, teachers 16; secondary, pupils 671, teachers 34.

Finance and Trade. Monetary unit: U.S. dollar. Budget (1975 actual): revenue $2,077,000; expenditure $3,435,684. Foreign trade (1974): imports $6,597,000; exports $563,000. Main exports: crayfish 73%; conch meat 25%.

TUVALU

The colony of Tuvalu comprises nine main islands, together with their associated islets and

reefs, located just south of the Equator and just west of the International Date Line in the western Pacific Ocean. Area: 26 sq km (9.5 sq mi). Pop. (1976 est.): 6,500. Seat of government: Funafuti (pop., 1976 est., 1,300).

Education. (1976) Primary, pupils 1,570, teachers 39; secondary, pupils 250, teachers 12.

Finance and Trade. Monetary unit: Australian dollar. Budget (1976 est.) balanced at A$1,687,- 000 (including British aid of A$839,000). Main export (1975) copra (valued at A$23,184).

UNITED KINGDOM and FRANCE

NEW HEBRIDES

The British-French condominium of the New Hebrides is located in the southwestern Pacific about 800 km W of Fiji and 400 km NE of New Caledonia. Area: 11,870 sq km (4,583 sq mi). Pop. (1977 est.): 99,300. Cap.: Vila (metropolitan area pop., 1976 est., 17,400).

Education. (1976) Primary, pupils 21,158, teachers 917; secondary, pupils 1,193, teachers 97; vocational, pupils 241, teachers 18; teacher training, students 137, teachers 15.

Finance. Monetary units: Australian dollar and New Hebrides franc, with (Sept. 19, 1977) a parity of NHFr 16.16 to the French franc and a free rate of NHFr 79.70 = U.S. $1 (NHFr 138.83 = £1 sterling). Condominium budget (1975): revenue NHFr 737 million; expenditure NHFr 1,028,000,- 000. British budget (1974–75 est.): revenue A$4,- 450,000; expenditure A$4,221,000. French budget (1975 est.) balanced at NHFr 9 million.

Foreign Trade. (1975) Imports NHFr 1,- 622,000,000; exports NHFr 789.7 million. Import sources: Australia 30%; France 25%; Japan 8%; New Caledonia 7%; U.K. 5%. Export destinations: France 43%; U.S. 28%; Japan 15%; New Caledonia 8%. Main exports: copra 43%; fish 33%; manganese 9%; beef and veal 8%; cocoa 5%.

Agriculture. Production (in 000; metric tons): copra (1976) c. 40; cocoa (1975) 0.7; fish catch (1975) c. 8. Livestock (in 000; 1975): cattle c. 104; pigs c. 63.

Industry. Production (in 000; 1975): manganese ore (metal content; exports; metric tons) 47; electricity (kw-hr) c. 13,000.

UNITED STATES

AMERICAN SAMOA

Located to the east of Western Samoa in the South Pacific, the unincorporated territory of American Samoa is approximately 2,600 km NE of the northern tip of New Zealand. Area: 197 sq km (76 sq mi). Pop. (1976 est.): 31,000. Cap.: Pago Pago (pop., 1974, 4,700).

Education. (1974–75) Primary, pupils 7,213, teachers 333; secondary, pupils 2,367, teachers 142; vocational, pupils 800, teachers 38; higher, students 909, teaching staff (1971–72) 32.

Finance and Trade. Monetary unit: U.S. dollar. Budget (1976 est.) balanced at $45.4 million (including U.S. federal grants of $41 million). Foreign trade (1974–75): imports $52.8 million (91% from U.S. in 1970); exports $50.4 million (95% to U.S. in 1970). Main exports (1970): canned tuna 90%; pet food 5%.

CANAL ZONE

The Canal Zone is administered by the U.S. under treaty with Panama and consists of a 16-km-wide strip on the Isthmus of Panama through which the Panama Canal runs. Area: 1,432 sq km (553 sq mi). Pop. (1976 est.): 44,000. Administrative headquarters: Balboa Heights (pop., 1970, 200).

Education. (1976) Primary, pupils 8,000; secondary, pupils 3,000; primary and secondary, teachers 427; higher, students (1975) 1,590, teaching staff (1971) 120.

Finance. Monetary unit: U.S. dollar (Panamanian balboa is also used). Budgets (1976): Canal Zone government, revenue $73,681,000, expenditure $71,595,000; Panama Canal Company, revenue $250,103,000, expenditure $257,461,000.

Traffic. (1975–76) Total number of oceangoing vessels passing through the canal 12,157; total cargo tonnage 117,212,000; tolls collected U.S. $134 million. Nationality and number of commercial vessels using the canal: Liberian 1,777; British 1,285; U.S. 1,064; Japanese 1,008; Panamanian 930; Greek 885; Norwegian 685; West German 626; Swedish 332; Dutch 300.

GUAM

Guam, an organized unincorporated territory, is located in the Pacific Ocean about 9,700 km SW of San Francisco and 2,400 km E of Manila. Area: 549 sq km (212 sq mi). Pop. (1975 est.): 107,400. Cap.: Agana (pop., 1974 est., 2,500).

Education. (1976) Primary, pupils 24,600; secondary and vocational, pupils 8,500; primary and secondary, teachers 1,402; higher, students (1975) 3,800, teaching staff (1971–72) 140.

Finance. Monetary unit: U.S. dollar. Budget (1974 est.): revenue $112.6 million (including U.S. federal grants of $11.5 million); expenditure $99.1 million.

Foreign Trade. (1973) Imports $211 million; exports $11 million. Tourism (1975) 492,000 visitors.

Agriculture and Industry. Production (in 000; metric tons; 1975): copra 1.1; fish catch 0.1; petroleum products (1974) c. 1,625; electricity (kw-hr; 1974) c. 1,250,000.

PUERTO RICO

Puerto Rico, a self-governing associated commonwealth, lies about 1,400 km SE of the Florida coast. Area: 8,897 sq km (3,435 sq mi). Pop. (1976 est.): 3,213,000. Cap.: San Juan (pop., 1975 est., 1,087,000).

Education. (1975–76) Primary, secondary, and vocational, pupils 812,445, teachers 29,600; higher, students 105,309, teaching staff (1971–72) c. 4,400.

Finance. Monetary unit: U.S dollar. Budget (1974–75 actual): revenue $2.4 billion; expenditure $2,545,000,000. Gross domestic product (1975–76) $8,735,000,000. Cost of living (1970 = 100; June 1977) 161.

Foreign Trade. (1975–76) Imports $5,432,000,-000 (62% from U.S., 10% from Venezuela); exports $3,346,000,000 (84% to U.S.). Main exports (1972–73): chemicals 20%; textiles 18%; machinery 9%; fish products 9%; petroleum products 9%. Tourism (1975–76): visitors 1,290,000; gross receipts $393 million.

Transport and Communications. Roads (1974) 16,827 km. Motor vehicles in use (1974): passenger 608,000; commercial (including buses) 124,500. Railways (1975) 96 km. Telephones (Jan. 1976) 474,000. Radio receivers (Dec. 1974) 1,755,000. Television receivers (Dec. 1974) 625,000.

Agriculture. Production (in 000; metric tons; 1976): sugar, raw value 279; yams (1975) c. 13; pumpkins (1975) 15; pineapples 38; bananas c. 114; oranges 32; coffee c. 12; tobacco (1975) 1.8; fish catch (1975) 81. Livestock (in 000; Jan. 1975): cattle 553; pigs 233; poultry 4,391.

Industry. Production (in 000; metric tons; 1976): cement 1,398; sand and gravel (1973) 6,786; stone (1973) 14,195; petroleum products (1974) 10,566; electricity (kw-hr) c. 14,830,000.

TRUST TERRITORY OF THE PACIFIC ISLANDS

The Trust Territory islands, numbering more than 2,000, are scattered over 7,750,000 sq km in the Pacific Ocean from 720 km E of the Philippines to just west of the International Date Line. Area: 1,-880 sq km (726 sq mi). Pop. (1976 est.): 123,000. Seat of government: Saipan Island (pop., 1972 est., 10,700).

Education. (1975–76) Primary, pupils 30,939, teachers (1973–74) 1,433; secondary, pupils 7,970, teachers (1973–74) 476; vocational, pupils 260, teachers (1973–74) 13.

Finance. Monetary unit: U.S. dollar. Budget (1972–73 est.): revenue $79,605,000 (including U.S. grant of $59.4 million); expenditure $62,812,000.

Foreign Trade. (1975) Imports c. $38 million (c. 50% from U.S.; c. 27% from Japan in 1972); exports $6.8 million (54% to Japan in 1972). Main exports: copra 47%; fish 44%.

Agriculture. Production (in 000; metric tons; 1975): sweet potatoes c. 3; cassava c. 6; bananas c. 2; copra c. 10. Livestock (in 000; June 1975): cattle c. 17; pigs c. 17; goats c. 7; chickens c. 167.

VIRGIN ISLANDS

The Virgin Islands of the United States is an organized unincorporated territory located about 60 km E of Puerto Rico. Area: 345 sq km (133 sq mi). Pop. (1976 est.): 96,000. Cap.: Charlotte Amalie, St. Thomas (pop., 1970, 12,200).

Education. (1976) Primary, pupils 23,600; secondary and vocational, pupils 6,700; primary and secondary, teachers 1,611; higher, students 2,079, teaching staff (1971–72) 50.

Finance. Monetary unit: U.S. dollar. Budget (1972 est.): revenue $90.7 million; expenditure $90,280,000. U.S. aid (1974–75) $195 million.

Foreign Trade. (1975) Imports $2,197,500,000; exports $1,933,200,000. Import sources: Iran 37%; Qatar 14%; U.S. 12%; Libya 8%; Nigeria 5%; Saudi Arabia 5%; Venezuela 5%. Export destinations: U.S. 97%. Main export petroleum products. Tourism (1972–73): visitors 1,312,000; gross receipts $100,020,000.

continued from page 302

hanging of two black men accused of murdering whites touched off three days of rioting and arson in December. Order was restored after imposition of a curfew and the arrival of 260 British troops to assist the police.

In the French Antilles poverty, strikes and lock-outs, and unemployment (about 60,000 persons) remained issues in Guadeloupe, with the local Communist Party pressing for independence. Martinique's sugar production declined; unemployment on the island totaled 30,000, and about 5,000 young people left for France annually. In the March municipal elections A. Césaire and his Martinique Progressive Party, supported by the Communist Party, won an overwhelming victory, interpreted as a vote for autonomy. In French Guiana (Guyane) the Socialist Party in September demanded a new constitution rather than immediate independence. The two-year-old plan to bring in 30,000 settlers failed to get off the ground.

In the Netherlands Antilles Aruba voted in a referendum to secede from the Netherlands Antilles Federation (to become independent in about 1980). Aruba believed that it could live off its oil refinery, petrochemical plant, tourism, and offshore companies, backed by Venezuela, and feared domination by Curaçao. In elections to the Netherlands Antilles Parliament, parties advocating independence gained. On Curaçao the right-of-centre Democratic Party staged a comeback. The Antilles government of Prime Minister Juancho Evertsz stepped down on September 29 in favour of a coalition.

Africa. In June, after consultation with five Western powers, South Africa agreed to abandon the arrangement made at the Turnhalle constitutional conference at Windhoek for a multiethnic transitional government in South West Africa (Namibia) in favour of administration by an administrator general (Justice Marthinus Steyn was appointed by South Africa in July), to be followed by UN-supervised elections. This arrangement was made on the condition that the South West Africa People's Organization participate in the elections, but the latter demanded the replacement of South Africans by UN troops. South Africa refused to relinquish the Walvis Bay enclave and its 13 offshore islands (with resources of guano, crayfish, and diamonds), which had been incorporated into South Africa by the Act of Union of 1910; though later administered from South West Africa, it was acknowledged by the League of Nations as not forming part of the mandated territory. The deepwater port was important strategically and was the centre of the region's fishing industry as well as the dispatch point for 90% of South West Africa's exports.

The former Spanish Sahara suffered the unique fate of being decolonized out of existence through its partitioned annexation by Morocco and Mauritania in 1976, but was still the scene of a struggle as the indigenous Polisario Front, with Algerian support, fought both countries in an effort to set

KEYSTONE

The harbour of the Walvis Bay enclave in Namibia was the subject of
dispute in the United Nations when
South Africa refused to relinquish its
administration.

up a "Saharan Arab Democratic Republic." Neither the Organization of African Unity (OAU) nor
the UN could achieve a settlement. (*See* MAURI-
TANIA; MOROCCO.)

In the Canary Islands, which form two metropolitan provinces of Spain, there was a demand
for greater autonomy for the one million inhabitants. Few supported the left-wing (OAU-backed)
movement from Cape Verde and its campaign of
terrorism, or the claim of its leader, Antonio
Cubillo, that the Canaries belonged to Africa.
Spain used the Canaries as a base for the forces
formerly in its Africa colonies.

Indian Ocean. In the Comoro Islands, Mayotte,
which had voted to stay French, was given special
territorial status and a deputy, Younoussa Bama-
nas, elected March 13 to the French Parliament.
Threats of invasion from the independent Comoro
regime did not materialize. Mayotte had the only
deep harbour in the islands.

Pacific. In Tuvalu, at elections for the 12 seats
in the House of Assembly held in August 1977,
most sitting members were returned. Toalipi Lauti
was reelected chief minister, and he was expected
to lead Tuvalu to independence from the U.K. in
1978. The Solomon Islands and the Gilbert Islands,
both enjoying internal self-government, also were
expected to attain complete independence in 1978,
and constitutional talks in London to this effect
ended in September 1977.

The long-drawn-out lawsuit, heard in the High
Court in London, by the inhabitants of Ocean Island (Banaba) resulted in the dismissal of their
£21 million claim for additional phosphate royalties (the offer of £6.4 million by Great Britain,
Australia, and New Zealand was rejected until
such time as independence for Ocean Island
should be granted). However, the island's constitutional future in relation to the Gilberts and Fiji
remained uncertain.

Two of Australia's eight external territories were
also concerned with constitutional change. Norfolk Island protested the findings of the Nimmo

Report of December 1976, which recommended increased integration of the island into the Australian Capital Territory. The islanders demanded a
referendum on the plan, objecting that it would
ruin their way of life and increase taxation. Controversy also took place concerning the future of
the 27 Cocos Islands, largely owned by the Clunies-Ross family. John Clunies-Ross refused all
Australian financial offers.

In the New Zealand dependencies the Cook Islands government faced a large deficit for 1977–78,
partly offset by surpluses carried forward and continuing aid from New Zealand. In 1976 the flow of
migrants to New Zealand reversed (because of
unemployment and inflation there), and the Cook
Islands had a net gain from immigration. Niue
Island experienced a net loss from migration. By
the end of 1977 there were fewer than 4,000 Ni-
ueans on Niue and some 8,000 in New Zealand.
Both Niue and the Cook Islands, as self-governing
members of the South Pacific Forum, intended to
declare 200-mi offshore economic zones in 1978. In
1976 a UN mission to the Tokelau Islands found
that a small population (1,600, declining through
migration), economic dependence, and remoteness caused the Tokelauans to oppose any plans for
self-government or independence.

In New Caledonia both the majority and opposition parties united in criticism of the French government, and feelings ran high in Nouméa in
June. In spite of warnings and advice the French
National Assembly modified the territory's electoral procedure; after its rejection by the Senate,
the reform gave place to a procedural battle and
was deferred. Olivier Stirn, French minister of
overseas territories, visited New Caledonia and an
additional deputy was created for it. The government's intervention assured the success of parties
opposed to independence, as was evidenced by the
election of Dick Ukeiwe as president of the Territorial Assembly.

In the New Hebrides, after a Franco-British
ministerial conference in Paris in July, further

Disasters:
see page 58

Disciples of Christ:
see Religion

Diseases:
see Health and Dis-
ease

Divorce:
see Demography

bilateral discussions were scheduled for December. It was decided that the archipelago would attain internal self-government early in 1978 as a stage toward complete independence, perhaps late in 1980. In French Polynesia in March the French government, the majority party, and the pro-independence autonomists reached agreement on a new draft constitution. The autonomists then won the elections of May 29, and in July the new constitution was adopted.

Indonesia continued to administer former Portuguese East Timor as its 27th province despite a UN protest. Though Portugal appeared to relinquish interest in Timor, Macau remained a Portuguese colony, for China seemed in no hurry to destroy that link with the West.

In Guam the 1976 referendum, which resulted in the maintaining of U.S. ties, developed into negotiations for improved status in 1977. A draft constitution granting control over local affairs was set forth. Guam showed some interest in joining the North Marianas, which were in the process of splitting off from the rest of Micronesia in order to become a U.S. commonwealth on the lines of Puerto Rico. Its draft constitution was approved in March 1977. American Samoa elected its governor for the first time.

(PHILIPPE DECRAENE; BARRIE MACDONALD; MOLLY MORTIMER; SHEILA PATTERSON)

See also African Affairs; Commonwealth of Nations; United Nations.

Djibouti

An independent republic in northeastern Africa, Djibouti is bordered by Ethiopia, Somalia, and the Gulf of Aden. Formerly called the French Territory of the Afars and Issas, Djibouti received its independence from France on June 27, 1977. Area: 23,-000 sq km (8,900 sq mi). Pop. (1976 est.): 226,000, most of whom are Cushitic Afars or Somali Issas; there are smaller Arabic and European communities. Capital: Djibouti (pop., 1976 est., 120,000). Language: Arabic and French (official); Saho-Afar and Somali are spoken in their respective communities. Religion: predominantly Muslim. President in 1977, Hassan Gouled Aptidon; premier to December 17, Ahmed Dini Ahmed.

On June 27, 1977, the French Territory of the Afars and Issas became independent as the Repub-

DJIBOUTI
  Education. (1975–76) Primary, pupils 10,469, teachers 336; secondary, pupils 1,644, teachers 96; vocational, pupils 67, teachers 59; teacher training, students 11, teachers 4.
  Finance. Monetary unit: Djibouti franc, with (Sept. 19, 1977) a free rate of DjFr 170 to U.S. $1 (DjFr 300 = £1 sterling). Budget (1973 est.) balanced at DjFr 2,955,000,-000.
  Foreign Trade. (1973) Imports DjFr 12,675,060,000; exports DjFr 3,498,540,000. Import sources: France 49%; Ethiopia 12%; Japan 6%; U.K. 6%. Export destinations: France 84%. Main exports: ships and boats 16%; leather and shoes 7%.
  Transport. Ships entered (1974) vessels totaling 4.4 million net registered tons; goods loaded 139,000 metric tons, unloaded 728,000 metric tons.

lic of Djibouti; more than 98% of the voters had asked for independence in a referendum on May 8. Hassan Gouled Aptidon (*see* BIOGRAPHY), former leader of the opposition party, the Popular African League for Independence (LPAI), was elected president of the republic and head of state on June 24; on July 12 he picked as premier his former colleague Ahmed Dini Ahmed, who had been elected president of the new Chamber of Deputies on May 13. The government, formed on July 15, preserved the balance between the new state's ethnic communities and its four chief political parties. However, acts of terrorism, including a hand-grenade attack on French soldiers, were blamed on an Afar movement. In December Ahmed Dini and four of his ministers, all Afars, resigned to protest what they called tribal oppression.

The war in Ethiopia severely affected the almost nonexistent national economy; rail traffic with Addis Ababa, Ethiopia, was stopped in June, and the port dues of Djibouti fell by half. Seven cooperation agreements were signed with France on June 27, and it was decided in August that a French force of 4,150 should remain to train a Djibouti force. (PHILIPPE DECRAENE)

Djibouti

Independence was celebrated in Djibouti as that former French territory became an independent state June 27. Girls in traditional dress perform a dance with daggers as part of the ceremony.

Dominican Republic

Dominican Republic

Covering the eastern two-thirds of the Caribbean island of Hispaniola, the Dominican Republic is separated from Haiti, which occupies the western third, by a rugged mountain range. Area: 48,442 sq km (18,704 sq mi). Pop. (1977 est.): 5 million, including (1960) mulatto 73%; white 16%; Negro 11%. Cap. and largest city: Santo Domingo (pop., 1977 est., 1 million). Language: Spanish. Religion: mainly Roman Catholic (94%), with Protestant and Jewish minorities. President in 1977, Joaquín Balaguer.

Failure to come to an agreement on sugar prices at an international meeting in Geneva had a negative effect on the ongoing recession affecting the Dominican economy. This situation was worsened by a drought that caused a reduction in the pro-

DOMINICAN REPUBLIC

Education. Primary (1972–73), pupils 833,439, teachers 15,216; secondary (1971–72), pupils 118,190, teachers 5,-381; vocational (1971–72), pupils 6,923, teachers 409; teacher training (1971–72), students 621, teachers 51; higher (1973–74), students 37,538, teaching staff 1,709.

Finance. Monetary unit: peso, at parity with the U.S. dollar, with a free rate (Sept. 19, 1977) of 1.74 pesos to £1 sterling. Gold, SDR's, and foreign exchange (June 1977) U.S. $102.1 million. Budget (1976 actual): revenue 583.9 million pesos; expenditure 555.2 million pesos. Gross national product (1975) 3,516,800,000 pesos. Money supply (April 1977) 378.6 million pesos. Cost of living (Santo Domingo; 1971 = 100; March 1977) 189.

Foreign Trade. (1976) Imports 878.1 million pesos; exports 716.4 million pesos. Import sources: U.S. 68%; Japan 9%. Export destinations: U.S. 70%; The Netherlands 7%; Switzerland 7%. Main exports: sugar 38%; coffee 14%; cocoa 7%; tobacco 5%.

Transport and Communications. Roads (1971) 10,467 km. Motor vehicles in use (1975): passenger 71,500; commercial (including buses) 35,600. Railways (including sugar estates; 1975) c. 1,700 km. Telephones (Jan. 1976) 108,000. Radio receivers (Dec. 1974) 185,000. Television receivers (Dec. 1974) 156,000.

Agriculture. Production (in 000; metric tons; 1976): rice c. 286; corn (1975) c. 53; sweet potatoes (1975) c. 102; cassava (1975) c. 209; sugar, raw value c. 1,315; dry beans c. 40; tomatoes c. 92; peanuts c. 60; oranges c. 70; avocados (1975) c. 131; mangoes c. 164; bananas c. 302; cocoa c. 37; coffee c. 51; tobacco c. 31. Livestock (in 000; June 1975): cattle c. 1,900; sheep c. 50; pigs c. 820; goats c. 345; horses c. 174; chickens c. 7,300.

Industry. Production (in 000; metric tons; 1975): cement 555; bauxite 785; electricity (kw-hr) 1,632,000.

duction of coffee, cocoa, and other export goods. A partial solution to this problem was the acceleration of small construction projects. The tourist industry was strengthened by the opening of a seaport-airport complex on the northern coast.

In the political arena public protests were raised to prevent the establishment of a political party by a son of the assassinated dictator Rafael Trujillo. Activities to prepare for the 1978 elections seemed to be running smoothly, with the participation of all political parties.

The Autonomous University of Santo Domingo experienced unrest, as students and teachers demanded an increase in its budget. Revisions of primary school curricula and an intensification of a campaign against illiteracy were the most significant achievements in the educational sector.

(RAFAEL EMILIO YUNEN)

Earth Sciences

GEOLOGY AND GEOCHEMISTRY

In the past geological research had been commonly associated with exploration. New rocks were discovered as geologists opened new frontiers in unknown terranes. Although geological research in 1977 was still associated with exploration, it was being conducted by a new breed of explorers who carried fewer hammers and who depended more upon complex instruments, theory, and the power of computers. The new frontiers were those parts of the Earth not accessible directly, such as the ocean floor and beneath the Earth's crust.

Plate Tectonics and Mountain Building. According to simple plate-tectonic theory, the uplift of Tibet and the Himalayas resulted from the collision of two rigid plates containing the continental masses of India and Asia. The past year saw completion of much research and accumulation of valuable evidence from interpretation of Landsat satellite imagery. The geology, structure, and evolution of Tibet and analogous regions was the subject of a Penrose Conference in March, where it was amply demonstrated that the collision between India and Asia could not be described simply in terms of two rigid plates.

Four different models were presented for the evolution of Tibet. In one, the Asian lithosphere behaved like a rigid plastic medium, indented by the rigid Indian plate, with Tibet analogous to the "dead triangle" observed in laboratory experiments with rigid plastic media. The slip-line fields emanating from a dead triangle correspond to the major strike-slip faults that are displacing China eastward, out of the way of the converging plates. The other models suggested that Tibet was heated and prepared for deformation by late Cretaceous subduction and convection in the asthenosphere, that Tibet was shortened like an accordion, with crustal thickening, or that India was thrust under the whole of Tibet. It was agreed at the conference that the best way to test the models was by detailed mapping of these poorly charted regions.

Plate Tectonics, Energy, and Mineral Resources. A review article with the above title, published in August, was subtitled "Basic research leading to a payoff." This hope had been expressed before, but it was possible that the Earth sciences were in a pivotal period when the emphasis of organized international research in geology was tipping from the theory of Earth dynamics toward natural-resource systems.

Whereas many papers have illustrated how the concepts of plate tectonics provide general guidelines to likely new regions of mineralization and energy resources, current research was directed toward making more precise predictions for the location of hydrocarbon deposits and specific types of ore. Refinement of the plate-tectonic model was needed for the design of prospecting programs.

An important aspect of this research involved exploration of the ocean floor. At divergent plate boundaries, where structural and thermal conditions favour penetration of basalt by seawater—with subsequent intense hydrothermal circulation—metalliferous sulfide bodies of hydrothermal origin are developed on and within the oceanic crust. Exploration for submarine hydrothermal activity and metal deposits in oceanic crust was being conducted by the Deep Sea Drilling Project (DSDP).

Scientific Ocean Drilling. The spectacularly successful DSDP, started in the U.S. in 1968, recently entered a new phase—the International Phase of Ocean Drilling, involving 14 institutions from six countries. The program included deep drilling to determine the structure of the ocean crust and the continental shelves, potentially significant sources of raw materials, together with a developing science of the paleoenvironment, involving the interaction among paleoclimatology, paleogeochemistry, paleo-oceanography, and the living Earth. Such remote exploration by drilling was being

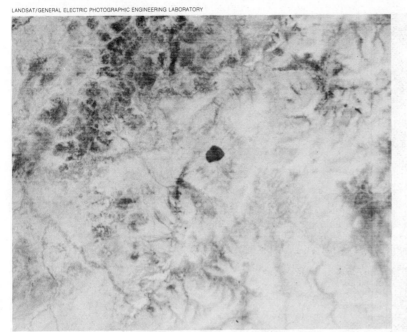

Satellite photos indicate that Sithylemenkat Lake in Alaska probably was created as a result of a meteor impact. If so, the meteor must have weighed approximately 50 million metric tons.

supplemented by direct visual contact and collection of specimens by geological explorers in submersible research vessels.

Planning committees were at work in 1977 preparing proposals for continuation to 1981. The prospect of supplementing the deep-drilling ship "Glomar Challenger" with a new ship, the "Glomar Explorer," offered an opportunity for drilling under poor weather conditions in high latitudes, and for drilling with riser control for deep penetration, which was necessary for some important drilling objectives.

Antarctic Research. During the winter of 1976–77, a joint U.S.-Japanese expedition from the U.S. base station near McMurdo Sound in Antarctica combined aspects of classical geological exploration with space research. This work was planned following discovery by Japanese explorers, in successive expeditions since 1969 on the opposite side of Antarctica, of about a thousand meteorite specimens with total weight of 100 kg. The latest expedition found concentrations of meteorites with total weight of 460 kg perched on the surface of windswept blue ice near the peaks of partially ice-buried mountain ranges.

The process of meteorite concentration was thought to begin when the infrequent falls of meteorites over the ice sheet become buried by new snow and are transported toward the continental margins within the ice. Normally the entrained meteorites become mixed and camouflaged with much larger quantities of Antarctic rock plucked from mountains through which the ice flows in marginal glaciers. In suitable locations, however, when barrier mountain ranges cause the ice to flow upward, fierce winds blow new snow away and erode the old ice, thus exposing the meteorites to easy view before they become mixed with other rocks.

McMurdo Station borders the Ross Ice Shelf, which probably rested on the ocean floor 6,000 years ago. Presently the shelf is floating, and there was evidence that it may be disintegrating. The Ross Ice Shelf Project was a major U.S. research program, and drilling was started into the shelf in late 1976 to determine its history and present condition. Flowing ice trapped the drill bits in the holes, but resumption of the project in December 1977 met with success; nearly 425 m (1,400 ft) of ice were pierced in just ten hours using a special drill tipped with a jet of hot gas. Subsequent observation via television cameras and lights lowered below the ice revealed the presence of a rich community of marine life despite the complete lack of sunlight and of direct contact with atmospheric oxygen.

If the Ross Ice Shelf disintegrated, it would cease to keep the ice of the Western Ice Sheet piled high above the Antarctic continent. Some glaciologists and geologists estimated that a catastrophic surge of the ice sheet could occur within 300 years. If the ice collapsed and melted into the ocean, sea levels would be raised by about 6–7 m (20 ft) worldwide with severe consequences for coastal cities. The prospect of large fluctuations within such a short time span had not generally been considered plausible before these recent studies.

Thermodynamics and Experimental Petrology. There have been several conferences dealing with thermodynamics during recent years, illustrating the increasing power of theoretical approaches to problems in geology and geochemistry. Calculations were hampered by inadequate thermochemical data, but new developments in high-temperature calorimetry of refractory rock-forming minerals were improving this situation. The combination of calorimetry and phase-equilibrium experimental studies was developing into a powerful approach, defining relationships with a clarity previously impossible.

New research programs were under way to determine the thermodynamic properties of silicate

WIDE WORLD

A huge lava flow spewed from Kilauea volcano in Hawaii after an eruption in September. The volcano suddenly ceased erupting and no serious property damage occurred.

liquids with the compositions of magmas. The high-temperature heat contents of silicate liquids were determined by calorimetry. An internally consistent set of volume, enthalpy, and entropy data for liquid silicate compounds was derived from the calorimetric data. These thermodynamic data were used to calculate the pressures and temperatures at which magmas equilibrated with stipulated source materials in the mantle. The results appeared to be reasonably consistent with experimentally determined phase diagrams.

Computers in Geology. The DSDP routinely processed by computer most of the quantitative data gathered. Numerous large data sets for many other research programs in geology and geochemistry also were stored in computers, and there was much activity in the applications of computers to simulation models for mine planning, estimating the reserves of ores, and optimization techniques in mineral industries. Many instruments became more efficient when coupled with a computer. The use of neodymium/samarium isotopes for geochronology and petrogenetic tracers became possible only through computer-controlled acquisition of high-precision mass-spectrometer data. Many calculations of mineral reactions were processed by computer, making possible complex calculations and predictions that formerly had been beyond the capability of geochemists.

(PETER JOHN WYLLIE)
[212.D–F; 213.D; 214.A.5; 222.A.3.a; 241.F–G]

GEOPHYSICS

Destructive earthquakes during the reporting period included one of magnitude 7.4 in the region of the Turkey-Iran-U.S.S.R. border, which occurred on Nov. 24, 1976, and killed 5,000 persons,

and a very damaging shock of magnitude 7.1, which occurred on March 4, 1977, near Bucharest, Romania, killing 1,570 persons and causing many injuries. (*See* ROMANIA.) The largest shock during the period had a magnitude of 7.7 to 8.7. Although it occurred in a remote area south of Sumbawa Island, Indonesia, it caused a destructive tsunami that reached heights of 30 m at several points and left 187 known dead.

Worldwide seismological research continued, with much of it aimed at eventual prediction capability. (*See* Special Report.) It had long been noted by seismologists that very large earthquakes are not adequately described by the Richter magnitude scale. The difference in Richter magnitude of an ordinary large shock and one of cataclysmically destructive proportions is often very minor, although the shocks are obviously of very different size. A recently published study by Hiroo Kanamori of the California Institute of Technology noted that the Richter magnitude scale is saturated when the rupture dimension of the earthquake exceeds the wavelength of the seismic waves used in the determination of the magnitude; this leads to an inaccurate estimate of the energy released by great earthquakes. He defined a new magnitude M_w based on the strain energy drop derived from the seismic moment and the area of the fault interface.

This concept had several important theoretical implications, but most importantly it provided a magnitude scale that coincided with the Richter magnitude for earthquakes with rupture dimensions of less than 100 km but provided greater resolution for determining the size of really large shocks. The largest magnitude assigned under the new system of determination was 9.5 for an earthquake in Chile in 1960 that had been given a Richter magnitude of 8.3. In contrast, the Kuril Islands shock of 1958 had been assigned a Richter magnitude of 8.7 but under the new scale was reduced to 8.3, whereas the great Alaska shock of 1964 was rated up from 8.4 to 9.2. Although these changes did not show a consistent upward trend, the new scale gave a much smoother, more direct correlation to other derived and observed effects of the relative severity of the great earthquakes.

Chinese Seismology. Successful predictions in February 1975 of a major Chinese earthquake in Liaoning Province saved thousands of lives and resulted in widespread interest among world seismologists. A special study delegation, headed by Barry Raleigh of the U.S. Geological Survey, visited China in 1976 in part to study the effects of the earthquake and the methods used in its prediction and in evacuation of the affected communities. Earlier visitors making similar studies were R. D. Adams from New Zealand and a Canadian seismological mission headed by Kenneth Whitham. The U.S. team found that the epicentral area was near the northern boundary of a highly seismic region and that a series of large shocks occurring progressively closer to the region prompted the Chinese to identify the province as long ago as 1970 as a region deserving special attention.

The first prediction in June 1974 postulated an intermediate-size shock in the area within the next one to two years. Then, on Jan. 13, 1975, a more definite prediction was made that a shock of magnitude 5.5–6.0 would occur in the first six months of 1975. Finally, the official warning of imminent earthquake was given a few hours prior to the actual shock. The long-term prediction was made on the basis of epicentre migration patterns and temporal periodicity. New equipment was installed, fault structures were investigated, the professional seismological staff was increased, and many nonprofessional observers were employed. The intermediate-term prediction was based on data collected through this increased effort. Then, on Feb. 1, 1975, a series of foreshocks of increasing frequency and magnitude began, lasting until six hours before the main shock on February 4 and culminating in a foreshock of magnitude 4.8. This activity was the final spur to the issuance of the prediction a few hours prior to the earthquake.

Continent Building. Plate-tectonic theory continued in the forefront of geophysical interest. Most of the results of recent studies tended to reinforce or expand upon the original concept, including a recently completed study of ancient rocks in Greenland. The age of the Earth has been inferred from the age of Moon rocks and meteorite materials, which are older than any rocks yet found on Earth, and from the decay sequences of several radioactive elements in terrestrial rocks. Although 4.6 billion years has been determined as the age of the Earth and the solar system, until recently the oldest rocks found on Earth were only about 2.6 billion years old. Stephen Moorbath and colleagues found rocks in Greenland that have an age of 3.8 billion years. From this evidence, which was corroborated by finds in other parts of the world, Moorbath constructed a sequence of continental

development that correlated with plate tectonics. The oldest rocks dated have even earlier inclusions, however, so they could not be inferred to be part of the original continental surface.

According to Moorbath, irreversible chemical differentiation of the mantle formed the first crust at least 3.8 billion years ago. This was followed by an episode of immense accretion lasting only 200 million years, during which the bulk of continental material was formed. He suggested that continent forming is episodic and gave evidence that these episodes occurred 3.8, 2.9–2.6, 1.9–1.7, and 1.1–0.9 billion years ago and most recently at the beginning of the present plate-tectonic cycle, 600 million years ago, when the supercontinent Pangaea began to break up.

(RUTLAGE J. BRAZEE)

[213.B; 223.B.1.c; 241.D–G]

HYDROLOGY

Droughts, floods, and the need for sensible governmental policies with which to meet their effects and those of increasing demands for water dominated hydrology in 1977.

The central and western U.S. experienced extensive droughts during most of the year. Seasonal rains, including some severe storms that caused flooding in the Midwest, eventually alleviated the situation in the central and northwest regions. Rains in California, however, particularly its central region, continued well below normal.

The major effect of the drought in California was on agriculture and power production. Local standby power supplies and the availability of electricity from the Northwest averted power shortages and made it feasible for farmers to revert to the use of groundwater to save agricultural production in the Central Valley. Thousands of water wells, previously abandoned to alleviate land subsidence when surface-water supplies were made available from California's reservoirs, were renovated. The effect of the renewed withdrawal of water from aquifers underlying land prone to subsidence remained to be proven. By the end of August reservoirs in California were carrying about 32% of their normal volume and the flows of many streams were the lowest of record.

The drought also affected water quality as well as quantity. Low flows in rivers, particularly those carrying sewage, were characterized by undesirable odours and heavy growths of algae. Fish and plants were affected where dissolved oxygen concentrations dropped and stream temperatures rose. For example, about one-tenth of the northern California salmon run were to be transferred from the Sacramento River, where water temperatures became too high for spawning. Declining groundwater levels allowed salt water to invade some coastal aquifers. Consequently some communities turned to bottled water as the quality of the groundwater on which they had depended declined to unsuitable levels.

International Activities. Two worldwide, UN-sponsored conferences considered problems of world water supply and of the encroachment of deserts (desertification). Both conferences were convened in the expectation that such attention

WIDE WORLD

Near empty reservoirs were a common sight in northern California. In a normal year the water level of the Pardee Reservoir (right) would be up near the catwalk on which superintendent Donn Wilson stands.

would galvanize governments to support the research and administrative adjustments required to reach needed methodologies and policies.

The UN Water Conference, held in Argentina, focused on the need to establish national water policies on the basis of water resources assessments. The participating countries agreed to seek assessments and to arrive at policy guidelines by 1990. These would be submitted to the UN Economic and Social Council for consolidation into a world assessment.

Subsequently Kenya was host to the UN Desertification Conference in Nairobi. The gathering outlined guidelines for an overall plan to combat and reverse the process of desertification, which some claimed was expanding desert areas at the rate of about 5,000 sq km per year. The causes of desertification generally were conceded to be manmade and thus should be subject to organized counteraction. They included overpopulation, overgrazing, overcultivation, deforestation, excessive lowering of shallow groundwater tables, soil degradation, and erosion. (*See* Feature Article: *Nor Any Drop to Drink.*)   (L. A. HEINDL)
[222.A.2; 232.C.5.a–c; 232.C.5.f]

METEOROLOGY

Weather and climate with their academic umbrella, the atmospheric sciences, were among the foremost subjects of public interest during 1977. Perhaps the most phenomenal advance in recent years in the field of forecasting was improved techniques for discovery and prediction of tropical cyclones; that is, hurricanes and typhoons. Only a quarter-century earlier, these fierce storms had brought certain death and destruction every year to ships at sea, to coastal cities and shores of the

Caribbean, Gulf of Mexico, West Indies, and southeastern U.S., and more frequently to lands of the western Pacific, the Indian Ocean, and adjoining waters. By 1977, although annual losses from tropical cyclones were still large, they were reduced to a small fraction of previous average totals. Prevention came primarily through timely storm warnings and advisory bulletins, which made it possible for inhabitants to find protection.

The underlying science and technology consisted mostly of combined use of hemispheral synoptic weather charts analyzed at least four times daily, aircraft reconnaissance, long-range radar, and computer processing. More than 20 of the member countries of the World Meteorological Organization (WMO) were contributing to these advances in protection against cyclones, in particular the National Hurricane Center in Miami, Fla., whose work was outstanding.

Understanding Climatic Changes. Record-breaking cold in the eastern half of the U.S. during the winter of 1976–77 and prolonged droughts in western states typified the world's weather abnormalities that spurred meteorologists to still greater studies. The British Isles, plagued in 1976 by the worst droughts in a century in many localities, recovered after return of near normal rainfall. Year after year similar anomalies in weather in one region or another on every continent emphasized the urgency of research and progress in meteorology.

Responding to these acute needs the scientific journals in 1977 focused on research for improving the accuracy and time range of predictions, especially on great changes in climate and weather. Again, the climatic effects of man-made pollutants were extensively investigated. Experiments in rainmaking by cloud seeding were continued over drought-stricken localities in many nations, particularly Australia, Brazil, Canada, China, France, India, Japan, Mexico, Norway, Sweden, the U.K., the U.S.S.R., and the U.S. Usually the results were controversial.

Apprehension over changes in weather and climate led WMO, the American Meteorological Society (AMS), and other concerned scientific bodies to organize study groups and symposia with participation by well-recognized world experts. Significant among their conclusions was the finding that such man-made pollutants as CO_2, dust, and effluents that attack the ozone layer could indeed modify the climate if continued for two or three decades at 1977 amounts. The jeopardy was accentuated by the divergence of expert opinions. Some thought the consequence would be a warming of the atmosphere, melting of the Earth's ice caps, and critical rise in sea level; other scientists found that the complex reactions would bring a colder atmosphere and earlier return of an interim ice age.

One symposium found reasons to be somewhat less optimistic about future use of rainmaking and methods of weather modification than had been predicted during the initial enthusiasm of the 1950s and 1960s. The WMO quarterly bulletin for January 1977 published conclusions of a world conference in Boulder, Colo., which confirmed that under certain conditions the seeding of clouds might add 10–20% precipitation on the ground.

Many successes were reported but also many failures. In hail suppression efforts the U.S.S.R. reported 50–90% successes, whereas many other nations experienced much poorer results. There was even some evidence that cloud seeding might increase hail. Methods and analysis of results were often questionable. Agreement on the qualified success of seeding to dissipate fog from airports gave an affirmative answer to at least this segment of weather modification.

(F. W. REICHELDERFER)

[224.A.3.e; 224.B.3.b; 224.C; 224.D.2 and 6]

OCEANOGRAPHY

Over the past decade, work by the Deep Sea Drilling Project has confirmed and described, worldwide and in impressive detail, the pattern of seafloor spreading. At mid-oceanic ridges, molten material from the Earth's interior rises and then spreads laterally as a crust of basalt, over which sediments gradually accumulate. The interior temperature of these sediments usually rises with increasing penetration, an indication that heat from the Earth's interior is diffusing outward into the oceans. Measurements made in this way generally show a smooth increase of outward diffusion toward the spreading centres.

During the past year, new and detailed studies of heat flow were made at one spreading centre,

the Galápagos Rift of the eastern equatorial Pacific. It was found that heat flow there also occurs when submarine hot springs vent warm water into the sea. Earlier studies had shown an abnormally high percentage of the rare isotope helium-3 in submarine hot springs at the bottom of the Red Sea, where another spreading centre is located. This extra helium-3 indicates that brine from the hot springs had spent a long time in contact with the basalts forming the ocean crust. During the year a similar excess of helium-3 was reported in the Galápagos Rift.

Researchers studied the region with undersea cameras that could be towed above the seafloor from shipboard while simultaneously monitoring water temperature for plumes of hot water. They then descended to the most promising sites in the deep-diving submersible "Alvin." At one location, water could be seen emerging from cracks in the lava. Unusual sea life around the vents included giant mussels, clams, and large anemones, as well as previously unidentified animals. These organisms evidently feed upon bacteria that are able to utilize hydrogen sulfide in the vented water.

As fossil fuels become scarcer and more expensive, alternate sources of energy become important. During the year large-scale engineering studies considered at least two oceanic sources of energy. One, harnessing the tides, was an old idea

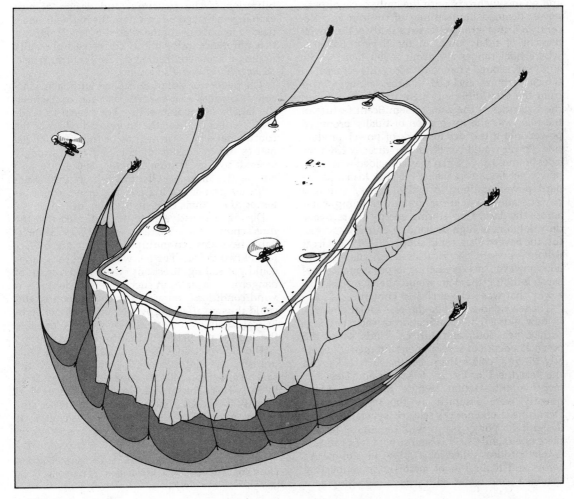

An artist's conception of one way to tow icebergs using tugs and helicopters. Large masses of ice from the polar caps could supply drought-stricken lands with abundant fresh water.

Whereas scant sea life and near-freezing temperatures are typical along most of the Galápagos Rift, large fissures such as that shown at right were thought to provide cold-water inlets for hot springs that emerge from the central rift valley. Giant clams (far right), some of them 12 inches long, are among the strange creatures that have evolved near these underwater geysers.

Eastern European Literature:
see Literature

Eastern Orthodox Churches:
see Religion

Ecology:
see Environment; Life Sciences

and was feasible only in places where the tidal range is high. Even there, if turbines are run directly from tides, the fact that tides do not come and go in synchrony with the daily cycle of peak power demand limits utility of the concept. Recently a British group released a study of the development of tidal power in the Severn Estuary, where tidal ranges are about seven metres. The study envisioned a dam built across the estuary, in which turbines enclosed in tubes extract power from the tidal difference in water level between the two sides of the dam. A significant feature of the plan was the integration of tidally produced power into a broader network of power production. Power would be withdrawn directly from the tides on those days when they coincided with peak power needs, thus reducing the peak load on standard power stations. At other times, standard power stations would run at night to pump water across the dam, thus storing energy for recovery during hours of high demand. If entirely successful, the Severn Dam could supply 10–20% of Great Britain's present electrical needs. A major problem, however, was predicting its performance, because building the dam would alter local tides in a way that was not yet clearly known.

The second idea is a popular one—solar power—in new guise. The combination of solar heating, surface heat loss, and surface winds keeps the ocean at a depth of several thousand metres generally 15–20° C colder than near the surface. During the year the U.S. Energy Research and Development Administration (whose functions subsequently were assumed by the newly created Department of Energy) selected several firms to design pilot power plants with the aim of testing the exploitability of this source on a large scale.

Current ideas called for a "pipe" tens of metres across and thousands of metres long connecting the deep, cold water with generating equipment

in the warm surface layers. The problems involved in producing operating power plants included fabrication and installation of such massive pipe, stabilization of the structure, and design of heat exchangers that could maintain the high efficiency needed to make use of the relatively small temperature difference in the highly corrosive and readily fouling marine environment. (*See* Feature Article: *Managing the World's Oceans*.)

The history of seafaring is filled with factual accounts of freak giant waves that can overwhelm the largest of modern ships. They seem to occur most frequently near the shoreward edges of the continental slopes (in depths of roughly 100–200 metres) where coastal currents tend to be strongly steered by the bottom. These regions are also among the most heavily traveled in the ocean; ships making or leaving port traverse them or attempt to use their currents to save fuel.

During the past year studies indicated that the interaction of these currents with otherwise navigable sea states can multiply wave height by factors of two to four. Further work along these lines could put sailing directions, which often warn of dangerous sea states in such waters under certain wind conditions, on a firm scientific footing and could thus greatly improve the utility of meteorological satellites to seafarers by making possible the routine prediction of catastrophic sea states.

The U.S. National Aeronautics and Space Administration continued with plans to launch the first oceanographically oriented satellite, Seasat A, by early 1978. The satellite would monitor sea level directly by radar altimetry and image the sea surface at microwave and infrared wavelengths. It would cover most of the world oceans every 36 hours. (MYRL C. HENDERSHOTT)

See also Disasters; Energy; Life Sciences; Mining and Quarrying; Physics; Space Exploration; Speleology.
[241.G; 721.A.3.a and c]

MOVING CLOSER TO EARTHQUAKE PREDICTIONS

by Walter Sullivan

Until a few years ago the idea of being able to predict earthquakes, much less control them, seemed utterly hopeless. Other great natural catastrophes, such as hurricanes or tornadoes, could be observed as they approached, but the only clue to earthquakes was their tendency to occur in some regions and not in others. For example, earthquakes of local origin are virtually unknown in Texas, but Californians are all too familiar with them. Indeed such familiarity applies to almost all who live around the rim of the Pacific, for reasons that have become evident in the new theory of plate tectonics.

Walter Sullivan is Science Editor of the New York Times

Plates in Motion. A crude way to predict quakes, therefore, was to look at the record of past occurrences in particular regions and seek out those sectors where a quake was "overdue." According to the theory of plate tectonics, the main body of the Pacific floor forms a giant plate of the Earth's surface that is moving inexorably northwest relative to the land surrounding it. The northern and western edges of the plate are descending under the volcanic island arcs along its boundary, including the Aleutians, the Kurils, the Marianas, and the Philippines. The process generates earthquakes under those islands as well as volcanic activity. A smaller section of the Pacific floor off South America is moving east, away from the East Pacific Rise that breaks the ocean's surface at a few points (including Easter Island). Its descent under South America produced the Andes Mountains, with their lofty volcanoes, and also causes the earthquakes that sometimes take thousands of lives along the coast.

Other plate movements, probably related to changes in the relative positions of Eurasia and Africa, account for the earthquakes north and east of the Mediterranean, as in Italy, Yugoslavia, Greece, and Turkey. A plate that includes India and Pakistan and was once attached to Australia and Antarctica has pushed north against the southern flank of Asia,

The awesome power of earthquakes was exhibited in San Francisco in 1906.

NOAA

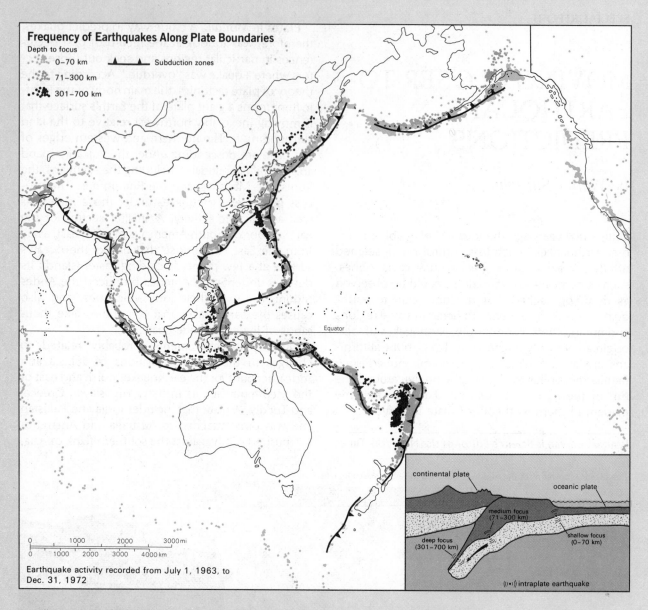

Frequency of Earthquakes Along Plate Boundaries

Depth to focus
- 0–70 km
- 71–300 km
- 301–700 km

Subduction zones

Equator

0   1000   2000   3000 mi
0   1000   2000   3000   4000 km

Earthquake activity recorded from July 1, 1963, to
Dec. 31, 1972

continental plate

oceanic plate

medium focus
(71–300 km)

deep focus
(301–700 km)

shallow focus
(0–70 km)

((•)) intraplate earthquake

Surveillance over the past 17 years provided the first precise information on the location of both deep- and shallow-
focus earthquakes in the Pacific region and elsewhere. Quakes were found to occur along belts that outline plate
boundaries. Subduction zones, where one plate dives beneath another (inset), are sites of high seismic activity.

thrusting up the Himalayas, Pamirs, and Hindu Kush, the highest mountains in the world.

Pressure-Wave Velocity. This same plate is continuing to move, and one of the resulting earthquakes led to a disaster that set in motion an intensive effort to find ways to predict a quake. In 1949 the town of Khait at the outlet of a deep, V-shaped valley in the Pamir Mountains of Tadzhikistan, a Soviet republic northeast of Afghanistan, was buried with its 12,000 inhabitants when a landslide released by a quake farther up the valley impounded water and then collapsed, allowing the town to be suddenly inundated.

Since the region, like many earthquake-prone areas, is frequently subject to tiny quakes, most of them observable only with instruments, it occurred to Soviet scientists that by monitoring such activity they might uncover some sort of warning sign. This led to the discovery that before the more severe quakes there is a slowing in the velocity of pressure waves (which include sound waves) traveling through that part of the Earth's crust where a quake is to occur. Earthquakes generate several forms of wave motion, but this effect seems applicable only to pressure waves.

The United States Geological Survey, which was also looking for ways to predict quakes, had set up a number of seismic stations along California's San Andreas Fault, each equipped with instruments capable of recording the various forms of ground motion produced by a quake. The Survey and cooperating institutions, such as the California Insti-

318

Buildings tumbled into a giant fissure in Alaska during a 1964 earthquake.

tute of Technology, began watching for the effect reported by the Soviets, and they also examined past records. It appeared that the slowing of pressure waves had, in fact, occurred before California's San Fernando quake of Feb. 9, 1971, which took 65 lives and did an estimated $500 million in damage north of Los Angeles.

Unfortunately, a change in pressure-wave velocity has not been recorded before all earthquakes, possibly because of difficulties in observing waves from a sufficient number of directions to catch those passing through the critical area. Based on the observations that have been made, scientists have concluded that a quake tends to occur not at the time of maximum slowing in wave velocity but when that velocity has returned to normal. The more prolonged the period of slowing before such recovery, the more severe the earthquake that follows.

Other Warning Signs. There are a number of other warning signs that are applicable, at least to some quakes in some areas. As strain accumulates toward the breaking point, the terrain may swell or tilt in an observable manner. In 1958 Japanese surveys in the vicinity of Niigata on the west coast of Honshu showed a rise in the landscape that in some areas approached five centimetres (two inches). In 1964 a severe earthquake struck the city. Changes in tilt have been recorded before quakes along the San Andreas Fault.

During the 1960s the Palmdale region some 50 mi north of downtown Los Angeles began to swell, and by the 1970s its central section had risen about ten inches. This "Palmdale Bulge" extended along 450 mi of the San Andreas Fault, though by 1977 it had begun to subside. Hundreds of small tremors were recorded in the vicinity of the uplift, but seismologists were reluctant to make any firm predictions concerning the imminence of a quake in the area.

A warning sign noticed by Soviet scientists is an increase in the radon content of water from deep wells. Radon is a radioactive gas with a half-life of 3.823 days. It is emitted by radium within the Earth, and because it decays rapidly very little is normally found in well water. When the crustal rocks are under stress, however, it appears that cracks open and allow a relatively rapid discharge of radon into a deep well.

Prediction in China. The most ambitious, and seemingly successful, effort at prediction has been carried out in China. The Chinese had strong motivation for such a program, for no other region of the world has suffered such devastating earthquakes. It is said that, following one in 1556, the emperor ordered an inventory of the casualties, and some 820,000 of those killed were recorded by name. The total deaths may have been a million. Estimates of the casualties in and near T'ang-shan from the earthquake of July 28, 1976, run to more than 650,000.

Slow movement along the San Andreas fault was demonstrated in Marin County, California, where a fence has become offset 8 1/2 feet by subterranean movement.

Rather than focusing on any one type of warning, the Chinese sought to watch all the reported indicators, ranging from unusual animal behaviour to changes in pressure-wave velocity. One of the most dramatic successes of the Chinese was their prediction of a serious earthquake at Hai-ch'eng on the Liaoning Peninsula in February 1975. An earlier warning, in December 1974, had caused the authorities to order people out of their homes. The populace slept in tents pitched on the snowy landscape, and no quake occurred. In February, therefore, considerable persuasion was needed to bring about another evacuation. This time a major quake did occur, and thousands of lives are believed to have been saved. There seem to have been some rather ambiguous warning signs before the devastating T'ang-shan quake, but in that instance no emergency measures were taken.

The Chinese have reported a variety of unusual forms of animal behaviour before quakes: snakes coming out of their holes, chickens refusing to roost, dogs barking incessantly. Such behaviour has also been observed elsewhere, leading to speculation that some animals may recognize warning sounds or other manifestations beyond the reach of human senses.

Future Prospects. It seems likely that it will eventually become possible to predict many, if not all, quakes and even to control some. How to make use of a prediction for a large city such as Los Angeles or San Francisco has been much debated during the past few years. Such measures as moving firefighting equipment out of doors and shutting off gas pipelines have been programmed, but evacuation of the population would be a formidable and highly disruptive operation.

The possibility of control came to light when it was discovered in the 1960s that small quakes tended to occur in the vicinity of Denver, Colo., whenever fluid (contaminated with chemical warfare agents) was injected into a 12,000-ft well at the U.S. Army's Rocky Mountain Arsenal. If quakes could be "turned on" by fluid injection, perhaps they could be "turned off" by withdrawing water. This proposition was demonstrated at the Rangely oil field in western Colorado, where water was being injected into some wells to drive oil upward in other nearby wells. The injections were causing local quakes, and when water was removed the quakes ceased.

Under consideration has been a tactic for relieving, by water injection, the stress that leads to major earthquakes. The method would only be applicable to areas, such as the San Andreas Fault, where the quakes occur at a shallow depth. A sector of the fault would be locked by water withdrawal at the ends of the sector. Water would then be injected into wells between the locked ends to produce a local earthquake of minor intensity. At this time, however, the controlling factors are not well enough understood to permit the use of such a strategy near any population centre, lest a major quake be induced rather than a minor one.

Economy, World

A mixed and somewhat disappointing performance in the world economy characterized the year 1977. By the end of 1976 it was clear that the recovery from the previous year's recession was beginning to falter and that several countries of the non-Communist world were not achieving their objective of a cautious but steady growth in output combined with a reasonable balance in overseas payments. The task for 1977, therefore, was to devise a world economic strategy that would boost the faltering growth rate and assist in the achievement of desirable external payments balances. This, however, was not possible. The tempo of growth remained sluggish and erratic. External imbalances became more pronounced, giving rise to instability in foreign exchange markets and to a growth in protectionist sentiments.

In 1976 growth in the 24 member countries of the Organization for Economic Cooperation and Development (OECD) was estimated at just over 5%. Although there was an encouraging acceleration in the growth rate in the U.S. during the first half of 1977, other countries failed to follow suit, and by the summer of 1977 it appeared that growth for the whole year would fall to about 4%. The main reason for this was that countries with balance of payments surpluses were reluctant to boost domestic demand, relying instead on exports to provide support to domestic activity. This policy, however, had the effect of reducing the potential for imports from the deficit countries, which, in turn, were forced to take a restrictive approach to domestic demand in order not to aggravate their balance of payments difficulties.

Thus, the West German government refused to provide a significant boost to the economy before September, despite a strong external balance and a continued decline in the rate of inflation. In a similar vein, Japan postponed action until the autumn despite a mounting and increasingly embarrassing trade surplus. As with those two countries, the United Kingdom, France, Italy, and others also adopted cautious monetary and demand management policies, although in their cases the motivation was the need to combat inflation and to reduce the external payments deficit. This led to a general weakening in the recovery, with virtually every non-Communist industrialized country expecting a slower growth in 1977 than during the previous year. The U.S. was projecting 5% as against 6.1%; the forecast for France pointed to a gain of 3% (compared with 5%); West Germany was looking forward to an advance of 4% (5.6%); and the outlook for the U.K. was no growth at all compared with a gain of just over 1% in 1976. Canada was also expected to do relatively poorly (3.5% as against 4.9%), as were the smaller OECD countries, where the growth rate was projected to fall from 3% to about 2.5%. The only major exception appeared to be Japan, where a slight acceleration in growth seemed likely, but this was largely the result of a strong export performance rather than domestic demand.

Under the circumstances, a sharp reduction in the level of unemployment could hardly be expected. In fact, most countries, with the notable exception of the U.S., registered a continuing increase, and the early indications were that the average unemployment rate for the larger OECD countries, amounting to 5.2% of the labour force in 1976, would not be materially different at the end of 1977. The magnitude of the task before governments was well illustrated by the fact that in 1974 the rate of unemployment had been 3.3%, which in itself compared unfavourably with the average of 2.8% during the preceding ten-year period.

An effect of 1976's poor economic growth was a persistent lack of business confidence. This had a particularly adverse influence on the level of investment expenditures, which in turn held back the growth of industrial production. In fact, in the OECD area industrial output grew by only about 2.5% in the first half of 1977, compared with an increase of 3% during the preceding six-month period. Once again the U.S. was an exception to the rule, but most other countries faced deteriorations in their performances. On the basis of the autumn returns, it was judged that OECD growth for the whole year could reach 5–6%, as against nearly 9% in 1976.

Nor did the trend of consumer prices give reason for much satisfaction. Despite the relatively sluggish growth in output, consumer prices in the OECD area rose at an annual rate of about 10% during the first half of 1977, compared with about 8% in the closing half of the preceding year. Although a significant part of the acceleration was

CHART 1

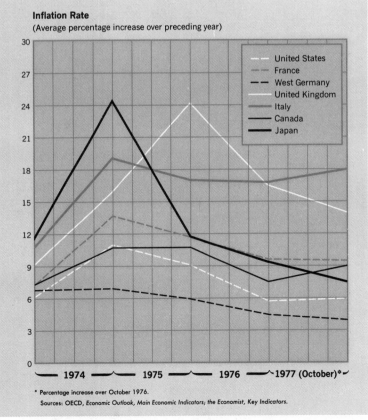

Inflation Rate
(Average percentage increase over preceding year)

United States
France
West Germany
United Kingdom
Italy
Canada
Japan

1974 — 1975 — 1976 — 1977 (October)*

* Percentage increase over October 1976.
Sources: OECD, *Economic Outlook, Main Economic Indicators;* the Economist, *Key Indicators.*

attributed to seasonal factors affecting food prices, by late 1977 the signs were pointing to a rise for the entire year of just over 8%, representing no improvement over 1976. The lowest rates of inflation were projected in Switzerland (1.5% compared with 2% in 1976) and West Germany (4% as against 4.5% in the previous year), but because of the double-digit increases expected in the U.K. and Italy, as well as in some smaller countries such as Finland, Ireland, Spain, and possibly Sweden, Denmark, and Norway, the average for Europe was projected at just over 10%. In Japan the autumn indicators pointed to a rise of about 7%, much the same as in the U.S. but 1–2% below the forecast for Canada.

As in the preceding year, widespread fluctuations in exchange rates took place in 1977. They were largely governed by foreign exchange policies and developments in external payments positions of individual countries. Faced with a rapidly growing trade surplus, Japan attempted to resist the pressure for monetary revaluation. It was forced to give way in the second half of the year, however, and by the end of November the yen's value against the dollar was some 20% higher than a year earlier. At the same time, mainly because of the mounting trade deficit of the U.S., the dollar recorded a decline in most countries, and its value against the trade-weighted average of important currencies fell by about 6% between January and November 1977. The West German mark and the Swiss franc continued to gain strength against virtually all other currencies, and the pound sterling —which was facing a major crisis in late 1976— improved its position against both the dollar (6%) and the weighted average of other important currencies (4.6%). The lira fell just about everywhere, and the Swedish krona was devalued by 10% in August 1977.

With the exception of the African continent, the less developed countries grew at the same rate in 1977 as in 1976. Although a cutback in oil production took place in 1977, this seemed to have been offset by relatively high levels of activity in other sectors of industry and a good increase in agricultural production. Inflation, although probably marginally slower than in 1976, remained a problem. Another adverse feature of the year was the decline in the level of commodity prices. Partly because of this, earlier hopes of a continuing reduction in the current account deficits of the non-oil-producing less developed countries remained largely unfulfilled.

NATIONAL ECONOMIC POLICIES

Developed Market Economies. UNITED STATES. The U.S. economy slowed down appreciably halfway through 1976, just as the presidential election campaign was getting into full swing. The annual increase in gross national product (GNP) fell from a rate of 9.2% in January–March to 4.5 and 3.9% in the two subsequent quarters, and the first results for the fourth quarter indicated a further reduction to 3%. This was later revised to 2.4%, which seemed to confirm fears that the economy was moving into recession once again.

A closer analysis, however, painted a more favourable picture. In fact, the rate of growth of sales for the final quarter of 1976 was the best for the entire year, and the reason for the poor overall performance was a cutback in inventory accumulation. This meant that industry was reducing stocks to more normal levels, thereby creating the opportunity for a sustained increase in industrial production.

Not altogether surprisingly, the economy rebounded during the first half of 1977, giving rise to a 7.5% advance in GNP in the first quarter and a 6.2% gain in the second. The recovery was initially fueled by an exceptionally strong consumer demand, which to a large extent was financed by a sharp depletion of savings and an increase in consumer credit.

The housing boom that began in 1976 gained further momentum in 1977, assisted by plentiful mortgage funds at reasonable interest rates. Nonresidential investment was also strong, especially during the first quarter when it rose at the fastest rate recorded in the current recovery. The strong

CHART 2

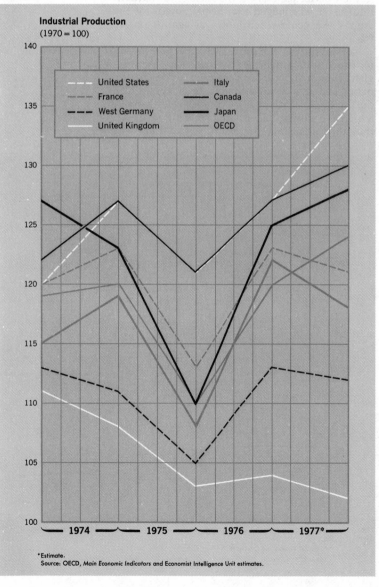

Industrial Production
(1970 = 100)

Legend: United States, France, West Germany, United Kingdom, Italy, Canada, Japan, OECD

1974 — 1975 — 1976 — 1977*

*Estimate.
Source: OECD, *Main Economic Indicators* and Economist Intelligence Unit estimates.

Table I. Real Gross National Products of OECD Countries*

% change, seasonally adjusted annual rates

Country	Average 1963–64 to 1973–74	From previous year 1976	From previous year 1977†	From previous half year 1977 first half	From previous half year 1977 second half†
United States	4.0	6.1	5.25	5.75	5.5
Japan	9.4	6.3	5.5	5.75	7.0
Germany, West	4.4	5.6	4.0	4.5	3.75
France	5.4	5.2	3.0	2.75	3.0
United Kingdom	2.7	1.4	1.0	0.0	2.25
Italy	4.7	5.6	2.25	2.0	0.25
Canada	5.4	4.9	3.0	4.25	3.5
Total major countries	5.0	5.6	4.25	4.5	4.75
Australia	5.1	3.6	2.0	...	...
Austria	5.2	5.2	3.75	...	...
Belgium	5.0	2.3	2.75	...	...
Denmark	4.3	5.5	1.0	...	...
Finland	5.2	0.2	2.0	...	...
Greece	7.1	6.0	5.0	...	...
Ireland	4.1	3.0	4.25	...	...
Netherlands, The	5.3	4.2	3.5	...	...
New Zealand	3.7	−1.1	−2.0	...	...
Norway	4.7	6.0	5.5	...	...
Spain	6.6	1.8	2.25	...	...
Sweden	3.6	1.5	1.0	...	...
Switzerland	3.6	0.5	1.75	...	...
Total OECD countries	5.0	5.2	4.0	4.5	4.75

*OECD countries are those listed above and Iceland, Luxembourg, Portugal, and Turkey.
† Estimate.
Source: Adapted from OECD *Economic Outlook*, July 1977.

demand spurred industrial output, which showed a gain of 9% in the first six months. The quality of this increase could be judged from the fact that it was accompanied by relatively low inventory formation. Not surprisingly, there was a noticeable improvement in the employment situation. The number of unemployed was cut to 6.7 million, or 6.9% of the labour force, by mid-1977, achieving Pres. Jimmy Carter's aim of reducing unemployment to below 7% six months early. After a hesitant start, some progress was also made in slowing down the rate of retail price rises, and by June the government's target of a maximum 5.5% increase by the end of the year looked achievable.

Two aspects of the economy, however, gave rise to concern. The trade deficit, influenced by additional imports of fuel necessitated by the severe winter, had risen to $9,780,000,000 in the five months to May 1977, compared with only $3,610,-000,000 in the same period of 1976. At the same time, government expenditure was unexpectedly sluggish. Actual outlays turned out to be below budget projections, and it was feared that a similar trend could weaken the level of economic activity during the second half of the year.

While the economy was getting into its stride in the spring, the money supply rose at a rapid rate, breaching the Federal Reserve Board's target figures. Encouraged by the bullish economy but worried about the outlook for inflation, the board's Open Market Committee raised the interest rate on federal funds to 5.5%. (Federal funds are moneys available to members of the Federal Reserve System for use as overnight loans to adjust their required reserves against deposits.) This step, however, had only a temporary effect, and, following the April spurt of the narrowly defined money supply (M1), there came another in July and another at the end of September. (M1 is cash in circulation plus checking account deposits.)

This pushed the average growth rate in the six months to October to about 9.5% in spite of a progressively tighter policy followed by the board since the spring. A result of this was that short-term interest rates moved up from 6.25% at the start of the year to 7.75% in November.

The Federal Reserve Board's increasingly restrictive stance, together with the stubborn inflation rate (about 6.5% annually) and the growth of the money supply, gave rise to fears of a further upward adjustment in interest rates, which might discourage the faltering revival in investment. However, in reply to his critics (the ranks of which were reinforced by the Carter administration in October), Federal Reserve Board Chairman Arthur Burns made it clear that it was not the board's intention to create conditions that might jeopardize the prospects for a continued economic recovery. Burns argued that, though the board was confident about the level of economic activity in the final quarter of 1977 and beyond, the still-uncertain outlook for inflation and the dollar necessitated firm monetary policies.

By comparison, the administration's fiscal policy was more expansionist. In early January President Carter proposed a two-year, $31.6 billion package of tax cuts and public works spending designed to stimulate the economy. In fiscal 1977 this would have resulted in a one-time tax rebate of $11.9 billion followed by the proposed additional public spending in 1978. The net result would have been an even larger budget deficit than that approved in the autumn. In April, however, the president—convinced by the bullish economic indicators and uncertain whether he could get the measure through the Congress—announced that the tax rebates were no longer necessary. The proposed stimulus for fiscal 1978, though, remained intact.

In April, too, came the announcement of the administration's energy policy. It could be argued that this was potentially more important to the U.S. and to the world economy than the abandoned tax concessions, for it struck at the root of the mounting current account deficit. (Since most of the U.S. deficit is with the Organization of Petroleum Exporting Countries [OPEC], and they are unable to spend this surplus quickly enough, it is a drag on world economic recovery.) The presi-

ROSS—ROTHCO

"My cartel doesn't understand me."

Table II. Percentage Changes in Consumer Prices in Selected OECD Countries

Country	Average 1963–73	1974	1975	1976	Latest month* 1977
United States	3.8	11.0	9.1	5.8	6.0
Japan	6.0	24.5	11.8	9.3	7.5
Germany, West	3.6	7.0	6.0	4.5	4.0
France	4.6	13.7	11.7	9.6	9.5
United Kingdom	5.6	16.0	24.2	16.5	14.0
Italy	4.6	19.1	17.0	16.8	18.0
Canada	3.9	10.8	10.8	7.5	9.0
Australia	4.3	15.1	15.1	13.5	13.0
Austria	4.4	9.5	8.4	7.3	...
Belgium	4.2	12.7	12.8	9.4	7.2
Denmark	6.4	15.3	9.6	9.0	11.4
Finland	6.3	16.9	17.9	14.4	13.3
Greece	3.8	27.0	13.4	13.3	11.7
Iceland	12.6	42.9	49.1	33.0	29.2
Ireland	6.7	17.0	20.9	18.0	13.9
Luxembourg	3.7	9.5	10.7	9.8	7.3
Netherlands, The	5.7	9.6	10.2	8.8	5.5
Norway	5.5	9.4	11.7	9.1	8.9
Portugal	6.3	29.2	20.4	19.3	35.0
Spain	7.3	15.7	16.9	17.6	22.4
Sweden	5.1	9.9	9.8	10.3	12.5
Total OECD countries	4.6	13.6	11.4	8.6	9.5

*Percentage increase from corresponding month of previous year.
Sources: OECD, *Economic Outlook*, July 1977; OECD, *Main Economic Indicators*; The Economist, *Key Indicators*.

dent's program was aimed at reducing the annual growth rate of energy by 2% between 1977 and 1985 and at encouraging domestic production of energy sources. This was to be achieved by the aid of a complex set of tax, price, subsidy, and rebate measures to be introduced from the beginning of 1978. The package progressed through the House of Representatives slowly, reaching the Senate in September 1977. Increasingly, it seemed unlikely to gain congressional acceptance, adding to the uncertainty of the business community. The other factors behind the autumn gloom were the economic slowdown, which, according to the pessimists, would deepen in 1978; the enormous current account deficit with little prospect of a reduction in 1978; the president's tax reforms, which were twice postponed; and finally the weakness of the dollar on the foreign exchanges.

There was no doubt that the growth of the economy slowed in the summer. The annual growth rate of GNP in the third quarter was down to 3.8%, which meant that growth for the year as a whole would be 0.5% lower than the administration's target of 5.5%. The weaker aspects of the economy in the closing quarters included a decline in retail sales, hardly surprising since consumers, having spent a tax rebate they did not in the end receive, had to catch their breath.

During the closing months of the year industrial production was showing some gains; unemployment was below 7%; inflation appeared steady at about 6%; and personal incomes were set on a gentle upward curve. The only weak spots were the trade balance and the erratic money supply.

At the end of 1977 a 4–4.5% growth rate in 1978 seemed assured, given the government spending programs already under way, the continuing large budget deficit, and the near certainty of a strong fiscal boost—up to $20 billion according to Secretary of the Treasury Michael Blumenthal.

UNITED KINGDOM. In 1976 the British economy experienced a modest growth of 1.2%, but by the end of the year inflation was once again accelerat-

ing and the external value of the pound sterling was falling rapidly. During 1977 gross domestic product (GDP) recorded no increase, but by the closing quarter inflation was on a definite downward curve, the current account of the balance of payments was in surplus, and sterling regained some of the ground lost in the previous year.

The beginnings of this remarkable transformation can be traced back to the end of 1976, when, in return for a standby facility of $3.9 billion designed to stabilize sterling's rapidly weakening position, the International Monetary Fund (IMF) imposed on the U.K. a substantial cut in the public sector borrowing requirement and a fairly restrictive ceiling on the growth of money supply. As these conditions could be met only with the aid of strict controls on private consumption and government spending, the chancellor of the Exchequer submitted a mini-budget in December 1976 which slashed official spending plans and increased indirect taxation. Not surprisingly, the level of GDP in the first quarter of 1977 was well below that of the preceding three months as well as that of the corresponding quarter of the previous year. Although faced with increasing agitation for a change of course from the left wing of the Labour Party, the government stuck to its strategy. In fact, the public sector borrowing requirement and monetary aggregates grew at a slower rate than that imposed by the IMF, and in March the authorities submitted a largely neutral budget.

The second quarter's GDP figures confirmed that the economy was static, if not slowly declining. By that time, it also had become clear that the government could pump more money into the economy without breaching the IMF conditions. Originally, the intention was to make any relaxation conditional on acceptance by the trade unions of a third phase of income restrictions with a ceiling on wage increases of about 10%. The unions, however, refused to support any formal or informal guidelines, but the chancellor—faced with a rise in unemployment and prospects of continuing stagnation in the economy—provided a mild stimulus in July. This was accomplished mainly by a small reduction in the standard rate of income tax and some increases in tax allowances, but there was no attempt to increase public spending or to boost the money supply.

These measures were too small (and came too late) to have a significant effect on the level of economic activity, with the result that GDP re-

Table III. Total Employment in Selected Countries
(1970=100)

Country	1973	1974	1975	1976	1977 First quarter	1977 Second quarter
Canada	111	116	118	121	117	123
United States	107	109	108	111	111	115
Japan	103	103	103	103	101	106
Australia	106	108	108	109	111	111
France	101	102	100	99	99	99
Germany, West	100	98	95	94	...	...
Italy	99	101	102	102	106	108
Sweden	101	103	105	106	105	107
United Kingom	101	101	101	100	100	...

Source: OECD, *Main Economic Indicators*.

Angry electronics workers, who faced massive layoffs resulting from sales of imported television sets in the U.S., carried their protests to the streets in Chicago's Loop.

mained largely static during the third quarter. However, the position of sterling strengthened remarkably during this quarter; although this was partly a reflection of the rapid weakening of the dollar, it was basically the result of the improvement in confidence in the U.K. by other nations. There were many reasons for this, but it seems that the principal factors were the improvement in the balance of payments situation (which, in turn, was due to increasing oil production and the competitive edge provided by the earlier decline in the external value of sterling) and the government's apparent determination to observe the fiscal and monetary constraints laid down by the IMF. Together with the effects of a weak domestic demand and the widespread observance of the Phase Two income restraint that expired in late summer, the upward climb of sterling had a distinctly beneficial effect on the trend of prices. Inflation, reflecting the weakness of sterling, rose steadily in the first half of the year, but between July and October the annual increase in the index of retail prices fell from a rate of 17.6 to 14.1%. All indicators pointed to a further decline well into 1978.

At the start of the second half of 1977 the public sector borrowing requirement and the increase in monetary aggregates were still well below the IMF limits. Encouraged by this and hoping that further concessions would persuade the labour movement to adopt a moderate approach to wage claims, the chancellor of the Exchequer provided an additional mild stimulus to domestic demand in October. This took the form of higher personal tax allowances, a tax-free year-end bonus for pensioners, and an upgrading of public expenditure plans for 1978. The government also maintained its policy of trying to encourage investment by a steady lowering of interest rates, which resulted in a decline in the minimum lending rate of the Bank of England from 14% in January to 5% at the end of October. During the subsequent month, however, the rate

was raised to 7% in an attempt to slow down the increase in the money stock, which received a significant boost from the inflow of foreign funds in September and October.

Faced with a gradual improvement in overseas confidence during the second half of the year, the Bank of England, wishing to maintain the competitiveness of British exports, attempted to resist a rise in the value of sterling by repeatedly reducing the minimum lending rate and by large-scale interventions in the foreign exchange market. The result of this policy, however, was a rapid increase in the level of foreign exchange reserves, which, in turn, led to an expansion in the money supply well in excess of the IMF ceiling during the autumn months. It was largely for this reason that the central bank announced at the beginning of October that it would no longer attempt to keep the rate down; the immediate consequence of this move was a further appreciation in the pound from U.S. $1.78 to $1.84. Although by the end of November the rate declined to $1.81, this still represented a

Table IV. Unemployment Rates in Selected OECD Countries*
% of civilian labour force, seasonally adjusted

Country	Average 1962–73	Peak 1955–73			1974	1975	1976	Latest month 1977
United States	4.9	7.5	July	1958	5.6	8.5	7.7	7.0
Japan	1.3	1.9	October	1955	1.4	1.9	2.0	2.1
Germany, West	1.3	4.9	March	1955	2.7	4.8	4.7	4.6
France	1.8	2.4	September	1972	2.3	4.0	4.2	...
United Kingdom	2.4	3.9	April	1972	2.5	3.9	5.4	6.1
Italy	3.6	5.5	April	1959	2.9	3.3	3.7	7.7
Canada	5.3	7.9	June	1958	5.4	7.1	7.2	8.2
Australia	1.6	2.6	August	1972	2.3	4.4	4.4	6.0
Belgium	2.1	4.0	February	1959	2.6	4.5	5.8	...
Denmark	...		...		2.5	6.0	6.1	...
Finland	2.4	5.0	January	1968	1.7	2.2	4.0	...
Netherlands, The	1.4	2.8	November	1972	3.3	4.7	5.1	...
Norway	0.9	2.1	December	1958	0.6	1.2	1.1	...
Spain	...		...		3.2	3.8	4.9	...
Sweden	2.1	2.9	November	1973	2.0	1.6	1.6	2.0

*Rates not comparable between countries.
Sources: OECD, *Economic Outlook*, July 1977; The Economist, *Key Indicators*.

significant improvement on the year's opening figure of $1.71.

Taking the year as a whole, most components of aggregate demand were sluggish. Consumers' expenditure, which was affected by the fall in real disposable incomes, was consistently weak in the wake of a modest rise during the previous year. Gross fixed investment, which had been falling steadily since 1973, was expected to register a further decline; indeed, the indications were that, despite a modest recovery in the manufacturing sector toward the end of the year, the overall loss would exceed the decline of 3.4% in 1976. Government current expenditures also decreased somewhat, although there was some evidence that stockbuilding would prove to be a positive influence. But the mainstay of the economy was overseas demand. Exports recorded a good increase in both halves of the year, and by November there was a good chance that the overall volume increase would match the previous year's gain of 7%. Combined with a somewhat slower expansion in imports and an improvement in the terms of trade, this was likely to ensure a spectacular drop in the trade deficit and the emergence of a small surplus on the current account for the first time since 1972.

JAPAN. During the 1976–77 fiscal year (ended March 1977), the Japanese economy recorded a 5.8% volume increase, compared with a gain of 3.4% in the previous year. Although this was one of the most impressive growth rates registered in the entire OECD area, the nation's authorities faced sustained pressure from both domestic business circles and other countries to adopt a more expansionist policy. Domestic business was particularly concerned with the fact that at the end of 1976–77 industry was still suffering from a large margin of excess capacity and that, at least in certain areas of the economy, there were some tentative signs of a slowdown. Japan's trading partners, on the other hand, were unhappy because during 1976–77 much of the gain in GDP came from high exports rather than an increase in domestic consumption, the result of which was a large and rapidly expanding balance of payments surplus. Somewhat reluctantly, the authorities gave way in April 1977 and introduced a much publicized, but modest, package, the main components of which were a reduction in the discount rate from 6 to 5% and an acceleration of the public expenditure programs already agreed upon for the year.

During the April–June quarter (the first quarter of the 1977–78 fiscal year), the volume of GNP rose by 1.9%. Although this was a somewhat smaller gain than in the previous three months, it was well in line with the authorities' target of a 6.7% advance for the year as a whole and provided some signs of a weakening in the trend of exports and a strengthening in the level of domestic demand. Nevertheless, pressure for more reflation continued, and in September the government was forced to take further action. The central bank's discount rate was reduced to 4.25% (the lowest since World War II), while public and related expenditure programs were upgraded by about $7.5 billion. Some of this additional expenditure was not expected to be incurred until the following

year, however, so that the true additional impact on demand during 1977–78 was estimated at only about $4.5 billion. Although this was equivalent to about 0.5% of GNP, it was hardly a major contribution to world economic growth as claimed by the government. Nevertheless, it was probably more than sufficient to ensure that the GNP growth target of 6.7% for 1977–78 would be reached, thus putting Japan once again at the top of the OECD growth league.

Thus, compared with the progress of the world economy and that of the larger industrial countries, Japan's overall growth performance was judged to be satisfactory. However, satisfaction was tempered by the fact that it was an unbalanced growth, failing to solve and even exacerbating some difficulties. Although full national accounts were not available, it was clear that some elements of demand failed to register a satisfactory increase. Private plant and equipment investments, which were relatively weak in the previous year, remained sluggish despite a steady downward trend in interest rates and the introduction of a range of investment incentives. This was largely explained by the fact that many industries faced an acute degree of overcapacity and weak consumer demand; the latter was largely the result of a small rise in wages and uncertainty about future prospects. By Japanese standards, unemployment also remained high; in July 1977 the wholly unemployed accounted for some 2.1% of the labour force, slightly more than the total at the beginning of the year.

At the same time, the trend of industrial production was relatively subdued and erratic. During the first nine months of 1977 its level was only about 3% above the average of the previous year, and some of the forecasts suggested that the gain for the entire year would not exceed 6%, compared with over 13% during 1976. By contrast, the level of inventories was on a rising trend, and the signs were that, unlike 1976, the year would finish with a modest increase. Not unexpectedly, these trends had an adverse influence on business results; after an uninterrupted increase in profits for two years, the half year to September 1977 showed an average decline for the large corporations of about 15%. The most buoyant areas of demand were public expenditure, house building, and exports. Public spending benefited from the successive demand-boosting packages and was expected to remain buoyant well into 1978–79. House building activities were stimulated by the government's policy of ensuring a good supply of housing loans, a policy that was reemphasized in the September reflationary package.

One of the most remarkable features of the economy was the growth of exports. In the 1977–78 fiscal year overseas shipments promised to register a gain from 1976–77 of about 17–18%, nearly three times the anticipated rate of growth in world trade. Caused largely by extremely aggressive Japanese foreign trade policies, this was responsible for a major part of the gain in GNP during the year. However, it also had the effect of impairing Japan's economic relations with other countries and of contributing to monetary instability and the rise of protectionist sentiments in the Western world. Even in 1976–77, the country had been under widespread attack for running a trade surplus of over $11 billion. Then, contrary to the government's prediction of a sharp reduction during 1977–78, the figures pointed to an increase in the surplus to about $15 billion–$16 billion.

Japan's strong export performance aggravated the deficits of some receiving countries and adversely affected their ability to stimulate their economies for fear of further weakening their external positions. Not surprisingly, this led to renewed pressures for, and the imposition of, restrictions on a range of Japanese exports. It also had the effect of forcing a sharp appreciation in the external value of the yen, which despite some initial resistance by the Bank of Japan moved from about 290 yen per U.S. $1 in November 1976 to about 240 yen per $1 by late November 1977.

WEST GERMANY. During 1976 West Germany recorded one of the highest growth rates among OECD countries, but by the end of the year signs of a slowdown were becoming apparent. As the year drew to a close, the Council of Economic Advisers warned that the economy was running out of steam and that an immediate stimulus to demand was appropriate. The government, however, took the view that some of the effects of the earlier reflationary packages (six in the three years to the end of 1976) were still to be felt and that an additional stimulus would achieve little more than higher inflation. It was on this basis that the policymakers mapped out their targets for 1977: a growth in GDP of 5%, an inflation level below 4%, a decline in unemployment to 800,000 (or 4% of the labour force), and a ceiling on the increase of wages and salaries of 7.5%. The Bundesbank's target for the growth of the money supply was set at 8%, the same as in 1976.

As the year unfolded, the economic indicators showed that, although there was a pickup in the level of business activity during the closing quarter of 1976, the underlying trend of the economy was generally sluggish. Industrial production, having risen sharply in January, remained stagnant for the next three months; order books were weak and inventories were on a gently rising trend. Construction activity was flat, as were industrial investment and retail sales. Nevertheless, the authorities maintained their antireflationary posture in the face of further criticism, this time from other European Economic Community countries.

At least partial justification was provided for this stance by the first quarter's GNP gain of 4%, which, while well below the advance of 6% during the preceding three months, was regarded as respectable. Additional support was provided by a reduction in the level of unemployment from 1.2 million in January to below 1 million in May and a deceleration in the rate of inflation to 3.8% by the early summer. During the second quarter, however, GNP was virtually stagnant, showing an increase of 0.5%. This unexpectedly sharp slowdown took West German economic policymakers by surprise. In July the government abandoned its opposition to an additional stimulus and in mid-

September announced a package intended to inject approximately DM 11 billion into the economy, mostly during 1978. This turnaround was all the more remarkable because as late as June the authorities were still trying to dispel any notion that the labour mobility and retraining incentives announced in May and the four-year program of public works projects revealed in March were dictated by a desire to stimulate economic activity in the short term.

The emphasis of the September measures, which went through Parliament after a lengthy wrangle, was on quick-acting tax cuts and higher depreciation allowances designed to boost flagging business confidence and revive private investment. Another turnaround in government thinking was seen in the approach to fiscal policy for the six months to May 1978, when it was decided to finance the measures just announced by a larger budget deficit. Furthermore, an even larger deficit for 1978–79 was in the cards, marking the end of the policy, at least temporarily, of returning to a balanced budget for 1981.

Some months before the government decided to reassess its policy, a gradual relaxation in the Bundesbank's monetary stance could be detected. Although the money supply appeared to be heading for a slightly higher growth rate than the 8% target projected for the year, the Bundesbank acted repeatedly to ease liquidity and encourage lower interest rates. In August, for instance, a 10% cut in the minimum reserve requirements and an immediate increase in rediscount quotas freed DM 6.5 billion.

Unfortunately, the government's fiscal measures and the abundance of cheap money did little to lift the gloom, which, if anything, deepened as the year drew to a close. This was not without some justification, for all the economic forecasts for the year as a whole pointed to an increase in GNP of 3.5–4%. Investment rose by only 3–4% for 1977 and did not seem likely to increase much faster in 1978. Unemployment was equally worrying because, on a seasonally adjusted basis, it moved back to above the one million mark. Another source of disappointment was the slow rise in ex-

OPEC ministers meeting in Stockholm in July tried to resolve existing price differences for medium and heavy grade oil among the members. No resolution of the disagreement was attained, and Saudi Arabia continued to charge lower prices for these grades than other Persian Gulf oil countries. Earlier, however, the price of light grade crude had been standardized by a 5% increase in Saudi and U.A.E. prices.

KEYSTONE

ports. At the start of the year double-figure increases were expected, but this was cut back to 7% on the basis of the first nine months. This could be partly explained by the slower than anticipated growth by West Germany's trading partners, but the decline in the value of the dollar in the summer was also likely to have played an important role. Pressure on costs, especially from wages which rose on average by 6.5–7% during 1977, threatened profit margins and reduced business confidence—which, in turn, weakened the climate for investment.

FRANCE. The French economy entered 1977 sedated by the powerful corrective medicine administered by Premier Raymond Barre during the previous September. Essentially, this consisted of a short-term price freeze and a moderately severe monetary squeeze aimed at halving the inflation rate to 6.5%, restoring the balance of trade, and consolidating the franc, while at the same time preventing the economy from lapsing into a deflation-induced stagnation. The economic indicators available up to November 1977 suggested that the "Barre plan" had been successful on two counts. The franc held up remarkably well against the turbulent international exchange markets; it appreciated against the dollar and its depreciation against the mark was less than might have been expected. A dramatic improvement was also seen in the trade deficit, which was reduced from Fr 3 billion in January to Fr 100 million in July. As a result, the trade deficit for the year as a whole was expected to be nearly halved from 1976's Fr 21 billion, with a similar recovery mirrored in the balance of payments.

In contrast, progress in combating inflation and stimulating the real economy was disappointing. In fact, halfway through the year the government was forced to downgrade its original forecast of economic growth to 3% from 4.8%. Most components of demand were sluggish throughout the year. As a result, industrial production followed an erratic course and seemed likely to finish the year with only a 2.5% overall increase. New investment was flat too, registering an increase of only 1.6%, compared with 2.5% in 1976 and a target of 7.5%.

The low level of investment in France, as in other OECD countries, was due to a lack of business confidence brought about by the weakness of demand, low utilization of capacity, declining orders, and uncertainties pertaining to the outcome of the general elections due in spring 1978. Calls by the government for increased investment (supported by direct measures in the shape of special loans) went largely unheeded. It was generally expected that the 1976–77 recovery would be stepped up in France, as in other European countries, by the engine of private investment. Its failure to do so put the authorities in a quandary because they could not resort to classical Keynesian demand stimulation without abandoning the restrictive demand management and monetary policies followed since September 1976. To do so would have risked runaway inflation, exchange crises, and, eventually, a slump.

This view could, to some extent, be justified by the slowness of inflation in responding to the September 1976 freeze and the cuts in value-added taxes that followed in January. Following the gradual dismantling of the controls in the spring, the index of retail prices began to rise and in the summer it was running at an annual rate of 10.2%. After the summer inflationary pressures eased off, thanks to a fall in commodity prices and slowdowns in the rise of wages and in the prices of public services. The outcome for the year was likely to be a gain of 8.5–9%, indicating that the battle was only half won and that there was no room for complacency.

The real weak spot of the French economy in 1977 was unemployment. In the wake of the failure of the economic recovery to pull through, unemployment rose from a base of just over 1 million at the beginning of the year to a postwar peak of 1,210,000 in August. At that level it was more than 20% higher than a year earlier. After August it improved somewhat, reflecting the relatively higher level of economic activity that could be partly attributed to the successive doses of mild reflation and the special measures introduced by the government. Toward the close of the year the number of unemployed stood at 1.1 million, a high level historically, but at least the trend was pointing in the right direction.

The strategy of the economic policymakers at the beginning of the year was to bring inflation under control, first by controlling prices and then by influencing wage rates against a background of fairly restrictive monetary policies. However, as the year unfolded and unemployment began to rise sharply (threatening the strategy of the government and its chances of winning the spring 1978 elections), emphasis shifted to slowing down the rise in unemployment and encouraging investment, without abandoning the basically restrictive monetary stance. The first of these "special measures" followed hard on the heels of the two-stage ending of the price freeze. A Fr 8 billion credit (equal to 2% of gross fixed investment) was introduced to support flagging investment expenditures. This was quickly followed in April by the second Barre plan, which addressed itself to social considerations, including youth unemployment, family allowances, and old-age pensions. A total of Fr 4 billion cautiously injected into the economy underlined the continuation of the original policy with only minor concessions.

The approaching general election, the gathering forces of unemployment, the possibility of a deeper recession in the wake of the summer slowdown in the U.S., and the continued sluggishness of the other two major OECD economies (West Germany and Japan) capable of rekindling world economic recovery persuaded Premier Barre to put together at the end of August yet another credit package (Fr 6 billion) within the framework of his overall strategy. The rise in the discount rate announced in September 1976 was reversed, and assistance was offered to the hard-hit construction sector. Loans to large companies for investment and assistance to companies in financial difficulties were its other features. Consumers benefited slightly through an increase in child allowances.

OTHER DEVELOPED ECONOMIES. The relatively sluggish growth of the larger Western countries had an adverse effect on the performance of most other developed market economies. Most of these faced balance of payments problems, and some were also concerned with a possible acceleration in inflation, especially in the early part of the year, and tended to follow restrictive or, at best, neutral fiscal and monetary policies. This was true of Italy, which also faced a steady decline in the value of its currency; Austria; Denmark; and Sweden, where the currency also had to be devalued. All these countries were expected to record a substantially slower growth in 1977 than during the previous year, with the Italian advance falling from 5.6 to about 2.5% and that of Denmark declining from 5.5 to a little over 1%. The Swedish growth rate was forecast at about 1%, only marginally poorer than in the previous year; Norway had also been expected to record a slowdown, but, largely because of lively North Sea oil activity, a comparatively large gain of about 5% seemed likely. Switzerland and The Netherlands had sizable current account surpluses, and indications were that Switzerland would accelerate its growth rate from 0.5% in 1976 to about 1.5% in 1977.

Outside Europe, Canada too was suffering from a large external payments deficit, as were New Zealand and Australia. Although Australia brought in a mildly expansionary budget in March, the underlying trend of the economy was weak and growth was not expected to reach the previous year's level. Canada and New Zealand were both subject to restrictive economic policies; in the latter case the effect of these was likely to be a decline in GNP for the second successive year.

The one encouraging feature of 1977 was that, despite signs of an acceleration in the first half of the year, inflation appeared to be falling marginally in most countries. As a result, many of the smaller European economies (except Ireland, Finland, and possibly Sweden) expected price rises averaging in the single digits in 1977. Australia and New Zealand were also expected to show some improvement compared with 1976, but their rates were projected to be in excess of 10%.

Developing Countries. The gradual process of adjusting to the economic setbacks of the mid-1970s continued among the developing countries. Taken as a group, their average growth rate improved markedly during 1976 (the latest year for which statistical data were available) and similar progress for 1977 was indicated by periodic surveys undertaken by such international organizations as the IMF and the World Bank. The developing countries, for the purposes of this article, may be divided into three groups (along the lines of the IMF classification): major oil-exporting countries, more developed countries, and less developed countries.

The major oil-exporting countries in 1976 continued the tighter demand policies adopted in 1975. Thanks to a deceleration in the rate of growth of government expenditure and an improvement in the supply situation, their average rate of inflation declined from 18% in 1975 to 15% in 1976. Slower increases in import prices and controls ex-

Table V. Economically Active Population
Latest census or estimate

Country	% in Agriculture [1]	% in Industry [2]	% in Services [3]
AFRICA			
Algeria	50.4	12.3	37.3
Angola	60.2	...	39.8[4]
Benin	47.5	...	52.5[4]
Botswana	83.1	...	16.9[4]
Burundi	95	1	4
Cameroon	80	10	10
Cape Verde Islands	40.1	1.2	58.7
Central African Empire	89	...	11[4]
Chad	96	4	...
Comoros	63.9	17.6	18.5
Congo	37.3	...	62.7[4]
Djibouti	50	...	50
Egypt	47.7	16.8	35.5
Equatorial Guinea	95	...	5
Ethiopia	81.2	...	18.8[4]
Gabon	84.1	7.0	8.9
Gambia, The	79.6	...	20.4[4]
Ghana	58.0	11.9	30.1
Guinea	82	...	18[4]
Guinea-Bissau	84.3	...	15.7[4]
Ivory Coast	86.4	1.9	11.7
Kenya	86.5	3.6	9.9
Lesotho	91	1	8
Liberia	76.4	5.9	17.7
Libya	22.8	23.1	54.1
Madagascar	80	2	18
Malawi	86	...	14[4]
Mali	88.7	...	11.3[4]
Mauritania	84.8	...	15.2[4]
Mauritius	32.8	23.1	44.1
Morocco	50.0	14.7	35.3
Mozambique	73.4	12.5	14.1
Niger	90.1	...	9.9[4]
Nigeria	55.9	12.1	32.0
Réunion	29.5	22.6	47.9
Rhodesia	60.8	...	39.2[4]
Rwanda	91.1	...	8.9[4]
Senegal	72.7	7.0	20.3
Seychelles	28.5	29.1	42.4
Sierra Leone	74.6	10.3	15.1
Somalia	82	...	18[4]
South Africa	28.0	26.9	45.1
Bophuthatswana	56.8	13.6	29.6
Transkei	78.5	7.6	13.9
South West Africa	58.5	10.2	31.3
Sudan	66.4	6.1	27.5
Swaziland	19.4	6.9	73.7
Tanzania	91.0	1.7	7.3
Togo	70.2	...	29.8[4]
Tunisia	41.0	17.1	41.9
Uganda	83	...	17[4]
Upper Volta	83.8	...	16.2[4]
Zaire	76.3	...	23.7[4]
Zambia	43.7	20.0	36.3
ASIA			
Afghanistan	77.0	8.2	14.8
Bahrain	6.6	31.4	62.0
Bangladesh	77.0	5.4	17.6
Bhutan	93.8	...	6.2[4]
Brunei	11.9	31.9	56.2
Burma	69.3	9.2	21.5
Cambodia	80.3	2.8	16.9
China	63	...	37[4]
Cyprus [6]	33.1	24.9	42.0
Hong Kong	2.5	48.7	48.8
India	72.0	11.2	16.8
Indonesia [7]	64.2	8.3	27.5
Iran	41.8	23.7	34.5
Iraq	55.3	6.9	37.8
Israel	6.3	32.0	61.7
Japan	14.0	34.2	51.8
Jordan	35.3	10.8	53.9
Korea, North	49.3	...	50.7[4]
Korea, South	49.1	21.9	29.0
Kuwait	2.5	20.6	76.9
Laos	75.8	...	24.2[4]
Lebanon	19.3	24.7	56.0
Macau	0.4	0.4	99.2
Malaysia	46.2	11.8	42.0
Mongolia	45.4	22.3	32.3
Nepal	94.4	1.2	4.4
Oman	82.7	4.0	13.3
Pakistan	57.3	16.3	26.4
Philippines	52	15	30
Qatar	...	...	...
Saudi Arabia	62.5	...	37.5[4]
Singapore	2.0	29.8	68.2
Sri Lanka	50.4	10.0	39.6
Syria	50.8	18.2	31.0
Taiwan	26.8	36.6	36.6
Thailand	74.3	5.3	20.4
Turkey	67.6	12.1	20.3
Vietnam	73	...	27[4]
Yemen (Aden)	62	...	38[4]
Yemen (San'a')	76.7	...	23.3[4]
EUROPE			
Albania	62.7	...	37.3[4]
Andorra	8.3	28.6	63.1
Austria	12.5	39.8	47.7
Belgium	3.4	36.6	60.0
Bulgaria	44.3	32.9	22.8
Channel Islands [8]	8.3	22.5	69.2
Czechoslovakia	16.4	48.0	35.6
Denmark	9.3	31.3	59.4

Country	% in Agriculture [1]	% in Industry [2]	% in Services [3]
Faeroe Islands	23.6	30.2	46.2
Finland	14.3	34.6	51.1
France	10.8	35.9	53.3
Germany, East	11.7	47.5	40.8
Germany, West	6.4	43.9	49.7
Gibraltar	...	42.2	57.8
Greece	40.6	25.7	33.7
Hungary	22.7	43.9	33.4
Iceland	16.8	36.1	47.1
Ireland	25.4	30.0	44.6
Isle of Man	6.1	25.1	68.8
Italy	15.1	41.1	43.8
Liechtenstein	6.2	56.6	37.2
Luxembourg	7.5	42.7	49.8
Malta	6.0	37.3	56.7
Monaco	0.2	20.0	79.8
Netherlands, The	6.1	35.8	58.1
Norway	9.9	33.4	56.7
Poland	34.6	37.3	28.1
Portugal	29.6	29.6	40.8
Romania	57.2	24.6	18.2
San Marino	8.5	54.1	37.4
Spain	22.3	35.9	41.8
Sweden	6.6	33.9	59.5
Switzerland	7.7	47.4	44.9
United Kingdom	2.5	40.9	56.6
Yugoslavia	44.6	22.2	33.2
NORTH AMERICA			
Antigua	10.6	20.0	69.4
Bahamas, The	6.9	17.7	75.4
Barbados	21.3	13.8	64.9
Belize	33.9	12.8	53.3
Bermuda	1.6	19.5	78.9
British Virgin Islands	7.5	34.8	57.7
Canada	5.5	26.6	67.9
Cayman Islands	10.9	27.6	61.5
Costa Rica	36.4	18.9	44.7
Cuba	30.0	26.3	43.7
Dominica	39.4	17.6	43.0
Dominican Republic	44.3	10.5	45.2
El Salvador	54.2	12.6	33.2
Greenland	18.6	28.2	53.2
Grenada	71.6	17.5	10.9
Guadeloupe	32.4	25.7	41.9
Guatemala	57.2	18.0	24.8
Haiti	61.5	5.9	32.6
Honduras	58.9	14.4	26.7
Jamaica	29.0	16.9	54.1
Martinique	28.1	20.4	51.5
Mexico	40.9	23.8	35.3
Montserrat	19.3	15.1	65.6
Netherlands Antilles	1.0	27.7	71.3
Nicaragua	51.0	14.7	34.3
Panama	38.4	13.8	47.8
Puerto Rico	7.7	29.3	63.0
St. Lucia	10.5	5.3	84.2
St. Pierre & Miquelon	11.3	17.5	71.2
Trinidad and Tobago	13.9	28.1	58.0
United States	3.8	29.7	66.5
Virgin Islands (U.S.)	1.2	25.5	73.3
OCEANIA			
American Samoa	5.1	29.2	65.7
Australia	7.4	32.5	60.1
Christmas Island	...	80.3	19.7
Cook Islands	34.1	24.1	41.8
Fiji	53.6	14.3	32.1
French Polynesia	37.1	22.3	40.6
Gilbert Islands [9]	65.5	3.8	30.7
Guam	0.7	22.8	76.5
Nauru	0.1	31.4	68.5
New Caledonia	29.1	25.8	45.1
New Hebrides	82.5	2.5	15.0
New Zealand	12.0	31.7	56.3
Niue	11.4	...	88.6
Norfolk Island	6.1	15.9	78.0
Papua New Guinea	56.4	4.5	39.1
Solomon Islands	23.2	12.5	64.3
Tonga	70.3	14.4	15.3
Western Samoa	66.9	6.5	26.6
SOUTH AMERICA			
Argentina	14.8	28.0	57.2
Bolivia	48	16	36
Brazil	44.3	17.4	38.3
Chile	21.4	17.8	60.8
Colombia	30.2	17.9	51.9
Ecuador	32.5	11.5	56.0
French Guiana	18.4	28.6	53.0
Guyana	29.6	23.1	47.3
Paraguay	47.7	18.2	34.1
Peru	40.9	18.3	40.8
Surinam	34.9	14.9	50.2
Uruguay	18.5	27.8	53.7
Venezuela	18.6	24.7	56.7
U.S.S.R.	26.3	45.1	28.6

[1] Includes forestry and fishing. [2] Includes mining and construction. [3] Includes all other economic activities, including government employment. [4] Includes all nonagricultural activities. [5] Excludes Herschel and Glen Grey districts. [6] Includes the period from January to June 1974 only. [7] Excludes East Timor. [8] Jersey only. [9] Includes Tuvalu (Ellice Islands).

ercised over wages were thought to have brought further benefits in 1977.

In spite of the restrictive stance of their economic policies, economic activity in the non-oil sectors of the oil exporters remained surprisingly high in 1976 and was likely to have increased at a faster rate during 1977. Oil production, however, rose less rapidly in 1977 than during the previous year. Total output of the oil-exporting countries was, therefore, likely to have grown at a slower pace than the exceptionally rapid rate achieved in 1976.

Although the more developed countries (including Finland, Greece, Turkey, Iceland, Ireland, Malta, Spain, and Portugal) had been less severely affected by the 1974–75 world recession than the industrialized countries, they lagged behind in the subsequent recovery. On the inflation front, too, their progress was poor. At the end of 1976 their inflation rate was twice that of the industrialized countries, and single-figure inflation in 1977 was unlikely to have been achieved. Part of the

reason why this group of countries lagged behind in the recovery was that in the initial stages of the recession, in order to maintain their economic activity levels, they borrowed heavily and thus artificially sustained imports and consumption. This policy, however, quickly led to large current account deficits and to higher budgetary deficits. To bring the ensuing upsurge in prices under control, demand-restraining measures were reluctantly enacted from late 1976 onward. The only countries not following such policies were those where political uncertainty and insecurity prevented decisive action by the authorities (for example, Turkey until after the summer 1977 elections).

Although the economic pattern of the less developed countries (LDC's) followed that of the industrialized world, their economic activity was less directly affected by the recession. Except for the very poor countries and regions caught in the downward spiral of poverty, a combination of economic adjustments, demand management policies, and good harvests resulted in an improvement in the rate of output growth in 1976, bringing it almost to pre-recession levels. A somewhat higher growth rate was expected in 1977.

Centrally Planned Economies. From June 21 to June 23, 1977, the 31st plenary session of the Council for Mutual Economic Assistance (CMEA; Comecon) was held in Warsaw. The discussions were dominated by three main problems: energy and raw materials; agriculture, food, and consumer durables; and further implementation of the "Target Programs."

It became clear during the year that all the countries of the Soviet bloc were faced with shortages of fuel and raw materials. This was due to two factors, rapid industrial growth and the high cost of investment in fuel and raw-material projects. For many years the Soviet Union has been the main supplier of raw materials to Eastern Europe; however, its known deposits were running low and it had become necessary to explore new fields. The Soviet Union demanded that other member countries should contribute to the investment needed for this exploration work, making this contribution a condition for any increase in supplies of raw materials to them. During the current five-year plan (1976–80), member countries were required to invest 9 billion to 10 billion transferable rubles in the fuel, energy, and raw material sectors. This program was to be greatly expanded in the following five-year plan (1981–85). All member countries would have to increase their financial

Table VIII. Output of Basic Industrial Products in Eastern Europe, 1976

In 000 metric tons except for natural gas and electric power

Country	Hard coal	Brown coal	Natural gas (000,000 cu m)	Crude petroleum	Electric power (000,000 kw-hr)	Steel	Sulfuric acid	Cement
Bulgaria	288	25,176	...	120	27,744	2,460	856	4,356
Czechoslovakia	28,272	89,472	8,304	132	62,628	14,688	1,236	9,552
Germany, East	456	246,888	...	...	89,148	6,732	956	11,340
Hungary	2,940	22,320	54,996	2,136	22,044	3,648	617	4,296
Poland	179,304	39,300	60,276	456	104,100	15,636	3,288	19,812
Romania	...	...	...	...	...	...	...	...
U.S.S.R.	711,996	...	3,026,784	519,996	1,110,960	144,996	20,016	123,960

Source: UN, *Monthly Bulletin of Statistics.*

UPI COMPIX

Phones rang furiously in currency brokers' offices in Frankfurt am Main, West Germany, during a period of currency turbulence in July.

contributions to joint investments in fuels and raw materials and also contribute labour, equipment, and services for constructing the facilities necessary for extracting and distributing them.

Most of the new projects were situated in the Soviet Union, but some joint developments were to be undertaken in Poland (coal) and in Cuba (nickel and cobalt). At the same time nuclear energy was to be jointly expanded; a general plan for specialization in nuclear engineering was drawn up. Joint nuclear complexes were being built on the Hungarian-Soviet and Hungarian-Czechoslovak borders. A program for the extension of a high-tension transmission line was discussed at the Warsaw plenary meeting, and all member countries emphasized the need to expand the use of lignite in the production of electricity. Soviet Premier Aleksey N. Kosygin suggested that a joint specialization plan should be developed with regard to mining. Bilateral agreements between the Soviet Union and Czechoslovakia and between East Germany and Poland already existed in this field.

The problem of adequate supplies of basic agricultural products to the member countries was thoroughly discussed. After a bad harvest in the Soviet Union and Poland, there was a growing demand for food that could not be met by the member countries. Because the Soviet Union supplied less meat per capita for the internal market than most other CMEA countries, it was clear that those countries could not rely on supplies of Soviet grain and fodder to the same extent as in previous years. Premier Kosygin said that CMEA member countries would have to improve their own fodder supplies and be more self-sufficient. Among CMEA countries, only Bulgaria, Hungary, and Romania were net food exporters.

The Target Programs had been formulated at the 29th CMEA plenary session, which was held in Budapest in June 1975. These programs covered five fields: energy and raw material supplies; machine-building industries; agriculture and food industries; industrial consumer goods; and

transport. Target Programs envisaged long-term coordination of planning aimed at joint management and production; in fact, they were designed as the main vehicles for economic integration.

At the 31st plenary session the only target planning that got under way was that dealing with energy and raw materials, but even in that field there emerged strong opposition. At the Warsaw meeting two opposing views on the problems of joint investments emerged once more. The Soviet Union held the view that the overall program of gradual integration within CMEA must be vigorously pursued. This program called for both joint investment and joint production through coordination of economic plans and implementation of Target Programs. Other countries, most notably Romania and Hungary, were less enthusiastic, arguing that too costly investments would have an adverse effect on the development of national economies and might favour the stronger and richer countries. Hungary for example, was committed to contribute 1.1 billion rubles to joint CMEA investments during the current five-year plan, a

Table IX. Rates of Industrial Growth in Eastern Europe*

Country	1956–60	1961–65	1971–75	1976	(1977 plan)
Bulgaria	15.9	11.7	9.0	8.0	9.2
Czechoslovakia	10.5	5.2	6.7	5.5	5.3
Germany, East	9.2	5.9	6.3	5.9	5.1
Hungary	7.5	8.1	6.3	4.1	6.0
Poland	9.9	8.6	10.5	10.7	6.3–7.3
Romania	10.9	13.0	13.1	11.5	10.5
U.S.S.R.	10.4	8.6	8.5	4.8	5.6

*Yearly average percentages.

Table X. Foreign Trade of Eastern Europe

In $000,000

Country	Exports			Imports		
	1974	1975	1976	1974	1975	1976
Bulgaria	3,833	4,601	5,382	4,322	5,309	5,626
Czechoslovakia	6,898	7,808	9,035	7,360	8,489	9,706
Germany, East	8,729	10,065	11,361	9,625	11,265	13,196
Hungary	4,817	5,355	4,932	5,148	6,223	5,528
Poland	8,321	10,289	11,050	10,489	12,545	13,867
Romania	4,863	5,329	6,100	5,132	5,330	6,100
U.S.S.R.	27,768	32,175	37,169	25,212	35,711	38,108

Source: UN, *Monthly Bulletin of Statistics.*

Table XI. Soviet Trade with Eastern European Countries

In 000,000 rubles, current prices

Country	Exports			Imports		
	1974	1975	1976	1974	1975	1976
Bulgaria	1,478.5	2,059.6	2,276.7	1,425.6	1,931.2	1,663.5
Czechoslovakia	1,511.1	2,019.5	2,320.5	1,518.4	1,891.5	1,648.6
Germany, East	2,164.6	2,980.3	3,217.9	2,150.7	2,643.1	2,275.9
Hungary	1,134.5	1,657.7	1,771.3	1,147.8	1,616.0	1,984.9
Poland	1,838.2	2,447.2	2,750.1	1,745.4	2,406.1	2,485.0
Romania	578.5	702.1	770.2	612.3	828.7	529.8

Source: Ministry for Foreign Trade of the U.S.S.R.

Table XII. Soviet Crude Petroleum and Products Supplied to Eastern Europe

In 000 metric tons

Country	1973	1974	1975	1976
Bulgaria	9,322	10,855	11,553	11,868
Czechoslovakia	14,340	14,836	15,965	17,233
Germany, East	12,985	14,424	14,952	16,766
Hungary	6,294	6,729	7,535	8,435
Poland	12,376	11,855	13,271	14,073

Source: Ministry for Foreign Trade of the U.S.S.R.

sum that represented approximately 10% of its total industrial investment. A well-known Hungarian economist, Rezso Nyers, expressed the opinion that there should be a limit on joint investments and that the program for extending the sphere of higher central planning, advocated by the Soviet Union, should be moderated.

At Warsaw, Hungarian Premier Gyorgy Lazar advocated the policy of developing industries that are not high energy consumers and locating such industries in countries that have rich fuel deposits, such as the Soviet Union and Poland. Czechoslovak Premier Lubomir Strougal referred to the difficulties that all member countries experience when they implement CMEA programs of integration. In view of such opposition, it was decided that specific measures designed to implement economic integration would be discussed at the next CMEA Council session, to be held in Bucharest in 1978.

All proposed Target Programs were based on joint investments. These investments represented a heavy burden on national economies at a time when all member countries were beginning to feel the adverse results of too rapid industrial expansion. Poland was perhaps the best example of this, but even Hungary, where the economic situation was more stable, found its commitments to joint CMEA investments almost intolerable.

INTERNATIONAL TRADE

As the recovery in most of the world's main economic areas lost momentum during 1977, there was a corresponding decline in the rate of growth in international trade. During the second half of 1976 demand for imports clearly slackened, and this trend intensified during 1977. By the third quarter it was apparent that expansion in world trade had come almost to a standstill.

The underlying developments that combined to produce this reversal of the previous trend were the sluggishness of economic growth in the industrial countries, the weakening of international prices for most of the commodity exports of primary producing countries, little increase in demand for oil, and the continuing low level of demand from the centrally planned economies of the Soviet bloc. On the basis of trends up to October it was expected that the increase in world trade in 1977 in real terms would be no more than 5% and possibly only 3%, dramatically lower than the 11% increase that took place in 1976.

In the industrial countries the business recovery in 1976, which was based in large part on restocking after the previous recession, failed to develop into sustained expansion during 1977. The effect on the foreign trade of these countries made itself felt increasingly as the year progressed. By mid-1977 imports into OECD countries were growing very slowly, and in volume terms the increase was negligible. In particular, imports of oil from OPEC sources—previously increasing rapidly as stocks were replenished ahead of the increase in OPEC posted prices expected at the beginning of 1977—grew more slowly, partly because of supplies available from the United Kingdom, Norway, and the United States. Exports by the industrial countries were affected by slacker demand from OPEC oil producers, which in 1976 had been an extremely buoyant element of total demand, and by the continuing lack of purchasing power in most non-oilproducing less developed countries.

During the early months of 1977 the oil-producing countries imported goods at a high level, but most of those shipments represented orders placed during 1976 when those countries' reserves were growing fastest. Activity in the first part of 1977 also reflected the progressive clearing of earlier orders held up by port congestion and internal distribution problems. By the third quarter it appeared that the current account surplus of the oil-exporting countries would fall below $39 billion, about 5% less than in 1976. Another indicator of the diminished buoyancy of import demand was provided by the rise in international borrowing in some OPEC countries, implying an insufficiency of oil earnings in relation to demand levels. Thus, in 1977 imports by the oil producers were no longer growing fast enough to offset the lack of buoyancy in other economies.

After a long period of rapid expansion in imports from third world countries, CMEA members were obliged to retrench in 1977 in order to correct their serious trading deficits. Nevertheless, the fulfillment of orders for machinery and equipment placed in 1976 and earlier produced relatively high activity during the first part of the year. Continuing, though diminishing, imports of agricultural produce to make up the shortfall in aggregate CMEA output also added their effect. The value of intra-CMEA trade continued to grow in terms of value at a rate similar to that achieved in 1976 (about 10%), but the volume increase was faster because of a slower rate of official price increases.

Final data revealed that the volume of world trade rose by 11.5% in 1976 as most major economies began to emerge from recession. It was notable that this rapid growth resulted almost entirely from an increase in demand from the industrial countries and the oil exporters. The volume of trade of the non-oil primary producers increased only nominally.

Primary Producing Countries. Though the only evidence that imports by OPEC states were growing more slowly in 1977 was derived from export data published by the industrial countries, it was plain from the increasing concern of national governments to control inflation that economic policies had undergone a fundamental change during the year. Exports, too, were strongly affected by relatively modest demand for OPEC oil as a result of the pause in economic growth in the major industrial countries and the increasing availability of alternative supplies.

In Saudi Arabia limiting inflation became the major preoccupation of the government, leading to the postponement or cancellation of some of the planned heavy industrial projects. The consequences for imports of this shift in official policy were substantial, though mitigated by a decision to concentrate development efforts on infrastructure, which still required heavy imports. Iran faced similar problems in selling its crude oil and in curbing the rate of domestic price increases. It is probable that the value of its oil exports in 1977 was some 10% lower than in 1976. The nation's strong reserves position, however, permitted its imports to grow by 6% during the year, including large volumes of foodstuffs and consumer goods as well as capital goods. The main suppliers were the U.S., West Germany, Japan, France, and the United Kingdom.

The decline in primary commodity prices undermined the capacity to import of most non-oil-producing less developed countries in 1977. Even the modest 1.5% growth in the volume of their imports during 1976 probably was not equaled because price increases of industrial products further eroded the purchasing power of their export earnings. Among specific countries, India's foreign trade position was strengthened by an improvement in agricultural production and by higher overseas sales of engineering products, leather goods, tea, and other foodstuffs. This meant that, after contracting in 1976, imports were able to rise again in 1977. In Indonesia buoyant oil, tin, and natural rubber exports made a large contribution to foreign trade turnover, though this was partly offset by sluggish demand for imports caused by domestic economic problems. Problems in disposing of its sugar, coconuts, and copper weakened export performance in the Philippines, but imports were lifted by heavy government spending on infrastructure and energy and development projects. South Korea, which achieved a massive 60% growth in exports in 1976, showed a more modest 20% increase in value in 1977, equivalent to about 13% in volume terms. There were indications that the trading positions of the less developed countries deteriorated further toward the end of the year as world demand for their major exports weakened in the face of the pause in the economic recovery in the industrial nations.

Industrial Countries. The evolution of import demand in the industrial countries during 1977 was against the trend foreseen by most experts at the beginning of the year. The slowness of the increase during the first part of the year turned out to be the consequence of something more funda-

mental than the ending of the inventory buildup as those countries completed the first phase of reexpansion after the recession. It became clear by the third quarter that the underlying trend in the growth of gross national products was still weak and that a lengthy pause was taking place in the process of economic recovery. The foreign trade data fully reflected this development, causing a downward revision of earlier estimates of the growth pattern.

Though economic expansion in the U.S. slowed as the year progressed, the growth rate there held up better than in Western Europe. This helped to sustain a continuing fast increase in imports, which on the basis of data for the first three quarters rose by 20% (in dollar terms) in 1977 as a whole; in volume terms the increase was about 12%. Exports, on the other hand, rose by only 6% in value and showed no increase in volume.

Aided by competitive prices, Japan's exports continued their steady and rapid growth in 1977. For the year the increase was 18% at current prices (expressed in new Special Drawing Rights, or SDR's, a currency created by the IMF and defined in terms of 16 major currencies), higher than the 15% rise in 1976. Imports, as had been the pattern for several years, grew at a slower rate (8.5%) in 1977. The Japanese government introduced various measures aimed at boosting imports, but their net effect amounted to only 600 million SDR's during 1977.

In West Germany the rate of growth in foreign trade declined during the second half of 1977. Both exports and imports increased by 18% during the first six months (in terms of SDR's) compared with the same period of 1976, but they both grew more slowly in the second half, bringing down the increase for 1977 as a whole to 13% at current prices for imports and to 12% for exports. The trade surplus during the first half of 1977 was slightly larger than in the corresponding period of 1976, and the evidence indicated that this trend continued to the end of the year.

Great Britain's foreign trade performance was strong in 1977, at least in relation to the trend in previous years. The volume of imports rose by 5.5%, compared with a 7% increase in exports. The latter was helped by the advantageous exchange rate for the pound sterling against other major currencies. Assuming a rise of 17% in export prices and 7% in import prices, the 1977 trade deficit would be the equivalent of 5 billion SDR's.

In Italy the value of exports rose by 37% in the first half of 1977. Allowing for price increases, overseas sales of goods increased by 10% in volume terms. The trend in imports, reflecting the slow rate of growth in general business activity, was almost stationary in volume, though the depreciation of the lira produced a large increase in terms of the local currency. The performance of the main economic indicators during the second half of the year implied a 6% growth in export volume for 1977 as a whole but only a nominal expansion in the volume of imports.

Contradictory trends in France's monthly trade figures up to June caused the final trade account for 1977 to be uncertain. It became clear, however,

CHART 3

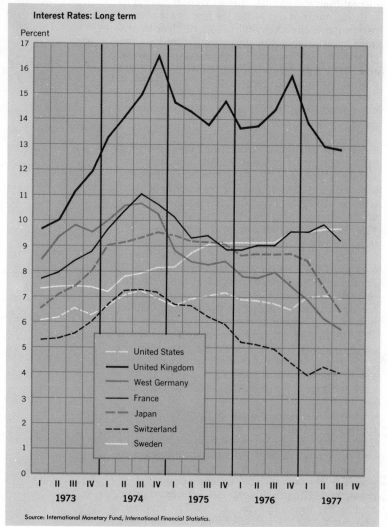

Interest Rates: Long term

Percent

	1973	1974	1975	1976	1977

United States
United Kingdom
West Germany
France
Japan
Switzerland
Sweden

Source: International Monetary Fund, *International Financial Statistics.*

with suppliers outside the CMEA was the large amount of machinery imports from France, West Germany, and Japan.

During the first six months of 1977 Poland's foreign trade turnover increased by 9%, most of which was attributable to an increase in imports. The large deficit in trade with industrial countries outside the CMEA was a source of concern to the government, which sought a solution by reorienting its purchases toward CMEA partners. On the basis of trends in the first half year, it seemed likely that Czechoslovakia's foreign trade achieved the authorities' fundamental objective of increasing exports faster than imports. Exports rose by about 14%, slightly ahead of the 13% rise in imports. Elsewhere in the CMEA area trade within the group grew faster than with nonmembers except in the case of Hungary.

Commodity Trade. During the first six months of 1977 increases in the prices of most primary commodities helped to push up the average unit value of the world's foreign trade. The most important in terms of its effect was the increase in the posted price of OPEC crude oil at the beginning of the year (followed by another increase at midyear). Increases, some large, in other items were widely spread over a broad range of products in all the main categories. Among particular items, cocoa, tea, coffee, vegetable oils, and oilseeds experienced strikingly large increases. On the other hand, world prices for sugar and grains fell.

In large part these increases were generated by the general quickening in economic activity in the main importing countries during 1976. As expansion lost momentum in early 1977, however, most commodity prices reacted sharply. Prices of primary products, except oil, fell by an average of about 8% in the third quarter. In particular, favourable harvests for a wide range of crops produced a marked decline in foodstuff prices, though these were on average still 17% higher than a year earlier, boosted by coffee and cocoa.

Commercial and Trade Policies. Discussions continued throughout the year on the possibility of establishing new commodity price stabilization schemes. The only clear achievement in this direction in 1977, however, was the success of the international sugar discussions. Other schemes that would cover cotton, tungsten, and copper had reached the preparatory stages by the end of the year.

There was no clear progress in liberalizing international trade within the framework of the existing international agencies such as the General Agreement on Tariffs and Trade (GATT), but at least the slackening of economic growth worldwide produced relatively few new trade restraints. Almost inevitably, industries under pressure from the slackening in the rate of growth in business activity sought protection from imports of competitors' products. European, Japanese, and Indian steel producers were the subject of complaints from the U.S. steel industry. The U.K. steel industry gained a degree of protection when its government tightened the system of licenses on steel imports from countries outside the European Economic Community. (EIU)

that the 1977 objectives set in the seventh national development plan would not be attained, and that growth in gross domestic product would probably not exceed 2.75%. There was little growth in imports after midyear, even at current prices, and for the full year it was probable that in constant price terms purchases of goods from foreign suppliers declined. Exports, however, appeared likely to expand by 4% in volume, reflecting the high level of shipments to CMEA and less developed countries.

Centrally Planned Economies. The complete Soviet trade returns for 1976 became available late in 1977, revealing a large deficit in hard currency trade amounting to U.S. $5 billion (incurred mainly with Western industrial countries). The official data, however, overstated the size of the deficit because of the omission of arms exports paid for in hard currencies and possibly totaling $1.5 billion. In the first half of 1977 the hard currency deficit with Western industrial countries was $1.9 billion, implying an adverse balance of approximately $3.8 billion for the full year. The deficit remained high as a result of continuing heavy purchases of grain under the agreement with the U.S., together with imports from Canada and Australia. Another factor contributing to the trade deficit

INTERNATIONAL EXCHANGE AND PAYMENTS

There was little change in the pattern of balance of payments deficits in 1977. Large deficits for the small industrial nations and the less developed countries, a surplus for the oil producers, and shifting but offsetting surpluses and deficits for the major countries could no longer be regarded as a temporary phenomenon. Compared with 1976, there was a shift in emphasis from proposals to stimulate the international economy by encouraging surplus countries to reflate to urging deficit countries to provide their own stimulus, with the realization that this requires continued deficits and efforts to find financing for them. This was partly because of growing recognition that the effects of reflation on trade would be too small to provide an effective stimulus.

The relatively rapid growth by the U.S. had little effect on other industrial countries (although import growth was rapid, this mainly affected oil), while the two principal surplus countries, Japan and West Germany, were either unable or unwilling to alter domestic policies sufficiently to provide a significant international economic stimulus. The sharp increase in 1977 in the number of restrictions on trade, which had the effect of blunting the international effects of any country's internal reflation, also reduced the potential effects of encouraging domestic reflation.

There was also, particularly in the second half of the year, a shift in international concern from reducing inflation to reducing (or at least not permitting further increases in) unemployment. In the spring, the rapid increase in primary product prices, particularly food, had prompted concern that renewed inflation would inevitably accompany the return to growth. The fall in these prices and the less rapid than expected growth in the summer were followed by a reaction against the policy of increasing confidence by reducing inflation to encouraging investment and growth directly. This change came too late for any reflation in the small countries to appear in 1977.

The change in the emphasis of policy was also encouraged by the fact that, contrary to some expectations, the commercial capital markets continued to be able to supply the finance needed for the deficits, at least at 1977 levels, although the official sources remained extremely limited. Nevertheless, although the aggregate volume of funds was sufficient, the distribution became progressively more uneven, producing wide variations in the growth possible for individual countries and creating the risk, among those less developed countries that had already reduced their imports sharply, of severe temporary difficulties in the face of any cut (or slow growth) of export earnings. The stability of the payments balances between 1976 and 1977 did not, therefore, indicate that a new equilibrium had been reached, with stable adjustment to the effects of the oil price rises of 1973–74 and the recession in the major countries.

Current Balances. For the OECD countries the virtually unchanged balance reflected a small increase in the deficit on trade in goods balanced by higher income on services. The largest change was the increase in the U.S. deficit by $20 billion. There was a large rise in the Japanese surplus; the U.K. and Italy moved from deficit into surplus; and the French deficit was sharply reduced. Most of the smaller countries had either increased deficits or lower surpluses. The change in the oil exporters' surplus was small because their exports were so much greater than their imports that small percentage rises in export volume and price were temporarily sufficient to balance the much larger percentage rises in the price and volume of imports. Nonetheless, the real value of their surplus was falling. The same effect in reverse held the value of the other less developed countries' deficit at a high level, although both the price and the volume of their exports rose rapidly at the end of 1976 and in early 1977. The centrally planned economies seemed likely to move back into surplus in 1977, mainly because of slow import growth.

Although merchandise trade was the principal explanation of changes in current balances, there were major changes in other parts of the balance, notably payments of interest and income from tourism. For the former, the main change was again the increase in payments by the less developed countries (directly to the industrial countries but indirectly to the oil exporters), while in tourism the main trends were a continuation of the general revival that began in 1976 and increased net income from the North American countries for most European countries.

CHART 4

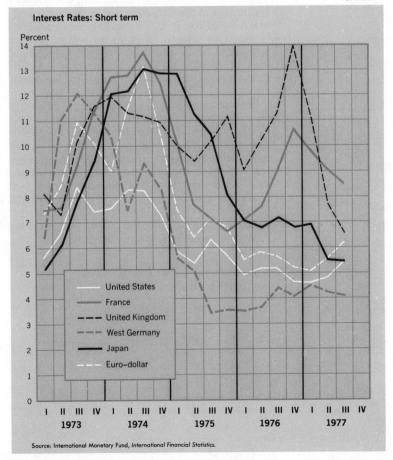

Source: International Monetary Fund, *International Financial Statistics.*

Capital Movements. Official capital has made little contribution to financing increased deficits since 1973, and in 1977 the use of credit from the IMF actually fell from the 1976 level. Only the developed countries, and within them, the U.K., were net users of credit in 1977. The World Bank remained a significant, although relatively small, source of development finance; the real value of its assistance had risen since the early 1970s. The money value of direct aid from OECD nations to less developed countries was the same in 1976 as in 1975; its real value thus fell further from the 1973 level.

The principal contribution to financing deficits of both developed and less developed countries in 1977 was, as it had been since 1974, commercial bank finance; its value probably rose above the level of about $60 billion recorded in 1976. The increase was largely because of increased borrowing by OPEC countries, although there were also smaller increases for the other less developed countries. Borrowing by the developed countries also increased; this group took over half the total lending, although the share may have declined in the second half of the year.

The countries that increased their borrowing almost all had surpluses or declining deficits. Countries with increasing deficits found borrowing more difficult. Among the less developed countries and the small OECD nations, some were no longer able to obtain new financing and were either unwilling or unable to meet the conditions for normal IMF credits. Both because of their own worries over credit risks and because of pressure from the Federal Reserve Board, U.S. banks became increasingly reluctant to lend to countries whose policies would not be approved by the IMF. Commercial lending therefore no longer provided as independent a source of alternative financing for deficit countries as it had between 1974 and 1976.

Because of the reduction in IMF funds following the exhaustion of the "oil facility" (money donated by OPEC to the IMF to help countries most seriously hurt by the high price of imported oil), as well as the increased caution of commercial lenders, there were efforts to increase IMF funds. In September the "Witteveen" facility (named after the IMF managing director) was set up. It consisted of $10 billion, of which $6 billion was to come from the industrial countries (the U.S., West Germany, Japan, Switzerland, Canada, Belgium, and The

Table XIV. Current Balances of Payments
In $000,000,000

Country	1974	1975	1976	1977*
Canada	−1.5	−4.9	−4.2	−6.3
France	−5.9	—	−6.1	−3.9
Germany, West	+9.6	+3.9	+3.4	+3.4
Italy	−7.8	−0.5	−2.9	—
Japan	−4.7	−0.7	+3.7	+10.5
Netherlands, The	+2.1	+1.7	+2.5	+1.4
Norway	−1.1	−2.2	−3.7	−5.3
United Kingdom	−7.8	−3.7	−2.5	+0.4
United States	−5.0	−11.6	−1.3	−16.1
OECD total	−37.9	−5.6	−26.5	−30.0
Other developed countries	−2.6	−3.4	−1.5	−3.0
Centrally planned economies*	−3.0	−4.0	−0.5	−2.0
Oil-exporting countries*	+66.5	+40.0	+43.0	+44.0
Other less developed countries	−23.0	−27.0	−14.5	−9.0

*Estimate.
Sources: International Monetary Fund, *International Financial Statistics*; national sources.

Netherlands) and the rest from OPEC ($2.5 billion from Saudi Arabia and the rest from Iran, Venezuela, and some smaller countries). The target date for its implementation was mid-1978, but it had not been ratified by the U.S. by the end of 1977. If ratified, it could offer loans for IMF credit for up to seven years instead of the usual three–five years. The OPEC contributors preferred that it be directed primarily to the less developed countries, which would be a change from the current distribution of IMF credit. The IMF also decided to attempt to increase its normal lending facilities by raising member countries' quotas.

Reserves and Exchange Rates. The increase in international reserves in 1977 was about the same as in 1976 and was approximately proportional to the rise in world trade. The share of U.S. liabilities in the total increased slightly, while that of U.K. liabilities was almost unchanged in spite of the conversion in the spring of some sterling liabilities into medium-term foreign currency bonds in order to reduce the vulnerability of sterling to short-term outflows. This was part of a long-term effort to end sterling's role as a reserve currency, but the immediate reason was the very low level of U.K. external reserves at the end of 1976. The large inflows, first as a result of borrowing and the capital controls and then because of increased confidence in the stability of the pound, combined with the policy until October of trying to prevent any rise in the pound to produce an increase in reserves of more than $13 billion. Italy also had a large rise in reserves as its balance improved and its capital controls became more effective.

After two years of slow growth, Iran among the oil exporters increased its reserves substantially, while the recorded reserves of Saudi Arabia rose more slowly than in recent years. Among the other less developed countries, almost the entire increase went to India, South Korea, Mexico, the Ivory Coast, and Kenya, all for special reasons (mainly import controls; the last two are coffee exporters). The increase did not, therefore, represent a general improvement in the position of the less developed countries.

Although changes in effective exchange rates for most countries were smaller than in 1976, fluctuations and intervention by governments to control

Table XIII. Global Structure of Current Account Balances
In $000,000,000

Area	Average 1967–72	1973	1974	1975	1976	1977	1967–72 average adjusted to 1977 prices and levels of real output
Major oil exporters	0.7	6	67	35	41	37	3
Industrial countries	10.2	12	−10	19	−1	−1	31
Other non-oil countries							
More developed	−1.7	1	−14	−15	−14	−12	−6
Less developed	−8.1	−11	−30	−38	−26	−25	−28
	1.1	8	14	—	—	—	

Source: Adapted from the International Monetary Fund, *Annual Report 1977*.

CHART 5

rates were more general in 1977. The changes that did occur reflected changes (actual or anticipated) in balances as well as the relative inflation rates, which had been important in 1976. Although the effective rate of the U.S. dollar changed relatively little, this was because of the importance of Canada (whose currency had also fallen) in U.S. trade. Relative to the European currencies, there was a large decline, about 8% through the year against the mark and over 12% against the Swiss franc.

Changes among the European currencies were generally smaller, except for the rises in the mark and the Swiss franc and the successive devaluations by the Scandinavian currencies; there were devaluations by Sweden, Denmark, Norway, and Finland in the spring and by Sweden in August when it left the EEC "snake" of floating currencies. Portugal, Spain, and Iceland also devalued during the year. After a small decline in January the Italian lira remained stable relative to the dollar, with its effective rate therefore falling. The U.K. attempted to pursue a similar policy of keeping the dollar rate constant, but abandoned this in the summer when capital flows increased. From July to October, it tried to maintain a constant effective rate, but this was again changed at the end of October. The policy remained broadly one of stability, although presumably within much wider bounds, but with priority given to domestic monetary policy.

The strong improvement in the Japanese current balance created pressure on the yen. Its effective rate rose through the year, particularly strongly at the end. By then, the policy was to hold it at 240 to the dollar, more than 20% above its level at the beginning of 1977. There was thus, as in the United Kingdom, no abandonment of the policy of attempting to manage the rate. The less developed countries continued to devalue slowly, with no general attempt to use this to correct their imbalances.

In April the IMF approved a set of principles for exchange-rate policies. They required that countries avoid engineering exchange-rate policies to obtain an "unfair" competitive advantage but permit intervention for short-term smoothing of fluctuations.

Short-term interest rates moved increasingly close together during 1977, with reductions in the relatively high rates of the U.K. and Italy and a small rise in that of the U.S. The change in the U.K. rate was partly because of exchange-rate policy. Except for that, European rates were somewhat higher than in 1976, while those of the U.S. and Japan were lower. The spread among long-term rates remained wide, with the sterling rates particularly high. French, Swedish, and U.S. rates rose, but those of West Germany, Japan, and Switzerland fell. Except for the U.K., the changes appeared to be increasingly associated not with exchange-rate management but with domestic developments.

The price of gold increased during 1977, from an average of $125 an ounce in 1976 to over $160 by the end of the year, for an average of about $145–$150. This was, however, still lower even in nominal terms than in 1975. (SHEILA A. B. PAGE)

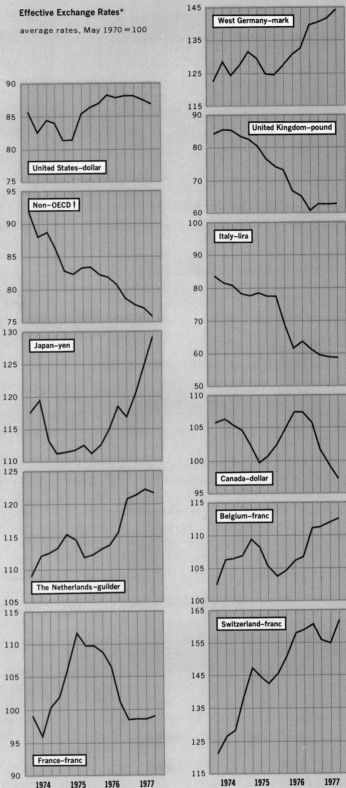

Effective Exchange Rates*

average rates, May 1970 = 100

* Measure of a currency's value relative to a weighted average of the value of the currencies of the country's trading partners.
† April 1971 = 100.
Sources: International Monetary Fund, *International Financial Statistics*; OECD, *Economic Outlook*; National Institute of Economic and Social Research (United Kingdom).

THE THIRD WORLD LOOKS TO ITS OWN

by Harford Thomas

During the past four or five years a new strategy for third world development has been taking shape. It springs from a growing realization that the benefits of development programs have not been getting through to the bulk of the people. Three-quarters of the population of the less developed countries are country folk living in villages. They are poor, they lack the basic services of decent living, and they are hard to reach. They remain unreached.

The philosophy of the United Nations' First Development Decade (1961–70) was to help install the infrastructure of Western industrialism. Roads, railways, docks, airports, oil refineries, steel mills, fertilizer plants, factories, city centre office buildings—all these were being built and expanded. This was to be the launching pad for economic takeoff; the benefits would trickle down and spread to the rest of the community. It did not happen. The poor in the villages and in the slums that surround most third world cities increased in numbers and stayed poor.

Early in the 1970s the failure of the "trickle down" theory came to be generally acknowledged. In 1973 the World Health Organization (WHO) reported: "In many countries the health services are not keeping pace with the changing populations either in quantity or in quality. It is likely that they are getting worse." In 1974 the UN Children's Fund (UNICEF) declared a world emergency for children because of the damaging effect of world price inflation.

Second Thoughts on Basic Needs. Meanwhile, the International Bank for Reconstruction and Development—the World Bank—which had been a leading agent of the trickle down theory, was having second thoughts. Under the leadership of Robert McNamara, its president, it began to change course. In a seminal speech at the World Bank meeting in Nairobi, Kenya, in September 1973, McNamara focused attention on rural poverty. He estimated that 40% of the population of less developed coun-

tries had neither shared in economic progress nor been able to contribute to economic growth.

By 1975 the World Bank, in a policy paper on rural development, had begun to formulate a new strategy. The emphasis was to be switched from capital-intensive development—frequently centred in the towns—to labour-intensive agricultural activity involving local participation. The bank became the largest single source of funds for agricultural development. This pointed the way, though the philosophy was still rather tentative.

A more radical change was still to come. It was to reverse the conventional assumption that development programs are planned at the top in government departments and proceed downward to the people in the villages. The first step is to discover what the people themselves want, what are their priorities, what are their "felt needs," as the jargon has it. The people themselves are then organized to take on their own development programs with the help of such training, materials, and money as they may need from the governmental system. By direct involvement, the people learn that they can improve the quality of their lives by their own efforts.

The evolution of this strategy of self-help has been most rapid in the agencies and government departments with most experience in the field. A comprehensive statement of the theory and practice of community-based self-help has come from UNICEF in a document called *A Strategy for Basic Services*, published early in 1977. WHO has worked with UNICEF in producing two reports, on alternative approaches to meeting basic health needs (1975) and on community involvement in primary health care (1977). A number of third world governments have also been making studies and acquiring experience with pilot projects, as have independent charitable organizations. The UN General Assembly ratified and recommended the new approach in a resolution adopted on Dec. 21, 1976.

It is surprising that this did not happen much earlier. There are hundreds of millions of poor people in the less developed countries, and very few trained experts. Yet the unspoken assumption until very recently has been that essential services—health, housing, education—are provided for people by official bodies. Obviously development is impossible if it is thought of in this way.

The involvement of the people themselves has been the missing link in development strategy. The executive director of UNICEF, Henry R. Labouisse, has said: "We stress using the prodigious untapped human resources in developing countries," and again, "It is better to do things *with* people than *for* people." The philosophy is crystallized in the title of a 1975 WHO report, *Health by the People.*

Formerly deputy and financial editor of The Guardian, *London, Harford Thomas has recently been studying third world problems at first hand in a number of African countries.*

Barefoot Doctors. The new thinking has achieved its most spectacular and best-known successes with the "barefoot doctors." The first considerable experiment along these lines seems to have been a village midwives project pioneered by two British nursing sisters in the Sudan as long ago as the 1920s. There must have been other similar schemes, for necessity mothers improvisation everywhere. But it was not until China in 1965 launched a village-based health care program that the "barefoot doctor" came to be talked about throughout the world.

It is a vivid phrase, but a misleading one, for he or she is neither a doctor in the professional sense nor necessarily barefoot. The official terminology varies, from country to country, but the most usual is "primary health worker." The essential features of the system are common to a large number of village-based health programs now operating in every continent. Primary health workers might be described as "first aiders," trained to recognize common symptoms that require simple treatment.

The primary health workers are chosen by the local community from among their own people. They are given a minimum basic training in diagnosis and treatment. This may take as little as two or three weeks followed by a further one day a week, although commonly the training period is from three to six months. Experience shows that local people, often illiterate, can quickly learn the necessary skills to treat the most common family diseases, ailments, and accidents. They can deal with vaccination and family planning. They have the additional advantage of being known to and trusted by their neighbours. Furthermore, it has been found that these primary health workers will give especially attentive care to their patients because they usually know them and their families personally.

The country's health service structures then have to be reorganized to serve a village- and urban community-based system. A district level of doctors and medical auxiliaries will provide supervision, advice, and the supply of necessary medicines, materials, and equipment. More serious cases can then be referred to regional and national hospital services.

The "Total Approach." By getting into the villages and the neglected urban slums another lesson is learned. It is not just health but poverty that is the problem. In a pamphlet called *Health for All by the Year 2000*, WHO says there must be a "total approach" to development. Thus WHO finds itself tackling the causes of ill health—polluted water, bad sanitation, inadequate food, wretched housing.

UNICEF has come to the same conclusion. Its responsibility for the welfare of children calls for a many-pronged approach, a combination of mutually supportive services. If the rights of the child are to

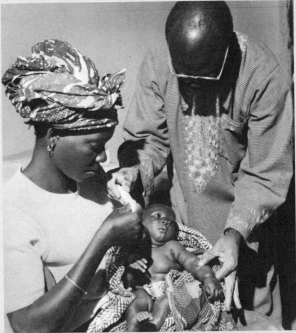

Oumar Diouf is a chicken farmer who also tends to the health needs of the villagers in Khinine, Senegal. He was selected by his fellow villagers to take a three-month health training course sponsored by UNICEF.

be met, they must include a decent home, adequate food, good health, education, the prospect of a job. In practice such a program will include food production from home gardens, health protection, safe water, and suitable vocational training. Similarly, the International Labour Organization (ILO), in framing its concept of basic needs for the 1976 World Employment Conference, could not isolate the right to work from a total approach.

It becomes clear that there are no frontiers to be drawn in third world development. It is not the exclusive concern of any one UN agency or any one government department. The participating, community-based approach must be integrated, multisectoral, interdepartmental. The international organizations are reflecting a growing consensus of views not only of their own fieldworkers but, more significantly, of the governments with which they work. Present trends in development strategies suggest the welling up of a worldwide commitment to a new philosophy.

"Barefoot Everything." It has been called "barefoot everything," although this too can be misleading. Sometimes it has been taken to imply an inferior, second-best style of development compared with Western industrialization. Experience shows, however, that to import an alien industrialism may create more difficulties than it solves. Conversely, direct involvement in the life of the community is coming to be the aspiration of over-centralized Western societies.

In practice, community-based self-help is a way of enabling people not only to improve their lot but to decide their own priorities. Education projects in which UNESCO has been involved are directed to providing the kind of teaching people want—less academic, more functional and informal, and better fitted to the needs of each particular community. Here again it is proving possible to train local teachers quickly and to rely on minimum local resources. In some climates an open-air class with a blackboard nailed to a tree can make more sense than rows of desks in a hot brick box.

Equally, there is a manifest case for appropriate technology rather than the technology imported from advanced countries, which is often utterly inappropriate for its intended purpose. If a water system is so complicated as to be beyond the resources of a village to maintain and repair, it is no aid to development. A simple pump capable of simple maintenance is a definite step forward. Hence the new interest in appropriate technology is actively supported by UNICEF, WHO, the Food and Agriculture Organization (FAO), the UN Development Program (UNDP)—indeed all the UN agencies—by all the nongovernmental development agencies, and by many government departments.

Not surprisingly, there has been resistance. The new approach challenges the interests of the city elites, of the bureaucracies, of jealously exclusive departments, of the professions. Highly qualified civil servants, teachers, doctors, and others will naturally question the quick minimum functional training now proposed for the villages and the city slums. It involves a tremendous social shake-up, the liberation of the illiterate, and, not least, the liberation of the women.

A Spreading Doctrine. Yet all this is on the move. To make a substantial impact it needs the backing of political will, as it has, for example, in China, with 1.3 million village health workers, and in Tanzania, with its *ujamaa* villages and Pres. Julius Nyerere's Arusha Declaration. The catalog of recent projects in community-based development involving central governments, state governments, UN agencies, and nongovernmental aid organizations is a long one. The UNICEF strategy report mentions 23 countries as having instructive basic services projects. They are widely differing countries in different parts of the world. Yet the main principles of the new approach can be applied in all of them, though the details will be particular to local customs and governmental methods.

This demonstrates a vital point. If a development strategy is to have real value it must involve more than a one-shot project; it must be repeatable and it must invite imitation. The common experience is that these prototype projects are being taken up by neighbouring countries. The message is being passed from one country to another.

Finally, it is an economical, cost-attractive as well as cost-effective approach. Local communities contribute in labour and local materials. Running costs are within the capacity of the communities and countries to meet. A UN estimate puts the cost of bringing basic services to the unserved areas of the third world at $1 billion a year over a period of 15 years. By way of comparison, the world spends about $1 billion a day on arms.

Ecuador

A republic on the west coast of South America, Ecuador is bounded by Colombia, Peru, and the Pacific Ocean. Area: 281,334 sq km (108,624 sq mi), including the Galápagos Islands (7,976 sq km), which is an insular province. Pop. (1977 est.): 7,550,000. Cap.: Quito (pop., 1977 est., 977,400). Largest city: Guayaquil (pop., 1974, 823,200). Language: Spanish, but Indians speak Quechuan and Jivaroan. Religion: Roman Catholic about 93%, others 7%. In 1977 the country was ruled by a military junta including Vice-Adm. Alfredo Poveda Burbano (Navy), Gen. Guillermo Durán Arcentales (Army), and Gen. Luis Leoro Franco (Air Force).

The 1977 political scene was dominated by preparations for the return to civilian rule; the military junta had announced in December 1976 that the referendum on a new constitution and the consequent presidential elections, previously scheduled for late 1977, would take place by early 1978 and mid-1978, respectively. A strike of teachers that began on May 18 led to the dismissal of 200 teachers in July.

In January the state petroleum company, CEPE, took over Gulf Oil's holdings in the Gulf-Texaco consortium. Disagreement on the final settlement delayed the official signing of the treaty until June and caused disruption that resulted in a lower petroleum output, with exports declining slightly in value. A reform of the Hydrocarbons Law was undertaken, with a view to offering incentives to foreign companies while maintaining "the reservation of oil as a national resource and the property of the state."

The economy performed well; the Central Bank estimated the 1977 gross domestic product growth rate at 10%, as compared with 6.5% in 1976. However, preliminary figures for the first half of 1977 showed a trade deficit of $76.2 million, as against

During a visit to Ecuador in June, U.S. first lady Rosalynn Carter visited a technical trade school in Quito.

UPI COMPIX

Ecuador

ECUADOR

Education. (1975–76) Primary, pupils 1,266,478, teachers 32,285; secondary, pupils 290,265, teachers 18,455; vocational, pupils 88,921, teachers 4,939; teacher training, pupils 960, teachers 140; higher (1972–73), students 43,743, teaching staff (1970–71) 2,867.

Finance. Monetary unit: sucre, with (Sept. 19, 1977) an official rate of 25 sucres to U.S. $1 (free rate of 43.35 sucres = £1 sterling). Gold, SDR's, and foreign exchange (June 1977) U.S. $582.1 million. Budget (1975 actual): revenue 12,617,000,000 sucres; expenditure 12,311,000,000 sucres. Gross national product (1976) 120,830,000,000 sucres. Money supply (Feb. 1977) 24,663,000,000 sucres. Cost of living (Quito; 1970 = 100; June 1977) 232.

Foreign Trade. (1976) Imports U.S. $993.1 million; exports U.S. $1,162,800,000. Import sources (1975): U.S. 40%; Japan 13%; West Germany 10%. Export destinations (1975): U.S. 47%; Panama 15%; Chile 8%; Peru 7%. Main exports: crude oil 49%; coffee 18%; bananas 15%.

Transport and Communications. Roads (1972) 18,345 km (including 1,392 km of Pan-American Highway). Motor vehicles in use (1974): passenger 43,600; commercial (including buses) 68,400. Railways (1974): 1,151 km; traffic 65 million passenger-km, freight 46 million net ton-km. Air traffic (1975): 301 million passenger-km; freight 6.7 million net ton-km. Telephones (Jan. 1976) 193,100. Radio receivers (Dec. 1971) 1.7 million. Television receivers (Dec. 1974) 250,000.

Agriculture. Production (in 000; metric tons; 1976): rice 367; barley c. 57; corn (1975) 260; potatoes c. 500; cassava (1975) 365; sugar, raw value c. 328; bananas c. 2,873; pineapples c. 234; oranges c. 275; coffee c. 78; cocoa c. 64. Livestock (in 000; 1975): cattle c. 2,800; sheep c. 2,050; pigs c. 2,200; horses c. 263; chickens c. 10,000.

Industry. Production (in 000; metric tons; 1975): crude oil 8,155; petroleum products 1,977; electricity (kw-hr) c. 1,290,000; cement 604; gold (troy oz; 1974) 7.7; silver (troy oz) c. 30.

a surplus of $54 million during the first half of 1976. Reserves were $541 million at the end of August 1977, compared with $514 million a year earlier. Both inside and outside Ecuador the increasing external public debt ($731 million at the end of 1976, as compared with $513 million in December 1975) was causing concern, and inflationary pressures (the cost of living index rose 13.2% in 1976) were contained with extreme difficulty. (FRANÇOISE LOTERY)

Education

The continued economic difficulties that afflicted most countries of the West in 1977 had two principal effects on their educational systems. One was to prevent any further expansion in education except where economic necessity demanded otherwise; the other was to initiate reappraisals of the goals of the system, with a resulting emphasis on standards of attainment and the need to obtain value for money. There was particular concern about the fate of the young unemployed, who appeared to be disproportionately increasing in numbers. Figures published by the Organization for Economic Cooperation and Development (OECD) in 1977 showed, for example, that in the United States in 1968, 7.6% of those in the 16–24 age range who were seeking work were unemployed, compared with 2.2% of those over 25. By 1976 the figures had become, respectively, 14.4 and 5.5%. In the United Kingdom the change had been even more dramatic. For the 16–24 age group in 1968 the percentage unemployed was 2.2% and for those

Ecumenical Movement:
see Religion

over 25 it was 2%. By 1976 the figures were, respectively, 12 and 3.8%. The same trends could be seen, according to the OECD, in Canada, France, West Germany, Italy, and Japan.

Although there was no total consensus on the causes of this phenomenon, most observers believed that the composition of the labour force was changing so that young people formed a smaller proportion of it. Thus, even if Western economies grew more buoyant the numbers of young persons unemployed would still remain high. In a conference held in May 1977 at Fère-en-Tardenois in France, under the aegis of the Carnegie Council on Policy Studies in Higher Education, a group of 20 academic leaders and administrators drawn from the U.S. and a number of European countries reflected the general view in the West that strong economic intervention was required by governments to sustain youth employment. The U.S. representatives suggested that since entry into what was described as the "primary labour market," the main area of employment protected by labour unions and legislation, is delayed until age 21 or 22, until that age the young should have the opportunity to carry out a whole range of jobs in social and environmental services that were not conventionally thought of as making a contribution to the gross national product.

There were strong differences of view on this, but it was clear by mid-1977 that most countries had programs of some kind for subsidizing the employment of youth. In the U.K., for example, there was a determined effort made by the government through its Manpower Services Commission to ensure that all unemployed persons leaving school had at some stage the opportunity of getting work. Implicit in any policy of this kind was the need to give priority to those at the bottom of the educational qualifications scale and to provide adult education so that the opportunity was always open to people to enhance their educational attainment and to acquire new vocational skills.

In the oil-rich countries education continued to be given a high priority, but there was concern in the Muslim nations that what were thought to be the less desirable attributes of Western life should not infiltrate the schools and colleges. Saudi Arabia, the guardian of the more conservative traditions of Islam, called the first world conference on Muslim education in Mecca in April. Great stress was placed at the conference on the need to follow the precepts of the Koran. There were, however, differences of opinion on quite how the Koran should be interpreted. Did it, for example, prohibit coeducation? According to the Saudis, most certainly yes. But in Egypt coeducation, particularly in the universities, is not uncommon. However, even in Egypt there were signs that the government wished to stress the significance of religious education. Pres. Anwar as-Sadat announced in February that "religion must be a basic and compulsory subject in our schools," though there were skeptics who said that this enthusiasm for Islam was not unconnected with the serious food riots in Cairo and the manifest attempts of President Sadat to court the support of the Muslim establishment.

If this was so, it was but one example of many where political considerations had a direct effect on educational policy. This was perhaps most important in China, where conventional educational values gained increasing support following the overthrow of the radical faction centred on Chiang Ch'ing, the widow of Mao Tse-tung. There was more and more evidence of the destructive side of the Cultural Revolution, especially the way in which it had undermined the teachers' morale. Following the congress of the Chinese Communist Party in August, greater emphasis was placed on examinations and academic qualifications, stricter class discipline, greater respect for teachers, and more enthusiasm for theoretical studies. The necessity for developments of this kind was well illustrated by the fact that, although China had some 200 million at school, it had about 500,000 at the university level, compared with some 5 million in the Soviet Union.

In South Africa there was some response to the growing hostility outside the country to its apartheid (racial separation) policies. The Indian University of Durban, for example, was allowed to open its courses to white students as part of the government policy of selective relaxation of academic apartheid. On the face of it there were also attempts to equalize the quality of education for black children, and black parents were allowed to have comparatively more say in their children's education. This did not, however, prevent continued unrest in Soweto, a black township of some one million inhabitants near Johannesburg, where rioting occurred in 1976 over the insistence on black schoolchildren learning Afrikaans.

"Reverse discrimination" was the key issue in U.S. education in 1977. The University of California at Davis had refused to admit Allan Bakke to its medical school in 1973 although he scored in the 90% range on admissions tests. His credentials were better than some of the minority-group students admitted under a special plan for increasing the number of blacks, Latinos, American Indians, and Asians in the student body. Under the plan, 16 of 100 openings in the medical school were reserved for minority-group students. The California Supreme Court ruled that Bakke's constitutional rights were violated when others were admitted on the basis of race. As the case went to the Supreme Court, it gained increased public attention, and dozens of briefs were filed, both pro and con.

The Supreme Court delayed making an immediate ruling, but in asking contending attorneys to analyze the case in terms of the 1964 U.S. Civil Rights Act, the court hinted that its eventual ruling would be based on that act, which is clearer than the Constitution in forbidding discrimination based on race.

School racial imbalances may be corrected by federal courts, but the solutions must be designed to undo past deliberate discrimination, according to a series of Supreme Court rulings. When racial imbalances are not the result of deliberate effort by school officials, court orders for massive busing are too sweeping, said the justices. The ruling was made about Indianapolis, Ind., where a metropoli-

Myrra Lenore Lee, a high-school teacher in La Mesa, Calif., was congratulated by Pres. Jimmy Carter during ceremonies at the White House in March after being named Teacher of the Year. The annual Teacher of the Year awards are sponsored by Encyclopædia Britannica companies, the Council of Chief State School Officers, and the *Ladies' Home Journal.*

tan government had been formed without including the city and county school districts.

In its decision concerning a Dayton, Ohio, case, the court concluded that a federal judge's requirement that there be citywide busing was excessive. The court did uphold the power of federal judges to order measures that improve learning of students penalized by past segregated schooling. In a Detroit, Mich., case the justices concluded that a federal judge there was correct in ordering the city of Detroit and the state of Michigan to split costs of remedial reading programs, changes in testing and counseling, and teacher preparation. The reforms were ordered to supplement busing efforts as part of a compensatory education program.

The U.S. Congress forbade the Department of Health, Education, and Welfare to cut federal support for schools that do not undertake busing to eliminate racial imbalances. The administration of Pres. Jimmy Carter seemed to be leaning toward busing and pairing (or clustering) schools to mix students from predominantly white or black schools. Under the pairing plan, an elementary school is formed from two or more different schools so that students will attend a racially mixed class even though they may reside in segregated neighbourhoods.

The U.S. Supreme Court went further than usual in its rulings on aid to parochial schools. The justices concluded that public funds may be used for busing handicapped and slow-learning students from private schools to remedial centres. All students may be transported to public centres for guidance counseling. The states may provide textbooks and certain services but still may not provide across-the-board aid. The court cited a three-part test for laws concerning public support of schools: they must have a secular purpose; their primary effect must neither advance nor inhibit religion; and they must not foster excessive government involvement in religion.

Elementary schools in the U.S. continued the slight enrollment declines of the 1970s, dropping 1½% to 33.3 million students as school opened in the fall of 1977. Secondary-school enrollments declined less than 1%, to 15.7 million, and colleges enrolled 11.3 million persons, up about 2½%. The number of graduates was expected to increase to 3,150,000 from high schools and to an all-time high of 969,000 receiving bachelor's degrees and 455,000, graduate and professional degrees.

Faced with job losses by more than 60,000 persons in the U.S., teacher groups pressed for better security for their members. The National Education Association found its members more dissatisfied than they had been since 1961, when it began surveying teachers. It estimated that some 300,000 teachers were looking for jobs.

The growing difficulty of providing effective government by the Christian Democrats without the cooperation of the Communist Party led to mutual discussion about educational reform in Italy. There was general agreement that compulsory education should be extended to the age of 15, that there should be less emphasis on classical and more on technical education, and that university teachers should work full time.

According to figures put out by UNESCO, if current trends continued the number of children between the ages of 6 and 11 in the third world countries who were not attending school would reach approximately 134 million by 1985, including 35 million in Africa, 90 million in Asia, and 9 million in Latin America. Addressing a ceremony at UNESCO headquarters in Paris on the occasion of the 12th International Literacy Day, John Fobes, deputy director-general of UNESCO, said that one adult in three could not read, write, or make a simple calculation in written form. He estimated that the absolute number of illiterates was increasing to approximately 800 million. Most progress in the middle 1970s in adult literacy training had occurred in Algeria, India, Iran, Mali, Tanzania, Burma, Brazil, Cuba, and Somalia.

Primary and Secondary Schools. The two countries of Western Europe in which there was almost continuous discussion of the school system in 1977 were France and the United Kingdom. In

Students attempted to catch up with their grade level in a "competency lab" in Portland, Oregon. High-school competency labs gave remedial instruction to students who lacked ability in basic educational skills.

France the so-called Haby reforms were introduced on September 15. Named after the French minister of education, they were aimed chiefly at making the secondary schools more comprehensive in character so that all children who left a primary school went on to the same type of secondary school. Another aim was to reduce average class size over a long period from 35 to 25. The emphasis on examinations was also much modified by the Haby reforms, and the examination taken at age 14—the *brevet*—was abolished.

In England and Wales (and to a lesser extent in Scotland) a "great debate" took place initiated by the prime minister, James Callaghan, in November 1976. A series of regional meetings was held, followed in July by a government statement called "The Green Paper"; this set out in rather vague terms the government's views on such matters as teacher training, scholastic standards, and the curriculum. The curriculum had never been centrally controlled in England and Wales and had always been a sensitive area of discussion, since teachers naturally resented an intrusion into what they considered to be their own preserve. The main concern of the Green Paper, however, was that the curriculum in many schools was not sufficiently matched to life in a modern industrial society, and that it had been overloaded to such an extent that the essentials, "the common core of the curriculum," were at risk of not receiving enough emphasis.

A study of the 14-year decline in the scores of tests used to predict suitability for college in the U.S. was front-page material in many newspapers. The facts were simple: scores on the Scholastic Aptitude Test (SAT) used by many colleges and universities to predict college success had fallen year after year. In making its report, a panel of citizens refused to make sweeping recommendations for halting the decline and cautioned against using its study to reach broad conclusions about the quality

of education for the majority of students, those who do not go to college.

The SAT study panel made several guesses about the causes of the decline. Prior to 1970 the major cause could have been the increased number of students taking the test, persons from segments of the population who historically have done less well on standardized tests. After 1970, when the number and kinds of students staying in high school and taking tests before applying for college became stable, the panel thought that the amount of time spent watching television, the trauma of the divisive war in Vietnam, turbulence in the nation's cities, and increased numbers of single-parent homes all contributed to the scoring decline. The panel also concluded that the schools, along with society in general, had been giving less attention to the mastery of skills and knowledge and also had weakened standards by giving automatic promotions from grade to grade, permitting grade inflation, tolerating increases in absenteeism, using textbooks with lowered demands, and cutting down on homework.

Critics of schools in the U.S. advocated high-school diplomas based on statewide standardized achievement testing and certifying a minimal level of academic competence. Some states tested for competency over a period of several years to determine strengths and weaknesses. Most such tests stressed basic subjects such as reading, while some required minimum competencies in citizenship, work, and leisure utilization.

Commonly called the most significant development since passage of the Elementary and Secondary Education Act of 1965, the Education for All Handicapped Children Act of 1975 was put into effect during the year by the U.S. Department of Health, Education, and Welfare. The far-reaching legislation banned segregation of the handicapped and required accessible classes wherever they are offered for other students. Federal funds were to be provided to help the states implement the act. Such plans were to be effected for ages 6–17 by September 1978, and implementation would be extended to ages 3–5 and 18–21 in subsequent years. The law is broadly applicable since it must be implemented in all elementary, secondary, and collegiate institutions that receive federal funds.

There was a noticeable trend in the U.S. toward wanting schools to emphasize teaching of the basics, defined as the traditional reading, writing, and arithmetic. Some thought that basics also include respect, manners, politeness, discipline, and similar virtues.

Reversing a long-held view that the best schools are in the large urban areas, many citizens in the U.S. during the year expressed their belief that small communities had the best schools. Many of these people advocated decentralization of school districts. Citizens generally preferred leaving policy and fiscal control in the hands of their elected school boards and believed that the federal government should avoid such control, even when federal funds were being spent on special programs.

In Sweden, long regarded as being in the vanguard of educational progress in Western Europe, particularly in secondary education, the economic

A Teenager's Greatest Influence: Mom and Dad?

Today's high-school students admire many celebrities, but have few heroes. John Wayne, Chris Evert, Kojak, and Pres. Jimmy Carter lead in the most-admired list. Those, however, who have the greatest influence on the students lives' are Mom and Dad.

The return to family influence on teenagers is significant. In a poll of some 2,000 high-school students in classrooms throughout the country, conducted by Encyclopædia Britannica Educational Corp., nearly 55% of those polled stated that at least one member of their family had greatly influenced their lives. A similar Britannica poll two years earlier, at the junior high-school level, showed that television was then the greatest single influence on teenagers' lives.

The greatest problems in the world today, according to the poll, are crime (25%) and unemployment (23%). But the reply by many to the question of "What worries you most today?" was the future and their own life in the years ahead.

One female junior high-school student stated, "The world is changing. I am afraid it may be changing too fast for me." A senior high-school male said that what worried him most was "being listed as a criminal by law just because he smoked pot every now and then." Many were concerned over the rising prices of "just about everything."

Young people are concerned primarily about their personal destinies (getting into college, finding a career, getting a job). World resources, crime, inflation, and war are secondary considerations. Yet 63% think that war is a serious threat and that the Middle East will be the area most likely to explode. While 90% think there are violations of human rights in the U.S., the majority believe that their nation should speak out against the violations of human rights occurring in other countries.

"While it is true that this year's poll was conducted among more mature teenagers (high school versus junior high school), the answers I believe reflect a serious concern over such all-encompassing interests and such controversial subjects as pornography and the ban on the Concorde," Ralph Wagner, president of Encyclopædia Britannica Educational Corp., stated. "It was interesting to me to find that quite a few boys and girls (nearly 40%) said nothing worried them. Lucky people."

"Of particular significance to Encyclopædia Britannica Educational Corporation is the overwhelming (95%) belief that films in classrooms help students to understand subjects better and (93%) that more films in their high school classes would be desirable," said Wagner.

crisis and a 10% devaluation in 1977 led to a severe curtailment of innovations. It was clear nonetheless that most countries in the Nordic group continued to follow Sweden's lead, especially in the introduction of a nine-year comprehensive school. This was already implemented in Norway and Denmark (as well as Sweden), and a report by the Nordic Council indicated that it would be instituted in Finland by 1981–82 and in Iceland by 1984. The Nordic Council also considered the possibility of lowering the starting age for compulsory schooling from seven, Europe's highest, to six.

In West Germany moves toward comprehensive schools made distinctly slow progress and were the subject of continued dispute. In North Rhine-Westphalia proposals were made for "cooperative schools" that would provide a common secondary education for two years and then separate students into the three familiar schools or streams—grammar (*Gymnasium*), intermediate (*Realschule*), and secondary modern (*Hauptschule*)—all at the same school centre.

In Ireland the change of government to the Fianna Fail led to some change of emphasis in educational policy. The minister of education, John Wilson, said that priority would be given to reduction in the pupil/teacher ratios in primary schools down to one teacher per 40 pupils and, in due course, one to 32. He also showed signs of encouraging interdenominational schools, despite opposition from some Roman Catholic interests.

The size of schools was a preoccupation in a number of countries and, although it was not always accepted that small was beautiful, large

schools were generally condemned. A report from the Ottawa (Ontario) Board of Education showed that vandalism in large schools was greater than in small. Taking schools with more than 1,000 students, the average property damage per school in Ottawa in 1975–76 was $6,500; for schools of less than 1,000 students it was $5,300. But there were differences of opinion about the desirability of maintaining small schools in rural areas with one or two teachers. In England and Ireland there were heated arguments that the closing down of these schools in rural hamlets led to the destruction of village life and that busing children long distances had serious disadvantages. Others argued that not to provide larger schools would reduce educational opportunity.

In countries where there was civil unrest the schools were, needless to say, among the first sufferers. Figures released by the secretary for African education in Rhodesia showed that the percentage of black pupils going on to secondary school had declined since 1974. Although a target of 25% of black primary-school children going on to secondary school was set for 1980—a modest figure since it stood at 22% in 1974—the proportion had in fact been reduced by 1976 to 19%.

Higher Education. Reversing a trend, job opportunities improved in 1977 for college graduates in the U.S. College placement officials said that job offers increased 41% on the bachelor's degree level, 43% on the master's degree level, and 33% on the doctoral level. From that standpoint the 1976–77 academic year was the best of the 1970s. Engineering graduates received the largest number of

World Education

Most recent official data

Country	1st level (primary) Students (full-time)	1st level Teachers (full-time)	1st level Total schools	General 2nd level (secondary) Students (full-time)	General 2nd level Teachers (full-time)	General 2nd level Total schools	Vocational 2nd level Students (full-time)	Vocational 2nd level Teachers (full-time)	Vocational 2nd level Total schools	3rd level (higher) Students (full-time)	3rd level Teachers (full-time)	3rd level Total schools	Literacy % of population	Literacy Over age
Afghanistan	694,240	19,158	...	166,361	7,376	197	10,061	871	...	9,339	1,264	...	8.0	15
Albania	518,002	20,555	1,374	23,229	1,318	46	62,212[1]	1,712[1]	85	28,668	1,153	5	71.0	9
Algeria	2,785,264	70,498	8,209	592,265	20,861	939	20,036	1,744	16	41,847	4,670	15	26.4	15
Angola	536,599	13,230	5,585	59,209	3,060	177	15,845	1,184	99	2,942	274	1	30.0	...
Argentina	3,601,243	199,256	20,590	445,397	59,765	1,679	837,659	109,939	3,206	601,395	42,007	412	92.6	15
Australia	1,842,101	81,747	8,007	1,118,149[1]	77,638[1]	2,239	...	...	...	184,343	20,848	101	...	...
Austria	985,286	52,466	5,920	167,904	11,624	...	267,426	14,517	995	84,349	10,607	35	98.0	15
Bangladesh	7,747,559	144,258	36,633	1,822,740	74,924	8,193	10,661	911	53[2]	68,075	7,201	138	22.2	15
Bolivia	912,998	39,835	...	124,092	8,044	...	43,394	1,032	80	34,030	2,270	16	39.8	15
Botswana	125,588	3,921	335	13,991	599	32	2,284	258	26	465	56	1	18.4	15
Brazil	15,837,283	525,628	186,563	4,077,506	266,328	9,323	1,053,550	105,936	...	668,857	64,479	...	79.8	15
Brunei	31,605	1,621	153	13,687	876	27	927	109	2[3]	...	...	...	64.0	15
Bulgaria	1,000,504	51,670	3,496	113,267	7,830	321	279,663	19,406	550	119,258	12,747	26	91.4	8
Burma	3,449,552	73,653	...	945,719	26,761	...	11,205	871	...	57,965	3,404	...	68.3	8
Cambodia	429,110	18,794	1,021	98,888	2,226	79	5,409	220	72	11,570	276	35	36.1	...
Cameroon	1,074,021	20,803	4,349	93,934	3,699	226	28,639	370	...	6,171	328	8	12.0	...
Canada	2,753,553	142,900[5]	16,500	2,577,190[1,6]	101,844[1,6]	...	...	...	...	613,120	50,003	254	95.6	14
Chile	2,243,274	57,164	8,156	307,946	19,341	597	157,989	11,509	272	147,049	8,835	8	88.2	15
China	90,000,000	2,600,000	...	8,520,000	...	...	850,000	...	...	820,000	...	...	40.0	...
Colombia	3,953,242	131,211	32,230	977,648	51,232	3,252	328,627	18,889	932	192,887	21,163	70	78.5	15
Congo	307,194	5,053	...	81,541	1,703	...	6,427	440	...	2,570	166	2	28.8	...
Costa Rica	377,111	14,808	...	114,816	5,229[6]	...	17,558	...	...	27,625	3,500	5	84.7	15
Cuba	1,923,290	78,451	15,547	337,524	26,504	642	117,536	9,008	136	76,900	5,725	4	...	...
Czechoslovakia	1,935,361	101,183	10,211	128,917	8,511	357	634,974[1]	27,050[1]	1,551	151,282	17,009	91	98.5	15
Denmark	559,745	58,405[4]	2,474	223,134	...	1,336	89,169	4,200	154	112,457	7,865	60	100	15
Dominican Republic	833,439	15,216	...	118,190	5,381	...	7,544	460	8	37,538	1,709	...	67.3	15
Ecuador	1,266,478	32,285	...	290,265	18,455	...	89,881	5,079	...	131,078	9,319	28	67.5	...
Egypt	4,120,936	112,649	...	1,697,382	35,635	...	410,635	27,049	...	419,750	19,300	...	44.0	14
El Salvador	759,725	15,665	3,103	29,559	1,546[6]	161	22,172	...	91	26,692	2,175	14	49.0	...
Fiji	135,092	4,229	...	26,202	1,103	...	2,221	224	...	1,031	145	...	72.7	15
Finland	405,809	27,773	4,396	391,788	19,598	1,002	114,079	11,600	536	71,526	4,420	24	100	15
France	4,579,602	173,493[5]	59,967	4,327,670	372,386[6]	6,282	713,921[11]	2,979[11]	4,478	777,348	38,000[2]	278	100	7
Germany, East	2,649,886	158,543[6]	5,636	47,854	...	285	412,785	44,213	979	293,238	33,570	292	100	15
Germany, West	6,287,642	236,356[1]	25,731[1]	3,331,159	152,594	...	2,270,516	59,455	4,249	877,328	93,841	3,301	99.0	15
Greece	925,495	29,921	9,738	504,031	16,595	1,137	133,361	...	...	97,131	5,068	137	86.0	15
Guatemala	618,544	17,171	6,010	104,492	7,073[6]	493	15,810	1,380	...	21,715	1,314	5	36.7	15
Honduras	460,744	13,045	4,245	65,527	3,104[6]	163	1,207	97[11]	1,394	10,635	648	2	60.4	10
Hong Kong	606,860	19,695	965	384,656	13,077	354	12,494	[7]	27	19,690	2,328	16	80.9	...
Hungary	1,072,000	68,425	4,214	99,656	6,663	285	110,820	7,751	251	64,000	12,233	48	98.2	15
India	66,000,000	2,560,000[4]	404,418	24,900,000	...	124,360	[7]	[7]	[7]	2,230,225	119,000	3,721	33.3	15
Indonesia	14,280,157	472,698	73,589	1,863,348	114,525	7,185	832,229	64,904	3,162	147,972	15,260	40	56.6	15
Iran	4,768,588	144,068	38,369	2,446,574	84,092	7,152	203,734	10,193	616	154,215	5,465	205	22.8	15
Iraq[2]	1,999,022	73,090	8,432	555,184	19,573	1,320	49,551	2,743	125	88,459	3,042	61	52.0	15
Ireland	550,078	18,023	3,750	267,141	15,555	831	3,814	217	56	33,148	2,957	48	100	15
Israel	578,658	31,835	1,924	77,943	5,732	362	74,441	7,652	367	74,731	13,981	...	92.4[8]	14[8]
Italy	4,741,650	292,062	32,867	2,869,120	246,674	9,949	1,558,117	144,633	4,026	746,323	42,639	73	93.9	...
Ivory Coast	681,735	14,403	2,697	102,500	3,959	...	8,165	620	...	6,274	368	...	20.0	...
Japan	10,364,846	415,071	24,650	7,488,201	463,054	14,334	1,655,275	47,696	1,419	2,057,986	105,314	933	99.7	...
Jordan	402,401	11,636	1,123	178,153	8,129	1,118	7,547	457	14[2]	15,735	811	13	67.6	15
Kenya	2,894,617	89,074	8,544	280,388	11,438[6]	1,160	8,668[11]	639[11]	11[3]	5,753[12]	...	2	40.0	15
Korea, South	5,503,737	109,530	6,405	3,370,311	87,142	3,174	507,430	16,536	484	313,608	14,730	194	88.5	13
Kuwait	111,820	5,444[2]	177	106,943	7,972[2]	199	3,528	784	16	1,858	269	5	64.0	10
Laos	273,357	7,320	2,125	14,633	613	37	5,977	413	27	875	136	3	58.8	...
Lebanon	497,723	32,901[4]	2,319	167,578	...	1,241	7,836[2]	...	159	50,803	2,313	13	88.0	15
Lesotho	221,932	4,228	1,081	15,611	605	60	547	66[3]	11[3]	847	130	9	56.5	15
Liberia	149,687	4,111	843	26,426	1,015	275	1,511	107	6	1,980	190	3	21.5	15
Libya	568,781	26,385	2,143	172,250	12,025	868	26,709	2,409	13	12,459	350	9	52.4	15
Luxembourg	34,980	1,711	472	8,086	763	15	14,513	994	44	440	136	2	100	15
Malawi	663,940	10,735	2,371	14,826	725	61	1,877	181	7	1,179	93	3	16.5	15
Malaysia	1,843,514	57,693	6,370	799,284	28,949	1,179	21,922	1,024	82	28,601	2,137	23	60.8	10
Mali	276,307	7,848	...	6,786	511	...	2,704	332	...	2,445	327	4	2.2	...
Mauritius	144,002	6,008	235	67,264	2,135	126	1,858	117	10	1,203	99	1	61.6	12
Mexico	11,461,415	255,939	55,618	2,141,127	123,607	8,778	797,845	46,174	1,494	543,112	47,529	149	76.2	9
Morocco	1,547,647	37,226	...	471,575	19,613	...	10,016	1,058	...	34,092	1,921	...	22.2	...
Mozambique	577,977	8,345	...	36,155	1,682	...	18,495	1,106	...	2,621	326	...	7.0	...
Nepal	401,034	19,851	...	221,583	7,749	...	14,902	1,568	...	21,760	1,800	...	12.5	15
Netherlands, The	1,536,831	60,740	...	766,391	48,193	1,514	517,194	43,000	1,955	231,383[9]	28,300[9]	224	100	15
New Zealand	525,323	21,187[9]	2,544	219,754	11,107[9]	396	2,387	11,136	21	35,078	4,502[6]	33	100	15
Nicaragua	350,519	8,817	2,297	76,763	1,578	251	6,945	429	44	11,618	694	6	57.6	15
Nigeria	4,889,857	144,351	14,676	498,744	19,409	1,343	71,333	3,480	66	5,921	2,361	6	25.0	15
Norway	391,079	19,613	2,970	264,030	14,240	695	69,998	6,214	695	66,628	5,651	86	100	15
Pakistan	5,150,000	121,200	53,204	1,621,000	95,000	7,895	33,833	2,915	183	251,532	12,935	428	26.7	10
Panama	342,043	11,185	2,171	81,928	3,472	70	43,563	2,170	138	26,289	1,022	2	81.3	15
Papua New Guinea	243,080	7,824	1,815	30,492	1,282	82	11,232	745	122	2,624	324	3	32.1	15
Paraguay	452,249	15,398	2,799	75,424	10,406	731	1,361	67	2	12,212	1,529[10]	4	79.7	15
Peru	2,970,708	76,645	20,055	758,320	30,051	1,560	250,788	10,320	446	320,038	16,095	629	71.6	15
Philippines	7,964,332	247,551	...	1,911,530	45,594	...	110,879	12,378	...	786,103	32,651	...	83.4	10
Poland	4,198,667	184,800	16,366	452,246	22,998	1,262	897,197	76,805	8,957	491,030	49,892	89	97.8	15
Portugal	1,254,364	61,398	13,790	334,944	15,715	485	137,469	15,045	208	73,525	7,619	71	71.0	...
Puerto Rico	418,419	14,096	1,357	303,702	10,016	476	...	3,097	71	111,311	1,042	13	87.1	15
Rhodesia	892,616	23,348	3,729	75,228	3,821	206	5,342	524	24	2,820	351	3	34.3	15
Romania	3,125,584	147,582	14,722	371,201	15,261	434	819,726	37,865	...	174,888	13,662	...	100	8
Rwanda	434,150	8,151	1,606	8,870[7]	707[7]	56	3,650	...	...	1,069	184	4	23.0	15
Saudi Arabia	625,733	28,989	2,711	159,938	10,964	749	19,249	1,587	78	19,773	1,181	20	5.2	...
Senegal	297,560	7,300	...	64,060	2,513	...	7,767	920	124	7,502	374	...	45.6	6
Singapore	316,265	11,432	379	177,992	7,592	126	12,941	813	12	15,609	990	4	77.6	10
South Africa	4,299,570	149,651	20,262	943,512	[4]	[4]	49,075	3,146	179	109,476	8,128	52	89.0	...
Soviet Union	36,800,000	2,399,000	167,000	14,165,000	...	...	4,525,000	218,000	4,302	4,854,000	317,000	865	99.7	10
Spain	6,393,804	193,370	191,101	818,403	48,694	2,351	376,083	21,156	1,631	461,076	26,565	175	90.1	15
Sri Lanka	1,367,860	98,925[4]	6,970	1,063,766	98,925	1,673	12,936	895	39	14,568	5,438	...	78.1	10
Sudan	1,257,339	28,926	4,440	231,311	8,651	1,075	12,447	1,073	37	22,204	750	20	20.0	9
Sweden	708,986	41,150	4,934	545,253	46,994	...	12,622[11]	843[11]	63	121,266	...	40	100	15
Syria	1,245,801	36,852	6,929	452,051	22,277	1,041	28,935	3,039	48	64,094	989	8	46.6	10
Taiwan	2,341,413	64,974	2,378	1,240,803	51,945	809	296,493	10,447	178	299,414	14,548	101	85.9	15
Tanzania	1,591,834	29,783	...	53,257[6]	2,606[6]	...	9,930[11]	612[11]	...	3,064	434[13]	...	...	...
Thailand	6,736,751	270,567	32,445	1,091,997	35,170	1,043	272,296[14]	15,050[14]	320	51,838[15]	7,757[15]	9[15]	81.8	10
Togo	362,895	6,080	1,199	59,162	1,358	112	5,428	276	23	2,353	236	2	10.5	...
Tunisia	910,532	22,225	...	49,798	8,902[7]	...	35,409	...	...	17,235	1,142	...	32.2	10
Turkey	5,324,707	156,476	...	1,363,188	37,899	2,933	376,131	15,146	563	218,934	14,561	...	54.7	6
Uganda	1,125,817	32,490	4,022	75,044	3,456	198	10,029	628	44	5,173	617	4	32.0	15
United Kingdom	5,965,702	249,191	27,116	4,604,900	273,385	5,885	538,242[3]	78,417[3]	888[3]	301,173	43,245	113	100	15
United States	25,046,264	1,167,008	...	19,441,373[6]	1,020,051[6]	...	...	...	...	10,087,000[1]	633,000[1]	...	98.8	14
Uruguay	355,328	13,935	2,327	143,852	9,668	261	42,340[2]	3,953[3]	23[11]	33,664	2,545	3	90.5	15
Venezuela	1,990,123	63,198	...	583,163	35,671	...	48,047	...	...	213,542	15,792	...	83.4	...
Western Samoa	40,490	1,322	150	8,258	376	37	695	77	8	249	9	1	98.3	10
Yugoslavia	2,866,847	127,988	13,661	217,294	9,887	450	581,908	12,096	1,640	393,801	19,197	149	83.5	10
Zaire	3,538,257	80,481	5,924	225,606	14,483[7]	2,511	109,597	...	...	19,294	2,550	36	15.0	15
Zambia	872,392	18,096	2,710	73,049	3,202	120	7,888	764	26	2,354	189	1	38.3	...

[1]Includes teacher training. [2]Public schools only. [3]Excludes teacher training. [4]Data for primary include secondary. [5]Includes preprimary education. [6]Includes vocational. [7]General includes vocational and teacher training. [8]Jewish population only. [9]Estimate. [10]Excludes private 3rd-level teacher training. [11]Teacher training only. [12]Kenyans only. [13]Universities only. [14]Includes teacher's college. [15]Excludes teacher's college.

job offers, and those from the social sciences and humanities the smallest.

As public pressures for better college instruction increased in the U.S., the institutions conducted faculty development efforts. Some 50% of the colleges reported to Educational Testing Service that they had programs under way. Providing small grants to faculty for study and innovation was the most common effort used by large institutions that could afford them. Smaller colleges reported that staff visits to other institutions were satisfactory and economical.

The Carnegie Council on Policy Studies in Higher Education surveyed colleges in the U.S. to discover what they were doing about grade inflation, flexible course requirements, and innovative courses. The colleges responded that they were returning to traditional course requirements and performance expectations for students. Colleges appeared to be shifting away from the values of the 1960s, when they were pressed to seek "relevance" to current social and political conditions.

Bitter arguments about the *numerus clausus* (a strict limit on the numbers of students entering particular academic fields) were a central issue in West Germany. The government announced that there would be a "hard core" of specialties to which entry would be limited, namely architecture, biology, dentistry, medicine, pharmacy, psychology, and veterinary surgery, with the restriction temporarily extended to agricultural science, biochemistry, domestic science, food chemistry, and surveying. But there was evidence that the entry of unlimited numbers into other fields was resulting in more graduate unemployment. It was predicted that by 1980 one-third of the lawyers who were graduating would not be able to find jobs.

The much-publicized U-68 reform of higher education came into effect in Sweden on July 1. Its aims were to make study opportunities recurrent (thus increasing enrollments among mature students), to strengthen links between education and working life, and to create a new administrative organization. Under the proposals, the country was divided into six regions, each based on one of the existing universities. Within each region several units of higher education were created, the idea being that all institutions in one town should form one administrative unit. The reform was planned eventually to bring higher education to 28 towns in Sweden. Although U-68 was initiated by a Social Democratic government, the new conservative coalition in Sweden committed itself to carrying it through. Unfortunately, U-68 got off to a troubled start in September. Far more would-be students applied for places than had been expected. In practice, therefore, university admissions had to be restricted because of lack of teachers and facilities.

In Denmark restricted entry was introduced to all departments of universities, which, curiously, reported a lower than expected demand. Copenhagen University, the largest, with 3,915 first-year places as against 4,860 in 1976, had only 3,490 first-choice applicants. The university in Denmark with a distinctly radical reputation, Roskilde, had only some 100 first-choice applicants, as compared with the 330 places on offer. The reverse, however, was true of technical and professional colleges, which had 13,200 first-choice applicants seeking some 10,000 places.

There was little perceptible change in university policy in Ireland following the electoral success of the Fianna Fail on June 16. The move to create separate universities in Dublin (the National University of Ireland), Cork, and Galway persisted. The separate existence of St. Patrick's College, Maynooth, which was currently linked with the National University of Ireland, was a subject of contention. Two lecturers on the staff of Maynooth were dismissed, chiefly for religious reasons, and this led to the first strike ever called by university professors in Ireland.

Important changes in higher education were introduced in Burma, where 17 regional colleges were opened, each offering two-year courses leading to a diploma. The objective of the Burmese government was to disperse students from the big cities, Rangoon and Mandalay, and at the same time to increase the numbers undergoing higher education so as to reach 185,000 in 1980 (50,000 in 1950). The courses at the regional colleges were planned to be partly ideological (teaching "Burmese socialism") and partly vocational.

Research. Research budgets contracted in most countries, and there was a sharp increase in emphasis on the practical applications of educational inquiry. In the Soviet Union, for example, the first deputy chairman of the Ministry of Education, F. Panachin, warned educators that they must not isolate the world of schooling from the social life of the country and condemned those who manifested "a childlessness and grayness" in their publications. This was seen as an attempt to check the emphasis in Soviet educational research on "the ideal pupil," "the ideal school leaver," and so on, which led to an overemphasis on measurement, evaluation, and assessment of performance.

Criticism of the psychological propositions of Jean Piaget, which had mounted since the early 1970s, was the subject of an important symposium in *The British Journal of Educational Psychology*. Particularly significant among the views presented were those of the internationally known Norwegian psychologist Jan Smedslund, who was for many years a "Piagetian" himself and worked for a time with Piaget in Geneva. He reported in the symposium on how he "gradually became aware of some major weaknesses" in the Piagetian tradition. Some of the tasks given by the Genevan school of psychology to young children to test their logical powers—classifying objects, matching shapes, and so on—were irrelevant to a child's real world, according to Smedslund. Therefore, when children appeared to fail logic tests, the real problem was that they simply did not understand what it was all about. It seemed that Piaget's main thesis that young children's ability to learn and understand things progressed in certain defined stages, which invariably succeeded each other in the same order for every child, had been effectively challenged.   (TUDOR DAVID; JOEL L. BURDIN)

See also Libraries; Motion Pictures; Museums.

WHY COLLEGE?

by Charles Van Doren

A trend that began to become evident early in the 1970s was definitely confirmed in 1977. College enrollments in the United States were down sharply and seemed likely to be headed further down in the years to come. One almost certain result will be the bankruptcy of scores, if not hundreds, of the nation's private colleges and universities. Even the great city and state universities of the U.S. are going to be in trouble.

The college-age population of the U.S. is also falling, but that is not the only reason for the decline in college enrollments. High-school graduates these days just do not seem to take college for granted, as their counterparts did a decade ago. Many young people who would have gone to college in the 1960s are now seriously considering entering a trade rather than one of the professions. Enrollment in vocational schools has increased as that in four-year colleges has decreased, and by 1977 many communities were under severe pressure to provide better vocational training opportunities for their young people.

This decline in enrollment should not be surprising to educators, who for a generation have been selling college to young people (and their parents) on the basis of its financial rewards. For a generation, that seemed to make economic sense. But now, with the cost of four years in a good liberal arts college approaching $40,000, there is serious question as to whether there are not better things to do with that kind of money. Money deposited at 6% interest, which is obtainable in tax-free bonds, doubles in 12 years. If one assumes that $40,000 is deposited for the benefit of a youth at age 16, the money will have grown to $160,000 by the time he is 40. A nest egg like that might make up for the lack of a college degree.

The above remarks are perhaps unnecessarily cynical. There are three very good reasons to go to college, and none of them has anything whatever to do with money or financial success.

Charles Van Doren attended one college, taught at another college, and has a daughter who attends a third. His son, now in high school, will probably choose a fourth.

Getting Away. The first reason is to get away from home. Almost everyone does this eventually, whether or not he goes to college, and so one might ask what college has to do with it. The answer is that there are better and worse ways to leave home, and better and worse times to do so. One should not leave home too early; it often stunts one's emotional growth. Nor too late, because then one never really learns to live in the world.

The ideal age is from 15 to 18, for both boys and girls. At that youthful age, even at 18, one should not simply spill out into the world willy-nilly and try to make one's way. One should seek to join an organization that will help to bridge the enormous gap between the family and the world. An army is such an organization, and over the centuries armies have performed this role for young men with considerable success. Once, too, there were other kinds of opportunities for boys, if not girls, through the institution of apprenticeship. Until recently the only escape for girls was to leap from one family to another, through the institution of marriage.

What remains is college, but it is by no means the least appetizing of the possibilities. Going to college is almost ideal for bridging the generational gap. As with the family, a college has two classes distinguished by a difference in ages; a benevolent despotism, it is organized for the benefit of both classes, not just one; it ordinarily exists in fairly congenial surroundings; and it usually tries to devote its efforts to fairly lofty goals. In all these respects the *collegium* (this old word for college means community in the modern sense) is like the family but unlike it, too, and most of the differences are for the better.

Learning to Think. The second reason to go to college is to learn to think. (Many colleges do not know this any more than the students do, but it is true nonetheless.) The purpose of going to college is not to study calculus but to learn to calculate; not to write themes and reports but to learn to write; not to read history or sociology or metaphysics but to learn to read; not to pass tests but to learn to answer difficult questions. Mathematics, English composition, history, sociology, philosophy, and the like are all merely vehicles for learning those skills that, together, mean that their possessor can think reasonably well and clearly.

If accounting or biology or coaching is what one wants to do, then college is more an obstacle than not. If one already knows how to think or could not care less about thinking, and is obsessed with doing medicine or mathematics or law, then one should try to enter a graduate or professional school as soon as possible. Such institutions teach one to be a mathematician, or a historian, or a sociologist, and

Students utilizing to good effect the Greek theatre at the University of Illinois Chicago Circle Campus.

so forth. A college, on the contrary, teaches one, or helps one, to become a full-fledged human being. (A human being is an animal that thinks.) The reason to go to college is to become a more excellent person—the most excellent person one can become. (In the old days they said, "to become a virtuous man," but that was before virtue had lost its value and before females began to insist, correctly, that they were human, too.) When one has become as excellent as one can, there will then be time to learn a trade or profession and to make a living as well as a good life.

Gaining Ideals. The third reason to go to college is to live in a community professing lofty ideals and to think well about them. The goals of infants and children are inevitably material. Babies start out with the goods of the belly and do not progress very far beyond them for years. There is nothing wrong with that. Babies must grow into children and children into adults. If physical development is stunted, intellectual and moral development will almost inevitably be stunted, too.

By college age, physical growth should be pretty well accomplished. Intellectual growth—if its foundations are laid during the college years—will continue throughout adult life. That is not true of moral development. The world is impatient with morals. Selfishness, lust, intemperance, to say nothing of anger, envy, and pride, are in fact what make the world go. (We naturally, as a consequence, have nicer names for these qualities, which used to be called vices or even sins—names like love and ambition and righteous indignation and leadership and patriotism.) But in a college, love can really be friendship, and ambition can really be a desire to excel. Moderation is not frowned upon by advertisers, and humility is not arrested and thrown into the

slammer, just for fun. And pride often, if not always, goeth before a fall.

The greatest educators have always known the abysmal difference between the *collegium* and the world. Robert M. Hutchins, a great educator who died in 1977, knew it very well, and his words to the graduating class of 1935 at the University of Chicago were accordingly sombre: "The most paralyzing danger you will face," he said, "is the danger of corruption. Time will corrupt you. Your friends will corrupt you; your social, political, and financial ambitions will corrupt you.

"Believe me," he said, "you are closer to the truth now than you will ever be again." And he warned the graduates not to "be reconciled to dishonesty, indecency, and brutality because gentlemanly ways have been discovered of being dishonest, indecent, and brutal. . . . Take your stand now before time has corrupted you. Before you know it, it will be too late."

The perceptive reader will have long since realized that in speaking of college as a place to which one can move gracefully away from home, as a place where one can learn to think, and as a place where one may be closer to the truth than at any other time in one's life, we are referring not to all colleges but only to the best ones. Most colleges are merely disguised trade schools which do not even do that job very well, and since they have no other justification for their existence doubtless they will deserve their coming fate. But the reasons for going to a good college are important. So important, in fact, that they justify our insisting that such colleges continue to exist and that students continue to attend them.

But are they worth $40,000 for four years? Ah, there is one of those questions that everyone must answer for himself.

349

Egypt

Egypt

A republic of northeast Africa, Egypt is bounded by Israel, Sudan, Libya, the Mediterranean Sea, and the Red Sea. Area: 1,002,000 sq km (386,900 sq mi). Pop. (1976 prelim.): 38,228,200. Cap. and largest city: Cairo (pop., 1976 prelim., 5,084,500). Language: Arabic. Religion: Muslim 93%; Christian 7%. President in 1977, Anwar as-Sadat; prime minister, Mamdouh Salem.

Foreign Affairs. After spending most of the year in an attempt to secure a resumption of the Geneva Middle East peace conference, Pres. Anwar as-Sadat (*see* BIOGRAPHY) dramatically launched an independent peace initiative with Israel late in 1977 that attracted worldwide attention and deepened the split within the Arab world. On November 9 Sadat, in a speech before the People's Assembly, proclaimed his willingness to go even to the Israeli parliament in pursuit of peace. The offer was taken up by Israeli Prime Minister Menahem Begin (*see* BIOGRAPHY), and on November 19 Sadat arrived in Jerusalem. Although his speech to the Knesset the following day largely repeated long-standing Arab demands, there was a widespread feeling that a breakthrough had been achieved.

On November 27 Sadat issued invitations to a conference in Cairo designed to clear away procedural barriers to the Geneva conference. Israel, the U.S., and the UN agreed to participate, but the U.S.S.R., all the Arab states, and the Palestine Liberation Organization (PLO) declined. In early December the PLO, Algeria, Libya, Syria, Iraq, and Yemen (Aden) met in Tripoli, Libya, to map an anti-Sadat strategy, and on December 5 Sadat broke relations with the five hard-line states and ordered the closing of all Soviet cultural centres and consulates in Egypt.

The Cairo meeting, which opened December 14, was shortly overshadowed by a summit meeting between Sadat and Begin in Ismailia on December 25–26, in which Begin presented a 26-point peace plan. No agreement was reached, but it was decided that negotiations would continue. Sadat later emphasized that while he could have reached agreement with Israel on the return of the Sinai to Egypt, he would not sacrifice the interests of the Palestinians. Meanwhile, denunciations of his efforts by the PLO and hard-line Arab spokesmen continued. Saudi Arabia, which had worked closely with Egypt in its attempt to reconvene the Geneva conference, maintained an attitude of public neutrality.

Throughout the year, Sadat had continued to maintain that the U.S. held 99% of the cards in the Middle East, and this had led to increasing disagreement with Syria as the latter accused Egypt of acceding too readily to U.S. pressure. Even Jordan disagreed with Sadat's proposal that a Jordanian-Palestinian link should be established before the Geneva conference. Sadat's public stance was that the PLO must represent the Palestinians at Geneva and he disagreed with U.S. Pres. Jimmy Carter's views on Israel's need for defensible borders. In contrast, relations with the U.S.S.R. did not improve. Sadat variously accused the U.S.S.R. of refusing to reschedule Egypt's debts, failing to provide promised arms supplies, and encouraging subversion in Egypt and troublemaking in Libya. On August 14 he announced a ban on further cotton sales to the U.S.S.R. in retaliation for the Soviet failure to supply arms he said had been paid for. Relations with the U.S.S.R. were exacerbated by President Sadat's vigorous support for conservative anti-Communist forces in Africa.

Deteriorating relations with Libya absorbed much of the Egyptian government's attention in 1977. In February and March several bombing incidents were blamed on Libya, which was accused of sending saboteurs and assassination squads into Egypt. Border restrictions imposed by both sides in March raised tension, and in May Libya accused Egypt of massing troops for invasion. An attempt at reconciliation in June led to nothing and finally open conflict developed on July 21. Egyptian troops advanced a short way into Libyan territory, and Egyptian planes bombed military airports and three Soviet-built radar stations. Fighting ended on July 24 with the help of Algerian Pres. Houari Boumédienne and mediation by PLO Chairman Yasir Arafat. Sadat said that he had been unable any longer to restrain his forces. After the fighting the propaganda war continued unabated.

Domestic Affairs. Two days of rioting in a Nile Delta town at the beginning of the year, caused by bitterness between peasants and landowners, led to arrests. Much more serious rioting broke out on January 18 and 19. Beginning with demonstrations outside the People's Assembly in Cairo by students and industrial workers from the suburb of Helwan, the disturbances spread to Alexandria and other major towns. Much of Cairo's restaurant and nightclub area was destroyed; approximately 80 were killed and 800 injured, and 900 were arrested in connection with the rioting. Troops were called in for the first time since the 1952 revolution. The rioting followed a government announcement that government subsidies covering many services and

Government-ordered price increases for various goods touched off riots in Cairo, Egypt. Thousands of people stormed through the streets battling police.

WIDE WORLD

products would be cut from $1.4 billion to $700 million per year in order to reduce the national budget deficit. Prices subsequently rose for many goods, including rice and sugar. The rioting caused the government to suspend the price increases on July 19, although it was later made clear that the government considered subsidy cuts essential if Egypt was to receive help from the International Monetary Fund and other Western sources.

Although the minister of the interior was blamed for not controlling the riots and was dismissed on February 1, President Sadat laid main responsibility for the disturbances on left-wing subversion with support from Libya, the U.S.S.R., and Israel. On February 11 severe restrictions on unlicensed political activity were put to a national referendum and approved by 99% of the voters. Of the 1,600 arrested during the riots, including some prominent journalists and intellectuals, more than half were released by May but some 700 were put on trial in June. The courts showed leniency; three of every four were acquitted and the rest received light sentences.

Government spokesmen not only implicated the illegal Egyptian Communist Party and Communist Labour Party in the riots but also the officially authorized left-wing National Progressive Union-

Egyptian Pres. Anwar as-Sadat examined a model of a new town being built near Cairo. When completed, the new town will have 500,000 inhabitants and will be named the Tenth of Ramadan.

ist Party. The left as a whole vigorously denied the charge and tried to fight back, with some student support. The right-wing former vice-president, Kamal Eddin Hussein, also strongly condemned the government for its handling of the crisis and was expelled from the People's Assembly.

The government's main action was taken against the left. The editors of the country's two remaining left-wing journals, *al-Talia* and *Rose al-Youssef*, were replaced. However, the regime was also challenged by the right and especially by Islamic extremist movements. On July 3 members of a group called al-Takfir Wa al-Hijra (Society for Repentance and Retreat from Evil) kidnapped and murdered Muhammad Hussein al-Zahabi, a former minister of *waqfs* (religious endowments) and prominent Islamic scholar who had previously attacked their movement; 54 members of the group were charged in connection with the case. Partly in response to this challenge and the charge that Egypt had ignored strict Islamic practice, various proposals were put before Parliament for the application of full Islamic Sharia law, including the death penalty for apostasy (*ridda*), stoning for adultery, and the amputation of thieves' hands. The proposal regarding apostasy aroused strong reaction among Egypt's Coptic Christian community.

The government sought to keep the organization of political life under its control. A draft bill to license political parties but limiting them to those with more than 20 supporters in Parliament provoked a walkout by both right- and left-wing

---

EGYPT

Education. (1975–76) Primary, pupils 4,120,936, teachers 112,649; secondary, pupils 1,697,382, teachers 35,635; vocational, pupils 377,495, teachers 24,294; teacher training, students 33,140, teachers 2,755; higher, students 419,-750, teaching staff 19,300.

Finance. Monetary unit: Egyptian pound, with (Sept. 19, 1977) an official rate of E£0.39 to U.S. $1 (free rate of E£0.67 = £1 sterling) and a tourist rate of E£0.70 to U.S. $1 (E£1.21 = £1 sterling). Gold, SDR's, and foreign exchange (April 1977) U.S. $405 million. Budget (1976 est.) balanced at E£5,976 million. Gross national product (1974) E£3,949 million. Money supply (April 1977) E£2,-476.9 million. Cost of living (1970 = 100; Jan. 1977) 155.

Foreign Trade. (1976) Imports E£1,489.9 million; exports c. E£550 million. Import sources (1975): U.S. 19%; France 11%; West Germany 8%; U.S.S.R. 6%; Italy 6%; U.K. 5%. Export destinations (1975): U.S.S.R. 43%; Czechoslovakia 7%; East Germany 6%; Romania 5%. Main exports (1975): cotton 37%; cotton yarn 11%; fruit and vegetables (1974) 6%.

Transport and Communications. Roads (1972) 25,976 km (including 12,100 km main highways). Motor vehicles in use (1975): passenger 215,500; commercial (including buses) 46,300. Railways (1974): 4,510 km; traffic 8,-671,000,000 passenger-km, freight 2,767,000,000 net ton-km. Air traffic (1975): 1,459,000,000 passenger-km; freight 21.4 million net ton-km. Shipping (1976): merchant vessels 100 gross tons and over 157; gross tonnage 376,066. Telephones (Jan. 1975) 503,200. Radio licenses (Dec. 1974) 5,115,000. Television licenses (Dec. 1974) 610,000.

Agriculture. Production (in 000; metric tons; 1976): wheat 1,960; barley 123; millet c. 800; corn c. 2,710; rice c. 2,530; potatoes c. 772; sugar, raw value c. 639; tomatoes c. 2,192; onions c. 700; dry broad beans (1975) 234; watermelons (1975) c. 1,150; dates c. 418; oranges c. 893; grapes c. 226; cotton, lint c. 386; cheese c. 229; beef and buffalo meat c. 246. Livestock (in 000; 1976): cattle c. 2,254; buffaloes c. 2,314; sheep c. 1,943; goats c. 1,438; asses (1975) c. 1,554; camels (1975) c. 105; chickens c. 26,375.

Industry. Production (in 000; metric tons; 1976): cement 3,294; iron ore (50% metal content) 1,243; crude oil (1975) 8,428; petroleum products (1975) c. 8,533; fertilizers (nutrient content; 1975–76) nitrogenous 151, phosphate 77; salt (1975) c. 500; sulfuric acid (1975) 232; cotton yarn (1975) 181; cotton fabrics (m; 1975) 562,000; electricity (kw-hr; 1975) 10,421,000.

members. The bill was passed on June 29 but with the modification that new parties no longer had to be approved by the Arab Socialist Union (ASU) Central Committee but rather by a newly constituted government committee. All organs of the ASU were abolished except the Central Committee, which was to have 476 members and include representatives of labour unions and professional associations as well as the 360 members of the People's Assembly. Against the express wishes of the government the prerevolutionary nationalist Wafd party reconstituted itself and elected Fuad Seraggedin, minister of the interior under the monarchy, as its leader.

The January riots underlined Egypt's urgent economic problems, and the Arab oil states consequently were inclined to be more generous. After a tour of those nations the finance minister was able to announce that Egypt would receive an immediate loan of U.S. $1.5 billion on easy terms. The minister also said, however, that Egypt's total debts amounted to $6.8 billion in addition to $3.7 billion owed to the U.S.S.R. and that Egypt really needed $2.8 billion for the coming three years. Egypt received new loans during the year from several non-Communist sources, including West Germany, France, Japan, and the World Bank. U.S. aid to Egypt was being maintained at about $900 million a year. Oil was expected to contribute some $932 million to the treasury in 1977, a 342% increase over 1973 when oil production-sharing agreements were introduced.

(PETER MANSFIELD)

El Salvador

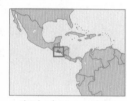

El Salvador

A republic on the Pacific coast of Central America and the smallest country on the isthmus, El Salvador is bounded on the west by Guatemala and on the north and east by Honduras. Area: 21,041 sq km (8,124 sq mi). Pop. (1976 est.): 4,123,300. Cap. and largest city: San Salvador (pop., 1976 est., 500,000). Language: Spanish. Religion: Roman Catholic. Presidents in 1977, Col. Arturo Armando Molina and, from July 1, Gen. Carlos Humberto Romero.

A presidential election, prosperity resulting from high world coffee prices, and a succession of violent acts made 1977 one of El Salvador's stormiest recent years. Gen. Carlos Humberto Romero (*see* BIOGRAPHY), the candidate of the conservative governing National Conciliation Party, was elected president on February 20. The losing National Opposition Union claimed fraud. Mass demonstrations and riots followed, and up to 100 demonstrators were killed by security forces. The government imposed a state of siege that lasted through June 30. General Romero was inaugurated July 1.

Foreign Minister Mauricio Borgonovo Pohl, a prominent member of the ruling oligarchy and second in political importance only to the president, was kidnapped April 19 by the leftist Popular Liberation Forces. When the government refused to meet a demand to release 37 political prisoners, he was murdered. There were at least

A disappointed youth attempts to knock down a poster of General Carlos Humberto Romero in San Salvador, El Salvador. General Romero had just won a hotly contested election for the presidency of the country.

six other leftist-generated abductions and one murder, as well as street assassinations of the national university's rector and a former president. From the right came attacks on the Jesuits, who were accused of inciting popular unrest. Two priests were murdered. (HENRY WEBB, JR.)

EL SALVADOR

Education. (1975) Primary, pupils 759,725, teachers 15,-665; secondary, pupils 29,559, teachers (including vocational) 1,491; vocational, pupils 21,552; teacher training, students 620, teachers 55; higher, students 26,692, teaching staff 1,275.

Finance. Monetary unit: colón, with (Sept. 19, 1977) a par value of 2.50 colones to U.S. $1 (free rate of 4.36 colones = £1 sterling). Gold, SDR's, and foreign exchange (June 1977) U.S. $402.6 million. Budget (1976 est.) balanced at 844 million colones. Gross national product (1976) 5,387,000,000 colones. Money supply (May 1977) 1,087,300,000 colones. Cost of living (1970 = 100; June 1977) 182.

Foreign Trade. (1976) Imports 1,762,400,000 colones; exports 1,803,500,000 colones. Import sources (1975): U.S. 31%; Guatemala 14%; Venezuela 8%; Japan 7%; West Germany 6%; Costa Rica 5%. Export destinations (1975): U.S. 27%; Guatemala 15%; West Germany 13%; Japan 12%; Costa Rica 6%; The Netherlands 6%; Nicaragua 6%. Main exports (1975): coffee 33%; sugar 16%; cotton 15%; chemicals 6%; textile 6%.

Transport and Communications. Roads (1974) 10,972 km (including 625 km of Pan-American Highway). Motor vehicles in use (1974): passenger 41,000; commercial (including buses) 19,100. Railways (1975) 1,031 km. Telephones (Jan. 1976) 55,800. Radio receivers (Dec. 1971) 350,000. Television receivers (Dec. 1974) 111,000.

Agriculture. Production (in 000; metric tons; 1976): corn 463; sorghum c. 164; rice (1975) 37; dry beans 42; sugar, raw value c. 256; oranges c. 42; coffee c. 198; cotton, lint 62; jute 5. Livestock (in 000; 1975): cattle 1,062; pigs c. 420; horses c. 81; poultry c. 8,900.

Industry. Production (in 000; metric tons; 1975): cement 340; petroleum products 630; cotton yarn (1974) 6.2; electricity (kw-hr) 1,068,000.

Energy

The energy scene in the United States during 1977 was dominated by the formulation and announcement of a national energy policy, and its passage through the legislative process. Shortly after his inauguration it became known that the establishment of such a policy would be one of the first and most important goals of Pres. Jimmy Carter. In April the president revealed the new policy in an address to the U.S. Congress and proposed a program to put it into effect. The aim of the program, the most comprehensive and far-reaching piece of energy legislation ever submitted to Congress, was to shift the energy consumption pattern of the U.S. from a major reliance on oil and gas (most of the former imported) to coal, nuclear power, and solar and geothermal energy, and to attain specific goals by 1985. To this end the program included strong emphases on energy conservation, taxes and price increases to discourage the use of oil products and natural gas and to encourage the use of coal, a speedup in the licensing of new nuclear power plants, the "reform" of electricity rates, and incentives for the development and use of solar and geothermal energy.

The proposals promptly evoked intense controversy, especially over the provision to impose a graduated excise tax on "gas guzzling" automobiles. Congressional consideration of the legislation, which extended over the remainder of the year, involved heated debate and the modification of much of the program as originally proposed. At the year's end a House-Senate conference committee was attempting to resolve the two remaining unsettled issues: the pricing of natural gas, and taxes on crude oil, on business use of oil and natural gas, and on gas guzzling cars.

On November 8, in a nationally televised address, President Carter attempted to ease the tensions that had developed between his administration and Congress over his energy proposals. "This is not a contest of strength between the President and the Congress, nor between the House and the Senate," he said. "What is being measured is the strength and will of our nation—whether we can acknowledge a threat and meet a serious challenge together."

A companion piece of legislation, submitted to Congress by President Carter on March 1, called for the extensive reorganization of those agencies in the executive branch of the government dealing with energy matters and their consolidation into a new Department of Energy. Although controversial, it was much less so than the energy program, and the new department came into existence on October 1. The department absorbed and took over the functions of the Federal Energy Administration, the Energy Research and Development Administration, and the Federal Power Commission, all of which were abolished. The FPC was replaced with a new Federal Energy Regulatory Commission under the secretary of energy. Also transferred to the new department were several administrative bodies for marketing power from federal dams (previously in the Department of the Interior) and Interior Department authority over offshore oil and gas operations, as well as selected functions related to energy in the departments of Commerce and Housing and Urban Development and the Interstate Commerce Commission.

The most severe winter of the century in the U.S. caused an energy crisis in many areas when natural gas and electricity capacities were unable to meet the demands. A severe storm in January followed by unprecedented low temperatures continuing into February created the worst energy crisis in the country's history. It was especially severe in Ohio and parts of the South; under emergency conditions factories were ordered to close to permit the available gas to be used in homes, but even so thousands went without heat. Efforts to obtain emergency supplies of fuel oil and liquefied petroleum gas were hampered by snow and ice, which disrupted land and water transportation. Congress quickly passed an Emergency Gas Act, which authorized the FPC to direct the transfer of natural gas from one pipeline to another and to exempt emergency sales from normal price regulations. It was estimated that the extreme cold raised the national bill for home heating in the 1976–77 winter by $5.5 billion.

The effect of the weather was felt equally severely by the electric utilities. Demand rose to the highest level ever at the same time that fuel

Congress debated late into the night in September on aspects of Pres. Jimmy Carter's energy proposals.

The U.S.'s first energy secretary, James Schlesinger, briefed reporters on September 9 on a proposed natural gas pipeline route from Alaska to the lower 48 states.

supplies became difficult to obtain, and generating plants were put out of action by weather effects. Utilities in six Southern states were forced to black out portions of their systems in sequence when demand exceeded capacity, and utilities throughout the eastern half of the U.S. and in Ontario reduced the voltage on their systems to increase the amounts of power they could send to those utilities in distress. (It was later revealed that for one day the entire electric system of the eastern U.S. was in danger of collapse.) Bulwarks of the systems were the nuclear power plants, which were unaffected by fuel supply problems.

Weather conditions of a different kind plagued much of the western U.S. The second year of a sustained drought reduced hydroelectric capacity, leading some utilities to reduce voltage by a few percent permanently and the governors of Washington, Oregon, Idaho, and Montana to call for a 10% voluntary reduction in electricity use.

In July still another freakish weather occurrence in the form of a thunderstorm knocked out transmission lines to New York City, causing a complete blackout of the city that lasted in some areas for 25 hours. Also during the summer a heat wave over much of the U.S. sent electricity output to a new high, eclipsing that of the previous winter.

As in previous years, the Organization of Petroleum Exporting Countries (OPEC) continued to make news with its oil price decisions. At a meeting in December 1976 the majority of OPEC members decided to raise prices on Jan. 1, 1977, by 10%, but to the surprise of everyone Saudi Arabia and the United Arab Emirates announced that on that date their prices would rise by only 5% while the 11 other OPEC members went ahead with the 10% increase. This was the first such "two-tiered" pricing in the history of the cartel. At the next semiannual meeting in July the world held its breath as it waited to see whether the announced intention of some OPEC members to raise prices still another 5% would be carried out. In a compro-

mise that restored unity, Saudi Arabia and the U.A.E. raised their prices by another 5%, and the other members retained their existing prices. Meeting in December in Venezuela, the OPEC oil ministers failed to reach agreement as to whether to raise oil prices in 1978.

With oil imports running at record levels (and causing a record trade deficit), the U.S. was heartened by the final startup of the trans-Alaska pipeline, nine years after oil was discovered at Prudhoe Bay on the shore of the Arctic Ocean. The first oil left Prudhoe Bay on June 20, and, after several accidents that interrupted the flow, reached Valdez, the southern terminal, on July 28. The first tanker load of crude oil from the pipeline left Valdez on August 1 and was delivered in California on August 9. Other Alaskan oil shipments began moving through the Panama Canal to refineries on the Gulf Coast, while controversy continued over the desirability of building a pipeline to move the oil from California to the East. On September 17 the first cargo of Prudhoe Bay crude oil was delivered by tanker to a Delaware refinery.

The oil- and gas-hungry East Coast of the U.S. watched a seesaw battle over the opening of the neighbouring continental shelf to petroleum exploration. After adverse administrative decisions and court appeals by environmental groups, a federal court finally gave approval to drilling on the first leases, which had been sold in 1976. The tracts involved are on the edge of the continental shelf southeast of New Jersey.

Still another development helping to reduce the vulnerability of the U.S. in its dependence on foreign oil was the beginning of the national Strategic Petroleum Reserve. The first shipment of crude oil was delivered to special storage facilities in a Louisiana salt dome in July. The Strategic Petroleum Reserve was intended to lessen the susceptibility of the U.S. to interruptions in oil imports such as occurred in 1973 and 1974 as a result of the Yom Kippur War by providing a cushion for emergency use. The first shipment of 412,000 bbl began the buildup to an eventual total of one billion barrels or more.

In natural gas matters a major decision was reached in September when the U.S. and Canadian governments announced an agreement on the route of a projected pipeline to carry natural gas produced along with the oil at Prudhoe Bay. The agreed-upon route, which parallels the Alaska Highway, was chosen over the alternatives of a route down the Mackenzie Valley (essentially an "all-Canada" route) and a parallel to the trans-Alaska pipeline (the "all-Alaska" route). The pipeline would run for 730 mi in Alaska and more than 2,000 mi in Canada, with 900 mi of connecting lines from the U.S. border.

In the North Sea two new gas pipelines began operation in September and October. A 275-mi line, the longest undersea gas transmission line in the world, began delivering gas from Norway's Ekofisk field to Emden, West Germany. Delivery from the Frigg field, astride the boundary of the Norwegian and United Kingdom sectors of the North Sea, began over the 270-mi line to Scotland.

A historic event affecting coal in the U.S. was the enactment in August of legislation establishing the first uniform federal controls over strip mining, previously a state matter. The law requires the restoration of stripped land so that it will serve the same function it did prior to mining; gives farmers and ranchers veto privileges over the mining of their own land even if they do not own the mineral rights; and sets up a $4.1 billion fund, financed by a federal tax on all coal, from both strip and underground mines, to restore previously stripped land that was not restored.

In a major nuclear policy pronouncement in April, President Carter announced that the U.S. would not reprocess spent fuel or recycle plutonium for the indefinite future, pending a resolution of the problems of waste disposal and international proliferation of nuclear weapons; and that the U.S. fast breeder reactor program would henceforth "give priority to alternative designs of the breeder other than plutonium." The effect of the latter was to deemphasize the Clinch River (Tenn.) breeder reactor project, until then the centerpiece of the U.S. breeder program.

In March the world's first commercial high temperature gas-cooled reactor (HTGR) began power production 45 mi N of Denver, Colo. The design of the 330-Mw HTGR is unusual in that it uses helium instead of water or sodium as the reactor coolant and a uranium-thorium mixture as fuel.

In the field of solar energy, after a two-year process of choosing among alternative sites, the U.S. Energy Research and Development Administration announced the establishment of the national Solar Energy Research Institute at Golden, Colo. The purpose of the institute would be to coordinate all solar energy research in the U.S. France, meantime, became the first country to generate electricity for commercial purposes with solar energy when it converted an experimental solar furnace in the Pyrénées Mountains into a solar generating plant with a capacity of 64 kw. The output of the plant was fed into the national grid.

(BRUCE C. NETSCHERT)

Towboats failed in their attempts to free coal-laden barges jammed in as much as ten feet of ice on the Ohio River during 1977's bitterly cold winter.

COAL

By 1977 many countries looked to coal to compensate for the shortages in oil and nuclear supplies expected before the end of the century. Oil companies maintained their financial interest in coal and its conversion into gaseous and liquid fuels. Interest was shown too in underground gasification of deep coal deposits not readily accessible by conventional methods. Coal-producing nations implemented plans to increase production. Countries with diminishing reserves invested in development of deposits in other countries.

A slow but steady increase in coal production continued. World hard coal production in 1976 reached 2,468,551,000 metric tons, 2.3% above 1975. Increases were reported from the U.S., U.S.S.R., China, Poland, South Africa, India, and Australia. Western European production fell by 3.5%, but Eastern European output increased by just under 2%.

CHINA. China produced 480 million metric tons, 10 million tons over the 1975 figure. Many coal-producing regions exceeded their official targets, benefiting from increased mechanization and the expansion of existing mines. The earthquake in July 1976 caused flooding of the mines in Hopeh Province, where full production was not resumed until early in 1977.

U.S.S.R. The Soviet Union planned to produce 733 million metric tons of raw coal and lignite in 1977, 21 million tons more than the output in 1976. Increased lignite production was expected to come from open pits in Siberia and Kazakhstan and increased hard coal production from the Donets and Kuznetsk basins. Output in 1976 was 1.6% over 1975. Lignite production fell slightly in 1976 to 162.8 million metric tons, while the output of coking coal rose by 5.2 million tons to 186,222,000 tons. Total hard coal production, including coking coal, was 541.9 million tons, 7 million tons over 1975.

UNITED STATES. Pres. Jimmy Carter's 1977 energy policy gave a clear-cut priority to coal production and to energy conservation. Substitution of coal for oil in electric power utilities and industry was a stated objective. In mid-1977 it was forecast that total coal consumption would increase by 6.6% above the 1976 figure to reach 700 million short tons: 638 million for domestic use and 62 million for export. Bituminous coal production was expected to increase by 1.1% over the 1976 figure of 665 million tons. Coal stockpiles, 133.7 million tons at the beginning of 1977, were to be used to cover shortages. Arctic weather early in 1977 caused a loss of between 20 million and 25 million short tons of production. Anthracite production at 6.4 million short tons showed its first increase in 14 years.

On Dec. 6, 1977, unionized coal miners in the U.S. went on strike. At issue were the rights of local unions of the United Mine Workers to call strikes against individual mines over local grievances. The coal operators wanted an end to such local union autonomy. The effects of the strike were not expected to be felt outside the industry for

COURTESY, GENERAL ELECTRIC RESEARCH AND DEVELOPMENT CENTER

"Logs" composed of coal dust and tar were developed at the General Electric Research and Development Center at Schenectady, New York. The logs are used as fuel in a pilot-scale coal gasification system which converts low-grade coal into fuel gas.

some time because large stockpiles of coal were on hand.

EUROPEAN ECONOMIC COMMUNITY. Total hard-coal production in 1976, at 240,662,000 metric tons, declined 9.5 million tons from 1975. The fall in production continued despite strenuous efforts in all member countries to stabilize output at current levels. Belgium's 7.2 million metric tons in 1976 was a drop of 3.2% from 1975. In France production fell by half a million tons to 21,880,000 metric tons. Lignite production was 3,140,000 metric tons. The participation of French coal-mining companies in the development of several overseas coalfields was announced during 1977.

Hard coal production in West Germany dropped by 3.1 million metric tons to 89.3 million tons, although lignite production increased by 11.2 million metric tons to 134.5 million tons. West Germany remained the world's third largest lignite producer.

West German consumption was only 83.5 million tons, adding some 6 million tons to the 12 million stockpiled in 1975. This situation would have been worse except that power stations burned 30.2 million tons, an increase of 29.6%.

The U.K.'s National Coal Board (NCB) finished a third consecutive financial year with a profit, £110 million for 1976–77. Productivity fell from 44.8 cwt per manshift in 1975–76 to 43.6 cwt per manshift in 1976–77. Deep-mined output, at 106.6 million long

tons, was down 5.9 million. Opencut operations increased by 1 million tons to 11.2 million. Production from licensed mines remained stable at 1.1 million tons.

The NCB planned to produce 120 million tons per year by 1985. With a new coalfield under development at Selby (10 million tons per year) and additional coalfields under investigation (Vale of Belvoir), the NCB seemed likely to reach the target provided planning permissions were granted and productivity improved.

POLAND. Hard coal production in Poland increased 4.5% over 1975 to reach a record level of 179.3 million metric tons. Exports, at 38.9 million tons, exceeded those for 1975. Brown coal production, at 39.3 million metric tons, was slightly below the 1975 figure. Poland's brown coal production was expected to double when the new opencut operation at Belchatow reached full capacity of 40 million tons per year. Some 3 million tons of brown coal were exported in 1976.

JAPAN. Japan's production of coal in 1976, 18.4 million metric tons, declined 500,000 tons from the 1975 figure. This was attributed to a disastrous gas explosion at Horonai and to labour troubles. Coal imports declined in 1976 for the second year in succession, to 60,760,000 metric tons, a fall of 1,350,000 metric tons. Australia remained the leading supplier with 26,290,000 tons. Next was the U.S. with 17.5 million tons, a decline of 22.1% from the

1975 figure. During the first four months of 1977, increased supplies were reported from Australia and fewer imports from the U.S. and Canada. South Africa moved into fourth place, with 981,886 tons, a significant increase from the 37,246 tons for the first four months of 1976.

INDIA. Approximately 100 million metric tons of hard coal were produced in 1976, 4.5 million metric tons more than in 1975. Low demand resulted in increased pithead stocks, which stood at 11.7 million tons by the end of the year. An active export policy more than tripled coal exports, which stood at 1.5 million metric tons for the 1976–77 financial year.

For the financial year 1978–79, revised five-year-plan targets were set at 124 million metric tons. Coal of India Ltd., which already produced 90% of the nation's output, announced plans for a 50% increase in production by 1985. The bulk of this increase was expected to result from further mechanization. Lignite production in 1976 was about 3.5 million tons. Plans were under way to increase this to 6.5 million by 1980–81.

SOUTH AMERICA. Coal production in 1976, at 8,615,000 metric tons, showed a modest increase of 192,000 metric tons over 1975. Colombia, with 3.6 million metric tons and 60% of Latin America's coal resources, was the largest producer. Brazil produced 2.6 million tons and Chile 1.4 million tons. Both Colombia and Brazil planned to increase production.

AFRICA. Of the estimated total of 78,887,-000 metric tons of hard coal mined in Africa in 1976, some 76.4 million metric tons were produced by South Africa, an increase of 10% over 1975. With the opening of the Richard's Bay export facility, South Africa's exports showed a dramatic 122% increase to just under 6 million tons. South Africa hoped to reach an output of 150 million metric tons by 1980, about half of it for export.

Rhodesia produced 2,820,000 metric tons. Mozambique, where production was barely over half a million tons in 1976, planned to increase annual output to 4 million tons by the early 1980s; setbacks were suffered there due to mine explosions in 1976 and 1977.

AUSTRALIA. Black coal production in 1976 exceeded the record level of 1975 to reach 73.9 million metric tons, an increase of some 7 million tons; 60% of it came from New South Wales and 35% from Queensland. Queensland's production came mainly from open pit operations. Lignite production, all from Victoria, totaled 30.4 million metric tons, an increase of 2.2 million. Exports increased by 4.2 million to 34.1 million metric tons, more than 75% of which went to Japanese steel mills.

Several Australian companies expressed interest in the conversion of low-grade coal into oil, and feasibility studies were commissioned. Overseas demand for Australian steam coal was expected to rise tenfold to more than 10 million metric tons a year by 1982. The federal government, concerned over increasing foreign financial control of Australia's coal resources, proposed that 50% of the equity should remain in Australian hands.

CANADA. In 1976 total coal production declined marginally to 25.3 million metric tons, a decrease of 218,000 metric tons. A miners' strike in British Columbia prevented the expected increase in production. Sub-bituminous and lignite output increased, but bituminous coal production fell 1.4 million metric tons. Exports remained at about the 1975 level of 11,760,000 metric tons, 90% of which went to Japan. Imports dropped 654,123 metric tons to 14.6 million metric tons.

Production in British Columbia fell by 2 million metric tons to 7.5 million tons. Alberta's total coal production, of all types, increased by 940,000 metric tons. Lignite production in Saskatchewan increased about 1,130,000 metric tons to 4,680,000 tons. Bituminous coal output in Nova Scotia increased slightly. In New Brunswick production remained at the same level as in 1975. Total coal production in Canada was expected to reach 28 million metric tons in 1977.

(R. J. FOWELL)

ELECTRICITY

The annual growth rate in the consumption of electricity throughout the world increased from the 1975 figure of 2.3% to slightly more than 5% in 1976, approaching the previously recorded 7.3% mean annual rise and proving that the measures that had been encouraged or even imposed in many countries in an attempt to conserve electricity were not too effective. Some countries, such as France, considered taking action to reinforce a policy of restraint by modifying or even abolishing certain off-peak and reducing-rate tariffs that cut the average price to the consumer as his consumption rose.

Electricity's very versatility was the main reason why it had proved so difficult to reduce consumption. Electricity could substitute for most other power sources, particularly for heating, and therefore any sudden spell of cold weather brought an upsurge in demand as supplementary heating appliances were brought into use. This was a prospect dreaded by producers because it often led to overloading on the grid and consequent power cuts.

However, it was not domestic heating

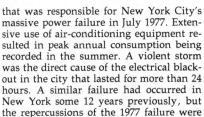

that was responsible for New York City's massive power failure in July 1977. Extensive use of air-conditioning equipment resulted in peak annual consumption being recorded in the summer. A violent storm was the direct cause of the electrical blackout in the city that lasted for more than 24 hours. A similar failure had occurred in New York some 12 years previously, but the repercussions of the 1977 failure were far more serious and estimates of losses ran to hundreds of millions of dollars.

Although it was hoped that such failures would remain the exception, some authorities feared that beginning in the early 1980s several producers would be obliged to impose power cuts because of a shortage of power plants. Several planned programs of investment had been substantially delayed, and because of the social and political implications governments were becoming ever more unwilling to give permission for the construction of new power stations. In 1977 there were confrontations, sometimes violent, at the sites of the Wyhl, Grohnde, and Brokdorf power stations in West Germany and on the site of the world's first commercial 1,200-Mw fast breeder reactor, the Super Phénix, near Grenoble in France. In the U.K. objections to the proposals of British Nuclear Fuels Ltd. to expand substantially facilities at Windscale for reprocessing irradiated oxide fuels from both British and non-British power stations had culminated in the 100-day-long Windscale inquiry; it was believed that several months would be needed to consider the substantial volume of evidence before a decision could be reached.

Following a visit to London in April, Pres. Jimmy Carter defined U.S. policy on nuclear matters and expressed the hope that other countries would follow suit. He condemned plutonium-producing systems in the interests of nonproliferation of nuclear weapons, and announced that he had decided to halt research aimed at perfecting

An experimental dairy farm fueled by solar energy was developed at the U.S. Department of Agriculture's Animal Genetics and Management Laboratory at Beltsville, Maryland.

Installed Capacity and Production of Electric Power in Selected Countries, 1975–76

Country	Hydroelectric power — Operating plants — Installed capacity (000 kw)	Production (000,000 kw-hr)	Total electric power — Installed capacity (000 kw)	Production (000,000 kw-hr)
World	...	...	...	6,438,900
Algeria	286*	346*	1,110	3,120*
Argentina†‡	1,531	5,196	9,259	25,404*
Australia	5,535*	15,217	19,506*	76,500
Austria	6,085	23,745	10,001	35,040
Bangladesh	80*	355*	818*	1,380*
Barbados	—	—	67	204*
Belgium†‡	503	430	11,127	47,352
Brazil	16,193	71,991	19,588	78,072
Bulgaria†‡	1,793	2,452	7,060	27,744
Burma	101	470	263	840*
Cameroon	197	1,135	225	1,190
Canada†‡	37,253	202,404	59,886	293,412
Central African Empire	11*	49*	17*	52*
Chad	—	—	22*	56*
Chile	1,462	6,135	2,620	9,332
Colombia	3,067	10,200	4,495	13,620*
Congo	15*	60*	32*	110*
Costa Rica	241	1,306	407	1,536
Cyprus	—	—	239	804
Czechoslovakia†‡	1,691	3,816	13,631	62,628
Denmark	9	24	6,273	19,248*
Dominican Republic	96*	194*	443	1,632
Egypt	2,445*	6,798*	3,893	10,421
El Salvador	108*	558*	306	1,068
Ethiopia	206	352	320	456*
Finland	2,336	12,189	7,395	29,316
France†‡	17,574	59,892	49,200	191,196
Gabon	—	8*	45*	240*
Germany, East†‡	679	1,272	16,928	89,148
Germany, West‡	5,573	17,111	74,356	333,648
Ghana	925	4,000	995	4,050
Greece	1,416*	2,006*	4,868	16,320*
Guatemala	124*	395*	279	1,100
Guyana	—	—	95*	384
Hong Kong	—	—	2,274*	8,340*
Hungary	48	161	4,291	22,044
Iceland§#	389*	2,206*	514	2,424*
India†‡	8,442	33,247	22,172	89,208*
Iran	850*	5,600	6,000	15,000
Ireland	531*	728*	1,986*	7,548*
Israel	—	—	2,181*	10,344
Italy†‡§#	16,995	42,116	43,305	160,560
Ivory Coast	224*	280*	350*	864*
Jamaica	21*	131	677	2,328
Japan†‡§#	24,853	85,906	112,285	475,800
Kenya	172	649	282	1,044*
Korea, South	621*	1,683*	5,135	23,112*
Kuwait	—	—	...	4,656*
Lebanon	246	800	608	1,848
Libya	—	—	300*	900*
Luxembourg	932*	...	1,157	1,548
Madagascar	40	173*	95	252*
Malawi	47	252	79	252*
Malaysia	...	...	1,177	6,480
Mauritania	—	—	39*	95*
Mauritius	25	40	121	276
Mexico§#	4,124	15,140	11,052	46,236
Morocco	399*	1,100*	730	3,168*
Mozambique	114*	293	393	552*
Netherlands, The†‡	—	—	13,982	58,056
New Zealand§#	3,471*	16,868*	4,901*	20,064*
Nigeria	320*	2,341*	860	3,216
Norway	16,928	77,496	17,090	82,188
Panama	15*	72*	275	1,164*
Papua New Guinea	45	180	250	969
Philippines	1,050	2,419*	3,019	10,404*
Poland	827	2,379	20,057	104,100
Portugal	1,954	6,437	3,149	9,600
Rhodesia	705	5,321	1,192	6,744
Romania	2,632	8,711	11,577	53,724
Senegal	—	—	120*	384*
Singapore	—	—	1,115*	4,608*
South Africa	169*	1,120	13,990	80,712
Spain†‡	11,955	28,750	24,534	90,600
Sri Lanka	195	1,002	281	1,149
Surinam	21	1,020	301	1,600
Sweden†‡	12,716	57,669	23,135	84,312
Switzerland†‡	9,800	33,069	12,816	34,836
Syria	—	—	616	1,668
Thailand	950*	2,550*	2,500	7,380*
Togo	2	4	25	118
Trinidad and Tobago	—	—	334	1,128*
Tunisia	29*	31*	426	1,344*
Turkey	1,770	5,886	4,165	18,252
U.S.S.R.†‡	40,515	125,987	217,484	1,110,960
U.K.†‡	2,456	4,948	78,911	276,972
U.S.†‡§#	66,285	303,195	524,270	2,117,628
Yugoslavia	4,801	19,317	9,043	43,572
Zaire	1,159	3,370	1,217	3,440
Zambia	759	5,940	1,031	6,192

*Public sector only. †Includes nuclear (in 000 kw): Argentina 340; Belgium 1,663; Bulgaria 880; Canada 2,666; Czechoslovakia 150; France 3,098; East Germany 950; West Germany 3,504; India 640; Italy 670; Japan 6,615; The Netherlands 524; Spain 1,120; Sweden 2,522; Switzerland 2,422; U.S.S.R. 5,600; U.K. 5,734; U.S. 38,943. ‡Includes nuclear (in 000,000 kw-hr): Argentina 2,517; Belgium 6,784; Bulgaria 2,554; Canada 11,858; Czechoslovakia 187; France 17,451; East Germany 2,740; West Germany 21,406; India 2,627; Italy 3,800; Japan 25,125; The Netherlands 3,335; Spain 10,000; Sweden 11,969; Switzerland 7,373; U.S.S.R. 11,200; U.K. 30,338; U.S. 171,363. §Includes geothermal (in 000 kw): Iceland 2; Italy 421; Japan 54; Mexico 79; New Zealand 192; U.S. 559. #Includes geothermal (in 000,000 kw-hr): Iceland 18; Italy 2,482; Japan 378; Mexico 491; New Zealand 1,272; U.S. 3,246.
Sources: United Nations, *Statistical Yearbook, 1976*; *Monthly Bulletin of Statistics.*

an experimental fast breeder and to abandon construction of factories to reprocess irradiated fuels. Though many commended Carter's motives, one result of worldwide compliance would be to give an effective monopoly lasting several years to U.S. ordinary water nuclear stations.

President Carter indicated that to save costs the U.S. would not construct additional production facilities using the gaseous diffusion method but would adopt the more economical and less cumbersome ultracentrifuge process. Such a decision hardly accorded with nonproliferation policies, since the ultracentrifuge process easily lends itself to widespread dispersal of facilities. The French Commissariat à l'Énergie Atomique (CEA) announced that, with nonproliferation in mind, a method of uranium enrichment said to require at least 30 years before military levels could be attained had been perfected.

President Carter's nuclear policy was greeted with considerable reservations by those countries directly affected and by various international organizations. Experts feared that the world's limited resources of uranium would barely suffice to meet energy needs until new sources such as solar energy and geothermal energy were ready to be utilized in 2010 or 2020; they suggested that the deliberate refusal to build fast breeders, which for an equal quantity of fissile material would be able to produce 50 times as much electricity as an ordinary reactor, or to construct processing plants for irradiated fuels so that recoverable elements could be recycled, involved considerable risks.

In October the U.S. made it clear that it did not wish to impose a particular policy on any other nation but that exporters of nuclear technology were expected to exercise some degree of self-discipline. Some 40 countries were invited to Washington, D.C., to take part in a conference to work out an international program to study the fuel cycle. Representatives from these nations met again in December in Vienna.

In July, France, West Germany, and other EEC countries signed a series of agreements setting up a joint company for research and development of fast breeder nuclear reactors and their marketing abroad. The French side of the venture, headed by the CEA, included the Creusot-Loire subsidiary Novatom and would hold a 65% majority share. A consortium of non-French firms led by West Germany's Interatom, part of the Siemens group, and including Belgonucléaire of Belgium, Neratoom of The Netherlands, and an Italian company, would hold a 35% stake, which in due course would be raised to 49% while the French share was reduced to 51%. The move was an implicit rejection of President Carter's suggestion that Europe follow the U.S. example in limiting fast breeder technology to avoid nuclear proliferation.

NUCLEAR ELECTRICITY. By January 1977 there were 196 nuclear power stations in service worldwide, representing a total capacity of 93,800 Mw. Of these, 165 stations, 84,600 Mw, were in 15 Western countries, and 31 stations, 9,200 Mw, in the U.S.S.R. or elsewhere in Eastern Europe. Ordinary pressurized water reactors (PWR) comprised 45% of the total capacity, boiling water reactors (BWR) 33%, and advanced gas-cooled reactors (AGR) 10%, with various other types accounting for the balance.

Electrical Power Production of Selected Countries, 1976
By source

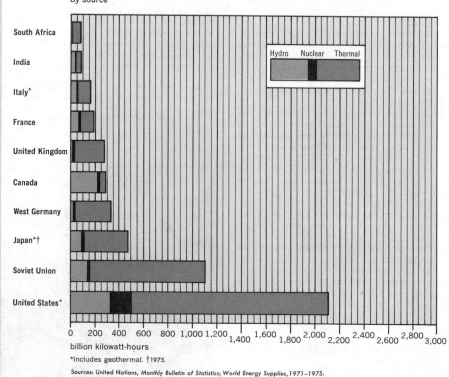

0 200 400 600 800 1,000 1,200 1,400 1,600 1,800 2,000 2,200 2,400 2,600 2,800 3,000
billion kilowatt-hours

South Africa · India · Italy* · France · United Kingdom · Canada · West Germany · Japan*† · Soviet Union · United States*

Hydro Nuclear Thermal

*Includes geothermal. †1975.

Sources: United Nations, *Monthly Bulletin of Statistics*; *World Energy Supplies, 1971–1975.*

In 1976 total production from Western nuclear power stations amounted to 390,000,000,000 kw-hr, or less than 6% of the world's total electricity production. More than 50% of this, 47,000 Mw of capacity, an output of 201,000,000,000 kw-hr, was produced in the U.S. The U.S. Nuclear Regulatory Commission granted six permits for operation for a total capacity of 5,477 Mw and nine permits for construction, 10,076 Mw. Electricity producers ordered three 1,200-Mw PWR's.

Four nuclear power stations, with a total capacity of 7,920 Mw, were under construction in the U.K., where the Central Electricity Generating Board (CEGB) planned to order two additional stations early in 1978. Despite a recommendation from the British National Nuclear Corporation in July 1977 that one AGR and one U.S.-designed PWR be built, it was virtually certain, in view of the delays that the introduction of any new system would involve, that the new stations would have AGR's. Two British AGR's already in commission, at Hinkley Point, Somerset, and Hunterston, Scotland, produced some of the cheapest electricity available from British power stations.

In West Germany a 300-Mw prototype breeder was under construction at Kalkar, near the Dutch border, with cooperation from Belgium and The Netherlands. Antinuclear protests had been particularly active there, but the federal government intended to continue with its program, although the original target had been reduced from 50,000 to 30,000 Mw.

In January the French nuclear program involved 21,980 Mw to be brought into operation in stages before 1983. The two 930-Mw PWR's at Fessenheim, the first power station in the program, went into operation, one in March, and the other in June.

In Sweden the five nuclear reactors in service, a total capacity of 3,300 Mw, were joined in March 1977 by a 580-Mw BWR. The government failed to keep past promises to call a halt to the nuclear program, and work continued on sites at Forsmark (two BWR's of 900 Mw) and Ringhals (two PWR's of 900 Mw). A bill introduced on reprocessing of irradiated fuels and stockpiling of radioactive wastes would impose such strict conditions as to be unrealizable in practical terms.

The U.S.S.R. considered raising the 7,200-Mw nuclear capacity currently in service to a total of 19,000–21,000 Mw by 1980. The program had originally been based on enriched uranium and ordinary water reactors, but growing interest was shown in fast breeders; a 350-Mw prototype was already in service with a 600-Mw unit nearing completion.

The world's first factory to use the ultracentrifuge process for uranium enrichment on an industrial scale, built by the Urenco consortium, a grouping of the U.K., West Germany, and The Netherlands, came into service in September 1977.

In June a U.S.-built 40-ton superconducting magnet, the largest of its kind, arrived in Moscow on indefinite loan for joint U.S.-Soviet experiments to find cheaper ways of producing electricity. Scientists would attempt to use the device, producing a field 250,000 times stronger than the Earth, for generating electricity by the magnetohydrodynamic (MHD) process. Gas at 2,400° C would be forced at velocities close to the speed of sound through ducts near the magnet, the moving gas replacing the rotating arm of a conventional generator. It was hoped that the MHD system would lead to power stations producing electricity almost twice as efficiently as current turbine generators. (LUCIEN CHALMEY)

NATURAL GAS

Total British gas reserves were slightly higher at the beginning of 1977. Proved reserves at 28.6 Tcf (trillion cubic feet) were almost exactly the same as they had been 12 months earlier. Proved U.S. gas reserves at the end of 1976 were about 216 Tcf, according to the American Gas Association (AGA) Committee on Natural Gas Reserves. A total of 1,164 Tcf was suggested by the U.S. Potential Gas Committee to include possible and speculative reserves. The AGA figure was a 5.3% decline from the previous year, the sixth successive yearly decline. Gas production in the U.S. declined 1.5% in 1976 to 19.8 Tcf. Demand from the household and commercial sector rose 7% and from utilities by an encouraging 12.4%, but fell 2.4% in industry.

In The Netherlands gas reserves fell 3% in 1976 to 83.9 Tcf, the first decline since the discovery of the Groningen field in 1959. Dutch gas production reached a record 3.5 Tcf in 1976, about half of it exported. Canada's gas reserves rose 6.9% in 1976. Most of the additions were in the Mackenzie Delta and the Arctic islands, where estimates of reserves increased 39.6% to 16.8 Tcf. Alaska agreed to sell 2.6 Tcf of its one-eighth royalty share of Prudhoe Bay gas to Tennessee Gas Transmission Co. over a 20-year period.

Potential gas discoveries in the U.S. Anadarko Basin were thought to be comparable to those that might be made in such frontier areas as the Arctic, offshore Alaska, and the outer continental shelves; 100% probability estimates were given for a total of 60 Tcf. Wells drilled on Canada's Labrador shelf 700 mi N of St. John's, Newfoundland, produced 9.8 million cu ft a day of gas and 235 bbl a day of condensate. A well in the U.S.S.R.'s Vaneivisskoe field, within the Arctic Circle, tested over 53 million cu ft a day of gas, and the discovery raised estimates for the field. Late in 1976 construction began on a third gas pipeline from the Messoyakha and Soleninskoe gas fields, the northernmost in the U.S.S.R. and 200 mi N of the Arctic Circle, 160 mi E to Noril'sk.

A well in the Caspian Sea and another off Turkmenistan each yielded 17.7 million cu ft a day of gas. Soviet gas production was thought to have reached a record 11.3 Tcf in 1976, nearly 10% higher than in 1975 and 3% above the target.

A total of 47,480 oil, gas, and dry wells were reported drilled in North America in 1976, an 8.7% increase over 1974. Texas had the largest number with 12,740 wells, followed by Oklahoma with 4,393. A record 26.5% of the wells produced oil and gas. A well drilled by Monsanto Co. in Fremont, Wyo., yielded 16 million cu ft a day.

India quadrupled oil and gas development budget expenditure estimates of $470 million for the 1974–79 period to $1.9 billion. Over half was to be used for developing the Bombay High and Bassein fields off the northwest coast. India's proved gas reserves were estimated at 3.5 Tcf, with potential reserves put as high as 265 Tcf. The first gas discovery ever made off Bangladesh was reported early in 1977. The well, 50 mi offshore in the Bay of Bengal in only 27 ft of water, tested at 17.9 million cu ft a day.

A well drilled in southwest Nigeria produced oil, condensate, and 10.9 million cu ft a day of gas. Although Nigeria produced 1.4 Bcf (billion cu ft) a day of gas from associated reserves (estimated to be around 70 Tcf), almost 98% of gas produced in 1974 was flared at the wellhead. Only 21.4 Bcf was utilized, but plans for the export of liquefied natural gas (LNG) to the U.S. and of liquid ethylene to Europe were in hand. Conversion to protein was thought to be another possible use.

Production began in late 1976 about 6½ mi off Niigata in the Sea of Japan from the Aga Oki field. Results were not yet available but a production rate of 60 million cu ft a day of gas was expected in 1977.

Thailand considered the construction of a 450-mi pipeline to Bangkok from offshore fields in the Gulf of Siam, with the British Gas Corporation aiding in offshore gas development. Reserve estimates in the Thai concessions were 1 Tcf.

Planned LNG projects reported during 1977 included additional gas shipments from Algeria to the U.S. One terminal, at Lorneville, New Brunswick, would receive and regasify up to 1 Bcf a day. Construction of the terminal would take four years and cost an estimated $350 million. Pipeline transmission project plans included a $4 million pipeline and compressor installation in Daggett County, Utah. Articles of agreement between Canada and the U.S. were signed in September 1977 for the $8 billion Alcan pipeline project to carry Alaskan natural gas across Canadian territory to markets in the midwestern and western U.S. The 5,500 mi of pipeline were scheduled to be operational in 1983. With rising energy prices, uneconomic supplies in remote regions became worth recovering, and there was talk of an icebreaking LNG tanker for small Arctic supplies not recoverable by other means.

At the end of 1976 reports of a 20-year contract between Czechoslovakia and the Soviet Union for the purchase of 134 Bcf a year of Iranian gas featured a planned pipeline 3,720 mi long from the Kangan field on the Persian Gulf into Europe. A $3 billion underwater and on-ground 1,500-mi pipeline from Hassi R'mel in Algeria to Bologna in northern Italy was to carry approximately 300 Tcf over 25 years.

An 806-mi offshore pipeline from Moomba in the Cooper Basin, South Australia, to Sydney was completed in late 1976. In late 1977 the new northern sections of the British transmission system were made ready for the first supplies from the Frigg field in the northern North Sea, and small quantities of gas started to come ashore in October —the first gas from the northern sector of British waters.

Various experiments in underground gasification of coal, and in the production of substitute natural gas from biological sources and from coal, were reported during the year. The year's most unexpected development was the suggestion by a British scientist that biological sediments on the ocean floors around Britain could yield enough methane gas to keep British Gas Corporation going for several generations.

(DAVID RICHARD BUTLER)

PETROLEUM

Emphasis in oil affairs moved during 1977 from the producing to the consuming countries. The controversy and bitterness within OPEC about the two-tier pricing system announced in 1976 was resolved in a compromise. The market price for Saudi Arabian light crude oil was aligned with that from other OPEC countries, but problems on differentials on heavier crudes remained. At a meeting of the OPEC oil ministers in Venezuela in December no agreement was reached on a new price structure.

The inability of oil production to keep pace with demand by the end of the century dominated discussion. U.S. dependence on foreign oil imports increased to 48% of total U.S. demand in the bitter winter months of 1976–77 and continued at record levels with record trade balance deficits, tripled in volume since 1973. During the first half of 1977 demand in the U.S. increased by 8.3% and in Japan by 6%. In Western Europe, however, demand fell by 1.3%. Refinery utilization, at two-thirds of capacity, reflected the slow economic recovery.

Exploration continued. Rig activity increased by 5% in 1976. Offshore deepwater-drilling records were set off southwestern Thailand at 3,461 ft and on the European continental shelf off Spain at 4,457 ft. Pipe laying was tested off Sicily at 1,850 ft. However, the spectacular blowout of the

Bravo well in the Ekofisk field in the North Sea in April, the rupture of the underground pipeline at the Saudi Arabian gathering centre at Abqaiq in May, and the fire at the Alaskan pumping station in July as crude oil filled the trans-Alaska pipeline for the first time all served to stress the risks inherent in oil production.

RESERVES. At the beginning of 1977 total world "published proved" reserves had again fallen, to 652,000,000,000 bbl, compared with 666,100,000,000 bbl for 1976. The Western Hemisphere share fell to 12% of the total, 78,700,000,000 bbl. Middle East reserves remained almost the same at 367,-300,000,000 bbl, 56.3% of the total. The U.S. share was 5.7% of the total, 37,-300,000,000 bbl. Western Europe had 3.8%, 24,900,000,000 bbl; the U.S.S.R. 12%, 78,100,000,000 bbl; Africa 9.3%, 60,-600,000,000 bbl; and China 3.1%, 20,000,-000,000 bbl.

PRODUCTION. World oil production in 1976 increased by 8.5% to 59,555,000 bbl a day, exceeding the previous high of 1974. In the Western Hemisphere production fell by 1.7% to 15,905,000 bbl a day, with North America down 3.4% and Latin America up 2.2%; the Western Hemisphere share amounted to 26.3% of the total, compared with 28.9% in 1975. The Middle East total of 37.4%, 22,175,000 bbl a day, the highest ever, was 13.1% more than in 1975, and only the Neutral Zone and Sharjah showed decreases. Saudi Arabia, with 14.4%, retained the largest share of the world total, 8,525,000 bbl a day. Iran had 10%, 5,920,000 bbl a day; Iraq 3.8%, 2,280,000 bbl a day; and Kuwait 3.4%, 1,-950,000 bbl a day. African production registered a 16.1% increase to 5,850,000 bbl a day. Libya had the largest increase, 30.9%, to 1,930,000 bbl a day, but Nigeria, with 2,065,000 bbl a day, 3.5% of the world total, was the largest producer. Southeast Asian production at 3.1% of the world total, 1,865,000 bbl a day, was 17.2% more

than for 1975. In the U.S.S.R., production increased to 10,315,000 bbl a day, but at 17.6% the share of the world total was fractionally down. In the U.K. production rose by 300% and in Norway by 49%.

CONSUMPTION. World petroleum consumption rose in 1976 to break new records at 58,790,000 bbl a day, an increase of 6.6%. Consumption was up 7% in both North and Latin America and 6.3% in Western Europe and in the Eastern Hemisphere. The U.S. consumed the most, 16,980,000 bbl a day for 28.6% of the world total, followed by the U.S.S.R. with 7,685,000 bbl a day, 13.2%; Japan with 5,195,000 bbl a day, 8.8%; West Germany with 2,885,000 bbl a day, 4.8%; and France with 2,385,000 bbl a day, 4.1%. The U.K., with 3.2% of the total, 1,870,000 bbl a day, was the only major country to register a drop in consumption. China registered the largest increase, at 18.7%, 1,320,000 bbl a day. Large increases were also registered by Turkey with 13.2%, 305,000 bbl a day, and The Netherlands with 13.1%, 800,000 bbl a day.

U.S. imports from the Middle East rose to 1,910,000 bbl a day in 1976. Imports from Latin America were 2,010,000 bbl a day, and from West Africa 1,085,000 bbl a day. Western Europe imported 13,725,000 bbl a day, including 9,405,000 bbl a day from the Middle East. Japan's imports rose to 5,320,-000 bbl a day, of which 3,955,000 bbl a day came from the Middle East.

Product demand did not change significantly. Gasolines predominated in the U.S., and middle distillates and fuel oil were much the same in Western Europe, 4,930,-000 bbl a day and 4,410,000 bbl a day, respectively. In Japan, middle distillates increased in relation to fuel oil. Excluding the U.S.S.R., Eastern Europe, and China, world gasoline consumption was 14,-230,000 bbl a day; middle distillates totaled 13,980,000 bbl a day; and fuel oil 12.8 million bbl a day.

REFINING. World refinery capacity increased by 4.7% in 1976 to 74,985,000 bbl a day. Important increases were in Indonesia, 24%, Mexico, 19.1%, Belgium, 14.9%, and Brazil, 12.4%. Western Hemisphere capacity at 26,665,000 bbl a day was 35.6% of the total. Western Europe, 21,205,000 bbl a day, had 28.2% of the world total, a 2.5% increase over 1975. Japan, with 7.1%, 5,345,000 bbl a day, had an even smaller increase, 1.4%. Total refining capacity for the U.S.S.R., Eastern Europe, and China was 17.3% of the world total, 13 million bbl a day. Refinery capacity of Western Europe surpassed that of the U.S. for the first time.

TANKERS. The world tanker fleet in 1976, 320.7 million tons deadweight (dw), was 29.3% over 1975. The Liberian-registered share, 31.1% of the total, increased by 10.1%. Japan had 10.1% of the total. The U.K.'s share fell by 1.9%. Japanese-registered tonnage became second largest for the first time. Of world tonnage, 41% was employed between the Middle East and Western Europe and 11% between the Middle East and Japan. The world tanker fleet had doubled in the five years to 1976. Surplus capacity at year's end was some 68 million tons dw.

(R. W. FERRIER)

See also Engineering Projects; Industrial Review; Mining and Quarrying; Transportation.

The supertanker "Arco Juneau" pulled away from a loading berth at Valdez, Alaska, on August 1 with the first load of oil from the trans-Alaska pipeline.

Engineering Projects

Bridges. A report published in 1977 by the U.S. Federal Highway Administration suggested that one-sixth of the existing bridges in the U.S. were unsatisfactory. Steel had rusted and concrete had chipped off to expose the reinforcement, which, in turn, had corroded. A prime cause of troubles in road bridges was found to be the deicing salt spread by the highway authorities themselves; the salt had seeped through the wearing surface to crack the concrete and corrode the steel. The report stated that of the 546,000 road bridges in the U.S., 75% had been built more than 40 years earlier, when truck loads and numbers of trucks and cars were a fractional proportion of current figures. In the earthquake belt, many minor bridges were found unlikely to survive a serious tremor and were thus a threat to rescue operations. In addition to those bridges that were structurally deficient, there were also those that were "functionally obsolete" because they were too narrow or had sharply curved approaches. Altogether more than 100,000 bridges, generally small structures, were found to be in need of significant repairs. This pattern was repeated, in varying degrees, in most parts of the industrial world.

The problems facing bridge engineers in the less developed countries were discussed at a symposium organized by the International Association of Bridge and Structural Engineering in Munich, West Germany, in October. Many speakers stressed the need to produce designs appropriate to the country concerned and to accept the idea that advanced practices as used in a technological society were rarely suited to third world countries. Standards of materials and workmanship, as well as climatic conditions and geology, were also likely to be different from those to which a designer was accustomed, and allowances should be made accordingly.

Japan was about to embark on the largest bridge-building project ever undertaken anywhere. Three road links were planned between Shikoku, the smallest of Japan's four main islands, and Honshu, the largest. Each link would be about 10 km (6 mi) long, and 19 major bridges would be required to provide the hops between the smaller islands that lie between Honshu and Shikoku. The channels were as much as 100 m deep, and currents ran at ten knots. Equipment was designed and built to place bridge foundations in 50 m of water. As of the end of 1977 only one of the three routes, for road and rail, was fully authorized, although three bridges on the other two routes were being built to aid local development and help reduce the 110,000 daily ferry trips made between the principal islands.

In Europe, too, plans were well advanced for bridging sea passages. The most advanced was the $1 billion Great Belt Bridge between Jutland and the island of Zealand, on which Copenhagen is located. One section would comprise 7.4 km of high-level viaduct with two bridges across two adjacent main shipping channels. The project at-

COURTESY, UNITED STATES STEEL CORPORATION

The New River Gorge Bridge, near Fayetteville, West Virginia, opened on Oct. 22, 1977, features the world's longest main steel arch span (shown under construction). The 518.5-metre (1,700-foot) span soars 267 metres (876 feet) above the river.

tracted the attention of all the leading European bridge engineers, and a choice was scheduled to be made in mid-1978.

Another European project likely to materialize in the next decade was the Messina Strait crossing between the toe of Italy and Sicily. Wind tunnel tests were being made on a new form of deck structure designed to carry both road and rail over a single suspended span of 3,000 m, more than twice as long as the main span of the Verrazano-Narrows Bridge (1,299 m) in New York or the Humber Bridge (1,410 m) due for completion in Britain in 1979. The proposed Messina deck, with air vents between each traffic lane, was designed to eliminate the aerodynamic stability problems that had troubled suspension bridge engineers in recent years. This would greatly reduce the need for a stiffening girder, thereby simultaneously reducing the dead load and simplifying the otherwise enormous problems of building such a long span.

Completed in Europe during 1977 were the Pont de Brotonne (France), a cable-stayed concrete bridge with a main span of 320 m, the longest in the world of this type; Puente de Rande, near Vigo (Spain), a steel cable-stayed bridge with a main span of 400 m; and the 525.5-m suspension bridge at Kvalsund, northern Norway. In Argentina, twin steel cable-stayed bridges, with main spans of 330 m, were completed as part of the Zarate Brazo Largo crossing to carry four road traffic lanes and two railway lines.

In the U.S. two notable long-span bridges were completed: the Francis Scott Key Bridge (main span 366 m) in Baltimore, a continuous steel truss bridge; and the New River Gorge Bridge, near Fayetteville, W.Va., a steel arch of 518.5-m span (the longest in the world).   (DAVID FISHER)

Buildings. Although economic recovery proceeded more slowly than anticipated, the flattening out of the recession during 1977 brought back a little of the long-missed buoyancy to the international construction world. While there was still much activity in the Middle East, the headlong spree of grandiose development plans that characterized the early years of the oil boom there was replaced by more rational and controlled expansion programs, often smaller in scale and more exactly defined. Paradoxically, oil money in some instances was flowing back to its source in the West and being employed to finance large-scale projects for urban renewal. An example was the rundown waterfront area of New Orleans, La., where Iran's government-controlled Bank Omran was backing a $500 million plan to turn the district into a modern complex of offices, hotels, housing, a huge shopping centre, and waterfront facilities including a cruise terminal and restaurants.

Another quite different aspect of the current building scene was the continuing concern about the economical use and reuse of materials. A welcome trend was the growing ability of designers to turn the demands of energy conservation to positive aesthetic advantage. The fashion for enclosing a building entirely in a skin of reflecting glass was a case in point. This reduced air-conditioning costs and acted as an environmental protection to the building, but still permitted unobstructed views from the inside. Aesthetically, the clear reflection of the external environment had the paradoxical effect of both negating and emphasizing the presence of the building in a new and surprising way. Perhaps the most spectacular use yet of the technique was in the head office building for Willis, Faber & Dumas Ltd., in Ipswich, England, where a low-rise solution on a very large irregular site resulted in a vast undulating vertical mirror that reflected a constantly changing panorama of its surroundings.

Another comparatively new building technique was the air-supported roof. A striking example was the Pontiac (Mich.) Metropolitan Stadium,

"Little sister" to the notable 210-metre (690-foot) Montparnasse tower in Paris, a 175-metre concrete-and-steel building rose toward completion over Lyon in 1977. Its top floors would house a hotel with a skylight-illuminated atrium.

KEYSTONE

where seating accommodations for 80,000 spectators were completely covered by a glass-fibre fabric roof 400,000 sq ft in area and measuring 722 ft × 552 ft. The fabric spanned the area between a network of steel cables anchored to a polygonal compression ring that consisted of 6-ft-deep plate girders and poured-in-place concrete. The ring was supported by two rows of columns at an elevation 100 ft above grade. Technically, there was no reason why much larger roofs of this type should not be erected, covering entire exhibitions, districts, or even cities.

While steel and concrete were being challenged by this unconventional material and technique, large timber domes were also being considered for stadiums in the U.S., their costs being comparable with those for the air-supported fabrics. The largest built example probably was the 502-ft-diameter Varax Dome for the Northern Arizona University multipurpose stadium. The 15,000-seat arena was sunken below ground level and completely covered by a circular dome meeting the ground on all sides. It consisted of a grid of glue-laminated timber ribs on intermeshing great circle arcs. The ribs formed triangles connected by 127 steel hubs, with grid members ranging in length from 19 ft 4 in to 61 ft 9 in.

A resurgence of interest in brick was perhaps most strikingly seen at the new Hillingdon Civic Centre in England. Although internally it was a relatively simple three-story, square, reinforced concrete structure, externally it presented an extremely striking and complicated profile. All the walls were elaborately modeled brickwork, and each floor was set back from the one beneath; the floors were connected by a multiplicity of tile roofs pitched at an angle of 45°. This interlocking torrent of brick and tile created an effect like a giant bungaloid fantasy, as if the homely model had been duplicated again and again both vertically and horizontally.

Reinforced concrete continued to be used in an almost limitless variety of situations, from the most mundane to the most prestigious. In the latter category, few buildings recently completed attracted more attention than the New National Theatre on London's South Bank. Every aspect of the theatre was dominated by the texture of board-marked concrete in horizontal bands, angled buttresses, and above all by the huge vertical masses of the fly towers for the two main auditoriums. The larger of the auditoriums, the Olivier Theatre, had an open stage around which the 1,160 seats were arranged in a bowl-like configuration. The smaller 900-seat Lyttleton Theatre had a conventional proscenium arch, and, in addition, there was a third, experimental theatre, the Cottesloe. This accommodated 400 people in a variety of arrangements ranging from a conventional stage/audience relationship to an open acting area completely circled by spectators.   (PETER DUNICAN)

Dams. In November 1977, the 40-year-old Toccoa embankment dam in Georgia suddenly collapsed, killing 39 people and destroying much of the Toccoa Falls Bible College campus. A preliminary report indicated that piping, the formation of a leakage path through the body of a dam or its foundation, was the likely cause. The water level before collapse was about 1.2 m below crest level. Georgia was one of six states in the U.S. with no dam safety regulations. An inventory of 49,500 dams in the U.S., completed by the Army Corps of Engineers in 1975, included 84 dams (the Toccoa among them) listed as "high hazard" in Georgia. When the inventory was submitted to Congress in November 1976 after the Teton Dam failure in Idaho in June of that year, it was claimed that in most states and some federal agencies dam safety programs were either nonexistent or inadequate to protect the public from the hazards created by dams. Repercussions of the Teton disaster included the resignation of the design and construction director of the U.S. Bureau of Reclamation. In December 1977 the Corps of Engineers began an inspection of 9,000 "high hazard" nonfederal dams listed in the 1975 inventory.

There was statistical evidence that dams are most at risk during and immediately after first impounding. However, there were many dams, both concrete and embankment, that were reaching an age when longevity could not necessarily be taken for granted. Neither form of construction was immune to the ravages of natural forces, and many had been built before some of the current princi-

ples of dam design had been established. Also, spillway capacities often were inadequate when judged by modern standards. There was an erroneous view in some quarters that only electrical and mechanical works required maintenance. But the regular inspection and maintenance of dam structures and other reservoir works were essential to prevent deterioration and the eventual creation of a hazard to life and property.

The assessment of safe spillway discharge capacity was the subject of much research, and a major contribution was the five-volume report of *Flood Studies* by the U.K. Natural Environment Research Council, published in 1975. The implementation of the design principles inherent in this report resulted in the provision of greater spillway discharge capacity than previously was considered necessary. Similarly, in the U.S., the Bureau of Reclamation found that recent severe floods, particularly those due to winter rain on snow-covered frozen ground, had made it necessary to design spillways to accommodate much higher peak discharges than had been done previously.

When embankment dams are in a cascade arrangement in the same valley, they are particularly vulnerable to freak storms. This was illustrated in January in Brazil, when 230 mm (9.2 in) of

Major World Dams Under Construction in 1977 [1]

Name of dam	River	Country	Type [2]	Height (m)	Length of crest (m)	Volume content (000 cu m)	Gross capacity of reservoir (000 cu m)
Agua Vermelha	Grande	Brazil	EG	90	3,990	19,641	10,978,200
Amaluza	Paute	Ecuador	A	170	410	1,157	119,600
Auburn	American (N. Fork)	U.S.	A	209	1,265	4,587	3,083,800
Balimela	Sileru	India	E	70	4,633	22,631	3,823,900
Bilandi Tank	Bilandi	India	EG	32	707	20,572	62,900
Chicoasen	Grijalva	Mexico	R	250	478	12,004	1,233,500
Fierze	Drin	Albania	R	158	400	700	2,620,000
Finstertal	Finstertalbach	Austria	R	158	620	4,390	60,400
Gura Apelor Retezat	Riul Mare	Romania	R	173	480	9,000	209,700
Hasan Uğurlu	Yeşil Irmak	Turkey	E	175	435	9,042	1,078,100
Inguri	Inguri	U.S.S.R.	A	272	766	3,798	988,000
Itaipu	Paraná	Brazil-Paraguay	ERG	177	7,900	27,001	28,999,600
Itumbiara	Paranaíba	Brazil	EG	100	6,700	36,002	17,029,700
Karakaya	Euphrates	Turkey	A	173	459	1,988	9,498,000
Kolnbrein	Malta	Austria	A	198	620	1,525	199,800
Kolyma	Kolyma	U.S.S.R.	R	130	750	12,550	14,802,000
La Grande No. 2	La Grande	Canada	ER	160	2,835	22,937	62,000,600
La Grande No. 3	La Grande	Canada	ER	98	3,901	22,937	61,200,100
La Grande No. 4	La Grande	Canada	ER	117	3,475	19,114	18,899,700
Las Portas	Camba	Spain	A	152	484	747	751,200
Miyagase	Nakatsu	Japan	G	154	411	1,950	206,000
Mornos	Mornos	Greece	E	126	816	17,000	779,600
Nader Shah	Maroon	Iran	E	175	220	7,201	1,619,600
Nurek	Vakhsh	U.S.S.R.	E	300	728	58,003	10,391,000
Olmapinar	Manavgat	Turkey	A	185	360	565	299,700
Oosterschelde	Vense Gat Oosterschelde	Netherlands, The	E	45	8,900	70,003	2,900,000
Patia	Patia	Colombia	R	240	550	23,601	18,899,700
Poechos	Chira	Peru	E	50	10,000	17,501	1,200,200
Raúl Leoni	Caroni	Venezuela	G	162	1,404	76,456	135,685,000
Rogunsky	Vakhsh	U.S.S.R.	E	325	764	70,340	11,699,700
Salto Grande	Uruguay	Uruguay-Argentina	EG	40	3,506	3,964	5,000,000
São Simão	Paranaíba	Brazil	ERG	120	3,611	27,388	12,539,800
Sayano-Shushenskaya	Yenisei	U.S.S.R.	A	245	1,067	9,110	31,272,900
Sobradinho	São Francisco	Brazil	ERG	42	3,900	13,200	34,168,000
Sterkfontein	Nuwejaarspruit	South Africa	E	93	3,060	17,001	2,655,700
Takase	Takase	Japan	R	176	362	9,643	76,500
Tedorigawa	Tedori	Japan	R	153	413	9,643	230,700
Thomson	Thomson	Australia	R	162	549	9,633	1,100,300
Toktogul	Naryn	U.S.S.R.	G	213	450	2,895	19,489,300
Tucurui	Tocantins	Brazil	E	91	8,047	...	44,406,000
Ukai	Tapi	India	EG	69	4,927	25,517	8,511,200
Ust-Ilim	Angara	U.S.S.R.	EG	105	3,565	8,702	59,331,400
Warm Springs	Dry Creek	U.S.	E	97	914	23,231	302,200
Yacyreta-Apipe	Paraná	Argentina-Paraguay	EG	38	49,987	70,003	17,366,400
MAJOR WORLD DAMS COMPLETED IN 1976 AND 1977 [1]							
Chivor	Batá	Colombia	R	237	280	10,800	815,300
Dartmouth	Mitta-Mitta	Australia	R	180	690	15,300	6,453,700

[1] Having a height exceeding 150 m (492 ft); or having a total volume content exceeding 15 million cu m (19.6 million cu yd); or forming a reservoir exceeding 14,800 x 10⁶ cu m capacity (12 million ac-ft).
[2] Type of dam: E=earth; R=rockfill; A=arch; G=gravity.

In Japan construction proceeded rapidly on a railway line which will carry "bullet trains" from Tokyo to northern Japan. These rapid transit trains attain speeds of 260 kilometres per hour.

rainfall in 24 hours caused the overtopping and consequent failure of the Euclides da Cunha Dam on the Pardo River. The dam withstood overtopping to a maximum depth of 1.2 m for seven hours before it was breached, causing the collapse within minutes of the Amando de Salles Oliveira embankment dam farther downstream; 4,000 homes and two hydroelectric power plants were destroyed in this disaster, but fortunately no lives were lost.

Dams are not usually covered by insurance except in cases where the hydroelectric generating plant installation is part of the dam. A major dam failure usually results in a national disaster being declared, and financial aid for relief programs is then forthcoming from government sources. With such a wide variety in type of dam, possible cause of failure, and potential for consequential damage, there was need for a "Reservoir Hazard Index" to provide a comparative measure of the risk potential involved in the project and to give some basis for an assessment of premiums for insurance purposes.   (J. C. A. ROSEVEARE)

Roads. In the current worldwide economic climate a growing problem facing many road authorities was the division of scarce resources between the construction of new and needed roads and the maintenance of existing facilities. The steadily increasing volume of road transport, particularly of trucks, called for increased maintenance, road improvements, and the strengthening of bridges. Consequently, it seemed likely that in the coming years new road construction would be mostly in the less developed countries, while the industrialized nations would endeavour to maintain their existing highways.

Financial support from the World Bank and regional organizations such as the African Development Fund and the Asian Development Bank provided a strong stimulus to road building in the less developed countries, many of which were devoting a large part of their national revenues to building roads to open up their hinterlands and also to provide international links.

While the year was not marked by the completion of any major road project, there was steady progress. In Europe, the length of the French expressway network in service reached 4,000 km (2,500 mi), an impressive figure as it represented the construction and entry into service of 3,000 km in the space of ten years. The construction program continued with about 350 km of expressway in the Rhône-Alps region. When completed, four interconnected expressways would link France with Switzerland and central Europe.

A major project in progress in Europe was the development of a north-south expressway system that eventually would link the Baltic to the Mediterranean and Black seas. When completed, it would be more than 5,000 km in length. Construction preparations for it were well advanced in Austria, Czechoslovakia, and Hungary. Elsewhere in Europe, major expressway developments were taking place in Spain. Plans were being developed for the next 10–15 years, and the objective was to link all the major cities, industrial areas, and ports. In West Germany, the road program up to 1980 involved an expenditure of $12.7 billion for 2,500 km of highways, 400 km of them being four-lane.

In the Middle East, Saudi Arabia's five-year plan comprised the addition of 14,000 km to the road network, 3,400 km of which would be main highways. In Iraq, a similar five-year plan covered construction of 5,000 km of new roads, including a 1,200-km expressway from the Syrian and Jordanian borders via Baghdad to the border of Kuwait. Jordan planned to construct at least 662 km of major highways by 1980, including main routes from Amman to the Syrian, Saudi Arabian, and Iraqi borders. In Egypt a five-year plan envisaged construction or reconstruction of 10,000 km of main roads and the construction of secondary roads in newly cultivated areas of Lower Egypt. Construction of a road tunnel under the Suez Canal was begun. (See *Tunnels,* below).

There was considerable construction activity in virtually all the African nations, largely financed from international funds. Work included both new road construction and the improvement of existing earthen roads to permit the passage of heavy traffic. Considerable efforts were being made to link national road networks with those of neighbouring countries to provide access to ports, 14 of the African countries being landlocked. Major developments centred on completion of the Trans-African Highway (linking Lagos, Nigeria, and Mombasa, Kenya) and the Trans-Sahara Route. The latter was expected to reach the border of Niger in 1978. Studies were also under way on the route to be selected for a Trans-East African Highway linking Cairo to Gaborone in Botswana. The 9,027-km route would pass through the Sudan, Ethiopia, Kenya, Tanzania, and Zambia and would link with the national networks in Swaziland, Chad, and Zaire.

In the U.S. there was a slight increase in highway spending during the year. Some 90% of the Interstate Highway System was open to traffic. A major project in the Americas was the Pan-American Highway. Completion of this continued to be delayed by difficulties in the Darien Gap section in Panama, where work was held up pending the settlement of disputes on environmental problems.

(IRF)

Tunnels. By 1977 work on the Seikan Tunnel in Japan was running three years behind schedule. High-pressure grouting through holes drilled up to 70 m ahead of the face proved successful, and world records were created with forward probe holes up to 2 km long. Japanese engineers made progress with the development of slurry shields as an alternative to compressed air for tunneling where groundwater was a major problem, and they proposed improved methods for sealing immersed tube elements for the Daiba Railway Tunnel. Post-tensioned cables were to seal the rubber joints between concrete sections to accommodate the estimated 1.2 m of final settlement.

In Melbourne, Australia, the original tunneling machine commissioned in 1974 for the underground railway contract had to be completely redesigned at a cost approaching £400,000. With the rebuilt machine, progress rates of up to 73 m a week were achieved. In Hong Kong, work began on the 2-km-long twin-tube Aberdeen Tunnel, scheduled for completion in 1980. Hong Kong engineers claimed a world record for the urban hole made when they removed 330,000 cu m for the Admiralty station on the new mass transit railway. Work commenced in Bangkok, Thailand, for the construction of 24 km of tunnel for the Metropolitan Water Works, where the use of precast, prestressed, segmental concrete linings was proposed.

In Egypt driving of the 4-m-diameter pilot tunnel for the Ahmed Hamdi Tunnel under the Suez Canal began. A precast concrete road deck was to be constructed concurrent with the tunnel drive. The main tunnel shield, weighing 700 metric tons, was capable of towing a trailer 130 m long carrying conveyors and lifting equipment.

In Europe, Italian engineers struggled to complete the 16-km-long Santo Marco Tunnel. Construction had taken more than 20 years, and completion was not expected before 1980. Wet clay and silty ground had to be frozen to enable the tunnel shield to advance. In Switzerland, excavation of the St. Gotthard Tunnel was completed. The 12.8-km-long Fréjus Tunnel linking Italy and France suffered major geologic problems as the rock continued to expand months after it had been exposed and rock-bolted. In the Austrian Alps, progress on the 14-km-long Arlberg road tunnel, Europe's second longest, was ahead of schedule, and completion was anticipated in 1978. Unique for a tunnel of this length was the use of rubber-tired transport up to the face of the eastern drive, where road speeds of up to 40 kph (25 mph) were achieved. Conventional rail haulage was used on the west drive.

In Belgium work proceeded on the construction of Antwerp's subway. A bentonite shield was to be used to drive 3.8 km of running tunnel, and one section of the drive was to have an in situ concrete lining placed immediately behind the shield; if successful, this would be a major breakthrough in tunnel construction. In Sweden, work proceeded

KEYSTONE

A bouncy road cushion was put down near Erding, Bavaria, where 25,000 old auto tires were cut in half to make a foundation for a new road.

on the Bolmer water supply tunnel; engineers claimed that higher productivity and better working conditions had resulted from the use of all-electrical equipment for driving. The Drecht Tunnel in The Netherlands, opened at the end of 1977, had precast concrete sections weighing 45,000 metric tons each and, with four tubes measuring 50 m in total, was the world's widest sunken-tube tunnel. Driving was completed on the U.K.'s second Dartford Tunnel under the Thames River.

In the U.S. work began on Chicago's new deep-tunnel sewerage project, one of the world's largest tunneling contracts. U.S. engineers claimed a world record for an advance of 506 linear metres during seven consecutive working days on a 2.59-m-diameter tunnel near Charleston, S.C.

(DAVID A. HARRIES)

Environment

Nuclear power was the dominant environmental issue of 1977. Debate over its use took place—sometimes angrily—in every Western, developed country whose government planned to introduce or expand the generation of electricity by this means. Certain older issues waned, most notably that of population growth. With indications that the populations of industrial countries were more likely to be falling than rising, some politicians began to urge a population increase.

For some years the environmental movement in many countries had been growing more overtly political. The French municipal elections in March saw environmental candidates emerge as a serious political force, polling between 10 and 13% in the first round of balloting. This was insufficient to take them into the second ballot, but it impressed the established parties. In Britain, where the Ecology Party had little success in the county council elections in May, other environmentalists courted the trade unions; the two movements agreed to collaborate over problems of lead pollution, transport policy, and toxic wastes.

HOUPLINE-ESCH—SIPA PRESS/BLACK STAR

One demonstrator died in a melee as antinuclear protesters tried to crash the Super-Phénix reactor site at Creys-Malville, France.

Environmentalists all over the world mourned the death of E. F. Schumacher, author of the best-selling book *Small Is Beautiful* (*see* OBITUARIES).

INTERNATIONAL COOPERATION

UN Environmental Program (UNEP). At the fifth meeting of the UNEP governing council, held in Nairobi, Kenya, in May, it was announced that $23 million of the U.S. $24 million pledged by governments for 1977 had been received. The main issues discussed were the danger to the ozone layer from nuclear explosions and supersonic aircraft and the Ekofisk oil platform blowout in the North Sea (*see* below). UNEP's executive director, Mostafa K. Tolba, introduced a set of 21 goals to be achieved by 1982. These included evaluation and publication of results from the Global Environmental Monitoring System; bringing the International Referral System into full operation; development of the International Register for Potentially Toxic Chemicals to a point where it could issue warnings and technical publications; finding approaches to economic development that enhance rather than damage the natural environment; and the reduction of pollution levels.

Several specialist conferences were held during the year. No concrete plan emerged from the UN Water Conference, held at Mar del Plata, Arg., in March. Third world delegates urged the creation of a special fund to provide better water supplies in less developed countries, but they were defeated by the industrial nations, which opposed any addition to the UN bureaucracy, and by the Arab nations, which would have had to provide the financing. The issues were referred back to the General Assembly.

Following regional preparatory conferences held earlier in the year in Chile, Portugal, Kenya, and India, the UN Conference on Desertification met in Nairobi during August 29–September 9 to discuss and produce a plan of action to combat the spread of the world's deserts. The Western industrial nations and the Arab nations continued to oppose the establishment of any new UN agency or fund, and it was agreed that future activities would be coordinated by a consortium of specialists from various UN agencies, private foundations, and government agencies concerned with aid and development. (*See* Feature Article: *Nor Any Drop to Drink.*) On September 19 the director general of the Food and Agriculture Organization, Edouard Saouma, warned that parts of the African Sahel zone were again facing drought and serious food shortages.

The sixth session of the UN Conference on the Law of the Sea, held in New York City (May 23–July 15), ended more optimistically than earlier sessions, with an agreed plan for a strong international authority to supervise the deep-sea mining activities of state and commercial organizations. UNEP was represented at the second International Conference on the Environmental Future, in Reykjavik, Iceland, in June, at which leading scientists and administrators discussed such perennial problems as population growth, climate changes, and food resources. The World Health Organization (WHO) sponsored a one-week symposium, July 25–August 1, at its Geneva headquarters, at which representatives from 19 countries and several UN agencies discussed environmental health in less developed countries. The conference noted that, five years after the UN Conference on the Human Environment, little progress had been made toward achieving even minimal standards of environmental health.

European Economic Community. In March officials from the European Commission's Environmental Service met representatives of the International Union of Local Authorities and of municipalities in Council of Europe member countries to discuss the progress made in implementing the EEC's first environmental program and expectations for the second, with particular reference to waste disposal, water purification, and rural management.

In April the Commission collaborated with WHO and the U.S. Environmental Protection Agency (EPA) to sponsor a seminar in Luxembourg, at which more than 60 international experts discussed the relationship between pollution and human health. They concluded that detection methods were sufficiently advanced to permit immediate application to a number of heavy metal pollutants, carbon monoxide, organochlorine pesticides, polychlorinated biphenyls (PCB's), and some other substances.

Marine Pollution. The Council of the Organization for Economic Cooperation and Development (OECD) announced, in September, a decision to create a multilateral consultation and surveillance mechanism to regulate the dumping of radioactive wastes at sea. Participating countries would be required to give at least six months' advance warning of each dumping operation, including details of the quantities and types of wastes, the site selected for dumping, and the procedure to be followed, and an assessment of the environmental impact, with further details to be supplied three months before the operation. This information would be assessed by the OECD Nuclear Energy Agency and circulated to all participating countries. The agency would supervise the dumping operation and then report back to the steering committee for nuclear energy and the environment committee. All OECD members except Australia, Austria, Japan, and New Zealand participated in the decision. Between 1967 and 1977 a total of 46,000 metric tons of radioactive wastes had been dumped into the Atlantic.

Representatives of the oil industry and the oil-producing countries met in Paris in March, under the auspices of UNEP, to discuss the effects of oil spillages at sea, a subject also discussed by the EEC Council of Ministers in Brussels in June. The UNEP meeting called for better training of tanker crews, while the EEC meeting suggested the creation of a Community data bank to store information on techniques for dealing with pollution incidents. The Soviet government announced in April that all the Soviet Black Sea ports were now equipped to distill and purify effluents and that by 1990 all Soviet ships would be fitted with separators to purify oil-contaminated discharge water, as well as garbage and food wastes. At an intergovernmental meeting sponsored jointly by UNEP and WHO and held in Athens, June 27–July 1, 18 Mediterranean countries agreed to launch a Mediterranean pollution monitoring and research program, consisting of seven pilot projects.

NATIONAL DEVELOPMENTS AND POLICIES

Nuclear Energy. Arguments over nuclear energy were quickened by the news, released on May 3, that several thousand pounds of uranium had been mislaid over the years in commercial nuclear plants in the U.S., that in 1965, 362 lb of highly enriched uranium had vanished from a plant in Apollo, Pa., and that 200 metric tons of uranium ore disappeared in 1968 en route from Antwerp, Belgium, to Genoa, Italy.

On April 20, U.S. Pres. Jimmy Carter presented his national energy plan to a joint session of Congress. Its emphasis on reducing energy demand through conservation was welcomed by environmentalists, but it encountered fierce opposition from those who argued that the energy crisis should be resolved by stimulating demand, and therefore production, especially of indigenous fuel resources. (*See* ENERGY.) A second aspect of the president's plan aimed to reduce the risks of nuclear proliferation by deferring indefinitely the development of a plutonium fast breeder reactor in the U.S. Such a deferment had been urged in a report published early in April by the Ford Foundation, which also called for a ban on the reprocessing of plutonium in the U.S. Carter vetoed a bill authorizing $80 million for development of a breeder reactor on the Clinch River in Tennessee, but at year's end attempts were being made in Congress to revive the project.

The public controversy was punctuated by mass demonstrations at nuclear plant construction sites. A group calling itself the Clamshell Alliance organized the occupation of a nuclear power plant site in Seabrook, N.H., which resulted in some 500 arrests. In West Germany further violent demonstrations followed that of November 1976 at Brokdorf, Schleswig-Holstein. On March 20, 1977, 12,000 demonstrators clashed with police outside the site of a proposed plant at Grohnde, Lower Saxony. An "antiatom village" set up by demonstrators at the Grohnde site in mid-June was cleared by police equipped with water cannons on August 23. At the Kalkar site, close to the Dutch border, 35,000 demonstrators staged a peaceful protest on September 24–25. In all, West German protesters halted construction on at least 18 nuclear power stations and brought the government's nuclear power program to a virtual standstill.

On May 28 more than 5,000 Swiss demonstrators began a march from Kaiseraugst to Goesgen, both proposed nuclear plant sites, and on June 25 several thousand demonstrators clashed with police when they tried to occupy the access routes to the Goesgen site. In France the official nuclear power program was threatened when a large cloud of highly corrosive uranium hexafluoride gas escaped from the nuclear plant at Pierrelatte, in the Rhône Valley, on July 1, causing considerable local alarm. The French government also had to deal with determined demonstrators, and on May 30 more than 500 scientists from Grenoble University issued an open letter to Pres. Valéry Giscard d'Estaing protesting against the Super-Phénix breeder reactor the government planned to build at Creys-Malville, near Lyon. Austria experienced a series of demonstrations against the country's only planned nuclear plant, at Zwentendorf. The opening of the plant, set for 1977, was postponed pending agreement on a site for the dumping of radioactive wastes.

In Australia the controversy centred on plans to

mine uranium ore. (*See* AUSTRALIA: *Special Report.*) Britain had no immediate plans to build more nuclear power plants, but spent fuel was being reprocessed at the Windscale, Cumbria, plant of British Nuclear Fuels Ltd. (BNFL). The application of BNFL for planning permission to build a new type of reprocessing plant was the subject of a public inquiry that opened on June 14 at Windscale and continued until November 4. The inquiry, which encompassed many of the wider ethical issues raised by nuclear power, became the most important part of a nationwide debate on the implications of the "plutonium economy."

The Seas and Beaches. The major oil pollution incident of the year occurred on April 22, when a blowout at the Ekofisk Bravo 14 oil platform in the Norwegian sector of the North Sea discharged about 20,000 tons of oil before it was sealed on April 30. The fact that the accident occurred at all, and the difficulty in controlling the flow, had political repercussions throughout northern Europe. The report of the official Norwegian inquiry into the incident, published on October 10, placed the blame on Phillips Petroleum, the company operating the platform, and on the Norwegian Petroleum Directorate. The large oil slick dispersed naturally, and the environmental consequences of the blowout were not severe. South Africa also narrowly escaped serious pollution after two Liberian-flag supertankers collided off the Cape of Good Hope in December.

The U.S. had suffered a record number of oil tanker accidents in or near its waters in 1976. On March 18, 1977, President Carter delivered a message to Congress calling for more stringent measures to reduce pollution from this source, to deal more swiftly and effectively with the spills that occurred, and to provide full and dependable compensation to the victims of oil pollution damage. Among the measures the president proposed were the introduction of construction and equipment standards for all oil tankers of 20,000 tons deadweight or more calling at U.S. ports, to be fully effective within five years; better training programs for tanker crews, leading to higher qualifications; and the right of the U.S. Coast Guard to board and inspect at least once a year all foreign tankers calling at U.S. ports.

Work began on April 4 to recover 910 drums containing 250 tons of tetraethyl lead from the wreck of the Yugoslav ship "Cavcat," which sank in the Adriatic in July 1974. In July 1977 the "Daphne," a small fishing vessel converted for research use, sailed from Italy to seek the sources of the blooms of toxic red algae threatening large areas of the Adriatic.

The condition of many European beaches was causing concern. On July 12 French authorities closed three out of five beaches near Cherbourg; a survey by local authorities showed that during 1975 and 1976, under existing French regulations, one beach in four should have been closed to bathers occasionally and one in 20 should have been closed permanently. Investigators believed that some Spanish and Italian beaches were even dirtier, but UN research teams felt the situation would improve as the coastal states adopted comparable standards and a coordinated approach to the problem under the 1976 Barcelona Convention.

Fresh Water. While Britain continued to disagree with its European partners over what it saw as needlessly high quality standards for fresh water, there was some disquiet over the safety of drinking water in a number of British towns. In May scientists from the Water Research Centre began an investigation into the quality of water in 150 towns, each with a population of more than 50,000, because of fears about the increased exposure to chemical contaminants that might occur through the use of recycled water.

Lead in water also raised doubts. About two million British homes received water with a lead content in excess of the EEC proposed upper limit, and in about 800,000 homes even the lower WHO limit was exceeded. These figures were revealed in a report published by the Department of the Environment in which it was argued that existing levels were tolerable. In July, however, the U.S. National Academy of Sciences published a report, *Drinking Water and Health*, recommending a safety limit for lead that was half the EEC limit and one-quarter of the WHO limit.

In June, under the provisions of the 1974 Safe Drinking Water Act, the purity of drinking water throughout the U.S. came under federal supervision. In January the EPA banned the discharge of PCB's into the nation's waters. Widespread PCB contamination continued to be a major problem. Consumers were warned not to eat fish caught in the Great Lakes more than once a week because of their PCB content.

The threat to Kenya's Lake Nakuru from a factory on its shores manufacturing copper oxychloride fungicide began to recede with the decision of the Kenyan government to resite the factory, owned by Copal Ltd., in an industrial area near Mombasa. This followed a prolonged campaign by the World Wildlife Fund, supported by the West German government, to have the factory closed.

The Ozone Layer. Much of the concern about air pollution during 1977 centred on threats to the ozone layer from aircraft and from propellants used in aerosol cans. A global monitoring program began in December 1976, when the Concorde aircraft in commercial service began measuring concentrations of 30 different atmospheric pollutants, including a range of chlorofluorocarbon compounds. The project, sponsored by the U.K. government's Central Unit on Environmental Pollution, was scheduled to last 18 months. The U.S. National Academy of Sciences began its own ozone monitoring program early in 1977, basing it on satellite measurements which were compared with readings made at ground stations. Both Britain and the U.S. planned to collect sufficient information for firm decisions on the future of chlorofluorocarbon aerosol propellants.

In the U.S. the sale of cans containing chlorofluorocarbon propellants was banned in Oregon, and the Food and Drug Administration and the Consumer Product Safety Commission decided to require warning labels on all chlorofluorocarbon-powered sprays as a step toward a complete ban. Moving more cautiously, Britain's Clean Air

Council officially endorsed the government policy, which was to take no action until monitoring programs were completed and data analyzed. Meanwhile, Robert Abplanalp, the inventor of the original aerosol spray-can valve, announced the invention of a new valve that used butane, isobutane, or propane gas as a propellant in place of chlorofluorocarbons.

It was reported that during the unusually hot weather of late June and early July 1976, ozone levels in the lower air over southeast England reached the highest values ever recorded, far exceeding the maximum that industrial workers continually exposed to ozone are permitted to breathe.

Arguments that the Concorde supersonic transport aircraft would damage the ozone layer faded during the year, but noise pollution arguments gained force. Local residents waged a vigorous campaign against British and French attempts to gain landing rights at New York's John F. Kennedy Airport. Late in the year, however, a U.S. federal court overruled the Port Authority of New York and New Jersey to permit trial service. (*See* TRANSPORTATION: *Aviation.*)

Seveso. The repercussions of the 1976 incident at Seveso, Italy, when a large area was contaminated with dioxin following an accident at the Icmesa chemical plant, continued in 1977. On February 22 Italian troops completed the secure fencing of the most heavily contaminated area, and on April 20 the Lombardy regional government decided to close off the grounds of 15 factories at Cesano Maderno, adjacent to the Seveso commune, in order to clean the factories and asphalt the grounds. On June 8 the Italian Senate approved the appointment of a special parliamentary com-

mission to investigate the incident. On June 13, Cesare Golfari, chairman of the regional administration, announced that 600 people evacuated from the area would be allowed to return by the end of August, while 200 more, evacuated from the most heavily contaminated area around the Icmesa factory itself, would be rehoused elsewhere in Seveso. The European Commission provided more than $175,000, over one-quarter of the total cost, for 14 research projects into ways of dealing with atmospheric pollution by dioxin.

THE URBAN ENVIRONMENT

At 9.34 PM on July 13 the electricity supply failed over a large part of New York City. The blackout lasted for 25 hours and was accompanied by extensive violence as looters and arsonists rampaged through impoverished, mainly black and Puerto Rican neighbourhoods; 3,200 people were arrested for looting and vandalism, most of them from the Bronx where the worst disorders occurred. There were complaints about the conditions under which the prisoners were held, especially in "The Tombs," a disused Manhattan prison reopened to accommodate the large numbers arrested.

There were parallel instances of violence in other cities across the world. In Britain, where violence at soccer matches increased to such an extent that the Manchester United team was almost disbarred from European competitions, the U.K. minister for sport, Denis Howell, had to intercede repeatedly to improve security arrangements. Political violence also occurred, as the National Front, a political party of the far right, held marches and public meetings that provoked angry responses from the equally extreme left-wing

YNNEDAL—SIPA PRESS/BLACK STAR

More than 2,500 metric tons of oil a day spewed from this North Sea oil rig before it was capped by U.S. oil fire specialist Red Adair in April. About 20,000 tons of crude oil were lost.

World's 25 Most Populous Urban Areas [1]

Rank	City and country	City proper Most recent population	City proper Year	Metropolitan area Most recent population	Metropolitan area Year
1	Tokyo, Japan	8,568,700	1977 estimate	27,037,300	1975 census
2	New York City, U.S.	7,453,600	1976 estimate	16,839,800	1976 estimate
3	Osaka, Japan	2,730,800	1977 estimate	16,772,900	1975 census
4	London, U.K.	7,028,200	1976 estimate	12,606,700	1974 estimate
5	Mexico City, Mexico	8,941,900	1977 estimate	12,578,400	1977 estimate
6	Shanghai, China	5,700,000	1970 estimate	10,820,000 [2]	1970 estimate
7	Los Angeles, U.S.	2,739,100	1976 estimate	10,468,000	1976 estimate
8	Ruhr, West Germany [3]	—	—	10,278,000	1975 estimate
9	São Paulo, Brazil	7,198,600	1975 estimate	10,041,100	1975 estimate
10	Nagoya, Japan	2,083,200	1977 estimate	9,417,500	1975 census
11	Paris, France	2,317,200	1975 census	8,614,600	1975 census
12	Buenos Aires, Argentina	2,980,000	1977 estimate	8,498,000	1975 estimate
13	Moscow, U.S.S.R.	7,563,000	1976 estimate	7,734,000	1976 estimate
14	Chicago, U.S.	3,150,000	1975 estimate	7,650,400	1976 estimate
15	Peking, China	. . .	. . .	7,570,000 [2]	1970 estimate
16	Rio de Janeiro, Brazil	4,857,700	1975 estimate	7,080,700	1975 estimate
17	Cairo, Egypt	5,084,500	1976 census	7,066,900	1976 census
18	Calcutta, India	3,148,700	1971 census	7,031,400	1971 census
19	Seoul, South Korea	. . .	. . .	6,964,900 [2]	1976 estimate
20	Jakarta, Indonesia	. . .	. . .	6,178,500 [2]	1977 estimate
21	Bombay, India	. . .	. . .	5,970,600 [2]	1971 census
22	Philadelphia, U.S.	1,824,900	1975 estimate	5,728,600	1976 estimate
23	Manila, Philippines	1,454,400	1975 census	5,369,900 [2]	1974 estimate
24	Teheran, Iran	. . .	. . .	4,496,200 [2]	1976 census
25	San Francisco, U.S.	666,100	1976 estimate	4,642,100	1976 estimate

[1] Ranked by population of metropolitan area.
[2] Municipality or other civil division within which a city proper may not be distinguished.
[3] A so-called industrial conurbation within which a single central city is not distinguished.

Socialist Workers Party. The first of these, at Lewisham, southeast London, on August 13, left some 100 persons injured and 214 under arrest, 202 of whom were charged.

Such violence was certainly not unrelated to the frustration of people compelled to live in declining urban areas, often with the past mistakes of planners—particularly the high-rise housing developments favoured in the 1950s and 1960s but now almost universally discredited. The plight of Britain's older cities was the subject of a White Paper, "Policy for the Inner Cities," and an official report, *Inner London: Policies for Dispersal and Balance*, both published in June 1977. On May 2, Peter Shore, secretary of state for the environment, had announced that the government would provide £57 million in aid to the inner cities, to be spent in London, Birmingham, Liverpool, and Manchester-Salford.

Many urban problems stemmed from the remoteness of planning authorities from the citizens whose lives they influenced. This was recognized in the communiqué issued at the end of a symposium on "Citizen Participation in Environment Planning," sponsored by the Council of Europe and held in Venice, Italy, March 8–10. The symposium concluded that "every planning project that directly affects the public's living conditions should be the subject of consultation between as many as possible of the inhabitants concerned, representatives of the local authorities and professionals in the matter."

In less developed countries, urban problems were different—and worse. In September the authorities began demolition of ramshackle dwellings around Buenos Aires, Arg., that had been inhabited by Bolivian migrants. About half a million Bolivians had gone to Argentina in search of better prospects, most of which proved illusory, and the Bolivian government was attempting to lure them back with free rail transport and guaranteed jobs. In March a team of experts invited to Bolivia by the government had presented the re-

sults of its four-month study, including comprehensive recommendations for urban improvements, especially those that would benefit the very poor. The team was supplied by the UN Habitat and Human Settlements Foundation, formed following the 1976 UN Conference on Human Settlements, with headquarters in Nairobi. On March 29, 1977, UN Secretary-General Kurt Waldheim named César Quintana as the foundation's first administrator. Its work would be supported by an advisory group of nongovernmental organizations, which met in Nairobi on May 4–6 under the chairmanship of Margaret Mead.

In the area of air pollution, studies made around Lancaster, England, where air was affected by an oil refinery discharging sulfur dioxide and a fertilizer factory discharging nitrous oxide, concluded that the effects of the two gases can be multiplied several times when they occur together. According to David Hall of the Greater London Council's Scientific Branch, air pollution levels, in London at least, were being underestimated. He published a report showing that 75 to 90% of London's "dark" smoke came from vehicle emissions, which were not controlled under the Clean Air Act, 1956.

An OECD report published on July 9, based on a five-year study, showed that Britain was Europe's major contributor of atmospheric sulfur dioxide, emitting 2.9 million tons a year. Much of it was carried to the north and northeast, so that while Britain received only 1 million tons, Norway, which emitted only 91,000 tons, received 250,000. The report implied a sharp criticism of the British policy of dealing with sulfur dioxide emissions mainly by building taller chimney stacks.

There were signs, in Britain at least, of a change in official attitudes to road transport. In February Secretary of State for Transport William Rodgers appointed a committee to examine the official traffic forecasts, used in calculating the need for new roads, and in April he canceled a key proposal for an expressway (motorway) between Manchester and Sheffield in favour of more modest improvements to existing roads. The British government's White Paper "Transport Policy," published in August, suggested more stringent rules for the safety and loading of heavy vehicles and greater protection for the environment. They were welcomed by the influential Committee for Environmental Conservation, which remained highly critical of road transport in general.

In France government and municipal policy was directed toward reducing traffic congestion in Paris by encouraging the use of public transport and possibly eventually banning private cars from some central city areas. In March Moscow traffic authorities, alarmed at the report of a 1976 study showing a rapid increase in the number of vehicles entering the city daily, banned all trucks, vans, and coaches from entering the city between 7 AM and 8 PM.

A more novel form of urban pollution was identified in San Francisco by Antony Fraser-Smith of the Stanford Radioscience Laboratory. Fraser-Smith found that the very large magnetic fields caused by underground trains generated electric currents in trees. He feared that the overall in-

Environment

crease in electromagnetic signals being added to the environment might generate currents in the human body, the long-term effects of which could be disruptive.

The Working Environment. Several steps were taken during the year to reduce health hazards in the workplace. Vinyl chloride monomer, used in the manufacture of polyvinyl chloride (PVC) and identified as a carcinogen, was the subject of new EEC regulations. In January the European Commission announced that materials coming into contact with food must contain no more than one milligram of vinyl chloride per kilogram, on the assumption that, at this level of concentration, no more than 0.05 mg would be absorbed by the food. This was the lowest concentration that could be detected by existing techniques. In September the Commission announced that factory workers must be exposed to no more than three parts per million of vinyl chloride; existing factories were given one year in which to make the necessary modifications.

In June the British Health and Safety Commission published a report explaining a new plan for screening chemicals for toxicity before they reach the workplace, based on tests to be carried out by manufacturers and reported in full to the Health and Safety Executive. The scheme was welcomed cautiously by the Chemical Industries Association, still more cautiously by trade unions, and was criticized sharply by independent scientists as being too lax in its testing requirements.

In May the U.S. secretary of labour, Ray Marshall, announced a change of focus for the much-criticized Occupational Safety and Health Administration. OSHA had come under fire for overemphasizing minor safety regulations while ignoring such major hazards as exposure of workers to dangerous chemicals. According to Marshall, the agency would concentrate on "the most serious dangers to human life and limb in high-risk workplaces."

What might well be the most comprehensive reform of working conditions ever attempted began early in the year at the Götaverken shipyard in Sweden, the world's largest shipyard outside Japan. Every working section, every worker, every chemical, and every aspect of ship design was being scrutinized. Quite early in the program 300 of the 600 chemicals used in the yard were banned as either harmful or superfluous.

THE NATURAL ENVIRONMENT

Alaska. Ever since the construction of a pipeline to carry oil to the south was first proposed, Alaska had been an environmental battleground. On Jan. 4, 1977, the battle entered a new phase when Rep. Morris K. Udall (Dem., Ariz.) introduced the Alaska National Interest Lands Conservation Bill into the House of Representatives; it was followed three weeks later by the introduction of almost identical legislation into the Senate by Senators Henry Jackson (Dem., Wash.) and Clifford Hansen (Rep., Wyo.). The aim of these bills was to bring 51 units of land, with a combined area of 114.9 million ac (the total area of Alaska is 375 million ac) into the various national conservation systems. Under ex-

ROB STAPLETON—THE NEW YORK TIMES

Part of the wilderness area near Sitka, Alaska, was included in a U.S. wilderness protection plan. Local residents who rely on lumbering were outraged by the proposal.

isting law, the land was administered by the Department of the Interior, but it was not part of any reserves and so was not protected against development. Opponents of the bills sought to limit the area to be reserved to 25 million ac, with a further 55 million ac to be administered jointly by the federal and state governments. In mid-September, Secretary of the Interior Cecil D. Andrus announced to Congress his decision to bring about 93 million ac into the reserves.

In May Justice Thomas Berger of the British Columbia Supreme Court submitted to the Canadian government the findings of a two-year inquiry into a proposed gas pipeline that would carry natural gas from Prudhoe Bay and the Mackenzie River Delta to southern Canada and the U.S. The report recommended a ten-year moratorium on pipeline construction, for social as well as environmental reasons, and urged that under no circumstances should a pipeline cross the ecologically sensitive Canadian Yukon. On September 8, however, Prime Minister Pierre Trudeau and President Carter announced agreement in principle on a route that would cross the southern Yukon on its way to British Columbia and Alberta, following the route of the Alaska (Alcan) Highway from Fairbanks, Alaska, to Calgary, Alta.

Dams, Reservoirs, and Canals. On February 23 the Soviet government announced a plan to build a canal linking the Volga and Pechora rivers to restore water levels in the Volga, which is used to feed extensive irrigation systems. The canal, which would not be completed until the end of the century, would also increase the amount of water in the Caspian Sea.

It had been known for some years that a causal relationship exists between large man-made reservoirs and the incidence of earthquakes. In December 1976 Soviet and U.S. geophysicists began an investigation into a reservoir on the Vakhsh River, Tadzhikistan, that, when filled, would serve the Nurek hydroelectric power station. The reservoir was being filled slowly, to lessen the rate of increase in subterranean pressure, but filling had to be stopped entirely when, just short of the halfway mark, seismic activity increased markedly. A network of Soviet-U.S. stations was being established to monitor the situation and to collect data for use in earthquake forecasting.

Large reservoirs may also cause changes in microclimates, perhaps with macroclimatic repercussions. A report published in the U.S.S.R. in August described studies of the Yenisey Basin hydroelectric scheme in Siberia, where the Yenisey and Angara rivers are dammed at several points. The rivers meet downstream of the cascade of dams and flow as a single river into the Arctic Ocean. The studies showed that away from Lake Baikal, the source of the Angara, water temperatures are reduced significantly by the dams. Since the rivers carry a substantial amount of heat into the Arctic, it was possible that the ice regime at the mouth of the Yenisey could be modified.

Wetlands. The protection of Europe's wetlands was the theme of the 1976–77 Wetlands Campaign of the Council of Europe's Information Centre for Nature Conservation. In Britain, the Norfolk Broads, the country's largest and most spectacular wetland area, was the subject of concern. With 210 mi of navigable water, the Broads are used by about 7,000 privately owned boats and a further 4,000 rented ones each year. Apart from the obvious physical pressure such numbers exert, the discharge of sewage from the shore led to the proliferation of algae, reducing the population of higher plants. This, in turn, allowed boats to approach closer to the banks, causing further damage. In September the Countryside Commission published four alternative courses of action designed to improve the long-term management of the Broads. The commission itself preferred that the area be designated as a national park under the control of an authority with additional powers to act as a navigational authority and to deal with problems peculiar to a wetland area.

Trees and Forestry. The 1976 drought, which had brought acute water shortages to many parts of Europe, led to the loss of large numbers of trees, especially shallow-rooting conifers. This loss was made worse by beech bark disease, which necessitated the felling of thousands of diseased British beeches, and by two parasites, a fungus (*Corineum cardinale*) and an insect (*Cinara cupressi*), which simultaneously attacked the cypresses of central and southern Italy. In the western U.S., two years of severe drought created a serious fire hazard, and during one period in August hundreds of fires, many ignited by lightning storms, burned over millions of acres of forestland. One fire, in Alaska, involved some 350,000 ac, and another, in northern Modoc County, Calif., was estimated to have destroyed at least $175 million worth of timber.

The most strenuous effort to save forest resources was made in the Philippines. In June, in what might well be the most original legislation of the year, the government issued a decree compelling every able-bodied man and woman and every child over the age of ten to plant one tree each month for five years—1.8 billion trees in all. A certificate would be issued for each tree planted, and failure to produce a certificate would be punished by a fine and loss of civil rights. Seedlings were being supplied free of charge and might be planted almost anywhere, but they must be tended for two years and replaced if they should die or become diseased or badly damaged. Within seven years, demand for timber for export had deforested nearly 3.5 million ac in the Philippines, exposing large areas to the risk of soil erosion, flash floods, and the silting up of dams and other water projects.   (MICHAEL ALLABY)

Wildlife. On Dec. 28, 1976, the U.S. became the fifth party to the Convention for the Conservation of Antarctic Seals. Two more signatories were needed to bring the convention into force.

In February Sir Dawda Jawara, president of The Gambia, chose the Gambian independence day to make his "Banjul Declaration," pledging his country to the cause of conservation of wildlife and natural habitats. On May 27 Guyana became the 36th state to accede to the Convention on International Trade in Endangered Species of Wild Fauna and Flora. Also in May, Kenya announced a ban on all hunting and followed this up in December

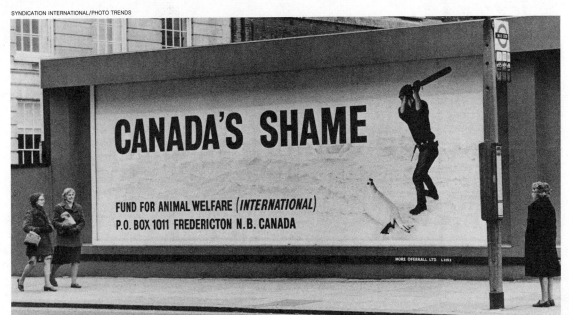

A giant billboard was used in an attempt to shame hunters from participating in the annual baby harp seal kill in the waters off Newfoundland.

with the announcement of a ban on the sale of animal trophies and game skins. However, the success of these bold moves to eliminate poaching would depend, to a large degree, on international cooperation in restricting markets for wildlife products. In the latter respect, a bad omen was the British government's action in entering a reservation on behalf of Hong Kong, the main world market for elephant tusks, to the inclusion of the African elephant in Appendix 2 of the endangered species convention.

In the U.S. Congress there were signs of restiveness over the 1973 Endangered Species Act, which directed the secretary of the interior to ensure that the "critical habitat" of any endangered species was not destroyed as the result of federal action. Some federal projects were blocked or delayed under this provision, the most controversial being the Tennessee Valley Authority's $116 million Tellico Dam, which would destroy the only known natural habitat of a minnow called the snail darter, and the Army Corps of Engineers' Dickey-Lincoln School Dam project in Maine, which threatened the Furbish lousewort, a flower thought to be extinct but rediscovered in 1976 along the St. John River. Several bills modifying the act were introduced in Congress, and many environmentalists feared that the law might be seriously weakened.

In May the Royal Forest and Bird Protection Society of New Zealand reported that, for the first time in the 20th century, the Chatham Island black robin (*Petroica australis*) had bred on Mangere Island and a chick had been reared. This robin, a bird of the flycatcher family, had been reintroduced from Little Mangere Island, where its numbers were falling and its habitat was deteriorating, in a last effort to save the species from extinction. Even more exciting was the discovery, by the New Zealand Wildlife Service, of a colony on Stewart Island, perhaps 20 strong, of the gravely endangered kakapo, or owl parrot.

During the spring, continued research in Great Britain into the connection between badgers and

bovine tuberculosis showed that the disease could be transmitted from badgers to cattle. Naturalists, therefore, reluctantly accepted the Ministry of Agriculture, Fisheries and Food's policy of gassing badger setts where badger populations were high and the badgers were infected.

In June the International Whaling Commission (IWC), meeting in Canberra, Australia, sharply reduced the quotas for killing sperm and Bryde's whales in the North Pacific and for killing sei and minke whales in the Southern Hemisphere. But quotas were increased for sperm whales in the Southern Hemisphere and for fin and minke whales in the North Atlantic. In a reversal of its 1976 position, the IWC called on its members to ban imports of whale products from nonmember countries—presumably an attempt to counter a "flags of convenience" position, under which IWC members could pay lip service to conservation but continue to import whale products without restraint. IWC had before it a statement from the International Union for the Conservation of Nature and Natural Resources (IUCN) which, among other things, deplored Japan's decision to allow the capture of 240 Bryde's whales "for scientific purposes." This and similar actions had confirmed the IUCN's opinion that all commercial whaling should stop until a true scientific analysis of the world's whale stocks and prospects had been made. In December, however, it was reported that the IUCN, under pressure from the Soviet Union and Japan, had raised the quota of sperm whales that could be killed in the North Pacific from 763 to 6,444. Members of Greenpeace, an environmental group seeking to protect whales, sailed to the Icelandic and Norwegian whaling grounds in late September with the intention of disrupting whaling by interposing their small vessel between the whalers and their prey, a technique they claimed had worked successfully in the Southern Hemisphere.

In July Britain's Royal Society for the Prevention of Cruelty to Animals drew attention in *RSPCA Today* to the huge illegal traffic in Australian birds and, to a lesser extent, in reptiles. The official report of the Australian House of Representatives Standing Committee on Environment and Conservation had shown that "The international smuggling of Australian native birds is a highly capitalized and organized activity involving an annual turnover estimated by some to exceed $1 million and by others to be several times that figure. The involvement of light aircraft and ocean-going yachts is an indication of the extent of huge profits available."

In July also came news that the whooping crane —long a symbol of endangered wildlife—was increasing in numbers, under careful protection, in Canada and the U.S. During the spring 28 chicks had been hatched, bringing the world population to 126.

The Getty Wildlife Conservation Prize for 1976 was awarded to Maj. Ian R. Grimwood, a vice-president of the Fauna Preservation Society.

(C. L. BOYLE)

See also Agriculture and Food Supplies; Energy; Fisheries; Historic Preservation; Life Sciences; Transportation. [335.D; 525.A.3.g and B.4.f.i; 534.C.2.a; 724.A; 737.C.1]

Equatorial Guinea

Equatorial Guinea

The African republic of Equatorial Guinea consists of Río Muni, which is bordered by Cameroon on the north, Gabon on the east and south, and the Atlantic Ocean on the west; and the offshore islands of Macías Nguema Biyogo and Pagalu. Area: 28,051 sq km (10,831 sq mi). Pop. (1977 est.): 322,-000. Cap. and largest city: Malabo, on Macías Nguema Biyogo (pop., 1970 est., 19,300). Language: Spanish. President in 1977, Francisco Macías Nguema.

Pres. Francisco Macías Nguema's ruthless regime drew little notice in 1977, apart from a luke-warm stricture from the UN Commission on Human Rights to the UN secretary-general. Although Spain was Equatorial Guinea's chief source of economic support (taking 90% of its exports), Macías attacked it in a speech and in March Spain temporarily suspended diplomatic relations.

Refugees from Equatorial Guinea reached record numbers, and on May 21, 28 people were killed in

---

EQUATORIAL GUINEA

Education. Primary (1973–74), pupils 35,977, teachers 630; secondary (1972–73), pupils 4,713; vocational (1972–73), pupils 586; teacher training (1972–73), students 201; secondary, vocational, and teacher training (1970–71), teachers 175.

Finance and Trade. Monetary unit: ekpwele, at par with the Spanish peseta, with (Sept. 19, 1977) a free rate of 84.63 ekpwele to U.S. $1 (147.42 ekpwele = £1 sterling). Budget (1970): revenue 709.4 million ekpwele; expenditure 589.3 million ekpwele (excludes capital expenditure of 650.7 million ekpwele). Foreign trade (1970): imports 1,472,100,000 ekpwele (80% from Spain); exports 1,740,900,000 ekpwele (91% to Spain). Main exports: cocoa 66%; coffee 24%; timber 9%. Trade with Spain (1976): imports 247,000,000 ekpwele; exports 140,-000,000 ekpwele.

Agriculture. Production (in 000; metric tons; 1976): sweet potatoes c. 30; bananas c. 12; cocoa c. 12; coffee c. 5; palm kernels c. 2; palm oil c. 5. Livestock (in 000; 1975): sheep c. 32; cattle c. 4; pigs c. 8; goats c. 8; chickens c. 82.

Epidemics:
see Health and Disease

Episcopal Church:
see Religion

---

the Bindung concentration camp, among them the former governor of the central bank, Jesus Buendi. Gen. Olusegun Obasanjo of Nigeria visited the 25,000 Nigerian workers who had left Guinea's forced labour camps in 1976 in their refugee camp near Owerri, Nigeria, and stated that Nigeria's labour agreements with Equatorial Guinea had been abrogated.

President Macías asserted in an interview that intellectuals were the problem of Africa. Dissident Equatorial Guinea intellectuals in exile, including the former health minister, Pedro Ekong, formed a united opposition and in July announced from Barcelona the establishment of the Organización Nacional de la Oposición de Guinea Ecuatorial en el Exilio.   (MOLLY MORTIMER)

Equestrian Sports

Thoroughbred Racing and Steeplechasing. UNITED STATES AND CANADA. Seattle Slew, the only undefeated winner of the Triple Crown (Kentucky Derby, Preakness, and Belmont), was voted horse of the year in 1977 to end Forego's three-year domination of that honour. Forego thus lost the opportunity of matching the feat of money-winning champion Kelso, which had been acclaimed horse of the year five consecutive times (1960–64), and also of surpassing Kelso in earnings.

Forego's campaign was shortened for the third consecutive year because of physical problems, but nonetheless he won six stakes under heavy weight assignments and came within $53,940 of passing Kelso's world record total of $1,977,896. The huge seven-year-old gelding, owned by the Lazy F Ranch, scored his most important victory in the Woodward Stakes while carrying 133 lb. Under 138 lb he lost the Suburban by a neck to Quiet Little Table (114 lb). Forego was expected to race again in 1978.

Seattle Slew, champion two-year-old colt of 1976, dominated the three-year-old division by winning the first six starts for his owners, Mickey and Karen Taylor and Jim and Sally Hill. He then suffered a shocking defeat, the only one of his career, in the $200,000 Swaps at Hollywood Park on July 3, his final start of the season. He finished fourth, beaten by 16 lengths as J. O. Tobin won easily. Seattle Slew was to be raced in 1978 but with a new trainer, Billy Turner and the colt's owners having parted.

Seattle Slew began his campaign by winning a seven-furlong allowance race at Hialeah Park by nine lengths and lowering the record for the distance by 0.4 sec to 1 min 20.6 sec. A free-running colt, he then scored front-running victories in the Flamingo and Wood Memorial before launching his assault on the Triple Crown.

The Kentucky Derby provided Seattle Slew with his most difficult race to date. He broke from the gate poorly, was squeezed back to last, and seemed in a hopeless position behind a wall of horses. Within a quarter of a mile, however, he had shouldered his way between rivals and was head-to-head with pacesetting For the Moment. They were still together at the top of the long Churchill

Downs stretch, and then Seattle Slew drew away to win handily. In the Preakness Seattle Slew engaged in a speed duel with Cormorant and again surged to victory in the stretch. The champion had his easiest race in the 1½-mi Belmont Stakes, taking the lead early and winning by four lengths.

Seattle Slew was voted the outstanding horse in the three-year-old colt division. Other award winners were Harbor View Farm's Affirmed in the two-year-old colt or gelding classification; Randolph Weinsier's Lakeville Miss, two-year-old filly; Calumet Farm's Our Mims, three-year-old filly; B. J. Ridder's Cascapedia, older filly or mare; Forego, older colt or gelding; Dana S. Bray, Jr.'s Johnny D., turf; Mrs. B. R. Firestone's What a Summer, sprinting; and Augustin Stables' Cafe Prince, steeplechasing.

The two-year-old division was highlighted by the rivalry between Affirmed and Calumet Farm's Alydar. The climactic race was the Laurel Futurity, in which Affirmed defeated his adversary by a neck to gain a four-to-two margin for the season.

Steve Cauthen (*see* BIOGRAPHY), 17-year-old native of Walton, Ky., had an astonishing season in his first full year as a jockey. He became the first rider to win awards as best apprentice and best journeyman in the same season. Despite missing one month because of injury he was first in the two most important riding categories: number of winners (487) and money earned by his mounts ($6,151,750). It was the first time a jockey's purse earnings had totaled more than $6 million in a single season. Cauthen was the regular rider for Affirmed and Johnny D. Other award winners were Max Gluck, owner; Lazaro Barrera, trainer (for the second consecutive year); and Edward Plunket Taylor, breeder.

In Canada, Sound Reason won the Queen's Plate, the first leg of the Triple Crown for three-year-olds. Dance In Time won the other two, the Prince of Wales Stakes and the Breeders' Stakes. Exceller triumphed in the Canadian International, and Northernette won the Canadian Oaks for three-year-old fillies.   (JOSEPH C. AGRELLA)

EUROPE AND AUSTRALIA. In 1976–77 followers of National Hunt racing in Britain saw Red Rum, owned by N. Le Mare, trained by D. McCain, and ridden by T. Stack, win the Grand National Steeplechase, from Churchtown Boy and Eyecatcher, for the third time. Red Rum became the first horse to achieve such a feat (on the other two of his five appearances he had been second), and he was also the first jumper to earn more than £100,000. The hurdler Night Nurse, owned by R. Spencer, trained by M. H. Easterby, and ridden by P. Broderick, bravely fought his way to victory over Monksfield and Dramatist in the Champion Hurdle. Also run in bad conditions, the Cheltenham Gold Cup was won by Davy Lad, owned by Mrs. J. McGowan, trained by M. O'Toole, and ridden by D. T. Hughes, from Tied Cottage and Summerville; all the favourites fell or were pulled up and one of the best of them, Lanzerote, had to be destroyed.

Wet weather caused the cancellation of more than 100 National Hunt meetings. Cancello won the Mackeson Gold Cup Steeplechase, and Zeta's

Son the Hennessey Gold Cup Steeplechase. The King George VI Steeplechase was won by Royal Marshal II; the Schweppes Gold Trophy Hurdle by True Lad; and the Whitbread Gold Cup Steeplechase by Andy Pandy. T. Stack was National Hunt champion jockey. In France the Grand Steeplechase de Paris, at Auteuil, was won by Corps-à-Corps; two horses had to be destroyed, one of them, Air Landais, had won the race in 1975.

The most powerful flat-racing empire of 1977 was that of the Irish trainer M. V. O'Brien, his principal owner, millionaire football-pools promoter Robert Sangster, and leading jockey, Lester Piggott (*see* BIOGRAPHY). Their three-year-old colt The Minstrel, after finishing third and second in the English and Irish Two Thousand Guineas, respectively, then won the Derby from Hot Grove in a driving finish, and afterward never looked back. But his racing career ended abruptly when he and several other horses were retired to stud in the U.S. hastily, in order to beat a ban on the importation of British Isles and French bloodstock imposed by the U.S. from September 16. The cause of the ban was an outbreak of contagious metritis, a genital infection that rendered infertile mares sent to infected stallions; it was first noticed in Ireland and England. The National Stud in Britain was closed on May 11, about two months before the end of the breeding season. Yet the Newmarket Houghton sales in October realized a record £7 million, an average of more than £14,000 a lot. The Minstrel was syndicated for a staggering $9 million and Blushing Groom for $6.4 million.

Because of The Minstrel's retirement, Alleged represented Sangster and O'Brien in the Prix de l'Arc de Triomphe at Longchamps, Paris. Winner of the Great Voltigeur Stakes, Alleged had been outstayed in the St. Leger by Queen Elizabeth II's Oaks winner, the filly Dunfermline, but he ran

Seattle Slew romps home to victory in the Belmont Stakes to win racing's coveted Triple Crown.

UPI COMPIX

Jumping into history was Red Rum who cleared the final hurdle to win his third Grand National victory at Aintree, England.

away with the Arc, chased home by Balmerino from New Zealand with Crystal Palace third. Among the stable's other important winners was the English season's best two-year-old, the unbeaten colt Try My Best, winner of Newmarket's Dewhurst Stakes.

Sagaro, Europe's best distance horse, won the Ascot Gold Cup for the third time and was the first horse to do so. The best of the middle-distance horses was Exceller, and of English three-year-olds, North Stoke. Lady Beaverbrook's consistent, top-class, seven-year-old miler Boldboy ended his career in glory by winning the Vernon's Sprint Cup, amassing more stakes money than any English gelding before him, £89,509. Of the sprinters, Gentilhombre won Newmarket's July Cup, Ascot's Diadem Stakes, and Longchamp's Prix de l'Abbaye, and Haveroid the William Hill Sprint Championship. Grey Baron won the Goodwood Cup and the Jockey Club Cup.

Among the two-year-olds, besides Try My Best, Super Concorde (winner of the Prix Morny and Grand Criterium) was outstanding in France; and the best in England were Formidable (Mill Reef Stakes, Middle Park Stakes) and the filly Cherry Hinton. Patrick Eddery was champion jockey for the fourth successive year, and O'Brien the leading trainer (£439,124). Roger Poincelet (see OBITUARIES), for many years France's leading jockey, died on November 1, aged 57.

In March representatives of 16 countries agreed on antidoping procedures at the International Conference on Doping, in Rome; later the English Jockey Club announced its new rules against doping.

In Australia the A$156,000 Melbourne Cup, run over 3,200 m, was won by the favourite, Gold and Black, trained by Australia's leading trainer Bart Cummings (his record sixth win in the race), from Reckless and the New Zealand horse Hyperno.

(R. M. GOODWIN)

Harness Racing. In the U.S. in 1977 pacer Governor Skipper captured the Little Brown Jug. Say Hello won the first heat of the $100,000 Fox Stake, while Spicy Charley won the second. All previous attendance figures and wagering figures were eclipsed by the Meadowlands Raceway in New Jersey. Meadowlands in 1977 staged the biggest race in Standardbred or Thoroughbred history with its $425,000 event for three-year-old pacers in July, in which the final went to Escort from Nat Lobell and Crash. Meadowlands also staged a $280,000 race for two-year-old pacers, won by No No Yankee. The $200,000 Roosevelt International Trot was won by the Italian entry Delfo from Bellino II of France and Dapper Dillon of Canada. Green Speed won the Hambletonian in the record time of 1 min 55.6 sec, but the U.S. trotting championship winner was Cash Minbar.

The New Zealand Cup was won by Sole Command, and the Auckland Cup went to Bolton Byrd. Sapling won the New Zealand Great Northern Derby. In Australia, New Zealand's Stanley Rio journeyed to Brisbane to win the Inter Dominion championship. The Craven Filter Miracle Mile went to the West Australian pacer Royal Force, and the Perth Cup was won by Pure Steel, which also won Melbourne's Hunter Cup. Rip Van Winkle won the New South Wales Pacers Derby, and Sammy Karamea took the Victorian Pacers Derby.

In Finland the fine trotting mare Charme Asserdal won the final of the Rihimeke Grand Prix. Express Pride rated 1 min 59.1 sec over 1,600 m in a great win at the Mikkeli track. Imported U.S. trotters dominated big feature races in Finland. The Danish Derby was won by Vixi Bird. Top Danish-bred filly Berthe's Pride and filly Betina Hadvang were both winners in fast times. The Danish Grand Prix was won by Osiris Salar; the Nordic championship went to Duke Iran; and the Danish Criterium to Asius C. The Swedish Derby was won by Express Gaxe.

In Rome an unusual match race was staged between Delfo and Cash Minbar. Delfo won both mile heats, by half a length and a length, respectively. Wayne Eden, winner of the Lottery Stakes, also won the Premio Locatelli. In the Campionato Europeo final Cash Minbar broke, and victory went to Last Hurrah.

In West Germany a "Fillies Derby" of $20,000 was won by Kenwood Lady Day, while the top two-year-old trot resulted in a win for the highly rated Skipper. Melodrama won the $40,000 Great Prize at Daglfing. Kenwood Lady Day also proved her class in winning the $42,000 Biddenbrook Stake in West Berlin. Unbeaten German three-year-old Corner, with ten wins in as many starts, by September had earned over $150,000.

The 1977 Prix d'Amérique in Paris was won for the third time by Bellino II, the $116,129 first prize bringing his lifetime earnings past $1,710,000. At the Vincennes, Paris, track the $70,000 European Invitational marked the final appearance in France of Bellino II, who was retired at the end of his tenth year. He made a gallant effort, only to be beaten by a nose by Fakir de Vivier. At The Hague Bellino II had shown he was still a great trotter by winning the $60,000 Netherlands Grand Prix.

The Soviet Union produced a fast trotter in Gladiolus and recorded 177 performers in under 2 min 10 sec. Most of the speedy times were credited to U.S.-imported sires. In Britain the 1977 Kendal Derby was won by the Scottish-bred filly Barn Beauty.

The world drivers' championship held in Europe was won by Ulf Thoresen (Norway) with Peter Wolfenden (New Zealand) second and Dieter Marz (Austria) third.   (NOEL SIMPSON)

Show Jumping. Johan Heins won the individual show jumping championship of Europe in Vienna in June 1977, riding the British-bred horse Severn Valley. Eddie Macken from Ireland was second by 0.1 sec; Anton Ebben placed third; and David Broome shared fourth place with Marc Roguet of France. Heins was also a member of the winning team from The Netherlands, which included Ebben (on Jumbo Design), Henk Nooren (Pluco), and Harry Wouters (Salerno). The British team finished second by 20.25 faults to 20, the fractional margin being a time fault. The British riders included David Broome (Philco), Harvey Smith (Olympic Star), Derek Ricketts (Hydrophane Coldstream), and Deborah Johnsey (Moxy). West Germany was third with 36 points.

At Burghley in Lincolnshire the U.K. won the European Three-Day Event championship. Lucinda Prior-Palmer retained the individual title with George. The British team consisted of Prior-Palmer (George), Jane Holderness-Roddam (Warrior), Clarissa Strachan (Merry Sovereign), and Christopher Collins (Smoky VI). The winning score was 151.25 penalty points; West Germany finished second and Ireland third. The individual silver medal was won by Karl Schultz of West Germany with Madrigal; the individual bronze went to Horst Karsten of West Germany with Sioux.

(PAMELA MACGREGOR-MORRIS)

Polo. The richly endowed Gould World Cup attracted six of the best teams in the North American continent, except Cotonel Suarez. It was played in September at the Oak Brook (Ill.) Polo Club. In the final match Chapaleufu from Argentina, represented by J. J. Alberdi (handicap 8), A. Heguy (10), G. Tanoira (10), and A. Harriott (10), beat Texas—C. Smith (7), T. Wayman (9), R. Armour (8), J. Batty (9)—by 10 goals to 7.

Early in the year an English team—A. Kent (4), H. Hipwood (8), P. Withers (7), and J. Horswell (5)—played a series of test matches in Australia. In the final England won by 7 goals to 3 against Australia—R. Marle-Brown (5), R. Walker (7), J. McGinley (6), and J. Gunn (5).

In three test matches between Peru and South Africa, the latter won the first 12–9, but Peru won the second and third by 11–9 on each occasion. M. Rizon-Petron (4), J. Pena (7), M. Pena (7), and F. Reusche (7) represented Peru, and J. Watson (6), A. Williamson (5), D. McDonald (5), and P. Potgieter (5) were the South African players. In the annual international match for the Coronation Cup, South America—L. Sosa Basualdo (6), G. Pierez (7), E. Moore (9), H. Crotto (6)—won 7–6 over England—A. Kent (4), S. Hill (8), H. Hipwood (8), P. Churchward (5).

(ANDREW HORSBRUGH-PORTER)

Major Thoroughbred Race Winners, 1977

Race	Won by	Jockey	Owner
United States			
Acorn	Bring Out The Band	D. Brumfield	Hickory Tree Stable
Alabama	Our Mims	J. Velasquez	Calumet Farm
Amory L. Haskell	Majestic Light	S. Hawley	O. M. Phipps
Arlington-Washington Futurity	Sauce Boat	S. Cauthen	J. M. Schiff
Beldame	Cum Laude Laurie	A. Cordero Jr.	D. M. Galbreath
Belmont	Seattle Slew	J. Cruguet	Wooden Horse Investments
Blue Grass	For the Moment	A. Cordero Jr.	Gerald Robins
Brooklyn	Great Contractor	A. Cordero Jr.	H. P. Wilson
Californian	Crystal Water	L. Pincay Jr.	Connie M. Ring
Champagne	Alydar	J. Velasquez	Calumet Farm
Coaching Club American Oaks	Our Mims	J. Velasquez	Calumet Farm
Delaware	Our Mims	J. Velasquez	Calumet Farm
Delaware Oaks	Cum Laude Laurie	J. Velasquez	D. M. Galbreath
Fall Highweight	What A Summer	J. Vasquez	Mrs. B. R. Firestone
Flamingo	Seattle Slew	J. Cruguet	Wooden Horse Investments
Florida Derby (two divisions)	Coined Silver	B. Thornburg	C. V. Whitney
	Ruthie's Native	C. Perret	Ruth A. Perlmutter
Frizette	Lakeville Miss	R. Hernandez	Randolph Weinsier
Futurity	Affirmed	S. Cauthen	Harbor View Farm
Gulfstream Park	Strike Me Lucky	J. D. Bailey	Maribel G. Blum
Hawthorne Gold Cup	On the Sly	G. McCarron	Balmak Stables
Hollywood Derby	Steve's Friend	R. Hernandez	Kinship Stable
Hollywood Gold Cup	Crystal Water	L. Pincay Jr.	Connie M. Ring
Hollywood Invitational	Vigors	J. Lambert	W. R. Hawn
Hollywood Oaks	Glenaris	W. Shoemaker	Mrs. A. W. Stollery
Hopeful	Affirmed	S. Cauthen	Harbor View Farm
Jockey Club Gold Cup	On the Sly	G. McCarron	Balmak Stables
Kentucky Derby	Seattle Slew	J. Cruguet	Wooden Horse Investments
Kentucky Oaks	Sweet Alliance	C. J. McCarron	Windfields Farm
Ladies	Sensational	M. Venezia	Mill House
Laurel Futurity	Affirmed	S. Cauthen	Harbor View Farm
Man o'War	Majestic Light	S. Hawley	O. M. Phipps
Marlboro	Proud Birdie	J. Vasquez	Marablue Farm
Matchmaker	Mississippi Mud	J. Tejeira	Mrs. B. Sharp
Matron	Lakeville Miss	R. Hernandez	Randolph Weinsier
Metropolitan	Forego	W. Shoemaker	Lazy F Ranch
Monmouth Invitational	Affiliate	M. A. Rivera	Harbor View Farm
Monmouth Oaks	Small Raja	M. Solomone	D. P. Reynolds
Mother Goose	Road Princess	J. Cruguet	Elmendorf
Norfolk	Balzac	W. Shoemaker	Mrs. H. B. Keck
Oak Tree Invitational	Crystal Water	W. Shoemaker	Connie M. Ring
Preakness	Seattle Slew	J. Cruguet	Wooden Horse Investments
Ruffian	Cum Laude Laurie	A. Cordero Jr.	D. M. Galbreath
Santa Anita Derby	Habitony	W. Shoemaker	A. W. Pejsa
Santa Anita Handicap	Crystal Water	L. Pincay Jr.	Connie M. Ring
Sapling	Alydar	E. Maple	Calumet Farm
Solima	Lakeville Miss	R. Hernandez	Randolph Weinsier
Sorority	Stub	R. Turcotte	Marcia W. Schott
Spinaway	Sherry Peppers	A. Cordero Jr.	T. B. Martin
Spinster	Cum Laude Laurie	A. Cordero Jr.	D. M. Galbreath
Suburban	Quiet Little Table	E. Maple	Meadowhill
Sunset	Today 'n Tomorrow	W. Shoemaker	Connie M. Ring
Swaps	J. O. Tobin	W. Shoemaker	G. A. Pope Jr.
Travers	Jatski	S. Maple	W. H. Murray
Turf Classic	Johnny D.	S. Cauthen	Dana S. Bray Jr.
United Nations	Bemo	D. Brumfield	Hickory Tree Stable
Vanity	Cascapedia	S. Hawley	B. J. Ridder
Vosburgh	Affiliate	C. Perret	Harbor View Farm
Washington (D.C.) International	Johnny D.	S. Cauthen	Dana S. Bray Jr.
Widener	Yamanin	G. Patterson	Hajime Doi
Wood Memorial	Seattle Slew	J. Cruguet	Wooden Horse Investments
Woodward	Forego	W. Shoemaker	Lazy F Ranch
England			
Two Thousand Guineas	Nebbiolo	G. Curran	N. Schibbye
One Thousand Guineas	Mrs. McArdy	E. Hide	Mrs. E. Kettlewell
Derby	The Minstrel	L. Piggott	R. Sangster
Oaks	Dunfermline	W. Carson	Queen Elizabeth II
St. Leger	Dunfermline	W. Carson	Queen Elizabeth II
Coronation Cup	Exceller	G. Dubroeucq	N. B. Hunt
Ascot Gold Cup	Sagaro	L. Piggott	G. Oldham
Eclipse Stakes	Artaius	L. Piggott	Mrs. G. Getty II
King George VI and Queen Elizabeth Diamond Stakes	The Minstrel	L. Piggott	R. Sangster
Sussex Stakes	Artaius	L. Piggott	Mrs. G. Getty II
Benson & Hedges Gold Cup	Relkino	W. Carson	Lady Beaverbrook
Champion Stakes	Flying Water	Y. Saint-Martin	D. Wildenstein
France			
Poule d'Essai des Poulains	Blushing Groom	H. Samani	Aga Khan
Poule d'Essai des Pouliches	Madelia	Y. Saint-Martin	D. Wildenstein
Prix du Jockey Club	Crystal Palace	G. Dubroeucq	Baron G. de Rothschild
Prix de Diane	Madelia	Y. Saint-Martin	D. Wildenstein
Prix Royal Oak	Rex Magna	P. Pacquet	Mme J. Couturie
Prix Ganay	Arctic Tern	M. Philipperon	Mrs. J. S. Knight
Prix Lupin	Pharly	M. Philipperon	A. Blasco
Prix du Cadran	Buckskin	Y. Saint-Martin	D. Wildenstein
Grand Prix de Paris	Funny Hobby	P. Pacquet	Mme T. J. Caralli
Grand Prix de Saint-Cloud	Exceller	F. Head	N. B. Hunt
Prix Vermeille	Kamicia	A. Badel	Mme H. Rabatal
Prix de l'Arc de Triomphe	Alleged	L. Piggott	R. Sangster
Ireland			
Irish One Thousand Guineas	Lady Capulet	T. Murphy	R. Sangster
Irish Two Thousand Guineas	Pampapaul	G. Dettori	H. Paul
Irish Guinness Oaks	Olwyn	J. Lynch	S. Vanian and P. J. Stokes
Irish Sweeps Derby	The Minstrel	L. Piggott	R. Sangster
Irish St. Leger	Transworld	T. Murphy	S. Fraser
Italy			
Derby Italiano del Galoppo	Sirlad	T. Di Nardo	Razza La Tesa
Gran Premio del Jockey Club	Stateff	S. Atzoni	Lady "M" Stable
West Germany			
Grosser Preis von Baden Baden	Windwurf	G. Lewis	Gestüt Ravensburg
Grosser Preis von Berlin	Windwurf	G. Lewis	Gestüt Ravensburg
Grosser Preis von Düsseldorf	Windwurf	G. Lewis	Gestüt Ravensburg
Grosser Preis von Europa	Ebano	R. Suerland	Gestüt Fährhof

Ethiopia

Ethiopia

A socialist state in northeastern Africa, Ethiopia is bordered by Somalia, Djibouti, Kenya, the Sudan, and the Red Sea. Area: 1,221,900 sq km (471,800 sq mi). Pop. (1977 est.): 28,556,400. Cap. and largest city: Addis Ababa (pop., 1977 est., 1,327,200). Language: Amharic (official) and other tongues. Religion: Ethiopian Orthodox (Coptic) and Muslim, with various animist minorities. Heads of state and chairmen of the Provisional Military Administrative Council in 1977, Brig. Gen. Teferi Benti to February 3 and, from February 11, Lieut. Col. Mengistu Haile Mariam.

Sept. 12, 1977, marked the third anniversary of the overthrow of the monarchy and the establishment of the Provisional Military Administrative Council (PMAC), otherwise known as the Dirgue. In his anniversary speech, the PMAC chairman, Lieut. Col. Mengistu Haile Mariam (*see* BIOGRAPHY), claimed progress toward implementation of the Dirgue's basic program for a socialist economy and society. He cited the formation of an All-Ethiopia Trade Union, which replaced the Council of Ethiopian Trade Unions in January 1977, and the formation of an All-Ethiopian Farmers' Association. But despite these claims, 1977 was more notable for the intensification of the political struggle.

Early in the year, the PMAC proclaimed the need to move from "the defensive to the offensive" in the fight against internal and external enemies, and in April the slogan "Motherland or Death" was issued by Mengistu in a radio broadcast. In part, these policies were a response to increased external pressures from secessionist groups in the Eritrean region, clashes along the Sudan border in the west, and growing problems in the southeast, which culminated in the open invasion of the Ogaden by Somalia, thinly disguised as support for the West Somalia Liberation Front (WSLF). But there was also strong internal opposition from dissenting underground Marxist groups, such as the Ethiopian People's Revolutionary Party (EPRP), and from dispossessed members of the old order, generally categorized as supporters of the opposition movements led by the Ethiopian Democratic Union (EDU), a refugee organization based in London, as well as dissension within the PMAC itself.

In January differences within the council over the Eritrean problem, the promotion of the National Democratic Revolution through formation of a national political party, and the relationship between the PMAC and its political arm, the Provisional Office for Mass Organizational Affairs (POMOA, controlled by a political group calling itself Me'isone, or the All-Ethiopian Socialist Movement), came to a head. On January 29 the then chairman of the PMAC, Brig. Gen. Teferi Benti, issued a call for unity in which, for the first time, EPRP was not mentioned as a major target. This was interpreted as a possible move within the PMAC to create a broader political front and move more rapidly toward civilian government, a main EPRP demand.

On February 3, after a shoot-out in the grounds of the old palace, Mengistu, then one of two PMAC vice-chairmen, declared that a counterrevolutionary plot had been uncovered and that "revolutionary justice" had been meted out to Teferi Benti and eight or so members of the Dirgue. On February 11 it was announced that Mengistu had been appointed PMAC chairman and head of state. Lieut. Col. Atnafu Abate remained as vice-chairman, various other posts were reshuffled, and a new structure for the Dirgue was announced. Mengistu and his supporters within the Dirgue succeeded in gaining support for a hard line in internal politics and in the prosecution of the war in Eritrea. No concessions were to be made to the Eritreans outside the 1976 Nine-Point Declaration, which offered some degree of regional autonomy.

This was the signal for a more aggressive internal policy. During March and April, Addis Ababa was torn by bloody strife between government forces and dissidents headed by EPRP supporters. A house-to-house search in the capital in March resulted in many deaths and arrests. Meanwhile, the opposition continued its campaign of assassinating government officials, particularly officials of the Urban Dwellers' Associations (*kebeles*) in Addis Ababa and other urban centres, and of killing leaders of workers' organizations. Government retaliation was severe. In early May, following street demonstrations mainly carried on by young people and students, it was reported that at least 300 EPRP supporters had been killed and large

ETHIOPIA

Education. Primary (1974–75), pupils 959,272, teachers (1973–74) 18,646; secondary (1973–74), pupils 182,263, teachers 6,181; vocational (1973–74), pupils 5,533, teachers 554; teacher training (1973–74), students 3,126, teachers 194; higher (1973–74), students 6,474, teaching staff 434.

Finance. Monetary unit: birr, with (Sept. 19, 1977) a par value of 2.07 birr to U.S. $1 (free rate of 3.61 birr = £1 sterling). Gold, SDR's, and foreign exchange (June 1977) U.S. $310.4 million. Budget (1975–76 est.): revenue 1,175,-000,000 birr; expenditure 1,331,000,000 birr. Money supply (April 1977) 996.7 million birr. Cost of living (Addis Ababa; 1970 = 100; June 1977) 172.

Foreign Trade. (1976) Imports 729.5 million birr; exports 580.6 million birr. Import sources (1975): Saudi Arabia 15%; Japan 12%; Italy 11%; West Germany 10%; U.K. 8%; U.S. 8%; France 5%. Export destinations (1975): U.S. 20%; Saudi Arabia 14%; Djibouti 10%; Egypt 9%; Japan 9%; West Germany 8%; Italy 5%. Main exports: coffee 56%; beans 10%; hides and skins 10%; oilseeds 5%.

Transport and Communications. Roads (1973) 23,000 km. Motor vehicles in use (1974): passenger 43,380; commercial (including buses) 12,000. Railways (1975): 988 km; traffic (including Djibouti traffic of Djibouti-Addis Ababa line; excluding Eritrea) 108 million passenger-km, freight 244 million net ton-km. Air traffic (1976): 523 million passenger-km; freight 20.2 million net ton-km. Telephones (Jan. 1976) 68,900. Radio receivers (Dec. 1974) 200,000. Television receivers (Dec. 1974) 20,000.

Agriculture. Production (in 000; metric tons; 1976): barley *c.* 800; wheat 694; corn *c.* 1,200; millet 329; sorghum 863; yams (1975) *c.* 270; potatoes *c.* 175; sugar, raw value 159; linseed *c.* 50; sesame seed *c.* 60; chick-peas 109; dry peas *c.* 52; dry broad beans (1975) *c.* 124; lentils (1975) *c.* 80; coffee *c.* 170; cotton *c.* 20. Livestock (in 000; 1976): cattle 25,963; sheep 23,065; goats 17,064; horses (1975) *c.* 1,500; mules (1975) *c.* 1,460; asses (1975) *c.* 4,000; camels (1975) *c.* 1,010; poultry *c.* 51,300.

Industry. Production (in 000; metric tons; 1975): cement 117; petroleum products *c.* 585; cotton yarn (1972–73) 11.7; cotton fabrics (sq m; 1972–73) 82,000; electricity (kw-hr) *c.* 660,000.

numbers had been arrested. These activities continued through a second widespread urban search campaign in May, in which it was claimed that large quantities of arms and ammunition had been seized, to a third, more selective, search in October of *kebele* areas that were thought to be centres of EPRP activity. Meanwhile, arms were issued to members of peasant associations, who were instructed to conduct "search and destroy" operations against dissident elements in the countryside, to factory workers, who were encouraged to take direct action against management, and to the *kebeles* which, in addition to taking over many normal security duties from the police, were involved in the search campaigns.

During April and May the government also began to organize the population against external threat. U.S. military missions in Ethiopia were closed down on April 23, and on May 28 the defense attachés of the U.S., Great Britain, and Egypt were expelled. On June 25 the first contingent of the People's Militia (recruited during May, largely from the southern provinces, and trained at a special camp northwest of Addis Ababa) paraded in the capital. Recruitment later included factory workers, civil servants, and *kebele* guards, and training was reported to have been assisted by Cuban advisers. A second Army/Militia parade was held in Addis Ababa in June, when the slogan "Red Campaign to Crush White Terror" was prominent. The People's Militia was deployed on both the northern and eastern fronts to bolster the much-extended regular Army. General mobilization was ordered on August 20.

On the war fronts, Somali forces, aided by their guerrillas in association with groups in the WSLF, had advanced by October to positions that menaced the old city of Harer but had not succeeded in neutralizing the key airstrip in Dire Dawa. Activity by dissident and Somali-backed groups had been reported for some time from the Hararghe, Bale, and Sidamo regions, but the military offensive itself began on July 23, moving from the south toward Kebre Dehar and Gode and from the east toward Jijiga and Dire Dawa. Gode and Jijiga were captured before the end of September. On August 2 the Ethiopian government brought its case to the Good Offices Committee of the Organization of African Unity in Libreville, Gabon, where the principle of the inviolability of African frontiers was reaffirmed. Diplomatic relations with Somalia were severed on September 7.

In the north the Eritrean Liberation Front and the Eritrean Popular Liberation Front controlled the bulk of Eritrea, with the major exception of Asmara. Earlier in the year, however, Ethiopian forces managed to regain control of positions along the Sudan border, including the larger settlements of Metmma and Humera, previously occupied by units of the EDU. In the east, supply lines from Assab and Djibouti were kept open despite sabotage to roads and rail lines and attacks on convoys.

Some indication of the continuing political differences within the government was given in April, when an Addis Ababa *kebele* chairman and his committee were executed for excessive zeal in arresting, torturing, and killing counterrevolu-

JEAN-PIERRE REY—SIPA PRESS/BLACK STAR

Eritrean Liberation Front troops practiced maneuvers before battling Ethiopian forces. The ELF was attempting to set up an independent Eritrean state.

tionaries. In August differences within the Dirgue on strategies for arming the popular organizations erupted in a political crisis, in which the reputedly hard-line leaders of Me'isone and the POMOA were eliminated. The most prominent personality in Me'isone, Haile Fida, was reported to be under arrest, and others went underground. The government declared, however, that the true Me'isone had not been repressed. It indicated a move toward a Marxist-Leninist party incorporating some five groups, among them Seded (Revolutionary Flame), strongly supported by the Army and now, it was rumoured, by Mengistu. After the August crisis, the POMOA was reorganized. A Central Revolutionary Operations Command with a National Operations Council under Mengistu was set up (August 26) and given absolute powers to coordinate the war effort with measures against antirevolutionaries. New government appointments were announced on September 9. In mid-November the Ethiopian press agency reported that Atnafu had been subjected to a "revolutionary measure," presumably execution.

The alignment of Ethiopia with the socialist world resulted in continued close relations with the U.S.S.R. Apparently abandoning their association with Somalia, the Soviets took over from the U.S. the task of supplying military equipment to Ethiopia. This was done partly through Eastern European associates, among whom East Germany was prominent. Mengistu headed a delegation to the U.S.S.R. in May. Earlier, in March, the Cuban president, Fidel Castro, had paid a three-day visit to Addis Ababa, after which Cuban assistance was reportedly extended beyond medical aid.

At the same time, some Western aid continued to reach Ethiopia in the form of support from the European Economic Community and for rural water projects. A 30 million birr agreement providing for the continuation of existing aid projects was concluded with the Swedish International Development Authority. Foreign balances and currency exchange rates remained virtually unchanged, but the cost of living increased, particularly in the towns. The price of basic commodities, such as grain, rose twofold; such goods as sugar, tea, and matches were rationed through the urban *kebeles*; and gasoline rationing became more strict. Although continued crop failures and food shortages caused by natural factors were reported from some areas, the overall indication was that total grain production had risen since the Land Reform Proclamation, and price increases appeared to be associated with lack of control over marketing and distribution. Income from coffee, the major export, was at a record level, and a large 1977 harvest was expected.

See also Somalia.

European Unity

Far-reaching questions dominated political and economic developments in Europe during 1977. Among them were the following: Could the European Economic Community (EEC) increase in size and still hope to achieve greater internal union? How could the economic divisions between the stronger and weaker economies within its common market be overcome? What should be the relations between the EEC and other Western European countries that were members of the European Free Trade Association (EFTA), as well as between the EEC and wider European bodies such as the Council of Europe? And what should be the links with the member states of the Council for Mutual Economic Assistance (CMEA; Comecon), the association of Eastern European Communist countries and the Soviet Union?

Few answers to these questions were forthcoming, but there was a growing realization that unless ways could be found to increase the cohesion of the European Community, its very existence could be called into question. The goal of political and economic integration—of a United Europe—seemed further off than ever. There were those who advocated a new, looser, more pragmatic association of the member states of the EEC as the best way to keep the Common Market in being. In some member states—notably Great Britain—there was a revival of opposition to the whole notion of membership.

Applications for Membership. During the year two new countries formally submitted applications to become full member states: Portugal on March 28 and Spain on July 28. This brought to three the number of candidate members. The Greek government had submitted Greece's membership bid in 1975, and formal negotiations with the European Commission in Brussels had begun in July 1976. They continued through 1977 amid growing debate about the implications of expanding the Community's membership from 9 to 12. There were fears about the ability of the Community to integrate three relatively poor southern European countries at a time of acute economic austerity. There was apprehension that enlargement would lead to the "political dilution" of the Community. And there were those who questioned whether the decision-making institutions, designed for the six original member states and strained in seeking agreement among the existing nine, could cope with further additions.

Suggestions that the Community should negotiate collectively with the three aspirant members were rejected, but the Commission made it clear that in its negotiations with Greece it would "have to have regard" for the implications of future agreements with Portugal and Spain. This was taken to mean that the EEC would not offer any special concessions to one applicant state that might be taken as a precedent by the others. Meanwhile, the negotiations with Greece proceeded fitfully through the year. By the end of the summer, both sides said they were now ready to begin the final, substantial, phase of the talks, aiming at agreement on how long Greece would be given to conform with all Community conditions of membership. The government in Athens was still confident that Greece would be a full member by the end of 1979 and would be allowed a subsequent transition period of between five and seven years. On the Community side there was less certainty.

The French government began to raise a number of difficulties immediately concerned with the Greek application but relating to enlargement generally. The main problem had to do with agriculture, and at one point in June France appeared to be blocking progress in the Greek talks. In the end, the French veto was withdrawn on condition that, before there was any enlargement of the Community, there should be major changes in the current EEC common agricultural policy (CAP). This gave benefits to northern dairy farmers through purchase of their products at fixed prices, irrespective of the state of supply or demand in the market. The French and Italian governments feared that with Greece, then Portugal and Spain, inside the EEC, there would be a further flood of cheap Mediterranean fruit, vegetables, and wine into a market where there were already substantial surpluses. The Commission promised a major reform that would not, however, concentrate on the CAP only but would extend to regional, industrial, and social aid for the Mediterranean regions of France and Italy.

Having received the Portuguese application, the Commission undertook a preliminary investigation of the prospects and problems involved. The results were not expected to be sent to the EEC Council of Ministers until early 1978, and if the Council did decide to open formal negotiations, these were unlikely to get under way before 1979. In the fall the Council also discussed Spain's application, which caused the most apprehension. Apart from the problems raised by Spanish agriculture, many member countries were convinced that Spain would make inordinate claims on the EEC's meagre budget for regional, social, and industrial aid to the less well-off parts of the Community.

These fears were increased in July, when the Council refused a Commission proposal to increase the 1978 budget by about 20% and suggested a budget that barely kept pace with the rate of inflation in the EEC during the previous year. However, the Community did agree to increase its aid for Portugal. There was concern that Portugal's deteriorating economic position might topple the Socialist government of Mário Soares and plunge the

European Economic Community:
see Economy, World; European Unity

country back into political chaos, and Soares' resignation late in the year was viewed with considerable anxiety.

The Economy. Enlargement was only one of the critical issues that confronted the new Commission, which took office in Brussels in January. Its new president, Roy Jenkins, a former British Labour Cabinet minister, pledged to restore confidence in the goal of a united Europe. He was also anxious to restore the diminishing political authority of the Commission. In the view of the new Commission, the most immediate threat posed to the prospects for European union remained the grave economic crisis.

The Commission insisted on being represented at the summit conference of the seven most important Western industrial nations (including Japan) in London on May 7–8. However, at the insistence of Pres. Valéry Giscard d'Estaing of France, Jenkins was only allowed to attend those sessions dealing with subjects strictly in the competence of the EEC. At the subsequent EEC heads of government summit in London in June, Jenkins unfolded a Commission plan to give the Community much greater powers to borrow money to lend to the weaker regions and to industries in dire need of restructuring. The plan met with a chilly response.

In spite of a slight overall decline in the rate of inflation in the Community in 1977—to around 9% per annum—the gap between the strong and weak economies continued to grow. A problem common to all the nine—and to many other countries in Europe—was unemployment. Despite special measures taken by national governments, supported on occasion by aid from the Community itself, the number out of work rose to between 5 million and 6 million at year's end. There was increased pressure on both governments and the Commission to protect jobs through import controls. During the year the Commission negotiated with Japan and a number of other countries, urging them voluntarily to restrict their exports to Europe in sensitive areas, but this had only limited success. During the summer, measures to restrict certain categories of textile imports were introduced throughout the EEC; earlier, agreement was reached on a plan to fix output and minimum prices for the steel industry.

The year saw growing friction with the U.S., the Community's principal trade partner. The EEC was alarmed at signs that the U.S. was adopting protectionist policies, while the administration in Washington charged the EEC with maintaining an unduly protectionist agricultural policy. Following high-level talks between the Commission and U.S. Pres. Jimmy Carter's special trade representative, Robert Strauss, in July, it was agreed to put more urgency into preparation for the Tokyo round of the General Agreement on Tariffs and Trade (GATT) trade liberalization talks.

There were few questions of internal economic policy that found the Community member states united. There were deep divisions on the eventual introduction of a common internal fisheries policy, although the Community did conclude a number of reciprocal fishing agreements with other countries following the general move to 200-mi national

AFP/PICTORIAL PARADE

(Top) The new Palace of Europe which will provide facilities for the 410 members of the European Parliament in Strasbourg, France. (Bottom) The Parliament room in the new building.

fishing limits. The nine made repeated fruitless efforts to agree on a site for the Community thermonuclear fusion process, the Joint European Torus, or JET, and for a time the whole project appeared in danger of collapse. However, in October, the EEC finally voted to build the JET project in Culham, England. The nine remained committed to the development of nuclear energy, but the policy met with widespread apprehension and some violent opposition, notably in France and West Germany. In September the Commission began a public inquiry into nuclear power developments, with special reference to the possible dangers to human life and the environment, and to the risk of proliferation of nuclear technical knowledge directed toward military purposes. Britain, concerned with its own need to curb inflation, continued its opposition to raising the prices of farm products. In April it did agree to a 2.9% devaluation of the "green pound" (i.e., the fixed exchange rates of farm products) and was granted a butter subsidy of 8½ pence per pound, to be phased out after April 1978.

One landmark recorded in July 1977 was the achievement of full free trade between the countries of the EEC and those in EFTA. The EFTA secretariat expressed its eagerness to increase cooperation between the two organizations. This

In May British Prime Minister James Callaghan was host to a "Downing Street summit" meeting with leaders of the U.S., France, West Germany, Italy, Japan, and Canada.

was welcomed by the EEC member states, but the Commission underlined the difference between EFTA, as a mere trade association, and the EEC, which was committed to achieving more fundamental union.

Internal and Foreign Policies. In the view of the Commission and many EEC member governments, the prospects for greater European unity were improved when the nine committed themselves to "use their best endeavours" to be ready to hold the first elections to the European Assembly, or Parliament, by May or June 1978. Doubts persisted, however, especially in view of continued opposition to direct election within the British Labour Party and also from French Gaullist party leader Jacques Chirac. In the event, defeat of the British government's direct elections bill, over the issue of proportional representation, in December 1977, meant that the elections would almost certainly have to be put off until 1979.

In February the executive committee of Comecon approached the EEC to suggest discussion of a commercial and economic cooperation agreement. On June 25 the EEC agreed to talks, but only about possible specific areas of cooperation. Major stumbling blocks to any more ambitious agreement remained the refusal of the Eastern-bloc countries to recognize formally either the EEC or the Commission and the reluctance of the nine to acknowledge that Comecon was comparable to the EEC.

On January 27 the European Convention on the Repression of Terrorism was signed at Strasbourg by 17 member countries of the Council of Europe, but with reservations by France, Norway, Italy, and Portugal and refusals by Malta and Ireland. Definitions of political crimes and the question of individual appeals to the European Commission on Human Rights proved difficult, and the document lacked real force. In April the EEC foreign ministers stated that the Community would promote majority rule and nonracial government in southern Africa. In June the EEC deplored the violation of human rights in Uganda and supported establishment of a Palestinian homeland and the right of Palestinians to participate in Middle East negotiations.　　　　(JOHN PALMER)

See also Defense; Economy, World.
[534.F.3.b.iv; 971.D.7]

Fashion and Dress

The winter of 1976–77 was quite mild in Europe, and the muffled look—a matter of survival in much of the U.S.—was more a fad there than a necessity. Shawls and hoods, all part of the still-popular ethnic look, were enhanced by lavish braid trimming or bright embroidered bands and enriched by quality fabrics. Coats—soft, unlined, and devoid of structure or tailoring—were merely functional and no longer the pivot of an outfit.

The basic trend in Paris, London, and New York was the bloused overjacket or blouson. With low hip-level drawstring, the inflated blouson appeared in quilted nylon, in plain poplin with jersey shoulder yoke, or in heavy hand knit. Many had huge muff pockets at the centre front. Pegged pants with a raised waist and rounded hipline made an appearance, but it was the long-legged look that scored with the younger generation. Pants were worn skin tight all the way from waist to boot top, and long johns and leggings were paired with high-heeled boots and puffed blousons, suggesting the look of a bulb strutting around on stilts. For resort wear, low-blousing blousons in gauze, crepon, fishnet, and mosquito netting were paired with boxer shorts.

With spring everything turned soft and fluid. The town silhouette became slimmer. Tailored jackets in plain velvet replaced the blousons, and pants gave way to a variety of skirts: the flared culotte skirt, the flared wrap skirt with knotted self-belt, the knife-pleated skirt in floral printed silk, and—the favourite—the gypsy skirt. As three-tiered, gathered petticoat skirts undulated along city sidewalks, the streets seemed to be alive with gypsies and palm readers. In cool weather this skirt was worn with a soft blouse and a tailored jacket. In the height of summer it accompanied romantic tops with drawstring necklines and billowy sleeves caught in at the wrist, or sleeveless tops with a deep ruffle covering one shoulder and baring the other. Crinkled Indian cotton was the preferred plain material, with paisley- or floral-patterned challis favoured for the printed versions.

Espadrilles with wedge soles in cord were again laced up the leg. Sandals with spike heels were back, and clogs were out. High-heeled sandals accompanied the pajama look, consisting of a soft, open-necked shirt tucked into slim pants of matching poplin. Another version featured pants gently bloused at the ankles and a knee-length loose chemise, all in silk crepe. At a much talked about summer wedding in Paris, a number of guests, both men and women, appeared in identical white poplin pajamas straight from the Saint Laurent menswear boutique.

Very full dirndl skirts ending just above ankles, without tiers, were paired with loose chemises and smocks. Lace-trimmed camisoles and petticoats were all part of the summer's romantic mood and lingerie look, often emphasized by a snug-fitting corselet with open V-neckline and ruffle trimming. Rippling ruffles were everywhere, at neck

Jean Patou interpreted the blouson for evening in gold-flecked and paisley-swirled chiffon with a matching cape and a velvet skirt.

and hem and peeking in twos and threes from under skirt hems.

The summer "must" was the shawl. Large and fluid, often printed or in see-through material and fringed, it might be wrapped around the throat Spanish fashion, slung over one shoulder as a sari, draped around the hips like a loincloth, or just worn lying on the shoulders and knotted at the side. In the fall the floral-printed wool challis shawl added a newsy detail to tailored jackets and chemise dresses.

As always, seaside resorts had their individual trends. Deauville's, based on navy and white, featured heavy seagoing sweaters. Well-pressed jeans in navy with white stitching were paired with long, striped overshirts. Pants were white with patch pockets in front at the thigh; for evening the preferred styles were in lacquered crepe, worn very tight. Cannes regulars preferred the low-backed jumpsuit, puffed at the ankles, in cotton satin for day and big floral prints for evening. They loved the Indian cotton "French Connection" dresses, white eyelet tops, handkerchief points and high slits in skirts, and, of course, the gypsy skirt. Large fruit prints gave Cannes bermudas a tropical flavour.

At Saint-Tropez, bathing suits and shorts were micro-size but tops were voluminous. The "look" consisted of a huge inflated shirt or T-shirt, belted under the hips, balloon style, over bare legs. Three-tiered skirts, corselets, old-fashioned petticoats with embroidered hem ruffles, and camisoles discovered at thrift shops were put together with flair. Neutral or white fishnet provided the desired transparency for tops. Bobby socks were worn with both high heels and Mary Jane sandals.

For the beach, a G-string was the last stepping-stone before total exposure.

The London streets had their share of gypsy skirts, often in hand-blocked Indian cottons, but there they were worn with tweed hacking jackets and waistcoats. On sunny days very loose separates—camisole or peasant top over gathered skirt—reflected the Paris picture. In London there was also much peasant prettiness, with guipure lace insets on cotton T-shirts and eyelet hem ruffles. More sporty were the big tops with a tweedy look. Some of the blousons were so inflated that they turned into mini-tunics, needing only matching socks over tights to complete the outfit.

The British sporting style and country classics in herringbone or dogtooth woolens crossed the Channel in the fall to be snatched up by Parisiennes. Hacking jackets in tweed appeared over fully gathered dirndl skirts, sometimes with matching waistcoat, occasionally with the flat tweed cap Londoners fancied. The tailored velvet jacket was carried over from spring, acquiring an autumn flavour with a deep brick colour that matched the falling leaves on the Champs Elysées. A counterpart to the tailored jacket was the loose, oversize blazer. The bulky proportions were attenuated by the softness of the woolen material but still allowed for the layered look of shirt plus waistcoat—or even a couple of sweaters—underneath. And there was still room for a huge floral print wool challis shawl to be slung over one shoulder.

The generous cut also applied to the full smocks worn over dirndl skirts and to the fluttering smock dresses with hem flounces, done in small figurative prints. A narrow ruffle edging the square shoulder yoke was repeated at the neck, cuffs, and hem, adding a Victorian flavour. Hemlines covered the calf, but the look was echoed by younger

Heavy ribbed tights and casual boots appeared in the Courrèges collection, worn with a lamb and lynx vest (left). A look popular both in the showrooms and on the streets (right) combined a soft pleated divided skirt and loose jacket, here in gray flannel by Jacques Estérel, with boots and a soft shawl.

FRED PERRY SPORTSWEAR

HEPWORTHS

The athletic influence in menswear was exemplified in the popular warm-up suit (left) worn for active sports and for leisure. The traditional British country look in tailored tweeds (right) was strong for both men and women.

women with a very full knee-length skirt. Roomy capes in soft mohair, angora jersey, or cashmere sported a ruffled tippet covering the shoulders, suggesting a Venetian masquerade.

Cosmetics and Hair Styles. Through the summer hair styles were in keeping with the gypsy look, uncombed, frizzy, kinky. Bows, slides, and combs in acid colours served as trimmings. For evening, hair was disciplined into ponytails or loose chignons and sprinkled with flowers. In the fall there was a switch toward a more boyish cut, freeing the neck and establishing better proportions with the voluminous new clothes.

Protective creams, which acted as filters for straining the sun's rays, were more in demand than oils for sun exposure. Helena Rubinstein's "Sun Treatment" provided a moisturizing protection for the face. Estée Lauder's "Ultra-Violet Screening Cream" allowed a slight tan.

Autumn makeup was tinged with russet and spice, like the clothes. Estée Lauder's "Spice Streaker" brush-on powder bestowed a golden patina, and "Silk Fashion Face Powder" from Helena Rubinstein boasted real silk particles to provide extra radiance. While lipsticks and nail polish continued to match in most cases, at Elizabeth Arden they were disconnected, with "Sultry Red" lipstick and "Mulberry Haze" nail polish.

(THELMA SWEETINBURGH)

Men's Fashions. In the course of 1977 Pres. Jimmy Carter of the U.S. and Prime Minister James Callaghan of the U.K. wore the first suits in a Huddersfield cloth, produced from 89% superfine 100's quality Merino wool and 11% cashmere, with their initials—"JC"—incorporated as a decorative stripe. For two of his new suits, Prince Charles chose gray patterns of a special Wain Shiell Silver Jubilee cloth in pure virgin wool. London's Savile Row made history by tailoring the first two-piece suits to cost over £500 ($870). But these

were the exceptions in a year of contrast and contradictions, when men's clothes generally had a lean look and a modest price in keeping with the economy.

The "lean and clean" look emerged at the spring menswear trade exhibitions in London, Paris, and Cologne, West Germany. The trend to economical elegance continued throughout the year and was confirmed at the autumn exhibitions in Cologne, Paris, Birmingham, England, and Florence, Italy. As designer Nino Cerruti noted: "Menswear is not searching for gimmicks . . . the styles are very simple." In Europe the simple Italian styles and the basic British-look suits were the leaders, with single-breasted styles more fashionable than double-breasted. Gray remained the best seller as a suiting shade, but more browns were introduced—warm, earth shades, often enhanced by lighter tones. Brown was also introduced for formal morning suits for the first time.

A strong military influence was seen in topcoats and raincoats. The sports jacket made a comeback in traditional tweeds such as Harris, Shetland, and Donegal; often it had suede elbow patches and suede trimming at the pockets. Country-look full- and semihacking jackets were worn by both men and women, as were checked caps. The Tattersall check was a popular choice for shirts.

Active sportswear was becoming more fashionable as leisure attire. Training "tops" and track suits, once worn only by athletes, were now worn regularly by men whose athletic activity went no further than walking behind a power-driven lawn mower.

The British Men's Fashion Association was formed during the year on the pattern of similar institutes already existing in most other Western European countries. (STANLEY H. COSTIN)

See also Industrial Review: *Furs.*
[451.B.2.b and d.i.; 629.C.1]

Fencing:
see Combat Sports

Field Hockey and Lacrosse

Field Hockey. Women's hockey was stimulated in 1977 by a decision of the International Olympic Committee to include a women's competition for the first time in the 1980 Olympic Games in Moscow. In addition, the Great Britain Hockey Board was formed and affiliated to the International Hockey Federation, so that it could arrange the participation of the British men's and women's teams in the 1980 Games.

In January Scotland won the British Indoor Tournament at Cardiff, Wales; England was second, followed by Wales and Ireland. Scotland also triumphed at the Sobell Sports Centre in London by defeating Belgium and England. These successes ensured that the indoor game would get strong Scottish support, including commercial sponsorship and television time. West Germany won the Women's European Indoor Cup.

Outdoors, at Lord's Cricket Ground in London, France, West Germany, and Spain joined with England in a two-day program in March; Germany defeated England and Spain, both of whom beat France. In other contests Scotland, Ireland, Poland, and Wales met in Glasgow, Scotland, and England, The Netherlands, Ireland, and Scotland faced each other in Dublin. In Amsterdam, The Netherlands sent its senior and junior national teams against visiting teams from England, West Germany, and Japan. Four national teams from England, France, West Germany, and The Netherlands competed in Limbourg, Belgium. On balance, West Germany and The Netherlands maintained their reputations as the most consistent teams in Europe. When Australia and New Zealand, both 1976 Olympic finalists, played four tests in September, Australia turned the tables dramatically on the Olympic gold medalists by making a clean sweep. During competition for the Inter-Continental Cup, Poland, Ireland, the U.S.S.R., and Belgium all qualified for the 1978 World Cup in Buenos Aires, Argentina.

(R. L. HOLLANDS)

Lacrosse. MEN. During 1977 international lacrosse was focused on the world series to be held in 1978 in England. The Stockport Club of England celebrated its centenary by sending a junior team to the U.S. Canada was by far the most enthusiastic lacrosse-playing country, with box lacrosse remaining the favourite game. The west coast clubs took all the major honours, including the Mann Cup (the Junior Trophy), which was won by the Victorian Club. The Mike Kelly Memorial, awarded to the best club player, went to Dave Durande of the New Westminster Club.

In the U.S., Cornell University successfully defended its National Collegiate Athletic Association title by defeating Johns Hopkins University 16–8. In the Collegiate All-Star Game, the North defeated the South 21–17. For the third consecutive year, the Mount Washington Club won the club championship. Eamon McEneaney of Cornell University received the most valuable player award.

The Australian state championship was held in Perth in July and was won by South Australia. The state championship clubs were: Victoria, Williamstown; South Australia, Glenelg; and Western Australia, East Fremantle. The winner of the Isaachsen Trophy, awarded to the best and fairest player in Australia, was won by Jim Wiles of the Stuart Club, South Australia.

The English club championship (Iroquois Cup) was won by Sheffield University, which defeated Hampstead 20–8. Sheffield also won the English Universities' Cup and the North of England Lacrosse Association senior flags competition by defeating Urmston 17–11 in extra time in a replayed match. Hampstead won the South of England Men's Lacrosse Association senior flags, defeating Lee 15–6.   (CHARLES DENNIS COPPOCK)

WOMEN. In the U.S., the invincible Philadelphia team defeated the South 8–4, thus retaining its national tournament title. The highlight of the season was the visit of the young Australian Touring Team, which was victorious over a Californian team but lost a close match to the U.S. Reserves and was easily defeated by the U.S. team. Although the Australians improved immeasurably, they were no match for the U.S. players, who ranked as the best in the world.

In Great Britain the 1976–77 season was dogged by rainy weather that caused the cancellation of the National Counties Tournament. An interesting development was the appointment of coaches and managers to most teams, who perceptibly improved the standard of play. South, the first territory to appoint a manager, won both major territorial events. South Reserves won the Reserves Tournament in January and later the South, in superb displays at all four matches, regained the territorial championship, having lost it to the Midlands in 1975–76. The North made a strong comeback to finish as runner-up.

WIDE WORLD

Bob Mathisen of Cornell (left) collides viciously with Mike Connor of Johns Hopkins as Cornell defeated Johns Hopkins 16–8 to win the NCAA lacrosse championship.

The All-England Clubs and Colleges Tournament in April was won by the vigorous team of Pendley Club, which made history by beating Bedford College of Physical Education in the final, thus interrupting the latter's long series of victories at Merton. The English team received its first official coach in Judy Harding, under whom England defeated Wales 23–0 and Scotland 22–1. England's greatest test came in a special Silver Jubilee fixture at Hurlingham, London, against England Reserves, which England won 9–6.

(MARGARET-LOUISE FRAWLEY)

Fiji

Finland

Fiji

An independent parliamentary state and member of the Commonwealth of Nations, Fiji is an island group in the South Pacific Ocean, about 3,200 km E of Australia and 5,200 km S of Hawaii. Area: 18,272 sq km (7,055 sq mi), with two major islands, Viti Levu (10,388 sq km) and Vanua Levu (5,535 sq km), and several hundred smaller islands. Pop. (1976 census): 588,100. Cap. and largest city: Suva (pop., 1976 census, 63,600). Language: English, Fijian, and Hindi. Religion: Christian and Hindu. Queen, Elizabeth II; governor-general in 1977, Ratu Sir George Cakobau; prime minister, Ratu Sir Kamisese Mara.

In the March-April 1977 elections the Alliance Party lost its majority. The Fiji National Party ("Fiji for the Fijians") challenged the Alliance's multiracial policies and, although winning only one seat, split the Fijian vote sufficiently to reduce the Alliance's seats in the 52-seat House of Representatives from 33 to 24. The Indian-dominated National Federation Party (NFP) won 26 seats. Because of dissension within the NFP, and on the grounds that its leader could not command a majority, the governor-general recalled Ratu Sir Kamisese Mara as prime minister. When a confi-

dence motion was defeated in June, Parliament was dissolved and new elections were held in September. The NFP divided into two factions and split the Indian vote. The Fijian National Party (whose leader, Sakeasi Butadroka, was serving a prison term for inciting racial hatred) polled poorly because its followers, now aware of the implications of splitting the Fijian vote, flocked back to the Alliance, which won 36 seats.

In its budget for 1977 the government relied on heavy overseas borrowing to meet its deficit. Tourism showed a slow but steady recovery from the slump of 1975. (BARRIE MACDONALD)

FIJI

Education. (1974) Primary, pupils 135,092, teachers 4,-229; secondary, pupils 26,202, teachers 1,103; vocational, pupils 1,715, teachers 174; teacher training, students 506, teachers 50; higher, students 1,031, teaching staff 145.

Finance and Trade. Monetary unit: Fiji dollar, with (Sept. 19, 1977) a free rate of F$0.92 to U.S. $1 (F$1.60 = £1 sterling). Budget (1975 actual): revenue F$107,490,000; expenditure F$128,550,000. Foreign trade (1976): imports F$236,940,000; exports F$124,870,000. Import sources: Australia 29%; Japan 18%; New Zealand 14%; U.K. 11%; Singapore 9%. Export destinations: U.K. 40%; Australia 18%; New Zealand 10%; Singapore 5%. Main exports (1974): sugar 54%; petroleum products 12%; coconut products 9%; gold 7%. Tourism (1975): visitors 162,000; gross receipts U.S. $75 million.

Transport and Communications. Roads (1975) 2,976 km. Motor vehicles in use (1975): passenger 21,500; commercial (including buses) 10,800. Railways (1975) 644 km (for sugar estates). Shipping (1976): merchant vessels 100 gross tons and over 31; gross tonnage 10,604. Shipping traffic (1976): goods loaded 446,000 metric tons, unloaded 725,000 metric tons. Telephones (Dec. 1975) 29,000. Radio receivers (Dec. 1974) 300,000.

Agriculture. Production (in 000; metric tons; 1976): sugar, raw value c. 318; rice (1975) c. 23; sweet potatoes and yams c. 20; cassava (1975) c. 90; copra c. 22. Livestock (in 000; Sept. 1975): cattle c. 173; pigs c. 31; goats c. 55; horses c. 34; chickens c. 575.

Industry. Production (in 000; 1975): cement (metric tons) 73; gold (troy oz) 61; electricity (kw-hr) 241,000.

Finland

The republic of Finland is bordered on the north by Norway, on the west by Sweden and the Gulf of Bothnia, on the south by the Gulf of Finland, and on the east by the U.S.S.R. Area: 337,032 sq km (130,129 sq mi). Pop. (1977 est.): 4,733,200. Cap. and largest city: Helsinki (pop., 1977 est., 493,324). Language: Finnish, Swedish. Religion (1975): Lutheran 98.6%; Orthodox 1.3%. President in 1977, Urho Kaleva Kekkonen; prime ministers, Martti J. Miettunen and, from May 15, Kalevi Sorsa.

The year 1977 was the third consecutive one of no growth in Finland, a fact that determined economic and political developments. Official figures issued in September showed increases from the previous year of 13% in consumer prices and only 8% in pay. The unemployment rate, peaking at more than 6% in late spring, persisted at a record high level.

The tone for the early months was set by tough wage negotiations, pursued industry by industry rather than on the familiar centralized basis. Though a two-year formula devised by government incomes negotiator Keijo Liinamaa was grudgingly accepted by most organized labour, several unions held out for more. The most adamant group was the Technical Employees' Federation, which backed a seven-week strike by power-station engineers and sympathy work stoppages by affiliated unions. Pres. Urho Kekkonen addressed trade unionists on April 16, contending that the strike weapon was obsolete and should be replaced by effective industrial democracy, but his comments failed to produce an immediate resumption of work.

The strike wave ended on May 12, and just three days later a new five-party left-centre government was installed. Headed by Social Democratic chairman Kalevi Sorsa, it replaced the seven-month-old minority administration of Martti Miettunen (Centre Party). With 152 of 200 members of Parliament behind it, Sorsa dubbed his coalition, which contained Communists, a "national recovery government." It quickly published an economic stimulation program for 1977–82, supported by the 1978 budget, supplementary budgets, and several separate measures meant to counteract unemployment and give Finnish industry a competitive edge abroad. Despite the divergent interests of the main parties a consensus existed on the chief priorities,

Education. (1974–75) Primary, pupils 405,809, teachers 27,773; secondary, pupils 391,788, teachers 19,598; vocational, pupils 112,210, teachers 11,200; teacher training, students 1,869, teachers 400; higher (including 11 universities), students 71,526, teaching staff 4,420.

Finance. Monetary unit: markka, with (Sept. 19, 1977) a free rate of 4.16 markkaa to U.S. $1 (7.25 markkaa = £1 sterling). Gold, SDR's, and foreign exchange (June 1977) U.S. $391.9 million. Budget (1977 est.): revenue 31,227,-000,000 markkaa; expenditure 32,161,000,000 markkaa. Gross national product (1976) 109,570,000,000 markkaa. Money supply (Dec. 1976) 9,268,000,000 markkaa. Cost of living (1970 = 100; June 1977) 227.

Foreign Trade. (1976) Imports 28,560,000,000 markkaa; exports 24,506,000,000 markkaa. Import sources: U.S.S.R. 18%; Sweden 16%; West Germany 15%; U.K. 8%; U.S. 5%. Export destinations: U.S.S.R. 20%; Sweden 17%; U.K. 14%; West Germany 9%. Main exports: paper 25%; machinery 14%; ships 8%; timber 8%; wood pulp 6%; clothing 6%.

Transport and Communications. Roads (1975) 73,548 km (including 174 km expressways). Motor vehicles in use (1975): passenger 996,284; commercial 128,451. Railways: (1975) 5,957 km; traffic (1976) 3,046,000,000 passenger-km, freight 6,546,000,000 net ton-km. Air traffic (1976): 1,376,400,000 passenger-km; freight 32,922,000 net ton-km. Navigable inland waterways (1975) 6,675 km. Shipping (1976): merchant vessels 100 gross tons and over 350; gross tonnage 2,115,322. Telephones (Dec. 1975) 1,834,-000. Radio licenses (Dec. 1975) 2,099,000. Television licenses (Dec. 1975) 1,336,000.

Agriculture. Production (in 000; metric tons; 1976): wheat 654; barley 1,553; oats 1,573; rye 178; potatoes 948; sugar, raw value (1975) 87; butter 80; eggs 82; timber (cu m; 1975) 30,860; fish catch (1975) 114. Livestock (in 000; June 1976): cattle 1,815; sheep 111; pigs 1,054; horses 33; poultry 7,767.

Industry. Production (in 000; metric tons; 1976): pig iron 1,321; crude steel 1,643; iron ore (metal content; 1975) 597; cement 1,725; sulfuric acid 1,022; petroleum products (1975) 7,763; plywood (cu m; 1975) 393; cellulose (1975) 3,370; wood pulp (1975) mechanical 1,605, chemical 3,569; newsprint 990; other paper and board (1975) 3,002; electricity (kw-hr) 29,319,000; manufactured gas (cu m) 26,800.

and a calmer political atmosphere prevailed because of the unanimous backing of the government partners and the opposition Conservatives for the reelection of President Kekkonen in early 1978.

Prompted by markdowns of the Swedish krona, the Finnish markka was devalued twice, by 5.7% on April 5 and by 3% on August 31. The total percentage appeared to fall just short of the "fundamental" level at which existing wage contracts would be liable to renegotiation. Praised by the Organization for Economic Cooperation and Development and the International Monetary Fund for dramatically cutting the current account deficit, the Bank of Finland maintained its tight credit policy, though a 1% reduction in the discount rate was applied from October 1. On June 30 the Central Bank signed a $300 million credit facility arrangement with 18 North American banks, replacing two previous agreements.

In a year marking the 60th anniversary of both Finnish independence and the Bolshevik Revolution (historically somewhat interrelated events), spectacular developments were chalked up in Finnish-Soviet relations. During an official visit Soviet Premier Aleksey Kosygin was co-inaugurator of Finland's first nuclear power station, largely Soviet-built, at Loviisa on March 23. A 15-year joint economic cooperation program was signed in Moscow on May 18, while President Kekkonen

was paying a state visit to the U.S.S.R. An estimated $680 million deal concerning Finnish participation in building a mining centre at Kostomuksha in Soviet Karelia was also completed.

An unanticipated Soviet arrival took place on July 10, when a Tu-134 airliner was hijacked to Helsinki while on a flight from Petrozavodsk, in Soviet Karelia, to Leningrad. During a 34-hour drama some of the 70 passengers and 7 crew escaped; the others were released by the two Soviet hijackers, who were then extradited to the U.S.S.R. in accordance with a bilateral antihijacking agreement signed in 1975.   (DONALD FIELDS)

Fisheries

Although the 1976–77 sessions of the third UN Conference on the Law of the Sea failed to produce a definitive convention, there was a broad consensus among participant nations in favour of an international 200-mi fisheries limit. This, it was generally agreed, would create zones extending 200 mi from coastlines in which coastal states would exercise control over fish and shellfish resources; be responsible for deciding the total allowable catch in any year; issue—for a fee—licenses to foreign vessels; and fix quotas and negotiate joint ventures with other countries, permitting them to take fish in excess of the coastal state's requirements or land fish for its own markets.

By mid-1977 most of the concerned states had either declared or given notice of their intention to establish such zones. In each case, the decision was motivated by the need to conserve or rebuild stocks, most of which were showing signs—often danger signs—of overexploitation. For states such as Britain whose fisheries were still in good condition, it was necessary to establish a 200-mi limit to protect grounds from an invasion by vessels displaced from other areas.

Those nations whose fleets had traditionally fished waters far from home—and whose distant-water fleets were unsuitable for any other role—found themselves excluded from one fishing

**Table I. Whaling: 1975-76 Season (Antarctic);
1975 Season (Outside the Antarctic)**

Number of whales caught

Area and country	Fin whale	Sei/ Bryde's whale	Hump-back whale	Minke whale	Sperm whale	Total	Percentage assigned under quota agreement[1]
Antarctic pelagic (open sea)							
Japan	118	1,316	—	3,017	146	4,597	52.8
Norway[2]							
U.S.S.R.	88	505	—	3,017	2,683	6,293[3]	47.2
Total	206	1,821	—	6,034	2,829	10,890[3]	100.0
Outside the Antarctic[4]							
Japan	129	1,288	—	—	4,110	5,527	
U.S.S.R.	33	653	—	—	3,750	4,611[5]	
South Africa	21	4	—	—	1,682	1,707	
Peru	5	545	—	—	793	1,343	
Australia	—	—	—	—	1,172	1,172	
Iceland	245	138	—	—	37	420	
Others	15	339	9	—	252	631[6]	
Total	448	2,967	9	—	11,796	15,411[5][6]	

[1] Antarctic only.
[2] Norway had no expeditions in the Antarctic in the 1975–76 season.
[3] Includes others (bottlenose, killer, gray, right, and blue whales).
[4] Excluding small whales.
[5] Includes 175 gray whales.
[6] Includes 16 other whales.
Source: The Committee for Whaling Statistics, *International Whaling Statistics*.

ground after another. Among such nations were Japan, South Korea, the U.S.S.R., Poland, East Germany, France, Britain, Spain, Portugal, and Romania, all of which had been negotiating fishing licenses or joint venture schemes with nations having more fish than they themselves could exploit. The Canadian Atlantic coast was a prime target, but Canada's determination to build up its depleted stocks, and its own fishing fleet, left little room for generous quotas. Some nations, including Britain, the U.S.S.R., and Japan, sought a foothold in the waters of New Zealand and Australia, while on the other side of the world the U.S. and Cuba amicably concluded an agreement on fishing rights in their overlapping zones.

The Netherlands, Britain, and even the U.S.S.R. talked of fleet reductions, although, for the Soviets, this was seen as a halt in the rate of fleet expansion rather than an actual cutback. Soviet fleet tonnage had grown by 50% in five years, and a record 13 million-metric ton catch in 1976 placed the U.S.S.R. ahead of Japan for the first time. Obviously, reduced access and the resultant reduced landings would call for a restructuring of fleets. During the year a number of modern trawlers were sold or redeployed, while old vessels were being scrapped and not replaced. It remained to be seen how this situation would affect the world catch, for grounds lost to distant-water fleets would not be replaced by others overnight.

The need for strict stock management by the state owning the resource was borne out during the year in the North Sea. There, despite biologists' warnings that herring were dangerously near extinction, agreement on drastic control could not be reached within the European Economic Community because The Netherlands was not prepared to accept the economic consequences of a total ban. Only after Britain had unilaterally applied such a ban in its 200-mi zone, on July 1, did the EEC as a whole support it.

Even such reluctant agreement between Britain and Brussels was rare where fisheries were concerned. There was no letup in the determination of

other EEC nations—France in particular—to invoke the "spirit of the Treaty of Rome," whereby all the partners would have equal access to the fishing grounds around the British Isles, constituting some 60% of the total Community fish stock. However, both Britain and Ireland had long disputed the validity of this clause, part of the EEC common fisheries policy package hastily "cobbled together" long before the days of 200-mi zones.

The diversion of distant-water fleets by Britain, France, West Germany, Italy, Belgium, and perhaps later Spain and Portugal could quickly ruin the carefully husbanded stocks around the British Isles. Claims by France that no increased catch was planned and by Brussels that Community conservation would be effective were met with derision from British and Irish fishermen and more polite disbelief on the part of fishermen's associations and members of Parliament. All were quick to point out the inability of the EEC to take effective action to save the North Sea herring.

The solution proposed by Britain and Ireland was a 50-mi exclusive national zone inside the 200-mi supranational zone, nicknamed the Community Pond. The proposal was backed by lobbying, propaganda, and an armada of fishing vessels that steamed up the Thames to London to dramatize the fishermen's demands. Ireland claimed—and enforced—the right to limit the size of vessels fishing within 50 mi and was prepared to argue its case in the highest courts of the EEC. But there was little sign of a change of heart in Brussels, other than a proposal to extend the life of the six-mile exclusive and six-mile privileged zones, due to be phased out in 1982. Meanwhile, Britain had to enforce the 200-mi limit it had claimed on Jan. 1, 1977, mainly against the incursions of Spanish fishermen who had long depended on British grounds.

The search for substitute species continued, with only some measure of success. Earlier experiments with new deepwater species such as grenadier had shown that they were costly to catch and difficult to process. Attention turned to a smaller species the size of a thin herring, known as blue whiting. This could be caught in large quantities by trawl, and the colour and flavour were acceptable to the cod-eating public once problems of machine filleting had been overcome. Initially, it was thought that blue whiting would be suitable for the new deboning machines which produced mince from fillets or even whole fish. However, fish mince had not proved so popular as had been hoped. In the case of blue whiting a satisfactory colour could be obtained only from skinned fillets, which fetched a better price unminced. The French had been fishing blue ling from relatively deep water with some success.

The abundant mackerel shoals off Britain's southwest coast were being fished by giant Soviet factory trawlers, British freezer stern trawlers, and Scottish purse seiners, all capable of catching hundreds of tons per trip. This had upset the traditional English and French small-boat line fishery, reducing prime fish to a bulk commodity for the fish-meal plant and upsetting both market prices and crews' earnings. The result was a licensing order introduced in September by Britain to limit

Porpoises struggle to escape death from drowning in the clutches of a tuna net. Thousands are killed unintentionally each year by tuna fishermen.

	Catch		Disposition of catch[2]	
Country	Total	Freshwater	Fresh marketed	Frozen, cured, canned, etc.
Japan	10,508.4	198.8	3,297.0[3]	7,210.0
U.S.S.R.	9,876.2	944.0	...	...
China	...	...		
Peru	3,447.5	7.9	125.5[4]	3,283.6[4]
United States	2,798.7	78.8	865.0	1,876.5
Norway	2,550.4	...	75.4	2,474.9
India	2,328.0	850.0	1,616.4	711.6
Korea, South	2,133.3	8.8	1,493.2[5]	641.7[5]
Denmark	1,767.0	16.4	151.9	1,615.0
Spain	1,532.9	14.2	625.1	754.9
Indonesia	1,389.9	402.7	...	...
Thailand	1,369.9	156.3	600.0[6]	1,028.0[6]
Philippines	1,341.6	106.2	1,073.3	268.3
South Africa	1,314.7	0.1	...	...
Chile	1,128.2	...	94.2[6]	1,032.4[6]
Canada	1,023.8	45.0	186.0	795.0
Vietnam	1,013.5	176.3		
United Kingdom	999.1	...	622.3[7][8]	532.8[7]
Iceland	994.8	...	36.8	947.5
France	805.8	...	...	...
Poland	800.7	23.3	...	...
Korea, North	800.0	...		
Brazil	674.5	89.9	...	...
Bangladesh	640.0	550.0	...	...
Nigeria	506.8	337.1	...	...
Mexico	499.3	17.8	167.6	331.7
Burma	485.1	130.0	121.3	363.9
Malaysia	473.6	2.5	333.3[4]	41.9[4]
Germany, West	441.7	15.0	87.7[9]	496.7[9]
Italy	405.7	19.1	344.6	61.2
Germany, East	374.5	13.1		
Portugal	368.6	0.1	195.4	173.1
Senegal	361.7	10.0	...	...
Netherlands, The	350.5	4.4	208.9	120.4
Faeroe Islands	285.6	...	44.7[6]	202.5[6]
Turkey	259.4	14.4	...	...
Ghana	254.5	41.9	...	...
Argentina	224.4	10.2	59.7	139.2
Sweden	215.3	10.4	69.0	132.0
Morocco	210.5	0.4	72.2	162.9
Pakistan	195.0	27.2	50.9	123.2
Angola	183.8	...	13.2[7]	454.0[7]
Tanzania	180.7	150.5	76.2	116.2
Uganda	169.7	169.7	134.1	33.3
Cuba	165.0	2.2	24.5[9]	101.6[9]
Bulgaria	158.1	7.8	...	...
Venezuela	153.4	15.2	120.4[7]	41.9[7]
Other	1,000.5	...	...	...
World total	69,732.2	10,394.0	20,700	28,000

[1] Excludes whaling.
[2] May include statistical discrepancy.
[3] Includes freezing.
[4] Excludes freshwater fish.
[5] Excludes aquaculture fisheries.
[6] 1974.
[7] 1973.
[8] Includes cured fish other than herring.
[9] Catch includes imports but excludes exports. Data refer to period between July 1, 1973 and June 30, 1974.
[10] 1971.
Source: United Nations Food and Agriculture Organization, *Yearbook of Fishery Statistics*, vol. 40 and 41.

catches by British boats to fish for human consumption.

This was only one of several reactions against the indiscriminate use of food fish for fish meal—a policy already blamed for the destruction of Scandinavian-Atlantic herring shoals, for the near destruction of North Sea herring, and to some extent for the decline of the Peruvian anchoveta fishery. During the year, Norway announced plans to divert fishing effort from the fish-meal plants to the food market, while Peru had been stepping up its food fishery and Canada talked of a "no herring for fish meal" policy.

The growing fear of fish famine was underlined by two reports on "alternative protein" issued by the UN Food and Agriculture Organization. One of these dealt with the use of seaweeds, either as a food source or as a source of alginates and agar, derivatives widely used in industrial society. The other dealt with squid, which offered a source of protein that some nations at least found acceptable.

The promise of Antarctic krill remained questionable. Processing trials of these shrimp-like creatures were not encouraging, according to the U.K. Torry Research Station, nor was any large market foreseen. Above all, the cost and logistics made fishing in the Antarctic impractical for northern nations not operating mother ships, although not perhaps for Australia and Argentina.

Greater consumption of tuna was forecast in Europe, where both Spain and France had been expanding their tuna-catching power. In the U.S. the tuna fleet remained in port from February until May to protest tough regulations imposed to reduce the mortality of porpoises incidentally caught in purse seine nets, and some owners threatened to transfer their boats to a foreign flag. A compromise was eventually negotiated, and the ships returned to sea.

The new 200-mi zone encouraged both U.S. and Canadian fisheries to initiate extensive investment programs. In Halifax, Nova Scotia, the biennial World Fishing Exhibition was welcomed by the government as a prelude to such a program, and its success seemed to prove the point. In Dakar, Senegal, West Africa's first fisheries exhibition was also seen as a curtain raiser for the expansion of fisheries in the region. In the Caribbean and Gulf of Mexico region, too, there was a mood of expansion; in Mexico the giant Zapata Corp. had invested heavily in anchoveta fishing, and the government had announced a 4 billion peso program. By the fall of 1977 preliminary reports suggested a reduced catch for many nations in the Northern Hemisphere, although this was offset to some extent by higher prices.

At the June meeting of the International Whaling Commission in Canberra, Australia, quotas were cut overall by 36%, though there was considerable variation according to species, but the quota for sperm whales in the northern Pacific was raised again at a December session in Tokyo. A limit of 12 was set on the catch of bowhead whales by Alaskan Eskimos, although Eskimo leaders claimed this was insufficient to meet their peoples' nutritional needs. The U.S.S.R. had already announced plans to withdraw from the whale fishery. (H. S. NOEL)

See also Food Processing.
[731.D.2.a]

Food Processing

The rising cost of health care in the U.S. and Britain led both governments to set up special committees to review the role of dietary factors in disease. The report of the U.S. Senate Select Committee on Nutrition and Human Needs, "Dietary Goals for the United States," made some sweeping recommendations, including reductions in saturated fat consumption, cholesterol intake, sugar consumption (by 40%), and salt intake (by 50–85%). More guarded recommendations appeared in a report of the British government's Expenditure Committee on "Preventive Medicine."

As an aftermath of the 1976 drought, nitrate levels of water in parts of Britain exceeded the limit

Floods:
see Earth Sciences; Engineering Projects

Donald Kennedy, commissioner of the U.S. Food and Drug Administration, explained to reporters a new label which the FDA proposed be made mandatory for all liquid protein diet products. A number of deaths had been traced by physicians to the use of liquid protein.

recommended by the World Health Organization, and purified water was supplied for the preparation of baby foods. It was reported that dioxin from Seveso, Italy, where a wide area had been contaminated as the result of an industrial accident in 1976, had reached the underground water reservoirs supplying Milan. In Michigan the accidental contamination of some animal feed in 1973 with a polybrominated fire-retardant preparation continued to have repercussions; some samples of breast milk were reported to contain detectable amounts. The contamination of animal and human milk by hormones, toxic metals, drugs, food additives, carcinogens, radionucleotides, pesticides, and other environmental contaminants was comprehensively reviewed by two British scientists in *Dairy Science Abstracts*. (*See* also ENVIRONMENT.)

The decision of the Canadian government to ban saccharin, followed closely by the announcement of a similar ban by the U.S. Food and Drug Administration (FDA), created a serious problem by removing the only remaining noncaloric sweetener. In the U.S., Congress responded to a public outcry by delaying the ban for 18 months, during which a broad investigation into food additives was to be conducted. European governments also delayed action pending further investigation. Researchers in Israel reported the commercial development of a sweetener made from citrus wastes that was 2,000 times sweeter than sugar; a British company announced the discovery of a chlorinated derivative of sucrose that was 500–600 times sweeter and free of aftertaste; and new technology made possible the production of syrups with enhanced fructose content and sweetness by the isomerization of corn syrups. However, production of these products in Europe was inhibited by discriminatory levies introduced by the European Economic Community in order to protect the sugar-beet industry. The use of xylitol in chewing gum was allowed in the U.S., but its reputation as a noncarcinogenic sweetener was clouded late in the year when a British testing firm announced that large doses had produced tumours in male mice.

Following representations by consumer groups,

the FDA stopped the use of mechanically deboned meat in foods. The EEC introduced regulatory proposals for emulsifying, stabilizing, and gelling agents, as well as for the labeling of foodstuffs for particular nutritional uses; the permissible amount of extraneous water in frozen poultry; and the permissible amount of erucic acid (present in rapeseed oil) in edible fats. A proposal that the term "ice cream" be restricted exclusively to dairy ices met with strong opposition in Britain, where nondairy-fat ices represented 87% of sales. The U.S. Academy of Sciences convened a forum on problems of food safety assessment, and numerous symposia were held in the U.S. on the repercussions of new regulatory measures and the industrial problems of coping with their interpretation and requirements. (*See* Special Report.)

Fruit, Vegetable, and Bakery Products. U.S. scientists developed new cabbage hybrids, containing 20% more dry matter, for sauerkraut manufacture. This improved the yield by 41% and reduced waste brine by 57%. A Swedish company developed a new type of ready-peeled potato that would remain fresh for six weeks. A British invention of an alternative to fermentation for pickling reduced processing time from several months to a few days and halved salt usage. A French development, so-called whirling-bed fluidization in a mixture of steam and air, made possible the blanching of vegetables with minimum leaching of nutrients and lower energy consumption.

A U.S. company introduced a heat-sensitive ink for coding cans as a safeguard against underprocessing, and a Swedish firm developed a plastic retortable container said to withstand temperatures as high as 135° C. It was lighter than tinplate, easy to open, and its rectangular shape saved 20% shipping space. An Australian-designed high-speed packaging machine that replaced the headspace air in cans with nitrogen was said to improve the shelf life of many canned foods. The Japanese developed an edible plastic from starch for use as a low-calorie ingredient in cookies.

In the Ivory Coast, a government organization developed new processes for the preparation of cassava and for processing coconuts. New plants were commissioned in Venezuela for processing fruit and vegetables, in Poland for pea canning, in Yugoslavia for vegetable canning, and in Egypt for processing exotic vegetables. The commercial development of a line of compressed freeze-dried foods of much reduced weight and volume was a spin-off of the U.S. space program. They were said to retain their full nutritional value and to reconstitute to their original appearance, texture, and flavour; 70 lb of beef with green beans was sufficient for 480 servings.

Dairy Products. Considerable research effort was being devoted to the economic utilization of cheese whey. Improvements in the recovery of whey proteins by reverse osmosis and ultrafiltration were reported by U.S., Belgian, British, French, Italian, and Norwegian workers. A wide range of beverages based on whey was developed by scientists in East Germany, the U.S., France, and Norway, and Swiss researchers developed some novel cheese from whey protein.

Criticisms of milk fat on health grounds and the growing problem of obesity stimulated the development of many low-butterfat products, including a low-fat Guernsey milk and reduced-fat flavoured milks produced in Denmark. A Scottish research institute reviewed the possibilities of modifying the composition of milk by genetic means. India introduced a national milk-distribution grid. A computerized dairy commissioned in Switzerland utilized the most advanced technology hitherto seen in the industry. A Dutch company developed a fully automated cheese-handling system including turning, shelf cleaning, packaging, weighing, and stock control.

Meat and Unconventional Protein Foods. Scientists in Kenya established that the oryx (a species of antelope) produces twice as much meat as cattle for the same weight of feed, is better adapted to arid conditions, and is immune to most cattle diseases. A process developed by British scientists for making spun-protein foods from meat wastes could potentially retrieve some 200,000 tons of protein annually.

Research continued into fermentation processes utilizing bacteria, yeasts, fungi, and algae, but their use in human food was being held back because of unresolved problems of toxicity and legislative hurdles. A further difficulty was that these processes were highly capital and energy intensive. There was renewed interest in the utilization of unconventional proteins from leaves, legumes (1,300 known species), cereals, and seeds, especially wild grasses, many of which grow under relatively arid conditions. U.S. workers obtained a high-protein product from alfalfa juice, and Nigerian researchers found cassava to be a particularly good source of leaf-protein concentrate.

Seafoods. With supplies of many commercially popular fish dwindling, wastage became a matter of serious concern. For example, around Britain some 50 species were landed, but many were not utilized because of lack of consumer interest. Clearly, more research was needed to develop acceptable processed products. Progress was made in salmon culture, and two plants established in Norway were reported to have a total capacity of 900,000–1.1 million kg annually. It was estimated that the warm water from power stations in the U.K. could support fish farms yielding 50,000 tons annually. Ghana began intensive fish farming and expected to be self-sufficient by 1980. South Africa introduced Chinese grass carp in reservoirs for the dual purpose of weed control and food.

New Foods. The—as yet unproven—possibility that deficiency of dietary fibre was a causative factor in heart disease, diabetes, obesity, and cancer led to the development of many new products containing bran. Bread reinforced with the bran removed from the flour during milling was widely introduced throughout Europe and America. Frozen yogurt achieved great popularity in Europe and the U.S. Its success depended on the enzymatic breakdown of the lactose into its component sugars to prevent grittiness. Low-calorie preparations for weight control continued to proliferate. A line of low-calorie dairy spreads was developed in Sweden, and an ice cream with 40% fewer calories than the normal product was successfully introduced in Britain. In 1974 the *Wall Street Journal* commented that "Most people have no taste. It's been lost in the process (fresh foods taste peculiar if you grow up eating instant, frozen or canned)." In 1977 this trend showed some signs of being reversed. Many new foods were based on the "natural" concept—bread from whole and cracked wheat grains with other grains like rye; carrot cake containing raw carrot, pineapple, and walnuts; breakfast foods based on spiced whole cereals. There was also a demand for spicier foods, and this led to the introduction of single serving sizes to satisfy individual preferences.

Other new foods included a spun-vegetable-protein product resembling roast meat in flavour, texture, and appearance, developed in Britain for the catering trade, and, in the U.S., a line of precooked meat products based on new technology whereby the meat is flaked instead of being minced or ground, making possible the preparation of very tender products that can vary from a hamburger texture to steaklike bites. A West German company developed a line of soups, pastries, and filled pancakes based on krill, and a Dutch company invented a line of nutlike products using soybeans as a substitute for almonds, hazelnuts, and peanuts. A U.S. company patented a solid sauce bar for reconstitution with water. A yeast-leavened rice bread developed by a U.S. company was especially suitable for people who were allergic to wheat, and high coffee prices inspired a coffee substitute made from corn. A Hungarian manufacturer successfully introduced to Western consumers a canned pickle made from patisson, a kind of gourd. The growing popularity of microwave ovens in the U.S. stimulated the development of products designed to overcome the problems of texture and lack of crispness and browning commonly encountered in microwave cooking.

(H. B. HAWLEY)

See also Agriculture and Food Supplies; Fisheries; Health and Disease; Industrial Review: *Alcoholic Beverages.*
[451.B.1.c.ii; 731.E–H]

TOO MANY WATCHDOGS?

by Everett Edgar Sentman

It started with an apple. If Adam had not eaten the Apple of Knowledge and thus violated God's law, according to Genesis 3, we might still all be living in the Garden of Eden.

History and legend are replete with examples of food laws. Joseph made a name for himself in Egypt by persuading the pharaoh to decree the storage of surplus grain from fat years to feed his people in lean years. Food laws have always been with us. But today there are more laws and regulations governing what we eat than ever before in history.

In the United States, dozens of federal agencies are concerned with food. The best known of them, because its actions are the most publicized, is the Food and Drug Administration (FDA). The U.S. Department of Agriculture (USDA) runs second, with its proliferation of agencies concerned with problems ranging from dairy inspection to the proportion of chicken and soybeans in hot dogs. The Environmental Protection Agency issues edicts and recommendations involving drinking water (water is a food, too), contamination of food by chemicals and drugs, and other matters. The Public Health Service is also concerned with drinking water, as well as with dairy products, caterers, taverns, and vending machines. Other food regulatory agencies include the Department of Defense, the Department of the Interior, the Department of Commerce, the Federal Trade Commission, and the General Services Administration. The Department of the Treasury monitors the quality of alcoholic beverages. No other country has so many agencies involved with the enforcement of food laws and regulations.

Congress can adopt food-law legislation approving or disapproving actions by the administrative agencies. It can also originate its own food laws, and it has scores of permanent and ad hoc committees studying food issues. Legislators agree that food issues are outstanding vote getters. In 1977, food-related bills accounted for about 50% of all legislation introduced in Congress.

Everett Edgar Sentman, a writer and editor, is president of Sentman Publishing Enterprises.

Add the state, county, and municipal food laws and enforcing agencies, plus conflicting stands taken by industry, professional groups, and activists, and the poor consumer grows dizzy wondering what to think—and what and what not to eat. Consistency has not been one of the conspicuous virtues of the food watchdogs.

The FDA and its predecessors have been in the food watching business longer than any other agency in the U.S. In 1906 Congress enacted the Pure Food and Drug Act after lobbying by Harvey Wiley, chief chemist of the U.S. Department of Agriculture, and a public outcry over filthy food stimulated by muckraking books and articles by such journalists as Upton Sinclair and Samuel Hopkins Adams. U.S. food quality had sunk so low that European countries had adopted laws barring imports of American meats. Until 1928 responsibility for enforcement of

---

100 Laws Govern a Can of Soup

Quality-control analysts for leading soup manufacturers in the U.S. point out that more than 100 federal laws apply to the production of a can of tomato soup. These laws are administered by a maze of federal agencies. In addition, there are many state, county, and municipal regulations and ordinances. A can of tomato soup has been through the wars before it ever reaches the consumer's can opener.

Food cans are made of steel with an inner plating of tin. For some food products such as coloured fruits this is enough, but for the great majority of foods an additional inner coating of enamel must be added. For acid foods, such as tomatoes or mixtures containing tomatoes, this coating must be an acid-resistant enamel. Federal laws govern the kind of can that may be used for each product.

Federal law specifies that pressure cooking of sealed cans must produce temperatures high enough to kill harmful bacteria. A #303 (1-lb) can of tomatoes must be cooked to 160° or 165° F (70° or 74° C). Other foods present special problems. For example, dry beans are a good insulator and despite heat can readily support harmful organisms of the botulism type. Therefore, pork and beans must be cooked 60 to 105 minutes at 240° F (117° C) and under ten pounds of pressure.

Several federal agencies are concerned about labeling of foods. The Food and Drug Administration insists that the ingredients largest in volume be listed first. If water is added, it too must be listed. If water is the first ingredient listed on the label, you may draw your own conclusion about the contents.

Food packers employ their own quality-control chemists to sample their packs for various qualities but especially for extraneous materials such as insect parts, rodent feces, or rodent hairs. The work of these chemists is followed up by FDA or USDA inspectors. In a recent case, on the basis of one-half of an insect larva in 100 millilitres of a canned product, the FDA seized and destroyed the pack. Federal courts frequently are called upon to make the decision whether contamination of the food is great enough to justify withdrawing it from the market.

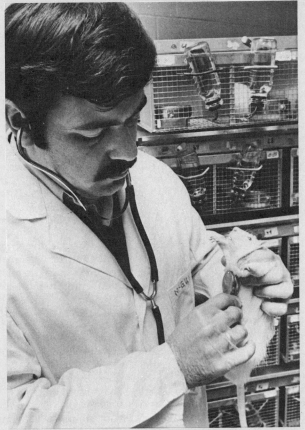

A rat being used in testing various food substances is examined by a researcher.

the act resided with the USDA. Then for a time an independent agency administered it. To counter pressure from industry, the FDA in 1940 was placed under the wing of the Federal Security Agency, renamed in 1953 the Department of Health, Education, and Welfare.

Today, the FDA is among the most shot-at agencies in the federal bureaucracy. Marksmen include members of Congress, former FDA employees, major industrial firms, pharmaceutical companies, Ralph Nader, citizens' groups, and, most recently, diabetics and dieters.

It is a small target. The FDA has only a few thousand employees and its budget is about $242 million a year, a drop in the U.S. budgetary bucket.

The FDA made news in 1970 when it banned the use of cyclamates because of a suspicion that they may cause cancer. Diabetics and others who use sugar substitutes in their food wrote indignant letters, but to no avail. Meanwhile, the drug companies filed their protests and concentrated on filling orders for cyclamates from abroad.

In 1976 the FDA banned the use of Red No. 2, the most widely used red-colour additive to foods, drugs, and cosmetics; and Red No. 4, used in maraschino cherries. Drinkers sighed and tried to adjust to the slightly paler Red No. 40 in the cherry in their manhattans. Early in 1977 the FDA indicated that Red No. 40 may also be banned because it causes cancer in mice. Another colour, Yellow No. 5, was said to be a threat because some people are allergic to it. In 1977 the FDA was seeking to establish a warning label for this additive.

Also in 1977, prodded by consumer activists, the FDA began to insist that food packers state solid weight on their labels, that is, the weight of the fruit or vegetable before the packing liquid is added. The National Canners Association replied that drained-weight labeling would cost consumers about $100 million a year. Meanwhile, knowledgeable shoppers proceeded to do what they had been doing since Nicolas Appert invented canning for Napoleon: shake various cans to see how much they slosh and choose the least sloshable.

The big travail for both the FDA and the public in 1977, however, was the ban on saccharin. The Delaney clause of the Food, Drug, and Cosmetic Act empowers the FDA to act against substances that are found to cause cancer in experimental animals. Diabetics and overweight people had been forced to give up cyclamates in favour of saccharin. Experiments with rats in Canada showed that saccharin, when given in heavy doses, caused bladder cancer, said the FDA.

Congress and the FDA received carloads of mail, nearly all opposed to the edict. In October committees of the U.S. House of Representatives and Senate agreed upon an 18-month delay in the ban on saccharin. Tongue in cheek, Rep. Andrew Jacobs, Jr. (Dem., Ind.), introduced a bill that would allow sales of saccharin-sweetened products under the label: "Warning: the Canadians have determined that saccharin is dangerous to your rats' health."

In Great Britain controversy continued over the food standards of "take-away (carryout) food shops." In addition, the Food Standards Committee urged that labeling standards be tightened. Various firms were fined for selling stale produce. Stricter controls were urged on lead, nitrites, and arsenic in foods by the Food Additives and Contaminants Committee. Industry warned against the stifling of enterprise through restrictive food measures.

In October 1977, food-quality officials in India were taken aback when Prime Minister Morarji Desai recommended in a speech to the Tuberculosis Association his therapy for cancer, tuberculosis, and cataracts: along with a vegetarian diet, a daily drink of one's own urine. Meanwhile, on an international basis, the Food and Agriculture Organization and the World Health Organization of the UN continued to work for improved food quality, especially in the less developed nations.

Football

Association Football (Soccer). The focal point during 1977 for almost all nations competing in association football was Argentina—and the World Cup finals scheduled there for June 1978. By the end of 1977 many countries had qualified for the finals. By September Brazil and Peru had booked their tickets from the South American qualifying groups, and Hungary had won its section to gain a play-off against Bolivia. Sweden also joined automatic qualifiers West Germany (defending champions) and Argentina (hosts) among the final 16.

Crowd problems persisted worldwide, and more and more countries were fencing in the hooligans. Barcelona, Spain, dug a moat at a cost of $150,000 to keep fans off the playing field, but there were no plans to fill it with alligators, piranha fish, or other exotic deterrents. But despite the occasionally unruly spectators the game maintained its popularity, with the Arab countries plowing large amounts of oil money into importing top coaches—including England manager Don Revie—to improve their standard of play.

In the United States the sport began to take a real hold, with as many as 70,000 attending contests in New York featuring the Cosmos, champions of the North American Soccer League. The legendary Brazilian Pelé, star of the Cosmos along with West Germany's Franz Beckenbauer, announced his retirement from soccer after giving the game in the U.S. the lift it needed.

EUROPEAN CHAMPIONS' CUP. Liverpool, the English champions, brought the cup back to England for only the second time since its inception in 1956.

Famed soccer player Pelé gave his traditional leap of joy after scoring one of the final goals of his career as his New York Cosmos defeated the Rochester Lancers in August.

UPI COMPIX

It did so by beating Borussia Mönchengladbach of West Germany 3–1 in Rome on May 25. Liverpool was helped to a degree by a below-par performance by Borussia and by the tremendous backing of Merseyside fans in the Olympic Stadium.

With Terry McDermott opening the scoring after 28 minutes from a Steve Heighway pass, Liverpool's method and determination carried it forward. However, an error by Jimmy Case let in the speedy Allan Simonsen, and he roared away from defenders Phil Neal and long-serving Tommy Smith to tie the score. Both Neal and Smith later atoned for this by scoring. Smith, who was playing his 600th game for Liverpool, moved in for a corner won and taken by Heighway and headed the ball past Wolfgang Kneib. Then, with only eight minutes remaining, Borussia captain Bertie Vogts brought down Kevin Keegan (who later joined SV Hamburg) as he was dashing through with the ball at his feet bound for the goal. A penalty was awarded, and Neal made no mistake with the kick. Without detracting from the Liverpool performance, which was cool, efficient, and controlled, the speculation was how Borussia would have fared with Jupp Heynckes and Simonsen fully fit and Herbert Wimmer not lost with a thigh strain midway through the first half. But the night and the trophy undoubtedly belonged to the red-shirted English club and marked the climax of a long, hard season.

EUROPEAN CUP-WINNERS' CUP. SV Hamburg maintained West German prominence in major European club competitions when, in the final at the Ajax Stadium in Amsterdam on May 11, it defeated the defending champions, Anderlecht of

Table I. Association Football Major Tournaments

Event	Winner	Country
European Super Cup	Liverpool	England
European Champions' Cup	Liverpool	England
European Cup-Winners' Cup	SV Hamburg	West Germany
UEFA Cup	Juventus	Italy
South American Champions' Cup	Boca Juniors	Argentina
UEFA Youth Cup	Belgium	
World Club Championship	Bayern Munich	West Germany

Table II. Association Football National Champions

Nation	League winners	Cup winners
Austria	SW Innsbruck	Austria/WAC
Belgium	FC Bruges	FC Bruges
Bulgaria	Levski Spartak	Levski Spartak
Czechoslovakia	Dukla, Prague	Lokomotiv Kosice
Denmark	BK 1903, Copenhagen	Esbjerg
England	Liverpool	Manchester United
Finland	Kuopion Palloseura	Lahden Reipas
France	FC Nantes	Saint-Étienne
Germany, East	Dynamo Dresden	Dynamo Dresden
Germany, West	Borussia Mönchengladbach	FC Cologne
Greece	Panathinaikos	Panathinaikos
Hungary	Vasas Budapest	Diosgyor
Iceland	Valur	Valur
Ireland	Sligo	Dundalk
Italy	Juventus	AC Milan
Luxembourg	Jeunesse D'Esch	Progrès Niedercorn
Netherlands, The	Ajax	Twente Enschede
Northern Ireland	Glentoran	Coleraine
Norway	Lillestrøm	Brann Bergen
Poland	Slask Wroclaw	Zaglebie Sosnowiec
Portugal	Benfica	FC Porto
Romania	Dinamo Bucharest	Univer. Craiova
Scotland	Celtic	Celtic
Spain	Atletico Madrid	Real Betis
Sweden	Halmstad	AIK Stockholm
Switzerland	FC Basel	Young Boys Bern
Turkey	Trabzonspor	Trabzonspor
U.S.S.R.	Dynamo Moscow	Dynamo Tbilisi
Wales		Shrewsbury Town
Yugoslavia	Red Star, Belgrade	Hajduk Split

Despite high-flying D. Watson, England lost the British Isles championship to Kenny Dalglish and his Scots teammates.

Belgium, 2–1. Hamburg captain Georg Volkert hammered home the opening goal from the penalty spot only 12 minutes before the game's end, after Ludo Coeck had brought down Hamburg's Arno Steffenhagen. Keystone of the SV victory was the shadowing of Anderlecht danger man Rob Rensenbrink out of the action by either Casper Memering or defender Manfred Kaltz, a more than capable sweeper. After the penalty Anderlecht was forced onto the attack if it was to salvage anything from its erratic season, and Rensenbrink slipped his shadows long enough to dash through and drill a shot just over the bar, six minutes before the end of the game. But then Volkert sped away from Gilbert Van Binst and crossed the ball for "Felix" Magath to divert past goalkeeper Jan Ruiter.

UEFA Cup. Juventus, the pride of Turin, finally clinched a major club tournament by winning on the away-goals rule in the two-legged UEFA Cup final against Atlético Bilbao when the aggregate score stood at 2–2 after the game in Spain on May 18. Marco Tardelli put Juventus ahead from Antonello Cuccureddu's cross after 15 minutes in the first leg at Turin on May 4. His goal was the culmination of a period of intense pressure by the Italians; they struck before the Spanish defense was welded into a solid barrier. Indeed, the Atlético goalkeeper, José Iribar, made some first-class saves to confine Juventus to that single goal. The loss of Roberto Boninsegna ten minutes from the halftime break robbed Juventus of much of its forward penetration, and the Italians could not add to their total.

Atlético Bilbao was without its strong man, Antonio Goicoechea, for the second leg in Spain a fortnight later and, by the time the defense had settled down, Roberto Bettega had dashed in to put Juventus two goals up for the series with a fine header from Tardelli's cross. On their own Campo San Mames, with the backing of some 45,000 fans, Atlético buckled to its task of pulling even, and within four minutes Javier Irrueta had halved the deficit with a stinging shot that Dino Zoff could not stop.

Bilbao did not persevere with an all-out offensive of sufficient power to ruffle the well-drilled Juventus defense. But Carlos Ruiz slammed in the Spaniards' second goal just 12 minutes before the game's end. This leveled the aggregate score, and so the rule counting away-from-home goals double was invoked. The Spanish players complained bitterly when they were not awarded a penalty after Ignacio Churruca had been brought down by Francesco Morini, but the referee, Erich Linemayr, was firm in his refusal.

BRITISH ISLES CHAMPIONSHIP. For the second year in succession Scotland triumphed in this competition, showing a much more marked cutting edge to its attack than did its British rivals. The Scots clinched the title in spectacular fashion by beating England 2–1 at Wembley, London, on June 4. Key figure in the triumph in a match that never reached great heights was Celtic's Kenny Dalglish, who was transferred later in the summer to Liverpool for a British record fee (between U.K. clubs) of £440,000. Gordon McQueen (Leeds United) and Dalglish scored for Scotland, while Mick Channon (Southampton) tallied for England from a penalty. After the final whistle some thousands of Scots, apparently the worse for alcohol, tore down the goals and dug out chunks of the playing field in a display of vandalism that soured the victory for Alistair MacLeod in his first year as the manager for Scotland.

Northern Ireland tied 1–1 with Wales in Belfast when Sammy Nelson (Arsenal) matched the goal scored by Wales' Nick Deacy (PSV Eindhoven). Wales thus missed its chance for the title after a 40-year blank; it had drawn 0–0 with the Scots in Wrexham and beaten England 1–0 at Wembley with a penalty by Leighton James (Derby County). Scotland hammered Northern Ireland 3–0, with goals from Dalglish (2) and McQueen. England struggled to defeat Northern Ireland in Belfast 2–1, with goals by Channon and Dennis Tueart (Manchester City).   (TREVOR WILLIAMSON)

Rugby. RUGBY UNION. The first tour of the 1976–77 period was that made by Japan to England, Wales, and Scotland in September and October 1976. The Japanese had a final record of won 3, lost 5, points for 158, points against 291. They did not meet the full England side but were beaten 58–13 by the England Under-23 team. The Pumas of Argentina also toured Wales and England and held "a Wales XV," which in all but name was the full Wales team, to a score of 20–19 at Cardiff. Their record was won 3, lost 3, points for 112, points against 111. Soon after the Pumas returned from Britain, they played host to a New Zealand team made up of players who had not just recently

SYNDICATION INTERNATIONAL/PHOTO TRENDS

England won its biggest Rugby Union victory ever when it defeated Scotland 26–6 during the home international championship at Twickenham in January.

toured South Africa with the All Blacks. The New Zealanders won all their eight games in Argentina, including two tests by 21–9 and 26–6. The Wallabies of Australia toured France in October and November 1976, playing nine matches that included two tests. Their final record was disappointing: won 3, lost 6, points for 98, points against 138. They lost the two tests 18–15 at Bordeaux and 34–6 in Paris.

The home international championship again had France and Wales as chief contenders, and this time France came out on top. Wales beat Ireland 25–9 at Cardiff, and England beat Scotland 26–6 at Twickenham. But while England was beating Ireland 4–0 in Dublin, Wales was outplayed 16–9 by France in Paris in what turned out to be the vital match of the championship. France went on to beat England 4–3 at Twickenham, Scotland 23–3 in Paris, and Ireland 15–6 in Dublin and so achieved the second grand slam in its history. Wales beat England 14–9 at Cardiff and Scotland 18–9 at Murrayfield, thus gaining the triple crown for the 14th time. England finished third.

Following the home international championship the Lions, a team of 30 players captained by Phil Bennett of Wales, managed by George Burrell of Scotland, and coached by John Dawes of Wales, played 25 matches in New Zealand. Aside from the four tests, they won every match but one, losing only to New Zealand Universities, 21–9, at Christchurch. In the test series, however, the Lions were beaten 3–1 by the All Blacks. The Lions took a long time to settle down, and defeat in the first test, at Wellington, was more complete than the score of

16–12 would suggest. But then, led by forward Terry Cobner of Pontypool, they won the second test at Christchurch 13–9. The All Blacks, gaining confidence under the captaincy of Tane Norton and the coaching of Jack Gleeson, scored some fine tries in winning the last two tests 19–7 at Dunedin and 10–9 at Auckland.

Meanwhile, France toured Argentina, winning the first test 26–3 and drawing the second 18–18. Canada beat the U.S. 17–6 at Vancouver, and Scotland toured the Far East, beating Japan 74–9.

The International Board, in London in March 1977, decided that technical infringements of the laws at scrums and line-outs would no longer be punishable by a direct kick at goal but only by an indirect free kick.

RUGBY LEAGUE. In the international championship, held in Australia and New Zealand in May and June 1977, Australia beat New Zealand 27–12, France 21–9, and Great Britain 19–5. Great Britain defeated France 23–4 and New Zealand 30–12. In the final, Australia beat Great Britain 13–12 in Sydney. New Zealand defeated France 28–20 and so won third place. France won the international triangular competition, beating Wales 13–2 at Toulouse and England 28–15 at Carcassonne.

(DAVID FROST)

U.S. Football. PROFESSIONAL. The Dallas Cowboys won the championship of the National Football League (NFL) by defeating the Denver Broncos 27–10 in the Super Bowl at New Orleans, La., on Jan. 15, 1978. Played indoors for the first time, in the Louisiana Superdome, the contest was the first victory for the National Football Conference (NFC) representative since 1972. Both defensive teams were outstanding, their mettle being frequently tested by the numerous offensive-unit turnovers. Denver quarterback Craig Morton (see BIOGRAPHY) was intercepted four times and there were ten fumbles in all, both Super Bowl records. Dallas scored on a 2-yd run by Tony Dorsett, a 45-yd pass from Roger Staubach to Butch Johnson, a 29-yd pass from Robert Newhouse to Golden Richards, and 35-yd and 43-yd field goals by Efren Herrera. Denver tallied on a 1-yd plunge by Rob Lytle and a 47-yd field goal by Jim Turner. Lytle's touchdown was set up by a 67-yd kickoff return by Rick Upchurch, another Super Bowl record.

Dallas dominated the NFC, finishing 12–2 and establishing the NFC's best records in total offense and rushing and total defense. Roger Staubach led NFC passers with 87.1 rating points (determined on the basis of number of completions, touchdowns, interceptions, and yards gained per attempt), and Tony Dorsett became the eighth NFL rookie to run for 1,000 yd, gaining 1,007 and scoring 13 touchdowns after not starting in Dallas' first nine games. In the play-off game for the conference championship Dallas easily defeated Minnesota 23–6.

The Broncos, however, were the most surprising NFL team. Denver took the American Conference (AFC) Western Division title away from the defending Super Bowl champion Oakland Raiders for the first time in five years and had the AFC's best record, 12–2. Oakland and Denver split their regular-season games and met for the AFC title after Denver beat the 9–5 Central champion Pittsburgh

Steelers 34–21 and Oakland, the AFC wild card team, beat the Baltimore Colts 37–31 in double overtime. In the title contest Denver outlasted the Raiders 20–17.

The Broncos, led by their "Orange Crush" defense that topped the AFC in halting the rush, had a much improved offense under new coach Red Miller and quarterback Morton, a previously undistinguished veteran who ranked second among AFC passers. They had to play nine games against teams that won at least half of their games but made the play-offs for the first time in their 18-year history.

Oakland's offense ranked first in the AFC in total and rushing yardage, and Mark van Eeghen's 1,273 yd rushing trailed only Walter Payton of the Chicago Bears. Kicker Erroll Mann led the league with 99 points, as did Ray Guy with a 43.3-yd punting average.

The Colts lost three in a row after a 9–1 start, but then overcame a 21–3 deficit against the New England Patriots to make the play-offs. A controversial apparent fumble was ruled to be a dead ball on a key play in that game, touching off more cries for officials to use television instant replays. Lyle Blackwood of Baltimore led the NFL with 10 interceptions, and Lydell Mitchell, the NFL reception leader with 71, also was the fifth best rusher.

The Miami Dolphins' 10–4 record was identical to Baltimore's, but the Dolphins missed the play-offs because their conference record was not as good. Still, coach Don Shula built a strong defense around five rookies, and Miami's offense featured Bob Griese, who led NFL passers with 88 rating points and 22 touchdown passes. Nat Moore's 12 touchdown catches also led the league.

The 10–4 Los Angeles Rams won their fifth straight Western Division title, going 8–2 after Joe Namath was replaced by second-year quarterback Pat Haden but losing in the play-offs 14–7 to the Minnesota Vikings. The Vikings' 9–5 record gave them their ninth Central Division title in ten years because they outscored the 9–5 Bears in their two contests, making the Bears the NFC wild-card team. Minnesota won only three of its last five regular-season games after losing injured quarterback Fran Tarkenton, holder of many NFL passing records, but Ahmad Rashad's 51 catches led the NFC.

During the season, a Chicago Bear fan asked one of Walter Payton's teammates just what it was that made Payton such an electrifying running back. Was it his strength? Or his fancy moves? Or his doggedness in breaking tackles? Or maybe his acceleration or his quick start or his instinct for picking the right holes?

"All of those," the teammate said.

After setting the NFL's single-game rushing record with 275 yd against the Vikings, Payton challenged O. J. Simpson's record of 2,003 yd in a season. He fell short with 1,852 yd, but that was the third highest total in NFL history and included ten 100-yd games. He led the league with 16 touchdowns, 14 on the ground, and the Bears began their season-ending six-game winning streak when Payton started carrying 30 times a game. Payton's 5.5-yd average per carry did not include

Chicago's Walter Payton demonstrates his style against the Minnesota Vikings in setting a new NFL single-game rushing record.

the Bears' 37–7 play-off loss to the Cowboys, when he was held to 60 yd in the team's first post-season game in 14 years. After the season Payton was voted most valuable player in the NFC.

The Washington Redskins' 9–5 record equaled that of the Vikings, but they missed the play-offs on the basis of the NFL's intricate tie-breaking formula. The NFL planned to add two weeks to the 1978 regular season and one week to the play-offs, accommodating two additional wild-card teams, but sentiment was strong that the extra play-off week should be used for breaking ties.

After three years without a labour contract, the NFL Players Association signed an agreement before the season that gave teams losing free agents the option of matching a free agent's best salary offer from another team or letting him go in exchange for a draft choice. Minimum salaries, play-off prizes, pension contributions, and fringe benefits also were increased. NFL teams had a financial windfall when the television networks committed themselves to an additional $5 million to $6 million per year for each team in the next five years.

COLLEGE. When Fred Akers was rebuilding the football program at the University of Wyoming, he drove up high in the Rocky Mountains on Saturday nights so that he could listen to games of the University of Texas football team, which he hoped someday to coach. He got his chance in 1977, and Texas won the Southwest Conference title with an 11–0 record after a 5–5–1 1976 season. The Longhorns were the only major unbeaten college team and were sure of being awarded the national championship if they could win the Cotton

Table III.
NFL Final Standings and Play-offs, 1977

AMERICAN CONFERENCE
Eastern Division

	W	L	T
*Baltimore	10	4	0
Miami	10	4	0
New England	9	5	0
New York Jets	3	11	0
Buffalo	3	11	0

Central Division

*Pittsburgh	9	5	0
Cincinnati	8	6	0
Houston	8	6	0
Cleveland	6	8	0

Western Division

*Denver	12	2	0
*Oakland	11	3	0
San Diego	7	7	0
Seattle	5	9	0
Kansas City	2	12	0

NATIONAL CONFERENCE
Eastern Division

*Dallas	12	2	0
Washington	9	5	0
St. Louis	7	7	0
New York Giants	5	9	0
Philadelphia	5	9	0

Central Division

*Minnesota	9	5	0
*Chicago	9	5	0
Detroit	6	8	0
Green Bay	4	10	0
Tampa Bay	2	12	0

Western Division

*Los Angeles	10	4	0
Atlanta	7	7	0
San Francisco	5	9	0
New Orleans	3	11	0

*Qualified for play-offs.

Play-offs
American semifinals
Oakland 37, Baltimore 31
Denver 34, Pittsburgh 21

National semifinals
Dallas 37, Chicago 7
Minnesota 14, Los Angeles 7

American finals
Denver 20, Oakland 17

National finals
Dallas 23, Minnesota 6

Super Bowl
Dallas 27, Denver 10

Bowl. But they were soundly beaten 38–10 by Notre Dame, which was subsequently voted the nation's best.

Notre Dame had been the preseason favourite but lost its second game to Mississippi and won four others by ten points or less. Until the Cotton Bowl the highlight of its 10–1 season was a 49–19 victory over Southern California when the Fighting Irish wore green jerseys for the first time since 1963. They ranked fifth nationally in total offense, sixth in scoring offense, and third in rushing defense.

Texas was led by its first Heisman Trophy winner ever as halfback Earl Campbell led the nation with 1,744 yd rushing on 267 carries, 19 touchdowns, and 168.6 all-purpose yards per game. Brad Shearer won the Outland Trophy as the nation's outstanding lineman. Texas had the most high national statistical rankings of any team: third in scoring, fourth in rushing, sixth in total offense, fourth in defending against the run, and fifth in total defense.

Although Texas had been a traditional powerhouse before its recent decline, its rapid rise to the top in 1977 was indicative of the increasing chances for mediocre teams to join the country's elite. An equalizing rule, which began to take noticeable effect in 1977, limited football scholarships to 105 per school.

Another balancing factor was the increase in regional scheduling by top teams. Some 10–1 teams lost their only games to teams they would not have played in past years. Alabama lost to Nebraska, Kentucky to Baylor, and Penn State to Kentucky. Ohio State (9–2) lost to Oklahoma in addition to Big Ten rival Michigan, and Texas A & M (8–3) lost to Michigan. Texas was the only team to beat Arkansas and Oklahoma, which it plays every year, and Michigan lost only to Big Ten opponent Minnesota.

The most intriguing bowl matchup was in the

Sugar, where Southeastern Conference champion Alabama easily defeated Big Ten runner-up Ohio State 35–6. Alabama was outstanding on both offense and defense. The coaches of the two teams, Paul ("Bear") Bryant of Alabama and Woody Hayes of Ohio State, were the patriarchs of their profession with 65 years' experience and 504 victories between them.

The well-balanced Pacific Eight Conference sent 7–4 Washington to the Rose Bowl, which it won against Michigan 27–20 in a rare appearance by a non-California Pac-Eight school. Stanford (8–3) had the conference's best overall record, the nation's second best total offense, and college football's best quarterback, Guy Benjamin, who completed 208 of 330 passes for 2,521 yd and 19 touchdowns. But Washington's 6–1 conference record was best after Southern California's last-minute victory over UCLA. The Washington triumph was the ninth for the west coast conference over the Big Ten in the last 11 Rose Bowls.

In the Fiesta Bowl Penn State beat Arizona State 42–30. Two 10–1 teams were matched in the Orange Bowl, where Southwest Conference runner-up Arkansas surprised Big Eight champion Oklahoma with a 31–6 trouncing. Arkansas was sparked by the running of sophomore fullback Roland Sales, who set an Orange Bowl record of 205 yd in 22 carries. Oklahoma ranked fourth in scoring, and its 328.9 yd rushing per game led the nation. Arkansas ranked fifth in pass defense and third in scoring defense.

Grambling College, one of the leading providers of black players to the NFL, led the country with 42 points per game, thanks largely to quarterback Doug Williams, the national total offense leader with 293.5 yd per game, and college punt return leader Robert Woods, who averaged 25.4 yd. North Carolina (8–2–1) ranked first in scoring defense with a 7.4-point average and edged Clemson (8–2–1) for the Atlantic Coast Conference title.

Notre Dame's Terry Eurick pushes on for a first-quarter touchdown against Texas in the Cotton Bowl. The 38–10 victory by the Fighting Irish was capped by their being chosen top college team by both the UPI and AP polls.

UPI COMPIX

GLOSSARY

audible: a signal at the line of scrimmage that changes the offensive play or the defensive coverage just before the ball is snapped.

blitz: to rush the passer with a linebacker or a defensive back along with the defensive linemen.

cornerback: one of two defensive backs on the outside of the field, whose responsibility is to cover a wide receiver on passes.

double zone: double coverage of each wide receiver on the outsides of the field, leaving the inside more vulnerable.

free safety: one of two defensive backs on the inside of the field, who usually does not cover a particular receiver and can help double-cover any receiver.

I formation: an offensive alignment with the quarterback, fullback, and halfback in a straight line.

monster man: a defensive player used by some college teams whose job is to follow the ball rather than cover a specific player or area.

nickel defense: a defense in passing situations in which one of the three linebackers is replaced by a fifth defensive back.

nose guard: a defensive player directly opposite the offensive center. Also called middle guard.

odd-front defense: any defense that uses a nose guard. Often it involves three linemen and four linebackers instead of the conventional four linemen and three linebackers.

play action pass: a fake run by a back on a passing play.

pocket: the area of protection from which a quarterback passes.

pro-set offense: a formation with two wide receivers split toward the sidelines and two running backs in a horizontal line behind the quarterback.

shotgun: an offensive formation in which the quarterback lines up several yards behind the center in passing situations.

slot back: a player lined up behind the line of scrimmage but outside the running backs. Also called wing back.

split: a position on the line or in the backfield close to a sideline and away from the greater concentration of players.

strong safety: one of two defensive backs on the inside of the field whose responsibility on passes usually is to cover the tight end.

strong side: the side of the field where the tight end lines up.

tight end: an offensive lineman who is an eligible receiver and who lines up next to the other linemen instead of near the sideline.

trap play: a move by an offensive lineman as though there would be a different play from the one being used, in order to coax a defensive player out of position.

veer offense: a popular college offense that uses a pro-set formation and option plays that enable the quarterback to pitch the ball to a running back or run with it himself.

veer running: cutting back against the pursuit of the defensive players. Also called cutback running.

weak side: the side of the field where the tight end is not lined up.

wide receiver: an eligible receiver, either a back or a lineman, who lines up near the sideline.

wishbone: a formation in which the quarterback, fullback, and halfbacks form a Y. The offensive philosophy built around this formation is called the triple option. It uses very few passes but gives the quarterback an option of handing to the fullback for a straight-ahead run, pitching to a halfback for a sideline run, or keeping the ball himself for an end run. (KEVIN M. LAMB)

Clemson improved from 3–6–2 under new coach Charley Pell, but lost to (8–2–1) Pittsburgh in the Gator Bowl 34–3.

Colgate dominated the Eastern schools with a 10–1 record, leading the nation with 486.1 yd total offense per game. Army ended Navy's four-game service academy winning streak with a 17–14 victory that protected its series lead of 37–35–6, and Yale's 24–7 victory in its 94th game against Harvard clinched the Ivy League title.

Other individual college leaders were Colgate's Paul Lawler with seven interceptions, Mississippi punter Jim Miller with a 45.9-yd average, Western Carolina's Wayne Tolleson with 73 receptions, Tennessee-Chattanooga kickoff returner Tony Ball with a 36.4-yd average, and Kent State field-goal kicker Paul Marchese with 18 in 27 tries. In the kicking-rich Southwest Conference, Steve Little of Arkansas and Russell Erxleben of Texas shared the National Collegiate Athletic Association (NCAA) record after kicking 67-yd field goals during the season; they broke the record of 65 yd set in 1976 by Tony Franklin of Texas A & M.

Canadian Football. A temperature of 16° F (−9° C) put a premium on kicking in the Canadian Football League's Grey Cup championship game at Montreal November 27, and Don Sweet of the Montreal Alouettes came through with a record six field goals in a 41–6 win over the Edmonton Eskimos. The field was partly covered with ice, but trying to melt it with salt was not a good idea. Besides aggravating open wounds, the salt made the ball slippery. Edmonton lost four fumbles and

four interceptions in the most lopsided Grey Cup game since 1956. Alouette quarterback Sonny Wade threw three touchdown passes and won his third most valuable player award for the game.

Jimmy Edwards of the Hamilton Tiger-Cats won the season's most outstanding player award, leading the league with 1,581 yd rushing and averaging 6.3 yd per carry for his last-place team. British Columbia centre Al Wilson and wide receiver Leon Bright were the most outstanding offensive lineman and rookie of the year, respectively. Ottawa tight end Tony Gabriel, the Eastern Conference reception leader with 65 for 1,362 yd, was named the best Canadian native. Edmonton linebacker Danny Kepley was the most outstanding defensive player. (KEVIN M. LAMB)

France

A republic of Western Europe, France is bounded by the English Channel, Belgium, Luxembourg, West Germany, Switzerland, Italy, the Mediterranean Sea, Monaco, Spain, Andorra, and the Atlantic Ocean. Area: 544,000 sq km (210,040 sq mi), including Corsica. Pop. (1977 est.): 53,094,000. Cap. and largest city: Paris (pop., 1975 census, 2,-317,200). Language: French. Religion: predominantly Roman Catholic. President in 1977, Valéry Giscard d'Estaing; premier, Raymond Barre.

Domestic Affairs. Throughout 1977 attention was focused on the parliamentary elections, due to take place in March of the following year and fore-

France

Foreign Aid:
see Economy, World

Foreign Exchange:
see Economy, World

Resplendent in the traditional sash of office, Jacques Chirac made his first official outing as mayor of Paris. He was the first elected mayor of the city in over 100 years.

the government). Admittedly, the latter held Paris and some very large cities, including Bordeaux, Rouen, Strasbourg, Lyon, Nice, Toulouse, and Nancy, but the opposition became the governing party in two-thirds of the major towns in France, including Bourges, Le Mans, Montpellier, Nantes, Rennes, Saint-Étienne, Lille, Reims, and Marseille. In towns with between 9,000 and 30,000 inhabitants, the opposition scored quite clear successes, with the majority parties losing 112 of the 350 towns they had formerly held. On the other hand, in communes with populations of less than 9,000 (accounting for nearly 53% of the electorate), the swing was less marked.

Under a law of Dec. 31, 1975, Paris had been given the same status as other communes, and this meant that, for the first time in over a hundred years, the capital would have an elected mayor, chosen by the new municipal council a few days after the second round of the municipal elections. In the first round, Chirac's list of candidates for the council led in 11 of the 18 districts, but there was some danger that the left would win because of the split among the majority parties. Accordingly, Chirac and d'Ornano reached an agreement whereby each would support the other's list in districts where he had led in the first round. The final result was: Chirac's list 50 seats, joint left-wing 40, d'Ornano's list 15, and other majority candidates 4. Chirac's election as mayor a few days later thus became a mere formality.

The victory was less decisive than appeared from these figures, however. In reality, it was decided by a very close margin in two districts. Moreover, with 45% of the vote in the second round, the united left was nearly 2% ahead of its total in Paris in the second round of the 1974 presidential elections. An interesting feature of the election was the strong showing in the first round of the Ecological Movement candidates (in theory apolitical), who obtained 10% of the vote.

The relative failure of the majority parties in the municipal elections led President Giscard to form a new government, specifically chosen with the parliamentary campaign in mind. In this second Barre government (March 30), the number of ministers was reduced from 17 to 14 (excluding the

seen as presenting a fundamental choice between "alternative forms of society." The opposition parties seemed to emerge as effective victors in the March 1977 municipal elections, thus confirming a swing to the left, but the failure of the attempt by the left-wing alliance (Socialists, Communists, and Left Radicals) to update its joint program in September threw the political scene once more into confusion. On January 19 Jacques Chirac (see BIOGRAPHY), president of the new Gaullist Rassemblement pour la République (RPR), which had replaced the Union des Démocrates pour la République, caused a political sensation by announcing his candidacy for the office of mayor of Paris—a direct challenge to Pres. Valéry Giscard d'Estaing, who had "launched" Michel d'Ornano, Independent Republican (IR) and minister of industry and research, as his candidate.

The swing to the left, evident in the 1971 municipal elections, was confirmed in the two rounds of the municipal elections on March 13 and 20. Of 221 towns with populations of more than 30,000, 56 were captured by the opposition from the "majority" parties (RPR, IR, Centre of Social Democrats or CDS, Radicals, and others supporting premier). Three ministers of state, Olivier Guichard (RPR), Jean Lecanuet (CDS), and Michel Poniatowski (IR), left the government. C. Bonnet (IR) took over internal affairs and d'Ornano replaced Françoise Giroud at culture and the environment. The new men in the government were Alain Peyrefitte (RPR), who became minister of justice, and René Monory, a Centre Party senator, who went to industry and commerce. The number of secretaries of state was increased from 19 to 25.

On April 26 Barre announced his new economic plan to the National Assembly. It involved measures designed to create new jobs, an extension of the preretirement system; increases in the minimum pension to Fr 10,000 a year on July 1 and to Fr 11,000 on December 1; an increase of 10.2% in family allowances on July 1; and the unfreezing of extensive credits for public investment. The costs were to be met by a rise in gasoline prices, earlier levying of certain taxes, a state loan of Fr 6 billion, and short- and medium-term Treasury loans of Fr 5.8 billion. Barre gained the "qualified" confidence of the Assembly, by 271 votes against 186 and 17 abstentions, but there was still considerable tension between the pro-Giscard forces and Chirac's RPR. The workers in the nationalized industries responded by calling for a strike on April 28, and gas and electricity supplies in Paris were cut off for an entire day. Giscard refused to be moved, however, and he announced on television that Barre would remain as premier until the 1978 elections.

By May signs of disunity had begun to appear within the left alliance, whose representatives were to meet during the summer to update their 1972 joint manifesto. During a television debate on May 12, Barre told François Mitterrand, secretary-general of the Socialist Party, that "The policy you are putting forward is a gigantic improvisa-

tion"—to Mitterrand's apparent discomfort. The next day, the stock exchange experienced a spectacular rise in share prices. Labour remained restive, however, and all the representative trade union organizations called a 24-hour general strike for May 24 in protest against the Barre plan's provision for wage restraints. There was a huge march in Paris, the largest mass demonstration since May 1968. Three-quarters of the country was paralyzed, with the large towns especially hard hit. The cost to the country was estimated at Fr 5 billion.

Also in May, Jean-Jacques Servan-Schreiber, parliamentary deputy for Meurthe-et-Moselle, once more became president of the Radical Party (an office he had voluntarily given up two years earlier); he was elected at the Radical Party congress by 465 votes against 340 for Edgar Faure, president of the National Assembly. His announced intention was to make the Radical Party the reformist wing of the majority. At about this same time, Jean-Pierre Soisson was elected secretary-general of the Republican Party (the new name adopted by the Independent Republicans) and resigned his post as secretary of state for youth and sports. Poniatowski, formerly minister of state and president of the Independent Republicans, was entrusted with a study mission abroad and withdrew from politics. The differences within the left alliance grew more pronounced, and in June Georges Marchais, secretary-general of the Communist Party, accused Mitterrand of personal ambition and power-seeking.

At the end of August, Barre held a Cabinet meeting, devoted to the question of employment, at which he announced various economic and financial measures intended to stimulate economic activity. Although the majority parties put forward

Chinese General Yang Ch'eng-wu reviewed an honour guard in Paris in front of the Tomb of the Unknown Soldier.

an election manifesto in September stating that "the time is not ripe for upheavals or risky experiments," Barre gained Cabinet approval for the draft 1978 budget, which projected a deficit for the first time in several years. Priorities remained foreign trade and maintenance of the franc. There was no question of relaxing the austerity which alone, in the long term, could save an economy undermined by inflation.

On September 14 the leaders of the left alliance held a "summit" meeting in an effort to escape the impasse over the updating of their joint program. Robert Fabre (*see* BIOGRAPHY), president of the Left Radicals, created a sensation by walking out of the meeting after quarreling with Marchais on the subject of nationalization. Fabre, who saw himself as the protector of small and medium-sized businesses, had hoped to suppress the clause in the program that would allow workers, should they wish, to demand nationalization of their firm. Mitterrand, meanwhile, continued to support moderate proposals for the nationalization of nine corporations named in the 1972 program, which Marchais rejected. At a second meeting, held a week later, the rift became complete. The three parties could not reconcile their differences over social proposals, nationalization, or defense policies. But the root of the quarrel seemed to lie in the Communist Party's frustration over losing its position as the strongest party of the left and in Mitterrand's determination to assert his position as leader of the largest party in France. In any event, the joint program, having symbolized the Union of the Left, now seemed rather to enshrine its disunity. Victory for the left in 1978, which had appeared almost certain after the spring municipal elections, now seemed much more doubtful.

The election at the end of September of one-third of the Senate (indirectly elected by *collèges électorals* in the départements) indicated stability. The majority parties, which had held two-thirds of the seats in the previous upper house, maintained a comfortable lead. Only the Socialist Party increased its representation, from 52 to 62. Of the 115 seats to be filled, 73 went to newly elected members, and many young men entered the Senate. There was a minor government reshuffle after the

election as several government members went into the upper house. In October opinion polls gave the left-wing parties 50% of the vote instead of the 53% registered in earlier samplings; the majority remained unchanged at 47%, and the ecologists accounted for 3%. The polls indicated that the public's "image" of both Giscard and Barre had improved.

During the spring session of Parliament, Barre had twice asked for a vote of confidence in the National Assembly, first over his economic plan, the second time on the bill concerning election to the European Parliament by universal suffrage, which was carried without a vote. In the autumn session, the National Assembly, in addition to passing the draft budget, voted by 289 to 176 (Socialists and Communists) for the draft bill on Information Processing and Individual Freedom. In September France's foreign trade balance was in surplus for the first time in nearly two years. On October 21, after six months of uninterrupted slump and four months of recovery, the Paris stock exchange regained the level of Jan. 1, 1977.

France did not escape the terrorism and violence that bedeviled other countries in 1977. The most notable incidents were the kidnapping of Luchino Revelli-Beaumont, director of Fiat-France, who was freed after three months in captivity, and the violent confrontation between antinuclear demonstrators and police at the site of the Super-Phénix fast breeder reactor at Creys-Malville in Isère, which resulted in one death and 100 injured. In Corsica explosions, presumably set off by separatists, deprived part of the island of television for several months, and bombs even damaged the underground basilica at Lourdes. The press, though still in decline, did see one success: the signing of an agreement between *Le Parisien Libéré* and the Communist-led Syndicat du Livre after two and a half years of disputes and intervention by the minister of labour. In the cultural field, Giscard inaugurated the Centre National d'Art et de Culture Georges Pompidou. (*See* ARCHITECTURE; MUSEUMS.)

Foreign Affairs. Europe and Africa were the two main fields of action for Giscard. The traditional Franco-West German summits allowed the

Paris Metro commuters who were entertained by concerts in subway stations earlier in the year later got a chance to watch as artists created murals for the city's rapid transit.

UPI COMPIX

two countries to intensify cooperation. The French head of state observed that, in the face of the growing "misunderstanding" between Washington and Moscow over human rights since the arrival of Pres. Jimmy Carter in the White House, Europe was adopting an increasingly unified attitude. This solidarity was confirmed during the hijacking of a Lufthansa jet to Mogadishu, Somalia, which gave Chancellor Helmut Schmidt the opportunity to hold talks with Barre in Bonn. In November the extradition to West Germany of Klaus Croissant, defense lawyer for the West German terrorist Baader-Meinhof gang, made amends for France's refusal to hand over Abu Daoud (*see* BIOGRAPHY), a Palestinian terrorist wanted in West Germany who was apprehended in Paris in January and then released. (*See* GERMANY, FEDERAL REPUBLIC OF.)

In Africa, Giscard made the first official visit of a French president to Mali since its proclamation of independence in 1960. Speaking on television, he affirmed that, by lending planes to Morocco and thus enabling it to assist Zaire, France wished to give Africans a "sign of security and solidarity." (*See* ZAIRE.) In Paris he held talks with Juvénal Habyalimana, president of Rwanda, Gen. Gaafar Nimeiry, president of the Sudan, and Kenneth Kaunda, president of Zambia. He also presided over the fourth summit of francophone African states in Dakar, Senegal. On June 27 France granted independence to its last African possession, the French Territory of the Afars and Issas, henceforth the Republic of Djibouti. Relations between France and Algeria became extremely tense in November when Algeria refused to release eight French hostages, kidnapped in Mauritania by the Polisario Front operating from bases in Algeria. In December the hostages were released to UN Secretary-General Kurt Waldheim in Algiers, but France continued to berate Algeria for its refusal to cooperate with the French government in the matter.

Vietnamese Premier Pham Van Dong paid an official visit to Paris during the year. The visit by Soviet leader Leonid Brezhnev in June confirmed Franco-Soviet agreement on questions of détente and nuclear nonproliferation. At the end of September Brezhnev received Giscard in Moscow for economic discussions. Other visitors to France were King Hussein of Jordan, Edward Gierek, first secretary of the Polish United Workers' Party, and President Tito of Yugoslavia. In November the welcome given to René Lévesque, the separatist premier of Quebec, was surrounded with so much ostentation that it inevitably recalled Gen. Charles de Gaulle's cry of "Vive le Québec Libre" during his visit to Canada in 1967. (JEAN KNECHT)

See also Dependent States.

Gabon

A republic of western equatorial Africa, Gabon is bounded by Equatorial Guinea, Cameroon, the Congo, and the Atlantic Ocean. Area: 267,667 sq km (103,347 sq mi). Pop. (1976 est.): 1,156,000. Cap. and largest city: Libreville (pop., 1975 est., 169,200). Language: French and Bantu dialects.

Religion: traditional tribal beliefs; Christian minority. President in 1977, Omar Bongo; premier, Léon Mébiame.

Pres. Omar Bongo (*see* BIOGRAPHY) devoted himself above all in 1977 to strengthening his country's ties with France and to establishing Gabon in an important position in the African scene by conducting various attempts at mediation. Bongo paid three visits to France, in February, July, and September, and met Pres. Valéry Giscard d'Estaing each time. Because it was believed to be responsible for a raid by mercenaries on Cotonou, Benin, on January 16, the Gabon government was regarded with suspicion by many African governments, which tried unsuccessfully to prevent the Organization of African Unity from holding its summit meeting at Libreville on July 2–5.

Gabon Pres. Omar Bongo (left) was on hand to greet Egyptian Pres. Anwar as-Sadat when Sadat arrived in Libreville to attend a summit meeting of the OAU in July.

GABON

Education. (1974–75) Primary, pupils 121,407, teachers 2,412; secondary, pupils 17,575, teachers 616; vocational, pupils 3,042, teachers (1971–72) 190; teacher training, students 382, teachers 34; higher, students 986.

Finance. Monetary unit: CFA franc, with (Sept. 19, 1977) a parity of CFA Fr 50 to the French franc (free rate of CFA Fr 246.50 = U.S. $1; CFA Fr 429.50 = £1 sterling). Budget (1976 est.) balanced at CFA Fr 193,113,000,000.

Foreign Trade. Imports (1976) c. CFA Fr 130 billion; exports CFA Fr 214,480,000,000. Import sources (1975): France c. 63%; U.S. c. 11%; Belgium-Luxembourg c. 5%. Export destinations (1975): France c. 21%; U.S. c. 19%; Spain c. 13%; The Bahamas c. 11%; West Germany c. 9%. Main export crude oil 82%.

Transport and Communications. Roads (1973) 6,848 km. Motor vehicles in use (1974): passenger c. 10,000; commercial (including buses) c. 7,300. Construction of a Trans-Gabon railway was begun in 1974, with planned completion of 670 km by 1980. Telephones (Dec. 1973) 11,000. Radio receivers (Dec. 1974) 90,000. Television receivers (Dec. 1974) 5,100.

Agriculture. Production (in 000; metric tons; 1975): sweet potatoes c. 3; cassava c. 179; corn c. 2; peanuts c. 2; bananas c. 10; palm oil c. 3; coffee c. 1; cocoa c. 5; timber (cu m) 2,600. Livestock (in 000; 1975): cattle c. 5; pigs c. 5; sheep c. 58; goats c. 62.

Industry. Production (in 000; metric tons; 1975): manganese ore (metal content) 1,115; uranium 0.8; petroleum products c. 810; crude oil (1976) 11,392; electricity (kw-hr) 235,000.

Gabon

At the fourth Franco-African summit conference, held at Dakar, Senegal, in April, President Bongo was entrusted by his fellow heads of state with the task of trying to persuade President Giscard to change his policy toward the Comoro Islands by allowing the Comoro government to take over the island of Mayotte, which had preferred to remain French. This effort failed, and Bongo met with no more success in his efforts at mediation between Chad and Libya and in the struggle between the Toubou rebels and the Chad government's forces. (PHILIPPE DECRAENE)

The Gambia

Gambia, The

A small republic and member of the Commonwealth of Nations, The Gambia extends from the Atlantic Ocean along the lower Gambia River in West Africa and is surrounded by Senegal. Area: 10,689 sq km (4,127 sq mi). Pop. (1976 est.): 538,-200, including (1973) Malinke 37.7%; Fulani 16.2%; Wolof 14%; Dyola 8.5%; Soninke 7.8%; others 15.8%. Cap. and largest city: Banjul (pop., 1975 est., 42,400). Language: English (official). Religion: predominantly Muslim. President in 1977, Sir Dawda Jawara.

In the April 4–5, 1977, general election, the People's Progressive Party won 27 out of 35 seats (with a later result and a by-election 29 out of 35). Sir Dawda Jawara became president again for a second five-year term. Four parties contested the election in a quiet poll with an 82% turnout, offering some evidence that poverty is not incompatible with stable democracy.

Britain remained the main source of aid and trade, supplying £1 million toward a passenger cargo ferry and 85% of the cost of improvements to Banjul harbour as well as a technical team for research on cotton, the planting of which had increased to 4,500 ac from 27 ac in 1969. Peanuts (groundnuts) remained the major crop and by far the greatest foreign exchange earner, though tourism, which had been stagnant in 1976, boomed after the publication of *Roots* by Alex Haley (*see* BIOGRAPHY). This book and the television film made from it purported to trace Haley's origins from the U.S. back to the Mandinka tribe in the Gambian village of Juffure (declared a national monument by the president) and helped to bring Gambia much-increased tourist trade.

(MOLLY MORTIMER)

GAMBIA

Education. (1975–76) Primary, pupils 24,617, teachers 948; secondary, pupils 1,896, teachers 107; vocational, pupils 4,282, teachers 197; higher (including teacher training), students 440, teachers 43.

Finance. Monetary unit: dalasi, with (Sept. 19, 1977) a free rate of 2.30 dalasis to U.S. $1 (par value of 4 dalasis = £1 sterling). Budget (1976-77 est.): revenue 42,963,-000 dalasis; expenditure 44,311,000 dalasis (excludes development expenditure of 59,464,000 dalasis).

Foreign Trade. (1976) Imports 164,330,000 dalasis; exports 75,710,000 dalasis. Import sources: U.K. 25%; China 13%; The Netherlands 6%; Japan 6%; France 5%; Burma 5%; West Germany 5%. Export destinations: U.K. 30%; The Netherlands 22%; France 10%; Italy 7%; Switzerland 6%; Portugal 5%. Main export peanut products 91%.

Gambling

Often described as the "growth industry of the 1970s," gambling, both legal and illegal, continued to flourish throughout the world. In the United States, federal government sources estimated that more than $50 billion was wagered legally in 1976; the breakdown included $32 billion on horse racing, $14 billion on lotteries, $2 billion on casinos, and the remainder on such sports and games as dog racing, jai alai, and bingo. In addition, authorities estimated that some $30 billion was bet illegally on major team sports such as football, baseball, and basketball. Several states during 1977 followed the lead of Delaware and made such gambling legal.

On June 2 Gov. Brendan Byrne of New Jersey signed legislation that permitted casino gambling in Atlantic City. The state's voters had approved this move in a referendum held the previous November. Property values quickly soared in the decaying resort city, and it was announced that developers planned to spend more than $1 billion for casino-hotel complexes there during the next ten years. Some 5,000 new hotel rooms were expected by 1981. Casino business continued to be good in Nevada, and several other states, including New York and Florida (where interest was

It was just more of the same as Doyle "Dolly" Brunson (standing, holding drink) watched friends gather up his $340,000 in winnings at the eighth annual World Series of Poker in Las Vegas. Brunson also won the big pot last year.

especially high in the Miami Beach area), were considering legalization of this form of gambling.

In Japan approximately U.S. $14 billion was gambled legally in 1976, including $5.7 billion on horse racing, $4.2 billion on bicycle and motorcycle racing, and $4.1 billion on boat racing. Government-run lotteries were increasing in popularity.

Gambling continued to attract large numbers of bettors in the U.K. About one-third of the nation's adult population wagered $400 million in 1976 on the weekly soccer pools. Of the total of $5.5 billion bet legally in Britain in 1976 the largest amount, $850 million, was wagered on dog races. Horse racing and bingo also attracted many players, and lavish private clubs in London continued to serve those who gambled for high stakes.

Horse racing was the most popular form of gambling in France; in 1975, the latest year reported, $2.6 billion was wagered. In West Germany the national lottery made up the largest part of the 1976 total of $4 billion, with lesser amounts bet on slot machines, electronic games, horse racing, and casinos. Of the $587 million bet in Italy in 1976, the weekly lottery game accounted for $298 million and soccer pools for $230 million.

Five national lotteries in the Soviet Union were that nation's major form of gambling; the only other type permitted was horse racing. Several countries in the Middle East, including Egypt, Syria, Jordan, and Lebanon, ignored the rule against gambling in the Koran and established national lotteries.   (DAVID R. CALHOUN)

See also Equestrian Sports.
[452.C.2]

Games and Toys

Skateboarding, which had enjoyed a big revival in the U.S. from the early 1970s onward, seemed set to become an established sport worldwide in 1977, with a fast-growing following in Europe (including the U.S.S.R.), Australia, New Zealand, and South Africa. In the U.K., where interest was fanned by a visit from the professional team of the U.S. manufacturer Hobie Skateboards, sales of boards were expected to reach the million mark by the year's end. The first skate parks built specifically for that purpose opened in London and other cities during the year.

The high cost of skateboarding equipment, which, besides the skateboard itself, included a safety helmet and protective clothing, inevitably had an effect on the rest of the toy industry, which, generally, was depressed in 1977. In Europe the toy fairs were much quieter than usual and showed little that was original and new. One amusing novelty at the Nürnberg, West Germany, fair was a toy van that obeyed orders and would turn left or right, stop, or go when told to do so in French, German, or English. The van was a U.S. invention being developed by the British Mettoy Co. Ltd.

The great success of the motion picture *Star Wars* led to a renewed demand for space toys after several years of relatively sluggish sales. The film's popularity took the industry by surprise, and action dolls based on its characters were not expected to be available until the spring of 1978.

The popularity of "The Muppet Show" on both sides of the Atlantic made Kermit the Frog (*see* BIOGRAPHY), Fozzie Bear, and Miss Piggy bestsellers among TV character toys. Action Man and Sindy continued to be favourite dress-up dolls for boys and girls and were joined by Bullet Man, Intruder, and Bionic Woman.

Video games proliferated in a wide range of sophistication, simulating, besides simple bat and ball games, automobile racing, aerial dogfights, and tank battles. The U.S. market was currently running at some seven million units (about $200 million) annually. Among board games a popular newcomer—based on an ancient Japanese game—was Othello. In the U.S. it was the success story of 1976, with some 500,000 sets sold. Mastermind, several variations of which were introduced, remained popular, as did such old favourites as Scrabble and Monopoly. (The 1977 Monopoly world championship, played in Monte Carlo, was won by Chung Seng Kwa of Singapore.)

When a simple skateboard is not enough, add a sail. Wind skates are capable of attaining high speeds for a skater who is willing to take the chance.

KEYSTONE

In the U.S. game arcades continued to flourish. One of their most popular offerings in 1977 was Foosball, a tabletop game for two or four players in which the contestants operate teams of mechanical men in an effort to get the ball into the opponent's goal. Pinball machines also grew rapidly in popularity, especially in the U.S. and Western Europe.

Hong Kong's grip on world toy markets remained strong. Its exports were expected to approach $700 million in 1977, a value greater than that of the total production of West Germany, the U.K., or France. While Hong Kong was likely to keep its supremacy for some time despite increasing competition from nearby Taiwan, there was a strong possibility of increasing competition from Communist countries. The Soviet Union, for example, was in the process of building a formidable toy industry to meet its considerable domestic demand and showed itself able to produce high-quality toys at prices considerably below those of Western manufacturers. Soviet-made toys were finding their way into Western markets because many of them were being manufactured with the aid of Western technology, and Soviet toys were being shipped to the West to help pay for this assistance.

The world's fastest expanding toy company was the British-owned Dunbee Combex Marx (DCM) group. DCM gained a firm foothold in the U.S., West Germany, and Hong Kong, through its acquisitions of Louis Marx Inc. and its Hong Kong factories and of Shuco in West Germany, and continued to be strong in Britain, France, and the Commonwealth. After taking over Louis Marx in 1976 DCM converted the company's $16 million annual losses to a profit within a year, more than doubling production of its popular Green Machine three-wheeler. DCM was also supplying the Soviet toy industry with a significant amount of tooling. It estimated that within ten years more than £50 million worth of tools would be supplied, against an original commitment to supply only £2.5 million.

One explanation put forward to account for the generally depressed level of toy and games sales worldwide during 1977 (in the U.K. retail sales in the first nine months were about 20% below the level of the previous year; in West Germany they were down about 7%) was that parents were buying "useful" things such as clothes for their children's birthday and Christmas presents instead of toys. This was a trend brought about by two factors. The first, inflation, meant that parents had to be more careful with purchases; the second was that children were maturing more quickly and, in fact, increasingly preferred clothes to toys, especially as clothing designs for children were now more interesting.   (GORDON A. WEBB)

Gardening

Severe drought in many sections of the U.S. caused serious concern in 1977. Speaking of one of the most seriously affected areas, J. B. Kendrick, Jr., director of the University of California Agricultur-

al Experiment Station and Cooperative Extension, stated: "In California, we now know we can no longer take for granted our water supply and its unrestricted use. Water has made our state what it is today and sound planning is essential for a secure future."

In keeping with the emphasis on conservation and more efficient use of water for farms and gardens, the idea of trickle irrigation (called drip irrigation in California and daily flow irrigation in Australia) was spreading. In this system, small amounts of water are applied to plants at frequent intervals. A main hose carries water to the garden or field; plastic tubes branching from it run along each row; and tiny plastic microtubes deliver a minute trickle of water to each plant. Only a narrow strip of soil is moistened, and very little water pressure is involved. The water merely drips or trickles into the soil. Water loss through runoff and evaporation is almost zero, and since water is applied only to the root zone of the plant, the areas between the rows tend to remain relatively weed-free. According to research reports from California, South Dakota, Arkansas, and Michigan, well-managed drip irrigation, used on certain crops, can save significant amounts of water with no reduction in crop yield.

Composting sludge from municipal waste treatment plants could help solve an urgent environmental problem, according to T. W. Edminster, administrator of the Agricultural Research Service, U.S. Department of Agriculture: "The composted sludge can be used as a fertilizer and soil conditioner on both agricultural and recreational land, benefiting farmer, gardener and the general public." The technique for composting sludge was developed by Agricultural Research Service scientists at Beltsville, Md. It dilutes heavy metal content, and the high temperature generated during composting kills most pathogens.

The rising cost of fuel for heating greenhouses was forcing European growers to introduce thermal screens, which can be pulled over growing crops at night to box in the heat. Fuel savings of up to 37% were demonstrated, and manufacturers were competing to produce porous materials that would combine good insulation with minimum restriction of light. Computer programs were developed by the U.K. Meteorological Office to collate weather information relevant to the development of such plant diseases as apple scab and potato blight. Timely warnings when weather conditions are conducive to the spread of the diseases would enable growers to apply protective sprays at the most sensitive period.

Color Magic, a pink hybrid tea rose, and Charisma, a red and yellow floribunda, were the All-America award-winning roses for 1978. The blooms of Color Magic change colour as they develop from buds to mature flowers and have a light, sweet fragrance. Charisma was notable for its brilliance and masses of blooms, which have good lasting quality, both as cut flowers and on the plant.

Fleuroselect, the European seed-testing organization, awarded bronze medals to *Alyssum maritimum* Wonderland (Hurst Gunson Cooper Taber),

Zinnia elegans Cherry Ruffles and Yellow Ruffles (Bodger), and *Salvia farinacea* Victoria (Ets L. Clause). At the Belfast International Rose Trials, the Uladh award for the most fragrant rose and the best hybrid tea was won by Evening Star, raised by Jackson and Perkins of the U.S. Dreaming Spires, raised by John Mattock of Nuneham Courtenay, near Oxford, England, won the best floribunda award. The 1977 Golden Rose of The Hague went to Helga, raised by G. de Ruiter of The Netherlands.

By 1977 plant tissue and cell culture propagation techniques were sufficiently advanced to permit their application in commercial nursery production. Their advantages include rapid plant propagation; eradication of viruses and other plant disease organisms from named cultivars (varieties); production of true breeding plants; longtime, low-cost storage of nursery crop germ plasm; and more efficient methods of plant breeding. A new culturing technique developed at the Scottish Horticultural Research Institute was used successfully to produce five new lily cultivars. By crossing an Asian cultivar such as Enchantment with a southeastern Asian species such as *L. lankongensis*, embryos are produced in the seedpods which, when cultured in a sterile nutrient, can be grown to produce a new plant. Two cultivars raised by this method were Ariadne, cream with a mauve blush, and Adonis, a dark, glossy red.

From the Regovan Horticultural Research Station near Sofia, Bulgaria, came a new race of carnations, raised from *Dianthus caryophyllus semperflorens*. The strongly fragrant blooms were available in a range of colours. A race of dwarf gerberas called Gergerellas was released in West Germany. A race of tetraploid pelargoniums developed in East Germany was available under the name Tetra-Pel-Hybride. The individual blooms are larger than those of diploid cultivars, and more resistant to bad weather.

In the U.K. four new cultivars of strawberries were released which combine yield, quality, and resistance to red core and verticillium wilt: Tantallon, Troubadour, and Saladin from the Scottish Horticultural Research Institute and Harvester from the John Innes Institute. Saladin flowers a few days later than usual, and it was hoped that it would be less susceptible to spring frost. The John Innes Institute was also using pea mutants obtained from the world's largest collection of pea cultivars in the U.S.S.R. to breed new varieties with stiffer stems, no leaves, and peas in pods that hang as if glued into position.

Radiation treatment can be used to overcome genetic barriers to the improvement of turf grasses, according to Jerrel B. Powell, an Agricultural Research Service geneticist, who succeeded in using gamma radiation to induce genetic mutations in commercial varieties of Bermuda grass. In the U.K. the Sports Turf Research Institute was comparing new cultivars of grass especially bred for sports turf and amenity purposes. Of particular interest were cultivars combining the toughness and recovery powers of ryegrass with the fine leaf, dwarf habit, and year-round colour usually associated with the fescues.

The seven-spotted ladybird beetle, a cousin of the American ladybug and the most important aphid predator in Europe, Asia, and North Africa, had become established in several parts of the U.S., according to Agricultural Research Service scientists. If sufficient numbers of the beetle could be obtained and established throughout the country, it might provide successful biological control for many species of aphids. The U.K. Glasshouse Crops Research Institute discovered a fungus, *Verticillium lecanii*, that under conditions of high humidity in greenhouses can infect and control aphids in a 10- to 12-hour period.

(J. G. SCOTT MARSHALL; TOM STEVENSON)

See also Agriculture and Food Supplies; Environment; Life Sciences.
[355.C.2-3; 731.B.1]

German Democratic Republic

German Democratic Republic

A country of central Europe, Germany was partitioned after World War II into the Federal Republic of Germany (Bundesrepublik Deutschland; West Germany) and the German Democratic Republic (Deutsche Demokratische Republik; East Germany), with a special provisional regime for Berlin. East Germany is bordered by the Baltic Sea, Poland, Czechoslovakia, and West Germany. Area: 108,328 sq km (41,826 sq mi). Pop. (1977 est.): 16,767,000. Cap. and largest city: East Berlin (pop., 1977 est., 1,106,300). Language: German. Religion (1969 est.): Protestant 80%; Roman Catholic 10%. First secretary of the Socialist Unity (Communist) Party and chairman of the Council of State in 1977, Erich Honecker; president of the Council of Ministers (premier), Willi Stoph.

East Germany made a relatively small concession to the demand for human rights before the Belgrade (Yugos.) review conference on the Helsinki agreements started on Oct. 4, 1977. Some 90 political prisoners were freed and sent to West

Cuban leader Fidel Castro was met by crowds of flag-waving spectators as he arrived for a tour of East Berlin in April.

UPI COMPIX

German Democratic Republic

Germany. Most of them, like the majority of East Germany's estimated 6,000 political prisoners, had been imprisoned for trying to escape to the West. This was good business for the East German government, because West Germany paid about DM 40,000 for each released prisoner. These prisoners-for-cash exchanges had been going on for some time, and about 1,200 political prisoners were let out of East Germany each year.

The East German government justified the arrangement on the ground that the money it got from West Germany was compensation for its investment in the education of the people it let go. But it showed no signs of liberalizing its emigration policy in other respects. Unless they were old pensioners or had urgent family business requiring their presence in the West, other East Germans did not get exit visas. Thirty or so intellectuals expelled during the year for dissident activity were in a different category from the political prisoners, and West Germany did not pay for their release. Taking a cue from the U.S.S.R., the East German government simply decided to get them out of the country as part of its policy of neutralizing its opponents by dispersing them.

A riot that occurred in East Berlin on October 7 was serious enough to bring the police into action with water cannons and batons. The incident was dismissed by the East German authorities as the work of drunken rowdies. The trouble started when police sealed off an area around Alexanderplatz, East Berlin's central square, where a crowd had gathered for a pop concert, and ordered a restaurant and discotheque to close after an incident in which eight people fell down a ventilator shaft. When the police appeared the crowd chanted the name of Wolf Biermann, a singer and writer of protest songs who was deprived of his East German citizenship while on a concert tour in West Germany in 1976. A report published by Amnesty International in September pointed out that the state retained "censorship of the press and communications, a heavily guarded frontier with West Germany, including the Berlin Wall, and severe restrictions on freedom of movement, expression and association."

Despite signs of deliberalization, it was not thought that the hawks in East Berlin had necessarily gotten the upper hand. Erich Honecker, the Communist Party leader, was regarded as a rela-

German Literature:
see Literature

tive dove, an impression strengthened by his statement in January that the relationship between the two German states should be guided by common sense and goodwill. Indeed, the East Germans made it clear that they would be prepared to consider further "easements" in their relations with West Germany—but at a price. They said it was illogical for the West German government, having recognized the sovereignty of East Germany, to hold onto the myth that there was only one German citizenship. This allowed East Germans in any part of the world to be issued West German passports with a minimum of formality. The East Germans contended that their citizens were sometimes bribed to accept such passports and claimed that, if this anomaly were removed, the border with the West would become more permeable and relations more normal.

East Germany's draft economic plan for 1978 set targets that appeared completely unrealistic—an increase in exports to the capitalist countries of an average 30% and a decrease in imports from these countries of 5%. This goal was believed to be a consequence of the Soviet Union's insistence that East Germany drastically reduce its indebtedness to the West, put at the colossal sum of DM 13.3 billion. Moscow feared that this risky credit business was not only economically unsound but could also force East Germany to surrender some of its political independence vis-à-vis the West. The authorities went to considerable lengths to obtain hard Western currencies. They greatly extended the chain of Intershops where a wide variety of high-quality Western goods could be bought with Western money, thus provoking strong criticism from some of the people who had none.

In August, Rudolf Bahro, a staunch Communist and a department head in an East Berlin factory, created a stir by launching a fierce attack on East Germany's brand of Communism in a book published in the West. Bahro faithfully defended the orthodox positions of Marxism-Leninism—just as they were taught in East Germany—but he accused the authorities of distorting this teaching when they came to put it into practice. He was particularly critical of the state's economic system. Immediately after excerpts from his book were published in *Der Spiegel*, Bahro was arrested and held in prison on charges of spying for the West.

(NORMAN CROSSLAND)

GERMAN DEMOCRATIC REPUBLIC

Education. (1975–76) Primary, pupils 2,649,886; secondary, pupils 47,854; primary and secondary, teachers 158,543; vocational, pupils 412,785; higher (including 7 universities), students 293,238, teaching staff (1974–75) 33,570.

Finance. Monetary unit: Mark of Deutsche Demokratische Republik, with (Sept. 19, 1977) a free commercial exchange rate of M 2.33 to U.S. $1 (M 4.05 = £1 sterling). Budget (1975 est.): revenue M 114,662,000,000; expenditure M 114,160,000,000. Net material product (at 1967 prices; 1975) M 141.7 billion.

Foreign Trade. (1976) Imports M 45,921,000,000; exports M 39,536,000,000. Import sources (1974): U.S.S.R. 30%; West Germany 9%; Czechoslovakia 7%; Poland 7%; Hungary 5%. Export destinations (1974): U.S.S.R. 33%; Czechoslovakia 10%; West Germany 10%; Poland 9%; Hungary 6%. Main exports (1975): machinery 31%; transport equipment 9%; chemicals; textiles.

Transport and Communications. Roads (1975) 126,933 km (including 1,561 km autobahns). Motor vehicles in use (1975): passenger 1,880,000; commercial 238,900. Railways: (1975) 14,298 km (including 1,454 km electrified); traffic (1976) 22,339,000,000 passenger-km, freight 51,801,000,000 net ton-km. Air traffic (1975): 1,490,000,000 passenger-km; freight 52,570,000 net ton-km. Navigable inland waterways (1975) 2,538 km; goods traffic 2,362,000,000 ton-km. Shipping (1976): merchant vessels 100 gross tons and over 446; gross tonnage 1,437,054. Telephones (Dec. 1975) 2,570,000. Radio licenses (Dec. 1974) 6,114,000. Television licenses (Dec. 1974) 5,096,000.

Agriculture. Production (in 000; metric tons; 1976): wheat c. 2,600; barley c. 3,300; rye c. 1,400; oats c. 600; potatoes c. 7,673; sugar, raw value c. 595; cabbage (1975) c. 371; rapeseed 318; apples c. 454; fish catch (1975) 375. Livestock (in 000; Dec. 1975): cattle 5,532; sheep 1,883; pigs 11,501; goats 53; horses (1975) c. 82; poultry 47,122.

Industry. Index of production (1970 = 100; 1976) 145. Production (in 000; metric tons; 1976): lignite 246,889; coal 456; electricity (kw-hr) 89,148,000; iron ore (39% metal content) 51; pig iron 2,529; crude steel 6,739; cement 11,345; potash (oxide content; 1974) 2,864; sulfuric acid 966; synthetic rubber 145; cotton yarn (1975) 59; rayon, etc., filaments and fibres 139; passenger cars (units) 164; commercial vehicles (units) 36.

Germany, Federal Republic of

A country of central Europe, Germany was partitioned after World War II into the Federal Republic of Germany (Bundesrepublik Deutschland; West Germany) and the German Democratic Republic (Deutsche Demokratische Republik; East Germany), with a special provisional regime for Berlin. West Germany is bordered by Denmark, The Netherlands, Belgium, Luxembourg, France, Switzerland, Austria, Czechoslovakia, East Germany, and the North Sea. Area: 248,620 sq km (95,993 sq mi). Pop. (1977 est.): 61,442,000. Provisional cap.: Bonn (pop., 1977 est., 285,000). Largest city: Hamburg (pop., 1977 est., 1,698,600). (West Berlin, which is an enclave within East Germany, had a population of 1,950,700 in 1977.) Language: German. Religion (1970): Protestant 49%; Roman Catholic 44.6%; Jewish 0.05%. President in 1977, Walter Scheel; chancellor, Helmut Schmidt.

The outbreak of urban terrorism in West Germany in 1977 presented the constitutional state with the most serious challenge it had had to face in its history. The way in which this challenge was met strengthened the position of the federal chancellor, Helmut Schmidt. Previously, economic difficulties had caused the government to lose ground.

Domestic Affairs. On April 7 Siegfried Buback, West Germany's chief public prosecutor, was murdered on the way to his office in Karlsruhe, together with his driver and a motor mechanic traveling with him. A terrorist group known as the Red Army Faction (RAF) claimed responsibility. Some four months later, on July 30, Jürgen Ponto, chairman of the Dresdner Bank, was killed while resisting the attempts of a group of terrorists to kidnap him at his home near Frankfurt am Main. On September 5 terrorists kidnapped the president of the employers' federation, Hanns-Martin Schleyer (see OBITUARIES), in Cologne and killed his driver and three bodyguards. Six weeks later, after the government had refused to give in to the kidnappers' demands, Schleyer's body was found in the trunk of a car in the French town of Mulhouse. He had been shot through the head.

With the arrest of the ringleaders of the Baader-Meinhof gang in the summer of 1972, it had been hoped that West Germany had got on top of terrorism. But the events of 1977 showed that a new generation of terrorists, more ruthless than their predecessors, had sprung up. The new attacks led to a chorus of demands for more law and order.

Since terrorism gained a foothold in West Germany in the late 1960s, the internal security forces had become markedly stronger and more effective. But the opposition, composed of the Christian Democratic Union (CDU) and the Bavarian Christian Social Union (CSU), insisted that more legislation was needed. For instance, it wanted to tighten the law on demonstrations, breaches of the peace, and criminal associations; have "dangerous objects" classified as weapons; increase the penalties for violent crime; and in certain cases allow a judge to listen to conversations between a defense lawyer and his client. It was strongly suspected that many lawyers representing terrorists had a conspiratorial relationship with their clients.

The kidnappers of Schleyer, again members of the RAF gang, demanded the release of 11 terrorists in West German prisons and that they be flown to a country of their choice. The 11 included the three remaining members of the Baader-Meinhof gang, Andreas Baader (see OBITUARIES), Jan-Carl Raspe, and Gudrun Ensslin, who were sentenced to life imprisonment in April for terrorist crimes. The government, a coalition of the Social Democratic Party (SPD) and the Free Democratic Party (FDP), hung a news blackout over its negotiations with the terrorists, but it was clear from the start that the authorities had no intention of surrendering.

On October 13 Arab terrorists launched a backup operation in support of their German comrades. The Arabs—two men and two women—hijacked a Lufthansa aircraft with 87 people on board during a flight from Majorca, Spain, to Frankfurt am Main. The plane was forced to fly to Rome, then to Cyprus, Bahrain, Dubai, and Aden, where the pilot was murdered, and finally, with the co-pilot at the controls, to Mogadishu in Somalia. In the early hours of October 18—with the Somali government's permission—it was stormed by a unit of Germany's crack antiterrorist force, known as GSG 9. All the hostages were freed, most of them physically unharmed. Three terrorists were killed, and the other, a woman, was seriously injured. But the government's joy at the outcome was rapidly overshadowed by the news that Baader, Ensslin, and Raspe had committed suicide on October 18 in their cells at Stammheim jail, near Stuttgart. Baader and Raspe had shot themselves, Ensslin had hanged herself from a window, and Irmgard Möller, another terrorist prisoner, had stabbed herself, but not fatally.

Not only had Baader and Raspe been able to conceal pistols in their cells, Raspe also had a transistor radio and had managed to build a primitive radio circuit to enable the prisoners to communi-

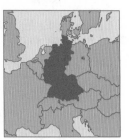

Federal Republic of Germany

West German police used barbed wire entanglements to prevent thousands of protesters from swarming onto the site of a nuclear power station under construction in Kalkar.

KEYSTONE

cate with one another. The autopsies, at which foreign medical observers were present, showed that the deaths were caused by suicide; there was no evidence of murder. The minister of justice in Baden-Württemberg, Traugott Bender, resigned, the prison governor was dismissed, and a full inquiry was ordered into the circumstances. The Stammheim affair was all the more alarming because it happened at a time when terrorist prisoners throughout the country had been barred from contact with each other and with the world outside under a special law. This controversial measure, passed by the Bundestag after the Schleyer kidnapping, also deprived prisoners of access to defense counsel.

Certain conclusions could be drawn from these events. Although the German terrorists had shown they could count on international support, so had Chancellor Schmidt. The chancellor succeeded more than any other statesman in persuading the world that terrorism was an international problem, the solution of which required international cooperation. Similarly, the chancellor managed to ensure that his every move had the support not only of his Cabinet colleagues but of the leaders of all political parties represented in the Bundestag. Schmidt, whose reputation as a man of action had been suffering in the face of obstinate unemployment and declining economic growth, was again at the top of the popularity table.

France, which in January had refused to extradite the Palestinian terrorist Abu Daoud (*see* BIOGRAPHY) to West Germany as requested, but instead had set him free, nevertheless extradited Klaus Croissant to West Germany on November 17. Croissant had been the Baader-Meinhof defense lawyer and was suspected of having established communication between the prisoners.

The end of the economic upswing, after just two years, took most German economists by surprise, although more modest growth had been expected in 1977 than in the previous year, when it reached 5.6%. In the event, the slowdown from the fourth quarter of 1976 to the first quarter of 1977 turned into virtual stagnation in the second quarter. Hopes that unemployment would average about

900,000 persons in 1977 as part of a steady decline were dashed. Instead the figure was likely to average at least 1 million for the year. The effects of the DM 16.5 billion medium-term investment program, designed mainly to help the chronically sick building industry, were disappointing. In September the government announced a package of tax cuts, so as to inject at least DM 10 billion into the economy in 1978. In October Count Otto Lambsdorff was appointed minister of economics in succession to Hans Friderichs, who resigned to take Ponto's former post as chairman of the Dresdner Bank.

Uncertainty about the country's nuclear energy program grew during the year. *Bürgerinitiativen*—"citizens' initiatives" created by environmentalists—played a big part in wrecking it. The future of the 300-Mw fast breeder reactor being built at Kalkar on the Lower Rhine, a joint venture with the Belgians and the Dutch, depended on the Federal Constitutional Court, which had been asked to rule whether fast breeder reactors conformed to West Germany's Basic Law. Work on six other (light water) breeder reactors was held up by litigation, a dozen were still being built, and nine, generating a total of 6,340 Mw—about 2% of West Germany's primary energy needs—were actually in operation. In March the plan to generate 45,000 Mw of nuclear energy by 1985 was slashed by one-third. Later it became clear that even the new, lower target was wildly optimistic.

Discord in the SPD made the future of the energy program all the more uncertain. By a majority of one vote, the national executive committee of the party recommended in September that no new stations be built until permission had been granted for work to start on a plant for the storage of nuclear waste and the reprocessing of nuclear fuel elements. The federal government wanted the waste to be stored in the subterranean salt dome structures of Lower Saxony, at Gorleben near the East German border. The Christian Democratic prime minister of Lower Saxony, Ernst Albrecht, who faced a state election in 1978, did not want the plant and argued that it would take two or three years to investigate the suitability of the site. The

---

GERMANY, FEDERAL REPUBLIC OF

Education. (1976–77) Primary, pupils 6,287,642, teachers (1975–76) 236,356; secondary, pupils 3,331,159, teachers (1975–76) 152,594; vocational, pupils 2,270,516, teachers (1975–76) 59,455; higher, students 877,328, teaching staff (1973–74) 93,841.

Finance. Monetary unit: Deutsche Mark, with (Sept. 19, 1977) a free rate of DM 2.33 to U.S. $1 (DM 4.05 = £1 sterling). Gold, SDR's, and foreign exchange (June 1977) U.S. $31,523,000,000. Budget (federal; 1976 actual): revenue DM 141,570,000,000; expenditure DM 171,660,000,000. Gross national product (1976) DM 1,135,100,000,000. Money supply (April 1977) DM 173.7 billion. Cost of living (1970 = 100; June 1977) 147.

Foreign Trade. (1976) Imports DM 210,590,000,-000; exports DM 256,640,000,000. Import sources: EEC 49% (The Netherlands 14%, France 12%, Belgium-Luxembourg 9%, Italy 9%); U.S. 8%. Export destinations: EEC 46% (France 13%, The Netherlands 10%, Belgium-Luxembourg 8%, Italy 7%, U.K. 5%); U.S. 6%; Austria 5%. Main exports: machinery 29%; motor vehicles 15%; chemicals 13%; iron

and steel 9%; textiles and clothing 6%. Tourism (1975): visitors 7,403,000; gross receipts U.S. $2,840,000,000.

Transport and Communications. Roads (1975) 464,000 km (including 6,200 km autobahns). Motor vehicles in use (1975): passenger 18,161,000; commercial 1,231,000. Railways: (1975) 32,006 km (including 10,323 km electrified); traffic (1976) 38,349,000,000 passenger-km, freight 59,202,-000,000 net ton-km. Air traffic (1976): 14,982,000,-000 passenger-km; freight 1,098,545,000 net ton-km. Navigable inland waterways in regular use (1975) 4,-381 km; freight traffic 47,565,000,000 ton-km. Shipping (1976): merchant vessels 100 gross tons and over 1,957; gross tonnage 9,264,671. Telephones (Dec. 1975) 19,603,000. Radio licenses (Dec. 1974) 20,909,000. Television licenses (Dec. 1974) 18,920,-000.

Agriculture. Production (in 000; metric tons; 1976): wheat 6,702; barley 6,487; oats 2,497; rye 2,-100; potatoes 9,808; sugar, raw value 2,217; apples 1,487; wine c. 795; cow's milk c. 20,495; butter 544;

cheese 642; beef and veal 1,334; pork 2,454; fish catch (1975) 442. Livestock (in 000; Dec. 1975): cattle 15,266; pigs 21,875; sheep 1,450; horses used in agriculture (1975) 325; chickens 89,119.

Industry. Index of production (1970 = 100; 1976) 114. Unemployment (1976) 4.6%. Fuel and power (in 000; metric tons; 1976): coal 89,270; lignite 134,-536; crude oil 5,526; coke (1975) 34,817; electricity (kw-hr) 333,652,000; natural gas (cu m) 19,030,000; manufactured gas (cu m) 15,585,000. Production (in 000; metric tons; 1976): iron ore (32% metal content) 2,255; pig iron 32,170; crude steel 42,413; aluminum 1,041; copper 446; lead 278; zinc 452; cement 34,-097; sulfuric acid 4,682; cotton yarn 208; woven cotton fabrics 199; wool yarn 60; man-made fibres 874; petroleum products (1975) 91,784; fertilizers (1975–76) nitrogenous 1,259, phosphate 649, potash 1,848; synthetic rubber 378; plastics and resins 6,443; passenger cars (units) 3,546; commercial vehicles (units) 330. Merchant vessels launched (100 gross tons and over; 1976) 1,874,000 gross tons. New dwelling units completed (1976) 392,000.

federal government accepted that work on new stations should not begin until the problem of waste disposal had been solved, but the chancellor did not agree that this meant waiting for the go-ahead at Gorleben.

A major spy scandal broke in December when the Ministry of Defense confirmed a newspaper report that two men and a woman, arrested in 1976 on charges of spying for East Germany, had had access to highly sensitive military documents, including NATO contingency plans. The official whose safe had contained the documents was suspended, and Chancellor Schmidt called for a thorough investigation of the affair.

In the late summer the West Germans indulged in an orgy of introspection. Whole pages of newspapers were devoted to reports about how West Germany looked to foreign eyes. One newspaper published a soul-searching article headed "Is Germany a Nightmare?" In the Bundestag the chancellor cited one commentator's suggestion that the kidnapping of Schleyer might be an expression not just of extremist madness but of a specifically German madness which was liable to break out periodically. This preoccupation with the theme of the unpopular German was prompted in large measure by three events. One was West Germany's refusal to extradite Herbert Kappler, the former Nazi police chief of Rome, who escaped from a hospital in Rome in August; Kappler had been serving a life sentence in Italy for war crimes. The others were a revival of West German interest in the Nazi period, inspired by a film and several books about Hitler, and a letter to the chancellor from his predecessor, Willy Brandt, expressing concern about the activities of right-wing extremists.

The Nazi past still accounted for a considerable measure of anti-German sentiment. The Third Reich was close enough for millions of Europeans to have vivid personal memories of an unparalleled outbreak of "German madness." But history alone could not explain recurring outbursts of anti-German feeling. One reason, of course, was envy and resentment of West Germany's economic power and suspicion of the political and even military power assumed to go with it.

Foreign Affairs. Chancellor Schmidt's visit to Washington, D.C., in July for talks with U.S. Pres. Jimmy Carter helped to iron out differences between the West German and U.S. governments. Some friction in this relationship had been caused by West Germany's undertaking to supply Brazil with eight nuclear power stations, a uranium enrichment plant, and an installation for reprocessing spent fuel elements. The Carter administration was utterly opposed to this transfer of the technology for the entire nuclear fuel cycle, especially the reprocessing plant, which produced plutonium that could be used to make nuclear warheads. West Germany argued that its credibility as an exporter of advanced technology was at stake, and it also suspected that the U.S., not content with being a superpower in weaponry, wanted to dominate the West in peaceful uses of atomic energy as well. The West German government refused to back down on the deal.

Commander Ulrich Wegener, chief of the commando unit that freed 86 hostages aboard a hijacked Lufthansa airliner at Mogadishu, Somalia, reviewed his victorious troops after their return to Bonn.

Schmidt's government was also skeptical about President Carter's stand on human rights. It feared that the spectacular championship of dissidents in the Communist world might only make the Communist regimes more repressive, as well as hampering the West's negotiations with them. The West German government claimed that its own quiet diplomacy had produced tangible, if modest, results. Many thousands of ethnic Germans had been allowed to leave Poland and other Eastern European countries; there was even a trickle of settlers from East Germany; and the situation in and around Berlin had improved, although annoying pinpricks from the East had been resumed in recent months.

The third bone of contention was the economy. President Carter's administration regarded West Germany as a main obstacle to revitalizing the world economy because, in Washington's view, it did not do enough to reflate. Schmidt was unmoved, and his ministers reeled off lists of good deeds the West Germans had done to help their partners' economies. In the tough recession year of 1975, they said, all other industrial countries cut back their imports by about 7% while West Germany's went up by 3%. In 1976 Britain, Japan, and the U.S. had stepped up their exports to West Germany by 20%, while German exports became dearer because of the mark revaluation. As for reflation, it sounded to German ears too much like inflation to be acceptable.

West Berlin. The East German government, with the blessing of the Soviet Union, took one or two significant steps in January to illustrate its thesis that quadripartite control really applied only to West Berlin. From January 1 foreigners and stateless persons crossing from West Berlin to East Berlin for the day needed a visa, obtainable for a fee of DM 5. After all, said the East German government, visas were required for journeys into the German Democratic Republic, so why should visits to its capital be treated differently?

The East Germans also removed the control posts of the People's Police on the boundary between East Berlin and East Germany to underline the argument that there was nothing special about

Ashanti chiefs greeted Prince Charles in royal style when the prince visited the Ashanti people during a trip to Ghana in March. Ghana was celebrating its 20th anniversary of independence from British rule during the prince's visit.

East Berlin's status. The Western allies did what was expected of them, spelling out once again that they shared responsibility for maintaining the status of greater Berlin with the Soviet Union and that this arrangement could be changed only with the agreement of the four powers.

The governing mayor of West Berlin, Klaus Schütz, resigned in May and was succeeded by Dietrich Stobbe, 39, formerly the city's senator for federal affairs. This followed the resignation of the senator for internal affairs, Kurt Neubauer. Neubauer had neglected to hand over to the city treasury a payment of DM 56,000, which he had received for his work as a member of the supervisory board of the Berlin Bank between 1972 and 1976. He said that his wife had forgotten to transfer the money. This was one of a number of affairs that in recent years had marred the reputation of the Berlin SPD. In the city elections in the spring of 1975, the party had lost its overall majority in the House of Representatives and had formed a coalition with the FDP. Schütz subsequently became West German ambassador to Israel.

(NORMAN CROSSLAND)

Ghana

Ghana

A republic of West Africa and member of the Commonwealth of Nations, Ghana is on the Gulf of Guinea and is bordered by Ivory Coast, Upper Volta, and Togo. Area: 238,533 sq km (92,098 sq mi). Pop. (1976 est.): 10,309,000. Cap. and largest city: Accra (pop., 1975 est., 716,600). Language: English (official); local Sudanic dialects. Religion (1960): Christian 43%; Muslim 12%; animist 38%. Chairman of the National Redemption Council and of the Supreme Military Council in 1977, Gen. Ignatius Kutu Acheampong.

Civil agitation and a severe economic crisis brought the military government to the brink of collapse in 1977. In May and June students demanding immediate return to civilian rule demonstrated against the government, and universities

were closed. More remarkably, professional bodies struck or threatened to strike, and Gen. Ignatius Acheampong reconstituted the 23-member National Redemption Council in order to include 5 new civilian commissioners. On July 1 Acheampong announced a return to civilian rule "as soon as possible," and on July 13 this was defined as being by July 1, 1979. The existing Koranteng-Addow ad hoc committee was to submit its report on "union government" within three months. A

GHANA

Education. (1974–75) Primary, pupils 1,051,012, teachers 35,334; secondary, pupils 509,627, teachers 21,099; vocational, pupils 15,940, teachers 903; teacher training, students 6,399, teachers 757; higher, students 8,022, teaching staff (1973–74) 952.

Finance. Monetary unit: new cedi, with (Sept. 19, 1977) an official rate of 1.15 cedi to U.S. $1 (free rate of 1.99 cedi = £1 sterling). Gold, SDR's, and foreign exchange (June 1977) U.S. $185 million. Budget (1975–76 est.): revenue 852.2 million cedis; expenditure 1,198,800,000 cedis. Gross national product (1974) 2,153,000,000 cedis. Money supply (April 1977) 1,534,400,000 cedis. Cost of living (Accra; 1970 = 100; March 1977) 590.

Foreign Trade. (1975) Imports 909.3 million cedis; exports 928,260,000 cedis. Import sources: U.S. 16%; U.K. 15%; West Germany 11%; Nigeria 7%; Japan 6%; Libya 5%. Export destinations: U.K. 15%; U.S. 11%; The Netherlands 10%; Switzerland 8%; West Germany 8%; Japan 7%; U.S.S.R. 7%; Yugoslavia 5%. Main exports (1975): cocoa 59%; timber 8%.

Transport and Communications. Roads (1974) 35,023 km. Motor vehicles in use (1974): passenger 55,500; commercial (including buses) 43,900. Railways: (1976) 953 km; traffic (1972) 431 million passenger-km, freight 305 million net ton-km. Air traffic (1975): 176 million passenger-km; freight 3.6 million net ton-km. Shipping (1976): merchant vessels 100 gross tons and over 84; gross tonnage 183,089. Telephones (Dec. 1975) 60,000. Radio receivers (Dec. 1974) 1,060,000. Television receivers (Dec. 1974) 33,000.

Agriculture. Production (in 000; metric tons; 1976): corn c. 395; cassava (1975) c. 1,800; taro (1975) c. 1,400; yams (1975) c. 800; millet c. 71; sorghum c. 81; tomatoes c. 110; peanuts c. 60; oranges c. 165; cocoa c. 320; palm oil c. 30; timber (cu m; 1975) c. 11,973; fish catch (1975) 255. Livestock (in 000; 1975): cattle c. 1,000; sheep c. 1,700; pigs c. 390; goats c. 2,000.

Industry. Production (in 000; metric tons; 1975): bauxite 325; petroleum products c. 1,183; gold (troy oz) 524; diamonds (metric carats) 2,328; manganese ore (metal content) 199; electricity (kw-hr) c. 4,050,000.

referendum on the type of government desired would follow in March 1978, after which a constituent assembly would create a draft constitution and elections would be held in June 1979.

The economic crisis triggered by rising food prices was aggravated by such factors as the two-year drought, smuggling, a shortage of foreign exchange, and a black market in currency. High cocoa prices did little to relieve inflation, and the budget deficit rose from £76 million in 1973 to £399 million in 1976. The International Monetary Fund offered aid for a 30% devaluation, but Acheampong refused to devalue the cedi. A new five-year development plan (6.7 billion cedis) aimed at full employment of all resources and agricultural rehabilitation, especially reorganization of the cocoa industry.   (MOLLY MORTIMER)

Golf

The golfing year of 1977 was memorable for the remarkable achievements of Tom Watson (*see* BIOGRAPHY), who won the Masters at Augusta, Ga., and the British Open at Turnberry and also won the most money on the U.S. tour. His total of $310,-653.16 enabled him to join Jack Nicklaus and Johnny Miller as the only golfers to have won over $300,000 in a year. In the Danny Thomas Memphis Golf Classic, Al Geiberger broke the Professional Golfers' Association (PGA) tour record for a single round by scoring a 59.

Nicklaus finished second to Watson in both the Masters and the British Open, prompting many to wonder whether the great man's reign over professional golf was at last beginning to decline. If so, it was only in relation to Watson. In the major championships and in most other events Nicklaus still cast the longest shadow in the minds of the other competitors, and he was easily second in the money list.

At the Masters Nicklaus began the last round three shots behind Watson and immediately launched a tremendous counterattack, but Watson did not yield. Although playing behind Nicklaus and thus in a good position to see what he was doing, Watson matched him shot for shot down the stretch until the 17th hole where he had a birdie to go one stroke ahead. As the cheers for this putt thundered over the course, Nicklaus was preparing to hit his second on the 18th hole and thinking that a par four would probably be good enough for a tie. When he heard the cheers, he knew that he must go for the birdie but hit the shot into a bunker. A moment later Watson made his par and won by two strokes.

Neither Watson nor Nicklaus was in the final pursuit for the U.S. Open title at Tulsa, Okla. This tournament developed into a contest between Lou Graham, the 1975 champion, and Hubert Green, who won by a stroke in spite of a threat to his life on the last day. Green was warned that he might be killed on the 15th hole but decided to continue. At the same time, he warned his playing partner and the caddies to keep away from him. His courage and presence of mind were rewarded with a final round of 70, which enabled him to resist Graham's great challenge. Graham finished with a pair of 68s. Tom Weiskopf was third, while Watson shared seventh place, a stroke ahead of Nicklaus.

The British Open was one of the most extraordinary championships ever played. Staged for the first time in the magnificent setting of Turnberry in western Scotland, it produced an astonishing climax. Watson's total of 268, 12 under par, beat by eight strokes the previous record, set by Arnold Palmer at Troon and later equaled there by Weiskopf. Never had the record been reduced by such a margin in one attempt. However, Watson beat Nicklaus by only one stroke. Green was the only other player to finish under par, and he was ten strokes behind Nicklaus. Not since Palmer and Kel Nagle had the last day to themselves in 1962 had the climax been such a private affair, but Palmer beat Nagle by six strokes. At Turnberry Watson and Nicklaus fought probably the greatest match ever seen in Open championship golf.

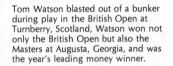

Tom Watson blasted out of a bunker during play in the British Open at Turnberry, Scotland, Watson won not only the British Open but also the Masters at Augusta, Georgia, and was the year's leading money winner.

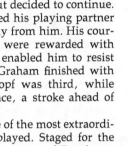
UPI COMPIX

The contest revealed the resourcefulness and unyielding courage of Watson. After four holes of the final round he was three behind. Immediately he countered with a birdie at the fifth and then, as on two other holes later, holed out in two shots from a bunker. He was still one behind on the short 15th, where he hit probably his worst shot of the round. It was fortunate not to land in a bunker, and Nicklaus seemed certain to be two or three strokes in front; but Watson, putting through light rough, holed from 20 yards.

This was a harsh blow for Nicklaus, who went behind for the first time at the 17th when his long iron shot missed the green; after Watson had played the hole perfectly, Nicklaus missed from four feet. The last hole was little short of miraculous. Nicklaus, pressing for a birdie, sliced within inches from being unplayable in a bush but managed to reach the green. Then, after Watson had hit a superb seven iron two feet from the hole, Nicklaus holed his long putt for a birdie. It was a heroic gesture, but Watson tapped in his putt and was British champion for the second time in three years.

The PGA championship, played for the first time at Pebble Beach, Calif., brought unexpected triumph to Lanny Wadkins and sad defeat for Gene Littler, who lost a six-stroke lead in the final round and a play-off on the third extra hole. Nicklaus finished one stroke behind the leaders.

To what extent Watson's performance was affected when it was discovered that some of his clubs had illegal markings cannot be determined. Although innocent of the minute flaw in the club

A little body English helped sink a putt for Chako Higuchi, a Japanese golfer who is known as the Oriental Express. She became the first Asian to win the U.S. LPGA championship.

WIDE WORLD

design, he was probably disconcerted and embarrassed by the affair, and tied for sixth. The tragedy, however, was Littler's. For a generation his superb swing and manner had been a model for all golfers, and his courage in recovering from a cancer operation was a source of admiration.

Wadkins, who caught and defeated Littler with great attacking golf, had also recovered from surgery that had set him back in 1976. Three weeks later he won the World Series of Golf at Akron, Ohio, with its first prize of $100,000. Weiskopf was second, five strokes behind. With his victory Wadkins gained an automatic place on the Ryder Cup team for the match at Royal Lytham St Anne's in England. This contest resulted in the usual comfortable victory for the United States by 12½–7½, but Great Britain and Ireland gave a better account of themselves than had been expected.

On the first day in the foursomes, where two partners play one ball with alternate shots, great putting by Dave Stockton turned one probable U.S. defeat into victory. As often before, the four-ball matches, in which two partners play separate balls, gave the U.S. a commanding lead. Nick Faldo, at 20 the youngest British player ever to appear in the tournament, and Peter Oosterhuis, who had won their foursome the previous day, again were the one successful British pair. Faldo, who had been a professional only 18 months, played with great poise. To beat Ray Floyd and Nicklaus was a rare achievement, and Faldo, who finished eighth in the European order of merit, proved to be the most promising British player in a decade.

In the singles Faldo beat Watson, and Oosterhuis won his match, but although the ten points were shared equally that day the U.S. team was always in sight of the three it needed for total victory. The same was true on the last afternoon of the Walker Cup match for amateurs at Shinnecock Hills, Long Island. There, the British, who lost 16–8, suffered their worst defeat in the U.S. since the matches were first played over 18 holes in 1963.

Basic errors, especially in the foursomes, cost the British dearly. Too many fairways on the magnificent course were missed, and the U.S. players were allowed to win too many holes in par. The U.S. was well served by John Fought, Scott Simpson, Lindy Miller, and Vance Heafner, products of college golf; they won all their matches, contributing ten points to the total. The British failed to fulfill their ability with a few exceptions, including Michael Kelley, Steve Martin, and Allan Brodie, who won three of his four matches.

Fought continued to play impressively strong golf in winning the U.S. Amateur championship at Aronomink in Pennsylvania, beating Doug Fischesser 9 and 8 in the 36-hole final. Three of the British golfers, British amateur champion Peter McEvoy, Sandy Lyle, and Kelley, reached the fifth round but none survived it. McEvoy fell to a long putt by Fischesser on the last green.

The European tour was dominated by Spanish golfers, who won eight tournaments. Severiano Ballesteros again was the outstanding European golfer, easily heading the order of merit for the second successive year. The Colgate (formerly Piccadilly) World match play championship was won by Graham Marsh of Australia, who beat Hubert Green, Hale Irwin, and Ray Floyd on his way to winning £30,000, the largest prize in Europe.

The women's professional tour in the U.S. again was dominated by experience. Judy Rankin remained leading money winner, with Joanne Carner also richer by more than $100,000. They were closely pursued by Jane Blalock and Kathy Whitworth, but the younger players continued to improve. Hollis Stacy won three events, including the U.S. Open, and Pat Bradley, Sally Little, and Jan Stephenson were well up on the money list. The most remarkable performance, however, was that of Debbie Austin who, after nine years on the tour without a victory, won five tournaments, a tally equaled only by Rankin. Hisako "Chako" Higuchi (*see* BIOGRAPHY) won the ladies' PGA championship to become the first Japanese woman to win a major U.S. tournament.

Within one autumn month the golf world lost three illustrious figures. Cecil Leitch, who was 86, dominated British women's golf around the time of World War I. Clifford Roberts (*see* OBITUARIES) ended his life at the Augusta National Club, which he had helped Bobby Jones to found and where his iron hand and devotion were greatly responsible for the Masters' being the unique event it is. And immediately after finishing a round of golf in Madrid, Bing Crosby (*see* OBITUARIES) died from a heart attack. Earlier in the summer Fred Corcoran (*see* OBITUARIES), one of the game's most famous entrepreneurs and the moving force behind the World Cup, died soon after attending the U.S. Open.

(P. A. WARD-THOMAS)

Greece

A republic of Europe, Greece occupies the southern part of the Balkan Peninsula. Area: 131,990 sq km (50,962 sq mi), of which the mainland accounts for 107,194 sq km. Pop. (1976 est.): 9,165,000. Cap. and largest city: Athens (pop., 1971, 867,000). Language: Greek. Religion: Orthodox. President in 1977, Konstantinos Tsatsos; prime minister, Konstantinos Karamanlis.

General elections were held in Greece on Nov. 20, 1977, a full year before they were due, although Konstantinos Karamanlis' government still enjoyed the unqualified support of its 215 out of 300 deputies in Parliament. The reason invoked by the prime minister for holding early elections was that the country's main foreign policy problems—Cyprus, the Aegean, and membership in the European Economic Community (EEC)—were expected to reach a critical phase in 1978; therefore, Greece needed a government armed with a fresh popular mandate. It was also likely that Karamanlis, facing threatening domestic problems, believed that his New Democracy Party would fare better if elections were held in 1977 rather than a year later.

The New Democracy Party retained its hold on power, but with a much reduced majority, obtaining 173 seats and 41.85% of the vote, as against 54% in 1974. Andreas Papandreou's Panhellenic

Greece

Socialist Movement, which won 92 seats (+77) and 25.33% of the vote, surpassed George Mavros' Democratic Centre Union to become the main opposition party. The Centre Union obtained only 15 seats (−42) and 11.95% of the vote. Two new parties, the rightist National Rally led by former prime minister Stephanos Stephanopoulos and the New Liberals of Konstantinos Mitsotakis, obtained 5 and 2 seats, respectively. The two factions of the deeply divided Communist Party stood separately for the first time. The Moscow-oriented Greek Communist Party won 11 seats, while 2 seats went to the Left Alliance, formed by the Communist Party of the Interior—the Greek version of Eurocommunism—and four other leftist groups.

The Greek-Turkish disputes over Cyprus and the Aegean made little headway toward settlement, but there was no major crisis. Both countries were preoccupied with electoral campaigns and premature elections which, in a sense, gave them legitimate grounds for stalling. U.S. Pres. Jimmy Carter, whose election was hailed in Greece and in Cyprus with unjustified exuberance, sent his personal envoy, Clark Clifford, to the area in Febru-

Great Britain:
see United Kingdom

Greek Pres. Konstantinos Tsatsos was a keynote speaker at the "Future of Democracy" conference in Greece.

ary to explore possible solutions. Clifford visited Athens, Ankara, and Nicosia, but with little result. The death in August of President Makarios of Cyprus, who in January had initiated a constructive dialogue with the Turkish Cypriots, gave rise to further complications and delays.

Hopes were revived toward the end of the year when the U.S. and Britain presented a fresh initiative. The plan was to commit Turkey, which was in the throes of a major economic crisis, to a predetermined and phased settlement of the Cyprus problem. In exchange, the U.S. would ratify the U.S.-Turkish defense cooperation agreement, pledging Turkey military credits worth $1 billion over four years. Further Greek-Turkish confrontations in the Aegean were avoided thanks to a protocol signed by the two sides in Bern, Switz., in November 1976, whereby they agreed to negotiate and refrain from any provocations. Three Greek-Turkish meetings on the Aegean continental shelf were held during the year, but no progress was made.

Efforts to improve Greek-U.S. relations suffered a serious setback in July when Athens, yielding to public pressure, asked Washington to cancel the appointment of William E. Schaufele as ambassador-designate to Greece. In the course of his confirmation testimony before a Senate committee, Schaufele had spoken of "unusual" past geographic settlements in the Aegean as the cause of the Greek-Turkish dispute, and the remark was construed as implying criticism of the international treaties that awarded the Aegean islands to Greece. The State Department gave full support to the ambassador, and the Athens post was deliberately left vacant for some time. Shortly afterward Greece agreed to initial the U.S.-Greek Defense Cooperation Agreement governing the use of military facilities in Greece by U.S. armed forces. The actual signing was left until after the Greek elections. Although Greece's alienation from the NATO mili-

tary structure continued to some extent, Greek naval and air force units participated in a NATO exercise for the first time since 1974.

Greek efforts to gain full membership in the EEC made good progress, but new obstacles emerged following a French request that negotiations with Greece be suspended until the Community carried out reforms in its common agricultural policy. The changes, designed to protect French and Italian growers of Mediterranean crops, were chiefly aimed at Spain, and the condition was eventually lifted. It became clear, however, that while negotiations would continue, the question of agriculture would not be broached until after the French elections in March 1978.

The Greek economy fared well, despite the heavy burden of military expenditure. The Bank of Greece estimated that per capita income would rise to $2,700 in 1977, and inflation would be held at below 13%. The balance of payments situation was satisfactory, despite a large trade deficit. The basic defects of the economy persisted, however. Unrestrained consumerism had inflated the trade deficit and diverted domestic investments to luxury goods, while productive investment was inhibited by international and domestic uncertainties, some of the latter due to clumsy government tactics that undermined the confidence of the economic establishment.

For the first time, perhaps, the Greeks became aware of a new enemy: pollution. It was eroding the ancient marbles of the Acropolis as well as the lungs of the Athenians, and clean beaches were becoming hard to find in a country that boasted 15,000 km of coastline. On January 10 UNESCO director general Amadou-Mahtar M'Bow, speaking at the Acropolis, launched an international appeal for $10 million to halt the decay of the monuments. At the same time, in order to reduce air pollution, the government banned the use of heavy fuels for heating in Athens.　　(MARIO MODIANO)

Grenada

A parliamentary state within the Commonwealth of Nations, Grenada, with its dependency, the southern Grenadines, is the southernmost of the Windward Islands of the Caribbean Sea, 161 km N of Trinidad. Area: 344 sq km (133 sq mi). Pop. (1974 est.): 106,200, including Negro 53%, mixed 42%, white 1%, and other 4%. Cap.: Saint George's (pop., 1974 est., 6,600). Language: English. Religion: Christian. Queen, Elizabeth II; governor-general in 1977, Leo de Gale; prime minister, Sir Eric Gairy.

After the December 1976 elections, at which his United Labour Party was returned with a reduced majority of nine seats to the opposition's six, Eric Gairy formed a new government. A court challenge was instituted over the election results, charging that the opposition coalition, the Peoples' Alliance, had been prevented from using the government radio station or loudspeakers in the streets. At an antigovernment, pro-human rights demonstration staged during the meeting of the Organization of American States in Saint George's in June, opposition senator MacDonald Grant said the knighthood recently conferred on Gairy was a "fitting honour" for a "well-deserving slave." The opposition was concerned about Gairy's cultivation of such friends as the Pinochet regime in Chile.

Grenada's economy remained in a parlous condition. Tourism was still crippled after the unrest of 1973–74, and the amount and value of banana exports were reduced by the decline in sterling. A trade deficit of £7.2 million was reported in 1976.

(SHEILA PATTERSON)

Grenada

In an attempt to increase its energy supply, Guatemala made plans to tap the geothermal potential of its volcanoes. The Moyuta volcano was selected as the site for a $22.3 million generating plant.

The upsurge of activity that followed the February 1976 earthquake, coupled with excellent export performances of coffee and cotton, led to continued economic progress in late 1976 and 1977; the growth rate reached 8% in 1976 (6.5% in 1975) and was estimated at 11% in 1977. Inflation remained a problem, despite a drop in the inflation rate from 20% in 1976 to a predicted 15%.

GRENADA

Education. (1971–72) Primary, pupils 29,795, teachers 884; secondary, pupils 4,470, teachers 182; vocational, pupils 497, teachers 10; teacher training, students 101, teachers 6.

Finance and Trade. Monetary unit: East Caribbean dollar, with (Sept. 19, 1977) a par value of ECar$2.70 to U.S. $1 (free rate of ECar$4.70 = £1 sterling). Budget (1976 est.) balanced at ECar$28 million. Foreign trade (1975): imports ECar$52.8 million; exports ECar$26.9 million. Import sources (1973): U.K. 27%; Trinidad and Tobago 20%; U.S. 9%; Canada 8%. Export destinations (1973): U.K. 33%; West Germany 19%; The Netherlands and possessions 14%; U.S. 8%; Belgium-Luxembourg 5%. Main exports (1974): cocoa 29%; nutmeg 28%; bananas 16%; mace 9%. Tourism (1975): visitors 21,000; gross receipts U.S. $8 million.

Guatemala

A republic of Central America, Guatemala is bounded by Mexico, Belize, Honduras, El Salvador, the Caribbean Sea, and the Pacific Ocean. Area: 108,889 sq km (42,042 sq mi). Pop. (1976 est.): 6,451,200. Cap. and largest city: Guatemala City (pop., 1973, 700,500). Language: Spanish, with some Indian dialects. Religion: predominantly Roman Catholic. President in 1977, Kjell Eugenio Laugerud García.

GUATEMALA

Education. (1974) Primary, pupils 618,544, teachers 17,-171; secondary, vocational, and teacher training, pupils 104,492, teachers 7,073; higher (1973), students 21,715, teaching staff (university only) 1,314.

Finance. Monetary unit: quetzal, at par with the U.S. dollar (free rate, at Sept. 19, 1977, of 1.74 quetzal to £1 sterling). Gold, SDR's, and foreign exchange (June 1977) U.S. $713.8 million. Budget (1976 actual): revenue 428 million quetzales; expenditure 524.6 million quetzales. Gross national product (1975) 3,526,000,000 quetzales. Money supply (April 1977) 647.8 million quetzales. Cost of living (1970 = 100; Jan. 1977) 179.

Foreign Trade. Imports (1976) 981.6 million quetzales; exports (1975) 640.9 million quetzales. Import sources (1975): U.S. 34%; Venezuela 11%; Japan 9%; El Salvador 8%; West Germany 8%. Export destinations: U.S. 23%; El Salvador 12%; West Germany 10%; U.K. 8%; Italy 6%; Costa Rica 6%; Nicaragua 5%; Japan 5%. Main exports (1975): coffee 26%; sugar 18%; cotton 12%; bananas 5%.

Transport and Communications. Roads (1975) 13,450 km (including 824 km of Pan-American Highway). Motor vehicles in use (1975): passenger 76,100; commercial (including buses) 40,100. Railways (1975): 904 km; freight traffic 127 million net ton-km. Air traffic (1976): 131.6 million passenger-km; freight 7,080,000 net ton-km. Telephones (Jan. 1974) 53,000. Radio licenses (Dec. 1974) 261,000. Television receivers (Dec. 1974) 106,000.

Agriculture. Production (in 000; metric tons; 1976): corn 686; sorghum c. 96; sugar, raw value c. 515; tomatoes c. 78; dry beans c. 93; bananas c. 571; coffee c. 153; cotton, lint c. 100. Livestock (in 000; March 1976): sheep c. 520; cattle (1975) c. 2,030; pigs (1975) c. 880; chickens c. 12,-290.

Industry. Production (in 000; metric tons; 1975): petroleum products 955; cement 341; electricity (kw-hr) 1,-100,000.

Guatemala

Economically, the country had almost completely recovered from the effects of the earthquake, although large numbers of the poor remained homeless. The construction of some 14,000 dwellings was undertaken in the metropolitan area at a cost of U.S. $7 million. The EXMIBAL nickel plant, which began operation in July, was expected to produce some 11,300 tons of nickel and provide U.S. $60 million in export earnings annually. Further discoveries in the Rubelsanto oil fields brought total estimated reserves to 27.3 million bbl; daily production of 5,000–6,000 bbl was forecast for 1978.

British troops were sent to Belize in June, when Guatemalan troop movements near the frontier led to fear of an imminent invasion. Talks with the U.K. on the future of Belize continued, but no solution to the problem was in sight. Guatemala broke off diplomatic relations with Panama in May as a result of the latter's support for Belize's claim to independence, and in December it rejected a similar conclusion by a ministerial meeting of Caribbean states. Various political coalitions were set up in preparation for the 1978 presidential election, but the ruling Partido Institucional Democrático was expected to maintain its position.

(FRANÇOISE LOTERY)

Guinea

Guinea

Guinea-Bissau

A republic on the west coast of Africa, Guinea is bounded by Guinea-Bissau, Senegal, Mali, Ivory Coast, Liberia, and Sierra Leone. Area: 245,857 sq km (94,926 sq mi). Pop. (1977 UN est.): 4,642,000; however, a census held on Dec. 30, 1972, reported 5,143,284 persons, of whom 1.5 million were living abroad. Cap. and largest city: Conakry (pop., 1974, 412,000). Language: French (official). Religion: mostly Muslim. President in 1977, Sékou Touré; premier, Louis Lansana Beavogui.

Discontent continued in 1977 in Conakry and in the provinces. During street demonstrations Pres. Touré reportedly was the target of stones and jeers; later Touré reportedly had 13 soldiers executed for refusing to break up the demonstrations. These stories were denied by the government, which stated in September, however, that foreign agents were stirring up trouble in various parts of the country to embarrass the regime.

The government's alleged savage repression had been exposed in October 1976 in *Prison d'Afrique* by Jean-Paul Alata, a former colleague of Touré. In France the book was seized by the authorities to please Touré; but, although Pres. Valéry Giscard d'Estaing received Guinea's minister of planning and cooperation, N'Faly Sangare, in Paris in January 1977, his own proposed visit to Guinea did not take place. Furthermore, the French government dismissed several requests by Guinea for the extradition of Alata from France. James Soumah, a member of the French Socialist Party, in June called upon the French left to denounce Guinea's "regime of terror." Touré reacted by comparing the Socialist leader, François Mitterrand, with Hitler. In November Guinea quietly ended Soviet reconnaissance flights from its territory.

(PHILIPPE DECRAENE)

Guinea-Bissau

An independent African republic, Guinea-Bissau has an Atlantic coastline on the west and borders Senegal on the north and Guinea on the east and south. Area: 36,125 sq km (13,948 sq mi). Pop. (1977 est.): 930,800. Cap. and largest city: Bissau (metro. area pop., 1970, 71,200). President in 1977, Luis de Almeida Cabral; premier, Maj. Francisco Mendès.

Regional councils were elected between Dec. 19, 1976, and mid-January 1977. These were the first elections held in Guinea-Bissau since independence in 1974, but, although everyone over the age of 15 was entitled to vote, less than 50% of the electorate went to the polls in some constituencies. The ruling African Party for the Independence of Guinea-Bissau and Cape Verde provided an official list of candidates, and in most districts an average of 80% voted for the list. In some areas, however, a majority preferred unofficial candidates.

The National Assembly, consisting of 150 members chosen from the regional councils, met on March 13 and reelected Luis de Almeida Cabral as president of the country and of the 15-member Council of State, with Maj. João Bernardo Vieira as vice-president and president of the National Assembly. Maj. Francisco Mendès was confirmed as premier and at once formed a new government.

GUINEA

Education. (1971–72) Primary, pupils 169,132, teachers 4,698; secondary, pupils 68,410, teachers (1970–71) 2,360; vocational (1970–71), pupils 2,013, teachers 150; teacher training (1970–71), students 1,478, teachers 275; higher (1970–71), students 1,974, teachers (1965–66) 95.

Finance. Monetary unit: syli, with a free rate (Sept. 19, 1977) of 22.03 sylis to U.S. $1 (38.38 sylis = £1 sterling). Budget (1972–73 est.) balanced at 4.5 billion sylis.

Foreign Trade. (1975) Imports c. 3.8 billion sylis; exports c. 3.3 billion sylis. Import sources: France c. 24%; U.S.S.R. c. 15%; U.S. c. 15%; Morocco c. 8%; Belgium-Luxembourg c. 7%; U.K. 5%. Export destinations: U.S. 16%; Spain c. 14%; U.S.S.R. c. 12%; Canada c. 9%; West Germany c. 8%; Cameroon c. 8%; Canada c. 8%; France c. 7%; Yugoslavia c. 6%; Switzerland c. 6%. Main exports (1971): alumina and bauxite 72%; pineapples 10%; coffee 6%; palm kernels 6%.

GUINEA-BISSAU

Education. (1975–76) Primary, pupils 84,711, teachers (including preprimary) 2,415; secondary, pupils 2,576, teachers 123; vocational, pupils 343, teachers 13; teacher training, students 127, teachers 14.

Finance and Trade. Monetary unit: Guinea-Bissau peso, with (Sept. 19, 1977) a par value of 0.85 peso to the Portuguese escudo (nominal free rate of 34.40 pesos to U.S. $1; 60 pesos = £1 sterling). Budget (1972 est.): revenue 433 million pesos; expenditure 408 million pesos. Foreign trade (1975): imports 965,360,000 pesos; exports 157,361,000 pesos. Import sources (1973): Portugal 56%; Spain 7%; U.K. 5%; Japan 5%. Export destinations (1973) Portugal 90%. Main exports (1973): peanuts 46%; transport equipment (transit) 21%; petroleum and products (transit) 8%; palm kernels 7%; metals 6%; timber 5%.

Agriculture. Production (in 000; metric tons; 1975): rice c. 32; peanuts c. 27; palm kernels c. 8; palm oil c. 5; timber (cu m) c. 530. Livestock (in 000; 1975): cattle c. 256; pigs c. 171; sheep c. 69; goats c. 181.

Guiana:
see Dependent States; Guyana; Surinam

Addressing the National Assembly, Cabral announced his government's intention to continue its policy of nonalignment and its membership in the Economic Community of West African States. As of March 1 Guinea-Bissau had its own currency, the peso, with the same value as the old escudo. (KENNETH INGHAM)

Guyana

A republic and member of the Commonwealth of Nations, Guyana is situated between Venezuela, Brazil, and Surinam on the Atlantic Ocean. Area: 215,000 sq km (83,000 sq mi). Pop. (1976 est.): 783,000, including (1970) East Indian 51.8%; African 31.2%; mixed 10.3%; Amerindian 4.9%. Cap. and largest city: Georgetown (pop., 1970, 63,200). Language: English (official). Religion: Protestant, Hindu, Roman Catholic. President in 1977, Arthur Chung; prime minister, Forbes Burnham.

Beginning in 1976, Guyana had experienced a serious economic downturn, but foreign exchange controls and import cuts began to bite by late 1977, and more austerity measures were announced for 1978. The International Monetary Fund made a loan and, as relations between Guyana and the new U.S. administration improved and the government's attitude toward foreign private enterprise softened, $12 million in U.S. aid was announced for 1978. A Cabinet reshuffle in the spring of 1977 placed leading technicians in posts where they could exert influence on the country's serious economic problems.

Early 1977 saw the collapse of the move toward unity between Burnham's People's National Congress (PNC) and Cheddi Jagan's opposition People's Progressive Party (PPP). At the August PNC congress, Burnham rejected a renewed appeal by Jagan for a "national patriotic front." Jagan's Guyana Agricultural Workers Union then called a strike in the sugar industry that threatened the autumn harvest. The PPP had been courting the ultraleft Working People's Alliance (WPA). Meanwhile, right-wing elements, including the new Liberator Party, were said to be regrouping.

(SHEILA PATTERSON)

GUYANA
Education. Primary (1973–74), pupils 132,023; (1974–75) secondary, pupils 64,314; primary and secondary, teachers 7,144; vocational, pupils 2,956, teachers 126; teacher training, students 640, teachers 89; higher, students 1,752, teaching staff 157.
Finance. Monetary unit: Guyanan dollar, with (Sept. 19, 1977) a par value of Guy$2.55 to U.S. $1 (free rate of Guy$4.44 = £1 sterling). Budget 1976 est.): revenue Guy$450 million; expenditure Guy$664 million.
Foreign Trade. (1975) Imports Guy $806.4 million; exports Guy$837.2 million. Import sources: U.S. 30%; U.K. 22%; Trinidad and Tobago 18%. Export destinations: U.K. 28%; U.S. 23%; U.S.S.R. 9%; Jamaica 6%; Trinidad and Tobago 5%. Main exports: sugar 50%; bauxite 24%; rice 10%; alumina 8%.
Agriculture. Production (in 000; metric tons; 1976): rice c. 270; sugar, raw value 371; oranges (1975) c. 10; copra c. 5. Livestock (in 000; 1974): cattle c. 275; sheep c. 106; goats c. 60; pigs c. 120.
Industry. Production (in 000; 1975): bauxite (metric tons) 3,198; diamonds (metric carats; 1974) 50; electricity (kw-hr) 393,000.

Gymnastics and Weight Lifting

Gymnastics. Nadia Comaneci of Romania continued to dominate women's gymnastics by winning the 1977 European all-around title at Prague, Czechoslovakia. After her victory the Romanian team refused to finish the finals of the individual events as a protest against "underscoring." Similar complaints had marred the Olympic competitions at Montreal. The head of the International Women's Gymnastics Technical Committee denied the charges, but spectators repeatedly manifested displeasure when the scores were posted. In the all-around competition the U.S.S.R. placed three gymnasts among the top five: Nelli Kim, Elena Muchina, and Maria Filatova. With Ludmila Tourischeva in retirement and Olga Korbut's future in doubt, these three led a field of at least 20 world class Soviet gymnasts who would vie for places on the team that was to defend the World Cup in 1978. In men's competition, Vladimir Markelov of the Soviet Union won the all-around European title. It was evident that the Soviets were developing male athletes for the 1980 Olympics and hoped to dethrone the Japanese men, who won the team gold medal at Montreal.

In competition for the American Cup in New York City, Kathy Johnson (U.S.) outscored Donna Turnbow (U.S.) to win first place. Third place went to Karen Kelsall, the Canadian champion, who was the youngest female gymnast to compete

Guyana

SYNDICATION INTERNATIONAL/PHOTO TRENDS

Teodora Ungureanu of Romania officially retained the women's title in the Champions-All Gymnastics tournament in London in April. She was, however, outscored in all events by Nadia Comaneci, who competed as a guest.

at Montreal. Mitsuo Tsukahara (Japan), a bronze medal winner at Montreal, captured the men's all-around crown. He was followed by Kurt Thomas, the U.S. champion, Toshiomi Nishiki (Japan), and Bart Conner (U.S.). During competitions sponsored by the U.S. Gymnastics Federation and the National Collegiate Athletic Association, fine performances were given by Peter Kormann, the first U.S. gymnast in 44 years to win an Olympic medal, by Kurt Thomas, and by Bart Conner. Teodora Ungureanu, generally considered Romania's finest woman gymnast after Comaneci, won the 1977 Champions-All Gymnastics title. Defending champion Kormann finished fifth in the men's division and relinquished his title to Sergei Khishniakov of the Soviet Union. Ann Carr, all-around champion during the 1975 Pan American Games, outscored fellow Americans Carrie Englert and Connie Jo Israel to win the all-around championship during a competition sponsored by the Association for Intercollegiate Athletics for Women. The national Amateur Athletic Union (AAU) elite class championships were won by Stephanie Willim and by Koji Sato, a Japanese living in the U.S.

In general, 1977 was a year during which gymnasts were given numerous opportunities to broaden their experience and polish their skills. The U.S. Gymnastics Federation, for example, prepared a full schedule of competitions and exhibitions at home and in many countries of Europe, Asia, and Africa. The Romanians made several tours, one of which carried them to the U.S. in October. Former Soviet Olympic champion Yuri Titov, president of the International Gymnastics Federation, confidently predicted that gymnastics would become even more spectacular in the future as athletes refined their techniques and developed more original and complicated exercises.

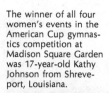

The winner of all four women's events in the American Cup gymnastics competition at Madison Square Garden was 17-year-old Kathy Johnson from Shreveport, Louisiana.

The agony of competition was etched deeply onto the face of Cuba's Roberto Urrutia who set a new weight lifting world record in the lightweight class with a total of 315 kg (693 lb) at the world championships in Stuttgart, West Germany.

Weight Lifting. Soviet weight lifter Vasily Alekseyev retained his world superheavyweight title at Stuttgart, West Germany, with a lift of 430 kg, which was 10 kg less than the total he raised in winning the gold medal in Montreal. The world championships were the first major international competition since the Olympic Games and introduced one new weight class that brought the total to ten. Although athletes from Japan, Cuba, and Bulgaria each won a single title, the Soviets took all the others. Roberto Urrutia of Cuba evidently profited from Soviet coaching. He finished seventh in the lightweight class at Montreal but at Stuttgart he bettered his Olympic performance by 22.5 kg and set a new world record of 315 kg. Valentin Khristov of Bulgaria, who finished first at Montreal but was disqualified for using anabolic steroids, won the second heavyweight division title. Jiro Hosotani of Japan took the bantamweight crown. The final standings at Stuttgart told much of the story. The U.S.S.R. led with 328 points, East Germany had 182, and Hungary 165.

Prospects for the U.S. in international competition continued to be poor. Mark Cameron finished fourth at Stuttgart in the newly created first heavyweight division and Bruce Wilhelm was fifth among the superheavyweights. In the national AAU championships, Curtis Lee White won the flyweight class and became the youngest national champion at age 14. Sam Walker won the superheavyweight division but was unchallenged by Wilhelm who was forced to withdraw because of a training injury.　(CHARLES ROBERT PAUL, JR.)
[452.R.4.f]

Haiti

The Republic of Haiti occupies the western one-third of the Caribbean island of Hispaniola, which it shares with the Dominican Republic. Area: 27,-700 sq km (10,695 sq mi). Pop. (1977 est.): 4,749,-000, of whom 95% are Negro. Cap. and largest city: Port-au-Prince (pop., 1976 est., 652,900). Language: French (official) and Creole. Religion: Roman Catholic; Voodooism practiced in rural areas. President in 1977, Jean-Claude Duvalier.

In June 1977, Pres. Jean-Claude Duvalier gained enough backing from the technocrats in his administration to secure the dismissal of Pierre Biamby as interior and defense minister and his replacement by the justice minister, Aurélien Jeanty. Biamby had been forced on him early in 1976 by old-guard supporters of his late father. The president also obtained the appointment of a technocrat, Edouard Berrouet, as agriculture minister. Andrew Young, the U.S. ambassador to the UN, visited Haiti as part of a Caribbean tour in August. Largely as a result of pressure from Washington in support of human rights, 104 political prisoners were released in September to celebrate the 20th anniversary of the Duvalier family's assumption of power on September 22. Civilian courts were established in June to try subversives, and measures to increase civilian participation in decision making were promised in September.

The economy showed some improvement. The growth rate rose from 2% in 1975 to 5% in 1976, largely as a result of high coffee prices, and the inflation rate fell from 17 to 9%. In August the International Monetary Fund made available a credit of $8.1 million. However, the four-year drought continued to affect large parts of the country; the corn, millet, and mountain bean crops failed, and electricity and water supplies, especial-

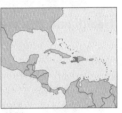

Haiti

ly to the capital, were at a reduced level. Food riots reportedly broke out in the city of Gonaïves on December 24.　　　　　　　(ROBIN CHAPMAN)

Health and Disease

International Aspects. A report of the World Health Organization (WHO) published in February described the general practitioner, "once the mainstay of medical care," as an endangered species, "just when a heightened awareness of the importance of the non-specialist had developed as a result of revised concepts of medical care." It stated that in countries in which students had a choice they mostly preferred to specialize. Special-

Sixty-one Haitians who pooled their money to buy a wooden sailboat were towed to Miami in August by the U.S. Coast Guard after losing their way and spending three days without food or water.

UPI COMPIX

Handball:
see Court Games

Harness Racing:
see Equestrian Sports

STAYSKAL—© 1977 THE CHICAGO TRIBUNE

"Rooms are $175 a day. Tests and medicine are extra. . . . And, oh, yes! Will you need a bed?"

ists were found to be less isolated and overworked, while their work carried greater prestige and reaped higher financial rewards. The report also noted that many Europeans wanted to avoid hospitalization wherever possible, especially for children, the mentally ill, and the aged, "whose treatment in hospitals may hinder rather than help the recovery process."

The call for a reassessment of priorities in medical care was repeated at WHO's 30th world assembly in May when its director general, Halfdan Mahler, said it was regrettable that both third-world and developed countries still allocated up to three-quarters of their health expenditures to highly sophisticated, disease-oriented institutional care of individual patients in capital cities, leaving large sections of the population unserved by primary health care provisions. One of the key programs to be mounted by WHO in its "Health for all by 2000" campaign was a worldwide immunization drive in an attempt to reduce the high toll of preventable disease still prevalent, especially in the third world.

The proportion of children in the developed countries receiving protective vaccinations of all kinds continued to fall, both because of publicity given to the possibility of adverse reactions to certain vaccines and because the dramatic fall in once common childhood infections achieved by mass inoculation programs had produced a false sense of security. In October the British secretary of state for health told a vaccination conference that in the U.K. the number of children vaccinated against polio, tetanus, and diphtheria had fallen from 80 to 75% in the last few years and that whooping cough vaccination had been halved from 78 to 39%. Polio vaccination had reduced the number of paralytic cases in England and Wales from an average of 5,000 a year to less than 5, but 14 cases of the disease occurred in the U.K. between January and October 1977, and fears of an epidemic were growing. In April the U.S. Department of Health, Education, and Welfare (HEW) announced a plan to launch a major national campaign to immunize by 1979 more than 90% of the 20 million American children who did not have complete protection against polio, measles, rubella, diphtheria, whooping cough, mumps, and tetanus.

The year provided several further reminders of

the fact that infectious diseases had by no means been conquered. France maintained its vigorous campaign against rabies, which continued to advance toward the Channel ports, and recently released figures showed that in the previous 12 months more than 2,000 rabid foxes had either been shot or found dead, and the disease had also been identified in some 60 dogs, 90 cats, nearly 200 cattle, and about 20 horses. Antirabies measures included the systematic gassing of fox dens with phosgene gas, financial support for hunting organizations for the purchase of equipment and cartridges, and a bounty of 30 francs for each fox tail handed in. About 75,000 were being "cashed" at local ministry offices each year. On the credit side, trials conducted by WHO's Collaborating Centre for Research in Rabies in Teheran, Iran, proved the efficacy of a new antirabies vaccine prepared by growing the virus in tissue cultures of human cells. Developed in Philadelphia and nearing widespread commercial availability, this so-called diploid vaccine conferred a high degree of immunity after only four shots followed by two booster doses.

India, like other countries in the region, suffered an explosive comeback of malaria. By October 450,000 cases (10% of the population) had been reported in New Delhi, and the countrywide figure was six million. The resurgence was due partly to the development of resistance by the malarial parasite and the malarial mosquito to the pesticides and drugs used to combat them, and partly to the recent slackening of the once intensive malaria eradication campaign. Kala-azar, spread by the sandfly, which was all but wiped out 20 years ago as a by-product of antimalarial measures, also returned, with over 100,000 cases and 4,000 deaths recorded in Bihar. Several Indian states reintroduced house-to-house spraying with DDT, a practice abandoned several years ago.

There also was a sharp rise in the number of malaria cases diagnosed in the U.K. Figures published during the year listed 1,177 cases in 1976, compared with 594 in 1975. The rise was due largely to Indian and Pakistani immigrants who, having lost their immunity during their stay in the U.K., returned to their own countries for holidays without realizing the need for some kind of prophylactic treatment. They then picked up the infection in their homelands and imported it on their return to the U.K.

Although WHO had hoped that 1977 would prove to be the year in which smallpox was finally eradicated from the world, this expectation was dashed when 192 cases were reported in Somalia during May. It now seemed possible that the virus could survive in burial grounds and elsewhere for months and perhaps many years; if true, it would be some time before the final disappearance of the disease could be assumed, even after a period during which no clinical cases were reported anywhere.

Medical Economics. The two major cost-saving proposals made in the health field by the U.S. government during 1977 called for imposition of an annual ceiling of about 9% on all hospital revenue increases and elimination of about 100,000 hospital beds, representing a 10% reduction, over the next seven years. The American Hospital Association (AHA) and the American Medical Association (AMA) attacked the revenue limitations as a revival of the wage-price freeze in an economy otherwise free of restraints. Opponents asserted that the ceiling would prove disastrous for many of the more efficient hospitals and result in a reduction of quality care.

The administration's proposals came as spending for health care in the U.S. shot up once again. The Social Security Administration put the national health bill at $139.3 billion for 1976, a rise of $17 billion above the previous year. A study by Arthur D. Little Co. estimated Americans would be spending $240 billion a year in 1987, a figure that included a leveling off of escalating costs. Speaking at the annual AMA convention in June, HEW Secretary Joseph Califano blamed "four classic problems in U.S. medicine" for the runaway expenditure. He said that health resources were neither economically nor fairly distributed; that health care was poorly organized, with doctors performing many services that could be performed as well and less expensively by other trained personnel; that the U.S. system emphasized acute care treatment at the expense of preventive health care; and that U.S. health insurance was "an expensive and inequit-

able patchwork quilt." Nearly half the population under 65, he said, did not have insurance sufficient to cover major medical expenses, and 18 million Americans had no health insurance.

In September a report by a House of Representatives subcommittee revealed that the number of operations performed on poor patients whose payments were provided by the government Medicaid scheme was about double that for the general population. The commonest operations were hysterectomies, tonsillectomies, mastectomies, and gall bladder removals. The implication was that U.S. doctors were performing hundreds of thousands of unnecessary operations knowing their fees were guaranteed.

A report from the Institute of Medicine of the U.S. National Academy of Sciences (NAS) called for a critical evaluation of the new and extremely expensive diagnostic technique of computerized axial tomography (CAT), in which electronically processed X-ray scans are used to produce cross-sectional images of the body. Pioneered by the British firm EMI, CAT scanning was sweeping the U.S. medical scene, 760 devices having been sold to U.S. hospitals and doctors since the first two were installed in 1973. Each cost as much as $700,-000 to buy and $370,000 annually to run. The NAS report reflected a growing doubt, worldwide, concerning the wisdom of devoting an ever larger slice of finite resources to high technology at the expense of basic health care and the implementation of more effective preventive measures.

The health insurance giant Blue Cross adopted a variety of cost-containment procedures, including an active program of fraud and abuse investigation and elimination of duplicate payments to subscribers who were covered by more than one health insurance policy. Its sister organization, Blue Shield, announced that its member plans would halt routine payment to physicians for 28 "inappropriate" surgical and diagnostic procedures, amounting to a potential savings of $27 million annually.

A report by a special committee of the NAS National Research Council recommended that the Veterans Administration health care system even-

Herpes Type II virus (below, left) appears as a cluster of circles in a photomicrograph. (Below) Charles A. Alford (right) and Richard J. Whitley, both of the University of Alabama, examine samples of tissue cultures in search of the virus responsible for herpes encephalitis. The two men led a successful effort to treat this often fatal infection with drugs.

423

Health and Disease

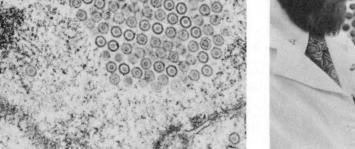

(LEFT) COURTESY, TOMMIE SUE TRALKA, NATIONAL CANCER INSTITUTE, NATIONAL INSTITUTES OF HEALTH; (RIGHT) COURTESY, NATIONAL INSTITUTES OF HEALTH tually be phased into the general delivery system. The report said the VA system was oversupplied with short-term hospital beds, was burdened with poorly allocated staff, lacked sufficient facilities for outpatient care, provided care of inconsistent quality, and faced an increasing demand for long-term care facilities. VA Administrator Max Cleland said that any plan to eliminate the VA system was contrary to the nation's history of providing for veterans' health care.

The Carter administration adopted a go-slow attitude on a national health insurance program because of other legislative priorities. Four bills were introduced in the opening days of the 95th Congress, but none came from the White House. A congressional budget-office report estimated the costs of a national plan to be a minimum of $108 billion by 1982. A 1977 Gallup Poll showed that the number of Americans who wanted such a federally controlled plan declined from 40 to 28%. Pat Cadell, head of the Cambridge Survey Research Corp. and a pollster for Pres. Jimmy Carter, found that only 18% of the American people favoured a nationalized system of health insurance in which the federal government would own all hospitals and pay doctors a salary.

In the U.K. both the British Medical Association and the recently formed Conservative Medical Society called for an introduction of fees into Britain's free health service as a method of raising additional revenue. They favoured charges for consultations and for hospital accommodation and a more realistic charge for drugs dispensed in place of the token payment required at present. These costs would be covered by health insurance schemes of the type common in many industrial countries.

General Developments. Life expectancy in the U.S. should increase to 81 years for women and 71.8 years for men by AD 2050, according to revised data of the Census Bureau. Previous rates were 76.5 years for women and 68.7 for men. The new figures followed a drop in the mortality rate from heart disease, which accounted for one of every three deaths. A nationwide study by the National Heart, Lung and Blood Institute found that the levels of cholesterol and fats in the blood also had dropped in recent years.

The cancer picture, however, remained discouraging. A 1977 National Cancer Institute report, comparing five-year survival rates of the ten most common cancers in the U.S. over three different periods between 1950 and 1973, showed little change. The lone bright spot was Hodgkin's disease, for which five-year survival averaged 54% for the period 1965–69, up from 30% in 1950.

The trouble-plagued swine (A/New Jersey) flu vaccination program was resumed on a limited scale in the U.S. early in 1977 after a moratorium was declared Dec. 16, 1976. The crowning blow bringing the temporary halt was a cluster of cases of Guillain-Barré syndrome, an unusual paralytic malady, among those who had received the vaccine. Several local health departments suspended their programs until the federal Center for Disease Control (CDC) in Atlanta, Ga., could determine that most of the Guillain-Barré cases were due to other causes, although it acknowledged that influenza vaccination might expose recipients to a higher risk.

After months of patient investigation, the CDC announced that the cause of Legionnaire's disease, the mysterious respiratory ailment that killed 29 people and hospitalized scores of others in 1976 after an American Legion convention in Philadelphia, was a previously unidentified rod-shaped bacterium. The organism was not considered contagious and its source was unknown. Sporadic cases of Legionnaire's disease continued during 1977, the first being a cluster of seven, including one death, in Ohio.

In August a team of U.S. medical investigators reported the first successful use of a drug against a major viral disease. A synthetic chemical originally designed as an antitumour agent, the drug— known as arabinosyladenine (ara-A) or vidarabine —proved 90% effective in clinical trials against herpes encephalitis, an often fatal infection characterized by severe inflammation of the brain. Drug treatment of viral diseases has been difficult because effective antiviral agents usually destroy unacceptable numbers of human cells in the process.

The long-time popularity of oral contraceptives was threatened by the rapidly growing attractiveness of sterilization. The latest fertility study in the U.S., by sociologist Charles F. Westoff of Princeton University, showed an estimated 6.8 million married couples had chosen surgical contraception, compared with 7.1 million on the Pill. Somewhat more female sterilizations (3.8 million) had been done than male vasectomies (3 million). Whereas the Pill remained the most popular method of contraception among young married women, the per-

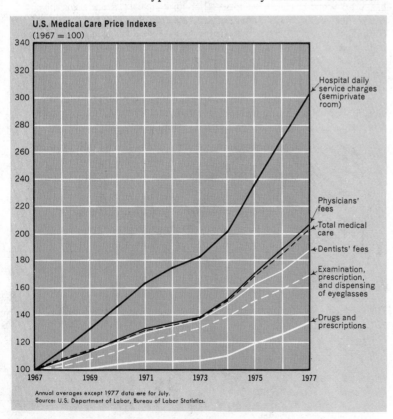

U.S. Medical Care Price Indexes
(1967 = 100)

Hospital daily service charges (semiprivate room)

Physicians' fees

Total medical care

Dentists' fees

Examination, prescription, and dispensing of eyeglasses

Drugs and prescriptions

Annual averages except 1977 data are for July.
Source: U.S. Department of Labor, Bureau of Labor Statistics.

centage declined among women married 15 years or more. Westoff also found that birth control practices of Roman Catholics were virtually the same as those of non-Catholics. More than nine out of ten Catholic married couples were using contraceptive methods forbidden by their church.

Two British reports published in October showed that women who used oral contraceptives were nearly five times as likely to die from circulatory disease as those who had never taken them, and that for users the risk of death from all causes was up 40%. This was an excess substantially greater than deaths from complications in pregnancy and was double the death rate from accidents. The risk of death was shown to increase with age, with cigarette smoking, and with the duration of use of oral contraceptives.

Regulation and Legal Matters. An end to U.S. federal funding for elective abortions that were not necessary to save the life of a woman was ordered by HEW in August. The Supreme Court had cleared the way for the action in June when it ordered lifting of a federal district court's prohibition against enforcement of the ban, which had been directed by Congress in 1976 as part of a fiscal appropriations bill. Victims of rape or incest were not affected by the ruling. Medicaid had been paying for about 300,000 of the 1.1 million legal abortions performed annually in the U.S. Individual states could pay the full cost of elective abortions if they so chose. In December, after months of bitter debate, both houses of Congress reached a compromise position on abortion. Use of federal funds was to be permitted only if continued pregnancy would endanger the life or severely affect the long-term health of the mother, or if pregnancy resulted from rape or incest that had been promptly reported to authorities.

Heated controversies developed in 1977 over two products ordered banned by the U.S. Food and Drug Administration (FDA). One was the artificial sweetener saccharin, banned on the grounds that it caused bladder tumours in animals. The other was a substance called laetrile, derived from apricot pits and purporting to be an effective treatment for cancer.

Based on a Canadian study that found tumours in male offspring of female rats given a 5% diet of saccharin during gestation, the FDA invoked the 1958 Delaney clause to the Food, Drug, and Cosmetic Act, which decrees eliminating any food or cosmetics additive shown to cause cancer in animals or man. In 1969 the FDA banned cyclamate as an artificial sweetener under this legislation.

The saccharin action, announced in March, stirred an unprecedented public outcry. Hundreds of complaints descended on Congress from diabetics and obese individuals who could not believe that the sweetening agent used for decades might cause cancer in human beings. Opposition also came from such health agencies as the American Heart Association, the American Diabetes Association, and the American Cancer Society. Later the FDA proposed forbidding addition of the drug to food, beverages, and cosmetics likely to be ingested (such as lipsticks), while still allowing its sale without prescription as a single ingredient drug,

Technicians readied syringes as they prepared to inoculate as many as 6,000 children in Detroit against major childhood diseases. Children lacking immunization shots were barred from school.

provided manufacturers could demonstrate its efficacy in medical uses. Nevertheless, public pressure compelled Congress to vote a delay of any FDA ban until it was decided whether to modify the rigid wording of the Delaney clause.

Although all major health agencies strongly supported the FDA ban on laetrile, legislatures in 13 states yielded to public pressure to enact laws permitting intrastate production and distribution of the compound. Legislation was stalled in several other states. In addition, a federal district court order in effect overturned the FDA ban by allowing importation from Mexico of laetrile by patients whose physicians certify them by affidavit as terminal cases.

At a court-ordered hearing conducted by the FDA, pro-laetrile forces called medical scientists "murderers" and opponents called the promoters "hoaxters and hucksters." A laetrile lobby, the Committee for Freedom of Choice in Cancer Therapy, testified that their apricot-pit extract was not a drug but a "natural vitamin and food supplement, vitamin B-17." Among pro-laetrile leaders were three men found guilty by a federal jury in San Diego, Calif., on five counts of smuggling and conspiring to smuggle laetrile from Mexico.

Donald Kennedy, the FDA commissioner, told a Senate hearing that laetrile was regarded by the overwhelming majority of qualified experts as "being of unproved safety and no effectiveness whatsoever." U.S. Surgeon General Julius Richmond warned that people who used laetrile to combat cancer ran the risk of death from cyanide poisoning because enzymes in the human digestive system could break down cyanide contained in the apricot pits.

In more than 30 U.S. states, right-to-die legislation was adopted or pending. Most of the bills were patterned after a ground-breaking California law, which had taken effect at the start of the year. New Jersey became the first state to adopt guidelines on when to let death take its course legally and ethically. The guidelines called for "prognosis committees" to determine at the request of the family or guardian whether an unconscious patient had a reasonable possibility of returning to a brain-functioning life. The committee would be composed of physician specialists and would exclude the attending physician on the case.

The Food and Drug Administration cautioned that women taking estrogen drugs should be made aware of the association of long-term use of these hormones with cancer of the uterus. A brochure was required of manufacturers advising women that estrogens were not effective in cases of nervousness or depression or for restoring youthfulness. Warning brochures also were required for progestins, hormones prescribed to prevent miscarriages. The FDA said progestins could increase the risk of birth defects.

The Massachusetts Supreme Court overruled the 1975 manslaughter conviction of physician Kenneth C. Edelin, who had been tried on charges that he attempted to smother a viable fetus in the uterus of an abortion patient and then took no steps to save the fetus after its removal from the uterus. The high court's reversal was greeted with relief by physicians who had feared they would be vulnerable to similar actions after performing midtrimester abortions. The court ruled that Edelin had no evil frame of mind, was actuated by no criminal purpose, and committed no wanton or reckless act in carrying out the medical procedure.

By the end of May the British firm Imperial Chemical Industries had accepted the claims of 2,000 victims of their drug Eraldin (practolol), a relatively new agent promoted as a unique contribution to the drug treatment of cardiac arrhythmias and hypertension, which had been withdrawn in 1975 following reports of serious side effects, including a form of peritonitis, eye damage, skin damage, and deafness. It was thought that the total number of patients in whom significant damage could be demonstrated might reach 5,000, and this cast doubt upon the efficien-

cy of the present system for monitoring adverse drug reactions. Great Britain's Department of Health funded a research project designed to test a new system called "recorded release" whereby family doctors would be allowed to prescribe some drugs only on condition that they recorded all significant adverse events. The FDA in the U.S. had refused to allow Eraldin to be put on general sale, and thus had indisputably avoided a major drug disaster.

(ARTHUR J. SNIDER; DONALD W. GOULD)
[425.D–E; 425.H; 425.I.2.e.i; 425.J]

MENTAL HEALTH

In 1977 mental illness remained a stigma, with attendant attitudes of shame, fear, and mystery. There was still inadequate emphasis on educating the populace, both in the community and in the schools. The year also saw continuation of the distinct movement away from hospitalization of the mentally ill, with focus being directed toward the community. In the U.S., community "outreach" programs ironically were unable to extend their reach far enough, as communities often lacked both financial resources and trained personnel to meet the needs of the emotionally disturbed.

Depression in all its forms increased as a major affective disorder. Whereas pharmacological aids (antidepressants) were prescribed frequently, experience was showing that usually only the depressive symptoms were alleviated. Resurgence of the disorder often followed once medication was stopped, and drug dependency became a common problem if medication was continued. One particular drug, the salt lithium carbonate, grew increasingly popular as an effective medication for the treatment of a specific diagnostic category, the manic-depressive. In this disorder the patient often suffers from widely fluctuating moods ranging from hyperactivity, even grandiose behaviour, to deep depressions. Lithium carbonate reduced the fluctuations of these moods and stabilized incapacitating emotional ups and downs.

Whether the cycle of treatment modalities would continue, and return verbal therapeutic methods to their previous position of favour, remained to be seen. There was an increase in research studies examining the outcome of differing psychotherapies. One such finding suggested that the longer psychotherapy was utilized, the greater the benefit derived. Short-term therapies, however, continued to flourish, pushed by professionals as well as patients who were anxious for results. Results, in the form of change, sometimes did occur but their stability was dubious.

An apparent increase in the respectability of verbal therapies was reflected in the introduction of legislation in the U.S. to allow psychologists, as nonmedical psychotherapists, to be recipients of third-party insurance payments. In 1977, for example, 47 of 50 U.S. states had legislation granting "freedom of choice" to the patient, who could choose his or her therapist regardless of professional affiliation (social workers were not yet included) and have partial insurance coverage (most insurance companies paid 50–80% of the bill).

There was a widespread popular demand for a

The limbic system (shown shaded) is believed to be closely linked to emotions in man. Recent investigations uncovered a family of naturally occurring morphinelike molecules concentrated in sensory nerve endings of this system, especially the amygdala, and in certain regions of the spinal cord.

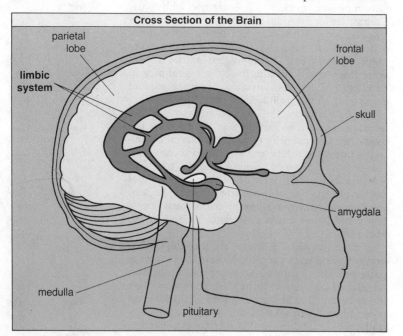

Cross Section of the Brain

parietal lobe

limbic system

frontal lobe

skull

amygdala

medulla

pituitary

curb on the use of electroconvulsive therapy (ECT), many lay and some medical people regarding the passage of an electric current through the brain as an irrational, ineffectual, and often dangerous procedure. Following his appearance on a television program, a British member of Parliament reported having received 80 letters from former patients and their relatives, of whom four testified to the beneficial effects of ECT and pleaded for its retention while 76 urged its banning or curtailment. He said that the most common specific criticisms were that the treatment produced substantial and permanent impairment of memory and that the procedure engendered a sense of terror beforehand and subsequent humiliation. A few patients thought that their psychiatrist had used ECT as a punishment.

A California law came into effect in January giving mental patients the right to refuse convulsive therapy and psychosurgery. The new law also required the psychiatrist proposing to use such treatment to obtain informed consent of the patient or, with the permission of the court, of a guardian. "Informed consent" was defined to mean that the patient must be told the reason for treatment, be warned of the possibility of side effects, and be made aware of the fact that there was a division of opinion concerning the efficacy of the therapy offered. Psychosurgery required, in addition, the unanimous agreement of a three-physician review committee. Following this legislation the number of patients in the state subjected to ECT fell dramatically, and during the first nine months of the year no psychosurgery was performed at all. In Great Britain a report by a special committee of the Royal College of Psychiatrists conceded that the value of ECT in the treatment of schizophrenia and mania was still not beyond dispute and required further research, but maintained that the therapy was safe and was an effective treatment for severe depressive illness.

The most highly publicized move concerning psychiatric abuse was a resolution narrowly approved at a meeting on August 31 of the World Psychiatric Association in Honolulu that condemned the Soviet practice of using compulsory psychiatric "treatment" as a means for dealing with political dissidents. U.S. delegates, however, stressed the fact that their protest was not limited to the Soviet Union, where the abuse of psychiatry was most apparent, "but to all other countries where such conditions exist."

(DONALD W. GOULD; ROBERT I. YUFIT)

[438.D]

DENTISTRY

During the past year the American Dental Association (ADA) reiterated its strong support of water fluoridation as an effective, economical, and safe public health measure to combat tooth decay. Testifying before a House subcommittee in September, ADA officials responded to allegations questioning the safety of fluoridation by quoting a review of fluoridation research by the Royal College of Surgeons in London. The college's findings concluded that studies in Great Britain and the U.S. failed to demonstrate any relationship between cancer mortality or cancer incidence and fluoride levels in water supplies.

Although test animals have been immunized successfully against tooth decay with a vaccine derived from a decay-causing strain of bacteria (*Streptococcus mutans*), an effective and safe vaccination process for human use still seemed at least a decade away. Addressing the 55th general session of the International Association for Dental Research in Copenhagen in March, Robert Genco of the State University of New York at Buffalo pointed out that the best possibilities for a vaccine lay in preparation of purified product from this organism. The whole-bacterium approach, which worked in animals, was not as desirable in people, and other approaches of inducing antibodies needed to be investigated.

Although the value of fluoride dentifrices in helping reduce tooth decay rate had been demonstrated extensively by clinical studies, a British study based only on normal home use recently reconfirmed the findings of the controlled trials. Results suggested that approximately 10% less decay or treated decay occurred in children who had used fluoride toothpaste for two years or longer, according to Malcolm N. Naylor of Guy's Hospital Dental School in London.

Anxious dental patients were treated safely without general anesthesia and yet without the memories of unpleasant surgical procedures, reported Stephen S. Gelfman, a scientist with the National Institute of Dental Research. His study showed that even the most anxious of 160 subjects could not remember being injected with local anesthetics when the oral injections followed intravenous injections of memory-erasing agents. Speaking at a meeting of the American Association for Dental Research in June, he declared that, although these sedatives prevented recall of surgery, the patients were sufficiently conscious to respond to questions, follow instruction readily, and breathe and cough effortlessly. (LOU JOSEPH)

See also Demography; Life Sciences; Nobel Prizes; Social and Welfare Services.
[422.E.1.a; 10/35.C.1]

Historic Preservation

A significant event in the development of international legislation for historic preservation was the first meeting, on June 27–July 1, 1977, of the committee established by the International Convention Concerning the Protection of the World Cultural and Natural Heritage, to which 33 UNESCO states were now parties. A system of fixed or voluntary contributions from the nations that subscribed to the World Heritage Fund would enable financing of preservation projects, and many activities were being considered. The committee decided that the first action to be taken would be nominations to the "World Heritage List" in the form of detailed case studies. It took into account that some countries might have neither the staff nor the documentation required in preparing nominations, and approved a budget from the fund that would permit sending experts or furnishing equipment to help in drafting the case studies called for.

Many of the international campaigns to safeguard historic monuments continued to make progress. In Philae, Egypt, all of the temple structures had been dismantled; work on reshaping Agilkia to resemble Philae was completed, foundations were laid, and the work of reassembly was under way. At Borobudur, Indonesia, the north and south faces of the pyramidal structure were completely dismantled; reinforced concrete foundations were constructed for the terraces, and work began on reassembling the structure after cleaning and restoration of the sculptured stones.

In Venice several private committees began new projects, such as the restoration of the Scuola di San Pasquale (Council of Europe); Casino Vernier (French committee); the facade of the Palace of Ateneo Veneto (Swedish committee); the Scuola di San Giovanni Evangelista, the Scuola Canton, and the Church of the Pietà (U.S. International Fund for Monuments); Church of St. Mary of Miracles (West Germany); St. Martin di Castello (Australia); and St. Stae (Swiss committee). The first proposals for the control of unusually high tides that menace the city from time to time were received by the Italian government. Plans for sewage disposal and for studies to aid in projects for the renewal of habitations were underway.

The Greek government adopted a budget equivalent to $15 million, required for safeguarding the Acropolis and its monuments. Greece counted upon UNESCO, through an international campaign, to aid in financing the scientific and analytic studies that would be required to ensure that the best possible techniques and materials were used to provide for the long-term preservation of the site.

An important trend was concern for the inner city areas where urban renewal projects often remove old buildings and replace them with high-rise structures. In reaction to the social and economic changes caused by such projects, movements were under way to restore such areas to their former appearance and role. Thus, in September 1977, the East German national committee of the International Council of Monuments and Sites organized a regional meeting on the theme "Contribution of young people to the preservation, care, presentation, and use of historic town centres." Representatives from 24 countries reported on youth involvement in inner-city preservation projects, and participants at the seminar were able to visit reconstruction and renewal projects in Rostock and neighbouring cities.

The need for legislative controls as well as an expansion of programs for the preservation of the cultural heritage became an increasingly important problem in many industrialized nations. In the U.S., for example, following the bicentennial celebrations of 1976, in which historic preservation projects were featured, Pres. Jimmy Carter's administration planned a program that would centralize and improve coordination of all federal government projects for the preservation of the nation's cultural heritage. These proposals were submitted to Congress in the fall of 1977.

BRYAN WHARTON—CAMERA PRESS/PHOTO TRENDS

One of the world's largest jigsaw puzzles confronted a worker in Thebes, Egypt. Each of the stone fragments is a piece of the ancient Egyptian temple of Queen Hatshepsut. It is being restored to its original glory by a team of Polish archaeologists.

In Washington, D.C., the Pennsylvania Avenue Development Corp. proposed a series of measures to improve conditions on the avenue—which links the White House with the Capitol—and these were approved by Congress. The avenue, now lined with many deteriorating buildings, was to have wide pedestrian walkways dotted with shops and lined with trees, and new housing units. Historic buildings of importance such as the old Willard Hotel and the 1899 Old Post Office Building together with many other 19th-century buildings were to be saved to "recreate the ambiance of turn-of-the-century Washington."

In Britain the Civic Trust, a private nonprofit organization that played an important role in the preservation of inner cities, celebrated its 20th anniversary. One of its first projects had been the cooperative face-lift of an entire street frontage—Magdalen Street in Norwich—in which shabby storefronts were transformed into a cohesive architectural group. Many other towns in England followed this example, and by 1977 an additional 300 such improvements were under consideration.

The sale of Mentmore Towers in Buckinghamshire, seat of the earl of Rosebery, and its contents (*see* ART SALES) called into question the adequacy of existing provisions in Britain for the acquisition and maintenance of properties forming part of the national heritage.   (HIROSHI DAIFUKU)

See also Architecture; Environment; Museums.

Honduras

A republic of Central America, Honduras is bounded by Nicaragua, El Salvador, Guatemala, the Caribbean Sea, and the Pacific Ocean. Area: 112,088 sq km (43,277 sq mi). Pop. (1976 est.): 2,-831,000, including 90% mestizo. Cap. and largest city: Tegucigalpa (pop., 1974, 270,600). Language: Spanish; some Indian dialects. Religion: Roman Catholic. President in 1977, Col. Juan Alberto Melgar Castro.

The military government moved steadily toward the right during the year, beginning in January with the removal of several reform-minded young officers from key governmental positions. The popular pro-union minister of labour was also fired, and in March the director of the National Agrarian Institute, frustrated over his inability to accelerate the land reform program, resigned.

Pres. Juan Alberto Melgar Castro's advisory council drafted regulations to govern a return to a constitutional regime in 1979. The trend appeared to be toward reinstatement of civilian rule by the traditional National and Liberal parties.

Freedom of press, speech, and assembly was unaffected by the rightist trend, and antigovernment sentiment abounded. Especially sharp criticism from the leftist-oriented national university spurred a movement to establish a second institution of higher learning. Antigovernment expression by organized labour was weakened by internal conflict. (HENRY WEBB, JR.)

Honduras

Hungary

HONDURAS

Education. (1975) Primary, pupils 460,744, teachers 13,-045; secondary and vocational, pupils 65,527, teachers 3,-104; teacher training, students 1,207, teachers 97; higher (university only), students 10,635, teaching staff 648.

Finance. Monetary unit: lempira, with (Sept. 19, 1977) a par value of 2 lempiras to U.S. $1 (free rate of 3.50 lempiras = £1 sterling). Gold, SDR's, and foreign exchange (May 1977) U.S. $195,650,000. Budget (1976 actual): revenue 352.7 million lempiras; expenditure 383.9 million lempiras. Gross national product (1976) 2,341,000,-000 lempiras. Cost of living (Tegucigalpa; 1970 = 100; May 1977) 154.

Foreign Trade. (1976) Imports 906.2 million lempiras; exports 783.7 million lempiras. Import sources (1975): U.S. 42%; Venezuela 16%; Japan 7%; Guatemala 6%. Export destinations (1975): U.S. 52%; West Germany 11%; Dominican Republic 5%. Main exports (1975): coffee 20%; bananas 16%; timber 14%; lead and zinc 8%; meat 6%; silver 5%.

Transport and Communications. Roads (1975) 6,595 km (including c. 150 km of Pan-American Highway). Motor vehicles in use (1974): passenger c. 14,700; commercial (including buses) 22,900. Railways (1975) 991 km. Air traffic (1975): 240 million passenger-km; freight 3.2 million net ton-km. Shipping (1976): merchant vessels 100 gross tons and over 57; gross tonnage 71,042. Telephones (Jan. 1976) 19,550. Radio receivers (Dec. 1974) 158,000. Television receivers (Dec. 1974) 46,000.

Agriculture. Production (in 000; metric tons; 1976): corn c. 289; cassava (1975) c. 46; coffee c. 57; sorghum c. 47; sugar, raw value (1975) c. 90; dry beans c. 55; bananas c. 1,629; oranges c. 25; cotton, lint (1975) c. 5; beef and veal (1975) c. 50; timber (cu m; 1975) c. 3,868. Livestock (in 000; 1975): cattle c. 1,690; pigs c. 510; horses c. 278; chickens c. 7,600.

Industry. Production (in 000; metric tons; 1975): petroleum products 598; silver 0.1; gold (troy oz; 1974) 2.1; lead ore (metal content) 23; zinc ore (metal content) 30; electricity (kw-hr) c. 480,000.

Hungary

A people's republic of central Europe, Hungary is bordered by Czechoslovakia, the U.S.S.R., Romania, Yugoslavia, and Austria. Area: 93,032 sq km (35,920 sq mi). Pop. (1977 est): 10,625,300, including (1970) Hungarian 95.8%; German 2.1%. Cap. and largest city: Budapest (pop., 1977 est., 2,081,700). Language (1970): Magyar 95.8%. Religion (1970): Roman Catholic about 60%, most of remainder Protestant or atheist. First secretary of the Hungarian Socialist Workers' (Communist) Party in 1977, Janos Kadar; chairman of the Presidential Council (chief of state), Pal Losonczi; president of the Council of Ministers (premier), Gyorgy Lazar.

During 1977 Janos Kadar successfully maintained his cautious policy of balance between East and West while ensuring the Hungarian people a tranquil and relatively prosperous life. The only jarring incident was the telegram of sympathy that some 30 intellectuals sent in January to the Czech and Slovak signatories of the Charter 77 manifesto. (*See* CZECHOSLOVAKIA.) They were reprimanded by members of the Hungarian Politburo, but no penalties were imposed. When Bohuslav Chnoupek, the Czechoslovak foreign minister, visited Budapest at the beginning of March, he expressed surprise at such leniency.

Kadar traveled abroad more widely than ever before. In March, accompanied by his premier Gyorgy Lazar, he paid a state visit to East Germany, and on March 24 he signed with Erich Honecker, the East German party leader and head of state, a 25-year treaty of friendship, cooperation, and mutual assistance to replace a similar one concluded on May 18, 1967. Under the new treaty the two countries, in recognition of the obligations created by the Warsaw Treaty, would render each other assistance, including military assistance, in the event either was attacked by another state or group of states.

The new planetarium in People's Park, Budapest, was inaugurated on August 20 to mark Constitution Day. The cupola of the planetarium has a diameter of 23 metres.

GÁBOR CSIKÓS—INTERFOTO MTI/KEYSTONE

The 977-year-old crown of St. Stephen, the symbol of Hungarian nationhood, had been held by the U.S. since the end of World War II. Pres. Jimmy Carter's plan to return it to Hungary met some opposition in the U.S.

In June Kadar was in Rome as the guest of the Italian government, and on June 9 he was also received by Pope Paul VI. At a press conference in Rome, Kadar admitted that the term "Eurocom-

---

HUNGARY

Education. Primary (1976–77), pupils 1,072,000, teachers 68,425; secondary (1975–76), pupils 99,656, teachers 6,663; vocational (1975–76), pupils 107,661; teacher training (1975–76), students 3,159; vocational and teacher training (1975–76), teachers 7,751; higher (including 18 universities; 1976–77), students 64,000, teaching staff 12,-233.

Finance. Monetary unit: forint, with (Sept. 19, 1977) a commercial free rate of 40.68 forints to U.S. $1 (70.86 forints = £1 sterling) and a noncommercial (tourist) rate of 19.70 forints to U.S. $1 (34.92 forints = £1 sterling). Budget (1977 est.): revenue 359.2 billion forints; expenditure 362.4 billion forints.

Foreign Trade. (1976) Imports 230,056,000,000 forints; exports 204,834,000,000 forints (before 1976 valued in "exchange" forints). Import sources: U.S.S.R. 27%; West Germany 10%; East Germany 9%; Czechoslovakia 6%; Austria 5%. Export destinations: U.S.S.R. 30%; East Germany 9%; West Germany 8%; Czechoslovakia 7%. Main exports: machinery 26%; motor vehicles 10%; chemicals 8%; iron and steel 6%; meat and meat preparations 5%; fruit and vegetables 5%.

Transport and Communications. Roads (1975) 99,767 km (including 181 km expressways). Motor vehicles in use (1975): passenger 579,900; commercial 120,960. Railways: (1975) 8,243 km; traffic (1976) 13,367,000,000 passenger-km, freight 22,553,000,000 net ton-km. Air traffic (1975): 500 million passenger-km; freight 5.6 million net ton-km. Inland waterways in regular use (1975) 1,302 km. Telephones (Dec. 1975) 1,048,000. Radio licenses (Dec. 1975) 2,537,000. Television licenses (Dec. 1975) 2,390,000.

Agriculture. Production (in 000; metric tons; 1976): corn c. 5,200; wheat 5,138; barley 746; rye 156; potatoes c. 1,700; sugar, raw value c. 410; cabbages (1975) c. 180; tomatoes c. 330; sunflower seed c. 115; green peas (1975) c. 210; dry peas c. 110; peaches (1975) c. 126; plums (1975) c. 230; apples c. 866; wine c. 480; tobacco c. 18; milk c. 2,052; beef and veal c. 153; pork c. 740. Livestock (in 000; March 1976): cattle 1,904; pigs 6,953; sheep 2,039; horses (1975) 163; chickens 53,390.

Industry. Index of production (1970 = 100; 1976) 141. Production (in 000; metric tons; 1976): coal 2,934; lignite 22,323; crude oil 2,141; natural gas (cu m) 6,083,000; electricity (kw-hr) 22,040,000; iron ore (24% metal content) 602; pig iron 2,227; crude steel 3,652; bauxite 2,919; aluminum 70; cement 4,298; petroleum products (1975) 9,579; sulfuric acid 617; fertilizers (1975–76) nitrogenous 453, phosphate 206; cotton yarn 58; wool yarn 10; commercial vehicles (units) 13.

---

munism," used by certain Western European Communist parties, was disturbing to the world Communist movement, but he was convinced that all the nations would enter on the road to socialism. In an interview for the *Frankfurter Rundschau* given on June 30 before he started on an official visit to West Germany on July 4, Kadar, while scouting Eurocommunism as a concept employed by antidemocratic forces in an attempt to divide Western from Eastern European Communism, conceded that every Communist party had the right to choose its own path toward socialism. However, Janos Berecz, head of the foreign section of the Central Committee of the Hungarian Socialist Workers' Party, wrote in the daily newspaper *Nepszabadsag* on July 24 that the slogan "Eurocommunism" was "the most dangerous instrument for dividing the Communist camp." Andras Gyenes, a secretary of the Politburo, writing in the July issue of *Tarsadalmi Szemle* ("Social Review"), attacked the U.S. administration for releasing a new wave of anti-Communist propaganda under the pretext of defending human rights.

On July 26 Kadar was received in the Crimea by Soviet party leader and head of state Leonid Brezhnev. It was announced on June 5 that Kadar and Nicolae Ceausescu, general secretary of the Romanian Communist Party, met at Oradea in northwestern Romania and at Debrecen in eastern Hungary. In September the *Magyar Nemzet*, organ of the Patriotic People's Front, revealed that the two leaders mainly dicussed the problem of the two million-strong Hungarian minority in Transylvania. *Magyar Nemzet* alleged that the Hungarians in Romania were victims of a "constant and all-embracing" policy of discrimination.

The American evangelist Billy Graham visited Hungary in September. For the first time he was allowed to preach in a Communist country. It was reported by a Polish daily newspaper, the *Kurier Polski*, that U.S. Pres. Jimmy Carter had authorized Graham to inform the Hungarian government that the Holy Crown of St. Stephen, entrusted to the U.S. government in 1945, would soon be returned to Hungary. The crown was given to King Stephen by Pope Sylvester II in AD 1000. At the end of World War II, as the Soviet Army was approaching Budapest, two Hungarian officers smuggled this national treasure out of the vaults of Buda Castle and brought it to western Austria, then under U.S. occupation. The plan to return it was opposed by Hungarian-American and other groups, but court suits brought to stop it were unsuccessful. At year's end it was announced that a U.S. delegation headed by Secretary of State Cyrus Vance would return the crown and other regalia on Jan. 6, 1978.   (K. M. SMOGORZEWSKI)

Ice Hockey

North American. Breaking a staggering number of records and collecting nearly every regular-season and postseason trophy, the Montreal Canadiens claimed their second straight Stanley Cup as the National Hockey League champions for the 1976–77 season. In 14 play-off games they dropped just two, both to the New York Islanders, winning four straight from the Boston Bruins in the final series. The Bruins had beaten the Philadelphia Flyers in the semifinals in four straight games including two sudden-death overtime victories, one of which ended at 10:07 of the second extra period on a goal by Terry O'Reilly. In the World Hockey Association the Quebec Nordiques defeated the defending champion Winnipeg Jets in seven games to take the AVCO World Trophy.

The Canadiens set ten NHL records and tied another during a spectacular year in which they lost just eight games, an unprecedented mark. They had the most points (132), most victories (60), and a record 34-game undefeated streak on their home rink. Guy Lafleur, their right wing, won the NHL scoring championship for the second straight season with 56 goals and 80 assists. Larry Robinson won the Norris Trophy as the league's outstanding defenseman, and Ken Dryden and Michel ("Bunny") Larocque shared the Vezina Trophy for best goalkeeping with a combined average of 214 goals against. Marcel Dionne, centre-right wing for the Los Angeles Kings, received the Lady Byng Trophy as the league's most gentlemanly player, and Willi Plett, right wing for the Atlanta Flames, won the rookie-of-the-year award. Runner-up in the latter category was the New York Rangers' Don Murdoch, who, after starting at a record-setting scoring pace, suffered an ankle injury in February that sidelined him for the season. Over the summer Murdoch again made the headlines when he was charged with possession of about one-fifth of an ounce of cocaine discovered in his luggage by a customs official at Toronto International Airport. He was the first NHL player to be charged with drug possession. At a hearing in September, action on the case was postponed until after the 1977–78 season.

In other legal action Don Saleski, Joe Watson, and Bob Kelly of the Philadelphia Flyers were found guilty of simple assault for their involvement with the crowd during a play-off game in Toronto the previous season. The sentences were suspended, and they were fined. Charges against Mel Bridgman for assaulting Toronto's Borje Salming during a game were dropped.

History was made in the World Hockey Association when Robbie Ftorek was named the league's most valuable player, making him the first U.S.-born winner of that award in either league. The little centre won the prize despite playing on the Phoenix Roadrunners, which finished with the worst record in the WHA. Anders Hedberg, the Winnipeg Jets' "Swedish Express," scored 51 goals in his first 47 games to better the standard of 50 goals in 50 games set by Maurice ("Rocket") Richard in 1944–45. Hedberg ended the season as the league's second leading scorer, ten points behind Real Cloutier of Quebec, who had 66 goals and 75 assists for 141 points. During the season 49-year-old Gordie Howe scored the 1,000th goal of his professional career. Howe and his sons Mark and Marty moved from Houston to the New England Whalers for the 1977–78 season. Quebec and Houston were winners of the Eastern and Western divisions, respectively.

Guy Lafleur (centre), the leading scorer of the Montreal Canadiens, was boxed in by two Boston defensemen during the Stanley Cup play-offs in May.

After 32 years as president of the NHL, 72-year-old Clarence Campbell retired, and John Ziegler, a 43-year-old attorney formerly with the Detroit Red Wings organization, became his successor. Ziegler immediately was faced with steering the board of governors through summer-long negotiations with the WHA concerning a possible merger of the two leagues. In the event the 18-member board voted not to expand the NHL to include the younger league.

Despite the rejection by the NHL the WHA continued operations. Following the shutdown of the Minnesota franchise in the middle of the 1976–77 season and the post-season folding of Phoenix and San Diego, the league opened its sixth season in 1977 with eight teams. An innovation in the 1977–78 WHA schedule called for each club to play one game against a touring Soviet All-Star team and one against a Czechoslovak national team, with the results to count in the WHA standings. Taking over from Bill MacFarland as new president of the league was Howard Baldwin, the 36-year-old New England Whaler president who had spearheaded his league's drive to merge with the NHL.

While the WHA had always included many European players, the NHL during the year began a serious raid of the overseas market. The New York Rangers signed Hardy Astrom and the New York Islanders obtained Göran Högosta, robbing the Swedish national team of its top goaltending pair.

Good news for the Rangers was a board of governors decision to adopt a wild-card system for the 1977–78 play-offs in which the top two teams in each of the four divisions would automatically gain a play-off berth. The remaining four berths would be awarded to the teams with the most points regardless of division. Under the previous system the weak Conn Smythe Division sent Minnesota with 64 points and Chicago with 63 points into the play-offs, while the Rangers in the com-

Hydroelectric Power:
see Energy; Engineering Projects

Hydrology:
see Earth Sciences

Czechoslovak skaters, celebrating their second successive world championship title, wave their trophy high at a victory ceremony in Vienna in May.

Table I. NHL Final Standings, 1976–77

	Won	Lost	Tied	Goals	Goals against	Pts.
Prince of Wales Conference						
JAMES NORRIS DIVISION						
Montreal	60	8	12	387	171	132
Los Angeles	34	31	15	271	241	83
Pittsburgh	34	33	13	240	252	81
Washington	24	42	14	221	307	62
Detroit	16	55	9	183	309	41
CHARLES F. ADAMS DIVISION						
Boston	49	23	8	312	240	106
Buffalo	48	24	8	301	220	104
Toronto	33	32	15	301	285	81
Cleveland	25	42	13	240	292	63
Clarence Campbell Conference						
LESTER PATRICK DIVISION						
Philadelphia	48	16	16	323	213	112
New York Islanders	47	21	12	288	193	106
Atlanta	34	34	12	264	265	80
New York Rangers	29	37	14	272	310	72
CONN SMYTHE DIVISION						
St. Louis	32	39	9	239	276	73
Minnesota	23	39	18	240	310	64
Chicago	26	43	11	240	298	63
Vancouver	25	42	13	235	294	63
Colorado	20	46	14	226	307	54

Table II. World Ice Hockey Championships, 1977

	Won	Lost	Tied	Goals	Goals against	Pts.
GROUP A Section 1						
Czechoslovakia	7	2	1	54	32	15
Sweden	7	3	0	43	19	14
U.S.S.R.	7	3	0	77	24	14
Canada	6	3	1	47	35	13
GROUP A Section 2						
Finland	5	5	0	45	43	10
United States	3	6	1	29	43	7
West Germany	2	7	1	23	58	5
Romania	1	9	0	20	84	2
GROUP B						
East Germany	8	0	0	57	16	16
Poland	6	2	0	39	22	12
Japan	5	2	1	30	21	11
Norway	4	2	2	30	30	10
Switzerland	4	4	0	35	33	8
Hungary	3	5	0	27	46	6
Yugoslavia	2	5	1	30	36	5
Netherlands, The	1	5	2	23	39	4
Austria	0	8	0	19	47	0
GROUP C						
Italy	5	0	1	64	6	11
Denmark	5	0	1	65	15	11
Bulgaria	4	2	0	47	25	8
France	3	3	0	37	23	6
Spain	1	5	0	17	65	2
Belgium	1	5	0	24	89	2
Great Britain	1	5	0	17	47	2

petitive Patrick Division did not make it with a 72-point finish.

Sitting out the last part of the season after trying to make a comeback, the celebrated defenseman Bobby Orr appeared in just 20 games for his new team, the Chicago Black Hawks, scoring 4 goals and assisting on 19 others. He planned to sit out the 1977–78 season and attempt another comeback the following year.

In the American Hockey League play-offs the perennially strong Nova Scotia Voyageurs, farm club of the Montreal Canadiens, defeated Rochester in six games to win the Calder Cup. Kansas City defeated Tulsa in four straight games to take the Central League championship, and the Grand Rapids Blades defeated defending champion Milwaukee for the United States Hockey League title. Saginaw defeated Toledo in seven games for the International Hockey League championship. Midway through the season the six-team Southern League folded. (ROBIN CATHY HERMAN)

European and International. During March, April, and May the 44th world championships—the second to admit professional players—were contested in three groups by 24 nations, three more than in 1976. Interest was heightened by the return of Canada, winner of the title a record 19 times, following a seven-year absence due to disagreement over the previous exclusion of professionals. The admission of Spain underlined the increased interest in the sport in that area. Belgium was the third additional entrant.

The eight title contenders competed in Group A in Vienna. Czechoslovakia retained the championship for its fifth win since the event's inauguration in 1920, thanks mainly to Sweden, the silver medalist, which beat the Soviet Union 3–1 in the final match; the U.S.S.R. had needed only a tie in that game to clinch the title. Third place was the lowest position for the Soviets since 1961. Although a point below the champions, the swift-skating Swedes were more impressive, beating the powerful Soviet squad twice, 5–1 and 3–1, the biggest upsets of the tournament. Roland Eriksson, who played during the season in North America for the Minnesota North Stars, scored all three goals for Sweden in the crucial last game. The overall top

scorers for the tournament were Soviet players Vladimir Petrov (21 points from 7 goals and 14 assists) and Boris Mikhailov (19 points, including the highest number of goals, 12). The outstanding goalie was Göran Högosta of Sweden. Fourth-placed Canada was not represented by all of the nation's best players, much talent being engaged in the Stanley Cup play-offs, and lacked team cohesion because of limited practice together. An 11–1 defeat by the Soviets was the worst suffered by Canada in the competition's history.

A format similar to that of the previous year divided the eight teams into two sections after each had played the other once, the top four then playing off a very open contest for the title while the others fought to avoid relegation to Group B. The Romanians were outclassed and moved down in exchange for East Germany, the well-drilled winners of Group B, contested by nine nations in Tokyo. Seven other countries participated in

Group C, played simultaneously in Copenhagen. (*See* Table II.)

Apart from the world championships, the season's most important international tournament was for the Izvestia Cup, in Moscow on Dec. 16–21, 1976, contested by the world's "top five." An early surprise defeat of the Czechoslovaks by Sweden left little doubt that the host country would win, and the Soviets settled the issue with a 3–2 victory over Czechoslovakia in the final match. Sweden was runner-up, followed by Czechoslovakia, Canada, and Finland.

In Vienna, the annual congress of the International Ice Hockey Federation (IIHF) agreed, subject to confirmation by all parties, that in subsequent seasons an annual World Cup club competition would be held, involving the two top European teams, including the European Cup holder, and the two top North American clubs, including the Stanley Cup holder. J. F. Ahearne, former British president of the IIHF, became the first European to be elected to membership in the Hockey Hall of Fame in Toronto.

The Brantford Alexanders of Canada beat the defending champion Spokane (Wash.) Flyers in the final of the Allan Cup. While this was perhaps still the most prestigious senior amateur club tournament, the quality of the competition continued to decline because of an increasing loss of talent to the professional ranks. At the junior level, the world under-21 title was retained by the U.S.S.R. Canada was runner-up and Czechoslovakia third among eight nations.   (HOWARD BASS)

Iceland

Iceland is an island republic in the North Atlantic Ocean, near the Arctic Circle. Area: 103,000 sq km (39,769 sq mi). Pop. (1977 est.): 221,000. Cap. and largest city: Reykjavik (pop., 1976 est., 84,500). Language: Icelandic. Religion: 97% Lutheran. President in 1977, Kristjan Eldjarn; prime minister, Geir Hallgrimsson.

Late in 1976 Iceland had achieved a major victory in its effort to gain exclusive control over its fishing waters when it succeeded in bringing about the departure of all British fishing vessels from inside the 200-mi zone on December 2. In the early months of 1977 the U.K. government sought to negotiate renewed entry for British fishing vessels under the auspices of the European Economic Community (EEC), which had taken over the question of fishing rights on behalf of all EEC countries. The EEC was not successful in negotiating a new agreement with Iceland, however. By Nov. 28, 1977, when West Germany's agreement with Iceland on fishing concessions for German trawlers within Iceland's 200-mi zone expired, Iceland had driven away virtually all foreign fishing vessels from Icelandic waters, allowing only a few to remain under special arrangements.

The departure of the large contingent of foreign fishing boats from Icelandic shores had an immediate and positive effect on Icelandic fisheries. The cod catch, which had declined alarmingly in recent years, improved considerably in 1977, though the state of the fish stock, an object of much concern since 1975, was still serious. Icelandic marine scientists called for drastic cutbacks in current fishing, even after the departure of foreign vessels, to save the seriously threatened stock of whitefish. The government instituted some moderate measures toward this end, including a temporary limitation on fishing by trawlers, the closing of several breeding areas for young whitefish, and limitations on catches of other species.

Volcanic activity in the Myvatn region was pronounced in 1977. Two eruptions, one on April 28 and another on September 8, began in that area. The lava flow was small, but considerable damage was done to a diatomite refining plant in the area, as well as to the Krafla power project, which depended upon geothermal steam from deep drill holes for its power source. The power project was all but paralyzed by the volcanic activity and associated earthquakes and would remain so for some time to come.

Unlike most Western European countries, Iceland experienced a pronounced economic upswing in 1977. Real gross national product (GNP) rose an estimated 4% and the terms of foreign trade improved sharply, leading to an estimated 7% increase in real gross national income. This compared with increases of 1.9% in real GNP and 5.4% in real gross national income in 1976. The sharp rise in real income was accompanied by very high inflation. Consumer prices rose by 34% in 1976 and were estimated to have increased by 31% in 1977. Wages and salaries were expected to rise by more than 40% in 1977. There was a series of strikes for higher pay in June, and a civil servants' strike in October brought the economy to a halt.

Iceland

ICELAND

Education. (1974–75) Primary, pupils 26,922, teachers 1,379; secondary, pupils 19,829, teachers 1,547; vocational, pupils 4,977, teachers 810; teacher training, students 222, teachers 56; higher, students (1975–76) 2,970, teaching staff 447.

Finance. Monetary unit: króna, with (Sept. 19, 1977) a free rate of 204.97 krónur to U.S. $1 (357.05 krónur = £1 sterling). Gold, SDR's, and foreign exchange (June 1977) U.S. $108.4 million. Budget (1976 est.): revenue 60,342,000,000 krónur; expenditure 58,857,000,000 krónur. Gross national product (1976) 255.7 billion krónur. Money supply (May 1977) 28,106,000,000 krónur. Cost of living (Reykjavik; 1970 = 100; May 1977) 503.

Foreign Trade. (1976) Imports 85,661,000,000 krónur; exports 74.5 billion krónur. Import sources: U.S.S.R. 12%; West Germany 11%; U.S. 11%; U.K. 10%; Denmark 10%; Norway 8%; Sweden 6%; The Netherlands 6%. Export destinations: U.S. 29%; U.K. 12%; West Germany 11%; Portugal 10%; U.S.S.R. 5%. Main exports: fish and products 73%; aluminum 17%. Tourism (1975): visitors 72,000; gross receipts U.S. $12 million.

Transport and Communications. Roads (1975) 11,533 km. Motor vehicles in use (1975): passenger 63,900; commercial 6,621. There are no railways. Air traffic (1976): 1,915,000,000 passenger-km; freight 29,470,000 net ton-km. Shipping (1976): merchant vessels 100 gross tons and over 370; gross tonnage 162,268. Telephones (Dec. 1975) 91,000. Radio licenses (Dec. 1974) 64,000. Television receivers (Dec. 1974) 50,000.

Agriculture. Production (in 000; metric tons; 1976): potatoes 7; hay 374; milk 126; mutton and lamb 15; fish catch 975. Livestock (in 000; Dec. 1976): cattle 61; sheep 871; horses 48; poultry 296.

Industry. Production (in 000): electricity (public supply only; kw-hr; 1976) 2,421,000; aluminum (metric tons; 1975) 59.

Ice Skating:
see Winter Sports

After record current account deficits in 1974 and 1975, the balance of payments improved sharply in 1976, when the current account registered a deficit of only U.S. $24.1 million, equivalent to 1.7% of GNP. In 1977 the current account deficit was expected to be of the order of $30 million–$35 million. The deficit was more than covered by foreign borrowing, leading to a marked rise in foreign exchange reserves. On August 30 Iceland devalued the króna by 2.4%, in line with Norwegian and Danish devaluations.

Construction of a 52,000-ton-per-year ferrosilicon plant was under way in 1977. The project was a joint venture of Elkem Spigerverket A/S and the Icelandic government.   (BJÖRN MATTHÍASSON)

India

India

Residents were forced to higher ground after severe storms and tidal waves in November caused damage to villages near Tiruchirappalli on the eastern coast of India. The final death toll was expected to exceed 20,000.

A federal republic of southern Asia and a member of the Commonwealth of Nations, India is situated on a peninsula extending into the Indian Ocean with the Arabian Sea to the west and the Bay of Bengal to the east. It is bounded (east to west) by Burma, Bangladesh, China, Bhutan, Nepal, and Pakistan; Sri Lanka lies just off its southern tip in the Indian Ocean. Area: 3,287,782 sq km (1,269,420 sq mi), including the Pakistani-controlled section of Jammu and Kashmir and the Himalayan state of Sikkim. Pop. (1977 est.): 615 million; Indo-Aryans and Dravidians are dominant, with Mongoloid, Negroid, and Australoid admixtures. Cap.: New Delhi (pop., 1971, 301,800). Largest cities: Calcutta (metro. pop., 1971, 7,031,400) and Greater Bombay (metro. pop., 1971, 5,970,600). Language: Hindi and English (official). Religion (1971): Hindu 83%; Muslim 11%; Christian 3%; Sikh 2%; Buddhist 0.7%. Presidents in 1977, Fakhruddin Ali Ahmed to February 11 and, from July 25, N. Sanjiva Reddy; prime ministers, Indira Gandhi to March 22 and, from March 24, Morarji Desai.

Domestic Affairs. The year 1977 was one of the most eventful in India's three decades of freedom, one in which the country thought the unthinkable and voted out Indira Gandhi and the Indian National Congress. The party lost control not only in New Delhi but also in 13 states.

On January 18 Prime Minister Indira Gandhi unexpectedly announced that elections would be held for the Lok Sabha (lower house) in March. A general release of thousands of political prisoners followed. Leaders of the Organization Congress, Jan Sangh, Bharatiya Lok Dal, and the Socialist Party—all of which had already decided to merge and form the Janata Party—met and reiterated their decision to fight the election on a single list with a common manifesto and a common symbol. Morarji R. Desai (see BIOGRAPHY) was elected provisional chairman of the party. With censorship suspended, newspapers began publishing reports and comments more freely. A vital blow against the Congress was struck on February 2 when Jagjivan Ram, agriculture minister and a government stalwart, decided to quit and form a new Congress for Democracy along with H. N. Bahuguna and Nandini Satpathy, former chief ministers of Uttar Pradesh and Orissa. The unexpected death of the president of the republic, Fakhruddin Ali Ahmed (see OBITUARIES), on February 11 added a new political uncertainty.

As electioneering gathered tempo, it became evident that sympathy for the leaders who had emerged from prison and revulsion against the political and administrative excesses committed during the emergency, especially the use of compulsion in sterilization, had turned the people in large parts of northern and eastern India against the Congress. Polling was spread over March 16 to 20, and some 194 million people in an electorate of 320 million exercised their franchise. The result was a landslide victory for the Janata Party, which secured 295 seats against 153 for the Congress (see POLITICAL PARTIES). In five northern states—Himachal Pradesh, Punjab, Haryana, Uttar Pradesh and Bihar—the Congress was unable to secure a single seat. Only in the south could it save face. The biggest humiliation for the party that had held power continuously for 30 years was the personal defeat of its masterful leader, Indira Gandhi, in Rae Bareli, where she lost to Raj Narain by a margin of 55,212 votes. Her son, the controversial Sanjay Gandhi, was also defeated. Along with the parliamentary election, polling was also held for the State Assembly in Kerala, where the coalition of Congress and the Communist Party of India (CPI) won handsomely. The last act of the outgoing central government was to lift the state of emergency and the ban on several groups that had been outlawed.

The victorious Janata members of Parliament, having sought the help of Jayaprakash Narayan and J. B. Kripalani in the choice of a leader, announced that the consensus was in favour of Desai, who was sworn in as prime minister on March 24. Next day he announced the names and portfolios of 19 Cabinet colleagues: Charan Singh (home, personnel), Jagjivan Ram (defense), L. K. Advani (information and broadcasting), P. S. Ba-dal (agriculture), H. N. Bahuguna (petroleum and chemicals), Sikandar Bakht (works, housing, and supply), Shanti Bhushan (law, justice, and company affairs), P. C. Chunder (education, culture, and social welfare), M. R. Dandavate (railways), Mohan Dharia (commerce and civil supplies), George Fernandes (communications), P. L. Kaushik (tourism and civil aviation), Raj Narain (health and family welfare), H. M. Patel (finance), Biju Patnaik (steel and mines), P. Ramachandran (energy), A. B. Vajapayee (external affairs), Ravindra Varma (labour and parliamentary affairs), and Brijlal Varma (industry). Fernandes, who had been accused in the Baroda dynamite case of causing a series of explosions on railways with the aim of overthrowing the government and had fought the election from prison, was soon assigned the industry portfolio, and Brijlal Varma moved to communications.

The national councils of the four constituent units of the Janata Party, as well as the Congress for Democracy, announced their disbandment in the last week of April, and Chandra Shekhar was elected chairman of the Janata Party. The Congress, in deep disarray, elected K. Brahmananda Reddy as its president in place of D. K. Borooah.

One of the first consequences of the Janata victory was the fall of the Congress government in Gujarat. A Janata Cabinet was sworn in there with B. J. Patel as chief minister. The central Janata leadership lost no time in calling elections in those states where Congress had been routed in the parliamentary poll. After a period of central rule, elections were held in June in ten states (Bihar, Haryana, Himachal Pradesh, Madhya Pradesh, Orissa, Punjab, Rajasthan, Tamil Nadu, Uttar Pradesh, West Bengal). Once again it was a triumph for the Janata Party, which won in all the states except West Bengal, where a Left Front led by the Communist Party of India (Marxist) won a runaway victory, and Tamil Nadu, where the All-India Anna Dravida Munnetra Kazhagam emerged successful. Elections were held a little later in Jammu and Kashmir. The National Conference gained 49 out of 76 seats, and Sheikh Abdullah formed a new Cabinet. In Sikkim the Congress en bloc merged in Janata. Congress governments fell in Manipur and Tripura, leaving the Congress with control of only six states.

The presidential election was held in July. With Congress cooperating with the ruling party, Neelam Sanjiva Reddy (*see* BIOGRAPHY) was unanimously elected. He was sworn in on July 25.

The outcome of the March-June elections was essentially a constitutional restoration—a return to the rule of law and the political rights and protections guaranteed in the constitution. The new government abolished press censorship, the Prevention of Publication of Objectionable Matters Act, and curbs on free reporting of parliamentary proceedings. It undertook not to use the Maintenance of Internal Security Act and retransferred High Court judges who had been posted to other states as a mark of executive displeasure. It also announced that all amendments to the constitution that had been introduced during the state of emergency would be rescinded, although the majority

enjoyed by the Congress in the Rajya Sabha (upper house) prevented the government from coming forward with the necessary bills.

Moving speedily, the government ordered inquiries into emergency excesses and misuse of authority. Other commissions were looking into the affairs of Sanjay Gandhi's Maruti company, the alleged embezzlement of funds from the State Bank of India by H. M. Nagarwala, a former aid of Mrs. Gandhi, and allegations against the Congress chief ministers of Karnataka and Andhra Pradesh and a former Orissa chief minister, a Janata leader.

The Central Bureau of Investigation arrested Indira Gandhi on October 3, but she was set free the next day. A New Delhi magistrate held that there were no grounds for believing that the accusation of misuse of office to obtain vehicles for electioneering was well founded, since no evidence, documentary or oral, had been collected. Mrs. Gandhi's resignation from the National Congress executive in December appeared to presage a split in the party into pro- and anti-Gandhi groups.

The Economy. With the lifting of curbs on trade union activity, industrial workers began to press demands for increases in wages, cost-of-living increases, and bonuses. The government rescinded the rule that salaried workers should deposit part of their cost-of-living increases in compulsory savings and restored the scheme whereby workers received a bonus payment of 8.33% whether a company made a profit or not.

The union government's budget for 1977–78, presented by the finance minister on June 17, envisaged revenue receipts of Rs 95,540,000,000 (including Rs 1.3 billion from new taxation), capital receipts of Rs 59,420,000,000 (including external

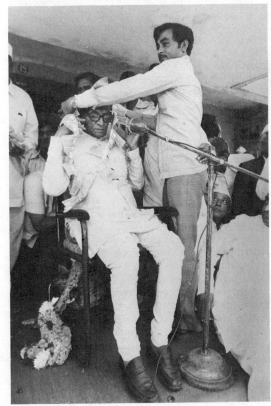

Morarji R. Desai received the regalia of office when he was invested as prime minister of India on March 24. The 81-year-old Desai succeeded Indira Gandhi in the post.

J. P. LAFFONT—SYGMA

INDIA

Education. (1975–76) Primary, pupils *c.* 66 million; secondary, pupils *c.* 24.9 million; primary and secondary, teachers *c.* 2,560,000; higher (1974–75), students 2,230,-225, teaching staff (1970–71) 119,000.

Finance. Monetary unit: rupee, with (Sept. 19, 1977) a free rate of Rs 8.69 to U.S. $1 (Rs 15.13 = £1 sterling). Gold, SDR's, and foreign exchange (May 1977) U.S. $4,431,000,000. Budget (central government; 1976–77 est.): revenue Rs 94,711,000,000; expenditure Rs 128,408,-000,000. Gross national product (1974–75) Rs 681,-090,000,000. Money supply (March 1977) Rs 151.5 billion. Cost of living (1970 = 100; May 1977) 173.

Foreign Trade. (1976) Imports Rs 44,333,000,000; exports Rs 44,632,000,000. Import sources (1975–76): U.S. 25%; Iran 9%; West Germany 7%; Japan 7%; U.S.S.R. 6%; Saudi Arabia 6%; U.K. 5%; Iraq 5%. Export destinations (1975–76): U.S. 13%; Japan 11%; U.S.S.R. 10%; U.K. 10%; Iran 7%. Main exports (1975–76): sugar 12%; jute fabrics 6%; tea 6%; iron ore 5%; cotton fabrics 5%; clothing 5%; leather 5%.

Transport and Communications. Roads (1974) 1,232,-300 km (including 28,750 km main highways). Motor vehicles in use (1975): passenger 756,500; commercial (including buses) 434,400. Railways: (1975) 60,357 km; traffic (1975–76) 134,747,000,000 passenger-km, freight 143,100,000,000 net ton-km. Air traffic (1975): 6,002,000,-000 passenger-km; freight 233.8 million net ton-km. Shipping (1976): merchant vessels 100 gross tons and over 526; gross tonnage 5,093,984. Telephones (Jan. 1976) 1,-817,000. Radio licenses (Dec. 1974) 14,848,000. Television licenses (Dec. 1974) 275,000.

Agriculture. Production (in 000; metric tons; 1976): wheat 28,336; rice *c.* 70,500; barley 3,196; corn *c.* 6,500; millet *c.* 9,600; sorghum *c.* 8,700; potatoes 7,432; cassava (1975) 6,328; sugar, raw value *c.* 4,630; sugar, noncentrifugal (1975) *c.* 7,000; chick-peas *c.* 5,360; mangoes *c.* 8,850; bananas *c.* 3,450; rapeseed *c.* 1,945; linseed *c.* 621; peanuts *c.* 5,700; tea *c.* 511; tobacco 347; cotton, lint *c.* 1,175; jute (including substitutes) 1,248. Livestock (in 000; 1976): cattle *c.* 180,637; sheep *c.* 40,000; pigs *c.* 7,301; buffaloes *c.* 61,534; goats *c.* 70,358; poultry *c.* 142,000.

Industry. Production (in 000; metric tons; 1976): coal 100,991; lignite 3,895; iron ore (63% metal content) 42,-647; pig iron 10,000; crude steel 9,144; aluminum 210; cement 18,499; cotton yarn 1,028; woven cotton fabrics (m; 1975) 8,034,000; petroleum products (1975) 20,285; sulfuric acid 1,689; caustic soda 504; gold (troy oz; 1975) 52; manganese ore (metal content; 1975) 575; electricity (excluding most industrial production; kw-hr) 88,092,000.

loans of Rs 8,940,000,000), revenue disbursements of Rs 94,870,000,000, and capital expenditure of Rs 60,810,000,000, leaving a deficit of Rs 720 million. The outlay on development was placed at Rs 88,-620,000,000, as compared with Rs 27,520,000,000 on defense.

The government's efforts to keep prices in check were helped by a good monsoon throughout the country and a grain reserve of nearly 20 million metric tons, which it inherited. The wholesale price index stood at 184.7 in the last week of October (1970–71 = 100), compared with 177.8 a year earlier. There were complaints during the year of a steep rise in the price of cooking oil. Thousands of acres of crops in Andhra Pradesh were destroyed in November by a cyclone that left thousands dead or homeless. (*See* DISASTERS.)

As a result of strict enforcement of the Foreign Exchange Regulation Act, which required indianization of a proportion of share holdings in industries not producing goods for export only, the Coca-Cola company and IBM decided to wind up their business in India.

Foreign Affairs. Foreign policy was not one of the issues in the election. In their very first statements, the prime minister and foreign minister

declared adherence to "genuine nonalignment." The warm references by U.S. Pres. Jimmy Carter to the restoration of democracy in India were welcomed, and there were exchanges of letters between him and Desai. Soon after the election, the Soviet Union sent Foreign Minister Andrey Gromyko to New Delhi, and Prime Minister Desai visited the Soviet Union in October. These exchanges provided an opportunity to reaffirm that there would be no weakening of Indo-Soviet friendship.

After protracted negotiations, an accord was reached with Bangladesh on September 29 on the sharing of Ganges waters below the barrage at Farakka for Calcutta port and on undertaking joint studies into the longer-term water needs of the region. There was speculation about initiatives to improve Sino-Indian relations, although Foreign Minister Vajapayee declared in November that dramatic developments should not be expected.

(H. Y. SHARADA PRASAD)

Indonesia

A republic of Southeast Asia, Indonesia consists of the major islands of Sumatra, Java, Kalimantan (Indonesian Borneo), Celebes, and Irian Jaya (West New Guinea) and approximately 3,000 smaller islands and islets. Area: 1,919,494 sq km (741,121 sq mi). Pop. (1977 est.): 138,133,500. Area and population figures include former Portuguese Timor. Cap. and largest city: Jakarta (pop., 1977

Palapa-B, Indonesia's second domestic communications satellite, was readied for its move to Cape Canaveral where it was launched in March. Solar cells surrounding the satellite were to provide most of its power once it was in orbit.

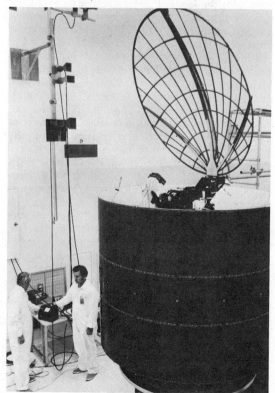

Indonesia

est., 6,178,500). Language: Bahasa Indonesia (official); Javanese; Sundanese; Madurese. Religion: mainly Muslim; some Christian, Buddhist, and Hindu. President and prime minister in 1977, General Suharto.

Indonesia's third general election in 32 years highlighted the country's affairs in 1977. The election was important as a demonstration of the Suharto government's adherence to constitutional procedures. The year was also marked by an improved economic situation and by the first move toward reestablishment of diplomatic relations with China, suspended following Indonesian charges of Chinese complicity in the abortive Indonesian Communist coup in 1965.

In May three parties contested for 360 of the 460 seats in the People's Representation Council. Under the constitution, 100 members of the Council are appointed directly by the head of state. As expected, the government-sponsored Joint Secretariat of Functional Groups (Sekber Golkar), a melange of civil servants and government-sponsored labour unions and peasant groups, triumphed at the polls. Golkar secured 62.1% of the popular vote (38 million) and 232 parliamentary seats. Its nearest rival, the United Development Party (PPP), consisting of several Muslim groups, polled 29.3% of the vote (18 million) and won 99 seats. The Democratic Party (PDI), a coalition of nationalist and Christian parties, fared poorly, winning 8.6% (5 million) and 29 seats.

The outcome assured the parliament's election of incumbent President Suharto in 1978 to another five-year presidential term. Golkar's opposition campaigned principally against acknowledged widespread official corruption and the perfunctory role of the parliament in the nation's quasi-military power structure. In a surprising development, the PPP won in Jakarta, the country's political, economic, and intellectual capital, in effect defeating the government on its own turf.

In 1977, after more than a decade of suspended relations resulting from China's alleged complicity in the 1965 coup attempt and its support of an Indonesian Communist Party (PKI) in exile, both countries moved toward a resumption of diplomatic relations. Direct trade between China and Indonesia resumed, and Chinese and Indonesian diplomats engaged in a nonpublicized dialogue in the autumn that was expected to lead toward further normalization in 1978.

The turnabout in Indonesia's attitude toward Peking followed on the death of Mao Tse-tung and the apparent entry of Vietnam into the Soviet bloc, coupled with Vietnam's absorption of Laos as a satellite and its pressures on Cambodia and Thailand. The U.S.S.R. reacted sharply to indications of a Sino-Indonesian détente. A Soviet-backed Communist Party of Indonesia Committee in Exile surfaced in Moscow as a warning to Jakarta against a rapprochement with Peking.

In May South Moluccan terrorists seized a train and school building in The Netherlands in an effort to persuade the Dutch government to help them gain independence for their islands from Indonesia (see NETHERLANDS, THE). Also seeking independence from Indonesia was the Free Papua Movement, which during the year engaged in guerrilla activities on the borders of Indonesia's West Irian province and Papua New Guinea.

Indonesia's economy displayed signs of recovering confidence in the wake of the notorious Pertamina Affair. Pertamina, the state-owned oil company, had accumulated a U.S. $10.6 billion foreign debt and was on the verge of bankruptcy when Suharto bailed it out. The affair put a severe strain on the economy. Nonetheless, in 1977 the annual rate of domestic inflation was trimmed to 12%, and the gross national product continued at an annual growth rate of 7%.

In a bid to combat widespread corruption and resultant social unrest, the Suharto government called on the Indonesian press to expose bribery by government officials as part of a nationwide campaign.

(ARNOLD C. BRACKMAN)

Industrial Relations

Economic conditions continued to exert a dominant influence on industrial relations in 1977. In most industrialized countries economic recovery continued to be somewhat hesitant. Unemployment reached record postwar levels in many of the developed countries and showed no sign of abating in the future. In this situation the main stresses in industrial relations continued to come from workers' efforts to maintain, and where possible to improve, their living standards and to retain their jobs. Because wages in a number of countries had been subject to restraints of one form or another, and fiscal and other policies had often been directed toward helping low-paid workers, some traditionally higher-paid groups believed their wages were now too low and made efforts to restore what they considered to be their justified level of pay.

Some industries and firms were particularly affected, most notably the steel industry. In most of the traditional producer countries plants were closed down or their operations cut back. Limitations on public expenditure curbed what had been, in many countries, an appreciable growth in public employment. Against such a background, governmental action in many countries was aimed at encouraging job creation, or at least job maintenance. For their part, labour unions did what they could to stop shutdowns and tended to pursue such policies as reduction of working hours, which they saw as providing work for more people, and the attainment of better job security through collective bargaining.

The Wages Scene. Given the prevailing economic conditions, there was little room for increases in real wages. In general, wage bargaining, though frequently hard fought, succeeded in escaping major crises and, thanks to the realism of negotiators, on the whole produced results compatible with the need to moderate inflationary pressures. This was certainly true in the U.S., Japan, and West Germany, the three countries regarded as most important in leading the way to renewed economic growth. France, too, weathered the year successfully, though there was some friction in the publicly owned sector of industry, where a number of collective agreements had provided built-in increases in real wages that were difficult to accommodate in the government's overall economic strategy.

In the U.K. the joint government-labour union policy of wage restraint, born of the "social contract" of 1974 and continued in policies worked out in 1975 and 1976, came under pressure from workers seeking to deal with what they regarded as wage inequities. By the summer of 1977 it was

clear that no further limitations could be implemented. The unions remained generally cooperative, however, and the Trades Union Congress (TUC) in September undertook to maintain the rule of a 12-month interval between successive settlements. The government urged that increases in earnings in forthcoming bargaining should not exceed 10% overall. Ireland was successful in achieving another national wage agreement, ratified in February.

Italy's economic problems resulted in a call for some limitation of labour costs. The unions rejected a demand for adjustment of the traditional cost-of-living payments — the *scala mobile* — but, in January, a "moderation" agreement was reached; subsequently, the government undertook, among other things, to shoulder part of the social security charges borne by employers. In Spain moderation in wage increases was secured in the framework of a general package of economic measures designed to alleviate the country's difficulties.

There were widespread strikes in The Netherlands before unions and employers' organizations reached agreement in February, when the employers agreed to maintain cost-of-living adjustments in 1977. Subsequent industry negotiations added some small general wage increases and other benefits.

Working Conditions and Workers' Participation. Although wages and job security were at the centre of the industrial relations stage in 1977, a number of countries continued to improve working conditions and strengthen workers' participation in management. In France three measures were introduced during the year; one limited overtime (which in France as elsewhere had been increasing appreciably in recent years); a second provided for medium-sized and large enterprises to make an annual "social report" to worker representatives; and a third offered special incentives for young manual workers to embark on savings schemes. Also in France, a central collective agreement on early retirement was signed in June, guaranteeing a proportion of income for workers in the private sector wishing to stop work between the ages of 60 and 65.

A new and comprehensive act concerning the protection of workers and the working environment came into force in Norway in July, and a new Institute for Research on Working Life was set up in Sweden in January. Ireland in March passed a bill permitting workers to serve on the boards of specified state enterprises.

In the U.K., although no legislation was passed, debate about participation was heated. The Bullock Committee on Industrial Democracy produced its report in January. The majority of the committee proposed continuation of the single-level British board of directors but recommended that the boards of large companies should comprise two equal groups, representing stockholders and workers, respectively (the workers being appointed through labour union machinery), and a smaller group of independent members jointly elected by the others. The employer members of the committee submitted a minority report proposing a much more restricted form of participation, in-

Idle cranes were visible evidence of a longshoremen's strike which crippled most U.S. ports in October and November.

WIDE WORLD

Four thousand helmeted policemen cleared the way through 11,000 pickets as a double-decker bus carrying nonstriking workers approached the Grunwick photo-processing plant in London. Although only 137 strikers were involved, the dispute aroused national attention in Britain.

cluding worker representation on the supervisory level of a two-tier board structure. The majority report, while generally welcomed by the TUC, met with little support and a great deal of strong opposition elsewhere. Employers, for their part, urged that innovation should start with participation at lower levels than the board.

National Developments. In the United States, Pres. Jimmy Carter's new administration put forward measures to strengthen collective bargaining, involving revision of procedures largely unchanged since passage of the Wagner Act of 1935 and the Taft-Hartley Act of 1947. The method of adjusting the national minimum wage was discussed by Congress, and a series of increases over several years was enacted. Also, varying somewhat from trends elsewhere except in Japan, Congress voted in favour of phased elimination of compulsory retirement under the age of 70.

Probably the most important negotiations in the U.S. during the year were those in the steel industry, in which a new three-year contract was signed in April. Apart from wage increases the contract strengthened supplementary unemployment benefits for long-service workers in the industry. An important outcome was renewal of steel's experimental negotiating agreement, providing for outside arbitration and no strike in the event of disputes between the union and the industry. Job security was the critical issue in the 44-day East Coast dockworkers' strike. The settlement included a program designed to protect workers against the effects of both the seasonality of the work and the increasing use of containerships.

In Britain a relatively small-scale but lengthy and bitter dispute, basically concerned with union recognition and the reinstatement of dismissed strikers at Grunwick, a firm in northwest London processing film by mail order and employing mainly immigrant labour, raised several important issues. Somewhat unusual for Britain, the firm proved able to continue operations using non-union labour. Action taken to support the strikers included a refusal by postal workers to handle mail for the firm, which raised issues as to the statutory

obligations of the postal services, and mass picketing, to an extent that raised serious questions about the adequacy of the existing law on picketing. The company's refusal to deal with the union seemed to point to loopholes in recent legislation intended to encourage collective bargaining.

In Australia a lengthy pay dispute concerning maintenance workers in power stations in Victoria caused widespread disruption of industry. It occurred at a time when industrial relations were already a political issue in the nation and after the government had introduced legislation to strengthen powers to act in industrial disputes.

Colombia and Peru both suffered general strikes, accompanied by some violence. Ghana experienced a strike by physicians, lawyers, and other professional workers in July. Physicians were also among workers taking industrial action in Malta during the summer. Iceland had an exceptionally turbulent year with general unrest followed by a strike of civil servants in October.

International Developments. Constraints on multinational enterprises continued to be the subject of consideration by several international bodies including the UN and the International Labour Organization (ILO). The European Commission set forth a code in relation to such enterprises operating in South Africa. With the Organization for Economic Cooperation and Development (OECD), which established guidelines in 1976, the unions raised a number of cases of alleged breach of the provisions. OECD had no judicial role in such matters, but its responsible committee took note of the allegations. The most notable of the cases, concerning the Belgian subsidiary of a U.S. company, was settled after discussion in the committee.

On Nov. 1, 1977, President Carter announced that the U.S. had decided to terminate its membership in the ILO.   (R. O. CLARKE)

R. O. Clarke is a principal administrator in the Social Affairs and Industrial Relations Division of the Organization for Economic Cooperation and Development, Paris. The views expressed in this article are his own and should not be attributed to the OECD.

See also Economy, World; Industrial Review.
[521.B.3; 534.C.1.g; 552.D.3 and F.3.b.iij]

Industrial Review

The year 1976 was one of industrial recovery. The deep recession of 1974–75 reached its trough by about the middle of 1975; in the second half of that year industrial output was already rising strongly in the United States, while Japan and Western Europe followed somewhat more slowly and at more moderate rates. In the first half of 1976 the

recovery was in full swing everywhere, but then it slowed down sharply. From the second quarter of 1975 to the same period in 1976 total industrial production in the nations belonging to the Organization for Economic Cooperation and Development (OECD) rose by 10%; this rate of growth was halved in the rest of 1976, and output continued to advance at about that pace in the first half of 1977.

Because the recession in 1975 was deeper than at any time in the years since the end of World War II, it might have been expected that the recovery would be faster and better sustained. Indeed, manufacturing output in the industrial nations, as well as in those less industrialized, recovered rapidly and in 1976 overtook the highest previous level, that of 1974. The speed of this initial recovery was not sustained, however. The reasons for the slowing down were many and included cautious policies stemming from concern over inflation, budgetary and external deficits, subdued business confidence, and, as a result, weakening demand.

Stocks of basic materials and of intermediate and finished products were severely reduced at all levels in the industrial countries during the recession; the rebuilding of them added to final demand in the initial periods of recovery but ceased to act as a stimulus later. OECD officials estimated that in the seven major countries stockbuilding accounted for more than 1% of real gross national product in the first half of 1976, but in the second half its contribution was negligible.

During the early months of 1976 many believed that the fast growth in the three strongest economies, the U.S., Japan, and West Germany, should exercise a widespread beneficial effect on the rest of the world. These hopes did not come to pass, however. Japan and West Germany never reached the growth expected from them by proponents of the theory and, although expansion in the U.S. was rapid, it could not generate enough demand for imports of primary products and manufactures to increase activity markedly elsewhere.

The above developments naturally influenced the course of manufacturing activity. Although in many branches of industry output rose from 1975

Table I. Index Numbers of Production, Employment, and Productivity in Manufacturing Industries
1970=100

Area	Relative importance [1] 1970	Relative importance [1] 1976	Production 1975	Production 1976	Employment 1975	Employment 1976	Productivity [2] 1975	Productivity [2] 1976
World [3]	1,000	1,000	114	125	...	...	...	...
Industrial countries	896	874	111	122	...	...	...	...
Less industrialized countries	104	126	141	152	...	...	...	...
North America [4]	409	409	113	125	...	...	...	...
Canada	27	27	121	126	103	104	117	121
United States	381	381	109	123	95	98	115	126
Latin America [5]	59	72	142	152	...	...	...	...
Mexico	13	14	137	139	...	...	...	...
Asia [6]	137	145	118	132	...	...	...	...
India	11	11	116	128	111	...	105	...
Iran	4	5	...	...	...	...	...	...
Japan	99	99	110	125	99	99	111	126
Pakistan [7]	3	(3)	120	111	...	...	...	...
Europe [8]	365	347	110	117	...	...	...	...
Austria	6	6	118	126	102	100	116	126
Belgium	11	11	111	122	...	...	...	...
Denmark	5	5	103	114	89	90	114	127
Finland	4	4	121	122	110	106	110	115
France	67	67	113	125	100	100	113	125
Germany, West	104	94	103	112	91	87	113	129
Greece	3	4	150	166	119	127	126	131
Ireland	1	1	117	129	94	96	124	134
Italy	37	36	108	120	107	108	101	112
Netherlands, The	13	12	109	115	88	86	124	134
Norway [9]	4	4	114	116	110	111	97	98
Portugal	3	3	132	140	...	...	...	...
Spain	12	15	144	153	115	116	125	132
Sweden	13	12	115	113	109	105	106	108
Switzerland	12	9	95	96	86	80	110	120
United Kingdom	54	45	102	103	90	88	113	118
Yugoslavia	13	16	149	154	124	128	120	120
Rest of the world [10]	30	27	...	...	...	...	...	...
Australia [7]	14	13	110	112	94	93	117	120
South Africa	6	6	124	123	117	118	106	104
Centrally planned economies [11]	...	...	154		...	...	...	...

[1] The 1970 weights are those applied by the UN Statistical Office; those for 1977 were estimated on the basis of the changes in manufacturing output since 1970 in the various countries.
[2] This is 100 times the production index divided by the employment index, giving a rough indication of changes in output per person employed.
[3] Excluding Albania, Bulgaria, China, Czechoslovakia, East Germany, Hungary, Mongolia, North Korea, North Vietnam, Poland, Romania, and the U.S.S.R.
[4] Canada and the United States.
[5] South and Central America (including Mexico) and the Caribbean islands.
[6] Asian Middle East and East and Southeast Asia, including Japan.
[7] Years beginning July 1.
[8] Excluding Albania, Bulgaria, Czechoslovakia, East Germany, Hungary, Poland, Romania, and the U.S.S.R.
[9] Employment and productivity based on 1972=100.
[10] Africa and Oceania.
[11] These are not included in the above world total and consist of Albania, Bulgaria, Czechoslovakia, East Germany, Hungary, Poland, Romania, and the U.S.S.R.

Table II. Industrial Pattern of Boom, Recession, and Recovery, 1973–76
Percent change from previous year

	World [1] 1973	World [1] 1974	World [1] 1975	World [1] 1976	Developed countries 1973	Developed countries 1974	Developed countries 1975	Developed countries 1976	Less developed countries 1973	Less developed countries 1974	Less developed countries 1975	Less developed countries 1976	Centrally planned economics 1973	Centrally planned economics 1974	Centrally planned economics 1975	Centrally planned economics 1976
All manufacturing	9	1	−6	10	9	0	−7	10	10	6	3	8	9	9	9	8
Heavy industries	12	2	−7	10	12	1	−8	10	13	10	1	10	11	11	10	9
Base metals	12	2	−15	9	12	1	−16	8	4	11	4	12	6	6	7	8
Metal products	13	1	−6	9	13	0	−7	10	18	14	2	12	12	12	12	9
Building materials, etc.	9	−1	−6	9	8	−2	−8	8	10	7	5	8	9	7	7	6
Chemicals	11	2	−5	12	11	1	−6	13	9	6	−1	7	11	11	10	9
Light industries	6	−1	−2	8	6	−2	−4	9	8	3	4	7	7	8	6	4
Food, drink, tobacco	5	3	0	6	5	3	−2	5	6	5	4	8	5	8	5	3
Textiles	5	−3	−2	8	6	−5	−4	9	6	0	4	6	7	6	6	5
Clothing, footwear	4	−2	1	11	2	−3	−1	9	13	6	9	12	6	7	7	7
Wood products	7	−3	−7	11	8	−4	−8	11	2	2	0	8	7	6	8	5
Paper, printing	6	0	−8	8	7	−1	−7	8	8	15	3	−5	−7	8	7	8	6

[1] Excluding centrally planned economies.
Source: UN, *Monthly Bulletin of Statistics*.

Table III. Output per Hour Worked in Manufacturing
1970=100

Country	1970	1972	1973	1974	1975	1976
France	100	114	121	125	121	134
Germany, West	100	111	117	121	126	136
Italy	100	113	122	120	121	129 [1]
Japan	100	114	133	136	131	148
U.K.	100	112	118	118	118	123
U.S.	100	110	113	116	118	124

[1] Estimate.
Source: National Institute, *Economic Review*.

Table IV. Manufacturing Production in the U.S.S.R. and Eastern Europe [1]
1970=100

Country	1974	1975	1976
Bulgaria [2]	140	154	164
Czechoslovakia	130	140	148
East Germany [2]	128	137	145
Hungary	131	137	142
Poland	151	168	184
U.S.S.R.	135	145	152

[1] Romania not available.
[2] All industries.
Source: UN, *Monthly Bulletin of Statistics*.

A computer-directed process for assembling wiring for 747 aircraft was developed at Boeing's Everett, Washington, plant. With the new process, the wiring job is completed 16 times faster than when it was done by hand.

to 1976 by 8–12%, this was somewhat illusory in that it started from a low level and partly concealed the still-low utilization of capacity. The pattern of recovery (Table II) reflected the importance of the personal sector. The food, textile, and clothing industries recovered at an early stage and relatively strongly. So did metal products, but their recovery was mainly due to the strong demand for automobiles in the first half of 1976.

These trends appeared to continue into 1977. During the first half of that year the disparities in the investment activity in the U.S. and Japan on the one hand and Western Europe on the other became particularly marked. The first two countries seemed to have been responsible for almost the entire increase in investment, estimated at 5–6%, for 1977. The fact that investment failed to recover in Europe reflected the depressed demand, the low capacity of plant utilization, the unsatisfactory level of post-tax profits (especially in countries where price controls were in operation), and the high nominal cost of borrowing.

The dominant source of demand for industrial products in the U.S. was the personal sector; consumers' expenditure rose by nearly 6% in real terms, and the rise was particularly marked in demand for cars, household durable goods, and dwellings. Stockbuilding was another major factor in raising the demand for manufactured goods. Business investment started to turn up later, becoming more important in 1977.

The Canadian manufacturing industry benefited from the U.S. recovery. The trends in that nation were similar to those in the U.S. except for business investment, which was expected to remain depressed for a longer time in view of the large amount of idle production capacity.

In Japan the main stimulus for growth was export performance. In a sense the drive to offset the weak internal demand by exports was too successful and led to serious complaints (and some action, even if it was weak) against Japanese import penetration in other OECD countries. Virtually all other components of demand, except housing, remained weak throughout 1976.

Manufacturing activity in the Western European industrial countries was dominated by the general trends described above; developments were nevertheless not uniform. In the majority of European countries the recovery of manufacturing was quite marked, and relatively high growth rates were achieved in 1976: 10–11% in Belgium, Denmark, France, Greece, Ireland, and Italy; 9% in West Germany; 6–7% in Austria, The Netherlands, Portugal, and Spain. In another, though smaller, group of countries the change was marginal, chiefly because of anti-inflationary or other restrictive policies (United Kingdom, Finland, Switzerland), while manufacturing output actually fell in Sweden.

In the major manufacturing countries of the Southern Hemisphere (outside Latin America) conditions were not favourable. There was a marginal increase in production in Australia and a fractional decline in South Africa.

One characteristic feature of the manufacturing industries in 1976 was that the recovery was achieved with generally very little addition to the employed labour force. The U.S. was an exception (the 13% output rise required a rise of 3% in employment); in most other industrial countries employment hardly changed, and in many of them it actually fell. As a consequence, productivity rose significantly in 1976 (Table III).

While manufacturing output in the industrial countries fell by 7% in 1975, that in the less industrialized nations avoided a decline; the effect of the recession was the reduction of their growth rate to 3%. Mainly because their decline was not so great in 1975, the less developed countries raised their manufacturing output by only 8% in 1976.

Although the centrally planned economies escaped the 1975 recession, the rate of growth of manufacturing production was reduced in all of them in 1976. In the Soviet Union manufacturing grew by 5%, following an 8% growth in each of the two preceding years. Among the other countries manufacturing production increased fastest in Poland (9%) and slowest in Hungary (4%).

(G. F. RAY)

Industrial Review

ADVERTISING

The use of advertising by professional associations was the major event in 1977. The American Hospital Association approved guidelines allowing hospitals to advertise as long as no comparisons were made with other hospitals and specific individuals on the hospital staff were not promoted. The National Society of Public Accountants modified its rules for its members, allowing them to advertise professional services if the advertisements were truthful about the accountant's education, the services offered, and the fees charged.

The big story of the year, however, was the Supreme Court ruling that lawyers could not be barred from advertising their fees for routine services. The American Bar Association revised its Code of Professional Responsibility to eliminate its ban on advertising and adopted guidelines on what attorneys could say in print and on radio broadcasts. The ABA recommended to its members that they limit their advertisements to such information as their field of law, names of clients represented, fee for initial consultation, contingent fee rates, range of fees for services, hourly rates, and fixed fees for specific legal services. The ABA established a Commission on Advertising to study developments at the state bar level and to review advertising in other professions. The Michigan Bar Association was the first to allow advertising of more than a

Dannon Milk Products filmed a series of yogurt commercials among the long-lived inhabitants of Soviet Georgia; the series was the first filmed in the U.S.S.R. for U.S. television.

name, address, and phone number in the telephone directory. Under new regulations passed at the state bar meeting, attorneys in Michigan could advertise in newspapers and on radio but could not use television.

The Federal Trade Commission (FTC) in 1977 brought a lawsuit against the American Medical Association and the American Dental Association to remove restrictions that prohibit physicians and dentists from advertising. In July 1977 the New York State Board of Regents ruled that physicians could place limited advertising in professional directories, newspapers, and magazines.

By allowing professions to advertise, the U.S. Supreme Court extended advertising's First Amendment status. In 1976 the court overturned a Virginia regulation that prohibited price advertising for proprietary drugs. In this case, the court concluded that commercial speech was protected. However, the court did not prevent regulation of advertising that was false, deceptive, or misleading.

In other areas of the economy in 1977 different types of advertising were being studied by governmental agencies and consumer groups. Congressmen introduced legislation that prohibited utilities from using their advertising expenses as a cost factor in determining electric and gas utility rates. The practice of eliminating such institutional advertising from rate hearings had already taken place in a number of states. The Civil Aeronautics Board considered regulations that would prevent institutional advertising from being treated as a cost in determining airline fares.

Advertising in the U.S. in 1977 rose 11% over 1976, to $37 billion. In 1976 advertising had reached $33.5 billion, 18% better than in 1975. Even with a raise in rates by the media, advertising in almost all product categories increased in 1976. Network television prices increased by 15%, while local spots on television increased 20%. Newspaper rates rose substantially; radio rates moved up with an increase in demand for broadcast time; and magazine rates rose by a small percentage. The strong demand for network television time continued, but there was less of a demand for local spots.

A new media measurement, RADAR XIV, showed that the gap between the numbers of listeners to AM and FM radio stations narrowed in 1977. In 1977 some 40% of radio listeners turned to FM stations, while 60% listened to AM stations. Comparable figures from 1976 had shown only 30% listening to FM stations. This change in listening habits caused advertisers to spend more money for sponsoring FM programs.

In August statistics published by *Advertising Age* indicated that the 100 largest national advertisers in the U.S. increased their advertising and promotion expenditures 20% in 1976, to $7.7 billion. This was the largest annual increase in the 22 years that *Advertising Age* had published these figures. Of the largest national advertisers, Procter and Gamble Co. maintained its number one position by spending $445 million. Others in the top five included General Motors Corp., General Foods Corp., Sears, Roebuck and Co., and Warner-Lambert Co. These five largest advertisers accounted for more than $1.4 billion of media

expenditures in 1976. The top three network television users in 1976 were Procter and Gamble, General Foods, and Bristol-Myers Co.

Several congressmen introduced legislation restricting the use of the telephone for advertising products and services. The proposed legislation would allow consumers who do not want to receive advertisements on the telephone to have their names removed from telephone company lists. Organizations planning to use the telephone for advertising purposes would need to obtain a master list from the telephone company before making calls.

Of major concern for advertisers in 1977 were three proceedings before the FTC on the advertising of food and drugs. The proceedings were concerned with nutritional claims, product claims for over-the-counter drugs, and warnings for over-the-counter antacids.

Since 1975 advertising in which competitive brands were named had given rise to considerable controversy. The results of a study reported in early 1977 showed that such commercials created a greater negative attitude toward advertising and did not create higher awareness of the sponsored brands. In addition, these advertisements led to greater misidentification of the sponsors' products, often to the benefit of the named competitors.

In late 1976 Sears Roebuck agreed to an FTC order banning the use of bait-and-switch tactics for selling major home appliances. The complaint that led to the consent agreement challenged advertising by Sears that offered sewing machines, washers and driers, and other major home appliances at low prices. The complaint alleged that these advertisements were not bona fide offers to sell but were made to get prospective customers to the stores. Sears was ordered to have sufficient quantities of advertised appliances available to meet reasonably anticipated demand. Copies of the advertisement had to be posted in the stores.

(EDWARD MARK MAZZE)

AEROSPACE

The most important events of 1977 involved air transport over the North Atlantic. A new agreement was signed between Britain and the U.S. to regulate traffic across a region that contained the world's most competitive air routes. Concorde concluded its first year of commercial operation. In the U.K., Freddie Laker (*see* BIOGRAPHY) began his controversial Skytrain service.

In June 1976 Britain had given the U.S. a year's notice of withdrawal from the 1946 Bermuda Agreement by which routes across the North Atlantic had been arranged. Britain argued that the original objectives of low cost, reasonable profitability, and economic use of resources were not being realized. Renegotiations dragged on, and Bermuda II (as it was called) was finally signed after the deadline had expired and with aircraft bound for London in doubt up to the very last moment as to whether they would be permitted to land at the city's airports.

The Anglo-French Concorde supersonic transport proved itself a technical success, with consistently high load factors on the London–Washington routes. But despite the efforts of two presidents and the weight

A Concorde supersonic airliner approaches the runway at John F. Kennedy Airport in New York City on October 19, having won a 19-month battle to gain permission to land.

of the U.S. judiciary, the Port Authority of New York and New Jersey continued to refuse Concorde landing rights into Kennedy Airport, regarded by Europe as the gateway to commercial America. Finally, in October, the U.S. Supreme Court turned down the Authority's request for a further delay, and British Airways and Air France began Concorde service on November 22.

Meanwhile, new routes began to open up. The U.S. airline Braniff made plans to take over British Airways' Concordes at Washington, D.C., in 1978 and to extend the route to Dallas, Texas. Similarly, Singapore International planned to take over the Concorde between Bahrain and Singapore, with Qantas perhaps completing the leg from Singapore to Melbourne.

Freddie Laker, entrepreneurial head of Britain's Laker Airways, after six years won his application to operate a cut-rate, "no-frills" service between London and New York. The first flight was on September 26. Pan Am, British Airways, TWA, and other carriers that had opposed the one-year trial period themselves filed applications to operate similar service on the North Atlantic route.

Another European triumph was the decision of Eastern Airlines to lease four A300 Airbus wide-body airliners for a six-month trial period to service the New York–Florida winter holiday route, with the option to buy. If successful, the operation could signal the introduction of the twin-engined jumbo jet in the U.S.

In March two Boeing 747s collided on the runway at the Tenerife airport in the Canary Islands, killing 582 people and setting a record for the world's worst aviation accident. By contrast, the loss of a Dan-Air

Boeing 707 the following month at Lusaka, Zambia, with only the crew aboard, created little stir. The latter accident, which was attributed to metal fatigue, might have some influence on the reequipment quandary that increasingly troubled the airlines: whether to reengine existing airplanes or to buy more expensive replacements.

Reequipment became a central question because the airlines were flying many planes that were 15–20 years old and due for retirement about 1982. DC-8s and DC-9s; Boeing 707s, 727s, and 737s; Lockheed Tridents; BAC One-Elevens; and others were thought to be too noisy and too thirsty for fuel for the 1980s, but development costs for new and untried designs had become so great that no manufacturer could afford to make mistakes in judging the market. The alternative, putting new engines in old airplanes, attracted little enthusiasm from the airlines.

The aircraft firms continued to tempt the airlines with a host of designs, Boeing, for example, with the 160-seat 7N7 and the 200-seat 7X7. Europe offered its equivalent BAC X-11 and A200 (a smaller version of the A300). But the world's best-selling transport remained the Boeing 727. Production of the 1960 design began a rise to an estimated 11 a month by mid-1978.

The main event of the year for Britain was the nationalization of the aerospace industry in March; this was part of the continuing plan to bring large private companies more directly under state control. After so many years of preparation the event caused little excitement, the main point at issue being the compensation to be paid out. Financial difficulties hit Fairey-Britten-Norman when a large number of

Islanders produced by its factory at Gosselies in Belgium were left unsold. One solution under investigation was the takeover of Islander and Trislander production by the Northern Irish firm of Shorts; the latter's twin-engined 30-seat commuter plane had made a modest penetration of the U.S. market.

France's nationally owned company, Aérospatiale, lost money, and the French government called for an investigation into the affairs of the privately owned Dassault company, with a view to restructuring the entire industry. In April the government formally ended the agreement between Aérospatiale and the U.S. company McDonnell Douglas to study a French airliner proposal, the Advanced Short/Medium Range transport (ASMR). France's anti-U.S. sentiments were confirmed in May at the Paris Air Show when Pres. Valéry Giscard d'Estaing, angered by, among other things, the failure to get ASMR launched and the persistent refusal of the United States to allow the Concorde to begin service to New York, overturned the policy announced at the 1975 show and declared that henceforth France would look to Europe for partners.

The 1977 Paris Air Show emphasized the U.S. lead in aviation technology. Europe had nothing like the two prototype transports by Boeing and McDonnell Douglas, which competed to replace the C-130 Hercules, or the Fairchild A-10 tank killer. The Soviet Union's new wide-body transport, the Ilyushin Il-86, made its first public appearance in the West. Equivalent in size to the DC-10 and L-1011 trijets, it lacked the quiet, economic high-bypass fan engines of the big Western transports; the Soviet Union sought to buy these engines from Rolls-Royce and General Electric.

A significant development was the totally unexpected cancellation by U.S. Pres. Jimmy Carter of the North American Rockwell B-1, designed to replace the nation's mighty but aging and subsonic B-52 strategic bombers. Already well along in its flight-test program, the B-1 was to have been one of the prongs in the U.S. "Triad" system of strategic manned bombers and intercontinental missiles launched from land and submarines. It was to be replaced by modernized B-52s carrying cruise missiles with a 1,500–2,000-mi range, and perhaps a new version of the swing-wing F-111 fighter/bomber. (MICHAEL WILSON)

ALCOHOLIC BEVERAGES

Beer. World beer production in 1976 reached an estimated total of 800 million hectolitres (hl), the first time this total had been attained since records began to be kept. This compared with 775 million hl a year earlier (1 hl = about 26.5 U.S. gal). West Germany retained world leadership in terms of per capita consumption, followed by Australia, Czechoslovakia, and Belgium. The U.S., although by far the world's biggest beer producer (about 190 million hl), dropped from 13th to 14th place. (*See* Table V.)

The 1977 malting quality barley crop looked promising in the U.S., but in Europe

Industrial Review

a bumper harvest was ruined by torrential rains just as the combines were due to begin reaping. Great Britain and most countries of northern Europe were affected by the rains and the harvest was seriously delayed. No one seemed willing to guess at the outcome, but there was all too much evidence that the abnormal weather conditions had caused the barleycorns to sprout while still on the plant and that much more grain had been spilled onto the ground. All this was in addition to the effect of the strong winds that accompanied the rain in much of Europe, flattening the grain to the ground and making the job of the combine harvesters almost impossible.

In 1976 almost all European continental countries, as well as Britain, boosted their beer sales during one of the longest, hottest, driest summers on record. Reckoned in terms of barrels, the British output for the first time exceeded the 40 million mark. European countries long ago had almost entirely abandoned ale in favour of lager, something that had not happened to the same extent in Britain. However, the hot weather of 1976 boosted lager sales in Britain until they were only a decimal point under 25% of the total brew.

Within the EEC malting barley prices rose in common with other grain and crop prices generally. The West Germans made good their supply shortages by buying from Britain at prices in excess of £105 per ton. Throughout the marketing period there was little of malting quality sold at under £100 per ton. Brewers and maltsters continued to be alarmed by the obstinately high nitrogen levels in barley samples submitted for acceptance as malting quality. High nitrogen meant high protein, and this meant lowered yield for brewing purposes. Thus, the brewer was faced with steeply

rising prices for his grain purchases and yet needed to buy more grain with which to produce a given quantity of beer.

(ARTHUR T. E. BINSTED)

Spirits. The spirits market continued to suffer from high taxation of its products. In Britain the government followed the 11% increase in excise duty imposed in 1976 with a second increase on Jan. 1, 1977, thereby taking £3.16 in excise duty alone from every bottle of whiskey sold in the home market. During the first nine months of 1977 sales of spirits declined 11.6% from the corresponding period of 1976. From January to June 1977 total sales were down 22%; among imported spirits rum, the biggest seller, rose 5% while noncognac brandy rose nearly 30%.

Sales of bonded Scotch whisky in the U.K. reached 17,292,000 proof gallons in the year ended Sept. 30, 1977, an increase of 7½%. Scotch whisky exports in the 12 months November 1976–October 1977 rose 5% to 95,340,000 proof gallons, an increase of 2.4% in value to £511,408,000.

The U.S. market remained practically static with a slightly more than 1% increase to 33,112,000 proof gallons. The trend continued toward white wines and away from darker spirits. Although Scotch held its position fairly well, bourbon had lost over 40% of its market share since 1965, and American blended whiskey had lost half its share, dropping to one-eight of the market. Vodka, by comparison, still continued its upward climb in sales throughout the world, while some industry observers considered that white rums were reaching a peak.

The consumer swing toward wine brought difficult times for U.S. and Canadian whiskey distillers. After a rapid expansion in distilling capacity in Canada in recent years, most distillers were shutting down for six months until mid–1978 to bring down existing inventories to more realistic levels. Many U.S. whiskey distil-

leries were shutting for a similar period. In general, however, sales of well-established brands appeared to be holding up well; the casualties were mainly among lesser brands.

(COLIN PARNELL)

Wine. World production of wine in 1977 was estimated at 280 million hl, a drop of 43 million hl, or 13%, from 1976. The decline was accounted for by the drop in European production from 252 million hl in 1976 to 212 million hl. France and Italy, which together accounted for 45% of world production, suffered markedly small harvests. In other continents, where annual variations are slight, North and South America produced about 50 million hl. This was about the same quantity as in 1976, a decrease of 5 million hl in Argentina being partly offset by a U.S. increase. Production in the major areas in 1977 was inferior to that of previous years and the wine of moderate quality only.

The French harvest reached 54 million hl, a shortfall of 19 million hl, or about 26%, the lowest level since 1969 and, in most places, of inferior quality. In Bordeaux the harvest was one of the smallest since World War II but of good quality; in Burgundy it was small and of poor quality, although the Beaujolais area produced more wine than in 1976 and of average quality; Alsace performed much as in 1976, as did the Champagne region.

Italy suffered from bad weather just before grape picking, and the harvest fell below expectation to 55 million hl (as against the 1966–75 average of 69 million hl). Quality varied according to the effects of the weather upon the particular region. Spain (25 million hl) and Portugal (7.5 million hl) also experienced small harvests, 30% below 1976. West Germany, however, had an above-average harvest (9 million hl) but of slightly inferior quality. The Soviet Union was estimated to have produced about 30 million hl, maintaining the previous years' high level.

Table V. Estimated Consumption of Beer in Selected Countries
In litres [1] per capita

Country	1974	1975	1976
Germany, West	146.9	147.8	150.9
Australia [2]	141.3	142.1	139.9
Czechoslovakia	142.1	143.4	139.4
Belgium [3]	132.9	130.6	138.0
New Zealand	126.1	133.2	131.0
Luxembourg	135	129.0	130.0
Germany, East	113.5	117.6	124.5
Ireland	130.0	128.6	123.0
United Kingdom	114.3	117.6	118.9
Denmark	111.96	117.46	118.68
Austria	105.4	103.8	102.0
Canada [4]	85.8	86.4	84.7
Netherlands, The	75.72	78.92	83.8
United States	80.1	81.7	82.5
Hungary	66.8	72.3	77
Switzerland	75.4	71.8	71.1
Sweden	58.3	60.2	59.1
Finland	56.2	54.7	54.6
Venezuela	40.4	50	...
France	44.19	44.9	48.66
Spain	44.3	47.0	47.9
Bulgaria	52	46	...
Norway	43.85	45.44	44.72
Colombia	35.3	32.8	39.9
Yugoslavia	39.1	39	...

[1] One litre = 1.0567 U.S. quart = 0.8799 imperial quart.
[2] Years ending June 30.
[3] Excluding so-called "household beer."
[4] Years ending March 31.

Table VI. Estimated Consumption of Potable Distilled Spirits in Selected Countries
In litres [1] of 100% pure spirit per capita

Country	1974	1975	1976
Poland	4.0	4.6	5.4
Luxembourg	3.1	3.5	4.1
Hungary	3.11	3.61	4.1
Germany, East	3.4	3.6	3.6
Yugoslavia	3.4	3.5	...
U.S.S.R.	3.3	3.3	3.3
Canada [2]	3.11	3.16	3.24
United States	3.12	3.1	3.12
Spain	2.5	2.6	3.1
Sweden	2.94	2.97	3.08
Finland	2.9	2.81	3.0
Czechoslovakia	2.72	2.88	3
Germany, West	2.64	3.04	2.83
France [3]	2.7	2.5	2.5
Netherlands, The	2.75	3.44	2.49
Iceland	2.65	2.4	2.31
Italy	2.1	2	2
Bulgaria	2	2	...
Ireland	1.91	2.03	1.98
Belgium	1.9	1.99	1.95
Denmark	1.58	1.74	1.9
Norway	1.82	1.84	1.87
Switzerland	2.15	1.94	1.8
Austria	1.96	1.65	1.7
South Africa	1.31	1.38	1.15

[1] One litre = 1.0567 U.S. quart = 0.8799 imperial quart.
[2] Years ending March 31.
[3] Including aperitifs.

Table VII. Estimated Consumption of Wine in Selected Countries
In litres [1] per capita

Country	1974	1975	1976
France [2]	104.1	103.7	101.3
Italy	109.2	103.9	99.7
Portugal	96.0	89.8	97.8
Argentina	77.2	83.7	84.8
Spain	77.0	76.0	71.0
Chile	40.0	43.46	47.84
Luxembourg	49.6	41.3	45.3
Switzerland [3]	46.0	43.9	43.5
Greece	36.5	38.0	39.8
Austria	35.4	35.1	36.3
Hungary	34.6	34.2	34.0
Romania	30.0	33.0	30
Yugoslavia	28.9	28.6	...
Uruguay	25.1	25.1	...
Germany, West	20.3	23.3	23.6
Bulgaria	19.98	20	...
Czechoslovakia	15.3	16.3	16.5
Belgium	15.8	17.2	15.7
U.S.S.R.	13	13.4	13.4
Denmark	9.66	11.48	12.53
Netherlands, The	10.37	10.25	11.34
Australia [4]	11.2	11.2	11.2
South Africa	11.34	10.41	9.82
New Zealand	9.2	8.8	8.8
Poland	6.7	7.5	8.5
United States	6.29	6.55	6.6

[1] One litre = 1.0567 U.S. quart = 0.8799 imperial quart.
[2] Excluding cider (c. 20 litres per capita annually).
[3] Excluding cider (c. 6 litres per capita 1975–76).
[4] Years ending June 30.

Source: Produktschap voor Gedistilleerde Dranken, *Hoeveel alcoholhoudende dranken worden er in de wereld gedronken?*

The first shipment of the Ford Fiesta, a minicar built in Europe for the North American and European markets, arrives in Nova Scotia in May to be sold in Canada.

Argentina continued as the major non-European producer with 23 million hl. The U.S. produced 16 million hl, maintaining a steady annual increase (14.4 million hl in 1976). In Australia the 1977 grape harvest was the largest ever recorded and production was estimated at 2,525,670 hl. The quality was good.   (PAUL MAURON)

AUTOMOBILES

The U.S. automobile industry's program to take pounds and inches out of its cars in order to make them more fuel-efficient entered its second stage in 1977 with the introduction of resized intermediates at General Motors Corp., all-new compacts at Ford Motor Co., and the elimination of its standard-size cars altogether at Chrysler Corp. American Motors Corp. (AMC), already the self-acclaimed small car specialist, continued to produce its smaller car lines and expanded its output of four-cylinder engines.

A year earlier GM had initiated the downsizing movement when it brought out its new line of standard-size cars that were as much as 1,000 lb lighter and a foot shorter than previous models. In the fall of 1977, when the 1978s appeared, mid-size models such as the Oldsmobile Cutlass, Pontiac Le-Mans and Grand Prix, Buick Century and Regal, and Chevrolet Malibu and Monte Carlo had lost 600 to 900 lb and from 8 to 18 inches in length.

While GM was scaling down its large models, Ford was working from the small ones up and brought out a new pair of compacts. The new Ford Fairmont and Mercury Zephyr were replacements for the Ford Maverick and Mercury Comet.

Chrysler, realizing that the days of the big car were numbered because of federally mandated fuel economy laws, simply dropped the full-size Dodge Royal Monaco

and Plymouth Gran Fury from its lineup because the company's budget did not allow it to spend the billions of dollars GM and Ford could on all-new lightweight cars.

The reason downsizing picked up momentum in the latter part of 1977 was that for the first time the federal government had dictated to the U.S. automakers that they must build a fleet of cars that obtained an average of 18 mi per gallon (mpg) or pay a penalty of $5 for every 0.1 mpg they fell short for every car sold during the entire year. If they sold a product mix that obtained 18 mpg for the first 11 months of the year but fell short the last month, the penalty would then be on all cars sold during the entire 12 months. The 18-mpg minimum was to move up to 19 mpg in 1979, 20 mpg in 1980, and 27.5 mpg in 1985.

Because of the potential monetary penalties, the U.S. auto industry adopted a new small-car pricing strategy. GM, Ford, and AMC priced their small cars lower in several Western states, where imports held a 40% share of the market, than elsewhere in the country. Cars under this system included the Chevrolet Chevette, Ford Pinto and Mustang II, Mercury Bobcat, and AMC Gremlin.

Prices in general, however, were several hundred dollars higher when the new 1978 models appeared in the fall. GM boosted prices an average of 5.7% or $387; Ford by 5.8% or $387; Chrysler by 5.8% or $354; and AMC by 2.7% or $103. As a rule the larger cars bore the brunt of the increases and the smaller ones were raised only minimally.

In 1977 the swing to big cars continued. Large cars accounted for about 27% of sales, mid-size for 33%, and small cars, including imports, 40%. This compared with 25% for large cars, 33% for mid-size, and 42% for small cars in 1976. As proof of large-car popularity, the full-size Chevrolet was once

again the industry's best-selling car, taking the crown away from the mid-size Oldsmobile Cutlass after the latter had enjoyed nearly a two-year reign at the top.

The U.S. industry sold 9,104,453 cars in the 1977 calendar year, up from 8,606,573 in 1976. In the 1977 model year, which ended on September 30, the domestic manufacturers sold 9,009,176 cars, up 6.1% from 1976. GM accounted for 57% of all sales, Ford for 27%, Chrysler for 13.7%, and AMC for 2.3%. The 1978 model year got off to a slow start, however, with new car sales in November and December trending steadily downward.

Imports had a field day in 1977. During the calendar year 1977 import sales totaled a record 2,069,891 units for an 18.5% share of the market. That compared with the previous sales record of 1.7 million units in 1973 and the market share record of 18.3% in 1975.

Among the U.S. manufacturers, new models introduced during the year included the Fairmont and Zephyr compacts at Ford along with a new import, the mini Fiesta, assembled in West Germany, Spain, and Great Britain. To commemorate its 75th year in business Ford also brought out the Diamond Jubilee editions of the Continental Mark V and the Ford Thunderbird. The Diamond Jubilee Mark V, which came complete with a leather-bound owner's manual and leather-wrapped tool kit, was priced at $20,099.

At GM the new cars included the above-mentioned restyled and downsized midsize models. GM also brought out a four-door Chevrolet Chevette, a glassy, fastback-style 25th-anniversary Chevrolet Corvette, diesel-engine versions of the Delta 88 and 98 Oldsmobiles, and a turbocharged Buick Regal and LeSabre sport coupe.

At Chrysler the emphasis was on small cars, and two new imports from Japan were introduced, the Plymouth Sapporo and Dodge Challenger. Two domestically built subcompacts, the Plymouth Horizon and Dodge Omni, were scheduled to appear early in 1978. They would be Chrysler's first domestically built subcompacts and would feature front-wheel drive in four-door hatchbacks. In the mid-size line Chrysler also brought out station wagon versions of the Dodge Diplomat and Chrysler LeBaron and a Magnum model with a front end that seemingly was borrowed from the classic Cord. AMC limited its new entries to a compact model Concord, a replacement for the former Hornet that bore a striking resemblance to the old model.

Automakers in other nations did not stand still either. Toyota, the best-selling import in the U.S. since 1975, unveiled a newly styled sporty Celica and a top-of-the-line luxury model Cressida with a unique four-speed automatic transmission; the fourth gear was an overdrive to achieve better fuel economy at highway speeds by means of reduced engine revolutions per minute. Datsun, the second best-selling import in the U.S., resurrected an old model designation, the 510, on a new family sedan and wagon.

Industrial Review

Volkswagen introduced a four-cylinder diesel engine for its Rabbit and sold 15,000 of these models during the year. Subsequently it raised its sales estimate for the following year to 45,000. The engine was a $170 option in 1977 that was boosted to $195 for 1978. VW also did some name changing and interior upgrading in its Rabbit line by adding a "C" model custom series and a top-of-the-line "L" model to its basic Rabbit hatchback. Volkswagen's Porsche-Audi division brought out a new five-cylinder engine replacement for the Audi 100LS, simply named the 5000, while Porsche introduced a new 928 2-plus-2 sports car.

Despite the inroads made in the U.S. by imports, Volvo announced that it had scrapped plans to build cars at a $150 million plant in Chesapeake, Va. VW, however, continued with plans to build Rabbits at its plant in Pennsylvania, starting in the spring of 1978. Honda announced plans to build motorcycles at a plant in Ohio.

In 1977 the U.S. automakers offered 252 models, down from 275 at the close of the previous year. This was the lowest total of models since 244 were available in 1960. At least a half-dozen midyear models were introduced in the spring, however.

An analysis of the remaining models and the prices they commanded revealed that there were 36 offered in the $3,000 to $4,000 range, down from 59 in that same category a year earlier. In the $5,000 to $6,000 range, meanwhile, there were 79 cars, compared with 64 the previous year.

One reason for higher prices was some new engines, the turbocharged V-6 engine at Buick and the diesel version of the 350 gasoline engine offered in Oldsmobile cars and Chevrolet and GMC trucks. The diesel engine was not entirely new to the market. Mercedes had long offered one and 50% of its U.S. sales were in diesel-engine cars. Peugeot as well had offered the diesel for several years, while Volkswagen introduced its diesel Rabbit at midyear.

The diesel operates differently from a gasoline engine in that instead of spark plugs used to ignite the air-fuel mix, glow plugs and the heat they generate do the work. Glow plugs, similar in the way they work to the coils on an electric stove, warm the air-fuel mix. This combustion process is the reason for the pinging sound made by diesel engines.

The advantages of a diesel engine are improved fuel economy because of a higher air-to-fuel mix, long life from fewer moving parts than in a gasoline engine, and the lower cost of diesel fuel as compared with gasoline. The disadvantages are diesel fumes; a long wait for combustion and ignition as the air-fuel mix heats, causing slow starts in cold weather; and slightly sluggish acceleration and overall performance. Also the combustion process is dirtier than with gasoline, and diesel cars require an oil change every 3,000 mi, as opposed to 6,000–7,500 mi for a gasoline-engine car.

The conversion to the turbocharged 231-cu in Buick V-6 engine was also not entirely new, having been done previously by GM. But it had become more important in 1977 because in the past the best way to ensure increased engine power was to build a bigger engine. With federal fuel economy laws, however, both the size of cars and the engines that power them had to become smaller. To get more power from a smaller engine, the turbocharger is ideal.

A turbocharger simply puts normally wasted exhaust gases to work to boost engine horsepower. But under normal engine operation the turbo is not utilized, allowing a V-6 engine to maintain its six-cylinder economy; however, when the power of a V-8 engine is needed the turbo can be put to use. When a driver needs that sudden burst of power he steps on the accelerator. This pumps a greater than normal air-fuel mix into the turbo's compressor. There it is compacted to make it more volatile in the cylinders. After combustion the normally spent exhaust gases are then directed to the turbine rather than allowed to escape through the exhaust manifold. The gas turns the turbine blades, which in turn keep the compressor going, and the cycle repeats itself continuously.

Though it did not offer a turbocharged engine, Ford was awarded a federal government contract that could total $110 million over eight years for development of the Stirling external combustion engine. In such an engine precombustion takes place in a chamber and that mix is then fed into the main cylinder for a second firing.

The government also chose five contractors to provide electric vehicle prototypes and awarded Chrysler and General Electric Co. a $5,980,000 contract to develop a small electric car with a range of 75 mi at speeds of up to 55 mph.

Because of the U.S. government ruling requiring an 18-mpg fuel economy average for an automaker's entire line of cars, six-cylinder engines were made standard in the mid-size line at GM; a 2.3-litre, four-cylinder engine was made standard on the new Fairmont and Zephyr from Ford; and Chrysler went to the smaller 225-cu in six-cylinder model instead of the 318-cu in V-8 as standard in its mid-size Dodge Diplomat and Chrysler LeBaron.

The EPA ratings were once again dominated by the imports. Of the top 20 cars on the list only 2 were domestics, the subcompact Ford Pinto (17th) and subcompact Mercury Bobcat (18th). Of the top 20, 17 were Japanese-built. Other than Pinto and Bobcat, the only other non-Japanese car in the EPA top 20 was the French Renault Le-Car, which finished 14th. The most economical car in the initial EPA ratings (Honda did not certify its cars in time to make the first listing) found the subcompact Datsun B-210 leading the field.

After a year-long controversy, GM agreed to pay some $40 million to customers who unknowingly bought Buicks, Oldsmobiles, and Pontiacs with Chevrolet engines. GM claimed that such interchanging among product lines was common practice in the industry, but its discovery early in the year had given rise to more than 250 government and private lawsuits.

Somewhat of a surprise during the year was the announcement by Volvo and Saab-Scania, two Swedish automakers, that they would call off merger talks. The marriage would have created one of Europe's largest car manufacturing firms.

A general overview of the automobile markets outside the U.S. revealed that most countries were experiencing slow but steady sales recoveries after the same recessionary pattern the U.S. had undergone in 1975. The total car market outside the U.S. was expected to be more than 20 million units, up from 19.3 million in 1976 and the first time that 20 million had ever been reached.

As a rule, European countries were experiencing a much healthier sales recovery than Japan. The Japanese were setting sales records with their cars in the U.S. market but at home were having troubles with a sluggish economy. Thus, the Japanese increased their exports to Europe and the U.S. to offset the softness at home.

So many Japanese cars started appearing in Great Britain that support grew for limiting Japanese cars there. One reason for the concern in that country was that total car sales in Great Britain rose from the previous year but sales of British cars declined. Imports took nearly 50% of the market.

In West Germany the economy became a bit healthier and auto sales were exceptionally strong. Volkswagen returned to profitability and once again topped Opel as the nation's best-selling car. And, ironically, while the Japanese were making so many inroads throughout the world, the second best-selling car in Japan was the VW Rabbit.

(JAMES L. MATEJA)

BUILDING AND CONSTRUCTION

The value of new construction put in place in the U.S. was at a seasonally adjusted annual rate of $170.7 billion in July 1977. The level of construction expenditures had moved up in successive months during 1977 and, with the added stimulus provided by the Housing and Community Development Act signed by the president in October, it was anticipated that construction outlays would continue at comparatively high levels throughout the remainder of the year. On a current dollar basis, the expectation was that construction expenditures for the year would be in excess of $165 billion, compared with the previous record of $147.5 billion in 1976.

When the dollar outlays for the years 1972 through 1977 were adjusted to the 1972 price level, however, a quite different picture emerged. For example, the peak level of activity in 1976 fell considerably below the levels of 1973 and 1974, and it was clear that, on this basis, the level of activity in 1977 would be significantly less than that achieved in 1973 and possibly 1974 as well.

The National Association of Home Builders reported that a new home in 1977 would cost the average U.S. purchaser about 8% more than in 1976. During the first seven months of 1977 the median price of new homes sold was $47,900, compared with $27,600 in 1972. A study by the MIT-Harvard Joint Center for Urban Studies noted that if housing prices continued to rise over the next five years as fast as they had from 1970 to 1976, a typical new home in 1981 would sell for $78,000. Given the slower growth of personal income, it was predicted that the U.S. would become less and less a nation of homeowners.

The inflationary conditions plaguing the industry were reflected in the various construction cost indexes. The U.S. Depart-

Housing project being constructed at Costa Mesa, California, in an area where new housing costs were suffering from severe inflation. New housing construction expenditures in the U.S. for 1977 were expected to be over $165 billion.

ment of Commerce composite cost index stood at 205 early in 1977 (1967 = 100), while the American Appraisal Co. index for residences reached 208.9. Wholesale prices of materials used in construction were major contributing factors, along with higher earnings for construction workers. In March 1977 the average hourly wage for construction workers was $7.85.

Housing investment declined in Canada in 1977. There was a large inventory of unsold new homes, and the number of houses started during the first four months of 1977 was 13% below the same period of 1976. In Great Britain investment in private dwellings during early 1977 was at its lowest level in 14 years, partly because of a shortage of mortgage funds. The rate of housing starts in the public sector was also down, and the construction industry remained in a state of acute recession after four years of decline.

The building industry was also depressed in most of the countries on the Continent. In West Germany the value of construction permits issued during the first four months of 1977 was 17% lower than in the corresponding period of 1976. In Denmark it was anticipated that the decline in residential construction would be greater than the small expected increase in industrial investment. In Japan private housing contributed significantly to the first quarter expansion in economic activity.

(CARTER C. OSTERBIND)

CHEMICALS

The U.S. chemical industry's performance in 1977 was much the same as in 1976. It registered solid gains in the first half of the year but showed evidence of slowing down in the third quarter and early part of the fourth quarter. In most other industrialized nations, the industry gains were falling short of early expectations. Overcapacity in man-made fibres was the principal culprit.

The U.S. Department of Commerce changed its base for gathering data on chemical shipments. Under the revised system, the value of U.S. shipments in 1975 totaled $90,370,000,000. In 1976 they increased 12.2% to $101,385,000,000. For the first half of 1977, they amounted to $57,581,000,000, 10.5% higher than in the corresponding period of 1976.

Chemical production increased 15% in 1976 as the Federal Reserve Board's index of chemical production averaged 169.4 (1967 = 100). The upward trend continued through the first half of 1977, increasing each month to reach 182.5 (seasonally adjusted) in June.

Although beset by high costs for raw materials, equipment, labour, and particularly for energy, chemical companies in 1976 had difficulty increasing prices for their products. In that year the U.S. Department of Labor's index of chemical prices averaged 187.2 (1967 = 100), 3.2% over the average in 1975. The situation was improving in 1977 as the index averaged 191.7 (not

seasonally adjusted) for the first six months, representing a 5.1% increase over 1976.

The U.S. chemical industry continued to spend heavily for expansion. The McGraw-Hill Department of Economics 1977 fall survey revealed that companies in the chemical industry planned to spend $7,160,000,000 in 1977, 7.1% more than they did in 1971. They were, moreover, planning an 8.9% increase in 1978 to $7.8 billion.

Chemicals made their customary positive contribution to U.S. trade. Net chemical exports in 1976 were $5,186,400,000 on total exports of $9,958,200,000 and imports of $4,771,800,000. That was a 3.8% boost over 1975. During the first half of 1977 chemical exports were $5,403,400,000 and imports totaled $2,788,200,000. The net export of chemicals, $2,615,200,000, was marginally below the $2,657,300,000 figure for the same period in 1976.

The Soviet Union made headway in reaching its production goals for 1977. During the first nine months of 1977 production of man-made fibres rose 6% over the same period of 1976, to 801,000 metric tons. Synthetic resin production increased 8% to 2.4 million tons; sulfuric acid, 6% to 15.4 million tons; and mineral fertilizer, 5% to 71.8 million tons.

In Europe and Japan the continuing recession in the man-made fibre industry caused chemical industries to miss growth targets. European man-made fibre operations appeared headed for another $1 billion loss in 1977. At the heart of the difficulty lay international overcapacity. In 1976 producers turned out 8.6 million metric tons of synthetic non-cellulosic fibres. But that was only 73% of their estimated capacity, and capacity was scheduled to increase 8.9% by

A General Electric physicist examines a new phosphor coating material for fluorescent tubes. The coating enables a 35-watt lamp to produce 97% as much light as a 40-watt lamp and reduces energy costs by about 14%.

the end of 1978. By the fourth quarter of 1977, plants were being shut down and governments were starting to take some steps to improve the situation. But it did not appear likely that producers would find significant relief before 1980.

In Japan the chemical industry was feeling some growing pains. Early figures for 1976 indicated chemical sales of $37 billion, and the industry was aiming at a 16% growth in 1977, to $43 billion. By the third quarter of the year, however, it was recognizing some problem areas. The country's largest fibre maker increased its earnings 154% in fiscal 1976 (which ended March 31, 1977). But its profit margin (as a percent of sales) was slightly under 1%. Most chemical and fibre makers in Japan, in fact, were having difficulty achieving profit margins of 1%.

Plants were operating at 75% of capacity on the average, and inventories were high. As a result, chemical companies were starting to shed unprofitable ventures, reduce outstanding debt, and move into more profitable lines. They were also slowing down their new capital outlays. For fiscal 1977 plans called for a capital expenditure of $2.1 billion, 6.4% below that for fiscal 1976. Despite these problems, chemical trade continued healthy. For the first half of 1977 Japan posted a $580 million chemical (excluding fibres) trade surplus on exports of $2,070,000,000 and imports of $1,490,000,-000.

West Germany's chemical industry was also having trouble meeting its targets. In 1976 chemical sales reached $36 billion, and early in 1977 the industry was looking toward a growth of 8%. This was later pared to 4%, and indications were that even the revised figure was proving difficult to meet. In 1976 West Germany's chemical trade surplus was approximately $6.8 billion on exports of $13.8 billion and imports of $7 billion. The exports were 38% of sales, and this heavy dependence upon selling its products abroad was one reason the industry was having trouble attaining its goals. The rising value of the mark in relation to the dollar was also making exports more expensive.

In the U.K. the chemical industry was beginning to face a similar problem. For years the weakness of the pound sterling had given British exports a competitive edge. However, this advantage started to erode in the second half of 1977 as the pound strengthened. Even so, the industry was finding grounds for optimism. The main cause for cheer was North Sea oil and gas. In August 1977 the U.K. sold enough of its oil to post a monthly balance of payments surplus of $535 million.

U.K. chemical sales in 1976 were $18.7 billion. Exports were $5.1 billion, and the favourable chemical trade balance totaled $1.9 billion. For the first half of 1977 the trade surplus reached $1 billion. The Chemical Industries Association had projected growth of 5.3% for the industry in 1977. That was lowered to 4–4.5% and then, by the end of the third quarter, to 3.5%. But with North Sea oil and gas and associated gas liquids to build on and with an improv-ing economic climate, British chemical companies were hopeful that they could reestablish their growth rates to levels more comparable to their healthy counterparts in Western Europe.

(DONALD P. BURKE)

ELECTRICAL

Worldwide optimism at the beginning of 1977 that the depression following the oil crisis of 1973 was over was replaced as the year wore on by more sober assessments indicating that a growth of 3 to 4% was the best that could be accomplished. In March the U.S. National Electrical Manufacturers Association had predicted that the industry's total 1977 production would increase 9.4% over that of 1976. Consumer electrical products, cable and wires, and industrial equipment were expected to grow at a rate of 10%; lighting equipment at 7.5% (4% in 1976); and power equipment at 5% (zero growth in 1976). The likelihood of these projections being achieved gradually evaporated. By October it was obvious that industrial investment was lower than had been expected and that increasing interest rates were holding up growth.

A similar slow pace of economic recovery in Western Europe was reflected in the generally disappointing results of major electrical companies for the first six months of the year, although buoyant overseas markets in the less developed countries, particularly in the Middle East, enabled firms to steer clear of serious trouble. The future remained full of doubts, and more workers were laid off.

During the first six months of 1977, sales in the foreign divisions of West Germany's Siemens empire rose by 11%. At home, business activity increased by 6%. AEG (Allgemeine Elektrizitäts-Gesellschaft) experienced a 4% decline in sales at home but

Developed by IBM scientists, the first fully operational "read/write" computer memory device using a lattice of magnetic bubbles for information storage appears as a parallelogram (centre) in the magnified view of an integrated circuit.

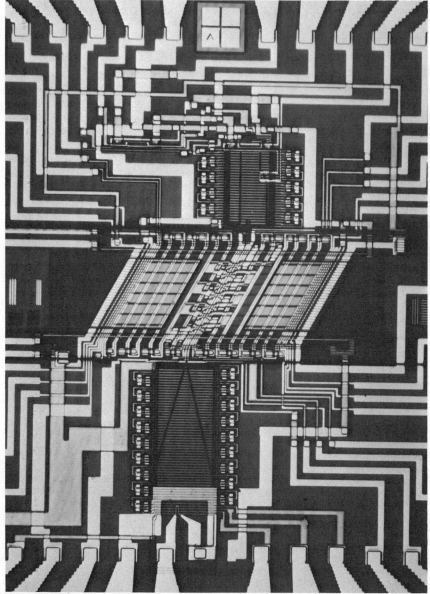

a 14% increase abroad. According to the West German electrical manufacturers association, ZVEI, electrical exports to members of the Organization of Petroleum Exporting Countries (OPEC) had increased by a record 48% in 1976. Such an explosive rate of growth was not expected to continue in 1977.

Exports of electrical products from Britain in 1976 were 31% higher than in 1975 (70% higher to OPEC countries), much of the increase being due to the decline in the value of the pound sterling in 1976. Disappointing results for the first half of 1977 were reported by Philips, the Dutch electrical giant. Sales rose by only 1% over the same period in 1976, and those of consumer goods did not increase at all. Investment goods improved, but sales again tailed off in the second quarter.

In France the electrical and electronics sectors fared better than other sectors of the economy in 1976, with an 18% increase in sales (23% in exports) over 1975. France occupied third place in the electrical equipment international export league with a 15% share of world exports (West Germany 23%; U.S. 20%).

Japanese industry expected orders for electrical power equipment to rise by 13% in 1977 compared with 1976. No large increase in exports was expected because of the high exchange rate value of the yen.

For many companies, an increasing proportion of investment was directed toward improving the quality and competitiveness of existing products. Designers were concerned with making existing technology as efficient as possible rather than with making dramatic technical advances.

Energy conservation was a main theme of new product development. The Danish Thrige-Titan energy-saving industrial motor, introduced in 1977, had an efficiency about 10% higher than was normally achieved by the popular induction machines. The motor's extra initial cost could be made up in a year or two, depending on the price of energy. In an average medium-sized production factory with about 100 motors in use, the saving in electricity demand would be about 15 kw.

There was a new energy-saving idea for domestic cookers. An induction coil placed under the hot plate induced eddy currents in the base of the cooking vessel. The coil itself did not heat up, and the working area temperature would be only as high as that of the vessel being heated. The system was claimed to be extremely safe and to cut electricity consumption in half by improving the 40% efficiency of conventional cookers to approximately 70%.

Much criticism came from the less developed countries concerning the low rate of technology transfer from the advanced countries. Manufacturers of nuclear reactors remained reluctant to disclose certain key component information, and governments were cautious about fuel supplies. But much of the criticism was unjustified. The British Chloride Group, for example, opened a new electric battery research and development centre in India that had three main objectives: to aid in the transfer of advanced technology, to develop the process of import substitution, and to carry out some basic research on its own behalf.

(T. C. J. COGLE)

FURNITURE

After a slow first half, the value of household furniture sales in the United States rose to $17 billion in 1977, 10% over the 1976 level. About half of the increase was due to inflation.

Upholstered furniture styles that showed exposed wood grew in popularity. In wood furniture, styles of the early 20th century, classed as "nostalgia," gained increasing acceptance.

In an industry that had not previously featured designers, a number of well-known fashion designers began creating furniture for national manufacturers. Modular wall systems constituted a notable growth segment of the industry as consumers sought to utilize more vertical storage space in apartments and homes.

The European-born taste for easy-to-assemble (knockdown or KD) furniture also grew in popularity. This so-called life-style furniture was made to carry home and was most popular with younger consumers.

The increase in housing starts and the fact that one family in four moves each year were considered the main reasons for the health of the furniture industry during the year.

(ROBERT A. SPELMAN)

FURS

Despite many economic and political problems, the fur industry experienced another excellent year in 1977. Fashion was again the major factor, as virtually every internationally known couturier included furs in his collection. Another element was the investment value of furs, as continuing inflation throughout the world eroded the value of money. Even the sharply higher price structure failed to dampen demand.

Humane societies and other pro-animal forces stepped up their campaigns against the industry on a broad front, particularly in the U.S. and Switzerland and, to a lesser extent, in West Germany and Canada. Outside the U.S. these campaigns were largely directed at the consumer through the media, but in the U.S., the antifur forces sought more permanent sanctions. As a result of their efforts, at least four states enacted laws prohibiting the use of the leghold trap, which had been the principal means of catching wild animals, and at year's end the battle had been carried to the important trapping state of Ohio. Possibly more significant was a ruling by a U.S. Court of Appeals granting such groups the right to legally represent animal interests on the ground that animals are "uniquely incapable of defending their own interests in court." The issue was being appealed to the U.S. Supreme Court.

In another situation, the U.S. Endangered Species Scientific Authority banned exports of lynx cats, bobcats, and otters, while the Interior Department continued to promote killing of the cats as part of its predator-control program. This not only threw the industry into confusion but also angered state conservation officials, who accused the federal government of usurping state powers.

A different problem appeared in some southern European countries, where political unrest and the possibility of a shift to Communism were causing the business and industrial communities to postpone expansion in their own countries and to in-

crease their investments abroad. Insofar as this dampened the economies of the nations in question, sales of such luxury items as furs would be affected.

The world crop of ranched mink rose somewhat in 1977. This would have little effect on the number of pelts reaching the open market in 1978, however, because virtually all of the increase was in the Soviet Union, which did not plan to increase its exports. U.S. mink ranchers, who bred more females for a larger crop, were foiled by poor feed and weather conditions; the 1977 U.S. crop was expected to be the same as or slightly less than the 3.1 million pelts produced in 1976. (SANDY PARKER)

GEMSTONES

The gemstone industry appeared to have had another good year in 1977. By the end of 1976 considerable softness had developed in the gem market, though Christmas sales brought temporary relief, and the weakness persisted into early 1977. Spring brought a rapid recovery, however, and by July over 80% of retailers, manufacturers, and wholesalers were predicting sales gains and higher profits for the second half of the year. Actual sales trends after July indicated, for the year as a whole, an 8% increase in profits for retail jewelers and 6% for wholesalers.

Diamonds, as always, continued to dominate the market. From January to May the value of cut and uncut gemstone imports into the U.S. totaled approximately $645 million, with diamonds accounting for over $600 million. The succession of price increases declared by the Central Selling Organization—3% in January 1976, 5.75% in September 1976, and an enormous jump of 15% in March 1977—pushed retail prices up as much as 40% for some sizes and qualities. For example, the median retail price per carat of a 1.00 carat, highest-quality (D-Flawless) diamond in July was $15,750; by August it was $16,276.

Total diamond sales by the Central Selling Organization in 1976 amounted to $1,550,000,000, a 47% increase over 1975, and 1977 sales promised to be even larger if supplies permitted. As an indication of what was happening, the De Beers group of mines produced a record 10,520,000 carats in 1976, but by the end of the year its stocks were down 25%. Among suppliers, the Soviet Union remained the world's largest single producer of diamonds, followed by Zaire, South Africa, Botswana, Ghana, and South West Africa (Namibia), in that order.

The great consumer love affair with coloured gemstones continued, but with considerable variation among different stones. At the start of the year prices were easing slightly for opal, ruby, tanzanite, and tourmaline and more steeply for emerald and chrysoberyl cat's-eye. Between July and August 1976 the keystone price for a good quality emerald had shot from a median of $4,000 to $6,000 per carat. A year later the median had slipped to $5,500, and prices for commercial and fair quality grades fell even more. Bucking the downward trend, prices for aquamarine, citrine, amethyst, peridot, and—especially—sapphire continued to rise. Overall, the price trend for coloured gems was stable to slightly higher, following the economy closely.

Peridot and pearls showed consistent and strong price rises. For pearls particularly, demand was heavy and supplies were scarce—partly because of pollution in the South Seas pearl beds. Brazil remained the largest single producer of coloured gemstones, but prices there were higher, quality was lower, and supplies were diminished. Excellent alexandrite gems in small sizes, good enough to wholesale at $1,000 per carat, continued to come from Malucacheta in the northern part of Minas Gerais state.

The general pattern for the industry appeared to be set for some time, barring abrupt shifts in the economy: a reduced and spotty supply of new gems in quantities inadequate for the constantly expanding market, causing continuously rising prices.

(PAUL ERNEST DESAUTELS)

GLASS

The glass industry was quiet in 1977, due to the worldwide depression, the consequent cutback in private housing, office, and industrial building, and a recession in automobile manufacture. Looking toward the future, companies took steps aimed at more efficient operation.

Three companies, the Swedish-owned Scanglas, operating in Denmark, the French-owned Emmaboda Glasverk in Sweden, and the Norwegian Drammens Glassverk, combined to form one Scandinavian company, Uniglas. Production would be concentrated in Denmark. The U.K.'s Pilkington Brothers planned to build a further float glass plant in South Africa and to invest £70 million in a replacement plant in the U.K.

Glass container manufacturers suffered from low demand and remained subject to environmental pressures. The first international recycling symposium was held in Sheffield, England, late in 1976. Many European glass container industries collectively operated waste glass collection systems, as did the industries of the U.S., Australia, and Japan. The technology of glass melting for glass containers moved toward the use of larger quantities of waste glass with primary raw materials. Provided that the waste glass contained no impurities, such as bottle caps, there were no problems, and a saving of energy could result. In Denmark, Kastrup og Holmegaards reported the closing of its Copenhagen works, citing declining consumption due to increased reuse of bottles. Denmark's policies on nonreturnable containers were strict; it was suggested that the use of beer and soft drink cans, already severely restricted, might be completely banned by 1982.

Energy saving remained important, both in the manufacturing process and in product lines. The cost of energy for melting glass could form as much as 10% of production costs, and further economies were sought. Well-designed windows, using coated and photochromic glasses, could contribute to heat saving in domestic and industrial installations. Pittsburgh Plate Glass Industries in the U.S. was particularly active in developing solar heating systems. The French National Research Centre opened a demonstration plant at Odeillo designed to interest the Mediterranean countries and the third world. The Corning Glass Works' 96% silica glass was used to coat most of the outer surface of the U.S. space shuttle.

Glass fibre continued to interest a wide range of associated industries. In Japan, Central Glass began to market a wall-cladding material made from glass-fibre-reinforced foamed gypsum. Asahi made a reciprocal agreement with Pilkington Brothers on glass-fibre-reinforced cement products.

Several companies interested themselves in the use of glass fibres for communications. Philips tested an optical fibre cable using laser beams in both West Germany and The Netherlands. The method, immune to electromagnetic interference, was seen as the best answer to the growing demand for large-band-width videophonic services, for example, at conferences. The International Telephone and Telegraph Co. carried out similar research in the U.K., and Bell Laboratories in the U.S. developed long lengths of thin glass fibres, stronger than stainless steel of the same dimensions, whose primary application was in modulated-light communications cables that would be highly resistant to accidental damage.

(CYRIL WEEDEN)

INSURANCE

The market for private insurance rose above $250 billion in annual sales in 1977; of this, the U.S. accounted for 50%; Japan and West Germany for 10% each; and France, Great Britain, and Canada, 5% each. Windstorm damage was relatively low during the year, but aircraft hijackings and terrorism led to major losses and a Canary Islands crash of two jumbo jets cost

Glass filaments that are stronger than steel were developed by Bell Laboratories, Murray Hill, New Jersey. Polished glass rods are fed into a laser and drawn into fibres for fibre-optic communications lines.

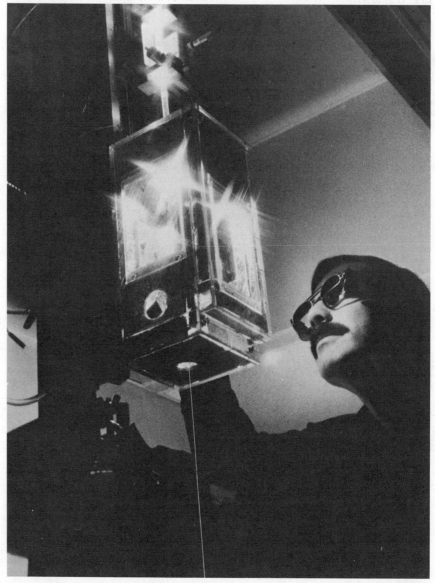

nearly 600 lives, the highest death toll in any single air disaster to date.

U.K. insurance companies reported in early 1977 that their worldwide annual premium income had increased almost 30% in general insurance and 23% in long-term (principally life) insurance. In spite of an overall underwriting loss on general business, investment income created a surplus, largely plowed back to finance reserve requirements, which rose rapidly with inflation.

Individual underwriting membership of Lloyd's of London exceeded 10,000 for the first time. In line with the movement toward increased consumer protection, insurance companies published statements of practice and the Insurance Brokers (Registration) Act, 1977 set new standards. Progress toward a common market for insurance in the EEC continued slowly. One directive enabled brokers and agents to use the provisions for freedom of establishment and services throughout the EEC area.

Total coverage in U.S. life insurance companies exceeded $2.5 trillion in 1977, with group life insurance purchased through employers accounting for more than $1 trillion. Premiums, interest earnings, and other income totaled approximately $100 billion. New life insurance protection of approximately $350 billion was purchased, and individual annuities grew rapidly as individual retirement accounts and liberalized Keogh plans were set up under the Employee Retirement Income Security Act. Many estate plan adjustments were made to meet new provisions of the U.S. Tax Reform Act.

A profit turnaround for U.S. property-liability insurers occurred in the second quarter of 1977, with statutory underwriting gains of approximately $300 million, the first such quarterly profit since mid-1973. However, overall first-half 1977 underwriting losses exceeded $100 million on $30 billion of premiums. Investment gains continued favourable, and total policyholder surplus increased by $1.2 billion, to more than $25 billion at midyear.

Fire insurance losses caused by arson, estimated at more than one in four, were combated with computerized loss data, harsher state penalties, and reward funds. The need for flood insurance was emphasized by a $40 million loss in Johnstown, Pa., while a controversy between the Department of Housing and Urban Development and the National Flood Insurers Association indicated major changes in 1978 for the government-private flood insurance program. Disorders during the July 13 blackout in New York City resulted in hundreds of millions of dollars in losses, only partially covered under riot insurance.

Liability insurance suffered increasing problems of market availability, particularly for products liability exposures. Corrective legislation was stalled or defeated in most of the 31 states where limited liability laws were introduced. A May fire in a Southgate, Ky., nightclub cost the lives of 164 persons and resulted in more than $300 million in lawsuits.

Several major auto insurers paid refunds during the year, and some homeowners' rates were decreased in selected states. A new commercial insurance manual was introduced in Florida and proposed for na-

tionwide use in 1978. Revised personal lines classifications were also expected in the near future. Four of the largest life insurance companies (Prudential, Metropolitan, Equitable, John Hancock) expanded their all-lines marketing to $800 million of annual property-liability premiums.

Federal regulation of auto no-fault laws and a proposal for dual federal-state regulation of insurance appeared to be stalled in Congress. The Department of Transportation mandated airbag restraint requirements for new cars in the 1980s. Continued hearings on national health insurance proposals were held in response to rising health care costs.

(DAVID L. BICKELHAUPT)

IRON AND STEEL

In 1977 depression conditions prevailed in the steel industries for the third year in succession, making the recent period by far the most difficult since World War I. The hope that the renewed decline in the autumn of 1976 might prove to be temporary was dashed. In retrospect, it was the revival in the first half of that year that was the brief aberration, albeit a highly welcome one. World crude steel production in 1976 showed only a 4.5% increase over the very depressed 1975 level of 646.3 million metric tons, and it was clear that output in 1977 would fall short of 700 million metric tons. Moreover, the traditional Western producers experienced a further decline in production, the modest rise in the world total being attributable to the Communist countries and to some less developed countries, especially Brazil and India among the larger producers and South Korea among the smaller ones.

The effects of the long-continued recession were considerable and would certainly be felt for some time to come. Most immediately, many of the world's major steel companies were suffering substantial and growing losses, especially those with few interests in other industrial sectors to cushion the financial consequences of the depression in the steel market. The depression affected companies' revenues and costs both through reduction in orders and associated uneconomic operating rates, and through persistent price weakness on the world market. Several large firms reached the point where substantial structural change was inevitable, and discussions to this end, involving governments and labour unions as well as steel producers, were proceeding in a number of countries.

Current financial pressures and highly uncertain future prospects induced retrenchment in investment expenditure in most producing areas, including the less developed countries, where a number of projects were postponed or effectively canceled. This retrenchment was in large measure inevitable and could in some respects be beneficial in contributing to restoration of a balance in the international steel market. However, it also carried the danger that installed capacity could later prove insufficient to meet demand, as it did as recently as 1973-74.

The pressures for some form of international regulation of the steel market or, failing that, for national protective measures grew markedly during the year. The U.S. producers, which had been most suc-

cessful in maintaining domestic prices but which had also experienced a large rise in competing imports, were active in this direction. By the end of the year several court cases had been brought against Japanese and European producers for "dumping" (selling a commodity on the world market at a price lower than the domestic price). Earlier in the year cases were also brought against overseas producers by some EEC steelmakers, while the U.S. administration took the initiative early in the summer in proposing discussions of the international steel situation within the Organization for Economic Cooperation and Development. These discussions continued throughout the year against a background of proposals for some form of "voluntary restraint" or of international oversight of the steel market.

The effects of the long recession were acutely felt in the EEC, where they reached crisis proportions. The European Commission, which, under the Community treaties, had a much more direct involvement with the coal and steel industries than with other industrial sectors, was active throughout the year. In the spring the Commission approved a wide-ranging countercrisis program. This included, on the one hand, short-term commercial measures intended to contribute to stabilization of the market in tonnage and price terms. The success of these efforts was, however, made difficult by the continued decline in the market. On the other hand, there were longer term measures designed to encourage restructuring of the steel industry, but the effects of these could not be known for some time. Meanwhile, in Sweden, which had perhaps the unhappiest experience of any producing country in 1977, major restructuring measures affecting both the commercial and special steel sectors already were under way.

In the U.S. there were reasonably satisfactory operating rates in the industry and some price rises during the early part of the year. However, the failure of demand from the construction and investment goods sectors to revive and the adverse economic effects of exceptionally severe winter weather in many areas, together with increasing pressure from imports, caused the situation to deteriorate later. Company profits declined sharply, and substantial layoffs and plant shutdowns were announced or foreshadowed by several firms during the fall.

The Japanese industry also failed to shake off the recession. Although prices rose in the domestic market in early summer, continued weakness of demand, especially from the private investment sector, and high inventory levels caused manufacturers to lower their production estimates for the year on several occasions. Output was unlikely to exceed the 1975 level, which was five million metric tons below that of 1976. The effect on company profits more than offset the earlier price increases. Even in Eastern Europe, whose exports had a seriously disruptive effect on the international market for certain products, the energy crisis and the prolonged recession in the West appeared to have had adverse

Table VIII. World Production of Crude Steel
In 000 metric tons

Country	1972	1973	1974	1975	1976	1977 Year to date	No. of months	Percent change 1977/76
World	630,100	697,100	707,800	646,300	676,500	—	—	—
U.S.S.R.	125,590	131,480	136,200	141,300	144,800	85,200	7	+ 0.5
U.S.	120,750	136,460	131,990	105,940	116,310	85,850	9	− 4.6
Japan	96,900	119,320	117,130	102,310	107,380	77,420	9	− 1.7
West Germany	43,700	49,520	53,230	40,410	42,410	29,550	9	−10.1
United Kingdom	25,390	26,720	22,400	19,840	22,460	15,700	9	− 5.8
France	24,050	25,270	27,020	21,530	23,230	16,800	9	− 2.2
China*	23,000	25,000	25,000	26,500	21,000	†		
Italy	19,810	21,000	23,800	21,870	23,460	17,500	9	+ 0.8
Belgium	14,530	15,520	16,230	11,580	12,150	8,540	9	− 7.6
Poland	13,420	14,060	14,560	15,100	15,340	10,410	7	+15.4
Czechoslovakia	12,730	13,160	13,640	14,320	14,690	8,800	7	+ 3.4
Canada	11,860	13,390	13,610	13,030	13,160	10,050	9	+ 1.6
Spain	9,530	10,800	11,500	11,100	10,980	8,240	9	+ 0.9
Romania	7,400	8,160	8,840	9,550	10,970	†		
India	6,860	6,890	7,070	7,990	9,360	7,430	9	+ 8.9
Australia	6,750	7,700	7,810	7,870	7,790	5,540	9	− 7.3
Brazil	6,520	7,150	7,520	8,390	9,250	8,250	9	+20.0
East Germany	6,070	5,860	6,170	6,480	6,740	3,980	7	+ 2.1
Netherlands, The	5,590	5,620	5,840	4,820	5,180	3,750	9	− 0.2
Luxembourg	5,460	5,920	6,450	4,620	4,570	3,240	9	− 7.4
South Africa	5,340	5,720	5,840	6,830	7,110	5,460	9	+ 3.2
Sweden	5,260	5,660	5,990	5,610	5,140	2,840	9	−25.4
Mexico	4,430	4,760	5,120	5,280	5,290	3,920	9	− 1.0
Austria	4,070	4,240	4,700	4,070	4,480	3,130	9	− 8.9
Hungary	3,270	3,330	3,470	3,650	3,650	2,120	7	− 0.7
Yugoslavia	2,590	2,680	2,840	2,920	2,750	2,360	9	+17.4
North Korea*	2,500	2,900	3,200	2,900	3,000	†		
Argentina	2,150	2,210	2,350	2,210	2,410	1,920	9	+ 0.2
Bulgaria	2,120	2,250	2,190	2,270	2,460	1,510	7	− 0.7
Turkey	1,560	1,350	1,590	1,700	1,970	1,390	9	− 4.2
Finland	1,460	1,620	1,660	1,620	1,650	1,550	9	+33.2
Greece	680	1,090	930	900	1,110	†		
South Korea	590	1,160	1,950	1,990	3,520*	3,030	9	+24.3
Taiwan	540	540	900	1,010	1,630	1,300	9	+12.1

*Estimated. †1977 figures not yet available.
Sources: International Iron and Steel Institute; British Steel Corporation.

Table IX. World Production of Pig Iron and Blast Furnace Ferroalloys
in 000 metric tons

Country	1972	1973	1974	1975	1976
World	454,200	500,000	504,900	469,900	490,400
U.S.S.R.	92,300	94,900	99,870	102,970	105,500
U.S.	82,860	93,520	87,010	72,510	79,210
Japan	74,060	90,000	90,440	86,880	86,580
West Germany	32,220	37,100	40,220	30,070	31,850
China*	21,000	21,000	22,000	22,000	23,000
France	19,400	20,750	22,520	17,920	19,030
United Kingdom	15,490	17,030	14,120	12,340	14,020
Belgium	11,780	12,660	13,150	9,070	9,870
Italy	9,630	10,270	11,760	11,410	11,690
Canada	8,720	9,740	9,580	9,310	10,050
Czechoslovakia	8,480	8,660	8,910	9,290	9,400
Poland	7,580	7,900	7,790	7,750	8,320
India	7,400	7,340*	7,410	8,440	9,780
Spain	6,100	6,570	6,910	6,840	6,610
Australia	6,010	7,180	7,520	7,510	7,310
Brazil	5,410	5,510	5,980	6,980	7,860
South Africa	4,900	4,890	4,660	5,210	5,850
Romania	4,890	5,710	6,080	6,600	6,650
Luxembourg†	4,670	5,090	5,470	3,890	3,750
Netherlands, The	4,290	4,710	4,800	3,970	4,270
Austria	2,850	3,010	3,440	3,060	3,320
Mexico	2,780	2,890	3,210	3,220	2,330
North Korea	2,600	2,700	2,700	2,900	3,200
Sweden	2,590	2,780	2,980	3,310	2,950
East Germany	2,150	2,200	2,280	2,460	2,530
Hungary	2,070	2,120	2,290	2,220	2,230
Yugoslavia	1,950	2,110	2,130	2,000	1,920
Bulgaria	1,560	1,610	1,530	1,510	1,550
Finland†	1,180	1,410	1,390	1,370	1,390
Turkey†	1,140	900	1,320	1,340	1,830
Argentina†	850	800	1,080	1,030	1,280
South Korea	—	460*	990	1,200	2,010

*Estimated. †Excluding ferroalloys.
Source: International Iron and Steel Institute.

effects on steel demand. Many of the Eastern European producing countries seemed likely to achieve smaller expansions of output in 1977 than in many recent years.

The prospects for 1978 were uncertain with few producers expecting much improvement. However, given the likelihood of some further growth in Eastern European output and in that of a number of less developed countries, it was expected that the world total would at least break the 700-million-metric-ton barrier for the first time since 1974. (TREVOR J. MACDONALD)

MACHINERY AND MACHINE TOOLS

In terms of dollar volume only, the U.S. machine tool industry's sales were expected to establish a record high in 1977. The previous high for net new orders was attained in 1973, when the total reached $2,-612,650,000. After the peak in 1973, orders fell off drastically to a low of $1,186,350,000 for 1975. However, the bottom was reached early in 1975 and the upward trend that began then continued through 1976 and was almost as sharp as the 1974 decline. This trend continued during 1977, and the total for the year was estimated at $2.8 billion.

The backlog of unfilled orders increased steadily and at the end of 1977 was about $2.2 billion. The increase in the backlog occurred because the industry was unable to expand its production to meet the current demand. Shortages of critical materials, components, and skilled labour and, in some cases, strikes contributed to these problems. In the past, when the backlogs of U.S. builders increased, the importation of machines likewise increased, but more slowly. Then, when the backlogs shrank, the imports also decreased, but after a lag

of about one year. Recently, however, this relationship between backlogs and imports changed. When backlogs rose in 1972 the increase in imports was simultaneous. And when the U.S. backlogs fell in 1975, imports remained at the same level. After each rise and fall in the business cycle the relative proportion of imports increased to the extent that in 1977 imports accounted for 21%

of the domestic sales of machine tools. This can be compared with only 7% in 1959, 4.5% in 1964, and an average of 7.5% from 1967 through 1973.

U.S. domestic sales of certain types of machines were more adversely affected than those of others. Milling, boring, gear-making, and metal-forming machines, as well as lathes, all experienced an import inva-

This giant water wheel, developed by Allis-Chalmers Corp., will generate 150,000 kw of electricity. The hydro-turbine runner will be installed in a power plant on the Snake River in the Washington-Oregon area.

sion of more than 20% of their market; in the case of gear-making machines, it amounted to 41%. Production of certain sizes of engine lathes virtually ceased in the U.S. as the foreign competition became increasingly difficult to overcome. The imported machines had been standard general-purpose models in the past, but in 1977 there was a notable increase in the importation of more sophisticated items, such as tape- and computer-controlled machines.

As happened in the steel industry, allegations of "dumping" were directed at the major countries exporting machine tools to the U.S. Prodded by the U.S. National Machine Tool Builders' Association (NMTBA), the U.S. government began to investigate these charges.

Sales promotion activities on the part of all countries building machine tools were carried on at a high level during 1977. The biggest event of the year was the biennial show sponsored by the European machine tool builders. This was held in September at Hannover in West Germany. With 1,500 exhibitors representing 27 countries, including the U.S., the show attracted an estimated 200,000 visitors.

The NMTBA increased its efforts to foster exports from the U.S. by conducting trade missions to several countries, including South Korea and China. However, numerous complaints were registered by U.S. exporters about nontariff barriers existing in some of their foreign markets. A particularly troublesome problem was the difficulty in obtaining export licenses for the shipment of equipment to the Communist countries, which represented a very large market for machinery.

No significant new developments occurred in machine-tool design during the year. The numerically controlled (tape) machines continued to increase their share of the market, but the trend away from tape- to computer-controlled machines also continued.   (EDWARD J. LOEFFLER)

NUCLEAR INDUSTRY

By the autumn of 1977 there were 184 operating nuclear power plants in the world (64 in the U.S.), 196 under construction (92 in the U.S.), and more than 130 firmly ordered with a similar number in the planning stage. Few orders were placed in 1977, the first in the U.S. not occurring until midyear with only another three expected. Unlike U.S. companies, West Germany's main nuclear constructor, Kraftwerk Union (KWU), was able to win orders mainly outside its home country. It gained an order from Iran at the end of 1977 for four 1,200-Mw reactors.

While industrial growth was generally stagnant throughout the world, there were some notable developments in the nuclear field. Two countries opened their first nuclear-power stations: South Korea began operating a Westinghouse-built station and Finland a Soviet-built one. Canada started operating the first two units at the nation's second nuclear power station at Bruce, Ont. France began operation of Fessenheim 1 & 2, the first of its massive program based on the Westinghouse pressurized water reactor (PWR).

The U.K. seemed to have conquered its problems in constructing advanced gas-cooled reactors (AGR). The first four units

(two in England and two in Scotland) operated successfully for more than one year. This might persuade the government to choose to build more AGR's in place of the steam-generating heavy water reactors that had been planned. A major study prepared by the National Nuclear Corp., in which the U.K. government was the major stockholder, concluded that steam-generating heavy water reactors were unproven and too expensive to build.

At the end of 1976 the nuclear industry's attention was focused on the U.S. elections. During his campaign Democratic presidential candidate Jimmy Carter emphasized several nuclear issues. Also, in six states propositions aimed at stopping the construction of nuclear stations were on the ballot. The propositions were defeated by an overall majority of 2 to 1, as had been the case in the first such referendum in California in June 1976.

Carter began his presidency by announcing the establishment of a Department of Energy under James Schlesinger, a past chairman of the now-defunct U.S. Atomic Energy Commission. While Carter saw the need for and actively promoted the expansion of a conventional reactor program, he was against fast breeder reactors (which produce large quantities of plutonium) and the reprocessing of spent fuel to recover the plutonium produced in reactors. Carter feared that the greater availability of plutonium would increase the risks of proliferation of nuclear weapons. Carter attempted to extend this policy to other countries but met widespread resistance from those who were unwilling to give up the possibility of greatly extending their energy supplies by utilizing plutonium.

Carter also attempted to stop the export of nuclear technology to nonnuclear countries. Brazil, for example, contracted with West Germany for the supply not only of power reactors but also of small reprocessing and uranium-enrichment facilities which in theory could be used to create weapons material. While West Germany would not cancel the contract, as Carter demanded, it did agree not to sell this technology to other countries. France was in a similar situation in selling a reprocessing plant to Pakistan, and it also agreed to embargo further exports.

Canada was faced with a near scandal when it was admitted that poor financing arrangements made by the Atomic Energy of Canada Ltd. (a crown corporation), in their Candu reactor sales to Argentina and South Korea, had cost the company tens of millions of dollars. Besides resulting in top-level management changes, the affair led to detailed examinations of the organization and operation of the corporation.

The Canadian government was also under pressure following disclosures that it was involved in the formation of an international cartel of uranium producers (outside the U.S. though involving U.S. companies), which up until 1975 had set a minimum price for uranium ore. This was mainly done to protect the industry from disaster. Westinghouse in the U.S. sued the mining companies involved, contending restraint of free trade. Generally, however, the availability of uranium improved and the prices stabilized.

The near monopoly by the U.S. in pro-

viding uranium-enrichment services was being successfully challenged by Urenco (set up by Britain, West Germany, and The Netherlands), which started operating its demonstration centrifuge enrichment plants in 1976. Subsequently, the U.S. dropped plans to build additional diffusion enrichment facilities and decided to devote its efforts to centrifuge development. France, however, was well advanced in the construction of its first commercial diffusion plant.

Generally in Europe and Japan, construction programs were continuing successfully and many new nuclear plants began operating. All countries, however, noted a decrease in projected growth, largely due to growing public concern over possible dangers to public safety and the environment. In France there were several demonstrations, including one at the Super Phénix reactor site where 20,000 demonstrators clashed violently with police, and one died. There were also several demonstrations in West Germany, including one by proponents of nuclear power. However, the opponents there were able to slow up and even stop some projects by means of lawsuits. The government was forced to announce a smaller program than it had previously proposed.

Fast breeder reactor prototypes (PFR) in France (Phénix) and Britain continued to prove out the technology, though Phénix had to be shut down several times because of leaks. Britain shut down its pilot fast breeder at Dounreay, Scotland, after operating it for 17 years; it was not needed after PFR started operating. President Carter tried to stop the U.S. prototype fast breeder project (Clinch River) and vetoed a congressional appropriation of $80 million for it.

Many governments and political parties demanded that an acceptable solution to the problem of nuclear waste disposal be found before any significant expansion in nuclear construction was allowed. A difficulty was that the people living near potential disposal sites blocked even testing of the area. West Germany found a site for a national waste management centre but would still have to apply for necessary permits.

Development of nuclear fusion was boosted when the EEC finally decided to place its advanced Tokomak project in the U.K. after nearly two years of argument. The Soviet Union and the U.S. had similar projects well under way.

Nuclear ship propulsion was taken a step forward when a British shipping company signed a letter of intent with a U.S. shipbuilder for three nuclear oil tankers. Also, the Canadian Coast Guard announced that it wanted to order a nuclear icebreaker; the Soviet Union's third nuclear icebreaker reached the North Pole, the first ship ever to do so.   (RICHARD W. KOVAN)

PAINTS AND VARNISHES

The paint industry experienced a marked recovery in 1977 in some of the countries where it had been hit by recession. U.S. sales reached 969 million gal (3,670,000,000 litres), an increase of 9% over the previous year, while value rose 16.5% to $4,-690,000,000. Sales value in Canada was 10% higher than in 1976, and output in Belgium rose 12.2% by volume and 16% by value. U.K. paint makers achieved sales worth £530 million, a gain of 17.6%, but this was mainly due to price increases in a stagnant market.

The lesson that in times of inflation prices must be raised in line with costs seemed to have been learned; 1976 saw improvements in profitability in all industrialized countries except Canada, Finland, and The Netherlands. South Africa's performance was outstanding, with a return of 24% on investment. The U.K. industry, aided by a depreciating currency, raised exports to about 10% of total production. West Germany remained the largest European exporter, while France was the leading importer at over 50,000 tons. In The Netherlands exports rose by 6.2% to 65,000 tons, but imports grew from 31,700 to 39,000 tons.

The paint and varnish industry in most developed countries continued to be beset by environmental and consumer pressures. In the U.S. there was concern over the new Toxic Substances Control Act and proposed tighter air-pollution controls in California, where current restrictions originated. After a long battle, the level of lead permitted in household paints was reduced in June 1977 to 0.06%. The industry claimed this was unnecessarily low on health grounds and would require unduly large increases in raw material costs.

In the U.K. the chaotic pricing situation in the retail sector led to an investigation by the Price Commission. The government's plans for partial public ownership of major suppliers of building materials posed a new long-term threat to the industry.

Final publication of EEC directives regulating the labeling of paints, varnishes, solvents, and other products was expected in the near future. Three related directives seemed likely to be published in incomplete form, subject to refinement during the two or more years before implementation. Of more immediate concern to the industry were directives on the average contents of containers (which differed from current practice in several countries) and on manufacturers' liability for defective products. The Council of Europe opened for signature a convention that would impose strict liability on manufacturers, without proof of negligence, in cases of death or personal injury.

Elsewhere, the industry also suffered from government restrictions. In Pakistan the excise duty of 22% on the retail selling price was described as a duty coupled with a tax on a tax. In Italy there was a dispute over the industry's statistics, which probably turned on the old problem of defining "paint."

Looking ahead, paint makers worked on waterborne finishing coats for the automotive industry, a major customer. Waterborne systems, in use in California since 1975 to meet air-pollution standards, required extensive air conditioning and very large capital expenditure. Vehicle builders in other areas seemed content to wait for the cost to come down or for legislation to catch up.   (LIONEL BILEFIELD)

PHARMACEUTICALS

For three decades U.S. pharmaceutical firms had appeared to be the major competitive force in world markets, setting the pace in antibiotics, steroids, oral contraceptives, and several other key categories. In much of Europe and in all the less developed countries, subsidiaries and licensees of U.S. firms had been the major influence in the pharmaceutical market or the bellwether most closely watched by domestically owned firms.

Some of this dominance had been challenged in recent years by the aggressive overseas marketing of tranquilizers, vitamins, and certain specialized antibiotics by Swiss and West German companies. But 1977 saw another profound change in the pharmaceutical "balance of power"—a full-fledged invasion of the U.S. market by West German and Swiss firms in search of major U.S. acquisitions, coupled with a series of agreements between U.S. and Japanese firms that might someday signify a similar Japanese beachhead.

Thus, in the waning months of 1977, West Germany's Bayer AG made a $253.4 million offer for Miles Laboratories and Alcon Laboratories was the target of a $268 million offer from Nestlé S.A. of Switzerland. Earlier in the year, major expansions of U.S. subsidiaries were announced by ICI Ltd. (Britain), Farbwerke Hoechst (West Germany), and Astra (Sweden). In August, Abbott Laboratories and Takeda Chemical Industries (Japan) announced formation of a joint venture to develop and market new drugs in the U.S.

This was, in fact, the second invasion of the U.S. market by European giants. Already profitably established in the U.S. were Beecham and Burroughs-Wellcome (from Britain), Knoll and Cutter (West German-owned), Organon and Fougera (Dutch), and Hoffmann-LaRoche, Sandoz, and Ciba-Geigy (all Swiss-owned).

Of some relevance to these developments was the so-called drug lag, the interval between the introduction of new drugs outside the U.S. and formal Food and Drug Administration clearance of the same drugs for the U.S. market. U.S. regulatory officials denied that such a "lag" existed (except where FDA insistence on safety data had served to prevent disaster, as in the barring of thalidomide, later shown to cause fetal deformities), but at the same time they suggested that FDA drug-clearance procedures could be streamlined and the entire process speeded up. Such a speedup, combined with accelerated introduction of European- and Japanese-developed drugs to the U.S. market, now appeared likely in the next few years.

According to the Pharmaceutical Manufacturers Association, 1976 sales of prescription and bulk drugs by U.S.-headquartered firms totaled about $8.1 billion in the U.S. and $14.3 billion worldwide. Over-the-counter drugs accounted for another $3.8 billion. Among ethical drugs, products acting on the central nervous system continued to lead all other categories, with slightly more than 25% of the total. This position had been main-tained for more than a decade, mainly on the strength of continued strong sales of tranquilizers. Companies with over $100 million in sales continued to dominate the U.S. industry. Such companies accounted for more than 83% of domestic sales and 91% of foreign sales in 1975, the most recent year for which figures were available.

(DONALD A. DAVIS)

PLASTICS

Against a background of stagnant world trade and a persistent lack of any reflationary lead from those countries with the strongest economies, the plastics industry failed to obtain even the modest growth that had been hoped for. Nevertheless, there was some solid progress. For once, a year passed without violent commercial disruption or cyclic swings. The main concern of major plastics materials manufacturers was that excessive capacity remained available and, consequently, profitability stayed low.

Predictions for the future varied widely. A well-reasoned set of figures from Imperial Chemical Industries Ltd. (ICI) of the U.K. covered the "commodity" thermoplastics; i.e., low-density polyethylene, high-density polyethylene, polypropylene, polystyrene and styrene copolymers (principally ABS), and polyvinyl chloride (PVC). The ICI estimate for world consumption of these materials (accounting for about 95% of all thermoplastics output) outside the Eastern European countries was 28 million metric tons in 1976, rising to 71 million tons by 1987. Western production of thermosetting plastics in 1976 was approximately 8 million–9 million tons, and production in Eastern Europe was estimated at 5 million tons. The overall total was 43 million tons for the year.

ICI expected usage of commodity thermoplastics in the West to grow at an average annual rate of some 9% over the next decade, with a higher, 10% rate until 1982 falling to 8% by the mid-1980s. This compared with an average annual growth of nearly 13% in the previous decade and a maximum of 20% in the early 1970s before the 1974–75 collapse following the oil crisis. The same study suggested that the considerable excess of production capacity that existed in some countries after 1974, particularly for low-density polyethylene and polystyrene, would take some years to correct. Production capacity for the commodity thermoplastics was put at 35 million tons, whereas estimated actual consumption was only 28 million tons. However, further capacity of some 40 million tons would be needed to achieve the 1987 forecasts, with associated investment in petrochemical plant to make the raw materials. Increases in capacity would need to be phased to match rises in demand.

Estimates for the individual thermoplastic material groups for 1976 and 1987, respectively, were: low-density polyethylene, 7.8 million tons rising to 19 million tons; high-density polyethylene, 3.5 million tons to 9.3 million tons; styrene polymers and copolymers, 5.1 million tons to 13 million tons; and PVC, 8.6 million tons to 18.6 million tons. The remaining "commodity" polymer, polypropylene, was expected to have the fastest growth of all, from 3.1 million tons to 11.3 million tons,

A plastic minisub for undersea oil exploration was developed by the Vickers group at Yorkshire, England. The plastic hull is said to be as strong as steel and rustproof.

an average annual rate of increase of about 13%.

Continuing progress with polypropylene was a marked feature of 1977, which saw important prospects opening for this versatile material in several sectors of packaging, such as thermoformed food containers, and in fine fibres, notably carpet face fabrics. Polypropylene was already firmly established for carpet backing and had achieved considerable success in structural foams, where a cellular core with a solid skin gives components an extremely favourable ratio of rigidity to weight. In Western Europe the attractions of polypropylene, made from feedstock that was both freely available and comparatively cheap, had resulted in a grossly excessive increase in installed capacity in 1977, with more to follow. In the short term, at least, competition would be damagingly intense.

Concentration on "fine tuning" of formulations based on existing polymers continued to be a predominant technical feature of plastics materials available to the processor. Such characteristics as flame retardancy were achieved through the use of improved additives. Much development work was associated with the ever increasing need to meet the specifications of governments and other regulatory bodies, made even more complicated by the variations from country to country. The purpose of such legislation was to protect workers in the industry and consumers of the products, but industry spokesmen were quick to point out that overly severe restrictions could inhibit progress and deprive society of real benefits.

The problem of the permissible level of vinyl chloride monomer in the atmosphere of plants manufacturing PVC appeared to be moving toward solution. Sweden had imposed a severe upper limit for vinyl chloride monomer concentration, one part per million (ppm), but in most of Europe the limit varied from 5 to 10 ppm. During the year Denmark refused to allow construction of its first PVC plant on the grounds that the authorities had yet to determine what the acceptable level should be. Overall, however, several question marks that had hung over the future of the immense PVC industry were dissipated. In Britain all four producers of PVC resin announced expansion plans; these would increase capacity by about 200,000 tons a year above the current 575,000 tons by 1980—a remarkable expression of confidence.

(ROBIN C. PENFOLD)

PRINTING

The world's biggest printing exhibition, held at Düsseldorf, West Germany, attracted almost 300,000 visitors in 1977, but relatively little that was shown was really new. Nonsilver films, from Mitsubishi in Japan and Coulter in the U.S., attracted attention as the first practicable means of avoiding the need for intermediate film stages between photographing of the original copy and platemaking. In photopolymer platemaking, du Pont's Cyrel and BASF's Nyloprint introduced materials for fine-detail flexographic printing. Daetwyler and Wifag in Switzerland cooperated to develop a wraparound copper gravure plate.

Optronics of the U.S., Dr.-Ing. Rudolf

Hell of West Germany, and Crosfield Electronics of the U.K. made progress in developing electronic systems combining phototypesetting, electronic scanning, and automatic merging of texts and pictures onto film or printing form. Graphicart introduced a new line of gravure cylinder preparation machines and chemicals. Sci-Tex of Israel designed an interface to link its Response 200 computer-aided design system to the engraver to provide a totally electronic magnetic tape-operated system of engraving cylinders.

In offset, Roland introduced computer-controlled inking to permit instant adjustment of inks to changing press conditions and, together with Grapho-Metronic, offered ink temperature control for offset printing. Sophisticated ink control systems were introduced by Heidelberg and FAG. With the introduction of the Crabtree-Vickers Dampaguide unit, electronic damping control and monitoring became possible.

The Fiat group acquired Italy's largest printing machine maker, Nebiolo. In web offset, small size presses triumphed, and a line of Albert machines from West Germany using a new mechanical system of ink control found instant success. MAN, departing from company tradition, presented the Uniman web offset press for budget-minded printers. Strachan & Henshaw of Britain, which claimed to have supplied the presses handling 80% of U.S. pocketbook printing, designed a new book press for short-run work using direct lithography. Wifag made a new press for Di-Litho printing that allowed later conversion to letterpress or web offset.

In rotogravure package printing, orders rose for inline printing and die-cutting. The Bobst Lemanic was the fastest such machine, although Rotomec of Italy claimed to print polythene film at speeds of up to 400 m per minute. In phototypesetting, simplification of designs coupled with top quality became possible on low-cost Bobst and Berthold machines and on compact Linofilm equipment. In Switzerland, Bobstgraphic's portable typewriter with electronic printout and mini-cassette recording enabled reporters to tape-record copy and play back stories via ordinary telephones for retyping at the office, eliminating the need for a copy taker. *U.S. News & World Report* began working with a fully computerized page-makeup system.

In the U.S., Canada, Austria, and West Germany, health authorities investigated the possible risks of electronic editing screens (visual display units). Following the death of a worker in Bristol, England, the unions called for a ban on TDI components of toluene-base gravure inks.

(W. PINCUS JASPERT)

RUBBER

The U.S. rubber industry made a remarkable comeback after the 141-day strike that ended in September 1976. By late 1977 the backlog of orders had been filled, and there were even some signs that tire sales were slowing. The rubber industry enjoyed record sales in the first half of 1977, due to the large number of new cars made and pent-

Industrial Review

up demand for replacement tires. The prices of tires and other rubber products increased by about the same percentage as the cost-of-living index.

In general, raw materials were readily available, with periodic price increases reflecting the costs of labour and feedstocks. Carbon black inventories in some grades went essentially to zero during the first quarter before supply and demand were reconciled. Guayule, a shrub native to Mexico and the southwestern U.S., was being cultivated as an alternate source of polyisoprene. With proper processing, the product was equivalent to natural rubber. A pilot plant had been in operation in Mexico for some time, and plans were under way for a plant capable of producing 5,000 tons per year. The U.S. National Academy of Sciences proposed a joint U.S.-Mexican effort. It was predicted that the price could be competitive with that of natural rubber by 1985, and if intensive cultivation were practiced, the U.S. could become self-sufficient in polyisoprene production.

Natural rubber was just one of the raw materials used in rubber manufacture to exhibit an upward trend in price during the year. On Oct. 1, 1976, the New York spot price was 40⅝ cents per pound for smoked sheets, and on Oct. 1, 1977, it was 44½ cents, reflecting a 10% increase. The price of non-oil-extended, 1500-type styrene-butadiene rubber (SBR), the most widely used synthetic, remained constant at 34 cents per pound.

World production of natural rubber in 1976 was estimated at 3,530,000 metric tons, an increase of 230,000 tons over 1975. Production for 1977 was estimated at 3.7 million tons, up 170,000 tons compared with 1976. The Management Committee of the International Rubber Study Group (IRSG) estimated natural rubber supplies at 3.7 million tons for 1977 and synthetic rubber at 8.7 million tons, while 3.8 million tons of natural rubber and 8.5 million tons of synthetic rubber would be turned into manufactured products. The predicted consumption of natural rubber was about 3% greater than predicted production, while synthetic rubber consumption was about 3% less. (*See* Tables X and XI.)

The U.S. continued to be the largest single buyer of natural rubber, purchasing 730,000 tons in 1976. World consumption of natural rubber latex (dry basis) was estimated at 267,000 tons. Statistics on world consumption of synthetic latexes were not complete, but U.S. consumption was 157,-000 tons (dry basis) of the SBR type. Consumption of both natural and synthetic rubber worldwide was estimated at 11.3 million tons in 1976. Production of reclaimed rubber continued to decline, from 227,561 tons in 1975 to 190,976 tons in 1976.

Reduction of tire rolling resistance was being studied by all the major manufacturers. The radial tire has less rolling resistance than the bias ply tire and hence decreases gasoline consumption, but Uniroyal and Goodyear demonstrated new types of tires with 6 to 10% improvement over the radial. Tire safety was being emphasized in Canada's new certification plan, which required a seal of safety on all tires by March 1, 1978. Tire tread designs were being changed to reduce the effect of the antiskid seams being ground into concrete pavement. After ten years' development, polynorbornene was

Table X. Natural Rubber Production
In 000 metric tons

Country	1974	1975	1976
Malaysia	1,549	1,478	1,639
Indonesia	855	825	848 [1]
Thailand	379	349	392
Sri Lanka	132	149	152
India	128	136	148
Liberia	86	83	76 [1]
Nigeria [1]	78	63	51
Philippines	32	35 [1]	36 [1]
Zaire	31	30 [1]	29 [1]
Brazil	19	19	20
Others	151	133	139 [1]
Total	3,440	3,300	3,530

[1] Estimate, or includes estimate.
Source: The Secretariat of the International Rubber Study Group, *Rubber Statistical Bulletin.*

Table XI. Synthetic Rubber Production
In 000 metric tons

Country	1974	1975	1976
United States	2,396	2,004	2,304
Japan	858	789	941
France	463	350	437
United Kingdom	336	261	320
Germany, West	372	316	380 [1]
Netherlands, The	245	216	247
Italy [1]	240	200	250
Canada	209	173	210
Germany, East	139	144	150 [1]
Brazil	155	129	164
Poland	101	108	117
Romania	92	99	147 [1]
Spain	67	53	...
Belgium	65 [1]	65 [1]	115
Mexico	66	60	69 [1]
Czechoslovakia	51	57	57 [1]
Argentina [1]	50	40	45
Australia	45	38	42
South Africa	32	32	35
Others	1,603	1,741	1,953
Total	7,585	6,875	7,983

[1] Estimate, or includes estimate.
Source: The Secretariat of the International Rubber Study Group, *Rubber Statistical Bulletin.*

The first U.S.-built natural gas tanker was dedicated May 27 at the General Dynamics shipyard in Quincy, Massachusetts. The vessel would be used to carry gas from Indonesia to Japan.

introduced as the world's newest rubber. A product of ring-opening polymerization, it is produced in a powder form found to be desirable for processing and yields vulcanized compounds covering a wide range of hardness. (JAMES R. BEATTY)

SHIPBUILDING

During 1977 governments took desperate measures to keep shipyards in operation. A price war developed in Japan between yards chasing orders. In the intense competition for a giant floating dock for Portland, Ore., expected to cost $35 million, one Japanese yard submitted a tender which, at $17.5 million, was $6 million less than the next nearest bid.

Prices quoted by South Korea for finished ships barely covered the cost of raw materials to British yards, resulting in a 50% difference in final cost. But British shipowners did support U.K. yards, which took more orders in the first nine months of 1977 than in the whole of 1976. Help also appeared in the form of £60 million of government funds pledged to narrow the gap between quoted prices and tenders from European yards, as well as sterling's lower rate of exchange. France, The Netherlands, Belgium, Spain, and West Germany all introduced some kind of financial assistance to the industry. There was little sign of any significant cutback in shipbuilding capacity except in Sweden, where there was a 30% reduction.

Government assistance took the form of preferential loans, interest rate subsidies, and guarantees to owners ordering from national yards. Shipbuilders were offered loans and subsidized interest, particularly for orders placed on behalf of less developed countries outside the scope of credit guidelines recommended by the OECD. Swedish yards introduced building for stock, although such an arrangement would only serve to make the cargo overcapacity situation worse.

By October 1977 the world order book for new tonnage had fallen to 3,050 vessels of 85.5 million tons deadweight (dw), compared with 3,651 vessels a year earlier; 43 million tons dw was for tankers and ore-bulk-oil carriers. There were 1,550 dry cargo vessels on order (15.4 million tons dw), 316 containerships (3.7 million tons dw), and 660 bulk carriers (23.8 million tons dw).

Japan took the lion's share of the new orders; 44% of the contracts and 56% of the deadweight tonnage in the year ended August 1977. Eastern European countries took 13.7% of all orders placed (3.1 million tons dw) and West Germany, 7%. Total orders placed for the period amounted to 1,648 ships and 27.3 million tons dw.

World shipbuilding capacity contracted to just under 35 million gross registered tons (grt), with Japan's potential capacity remaining at near 17 million grt. By October 1977 orders placed had risen to 27.3 million tons dw (about 13 million grt), but the situation remained bleak.

In October the U.K. and Polish governments announced that a new joint U.K.-Polish shipping company would order 24 ships from the state-owned British Shipbuilders, which formally came into existence on July 1. The ships would be bare-board-chartered to the Polish State Shipping Company for 15 years. The deal was reputed to be worth over £115 million, but more than £20 million of the U.K. government's intervention fund had to be allocated to obtain it.

Some European commercial yards prepared and sold designs for small naval craft, and about 40 orders were placed worldwide for naval support and patrol vessels. As more countries adopted 200-mi protected zones around their coastlines, there were hopes of orders for fishery and coastal protection vessels. U.S. shipbuilders expected an upturn in their order books if Congress approved the proposed oil cargo preference bill, which would have required 9.5% of all oil imported into the U.S. to be moved in U.S. flag tankers, but the bill was defeated in the House of Representatives in October. Such a step on the part of the U.S. would have served to accentuate the crisis situation in the Scandinavian and other European yards and put back any hope of equilibrium in the tanker market to the late 1980s. In the year ended October 1977, U.S. yards took 17 orders for 2 million tons dw, including an unconfirmed order for three 600,000-tons-dw nuclear-powered tankers.

The general shipbuilding picture continued dark, and for many yards the gloom was only slightly relieved by government assistance. If the proposal for all tankers of 70,000 tons dw and over to be fitted with segregated ballast tanks (to reduce oil pollution at sea) should become a reality and gain government support, there would be a much-needed increase in shipbuilders' work. More tankers could be scrapped, new orders could be placed, and many vessels in service would have to be retrofitted. With the tanker market likely to remain depressed at least until 1980, however, shipbuilders would have to continue to depend on the market for dry cargo ships and small bulk carriers of between 4,000 and 20,000 tons dw. (W. D. EWART)

TELECOMMUNICATIONS

Following close on the heels of field trials in 1976, both the American Telephone and Telegraph Co. (AT&T) and General Telephone & Electronics Corp. (GTE) installed fibre-optic systems that carried actual telephone traffic over tiny, hair-thin glass fibres encased in protective sheaths under the streets of Chicago and Santa Monica, Calif. Satellite networks handled an increasing proportion of domestic communications in both industrialized and less developed nations, as well as being used to predict weather patterns and to detect potentially dangerous storms. Pocket pagers, commonly called beepers, allowed people on the move to keep in touch, and applications for citizens band (CB) radio licenses continued to rise. U.S. telephone companies made it easier for consumers to buy telephones in a wide assortment of models. Other developments during the year included the use of circularly polarized television signals to minimize "ghosts," installation of a trial mobile radiotelephone system that could accommodate an increased number of users, and transmission of stereo music over commercial AM stations.

Table XII. Countries Having More Than 100,000 Telephones

Telephones in service, 1976

Country	Number of telephones	Percentage increase over 1966	Telephones per 100 population	Country	Number of telephones	Percentage increase over 1966	Telephones per 100 population
Algeria	250,424	75.0	1.46	Kuwait	128,751	394.4	12.49
Argentina	2,469,250	64.9	9.66	Lebanon [3]	227,000	221.1	7.67
Australia [1]	5,266,843	87.4	39.01	Luxembourg	146,869	68.7	41.14
Austria	2,132,758	111.4	28.13	Malaysia	291,968	121.7	2.42
Belgium	2,776,882	77.5	28.34	Mexico	2,914,531	254.1	4.76
Brazil	3,371,284	150.7	3.08	Morocco	198,500	38.7	1.15
Bulgaria	777,127	178.3	8.90	Netherlands, The	5,047,117	114.6	36.75
Canada	13,142,235	76.5	57.15	New Zealand	1,570,784	53.2	50.18
Chile	455,169	68.9	4.40	Nigeria [1]	111,478	84.5	0.16
Colombia	1,285,670	190.2	5.45	Norway	1,406,995	55.0	35.03
Costa Rica	111,812	367.1	5.61	Pakistan	239,600	64.5	0.33
Cuba [2]	274,949	22.9	3.16	Panama	142,159	196.4	8.52
Czechoslovakia	2,614,761	75.3	17.62	Peru [1]	333,346	151.8	2.14
Denmark	2,316,208	69.8	44.97	Philippines	489,717	197.1	1.17
Dominican Republic	108,023	242.7	2.40	Poland	2,577,636	99.2	7.54
Ecuador	193,066	338.8	2.94	Portugal	1,065,974	83.2	12.30
Egypt [1]	503,200	67.0	1.37	Puerto Rico	474,333	133.6	15.19
Finland	1,833,993	119.5	38.89	Rhodesia	182,594	72.9	2.84
France	13,833,346	126.2	26.20	Romania [1]	1,076,566	152.4	5.10
Germany, East	2,570,113	54.9	15.23	Singapore	317,932	237.9	14.04
Germany, West	19,602,606	122.7	31.70	South Africa	2,072,131	64.4	8.10
Greece	2,008,522	295.2	22.12	Spain	7,835,970	156.6	21.98
Hong Kong	1,033,735	295.3	33.60	Sweden	5,422,795	51.8	66.07
Hungary	1,048,090	85.2	9.91	Switzerland	3,912,971	63.4	61.09
India	1,816,901	106.1	0.30	Syria [4]	143,320	83.7	2.08
Indonesia	305,455	83.6	0.23	Taiwan	1,117,989	570.6	6.92
Iran	688,396	231.7	2.00	Thailand [1]	312,312	263.1	0.74
Iraq	184,924	184.5	1.69	Tunisia	126,750	137.7	2.26
Ireland	444,000	93.0	14.07	Turkey	1,011,790	162.4	2.52
Israel	796,348	211.3	22.80	U.S.S.R.	16,949,000	120.1	6.63
Italy	14,495,677	142.4	25.88	United Kingdom	21,035,602	86.3	37.51
Jamaica	100,000	102.9	5.00	United States	149,011,685	50.8	69.49
Japan	45,514,709	225.1	40.47	Uruguay	249,655	49.3	8.97
Kenya	121,910	127.5	0.91	Venezuela	649,603	129.9	5.34
Korea, South	1,400,103	410.3	4.03	Yugoslavia	1,301,219	187.7	6.06

[1] 1975. [2] 1973. [3] 1972. [4] 1974.

Sources: American Telephone and Telegraph Company, *The World's Telephones, 1976*; Statistical Office of the United Nations, *Statistical Yearbook, 1967*.

Industrial Review

Satellites. A domestic U.S. communications satellite system jointly owned and operated by AT&T and GTE, the largest non-Bell telephone company, was completed during the year. The satellite network was the first to carry long-distance telephone calls within the 48 contiguous states and between the mainland and Hawaii. In addition, satellite systems were bringing television programming to numerous new locations. The Public Broadcasting System was interconnecting TV stations throughout the U.S., Alaska, Hawaii, Puerto Rico, and the Virgin Islands. Meanwhile, a European consortium launched the fourth of a planned five-satellite network, part of the UN's Global Atmospheric Research Program to gather worldwide weather data.

Telephones. During 1977 the Bell System and GTE increased the number of "phone stores" where consumers could choose a phone from a wide selection of styles. The phone could be installed by the customer in company-provided telephone jacks.

A Federal Communications Commission (FCC) ruling that would eliminate paying the telephone companies for the required interconnect device when plugging in oth-

er than company-supplied phones was stayed, pending an appeal by the phone companies, which objected to having "foreign devices" plugged into the network. Later, AT&T modified its position, requiring only that at least one company instrument be on the customer's premises. In October the New York State Public Service Commission, which regulates telephone rates for the state's 49 telephone companies, ordered them to allow subscribers to buy and install their own phones instead of renting them from the companies.

Rep. Lionel Van Deerlin (Dem., Calif.), chairman of the U.S. House subcommittee that was rewriting the Communications Act of 1934, conceded late in the year that there was little chance of any revision occurring in 1978. The bill would influence the future of communications in the United States, but the issues were complex and the broadcasting industry generally opposed changes.

Mobile Communications. Both AT&T and Motorola were readying a "cellular system" that would allow more efficient use of the radio spectrum. The system multiplies the number of users that can be served by dividing metropolitan areas into clusters of cells, each with its own transmitter. Each channel can be used many times by coordinated reuse over the entire area. The cells are connected by control and switching centres over land lines.

As of January 1, CB users were allowed 40 channels instead of the previous 23. The FCC reported over three million applications for CB licenses during the first half of the year.

A major advance in CB radio was Texas Instruments' 40-channel microprocessor-controlled AM and single-sideband transceiver. Both mobile and base stations use two tiny computers to monitor and control transmitter and receiver functions. Pocket pagers had previously been confined to short ranges, but in 1977 callers were able to bounce their beeps from New York to Chicago to the West Coast via satellite.

A small company, Digital Broadcast Corp. of Vienna, Va., developed a system that lets a user send a written message almost anywhere in the U.S. in less than a minute for about the cost of first-class postage. A message received at the central switching centre is sent over telephone lines to a commercial FM broadcast station within 75 mi of the destination. The message is then transmitted digitally along with the station's regular programming and picked up by a receiver at the customer's location, where it is decoded and displayed either on a TV screen or as a printout.

The British Post Office offered a Viewdata/Teletext service that allows customers to select and view newspaper pages, stock market prices, reference works, and similar matter on their television sets. The information is sent over telephone lines.

(RICHARD G. GUNDLACH)

TEXTILES

Some recovery in the world textile trade had been expected in 1977, but there was little improvement, although the spring saw a slight increase in purchasing by U.S. buyers. Manufacturers in a number of countries, particularly in the industrialized nations, went out of business, including one Irish ultramodern cotton spinner where open-end spinning capacity had been installed as an alternative to classical ring-spinning processes. Much of the decline in Western textile manufacturing was attributed to competitive pressure from manufacturers in Korea, Hong Kong, Taiwan, and India.

Replacement of old-style shuttle looms by modern systems continued, but at a slower rate. In Czechoslovakia a new style of fabric manufacture, called Metap, combined weaving and knitting. In East Germany the search for new products and processes produced Malifol, a system for reusing waste polyester by converting it into an inexpensive new type of textile with possible applications as an insulation material and as high quality packaging.

In spinning, open-end machine builders suffered from overcapacity. A new system from Austria offered great potential for producing medium to coarse yarns from wool and seemed suitable for other fibres. Renewed interest was shown in electrostatic spinning. Yarns assembled with the aid of an electrostatic field could be produced at very high speeds.

(PETER LENNOX-KERR)

Wool. Because of the fluctuation in currencies in 1977, no consistent trend in wool prices could be discerned. Allowing for this currency-induced variability in price, how-

A Bell System telephone lineman displays an experimental cable of glass fibres capable of carrying on a beam of light the same volume of signals as the much bulkier electrical lines currently in use.

ever, the year was a relatively steady one. Wool made some gains as against man-made fibres, despite some price changes making wool relatively more expensive.

Prices generally eased to a slightly lower basis, associated with disappointment in wool textile activity and consumption in particular countries, notably Japan. At the same time there was no return to the depths of recession reached in 1974–75. The year therefore ended with the wool industry in neither boom nor slump nor convincingly pointed in either direction.

There was an apparent development of recession in trade before the 1977–78 selling season opened in Australia and New Zealand in August, but this was largely counteracted by a burst of better, probably covering, demand in September and October. Wool production in Australia was estimated at 672 million kg in the 1977–78 season (709 million in 1976–77), and the downward adjustment in supply there and elsewhere, coupled with lower commercial stocks, helped to create more strength and confidence later in the year.

(H. M. F. MALLETT)

Cotton. World output of raw cotton rose by some 3 million bales in 1976–77 to nearly 58 million bales. Most of the gain was attributable to an increase in planted acreage. Demand for textiles remained slack and consumption, at around 61.5 million bales, was more than a million bales below the 1975–76 record. Worldwide carry-over stocks at the start of the 1976–77 season totaled 22.7 million bales. By August 1977 they had fallen to 19.3 million bales, some three and a half months' consumption at current levels and the lowest total in decades.

U.S. production remained significant, but crops in the U.S.S.R. and China began to compete for supremacy. Soviet output rose to 12.2 million bales in 1975–76, with improved yields accounting for much of the gain. China's output fell slightly.

The Liverpool index of average values, which began the 1976–77 season at 84.6 cents a pound and touched 88 cents in November 1976, had fallen to 86.3 cents by the year's end. The quotation improved to over 87 cents in March 1977 but then declined steadily, falling below 60 cents in September for the first time since 1975.

Worldwide, average yield per acre improved, from 158.4 kg to an estimated 161.6 kg. Plantings for 1977–78 were increased considerably, and a substantial rise in output, perhaps as much as 10%, was anticipated. (ARTHUR TATTERSALL)

Silk. The steady growth of demand for silk throughout the West continued in 1977, justifying China's spending on promotion. However, demand in Europe and America could not significantly influence world prices. Japan remained the world's largest single producer, consumer, and importer of silk, despite slipping living standards and a new frugality in shopping habits. For the younger woman in particular, silk had become a luxury.

To support the quarter of a million farming families engaged in cocoon production, Japan had virtually banned the import of raw silk in 1974. The violence of the repercussions could scarcely have been foreseen. The high prices of the boom years had attracted a surge of imports, and overnight producing countries such as China and South Korea lost a large share of their raw silk market. China and Korea negotiated terms, and a licensing system for yarns was introduced in Japan in May 1977.

The free market saw little movement in prices. For nine months China held firm at 45 yuan per kilo for 3A 20/22 denier, and in July 1977 there was a modest upward adjustment of 1.5%. With Korea and Brazil seeking to replace what had been lost in Japan, competition was keen and the West enjoyed a period of stable prices.

(PETER W. GADDUM)

Man-Made Fibres. The catastrophic situation within the industry continued through 1977, and the pressure on prices, despite very substantial rises in the costs of the main raw materials, was maintained. Several old factories were scrapped, and some producers closed production lines.

In Britain, ICI and Courtaulds had taken preventive action early in the recession and were better equipped to meet the continuing depressed market than most other Western European manufacturers. Italian plans to bring vast new fibre plants on stream and the ever greater capacities under construction in Eastern Europe would inevitably increase pressures in Western markets. With the collapse of the market for textured filament yarns, polyester-producing plants had been put up for sale, scrapped, or savagely cut back in output, and projected price increases would do little to restore business. Major companies were concerned about the prospects of an upturn in the textile trade before surplus capacity could be fully reduced.

A steady rise in the production and consumption of polypropylene fibres in 1976–77 had been achieved at the expense of the acrylics. Much of the growth was in domestic textiles, particularly upholstery fabrics, but there were signs that the fibre could offer some interesting properties for clothing manufacture. (PETER LENNOX-KERR)

TOBACCO

World tobacco production rose an estimated 1% in 1976, to a record 11,900,000,000 lb. Leading producers were China (2,160,508,000 lb); the U.S. (2,118,560,000); India (837,748,000); the U.S.S.R. (639,334,000); Turkey (573,636,000); Brazil (557,816,000); Japan (364,244,000); Bulgaria (319,667,000); Greece (279,168,000); Italy (239,419,000); South Korea (238,996,000); and Poland (220,812,000).

Prices charged to importers of leaf tobacco continued to rise steeply, following a trend begun in the early '70s, while prices paid to growers, although increasing, had not kept pace with the cost of living in many producing countries. The picture varied widely, however; between mid-1974 and mid-1976 the index of U.S. farmers' earnings dropped from 128 to 95 (1970 = 100), while Japanese farmers' earnings rose from 130 to over 140.

In the U.S. there was increasing pressure on the tobacco industry. Attempts were being made to force the government to drop its price-support program for tobacco and to levy prohibitive taxes on high-tar cigarettes. Various groups were also lobbying for a complete ban on cigarette advertising. Three-fifths of the states had some form of restriction on smoking in public places. In late November the CAB announced that a ban on cigar and pipe smoking on airplanes would go into effect in 30–60 days, and a ban on cigarettes was expected. Manufacturers had responded to public opinion by concentrating on low-tar brands, a sector of the industry that had increased its market share from 10.9% in 1975 to an estimated 15.8% in 1976. It was expected that the market share would reach 20% in 1977.

In Europe the industry faced similar pressures. Most countries had implemented

Vintner Frederic Chandon de Briailles (left) and cigar maker Zino Davidoff (right) toast a new cigar made of Cuban tobacco, which their associated companies planned to market in France.

Industrial Review

selective smoking prohibitions or were in the process of doing so. Active antismoking campaigns had been mounted with government backing in many countries, although enforcement of recently introduced "no-smoking" laws was patchy. A closely watched development in the U.K. was the introduction of cigarettes containing substitute tobacco. Eleven brands launched in June by three manufacturers contained either 25 or 40% substitute produced from wood cellulose. Vast amounts of money were being spent on promotion, and manufacturers were hoping for around 10% market penetration. It was estimated that the new cigarettes reached about 8% of sales at one point but then fell back to under 5%.

Sales of tobacco goods in the U.K. fell from 111,547,800 kg in 1975 to 108,142,800 kg in 1976, but manufacturers continued to turn increased profits. This was achieved despite severe price competition in the king-size sector. It was this sector of the market that was growing, having risen from just over 9% of sales in 1975 to more than 25%. During the same period sales of low-tar cigarettes increased from 5.4 to 11.7%. With EEC tax harmonization due to take effect in the U.K. on Jan. 1, 1978, manufacturers were fighting hard to increase and consolidate their share of the king-size market. The effect of harmonization would be to make king-size brands relatively cheaper than smaller cigarettes.

Canada's share of world leaf production continued to fall, and the government commissioned a study of a two-price system designed to keep Canadian leaf prices in line with those of competing producers. In Nigeria, where sales of cigarettes rose nearly 25% between 1973 and 1976, the government began a crackdown on smuggling. Italy rescinded a four-year ban on the import of cigarettes, with the result that the Tobacco Monopoly inscribed 59 new brands of tobacco product; however, the government remained under pressure to restrict imports. In France, Seita lost its right to a monopoly over the import and distribution of tobacco products from EEC countries but retained its monopoly over tobacco products from third-party countries. In general, tobacco taxes throughout the world continued to increase, but there was no marked effect on consumption.

(PETER BARBER)

TOURISM

International tourism broke new records in 1977. Worldwide receipts reached U.S. $50 billion and international arrivals numbered 240 million, representing substantial increases over 1976 figures.

Growth was sustained in Europe and Asia. Tourism recovered strongly in Cyprus and Portugal, where arrivals were one-third higher than in 1976. Arrivals in Spain, at well over 30 million, surpassed the record of 1973. The U.K. welcomed over 12 million foreign visitors. Romania's Black Sea tourist resorts were filled to capacity, and tourism provided 6% of Romania's foreign earnings. Hong Kong, India, and Sri Lanka all saw arrivals grow by more than 15%, but tourism in Thailand marked time.

The first U.S. tour group to visit Havana since 1961 visited the historic buildings of old Havana in May.

Severe winter conditions in parts of North America curbed travel growth in the early months of the year. The Bicentennial had boosted tourism in 1976, when arrivals in the U.S. grew by 12% to 17.5 million. In 1977, however, the increase fell to a respectable but modest 5%. Uncertain economic prospects clouded Canadians' travel intentions, and fewer planned to take a vacation. Intentions of the much larger U.S. market reached an 18-month high in the spring, when 4.3% of households planned to travel abroad.

Arrivals in the Caribbean for 1977 reflected a disappointing winter season. The Bahamas showed no growth, and Jamaica recorded a one-third decline. The year saw at least one Caribbean breakthrough, however; the first U.S. travelers in more than a decade and a half reached Cuba direct from a U.S. port aboard a Greek ship. (See CUBA: Special Report.)

There was an unexpected upsurge of arrivals in The Gambia and Senegal. The best-selling book Roots by Alex Haley (see BIOGRAPHY) and the television series based on it had moved thousands of black Americans to seek their own origins in the old slavery heartlands of West Africa. "Roots tours" and "Roots Pilgrimages" became a vogue, and new types of tour were developed. For example, arrangements were made for small groups of visitors to join in the everyday life of an African village.

Africa was also the focus of a major study by the International Civil Aviation Organization (ICAO), the results of which were published in 1977. The ICAO saw air transport, both passenger and freight, as playing a key role in the economic development of the continent, but it noted that there were still too few services linking African destinations and too many routed via Europe. Kenya announced a move to ban hunting in the game parks, where annual earnings of $80 million came from foreign tourists who wished to view and photo-

graph—but not shoot—wild animals in their natural habitat.

In expectation of a peace settlement in the Middle East, development proceeded on such ambitious projects as the holiday city at Habbaniyah Lake, near Baghdad, Iraq, and the marina at Aqaba in Jordan. Airlines serving the oil-rich Gulf states reported a tourist boom, with 500–600% increases in passengers carried since 1973.

Member airlines of the International Air Transport Association (IATA) made an operating profit in 1976 (after suffering a loss in 1975) but warned that it was inadequate to finance the planned program of reequipment. Introduction of Laker Airways' cut-price, no-frills, no reservation Skytrain service between London and New York brought that much closer the possibility that travelers would "casually" cross the Atlantic. Laker's chairman, Freddie Laker (see BIOGRAPHY), went on to draw up plans for a Europe-to-Australia Skytrain service. (See TRANSPORTATION: Aviation.)

French market researchers confirmed something already known in North America—that women now traveled more than men and that women usually made the decisions about family vacations. They noted the strong preference of women for hotel and holiday village accommodations where they did not have to do household chores, but did not say whether the housewife's keen sense of a bargain was responsible for the international tourist's increasing sensitivity to price.

Major tourist destinations showed a strong interest in price indices and price comparisons in 1977. The U.S. Travel Data Center reported the U.S. travel price index was rising at a rate of nearly 7%. In Europe a hotel survey reported rates were up by 39% in Brussels, 30% in Venice, 27% in Amsterdam, 17% in London, 9% in Paris, and 4% in Geneva. Spanish hoteliers were allowed to renegotiate tour contracts following Spain's 20% devaluation of the peseta in July and a short-lived but much publicized strike of hotel employees on the Costa del Sol protesting against low wages, long workweeks, and seasonal unemployment.

A strong attack on tourism as a form of "neocolonialism," published in June 1977 in the UN's *Development Forum,* stimulated a lively discussion of the costs and benefits of tourism to less developed countries. The article suggested that earnings were not used to benefit the populations of receiving countries, that foreign tour operators effectively controlled governments, and that citizens of less developed countries working in the tourist industry degenerated into "flunkies."

The attack provoked a number of forceful defenses of tourism. Counterarguments were put forward affirming that "Tourism is an industry. That it is an early choice of third world countries is understandable. It is a way to quickly generate an inflow of foreign currency, upgrade facilities, provide jobs and spawn attendant industries and services." It was also noted that tourism had brought long-standing and significant benefits to such rich industrialized countries as Austria and Switzerland, and no one would suggest that the people there had degenerated into menials. There was a call to give less developed nations a greater feeling of "belonging" to the industry.

Delegates from the World Tourism Organization's 100 member states, attending the organization's second General Assembly at Torremolinos, Spain, in 1977, resolved to hold a "World Tourism Conference" in Manila in 1980.

(CAMILLE SHACKLEFORD)

WOOD PRODUCTS

In the U.S. a boom in home building, the major market for structural wood products, pushed lumber and plywood demand and prices to high levels in 1977. Production of paper and allied products also reached record volume, but demand for many paper-related products was mixed. Overall, the year saw healthy growth for forest-based products in the U.S., despite domestic and foreign developments that put severe pressure on prices and on the profits of some companies.

With residential construction at an annual rate of over two million starts during the year, production of lumber and softwood plywood reached near-capacity levels. According to the National Forest Products Association, U.S. lumber production in 1977 totaled about 37,900,000,000 bd-ft, the highest level since 1973, while softwood lumber, representing 83% of total output, reached a production level of 31,600,000,000 bd-ft, not exceeded since 1926. Lumber imports, mainly from Canada, rose to 10,500,000,000 bd-ft, about 30% above 1976.

U.S. exports were down slightly from 1976. Plywood exports fell in the face of soft demand in Europe and a devaluation of the Canadian dollar that helped Canada get a bigger share of the business. Total 1977 consumption of softwood plywood was expected to top 19,000,000,000 sq ft (3/8-in basis), 14% above the preceding year.

The forest products industry was turning increasingly to wood-based waste as a partial answer to its energy needs. A growing number of companies were installing equipment to burn sawdust, bark, and other residues as fuel. By 1977 the paper industry had become about 45% energy self-sufficient, representing a saving of more than 100 million bbl of oil a year.

Historically, paper consumption in the U.S. has closely followed GNP, but in 1976 and 1977 consumption fell below this basic economic trend line. U.S. production of paper and paperboard in 1977 was expected to reach 62 million tons, surpassing the record 1974 output of 61 million tons. However, demand for different kinds of paper products varied widely. Consumption of coated paper used for magazines rose strongly, as did that of such products as tissues and disposable diapers, but demand for wrapping and packaging papers was soft. Operating results varied within the industry, with some companies registering record earnings while other companies experienced declines.

Woodpulp production, at more than 50 million tons in 1977, exceeded the record volume of the previous year, but sales were affected by a large worldwide pulp inventory. Most U.S. pulp is produced by companies that use it themselves to make paper and paperboard and so does not enter the commercial mainstream. Only about five million tons of market pulp were shipped by U.S. companies in 1977, and about four million tons were imported. U.S. companies exported about 2.8 million tons of market pulp in 1977, but they faced serious problems: the worldwide glut of pulp, foreign economies still sluggish from the global recession of 1974–75, and a 10% devaluation of the Swedish krona that made the price of Swedish market pulp even more competitive.

The U.S. forest products industry faced continued high costs in 1977, resulting from environmental regulations on the one hand and raw material supply problems resulting from federal land-use policies on the other. The paper industry was expected to spend $400 million for pollution-abatement equipment during the year. These costs were moving down as national clean water goals were met, but paper mills were under pressure to convert from oil and gas to coal, and this, together with increased outlays for safety measures, would raise both capital and operating costs. Meanwhile, several West Coast sawmills and plywood mills that bought timber from the national forests closed down, and others were put up for sale in the face of rising costs and unpredictable supply. The government was proposing that several million acres of national forest lands be set aside as wilderness areas where no more timber could be cut.

(TAIT TRUSSELL)

See also Agriculture and Food Supplies; Computers; Consumerism; Economy, World; Energy; Food Processing; Games and Toys; Industrial Relations; Materials Sciences; Mining and Quarrying; Photography; Television and Radio; Transportation.

The first half of a floating paper pulp processing plant was launched in Japan on September 1. When the other half of the plant is completed the two units will be towed to Brazil.

WIDE WORLD

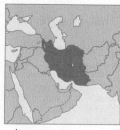

Iran

Iran

A constitutional monarchy of western Asia, Iran is bounded by the U.S.S.R., Afghanistan, Pakistan, Iraq, and Turkey and the Caspian Sea, the Arabian Sea, and the Persian Gulf. Area: 1,648,000 sq km (636,000 sq mi). Pop. (1976 census): 33,-591,900. Cap. and largest city: Teheran (pop. 1976 est., 4,002,000). Language: Farsi Persian. Religion (1972 est.): Muslim 98%; Christian, Jewish, and Zoroastrian minorities. Shah-in-shah, Mohammad Reza Pahlavi Aryamehr; prime ministers in 1977, Emir Abbas Hoveida and, from August 7, Jamshid Amouzegar.

Throughout 1977 the government, with the support of the Majles (Parliament), pressed ahead with the program of raising the living standards of the rural masses, in part by breaking up great estates and distributing land to the peasants. Communications by road and by air were systematically improved, and outlying parts of the country, which had formerly been ruled largely by local magnates, were brought under the control of the central government. The driving force behind all this progress was Shah Mohammad Reza Pahlavi, who personally supervised the activities of the government. Toward the end of 1976 and in February 1977 he effected the reorganization of the Cabinet to increase the technical expertise at its disposal; and on August 7, after Prime Minister Emir Abbas Hoveida had come under criticism for shortcomings in the electrical and other services, the shah appointed him minister in waiting and appointed as prime minister Jamshid Amouzegar (see BIOGRAPHY), who had championed Iran's interests at meetings of the Organization of Petroleum Exporting Countries (OPEC).

Some underground opposition to the regime continued, inspired partly by disgruntled vested interests, partly by the banned Tudeh Party, and partly by what the government described as "Islamic Marxists." There were several political assassinations and some abortive insurrectionary movements. (On September 13, the shah's sister, Princess Ashraf Pahlavi, escaped assassination when her car was fired upon near Cannes on the

French Riviera.) All opposition movements were defeated by the vigilance of the security agencies, which operated not only in Iran but also in some of the Iranian diplomatic missions abroad. This led to occasional difficulties with the host countries and aroused unfavourable comment in sections of the Western press, which accused the shah of violating human rights in his suppression of dissident elements. A Red Cross delegation, by invitation—the first such to be made—visited about 20

President and Mrs. Carter wipe tears from their eyes at a reception for the shah of Iran on the White House lawn on November 15. Tear gas that was being used to disperse demonstrators across the street wafted onto the lawn.

prisons holding 3,087 prisoners and made recommendations to the Iranian government.

Plans for the betterment of the people of Iran largely depended upon the financial strength derived from oil revenues. Two factors combined to threaten the adequacy of those revenues: the efforts of Western countries to diminish their dependence upon imported oil, and the higher prices that Iran, like other less developed countries, had to pay for essential imported goods and services because of widespread inflation in the Western world. Iran thus had been a leader among the OPEC countries favouring an increase in the price of oil to meet the changed situation. However, during a visit to the U.S. in November that included talks with U.S. Pres. Jimmy Carter (who returned the visit at year's end during his international tour), the shah told a press conference that Iran would actively oppose an oil price increase during the next year, and at the December OPEC meeting in Caracas, Venezuela, Iran joined Saudi Arabia in supporting a price freeze for 1978. A deficit in the Iranian budget was forecast in early 1977, and efforts were made to conclude trade agreements with Western countries that would allow payment in oil instead of cash. Nevertheless, in the U.S. and later in France, the shah emphasized his country's continuing need for Western goods.

Iran continued to play an important part in the stabilization of the areas that affected its interests. The shah's influence assisted the maintenance of improved relations between Afghanistan and Pakistan, and between Pakistan and India. Important steps were taken under the shah's inspiration to strengthen and improve the Regional Cooperation for Development, which linked Iran, Turkey, and Pakistan. A formal treaty between the three countries was signed in March in Teheran finalizing arrangements for the importation from the West of technical skills and modern machinery.

(L. F. RUSHBROOK WILLIAMS)

Iraq

A republic of southwestern Asia, Iraq is bounded by Turkey, Iran, Kuwait, Saudi Arabia, Jordan, Syria, and the Persian Gulf. Area: 437,522 sq km (168,928 sq mi). Pop. (1976 est.): 11,505,000, including Arabs, Kurds, Turks, Assyrians, Iranians, and others. Cap. and largest city: Baghdad (pop., 1975 est., 2,987,000). Language: Arabic. Religion: mainly Muslim, some Christian. President in 1977, Gen. Ahmad Hassan al-Bakr.

During 1977 Iraq's Baathist regime continued to oppose efforts by other Arab states to reach a negotiated settlement with Israel, but it showed special enmity toward the rival Baathist government in Syria. Internally there were signs of dissension within the Baath high command and also of troubles among the Kurdish and Shi'ah Muslim minorities.

The first regional congress of the Baath Party in three years was held in Baghdad in January, and the party leadership was increased from 13 to 21. On January 23 a major government reshuffle raised the number of Cabinet members from 30 to 40

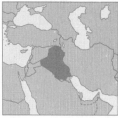

Iraq

IRAQ

Education. (1974–75) Primary, pupils 1,523,955, teachers 57,621; secondary, pupils 457,763, teachers 16,862; vocational, pupils 21,033, teachers 1,508; teacher training, students 8,540, teachers 306; higher, students 73,991, teaching staff 2,577.

Finance. Monetary unit: Iraqi dinar, with (Sept. 19, 1977) an official rate of 0.296 dinar to U.S. $1 (free rate of 0.515 dinar = £1 sterling). Gold, SDR's, and foreign exchange (June 1977) U.S. $5,361,600,000. Budget (1973–74 rev. est.): revenue 1,018,000,000 dinars; expenditure 698.9 million dinars (includes development expenditure of 244 million dinars). Gross national product (1975) 3,907,400,-000 dinars. Money supply (March 1977) 785.4 million dinars. Cost of living (Baghdad; 1970 = 100; April 1977) 165.

Foreign Trade. (1976) Imports 1,026,900,000 dinars; exports 2,621,200,000 dinars. Import sources (1975): Japan 18%; West Germany 18%; U.S. 9%; France 6%; U.K. 6%; Brazil 5%. Export destinations (1975): Italy 17%; France c. 11%; Brazil c. 6%; Turkey c. 5%; U.S.S.R. c. 5%; Spain c. 5%. Main export crude oil 98%. Tourism (1975): visitors 482,000; gross receipts U.S. $78 million.

Transport and Communications. Roads (1975) 11,859 km. Motor vehicles in use (1975): passenger 118,300; commercial 65,500. Railways: (1975) 1,955 km; traffic (1974–75) 645 million passenger-km, freight 1,871,000,000 net-ton-km. Air traffic (1975): 533 million passenger-km; freight 7.5 million net ton-km. Shipping (1976): merchant vessels 100 gross tons and over 87; gross tonnage 748,774. Telephones (Jan. 1976) 185,000. Radio receivers (Dec. 1974) 1,250,000. Television receivers (Dec. 1973) 520,000.

Agriculture. Production (in 000; metric tons; 1976): wheat c. 1,312; barley c. 579; rice 163; aubergines (1975) c. 117; cucumbers (1975) c. 140; watermelons (1975) c. 551; melons (1975) c. 180; tomatoes c. 422; dates c. 501; tobacco c. 6; cotton, lint (1975) c. 15. Livestock (in 000; 1976): sheep c. 16,517; goats c. 2,766; cattle c. 2,183; buffaloes c. 345; camels c. 338; horses c. 130; asses c. 607.

Industry. Production (in 000; metric tons; 1975): cement c. 1,800; crude oil (1976) 112,415; petroleum products c. 5,000; electricity (excluding most industrial production; kw-hr) c. 3,400.

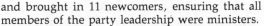

and brought in 11 newcomers, ensuring that all members of the party leadership were ministers.

Early in February there were serious disturbances within the Shi'ah Muslim community following the annual pilgrims' march from Najaf to Karbala. The government blamed Syrian agents for provoking the trouble. A special three-man tribunal, set up on February 23 under a prominent minister, Izzat Mustafa, to try those responsible, at once condemned 8 to death and 15 to life imprisonment. On March 23, however, Mustafa and a colleague were dismissed from all their posts, reportedly because other members of the Revolutionary Command Council (RCC) felt they had been insufficiently severe.

From January there were signs of renewed activity by a reorganized Kurdish Democratic Party. Kurdish partisans kidnapped some Polish specialists in December 1976 and some Frenchmen in February, but later released them. Kurdish émigré sources claimed that 300,000 Kurds had been forced to move to the south, although some had been allowed to return, and that 63 Kurdish villages had been destroyed.

Bad relations with Syria were exacerbated by the inauguration in January of a major oil pipeline to the Turkish port of Dortyol, bypassing Syria and depriving it of substantial revenues. Charges and countercharges of subversion were exchanged by the two regimes throughout the year. Support for the Palestinian hard-line "rejection front" was vigorously maintained, and some of its leaders visited

Baghdad in March. The Baath strong man and deputy chairman of the RCC, Saddam Hussein, visited Moscow from January 31 to February 2. There were tentative moves toward a rapprochement with the U.S., and in May U.S. Undersecretary of State Philip Habib became the first senior U.S. official to visit Baghdad in several years. However, the government later denied that renewal of relations with Washington was imminent.

To back up Iraq's policies in Arabia, the minister of the interior led a delegation to the Gulf states and Saudi Arabia in April, and the vice-president visited Somalia and the two Yemens in June. Iraq expressed strong support for Eritrean and Somali forces fighting Ethiopia. A visit to Iraq by the Kuwaiti minister of the interior, June 27–July 23, led to an agreement to settle the long-standing border dispute. Troops were withdrawn from both sides of the border, which was reopened on July 23. Iraq attended the Tripoli, Libya, meeting of hard-line Arab countries called in December to counter Egyptian Pres. Anwar as-Sadat's peace initiative toward Israel; however, the Iraqi delegation walked out before the conference ended in protest against its failure to adopt stronger measures. Subsequently, Egypt broke diplomatic relations with Iraq.

Oil output in the first quarter of 1977 averaged 1.7 million bbl a day, compared with a projected 2.4 million bbl a day. Iraq favoured a compromise in the oil-pricing dispute within the Organization of Petroleum Exporting Countries, and on June 29 it finally decided to forgo its further planned increase (from July 1) of 5% in oil export prices. The 1977 investment program of $7,990,000,000 represented a 58% increase over 1976, with the main allocations going to education (+84%) and social services (+90%).   (PETER MANSFIELD)

Ireland

Separated from Great Britain by the North Channel, the Irish Sea, and St. George's Channel, the Republic of Ireland shares its island with Northern Ireland to the northeast. Area: 70,283 sq km (27,-

Ireland

IRELAND

Education. (1975–76) Primary, pupils 550,078, teachers 18,023; secondary, pupils 267,141, teachers 15,555; vocational, pupils 3,814, teachers 217; higher, students 33,148, teaching staff 2,957.

Finance. Monetary unit: Irish pound, at par with the pound sterling, with a free rate (Sept. 19, 1977) of U.S. $1.74 = £1. Gold, SDR's, and foreign exchange (June 1977) U.S. $1,697,000,000. Budget (1976 actual): revenue £1,551 million; expenditure £2,042 million. Gross national product (1976) £4,420 million. Money supply (May 1977) £874.5 million. Cost of living (1970 = 100; May 1977) 250.

Foreign Trade. (1976) Imports £2,332.3 million; exports £1,857.3 million. Import sources: EEC 69% (U.K. 49%, West Germany 7%, France 5%); U.S. 8%. Export destinations: EEC 76% (U.K. 49%, West Germany 9%, The Netherlands 6%, France 5%); U.S. 7%. Main exports: machinery 12%; dairy products 11%; beef and veal 9%; chemicals 9%; textile yarns and fabrics 6%, livestock 6%. Tourism (1975): visitors 1,688,000; gross receipts U.S. $216 million.

Transport and Communications. Roads (1975) 89,006 km. Motor vehicles in use (1975): passenger 510,700; commercial 52,400. Railways: (1975) 2,006 km; traffic (1976) 739.3 million passenger-km, freight 523.4 million net ton-km. Air traffic (1976): 1,527,000,000 passenger-km; freight 74,810,000 net ton-km. Shipping (1976): merchant vessels 100 gross tons and over 96; gross tonnage 201,965. Telephones (Jan. 1976) 444,000. Radio licenses (Dec. 1974) 886,000. Television licenses (Dec. 1974) 550,000.

Agriculture. Production (in 000; metric tons; 1976): barley c. 973; wheat 216; oats c. 123; potatoes c. 1,280; sugar, raw value c. 184; cow's milk c. 4,300; butter c. 98; cheese c. 48; beef and veal c. 303; pork c. 115; fish catch (1975) 85. Livestock (in 000; June 1976): cattle 6,688; sheep c. 3,796; pigs c. 1,000; horses (1975) c. 94; chickens c. 9,711.

Industry. Production (in 000; metric tons; 1975): coal 48; cement 1,560; petroleum products c. 2,340; electricity (kw-hr; 1976) 8,190,000; manufactured gas (cu m) 277,000; beer (hl; 1973–74) c. 5,050; wool fabrics (sq m; 1973) 5,-000; rayon, etc., fabrics (sq m; 1972) 7,300.

136 sq mi), or 84% of the island. Pop. (1977 est.): 3,199,000. Cap. and largest city: Dublin (pop., 1971, 567,900). Language (1971): mostly English; 28% speak English and Irish or Irish only. Religion: 94% Roman Catholic. President in 1977, Patrick J. Hillery; prime ministers, Liam Cosgrave and, from July 5, John Lynch.

From early 1977 the dominant issue was the general election, variously predicted for spring, summer, and autumn. Thus it came as no great surprise when the prime minister, Liam Cos-

Canvas shrouds bullet holes in the car in which Seamus Costello, leader of the Marxist Irish Republican Socialist Party, was killed in October on a Dublin street.

Jack Lynch and his Fianna Fail party scored an upset election victory in June in Ireland.

grave, dissolved the Dail (parliament) on the evening of May 25 and fixed the election for June 16.

A comfortable victory for Cosgrave's National Coalition government was predicted throughout the campaign, which was waged mainly on inflation and job-creation issues. Handicapped by alleged internal divisions, by an uncertain performance in opposition, and by a careful drawing of the constituencies in favour of coalition candidates, the main opposition party, Fianna Fail, led by Jack Lynch, fought a hard, intelligent, and carefully prepared campaign. The party issued a detailed manifesto, with many specific promises, and also organized a countrywide campaign by the party leader, whose personal appeal was a major factor in the result.

The outcome was the most substantial reversal in Irish political history: Fianna Fail was returned to power with its biggest majority ever, while the National Coalition suffered a humiliating defeat. Fianna Fail gained a total of 84 seats; Fine Gael won 43; Labour captured 17; and there were four independents. Three outgoing ministers, Conor Cruise O'Brien (posts and telegraphs), Justin Keating (industry and commerce), and Patrick Cooney (justice), lost their seats. Cosgrave resigned as Fine Gael party leader, and Brendan Corish, who had been deputy prime minister, relinquished the leadership of the Labour Party. They were succeeded by Garret FitzGerald, the former foreign minister, who became Fine Gael leader and therefore leader of the opposition, and Frank Cluskey, who became leader of the Labour Party.

Prior to the general election, the prime minister had been consistently advised to delay the dissolution because of a likely upturn in the economy. It was debatable whether this would have any marked impact on an electorate that had witnessed unprecedented inflation during the National Coalition's term of office. Nevertheless, the economy did pull out of its deepest recession during the second half of the year, and there was an improvement in the employment figures and in the inflation rate.

The new administration immediately set about honouring its election promises, which included

an end to taxes on cars and to house rates (property taxes) and a general reduction in personal taxation. It was slower to announce plans for the creation of a promised 20,000 new jobs, and it postponed outlining its general economic development program until the end of the year. Political debate in the autumn centred around the crucial issue of how the government was to achieve the 5% wage ceiling on which its manifesto promises were based. In September the government announced the creation of a new Department of Tourism and Transport, to be headed by Patrick Faulkner, formerly minister for transport and power and for posts and telegraphs; he would remain minister for posts and telegraphs, but responsibility for power would be transferred to the Department of Industry and Commerce.

On September 28 Lynch met the British prime minister, James Callaghan, for general discussions covering Northern Ireland, the European Economic Community, and, particularly, fishing policy. There was no pressure on the British leader for a unilateral declaration of intent to withdraw from Northern Ireland. In a wider context, Garret FitzGerald, while foreign minister, visited the U.S. in March and obtained from the Carter administration assurances of support for Ireland's policy as regards Northern Ireland. Reports had been published in Ireland and the U.K. that a U.S. group supporting the Irish Republican Army (IRA) had gained access to high administration circles. At the same time, FitzGerald praised a statement issued by four prominent Irish-Americans, Senators Edward Kennedy of Massachusetts and Daniel Moynihan of New York, Gov. Hugh Carey of New York, and Thomas ("Tip") O'Neill, speaker of the House of Representatives, urging U.S. citizens not to give the IRA financial support.

In February Ireland claimed rights over economic resources within 200 mi of the uninhabited British island of Rockall in the North Atlantic, and the British Foreign Office agreed to arbitrate the dispute. The Irish claim, which was prompted by Great Britain's grant of permits for oil exploration in the area to two British firms, was based upon the legality of using uninhabited islands to claim an economic zone. Britain regarded Rockall as part of its continental shelf. (Denmark had already claimed fishing rights within the area.)

On April 17, William Cardinal Conway (*see* OBITUARIES), the Irish primate, died at Armagh at the age of 64. He was succeeded by Tomas O Fiaich (*see* BIOGRAPHY), president of the ecclesiastical college at Maynooth.   (BRUCE ARNOLD)

See also United Kingdom.

Israel

A republic of the Middle East, Israel is bounded by Lebanon, Syria, Jordan, Egypt, and the Mediterranean Sea. Area (not including territory occupied in the June 1967 war): 20,700 sq km (7,992 sq mi). Pop. (1977 est.): 3,590,700. Cap. and largest city: Jerusalem (pop., 1977 est., 366,300). Language: Hebrew and Arabic. Religion: predominantly Jewish (1976 est., 84.9%) with Muslim, Christian, and other minorities. President in 1977, Ephraim Katzir; prime ministers, Yitzhak Rabin and, from June 21, Menahem Begin.

The return to high office of Moshe Dayan with his Kissinger-like influence on the foreign policies of the new Begin administration marked the year 1977. Popular discontent with the domestic failures of the previous regime led to that government's downfall in the general election in May. However, it was the foreign policy of the Begin-Dayan administration that carried it to the crest of popularity by the end of the year, reaching a startling climax in the visit to Israel in November of Egypt's president, Anwar as-Sadat, and the subsequent Egyptian-Israeli negotiations. At the same time the government faced labour unrest over its New Economic Policy.

The year began with an impending general election. Yitzhak Rabin's government had resigned on Dec. 20, 1976, so that the date of the election could

be advanced from November 1977 to the early summer. On January 1 Rabin's deputy, Defense Minister Shimon Peres, announced that he would be a candidate for the Labour Party leadership at the party convention in February, and on January 3 the former foreign minister, Abba Eban, announced that he also would maintain his own candidacy for the Labour Party leadership. On the same day, the Labour Party was shocked when one of its stalwarts, Housing Minister Avraham Ofer, committed suicide after leaving a note accusing Israel's press and television of hounding him with unfounded rumours and charges that he had been guilty of financial improprieties.

Meanwhile, Israel's politicians, press, and public had another opportunity to engage in a reading of the political intentions of the new U.S. administration in Washington. In record time, Israel and U.S. Pres. Jimmy Carter went through the traditional gamut of emotions—high hope, qualification, crisis and disappointment, and, finally, understanding—not always helped by the heavy-handed intervention of Israel's friends in the U.S. or by vociferous expressions of the more extreme partisans of the new regime in Israel. Eventually these handicaps were overcome by the understanding that quickly developed between President Carter and Prime Minister Menahem Begin (*see* BIOGRAPHY) and, more especially, between Carter and Israel's foreign minister, Moshe Dayan. But between President Carter's inauguration in January and President Sadat's visit to Jerusalem in November, there were many traumatic moments in U.S.-Israeli relations.

As the year opened, however, it was strife within the Labour Party and the so-called financial scandals affecting some of its leading members that preempted the political stage. On February 14 Asher Yadlin, a pillar of the Labour establishment who had been nominated by Rabin to the vacant post of governor of the Bank of Israel, pleaded

Menahem Begin, leader of the Likud Party, applauds as returns show his party has defeated the ruling Labour Party in Israeli elections in May.

UPI COMPIX

Israel

guilty to charges of fraudulent misuse of the funds of the powerful and wealthy Histadrut Sick Fund. Yadlin claimed that the money had been diverted on instructions from leading figures of the Labour Party to help pay for the 1973 election campaign. This was denied, and on February 22 Yadlin received a five-year prison sentence. But though the judge did not believe Yadlin's defense, such a trial could not have come at a worse moment for Labour. The party's critical convention opened in Jerusalem on February 22 and, amid considerable tension, the leadership vote was taken the following day. Of 2,870 votes cast (of a possible 3,018), Rabin received 1,445, Peres 1,404, and 21 were blank. On March 7 Rabin was in Washington, making his first contact with the new president and his advisers.

The Washington talks went reasonably well, but as Rabin departed for home President Carter gave the first of a number of press conferences that disoriented the Israelis and the American Jewish leadership. The president formulated new ideas and restated old ones in an unfamiliar way. Moreover, partial and garbled texts in the Israeli media gave the impression that the U.S. was backtracking on its commitments to Israel. While the implications of Carter's remarks about a future peace settlement that would allow Israel a form of "defensible borders" beyond the recognized frontier were still being debated, Carter added yet another discomfiting formulation. Answering a question posed at a town meeting at Clinton, Mass., on March 16, the president said that, while the Palestinians must be prepared to recognize Israel, "there has to be a homeland provided for the Palestinian refugees who have suffered so many, many years." It was a phrase that was to haunt U.S.-Israeli diplomacy and public debate throughout the year.

It was almost midnight on April 7 when Rabin announced on Israel television that he was standing down from the leadership of the Labour Party and would relinquish the premiership because of the technical irregularity under which he and his wife had maintained a bank account in Washington. Under normal circumstances, he said, this would have been considered a minor matter, but he did not want it to have any repercussions on Labour's election chances. There was regret among the general public. Among the politicians there were signs of confusion, self-righteous pronouncements from Rabin's old associates, and talk of corruption from the opposition Likud. Peres reached an agreement with Foreign Minister Yigal Allon and with Eban that they would not contest his succession to the leadership.

In the early hours of May 18 the computer predictions of the election outcome were broadcast from Jerusalem. The confirmed results, which came later, bore out the awesome computer message: the Labour Party, which had ruled Israel since its establishment, had lost. The result was as follows (seats in the previous Knesset in parentheses): Likud 43 (39); Labour Alignment 32 (51); Yigael Yadin's Democratic Movement for Change (DMC) 15 (none); National Religious Party 12 (10); Torah Front 5 (5); Ariel Sharon's Shlomzion 2 (none); and Shmuel Flatto-Sharon 1 (none) (these last three supported Likud). Subsequently, Moshe Dayan resigned from the Alignment and remained in the Knesset as an independent member supporting the Likud government. In all, 1,771,726 votes were cast, representing 79.2% of the electorate. Likud received 33.4% of the vote; the Labour Alignment 24.6% (as against 40% in the last election), and the DMC 11.6%. The combined vote of the religious parties accounted for 14% of the votes cast. The Knesset approved the new government by 63 to 53 on June 21. Begin was the new prime minister; Simha Ehrlich, the minister of finance; Ezer Weizman, defense; and Moshe Dayan, foreign affairs. On October 24, following the decision of the DMC to join the coalition, the Knesset approved the appointment of four DMC ministers, of whom Yigael Yadin (see BIOGRAPHY) was deputy prime minister.

The Labour Alignment did better against the Likud assault on the Histadrut, the Trade Union Federation. In a nationwide election for the Histadrut Council on June 21, the Labour Alignment won 55.3% of the votes cast (58.3% at the last election); Likud won 28.2% (22.8%); the DMC, 8.2%; and the combined left-wing and Communist groups, 2.4%.

With the northern border on constant alert, in view of conditions in southern Lebanon and Israel's declared interest that the Christian villages near the border remain unmolested and that Palestine Liberation Organization or Syrian Army units

---

ISRAEL

Education. (1976–77) Primary, pupils 578,658, teachers 31,835; secondary, pupils 77,943, teachers 5,732; vocational, pupils 74,441, teachers 7,652; higher, students 74,371, teaching staff (1973–74) 13,981.

Finance. Monetary unit: Israeli pound, with (Sept. 19, 1977) a free rate of I£10.07 to U.S. $1 (free rate of I£17.54 = £1 sterling). Gold, SDR's, and foreign exchange (May 1977) U.S. $1,440,400,000. Budget (1976–77 est.) balanced at I£67,300 million. Gross national product (1976) I£95,317 million. Money supply (Dec. 1976) I£13,486 million. Cost of living (1970 = 100; June 1977) 499.

Foreign Trade. (1976) Imports I£46,087 million (including I£12,886 million military goods); exports I£19,388 million. Import sources: U.S. 22%; U.K. 16%; West Germany 10%; The Netherlands 6%. Export destinations: U.S. 18%; West Germany 8%; U.K. 8%; The Netherlands 7%; Hong Kong 6%; France 6%; Iran 5%. Main exports: diamonds 33%; chemicals 10%; citrus fruit 7%; machinery 7%; metal manufactures 6%; clothing 5%. Tourism (1975): visitors 559,000; gross receipts U.S. $234 million.

Transport and Communications. Roads (1974) 10,657 km. Motor vehicles in use (1975): passenger 287,300; commercial 96,100. Railways: (1976) 902 km; traffic (1974) 323 million passenger-km, freight 464 million net ton-km. Air traffic (1976): 4,020,000,000 passenger-km; freight 131,660,000 net ton-km. Shipping (1976): merchant vessels 100 gross tons and over 68; gross tonnage 481,594. Telephones (Dec. 1975) 813,000. Radio receivers (Dec. 1972) 680,000. Television receivers (Dec. 1974) 441,000.

Agriculture. Production (in 000; metric tons; 1976): wheat 203; barley (1975) 27; potatoes c. 170; peanuts 24; watermelons (1975) c. 109; tomatoes c. 210; onions c. 56; oranges c. 1,200; grapefruit c. 460; grapes c. 80; apples c. 80; olives c. 30; bananas c. 56; cotton, lint c. 52; fish catch (1975) 24. Livestock (in 000; 1975): cattle 300; sheep 197; goats 138; pigs c. 79; chickens c. 11,200.

Industry. Production (in 000; metric tons; 1976): cement 2,042; petroleum products (1975) c. 6,520; sulfuric acid 208; salt c. 117; potash (oxide content; 1974–75) c. 570; electricity (kw-hr) 10,344,000. New dwelling units completed (1975) 53,800.

It was a historic occasion as Egyptian Pres. Anwar as-Sadat addressed the Israeli Knesset on November 20. Knesset Speaker Yitzhak Shamir (right) listens intently to a translation.

Italy

Italian Literature:
see Literature

not come south of the Litani River, the focus of attention remained on the Begin government's standing in Washington. When he arrived in Washington on July 19 for his meeting with Carter, Begin had to overcome two preconceptions about himself: that of the Arab-hating Jewish terrorist widely publicized by a pro-Arab lobby and that of the all-wise, kindly, liberal Jewish father-figure, somewhat oversold by Begin's supporters and by Begin himself. In the event, Begin disarmed all but the most skeptical of critics. He agreed with Carter on the objectives of the much-discussed Geneva peace conference without unduly dwelling on the means of getting there. This was to be left to discussions between U.S. Secretary of State Cyrus Vance and Dayan and between Vance and the Arab foreign ministers when they met in New York in September for the UN General Assembly.

Within 24 hours of his return from Washington, however, Begin authorized the legalization of three Jewish settlements on the West Bank of the Jordan River. Suddenly all had changed. On August 4 the *Jerusalem Post* headlined its defense correspondent's account "War more likely than Geneva," and on August 10 it reflected the general misreading of U.S. intentions with a boldface "U.S. closes gap with Arabs in attempt to isolate Israel." On August 14 the Cabinet decided to extend current Israeli social services to the occupied West Bank and Gaza, again producing adverse comment from Washington and around the world. On August 25 Begin visited Romania but brought back few laurels, and it was left for Dayan to pick up the pieces when he met President Carter on September 19. Against a background of mutual U.S.-Israeli press recrimination, the two leaders produced an agreed working paper setting out terms for resumption of the Geneva conference, later approved by both the Cabinet and the Knesset.

It was more effective as a means of healing the threatening U.S.-Israeli rift than of bringing Arab leaders to Geneva, but it did open the way for

unexpected events in another quarter. In November President Sadat invited himself to Jerusalem and Begin proffered a welcoming hand; a formal invitation, approved by the Knesset on November 15, was sent and accepted; and on the evening of November 19 an Egyptian 707 with Sadat aboard touched down at Ben-Gurion Airport, to be greeted by thousands of Israelis waving Egyptian flags. Sadat spent his two nights in Israel at Jerusalem's King David Hotel, bombed by Begin's underground group in the days of the British mandate, and prayed at al-Aqsa Mosque on the Temple Mount, where King Abdullah of Jordan was assassinated in 1951 by an Arab fanatic for his "soft" attitude toward Israel.

The momentum continued as Sadat called a meeting at Cairo to prepare for Geneva, and on December 14 Egyptian and Israeli delegates began discussions, with the U.S. and the UN as observers. (The other front-line Arab states, the PLO, and the U.S.S.R. declined Sadat's invitation.) At the same time, Begin flew to the U.S. for a conference with Carter, arranged on short notice so that he could present his peace proposals. These included a phased return of the Sinai to Egypt and a form of civil autonomy for the West Bank and the Gaza Strip, but with Israel retaining a military presence. The proposals were later approved by the Knesset, in its longest session on record, but at a meeting between Sadat and Begin at Ismailia on December 25–26, Sadat reiterated his determination to secure complete self-determination for the Palestinians and the withdrawal of Israel from all occupied territories. The two leaders did agree to set up ministerial-level committees, which would open discussions early in the new year.

There was a feeling that the Middle East would not be the same again, but whether the change would be for better or worse was unclear. In the short term, the peace initiative did help to defuse escalation of incidents across the Lebanese border after the firing of rockets from PLO bases in the Lebanon into northern Galilee and Israel's reprisal air raids. But even the accompanying euphoria did not quite succeed in taking Israeli minds off the possible consequences of the New Economic Policy announced by Finance Minister Ehrlich on October 28, in effect a 44% devaluation accompanied by cuts in subsidies and a sharp increase in prices.

(JON KIMCHE)

Italy

A republic of southern Europe, Italy occupies the Apennine Peninsula, Sicily, Sardinia, and a number of smaller islands. On the north it borders France, Switzerland, Austria, and Yugoslavia. Area: 301,245 sq km (116,311 sq mi). Pop. (1977 est.): 56,324,700. Cap. and largest city: Rome (pop., 1977 est., 2,884,000). Language: Italian. Religion: predominantly Roman Catholic. President in 1977, Giovanni Leone; premier, Giulio Andreotti.

A new political pact between the Communist Party and the governing Christian Democrats, who had ruled Italy uninterruptedly since World

ITALY

Education. (1976–77) Primary, pupils 4,741,650, teachers 292,062; secondary, pupils 2,869,120, teachers 246,674; vocational, pupils 1,357,094, teachers 125,712; teacher training, students 201,023, teachers 18,921; higher, students 746,323, teaching staff (1974–75) 42,639.

Finance. Monetary unit: lira, with (Sept. 19, 1977) a free rate of 884 lire to U.S. $1 (1,540 lire = £1 sterling). Gold, SDR's, and foreign exchange (June 1977) U.S. $9,737,000,000. Budget (1976 actual): revenue 31,942,000,000,000 lire; expenditure 42,367,000,000,000 lire. Gross domestic product (1976) 142,128,000,000,000 lire. Money supply (March 1977) 80,300,000,000,000 lire. Cost of living (1970 = 100; June 1977) 236.

Foreign Trade. (1976) Imports 36,310,000,000,000 lire; exports 30,903,000,000,000 lire. Import sources: EEC 44% (West Germany 17%, France 14%, The Netherlands 5%); U.S. 8%; Saudi Arabia 6%. Export destinations: EEC 48% (West Germany 19%, France 15%, U.K. 5%); U.S. 6%. Main exports (1975): machinery 24%; motor vehicles 9%; chemicals 8%; iron and steel 7%; textile yarns and fabrics 6%;

petroleum products 5%; clothing 5%. Tourism (1975): visitors 13,234,000; gross receipts U.S. $3,258,000,000.

Transport and Communication. Roads (1974) 289,840 km (including 5,177 km expressways). Motor vehicles in use (1975): passenger 15,061,000; commercial 1,149,000. Railways: state (1975) 16,077 km, other (1974) 4,099 km; traffic (1976) 39,646,000,000 passenger-km, freight 16,673,000,000 net ton-km. Air traffic (1976): 10,780,000,000 passenger-km; freight 468,240,000 net ton-km. Shipping (1976): merchant vessels 100 gross tons and over 1,719: gross tonnage 11,077,549. Telephones (Jan. 1976) 14,496,000. Radio licenses (Dec. 1974) 12,641,000. Television licenses (Dec. 1974) 11,817,000.

Agriculture. Production (in 000; metric tons; 1976): wheat 9,528; corn 5,082; barley c. 760; oats 440; rice 976; potatoes 3,043; lettuce (1975) 777; cabbages (1975) 640; cauliflowers (1975) 611; onions 483; sugar, raw value 1,630; tomatoes 3,015; grapes 10,250; wine c. 6,500; olives 2,150; oranges 1,624; mandarin oranges and tangerines 355; lemons 817;

apples 2,048; pears (1975) 1,453; peaches (1975) 1,139; figs (1975) c. 123; tobacco c. 113; cheese c. 552; beef and veal c. 1,006; pork c. 790. Livestock (in 000; Jan. 1976): cattle c. 8,251; sheep c. 8,056; pigs c. 9,592; goats c. 958; poultry c. 110,000.

Industry. Index of production (1970 = 100; 1976) 122. Unemployment (1976) 3.7%. Fuel and power (in 000; metric tons; 1976): lignite 1,222; crude oil 1,108; natural gas (cu m) 15,370,000; manufactured gas (cu m) 3,508,000; electricity (kw-hr) c. 161,400,000. Production (in 000; metric tons; 1976): iron ore (44% metal content) 524; pig iron 11,889; crude steel 23,447; aluminum 213; lead 45; zinc 201; cement 36,323; cotton yarn 164; man-made fibres (1975) 396; fertilizers (nutrient content; 1975–76) nitrogenous 1,000, phosphate 370, potash 142; sulfuric acid 2,887; petroleum products (1975) 94,553; passenger cars (units) 1,469; commercial vehicles (units) 119. Merchant vessels launched (100 gross tons and over; 1976) 715,000 gross tons. New dwelling units completed (1976) 184,500.

War II, highlighted a year in which Italy enjoyed relative political stability under the premiership of Giulio Andreotti. At the same time, there was an alarming rise in street violence by students and political extremists, and the escape from a Rome military hospital of the Nazi war criminal Herbert Kappler caused international repercussions.

Domestic Affairs. By astute political maneuvering, Andreotti managed to survive, despite his apparently weak position as head of a minority Christian Democrat government. One reason was simply that no one could think of a better practical alternative. Although the right wing of the ruling party pressed for a new general election, the consensus among the two leading parties, the Christian Democrats and the Communists, was that new elections would do nothing to solve basic political problems. Local elections scheduled for November were postponed until the spring of 1978.

The early part of the year was taken up by delicate negotiations with the International Monetary Fund (IMF) for a $530 million standby loan to tide the country over its economic difficulties. The loan was finally signed in April, but Andreotti had to agree to conditions that severely limited his freedom of action in the political and economic fields. This was followed by negotiations between the party secretaries of the Christian Democrats and the Communists, together with the secretaries of four smaller parties that had been members of previous coalition governments (Socialists, Social Democrats, Republicans, and Liberals), for a joint-action program to tackle serious economic and social problems. The agreement came to fruition in July when Parliament approved a joint-action pact that brought the Communists nearer to government than at any time since the immediate post-World War II period.

One of the key sections of the agreement was the implementation of a devolution law transferring wide powers from the government in Rome to Italy's 20 regional administrations. From Jan. 1, 1978, control over funds for welfare, education, and health, plus many other social services, would

pass to local government. Since most regional and city administrations in the richer industrial half of the country were now run by Communist-led coalitions, many Christian Democrats vehemently opposed the idea that large funds, until now distributed according to a hallowed tradition of political patronage, would be handed over to the Communists. The devolution bill became law only after an 18-hour Cabinet session, the longest in the history of the Italian republic, on July 9–10.

A new abortion law that would have been one of the most liberal in Europe passed by a narrow majority in the Chamber of Deputies on January 21, but was defeated by an even narrower majority in the Senate on June 7. The Vatican organized a campaign of bitter opposition to the abortion bill, and a national referendum was due to be held on the subject in 1978. An agreement was reached between the Italian government and the Vatican for a revision of the Concordat signed between the Roman Catholic Church and Benito Mussolini in 1929. The Vatican agreed in principle to the ending of the church's special status and of certain fiscal

After the Italian government imposed a 40-day ban on demonstrations in Rome, radical groups erupted. A young woman was accidentally killed in this riot on May 13.

MARCELLI—SYGMA

Towns in northern Italy resembled Venice after floods hit the region in October. The town of San Zenone Po was flooded by the Po River.

privileges enjoyed under the old treaty. A referendum on the subject was proposed, also for 1978.

There was ferment in Italy's overcrowded universities. Rome University, built for 20,000 students but with an enrollment of almost 180,000, was closed three times during the academic year after serious street clashes between police and students. There were also riots in Bologna during March following the death of a left-wing student, allegedly shot by police although this was never proved. The students were protesting against unemployment and the failure of the government to implement promised teaching reforms. Terrorist activity by left-wing organizations and by the Mafia in Calabria also made news. The preservation of law and order became a priority for the government, which voted $100 million for improved riot-control equipment for the police. Over 60 major kidnappings were reported by the end of October, and police estimated that the equivalent of about U.S. $150 million in ransom had been paid by victims' families. The courts faced a backlog of over two million cases, and more than half the prison population were awaiting trial.

On October 6 freak rainstorms hit northwestern Italy, causing 18 deaths and hundreds of million of dollars' worth of damage to property and communications. Hundreds of square miles of land in the Po Valley were flooded.

Foreign Affairs. In the hope of ensuring continued financial help, Premier Andreotti visited Bonn in January to reassure the West German government of his country's stability. West Germany was a major participant in both the IMF loan and a European Economic Community (EEC) loan.

Widespread anti-German feeling erupted following the escape of the Nazi war criminal Her-

bert Kappler from the Celio Military Hospital in Rome on August 15. Kappler had been sentenced to life imprisonment in 1948 for the 1944 Ardeatine Caves massacre, in which 335 Italians were shot by German troops. A scheduled meeting in Italy between Andreotti and the West German chancellor, Helmut Schmidt, was canceled, and relations between the two governments became tense when Bonn rejected an Italian request to extradite Kappler, who had fled to West Germany. Kappler had been taken to the hospital from prison because he was said to be dying of cancer, but in the course of official inquiries into the escape doubts were expressed about the true state of his health. The Italian defense minister, Vito Lattanzio, who had been responsible for the security of Italy's last war criminal but one (Walter Reder, an Austrian subject, remained in detention), was transferred to another ministry. In October further anti-German demonstrations took place all over Italy following the reported suicides of members of the Baader-Meinhof terrorist group in a West German prison.

The first official visit by a Spanish monarch to Italy in over 50 years took place February 9, when King Juan Carlos and Queen Sofia of Spain arrived in Rome. Their visit was followed later in the year by that of the Spanish premier, Adolfo Suárez, who tried to gain Italian support for Spain's entry into the EEC. U.S. Vice-Pres. Walter Mondale spent a day in Rome in January during his European tour. In July Andreotti returned his visit and was received by Pres. Jimmy Carter. The British prime minister, James Callaghan, paid an official visit to Italy in September.

The Economy. The Italian economy was dominated by the aftermath of the 1976 lira crisis, during which the currency suffered a 30% devaluation. The government relaxed some of the stiffer emergency measures imposed to protect the lira but was forced to introduce other price, money, and tax controls to keep the lira stable. In the event, the lira held up well against the dollar, helped by a big increase in tourist receipts during the summer, but there were signs of a new recession.

A reduction in consumption was reflected by a 7.7% decline in industrial production in July, the first in two years, and there were indications that the downward trend continued in August and September. The trade unions and employers pressed the government to reflate the economy, but the government's hands were tied by the conditions imposed by the IMF, including strict limits on public expenditure and the amount of credit to be granted in industry. Andreotti also had to promise to try to bring the inflation rate down to 12% by March 1978. Economists felt it was unlikely that the government would be able to stick to the exact limits laid down in its "letter of intent" if the estimated growth rate of 2% was to be achieved in the current year.

Official Italian unemployment statistics had long been suspect because they failed to take underemployment into account. In 1977 the government Central Statistical Agency (ISTAT) revised the base for computing such figures and estimated current unemployment at 1.7 million, or 8% of the labour force; 75% of the jobless were under the age of 30.

The balance of payments figures improved dramatically in comparison with 1976, partly because of increased borrowing abroad and partly because of the increased value of exports. Currency reserves reached a record $7,140,000,000. Measures were introduced to stimulate stock exchange investment after the Milan bourse index touched an all-time low.   (DAVID DOUGLAS WILLEY)

In April thousands of angry Italian feminists gathered and raised their hands in the "woman" symbol outside the Palace of Justice in Rome where seven youths were on trial for raping a young woman. All the defendants were found guilty; three received jail sentences of three to four years and the others received suspended sentences.

UPI COMPIX

Ivory Coast

Ivory Coast

A republic on the Gulf of Guinea, the Ivory Coast is bounded by Liberia, Guinea, Mali, Upper Volta, and Ghana. Area: 322,463 sq km (124,504 sq mi). Pop. (1975 census): 6,714,000. Cap. and largest city: Abidjan (pop., 1975, 685,800). Language: French (official) and local dialects (Akan 41%, Kru 17%, Voltaic 16%, Malinke 15%, Southern Mande 10%). Religion: animist 65%; Muslim 23%; Christian 12%. President and premier in 1977, Félix Houphouët-Boigny.

On July 20, 1977, Pres. Félix Houphouët-Boigny announced Cabinet changes, and nine ministers were dismissed. A few days later the president donated all his coffee and cocoa plantations to the country, to set an example in the campaign against official corruption.

A spectacular economic recovery took place during the year, with coffee and cocoa reaching record production levels of 308,000 and 300,000 metric tons, respectively. The high world price of those commodities led to a trading surplus of approximately CFA Fr 10 million. Forestry and cotton and rice cultivation flourished in the north, and indications that there might be petroleum deposits raised hopes of an "economic miracle." Of the country's 122,000 visitors in 1976, 44% were businessmen attracted by its economic possibilities; the construction of an urban subway at Abidjan was even discussed.

The country's political stability contrasted with conditions in neighbouring states. Student agitation at Abidjan cast the only shadow and required the president's intervention, notably in January.

Committed to encouraging dialogue between adversaries, Houphouët-Boigny sought to establish grounds of agreement in the Middle East. In January he met with Issam Sartoui, emissary of Palestinian leader Yasir Arafat, and in February with Israeli Prime Minister Yitzhak Rabin.

   (PHILIPPE DECRAENE)

IVORY COAST
  Education. (1975–76) Primary, pupils 681,735, teachers (1974–75) 14,403; secondary, pupils 102,500, teachers (1974–75) 3,959; vocational (1974–75), pupils 8,165, teachers 620; higher, students 6,274, teaching staff (1973–74) 368.
  Finance. Monetary unit: CFA franc, with (Sept. 19, 1977) a parity of CFA Fr 50 to the French franc (free rate of CFA Fr 246.50 = U.S. $1; CFA Fr 429.50 = £1 sterling). Gold, SDR's, and foreign exchange (May 1977) U.S. $416.7 million. Budget (1976 est.) balanced at CFA Fr 140.2 billion. Money supply (April 1977) CFA Fr 321,720,000,000. Cost of living (Abidjan; 1970 = 100; June 1977) 222.
  Foreign Trade. (1976) Imports CFA Fr 311,610,000,000; exports CFA Fr 392.5 billion. Import sources: France 38%; U.S. 7%; West Germany 7%; Japan 5%. Export destinations: France 25%; The Netherlands 13%; U.S. 10%; Italy 9%; West Germany 7%. Main exports: coffee 34%; cocoa 24%; timber 20%.
  Agriculture. Production (in 000; metric tons; 1976): rice c. 450; corn (1975) c. 100; millet c. 50; yams (1975) c. 1,700; cassava (1975) c. 620; peanuts c. 45; bananas c. 210; pineapples c. 250; palm kernels c. 40; palm oil c. 176; coffee c. 270; cocoa c. 190; cotton, lint c. 26; rubber c. 19; timber (cu m; 1975) c. 9,350. Livestock (in 000; 1975): cattle c. 500; sheep c. 980; goats c. 980; pigs c. 200; poultry c. 6,600.

Jai Alai:
see Court Games

Jamaica

Japan

Jamaica

A parliamentary state within the Commonwealth of Nations, Jamaica is an island in the Caribbean Sea about 90 mi S of Cuba. Area: 10,991 sq km (4,244 sq mi). Pop. (1977 est.): 2,085,200, predominantly Negro, but including Europeans, Chinese, Indians, and persons of mixed race. Cap. and largest city: Kingston (pop., 1974 est., 169,800). Language: English. Religion: Christian, with Anglicans and Baptists in the majority. Queen, Elizabeth II; governor-general in 1977, Florizel Glasspole; prime minister, Michael Manley.

The People's National Party (PNP), which had already won the general election of December 1976, had an even more sweeping success in the local elections of March 1977, winning control of all 13 of the island's parishes and 68% of the votes. The war of words between right and left con-

tinued, with the Castro-Communist bogey being kept alive by the *Daily Gleaner* to counter Manley's "democratic socialism." The issue also flared up within the ruling PNP, where right-wingers in September forced the resignation of a leading young leftist, D. K. Duncan. In October, Cuban Pres. Fidel Castro's twice-postponed visit to Jamaica took place. Cuban-Jamaican cooperation grew during the year; at the same time, U.S. relations with Jamaica were becoming more cordial.

Jamaica's economy remained in severe straits, but international funds began to flow again, at the price of a substantial devaluation of the Jamaican dollar and a pledge of domestic economic restraint. The state of public emergency imposed in 1976 was lifted in June. The government took over three banks and 51% of Kaiser Bauxite and Reynolds Jamaica Mines. The country's first prime minister, Sir Alexander Bustamante (*see* OBITUARIES), died on August 6.   (SHEILA PATTERSON)

JAMAICA

Education. (1976–77) Primary, pupils 367,525, teachers 10,002; secondary, pupils 213,621, teachers 8,377; vocational, pupils 5,321, teachers 355; teacher training, students 6,017, teachers 291; higher, students 10,305, teaching staff (1973–74) 638.

Finance and Trade. Monetary unit: Jamaican dollar, with (Sept. 19, 1977) a par value for essential imports of Jam$0.91 to U.S. $1 (free rate of Jam$1.58 = £1 sterling) and for other imports, exports, and tourism of Jam$1.25 to U.S. $1 (free rate of Jam$2.18 = £1 sterling). Gold, SDR's, and foreign exchange (June 1977) U.S. $49 million. Budget (1976–77 est.): revenue Jam$645,871,000; expenditure Jam$1,063,113,000.

Foreign Trade. (1976) Imports Jam$850.5 million; exports Jam$547.5 million. Import sources: U.S. 37%; Venezuela 14%; U.K. 11%; Canada 6%; Netherlands Antilles 6%. Export destinations: U.S. 43%; U.K. 17%; Norway 12%; Sweden 5%. Main exports: alumina 43%; bauxite 23%; sugar 9%. Tourism (1975): visitors 396,000; gross receipts U.S. $133 million.

Agriculture. Production (in 000; metric tons; 1976): sugar, raw value c. 379; bananas c. 140; oranges c. 40; grapefruit c. 30; sweet potatoes (1975) c. 21; yams (1975) c. 134; cassava (1975) c. 15; corn (1975) c. 10; copra c. 6. Livestock (in 000; 1975): cattle c. 280; goats c. 300; pigs c. 233; poultry c. 3,841.

Industry. Production (in 000; metric tons; 1976): bauxite 10,310; cement 365; petroleum products (1975) 1,484; electricity (kw-hr; 1975) 2,331,000.

Cuban-Jamaican relations improved after Cuba's Fidel Castro (right) visited Jamaica in October. Jamaican Prime Minister Michael Manley applauds Castro's speech on arrival.

WIDE WORLD

Japan

A constitutional monarchy in the northwestern Pacific Ocean, Japan is an archipelago composed of four major islands (Hokkaido, Honshu, Kyushu, and Shikoku), the Ryukyus (including Okinawa), and minor adjacent islands. Area: 377,582 sq km (145,785 sq mi). Pop. (1977 est.): 113,860,000. Cap. and largest city: Tokyo (pop., 1977 est., 8,568,700). Language: Japanese. Religion: primarily Shinto and Buddhist; Christian 0.8%. Emperor, Hirohito; prime minister in 1977, Takeo Fukuda.

Domestic Affairs. The general election for the (lower) House of Representatives in December 1976 marked the end of more than 20 years of uninterrupted majority-party rule by the Liberal-Democratic Party (LDP). As a result of the election the party standings in the lower house were as follows (pre-election strengths in parentheses): LDP 249 (265), Japan Socialists (JSP) 123 (112), Komeito 55 (30), Democratic Socialists (DSP) 29 (19), Japan Communists (JCP) 17 (39), New Liberals 17 (5), independents 21 (4), vacancies 0 (17); total 511 (491). Although the number of seats had been increased to 511 by a revision of the election law, only the support of some of the independents allowed the LDP to form a Cabinet. In the Diet the LDP faced for the first time the problems of coalition politics in the various committees.

On Dec. 23, 1976, Takeo Fukuda (*see* BIOGRAPHY) was chosen president of the LDP to succeed Takeo Miki, whose Cabinet resigned on December 24. Fukuda was elected Japan's 13th postwar prime minister at a plenary session of the (lower) House of Representatives and (upper) House of Councillors on the afternoon of December 24. That evening the Fukuda Cabinet was inaugurated, with more than one-third of those appointed to the 20 Cabinet posts given portfolios for the first time. A junior upper house member, Iichiro Hatoyama, held the key post of foreign minister. Hideo Bo became the finance minister and Tatsuo Tanaka the minister of international trade and industry. Almost immediately the LDP began preparations for the upper house election, scheduled for July.

Meanwhile, the Lockheed scandal, which had so adversely affected the LDP during 1976, began to reach a climax in the courts. On Jan. 21, 1977, the Tokyo district prosecutor's office announced the indictment of Yoshio Kodama, a wealthy ultrarightist, on charges of tax evasion and violation of foreign exchange regulations in connection with the Lockheed case. This brought to an end the year-old preliminary investigation.

On January 27, in the Tokyo district court, former prime minister Kakuei Tanaka pleaded innocent at his first hearing, essentially denying that he had accepted 500 million yen from Lockheed to influence favourably Japan's purchase of aircraft. Toshio Enomoto, his former secretary, and three former executives of the Marubeni company (representing Lockheed) also issued denials. The prosecution, however, made a formidable case with its list of dates, times, places, and names. On June 2 Kodama emerged from 16 months of seclusion to attend his first hearing and denied charges of bribery. Kenji Osano, a wealthy transport and real estate figure, became the 17th and last defendant when he was brought to trial on July 21. All proceedings promised to be lengthy.

On January 13 the new Cabinet approved estimates of 28,510,000,000,000 yen (U.S. $95 billion) for the 1977 fiscal budget. This was 17% higher than the budget of the previous year, and placed priority on expansion of the economy through public works projects and record borrowing. On March 10 LDP secretary Masayoshi Ohira reached a compromise with opposition parties, which resulted in an additional income tax cut of 300 billion yen and special welfare grants of 63 billion yen.

Nonetheless, the Cabinet had a struggle to obtain an extension of the 80th regular Diet just a few hours before it was due to expire on May 28. When the Diet adjourned on June 9 it had to pass along to the next session such important bills as the increase in Japan National Railway fares and development of resources on the continental shelf between Japan and Korea. The legislature thus witnessed a significant shift from "LDP-opposition confrontation" to "compromise through talk."

A grim-faced Kakuei Tanaka, former prime minister of Japan, arrives at the Tokyo District Court in January to answer charges concerning his involvement in the Lockheed payoff scandal.

All parties cited the approaching critical election for the upper house as the reason for not remaining in session any longer. In May some 100 scholars, novelists, artists, and television actors announced formation of the new United Progressive Liberal (UPL) party. Its first two candidates were Moeko Tawara, 46, a women's liberation leader, and Takeshi Nakamura, 68, a popular novelist and crusader on housing problems. Formal campaigning for the 11th Councillors election opened in rainy weather on June 17, with the UPL and another new political group, the Socialist Citizens League (SCL), entering the race. In the election

JAPAN

Education. (1975–76) Primary, pupils 10,364,846, teachers 415,071; secondary, pupils 7,488,201; vocational, pupils 1,655,275; secondary and vocational, teachers 463,054; higher (including 40 main national universities), students 2,057,986, teaching staff 105,-314.

Finance. Monetary unit: yen, with (Sept. 19, 1977) a free rate of 268 yen to U.S. $1 (467 yen = £1 sterling). Gold, SDR's, and foreign exchange (June 1977) U.S. $16.1 billion. Budget (1976–77 est): revenue 26,026,000,000,000 yen; expenditure 33,-505,000,000,000 yen. Gross national product (1976) 164,470,000,000,000 yen. Money supply (May 1977) 53,291,000,000,000 yen. Cost of living (1970 = 100; June 1977) 204.

Foreign Trade. (1976) Imports 19,229,000,-000,000 yen; exports 19,930,000,000,000 yen. Import sources: U.S. 18%; Saudi Arabia 12%; Australia 8%; Iran 7%; Indonesia 6%. Export destinations: U.S. 24%; South Korea 4%. Main exports: machinery 25% (telecommunications apparatus 7%); iron and steel 18%; motor vehicles 18%; ships 10%; chemicals 8%; instruments 6%; textile yarns and fabrics 6%.

Transport and Communications. Roads (1975) 1,067,643 km (including 1,615 km expressways). Motor vehicles in use (1975): passenger 17,236,000; commercial 10,651,000. Railways: (1974) 28,024 km; traffic (1976) 321,100,000,000 passenger-km, freight 47,851,000,000 net ton-km. Air traffic (1976): 18,674,000,000 passenger-km; freight 1,004,500,000 net ton-km. Shipping (1976): merchant vessels 100 gross tons and over 9,748; gross tonnage 41,663,188. Telephones (March 1976) 45,515,000. Radio receivers (Dec. 1972) 70,794,000. Television licenses (Dec. 1975) 25,832,000.

Agriculture. Production (in 000; metric tons; 1976): rice 15,292; wheat c. 222; barley c. 210; potatoes c. 3,200; sweet potatoes (1975) 1,418; sugar, raw value (1975) 464; onions c. 1,030; shallots (1975) c. 610; tomatoes c. 1,165; cabbages (1975) c. 3,700; cucumbers c. 1,000; aubergines (1975) 650; watermelons (1975) c. 1,200; apples c. 900; pears (1975) c. 499; mandarin oranges and tangerines 3,-938; grapes c. 314; tea c. 105; tobacco c. 171; milk c. 5,307; eggs 1,815; pork c. 1,077; timber (cu m; 1975) 36,548; fish catch (1975) 10,508; whales (number; 1974–75) 9.4. Livestock (in 000; Feb. 1976):

cattle c. 3,700; sheep c. 10; pigs c. 8,000; goats c. 100; chickens c. 245,000.

Industry. Index of production (1970 = 100; 1976) 125. Fuel and power (in 000; metric tons; 1976): coal 18,396; crude oil 580; natural gas (cu m) 2,813,000; manufactured gas (cu m) 6,500,000; electricity (kw-hr; 1975–76) 475,794,000. Production (in 000; metric tons; 1976): iron ore (54% metal content) 770; pig iron 88,612; crude steel 107,383; petroleum products (1975) c. 205,300; cement 68,712; cotton yarn 498; woven cotton fabrics (sq m) 2,237,000; man-made fibres 1,621; sulfuric acid 6,103; fertilizers (nutrient content; 1975–76) nitrogenous 1,557, phosphate 585; cameras (35 mm; units) 5,447; wrist watches (units) 34,001; radio receivers (units) 16,771; television receivers (units) 15,103; passenger cars (units) 5,028; commercial vehicles (units) 2,814; motorcycles (units) 4,235. Merchant vessels launched (100 gross tons and over; 1976) 14,524,000 gross tons. New dwelling units started (1976) 1,719,000.

In an attempt to prevent the opening of a new international airport near Tokyo, student radicals burn automobile tires near the runway.

held on July 10 (for half the house seats) the LDP managed to maintain a razor-thin majority in the upper house by winning 63 seats and then adding 3 pro-LDP independents to its roster. In the national constituency, once again the LDP share of the popular vote was further eroded to 18,160,060 (35.8%), down from the 23,332,773 votes (44.3%) that it received in 1974. When the results of individual contests for the upper house were tallied, notable shifts in party strengths were evident. The following figures indicate the number of contested seats won by the various parties, their new totals, and in parentheses their pre-election strengths: LDP 63, 124 (126); JSP 26, 55 (61); Komeito 14, 28 (24); JCP 4, 15 (20); DSP 6, 11 (10); New Liberals 3, 4 (1); SCL 1, 1 (0); UPL 1, 1 (0); independents 8, 12 (7). In all, 126 of the 252 upper house seats were contested, but one of the three pre-election vacancies was not filled; as a consequence, the total number of active members in the upper house stood at 251 when the election results were posted.

The opposition parties (JSP, JCP, Komeito) lost their coalition majority in the Tokyo Metropolitan assembly as conservatives (LDP, NLC) took control. Long-time governor Ryokichi Minobe, 73, announced that he would not stand in the 1979 election. As a result of the poor JSP showing in both elections, Secretary Masashi Ishibashi and three Diet members bolted the party on September 27. On the following day the strife-torn JSP wound up its 41st regular convention by leaving Tomomi Narita as its caretaker party chairman.

Prime Minister Fukuda, noted for his economic skill, spent most of 1977 fighting a stubborn recession. Effective March 12, the Bank of Japan cut the official discount rate from 6.5 to 6% as part of a package to stimulate business. The rate of inflation, however, kept pace, and the official discount rate was further reduced to 5% on April 18 and to 4.25% on September 4. The nation's consumer price index (CPI) rose 0.6% in March, a total of 9.4% for fiscal year 1976–77, thus frustrating the government's effort to hold down the annual rate to 8.6%. In April the CPI for Tokyo was 8.4% above the level of the previous year. Unemployment totaled over one million (2.4% of the labour force) in March, the highest recorded since 1959.

In fiscal 1976–77 Japan's gross national product (GNP) rose by 5.8% over the previous year, to a total of 98,678,200,000,000 yen ($329 billion), thus exceeding the government target of 5.7%. On September 6 Fukuda proposed a 2,000,000,000,000 yen supplementary budget, designed to achieve a promised 6.7% rise in the GNP for fiscal 1977. Buoyed by public works spending, the increase in GNP for the second quarter (through September) was running at an inflation-adjusted annual rate of 7.6%. Of greater concern to Japan's trading partners, however, was the state of the nation's foreign exchange reserves, which by the end of April reached $17,317,000,000.

On November 28, in an effort to stabilize Japan's economy, Fukuda announced a major revision of his Cabinet. Nobuhiko Ushiba was named to the new post of minister for external economic affairs; Toshio Komoto was appointed minister for international trade and industry; Tatsuo Murayama became finance minister; and Sunao Sodona was given the post of foreign minister. In mid-December, when Ushiba visited the U.S., Japan pledged to boost its growth by 7% during the next fiscal year to stimulate demand for foreign goods; it also agreed to increase quotas for certain imported goods and reduce tariffs on others—"the maximum possible concession at this time." But U.S. negotiators insisted this was not enough to rectify the situation created by Japan's estimated $16 billion trade surplus for the year.

The Fukuda government was also plagued by a series of terrorist activities. On March 4 four armed men surrendered after occupying a Tokyo office of the Federation of Economic Organizations (*Keidanren*). These right-wing terrorists were former members of the Tatenokai, a private army organized by Yukio Mishima (the writer who committed ritual suicide in 1970). On May 6 violence again occurred at Narita, the site of the new Tokyo international airport, when authorities in a surprise action demolished steel towers that had been erected by left-wing youths to block the runways. Meanwhile, terrorist activity assumed international importance.

Foreign Affairs. On September 28 a Japan Air Lines (JAL) DC-8, on a flight from Paris to Tokyo, was hijacked over India by five Japanese Red Army members and ordered to land at Dacca, Bangladesh. After negotiations, the plane flew to Kuwait and then to Algiers on October 3. The next day, having received $6 million in ransom and having welcomed six comrades released from jail in Tokyo, the hijackers surrendered to Algerian authorities and were removed to an undisclosed destination. All passenger-hostages were released.

Questions of trade dominated Japan's relations with its chief partner, the U.S. On January 30 U.S. Vice-Pres. Walter Mondale arrived in Tokyo to initiate the first contact between the Carter administration and the Fukuda government. Mondale said the U.S. president wanted Japan to know that close ties with Japan were one of the cornerstones of his administration and that a satisfactory handling of international financial problems depended on this relationship. The governments agreed that Fukuda would visit Washington in March and that there was a need for a third global summit conference of advanced nations in May. Mondale also asked for voluntary restraints on Japan's exports. In a joint communiqué issued after their meeting in Washington, Fukuda and Carter recognized a responsibility to reinvigorate the economies of the "three engine countries" (U.S., Japan, West Germany). There was, however, disagreement over Japan's program for developing nuclear energy. Whereas Carter emphasized the need to restrict the spread of technology that could lead to the production of nuclear weapons, Fukuda pointed out that Japan had signed the nuclear non-proliferation treaty of 1976 and that nuclear power would help solve its problem of oil imports. Carter promised to give "full consideration" to Japan's energy needs.

On June 11 former U.S. senator Mike Mansfield presented his credentials as the 22nd U.S. ambassador to Japan. Asked about U.S.-Japan relations during his first Tokyo press conference, he said there was "no junior partnership between our two countries," and was confident that a settlement of the nuclear issue would be reached. In his first public speech on July 24, he warned that the $5 billion U.S. trade deficit vis à vis Japan was "a disturbing figure" and provided "much ammunition to the advocates of protectionism." On August 27 U.S. Secretary of State Cyrus Vance and Japan's Foreign Minister Hatoyama reaffirmed that their respective countries were striving to resolve the nuclear dispute. On September 1, Gerard Smith, representing Carter on a visit to Tokyo, provisionally approved a two-year demonstration operation of the Tokai nuclear reprocessing plant.

On September 12 in Tokyo Richard Cooper of the U.S. State Department again called on Japan to reduce its current account surplus, estimated at $6 billion–$7 billion. Later in September U.S. Steel Corp. filed a complaint in Washington against alleged dumping of steel products by six Japanese manufacturers. The U.S. Treasury Department decided to proceed with an investigation, but the International Trade Ministry in Tokyo agreed to cut back on steel exports to the U.S. if the dumping complaint was withdrawn.

Another major issue between the two nations arose over the question of diplomatic security and involved the U.S., Japan, and the Republic of Korea. Regarding the withdrawal of U.S. troops from South Korea, Mondale explained during his visit to Japan that Carter's campaign promise would be carried out only after "close consultation" with Seoul and Tokyo. At the March summit meeting in Washington, Carter reassured Fukuda that the U.S. intended to maintain a "balanced and flexible military presence" in the Western Pacific. Similar assurances were given on May 30 by Gen. George Brown of the Joint Chiefs of Staff, and on July 27 by Secretary of Defense Harold Brown in Tokyo.

On September 5 Japan and South Korea opened their ninth ministerial conference in Tokyo to discuss the U.S. plans for troop withdrawal, Japanese economic assistance to South Korea, and an accord

for development of the continental shelf that lies between the two countries. Tokyo was reluctant to appear openly pro-Seoul because of Korean CIA activities in Japan and because of U.S. criticism of Pres. Park Chung Hee and his regime.

After three months of hard bargaining, Japan and the U.S.S.R. signed a bilateral fisheries agreement on May 27 covering operations within the Soviet 200-mi coastal zone. Tokyo accepted a severely limited 455,000-ton catch quota for a period of six months. On June 20, however, Fukuda declined Soviet Communist party leader Leonid Brezhnev's proposal for a treaty of friendship because it would have ignored Japan's claims to the "northern territories" (islands off Hokkaido held by the U.S.S.R. since World War II). During the year Japan did not move much closer to a Sino-Japanese treaty of peace, despite the fact that diplomatic relations with Peking had been normalized in 1972. Negotiations toward a treaty remained stalled over Peking's insistence on an "antihegemony" clause (not too subtly aimed at the U.S.S.R.). On August 9 Fu Hao became China's second envoy posted to Tokyo.

Fukuda concluded a 13-day, six-nation tour of Southeast Asia by announcing the "Fukuda Doctrine" in Manila on August 18. The statement contained three principles: the determination of Japan to remain pacifist, to foster mutual trust among Southeast Asian nations, and to cooperate with them as mutual partners. On August 7, in Kuala Lumpur, Malaysia, Fukuda pledged $1 billion in assistance for joint industrial projects with the Association of Southeast Asian Nations (ASEAN). The previous day he had called for peaceful coexistence between non-Communist ASEAN nations and Indochinese Communist countries.

Effective July 1, Japan expanded its territorial sea from 3 to 12 mi and established a 200-mi exclusive fishery zone off its coast. Excluded were international straits between Honshu and Hokkaido (Tsugaru), between Japan and South Korea (Tsushima), and between Hokkaido and Sakhalin (Soya).   (ARDATH W. BURKS)

Jordan

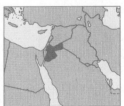

Jordan

A constitutional monarchy in southwest Asia, Jordan is bounded by Syria, Iraq, Saudi Arabia, and Israel. Area (including territory occupied by Israel in the June 1967 war): 95,396 sq km (36,833 sq mi). Pop. (1976 est.): 2,779,000. Cap. and largest city: Amman (pop., 1976 est., 691,100). Language: Arabic. Religion (1961): Muslim 94%; Christian 6%. King, Hussein I; prime minister in 1977, Mudar Badran.

In 1977 Jordan continued to enjoy internal stability and considerable economic prosperity despite serious inflation, but the king and his government remained pessimistic about the prospects of a Middle East settlement and about the dangers of a new Arab-Israeli war. Some steps were taken toward a reconciliation between the regime and the Palestine Liberation Organization (PLO). In January King Hussein received a delegation led by the Palestine National Council chairman, who returned in February with other PLO officials. In March the king had a meeting with PLO chairman Yasir Arafat during the Afro-Arab summit conference in Cairo, but a later projected visit by Arafat to Jordan did not take place.

In policy statements King Hussein stood by Jordan's commitment to the Arab decision to recognize the PLO as the sole legitimate representative of the Palestinians, and he publicly differed with Pres. Anwar as-Sadat of Egypt, who recommended the establishment of a Jordanian-Palestinian link before a Geneva Middle East conference was held. The king's view was that Israel must first evacuate the West Bank and Gaza so that the Palestinians could decide freely for themselves. He said, however, that Jordan would speak for the Palestinians at Geneva if asked to do so by the Palestinians. The PLO remained suspicious that the king had not abandoned his earlier project for a United Arab Kingdom of the East and West Banks of Jordan.

Hussein visited Cairo in January and July, as well as in March. He also traveled to Damascus in February and June, and senior Syrian ministers came to Amman several times during the year. Although Hussein said that Jordan and Syria were looking toward full federation, there were some signs that the close cooperation between the two countries established over the last two years was waning. However, some social and economic measures were taken; the Syrian and Jordan electric power grids were linked in March, and close collaboration was arranged between the two national news services.

In press interviews the king constantly warned against excessive optimism about a Geneva conference and suggested that Israel might be planning a preemptive strike to improve its position. He accused the Arab oil states of failing to provide the amount of aid they had promised to those Arab

JORDAN

Education. (1976–77) Primary, pupils 402,401, teachers 11,636; secondary, pupils 178,153, teachers 8,129; vocational, pupils 7,547, teachers 457; higher, students 15,735, teaching staff 811.

Finance. Monetary unit: Jordanian dinar, with (Sept. 19, 1977) a free rate of 0.32 dinar to U.S. $1 (0.57 dinar = £1 sterling). Gold, SDR's, and foreign exchange (June 1977) U.S. $563.6 million. Budget (1976 actual): revenue 155 million dinars (including foreign aid and loans of 44 million dinars); expenditure 224 million dinars. Gross national product (1975) 394.9 million dinars. Money supply (May 1977) 283,910,000 dinars. Cost of living (Amman; 1970 = 100; June 1977) 274.

Foreign Trade. (1976) Imports 307,060,000 dinars; exports 68,710,000 dinars. Import sources: West Germany 17%; U.S. 9%; U.K. 8%; Japan 7%; Italy 6%. Export destinations: Saudi Arabia 11%; Syria 9%; Iran 9%; Kuwait 5%. Main exports (1975): phosphates 40%; oranges 11%; vegetables 6%. Tourism (1975): visitors 707,600; gross receipts U.S. $101 million.

Transport and Communications. Roads (excluding West Bank; 1975) 4,095 km (including 40 km expressways). Motor vehicles in use (1975): passenger 31,500; commercial 9,700. Railways (1975) 618 km. Air traffic (1975): 711 million passenger-km; freight 13.5 million net ton-km. Telephones (Dec. 1973) 40,000. Radio receivers (Dec. 1974) 529,000. Television licenses (Dec. 1974) 85,000.

Agriculture. Production (in 000; metric tons; 1976): wheat 67; barley (1975) c. 16; lentils (1975) c. 31; tomatoes c. 145; aubergines (1975) c. 32; watermelons (1975) c. 40; olives c. 30; oranges c. 6; grapes c. 20; tobacco c. 2. Livestock (in 000; 1975): cattle c. 49; goats c. 400; sheep c. 792; camels c. 16; asses c. 44; chickens c. 2,740.

Industry. Production (in 000; metric tons; 1975): phosphate rock 1,353; petroleum products 756; cement 572; electricity (kw-hr) 443,000.

nations bordering Israel. The king was embarrassed by reports in the *Washington Post* on February 18 that he had been receiving secret U.S. Central Intelligence Agency funds since 1957 in return for allowing U.S. intelligence agencies to operate freely in Jordan. The report coincided with the visit of U.S. Secretary of State Cyrus Vance to Jordan in February. The king denied that the funds were for his personal use. In April he visited the U.S. and Britain. U.S. aid to Jordan was substantially increased in 1977 to $93 million, as compared with the $33 million that had been promised earlier by Pres. Gerald Ford. Hussein maintained neutrality in the inter-Arab disputes that followed President Sadat's peace initiative late in the year. In December he visited Damascus and Riyadh to discuss ways of ending Arab differences.

Economic expansion continued despite a poor average harvest in 1976. Phosphate exports reached record levels. The visible trade deficit had increased by 50% in 1976, but foreign exchange reserves were rising because of foreign aid and the continuing high level of remittances from Jordanians abroad. In 1977 it was reported that there were 174,000 Jordanians in Kuwait alone. The cost of living continued to rise by about 30% a year.

On January 20 the king told visiting journalists that Jordan would return to "full political life" with a reconvened Parliament in the shortest possible time, but he gave no date. March 27 marked the opening of the celebration of Hussein's silver jubilee on the throne, which continued during the summer. The king's personal life was shadowed by the death of his third wife, Queen Alia, on February 9 (*see* OBITUARIES).   (PETER MANSFIELD)

See also Middle Eastern Affairs.

King Hussein of Jordan strikes a regal pose for foreign journalists during celebration of his silver jubilee.

TERRY FINCHER—PHOTOGRAPHERS INTERNATIONAL/PICTORIAL PARADE

Kenya

An African republic and a member of the Commonwealth of Nations, Kenya is bordered on the north by Sudan and Ethiopia, east by Somalia, south by Tanzania, and west by Uganda. Area: 582,646 sq km (224,961 sq mi), including 13,395 sq km of inland water. Pop. (1976 est.): 13,847,000, including (1969) African 98.1%; Asian 1.5%. Cap. and largest city: Nairobi (pop., 1975 est., 700,000). Language: Swahili (official) and English. Religion: Protestant 36%; Roman Catholic 22%; Muslim 6%; others, mostly indigenous 36%. President in 1977, Jomo Kenyatta.

The year 1977 began with encouraging news of the economy, largely the result of high prices for coffee and tea. This favourable situation encouraged some sections of industry to increase their output. The estimated budget deficit for 1976–77 was higher than for the previous year, however, and the country continued to rely on external aid to finance it. External aid also financed various development programs. As a result of 1976 legislation authorizing the Kenya Pipeline Company to seek foreign capital for construction of an oil pipeline from the refineries in Mombasa to Nairobi, with government guarantees for loans, the company was able to obtain $10 million from the Citibank of North America. In mid-1977 it was announced that Sweden would provide capital and technical assistance amounting to $37 million during the next two years, mainly to assist the rural population. Denmark offered financial aid to the Ministry of Health, and an agreement was signed with Sudan and Norway to investigate construction of a road between Kenya and Sudan.

Distrust among the members of the East African Community (EAC) surfaced again in January when Kenya insisted that the East African Airways Cor-

Kenya

poration restrict some of its long-distance flights because Tanzania and Uganda had failed to make adequate contributions to the upkeep of the airline. Tanzania retaliated in February by closing its border with Kenya, a decision which, two months later, was stated to be permanent. By the end of June the EAC had effectively ceased to exist. As a result, Kenya was deprived of the raw materials, mainly cotton, normally imported from Tanzania. The last link between the two countries was cut November 1, when Kenya suspended flights between Nairobi and Dar es Salaam.

Toward the middle of the year Pres. Idi Amin's announcement that Uganda would provide a large military base for the U.S.S.R. and would acquire a modern nuclear reactor caused great concern in Kenya. With the Soviet Union already active in Somalia on Kenya's northeastern frontier and against a background of economic and ideological opposition from Tanzania in the south, developments in Uganda to the west threatened Kenya with encirclement by unfriendly states. A raid by 3,000 Somali soldiers over the northeastern border in June heightened the tension, but Kenya and Somalia agreed to set up a border commission to restore peace along the frontier. Somalia, however, did not renounce its claim to Kenya's northeastern province.

In March, Oginga Odinga's campaign to become vice-president of the Kenya African National Union (KANU), and possibly put himself in line to be Pres. Jomo Kenyatta's successor, received a setback when Kenyatta barred him from elections because he had not been cleared after his association with the Kenya People's Union. In the event, the KANU elections, due on April 3, were postponed indefinitely, but party members and MP's belonging to Odinga's own tribe, the Luo, unanimously elected him as leader of the Luo group within KANU. Oginga's arrest was reported in early December. Another MP, George Anyona, who

A new airline came into being on February 3 when Kenya inaugurated Kenya Airways. Kenya had previously been a partner in the East African Airways Corporation, but withdrew and formed its own airline.

CAMERAPIX/KEYSTONE

KENYA

Education. (1976) Primary, pupils 2,894,617, teachers 89,074; secondary and vocational, pupils 280,388, teachers 11,438; teacher training, students 8,668; teachers 639; higher, students 5,753.

Finance. Monetary unit: Kenyan shilling, with (Sept. 19, 1977) a free rate of KShs 8.30 to U.S. $1 (KShs 14.44 = £1 sterling). Gold, SDR's, and foreign exchange (May 1977) U.S. $493.3 million. Budget (1975–76 actual): revenue KShs 5,037,000,000; expenditure KShs 6,614,000,000. Gross domestic product (1975) KShs 23,292,000,000. Cost of living (Nairobi; 1970 = 100; March 1977) 209.

Foreign Trade. (1976) Imports KShs 8,138,000,000; exports KShs 6,629,000,000. Import sources: U.K. 19%; Iran 17%; Japan 11%; West Germany 10%; Saudi Arabia 6%; U.S. 6%. Export destinations: West Germany 13%; U.K. 11%; Tanzania 10%; Uganda 10%; U.S. 6%; The Netherlands 5%. Main exports: coffee 37%; petroleum products 12%; tea 12%; fruit and vegetables 6%. Tourism (1975): visitors 407,400; gross receipts U.S. $98 million.

Transport and Communications. Roads (1975) 49,521 km. Motor vehicles in use (1975): passenger 142,000; commercial 20,900. Railways (1975): 2,073 km; freight traffic 2,120,000,000 net ton-km. Air traffic (apportionment of traffic of East African Airways Corporation; 1975): 694 million passenger-km; freight 17.7 million ton-km. Telephones (Dec. 1975) 122,000. Radio receivers (Dec. 1974) 510,000. Television receivers (Dec. 1974) 37,000.

Agriculture. Production (in 000; metric tons; 1976): corn c. 1,360; wheat c. 158; millet and sorghum c. 360; sweet potatoes (1975) c. 550; cassava (1975) c. 650; sugar, raw value (1975) c. 179; coffee c. 80; tea c. 62; sisal 33; cotton, lint c. 6; fish catch (1975) 27. Livestock (in 000; May 1976): cattle c. 7,810; sheep c. 3,200; pigs c. 71; goats (1975) c. 3,900; camels (1975) c. 530; chickens (1975) c. 15,239.

Industry. Production (in 000; metric tons; 1975): cement 897; soda ash 95; petroleum products c. 2,750; electricity (kw-hr; 1976) 1,040,000.

had frequently criticized the government, was detained early in May after denouncing the cancellation of a Canadian firm's tender for the supply of railway freight cars after it had already been accepted. He claimed the change of policy was the result of pressure from ministers and from the British high commissioner.

Almost 40,000 people in Nairobi and near the shores of Lake Victoria were rendered homeless in April and May by floods, which followed the heaviest rains in 25 years.

The trade unions expressed their anxiety at the slow replacement of expatriates by Kenya nationals. Unemployment remained high, and doubts were expressed about the way in which expatriates retained to train Kenyans were fulfilling their obligations. (KENNETH INGHAM)

Korea

A country of eastern Asia, Korea is bounded by China, the Sea of Japan, the Korea Strait, and the Yellow Sea. It is divided into two parts roughly at the 38th parallel.

Korea went into a holding pattern during 1977 following the U.S. government's decision, announced on February 1 in Tokyo by Vice-Pres. Walter Mondale, to withdraw some 33,000 U.S. ground forces from the peninsula within five years. While the decision touched off a major controversy within the U.S., there was uncertainty in both halves of Korea. The South was worried about its repercussions on security, while the

Khmer Republic: *see* Cambodia

North was uncertain as to whether it meant a Western abandonment of Seoul or only a lowering of profile by the U.S. In the meantime, both governments launched heavy military buildups.

The U.S. tried to suggest that its commitment to South Korea remained unshaken. A series of top officials traveled to Seoul to demonstrate this, one of them being Secretary of Defense Harold Brown. A senior official in his party even said that he "would not want to rule out" the return of U.S. ground forces in case of attack by the North. For the present, the agreement was to leave a joint U.S.-Korean command structure in the South. The North, none too happy about that, kept up its pressure to get the U.S. out of the peninsula. In October North Korean Pres. Kim Il Sung said that, if U.S. troops were completely withdrawn, his country was ready "to make arrangements" with the U.S. to remove the danger of a future Korean war.

The annual custom of peace feelers continued in 1977. South Korean Pres. Park Chung Hee's new-year overture took the form of a proposal for a nonaggression pact. The North promptly dismissed it as "empty talk" and countered with its own call for a disarmament conference followed by talks aimed at reunifying the country. In June the South's foreign minister, Park Tong Jin, called on the North to resume the suspended dialogue between the two governments, but the North did not seem to hear.

In the midst of all the political-diplomatic fencing, the two states indulged in less war talk during the year. There were also fewer border incidents.

Mystery man Park Tong Sun emerges in Seoul in August after disappearing from Washington in late 1976. Park was accused of being a key figure in a Korean plot to buy influence with U.S. congressmen.

UPI COMPIX

What might have been a serious military incident was defused before it could develop into anything big. This involved the shooting down by North Korea of a U.S. Army Ch-47 Chinook helicopter on July 13. Both the U.S. and South Korea said that the craft had strayed by mistake into the demilitarized zone. The crewmen apparently tried to escape, there was shooting, and only one of the four men survived. The U.S., however, did not play up the incident, and North Korea responded by also staying cool. The "unhappy incident" would not have happened had the crew simply heeded the warning shots, said the North Koreans.

Republic of Korea (South Korea). Area: 98,799 sq km (38,146 sq mi). Pop. (1977 est.): 36,436,400. Cap. and largest city: Seoul (pop., 1975 prelim., 6,879,100). Language: Korean. Religion: Buddhist; Christian; Confucian; Tonghak (Chondokyo). President in 1977, Gen. Park Chung Hee; prime minister, Choi Kyu Hah.

Relations with the U.S. were the dominant preoccupation in South Korea during 1977. They figured in a series of emotional issues—the Asian policy of Pres. Jimmy Carter, charges of corrupt Korean lobbying in Washington, D.C., and human rights.

The Carter troop withdrawal plan created considerable dismay among South Koreans. The general feeling was that the U.S. "has let us down." Interestingly, the Korean dismay was shared by several Asian governments as well as the U.S.'s own military leaders. Singapore Prime Minister Lee Kuan Yew saw the Carter plan as "a monumental decision" that would have profound consequences for northern Asia. Among a number of U.S. generals who said the withdrawal could pave the way for a new Korean war, the most prominent was Gen. John Singlaub, chief of staff of the U.S. 8th Army in Korea. On the ground that his open criticism of the plan was a serious breach of propriety, he was recalled from Korea.

President Park himself adopted, publicly at any rate, a stoic attitude to the withdrawal question. "We cannot ask them to stay here forever," he said. "They have to leave sooner or later. After all, the defense of our country is our responsibility." But Park was clearly hoping that U.S. congressional opinion would at least delay U.S. withdrawal long enough for him to reinforce his 650,000-man armed forces. A $5 billion military modernization program had been drawn up, and all indications were that the U.S. would help implement it. The program included establishing local industrial capability to produce, before the end of 1980, all essential weaponry except combat aircraft and some highly advanced electronic weapons. South Korea seemed confident that by 1980 it would attain economic and military self-sufficiency.

The popular resentment generated by the troop withdrawal decision was overshadowed in midyear by what became known as "Koreagate"—a case involving an alleged Korean bid to bribe U.S. congressmen. It surfaced over U.S. investigations into the activities of Korean businessman Park Tong Sun (see BIOGRAPHY), who had lived lavishly in Washington for 25 years. In August a U.S. grand jury secretly indicted him on charges of of-

fering up to $1 million a year in inducements to various U.S. dignitaries. By that time Park was in Seoul, denying all charges and insisting that whatever he had done was in his private capacity as a businessman and never as a lobbyist for the South Korean government. Subsequent maneuvers over the question of persuading Park to return to the U.S. brought U.S.-Korean relations to a low ebb, but in December the U.S. Department of Justice announced an agreement whereby Park would be questioned in Seoul and would return to the U.S. to testify at trials resulting from the "Koreagate" investigation. If he testified truthfully, the U.S. would drop all charges against him.

On the human rights issue, U.S. criticisms of South Korea were less vehement in 1977 than in some previous years. But the very fact that the issue had been made a major plank of the Carter administration was enough to keep it alive. In July President Park released 14 political prisoners, and in August, marking the 32nd anniversary of the nation's liberation from Japanese colonial rule, 2,-123 prisoners were released, among them 17 political detainees. But the star detainee, former opposition leader Kim Dae Jung, was not one of them. In October there were student riots.

The one area where South Korea was full of confidence was the economy, which clearly was booming. A surplus of $385 million in current accounts was announced for the first quarter of 1977. By the end of March the foreign exchange holdings had already hit an all-time high of $3,290,000,000 and were still rising. In midyear the U.S. Department of Commerce said that the gross national product growth in 1977 would be maintained at 10%, as against 15.5% in real terms the previous year. Inadequate employment opportunities, however, remained a source of worry.

Democratic People's Republic of Korea (North Korea). Area: 121,200 sq km (46,800 sq mi). Pop. (1977 est.): 16,665,000. Cap.: Pyongyang (metro. pop., 1976 est., 1.5 million). Language: Korean. Religion: Buddhist; Confucian; Tonghak (Chondokyo). General secretary of the Central Committee of the Workers' (Communist) Party of

Korea

Three U.S. airmen were killed when their helicopter strayed into North Korean airspace and was shot down. A fourth airman, Glenn W. Schwanke, of Spring Green, Wisconsin, survived and was released to U.S. authorities at Panmunjom on July 16 after intensive questioning.

UPI COMPIX

An unidentified man grieves for his family who were buried in a mudslide near Seoul in July. Mudslides which followed torrential rains killed 180 and wiped out several villages.

People's Assembly opened in April, the all-important government list did not include son Kim or the president's younger brother Kim Young Ju, a potential contender for the succession. After Pres. Kim Il Sung were listed three vice-presidents, the premier, and the defense minister. In December Cabinet changes were announced, apparently aimed at boosting the economy. Several young technocrats received appointments, and Li Jong Ok, an economic expert, was named premier.

The U.S. Department of Defense claimed in May that North Korea had improved its military capabilities significantly. According to its figures, North Korea had ground forces totaling 440,000 men, a Navy of 27,000 men, and an Air Force of 45,000 men. The figures also showed big increases in the number of tanks, antitank weapons, combat ships, and transport aircraft. Some military experts in the U.S. were skeptical about those figures, claiming that the Pentagon was only trying to scare President Carter into reversing his troop withdrawal plans.

It was an important year for contacts with other Communist countries. Kim played host to Yugoslavia's Tito, Laos' Kaysone Phomvihan, and Cambodia's Pol Pot. In September Foreign Minister Ho Dam went to New York, ostensibly to attend the UN General Assembly. Since it was the first visit to the U.S. by a senior North Korean leader, there was speculation as to whether talks with U.S. and South Korean ministers were planned during the visit. On the record, Ho said that the North had no intention of invading the South and that he was disappointed by the slow pace of the U.S. pullout there.

Indicative of its continuing desire to strengthen relations with economically important Japan, North Korea dispatched a parliamentary delegation to Tokyo in May. During the ten-day visit the North Koreans discussed trade and fishery problems preparatory to concluding a private trade agreement to replace one that had expired the previous December.

Korea and president in 1977, Marshal Kim Il Sung; chairmen of the Council of Ministers (premiers), Pak Sung Chul and, from December 15, Li Jong Ok.

Early in the year rumours gained currency in Japan that Pres. Kim Il Sung had installed his 36-year-old son Kim Chong Il as his successor. In April Western sources reported from Peking that North Korea had bought 40,000 Swiss gold watches with portraits of father and son on the faces to be distributed to trusted party workers on the president's 65th birthday on April 15.

But the official announcement expected on that day did not materialize. In fact, if reports of the son's elevation were true, the leadership was keeping it a secret in order to prevent family wrangles such as were reported in 1976. When the Supreme

(T. J. S. GEORGE)

KOREA: Republic

Education. (1975–76) Primary, pupils 5,503,737, teachers 109,530; secondary, pupils 3,370,311, teachers 87,142; vocational, students 507,430, teachers 16,536; higher, students 313,608, teaching staff 14,730.

Finance. Monetary unit: won, with (Sept. 19, 1977) an official rate of 485 won to U.S. $1 (free rate of 845 won = £1 sterling). Gold, SDR's, and foreign exchange (May 1977) U.S. $3,519,400,000. Budget (1976 actual): revenue 2,751,700,000,000 won; expenditure 2,700,000,000,000 won. Gross national product (1976) 12,108,800,000,000 won. Money supply (May 1977) 1,654,500,000,000 won. Cost of living (1970 = 100; June 1977) 258.

Foreign Trade. (1976) Imports 4,246,500,000,000 won; exports 3,734,400,000,000 won. Import sources: Japan 35%; U.S. 22%; Saudi Arabia 8%; Kuwait 8%. Export destinations: U.S. 32%; Japan 23%; West Germany 5%. Main exports (1975): clothing 23%; textile yarns and fabrics 13%; electrical machinery and equipment 9%; fish 7%; iron and steel 5%. Tourism (1975): visitors 633,000; gross receipts U.S. $141 million.

Transport and Communications. Roads (1975) 44,905 km (including 1,142 km expressways). Motor vehicles in use (1975): passenger 84,200; commercial (including buses) 104,700. Railways: (1975) 5,640 km; traffic (1976) 13,890,000,000 passenger-km; freight 9,486,000,000 net ton-km. Air traffic (1975): 3,673,000,000 passenger-km; freight 299 million net ton-km. Shipping (1976): merchant vessels 100 gross tons and over 936; gross tonnage 1,796,106. Telephones (Dec. 1975) 1.4 million. Radio receivers (Dec. 1974) 4,812,000. Television receivers (Dec. 1974) 1,619,000.

Agriculture. Production (in 000; metric tons; 1976): rice 7,250; barley c. 1,759; potatoes c. 650; sweet potatoes (1975) c. 1,500; soybeans c. 329; cabbages (1975) c. 850; watermelons (1975) c. 175; onions c. 149; apples c. 319; tobacco c. 108; fish catch (1975) 2,133. Livestock (in 000; 1975): cattle 1,778; pigs 1,818; goats 253; chickens 18,814.

Industry. Production (in 000; metric tons; 1976): coal 16,428; iron ore (56% metal content) 621; steel 2,698; cement 11,872; tungsten concentrates (oxide content; 1975) 3.3; zinc (1975) 21; gold (troy oz; 1975) 12; silver (troy oz; 1975) 1,480; sulfuric acid 639; petroleum products (1975) 16,100; electricity (excluding most industrial production; kw-hr) 23,118,000.

KOREA: People's Democratic Republic

Education. (1973–74 est.) Primary, pupils c. 1.5 million; secondary and vocational, pupils c. 1.2 million; primary, secondary, and vocational, teachers c. 100,000; higher, students c. 300,000.

Finance and Trade. Monetary unit: won, with (Sept. 19, 1977) a nominal exchange rate of 0.97 won to U.S. $1 (1.68 won = £1 sterling). Budget (1976 est.) balanced at 12,513,000,000 won. Foreign trade (approximate; 1975): imports c. 1.4 billion won (c. 30% from China, 20% from U.S.S.R., 13% from Japan); exports c. 1.2 billion won (c. 60% to China, 17% to U.S.S.R.; 5% to Japan). Main exports (1965): metals (zinc, lead, magnesite, steel) 50%; minerals 12%; farm produce 11%.

Agriculture. Production (in 000; metric tons; 1976): rice c. 3,900; corn c. 2,100; barley c. 370; millet c. 410; potatoes c. 1,210; sweet potatoes (1975) c. 320; soybeans c. 300; apples c. 162; tobacco c. 40; fish catch (1975) c. 800. Livestock (in 000; 1975): cattle c. 781; pigs c. 1,520; sheep c. 211; goats c. 181; chickens c. 22,300.

Industry. Production (in 000; metric tons; 1975): coal c. 35,000; iron ore (metal content) c. 3,760; pig iron c. 2,900; steel c. 2,800; lead c. 95; zinc c. 138; magnesite c. 1,700; silver (troy oz) c. 700; tungsten concentrates (oxide content) c. 2.7; cement c. 6,000; electricity (kw-hr; 1965) 13,300,000.

Kuwait

An independent constitutional monarchy (emirate), Kuwait is on the northwestern coast of the Persian Gulf between Iraq and Saudi Arabia. Area: 16,918 sq km (6,532 sq mi). Pop. (1975 census): 994,800. Cap.: Kuwait (pop., 1975 census, 78,000). Largest city: Hawalli (pop., 1975 prelim., 130,300). Language: Arabic. Religion (1975): Muslim 94.9%; Christian 4.5%. Emir until Dec. 31, 1977, Sheikh Sabah as-Salim as-Sabah; prime minister, Crown Prince (from December 31, Emir) Sheikh Jabir al-Ahmad al-Jabir as-Sabah.

Kuwait's constitution remained suspended in 1977, and plans for its revision were postponed until 1978. Several newspapers were closed temporarily, and there were signs of protest among university students. The government was concerned about internal security and the illegal entry of non-Kuwaitis. In foreign policy Kuwait emphasized its independence and even criticized Egypt and Saudi Arabia for allegedly aiming toward a U.S. rather than an Arab solution in the Middle East. Emir Sheikh Sabah (see OBITUARIES) died on December 31 and was succeeded by Crown Prince Sheikh Jabir.

In July the long-standing border dispute with Iraq was settled, and a two-kilometre buffer zone was created. A Japanese company was engaged to build a naval base. In March an arms deal with the Soviet Union, including SAM-7 ground-to-air missiles, was concluded. Oil production stood at about 1.6 million bbl a day in the first half of the year, compared with 2.2 million in 1976, but a government offer of a discount to contract customers in September helped to raise production. In September the government nationalized the independent U.S. oil company Aminoil. Kuwait still had a large budget surplus. About half of its aid in 1977 went to Arab states, but $200 million was offered to black African states.   (PETER MANSFIELD)

KUWAIT
   Education. (1975–76) Primary, pupils 111,820, teachers (1974–75) 5,729; secondary, pupils 106,943, teachers (1974–75) 8,227; vocational, pupils 3,528, teachers 784; higher, students 1,858, teaching staff 269.
   Finance. Monetary unit: Kuwaiti dinar, with (Sept. 19, 1977) a free rate of 0.28 dinar to U.S. $1 (0.49 dinar = £1 sterling). Gold, SDR's, and foreign exchange (June 1977) U.S. $1,350,600,000. Budget (1975–76 est.): revenue 1,737,000,000 dinars; expenditure 924 million dinars. Gross national product (1974–75) 3,198,000,000 dinars. Money supply (April 1977) 434.2 million dinars. Cost of living (1972 = 100; March 1977) 148.
   Foreign Trade. (1976) Imports 969.8 million dinars; exports 2,866,700,000 dinars. Import sources (1975): U.S. 18%; Japan 16%; West Germany 11%; U.K. 10%; Italy 5%. Export destinations (1975): Japan 25%; The Netherlands 9%; U.K. 8%; France 6%; Brazil 5%. Main exports: crude oil 75%; petroleum products 17%.
   Transport. Roads (1974) c. 1,920 km. Air traffic (1975): 955 million passenger-km; freight 24.5 million net ton-km. Shipping (1976): merchant vessels 100 gross tons and over 182; gross tonnage 1,106,816. Shipping traffic (1975): goods loaded 107,233,000 metric tons, unloaded 2,532,000 metric tons.
   Industry. Production (in 000; metric tons; 1976): crude oil 108,562; natural gas (cu m) 5,580,000; petroleum products (1975) c. 13,700.

Laos

A landlocked people's republic of Southeast Asia, Laos is bounded by China, Vietnam, Cambodia, Thailand, and Burma. Area: 236,800 sq km (91,400 sq mi). Pop. (1977 est.): 3,462,000. Cap. and largest city: Vientiane (pop., 1973, 176,600). Language: Lao (official); French and English. Religion: Buddhist; tribal. President in 1977, Prince Souphanouvong; premier, Kaysone Phomvihan.

Despite the high visibility of Premier Kaysone Phomvihan, Laos remained well in the background for much of 1977. The government had to cope with a serious problem of internal rebellion, overwhelming external influence, and an economic shambles.

The activities of rebels were reported frequently by Thailand, which said it received a regular flow of Laotian refugees, some of them alleged to be ranking officials of the Communist regime. If these reports raised a degree of skepticism, observers seemed convinced that internal disorder at some level was a reality. Widespread arrests were said to have taken place, and at least three pilots escaped into Thailand with their craft. In March there were reports that former King Savang Vatthana had been arrested for his part in the resistance. Subsequently it was rumoured that he had escaped or—conversely—had been sentenced to death, but there were no official indications as to his fate or whereabouts. Rightist rebels gained more headlines when they captured two small Mekong River islands in April. Laos formally protested to Thailand and three days later said its forces had repossessed the islands after killing a small band of rebels. Premier Kaysone, visiting North Korea in June, told North Korean Pres. Kim Il Sung that efforts to quell plots by reactionaries were continu-

LAOS
   Education. (1972–73) Primary, pupils 273,357, teachers 7,320; secondary, pupils 14,633, teachers 613; vocational, pupils 1,946, teachers 186; teacher training, students 4,031, teachers 227; higher (1973–74), students 875, teaching staff 136.
   Finance. Monetary unit: new kip, with (Sept. 19, 1977) an official exchange rate of 200 new kip to U.S. $1 (official free rate of 348.40 new kip = £1 sterling). Budget (1974–75 est.): revenue (excluding foreign aid) 980 million new kip; expenditure 1,852,000,000 new kip (including defense expenditure of 650 million new kip).
   Foreign Trade. (1974) Imports 1,943,000,000 new kip; exports 340 million new kip. Import sources: Thailand 49%; Japan 19%; France 7%; West Germany 7%; U.S. 5%. Export destinations: Thailand 73%; Malaysia 11%; Hong Kong 10%. Main exports: timber 81%; tin 11%.
   Transport and Communications. Roads (1974) 7,412 km (including 3,412 km all-weather). Motor vehicles in use (1974): passenger 14,100; commercial (including buses) 2,500. Air traffic (1975): 22 million passenger-km; freight 500,000 net ton-km. Inland waterways (Mekong River) 715 km. Telephones (Dec. 1973) 5,000. Radio licenses (Dec. 1974) 125,000.
   Agriculture. Production (in 000; metric tons; 1975): rice c. 910; corn c. 28; onions c. 29; melons c. 21; oranges c. 18; pineapples c. 27; coffee c. 2; tobacco c. 4; cotton, lint c. 2; timber (cu m) 3,154. Livestock (in 000; 1975): cattle c. 476; buffalo c. 1,072; pigs c. 1,313; chickens c. 14,112.
   Industry. Production (1975): tin concentrates (metal content) 518 metric tons; electricity (excluding most industrial production) c. 255 million kw-hr.

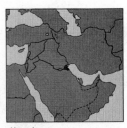

Kuwait

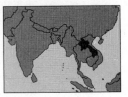

Laos

Labour Unions: see Industrial Relations

Lacrosse: see Field Hockey and Lacrosse

Thousands of Laotian civilians were pressed into service by the government to dig an irrigation canal near Vientiane. Even Premier Kaysone Phomvihan was given a shovel and put to work.

ing. According to Pyongyang Radio, however, Kaysone was confident that the difficulties would be overcome.

The impression that the country was essentially shaky was reinforced by uncertainties in its relations with other Communist states. Although Kaysone visited several countries, including China and the Soviet Union, Soviet influence was considered dominant. Hundreds of Soviets were living in Vientiane, and Soviet movies were regularly shown in local cinemas. The delivery of 20 MiG-21s by Moscow in October prompted the suspicion among Western experts that the Soviet Union was planning to make Laos its forward base in Southeast Asia. China, however, was making good use of its advantage gained many years earlier as the builder of strategic roads in northern Laos. Numerous Chinese technicians were still guarding completed roads and building new ones.

Laos' foreign relations were dominated, however, by its immediate neighbour Vietnam. Significant numbers of Vietnamese troops were known to be stationed in Laos—according to one estimate, between 30,000 and 40,000 army regulars. Travelers as well as diplomatic sources said the Vietnamese were directly helping Lao soldiers put down pockets of resistance, particularly in the mountain strongholds of the Meo tribesmen.

The impression that Vietnam had a firm hand in the affairs of Laos was strengthened when a 25-year treaty of friendship and cooperation was signed by the two countries in Vientiane in July, with much fanfare and repeated pledges that "Laos and Vietnam are linked forever." The treaty provided for cooperation in defense, development, and even the arts and sciences and sports. The common border between the two countries was called a "frontier of fraternal friendship."

Laos' economic plight would have given it little

choice even if it wanted to avoid such a relationship. Even before the Communist takeover, Laos had an artificial economy maintained by Western aid, and dependence on Communist allies became total when traffic from Thailand was closed. Laos accepted a Vietnamese offer to cut a new road to the sea from Vientiane east across Vietnam. In September there were reports of famine. Although some sources doubted this, widespread shortages were known to exist, and international appeals for aid were raised at the UN level.

(T. J. S. GEORGE)

Latin-American Affairs

Some of the most important events in Latin-American affairs in 1977 took place in Washington, D.C. In January Jimmy Carter assumed the office of president of the United States, having been elected with a program including strong concern for human rights and nuclear proliferation. The new government continued to press these and other global pre-election policies in its relationships with other nations, but over time they became tempered by the pragmatic restraints which imposed themselves on each set of bilateral relations.

These overall aspects of U.S. policy combined with the declared intention of dropping previously held attitudes toward Latin America, which amounted to almost "benign neglect" in the views of some commentators, had considerable effects and repercussions in Latin America. The human rights debate took up considerable time at the Organization of American States (OAS) meeting held in Grenada in June. This followed the rejection of U.S. military aid and assistance agreements by Argentina, Uruguay, Brazil, El Salvador, and Guatemala because of reports made to the U.S. Congress on human rights in those countries, an action which the latter regarded as an intolerable interference in their domestic affairs.

The attitude that the U.S. was guilty of interference was also adopted by Brazil when, as a safeguard against nuclear proliferation, the U.S. exerted pressure on that country and West Germany to modify their 1975 nuclear technology agreement. The talks broke down on March 2 after only one session. Brazil professed interest in only peaceful uses of nuclear energy and regarded attempts to have the agreement changed as an unwarranted interference in an independent state's right to acquire the latest advanced technology. Virtually all other Latin-American countries supported Brazil's stand, which U.S. Secretary of State Cyrus R. Vance's visit to Argentina, Brazil, and Venezuela in November left unchanged.

Panama Canal Treaties. Despite other difficulties the most symbolic issue in inter-American relations appeared to take a significant step toward resolution on September 7 when President Carter and the Panamanian leader, Brig. Gen. Omar Torrijos Herrera (*see* BIOGRAPHY), signed the new Panama Canal treaties in Washington. These provided for the U.S. to hand over the canal to Panama in the year 2000 (at noon, Panama time, Dec. 31, 1999) and to defend it before and after that date.

The handling of the Panama Canal problem was regarded by Latin-American nations as the touchstone of U.S. intentions toward the southern continent and the most symbolic issue between the two areas. The peculiar status of the canal problem might only become widely apparent in 1978 with the possibility of rejection of the treaties by the U.S. Senate, or, should the treaties be successfully ratified by both parties, by the practical effects of implementation as canal tolls were increased to provide greater revenue for Panama. Such increases could adversely affect the commercial interests of other Latin-American states.

The signing of the treaties in Washington was attended by nearly all the Latin-American heads of state, allowing for extensive consultation with the U.S. authorities. These consultations complemented those undertaken by a number of ranking ad-

ministration officials during their visits to Latin America and by Rosalynn Carter, the U.S. president's wife, during her June tour of Latin-American countries. The consultations covered all aspects of bilateral relations, including, once again, human rights. The fragile state of civic rights in Latin America was illustrated at the October annual meeting of the Inter-American Press Association, which singled out only four countries —Venezuela, Colombia, Costa Rica, and the Dominican Republic—as having a completely free press.

Commercial Relations. Also of immediate interest to the Latin-American states during the year were their commercial relations with the U.S., particularly the issues of protectionism and open markets in the industrialized countries for the growing range of exports from the less developed countries. This formed one of the strands of the North-South dialogue carried on between industrial and less developed countries at the meeting of the Conference on International Economic Cooperation held in Paris in June. The conference reflected the more general problems of relations between the less developed and industrialized nations in matters of trade policy, balance of payments problems, development finance, debt, and technology transfer, but achieved no conclusive agreements.

Given the world economic situation in 1977 and the increasingly gloomy prospects for 1978, the lack of substantial progress on these issues was not surprising. Nevertheless, the steps taken by the U.S. and Cuba toward a resumption of full diplomatic relations, namely the reopening of missions in each other's capitals on September 1 after a break of more than 16 years, gave evidence of a new spirit of accommodation, even though relations at the ambassadorial level were unlikely to be established for some time.

Integration Movements. The continued moribund status of the majority of the regional integration movements, at least from the viewpoint of their loftier ideals, was again in evidence in 1977. The OAS Grenada conference in June showed the usefulness of that body as a forum for discussion but as little else. The Latin American Free Trade Association and Latin-American Economic Sys-

The seventh General Assembly of the Organization of American States gathered June 14 in Grenada with delegates from 25 member nations attending.

UPI COMPIX

tem, although undertaking useful work in peripheral technical areas, did not produce any major advances in regional integration. The Andean Pact, weakened by Chile's withdrawal in 1976, did perhaps overcome a major crisis in 1977. A threatened withdrawal by Bolivia was averted through Decision 119, which instituted a special aid program for that country. The proposed reorganization of the Central American Common Market (CACM) continued to be under discussion.

In comparison, integration movements with more limited aims achieved some success in 1977. The finance fund of the River Plate Basin Group began operations, and members submitted plans for infrastructure projects to the fund. Brazil's proposal for an Amazon Pact, again aimed largely at achieving integration in terms of infrastructure projects and economic cooperation, received a favourable response from all Amazon basin states, and substantial negotiations took place before the end of the year. Commodity groups made some headway in protecting the interests of Latin-American producers. A multinational banana marketing organization, Comunbana, was formed in March by the member countries of the Unión de Paises Exportadores de Banano (Colombia, Costa Rica, Guatemala, Honduras, Panama, and the Dominican Republic). During the second half of the year Latin-American coffee producers had several meetings to coordinate policy in the face of the falling world prices for coffee. In mid-October ten producers—Mexico, Costa Rica, Ecuador, Guatemala, Honduras, Nicaragua, the Dominican Republic, Venezuela, Panama, and El Salvador—suspended sales abroad in an effort to halt the price decline. In September, 19 Latin-American countries established the Latin American Export Bank, scheduled to start operations in April 1978.

The failure of the integration movements in Latin America to achieve greater success was in large measure due to the disparate nature and aims of the countries that form the region. Apart from the general ideological differences between the few re-

maining democratically governed countries, such as Colombia and Venezuela, and the military regimes, during 1977 there also remained several unresolved disputes between various nations. These included the Beagle Channel question between Argentina and Chile (see LAW: *International Law*) and the trilateral problems involving Chile, Bolivia, and Peru over Bolivia's access to the Pacific, and Argentina, Brazil, and Paraguay over the use of the Paraná River. Farther north a final settlement of the Honduras-El Salvador conflict was still awaited, while the question of independence for Belize (British Honduras) divided the region with only Nicaragua, Honduras, El Salvador, and Argentina (in dispute with Britain over the Falkland Islands) as strong supporters of Guatemala's claim to the British colony.

Economic Developments. Given the faltering nature of the world economy in 1976 and 1977, the region showed progress that was steady but not sufficiently dynamic to make a significant impression on the problems, such as rapid population growth, that faced it. A UN Economic Commission for Latin America report revealed that in 1976 the region achieved a surplus in its trade balance of some $600 million (as against a deficit of more than $5 billion in 1975) and succeeded in reducing the deficit on its current account to $4.5 billion (from $8.5 billion). A factor contributing to the overall surplus was the influx of $13.7 billion of private capital into the region. The growth in regional gross domestic product in 1976 was 4.5–5.0%, roughly double that of the previous year.

In January 1977 three new members joined the Inter-American Development Bank (IDB), Austria, France, and The Netherlands. Loans made by the IDB totaled $1,528,000,000 in 1976, bringing cumulative net lending to more than $10 billion; grants and technical cooperation in 1976 amounted to $30.9 million. The IDB raised $550 million in the world's capital markets, and earnings from its own resources in 1976 totaled $122 million; loan repayments in that year totaled $229 million.   (JOHN HALE)

See also articles on the various political units.
[971.D.8; 974]

Law

Court Decisions. Decisions from various courts throughout the world on questions of abortion, marriage, contraception, family property, and other matters commonly lumped together under the heading of family law were considered by legal scholars to be the most important judicial developments of 1977. Other important cases involved criminal law and the "Watergate" scandal.

FAMILY LAW. In *Maher* v. *Roe*, the Supreme Court of the United States held that the equal protection clause of the Constitution does not require a state to pay the expenses incident to a nontherapeutic abortion for indigent women simply because it has adopted a policy of paying the expenses incident to childbirth for such women. It was admitted by all parties to the litigation that the Constitution imposes no obligation on the states to

LURIE'S OPINION

LURIE—© 1977 KING FEATURES SYNDICATE, INC.

In October an unusual plea of "involuntary intoxication" caused by watching too much violence on TV failed to convince a Miami, Florida, jury, which convicted 15-year-old Ronny Zamora of killing an elderly neighbour.

through a "conspiracy of silence," police payoffs, and because prosecuting officers cannot do their job effectively in the face of the overwhelming number of abortions performed.

In *Carey* v. *Population Services International*, the U.S. Supreme Court held unconstitutional a New York law that prohibited the distribution of contraceptives to minors. Some writers and others found this decision inconsistent with the thrust of *Maher* v. *Roe*, but most legal scholars were able to reconcile the two decisions. In the *Carey* case, the court pointed out that the decision whether or not to beget or bear a child is an important right protected by the Constitution. Therefore, a state may not prohibit the distribution of contraceptives. Consistently, in *Maher* v. *Roe*, the court reaffirmed its position that a woman is entitled to an abortion, and no state may deny her that right. But she may have to pay for the abortion out of her own funds, just as a person may have to pay for his or her own contraceptives.

In other important developments in the family law area, the Supreme Court of Cyprus held that a civil marriage performed in England by Cypriot resident domiciliaries who were of the Greek Orthodox faith was void. The Federal Constitutional Court of (West) Germany held that matrimonial assets do not include one spouse's lottery winnings. The Supreme Court of New Zealand ruled that a wife who was the business partner of her husband had no action against him for business losses. The U.S. Supreme Court held that children can be subjected to corporal punishment in school; regardless of the severity of the punishment, laws providing for, or permitting it violate neither the

pay the pregnancy-related expenses of indigent women, or indeed to pay any of the medical expenses of indigents. It was also admitted that when a state decides to provide some medical assistance to indigents it must make its dispensation within constitutional limitations.

In this connection it was contended that a state that provides medical assistance for childbirth must accord equal treatment for abortion. In other words, it was asserted that the equal protection clause of the Constitution requires that states may fund, or refuse to fund, medical costs of childbirth and abortions, but that they may not fund one without funding the other since both relate to the same kind of matter.

The majority of the court did not agree with this argument, pointing out that there was a reasonable basis for a policy favouring childbirth, even though no such favouritism is shown toward abortions. The court made clear that the Constitution does not proscribe the enactment of laws funding abortions, but neither does it require such funding merely because a state has decided to pay for the medical costs of childbirth for indigents. The decision was sharply criticized by many liberals and women's rights organizations. As the year ended, Congress was in the process of enacting legislation to fund abortions under certain circumstances.

In some other countries, legislatures were also concerned with the matter of abortion. The Italian Chamber of Deputies legalized abortion on demand but the law was defeated in the Senate in June, and the Israeli Knesset enacted a law permitting an abortion to be performed on the approval of a three-member committee consisting of two medical doctors and a social worker. A UN report dealing with abortions in Brazil pointed out that they are illegal in that country but extremely common. It suggested that abortionists operate freely

Pickets marched around Detroit's Federal Building in October to protest a suit filed by Allan Bakke, a white student who claimed that he was the victim of reverse discrimination by being denied admission to a medical school in California.

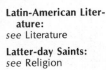

"cruel and unusual punishment" nor "due process" clause of the Constitution. The possibility of suit against the teacher under state tort law for excessive punishment satisfies the due process requirement.

CRIMINAL LAW. The U.S. Supreme Court continued in 1977 to wrestle with the constitutional implications of the death penalty. In 1976 the court had held in *Gregg* v. *Georgia* that the death penalty is not necessarily a cruel and unusual punishment proscribed by the Eighth Amendment to the Constitution, but that each statute under which the death penalty is imposed must be separately reviewed to determine whether it meets constitutional standards. Pursuant to this holding, the court reviewed a Georgia statute which was used as the basis for the imposition of a death penalty for the crime of rape. In *Coker* v. *Georgia*, the court, in a divided opinion, concluded that the sentence of death for the crime of rape is grossly disproportionate and excessive and therefore constitutes "cruel and unusual punishment" in violation of the Eighth Amendment.

In the plurality opinion, written by Justice Byron White and adopted by Justices Potter Stewart, Harry Blackmun, and John Paul Stevens, the court held that the Eighth Amendment bars not only those punishments that are barbaric but also those that are excessive in relation to the crime committed. It found that the death penalty is grossly out of proportion to the severity of the crime of rape. Justice Lewis Powell concurred, opining that death is disproportionate punishment for the crime of raping an adult woman when, as in the case at hand, the crime was not committed with excessive brutality and the victim did not sustain serious or lasting injuries.

Justices William Brennan and Thurgood Marshall concurred in the result of the decision, but for vastly different reasons. Reiterating their past positions, each concluded that the death penalty is in all circumstances cruel and unusual punishment prohibited by the Constitution. Finally, Chief Justice Warren Burger and Justice William Rehnquist dissented, opining that rape is not a crime "light-years removed from murder in the degree of its heinousness." Since murder is properly punishable by death where that is the considered judgment of the legislators, the dissenters thought that legislatures could properly impose that sentence for rape, a crime that "poses a serious potential danger to the life and safety of innocent victims—apart from the devastating psychic consequences." Legal scholars felt that the decision cast some doubt on the constitutionality of a variety of federal and state statutes authorizing imposition of the death penalty, under some circumstances, upon conviction for serious crimes—such as treason, airplane hijacking, and kidnapping—that may not necessarily result in any immediate death.

In India, the Supreme Court held that the execution of criminals is a matter left entirely to the legislature. The case arose on a petition to stay the execution of an arguably insane convict. The court said it had no common law or natural law power to grant relief.

Two significant decisions involving prisoners'

rights were handed down in West Germany and the U.K. The Oberlandesgericht Koblenz held that German constitutional law does not prohibit the forced feeding of detainees on hunger strikes. The English Court of Appeal held that a prisoner has no right to require reasons for his classification as a particular type of prisoner. The French Constitutional Council held unconstitutional legislation authorizing the police to search vehicles on grounds of suspected banditry or drug trafficking. The council stated that the legislation was ill defined and did not meet constitutional standards designed to safeguard privacy.

WATERGATE SCANDAL. In *Nixon* v. *Administrator of General Services*, the U.S. Supreme Court upheld the constitutionality of the Presidential Recordings and Materials Preservation Act. After Richard Nixon had resigned as president, he executed a depositary agreement with the administrator of the General Services Administration (GSA) under which his presidential materials, estimated to consist of 42 million documents and 880 tape recordings, were to be stored near his retirement home in California. Under the agreement, neither Nixon nor the GSA could gain access to the materials without the consent of the other. The public announcement of the agreement created considerable furor. Its defenders pointed out that, historically, every president prior to Nixon had been regarded as the owner of materials accumulated during his tenure in office, and that Nixon should be treated no differently. Against this, it was alleged that Nixon's agreement with the GSA had the effect of removing important evidence from the various trials stemming from the Watergate scandal.

The Watergate special prosecutor advised Pres. Gerald Ford of his continuing need for the materials, and Congress quickly intervened and enacted the Presidential Recordings and Materials Preservation Act. This act nullified the GSA-Nixon agreement and directed the GSA to keep the Nixon presidential papers in Washington and make them available for use in judicial proceedings. It did not direct the GSA to recover the presidential papers of former presidents, nor did it direct it to sequester the papers of future presidents, but, in this connection, it established a study commission to examine the question of whether or not future presidents should be deemed to own the materials accumulated during their tenure. Nixon brought an action challenging the constitutionality of the act and, in a landmark decision, the court held the act constitutional. In the court's opinion, (1) the act did not violate the principle of separation of powers; (2) it did not work an impermissible intrusion on the doctrine of presidential privilege; (3) it did not infringe on the privacy of former president Nixon; (4) it did not impair his right of association; and (5) it did not constitute a bill of attainder.

The bill of attainder point was the one constitutional law experts found most interesting, because the Supreme Court has had few occasions to decide cases involving this matter. The Constitution prohibits the Congress and state legislatures from passing bills of attainder; that is, legislation that determines the guilt of, and inflicts punishment on, an identifiable individual without provision for a judicial trial. Nixon argued that, in passing the act in question, Congress had acted on the premises that he had engaged in misconduct, was an unreliable custodian of his papers, and generally deserved the judgment of blameworthiness. Therefore, the act, in his view, was punitive, and since it singled him out for treatment ("punishment") not meted out to other presidents, it met the other requirements of the bill of attainder.

Most members of the court disagreed with this analysis, holding that the act was not punitive and that it is permissible to enact legislation aimed at a single individual, here Nixon, as long as that individual constitutes a "legitimate class." Because Nixon had resigned his office under unique circumstances and accepted a pardon for offenses committed while in office, he placed himself in a different class from all other presidents and, "as a class of one," was subject to legitimate congressional action aimed only at him.

(WILLIAM D. HAWKLAND)

International Law. In the field of international law, 1977 was an unusually quiet year. No great initiatives were taken, and no major conventions were concluded. The most newsworthy events were political rather than legal.

TERRITORY AND SOVEREIGNTY. Of considerable potential legal significance was a perceptible change in policies relative to the polar regions. The existing quiescence in Antarctica was likely to be affected by the worldwide extension of fishery limits and the simultaneous discovery that direct fishing of Antarctic krill might be economically feasible.

At the other pole, the tension between Norway and the U.S.S.R. over the "gray zone" in the Barents Sea—involving a dispute over whether the equidistance line or the sector principle should be used to demarcate the boundary between the fishery and continental shelf areas of the two states —led to some gunboat diplomacy directed against fishing vessels. By year's end, however, the matter seemed to be moving toward a diplomatic settlement. The related problem of Svalbard (Spitsbergen) was more difficult. This concerned both the unsuccessful attempt by the Norwegian authorities to exercise their territorial sovereignty over the Soviet "settlements" on the island, and the Norwegian claim to a 200-mi Exclusive Economic Zone (EEZ) and continental shelf around the island that would be purely Norwegian and not subject to the open-sharing system applicable to the land territory under the Svalbard treaty of 1920 (to which the U.S.S.R. acceded in 1925).

The equatorial states of Brazil, Colombia, Ecuador, the Congo, Zaire, Kenya, Uganda, and Indonesia claimed under the *usque ad coelum* ("up to the sky") principle that their air sovereignty extended up beyond the ionosphere so as to embrace any geostationary satellites positioned above their territories; this could have serious consequences in years to come. Other outer space developments included the adoption by the International Telecommunication Union of an agreement on the broadcasting satellite service for the whole world, except the Western Hemisphere, and a rearrange-

ment of the Radio Regulations, both of which would come into force in 1979. Later in the year, the U.S.S.R. and the U.S. signed an agreement, to replace that of 1972, on cooperation in the exploration and use of outer space for peaceful purposes. The Convention on Registration of Objects Launched into Outer Space, which was opened for signature in 1975, came into force.

The International Court of Justice was quiet, but there were two important arbitrations during the year, both (as usual) concerning boundaries. The Beagle Channel arbitration, between Argentina and Chile, resulted in an award in favour of Chile. The 1881 treaty was interpreted so as to draw the eastern sea exit of the channel in such a way that the three disputed islands of Nueva, Picton, and Lennox form part of Chilean territory. The award was not accepted by Argentina. In the English Channel and Western Approaches, the dispute between the U.K. and France concerned the continental shelf boundary and the effect on it of the various island groups, particularly the Scilly Isles and the Channel Islands. The award minimized that effect, and indeed restricted the shelf appurtenant to the latter group to a 12-mi belt. However, the surveyor appointed by the tribunal to draw the cartographic lines expressing the award used a Mercator projection instead of a great circle, thus producing a long narrow strip of sea still in dispute, and the British government returned the matter to the tribunal for clarification.

Among other boundary settlements were the Ghana-Upper Volta treaty demarcating 135 mi of joint border; an agreement between Iran and Afghanistan on the sharing of the waters of the Helmand River; a similar agreement between Portugal and Spain on the use of the Mino, Limia, Tajo, Guadiana, and Chanza rivers; and an agreement between Mexico and the U.S. approving a proposal of the International Boundary and Water Commission, under the Boundary Treaty of 1970, for the transfer of jurisdiction over some 2,340 ac. Of greater significance was the signature by the U.S. and Panama in September (subject to ratification) of a new Panama Canal treaty, which would transfer to Panama by the year 2000 full control and jurisdiction over the canal. (*See* PANAMA.)

ENVIRONMENTAL PROTECTION. In this field the most important development was the adoption by the UN General Assembly in May of the Convention on the Prohibition of Military or Any Other Hostile Use of Environmental Modification Techniques. Modification of the environment for peaceful purposes was expressly permitted, however, and cooperation in such matters was encouraged. On the internal domestic level, the prolonged drought in the western U.S. had led to the development of cloud-seeding to make rain and to accusations by some states of "cloud grabbing." The legal implications on a national level were complicated enough; internationally, as with other environmental modifications, the position would be even more difficult.

In December 1976 three Rhine Pollution conventions were signed by the five riparian states (and in one case by the European Economic Community [EEC] as well). The conventions regulated the dis-

Spencer Sacco (centre), grandson of Nicola Sacco, received a proclamation in Boston in July from Massachusetts Gov. Michael Dukakis stating that his grandfather, together with Bartolomeo Vanzetti, had been improperly tried for murder. Sacco and Vanzetti were executed in 1927 for a crime they maintained they did not commit.

charge of chlorides and the pollution of the Rhine by chemicals, and also entitled the EEC to become a party to the existing convention concerning, and a member of, the International Commission for the Protection of the Rhine against Pollution.

SOCIAL LAW. The growing international influence of labour unions was reflected in a number of new instruments relating to "social law." These included new International Labour Organization (ILO) conventions on substandard ships and the working conditions of merchant seamen (October 1976) and on the training and working conditions of nurses and the protection of employees against air pollution, noise, and vibration at the place of work (June 1977). The ILO also prepared, for consideration at its 1978 conference, draft standards on freedom of association and working conditions of public servants. The U.S. withdrew from the ILO November 1. The Council of Europe Social Security Convention came into force during the year, and a new convention that would give migrant workers a legal status ensuring them rights and protection in the contracting states was opened for signature.

MARITIME AFFAIRS. The UN Conference on the Law of the Sea (UNCLOS) held further sessions during the year, and progress was made in reaching a new "Informal Composite Negotiating Text." Intended merely as a basis for negotiation, it replaced the earlier informal single negotiating text and the revised single negotiating text. A further session was to be held in the spring of 1978.

Unwilling to wait for the conclusion of UNCLOS, the international community tacitly agreed on the basic lawfulness of a 12-mi territorial sea and a 200-mi EEZ, although state practice still varied in detail. There was an almost universal extension of fishery limits to 200 mi (as a partial EEZ) or claims of a full EEZ over 200 mi. The consequent problems of access to traditional fishing grounds by foreign fishermen led during the year to a vast number of bilateral fishery treaties.

After all the EEC member states had introduced 200-mi fishing limits on Jan. 1, 1977, the EEC took over the international negotiating powers of its member states in fishery matters. This particularly affected the North Sea. Because the North Sea is part of the North East Atlantic Fisheries Commission area, the powers and function of the latter came into question. Between August 1976 and February 1977, all the EEC members of the commission gave one year's notice of withdrawal from it, and a diplomatic conference was held in April to consider, without success, a new draft convention to replace the existing one. Paradoxically, several states in other parts of the world (Cuba, Finland, the U.S.S.R.) had become members of the commission during the previous year.

Other fishery commissions were also coming under pressure. The U.S. withdrew from both the North Pacific Fisheries Convention and the International Convention for the Northwest Atlantic Fisheries, effective February 1978 and January 1977, respectively. The former would thereupon be completely dissolved, but the latter continued in being, with its local management function transferred to Canada. (See FISHERIES.)

EUROPEAN ECONOMIC COMMUNITY. The legal activity of the EEC was moving into areas of great substantive importance on all levels. On the constitutional level, the European Audit Court and Budgetary Powers Treaty of July 1975 came into force, and the first members of the court were appointed. The Direct Elections Act of September 1976 was ratified by all the member states except the U.K., and implementation legislation (intended to be in time to allow direct elections for the European Assembly in May 1978) was far advanced in most member states by year's end. The opinion of the European Court of Justice on the proposed Rhine Agreement on a Laying-Up Fund for barges was also of great constitutional significance, both internally (equality of participation of member states in international arrangements involving the Community as such—i.e., balance of powers between states and Community organs) and externally (the court accepted supranational executive powers, while leaving open the possibility of supranational legislative powers).

Significant legislative developments included the 6th Value-Added Tax (VAT) Directive, which unified most aspects (except actual rates) of that consumer tax and also made it possible to introduce the VAT part of the Community's "own resources" revenue system as of January 1978. The 2nd Company Law Directive (December 1976) unified many aspects of the law relating to public companies. The European and Community Patent Conventions of 1973 and 1975 were ratified, and the European Patent Office would be able to open in Munich, West Germany, in mid-1978. Full freedom of establishment (under the 1975 directive) for doctors and nurses was now in force, as well as a new directive on freedom of lawyers to supply services. The European Court of Justice extended the rights of establishment in professions generally where the host state has in fact recognized an equivalence of qualifications.

(NEVILLE MARCH HUNNINGS)

See also Crime and Law Enforcement; Prisons and Penology; United Nations.

AMERICA'S LITIGIOUS SOCIETY

by David C. Beckwith

Early in the summer of 1977, four coeds and a male professor at Yale University filed a civil suit in U.S. District Court, New Haven, Conn. The women charged they had been victims of "sexual harassment" by teachers, and the professor alleged that the resulting "atmosphere poisoned by distrust" interfered with his ability to teach. The plaintiffs asked not for the traditional money damages but for a judicial order forcing Yale to establish a formal grievance procedure to handle complaints of sexual harassment in the future.

A bizarre incident? Hardly. The case was all too typical of an accelerating trend in U.S. life: the dumping of all problems, major and inconsequential, into the courts. Although Americans have long been noted for litigiousness (Alexis de Tocqueville observed in 1835 that "There is hardly a political question in the U.S. which does not sooner or later turn into a judicial one"), the march to the courts in recent years has turned into a near stampede.

An estimated ten million civil cases were docketed in trial courts nationwide in 1977, more than double the total of 15 years earlier. This backlog, combined with an unprecedented upsurge of criminal cases (incidence of crime has risen by more than 180% since 1960, with a corresponding increase in court-processed arrests), has left courts staggering under the work load. Delays of a year in hearing even routine civil cases are the norm in most major city court systems. In Cook County (Chicago), Ill., for example, a negligence case usually takes four years to get to trial. And the trend shows no sign of abating, as both citizens and public officials demonstrate a continuing willingness to turn over to the courts questions that were once decided by legislatures, citizens, teachers, parents, and executives—or not decided at all.

The Tilting Balance of Powers. The situation is deeply troubling. On one level, the litigation explosion is producing a whole litany of undesirable side effects. Distressing delays become routine as the legal process is stretched out, all too often benefit-

---

David C. Beckwith is a correspondent and writer for Time *magazine.*

ing the guilty or the party at fault. Court costs, attorney fees, and stenographer bills mount, tilting the scales of justice toward the litigant with the deeper pockets. Attorneys, usually paid by the hour, find new ways to delay cases with discovery, postponement, appeal, and motion after new motion. In the process, a mood of intransigence and stubbornness replaces conciliation and compromise. Criminals are freed with wrist-tapping sentences under plea-bargain arrangements so that courts can turn attention to the next defendant copping a plea.

On a more important level, however, the trend represents a basic challenge to democracy itself. Officials elected by the people have found it increasingly convenient to abdicate their toughest decisions to nonelected judges. As *New York Times* columnist Russell Baker aptly observed, "The Supreme Court's desegregation decision of 1954 opened a new way out for the politicians. If the courts could be forced to make the more troublesome political decisions, the politicians could escape retribution, at least in this world, and even profit from denouncing those court decisions which particularly annoyed the electorate." Thus, in Alabama, U.S. District Judge Frank Johnson found it necessary virtually to take over the state's prisons, mental hospitals, and public hiring procedures after the state legislature refused to take the responsibility for making needed reforms. Dean Roger Cramton of the Cornell University law school summarized: "The critical question in a republic is how government by non-elected officials can be squared with representative democracy."

Nonetheless, the lure of the courthouse has proved increasingly irresistible. In some eyes, the litigious trend represents little less than a desirable silent revolution in American life, an unexpected heritage from the Warren court's civil rights decisions of the 1950s and 1960s. According to this view, Americans have become aware that they have rights lying dormant in a properly functioning constitutional democracy and are moving to have them articulated and enforced. Others see it in somewhat different terms: judges, encouraged by the heady activism of the Warren court, are showing an increased willingness to expand individual rights to match the growth of governmental power, roaming widely in search of equitable solutions. Certainly a lawsuit can be a cheaper and more decisive vehicle for law reform than an expensive and time-consuming lobbying effort. And so, often using the Fourteenth Amendment's guarantee of "equal protection of the laws" as a rallying cry, Americans are engaged in a push for their rights—or in a fight to persuade judges to declare new rights—through the mechanism of judicial review.

A legal aid office in a low-income neighbourhood in Cambridge, Mass., where residents had once been "legally deprived."

Legions of Lawyers. Abetting this process is a flood of new, young lawyers. The 445,000 established attorneys in the U.S. are joined every year by nearly 30,000 law school graduates, and many have litigation on their minds. The wealthy have always had access to legal assistance. Now, expanded federally financed legal aid programs for the poor service hundreds of localities nationwide, and prepaid group legal service plans (one million Americans already have this "legal insurance"), plus advertising (made possible by a Supreme Court decision in 1977) and bar assistance programs, are gradually bringing routine legal care within reach of the middle class. Are these lawyers helping to extend equal justice to a long-deprived public, or are they merely stirring up trouble? Critics love to tell the apocryphal story of the attorney who was starving as the only lawyer in a small town until another lawyer hung out his shingle across the street; then they both prospered as their clients sued each other.

Charges of solicitation aside, however, there is little doubt that the demand for legal assistance is both strong and growing. Thanks to recent court decisions, any criminal defendant subject to incarceration must now have access to a lawyer, publicly paid if necessary. Even more important is the headlong growth of government. An estimated 150,000 new laws and countless regulations are passed by various legislative and administrative bodies annually, and each one is the subject of possible legal action. Just one seemingly innocent law—Title VII of the 1964 Civil Rights Act, prohibiting job discrimination on the basis of sex, race, or religion—has produced a three-year backlog of 128,000 complaints at the federal Equal Employment Opportunity Commission and thousands of court cases annually. According to a U.S. Supreme Court justice: "Just about anybody who doesn't get a job can take the matter to court under that law. It's just staggering." The burgeoning maze of government bureaucracy has made the hiring of an expensive lawyer-lobbyist in the state or national capital a necessary cost for the prudent businessman. Before taking a Cabinet post in the Carter administration, Joseph Califano, Jr., revealed that he had earned $505,490 in 1976 as a topflight Washington attorney, demonstrating just how expensive that legal advice can be.

Thanks largely to probing assaults by imaginative lawyers, whole new fields of legal action have sprung up that were undreamed of a generation ago, and their future growth appears limited only by the ingenuity of those same attorneys. Hispanics, Indians, and the poor generally are demanding their own versions of legal rights granted to blacks. Children, military personnel, and prisoners are discovering that they, too, have rights. Consumers and environmentalists, virtually powerless in courtrooms only a few years ago, are flexing awesome legal muscles today. Medical science and technology have made new claims possible—over the "right to die," genetics, microbiology, and even the influence of television on a murder defendant's sanity. Even sports, the traditional outlet for aggressive competitiveness, has been swept into legal combat. A player injured in a brawl on the field or a college suspended for recruiting irregularities no longer accepts the event stoically as one of the vicissitudes of a risky enterprise. Instead, the matter may go to court. And increased urbanization, crowding people together, promises still more knotty legal problems for the future.

Block That Lawsuit! Not surprisingly, this steady accumulation of decision-making power by lawyers and judges has given rise to a strong adverse reaction. An outspoken critic of the trend is U.S. Chief Justice Warren E. Burger, who has sought alternatives to court settlement of grievances while decrying the spectre of "a society overrun by hordes of lawyers, hungry as locusts, . . . and brigades of judges in numbers never before contemplated." And the attack has not been merely vocal. The U.S. Justice Department and other critics have accused bar associations of attempted monopolization and price-fixing, successfully overturning (in court, of course) the bar's title-search requirements, advertising restrictions, and minimum fee schedules. Several states have enthusiastically embraced "delawyering" proposals. Wisconsin in 1977 enacted laws encouraging individuals to handle their own court business. The New York legislature approved a law requiring contracts and bank loan applications, beginning in 1978, to be written in simple English understandable to laymen as well as lawyers. Five Midwestern states have drastically simplified their probate laws in an attempt to prevent attorneys from skimming off unconscionable fees. And serious efforts to remove the disciplining of errant lawyers from the sole control of attorneys themselves are under way in a number of states.

A movement to decriminalize so-called victimless crimes, such as drunkenness, marijuana possession, prostitution, gambling, and sexual intercourse among consenting adults, has made significant headway in recent years, reducing court logjams in some states. Other targets of court uncloggers are some probate, child custody, adoption, and name-change procedures where no real dispute exists; increasingly, these matters are being transferred to administrative clerks. Still other programs are aimed at channeling minor disputes to mediators or arbitrators rather than judges, or even to neighbourhood tribunals—a practice developed in China and Cuba.

The concept of "no-fault," approved by 23 states for automobile accident insurance, theoretically permits immediate payment to victims without red tape and courtroom delays. Some legal reformers want the concept extended to cover medical malpractice cases and other disputes where swift compensation to the victim is vital. And some states are reviving and strengthening their small claims courts as places where consumers and "small" litigants can get fast adjudication of complaints without becoming fouled in the legal process.

But if these efforts are symptomatic of public dissatisfaction with the increasing pervasiveness of lawyers, they do not address the underlying problem. Significant reforms aimed at stanching the flow of societal disputes into the nation's courtrooms have proved to be difficult and, thus far, largely ineffective. Americans have unmatched respect for the law. In no other country do lawyers and judges have more power, and nowhere else are courts held in such high regard. But the citizenry's esteem for the law threatens its very existence. Unless ways are found to lighten the burden and shift decision-making away from judges, the system may well break down from overuse.

"Do we really believe that judges have any special aptitude which makes them suitable custodians for the solution of our social problems?" asks former U.S. judge Simon H. Rifkind. The concept of judicial review, firmly planted in the young republic by Chief Justice John Marshall and the early U.S. Supreme Court, is being stretched to the breaking point; it can give judges the last word on virtually every question, and it is being abused to the point where courts are overburdened with too many controversies that should be resolved elsewhere. More fundamental reforms than those already proposed— perhaps even reaching the prevalent "sue the bastards" attitude permeating the national consciousness—will have to be found if the delicate system of U.S. government is to be kept in balance.

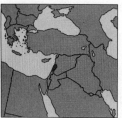

Lebanon

Lebanon

A republic of the Middle East, Lebanon is bounded by Syria, Israel, and the Mediterranean Sea. Area: 10,230 sq km (3,950 sq mi). Pop. (1976 est.): 2,961,-000. Cap. and largest city: Beirut (metro. pop., 1975 est., 1,172,000). Language: Arabic. Religion: recently released 1965 census figures, of questionable reliability, show Christians: 54.5%; Muslims 45.5%. President in 1977, Elias Sarkis; prime minister, Selim al-Hoss.

In 1977 Lebanon made a slow and partial recovery from the effects of the 1975–76 civil war, but the conflict between Christian rightist forces and Palestinians near the southern borders remained unresolved, and there were periodic resumptions of sectarian violence.

The Syrians, as by far the largest element in the Arab Deterrent Force, continued to play a major role in the country's political life. A four-power committee of representatives of Syria, Saudi Arabia, Egypt, and Kuwait, presided over by Pres. Elias Sarkis, tried to ensure disarmament and the handing over of all heavy weapons to the Arab Deterrent Force, but with only limited success. In late January, Syrian troops advanced to Nabatiya, within 15 km of the Israeli border, but they stopped short of the Litani River to avoid provoking Israeli intervention. Fierce fighting between Christian rightists and Palestinians centred on Marjayoun and Khiam in late February and continued sporadically throughout the summer. Israel, alleging a Palestinian buildup in the area, supported the Christian forces with artillery and later with tanks. The Lebanese Army was being rebuilt but was still incapable of controlling the southern borders.

The Lebanese Front, comprising Maronite political and religious leaders, insisted that all Lebanese territory must be "liberated from Palestinian occupation," but there was a division within the Maronite leadership. The Falangist leader, Pierre Jemayel, showed greater willingness to compromise than the National Liberal Party lead-

Leftist guerrillas took cover from Christian rightist forces near the town of Marjayoun as the conflict between the two forces continued in southern Lebanon.

UPI COMPIX

er, former president Camille Chamoun. This became apparent in March when Jemayel refused to support a general strike called by Chamoun to protest President Sarkis' replacement of the army commander by a moderate more acceptable to Lebanese Muslims. Sarkis pursued his policy of building up the authority of his regime and of the government's security forces. Press censorship was imposed in January and later extended to foreign correspondents in Lebanon. Although the censorship was later partially relaxed, several newspapers were temporarily banned.

Apart from the explosive situation in the south, the worst danger for the government was the revival of sectarian violence. A series of explosions in the rightist Christian areas of Beirut in January was followed by retaliations against Muslims. The murder by unidentified assassins of the Druze leftist leader Kamal Jumblatt (see OBITUARIES) on March 16 was followed by Druze attacks on Christian villagers and counterreprisals. Similar incidents, often exaggerated by rumours, continued throughout the year. Kamal Jumblatt was succeeded as head of the Progressive Socialist Party by his son Walid, but the leftist forces in the country were at least as divided as the right, especially in their attitude toward the Syrian occupation.

In June, President Sarkis called for an Arab summit meeting to reach a final settlement of the Lebanese problem, but there was no consensus favouring such a meeting among the Arab states. Similarly, a proposal by several leading Lebanese politicians to station a UN force on the border with Israel elicited no response. Finally, a meeting of Lebanese-Syrian and Palestinian representatives

The rubble of Beirut's commercial district was clearly evident when UN Secretary-General Kurt Waldheim (centre) and his delegation visited Lebanon in February.

in Shtoura on July 25 reached an agreement to carry out the terms of the 1969 Cairo agreement on Lebanese-Palestinian relations in all areas, including the south. Official details were not fully disclosed, but it was reported that armed Palestinians would not be allowed to leave the refugee camps and all Palestinian heavy weapons would be withdrawn from the camps under the supervision of the Arab Deterrent Force. Supervision of the agreement remained a problem because the Lebanese Army was still inadequate and the Syrian forces could not advance into the crucial border areas. A cease-fire involving the Lebanese rightists, Palestinians, and Israel, arranged through U.S. mediation at the end of September, did not hold. In December, Egyptian Pres. Anwar as-Sadat's peace initiative brought demonstrations and strikes from both Christians and Palestinians who feared a separate Egyptian-Israeli peace without settlement of the Palestinian problem.

Selim al-Hoss's government of nonpolitical technocrats concentrated much of its effort on economic recovery. The prime minister estimated losses from the civil war at between $1.7 billion and $2.7 billion in material destruction and a further $6.7 billion to $16.7 billion in lost revenues. In January he toured the Arab oil states to seek aid, but in May he admitted there had been only a slow and limited response. On January 17 it was announced that full banking operations were being resumed, and during the year Beirut international airport gradually recovered its pre-civil war traffic. The formation of a Reconstruction and Development Council was announced on March 21, and one of

its first duties was to negotiate with the World Bank for major infrastructure projects. In February a French company announced plans to reconstruct Beirut's devastated business centre and port.

Inflation was the most serious immediate problem facing the government. Prices rose by over 80% in 1976, and some food products cost over 400% more than before the civil war. A government survey in April showed that of 625,760 Lebanese who left the country during the civil war, 353,260 had returned. In February the government announced that all citizens must obtain new passports as a measure to eliminate the many illegal passports believed to have been obtained during the civil war. A special parliamentary session was convened, July 18–August 4, to enable deputies to vote the government a further six-month period with powers to legislate by decree, the first period having expired on June 30. Although the powers were granted by an overwhelming vote on August 4, deputies expressed fierce criticisms of the government's performance.   (PETER MANSFIELD)

Lesotho

A constitutional monarchy of southern Africa and a member of the Commonwealth of Nations, Lesotho forms an enclave within the republic of South Africa. Area: 30,355 sq km (11,720 sq mi). Pop. (1976 prelim.): 1,230,000. Cap. and largest city: Maseru (pop., 1976 prelim., 14,700). Language: English and Sesotho (official). Religion: Roman Catholic 38.7%; Lesotho Evangelical Church 24.3%; Anglican 10.4%; other Christian 8.4%; non-Christian 18.2%. Chief of state in 1977, King Moshoeshoe II; prime minister, Chief Leabua Jonathan.

In February 1977 Lesotho accused South Africa of withdrawing a R 2.5 million corn and wheat subsidy and claimed sovereignty over the whole of the Orange Free State, small parts of Natal and Transvaal, and territory occupied by the Southern Sotho "fraudulently taken in the Basuto wars." Relations between Lesotho and South Africa had already become embittered by the end of 1976 as a result of Lesotho's refusal to recognize the independence of Transkei and Transkei's closure of border posts.

Though the UN Security Council in May approved a plan to rescue Lesotho from dependence on South Africa, the necessary development aid,

Lesotho

LESOTHO

Education. (1975) Primary, pupils 221,932, teachers 4,-228; secondary, pupils 15,611, teachers 605; vocational, pupils 547, teachers 66; higher, students 847, teaching staff 130.

Finance and Trade. Monetary unit: South African rand, with (Sept. 19, 1977) an official rate of R 0.87 to U.S. $1 (free rate of R 1.52 = £1 sterling). Budget (1974–75 est.): revenue R 17,251,000; expenditure R 16,008,000. Foreign trade (1974): imports R 84.7 million; exports R 9.7 million. Main exports: wool 35%; mohair 16%; livestock 16%; diamonds 9%. Most trade is with South Africa.

Agriculture. Production (in 000; metric tons; 1975): corn c. 100; wheat c. 51; sorghum c. 60; dry peas c. 8; wool c. 1.6. Livestock (in 000; 1975): cattle c. 550; goats c. 900; sheep c. 1,610.

Law Enforcement:
see Crime and Law Enforcement

Lawn Bowls:
see Bowling

Lawn Tennis:
see Tennis

estimated at over $110 million, was slow in coming, nor could Lesotho provide manpower to carry out the plan. A $23 million five-year plan, largely financed by Britain and West Germany, was already under way. The Lesotho National Development Corporation announced the expenditure of R 20 million over four years with the help of the European Economic Community, the Commonwealth Development Corporation, Canada, and Kuwait. Nevertheless, Lesotho remained linked to South Africa, which marketed its wool exports (two-thirds of total exports in value) and employed more than 90,000 Lesotho miners.

(MOLLY MORTIMER)

Liberia

Liberia

A republic on the west coast of Africa, Liberia is bordered by Sierra Leone, Guinea, and Ivory Coast. Area: 111,400 sq km (43,000 sq mi). Pop. (1977 est.): 1,553,900. Cap. and largest city: Monrovia (pop., 1977 est., 172,100). Language: English (official) and tribal dialects. Religion: mainly animist. President in 1977, William R. Tolbert, Jr.

Liberia in 1977 experienced a year of progress and prosperity under Pres. William Tolbert's system of "Human Capitalism," which emphasized the right to acquire by initiative and the duty to share with the less fortunate. In his annual message, on January 28, Tolbert saw 1977 as dedicated to self-help. The $415 million National Socio-Economic Development Plan (1976–80), over 40% internally funded, concentrated on self-sufficiency in rice, although Liberia did not have the food problems of many African countries.

The 1977–78 budget emphasized a move from dependence on revenue to profit-sharing, result-

> **LIBERIA**
> **Education.** (1974) Primary, pupils 149,687, teachers 4,-111; secondary, pupils 26,426, teachers 1,015; vocational, pupils 1,087, teachers (1970) 66; teacher training, students 424, teachers 41; higher (university only; 1976), students 1,980, teaching staff 190.
> **Finance.** Monetary unit: Liberian dollar, at par with the U.S. dollar, with a free rate (Sept. 19, 1977) of L$1.74 to £1 sterling. Budget (1975 actual): revenue L$154.5 million; expenditure L$146.6 million.
> **Foreign Trade.** (1976) Imports L$399.3 million; exports L$459,960,000. Import sources: U.S. 30%; Saudi Arabia 13%; West Germany 12%; U.K. 8%; Japan 7%; The Netherlands 6%. Export destinations: West Germany 28%; U.S. 19%; Italy 14%; France 8%; Belgium-Luxembourg 8%; The Netherlands 6%; Spain 5%. Main exports: iron ore 72%; rubber 12%.
> **Transport and Communications.** Roads (state; 1975) 7,266 km. Motor vehicles in use (1974): passenger 12,100; commercial (including buses) 10,000. Railways (1975) 493 km. Shipping (1976): merchant vessels 100 gross tons and over 2,600 (mostly owned by U.S. and other foreign interests); gross tonnage 73,477,326. Telephones (Dec. 1974) 7,000. Radio receivers (Dec. 1974) 261,000. Television receivers (Dec. 1973) 8,500.
> **Agriculture.** Production (in 000; metric tons; 1976): rice c. 230; cassava (1975) c. 260; bananas c. 64; palm kernels c. 15; palm oil c. 20; rubber c. 90; cocoa c. 3; coffee c. 4. Livestock (in 000; 1975): cattle c. 34; sheep c. 172; goats c. 170; pigs c. 90.
> **Industry.** Production (in 000; metric tons; 1975): iron ore (metal content) 16,923; petroleum products c. 505; diamonds (exports; metric carats) 406; electricity (kw-hr) c. 870,000.

ing from a new agreement with the Firestone Tire and Rubber Co. abolishing its tax privileges and increasing its contributions by $1 million a year. The government made a 50% profit-sharing agreement with the Liberian Iron and Steel Co. consortium at the Wologisi iron mine. Other healthy economic signs included foreign investment at about $2 billion, with more to come in the new Industrial Development Park free zone, inflation down to 11.4%, gross domestic product up by 10.7% ($733 million in 1976), and a trade surplus of $98.3 million. The Mano River customs union, under a joint commission and secretariat with Sierra Leone, was agreed on in April. (MOLLY MORTIMER)

Libraries

The International Federation of Library Associations and Institutions (IFLA) celebrated its 50th anniversary in September 1977 at a congress in Brussels. The gathering, which was attended by about 1,800 librarians from over 100 countries, marked the first time IFLA had met under its new statutes. Preben Kirkegaard of the Royal School of Librarianship, Copenhagen, was reelected president for a second term of three years. The theme of the congress was "Libraries for All," and in the specialized meetings it became evident that, after some years of concentration on universal bibliographical control, it was now even more important to work on the universal availability of publications. A special number of the *IFLA Journal* on contemporary library problems and a commemorative volume on IFLA were issued for the congress. Also published were four international standard bibliographical descriptions and UNIMARC, a standard for mechanized bibliographical exchange.

The March–April 1977 *Unesco Bulletin for Libraries* gave details of the new General Information Programme (PGI) adopted at UNESCO's 19th General Conference in November 1976, when a PGI division was established. Its purpose was to promote international, national, and regional information systems, with special attention to the less developed countries. There were further national responses in 1977 to UNESCO's national information systems (NATIS) program. An international congress on national bibliographies was held in Paris in September, and plans for national information and library systems were developed in Algeria, Canada, Italy, Jordan, Libya, Indonesia, Pakistan, and Australia. Important reports appeared on existing library and information networks in the U.S. and the U.S.S.R.

The Royal Library of Sweden began its reorganization. The final report of the consultants on the plan for the new Pahlavi National Library appeared in Iran. The National Library of Canada published a detailed review of its role and services, and a general policy statement on national libraries by their directors appeared in the *Unesco Bulletin for Libraries* for January–February.

The Library Association of the U.K. celebrated its centenary in October at a conference at the Royal Festival Hall, London, attended by about 1,000 librarians. In June the American Library Associa-

Chicago's outmoded public library was converted at a cost of $4 million into a richly decorated cultural centre. Years' accumulation of grime were removed from bright, colourful mosaics and from carved ceilings.

tion (ALA) welcomed over 7,000 librarians to its conference at Detroit on the theme "First step into ALA's second century." The film *The Speaker*, produced by the ALA's Intellectual Freedom Committee, was shown for the first time. In May U.S. Pres. Jimmy Carter had agreed to allocate $3.5 million for the White House Conference on Library and Information Services, to be held in 1979. The new Bibliothèque Publique d'Information in the Centre Georges-Pompidou in Paris continued to develop, and a special exhibition advertised its audiovisual services.

Important events in the field of academic and specialized libraries included the 150th anniversary of the Library of the Hungarian Academy of Sciences; the 200th anniversary of the Universitätsbibliothek in Vienna; and the efforts of the library of the Royal Institute of British Architects, London, one of the greatest architectural collections in the world, to maintain its services. A model children's library was opened at Kampala, Uganda, to serve as an example for schools. The International Youth Library in Munich, West Germany, published an enlarged edition of its catalog *The Best of the Best*, listing recommended works from over 100 countries. The ALA awarded the Caldecott Medal for children's literature to Leo and Diane Dillon, illustrators of *Ashanti to Zulu: African Traditions*.

General classification systems were the subject of a symposium in Brussels in late November 1976 held by the International Federation for Documentation, at which papers were presented on the Dewey and Universal Decimal systems. The London Classification of Business Studies, compiled by K. Vernon and V. Lang, was revised by Liverpool Polytechnic's department of library and information science; and the INSPEC classification (Institution of Electrical Engineers, London) produced a concordance of revisions since 1969. The first Ranganathan Award for Classification Research was presented to Derek Austin for pioneer work on the Preserved Context Index System; and

UNESCO published its *UNISIST Guidelines for Multilingual Thesauri.*

France announced plans for a national lending collection at Le Mans as a division of the Bibliothèque Nationale. The U.S. announced plans for a national serials data base for the humanities and for a national collection of serials. The National Library of Scotland was studying projects for an on-line bibliographical network to be linked with the British Library. Problems of copyright arose again: the ALA held sessions on the implementation of the new U.S. copyright law at its conference in June, and in the U.K. the Whitford report provoked protests from many librarians because it rejected the principle of allowing single copying for study and research and recommended a system of blanket licensing instead.

(ANTHONY THOMPSON)

[441.C.2.d; 631.D.1.a; 735.H]

Libya

A socialist republic on the north coast of Africa, Libya is bounded by the Mediterranean Sea, Egypt, the Sudan, Tunisia, Algeria, Niger, and Chad. Area: 1,749,000 sq km (675,000 sq mi). Pop. (1975 est.): 2,444,000. Cap. and largest city: Tripoli (pop., 1973 census, municipality, 551,000). Language: Arabic. Religion: predominantly Muslim. Leader of the Revolutionary Command Council to March 2, 1977, and then Secretary-General of the General People's Congress, Col. Muammar al-Qaddafi.

War on the Libyan-Egyptian border dominated world news during the last week of July 1977 and the first week of August. There had been a brief halt in the public and reciprocal haranguing by Libyan Pres. Muammar al-Qaddafi and Pres. Anwar as-Sadat of Egypt (*see* BIOGRAPHY) in early June and then again when the president of Togo offered to mediate on July 7 in Lomé. Libya ceased its propaganda campaign against Egypt, and high-

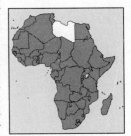

Libya

A Libyan soldier searches through the ruins of a building after an Egyptian-Libyan border clash near Tobruk in July.

level ministerial meetings were arranged. But the short-lived reconciliation was shattered by a four-day war which started on July 21 and led to great economic and personal disruption in Libya. The return home of many of the 250,000 Egyptians working in Libya in agriculture, industry, private and public services, and especially in education

left many organizations acutely short of personnel, especially when their departure came on top of the mobilization of Libyan manpower into the armed services. After Egyptian troops advanced a short distance into Libya, the armed conflict ended with the help of Pres. Houari Boumédienne of Algeria, but the propaganda war continued. Sadat's visit to Jerusalem in November was denounced by Qaddafi, who was host to a "rejection front" conference in Tripoli, December 2–5, attended by Algeria, Iraq, Syria, Yemen (Aden), and the Palestine Liberation Organization.

Demand for Libyan oil remained steady despite the world surplus of crude oil, and as a result the nation's economy was strong. Massive investments in the infrastructure continued, and huge allocations were being made for arms purchases, mainly from the Soviet Union, which seemed to be Libya's sole ally during the year. Poor relations continued with most Arab countries and especially with Egypt and Sudan. In that region Soviet and Libyan interests moved together, and in the Horn of Africa they worked against Sudan and Somalia on behalf of Ethiopia; this was a strange shift in policy for Libya, which had previously promoted the cause of Arab unity in Eritrea against the Ethiopian regime. Libya and Chad clashed sharply at the July meeting of the Organization of African Unity, with Chad alleging that Libya had armed the rebels in Chad and had occupied large areas of northern Chad that might contain significant mineral resources. Relations with Tunisia were dominated by disputed offshore oil rights.

At home President Qaddafi further implemented his "Universal Theory," which advocated mass participation in government through public debate in a hierarchy of popular committees. In the spring a new generation of young people participated in nationwide debates, many of which were shown on television, with the main issue being the name of the country. A meeting of the General People's Congress declared the new name

---

LIBYA

Education. (1976–77) Primary, pupils 568,781, teachers 26,385; secondary, pupils 172,250, teachers 12,025; vocational, pupils 4,990, teachers 403; teacher training, students 21,719, teachers 2,006; higher, students 12,459, teaching staff 350.

Finance. Monetary unit: Libyan dinar, with (Sept. 19, 1977) a par value of 0.296 dinar to U.S. $1 (free rate of 0.516 dinar = £1 sterling). Gold, SDR's, and foreign exchange (June 1977) U.S. $3,709,000,000. Budget (1974 actual): revenue 2,067,000,000 dinars (including petroleum revenue of 1,442,000,000 dinars); expenditure 2,062,000,000 dinars. Gross domestic product (1974) 3,636,000,000 dinars. Money supply (Dec. 1976) 1,139,400,000 dinars. Cost of living (Tripoli; 1970 = 100; March 1977) 138.

Foreign Trade. (1976) Imports (fob) c. 1,276,000,000 dinars; exports 2,487,100,000 dinars. Import sources (1975): Italy 26%; West Germany 12%; France 9%; Japan 8%; U.K. 5%. Export destinations: U.S. 22%; Italy 22%; West Germany 19%; Spain 5%. Main export crude oil 100%.

Transport and Communications. Roads (with improved surface; 1972) c. 5,200 km (including 1,822 km coast road). Motor vehicles in use (1975): passenger 263,100; commercial (including buses) 131,300. Air traffic (1975): 556 million passenger-km; freight 5.1 million net ton-km. Shipping (1976): vessels 100 gross tons and over 34; gross tonnage 458,805. Ships entered (1975) vessels totaling 6.4 million net registered tons; goods loaded 72,994,000 metric tons, unloaded 9,619,000 metric tons. Telephones (Dec. 1971) 42,000. Radio licenses (Dec. 1974) 105,000. Television licenses (Dec. 1974) 6,000.

Agriculture. Production (in 000; metric tons; 1976): barley c. 200; wheat c. 70; potatoes (1975) c. 67; watermelons (1975) c. 101; tomatoes c. 208; onions c. 40; oranges c. 28; olives c. 100; dates c. 62. Livestock (in 000; 1975): goats c. 1,109; sheep c. 3,329; cattle c. 121; camels c. 120; asses c. 73.

Industry. Production (in 000; metric tons; 1975): petroleum products c. 1,850; crude oil (1976) 92,773; electricity (Tripolitania; excluding most industrial production; kw-hr) c. 900,000.

to be the People's Socialist Libyan Arab Jamahiriyah; the last word was coined and means "government through the masses."　(J. A. ALLAN)

Liechtenstein

A constitutional monarchy between Switzerland and Austria, Liechtenstein is united with Switzerland by a customs and monetary union. Area: 160 sq km (62 sq mi). Pop. (1976 est.): 23,900. Cap. and largest city: Vaduz (pop., 1975 est., 4,500). Language: German. Religion (1970): Roman Catholic 90%. Sovereign prince, Francis Joseph II; chief of government in 1977, Walter Kieber.

For the first time in the history of the principality women were able to vote on April 17, 1977, when they took part in communal elections in Vaduz. This had been made possible by the introduction in 1976 of a constitutional law empowering communes to grant women the vote at the local level.

On June 27 the government and the principality's bank association, following the example of Switzerland, signed an agreement to improve identification of clients and funds in order to counter money-switching movements. This followed the improper channeling of SFr 217 million of clients' funds from the Chiasso branch of Crédit Suisse into the Liechtenstein holding company Texon-Finanzanstalt, in possible contravention of tax, currency, and banking regulations. Earlier, on May 11, the Liechtenstein prosecutor investigating the affairs of Texon-Finanzanstalt had indicated there was no reason to suppose that offenses against local laws had been committed by directors and former directors resident in the principality, and had added that it had not been possi-

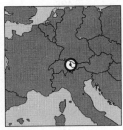

Liechtenstein

LIECHTENSTEIN
Education. Primary (1977), pupils 2,122, teachers 90; secondary, pupils 1,616, teachers 79.
Finance and Trade. Monetary unit: Swiss franc, with (Sept. 19, 1977) a free rate of SFr 2.38 to U.S. $1 (SFr 4.15 = £1 sterling). Budget (1977 est.): revenue SFr 189,670,000; expenditure SFr 182,240,000. Exports (1975) SFr 522.3 million. Export destinations: Switzerland 41%; EEC 27%; EFTA (other than Switzerland) 9%. Main exports: metal manufactures, furniture, pottery. Tourism (1975) 78,550 visitors.

ble to establish the nature of Texon's activity because none of the local directors participated in any of the company's transactions.

(K. M. SMOGORZEWSKI)

Life Sciences

An important feature of 1977 was the continuing interaction of the biological sciences and public affairs. In many matters of national and international concern, such as fisheries control, pollution, and energy, the biological facts of life upon which permanent policies depended were subordinated to temporary political and economic considerations. Other matters, too, such as research on genetic engineering (see Special Report), forced biologists into the public arena. One striking example of this kind of involvement occurred in France, where wide support for a well-organized "ecology party" posed a serious threat to the established parties.

In becoming political, biologists ceased to be concerned only with isolated problems of conservation. Consequently, they needed a comprehensive, practical political philosophy directed to a

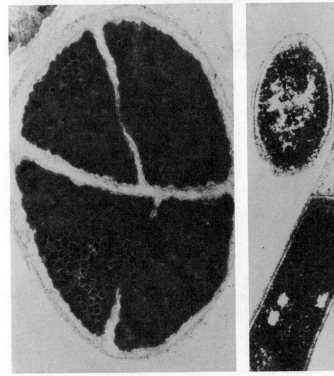

In 1977 scientists reported that methanogens, shown here in an electron micrograph, are a unique life form evolutionarily distinct from bacteria, plants, or animals.

Life Insurance:
see Industrial Review

stable relationship with man's terrestrial environment, rather than to the continual acceleration of its exploitation. The urgency of this outlook was stressed notably at the second International Conference on the Environmental Future in Reykjavik, Iceland, and at the influential UNESCO round table on "The Challenge of the Year 2000" in Paris in June.

Unfortunately, opposition was not limited to the entrenched political, economic, and military interests but came from much of the public, including many so-called ecologists to whom scientific biology was equated with its technological abuses with respect to drugs, food additives, fertilizers, and pesticides, to say nothing of test-tube babies and biological warfare. Memories of the misuses of Charles Darwin's principle of "survival of the fittest" and of Gregor Mendel's genetics to justify war, racism, and unpopular forms of elitism had given biology an evil reputation in some quarters. This attitude was strengthened by such recent, widely read popularizations as Konrad Lorenz' *On Aggression* (1966) and Robert Ardrey's *The Territorial Imperative* (1966), which caused many people to regard the ideas of human evolution and ethology as being hostile to the establishment of a humane society instead of being essential to a true understanding of man's place in nature.

Well-preserved microfossils resembling blue-green algae, the oldest form of life on Earth for which evidence exists, were discovered within 3,-400,000,000-year-old rocks from South Africa. The find adds 100 million years to the age of the earliest known evidence of life, which is nearly 3,000,000,000 years before the start of the Cambri-an Period, when prolific, easily visible fossils first appear in the rock record.

Working with primitive microorganisms previously thought to be a type of bacteria, scientists at the University of Illinois, Urbana, reported evidence during the year that these organisms are in fact a separate form of life, genetically and structurally distinct from either present-day bacteria or the more complex cells of plants and animals. Referred to informally as methanogens, they were known to exist in nature only in oxygen-free environs—*e.g.*, in deep, hot (170° F) geothermal springs and in decaying material in the bottom mud of seas and bays—where they utilize carbon dioxide and evolve methane as a waste product. Through investigations that placed their unique structure within the larger framework of molecular evolution and from their ability to thrive in an environment similar to that of the Earth of perhaps 3,500,000,000–4,000,000,000 years ago, it was suggested that organisms of this type were among the earliest offspring of the primordial spark of life from which all extant organisms were believed to derive. (HAROLD SANDON)

[312.A.3–4]

ZOOLOGY

The past year saw publication of several interesting reports describing the effects of environmental pollution on animals. F. L. Rose of Texas Tech University, Lubbock, and J. C. Harshbarger of the Smithsonian Institution, Washington, D.C., studied the incidence of skin lesions in tiger salamanders (*Ambystoma tigrinum*) from a sewage sedimentation lagoon on a Texas air base. They

Indiscriminate insecticide spraying, as shown at right, in Wenatchee, Washington, has come under heavy attack from environmentalists because of its potential ill effects on forest animals.

discovered that about one-third of the animals had skin lesions, 84% of which were cancerous. All of the salamanders were also neotenic; *i.e.*, they failed to metamorphose from larvae into adults. By contrast, tiger salamanders from nearby uncontaminated lagoons metamorphosed and were free of skin lesions. The neotenic condition was found to be related to appearance of the cancers, because it allowed passage of the 14–17 months that are required for larval skin to develop cancer. Whereas the sewage contamination could not be related to the development of the cancers, polycyclic aromatic hydrocarbons, which might have arisen from runway washing or jet exhausts, were found in the water. Such chemicals were known to cause cancer in rats and mice. These results suggested that tiger salamanders might be sensitive indicators for carcinogens released into the environment.

Two other studies dealt with the biological effects of oil pollution. C. T. Krebs of St. Mary's College, St. Marys City, Md., and K. A. Burns of the Marine Chemistry Unit, Melbourne, Australia, examined the long-term effects of a fuel-oil spill in 1969 on populations of the saltmarsh fiddler crab (*Uca pugnax*) in Massachusetts. Comparing crabs from an oil-spill region with those from a similar, spill-free region, they found the spill to be associated with reduced crab density, a reduced ratio of females to males, reduced settlement of juveniles, heavy overwinter mortality, incorporation of oil into tissues, and behavioural disorders; *e.g.*, problems of movement and abnormal burrow construction. Juveniles were found to be ten times as sensitive as adults to the direct killing effect of the oil. Reduction of the number of crabs was of ecological importance because these animals play a role in the energy flow both within the salt marshes and between marshes and coastal waters.

The second study involved feeding of fuel oil to Japanese quails (*Coturnix coturnix japonica*) by C. R. Grau and co-workers at the University of California, Davis, as a follow-up to the well-known catastrophic effect of oil pollution on seabirds. They found that a single oil dose of 200 mg resulted in abnormal yolk deposition for the next 24 hours. During the next four days, oil-treated birds laid fewer eggs than controls and hatchability was greatly reduced. Mineral oils did not have the same effects. It was speculated that the observed abnormalities resulted either directly from toxins deposited in the yolk or indirectly from an inhibition of sodium and potassium absorption by the gut. Although this study did not involve seabirds, its results seemed applicable to them.

The general field of adaptation to background and mimicry was the subject of three interesting studies. The first involved the discovery of infrared reflectance in four species of leaf-sitting neotropical frogs by P. A. Schwalm and P. H. Starrett of the University of Southern California, Los Angeles, and R. W. McDiarmid of the University of South Florida, Tampa. As had long been known, certain frogs adjust their coloration to that of their background to reduce their visibility to predators; called cryptic or protective coloration, this phenomenon with few exceptions was thought to involve only visible light. Although it was known

that the Australian tree frog (*Hyla coerulea*) is cryptically coloured in infrared light and thus inconspicuous to an infrared detector, the four neotropical frogs studied exhibited this same feature, blending into a leaf when photographed in infrared light. It was felt that these frogs would be inconspicuous to a predator having an infrared receptor; *e.g.*, any of certain birds and snakes.

The second study involved a case of Batesian mimicry, wherein a species that is desirable to predators (the mimic) resembles another species that is undesirable to predators (the model). J. E. McCosker of San Francisco's Steinhart Aquarium found that, when frightened, the Pacific reef fish *Calloplesiops altivelis* adopts an appearance that mimics the head of a noxious moray eel (*Gymnothorax meleagris*). In such a posture, the hind region of the fish remains exposed beyond the rock or coral that it seeks for protection, and an eyespot (ocellus) on its skin imitates the eye of the moray eel. Such behaviour is quite unusual for a reef fish, most of which hide when threatened. Presumably the mimicry evolved because it allowed the mimic more time for productive activities by reducing the time lost in hiding from predators.

The third study, by R. B. Huey of the University of California, Berkeley, and E. R. Pianka of the University of Texas, Austin, also involved Batesian mimicry and was possibly the first reported case of a terrestrial vertebrate mimicking an invertebrate. Both the model, a noxious beetle (*Anthia* species), and the mimic, a juvenile lizard (*Eremias lugubris*), are found in the Kalahari semidesert of southern Africa. The juvenile lizards, which are jet black above and below with broken light lateral and dorsal stripes, walk stiffly and jerkily, with arched backs and tails pressed to the ground. In this posture they mimic their model so closely that the investigators occasionally mistook lizards for beetles. Among indirect evidence that this mimicry reduces the likelihood of predator attack was the finding that these lizards have the lowest frequency of broken tails of all juvenile lizards of their genus in the southern Kalahari. As was well known, certain lizards shed their tails when attacked.

Some intriguing findings involved specialized animal senses. R. Fox and his co-workers at Vanderbilt University, Nashville, Tenn., demonstrated that falcons actually have stereoscopic vision. Previously this type of vision had been thought peculiar to mammals, although recent work had indicated that some birds have brain patterns in their visual systems that would permit extensive interaction between the eyes. An American kestrel (*Falco sparverius*) was trained to select a stereoscopic form in a two-choice discrimination test. The test was designed so that both eyes were required to make the stereoscopic choice, each eye seeing one-half of a stereogram in a different colour. The bird made the stereoscopic choice about 80% of the time. This ability was lost when the bird was allowed only a monocular view of the form. Fox also found that the falcon's threshold for stereo perception was of the same order as that of humans. These results suggested that many other nonmammals might also have binocular vision and some of these might be suited for studies of the physiology and pathology of stereoscopic vision.

Another study, on the mechanism of species identification of cowbirds, approached an unsolved problem. The parasitic brown-headed cowbird (*Molothrus ater*) lays its eggs in the nests of about 200 other species; thus, the young are reared by "strangers" and are not exposed to their own species during their formative period. A. P. King of Cornell University, Ithaca, N.Y., and M. J. West of the University of North Carolina, Chapel Hill, reared a female cowbird in complete auditory and visual isolation from other cowbirds. They discovered that at eight months of age she developed a copulatory response posture when played a recording of a male cowbird courtship song. This response did not occur with other bird songs; *e.g.*, the cowbird flight song or the song of the red-winged blackbird. They also found that male cowbirds reared in isolation developed slightly different songs from males reared in the company of male peers and adults. This abnormal song was even more potent than the normal song in triggering copulatory behaviour in females reared in isolation. These results demonstrated that cowbirds do not require prior experience with adult cowbirds in order for species identification to occur.

(RONALD R. NOVALES)

[312.C.3.b; 333.B.1; 342.A.6.e.iii]

Entomology. Late in 1976 the UN Food and Agriculture Organization announced the successful use of surveillance satellites in control of the desert locust (*Schistocerca gregaria*). Development of locust swarms, from West Africa to northwest Asia, depends on sufficient rains during egg laying to provide water for absorption by the developing eggs, and subsequent growth of enough vegetation to see the hoppers through to maturity. In a pilot study, weather satellites indicated where rains had been plentiful, Landsat satellite data evidenced vegetation cover, and together they pinpointed potential breeding areas at a cost that promised to cut by a quarter the previous $20 million spent annually by 45 countries on surveillance and control.

During 1977 another devastating invader made its appearance in Australia. In March the spotted alfalfa aphid, *Therioaphis trifolii*, was recognized near Brisbane, and by May forerunners were recorded 1,500 km (930 mi) away in South Australia. During the interval, thousands of hectares of alfalfa were destroyed by the pest in the sweep of pasture land lying west of the Great Dividing Range. What made the insect deadly was its exceptional ability to multiply and its apparent toxicity to susceptible plants. Originating in the Near East, it had made a forceful appearance in the U.S. in the 1950s, and hence the Australians were able to draw on U.S. experience with resistant plant varieties and successful parasites. A serious complication soon arose, however, when another globe-trotter was found, again near Brisbane, the blue-green aphid, *Acyrthosiphon kondoi*. Originating in Asia, it had not been a recognized pest until it arrived in the U.S. in 1975, where, like *Therioaphis*, it attacked a range of legumes including alfalfa and was reputedly toxic; but little was yet known about its control.

In a remarkable turnabout in insect-human interactions, the Chinese were proving the effectiveness of mass attacks on pest species by man. Robert Metcalf of the University of Illinois reported that while on a visit to China in 1975 he had checked on the success of its much-publicized fly-catching campaign. He found that, with such simple methods as light traps, persistent and massive community involvement across the countryside was coping successfully with a number of insect pests, and providing useful animal feed in the process.

In the southern U.S., where the battle against the imported fire ant (*Solenopsis invicta*) had not proceeded well, Wendell L. Morrill of the University of Georgia predicted that the insect, which had spread from Texas to North Carolina, could well extend its range to New York, Kentucky, Arizona, California, and Washington. Although primarily adapted to warm, humid regions, it could survive cold weather as long as the brood did not freeze. The chief weapon against the ant so far had been the insecticide Mirex, but after six years

A "scout" ant (*Harpagoxenus sublaevis*) leads a recruit in a raid on a colony of another ant species. These ants steal pupae, which then grow to become slaves in their adoptive colony.

A scientist adjusts a sensitive microphone used to record birdcalls. The Hungarian Academy of Science was making a collection of birdcalls heard in the Hungarian woods.

of politicking the U.S. Environmental Protection Agency and the state of Mississippi agreed to phase out its use over an 18-month period. Mirex had proved to be one of the most persistent, and hence polluting, of insecticides. Yet its usefulness was limited by the four-day effective life of the soybean-oil and corn-grits bait in which it was incorporated. To overcome this problem Earl Alley at Mississippi State University was seeking shorter lived compounds that were similar to Mirex in their toxicity to the ants.

Many research centres continued to work on pheromones, the chemicals by which insects communicate with one another. A. K. Minks of the Laboratory for Research on Insecticides at Wageningen, Neth., and co-workers found that synthetic optical isomers of sex pheromones could act as their inhibitors. The natural sex pheromone of the summer fruit tortrix moth (*Adoxophyes orana*) is a 9:1 mixture of *cis*–9- and *cis*–11-tetradecenyl acetate, and even a 10% admixture of the *trans* isomers in the same ratio blocked attraction. Used in the field in microcapsules of gelatin, the blocking agents so disrupted mating behaviour that the subsequent generation fell by 75%, compared with that in an untreated control area.

New research threw doubt on the generally accepted belief that production of the molting hormone of insects is essentially due to the prothoracic (ventral) gland—a structure that disappears in adults, which then molt no more. In cockroaches at least, some juvenile females still became adults after the prothoracic gland had been removed, according to M. Gersch and H. Eibisch of the Friedrich-Schiller University in East Germany, who found that molting hormone was then supplied by other tissues.   (PETER W. MILES)

[321.B.9.c.i; 321.E.2.a; 342.A.6.d.ii]

Ornithology. An up-to-date survey of tool use by birds showed that 28 species were known to wield external objects as implements. Among captive birds, five members of the parrot family were observed to use various objects as "back scratchers" to help them preen, or to use small tins or even a briar pipe to bail water. A captive female striped owl gathered pieces of dried leaf and used them as towels to wipe blood from her young, who had become soiled by their fleshy food. A captive bald eagle repeatedly threw an object at its keeper to attract his attention.

Among birds in the wild 16 species were known to have picked up objects in their bills as prods or levers to find food. The wild Egyptian vulture commonly breaks open ostrich eggs by the aimed throwing of stones or by using a stone as a hammer. A wild blackbird was reported to have used a small stick to clear snow from a small area in a garden, presumably in search of food. Similarly, an American robin used a twig to scatter autumn leaves. When painting its bower with a suspension of chewed charcoal in saliva, the satin bowerbird of Australia uses fragments of bark to manufacture a small oval pellet that is held near the end of the bill, where it acts as a sponge to help retain the "paint" and also as a wedge and a stopper.

Most remarkable of all, two bird species were shown to be toolmakers, modifying objects to render them more effective as implements. One is the classic avian tool user, the Galápagos woodpecker finch, which was seen to shorten a twig and to nip off side shoots so that it could be used as a probe. The other is the northern blue jay. Caged birds of this species tore off pieces of newspaper and used them to rake in food situated just outside the cage. Whereas tool use was also known in insects, spiders, and fish as well as in mammals, the actual making of tools was previously thought to be confined to man and a few nonhuman primates.

In certain songbird species, individual males each have a wide repertoire of different songs. A number of hypotheses have been put forward to explain this phenomenon; for example, that distinctive repertoires enable different cocks to identify one another as individuals. A new and fascinating explanation, dubbed the "Beau Geste hypothesis," was advanced by John R. Krebs, who suggested that a great tit which sings a variety of songs gives the impression that more great tits are present than is in fact the case, and thus decreases the apparent suitability of its territory to new birds looking for land to occupy.

The evolution of clutch size and of male "chauvinism" in the white-bearded manakin was investigated by A. Lill. Male manakins attend a courting ground and compete for females with whom they copulate promiscuously. They subsequently play no part in rearing the young. This male liberation was explained by the small size of the clutch, which usually results in a brood of two that the female can raise alone. The small clutch size was explained in turn by the need for a small nest inconspicuous to predators.

Because in recent years an average of only one new bird species has been found annually, and usually in the tropics, considerable significance attached to the Kabylie nuthatch (*Sitta ledanti*) discovered in Algeria by J. P. Ledant, a Belgian agronomist.

A masterly analysis of avian vagrancy by J. T. R. and E. M. Sharrock in their *Rare Birds in Britain and Ireland* showed among other features that American birds were visiting Europe more frequently than before. It was believed that, although a few might be ship-assisted, most were crossing under their own power. Prime among them were shorebirds (waders) like the pectoral sandpiper and land birds like the American robin. It was postulated that a change in weather patterns was responsible for the increase.

Other major works of the year included *Birds of the Western Palearctic* (edited by Stanley Cramp and K. E. L. Simmons), first volume of a seven-volume *Handbook of the Birds of Europe, the Middle East, and North Africa*; the second and third volumes of the *Handbook of North American Birds*, dealing with ducks, geese, and swans, edited by Ralph S. Palmer; and Poul Bondesen's *North American Bird Songs—A World of Music*, which for the first time gave sound spectrograms of most of the birds' vocalizations.   (JEFFERY BOSWALL)
[313.J.6; 342.A.6.e.iii; 342.B.1.b.vi]

MARINE BIOLOGY

Industrial and domestic wastes posed an increasing threat to the marine environment. Blooms of phytoplankton (the plant or plantlike component of minute, water-dwelling organisms collectively known as plankton) were related to sewage discharges, particularly near urban complexes in enclosed estuaries in Norway and Japan. On a larger scale, organic material from New York's discharges seemed to be related to annual phytoflagellate blooms in Lower New York Bay and New Jersey coastal waters. Many phytoflagellate blooms are benign but some have adverse effects, including possible fish mortality, respiratory discomfort among bathers, and diminished aesthetic value of beaches. Feasibility studies were carried out successfully at the Woods Hole Oceanographic Institution in Massachusetts on mass culture of marine phytoplankton in a mixture of sewage and seawater as a method of wastewater treatment. Follow-up work also demonstrated the possibility of growing oysters (*Crassostrea gigas* and *Ostrea edulis*) in such a recycling system.

In considering the energy balance of marine ecosystems, usually little attention is paid to heterotrophic microplankton (especially bacteria and protozoans), which require complex organic nutrients. Soviet work emphasized the importance of these organisms in the Sea of Japan; they occur in large numbers in summer as a heterotrophic phase of plankton succession that utilizes the energy from organic matter synthesized by phytoplankton during the spring outburst of autotrophic metabolism, which requires only simple inorganic

A giant 200-foot doughnut-shaped tank that maintains a steady three-knot current was built at San Francisco to study the movement of tuna, large sharks, and other fast-swimming fishes that cannot survive in rectangular tanks without colliding with the walls.

PAUL HARRISON—CAMERA PRESS/PHOTO TRENDS

A researcher examines "super plants" at the International Centre for Tropical Agriculture in Colombia. These specially bred cassava plants, grown without fertilizer, deliver five to six times the yield of ordinary cassava plants, and more food value per acre than rice or wheat.

compounds. New work in the Antarctic showed that herbivorous zooplankton (the animal component of plankton) in polar seas synthesize large lipid stores from their food to sustain them over the winter, thus explaining why cold-water forms appeared to have higher lipid contents than their low-latitude relatives.

Primary productivity of coral reefs is high despite low phytoplankton concentrations, productivity deriving particularly from a group of symbiotic protozoans (zooxanthellae) in reef corals and other invertebrates. Australian work ascertained that the zooxanthellae fix carbon at three times the rate of phytoplankton production. Zooplankton is also scarce as a food resource over coral reefs, but hitherto its availability appeared to have been underestimated, having been assumed to depend solely on organisms drifting in from the surrounding, relatively unproductive open ocean. Many plankton organisms were now known to be resident on coral reefs, hiding by day and emerging at night.

Chitin is the major skeletal component of many invertebrates in the sea; yet, unlike other skeletal compounds, it has never been reported to occur in large accumulations on the seabed. It must be rapidly degraded and recycled, and it was estimated that a population of buffalo sculpin (*Enophrys bison*) numbering 500,000 fish decomposes about 16 metric tons of chitin annually by digestion.

Recent work in Mexico explained why inshore sponges in tropical regions tend to be distasteful or toxic, while occurrence of toxicity is rarer in high latitudes. Sponges are often grazed upon by fish, which in tropical regions are numerous and diverse and show a wide variety of specialized feeding habits. This competitive pressure presumably has been met by the evolution of a variety of defensive mechanisms in prey organisms; for example, by the development of toxicity in sponges.

Similarly, gastropod mollusks respond with defensive behaviour to predatory starfish. It was shown that the normal pattern of emergence of the snail *Olivella biplicata* from sand at night could be disrupted by introducing specimens of the starfish *Pisaster brevispinus* upstream of the snails. In an aquarium, snails located as much as one meter from a tethered starfish burrowed within seconds in response to a waterborne chemical stimulus from the predator.

Further evidence of the adaptability of marine organisms in dealing with toxic materials came from work on barnacles, which in a copper-polluted region accumulate potentially toxic copper within an organic complex, thus forming granules. This immobilization of copper offered another example of the biological detoxification of heavy metals, for copper-rich granules of this kind are biologically inert. (ERNEST NAYLOR)
[354.B.2 and 4]

BOTANY

The ability of certain procaryotic microorganisms, whether free-living or in symbiotic association with a eucaryotic partner, to fix atmospheric nitrogen attracted much attention in 1977, attention that focused not only on the nature of the processes involved but also on the possibility of modifying these as a means of increasing the availability of nitrogen to crop plants and improving food production. In species of nitrogen-fixing bacteria, blue-green algae, and bacteroids that inhabit legume root nodules, the enzyme complex nitrogenase reduces atmospheric nitrogen to ammonia. Evidence presented in 1977 indicated that whereas free-living forms of these organisms assimilate the ammonia into their own amino-acid pools, in symbiotic associations the fate of the ammonia is controlled by enzymes of the non-nitrogen-fixing partner.

In lupine root nodules the ammonia synthesized by bacteroid nitrogenase was found to be assimilated first into the amino acid glutamine and then into asparagine, the form in which the nitrogen is transported in the plant; the enzymes catalyzing these steps were shown to develop in the plant part of the root nodule and not within the bacteroid. In *Nostoc*, a blue-green alga found both free and in lichen symbiosis with a fungus, it was demonstrated that in the free-living form the activity of the key enzyme for the formation of glutamine from ammonia is high, but is reduced by more than 90% when *Nostoc* is associated with the fungus. In the latter case the ammonia is secreted by the blue-green alga for sequestering by fungal enzymes. Thus the biochemistry of at least some nitrogen-fixing organisms appeared to be modified by the symbiotic partner in a way that ensures a continuing supply of available nitrogen.

Various methods of improving nitrogen fixation in crop practice were discussed at a symposium held at Brookhaven National Laboratory in New York. For example, it was reported that strains of *Rhizobium* bacteria had been isolated that could fix nitrogen in soybean root nodules without the concomitant, energy-wasting production of hydrogen that is chacteristic of *Rhizobium*-legume nodules. The recently developed techniques of molecular cloning were also employed. In one such instance genes responsible for nitrogen fixation were introduced into a plasmid (functional extranuclear genetic material) and cloned; the cloned DNA then endowed recipient bacteria with nitrogen-fixing capability. The possibility that such genes might

Well-preserved green leaves 30 million years old were found compressed within volcanic ash in Oregon. Samples included *Zelkova* species (at right), a member of the elm family. A leaf from living *Zelkova*, which survives in modern times only in the Old World, is shown at top left for comparison.

be introduced directly into plant cells, however, was thought to be remote for at least several years.

Plasmids of a different type were also shown to be of importance to plants. The discovery that crown gall disease of plants is caused by strains of *Agrobacterium tumefaciens* carrying a specific plasmid was followed by demonstrations that the plasmid could be transmitted to nonvirulent strains (thereby conferring virulence) and that it could be detected in infected plant cells that had been transformed to the tumorous state. These observations appeared to have established a case of natural transfer of bacterial genes into plant cells. Further support for the hypothesis that transfer of the plasmids from bacterial to plant cells was necessary for tumour induction came with the demonstration that conjugation transfer of the plasmids from virulent to nonvirulent strains of *Agrobacterium* is heat sensitive in the same temperature range as is tumour induction itself.

Much of the exchange of CO_2 and water vapour between the plant and the atmosphere occurs via the stomata, pores in the leaf epidermis bordered by specialized guard cells that control stomatal opening and closing. The isolation of protoplasts from guard cells of onion and tobacco leaves was recently achieved, suggesting a novel approach to investigating the cellular basis of control of stomatal opening and closing. This suggestion was confirmed when isolated guard-cell protoplasts were shown to respond to blue light by swelling; blue light was known to be effective in inducing stomata to open. The swelling was also found to be dependent on the presence of potassium ions, which were believed to be involved in turgor pressure changes in guard cells that cause stomata to open and close. These experiments indicated that the effects of light on stomatal opening and closing are mediated not only by changes in photosynthetic rates but also by the absorption of light by a receptor in the guard cell, a receptor believed to be located in the tonoplast (the membrane that bounds the central vacuole of plant cells).

The study of chemical evolution in plants, hitherto dependent on analysis of present-day forms, received a boost with the "rediscovery" of still green, well-preserved leaves that had survived for 30 million years in volcanic ash deposits in Oregon. At least 50 different compounds were detected in the leaves, including flavonoids, pigments that were under extensive study in extant plants. It was hoped that subsequent specimens from such deposits would provide additional information on evolution in flowering plants. (*See also* GARDENING.)

(PETER L. WEBSTER)
[322.A and C]

MOLECULAR BIOLOGY

Muscle Contraction. A large fraction of the body weight of most animals is given over to skeletal muscle tissue, whose specialty is a forceful shortening that is converted by ingenious systems of levers and joints into all of the macroscopic movements of life. It was known that the contractile structure of skeletal muscle is composed of parallel, interpenetrating arrays of thick and thin protein filaments, and that forceful contraction involves the creeping of thick filaments over thin filaments. Figure 1 illustrates the arrangements of these filaments in both relaxed and contracted muscle and Figure 2 presents such additional details as the cross bridges, whose "rowing action" was known to pull the thick filaments over the thin ones. Figure 2 also shows cross-sectional views that clarify the hexagonal arrangement of the filaments. Where thin filaments and thick filaments overlap, each thick filament is surrounded by six thin filaments. Thick filaments are composed of myosin, a long protein molecule with a rodlike portion and a head or paddle at one end. Myosin is 0.15 microns (1.5×10^{-7} m) long, only one-third the wavelength of blue light. It takes 350 myosin molecules to make one thick filament and there are, for instance, 9.6×10^{16} thick filaments in each cubic centimetre of rabbit skeletal muscle. Myosin molecules associate in parallel with a staggering overlap, much as one would overlap short threads in twisting a long rope. The heads of myosin molecules project from this thick filament in a spiral pattern, with six projections per turn. This count matches that of the thin filaments, six of which surround each thick filament.

Each thick filament is bipolar, with myosin molecules arranged antiparallel or tail-to-tail at its middle but in parallel on both sides of this middle.

It is as though the rowers at two ends of a long boat sat facing each other and rowed in opposite directions. Whereas this arrangement would not be sensible in a boat, in muscle the rowing motions of the myosin heads pull the thin filaments from both ends toward the middle, shortening the entire array.

The thin filaments, which are shown in Figures 1 and 2 firmly anchored to a flat protein structure called the Z line and projecting in both directions from it, are composed primarily of three proteins. One is actin, a globular protein that associates in long strings, rather like a strand of pearls; two of these strands are twisted together to create a thin filament. There is also tropomyosin, an elongated protein whose length is seven times greater than the diameter of an actin globule. Tropomyosin binds lengthwise to strands of actin. The third major component of thin filaments is troponin, which binds to tropomyosin on a one-to-one basis.

Muscle is a transducer in that it converts chemical energy into mechanical work. Hydrolysis of the high-energy compound adenosine triphosphate (ATP) provides the energy, and the myosin head, in association with actin, has the power to catalyze this hydrolysis. But muscles must contract only upon demand; hence ATP must be hydrolyzed only when necessary to answer that demand. Calcium,

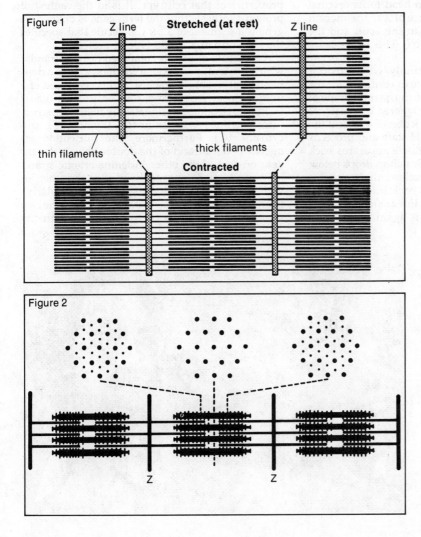

Figure 1 — Stretched (at rest) — Z line ... Z line — thin filaments — thick filaments — Contracted

Figure 2 — Z — Z

troponin, and tropomyosin interact to provide the essential controls on muscle action. The calcium in a resting muscle is 99.9% sequestered into a system of little sacs called the sarcoplasmic reticulum. A nerve impulse, arriving at a muscle, triggers a sudden increase in the permeability of the membranes of this reticulum and calcium diffuses out. The calcium binds to troponin and changes its conformation in a way that allows the attached tropomyosin to move into the groove between paired strands of actin globules. This movement uncovers sites on the actin molecules that can interact with myosin heads. The resultant association of myosin heads with actin establishes the ability to catalyze the hydrolysis of ATP, and at each myosin head this hydrolysis causes a rowing action.

Although by 1977 the more intimate details of this rowing action were not yet known, it was clear that each stroke of each myosin head is associated with the hydrolysis of one ATP molecule. It appeared that ATP binds to the myosin head and is promptly hydrolyzed, resulting in an energized myosin that retains the products of ATP hydrolysis. The energized myosin binds onto the nearest actin molecule and rows one stroke without detaching from that actin. The binding of another molecule of ATP then releases the myosin from that actin and returns the myosin head to its original cocked position. In the absence of ATP the myosin heads would remain bound to the actin and the muscle would not be extensible. This is the cause of rigor mortis.

Once the muscle has dutifully contracted, it must return to the resting state in readiness for the next nerve signal. The change in the membrane of the endoplasmic reticulum, triggered by the nerve impulse, is transitory. In a fraction of a second the membrane returns to its usual state and proceeds to pump calcium from the muscle apparatus back into the reticulum. When the calcium drops below a certain threshold concentration, the troponin-tropomyosin complex moves back into the blocking position, actin-myosin interaction becomes impossible, and the muscle is again relaxed and ready for the next impulse.

Actin and myosin together constitute fully half of the total protein of skeletal muscle and were first isolated from and studied in that tissue. Indeed it was long thought that these proteins of contraction were only found in muscle. Recently, however, actin and myosin were recognized in and isolated from dozens of cells including free-living amoebas and the phagocytes and platelets of human blood. The actins and myosins so obtained were very similar to those found in muscle, and calcium appeared always to be involved in regulating their associated action. Hence it was becoming evident that the cell's internal mechanism of protoplasmic movement (streaming) or of pinching into two daughter cells during cell division is not basically different from that of muscular contraction, and that the ability of actin and myosin to convert chemical energy into a mechanical movement must have predated muscle by hundreds of millions of years.

Genetics. Since its identification as the genetic substance in the late 1940s and early 1950s, DNA has continued to intrigue biologists. Chromosomes are composed of extraordinarily long molecules of DNA, with each molecule containing many genes. In terms of function within the cell, DNA serves to specify the structure of proteins, which in turn virtually determine the metabolic and structural properties of that cell type. It is in the context of protein synthesis that the term gene is defined. A gene is a segment of a DNA molecule that specifies the structure of a single type of protein.

A molecule of DNA is composed of two strands, which are wrapped about a common axis in a double-helical structure. Each strand is composed of a unique linear sequence of four basic constituents (called nucleotides) designated by their base structures: adenine (A), guanine (G), thymine (T), and cytosine (C). Furthermore, the nucleotide sequence of one strand of the double helix is dependent on that of the other. Adenine on one strand is always located opposite thymine on the other, to which it is joined by hydrogen bonds. Similarly, guanine is always opposite cytosine. Thus, the two strands are said to be complementary, with the

continued on page 510

George Pieczenik of Rutgers University studies radiograph of DNA sequence in efforts to understand the early evolution of protein-synthesizing mechanisms within the living cell.

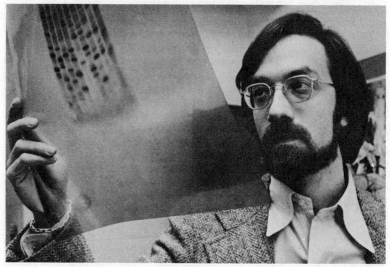

DNA RESEARCH
AND THE LAW

by Arthur J. Snider

Not since the 1940s, when significant advances in physics stimulated warnings that technology was outrunning man's ability to control it, has there been as much public and political concern over a new development in science. Three decades ago the issue was nuclear energy, a development with great potential for good or evil. In 1977 the debate centred on the capability of transplanting genetic material of one cell into a cell of a wholly different species, thereby creating a new organism; again the potential for good or evil appeared to be great.

The "gene splicing" technique consists of cutting into small pieces the long, threadlike molecules of DNA (deoxyribonucleic acid), the transmitter of genetic information, then recombining these segments with the DNA of a suitable carrier molecule and inserting the combination into an appropriate host cell, such as a bacterium. The recombinant DNA changes and controls the hereditary characteristics of the host bacteria.

Thus, recombinant DNA technology places in hu-

Arthur J. Snider is science editor of the Chicago Daily News.

man hands the capability of redesigning living organisms that have evolved over millions of years. While DNA has been combining naturally for aeons and by artificial means in plant and animal breeding for decades, the new feature offered by recombinant DNA technology is the possibility of bringing together pieces from organisms that may not normally breed with one another and thereby producing a hybrid that very probably would not have occurred in nature.

Benefits. Proponents contend that the technique not only can be a valuable tool for understanding nature but also can provide a number of practical benefits. They envision the capability of constructing bacterial strains that will revolutionize the production of biologically important substances such as antibiotics, vitamins, and medically and industrially useful chemicals. An antibiotic now is manufactured by growing large numbers of microorganisms and extracting from them a small amount of the drug, an expensive and energy-consuming process. A bacterium with an antibiotic-producing gene could manufacture the drug more efficiently.

The recombinant technique can also make possible the synthesis of large quantities of proteins, growth hormones, blood-clotting factors, and immunological agents. A research team at the University of California at San Francisco moved biochemical copies of insulin genes from a rat into the bacterium *Escherichia coli*. And although the new host did not immediately make any insulin, the California scientists were confident that such gene expression could occur. They also believe that by means of this same process they can use nucleic acid from humans to produce insulin, now available only from the pancreas of cattle or hogs. At

Demonstrators protested against unregulated DNA research at a U.S. National Academy of Sciences meeting early in the year.

PAUL S. CONKLIN

a minimum, they believe that animal experiments with rat insulin genes will shed light on the mechanism of diabetes.

In agriculture, food crops could be given the genetic ability to convert nitrogen from the air directly into chemicals essential for growth, a process known as nitrogen fixation. This could reduce world dependence on expensive fertilizers.

Risks. Critics acknowledge the potential benefits but state that they might be outweighed by unforeseeable risks. Since the DNA fragments may combine in many different ways in a given recombinant experiment, it is necessary to create vast numbers of cells with unknown genetic alterations in order to obtain a cell containing a specific recombinant DNA. Such experimentation may produce a self-perpetuating malignant "Andromeda strain" that cannot be recalled. There is no way to test for the danger. The scientist does not know what he has done until he has analyzed the newly created cells, at which time it may be too late.

From the point of view of public health, the *E. coli* bacterium chosen for most of the experiments is the worst of all possible choices. *E. coli* is a normal inhabitant of the human digestive tract and easily enters the body through the mouth or nose. Any worker harbouring *E. coli* could spread a dangerous recombinant to the rest of the world. Scientists chose *E. coli* for research because they knew more about its genetics than about those of any other cell.

Actually, it was the scientists themselves, in an act of moral initiative, who first sounded the alarm when it became apparent that these new opportunities in genetic research could lead to tampering with DNA and creating uncontrollable strains of disease-causing bacteria. Concerns were first expressed at the Gordon Conference, a scientific meeting on nucleic acids, held in New Hampton, N.H., in the summer of 1973. An open letter was sent to the journal *Science* in 1974 requesting the National Academy of Sciences to appoint a committee to study various problems of recombinant DNA. The committee recommended that a moratorium be placed on certain forms of recombinant DNA research, the first such voluntary move since physicists in the 1930s voluntarily stopped publishing nuclear energy data lest they give potential enemies information that could be used for military purposes.

Guidelines. The committee also requested that the National Institutes of Health (NIH) set up an advisory group to develop guidelines. In February 1975 the scientists went public with an international conference also attended by laymen at the Asilomar Conference Center in Pacific Grove, Calif. The conference agreed to lift the voluntary moratorium in favour of guidelines developed by the NIH.

The guidelines, governing federally supported work only, established four levels of estimated risk and prescribed combinations of suitable physical and biological containment conditions. At the low-

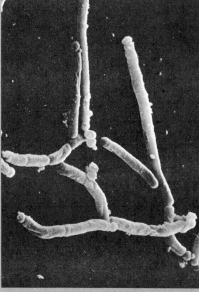

Howard M. Goodman of the University of California (right) explains a diagram of the rat insulin molecule and its gene, or DNA sequence. Goodman's research team transferred the animal gene into a special strain of *Escherichia coli* bacterium (above).

est level, experiments judged to present an insignificant risk require only the safeguard of good laboratory practice. At the highest level, the containment must be equivalent to that applied to dangerous pathogens or a chemical warfare laboratory.

But instead of allaying fear, the Asilomar conference and the guidelines that followed only fanned public anxiety. What began as an act of responsibility on the part of scientists became a breeding ground for scare scenarios. The caution adopted by scientists was widely interpreted as implying the likelihood of danger. A few leading scientists supported the ranks of the doubters and provoked even greater reaction. These scientists, joined by politicians, began questioning whether molecular biologists should do their own policing.

Public hearings, held by the city council in Cambridge, Mass., resulted in a moratorium on research at Harvard University and the Massachusetts Institute of Technology. The moratorium was lifted in February 1977, permitting the research to be resumed under standards slightly stricter than NIH guidelines. While Cambridge was the first city to regulate recombinant DNA research, several other cities with university laboratories, and some state legislatures, held hearings seeking reassurances.

Acrimonious debate continued through 1977 as federal legislative proposals were drawn up in Congress. The vast majority of scientists were fearful that the new laws might be too restrictive and impede scientific research, while critics were concerned about the spread of unpredictably virulent organisms that might threaten the public health and the environment. Critics said that the time had come for scientists to abandon their belief that they should be free to pursue the acquisition of new knowledge, regardless of possible consequences.

Scientists responded by pointing out that humanity continues to be buffeted by disease, malnutrition, and pollution, areas in which recombinant DNA research offers reasonable expectations of a partial solution. To allow preoccupations and conjecture about potential but unknown hazards limits scientific ability to deal with hazards that do exist. In addition, many scientists are convinced that the hazards of the new research have been overestimated, particularly because a newly weakened strain of *E. coli* now used in research cannot survive outside the laboratory environment.

A flood of letters and visits to congressmen by scientists and others slowed federal regulatory legislation on recombinant DNA during 1977. The Senate and House bills differed in the amount and nature of the penalties prescribed for violations and in the source of the licensing authority. Scientists feared proposed provisions that would allow local communities to impose regulations stricter than the federal law. They also argued that local option would set a dangerous precedent for regulation of other basic research.

A researcher uses suction to lift a solution of DNA segments and deposit it in a device for analysis

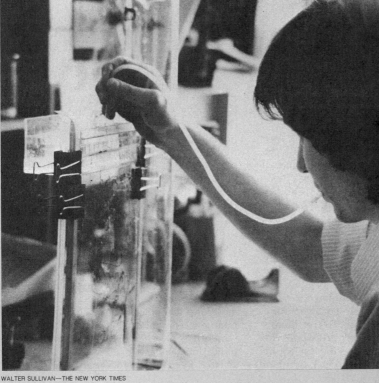

continued from page 506

nucleotide sequence of one being sufficient to specify the sequence of the other.

It is the sequence of nucleotide pairs in DNA that encodes the information for protein structure and for the regulation of gene expression. Consider, for example, how a gene codes for the structure of a protein. Proteins, like DNA, are assembled from a set of basic building blocks. These are the 20 amino acids, which in a protein are joined together in various combinations in a linear fashion.

Coding works in the following way. Each amino acid is specified by a set of three nucleotide pairs; *e.g.*, the first amino acid in a protein is specified by the first-through-third nucleotide pairs of the gene, the second amino acid by the fourth-through-sixth pairs, etc. Hence, the first triplet of nucleotides within the gene is said to set the reading frame for the rest of the nucleotides in the gene and these are decoded in a nonoverlapping fashion, in groups of three at a time. The basic triplet coding units in DNA are referred to as codons, there being 64 different codons of unique sequence. The beginning of a protein chain is signaled by one of two specific codons, whereas three different codons each function to terminate a protein. The remaining codons each designate one of the 20 amino acids, with almost every amino acid being specified by more than one codon.

However, DNA does not participate directly in the process of protein synthesis. Rather, a working copy of the nucleotide sequence of the gene is made in the form of RNA, which acts as messenger to carry the nucleotide sequence from the nucleus to the protein-synthesis apparatus in the cytoplasm, where it is decoded by the triplet method outlined above. The existence of this messenger RNA (mRNA) is fundamental to understanding the phenomenon of regulated gene expression. Evidence obtained from a variety of organisms demonstrated that a primary control governing gene expression operates at the level of synthesis of this "active" gene copy. The enzyme responsible for synthesis of mRNA, RNA polymerase, initiates synthesis at unique points on DNA, called promoters, which are located before the beginnings of genes. Synthesis proceeds along the gene and somewhat beyond to a point where the RNA chain is terminated and released.

What are promoters and how is synthesis of RNA gene copies from such points regulated? Again the answer appeared to lie in the nucleotide sequence of DNA. It was thought that RNA polymerase identifies promoter sites in DNA by virtue of its ability to specifically recognize nucleotide sequences characteristic of such sites. Furthermore, it was known that different promoter sites can differ in the efficiency with which they are recognized by RNA polymerase. Such promoter sites presumably contain subtle differences in their nucleotide sequences. Consequently the expression of genes under control of these sites may be regulated to some extent by the sequences of their corresponding promoters. In addition, proteins were identified that, depending on the metabolic state of the cell, are capable of recognizing specific nucleotide sequences adjacent to promoter regions. Binding of

such a protein to its recognition sequence leads in some cases to activation and in some cases to inactivation of the adjacent promoter.

During the past several years direct methods for determination of DNA sequences became available through two major developments. The first was the identification in several laboratories of a set of enzymes called restriction endonucleases. Each enzyme in this set recognizes a specific sequence in DNA, between four and six nucleotide pairs in length, and cleaves the DNA within that sequence. Use of these enzymes permits reduction of a large DNA molecule into a unique set of smaller fragments more amenable to sequence analysis. The second development, by Frederick Sanger and his colleagues in Cambridge, England, and by Walter Gilbert and his colleagues at Harvard University, was of techniques for determining the nucleotide sequence of these short DNA fragments.

A spectacular consequence of this work was the determination by Sanger's group of the entire nucleotide sequence of the chromosome of the small virus phiX174, which attacks the intestinal bacterium *Escherichia coli*. The DNA of this virus contains 5,375 nucleotide pairs and codes for nine proteins designated A through J (the letter I was not used). This determination made it possible to view the viral chromosome as a giant molecule of known structure and to relate this structure to the function of individual genes. Most striking in this work was the discovery that two genes can occupy the same segment of DNA. Gene B, together with its probable promoter, is contained entirely within the larger gene A, with the codons for the two genes being one nucleotide out of phase. Similarly, gene E is one nucleotide out of phase with and contained entirely within gene D. Thus, by utilizing two different reading frames, the same segment of DNA is used to specify two distinct protein products. It had generally been thought that genes were always contiguous and nonoverlapping.

Virtually all the information described above was obtained from studies on the bacterium *E. coli* and several of its viruses. What is the feasibility of extending such studies to more complex organisms? To put this problem in perspective, consider that, whereas the chromosome of phiX174 contains 5,375 nucleotide pairs, the chromosome of *E. coli* contains 3.2×10^6 nucleotide pairs and the haploid DNA content of the human cell is 2.9×10^9 nucleotide pairs. Although the problem might seem impossible, recent developments in recombinant DNA technology (*see* Special Report) could provide the major breakthrough in this field in much the same way that restriction endonucleases facilitated DNA sequencing methods.

In recombinant experiments large DNA molecules are cleaved into smaller fragments (typically about 5,000 nucleotide pairs in length). These fragments then are individually attached to a vector, a piece of DNA capable of autonomous replication in the cytoplasm of *E. coli*. Next these hybrid DNA molecules are placed into *E. coli* cells, where the fragment is replicated along with the vector to which it is attached. This technique permits amplification of a particular fragment that can then be isolated in quantity and analyzed.

In recent, independent studies Ronald Davis and his colleagues at Stanford University and John Carbon and his co-workers at the University of California, Santa Barbara, cloned gene-containing segments derived from yeast DNA in *E. coli*. Of major significance was the finding in both laboratories that at least some yeast genes were capable of producing active protein products in the *E. coli* cell. Successful efforts to induce higher-order gene expression in bacteria were announced late in the year by Herbert Boyer of the University of California, San Francisco, and co-workers who inserted into a strain of *E. coli* a viable artificial gene fragment that coded for a modified form of the mammalian hormone somatostatin. A two-gallon culture of the altered bacterium subsequently yielded about five milligrams of the hormone, a striking demonstration that all the genetic information needed to produce an animal protein could be transferred to a bacterium for the rapid manufacture of a desired gene product.

(IRWIN FRIOVICH; PAUL LAWRENCE MODRICH) [323.D; 339.C]

See also Earth Sciences; Environment.

Literature

The 1977 Nobel Prize for Literature went to the 79-year-old Spanish poet Vicente Aleixandre, one of those unpredictable choices with which the Swedish Academy astounds the Anglophone literary world in particular. The frail survivor of a lifetime's serious ill health, the Spanish Civil War, and the ensuing isolation and suppression seemed as surprised as anyone. But if others had more fame abroad, no one had had more influence on succeeding generations of Spanish poets than Aleixandre, with his flashing metaphors and profound meditations on man's uneasy homesteading in the natural world. (*See* NOBEL PRIZES.)

The year saw the deaths of Vladimir Nabokov and Robert Lowell (*see* OBITUARIES), certainly the most accomplished novelist and poet of the time not to have been awarded a Nobel Prize. Each seemed to have summed up, if not concluded, a tradition in his work, Lowell the American patrician line, and Nabokov a whole complex of traditions—of the Russian line of fantasy stemming from Gogol, which went underground in the Soviet Union after Mikhail Bulgakov, and of the main branches of modernism in the novel stemming from Joyce and Kafka.

It was not difficult to see these deaths as emblematic in a year in which thoughtful observers, like the Swedish publisher Per Gedin, reported declining standards in Western publishing practice and reading habits. In *Literature in the Market Place*, Gedin described how in Sweden, culturally and economically "a kind of pilot country," the effects of increased economic specialization had reduced the literary and historical content of educational syllabi in the interests of relevance and productivity, with the result that classic texts, deprived of a secure educational market, were being allowed to go out of print at an alarming rate.

A former New York publisher, the novelist W. J. Weatherby, described the structural changes that were reinforcing this harsh commercialism: a growing reluctance to publish books at all unless paperback rights could be sold in advance; the declining status of editors and the growing power of salesmen, from whose ranks top publishing executives were increasingly chosen. "Inflation and recession have imposed their own form of censorship," he concluded.

Blunter forms of censorship were practiced on publishers arriving for the new Moscow Book Fair who had books and catalogs impounded by Soviet customs men. In Prague the playwrights Vaclav Havel (*see* BIOGRAPHY) and Pavel Kohourt were brought to trial on charges of "subversion." (See *Eastern European Literature*, below.)

The *Times Literary Supplement* celebrated its 75th anniversary with a feature, "Reputations Revisited," in which a distinguished international band of intellectuals offered an interesting set of brief revaluations. Freud, Gide, Malraux, Toynbee, E. M. Forster, and the Bloomsbury writers generally were thought to have been overrated and H. G. Wells, Ford Madox Ford, Thomas Mann, and Raymond Queneau to be currently undervalued.

Liquors, Alcoholic:
see Industrial Review

Vicente Aleixandre, Spanish poet and winner of the 1977 Nobel Prize for Literature.

© LÜTFI ÖZKÖK

ENGLISH

United Kingdom. Although the nation's financial books seemed to be coming into balance at last, there were some fairly spectacular crashes on the British literary stock market in 1977, such gilt-edged reputations as John Fowles, Ted Hughes, and the late J. R. R. Tolkien (*see* OBITUARIES) being among those marked down heavily in the reviewing columns.

"The most massively awaited work since the return of Sherlock Holmes from the Reichenbach Falls" *The Guardian's* reviewer called Tolkien's posthumous epic, *The Silmarillion* (not unreasonably, since well over half a million copies were subscribed before publication). And the novelist Margaret Drabble recalled how, waiting for the last volume of *The Lord of the Rings* 20 years earlier, she "used to include Tolkien in my prayers at night." Even so devout a reader, however, found herself describing these ruins of the author's lifelong work on an English creation myth as "pretentious," while *The Spectator's* reviewer confessed that, "not for want of trying," he found the book "literally unreadable."

FICTION. Pretentious was a common verdict, too, on John Fowles's long novel *Daniel Martin,* an attempt, inflated in every way, at a representative statement about the diseased consciousness of his generation, as witnessed by a highly successful playwright and scriptwriter. Drabble's *The Ice Age,* another diagnostic novel about current strains of English sickness by a writer also given to lecturing her readers—and characters—was similarly, though less drastically, deplored.

If it was not a vintage year for fiction this was hardly the fault of Anthony Burgess, who published two novels within four months. *Beard's Roman Women,* a strange piece of self-haunting, was full of angry and ironic parodies of episodes from

his own life and fictions. "He has begun to do fictional 'turns,'" wrote Paul Theroux, "bringing vaudeville into the novel." *Abba, Abba* showed Burgess the wordman in spate, providing first a meeting between the dying Keats and the scatological Roman dialect poet Giuseppe Belli (about to become Vatican censor), then a mock note on and translations of 75 of Belli's biblical sonnets. Theroux himself produced *The Consul's File,* a linked set of 20 stories of the life of a small Malaysian town observed by a quiet young American, a characteristically cool and intelligent performance.

Beryl Bainbridge's *Injury Time* was characteristic, too: a brief, funny, and painful, even cruel, account of a middle-aged affair disrupted by the intrusion of a gang of villains; characteristic also in making one wish she would risk a little more by attempting something more humanly comprehensive than these intriguingly freaked but rather bleak little tales of hers. *Johnny, I Hardly Knew You,* on the other hand, made one wish for rather less of Edna O'Brien, whose latest creature of excess, Nora, was like a parody of some of her earlier, likelier girls. There were better Irish novels: Jennifer Johnston's *Shadows on Our Skin,* for example, which kept civil war in its place while her hero grappled with the dire enough complexities of growing up; or Aidan Higgins' rather mood-drunk reordering of a life in memory, *Scenes from a Receding Past.*

Certainly Dan Jacobson's *The Confessions of Josef Baisz* was one of the most ponderable novels of the year, a darkly ambiguous study of a totalitarian apparatchik, set in a vividly registered nightmare country that owed something to the author's native South Africa and something to the atmosphere of Eastern European totalitarianism in one of its darker episodes.

Two very different serial works of fiction were concluded and a new one begun. Christopher Isherwood's lifelong friend and critic Edward Upward ended his trilogy *The Spiral Ascent* with a volume called *No Home but the Struggle.* One might doubt the conviction of his dialectical resolution—back to political hope after recovering the imaginative moments of early life in a long poem—but Upward's dogged and vulnerable exploring of a kind of writing and thinking neglected in England, no less than the sometimes eerie relationship of his work to that of Isherwood and W. H. Auden, had won him a place in literary history.

Michael Moorcock's Jerry Cornelius tetralogy, completed with *The Condition of Muzak,* engaged more closely with the imaginative life of the times than many more solemn works, rather as H. G. Wells's scientific fantasies did in the early years of the century. A cleverly chosen collage of quotations helps to structure the novel's glittering episodes, and one of them, from the historian George Dangerfield, defines its character quite precisely: "Very minor literature . . . is the Baedeker of the soul, and will guide you through the curious relics, the tumbledown buildings, the flimsy palaces, the false pagodas, the distorted and fantastical vistas which have cluttered the imagination of mankind at this or that brief period of its history." Not so minor either, perhaps.

John Fowles, author of *Daniel Martin.*

The new start was that of Olivia Manning, who, in *The Danger Tree*, stylishly relaunched Guy Pringle, the admirable hero of her Balkan trilogy, on a new series of adventures in wartime Egypt—familiar territory to which P. H. Newby also returned with a darkish comedy of sexual manners in a novel called *Kith*.

The year's Booker Prize for fiction was awarded to Paul Scott, who in *Staying On* poignantly portrayed an elderly English couple, left-overs of the British Raj, living in the new India.

LETTERS, LIVES, HISTORY. Martin Green's *Children of the Sun* essayed English cultural history since World War I in terms of opposed traditions of "dandyism" and what he had called "decency" in an earlier book. The shrill hostility and rude glee provoked by its account of the "dandy" tradition, which provided England's dominant cultural models for more than three decades, showed that it touched on still raw nerves. This "saga of snobbery, sodomy, and epideictic incontinence," wrote Dennis Potter, ". . . makes *Children of the Sun* more than just another book about books." E. M. Forster's homosexuality was hardly of the exhibitionistic kind common among Green's "dandy-aesthetes," but P. N. Furbank's *E. M. Forster: A Life* made plain the importance of his sexual history to Forster himself and to the nature of his art in a sympathetic account of the 30 years spent, as Hynes observed, living "the life of an aunt in Surrey"—and a maiden aunt at that.

Although Isherwood claimed Forster as his spiritual father and the leader of his English "tribe," there was nothing aunt-like about *Christopher and his Kind*, an account of his own life and loves in Herr Issyvoo's world of the 1920s and '30s (oddly transposed into the third person). *Ruling Passions* was the uncompleted autobiography of an unhappier member of the "tribe," Evelyn Waugh's contemporary at Lancing and Oxford, Tom Driberg, the man who introduced Auden to *The Waste Land* and later became a dedicated servant of the Labour Party. Hardly anything emerged of this part of his career; much, of a desperately exhibitionist kind, of his adventures in alleyways and public lavatories. Some vivid gossip did little to lighten the bitter pathos of this gifted man's self-portrait. Robert Hewison's *Under Siege* and Derek Stanford's *Inside the Forties* were collective portraits, covering the half-forgotten ground of the decade from the pubs and pads of Fitzrovia to the maneuvers of the small army of literary firemen and their little magazines.

V. S. Pritchett wrote a good study of Turgenev (*The Gentle Barbarian*), and there was an excellent reappraisal of an eminent and underprized Victorian, *Thackeray: Prodigal Genius*, by John Carey, a young Oxford don who emerged as one of the most effective polemicists on the English literary scene. *Caught in the Web of Words* was an affectionate and informative study of James Murray, the dour dominie who became lexicographer extraordinary of the great *Oxford English Dictionary*, by his granddaughter K. M. Elisabeth Murray; and Eric Partridge, a surviving lexicographer almost as remarkable, produced *A Dictionary of Catch Phrases* which, as Paul Theroux wrote, could be read "for

the sheer fun of it" but was invaluable for what it recorded of the oral tradition in social history.

A historian wrote the most important literary study of the year—Christopher Hill's *Milton and the English Revolution*, which brought the living complexity of the poet's interaction with his times into focus as no previous work had done. It seemed appropriate since, while literary criticism was in the doldrums, Britain was clearly in the middle of a great period of historical writing, with brilliant scholars of a younger generation emerging. One of these, Theodore Zeldin, completed his astonishing single-handed history of modern France with a second volume, *France, 1848–1945: Intellect, Taste and Anxiety*. *Patriots and Liberators*, a densely peopled study of the late 18th-century revolutionary period in The Netherlands, showed Simon Schama to be in the same brilliant class. Tom Nairn's *The Break-up of Britain* was one of the most effective polemics the new British New Left had produced on domestic politics, as Paul Thompson's revised edition of his biography of *William Morris* was the noblest work of the old New Left.

POETRY. With Ted Hughes's *Gaudete*, the first problem was to determine the genre: poetic novel, narrative poem, verse play? It was in fact derived from an abandoned film scenario, as many powerful visual setpieces attested. But that was the least of critical problems with this extraordinary account of the pastoral visiting of the Rev. Nicholas Lumb in an English village that sometimes sounded uncomfortably like the parish of Stella Gibbons' *Cold Comfort Farm*. Martin Dodsworth cut most cleanly through the murk. *Gaudete*, he wrote, had "careless strokes of genius on most pages, all at the level of registering sensation . . . But Hughes can't or won't think. The sex and violence give way to nothing else and so don't liberate." More attention might have been paid instead to *Mother Poem*, the beginning of a new sequence by a master of the long poem, Edward Braithwaite, who here celebrated the people and culture of his native Barbados and his own return to it. Michael Hamburger's *Real Estate* was another collection that repaid attention, the mature work of a fine, melancholy poet who was also Britain's most accomplished translator of German poetry.

(W. L. WEBB)

United States. FICTION. In 1977 the novel found itself in the midst of the post-modern crisis in fiction. Writing in the shadow of Nabokov, Beckett, and Borges, novelists searching new themes confronted endless intellectual deadends. Master parodists, versatile in style and skeptical of temper, they located their home in a region where irony and fancy discovered their largest freedom of expression. Dealing with the crippling excesses of consciousness in a world deprived of moral values, they still managed to make art of nihilistic themes.

Their contemporary fictions, taking forms of pastiche, mock history, and droll allegory, supported heroes who were lovers of reality attempting to discover—with the medium of a protean language—some balm for the ache of consciousness. They went still further in decreating the forms of fiction and in reconstructing myth, litera-

© THOMAS VICTOR

Jerzy Kosinski.

ture, even technology, so as to discover glimmers of values that a post-modern artist might still hold.

In 1972 Philip Roth told how the mature David Kepesh turned into *The Breast*; in *The Professor of Desire* he describes Kepesh's earlier, less symbolic guises — child of the Borscht Belt, scholar of Kafka, wrestler with temptation. Believing that "my desire is *desire*, it is not to be belittled or despised," young David becomes a "visiting fellow in erotic daredevilry" in the Swedish company of anything-goes Birgitta and secretly shy Elisabeth. Saddled with the guilt of having corrupted Elisabeth, David moves on and West — to "hopeless misalliance" with wife Helen, "runnerup for Queen of Tibet." An inertial move back East to analysis: "I cannot maintain an erection, Dr. Klinger. I cannot maintain a smile, for that matter." And finally school-teacher Claire, who, if Birgitta represented a lust-indulging "more," represents the comforts of "enough."

But is enough enough? And will it last? Even forgetting *The Breast*, probably not, for David Kepesh is a direct descendant of Alex Portnoy, doomed to *kvetch* his lonely way out of any possible happiness. And if this gravity makes David's self-pitying narcissism somewhat indigestible, it also allows Roth to find quieter music in Jewish word-rhythms that have blared raucously before. And David's musings on Kafka, though not shedding light on his own groinal angst, make him a more substantial schlemiel than his precursors. From the waist down, then, the same old story, sans laughs; but, in head and heart, a subdued and seductive tour de force.

A year after the unanticipated success of *Fear of Flying*, Erica Jong, Roth's closest confessional imitator, the uncanonized "matron Saint of Adulteresses," had already programmed her next zipless book, *How to Save Your Own Life*. Isadora Wing of *Fear of Flying*, otherwise Candida of *Candida Confesses*, otherwise Erica, plans to abandon her coop and her glum, methodical, Oriental psychiatrist husband. In the same off-the-wall fashion as in the earlier books, this ultimate *femme sensuelle* ("Someday every woman will have orgasms — like every family has color TV") vamps identical material.

With Jerzy Kosinski's *Blind Date*, it is once more with horror as another Kosinskian foreign-born American — George Levanter of "Investor's International" — goes out on a taut, unconnected series of international "blind dates" with violence and debasement. Whether Levanter is victim (blackmailed by corrupt cops) or avenger (skewering a Communist spy in a homosexual bath-house), he is "removed from the act." A master of secret-keeping and of enticingly neutral prose — never ironic, flushed, or crude — Kosinski guides his reader into dark places otherwise avoided and elicits shudders otherwise suppressed in advance in this refined inventory of human abuse.

In the genre of seriocomic myth-fantasy, 1977 was the year of the detective. *Dreaming of Babylon* found Richard Brautigan at his breeziest — inside the mind of C. Card, the worst shamus in 1942 San Francisco, bereft of clients, cash, and companionship. A cartwheeling fantasy, more like a sentimental comic book without pictures, the Babylonian pipedreams and whimsies do their tricks without keeping C. Card from getting where he's going, which is nowhere.

In *Fata Morgana*, William Kotzwinkle's lyrical star twinkled above Second Empire Paris, where Inspector Paul Picard, after bungling an arrest, is put on a con-artist case. Ric Lazare's salon attracts the choicest billfolds, breasts, and pedigrees; they come for the glitz, for decolletage, but, above all, for Ric's fortune-telling machine: a complex, deadly, pornographic toy telegraph that never errs.

Thomas Berger, the seriocomedian of *Little Big Man* and the Reinhart trilogy, kissed serio goodbye in *Who Is Teddy Villanova?* as private eye Russel Wren slides from seedy idleness into 72 hours of justifiable paranoia and incorrigible wordplay. Clues: a bullet in a brownie, a black lace brassiere. Suspects: Boris the pedophile, Natalie "Pick up a Czech" Novotny of the Treasury Department, a busful of Lolitas, and the Gay Assault Team.

In women's movement fiction: more sad songs — replay them as they lay — in the shimmering oblivion of empty glasses and empty beds. *A Book of Common Prayer* by Joan Didion (*see* BIOGRAPHY) offered another lost lady, a dim survivor named Charlotte: about to be killed, carrying a child who will· never see life, formerly married to Warren dying of cancer, waiting for daughter Marin who is wanted by the FBI — all bound together with decorative sophistication.

More desperate intimacy and all-too-self-fulfilling martyrdom were visible in Anne Roiphe's *Torch Song*, another negative commitment, about the submissive, masochistic, and sexually morti-

© THOMAS VICTOR

Coming into the Country by John McPhee reported on an eastern American's encounters with the Alaskan landscape and its inhabitants.

fying love of Marjorie Weiss—assimilated Park-Avenue Jewish—for Jim Morrison, wasp homosexual with very peculiar habits.

Sandra Hochman's *Endangered Species* discovered Woman in Transition about to emerge, in disjointed recollections, from a tent of past secrets: divorced parents who never truly parented, marriage to a salesman, travel, divorce, and affairs all those lib-long nights. Other remote, self-contained persons populated Shirley Ann Grau's *Evidence of Love*, where the evidence is nowhere to be seen. The novel leads down, in fastidiously curious steps, from birth ("the evidence") to death ("the community of blood").

"One simply does not marry men who are Siamese twins!" was the premise of Judith Rossner's novel, *Attachments*. But Nadine and Diane do—and what begins as prurient interest in "academic" sexual positions becomes a rather conventional *ménage à quatre* rife with frustrations and complaints about who's washing all the dishes.

On the popular front, John Cheever's (*see* Biography) broad metaphysics of life and death, always in mysterious tandem, were constants in *Falconer*. In a prison redolent of Genet sits Farragut, a fratricide and drug addict, awaiting salvation. The shrewdest Washington novel since *Advise and Consent*, William Safire's *Full Disclosure* was about a president blinded in an air attack and a campaign to replace him (using the ambiguous 25th Amendment on presidential disability) with a Throttlebottom-of-the-barrel VP.

History, Biography, and Belles Lettres. In *The Age of Uncertainty*, John Kenneth Galbraith scored a major achievement. After dollops of Smith, Ricardo, and Malthus and heartier servings of Marx and Keynes, the work gathers force as Galbraith, leaving the confines of history, deals with the modern corporation, the causes and cure of poverty, the urban quandary, and live politics.

The Wolf by the Ears, by distinguished academic historian J. C. Miller, examines Thomas Jefferson's political and personal views of slavery, finding him an increasingly committed defender of the system's expansion after his efforts in the 1780s to ban it from the western territories. Another 18th-century effort was *The Empire of Reason*, an essay by Henry Steele Commager, a dean of American historiography, contrasting the European profession of the Enlightenment with down-to-earth American accomplishments.

More contemporary was George Kennan's *The Cloud of Danger*, offering a "grand design" for meeting the overall needs of U.S. foreign policy on a region-by-region basis, including forceful arguments advocating détente with the Soviet Union.

John Cheever, reclining.

© THOMAS VICTOR

© THOMAS VICTOR

Susan Sontag published *On Photography*, an analysis both of the artistic elements of photographic art and of the effects of photojournalism on the perception of reality.

America's leading poet, Robert Lowell, who died in 1977. His *Day by Day* appeared during the same year.

© THOMAS VICTOR

Even more topical was Richard Reeves's *Convention*, an adrenalin-rush entry in new journalism—a frenzied, hysterical circus with hundreds of private campaigns going on even as the delegates prepare to nominate the candidate from Georgia. Amid the spectacle, Reeves has time to wonder if Jimmy Carter with his ritual laying on of hands represents some new kind of political force, if the convention bespeaks a day when candidates and presidents may lead via primitive symbolism.

From the Puritan veneration of the elders to present-day gerontophobia, David Fischer, a resourceful and incisive social historian, traces America's changing attitudes toward the aged in *Growing Old in America*. In a radical departure from prevailing sociological wisdom, Fischer disputes the notion that the breakup of the family led to the disesteem for and isolation of the old. In behavioural science, *Toys and Reasons* by Erik Erikson contains intricate ruminations on the relation of play to reality during different stages of life and in various aspects of human experience. Exploring the interplay between inner experiences and social/political behaviour, Erikson attributes critical importance to early visual associations and to vision as a perceptual modality throughout life.

More dramatic, in what could be called the big bang theory of consciousness, Princeton University psychologist Julian Jaynes asserts in *The Origin of Consciousness in the Breakdown of the Bicameral Mind* that up to the end of the second millennium BC there was no such thing as consciousness. People heard voices—the commands of the gods or of their authoritarian emissaries. Such auditory hallucinations dictated the decisions that ruled lives. The two sides of the brain neatly embody this order, Jaynes argues: "the language of men was involved with only one hemisphere in order to leave the other free for the language of god"—an extraordinary, not to say radical, hypothesis.

In the genre of literary biography, Jonathan Yardley's *Ring* charts the development of the wise-boob persona and the ungrammatical, misspelled vernacular style that became Ring Lardner's trademark and, arguably, one of the prime sources of "talking" prose in modern American letters. In *Nabokov: His Life in Part*, Andrew Field parlays his expertise into an elegant homage, discursive and elliptical, anecdotal and analytic, precious and profound, buddy-buddy but nevertheless ultimately impersonal.

Two worthy political biographies also appeared: *Harry Hopkins* by Henry Adams examines Franklin Roosevelt's all-round troubleshooter, adviser, and personal liaison during World War II with Winston Churchill, who dubbed him "Lord Root of the Matter." And Gerald Dunne's *Hugo Black and the Judicial Revolution* shares its subject's unabashed spirit and size. Born in farm country, with populist background, Black befriended such patrician Fabians as Harold Laski in his ascent to the U.S. Supreme Court. This Fabianism, defined by Dunne as "procedural change to effect social transformation from above," came to permeate the court as a whole.

In a year more notable for memoir than for biography, several major autobiographies appeared. *Philosopher at Large*, by intrepid encyclopaedist Mortimer Adler, impressed, revealing a dedicated philosopher possessed of self-effacing wit and winning charm. Adler describes with candour, humour, and much detail his role in the expansion of the "great books" idea and the creation of the major new revision of the *Encyclopaedia Britannica*.

In a major Vietnam memoir, entitled *A Rumor of War*, Philip Caputo's supreme achievement was to make the war psychologically comprehensible to those who can only blame or mourn—a clearsighted, unsentimental record of a legacy that will not relinquish its hold. Less solemn, *Talking to Myself: A Memoir of My Times* reveals Studs Terkel as ever laconic, wry, often baffling ("I tape therefore I am"). The inflections and sensibility are all Chicago, and Terkel keeps it taut all the way through.

When America's greatest living humorist turned travel correspondent from Europe, Asia, and darkest Los Angeles, his chewy muse only slightly stifled by the duty to play it straight, the result was S. J. Perelman's *Eastward Ha!* Also noteworthy were *Clearing the Air* by Daniel Schorr, a dignified account of his fall from corporate grace, and *The Names*, N. Scott Momaday's poetic recollections of his Kiowa Indian childhood in the Southwest. Two important belletristic volumes were Edmund Wilson's *Letters on Literature and Politics, 1912–1972*, edited by Elena Wilson, and *Selected Letters of William Faulkner*, edited by Joseph Blotner.

POETRY. As if culminating Robert Lowell's personal and poetic drama, *Day by Day* appeared: "heightened from life,/yet paralyzed by fact." Perhaps Lowell (*see* OBITUARIES), in his mood of valediction, had made peace with the entropy that saturates this volume.

Other major contributions included: John Ashbery's *Houseboat Days*; A. R. Ammons' *The Snow Poems*; *This Body is Made of Camphor and Gopherwood* by Robert Bly; and Allen Tate's *Collected Poems*. Most significant was John Berryman's *Henry's Fate and Other Poems, 1967–1972*, the first posthumous volume of his poems, containing 45 previously unpublished Dream Songs.

(FREDERICK S. PLOTKIN)

Canada. The great question facing Canada in 1977 was national unity, but this would have been difficult to ascertain if one read only its English-language literature. Rudy Wiebe's *The Scorched Earth People* did deal with some of the historical events behind the crisis, and Matt Cohen's *The Colours of War* was set during a civil war, but neither reflected the current situation.

Margaret Atwood's first collection of short stories, *Dancing Girls*, displayed again her ability to present the inner world of her characters. Jane Rule, in *The Young in One Another's Arms*, demonstrated once more why she deserved recognition as a writer rather than notoriety as a lesbian. *Personal Fiction*, an anthology of stories by Alice Munro, Rudy Wiebe, Audrey Thomas, and Clark Blaise, edited by Michael Ondaatje, combined each author's theories on their art with samples of their mastery of it. Audrey Thomas explored the complex interactions of the sexes in *Ladies and Escorts* by assuming now the Lady's role, now the Escort's. Constance Beresford-Howe ventured onto this same terrain in *A Population of One*, but her excursion was more that of a soldier preparing to assault a machine-gun nest.

In nonfiction, *Broken Promises* by J. L. Granatstein and J. M. Hitsman deals with the high political price paid for conscription. In *A Terrible Beauty* Heather Robertson collected prose, poetry, drawings, and paintings that superbly realize her title. *Out of the Shadows* by W. A. B. Douglas was a sober analysis of Canada's contribution in World War II. In Charles Taylor's *Six Journeys*, such disparate

Pierre Berton brought the sensation of a spectacular event of Canadian history back to life in *The Dionne Years.*

figures as Emily Carr and Bishop William White are brought within his conception of a Canadian pattern. Pierre Berton used the sensation caused by the Dionne quintuplets as a paradigm of life in Canada during the '30s in *The Dionne Years*. In Volume 3 of *One Canada*, John Diefenbaker presented his version of the fall of his administration. *The Neglected Majority*, edited by Susan Mann Trofimenkoff and Alison Prentice, details the contribution of Canadian women from the early days of the fur trade to the present.

After a long silence Leonard Cohen was heard again in *Death of a Ladies' Man*, pursuing his themes in both prose and poetry. Earle Birney had three new books—*Alphabeings and Other Seasyours*, in which he played with visual poetry; *The Damnation of Vancouver*, a satire on the modern city; and *Ghost in the Wheels*, a selection of poems from 1920 to 1976. *A Stone Diary*, Pat Lowther's last book, reaffirmed the loss to Canadian letters in this fine poet's untimely death. In *Extra Innings* Ray Souster was back at what he does best, observing the small significant moments of contemporary life.

(ELIZABETH WOODS)

FRENCH

France. The trend among younger novelists was away from the complexities of the "new novel" and toward the construction of solemn fantasies, typified by Didier Martin's *Un Garçon en l'air*. As a child, the narrator discovers he can fly. Though this talent gives him great satisfaction, it has no practical use and isolates him even from those who share his ability. While denying analogies with anything outside the novel, the writer allows flight to serve as a paradigm for various human conditions and impulses, from religious and sexual emotions to artistic creation.

A still more sombre account of the discontinuity between the everyday world and a child's poetic vision was given in Myrielle Marc's undervalued novel *Petite Fille rouge avec un couteau*. Sustained fantasy also inspired Pascal Bruckner's story of a group of children who terrorize the Paris métro, *Allez jouer ailleurs*, and Patrick Thévenon's *L'Artefact*, in which the hero makes a work of art of his own body and pursues the process of self-effacement in his creation to its ultimate conclusion.

American literature had clearly inspired some of these trends among younger writers, and America itself offered a pasture for the imagination as well as an intellectual challenge. Yves Berger had explored the possibilities of its mythology in the previous year with *Le fou d'Amérique*. Georges Walter's *Le Faubourg des Amériques* played on the continuities and contrasts between Puritan past and Hollywood present, and Didier Decoin, in *John l'Enfer* (the year's Goncourt prizewinner), examined New York through the eyes of an American Indian window cleaner. All these novels, despite their differences, chose to fantasize about the New World rather than to study the actuality of the United States.

Most of this was very far from the textual density one had come to associate with the French novel, illustrated, for example, in 1977 by Jean Ristat's *Lord B.* and finding theoretical expression in the work of the critic Roland Barthes, whose *Fragments d'un discours amoureux* was one of the surprise successes of the year. But in general the public continued to prefer the straightforward traditional novel and was given plenty of opportunity to appreciate its strengths and weaknesses. Henri Troyat (*Le Front dans les nuages*) and Gilbert Cesbron (*Mais moi je vous aimais*) were among the many well-established writers to publish new works. Marcel Pagnol's posthumously published fourth volume of autobiography, *Le Temps des amours*, gained a predictable success. Another bestseller was Michel Déon's *Les vingt ans du jeune homme vert*. Mixing humour and pathos in its story of one man's survival under the World War II German occupation, it appealed to a fashion for nostalgia which admitted even the less enchanting moments of the past. If Patrick Modiano, exploring the theme of Jewishness during and after the war in the pseudo-autobiographical *Livret de Famille*, gave a very different picture of the Occupation, the real contrast between his work and that of Déon lay in the demands made on the reader.

Modiano's book was one of a number that mixed fiction and autobiography. Pierre Goldman's *L'ordinaire Mésaventure d'Archibald Rapoport* also begins under the Occupation and analyzes violent rebellion against the established order in a manner reminiscent of Jean Genet. There was also an element of self-analysis in Régis Debray's novel about a European among left-wing guerrilla fighters in South America, *La Neige brûle* (awarded the Prix Fémina). While Debray had turned from political writing to fiction, the country's mood of political scepticism was best expressed in such works as Roger-Gérard Schwartzenberg's *L'État spectacle* and in the soothsaying of *Les 180 Jours de Mitterrand*, where a group of journalists cynically predict the outcome of a left-wing victory in the March 1978 elections.

In October a conference in London discussed the situation of poetry in France and Britain. Reaching much the same conclusions as a survey in the magazine *Les Nouvelles littéraires* earlier in the same month, participants suggested that major publishing houses in both countries were increasingly unwilling to take on work by lesser-known poets, who were obliged to turn to the little magazines and small presses. For some, this picture of too many poets and not enough readers was discouraging, while others, mistrusting the literary establishment, found the vitality of the small presses exhilarating. The work they published ranged through every stage from the tediously conventional to the merely bizarre. But among poets who no longer had to rely on their services, the trend was toward the adoption of elaborate formal constraints, as in Georges Pérec's *Alphabets* and in the "found" poetry of Jacques Roubaud's *Autobiographie, chapitre dix*.

Alain Peyrefitte, the novelist, historian, and essayist who in 1977 was also minister of justice, was among new members of the Académie Française. From October, Marcel Arland handed over the editorial chair of the *Nouvelle Revue française* to Georges Lambrichs, who promised both an eclectic approach and one that he hoped would attract young readers to the French literary establishment's most eminent periodical. Among writers who died in 1977 was the poet and screenwriter Jacques Prévert (*see* OBITUARIES).

(ROBIN BUSS)

Canada. Noteworthy developments in 1977 included the reissue of several old works, among them *Le Débutant*, an early 20th-century novel by Arsène Bessette, whose original publication caused something of a scandal. The publication of the *Lettres d'une paysanne à son fils*, collected by Jeanne L'Archevêque-Duguay, was a long-awaited event. The letters, written between 1908 and 1927, provide a carefully detailed account of country life.

Several novels merited mention: Roger Fournier's *Les Cornes sacrées*, recounting the adventures of a young peasant boy much attached to his pet bull; Roch Carrier's *Il n'y a pas de pays sans grandpère*, in which an old man attempts to relate his thoughts to his grandson and, in so doing, give the boy a sense of historical continuity; Jean-Paul Filion's *Les Murs de Montréal*, a chronicle of the author's working-class youth; Gabrielle Roy's *Ces enfants de ma vie*, in which the author relives her days as a teacher in Manitoba; and Alain Pontaut's *La Sainte Alliance*, a brilliant work on certain levels, which uses an allegorical tableau to trace a portion of Quebec's history.

In poetry, the long-awaited, posthumous volume of Claude Gauvreau, *Oeuvres créatrices complètes*, sustained the beauty, depth, and hermeticism of his other poetry and plays. *La Traversée du réel* represented some of Michel Leclerc's most beautiful poetry in recent years. *Retailles* by Denise Boucher and Madeleine Gagnon approaches the form of oral discourse more closely than that of poetry, allowing the reader to focus on the two women's political lament.

Among collections of essays, *L'Homme gratuit*

was a long, systematic, and perceptive interrogation on the human condition. *Blocs erratiques*, a posthumous work by Hubert Aquin, included a selection of unedited texts written between 1948 and 1977. *Souvenirs et impressions du premier âge, du deuxième âge, du troisième âge—Mémoires humouristiques et littéraires*, the memoirs of François Hertel, educator and controversial philosopher of the 1930s and '40s, marked the author's return to public life after more than 20 years' exile in France. André G. Bourassa's *Surréalisme et littérature qúebécoise* studies the influence of surrealism on French-Canadian literature through an examination of the works of such authors as Grandbois, Gauvreau, and Giguère.

(ROBERT SAINT-AMOUR)

GERMAN

Writers had a bad time in 1977. In the East the storm surrounding protest singer Wolf Biermann's expulsion continued to send forth waves on which, among others, Reiner Kunze and Sarah Kirsch landed in the Federal Republic. In the West the kidnapping and murder of industrialist Hanns-Martin Schleyer provoked the right-wing press to accuse people like Günter Grass and Heinrich Böll of "sympathizing with terrorists."

In the West the book of the year was undoubtedly Grass's *Der Butt*, his first novel since 1969. A Rabelaisian work in many senses, it covers the history of woman's social role since the Stone Age, mingling politics with recipes, poems with anecdotes, the whole bound together by the nine months of the narrator's wife's pregnancy and an old tale of a fisherman and his wife.

Other works appeared slight or lifeless by comparison. Gisela Elsner's *Der Punktsieg* was an entertaining novel of manners set in the world of aesthetes and rich industrialists whose Social Democratic affiliations do not prevent them from laying off their workers. Both W. E. Richartz (*Büroroman*) and Wilhelm Genazino (*Abschaffel*) exploited the unpromising material of office life. Günter Herburger's 700-page *Flug ins Herz* moved into unreality with its story of a social experiment, the coupling of a kidnapped capitalist with a proletarian wench. Most effective was Otto F. Walter's *Die Verwilderung*, which relates an attempt to establish a commune in Switzerland against the opposition of the local inhabitants and incorporates a montage of actual and imaginary press clippings, reflective passages on historical anthropology, and extracts from a novella by Gottfried Keller.

Other writers concentrated on the personal problems and relationships of individuals, while hinting at the social or political forces that contributed to these problems. Nicolas Born's *Die erdabgewandte Seite der Geschichte* was an impressive-depressing evocation of life as it impinges, as if for the first time, on a consciousness shaken out of its equilibrium. In Dieter Wellershoff's *Die Schönheit des Schimpansen*, social factors, notably the half-criminal underworld, and the pathological were more prominent.

Historical fiction, often linked with autobiography, enjoyed a certain vogue. Horst Bienek's *Sep-temberlicht* continued where his previous novel left off—in Silesia on the eve of World War II. Angelika Mechtel's *Wir sind arm, wir sind reich* evokes the 1950s, while Hermann Kinder's *Der Schleiftrog* covers, at breakneck speed, the years 1960 to the present from the perspective of schoolboy and student. Conventional autobiographies included Elias Canetti's enormously successful *Die gerettete Zunge*, on his youth in Bulgaria, England, Austria, and Switzerland, and Oda Schaefer's *Die leuchtenden Feste*, on the years 1945–50. Peter Handke's *Das Gewicht der Welt*, diary entries of the past few years, impressed even his opponents. In perhaps the most exciting event of this kind, Wolfgang Koeppen broke his silence with *Jugend*, impressionistic scenes from his early years around the time of World War I. Of international interest was the publication of Cosima Wagner's diaries of the years 1869–83. Collections of shorter fiction included Günter Radtke's *Der Krug auf dem Weg zum Wasser*, Mario Szenessy's posthumous *In Paris mit Jim*, and Urs Widmer's *Vom Fenster meines Hauses aus*.

The continuing trend in lyric poetry was to register everyday observations in a precise, matter-of-fact manner, as in Karl Krolow's *Der Einfachheit halber* and Rolf Haufs' *Die Geschwindigkeit eines einzigen Tages*. Herbert Asmodi's *Jokers Farewell* consists of understated but wholly sympathetic poems on aging and death. In an older, more hymnic and hermetic tradition were the poems in *Zeit, Überzeit* by Gotthard de Beauclair.

In East Germany historical fiction continued to be popular. Martin Stade's *Der König und sein Narr*, set in 18th-century Prussia but with many implied parallels with the present, had considerable success. Erich Köhler's *Hinter den Bergen* describes the fluctuating postwar fortunes of a remote community in a curious mixture of realism and allegory.

© LÜTFI ÖZKÖK

Günter Grass.

Christa Wolf.

Two important novels took up the thorny question of Polish-German relations: Hermann Kant's *Der Aufenthalt*, written in his familiar racy style, was based on his experiences as a prisoner of war in Poland; Christa Wolf's *Kindheitsmuster*, describing an extraordinarily honest search for the everyday reality of life under the Nazis in what is now Gorzow, was undoubtedly the most important work to appear in East Germany in recent years. Stefan Heym's short stories *Die richtige Einstellung* also included historical themes. However, in this genre Hans Joachim Schädlich's *Versuchte Nähe* was outstanding: scenes from East German life written in impressively dense and concise style; stories which, however, could appear only in the West, like emigré Thomas Brasch's bitterly critical *Vor den Vätern sterben die Söhne*.

Paul Günter Krohn's *Alle meine Namen* collected poems from 20 years on individuality and the collective will, while Sarah Kirsch consolidated her reputation as the most important female lyricist of her time with the love poems *Rückenwind*.

(J. H. REID)

SCANDINAVIAN

Danish. Two of Denmark's major writers died in 1977: Frank Jaeger, whose impact was mainly in the 1950s, and Leif Panduro, whose high reputation as a novelist and, more especially, as a writer of television plays, was steadily increasing. One of Jaeger's contemporaries, Tage Skou-Hånsen, analyzed the contradictions of modern Danish society in *Den hårde frugt*. The prolific Klaus Rifbjerg published a thought-provoking novel, *Et bortvendt ansigt*, portraying the efforts of a middle-aged architect to overcome the barriers of age and class, and the semiautobiographical *Drengene*. In contrasting vein was Karen Blixen's hitherto unpublished essay "Moderne aegteskab og andre betragtninger" (in the second volume of *Blixeniana*), which takes a critical look at modern concepts of marriage.

More books written by women were appearing.

A newcomer was Ellinor Kotyza Rich, whose "lyrical collage-novel" *Vi ses naeste torsdag* was a mixture of poetry and reflection with only slight action to keep them together. Jytte Borberg produced an entertaining historical novel in *Eline Bessers laeretid*.

Memoirs included Karoline Jensen's *Jomfru Jensens erinderinger* (1976), Frode Jakobsen's *Da leret tog form* (1976), Terkel Terkelsen's *Fra pålidelig kilde. Kapitler fra et bevaeget journalistliv*, and Aage Dons' *Uden at vide hvorhen* (1976) and his largely autobiographical essays, *Den arabiske pulver* (1976). William Heinesen's *Tarnet Vid Verdens Ende* (1976), a mixture of biography and fantasy in the true

Klaus Rifbjerg.

(Left) William Heinesen;
(right) Peter Holm.

Heinesen tradition, continued the semiautobiographical late works of this distinguished author.

Among much poetry to appear in 1977 were Charlotte Strandgaard's *Naesten kun om kaerlighed*, Vita Andersen's *Tryghedsnarkomaner*, Jørgen Gustava Brandt's *Ophold*, and Jess Ornsbo's *Digte uden arbejde*. The novelist Vagn Lundbye published his first poems, *Digte 1977*, revealing a love of nature and concern for the way it is being treated.

Winner of the Danish Academy's 1977 literature prize was Peter Seeberg, whose analysis of provincial life, *Argumenter for benådning*, appeared late in 1976.

(W. GLYN JONES)

Norwegian. Rolf Sagen received a well-deserved Norwegian Critic's Prize for his remarkable novel *Mørkets gjerninger*, in which he managed to weave social satire into an amusing story of a day in the life of a 19-year-old youngster. Considerable stir was caused by the winner in a publisher's thriller competition, the documentary *Jernkorset* by Jon Michelet, which saw Nazism as a force still very much alive in Norway. Odd Winger's ironic meta-novel *Romanen* was an elegant survey of the contemporary Norwegian intellectual climate. Autobiographical material formed the basis of two humorous regional novels set around 1930, *Avikfjord* by Terje Stigen and *De lange mil til paradiset* by Kåre Holt. Childhood reminiscences from the early years of the 20th century were explored in Finn Havrevold's novel *I fjor sommer*. Male attitudes toward women formed a leading theme in Gunnar Lunde's novel *Benken ved jernbanestasjonen* and Finn Carling's collection of short stories, *Marginalene*.

Johan Borgen's 75th anniversary was marked by the publication of four volumes of his shorter prose works, *Noveller og annen kortprosa I-IV*, as well as a two-volume collection of his articles on writers and books, *Borgen om bøker I-II*. Vera Henriksen's

historical novel *Skjaersild* concluded a cycle of five volumes centred round the 16th-century figure Bent Jonsson. Among poetry collections were Gunvor Hofmo's *Hva fanger natten*, Hans Børli's *Vinden ser aldri pa veiviserne*, Stein Mehren's *Det trettende stjernebilde*, and Sigmund Skard's *Ord mot mørkret*. Love poetry was central in Jan Magnus Bruheim's *Lyrespelaren* and, with refreshing irony, in Helge Vatsend's *Livets bok*. Irony and humour were ingredients in Peter R. Holm's *I disse bilder*.

Critical works included Jørgen Haugan's detailed analysis of six Ibsen plays, *Henrik Ibsens metode*; Ase Hiorth Lervik's *Menneske og miljø i Cora Sandels diktning*; and Bjarte Birkeland's *Olav Duuns soger og forteljingar*.

(TORBJØRN STØVERUD)

Swedish. Sara Lidman, one of Sweden's most powerful novelists of the 1950s, had abandoned fiction for almost a decade of dedicated political activity. In her new novel, *Din tjänare hör*, she embarked on a trilogy, with the year 1867 as starting point and the inhabitants of an isolated community as her subject. The relationship of individuals to society was a theme in several works: in Karl Rune Nordkvist's *Hösten lang*, a prematurely retired construction worker bitterly reviews his life in light of the nonsocialist parties' victory in the 1976 general election; in Lennart Frick's *Sprängningen*, an old worker looks back over a life of dedicated party adherence only to ask himself what became of the brotherhood the early socialists dreamed of. Provocatively critical of the political establishment was young Henning Mankell's novel *Vettvillingen*, which built on the internment of Communists in northern Sweden during the early 1940s.

Heidi von Born's *Simulantens liv* was a skillful study of an elderly hypochondriac, unable to deal with his real relationships but engrossed in identifying with a famous dying man several thousand miles away. In Per Gunnar Evander's *Fallet Lillemor*

Karl Rune Nordkvist.

Holm, a middle-aged psychotherapist reviews the case of a young clairvoyant patient who committed suicide. The book aroused considerable discussion when it transpired that the girl's own account of her life had appeared under the title *Lungsnäckan* earlier in the year, conceivably edited by Evander himself. In Sven Delblanc's *Grottmannen,* human passion is seen as a mystical experience. Rune Pär Olofsson, a former parson, wrote an allegory of God captive at the hands of the church in *Morgonlandet.* On the poetic front, Lars Gustafsson's *Sonetter* aroused interest, as did Per E. Rundquist's collection *Men störst av allt är kärleken till vem.* A posthumous selection from Pär Lagerkvist's notebooks was published in *Antecknat.*

(KARIN PETHERICK)

Heidi von Born.

ITALIAN

Italian writers' concern for the country's persistent state of general tension was again central to much of the year's literature. *I ratti d'Europa* by Mario Lunetta was a very dense, somewhat allegorical novel, experimental in form, recounting the peregrinations, intellectual and moral as well as physical, of a contemporary left-wing militant, kidnapped and subjected to continuous violence all over Western and Eastern Europe by the mysterious agents of the "strategy of tension." A historical antecedent of this kind of strategy was closely examined by Leonardo Sciascia in his documentary work *I pugnalatori.* The book was written with one eye on a historical event—the simultaneous stabbing to death of 13 apparently unconnected people in Palermo in 1862, commissioned by powerful and untouchable supporters of the return of the Bourbons—and the other on the contemporary political situation of the country, where a long-term strategy of disseminating panic among ordinary citizens seemed to be employed with the aim of weakening both the country's democratic institutions and the determination of its people to oppose any kind of authoritarian solution.

A more universal feeling of dissatisfaction inspired the last, posthumously published, novel by Guido Morselli, *Dissipatio H.G.,* whose narrator, a lonely middle-aged intellectual, discovers on surviving his own suicide attempt that mankind has entirely vanished from the face of the earth. The tradition of socially inspired regional novels was well sustained by Gavino Ledda, whose success with *Padre padrone: l'educazione di un pastore,* the autobiographical story of a lonely, self-taught Sardinian shepherd who becomes a professor of linguistics, was confirmed by *Lingua di falce,* a new novel on a similar theme but perhaps more carefully and more sensitively structured. Saverio Strati's *Il selvaggio di Santa Venere* was an impressive portrait of the tragic reality of Calabrian peasant life.

Memorie di una dilettante by Rossana Ombres, *La spiaggia del lupo* by Gina Lagorio, and *La condizione sentimentale* by Carla Cerati, three novels with different social settings and characters, well represented the contemporary predicament of Italian women, caught between their traditional role and the progressive affirmation of a feminist consciousness. But the most controversial book of the year was *Porci con le ali,* an anonymous diary in which the alternating narrators, a boy and a girl in their teens, explicitly use an utterly uninhibited language to describe their sexual experiences against a background of crumbling families and the chaotic activities of young left-wing militants.

The best works of the year were perhaps to be found outside the areas of topical literature. Fulvio Tomizza's novel *La miglior vita* was ostensibly a diary kept by the sexton of his community through two world wars, Fascism, the Resistance, and socialism under Tito. The seven parish priests he served provide a splendid gallery of human characters and attitudes and, although the "better life" of the title is that which comes after death, the novel avoids moralistic pitfalls. Memory was also central to Luigi Meneghello's *Fiori italiani,* where it was focused on the protagonist's educational experiences in Fascist Italy. The book shows how the youth of that generation was easily manipulated by the regime's cultural policies, at least until the crisis of World War II. More significantly, it shows that Italian culture was traditionally well suited to warp even the best minds long before Fascism inherited it.

New poetry included Maria Luisa Spaziani's *Transito con catene*, Bartolo Cattafi's *Marzo e le sue idi*, and Giovanni Giudici's *Il male dei creditori*. Tommaso Landolfi, better known as a novelist, again tried his hand at poetry and achieved considerable success with *Il tradimento*. Perhaps overshadowing these was Eugenio Montale's *Quaderno di quattro anni*, a collection of more than 100 new poems, written after *Diario del '71 e '72*, in which the poet seems to reconfirm his definitive awareness of the absurdity of existence and his profound conviction of the necessity of man's allegiance to an ideal of moral dignity.

(LINO PERTILE)

SPANISH

Spain. The award of the 1977 Nobel Prize for literature to Vicente Aleixandre was a tribute to the dedication of a poet given over entirely to the full practice of his art. Though he was not politically motivated in his work, Aleixandre's home had been a refuge for other writers, many of whom had been leading dissidents. He had also greatly influenced the younger poets of the country. Worthy as the judges' choice was, it displayed a certain bias: the clearly great Spaniards had been overlooked. Passed over through the years were such masters as Unamuno, Ortega y Gasset, Antonio Machado, Pío Baroja, even the very much alive Camilo José Cela and Jorge Guillén. (*See* NOBEL PRIZES.)

Cela busied himself during the year with his *Enciclopedia del Erotismo* and put an end to it with No. 60 of the series, published as a part work. The most readable of the year's novels was perhaps Gonzalo Torrente Ballester's *Fragmentos de Apocalipsis*, though it was not up to the standard established by *La Saga/fuga de J.B.* A noteworthy verse collection was Francisco Brines' *Insistencia en Luzbel*. Another meaningful book was José María Valverde's *Ser de palabra*; Valverde himself returned to Spain from years of exile in Canada. The Premio de la Crítica was awarded, for a novel, to Rosa Chacel, author of *Barrio de maravillas*, and for poetry to Octavio Paz.

(ANTHONY KERRIGAN)

Latin America. Three major figures died during 1977: Juan Marinello of Cuba and Carlos Pellicer and Martín Luis Guzmán, both of Mexico. Guzmán's "novel" *The Eagle and the Serpent (El Águila y la Serpiente)*, first published in 1928, remained one of the classic eyewitness accounts of the Revolution. Pellicer and Marinello both belonged to the iconoclastic avant-garde of the 1920s. The first, best known for his poems of tropical America, became the first president of the Association of Latin-American Writers. Marinello was one of the founders of the influential Cuban journal *Revista de Avance*.

Publishing remained depressed in Latin Ameri-

© LÜTFI ÖZKÖK

Leonardo Sciascia.

ca, where censorship was a fact of life, but thanks to a small boom in Spanish publishing the year was a good one for the major Latin-American writers. Perhaps the main event, however, was the awarding of the Rómulo Gallegos Prize in Venezuela, given only once every five years. The most serious contenders were the Paraguayan Augusto Roa Bastos, Gabriel García Márquez, and Carlos Fuentes, who finally received the award for his monumental novel *Terra Nostra*. *World Literature Today* (formerly *Books Abroad*) honoured Mario Vargas Llosa, currently president of the International Pen Club. The Cuban *Casa de las Américas* prizes, always an interesting sign of new literary talent, went to Manlio Argueta (El Salvador) for his novel *Caperucita en la zona roja*, Eugenio Hernández Espinoza (Cuba) for his play *La Simona*, Jorge Musto (Uruguay) for a poetry collection, *El pasajero*, and Guillermo Samperio (Mexico) for his short-story collection *Miedo ambiente*.

In fiction the main trend was toward themes involving both politics and mass culture. Julio Cortázar, despite his experiments in pop and comic strip, was one of the exceptions, returning to the kind of short story he wrote in the early '60s. Nevertheless, his new collection, *Alguien que anda por ahí*, was not entirely devoid of political references. Mario Vargas Llosa, on the other hand, seemed to prefer the lighter vein; his new novel, *La tía Juana y el escribidor*, is set in the 1950s and has a radio soap opera scriptwriter as its protagonist. Manuel Puig, the Argentine writer who helped set the trend of pop narrative, turned to weightier matters. His *El Beso de la mujer araña* uses pop elements, tape recordings, and legal documents, but its axis is a dialogue between a homosexual and a political militant, confined to the same prison-cell. This allows Puig to confront, from opposing standpoints, problems of personal and social liberation.

The important Peruvian writer Julio Ramón Ribeyro also turned to politics in *Cambio de guardia* which, like Vargas Llosa's earlier *Conversation in the Cathedral*, takes place during the Odría dictatorship. Other novels mingling pop culture with narrative were Osvaldo Soriano's *Triste, solitario y fina final*, a fantasy that brings in Laurel and Hardy and characters from Raymond Chandler; and Luis Rafael Sánchez's *La guaracha del macho Camacho*, in which a popular song links diverse characters to form a panorama of Puerto Rican life. Among Mexican novelists, Jorge Ibargüengoitia's *Dos muertas* related the lives of two prostitutes, while José Agustín brought out *La mirada en el centro*. From Puerto Rico, Rosario Ferré, the brilliant young editor of the literary journal *Zona de carga y descarga*, published her first short-story collection, *Papeles de Pandora*. In a more traditional mode, Juan José Hernández of Argentina brought out *La favorita*, a collection of stories centering mainly on provincial life.

The prize for the best young Peruvian poet was awarded to Jesús Cabel for *Cruzando el infierno*. Also in Peru, there appeared a fine edition of a new book of poems by Antonio Cisneros, *El libro de dios y de los húngaros*. In Mexico two major poets published collections: Jaime Sabines was represented by *Nuevo recuento de poemas* and Efraín Huerta by *Circuito interior*. Among young poets, David Huerta's *Cuadernos de noviembre* showed special promise.

(JEAN FRANCO)

PORTUGUESE

Portugal. Concern with the debasement of post-revolutionary language to catchwords, clichés, and slogans might account for the metalinguistic or metaliterary character of almost every significant work of the year. Herberto Helder's *Cobra*, opening with a poem redefining poetry and closing with one calling for the abolition of "texts," explored the antithesis of word and silence, as did the somberly sensual poems of António Ramos Rosa's *Boca Incompleta*, relating word and silence to presence and absence. Sophia Andresen ended five years' silence in *O Nome das Coisas*, interspersing grave mediations on love and time with "metapoems" in praise of other poets and of the word in peril. Fiama Brandão's *Homenagem à Literatura* likewise included poetic tributes to poets, from the 15th-century Sá de Miranda to the contemporary American Lawrence Ferlinghetti. In *Distância*, by Liberto Cruz, the erotic and semiotic were inextricably intertwined. But the revelation of the year was the fastidious poet and retired professor Vitorino Nemésio's scrupulous and unflinching analysis of physical passion in old age, *Sapateia Açoriana*, endowing a potentially embarrassing theme with a dignity and even a paradoxical delicacy that put him as much in the company of a Yeats or an Ungaretti as of the Camões and Goethe he specifically invoked.

Fiction was, on the whole, less impressive. Olga Gonçalves's short novel *Mandei-lhe uma Boca* tape-recorded the impoverished language (and corresponding emotional impoverishment) of middle-class Lisbon adolescents, cut off by changing times from their families and by class from the mass of their contemporaries. Linguistic brilliance and structural complexity failed to redeem two more ambitious novels from a hint of pretentiousness. *Os Lusíadas* by M. da Silva Ramos and Alface was

apparently a reworking of Camões' epic, analogous to Joyce's of the *Odyssey*. *Casas Pardas* by Maria Velho da Costa(most gifted of the three authors of the celebrated *New Portuguese Letters* and perhaps the subtlest prose writer of her generation) seemed excessively clever and suffered by comparison with her earlier *Maina Mendes*.

(STEPHEN RECKERT)

Brazil. Jorge Amado's *Tieta do Agreste* was the most acclaimed novel published in 1977. A masterful yarn about the grandiose banality of life in the northeastern town of Agreste, its madcap conflicts, revolving around pollution and power, are developed in Amado's typical thought-provoking yet entertaining manner. Josué Guimarães' *Os tambores silenciosos*, which deals with the rise of a dictatorship in Río Grande do Sul, was involved in a censorship dispute after being awarded the first Érico Veríssimo Prize. Nonfiction fiction of a journalistic nature was abundant, the most notable examples being José Louzeiro's *Acusado de homicídio* and Aguinaldo Silva's *República dos assassinos*. Paulo Francis's first novel, *Cabeça de papel*, views the disillusionment of a sector of Brazilian society as a result of the 1964 military coup.

Short fiction continued to be extremely popular. Lygia Fagundes Telles's new collection, *Seminário dos ratos*, has one bordering on a gothic horror tale, while the title story (this year's quota of metaphorical Brazilian rats) is an effective political satire. Interest in certain national "minorities" gave rise to the collection *Malditos escritores*, which includes stories by major figures on a variety of social situations, from pornography to soccer.

Two new volumes of poetry reflected the continued importance of concretism: Carlos Nejar' *Árvore do mundo* and Décio Pignatari's *Poesia/Pois é/Poesia*. Pignatari also published a theoretical volume on poetry, *Comunicacao poética*. An anthology of poems by the late Murilo Mendes was organized by João Cabral de Melo Neto with a study by José Guilherme Merquior.

Many notable critical works appeared: collections of general criticism by Ledo Ivo, Miroel Silveira (on theatre), and Almeida Fisher; a volume of the major critical studies on Drummond de Andrade; and an edition of Mário Faustino's literary theories and criticism. Raul Bopp, who received the Machado de Assis Prize, published an "inside story" of the modernist movement, *Vida e morte da antropofagia*. The first volume of Roberto Schwarz's *Ao vencedor as batatas* discusses the literary role of Alencar (whose centenary was celebrated in 1977) and studies Machado de Assis's first prose works.

(IRWIN STERN)

RUSSIAN

Soviet Literature. With 1977 marking the 60th anniversary of the October Revolution, many of the 7,000 or so works of fiction and poetry published in the U.S.S.R. during the year were devoted to this theme. Afanasy Koptelov, who had already written two interesting novels on Lenin's life and work, published a third, *Fulcrum*, recounting Lenin's early revolutionary activities, his exile in Siberia, and the struggle to create the newspaper *Iskra* and a Marxist party in Russia.

Anatoly Ivanov's two-part novel *Eternal Call* was well received, reviewers praising in particular his skill in portraying complex characters. The book's first volume covered the period of social transformation in rural life during the 1920s. In the second volume, Ivanov probed the inner world of his characters within the framework of historical development through World War II (the Great Patriotic War) and the difficult years of the immediate postwar period.

The Bank of Love, a novel by the Ukrainian writer Oles Gonchar, was set in the present and was concerned, on one level, with the daily life of Ukrainian farmers and on another, with man's creative quest in life. The evocation of steppeland nature was particularly fine. Pyotr Proskurin scored a popular success with *Destiny*, a novel dwelling on the fate of his own generation, the emergence of the collective farm system in the Soviet countryside, and the people's exploits during the grim years of the Great Patriotic War. In a new novel, *Your Name*, Proskurin depicted postwar life and its challenges.

While the heroic years of the Great Patriotic War retreated ever further into the past, the exploits of this period were not forgotten. In *Sevastopol Chronicle*, Pyotr Sazhin, a former seaman in the Soviet Navy, wrote about those who had defended the besieged city in 1942 and about meetings with his former front-line comrades. Other writers who dwelt on the military theme were Iosif Gerasimov, Ilya Turichin, and Yury Ilyinsky.

The year's poetry included collections by such established poets as Stepan Shchipachev, Yevgeny Yevtushenko, Valentin Sorokin, and Arkady Kuleshov. Among lesser known poets who attracted attention were Konstantin Vanshenkin, Bella Akhmadulina, Anatoly Zhigulin, Rimma Kazakova, Viktor Bokov, Maya Borisova, and Stanslav Zlotsev.

In the field of literary studies and criticism, the outstanding Soviet literary scholar Mikhail Khrapchenko published *Artistic Creative Endeavour, Reality, Man*, representing a summation of the reflections of one who for half a century had stood in the vanguard of Soviet literary historians and theoreticians but who preferred to dwell on the present rather than the past. Other scholarly publications included a new edition of Lenin's writings *On Literature and Art*.

Soviet letters suffered a major loss with the death in July of Konstantin A. Fedin (*see* OBITUARIES).

(ALEKSEY OVSYANNIKOV)

Expatriate Russian Literature. The two most important works of Russia's alternative literature to emerge during the year were linked in a strange cousinage. Aleksandr Solzhenitsyn's crude but powerful narrative poem *Prussian Nights*, composed, much of it, in his head during the worst of his time in the camps, recalls vividly his experiences as an officer in the Soviet army that entered enemy territory early in 1945, shortly before his arrest. The autobiography of his contemporary, Lev Kopelev, *To Be Preserved Forever* (called *No Gaol Without Thought* in the London edition), begins with its author's arrest on the same East Prussian front after he had irritated his superiors with

protests against the same brutal treatment of German civilians that Solzhenitsyn bears witness to in his poem. Two years later the two men met as privileged prisoners at the same *sharashka* (research institution), which Solzhenitsyn was to use as the setting for *The First Circle*, and Kopelev became the model for the character of Lev Rubin—"a Jew and a Communist . . . [who] felt that his own position here was tragic in the Aristotelian sense. He had been struck down by something he loved more than anything else." That indeed was the situation Kopelev describes in his account of how the enthusiasm was wrung out of him as he went through the Stalinist mill—though even at his most bitter he makes the whole appalling history seem humanly comprehensible, as the God-intoxicated Solzhenitsyn often does not.

During the Thaw and after, the complex relationship between the two men continued. It was Kopelev, Solzhenitsyn disclosed in *The Calf Butted the Oak*, who persuaded him to take the manuscript of *One Day in the Life of Ivan Denisovich* to Aleksandr Tvardovsky, the editor of *Novy Mir*, who first published it, with Khrushchev's approval. And it was Kopelev, now doyen of the dissidents' corps in Moscow, who contributed an essay to a collection of "voices of the socialist opposition in the Soviet Union" published in April (*Samizdat Register I*, edited by Roy Medvedev), rebuking Solzhenitsyn for some of the bad history and dark argument of his *Letter to the Soviet Leaders*, especially his demonizing of Marxism as if it were synonymous with Stalinism.

(W. L. WEBB)

EASTERN EUROPEAN LITERATURE

"Big nations make history, small ones receive its blessings," wrote the Czech novelist Milan Kundera in the magazine *Index*. "A small nation does not see history as its property and has a right not to take it seriously." In 1977, a year in which history continued to bear down harshly on Czechoslovakia, many of its writers were hard put to it to count their meagre blessings in the wry Czech way. Vaclav Havel (*see* BIOGRAPHY), the country's most gifted dramatist, spent more than three months in prison and then received a 14-month suspended sentence on charges of "subversion" (for sending or attempting to send out of the country material the authorities would not allow to be published at home and did not wish to be published abroad).

Nevertheless, work of value continued to be published in Prague, both officially and in the *samizdat* form known locally as "the padlock press." Novelist Ludvik Vaculik (also subject to police harassment for his sponsorship of Charter 77, the human rights manifesto circulated in January 1977) called on his friends to revive the characteristic local form of the feuilleton, formerly an important feature of the Czech press and one of the ways in which the nation had talked to itself since the days of the 19th-century nationalist writer Jan Neruda. By the end of the year about 30 of these reflective little essays-with-a-moral were circulating in typescript bundles, some of Vaculik's own contributions appearing in translation in the West German weekly *Die Welt*. Occasionally work by a

Jerzy Andrzejewski.

© LÜTFI ÖZKÖK

writer previously banned would suddenly appear from official presses: *Postriziny* ("Cuttings"), for example, a novella by the surrealist writer Bohumil Hrabal (known best as the author of *Closely Watched Trains*) celebrating episodes in the life of his eccentric mother. Jiri Sotola, a gifted poet largely unpublished since 1969, was allowed to bring out *Kure na rozni* ("Chicken-on-a-Spit"), a vivid historical novel.

New forms of *samizdat* also appeared in Poland, most significantly in the magazine *Zapis*, which specialized in good work turned down by the official magazines and publishing houses. These included an extract from Jerzy Andrzejewski's massive new novel *Pulp*, based on Boris Pasternak's famous telephone call from Stalin, and poems and stories by Kazimierz Brandys, Stanislaw Barancak, and Marek Nowakowski. In Hungary writers mourned the death of Tibor Déry (*see* Obituaries), the nation's finest modern novelist. Published abroad was *A Worker in a Workers' State*, a remarkable account, suppressed after fierce debate, of the effects on workers of the piece-rate system as it operated in a Hungarian factory, written by the young poet Miklos Haraszti after several months spent working on the shop floor.

(W. L. WEBB)

JEWISH

Hebrew. The literary event of the year in Israel was the ongoing celebration of U. Z. Greenberg's 80th birthday, marked by an extensive exhibit at Jerusalem's National and University Library. Other anniversaries noted were the 75th birthday of Dov Sadan, the 80th of Abraham Regelson, M. Bernstein, and Nathan Bistritsky, and the 90th of D. Zackai.

The year saw the demise of the prominent journal *Keshet* and the birth of two "little magazines,"

Itton and *Proza*. The venerable *Moznayim* published an index to its volumes for 1929–69. Now with seven volumes, *Siman Kri'a* had become Israel's central literary periodical, energizing the literary scene with continued high-quality and forceful aesthetic (and often political) manifestos. As a result, a minor Kulturkampf developed, with vigorous exchanges on "realism" versus "aestheticism." Certainly the recent changes in Israel's political leadership contributed to these debates.

Major poetry publications included books by the veteran poets Yonothan Ratosh, Avot Yeshurun, Shin Shalom, and Gabriel Preil, posthumous works by Zussman and Nathan Alterman, and the collected poems and works of Simon Halkin and Shimshon Meltzer. New collections appeared by Yehuda Amichai, Abba Kovner, T. Carmi, and Tuvia Ruebner. Important younger poets with new works were Mier Wieseltier, O. Bernstein, Hurvitz, Dalia Ravikovitch, and Y. Wallach (her collected poetry)—most from the *Siman Kri'a* circle. Major prose publications included S. Y. Agnon's *Pithei Devarim*, Kahana-Carmon's *Sadot Magnetiyim*, A. B. Yehoshua's *Hame'ahev*, and novels by D. Shajar, A. Megged, D. Tselka, H. Lazar, and Y. Levitas. Impressive new writers were A. Rodriguez and "Gabi Daniel." New plays were penned by H. Levin, Y. Sobol, A. Raz, and Moshe Shamir. Eminent translations included Ephraim Broido's *Sonnets* by Shakespeare and M. Wieseltier's *To the Lighthouse* by Virginia Woolf. Critical works appeared on Sholem Aleichem, Hayyim Bialik, J. H. Brenner, Saul Tchernichowsky, and Yitzhak Shenhar.

(WARREN BARGAD)

Yiddish. In *Whither Daniel?*, Benjamin Schlevin produced a political novel dealing with Jewish youth in Paris searching for the meaning of existence. Flashbacks describe life in postwar Poland and ill-fated attempts to reconstruct Jewish life there. Jehiel Mohr, in *A Haluts from Poland*, portrays the struggles of Jewish youth to settle in Palestine in the 1920s. Aron Pacht in *Two Households* returns to Jewish shtetl life in Poland between the two world wars. Family struggles and conflict are dealt with in Leizer Treister's *By the Rivers of New York*.

Kalman Segal, an Israeli, in his collection of stories, *Privacy*, writes in an ironic mode about alienated Jews. Israel Kaplan in his collection, *Harvest of Time*, captures prewar Lithuania and the life of the extremely pious Jews of Jerusalem. Meir Yelin's *The Price of that Bread* describes the suffering in Lithuania during the Holocaust. Mordkhe Tsanin's *The Insurrection of Mezhibosh*, the latest addition to his multivolume epic novel *Artapanos Comes Home*, depicts the rise of Hasidism with clarity and sympathy.

In poetry, Avrom Sutzkever's exceptional *Poems from My Diary* reveals mastery of form and maturity achieved through years of creativity. Part of Josl Lerner's *Till Dawn Breaks* consists of poems written in a German-Romanian death camp during World War II. Motl Saktzier's *With a Burned Pencil* describes his experiences in various Soviet *gulags*. Chaim Maltinsky conjures up his native Vitebsk in *My Mother's Resemblance*. Shloyme Roitman offers magnificent sonnets in *My Israel Shofar*, and Efraim Roitman, delicately constructed, polished poems in *The Earth Sings*. Hirsh Osherovitch's *Song in a Labyrinth* contains unpublished poems written in the Soviet Union and others composed in Israel. Rajzel Zychlinska displays astonishing craftsmanship in *The Sun of November*. M. M. Shaffir, in *Words of Endearment*, elegantly reworks traditional themes in a *folkstimlekh* manner. An important two-volume selection of the work of David Hofshteyn, a major poet and one of Stalin's last victims, was published in Israel.

(ELIAS SCHULMAN)

CHINESE

The literary mood in Taiwan in 1977 seemed to be less serious and more disposed toward entertainment. Whether the stories were set in the imperial past, as in Kao Yang's *The Iron Justice* and Chang Sou-han's *The Jade Dragon*, or in the contemporary milieu of bar girls, nuns, and characters from the lower class, as in Ts'eng Hsin-i's *I Love Doctor* and Chiang Kuei's *The World of Su Pu-chin* and *The Seed Forms When the Petals Fall*, the reader's interest was sustained by complicated plots and surprising turns of fortune. Typical was Chiang Kuei's *The Seed Forms*, which describes the stories of three nuns whom the author met on one of her journeys. But while the theme might owe something to Liu O's *The Travels of Lao Ts'an*, *Seed* has none of that work's psychological and formal complexity. Against these entertaining pieces, Ch'i Tengsheng's *White Horse* stood out as a more artistically ambitious collection of short stories, each one a poetic vignette cast in spare, lucid language.

With the first signs of cultural liberation in China came an abundance of historical evaluation in fiction, drama, and poetry. The Korean War forms the setting for Ch'en Li-te's *On Wings*, while the Japanese invasion of China in World War II provides the backdrop for such novels as Lin Ching-jan's *Mighty Ch'ing Lüan Mountains*, Ma Yun-p'eng's *The Fort Eagle Guerrilla Troop*, and Ch'u Po's *The Mountains Beckon and the Sea Calls* and for the modern revolutionary opera *Storm on August 1st*, all recounting the selfless struggle of deprived heroes to unite the masses and direct their efforts against the common enemies. In these works, not only is the literary structure formalized but also the subject matter, so that the link with reality is weak and the scope for creative originality limited. An exception was Yang Ta-ch'un's *Mountain Swallow*, the name of the heroine, who is sent with a small band of intellectuals to work in a remote mountain village. Through this attention to detail, the author manages to portray realistically the sociopolitical forms within which the individual has to be defined.

The quality of revolutionary verse was exemplified in two volumes: the versified heroics of Wen Wu-pin's *Battle Songs of Tachai*, which contains such titles as "What the Gang of Four Hate, I Love More," "Tachai Forever Remembers Chairman Mao," and "Remembering How Our Heroes Battle the Villainous Four," and the rhetorical romanticisms of Chen Yi's *Selected Poems*.

(JOHN KWAN-TERRY)

JAPANESE

The honour of a dead novelist and the privacy of his personal life provided one of the most controversial literary items of the year. Yasunari Kawabata, who became Japan's first Nobel laureate in literature in 1968, had committed suicide in 1972. Since Kawabata was highly respected and even idolized by a large segment of the Japanese public, there was considerable shock when Yoshimi Usui (*see* BIOGRAPHY), a literary critic turned novelist, published *Circumstances of the Incident*, in which Kawabata's suicide was attributed to despondency when his love for a teenage maidservant was rebuffed. Even though the story was presented as fiction and had no special literary qualities to recommend it, it created a sensation.

There are two senses in which this literary incident could be taken as significant or symptomatic. Preoccupation with the personal aspect of life has been one of the most salient features of Japanese literature since the female diarists of the Heian period, and Usui's *succès de scandale* seemed to show that this characteristically Japanese preoccupation was still alive. In another sense, the incident could be taken as a literary echo of the debunking mood inaugurated by the Lockheed scandal.

Though Masahiro Mita's novelette *What Am I?* was set during one of the student riots of the later '60s, it was not a "political" novel at all. The hero is a weak, innocent boy, fresh from the country, who moves from one sect to another at the mercy of circumstances and at the beck and call of an attractive coed. The tone of the novel is witty, comical, and movie-esque, and it could be characterized as a mildly satirical debunking of the radical student activists of the 1960s. It was awarded the Akutagawa Prize, together with the *Dedicated to the Aegean Sea* of Masuo Ikeda, a well-known woodcut artist and printmaker working in New York.

There was nothing topical about Toshio Shimao's *Thorn of Death*. The theme is the jealousy of a betrayed wife, and the narrator-husband could be identified with the author himself. A typical example of the characteristically Japanese first-person novel, it was the year's most impressive achievement. Kunio Tsuji's *Coronation in Spring* was an attractive novel set in 16th-century Florence. The prose is fluent and evocative, and several historical figures are vividly portrayed. Three novels by women authors should be mentioned: Tsuneko Nakasato's *Shigure Chronicle*, an elegant love story; Fumiko Enji's Japanese-gothic *Motley Mist*; and Minako Ohba's *Urashima-gusa*, concerned with the response of Japanese exiles to native tradition. Two noteworthy books of biographical criticism were Kohei Hata's on Junichiro Janizaki and Junko Shindo's on Kawabata. Gozo Yoshimasu's *River, Written in Cursive Characters* and Yasuo Irisawa's *Moon and Other Poems* were impressive books of poetry.

(SHOICHI SAEKI)

See also Art Sales; Libraries; Nobel Prizes; Publishing; Theatre.
[621]

CHILDREN'S LITERATURE IN THE SEVENTIES

by Natalie Babbitt

Once upon a time, in the first half of this century, children's books celebrated honesty, perseverance, generosity, hard work, good manners, and the value of success. They were, that is, lessons in how to live, their moral stance always evident, their message unmistakable. The world has changed drastically since those good old days, but the central purpose of children's books remains essentially unchanged. The modern tale is still a lesson in how to live and though its setting now is sometimes hostile rather than paternalistic, the message is still the same. Delivered with a beam or a glower, it carries the old exhortation: learn to live right or else.

The changes that have come lie in the flesh of the new books if not in the supporting bone—in their appearance, in their prose style, often in their subject matter. For the lessons keep widening their scope. Daily, it seems, new pitfalls yawn for the unwarned young. World War II shrank the globe, opened up exchanges of ideas, invigorated the economy, and forced adults to look at their lives through different filters. A swell of interest in behavioural psychology strongly affected theories about raising and educating children, while the new affluence, coupled with a compulsion on the part of parents to give their children all the things they themselves had done without during the Spartan '30s and '40s, altered the earlier idea that children should be seen and not heard. Teenagers, all at once a separate community, became an economic and social power in themselves.

Parents and educators, less satisfied with old solutions to the problems of children but far from confident about finding new and better ones, found themselves often in a quandary, often polarized. For the postwar period brought with it conflicts that remain unresolved. Was the world kindly or hostile? Was it all-wise or all-absurd? Did the old values still

Natalie Babbitt is a writer and illustrator of books for children. Among her books are Tuck Everlasting *(1975) and* The Eyes of the Amaryllis *(1977).*

hold true or were they obsolete? Dr. Spock suggested that parents relax and try a little indulgence at the very moment when the Soviet Sputnik suggested that life for free-world youngsters was dangerously relaxed already. Television, solidly established by 1950, offered cheap and continuous home entertainment while at the same time creating a vague puritan discomfort with the idea that entertainment should be so readily available, at least for children. The rush to fathom child psychology compelled parents and teachers to attempt to see life from a child's point of view—always a difficult feat for adults and now, with changing standards of discipline, increasingly a source of confusion. And all at once, whether or not Johnny could read became a hotly debated question.

The Compartmentalized Child. All these contradictions are evident in the children's books of the last 25 years. While popular fiction for adults celebrated disillusion, blurring old definitions of good and evil and presenting only antiheroes, and while films and television echoed that attitude against backgrounds of increasing violence, children's books sought a balance between sugar and gall and settled uneasily on a childhood-spanning menu that began with the former and ended with the latter.

As we attempted to understand young psyches, it seemed helpful to define clear stages of development. From this followed fiction similarly compartmentalized. No pea under the mattress of childhood was too insignificant to provide a story line. We were faced with a great flow of books so assigned as to suggest that growing up was a process whereby a child made mighty leaps from rung to rung of a ladder, rather than progressing in fits and starts up an inclined ramp. No matter what age the child, there was a book just for him: the preschool picture book, the "easy reader," the K-through-four storybook, the junior novel for grades four through six, and finally a type of story brand new for our brandnew adolescents, the teenage novel.

Of these new designations, the stories assigned to children in grades four through six have changed the least. Most of the so-called children's classics, holdovers from the first half of the century and still much loved, have been filed here, while new stories being written for this age group attempt to follow their venerable example. It is as if we had decided that this span of years is the golden one for all the long stories in the fantasy category, since children at this stage must be relatively sophisticated in their reading ability and yet, being prepubescent, are still innocent enough to be interested in the broader, less personal aspects of life with which fantasy most often deals. Here is to be found everything from *Alice in Wonderland* to new novels like *Charlie and the Chocolate Factory*—the books most appropriately defined as literature and once thought good for any age.

The Picture Book Explosion. It is in the areas of picture books and teenage novels that dramatic changes in the flesh of young people's fiction are visible. Picture books, most simply defined as books with more pictures than text, have inherited the fruits of two trends that have nothing at all to do with children. The first is the technology that has made it possible to reproduce, with speed and relative cheapness, illustrations in full colour.

The second is more complex. Before and during World War II, there were always short stories in the weekly and monthly magazines, and they were always lavishly illustrated. A whole new kind of artist had been found to supply such illustrations. He was not, traditionally speaking, a *painter*. He was a *commercial* artist, and his subject matter was primarily homespun and/or romantic in nature at a time when "painting" was growing increasingly personal and experimental. When, in mid-century, magazine fiction died, many of these illustrators turned to children's picture books.

The result has been that the modern picture book is very often remarkably beautiful, with illustrations that have found a special place in the arts. They have grown ever more experimental themselves, inheriting and redefining all the various movements that have shaken up the world of fine arts. In addition, they have extracted, from film and television animation and from the comic books, modes of expression that are an amalgam of both and yet something quite unique. The children themselves have not necessarily benefited. The new illustrations sometimes require a visual sophistication far beyond the capabilities of a small child. And since picture books belong to the illustrators, their texts are all too often only vehicles for the pictures and tend to be weak.

Two spin-offs from picture books have created their own subcategories. With the cheaper printing processes, some publishers have made a big business of very inexpensive, mass-produced, cardboard-bound books which are sold in high-volume locations such as supermarkets and drugstores. These books, attracting for the most part neither the best writers nor the best illustrators, have come to be anathema to anyone in the field who strives for quality. However, with the rapid increase in prices, they may well be the only hardbound books many parents can afford.

Another spin-off is a new kind of picture book called an easy reader. Here a limited vocabulary list ensures a text that beginning readers can manage all by themselves. Although it presents little challenge —overlooking as it does the fact that new and harder words can often be understood from their context and are necessary to a growth of language skills —and although some writers have taken advantage of the demand by producing thin Dick-and-Jane stories of no value beyond the fact that they are easy, many other writers have managed to create tales of great charm and appeal.

Problem Novels and Paperbacks. At the opposite end of the field, teenage novels are proliferating. To reach that newly minted audience, writers have assumed—perhaps correctly, perhaps not—that it is essential to comment on every social phenomenon that appears likely to catch their attention in a rapidly changing environment. Many of these novels have adopted the viewpoint of recent adult fiction: the world is hostile and often absurd, and the old values are due for a hard look. Story lines deal openly with such problems as divorce, premarital sex, drugs, homosexuality, and simple alienation, with the young protagonist always the victim but always able, by virtue of living right, to cope.

Unless written with enormous sensitivity, these books slide to the very edge, and sometimes over the edge, of prurience, and some seem to have been written and published solely for their commercial value. Others, however, answer a real need for honesty and candour and can help to relieve some of the anxiety and loneliness a young person may feel when he is confronted with the complex society of junior high and high school.

In all categories, as the price of book production rises and the post-postwar economy falters, paperbound editions are growing in numbers and popularity. They are, of course, exactly as various in quality as the hardbound texts they reproduce.

However, whether picture book, junior novel, or teenage novel, whether hardbound or paperback, fiction for the young continues to be primarily instructional at bottom. Stories that merely share ideas rather than promoting them are as rare now as they were in 1900. As long as adults continue to see themselves as all-wise and children as all-fallible, the instruction will go on, social change notwithstanding, and the message will continue clear: learn to live right or else.

The only remaining question is the most painful question of all. Though there are more books for children now than ever before, will the children bother to read them? For many reasons, reading, as a beloved leisure-time activity, is decidedly on the wane. For most young people, it is done now in response to classroom assignments and is thereby defined as work rather than pleasure. It remains to be seen whether further change will bring young people around full circle and reinstate the appeal of curling up with a good book.

Luxembourg

Madagascar

Luxembourg

A constitutional monarchy, the Benelux country of Luxembourg is bounded on the east by West Germany, on the south by France, and on the west and north by Belgium. Area: 2,586 sq km (999 sq mi). Pop. (1976 est.): 358,400. Cap. and largest city: Luxembourg (pop., 1975 est., 78,300). Language: French, German, Luxembourgian. Religion: Roman Catholic 97%. Grand duke, Jean; prime minister in 1977, Gaston Thorn.

At the beginning of September 1977 a group of Belgian steelworkers from the Belgian frontier town of Athus threatened to invade Luxembourg in an attempt to protect their jobs at the Minière et Métallurgique de Rodange-Athus complex, situated in the frontier towns of Rodange (in Luxembourg) and Athus (in Belgium) and employing more than 3,000 Belgian workers, mostly at Athus. The Luxembourg firm proposed to restrict production at Athus while maintaining that of Rodange. (*See* BELGIUM.)

René Urbany, chairman of the Luxembourg Communist Party, was received in Moscow on July 25 by Boris Ponomarev, a candidate member of the Central Committee of the Communist Party of the Soviet Union.

The grand duke and grand duchess of Luxembourg were present at the Sovereign's Parade at the Royal Military Academy, Sandhurst, England, on August 5, when their son Prince Jean, a cadet at the academy, was among those who received their officers' commissions. Prince Charles of Bourbon-Parma, the grand duke's younger brother, died on July 26. (K. M. SMOGORZEWSKI)

The Luxembourg embassy in Brussels was seized in August by striking steelworkers from a jointly owned Luxembourg-Belgium steel plant. The workers were protesting the threatened closure of the Athus plant in Belgium.

WIDE WORLD

Madagascar

Madagascar occupies the island of the same name and minor adjacent islands in the Indian Ocean off the southeast coast of Africa. Area: 587,041 sq km (226,658 sq mi). Pop. (1976 est.): 8,266,000. Cap. and largest city: Antananarivo (pop., 1975 est., 438,800). Language: French and Malagasy. Religion: Christian (about 50%) and traditional tribal beliefs. President in 1977, Didier Ratsiraka; prime ministers, Justin Rakotoniaina and, from July 31, Lieut. Col. Désiré Rakotoarijaona.

In 1977 Pres. Didier Ratsiraka concentrated on

strengthening his personal authority and extending state control over most of the national economy. In March he became president of the National Front for the Defense of the Revolution (FNDR), a coalition of the principal political parties. Elections on June 30 gave the FNDR control of the provincial assemblies, with over 90% of the votes cast. On July 28 Justin Rakotoniaina was relieved of his post of prime minister and on July 31 was replaced by Lieut. Col. Désiré Rakotoarijaona. The Supreme Council was reshuffled and raised to 18 members.

Madagascar became involved in long-drawn-out negotiations with the Comoro government over the repatriation of Comoro nationals who had been the target in communal violence at Majunga in December 1976. In September 1977 a Malagasy mediation mission of the Organization of African Unity failed to obtain a cease-fire in Ogaden between Somali and Ethiopian forces. Improved Franco-Malagasy relations were presaged when France's minister of cooperation, Robert Galley, attended meetings of a joint commission in Antananarivo in November.

On July 30, some 400 km from Antananarivo, a giant meteorite fell near the town of Fianarantsoa and dug a crater over 240 m in diameter.

(PHILIPPE DECRAENE)

Malawi

A republic and member of the Commonwealth of Nations in east central Africa, Malawi is bounded by Tanzania, Mozambique, and Zambia. Area: 118,573 sq km (45,781 sq mi). Pop. (1976 est.): 5,-175,000. Cap.: Lilongwe (pop., 1976 est., 75,000). Largest city: Blantyre (pop., 1976 est., 219,000). Language: English (official) and Nyanja (Chichewa). Religion: predominantly traditional beliefs. President in 1977, Hastings Kamuzu Banda.

Malawi

In January 1977 an assassination plot against Pres. Hastings Banda was uncovered, the second in less than a year. Charged with participation in the plot and sentenced to death were Albert Muwalo Nqumayo, minister of state in the president's office and secretary-general of the Malawi Congress Party (MCP), who had been mentioned as his probable successor, and Focus Gwede, head of the special branch. Both men had been prominent in the purges of lawyers, teachers, and civil servants after an assassination plot in May 1976, and more than 1,000 of their victims were released from prison after the two men's arrest.

Malawi's economic prosperity might have emboldened the president to take a more lenient attitude toward his critics. The harsh import control of the previous three years had combined with increased production of the country's export crops and the high prices offered for tobacco and tea to restore financial strength and sharply reduce the rate of inflation.

In July Banda dismissed his Cabinet and dissolved the MCP's executive committee. Almost immediately he announced a new Cabinet in which there were only three changes while the whole of the Executive Committee was reinstated.

(KENNETH INGHAM)

Malaysia

A federation within the Commonwealth of Nations comprising the 11 states of the former Federation of Malaya, Sabah, Sarawak, and the federal territory of Kuala Lumpur, Malaysia is a federal constitutional monarchy situated in Southeast Asia at the southern end of the Malay Peninsula (excluding Singapore) and on the northern part of the island of Borneo. Area: 329,747 sq km (127,316 sq mi). Pop. (1976 est.): 12,300,000. Cap. and largest city: Kuala Lumpur (pop., 1975 UN est., 557,-000). Official language: Malay. Religion: Malays are Muslim; Indians mainly Hindu; Chinese mainly Buddhist, Confucian, and Taoist. Supreme head of state in 1977, with the title of *yang di-pertuan agong,* Tuanku Yahya Putra ibni al-Marhum Sultan Ibrahim; prime minister, Datuk Hussein bin Onn.

Malaysia

In September 1977 a series of political crises erupted within the ruling National Front coalition at the state government level. In Malacca there was an attempt to oust the chief minister, Abdul Ghani Ali, and in Perak disagreement between the sultan and Chief Minister Tan Sri Ghazali Jawi led to the latter's resignation. Most contentious was the conflict in Kelantan, where the dismissal in October of the chief minister, Datuk Mohamed Nasir, provoked rioting in Kota Bahru, the imposition of a state of emergency, and passage of a law authorizing federal rule of the state. In each case, allocation of land was a factor. In November the Islamic Party, whose power base was in Kelantan, withdrew from the coalition in protest against the imposition of federal rule. The party's president, Datuk Haji Mohamed Asri, was federal minister for land and regional development.

Malaysian security forces crossed the border

MALAYSIA

Education. *Peninsular Malaysia.* (1975) Primary, pupils 1,593,804, teachers 49,225; secondary, pupils 789,031, teachers 28,255; vocational, pupils 21,134, teachers 930; higher (1974–75), students 32,295, teaching staff 2,986. *Sabah.* (1974) Primary, pupils 123,419, teachers 4,764; secondary, pupils 43,257, teachers 1,702; vocational, pupils 285, teachers 30; teacher training, students 599, teachers 56. *Sarawak.* (1974) Primary, pupils 165,484, teachers 4,-753; secondary, pupils 50,202, teachers 1,886; vocational, pupils 293, teachers 25; teacher training, students 695, teachers 68.

Finance. Monetary unit: ringgit, with (Sept. 19, 1977) a free rate of 2.46 ringgits to U.S. $1 (4.28 ringgits = £1 sterling). Gold, SDR's, and foreign exchange (April 1977) U.S. $2,480,000,000. Budget (1977 est.): revenue 5,-208,000,000 ringgits; expenditure 5,341,000,000 ringgits. Gross national product (1975) 21,747,000,000 ringgits. Money supply (Feb. 1977) 5,412,000,000 ringgits. Cost of living (Peninsular Malaysia; 1970 = 100; April 1977) 150.

Foreign Trade. (1976) Imports 10,066,000,000 ringgits; exports 13,419,000,000 ringgits. Import sources: Japan 21%; U.S. 13%; Singapore 9%; U.K. 7%; Australia 7%; West Germany 6%. Export destinations: Japan 21%; Singapore 18%; U.S. 16%; The Netherlands 7%; U.K. 5%. Main exports: rubber 23%; tin 11%; palm oil 9%; timber 18%; crude oil 13%.

Transport and Communications. Roads (1974) c. 18,-100 km. Motor vehicles in use (1974): passenger 430,400; commercial (including buses) 140,300. Railways: (1974) 1,-814 km; traffic (including Singapore; 1976) 1,138,000,000 passenger-km, freight 1,007,700,000 net ton-km. Air traffic (1976): 1,815,000,000 passenger-km; freight 36,470,000 net ton-km. Shipping (1976): merchant vessels 100 gross tons and over 150; gross tonnage 442,740. Telephones (Jan. 1976) 292,000. Radio licenses (Dec. 1974) 365,000. Television licenses (Dec. 1974) 390,000.

Agriculture. Production (in 000; metric tons; 1976): rice c. 1,880; rubber c. 1,590; copra c. 166; palm oil 1,393; tea c. 3; bananas c. 431; pineapples c. 257; pepper (Sarawak only; 1975) 30; tobacco c. 10; timber (cu m; 1975) 26,991; fish catch (1975) 474. Livestock (in 000; Dec. 1974): cattle c. 423; pigs c. 1,069; goats c. 349; sheep (Peninsular Malaysia only) c. 43; buffalo c. 285; chickens c. 43,688.

Industry. Production (in 000; metric tons; 1976): tin concentrates (metal content) 63; bauxite 660; cement 1,-733; iron ore (56% metal content) 308; crude oil 8,024; petroleum products (Sarawak only; 1975) c. 830; gold (troy oz; 1975) 3.6; electricity (kw-hr) 6,474,000.

The five heads of government of the Association of Southeast Asian Nations (ASEAN) met in Kuala Lumpur in August to commemorate the tenth anniversary of the organization. During the meeting Philippine Pres. Ferdinand E. Marcos announced his country's intention to abandon its claims to territory in North Borneo.

with Thailand in January to take part in an unprecedented joint operation against Communist insurgents. The operation (Big Star), which was in two phases, concentrated on the western sector north of the border in Sadao district of Songkhla Province, where the Revolutionary Faction of the fractured Malayan Communist Party had been deployed. Prime Minister Datuk Hussein bin Onn visited Bangkok in March and signed a new joint border agreement, which provided for hot pursuit but not for the permanent stationing of one country's security forces on the other's territory. In July a second joint operation (Sacred Ray), also in two phases, was launched in the Betong and Weng districts along the central and eastern sectors north of the border, with the object of disrupting a long-established Communist insurgent infrastructure.

In January Datuk Harun Idris, the former chief minister of Selangor, was sentenced to six months' imprisonment on forgery charges arising from the promotion of a world heavyweight boxing contest between Muhammad Ali and Joe Bugner in Kuala Lumpur in 1975. In June this sentence, together with another of two years levied in May 1976, was upheld on appeal by the Federal Court, although leave was granted to appeal further to the Privy Council. Also in January the controversial former secretary-general of the United Malays National Organization (UMNO), Tan Sri Syed Jaafar Albar, died. In July 1976 he had been elected, at the age of 62, to the leadership of the UMNO's youth wing.

In February two former deputy ministers, Abdullah Ahmad and Abdullah Majid, confessed on television to Communist sympathies, which, however, they claimed to have recanted. They also implicated officials of the Soviet embassy for working with them to promote Communist interests. A 14-year-old Malaysian Chinese boy was sentenced to death in August for unlawful possession of a pistol and ammunition under a mandatory provision of the amended Internal Security Act. The rejection of his appeal in October caused considerable controversy among the legal profession, although further appeal would take place before the Privy Council.

The five heads of government of the Association of Southeast Asian Nations (ASEAN) met in Kuala Lumpur in August to commemorate the tenth anniversary of the association's founding. The occasion had additional significance for Malaysia, since it was marked by Philippine Pres. Ferdinand E. Marcos' announcement that he was taking definite steps to terminate the long-standing Philippine territorial claim to Sabah in North Borneo. He and Mme Marcos visited Sabah after the conclusion of the Kuala Lumpur summit, the first visit ever made by a Philippine head of government to the disputed territory. Malaysia's attempt to act as a bridge between the ASEAN states and the Communist countries of Indochina was exemplified by the visit to Kuala Lumpur in March of Cambodia's foreign minister, Ieng Sary, and that of Malaysia's foreign minister, Tunku Ahmad Rithauddeen, to Hanoi in May.

The Malaysian economy continued buoyant, if without significant structural change. The trade surplus for the year was based on such traditional sources of revenue as natural rubber, palm oil, tin, and sawn timber. Increased earnings did arise from the export of textiles, wood products, petroleum products, and machinery, but they accounted for less than 20% of export income.

(MICHAEL LEIFER)

Maldives

Maldives, a republic in the Indian Ocean consisting of about two thousand small islands, lies southwest of the southern tip of India. Area: 298 sq km (115 sq mi). Pop. (1976 est.): 132,000. Cap.: Male (pop., 1974, 16,700). Language: Divehi. Religion: Muslim. Sultan, Emir Muhammad Farid Didi; president in 1977, Ibrahim Nasir.

More than 20 countries, including the U.S.S.R., China, and Iran, established diplomatic missions in Maldives in 1977. Trade agreements were reached with India and Japan, and offshore oil rights were granted to the Santiago Mineral Co. A five-year development plan gave priority to the fishing industry, with Japanese aid. India, already establishing canning factories and building seagoing boats, helped with public health and education. Aid and training opportunities were offered under the Colombo Plan.

During his visit to India, Vice-Pres. Amir Ahmed Hilmy Didi stated that the former British air base on Gan Island would be leased to "an agency which will use the facilities in a manner beneficial to the inhabitants," but an offer from the U.S.S.R. was refused in October by the government, unwilling to accept the presence of a superpower. Though the closing of the base by the British was welcomed by the government as a step toward ending great-power rivalry, it dismayed the 17,000 people of Addu Atoll, long at odds with Pres. Ibrahim Nasir. The government stripped Gan of facilities and destroyed the Hitadu Island station, also in Addu Atoll. The British government offer to keep the hospital on Gan running and to train local assistants was refused.

(MOLLY MORTIMER)

MALDIVES
  Education. (1977) Primary, pupils 4,411, teachers 30; secondary, pupils 641, teachers 55; teacher training, students 30, teachers 11.
  Finance and Trade. Monetary unit: Maldivian rupee, with (Sept. 19, 1977) a free rate of MRs 3.93 to U.S. $1 (MRs 6.85 = £1 sterling). Budget (1975) expenditure MRs 26.5 million. Foreign trade (1975): imports MRs 26,533,000; exports (main) MRs 6,940,000. Main destinations: Sri Lanka and Japan. Main exports (metric tons): fresh fish 5,870; dried fish 1,960; fish meal 75; shells 62.

Mali

A republic of West Africa, Mali is bordered by Algeria, Niger, Upper Volta, Ivory Coast, Guinea, Senegal, and Mauritania. Area: 1,240,142 sq km (478,822 sq mi). Pop. (1976): 6,035,300. Cap. and largest city: Bamako (pop., 1976, 404,022). Language: French (official); Hamito-Semitic and various tribal dialects. Religion: Muslim 65%; animist 30%. Head of the military government in 1977, Col. Moussa Traoré.

The official visit to Mali of the French president, Valéry Giscard d'Estaing, in February 1977 had barely ended when student agitation arose and became almost continual. In February and May

MALI
  Education. (1974–75) Primary, pupils 276,307, teachers 7,848; secondary, pupils 6,786, teachers 511; vocational, pupils 2,704, teachers (1970–71) 332; teacher training, students 1,839, teachers 126; higher, students 2,445, teaching staff 327.
  Finance. Monetary unit: Mali franc, with (Sept. 19, 1977) a par value of MFr 100 to the French franc and a free rate of MFr 493 to U.S. $1 (MFr 859 = £1 sterling). Gold, SDR's, and foreign exchange (April 1977) U.S. $8 million. Budget (1976 est.) balanced at MFr 49,272,000,000.
  Foreign Trade. (1976) Imports MFr 71,510,000,000; exports MFr 47,120,000,000. Import sources (1974): France 24%; U.S. 13%; Ivory Coast 9%; China 9%; U.S.S.R. 7%; West Germany 7%; Senegal 5%; Pakistan 5%. Export destinations (1974): France 27%; China 17%; Ivory Coast 15%; Senegal 11%; West Germany 5%. Main exports (1972): cotton 34%; livestock 25%; peanuts 6%; fish 6%; textile yarns and fabrics 5%.
  Agriculture. Production (in 000; metric tons; 1976): millet and sorghum c. 804; rice (1975) c. 90; corn (1975) c. 60; peanuts c. 200; sweet potatoes (1975) c. 60; cassava (1975) c. 121; cotton, lint c. 24; beef and veal (1975) c. 37; mutton and lamb (1975) c. 29. Livestock (in 000; 1975): cattle c. 3,886; sheep c. 4,000; goats c. 3,800; camels c. 160; horses c. 123; asses c. 340.

their opposition was especially bitter, as schoolboys and students protested against the entrance examinations established for institutions of higher education.

In May the death of Modibo Keita (see OBITUARIES), former president of Mali who had been imprisoned after the coup of Nov. 19, 1968, was announced in a brief communiqué which made no reference to his earlier career. Several thousand people attended the funeral, which the Military Committee of National Liberation (CMLN) had wished to be almost secret.

Mali, with its 1,250 mi of common frontier with Mauritania, was used several times as a base for attacks on the latter's territory by elements of the Polsario Front in its struggle for the Western Sahara. Lieut. Col. Tiekoro Bakayoko of the CMLN visited Nouakchott to concert measures against the Front, but in June a fierce engagement between Mauritanian forces and Polisario guerrillas spilled over into Mali.

In a broadcast on September 22, Col. Moussa Traoré said that political activity would be restored in 1978. In December, with the presidents of Mauritania and Senegal, he visited Kuwait to seek development funds.   (PHILIPPE DECRAENE)

Malta

The Republic of Malta, a member of the Commonwealth of Nations, comprises the islands of Malta, Gozo, and the Comino in the Mediterranean Sea between Sicily and Tunisia. Area: 316 sq km (122 sq mi), including Malta, Gozo, and Comino. Pop. (1977 est.): 322,000. Cap.: Valletta (pop., 1977 est., 14,100). Largest city: Sliema (pop., 1977 est., 20,100). Language: Maltese and English. Religion: mainly Roman Catholic. President in 1977, Anton Buttigieg; prime minister, Dom Mintoff.

Throughout 1977 the government actively pursued its avowed policy of eliminating foreign military bases in Malta after March 1979 and converting the island into a nonaligned centre for

Maldives

Mali

Malta

regional cooperation in the Mediterranean, with its neutrality guaranteed politically and economically by Italy and Libya, France and Algeria. High-level talks were held with these and other interested European countries. Negotiations with the European Economic Community to amend the existing agreement with Malta brought about substantial changes to Malta's advantage. An economic and technical cooperation agreement with China was concluded during Dom Mintoff's visit to the Far East in November, by which China promised to construct a breakwater at Malta's Marsaxlokk harbour. At an official banquet in Peking the Soviet ambassador walked out when Mintoff criticized the Soviet Union's stinginess toward Malta.

Following the resignation of G. Borg Olivier, Edward Fenech Adami became leader of the Nationalist Party and of the official opposition. The budget for 1977–78 envisaged expenditure of M£103 million, including M£32.3 million on capital account. The minimum weekly wage went up by M£1.50. Strikes by bakers and bank employees ended after several weeks, but disputes with doctors and Telemalta employees remained unsettled by mid-November after six months of confrontation. The government imported foreign doctors to substitute for those suspended or dismissed. (ALBERT GANADO)

MALTA

 Education. (1975–76) Primary, pupils 29,834, teachers 1,319; secondary, pupils 28,022, teachers 1,877; vocational, pupils 4,387, teachers 447; higher, students 1,023, teaching staff 191.
 Finance. Monetary unit: Maltese pound, with (Sept. 19, 1977) a free rate of M£0.42 to U.S. $1(M£0.74 = £1 sterling). Gold, SDR's, and foreign exchange (June 1977) U.S. $637.9 million. Budget (1975–76 actual): revenue M£85.2 million; expenditure M£82 million.
 Foreign Trade. (1976) Imports M£179,920,000; exports M£97,410,000. Import sources: U.K. 24%; Italy 17%; West Germany 10%; U.S. 10%; France 5%. Export destinations: West Germany 24%; U.K. 18%; Libya 13%; Italy 5%. Main exports: clothing 42%; petroleum products 7%; food 6%; textile yarns and fabrics 5%; ships 5%. Tourism (1975): visitors 334,500; gross receipts U.S. $73 million.
 Transport and Communications. Roads (1974) 1,267 km. Motor vehicles in use (1975): passenger 54,000; commercial 11,900. There are no railways. Air traffic (1976): 340.3 million passenger-km; freight 3,783,000 net ton-km. Shipping (1976): merchant vessels 100 gross tons and over 32; gross tonnage 39,140. Ships entered (1975) vessels totaling 1.7 million net registered tons; goods loaded (1976) 133,100 metric tons, unloaded 1 million metric tons. Telephones (Dec. 1975) 49,000. Radio licenses (Dec. 1973) 129,000. Television licenses (Dec. 1974) 75,000.

Materials Sciences

Ceramics. Although many of its products were essential for the efficient generation and conservation of energy, the ceramic industry was also a major energy consumer. A Federal Energy Administration study showed that in the U.S. the stone, clay, and glass industry grouping ranked fifth among all manufacturing industries in energy consumption. Faced with increasing costs and shortages of fuel, many companies sought protective measures. Because virtually all ceramics are fired to high temperatures to achieve hardness, strength, and durability, most efforts focused on

Manufacturing:
see Economy, World;
 Industrial Review

Marine Biology:
see Life Sciences

kiln and furnace improvements, including better insulation and burner maintenance and shortened firing schedules.

Production capacity for industrial and residential insulating fibres increased, but shortages were still evident. Typical of emphasis on conservation in building construction was PPG Industries' introduction of insulating glass panels containing a thin, reflective gold coating to reduce peak solar heat gain on a building's sunward surfaces as much as 86% on a typical summer day.

Ceramic electrodes and insulators for magnetohydrodynamic (MHD) generators, which extract electricity very efficiently from a moving hot gas (plasma), were also studied. A cooperative U.S.-U.S.S.R. program tested the ability of ceramics to withstand the extremely corrosive MHD environment in the U-25 combined MHD-steam turbine power plant operating in Moscow. Doped zirconia, silicon carbide, and various spinels were tested with modest success in limited duration runs. Some experts felt that an industrial 1,000-megawatt generating plant incorporating an MHD generator would be built in the U.S.S.R. by the early 1980s.

In ceramics for gas turbines, Ford Motor Co. passed a major milestone by successfully running an uncooled, aerodynamically loaded ceramic turbine rotor at 2,500° F (1,370° C) for more than 1.5 hours. Ford's all-ceramic rotor, using both ceramic blades and a ceramic disk, was an extremely challenging design, material, and component-production task, but it offered great potential as a low-cost turbine for mass-produced automobile use. Scientists of Pratt and Whitney Aircraft and Garrett AiResearch Co. made similar strides in the design, fabrication, and testing of hybrid turbine rotors, consisting of ceramic blades retained in metal disks, for use in small, limited-life engines for aircraft and missile applications.

The Swedish company ASEA, which had experimented with hot isostatic pressing (HIP) of ceramics for several years, announced that it had successfully densified silicon nitride, the leading ceramic candidate for turbine components. At a pressure of 250 megapascals (MPa; 35,000 lb/sq in) and a temperature of 3,180° F (1,750° C) high-purity silicon nitride was pressed to near theoretical density with only 0.5% yttria by weight as a pressing aid (compared with 8% yttria in conventionally hot-pressed silicon nitride). Reduction of the pressing-aid content should significantly improve the high-temperature strength and durability of this important material. Indeed, ASEA's results indicated much lower creep rates and much less scatter in high-temperature strengths for HIP-processed specimens, and opened the exciting possibility of low-cost, high-quality silicon nitride blades and perhaps even integral rotors, produced by densifying directly to net shape.

A major problem in fibre-optic communications research was the difficulty of producing long lengths of strong glass fibres and the tendency of such material to weaken rapidly when handled or exposed to moisture. Scientists at Bell Laboratories recently announced development of a protective resin coating that allowed their fibres to retain

A use for waste fume from steel-making furnaces was developed by Bethlehem Steel technicians who devised a way to convert the fumes into pellets to be reused in the steel-making process.

strengths as high as 4,137 MPa (600,000 lb/sq in) for many years.   (NORMAN M. TALLAN)
[724.C.5.c]

Metallurgy. During 1977 reduction of production costs in terms of money and energy was of prime concern. Problems with increasingly strict environmental protection and safety requirements and the rapid rise in product liability litigation demanded a great deal of attention, much of it at the expense of metallurgical development. Many previously announced plans for new plants or major expansion were abandoned because of increasing difficulty in obtaining capital, rising costs, and unfavourable political situations in many countries. The risk of metal shortages in the near future also continued to increase.

Two large plants did start production of nickel sulfide matte from abundant, though largely unexploited, laterite ore. In these plants the oxide ore is roasted with sulfur, converting the nickel to a sulfide that is then smelted in a fairly conventional way to obtain the metal. The higher energy requirements expected of any alternative leaching and electrowinning process might well have been a factor in the choice of the smelting process, in spite of its SO_2 generation problem.

A large aluminum pilot plant came into operation using an aluminum chloride process that potentially expended 30% less energy than the Hall process. Actual efficiency of the plant, however, had not yet been determined. Aluminum chloride eventually might be derived from aluminum-containing municipal waste; research at the U.S. Bureau of Mines produced volatile aluminum and other metal chlorides by roasting samples of a high-density nonmagnetic fraction of separated waste in a chlorine atmosphere.

The use of direct reduction of iron ore without melting continued to grow. One new process was adaptable to a wide variety of reducing agents, and its application in a Brazilian plant was the first use of gasified heavy fuel oil for iron reduction. Because the iron was discharged while hot, charg-ing it directly into the steel-making furnace could save energy. Alternately, the hot sponge iron could be pressed into dense briquettes, which could be stored outdoors without serious reoxidation.

The argon process for removing gases from steel was modified by adding finely divided calcium or magnesium to the gas blown through molten steel to reduce sulfur content to less than 0.01%. Remaining sulfur occurred as spherical rather than elongated particles, and low-temperature properties of the steel were improved. A 12.5% nickel steel to which was added a small amount of a reactive metal to remove carbon and nitrogen exhibited excellent toughness at cryogenic temperatures; with essentially zero carbon this steel permitted strong, nonbrittle welds. High-strength, low-alloy steel suitable for use at low temperature was obtained by adding a few hundredths of a percent columbium or vanadium and using temperature-controlled rolling to give a fine grain structure of satisfactory toughness.

Fuel-conscious demands for weight reduction in automobiles were giving the aluminum industry expectations of an increased share in this market. Two new aluminum alloys developed in Europe for auto-body sheet combined good formability and the dent resistance needed for satisfactory service. Another new aluminum alloy was suitable for making stamped wheels on the same machines used with steel, a very important cost consideration where material substitution is involved. Aluminum wheels at present are cast.

Melt welding was becoming competitive with spot welding. In a typical operation, a 400-kilohertz induction heater melted a small region of the weld at a time. Only light pressure was needed to hold the parts, thin metal could be joined to thick, and such unlikely welds as aluminum to steel were sometimes possible.   (DONALD F. CLIFTON)
[725.B]

See also Industrial Review: *Glass; Iron and Steel; Machinery and Machine Tools; Mining and Quarrying.*

Mathematics

Although no single issue dominated mathematics in 1977, topics deserving of special mention included one from mathematics education and two involving solutions of long-standing conjectures.

Every summer teams of high school mathematics students from various nations convene for an intensive competition in which they attempt to solve challenging problems from elementary mathematics. This event, called the International Mathematical Olympiad, was established nearly 20 years ago among countries of Eastern Europe; the U.S. first entered the competition in 1974.

In 1977 the two-day contest was held July 5–6 in Belgrade, Yugos., and for the first time the U.S. team won. Its eight members achieved a total of 202 points, including two perfect papers by Randall Dougherty of Fairfax, Va., and Michael Larsen of Lexington, Mass. Second place went to the U.S.S.R., whose team scored 192 points.

The U.S. team was selected through a two-step national competition that began with more than 340,000 high school students and climaxed in a U.S. olympiad in May. Following their selection, team members trained for three weeks in June at West Point with their coaches, Samuel L. Greitzer of Rutgers University, New Brunswick, N.J., and Murray S. Klamkin of the University of Alberta, Edmonton. The International Olympiad comprised six problems (displayed in the accompanying box with their countries of origin) that were solved in two four-hour sessions.

Schoolchildren are taught that area and volume measurements are based on the more primitive concept of length. Mathematicians call a measure of length (or distance) a metric and frequently derive from it the higher dimensional measures of area and volume. The relation between distance and volume (or, in technical terms, between metrics and measures) is of crucial importance in differential geometry, that part of geometry that is concerned with the properties of curved, higher dimensional spaces.

About 25 years ago Eugenio Calabi (presently at the University of Pennsylvania) conjectured that not only do distances determine the way volume is measured but also that measures of volume frequently determine how distance can be measured. He provided a strong but incomplete argument that the natural measure of volume on certain complex manifolds—curved spaces whose coordinates are complex numbers—determines a unique metric, called a Kähler metric, that is intrinsically related to the geometry of the manifold.

In 1977 the final link in Calabi's chain of reasoning was closed by Shing-Tung Yau of Stanford University. By solving a complicated system of nonlinear partial differential equations, Yau not only confirmed the Calabi conjecture but also yielded new insight into the relation between partial differential equations—a key tool of theoretical physics—and the geometry of surfaces.

In 1955 the influential French mathematician Jean-Pierre Serre published a lengthy paper that

---

1977 International Mathematical Olympiad

1. Equilateral triangles ABK, BCL, CDM, DAN are constructed inside the square $ABCD$. Prove that the midpoints of the four segments KL, LM, MN, NK and the midpoints of the eight segments AK, BK, BL, CL, CM, DM, DN, AN are the 12 vertices of a regular dodecagon.

(The Netherlands)

2. In a finite sequence of real numbers the sum of any 7 successive terms is negative and the sum of any 11 successive terms is positive. Determine the maximum number of terms in the sequence.

(Vietnam)

3. Let n be a given integer > 2, and let V_n be the set of integers $1 + kn$, where $k = 1, 2, \ldots$. A number $m \epsilon V_n$ is called *indecomposable in V_n* if there do not exist numbers $p, q \epsilon V_n$ such that $pq = m$. Prove that there exists a number $r \epsilon V_n$ that can be expressed as the product of elements indecomposable in V_n in more than one way. (Expressions which differ only in the order of the elements of V_n will be considered the same.)

(The Netherlands)

4. a, b, A, B are given constant real numbers and $f(\theta) = 1 - a \cos \theta - b \sin \theta - A \cos 2\theta - B \sin 2\theta$. Prove that if $f(\theta) \geq 0$ for all real θ, then $a^2 + b^2 \leq 2$ and $A^2 + B^2 \leq 1$.

(Great Britain)

5. Let a and b be positive integers. When $a^2 + b^2$ is divided by $a + b$, the quotient is q and the remainder is r. Find all pairs (a,b), given that $q^2 + r = 1977$.

(West Germany)

6. Let $f(n)$ be a function defined on the set of all positive integers and taking on all its values in the same set. Prove that if $f(n + 1) > f(f(n))$ for each positive integer n, then $f(n) = n$ for each n.

(Bulgaria)

---

revealed profound logical connection between two esoteric theories: algebraic topology and algebraic geometry. This paper, universally referred to by its initials FAC (for "Faisceaux algébriques cohérents"), contained a major unproved conjecture on the structure of generalized vector spaces. Since FAC appeared, its main themes have strongly influenced the shape of mathematical theories and, in the process, increased the importance of Serre's conjecture.

The 20-year search for a proof (or counterexample) concluded last year with two quite different proofs discovered independently by Daniel Quillen at the Massachusetts Institute of Technology and A. A. Suslin of Leningrad State University. Each only four pages long, these proofs confirm that all abstract spaces of a certain common type are constructed in direct analogy with two- and three-dimensional Euclidean space. (In exact language, every projective module over a polynomial ring is free.) Upgraded to a theorem, Serre's conjecture joined a long list of major results at the core of mathematics that reveal common structure among apparently different objects.

(LYNN ARTHUR STEEN)

ANSWERING ROTA'S QUESTION

by R.L. Graham

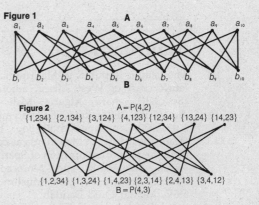

Figure 1

Figure 2

A = P(4,2)

{1,234} {2,134} {3,124} {4,123} {12,34} {13,24} {14,23}

{1,2,34} {1,3,24} {1,4,23} {2,3,14} {2,4,13} {3,4,12}

B = P(4,3)

A basic concept in mathematics is the idea of a matching, which can be described as follows. Suppose there exist two collections (or sets) of objects, A and B, so that to each object *a* that belongs to A, there is associated some subset contained in B. A matching of A into B is simply a selection, for each object *a* in A, of some unique object *b* in that subset of B. A typical interpretation is to imagine A to be a set of men and B to be a set of women. For each man *a* in A, there exists a subset that corresponds to the set of women he knows. A matching of A into B is just a way of pairing up each man with a specific woman from his associated subset.

The most famous result dealing with matchings is the so-called Marriage Theorem, discovered by the English mathematician Phillip Hall in 1935. It asserts that, in order for there to be a matching of a set A of men into a set B of women, it is both necessary and sufficient that, for any given number *k*, any subset of *k* men know altogether at least *k* women. An example of this is shown in Figure 1.

It can be checked in the figure that every *k* men know at least *k* women. For example, the three men a_1, a_3, and a_8 know the seven women b_1, b_2, b_3, b_4, b_6, b_7, and b_{10}. Therefore, by the Marriage Theorem this implies that there must exist a matching of A into B. Although the theorem does not indicate how to find it, one such matching is a_1—b_1, a_2—b_4, a_3—b_2, a_4—b_3, a_5—b_7, a_6—b_9, a_7—b_8, a_8—b_{10}, a_9—b_5, and a_{10}—b_6.

Mathematicians usually refer to the type of structure shown in Figure 1 as a bipartite graph. The partition graph $G(n,k)$, one of the most fundamental classes of bipartite graphs, is formed as follows. For any given numbers *n* and *k*, the set of objects (or points) A of $G(n,k)$ consists of all possible partitions of the numbers from 1 to *n* into exactly *k* pieces, or blocks. This set A is denoted by P(n,k). For example, for *n* = 4 and *k* = 2, A = P(4,2) and consists of the seven partitions [1,234], [2,134], [3,124], [4,123], [12,34], [13,24], and [14,23]. Similarly, the set of points B of $G(n,k)$ is defined as P(n,k + 1); i.e., all

R. L. Graham, a leading expert in combinatorics, is head of the Discrete Mathematics Department at Bell Laboratories, Murray Hill, New Jersey.

possible partitions of the numbers from 1 to *n* into exactly *k* + 1 blocks. In the above example, B = P(4,3) and is the set of the six partitions [1,2,34], [1,3,24], [1,4,23], [2,3,14], [2,4,13], and [3,4,12].

The lines of this partition graph are placed between a partition p_A in A and a partition p_B in B provided each block of p_B is contained in some block of p_A. In this case it is said that p_B refines p_A. See Figure 2. For example, the partition [1,2,34] in B refines [12,34] in A, but it does not refine the partition [13,24] because the block 34 of [1,2,34] is not contained in any block of [13,24].

A long-standing question, first raised some 15 years ago by the mathematician G.-C. Rota, is whether for every such partition graph $G(n,k)$ there is always a matching of the smaller of its two sets A and B into the larger set. Although for many years it was generally believed that the answer was in the affirmative, researchers were frustrated in their attempts to prove mathematically that there would always be such a matching for every choice of *n* and *k*. It should be pointed out that even for moderate values of *n* and *k*, the size of P(n,k), which is denoted by S(n,k), is awesome.

In 1977 Rota's question was finally settled in a very unexpected way by E. Rodney Canfield of the University of Georgia, who showed that the answer to Rota's question is in the negative! In particular he proved that, once *n* becomes large enough, none of the partition graphs will have the desired matching, whenever *k* is chosen so that S(n,k) assumes its largest values.

It seemed unlikely, however, that the smallest value of *n* for which this happens would ever be known. The best estimates Canfield offered for the first time his technique works is when *n* approximately equals 6.52608×10^{24}. For such values of *n*, the corresponding values of S(n,k) can be truly astronomical, exceeding, for example, 10 raised to the 10^{20} power. It may well be that Canfield's answer to Rota's question belongs to the growing collection of mathematical results that serve as pointed reminders of the limits of human thought.

Mauritania

Mauritius

Mauritania

The Islamic Republic of Mauritania is on the Atlantic coast of West Africa, adjoining Western (Spanish) Sahara, Algeria, Mali, and Senegal. Area: 1,030,700 sq km (398,000 sq mi). Pop. (1976): 1,481,000. Cap.: Nouakchott (pop., 1976, 135,000). (Data above refer to Mauritania as constituted prior to the purported division of Spanish Sahara between Mauritania and Morocco.) Language: Arabic, French. Religion: Muslim. President in 1977, Moktar Ould Daddah.

While Morocco and Mauritania strove to get some return from their acquisition of the Western Sahara, the Polisario Front maintained a vigorous diplomatic military offensive in 1977 that largely frustrated their efforts. Polisario's most spectacular raid took place May 1 against Zouerate, the Mauritanian iron-ore centre, when six French nationals were taken and held as hostages by the

MAURITANIA

Education. (1974–75) Primary, pupils 47,000, teachers 1,768; secondary, pupils 5,493, teachers (1973–74) 200; vocational, pupils 1,591, teachers (1973–74) 117; teacher training (1971–72), students 145.

Finance. Monetary unit: ouguiya, with (Sept. 19, 1977) a free rate of 49.44 ouguiya = U.S. $1 (86.13 ouguiya = £1 sterling). Gold, SDR's, and foreign exchange (June 1977) U.S. $52.2 million. Budget (1976 est.) balanced at 6,125,-000,000 ouguiya.

Foreign Trade. (1976) Imports 8,072,000,000 ouguiya; exports 8,013,000,000 ouguiya. Import sources (1975): France c. 56%; U.S. c. 8%; West Germany c. 8%; Senegal c. 5%; U.K. c. 5%. Export destinations (1975): France c. 20%; U.K. c. 16%; Italy c. 13%; Japan c. 11%; Spain c. 11%; Belgium-Luxembourg c. 8%; West Germany c. 5%. Main export (1975) iron ore 82%.

guerrillas. Robert Galley, the French minister of cooperation, visited Nouakchott and promised an increase of French military aid.

The Mauritanian economy suffered a blow in June, when Spanish technicians abandoned the phosphate mines at Bou Craa. Polisario attacked Nouakchott on July 3 but disclaimed responsibility for an attempt on the life of the Mauritanian ambassador in Paris on July 7. After another Polisario raid on Zouérate on July 16, Moroccan troops reinforced the installations there. In August an attack on Aoucert cost the Mauritanians 40 dead. Later, the fighting became more extensive. After prolonged negotiations, on December 23 eight French hostages (including two railway engineers captured in October) were released to UN Secretary-General Kurt Waldheim in Algiers. Meanwhile, Polisario alleged French Air Force involvement.

On August 4 Pres. Moktar Ould Daddah reorganized his Cabinet, reducing it from 28 to 17 members. (PHILIPPE DECRAENE)

See also Morocco.

Mauritius

The parliamentary state of Mauritius, a member of the Commonwealth of Nations, lies about 800 km E of Madagascar in the Indian Ocean; it includes the island dependencies of Rodrigues, Agalega, and Cargados Carajos. Area: 2,040 sq km (787.5 sq mi). Pop. (1977 est.): 908,200, including (1972) Indian 66%; Creole (mixed French and African) 31%; others 3%. Cap. and largest city: Port Louis (pop., 1977 est., 141,300). Language: English (official); French has official standing for certain legislative and judicial purposes; and Creole is the lingua franca. Religion (1974 est.): Hindu 51%;

A French couple was killed and six French nationals taken hostage at Zouerate, the Mauritanian iron-mining town, when the Polisario Front attacked the site in May. The town was occupied by French technicians who ran the government-owned mining complex.

Christian 30%; Muslim 16%; Buddhist 3%. Queen, Elizabeth II; governor-general in 1977, Sir Abdul Rahman Muhammad Osman; prime minister, Sir Seewoosagur Ramgoolam.

With support from Gaëtan Duval's right-wing Social Democratic Party after the December 1976 elections, the prime minister, Sir Seewoosagur Ramgoolam, announced that he would head a coalition government with policies oriented toward the nonaligned left. A referendum on whether Mauritius should become a republic or not was promised. The Citizenship Act, passed in April, permitted the withdrawal of citizenship from a resident of foreign origin, and measures to make Mauritius less economically dependent upon South Africa and the U.K. and closer to radical black Africa were propounded. Despite a state of emergency and such measures as a Public Order Act, Mauritius remained a multiparty democracy. Paul Bérenger's Mauritius Militant Movement still pressed for the taking over of 5 of the 21 large sugar estates owned by white Franco-Mauritians.

Disease damaged much of the 1977 sugar harvest, reducing it to 675,000 metric tons (715,000 metric tons in 1976), of which 500,000 metric tons were exported to European Economic Community (EEC) countries at a guaranteed £220 a ton. The need for crop diversification intensified.

(MOLLY MORTIMER)

Mexico

A federal republic of Middle America, Mexico is bounded by the Pacific Ocean, the Gulf of Mexico, the U.S., Belize, and Guatemala. Area: 1,972,546 sq km (761,604 sq mi). Pop. (1977 est.): 64,594,400, including about 55% mestizo and 29% Indian. Cap. and largest city: Mexico City (pop., 1977 est., federal district 8,941,900, metro. area 12,578,400). Language: Spanish. Religion: predominantly Roman Catholic. President in 1977, José López Portillo.

The universities were sources of trouble throughout 1977, mainly as a result of conflicts between the state governors and university members. In Oaxaca the appointment of a right-wing

rector by the state governor led to violent demonstrations, and the governor subsequently resigned. In June there was a strike at the Universidad Nacional Autónoma de México over the formation of a new union, which would encompass both teaching and nonacademic staff, be in charge of collective bargaining, and demand a 20% wage increase. The government recognized the union and its bargaining position, but without giving in to its wage claims.

Mexico

In April Pres. José López Portillo reaffirmed his intention to bring about electoral reforms that would allow minority parties greater representation and provide a more meaningful opposition. In his presidential message on September 1, he outlined a plan for a Chamber of Deputies with some 400 seats (as against the current 250), 300 of which would be up for election, with 100 reserved for minority opposition parties voted in by proportional representation. A minority party would be legally recognized if it had 65,000 members in at least half of Mexico's states and territories or obtained a minimum of 1½% of the vote in the first national election in which it participated.

About 20 bomb attacks in Guadalajara, Mexico City, and Oaxaca were attributed to the Union del Pueblo, a hitherto unknown political element. A scandal broke out in September when Félix Barra García, agrarian reform secretary under the previous administration, was charged with having extorted the equivalent of U.S. $450,000 from a farmer whose land was being expropriated. Some 72 landowners, whose land had been redistributed by the authorities but who had contested the case through the courts, finally received approximately 189 million pesos in compensation.

In April a former president, Gustavo Díaz Ordaz, was appointed ambassador to Madrid. This prompted the resignation of the ambassador-writer in Paris, Carlos Fuentes, because of Díaz Ordaz's association with the massacre of university

A worker makes adjustments on a drilling platform at one of the many new oil wells drilled in Mexico during the administration of former president Luis Echeverría. Crude oil reserves in southeastern Mexico were estimated at 60,000,000,000 barrels, six times those of the North Slope deposits in Alaska.

WIDE WORLD

Peasants demanding more equitable
land reform marched through towns
and villages of northern Mexico.
Many peasant farms are still un-
economically small despite the government's land redistribution
programs.

students in Mexico City before the 1968 Olympics.
Díaz Ordaz himself later resigned. In September
President López Portillo paid an official visit to
Spain—the first Mexican leader to do so since the
Spanish Civil War—and a cooperation treaty was
signed. An agreement with the U.S. granted Mex-
ico reciprocal rights to fish within the 200-mi
fishing limit claimed by the U.S.

The economy grew about 2% in 1976 in real
terms, compared with 4% in 1975. The main cause
of the slowdown was a recessionary trend reinforced by the peso devaluation of August 1976.
Overall growth in the gross domestic product in
1977 was forecast at some 2%. The consumer price
index rose 27% in 1976, mostly after the devaluation, when wage increases were granted and
prices rose because of speculative buying. In the
first eight months of 1977, however, the rate was
held to about 15%. Labour kept wage increase demands to around 10%, although there were some
wage-related strikes in major industries, such as
steel. As part of a medium-term stabilization program, borrowing was restricted to $3 billion net in
1977 and $1.7 billion in 1978. An Alliance for Pro-
duction scheme was set up by the government and
about 140 private companies under which some $5
billion would be invested to develop industry and
encourage exports and import substitution.

Boding well for the future was the announcement that proven petroleum reserves stood at 16,-
800,000,000 bbl—or 30 years' supply—and
estimated reserves at more than 60,000,000,000
bbl. The existence of large gas deposits encouraged
plans for a gas pipeline to the U.S. This would
make possible the export of 1,000,000,000 cu ft
daily by 1979 and double that by 1981.

(BARBARA WIJNGAARD)

Middle Eastern Affairs

Arab-Israeli Dispute. The year saw considerable
international diplomatic activity aimed at resumption of the Geneva Middle East peace conference;
some progress was achieved on procedural matters, but there was no narrowing of the gap on
substantive questions. The initiative of Pres. Anwar as-Sadat of Egypt (*see* BIOGRAPHY) in accepting an invitation from Israeli Prime Minister
Menahem Begin (*see* BIOGRAPHY) to come to Israel
was in itself a momentous novelty. Nothing very
new appeared to have been said during the visit,
which took place November 19–21, but the Israelis
and Sadat succeeded in creating an atmosphere of
goodwill. Further Egyptian-Israeli talks, attended
also by U.S. and UN representatives, took place in

MEXICO
    Education. (1975–76) Primary, pupils 11,461,415,
teachers 255,939; secondary and vocational, pupils
2,827,470, teachers 161,385; teacher training, students 111,502, teachers 8,396; higher (including 44
universities), students 543,112, teaching staff 47,529.
    Finance. Monetary unit: peso, with (Sept. 19,
1977) a free rate of 22.85 pesos to U.S. $1 (free rate
of 39.80 pesos = £1 sterling). Gold, SDR's, and foreign exchange (March 1976) U.S. $1,388,000,000.
Budget (1976 est.) balanced at 392.4 billion pesos.
Gross domestic product (1975) 987.7 billion pesos.
Money supply (Nov. 1976) 141,070,000,000 pesos.
Cost of living (1970 = 100; May 1977) 258.
    Foreign Trade. (1976) Imports 90,989,000,000
pesos; exports 51,935,000,000 pesos. Import
sources: U.S. 63%; West Germany 7%; Japan 5%.
Export destinations: U.S. 56%; Brazil 5%. Main exports: crude oil 16%; coffee 10%; chemicals 9%;
cotton 8%; metals and ores 8%; machinery 6%;
shrimps 5%; textile yarns and fabrics 5%. Tourism

(1975): visitors 3,217,900; gross receipts U.S.
$2,142,000,000.
    Transport and Communications. Roads (1975)
187,660 km (including 1,070 km expressways). Motor vehicles in use (1975): passenger 2.3 million;
commercial 816,400. Railways: (1974) 24,700 km;
traffic (principal only; 1975) 4,198,000,000 passenger-km, freight 32,542,000,000 net ton-km. Air traffic
(1976): 7,954,000,000 passenger-km; freight 88,871,-
000 net ton-km. Shipping (1976): merchant vessels
100 gross tons and over 290; gross tonnage 593,875.
Telephones (Dec. 1975) 2,915,000. Radio receivers
(Dec. 1974) 17,514,000. Television receivers (Dec.
1974) 4,885,000.
    Agriculture. Production (000; metric tons; 1976):
corn 8,945; wheat 3,354; barley c. 460; sorghum c.
3,350; rice c. 450; potatoes c. 640; sugar, raw value
c. 2,750; dry beans 1,149; tomatoes c. 1,409; bananas
c. 1,200; oranges c. 2,500; lemons c. 600; safflower
seed (1975) 531; coffee c. 258; tobacco 68; agaves

(1975) 155; cotton, lint c. 207; fish catch (1975) 499.
Livestock (in 000; Dec. 1975): cattle c. 28,700; sheep
c. 5,300; pigs c. 12,100; goats 8,800; horses (1974)
5,664; mules (1974) c. 2,500; asses (1974) c. 2,891;
chickens c. 164,174.
    Industry. Production (in 000; metric tons; 1976):
cement 12,477; crude oil 40,840; coal (1975) 5,128;
natural gas (cu m) 23,980; electricity (kw-hr) 46,238,-
000; iron ore (metal content) 3,654; pig iron 3,545;
steel 5,124; sulfur (1975) 2,164; petroleum products
(1975) c. 30,780; sulfuric acid 1,805; fertilizers (nutrient content; 1975–76) nitrogenous c. 581, phosphate
c. 220; aluminum 42; copper (1975) 74; lead (1975)
154; zinc (1975) 154; antimony ore (metal content;
1975) 3.1; manganese ore (metal content; 1975) 154;
phosphate rock (1975) 282; gold (troy oz; 1975) 144;
silver (troy oz; 1975) 38,030; cotton yarn (1975) 158;
woven cotton fabrics (1974) 150; wool yarn (1975)
37; man-made fibres (1975) 181.

In an attempt to form a united front against Egyptian peace moves toward Israel, heads of five Arab states met on December 5 at Tripoli, Libya. The leaders failed to agree on a joint resolution.

Cairo in December, and on December 25–26 Begin and Sadat met again, at Ismailia in Egypt. At this meeting Sadat rejected Begin's initial proposals for limited self-rule in the Israeli-occupied areas and held that full Israeli withdrawal was essential.

Sadat's initiative startled some Arab leaders—particularly in Syria and the Palestinian Liberation Organization (PLO)—into bitter expostulation. At the invitation of Libya's Col. Muammar al-Qaddafi (*see* BIOGRAPHY), a summit meeting of "rejectionist" Arab states—Algeria, Iraq, Libya, Yemen (Aden), and Syria—and the PLO met in Tripoli on December 2–5. Iraq left the meeting before its conclusion, condemning it as "an umbrella for the peacemakers," but the other participants signed a declaration proclaiming a "Pan-Arab front for steadfastness and confrontation" and calling for the freezing of political and diplomatic relations with Egypt.

At the beginning of the year the way had seemed open for a new Middle East peace initiative; a new U.S. administration had taken office, and the Arab summit meetings in October 1976 had settled outstanding inter-Arab differences over Lebanon. President Sadat was foremost among Arab leaders in trying to persuade the U.S. to make the first move. At the end of December 1976 he proposed that a link be established between the Palestinians and Jordan before the Geneva conference, but other Arab leaders, including King Hussein of Jordan, were unenthusiastic. All the Arab states continued to insist that the PLO should speak on behalf of the Palestinians at Geneva, and this proved a major stumbling block since Israel still refused to negotiate with the PLO.

In February 1977 both UN Secretary-General Kurt Waldheim and U.S. Secretary of State Cyrus Vance visited the Middle East to sound out possibilities for a resumption of the Geneva talks. Waldheim later said he had detected an evolution in Palestinian thinking toward acceptance of a Palestinian "mini-state" on the West Bank of the Jordan River and in the Gaza Strip, as opposed to the declared PLO aim of a secular Arab-Jewish state in the whole of Palestine. Vance said in Israel that the PLO should amend its Charter to make this

plain. It was apparent, however, that little further progress could be made until after the Israeli elections of May 17.

U.S. Pres. Jimmy Carter unexpectedly divulged the outline of his administration's plans for a Middle East peace settlement in a speech on March 9, in which he spoke of the need for an Israeli withdrawal from occupied territory except for "minor adjustments," but with a possible interim stage of four to eight years in which Arab-Israeli relations might gradually improve. He also spoke of the possibility of Israel's having defense lines that need not conform to its legal borders.

The Palestine National Council (PNC) held its first meeting since 1974 in Cairo, March 12–20. The council's membership was increased from 182 to 292, including representatives from Jordan, the West Bank, and Gaza, as well as some 20 delegates from the hard-line "rejection front" groups. In general, the moderates were in the ascendant, and the rejectionist Popular Front for the Liberation of Palestine was kept off the newly elected 15-member PLO executive committee. But the 15-point political program issued by the PNC showed little sign of compromise; it specifically rejected UN Security Council Resolution 242 of Nov. 22, 1967, which called for Israel's withdrawal from occupied territories but referred to a "refugee problem," not to national Palestinians.

On March 17 President Carter carried U.S. Middle East policy a step further by declaring the need for a Palestinian homeland—a statement that was welcomed by PLO leader Yasir Arafat. President Carter also said Arab attitudes toward Israel were very moderate as compared with previous years. In the spring he met with President Sadat and, later, King Hussein in Washington, with Pres. Hafez al-Assad of Syria in Geneva, and with Crown Prince Fahd of Saudi Arabia in Washington. Prince Fahd denied that Saudi Arabia would use the "oil weapon" against the U.S., but he and other Saudi spokesmen made it clear that they expected the U.S. to put strong pressure on Israel to withdraw from all occupied Arab territories.

The victory of the right-wing Likud Party in the Israeli elections and Begin's subsequent accession to the premiership provoked strong reactions from the Arab states. Many Arab leaders prophesied war, especially when Begin referred to the West Bank as "liberated territory" and announced his support of Jewish settlements there. The U.S. State Department confirmed its view of the need for an Israeli withdrawal, and a major U.S.-Israeli policy clash seemed inevitable, although the U.S. constantly asserted that it would not use its military and financial aid to Israel as a means of exerting pressure. However, Begin's visit to the U.S. on July 16–24 avoided a confrontation, at least temporarily.

Attention then focused on the means of reconvening the Geneva conference. Vance paid a second visit to the Middle East in August, but without any positive results. His joint proposal with Egypt that a "working group" of the foreign ministers of the Arab front-line states and Israel should meet before Geneva was dropped after it was rebuffed by Syria. Vance suggested that if the PLO were to accept UN Resolution 242, the U.S. diplomatic boycott of the PLO might end. But despite Saudi-Egyptian pressure, the majority of the PLO continued to reject it.

September saw renewed diplomatic activity coinciding with the opening of the UN General Assembly session. On September 12 the U.S. introduced a new element by stating that it was essential for the Palestinians to take part in the peace process. Some progress seemed to be made when the Israeli Cabinet agreed, on September 25, that a unified Arab delegation could negotiate at Geneva and that Palestinians should attend a resumed Middle East peace conference. It continued to reject the participation of the PLO, but agreed not to look too closely at the antecedents of the Palestinians

involved. Yet a large gap remained between Arabs and Israelis, and prospects of resuming the Geneva conference before the end of the year receded. There was also considerable international concern about activity in southern Lebanon, where Israel was becoming increasingly involved on the side of the Lebanese rightists.

On October 1 a joint U.S.-Soviet statement on the Middle East outlined the principles and objectives for a full Arab-Israeli peace settlement and a common approach to Geneva. The statement included the phrase "the legitimate rights of the Palestinian people"—the first occasion on which the U.S. had officially subscribed to the term. The Arabs expressed qualified approval, but the Israeli reaction was strongly hostile. Israel's apprehensions were considerably allayed by an agreement reached between Secretary of State Vance and the Israeli foreign minister, Moshe Dayan, on a new approach to Geneva. Dayan, however, confirmed that Israel would not negotiate with the PLO or discuss a separate Palestinian state, and Arab doubts rose correspondingly.

In the autumn there were many signs of growing Arab impatience. Even the Saudi foreign minister openly criticized what was regarded as excessive Egyptian dependence on U.S. diplomacy, and the Syrians launched a diplomatic offensive to persuade the Arabs to close ranks in the face of what they saw as a new threat of war with Israel. It was at this point that President Sadat started his own campaign to try to save the Geneva conference.

During the year there were sporadic incidents of sabotage inside Israel, for which al-Fatah and other guerrilla groups claimed responsibility. The efforts of the Arab states to secure international

A guard with a submachine gun kept watch over a new Israeli settlement in the disputed West Bank area of Jordan. The colony, which housed 40 families, consisted of prefabricated units set up around the old Jordanian police station.

KAREL—SYGMA

Israeli tanks crossed back into Israel on September 26 after Israel withdrew its armed forces from Lebanon after a peacekeeping mission between Palestinians and Christians in that country.

condemnation of Israel's occupation of Arab territory and the establishment of new Jewish settlements bore fruit when a resolution condemning Israel passed the UN General Assembly on October 28 by an overwhelming majority. However, the U.S. abstained from voting on the ground that the resolution would prejudice negotiations, despite the fact that President Carter and other U.S. spokesmen had repeatedly deplored the Jewish settlements.

The nine European Economic Community (EEC) countries voted in favour of the UN resolution. This was in line with the joint statement by the EEC heads of state on June 29, calling on Israel to "recognize the legitimate rights of the Palestinian people" and stating that a resolution was possible only if the need for a Palestinian homeland was taken into account. However, Arab efforts to persuade the EEC states to give the PLO formal recognition were unsuccessful.

Inter-Arab Relations. The new entente between the Arab front-line states resulting from the October 1976 summit meetings did not openly break down during 1977, but there were signs of increasing strain below the surface. Although neither Egypt nor Saudi Arabia disputed Syria's dominant role in Lebanon, there were indications that Saudi Arabia had doubts about Syrian aggrandisement and its efforts to form a close association with Jordan. The Syrians, in turn, resented the reduction in promised Saudi aid and deplored what they regarded as Saudi and Egyptian subservience to U.S. wishes. The Lebanese government's attempts to have the dangerous situation in southern Lebanon discussed by all the Arab states were unsuccessful.

All the Arabs were concerned over Israel's intervention in the area, but they were unable to prevent it. Experts agreed that Israel's military superiority was greater than before the 1973 war, and a unified Arab approach was made difficult by the Arab states' differing approaches to a peace settlement and Egypt's continued failure to achieve a rapprochement with the U.S.S.R. Egypt's mounting economic problems and the severe food riots in January raised fears among the Arab oil states that the Egyptian regime might be replaced

by a more radical one. Accordingly, aid to Egypt was increased substantially.

The two leading rejection front states, Iraq and Libya, were in open dispute with their Arab neighbours in 1977. Iraq's relations with Syria went from bad to worse as the two Baathist regimes exchanged charges and countercharges of subversion and sabotage. Iraq, however, settled its outstanding problems with Kuwait and remained on fairly friendly terms with Saudi Arabia. Libya, on the other hand, was in dispute with almost every Arab state except Algeria. Egypt's relations with Libya deteriorated into open warfare in late July when Egyptian planes bombed Libyan airfields. The fighting was ended with the help of Algerian and PLO mediation, but relations remained extremely tense. Following the Tripoli summit in December, Egypt broke off diplomatic relations with Algeria, Libya, Yemen (Aden), and Syria. In contrast, Egypt moved closer to Sudan, a full union being mooted.

The Egyptian-Sudanese axis could also be seen as part of a wider move by conservative Arab regimes in Africa and the Middle East to exclude Soviet influence. Saudi diplomacy was active in this direction; the Saudis sponsored a meeting of the heads of state of Sudan, Somalia, and the two Yemens in Taiz in March, and in general attempted to wean both Yemen (Aden) and Somalia away from Soviet influence and dependence on Soviet arms supplies. A number of Arab states, including Iraq, gave open support to the Eritreans and Somalis fighting against the Marxist regime in Ethiopia. In this respect, as in many others, Libya was the exception in expressing support for Ethiopia.

(PETER MANSFIELD)

See also Energy; articles on the various political units.

Migration, International

There was a slowdown and in some cases a near-halt in 1977 in migration to the traditional migrant-receiving areas in North America, Australia and New Zealand, and Western Europe. This was associated with a continuing shortage of jobs and more stringent migration controls. National and international concern was increasingly focused on plans to improve conditions for migrants and their families. Among such initiatives were the Council of Europe's projected convention to give migrant workers a legal status assuring their rights and protection in the council's 19 member countries; the European Economic Community's (EEC's) comprehensive Action Program for migrant workers and their families with a directive on the education of migrant children, to provide also mother-tongue and native culture teaching; and the International Labour Organization's worldwide concern with social security for migrant workers.

In the EEC and other developed Western European countries, an estimated two million migrant workers (three in every ten) lost their jobs in the years after the 1974 oil crisis. France, Belgium, The Netherlands, Luxembourg, West Germany, Austria, and Switzerland remained the seven main employers of migrant labour, but there was little demand for new workers and West Germany, Austria, and The Netherlands appeared, though less publicly, to agree with the Swiss decision to reduce the size of the foreign population.

In West Germany, the total of migrant workers was reduced from nearly 2.6 million in 1973 to just over 1.9 million in 1977. One-quarter of these were Turks. In June, France with nearly two million foreign workers, not counting families, the largest single percentage from Portugal, offered migrants

their fare home and $2,000 in cash to leave and not return. U.K. statistics for 1976 showed a slightly reduced total of immigration, 80,745 compared with 82,405 for 1975. Of this total, 60,981 were from the Commonwealth and Pakistan.

In Italy the numbers of reentrants exceeded the number of emigrants for the fourth consecutive year. In 1971, 167,000 left Italy, but in 1976 only 90,000 did so. Returning migrants faced competition for work in Italy from Ethiopians, Somalians, and refugees from the Portuguese colonies. Unofficial figures for Spain estimated that 300,000–400,000 migrants had returned since 1974 from Western Europe, Morocco, and the Spanish Sahara. Of the three million Greek workers, businessmen, and professionals abroad, over 100,000 were reported to have returned to Greece during 1974–77, but no problems of absorption were noted.

Algeria began operating a plan to encourage the return of nationals, particularly the 60,000–80,000 qualified workers needed at home. More than 60,000 migrants and their dependents returned in 1976, up tenfold from 1975. About 800,000 Turks were living in Western Europe in 1976. Temporary immigration rose in the oil-rich Persian Gulf states, mainly from Islamic areas in the Middle East or the Indian subcontinent. Numbers were unreliable because of high illegal immigration.

Because of high unemployment, Australia's immigration target dropped from 110,000 in 1973 to 70,000 in 1977. The nation registered a net gain of only 21,000 persons in 1976, the lowest figure since 1945. Between 30,000 and 50,000 left, 20,000 being migrants unable to settle while another 15,000 were Australians opting for a new life elsewhere. In early 1977 the government issued a Green Paper on "Immigration Policies and Australia's Population." In New Zealand the total of new permanent arrivals for 1976 was 14,706, of which 4,940 were from the U.K., 882 from Europe, 804 from Asia, and 8,080 from other countries.

In Canada the number of immigrants admitted in 1976 was 149,429, a decrease of 20.5% from 1975. Of this total 41.1% were destined for the labour force, nearly one-third of them being in the professional or managerial categories. Nearly one-half of the total went to Ontario. Immigrants from Britain numbered 21,548 (14.4% of the total). Other large groups came from the U.S., 17,315 (11.6%); Hong Kong, 10,725 (7.2%); Jamaica, 7,282 (4.9%); Lebanon, 7,161 (4.8%); India, 6,733 (4.5%); Philippines, 5,939 (3.9%).

In the U.S. estimates of the number of illegal immigrants from Mexico already in the country ranged from 6 million to 12 million. Nearly 900,000 were apprehended in 1976. In August 1977 Pres. Jimmy Carter proposed a complex package of measures, including increased border security, possible increased economic assistance to countries like Mexico, fines on employers hiring illegal aliens, and the granting of permanent or temporary alien status to illegals who had entered before Jan. 1, 1970, or Jan. 1, 1977, respectively, with deportation of any who entered thereafter.

(SHEILA PATTERSON)

See also Refugees.
[525.A.1.c]

Immigration and Naturalization in the United States

Year ended June 30, 1976

Country or region	Total immigrants admitted	Quota immigrants	Nonquota immigrants Total	Nonquota immigrants Family— U.S. citizens	Aliens naturalized
Africa	7,723	5,735	1,988	1,797	2,974
Asia [1]	149,881	102,258	47,623	44,239	46,759
China [2]	18,823	14,404	4,419	4,036	9,326
Hong Kong	5,766	5,002	764	674	...
India	17,487	16,462	1,025	839	3,564
Iran	2,700	1,825	875	857	567
Iraq	3,432	3,264	168	164	482
Israel	2,982	2,134	848	731	1,863
Japan	4,258	2,062	2,196	1,862	1,408
Jordan	2,566	2,074	492	471	1,312
Korea, South	30,803	20,011	10,792	10,045	7,450
Lebanon	2,840	2,346	494	466	947
Philippines	37,281	20,978	16,303	15,601	14,765
Thailand	6,925	1,782	5,141	4,805	683
Vietnam	3,048	1,027	2,021	1,787	1,411
Europe [3]	72,411	51,374	21,037	18,798	49,322
Germany, West	5,836	1,613	4,223	3,796	5,056
Greece	8,417	6,338	2,079	1,938	6,595
Italy	8,380	6,202	2,178	1,956	8,696
Poland	3,805	2,742	1,063	973	2,904
Portugal	10,511	9,309	1,202	1,065	4,117
Spain	2,254	1,341	913	788	902
U.S.S.R.	8,220	7,998	222	188	518
United Kingdom	11,392	6,649	4,743	4,186	8,695
Yugoslavia	2,820	2,253	567	527	3,008
North America	142,307	107,110	35,197	29,879	34,676
Canada	7,638	3,475	4,163	3,463	3,384
Cuba	29,233	27,999	1,234	476	15,138
Dominican Republic	12,526	10,464	2,062	1,799	1,538
El Salvador	2,363	1,667	696	642	386
Haiti	5,410	4,805	605	553	2,088
Jamaica	9,026	7,398	1,628	1,490	2,535
Mexico	57,863	39,459	18,404	15,392	5,602
Trinidad and Tobago	4,839	4,040	799	724	1,012
Oceania	3,591	2,381	1,210	1,066	592
South America	22,699	15,914	6,785	6,240	6,764
Argentina	2,267	1,663	604	513	1,277
Colombia	5,742	3,542	2,200	2,024	1,711
Ecuador	4,504	3,633	871	824	796
Guyana	3,326	2,895	431	407	638
Peru	2,640	1,624	1,016	977	701
Total, including others	398,613	284,773	113,840	102,019	142,504

Note: Immigrants listed by country of birth; aliens naturalized by country of former allegiance.
[1] Includes Turkey. [2] Taiwan and People's Republic. [3] Includes U.S.S.R.
Source: U.S. Department of Justice, Immigration and Naturalization Service, 1976 Annual Report.

Mining and Quarrying

The world copper mining industry, mildly depressed at the beginning of 1977, went into a decline after the first quarter. In the United States after labour agreements with the United Steelworkers of America, which served most of the copper industry, expired at midyear, there were a number of strikes, some lasting longer than two months. Even so, weak demand and price for copper caused most companies to cut back production or to recess operations for various periods. Mines in Africa and South America continued to produce at capacity, causing the price to fall and remain depressed.

Copper was not alone. Iron ore was in equally bad shape because of the low level of steel production throughout the world. On August 1 the United Steelworkers struck the Minnesota and Michigan mines.

Nickel and zinc were also in depressed circumstances, but aluminum showed strength with the reappearance in 1977 of plans to expand capacity. Activity in uranium and coal was strong, with many new mines and processing facilities in progress or planned. Nevertheless, the coal industry was not successful in boosting U.S. production principally because of wildcat strikes that plagued the eastern coalfields most of the year. Other factors included reduced productivity because of health and safety legislation and the difficulty and delay in getting new mines started because of the need for government permits.

The Surface Mining Control and Reclamation Act, known as the "strip mining bill," was signed in early August. Within 36 months the individual states must either adopt surface mine control plans meeting or surpassing minimum regulations established by the U.S. Department of the Interior or else yield jurisdiction over their surface mines to the new federal Office of Surface Mining Reclamation and Enforcement.

Industry Developments. The U.S. Federal Trade Commission approved the sale of Peabody Coal Co., the largest coal company in the U.S., by Kennecott Copper Corp. for $1.2 billion to a consortium composed of Newmont Mining Co., the Williams Companies, the Boeing Co., Bechtel Corp., Fluor Corp., and Equitable Life Assurance Society of the United States. Proceedings by the FTC had begun in August 1968, although divestiture of Peabody was not ordered until 1971.

The merger of Molycorp Inc. into Union Oil Co. of California was consummated by the exchange of 1.035 Union Oil common shares for each Molycorp common share. Molycorp was to operate as a subsidiary. The company has rare-earth, molybdenum, and niobium (columbium) mines in the U.S. and Brazil. The transaction, valued at $240 million, illustrated the continuing trend of diversification of oil companies into minerals.

In Canada, the province of Quebec announced that it would make a public offer to buy the shares of Asbestos Corp. This followed an announcement in January by Premier René Lévesque in which he indicated that Quebec would take closer control of foreign investors. Asbestos Corp. was owned 55% by the U.S. corporation General Dynamics. In another move to suppress foreign interest in Canadian mining, the Potash Corp. of Saskatchewan purchased Alwinsal Potash of Canada, owned by French and West German interests, for $76.5 million.

Westinghouse Electric Corp. agreed in principle during the year to settle the uranium supply dispute with the Duquesne Light Co., Ohio Edison Co., and Pennsylvania Power Co. This dispute arose in 1975 when Westinghouse, faced with rapidly rising uranium prices, declined to meet various uranium supply commitments; this resulted in numerous lawsuits. By the terms of agreement the plaintiffs received cash, new equipment, and en-

NORTON PEARL PHOTOGRAPHY

Peru's new Cuajone copper strip mine, which began production in mid-1976, was expected to produce about 180,000 tons of blister copper a year. Over 14 million tons of rock had to be removed to get to the ore.

gineering and technical services from Westinghouse, which presumably amounted to less than the uranium supply obligation.

Westinghouse also reached an agreement with Farmland Industries, Bartow, Fla., to build a plant to extract 400,000 lb per year of uranium concentrate from phosphoric acid. Freeport Minerals Co. began construction of a similar 690,000-lb-per-year plant at Uncle Sam, La.

Louisiana Land & Exploration Co. and Superior Oil Co. made a surprising mineral discovery in the state of Maine in October. Although only three exploratory holes were drilled, each intersected thick sections of sulfide mineralization and one averaged 5.3% zinc, 0.82% copper, 2.57 ounces of silver per ton, and 0.04 ounces of gold per ton. This strike was an excellent prospect in an unusual location and could start a surge of exploration in the northeastern U.S.

Amax's $500 million Henderson molybdenum mine and concentrator was inaugurated in June. The project was notable for receiving environmental awards. One-fifth of the total investment was in the rail haulage system, which was necessary in order to locate the ore-processing facilities in an environmentally acceptable area 14 miles from the mine.

The Mt. Hope iron ore mine in northern New Jersey, owned by Halecrest Co., was reopened on October 26 after being closed since 1959. Records show that mining was in progress at Mt. Hope as early as 1640.

With environmentalists' suits settled, coal strip mines went back into operation in Wyoming.

BARRY STAVER—THE NEW YORK TIMES

Ireland got a new zinc mine during the year at Navan in County Meath. Rated at 2.5 million tons per year of ore capacity, its yield was expected to be 220,000 metric tons of zinc and 42,000 metric tons of lead. The mine was brought into production 6½ years after discovery at a cost of $150 million. Owned by Tara Exploration & Development Co., Ltd. (75%), and the government of Ireland (25%), it was to be the largest zinc and lead producer in Europe.

Exmibal, a joint venture of Inco Ltd. and Hanna Mining Co., went into operation in 1977 after 17 years of development. Lateritic nickel ores from Lake Izabal in Guatemala were treated to make 28 million lb per year of nickel in the form of 75% nickel matte. The project cost $224 million.

Liberia Mining Co. made its last shipment of iron ore in August from the Bomi Hill mine. A total of 59 million tons of ore was produced during the lifetime of the mine. As of 1977 Liberia shipped 23 million to 24 million tons of iron ore per year from five mining operations.

Gold Fields of South Africa, Ltd. and Phelps Dodge Corp. signed an agreement for the development of a $191 million mineral project to produce 132,000 tons of lead, 35,000 tons of zinc, and 22,-000 tons of copper in concentrate form per year from 1,130,000 tons of ore. In addition, about 113,-000 kg of silver were expected to be recovered. The deposit, located in the northern part of the Cape of Good Hope Province in South Africa, was expected to be in operation by 1980.

Gold shipments began from the new Telfer mine in the Paterson Range of Western Australia. The mine was a joint venture of the U.S. firm Newmont Mining Co. and Australia's Broken Hill Pty.

The giant Soroako nickel project came into production and was inaugurated on March 31 in a ceremony attended by Indonesian Pres. Suharto. The development was by PT International Nickel Indonesia, a subsidiary of Inco Ltd., which agreed with the government of Indonesia in 1968 to explore and develop lateritic deposits on the island of Sulawesi. The project necessitated construction of mining and ore-processing facilities to produce 35 million lb per year of nickel matte. Work was begun in 1975 on an expansion of the facility to bring output to 100 million lb of nickel matte per year by 1978.

Technological Developments. Marion Power Shovel Co. introduced an aluminum boom for draglines. The light weight of the boom increased productivity 7–15% and also yielded benefits of reduced maintenance and downtime. The lighter weight boom cut down deadweight, allowing the use of either buckets with larger capacity or a longer boom giving greater reach.

The impact breaker, used to reduce large rocks without drilling and blasting, gained increasing acceptance at mining operations. Proponents claimed cost saving and greater safety. These machines, which generate a blow of approximately 20,000 ft-lb, were being used underground at draw points and in surface mines. In one design liquefied nitrogen "explodes" to a gas, propelling a ram into a pool of oil that transfers the energy directly to the hammerhead.

A new underground mining method called vertical crater retreat eliminated many of the development excavation steps required to prepare blocks of ore for extraction. In addition, it minimizes damage to walls and roofs in mining areas. The technique was made possible by the introduction of large-diameter (6½-in) vertical blastholes, which permitted the placement of spherical charges in the holes. A horizontal slice of ore is blasted downward into a previously mined area. This procedure is repeated until the block of ore is mined to its full height. (JOHN V. BEALL)

Production. Most mineral commodities that experienced production cutbacks during 1975 recovered during 1976 and early 1977, although often only to regain old ground. A few commodities, however, were able to establish new highs in extraction or refining during 1976; they included refined aluminum, chromite, energy-related commodities such as natural gas and petroleum (but particularly coal), cobalt, manganese, molybdenum, platinum-group metals, and salt.

Because of the effects of the energy crisis and the fact that most mining development requires the expenditure of considerable sums at every stage, a trend appeared to be developing among the larger private companies toward concentrating development expenditure on large, high-return projects. Development of smaller, financially less well-assured projects became increasingly difficult in the period 1975–77 because of the considerable price instability of many commodities, even where the establishment of an international control group (bauxite, tin, iron, petroleum, etc.) or of buffer stocks indicated the willingness of member countries to subordinate their immediate interest to a longer-term goal.

Since many mineral exploitation operations are governmental and therefore not subject to normal market restraints, the effects of the recent energy and price crises were much less apparent among the centrally planned and less developed economies, where governmental control was the preferred means of development. In such situations stable employment levels and predictable supplies were often more important than return on investment; thus, as the table indicates, in all sectors except petroleum, production in the centrally planned and developing countries was far ahead of the market economies of the West. Indeed, these indexes imply enormous structural change in world employment, trade, and allied industries, most of it at the expense of the private, Western mining operations.

As the table indicates, mining worldwide (including the government-controlled operations) is continuing to lose ground against manufacturing. Where, for example, the 1972 index for manufacturing had been only 112 against mining's 107, by the first quarter of 1977 mining had risen to 123, but manufacturing had risen to 141. There was, in late 1977, no prospect for early change in any of these trends, except perhaps in the area of coal production. There, despite environmental problems, coal might be expected to provide both long- and short-term solutions to problems brought on by the continuing energy crisis.

Aluminum. World production of bauxite, the primary ore of aluminum, was estimated to have fallen off slightly during 1976, declining by about 2.8% from 81.9 million metric tons in 1975 to approximately 79.6 million tons in 1976. The major producer was Australia, as it had been since 1971, with some 21.1 million tons, about a 4.8% decline from its record production levels of 1975. Other major producers were Guinea 11,728,000 tons, Jamaica 11,-266,000 tons, the U.S.S.R. 6 million tons, Surinam 4,588,000 tons, Guyana 3,108,000 tons, and Greece 2,953,000 tons. Output of aluminum metal rose slightly in 1976, increasing by about 0.6%, to some 12,721,000 tons the major producers were the U.S. 3,850,-000 tons, the U.S.S.R. 2,130,000 tons, and Japan 920,000 tons.

Antimony. Production of antimony worldwide in terms of contained metal was estimated to have risen by approximately 3.2% during 1976, from 67,810 metric tons the previous year to an estimated 69,950. According to preliminary data, Bolivia had become the major producer, exporting a new high of 17,398 tons; South Africa appeared to be second with about 15,400 tons, followed by an estimated 11,800 tons for China. Primary consumption of antimony was down about 6.8% in the U.S. World prices in late 1977 were nearly 30% below those of a year earlier, although prospects for increased demand in 1978 and shorter ore supplies resulting from Bolivia's new smelting facility were expected to permit prices to recover during 1978.

Arsenic. Total world production of arsenic was estimated to have declined slightly during 1976, from 46,500 metric tons to about 45,350, a decline of about 2.5%; major producers were Sweden, the leader, at 15,400 tons, followed by France, the U.S.S.R., Mexico, and South West Africa, all ranging between 6,300 and 8,200 tons, according to U.S. Bureau of Mines estimates, although detailed data were not available.

Cadmium. Preliminary data from the U.S. Bureau of Mines indicated a strong recovery of production from the sharp decline of 1975. Production in 1976 was 15,373 metric tons, up 10.9% from the preceding year. Major producers of cadmium metal were Japan, at about 2,630 tons, the U.S.S.R an estimated 2,450 tons, and the U.S. 1,804 tons; three countries also producing more than 1,000 tons were West Germany, Canada, and Belgium.

Cement. World production of cement rose slightly, by about 1.2%, from 703 million metric tons in 1975 to an estimated 712 million in 1976. The U.S.S.R. was the largest producer, at 124 million tons, almost twice as many as the next largest producer, Japan, at 68.7 million; other important producers included the U.S. 61,430,000 tons, Italy 36.3 million tons, West Germany 33,980,000 tons, France 29 million tons, Spain 25.3 million tons, Poland 19.8 million tons, and India 18.5 million tons. Because production of cement requires considerable energy, conversions of U.S. production facilities to coal from oil and gas had reached 48% of capacity by 1976 and were expected to reach 90% within 15 years. U.S. cement, although expensive in the world market, continued to show strong growth (356% during 1973–76) in nearby markets, especially Canada, Mexico, the Dominican Republic, and Venezuela. Despite a gloomy medium-term outlook in the U.S. industry, construction began in 1977 on a 1.5 million-ton-per-year plant at Theodore, Ala.

Chromium. Total production of chromite, the principal ore of chromium, rose in 1976, showing a 1.8% increase over 1975 (from

Indexes of Production, Mining, and Mineral Commodities

(1970 = 100)

	1972	1973	1974	1975	1976	1977 I	1977 II
Mining (total)							
World [1]	107	114	116	115	120	123	...
Centrally planned economies [2]	111	118	124	132	138	143	144
Developed market economies [3]	101	105	104	102	104	107	107
Less developed market economies [4]	110	123	125	114	125	127	...
Coal							
World [1]	96	96	96	99	100	101	...
Centrally planned economies [2]	105	108	110	114	116	117	120
Developed market economies [3]	89	86	83	85	85	85	84
Less developed market economies [4]	104	104	112	122	124	138	...
Petroleum							
World [1]	112	122	124	121	129	134	...
Centrally planned economies [2]	113	122	130	140	148	159	158
Developed market economies [3]	110	112	112	114	114	122	119
Less developed market economies [4]	113	129	129	117	129	130	...
Metals							
World [1]	101	106	108	103	106	107	...
Centrally planned economies [2]	112	118	119	122	123	127	129
Developed market economies [3]	96	101	100	94	96	94	97
Less developed market economies [4]	102	106	111	103	108	112	...
Manufacturing (total)	112	123	127	126	137	141	...

[1]Excluding Albania, China, Mongolia, North Korea, Vietnam.
[2]Bulgaria, Czechoslovakia, East Germany, Hungary, Poland, Romania, U.S.S.R.
[3]North America, Europe (except centrally planned), Australia, Israel, Japan, New Zealand, South Africa.
[4]Caribbean, Central and South America, Africa (except South Africa), Asian Middle East, East and South East Asia (except Israel and Japan).
Source: UN, *Monthly Bulletin of Statistics* (November 1977).

7,930,000 metric tons to an estimated 8.1 million). The major producers were thought to be South Africa and the U.S.S.R., although chromium's position as a strategic metal made detailed data difficult to obtain. These two countries probably produced in excess of 2.1 million tons each; the next largest producers were probably Albania, Turkey, and Rhodesia in that order, all in the 600,000- to 750,000-ton-per-year range. Work continued on the U.S.S.R.'s beneficiation facility at Donskoye, the first stage of which entered production in 1974; completion was scheduled for 1980.

Cobalt. A strong increase in production levels of cobalt worldwide was indicated by preliminary figures: a 7.5% increase from 32,914 metric tons to an estimated 35,400 tons. More than half of the production originated in Zaire, about 17,000 tons; other producers all appeared to have shown increases during 1976, including Zambia, Australia, Morocco, New Caledonia, the U.S.S.R., and Canada, all within the 2,000- to 3,000-ton-per-year production range. Sumitomo began construction in late 1977 of a seabed nodule mining test facility at Niihama, Japan.

Copper. World mine production of copper was estimated to have fallen by approximately 3.5%, from 7,296,000 metric tons in 1975 to 7,040,000 tons in 1976. The major producers were the U.S. 1,212,600 tons, Chile 1,005,000 tons, the U.S.S.R., estimated at about 900,000 tons, Canada 747,000 tons, Zambia 711,000 tons, and Zaire 443,000 tons. The largest increase in production of the major producers was shown by Chile, some 22.4% over 1975, most of the increase attributable to the Chuquicamata mine, where milling of much high-grade ore was responsible for the increase. The early settlement of the July–August 1977 strike in the U.S. surprised many consumers, who had stockpiled against a much longer strike; utilization of these stockpiles in the second half of 1977 kept demand weak. Smelter production of copper fell in 1976 by about 2.0%, from 7,276,000 metric tons the preceding year to about 7,-129,000 tons. The U.S. continued to be the world's major producer, with approximately 1,195,000 tons, followed by Japan 1,009,000 tons, the U.S.S.R. about 900,000 tons, Chile 856,000 tons, Zambia 706,000 tons, and Zaire 408,000 tons.

Gold. World mine output of gold showed a slight increase in 1976, rising from 38,574,000 troy ounces in 1975 to an estimated 39,080,000 in 1976, an increase of about 1.3%. The major producer was South Africa with 22,056,000 troy ounces, followed by the U.S.S.R. with an estimated 7.7 million, Canada 1,686,000, and the U.S. 1,030,000. In August 1976, gold prices had dropped to little more than half of 1974 levels ($103.05); they subsequently recovered, and the recovery was reflected in the 1977 International Monetary Fund gold auction prices which reached $160.03 at the Dec. 7, 1977 IMF auction.

Iron. According to preliminary figures of the U.S. Bureau of Mines, world production of iron ore was virtually identical in 1975 and 1976, at 873 million metric tons. The major producer was the U.S.S.R. with some 234 million tons, followed by Australia 100 million, the U. S. 78 million, Brazil 74 million, China 65 million, Canada 57 million, France 43 million, and India 40 million. Each of these figures was consistent with previous production levels; Brazil, Canada, Australia, and the U.S.S.R. represented gains from 1975, India was constant, and the remainder showed losses.

World pig iron production was estimated to have gained about 3.8%, up to 489.6 million metric tons in 1976 compared to 471.8 million in 1975. The leading producer was the U.S.S.R. at 105.5 million metric tons, followed by Japan 96.5 million tons, the U.S. 80,626,000 tons; among other producers only West Germany exceeded 30 million tons.

Lead. World mine production of lead declined about 1.4% during 1976, falling from 3,405,000 metric tons to approximately 3,-358,000 tons. The major producers were unchanged with the U.S. the world leader at 553,000 tons, followed by the U.S.S.R. at an estimated 470,000 tons, Australia 399,000 tons, Canada 259,000, and Mexico 200,000. Five other countries that produced more than 100,000 tons were Peru, Yugoslavia, North Korea, Bulgaria, and China. The most notable changes in production levels occurred in Canada (down 23.8%) and Mexico (up 12%), the former almost entirely as a result of strikes. The burgeoning of the Mexican industry was visible in the recent expansions of the Chihuahua and Torreon smelters.

Smelter production of lead registered a strong 3.7% increase, from 3,314,000 tons in 1975 to 3,438,000 tons in 1976. The U.S. led with 592,000 tons, followed by the U.S.S.R. 500,000 tons, Australia 343,000 tons, Japan 219,000 tons, Mexico 190,000 tons, Canada 175,000 tons, and France, the only major smelter not also a major producer, 159,000 tons.

Manganese. World mine production of manganese ore was estimated to have risen approximately 3.8% in 1976, up to 24.6 million metric tons. The leading producers were the U.S.S.R. at 8.8 million metric tons, followed by South Africa at 5,715,000 tons; five lesser producers ranged between 1 million and 1.6 million tons: Australia, Brazil, India, Gabon, and China. Because 95% of manganese consumption is tied to steelmaking, the manganese market stagnated in 1976 together with steel; the only active area in the industry was the development of technology to mine and process submarine manganese nodules.

Mercury. It became apparent from studies released in 1977 that the U.S.S.R. had replaced Spain as the world's leading producer of mercury. World production in terms of 34.5-kg (76-lb) flasks was estimated by the U.S. Bureau of Mines to have declined from 251,226 flasks in 1975 to about 242,300 in 1976, continuing the trend apparent since 1971 and indicating that environmental risks, particularly in paints, pharmaceuticals, and agricultural applications, continued to limit growth of the industry.

Molybdenum. Total world production of molybdenum was estimated to have increased by 6.3% in 1976, up from 81,140 metric tons in 1975 to an estimated 86,266 tons in 1976; the major producer was the U.S., which accounted for approximately 60% of world production, with 51,250 tons; the only other important producers were Canada 14,416 tons, followed by Chile and the U.S.S.R., both with about 9,100 tons. Future U.S. production levels were probably tied to the Henderson mine in Colorado, where processing of ore began in July 1976 and production from caved ore began in January 1977; for the present, however, the Climax mine, also in Colorado, continued to be the major producer. It could continue present production levels until the year 2005.

Nickel. Mine production of nickel ore declined by an estimated 4.8% in 1976, down to 697,600 metric tons from 732,900 the year before. The major producer was Canada with 262,000 metric tons in 1976, a substantial increase above the 243,000 tons in 1975; after Canada, the major producers were the U.S.S.R. at an estimated 125,000 tons and Australia 83,000 tons. Three other countries, Cuba, the Dominican Republic, and South Africa, produced between 20,000 and 40,000 tons. Overall consumption worldwide fell by 10% during 1976 and was expected to decline further in 1977, resulting in serious oversupply of both ore and refinery capacity. Production of refined metal fell 15.7% in 1976, from 699,900 metric tons in 1975 to less than 590,000 tons, over half of the total being accounted for in Canada, which experienced a 32.6% decline. No recovery was expected during 1977 or 1978.

Phosphate Rock. World production of phosphate rock remained at 1975 levels; 1976 production was estimated at 106,537,-000 metric tons, compared to 106,563,000 in 1975. The major producer was the U.S. with 44,146,000 tons, followed by the U.S.S.R. with 24,230,000 tons, Morocco 15,293,000 (still well below 1974 production because of the success of Polisario guerrillas at several production and shipping points controlled by Morocco); a group of lesser producers, including China, Tunisia, Togo, Senegal, Jordan, South Africa, Vietnam, and Christmas Island ranged between 1 million and 4 million tons. Despite the worldwide slump in the phosphate market, active U.S. operations were producing at about 95% of available capacity. The slump, however, was not seen as permanent, and in North Africa both Morocco and Tunisia planned substantial increases in capacity for 1980 to 25 million tons per year and 7 million tons per year, respectively.

Platinum-Group Metals. Production of the several platinum-group metals (platinum, palladium, iridium, osmium, rhodium, and ruthenium) rose in 1976 by about 3.1%, from 5,763,000 troy ounces in 1975 to an estimated 5,940,000 ounces in 1976. The output was almost entirely from two countries, the U.S.S.R. and South Africa, both producing about 2.7 million ounces in 1976; the only other important producer was Canada with 430,000 ounces.

Potash. World production of potash declined somewhat in 1976, reaching a production level of approximately 23,926,000 metric tons compared to 24,453,000 in 1975 (about a 2.2% reduction); the major producer was the U.S.S.R., with some 8,250,000 tons compared to 7,944,000 in 1975, followed by Canada 5,126,000 tons, East Germany 3,160,000 tons, the U.S. 2,205,000 tons, West Germany 2,036,000 tons, and France 1,603,000 tons. The 1975 and 1976 production levels for the U.S.S.R. represented a remarkable 20% increase in the final year of the 1971–75 Five Year Plan and in the first year of the 1976–80 plan.

Silver. World mine production of silver, according to the U.S. Bureau of Mines, was estimated to have risen by about 2.6% in 1976, up to 303 million troy ounces compared to 295.3 million in the preceding year. Production was not dominated by any one country, five producing in the 30 million- to 45 million-ounce range: the U.S.S.R. probably led with about 42 million; Canada followed with 40,887,000, and was trailed closely by Mexico and Peru 40 million each, and the U.S. 34 million. Consumption in the U.S. (about 56% of the world total) rose by about 6% in 1976 and world consumption by about 7%. World supplies were unexpectedly increased in 1976 when about 28 million ounces of West German coins were demonetized and melted down. The Silver Institute produced data showing that the number of countries utilizing silver in their coinage had risen from 56 in 1973 to 73 in 1976, although it was not believed that this necessarily presaged increased demand in the near future.

Tin. World mine production of tin was estimated to have increased by about 3% in 1976, about 231,000 metric tons having been produced in that year compared to 224,800 in 1975; the leading producer was Malaysia, with about 66,000 tons. The U.S.S.R. probably produced about 30,000 tons and was followed by Bolivia 24,915, Indonesia 24,000, China 22,000 (estimated), and Thailand 21,000.

Smelter production of tin declined from 228,300 metric tons to about 225,500 tons; Malaysia was the world leader, producing about 80,000 tons; the U.S.S.R. and China, two countries for which hard data were not available, followed, probably at about 30,000 and 20,000 tons, respectively. Bolivia's acceptance of the Fifth International Tin Agreement in March 1977 brought into force that agreement, intended to stabilize the world market.

Titanium. Production of titanium rutile concentrates declined slightly (3.6%) in 1976; virtually all of the world's production originated in Australia, where 1976 production amounted to about 321,000 metric tons of the world total of 337,000. The only other significant producers were the U.S., at about 10,000 tons, and India and Sri Lanka, which together produced about 6,300 tons. Production of titanium ilmenite concentrates increased by about 7.5% to a total of about 3,577,000 metric tons; the major producer was Australia with production of about 976,600 tons; the only other important producers were Canada 816,000 tons, Norway 590,000 tons, and the U.S. 562,000 tons.

Tungsten. World production of tungsten rose about 4%, from 37,450 metric tons in 1975 to 38,900 in 1976. China led the U.S.S.R. with about 8,500 tons, followed by the U.S. with 2,720 tons, Bolivia 2,551 tons, and South Korea 2,427 tons. 1977–78 was expected to see the start-up of new mines at Mittersill, Austria; TBBM in Brazil; Tempiute and Strawberry in the U.S.; and at Uludag, Turkey.

Uranium. No data were available for uranium production in socialist countries, but available data for the West indicated that mine production of uranium oxide had risen by about a quarter from 1975, to an estimated 13,900 tons. Of these, about 6,120 (or 45%) originated in the U.S.; the only other major producer was Canada with 6,058 tons. Tensions were aroused in Australia when the government legalized exportation of uranium oxide there.

Zinc. Production of zinc ore in terms of contained metal rose about 1% in 1976, from 5,833,800 metric tons in 1975 to about 5,892,000 tons in 1976. Canada was by far the major producer with 1,039,700 metric tons, followed by the U.S.S.R. with about 720,000 tons, Australia 464,000 tons, the U.S. 439,500 tons, and Peru 421,300 tons. World production of zinc metal, however, rose by approximately 7% in 1976 to an estimated total of 5,426,850 tons, of which the major producers were Japan at 742,000 tons, based on imported ore; the U.S.S.R. at 720,000 tons, Canada 473,000 tons, the U.S. 453,000 tons. Five countries with outputs between 230,000 and 300,000 tons were West Germany, Australia, Poland, Belgium, and France. Strong production gains were noted in France (28.8%), Australia (25.5%), and in the U.S. (13.9%).

(WILLIAM A. CLEVELAND)

See also Earth Sciences; Energy; Industrial Review: *Gemstones; Iron and Steel*; Materials Sciences.

Monaco

A sovereign principality on the northern Mediterranean coast, Monaco is bounded on land by the French département of Alpes-Maritimes. Area: 1.89 sq km (0.73 sq mi). Pop. (1976 est.): 25,000. Language: French. Religion: predominantly Roman Catholic. Prince, Rainier III; minister of state in 1977, André Saint-Mleux.

A year that began with a 50 million cruzeiro damage suit filed in Brazil by Prince Rainier III against a Brazilian industrialist's son, Francisco Scarpa, for libeling his eldest daughter, Princess Caroline, in a television interview, continued on a happier note. The engagement of the 20-year-old Princess Caroline to Philippe Junot, a descendant of Marshal Andoche Junot, duke of Abrantès, one of Napoleon's companions, was officially announced on Aug. 25, 1977. Junot was a 37-year-old Paris insurance broker. The wedding would take place in June 1978 to permit Princess Caroline to complete her philosophy studies at the Paris Institute of Political Sciences.

In August it was reported that the principality was willing to sell some of its shares in the Société des Bains de Mer, the holding company that controls most of Monaco's tourist business. Control of the Société had been acquired from the late Aristotle Onassis a decade earlier.

(K. M. SMOGORZEWSKI)

Monaco

Mongolia

A people's republic of Asia lying between the U.S.S.R. and China, Mongolia occupies the geographic area known as Outer Mongolia. Area: 1,565,000 sq km (604,000 sq mi). Pop. (1977 est.): 1,532,000. Cap. and largest city: Ulan Bator (pop., 1976 est., 331,800). Language: Khalkha Mongolian. Religion: Lamaistic Buddhism. First secretary of the Mongolian People's Revolutionary (Communist) Party in 1977 and chairman of the Presidium of the Great People's Hural, Yumzhagiyen Tsedenbal; chairman of the Council of Ministers (premier), Zhambyn Batmunkh.

Chairman Yumzhagiyen Tsedenbal paid a state visit to East Berlin in 1977 and, on May 6, signed a 25-year treaty of friendship and cooperation with East Germany. On June 19 a new, ninth Great People's Hural was elected, and on June 27 an 11-member Presidium was elected, with Tsedenbal remaining as chairman. Also on June 27, a new 38-member Council of Ministers, including Zhambyn Batmunkh as chairman, was appointed.

On August 12 Leonid Brezhnev, general secretary of the Communist Party of the Soviet Union, received Tsedenbal at his summer villa in the Crimea. Mangalyn Dugersuren, the Mongolian minister of foreign affairs, visited Yugoslavia and Romania in May.

The "Erdenet," a copper-molybdenum-dressing

Mongolia

MONACO

Education. (1971–72) Primary, pupils 1,486, teachers 71; secondary, pupils 2,089, teachers 165; vocational, pupils 458, teachers 61.

Finance and Trade. Monetary unit: French franc, with (Sept. 19, 1977) a free rate of Fr 4.93 to U.S. $1 (Fr 8.59 = £1 sterling). Budget (1975 rev. est.): revenue Fr 427 million; expenditure Fr 386 million. Foreign trade included with France. Tourism (1975) 139,000 visitors.

MONGOLIA

Education. (1974–75) Primary, pupils 127,986, teachers 4,144; secondary, pupils 161,309, teachers 6,511; vocational, pupils 12,718, teachers 755; teacher training, students 1,461, teachers 157; higher (1972–73), students 8,900, teaching staff (1971–72) 710.

Finance. Monetary unit: tugrik, with (Sept. 19, 1977) a nominal exchange rate of 3.35 tugriks to U.S. $1 (5.80 tugriks = £1 sterling). Budget (1976 est.): revenue 2,987,000,000 tugriks; expenditure 2,972,000,000 tugriks.

Foreign Trade. (1975) Imports U.S. $547 million; exports U.S. $219 million. Import sources U.S.S.R. 90%. Export destinations: U.S.S.R. 79%; Czechoslovakia 6%. Main exports: livestock 27%; meat 19%; wool 16%.

Transport and Communications. Roads (1970) *c.* 75,000 km (including *c.* 9,000 km main roads). Railways (1975) *c.* 1,520 km. Telephones (Jan. 1976) 31,000. Radio receivers (Dec. 1974) *c.* 200,000. Television receivers (Dec. 1974) *c.* 27,000.

Agriculture. Production (in 000; metric tons; 1975): wheat *c.* 366; oats *c.* 49; barley *c.* 34; potatoes *c.* 23; milk *c.* 244; beef and veal *c.* 63; mutton and goat meat *c.* 120. Livestock (in 000; Dec. 1975): sheep 14,458; goats 4,595; cattle (1974) *c.* 2,365; horses (1974) *c.* 2,264; camels (1974) *c.* 670.

Industry. Production (in 000; metric tons; 1975): coal 171; lignite 2,549; salt *c.* 11; cement 159; electricity (kw-hr) 818,000.

---

complex being built with Soviet assistance, was expected to start production in 1978. It would be one of the largest of its kind in the world, and a town of 27,000 inhabitants had sprung up with it.

(K. M. SMOGORZEWSKI)

Morocco

Morocco

A constitutional monarchy of northwestern Africa, on the Atlantic Ocean and the Mediterranean Sea, Morocco is bordered by Algeria and Western (Spanish) Sahara. Area: 458,730 sq km (177,117 sq mi). Pop. (1975 est.): 17,305,000. Cap.: Rabat (pop., 1975 UN est., 654,000). Largest city: Casablanca (pop., 1975 est., 1,864,400). Data above refer to Morocco as constituted prior to the purported division of Western (Spanish) Sahara between Morocco and Mauritania. Language: Arabic; Berber. Religion: Muslim. King, Hassan II; prime minister in 1977, Ahmed Osman.

In 1977 the Moroccan Army was increased to 90,000 men, 15,000 of whom were permanently stationed in the new Saharan provinces, and military spending rose from $533 million in 1976 to $773 million. At the beginning of 1977 a bond drive was launched throughout the country to raise $227 million to develop the Western Sahara. Nevertheless, the Popular Front for the Liberation of Saguia el Hamra and Río de Oro (Polisario Front) guerrilla movement, operating from bases around Tindouf in Algeria, was able to tie down Moroccan forces around the major Western Saharan towns and keep the phosphate mining installations at Bu Craa out of action. Morocco, acting under the terms of its mutual defense pact with Mauritania, airlifted 600 troops to aid the Mauritanian Army after a second Polisario attack on the iron-ore centre of Zouerate in July.

A Polisario Front delegation was admitted to the Organization of African Unity (OAU) meeting at Lomé, Togo, in February, causing Morocco and Mauritania to walk out, but the two countries attended the OAU summit at Libreville, Gabon, in July, from which the Front was excluded. In February Morocco angrily rejected an accusation that it had organized the mysterious mercenary attack

Keeping a wary eye on the sky for enemy planes, Moroccan troops moved toward the village of Mutshatsha, in Zaire's Shaba Province, which had been captured by the Katangan rebels in March and virtually abandoned one month later.

MOROCCO

Education. (1975–76) Primary, pupils 1,547,647, teachers (state only) 37,226; secondary, pupils 471,575, teachers (state only) 19,613; vocational (1970–71), pupils 6,986, teachers 572; teacher training, students 4,030, teachers 486; higher, students (1974–75) 34,092, teaching staff 1,-921.

Finance. Monetary unit: dirham, with (Sept. 19, 1977) a free rate of 4.50 dirhams to U.S. $1 (7.84 dirhams = £1 sterling). Gold, SDR's, and foreign exchange (May 1977) U.S. $592 million. Budget (1974 actual): revenue 7,-326,000,000 dirhams; expenditure 8,748,000,000 dirhams. Gross national product (1975) 31,820,000,000 dirhams. Money supply (April 1977) 14,938,000,000 dirhams. Cost of living (1970 = 100; March 1977) 170.

Foreign Trade. (1976) Imports 11,555,000,000 dirhams; exports 5,579,000,000 dirhams. Main import sources: France 29%; U.S. 9%; West Germany 8%; Spain 6%; Italy 6%; Iraq 5%. Main export destinations: France 24%; West Germany 10%; Italy 7%; U.K. 6%; Belgium-Luxembourg 6%; Spain 5%; Poland 5%. Main exports: phosphates 39%; citrus fruit 11%. Tourism (1975): visitors 1,245,000; gross receipts U.S. $296 million.

Transport and Communications. Roads (1973) 25,400 km. Motor vehicles in use (1975): passenger 320,100; commercial (including buses) 127,200. Railways: (1975) 2,071 km; traffic (1976) 863.4 million passenger-km, freight 3,-131,000,000 net ton-km. Air traffic (1976): 1,228,000,000 passenger-km; freight 18.1 million net ton-km. Shipping (1976): merchant vessels 100 gross tons and over 67; gross tonnage 136,596. Telephones (Dec. 1975) 168,000. Radio receivers (Dec. 1974) 1.3 million. Television licenses (Dec. 1974) 382,000.

Agriculture. Production (in 000; metric tons; 1976): wheat 2,190; barley 2,862; corn c. 430; potatoes c. 207; sugar, raw value c. 310; dry broad beans (1975) 213; tomatoes c. 315; grapes c. 280; oranges 566; mandarin oranges and tangerines c. 140; olives c. 312; figs (1975) c. 67; dates c. 102; fish catch (1975) 210. Livestock (in 000; 1975): cattle c. 3,500; sheep c. 16,000; goats c. 6,800; horses c. 300; mules c. 373; asses c. 1,202; camels c. 190; poultry c. 23,590.

Industry. Production (in 000; metric tons; 1976): coal 702; crude oil c. 10; cement 2,108; iron ore (55–60% metal content) 343; phosphate rock (1975) 14,119; manganese ore (metal content; 1975) 105; lead concentrates (metal content) 68; zinc concentrates (metal content) 17; petroleum products (1975) c. 2,415; electricity (kw-hr; 1975) c. 2,950,000.

on Cotonou, Benin. (See BENIN.) On April 7, 1,500 Moroccan troops were airlifted, with French help, to Zaire to repel an invasion of Shaba Province. (See ZAIRE.) By the end of May, King Hassan was able to recall his victorious troops, and in mid-June a joint Moroccan-Zairian victory parade was held in Casablanca.

In the Assembly elections held June 3 and June 21, the monarchist Independents and royalist parties won 185 of the 264 seats. Just before the new Assembly met in October, King Hassan dissolved his government and instructed his previous prime minister, Ahmed Osman, to form a new one.

The Moroccan economy suffered from the effects of a 20% inflation rate and from the strains imposed by the Saharan conflict and low world phosphate prices. The rate of growth was below the expected 7½%, the poor 1977 harvest meant that stocks would have to be bought on the world market, and income from tourism also fell. Nevertheless, the 1977–78 budget, published in June, proposed a 19% increase in investment in development. The U.S.S.R. and Morocco signed an agreement whereby the U.S.S.R. would invest in phosphate treatment plants in Morocco in return for 25–30 years of phosphate exports for Soviet domestic use.

(EMIL G. H. JOFFÉ)

Motion Pictures

Sir Charles Chaplin, perhaps motion pictures' greatest pioneer, died on Dec. 25, 1977 (*see* OBITUARIES). The many and lengthy tributes in the world press, regardless of political barriers, testified to the universality of his unique creation, the little tramp Everyman who appeared in different guises in all his best-loved films, from the early shorts to *The Great Dictator*, and became the cinema's most enduring symbol.

English-Speaking Cinema. UNITED STATES. The outstanding commercial success of the year was *Star Wars*, written and directed by George Lucas (*see* BIOGRAPHY). A science-fiction fairy tale with outstanding special effects, its attraction for audiences seemed to lie in its elemental confrontation of good and evil. It drew large crowds in the U.S. and Europe and became one of the biggest moneymakers in movie history. Opening late in the year was Steven Spielberg's *Close Encounters of the Third Kind*, also rich in special effects, about UFO's landing on the Earth.

Hollywood was much taken up with its usual strategy of cashing in on past successes. There was an *Airport 77*; and to follow *Walking Tall* and *Part 2, Walking Tall* there was *Final Chapter—Walking Tall*. Clint Eastwood reappeared as the tough policeman, Harry Callahan, in *The Enforcer*. There were ambitious remakes of *King Kong* (directed by John Guillermin) and *A Star Is Born* (directed by Frank Pierson and starring Barbra Streisand and Kris Kristofferson), both of which lost the essence of their originals.

Several Hollywood films reflected a continuing fascination with Satanism and the occult. These included Michael Winner's *The Sentinel*, Robert Wise's *Audrey Rose*, and John Boorman's *Exorcist II: The Heretic* (bearing little relation to the original *The Exorcist*). Donald Cammell's bizarre *Demon Seed* merged science fiction and the occult in a story

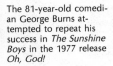

The 81-year-old comedian George Burns attempted to repeat his success in *The Sunshine Boys* in the 1977 release *Oh, God!*

about a supercomputer that seeks to reproduce itself by human means of generation.

The "disaster" film seemed in decline. Two survivors of the genre, Larry Peerce's *Two-Minute Warning* and John Frankenheimer's *Black Sunday*, both chose similar settings—crowded sports stadiums threatened respectively by a crazy sniper and a terrorist gang determined to drop a powerful explosive weapon. Real-life terrorists apparently provided greater attractions. William Graham's *21 Hours at Munich* reconstructed the 1972 Olympic Games massacre. The Israeli commando raid on Entebbe Airport (Uganda) in July 1976, to free the Israeli hostages held there by terrorists, provided the subject for two films, *Victory at Entebbe* directed by Marvin Chomsky, and Irvin Kershner's *Raid on Entebbe*. The choice between the two films was largely a matter of preference for the cast, and it remained for Israel to provide a more believable reconstruction of the event (*see* below).

After several years of movies describing friendships between men, two films in 1977 focused on close relationships between women. Fred Zinnemann's *Julia*, with Jane Fonda and Vanessa Red-

Mormons:
see Religion

The robot Artoo-Detoo (R2-D2) was one of the star attractions of the movie *Star Wars*.

Annual Cinema Attendance[1]		
Country	Total in 000	Per cap-ita
Afghanistan	19,200	1.1
Albania	9,000	4.1
Algeria	48,400	3.0
Angola	3,700	0.6
Argentina	82,300	3.3
Australia	32,000	3.0
Austria	28,000	3.7
Bahrain	2,000	8.2
Barbados	1,800	7.4
Belgium	25,400	2.6
Benin	1,200	0.4
Bolivia	3,200	0.9
Brazil	195,400	1.9
Brunei	2,900	20.4
Bulgaria	114,300	13.1
Burma	222,500	8.1
Cambodia	20,000	3.0
Cameroon	6,200	1.0
Canada	89,000	3.9
Chile	44,600	5.0
Colombia	163,600	6.8
Cuba	124,300	14.2
Cyprus	6,100	9.5
Czechoslovakia	87,700	6.0
Denmark	19,900	3.9
Dominican Republic	5,200	1.2
Ecuador	38,700	5.6
Egypt	65,000	1.9
El Salvador	14,100	3.5
Finland	9,600	2.0
France	178,500	3.4
Germany, East	79,500	4.6
Germany, West	136,200	2.2
Ghana	18,700	2.0
Guam	1,000	10.3
Guatemala	15,400	2.8
Guyana	8,700	11.2
Haiti	1,500	0.3
Hong Kong	63,000	14.8
Hungary	74,000	7.0
Iceland	2,000	9.2
India	2,424,000	4.1
Iran	110,000	3.3
Iraq	8,300	1.3
Ireland	38,000	13.0
Israel	28,500	8.4
Italy	546,100	9.8
Ivory Coast	11,500	2.5
Japan	171,000	1.5
Jordan	4,300	1.6
Korea, South	99,900	3.0
Kuwait	4,700	4.7
Lebanon	49,700	18.0
Liberia	1,000	0.6
Luxembourg	1,100	3.2
Macau	2,400	8.9
Madagascar	2,900	0.4
Malaysia	95,400	8.2
Mali	2,500	0.5
Malta	3,100	9.4
Martinique	2,100	6.0
Mauritius	16,000	18.3
Mexico	238,600	4.1
Morocco	29,000	1.7
Mozambique	4,600	0.5
Netherlands, The	26,100	1.9
New Zealand	15,000	5.0
Nicaragua	7,700	7.7
Norway	17,900	4.5
Pakistan	194,800	3.0
Panama	7,100	4.8
Philippines	38,000	7.6
Poland	144,200	4.2
Portugal	35,700	4.1
Puerto Rico	6,800	2.2
Romania	191,200	8.9
Senegal	5,200	1.2
Singapore	41,300	18.4
Somalia	4,700	1.7
Spain	262,900	7.5
Sri Lanka	53,500	3.9
Sudan	24,000	1.4
Surinam	1,700	5.0
Sweden	25,400	3.1
Switzerland	27,000	4.2
Thailand	71,000	1.7
Trinidad and Tobago	8,400	8.0
Tunisia	12,500	2.3
Turkey	246,700	6.7
U.S.S.R.	4,497,000	17.7
United Kingdom	116,000	2.1
United States	1,032,800	4.8
Upper Volta	1,000	0.2
Venezuela	36,100	3.1
Yemen (San'a')	3,500	2.4
Yugoslavia	80,000	3.7
Zaire	1,700	0.1

[1] Countries having over one million annual attendance.
Source: United Nations, *Statistical Yearbook 1976*; various country publications.

Rudolf Nureyev, as Valentino (right), danced with the legendary Nijinsky (Anthony Dowell) in Nureyev's acting debut in the movie *Valentino*.

grave, was adapted from a memoir by Lillian Hellman, and Herbert Ross's *The Turning Point* starred Anne Bancroft and Shirley MacLaine in a story dealing with the world of ballet. Another film having a woman as the central character was Richard Brooks's adaptation of the Judith Rossner novel *Looking for Mr. Goodbar*, in which Diane Keaton sensitively portrays a young woman who teaches deaf children by day and collects men in singles bars at night.

Biographical films enjoyed a revival. Hal Ashby's *Bound for Glory* was an attractive if somewhat rosy re-creation of the career of the folk singer Woody Guthrie (with a fine performance by David Carradine). Michael Schultz's *Greased Lightning* traced the career of the first black automobile racer, Wendell Scott, played by Richard Pryor. In *The Greatest*, the subject, Muhammad Ali, played his own role, revealing himself as an actor of natural talent and resource. The director was Tom Gries, who died shortly after shooting the film.

Sport—or at least a somewhat jaundiced view of it—was also the subject of *Slap Shot* (director George Roy Hill), a tale about a failing ice hockey team that regains public favour by introducing foul play and violence into its games; and of Lamont Johnson's *One on One*, the story of a dedicated college basketball player who finds that corruption and exploitation are an inescapable fact of sporting life. Michael Ritchie's *Semi-Tough*, adapted from the novel by Dan Jenkins, satirized the human potential movement against a backdrop of professional football.

Sport, too, was the theme of one of the year's runaway successes, *Rocky*, directed by John G. Avildsen but essentially the creation of the writer and star, Sylvester Stallone (*see* BIOGRAPHY). A fairy tale about an unsuccessful boxer who gets and seizes the chance of a lifetime, the film was also Stallone's real-life fairy tale of overnight success after hard battles to convince a producer to undertake his script.

Of older-generation directors, Sidney Lumet adapted Peter Shaffer's play *Equus*, which benefited from the literal context in which the cinema was able to place it. Otherwise, it was a year for directors who had made their names in the 1970s. John Schlesinger made an effective if unappetizing political thriller, *Marathon Man*. Martin Scorsese abandoned the streets of Little Italy for the claustrophobia of the studio and reexamined all the character and situation clichés of the musical genre in *New York, New York*, the story of the love of band singer Liza Minnelli and saxophone player Robert DeNiro (*see* BIOGRAPHY) in the post-World War II years. Woody Allen combined his singular comic talent with sensitive insight and autobiographical poignancy in *Annie Hall*, a recollection of a love affair that had cooled into friendship.

In a year not rich in comedy, Carl Reiner's *Oh, God!* featured George Burns in the title role, an understated deity who made his presence known to a supermarket manager, and Arthur Hiller rather mechanically parodied the disaster genre in *Silver Streak*. Creative documentary continued to flourish. The brilliant Fred Wiseman's now annual study of an aspect of U.S. life was *Canal Zone*, a subtle and understated picture of a fringe society in which the values of the homeland are feverishly exaggerated. Barbara Kopple's *Harlan County, U.S.A.* was a revealing study of a Kentucky miners' strike. In contrast, George Butler's *Pumping Iron* patently manipulated its facts in a witty portrayal of the sport of body-building.

At the annual award ceremony of the U.S. Academy of Motion Picture Arts and Sciences, the Oscars for best film, best direction, and best editing (Richard Halsey and Scott Conrad) went to *Rocky*. *Network* took four prizes, for best actor and actress (Peter Finch—the first artist to receive a posthumous Oscar award—and Faye Dunaway); for best screenplay (Paddy Chayefsky); and for best supporting actress (Beatrice Straight). Alan Pakula's *All The President's Men* also received four awards: for best adapted screenplay (William Goldman), for best supporting actor (Jason Robards, as Ben Bradlee, the *Washington Post*'s executive editor), best sound, and best art direction. *Bound for Glory* received awards for best adapted score (Leonard Rosenman) and best camerawork (Haskell Wexler). The best original music score was Jerry Goldsmith's for *The Omen*, and the best original song was "Evergreen" by Paul Williams and Barbra Streisand, from *A Star Is Born*. The best foreign-language film was the French *Black and White in Colour*, directed by Jean-Jacques Annaud.

BRITAIN. The declining production and generally unhealthy economic state of the British film industry was a continuing cause for alarm and was the concern of a committee set up under Sir Harold Wilson. Meanwhile, too, a Home Office departmental committee on obscenity had a special assignment to consider the laws applying to film censorship. This was of particular relevance at a time of a stern moral "backlash" in Britain; in the summer, Pier Paolo Pasolini's powerful last work, *Salo*, was seized by police from the London cinema club where it was being shown.

By and large production was based on spin-offs of popular television series (*Are You Being Served?*), soft-core sex (*Come Play with Me*), recapitulation of old triumphs like the James Bond cycle (Lewis Gilbert's *The Spy Who Loved Me*), and participation in huge international co-productions (Sam Peckinpah's *Cross of Iron*; George Pan Cosmatos' *The Cassandra Crossing*). Of the year's major productions, Tony Richardson's ill-formed *Joseph Andrews*, failing to recapture the spirit of *Tom Jones*; Ken Russell's vulgar, flamboyant, and unhistorical *Valentino* (notable only for the acting debut of Rudolf Nureyev); and Richard Attenborough's overinflated, star-laden story of the World War II Arnhem airborne operation, *A Bridge Too Far*, were equally disappointing.

The most interesting commercial films of the year were two police thrillers that made ingenious use of British locations, Michael Apted's *The Squeeze* and David Wickes' *Sweeney!*; Terry Gilliam's zany medieval fairy tale *Jabberwocky*, in the comic vein of *Monty Python*; and Anthony Simmon's *Black Joy*, a lively musical about immigrant life in London. At the Cannes Film Festival Ridley Scott's *The Duellists* took a special prize for best first film, though it seemed an over-glossy and superficial treatment of the Joseph Conrad story from which it was adapted.

If the prospects of the commercial cinema were gloomy, there were encouraging signs of activity among low-budget independent productions financed with the aid of bodies like the Arts Council, the British Film Institute, and the Regional Arts Association. Among these Peter Wollen's and Laura Mulvey's feminist pamphlet *Riddles of the Sphinx* attracted a good deal of attention, while the 1977 London Film Festival was able to devote a special section to British independents, showing no less than 24 feature- or medium-length films and a large group of animated short subjects.

AUSTRALIA. Despite financial uncertainties, the Australian cinema went from strength to strength, a sturdily emergent cinema rapidly establishing an identity. John Power's *The Picture Show Man* was an endearing picaresque about a traveling film show in the 1920s. Set in the same period, Ken Hannam's *Break of Day* was a low-key love story of a smalltown newspaper proprietor and a "Bohemian" in Victoria. The eclectic Peter Weir (*see* BIOGRAPHY) followed his *Picnic at Hanging Rock* with *The Last Wave*, about a lawyer who gains a greater understanding of tribal psychology when engaged in a trial involving Aboriginals.

CANADA. English-language Canadian filmmakers evinced a taste for horror and violence in 1977 (*Squirm, Death Weekend, Rituals, The Uncanny*), but the best films of the year showed a healthy variety of approach. Robin Spry's *One Man* related a newspaperman's lone fight against pollution and the corruption of secrecy. Donald Shebib's *Second Wind*

Lavishly expensive sets were a feature of the James Bond thriller *The Spy Who Loved Me.*

Rocky, a low budget but award-winning film, was one of the biggest money-makers at U.S. box offices. The movie featured Sylvester Stallone and Talia Shire.

portrayed a young stockbroker with an obsession for competitive running. Silvio Narizzano's *Why Shoot the Teacher* adapted a novel about prairie life in the 1930s. Two auspicious debuts were those of Toronto filmmaker Richard Benner with *Outrageous*, a touching story about the mutual dependence of a plump homosexual transvestite and a deeply neurotic girl, and Vancouver director Zale R. Dalen with *Skip Tracer*, an acute, realistic portrait of a professional debt collector.

From the Quebec cinema came Jean Pierre Lefebvre's politically charged exploration of the relationship of Canadians to French, *Le Vieux Pays ou Rimbaud est mort*, and a ribald gangster comedy, Jean-Guy Noel's *Ti-Cul Tougas*.

Western Europe. FRANCE. Two of the great veterans remained at work. With *Cet Obscur Objet du Désir* Luis Buñuel realized a very old ambition, an adaptation of Pierre Louys' *La Femme et le Pantin*. Robert Bresson's *Le Diable, Probablement*, a sombre, riveting portrayal of a boy who can find no grace except suicide in a world of physical and moral pollution, won the Jury prize at the Berlin Film Festival in June. The middle generation of the New Wave directors was less in evidence. François Truffaut's *L'Homme qui aimait les femmes* (The Man Who Loved Women) was a slight piece; and Alain Resnais's *Providence*, even with fine design and a notable performance by John Gielgud as a decaying author weaving night fantasies about his family relationships, failed to conceal a pretentious quality in David Mercer's screenplay.

Among directors who had emerged in the last decade, the indefatigable Marguerite Duras released no fewer than three films during the period under review, continuing to explore cinema as an extension of her work in the novel. To a greater or lesser extent the "minimal" cinema of films like *Des Journées entières dans les arbres* (adapted from her own prizewinning play), *Baxter, Vera Baxter* (unraveling the life and psyche of a woman in stress as she sits in an elegant villa), and *Le Camion* (in which Duras simply discusses with her actor, Gérard Depardieu, the construction of a projected film about a middle-aged woman hitching a lift in

a truck) was a minority taste, but its devotees were passionate.

Another woman director, Agnès Varda, made her first feature film in nine years: *L'Une chante, l'autre pas*, with a feminist theme but an overriding human feeling for its characters—two girls whose ups and downs and periodic meetings are chronicled over the years 1962–77.

ITALY. At the close of 1976 the outstanding commercial success was Valerio Zurlini's adaptation of Dino Buzzati's novel *Il Deserto dei Tartari*, set in the Austro-Hungarian Army at the end of World War I. The outstanding artistic success of the year, however, *Padre Padrone*, directed by the brothers Paolo and Vittorio Taviani, was an important sign of the times (in an inflation economy, and a cinema of declining prosperity), having been made in collaboration with television on a minimal budget. The Tavianis' soaring imagination nevertheless gave epic quality to their factual story of a Sardinian shepherd, put to work in the fields at 6 and remaining illiterate till he was 20, when he revolted against a patriarchal system, learned to read, and finally took a university degree. The film was the first to win both the Grand Prize and the International Critics' Prize at the Cannes Film Festival.

Federico Fellini's long-awaited *Casanova* proved disappointing, a formless and uninvolved picaresque with a few dazzling set pieces and a Casanova whose much-vaunted conquests are ultimately so ineffectual that his memory of the perfect partner remains that of a robot he once encountered in Venice. Italian festival entries during the year seemed slight: Ettore Scola's *Una Gionata Particolare*, a wan, brief encounter between Italy's middle-aged idols Sophia Loren and Marcello Mastroianni, set on the momentous day of Hitler's 1938 state visit to Rome; and Mario Monicelli's *Un Borghese Piccolo Piccolo*, a bizarre and brutal parable about a mild little man who kills the man who was the cause of his son's death.

WEST GERMANY. Hitler loomed large as a preoccupation with filmmakers. Joachim C. Fest's documentary *Hitler—Eine Karriere*, with its compilation of superb film footage of the pomp and panoply of

Michael Palin and Annette Badland starred in *Jabberwocky*, a comedy film directed by Terry Gilliam, creator of the famed *Monty Python*.

the Third Reich, unwittingly painted so glamorous a picture that its showings incited storms of protest. Hans-Jürgen Syberberg's six-hour *Hitler — A Film Made in Germany* employed the director's now-familiar style of tableaux played against projected backgrounds to explore Hitler's ideas as well as his career. Ulli Lommel's *Hitler and Marlene* was a joyously tasteless speculation on an imagined infatuation for the star on the part of the dictator; it stirred angry protests and threats of litigation from Marlene Dietrich.

The major figures of the new generation of German filmmakers were all in full activity. Wim Wender's *The American Friend* was an adaptation of the novel *Ripley's Game* by Patricia Highsmith, a favourite author with filmmakers since Alfred Hitchcock's *Strangers on a Train*. Rainer Werner Fassbinder, who spent much of the year on his first big international production *Despair*, starring Dirk Bogarde, filmed Oskar Maria Graf's *Bolweiser*, a small-town melodrama originally made in two episodes for television but later adapted for the theatrical cinema by the director himself.

In *Stroszek* Werner Herzog made an uncharacteristically funny and sardonic film about an old jailbird who takes off for the New World with his prostitute girl friend and a crazy old man, only to find that it is not at all the paradise he had thought. Herzog also made two striking documentaries, *La Soufrière*, about the nonchalance of the inhabitants of a volcanic island facing imminent destruction, and *How Much Wood Would a Woodchuck Chuck*, about a U.S. auctioneering contest.

SWITZERLAND. Claude Goretta's *La Dentellière* adapted Pascal Lainé's prizewinning novel about a good, simple, inarticulate girl who falls in love with a student more intellectual than she but no better able to express his feelings. As in his earlier *L'Invitation*, Goretta revealed a rare sensitivity to human sentiments and relationships. Completed late in 1976, Alain Tanner's *Jonas qui aura 25 ans en l'an 2000*, co-scripted by Tanner and John Berger, concerned a group of eight characters trying to come to terms with themselves and their world after the traumas of 1968.

SCANDINAVIA. From Sweden, Bo Widerberg's *Man on the Roof* compromised ambitions to be a hard-hitting, realistic picture of a police investigation to settle for a conventional suspense melodrama about a sniper in the city. A more interesting work, Stellan Olsson's *Sven Klang's Combo*, was a slight, nostalgic, and sharply observed picture of a small dance band in the 1950s that goes to pieces under the strain of absorbing a genuinely dedicated new musician. From Denmark, Anders Refn's first film, *Cops*, proved a gripping little thriller with political undertones. From Norway, another new director, Vibeke Lokkeberg, made *The Revelation*, a feminist film whose innovation was to present a heroine gifted with neither looks nor intelligence.

SPAIN. The Spanish cinema was still rejoicing in emancipation after years of censorship. There were new films in the Galician and Basque languages, private experiments and public follies (*The Shirley Temple Story*), outspoken political documents such as Basilio Martín Patiño's *Caudillo*, and Manuel Gutiérrez Aragón's story of the making of a right-wing terrorist, *Camada Negra*.

PORTUGAL. The Portuguese cinema was also enjoying the euphoria of deliverance from dictatorship, though its manifestations were mainly in the area of documentary. Alberto Seixas Santos' *Sweet Customs* and Rui Simoes' *God, Fatherland, Authority* explored the history of the Salazar era; films such as Antonio da Cunha Telles' *Living On* discussed post-revolutionary problems.

Eastern Europe. U.S.S.R. Several new productions hinted at less rigorous official attitudes toward the content of Soviet films. Larissa Shepitko's *The Ascent*, which won the main prize at the Berlin Festival, drew parallels between Christ at Calvary and the agonies of a group of World War II partisans. Another unexpected and attractive war film, Valery Rubinchek's *The Crown of Sonnets*, viewed the last days of World War II through the eyes of two young Army musicians. Two other films, Igor Maslenikov's *A Sentimental Story*, about the erosion of idealism in a young man in the early days of revolution, and Gleb Panfiolov's *I Demand to Speak*, about the disillusionment of a housewife who is elected mayor of a community, were exceptional as admitting a possibility of human imperfectibility.

CZECHOSLOVAKIA. The Czechoslovak cinema continued to suffer from an oppressive bureaucracy. Vera Chytilova's vivacious satirical comedy, *The Apple Game*, perhaps the only film of note during the year, was unaccountably withdrawn from the Berlin Festival.

EAST GERMANY. Konrad Wolf's *Mama Ich Lebe* was a humane and sympathetic story of German soldiers of leftist tendencies who join up with the Soviet Army at the end of the war. Egon Günther made a brave but doomed effort to modernize the sentiments but not the setting of *Die Leiden des Jungen Werthers*.

HUNGARY. Hungary continued to maintain the most consistent standard of filmmaking among the socialist countries. The established Hungarian directors tended to pursue their own distinctive lines of activity. Thus, Istvan Szabo, in *Budapest Tales*, developed his preoccupation with the popular sentiments underlying the history of his times, through the metaphor of a ragged group of survivors after World War II for whom an abandoned streetcar becomes vehicle, home, fortress, and link with civilization. Marta Meszaros continued her series of studies of women in Hungarian society with *Nine Months*, the story of a young woman who revolts against conformity to male stereotypes of womanhood and decides to go it alone with her new baby.

POLAND. The only film to achieve international notice during the year was Krysztof Zanussi's *Camouflage*, a funny and satirical story of a young liberal professor who finds himself at odds with the academic bureaucracy.

Donald Sutherland was Casanova and Adele Angela Lojodice played the Doll Woman in Federico Fellini's version of *Casanova*.

KEYSTONE

Asia. JAPAN. The decline from the peak in 1960, when Japanese production reached 550 films, seemed to have stabilized at an annual output of approximately 300 films; included were "eroductions," cheaply made pornographic pictures of barely more than one hour in length. During a generally mediocre year Kaneto Shindo's *The Life of Chikusan*, a semidocumentary reconstruction of the 50-year wanderings of a blind folk singer, was notable. The annual award for the most successful film of 1976 went to the first feature film of Kazujiko Hasegawa, *Murderer of Youth*, not seen in the West until 1977. Based on a recent incident, the film begins with the young hero murdering, seemingly without motive, his parents, and then attempting self-immolation. The bloody incidents are viewed as an indictment of the effect on the young of the U.S. presence in Japan and the aftermath of the revolutionary mood of 1968.

INDIA. India's greatest director, Satyajit Ray, adapted a story by Munshi Premchand, *The Chess Players*, about two viceroys in India during the 1850s, oblivious to the encroachments of British imperialism and filling their time by playing chess. Shyam Benegal, a director dedicated to reaching a popular audience through serious films, financed *The Churning* with the aid of the farmers of Gujarat; in it he effectively dramatized an apparently unpromising subject, the establishing of a milk cooperative in a remote village. Girish Karnad, a Karnataka filmmaker who shared Benegal's ambition, followed his excellent *Kaadu* with an exciting martial-arts film, *Once upon a Time*.

Africa and the Middle East. ISRAEL. Two films from Israel were notable. A co-production with France, *The 81st Blow*, was among the most complete film studies of the Nazi plan to exterminate the Jews. Old archive films—some familiar, others newly unearthed; some professional, other sections raw home movies made by Nazi soldiers—were assembled together with first-hand commentaries by survivors of the Warsaw ghetto and the concentration camps into a devastating narrative. Turning to more recent history, Menahem Golan's *Operation Thunderbolt* was the best of the year's three competing reconstructions of the Israeli commando attack on Entebbe Airport in July 1976.

SENEGAL. In *Ceddo*, Ousmane Sembene, undisputed master of the African film, told a story of political and religious squabbling in a tribe torn by the conflicting appeals of Christianity, Islam, and local religion.

NORTH AFRICA. Allouache Merzak, a new Algerian director, revealed a lively sense of social comedy in *Omar Gatlato*, the story of a would-be *macho* who finds his boasted virility something of a liability. From Morocco, Souhel Ben Barka, adapting Federico García Lorca's *Blood Wedding*, shifted the scene from Spain to Morocco, a locale that seemed ideally suited to the overheated drama.   (DAVID ROBINSON)

Nontheatrical Motion Pictures. U.S. documentary films gained new stature in 1977. Robin Lehman's *End of the Game*, on animal interdependence in Africa, continued to win prizes. In addition to its earlier record of 11 international awards, it took top prizes during 1977 in Spain and Finland plus a blue ribbon in the American Film Festival.

Harlan County, U.S.A., a gripping documentary of the coal miners' struggle in a Kentucky county, won for director Barbara Kopple the American Film Festival's highest recognition, the Emily Award. Encyclopædia Britannica's *Volcano* was the top film at the International Scientific Film Association Congress in Venice, Italy.

Francis Thompson's *To Fly* was a giant-screen spectacular featured at the National Air and Space Museum in Washington, D.C. Sponsored by Continental Oil Co., *To Fly* was chosen in Berlin for the Inforfilm Award at the International Industrial Film Festival. Another film on flight, *Universe*, by Lester Novros for the U.S. National Aeronautics and Space Administration, took honours home and abroad.

The new copyright law brought shivers to many filmmakers who feared that their films could be legally copied on videotape. After the law went into effect on Jan. 1, 1978, producers watched for legal interpretations of it.   (THOMAS W. HOPE)

See also Photography; Television and Radio.
[623; 735.G.2]

Motor Sports

Grand Prix Racing. Not much technical change took place in grand prix competition in 1977, modern Formula One (F1) racing being mostly a matter of subtle technical advance and the skill and bravery of the drivers. Renault, the French company that won the first of the current series of grand prix in 1906, returned to top-class racing with an ambitious turbocharged car, on Michelin tires, but regarded the 1977 season only as a tryout.

On January 9 the first race was contested at Buenos Aires, although there had been no Argentine Grand Prix in 1976. Most of the teams were using the same cars as in 1976, but Lotus, Wolf, Ensign, and Ligier had new ones. Jody Scheckter of South Africa in a Wolf WR1 won a rather lucky victory, at 189.44 kph, from Carlos Pace of Brazil in a Brabham BT45/5 with a flat-12-cylinder Alfa Romeo engine. Carlos Reutemann of Argentina finished third driving a Ferrari 312T2 flat-12. James Hunt of Great Britain, the 1976 world champion, drove the fastest lap in a McLaren M23 at 193.46 kph but crashed when the rear suspension broke.

The competition then moved to Brazil, where in a race fraught with crashes and carnage only 7 cars completed the Interlagos course, although 22 had started. Reutemann won for Ferrari, averaging 181.73 kph, while Hunt finished second and Niki Lauda of Austria, who had recovered from a near-fatal accident toward the end of 1976, brought the other Ferrari home in third. Hunt again made the fastest lap, at 185.43 kph.

Before moving to Europe the F1 drivers contested the South African Grand Prix at Kyalami, and there Lauda was fully back in form, winning for Ferrari at 187.63 kph, although it was Britain's John Watson who drove the fastest lap, in a Brabham, at 190.3 kph. Second place went to Scheckter (Wolf) and third to France's Patrick Depailler (Tyrrell P34). The race was marred by a crash

James Hunt, in his McLaren-Ford, won the non-championship Race of Champions at Brands Hatch, England, on March 20 with a speed of 187.26 kph.

that caused the deaths of Welsh driver Tom Pryce and a race marshal struck by Pryce's car.

At Brands Hatch, England, a non-championship race was won before a large crowd of his supporters by Hunt, who averaged 187.26 kph. At Long Beach, Calif., the U.S. Grand Prix West was a hard-fought contest between the winner, Mario Andretti of the U.S. in the new Lotus 78, who averaged 139.83 kph, and Scheckter, who was defeated by a deflating front tire on his Wolf and finished third, behind Lauda's Ferrari.

The drivers then returned to Europe for the Spanish Grand Prix, where Andretti showed true prowess to bring his Lotus 78 home ahead of Reutemann's Ferrari and Scheckter's Wolf, at 147.73 kph. Fastest round the little Jarama circuit had been Jacques Laffite of France in a Ligier JS7, at 151.66 kph. Scheckter at 128.12 kph triumphed at Monaco; Lauda was second and Reutemann was third. In Belgium, at Zolder, Lotus scored again, Sweden's Gunnar Nilsson winning by 14.19 sec over Lauda's Ferrari. The Lotus also had the fastest lap, at 175.35 kph. Ronnie Peterson of Sweden kept Tyrrell in the picture, with third place.

The Swedish Grand Prix at Anderstorp was won by Laffite, who had an easy victory at 162.3 kph, from West Germany's Jochen Mass (McLaren) and Reutemann (Ferrari), although the Lotus 78 showed its superiority with the quickest lap, in Andretti's hands. The French Grand Prix at Dijon was a comparatively tame affair, which Andretti won by 1.55 sec, at 183.01 kph, when Watson's leading Brabham ran out of fuel with an unchallenged victory in sight. Hunt was third, and Andretti drove the fastest lap at 185.62 kph. In contrast, the British Grand Prix at Silverstone was an enormous festival of speed and spectator entertainment, out of which Hunt emerged the winner, at 209.79 kph; Lauda finished second and Nilsson third. Hunt had also lapped fastest, at 213.4 kph.

At the German Grand Prix at Hockenheim only 8 of the 24 contestants finished, Lauda leading Scheckter and West German Hans-Joachim Stuck (Brabham) home at 208.5 kph, with a fastest lap at 210.68 kph. In the Austrian Grand Prix at Zelt-

Motorboating:
see Water Sports

Motor Industry:
see Industrial Review

UPI COMPIX

Patrick Tambay, in his Haas/Hall Lola T/333 CS, won the SCCA Citicorp Can-Am race in Watkins Glen, New York, on July 10.

weg Alan Jones of Australia in a Shadow DN8 enjoyed a well-earned victory, at 197.49 kph; Lauda continued to amass championship points with another second place, and Stuck finished third. Zandvoort was the site of the Dutch Grand Prix where Lauda won easily from Laffite and Scheckter at an average speed of 186.88 kph in the Ferrari 312T. He also had the fastest lap. It then appeared that the courageous Lauda would be the world champion driver, as he was in 1975, because in the Italian Grand Prix at Monza he again placed second. Andretti won the event in a Lotus 78 at 206.01 kph, and also had the best lap at 210.7 kph, while Jones came in third.

The drivers then returned to North America for the U.S. Grand Prix at Watkins Glen, N.Y. There, Hunt exhibited wet-weather skills that brought him home ahead of Andretti and Scheckter, while Peterson had the fastest lap at 174.92 kph. There was a dramatic twist to the Canadian Grand Prix at Mosport Park, when the Cosworth engine of Andretti's Lotus 78 blew up while leading three laps from the finish. The final placings were Scheckter, Depailler, and Mass, and the race average was 187.76 kph. Andretti established a new single-lap record of 194.63 kph.

The season ended in Japan, where Hunt won at Fuji Speedway from Reutemann and Depailler, averaging nearly 130 kph. Scheckter had the fastest lap. Misfortune struck as the Ferrari of Gilles Villeneuve of Canada ran into the crowd, killing two people. Lauda won the championship, by 72 pt to Scheckter's 55 and Andretti's 47, while Enzo Ferrari, with his own engine in his own cars, took the constructors' world championship, scoring 95 pt to 62 by Lotus-Ford and 60 by McLaren-Ford.

(WILLIAM C. BODDY)

U.S. Racing. Though 1977 was a year for the old reliables in U.S. auto racing, in all the major forms of competition the gradual changing of the guard could be seen clearly. A. J. Foyt, winner of more United States Auto Club (USAC) championship

races than any other driver in history, became the first to win the Indianapolis 500 four times. The Texan gained his 58th championship victory in his 20th start at Indy. He averaged a nonrecord 161.331 mph to earn $252,278. Only 10 of the 33 starters were running at the finish.

But a rising star, ex-schoolteacher Tom Sneva, won USAC's season crown. Sneva, who finished second at Indianapolis, had driven his Penske Offenhauser to pole position at 198.884 mph, including a record lap of 200.535 mph. Sneva had recorded his first big car victory at another USAC Triple Crown event, the Schaefer 500 at Mt. Pocono, Pa. The consistent Michigan native then finished third at the California 500 at Ontario (won by veteran Al Unser with Foyt second) to also win the Olsonite Triple Crown Cup. In the three events Sneva earned $213,680, more than he had during his entire previous work life.

In National Association for Stock Car Auto Racing (NASCAR) events veteran Cale Yarborough piloted the Chevrolet of ex-driving great Junior Johnson to win the Winston Cup season title as well as the Daytona (Fla.) 500, richest race of the season. Rising young star Darrell Waltrip, also in a Chevrolet, won the Rebel 500 at Darlington, S.C., and the Winston 500 at Talladega, Ala., thus amassing as many victories for the season as all-time NASCAR winner Richard Petty. However, after winning the pole position, Waltrip lost the oldest stock-car classic, the Darlington Southern 500, to David Pearson and his Mercury.

Al Holbert, driving a Chevrolet Monza, won the International Motor Sports Association (IMSA) Camel GT road racing championship. Don Devendorf with a Datsun B210 clinched the Executive Motorhome Racing Stock title. In the IMSA-sponsored 24 Hours of Daytona Porsche's Hurley Haywood, Dave Helmick, and John Graves won. At the Sebring 12-Hour race, Porsches also totally dominated, led by George Dyer and Brad Frisselle of the U.S.

Sports Car Club of America (SCAA), which sanctions the two U.S. Grand Prix, reinstituted the Can-Am Challenge series, and a Frenchman, Patrick Tambay, won. The former ski star stepped into the Haas/Hall Lola T/333 CS when Brian Redman injured his back in the series' first race. Tambay drove to six victories and won the SCCA Citicorp Cup. Peter Gethin of the U.K., also in a Lola, finished second.

SCCA's Championship Runoffs at Road Atlanta crowned 23 national class champions and for the first time included the three Showroom Stock (SS) categories. D. J. Fazekis of Indianapolis won SSA in a Datsun; Tom Kersey of Ann Arbor, Mich., in an Alfa Romeo won SSB; and Douglas Farrow of Shoreview, Minn., won SSC in a Capri II. A rotary-engined Mazda gained its first national title when Stu Fisher of San Rafael, Calif., scored in the B Sedan category.

Janet Guthrie of New York City became the first woman to qualify for and race in the Indianapolis 500. Starting 26th with a speed of 188.403 mph, she lasted 27 laps before engine woes halted her.

Champions in other series included veteran Paul Feldner in USAC stock cars, Jerry Cook in NASCAR Modified, Jaguar's Bob Tullius in SCCA Trans-Am category I, and Mel Kenyon in USAC Midgets.

(ROBERT J. FENDELL)

Motorcycles. Britain's 27-year-old Barry Sheene (Suzuki) won the 500-cc world road-race title for the second successive year, followed by Steve Baker of the U.S. (Yamaha) and Pat Hennen of the U.S., riding for Sheene's Suzuki Great Britain team. Other class winners in the world championship were Angel Nieto of Spain (Bultaco), 50 cc; Pierpaolo Bianchi of Italy (Morbidelli), 125 cc; Mario Lega of Italy (Morbidelli), 250 cc; Takazumi Katayama of Japan (Yamaha), 350 cc; and George O'Dell and Kenny Arthur, both of Great Britain (Yamaha), sidecar.

In the Isle of Man Tourist Trophy (TT) races Phil Read of Great Britain won the Formula One event on a Honda at 97.02 mph and the 500-cc TT race on a Suzuki, at 106.97 mph. Mick Grant of Great Britain (Kawasaki) won the International Classic 1,000-cc event at a record 110.76 mph. At the British Grand Prix, Hennen (Suzuki) won the 500-cc event; Ron Haslam of Great Britain (Honda) Formula 1; Kork Ballington of South Africa (Yamaha) 250-cc and 350-cc; and Werner Schwarzel and A. Huber, both of West Germany (Aro), the sidecar. Steve Baker (Yamaha) became the first U.S. champion in a European race series by winning the Formula 750 championship. The chief amateur road-race event was the Manx Grand Prix, in which S. Davies (Yamaha) won the senior race, K. Riley (Yamaha) the junior, and D. Hickman (Yamaha) the lightweight.

In world motocross, the 500-cc class was won by Heikki Mikkola of Finland and the 250-cc class by Gennady Moisseev of the U.S.S.R. In the 52nd International Six-Days' Trial Czechoslovakia won the World Trophy competition for the 13th time and the secondary Silver Vase section for the 17th time. (CYRIL J. AYTON)

See also Water Sports.
[452.B.4.c]

Mountaineering

The highlight of the 1976 post-monsoon season in the Himalaya was the October ascent of the west face of Changabang (22,520 ft) in Garwhal by Britain's Peter Boardman and Joe Tasker. This ultralightweight, low-cost two-man ascent could be considered the hardest climb, technically, made in the Himalaya to date. Boardman and Tasker's elation was damped immediately afterward, however, by the duty of reaching and burying the bodies of three Americans and a Mexican killed on nearby Dunagiri. The American Bicentennial Everest Expedition was more fortunate, and two members reached the summit by the South Col route. Another U.S. expedition climbed Nanda Devi (25,645 ft) by the northwest face and north ridge. In Antarctica three British polar mountaineers disappeared after climbing Mt. Peary (6,100 ft).

In the pre-monsoon period in 1977, major new expeditions were the Japanese ascent of the west ridge of Nuptse; the ascent of the east ridge of Kangchenjunga by an Indian Army party; the first ascent of Baintha Brakk ("the Ogre," 23,900 ft) in the Karakoram by a British expedition; German ascents of Lhotse and Trisul; and a British ascent of Nanda Devi.

The Union Internationale des Associations d'Alpinisme (UIAA), at its meeting in Barcelona, Spain, in October 1976, considered mountaineering competitions. Such competitions were a feature of Soviet mountaineering; rock-climbing speed competitions were held, and awards were made for the best high mountain ascents. The U.S.S.R., backed by Poland and Czechoslovakia, proposed international competitions along these lines, with the ultimate aim of acquiring Olympic status, but most Western mountaineers felt that this would be alien to the ethic of climbing as practiced in the West. The proposals were remitted for study by a working party, and the issue re-

Veteran mountaineer Sir Edmund Hillary (centre) had to be rescued by helicopter after he became ill while climbing in the Himalayas.

UPI COMPIX

mained unresolved at the 1977 UIAA assembly which met in Mexico City.

The UIAA also considered a proposal for international reciprocity in the use of climbing huts and the formation of a mountain water charter. An agreement was reached between the UIAA and the Commission Internationale de Secours Alpine, the international mountain rescue organization, for closer future cooperation, in particular on insurance problems for mountain rescue teams and on field tests of electronic equipment for avalanche rescue.

New designs for nuts used in cracks for safeguarding were developed, a noteworthy example being the Clog Cog; another was the Salewa adjustable chock, which would fit in cracks of various widths. Salewa also produced a revolutionary new design of carabiner, of light alloy with a high breaking strain. (JOHN NEILL)

Mozambique

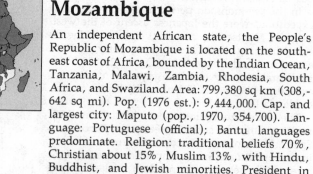

Mozambique

An independent African state, the People's Republic of Mozambique is located on the southeast coast of Africa, bounded by the Indian Ocean, Tanzania, Malawi, Zambia, Rhodesia, South Africa, and Swaziland. Area: 799,380 sq km (308,-642 sq mi). Pop. (1976 est.): 9,444,000. Cap. and largest city: Maputo (pop., 1970, 354,700). Language: Portuguese (official); Bantu languages predominate. Religion: traditional beliefs 70%, Christian about 15%, Muslim 13%, with Hindu, Buddhist, and Jewish minorities. President in 1977, Samora Machel.

At the third conference of the Mozambique Liberation Front (Frelimo), which was held in Maputo in February 1977, Pres. Samora Machel

---

MOZAMBIQUE

Education. (1972–73) Primary, pupils 577,997, teachers 8,345; secondary, pupils 36,155, teachers 1,682; vocational, pupils 17,216, teachers 984; teacher training, students 1,279, teachers 122; higher, students 2,621, teaching staff 326.

Finance and Trade. Monetary unit: Mozambique escudo, with (Sept. 19, 1977) a free rate of 33.40 escudos to U.S. \$1 (58.18 escudos = £1 sterling). Budget (1976 est.): revenue 7.1 billion escudos; expenditure 9.3 billion escudos. Foreign trade (1975): imports 10,472,000,000 escudos; exports 5,357,000,000 escudos. Import sources (1974): South Africa 20%; Portugal 17%; West Germany 14%; Japan 7%; U.K. 6%; U.S. 6%; France 5%; Saudi Arabia 5%. Export destinations (1974): Portugal 33%; U.S. 11%; South Africa 9%; India 6%; The Netherlands 5%. Main exports (1974): sugar 22%; fruit and nut preserves 14%; cotton 11%; copra 8%; cashew nuts 6%; petroleum products 5%.

Transport and Communications. Roads (1974) 39,173 km. Motor vehicles in use (1972): passenger 89,300; commercial (including buses) 21,500. Railways (1975): 4,161 km; traffic 210 million passenger-km, freight (1974) 2,180,-000,000 net ton-km. Telephones (Jan. 1976) 49,800. Radio licenses (Dec. 1974) 176,000. Television receivers (Dec. 1974) *c.* 1,000.

Agriculture. Production (in 000; metric tons; 1976): corn *c.* 450; sorghum *c.* 250; cassava (1975) *c.* 2,300; peanuts *c.* 100; sugar, raw value *c.* 264; copra *c.* 83; bananas *c.* 65; cashew nuts (1975) *c.* 180; tea *c.* 13; cotton, lint *c.* 35; sisal *c.* 15. Livestock (in 000; 1975): cattle 1,390; sheep 130; goats 568; pigs 180; chickens *c.* 15,500.

Industry. Production (in 000; metric tons; 1975): petroleum products *c.* 750; cement (1974) 465; bauxite *c.* 2; electricity (kw-hr) *c.* 717,000.

---

reaffirmed the country's adherence to a Marxist-Leninist program. The conference was attended by representatives from the U.S.S.R., East Germany, Romania, and Bulgaria, who pledged the support of their countries for Mozambique's efforts. East Germany had already signed a consular agreement with Mozambique after a visit by the East German foreign minister, Oskar Fischer, while Pres. Nikolay Podgorny of the U.S.S.R. also visited the country in March. Acknowledging the realities of the economic situation, however, Machel paid an official visit in May to Sweden, Mozambique's leading Western benefactor. Sweden had provided \$50 million in aid since Mozambique achieved independence, and Machel's visit was intended to strengthen still further the relations between the two countries.

Mozambique's economy was, indeed, in a serious condition. Floods in the Limpopo River basin in February, following the severe drought of 1976, added greatly to the country's burdens, while the departure of many experienced Portuguese farmers exacerbated the problems arising from the unbalanced economy that Mozambique had inherited from the colonial era. Pres. Jomo Kenyatta of Kenya sent a large supply of corn to assist the victims of the floods, but offers of \$100 million in aid from world sources, although important in overcoming some immediate problems, only added in the long term to the burden of the country's debts. May 16 was the deadline (later postponed) by which all residents who had renounced Mozambique nationality after independence were required to leave the country, and more than 20,-000 people tried to get away. This led to serious congestion at Maputo and Beira airports. In an attempt at self-help the government made plans to increase the output of coal and to exploit the mineral resources of the Manica region, but the results of these endeavours were not expected to be seen for some time.

The Cabora Bassa Dam began to supply electricity to South Africa early in the year, but relations with South Africa became less friendly when Soviet arms began to flow into Mozambique. Many of these arms were intended for use by the guerrilla forces fighting against the Smith regime in Rhodesia, and Machel's continuing support for the guerrillas led to claims and counterclaims about raids across the border by Frelimo and Rhodesian troops. In June Machel appealed to the UN secretary-general to convene the Security Council to discuss the threat to peace arising from the actions of Rhodesian troops.

In May more than 80 nations were represented at a conference in Maputo to discuss the problems of the black people of Rhodesia and South West Africa, and many of those present praised Machel's efforts in this cause. Within Mozambique itself, however, support for the president was not unanimous. Rebel forces controlled by a number of former Frelimo leaders, disappointed with the outcome of independence and opposed to Machel's socialist policies, carried out raids in various parts of the country. Mozambique, Machel's critics claimed, had become an economic dependency of South Africa and a political satellite of the

U.S.S.R., and true independence had been sacrificed. Most of the opposition drew its strength from traditional tribal loyalties resistant to the overriding doctrines of Frelimo, but the ruling party went ahead with plans for a general election organized so as to offer little scope for opposition activities. (KENNETH INGHAM)

Museums

The Centre National d'Art et de Culture Georges Pompidou (popularly known as the Centre Pompidou or Centre Beaubourg after the district of Paris in which it was situated) housed a display of modern art that was intended eventually to regroup and assemble the collections of modern art from other museums and galleries in Paris; not only a museum, the centre also contained a public reference library and the Institut de Recherche et de Coordination Acoustique-Musique (IRCAM) with its concert hall. Its opening by Pres. Valéry Giscard d'Estaing on Jan. 31, 1977, was the event of the museum year. (See ARCHITECTURE.)

In Britain, the new Museum of London was opened by Queen Elizabeth II in December 1976, amalgamating the London Museum formerly at Kensington Palace and the Guildhall Museum. The new facility presented the story of London and Londoners from prehistoric times to the present day, and each section had its own distinct character. The Natural History Museum, London, opened a new Hall of Human Biology.

In New York City, the New York Cultural Center, established as the Hartford Museum and adrift for several years since it was given up by the Hartford Foundation, was purchased by Gulf and Western Industries and donated to the city of New York for use as a cultural centre. The Museum of Modern Art in New York went ahead with its plans to build an income-producing, high-rise residential structure over its present museum facilities; also in New York, the Frick Collection opened its new $3 million wing.

In Detroit, the Institute of Arts opened its new Italian galleries; recently redesigned, they held the third largest collection of Italian art outside of Europe, 150 paintings and 50 sculptures. The Honolulu Academy of Arts celebrated its 50th anniversary by announcing the new $1.5 million Clare Boothe Luce Wing. The first state-sponsored art museum in the United States, the Virginia Museum of Fine Arts in Richmond, added a north wing.

The Yale Center for British Art opened in April in New Haven, Conn. Built to house Paul Mellon's extensive collection of British paintings, prints, drawings, and rare illustrated books, it made Yale the most important centre for the study of British art outside England.

In September the new Canadian wing of the Art Gallery of Ontario opened. It cost $7.7 million and provided a home for the gallery's Canadian collection. New departments of photographs opened in Washington, D.C., at the National Portrait Gallery and in London at the Victoria and Albert Museum.

The Yale Center for British Art at New Haven, Conn., formally opened its doors in April.

Appeals and Grants. In England, the Birmingham City Museums and Art Gallery was trying to raise £400,000 to purchase Giovanni Bellini's "Madonna and Child Enthroned," formerly in the Watney collection at Cornbury Park, Oxfordshire, which had been on loan to the gallery for ten years. The Tate Gallery raised an appeal to save two canvases by the 18th-century English painter of animals George Stubbs for the nation. They were "The Haymakers" and "The Reapers," and the full price for the two was £774,000.

Through the museum program of the National Endowment for the Arts, federal support to U.S. museums was increased; $27 million was awarded, for the most part as matching grants, to 59 institutions. The Business Committee for the Arts reported that of the $221 million in projects, cash, and services awarded to the arts by the 2,000 business organizations responding to its survey in 1976 the largest share, 21%, had gone to museums.

Against the possibility of "commercialization" of the museum, the museum store was becoming an important source of income. The Metropolitan Museum of Art in New York City clearly acknowledged its need of this facility by planning a five-story expansion of its existing store at a cost of $3 million.

Acquisitions. The National Gallery, London, acquired a portrait of Madame de Pompadour from the Mentmore collection. It was painted by François-Hubert Drouais shortly before Pompadour's death. The gallery also purchased "Portrait of a Collector" by Parmigianino for £650,000.

In the U.S. the Chrysler Museum at Norfolk, Va., received a number of notable gifts, including a fine oil by Eugène Boudin entitled "Le Bac à Trouville," a wonderfully decorative woven textile of 1949 by Henri Matisse, and a self-portrait of 1964 by the Spanish Surrealist painter Salvador Dalí. The Art Institute of Chicago acquired a great painting by the 19th-century French painter J.-F. Millet entitled "Horse." This unusual subject for Millet was originally commissioned as a trade "sign" by a veterinarian.

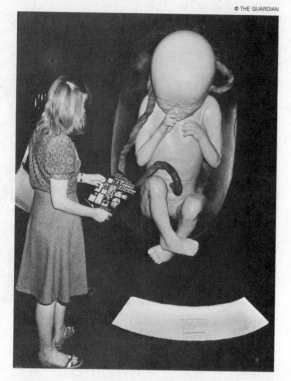

A visitor was fascinated by a model of a human fetus in the new Hall of Human Biology which opened in the Natural History Museum in London.

Other acquisitions included the Metropolitan Museum's purchase, made possible by a gift of "several million dollars" by Mr. and Mrs. Charles Wrightsman, of a double portrait by Jacques-Louis David, "Lavoisier and His Wife." The Cleveland Museum of Art obtained a rare oil painting by the Dutch 17th-century artist Hendrik Terbrugghen, "The Weeping Heracleitus." The Detroit Institute of Arts bought both a large mid-19th-century landscape, "Cotopaxi," by the U.S. painter Frederick Church, and also an African sculpture, a Congolese nail fetish, for $275,000, the highest price ever paid in the U.S. for African art. In Chicago, the Art Institute was presented with a major 18th-century French work by Jean-Honoré Fragonard, "Portrait of a Man as Don Quixote." The Art Institute also unveiled its gift from Marc Chagall, the three stained-glass "American Windows."

(JOSHUA B. KIND; SANDRA MILLIKIN)

See also Art Exhibitions; Art Sales.
[613.D.1.b]

Music

An important cultural event of 1977 was the opening of France's Centre National d'Art et de Culture Georges Pompidou in Paris. (*See* ARCHITECTURE; MUSEUMS.) Its main musical activity, housed deep underground, was the Institut de Recherche et de Coordination Acoustique/Musique (IRCAM), headed by Pierre Boulez, where "all the problems of contemporary music that do not lend themselves to individual solution can be dealt with"—a rather ambitious not to say rarefied aim.

The institute was not altogether completed in 1977, but when finished it would comprise a maze of offices, rehearsal rooms, and studios, separate but interlinked, with each controlled by an administrator well-known in the avant-garde field. Luciano Berio would be in charge of the electro-acoustical department, Vinko Globokar of the instrumental and field, and Jean-Claude Risset of the computer rooms. Most startling of all would be the Salle Polyvalente, a big concert hall and research area with motorized movable walls and ceilings and movable seating.

Research was IRCAM's main raison d'être according to Boulez, but while awaiting completion of its headquarters, it presented various adventurous programs, grouped under the general title "Passage du XXe siècle." These included concerts, ateliers, and lectures, given in nine different venues around Paris by seven orchestras, 11 choirs, several ensembles (including Boulez' own new Ensemble I Intercontemporain), and 17 conductors. "Passage" managed to cover the work of some 120 composers, most of them living. Boulez conducted the first European performance of Elliott Carter's *Symphony of Three Orchestras* in October on the stage of the Paris Opéra. There was also a special IRCAM audiovisual production called *La Voix des voies*, prepared by Berio and realized by the Centre Pompidou's audiovisual department, which played thrice daily on one of the centre's basement levels. It proved to be a survey of electronic music, taking in split screens, with projectors controlled by a computer and synchronized with a sound track. This rather glib presentation suggested the dangers of the new ideas while at the same time pointing the way forward to experiences of possibly greater substance. Meanwhile, some 6,000 mi away, Boulez was present at the opening of another kind of centre—the Schoenberg Institute on the campus of the University of Southern California, the brainchild of Schoenberg's three children by his second marriage, of his admirers in the part of the world where he spent his later years, and of four universities in the area. The city of Berlin also made a generous donation. The institute housed most of the composer's manuscripts, books and scores with his annotations, tapes and records, and a wide selection of memorabilia. At the opening on February 20, *Fanfare on the Motifs of Gurrelieder* was played in the institute's hall.

Opera. The Metropolitan Opera in New York City went from strength to strength (despite union disputes that threatened to stop its activities) under the aegis of its triumvirate of directors, Anthony Bliss (executive), James Levine (music), and John Dexter (productions). *Le Prophète* of Meyerbeer returned to the repertory in January, produced by Dexter with a good measure of success. Marilyn Horne scored a personal triumph as Fidès. This was followed by Poulenc's *Dialogues des Carmelites* in February, with Régine Crespin as the old Prioress, and a new production of *La Bohème*, conducted by Levine. Dexter produced Berg's *Lulu* in March with Levine in the pit. A revival of *La forza del destino* in March was given an all-star cast—Leontyne Price, Placido Domingo, Cornell MacNeil, and Martti Talvela. Talvela was also heard as *Boris Godunov* at the opening of the 1977–78 season in October. That was followed by a new production of *Rigoletto*, with the Dexter-Levine duo in charge and Ileana Cotrubas, Domingo, and Mac-Neil in the main parts.

At the nearby State Theatre, the New York City Opera gave the premiere of Leon Kirchner's *Henderson the Rain King* in April, with the composer conducting. His 1950-ish idiom did not exclude the use of speech, taped sounds, and taped music. The result was a qualified success. The 1977–78 season began with a revival of Arrigo Boito's *Mefistofele*, with Samuel Ramey in the title role. Thea Musgrave's *The Voice of Ariadne* had its first U.S. performance on September 30. It was preceded by *Die Fledermaus* with Beverly Sills as Adele. In November Maralin Niska sang Minnie in a new production of Puccini's *La fanciulla del West*.

At San Francisco the 1977 season opened September 9 with a new production of Cilea's *Adriana Lecouvreur*, with Renata Scotto in the title role and Elena Obraztsova as the Princesse de Bouillon, a formidable antagonist. Obraztsova had also made an impression during the year in a variety of parts at the Metropolitan. *Adriana* was followed by Jean-Pierre Ponnelle's production of *Idomeneo*, with John Pritchard (newly appointed musical director of the Cologne Opera) in the pit and Eric Tappy impressive in the title part. Günther Rennert produced Janacek's *Katya Kabanova* with Elisabeth Söderström in the title role, which she also recorded during the year with the Vienna Philharmonic. At Boston in March, Sarah Caldwell produced Glinka's rarely heard *Russlan and Ludmila*, and in Santa Fe, N.M., Nino Rota's *The Italian Straw Hat* had its first U.S. performance.

The Australian Opera opened its 1977 season with Joan Sutherland in a new production of *Lucrezia Borgia*, and she also appeared in the title role of *Suor Angelica*. In September she sang Sita in a revival at Vancouver, B.C., of Massenet's *Le Roi de Lahore*. In the same month, at Toronto, Canadi-

DON HOGAN CHARLES—THE NEW YORK TIMES

One of two recipients of the Avery Fisher prizes was pianist André-Michel Schub shown performing at Avery Fisher Hall.

an Opera opened its season with a production of the original French version of Verdi's *Don Carlos.*

In Britain, at Covent Garden, Götz Friedrich produced *Der Freischütz*, conducted by Colin Davis (whose contract as musical director was extended until 1982). In July came the premiere of Sir Michael Tippett's latest opera, *The Ice Break*, produced by Sam Wanamaker and conducted by Davis; it was a qualified success. In May Zubin Mehta conducted a new production of *La fanciulla del West*. The 1977–78 season began with a revival of *Les Troyens*. Unfortunately, an industrial dispute involving chorus and orchestra meant that only the second part of the work could be given, and the contract difficulties also affected the finely cast

MARTHA SWOPE

A dragon breathed fire in this scene from the Boston's Opera production *Russlan and Ludmila* by Mikhail Glinka.

revival of *Don Carlos*. A new *Lohengrin*, produced by Elijah Moshinsky and conducted by Davis, was given in November. Weber's *Euryanthe*, which so influenced Wagner's opera, was given by the English National Opera at the Coliseum a few weeks earlier, where it was produced, rather lamely, by John Blatchley and conducted by Sir Charles Groves, the company's musical director as of January 1978.

The company produced two new operas during the year, Iain Hamilton's *The Royal Hunt of the Sun*, based on Peter Shaffer's play, and David Blake's *Toussaint*, about the hero of the Haitian revolution. In March Dame Janet Baker sang Charlotte with great success in *Werther*, produced by John Copley and conducted by Charles Mackerras. Jean-Claude Auvray left Paris to stage *La Bohème* in September, a production that attempted to place the work in its authentic milieu. At the St. Magnus Festival in the Orkneys, the premiere of Peter Maxwell Davies' *The Martyrdom of St. Magnus* was given on June 18. It proved a work of austere, economic power. The BBC presented two premieres during the year: Iain Hamilton's *Tamburlaine* and William Alwyn's *Miss Julie*.

At Glyndebourne there was a forceful new production of *Don Giovanni* by Sir Peter Hall (*see* BIOGRAPHY), followed by John Cox's production of Richard Strauss's *Die schweigsame Frau* and a revival of his brilliant staging of *The Rake's Progress*. Kent Opera gave Jonathan Miller's production of

Ras Karbi, a leading composer and performer of reggae, was featured in a television special exploring Rastafarianism and the inspired music of the West Indies.

NBC PHOTO

Eugene Onegin and Norman Platt's of *Iphigenia in Tauris*. At the Wexford Festival at the end of October, Wolf-Siegfried Wagner produced, in a modern style, the original Vienna version of Gluck's *Orfeo ed Euridice*, and Massenet's *Hérodiade* was revived after long neglect everywhere except in France. At the Edinburgh Festival Teresa Berganza sang her first Carmen in a marvellous production of Bizet's work by Piero Faggioni.

The "Richard Strauss Festival Days" at the Vienna State Opera in January included a significant revival of *Die Frau ohne Schatten*, conducted by Karl Böhm. *Norma* was given a new production, by Faggioni, with Montserrat Caballé in the title role. Riccardo Muti (who conducted a splendid revival of *Aida* at Covent Garden in July) was in the pit. Filippo Sanjust staged the first new production of the 1977–78 season, Bellini's *I Capuleti ed i Montecchi*, in October, with Agnes Baltsa as Romeo. Herbert von Karajan revived his production of *Il trovatore* at the Salzburg Easter Festival, and at the summer festival there he conducted and produced *Salome*, with Hildegard Behrens in the title role. Böhm conducted a new production by Ponnelle of *Don Giovanni*, with Sherrill Milnes in the title role.

At Bayreuth, West Germany, Colin Davis, in charge of the revival of Götz Friedrich's production of *Tannhäuser*, became the first British conductor ever to appear at the festival. There were no new productions, but Patrice Chéreau's controversial *Ring* was repeated, while at Stuttgart in the autumn Ponnelle began what promised, judging by *Das Rheingold*, to be another modern concept of Wagner's tetralogy. At the Maggio Musicale in Florence, Italy, Luca Ronconi gave a new interpretation of Verdi's *Nabucco*, conducted by Muti. The bicentennial celebration of La Scala, Milan (the 200th anniversary would actually fall in 1978), began December 7 with a new production by Giorgio Strehler of *Don Carlos*, conducted by Claudio Abbado.

Symphonic Music. In February the New York Philharmonic under Boulez gave the premiere of Elliott Carter's *Symphony of Three Orchestras*. The orchestra also gave first performances of works by Takemitsu and Michael Colgrass during a year that saw the end of Boulez' reign as its musical director. He bowed out with Berlioz' *La Damnation de Faust* on May 12. His successor was Zubin Mehta. Other important premieres in the U.S. included Takemitsu's *Quatrain* by the Boston Symphony Orchestra and Jacob Druckman's *Chiaroscuro* by the Cleveland Orchestra under its chief conductor, Lorin Maazel. Harold Farberman's *War Cry* was given by the Colorado Springs Orchestra in November, and Sir Michael Tippett's Fourth Symphony by the Chicago Symphony in October.

On April 2 at Vancouver, B.C., the Orpheum opened as the new home of the Vancouver Symphony Orchestra. A former cinema converted at a cost of over $7 million, it was the largest hall in Canada, seating 2,788. The acoustics proved to be excellent. The program included the first performance of Pierre Mercure's *Triptique*.

In London two important appointments were announced in November: Gennady Rozhdestvensky as principal conductor of the BBC Symphony Orchestra and Sir Georg Solti as principal conductor of the London Philharmonic; Solti would retain his position as musical director of the Chicago Symphony. The Malvern Festival was inaugurated in May with programs of two figures associated with the town—George Bernard Shaw and Sir Edward Elgar. The music of John Taverner was given special prominence at the Bath Festival in June. The Benson and Hedges Festival was inaugurated at Aldeburgh in September with emphasis on the chamber music and songs of Britten and Schubert. A Liszt Festival took place during the autumn in London, reaching its climax with the first British performance of his vast oratorio, *Christus.*

The centenary of the Edison phonograph was celebrated in several British and U.S. centres. The 21st International Festival of Contemporary Music took place at Warsaw in September and the Styrian Autumn (also dealing with modern music), at Graz, Austria, in October.

Among notable musicians who died during the year were the composers Alexander Tcherepnin and Grace Williams, Maria Callas, Leopold Stokowski, and E. Power Biggs. (*See* also OBITUARIES.)   (ALAN BLYTH)

Jazz. A curious and not altogether reassuring aspect of jazz history which became more apparent than ever during 1977 was that as its population of authentic masters continued to shrink, so the process of proselytization across national frontiers became progressively more successful. A newcomer examining the phenomenon of jazz music for the first time might have been pardoned for wondering exactly where the heartlands were. The days when the music was a local dialect had long passed, of course; after the end of World War II the musical colonization of foreign cultures by U.S. soldiers had transformed a state like West Germany into one of the world's major potential jazz consumers. Even more spectacular had been the conversion of the Japanese, who by the 1970s could number themselves among the most sophisticated responders to the music.

This genuine internationalism was stressed during 1977 at a far deeper level than mere audience reaction, in an interchange of nationalities among exponents. American virtuosi like vibraphonist Milt Jackson and trombonist J. J. Johnson, usually thought of in terms of a club context, were among many outstanding instrumentalists who appeared before capacity audiences in Japan. Live recordings of those events, preserving the swift, audible response of audiences to some subtle improvisatory stroke, bore witness to the truism that, as far as appreciation of jazz is concerned, it would appear that the whole world consists of New Yorkers. At the Montreux (Switz.) Festival in July, dominated by several concerts sponsored by Norman Granz's Pablo label, the name of Ronnie Scott was to be found among those of American celebrities like Count Basie, Dizzy Gillespie, Clark Terry, Eddie "Lockjaw" Davis, Ray Brown, and Canadian Oscar Peterson. Scott, a London-born and London-based tenor saxophonist and proprietor of the most influential jazz club in Europe, had long been considered by informed judges in terms of international standards, but his appearance among his peers at Montreux was a symbolic event in the general advance of the rest of the world toward the standards of the best Americans.

The British singer Cleo Laine, although not purely a jazz phenomenon, remained closely enough linked to the jazz world to be mentioned in this context. After a distinguished local career in harness with her husband, the saxophonist-composer John Dankworth, Laine suddenly flowered during 1976–77 as a major American recording and concert attraction, using her freakishly wide range and extraordinarily broad repertoire to establish herself as one of the world's most original vocal performers. The outstanding female figure in jazz, however, remained Ella Fitzgerald. Since surgery had been performed to preserve her fading eyesight, Ella had made fewer public appearances, but if the quantity of her concerts lessened, there was no discernible slump in quality. Now in her 60th year, Ella had become an astonishing example of an aging artist whose art remained not only vigorous but positively youthful. The timbre of her voice and the unique sweetness of her interpretation enabled her to retain the lullaby quality that was so potent a weapon in her campaign to lend jazz the gloss of commercial blandishment without diluting its intensity.

Other aspects of the commercialization of the music tended to be less happy. The furor over Alex Haley's book *Roots*, which purported to trace the evolution of the African slave into the U.S. city dweller, might have been expected to contain at least peripheral observations about the origins of the music, but none was apparent. Ironically, the most interesting commercial manifestation of jazz was contained in an otherwise relentlessly mediocre movie, *New York, New York*. Since the story concerned the experiences of a white American jazz musician between 1945 and the present, the soundtrack required the services of a saxophonist who was at least competent. In the event, the considerable amount of improvised saxophone playing was performed by George Auld, who also played a supporting role. Auld would be remembered as one of the very best white imitative players of the 1940s, with groups of his own and, particularly, in the big band and sextet of Benny Goodman during World War II. His contribution to *New York, New York* made that otherwise indifferent production one of the most gratifying jazz bonuses of the year.

Among outstanding figures who died during the year were the Chicago trombonist Bennie Green, who had been prominent in the early years of modernism; Milt Buckner, the pianist-organist generally thought of in connection with extrovert leaders like Lionel Hampton and Illinois Jacquet; and the ultracommercial bandleader Guy Lombardo who, although his music had not the remotest connection with jazz, retained a curious kind of prestige among some players, particularly Louis Armstrong. The most grievous loss of 1977 was perhaps that of the saxophonist Roland Kirk. Through an ingenious combination of mechanical contrivance and manual ingenuity, Kirk could play two and even three saxophones at once, thus

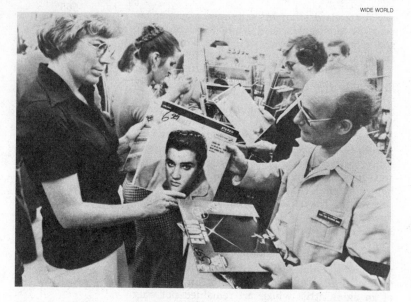

The death of Elvis Presley in August unleashed a flood of reissues of Presley albums.

becoming the first saxophonist in jazz history able to express explicitly the harmonies on which his improvisations were based. Although in recent years his performances had showed a leaning toward the bizarre, Kirk remained to the end of his life one of the most extraordinary of all jazz artists. (*See* also OBITUARIES.) (BENNY GREEN)

Popular. Punk rock, or "new wave," swept the music business in 1977, bringing raw energy, controversy, and new blood. It was essentially urban music, reflecting its cynical and violent times. In Britain the London bands were the most publicized—notably The Sex Pistols, who between October 1976 and April 1977 hit the headlines for using foul language on television, lost two recording contracts, and had their concerts banned. Their notoriety rebounded on other new bands, but around April the tide turned and the Pistols (with a new contract) reached the Top Twenty, blazing a trail for The Stranglers, The Jam, and Adverts. American developments were similar, with audiences at first wary but finally enthusiastic. New York bands included The Ramones, Television, and Blondie; CBGB's club was the main venue. The Sex Pistols' first U.S. tour, planned to begin in Pittsburgh, Pa., December 30, was delayed by the initial refusal of U.S. visas because the members had minor criminal records.

The major record companies' initial reluctance to sign punk bands led to the formation of independent labels, such as Stiff. A punk fashion style (torn clothes, garishly coloured hair, razor blades and safety pins as ornaments) arose, and punk "fanzines" (magazines) such as *Sniffin' Glue* proliferated. However, not all new talent was new wave. Jonathan Richman from Boston, Mass., had a musical style rooted in teen-beat pop. Established lyricist Carole Bayer Sager turned hit singer ("You're Moving Out Today"). And there was still room for romantic singers such as David Soul, who had three hits in 1977, and Mary MacGregor, whose "Torn Between Two Lovers" topped singles charts internationally.

Record prices remained high, and even established stars' sales were disappointing; the excep-

Namibia:
see Dependent
States; South Africa

NATO:
see Defense

Navies:
see Defense

tion was Stevie Wonder, whose "Songs in the Key of Life" topped the album charts within a week of release. Two "live" Beatles albums were issued, one recorded during their formative days in Hamburg, West Germany, the other at the Hollywood Bowl during 1964–65. Fleetwood Mac's "Rumours" topped the U.S. LP charts for 21 consecutive weeks. Interesting releases included David Bedford's musical interpretation of the *Odyssey* and Alan Parsons' futuristic narrative "I Robot," but Japanese synthesist Isao Tomita was prevented from releasing his version of Gustav Holst's *The Planets* following an objection from the composer's daughter. Disco music continued very popular; Donna Summer's sensuous vocalizing and the rich harmonies of Tavares made them favourite artists in this field.

The punk invasion provided a challenge to which many established artists responded enthusiastically. Yes's new album, "Going for the One," yielded a hit single, "Wondrous Stories." Former 10cc members Kevin Godley and Lol Creme produced "Consequences," a complex work introducing the gizmo, a device enabling one guitar to produce a wide variety of sounds. Abba of Sweden continued to be the undisputed leaders of European pop.

Reggae became increasingly profound and socially outspoken. In December 1976 leading reggae musician Bob Marley was the victim of a politically motivated shooting, but he recovered and toured Europe in the summer of 1977. Country music was very diverse. Don Williams' "I Recall A Gypsy Woman" was an international hit, and Guy Clark's invigorating songs were popular with other singers. Dolly Parton, already a U.S. favourite, made a successful British tour. Western swing was revived in entertaining style by the group Asleep At The Wheel.

Many major artists appeared "live," including Steely Dan, Peter Gabriel, and Dory Previn. Concert staging became extremely elaborate; Genesis, on their U.S. tour, required a jumbo jet to transport their equipment. Increased personnel added to tour costs, ticket prices rose, and sales suffered. Emerson, Lake & Palmer, having organized a world tour, ran up such debts that they were forced to dismiss their 70-piece orchestra and completely revise their show—but the success of their album "Works" (including Keith Emerson's Piano Concerto) provided consolation. Poor ticket sales were believed to have been the reason for the sudden cancellation of The Beach Boys' U.K. tour. In San Francisco Bill Graham, in addition to continuing his "Days on the Green," presented a charity concert in February.

Early in 1977 Tony Palmer's controversial film series chronicling the history of popular music, *All You Need Is Love,* appeared on British television. In a lighter vein, "The Muppet Show" superseded The Wombles as a near-cult, spawning lighthearted hits. Record album covers were fast becoming an art form, with designers going to extraordinary lengths to achieve effects. During photographic sessions for Pink Floyd's "Animals," an inflatable "flying pig" broke loose from its moorings between the chimneys of Battersea Power Station and drifted off over London, to be captured eventually by a Kent farmer. Dick Clark, presenter of the influential "American Bandstand" show, celebrated 25 years as a television host.

On August 16 Elvis Presley died at his Memphis home, and two months later Bing Crosby died in Spain. Other leading figures who died in 1977 were former CBS president Goddard Lieberson, under whose auspices many Broadway shows were recorded, and British rock star Marc Bolan. (*See* OBITUARIES.) Both Crosby and Presley in their times created a style of popular music. The punk-new wave phenomenon had no such single instigator. It was a group movement, and perhaps its most encouraging aspect was the anticipated development of new musicians.   (HAZEL MORGAN)

See also Dance; Motion Pictures; Television and Radio; Theatre.

Nauru

An island republic in the Pacific Ocean, Nauru lies about 1,900 km (1,200 mi) E of New Guinea. Area: 21 sq km (8 sq mi). Pop. (1977 est.): 7,100 (Nauruans, 3,950). Capital: Yaren. Language: English and Nauruan. Religion: Christian. President in 1977, Bernard Dowiyogo.

In 1977 Nauru's new president, Bernard Dowiyogo, presided over the island's most difficult year since independence. Phosphate returns leveled out because of the world recession, and the new administration, while paying tribute to former president Hammer DeRoburt's "imperishable place in Nauru's history as the founding father of independence," was determined to adopt a more vigorous economic policy.

A key element in the new economic policy was the earning of income from real estate investments in Australia; Nauru House in Melbourne was opened on April 15, 1977, but a local real estate slump resulted in less immediate return than had been expected. Described ironically as Nauru's "colony" in Australia, the 51-story office building had accommodated a population bigger than that of Nauru. Opening the building, which cost A$45 million, President Dowiyogo pointed out that although it was often said that on a per capita basis Nauru was one of the richest nations in the world, the truth of the matter was that phosphate rock was Nauru's capital and the only income available was that derived from the capital as the phosphate was sold.   (A. R. G. GRIFFITHS)

Nepal

A constitutional monarchy of Asia, Nepal is in the Himalayas between India and the Tibetan Autonomous Region of China. Area: 145,391 sq km (56,136 sq mi). Pop. (1976 est.): 13,289,400. Cap. and largest city: Kathmandu (pop., 1976 est., 171,400). Language: Nepali (official); also Newari and Bhutia. Religion (1971): Hindu 89.4%; Buddhist 7.5%. King, Birendra Bir Bikram Shah Deva; prime ministers in 1977, Tulsi Giri and, from September 12, Kirti Nidhi Bista.

On Sept. 12, 1977, former prime minister Kirti Nidhi Bista was again chosen by King Birendra to head the government. He replaced Tulsi Giri, whose tough attitude toward reform leader B. P. Koirala was generally thought to have cost him his post. The king's decision to release Koirala, a former prime minister, from jail in June, along with several of his colleagues from the Nepalese Congress, was seen as a move toward liberalization.

While relations with China remained on an even keel, those with Nepal's southern neighbour, India, underwent a strain as a result of the new Janata government's open concern over the continued detention of Koirala. His release and the subsequent visit to Kathmandu by Indian External Affairs Minister A. B. Vajpayee helped to improve the situation, and India promised to continue development aid on the same level as under the previous government. In November Koirala was rearrested on returning from medical treatment in the U.S., but Indian Prime Minister Morarji Desai's visit to Nepal in December, and international concern, increased pressure for a royal pardon.

The economy continued to suffer from high inflation, resulting from a 34.5% increase in money supply in the first eight months of the year. The government budgeted for NRs 3,087,000,000 (about U.S. $247 million) in expenditure for 1977–78, about $89.6 million of which represented foreign aid and credits.   (GOVINDAN UNNY)

Nauru

Nepal

The Netherlands

Food and emergency supplies were wheeled into a school building near Assen, Neth., where more than 100 children and 5 teachers were held hostage for more than two weeks by South Moluccan terrorists.

Netherlands, The

A kingdom of northwest Europe on the North Sea, The Netherlands, a Benelux country, is bounded by Belgium on the south and West Germany on the east. Area: 41,160 sq km (15,892 sq mi). Pop. (1977 est.): 13,814,500. Cap. and largest city: Amsterdam (pop., 1977 est., 738,400). Seat of government: The Hague (pop., 1977 est., 471,100). Language: Dutch. Religion (1971): Roman Catholic 40.4%; Dutch Reformed 23.5%; no religion 23.6%; Reformed Churches 9.4%. Queen, Juliana; prime ministers in 1977, Joop den Uyl and, from December 19, Andries van Agt.

The longest crisis in Dutch parliamentary history ended on Dec. 19, 1977, when a new, right-of-centre, Christian Democratic-Liberal government was sworn in, with the Christian Democratic Appeal leader, Andries van Agt, as prime minister.

In March van Agt, then minister of justice in former prime minister Joop den Uyl's Socialist-dominated coalition with the Democratic and Liberal parties, had refused to support a land expropriation bill because of certain objections by his party. On March 22 this conflict within

the Cabinet culminated in the resignation of the six Christian Democratic ministers, which in turn brought about the resignation of the government. Prime Minister den Uyl's Cabinet continued in a caretaker capacity and prepared for the dissolution of the lower house. General elections were fixed for May 25.

The election turnout was high, with 87.53% of the electorate going to the polls. The Socialist Party (PvdA) made the greatest gains (from 43 to 53 seats in the 150-seat lower house), together with the opposition Liberal Party (VVD; from 22 to 28 seats). The Christian Democratic Appeal remained more or less stable (from 48 to 49 seats). Most other parties, with the exception of the Democratic Party (D'66), suffered heavy losses. Den Uyl (Socialist Party) was asked to form a government.

The ensuing negotiations were characterized by disagreements on program, procedures, and persons, especially between the Socialists and Democrats on the one hand and the Christian Democrats on the other. They continued throughout the summer and autumn, with socioeconomic policy, abortion legislation, and the choice of ministers the main issues in dispute. Finally, on December 8, Queen Juliana asked van Agt to form a government. This he was able to do after reaching agreement with the Liberals.

Two days before the elections the country was startled by the seizure of a train and the occupation of a school, both in the province of Drenthe, by nationalist members of The Netherlands' South Moluccan community seeking independence of their islands from Indonesia. Fifty-four passengers on the train and more than 100 children and 5 teachers in the school were held hostage. The terrorists demanded the release of imprisoned fellow-South Moluccans and a safe conduct by air to an unknown destination. On June 11 both dramas were ended by military intervention. Six South Moluccans and two passengers were killed in the assault on the train, and seven other terrorists were captured; there were no casualties in the attack on the school.

From February 28 to March 2 the minister of foreign affairs, Max van der Stoel, visited Prague, and while there he received Jan Patocka (see

NETHERLANDS, THE

Education. (1975–76) Primary, pupils 1,536,-831, teachers 60,740; secondary, pupils 766,391, teachers 48,193; vocational, pupils 506,364, teachers 42,100; teacher training, students 10,830, teachers 900; higher (including 11 main universities, students 231,383, teaching staff (university only) 28,300.

Finance. Monetary unit: guilder, with (Sept. 19, 1977) a free rate of 2.47 guilders to U.S. $1 (4.30 guilders = £1 sterling). Gold, SDR's, and foreign exchange (June 1977) U.S. $6,519,000,000. Budget (1977 est.): revenue 71,642,000,000 guilders; expenditure 85,719,000,000 guilders. Gross national product (1976) 232,850,000,000 guilders. Money supply (March 1977) 52,450,000,000 guilders. Cost of living (1970 = 100; June 1977) 176.

Foreign Trade. (1976) Imports 107,267,000,000 guilders; exports 105,644,000,000 guilders. Import sources: EEC 55% (West Germany 24%, Belgium-Luxembourg 13%, France 7%, U.K. 6%); U.S. 9%. Export destinations: EEC 71% (West Germany 31%, Belgium-Luxembourg 15%, France 11%, U.K. 8%,

Italy 5%). Main exports: food 19%; chemicals 15%; machinery 13%; petroleum products 12%; transport equipment 6%; natural gas 5%. Tourism (1975): visitors 2,819,000; gross receipts U.S. $1,107,000,000.

Transport and Communications. Roads (1975) 86,052 km (including 1,530 km expressways). Motor vehicles in use (1975): passenger 3.4 million; commercial 312,000. Railways: (1975) 2,832 km (including 1,712 km electrified); traffic (1976) 8,306,000,000 passenger-km, freight 2,695,000,000 net ton-km. Air traffic (1976): 10,634,000,000 passenger-km; freight 663,370,000 net ton-km. Navigable inland waterways (1975): 4,366 km (including 1,344 km for craft of 1,500 tons and over); goods traffic 29,597,000,000 ton-km. Shipping (1976): merchant vessels 100 gross tons and over 1,325; gross tonnage 5,919,892. Ships entered (1975) vessels totaling 160.8 million net registered tons; goods loaded (1976) 82,530,000 metric tons, unloaded 255,785,000 metric tons. Telephones (Dec. 1975) 5,047,000. Radio licenses (Dec. 1975) 3.9 million. Television licenses (Dec. 1975) 3,-646,000.

Agriculture. Production (in 000; metric tons; 1976): wheat 710; barley c. 263; oats 103; rye 65; potatoes 4,717; tomatoes c. 370; onions c. 432; sugar, raw value c. 924; cabbages (1975) 236; cucumbers (1975) 330; carrots (1975) c. 150; apples 380; rapeseed 34; milk c. 10,415; butter c. 216; cheese c. 377; eggs c. 336; beef and veal c. 394; pork 922; fish catch (1975) 351. Livestock (in 000; May 1976): cattle 4,-969; pigs 7,506; sheep c. 777; chickens c. 66,527.

Industry. Index of production (1970 = 100; 1976) 125. Production (in 000; metric tons; 1976): crude oil 1,372; natural gas (cu m) 97,300,000; manufactured gas (cu m) 1,010,000; electricity (kw-hr) 58,059,000; pig iron 4,267; crude steel 5,190; cement 3,481; petroleum products (1975) 52,249; sulfuric acid 1,463; fertilizers (nutrient content; 1975–76) nitrogenous c. 1,153; phosphate c. 179; cotton yarn 33; wool yarn 11; rayon, etc., filament yarn and fibres 36; nylon, etc., filament yarn and fibres (1972) 113. Merchant vessels launched (100 gross tons and over; 1976) 634,000 gross tons. New dwelling units completed (1976) 107,000.

OBITUARIES), spokesman of the Czechoslovak human rights group, Charter 77. Pres. Gustav Husak showed his displeasure by canceling a meeting with van der Stoel on the last day of his visit.

The socioeconomic climate in The Netherlands remained depressed in 1977. Employers and trade unions came into conflict over the system of automatic wage indexing. After a series of strikes in February, both parties eventually reached a compromise whereby the disputed system would be maintained during the year.

On December 14, after an eight-month trial, Pieter N. Menten, a 78-year-old Dutch millionaire art collector, was sentenced to 15 years' imprisonment by an Amsterdam court for his part in the World War II massacre of Polish nationals, mostly Jews, at Podhorodce, Poland (now in the Soviet Union).   (GERARD P. NOORDZIJ)

See also Dependent States.

New Zealand

New Zealand, a parliamentary state and member of the Commonwealth of Nations, is in the South Pacific Ocean, separated from southeastern Australia by the Tasman Sea. The country consists of North and South islands and Stewart, Chatham, and other minor islands. Area: 268,704 sq km (103,747 sq mi). Pop. (1977 est.): 3,105,200. Cap.: Wellington (pop., 1976 census, 139,600). Largest city: Christchurch (pop., 1976 census, 172,000). Largest urban area: Auckland (pop., 1976 census, 797,400). Language: English (official), Maori. Religion (1976): Church of England 35%; Presbyterian 22%; Roman Catholic 16%. Queen, Elizabeth II; governors-general in 1977, Sir Denis Blundell and, from September 27, Sir Keith Holyoake; prime minister, Robert David Muldoon.

When he arrived from the International Monetary Fund-World Bank meetings in Washington, D.C., in October, Prime Minister Robert Muldoon reported that the inflation rate (15.6% in 1976) seemed to be coming down; however, less activity in major economies and rising protectionism around the world forecast another tough economic year for New Zealand. Oil price rises were still affecting the country's cost structure, so that even improved prices for farm exports were unable to match the rising cost of the most stringently checked imports. In the year ending March 1977 import costs had exceeded export receipts by NZ$371 million.

In March the Wage Hearing Tribunal ordered a 6% wage increase for all workers (12.8% had been applied for). That move, along with strikes in 1976 that were the worst in 25 years, and the initial explosive effect of the lifting of the wage and price freeze in September did not help the fight for economic stability.

Food (up 16.8% in 12 months) and other prices rose sharply, 23,000 more migrants left than arrived in the 12 months to July 31 — four times more than in the previous year — and by the end of September the figures for registered unemployed totaled 8,075 and were rising sharply. On October 28 Muldoon in an additional mini-budget granted a 5% tax cut effective as of February 1978 and took measures against unemployment, particularly of the young.

Among the Cabinet appointments, G.F. Gair was named secretary of a new department that comprised energy resources, electricity and mines, and national and regional development. Sir Keith Holyoake (*see* BIOGRAPHY), a former leader of the party and prime minister, left the post of minister of state and his parliamentary seat to accept appointment as governor-general; it was a controversial choice because it set a precedent for a serving politician to be called to Government House.

The prime minister was able to entertain Queen Elizabeth II during her Silver Jubilee world tour at a new official residence, Vogel House in Lower Hutt, but had limited residence there himself during a year in which he was away overseas six times. The agreement on contact with South Africa reached at the meeting of Commonwealth heads of government held at Gleneagles, Scotland, in June defused a race-relations embarrassment built up by opponents of South Africa's racial segregation policies, and caused the Muldoon government to be more positive in recommending its sportsmen to steer clear of racially selected South African teams.

The government had popularity tests in March and April. It watched helplessly as the Mangere seat, vacant through the resignation of former

New Zealand

agriculture minister Colin Moyle, went more emphatically to the Labour Party opposition because of the strong candidacy of David Lange; spirits revived when the National Party stronghold of Pahiatua remained firm even for a novice candidate, John Falloon. Both by-elections followed uproars: in the Labour seat, following Moyle's misleading the House of Representatives by denying allegations concerning a police inquiry; in the National seat, following the controversial appointment of Holyoake as governor-general.

Political controversies that distracted from the worsening economy revolved around a government move to maintain a trend toward liberalizing grounds for abortion and an attempt to provide rules for security wiretaps and to outlaw the disclosure of New Zealand security agents' identity. A depressingly wet winter, which followed the wettest summer in more than 100 years, brought ruinous landslides on urban and farm properties.

(JOHN A. KELLEHER)

See also Dependent States.

Nicaragua

Niger

Nicaragua

The largest country of Central America, Nicaragua is a republic bounded by Honduras, Costa Rica, the Caribbean Sea, and the Pacific Ocean. Area: 128,875 sq km (49,759 sq mi). Pop. (1976 est.): 2,-233,000. Cap. and largest city: Managua (pop., 1974 est., 313,400). Language: Spanish. Religion: Roman Catholic. President in 1977, Anastasio Somoza Debayle.

NICARAGUA

Education. (1974–75) Primary, pupils 350,519, teachers 8,817; secondary, pupils 76,763, teachers (1972–73) 1,578; vocational and teacher training (1972–73), pupils 6,945, teachers 429; higher (1972–73), students 11,618, teaching staff 694.

Finance. Monetary unit: córdoba, with (Sept. 19, 1977) a par value of 7 córdobas to U.S. $1 (free rate of 12.20 córdobas = £1 sterling). Gold, SDR's, and foreign exchange (May 1977) U.S. $208,630,000. Budget (1977 est.) balanced at 2,652,000,000 córdobas. Gross national product (1976) 12,398,000,000 córdobas. Money supply (May 1977) 1,917,100,000 córdobas. Cost of living (Managua; 1974 = 100; May 1977) 126.

Foreign Trade. (1976) Imports 3,738,900,000 córdobas; exports 3,807,500,000 córdobas. Import sources (1975): U.S. 32%; Venezuela 12%; Japan 7%; Costa Rica 7%; Guatemala 7%; West Germany 6%; El Salvador 6%. Export destinations (1975): U.S. 28%; Japan 13%; Costa Rica 10%; West Germany 9%; Guatemala 6%; El Salvador 6%. Main exports: cotton 24%; coffee 22%; sugar 10%; meat 7%.

Transport and Communications. Roads (1973) 12,902 km (including 485 km of Pan-American Highway). Motor vehicles in use (1975): passenger 32,400; commercial (including buses) 18,300. Railways: (1975) 373 km; traffic (1972) 28 million passenger-km, freight 14 million net ton-km. Air traffic (1975): 83 million passenger-km; freight 2 million net ton-km. Telephones (Jan. 1976) 22,000. Radio receivers (Dec. 1974) 126,000. Television receivers (Dec. 1974) 75,000.

Agriculture. Production (in 000; metric tons; 1976): corn 201; rice (1975) 84; sorghum 55; dry beans c. 47; sugar, raw value (1975) 199; bananas (1975) c. 314; oranges c. 52; coffee c. 53; cotton, lint c. 124. Livestock (in 000; 1975): cattle c. 2,500; pigs c. 600; horses c. 175; chickens c. 3,514.

Industry. Production (in 000; metric tons; 1975): petroleum products 626; cement 193; gold (exports; troy oz) 69; electricity (kw-hr) c. 835,000.

Pres. Anastasio Somoza Debayle was flown to Miami, Fla., on July 29 for treatment following a heart attack. He returned to Nicaragua early in September to convalesce and, working on a curtailed schedule, to continue his tight rule as the nation's chief of state.

Accusations of violations of human rights by Nicaragua were made in hearings before a U.S. House of Representatives subcommittee in April. Responding apparently to those charges and to the U.S. government's views on human rights in general, the Nicaraguan government, while denying all charges, lifted a three-year-old state of siege on September 19. The U.S. signed an agreement soon thereafter to provide $2.5 million for military assistance, with implementation on a piecemeal basis contingent upon continued improvement in the human rights situation.

The capture or killing of top leaders of the Sandinista guerrilla army late in 1976 and throughout 1977 did not reduce the activities of clandestine opposition forces, and numerous shoot-outs took place, with fatalities occurring on both sides. In October the Sandinistas and other groups launched a major offensive with the declared intention of overthrowing the Somoza regime and establishing a broadly based democracy.

(HENRY WEBB, JR.)

Niger

A republic of north central Africa, Niger is bounded by Algeria, Libya, Chad, Nigeria, Benin, Upper Volta, and Mali. Area: 1,186,408 sq km (458,075 sq mi). Pop. (1977 est.): 4,850,000, including (1972 est.) Hausa 53.7%; Zerma and Songhai 23.6%; Fulani 10.6%; Beriberi-Manga 9.1%. Cap. and largest city: Niamey (pop., 1975 est., 130,000). Language: French (official) and Sudanic dialects. Religion: Muslim, animist, Christian. President in 1977, Lieut. Col. Seyni Kountché.

In his anniversary speech to the nation of April 14, 1977, Pres. Seyni Kountché announced wage

NIGER

Education. (1975–76) Primary, pupils 142,182, teachers 1,195; secondary, pupils 13,621, teachers 640; vocational, pupils 233, teachers 25; teacher training (1974–75), students 485, teachers 51; higher, students 1,255, teaching staff 34.

Finance. Monetary unit: CFA franc, with (Sept. 19, 1977) a par value of CFA Fr 50 to the French franc (free rate of CFA Fr 246.50 = U.S. $1; CFA Fr 429.50 = £1 sterling). Gold, SDR's, and foreign exchange (May 1977) U.S. $84.3 million. Budget (1975–76 est.) balanced at CFA Fr 24.3 billion.

Foreign Trade. (1975) Imports CFA Fr 18,735,000,000; exports CFA Fr 18,203,000,000. Import sources (1974): France 37%; U.S. 13%; Nigeria 9%; West Germany 8%. Export destinations (1974): France 54%; Nigeria 27%; West Germany 7%. Main exports (1974): uranium 50%; livestock 17%; peanut oil 9%; textile yarns and fabrics 5%.

Transport and Communications. Roads (1975) 6,985 km. Motor vehicles in use (1975): passenger 15,200; commercial 2,800. There are no railways. Inland waterway (Niger River) c. 300 km. Telephones (Dec. 1975) 5,000. Radio receivers (Dec. 1971) 150,000.

Agriculture. Production (in 000; metric tons; 1976): millet c. 1,195; sorghum 308; rice (1975) 35; cassava (1975) 295; dry beans c. 175; onions c. 40; peanuts 95; goat's milk c. 104. Livestock (in 000; 1975): cattle c. 2,500; sheep c. 2,200; goats c. 5,000; camels c. 250.

increases and a housing policy; a priority of the development plan was to increase food production and water supplies.

In mid-March a conference of heads of states bordering the Sahara was held at Niamey and was attended by the presidents of Algeria, Chad, and Mali and the Libyan prime minister. The conference stressed the need for economic cooperation and affirmed adherence to the principle of self-determination. However, none of the frontier disputes that bedeviled relations between the Saharan states was touched upon: Libya's seizure of Niger's wells at Toummo, the question of the western Sahara, and the disagreement between Libya and Chad. In May Niger made two agreements with Chad, for neighbourly relations and for cooperation in mining.

Mining production intensified, with uranium mining and prospecting in the north and petroleum and phosphate prospecting in the east and west, respectively. Production of uranium had risen from 410 tons in 1971 to 1,600 tons in 1976, and in 1975 uranium mining provided about 14% of government income. (PHILIPPE DECRAENE)

Nigeria

A republic and a member of the Commonwealth of Nations, Nigeria is located in Africa north of the Gulf of Guinea, bounded by Benin, Niger, Chad, and Cameroon. Area: 923,800 sq km (356,700 sq mi). Pop. (1976 est.): 76.6 million, including Hausa 21%; Ibo 18%; Yoruba 18%; Fulani 10%. Cap. and largest city: Lagos (metro. pop., 1977 est., 3.5 million). Language: English (official). Religion (1963): Muslim 47%; Christian 34%. Head of the provisional military government in 1977, Lieut. Gen. Olusegun Obasanjo.

Elections for Nigeria's new local government councils, for which women candidates were eligible, were held on Dec. 28, 1976. The councils in turn elected the national Constituent Assembly on Aug. 31, 1977. The 203-member Assembly, chosen by the 19 states, held its opening session on October 6. The candidates, who had to be Nigerian citizens at least 18 years of age and not members of the armed forces, police, or civil service, stood as independents. It was hoped that party politics would be resumed in October 1978, after a year's work by the Assembly on the draft constitution (which had been delivered on Oct. 7, 1976), and that the country could return to civilian rule early in 1979. The draft constitution provided for a two-house Parliament and a nationally elected executive president, who would also be head of the armed forces; he had to be at least 40 years of age and could serve a maximum of two four-year terms.

Evident during 1977 was the return of the old politicians to various key positions, as the Supreme Military Council (SMC) found it necessary to make use of civilian experience. There was limited demobilization of the Army, but mass demobilization was not practical in the absence of sufficient employment opportunities. As of 1977 the Army had reached an expensive total of 250,000

men. More than 90% of the Army budget went for pay, and the privileges accorded to soldiers led to friction with civilians.

In October Lieut. Gen. Olusegun Obasanjo paid a state visit to the U.S., where his talks with Pres. Jimmy Carter centred on the Rhodesian conflict. Brig. Joseph N. Garba, the external affairs commissioner and an exponent of aggressive foreign policy, took the initiative in trying to settle the Kenya-Tanzania and Zaire-Angola disputes. Nigeria provided aid for the poorer members of the Economic Community of West African States, in particular the four francophone countries, partly to wean the latter from France. Aid in the form of cheap gasoline was given to Zambia and other landlocked states. Nigeria's oil reserves were estimated at 50,000,000,000 bbl, but its refining capacity was small and about half its domestic requirement was imported.

Nigeria

The second World Black and African Festival of Arts and Culture, Festac 2, postponed twice since 1970, opened in mid-January at the staggering cost of about £1,000 million. Though ostensibly cultural, it marked a turning point in African politics, with its pan-Africanism, black racialism, and obsessive concern with an anti-southern Africa crusade. The festival attracted 80,000 visitors from member countries of the Organization of African Unity, liberation movements, and black communities all over the world. The U.S. was represented by its ambassador to the UN, Andrew Young (see BIOGRAPHY).

Nigerian-British relations improved (there were over 10,000 Nigerian students in Britain in 1977). Trade between the two countries had reached record levels in 1976, with the balance swinging to Britain, Nigeria's main trading partner (25% of foreign trade). Lieut. Gen. Obasanjo took a sober view of national finance in his March budget speech, notwithstanding the accumulation of foreign reserves, a fall in the inflation rate from

---

NIGERIA

Education. (1973–74) Primary, pupils 4,889,857, teachers 144,351; secondary, pupils 498,744, teachers 19,409; vocational, pupils 22,117, teachers 1,120; teacher training, students 49,216, teachers 2,360; higher, students 25,921, teaching staff 2,361.

Finance. Monetary unit: naira, with (Sept, 19, 1977) a free rate of 0.66 naira to U.S. $1 (1.15 naira = £1 sterling). Gold, SDR's, and foreign exchange (June 1977) U.S. $4,-266,000,000. Federal budget (1976–77): revenue 5,756,000,000 naira; expenditure 9,792,000,000 naira (including 7,378,000,000 naira capital expenditure). Gross domestic product (1973–74) 9,120,000,000 naira. Money supply (April 1977) 4,550,400,000 naira. Cost of living (Lagos; 1970 = 100; Feb. 1977) 246.

Foreign Trade. (1976) Imports 5,139,700,000 naira; exports 6,622,400,000 naira. Import sources (1975): U.K. 23%; West Germany 15%; U.S. 11%; Japan 10%; France 8%; Italy 6%. Export destinations (1975): U.S. 29%; U.K. 14%; The Netherlands 11%; France 11%; Netherlands Antilles 7%; West Germany 7%. Main export crude oil 94%.

Transport and Communications. Roads (1974) 97,000 km. Motor vehicles in use (1973): passenger c. 150,000; commercial (including buses) c. 82,000. Railways: (1975) 3,524 km; traffic (1974–75) 785 million passenger-km, freight 972 million net ton-km. Air traffic (1975): 430 million passenger-km; freight 7.9 million net ton-km. Shipping (1976): merchant vessels 100 gross tons and over 92; gross tonnage 181,565. Telephones (Jan. 1975) 111,000. Radio receivers (Dec. 1974) 5 million. Television receivers (Dec. 1974) 110,000.

Agriculture. Production (in 000; metric tons; 1976): millet c. 3,200; sorghum c. 3,680; corn c. 1,050; rice c. 405; sweet potatoes (1975) c. 190; yams (1975) c. 15,000; taro (1975) c. 1,800; cassava (1975) c. 10,000; cowpeas (1975) c. 850; tomatoes c. 230; peanuts c. 700; palm oil c. 510; cocoa c. 180; cotton, lint c. 69; rubber c. 85; fish catch (1975) 507. Livestock (in 000; 1976): cattle c. 11,300; sheep c. 7,900; goats c. 23,000; pigs c. 680; poultry c. 90,000.

Industry. Production (in 000; metric tons; 1975): cement 1,383; crude oil (1976) 102,655; natural gas (cu m) 661,000; tin 4.7; petroleum products c. 2,430; electricity (kw-hr) 3,211,000.

35% in 1976 to 20% in 1977, economic growth of 10%, and increases of 14.8% in oil output and 3% in agricultural production. Trade had grown (exports rose 36% and imports 38%), but the balance of trade had moved into deficit. Expenditure for 1977–78 was estimated at 8.6 billion naira and revenue at 7,650,000,000 naira. Defense was allocated the largest slice of the budget (817 million naira), followed by education (239 million naira). The Indigenization Decree, promulgated on January 17, and the national development plan (1975–80) stressed agriculture and local industry and greatly increased local shareholding in foreign companies. Stern penalties, including death, were imposed on smuggling, which in 1976 cost the nation over 300 million naira in lost revenue.

(MOLLY MORTIMER)

Norway

Norway

A constitutional monarchy of northern Europe, Norway is bordered by Sweden, Finland, and the U.S.S.R.; its coastlines are on the Skagerrak, the North Sea, the Norwegian Sea, and the Arctic Ocean. Area: 323,886 sq km (125,053 sq mi), excluding the Svalbard Archipelago, 62,048 sq km, and Jan Mayen Island, 373 sq km. Pop. (1977 est.): 4,035,200. Cap. and largest city: Oslo (pop., 1977 est., 462,500). Language: Norwegian. Religion: Lutheran (94%). King, Olav V; prime minister in 1977, Odvar Nordli.

Saving Norway from the mass unemployment prevailing elsewhere in Europe was one of the Labour government's main goals in 1977. It maintained tax and subsidy policies that allowed real disposable incomes to continue rising and gave substantial help to export industries in the form of low-interest loans, loan guarantees, and some direct grants. Key industries that received such aid included shipbuilding and forest and fish products. Some 110,000 workers, 7% of the labour force, who might otherwise have been laid off, were thus supported. The outlook for Norway's merchant fleet was bleak. As the depression on the world freight market entered its fourth year, more than one-fifth of the fleet was laid up. (See TRANSPORTATION: *Shipping and Ports*.)

The government's policies did succeed in holding down unemployment, which remained below 1% of the total labour force. The counterrecession strategy had some undesirable side effects, however. One was a steady upward pressure on wages and costs, which made Norwegian goods less and less competitive, both abroad and on the home market. This, coupled with a continuing consumer boom, helped push Norway's payments deficit to record levels. By October it appeared that the deficit for 1977 would reach 27,500,000,000 kroner, more than double the figure foreseen in the national budget. Previously, the government had assumed that the international recession would be relatively short-lived. Many of the counterrecessionary measures were intended to be only temporary, keeping people at work until the slump ended. The money to finance them was easily raised by borrowing abroad, against future income from Norway's offshore oil and gas. During 1977, however, it became clear that no early upturn was likely. Official policymakers became concerned that Norwegian goods would price themselves out of traditional markets if rising costs were not curbed.

In campaigning for the September 11–12 parliamentary election, Labour Party leaders warned that the budget for 1978 would have to be considerably tougher than originally planned. The election gave a one-seat majority in the Storting (parliament) to the two Socialist parties—Labour and the Socialist Left (SV)—thus enabling Nordli's minority Labour government to continue for four more years. An important trend was an increase in the strength of the two largest parties, Labour and the Conservatives, at the expense of the smaller parties of the far left, far right, and centre. (See POLITICAL PARTIES.)

The offshore oil and gas industry suffered a setback in April, when a blowout occurred on Norway's only producing field, Ekofisk. It took a week to get the well under control again, at enormous

Norwegian Finance Minister Per Kleppe snipped a piece off a 1,000-kroner bill held by Prime Minister Odvar Nordli to symbolize Norway's devaluation of the krone.

UPI COMPIX

cost. Some 7.5 million gal of oil were spilled into the sea, and production was cut back for some time afterward. Output rose sharply in September, when the gas pipeline from Ekofisk to Emden in West Germany came into operation, but in October the field was again closed down briefly pending a safety inquiry. September also saw the start of production from the Anglo-Norwegian Frigg gas field. Gas from Frigg began flowing through a subsea pipeline to St. Fergus in Scotland, thus further increasing Norway's total petroleum output.

In June, Norway unilaterally established a 200-mi fisheries protection zone around the Svalbard Archipelago. Sovereignty over the archipelago had been granted to Norway by the treaty of 1925, with equal right of access for peaceful purposes given to the 40 signatory powers. The Soviet Union upheld its right to fish in the zone while the Western countries concerned, including the U.S. and U.K., reserved their positions. Norway was also in dispute with the Soviet Union over a fisheries dividing line in the Barents Sea.

(FAY GJESTER)

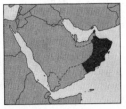

Oman

Oman

An independent sultanate, Oman occupies the southeastern part of the Arabian Peninsula and is bounded by the United Arab Emirates, Saudi Arabia, Yemen (Aden), the Gulf of Oman, and the Arabian Sea. A small part of the country lies to the north and is separated from the rest of Oman by the United Arab Emirates. Area: 300,000 sq km (120,000 sq mi). Pop. (1976 UN est.): 791,000; for planning purposes the government of Oman uses an estimate of 1.5 million. No census has ever been taken. Cap.: Muscat (pop., 1973 est., 15,000). Largest city: Matrah (pop., 1973 est., 18,000). Language: Arabic. Religion: Muslim. Sultan in 1977, Qabus ibn Sa'id.

At the end of March 1977, Britain relinquished its military air-staging base on Oman's Masirah Island. Reports that it would be replaced by a U.S. base were strongly denied by Sultan Qabus.

With the Dhofar rebellion virtually ended, work proceeded on the development of the southern region, although the Popular Front for the Liberation of Oman (PFLO) continued to issue communiqués in which it claimed to have inflicted casualties on the Omani forces. Efforts to mediate between Oman and Yemen (Aden), including one by Sudan's Pres. Gaafar Nimeiry who visited Oman in March, were without result. The bulk of the 3,000 Iranian troops in Oman were withdrawn, although the Iranian Air Force continued its overflights.

While oil revenues remained the main source of development funds, the five-year plan provided for the exploitation of copper and coal.

(PETER MANSFIELD)

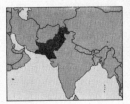

Pakistan

Pakistan

A federal republic, Pakistan is bordered on the south by the Arabian Sea, on the west by Afghanistan and Iran, on the north by China, and on the east by India. Area: 796,095 sq km (307,374 sq mi), excluding the Pakistani-controlled section of Jammu and Kashmir. Pop. (1976 est.): 72,368,000. Cap.: Islamabad (pop., 1972, 77,300). Largest city: Karachi (metro. area pop., 1975 est., 4,465,000). Language: Urdu and English. Religion: Muslim

90%, Hindu and Christian minorities. President in 1977, Chaudhri Fazal Elahi; prime minister, Zulfikar Ali Bhutto to July 5; chief martial law administrator from July 5, Gen. Mohammad Zia-ul-Haq.

By the beginning of 1977 Pakistan, under the firm guidance of Prime Minister Zulfikar Ali Bhutto and his Pakistan People's Party (PPP), had regained much of the standing in international affairs that had been lost after the breakaway of Bangladesh five years earlier. Relations with other Muslim states, particularly Iran, Saudi Arabia, and the Persian Gulf emirates, were close and cordial. The good understanding with Afghanistan noted in 1976 was maintained, while with India, relations established with the new Janata government brought about the full resumption of transit by road, rail, and air.

With Western nations, relations remained good, with the single exception of the U.S., where Pres. Jimmy Carter viewed with disfavour Pakistan's insistence on purchasing a nuclear fuel reprocessing plant from France. Moreover, a marked change took place in the former U.S. belief that Pakistan might be a valuable ally in countering the growth of Soviet influence in South Asia, partly because of the relaxation of tension between the two superpowers and partly because the new Indian government was at pains to modify the dependence on Soviet assistance that had marked the outlook of Indira Gandhi and her government. A new friendship sprang up between the U.S. and India, and many U.S. leaders made no secret of their belief that it was India that mattered in the subcontinent.

It was the domestic politics of Pakistan, however, that attracted most attention from foreign observers during 1977. At the beginning of the year, Bhutto and his PPP seemed firmly in control, but

when he announced that he would "seek a new mandate from the people" by holding elections on March 7, it became clear that his steamroller methods of land distribution and nationalization of small as well as large enterprises had created a formidable opposition movement. This had been driven underground by his drastic dealing with opponents both inside and outside the PPP and by use of the Federal Security Force as a kind of party police. Nine separate groups, covering almost every range of political view, financial interest, and Islamic ideology, came together to form the Pakistan National Alliance (PNA) to oppose Bhutto in the March elections.

When in March the PPP captured all but 45 seats in the National Assembly, the PNA mounted a furious campaign of protest against "vote rigging" and demanded new elections. PPP and PNA supporters turned the streets of the main cities into battlegrounds, and there were more than 200 deaths. Martial law was proclaimed in several cities without much effect on the general chaos. The economic consequences were disastrous to Pakistan's slowly improving growth rate; it was calculated in June that Rs 5 billion worth of production had been lost. Later, destructive floods

Just minutes after this picture was taken of protesters demonstrating in Lahore, Pakistan, against Prime Minister Bhutto, Army troops fired into the crowd, killing three and injuring several others.

WIDE WORLD

PAKISTAN

Education. (1974–75) Primary, pupils 5,150,000, teachers 121,200; secondary, pupils 1,621,000, teachers 95,000; vocational, pupils 26,950, teachers 2,161; teacher training, students 16,883, teachers 754; higher, students 257,051, teaching staff 13,248.

Finance. Monetary unit: Pakistan rupee, with (Sept. 19, 1977) a par value of PakRs 9.90 to U.S. $1 (free rate of PakRs 17.25 = £1 sterling). Gold, SDR's, and foreign exchange (June 1977) U.S. $438 million. Budget (1976–77 est.): revenue PakRs 20,478,000,000; expenditure PakRs 35,854,000,000. Gross national product (1974–75) PakRs 111,890,000,000. Money supply (June 1977) PakRs 35,709,000,000. Cost of living (1970 = 100; April 1977) 260.

Foreign Trade. (1976) Imports PakRs 21,130,000,000; exports PakRs 11,512,000,000. Import sources (1975–76): U.S. 19%; Japan 12%; Saudi Arabia 8%; U.K. 8%; West Germany 6%; United Arab Emirates 5%. Export destinations (1975–76): Hong Kong 11%; Saudi Arabia 7%; Japan 7%; U.K. 6%; U.S. 6%; West Germany 5%; Iraq 5%. Main exports (1975–76): rice 22%; cotton yarn 13%; cotton fabrics 12%; leather 9%; cotton 9%; carpets 6%.

Transport and Communications. Roads (1976) 49,936 km (including 27,158 km all-weather). Motor vehicles in use (1975): passenger 192,300; commercial (including buses) 95,300. Railways: (1976) 8,808 km; traffic (1975–76) *c.* 12,900,000,000 passenger-km, freight *c.* 8,700,000,000 net ton-km. Air traffic (1976): 3,411,000,000 passenger-km; freight 148.3 million net ton-km. Shipping (1976): merchant vessels 100 gross tons and over 83; gross tonnage 483,433. Telephones (Jan. 1976) 240,000. Radio licenses (Dec. 1974) 1,015,000. Television receivers (Dec. 1974) 125,000.

Agriculture. Production (in 000; metric tons; 1976): wheat 8,636; barley 130; corn *c.* 711; rice 3,942; millet *c.* 350; sorghum *c.* 325; sugar, raw value *c.* 565; sugar, non-centrifugal (1975) 1,400; chick-peas *c.* 535; onions *c.* 304; rapeseed *c.* 267; mangoes *c.* 648; tobacco *c.* 60; cotton, lint *c.* 550. Livestock (in 000; 1976): cattle *c.* 13,621; buffalo *c.* 10,812; sheep *c.* 19,300; goats *c.* 14,174; camels (1975) *c.* 850.

Industry. Production (in 000; metric tons; 1976): cement 3,190; crude oil 341; coal and lignite *c.* 1,100; natural gas (cu m; 1975) *c.* 5,000,000; petroleum products (1975) 3,340; electricity (excluding most industrial production; kw-hr; 1975) *c.* 8,800,000; sulfuric acid 42; caustic soda 30; soda ash (1974–75) 77; nitrogenous fertilizers (nutrient content; 1975–76) 316; cotton yarn 325; woven cotton fabrics (m; 1974–75) 608,000.

added further to the difficulties of the situation.

Many people began looking to the Army for salvation. The military authorities begged the rival factions to compose their differences, but when this could not be done they stepped in on July 5 and interned the leaders on both sides. Gen. Mohammad Zia-ul-Haq (*see* BIOGRAPHY), who headed the new military administration, sought reliable civilian assistance and announced that he hoped a "cooling-off period" would enable elections to be held in October to replace the national and provincial assemblies elected under the PPP regime. After this, he proposed to hand over power to a new civilian government. Difficulties arose because a number of serious criminal charges were brought against Bhutto and several of his colleagues, and General Zia decided that elections could not be held until the judiciary had pronounced upon their guilt or innocence.

(L. F. RUSHBROOK WILLIAMS)

Panama

A republic of Central America, bisected by the Canal Zone, Panama is bounded by the Caribbean Sea, Colombia, the Pacific Ocean, and Costa Rica. Area: 75,650 sq km (29,209 sq mi). Pop. (1977 est.): 1,771,300. Cap. and largest city: Panama City (pop., 1977 est., 427,700). Language: Spanish. Religion (1974 est.): Roman Catholic 87.2%. President in 1977, Demetrio Lakas Bahas.

While efforts to obtain a new canal treaty with the U.S. captured the headlines in 1977, the downward trend in Panama's economy continued unabated. The signs were evident: luxury apartment buildings unoccupied on many floors, office buildings uncompleted, fewer tourists and more thieves, higher living costs and lower employment, more costly oil imports and less profitable exports of bananas, rice, and other commodities. The basic problem lay in the noncompetitiveness of production in a country that maintained the highest wage levels of Central America.

The economic uncertainties impelled banking interests to hold back on new investments, and to fill the void the government of strong man Omar Torrijos Herrera (*see* BIOGRAPHY) continued its program of public works. Many millions were borrowed to construct, in Chiriqui Province, a hydroelectric plant designed to double the country's available electricity. A new modern airport neared completion, and an oil pipeline paralleling the canal was in the blueprint stage. For the fishing industry, Torrijos planned a new port with dry-dock facilities that would make Panama a centre for ship repairing.

The results of the public works programs were not encouraging. Their stimulative effect was negated by the costs they implied, and the national debt reached $1.2 billion. Hence the government took other measures to combat the decline: a 5% sales tax (food, fuel, and medicines exempted) and an increase in telephone and electricity rates. Changes in the labour code were initiated, including elimination of seniority rights, reduced guarantees against dismissal, a freeze on labour

contracts, and compulsory arbitration. Wage and price controls reduced the pay of government employees and rolled back the prices of bread, beans, and other staples. The use of telephones and air conditioners in government offices was limited.

Panama

These measures aroused resentment and suspicion. The National Workers' Council demanded a policy reversal, and banana workers went on strike. The resulting tensions flared into violence, and there were bombing incidents in October 1976, a shadowed reenactment in January 1977 of the bloody riots of 1964, and boisterous demonstrations in June commemorating the death of a student for which the U.S. Central Intelligence Agency was blamed. But although demonstrators desecrated the American flag and swarmed over the Canal Zone boundary, the National Guard did nothing to restrain them and the U.S. civil and military authorities issued only verbal protests.

Some observers believed the Panamanian government may have supported these incidents in an effort to impress if not to intimidate the U.S. negotiators, legislators, and public into a speedy acquiescence in Panama's treaty demands. Following U.S. Pres. Jimmy Carter's inauguration, Sol M. Linowitz, an experienced Latin-America hand, joined the U.S. negotiating team, while Aquilino Boyd, a fiery exponent of Panama's extreme claims, vanished from the Panamanian side. The discussions, which had been held intermittently over the past 13 years, reached a spectacular conclusion on September 7, when representatives of 26 American nations witnessed the signing of the new treaties by Carter and Torrijos at a gala ceremony in Washington.

The settlement consisted of two agreements, a lengthy general treaty and a neutrality pact. The former stipulated the repeal of the Hay–Bunau-

Panamanian activists hauled down an American flag in the U.S. zone in June and hoisted a Panamanian flag in its place.

Palestine:
see Israel; Jordan

UPI COMPIX

U.S. Senator Donald W. Riegle inspected the Pedro Miguel locks as a member of a Senate fact-finding mission which visited the Panama Canal Zone in November.

Varilla Treaty of 1903, which granted the U.S. exclusive rights to the canal, and several later agreements, and it provided for the continued operation, maintenance, and defense of the canal by the U.S., with increased sharing of responsibility with Panama, until the year 2000. At that time full control and responsibility were to be transferred to Panama. Shortly after ratification of the agreements, the U.S. was to convey to Panama those lands and waters of the Zone that were not regarded as vital to the operation of the canal, and Panama would assume jurisdiction, applying its law and controlling schools, police, the post office, and other public services.

Under the new agreement Panama would receive 30 cents out of a toll of $1.29 per canal ton and a percentage of the revenue from ship repair, docking, and other facilities. (It was estimated that this income could reach $60 million to $80 million yearly.) In a separate understanding Panama was assured of loans from international banking institutions amounting to some $300 million over a period of several years. The two countries would join in any feasibility study of a sea-level canal. The neutrality treaty provided, albeit in vague language, for the transit of naval and merchant vessels of all nations at all times but appeared to give the U.S. an indefinite unilateral right to defend the canal.

These agreements required ratification by a plebiscite of the voters in Panama and by a two-thirds vote of the U.S. Senate. On October 23 the Panamanians voted decisively in favour of the treaties, over the intense objections of leftist and nationalist groups. In the U.S., where a possible "giveaway" of the canal had been an issue in the 1976 presidential campaign, widespread and vocal opposition developed, and an air of caution and doubt pervaded the initial Senate committee hearings on the subject. Proponents of the treaties asserted that they would ensure an open, secure,

and efficiently operated canal, but many Americans believed the existing arrangement provided just that, and they discounted claims of general Latin-American support for the treaties and the threat of possible sabotage if they were not ratified. On October 14 Carter and Torrijos announced an agreement interpreting the U.S. right to defend the canal as not extending to intervention in the internal affairs of Panama and construing the right of U.S. war vessels to expeditious transit as priority of passage through the canal. This did not appear to satisfy the opposition.   (ALMON R. WRIGHT)

Panama Canal Zone:
see Dependent
States; Panama

Paper and Pulp:
see Industrial Review

PANAMA

Education. (1975) Primary, pupils 342,043, teachers 11,-185; secondary, pupils 81,928, teachers 3,472; vocational, pupils 37,713, teachers 1,926; teacher training, students 5,850, teachers 244; higher, students 26,289, teaching staff 1,022.

Finance. Monetary unit: balboa, at par with the U.S. dollar, with a free rate (Sept. 19, 1977) of 1.74 balboas to £1 sterling. Budget (1976 actual): revenue 282 million balboas; expenditure 445.8 million balboas. Gross national product (1976) 2,006,000,000 balboas. Cost of living (Panama City; 1970 = 100; June 1977) 159.

Foreign Trade. (1976) Imports 838.4 million balboas; exports 226,550,000 balboas. Service receipts from Canal Zone (1974) 145 million balboas. Import sources (1975): U.S. 27%; Saudi Arabia 17%; Ecuador 15%; Venezuela 8%; Japan 5%. Export destinations (1975): U.S. 59%; Canal Zone 12%; West Germany 6%; Italy 5%. Main exports: petroleum products 29%; bananas 27%; shrimps 15%; sugar 12%.

Transport and Communications. Roads (1974) 7,128 km. Motor vehicles in use (1974): passenger 69,800; commercial 16,100. Railways (1975) 391 km. Shipping (1976): merchant vessels 100 gross tons and over 2,680 (mostly owned by U.S. and other foreign interests); gross tonnage 15,631,180. Telephones (Jan. 1976) 142,000. Radio receivers (Dec. 1974) 260,000. Television receivers (Dec. 1974) 183,000.

Agriculture. Production (in 000; metric tons; 1976): rice 111; corn (1975) c. 61; sugar, raw value (1975) 131; bananas c. 989; oranges 62; coffee c. 5. Livestock (in 000; 1975): cattle 1,348; pigs c. 181; horses c. 164; chickens c. 3,880.

Industry. Production (in 000; metric tons; 1975): petroleum products c. 3,770; cement 277; manufactured gas (cu m) c. 12,000; electricity (kw-hr) c. 1,162,000.

Papua New Guinea

Papua New Guinea is an independent parliamentary state and a member of the Commonwealth of Nations. It is situated in the southwest Pacific and comprises the eastern part of the island of New Guinea, the islands of the Bismarck, Trobriand, Woodlark, Louisiade, and D'Entrecasteaux groups, and parts of the Solomon Islands, including Bougainville. It is separated from Australia by the Torres Strait. Area: 462,840 sq km (178,704 sq mi). Pop. (1976 est.): 2,829,000. Cap. and largest city: Port Moresby (pop., 1976 est., 113,400). Language: English, Police Motu (a Melanesian pidgin), and Pidgin English (or Neo-Melanesian) are official, although the latter is the most widely spoken. Religion (1966): Roman Catholic 31.2%; Lutheran 27.3%; indigenous 7%. Queen, Elizabeth II; governors-general in 1977, Sir John Guise and, from February 17, Sir Tore Lokoloko; prime minister, Michael T. Somare.

In June–July 1977 Papua New Guinea faced its first general election since independence (1975) in a mood of constitutional crisis. The governor-general, Sir John Guise, resigned to contest the election and, at the head of a party called the National Alliance, unsuccessfully challenged Michael Somare for the prime ministership. He was by no means the only thorn in Somare's side. The Pangu Party (the senior party in the coalition government) was also challenged by the United Party (the main opposition), the People's Progress Party, the National Party, the Country Party, and Papua Besena. As the *Pacific Islands Monthly* commented, "the party system as much as the candidates" was being tested. Somare and the party system were both successful.

While political affairs were agitated, Papua New Guinea continued on the sound economic lines developed by Somare. Papua New Guinea's

inflation rate stood at only 5% at the beginning of 1977. In August, however, Finance Minister Julius Chan revalued the kina 1.01% against the Australian dollar (devalued on August 3). The kina was pegged to the Australian dollar and would have been automatically devalued if Chan had not acted.

During the year relations with Indonesia were threatened by the guerrilla activities in border areas of a Free Papua Movement seeking independence for the Indonesian province of West Irian.

(A. R. G. GRIFFITHS)

Papua New Guinea

Paraguay

A landlocked republic of South America, Paraguay is bounded by Brazil, Argentina, and Bolivia. Area: 406,752 sq km (157,048 sq mi). Pop. (1977 UN est.): 2,805,000. Cap. and largest city: Asunción (pop., 1975 est., 434,900). Language: Spanish (official), though Guaraní is the language of the majority of the people. Religion: Roman Catholic (official). President in 1977, Gen. Alfredo Stroessner.

The Feb. 6, 1977, elections for a constitutional convention were won by the governing Partido Colorado, and the elected convention in March amended the 1967 constitution to permit a president to hold office for any number of consecutive terms (Gen. Alfredo Stroessner was in his fifth consecutive term). At the beginning of 1977 some political prisoners were released or put on trial.

PAPUA NEW GUINEA

Education. (1975) Primary, pupils 243,080, teachers 7,-824; secondary, pupils 30,492, teachers 1,282; vocational, pupils 9,031, teachers 569; teacher training, students 2,201, teachers 176; higher, students 2,624, teaching staff 324.

Finance. Monetary unit: kina, with (Sept. 19, 1977) a par value of 0.882 kina to the Australian dollar and a free rate of 0.80 kina to U.S. $1 (1.38 kina = £1 sterling). Budget (1975–76 rev. est.): revenue 432 million kinas (including Australian grants of 128 million kinas); expenditure 408 million kinas.

Foreign Trade. (1975–76) Imports 356.3 million kinas; exports 368.9 million kinas. Import sources (1975): Australia 46%; Japan 14%; U.S. 9%; U.K. 5%. Export destinations (1975): Japan 30%; West Germany 29%; Australia 14%; U.K. 6%; U.S. 6%; Spain 5%. Main exports (1974–75): copper ores 56%; cocoa 9%; coffee 8%; copra 7%.

Transport. Roads (1975) 18,188 km. There are no railways. Shipping (1976): merchant vessels 100 gross tons and over 57; gross tonnage 15,329.

Agriculture. Production (in 000; metric tons; 1976): cocoa *c.* 35; coffee *c.* 41; copra *c.* 132; cassava (1975) *c.* 84; taro (1975) *c.* 219; yams (1975) *c.* 168; tea *c.* 6; rubber *c.* 6; timber (cu m; 1975) *c.* 5,494. Livestock (in 000; March 1975): cattle *c.* 130; pigs *c.* 1,166; goats *c.* 15; chickens *c.* 1,069.

Industry. Production (in 000; 1974–75): gold (troy oz) *c.* 630; silver (troy oz; 1973–74) 1,254; copper ore (metal content; metric tons) 172; electricity (kw-hr) 969,000.

PARAGUAY

Education. (1975) Primary, pupils 452,249, teachers 15,-398; secondary, pupils 75,424, teachers 10,406; vocational, pupils 1,361, teachers 67; higher (1973), students 12,212, teaching staff 1,529.

Finance. Monetary unit: guaraní, with an official rate (Sept. 19, 1976) of 126 guaranis to U.S. $1 (free rate of 218 guaranis = £1 sterling). Gold, SDR's, and foreign exchange (June 1977) U.S. $235.3 million. Budget (1976 actual): revenue 19,384,000,000 guaranis; expenditure 18,465,000,000 guaranis. Gross national product (1976) 210.6 billion guaranis. Money supply (April 1977) 26,518,-000,000 guaranis. Cost of living (Asunción; 1970 = 100; June 1977) 200.

Foreign Trade. (1976) Imports 27,589,000,000 guaranis; exports 22,423,000,000 guaranis. Import sources: Argentina 21%; Brazil 17%; Algeria 13%; U.S. 10%; West Germany 8%; U.K. 8%; Japan 5%. Export destinations: The Netherlands 15%; U.S. 12%; West Germany 11%; Argentina 10%; Switzerland 10%; U.K. 6%; France 6%; Brazil 6%; Uruguay 5%. Main exports: cotton 19%; meat 12%; vegetable oils 9%; tobacco 8%; timber 7%.

Transport and Communications. Roads (1973) 15,956 km. Motor vehicles in use (1975): passenger 22,500; commercial (including buses) 19,800. Railways: (1976) 498 km; traffic (1973) 26 million passenger-km, freight 30 million net ton-km. Navigable inland waterways (including Paraguay-Paraná River system; 1975) *c.* 3,000 km. Telephones (Dec. 1975) 37,000. Radio receivers (Dec. 1974) 176,000. Television receivers (Dec. 1974) 53,000.

Agriculture. Production (in 000; metric tons; 1976): corn *c.* 371; cassava (1975) *c.* 1,134; sweet potatoes (1975) *c.* 90; soybeans 260; sugar, raw value (1975) *c.* 78; tomatoes *c.* 53; oranges *c.* 128; mandarin oranges and tangerines *c.* 32; bananas *c.* 260; palm kernels *c.* 14; tobacco *c.* 34; cotton lint *c.* 33; beef and veal (1975) 91. Livestock (in 000; 1975): cattle 4,936; sheep *c.* 355; pigs *c.* 800; horses *c.* 315; chickens *c.* 8,500.

Industry. Production (in 000; metric tons; 1975): petroleum products *c.* 200; cement 138; cotton yarn (1974) 24; electricity (kw-hr) *c.* 510,000.

Paraguay

Parachuting: *see* Aerial Sports

The opposition was still fragmented, and the Partido Liberal Unido (PLU) — formed by the merger of the Partido Liberal Radical and the Partido Liberal on January 24 — faced difficulties when it was soon declared illegal.

The 1977 economic growth rate was estimated at 8% (6.5% in 1976). The foreign trade position improved, the January–June trade balance showing a surplus of U.S. $29.8 million as compared with a deficit of $26.8 million in the first half of 1976. Cotton remained the main export, and meat, timber, vegetable oil, and oilseeds contributed to the improvement. A balance of payments surplus of $65 million and international reserves of $250 million were forecast. Inflation was thought to average 7% over the year, as against 6.5% in 1976.

(FRANÇOISE LOTERY)

Peru

Peru

A republic on the west coast of South America, Peru is bounded by Ecuador, Colombia, Brazil, Bolivia, Chile, and the Pacific Ocean. Area: 1,285,215 sq km (496,224 sq mi). Pop. (1976 est.): 16,090,000, including approximately 52% whites and mestizos and 46% Indians. Cap. and largest city: Lima (metro. area pop., 1975 UN est., 3,901,000). Language: Spanish and Quechua are official; Indians also speak Aymara. Religion: Roman Catholic. President of the military government in 1977, Francisco Morales Bermúdez.

At the beginning of February 1977 the government announced its 1977–80 Túpac Amaru Plan, which emphasized the trend toward political moderation begun in the previous year. The plan proposed the drafting of a new constitution that would permit the holding of general elections after 1980, would decentralize the economy, and would introduce new schemes to rid Peru of its financial difficulties, including the conversion of government-owned enterprises into cooperative, profit-oriented businesses. A recommendation was also

Giant trucks laden with sugarcane await their turn to unload at a refinery in Peru. Huge worldwide cane crops and reduced demand resulted in lower sugar prices.

UPI COMPIX

PERU

Education. (1975) Primary, pupils 2,970,708, teachers 76,645; secondary, pupils 758,320, teachers 30,051; vocational, pupils 250,788, teachers 10,320; higher, students 320,038, teaching staff 16,095.

Finance. Monetary unit: sol, with (Oct. 12, 1977, following the floating of the currency) a free rate of 85.25 soles to U.S. $1 (148.50 soles = £1 sterling). Gold, SDR's, and foreign exchange (April 1977) U.S. $343.7 million. Budget (1976 actual): revenue 111,305,000,000 soles; expenditure 137,655,000,000 soles. Gross national product (1976) 759 billion soles. Money supply (Jan. 1977) 143,520,000,000 soles. Cost of living (Lima; 1970 = 100; May 1977) 312.

Foreign Trade. Imports (1975) 104,824,000,000 soles; exports (1976) 73,969,000,000 soles. Import sources (1974): U.S. 31%; Japan 12%; West Germany 10%; Ecuador 5%. Export destinations (1974): U.S. 36%; Japan 13%; West Germany 8%; China 5%. Main exports: copper 17%; fish meal 13%; zinc 11%; silver 11%; coffee 9%; sugar 7%; cotton 6%; iron ore 5%.

Transport and Communications. Roads (1975) 56,416 km. Motor vehicles in use (1974): passenger 266,900; commercial (including buses) 139,900. Railways: (1972) 2,218 km; traffic (1973) 270 million passenger-km, freight 735 million net ton-km. Air traffic (1975): 1,132,000,000 passenger-km; freight 22,700,000,000 net ton-km. Shipping (1976): merchant vessels 100 gross tons and over 681; gross tonnage 525,137. Telephones (Jan. 1975) 333,000. Radio receivers (Dec. 1974) 2,010,000. Television receivers (Dec. 1974) 425,000.

Agriculture. Production (in 000; metric tons; 1976): rice 570; corn *c.* 670; wheat *c.* 148; barley *c.* 165; potatoes *c.* 1,930; sweet potatoes (1975) 785; cassava (1975) 470; sugar, raw value *c.* 950; onions *c.* 187; apples *c.* 80; oranges *c.* 257; lemons *c.* 96; coffee *c.* 60; cotton, lint *c.* 76; fish catch (1975) 3,447. Livestock (in 000; 1976): cattle *c.* 4,270; sheep *c.* 17,453; pigs *c.* 1,900; goats *c.* 1,960; horses (1975) *c.* 734; poultry *c.* 25,000.

Industry. Production (in 000; metric tons; 1975): coal *c.* 85; crude oil (1976) 3,708; natural gas (cu m) *c.* 550,000; cement 1,936; iron ore (metal content) *c.* 5,067; pig iron 307; crude steel 443; lead 70; zinc 67; copper 53; tungsten concentrates (oxide content) 0.7; gold (troy oz) 86; silver (troy oz) *c.* 38,000; fish meal 687; petroleum products *c.* 5,470; electricity (kw-hr) *c.* 8,300,000.

made to allow foreign investment in the development of natural resources where this would help the country and to improve diplomatic relations with neighbouring nations.

Political activity in general in 1977 centred on the country's economic performance because of the worsening of the trade position in the previous two years. This had been mainly due to low world copper prices and, more recently, to a comparatively small anchovy catch. This had prompted the government to borrow some U.S. $400 million abroad to help support the balance of payments. In 1977 foreign banks made further financing conditional on the approval of the International Monetary Fund (IMF) of any recovery measures. The minister of finance at that time, Luis Barúa Castañeda, prepared a deflationary program, but he encountered opposition from a government commission led by the minister of industry and tourism, Gen. Gaston Ibáñez O'Brien. The commission's proposals, which included wage increases, credit expansion, and generally reflationary policies, were diametrically opposed to Barúa's, and as a consequence he resigned.

Barúa was replaced in May by Walter Piazza Tangüis, an influential member of the business community and the first from that sector to be appointed to a ministerial post for eight years. In June Piazza introduced several emergency measures, including higher prices for food and gasoline, which were the source of some unrest in the provinces, especially in the south. At the same time, he tried to set up a program that would help secure the loans with a compromise, including not only further austerity measures but also a proposal for a devaluation of the sol to 90 soles=U.S. $1 by the end of 1977 rather than the original demand of 100 soles=$1. General Ibáñez again opposed this measure, causing Piazza and, soon after, the president of the Central Bank, Carlos Santisteban, to resign in July. Piazza was replaced by Gen. Alcibíades Sáenz Barsallo, a close associate of Pres. Francisco Morales Bermúdez, in mid-July.

A wave of disorders and strikes broke out on July 19 as a result of the increasing discontent of the population over the imposed emergency measures. The Workers' Central of the Peruvian Revolution (CTRP), the National Confederation of Peru (CNP), and the General Confederation of Workers of Peru (CGTP), whose secretary-general was later arrested, were involved. Six people were killed during the unrest, and some 500–700 union activists imprisoned.

Soon after these events the government announced that a constituent assembly would be set up in July 1978 (with the date for elections to it later set at June 4) and that general elections would be held in 1980 with the military still exercising some legislative power. Subsidies on basic foodstuffs and wage increases were subsequently reintroduced. On August 28 the state of emergency originally imposed on July 1, 1976, was lifted and constitutional guarantees were reintroduced. Certain progressive journals were again permitted to appear. On October 9 the government announced a revised Túpac Amaru Plan, which included the reorganization of universities to allow greater participation of students in decision making. In general, government policies toward the end of the year were designed to avoid further social upheaval.

Steps were taken in October to remove exchange controls and float the sol, with an expected immediate devaluation of 25–30%. By agreement with the IMF in September, austerity measures (public spending to be cut, foreign borrowing restricted, wages pegged) would be imposed and in return the IMF would provide a standby credit of $120 million.   (BARBARA WIJNGAARD)

Philately and Numismatics

Stamps. Rare classic stamps, unused and used (especially when on the original envelopes), rose sharply in value in 1977. The extreme example was a heavily postmarked Mauritius 1847 one-penny "Post Office." Purchased in a London auction in November 1976 for £50,000, it was offered in an auction at Hamburg, West Germany, in April 1977 and reportedly sold for £82,500. All the major British and U.S. auctioneers recorded heavy increases in turnover for the 1976–77 season ended in July. Results announced were: Stanley Gibbons (including Stanley Gibbons Merkur, Frankfurt, West Germany), £2,765,296; Harmers (London, New York, and Sydney, Australia), £6,232,868; Robson Lowe International, £5,321,000. The out-

A printer's error made this 1918 stamp one of the world's most expensive. A collector bid $62,500 for it at an auction in San Francisco.

WIDE WORLD

standing one-country auction was the sale of the Michael Sacher collection of the stamps and postal history of Palestine by Robson Lowe, which realized £187,000. All auctioneers agreed that there was an increasing trend for classic stamps to be bought by nonphilatelists seeking a hedge against inflation. While this affected genuine collectors adversely, it also meant that capital in the trade was released and that the investors intended to return their stamps to the market rather than housing them indefinitely in collections.

The major "omnibus" issue was that for the Silver Jubilee of the accession of Queen Elizabeth II of the U.K. The single design of the issue for Great Britain aroused considerable public criticism, but the issues produced by the crown agents for many Commonwealth territories were well received. Conversely, some of the independent Commonwealth countries exploited the situation with the issue of unnecessary "sidelines" such as perforated and imperforate miniature sheets of high-value stamps and commemorative stamp booklets.

The Royal Philatelic Society, London, of which the queen is patron, held a Silver Jubilee exhibition on September 22–24. Among the outstanding exhibits was a selection from the Royal Collection at Buckingham Palace. The invited exhibits included a collection of 1847 and 1848 stamps of Mauritius valued at nearly £1 million, owned by Hiroyuki Kanai of Japan. The overall value of the 50-frame exhibition was put at £3 million.

The year's major international exhibition was Amphilex 77, held in Amsterdam in June. The International Philatelic Federation's Grand Prix d'Honneur was won by Gary Ryan (U.K.) with a highly specialized collection of classic Hungarian stamps.

The merger of the Philatelic Congress of Great Britain (founded 1909) and the British Philatelic Association (founded 1925) was completed, and the new British Philatelic Federation met at Blackpool, Lancashire, in June. New signatories to the Roll of Distinguished Philatelists were Donnar Dromberg (Finland), Enzo Diena (Italy—the fifth Italian, and the third member of his family, to sign), Derek Palmer (Chile's first signatory), and Sigge Ringström (Sweden). The Philatelic Congress Medal was awarded to James Dowell Todd of Sunderland, England, at 84 still active in philately. The Lichtenstein Medal, awarded by the Collectors Club of New York for services to phi-

9ᴾ Hedgehog *Erinaceus europaeus* 9ᴾ Hare *Lepus capensis* 9ᴾ Red Squirrel *Sciurus vulgaris* 9ᴾ Otter *Lutra lutra* 9ᴾ Badger *Meles meles*

Pictures of various wild animals adorn stamps issued in Britain as part of a postal effort to increase awareness of British wildlife.

lately, went to F. Burton Sellers, chairman of Interphil 76, held in Philadelphia to mark the U.S. Bicentennial. (KENNETH F. CHAPMAN)

Coins. In early 1975 the U.S. Bureau of the Mint, in cooperation with the Federal Reserve Board of Governors, began studying the overall coinage requirements of the United States during the remainder of the 20th century. By the end of 1977 no decisions had been made, although elimination or change in composition of the cent was a probability, as were elimination of the half dollar and introduction of a smaller size dollar coin. The market price of metals and coinage production costs were likely to dictate the timing of changes that seemed to be inevitable.

Private mints continued to produce commemorative medals and a few special coins for governments, largely for collectors. Two medals, issued late in 1976, marked the landing of the Viking 1 and Viking 2 spacecraft on Mars earlier that year. There were several medals commemorating the 50th anniversary of Charles Lindbergh's 1927 solo transatlantic flight.

At least two medals relating to the American Revolution were issued: one commemorated the 200th anniversary of George Washington's crossing of the Delaware River and one, by the Friends of Valley Forge, commemorated the 200th anniver-

In March Britain issued the Jubilee crown, a coin specially minted to commemorate the queen's Silver Jubilee.

sary of Washington's 1777–78 winter encampment at Valley Forge, Pa.

Many nations throughout the world issued FAO (Food and Agriculture Organization of the United Nations) coins to help stimulate production of food for the world's growing population. The FAO itself issued medals in sterling silver and 18-karat gold, the latest one depicting a profile bust of Princess Grace of Monaco.

Representative new coins of nations of the world included: in observance of the Silver Jubilee of Queen Elizabeth II, a newly designed crown dated 1977 in copper-nickel for circulation and sterling for collectors, an Australian copper-nickel 50-cent coin, and crowns by Gibraltar, Guernsey, Jersey, Mauritius, St. Helena, and the Isle of Man, the latter having issued a 1976 crown in observance of the U.S. Bicentennial; Botswana, 1976, 0.500 fine silver 5 pula commemorating its tenth anniversary of independence; Chile, 1976, 5 and 10 pesos copper-nickel, and 100 pesos, 0.900 fine gold; Italy, dated 1974 but struck in 1976–77, 0.835 fine silver 500 lire honouring Guglielmo Marconi, inventor of radio; and West Germany, 1977, silver 5 marks commemorating the 200th anniversary of the birth of Carl Friedrich Gauss, famous astronomer-mathematician.

Among the unusual issues was the second in a series of Hong Kong gold coins relating to the ancient Chinese lunar cycle, 1977 being the Year of the Snake. The half-ounce, 22-karat gold coin had a value of 1,000 Hong Kong dollars (about $215 U.S.). Another was a several coin set by Pakistan in 1976 and 1977, ranging from 50 paise (one-half rupee) to 1,000 rupees and characterized by lengthy legends in several languages, mostly relating to the Islamic religion.

A new coin introduced by Mexico in 1977, its first silver 100-peso coin, bore a likeness of José María Morelos, a leader in Mexico's war for independence from Spain. The coin contained 27.778 grams of 0.720 fine silver, equivalent to only one-fifth gram of pure silver per peso. Erosion of the peso's value (inflation) could be seen by comparing this coin with a 1910 peso, the first of Mexico's modern coinage, which contained nearly 24.5 grams of pure silver. Measured in silver, the 1977 peso had less than 1% (0.818%) of its value 67 years earlier. (GLENN B. SMEDLEY)

[452.D.2.b; 725.B.4.G]

Philippines

Situated in the western Pacific Ocean off the southeast coast of Asia, the Republic of the Philippines consists of an archipelago of about 7,100 islands. Area: 300,000 sq km (115,800 sq mi). Pop. (1976 est.): 43,751,000. Cap. and largest city: Manila (pop., 1975 prelim. census, 1,454,400). Language: Pilipino (based on Tagalog), English, Spanish, and many dialects. Religion (1970): Roman Catholic 85%; Muslim 4.3%; Aglipayan 3.9%; Protestant 3.1%; others 2.4%. President in 1977, Ferdinand E. Marcos.

Negotiations with Muslim separatists in the southern Philippines broke down on April 30, 1977, and later in the year major clashes occurred between government troops and guerrilla forces. A cease-fire had been arranged on Dec. 23, 1976, in Tripoli, Libya, between the government and the Moro National Liberation Front. It provided for 13 southern provinces to have regional autonomy that would permit them to control their own administration, education, and economy within some limits of residual power held by the national government. Pres. Ferdinand Marcos announced on March 26 that a referendum on autonomy would be held in the provinces.

The Liberation Front opposed the referendum and said that it would boycott it and refuse to

Philippines

accept the results. Muslims formed a majority in only five of the provinces, and in the whole region Christians comprised about 70% of the population. The Front argued that Muslims were the original inhabitants and therefore should have a larger voice than recent Christian immigrants into the south. In the referendum on April 17, nearly 98% of those who voted opposed autonomy. This impasse led to the breakdown of negotiations two weeks later.

Guerrilla attacks increased. On September 17 a land mine exploded on Basilan Island, killing 25 civilians and instigating fighting that took more than 80 lives in the following few weeks. The general commanding the Philippine 1st Division and 33 others were killed on October 10 on Jolo Island in what the government said was a guerrilla ambush at a truce meeting.

At a memorial service for the general, Marcos said that the renewed fighting "convinces me that it is not yet time to lift martial law," which he had imposed on the country in 1972. In Manila on August 25, demonstrations against martial law, which police broke up with an estimated 100 injured, had already caused Marcos to warn that his emergency rule would be extended if trouble continued. In a referendum in December—the fifth since martial law was proclaimed—Marcos again received a mandate to remain in power.

Elections, promised repeatedly since 1972, continued to be postponed. Marcos had said in 1976 that he intended to call elections in 1977 for the first parliamentary body since Congress was abolished under martial law. However, opening a World Peace Through Law conference in Manila on August 22, Marcos promised only to hold elections for local officials "not later than next year."

The conference focused criticism on the martial-law regime. Defending it, the chief justice of the Philippines, Fred Ruiz Castro, said it "has been imposed and administered here with a benignity and a grace that have confused and confounded both hostile and friendly observers." After the conference, Marcos released 500 martial-law prisoners, and he said that between 1972 and 1976, 64,500 detainees had been freed. The number arrested was not disclosed.

The U.S. Department of State reported to Congress in January that the Philippines was among countries violating human rights. The International Commission of Jurists reported on July 31 that it had found a failure to take "effective steps to prevent the use of torture" by security forces. The people were denied elected government, free speech and press, and habeas corpus, the report said, and Marcos was continuing martial law "to perpetuate the personal power of the president and his collaborators and to increase the power of the military to control Philippines society."

Marcos threatened to break military ties with the United States because of the State Department report, but throughout the year he showed sensitivity to U.S. criticism. After prolonged negotiations, agreement in principle on the continued U.S. use of Clark Air Force Base and Subic Bay Naval Station in the Philippines was announced in mid-November.   (HENRY S. BRADSHER)

PHILIPPINES

Education. (1973–74) Primary, pupils 7,964,332, teachers (1972–73) 247,551; secondary, pupils 1,911,530, teachers (1972–73) 45,594; vocational, pupils 110,879, teachers (1972–73) 12,378; higher, students 786,103, teaching staff (1972–73) 32,651.

Finance. Monetary unit: peso, with (Sept. 19, 1977) a free rate of 7.40 pesos to U.S. $1 (12.88 pesos = £1 sterling). Gold, SDR's, and foreign exchange (June 1977) U.S. $1,531,000,000. Budget (1976 actual): revenue 21,026,000,000 pesos; expenditure 23,266,000,000 pesos. Gross national product (1976) 129,610,000,000 pesos. Money supply (June 1977) 13,144,000,000 pesos. Cost of living (1970 = 100; June 1977) 230.

Foreign Trade. (1976) Imports 29,414,000,000 pesos; exports 18,696,000,000 pesos. Import sources: Japan 27%; U.S. 22%; Saudi Arabia 8%; Kuwait 6%. Export destinations: U.S. 36%; Japan 24%; The Netherlands 8%. Main exports: sugar 18%; coconut oil 12%; copper ores 10%; timber 8%; fruit and vegetables 7%; copra 6%.

Transport and Communications. Roads (1975) 112,870 km. Motor vehicles in use (1974): passenger 362,500; commercial (including buses) 247,300. Railways: (1974) 1,169 km; traffic (1975) 953 million passenger-km, freight 66 million net ton-km. Air traffic (1975): 2,580,000,000 passenger-km; freight 78.9 million net ton-km. Shipping (1976): merchant vessels 100 gross tons and over 457; gross tonnage 1,018,065. Telephones (Jan. 1976) 490,000. Radio receivers (Dec. 1974) 1,825,000. Television receivers (Dec. 1974) 711,000.

Agriculture. Production (in 000; metric tons; 1976): rice c. 6,439; corn c. 2,710; sweet potatoes (1975) c. 704; cassava (1975) c. 485; sugar, raw value 2,735; bananas c. 1,732; coffee c. 57; copra 2,600; tobacco c. 60; rubber c. 35; manila hemp (1975) c. 47; pork c. 397; timber (cu m; 1975) c. 30,435; fish catch (1975) 1,342. Livestock (in 000; March 1976): cattle c. 2,276; buffalo c. 5,280; pigs c. 9,700; goats c. 1,380; horses c. 310; chickens c. 51,000.

Industry. Production (in 000; metric tons; 1975): iron ore (metal content) 839; chrome ore (oxide content) 189; copper ore (metal content) 226; gold (troy oz) 502; silver (troy oz) 1,600; cement 4,351; petroleum products c. 8,790; sulfuric acid (1976) 280; coal (1976) 149; electricity (kw-hr) 12,359,000.

Photography

As an industry, still photography experienced an equivocal year, with sales of its products and services generally increasing despite lingering recessionary factors, but with profits mostly down. A few manufacturers, including Miranda, went out of business or, as in the case of GAF and Honeywell, removed themselves from the consumer photographic market. In its cultural aspects 1977 was not a vintage year either, some of the steam apparently having gone out of the boom for collecting photography. A number of galleries continued to thrive, but others struggled to survive or even failed, suggesting that at least a temporary saturation point had been reached. Some of the most interesting and successful photographic books and exhibitions dealt with photography's past. Among contemporary photographers experimentation continued — with a conceptual approach; with the creation of fantasy by collage, darkroom manipulation, and mixed-media effects; and with extensions of the snapshot aesthetic.

Cameras and Lenses. For many manufacturers of 35-mm single-lens-reflex (SLR) cameras, the year was one of coping with the challenge of Canon's AE-1, a competitively priced, highly automated design that proved quite successful following its introduction in 1976. Of particular interest among post-AE-1 models was Minolta's XD-11 (designated XD-7 in Europe and Japan), the first automatic-exposure SLR to reach the market with a choice of three modes of operation: shutter priority (the user preselects the shutter speed, and the lens opening is chosen automatically), aperture priority (the reverse situation), and manual control. A moderately compact camera, the new Minolta had an electronically governed shutter with speeds from 1 to 1/1,000 sec. A new series of MD Rokkor lenses was being made available for use in all modes; existing MC lenses could be used only in aperture-priority or manual modes.

Nikon introduced a compact 35-mm SLR, the FM, which used a mechanically governed version

Remarkably detailed life-size colour copies of art objects are the specialty of a room-sized camera invented by Polaroid Corp. founder Edwin H. Land. Basically a huge light-tight box, the device is equipped with a lens and a giant easel-like mechanism holding negative and positive print materials and developing chemicals common to Polaroid's conventional instant-colour process.

Polaroid inventor Edwin H. Land displayed his new instant motion picture system, Polavision, in April. The system develops pictures immediately after they are taken and projects them on a screen.

WIDE WORLD

of the new CCS (Copal compact shutter) with speeds of 1 to 1/1,000 sec plus B and provided semiautomatic exposure control with a selected-area, through-the-lens metering system utilizing two gallium photodiodes. The basic lens was a 50-mm Nikkor $f/2$ or $f/1.4$ in a new AI (automatic-indexing) mount that eliminated the necessity in previous models for rotating the aperture control to engage a prong that signaled the maximum aperture of the lens. The new mount allowed simple bayoneting of the lens to the camera. Also introduced were a modified Nikon F2 Photomic (the A) and a modified version of the Nikkormat ELW, redesignated the Nikon EL-2, both of which accepted the new line of AI-Nikkor lenses. The new lenses were fully compatible with old Nikon and Nikkormat cameras; non-AI lenses could be used in a stop-down mode with the new camera models or (in most cases) modified for full compatibility at modest cost by Nikon.

Possible harbinger of a new stage in camera automation was Konica's C35AF, the first still camera to provide automatic focusing. A modified version of the C35EF, this compact, nonreflex 35-mm camera incorporated Honeywell's Visitronic sensing and control module announced two years previously. Functioning on a rangefinder principle, the Visitronic device photoelectronically detected the distance of any subject located within a 12° central spot in the viewfinder. This information was conveyed by electronic and mechanical means to the lens mount, where it stopped the lens at the appropriate focusing position. The lens mount was powered by a spring that was tensioned each time the film was advanced. No provision for manual focusing was provided on this model, and the device could only focus on a centrally located subject, but its operation seemed effective with typical snapshot subjects. De-

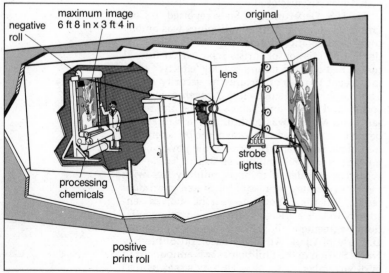

negative roll

maximum image 6 ft 8 in x 3 ft 4 in

original

lens

strobe lights

processing chemicals

positive print roll

COURTESY, POLAROID CORPORATION

signed as a point-and-shoot amateur camera, the C35AF had a 38-mm Konica Hexanon $f/2.8$ lens and provided full exposure automation with shutter speeds of 1/60, 1/125, and 1/250 sec.

An impressive addition to large-format equipment was the Hasselblad 2000FC SLR with a focal-plane shutter having a top speed of 1/2,000 sec and five new shutterless lenses, ranging from a 50-mm Zeiss Distagon $f/2.8$ to a 150-mm Zeiss Sonnar $f/2.8$ plus a Schneider 140–280-mm Variogon F $f/5.6$ zoom. The 2000FC also could be used with all older Synchro-Compur shuttered lenses.

Films and Papers. Advances in film technology during the year were potentially of major, long-range significance. Eastman Kodak, Sakura (manufactured by Konishuroku in Japan), and 3M Co. introduced ASA 400 colour negative films. Available in 110- and 35-mm formats (plus 120-size format from Kodak), these films provided the user with unprecedented freedom to expose colour negative film in low-light situations without flash.

Of considerable interest was the announcement and subsequent marketing of Polaroid's Polavision system, a new concept in motion pictures with possible applications to still-photography technology as well. The system consisted of a lightweight automatic camera, similar in size and operation to a conventional Super-8 camera; a film cassette containing a Super-8-size film yielding a little more than 2½ minutes worth of filming; and a Polavision player, which resembled a television set and projected the developed film onto a nearly 12-in diagonal screen for viewing by a small group in an undarkened room. The Polavision film incorporated technology developed by Edwin H. Land (*see* BIOGRAPHY) and associates over nearly 30 years. Based on an additive-colour concept, the film was processed, dried, and ready for projection within about 1½ minutes after the exposed cassette was plugged into the player, and only 12 drops of processing fluid were required.

Continuing its transition to E-6 processing of colour films, Kodak added three new "amateur" Ektachromes to its four previously introduced E-6 "professional" Ektachromes. The new films included Ektachrome 64 (daylight), Ektachrome 200 (daylight), and Ektachrome 160 (tungsten). Kodak also offered an Ektachrome Special Processing service that enabled the user to double the exposure rating of the latter two films.

In the field of printing papers, manufacturers were most active in modifying and enlarging lines of resin-coated (RC) material. However, some professionals and art photographers expressed concern over the cutback and threatened disappearance of esteemed fibre-based papers. In Great Britain, for example, Agfa discontinued sale of all its black-and-white materials including Brovira, a favourite of many serious printers.

Cultural Trends. In many ways 1977 was a year of rediscovering and reevaluating achievements of the past along with concern for contemporary work. For Great Britain in particular it was the year of pioneer photographer William Henry Fox Talbot, with many activities celebrating the centennial of his death including a "Sun Pictures" exhibition of calotypes recently made from original Talbot negatives. In Paris at that city's 32nd Salon of Photography an attractive exhibition was presented of little-known images by French documentarian Eugène Atget, printed by Pierre Gassmann from glass plates selected by Romeo Martinez from French archives. In New York City the International Center of Photography presented a major retrospective exhibition, simultaneous with the publication of a book of the photographs of Arthur Fellig, better known as "Weegee," who chronicled Manhattan fires, murders, high society, and Bowery low life during the 1940s.

Among other major exhibitions were Garry Winogrand's "Public Relations" at New York City's Museum of Modern Art, an ironic, sometimes amusing, sometimes biting comment on the reaction of Americans to public events; and Peter Beard's "The End of the Game," at the International Center of Photography, a collection of searing images dramatizing the destruction of African wildlife.

In photojournalism, Stanley Foreman of the *Boston Herald American* became the first photographer to win a Pulitzer Prize for photography two years in a row with his photograph of an American flag being used as a weapon during a demonstration in Boston. At the Pictures of the Year Competition co-sponsored by the University of Missouri School of Journalism and the National Press Photographers Association, the Newspaper Photographer of the Year award went to Bruce Bisping of the *Minneapolis Tribune*; Robert Madden of *National Geographic* was named Magazine Photographer of the Year. Top winner in the World Press Photo competition in Amsterdam was Françoise Demulder of Gamma (press agency).

Notable books of the year included Brassai's *The Secret Paris of the 30's*, depicting the seamier side of Paris after dark in the pre-World War II era; *After Ninety*, a collection of portraits by the late Imogen Cunningham; and *On Photography*, by Susan Sontag, a selection of essays severely critical of photography's artistic and social role in Western culture.

(ARTHUR A. GOLDSMITH)

See also Motion Pictures.
[628.D; 735.G.1]

KEYSTONE

This dramatic photomontage titled "Rivals," created by Wilfried Graf, was the winner of a photo contest sponsored by a West German publishing house.

Physics

Elementary Particles. For many years theoretical physicists have laboured to reduce the universe of matter into two sets of elementary particles: leptons (which include the electron, muon, and their associated neutrinos) and quarks (simple, point-like objects that were thought to constitute baryons—e.g., the proton and neutron—and mesons). Whereas the existence of leptons has been confirmed beyond doubt, experimental physicists have sought in vain for quarks. In 1977 it was not even clear what charge the quarks might carry; there were two schools of thought, one involving fractionally charged quarks that are not allowed to exist singly and a second in which free quarks with integral charge are allowed.

Since theoreticians were so confident of the existence of quarks, it was widely assumed that because they had not been experimentally observed, they do not exist singly and so must be fractionally charged. The value of charge was thought to be either $+\frac{2}{3}$ or $-\frac{1}{3}$ that of the proton. However, preliminary experimental evidence reported during the year indicated that quarks might well exist as free particles and be fractionally charged. The work was carried out by William Fairbank, Arthur Hebard, and George LaRue of Stanford University using a technique strongly reminiscent of one employed in 1911 by U.S. physicist R. A. Millikan. The original Millikan experiment measured the charge on the electron by observing the motion of very small drops of oil suspended against gravity in an electric field and assuming the oil drops possessed a multiple of the electronic charge.

Fairbank and co-workers made use of the perfectly diamagnetic properties of superconducting niobium to levitate tiny balls of the element in a magnetic field between electrically charged plates. After equal numbers of protons and electrons in the balls had been accounted for, two of eight balls tested retained a nonzero charge; their values were found to be about $+\frac{1}{3}e$ and $-\frac{1}{3}e$, in which e is the electronic charge. These two balls had been previously annealed on a tungsten plate, whereas five of the six showing zero charge had been annealed on niobium. It was not clear why free quarks should exist in tungsten that presumably migrated to the niobium balls during annealing, but not in niobium itself or in graphite, iron, and steel, which had also been tested by other experimenters. It was certain that much research activity in the near future would be devoted to reproducing these preliminary results.

Of the several different quarks thought to exist, one was differentiated by the property known as charm, a quantum number that must be conserved during any interaction among particles. The year was notable for a series of experimental results that all tended to confirm the existence of charm. Initially there was evidence in 1976 that electron-positron collision experiments at the Stanford (Calif.) Linear Accelerator Center (SLAC) had produced a meson that possessed charm. Since charm must be conserved in any such process, charmed particles should be produced in pairs, in which the second particle possessed a charm quantum number opposite to the first. This was confirmed by the energy threshold of the reaction, 3.9 GeV (billion electron volts), which was far in excess of the energy required to produce just one meson.

This result was quickly followed by experiments at the Fermi National Accelerator Laboratory (Fermilab) near Batavia, Ill., where high-energy photon beams directed at beryllium targets produced a new particle with a mass of 2.26 GeV, which was consistent with predictions for a charmed baryon. More recently SLAC experimenters observed charmed-meson decay and showed that parity (the equal likelihood of occurrence of a particle interaction and its mirror image) was not conserved during the decay process. Such behaviour was exactly what was required if a charmed quark was involved in the process.

Using a 400-GeV proton beam directed at metal targets, a collaboration of scientists at Fermilab observed an increase in the production of muon pairs at a combined mass of 9.5 GeV, suggesting that a particle which decayed into muons existed briefly at that mass. Called upsilon, the particle had about ten times the mass of the proton and, according to one interpretation of its nature, might contain yet another kind of quark with a unique quantum property. Subsequent evaluation of colliding-proton experiments at Fermilab also strongly supported the existence of the upsilon particle.

X-ray Lasers. During the year development of an X-ray laser, which would have particular application to crystallography and medical holography, progressed along two separate routes. The first involved the production of extreme ultraviolet radiation from a laser-created plasma, whereas the second took the gradual approach of reducing the output wavelength step-by-step by harmonic generation from an incident laser beam.

The plasma technique was employed by four

The first recorded track of a suspected charmed particle was captured in three-dimensional nuclear emulsion at the Fermi National Accelerator Laboratory near Batavia, Illinois, by a multinational collaboration of physicists.

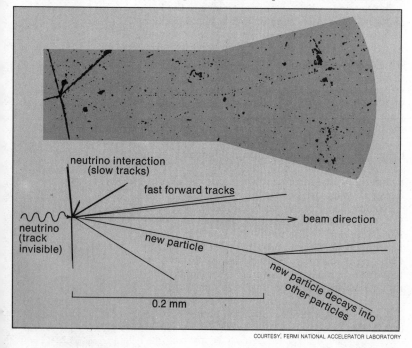

neutrino interaction (slow tracks)

fast forward tracks

beam direction

neutrino (track invisible)

new particle

new particle decays into other particles

0.2 mm

physicists of the University of Hull, England, to produce a population inversion at 182 Å (angstroms; 1 Å = 10^{-8} cm). They used a neodymium-glass laser giving a double-pulse output incident on a carbon fibre. The first pulse, or prepulse, produced a cold, dense plasma that filled the focal spot of the main laser pulse, which followed 200 picoseconds (2×10^{-10} second) later. Lasing action was observed by spectrograph to occur about 100 microns (1 micron = 10^{-6} m) from the fibre centre. R. J. Dewhurst and co-workers predicted that a workable laser could give a 1-millijoule (10^{-3}-joule) output using a carbon fibre. Shorter wavelength could be obtained by using targets of higher atomic number, but this demanded a higher density plasma and led into the problem of plasma confinement so familiar to fusion researchers.

The technique of harmonic generation was exploited by two groups. One, of the Imperial College, London, used a xenon excimer laser with output at 1,710 Å that was frequency-tripled in argon to produce laser output at 570 Å. Shortly afterward scientists of the U.S. Naval Research Laboratory and Colorado State University reported an output at 532 Å using a neodymium–yttrium-aluminum-garnet laser at 1.06 micron as parent. The laser was first frequency-doubled in potassium dihydrogen phosphate and then doubled again in potassium dideuterium phosphate. The resulting laser output at 2,661 Å was converted to the fifth harmonic, 532 Å, in a helium atmosphere. More recently the group reported obtaining the seventh harmonic of the 2,661 Å line, or 380 Å. Hence, the soft X-ray upper limit of 100 Å seemed within reach.

Time. In 1976 Robert Ehrlich of the State University of New York College at New Paltz suggested that time may well be quantized, with the quantum of time, the chronon (T_{ch}), being the lifetime of the rho meson. The mean lifetimes of the baryon and meson states that Ehrlich studied were all very close to integer multiples of the lifetime of the rho meson. This idea was supported during the year by F. Schwarz and P. Volk in West Germany, who showed that if Ehrlich was correct there should be a fundamental mass $m = h/(T_{ch}c^2)$, in which h is Planck's constant and c is the velocity of light. Using Ehrlich's value for T_{ch} produces a mass identical to the rest mass of the proton; *i.e.*, the rest mass of the heaviest stable elementary particle. The accuracy of four significant figures lent support to the idea that the smallest allowed time interval is $T_{ch} = 4.40 \times 10^{-24}$ second.

Superconductivity. The competing claims of magnetism and superconductivity in a particular material were probed during the year in work on ternary superconductors. Ternary (three-element) compounds in themselves were promising superconductors; for example, tin and lead compounds with molybdenum sulfide had high critical temperatures (15 K or −432° F) and high critical magnetic fields (50–70 tesla). However, the ternary series XRh_4B_4, in which X is a rare-earth element, was posing many problems. Investigating the rare-earth series, scientists from the University of California, San Diego, and Bell Laboratories found that, when X = Gd, Tb, Dy, or Ho, the

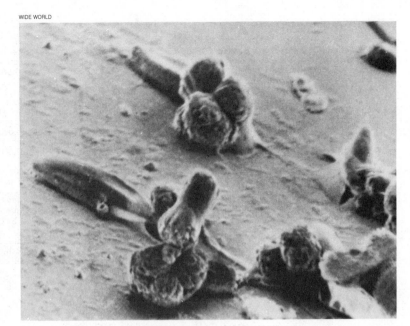

ternary compound is ferromagnetic at low temperature, but, when X = Er or Tm, the compound is a superconductor. $ErRh_4B_4$ was found to lose its superconductivity on cooling to 0.9 K, the first reported observation of such behaviour in an ordered superconductor.

Another ternary compound, $Gd_{1.2}Mo_6Se_8$, appeared to exhibit both antiferromagnetic ordering and superconductivity simultaneously below 3.5 K. Neutron confirmation of the magnetic ordering was eagerly awaited. (S. B. PALMER)

See also Nobel Prizes.
[111.H; 124.G.1; 125.D.8; 128.B.4]

Magnetic bacteria that are attracted by the south pole of a bar magnet were photographed through an electron microscope. Such bacteria had never before been observed.

Poland

A people's republic of eastern Europe, Poland is bordered by the Baltic Sea, the U.S.S.R., Czechoslovakia, and East Germany. Area: 312,677 sq km (120,725 sq mi). Pop. (1977 est.): 34,527,900. Cap. and largest city: Warsaw (pop., 1977 est., 1,463,-400). Language: Polish. Religion: predominantly Roman Catholic. First secretary of the Polish United Workers' (Communist) Party in 1977, Edward Gierek; chairman of the Council of State, Henryk Jablonski; chairman of the Council of Ministers (premier), Piotr Jaroszewicz.

In December 1976 important decisions to improve the supply of goods and services and step up housing construction were taken by the plenary session of the party Central Committee. There were three promotions in the party's key bodies. Stefan Olszowski, a member of the Politburo, passed his portfolio of foreign affairs to Emil Wojtaszek and was appointed a member of the party secretariat to carry out tasks connected with foreign policy, ideology, and information, and Alojzy Karkoszka, an economics expert, ceased to be deputy premier and joined the party secretariat. In April Zbigniew Zielinski, a member of the Central Committee, joined the party secretariat as head of the heavy industry department.

Poland

Pipelines:
see Energy; Transportation

Plastics Industry:
see Industrial Review

Poetry:
see Literature

Education. (1976–77) Primary, pupils 4,198,667, teachers 184,800; secondary, pupils 452,246, teachers 22,998; vocational (1975–76), pupils 1,879,575, teachers 74,554; teacher training, students (1975–76) 17,622, teachers (1971–72) 2,251; higher (including 10 main universities), students 491,030, teaching staff 49,892.

Finance. Monetary unit: zloty, with (Sept. 19, 1977) a basic rate of 3.32 exchange zlotys to U.S. $1 (5.90 exchange zlotys = £1 sterling), a commercial rate of 19.19 zlotys to U.S. $1 (33.40 zlotys = £1 sterling), and a tourist rate of 34 zlotys to U.S. $1 (59 zlotys = £1 sterling). Budget (1977 est.): revenue 940.1 billion zlotys; expenditure 869 billion zlotys.

Foreign Trade. (1976) Imports 46,145,000,000 exchange zlotys; exports 36,710,000,000 exchange zlotys. Import sources: U.S.S.R. 26%; West Germany 9%; East Germany 8%; U.S. 6%; Czechoslovakia 6%; France 6%; U.K. 5%. Export destinations: U.S.S.R. 30%; East Germany 10%; Czechoslovakia 8%; West Germany 6%. Main exports: machinery 44%; fuel and energy 18%; textiles and clothing 9%; chemicals 9%; food 7%.

Transport and Communications. Roads (1975) 297,822 km (including 139 km expressways). Motor vehicles in use (1975): passenger 1,077,700; commercial 425,000. Railways: (1975) 23,766 km (including 5,588 km electrified); traffic (1976) 42,800,-000,000 passenger-km, freight 130,956,000,000 net ton-km. Air traffic (1976): 1,426,000,000 passenger-km; freight 14,193,000 net ton-km. Shipping (1976): merchant vessels 100 gross tons and over 733; gross tonnage 3,263,206. Telephones (Dec. 1975) 2,578,-000. Radio licenses (Dec. 1975) 8,127,000. Television licenses (Dec. 1975) 6,472,000.

Agriculture. Production (in 000; metric tons; 1976): wheat c. 5,741; rye c. 6,914; barley c. 3,608; oats c. 2,696; potatoes c. 47,411; sugar, raw value c. 1,700; rapeseed c. 960; cabbages (1975) c. 1,440; onions c. 340; tomatoes c. 442; carrots (1975) c. 460; cucumbers (1975) c. 390; apples c. 841; tobacco c. 102; flax fibre (1975) c. 50; butter c. 253; cheese c. 364; hen's eggs c. 455; beef and veal c. 780; pork c. 1,793; timber (cu m; 1975) 21,820; fish catch (1975) 801. Livestock (in 000; June 1976): cattle 12,879;

pigs 18,853; sheep 3,430; horses (1975) 2,237; chickens c. 163,800.

Industry. Index of industrial production (1970 = 100; 1976) 181. Fuel and power (in 000; metric tons; 1976): coal 179,303; brown coal 39,302; coke (1975) 17,254; crude oil 460; natural gas (cu m) 5,963,000; manufactured gas (cu m; 1975) 7,337,000; electricity (kw-hr) 104,095,000. Production (in 000; metric tons; 1976): cement 19,808; iron ore (metal content; 1975) 376; pig iron 8,323; crude steel 15,641; aluminum 103; copper 270; lead 81; zinc 238; petroleum products (1975) 12,489; sulfuric acid 3,187; fertilizers (nutrient content; 1975) nitrogenous 1,533, phosphate 929; cotton yarn 219; wool yarn 106; manmade fibres 228; cotton fabrics (m) 948,000; woolen fabrics (m) 106,000; rayon and synthetic fabrics (m; 1975) 101,000; passenger cars (units) 216; commercial vehicles (units) 75. Merchant vessels launched (100 gross tons and over; 1976) 518,000 gross tons. New dwelling units completed (socialist sector; 1976) 211,000.

Poland was the last Eastern European country to formulate a final version of the 1976–80 five-year plan; the Sejm (parliament) passed it on Dec. 18, 1976. The delay was due in part to uncertainty about the future course of prices but mainly to prolonged debate within the key party bodies on the reallocation of investment funds among different branches of the national economy. The rate of investment was to be reduced from 32% of the national income in 1975 to 26% in 1980. Less would be invested in the machine-building sector, and the growth targets for 1980 were to be national income, industrial production, agricultural production, and real wages and rural incomes.

Short-term domestic difficulties coupled with a considerable trade deficit ($470 million in 1976 alone) highlighted the 1977 situation. According to Western sources, Poland's foreign debts amounted to about $10.5 billion at the end of 1976, and debt servicing reached 25% of hard-currency earnings. First Secretary Edward Gierek defended his "specific economic maneuver" of 1971–75. Assuming that prosperity in the West would continue, he had not hesitated to seek large foreign credits to buy plant for the long-overdue modernization of Polish industry. Because wages in Poland were lower than in the West and energy and raw materials were abundant and cheaper, it seemed reasonable to expect a competitive edge for Polish exports in Western markets. Unfortunately, recession, inflation, and unemployment in the West posed a dilemma. In November an agreement was signed in London providing for 22 ships and dockyard equipment to be built in British shipyards for a joint Polish-British Shipping Company.

Agriculture presented further problems. In 1976 Poland had suffered its third successive bad harvest. Cattle and pig numbers declined as a result of lack of fodder, although there was some increase after January 1977. Between 1970 and 1976 yearly imports of feedstuffs had risen from 2.7 million to 6.1 million tons, and poor weather and floods in 1977 would force Poland to import about 8 million tons of grain. Natural calamities, however, were only part of the reason meat was in short supply;

the other part was the need to export increasing quantities of foodstuffs, particularly meat.

During the year four heads of state visited Poland: Pres. Nicolae Ceausescu of Romania (May 17–19); the shah of Iran (August 22–26); King Baudouin of Belgium (October 10–14); and U.S. Pres. Jimmy Carter (December 29–31). Another prominent visitor was West German Chancellor Helmut Schmidt (November 21–25). Gierek visited East Germany, Czechoslovakia, France, Italy, and the Vatican, where on December 1 he was received in audience by Pope Paul VI.

(K. M. SMOGORZEWSKI)

Political Parties

The following table is a general world guide to political parties. All countries that were independent on Dec. 31, 1977, are included; there are a number for which no analysis of political activities can be given. Parties are included in most instances only if represented in parliaments (in the lower house in bicameral legislatures); the figures in the last column indicate the number of seats obtained in the last general election (figures in parentheses are those of the penultimate one). The date of the most recent election follows the name of the country.

The code letters in the affiliation column show the relative political position of the parties within each country; there is, therefore, no entry in this column for single-party states. There are obvious difficulties involved in labeling parties within the political spectrum of a given country. The key chosen is as follows: F—fascist; ER—extreme right; R—right; CR—centre right; C—centre; L—non-Marxist left; SD—social-democratic; S—socialist; EL—extreme left; and K—Communist.

The percentages in the column "Voting strength" indicate proportions of the valid votes cast for the respective parties, or the number of registered voters who went to the polls in single-party states.

[541.D.2]

Police:
see Crime and Law Enforcement

COUNTRY AND NAME OF PARTY	Affili-ation	Voting strength (%)	Parlia-mentary represen-tation
Afghanistan			
Presidential rule since July 17, 1973	—	—	—
Albania (October 1974)			
Albanian Labour (Communist)	—	99.9	250 (214)
Algeria (February 1977)			
National Liberation Front	—	99.95	261
Angola, People's Republic of			
Movimento Popular de Libertaçao de Angola (MPLA)	—	—	—
Argentina			
Military junta since March 24, 1976	—	—	—
Australia (December 1977)			
Liberal-Country	CR	...	86 (92)
Australian Democrats	C	...	0 —
Australian Labor	L	...	38 (35)
Austria (October 1975)			
Freiheitliche Partei Österreichs	R	5.4	10 (10)
Österreichische Volkspartei	C	42.9	80 (80)
Sozialistische Partei Österreichs	SD	50.4	93 (93)
Kommunistische Partei Österreichs	K	1.2	0 (0)
Bahamas, The (July 1977)			
Progressive Liberal Party	CR	55.0	30 (30)
Bahamian Democratic Party	L	...	5 (8)
Free National Movement	L	...	2 —
Vanguard Party	SD	...	0 —
Bahrain			
Emirate, no parties	—	—	—
Bangladesh			
Military government since Nov. 6, 1975	—	—	—
Barbados (September 1976)			
Democratic Labour	C	...	7 (18)
Barbados Labour	L	...	17 (6)
Belgium (April 1977)			
Front Démocratique Francophone } Rassemblement Wallon	R	7.0	15 (22)
Volksunie (Flemish)	R	10.1	20 (22)
Parti de la Liberté et du Progrès	CR	15.7	33 (33)
Parti Social Chrétien	C	36.0	80 (72)
Parti Socialiste Belge	SD	27.1	62 (59)
Parti Communiste Belge	K	2.7	2 (4)
Benin (Dahomey)			
Marxist-Leninist military government since Oct. 26, 1972	—	—	—
Bhutan			
A monarchy without parties	—	—	—
Bolivia			
Military junta since Nov. 9, 1974	—	—	—
Botswana (October 1974)			
Botswana Democratic Party	C	...	27 (24)
Botswana People's Party	L	...	2 (3)
Botswana National Front	EL	...	2 (3)
Brazil (November 1974)			
Aliança Renovadora Nacional (ARENA)	CR	...	199 (223)
Movimento Democrático Brasileiro (MDB)	L	...	165 (87)
Bulgaria (May 1976)			
Bulgarian Communist Party } Fatherland Front			272 (266)
People's Agrarian Union }	—	99.9	100 (100)
Nonparty }			28 (34)
Burma (February 1974)			
Burma Socialist Program Party	—	99.0	...
Burundi (October 1974)			
Tutsi ethnic minority government	—	—	—
Cambodia, People's Republic of (March 1976)			
People's Kampuchea Revolutionary Party	—	—	—
Cameroon (May 1973)			
Cameroonian National Union	—	...	120
Canada (July 1974)			
Social Credit	R	5.0	11 (15)
Progressive Conservative	CR	35.6	95 (107)
Liberal	C	42.9	141 (109)
New Democratic	L	15.6	16 (31)
Independents	—	...	1 (2)
Cape Verde Islands (June 1975)			
African Party for the Independence of Guinea-Bissau and Cape Verde (PAIGC)	—	84.0	56
Central African Empire			
Military government since Jan. 1, 1966	—	—	—
Chad			
Military government since April 13, 1975	—	—	—
Chile			
Military junta since Sept. 11, 1973	—	—	—
China, People's Republic of			
Communist (Kungchantang)	—	—	—
Colombia (April 1974)			
Partido Conservador	R	...	66 } (90)
Partido Liberal	C	...	113 }
Others		...	20 (72)
Comoro Islands (December 1974)			
Single party rule from Aug. 3, 1975	—	—	—
Congo			
Military government since Sept. 1968	—	—	—
Costa Rica (February 1974)			
Partido de Liberación Nacional	R	...	27 (32)
Partido de Unificación Nacional	C	...	16 (22)
Others (six parties)		...	8 (3)
Cuba (November 1976)			
Partido Comunista Cubano	—	...	481
Cyprus			
De facto partition in two parts	—	—	—
Czechoslovakia (October 1976)			
Communist Party of Czechoslovakia }			
Czechoslovak People's Party }			
Czechoslovak Socialist Party } — National			
Communist Party of Slovakia } Front	—	...	...
Slovak Freedom Party }			
Party of Slovak Revival }			
Denmark (February 1977)			
Conservative	R	8.5	15 (10)
Liberal Democratic (Venstre)	CR	12.0	21 (42)
Christian People's	CR	3.4	6 (9)
Progress (M. Glistrup)	C	14.6	26 (24)
Radical Liberal (Radikale Venstre)	C	3.6	6 (13)
Justice (Retsforbund)	C	3.3	6 (0)
Centre Democrats (E. Jakobsen)	L	6.4	11 (4)
Social Democrats	SD	37.0	65 (53)
Socialist People's	EL	3.9	7 (9)
Left Socialists	EL	2.7	5 (4)
Communists	K	3.7	7 (7)
Djibouti (May 1977)			
Ligue Populaire Africaine pour l'Indépendance (mainly Somali)	C	...	33
Front de Libération de la Côte des Somalis	L	...	30
Dominican Republic (May 1974)			
Partido Quisqueyano Demócrata	ER	...	...
Partido Reformista (J. Balaguer)	R	...	...
Partido Revolucionario Social-Cristiano	C	...	...
Partido Revolucionario Dominicano	L	...	...
Partido Demócrata Popular	L	...	...
Ecuador			
Military junta since Feb. 15, 1972	—	—	—
Egypt (November 1976)			
Arab { Social Democrats	—	...	12
Socialist { Egyptian Arab Socialists	—	...	336
Union { National Progressives	—	...	2
El Salvador (March 1976)			
Partido de Conciliación Nacional	R	...	52 (32)
Union Nacional de Oposición	C	...	0 (14)
Partido Popular Salvadoreño	L	...	0 (6)
Frente Unido Democrático Independiente	—	...	0
Equatorial Guinea			
Partido Único Nacional de los Trabajadores	—	—	—
Ethiopia			
Military government since 1974	—	—	—
Fiji (March-April 1977)			
Alliance Party (mainly Fijian)	—	...	24 (33)
National Federation (mainly Indian)	—	...	26 (19)
Others	—	...	2 —
Finland (September 1975)			
Conservative Party	R	18.4	34 (33)
Swedish People's Party	R	4.7	10 (11)
Centre Party (ex-Agrarian)	C	17.7	39 (35)
Liberal Party	C	4.4	9 (6)
Christian League	C	3.3	9 (4)
Rural Party	L	3.6	2 (5)
Social Democratic Party	SD	25.0	54 (55)
People's Democratic League	K	19.0	41 (37)
Others		4.0	2 (14)
France (March 1973)			
Union des Démocrates pour la République	R	31.3	185 (292)
Independent Republicans	CR	7.7	54 (61)
Centre Démocratie et Progrès	C	3.9	21 (33)
Other majority coalition	C	3.2	15 (0)
Radicals	L	3.8	12 (0)
Socialists	SD	21.9	89 (57)
Parti Socialiste Unifié	EL	0.3	3 (10)
Communists	K	20.6	73 (34)
Others	—	...	38 (3)
Gabon (February 1973)			
Parti Démocratique Gabonais	—	...	70
Gambia, The (April 1977)			
People's Progressive Party	C	...	29 (28)
United Party	L	...	2 (3)
German Democratic Republic (October 1976)			
Sozialistische Einheitspartei }			
Christlich-Demokratische Union }			
National-Demokratische Partei } National			
Liberal-Demokratische Partei } Front	—	99.9	500 (434)
Demokratische Bauerpartei }			
Germany, Federal Republic of (October 1976)			
Christlich-Demokratische Union	R	38.0	190 (177)
Christlich-Soziale Union	R	10.6	53 (48)
Freie Demokratische Partei	C	7.9	39 (41)
Sozialdemokratische Partei Deutschlands	SD	42.6	214 (230)
Deutsche Kommunistische Partei	K	0.3	0 (0)
Ghana			
Military government since 1972	—	—	—
Greece (November 1977)			
National Rally	R	6.82	5 (0)
New Democracy Party	CR	41.85	172 (215)
Democratic Centre Union	C	11.95	15 (57)
New Liberals (mainly in Crete)	C	1.08	2 (0)
Panhellenic Socialist Party	SD	25.33	93 (15)
Left Alliance (Eurocommunist)	EL	2.72	2 (6)
Greek Communist Party (pro-Moscow)	K	9.36	11 (5)
Others		0.89	— (2)
Grenada (December 1976)			
United Labour Party	L	...	9 (13)
People's Alliance (coalition parties)		...	6 (2)
Guatemala (March 1974)			
Partido Institucional Democrático } Movimiento de Liberación Nacional }	CR	41.2	...
Frente Nacional de Oposición } Partido Demócrata Cristiano }	C	35.7	...
Partido Revolucionario } Frente Democrático Guatemalteco }	L	23.1	...
Guinea (December 1974)			
Parti Démocratique de Guinéa	—	100.0	150

COUNTRY AND NAME OF PARTY	Affili-ation	Voting strength (%)	Parlia-mentary represen-tation
Guinea-Bissau (1975)			
African Party for the Independence of Guinea-Bissau and Cape Verde (PAIGC)	—	...	92
Guyana (July 1973)			
People's National Congress	C	...	37 (30)
People's Progressive Party	EL	...	14 (19)
Others	—	...	2 (4)
Haiti			
Presidential dictatorship since 1957	—	—	—
Honduras			
Military junta since Dec. 4, 1972	—	—	—
Hungary (June 1975)			
Hungarian Socialist Workers' Party	} Patriotic People's Front		
Young Communist League			
National Council of Women		97.6	352
Hungarian Federation of Partisans			
Federation of National Minorities			
Iceland (June 1974)			
Independence (Conservative)	R	42.7	25 (22)
Progressive (Farmers' Party)	C	24.9	17 (17)
Union of Liberals and Leftists	L	4.6	2 (5)
Social Democratic	SD	9.1	5 (6)
People's Alliance	K	18.3	11 (10)
India (March 1977)			
Janata (People's) Party and allies:			
Janata (including Jan Sangh, Opposition Congress, Swatantra, Samyukta, and Praja Socialist parties)	—	...	295 (53)
Akali Dal (Sikh Party)	C	...	9 (1)
Dravida Munnetra Kazhagam	R	...	1 (23)
Communist-Marxist (pro-Chinese)	K	...	22 (25)
Five other parties	—	...	14 (3)
Congress Party and allies:			
Congress	C	...	150 (350)
Anna Dravida Munnetra Kazhagam	R	...	19 —
Communist (pro-Soviet)	K	...	7 (23)
Four smaller parties	—	...	7 (9)
Four independent parties	—	...	14 (28)
Indonesia (May 1977)			
Sekber Golkar (Functional Groups)	—	62.1	232 (236)
United Development Party (merger of four Islamic parties)	—	29.3	99 (94)
Partai Demokrasi Indonesia (merger of five nationalist and Christian parties)	—	8.6	29 (30)
Iran (June 1975)			
Rastakhiz (National Resurgence) Party	—	52.0	268
Iraq			
Military and Baath Party governments since 1958	—	...	...
Ireland (June 1977)			
Fianna Fail (Sons of Destiny)	C	...	84 (69)
Fine Gael (United Ireland)	C	...	43 (54)
Irish Labour Party	L	...	17 (19)
Sinn Fein (We Ourselves)	L	...	0 (0)
Others	—	...	4 (2)
Israel (May 1977)			
Likud (Herut, Liberal Alignment, La'am, and Free Centre)	R	33.4	43 (39)
Torah Front (Agudat Israel and Poalei Agudat Israel)	CR	4.8	5 (5)
National Religious	C	9.2	12 (10)
Democratic Movement for Change	C	11.6	15 —
Independent Liberal	C	1.2	1 (4)
Civil Rights Movement	L	1.2	1 (3)
Labour Alignment (Mapam, Mapai, Rafi, and Achdut Ha'avoda)	SD	24.6	32 (51)
Democratic Front for Peace and Equality (pro-Soviet)	K	4.6	5 (4)
United Arab List	—	1.2	1 (3)
Others	—	8.0	5 (1)
Italy (June 1976)			
Movimento Sociale Italiano	F }	6.1	35 (56)
Partito di Unità Monarchica	R		
Partito Liberale Italiano	CR	1.3	5 (20)
Democrazia Cristiana	C	38.7	262 (267)
Partito Repubblicano Italiano	C	3.1	14 (15)
Partito Social-Democratico Italiano	L	3.4	15 (29)
Partito Socialista Italiano	SD	9.6	57 (61)
Democrazia Proletaria	EL	1.5	6 (0)
Partito Comunista Italiano	K	34.4	228 (179)
Südtiroler Volkspartei	—	0.5	3 (3)
Others	—	1.4	5 —
Ivory Coast (November 1970)			
Parti Démocratique de la Côte d'Ivoire	—	99.9	100
Jamaica (December 1976)			
People's National Party	L	...	48 (35)
Jamaica Labour Party	S	...	12 (18)
Japan (December 1976)			
Liberal-Democratic	R	41.8	249 (271)
Komeito (Clean Government)	CR	10.9	55 (29)
New Liberals	CR	4.2	17 —
Democratic Socialist	SD	6.3	29 (19)
Socialist	S	20.7	123 (118)
Communist	K	10.4	17 (38)
Independents and others	—	5.7	21 (16)
Jordan			
Royal government, no parties	—	—	60
Kenya (October 1974)			
Kenya African National Union	—	...	158 (171)
Korea, North (November 1977)			
Korean Workers' (Communist) Party	—	100.0	579

COUNTRY AND NAME OF PARTY	Affili-ation	Voting strength (%)	Parlia-mentary represen-tation
Korea, South (February 1973)			
Democratic Republican	CR	38.7	73
New Democratic	L	32.6	52
Democratic Unification	S	10.1	2
Independents	—	18.6	19
Kuwait			
Princely government, no parties	—	—	30
Laos, People's Democratic Republic of			
Lao People's Revolutionary Party	—	...	...
Lebanon (April 1972)			
Maronites (Roman Catholics)	—	...	30
Sunni Muslims	—	...	20
Shi'ite Muslims	—	...	19
Greek Orthodox	—	...	11
Druzes (Muslim sect)	—	...	6
Melchites (Greek Catholics)	—	...	6
Armenian Orthodox	—	...	4
Other Christian	—	...	2
Armenian Catholics	—	...	1
Lesotho			
Constitution suspended Jan. 30, 1970	—	—	—
Liberia (October 1975)			
True Whig Party	—	...	41
Libya			
Military government since Sept. 1, 1969	—	—	—
Liechtenstein (February 1974)			
Vaterländische Union	CR	...	7 (8)
Fortschrittliche Bürgerpartei	C	...	8 (7)
Christlich-Soziale Partei	C		0
Luxembourg (May 1974)			
Parti Chrétien Social	CR	28.0	18 (21)
Parti Libéral	C	22.1	14 (11)
Parti Ouvrier Socialiste	SD	29.0	17 (15)
Parti Social Démocratique	S	9.1	5 (6)
Parti Communiste	K	10.4	5 (6)
Madagascar (June 1977)			
Avant-garde de la Révolution Malgache	C	...	112
Parti du Congrès de l'Indépendance	L	...	16
Others	—	...	9
Malawi			
Malawi Congress Party	—	...	58
Malaysia (August 1974)			
Barisan Nasional (National Front, 12 mainly Malay parties)	—	61.6	120 (125)
Democratic Action Party (mainly Chinese)	L	...	9 } (19)
Pekemas (Social Justice Party)	K	...	1
Maldives			
Government by the Didi family	—	—	—
Mali			
Military government since Nov. 19, 1968	—	—	—
Malta (September 1976)			
Nationalist Party	R	48.7	31 (27)
Labour Party	SD	51.3	34 (28)
Mauritania (August 1971)			
Parti du Peuple Mauritanien	—	95.1	50
Mauritius (December 1976)			
Independence Party (Indian-dominated)	C	...	28 (39)
Parti Mauricien Social-Démocrate	L	...	8 (23)
Mauritius Militant Movement	K	...	34
Mexico (July 1976)			
Partido Revolucionario Institucional	CR	94.4	...
Partido Acción Nacional	C	...	...
Partido Auténtico de la Revolución Mexicana	L	...	...
Partido Popular Socialista	S	...	...
Partido Comunista Mexicano	K	...	...
Monaco (August 1970)			
Union Nationale et Démocratique	—	...	18
Mongolia (June 1977)			
Mongolian People's Revolutionary Party	—	99.99	336 (295)
Morocco (June 1977)			
Independents (pro-government)	CR	44.7	141 (159)
Popular Movement (rural)	CR	12.4	44 (60)
Istiqlal (Independence)	C	21.6	49 (8)
National Union of Popular Forces	L	14.6	16 (1)
Others	—	...	14 (12)
Mozambique, People's Republic of (1975)			
Frente da Libertaçao do Moçambique (Frelimo)	—	...	...
Nauru			
No political parties	—	—	—
Nepal			
Royal government since December 1960	—	—	—
Netherlands, The (May 1977)			
Christian Democratic Appeal (Anti-Revolutionaire Partij, Christelijk-Historische Unie, and Katholieke Volkspartij)	CR	31.9	49 (48)
Boerenpartij (Farmers' Party)	CR	0.8	1 (3)
Volkspartij voor Vrijheid en Democratie	C	18.0	28 (22)
Democrats 1966	C	5.4	8 (6)
Democratische-Socialisten '70	L	0.7	1 (6)
Partij van de Arbeid	SD	33.8	53 (43)
Communistische Partij van Nederland	K	1.7	2 (7)
Seventeen other parties	—	...	8 (15)
New Zealand (November 1975)			
National (Conservative)	CR	...	53 (31)
Labour Party	L	...	34 (56)
Nicaragua (September 1974)			
Partido Liberal Nacionalista (A. Somoza)	R	60.0	42 (35)
Partido Conservador de Nicaragua	R	...	11 (17)
Others	—	...	0 (1)
Niger			
Military government since April 17, 1974	—	—	—
Nigeria			
Military government since Jan. 15, 1966	—	—	—

COUNTRY AND NAME OF PARTY	Affiliation	Voting strength (%)	Parliamentary representation
Norway (September 1977)			
Høyre (Conservative)	R	24.7	41 (29)
Kristelig Folkeparti	CR	12.1	22 (20)
Senterpartiet (Agrarian)	C	8.6	12 (21)
Venstre (Liberal)	C	3.2	2 (1)
New People's Party	C	1.7	0 } (2)
Party of Progress	C	1.9	0 }
Arbeiderpartiet (Labour)	SD	42.5	76 (62)
Sosialistisk Venstreparti (Socialist Left)	S	4.1	2 } (16)
Kommunistiske Parti	K	0.4	0 }
Oman			
Independent sultanate, no parties	—	—	—
Pakistan			
Military government since July 5, 1977	—	—	—
Panama			
No-party assembly of "corregidores"	—	—	—
Papua New Guinea (1972)			
United Party	...	...	40
Pangu Party (M.T. Somare) } National	...	...	24
People's Progress Party } coalition	...	...	12
National Party	...	...	12
Paraguay (February 1977)			
Partido Colorado (A. Stroessner)	R	69.0	...
Opposition parties	—	31.0	...
Peru			
Military junta since Oct. 3, 1968	—	—	—
Philippines			
Martial law since Sept. 23, 1972	—	—	—
Poland (March 1976)			
Polish United Workers' Party } Front of			255 (255)
United Peasants' Party } National	—	99.4	117 (117)
Democratic Party } Unity			39 (39)
Nonparty			49 (49)
Portugal (April 1976)			
Centro Democrático-Social	CR	15.9	41 (16)
Partido Popular-Democrático	C	20.0	71 (80)
Partido Socialista	SD	35.0	106 (116)
União Democrática Popular	EL	1.7	1 (5)
Partido Comunista Português	K	14.6	40 (30)
Eight other parties	—	...	0 (0)
Qatar			
Independent emirate, no parties	—	—	—
Rhodesia (August 1977)			
Rhodesian Front (European)	R	85.0	50 (50)
Rhodesian Action Party	—	9.0	— —
National Unifying Force	—	6.0	— —
Romania (March 1975)			
Communist-controlled Socialist Unity Front	—	99.9	349
Rwanda (July 1975)			
National Revolutionary Movement	—	—	—
San Marino (September 1974)			
Partito Democratico-Cristiano	CR	...	25 (27)
Partito Social-Democratico	SD	...	9 (11)
Partito Socialista	S	...	8 (7)
Partito Comunista	K	...	15 (14)
Others	—	...	3 (1)
São Tomé and Principe (1975)			
Movimento Libertaçao	—	—	—
Saudi Arabia			
Royal government, no parties	—	—	—
Senegal (January 1973)			
Union Progressiste Sénégalaise	CR	99.9	100
Parti Démocratique Sénégalais	L	...	0
Seychelles			
People's United Party (alone in power after the June 5, 1977, coup)	—	—	—
Sierra Leone (May 1977)			
All People's Congress	CR	...	70 (84)
Sierra Leone People's Party	L	...	15 ...
Singapore (December 1976)			
People's Action Party	CR	...	69 (65)
Six opposition parties	—	...	0 (0)
Somalia			
Somalian Revolutionary Socialist Party	—	—	—
South Africa (November 1977)			
Herstigte Nasionale Partij	ER	3.2	0 —
National Party	R	64.8	134 122
South African Party	CR	1.7	3 —
New Republic Party	C	11.8	10 —
United Party	C		— 41
Progressive Federal Party	L	16.7	17 —
Progressive Reform Party	L	—	— 7
Others	—	...	— 1
Vacant	—	...	1 —
Spain (June 1977)			
Alianza Popular	R	8.1	16
Unión Centro Democratico	CR	34.3	165
Partido Socialista del Pueblo	L	4.3	6
Partido Socialista Obrero Español	SD	28.5	118
Partido Comunista Español	K	9.0	20
Catalans (two parties)	—	...	13
Basques (two parties)	—	...	9
Independents	—	...	3
Sri Lanka (July 1977)			
United National Party	R	...	139 (19)
Freedom Party	C	...	8 (91)
Tamil United Liberal Front	C	...	17 (12)
Lanka Sama Samaja (Trotskyists)	K	...	0 (19)
Communists (pro-Soviet)	K	...	0 (7)
Others	—	...	2 (18)
Sudan			
Military government since 1969	—	—	—
Surinam (November 1977)			
National Party Alliance (H. Arron)	—	...	24 (22)
United Democratic Party (J. Lachmon)	...	...	15 (17)
Swaziland			
Royal government, no parties	—	—	—
Sweden (September 1976)			
Moderata Samlingspartiet (ex-Höger)	R	15.6	55 (51)
Centerpartiet (ex-Agrarian)	CR	24.1	86 (90)
Folkpartiet (Liberal)	C	11.0	39 (34)
Socialdemokratiska Arbetarepartiet	SD	42.9	152 (156)
Vänsterpartiet Kommunisterna	K	4.7	17 (19)
Others	—	1.7	0 —
Switzerland (October 1975)			
Christian Democrats (Conservative)	R	20.6	46 (44)
Republican Movement	R	3.0	4 (7)
Evangelical People's	R	2.0	3 (3)
National Action (V. Oehen)	R	2.5	2 (4)
Swiss People's (ex-Middle Class)	CR	10.1	21 (23)
Radical Democrats (Freisinnig)	C	22.2	47 (49)
League of Independents	C	6.2	11 (13)
Liberal Democrats	L	2.3	6 (6)
Social Democrats	SD	25.4	55 (46)
Socialist Autonomous	EL	1.3	1 (0)
Communist (Partei der Arbeit)	K	2.2	4 (5)
Others	—	2.2	0 —
Syria (August 1977)			
National Progressive Front (dominated by Baath Party)	—	...	159
Others	—	...	36
Taiwan (Republic of China)			
Nationalist (Kuomintang)	—	...	773
Tanzania (October 1975)			
Tanganyika African National Union	C	93.2	218
Zanzibar Afro-Shirazi (nominated)	L		52
Thailand			
Military dictatorship since Oct. 6, 1976	—	—	—
Togo			
Military government since 1967	—	—	—
Tonga (June 1972)			
Legislative Assembly (partially elected)	—	—	21
Trinidad and Tobago (September 1976)			
People's National Movement (E. Williams)	C	...	24 (36)
Democratic Action Congress	—	...	2
United Labour Front	L	...	10
Tunisia (November 1974)			
Parti Socialist Destourien	—	99.0	112 (101)
Turkey (June 1977)			
National Action (A. Turkes)	ER	6.4	16 (3)
National Salvation (N. Erbakan)	R	8.6	24 (48)
Turkish Justice (S. Demirel)	CR	36.9	189 (149)
Democratic	C	1.8	1 (45)
Republican Reliance (T. Feyzioglu)	C	1.9	3 (13)
Republican People's (B. Ecevit)	L	41.4	213 (185)
Others	—	...	4 (7)
Uganda			
Military dictatorship since Jan. 25, 1971	—	—	—
Union of Soviet Socialist Republics (1974)			
Communist Party of the Soviet Union	—	99.8	767
United Arab Emirates			
Federal government of seven emirates			
United Kingdom (October 1974)			
Conservative	R	35.8	276 (296)
Liberal	C	18.3	13 (14)
Labour	L	39.3	319 (301)
Communist	K	...	0 (0)
Scottish National Party	—	...	11 (7)
United Ulster Unionists	—	...	10 (11)
Plaid Cymru (Welsh Nationalists)	—	...	3 (2)
Others	—	...	3 (4)
United States (November 1976)			
Republican	CR	...	143 (144)
Democratic	C	...	292 (291)
Upper Volta			
Military government since Feb. 8, 1974	—	—	—
Uruguay			
Rule by Council of State as of June 1973	—	—	—
Venezuela (December 1973)			
Cruzada Cívica Nacional	ER	4.3	7 (21)
Unión Republicana Democrática	R	3.2	5 (17)
COPEI (Social Christians)	C	30.2	64 (57)
Acción Democrática	L	44.3	102 (68)
Movimiento al Socialismo	SD	5.3	9 (10)
Fuerza Democrática Popular	S	1.2	2 (5)
Movimiento Electoral del Pueblo	EL	5.0	8 (27)
Partito Comunista Venezolano	K	1.2	2 (5)
Others (four parties)	—	...	4 —
Vietnam, Socialist Republic of (April 1976)			
North: Lao Dong (Communist Party)	K	...	249
South: National Liberation Front			243
Western Samoa			
No political parties	—	—	—
Yemen, People's Democratic Republic of			
National Liberation Front	—	—	—
Yemen Arab Republic			
Military government since June 13, 1974	—	—	—
Yugoslavia (May 1974)			
Communist-controlled Federal Chamber	—	...	220
Zaire (November 1975)			
Mouvement Populaire de la Révolution	—	98.0	420
Zambia (December 1973)			
United National Independence Party	—	80.0	125

(K. M. SMOGORZEWSKI)

Portugal

Portugal

A republic of southwestern Europe, Portugal shares the Iberian Peninsula with Spain. Area: 91,-632 sq km (35,379 sq mi), including the Azores (2,335 sq km) and Madeira (796 sq km). Pop. (1976 est.): 9,694,100, excluding about 550,000 refugees (mostly from Africa). Cap. and largest city: Lisbon (pop., 1976 est., 847,300). Language: Portuguese. Religion: Roman Catholic. President in 1977, Gen. António dos Santos Ramalho Eanes; premier, Mário Soares.

The voting pattern of the legislative elections of April 1976 was confirmed in the municipal elections of December 1976. The Socialist Party (PSP) maintained its position as the leading party, but in an overall minority position. The other parties retained percentages of the vote similar to those obtained in April, with the exception of the Communist Party, which rose from 14.4 to 17.7%. After the December elections, Premier Mário Soares pursued his strategy of declining to form a coalition government, partly because of fears that this might endanger the PSP's own political unity and also because of ideological and personal differences with the other parties which might have imposed restrictions on executive decisions.

Since taking office, one of Soares' chief aims had been to restore confidence abroad, badly shaken by the confusion of developments since the April 1975 elections. Late in February 1977, after seven months in office, his government introduced a package of austerity measures, designed to tackle the major problems posed by the balance of payments deficit, inflation (at 30%), and unemployment (about 15% of the working population). On February 25 the escudo was devalued by 15% against the European Unit of Account, taxes and interest rates were raised, and price controls were introduced on 16 staple items. Strict import quotas were also introduced, and surcharges of 30–60% were imposed on the import of many items.

In an extended parliamentary session that lasted until July, the PSP tried to obtain the support of the other parties for much-needed legislation. By June, when the normal session ended, many of the most important measures (including the amended agrarian reform plan, compensation for nationalization, revision of the budget, and local government and labour laws) were still in committee awaiting the necessary support to be canvassed from the opposition. The Christian (CDS) and Social-Democrat (PSD) parties agreed to cooperate with the government in return for legislative concessions and regular consultations, and the Communists (PCP) gave their support on several measures with a view to stopping formation of a right-wing coalition. Thus, by the end of July, most legislation had been passed, except for a medium-term economic plan and a law on worker participation, which went back to Parliament to be debated in October. However, Soares owed his survival in office to the selective support of the opposition, and it was clear that they might not support him when Parliament reconvened.

The costs of the extended session proved high to the Socialists in other respects. The compromises opened up political splits within the party, leading to the resignation of the ministers for agriculture and foreign affairs. In October it was reported that Fraternidad Obrera, with 300 militants, had been expelled from the party, while the Socialists' appeal to their constituency was reduced by their swings in policy. The session also hardened opposition attitudes. Both the PCP and the CDS were alienated by the Agrarian Reform Law (passed by Parliament on August 10); the left, because of its loss of power, and the right, because the amended law did not offer enough compensation. There remained only the PSD, whose leader, Francisco Sá Carneiro, resigned on November 8 after a disagreement with the party's left wing over his refusal to negotiate a coalition with either the Socialists or the Communists.

As it became clear that the austerity package of February was not producing the desired effect, the authorities announced a further set of measures on August 25, including a 1% "crawling" depreciation of the escudo, another general round of raising interest rates and energy prices to encourage saving, and stronger import quotas. It was reported that by August the trade deficit had doubled from its 1976 level and that the government was coming under pressure from the International Monetary Fund to follow a more restrictive and conservative financial policy. A promised U.S. $750 million loan from the Organization for Economic Cooperation and Development depended largely on the outcome of negotiations with the IMF on a second slice of a standby $50 million credit.

The agricultural sector became the focus of a struggle between the PCP and the authorities. The leader of the PCP, Alvaro Cunhal, promised that the return of land to its former owners would encounter resistance. However, the presence of the National Guard maintained order, if not peace. There were violent clashes in southern Portugal and, in September, the simultaneous bombing of the Agrarian Reform Institutes in Lisbon and in central and southern Portugal. The PCP and the farm labourers' unions denied responsibility for the bombings, but the records of land seizures and the farming cooperatives' accounts were reportedly destroyed, thus delaying the proposed land reform, perhaps for years. The need for some form of coherent land-utilization policy was pressing, however. Over 50% of human and animal feedstuffs was being imported, at a cost of some $3 million a day.

In October, in an effort to restore some confidence in the authorities' ability to run the economy, Pres. António Eanes appointed a commission to report to him, including João Salgueiro, head of the Banco de Fomento and a junior minister in the Caetano government. The commission would put the president in a strong position to intervene in economic management.

After several weeks of political maneuvering, during which the CDS and PSD refused to support Soares' program of additional austerity measures unless they were given a role in government and Soares maintained his opposition to forming a coalition, the premier called for a vote of confidence on December 6. It was uncertain until the last minute whether the Communists would support the government, but when the vote was finally taken in the early hours of December 8, after a 44-hour debate, Soares received the votes of only 100 Socialist deputies, as against 159 for the opposition. With no break in the deadlock among the parties in sight, President Eanes, on December 28, asked Soares to try to form a new government, although he was not actually picked as premier designate.

(MICHAEL WOOLLER)

See also Dependent States.

Prisons and Penology

The year opened dramatically with the execution of Gary Gilmore at the Utah state prison on January 17—the first execution in the U.S. since 1967. There was worldwide comment because of the special nature of the case (Gilmore, a convicted murderer, had resisted efforts to save him) and the extraordinary degree of publicity that surrounded

the execution when it was finally carried out. Legislation introduced or adopted in some states, such as Oklahoma, provided for the death penalty to be carried out by intravenous injection on the ground that it was more humane than other methods. However, some doctors opposed a procedure that, initially, would appear similar to the anesthesia required for potentially lifesaving surgery.

A Harris Poll carried out in February showed that two out of three Americans were in favour of capital punishment. In June, however, the U.S. Supreme Court held that a state must not make the death penalty mandatory. In the same month Jérome Carrein, a child-murderer, was guillotined in France despite Pres. Valéry Giscard d'Estaing's "profound aversion" to capital punishment. This was only the second execution since he had assumed office, and it occurred after a long series of controversial life sentences and presidential reprieves. A third execution, of a 28-year-old Tunisian convicted of murdering a woman friend, took place in September.

Crime and violence continued to increase almost everywhere, as documented in numerous reports and in such academic studies as Sir Leon Radzinowicz' and Joan King's *The Growth of Crime* (1977). Small, closely knit communities often had been able to develop effective social controls. But many of the conditions of modern life—the population explosion, rapid technological and social change, the growth of large cities, the physical and psychological distance between administrators and administered (mentioned in the report on violence published by the French Ministry of Justice in July), unemployment, and the fact that expectations had risen faster than available resources—precluded such controls and may well have contributed to the rising crime rate. This meant that penal systems were under greater pressure than ever.

Escapes from overcrowded prisons in Italy, at one time running at the rate of one every 19 hours, were again prevalent. One escaped prisoner, holding a family of five hostage, demanded that the pope volunteer to take the place of the children. In May the Italian Cabinet approved measures to combat attacks on judicial officers and interference with the process of law. Three months later, over 900 terrorists and other dangerous prisoners were transferred to two island fortress prisons.

Proposals for similar moves were turned down by the inspector general of prisons for England and Wales in a report concerning the riot at Hull prison the previous year. It was thought preferable to continue mixing relatively small numbers of potentially violent prisoners with other less dangerous ones. Given sufficient and experienced staff, this would permit the necessary control and yet retain humane conditions. An amnesty, also mooted in Italy, was criticized as a way of avoiding overdue reforms. In Spain the government did announce an amnesty for certain political prisoners. The remaining inmates, notably in Madrid's Carabanchel prison, rebelled, resenting the fact that mere thieves and robbers were being kept in while others, some of whom had killed, were being released.

Prisons and Penology

Five hundred inmates of Madrid's Carabanchel prison took over the prison roof and demanded improved conditions and an extended amnesty program. The mutiny later spread to other prisons in Spain.

Many countries tried new ways of dealing with less serious offenders in the community. But while these measures helped to reduce the pressure on penal institutions and were cheaper than detention, they proved no more effective than imprisonment in preventing relapse into further crime. They also forced the prisons to deal with a higher concentration of more difficult offenders.

There were signs of a reversal of this policy of decarceration. The Canadian province of Alberta, for example, had done away with custodial treatment for juveniles, but the increase in crime among this age group was such that reintroduction of penal institutions for roughly 150 hard-core culprits was being examined. In various international penological conferences, such as that held at the University of Kent at Canterbury, England, by the Howard League for Penal Reform to mark the bicentenary of the publication of John Howard's *The State of the Prisons*, the debate about the purpose of imprisonment particularly and punishment generally continued.

For some time the notion of rehabilitation had been under attack by the general public, which disliked the idea of being "soft on criminals." (*See* Special Report.) Now it was being criticized by penologists as well. They saw indeterminate sentences and treatment designed to modify criminal behaviour as conceivably leading to longer detention than might otherwise have been the case. Apart from the fact that this conflicted with basic ideas of justice, it was a luxury that could not be afforded at a time when institutions were already overextended.

These so-called antirehabilitative ideas were brought together most clearly in the concept of "humanistic deterrence," as expounded by Philip Bean of the University of Nottingham, England. This concept implied that attempts to make offenders better persons ought not to be the business of the penal system. Deprivation of liberty should result only from decisions arrived at openly in a court of law. The length of any sentence should be determined there and then and should be subject to clear rights of appeal. Sentences ought to be as short as was compatible with all the circumstances, but there should be as little subsequent interference by the executive as possible.

This, however, would mean the virtual disappearance of any form of conditional release and would make it difficult to adapt treatment forms to new circumstances that might arise during the sentence. Certain kinds of special treatment did give good results, some penologists argued, though precise assessment was difficult. Experience also showed that there were prisoners who could not survive long sentences without the aid of treatment experts, such as clinical psychologists, to combat periods of apathy and depression. And who could seriously argue against the acquisition of new social skills or better self-control?

Penologists agreed that when crime is on the increase, society's response has usually been to look to tougher sanctions. But history showed that severity of punishment did not itself reduce crime. At the beginning of the 19th century, more than 200 offenses, some of them very minor, had been punishable by death in England, yet crime flourished. Even attempts to deter future wrongdoing by demonstrating the severity of punishment were unlikely to be very effective. In 1977 such an attempt was made at Rahway state prison in New Jersey, where long-term prisoners told budding young lawbreakers of the misery of their existence. Yet 160 years earlier, when pickpockets were publicly executed in England in an attempt to deter would-be criminals by example, the very crowds engrossed in watching the grisly spectacle had their purses regularly removed by long-fingered thieves. (HUGH J. KLARE)

See also Crime and Law Enforcement; Law.
[521.C.3.a; 543.A.5.a; 10/36.C.5.b]

CHANGING ATTITUDES TOWARD CRIMINALS

by Richard Whittingham

In the early months of 1977, four men in Saudi Arabia were convicted of rape. In other parts of the world—or for that matter even in Saudi Arabia a few years ago—the four would ordinarily have been sent to prison for a certain number of years and eventually been paroled or otherwise released back into society. Not so with these four. Three of the men were married, compounding their crime of rape with that of adultery; they were buried to their waists in sand and slowly stoned to death. The unmarried man, guilty of just the single crime of rape, was simply beheaded.

Saudi Arabia is only one of a number of Middle Eastern countries that are radically changing their attitudes toward criminals by reinstating the harsh punishments prescribed in the Koran. Thus, convicted thieves now find that they may have a hand cut off, and death may be the punishment for a variety of crimes that would not normally be looked upon as deserving of capital punishment. The Saudi Arabi-

ans and other Middle Easterners have decided that the milder ways of Western justice have not worked as deterrents to crime there; they believe that the old "eye-for-an-eye" system, replete with death sentences, dismemberments, and public punishment, will work better.

A New Hard Line. The countries of the Middle East may be somewhat extreme in their approach to judicial punishment, but they are certainly not the only nations where attitudes toward criminals are being altered and redefined. While the Saudis were putting to death their four convicted rapists, Gary Gilmore, in a circuslike atmosphere in Utah, faced a firing squad and became the first person to be executed for a crime in the United States in more than ten years. At the same time a number of states rushed to readapt and reinstitute their death penalty laws in conformance with the U.S. Supreme Court rulings on the subject in 1976. And a recent (1976) Gallup Poll showed that more than 65% of those polled in the U.S. preferred to have an operative death penalty.

Capital punishment, however, is not the only area where people are seeking to harden the line taken with criminals. Petty thieves, drug pushers, and even the so-called white-collar criminals have begun to feel the effects of a sterner attitude, one that wants the convicted criminal off the street and in prison.

Horror story after horror story of dangerous criminals sent back into society on bail or parole from a penitentiary or (in many cases) release from a mental institution to commit further crimes have forced people to say that enough is enough. The consensus seemed to be that there must be no repetition of such situations as the one described by *Chicago Sun-Times* columnist Roger Simon in a Sept. 4,

Richard Whittingham is the author of numerous books, including Martial Justice: The Last Mass Execution in the United States *(1971).*

A prisoner crouched in front of a religious judge before being flogged by soldiers in Saudi Arabia.

FRED PEER—CAMERA PRESS/PHOTO TRENDS

1977, article about a man who had just been convicted of a particularly despicable crime:

> He had been arrested at least 22 times before. He had killed a man with a knife and been given probation. While on probation he had beaten his wife twice and been charged with battery. He made bail, got into a bar fight and put 90 stitches in a man's head. He was charged with aggravated assault and made bail again.
>
> While on this bail, he attacked the cab driver. He was charged with aggravated kidnapping, deviate sexual assault, armed violence and armed robbery. . . .

Permissive Era. The new attitude is, of course, a reaction to such situations. Violent crime—murder, rape, assault, armed robbery—rose rapidly in the 1950s and 1960s. At the same time, a prevailing attitude of protection and permissiveness regarding criminals and prisoners developed. Rehabilitation was the keynote in the treatment of convicted criminals. "Punishment" was a word *not* to be used in relation to the incarceration of prisoners. Human and civil rights were the considerations to be reckoned with in the handling of arrested persons. The Miranda and Escobedo cases of the mid-1960s (the rights of suspects and the warnings that must be given to them before questioning) often caused policemen and prosecuting attorneys to feel that they were dealing with a visiting dignitary rather than a thug who had just beaten up a little old lady while attempting to steal her purse.

Not only was it difficult to get a criminal into the courtroom, it was also problematic whether he would be sentenced adequately once he was there. There was often a distinct reluctance on the part of the courts to put convicted criminals in jail or at least to put them there for very long.

Rehabilitation Policy Questioned. Crime continued to escalate in the early 1970s, but as it did the view taken of it by various authorities and people in general changed decidedly. In 1975 Robert Martinson, a sociologist, published the results of a study he had made in New York regarding the rehabilitation of prisoners. Among the conclusions he drew: "The prison which makes every effort at rehabilitation succeeds no better than the prison which leaves its inmates to rot. . . . The certainty of punishment, rather than the severity, is the most effective crime deterrent. We should make plain that prisons exist to punish people for crimes committed."

In California another study, from the Rand Corporation, also suggested that keeping habitual criminals locked up would do more to reduce crime than any rehabilitation efforts. Despite treatment or preventive measures, habitual criminals commonly go back to crime after they are released from prison, the study showed. In addition, the study found that deterrence to crime was in direct proportion to the relative certainty of going to jail after being caught.

Even the U.S. Supreme Court was affected, and several of its decisions in the last few years (*Harris* v. *New York*, 1971; *Michigan* v. *Mosley*, 1975; *Oregon* v. *Mathiason*, 1977) substantially eroded what was often viewed as the "overprotection" of suspects' rights. The Miranda and Escobedo decisions were not reversed, but they were perhaps no longer the sacred pronouncements they once had been.

The result of these changing attitudes has been that more convicted criminals have been going to jail. In 1976 the U.S. prison population reached an all-time high, and it is increasing steadily; even more significantly, it grew by more than 33,000 convicts in that year, the largest annual increase on record. As this was taking place, violent crime in the United States was declining, the first decrease since the mid-1950s. This provided corroboration, in the view of many penologists, that the certainty of prison can serve as a deterrent to crime.

Lessening of Guilt. Although violent crime was on the downgrade, other types of criminal activity remained at a high level. The most striking example of this was the flagrant disregard for law and order during the New York City blackout of 1977. People looted with abandon, stealing everything from expensive cars off automobile showroom floors to an entire storeful of prayer shawls and Bibles. Newspaper and magazine reporters interviewed many of the looters, who explained simply and almost universally that they did it because everybody else in the country was stealing something—especially the rich and the politicians—and therefore they were just getting their rightful share.

Sociologists point out that one of the principal reasons for this attitude is that people in the U.S. have been exposed to premeditated crime on the highest levels of government in recent years. Bribery, political corruption, and efforts to subvert justice by those sworn to uphold it have become increasingly common. This has contributed to the growth of a national "lessening-of-guilt" feeling about crime, an attitude that worries many jurists and behavioural scientists.

The changing attitudes toward punishment in the U.S. have raised a new question. With more people being put in prison generally for longer periods of time, are the nation's prison systems prepared to handle the new influx of offenders? Everything—investigations, studies, statistics—points to the fact that they are not. The prisons today throughout the U.S. are overcrowded, underequipped, and inadequately staffed even to handle the present prison population, much less a fast-rising one. Thus, the solution to one problem, deterring violent crime, spotlights another, the need for additional facilities and manpower to run the penal systems.

Publishing

With the review conference on the Helsinki agreements on security and cooperation in Europe in progress in Belgrade, Yugos., during the latter part of the year, the free flow of information was an issue that commanded much attention in 1977. Western publishers were moderately encouraged by the first Moscow International Book Fair as a Soviet gesture toward greater openness, but since the Helsinki accords were signed in 1975, sales of Western newspapers in Eastern Europe appeared to have risen only marginally. Nor was the issue solely an East-West one. The less developed countries continued to complain, through UNESCO and in other forums, of the handling of third world news by Western news agencies, and they pressed for a "new information order" as essential for achieving a new international economic order. On the other hand, delegates to the annual general assembly of the International Press Institute (IPI) in Oslo, Norway, in June criticized UNESCO for its efforts to replace the free flow of information by a so-called balanced flow.

The IPI assembly expressed "grave concern at the increasing harassment and persecution of the press . . . particularly in Latin America, Asia, and Africa." Notable among the actions of individual countries was the South African government's banning, in October, of *The World*, which had been almost the sole source of information from within black townships. UNESCO, for its part, formed a commission to examine press freedom in all UN member countries, headed by Sean MacBride, winner of the Nobel (1974) and Lenin (1977) peace prizes, which held its first meeting in December.

Newspapers. It was a remarkable year for the press in Britain. Leading business entrepreneurs vied for a share of the supposedly ailing national newspaper business, while laws long unused were invoked by private individuals to put magazine editors in fear of prison sentences. In one instance the same entrepreneur was bidding with one hand and prosecuting with the other.

The main target for bids was Beaverbrook Newspapers Ltd., publishers of the *Daily Express*, *Sunday Express*, and the London-area *Evening Standard*. In the 1950s the *Daily Express* had been the leader of modern popular journalism in Britain, but it failed to change with the times, and a combination of rising costs, increased competition, and shrinking readership produced a steady slide of sales and profitability. The last three years had seen some desperate changes of editor and style, but sales in mid-1977 were down to 2.5 million and the group's profitability had disappeared. Lord Beaverbrook's heirs, the Aitken family, started a desperate hunt for solutions, which included the possible sale of their empire to their great rivals, Associated Newspapers Ltd., owners of the *Daily Mail* and London *Evening News*.

Known, invited, or rumoured bidders included several of the parties who, less than a year earlier, had been seeking control of *The Observer*, including Australian newspaper magnate Rupert Murdoch (*see* BIOGRAPHY) and an alliance of Sir James Goldsmith, Anglo-French head of Cavenham Foods Ltd. and Générale Occidentale SA, and "Tiny" Rowland of the multinational conglomerate Lonrho Ltd. But on June 30 Nigel Broackes's Trafalgar House property group, whose interests included the Cunard shipping line but no publishing, emerged as the winner. The group's chief executive, Victor Matthews (*see* BIOGRAPHY), gave the papers three years to become profitable. (See *Magazines*, below.)

For the rest of Fleet Street there was less drama but continuing anxiety. The *Daily Mail* continued to build up circulation, but failure to win Beaverbrook gave Associated Newspapers Ltd. no respite from its own problems, including the ailing *Evening News*. Nearly every national daily was taken off the streets at some time by strike action. Early in the year publishers and printing union leaders had worked out a scheme for bringing in labour-saving, cost-cutting techniques while making orderly arrangements for retraining, retirement, and layoffs. The plan was rejected by the workers, however, and managements were left to negotiate piecemeal with their own staffs.

Labour troubles disrupted the press elsewhere in Europe. In Denmark, Copenhagen's leading daily, the 228-year-old *Berlingske Tidende*, ceased publication on January 31 for over four months because of a dispute over work schedules and new technology. In France a 29-month strike against

The final edition of the *Long Island* (New York) *Press* bade farewell to its readers on March 25.

Profits:
see Economy, World

Protestant Churches:
see Religion

Psychiatry:
see Health and Disease

World Daily Newspapers and Circulations, 1976–77[1]

Location	Daily newspapers	Circulation per 1,000 population	Location	Daily newspapers	Circulation per 1,000 population
AFRICA			**ASIA**		
Algeria	4	17	Afghanistan	17	...
Angola	4	13	Bangladesh	21	4
Benin	1	0.3	Burma	7	11
Botswana	1	20	Cambodia	17	10
Cameroon	3	6	China	392	...
Central African Empire	1	0.3	Cyprus	12	123
Chad	4	0.4	Hong Kong	107	346
Congo	3	1	India	822	16
Egypt	14	21	Indonesia	170	...
Equatorial Guinea	1	4	Iran	28	25
Ethiopia	7	2	Iraq	7	17
Gabon	1	1	Israel	25	180
Ghana	4	38	Japan	180	374
Guinea	1	1	Jordan	4	22
Guinea-Bissau	1	12	Korea, North	11	...
Ivory Coast	3	10	Korea, South	30	125
Kenya	3	8	Kuwait	6	86
Lesotho	1	1	Laos	8	...
Liberia	1	2	Lebanon	37	...
Libya	3	...	Macau	7	...
Madagascar	12	...	Malaysia	31	89
Malawi	2	2	Mongolia	1	75
Mali	2	...	Nepal	26	...
Mauritius	11	117	Pakistan	93	...
Morocco	7	14	Philippines	13	18
Mozambique	5	9	Saudi Arabia	11	11
Niger	2	0.5	Singapore	12	239
Nigeria	19	...	Sri Lanka	15	33
Réunion	1	46	Syria	5	9
Rhodesia	3	15	Taiwan	31	...
Senegal	2	...	Thailand	15	20
Seychelles	2	41	Turkey	450	...
Sierra Leone	2	9	Vietnam	29	8
Somalia	1	...	Yemen (Aden)	2	7
South Africa	24	...	Yemen (San'a')	6	10
Sudan	4	...	Total	2,648	
Tanzania	3	...			
Togo	1	3			
Tunisia	5	35			
Uganda	2	3	**EUROPE**		
Upper Volta	1	0.2			
Zaire	6	...	Albania	2	48
Zambia	2	21	Austria	30	308
Total	180		Belgium	58	...
			Bulgaria	14	238
			Czechoslovakia	29	288
			Denmark	50	341
			Finland	60	450
NORTH AMERICA			France	103	220
			Germany, East	40	452
Antigua	1	4	Germany, West	411	404
Bahamas, The	3	159	Gibraltar	2	173
Barbados	1	98	Greece	105	107
Belize	1	29	Hungary	29	266
Bermuda	1	211	Iceland	5	429
Canada	117	227	Ireland	10	246
Costa Rica	6	97	Italy	79	126
Cuba	16	...	Liechtenstein	1	325
Dominican Republic	10	43	Luxembourg	7	365
El Salvador	12	...	Malta	6	...
Guadeloupe	2	72	Netherlands, The	93	311
Guatemala	11	...	Norway	80	412
Haiti	7	21	Poland	44	237
Honduras	7	...	Portugal	32	91
Jamaica	3	90	Romania	32	170
Martinique	2	77	Spain	115	97
Mexico	249	...	Sweden	112	540
Netherland Antilles	5	197	Switzerland	97	385
Nicaragua	6	42.3	U.S.S.R.	650	323
Panama	6	76	United Kingdom	134	...
Puerto Rico	4	114	Vatican City	1	...
Trinidad and Tobago	3	131	Yugoslavia	25	87
United States	1,762	283	Total	2,456	
Virgin Islands (U.S.)	2	152			
Total	2,237				
			OCEANIA		
SOUTH AMERICA			American Samoa	1	166
			Australia	58	386
Argentina	167	...	Cook Islands	1	48
Bolivia	14	25	Fiji	2	...
Brazil	280	39	French Polynesia	3	...
Chile	45	...	Guam	1	183
Colombia	36	69	New Caledonia	1	62
Ecuador	22	41	New Zealand	37	317
French Guiana	1	26	Niue	1	60
Guyana	2	71	Papua New Guinea	1	8
Paraguay	11	...	Total	106	
Peru	67	...			
Surinam	3	...			
Uruguay	30	...			
Venezuela	47	...	Grand total	8,352	
Total	725				

[1]Only newspapers issued four or more times weekly are included.
Sources: UN, *Statistical Yearbook 1976* (1977); *1977 Editor & Publisher International Year Book* (1977); *Europa Year Book 1977, A World Survey*; various country publications.

the right-wing *Le Parisien Libéré*, whose proprietor, Émilien Amaury, died in January (*see* OBITUARIES), ended in August; using nonunion labour, it had often been the only paper not touched by widespread sympathy strikes against it.

The year brought Paris two additional newspapers, but one proved short-lived. *Le Matin de Paris* (later shortened to *Le Matin*), a new left-wing daily tabloid, was launched by Claude Perdriel, publisher of the successful weekly *Le Nouvel Observateur*. Former Gaullist minister Joseph Fontanet's afternoon paper *J'Informe* ceased publication after only three months, during which it was said to have been losing the equivalent of $6,000 a day. Fontanet had hoped to capture the conservative readership felt to be unhappy with the leftward swing of *Le Monde*. This swing brought problems within *Le Monde* itself in November, when staff expressed their unhappiness at what was seen as support by the paper for the Baader-Meinhof terrorist group in West Germany. In June the other leading serious French newspaper, *Le Figaro*, also experienced staff eruptions, when its editor in chief, Jean d'Ormesson, and its political director, Raymond Aron, resigned to protest interference by the proprietor (since 1975), Robert Hersant.

In Italy, Piero Ottone resigned after five years as editor of the influential Milan-based *Il Corriere della Sera*, to be replaced by a former news editor, Franco Di Bella. The move was taken to indicate a conservative swing. In August the Rome-based English-language newspaper, the *Daily American*, closed, but three months later a new one, the *International Daily News*, was launched, with a print order of 40,000 copies. (PETER FIDDICK)

In the U.S. total daily circulation, which had slipped to a ten-year low in 1976, rose by 0.5% to 60,977,011, according to the 1977 *Editor & Publisher International Yearbook*. Evening circulation fell 0.1% to 35,118,625, but morning circulation increased by 1.4% to 25,858,386. The total number of daily newspapers rose by 6 to 1,762, the highest number since 1973. According to the McCann-Erickson, Inc., advertising agency, newspaper advertising revenues amounted to $11.1 billion, 12% over the previous year.

One factor in the improved economic picture was the introduction by many newspapers of regular supplements devoted to coverage of entertainment, fashion, food, home furnishings, and other nonnews subjects. Papers as large as the *New York Daily News* (circulation two million) and as small as the *Albuquerque* (N.M.) *Journal* (75,000) launched such "life-style" supplements, often with resulting increases in readership. At the *New York Times* average daily circulation rose by 33,000 within months after the paper introduced the first of three such weekly supplements. Despite the popularity of these magazine-like inserts with readers and advertisers, however, some journalists saw the trend as a retreat from serious news coverage.

A related and equally controversial trend was a growing use by publishers of outside consultants to help reorganize and restyle the content of newspapers. Typically, the consultants made their recommendations after extensive polling to determine what features were most popular with readers, and in many cases the result was less news and more self-help features and entertainment listings. By 1977 most major U.S. dailies were said to have hired news consultants for one reason or another.

Despite the overall health of the industry, there were a few notable casualties. The *National Observer*, one of the few general interest newspapers circulated nationwide, was discontinued by its owner, Dow Jones & Co., Inc., after 15 years of successive losses. The Newhouse chain folded its *Long Island* (N.Y.) *Press*, founded in 1820. In other major transactions, Rupert Murdoch paid more than $30 million to buy the *New York Post* from its longtime owner, Dorothy Schiff. Capital Cities Communications, Inc., a Manhattan-based owner of broadcast stations, magazines, and small newspapers, bought the Kansas City Star Co., publisher of the local *Star* and *Times*, for $125 million, thought to be the highest price ever paid for a one-city newspaper group.

The Federal Trade Commission (FTC) picked the *Los Angeles Times* as its initial target in a move to outlaw volume rate discounts to major advertisers, a standard practice at U.S. dailies. The FTC charged that volume discounts systematically discriminate against smaller advertisers, but publishers feared the FTC action, if sustained, could drive large advertisers to other media. A federal court of appeals ordered the government to draw up rules forbidding a newspaper from owning a broadcast station in the same city. The ruling, which was appealed to the U.S. Supreme Court, would affect as many as 64 U.S. newspapers.

Continuing a trend of recent years, Pulitzer Prizes for 1977 emphasized "investigative reporting." The Pulitzer Gold Medal for Public Service went to the *Lufkin* (Tex.) *News* for a series of articles and editorials inquiring into the death of a 20-year-old Lufkin man at a Marine Corps training camp. Other investigative reporters to win Pulitzers were Margo Huston of the *Milwaukee* (Wis.) *Journal* for a series of articles on nursing homes and health care for the elderly, and Acel Moore and Wendell Rawls, Jr., of the *Philadelphia Inquirer* for an investigation into conditions at a local hospital for the criminally insane. Walter Mears of the Associated Press won a prize for his coverage of the 1976 presidential election campaign, syndicated columnist George Will was cited for his commentary, and Paul Szep received an award for his editorial cartoons in the *Boston Globe*. For the first time no award was given for international reporting. Nor was an award made for fiction, though Alex Haley (*see* BIOGRAPHY) received a special Pulitzer for his best-selling *Roots*.

Two investigative reporting efforts seemed certain to provoke continuing controversy, though both came too late for any 1977 awards. One was a year-long inquiry into organized crime in Arizona by Investigative Reporters and Editors, Inc., headed by Robert Greene (*see* BIOGRAPHY). The other was an article by former *Washington Post* staff writer Carl Bernstein in *Rolling Stone* in which he claimed that over the past 25 years at least 400 U.S. journalists worked directly or informally for the CIA. (DONALD MORRISON)

With newspapers on strike in Copenhagen, Denmark, readers were forced to get their news from wall posters.

Magazines. The major development in Britain was the £20 million takeover of Morgan-Grampian Ltd., a large and profitable publisher of mainly specialist and industrial magazines, by Trafalgar House, less than five months after the latter had acquired the Beaverbrook newspaper group. This created a potential rival for the International Publishing Corp. (IPC) group. Morgan-Grampian was already moving further into the consumer fields, having bought the independent *Over 21* women's monthly and, in 1977, used it as a base for an English version of *Weight Watchers*, as well as launching *Hi-Fi Weekly* into a crowded market.

One of the more interesting phenomena in magazine publishing was the activity of Sir James Goldsmith. In addition to his unsuccessful bid for Beaverbrook Newspapers, he purchased, in February, a 45% interest in Jean-Jacques Servan-Schreiber's *L'Express*, the French weekly news magazine. Meanwhile, he was still pursuing his criminal and civil libel actions against *Private Eye*, the British satirical magazine, its publishers, printers, and distributors. On May 16 the private prosecution was dropped and a not guilty verdict ordered, and the civil actions were settled by an apology and payment of £30,000 costs by the magazine.

In another widely publicized legal case, *Gay News* was faced with a private prosecution for blasphemous libel, the first for 55 years, in an action initiated by antipornography campaigner Mary Whitehouse (*see* BIOGRAPHY). The cause was a poem, by a professor of English, about a homosexual Roman centurion's feelings toward Christ. The magazine was fined £1,000, and its editor, Denis Lemon, fined £500 and given a suspended nine-month jail sentence.

Prima, a women's magazine launched in 1976, folded in September 1977, but in March IPC began its own new monthly, *Woman's World*. There was upheaval at the English original of Bob Guccione's *Penthouse* empire. He dispatched a U.S. director to sack the editor and half the staff because English *Penthouse* looked "tatty." (PETER FIDDICK)

The most dramatic story in the U.S. was the takeover of Clay S. Felker's *New York* magazine, *New West*, and the *Village Voice* by Rupert Murdoch after an involved financial imbroglio. Six months later, the *New York Times* noted: "One press lord taketh away from Felker, but another helpeth to restore." In August Felker purchased *Esquire* with financial backing from one of Murdoch's British newspaper competitors.

In Cincinnati, Ohio, Larry Flynt (*see* BIOGRAPHY), publisher of the comparatively hard-core pornographic magazine *Hustler*, was found guilty of "pandering obscenity." The case came four years after the U.S. Supreme Court ruled that local juries must decide what is obscene for their own communities. A Cincinnati jury found *Hustler* obscene and sentenced Flynt to 7 to 25 years in prison. He appealed immediately. Meanwhile, the circulation of *Hustler* increased to more than two million.

In the words of a writer for *U.S. News and World Report*, "trivia, gossip, sex and leisure currently make up the 'hot' subjects for today's magazines." Popular titles, such as *People* and its carbon copy, *Us*, were strong on photographs and celebrities, short on editorial material. Both *People* and *Us* were doing well. One good effect was the rebirth of photojournalism, and not since the early days of *Life* had there been such interest in photography and magazine format. Still, there were millions of serious readers. Circulation of major magazines, among them nonpicture types, had risen from 147 million in 1950 to close to 260 million in 1977.

Most of this increase had been in specialized journals, and approximately 300 new consumer and business magazines began publishing in 1977, the majority appealing to special interest groups. There were *Skateboard World* and *Moped Biking*, while *Nuestro* served the special needs of Latinos in the U.S. Among the less esoteric titles were *Human Nature*, a takeoff on *Psychology Today*, with a newsstand price of $1.75 a copy, and *Quest*, featuring lively photographs for the whole family, at $2 a copy. *Horizon* changed to a soft-cover format, at $2.50 a copy.

While average magazine prices hovered around $1, the increased reliance of publishers on subscribers and newsstand purchases was expected to nudge prices up in 1978. The Magazine Publishers Association noted that the percentage of magazine revenue from circulation had risen from 30% in 1966 to 50%. Publishers saw this as a healthy development, making them less dependent on advertisers. Significantly, almost 50% of the total sales of consumer magazines were at supermarkets and related outlets.

The general magazine improved its economic position in 1977. According to an estimate by the U.S. Department of Commerce, revenues would increase 10 to 15% over 1976, itself a good year. At the same time, publishers continued to find ways to meet the challenge of higher production costs and postal rates. One cost-saving trick was to switch to lighter paper and to a smaller page size. Another, still to be thoroughly explored, was to go around the post office. *Reader's Digest,* for example, delivered three million copies by special home delivery in 1976. Publishers believed that by 1980 some 25 to 50% of their subscriptions might be delivered by alternative postal means.

(WILLIAM A. KATZ)

Books. INTERNATIONAL DEVELOPMENTS. Implementation of the U.S. Copyright Act of 1976 on Jan. 1, 1978, was expected to have a powerful effect on other national and international copyright laws, and new legislation was foreseen in several countries, including Australia, the U.K., Canada, and West Germany. In anticipation of full implementation of the human rights provisions of the 1975 Helsinki agreements on security and cooperation in Europe, international publishing circles campaigned vigorously for freedom to publish throughout the world. The International Publishers Association successfully interceded on behalf of two Argentine publishers who had been imprisoned. More than 50 countries participated in the first Moscow International Book Fair, held September 6–14, an initiative that reflected a Soviet wish to expand book circulation in the U.S.S.R. The fair was a success from the standpoint of sales and copyright purchases, in the participation of Soviet writers and public, and as a demonstration of at least relative freedom of expression.

At the 77th annual convention of the American Booksellers Association (ABA), held May 28–31 in San Francisco, representatives of non-U.S. publishers—from Australia, Canada, France, Japan, The Netherlands, the U.K., and West Germany—attended for the first time. In the future the ABA convention would be an international event.

The Frankfurt (West Germany) Book Fair, held October 12–17, once again attracted extraordinary interest. Seventy-five countries were represented, with more than 4,500 publishers and 300,000 titles. Copyright dealings were at the usual high level, with increased participation by less developed countries. Among titles on offer that drew keen interest were film star Greta Garbo's memoirs. Two notable aspects were the substantial scientific output from Brazil and the growing interest of Arab countries in publishing. Although China was not represented as it had been in 1976, Japanese and U.S. publishers' missions that visited China in 1977 were assured that the new Chinese government would be making substantial purchases of books and rights from other countries.

For British publishers 1976 was a good year for exports, with sales rising from £139 million to £175 million and exports rising from 40.48% to 43.15% of turnover. As domestic inflation matched the dramatic decline in the value of the pound sterling, British books became more attractive to importers, many of whom made large currency profits.

In the British home market, which increased from £204 million to £231 million, there was probably some decline in unit sales. There were indications, however, that the effects of public spending cuts were not fully felt in 1976 and that pressure on budgets would be more acute in 1977–78. Publishers of academic books were particularly concerned that this could have a severe effect on already shortening print runs and could further inflate prices of specialized books.

There was a surprisingly small decrease in the number of titles published in the U.K. in 1976. School textbooks suffered the most significant drop, from 2,099 titles to 1,622. Increases were recorded in medical science, plays, poetry, and religion and theology.

In Australia a crucial event was the publication at the end of December 1976 of the report of the Copyright Law Committee on Reprographic Reproduction (the Franki report), which showed a disturbing bias in favour of copyright users and against the interests of copyright owners. At its annual meeting in March 1977 the Australian Book Publishers' Association (ABPA) condemned the report outright, suggesting that implementation of its recommendations could lead to the destruction of Australian scholarly and educational publishing. All interested parties subsequently held discussions with the Australian attorney general's department, and no legislation was introduced during the year to amend the Australian Copyright Act.

The first major results of the consent decree that abolished the so-called British Traditional Market Agreement surfaced in 1977. Colleen McCullough's best-seller *The Thorn Birds* was published simultaneously in Australian and U.S. editions, and a British publisher bought the rights exclusive of the Australian and New Zealand markets. To counterbalance this kind of problem, four U.K. publishers, previously only represented in Australia, established Australian companies and joined the ABPA.

(MARTIN BALLARD; ANDREW FABINYI; JOSEPH A. KOUTCHOUMOW)

UNITED STATES. For U.S. book publishers and retailers 1977 was a banner year. The Carter administration ended its first year in office with appropriations for education, including book and library programs, at slightly higher levels than in 1976. Book sales for the first ten months of 1977 increased in all categories, and retailers looked forward to a record-breaking Christmas season, with gains of 10–40%. Industry sales in 1976 rose 8.7% to $4,185,000,000, which represented a new high and a better-than-average annual gain over the past several years.

Net sales of books in all categories during January–October 1977 were ahead of those in the same period of 1976, according to the Association of American Publishers. Adult trade hardcover book sales were up 11.7%; adult trade paperbacks rose 22.2%; juvenile hardcovers rose 11.2%; and juvenile paperbacks increased 7.5%. A slight increase of 0.1% in university press hardcovers; a 16.5% advance in university press paperbacks; and a 5.3% increase in college textbooks were also registered. Double-digit increases were the lot of all categories including Bibles, testaments, and hymnals; mass market paperbacks; book clubs; mail-order publications; technical, scientific, medical, and business books; and elementary and high school textbooks.

The largest gains for 1976 were in mass market paperbacks, 16.6%; mail order publications, 24.7%; book clubs, 13.1%; professional books, 11.5%; and subscription-reference books, 11%. Trade book sales increased 4.4% in 1976; this included adult hardcovers, with a 5.6% gain, and adult trade paperbacks, up 5.9%. Only two categories showed a decline in sales, and both were slight —0.5%. These occurred in the industry's elementary and secondary division, the largest segment of publishers' dollar receipts.

The overall U.S. book title output for 1976 declined 10.1% in new books and approximately 12.2% in new and revised editions, for a total drop of about 10.7%. Publishers produced 35,141 titles in 1976, of which 26,983 were new books and 8,158 were new editions. The 1975 total book output

For avid readers, the 29th Frankfurt Book Fair had 300,000 books on display from some 4,500 publishing houses worldwide.

KEYSTONE

was 39,372, of which 30,004 were new books and 9,368 were new editions. The decline in number of published titles occurred in all subject categories except history and agriculture.

Two former U.S. presidents commanded substantial fees for their political memoirs. Richard M. Nixon's still uncompleted memoirs were purchased in 1974 by Warner Books; Warner bought worldwide rights and in 1977 found a hardcover publisher, Grosset & Dunlap. The price of the original rights was estimated at about $2 million. Former president Gerald R. Ford and Betty Ford contracted to write separate memoirs under a joint program with Harper & Row and Reader's Digest Association, Inc. Industry estimates put the price of the contracts at about $1 million.

One of the fastest selling hardcover books in publishing history was J. R. R. Tolkien's *The Silmarillion*, a fantasy whose unprecedented groundswell of demand caused its publisher, Houghton Mifflin, some consternation. More than one million copies were printed and sold in a period of two and a half months. Tolkien books were also the vanguard of Christmas best-sellers for most retailers. A $30 edition of Tolkien's *The Hobbit* from Abrams, with illustrations based on an animated NBC television special, was possibly the most expensive fiction title ever to hit a national best-seller list.

Among the major mergers of the year was the acquisition of Fawcett Publications, one of the last family-run publishing giants, by CBS. The transaction, which involved an estimated $50 million in cash, was one of the largest of its kind in publishing history. Fawcett was one of the larger mass market paperback publishers, and CBS already owned other publishing businesses, including the hardcover firm Holt, Rinehart and Winston and Popular Library, a paperback publisher.

(DAISY MARYLES)

See also Literature.
[441.D; 543.A.4.e]

Qatar

Qatar

An independent emirate on the west coast of the Persian Gulf, Qatar occupies a desert peninsula east of Bahrain, with Saudi Arabia and the United Arab Emirates bordering it on the south. Area: 11,400 sq km (4,400 sq mi). Pop. (1975 est.): 180,-000. Capital: Doha (pop., 1975 est., 130,000). Language: Arabic. Religion: Muslim. Emir in 1977, Sheikh Khalifah ibn Hamad ath-Thani.

Qatar's constitutional future was settled with the emir's decree of May 31, 1977, appointing his son Maj. Gen. Sheikh Hamad ibn Khalifah ath-Thani, commander in chief of the armed forces, to the newly created posts of crown prince and minister of defense.

Economic expansion continued at a high level, with imports continuing to rise rapidly. Development expenditure in the 1977 budget amounted to $1.6 billion, with the main emphasis on electricity, education, housing, and health. There was continued concern over the need to diversify. Plans were laid to expand the cement and liquid

---

QATAR
 Education. (1974–75) Primary, pupils 20,152, teachers 1,068; secondary, pupils 6,985, teachers 620; vocational, pupils 190, teachers 46; teacher training, students 307, teachers 47.
 Finance. Monetary unit: Qatar riyal, with (Sept. 19, 1977) a free rate of 3.93 riyals to U.S. $1 (6.85 riyals = £1 sterling). Gold, SDR's, and foreign exchange (Dec. 1976) U.S. $118.6 million. Budget (1975 actual): revenue 7,135,000,000 riyals; expenditure 5,302,000,000 riyals.
 Foreign Trade. (1976) Imports 3,290,400,000 riyals; exports 8,683,400,000 riyals. Import sources (1975): U.K. 21%; Japan 15%; U.S. 13%; West Germany 9%. Export destinations (1975): U.K. *c.* 18%; U.S. Virgin Islands *c.* 17%; France *c.* 11%; Italy *c.* 7%; West Germany *c.* 6%; Thailand *c.* 6%. Main export crude oil 96%.
 Industry. Production (in 000; metric tons): crude oil (1976) 23,534; petroleum products (1975) 171.

gas industries to serve the whole Gulf region, but a project to enlarge the oil refinery to 150,000 bbl a day was scaled down to 50,000 bbl a day, which would serve Qatar's needs only. On February 9 agreement was reached with Royal Dutch-Shell for the takeover of its remaining 40% share in Shell Co. of Qatar; compensation was reported to be $23.8 million.

Qatar was actively engaged in mediation to end the two-tier price system within the Organization of Petroleum Exporting Countries. At the Afro-Arab summit conference in Cairo in March, Qatar pledged $77 million to African states. In March the emir issued a decree establishing Qatar's first university.

(PETER MANSFIELD)

Race Relations

The year saw widespread deterioration in racial and ethnic relations in many areas of the world. Human rights figured largely on the international agenda but were often infringed in practice. A tendency to ethnic separatism was also noted.

Europe. In Western European countries the influence of ultraleft groups, visible in strikes, demonstrations, and street violence that were widely reported in the media, remained stronger than that of the fragmented neo-Nazi or fascist groups. In London major confrontations took place during a National Front march and antiracialist counterdemonstration at Lewisham and at Notting Hill's annual black street carnival. To a large degree, Britain's antiwhite and antipolice subculture had its roots in widespread youth unemployment, especially among blacks. The number of coloured Commonwealth immigrants fell slightly, and birth statistics showed that West Indian and Asian women were having fewer children, thus conforming to the usual demographic pattern for Western urban societies. By 1976 Britain's estimated population of New Commonwealth and Pakistani origin was 1,771,000, or 3.3% of the total. The new Commission for Racial Equality replaced the Community Relations Commission and the Race Relations Board.

In Western Europe most of the problems were nationalistic rather than racial. The post-Franco regime in Spain restored the ancient Catalan

Generalitat, but military extremists in the three Basque provinces were still active despite a partial amnesty. In France Breton extremists continued active, and there was strong support for autonomy in Corsica. The long-standing problem of Flemish-Walloon relations in Belgium moved toward a possible political accommodation with agreement on a *pacte-communautaire*, in effect a detailed blueprint for a federal arrangement. The Netherlands' main ethnic problems were the integration of its Surinamese immigrants and the pacification of the more intransigent young South Moluccans, who seized hostages in a train and school in May. (See NETHERLANDS, THE.) Violence was also reported from Carinthia, Austria, where the Slovene-speaking minority claimed the government had failed to uphold the rights guaranteed to minorities by the 1955 Austrian state treaty. In Eastern Europe there was concern in Budapest about the fate of the large Hungarian minority in Romanian Transylvania, said to be facing the threat of forced assimilation. In the Soviet Union Jews were the most conspicuously threatened racial minority.

Asia. Perhaps the most intractable problem in Asia was that of India's 90 million Harijans (untouchables), most of them landless peasants. A campaign of violence led by Brahmin priests was reported, particularly from Bihar. There were warnings that Harijans might launch a U.S.-style civil rights movement. To another defiant minority, the Nagas, the new Indian prime minister, Morarji Desai, declared that he would "exterminate all Naga rebels." Karen separatists in Burma appealed to Britain to uphold their sovereignty and to raise the issue at the UN.

Mrs. Florrie Adams and three of her children posed outside their home in Salisbury, Rhodesia. The Adams family faced eviction because they are of mixed race and their home is in a white-reserved area.

Communal violence flared between Sinhalese and Tamils in Sri Lanka in August. At least 25,000 Tamils in Sinhalese areas were evacuated at their own request, many to the north, and the Tamil United Liberation Front demanded a separate Tamil state of Tamil Eelam. In Malaysia there was Malay pressure for a strict Muslim state, while the more affluent Chinese and Indian communities resented increasing discrimination on behalf of Malays in universities, jobs, and government service. In Sabah and Sarawak, where Malays were in a minority, the two largest native ethnic groups, the Ibans and the Kadazans, resented the extension of Malay political supremacy. In Fiji, where just over half the population was Indian, the multiracial Alliance Party swept to a landslide election victory in September.

Africa. Ethiopia, still in the throes of a military takeover, faced attacks from separatist forces and guerrillas, chiefly in Eritrea and the Ogaden, where Somalia supported the indigenous Somalis. In Uganda the situation continued to deteriorate as the government of Pres. Idi Amin pursued its tribal and political enemies. The National Union for the Total Independence of Angola, the Ovimbundu-based liberation movement in the south and central parts of the country, claimed in November that fighting was going on in 10 of Angola's 16 provinces.

In Rhodesia, Prime Minister Ian Smith used a general election in August to consolidate white opinion behind him and then, in November, made concrete proposals for an internal solution to the country's white-black problem. South Africa's Prime Minister B. J. Vorster also called a general election, on November 30, in which his National Party secured an increased majority in a show of white support for his apartheid policies. The reaction to international hostility—including the U.S. administration's human rights campaign and the UN Security Council's mandatory arms embargo —was such that even Colin Eglin, head of the Progressive Federal Party, the only party advocating a multiracial franchise, had to declare his opposition to U.S. pressure.

Ku Klux Klansmen showed their opinion of the Carter administration by staging a rally in July at Plains, Georgia.

The climate in South Africa made a continuing hard-line policy toward blacks seem inevitable, although some concessions were planned in the shape of constitutional proposals providing parliaments for Coloureds and Indians as well as whites. However, the new proposals could also sweep away such existing safeguards as a formally independent judiciary and press. It had been a bad year for South Africa; violent action by young urban blacks and Coloureds had triggered repressive counteraction, arrests and bannings of political dissidents by the police, and crackdowns against black and white editors and churchmen, climaxed by an international furor over the death in detention of the moderate young black leader Steven Biko (*see* OBITUARIES).

Amerindians and Eskimos. At a UN Human Rights conference in Genéva in September, over 100 Indians from the Americas were present to voice claims of genocide in South America and the U.S., colonialism in Canada, and the stealing of natural resources from the native peoples. Demands were also made for self-determination, but without success. Meanwhile, the U.S. was proceeding to more favourable mineral-exploration agreements for the Navajo, and the Canadian government wished to regularize its land settlement position with the Indians and Eskimos. In June 200 delegates representing U.S., Canadian, and Greenland Eskimos met at a conference on the problems (*e.g.*, pollution) of the Eskimo region in Alaska. Siberia's Eskimos were invited but, predictably, did not come. Eskimos in northern Quebec protested against the province's French language legislation, and some threatened to secede if Quebec became independent. In Latin America the situation of Indian tribes was much more precarious. In Brazil, where only 180,000–200,000 Indians re-

mained, the controversy over assimilation versus preservation on reserves continued.

Canada. The very survival of Canada as a federal entity came into question as the separatist Parti Québécois government in Quebec passed Bill 101, aimed at making French the official language in the province. The federal government set up a task force to support efforts toward Canadian unity and to advise the government on a third option as between the status quo and the *souveraineté-association* desired by Quebec Premier René Lévesque. In November relations between Quebec and the rest of Canada were further strained when the French government received Lévesque with honours usually reserved for a visiting head of state.

United States. Black voters had helped U.S. Pres. Jimmy Carter to victory in 1976, and in February 1977 he announced that he had appointed twice as many blacks to sub-Cabinet positions as the Ford administration had done. On the Cabinet level, his appointments included Andrew Young (*see* BIOGRAPHY) as U.S. ambassador to the UN. By summer, however, Carter's administration was coming under criticism from black leaders for not fulfilling its pre-election promise to help the poor find jobs. Meanwhile, the feeling among many whites that the government had long been favouring poor blacks and Latinos against the interest of "Middle America" came to a head in the Bakke case, argued before the U.S. Supreme Court in the fall. Allan Bakke, a white man, had sued the University of California for rejecting his application to medical school while admitting less qualified blacks in order to fill a racial quota. (*See* EDUCATION.) (SHEILA PATTERSON)

See also Feature Article: *The New Nationalism: Conflicts and Hopes.*
[522.B]

In spite of massive police protection, a huge brawl erupted when members of the extreme rightist National Front paraded in South London. A battle between the Front and its opponents left scores injured.

GIVE IT BACK TO THE INDIANS

by Thomas N. Tureen

In October 1976 the town of Millinocket, Maine, learned that its proposed $1 million municipal bond offering had been indefinitely postponed. The reason, the town was told, was that the prestigious Boston law firm of Ropes & Gray had refused to provide the necessary certification that the town had the unquestioned right to collect the taxes that would repay the bonds. Two days later a much larger bond offering by a consortium of Maine communities was withdrawn because it too was unable to obtain the necessary certification. The reason was a claim by two small Indian tribes to over half of the state of Maine. Since Indian property cannot be taxed, Ropes & Gray reasoned that if the claims were valid, the municipalities would not have power to collect the taxes. So it was that claims that had lain dormant since 1794, and had been in court since 1972, first began to be taken seriously.

Basis for the Claims. The claims of the Passamaquoddy and Penobscot tribes of Maine are based on aboriginal title, a property interest that Indians have under the American legal system by virtue of their use and occupancy of land since time immemorial. Although the Europeans who discovered the New World claimed the right to terminate the Indians' aboriginal possessory rights at will, until those rights were actually terminated they were good against all but the sovereign. In 1790 the United States put this doctrine into statutory form when it adopted the Indian Nonintercourse Act, which provided that no state or individual could obtain any interest in any land held by any Indian tribe without the consent of the United States. The Passamaquoddy and Penobscot tribes claimed that they were among a handful of tribes in the United States that still possessed aboriginal territory as of 1790, had their land taken from them in nonfederally approved transactions after that date, and thus were legally entitled to the return of the land, plus money damages for the time the land was illegally withheld.

Thomas N. Tureen, an attorney, acted as legal advocate for the Passamaquoddy and Penobscot tribes in the suit pressing their claims.

The Passamaquoddy and Penobscot tribes claimed to have occupied between five million and ten million acres of land in eastern and northern Maine during colonial times. The tribes played a crucial role as allies of the colonists during the Revolutionary War, and in return the superintendent of the federal government's Eastern Indian Agency promised in 1777 that the government would forever protect their hunting grounds and provide them with supplies in time of need. But the treaty in which these promises were made was never ratified, and after the war the tribes were left to shift for themselves. Massachusetts (of which Maine was then a part) was anxious to repay its soldiers with land grants, and the pressure for white settlement of the aboriginal territory became intense.

In 1792 the Passamaquoddies, having failed to get any help from the federal government, turned to Massachusetts in the hope of getting their lands protected. Massachusetts obliged with a 1794 treaty in which the tribe relinquished its claim to all of its land in return for clear title to only 23,000 ac. No money was paid; no services were promised. The Penobscots fared little better. In 1796 and 1818 Massachusetts obtained treaties from them in which they relinquished over five million acres in return for a yearly annuity of goods valued at about $1,500.

The claims of the Maine Indians, however, are not based on the unfairness of the treaties. The distinguishing feature of the Maine Indian claims is the allegation that the transactions violated federal law and that, under the white man's law, the Indians are legally entitled to recover.

The Passamaquoddies versus Morton. The present claims date from Feb. 22, 1972, when the tribes asked the federal government for help in getting their land back. The commissioner of the federal Bureau of Indian Affairs (which had not assisted

Indian land claims in the northeastern United States.

the Maine Indians since 1832 when the benefits for a local Indian school were discontinued after the Catholic priest got into a dispute with the federally funded Protestant school teacher) supported the tribes' request. The commissioner, however, was overruled by the secretary of the interior, who took the position that the federal government had no trust obligation to assist these Indians because the Nonintercourse Act only applied to "federally recognized tribes," and they were not "federally recognized." The tribes then brought suit against the secretary in an action titled *Joint Tribal Council of the Passamaquoddy Tribe* v. *Morton* and asked the federal court both to determine whether the Nonintercourse Act applied to them and to state whether it created a trust relationship between them and the United States. The tribes also asked the court for an order directing the government to file at least a part of their claims before a federal statute of limitations on old claims expired on July 18, 1972.

The federal court granted the order directing the government to file a portion of the suit before the statute expired and then, after three years of litigation, ruled that the Nonintercourse Act protects the tribes and creates a trust relationship between them and the federal government. The U.S. Court of Appeals for the First Circuit unanimously affirmed the decision in an opinion rendered Dec. 23, 1975. The case became final when the time for appeal to the Supreme Court expired in the spring of 1976.

While the tribes had not asked the court to order the government to actually litigate their claims, the Court of Appeals said that the trust relationship created by the act meant, at minimum, that the government had a duty to investigate the tribal claims and take such action as was appropriate. The decision was also crucially important because it addressed the single most significant question in the claim as a whole: whether the Nonintercourse Act applied to these particular Indians. While there had been other Nonintercourse Act claims in the past, no court had directly addressed the question of whether the act itself protected so-called "unrecognized tribes." This was certain to be a threshold issue in the claims themselves.

Judge Gunter's Recommendation. The federal government spent a year investigating the claims, and on Feb. 28, 1977, the Justice Department announced that it had concluded that the two tribes had valid claims for the return of over five million acres and would proceed to file suit against the largest landowners in the claim area by July 1, 1977, unless a settlement could be reached before that time. The government also indicated that it was studying a possible claim on behalf of the tribes for an additional three million acres. It announced that

it was taking no action on a possible further claim for two million acres that were actually occupied by homes and small businesses, since the tribes had said that they did not want to put anyone out of his home and would accept a substitute claim for the monetary value of their claims against small land-owners. At the same time, the Justice Department suggested that the White House and Congress seek a settlement of the dispute. Pres. Jimmy Carter responded by appointing Justice William B. Gunter, a retired justice of the Georgia Supreme Court, to evaluate the situation.

Judge Gunter concluded that an out-of-court settlement was the most appropriate course. He also concluded that responsibility for such a settlement lay both with the federal government, which was morally to blame for not having prevented the sales in the first place, and with the state of Maine. Private landowners should not be obliged to contribute to a settlement. He recommended that the federal government pay the Indians $25 million for their claim against private landholders (90% of their claim) and that Maine give the Indians 100,000 ac in lieu of the tribes' 530,000-ac claim against the state.

From the tribes' point of view, the problem with the recommendation was that it seemed to be made in the form of an offer that they could not refuse; the judge recommended that the president ask Congress to extinguish all of the tribal claim to privately held land without any compensation if the Indians did not voluntarily accept the $25 million. From the state of Maine's position, the problem was that it did not want to negotiate with the tribe at all and preferred to risk its land in court. As of mid-October 1977 it appeared that both parties would get some satisfaction. The White House announced appointment of a three-member task force to work out a consensual agreement with the tribes on a settlement package for their claims against private landowners, and the Justice Department and the Indians were planning to proceed against the state of Maine in court for the 530,000 ac of state-held land.

The following eastern Indian tribes were also pursuing claims under the Nonintercourse Act: the Mashpee (16,000 ac) and Gay Head (2,600 ac) Wampanoag tribes in Massachusetts; the Schaghticoke (1,300 ac), Western Pequot (800 ac), and Mohegan (1,700 ac) tribes in Connecticut; the Narraganset (3,-200 ac) in Rhode Island; the Mohawk (15,000 ac), Oneida (246,000 ac), Cayuga (45,000 ac), and Shinnecock (3,200 ac) in New York; and the Catawba (144,000 ac) in South Carolina. The claims in Maine are the largest in terms of acreage, and because the federal government itself concluded practically all Indian land transactions in the West, such claims were not expected to spread across the country.

Racket Games

Badminton. Top players from the 58 member nations of the International Badminton Federation traveled to Malmö, Sweden, to participate in the first official World Badminton Championships, held May 3–8, 1977. This triennial event replaced the All-England championships as the most prestigious in the world. Thomas Kihlstrom, an unseeded player from Sweden, pulled off the greatest upset of the tournament by defeating co-favourite Liem Swie King of Indonesia 15–9, 9–15, 15–12 in the third round of the men's singles. Top-seeded Flemming Delfs of Denmark, the All-England champion, narrowly escaped defeat in an early round before defeating Kini Zeniha of Japan 7–15, 17–15, 15–12. Delfs went on to win the world title with a lopsided 15–5, 15–6 victory over his fellow countryman Svend Pri. In women's competition, Gillian Gilks of England upset top-seeded Hiroe Yuki of Japan in a semifinal match 11–4, 11–7. When the two faced each other earlier in the year for the All-England title, Yuki triumphed 12–10, 11–8. Lene Koppen of Denmark was crowned world singles champion after defeating Gilks 12–9, 12–11 in the final. In the men's doubles, top-ranked Tjun Tjun and Johan Wahjudi played true to form and handily overcame Christian and Ade Chandra 15–6, 15–4 in an all-Indonesian final. Etsuko Toganoo and Emiko Ueno of Japan captured the women's doubles with two straight wins over Joke van Beusekom and Marjan Ridder of The Netherlands, 15–10, 15–11. The mixed doubles title went to Steen Skovgaard and Lene Koppen of Denmark who edged Derek Talbot and Gilks 15–12, 18–17. (JACK H. VAN PRAAG)

Squash Rackets. In 1977 the International Squash Rackets Federation admitted Singapore to membership, rejected Nigeria's resolution to expel South Africa, agreed to review the rules governing amateur status, and consented to evaluate the possibility of open tournaments. In September Pakistan won its first international amateur team championship in Canada and in the all-Pakistani singles final Maqsood Ahmad defeated his elder brother M. Saleem. The international, or softball, version of squash made strides in Canada where Bruce Brownlee of New Zealand won the national championship. During the year Sharif Khan captured his eighth North American Open championship and T. Page won the U.S. crown. The British Open championship was won by G. Hunt of Australia and the British Amateur by Brownlee. In women's squash, Heather McKay won her 16th consecutive British Open championship, losing only six points in the final to fellow Australian Barbara Wall. Pakistan International Airways financed a large squash complex in Karachi and in December 1976 sponsored a Masters Tournament won by Hunt. The 1977 Hashim Khan Trophy tournament was canceled because of political instability in Pakistan. (JOHN H. HORRY)

Rackets. In March 1977 William Surtees retained his world championship with a victory over Howard Angus, the British Open champion. Surtees, who had already built up a 4–0 lead on the first leg of the match in Chicago, quickly secured the one additional game he needed when the match was resumed at Queen's Club, London. Two British titles also changed hands at Queen's Club. John Prenn won his first Louis Roederer British Open title by defeating William Boone 4–1. Top-seeded Surtees and second-seeded Angus were both upset in the semifinals. The British amateur singles title was won by Charles Williams, who dethroned Boone in the final.

Real Tennis. Howard Angus retained his world championship with a 7–2 victory over Eugene Scott, the U.S. Open and U.S. Amateur titleholder. Angus also won the amateur singles title for the 12th straight year, edging Alan Lovell 3–2 in the closest final match of his illustrious career. Angus and David Warburg, however, lost their amateur doubles title to Lovell and Andrew Windham. The Cutty Sark British Open doubles title went to Lovell and Norwood Cripps, a Queen's Club professional. Angus also won the Grand Prix de Paris, retained the MCC Gold Racket at Lord's for his 12th straight victory, and successfully defended his Cutty Sark Open invitation singles title. (CHRISTINA WOOD)

[452.B.5.h.xxii; 452.B.4.h.xxvii]

Radio:
see Television and Radio

Railroads:
see Transportation

Recordings:
see Music

Reformed Churches:
see Religion

Howard Angus, the reigning champion of real tennis, retained the world championship and won the amateur singles championship for the 12th consecutive year. "Real" tennis (from the Spanish word for "royal") is regarded by its devotees as more difficult than lawn tennis.

LONDON DAILY EXPRESS/PICTORIAL PARADE

Refugees

Protecting the human rights of refugees and helping them to take up normal lives—the two tasks of the United Nations High Commissioner for Refugees (UNHCR)—continued to require action on a global scale in 1977. Efforts were made to promote accessions to international agreements affecting refugees, particularly the 1951 Convention relating to the Status of Refugees and the 1967 Protocol. By mid-November, 69 and 64 states, respectively, had become parties to these instruments. The high commissioner also intervened vigorously on behalf of refugees whenever they were subject to violations of their rights of asylum or *non-refoulement* (not being driven back) or were exposed to risk of personal violence.

The UN General Assembly convened a plenipotentiaries' conference on territorial asylum in Geneva from January 10 to February 4. The conference was unable to draft a convention within the allotted time, but it recommended that the General Assembly, at its 32nd session, consider the question of convening a further session.

Refugees continued to require major programs of assistance, particularly in Africa, Asia, and Latin America, where expenditure on all programs totaled some $72 million in 1977.*

Southern Africa saw considerable influxes of refugees, mainly from Namibia, South Africa, and Rhodesia (Zimbabwe) into neighbouring countries. In April UN Secretary-General Kurt Waldheim designated UNHCR to coordinate UN assistance for southern African student refugees, and the high commissioner launched an appeal to

Refugees from Vietnam aboard an old mine-sweeper searched desperately for a country to admit them. They were allowed to tie up temporarily at a Malaysian port.

SVEN SIMON/KATHERINE YOUNG

governments for $16 million to meet the needs of more than 50,000 refugees in the area. At the same time, the high commissioner addressed an appeal to African countries for places for these students in their educational systems, coupled, where possible, with scholarships.

New UNHCR assistance programs were required in Djibouti and Gabon, and assistance programs continued in Angola, Kenya, Mozambique, Sudan, and Zaire. At the request of the UN secretary-general, the high commissioner also continued to provide assistance to Saharawis in the Tindouf area of Algeria.

In Asia the backwash of the Vietnam war continued to generate major refugee problems. Assistance aimed toward rehabilitating displaced persons in Laos and Vietnam continued, albeit on a diminishing scale. The flow of Indochinese into Thailand—where they now numbered some 95,000—required a sustained assistance effort. A further problem was that of the so-called boat people, who left their countries in unseaworthy vessels to seek landfalls around the South China Sea. In the first six months of 1977 more than 10,600 such persons arrived, mainly in Thailand and Malaysia but many also in Hong Kong, Indonesia, the Philippines, Singapore, and even Australia and Japan. Still others were rescued on the high seas by passing ships and taken to the first port of call. On numerous occasions, the high commissioner called attention to the plight of these people and undertook intensive efforts to assure them temporary asylum, while urging governments to offer generous resettlement possibilities.

Elsewhere in Asia, the Malaysian government, in June, requested assistance for up to 90,000 Muslim refugees from the southern Philippines who had entered the state of Sabah. Arrangements were made for a rehabilitation program leading to local integration in Malaysia. In Lebanon UNHCR undertook a special program in cooperation with the authorities to assist displaced persons within the framework of overall UN action.

Some 16,000 Latin-American refugees had been resettled in 43 countries after the fall of the Salvador Allende government in Chile in 1973, but the need for resettlement opportunities persisted. Meanwhile, the desperation of those left behind grew more intense and sometimes found explosive release, on two occasions in the forcible occupation of UNHCR field offices. UNHCR strengthened its presence in Latin America and in 1977 spent $5 million on operations there. As coordinator of UN humanitarian assistance in Cyprus, UNHCR in 1977 channeled some $18 million in aid for displaced persons throughout the island.

During 1977 the traditional immigration countries of North America and Oceania and, in Western Europe, France and Scandinavia provided most of the resettlement opportunities for refugees and displaced persons, mainly from Southeast Asia and Latin America.

On December 8 the UN General Assembly designated Poul Hartling, former prime minister of Denmark, to succeed Sadruddin Aga Khan as high commissioner.   (UNHCR)

See also Migration, International.

Religion

Religious authority was put to the test many times, in many places, and in many different ways in 1977. The battles took place in civil courts, ecclesiastical courts, a kangaroo court or two, and the court of public opinion. Sometimes the disputes were between church and state. Sometimes the disagreements divided co-believers. At other times the battle lines were formed in private homes as parents fought with children over the demands of religious cults.

In the U.S. the traditional wall of separation between church and state proved to be no neat and well-defined boundary. Several legal questions became the source of border disputes.

Does the Internal Revenue Service have the right to require the submission of annual informational returns by organizations that are not "integrated auxiliaries" of the church? "Yes," said government attorneys. "No," replied many church leaders, who argued that the term "integrated auxiliaries" placed government bureaucrats in the constitutionally untenable position of defining what "religion" is.

Does the National Labor Relations Board have the right to rule that Roman Catholic bishops must bargain with unions representing lay teachers in their dioceses? A U.S. Court of Appeals judge ruled against the NLRB on the ground that bishops, under the First Amendment to the Constitution, have the authority to maintain parochial schools in accordance with ecclesiastical norms.

Should church employees who are working with radical groups be required to tell a federal grand jury what they know about those groups' activities? Definitely, said a New York judge, who jailed staff members of the Episcopal Church's National Commission on Hispanic Affairs on contempt of court charges. Definitely not, contended defense lawyers, who charged that the grand jury was involved in an unlawful "fishing expedition" for information.

Church-state tensions in the U.S. were mild, however, compared with those elsewhere. In South Korea, the Philippines, and El Salvador, Christian missionaries who regarded themselves as "partisans for the poor and oppressed" were expelled. As racial tensions mounted in Rhodesia and South Africa, churchmen were caught between opposing forces. After being found guilty of failing to report the presence of suspected black guerrillas in his diocese, Roman Catholic Bishop Donal Lamont was driven out of Rhodesia, while in the border areas of the country seven white missionaries were shot, allegedly by black liberationists. In South Africa the regime of Prime Minister B. J. Vorster continued its crackdown on churchmen who opposed apartheid. In Uganda, meanwhile, Anglican Archbishop Janani Luwum was slain after Pres. Idi Amin charged at a public rally that the prelate had masterminded a plot to overthrow the government. It was not an easy year for Christians to decide when to "obey God" and when to "obey Caesar."

U.S. civil courts also were involved in attempts to settle a growing number of internal church controversies. As "moderates" in the doctrinally divided Lutheran Church—Missouri Synod broke away from the parent body to join the Association of Evangelical Lutheran Churches, disputes flared over ownership of church property. Episcopalians went to court over similar issues after opponents of women's ordination to the priesthood and revisions in the Book of Common Prayer started a schismatic movement.

In other courts youthful members of new religious cults filed suits charging their parents with harassment and parents filed suits accusing cult leaders of brainwashing their children. A California judge, supporting parental rights of conservatorship, released into the custody of their parents five members of the Rev. Sun Myung Moon's Unification Church. Subsequently, four of the five "Moonies," who ranged in age from 21 to 26, left the church. Faced with a similar issue, a federal judge in Vermont dismissed a suit against the Unification Church on the ground that the parents did not have the right to represent their adult daughter. In October a New Jersey court

In March a California judge granted temporary custody rights to the parents of a number of young adults said to be under the influence of the Rev. Sun Myung Moon's Unification Church.

ruled that Transcendental Meditation courses, when offered in public schools, are unconstitutional. The TM people claimed the courses were not "religious," but the judge, citing Hindu aspects of the "puja" ceremony, decided to the contrary. All in all, it was obvious that the Rev. Eugene Kennedy, a priest and psychologist, had reason for characterizing the current period as "an age of litigation" —in church and in society. (*See* LAW: *Special Report*.)

Two major decisions were made by the U.S. National Conference of Catholic Bishops, but it was difficult to determine whether they were thereby showing their authority or acknowledging the authority of the people in the pews. They voted to rescind a 93-year-old church law excommunicating Catholics who divorce and remarry without church approval. An advocate of the change admitted the law was no longer enforceable. The bishops also favoured a measure permitting Catholics to decide for themselves whether they wish to receive communion in the hand or on the tongue. It was commonly known that many priests had been serving communion in the hand long before the bishops decided to authorize it.

Changing sexual mores constituted another major challenge to religious authority. In 1976 the Vatican issued a 6,000-word *Declaration on Certain Questions Concerning Sexual Ethics*. It reaffirmed traditional teachings condemning premarital sex, homosexuality, and masturbation. Not content to let the Vatican have the last word, the Catholic Theological Society of America in 1977 published a book, *Human Sexuality*, in which the theologians proposed "pastoral guidelines" stressing the "natural goodness and sacredness of human sexuality as a creative and integrative force."

The contrast between the old and new approaches was clearly illustrated by the two points of view on masturbation. In its *Declaration* the Vatican stated: "Whatever the force of certain arguments of a biological and philosophical nature . . . both the magisterium of the Church . . . and the moral sense of the faithful have declared without hesitation that masturbation is an intrinsically and seriously disordered act." In contrast, the American theologians asserted: "Masturbation is a subtle and complex phenomenon. To condemn every act of masturbation harshly as mortal sin or to dismiss it lightly as of no moral consequence fails to do justice to the symptomatic nature of masturbation capable of many meanings."

Homosexuality posed an especially vexing question for ethicists in all denominations. Many were torn between loyalty to traditional formulations and the desire to be open to new truths. The only religionists free from the struggle were fundamentalists like the pop singer Anita Bryant (*see* BIOGRAPHY), whose "Save Our Children" crusade in Dade County, Fla., led to the repeal of an ordinance protecting homosexuals from discrimination in housing, jobs, and public accommodations.

Others found the issue more complicated. In New York City, Bishop Paul Moore ordained Ellen Barrett, an avowed lesbian, as a deacon. His action cheered some Episcopalians and appalled many others. The American Lutheran Church reaffirmed its conservative view of homosexuality, explaining that it was not the church's task to be swept along by "the spirit of the times." Although the Vatican, in its 1976 *Declaration*, had stated that "homosexual acts are intrinsically disordered and cannot be approved of," the Catholic Theological Society study held that homosexuals cannot be "bound to the morally impossible and confined to a life of continence not expected of heterosexuals."

Religious leaders were more united on another front. Liberals and conservatives alike joined in a chorus of denunciation aimed at television producers and advertisers responsible for showing violence and explicit sex on prime time TV. Shortly before the fall TV season began, churchmen, with Southern Baptists in the vanguard, pressured sponsors to withdraw their support from such programs as "Soap," a new ABC series aimed at adult audiences. The churchmen seemed to enjoy finding a cause that united rather than divided their constituencies.

On most issues, it was evident that religious leaders, sensing the conservative mood of the times, were determined not to get too far in front of their followers, as some suspected they had done in the 1960s. Willingly or unwillingly, they had come to terms with the fact that they were living in a populist age when, as often as not, authority came from "below" rather than from "above." They knew how easy it was to assert their authority and how hard it was to have their authority acknowledged.

In the declining years of the 1970s, American religionists appeared to be moving along two paths which sometimes paralleled each other and at other times intersected. Some followed the path of official religion with its properly ordained leaders, its fully accredited seminaries, its officially sanctioned liturgies, and its well-staffed boards, agencies, divisions, and subdivisions. Others followed the path of populist religion, where much took place without benefit of clergy. Unable to exercise bureaucratic control over these unpredictable movements of the spirit, church authorities usually adopted policies of benign containment.

At a Kansas City, Mo., stadium in July, a folk festival of populist religion attracted 45,000 celebrants from all parts of the U.S. Called a Charismatic Renewal Conference, it brought together charismatic Catholics, traditional Protestant Pentecostalists, and "spirit-led" charismatics from main-line Protestant denominations. For five days they studied the Bible, attended workshops, participated in worship services, and bore witness to their conviction that they had been "baptized in the Holy Spirit." It was a major ecumenical event. It also differed from most ecumenical gatherings— assemblies of the National and World Councils of Churches, for example—which are dominated by "professional" churchmen. If it looked like a new kind of know-nothingism to some, it felt like the real thing to others.

Everything considered, in the year 1977 it was no mean feat for religious authority figures to stay on top of their situations. The pragmatic ones went barefooted; this made it easier for them to feel the grass roots stirring. (ROY LARSON)

PROTESTANT CHURCHES

Anglican Communion. The Most Rev. Janani Luwum, archbishop of Uganda, died on Feb. 16, 1977, after being arrested for alleged complicity in a plot against Pres. Idi Amin. The Ugandan authorities claimed that he died in a car crash while trying to escape, but reports that he had been shot in cold blood were widely accepted. Earlier, Luwum and Uganda's other Anglican bishops had written Amin expressing concern over the activities of the security forces. Subsequent reports indicated that the Ugandan church was continuing preparations for its centenary celebrations. When a kinsman of Amin's (the Most Rev. Silvanus Wari) was appointed to succeed Luwum, local churchmen asserted that he had been freely elected.

The archbishop of Canterbury, Donald Coggan, paid several important visits: in April–May to Christendom's leaders in Rome, Istanbul, and Geneva and, in September, a ten-day visit to the Soviet Union. There was an exchange of views with the ecumenical patriarch at Istanbul about women priests, whose increasing acceptance by Anglicans threatened to wreck the official talks between the Anglican and Orthodox churches. Orthodox unhappiness was restated, at another session held in Cambridge, England, in July, but the dialogue survived, at least for the time being. (See *Roman Catholic Church*, below.)

The first schism in the Anglican Communion over women priests (and other liberal policies) occurred in the U.S., where dissidents meeting at St. Louis, Mo., in September confirmed moves to establish a breakaway "Anglican Church in North America." The dissidents sought to maintain official links with Canterbury. In New Zealand the introduction of women priests was delayed by a challenge to the validity of the ordination statute, but in Australia the General Synod in August accepted the ordination of women in principle.

A controversial book, *The Myth of God Incarnate*, essays by seven prominent British theologians published in 1977, challenged the traditional concepts of Christ's divinity; the archbishop of Canterbury judged that it had created "more hubbub than it is worth."　(SUSAN YOUNG)

A court-appointed clerk checked ballots as members of an Episcopal parish voted whether to secede from the national church.

Baptist Churches. Baptists in North America totaled 29,016,036 in 1977, according to Carl W. Tiller, associate secretary of the Baptist World Alliance. If all the congregations had reported, Tiller said, the total North American "Baptist community" would be approximately 37,242,955. At the same time, Tiller noted that the growth of Baptists of South America had come to a standstill. Three new congregations were established in Moscow, bringing the total there to 17.

The Southern Baptist Convention, the largest non-Catholic church body in America, held its annual meeting in Kansas City, Mo. More than 16,000 messengers (delegates) attended. On the positive side, as part of its $63.4 million general budget, the Convention earmarked more than $8 million for a program to "evangelize the nation by 1980." But for the second time in little more than a decade the Convention became embroiled in a controversy over "verbal inerrancy" of the Scriptures. Mod-

erates prevailed, as was indicated by the election of the Rev. Jimmy Allen, pastor of the First Baptist Church, San Antonio, Texas, as the new president. The Convention approved a "call" for 5,000 short-term missionaries to augment the present contingent of 5,000 missionaries in the field. The new missionaries were to be recruited by 1982. The messengers gave Anita Bryant an ovation for her "courageous stand against the evils inherent in homosexuality." Several resolutions were passed opposing government interference in religion.

At the biennial meeting of the American Baptist Churches, U.S.A. (northern), in San Diego, Calif., retiring president Charles Z. Smith, a black, noted that since 1968 the church had demonstrated an "affirmative inclusion and participation across ethnic and racial lines." The American Baptists had the largest number of blacks of any predominantly white denomination. Among smaller Baptist groups, the Seventh Day Baptists withdrew their support from the World Council of Churches. At their annual meeting in Duluth, Minn., the Baptist General Conference (Baptists of Swedish extraction) sent a letter of commendation to Anita Bryant.

Mass baptisms continued in Angola despite civil strife. In Lisbon, pastor Antonio Tiago and his wife were commissioned by the Portuguese Baptist Convention as the first missionaries to France. The Tiagos would work primarily with Portuguese immigrants.　(NORMAN R. DE PUY)

Christian Church (Disciples of Christ). The 1.3 million-member church gave the largest amount, $200,000, of 92 church bodies to initiate the Ecumenical Development Cooperative Society. Based in Geneva, the society would make high-risk business loans to poor people of the third world.

In July the church began a unique program whereby four persons were put to work full-time pointing out human rights violations around the world. Three of them were missionaries who had been ejected from the Philippines and Paraguay. At the same time, the church faced a flood of protest from members over leadership support for the civil rights of homosexuals and a study that questioned biblical interpretations that homosexuality was sin.

At their General Assembly in Kansas City, Mo., Disciples voted to begin two years of preliminary exploration of union with the United Church of Christ. The word "provisional" was voted out of the title of the church's nine-year-old governing document, which would serve in lieu of a constitution for the time being. In September the Disciples began talks with the Roman Catholic Church, aimed at sharing views on the faith.

　(ROBERT LOUIS FRIEDLY)

Churches of Christ. More than 120 campus ministry programs were active in the U.S. in 1977. Church leaders from all over the U.S. gathered in "Soul-Winning" workshops, with thousands attending the largest ones in Tulsa, Okla., and Sacramento, Calif. The fastest growing churches were in the Southwest and South. In Lubbock, Texas, alone, three churches were construct-

Archbishop of Canterbury Donald Coggan (left, seated) paid his first visit to Pope Paul VI at the Vatican in April.

ing auditoriums that would seat over 2,000, and the five-year-old Bramel Road Church in Houston, Texas, collected over $1 million on one Sunday.

Six hundred new ministers were entering the field annually. Harding Graduate School of Religion in Memphis, Tenn., introduced a doctor of ministry degree. Outside the U.S., 200 countries were being served by 1,296 missionaries, the third largest number among U.S. religious groups; 300 graduates of the preacher training school in Addis Ababa, Eth., had helped convert 15,000 people during the past eight years.

Ira North succeeded B. C. Goodpasture as editor of the oldest weekly publication, the *Gospel Advocate.*   (M. NORVEL YOUNG)

Church of Christ, Scientist. Addressing the denomination's annual meeting in June, David E. Sleeper, chairman of the Christian Science Board of Directors, said it was time for members around the world "to unite in good, strong prayer" and to look beyond mere surface conditions in society.

The denomination had about 3,000 branches throughout the U.S. and overseas. Church officers acknowledged membership shifts away from the inner city and toward new and often growing congregations in the suburbs. But the most important growth needed, according to James Spencer, elected president of the church for the coming year, was in terms of "increased spiritual vision, greater Christian discipline, and much more patience, love, courage, and integrity."

For the first time, the First Church of Christ, Scientist, in Boston named a woman to be first reader, one of two lay members responsible for conducting worship and testimonial services.

(J. BUROUGHS STOKES)

Church of Jesus Christ of Latter-day Saints. Church membership approached four million by the end of 1977, with particularly rapid growth in Mexico, western South America, and the western U.S. Stakes (dioceses) were formed in Honduras, Venezuela, and Norway.

Partly because of the needs created by the church's growth, a major restructuring of church administration took place in late 1976 and 1977. The office of assistant to the Quorum of Twelve Apostles was discontinued, and the 21 former assistants were added to the First Quorum of Seventy, which then assumed a more comprehensive role as a major governing body of the church. Within the First Quorum of Seventy, a seven-man presidency composed primarily of former assistants to the Twelve replaced the First Council of Seventy, formerly the executive body of the Quorum.

During 1977 Mormon leaders realigned general church administrative responsibilities by placing ecclesiastical functions, including education, under the direction of the Council of Twelve and "temporal" functions under the three-man Presiding Bishopric. Revisions of the young men's and young women's programs on both the general and local level were aimed at providing more effective adult leadership. Church programs for single adults were unified.

In October 1976 the church's First Presidency affirmed that men and women were "equally important before the Lord," but that they had inherent biological, emotional, and other differences. They deplored injustices to women but recommended the adoption of legislation against specific abuses rather than the proposed Equal Rights Amendment to the U.S. Constitution. During 1977 leaders of the church's women's organization, the Relief Society, encouraged its members in the U.S. to participate in the state-level International Women's Year meetings. In several states and the District of Columbia, Mor-

mon women wielded an unexpectedly strong influence reinforcing opposition to abortion on demand and ERA.

(LEONARD J. ARRINGTON)

Jehovah's Witnesses. An international society of Christian evangelizers, Jehovah's Witnesses in 1977 numbered 2,223,538 individuals associated with 40,155 congregations in 216 lands; 124,459 new evangelizers were baptized after completing a course of Bible study. Witnesses carried on their preaching and teaching activity for a total of 321,425,305 hours, which included calling door to door. A series of four-day "Joyful Workers" assemblies held in the U.S. and Canada had an attendance of 1,058,596. The theme of the public lecture was "How God's Kingdom Can Benefit You." Hundreds of thousands more attended assemblies outside North America. *The Watchtower*, the official journal of Jehovah's Witnesses, had a circulation of 10.4 million copies in 79 languages, and its companion magazine, *Awake!*, 10,125,000 copies in 32 languages.

On June 22, Frederick W. Franz was elected president of the Watch Tower Bible and Tract Society, the legal corporation of Jehovah's Witnesses, by unanimous vote of the board of directors. He replaced Nathan H. Knorr (*see* OBITUARIES), president for 35 years, who died on June 8.

(FREDERICK W. FRANZ)

Lutheran Churches. The sixth Assembly of the Lutheran World Federation (LWF) was held in Dar es Salaam, Tanzania, June 13–26, the first time such a meeting had been held outside Europe or North America. About 250 voting delegates, plus twice that number of consultants, observers, and press attended. The theme was "In Christ—A New Community," and a strong declaration was issued on behalf of human rights. Bishop Josiah M. Kibira of Bukoba, Tanzania, was elected LWF president, the first African to hold that post. In accepting the office, he gave notice that the churches in Africa, Asia, and Latin America would continue their drive for equal partnership in the decision-making processes of world Lutheranism, even as they were forced to accept some financial and personnel support from the more affluent Western churches.

Lutheranism remained the largest Protestant confessional grouping in the world, with some 70.5 million members. About 54 million were in the 95 church bodies affiliated with the LWF. Among Lutheran churches outside the LWF, the largest was the Lutheran Church—Missouri Synod (LCMS).

A battle of many years between "moderates" and "conservatives" in the LCMS came to an end as conservatives took firm control. While many moderates remained with the Synod, about 100,000 broke away and were active in the year-old Association of Evangelical Lutheran Churches. Another phase of the controversy ended with the expulsion from the Synod of John H. Tietjen, the symbolic leader of the moderates, once president of the church's Concordia Seminary and now head of Concordia Seminary in Exile (Seminex). Charges of false doctrine against him were upheld, and he refused to appeal.

While the LCMS retained its membership in the Lutheran Council in the U.S.A.,

American evangelist Billy Graham (left) was photographed wearing a sheepskin coat and eating goulash on a visit to Budapest, Hungary, in September.

cooperating in a variety of programs with the American Lutheran Church (ALC) and the Lutheran Church in America (LCA), it pulled back significantly in two areas. A convention declaration of "fellowship in protest" with the ALC was adopted; this meant that while a sharing of communion and pulpits by the two churches was still permissible, the LCMS seriously questioned the relationship. Also, the LCMS decided to postpone its participation with the ALC, LCA, and the Evangelical Lutheran Church of Canada in the publication of a new *Lutheran Book of Worship*. The other churches gave final approval to the book and continued plans to make it available to congregations by the fall of 1978.

Lutheran and Roman Catholic theologians in the U.S. scheduled a ninth dialogue session on papal infallibility for 1978, when it was anticipated that a common statement would be completed. A series of conversations with Methodists was under way in the U.S., and a world-level dialogue was begun by the LWF and the World Methodist Council. The Lutheran Council in the U.S.A. was exploring the possibility of conversations with representatives of the Pentecostal community.

(NEIL B. MELLBLOM)

Methodist Churches. The Executive Committee of the World Methodist Council, meeting in Switzerland in September 1977, published figures showing that the Methodist community, worldwide, had increased from 45,776,638 in 1971 to 49,554,084 in 1976. The committee approved a four-year plan for world evangelism. A worldwide Lenten study of St. Mark's Gospel, using a study guide entitled *Christian Discipleship—the Hard Way*, was in preparation for 1978.

Pursuing a decision to seek conversations with the Orthodox Church, officers of the World Methodist Council met with the ecumenical patriarch in Istanbul, and with Metropolitan Juvenaly, head of interchurch relationships for the Russian Orthodox Church, in Moscow. Conversations with the Lutheran churches were also being planned, in addition to the already existing conversations with the Roman Catholic Church.

In June 1977 the Methodist Church of Australasia became a part of the Uniting Church in Australia by union with Congregational and Presbyterian churches. Although all local Methodist churches entered into union, many Congregational and Presbyterian churches voted to stay out, so that Methodists formed a majority in the new church. The Methodist churches of Fiji, Samoa, and Tonga, which had been associated with the Australian Conference, decided to remain Methodist and so became autonomous churches. The Rhodesian District of the British Methodist Church was granted autonomy by the British Conference in 1977. This opened the way for union with the United Methodist Church (UMC) in Rhodesia, linked with the UMC in the U.S. At its 29th session, the Central Conference of the Methodist Church in Southern Asia, which was also linked with the UMC and had not joined with other Methodists in the United Church of South India, passed a resolution to establish the "Methodist Church in India."

Gifts totaling some £700,000 from Meth-

odists all over the world had been received toward the restoration of Wesley's Chapel in City Road, London, the "Mother Church of World Methodism," which had been closed for five years.

(PETER H. BOLT)

Pentecostal Churches. The outstanding event of 1977 for American Pentecostals and charismatics was the Conference on Charismatic Renewal in the Christian Churches, which met in Kansas City, Mo., in July. Nearly 50,000 persons registered for the conference, almost half of them Roman Catholics. (See *Introduction*, above.)

The Pentecostal denominations took strong conservative positions on several social questions. The General Conference of the Pentecostal Holiness Church opposed abortion on demand, legalization of marijuana, the Equal Rights Amendment, violence and sex in the media, homosexuality, and pornography. The Assemblies of God took similar positions at its General Council, and the Church of God (Cleveland, Tenn.) sponsored a churchwide boycott to protest violence, sex, and obscenity on network television.

The Assemblies of God General Council reelected Thomas F. Zimmerman as general superintendent, despite opposition stemming from an article by columnist Jack Anderson, which implied a conflict of interest involving a bank Zimmerman directed in Springfield, Mo.

The second five-year cycle of the Roman Catholic-Pentecostal dialogue began in Rome in October with both parties discussing "speaking in tongues."

(VINSON SYNAN)

Presbyterian, Reformed, and Congregational Churches. A modest consultation rather than a large world assembly marked the centenary of the World Alliance of Reformed Churches (WARC) in 1977. Held in St. Andrews, Scotland, August 22–28, under the theme "the glory of God and the future of man," it brought together 200 participants from 43 countries. The consultation's findings and reports were remitted for endorsement to the newly elected WARC executive committee, which met August 29–30. The committee agreed, among other things, to appeal to the South Korean government to release all political prisoners and to call upon member churches to urge their governments to join in a general boycott of South Africa. James I. McCord, president of Princeton Theological Seminary, was chosen as the new president of the WARC, in succession to William P. Thompson, who had held office since 1970.

Reports on completed dialogues with the Baptist World Alliance and with the Secretariat for Promoting Christian Unity of the Roman Catholic Church were received and sent to the member churches for reaction and comment.

Three new churches were received into Alliance membership: the Presbyterian Church in North East India, the Lithuanian Evangelical Reformed Church in the U.S., and the Uniting Church in Australia. The latter was inaugurated on June 22 when the Congregational Union of Australia, the Presbyterian Church of Australia, and the Methodist Church of Australasia united. Total Alliance membership now stood at 144.

Church union negotiations continued,

though with an apparent slowdown in talks between the United Presbyterian Church in the U.S.A. and the Presbyterian Church in the U.S. The United Congregational Church in Southern Africa and the Tsonga Presbyterian Church agreed to unite "as soon as possible," with September 1978 as the target date.

In London on July 18, 22 Congregational and Presbyterian churches in 18 countries formed a new-style Council for World Mission (CWM), in which all were members with equal status. The new CWM was the successor to three former British missionary agencies, the London Missionary Society (founded 1795), the Commonwealth Missionary Society (1836), and the Overseas Mission (1847) of the former Presbyterian Church of England.

(FREDERIK H. KAAN)

Religious Society of Friends. For American Friends the most important event of 1977 was the Conference of Friends in the Americas, held at Wichita, Kan., at the end of June. Since the last century, American Quakers had gone their different ways, and many groups had little or no contact with others. The Wichita conference, although not intended to promote any kind of organic unity, achieved greater representation than ever before.

Among the concerns of British Friends were support for Amnesty International's campaign against torture and involvement in a joint campaign to draw public attention to the arms trade. They also joined in public discussion of Britain's nuclear energy policy and testified at the Windscale inquiry into plans to build a nuclear reprocessing plant. A recently formed Quaker group in Brussels proposed that a Quaker representative be maintained there, in view of the city's growing importance in international affairs. The proposal received some support from British Friends and scattered Quaker groups on the continent, but hesitations were also expressed, particularly by Scandinavian Friends.

The Quaker office in Nairobi, Kenya, established in 1976, brought together Friends from many parts of Africa in a seminar at Gaborone, Botswana, in August to discuss the role of nonviolent action in achieving social justice, particularly in southern Africa.

(DAVID FIRTH)

Salvation Army. In April 1977 the ninth High Council of the Salvation Army, meeting at Sunbury-on-Thames, England, elected Canada's territorial commander, Commissioner Arnold Brown (*see* BIOGRAPHY), to succeed Gen. Clarence Wiseman, who retired on July 4, as the Army's 11th world leader.

Emergency relief teams continued to provide aid in Bangladesh. Earthquake relief work in Guatemala led to the establishment of permanent social and evangelical centres there. In Britain social service centres in Bradford, Leeds, and Cardiff were replaced and/or extended.

The Army's 200,000-circulation international weekly *War Cry* was converted to colour printing but proclaimed that it would retain its black-and-white policy of backing virtue and blacking vice.

Joshua Ngugi, head of the Salvation Army in East Africa, was appointed commissioner, the first African to hold the rank. (JOHN M. BATE)

Seventh-day Adventist Church. Two major international meetings were conducted by the church in 1976–77. The World Congress for the Prevention of Alcoholism, in Acapulco, Mexico, attracted 350 delegates from 35 countries. In March the first World Congress on Religious Liberty, in Amsterdam, Neth., was attended by 350 delegates from 30 countries, including Eastern Europe.

World membership in the church at the end of 1976 was 2.8 million, 5.4% above 1975. Approximately 1,150 new or returning workers were sent outside North America. Church leaders visited congregations in the U.S.S.R. during 1977, and thousands attended meetings in Moscow and other cities. Church leaders in India reported that 300 churches in south India had been built and dedicated, completing a campaign begun in 1974.

On February 28 Huguley Memorial Hospital was opened in Fort Worth, Texas, the latest addition to the church's worldwide network of 420 health-care institutions. The denomination selected Andrews University, Berrien Springs, Mich., as its primary aviation centre. A fleet of 77 small planes served the church in the Americas, Africa, Southeast Asia, and Oceania.

(KENNETH H. WOOD)

Unitarian (Universalist) Churches. After many years of emphasizing black rights, churches of the Unitarian Universalist Association throughout North America turned their energies toward the elimination of discriminatory practices against women. Thirty women ministers now occupied pulpits, half of them having been settled within the past two years, and a substantial number of the 153 students currently preparing to enter the ministry were female.

The 16th annual General Assembly attracted 1,243 delegates and about 1,000 observers to the campus of Cornell University, Ithaca, N.Y., June 20–26. The Rev. Paul N. Carnes and Sandra M. Caron were elected to four-year terms as president and moderator, respectively. Reflecting the movement's traditional dedication to social concerns, resolutions were passed on disarmament, energy, world hunger, nuclear proliferation, human rights in El Salvador, women's rights, abortion, homosexual rights, and the environment, among other subjects.

Similar concerns emerged during the mid-April annual meetings of the British General Assembly in London, which took stands on equal status for women, an end to discrimination against homosexuals, repeal of Britain's Race Relations Act, world development, and lifting restrictions on the right to trial by jury. The Rev. Peter B. Godfrey, at 46, became the youngest president in the history of the British movement.

The Canadian Unitarian Council attracted almost 200 delegates to Ottawa, May 20–22. A task force was set up to produce Canadian religious education materials that would replace U.S. curricula. Amnesty International, energy policies that respect social and environmental needs, and the rights of the elderly were supported in resolutions.

Harold J. Hadley was named executive secretary and Paul H. Beattie was elected president of the Fellowship of Religious Humanists at that body's annual conference, held October 22–24 in St. Louis, Mo. The annual Meadville/Lombard Winter Institute, in Chicago in January, attracted 125 clergy, religious educators, and lay persons. Discussions centred on the place of social responsibility in the covenant that unites members of the Unitarian movement. (JOHN NICHOLLS BOOTH)

United Church of Canada. Conversations continued during 1977 with the Christian Church (Disciples of Christ), the Presbyterian Church in Canada, and the Roman Catholic Church. Recognizing the need to emphasize both social activism and personal spiritual growth, along with its special mission to the alcoholic, the poverty-stricken, the hungry, and the delinquent, the United Church was exploring the possibility of setting up a United Church investment corporation to invest in ministries to the cities.

The situation in Quebec was a source of concern. Whether the outcome was independence for Quebec or some other form of autonomy, it was clear that the English-speaking community in that province—many of them members of the United Church—would have to learn to live as a minority within an increasingly vigorous and assertive French-speaking community. The crux of the issue was whether that minority would possess sufficient vision to act responsibly and creatively.

Twenty-five countries received aid from the United Church in 1977, including 19 missionary countries, and 79 missionaries, including wives, were active overseas. Within Canada, there were 34 ethnic congregations that did not use either English or French. Well over a hundred women had been ordained.

(ARTHUR GUY REYNOLDS)

United Church of Christ. The 11th biennial General Synod, which met in Washington, D.C., in July 1977, considered pronouncements on "Exploitative Broadcasting," "Racism and Sexism," "The Church and the Handicapped," "The Right to a Useful and Remunerative Job," and "The Quality of Life in Rural America."

Ten priorities were adopted for the ensuing biennium: "Aging," involving ministries with and to the elderly; "The Church and Persons with Handicaps," proposing that persons with physical, mental, or emotional handicaps be fully integrated into the life of the church; "Criminal Justice and Penal Reform," urging changes that would make the U.S. criminal justice and penal systems more equitable, humane, and nondiscriminatory; "Evangelism and the Search for Faith"; "Exploitative Broadcasting," advocating a responsible broadcasting industry and seeking to minimize such practices as the use of gratuitous violence and exploitation of sex; "Family Life"; "Human Rights," including racial and economic justice; "Local Church," including Christian education and stewardship; "Women in Church and Society," proposing a systematic approach to the elimination of institutional and cultural sexism; and "World Hunger," with emphasis on long-term action.

The General Synod also elected the Rev. Avery D. Post as the fourth president of the United Church. He succeeded the Rev. Joseph H. Evans, who had been elected by the Executive Council following the death of Robert V. Moss, Jr., in October 1976.

(JOSEPH H. EVANS)

[827.D; 827.G.3; 827.H; 827.J.3]

ROMAN CATHOLIC CHURCH

Pope Paul VI reached his 80th birthday on Sept. 26, 1977, amid mounting rumours that he would resign. Resignation was always unlikely; the pope saw his office as the cross he had to bear, believed that "universal paternity" could not be resigned, and did not wish to set precedents for the future. In his discourses throughout the year, he continued to steer a middle course, denouncing liturgical innovations and experimenters as much as the traditionalist Archbishop Marcel Lefebvre.

In one sense, however, Pope Paul might be said to have completed preparations for the election of his successor. On June 27 he created five new cardinals, thus bringing the effective electoral college to 120. One of the most significant appointments was that of Giovanni Cardinal Benelli, previously the energetic chief of the Vatican bureaucracy, to be archbishop of Florence. Benelli was expected to become the next president of the Italian Episcopal Conference and to give it a more vigorously anti-Communist line.

One modest innovation helped to give some content to "collegiality," the idea that pope and bishops together were responsible for the church. The French bishops, instead of making their periodic *ad limina* visits to Rome individually, went in regional groups for working sessions around a table. But on one of these occasions the pope rebuked Bishop Guy-Marie Riobé of Orléans for reopening the question of priestly celibacy: the idea of married priests in the Western Church had been examined and found "inopportune," and so "impossible or illusory suggestions" should not be advanced.

Similar language was used in rejecting the ordination of women. On January 27 a 6,000-word document, published by the Congregation for the Doctrine of the Faith, said that women could not be ordained because there was no tradition of ordaining them. It tried to base an argument on appropriateness: "Because a priest truly acts in the person of Christ, there ought to be a natural resemblance between Christ and his minister." Women's organizations, especially in the U.S., were quick to point out that this argument reduced "natural resemblance" to "sexual resemblance." There were many protests: 23 professors and administrators of the Jesuit College of Theology at Berkeley, Calif., wrote an open letter to Archbishop Jean Jadot, apostolic delegate in Washington, D.C., to express their "disappointment and disagreement."

Collegiality in the sense of consultation was illustrated by the American "Call to Action" program. After 1,200 delegates had met in Detroit in October 1976 and passed 182 resolutions in three days, the response

More than 45,000 Roman Catholics attended a charismatic conference in Montreal in June.

communion now" and said that it was already happening. This, though true, was felt to be tactless.

The synod meeting in Rome in October was concerned with youth and catechetics. It refused to endorse a thoroughgoing "theology of liberation," which would turn the church into a political instrument, but it also rejected the conservative view that literal orthodoxy was more important than relevance. In other words, the synod was "moderate," the watchword for the year and for the pontificate.

(PETER HEBBLETHWAITE)
See also Vatican City State.
[827.C; 827.G.2; 827.J.2]

THE ORTHODOX CHURCH

United in faith and basic principles of canonical discipline, the Orthodox Church comprises a number of administratively independent ecclesiastical provinces called autocephalies or autocephalous churches, which correspond either to ancient centres of Christianity in the Middle East, to nations subsequently converted, or to newer communities created in modern times. These churches recognize an honorary primate in the person of the Greek ecumenical patriarch of Constantinople (Istanbul), whose community in Turkey is rapidly dwindling and whose activity is frequently impeded by political tensions between Greece and Turkey. Pressures by Communist governments in Eastern Europe—where 90% of Orthodox Christians live—constitute another serious obstacle to united action. It was therefore remarkable that, in spite of such adverse conditions, the Orthodox Church succeeded in 1976–77 in several efforts to establish a common stand.

These efforts included the meeting, on Nov. 21–28, 1976, in Chambésy, Switz., of a preconciliar conference, with the task of preparing a formal Great Council of the entire church. The conference approved a preliminary agenda, which would be studied by the local churches before being presented for decision at the future council. Its points included the burning issue of the Orthodox "dispersion," *i.e.*, those areas where, as in America, Western Europe, and Australia, the jurisdictions of various churches overlap; the order to be followed in establishing new independent churches; and problems related to the ecumenical movement.

Several commissions met to discuss issues of common concern, including the date of Easter and the dialogue with the Roman Catholic Church. The dialogue with the Anglican Communion was pursued at two general meetings of the mixed Anglican-Orthodox Commission, but it was clouded by the decision of some Anglican provinces to ordain women to the priesthood. That decision drew a unanimously negative response on the Orthodox side. However, the Orthodox recognized the need of furthering the role of women in the church, and a special conference of Orthodox women met in Agapia, Romania (September 1976), with a follow-up in Crestwood, N.Y. (April 30, 1977).

The death of Patriarch Justinian of Ro-

of the bishops to the pleas for greater social involvement and increased participation of the laity in church government was received in May 1977. On the whole the U.S. bishops approved the social orientation of the "Call to Action" but were cool on the more radical proposals which seemed to challenge their teaching authority.

Archbishop Lefebvre continued to cause trouble by his opposition to the vernacular mass and modernism in the church. In February his Parisian supporters occupied the church of Saint-Nicolas-du-Chardonnet and held it for many months. On June 29 Lefebvre ordained 14 priests at Econe, Switz.; hints had been dropped that he might be excommunicated, but despite a provocative sermon, in which he declared that Communists, Freemasons, and—somewhat oddly—the Orthodox were infiltrating the church, no further disciplinary measures were taken.

Demonstrators against the Vatican's cautious *Ostpolitik* were out in St. Peter's Square in Rome on June 9 when Janos Kadar, first secretary of the Hungarian Communist Party, had an audience in the pope's private library. There was an exchange of gifts and banalities about "mutual efforts at securing peace." The Hungarian cardinal, Laszlo Lekai, had already shown much more flexibility than his tough-minded predecessor, Jozsef Cardinal Mindszenty. But the appearance of harmony was disturbed in August when a group of Hungarian priests protested against the restrictions placed on them in catechism classes. In Poland the church was less reliant on Vatican diplomacy. Stefan Cardinal Wyszynski preached in support of the imprisoned Radom workers and discreetly backed the human rights movement. In May a hunger strike in St. Martin's Church, Warsaw, brought together, for the first time, workers, Catholic intellectu-

als, and dissident Marxists. By a quirk of Polish law, the "right of sanctuary" still existed: some saw this as a parable of the church as a place where the truth could be spoken without fear.

Elsewhere church-state conflicts were intensified. In Rhodesia, Bishop Donal Lamont, a fiery Irish Carmelite, was hurried off into exile. There he denounced the Smith regime and continued to act as bishop of Umtali as far as possible. In Brazil, Father João Burnier was shot dead before the eyes of his bishop when they went together to protest about a case of arrest and torture. The Brazilian bishops had said in a long collective pastoral letter in November 1976 that "national security" was made the pretext for setting aside elementary civil rights and for using torture.

The most positive ecumenical event of the year was the publication on January 19 of *Authority in the Church*, a product of the Anglican-Roman Catholic joint theological commission. Though it did not conceal Anglican hesitations about the pope's claims to infallibility and "universal jurisdiction," it also said that Anglicans could recognize the pope's primacy. Taken with previous agreements on Eucharist and ministry, *Authority in the Church* paved the way for full communion between the two churches. In August, Michael Ramsey, former archbishop of Canterbury, predicted that union would be achieved by the end of the century, but this kind of euphoria received setbacks. The document against the ordination of women appeared only a week after *Authority in the Church* and seemed like a deliberate blow to the hopes of agreement, since some Anglican provinces had already decided to ordain women. This soured the atmosphere for the visit of Donald Coggan, archbishop of Canterbury, to Rome, April 27–29. It was not a great success. Coggan preached a sermon on the need for "inter-

mania (March 26) was followed by the election, on June 12, of Patriarch Justin, formerly metropolitan of Moldavia. The death of Archbishop Makarios of Cyprus led to the election of a temporary head of the church, Metropolitan Chrysostomos of Paphos, whose position would not involve direct political responsibilities since a layman succeeded Makarios as president. Metropolitan Ireney, the aged primate of the autocephalous church in America, resigned effective October 25. His successor, Bishop Theodosius of Pittsburgh, was the first U.S.-born metropolitan of the American church. (JOHN MEYENDORFF)

EASTERN NON-CHALCEDONIAN CHURCHES

The church of Ethiopia remained in turmoil. Abuna Tekle Haimanot, "elected" on July 7, 1976, by 317 electoral votes out of 1,549 while his predecessor, Theophilos, was still imprisoned without trial, was still nominally in charge, while the traditional structures of the church had been thrown into confusion by the secularization of church properties and the civil war.

In the Armenian church, the former head of the American diocese, Archbishop Karekin Sarkissian, was elected, on May 22, 1977, as catholicos-coadjutor of the see of Cilicia (now in Antelias, Lebanon), after the practical retirement of the reigning catholicos, Khoren. The see of Cilicia stood in opposition (mainly on political grounds) to the "supreme" catholicos in Echmiadzin (Soviet Armenia). Contacts between the Oriental Non-Chalcedonian churches and the Western world were fostered by an unofficial meeting of their representatives with Roman Catholic theologians in Vienna in September 1976 and by the extended visit to the U.S. of Patriarch Shenouda III of the Coptic Church of Egypt in April 1977. (JOHN MEYENDORFF)

[827.B; 827.G.1; 827.J.1]

Patriarch Shenouda III of the Coptic Church of Egypt conducted services at the Coptic Orthodox Church of St. Mark in Jersey City, New Jersey, during a visit to the U.S. in April.

JUDAISM

Contemporary Judaism frames issues for discussion around questions that, among other religious groups, appear to be principally of political, rather than theological, interest. But Judaism deems the Jewish people to be a fundamental theological category, and it follows that for Judaism the fate of the Jewish people and the faith of Judaism are intertwined. Political issues, accordingly, bear theological dimensions.

One such issue was the character of the relationship of world Jewry to the state of Israel. In the spring of 1977 a concerted effort to call into question the acceptability of a small, dissident group, Breira ("Alternative"), raised once more the perennial issues of statehood and peoplehood in Judaism. Breira's advocates maintained that criticism of Israeli policies is legitimate in the Diaspora. Its critics accepted that proposition but argued that Breira's particular positions threaten the security of the Jewish state. In this regard, the comment of Leonard Fein (*Moment*, May 1977) was representative: "Is it not an act of unseemly arrogance for Americans . . . to announce that one set of risks rather than another is the more acceptable? Acceptable to whom? To those who make the announcement, or to those who will have to live or die according to their wisdom?" Fein further accused Breira of being a "one-issue organization." Breira came into being, others pointed out, to influence the media, and the concerted attacks on it that appeared in the media in 1977 seemed an appropriate response.

But Zionism, it was agreed in 1977, does require a fresh interpretation. This was the view of Shemaryahu Talmon of Hebrew University, expressed in *Jewish Observer* and *Middle East Review*. A Zionist, Israeli, and a Jew, Talmon maintained that Zionist ideology requires reexamination as a concept, not merely as politics. In particular, Talmon took the position, contrary to much Zionist thought, that the Diaspora—the communities of Jews living outside the state of Israel—must flourish and should not be deemed merely an instrument of convenience to the state. "I have come to the conclusion that a viable and flourishing diaspora is providential and a necessity for the viability of the State of Israel." Zionism, moreover, stresses the group. But, Talmon points out, "The more you stress the value of the individual, the more you undermine his readiness to realize an idea linked with the group concept." He concluded, "To me Zionism remains a national renaissance movement which has not fulfilled itself by the mere establishment of the sovereign State of Israel. I see the State as a vehicle to be used to try to develop again a Jewish culture."

American Judaism, for its part, raised questions about its own institutional development. In an important statement, *Agenda for American Jews: Federation and Synagogue*, Samuel H. Dresner pointed out that American Jews should form a holy community—*kehillah kedoshah*—a sacred people. But instead the classical religious values of Torah and commandments are lacking. Part of the problem, Dresner maintained, is that the two leading institutions of Judaism, the synagogues and the federations of Jewish philanthropies, do not cooperate with one another. The synagogues see philanthropic organization as secular; federations see synagogues as ineffective. But Dresner saw the failure of secularism and the renewal of faith as reasons for hope.

In the 1960s and early 1970s, a number of radical experiments in Judaism flourished, in the form of *havurot*, or religious fellowships, and *batim*, or Jewish residence houses. Writing in *Sh'ma*, Michael A. Monson noted that the young founders of the *havurot* and *batim* are "not so young anymore," and the students of the present period are "more private." "The generation of five years ago threw off the institutional helping hand. . . . Now the students want others to do things for them."

In synagogues, on the other hand, the *havurot*, developing as a result of the needs of synagogue members, continue to flourish. Lewis E. Bogage, also writing in *Sh'ma*, said that *havurot* "reduce the hollowness and loneliness of the temple as an institution and create family groups which can assist their members in the celebration of significant moments." These groups create "a contagious sense of friendship and vitality wherever they have been allowed to grow." But he also pointed out that *havurot* do not flourish under all circumstances. Some become elitist and separate from the larger synagogue body of which they are a part. Rabbis sometimes fail "to understand the independent, democratic nature of a *havurah* group . . . *Havurah* programming cannot be . . . organized from the top, but most of our temples are organized in this fashion." These comments suggest that while the promise of the late 1960s and early 1970s had not been fully kept, it had not been entirely fraudulent.

The year was marked by the transfer of leadership in important religious institutions. Rabbi Norman Lamm was elected president of Yeshiva University, the centre of American Orthodox Judaism. Rabbi Emanuel Rackman, City University of New York, took up the post of president of Bar Ilan University, the Orthodox Jewish university in Israel. (JACOB NEUSNER)

[826]

Millions of Hindu pilgrims bathed in the Ganges River during a huge religious festival in January.

BUDDHISM

In the immediate post-World War II period, Asian Buddhist leaders, who had actively cooperated in the movements for political independence, had high hopes that Buddhism would play a decisive role in the new social and political order. Recent developments, however, have indicated that Buddhism now faces a markedly different political atmosphere, ranging from mild antagonism to hostility.

In Sri Lanka a coalition of leftist parties toppled the regime of Prime Minister Sirimavo Bandaranaike, who had been an outspoken supporter of Buddhism. From Burma it was reported that over 10,000 technocrats and intellectuals, including Buddhist monks, had left the country. In 1976 hostility between two groups of Burmese refugee monks in Thailand had erupted when some Shan (one of Burma's ethnic minority groups) monks set fire to a temple in Bangkok where Burmese monks lived, causing several deaths. Former Thai dictator Thanom Kittikachorn, who returned from Singapore in 1976 ostensibly to enter the Buddhist priesthood, left the monastery early in 1977, causing much speculation.

The fate of Buddhism in Indochina was a matter of great concern. In Vietnam it was difficult to estimate how many persons, including Buddhist lay leaders and priests, had been sentenced to reeducation camps. In Laos, where Buddhism traditionally had been supported by the monarchy, King Savang Vatthana was reported to be learning Marxism-Leninism in a reeducation centre. The Cambodian constitution guaranteed the right to worship according to any religion, but "reactionary religion" was forbidden. There was every indication that Buddhism was being treated as such a "reactionary" religion; a French observer reported in 1976 that Buddhist pagodas were being used as storehouses and that the areas around Buddhist temples had been converted into pigsties.

The number of Buddhist meditation centres and educational institutions in Europe, the Americas, and the Southern Hemisphere continued to grow. Early in 1977 the supreme head of the Kagyu order of Tibetan Buddhism, Gyalwa Karmapa, visited the U.S. Two 7th-century Buddhist temples were unearthed in Soviet Central Asia by archaeologists of the Tadzhik Academy of Sciences.   (JOSEPH MITSUO KITAGAWA)
[824]

HINDUISM

Although India is constitutionally a secular state, the continuing importance of religion, especially Hinduism, in Indian politics was evident in 1977 in the effective role played by right-wing and nationalistic Hindu groups in the defeat of Prime Minister Indira Gandhi. (See INDIA.) These groups had strongly opposed government policies which they saw as undermining the traditional values of Indian society.

During 1977 the Indian government sought to enforce the Protection of Civil Rights Act, passed at the end of 1976, which specifically strengthens and extends the constitutional prohibitions against the ancient Hindu practice of "untouchability." The practice had continued in many parts of India despite the constitutional provisions, and the new law was intended to eliminate it altogether. It prescribes severe penalties for advocating or preaching untouchability and for compelling anyone to do tasks regarded by Hindus as "unclean." Also, whereas the constitution opened public temples and shrines to the lowest castes, the new law makes private places of worship accessible as well.

A notable event for Hindu scholarship was the publication by the International Academy of Indian Culture, New Delhi, of a facsimile edition of the Kashmiri text of the Bhagavata-Purana, one of the most popular and important Hindu scriptures. The Kashmiri text, which dates from the 14th century and is considered the purest form of the Purana, was reconstructed from badly damaged and fragmented bark manuscripts and required 12 years of painstaking labour by a team of German and Indian scholars.

The year also saw the continued growth of some 125 Hindu organizations throughout the world (nearly one quarter of them in the U.S.) offering a variety of doctrines and yogic, meditational, and devotional practices. The International Meditation Society, founded and led by the Maharishi Mahesh Yogi, drew special attention in 1977 with its claim that advanced meditators might attain classical yogic powers (siddhis), such as levitation and invisibility.
(H. PATRICK SULLIVAN)

[823]

ISLAM

The Hanafi Muslim takeover of three buildings in Washington, D.C., in March 1977 was best understood in relation to changes within the American Black Muslim movement (now called the World Community of Islam in the West). Hamaas Abdul Khaalis (see BIOGRAPHY), leader of the Hanafis, had been a member of the Black Muslims until 1958; in the later 1960s, he started his own group in New York City. He attracted basketball star Kareem Abdul-Jabbar, who apparently encouraged the Hanafis to move to Washington, D.C. In 1973 the Hanafi residence in Washington was attacked by gunmen, and seven people were killed. As with the murderers of Malcolm X in 1965, the men found guilty in the 1973 attack were alleged to have been members of the Black Muslim movement. In 1975 Wallace Muhammad (see BIOGRAPHY) succeeded his father, the late Elijah Muhammad, as leader of the Black Muslims, and a number of substantial doctrinal and organizational changes subsequently took place in that group. At a rally held early in March 1977, Wallace Muhammad reiterated the new tenets, which more closely reflect traditional Islamic beliefs and practices.

In their March takeover, the Hanafis demanded that the men convicted for the 1973 attack be delivered to them, and that the film Mohammad, Messenger of God, then opening in New York City and Los Angeles, be withdrawn. The film had been endorsed by certain Middle Eastern Muslim dignitaries and was also supported by the World Community of Islam, but a number of Muslim groups objected to it.

Muslims crowded into Mecca, Saudi Arabia, during the annual pilgrimage (hajj). The large structure in the centre of the courtyard is the Ka'bah, representing the physical axis of the Muslim world.

WORLD CHURCH MEMBERSHIP

Reckoning religious membership throughout the world remains one of the least exact of sciences for several fundamental reasons. First, different religions have differing theories and methods of counting and reporting. Some simply depend upon the population statistics issued by governments. Others, such as Wahhabi Muslims, conscientiously object to "numbering the people." Some reckon only adults or heads of families; others count children, servants, and retainers.

Second, the language varies between religious communities. Some count "members," others reckon "adherents" or "communicants" or "constituents." Procedures vary from country to country within the same religion; quite exact statistics are available as to Buddhist membership in Hawaii, but only estimates can be made for Burma and Sri Lanka. Third, where religious adherence is enforced by law, it is customary to count virtually the entire population in the statistics of a single religion. Fourth, where ideological regimes have been established which are opposed to all "religion," as in most countries under Communist control, it is difficult to obtain reliable estimates as to the staying power of the older world views. Fifth, the usual tabulations make no provision for several religions that have gained ground since the sociologists of religion established certain typologies and categories. There is no reckoning of Baha'i, of Chondokyo in Korea, of the Spiritualist Church in Brazil, of Jainism in India.

Finally, each year war sees substantial movements of refugees. Refugee figures are at best estimates, and the incorporation of the refugees in other, and perhaps religiously quite different, countries is slow to appear in statistical reports. The reader is therefore advised to reflect carefully upon the statistics and to refer to the articles discussing the different countries and the different religions when pursuing the subject in depth. (FRANKLIN H. LITTELL)

After two days of negotiations in which the ambassadors from Egypt, Iran, and Pakistan played key roles, the Hanafis surrendered. The showing of the film had been temporarily suspended. In July the Hanafis involved were convicted of second-degree murder, conspiracy, and kidnapping. In September they were sentenced to prison.

The strength of Islam in the U.S. was growing rapidly, largely as a result of immigration. In March, Muhammad Abdul Rauf, director of the Islamic Center in Washington, estimated the number of Muslims currently in the U.S. at two million. In early May more than 200 Muslim organizations in North America met in New Jersey under the sponsorship of the World Muslim League, which has headquarters in Mecca; the Islamic Conference of North America was recognized as the general coordinating body for these groups.

In Muslim countries political and religious developments continued to be inextricably fused (see MIDDLE EASTERN AFFAIRS; PHILIPPINES; THAILAND), but the vitality of Islamic movements was evident in a number of less politically related activities. In March, Bedouin sculptor Saleem Hamad Aouda was allowed by tribal elders to continue his art carvings in Sinai, provided it was clear no one would consider them as idols. The Bedouin have been among the most conservative of Muslims in their attitude toward the visual arts. The number of Muslims making the pilgrimage to Mecca was now well over one million, and Saudi Arabia expressed concern about the number of pilgrims who stayed in that country and sought jobs. Saudi Arabia announced support of a five-year project for a modern biography of the Prophet Muhammad. (R. W. SMITH)

Estimated Membership of the Principal Religions of the World

Religions	North America [1]	South America	Europe [2]	Asia [3]	Africa	Oceania [4]	World
Total Christian	231,099,700	158,980,000	348,059,300	89,909,000	137,460,300	18,112,600	983,620,900
Roman Catholic	131,631,500	147,280,000	182,514,300	47,046,000	53,740,000	4,475,000	566,686,800
Eastern Orthodox	4,189,000	552,000	50,545,000	1,894,000	15,255,000 [5]	380,000	72,815,000
Protestant [6]	95,279,200	11,148,000	115,000,000	40,969,000	68,465,300 [7]	13,257,600	344,119,100
Jewish	6,641,118	727,000	4,082,400	3,203,460	294,400	84,000	15,032,378
Muslim [8]	249,200	238,300	8,283,500	433,001,000	134,285,200	103,000	576,160,200
Zoroastrian	250	2,000	6,000	224,700	600	——	233,550
Shinto [9]	60,000	92,000	——	55,004,000	——	——	55,156,000
Taoist	16,000	12,000	——	31,088,100	——	——	31,116,100
Confucian	96,100	85,150	25,000	173,940,250	500	42,200	174,189,200
Buddhist [10]	155,250	195,300	200,000	260,117,000	2,000	16,000	260,685,550
Hindu [11]	81,000	782,300	260,000	515,449,500	483,650	841,000	517,897,450
Totals	238,398,618	161,114,050	360,916,200	1,561,937,010	272,526,650	19,198,800	2,614,091,328
Population [12]	353,560,000	230,139,000	738,746,000	2,355,700,000	423,655,000	22,157,000	4,123,957,000

[1] Includes Central America and the West Indies.

[2] Includes the U.S.S.R. and other countries with established Marxist ideology where continuing religious adherence is difficult to estimate.

[3] Includes areas in which persons have traditionally enrolled in several religions, as well as mainland China with an official Marxist establishment.

[4] Includes New Zealand and Australia as well as islands of the South Pacific.

[5] Includes Coptic Christians.

[6] Protestant statistics usually include "full members" (adults) rather than all baptized persons and are not comparable to those of ethnic religions or churches counting all constituents.

[7] Including many new sects and cults among African Christians.

[8] The chief base of Islam is still ethnic, although some missionary work is now carried on in Europe and America (viz. "Black Muslims"). In countries where Islam is established, minority religions are frequently persecuted and their statistics are hard to come by.

[9] A Japanese ethnic religion, Shinto has declined markedly since the Japanese emperor gave up claim to divinity (1947).

[10] Buddhism has several modern renewal movements which have gained adherents in Europe and America and other areas not formerly ethnic-Buddhist. In Asia it has also made rapid gains in recent years and shown greater staying power under persecution than Taoism or Confucianism.

[11] Hinduism's strength in India has been enhanced by nationalism. Modern Hinduism has also developed renewal movements that have reached Europe and America for converts.

[12] United Nations, Department of Economic and Social Affairs; data refer to midyear 1977.

(FRANKLIN H. LITTELL)

THE MODERN MARTYRS

by Martin Marty

Critics of American religion in the 1970s frequently claimed that believers were interested in nothing but their own spiritual welfare or the health of their local congregations. Suddenly, during 1977, events around the world brought home to the Americans an awareness of the repression of believers and began to lead them to identify again with sufferers of whatever faith in many nations. To many Americans words like persecution, torture, martyrdom, and pogrom had belonged to remote Christian and Jewish pasts. Now they began to learn that the realities these words represent are very much present in today's world.

The Fallout of Helsinki. One of the most tense situations developed over the issue of human rights, especially religious rights, in the Soviet Union. Debates over Soviet harassment of religious groups were not new; for several years American Jews and their friends had expressed agitation over "the plight of Soviet Jewry." The fresh element in the campaign appeared early in the year when the new U.S. president, Jimmy Carter, declared that he would speak up for human rights even though the direct effects of his advocacy would necessarily be minor and even if it set back progress in the strategic arms limitation talks.

President Carter based his protests on the Helsinki accords of 1975, whereby the signers—including the Soviets—had agreed to assure civil, religious, and other basic rights to their citizens. Soviet reaction to Carter's statements only gave increased visibility to the difficulties of religious groups in much of Eastern Europe. In Brussels late in 1976, Archbishop Basil Krivocheine of the Russian Orthodox Church complained that the World Council of Churches had failed to recognize the problems of Soviet Christians. He also charged that the Russian church hierarchy had been guilty of passivity and even of complicity with the authorities in their antireligious activities.

During the year the Institution of Scientific Atheism in the Soviet Union acknowledged for the first

Martin Marty is professor of the history of modern Christianity at the University of Chicago and associate editor of The Christian Century.

time that the number of sectarian and even underground groups in the U.S.S.R. was growing rapidly. M. K. Tepliakov, signer of the report, observed that half the believers were under 40 and thus represented a problem for the future. Now and then individual Christians received attention, as in the case of Georgi Vins, an imprisoned Soviet Baptist pastor. There were rumours that he had been released, but it was learned later that he was still confined for his religious activities.

From Right and Left. A second front of global interest divided American religious and civil rights advocates into left and right flanks. Conservatives complained about the frequency of liberal protests against religious persecution on the part of right-wing regimes, especially those supported by the U.S. government. Typical among these were the South Korean and Chilean governments. Such attacks, said people on the right, constituted a case of selective indignation, since they were not matched by equally constant notice given to Soviet, South Vietnamese, or Cambodian repression.

The South Korean case received the most attention. A dozen prominent U.S. Christians, including heads of the National Council of Churches and of some Roman Catholic religious orders, approached President Carter through UN Ambassador Andrew Young, asking him to use his personal prestige to criticize Pres. Park Chung Hee for alleged "harassment or persecution of Christian leaders."

Debates about human rights also divided the former antiwar forces from Vietnam war days. Virtually all dissenters against that war had feared that the North Vietnamese and Viet Cong, once they

Jews in London held a religious ceremony outside the Soviet Aeroflot offices in Piccadilly to protest Soviet harassment of Jews.

KEYSTONE

617

achieved victory, would "reeducate" and punish the defeated South Vietnamese. But now that it was actually happening, some explained away persecutions as an inevitable part of the aftermath of war while others wanted to include South Vietnamese Christian and Buddhist dissenters in their appeals for human rights.

James H. Forest, co-chairman of the Catholic Peace Fellowship, and over a hundred peace activists from numerous religious groups charged throughout the year that the victorious Vietnamese had gone back on their promises to respect human rights. Critics of Forest and his colleagues quoted the conservative Roman Catholic archbishop of Saigon, Nguyen van Binh, to the effect that there was no religious persecution. Paul McCleary, the executive director of Church World Service, complained that the strong appeal by the activists made future efforts for peace and freedom more difficult.

The Martyrs of Africa. Africa, especially Uganda and southern Africa, received the most notice. Idi Amin, the president of Uganda, was a Muslim with a special distaste for members of non-Muslim tribes in general and for Christians in particular. On February 5 Amin's police broke down the fence surrounding the home of Anglican Archbishop Janani Luwum, an outspoken advocate of human rights, threatened him, and searched his house. A week later Luwum delivered a letter of protest to Amin, and on February 16 he was killed, after having been tried in a mock court for allegedly helping plot Amin's assassination. Presumably he was the latest among the 100,000 people reportedly killed during Amin's six-year reign.

Luwum's death did not end the problems for Ugandan church people. Late in 1976 Bishop Festo Kivengere of the Anglican diocese of Kigezi had told New Yorkers that there was no organized campaign to persecute Christians in his country. Then early in 1977, finding that he was on the list of targets, he himself had to flee. Rabbi Marc Tanenbaum of the American Jewish Committee criticized the Christian missionaries for having said little about persecution until it touched prominent leaders. Tanenbaum showed particular interest because of Amin's flagrant anti-Semitism.

In the struggles between black and white in Rhodesia and South Africa, some Christians were simply caught in the crossfire. Thus, early in the year, seven nuns and priests were murdered in the Rhodesian bush country by Marxist guerrillas, though Bishop Abel T. Muzorewa of the Methodist Church in Rhodesia later claimed that new evidence exonerated the black nationalists. He blamed the security forces of Prime Minister Ian Smith. Smith banned *Umbowo*, the monthly paper of the Chris-

tian Council of Rhodesia, for being critical of his government, and Muzorewa subsequently announced that he could no longer adhere to his advocacy of nonviolent change.

In South Africa only the official Dutch Reformed Church and some small fundamentalist groups supported the white supremacist government. Robert G. Nelson, the Africa executive of the Christian Church (Disciples of Christ), reported to his church body that arrests and detentions of South African church leaders were resulting in greater unity among the churches, across the boundaries of denomination and race.

A Widening Threat. Right-wing terrorists warned the Jesuits to leave El Salvador on pain of "immediate and systematic execution" because, their persecutors claimed, they supported Communism. Six times the terrorists bombed the Jesuit-run university, and at least two Jesuits were killed. The U.S. State Department warned Gen. Carlos Humberto Romero, the country's leader, to provide protection for the Jesuits, but few expected much response as long as they supported a bill that would redistribute some farmland to peasants. While the Jesuits, who stopped wearing their clerical garb in the face of great dangers, continued their activities, many conservative Salvadoran Protestants continued to support the government.

Though many evangelicals tended to link anti-Communism with Christianity, U.S. evangelist Billy Graham, in a major reversal, accepted an invitation to preach in September as a guest of the Council of Free Churches in Hungary. Long an outspoken foe of Communism and every form of socialism, Graham later moderated his old criticisms enough to say that, while he would continue to avoid making political references in his preaching, he did observe that in moderate Communist regimes Christians could coexist with many kinds of socialism.

Viewing the whole scene of persecutions and tortures, German Protestant theologian Jürgen Moltmann, at the World Alliance of Reformed Churches meeting at St. Andrews, Scotland, summarized the trend: "It is as if we are sliding towards medieval times . . . . It is going on all over the world, and the means are more and more sophisticated to bring pain to people." At the very least, news of the repressions awakened American church people. Many of them gave support to the First World Congress on Religious Freedom, which drew 350 delegates from 50 countries to Amsterdam in March. The congress would certainly not be the last effort on a worldwide basis to speak up for those, whether Jewish, Christian, or members of any other persecuted group, who suffered for their religion in the late 20th century.

Rhodesia

Though Rhodesia declared itself a republic on March 2, 1970, it remained a British colony in the eyes of many other nations. It is bounded by Zambia, Mozambique, South Africa, and Botswana. Area: 390,245 sq km (150,674 sq mi). Pop. (1977 est.): 6,740,000, of whom 96% are African and 4% white. Cap. and largest city: Salisbury (urban area pop., 1977 est., 566,000). Language: English (official) and various Bantu languages (1969 census, Shona 71%, Ndebele 15%). Religion: predominantly traditional tribal beliefs; Christian minority. President in 1977, John Wrathall; prime minister, Ian D. Smith.

Early in 1977 negotiations for a constitutional settlement reached a stalemate. The task was later taken up by the new British foreign secretary, David Owen (*see* BIOGRAPHY), who from the outset worked in close consultation with the new U.S. administration. After visiting southern Africa in April, Owen firmly concluded that Ian Smith must hand over power and the Patriotic Front must stop fighting. In January, however, the presidents of Tanzania, Zambia, Mozambique, Botswana, and Angola had already announced their support for the Patriotic Front, led by Joshua Nkomo and Robert Mugabe (*see* BIOGRAPHY), which was conducting guerrilla activities from bases in Mozambique. This decision in no way affected Smith's resolve to have no dealings with the guerrilla leaders, and the Rhodesian armed forces conducted vigorous retaliatory measures, involving at times sharp incursions over the border into Mozambique. Both sides inflicted casualties, not only upon those involved in the fighting but also upon the civilian population.

At the end of May the Rhodesian forces carried out a raid deep into Mozambique, which led to suggestions that Smith was trying to provoke an international conflict. On the western border Rhodesia accused Botswana of harbouring schoolchildren who had been abducted at the end of January by guerrillas, with a view to training them to fight against the Rhodesian government. The majority of the children subsequently claimed that they had crossed the border voluntarily and were allowed to remain.

As a result of the guerrilla warfare there was a steady departure of whites from Rhodesia, including young men who left to avoid military service. In addition, the involvement of so many people in military activities had an adverse effect upon the economy, the output of both agriculture and industry being lower than in 1976, while 26% of the national budget was devoted to supporting military operations. The Rhodesian dollar was devalued by 3% in October.

In spite of the apparently hard line that Smith was taking with regard to future developments, there were those within his own party who believed he should adopt a still more rigid policy. They were critical of his proposals to soften some of the discriminatory race laws, and they were totally opposed to any form of negotiations that

Rhodesia

might lead to black majority rule. The prime minister reacted on April 29 by expelling his opponents from the Rhodesian Front party, and they in turn formed the right-wing Rhodesian Action Party. Their fears had been in part aroused by discussions that took place in March between Smith and Bishop Abel Muzorewa (*see* BIOGRAPHY), after which both claimed that they were willing to hold a referendum to see which of the African leaders commanded the greatest support. This plan did not meet with the approval of the Patriotic Front, which claimed that it alone should take control of an interim African government prior to any elections.

The Patriotic Front was recognized as the leading force in the independence campaign by the Organization of African Unity at its summit meeting in Libreville, Gabon, early in July. This was a blow both to Smith and to Muzorewa, and although Nkomo said that the bishop and his supporters were welcome to join the Patriotic Front his offer did not meet with an enthusiastic response. Smith, meanwhile, continued to refuse to deal with the Patriotic Front. To demonstrate the support he still had in the country he announced parliamentary elections for August 31. Both the Patriotic Front and Muzorewa's party refused to have any part in this move, and Smith won an overwhelming victory over the Rhodesian Action Party.

In spite of their refusal to take part in any government that Smith might set up after the elections, Muzorewa and the hitherto hard-line Ndabaningi Sithole (*see* BIOGRAPHY) had talks with Smith with a view to creating a majority government of a moderate political outlook. Sithole in particular reversed his former line, calling for cooperation between the races, while Muzorewa was prepared to modify his earlier demand for one man, one vote. Such unlikely cooperation was, however, undermined by the new proposals drafted by Owen and the U.S. secretary of state, Cyrus Vance, and published on September 1. Their plan accepted the leading role that must be played by the Patriotic Front and proposed that the armed forces of an independent Zimbabwe should be based upon the guerrilla armies, together with such elements of the existing Rhodesian armed forces as might be deemed acceptable. In addition, there would be a UN force to help the peacekeeping operation in the interim period before independence, while during that time power would be in the hands of a special resident commissioner appointed by the British government.

The plan had a lukewarm reception in all quarters, though gradually most of the leading figures said they were prepared to accept it as a basis for negotiation. All parties were wary of the proposal on the composition of the Army. Muzorewa, meanwhile, modified his policy and came out in sharp opposition to any dealings with Smith.

On November 24 Smith announced that he was prepared to accept the majority-rule principle of one man, one vote for Rhodesia as a basis for further negotiations with black leaders. Smith continued to insist, however, that he would meet only with the black nationalists inside Rhodesia and would not deal with the militant guerrilla organizations banned inside the country. He thereby excluded Mugabe and Nkomo from the talks. On December 2 Smith, Muzorewa, Sithole, and Sen. Jeremiah Chirau of the Zimbabwe United People's Organization met for the first of a series of conferences that continued throughout the month. The major problem, unresolved at the year's end, was whether and how to give minority whites veto powers in a black-dominated Parliament.

(KENNETH INGHAM)

See also African Affairs.

An angry horse tried to bite rodeo rider Joe Alexander's leg during the bareback bronc event at the Calgary Stampede in July.

CALGARY HERALD

Rodeo

Professional rodeo, which first took shape in 1936 with the formation of the Cowboys Turtle Association ("a turtle never gets anywhere if he doesn't stick his neck out"), continued to grow in 1977. One sign of growth was evident at the headquarters of the Professional Rodeo Cowboys Association (PRCA) in Denver, Colo., where computers made it possible for cowboys to enter any North American rodeo merely by calling a specific telephone number; rodeo stock for each contestant was also selected by computer. In 1977 the PRCA sanctioned some 600 rodeos in North America with prize money amounting to almost $7 million. Membership edged toward 4,000 as thousands of apprentice cowboys strove to gain full professional status by winning their first $1,000. During the year Major League Rodeo, Inc., of Los Angeles came into existence and sought the PRCA's sanction for a series of rodeo team franchises. Though no final PRCA decision was made, the new organization began drafting cowboys and drew up an 84-game schedule involving six teams: Los Angeles, Denver, Kansas City, San Antonio, Salt Lake City, and Tulsa. The first team competition was set for April 1, 1978.

When the PRCA regular season ended on November 6, the following cowboys were crowned champions on the basis of their yearly earnings: Tom Ferguson of Miami, Okla., all-around winner with $65,981; Bob Berger of Norman, Okla., in saddle bronc riding with $25,436; Joe Alexander of Cora, Wyo., in bareback riding with $41,555; Don Gay of Mesquite, Texas, in bull riding with $35,053; Roy Cooper of Durant, Okla., in calf roping with $45,713; Larry Ferguson of Miami, Okla., in steer wrestling with $27,437; and Jerold Camarillo of Oakdale, Calif., in team roping with $18,454. In barrel racing, Jimmie Gibbs of Valley Mills, Texas, won $21,894 and with it the PRCA women's title.

In early December Oklahoma City was the site of the world championships. Only the year's top 15 finishers in each event were allowed to compete in the ten go-arounds. When the dust settled, the following were declared world champions: Tom Ferguson in all-around with $10,749; J. C. Bonine of Hysham, Mont., in saddle bronc riding with $7,453; Jack Ward of Springdale, Ark., in bareback riding with $6,987; Don Gay in bull riding with $6,521; Jim Gladstone of Cardston, Alberta, in calf roping with $7,166; and Tom Ferguson in steer wrestling with $7,883. The $8,322 team roping prize was shared by two brothers, David Motes of Fresno, Calif., and Dennis Motes of Nasa, Ariz. Jackie Jo Terrin won the women's barrel racing title and $3,610. Once again Tom Ferguson was the top money winner of the year with a grand total of $97,080, which included $20,350 in bonuses. In retrospect, 1977 turned out to be a very satisfying year for rodeo executives, professional riders, apprentice cowboys, and fans who either attended the events or followed the action on their television sets.

(RANDALL E. WITTE)

Romania

A socialist republic on the Balkan Peninsula in southeastern Europe, Romania is bordered by the U.S.S.R., the Black Sea, Bulgaria, Yugoslavia, and Hungary. Area: 237,500 sq km (91,700 sq mi). Pop. (1977): 21,559,400, including (1966) Romanian 88.1%; Hungarian 7.9%; German 1.6%. Cap. and largest city: Bucharest (pop., 1977, 1,807,000). Religion: Romanian Orthodox 70%; Greek Orthodox 10%. General secretary of the Romanian Communist Party, president of the republic, and president of the State Council in 1977, Nicolae Ceausescu; chairman of the Council of Ministers (premier), Manea Manescu.

At 9:21 PM on March 4, 1977, Romania was struck by an earthquake of unusual force (7.1 on the Richter scale). Bucharest and other towns, including Craiova in the west and Iasi in the north, were severely affected. At the time of the earthquake Pres. Nicolae Ceausescu was on an official visit in Nigeria. Having decreed a state of emergency, he flew back to Bucharest, where he landed on the morning of March 5. At a joint meeting of the Romanian Communist Party and the Grand National Assembly, Ceausescu revealed that 1,570 people had been killed and 11,300 injured and that the collapse or damaging of 39,000 dwellings had left almost 35,000 families homeless; 763 economic units in basic sectors of industry, construction, and transport were hit. Ceausescu estimated the cost to Romania's economy at 10 billion lei.

Ten days after the earthquake life in Bucharest had begun to be almost normal. Most of the postwar buildings survived, and of nearly one million dwellings built during the previous 15 years only a few apartment buildings collapsed—two of them in Bucharest where, however, a number of noted artists and writers perished. Many countries hastened to send help, and in thanking them Ceausescu expressed the hope that, in spite of the earthquake, industrial and agricultural production would be able to maintain the rate of growth of Romania's foreign trade in 1977.

The executive Political Committee was enlarged from five to nine members on January 25 with the election of Mme Elena Ceausescu (the general secretary's wife), Cornel Burtica, Gheorghe Radulescu, and Ilie Verdet.

On May 9 Romania celebrated the 100th anniversary of the proclamation of its full independence. At the end of May Ceausescu visited Dobruja to inspect the digging of the Danube–Black Sea Canal, which would run south of the Cernavoda–Constanta railway. Started in November 1949 and abandoned in 1953, the huge project was restarted in 1973. By May 1977, 16 km at the western end of the canal were already completed. On the same occasion Ceausescu declared completed the reconstruction of a triumphal monument erected at Adamclisi, not far from the Bulgarian border, in the 2nd century AD by Roman legions to the memory of the emperor Trajan, conqueror of Dacia and instigator of the long process of romanization of its people. At Constanta

Romania

ROMANIA

Education. (1976–77) Primary, pupils 3,125,584, teachers 147,582; secondary, pupils 371,201, teachers 15,261; vocational, pupils 800,265, teachers 36,574; teacher training (1974–75), students 19,461, teachers 1,291; higher (including 12 universities), students 174,888, teaching staff 13,662.

Finance. Monetary unit: leu, with (Sept. 19, 1977) a commercial rate of 4.97 lei to U.S. $1 (8.65 lei = £1 sterling) and a tourist rate of 12 lei = U.S. $1 (20.50 lei = £1 sterling). Budget (1977 est) balanced at 283.3 billion lei.

Foreign Trade. (1975) Imports 26,548,000,000 lei; exports 26,547,000,000 lei. Import sources: U.S.S.R. 17%; West Germany 11%; East Germany 6%; Switzerland 5%; Czechoslovakia 5%. Export destinations: U.S.S.R. 20%; West Germany 8%; East Germany 5%. Main exports: machinery and transport equipment 25%; petroleum products and metals 22%; chemicals 11%; food 11%.

Transport and Communications. Roads (1975) c. 95,000 km (including 96 km expressways). Motor vehicles in use (1975): passenger c. 138,000; commercial c. 50,000. Railways (1975): 11,039 km; traffic 22,380,000,000 passenger-km, freight 64,803,000,000 net ton-km. Air traffic (1976): 769 million passenger-km; freight 10,580,000 net ton-km. Inland waterways in regular use (1975) 1,628 km. Shipping (1976): merchant vessels 100 gross tons and over 161; gross tonnage 994,184. Telephones (Dec. 1974) 1,076,566. Radio licenses (Dec. 1974) 3,066,000. Television licenses (Dec. 1974) 2,405,000.

Agriculture. Production (in 000; metric tons; 1976): wheat c. 6,730; barley c. 1,400; corn c. 11,700; potatoes c. 2,716; cabbages (1975) c. 620; onions c. 280; tomatoes c. 1,286; sugar, raw value c. 743; sunflower seed c. 800; soybeans c. 250; plums (1975) 560; apples c. 270; grapes c. 1,200; linseed c. 43; tobacco c. 45. Livestock (in 000; Jan. 1976): cattle c. 5,915; sheep 13,867; pigs c. 8,812; horses (1975) 557; poultry c. 78,611.

Industry. Fuel and power (in 000; metric tons; 1976): coal 7,320; lignite 19,771; coke c. 1,850; crude oil 14,590; natural gas (cu m) c. 32,000,000; manufactured gas (cu m) c. 950,000; electricity (kw-hr) 53,720,000. Production (in 000; metric tons; 1975): cement 11,520; iron ore (metal content) 779; pig iron 6,602; crude steel 9,549; petroleum products c. 17,680; sulfuric acid 1,448; fertilizers (nutrient content) nitrogenous 1,292, phosphate 404; cotton yarn 145; cotton fabrics (sq m) 591,000; wool yarn 51; woolen fabrics (sq m; 1974) 94,000; man-made fibres 148; newsprint 44; other paper 605. New dwelling units completed (1975) 178,000.

Ceausescu presided over the launching of the largest ship of the Romanian merchant fleet, the 150,000-ton oil tanker "Independenta."

On August 5 Ceausescu visited the Soviet leader Leonid Brezhnev in the Crimea. Ceausescu also paid state visits to Poland in May, to East Germany in June, and to Bulgaria in September; at that time the Romanian and Bulgarian heads of state agreed to begin construction of the Turnu Magurele-Nikopol hydropower project in 1978 and discussed a similar project on the Danube in the Calarasi-Silistra area. In June Ceausescu met the Hungarian leader Janos Kadar in Hungary.

The novelist Paul Goma, one of the dissidents who on February 14 had signed an open letter appealing to the authorities to show greater regard for human rights, was arrested in early April but was released in May under a general amnesty. On July 5 the official Communist Party newspaper *Scinteia* defended the Eurocommunist position. On January 7, in Rome, Ceausescu had reiterated his belief in the right of all Communist parties to total independence.

Justinian Moisescu, archbishop of Moldavia, was elected patriarch of the Romanian Orthodox Church to succeed Patriarch Justinian Marina, who died on March 26.   (K. M. SMOGORZEWSKI)

Roads:
see Engineering Projects; Transportation

Rockets:
see Defense; Space Exploration

Roman Catholic Church:
see Religion

Rowing

Rwanda

East Germany continued to dominate world rowing in 1977, winning 15 of the 25 men's, women's, and junior events. West Germany with three victories and Great Britain with its first two gold medals in 20 years were also impressive. The five other countries to win world titles were Bulgaria, France, Poland, Switzerland, and the U.S.S.R.

In the men's finals 19 medals went to five Eastern European countries, leaving Great Britain and West Germany with two each and New Zealand with one. The finals were marred by a shifting wind, which produced some inequality between lanes. There were no records, but one did fall in single sculls in the semifinal round when Nikolay Dovgan (U.S.S.R.) rowed to victory in 6 min 49.69 sec to break the 1976 Olympic record of Sean Drea (Ireland) by 2.77 sec. In the final of this event Joachim Dreifke of East Germany had the most sheltered lane and, taking an early lead, won by 3.31 sec from Olympic champion Pertti Karppinen of Finland. Dovgan finished third.

The closest contest was the triumph by 1.88 sec of Mike Hart and Chris Baillieu of the U.K. in the double sculls. In the coxless pairs the U.S.S.R. held off Great Britain, which beat East Germany for the silver medal and was closing fast on the Soviets at the finish line. The only other gold medal to escape East Germany was in the coxed pairs, which Bulgaria won by 2.88 sec to capture its first world title. Most of the five East German victories were clearcut, although in the coxed and coxless fours West Germany and New Zealand, respectively, finished a close second.

In the women's events five Eastern European countries collected all but 4 of the 18 medals. East Germany won all six events for the first time, but had to race hard to win. Bulgaria and the U.S.S.R. both won two silver medals, and the others went to The Netherlands and Romania. Canada did well to win two bronze medals while Bulgaria, Hungary, Romania, and the U.S. shared the remainder.

Eight countries shared the medals in three lightweight events, which were held for the third time but were still not contested by the Eastern European countries. France continued its unbroken run of success in coxless fours; Switzerland produced the winning sculler, Reto Wyss, for the second time; and Great Britain recorded its first win in an international eight-oared event since 1951.

In the eight events at the world junior championships in Tampere, Fin., East Germany lost its stranglehold on junior rowing, retaining only four of the seven titles it had held. West Germany won three gold medals, and the eighth went to Poland. The East Germans finished second in the four events they failed to win, and West Germany also won three silver medals.

At the Henley Royal Regatta in England five trophies went abroad. The University of Washington won the Grand Challenge Cup (eights) and Visitors' Cup (coxless fours); Ridley College, Canada, took the Princess Elizabeth Cup (eights) for the third time in seven years; Trinity College, Dublin, won the Ladies' Plate (eights); and Garda Siochana, the Irish police, gained the Prince Philip Cup (coxed fours). Oxford scored its biggest win in 79 years in the 148-year-old University Boat Race, defeating Cambridge by seven lengths. Cambridge, however, still led in the series with 68 wins to Oxford's 54.　　　(KEITH OSBORNE)

Rwanda

A republic in eastern Africa, and former traditional kingdom whose origins may be traced back to the 15th century, Rwanda is bordered by Zaire, Uganda, Tanzania, and Burundi. Area: 26,338 sq km (10,169 sq mi). Pop. (1977 est.): 4,449,000, including (1970) Hutu 90%; Tutsi 9%; and Twa 1%. Cap. and largest city: Kigali (pop., 1977 est., 90,-000). Language (official): French and Kinyarwanda. Religion: Roman Catholic 41%; most of the remainder are animist; there are small Protestant and Muslim minorities. President in 1977, Gen. Juvénal Habyalimana.

As current chairman of the Common African and Mauritian Organization (OCAM), Pres. Juvé-

The Oxford University boat surged ahead to beat the Cambridge crew by seven lengths in the 148-year-old University Boat Race on the River Thames.

CENTRAL PRESS/PICTORIAL PARADE

nal Habyalimana took an active part in the Franco-African summit conference at Dakar, Senegal, in April 1977 and at OCAM's own summit there immediately afterward. He expressed the need for OCAM to open its activities to other groups and supported French intervention in Zaire (repeating this during a visit to Gabon).

The World Bank estimated Rwanda to be the poorest country in the world, as well as one of the most densely populated. With little but subsistence agriculture, Rwanda found a bright spot in high world coffee prices and its own increasing coffee exports (430,000 bags in 1976, compared with 184,000 in 1972). The March 1977 budget, at RwFr 6 billion, was 22.8% above that of 1976; foreign aid, principally Belgian, provided 40% of government revenue. The Tanzania-Rwanda Commission agreed on a rail link from Kigali, and Zaire turned over the jointly owned Ntaruka hydroelectric power station, after 17 years of dispute, as a gesture of goodwill. Attempts to diversify crops with banana resulted in much unlooked-for conversion into banana beer, and annual per capita consumption reached 735 pints.

(MOLLY MORTIMER)

Sailing

Early in 1977 the 12-m and the Southern Ocean Racing Conference (SORC) series in the Caribbean kept the top design teams and sailmakers busy in a warm-up for the America's Cup series. In the 12-m field the Australians and Swedes produced interesting designs, while the Americans introduced two new boats. The SORC series featured one outstanding boat, the 39-ft "Imp," designed by Ron Holland and nicknamed "The Bionic Baby" by opponents. Lightly built, using a tubular alloy framework for strength, and owned by Dave Allen, it went fast in all conditions and won the series easily. Another newcomer, "Bay Bea," a Britton Chance centreboarder, showed flashes of brilliance, but breakages eliminated its chance. For the big-boat spot in the team the U.S. finally chose "Scaramouche," a craft that was very good in heavy winds.

By June the 12-m elimination series for both the U.S. defender of the America's Cup and the challengers from France, Australia, and Sweden were under way, off Newport, R.I. In the U.S. selection trials, Ted Turner (see BIOGRAPHY), self-proclaimed as the only amateur among the professionals, won the competition with the revamped "Cou-

The American yacht "Courageous" made it four straight over the Australian entry "Australia" in the America's Cup best-of-seven series. The American boat was piloted by Ted Turner.

rageous" against the new boats "Independence" and "Enterprise." Meanwhile, the French had been eliminated, and the Australians and Swedes fought out the final series. The Swedish team headed by Pelle Petterson, who designed and sailed "Sverige," unluckily broke a mast.

Thus, the Australians challenged for the cup with "Australia," and confidently approached the series because "Courageous" was an old boat. But the skills and experience that Turner and his crew gained in the prolonged U.S. trials gave "Courageous" the edge in both boat speed and handling techniques. The Americans retained the trophy yet again for the New York Yacht Club, with a clear-cut 4–0 victory.

In England the Admiral's Cup at Cowes, Isle of Wight, had become an event that attracted big money and had outgrown its original concept of encouraging big yachts to attend "Cowes week." Crowded conditions on the downwind led to inevitable collisions and chaos, which, with the consequent damage and disqualifications, soured the series. The orders to the British team to "keep out of trouble" lost places in individual races for the British boats but led to a trouble-free series and a victory over the U.S., with Hong Kong third.

On August 27 the first leg of the round-the-world race began. First to reach Cape Town, South Africa, the first stop, was the aptly named Dutch yacht "Flyer."

In the Ton Cup events, sailors from the Flying Dutchman class took both the quarter-ton championship, with Rodney Pattisson sailing a Span-

World Class Boat Champions		
Class	Winner	Country
Fireball	S. Benjamin	U.S.
O.K.	P. Lester	New Zealand
Soling	G. Dexter	Canada
Flying Dutchman	J. Hotz	Switzerland
Contender	D. Pitman	U.K.
Hornet	K. Herve	U.K.
Tempest	J. Albrechtson	Sweden
Cadet	S. Girven	U.K.
Optimist	P. Mark	Sweden
505	P. Colclough	U.K.
Star	D. Connor	U.S.
6-m	P. Petterson	Sweden
Tornado	J. Spengler	West Germany

Britain's "Marionette" (left) led West Germany's "Pinta" at the start of the Admiral's Cup in Cowes, England. Britain won the series, with the U.S. second and Hong Kong third.

ish-entered new Holland design, and the three-quarter-ton series, with Yves Pajot sailing a Farr design. In the dinghy and small-keel boat classes John Albrechtson won the Tornado class for Sweden, Dennis Connor the Star class for the U.S., and Jorg Spengler the Tornado catamarans for West Germany.

In 1977 the first women's world championships were held, sailed in 420s and Lasers. The winners of the two-handed event were Jan and Pat O'Malley (U.S.), and the winner of the single-handed event was Lyndall Coxon from Australia.

(ADRIAN JARDINE)

[452.B.4.a.ii]

San Marino

San Marino

A small republic, San Marino is an enclave in northeastern Italy, 5 mi SW of Rimini. Area: 61 sq km (24 sq mi). Pop. (1977 est.): 20,400. Cap. and largest city: San Marino (metro. pop., 1976 est., 4,600). Language: Italian. Religion: Roman Catholic. The country is governed by two *capitani reggenti*, or co-regents, appointed every six months by a Grand and General Council. Executive power rests with two secretaries of state: foreign and political affairs and internal affairs. In 1977 the positions were filled, respectively, by Giancarlo Ghironzi and Clara Boscaglia.

San Marino experienced a government crisis at the end of 1977 when the Socialists left the governing coalition, accusing the Christian Democrats of failing to solve the country's economic problems. On December 29 the co-regents asked the

São Tomé and Príncipe

Communists (who had received 23% of the vote in the 1974 general election) to form a government, but on December 29 they fell one vote short in the 60-seat Parliament and gave up the attempt. It was expected that the Socialists might be asked to form a coalition or, failing that, that elections would be called in the spring.

In June 1977 Giancarlo Ghironzi, secretary of state for foreign affairs of the republic, paid an official visit to Romania. He was received by Pres. Nicolae Ceausescu, who asked him to convey his greetings and friendly wishes to the co-regents of the republic, Alberto Lonfernini and Antonio Volpinari. Ghironzi also had talks on international issues with George Macovescu, the Romanian foreign minister. (K. M. SMOGORZEWSKI)

São Tomé and Príncipe

An independent African state, the Democratic Republic of São Tomé and Príncipe comprises two main islands and several smaller islets that straddle the Equator in the Gulf of Guinea, off the west coast of Africa. Area: 964 sq km (372 sq mi), of which São Tomé, the larger island, comprises 854 sq km. Pop. (1977 est.): 82,000. Cap. and largest city: São Tomé (pop., 1977 est., 20,000). Language: Portuguese. Religion: mainly Roman Catholic. President in 1977, Manuel Pinto da Costa; premier, Miguel Trovoada.

São Tomé and Príncipe was represented as an observer at the 28th general assembly of the Cocoa Producers' Alliance at Abidjan, Ivory Coast, Feb. 25–March 2, 1977, and there were hopes that it would subsequently be admitted to membership. Cocoa was São Tomé's principal crop; production had amounted to 7,900 tons in 1974–75 and was expected to increase. In an effort to diversify crops, North Koreans were invited to advise on rice-growing techniques, farmers were encouraged to grow vegetables, and the cattle and fishing industries were promoted. A deepwater harbour and an extension of the airport to take long-range aircraft were projected.

Earlier, the Council of Ministers of the Organization of African Unity, meeting at Lomé, Togo, February 21–28, exempted São Tomé and Príncipe (along with Mozambique, Cape Verde, Guinea-Bissau, and Angola) from making contributions to the organization's budget for 1977–78.

SAN MARINO
Education. (1974–75) Primary, pupils 1,698, teachers 107; secondary, pupils 1,140, teachers 96; vocational, pupils 476; teacher training, pupils 71; higher, students 289.
Finance. Monetary unit: Italian lira, with (Sept. 19, 1977) a free rate of 884 lire to U.S. $1 (1,540 lire = £1 sterling); local coins are issued. Budget (1976 est.) balanced at 29,-148,000,000 lire. Tourism (1975) 2,426,000 visitors.

SÃO TOMÉ AND PRÍNCIPE
Education. (1972–73) Primary, pupils 10,015, teachers 303; secondary, pupils 2,114, teachers 86; vocational, pupils 256, teachers 30.
Finance and Trade. Monetary unit: São Tomé and Príncipe escudo, with (Sept. 19, 1977) a free rate of 40.50 escudos to U.S. $1 (70.50 escudos = £1 sterling). Budget (1974 est.) balanced at 150 million escudos. Foreign trade (1975): imports 288,469,000 escudos; exports 180,432,000 escudos. Import sources: Portugal 61%; Angola 13%. Export destinations: The Netherlands 52%; Portugal 33%; West Germany 8%. Main exports (1973): cocoa 87%; copra 8%.
Agriculture. Production (in 000; metric tons; 1976): cocoa c. 8; copra c. 5; bananas c. 2; palm kernels c. 2; palm oil c. 1. Livestock (in 000; 1975): cattle c. 4; pigs c. 3; sheep c. 2; goats c. 1.

Saudi Arabia

A monarchy occupying four-fifths of the Arabian Peninsula, Saudi Arabia has an area of 2,240,000 sq km (865,000 sq mi). Pop. (1974 census): 7,012,600. Cap. and largest city: Riyadh (pop., 1976 est., 667,000). Language: Arabic. Religion: Muslim. King and prime minister in 1977, Khalid.

Foreign Affairs. Saudi Arabia's prime political objective during 1977 was to secure a resumption of the Geneva Middle East peace conference. To this end it tried to influence the Palestine Liberation Organization (PLO) to be more flexible and to persuade the U.S. to exert pressure on Israel to withdraw from occupied Arab territory. When Crown Prince Fahd visited Washington on May 24–25 for talks with Pres. Jimmy Carter, he discussed, according to a White House spokesman, "the process by which a Palestinian homeland with recognized boundaries could be established beside an Israel of guaranteed borders." Although Prince Fahd publicly denied claims by other Arab states that he had threatened the U.S. with another oil embargo, the Saudi government did not hide its intention of using its oil resources to influence events.

In March it was announced that the U.S. administration was undertaking a detailed review of the previously approved sale of $1,140,000,000 worth of antiaircraft missiles to Saudi Arabia.

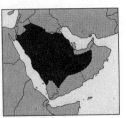

Saudi Arabia

Some U.S. congressmen hostile to the sale claimed that Saudi Arabia would then have a total of 1,200 missiles, which would alter the balance of power in the area. Another source of friction was the U.S. action taken against the Arab boycott of U.S. companies doing business with Israel. The Saudi view was that the boycott had to continue until the Middle East dispute was settled.

Throughout the year Saudi Arabia engaged in active diplomacy to encourage unified action on the part of the Arab front-line states—Egypt, Syria, and Jordan. The foreign ministers of these states and a PLO representative met in Riyadh in January, and the presidents of Egypt and Syria met King Khalid in Riyadh in May. Regular contact was maintained with the PLO chairman, Yasir Arafat, who also visited Riyadh in June. Although Saudi Arabia had played a major role in the Lebanese settlement and the reconciliation between Egypt and Syria that resulted from the Arab summit meetings in October 1976, there were signs of strain in Saudi relations with Syria. Saudi Arabia was thought to be alarmed by the extent of Syrian Pres. Hafez al-Assad's ambitions to dominate a revived Greater Syria (to include Lebanon and Jordan). In September Syrian spokesmen were publicly accusing Saudi Arabia and Egypt of conspiring with the U.S. to bring Syria to its knees by reviving the Lebanese civil war. The Saudi intention was certainly to exclude the Soviet Union as far as possible from the Middle East peacemaking process. The Saudis made no formal comment on the Egyptian peace initiative at year's end, though they were known to oppose any attempt by Egypt to reach a separate peace with Israel.

Saudi Arabia continued to play a leading role in the affairs of the Arabian Peninsula. In May the Kuwaiti crown prince and the rulers of Bahrain and Sharjah visited Riyadh. Saudi Arabia was increasingly concerned with events in the Red Sea area and the Horn of Africa, and it was a major influence behind the meeting of the heads of state of Sudan, Somalia, the Yemen Arab Republic (San'a'; North Yemen), and the People's Democratic Republic of Yemen (Aden; South Yemen) in Taiz in March. Saudi Arabia feared the development of a Soviet-backed confederation of Ethiopia, Somalia, and the newly independent Djibouti, and its efforts were directed toward weaning Somalia away from its alliance with the Soviet Union and securing a pro-Arab Djibouti, with the overall objective of making the Red Sea an Arab Lake.

Throughout the year Saudi Arabia kept in close contact with the Sudanese regime and encouraged the reconciliation between Pres. Gaafar Nimeiry and the Sudanese opposition leader Sadik al-Mahdi. Efforts to divert South Yemen from its Marxist policies were less successful, despite the two countries' decision in March 1976 to normalize their relations and establish diplomatic ties. However, some Saudi aid was provided to the Aden regime; the Saudi foreign minister, Prince Saud al-Faisal, visited Aden on April 10–12; and Pres. Salem Ali Rubayyi of South Yemen made his first visit to Saudi Arabia, July 31 to August 2. In a joint statement with King Khalid, Rubayyi referred to continuing improving relations "within a framework

---

SAUDI ARABIA

Education. (1974–75) Primary, pupils 625,773, teachers 29,989; secondary, pupils 159,938, teachers 10,964; vocational, pupils 5,150, teachers 550; teacher training, students 14,099, teachers 1,037; higher, students 19,773, teaching staff 1,818.

Finance. Monetary unit: riyal, with (Sept. 19, 1977) a free rate of 3.52 riyals to U.S. $1 (6.13 riyals = £1 sterling). Gold, SDR's, and foreign exchange (June 1977) U.S. $26,188,000,000. Budget (1976–77 est.) balanced at 110,935,000,000 riyals (including development expenditure of 74,433,000,000 riyals). Gross national product (1974–75) 131,325,000,000 riyals. Money supply (Nov. 1976) 24.3 billion riyals. Cost of living (1970 = 100; 3rd quarter 1976) 282.

Foreign Trade. (1976) Imports (fob) c. 37,740,000,000 riyals; exports 127,380,000,000 riyals. Import sources (1974): U.S. 17%; Japan 16%; Lebanon 15%; West Germany 6%; U.K. 5%. Export destinations (1974): Japan 16%; France 12%; Italy 10%; U.K. 9%; Spain 6%. Main exports: crude oil 94%; petroleum products 6%. Tourism (1975) gross receipts U.S. $509 million.

Transport and Communications. Roads (main; 1975) 18,404 km. Motor vehicles in use (1975): passenger 177,400; commercial 140,800. Railways (1974): 612 km; traffic 72 million passenger-km, freight 66 million net ton-km. Air traffic (1975): 1,750,000,000 passenger-km; freight 44.7 million net ton-km. Shipping (1976): merchant vessels 100 gross tons and over 84; gross tonnage 588,745. Telephones (Jan. 1974) 85,000. Radio receivers (Dec. 1975) c. 245,000. Television receivers (Dec. 1975) c. 130,000.

Agriculture. Production (in 000; metric tons; 1976): millet c. 150; sorghum c. 200; wheat (1975) c. 175; barley (1975) c. 22; tomatoes c. 120; onions (1975) c. 38; grapes c. 34; dates c. 264. Livestock (in 000; 1975): cattle c. 311; sheep c. 3,102; goats c. 7,722; camels c. 606; asses c. 148; poultry c. 9,267.

Industry. Production (in 000; metric tons; 1975): petroleum products c. 23,800; crude oil (1976) 424,232; natural gas (cu m) c. 3,300,000; electricity (excluding most industrial production; kw-hr) c. 1,988,000; cement (1974) 1,056.

of Arab and Islamic solidarity." Relations with North Yemen remained very close, and Saudi aid was responsible for that country's greatly increased economic activity.

Domestic Affairs. King Khalid, who was known to suffer from poor health, left on February 19 for a London hospital, where he had two operations on his left thigh. This gave rise to widespread reports of his imminent abdication or at least his withdrawal from active public life. However, the reports were strenuously denied, and on April 30 the king returned to Saudi Arabia, where he resumed his public activities. The appointment of Prince Ahmed ibn Abdul Aziz as deputy minister of the interior was announced on July 10; this meant that the seven sons of the late King Ibn Saud by the same mother, known as the Sudairi Seven, were all now members of the Cabinet.

At the end of June, Saudi Arabia officially announced that the long-standing negotiations with the Arabian-American Oil Co. (Aramco) for the takeover of the company's remaining 40% share of assets and its production operations had been completed. Saudi Arabia was to give priority as customers to the four U.S. companies then partly owning Aramco. A Saudi Arabian National Oil Company was to be established to control production and marketing of Saudi oil.

The Saudi government stood by its decision to freeze its oil price rise at 5% on July 1, provided the other members of the Organization of Petroleum Exporting Countries agreed to forgo their planned further 5% increase. Oil production in the first two months of 1977, at 8.3 million bbl a day, was well below the projected target of 10 million bbl a day. It rose to a record of over 9 million bbl a day in March and April, but fell back again sharply in May and June as the result of a major explosion and fire in the Abqaiq field in May, which cost an estimated $100 million in damages. In its annual report Aramco said new oil discoveries in 1976 had raised proved oil resources by 2,-300,000,000 bbl to 110,200,000,000 bbl and probable reserves to 177,500,000,000 bbl.

The Saudi budget for 1977–78, the third year of the country's second five-year plan, showed an estimated surplus of U.S. $10 billion, compared with a balanced budget in 1976–77. Of the total estimated state expenditure of $31.5 billion, about 32% was allocated to infrastructure development and about 30% to military expenditure.

In February the Saudi Council of Ministers issued an official protest alleging that some international companies, taking advantage of Saudi Arabia's desire to implement its development program rapidly, had raised prices in various ways. The council said that companies that overcharged would be blacklisted. The minister of industry and power later visited India, Pakistan, and Taiwan, and said Saudi Arabia would give joint contracts to less developed countries that could compete at "reasonable prices." The minister of finance and national economy claimed that the rate of inflation, which had risen in 1976 and the first quarter of 1977 (to a rate reportedly well over 30%), had begun to decline in the second quarter, although by an unspecified amount.

Saudi aid for Arab Islamic and third world countries continued at a high level. An official Saudi report said it had totaled $11,780,000,000 to 24 countries in 1973–76—equivalent to about 3% of the gross national product. At the Afro-Arab summit meeting in Cairo in March, Saudi Arabia promised $1 billion in aid to black African states in addition to the $600 million already pledged. Saudi Arabia agreed to contribute to the International Monetary Fund's projected fund of 14 billion Special Drawing Rights (about U.S. $16.5 billion) to help less developed countries in financial difficulties. Although the IMF was said to be hoping the Saudi contribution would be $4 billion, it was reported that Saudi Arabia had agreed to contribute only $2.9 billion, apparently because it believed the terms on which the money would be lent were too hard.

A First National Bank of Chicago report in August estimated that Saudi Arabia's foreign assets had increased from $785 million to $49.6 billion between 1969 and 1976, and that income from these assets had risen from $59 million to $3.8 billion in the same period. The report estimated that, according to current trends, this income would increase to $10 billion by 1981.

(PETER MANSFIELD)

Senegal

A republic of northwestern Africa, Senegal is bounded by Mauritania, Mali, Guinea, and Guinea-Bissau, and by the Atlantic Ocean. The independent nation of The Gambia forms an enclave within the country. Area: 196,722 sq km (75,955 sq mi). Pop. (1976 prelim.): 5,085,400. Cap. and largest city: Dakar (pop., 1976 prelim., 798,800). Language: French (official); Wolof; Serer; other tribal dialects. Religion: Muslim 80%; Christian 10%. President in 1977, Léopold Sédar Senghor; premier, Abdou Diouf.

Renamed the Socialist Party in December 1976, the government party had to face increased competition in 1977, when it was announced officially in September that a fourth party would be formed, the Senegalese Republican Movement (MRS), with right-wing affiliations. Opposition to Pres. Léopold Sédar Senghor became active; in July former premier Mamadou Dia launched an opposition newspaper, and in September some hundreds of

Senegal

SENEGAL

Education. (1974) Primary, pupils 297,560, teachers 7,-300; secondary, pupils 64,060, teachers 2,513; vocational, pupils 5,841, teachers (1972–73) 465; teacher training, students 1,926, teachers 455; higher (1974–75), students 7,-502, teaching staff 374.

Finance and Trade. Monetary unit: CFA franc, with (Sept. 19, 1977) a par value of CFA Fr 50 to the French franc (free rate of CFA Fr 246.50 = U.S. $1; CFA Fr 429.50 = £1 sterling). Budget (1976 est.) balanced at CFA Fr 96 billion. Foreign trade (1975): imports CFA Fr 124,620,000,000; exports CFA Fr 99.1 billion. Import sources (1974): France 41%; West Germany 6%; U.S. 6%; Nigeria 6%. Export destinations (1974): France 50%; The Netherlands 7%; U.K. 6%; Ivory Coast 6%; Mauritania 5%. Main exports (1974): phosphates 28%; peanut oil 22%; fish and products 7%; peanut oil cake 7%.

intellectuals published, in Europe, a manifesto calling for a return to truly multiparty politics. The Senegalese Democratic Party let it be known that it would put forward its leader, Abdoulaye Wade, as a candidate against Senghor in the presidential elections scheduled for February 1978.

Student unrest persisted during the year, especially in Dakar. In January high-school youths in the capital were arrested. From March to May a student strike movement spread over a part of Dakar University, and in July some 15 student activists were pressed into the Army.

On April 20–21 Dakar was host to the fourth French-African summit conference. It was attended by most of the heads of state from French-speaking Africa and by the French president, Valéry Giscard d'Estaing. In Paris in September Senghor rejected any dialogue with South Africa. During the same month he received a white South African opposition leader, Colin Eglin.

(PHILIPPE DECRAENE)

Seychelles

A republic in the Indian Ocean consisting of 89 islands, Seychelles lies 1,450 km from the coast of East Africa. Area: 443 sq km (171 sq mi), of which 166 sq km includes the islands of Farquhar, Desroches, and Aldabra. Pop. (1977 est.): 62,000, including Creole 94%, French 5%, English 1%. Cap. Victoria, on Mahé (pop., 1976 est., 14,500). Language: English and French are official, creole patois is also spoken. Religion: Roman Catholic 91%, Anglican 8%. Presidents in 1977, James R. Mancham and, from June 5, Albert René; prime minister till June 5, René.

The coalition government ended on June 5, 1977, with the overthrow of Pres. James R. Mancham during his absence in London to attend the meeting of Commonwealth heads of government. He was replaced as president by Prime Minister Albert René (who denied complicity in the plot). An exclusively Seychelles People's United Party Cabinet was formed, which announced that a constitutional committee would be set up, to be followed by elections in June 1979. René said fear that Mancham's Seychelles Democratic Party would postpone elections and make Mancham president for life had caused the coup. He denied Soviet connivance while admitting a "close affinity with Tanzania."

While encouraging tourism, René planned to concentrate on housing, fishing, and agriculture. The minister for foreign affairs, Guy Sinon, stated that Seychelles would be nonaligned, would continue its membership in the UN and the Organization of African Unity, and would honour international obligations. Closer relations would be sought with countries of the Indian Ocean seaboard, while good relations would be maintained with Britain, the U.S., and France.

(MOLLY MORTIMER)

Seychelles

Sierra Leone

Sierra Leone

A republic within the Commonwealth of Nations, Sierra Leone is a West African state on the Atlantic coast between Guinea and Liberia. Area: 71,740 sq km (27,699 sq mi). Pop. (1976 est.): 3,111,000, including (1963) Mende and Temne tribes 60.7%; other tribes 38.9%; non-African 0.4%. Cap. and largest city: Freetown (pop., 1974, 314,340). Language: English (official); tribal dialects. Religion: animist 66%, Muslim 28%, Christian 6%, according to outdated statistics; it appears that Islam is gaining animist converts rapidly, however. President in 1977, Siaka Stevens; prime minister, Christian A. Kamara-Taylor.

A state of emergency was declared on Feb. 1, 1977, after clashes between government supporters and students who were demanding Pres. Siaka Stevens' resignation and political reform. Parliament, in which all members were of the ruling All People's Congress Party (APC), was prorogued and elections were called for May 6. The APC was again returned, with 70 seats as against 15 for the Sierra Leone People's Party (SLPP). Because of civil disturbances, the elections for eight Bo area seats were postponed.

At the opening of Parliament, Stevens said the time had come to institute a one-party state. The speaker of the house, while accepting Salia Jusu-Sheriff as leader of the SLPP, ruled that he could not be called leader of the opposition because there were not enough SLPP members to form an alternative government.

Stevens' address to Parliament emphasized chiefs' participation in local government but concentrated on the poor state of the economy. The trade deficit had reached a record 70 million leones in 1976, the output of traditional foreign exchange earners, such as diamond and bauxite, had declined, agricultural production remained stagnant, inflation was running at 26% in 1976, and government debt had doubled between 1974 and 1976. (MOLLY MORTIMER)

Singapore

Singapore

Singapore, a republic within the Commonwealth of Nations, occupies a group of islands, the largest of which is Singapore, at the southern extremity of the Malay Peninsula. Area: 602 sq km (232 sq mi). Pop. (1977 est.): 2,308,200, including 76% Chinese, 15% Malays, and 7% Indians. Language: official languages are English, Malay, Mandarin Chinese, and Tamil. Religion: Malays are Muslim; Chinese, mainly Buddhist; Indians, mainly Hindu. President in 1977, Benjamin Henry Sheares; prime minister, Lee Kuan Yew.

General elections were held on Dec. 23, 1976, for an enlarged Parliament of 69 seats. The governing People's Action Party won all of the seats for the third consecutive time and increased its share of the popular vote in contested constituencies to 72.4%.

In January, Ho Kwon Ping, correspondent of the *Far Eastern Economic Review*, was arrested for possessing and disseminating "sensitive information." He resigned after being heavily fined. In February a prominent lawyer, G. Raman, was detained and accused of working through the Socialist International to secure the release of hard-core

Communist detainees. Among those named by Raman as associates engaged in pro-Communist activities was Arun Senkuttuvan, a correspondent for the London *Financial Times* and *The Economist*. Ho Kwon Ping was later rearrested, but he was released in April together with Senkuttuvan, whose citizenship was taken away.

In January, British financier Jim Slater was cleared in London of six charges of fraud and conspiracy brought against him by the Singapore government over profits made on share dealings; in April, Singapore once again unsuccessfully sought his extradition, but on July 30 it secured the extradition of his business associate Richard Tarling. (MICHAEL LEIFER)

SINGAPORE

Education. (1976) Primary, pupils 316,265, teachers 11,-432; secondary, pupils 177,992, teachers 7,592; vocational, pupils 11,751, teachers 704; teacher training, students 1,-190, teachers 109; higher, students 15,609, teaching staff 990.

Finance. Monetary unit: Singapore dollar, with (Sept. 19, 1977) a free rate of Sing$2.44 to U.S. $1 (Sing$4.26 = £1 sterling). Gold, SDR's, and foreign exchange (April 1977) U.S. $3,482,300,000. Budget (1976–77 est.): revenue Sing$3,108,000,000; expenditure Sing$2,479,000,000 (excluding transfer to development fund of Sing$625 million). Gross national product (1976) Sing$14,419,000,000. Money supply (May 1977) Sing$4,076,000,000. Cost of living (1970 = 100; June 1977) 165.

Foreign Trade. (1976) Imports Sing$22,406,000,000; exports Sing$16,267,000,000. Import sources: Japan 16%; Saudi Arabia 16%; Malaysia 14%; U.S. 13%. Export destinations: Malaysia 15%; U.S. 15%; Japan 10%; Hong Kong 8%; Australia 5%. Main exports: petroleum products 23%; machinery 19%; rubber 12%; ship and aircraft stores 7%; food 6%. Tourism (1975): visitors 1,324,000; gross receipts U.S. $335 million.

Transport and Communications. Roads (1975) 2,167 km. Motor vehicles in use (1975): passenger 149,000; commercial (including buses) 46,300. Railways (1975) 26 km (for traffic *see* Malaysia). Air traffic (1976): 6,330,000,000 passenger-km; freight 193,480,000 net ton-km. Shipping (1976): merchant vessels 100 gross tons and over 722; gross tonnage 5,481,720. Shipping traffic (1976): goods loaded 20.6 million metric tons, unloaded 38,303,000 metric tons. Telephones (Dec. 1975) 290,000. Radio licenses (Dec. 1974) 320,000. Television licenses (Dec. 1974) 252,-000.

Social and Welfare Services

During 1977 recession and unemployment continued to exert an important influence on social security developments in the nonsocialist world. Many governments introduced austerity measures of one kind or another, and social security in general did not escape their effect. Employers, anxious to keep labour costs down, resisted higher social security contributions and indeed sometimes campaigned for them to be reduced; on the other hand, workers, facing great economic uncertainty, pressed for improved protection.

International Developments. The branch of social security most directly affected by the state of the world economy was unemployment insurance. During 1977 the trend toward wider coverage and longer periods of benefit continued. In Denmark, for example, insurance was extended to persons in military service, and in light of the problem of youth unemployment, the enlistment age was lowered; in France, basic unemployment assistance became available to ex-prisoners; and in Japan, there was an extension of 360 days in the duration of benefits paid to workers between 55 and 64 who had reached the compulsory retirement age fixed by their companies, and to unemployed workers between 45 and 55 who lived in areas with severely limited employment opportunities. On the other hand, in Canada, where the current rate of unemployment was over 8%, legislation was passed that lengthened the period of employment required to qualify for benefit and shortened the period during which benefits may be paid.

Given the intractable problems that unemployment poses for older workers, many governments considered not only unemployment insurance but also early retirement. In some countries, notably France, this led to the introduction of benefits known as "pre-pensions," administered by unemployment insurance and payable on condition that the worker leave the labour force. Excluded from receiving the pre-pension were workers entitled to receive a full pension from the General Scheme at age 60; that is, those with long insurance records and a history of work in arduous manual occupations. Given the relatively high level of the pre-

Help for the Handicapped

Physically handicapped persons in the United States benefited in 1977 from regulations made effective in June by the Department of Health, Education, and Welfare. Implementing a section of the Rehabilitation Act of 1973, the new rules sought to prevent discrimination of the physically disabled in programs, activities, and facilities receiving federal funds.

Applications of the regulations took a variety of forms. In terms of site development for new structures, the ground must be graded so that it is level with a normal entrance. Public walks should not have a gradient greater than 5% and should not be interrupted by steps or sudden changes in level. In parking lots, spaces close to buildings should be set aside and identified for use by the physically disabled.

In regard to buildings, at least one primary entrance has to be designed so that it can be used by persons in wheelchairs and also so that it is on a level allowing accessibility to elevators. Stairs are required to have handrails 32 in high and extending at least 18 in beyond both the top and bottom steps. Some public telephones in a building should be designed so that they can be used by persons in wheelchairs.

For the blind, raised letters or numbers are to be used to identify rooms or offices, and doors not intended for normal use should be made identifiable to the touch by knurling the handle or knob. For the deaf, visual warning signals would simultaneously accompany audible ones. Other regulations dealt with improving educational programs and employment opportunities.

pension, these workers, deemed by legislation to be specially deserving, were, paradoxically, penalized.

The question of retirement age appeared in rather a different context in the U.S., where the House of Representatives approved a bill that would raise from 65 to 70 the age at which private employers could require their workers to retire and would eliminate altogether any compulsory retirement age in the government sector. The issue had been approached mainly in terms of civil rights for the elderly.

Legislation was passed in West Germany to slow down the rise in pension and health costs. The next annual pension adjustment was postponed by six months, and a change in the basis of assessment would result thereafter in slightly lower increases than under the previous method.

In France the deficit recorded in 1976 was eliminated in 1977, due mainly to a slowdown in the consumption of medical care and to the reduction of the value-added tax on pharmaceutical products. Nevertheless, it was expected that French social security would again be in deficit in 1978. In the United Kingdom pension adjustments were based on the government's forecast of inflation rather than on actual inflation, which in the event was higher; this helped to increase the National Insurance Fund surplus.

Maternity benefits had undergone widespread improvements in recent years. Benefits in many countries were set at, or near, 100% of earnings; also, some schemes extended the period during which benefits were payable. For example, in 1977 the Philippines integrated maternity benefits, previously provided by the employer, into the social security system; the benefit period was extended to 45 days and the period of employment required to qualify reduced from six to three months in the year preceding the birth.

The question of providing social security protection for housewives continued to be widely discussed. In Israel housewives were covered by a disability insurance scheme. Women residents in Israel who are unable to perform the role of housewife as a result of a physical, intellectual, or mental defect due to illness, accident, or birth were eligible for a full disability pension as well as an increment for dependents. They were exempt from contributions and from the qualifying period. In the U.K. a slightly different measure was implemented, allowing disabled housewives to receive the "noncontributory invalidity pension," a benefit for those not covered by the contributory insurance scheme. Although married women were initially excluded when the benefit was introduced in 1976, they became eligible in 1977.

In the field of pensions, perhaps the most noteworthy change in 1977 was the introduction in New Zealand of the National Superannuation Scheme. Since the 1938 Social Security Act, New

TATINER—LIAISON

Yielding to demands from handicapped persons, HEW Secretary Joseph Califano agreed to implement legislation prohibiting discrimination against the handicapped.

OLIPHANT—THE WASHINGTON STAR

"First the good news . . . When you were a boy your Uncle Franklin D. set up a trust fund for your retirement years. The bad news is some scoundrel seems to have spent it all!"

Zealand had had two systems of income maintenance for the elderly: the Age Benefit, payable to people aged 60 with 10 years of residence in the country and subject to an income test; and the Superannuation Benefit, for people aged 65 and over with 20 years of residence and not subject to an income test. In February 1977 these two benefits were replaced by the National Superannuation Scheme, which awards flat-rate pensions. The benefit for a married couple was fixed at 70% of the national average weekly wage, to be increased to 80% in August 1978. The rate for a single person was 60% of the married-couple rate. To qualify for the benefit, applicants must be aged 60 and have resided in New Zealand for ten years.

(ISSA)

U.S. Developments. In the United States, 1977 was a year of reform in the social welfare field. Sweeping changes were enacted or proposed in three major programs: Social Security, food stamps, and welfare.

A prime target was the Social Security system, which in recent years had been paying out more in benefits than it collected in payroll taxes. Pres. Jimmy Carter proposed major changes in May, and Congress enacted legislation in December.

The bill provided for the biggest peacetime tax increase in U.S. history—some $227 billion over the next ten years. That massive increase was needed to guarantee the solvency of the Social Security trust fund, which had been reduced by inflation-fed increases in benefits and a growing number of retirees.

Despite the big boost in taxes, the basic structure of the system would remain the same, with employers and workers paying equally and providing the entire income for the trust fund. President Carter had proposed that employers pay higher taxes than employees and that general Treasury revenues be used to supplement the payroll taxes. Congress rejected both ideas.

The new law provided that:

There would be no additional increases in 1978 Social Security taxes, which previously had been scheduled to rise to 6.05% on the first $17,700 of an employee's earnings (compared with 5.85% on the

first $16,500 in 1977). But between 1978 and 1987 the tax rate would rise in steps to 7.15%, and the maximum salary tax would go to $42,600. That meant the maximum Social Security tax levied on a worker would increase from $965 in 1977 and $1,071 in 1978 to $3,046 in 1987. Increases would not be as steep for low- and middle-income wage earners.

The amount of money a retiree could earn without losing part of his or her benefits would increase to $4,000 in 1978, $4,500 in 1979, and $6,000 in 1982. It was $3,000 in 1977. After 1982 automatic increases would keep pace with inflation. The earnings ceiling would be eliminated altogether for persons over 70 beginning in 1982.

A new formula would ensure that the average worker received a pension equal to about 41% of earnings just before retirement. The current average was 44%.

Widows over 60 who remarried would not lose any benefits.

Congress completed action on and President Carter signed the most far-reaching revision of the food stamp program since it became permanent in 1964. The major change was the elimination of the requirement that food stamp recipients must pay cash for a portion of their coupons. This was expected to expand participation among the very poor.

The new law also revised eligibility requirements. Only families with net incomes at or below the official poverty level would be eligible to receive food stamps. In figuring net income, the complicated deduction system used in the past was scrapped in favour of three basic deductions from gross income: (1) a standard $60 a month for every household; (2) a deduction equal to 20% of earned income for working families; (3) a deduction of up to $75 a month for working families for high shelter costs or child care expenses. Eligibility requirements for students and aliens were tightened, but strikers and their families would still be permitted to receive food stamps.

The most comprehensive, potentially most significant reform proposal, but one which only reached the debating stage in 1977, involved welfare. In August President Carter unveiled a plan that would do away entirely with the existing welfare and public jobs programs and replace them with a single system emphasizing work incentives and public service jobs. In place of Aid to Families with Dependent Children, Supplemental Security Income (SSI), and food stamps, there would be two basic types of payments in the Carter proposal. The first consisted of income support for the aged, blind, disabled, and single-parent families with young children. Such people would not be required to seek or hold jobs as a condition for receiving federal payments. Benefits would depend on the size of the family, with a basic stipend of $4,200 for a family of four. The second type of payment was a work benefit plan under which two-parent families, single people, childless couples, and one-parent families with no children under 14 would be expected to work full time. Cash supplements would be paid to those whose incomes were below $8,400 a year.

The Carter plan also would create 1.4 million full-time public service jobs, relieve states of $2.1 billion in welfare payments, and expand earned income tax credit for the poor. The administration set Oct. 1, 1980, as the target date for starting its program and estimated that it would cost about $30.7 billion the first year, $2.8 billion more than the cost of existing welfare programs.

Other measures passed by Congress in 1977 in the social welfare field included an urban aid bill authorizing $12,450,000,000 over the next three years to rebuild neighbourhoods through community-development block grants; a $4 billion emergency public works jobs bill that was expected to create between 160,000 and 300,000 new jobs, mainly in the building trades; a bill increasing the federal minimum wage from $2.30 an hour to $2.65 in January 1978, $2.90 in 1979, $3.10 in 1980, and $3.35 in 1981; and a bill aimed at reducing fraud and abuse in Medicare and Medicaid through tougher penalties and stronger oversight responsibilities of professional standards review organizations.

One of the most divisive issues in the social services field continued to be government funding of abortions for the poor. In 1976, after a battle between the House of Representatives and the Senate, Congress passed a bill barring all federal financing of abortions under Medicaid except when the life of the mother was endangered. That ban was challenged in court and did not take effect until after the U.S. Supreme Court ruled in June 1977 that states (and, by extension, the federal government) are not required to fund nontherapeutic abortions. The decision left state governments free to finance abortions if they chose, and a minority continued to do so. (*See* LAW.)

The fight was resumed in 1977 when the House and Senate again passed differing versions of abortion funding. After a five-month deadlock in conference committee, a compromise was adopted permitting Medicaid abortions when (1) the mother's life would be endangered if she gave birth; (2) two doctors agreed that she would suffer severe and long-lasting health damage if she gave birth; and (3) there had been rape or incest which was promptly reported to the proper authorities. It was estimated that these restrictions would allow about 100,000 Medicaid abortions a year.

(DAVID M. MAZIE)

See also Education; Health and Disease; Industrial Review: *Insurance.*
[522.D; 535.B.3.e; 552.D.1]

Somalia

Somalia

A republic of northeast Africa, the Somali Democratic Republic, or Somalia, is bounded by the Gulf of Aden, the Indian Ocean, Kenya, Ethiopia, and Djibouti. Area: 638,000 sq km (246,300 sq mi). Pop. (1976 est.): 3,261,000, mainly Hamitic, with Arabic and other admixtures. Cap. and largest city: Mogadishu (pop., 1976 UN est., 286,000). Language: Somali. Religion: predominantly Muslim. President of the Supreme Revolutionary Council in 1977, Maj. Gen. Muhammad Siyad Barrah.

In June 1977 the conflict with Ethiopia over the Ogaden, the Ethiopian province inhabited by Somali nomad herdsmen and claimed by Somalia since independence in 1960, broke into open war. The fighting was between the Ethiopian Army and the West Somalia Liberation Front (WSLF), a guerrilla organization founded in 1974 and unofficially supported and armed by Somalia. How deeply the Somali Army was actually involved was disputed; the WSLF, though alleged by Ethiopia to be no more than a cover organization, was strongly based among the province's Somali population. The Somali government position was that the Ogaden should be granted self-determination.

By July the WSLF had cut the Addis Ababa-Djibouti railway, running through the north of the province, and was in control of much of the countryside. In late September the town of Jijiga

---

SOMALIA

Education. (1973–74) Primary, pupils 69,493, teachers 1,789; secondary, pupils 37,910, teachers 1,693; vocational, pupils 1,798, teachers 133; teacher training, students 954, teachers 44; higher (1971–72), students 958, teaching staff 51.

Finance. Monetary unit: Somali shilling, with (Sept. 19, 1977) an official rate of 6.23 Somali shillings to U.S. $1 (free rate of 10.86 Somali shillings = £1 sterling). Gold, SDR's, and foreign exchange (June 1977) U.S. $84.6 million. Budget (1975 est.): revenue 667 million Somali shillings; expenditure 583 million Somali shillings. Cost of living (Mogadishu; 1970 = 100; May 1977) 180.

Foreign Trade. Imports (1975) 1,021,200,000 Somali shillings; exports (1976) 535.6 million Somali shillings. Import sources (1974): Italy 38%; U.S.S.R. 17%; China 9%; Kenya 7%; France 5%; Thailand 5%; Japan 5%; U.K. 5%; West Germany 5%. Export destinations (1974): Saudi Arabia 65%; Italy 12%; Iran 7%; U.S.S.R. 6%; Kuwait 5%. Main exports: livestock 61%; bananas 16%; hides and skins 8%.

Transport and Communications. Roads (1971) 17,223 km. Motor vehicles in use (1972): passenger 8,000; commercial (including buses) 8,000. There are no railways. Air traffic (1975): 19 million passenger-km; freight 200,000 net ton-km. Shipping (1976): merchant vessels 100 gross tons and over 255; gross tonnage 1,792,900. Telephones (Jan. 1971) *c.* 5,000. Radio receivers (Dec. 1974) 67,000.

Agriculture. Production (in 000; metric tons; 1975): corn *c.* 168; sorghum *c.* 100; cassava *c.* 28; sesame seed *c.* 25; sugar, raw value *c.* 39; bananas *c.* 130. Livestock (in 000; 1975): cattle *c.* 3,056; sheep *c.* 3,922; goats *c.* 5,100; camels *c.* 3,089.

Soil Conservation:
see Environment

CAMERAPIX/KEYSTONE

Somali women parade with swords in a show of strength. Somalia was engaged in continuing bitter strife with Ethiopia throughout the year.

fell to the guerrillas, leaving the Ethiopians holding only the ancient city and provincial capital of Harer and the nearby railway town of Dire Dawa. Both parties relied on Soviet arms, and Soviet support for the Ethiopian revolutionary regime caused bitterness in Somalia, a Soviet ally since 1969. At the end of October the Somali government, which had previously threatened to send in regular troops if foreign forces entered the Ogaden conflict, claimed that Cuban troops were supporting the Ethiopian Army. A final break came on November 13 when the government expelled all Soviet advisers, withdrew the use of military facilities, and renounced the Soviet-Somali treaty of friendship. At the same time, it broke diplomatic relations with Cuba and ordered all Cubans to leave the country within 48 hours.

When Djibouti, also part of Somalia's irredentist claims, became officially independent of France on June 27, Somalia undertook to respect its territorial integrity, though Radio Mogadishu welcomed the event as "paving the way for the freedom of the Somali nation as a whole."

In February the Ministry of the Interior was replaced by a new Directorate-General of Local Government and Rural Development, directly under the presidency. This brought the police force under direct presidential control. In November 1976 the four crew members of a yacht that ran aground on the northern coast had been arrested on espionage charges. They included an Englishwoman, Jane Wright. In June they were acquitted of espionage but were fined and sentenced to a year's imprisonment for illegal entry. They were released on July 2. The Somali government was widely applauded when it permitted a West German commando team to storm a Lufthansa airliner, hijacked from Majorca and finally brought to Mogadishu airport, on October 18. The pilot had been killed before the raid, but the remaining 86 hostages were rescued. In November West Ger-

many increased its aid to Somalia. Smallpox, which was thought to have been virtually eradicated, broke out again in Somalia; 192 cases were reported between May 22 and 28.

(VIRGINIA R. LULING)

See also Ethiopia.

South Africa

The Republic. Occupying the southern tip of Africa, South Africa is bounded by South West Africa (Namibia), Botswana, Rhodesia, Mozambique, and Swaziland and by the Atlantic and Indian oceans on the west and east. South Africa entirely surrounds Lesotho and partially surrounds the two former Bantu homelands of Transkei (independent Oct. 26, 1976) and Bophuthatswana (independent Dec. 6, 1977), although the independence of the latter two is not recognized by the international community. Walvis Bay, part of Cape Province since 1910 but administered as part of South West Africa since 1922, was returned to the direct control of Cape Province on Sept. 1, 1977. Area (including Walvis Bay but excluding the two former homelands): 1,140,943 sq km (440,521 sq mi). Pop. (1976 est.): 23,056,000, including (1970 census, adjusted for exclusion of the two homelands) Bantu 66.2%, white 19.8%, Coloured 10.7%, Asian 3.3%. Executive capital: Pretoria (pop., 1976 est., 634,400); judicial capital: Bloemfontein (pop., 1976 est., 234,900); legislative capital: Cape Town (pop., 1976 est., 842,600). Largest city: Johannesburg (pop., 1976 est., 1,371,-000). Language: Afrikaans and English (official); Bantu languages predominate. Religion: mainly Christian. State president in 1977, Nicolaas J. Diederichs; prime minister, B. J. Vorster.

DOMESTIC AFFAIRS. South Africa held a general election, both parliamentary and provincial, on Nov. 30, 1977—18 months ahead of the due date.

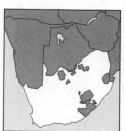

South Africa

Two main reasons were given by Prime Minister B. J. Vorster for calling an early election at that stage. The first was to demonstrate to the world that South Africa would present a united national front against outside pressures, particularly from the West, to bring about changes in the country's internal race policies. The second was that the government was seeking wide public support for proposed constitutional changes affecting the white, Coloured (mixed race), and Indian populations. These proposals had been framed by the Cabinet committee set up in 1976. The committee proposed the establishment of three parliaments, for the whites, the Coloureds, and the Indians respectively, each with power to legislate on matters concerning its own community and with its own Cabinet. On matters of national and common interest, the decision-making powers would rest in the hands of a Council of Cabinets, on which all three groups would be represented in proportion to their numbers, with the whites having a majority role. The ultimate authority would be vested in a state president with effective executive powers, functioning in conjunction with the Council of Cabinets and President Council.

The plan, which was submitted to and approved by all the provincial congresses of the ruling National Party, made no provision for the black population, whether in or outside the African homelands. This gave rise to the strongest criticism of the proposals, especially from sections of the Coloured and Indian communities, and led to its rejection by the majority Labour Party in the Coloured Persons' Representative Council. The party, under its leader Sonny Leon, regarded the scheme as an attempt to perpetuate white domination and refused to join in discussions on its details. The party demanded a referendum on the issue or a special council election to coincide with the general election on November 30—a demand turned down by Vorster. As in the past, the Labour Party declined to pass the council's budget for the current year.

The November general election was preceded, among the white electorate, by a realignment of opposition parties. The official opposition, the United Party, was dissolved after abortive attempts to form a new party in alliance with the Progressive Reform Party constituted in 1976. A small group of United Party members formed themselves as the South African Party (SAP). Another group joined the Progressive Reform Party to constitute the Progressive Federal Party (PFP) under the leadership of Colin Eglin. The bulk of the United Party established the New Republic Party (NRP) under the interim leadership of Sir De Villiers Graaff, the former leader of the opposition, who was later replaced by Radclyffe Cadman. Broadly speaking, the NRP stood for a middle-of-the-road policy on race relations, with equal participation by all races, no discrimination, and preservation of ethnic identities. The PFP advocated political equality for all races, the removal of all discrimination, voluntary integration, and a multiracial society that would provide full scope for cultural and similar identities. The SAP, while opposed to racialism and conceding the right of all

groups to have a say in the government of the country, was essentially conservative.

In the election the National Party won an overwhelming victory, gaining 64.8% of the popular vote and 134 of the 165 seats in the House of Assembly, as compared with 122 previously. Of the opposition the PFP fared the best. Cadman, the NRP leader, was defeated.

The government pursued its declared purpose of moving away from discrimination based on race or colour. Customary or legal restrictions on mixed sports and various other forms of social contact across the colour bar were removed in some, though not in all, cases. Apartheid signboards disappeared in many public places. Racial barriers to employment in jobs traditionally reserved for whites were lifted to a growing extent, often with labour union consent. More facilities for the technical training of black workers were made available in both the private and public sectors. A commission of inquiry into existing labour legislation was appointed in the latter part of 1977, and a parallel investigation was initiated by a Cabinet committee into various aspects of the working and other conditions of the urban black population.

Such steps were seen even by government supporters as not meeting the basic problems of black participation. The Urban Bantu Councils in such townships as Soweto (near Johannesburg) and Langa (Cape Town), which between them accommodated large permanent black populations, did not satisfy that need, as their powers and authority were too circumscribed. Under legislation passed in 1977 provision was made for the replacement of the Urban Bantu Councils by community councils with wider powers and a greater measure of autonomy in communal matters, as a step toward full local government. In the major townships like Soweto, with a population of close to a

WIDE WORLD

The editor of South Africa's largest black paper posed in front of his office in October after the paper was shut down by the South African government. Editor Percy Qoboza was later arrested.

million, the community council system encountered considerable opposition, on the grounds that the councils were still subject to the control of the Department of Bantu Administration and its agencies and left too little effective responsibility to the inhabitants. Members of many of the Urban Bantu Councils resigned before community councils were elected, and the townships concerned were left virtually leaderless. In Soweto a self-appointed Committee of Ten attempted to fill the gap but was denied recognition by the government, its members being later banned under the security laws.

The plans for the introduction of community councils in Soweto and elsewhere proceeded against a background of renewed serious unrest in black residential areas, coinciding with the first anniversary of the June 1976 riots and again accompanied by violence, the destruction of property, loss of life, and wholesale arrests. Starting in Soweto and, as in 1976, involving tens of thousands of schoolchildren and other students, the disturbances spread to other centres, notably Pretoria, western and eastern Cape Province, and some of the homelands. In Soweto in particular organized school boycotts continued, and, under pressure from students' organizations, school boards responsible for the running of the state-subsidized community schools resigned. The students demanded equal educational facilities, greater per capita expenditure on the education of black children, and higher standards of teaching. Efforts by the Department of Bantu Education, supplementing large-scale police action, to restore normal conditions failed. A total takeover by the state of all 40 secondary schools in the area and a threat to close them down if attendance did not improve had little effect. All the 700 high school teachers resigned on September 6, and post-primary education in Soweto virtually ceased.

The situation was aggravated when a former student leader, Steven Biko (*see* OBITUARIES), who had been detained by the Security Police in Port Elizabeth, died in a Pretoria jail while reportedly on a hunger strike. The incident helped to fan the unrest, especially in the Ciskei and eastern Cape Province. Students at several black universities joined in the protests. The minister of justice, J. T. Kruger, invoked the security laws to ban organizations, including the Soweto Committee of

Ten and the Soweto Teachers' Action Committee, as well as a number of black students' and youth bodies and the multiracial Christian Institute of Southern Africa. Two black newspapers, the *World* and the *Weekend World*, and the Christian Institute's journal, *Pro Veritate*, were banned, and banning orders were imposed on their editors and on the editor of the East London *Daily Dispatch*, Donald Woods. More than 40 other persons were restricted or detained, including the director of the Christian Institute, C. F. Beyers Naudé, and members of his staff. An inquest two months after Biko's death found that, contrary to earlier reports, he died from head and brain injuries incurred in a scuffle with the Security Police during interrogation. No one, the court found, could be held criminally responsible for his death. The matter was referred to the Transvaal attorney general for any further action deemed necessary.

The government's actions aroused worldwide reaction, and the issue came before the UN Security Council in the form of a demand for action against South Africa. The government defended its actions on the ground that the safety of the state was endangered by the activities of "Black Power" and other movements, by the intimidation of peaceful citizens, and by incitement from abroad. There was evidence of planned urban terrorism, it was stated. During the year trials under the Terrorism Act were heard in several centres.

FOREIGN AFFAIRS. In South West Africa (Namibia) the Windhoek Turnhalle conference on the territory's future, attended by representatives of all the region's 11 ethnic groups, continued its deliberations with the objective of full independence by the end of 1978. The conference, under the chairmanship of a white delegate, Dirk Mudge, failed to reach agreement on the division of functions between the proposed three tiers of government and on certain other details.

Meanwhile, a mission from the five Western members of the UN Security Council, representing the U.S., Great Britain, France, West Germany, and Canada, negotiated with South Africa on a possible settlement acceptable to the UN. It was decided, with the consent of the Turnhalle delegates, that elections should be held under UN supervision and with the inclusion of the South West Africa People's Organization (SWAPO), led

---

SOUTH AFRICA

Education. (1977) Primary, pupils 4,299,570, teachers 149,651; secondary, pupils 943,512; vocational, pupils 49,075; secondary and vocational, teachers 3,146; higher, students 109,476, teaching staff 8,128.

Finance. Monetary unit: rand, with (Sept. 19, 1977) an official rate of R 0.87 to U.S $1 (free rate of R 1.52 = £1 sterling). Gold, SDR's, and foreign exchange (June 1977) U.S. $936 million. Budget (1976–77 est.): revenue R 6,052,000,000; expenditure R 7,832,000,000. Gross national product (1976) R 27,733,000,000. Money supply (June 1977) R 4,649,000,000. Cost of living (1970 = 100; June 1977) 192.

Foreign Trade. (1976) Imports R 6,343,800,000; exports R 7,874,000,000. Import sources: U.S. 22%; West Germany 18%; U.K. 18%; Japan 10%. Export destinations (excluding gold): U.K. 25%; Japan 13%; West Germany 12%; U.S. 12%; Belgium-Luxembourg 5%. Main exports: gold specie c. 34%; food

8%; diamonds 8%; iron and steel 7%; gold coin 5%.

Transport and Communications. Roads (1975) c. 370,000 km (including 185,031 km main roads). Motor vehicles in use (1975): passenger 2,117,000; commercial 800,300. Railways: (excluding Namibia; 1975) 20,090 km; freight traffic (including Namibia; 1976) 68,114,000,000 net ton-km. Air traffic (1976): 6,012,000,000 passenger-km; freight 160.4 million net ton-km. Shipping (1976): merchant vessels 100 gross tons and over 275; gross tonnage 477,011. Telephones (Dec. 1975) 1,936,000. Radio receivers (Dec. 1974) 2,335,000. Television receivers (Jan. 1976) c. 250,000.

Agriculture. Production (in 000; metric tons; 1976): corn 7,312; wheat 2,060; sorghum 260; potatoes c. 750; tomatoes c. 260; sugar, raw value c. 2,007; peanuts c. 153; sunflower seed c. 255; oranges c. 650; grapefruit c. 128; pineapples c. 190; apples c.

310; grapes c. 1,150; tobacco 34; cotton, lint c. 27; wool c. 52; meat (1975) 807; milk c. 2,564; fish catch (1975) 1,315. Livestock (in 000; June 1976): cattle c. 12,700; sheep c. 31,500; pigs c. 1,380; goats c. 5,200; horses (1975) 225; chickens c. 25,400.

Industry. Index of manufacturing production (1970 = 100; 1976) 123. Fuel and power (in 000; 1976): coal (metric tons) 75,730; manufactured gas (cu m; 1975) c. 1,865,000; electricity (kw-hr) 78,056,000. Production (in 000; metric tons; 1976): cement 7,048; iron ore (60–65% metal content) 15,684; pig iron 6,631; crude steel 7,155; antimony concentrates (metal content; 1975) 16; copper ore (metal content; 1975) 179; chrome ore (oxide content; 1975) 906; manganese ore (metal content; 1975) 2,006; uranium (1975) 2.6; gold (troy oz) 22,800; diamonds (metric carats; 1975) 7,295; asbestos (1975) 355; petroleum products (1975) c. 13,920; fish meal (including Namibia; 1975) 250.

by Sam Nujoma (*see* BIOGRAPHY), in order to choose a constituent assembly that would frame a constitution for independence. The existing administration was replaced by an administrator general appointed by South Africa and invested with full legislative and executive powers, M. T. Steyn, a South African Supreme Court judge. He repealed the Mixed Marriages Act, the discriminatory Immorality Act, and the pass laws. The SWAPO-backed demand for the withdrawal of South African forces from the territory and for their replacement by a UN peacekeeping force met with opposition in South Africa and in South West Africa itself, while a split developed among the whites in the territory, one section of the National Party of South West Africa forming an alliance with other ethnic groups in the Turnhalle.

South Africa, in anticipation of South West Africa's independence, asserted a historical claim to Walvis Bay, administered before the mandate by the Cape and since then as part of South West Africa. The claim was disputed at the UN and by SWAPO. On the dissolution of the Turnhalle conference in November, without reaching consensus on major constitutional issues, the Democratic Turnhalle Alliance was formalized between the new Republican Party founded by Mudge and the ten other ethnic groups. The National Party of South West Africa was excluded.

Toward achieving a settlement in Rhodesia, South Africa was urged to apply pressure on the Rhodesian regime or else face, among other things, an oil embargo to prevent oil from reaching Rhodesia. South Africa consistently rejected such demands. Resolutions calling for a mandatory embargo on the sale of arms to South Africa and on nuclear cooperation were submitted to the UN Security Council, and the embargo was passed unanimously by the Security Council on November 4. The resolutions stopped short at economic sanctions, for the U.S. and the other Western powers wished to continue relations and dialogue with South Africa on its internal policies. Nonetheless, relations between the U.S. and South Africa became increasingly strained.

Bophuthatswana. The republic of Bophuthatswana consists of six discontinuous, landlocked geographic units, one of which borders Botswana on the northwest; it is otherwise entirely surrounded by South Africa, from which it obtained its independence on Dec. 6, 1977. Area: 40,-430 sq km (15,610 sq mi). Pop. (1976 est.): 1,039,000, including 99.6% Bantu, of whom Tswana 67.8%, Northern Sotho 7.5%. Capital: Mmabatho. Largest city: Ga-Rankuwa (pop., 1973 est., 64,200). Languages (official): Central Tswana, English, Afrikaans. Religion: predominantly Christian (Methodist, Lutheran, Anglican, and Bantu Christian churches). President in 1977, Lucas Mangope.

The most important political development was the attainment of independence as a republic by Bophuthatswana, the second homeland, on December 6, little more than a year after Transkei. During the final negotiations between Vorster and Bophuthatswana's chief minister and future president, Lucas Mangope, two key

UPI COMPIX

A woman held aloft a picture of black African leader Steven Biko as an inquest was opened into the cause of his death.

BOPHUTHATSWANA
Education. (1973) Primary, pupils 288,827, teachers 4,-537; secondary, pupils 22,436; vocational, students 471, teachers 37; teacher training, students 2,140; secondary and teacher training, teachers 771; higher, students 167.
Finance and Trade. Monetary unit: South African rand. Budget (homeland; 1973-74): revenue R 20.2 million; expenditure R 20.1 million. Foreign trade included in South Africa.

issues had to be ironed out. One was the question of the post-independence citizenship of Tswanas in South Africa who wished to remain South African nationals. The other was the consolidation of the six separate areas comprising the territory of the homeland into a cohesive unit. The citizenship issue was resolved by a compromise arrangement, which, in effect, would enable Tswanas to retain South African citizenship by way of other homelands not yet independent. The land consolidation question was left for future negotiation.

Attention was increasingly focused on the problems of greater economic viability, the utilization of natural resources, and the attraction of capital from abroad. A new capital, Mmabatho, replaced Mafeking as the seat of government. A 99-member Legislative Assembly, half elected and half nominated, was chosen to take over on December 6, nearly all seats being held by the ruling party under Lucas Mangope. The constitution guaranteed equal rights for persons of all races in the territory. At independence the state had an estimated Bantu population of over one million. About two-thirds of the Tswana population lived permanently or as migrants in white areas.

Transkei. Bordering the Indian Ocean and surrounded on land by South Africa, Transkei comprises three discontinuous geographic units, two of which are landlocked. Area: 41,002 sq km (15,-831 sq mi). Pop. (1976 est.): 2,061,000, including (1970) Bantu 99%, of whom 95% were Xhosa. Capital and largest city: Umtata (pop., 1976 est., 28,800). Language: Xhosa (official); English and

Bophuthatswana

Transkei

TRANSKEI
   Education. Primary, pupils 455,326, teachers 7,678; secondary, pupils 30,560; vocational, pupils 507, teachers 45; teacher training, students 1,933; secondary and teacher training, teachers 949; higher, students 344.
   Finance and Trade. Monetary unit: South African rand. Budget (1976–77 est.) balanced at R 136 million. Most trade is with South Africa.
   Agriculture. Production (in 000; metric tons; 1974): wool 2; mohair 0.03. Livestock (in 000; 1976): cattle 1,300; sheep 2,500; goats 1,250.

Sesotho may be used for official purposes as well. Religion: Christian 65.8%, of which Methodist 25.2%; non-Christians 13.8%. President in 1977, Paramount Chief Botha Sigcau; prime minister, Kaiser Daliwonga Matanzima.

In Transkei, the first independent homeland, Prime Minister Kaiser Matanzima called for its international recognition as an independent state. Efforts were made to attract outside investment capital. The problem of citizenship of Transkeians settled in South Africa and Transkei's land claims ruffled relations with South Africa. Transkei repealed several former apartheid measures and dissociated itself from that policy.　　(LOUIS HOTZ)

See also Dependent States.

Southeast Asian Affairs

After long incubation the concept of regionalism took firm root in Southeast Asia during 1977. It reflected government leaders' perceptions about a string of recent developments: a lowered Asian profile by the new U.S. administration of Pres. Jimmy Carter, uncertainties about the state of security in general and the Indochinese Communists' intentions in particular, continuing internal insurgencies, and the emergence of rapid economic progress as the only effective solution to Asia's endemic problems.

Policies of the Major Powers. Misgivings about Carter's Asia policy were generated primarily by his decision to withdraw U.S. ground forces from South Korea. Many saw this as a possible encouragement to the Communists. Their worries persisted despite some attempts by U.S. spokesmen to reassure Asian leaders. One of the more positive statements came from John Holdridge, U.S. ambassador to Singapore. Opening a conference of U.S. agricultural attachés in the region in June, he noted that Southeast Asian countries had identified two major points of interest: the actions and statements of the Soviet Union, China, and Vietnam, and the posture and policies of the Carter administration toward Southeast Asia. "In this respect," he said, "we have given firm assurances to the leaders of the region that there is a continuing U.S. foreign policy and that we fully intend to maintain a strong, flexible military presence in the region."

The impression in Southeast Asia, however, was that Carter's attention was fully engaged in the Middle East, Africa, and Latin America and that there was a marked inclination not to get involved in Asia. The main thrust of U.S. policy in

Asia, it was felt, was to gain for Japan an increasingly central role by enlarging its economic and defense responsibilities in the region. Some experts believed that the U.S. was reviewing its Asia policy every month, possibly with a view to avoiding any situation that would push it toward a new embroilment. In any case, Asian leaders sensed a lack of firmness in Washington's stance and were apprehensive that this could adversely affect the region's economic and security interests.

Nothing specific happened during the year to mount an immediate security threat. Yet Southeast Asians felt that the sagging of U.S. interest in their region was not matched by any letup in Sino-Soviet interest. Singapore Foreign Minister Sinnathamby Rajaratnam said in February that the Soviet Union had increased its presence in the region since the end of the Vietnam war. This was the result of Moscow's capitalizing on the withdrawal of Western powers. The West, he said, identified Southeast Asia with Vietnam, while the Soviets were more farsighted. As a result one-power preeminence could develop, and if the region adjusted itself to such a monopoly completely, "it will take the Western world a long, long time to reassert its presence in the consciousness of Southeast Asians."

Apprehensions about China were not so openly expressed in the region, and individual countries continued their efforts to build bridges to Peking. But there were nagging fears that their mutual rivalry could cause China and the U.S.S.R. to use the new Communist states of Indochina as well as underground forces in other countries to promote subversion plans. Vietnam's emergence as the third-largest Communist power in the world was considered an unsettling factor because there were no signs that it was about to join hands with its neighbours in cooperative regionalism.

Most Southeast Asian leaders saw a direct link between the huge quantities of arms and ammunition left by the U.S. in Vietnam and the hard strikes by insurgents in several nearby countries. The Communist underground in the Philippines was said to have gained some strength, while that in Malaysia made its presence felt despite government claims that its back had been broken. In Thailand there were widespread fears of the insurgents' gaining ground in districts adjoining the nation's Communist neighbours. In all, the rebel movements were strong enough to convince governments that concerted long-term plans were necessary to counter them.

ASEAN. The cumulative effect of these developments was felt when Southeast Asian leaders gathered in Kuala Lumpur, Malaysia, on August 4 for the second summit meeting of the Association of Southeast Asian Nations (ASEAN). It was a gala occasion, the glitter of which attracted some criticism. But behind the pomp, a good deal of work was done, prompting commentators in the region to say that "ASEAN has come of age."

The major political news that came out of the summit was an indication of the extent to which attitudes had changed. The Philippines won all-round approbation by announcing that it was prepared to withdraw its historical claim on Sabah, an east Malaysian state on the Borneo coast. It was the first time a member country publicly abridged its nationalism in the interest of regionalism.

But the focus of the summit was economic cooperation. In this area also one solid achievement overshadowed the progress made on a wide front. The governors of the central banks of the five member countries (Indonesia, Malaysia, the Philippines, Singapore, and Thailand) signed an agreement to create a standby credit facility of $100 million to help any of them who faced short-term international liquidity problems. Called "swap" (the credit was to be arranged by a member swapping its domestic currency for U.S. dollars), the arrangement was to be coordinated by each of the central banks acting as agent in rotation, beginning with the Bank Indonesia.

There were disagreements, too, stemming from the different levels of economic development in the member countries. This was seen in the areas of trade and industrial projects. The five leaders had agreed to lower tariffs for intraregional trade on 71 items. However, bilateral negotiations by Singapore, Thailand, and the Philippines led to the list's being extended to 1,758 items as far as the three countries were concerned. The reservations of the others were reflected in Indonesian Foreign Minister Adam Malik's statement that "the needs of 140 million must take precedence over those of two million"—a reference to the feeling that free trade would benefit Singapore at the expense of less-developed Indonesia.

The 1977 summit derived extra significance from the fact that the prime ministers of Japan, Australia, and New Zealand attended it in extended sessions. This was the direct result of an agreement by the ASEAN leaders that rapid economic progress was the key to the security of the region. They recognized the need for an Asian "Marshall Plan" to achieve this and welcomed the opportunity to get the three advanced countries in the area intimately involved with ASEAN.

Nothing like a Marshall Plan materialized, however. Japan was in no mood to relax its own stiff trade barriers, and its aid programs were organized on a bilateral basis. For domestic political reasons Australia also was not able to come up with significant proposals, while New Zealand's participation was expected to be relatively limited to begin with. It was agreed on all sides, however, that Japan would not be able to hold out much longer and that fairly large programs of economic cooperation would eventually be achieved.

The spirit that moved the summit leaders toward cooperative agreements had effects in a number of areas. In its quest for regional independence the Federation of ASEAN Shippers Councils took on such established and influential organizations as the European-dominated Far East Freight Conference. In a series of meetings, the council initiated moves to reduce dependence on foreign shipping lines and to "promote regional trade at reasonable freight rates." In March the five countries worked out a formula for an emergency sharing of oil that could be immediately activated if a member country ran into a crisis. Indonesia and Malaysia were the only oil producers in ASEAN.

UPI COMPIX

An employee of the Southeast Asia Treaty Organization (SEATO) was loaded down with flags of the eight member nations after the 23-year-old Asian alliance went out of existence on June 30.

Against the background of burgeoning regionalism, government leaders sometimes found it necessary to declare that the interests of foreign investors would be safeguarded. This was particularly so in the field of oil, where ASEAN countries continued to encourage foreign corporations. Indonesian Mining Minister Mohammad Sadli said in Brussels in April that nationalization of Western oil facilities in Southeast Asia was unlikely because the region depended on foreign knowhow for exploration and production.

Though the countries of Southeast Asia laid considerable emphasis in 1977 on attracting foreign investment, such investment was clearly distinguished from what Asian governments perceived as traditional Western exploitation of raw materials. During the Brussels talks, Malaysia's trade and industry minister, Datuk Hamzah Abu Samah, said that ASEAN states in fact wanted gradually to phase out their export to Europe of primary commodities in order to boost their own industries.

SEATO. The Southeast Asia Treaty Organization (SEATO), slowly dying for more than three years, finally folded on June 30. In a parting blast, outgoing Secretary-General Sunthorn Hongladarom of Thailand told reporters in Bangkok that SEATO's dissolution meant the departure of a deterrent against the Communists. The Communist superpowers, he warned, had not reduced their efforts to establish more influence in the region, nor had they decreased their stockpiling of weaponry. (T. J. S. GEORGE)

See also articles on the various countries.
[976.B]

Southern Rhodesia:
see Rhodesia

South West Africa:
see Dependent States; South Africa

Soviet Literature:
see Literature

Soviet Union:
see Union of Soviet Socialist Republics

Space Exploration

Soon after the new Democratic administration took office in the United States in 1977, it became apparent that there would be no major new U.S. space efforts, as there had been none during the two preceding Republican administrations. In particular, manned space ventures were ruled out other than those associated with the space shuttle. Later in the year U.S. Pres. Jimmy Carter nominated Robert A. Frosch, associate director for applied oceanography at the Woods Hole (Mass.) Oceanographic Institution, as the new administrator of the National Aeronautics and Space Administration (NASA). He was subsequently confirmed by the U.S. Senate.

On June 16 Wernher von Braun, a pioneer in rocketry and space exploration, died (see OBITUARIES).

By midyear NASA had received more than 8,000 applications in response to its advertisement for 30–40 space shuttle pilots and mission specialists. Included in the total were more than 1,500 women.

Elsewhere, activities in astronautics moved ahead. In August Czechoslovakia began construction of a large space laboratory. At the same time, the Japanese Space Activities Commission's Long-range Program Study Committee announced an extremely ambitious future plan. It included participation in the U.S. space shuttle, development of a booster capable of placing 10,000-kg (22,000-lb) payloads into Earth orbit by 1990, a probe to return lunar soil samples by 2000, and unmanned probes to Venus and Mars after 2000.

Another country with an eye toward a future in space was China, representatives of which visited Paris in September and received a two-day briefing on the operations and plans of the European Space Agency. The ESA presentation was followed by visits to member nations of the agency and further talks on national space programs and capabilities.

Manned Flight. The year was frustrating for the manned space program of the U.S.S.R. Lieut. Col. V. D. Zudov and Lieut. Col. V. I. Rozhdestvenskiy,

The space shuttle orbiter "Enterprise" takes off perched on the back of its 747 mother ship.

UPI COMPIX

the crew of Soyuz 23, were launched on Oct. 14, 1976, but were unable to dock with the Salyut 5 space station. After an additional day in space they returned to the Earth and made a hazardous landing in Lake Tengiz in freezing weather at night in a deep fog. Soyuz 24 had better luck. Launched Feb. 7, 1977, with a crew of Col. V. V. Gorbatko and Lieut. Col. Y. N. Glazkov, it successfully docked with Salyut 5 on the following day. For 18 days the two cosmonauts performed a series of scientific, engineering, and military observations and experiments. The two also completely replaced the cabin air with a fresh supply brought up from the Earth.

On October 9 Lieut. Col. Vladimir Kovalenok and flight engineer Valery Ryumin were launched aboard Soyuz 25 for a rendezvous with the Salyut 6 space station, which had gone into orbit on September 29. Approaching within 100 m of the station but failing to dock with it because of unspecified troubles, Soyuz 25 returned to Earth after 49 hours in orbit. On December 11, however, Lieut. Col. Yuri Romanenko and Georgi M. Grechko successfully docked Soyuz 26 with Salyut 6, where they remained at the year's end.

Launch Vehicles. In the U.S. the success of the first flights of the space shuttle orbiter was clouded by two catastrophic failures of previously reliable rocket launch vehicles. After preliminary taxi tests on the runway and flights mated to its Boeing 747 jet carrier plane, the shuttle orbiter "Enterprise" was pronounced ready for release from its mother plane. On August 12, at Edwards Air Force Base in California, astronauts Fred W. Haise, Jr., and C. Gordon Fullerton guided the "Enterprise" to a "superslick" landing on the floor of Rogers Dry Lake 5 minutes and 23 seconds after being released from the 747. A second flight, with astronauts Joe H. Engle and Richard H. Truly, on September 13 was equally successful. Haise and Fullerton put the "Enterprise" through yet another landing ten days later. However, all of these tests were conducted with a special aerodynamic shield, or tail cone, over the aft end of the craft. The shield was removed and dummy engines installed to see how the ship would handle as it would when actually returning from space. The first flight with the shield off was made successfully by Engle and Truly on October 12.

An ill omen appeared at the Kennedy Space Center in Florida in mid-May, when a small, strap-on solid-propellant booster rocket fell from its bracket on the first stage of a Delta vehicle and damaged it. The booster was being prepared to launch the Orbital Test Satellite for ESA. The satellite was destroyed on September 13 when its Delta launch vehicle exploded one minute after lift-off, apparently because one of its solid-propellant strap-on rockets detonated. Only 16 days later, a Centaur booster with an Intelsat 4A communications satellite on board also went up in flames only one minute after launch.

In view of such launch failures it was reasonable to assume that competitors to the NASA rockets might become available in the near future. Early in February the board of governors of the International Telecommunications Satellite Consortium

Major Satellites and Space Probes Launched Oct. 1, 1976–Sept. 30, 1977

Name/country/ launch vehicle/ scientific designation	Launch date, lifetime*	Physical characteristics					Orbital elements			
		Weight in kg†	Shape	Diam- eter in m†	Length or height in m†	Experiments	Perigee in km†	Apogee in km†	Period (min)	Inclination to Equator (degrees)
Soyuz 23/U.S.S.R./A II/ 1976-100A	10/14/76 10/16/76	6,570 (14,484)	sphere and cone	2.3 (7.55)	7.5 (24.61)	Manned spacecraft	188 (117)	224 (139)	88.6	51.6
Marisat 3/U.S./Delta/ 1976-101A	10/14/76	655 (1,444)	cylinder	1.9 (6.23)	2.4 (7.87)	Communications satellite	35,051 (21,780)	36,525 (22,696)	1,436.2	2.6
Meteor 26/U.S.S.R./A I/ 1976-102A	10/15/76	2,750 (6,063)	cylinder	1.5 (4.92)	5 (16.4)	Meteorological satellite	857 (533)	891 (554)	102.4	81.2
Ekran (Statsionar 1)/U.S.S.R./ D Ie/1976-107A	10/26/76	‡	‡	‡	‡	Television communications satellite	35,600 (22,121)	35,600 (22,121)	1,422	0.3
Prognoz 5/U.S.S.R./A IIe/ 1976-112A	11/25/76	910 (2,006)	‡	‡	‡	Radiation research by French, Czechoslovak, and Soviet scientists	1,584 (984)	197,754 (122,879)	5,728	65.9
Molniya 2/U.S.S.R./A IIe/ 1976-116A	12/2/76	1,250 (2,756)	cylinder and cone with six panels	1.6 (5.25)	4.2 (13.78)	Communications satellite	597 (371)	39,746 (24,697)	717.5	63
CS-7/China/CSS-X-3/ 1976-117A	12/7/76 1/2/77	‡	‡	‡	‡	‡	172 (107)	489 (304)	89.0	59.4
Molniya 3/U.S.S.R./A IIe/ 1976-127A	12/28/76	1,500 (3,307)	cylinder and cone with six panels	1.6 (5.25)	4.2 (13.78)	Communications satellite	634 (394)	39,717 (24,679)	717.7	62.9
Meteor 2/U.S.S.R./A I/ 1977-002A	1/6/77	2,750 (6,063)	cylinder with two panels	1.5 (4.92)	5 (16.4)	Meteorological satellite	890 (553)	904 (562)	102.9	81.2
NATO 3-B/NATO/Delta/ 1977-005A	1/28/77	376 (830)	cylinder	2.2 (7.22)	3.1 (10.17)	Communications satellite	35,463 (22,036)	35,962 (22,346)	1,432	2.8
Soyuz 24/U.S.S.R./A II/ 1977-008A	2/7/77 2/25/77	6,570 (14,484)	sphere and cone	2.3 (7.55)	7.5 (24.61)	Ferried crew to Salyut 5	173 (107)	323 (201)	89.5	51.6
Molniya 2/U.S.S.R./A IIe/ 1977-010A	2/11/77	‡	cylinder and cone with six panels	1.6 (5.25)	4.2 (13.78)	Communications satellite	484 (301)	39,888 (24,785)	735	62.8
Tansei 3 (MS-T3)/Japan/ Mu-3H/1977-012A	2/19/77	134 (295)	polyhedral cylinder	1 (3.28)	1 (3.28)	Engineering test satellite	795 (494)	3,814 (2,370)	134.1	65.7
Kiku 2 (ETS-2)/Japan/ Nu/1977-014A	2/23/77	130 (287)	polyhedral cylinder	1.4 (4.59)	1 (3.28)	Engineering test satellite	34,035 (21,148)	35,756 (22,218)	1,390.8	0.5
Palapa 2/Indonesia/Delta/ 1977-018A	3/10/77	575 (1,268)	cylinder	1.9 (6.23)	3.7 (12.14)	Communications satellite	35,764 (22,223)	35,809 (22,251)	1,436.1	0.1
Molniya 1/U.S.S.R./A IIe/ 1977-021A	3/24/77	‡	cylinder with two panels	1.6 (5.25)	3.4 (11.15)	Communications satellite	484 (301)	40,816 (25,362)	717.5	62.8
Meteor 2/U.S.S.R./A I/ 1977-024A	4/5/77	2,200 (4,850)	cylinder with two panels	1.5 (4.92)	5 (16.4)	Meteorological satellite	853 (530)	897 (557)	102.4	81.2
Geos 1/ESA/Delta/ 1977-029A	4/20/77	573 (1,263)	cylinder	1.6 (5.25)	1.1 (3.61)	Magnetosphere research	2,131 (1,324)	38,498 (23,922)	720	26.9
Molniya 2/U.S.S.R./A IIe/ 1977-032A	4/28/77	1,500 (3,307)	cylinder and cone with six panels	1.6 (5.25)	4.2 (13.78)	Communications satellite	467 (290)	40,817 (25,363)	736	62.8
Intelsat 4A/U.S./Centaur/ 1977-041A	5/26/77	762 (1,680)	cylinder	2.38 (7.81)	2.82 (9.25)	Communications satellite	35,784 (22,235)	35,790 (22,239)	1,436.1	0.0
Signe 3/France/C-1/ 1977-049A	6/17/77	102 (225)	‡	‡	‡	Space radiation experiments	457 (284)	523 (325)	94.3	51.7
Molniya 1/U.S.S.R./A IIe/ 1977-054A	6/24/77	‡	cylinder and cone with six panels	1.6 (5.25)	3.4 (11.15)	Communications satellite	480 (298)	39,016 (24,243)	700	62.9
Meteor 2/U.S.S.R./A I/ 1977-057A	6/29/77	2,200 (4,850)	cylinder	1.5 (4.92)	5 (16.4)	Meteorological satellite	602 (374)	685 (426)	97.4	98
Gima-1 (Himawari)/Japan/ Delta/1977-065A	7/14/77	‡	cylinder with two antennae	2.26 (7.4)	1.34 (4.4)	Meteorological satellite	35,771 (22,227)	35,804 (22,248)	1,436.2	1.1
Raduga 3 (Statsionar 2)/ U.S.S.R./D Ie/1977-071A	7/24/77	5,000 (11,023)	cylinder	‡	‡	Television communications satellite	35,757 (22,218)	35,820 (22,258)	1,436.2	0.3
Cosmos 936/U.S.S.R./D Ie/ 1977-074A	8/3/77 8/22/77	2,268 (5,000)	sphere	3 (9.84)		International biomedical research satellite	224 (139)	419 (260)	90.7	62.8
HEAO 1/U.S./Centaur/ 1977-075A	8/12/77	2,566 (5,657)	rectangular box with two panels	2.35 (7.7)	5.79 (19)	X-ray astronomy satellite	431 (268)	456 (283)	93.5	22.7
Voyager 2/U.S./Titan IIIe/ 1977-076A	8/20/77	825 (1,819)	10-sided base with parabolic antenna	1.78 (5.84)	0.47 (1.54)	Flyby of planets Jupiter and Saturn	Interplanetary trajectory			
Sirio/Italy/Delta/ 1977-080A	8/25/77	398 (877)	cylinder	1.4 (4.59)	2 (6.56)	Communications satellite	34,210 (21,257)	36,327 (22,573)	1,409.7	0.2
Molniya 1/U.S.S.R./A IIe/ 1977-082A	8/30/77	‡	cylinder and cone with six panels	1.6 (5.25)	3.4 (11.15)	Communications satellite	480 (298)	40,800 (25,352)	736	62.8
Voyager 1/U.S./Titan IIIe/ 1977-084A	9/5/77	825 (1,819)	10-sided base with parabolic antenna	1.78 (5.84)	0.47 (1.54)	Flyby of planets Jupiter and Saturn	Interplanetary trajectory			
Ekran 2/U.S.S.R./‡/ 1977-092A	9/20/77	‡	‡	‡	‡	Television communications satellite	35,767 (22,225)	35,802 (22,246)	1,436	0.4
Prognoz 6/U.S.S.R./A IIe/ 1977-093A	9/22/77	910 (2,006)	‡	‡	‡	Scientific experiments in interplanetary space	498 (309)	197,900 (122,969)	5,688	65
Intercosmos 17/U.S.S.R./ B 1/1977-096A	9/26/77	700 (1,543)	octagon	1.1 (3.61)	2.5 (8.2)	International scientific research in charged particles and micrometeorites	468 (291)	519 (322)	94.4	83
Salyut 6/U.S.S.R./D Ih/ 1977-097A	9/29/77	19,000 (41,888)	cylinder with solar panels	4 (13.12)	10 (32.81)	Manned space station	219 (136)	275 (171)	89.1	51.6

*All dates are in universal time (UT).
†English units in parentheses: weight in pounds, dimensions in feet, apogee and perigee in statute miles.
‡Not available.

(MITCHELL R. SHARPE)

(Intelsat) was given a briefing on the payload capabilities of the Ariane, being developed by ESA and the French Centre National d'Etudes Spatiales. Recent improvements in the Ariane propulsion system made it seem likely that the new vehicle could put the 1,700-kg Intelsat 5 into the required orbit.

Unmanned Satellites. As 1976 ended, China announced that it intended to join Intelsat, and in August it became the 98th member nation. Taiwan had withdrawn from the group on December 10. At the same time, an ominous note was sounded in regard to the uses of unmanned satellites. On December 27, the U.S.S.R. for the fourth time in 1976 demonstrated its killer satellite system. Cosmos 886 passed close to Cosmos 880 and was detonated.

As 1977 began, Japan launched its first geosynchronous satellite on February 23. Kiku 2 was an engineering test vehicle launched by a Nu rocket. Two months later ESA managed to salvage what could well have been a costly failure of a Delta launch vehicle. On April 20 the second stage of the Delta malfunctioned, and ESA's Geos satellite went into an eccentric orbit with a perigee of 240 km and an apogee of 10,074 km instead of the planned 230 km by 35,811 km (1 km = 0.62 mi). On April 25, however, commands sent by ESA placed the satellite into an orbit of 2,131 km by 38,498 km, which should provide maximum scientific data from the satellite.

Space cooperation between the U.S.S.R. and U.S. continued during the year. On August 3 Cosmos 936 was launched from Plesetsk in the Soviet Union. The U.S. had seven experiments aboard it,

The thrust of a powerful rocket pushed Voyager I off on a journey that would carry it past Jupiter in early 1979.

four of which had Soviet coinvestigators. Additionally, experiments from France, Czechoslovakia, Poland, Romania, Bulgaria, Hungary, and East Germany were in the satellite. The spacecraft landed after 19 days, and biological specimens were turned over to investigators in Moscow.

NASA's HEAO 1 scientific satellite, launched on August 12, soon proved its worth by spotting an X-ray nova in the constellation Ophiuchus and reporting its position to observatories on the Earth. Optical telescopes in Australia and Arizona soon identified it as an extremely dim star that was not visible on photographic plates made a few weeks earlier. On October 21 the Delta restored confidence to potential users by successfully placing two International Sun-Earth Explorer satellites into highly eccentric orbits about the Earth.

Space Probes. Mars continued to reveal itself to Vikings 1 and 2 during the year. However, mission controllers had some bad moments in January when the command receiver of the Viking 1 lander failed to acknowledge transmissions from the Earth. The trouble eventually cleared up in February, and activity resumed. The Viking 1 orbiter was shifted so that its orbit took it within 70 km of Phobos to photograph that Martian natural satellite. On Nov. 25, 1976, the Viking 2 lander sensed an event that might have been a Marsquake, the second since it descended to the surface. While the primary mission of the two landers ended in that month, extended missions began in mid-December to run through May 31, 1978.

On March 12 commands were sent to the Viking 1 lander to turn off its gas chromatograph mass spectrometer; a failure in its power supply had made it inoperative. The instrument earlier had detected no organic components of the Martian soil, the task for which it was designed. It had also determined the composition of the atmosphere at the planet's surface, discovering argon isotopes in it. Malfunctions also plagued the soil sampler arm of the Viking 2 lander on March 22. It failed to respond fully to a command to deploy to a position on the surface where it would scoop up a sample for analysis by the pyrolytic release experiment. Having completed their tasks and used up their high-pressure helium, nutrients, and other consumables, the biological experiments on both Viking landers were turned off in May.

Voyager 2 was launched on its trip to Jupiter and Saturn from Kennedy Space Center on August 20. The 825-kg probe was scheduled to fly by Jupiter in July 1979, and then continue to a meeting with Saturn in August 1981. If all went well, the craft could visit Uranus and Neptune as well. Voyager 1 was launched on September 5. It was targeted to pass Jupiter in March 1979 and Saturn in November 1980. Because of different trajectories, it would overtake the craft launched earlier.

Pioneer 11, on its way to a meeting with Saturn in September 1979, crossed the orbit of Jupiter for the second time on June 10. The first crossing occurred in December 1974. (MITCHELL R. SHARPE)

See also Astronomy; Defense; Earth Sciences; Industrial Review: *Aerospace; Telecommunications;* Television and Radio.
[738.C]

Spain

A monarchy of southwest Europe, Spain is bounded by Portugal, with which it shares the Iberian Peninsula, and by France. Area: 504,750 sq km (194,885 sq mi), including the Balearic and Canary islands. Pop. (1977 est.): 36,229,900, including the Balearics and Canaries. Cap. and largest city: Madrid (pop., 1977 est., 3,870,900). Language: Spanish. Religion: Roman Catholic. King, Juan Carlos I; premier in 1977, Adolfo Suárez González.

The positive vote in the Dec. 15, 1976, referendum and the approval of the Cortes made the Political Reform Law a fundamental law and laid down the future course of Spain's political development. The Movimiento Nacional, the Francoist organization that had enjoyed a monopoly of political power, was finally disbanded on April 1, 1977. In February political parties began to register with the authorities and were thereby legalized. The partial amnesty of July 1976 was extended to most political prisoners in March 1977 and was made practically all-inclusive in October. The electoral law, promulgated on March 15, set procedures for the election of a lower and upper house of the Cortes, with a term of four years. A law passed on March 30 legalized trade unions after official registration, subject to the union's not being under a political party or association. A decree in March regulated workers' rights with regard to job actions. Under the decree workers could not be dismissed for recognized strikes, but wildcat strikes remained illegal.

Premier Adolfo Suárez legalized the Communist Party (PCE) on April 9. The minister for the Navy,

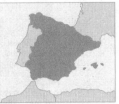

Spain

with the support of colleagues, resigned when the party was legalized, and was replaced by a retired officer, Adm. Pascual Pery Junquera. Meanwhile, the Supreme Council of the Army issued a communiqué stating its repugnance at the legalization but declaring that the Army would accept the accomplished fact. Parties of the right staged demonstrations, but the government made it clear that it alone would be responsible for political decisions.

Elections were fixed for June 15. Because of the ban on political party activity since the end of the Civil War, only three of the major parties could claim an "electorate": the Socialists (PSOE), the Communists, and the Falange. The other 52 parties and groups taking part in the elections were improvised alliances. Premier Suárez stood for the Unión del Centro Democrático (UCD), an alliance of 12 parties with right-of-centre ideologies ranging from conservative to social-democratic. Given the short campaigning time, the effect of personalities was a major influence. The leaders of the Socialist and Communist parties, Felipe González and Santiago Carrillo (see BIOGRAPHY), respectively, both toured the country.

Suárez' contribution to the UCD could hardly be overestimated. He was admired as the man who had brought Spain to the polls, his position in the government lent certain guarantees of stability, and he presented an electoral choice that avoided a dangerous polarization of forces between the right-wing Alianza Popular and the left, represented by the PSOE and the PCE, which many felt was unprepared to take power.

The UCD gained 34.3% of the 17.5 million votes cast (165 seats in the Cortes). Next came the PSOE with 28.5% (118 seats). The PSOE gained more votes than the UCD in the largest cities, the indus-

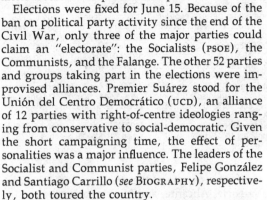

Amid ancient splendour, the first democratically elected Spanish Cortes (parliament) in more than 40 years was inaugurated July 22 in Madrid. King Juan Carlos and Queen Sofía presided at the ceremony.

Education. (1975–76) Primary, pupils 6,393,804, teachers 193,370; secondary, pupils 818,403, teachers 48,694; vocational, pupils 305,254, teachers 28,-283; teacher training, students 70,829, teachers 2,873; higher, students 461,076, teaching staff 26,565.

Finance. Monetary unit: peseta, with (Sept. 19, 1977) a free rate of 84.63 pesetas to U.S. $1 (147.42 pesetas = £1 sterling). Gold, SDR's, and convertible currencies (June 1977) U.S. $3,916,000,000. Budget (1976 actual): revenue 884 billion pesetas; expenditure 912 billion pesetas. Gross domestic product (1975) 5,800,000,000,000 pesetas. Money supply (May 1977) 2,345,000,000,000 pesetas. Cost of living (1970 = 100; April 1977) 245.

Foreign Trade. (1976) Imports 1,170,400,000,000 pesetas; exports 583.5 billion pesetas. Import sources: EEC 33% (West Germany 10%, France 8%, U.K. 5%, Italy 5%); U.S. 14%; Saudi Arabia 9%; Iran 5%. Export destinations: EEC 46% (France 14%, West Germany 11%, U.K. 7%, The Netherlands 5%); U.S. 10%. Main exports: machinery 12%; iron and steel 10%; fruit and vegetables 10%; chemicals 9%;

motor vehicles 7%; footwear 6%; textiles and clothing 5%; ships and boats 5%. Tourism (1975): visitors 30,122,500; receipts U.S. $3,481,000,000.

Transport and Communications. Roads (1975) 144,532 km (including 800 km expressways). Motor vehicles in use (1975): passenger 4,806,800; commercial 1,001,100. Railways: (1975) 15,839 km (including 4,220 km electrified); traffic (1976) 16,684,000,000 passenger-km, freight 10,767,-000,000 net ton-km. Air traffic (1976): 11,129,000,-000 passenger-km; freight 289,673,000 net ton-km. Shipping (1976): merchant vessels 100 gross tons and over 2,792; gross tonnage 6,027,763. Telephones (Dec. 1975) 7,836,000. Radio receivers (Dec. 1974) 8,050,000. Television receivers (Dec. 1974) 6,-125,000.

Agriculture. Production (in 000; metric tons; 1976): wheat 4,176; barley 5,163; oats 505; rye 209; corn 1,543; rice c. 392; potatoes 5,615; dry broad beans (1975) 119; sugar, raw value c. 1,296; tomatoes 2,103; onions 785; cabbages (1975) 664; melons (1975) 731; watermelons (1975) 423; apples 1,007; pears (1975) 405; peaches (1975) 281; oranges 1,702;

mandarin oranges and tangerines 662; lemons 210; sunflower seed 334; bananas 337; olives 220; olive oil 455; almonds (1975) 252; wine 2,475; tobacco 29; cotton, lint c. 48; cow's milk c. 5,393; hen's eggs 507; meat 1,959; fish catch (1975) c. 1,533. Livestock (in 000; 1976): cattle 4,408; pigs 8,583; sheep 15,745; goats 2,339; mules (1975) 352; asses (1975) 280; chickens c. 48,318.

Industry. Index of industrial production (1970 = 100; 1976) 152. Fuel and power (in 000; metric tons; 1976): coal 10,483; lignite 4,140; crude oil 1,982; manufactured gas (cu m) c. 2,650,000; electricity (kw-hr) 90,595,000. Production (in 000; metric tons; 1976): cement 25,291; iron ore (50% metal content) 7,609; pig iron 6,952; crude steel 10,910; aluminum 210; copper 150; lead 76; zinc 158; petroleum products (1975) c. 41,503; sulfuric acid 2,414; fertilizers (nutrient content; 1975–76) nitrogenous 825, phosphate 458, potash 506; cotton yarn 71; cotton fabrics 64; wool yarn 29; man-made fibres 201; passenger cars (units) 755; commercial vehicles (units) 110. Merchant vessels launched (100 gross tons and over; 1976) 1,624,000 gross tons.

trialized provinces of the north, and in Zaragoza, Valencia, Alicante, and Murcia, as well as in the Andalusian provinces. The PCE was successful in the same areas as the PSOE, with the exception of Vizcaya and Guipúzcoa; a major portion of the PCE's vote came from Barcelona, followed by Madrid. On the right, the Falangists obtained only 0.35% of the vote and no seats, while the Alianza Popular, which gained 8%, did moderately well in backward regions (Galicia) and in the major cities. In the Senate, besides the 41 appointments by the king, the largest representations among the 207 elected senators were the UCD 106 (1 elected in October) and the PSOE 35, followed by groupings of the left-wing and centre independent parties.

The government's post-election priority was the economic crisis: a rate of inflation at about 30% in 1977; unemployment at over 5%; and a balance of payments deficit of about U.S. $5 billion (25% of the import bill was spent on petroleum). The peseta was devalued by 19.8% on July 12, and measures to combat unemployment and short-term austerity schemes were introduced.

The UCD and the Cabinet disagreed over economic policy. The minister of economy aimed to bring down the high rates of inflation with a credit and money supply squeeze, while modernization of the tax system, the introduction of a wealth tax, and surcharges on high incomes would increase revenue. In return for a reform of the financial system, the government hoped for the cooperation of labour, but the delay in laying down firm lines for wage settlements led to exaggerated wage claims and wildcat strikes. To help resolve the crisis, the premier held meetings in mid-October between himself, the opposition, and the unions in an effort to obtain political support in curtailing wage demands until his packet of reforms had a chance to work. On October 25 all parties signed a pact agreeing to economic austerity measures.

In regional affairs, the government legislated for a general council for Catalonia and provided administrative arrangements for the four Catalan provinces. On September 29 it allowed the reestablishment of the Generalitat, the traditional form of

Catalan government. Although a campaign of violence continued in the Basque provinces, a decree-law was issued in March restoring the Juntas Generales of Guipúzcoa and Vizcaya, and the Basque language and flag were officially recognized. The murder of Vizcaya's provincial governor and members of the Guardia Civil in October, though causing outrage throughout the nation, failed to stop the proclamation of an amnesty by the king. With demonstrations in the Basque provinces set for Jan. 4, 1978, the government on December 31 approved a statute giving provisional limited autonomy to Guipúzcoa, Vizcaya, and Álava. The fourth Basque province, Navarre, was divided on the question of autonomy and would eventually decide the issue by referendum.

Spain's applications to join the Council of Europe and the European Economic Community (EEC) were accepted in principle, but the EEC Commission stated entry negotiations were unlikely to begin before 1980. To gain support for Spain's application, the premier visited EEC capitals in September and October.   (MICHAEL WOOLLER)

See also Dependent States.

Speleology

The world's longest cave, the combined Flint Ridge and Mammoth Cave system in Kentucky, was extended by steady exploration to more than 322 km (200 mi) by 1977. In Switzerland the Hölloch remained the second longest, and successive winter expeditions, when the reduced flow of meltwater made the passages accessible, increased its length to 129.5 km (80.5 mi). Meanwhile, the mazelike gypsum cave of Optimistitscheskaya in the Ukraine, the longest in the U.S.S.R., reached 109.3 km (67.9 mi) and became the third longest in the world. Discovery of another extension of the Gouffre de la Pierre Saint-Martin, French Pyrenees, which is also the deepest known (at 1,332 m [4,370 ft]), increased its length to 31 km (19 mi), making it the 17th longest.

The Kievskaya Cave (formerly known as Kilsi)

in the U.S.S.R. was explored by a large Soviet expedition to a depth of 1,030 m (3,380 ft), thus making it the fourth deepest in the world. The deepest cave in the Western Hemisphere (and 16th deepest altogether) was the Sotano de San Agustín in Mexico. Successive expeditions there reached a sump at 862 m (2,828 ft). In the course of one of the explorations a man was injured some 396 m (1,300 ft) below the surface, and his rescue took 31 hours.

In Austria the bottom of the Hochlecken Grosshöhle was reached 775 m (2,542 ft) below the entrance, but because the highest point in the cave was 102 m (335 ft) above the entrance, its total vertical extent became 877 m (2,877 ft); thus, it became the second deepest cave in Austria and the 15th in the world. Somewhat similarly, the Austrian Lamprechtsofen was explored to a height of 810 m (2,657 ft) above the entrance, and so it became the 20th "deepest" in the world. Also in Austria, the depth of the Schönbergschacht, or Kacherlschacht, was increased from 708 m (2,323 ft) to 730 m (2,395 ft). The same depth (730 m) was measured in the recently discovered Abisso Coltelli in the Apuan Alps of Italy, and so the two shared 30th place in the world list.

At the end of 1976 a Swiss group explored the Faustloch to a depth of 690 m (2,264 ft), making it the second deepest cave in Switzerland. Near the French Alps the Grotte de la Diau was linked with the Tanne du Bel Espoir, giving a combined depth of 613 m (2,011 ft). The deepest cave in Romania, Pestera de la Izvorul Tausoarelor, was descended to 415 m (1,362 ft), while the Pestera Vintului reached a length of 20.8 km (12.9 mi). The Japanese cave of Byakurendo was explored to 520 m (1,706 ft) to become that country's deepest. A Polish expedition visited Colombia and explored several caves, including the Hoyo del Aire, near La Paz, whose 200-m (656-ft) entrance shaft led on to a final sump at 280 m (919 ft).

The seventh International Speleological Congress (a quadrennial event) was held in England for the first time, in Sheffield. David Brook received the Royal Geographical Society's Cuthbert Peak Award for "exploration in speleology," particularly in Britain and New Guinea.

(T. R. SHAW)

Sri Lanka

An Asian republic and member of the Commonwealth of Nations, Sri Lanka (Ceylon) occupies an island in the Indian Ocean off the southeast coast of peninsular India. Area: 65,610 sq km (25,332 sq mi). Pop. (1976 est.): 14,270,000, including Sinhalese about 72%; Tamil 21%; Moors 7%. Cap. and largest city: Colombo (pop., 1974 est., 592,000). Language: Sinhalese (official), Tamil, English. Religion (1971): Buddhist 67%; Hindu 18%; Christian 7%; Muslim 7%. President in 1977, William Gopallawa; prime ministers, Mrs. Sirimavo Bandaranaike and, from July 23, J. R. Jayawardene.

The United National Party (UNP) won a sweeping election victory in July 1977, gaining 139 seats in Parliament to 8 for Mrs. Sirimavo Bandaranaike's Freedom Party (previously 19 to 91). A

Sri Lanka

SRI LANKA

Education. (1974) Primary, pupils (state only) 1,367,860; secondary, pupils (state only) 1,063,766; primary and secondary (1973), teachers 98,925; vocational (1973), pupils 3,648, teachers 302; teacher training (1973), students 9,288, teachers 593; higher, students 14,568, teaching staff 5,438.

Finance. Monetary unit: Sri Lanka rupee, with (Sept. 19, 1977) a free rate of SLRs 8.60 to U.S. $1 (SLRs 14.98 = £1 sterling). Gold, SDR's, and foreign exchange (June 1977) U.S. $127 million. Budget (1976 actual): revenue SLRs 5,739,000,000; expenditure SLRs 8,653,000,000. Gross national product (1976) SLRs 26,043,000,000. Money supply (Feb. 1977) SLRs 4,393,000,000. Cost of living (Colombo; 1970 = 100; June 1977) 147.

Foreign Trade. (1976) Imports SLRs 4,846,000,000; exports SLRs 4,805,000,000. Import sources (1975): China 13%; Saudi Arabia 12%; Japan 9%; Pakistan 6%; Australia 8%; France 8%; Thailand 7%; U.S. 6%; West Germany 5%. Export destinations (1975): China 13%; Pakistan 10%; U.K. 9%; U.S. 6%; Iraq 5%; Japan 5%. Main exports: tea 44%; rubber 18%; coconut products 8%.

Transport and Communications. Roads (1975) 30,983 km. Motor vehicles in use (1975): passenger 91,700; commercial 34,400. Railways: (1975) 1,534 km; traffic (1974–75) 2,898,000,000 passenger-km, freight 296 million net ton-km. Air traffic (1976): 305 million passenger-km; freight 2,658,000 net ton-km. Telephones (Jan. 1976) 72,000. Radio receivers (Dec. 1974) 505,000.

Agriculture. Production (in 000; metric tons; 1976): rice 1,253; cassava (1975) c. 727; sweet potatoes (1975) 160; onions c. 42; mangoes c. 64; pineapples c. 48; copra c. 200; tea 197; coffee c. 9; rubber c. 150. Livestock (in 000; June 1975): cattle c. 1,718; buffalo c. 736; sheep c. 30; goats c. 547; pigs 49; chickens c. 6,770.

Industry. Production (in 000; metric tons; 1975): salt 119; cement (1976) 421; graphite (1974) 9.4; petroleum products c. 1,560; cotton yarn (1974) 5.6; electricity (kw-hr) c. 1,149,000.

month later Tamil-Sinhalese communal violence erupted, seriously threatening to strain Sri Lanka's relations with India. A sympathetic approach to the problem by the Indian government and deft handling of the situation by the new prime minister, J. R. Jayawardene (see BIOGRAPHY), helped to restore normality, although the problem of Tamil separatism remained.

A package of measures announced by the UNP government before the parliamentary session provided for an increase in the rice ration from six to eight pounds per adult per week, a reduction of 25% in the prices of flour and bread, and an increase in the sugar ration of 50%. Constitutional changes establishing a French-style presidential system were approved and would go into effect in January 1978.

A trade agreement was signed in September with China, which would purchase 49,200 tons of sheet rubber in exchange for 200,000 tons of rice. With tea, the major export commodity, fetching higher prices, the economy showed some signs of improvement.

(GOVINDAN UNNY)

Stock Exchanges

Stock exchanges throughout the world generally experienced broad-based declines in 1977, while commodity prices recorded mixed results. Ten of the world's 16 major stock price indexes were lower at the end of 1977 than at the end of 1976 (Table I). Selected commodity price indexes fell in London and in Tokyo. Gold, traditionally a haven for

Squash Rackets:
see Racket Games

Stamp Collecting:
see Philately and Numismatics

Steeplechasing:
see Equestrian Sports

money fleeing from economic or political uncertainties, rose in price.

During 1977 the world economy suffered through sporadic periods of four different types of economic conditions: stagflation (slowing "real" growth and accelerating inflation), hesiflation (a stuttering economic growth pattern combined with strong inflationary pressures), disinflation (a selective slowing down but not elimination of inflation), and deflation (sharp price declines in certain economic sectors). The inability of the global economy to sustain vigorous economic growth following the 1974–75 worldwide recession was due mainly to imbalances created by the surplus income that the Organization of Petroleum Exporting Countries (OPEC) had collected from oil prices each year since 1973. While several major non-oil-producing nations enjoyed large balance of payments surpluses, many industrial countries that import oil experienced substantial deficits in their external payments accounts. Moreover, most countries in a deficit position had high inflation rates that necessitated cautious economic policies. These policies, in turn, precluded any meaningful reduction in the relatively high levels of unemployment prevailing in most developed countries.

While these trends were likely to have a major effect on stock prices in the long run, stock markets often act in a perverse manner over the short term. That is because stock prices often anticipate trends in economic activity and are influenced by a myriad of psychological factors. Particularly important to the market's short-run behaviour are the age of the economic cycle, the level and direction of interest rates, and investors' perceptions of the outlook for higher prices. For example, stock prices typically decline before a business slump begins and tend to rise before business starts to recover, while interest rates tend to be relatively high before economic activity turns down and relatively low before an economic recovery.

As 1977 drew to a close, the road to sustained worldwide prosperity was paved with obstacles. Large and small nations alike were faced with the challenge of adjusting their economies to a stable growth pattern that would not reignite inflation but would gradually cut unemployment and avoid protectionist policies. Their success would likely determine the ability of stock markets to generate upward price movements in 1978.

(ROBERT H. TRIGG)

United States. The U.S. stock market in 1977 displayed all of the characteristics of a bear market as blue-chip stock prices fell spasmodically month after month in the face of a generally healthy U.S. economy and a continuing rise in corporate profits and dividends. The Dow Jones industrial average, which ended 1976 at a level of 1004.65, dropped to a low of 800.85 on Nov. 2, 1977. A slight rally brought the year-end average to 831.17. The 17.3% decline was matched by similar results on other leading indexes of highest-grade common stocks. In 1977 approximately $75.3 billion of stock values on the New York Stock Exchange were wiped out. Among the generally lesser-grade securities traded on the American Stock Exchange (Amex) and over the counter, however, a contrary trend was observed. The Amex index rose 16.4% in 1977, and the composite index for over-the-counter stocks was up 7.3%. The increase in market value on the Amex was $2.8 billion; in the over-the-counter system, the gain was $2,250,000,000.

Overall, U.S. stockholders were poorer on paper at the end of 1977. Experiencing the sharpest fall was Eastman Kodak; the market value of its outstanding shares dropped from $13.9 billion to less than $8.3 billion. Kodak's loss about equaled the combined gains of all of the 30 biggest market-value gainers on the New York Stock Exchange. General Motors had the second largest value decline, nearly $4.5 billion. The New York Stock Exchange composite index closed 1976 at 57.88 and 1977 at 52.50, for a decline of 9.3%.

The paradoxical behaviour of stock prices in the face of a strong economy was explained by concerns about inflation, moves by managers of pension funds to diversify their portfolios, and anxiety about the erosion of the value of the dollar in foreign markets. The small stockholder continued to withdraw from the stock market and instead invested in bonds, real estate, or

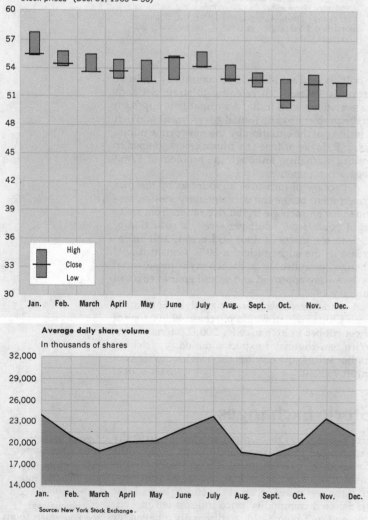

New York Stock Exchange Composite Index, 1977

Stock prices (Dec. 31, 1965 = 50)

High
Close
Low

Jan. Feb. March April May June July Aug. Sept. Oct. Nov. Dec.

Average daily share volume

In thousands of shares

Jan. Feb. March April May June July Aug. Sept. Oct. Nov. Dec.

Source: New York Stock Exchange.

savings-and-loan accounts. A record $44.9 billion of new tax-exempt bonds were sold to the public in 1977, a gain of 33% above the 1976 level, according to the *Daily Bond Buyer*.

The volume of trading on the New York Stock Exchange was 5,273,480,000 shares in 1977, virtually unchanged from the level of 5,263,496,000 the previous year. On the American Stock Exchange the volume was 653,128,700 in 1977, compared with 648,297,321 in 1976. In the over-the-counter market, as reported by the National Association of Securities Dealers, the trade volume in 1977 was 1,932,005,322 for 1977; in 1976 the comparable figure was 1,683,932,674. The volume in this market represented a healthy 15% increase over the previous year. The small investor's withdrawal from the market in 1977 was reflected in the decline of mutual fund sales and odd-lot volume. Also during 1977 the proportion of the cash flow from corporate pension funds into equities was only 23% in the first quarter and 31% in the second. This compared with 57% for all of 1976.

Market activity was so sluggish during 1977 that many brokers were compelled to retrench, and there was a greater wave of mergers of New York Stock Exchange firms than in many years. The price of a seat on the exchanges fell, sometimes sharply. In the case of the Pacific Stock Exchange, a seat that sold for $70,000 in 1970 could be purchased for only $600 at the end of 1977. A seat on the New York Stock Exchange sold for $45,000 on Dec. 31, 1977, the lowest level in years.

Average prices on the New York Stock Exchange declined irregularly throughout 1977 (Table II). The 500 stocks in Standard and Poor's composite index began the year at 103.81, fell rapidly in February and March to 100.57, and continued to slide to 98.76 in May. After a brief rally in June and July, the decline resumed, reaching a level of 93.74 in October, with continuing declines thereafter. The high for the year was 107.00, achieved in January 1977, and the low was 90.71 in December. The 400 stocks in the industrial index showed a more marked trend, beginning the year at 115.17 in January and falling with only a brief interruption in June and July to a level of 103.18 in October. The high for the year was 118.92 and the low 99.88.

Public utility stock prices were stable during 1977, starting the year at 54.01 and trading within a very narrow range throughout the year. The high for 1977 was 57.56, and the low was 51.60. These prices were substantially above their corresponding levels in 1976.

The railroad index declined during 1977 from an initial level of 50.24 in January to 49.27 in February, and after a brief recovery in the spring and summer slid back to 49.19 in August and down to 46.23 in October. On a year-to-year basis, railroad stock prices were higher in every month of 1977 than in 1976.

By contrast with the experience on the New York Stock Exchange, the Amex index closed 1976 at 109.84 and 1977 at 127.89, a gain of 16.43%. The over-the-counter composite index closed 1976 at 97.88 and 1977 at 105.05 for a gain of 7.33%.

The best performing industry groups in 1977 included cable television firms, the stock prices of which recorded an average gain of 62.5%; hospital and nursing home stocks, up 58.7%; computer leasers, up 46.8%; hotel and lodging companies, up 46.4%; and oil and gas field service stocks, up 39.3%. The worst performers were the copper mining companies, down 21.4%; bituminous coal mining firms, down 15.3%; radio and television stocks, down 14.5%; and lumber and wood products companies, down 12.9%. Other prominent losers were automobile manufacturers, down

Table I. Selected Major World Stock Price Indexes*

Country	1977 range High	1977 range Low	Year-end close 1976	Year-end close 1977	Percent change
Australia	477	419	431	477	+11%
Austria	2,674	2,282	2,522	2,297†	− 9
Belgium	99	91	96	91	− 5
Denmark	108	96	100	96	− 4
France	58	44	57	53	− 7
Germany, West	813	713	739	788	+ 7
Hong Kong	425	404	448	404	−10
Italy	74	55	75	56	−25
Japan	5,288	4,597	4,991	4,866	− 3
Netherlands, The	93	76	83	80	− 4
Singapore	268	242	255	264	+ 4
South Africa	211	169	184	211	+15
Spain	102	63	100	67	−33
Sweden	417	287	394	323	−18
Switzerland	319	281	290	301	+ 4
United Kingdom	549	358	355	485	+37

*Index numbers are rounded, and limited to countries for which at least 12 months' data were available on a weekly basis.
†As of Dec. 23, 1977.
Sources: *Barron's*, *The Economist*, *Financial Times*, and *The New York Times*.

Table II. U.S. Stock Market Prices

Month	Railroads (10 stocks) 1977	1976	Industrials (400 stocks) 1977	1976	Public utilities (40 stocks) 1977	1976	Composite (500 stocks) 1977	1976
January	50.24	41.42	115.17	108.45	54.01	46.99	103.81	96.86
February	49.27	43.40	112.14	112.96	52.88	47.22	100.96	100.64
March	50.21	44.54	111.88	113.73	52.14	45.67	100.57	101.08
April	52.83	44.91	109.89	114.67	52.57	46.07	99.05	101.93
May	54.14	46.09	109.10	113.76	53.68	45.69	98.76	101.16
June	53.06	46.56	109.46	114.50	55.29	46.51	99.29	101.77
July	53.12	47.75	110.12	116.90	56.95	47.49	100.18	104.20
August	49.19	46.90	107.50	115.63	55.42	48.81	97.75	103.29
September	48.11	46.59	105.94	118.15	54.61	50.63	96.23	105.45
October	46.23	44.89	103.18	114.03	54.26	50.18	93.74	101.89
November	...	46.93	...	112.96	...	50.55	...	101.19
December	...	50.48	...	116.33	...	53.01	...	104.66

Sources: U.S. Department of Commerce, *Survey of Current Business;* Board of Governors of the Federal Reserve System, *Federal Reserve Bulletin*. Prices are Standard and Poor's monthly averages of daily closing prices, with 1941−43=10.

Table III. U.S. Government Long-Term Bond Prices and Yields
Average price in dollars per $100 bond

Month	Average 1977	1976	Yield (%) 1977	1976	Month	Average 1977	1976	Yield (%) 1977	1976
January	59.73	55.75	6.68	6.94	July	57.48	58.38	6.97	6.85
February	56.23	57.86	7.15	6.92	August	57.30	58.88	7.00	6.79
March	55.83	58.23	7.20	6.87	September	57.77	59.54	6.94	6.70
April	56.31	59.33	7.14	6.73	October	56.68	59.93	7.08	6.65
May	56.06	57.38	7.17	6.99	November	...	60.21	...	6.62
June	57.38	57.86	6.99	6.92	December	...	62.05	...	6.39

Source: U.S. Department of Commerce, *Survey of Current Business*. Average prices are derived from average yields on the basis of an assumed 3% 20-year taxable U.S. Treasury bond. Yields are for U.S. Treasury bonds that are taxable and due or callable in ten years or more.

Table IV. U.S. Corporate Bond Prices and Yields
Average price in dollars per $100 bond

Month	Average 1977	1976	Yield (%) 1977	1976	Month	Average 1977	1976	Yield (%) 1977	1976
January	60.3	57.0	7.96	8.60	July	60.0	57.1	7.94	8.56
February	59.4	57.1	8.04	8.55	August	60.1	57.9	7.98	8.45
March	59.1	57.3	8.10	8.52	September	60.4	58.8	7.92	8.38
April	59.4	58.2	8.04	8.40	October	59.5	59.1	8.04	8.32
May	59.2	56.5	8.05	8.58	November	...	59.2	...	8.25
June	60.1	56.8	7.95	8.62	December	...	61.3	...	7.98

Source: U.S. Department of Commerce, *Survey of Current Business*. Average prices are based on Standard and Poor's composite index of A1+ issues. Yields are based on Moody's Aaa domestic corporate bond index.

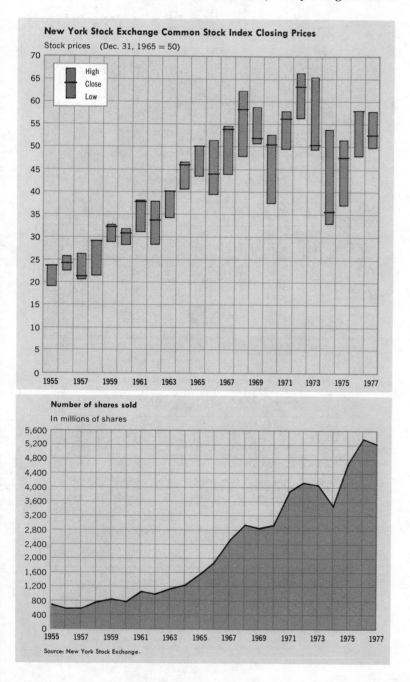

11.9%, and brokerage firms, off 11.6%. The price-earnings ratio on the Dow Jones industrial average dropped to 8.6 in December 1977, from 10.1 at the beginning of the year.

Long-term government bond prices traded within a narrow range during the year, starting at an average of 59.73 and slipping irregularly to a level of 56.68 in October (Table III). Except for the month of January 1977, the level of government bond prices was lower month by month than it had been the previous year. This was also reflected by the relative yields, which moved up into the 7% range during most months of 1977, whereas that level was not achieved during the previous year.

Corporate bond prices held firm during 1977 with a level of 60.3 in January being sustained

New York Stock Exchange Common Stock Index Closing Prices

Stock prices   (Dec. 31, 1965 = 50)

High
Close
Low

Number of shares sold

In millions of shares

Source: New York Stock Exchange.

within a narrow range during most of the year. On a year-to-year basis, these prices were above those of 1976 (Table IV). Yields were somewhat below those of the previous year with a high of 8.1% achieved in March 1977, contrasted with a 1976 high of 8.62% recorded in June of that year. Bond volume on the New York Stock Exchange was $4,646,354,000, down 13% from the previous year's level of $5,262,106,900. On the Amex bond trading volume declined to $284,930,000 from $301,095,000 in 1976, a drop of 6%.

Options trading continued to escalate sharply in the U.S. with the leadership continuing to come from the Chicago Board Options Exchange launched in 1973. Five major stock exchanges—American, Midwest, Pacific, Chicago, and Philadelphia—listed a variety of stock options for trade. Interest in the options market was widespread despite some evidence of market rigging by a few specialists. Nine option specialists on the American Stock Exchange were charged with filing fictitious market transactions and falsifying business records in New York. The indictment was a culmination of various investigations of the practices of options traders carried on by the Exchange itself. During the year the Exchange censured 36 specialists in options, fining them a total of $195,500 and ordering some suspensions from Exchange membership of from one to four weeks.

Canada. Canadian stock prices were much more volatile than their U.S. counterparts during 1977. The Toronto Stock Exchange composite index closed at 1059.59, up 60 from the end of 1976. In a sawtooth trend, stock prices rose from their January level through February and March, achieving an interim peak of 1025 before falling back to 980 in May, recovering to another peak of 1060 in July, retreating to 950 by October, and then moving ahead to close December near the highest level of the year. Performing best were the oil and gas securities and the gold-based stocks. The oil and gas group index was at 1075 in January and closed 1977 at a level of 1500, a gain of 40% during the year. The gold stocks moved from a low of 850 in January into a zigzag pattern during the first half of the year and then zoomed to 1300 by the end of the year for a gain of 53%. Metals and minerals stocks performed poorly, falling from a level of 1175 in February to 800 in November and then improving slightly to close the year at an index average of 900.

Short-term interest rates were stable during the first part of 1977, but rose fairly rapidly after April. The rise in short-term rates was attributed in part to the large increase in the demand for funds during the year. Long-term rates, on the other hand, were relatively stable throughout 1977. Average yields on the highest rated corporate bonds, for example, varied between 7.88 and 8.12% between January and November, with both the high and low occurring in the first three months of the year. Average stock yields, which were 6.24% in 1976, declined to an average of 5.88% by the end of 1977.

(IRVING PFEFFER)

Western Europe. The largest gain among the major world stock market indexes in 1977 was enjoyed by Great Britain. The *Financial Times* index of

30 industrial issues traded on the London Stock Exchange increased 37% from the end of 1976 to the end of 1977. This strong performance occurred despite a low rate of economic growth, high levels of unemployment, and severe wage and price inflation. However, the attractiveness of equity investments was enhanced by an easing of inflation rates, a decline in interest rates, and a surge in liquidity as foreign capital poured into the country.

Stock prices began 1977 on a strong uptrend, a continuation of the trend that started in October 1976. By mid-May the gain in equity values since January totaled 28%. Investors' confidence was buoyed by the announcement that the International Monetary Fund would lend Great Britain nearly $4 billion in return for budget restraints. In addition, the government reached agreement with the U.S. regarding a "safety net" system for sterling balances. Both of these developments promised to lift downward pressures on the depressed British pound, thereby generating renewed demand from foreign investors for sterling.

At the same time, the Bank of England's minimum lending rate, after reaching a record 15% on Oct. 7, 1976, was cut 21 consecutive times, sinking to 5% by October 1977. Investors also placed great weight on the significance of the North Sea oil flow beginning in 1978 and the possibility that Britain could show its first current account surplus since 1971. Restraining influences included a relatively high inflation rate (17.5%) and concern that labour unions might not accept a third year of wage limitation, scheduled to begin on August 1.

During July the British government unveiled a package of tax cuts and spending proposals designed to reduce the unemployment rate, which was at a postwar high, and to persuade major unions to hold down their wage demands. The stock market, which was in the process of consolidating its earlier gains, initially greeted the news with indifference. Within a matter of weeks, however, stock prices launched an uptrend of major proportions. On August 31 stock prices broke through the 500 barrier for the first time since January 1973. News that the nation in August achieved its first monthly trade surplus since 1972 sent the stock market into new high territory. From July 8 to September 14 the *Financial Times* index gained 24%, surpassing the record levels set in May 1972. But euphoria was soon to evaporate. After drifting aimlessly during October, stock prices were pushed sharply downward.

Triggering the change of direction was the decision by the British government to abandon its efforts to keep the British pound from rising in foreign exchange markets. Without such support, the pound leaped to U.S. $1.84 from $1.77. Stock prices weakened because of fears that the boost in the pound would hurt the nation's exports. This was followed by news that the British miners had rejected a new contract and that the Bank of England had increased the minimum lending rate from 5 to 7%. From September 14 to the end of the year stock prices plunged 12%. U.S. dollar weakness in international currency markets caused the pound to be worth $1.92 at the end of 1977.

The West German stock market was generally strong in 1977. Prices on the Frankfurt Stock Exchange at the end of December were 7% higher than at the beginning of the year. The relatively narrow fluctuations in equity prices during 1977 reflected the conservative economic policies of Chancellor Helmut Schmidt. Those policies were developed in the belief that economic stability would contribute more toward overcoming worldwide recession than would policies of rapid economic expansion.

After a hesitant start, stock prices rose steadily throughout March and April. By early May equity values were 7% above the 1976 close. The upturn was fueled by declining interest rates, moderate price inflation, and steady demand for West German exports. However, investor realization that economic activity would fall below government forecasts dampened confidence. The resulting decline in equity values reduced earlier gains by two-thirds before the beginning of July.

Tangible indications of the economy's flagging pace during the summer caused stock market rallies to sputter. Gross national product grew only 2% in the second quarter, compared with 4% in the first quarter and 6% in the final quarter of 1976. Moreover, registered unemployment in August was 4.3% of the labour force, a relatively high rate for West Germany, while business spending on new plant and equipment was disappointing. On the plus side, the nation's foreign trade surplus exceeded $1 billion in August, and the international value of the mark traded at an all-time high in foreign exchange markets. But the increasing value of the mark raised fears that West German exporters eventually would meet greater competition in world markets.

Following the government's announcement in September of a relatively mild economic stimulus package, the rush to buy stocks picked up. The subsequent rally carried equity values above the levels reached in April. Investor bullishness was based on the belief that economic stimulation would not cause the country's 4.5% annual inflation rate to accelerate. At the year's close, stock prices were only 3% below the November highs and 11% above the March lows.

In Switzerland the stock market rose 4%, on average, in 1977. The increase from the March 3 low to the high on October 14 was 14%. The Swiss inflation rate, at less than 2%, was the lowest in the non-Communist world. The government's determination to fight inflation was evidenced by its announcement in August that certain food subsidies would be eliminated and taxes raised on tobacco to reduce budget deficits. Reflecting worldwide demand for Swiss francs, the value of the U.S. dollar fell to SFr 2.01 at the end of 1977 from SFr 2.4505 at the end of 1976, a loss of 18%. As a result of the appreciation of the Swiss franc, selected controls were imposed to reduce speculative enthusiasm for the currency.

In Spain the price index of shares traded on the Madrid Stock Exchange finished 1977 with the largest average loss (−33%) among the major world stock price indexes. Moreover, this followed a 29% decline in 1976. Spain was confronted by

A foot-wide ribbon 150 feet long was cut to symbolize the opening of the new Commodities Exchange Center in New York on July 5.

stagflation, and the nation's progress toward instituting democratic reforms was being threatened by widespread labour strikes and public disorder. Despite price controls on basic consumer goods, the annual rate of inflation exceeded 25%. Efforts to hold down government spending and wage increases, however, were opposed by the Spanish left. Finally, Premier Adolfo Suárez González in July announced a 20% devaluation of the peseta against the U.S. dollar, higher taxes, and restrictions on wage increases in hopes of cutting the 8% unemployment rate and reducing the nation's $5 billion balance of payments deficit. These steps, however, did not seem to arrest the bear market. After a brief rally in the final weeks of 1977, equity values ended the year 6% above the December 9 lows.

The Financial Times Industrial Ordinary Share Index
Annual averages, 1955–77

Source: The Financial Times.

Stock prices in Italy took a beating in 1977. Equity values fell sharply in each month from January to May. Then, after rising 5% in June, they dropped 8% in July. At that time, equity values were 21% below the 1976 close. Inflationary pressures were pushing price indexes up at an annual rate of 20%. However, labour unions accepted the austerity program imposed by the International Monetary Fund to limit inflation. Reflecting the implementation of deflationary policies, industrial production in July tumbled nearly 8% from year-earlier levels. In an attempt to halt the faltering stock market, the Italian government announced a reduction in dividend withholding taxes and other measures designed to increase the attractiveness of equity securities. This set the stage for a strong rebound in stock prices, which added 16% to equity values. The downtrend later resumed, however, as investors realized that the economic recession experienced in 1977 would continue into 1978. Stock prices at the end of December were 25% lower than at the end of 1976, only slightly above their yearly lows.

Stock prices also followed a bearish pattern in Sweden. The decline in the price index of shares traded on the Stockholm Exchange was 18% from the end of 1976 to the end of 1977. After reaching their high on March 22, equity prices fell on average until late November. As 1977 came to a close, however, prices experienced a strong rally, which added 13% to equity values. To cope with an economy that was experiencing double-digit inflation, weak productivity, and a huge international trade deficit, Sweden devalued its currency 6% in April and 10% in August. In addition, consumer and industrial prices were frozen from September through October, while employer payroll taxes were reduced from 4 to 2% as of Jan. 1, 1978.

In Austria the price index of issues traded on the Vienna Stock Exchange declined 9% in 1977. The Austrian economy was operating at full employment, with price inflation at about 5%. Although the inflation rate was moderate and trending downward, it still was significantly higher than in West Germany and Switzerland, the country's major trading partners. As a result, Austria's balance of payments deficit exerted considerable pressure on the Austrian schilling in world foreign exchange markets. Uncertainty about the remedies that might be adopted to cope with the uncompetitiveness of Austrian industry in international markets added to investor bearishness as 1977 came to a close.

Economic and political crises had a dominant influence on stock price movements in France. After experiencing a general decline in share prices of 17% in 1976, prices on the Paris Bourse fell another 7% in 1977. The decline of 1976 accelerated into 1977. From January through March, the Paris Bourse index of equity values dropped nearly 15%. The decline was mainly due to social turmoil and widespread expectations that the Socialist-Communist coalition would gain political leadership in the national elections scheduled for March 1978. Beginning in May, the political climate began to shift. Premier Raymond Barre, the architect of the government's wage-limitation policy, won a clear-cut victory in a televised debate with Socialist leader François Mitterrand. Then the Socialist-Communist coalition unexpectedly failed to agree on common economic policies. The rift within the coalition was subsequently reflected in political polls, which showed only 50% of the electorate supporting it in October, down from 54% in March. As a result, equity prices rose 23% from the end of April to the end of November. Although stock prices had recovered from an oversold condition, the long-term outlook for the French stock market seemed clouded. Bond yields averaging 12% for new private issues and 11% for government-backed securities were a major factor inhibiting higher equity prices.

The Belgian stock market finished 1977 with a loss of 5%, after declining 9% in 1976. The index of prices on the Brussels Bourse moved within a fairly narrow range throughout 1977. During the first quarter prices dropped 2%, but the market regained the losses in the second quarter. In June the market experienced its best rally of the year, rising 3%. After sinking slightly more than 1% in the third quarter, the market attempted a comeback near the end of the year, but the rebound was not strong enough to wipe out earlier losses.

Denmark experienced an average 4% decline in stock prices during 1977. Equity values on the Copenhagen Stock Exchange rose nearly 8% in the first three months of the year. The substantial gains made by Prime Minister Anker Jørgensen's Social Democrats buoyed investor hopes that progress would be made in cutting unemployment and the deficit in the trade balance. However, stock prices retreated from April through July, erasing all but 2% of the first-quarter gains. Pessimism over the 3% devaluation of the Danish krone in April added to the decline. Following a small gain in August, stock prices resumed their downtrend. The year ended with equity prices at their lowest level.

In The Netherlands the seesaw movement of stock prices resulted in a net decline in the leading stock averages. From year-end 1976 to year-end 1977 the loss amounted to 4%. For the first time since World War II, the Dutch economy was disrupted by a series of "phased" labour union strikes, and the country suffered through a political crisis that left the government without a Cabinet for seven months. Although the political situation was resolved in December when Prime Minister Andries van Agt assumed office, uncertainty over whether his government could cope with militant labour unions dampened investor enthusiasm for equity securities.

Other Countries. Stock market declines were experienced in Japan and Hong Kong. The Tokyo Exchange's index of 225 common stocks, which had gained 14% in 1976, began 1977 in a bullish atmosphere. Japan's economy was growing at a rate that exceeded that of the U.S. and major European industrial nations. However, Japanese manufacturers were operating their plants at an average of only 77% of capacity. Thus, when Prime Minister Takeo Fukuda announced in mid-January that the government's budget would be increased by 17%, mainly for public works projects, the general feeling was that economic recovery would accelerate. But by the end of February stock prices had risen only 2%, reflecting the slowing pace of economic activity as well as growing concern over the steady depreciation in the value of the Japanese yen against the U.S. dollar. Over the next four months, huge trade surpluses were reported, causing the yen to decline 6% relative to the U.S. dollar. The stock market reacted by trading without any apparent direction until June, when prices fell fractionally below year-end 1976 levels.

During the summer, a strong rally caused equity prices to gain 18% in value from July 29 to August 26. This surge may have been in anticipation of the government's economic stimulus program, announced on September 5. That consisted of a cut in the discount rate to 4.75% from 5% and public works spending totaling $7.5 billion. Stock prices, however, turned down in late September, chiefly due to the increasing value of the yen in international currency markets. By the end of December, stock prices were down 3% from the 1976 close and 9% below their all-time high set in January 1973, while the foreign exchange rate of the yen in relation to the U.S. dollar fell to new lows, 18% below 1976 closing levels.

The decline on the Hong Kong Stock Exchange was about 10% in 1977. The Hang Seng index of 33 issues reached its high on January 6 and its low on the final trading day of 1977.

In Australia stock prices rose 11%. Prices were up 6% during the first six months, but the gains were wiped out by the end of August. Australia's deteriorating balance of payments position and rampant labour union militancy caused a loss of confidence in the Australian dollar in world foreign exchange markets. Political uncertainty was also responsible for investors' lack of enthusiasm for equities. This bearish sentiment was lifted, however, when Prime Minister Malcolm Fraser's government won the national elections on December 10. The rally from the end of November until the end of December added 8% to equity values.

Stock prices in South Africa were up in 1977. Industrial share prices on the Johannesburg Stock Exchange jumped 15%, after sinking 13% in 1976. Strength in the South African mining and agricultural sectors was largely responsible for the bullish trend.

Commodity Prices. The year 1977 was one of volatile commodity markets. Based on the Reuters United Kingdom commodity index of 17 primary commodities weighted by their relative performance in international trade, the average fell from 1569 at year-end 1976 to 1421 at year-end 1977, a drop of 9%. This index, first developed in 1931, reached an all-time high on March 22, 12% above the 1976 close. At that time, the index was nearly double the level recorded for the same date in 1973.

The sharp overall increase in early 1977 mainly reflected surging selected metals quotations, especially for tin and lead, as well as sharply higher prices for soybeans and cocoa. Nearly half of the index's rise, however, was erased before the end of May. It then dropped 5% in June, 3% in July, and 2% in August. Following a technical rally in September, commodity prices resumed their decline.

On December 28 the index touched bottom, 19% below the March high.

The weakness in overall commodity prices was attributable both to more abundant supplies and to a slackening of demand, reflecting the economic slowdown in industrialized nations. The rise in the value of the pound sterling against the U.S. dollar also contributed to downward pressures on commodity prices. Metal prices were particularly hard hit. Copper, which rose in price early in the year in anticipation of a possible strike in the U.S., plunged sharply when a settlement was reached without a work stoppage. The price of tin, which jumped 40% from the end of 1976 to early December, eventually collapsed, ending the year with a gain of 20%.

The Nikkei Index of Commodity Prices, covering 17 major commodities traded in Tokyo, dropped 6% from the end of 1976 through December 23. The index reached its peak on May 14, nearly 17% above the 1976 close, but declined steadily until mid-September. After a brief rally, renewed selling pressure carried the index to a 1977 low on December 7 before rebounding.

The price of gold also experienced sharp fluctuations during 1977. At the end of 1976 gold closed in the London market at $134.75 an ounce. It climbed to $153.55 on March 25 but then slid to $138.40 on June 13. Over the next five months, the London gold quote rose steadily, reaching $167.95 on November 11. After declining to $156.15 on November 21, it moved higher again and reached $164.95 at the end of December for a net gain of 22% for the year. (ROBERT H. TRIGG)

See also Economy, World.

Sudan

Sudan

A republic of northeast Africa, the Sudan is bounded by Egypt, the Red Sea, Ethiopia, Kenya, Uganda, Zaire, the Central African Empire, Chad, and Libya. Area: 2,505,813 sq km (967,500 sq mi). Pop. (1976 est.): 16,126,000, including Arabs in the north and Negroes in the south. Cap. and largest city: Khartoum (pop., 1973 est., 321,700). Language: Arabic; various tribal languages in the south. Religion: Muslim in the north; predominantly animist in the south. President in 1977, Maj. Gen. Gaafar Nimeiry; prime minister, Rashid Bakr.

Pres. Gaafar Nimeiry consolidated his government's stability with bold moves in domestic and foreign politics in 1977. In May he invited back political exiles ready to contribute to their country's welfare and, after confidential negotiations, even welcomed the return in September of Sadik al-Mahdi, a former prime minister sentenced to death in 1976 for masterminding a Libyan-backed coup attempt. Yet Mahdi's return and the formation of a predominantly right-wing Muslim Committee to revise the country's legal system to conform with Islamic principles aroused anxiety among African southerners and liberals. Nimeiry subsequently made the committee more representative and orchestrated compromises acceptable to most outside the extreme left. In December Nim-

Surinam

Strikes:
see Industrial Relations

Sumo:
see Combat Sports

Surfing:
see Water Sports

eiry announced that elections for the People's Assembly would be held early in 1978.

Sudan moved away from the Soviet bloc in 1977, with support in January for the guerrillas seeking the secession of the province of Eritrea from Ethiopia; some 90 Soviet military advisers were expelled from Khartoum in May. Later, Sudan made conciliatory overtures to Libya and Ethiopia. In November Nimeiry broke with most of the Arab world by expressing support of Egyptian Pres. Anwar as-Sadat's trip to Israel. With Saudi financial aid, Sudan sought sophisticated defense systems and weaponry from the West, notably from the U.S., France, and Britain. In late December the U.S. indicated that it was willing to sell the Sudan a squadron of 12 F-5 fighter aircraft.

(ALAN J. H. DARBY)

Surinam

An independent republic of northern South America, Surinam is bounded by Guyana, Brazil, French Guiana, and the Atlantic Ocean. Area: 181,455 sq km (70,060 sq mi). Pop. (1975 est.): 350,000, including (1971) Hindustanis 37%, Creoles 30.8%, Indonesians 15.3%, Bush Negroes 10.3%, Amerindians 2.6%. Cap and largest city: Paramaribo (pop., 1971, 102,300). Language: Dutch (official); English and Sranan (a creole) are lingua francas; Hindi, Javanese, Chinese, and various Amerindian languages are used within individual ethnic communities. Religion: predominantly Hindu, Christian, and Muslim. President

SURINAM

Education. (1974–75) Primary, pupils 91,769, teachers 3,005; secondary, pupils 25,524, teachers c. 1,620; vocational, pupils 2,815, teachers 168; teacher training, students 2,138; higher (university only), students 550, teaching staff 34.

Finance. Monetary unit: Surinam guilder, with (Sept. 19, 1977) a free rate of 1.78 Surinam guilder to U.S. $1 (3.12 Surinam guilders = £1 sterling). Budget (1977 est.): revenue 541 million Surinam guilders; expenditure 581 million Surinam guilders.

Foreign Trade. (1975) Imports 467 million Surinam guilders; exports 495 million Surinam guilders. Import sources (1974): U.S. 24%; The Netherlands 10%; Trinidad and Tobago c. 6%; Japan 5%. Export destinations (1974): U.S. 19%; West Germany 8%; The Netherlands 7%; Norway 6%. Main exports: alumina 43%; bauxite 18%; aluminum 8%.

Transport and Communications. Roads (1975) c. 2,000 km. Motor vehicles in use (1975): passenger 18,200; commercial (including buses) 5,200. Railways (1975) c. 50 km. Telephones (Dec. 1975) 18,000. Radio receivers (Dec. 1974) 109,000. Television receivers (Dec. 1974) 33,000.

Agriculture. Production (in 000; metric tons; 1975): rice c. 176; oranges c. 4; grapefruit c. 3; bananas c. 46; sugar, raw value c. 1. Livestock (in 000; Jan. 1975): cattle c. 43; pigs c. 13; chickens c. 870.

Industry. Production (in 000; metric tons; 1975): bauxite 4,751; aluminum 35; gold (troy oz) 0.1; electricity (kw-hr) c. 1,600,000 (64% hydroelectric).

in 1977, Johan Ferrier; prime minister, Henk Arron.

Political life in Surinam was characterized by various accusations of corruption and by the first general elections in the country's history as an independent state. In March Willy Soemita (Javanese Party, or KTPI), minister of agriculture, was accused of being involved in a corruption scandal. After his refusal to resign, Parliament initiated his impeachment. Thereupon the KTPI left the government coalition. Consequently, the government no longer commanded a majority in Parliament. Prime Minister Henk Arron refused to resign or dissolve Parliament, however, and in April the ties between the former coalition partners were strengthened again.

The selection of the list of candidates for the general elections of October 31, however, led to new difficulties. Two Creole parties (NPS and PNR) refused to continue to cooperate within the National Party Alliance (NPK), the ruling coalition in Parliament. On August 20 a new NPK was established, combining Prime Minister Arron's NPS Creole party, the Javanese KTPI, and two progressive parties. This new alliance won the general elections, receiving 24 out of the 39 parliamentary seats. The opposing coalition (United Democratic Party) of Jaggernath Lachmon got 15 seats.

(GERARD P. NOORDZIJ)

Swaziland

A landlocked monarchy of southern Africa, Swaziland is bounded by South Africa and Mozambique. Area: 17,364 sq km (6,704 sq mi). Pop. (1977 est.): 496,000. Cap. and largest city: Mbabane (pop., 1975 est., 24,000). Language: English and siSwati (official). Religion: Christian 60%; animist 40%. King, Sobhuza II; prime minister in 1977, Col. Maphevu Dlamini.

SWAZILAND

Education. (1975) Primary, pupils 89,528, teachers 2,363; secondary, pupils 16,227, teachers 739; vocational, pupils 625, teachers 43; teacher training, students 396, teachers 52; higher, students 1,086, teaching staff 158.

Finance and Trade. Monetary unit: lilangeni (emalangeni for more than 1), at par with the South African rand, with (Sept. 19, 1977) a par value of 0.87 lilangeni to U.S. $1 (free rate of 1.52 lilangeni to £1 sterling). Budget (1976–77 est.): revenue 70 million emalangeni; expenditure 75 million emalangeni. Foreign trade (1975): imports 134,566,000 emalangeni; exports 132,145,000 emalangeni. Export destinations (1970): U.K. 25%; Japan 24%; South Africa 21%. Main exports: sugar 54%; wood pulp 9%; iron ore 9%; asbestos 7%.

Agriculture. Production (in 000; metric tons; 1975): corn 120; rice c. 5; potatoes c. 7; sugar, raw value (1976) c. 222; pineapples c. 15; cotton, lint c. 5. Livestock (in 000; 1975): cattle c. 623; sheep c. 41; pigs c. 16; goats c. 282.

Industry. Production (in 000; metric tons; 1975): coal 127; iron ore (metal content) 1,417; asbestos 38; electricity (kw-hr) 112,000.

Swaziland

King Sobhuza II abolished Swaziland's multiparty parliamentary constitution in March 1977 and replaced it by a system, based on tribal tradition, called Tinkhundla. Ambrose Zwane, former leader of the defunct opposition, said this move had "put our country back a thousand years." Students staged violent demonstrations for several days in October, in support of their teachers who had gone on strike in a dispute over wages.

As commander in chief, the king announced that the Army would be enlarged into a full defense force, in light of the political realities of southern Africa. More than 80% of exports still passed along the unreliable Mozambique rail link, and a close economic link with South Africa, including a customs union, remained.

In May the finance minister announced a record 1977–78 budget at 118 million emalangeni (six times that of 1972–73), with revenue estimated at 79.5 million emalangeni (an increase of 38.5 emalangeni over 1976–77, largely from the South African customs union). International reserves reached a record 76 million emalangeni, and Swaziland absorbed the entire Commonwealth Development Corporation commitment of £4,320,000 for southern Africa. The economy remained buoyant for both minerals and agriculture. A rail link to South Africa through Golela was planned as insurance against disruption by Mozambique.

(MOLLY MORTIMER)

Sweden

A constitutional monarchy of northern Europe lying on the eastern side of the Scandinavian Peninsula, Sweden has common borders with Finland and Norway. Area: 449,964 sq km (173,732 sq mi). Pop. (1977 est.): 8,236,200. Cap. and largest city: Stockholm (pop., 1977 est., 661,300). Language: Swedish, with some Finnish and Lapp in the north. Religion: predominantly Lutheran. King, Carl XVI Gustaf; prime minister in 1977, Thorbjörn Fälldin.

During 1977 the economic crisis overshadowed the nuclear debate that had brought about the previous year's change of government in Sweden.

Sweden

SWEDEN

Education. (1976–77) Primary, pupils 708,986, teachers 41,150; secondary, pupils 545,253, teachers 46,994; teacher training, students (1975–76) 12,622, teachers 843; higher (including 9 universities), students 121,266.

Finance. Monetary unit: krona, with (Sept. 19, 1977) a free rate of 4.85 kronor to U.S. $1 (8.45 kronor = £1 sterling). Gold, SDR's, and foreign exchange (June 1977) U.S. $2,945,000,000. Budget (1976–77 est.): revenue 103,914,000,000 kronor; expenditure 112,076,000,000 kronor. Gross domestic product (1976) 322,860,000,000 kronor. Money supply (May 1977) 32,210,000,000 kronor. Cost of living (1970 = 100; June 1977) 181.

Foreign Trade. (1976) Imports 83,657,000,000 kronor; exports 80,239,000,000 kronor. Import sources: West Germany 19%; U.K. 11%; Denmark 7%; U.S. 7%; Norway 6%; Finland 6%. Export destinations: U.K. 11%; Norway 11%; West Germany 10%; Denmark 10%; Finland 6%; France 5%; U.S.

5%. Main exports: machinery 26%; motor vehicles 10%; paper 9%; ships and boats 7%; wood pulp 7%; iron and steel 7%; timber 5%; chemicals 5%.

Transport and Communications. Roads (1975) 124,798 km (including 692 km expressways). Motor vehicles in use (1975): passenger 2,760,300; commercial 156,600. Railways: (1975) 12,070 km (including 7,484 km electrified); traffic (1976) 5,363,000,000 passenger-km, freight 15,458,000,000 net ton-km. Air traffic (including Swedish apportionment of international operations of Scandinavian Airlines System; 1976): 4,042,000,000 passenger-km; freight 172,516,000 net ton-km. Shipping (1976): merchant vessels 100 gross tons and over 764; gross tonnage 7,971,246. Telephones (Dec. 1975) 5,423,000. Radio licenses (Dec. 1975) 3,140,000. Television licenses (Dec. 1975) 2,909,000.

Agriculture. Production (in 000; metric tons; 1976): wheat 1,788; barley 1,831; oats 1,281; rye 418; potatoes c. 900; sugar, raw value 308; rapeseed

280; apples c. 96; cow's milk c. 3,245; butter c. 54; cheese c. 87; beef and veal c. 149; pork c. 292; timber (cu m; 1975) 52,415; fish catch (1975) 215. Livestock (in 000; June 1976): cattle 1,874; sheep (1975) c. 402; pigs c. 2,463; horses (1975) c. 52; chickens (1975) c. 13,291.

Industry. Index of industrial production (1970 = 100; 1976) 113. Production (in 000; metric tons; 1976): cement 2,800; electricity (kw-hr) 84,305,000 (72% hydroelectric in 1975); iron ore (60–65% metal content) 30,526; pig iron 2,991; crude steel 5,206; silver (troy oz; 1975) 4,500; petroleum products (1975) c. 11,980; sulfuric acid (1974) 940; man-made fibres (1975) 20; wood pulp (1975) mechanical 1,626, chemical 6,718; newsprint 1,135; other paper (1975) 3,259. Merchant vessels launched (100 gross tons and over; 1976) 2,367,000 gross tons. New dwelling units completed (1976) 55,800.

The gross national product was expected to fall for the first time since 1945. The crisis, simply stated, was brought about by the sudden stagnation or even collapse of key Swedish export industries. The bottom had fallen out of shipbuilding in 1976, partly as a result of high wage and production costs. A state-owned shipping group was formed on July 1, 1977, which would receive some 3 billion kronor in subsidies and 10 billion kronor in state credit guarantees. Other export-oriented industries, such as timber, paper, and pulp, were suffering because of uncompetitive production costs and failure to develop new technologies. The important iron-ore industry saw its market position snatched by foreign competitors—again because of pricing. Mass layoffs were announced by the state mining concern, LKAB. Volvo, Sweden's biggest industrial undertaking, reported sharply reduced profits in 1977, with car production at about the same level as in the previous year. In August Volvo broke off merger talks with Saab-Scania because of clashes of management styles, raising doubts about the future of the Swedish automotive industry.

The official unemployment rate of slightly over

2%—which disguised mammoth manpower-retraining programs—started to rise sharply in late 1977 with the onset of the long Scandinavian winter. Official forecasts of industrial investments suggested a decline of 6.5%, while overall liquidity suffered a set of shocks resulting from successive tightenings of monetary policy. The centre-right government, clearly shaken by the economic debacle, devalued the once-proud krona by 10% on August 29 and decided to leave the European currency "snake." Explaining the latest devaluation, Prime Minister Thorbjörn Fälldin said that "structural crises are threatening employment in many companies" and that Swedish products were in danger of being priced out of world markets. His government noted that inflation was running at nearly 17% while industrial production and investments were declining. The current account deficit estimate was re-forecast upward to 16 billion kronor, an astronomical sum for a nation of eight million. In further moves to assist industry the government abolished the general payroll tax to counteract the effects of higher costs for foreign components and other expenditures. A general price freeze was clamped on the economy until October 31, when prices soared once again.

Companies generally blamed the crisis on high labour costs, but many economists believed the real Swedish sickness was related to managements themselves and their particular slowness in opening up new markets. Sweden's impressive technological lead resulting from wartime neutrality had vanished in later years, and in many firms insufficient attention was paid to developing well-financed research and development programs.

Swedish foreign policy, under the direction of Foreign Minister Karin Söder (*see* BIOGRAPHY), continued to maintain close and generous links with the third world, notably in Africa. Indeed, Sweden had set aside 1% of its gross national product for development assistance. In the UN, Sweden called for a ban on investment in South Africa; there had not been any fresh Swedish investment in that country from the mid-1970s onward. Disarmament initiatives and positive pressure on the human rights issue figured prominently in Swedish West-East diplomacy.

In September nearly 20,000 demonstrators

The young princess dressed up for her christening was held by her father, Sweden's King Carl XVI Gustaf, while her mother, Queen Silvia, looked on. The princess was christened Victoria Ingrid Alice Desirée.

KEYSTONE

marched on the Barsebäck atomic power station near Malmö to protest the failure of the Fälldin government to honour its antinuclear campaign promises. It appeared that Fälldin lacked sufficient political muscle within his coalition to stop the nuclear program, which called for 13 reactors by 1985. Significantly, the youth wing of Fälldin's own Centre Party took part in the Barsebäck march. (ROGER NYE CHOATE)

Swimming

After the 1976 Olympic Games, during which 22 world records were set, a letdown in swimming was expected in 1977. But no one anticipated that there would be so few new marks. Men and women swimmers could set but five each, and three were in events not contested in the 1976 Olympics.

The U.S. national team, selected at the Amateur Athletic Union (AAU) national championships in August, was hard pressed to defeat East Germany at East Berlin's Karl Friedrich Friesen pool, August 27–28. In their first meeting in 1971, the victory margin for the U.S. was 100 points. Their second meeting in 1974 was a bit closer, as the U.S. won by 50 points. In 1977, before worldwide television and with 17,000 Germans looking on, the U.S. rallied to come from behind on the final day to eke out an eight-point victory, 176–168. Five of the world records were achieved in that dual meet.

The year's highlight occurred in the U.S.-East German dual meet when Joseph Bottom, a 22-year-old University of Southern California graduate, bettered the oldest world record currently in the book, that in the 100-m butterfly set by Mark Spitz. Spitz's mark, 54.27 sec, withstood all challengers for five years before Bottom clocked 54.18 sec for his first world record. Bottom also joined Jim Montgomery, Jack Babashoff, and Rick DeMont to erase the 400-m freestyle relay world record as they combined to clock 3 min 21.11 sec.

Brian Goodell, 18, of Mission Viejo, Calif., the 1976 Olympic champion and world record holder in the 400-m and 1,500-m freestyle, continued to dominate the distance events. He lowered his 400-m freestyle mark by 0.37 sec to 3 min 51.56 sec.

Ulrike Tauber, 19, of East Germany was in a class by herself in the individual medley. Three times during the year she lowered her world standard in the 200-m event, saving her best for the

A new world record of 54.18 sec for the 100-m butterfly was set by U.S. swimmer Joe Bottom in East Berlin in August.

U.S.-East German dual meet when she clocked 2 min 15.85 sec. With East Germany's retired Olympic champion Kornelia Ender looking on, Christiane Knacke, 15, became the first woman to break the one-minute barrier for the 100-m butterfly as the East German swimmer stunned the U.S. competitors with a 59.78-sec clocking. It was the first major win for the new world record holder.

The U.S. defeated the Soviet Union on September 3–4 in Leningrad, 212 to 132. The Soviet male swimmers were stronger than in 1976, but continued to be dominated by the U.S.

East Germany won the 14th European Championships at Jönköping, Sweden, August 15–21, scoring 297 points to the Soviet Union's 231 and West Germany's 169. Petra Thumer, 16, of East Germany set her second world mark of the year by winning the 400-m freestyle in 4 min 8.91 sec. Earlier, at the East German national championships, she had lowered her own world standard in the 800-m freestyle to 8 min 35.04 sec to lay claim to being the best in the world in distance swimming. Gerald Morken, 18, of West Germany established himself as the world's premier breaststroke swimmer when he shattered Olympic champion John Hencken's world 100-m record with a 1-min 2.86-sec performance.

The East Germans garnered a total of 34 medals, only one less than three years earlier in Vienna. Sixteen of these were for first place and 11 were for second.

In the Canadian championships, Graham Smith, 19, set a new world mark in the 200-m individual medley, 2 min 5.31 sec. Alice Browne, 14, of Mission Viejo, Calif., was the only U.S. girl to achieve a world record, clocking 16 min 24.60 sec for the 1,500-m freestyle on August 21, in the AAU championships.

Diving. The U.S. divers competed in two international dual diving competitions. In East Germany the hosts, led by Falk Hoffman's 3-m

World Records Set in 1977

Event	Name	Country	Time
MEN			
400-m freestyle	Brian Goodell	U.S.	3 min 51.56 sec
100-m breaststroke	Gerald Morken	W. Ger.	1 min 02.86 sec
100-m butterfly	Joseph Bottom	U.S.	54.18 sec
200-m individual medley	Graham Smith	Canada	2 min 05.31 sec
400-m freestyle relay	U.S. national team (Jack Babashoff, Joseph Bottom, Rick DeMont, James Montgomery)		3 min 21.11 sec
WOMEN			
400-m freestyle	Petra Thumer	E. Ger.	4 min 08.91 sec
800-m freestyle	Petra Thumer	E. Ger.	8 min 35.04 sec
1,500-m freestyle	Alice Browne	U.S.	16 min 24.60 sec
100-m butterfly	Christiane Knacke	E. Ger.	59.78 sec
200-m individual medley	Ulrike Tauber	E. Ger.	2 min 16.96 sec
			2 min 15.95 sec
			2 min 15.85 sec

Swedish Literature: *see* Literature

WIDE WORLD

The one-metre springboard title of the AAU national indoor diving championships in Texas was captured by Cynthia McIngvale, who was a 1976 U.S. Olympic team member.

springboard and platform wins, defeated the U.S. 25–19. Kerstin Krause and Christa Kohler won the women's platform and springboard, giving the East Germans a sweep of the first places.

At Leningrad, the Soviet team defeated the U.S. 52–36. Cynthia McIngvale won the 3-m springboard to prevent a Soviet sweep, as Elena Vaytsekhovskaia won the women's platform and Aleksandr Kosenkov and Sergei Nemtsanov won the men's springboard and platform, respectively.

At the European Championships the Soviet Union outscored its East German rivals 56–40. West Germany was a distant third.

(ALBERT SCHOENFIELD)

[452.B.4.a.i]

Switzerland

Switzerland

A federal republic in west central Europe consisting of a confederation of 25 cantons, Switzerland is bounded by West Germany, Austria, Liechtenstein, Italy, and France. Area: 41,293 sq km (15,943 sq mi). Pop. (1976 est.): 6,346,000. Cap.: Bern (pop., 1976 est., 148,600). Largest city: Zürich (pop., 1976 est., 387,900). Language (1970): German 65%; French 18%; Italian 12%; Romansh 1%. Religion (1970): Roman Catholic 49.4%; Protestant 47.7%. President in 1977, Kurt Furgler.

The Swiss banking industry was shaken by scandal when, in April 1977, improper financial transactions, conducted chiefly via a Liechtenstein

holding company from the Chiasso branch of the Crédit Suisse, one of the country's three foremost banks, were revealed. An offer of help to the amount of SFr 3 billion from the central banks and two other large banks showed the magnitude of the transactions involved. The Crédit Suisse declined the offer, however, stating that it could meet the losses from its own reserves. In June it filed suit against the holding company for $680 million. Meanwhile, Parliament took measures to intensify control of banking activities, and the banking industry itself announced an agreement to exercise greater vigilance against use of its facilities for questionable activities.

The "total revision" of the constitution advanced slowly at an academic level in 1977. In March voters rejected, by almost three to one, initiatives designed to limit the number of foreign workers in the country and proposing a limitation on the annual number of naturalizations. An initiative calling for an optional, retroactive popular referendum on the conclusion of treaties with foreign countries and international organizations was defeated by more than a two-to-one margin, whereas the government-sponsored counterproject (compulsory plebiscites on treaties calling for Swiss membership in international organizations) was adopted. The results represented a clear

SWITZERLAND

Education. (1975–76) Primary, pupils 519,458, teachers (excluding craft teachers; 1961–62) 23,761; secondary, pupils 364,800, teachers (full time; 1961–62) 6,583; vocational, pupils (1974–75) 155,172; teacher training, students 18,585; higher (including 10 universities), students 57,900, teaching staff (universities only) 2,850.

Finance. Monetary unit: Swiss franc, with (Sept. 19, 1977) a free rate of SFr 2.38 to U.S. $1 (SFr 4.15 = £1 sterling). Gold and foreign exchange (June 1977) U.S. $10,450,000,000. Budget (1976 actual): revenue SFr 13,781,000,000; expenditure SFr 15,185,000,000. Gross national product (1976) SFr 147.9 billion. Money supply (May 1977) SFr 61,220,000,000. Cost of living (1970 = 100; June 1977) 149.

Foreign Trade. (1976) Imports SFr 36,874,000,000; exports SFr 37,015,000,000. Import sources: EEC 67% (West Germany 28%, France 13%, Italy 10%, U.K. 7%); U.S. 7%. Export destinations: EEC 45% (West Germany 16%, France 9%, Italy 7%, U.K. 6%); U.S. 7%; Austria 5%. Main exports: machinery 31%; chemicals 22%; watches and clocks 8%; textile yarns and fabrics 6%. Tourism (1975): visitors 6,199,000; gross receipts U.S. $1,930,000,000.

Transport and Communications. Roads (1975) 61,635 km (including 662 km expressways). Motor vehicles in use (1975): passenger 1,794,300; commercial 167,300. Railways: (1974) 4,969 km (including 4,939 km electrified); traffic (1976) 8,130,000,000 passenger-km, freight 5,659,000,000 net ton-km. Air traffic (1976): 8,493,000,000 passenger-km; freight 345,780,000 net ton-km. Shipping (1976): merchant vessels 100 gross tons and over 28; gross tonnage 212,526. Telephones (Jan. 1976) 3,913,000. Radio licenses (Dec. 1975) 2,076,000. Television licenses (Dec. 1975) 1,759,000.

Agriculture. Production (in 000; metric tons; 1976): wheat c. 405; barley c. 193; oats c. 55; corn (1975) c. 120; potatoes c. 900; rapeseed c. 24; apples c. 200; pears (1975) c. 175; sugar, raw value (1975) 66; wine c. 122; milk c. 3,460; butter c. 35; cheese c. 111; beef and veal c. 147; pork c. 238. Livestock (in 000; April 1976): cattle 2,005; sheep (1975) c. 360; pigs 2,006; chickens (1975) 6,121.

Industry. Index of industrial production (1970 = 100; 1976) 98. Production (in 000; metric tons; 1975): aluminum 79; cement 3,765; petroleum products c. 4,445; man-made fibres 76; cigarettes (units) 26,726,000; watches (units) 47,191; manufactured gas (cu m) 122,000; electricity (kw-hr; 1976) 34,897,000.

A historic occasion in Switzerland occurred in May when Elisabeth Blunschy assumed the "highest chair" as president of the National Council and also of the Federal Assembly.

victory over the xenophobic tendencies of a vociferous minority.

In June the people were called upon to decide about a government-sponsored comprehensive program of fiscal reforms, involving replacement of the sales (turnover) taxes by value-added taxes. Most political parties favoured this "package," but the voters defeated it, reportedly for fear of price rises. At the same time, voters approved a government proposal for uniform federal tax scales in all cantons. As a result the government had to raise taxes on selected consumer goods and to adopt makeshift measures to reduce federal expenditures.

In September an initiative for "better protection of rent payers," requiring increased government intervention in housing, was defeated. Also defeated was the so-called Albatros initiative calling for severe measures designed to reduce air pollution by motor vehicles. An initiative that would have legalized abortion within the first three months of pregnancy was narrowly defeated (994,677 to 929,239).

On December 4, with the participation of 38% of the enfranchised citizens—rather below the usual percentage—the people rejected (801,925 to 638,559) a so-called "tax-the-rich" initiative, which would have equalized cantonal and federal taxation and increased taxes on higher income groups. An initiative calling for a substitute civil service for conscientious objectors also failed (886,821 to 534,297). A proposed federal law reorganizing and redefining the political rights of citizens was approved (810,674 to 553,495), as was a federal law setting forth economy measures designed to balance the federal budget.

In February the constituent assembly of the proposed new canton of Jura adopted a fundamental charter, or constitution, which 80% of the citizens concerned approved in a plebiscite in March. The so-called "reunifications" article of this constitution, opening the way to ultimate adherence to the new canton by the areas that previously had

voted to remain with the old canton of Bern, was considered provocative by the (Bernese-inspired) antiseparatist forces.

The building industry recovered some ground through a partly subsidized building renovation boom. The departure of several hundred thousand foreign workers "solved" the employment problem to a considerable extent. The rate of inflation was still the lowest among industrialized countries (around 1½%). Progress toward the elaboration of constitutional provisions for a comprehensive system of government economic policies was slow. Widespread opposition to additional nuclear power plants slowed their construction. (*See* ENVIRONMENT.)

In June Jean-Louis Jeanmaire, a high-ranking army officer convicted of having passed important secret military information to the Soviet Union over a period of years, was sentenced to 18 years' imprisonment. (MELANIE STAERK)

Syria

A republic in southwestern Asia on the Mediterranean Sea, Syria is bordered by Turkey, Iraq, Jordan, Israel, and Lebanon. Area: 185,180 sq km (71,498 sq mi). Pop. (1976 est.): 7,595,000. Cap. and largest city: Damascus (pop., 1976 est., 1,054,-000). Language: Arabic (official); also Kurdish, Armenian, Turkish, and Circassian. Religion: predominantly Muslim. President in 1977, Gen. Hafez al-Assad; premier, Abdul Rahman Khleifawi.

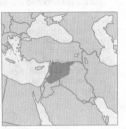

Syria

SYRIA

Education. (1975–76) Primary, pupils 1,245,801, teachers 36,852; secondary, pupils 452,051, teachers 22,277; vocational, pupils 21,606, teachers 2,407; teacher training, students 7,329, teachers 632; higher (1974–75), students 64,094, teaching staff 989.

Finance. Monetary unit: Syrian pound, with (Sept. 19, 1977) a par value of S£3.925 to U.S. $1 (free rate of S£6.84 = £1 sterling). Gold, SDR's, and foreign exchange (Dec. 1976) U.S. $346 million. Budget (1977 est.) balanced at S£17,050 million. Gross domestic product (1976) S£22,569 million. Money supply (Dec. 1976) S£8,599 million. Cost of living (Damascus; 1970 = 100; April 1977) 214.

Foreign Trade. (1976) Imports S£9,211.2 million; exports S£4,141.2 million. Import sources (1975): West Germany 13%; Italy 9%; France 7%; U.S. 6%; Japan 5%; Brazil 5%. Export destinations (1975): Italy 18%; Belgium-Luxembourg 11%; West Germany 10%; U.K. 8%; U.S.S.R. 7%; Yugoslavia 6%; Greece 6%. Main exports: crude oil 62%; cotton 15%.

Transport and Communications. Roads (1973) 13,575 km. Motor vehicles in use (1975): passenger 50,200; commercial (including buses) 34,400. Railways (1976): 1,761 km; traffic 165.7 million passenger-km, freight 305.2 million net ton-km. Air traffic (1975): 636 million passenger-km; freight 5 million net ton-km. Telephones (Dec. 1974) 152,000. Radio receivers (Dec. 1972) 2.5 million. Television receivers (Dec. 1974) 224,000.

Agriculture. Production (in 000; metric tons; 1976): wheat 1,790; barley c. 1,059; potatoes (1975) 120; pumpkins (1975) c. 124; cucumbers (1975) c. 140; tomatoes 450; onions c. 150; watermelons (1975) 300; melons (1975) c. 153; grapes c. 280; olives c. 170; cotton, lint c. 145. Livestock (in 000; 1976): sheep c. 6,200; goats c. 750; cattle (1975) 504; horses (1975) c. 60; asses (1975) c. 251; chickens c. 8,572.

Industry. Production (in 000; metric tons; 1976): crude oil 9,976; petroleum products (1975) c. 2,410; cement (1975) 994; cotton yarn 32; electricity (kw-hr; 1975) 1,673,-000.

In one of their last meetings before Egyptian Pres. Anwar as-Sadat's historic visit to Israel, Sadat (left) and Syrian Pres. Hafez al-Assad met on November 16 in Damascus.

Throughout 1977 Syria was obliged to maintain a major part of its armed forces in Lebanon. It indicated interest in a resumption of the Geneva Middle East peace conference, but it also expressed increasing reservations about Egyptian and U.S. diplomacy and denounced Egyptian Pres. Anwar as-Sadat's visit to Jerusalem in November. At home there were some serious signs of unrest.

Pres. Hafez al-Assad and his senior officials held frequent meetings with Lebanese and Palestinian leaders with the aim of settling the dangerous situation in southern Lebanon. While strongly denouncing Israeli intervention on behalf of the Lebanese Christian rightists, Syria kept its troops north of the Litani River. The Syrian-Lebanese-Palestinian agreement reached in Shtoura, Lebanon, in July and the cease-fire in south Lebanon in late September were not sufficiently effective to permit withdrawal of Syrian troops, which formed the main element in the Arab Deterrent Force.

Syria joined Egypt in attempting to resume the Geneva peace conference. President Assad had a friendly meeting with U.S. Pres. Jimmy Carter in Geneva on May 9, and a meeting of the heads of state of Syria, Egypt, and Saudi Arabia followed in Riyadh on May 19. However, differences of emphasis and approach became apparent, and Syrian spokesmen grew increasingly critical of what they construed to be excessive Egyptian-Saudi deference to U.S. wishes. Syria was openly critical of the Arab oil states for failing to provide promised aid. Relations with the Soviet Union were friendly, and Soviet arms supplies were maintained. Syria made clear its belief that Sadat's peace initiative was a betrayal of the Arab cause. It signed the anti-Sadat communiqué issued by the conference of hard-line Arab states in Tripoli, Libya, in early December, and Assad toured the Arab oil states in an effort to enlist their support against the Egyptian president.

The close relationship with Jordan was maintained and strengthened in the social and economic fields, though it stopped short of political federation. In contrast, relations with the rival Baathist regime in Iraq were extremely bad. In January Syria bitterly denounced Iraq over the opening of the Iraq-Turkey oil pipeline, which bypassed Syria and deprived it of substantial revenues. Iraq charged Syria with implication in acts of sabotage in February and with abetting the Kurdish rebels, and Syria countercharged that Iraqi agents were responsible for a series of assassinations and bomb outrages in Syria during the summer. Meanwhile, it became increasingly apparent that Syria was suffering from internal unrest, widely attributed to dislike of the Alawite minority, to which Assad belonged and which, although forming only 11% of the population, held 18 of 25 army commands. The regime responded with a series of measures designed to combat corruption and inefficiency in the administration. Assad and all senior officials announced they were handing over their property to the state.

The four-year term of the People's Council ended on June 9, and general elections were held on August 1, with 694 candidates contesting 195 seats. Public interest was so low that the balloting had to be continued the following day in the 12 out of 15 electoral districts where less than the statutory 51% of the electorate had voted. The ruling Baathists won 125 seats and allied parties in the National Progressive Front, 34 seats. Most of the remaining 36 seats were won by rightist candidates.

The decline in aid from the Arab oil states and oil pipeline transit revenues and the cost of maintaining troops in Lebanon caused a sharp economic recession. Development spending in 1977 was estimated at U.S. $2 billion—the same as in 1976 but half that of 1974 and 1975.   (PETER MANSFIELD)

Table Tennis

The 34th biennial world table tennis championships were staged in the newly opened National Exhibition Centre in Birmingham, England, from March 26 to April 5, 1977. In team competition, China retained both the Swaythling Cup, awarded to the men, and the Corbillon Cup, given to the women. Runner-up Japan was followed by Sweden, Hungary, and East Germany in the men's team competition. South Korea placed second in the women's standings, ahead of North Korea, Japan, and Hungary. The men's singles title was captured by Mitsuru Kono (Japan), who defeated Kuo Yao-hua (China) 3–1 in the final. Pak Yung Sun (North Korea) successfully defended her world title by sweeping to a 3–0 victory over Chang Li (China). In the men's doubles, which featured four Chinese finalists, Li Chen-shih and Liang Ko-liang took three straight games from Huang Liang and Lu Yuan-sheng. The team of Pak Yong Ok (North Korea) and Yang Ying (China) won 3–1 over Chu Hsiang-yun and Wei Li-chieh, both of China, to take the women's doubles title. France won its first world table tennis championship when Jacques Secretin and Claude Bergeret teamed up to defeat Tokio Tasaka and Sachiko Yokota of Japan 3–0 in the mixed doubles. Drug tests, used for the first time during world championship play, were all negative.

WIDE WORLD

The driving forehand of Mitsuru Kono of Japan was a plus in his victory over Kuo Yao-hua of China in the men's singles in the world table tennis championships at Birmingham, England, on April 5.

During the tournament the International Table Tennis Federation (ITTF), which celebrated its 50th anniversary with an exhibition of memorabilia, overwhelmingly approved a request to have table tennis recognized as an Olympic sport. The venue of future world championships was offered to North Korea (1979), to China (1981), and to Japan or Yugoslavia (1983).

The fourth Commonwealth championships, held in St. Peter Port, Guernsey, were dominated by players from Hong Kong, who won both the men's and women's team titles, the men's doubles, and the mixed doubles. England captured the women's doubles crown.

Egypt thoroughly dominated the fifth Arab table tennis championships, which took place in July at Rabat, Morocco. Its players won every title and monopolized the finals of the men's and women's singles and the women's mixed doubles.

The European League winners for 1976–77 were Hungary in the Super Division, The Netherlands in Division 1, Luxembourg in Division 2, and Finland in Division 3.   (ARTHUR KINGSLEY VINT)

1977 World Rankings

MEN	WOMEN
1. Mitsuru Kono (Japan)	1. Pak Yung Sun (North Korea)
2. Kuo Yao-hua (China)	2. Chang Li (China)
3. Huang Liang (China)	3. Chang Te-ying (China)
Liang Ko-liang (China)	Ko Hsin-ai (China)
5. Dragutin Surbec (Yugos.)	5. Chu Hsiang-yun (China)
6. Jacques Secretin (France)	6. Chung Hyan Sook (South Korea)
7. Stellan Bengtsson (Swed.)	7. Beatrix Kishazi (Hung.)
8. Istvan Jonyer (Hung.)	8. Ursula Hirschmuller (W. Ger.)
Milan Orlowski (Czech.)	9. Ilina Uhlikova (Czech.)
10. Gabor Gergely (Hung.)	

Taiwan

Taiwan, which consists of the islands of Formosa and Quemoy and other surrounding islands, is the seat of the Republic of China (Nationalist China). It is north of the Philippines, southwest of Japan, and east of Hong Kong. The island of Formosa has an area of 35,779 sq km (13,814 sq mi); including its 77 outlying islands (14 in the Taiwan group and 63 in the Pescadores group), the area of Taiwan totals 35,982 sq km (13,893 sq mi). Pop. (1977 est.): 16,678,100. Cap. and largest city: Taipei (pop., 1977 est., 2,117,800). President in 1977, Yen Chia-kan; president of the Executive Yuan (premier), Chiang Ching-kuo.

On Oct. 10, 1977, when the Chinese Nationalist government celebrated the 66th anniversary of the founding of the Republic of China, the number of countries continuing to recognize it as the legal government of all China had been reduced to 23. Saudi Arabia and the United States were the only two major countries maintaining diplomatic, economic, and financial ties with Taiwan. Sharing a strong distrust of Communists, Saudi Arabia and Taiwan further strengthened their ties following Pres. Yen Chia-kan's visit to Jidda in July at the invitation of King Khalid. The broad program of economic and financial cooperation between the two countries was expanded.

The U.S., seeking to establish full diplomatic relations with mainland China, downgraded its alliance with Taiwan. Vice-Premier Teng Hsiao-p'ing disclosed on September 6 that because of the Taiwan issue, efforts to normalize relations with the U.S. had suffered a setback during Vance's China trip. Later, a meeting that Vance scheduled with James Shen, ambassador to the U.S. from Taiwan, on September 10 was seen as a diplomatic message to Peking, since it was the first time in more than three years that Shen had been able to see a secretary of state.

The decline in the diplomatic relationship between the U.S. and Taiwan did not affect their close economic and trade ties. The U.S. remained the number one trade partner of Taiwan, and total U.S. investment in the republic was estimated at $2.5 billion.

On June 29 Vance declared, without any reference to U.S. commitments to or interests in Taiwan, that full normalization of relations with

Taiwan

A Taiwan Air Force officer climbed up on an MiG-19 to greet a Chinese pilot who had defected and flown his aircraft to Taiwan in July.

mainland China was a central part of U.S. foreign policy. Taiwan's foreign minister, Shen Changhuan, took exception to the statement and warned that friendly U.S. relations with Peking might lead to a new threat of war between Taiwan and the mainland.

The moral support of the U.S. people for the Nationalist position was reflected in public opinion polls and in resolutions adopted by a number of state legislatures and municipal councils urging the federal government to maintain its diplomatic ties with Taiwan. A public opinion survey conducted in March 1977 showed that 80% of the U.S. public favoured maintaining diplomatic ties with Taiwan; 74% were for adherence to the defense treaty; and 77% opposed breaking relations with Taiwan as the condition for full normalization with mainland China. The morale and confidence of the Nationalists were raised by the defection of the Chinese Air Force squadron leader Fan Yuanyen, who flew with his MiG-19 jet to Taiwan on July 7 and described discontent and disillusionment on the mainland.

In local elections in November, marred by rioting in the city of Chungli, candidates of the ruling Kuomintang (KMT) won 85% of the contested posts, but non-KMT candidates gained an unprecedented four mayoral posts and 21 of 77 contested seats in the Provincial Assembly. Two devastating typhoons during the summer caused considerable damage to production facilities and affected agricultural and industrial output. Nevertheless, Taiwan's remarkable economic growth continued. By 1977 the republic had become a semi-industrial power with foreign trade as the backbone of its economy. The 1976 economic growth rate was 11%, which raised the gross national product to over U.S. $17 billion and per capita income to more than $800.　　　　　　　　　　(HUNG-TI CHU)

See also China.

TAIWAN

Education. (1976–77) Primary, pupils 2,341,413, teachers 64,974; secondary, pupils 1,240,803, teachers 51,945; vocational, pupils 296,493, teachers 10,447; higher, students 299,414, teaching staff 14,548.

Finance. Monetary unit: new Taiwan dollar, with (Sept. 19, 1977) a par value of NT$38 to U.S. $1 (free rate of NT$66.20 = £1 sterling). Gold and foreign exchange (June 1977) U.S. $1,411,000,000. Budget (1974–75 est.): revenue NT$127,083,000,000; expenditure NT$119,-540,000,000. Gross national product (1976) NT$651,-460,000,000. Money supply (June 1977) NT$146,-880,000,000. Cost of living (1970 = 100; June 1977) 195.

Foreign Trade. (1976) Imports NT$288,540,000,000; exports NT$309,580,000,000. Import sources: Japan 32%; U.S. 24%; Kuwait 9%; Saudi Arabia 5%; West Germany 5%. Export destinations: U.S. 38%; Japan 14%; Hong Kong 7%; West Germany 5%. Main exports (1975): clothing 17%; electrical machinery and equipment 13%; textile yarns and fabrics 12%; footwear 6%; fruit and vegetables 5%; sugar 5%.

Transport and Communications. Roads (1975) 16,197 km. Motor vehicles in use (1975): passenger 159,000; commercial (including buses) 71,300. Railways (1975): 4,300 km; traffic 8,287,000,000 passenger-km, freight 2,702,000,-000 net ton-km. Air traffic (1970): 954 million passenger-km; freight 25,175,000 net ton-km. Shipping (1976): merchant vessels 100 gross tons and over 438; gross tonnage 1,483,981. Telephones (Dec. 1975) 1,118,000. Radio licenses (Dec. 1975) 1,486,000. Television licenses (Dec. 1975) 913,000.

Agriculture. Production (in 000; metric tons; 1975): rice 2,494; sweet potatoes 2,403; corn c. 85; cassava (1974) c. 330; peanuts c. 91; sugar, raw value c. 716; citrus fruit 348; bananas 197; pineapples 319; tea 26; pork 380. Livestock (in 000; 1975): cattle 249; pigs 3,315; goats 191; chickens 24,756.

Industry. Production (in 000; metric tons; 1975): coal 3,141; crude oil 215; natural gas (cu m) 1,574,000; electricity (kw-hr) 22,894,000; cement 6,796; crude steel 956; sulfuric acid 396; petroleum products c. 4,000; cotton yarn 131; man-made fibres 284; paper 422.

Tanzania

This republic, an East African member of the Commonwealth of Nations, consists of two parts: Tanganyika, on the Indian Ocean, bordered by Kenya, Uganda, Rwanda, Burundi, Zaire, Zambia, Malawi, and Mozambique; and Zanzibar, just off the coast, including Zanzibar Island, Pemba Island, and small islets. Total area of the united republic: 945,087 sq km (364,900 sq mi). Total pop. (1976 est.): 15,607,000, including (1966 est.) 98.9% Africans and 0.7% Indo-Pakistani. Cap. and largest city: Dar es Salaam (pop., 1977 est., 460,000) in Tanganyika. Language: English and Swahili. Religion (1967): traditional beliefs 34.6%; Christian 30.6%; Muslim 30.5%. President in 1977, Julius Nyerere.

On Jan. 21, 1977, a convention of delegates from both the Tanganyika African National Union and the Afro-Shirazi Party of Zanzibar agreed that the two parties should be amalgamated to form the Revolutionary Party (CCM). No merger of the mainland and Zanzibar governments was envisaged, and a new draft constitution adopted on April 25 guaranteed Zanzibar's autonomy and strengthened the position of Zanzibar's leader, the first vice-president, Aboud Jumbe, by abolishing the office of second vice-president.

In the middle of the year the East African Community, consisting of Tanzania, Kenya, and Uganda, ceased to exist. After lengthy recrimina-

Tanzania

TANZANIA

Education. (1975–76) Primary, pupils 1,591,834, teachers 29,783; secondary and vocational, pupils 53,257, teachers 2,606; teacher training, pupils 9,930, teachers 612; higher, students 3,064, teaching staff (universities only) 434.

Finance. Monetary unit: Tanzanian shilling, with (Sept. 19, 1977) a free rate of TShs 8.34 to U.S. $1 (TShs 14.52 = £1 sterling). Gold, SDR's, and foreign exchange (June 1977) U.S. $238.1 million. Budget (1975–76 actual): revenue TShs 4,063,000,000; expenditure TShs 6,325,000,000. Gross national product (1975) TShs 18,529,000,000. Money supply (April 1977) TShs 5,128,000,000. Cost of living (1970 = 100; 1st quarter 1977) 232.

Foreign Trade. (1976) Imports TShs 5,350,000,000; exports TShs 4,108,000,000. Import sources: U.K. 12%; Kenya 11%; Iran 9%; West Germany 8%; Japan 7%; China 6%; U.S. 6%. Export destinations: West Germany 14%; U.K. 13%; U.S. 9%; Singapore 7%; Italy 6%; Kenya 6%; Hong Kong 5%; India 5%. Main exports: cotton 16%; coffee 13%; cloves 8%; sisal 6%; tobacco 5%; cashew nuts 5%; petroleum products 5%.

Transport and Communications. Roads (1975) c. 35,000 km (including c. 16,000 km main roads). Motor vehicles in use (1974): passenger c. 39,100; commercial (including buses) c. 42,300. Railways (1976): 3,536 km (including c. 970 km of the 1,870-km Tanzam railway linking Dar es Salaam with Kapiri Mposhi in Zambia). Air traffic (including apportionment of traffic of East African Airways Corporation; 1975): 172 million passenger-km; freight 3.5 million net ton-km. Telephones (Jan. 1976) 63,000. Radio receivers (Dec. 1974) 231,000. Television receivers (Dec. 1974) c. 5,000.

Agriculture. Production (in 000; metric tons; 1976): corn 1,619; millet c. 130; sorghum c. 460; rice c. 430; sweet potatoes (1975) c. 305; cassava (1975) c. 3,560; sugar, raw value (1975) 110; dry beans 146; mangoes c. 176; bananas c. 770; cashew nuts (1975) c. 165; coffee c. 55; tobacco 19; cotton, lint c. 68; sisal c. 100; timber (cu m; 1975) c. 33,862; fish catch (1975) 181. Livestock (in 000; 1975): cattle c. 12,000; sheep c. 2,900; goats c. 4,600; asses c. 160; chickens c. 20,000.

Industry. Production (in 000; metric tons; 1975): cement 266; salt 44; diamonds (metric carats) 896; petroleum products 669; electricity (kw-hr) c. 636,000.

tions between Kenya and Tanzania the Kenya government had restricted the international operations of the East African Airways Corporation because, it claimed, the other two countries were not providing adequate financial support. In retaliation, Tanzania in February closed its borders to all traffic from Kenya by land, sea, and air. In April the border closing was declared to be permanent, and flights between Nairobi and Dar es Salaam ended in October. In December the two countries drew up an agreement on the eventual reopening of the border, but it was unclear how much time was expected to elapse before it could be implemented.

Nyerere continued to play an important role in African affairs, particularly in the negotiations regarding the future of Rhodesia. In August he paid a visit to the U.S., while visitors to Tanzania included Presidents Fidel Castro of Cuba and Nikolay V. Podgorny of the U.S.S.R.

(KENNETH INGHAM)

Target Sports

Archery. The 29th world archery championships were held in Canberra, Australia, in February 1977. A total of 66 men and 43 women representing 24 nations took part in the competition. Inasmuch as it was only the second time that the Inter-

national Archery Federation (FITA) had scheduled the event outside Europe, it was an uncommon gathering. The U.S. won both the men's and women's team titles and captured both individual championships. Richard McKinney shot his way to the men's world title and Luann Ryon made it a U.S. sweep by triumphing over her female competitors.

During the year seven new world records went into the books. Both single FITA round records fell. Giancarlo Ferrari of Italy scored 1,318 points, two points better than the record set by Darrell Pace of the U.S. in 1975, and Zebeniso Rustamova of the U.S.S.R. scored 1,304 points, 22 better than the record set in 1976 by Ryon. Rustamova also set two additional world records, amassing 315 points at 70 m and 348 at 30 m. The U.S. women raised the world record team score from 3,670 to 3,741. The sixth and seventh world records were set in distance shooting. Don Brown of the U.S. sent an arrow 3,492¾ feet and April Moon, also of the U.S., covered 2,431¾ ft.

Indoor archery, for many years popular only in the U.S., was incorporated into the archery programs of many nations. The competition includes two rounds: FITA I, which specifies 60 arrows at 18 m with a 40-cm target, and FITA II, which specifies 60 arrows at 25 m with a 60-cm target. The perfect score for each round is 600. Archers in the Western Hemisphere were elated to learn that their sport would be included in the Pan American Games for the first time; they were scheduled to be held in Puerto Rico in August 1979.

(CLAYTON B. SHENK)

Shooting. During the second Confederation of Americas championships held in Mexico City in November, U.S. shooters set three world records

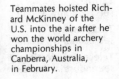
Teammates hoisted Richard McKinney of the U.S. into the air after he won the world archery championships in Canberra, Australia, in February.

WIDE WORLD

and won gold, silver, or bronze medals in every event but one. Sixteen nations participated. At the Benito Juárez international shooting championships, also held in Mexico City, the 55-member U.S. team garnered 24 gold, 10 silver, and 4 bronze medals. The Cuban team earned 13 medals, and Canada 9. Other major tournaments included the Roberts Trophy matches in England, the World Skeet and Clay Pigeon championships in France, and the European shooting championships, which were held in several locations, including Switzerland, Romania, and Andorra.

TRAP AND SKEET. During the Confederation of Americas competition, Joe Clemmons (U.S.) broke 199 of 200 skeet targets, his only miss occurring on the final round of 25. The previous record of 197 was set earlier in the year. The U.S. Open skeet team scored 586 out of 600 and broke the U.S.S.R. record of 577. Hugh Bowie (U.S.) took the individual gold medal in trap with a score of 197, and the U.S. team won the trap championship with 586. At the Benito Juárez tourney in April, John Satterwhite (U.S.) took the individual skeet title with 197, edging out Roberto Castrillo (Cuba) by a single point. At the World Skeet and Clay Pigeon championships, the individual gold medal was won by Benny Seiffert (Denmark) with 196, but the team event was taken by the U.S. with 577. The clay pigeon (trap) individual gold medal was won by Esteban Azkue (Spain) with 197 and the team title by Italy with 575. During the Grand American trapshooting tournament, traditionally held at Vandalia, Ohio, Roger Smith broke 965 out of 1,000 targets to win the men's overall title. Loral I. Delany won the women's crown with 924.

RIFLES. The third world record set at the Confederation of Americas championships occurred in the free rifle event when Lones Wigger (U.S.) scored 1,159 points. Other winners of individual events were Helmut Bellingrodt (Colombia) in running boar with 574×600; Edward Etzel (U.S.) in the three-position with $1,166 \times 1,200$; and Arne Sorensen (Canada) in the air rifle event with 384×400. Miguel Valdez (Cuba) won the English Match. Though Wigger also had a score of 596, Valdez was declared winner, under the rules, because he had the higher score in the last series of 100 shots. Gold medal team winners included the U.S., which fired $4,566 \times 4,800$ with the free rifle, 4,633 in the three-position, and $2,372 \times 2,400$ in the English Match. The running boar team title went to Colombia with $1,492 \times 1,600$. Canada took the team championship in air rifle with $1,511 \times 1,-600$.

At the Benito Juárez matches, gold medals were won by Mike Therimer (U.S.), who scored 556 in running boar, and by Vic Auer (U.S.), who shot 599 in the English Match. The Roberts Trophy match, a small-bore event fired between ten-man British and U.S. teams, took place in England in 1977. The U.S. outscored Britain 3,926 to 3,924. At the European shooting championships in Switzerland, Gennadi Luschtschikow (U.S.S.R.) won the free rifle competition with 1,147, the standard rifle event with 566, and led the Soviets to victory in both team events: the free rifle with 4,523 points and the standard rifle with 2,251. Winners at the

World Archery Records

Event	Winner	Year	Record	Old record	Maximum possible
Single FITA Round					
MEN					
FITA	G. Ferrari (Italy)	1977	1,318	1,316	1,440
90 m	D. Pace (U.S.)	1976	309	303	360
70 m	D. Pace (U.S.)	1975	333	325	360
50 m	S. Spegarelli (Italy)	1976	340	331	360
30 m	D. Pace (U.S.)	1975	354	350	360
Team	United States	1976	3,812	3,775	4,320
WOMEN					
FITA	Z. Rustamova (U.S.S.R.)	1977	1,304	1,282	1,440
70 m	Z. Rustamova (U.S.S.R.)	1977	315	310	360
60 m	V. Kovpan (U.S.S.R.)	1976	327	324	360
50 m	L. Sjoholm (Sweden)	1975	319	311	360
30 m	Z. Rustamova (U.S.S.R.)	1977	348	344	360
Team	United States	1977	3,741	3,670	4,320
World Distance Record					
MEN					
	D. Brown (U.S.)	1977	$3,492\frac{3}{4}$ ft		
WOMEN					
	A. Moon (U.S.)	1977	$2,431\frac{3}{4}$ ft		

World Indoor Archery Records

MEN					
FITA I					
18 m	G. Ferrari (Italy)	1976	586	583	600
FITA II					
25 m	D. Pace (U.S.)	1976	586	581	600
WOMEN					
FITA I					
18 m	L. Ryon (U.S.)	1977	573	567	600
FITA II					
25 m	L. Dashirabdanova (U.S.S.R.)	1977	573	561	600

seventh European air weapon championships held in Andorra included junior shooter Kurt Hillenbrand (West Germany), whose individual score of 387 bettered by one point the highest overall score by a senior shooter.

HANDGUNS. U.S. marksmen dominated the pistol events at the two matches in Mexico City. Melvin Makin won both individual standard pistol events with scores of 567 and 574. The centre-fire winners were Jerry Wilder at the Confederation tourney, who scored 588, and Frank Higginson at the Benito Juárez match, who scored 584. At the Confederation matches, Ruben Ariza (Colombia) took the free pistol event with 556, and Terry Anderson took the individual gold medal for rapid-fire with 590. Charles Wheeler (U.S.) won the air pistol title at the Juárez competition with a score of 381, but during the Confederation tournament Kenneth Buster (U.S.) triumphed with 383. The team title went to Cuba with a score of 1,485. Harald Vollmar (East Germany) won the individual European air pistol title at Andorra with a score of 386, and East Germany captured the team title with 1,539.

(ROBERT N. SEARS)

Television and Radio

Approximately 1,136,975,000 television and radio sets were in use throughout the world in 1977. No major nation lacked either TV or radio service in some form. There were about 788 million radio sets in use, of which 425.3 million, or 54%, were in the U.S., and approximately 348,975,000 television receivers, of which 127,575,000, or 37%, were in the U.S.

The Soviet Union ranked next to the U.S. in television sets with 60 million, according to *Broadcasting* magazine, and Japan was third with 27 million. Other *Broadcasting* estimates included West

Germany, 19 million; France, 14.5 million; Italy, 11.5 million; Brazil, 10.5 million; Canada, 8.5 million; Spain and Poland, 6.8 million each; East Germany, 5.3 million; Australia, 5.2 million; Mexico, 5 million; and Argentina and The Netherlands, 4 million each.

About 6,695 television stations were on the air throughout the world. Approximately 2,200 were in the Far East, 2,110 in Western Europe, 1,039 in the U.S., 920 in Eastern Europe, 180 in South America, 105 in Mexico, 96 in Canada, and 45 in Africa. There were about 15,090 radio stations, mostly amplitude modulation (AM) but with a growing proportion of the frequency modulation (FM) type. The U.S. had 8,656, of which 4,101 were FM.

Organization of Services. During 1977 The Bahamas and Guinea started television services, bringing the world's total of countries with television to 121 out of 156. Egypt, Colombia, Spain, and India were notable for starting major expansions of their television coverage and broadcasting hours. The established services continued to attract audiences (except in the U.S. and Australia), but only at much higher costs. Broadcasters that were allowed to sell advertising time were able to increase rates and show a profit, but many broadcasters that depended on government grants or license fees incurred serious losses. The commercial U.S., Japanese, and Australian networks again showed record profits. The British commercial Independent Television (ITV) companies were exceptionally rich, and some doubled or tripled the previous year's income. But the British Broadcasting Corporation (BBC), desperately poor, was given an increase in the license fee of only a few pounds (less than inflation had accounted for). In Australia, too, the commercial networks were buying TV rights to cricket and tennis events at such high prices that the non-profitmaking Australian Broadcasting Commission (ABC) could not even broadcast the all-important England-Australia test cricket matches. The new South Africa TV service decided to allow advertising as of Jan. 1, 1978.

New technologies were substantial challenges to the broadcasters' traditional monopoly over the supply of TV programs. Sony Corp. introduced Betamax, the first home video-cassette unit capable of recording a two-hour-long program, and other manufacturers followed suit. Video games became popular throughout North America, Europe, and Japan and occasionally attracted 2% of peak-time audience with some stations reporting lost revenue. Cable television continued to spread in North America, but developments in Europe were negligible.

Private and government-owned broadcasting organizations continued to exchange major news coverage by satellite. U.S. Pres. Jimmy Carter's inauguration and long segments of Egyptian Pres. Anwar as-Sadat's historic visit to Israel were among the broadcasts most widely distributed throughout the world. On a day-to-day basis, pickups of important "spot" news coverage by television systems throughout the world were commonplace.

The long-standing feud between cable operators and broadcasters intensified in 1977 when a U.S. Court of Appeals held that the Federal Communications Commission (FCC) had gone too far in protecting broadcasting from pay cable. The decision, which the U.S. Supreme Court in October refused to review, overturned the FCC's rules denying to pay cable specific sports events such as the baseball World Series and the football Super Bowl; putting restrictions on the amount of regularly scheduled sports events pay-cable systems might carry; generally limiting the films they might present to those that were less than three or more than ten years old; barring pay-cable operators from devoting more than 90% of their time to sports and films; and forbidding them to carry commercials. The court did not prohibit the FCC from adopting pay-cable rules but said that the commission had not justified the rules in question.

Over the protests of ABC and CBS, a federal judge in late 1977 approved a settlement between NBC and the U.S. Department of Justice covering NBC's part of a six-year-old civil antitrust suit that charged each of the three networks with illegally monopolizing prime-time entertainment programming. The consent decree limited the time for which NBC could retain exclusive broadcasting rights to any particular program and, among other things, forbade NBC to obtain any interests, except network broadcast rights, in programs produced by others. But several key elements of the accord—including restrictions on the amount of self-produced programming NBC can broadcast—were to take effect only if the suits against the other two networks were similarly resolved.

The Carter administration introduced in Congress in October a bill providing for federal funding of public broadcasting for five years beginning in 1981. The bill would authorize $180 million in matching federal funds during the first year and $200 million in each of the next four, as compared with $160 million authorized and $152 million actually appropriated for fiscal 1980. The formula for matching grants would be reduced under the bill;

LeVar Burton, as Kunta Kinte, waits to be auctioned into slavery in the ABC TV miniseries "Roots," based on Alex Haley's book. The series was watched by approximately 80 million viewers.

LIAISON

Jim Henson with his creations on "The Muppet Show" became a smash hit on Britain's TV screens in 1977 with about 14 million viewers. The Muppets had previously attained popularity in the U.S.

stitutional Court had ruled that the monopoly of Radiotelevisione Italiana (RAI) did not extend to private local stations. The complexities were exacerbated by the ending in 1977 of the system whereby RAI was controlled by the ruling political establishment.

In tune with the nation's increasing liberalization, the Spanish government started a major expansion of the second TV channel. Also, in a significant political move, it allowed all radio stations, for the first time in approximately 35 years, to broadcast their own news bulletins.

In Australia the Green Report proposed a major restructuring of both the ABC and commercial broadcasting. The government rejected most proposals but did set up a new Broadcasting Tribunal and, after some delay, gave it the power to grant and alter station licenses. Meanwhile, amid some acrimony, the government withdrew federal funds from the ABC's community 3ZZ station in Melbourne because it was considered to be too outspoken. In New Zealand the new National government reversed its predecessors' 18-month-old reform, which had increased autonomy and decentralization, and reinstated the New Zealand Broadcasting Corporation.

Programming. The international flow of television programs increased dramatically in 1977 in quantity if not in quality, with certain aspects causing major political controversy. In the early 1970s the international programs market was worth about $200 million, with the vast bulk of the business being done by the U.S. In 1977 the total was about $400 million and the increase was almost entirely due to the successful efforts of the Europeans, with Australia, Japan, and Mexico doing good business as well. Almost anything on celluloid or tape that moved was sold, but increases were especially noticeable in animation and children's programs. Prices were up from recent averages of U.S. $10,000 an hour in the top markets to about $15,000. Alongside sales of completed programs, the number of co-productions increased notably, especially between the European noncommercial organizations (with French-German-Italian consortia being most common) and between them and Australia and/or Canada.

The regional broadcasting unions continued to exchange ever larger quantities of news items. Many arrangements were made for the exchange of complete programs. Spanish TV started a program, "300 Millions," which was sent every Sunday to 300 million Spanish-speaking people in Europe and Latin America, as well as to 30 U.S. stations. The first East-West talk show took place on May 16 when the BBC's Jimmy Young broadcast a mixture of music and talk from a Moscow studio to the U.K.

Westerns, mysteries, and comedies produced in the U.S. were staple entertainment programming in many countries. *Broadcasting* estimated that foreign sales of U.S. television programs and movies totaled $180 million in 1976, an all-time high. The 1977 total was expected to approach $200 million. "The Six Million Dollar Man," "Kojak," "The Hardy Boys/Nancy Drew Mysteries," "Rich Man, Poor Man," "The Odd Couple," "Happy Days,"

instead of having to raise $2.50 in nonfederal funds for each $1 of federal money, public broadcasting would have to raise only $2.25.

The measure also was designed to eliminate frictions and overlap that had existed between the Corporation for Public Broadcasting (CPB) on the one hand and the Public Broadcasting Service (PBS) and National Public Radio (NPR) on the other. It would do this largely by restricting CPB's program responsibilities to the making of block grants for categories of programs—public affairs, science, arts, and the like—rather than for specific programs.

The major topic in Europe was the retransmission over existing cable systems of other countries' programs. The financial and copyright problems were complex, and no solution was near. The BBC's Ceefax and ITV's Oracle Teletext systems, each showing lines of text on a home TV screen, were given the status of permanent services by the government. TV sets with Teletext decoders were on sale for the first time in London at £700. The Post Office's Teletext system, with a two-way capability, called Viewdata, was being developed rapidly with a major test in 1,000 homes and was sold during the year to West Germany and Finland. France developed a separate but sophisticated system, and Australia's ABC a rather more simple one.

In Britain the report of the Committee on the Future of Broadcasting, chaired by Lord Annan, was received with considerable interest. Its main findings were that a new "open" broadcasting authority should be set up to run the much-discussed fourth British television channel; that a local broadcasting authority should take over all local radio services after 1979; and that a public inquiry board (to meet every seven years) and a broadcasting complaints commission should be established.

Broadcasting in Italy became increasingly chaotic. About 1,200 radio stations and 300 TV stations continued to operate in a legal vacuum. The Con-

"The Mary Tyler Moore Show," "M*A*S*H," "Hawaii Five-O," "Starsky and Hutch," "Mod Squad," "Police Woman," and "Charlie's Angels" were among the most popular U.S. exports.

In the U.S. the 1977–78 network television season got off to an early—and frantic—start. ABC, CBS, and NBC had planned to start introducing their new prime-time programming about September 19, as usual. Then, hoping for an early advantage to help it hold or extend its established lead in the prime-time audience ratings, ABC scheduled "Washington: Behind Closed Doors," a made-for-television miniseries based in part on Watergate figure John Ehrlichman's book *The Company*, across six consecutive nights starting September 6. The other networks responded by moving up the introductory dates of their own programs—and by scheduling specials of their own—so that in the 44 hours of prime-time programming in the two weeks preceding the originally scheduled September 19 starting date about 80% of the offerings on each network consisted of new or special programs.

Specials and miniseries dotted the schedules of all three networks throughout the rest of 1977. NBC was most prolific in this respect, followed by CBS and then by ABC, whose first-place position in the ratings did not require so much support from so-called "blockbuster" specials. In November alone, according to a tally by *Broadcasting*, almost 60 hours of specials were presented on the three networks. Through the rest of the 1977–78 season each of the networks planned to present up to 100 hours or more of specials. Such programming was costly; in the first two weeks alone it cost the three networks at least $45 million more than they normally spent in that period.

Just how productive the specials were in terms of audience ratings was not clear. ABC retained and even increased the first-place lead it had won in 1976–77, though it did so with fewer specials and miniseries than the others.

In preparing for the 1977–78 season ABC and NBC each canceled six series from the 1976–77 year, and CBS canceled ten. In recognition of growing public criticism of television violence, they dispensed with many of their action shows, replacing them for the most part with comedies. The few action shows that remained, such as "Starsky and Hutch" and "Baretta," were reoriented to put more emphasis on personal relationships and humour.

The largest audience in television history was won by "Roots," a made-for-television drama based on the search by author Alex Haley (*see* BIOGRAPHY) for his ancestors and presented by ABC as a miniseries across eight consecutive nights in January. A single episode attracted 71% of the television audience, exceeding the total who watched on either of the two nights on which *Gone with the Wind*, the previous winner, was presented in 1976. Seven episodes of "Roots" were the seven highest-rated programs of that week in the audience measurements, and seven of the eight also were among the ten highest-rated programs of all time.

Another widely seen series comprised the first four David Frost interviews with former U.S. president Richard Nixon. Not carried on any of the large networks, the series was sold directly to 163 stations capable of reaching, together, 96% of all U.S. TV homes. The first interview, dealing with the Watergate scandal, may have been the most widely watched syndicated show in television history. In some major cities its share of the audience ranged from 42 to 61%. Subsequent episodes did not do as well and when a fifth interview was put together later in the year the number of station buyers dropped to about 50.

The movement toward "fourth networks," groups of stations assembled for the presentation of limited numbers of special shows, continued in 1977, but in some cases the progress was slower than the participants had expected. A group of almost 100 stations underwrote and presented "Testimony of Two Men" in May, achieving an average rating of 16. Paramount Television Distribution, however, moved back the date of its "fourth network" project. Paramount planned to offer 22 new one-hour episodes of the "Star Trek" science-fiction series, 21 new made-for-TV movies, and several specials on 60 or more stations for three hours a week for 52 weeks, but it deferred the starting date from the spring of 1978 to sometime in the 1978–79 television season.

Programming for children was a continuing concern of networks and stations. In many cases,

Former and present members of TV's "Today" show got together on January 14 to celebrate the show's 25th anniversary. Former cast members (seated, left to right) are Dave Garroway, Jack Lescoulie, and Frank Blair. Present cast members, standing behind them, are Gene Shalit, Tom Brokaw, Floyd Kalber, Jane Pauley, and Lew Wood.

WIDE WORLD

stations worked together, pooling resources to produce a program or series more elaborate than they could afford individually. Under the auspices of Teachers Guides to Television Inc., a series of seminars to help parents and teachers "use" television for the benefit of children was begun in many cities throughout the U.S. in 1977 and was scheduled to continue in 1978.

In daytime programming, serials and game shows were the dominant formats. In early November, a count by *Broadcasting* showed 12 serials, 11 games, and reruns of five former primetime series. The trend toward expansion of serials to 60 minutes continued. "The Guiding Light" expanded to an hour, and "One Life to Live" and "General Hospital" were to go to an hour in January 1978. A new one-hour serial, "For Richer, For Poorer," was introduced in December.

In the 29th annual Emmy Awards, the Academy of Television Arts and Sciences (formerly the National Academy of Television Arts and Sciences) voted "Roots" the outstanding limited series of the year. "The Mary Tyler Moore Show," which voluntarily went off after the 1976–77 season, was named the outstanding comedy series, and "Upstairs, Downstairs" was voted the outstanding drama series. "Eleanor and Franklin: The White House Years" and "Sybil" were tied for the outstanding drama special, while "Van Dyke and Company" was chosen as the outstanding comedy-variety or music series and "Ballet Shoes" the outstanding children's special. Carroll O'Connor of "All in the Family" and Beatrice Arthur of "Maude" were named outstanding lead actor and actress in a comedy series. CBS's "NFL Today" was cited as the outstanding live sports series, and ABC received four awards for individual achievement in connection with its coverage of the 1976 Olympic Games, which were voted outstanding live sports special of the year.

Sports remained one of the most popular program formats, and one of the most expensive. *Broadcasting* estimated that television and radio networks and stations paid $82,555,292 for rights to cover professional and college football games in 1977 and $52,110,000 to cover major league baseball games. And the prices, especially for football, were going up. ABC signed a new contract for National Collegiate Athletic Association football games and agreed to pay $29.5 million a year for four years, up from $18 million a year under the old two-year contract. Audiences for football and baseball remained high. The Super Bowl football game in January 1977 was the highest rated sports event in television history to that time, reaching more than 31 million homes.

News and public affairs were basic television fare in 1977 as in prior years. The FCC reported that commercial television stations devoted an average of 24.2% of their air time to news, public affairs, and "other nonentertainment, nonsports" programming in 1976, and there was no apparent slowdown in 1977.

The Public Broadcasting Service introduced six new public-affairs series at the start of its 1977–78 season and also planned a number of new documentaries, more live coverage of important special

events, and what it called target-audience series for older persons, minority groups, and the handicapped. Among the new shows were "Over Easy," called "the first major television series specifically intended for Americans over 55"; "As We See It," a look at school desegregation from the perspective of high-school students; and "Eyewitness," a series of four one-hour dramatizations of recent events in the news.

In Europe the year was notable for hard-hitting social realism. The winners of the Prix Italia, perhaps the world's premier event for high-class programs, had typically downbeat titles: "It'll Work Out" (Sweden's winning drama production); "In a Mess" (Dutch TV's winner); and "Day-by-Day" (a Polish documentary). The BBC's documentary entry, "Spend, Spend, Spend," about a pools-winner who did exactly that, was enjoyed more and was probably more memorable, but on a final 6–4 vote the jury favoured the dour Swedish entry, about the closing of a factory and unemployment.

A major issue of the Prix Italia and elsewhere during the year was the nature of drama-documentary: how much producers in this genre (and their audience) should work within the traditions of fiction, and how much within those of documentary and reportage. There was some concern that audiences were not always informed, or aware, of the difference.

Often, public (and critical) discussion of such a program focused not on its content but on whether it had offended against one or other canon or convention of production style. ATV's "Dummy," a harrowing drama-documentary about a deaf-mute girl who became a prostitute, provoked a fairly typical reaction. Public and industry responses centred not on the questions raised by the story of the girl (*e.g.*, the education of severely handicapped people) but on the questions of taste raised by the decision to make and then transmit such a version of it.

A happier note was struck in the U.K. by the queen's Silver Jubilee celebrations, which received massive coverage and stimulated many related programs. The most substantial was the BBC's "Royal Heritage," in which Sir Huw Wheldon presented a vivid and impressive account of the royal family's nine centuries of collecting buildings, paintings, and objets d'art.

John Kenneth Galbraith attempted to follow in the footsteps of Lord Clark (art), Jacob Bronowski (human evolution), and Alastair Cooke (U.S. history) by giving a profusely illustrated, globetrotting, populist account of something the ordinary viewer was supposed to know little about, which in Galbraith's case was economics. The glossy 13-part "Age of Uncertainty," however, generally failed to attract viewers or to explain economics. More successful programs were the BBC's "Marie Curie," the dramatized life of the discoverer of radium, by Peter Goodchild, and London Weekend Television's "All You Need Is Love," a history of popular music by Tony Palmer.

Several expensive religious projects were finished during the year. Lord Grade's mammoth six-hour "Jesus of Nazareth" was written by Anthony Burgess, directed by Franco Zeffirelli, and starred Robert Powell. ATV also produced "Moses — the Lawgiver," with Burt Lancaster. Two historical series, Granada's "The Christians," presented by Bamber Gascoigne, and the BBC's "The Long Search," with Ronald Eyre, covered much the same ground; Eyre's series, however, dealt less with the politics of the church and more with matters of faith and ideas.

No British viewer could help noticing that Kermit the Frog (see BIOGRAPHY) had arrived. ATV's "The Muppet Show," originally an offshoot from "Sesame Street," had faltered uncertainly in its early days, but became a runaway success throughout Europe and the U.S. In Britain the Muppets won the British Academy of Film and Television Arts award for best light entertainment show, and also took the coveted Golden Rose award at the Montreux Festival. Another accolade went to Angela Rippon (see BIOGRAPHY), the BBC's most viewable news reader. She was named Show Business Personality of the Year by the Variety Club of Great Britain.

Radio's minority audience remained loyal, and program quality varied. Though the Annan report was critical of their organization, the local radio stations run by the BBC and the independents were well established, providing a mixture of news, music, phone-ins, and programs of regional and specialist interest. The BBC continued its experiments in quadraphonic sound.

The third French channel, France-3, again produced the most innovative programs in that country. They included "Vendredi," an outstanding documentary series, and a new 90-minute slot, "Cinéma 16," for independent filmmakers working in 16 mm.

(RUFUS W. CRATER; JOHN HOWKINS; SOL J. TAISHOFF; BRIAN WILLIAMS)

Amateur Radio. The number of amateur radio operators increased sharply in 1977. The American Radio Relay League (ARRL), the leading organization of amateur, or "ham," radio operators, reported 321,163 amateur radio licenses outstanding in the U.S. as of Aug. 1, 1977, a 17% gain in 12 months. By October 1 the number had reached 324,148. Much of the increase was attributed to the boom in the Citizens Radio Service (citizens band or CB), even though that boom cooled in 1977. Many CBers, it was believed, were becoming interested in the greater sophistication of amateur radio, in which operators may use internationally allocated frequencies throughout the radio spectrum. The number of ham operators throughout the world was expected to reach one million by late 1977 or early 1978, a 25% increase in little more than a year.

In times of trouble ham operators have played vital roles in providing communications facilities when other lines were down. In 1977 hams served as the only communications links with the rest of the world for several isolated communities in West Virginia, Kentucky, and Virginia when disastrous floods struck those areas.

(RUFUS W. CRATER; SOL J. TAISHOFF)

See also Industrial Review: Advertising; Telecommunications; Motion Pictures; Music.
[613.D.4.b; 735.I.4–5]

Tennis

Official sanction was given to current usage when, at the annual general meeting of the International Lawn Tennis Federation in Hamburg, West Germany, in July 1977, the name of the sport was changed from "lawn tennis" to "tennis" and the title of the world governing body to the International Tennis Federation (ITF). With this action the ITF followed a precedent set by the U.S. Tennis Association and by the Fédération Française de Tennis. The ruling body of the sport in Great Britain, the Lawn Tennis Association, opposed the move.

Large sums in prize money continued to be awarded to successful players in the leading tournaments. The U.S. Tennis Association estimated that during 1976, 17 men and 5 women each earned more than $100,000 in prize money alone. The prize winnings of Jimmy Connors of the U.S. were assessed at $687,335 and those of the top woman, his compatriot Chris Evert, at $343,165. The earnings of Connors were, however, enhanced by his participation in some exceptionally lucrative "winner take all" contests supported by television networks. The credibility of this form of tennis suffered a setback in mid-1977 when it was revealed that players in such matches had received fixed sums irrespective of status as winner or loser.

The Wimbledon tournament, first held in 1877, marked its centenary on the Centre Court at the All England Lawn Tennis and Croquet Club on the opening day, June 20, when past champions were presented with silver medals by the duke of Kent. The most senior singles champions among 41 present were Jean Borotra of France (born Aug. 13, 1898) and Kitty McKane-Godfree of the U.K. (born May 7, 1897), both of whom won in 1924 and 1926. With them, two doubles champions, "Toto" Brugnon and Elizabeth Ryan, also received medals.

The U.S. Tennis Association planned that from 1978 on the U.S. Open championships, held at the West Side Tennis Club at Forest Hills, N.Y., since 1915, would be staged at a new club. It was to be developed in Flushing Meadows, a few miles from Forest Hills, in the same New York City borough of Queens.

Men's Competition. Raúl Ramírez (Mexico) won the Grand Prix at the end of 1976 although he was a singles champion in only two of the qualifying tournaments, Gstaad, Switz., and the Dewar Cup, which was staged for the last time, in London. His total prize earnings for the year were $465,942. The subsequent Grand Prix Masters' tournament, held in Houston, Texas, in December, was won by Manuel Orantes (Spain), who beat Wojtek Fibak (Poland) in a five-set final. The most successful competitor in the circuit organized by World Championship Tennis (WCT) was Connors. His rivalry with his compatriot Dick Stockton was close. Stockton beat Connors in a five-set final of the Philadelphia indoor event, but in a four-set final at the Dallas tourament, the climax of the WCT series, Connors won 6–7, 6–1, 6–4, 6–3. U.S. left-hander Roscoe Tanner won the Australian championship at Melbourne in early January 1977. His most difficult match was in the semifinal against 42-year-old Ken Rosewall (Australia) with a score of 6–4, 3–6, 6–4, 6–1. Tanner beat Guillermo Vilas (Argentina) in the final 6–3, 6–3, 6–3.

Paolo Bertolucci (Italy) won the West German championship at Hamburg in May. He beat Orantes 6–3, 4–6, 6–2, 6–3 in the final. In the Italian championship, held in Rome the following week, Vitas Gerulaitis (U.S.) was the victor. Gerulaitis beat the defending champion, Adriano Panatta (Italy), 1–6, 7–6, 6–3 in the quarterfinal, Brian Gottfried (U.S.) 6–2, 7–6, 4–6, 7–5 in the semifinal, and Antonio Zugarelli (Italy) 6–2, 7–6, 3–6, 7–6 in the final.

In the French championship at Paris in June Panatta, the defending men's singles champion, was beaten by Ramírez in the quarterfinal. The title was won by Vilas, who dropped only one set in seven matches, crushing among others Stan Smith (U.S.), Fibak, Ramírez, and, in the final, Gottfried 6–0, 6–3, 6–0.

Björn Borg (Sweden) retained his singles championship at Wimbledon. He won in the quarterfinal against Ilie Nastase (Romania), in the semifinal against Gerulaitis 6–4, 3–6, 6–3, 3–6, 8–6 (acclaimed as one of the best contests seen in years), and in the final against Connors 3–6, 6–2, 6–1, 5–7, 6–4.

In the U.S. Open championship Borg withdrew during a fourth-round match against Dick Stockton (U.S.) because of an injured chest muscle. Connors and Vilas reached the final without losing a set, the first four rounds being played over the best of three sets. Vilas played a splendid final and beat Connors 2–6, 6–3, 7–6, 6–0.

DOUBLES. The doubles only tournament, organized by WCT in Kansas City as a separate doubles climax to its tournament series, failed to produce more than mundane-quality matches between inexperienced partnerships. Vijay Amritraj (India) and Dick Stockton (U.S.) were the winners. The Grand Prix Masters' tournament final in Houston at the end of 1976 was won by the established pair Sherwood Stewart (U.S.) and Fred McNair (U.S.) against an even more practiced partnership, Gottfried and Ramírez.

The Australian title went to Arthur Ashe (U.S.) and Tony Roche (Australia). Gottfried and Ramírez were victors in both Rome and Paris. At the Wimbledon meeting they were seeded first but lost in the first round. The title was taken by two Queenslanders, Ross Case and Geoff Masters, who beat the Australians John Alexander and Phil Dent, also unseeded, in the final. Bob Hewitt and Frew McMillan of South Africa won the U.S. Open title, losing only one set in the semifinal to Bob Carmichael (Australia) and Brian Teacher (U.S.). In the final they beat Gottfried and Ramírez 6–4, 6–0.

DAVIS CUP. In the American Zone final at Buenos Aires in May, Argentina, led by Vilas, beat the U.S. 3–2. Australia won the Eastern Zone without losing a rubber. Represented by Mark Edmondson and John Alexander in singles and by Alexander and Phil Dent in doubles, they beat India and then New Zealand.

In Section A of the European Zone the U.S.S.R. was disqualified for one year because of its withdrawal from the tournament for political reasons in 1976. France won the zone section with a 3–2 win against Romania in Paris. Italy, holder of the Davis Cup, won Section B of the European Zone. They beat Sweden 4–1 in Båstad and Spain 3–2 in Barcelona.

In the interzone competition Italy advanced to the Cup finals by defeating France 4–1. Australia

Winners of the women's and men's singles at Wimbledon in June were Britain's Virginia Wade (left), who defeated Betty Stove of The Netherlands in the final, and Sweden's Björn Borg, who triumphed over Jimmy Connors of the U.S.

KEYSTONE

SYNDICATION INTERNATIONAL/PHOTO TRENDS

Textiles:
see Industrial Review

won the other interzone contest 3–1 over Argentina, the last match ending in a draw. In the Davis Cup finals, held at Sydney in December, Australia regained the trophy from defending champion Italy 3–1, with the final match abandoned by mutual agreement. The key victory for Australia was Alexander's 6–4, 4–6, 2–6, 8–6, 11–9 triumph over Panatta, played over 3 hours 54 minutes.

Women's Competition. Chris Evert (U.S.) was the most successful competitor in the Virginia Slims series of tournaments. Martina Navratilova, who had left her native Czechoslovakia, was a close rival and so were two British players, Virginia Wade (*see* BIOGRAPHY) and Susan Barker. Barker qualified for the final of the climax tournament in New York, where she lost to Evert 2–6, 6–1, 6–1. The leading championships in Europe, those of West Germany, Italy, and France, attracted women competitors of less than top class. Laura DuPont and Janet Newberry of the U.S. won the singles in Hamburg and Rome, respectively. The French title was taken by Mima Jausovec of Yugoslavia.

The Wimbledon championship was won, amid much patriotic fervour, by Wade. She played spectacularly well in the semifinal and beat Evert 6–2, 4–6, 6–1. At the same stage Betty Stove (The Netherlands) beat Barker 6–4, 2–6, 6–4. In the final Wade beat Stove 4–6, 6–3, 6–1. A popular match in the third round of singles was Evert's 6–1, 6–1 win against the Californian Tracy Austin. The latter (born Dec. 12, 1962) was the youngest competitor at Wimbledon within living memory.

Evert won the U.S. Open championship easily, for the third successive year. Her hardest match was the final against the Australian Wendy Turnbull, whom she beat 7–6, 6–2. Turnbull had beaten Wade in the quarterfinal 6–2, 6–1 and the second-seeded Navratilova 2–6, 7–5, 6–4 in the semifinal. In the first round Wade beat the 43-year-old Renee Richards 6–1, 6–4. Richards, a transsexual, competed in the men's singles in the 1950s as Richard Raskind. She gained acceptance as a female competitor only after legal action.

The Federation Cup was staged in June at Devonshire Park, Eastbourne, England. Czechoslovakia, Hungary, the U.S.S.R., and the Philippines were excluded because of their withdrawal in 1976. The U.S., represented by Billie Jean King, Evert, and Rosemary Casals, won for the second straight year and for the sixth time in all. In the semifinal they beat South Africa 3–0 and in the final Australia 2–1. (LANCE TINGAY)

Thailand

A constitutional monarchy of Southeast Asia, Thailand is bordered by Burma, Laos, Cambodia, Malaysia, the Andaman Sea, and the Gulf of Thailand. Area: 542,373 sq km (209,411 sq mi). Pop. (1977 est.): 43,213,700. Cap. and largest city: Bangkok (pop., 1977 est., 4,545,600). Language: Thai. Religion (1970): Buddhist 95.3%; Muslim 3.8%. King, Bhumibol Adulyadej; prime ministers in 1977, Thanin Kraivichien to Oct. 20, 1977, and, from November 12, Gen. Kriangsak Chamanand;

chairman of the Revolutionary Council from October 20 and of the National Policy Council from November 12, Adm. Sa-ngad Chaloryu.

Thailand experienced another disruptive year in 1977. The Thanin Kraivichien administration, unbending in its opposition to dissent, proved unpopular both with the people and with the generals who had installed it in office in the first place. Before it could complete one year, it was dismissed by its mentors, bringing Thailand once again under direct military rule. This was the seventh change of government in six years.

One of the factors that led to the change was concern over security. The Communists in the northern and northeastern provinces generally stayed out of the limelight, but it was known that they were steadily building up their strength. Their ranks had been increased by a number of intellectuals and student leaders driven underground by the heavy-handed policies of the government. An apparent slowdown in the inflow of foreign investments was attributed to uncertainty over security. Meanwhile, Muslim rebels in the south were unusually active. In September some of them managed to explode two homemade bombs near King Bhumibol and Queen Sirikit when they were visiting the border provinces.

The security picture was further clouded by the hostility of Thailand's three Communist neighbours. Although some high-level meetings took place, relations remained tense, and Cambodia staged a series of bloody border raids that kept Thailand on war alert. According to some critics, any chance of a working relationship with the Indochinese states was negated by Bangkok's uncompromising anti-Communism. In December Thailand and Vietnam announced plans to establish diplomatic relations, but no time was set for the exchange of ambassadors.

The government was equally tough with domestic troublemakers. A grim warning to drug pushers was meted out in April when a 44-year-old man, found with heroin, was executed in prison. A rapist was also executed in another attempt to set an example. The most prominent victim of the new summary justice was a former general who led an abortive coup in March. Even Thais used to coups found the attempt made by Chalard Hiranyasiri bizarre. Sacked from the Army following the October 1976 takeover by the armed forces, Chalard, who had become a Buddhist monk, left his monastery to stage the coup. It involved some 300 troops brought in from outside Bangkok, Chalard's son, a major, and some of his middle-rank officer friends. The troops surrendered after ten hours of uncertainty. After a three-week inquiry, Chalard was executed, and his son and friends were sentenced to life imprisonment.

Eight months later it was a very different story. There was no air of crisis as military chiefs, without even ordering tanks into the streets, announced the removal of the Thanin government on October 20 on the grounds that it had caused disunity, divisiveness, and lack of public cooperation. A 23-man Revolutionary Council assumed power, with Adm. Sa-ngad Chaloryu as chairman and Gen. Kriangsak Chamanand as the key policy-

Thailand

THAILAND

Education. (1976–77) Primary, pupils 6,736,751, teachers 270,567; secondary, pupils 1,091,997, teachers 35,170; vocational, pupils 198,282, teachers 9,411; teacher training, students 44,156, teachers 5,639; higher, students 81,696, teaching staff (universities only) 7,757.

Finance. Monetary unit: baht, with (Sept. 19, 1977) a par value of 20 baht to U.S. $1 (free rate of 35.27 baht = £1 sterling). Gold, SDR's, and foreign exchange (June 1977) U.S. $1,978,000,000. Budget (1976–77 est.): revenue 48,082,000,000 baht; expenditure 67,364,000,000 baht. Gross national product (1976) 323,980,000,000 baht. Money supply (May 1977) 42,440,000,000 baht. Cost of living (Bangkok; 1970 = 100; April 1977) 168.

Foreign Trade. (1976) Imports 73,178,000,000 baht; exports 60,890,000,000 baht. Import sources: Japan 32%; U.S. 13%; Saudi Arabia 8%; Qatar 6%; West Germany 5%. Export destinations: Japan 26%; The Netherlands 13%; U.S. 10%; Singapore 7%; Indonesia 5%; Hong Kong 5%. Main exports: rice 14%; tapioca 12%; sugar 11%; corn 9%; rubber 9%; tin 5%. Tourism (1975): visitors 1,180,000; gross receipts U.S. $220 million.

Transport and Communications. Roads (1975) 37,218 km. Motor vehicles in use (1975): passenger 329,900; commercial 249,700. Railways (1975): 3,767 km; traffic 5,700,000,000 passenger-km, freight 2,340,000,000 net ton-km. Air traffic (1976): 4,663,000,000 passenger-km; freight 130 million net ton-km. Shipping (1976): merchant vessels 100 gross tons and over 90; gross tonnage 194,993. Telephones (Dec. 1975) 312,000. Radio receivers (Dec. 1974) 5,111,000. Television receivers (Dec. 1974) 715,000.

Agriculture. Production (in 000; metric tons; 1976): rice 14,900; corn c. 2,700; sweet potatoes (1975) c. 334; sorghum 231; cassava (1975) 6,358; dry beans c. 338; soybeans 125; peanuts 169; sugar, raw value c. 1,630; pineapples c. 500; bananas c. 1,300; tobacco 48; rubber c. 400; cotton, lint c. 12; jute c. 9; kenaf 233; timber (cu m; 1975) 20,719; fish catch (1975) 1,370. Livestock (in 000; 1976): cattle c. 5,078; buffalo c. 5,869; pigs c. 5,224; chickens c. 68,215; ducks c. 7,500.

Industry. Production (in 000; metric tons; 1975): tin concentrates (metal content) 16; tungsten concentrates (oxide content) 2; lead concentrates (metal content) 1.4; manganese ore (metal content) 9; cement 3,959; petroleum products 7,356; electricity (kw-hr) c. 7,910,000.

maker. The junta lifted press controls and began recruiting technocrats as advisers to the government. The emergence of the military as a liberalizing influence was described by commentators as an "elegant paradox."

Three weeks after the coup, the military leaders announced an interim constitution, Thailand's 11th since absolute monarchy was abolished in 1932. They also announced a new government with General Kriangsak as prime minister. With 33 members, the Cabinet was the largest in Thailand's constitutional history. Admiral Sa-ngad became chairman of the National Policy Council with powers to recommend the removal of the prime minister. A permanent constitution and elections were envisaged before the end of 1979.

(T. J. S. GEORGE)

Theatre

Improving national economies benefited many theatres in 1977, though by no means all. Because the total grant from the government to the Arts Council of Great Britain (£41.2 million for 1977–78) was increased by only 14.4% while the rate of inflation was 21%, the council could not help out the National Theatre (NT) when unforeseen building delays caused a loss of £400,000 added to a revenue loss of £230,000. The NT's main troubles arose because the costly new complex (annual upkeep £1 million) was not ready for full occupancy until March 1977, when the experimental Cottesloe Theatre was first brought into use. After that 2,500 seats were filled to 90% capacity daily, excluding late-night shows and events staged on the forestage of the Lyttelton Theatre or the Olivier Theatre in the early evenings.

The financial threat to the Royal Shakespeare Company (RSC) was successfully met by a greater number of productions, foreign touring, filming, and transfers of successful plays to commercial theatres, and Trevor Nunn was thus able to open an experimental stage (the Warehouse) in London on the lines of Stratford's The Other Place. In August, 19 RSC plays could be seen at one time in six theatres (including two transfers), and the tryout season at Newcastle was highly successful. All in all, attendance reached a record figure of 500,000, while income from box-office and other sources came to just under £2 million. For the first time in years, the RSC had broken even.

On the darker side were the cutback in the Arts Council Building Fund and the withdrawal or curtailment of subsidies to worthy bodies such as the English Music Theatre (founded 30 years before as the English Opera Group by Benjamin Britten). In the U.K. outside of London several famous "touring theatres" faced sale or demolition or both. Approximately 50% of them, however, were expecting to be bought by the municipality or the Arts Council or both.

The actors' trade union, Equity, launched an "Arts in Danger" campaign. The government formed the privately funded "Theatre Trust," and a further move to ease the financial burden of the commercial theatre was the creation of the Association for Business Sponsorship of the Arts. New theatres, or converted motion picture houses, like the Astoria in the West End of London, were still being opened by private enterprise. A future home for the Theatre Museum was found in Covent Garden, and the British Theatre Institute began to function.

In France Michel d'Ornano, the new minister of culture, announced the creation of eight new regional dramatic centres in a year when the state had spent more than U.S. $170 million setting up the ultramodern Centre National d'Art et de Culture Georges Pompidou in Paris (see ARCHITECTURE; MUSEUMS). The five subsidized theatres in Paris flourished, though some 50 private theatres still felt the pinch; the new mayor of Paris, Jacques Chirac, was criticized for wishing to withdraw the grants from three of the city's small experimental companies and for cutting back the subsidy to the Théâtre National de Chaillot to some $3.5 million, thereby forcing it to forgo production and present visiting troupes only. The coming expiration of Jean-Louis Barrault's lease at the Théâtre d'Orsay and the government decision to convert it into an art museum posed serious new problems in light of the renewal of his mandate as director of the Theatre of the Nations, staged in Paris in the summer under his auspices.

In West Germany attempts to attract theatre audiences with a provocative repertoire led to political interference. A victim was Peter Ebert, opera director and head of the Wiesbaden Hessian State Theatre, who, accused of left-wing bias, moved to Glasgow as the Scottish Opera's new administrator. The annual "merry-go-round" of managers of West German theatres claimed a number of victims, among them Peter Stoltzenberg, adventurous head of the Bremen Theatre, and Hans Hollmann of Basel (Switzerland) and Peter Zadek of Bochum. Though leaving Sweden in 1976 in disgust after his battle with the tax authorities and settling in Munich, Ingmar Bergman promised to return in 1978 to finish rehearsals at Stockholm's Royal Dramatic Theatre of the Strindberg play he had been prevented from staging.

In connection with the Charter 77 movement for human rights, a number of Czechoslovak writers and directors were held in custody or jailed on charges of "antistate activities." Yuri Liubimov's Taganka Theatre in Moscow was allowed to visit France and to take part in the Paris Autumn Festival. Some dissident performers, directors, designers, and writers were encouraged to emigrate or were expelled from East Germany. The Swiss-born former Bertolt Brecht pupil, Benno Besson, left as head of the East Berlin People's Theatre. A victim of the political violence in Italy was the Parioli Theatre in Rome, which was burned down by right-wing extremists.

Great Britain and Ireland. Britain's NT came in for criticism, but its director, Sir Peter Hall (*see* BIOGRAPHY), was vindicated by the excellence and variety of the performances in its three constituent theatres and the booming attendances. For all that, the only award from the Society of West End Theatre (SWET) to the National went to Michael Bryant, as the actor of the year in a new play, for his authentic interpretation of Lenin in Robert Bolt's semidocumentary *State of Revolution*, staged at the Lyttelton by Christopher Morahan. Hall's biggest hits were Ben Jonson's *Volpone*, William Wycherley's *The Country Wife*, and Alan Ayckbourn's *Bedroom Farce*. Almost as worthy were Harley Granville Barker's *The Madras House* (director, William Gaskill); the first British production of a play by Ödön von Horváth, *Tales from the Vienna Woods* (director, Maximilian Schell, from Vienna); Sean O'Casey's *The Plough and the Stars* (starring Cyril Cusack); and Georges Feydeau's *The Lady from Maxim's* (director, Morahan). At the Cottesloe were seen Julian Mitchell's *Half-Life* with Sir John Gielgud, the unusual *Strawberry Fields* by resident writer Stephen Poliakoff, Bill Bryden's satirical *Old Movies*, and the medieval *The Passion*, performed in the round. The Lyttelton welcomed its first three foreign troupes, Roger Planchon's from Lyon, France, Peter Stein's from Berlin, and Nuria Espert's from Madrid.

The Warehouse, seating 100 in a converted rehearsal room, put on transfers from Stratford, such as Edward Bond's *Bingo*, a gripping two-hour version of *Macbeth* (director, Trevor Nunn) starring Ian McKellen and SWET-prizewinner Judi Dench, and new works by C. P. Taylor, Howard Barker, Barrie Keeffe, James Robson, and Bond. At the Aldwych Theatre the RSC transferred *King Lear*, with Donald Sinden, which won John Na-

pier the stage-design award; six other classical transfers there included Nunn's two hilarious winners, the SWET-prizewinning *The Comedy of Errors*, done as a musical, and Ben Jonson's *The Alchemist*. The new productions included Peter Nichols' *Privates on Parade*, which won three prizes, as the comedy of the year and for Denis Quilley's and Nigel Hawthorne's performances; Ibsen's *Pillars of the Community* (director, John Barton), for which Ian McKellen got the acting award; and the British premiere of Brecht's *The Days of the Commune*. Clifford Williams was voted director of the year for the West End (London commercial) transfer of the hilarious *Wild Oats* by John O'Keeffe. The other RSC West End success was Shaw's *Man and Superman*.

The production by the enterprising London-based touring company, the Joint Stock, of the scabrously provocative *A Thought in Three Parts* by U.S. playwright Wallace Shawn at the Institute of Contemporary Arts drew the fire of puritan objectors for its nude display, but in their no less revealing *A Mad World My Masters*, by Barrie Keeffe, and *Epsom Downs*, by Howard Barker, the audience's laughter was enough to prevent similar objections. Other plays by Keeffe, a social critic and Britain's most prolific writer of the year, were seen in many established and fringe theatres, notably at the National Youth Theatre's home.

Outstanding events outside London were the uproarious guest production of Gogol's *The Government Inspector* in Sheffield by Moscow's Oleg Tabakov, and the world premiere, set and staged by Philip Prowse, at Glasgow Citizens' Theatre, of Noel Coward's rediscovered, 50-year-old, outspoken *Semi-Monde*. The year at the Mermaid included Willy Russell's *Breezeblock Park*, which moved to the West End, and the English premiere of Henry de Montherlant's *La Ville dont le prince est*

© OSSIA TRILLING

Alexis Minotis played the title role in his own production of Sophocles' "Philoctetes" at the 1977 Epidaurus Festival of the Greek National Theatre.

un enfant (director, Sir Bernard Miles), which, as *The Fire That Consumes*, won the Play of the Year award.

Leading productions of the purely commercial season included a revival of Sir Terence Rattigan's (*see* OBITUARIES) *Separate Tables* and the stage version of his radio play based on the notorious Rattenbury murder trial, *Cause Célèbre*, with Glynis Johns; Ayckbourn's acid *Just Between Ourselves*; *The Kingfisher*, a study of old love by William Douglas Home; stunning revivals of *Hedda Gabler*, with Janet Suzman, *The Apple Cart* (from the Chichester Festival), with Keith Michell, *Rosmersholm*, with Claire Bloom, and Lionel Bart's *Oliver!*; the farcical comedy *Shut Your Eyes and Think of England* by John Chapman and Anthony Marriott; Eduardo De Filippo's *Filumena*, with Joan Plowright; Alan Bennett's *The Old Country*, with Sir Alec Guinness; and Hugh Whitemore's biographical *Stevie*, with Glenda Jackson, which won Mona Washbourne the supporting actress award. Other British musicals were *Fire Angel*, a rock version of Shakespeare's *The Merchant of Venice*; the spectacular *Dean*, based on the life of James Dean; and *Elvis*, based on the Presley musical canon.

The Dublin Abbey Theatre, with two stages and a £1,250,000 subsidy, played to 75% capacity with new plays by Thomas Kilroy and Brian Friel, the Irish premiere of O'Casey's anticlerical *Cock-a-Doodle Dandy*, and Tom Stoppard's *Travesties*, with Desmond Cave as Joyce. Brian Friel's *Living Quarters*, with Ray McAnally as a modern Agamemnon, was much praised at the Dublin Festival alongside Peter Sheridan's critique of the prison system, *Liberty Suite*, and Kilroy's *Talbot's Box*, about the 19th-century saintly eccentric Matt Talbot. Belfast's Lyric Players put on *Black Man's Country*, a drama of Africa by Desmond Forristal, and Edna O'Brien's drama of a vicious family reunion, *The Gathering*.

France. Noteworthy at the Comédie Française's two theatres were Terry Hands's first try with a French play, Corneille's *Le Cid*, with Ludmila Mikael as Chimène; Jacques Rosner's new *Figaro*, with Alain Pralon; and *The Bacchae*, directed by Michel Cacoyannis. The Théâtre de l'Est Parisien featured Guy Rétoré's productions of *Saint Joan of the Stockyards* and Paul Claudel's *The Hostage*, staged in its entirety for the first time, Schiller's *The Brigands*, and Rezvani's epic drama of Catherine II of Russia, *La Mante Polaire* (director, Jorge Lavelli), with sumptuous decor by Ezio Frigerio and starring Maria Casarès. The Nouveau Carré presented *The Lady from the Sea* with Silvia Monfort, and at Barrault's Théâtre d'Orsay there were Villiers de l'Isle Adam's U.S.-centennial drama of 1876, *The New World*, Yukio Mishima's *Madame de Sade*, and Marguerite Duras' riveting childhood recollection drama *Eden Cinema* (director, Claude Régy), with Madeleine Renaud.

New dramas of merit were *The War of the Swimming Pools*, by Yves Navarre, Gérard Oury's *Stop Your Cinema*, Roland Dubillard's absurdist *The Steam Bath*, Yves Jamiaque's science-fiction thriller *The Vertical Journey*, Gabriel Arout's wartime *Yes*, Antoine Vitez' multimedia adaptation of the Charles Perrault tale of *Griselda*, Jean Anouilh's

latest pseudo-historical burlesque *Long Live Henry IV*, with Daniel Ivernel, and Françoise Dorin's seventh consecutive box-office hit, *If You're Cute, You Must be Dumb*. There were of course revivals and other foreign importations. The adventurous Odin Theatre from Denmark appeared both at the Paris Autumn and the Fourth Rennes Festival of Café-Théâtre and Onward Theatre.

Switzerland, Germany, Austria, Belgium. Harry Buckwitz' last season at the Zürich Schauspielhaus featured Stoppard's *Travesties* (director, Leopold Lindtberg), the world premiere of Friedrich Dürrenmatt's macabre comedy *Time Gained* (director, Kazimierz Dejmek, from Poland) about a dying dictator, and Buckwitz' farewell production of *The Dreyfus Affair*. Basel City Theatre staged the world premiere of *Nostalgia*, a drama of frustration by Austrian writer Gerhard Rothe. In West Berlin Peter Stein built the Forest of Arden in a remote disused film studio for a fanciful version of *As You Like It*. Other highlights of the year there were *A Doll's House* (director, Rudolf Noelte) with Cordula Trantow and *Hedda Gabler* (director, Niels-Peter Rudolph) with Gisela Stein. In East Berlin Manfred Wekwerth began a promising new regime at the Berliner Ensemble by staging Brecht's *The Tutor*, with Hans-Peter Minetti.

Outstanding productions elsewhere were Peter Zadek's updated *Hedda Gabler*, with Rosl Zech, and a *Hamlet* in a disused factory in Bochum; Ingmar Bergman's West German debut, in Munich, with Strindberg's *A Dream Play*; Strehler's first German production in 20 years, *The Good Woman of Setzuan*, with Andrea Jonasson, in Hamburg; Otomar Krejča's first Düsseldorf season, with *Hamlet* and Chekhov's *Platanov*; and *Faust*, parts 1 and 2, in Stuttgart, staged by Claus Peymann in Achim Freyer's splendid sets.

The Vienna Burgtheater presented Otto Schenk's *Juno and the Paycock* and Lindtberg's double bill of Gotthold Lessing's *The Jews* and Max Frisch's *Biedermann and the Firebugs*. The Belgian National Theatre's annual crop included *Poor Assassin* by Pavel Kohout of Czechoslovakia and a challengingly new view of a corrupt Berlin of the 1920s in Henri Ronse's version of Brecht's *The Threepenny Opera*.

Italy, Greece, Scandinavia, Eastern Europe. The new manager of Rome's Teatro Eliseo, Romolo Valli, appeared in Pirandello's *Henry IV* (director, Giorgio De Lullo), and Giancarlo Sbragia, heading the new Gli Associati ensemble, played the title role in a new play by Diego Fabbri about the poet Gioacchino Belli. Other productions included Ruth Wolff's *Abdication* (director, Giuseppe Patroni Griffi), an adaptation of *Antony and Cleopatra*, with Giorgio Albertazzi and Anna Proclemer (director, Roberto Guicciardini), and Giovanni Testori's *Oedipus*, with Franco Parenti. The wildly applauded production of *Philoctetes* at the Epidaurus Festival in Greece by Alexis Minotis, who played the protagonist, marked the Greek actor's welcome return as head of his old National Theatre after years of self-exile.

At Stockholm's Royal Dramatic Theatre Alf Sjöberg staged *Erik XIV* with Tommy Berggren, and Lars Göran Carlsson produced *The Caucasian Chalk*

Circle, with its action laid in a Swedish factory. A musical version, with puppets, of *A Dream Play*, using the original title of *The Growing Castle*, was revived at the City Theatre. At Oslo's National Theatre Swedish guest-director Eva Sköld staged Georg Bücher's *Danton's Death*, which Ralf Långbacka also chose as his farewell production at the Turku City Theatre in Finland. At the Helsinki National Theatre the highlights were Juhani Peltonen's historical *Toward the Heart of the World* and Hella Wuolijoki's *The Young Woman of Niskavuori*.

Moscow theatre highlights included Liubimov's adaptation at the Taganka of Mikhail Bulgakov's 1930s novel of diabolism, *The Master and Margarita*; Aleksey Arbuzov's resistance drama, *Expectations*, at the Vakhtangov; Aleksandr Gelman's *Feed-Back*, about the scientific revolution, at two theatres; Ion Drutze's Moldavian village drama, *Holy of Holies*, at the Soviet Army; and Anatoli Efros' production of *A Month in the Country* at the Malaya Bronnaya. The main events in Poland were Jerzy Jarocki's prizewinning production of *King Lear* at the Warsaw Dramatic, with Gustaw Holoubek; Erwin Axer's revival of *Kordian* at the Contemporary; and, at the Krakow Stary, Andrzej Wajda's version of *The Idiot*. Renamed the People's Theatre after joining with the Deryné Touring Theatre, the 25th Theatre staged Endre Fejez's Pirandellian *The Marriage of Margit Czerepes*, with Mari Töröcsik, in Budapest, where new plays by Istvan Örkeny, Gyula Hernádi, and Tibor Gyurkovics were also seen. The Belgrade Atelje 212 put on a historical first play by Zorica Jevremović, called *Ah Serbia, Nowhere Is There Respite*. Liviu Ciulei staged *The Seagull* at the Bucharest Bulandra.

(OSSIA TRILLING)

U.S. and Canada. In 1977 theatregoers became increasingly aware of a whole new "generation" of promising young U.S. playwrights. The names most often mentioned were David Mamet, Michael Cristofer, Albert Innaurato, and Christopher Durang.

American Buffalo, Mamet's major work, opened on Broadway in February after previous productions in Chicago and off-off-Broadway. Set in a junk shop and centred on an abortive burglary, it dealt with the conflict between the ethic of friendship and the ethic of business; with the relationship between the corruption of feeling and behaviour in general, and the corruption of language in particular; and with the banality of evil. It was easily the most controversial play of the year, attacked for the obscenity of its language and for its lack of overt action; many people simply could not grasp what was going on in it. It won the New York Drama Critics Circle Award as the best U.S. play of 1976–77, but in spite of taut staging by Ulu Grosbard and a powerful performance by Robert Duvall it did not run long.

Mamet was nothing if not prolific. In 1977 his double bill, *Sexual Perversity in Chicago* and *Duck Variations*, finished its run off-Broadway and went on tour. His children's play, *The Revenge of the Space Pandas—or—Binky Rudich and the Two-Speed Clock*, was produced off-off-Broadway and in Chicago. *Reunion* was produced by the Yale Repertory Theatre in New Haven, Conn., after a 1976

MARTHA SWOPE

Frank Langella was a stunning and compelling Dracula in the latest production of the venerable melodrama in New York at the Martin Beck Theatre. Lucy was played by Ann Sachs.

production in Chicago. Three other plays, *The Water Engine* (about an inventor), *A Life in the Theatre* (about actors), and *The Woods* (a love story), were staged in 1977 in Chicago, Mamet's home town. Another production of *A Life in the Theatre*, starring Ellis Rabb, was favourably received off-Broadway, and *The Water Engine* was produced by Joseph Papp at the New York Shakespeare Festival Public Theater's new Cabaret.

The Shadow Box by Michael Cristofer concerned three terminal cancer patients. It was first produced at the Mark Taper Forum in Los Angeles in 1975; with the same director (Gordon Davidson) and two of the same actors, it came to the Long Wharf Theatre in New Haven in January 1977, and then, in March, traveled to Broadway. It won the Tony Award as the best play of 1976–77 and the 1977 Pulitzer Prize.

Albert Innaurato's fiercely grotesque one-act, *The Transfiguration of Benno Blimpie*, was about the sufferings of a sensitive, intelligent young man weighing 500 lb. It was produced off-off-Broadway in 1976 and given a new production starring James Coco that opened off-Broadway in March 1977. Innaurato's comedy *Gemini*, in which a young Italian-American comes home from Harvard University to a working-class neighbourhood in Philadelphia, went from off-off-Broadway (December 1976) to the PAF Playhouse in Huntington, N.Y. (January 1977), to the Circle Repertory Theatre off-Broadway (March) to Broadway (May). Another comedy, *Ulysses in Traction*, opened at the Circle Rep in December 1977.

Christopher Durang wrote *A History of the American Film*, which comments satirically on U.S. images and attitudes through a montage of film parodies, from D. W. Griffith to contemporary pornography. In the spring of 1977 it was produced almost simultaneously by the Hartford Stage Company (Hartford, Conn.), the Mark Taper Forum, and the Arena Stage (Washington, D.C.); it was scheduled for Broadway in 1978.

None of these four playwrights really belonged to Broadway; all of them emerged through off-off-Broadway or regional theatres, and none had yet had a big commercial success. But even without them the U.S. commercial theatre continued its resurgence. For both Broadway and "the road," gross receipts for the 1976–77 season were the highest on record, according to *Variety*, the theatrical trade paper. Nor was this merely the result of inflation, as total attendance at Broadway theatres was 8,815,995, up 22.57% from 1975–76. There were more Broadway openings (63) than in any season since 1968–69.

Among the Broadway hits of 1977, the biggest splash was made by *Annie*, a sentimental, nostalgic, yet razzle-dazzle musical, based on the "Little Orphan Annie" comic strip. It won the Tony and the Critics Circle awards as best musical. *I Love My Wife*, a small-scale musical about wife-swapping in Trenton, N.J., was also popular. *The Act*, extensively revamped on the road, was a vehicle for Liza Minnelli, thinly disguised as a musical. It set a Broadway record with its top price of $25 on Saturday nights and $35 for opening night and New Year's Eve.

Among other Broadway hits were *Golda* by William Gibson, in which Anne Bancroft played former Israeli prime minister Golda Meir, and *Chapter Two*, Neil Simon's play about his own second marriage. The saddest of failures was *The Merchant* by Arnold Wesker; Zero Mostel, who was to have played the title role, died in Philadelphia during the tryout tour (*see* OBITUARIES).

Joseph Papp, producer of the New York Shakespeare Festival, continued, for a while, his policy of matching avant-garde directors with classical plays at the Vivian Beaumont Theatre in Lincoln Center. Andrei Serban's antinaturalistic production of Chekhov's *The Cherry Orchard*, played with sweeping movements against wide white horizons, was favourably received. Then in June, Papp suddenly announced that when *The Cherry Orchard* completed its run, the Shakespeare Festival would withdraw from Lincoln Center. Thus, the Vivian Beaumont, designed to be the home of a great U.S. repertory company, went dark, and by the end of 1977 the Lincoln Center authorities had not yet figured out how to reopen it.

Meanwhile, at his own Public Theater, Papp was not inactive. With the Manhattan Theatre Club he co-produced *Ashes* by the British playwright David Rudkin. He presented two plays by John Guare: *Marco Polo Sings a Solo* and (in cooperation with the Academy Festival Theatre, Lake Forest, Ill.) *Landscape of the Body*. In *Miss Margarida's Way* by a young Brazilian, Roberto Athayde, Estelle Parsons played a schoolteacher and the audience played her class; a personal triumph for Parsons, it was transferred to Broadway. The new Public Theater Cabaret opened with an adaptation of Martin Buber's *Tales of the Hasidim*.

Among the new theatrical organizations that began operations in 1977 were the Alaska Repertory Theatre in Anchorage, the BAM Theatre Company at the Brooklyn Academy of Music in New York, and the Massachusetts Center Repertory Company in Boston. On the other hand, the American Shakespeare Theatre at Stratford, Conn., ran out of money and canceled its 1977 season. New U.S. plays produced in regional theatres included *Counting the Ways* and *Listening*, a double bill by Edward Albee (Hartford Stage Company), and *Angel City* by Sam Shepard (McCarter Theatre, Princeton, N.J., and Mark Taper Forum after a previous production at the Magic Theatre in San Francisco).

In Canada artistic directors of theatres played musical chairs in 1977. Jean Gascon, formerly of the Stratford Festival, took over as director of theatre at the bilingual National Arts Center in Ottawa, with John Wood as director of English-speaking theatre. John Neville was to replace John Wood at the Neptune Theatre in Halifax, and Peter Coe would succeed John Neville at the Citadel Theatre, Edmonton. Arif Hasnain became the new artistic director of the Manitoba Theatre Centre in Winnipeg. Paxton Whitehead resigned as artistic director of the Shaw Festival at Niagara-on-the-Lake, Ont.; Richard Kirschner, who had been executive director, became producer, with artistic as well as administrative responsibilities.

Among the year's new plays was *Les Canadiens* by Rick Salutin, in which the recent history of Canada was interwoven with the fortunes of the Montreal Canadiens ice hockey team. Written in English and produced in Montreal and Toronto, it took on special significance from the separatist shadows that loomed over Quebec.

(JULIUS L. NOVICK)

See also Dance; Music.

[622]

The comic strip characters Little Orphan Annie, Daddy Warbucks, and Sandy came to the Broadway stage in a musical "Annie" in April.

MARTHA SWOPE

Theology:
see Religion

Timber:
see Industrial Review

Tobacco:
see Industrial Review

Tobogganing:
see Winter Sports

Togo

A West African republic on the Bight of Benin, Togo is bordered by Ghana, Upper Volta, and Benin. Area: 56,785 sq km (21,925 sq mi). Pop. (1976 est.): 2,283,000. Cap. and largest city: Lomé (pop., 1976 est., 229,400). Language: French (official). Religion: animist; Muslim and Christian minorities. President in 1977, Gen. Gnassingbe Eyadema.

As a result of a government reshuffle on Jan. 31, 1977, Gen. Gnassingbe Eyadema's Cabinet became entirely civilian. Yao Kunale Eklo was replaced as minister of the interior by Kpotivi Laclé, one of Eyadema's closest followers, who was generally considered more liberal and less of a rabble-rouser than his predecessor. Well aware of the desire of the members of the Ewe tribe in Ghana to reunite with their brothers in Togo, Eyadema agitated for a "return to natural frontiers"—that is, for Ghana's "return" of the region east of the Volta River to Togo. To strengthen Togo's forces, five Alpha jet fighters were purchased from France in May. Although relations with Ghana were necessarily cool, Togo cooperated closely with Nigeria and was active in the Economic Community of West African States.

The Council of Ministers of the Organization of African Unity met in Lomé in February to confer about southern Africa. Eyadema attended the fourth Franco-African summit conference at Dakar, Senegal, in April, and visited France and West Germany privately in September. A plot to kill Eyadema, supposedly involving British mercenaries, was uncovered by the British Foreign and Commonwealth Office in October.

(PHILIPPE DECRAENE)

TOGO

Education. (1975–76) Primary, pupils 362,895, teachers 6,080; secondary, pupils 59,162, teachers 1,358; vocational, pupils 5,118, teachers 251; teacher training, students 310, teachers 25; higher, students 2,353, teaching staff 236.

Finance. Monetary unit: CFA franc, with (Sept. 19, 1977) a par value of CFA Fr 50 to the French franc (free rate of CFA Fr 246.50 = U.S. $1; CFA Fr 429.50 = £1 sterling). Budget (1976 est.) balanced at CFA Fr 50,019,000,000.

Foreign Trade. (1975) Imports CFA Fr 37,270,000,000; exports CFA Fr 26,962,000,000. Import sources: France 35%; U.K. 11%; West Germany 11%; The Netherlands 7%; U.S. 5%. Export destinations: France 39%; The Netherlands 32%; West Germany 10%; Belgium-Luxembourg 6%. Main exports: phosphates 65%; cocoa 17%; coffee 7%.

Tonga

An independent monarchy and member of the Commonwealth of Nations, Tonga is an island group in the Pacific Ocean east of Fiji. Area: 748 sq km (289 sq mi). Pop. (1976): 90,100. Cap.: Nukualofa (pop., 1976, 18,400). Language: English and Tongan. Religion: Christian. King, Taufa'ahau Tupou IV; prime minister in 1977, Prince Tu'ipelehake.

Low prices for agricultural commodities, declining production in some sectors, limited potential

TONGA

Education. (1974) Primary, pupils 16,932, teachers 668; secondary, pupils 10,420, teachers 474; vocational, pupils 230; teacher training, students 110, teachers (1973) 12.

Finance and Trade. Monetary unit: pa'anga, with (Sept. 19, 1977) a free rate of 0.88 pa'anga to U.S. $1 (1.53 pa'anga = £1 sterling). Budget (1975–76 est.): revenue 5,257,000 pa'anga; expenditure 5,897,000 pa'anga. Foreign trade (1976): imports 11,655,000 pa'anga; exports 3,348,000 pa'anga. Import sources: New Zealand 40%; Australia 22%; U.K. 11%; Japan 6%; Fiji 5%. Export destinations: The Netherlands 30%; Australia 29%; New Zealand 19%; West Germany 11%; U.K. 6%; Fiji 5%. Main exports: copra 54%; desiccated coconut 11%; bananas 8%; kava 6%; watermelons 5%.

Togo

Tonga

for development because of sparse resources, and one of the fastest population growth rates in the world all combined in 1977 to give Tonga a bleak economic outlook. Because the government was facing liquidity problems in the latter part of 1976, the pa'anga was devalued 6% against the Australian dollar; back pay for civil servants was deferred; and severe economy measures were introduced into all government departments. Earnings from tourism increased, but those from remittances were cut because New Zealand reduced immigration from the Pacific Islands and repatriated many Tongans who had overstayed their permits. Random police checks on Polynesians in New Zealand caused a political furor and generated Tongan hostility. In July 1977 Tonga suffered a serious earthquake. Several buildings were destroyed, but there was no loss of life.

Together with other South Pacific Forum countries, Tonga decided to declare a 200-mi offshore economic zone in 1978 and to share the services of a common agency for policing and controlling the use of resources. Although suggestions of a Soviet fishing base faded, Soviet envoys visited Tonga for talks on trading arrangements. On her Silver Jubilee visit to Tonga in February, Queen Elizabeth II installed King Taufa'ahau Tupou IV as a knight Grand Cross of St. Michael and St. George.

(BARRIE MACDONALD)

Track and Field Sports

Inauguration of the first non-Olympic worldwide competition highlighted the 1977 track and field season. The World Cup proved to be a popular innovation in a year during which world records fell in a dozen standard events, seven men's and five women's.

Men's International Competition. Before 1977 track and field athletes from all over the world competed together only in the quadrennial Olympic Games, the last being in Montreal in 1976. The World Cup contest was designed to meet the need for more frequent competition and was scheduled to be held every other year. Unlike the Olympic Games, to which every country is entitled to send at least one athlete in each event, the World Cup allowed a maximum of eight participants in each event. Each competitor belonged to a team, thereby introducing team scoring to worldwide competition. Three teams came from Europe: East

Tourism:
see Industrial Review

Toys:
see Games and Toys

Germany and West Germany as the first and second finishers in the biennial European Cup and an all-star squad picked from among the remaining countries. The Americas had two entries, the United States and an all-star team, and there were groups from Africa, Asia, and Oceania. All Olympic events except the marathon, walk, and decathlon were included and scored with nine points for first, seven for second, six for third, and so on.

Held at Düsseldorf, West Germany, on September 2–4, the first World Cup produced a dramatic confrontation between the U.S., demonstrably the leader in track and field from the beginning of international competition, and East Germany, the fast-rising challenger. East Germany squeezed out a narrow win, 127–120, as U.S. hopes were shattered in the final event. Trailing by two points and favoured to win the 1,600-m relay, with East Germany expected to place no better than fourth, the U.S. was leading the relay in its final stages. Maxie Parks, running the final lap, was ahead when he suddenly pulled up lame and fell to the ground, out of the race. That accident resulted in no points in the relay and a second-place finish for the U.S. West Germany was third with 112 points, trailed by Europe III with 111, America II with 92, Africa 78, Oceania 48, and Asia 44.

In the other relay, the 400 m, the U.S. put together its usual group of swift sprinters and produced the lone world record of the meet. Bill Collins, Steve Riddick, Cliff Wiley, and Steve Williams covered the distance in 38.03 sec, knocking 0.16 sec off the mark set by another U.S. four-

some in the 1972 Olympics. Williams also won the 100 m to become one of three runners to score double victories.

A double triumph was a familiar achievement for Cuba's Alberto Juantorena, who captured the 400-m and 800-m runs just as he had a year earlier in the Olympics. Both races were memorable. In the 400 m, the big Cuban was the key figure in the most controversial action of the Cup. He got off to a very slow start and finished only third in an event he was supposed to win. But he angrily maintained that he had not heard the starting gun, and officials eventually allowed his protest and ordered the race rerun the next day. On that occasion Juantorena won handily in 45.36 sec. Earlier, Juantorena had triumphed in the hardest fought of all the races, barely edging Mike Boit of Kenya, 1 min 44.0 sec to 1 min 44.1 sec, in an 800-m struggle that was not decided until the final 10 m.

The other double winner was tiny Miruts Yifter of Ethiopia, a hard-luck athlete who finally won in big-time competition. Yifter had, among other things, stopped running a lap too soon while

A new world record in the women's 10,000-metre run was established June 9 by Peg Neppel of Iowa at the national AAU outdoor track-and-field championships in Los Angeles. She ran the distance in 33 minutes 15.1 seconds.

UPI COMPIX

Table I. World 1977 Outdoor Records—Men

Event	Competitor, country, date	Performance
800 m	Alberto Juantorena, Cuba, August 21	1 min 43.4 sec
5,000 m	Dick Quax, New Zealand, July 5	13 min 12.9 sec
10,000 m	Samson Kimombwa, Kenya, June 30	27 min 30.5 sec
110-m hurdles	Alejandro Casanas, Cuba, August 21	13.21 sec
400-m hurdles	Edwin Moses, U.S., June 11	47.45 sec
400-m relay	United States, September 3	38.03 sec
High jump	Vladimir Yashchenko, U.S.S.R., July 3	2.33 m (7 ft 7¾ in)
Nonstandard events		
20,000-m walk	Daniel Bautista, Mexico, May 14	1 hr 23 min 32 sec
50,000-m walk	Enrique Vera, Mexico, May 16	3 hr 56 min 39 sec
800-m relay	Arizona State University, April 30	1 min 21.4 sec
6,000-m relay	West Germany, August 17	14 min 38.8 sec

Table II. World 1977 Outdoor Records—Women

Event	Competitor, country, date	Performance
100 m	Marlies Oelsner, East Germany, July 1	10.88 sec
High jump	Rosemarie Ackermann, East Germany, July 3	1.96 m (6 ft 5¼ in)
	Rosemarie Ackermann, East Germany, August 14	1.97 m (6 ft 5½ in)
	Rosemarie Ackermann, East Germany, August 26	2.00 m (6 ft 6¾ in)
Shot put	Helena Fibingerova, Czechoslovakia, August 20	22.32 m (73 ft 2¾ in)
Javelin	Kate Schmidt, U.S., September 11	69.32 m (227 ft 5 in)
Pentathlon	Nadyezhda Tkachenko, U.S.S.R., September 18	4,839 pt
Nonstandard events		
1 mi	Natalia Maracescu, Romania, May 21	4 min 23.8 sec
5,000 m	Natalia Maracescu, Romania, March 15	15 min 41.4 sec
	Jan Merrill, U.S., July 6	15 min 37.0 sec
10,000 m	Loa Olofsson, Denmark, March 19	33 min 34.2 sec
	Peg Neppel, U.S., June 9	33 min 15.1 sec
Marathon*	Chantal Langlace, France, May 1	2 hr 35 min 15 sec
	Christa Vahlensieck, West Germany, September 10	2 hr 34 min 48 sec
400-m hurdles	Tatyana Storosheva, U.S.S.R., June 26	55.74 sec
	Karin Rossley, East Germany, August 13	55.63 sec
800-m relay	U.K., August 20	1 min 31.6 sec

*World best; no official record

Vladimir Yashchenko of the Soviet Union cleared 2.33 metres (7 feet 7-3/4 inches) to set a world high jump record July 3 in the U.S. *v.* U.S.S.R. Juniors competition in Richmond, Va.

ahead in the 1971 U.S. *v.* Africa 5,000-m race and also had reported to the wrong gate at the 1972 Olympic Games. This time there were no mistakes as his justly famed finish gave him runaway wins, first in the 10,000 m, in 28 min 32.3 sec, and then, two days later, in the 5,000 m, in 13 min 13.8 sec.

The best individual performance of the Cup was achieved by Edwin Moses of the U.S., who won the 400-m hurdles in 47.58 sec, the second fastest time ever. On June 11 he had broken his own world mark by running 47.45 sec at Los Angeles. Juantorena also achieved a new international record earlier in the year, bettering his own standard when he raced 800 m in 1 min 43.4 sec at Sofia, Bulg., to win the World University Games on August 21. Records also fell in the two longest runs, the 5,000 m and 10,000 m. New Zealand's Dick Quax, who missed the 5,000-m record by only 0.1 sec in 1976, bettered it by the same slim margin in 1977. He ran the race in 13 min 12.9 sec at Stockholm, Sweden, on July 5. The 10,000-m record of 27 min 30.5 sec was a surprising triumph for Samson Kimombwa of Kenya on June 30 at Helsinki, Fin. Alejandro Casanas gave Cuba its second world record holder when he sped over the 110-m hurdles in 13.21 sec at Sofia on August 21. The lone field event record was also the biggest surprise of the season as little-known Vladimir Yashchenko of the Soviet Union, just 18 years old, cleared 2.33 m (7ft 7¾ in) in the high jump.

Next to the World Cup, the most important international competition of the year was the European Cup, contested at Helsinki August 13–14. The usually spirited contest was further enlivened because the meet served as the qualifying test for the World Cup. East Germany won this meet too, and more handily, scoring 123 points to 110 for West Germany, 99 for the U.S.S.R., 93 for Great Britain, 91 for Poland, 82 for Finland, 68 for France, and 52 for Italy. The European Cup decathlon championships, held at Lille, France, on September 17–18, produced both team and individual winners for the Soviet Union. The U.S.S.R. outscored West Germany, 24,303 points to 24,049, while Aleksandr Grebenyuk was the

individual champion with 8,252 points. Indoors, the European Championships were highlighted by the world record of Thomas Munkelt of East Germany, who ran the 60-m hurdles in 7.62 sec.

Women's International Competition. East Germany's fortunes were reversed in the women's competition for the World Cup. Strongly favoured to win, the East Germans lost form on the final day, dropping into second behind the European all-star aggregation, 107–102. The U.S.S.R. had 89, the U.S. 59, America II 55, Oceania 45, Africa 31, and Asia 29. The leading performer was veteran Irena Szewinska of Poland, who had won the 400 m in the 1976 Olympic Games. In the World Cup she won the 200 m handily in 22.72 sec, won the 400 m in 49.52 sec, the second fastest time ever, and ran a relay leg in 49.9 sec for the second-place Europe all-star quartet. On the field, the top performance was by East Germany's peerless high jumper, Rosemarie Ackermann. The Olympic champion and world record holder jumped 1.98 m (6 ft 6 in), the second best performance ever.

Ackermann, who jumped straddle style rather than the more widely used flop, was the outstanding woman athlete of the season. Competing in only six meets, she broke the world mark three times. She jumped 1.96 m (6 ft 5¼ in) in July and 1.97 m (6 ft 5½ in) and 2.00 m (6 ft 6¾ in) in August.

Perhaps the biggest surprise among the world record breakers was Kate Schmidt of the United States. Third in the last two Olympic javelin contests, Schmidt was not having a particularly good year until after the World Cup, where she finished fourth. Suddenly, at Fürth, West Germany, on September 11, she hurled the javelin 69.32 m (227 ft 5 in). It was the first international record by an American woman since 1968. The shot put standard fell to Helena Fibingerova of Czechoslovakia, who reached 22.32 m (73 ft 2¾ in) in mid-August. The women's 100-m record dipped under 11 sec for the first time when Marlies Oelsner of East Germany sprinted to a 10.88-sec clocking on July 1. Because the pentathlon was a new event, the 800-m run having been substituted for the 200-m dash, records were set several times. The best score of the year, and the new world record, was 4,839 points achieved by Nadyezhda Tkachenko of the Soviet Union in September.

New rules resulted in fewer records in the running events than might have been expected. For men and women both, all events measured in units other than metres, except for the mile run, were eliminated from consideration as world records. Another new rule required that all events of 400 m or less must be timed automatically in order to be accepted as world marks.

East Germany's strong team, which easily dominated the 1976 Olympic Games, was an overwhelming winner of the European Cup. Led by world records from Ackermann (1.97 m) and Karin Rossley (55.63 sec for the 400-m hurdles), East Germany piled up 114 points to 93 for the Soviet Union and 67 each for Great Britain and West Germany.

In the Pacific Conference Games, held in December in Canberra, host country Australia won 17 gold medals; the U.S. was runner-up with 10. Denise Robertson of Australia won four individual golds, for the 100 m and 200 m and as a member of Australia's 400-m and 1,600-m relay teams.

Indoors, there were two world marks in the European Championships. Marita Koch of East Germany covered 400 m in 51.14 sec while Jane Colebrook of Great Britain ran 800 m in 2 min 1.1 sec. Elsewhere indoors, Ackermann jumped 1.95 m (6 ft 4¾ in) and Fibingerova put the shot 22.50 m (73 ft 9¾ in), both all-time international bests.

U.S. Competition. World record production was at a low ebb for the U.S. men. Only Moses, the national 400-m relay team, and Arizona State University were able to put their names on the current list. Arizona State's mark came in the seldom-contested 800-m relay, which was run in 1 min 21.4 sec at the Penn Relays in Philadelphia on April 30. Gary Burl, Tony Darden, Gerald Burl, and Herman Frazier carried the baton.

Several U.S. records were set, with the 3,000-m steeplechase and 5,000-m run marks falling twice each. George Malley of Penn State ran the steeplechase in 8 min 22.5 sec at Los Angeles on June 11 but lost the record to Henry Marsh of Brigham Young, who completed the event in 8 min 21.6 sec at Stockholm on July 5. Veteran Marty Liquori ran 5,000 m in 13 min 16 sec at Zürich, Switz., on August 21 and in 13 min 15.1 sec in the World Cup, finishing second in the latter race. In a notable performance at Boston on August 9, Bill Rodgers, U.S. record holder in the marathon, set four national marks. He covered 12 mi 1,351 yd in 1 hr and was timed in 43 min 39.8 sec for 15,000 m, 46 min 35.8 sec for 10 mi, and 58 min 15 sec for 20,000 m. The final mark was 15 min 9.4 sec in the 6,000-m relay set by a University of Tennessee team composed of John Wright, Keith Young, Sam James, and Dave Lapp.

Aside from the World Cup, the U.S. won most of its international competitions. The national team beat Italy 127–94; the U.K. 135–86; West Germany 118–104; and lost to the Soviet Union 118–105. The U.S. won the decathlon team match with the Soviets 46,724 to 46,235, as Fred Dixon had the highest score of the year, 8,393 points.

National Collegiate Athletic Association titles were won by Arizona State in Division I, Hayward State of California in Division II, and Southern University of New Orleans in Division III. Jackson State of Mississippi captured the National Association of Intercollegiate Athletics title, and the University of Kansas won the U.S. Track and Field Federation (USTFF) meet. U.S. juniors beat the Soviet juniors, 135–96, at Richmond, Va., on July 2–3.

U.S. women's records fell more rapidly than did the men's. In addition to Schmidt's world javelin mark there were the following national standards: 200 m, 22.62 sec by Evelyn Ashford of UCLA, Los Angeles, June 10; 1 mi, 4 min 28.2 sec by Francie Larrieu-Lutz, Pacific Coast Club, Mainz, West Germany, June 28; 3,000 m, 8 min 46.6 sec by Jan Merrill, Age Group Athletic Association, Düsseldorf, September 4; 5,000 m, 15 min 37.0 sec, Merrill, Ingelheim, West Germany, July 6; 100-m hurdles, 13.24 sec, Jane Frederick, Los Angeles Track Club, Sofia, August 19; 400-m hurdles, 56.61 sec, Mary Ayers, Prairie View, Los Angeles, June 11; marathon, 2 hr 37 min 57 sec, Kim Merritt, Wisconsin/Parkside, Eugene, Ore., September 11; discus, 57.04 m (187 ft 2 in), Lynne Winbigler, Oregon Track Club, Los Angeles, June 10; pentathlon, 4,625 points, Frederick, Sofia, August 20.

In team competition, the U.S. women defeated Italy 85–61 but lost to West Germany 84–61 and to the Soviet Union 89–66. The junior team beat the U.S.S.R. 79–67, but the Soviets won the pentathlon match and the indoor meet 61–59. UCLA won the Association of Intercollegiate Athletics for Women title, while Tennessee State took the USTFF championships. (BERT NELSON)

[452.B.3.b]

Transportation

The continued gradual recovery of the world economy in 1977 led to a slow growth in demand for transportation. This, coupled with higher than average inflation rates, meant that a growing number of countries were spending 20% of their gross national product on transportation or were fast approaching that figure. In contrast to 1974 and 1975, the inflation of transport costs resulted not so much from higher fuel prices as from higher costs of labour and materials such as steel.

As the near panic that followed the oil crisis subsided, governments came to realize that long-term programs for energy efficiency/conservation

World Total International and Domestic Air Traffic

	Passengers		Passenger-km		Freight (metric ton-km)		Total (metric ton-km)	
Year	In 000,000	Annual increase (%)	In 000,000	Annual increase (%)	In 000,000	Annual increase (%)	In 000,000	Annual increase (%)
1972	450	9.6	560,000	13.4	15,020	13.6	68,160	12.7
1973	489	8.7	619,000	10.4	17,540	16.8	75,810	11.2
1974	514	5.1	654,000	5.8	19,010	8.4	80,550	6.3
1975	536	4.2	691,000	5.6	19,110	0.5	83,930	4.2
1976	578	8.3	765,000	9.8	21,250	9.8	92,900	9.7

Note: Includes U.S.S.R.; excludes China and some small states not affiliated with the ICAO.
Source: International Civil Aviation Organization.

were needed. Increasingly, energy conservation was being incorporated into the national transport policies of the industrialized nations, and a small but growing number of initiatives for reducing the energy (particularly oil) needs of transport and producing oil substitutes were apparent. At the same time, environmental considerations seemed to have been relegated, perhaps temporarily, to a position of secondary importance.

The year had its share of notable events, among them the opening of the trans-Alaska pipeline, scheduled air services across the Atlantic via Concorde, the Sydney, Australia, rail disaster (*see* DISASTERS), and the opening of two new 200-kph rail services. But it was the less dramatic changes— the creation of new low-price transatlantic air fares at one extreme and the laying out of local dirt roads in the poorer African countries at the other—that most affected the lives of ordinary people.

(DAVID BAYLISS)

AVIATION

As 1977 drew to a close, the international airline scene was in turmoil, caused by increasing U.S. pressure for far-reaching economic liberalization of the industry. Since World War II the international scheduled airlines had in most cases agreed on international scheduled air fares among themselves, working through the International Air Transport Association (IATA). The fares had then been approved by the governments concerned. Pres. Jimmy Carter stated his views on this situation in an October 6 letter to the U.S. secretary of transportation. "Our central goal," he said, " . . . should be to move toward a truly competitive system." He called for the removal of restrictions on low fares and on the capacity offered by airlines: market forces should determine the variety, quality, and price of air service. In November, the possibility was raised that the U.S. Civil Aeronautics Board would remove the antitrust-law exemption that allowed U.S. carriers to participate in IATA rate-making conferences. The U.S. view was not shared by other countries. In April a special conference convened by the International Civil Aviation Organization (ICAO) had taken a conservative line on economic regulation and had come out in favour of capacity controls.

In 1976 the U.K. had given notice of its intention to renegotiate the bilateral Bermuda Agreement governing air services with the U.S. The negotiations ran to the brink of expiry before an 11th-hour agreement was reached on June 22, 1977. It provided for control of North Atlantic capacity, with prior scrutiny of airlines' schedules (something not enshrined in the original agreement), certain new routes, and single designation (one carrier only from each country) on most routes, the chief exception being London–New York. Many countries that had bilateral negotiations pending with the U.S. (notably Japan and Italy) watched the Bermuda II negotiations anxiously. Signature of the agreement in July, however, brought no lessening of the U.S. drive for liberalization.

The next landmark in transatlantic air transport was the commencement, on September 26, of Laker Airways' Skytrain walk-on, no-reservations service between London and New York, planned some years earlier but delayed by political factors in the U.K. Skytrain offered a fare of $135 eastbound and $103 westbound. The airline claimed a profit of $100,000 in the first two weeks. The IATA airlines countered with standby fares set marginally higher than Skytrain but including (unlike Skytrain) meals. Other low transatlantic fares were planned. One outcome of IATA's annual general meeting, in Madrid, November 7–11, was the establishment of a committee to review fare-making procedures and report back by June 1978.

According to preliminary reports, IATA airlines carried 6,955,422 passengers on scheduled North Atlantic services in the first eight months of 1977, a gain of 4.4% over the same period of 1976. Freight, at 400,993 tons, was up 7.4%. At the same time, passenger traffic on IATA airlines' North Atlantic charter flights declined 5.8%. IATA scheduled passenger traffic also rose in the much smaller mid-Atlantic and South Atlantic markets, by 8.1 and 5.9%, respectively. Traffic of U.S. scheduled airlines in the first eight months of 1977 totaled 126,375,733,000 revenue passenger-miles, an increase of 6.1% over the same period in 1976. The strongest gain—10.1%—was shown by local service airlines.

ICAO statistics for world air traffic during 1976 showed growth rates close to the ten-year average, representing, according to the organization, a "strong recovery" from 1974 and 1975. (*See* Table.) Among individual ICAO contracting states, the U.S. again led in traffic, with 35,000,000,000 metric ton-km performed on scheduled services; the U.S.S.R. was second with 14,750,000,000. Preliminary ICAO figures for 1976 indicated that scheduled carriers were regaining some of the share of the charter market lost to nonscheduled airlines during the previous five years. Total nonscheduled traffic in 1976 was estimated at 103,300,000,000 metric ton-km, 3% over 1975.

The first eight months of 1977 saw greatly increased profitability for the five largest U.S. carriers, American, Eastern, Pan American, TWA, and United. Their combined profit was $268.5 million, compared with $136.4 million in the correspond-

Mopeds jumped into popularity in the U.S. where thousands of the vehicles were sold. Basically a bicycle with a one-cylinder-engine, a moped can travel 120–200 miles on a gallon of gasoline.

GRANT COMPTON—PHOTO TRENDS

World Transportation

Country	Railways Route length in 000 km	Railways Traffic Passenger in 000,000 pass.-km	Railways Traffic Freight in 000,000 net ton-km	Road length in 000 km	Motor transport Vehicles in use Passenger in 000	Motor transport Vehicles in use Commercial in 000	Merchant shipping Ships of 100 tons and over Number of vessels	Merchant shipping Gross reg. tons in 000	Air traffic Total km flown in 000,000	Air traffic Passenger in 000,000 pass.-km	Air traffic Freight in 000,000 net ton-km
EUROPE											
Austria	6.5	6,680	10,540	102.8	1,721.0	146.0	48	83	15.0	824	9.8
Belgium	4.0	8,203	6,638	93.6	2,577.0	235.0	258	1,499	47.8	3,893	325.8
Bulgaria	4.3	7,500	17,055	36.2	c.198.0	c.43.0	176	933	9.5	398	7.0
Cyprus	—	—	—	9.5[1]	68.7	14.3	765	3,114	2.4	304	6.6
Czechoslovakia	13.2	18,470	70,747	145.5[1]	1,401.0	261.0	14	149	26.0	1,325	17.2
Denmark	2.0[2]	3,250[2]	1,860[2]	66.1	1,297.0	225.0	1,413	5,143	36.7[3]	2,413[3]	111.1[3]
Finland	6.0	3,046	6,546	73.5	996.3	128.5	350	2,115	30.3	1,376	32.9
France	34.3	51,170	68,518	794.7	15,520.0	2,150.0	1,388	11,278	252.3	25,187	1,376.0
Germany, East	14.3	22,339	51,801	126.9	1,880.0	238.9	446	1,437	26.9	1,490	52.6
Germany, West	32.0	38,349	59,202	464.0	18,161.0	1,231.0	1,957	9,265	174.7	14,982	1,098.5
Greece	2.5	1,553	931	36.5	414.1	196.8	2,921	25,035	35.1	4,623	57.9
Hungary	8.2	13,367	22,553	99.8	579.9	121.0	18	55	10.2	500	5.6
Ireland	2.0	739	523	89.0	510.7	52.4	96	202	18.8	1,527	74.8
Italy	16.1[2]	39,646	16,673	289.8[1]	15,061.0	1,149.0	1,719	11,078	133.1	10,780	468.2
Netherlands, The	2.8	8,306	2,695	86.1	3,400.0	312.0	1,325	5,920	95.3	10,634	663.4
Norway	4.2	1,990	2,774	77.1	953.7	138.5	2,759	27,944	45.9[3]	3,179[3]	118.9[3]
Poland	23.8	42,800	130,956	297.8	1,077.7	425.0	733	3,263	24.4	1,426	14.2
Portugal	3.6	4,856	856	46.2[1]	937.0	71.6[1]	431	1,174	41.5	3,312	74.6
Romania	11.0	22,380	64,803	c.95.0	c.138.0	c.50.0	161	994	14.2	769	10.6
Spain	15.8	16,684	10,767	144.5	4,806.8	1,001.1	2,792	6,028	132.9	11,129	289.7
Sweden	12.1	5,363	15,458	124.8	2,760.3	156.6	764	7,971	59.0[3]	4,042[3]	172.5[3]
Switzerland	5.0[1]	8,130	5,659	61.6	1,794.0	167.3	28	213	83.1	8,493	345.8
U.S.S.R.	266.2[1]	312,517	3,300,000	1,403.0	c.4,730.0	c.5,115.0	7,945	20,668	...	122,402	2,580.3
United Kingdom	18.1[4]	36,840[4]	20,448[4]	c.368.0	13,950.0	1,775.0	3,549	32,923	286.7	30,948	914.5
Yugoslavia	10.1	9,884	21,006	c.112.0	1,536.7	142.5	423	1,944	29.1	2,151	20.4
ASIA											
Bangladesh	2.9	3,331[1]	639[1]	10.2[1]	17.5[1]	9.4[1]	127	147	4.4[1]	300	1.8
Burma	4.3[1]	2,847	421	21.7[1]	36.3[1]	39.3[1]	39	69	5.0	187	2.5
Cambodia	0.6[1]	54[1]	10[1]	c.11.0	27.2[1]	11.0[1]	2	1	0.8	42	0.4
China	c.48.0	45,670[1]	301,000[1]	c.750.0	c.37.0	c.675.0	551	3,589	...	64[1]	2.0[1]
India	60.4	134,747	143,100	1,232.3[1]	756.5	434.4	526	5,094	71.7	6,002	233.8
Indonesia	7.9	3,525	966	84.9[1]	383.1	231.5	882	1,046	53.9	3,055	47.5
Iran	4.5	2,126[1]	4,917[1]	52.0	589.2[1]	111.2[1]	168	683	28.9	2,318	40.8
Iraq	2.0	645	1,871	11.9	118.3	65.5	87	749	7.8	533	7.5
Israel	0.9	323[1]	464[1]	10.7[1]	287.3	96.1	68	482	28.8	4,020	131.7
Japan	28.0[1]	321,100	47,851	1,067.6	17,236.0	10,651.0	9,748	41,663	268.4	18,674	1,004.5
Korea, South	5.6	13,890	9,486	44.9	84.2	104.7	936	1,796	35.3	3,673	299.0
Malaysia	1.8	1,138[5]	1,008[5]	c.18.1[1]	430.4[1]	140.3[1]	150	443	28.7	1,815	36.5
Pakistan	8.8	c.12,900	c.8,700	49.9	192.3	95.3	83	483	31.3	3,411	148.3
Philippines	1.2[1]	953	66	112.9	362.5[1]	247.3[1]	457	1,018	37.0	2,580	78.9
Saudi Arabia	0.6[1]	72[1]	66[1]	18.4	177.4	140.8	84	589	26.0	1,750	44.7
Syria	1.8	166	125	13.6[1]	50.2	34.4	17	10	8.3	636	5.0
Taiwan	4.3	8,287	2,702	16.2	159.0	71.3	438	1,484	18.0[1]	954[1]	25.2[1]
Thailand	3.8	5,700	2,340	37.2	329.9	249.7	90	195	34.3	4,663	130.0
Turkey	8.1	4,736	7,355	188.1	393.8	205.6	405	1,079	19.2	2,019	17.3
AFRICA											
Algeria	3.8	1,058[1]	1,901[1]	78.4[1]	204.1[1]	103.1[1]	86	463	20.0	1,039	6.5
Congo	0.8[1]	246	508	c.11.0	19.0[1]	10.5[1]	13	2	2.6[6]	118[6]	12.4[6]
Egypt	4.5[1]	8,671	2,767	26.0[1]	215.5	46.3	157	376	17.6	1,459	21.4
Ethiopia	1.0	108[7]	244[7]	23.0[1]	43.4[1]	12.0[1]	23	25	11.2	523	20.2
Gabon	—	—	—	6.8[1]	c.10.1[1]	c.7.3[1]	14	98	3.3[6]	134[6]	12.2[6]
Ghana	1.0	431[1]	305[1]	35.0[1]	55.5[1]	43.9[1]	84	183	3.8	176	3.6
Ivory Coast	0.8[1]	918[1]	529[1]	45.2	75.9	13.7	53	114	2.2[6]	114[6]	12.2[6]
Kenya	2.1	...	2,120	49.5	142.0	20.9	19	15	10.9[8]	694[8]	17.7[8]
Liberia	0.5	...	4,396[1]	7.3	12.1[1]	10.0[1]	2,600	73,477	—	—	—
Malawi	0.6	61	228	11.0	10.5	8.5	—	—	3.8	122	4.7
Mali	0.6	100	156	14.7	15.8	2.6	—	—	1.7	85	1.3
Morocco	2.1	863	3,131	25.4[1]	320.1	127.2	67	137	15.2	1,228	18.1
Nigeria	3.5	785	972	97.0[1]	c.150.0[1]	c.82.0[1]	92	182	9.5	430	7.9
Rhodesia	3.4	...	6,230[9]	78.9[1]	c.180.0[1]	c.70.0[1]	...	...	5.8	259	2.4
Senegal	1.0[1]	220[1]	392[1]	13.3[1]	48.0[1]	25.0[1]	65	27	2.4[6]	119[6]	1.5[6]
Somalia	—	—	—	17.2[1]	8.0[1]	8.0[1]	255	1,793	1.1	19	0.2
South Africa	20.1	...	68,114[10]	c.370.0	2,117.0	800.3	275	477	59.2	6,012	160.4
Sudan	4.6	...	2,288[1]	c.50.0	c.50.0	c.25.0	14	46	7.5	320	7.4
Tanzania	3.5	...	...	c.35.0	c.39.1[1]	c.42.3[1]	20	35	4.6[7]	172[7]	3.5[8]
Tunisia	2.1	641	1,277	21.3	99.4	59.9	31	63	10.7	968	7.5
Uganda	1.3	...	...	24.3	27.0[1]	14.1[1]	1	6	2.6[8]	151[8]	6.2[8]
Zaire	5.2	447[1]	3,017[1]	c.145.0[1]	84.8[1]	76.4[1]	32	107	15.5	691	66.8
Zambia	c.2.2	320[1]	897[1]	35.0[1]	86.0[1]	62.0[1]	1	6	9.7	343	19.7
NORTH AND CENTRAL AMERICA											
Canada	70.7	2,650	193,526	834.2	8,472.0[1]	2,161.0[1]	1,269	2,639	302.4	24,000	630.0
Costa Rica	1.4	c.97[1]	c.20[1]	21.7[1]	55.1[1]	34.4[1]	15	6	6.0	326	13.5
Cuba	5.2[1]	946[1]	1,617[1]	27.1[1]	c.70.0[1]	c.33.0[1]	294	604	8.4	517	15.5
El Salvador	1.0	...	...	11.0[1]	41.0[1]	19.1[1]	3	2	...	...	...
Guatemala	0.9	...	127	13.4	76.1	40.1	6	8	3.8	132	7.1
Honduras	1.0	174[1]	3[1]	6.6	c.14.7[1]	22.9[1]	57	71	5.8	240	3.2
Mexico	24.7[1]	4,198[11]	32,542[11]	187.7	2,300.0	816.4	290	594	93.1	7,954	88.9
Nicaragua	0.4	28[1]	14[1]	12.9[1]	32.4	18.3	27	26	2.3	83	2.0
Panama	0.4	...	...	7.1[1]	69.8[1]	16.1[1]	2,680	15,631	...	...	...
United States	331.3	15,715[11]	1,101,870[11]	6,139.6[1]	106,712.5	24,837.0	4,616	14,908	3,605.4	288,020	9,083.8
SOUTH AMERICA											
Argentina	39.8	14,390	10,680	311.9	2,446.0	1,050.0	379	1,470	62.5	4,161	103.0
Bolivia	3.7	270[1]	365[1]	37.3[1]	29.6[1]	33.0[1]	...	...	6.0	444	4.3
Brazil	33.0	10,603[1]	42,698[1]	1,397.4	5,118.0	635.0	520	3,096	170.2	10,364	478.0
Chile	9.8[1]	2,101[1]	1,926[1]	65.4	197.8[1]	151.4[1]	142	410	21.6	1,276	59.0
Colombia	3.4[1]	511	1,247	49.2	305.0	56.0	53	212	48.1	2,778	126.3
Ecuador	1.2[1]	65	46	18.3[1]	43.6[1]	68.4[1]	46	181	10.4	301	6.7
Paraguay	0.5	26[1]	30[1]	16.0[1]	22.5	19.8	26	22	...	...	...
Peru	3.2[1]	270[1]	735[1]	56.4	266.9[1]	139.9[1]	681	525	21.8	1,132	22.7
Uruguay	3.0	358	281	49.6[1]	c.151.6[1]	c.85.7[1]	43	151	2.7	83	0.2
Venezuela	0.2	42[1]	15[1]	65.7[1]	820.0[1]	295.0[1]	165	543	37.2	2,535	76.8
OCEANIA											
Australia	40.6[1,2]	...	29,800	864.0[1]	4,899.7	1,138.0	424	1,247	207.8	18,084	361.3
New Zealand	4.8	520	3,659	92.6	1,194.0	225.7	102	164	51.8	4,078	119.6

Note: Data are for 1975 or 1976 unless otherwise indicated. (—) Indicates nil or negligible; (...) indicates not known; (c.) indicates provisional or estimated.
[1] Data given are the most recent available. [2] State system only. [3] Including apportionment of traffic of Scandinavian Airlines System. [4] Excluding Northern Ireland.
[5] Including Singapore. [6] Including apportionment of traffic of Air Afrique. [7] Including Djibouti traffic. [8] Including apportionment of traffic of
East African Airways Corp. and Caspair Ltd. [9] Including traffic in Botswana. [10] Including Namibia. [11] Principal railways.
Sources: UN, *Statistical Yearbook 1976, Monthly Bulletin of Statistics, Annual Bulletin of Transport Statistics for Europe 1975;* Lloyd's Register of Shipping, *Statistical Tables 1976;*
International Road Federation, *World Road Statistics 1976.*

(M. C. MacDONALD)

ing period of 1976. Operating revenues were up 12%, to $8.2 billion, and operating expenses rose 11.6% to $7.9 billion. IATA member airlines reported a preliminary net profit of $400 million in 1976, compared with a net loss of $350 million in 1975.

The safety record of scheduled services deteriorated slightly in 1976 but remained the second best in 20 years. There were 20 fatal accidents (U.S.S.R. excluded) in which 726 passengers died; comparable figures for 1975 were 19 and 441. The passenger fatality rate was 0.11 per 100 million passenger-km (0.08 in 1975), and the fatal accident rate was 0.20 per 100,000 aircraft landings (the same as in 1975).

Supersonic passenger service into New York's Kennedy International Airport was begun November 22 by Concorde, which had been operating into Washington's Dulles International Airport since 1976 but had been barred from New York pending the outcome of legal action. The Soviet Union's supersonic transport, the Tu-144, entered passenger service with a flight from Moscow to Alma Ata on November 1.

(DAVID WOOLLEY)

SHIPPING AND PORTS

The efforts of the world shipping industry to achieve a balance between demand for tonnage and availability continued to be thwarted by the policies of a number of leading shipbuilding countries. In a desperate effort to preserve their shipbuilding capability, some Western European governments granted subsidies for the construction of ships that were not required. The result would undoubtedly be to prolong the current shipping crisis into the early 1980s.

At mid-1977 the world merchant fleet totaled 397 million gross registered tons (grt), equivalent to nearly 610 million tons deadweight (dw), of which 326 million tons dw represented tanker tonnage. More than 40 million grt of shipping were laid up, including 31.2 million grt of tankers, and many tankers were operated at reduced speed. Though more than 82 million tons dw in tankers alone had been canceled since 1973, vessels totaling 27 million tons dw were on order and due for delivery before the end of 1978. There was worldwide relief when the U.S. House of Representatives quashed a bill that would have required 9.5% of all oil imported into the U.S. to move in U.S. owned and registered tankers.

One of the few sectors to operate with a small degree of profit was the container group. Fewer ports of call for the larger containerships meant an upsurge of interest in smaller, feeder-type containerships, more than 150 of which were ordered between August 1976 and August 1977. Initially the impetus for roll-on/roll-off vessels had been the high level of port congestion in the Middle East; this had been reduced to modest proportions, but the economics of the large ro/ro's were attractive enough to justify many orders. After a bad period the liquefied natural gas market picked up, boosting demand for gas carriers. Recession had also hit the chemical carriers, but the slight improvement in the world economy helped this sector.

KEYSTONE

Freddie Laker, president of Laker Airways, waved a flag amid a group of delighted passengers before his airline's first scheduled flight from London to New York on September 26. Laker Airways was the first to offer low-cost, no-reservation transatlantic service.

With the exception of the Middle East, port development slowed in 1977, and there was less haste to increase roll-on/roll-off facilities. More than two years after it was reopened, the Suez Canal was again asserting some influence on world shipping patterns, but most of the volume was dry cargo rather than oil. Dry cargo shipped through Suez in 1976 totaled 42.2 million metric tons, most of it moving south to the oil-producing nations on the Gulf. Meanwhile, the Panama Canal recorded another decline in annual revenue, and the average number of ships using the canal daily fell from 40 to 32.

(W. D. EWART)

FREIGHT AND PIPELINES

World freight traffic continued to grow, with the greatest increase on roads rather than railways. Many railways had been able to maintain their carryings, but their market share continued to decrease. The chief development in road freight was the continued growth in the number of very large trucks capable of carrying more than 20 tons. The railways continued to introduce a number of important improvements, including high-speed, air-braked freight-car fleets, freight car identification and control systems, and automated marshaling yards. Better integration of road and rail services was opening up wider rail traffic opportunities.

A freight forecasting study for the European Economic Community countries and Spain, looking to the years 1985 and 2000, was almost complete. It would be combined with the European long-distance passenger transport study to produce a complete picture of Europe's future transport needs and possibilities. In the shorter term the EEC requirement to fit tachographs in truck cabs was being deferred in the U.K., and the question of maximum vehicle axle weights remained unresolved. In the U.K. the government decided to increase taxation on heavy trucks. Views of maximum axle weights for road vehicles appeared to be changing in some countries; Australia was considering raising the limit, and a stronger economic case for modest increases was being made in the U.S.

Probably the most important freight transport innovation in 1977 was the opening of the trans-Alaska pipeline. (*See* ARCTIC REGIONS.) Plans were made to convert a natural-gas pipeline to the carriage of oil between Los Angeles and Texas, and several major pipelines were being built for the movement of natural gas and oil from the North Sea fields. Other major projects were under way in the Middle East.

Interest in freight complexes was growing, although it seemed unlikely that many more would be built on the giant scale of Garonor near Paris. Planning for London's first freight complex was under way, and other cities were considering similar projects.

ROADS AND TRAFFIC

The world's road vehicle fleet continued to grow with the U.S. total in excess of 130 million and Japan's exceeding 30 million. Ownership rates varied enormously between countries such as Australia and the U.S., where the number of cars was approaching one for every two people, and such places as Paraguay and China where trucks were few and cars available only to a tiny minority.

Road building and maintenance absorbed the greatest proportion of public spending on transport, particularly in the less industrialized regions where railways were uncommon. Emphasis on the construction of major intersettlement trunk routes had been reduced in recent years. The industrial

nations were moving from a total network approach to something more selective, while in less developed areas more effort was being put into low-cost feeder roads needed for rural development. The growth of car ownership in Eastern Europe had produced a need for road construction, and a number of these countries were involved in substantial programs. Similar pressures were developing in the Middle East and the wealthier South American countries.

"Transportation Systems Management" (TSM) had become part of the highway and transport engineers' vocabulary. It included traffic management, public transport priorities, parking controls, car pooling, shifting of travel hours, public transport pricing, car-free areas, and even area-wide traffic restraint. Examples of TSM schemes were to be found in Besançon, France; Göteborg, Sweden; Singapore; Munich, West Germany; Nagoya, Japan; and, on a less dramatic scale, in London. Success had been mixed—Nottingham, England, demonstrated that trying to do too much too quickly could lead to failure—but there was little doubt that some variant of TSM would become standard in all major cities.

The prospect of oil scarcity had led to a search for alternative ways of propelling vehicles which, apart from energy conservation, had taken two forms: synthesis of petroleum-type fuels from non-oil sources and electric-battery vehicle traction. In the U.S. a $175 million program to build 7,500 battery cars for official and private use was in progress, and in London a trial of 75 electric vans of several different types was begun.

INTERCITY RAIL

During 1977 full high-speed train services between London and South Wales were introduced by British Railways. Unlike the Japanese Shinkansen bullet train services, the HST operated on upgraded existing tracks at speeds of up to 200 kpm, using diesel-electric power units. The Shinkansen was being extended to northern Honshu, and extensive track repairs and maintenance were being carried out on existing sections of trunk routes. The upgrading and extension of the Japanese National Railways had resulted in a massive debt of about U.S. $20 billion, but there was strong resistance to fare increases. The Soviet railways introduced a high-speed service between Moscow and Leningrad, using trains that could travel at 200 kpm. Both the Soviet Union and China had undertaken railway improvement and extension programs, some of which were substantial in scale. The Indian railways also had expansion programs.

Other major corridor improvements included those between Boston and Washington, D.C., in the U.S. and between Paris and Lyon in France. Amtrak was spending almost $2 billion upgrading the Boston–Washington route, and service improvements were introduced between Los Angeles and San Diego, Calif., Washington and Cincinnati, Ohio, and New York and Newport News, Va. Nevertheless, Amtrak continued to lose money, and only a last-minute government grant in November saved the quasi-governmental body from making the first cancellation of a major train

High-speed hydrofoil services began during the year between London and Zeebrugge, Belgium.

COURTESY, P. & O. INTERNATIONAL RELATIONS DIVISION

since it took over intercity passenger service in the U.S. Between Paris and Lyon, plans were being implemented to introduce a service with a top speed of 260 kpm in place of the existing 200-kpm service; 260-kpm trains (the Advanced Passenger Trains) were also being built by British Railways for introduction on the London to Glasgow run. Few new lines were being built in Europe, those joining The Hague with Zoetermeer and Utrecht with Rhenen (Neth.) being exceptions.

Operating losses on the European railways continued to grow, although not so fast as in the recession period following the 1973–74 oil crisis. Controls over public expenditure formed an element in the economic strategies of most European governments, leading to a hardening attitude toward heavy railway losses. In the U.K. it was decided to eliminate subsidies for freight and to hold those for passenger services at current levels.

URBAN MASS TRANSIT

New, extended, and upgraded metros (subways) continued to be the most glamorous objects on the urban public-transport scene. Major recent developments included completion of the east–west regional metro across Paris (RER), the opening of the second stage of the Washington, D.C., Metro and the first stage of the Marseille (France) metro, new starts in Kobe and Osaka, Japan; Oslo, Norway; and São Paulo, Brazil, and extensions to several other systems.

Suburban rail systems, though less spectacular, were nevertheless important. In London, for example, the suburban rail network was almost eight times as long as the Underground and carried two and a half times as many passenger-miles. Most investment in these systems had gone for renewal and modernization of track signaling and rolling stock, although there had been a few route extensions (*e.g.*, the $260 million line to Bondi in Sydney). Interest continued in light rail systems, ranging from the "pre-metros" of such cities as Bonn and Brussels to revived streetcar (tram) systems and very light systems, such as those at airports. Given the astronomical cost of full metros, more cities were turning to light rail and to streetcars, which had virtually disappeared outside of three or four European countries.

Most urban public transport, however, continued to be by road vehicles, mainly buses. Fleet modernization and reequipment were being carried on in many parts of the world, and competition between the major manufacturers was intense, especially as the practice of providing government grants for replacement became widespread. Programs to give traffic priority to buses and other high-occupancy vehicles continued to be introduced, although some of the more adventurous schemes had to be withdrawn because of strong adverse reaction from other road users. Perhaps the most interesting innovation was the Pittsburgh (Pa.) busway, a four-and-a-half-mile route using an existing streetcar tunnel.

Little progress was made with the introduction of completely new systems, although it was decided to go ahead with the second stage of the Morgantown, W.Va., "horizontal lift" system and to

build "Downtown People Movers" in Cleveland, Ohio; Houston, Texas; Los Angeles, and São Paulo. The most substantial aid to pedestrian movement was probably the system of pedestrian subways with over half a mile of moving walkways at London's Heathrow airport, connecting the three passenger terminals with each other and with the concourse of a new Underground station. Perhaps the most interesting innovation was the two-thirds-of-a-mile-long aerial tramway connecting Manhattan with Roosevelt (formerly Welfare) Island in the East River.   (DAVID BAYLISS)

See also Energy; Engineering Projects; Environment; Industrial Review: *Aerospace; Automobiles.*
[725.c.3; 734; 737.A.3]

A large articulated bus demonstrated its maneuverability in a crowded bus terminal in London.

Trinidad and Tobago

A republic and a member of the Commonwealth of Nations, Trinidad and Tobago consists of two islands off the coast of Venezuela, north of the Orinoco River delta. Area: 5,128 sq km (1,980 sq mi). Pop. (1976 est.): 1,149,000, including (1970) Negro 43%; East Indian 40%; mixed 14%. Cap. and largest city: Port-of-Spain (pop., 1973 est., 60,400). Language: English (official); Hindi, French, Spanish. Religion (1970): Christian 64%; Hindu 25%; Muslim 6%. President in 1977, Sir Ellis Clarke; prime minister, Eric Williams.

Trinidad and Tobago continued to ride the crest of its oil boom in 1977. Monetary reserves reached over U.S. $2 billion in 1976, with oil accounting for more than 90% of exports. The country also uncovered a gas bonanza; potential reserves of dry natural gas were estimated in September 1977 at 15 trillion standard cu ft. These resources were increasingly government owned or controlled, with U.S. capital promoting industrial expansion. A huge industrial estate taking shape at Point Lisas on the west coast would produce liquid ammonia, fertilizer, iron and steel, aluminum, liquid natural gas, and methanol.

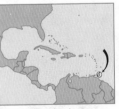

Trinidad and Tobago

Trapshooting:
see Target Sports

TRINIDAD AND TOBAGO

Education. (1975–76) Primary, pupils 200,095, teachers 6,471; secondary (1972–73), pupils 48,858, teachers 2,089; vocational, pupils 1,395, teachers 114; teacher training, students 1,188, teachers 116; higher, students 1,471, teaching staff 221.

Finance and Trade. Monetary unit: Trinidad and Tobago dollar, with (Sept. 19, 1977) a par value of TT$2.40 to U.S. $1 (free rate of TT$4.18 = £1 sterling). Budget (1977 est.) balanced at TT$2,431,000,000. Foreign trade (1976): imports TT$4,826,900,000; exports TT$5,407,400,000. Import sources: Saudi Arabia 26%; U.S. 20%; Indonesia 16%; Iran 11%; U.K. 8%. Export destinations: U.S. 69%; U.K. 5%. Main exports: petroleum products 58%; crude oil 34%.

Transport and Communications. Roads (1973) 6,100 km. Motor vehicles in use (1975): passenger 101,300; commercial (including buses) 25,700. There are no railways in operation. Air traffic (1976): 1,040,000,000 passenger-km; freight 24.2 million net ton-km. Ships entered (1974) vessels totaling 32,250,000 net registered tons; goods loaded 28,877,000 metric tons, unloaded 18,809,000 metric tons. Telephones (Dec. 1975) 67,000. Radio licenses (Dec. 1974) 250,000. Television receivers (Dec. 1974) 100,000.

Agriculture. Production (in 000; metric tons; 1975): sugar, raw value *c.* 163; rice 20; tomatoes *c.* 11; oranges *c.* 12; grapefruit *c.* 19; copra *c.* 9; coffee *c.* 4. Livestock (in 000; 1975): cattle *c.* 56; pigs *c.* 56; goats *c.* 41; poultry *c.* 6,200.

Industry. Production (in 000; metric tons; 1976): crude oil 10,992; natural gas (cu m; 1975) 1,320,000; petroleum products (1975) 11,682; cement 241; nitrogenous fertilizers (nutrient content; 1975–76) *c.* 57; electricity (kw-hr) 1,288,000.

TUNISIA

Education. (1975–76) Primary, pupils 920,924, teachers 23,181; secondary, pupils 149,798; vocational, pupils 34,-352; secondary and vocational, teachers 8,769; teacher training, students 1,057, teachers (1974–75) 133; higher, students 17,235, teaching staff 1,142.

Finance. Monetary unit: Tunisian dinar, with (Sept. 19, 1977) a free rate of 0.43 dinar to U.S. $1 (0.75 dinar = £1 sterling). Gold, SDR's, and foreign exchange (June 1977) U.S. $179 million. Budget (1976 est.) balanced at 641 million dinars. Gross domestic product (1976) 1,904,800,000 dinars. Money supply (April 1977) 521,160,000 dinars. Cost of living (Tunis; 1970 = 100; April 1977) 140.

Foreign Trade. (1976) Imports 656,720,000 dinars; exports 338,260,000 dinars. Import sources (1975): France 35%; Italy 9%; West Germany 8%; U.S. 7%; U.K. 5%. Export destinations (1975): France 19%; Italy 17%; Greece 14%; U.S. 10%; West Germany 8%; Libya 6%. Main exports: crude oil 41%; phosphates 11%; olive oil 11%. Tourism (1975): visitors 1,014,000; gross receipts (1974) U.S. $190 million.

Transport and Communications. Roads (1975) 21,309 km. Motor vehicles in use (1975): passenger 99,400; commercial 59,900. Railways: (1975) 2,089 km; traffic (1976) 641 million passenger-km, freight 1,277,000,000 net ton-km. Air traffic (1976): 967.8 million passenger-km; freight 7,460,000 net ton-km. Telephones (Dec. 1975) 129,000. Radio receivers (Dec. 1974) 277,000. Television receivers (Dec. 1973) 147,000.

Agriculture. Production (in 000; metric tons; 1976): wheat *c.* 919; barley *c.* 230; potatoes (1975) 128; tomatoes *c.* 269; watermelons (1975) *c.* 150; wine *c.* 110; dates *c.* 45; olives *c.* 530; oranges 86. Livestock (in 000; 1975): sheep *c.* 3,400; cattle *c.* 870; goats *c.* 661; camels *c.* 211; poultry *c.* 13,611.

Industry. Production (in 000; metric tons; 1976): crude oil 3,712; natural gas (cu m) 214,000; cement 478; iron ore (53% metal content) 494; phosphate rock (1975) 3,512; lead 23; petroleum products (1975) 1,135; sulfuric acid *c.* 1,060; electricity (excluding most industrial production; kw-hr) 1,340,000.

Government wealth was being funded for long-term development. Meanwhile, public utilities were chaotic, inefficiency and corruption widespread, and land and house prices soaring. Unemployment stood at 15%, and income distribution remained very uneven. The People's National Movement (PNM) faced what seemed to be its first credible opposition, the United Labour Front (ULF), representing interracial working-class interests as against the PNM's increasingly middle-class supporters. Its prospects were damaged, however, when the ULF left wing ousted Basdeo Panday (sugar production workers) as leader of the opposition and replaced him with Raffique Shah (cane farmers' union and leader of the 1970 army mutiny). (SHEILA PATTERSON)

Tunisia

Tunisia

A republic of North Africa lying on the Mediterranean Sea, Tunisia is bounded by Algeria and Libya. Area: 164,150 sq km (63,379 sq mi). Pop. (1976 est.): 5,737,000. Cap. and largest city: Tunis (pop., 1975 census, city proper 550,404; governorate 944,100). Language: Arabic (official). Religion: Muslim; Jewish and Christian minorities. President in 1977, Habib Bourguiba; prime minister, Hedi Nouira.

The succession to Pres. Habib Bourguiba's office seemed more open than ever in 1977, and Prime Minister Hedi Nouira had to face increasingly aggressive opposition from students, trade unionists, and organized political parties. On February 24 there were violent confrontations with the police at the University of Tunis; some of those arrested were freed in March. At the 20th congress of the Union of Tunisian Students the government was criticized fiercely, and disturbances broke out

outside the University of Tunis at Bardo in May.

In March Habib Achour was reelected secretary-general of the General Union of Tunisian Workers, a central directing organization over which authorities were unable to establish complete control. Although in September some responsible unions declared that they were ready to work with the government, during the following month police and strikers clashed at the small southern town of Ksar Hellal. In November waves of strikes and demonstrations occurred throughout the country to protest the threats made against Habib Achour.

Some 20 political colleagues of Ahmad Ben Salah, former minister of finance and planning, were arrested in March. His Movement of Popular Unity (MUP), founded in May 1973, had maintained an atmosphere of unrest. In June the trial of 32 persons connected with MUP and accused of wanting to overthrow the regime began. It resulted on August 19 in nine acquittals and sentences of from six months to eight years of imprisonment for the remainder.

There was restlessness among intellectuals throughout the year. In April 168 prominent leaders among them called for the summoning of a national conference on public liberties. In May the establishment of the League for Human Rights was authorized in Tunisia, and during the following month a National Council for the Defense of Public Liberties was created. This latter body at once issued a manifesto demanding the release of all political detainees.

On December 26 a new government was formed, in which Nouira remained as prime minister. Technocrats replaced a number of ministers who had resigned because of disagreements with Nouira, and Tahar Belkhodja, a proponent of greater liberalization, was ousted as minister of the interior. His duties were temporarily taken over by the minister of defense, Abdallah Farhat.

In foreign policy, links with France were strengthened during the year. In February Foreign Minister Habib Chatti visited Paris. He was followed by Nouira, who was received by the French premier, Raymond Barre. Relations with Libya had been normalized by the end of the year after coming near to breakdown once again. Two matters of contention troubled the two nations: the conditions under which immigrant Tunisian workers lived in Libya, and the demarcation of the territorial waters of the two countries. In June both sides again agreed to refer the demarcation question to the International Court of Justice at The Hague. (PHILIPPE DECRAENE)

Turkey

A republic of southeastern Europe and Asia Minor, Turkey is bounded by the Aegean Sea, the Black Sea, the U.S.S.R., Iran, Iraq, Syria, the Mediterranean Sea, Greece, and Bulgaria. Area: 779,452 sq km (300,948 sq mi), including 23,698 sq km in Europe. Pop. (1975 prelim.): 40,197,700. Cap.: Ankara (pop., 1975 prelim., 1,994,900). Largest city: Istanbul (pop., 1975 prelim., 2,634,-800). Language: Turkish, Kurdish, Arabic. Religion: predominantly Muslim. President in 1977, Fahri Koruturk; prime minister, Suleyman Demirel.

Economic difficulties, a feud between leftist and rightist militants that paralyzed university education and caused many deaths, and disagreements with his coalition partners led Prime Minister Suleyman Demirel, leader of the Justice Party (JP), to advance the general elections from October to June 5, 1977. The campaign was violent. More than 30 people were killed (mostly trampled to death) in Istanbul when extreme leftists opened fire at a May Day rally organized by the Marxist trade union confederation. Riots attended several provincial visits by the opposition leader, Bulent Ecevit of the Republican People's Party (RPP).

Election results were again inconclusive. The RPP advanced from 185 to 213 seats (41% of the poll) in the 450-seat Assembly, the JP from 149 to 189 (37%), and the JP's coalition partner, the National Action Party (NAP), from 3 to 16 (6%), while another coalition party, the religious National Salvation Party (NSP), fell from 48 to 24 (9%). The rightist Republican Reliance Party (RRP) and the Democratic Party dropped from 13 to 3 and from 45 to 1, respectively. In the Senate the RPP won an absolute majority, taking 28 seats, against 21 for the JP and 1 for the NSP, in elections for one-third of the membership.

Pres. Fahri Koruturk first asked Ecevit to form the new government. A minority RPP administration assumed office on June 21 but was defeated in

Turkey

the Assembly on July 3 and resigned. It was succeeded on July 21 by a second Nationalist Front coalition (JP, NSP, and NAP, but excluding the much-reduced RRP) under Demirel. The coalition, in which the JP had 16 members, the NSP 8, and the NAP 5, was confirmed in office by the Assembly on August 1 by 229 votes to 219.

The coalition was faced with immediate difficulties. Political killings continued, and when the universities reopened in November, classes were again disrupted. Inflation, unemployment, and an acute lack of foreign exchange plagued the economy; the external payments deficit had grown from U.S. $2 billion in 1975 to $2.4 billion in 1976 and $2.9 billion in 1977. With production and investment hampered by inability to import machinery and raw materials, the government called in the International Monetary Fund to obtain urgent credits. A package of austerity measures, including price increases of state-produced goods and a 10% devaluation of the lira, was announced in September; a further 3.4% devaluation came on December 1. On October 14 three JP ministers resigned. The RPP made substantial gains in local elections in mid-December, and shortly thereafter several members of the Assembly resigned from the JP, reducing the number of seats held by the coalition below 50%. On December 31 Demirel's government resigned after losing a vote of confidence, presumably opening the way for Ecevit to make another attempt to form a government.

The foreign exchange crisis was aggravated by the continued refusal of the U.S. Congress to ratify the $1 billion defense cooperation agreement signed in 1976. Ratification was tied to progress toward a solution in the Cyprus dispute, but despite extensive negotiations the situation remained frozen. There was some relaxation in relations between Greece and Turkey, however. The Aegean seabed dispute was again taken up by Greek and Turkish envoys in Paris at the end of May, and agreement was reached to avoid provocative action. Consequently, Turkey did not resume oil prospecting in disputed waters. Both Greece and Turkey took part in a NATO exercise in September, for the first time since 1974. Also in September, an agreement was reached for the sale of $55 million in U.S. military equipment to Turkey as part of the $125 million military aid program to Turkey for 1977. The Turkish foreign minister visited Moscow in March, but a promised summit meeting to sign a political document on friendly relations and cooperation did not take place.

An oil pipeline from Kirkuk in Iraq to the gulf of Iskenderun on Turkey's Mediterranean coast was inaugurated in January.   (ANDREW MANGO)

See also Cyprus.

Uganda

Uganda

A republic and a member of the Commonwealth of Nations, Uganda is bounded by Sudan, Zaire, Rwanda, Tanzania, and Kenya. Area: 241,139 sq km (93,104 sq mi), including 44,081 sq km of inland water. Pop. (1977 est.): 12,352,500, virtually all of whom are African. Cap. and largest city: Kampala (pop., 1975 UN est., 542,000). Language: English (official), Bantu, Nilotic, Nilo-Hamitic, and Sudanic. Religion: Christian, Muslim, traditional beliefs. President in 1977, Gen. Idi Amin.

At the beginning of 1977, to mark the sixth anniversary of his seizure of power, Pres. Idi Amin appointed Maj. Gen. Mustapha Adriki as vice-president. Shortly afterward, in February, there was an international outcry when it was learned that the Anglican archbishop, Janani Luwum, and two government ministers had been murdered by Amin's State Research Unit after being accused of involvement in a plot to overthrow the government. The murders were followed by a new wave of attacks against members of the Acholi and Langi tribes in which many were killed. There were also some persecutions of Christians, and threats against U.S. residents in Uganda brought a U.S. naval force into the vicinity of Mombasa.

A number of resistance groups had indeed grown up, both inside and outside the country, but attempts (at least four) to assassinate the president or to sabotage the economy were prevented

UGANDA

Education. (1976) Primary, pupils 1,125,817, teachers 32,490; secondary, pupils 75,044, teachers 3,456; vocational, pupils 3,701, teachers 264; teacher training, students 6,328, teachers 364; higher, students 5,173, teaching staff 617.

Finance and Trade. Monetary unit: Uganda shilling, with (Sept. 19, 1977) a free rate of UShs 8.30 to U.S. $1 (UShs 14.45 = £1 sterling). Budget (1976–77 est.): revenue UShs 3,111,000,000; expenditure UShs 2,180,000,000. Foreign trade (1976): imports UShs 1,342,000,000; exports UShs 3,006,000,000. Import sources: Kenya 50%; U.K. 15%; West Germany 9%. Export destinations: U.S. 33%; U.K. 20%; France 6%; Italy 6%; Japan 6%. Main exports: coffee 83%; cotton 6%.

Transport and Communications. Roads (1975) 24,310 km. Motor vehicles in use (1974): passenger 27,000; commercial 14,100. Railways (1975) 1,301 km. Air traffic (including apportionment of traffic of East African Airways Corporation; 1975): 151 million passenger-km; freight 6.2 million net ton-km. Telephones (Jan. 1976) 45,000. Radio receivers (Dec. 1974) 250,000. Television licenses (Dec. 1972) 15,000.

Agriculture. Production (in 000; metric tons; 1976): millet *c.* 650; sorghum 538; corn (1975) 870; sweet potatoes (1975) *c.* 650; cassava (1975) *c.* 1,000; peanuts 220; dry beans *c.* 173; coffee 211; tea *c.* 21; cotton, lint 41; timber (cu m; 1975) *c.* 14,675; fish catch (1975) 170. Livestock (in 000; Dec. 1974): cattle *c.* 4,200; sheep *c.* 700; goats *c.* 2,050; pigs *c.* 74; chickens *c.* 11,500.

Industry. Production (in 000; metric tons; 1975): cement 98; copper, smelter 8; tungsten concentrates (oxide content) 0.07; phosphate rock 15; electricity (kw-hr) *c.* 830,000.

by the vigilance of Amin's security forces, in which Palestinians and Sudanese played an important role. In August representatives of several resistance groups met in Lusaka, Zambia, with a view to setting up a united front. Former president Milton Obote, himself in exile in Tanzania, protested against the meeting, claiming that he was still the rightful head of state and that other claimants had no authority to act without him. The steady flow of arms from the U.S.S.R. further strengthened Amin's position while causing concern to his immediate neighbours. In April, however, Amin offered troops to assist Zaire's Pres. Mobutu Sese Seko (*see* BIOGRAPHY) in dealing with the rebels who had invaded Shaba Province.

A stream of refugees, many of them leading citizens and some of them government ministers, continued to leave Uganda, bearing tales of atrocities carried out by the regime and even by the president himself. International concern at these reports was reflected in Ghana's decision in May to suspend diplomatic relations with Uganda. Other Commonwealth nations experienced a similar revulsion, and this led to Britain's decision, taken after consultation with other Commonwealth countries, to prevent Amin from attending the meeting of Commonwealth heads of state in London in June. In the event, Amin made no attempt to attend, although he maintained until the last minute that he meant to do so. Pres. Kenneth Kaunda of Zambia, in London for the conference, roundly condemned Amin's actions in Uganda, and his views were endorsed by other Commonwealth leaders. Nevertheless, when Amin attended the Organization of African Unity summit conference in Libreville, Gabon, in July, he was given a friendly welcome.

The disintegration and final collapse of the East

African Community created further difficulties for Uganda's already disrupted economy. The export of coffee was held up because of difficulty in obtaining rail transport to Mombasa, and the president sent to Britain to buy two more aircraft to assist in airlifting coffee out of the country. At the same time, arrangements were made to fly out more coffee via Djibouti in planes chartered by a U.S. company. In Britain there was a sharp protest against the use of Stanstead airport as a base from which to fly luxuries to Uganda, used by Amin to maintain the loyalty and support of his troops. The British crown agents also came under criticism for continuing to supply goods to Uganda, including an order for Bedford trucks capable of being used for military purposes. After the collapse of the East African Community, more than 100 Ugandan employees at the Community's headquarters in Arusha, Tanzania, refused to obey Amin's order to return to Uganda and petitioned Pres. Julius Nyerere's government to be allowed to remain.

(KENNETH INGHAM)

Union of Soviet Socialist Republics

The Union of Soviet Socialist Republics is a federal state covering parts of eastern Europe and northern and central Asia. Area: 22,402,200 sq km (8,-649,500 sq mi). Pop. (1976 est.): 256.7 million, including (1970) Russians 53%; Ukrainians 17%; Belorussians 4%; Uzbeks 4%; Tatars 2%. Cap. and largest city: Moscow (pop., 1976 est., 7,734,000). Language: officially Russian, but many others are spoken. Religion: about 40 religions are represented in the U.S.S.R., the major ones being Christian denominations. General secretary of the Communist Party of the Soviet Union in 1977, Leonid Ilich Brezhnev; chairmen of the Presidium of the Supreme Soviet (presidents), Nikolay V. Podgorny and, from June 16, Leonid Ilich Brezhnev; chairman of the Council of Ministers (premier), Aleksey N. Kosygin.

In 1977 the long-awaited decision to replace the 1936 constitution, associated with the name of Stalin, represented a significant step in the process of breaking with the past. It also served to underline the personal ascendancy of Leonid I. Brezhnev (*see* BIOGRAPHY), who played a leading role in the preparation and public presentation of the new constitution, published on June 4. In reality, of course, little had changed. Thus, for example, the 15 republics that constitute the Union of Soviet Socialist Republics retained the right to secede from the union, but the procedure for doing this was not spelled out. As before, a Soviet citizen's enjoyment of his rights depended much more on the political climate of the moment than on the written guarantees contained in a constitution.

Nevertheless, the new constitution was of some documentary interest. The draft was produced for public discussion in May by a special commission chaired by Brezhnev. The legal formulations of the basic freedoms remained largely unchanged; as in the previous constitution these were to be prac-

ticed "in conformity with the interests of working people and the socialist system." In a speech to the Central Committee of the Soviet Communist Party on May 24, Brezhnev said that there could be no return to the "illegal repression" that had disfigured life in the Soviet Union in the years after the promulgation of the 1936 constitution, but he also stressed that the "rights and freedoms of citizens cannot and must not be used against our social system."

On the whole the provisions of the new constitution placed more emphasis upon the obligations and duties of the citizen, but government departments and mass organizations were told to respect the rights of the individual. The leading role of the Communist Party, described as "the nucleus of the political system," was stressed more than before. The new constitution was much more specific about the actual functions and policy of the Soviet state: it mentioned the socialist management of the economy, required the state to protect the environment, reaffirmed "the principles of peaceful coexistence," and prohibited "aggressive wars." One of the provisions added after four months of public discussion stated that "the U.S.S.R. seeks general and complete disarmament."

Domestic Affairs. Some of the changes that occurred in the leadership of both the Soviet state and party were linked to the provisions of the new constitution. Brezhnev, whose health had been reported to be poor for some time, emerged unimpaired as formal head of state, and he appeared to be as active and forceful as ever. An unexpected move was the removal of Nikolay V. Podgorny from the post of chairman of the Presidium of the Supreme Soviet and from the Politburo. No explanation was offered. He was replaced in June by Brezhnev himself, who then combined the position of head of state with that of general secretary of the Soviet Communist Party—the first man to do so. Addressing the Supreme Soviet, Brezhnev stressed that his appointment had "deep political meaning" because it underlined the Communist Party's leading role in the state. The new constitution created the post of first deputy chairman of the Presidium of the Supreme Soviet, a sort of

Moscow citizens clustered around a sidewalk newspaper stand to read the new Soviet constitution which was published June 4.

Union of Soviet Socialist Republics

Unemployment:
see Economy, World; Social and Welfare Services

On August 26–27 smoke and flames billowed from the top floors of the U.S. embassy in Moscow. Sensitive communications areas were involved in the blaze, but it was believed no classified material was compromised.

nists was not extremely youthful at 44, but his age must be seen in relation to the men who stood at the summit of power. Brezhnev was 71; Kosygin, the premier, was 73; the new first deputy chairman of the Presidium, Kuznetsov, was 76; the minister of defense, Marshal Dmitry Ustinov, 69; and Mikhail Suslov, the principal ideologue in the Politburo, 75.

Also in June, the Conference on Security and Cooperation in Europe opened in Belgrade, Yugos., to review the implementation of the final act of its 1975 Helsinki session, which was an agreement to facilitate the free movement of people and ideas across the East-West divide. Attention at Belgrade was concentrated on the question of human rights; the Soviet authorities seemed at one time to be determined to eliminate, in time for the Belgrade meeting, the most articulate among the dissidents who had plagued them with much greater persistence since the Helsinki agreement. Unofficial groups, dedicated to monitoring the implementation of Helsinki, were reported not only in Moscow and Leningrad but also in the Ukraine, Armenia, Lithuania, and Georgia. Early in the year, in February, the Central Committee passed a widely publicized resolution calling for a more concentrated mass propaganda effort to combat "ideological laxity" and "relaxation of discipline" in the party.

The Soviet Communist Party was obviously worried about the risk of ideological feedback from some of the Eastern European countries. In January it sent one of its principal ideological hardliners, Z. K. Zimyanin, to Warsaw for consultation, and in March a conference of Eastern European party secretaries responsible for questions of ideology met in Sofia with their comrades from Cuba and Mongolia. A communiqué issued by the conference did not mention "Eurocommunism," although the meeting in the Bulgarian capital coincided with a conference of leaders of the major Western European Communist parties in Madrid. The Eurocommunists in their turn behaved with discretion by not mentioning the problem of dissent in the Soviet Union. The Soviet leadership demonstrated its displeasure with the indepen-

vice-president whose duties were expected to be mainly ceremonial. In October this post was filled by Vasily Kuznetsov, an experienced diplomat who had served as first deputy minister of foreign affairs since 1955.

Other important personnel changes served to strengthen Brezhnev's position, as the promotions generally involved men close to him. Kuznetsov and Konstantin Chernenko, a recently appointed secretary of the party's Central Committee, became candidate members of the Politburo in October. In March, Konstantin Katushev, previously a secretary of the Central Committee, became deputy premier and in May his place in the Secretariat was taken by Konstantin Rusakov. In May, Evgeny Tyazhelnikov was appointed as secretary of the Central Committee of the Soviet Communist Party with special responsibility for propaganda work; Boris Pastukhov became head of the Komsomol, the Communist League of Youth, in his stead. The new leader of the young Commu-

---

U.S.S.R.

Education. (1975–76) Primary, pupils 36.8 million; secondary, pupils 14,165,000; primary and secondary, teachers 2,399,000; vocational, pupils 4,525,000, teachers 218,000; higher, students 4,854,000, teaching staff 317,000.

Finance. Monetary unit: ruble, with (Sept. 19, 1977) a free rate of 0.72 ruble to U.S. $1 (1.25 ruble = £1 sterling). Budget (1977 est.): revenue 238.8 billion rubles; expenditure 238.6 billion rubles.

Foreign Trade. (1976) Imports 28,731,000,000 rubles; exports 28,022,000,000 rubles. Import sources: Eastern Europe 43% (East Germany 10%, Poland 9%, Czechoslovakia 8%, Bulgaria 8%, Hungary 6%); U.S. 7%; West Germany 7%; Cuba 5%; Japan 5%. Export destinations: Eastern Europe 47% (East Germany 11%, Poland 10%, Czechoslovakia 8%, Bulgaria 8%, Hungary 6%); Cuba 5%. Main exports: machinery and transport equipment 19%; crude oil 18%; petroleum products 9%; iron and steel 7%; timber 5%.

Transport and Communications. Roads (1975) 1,403,000 km (including 660,500 km surfaced). Motor vehicles in use (1975): passenger c. 4,730,000; commercial c. 5,115,000. Railways: (1974) 266,200

km (including 137,500 km public and 128,700 industrial); traffic (1975) 312,517,000,000 passenger-km, freight (1976) 3,300,000,000,000 net ton-km. Air traffic (1975): 122,402,000,000 passenger-km; freight 2,580,300,000 net ton-km. Navigable inland waterways (1975) 145,400 km; traffic 221,700,000,000 ton-km. Shipping (1976): merchant vessels 100 gross tons and over 7,945; gross tonnage 20,667,892. Telephones (Dec. 1975) 16,949,000. Radio receivers (Dec. 1974) 116.1 million. Television receivers (Dec. 1974) 52.5 million.

Agriculture. Production (in 000; metric tons; 1976): wheat c. 96,900; barley c. 69,500; oats c. 17,000; rye c. 12,000; corn c. 10,300; rice c. 2,100; millet c. 4,500; potatoes c. 90,784; sugar, raw value 9,196; tomatoes c. 3,691; watermelons (1975) c. 3,100; sunflower seed 5,200; linseed c. 360; dry peas c. 6,700; soybeans c. 510; wine c. 2,965; tea c. 88; tobacco c. 312; cotton, lint c. 2,800; flax fibres (1975) 478; wool 285; hen's eggs c. 3,289; milk 88,700; butter c. 1,300; cheese 1,435; meat c. 13,300; timber (cu m; 1975) c. 387,600; fish catch (1975) 9,876. Livestock (in 000; Jan. 1976): cattle 111,034; pigs 57,899; sheep 141,-

436; goats 5,655; horses (1975) 6,749; chickens c. 777,000.

Industry. Index of production (1970 = 100; 1976) 150. Fuel and power (in 000; metric tons; 1976): coal and lignite 712,000; crude oil 520,000; natural gas (cu m; 1975) 289,000,000; manufactured gas (cu m; 1975) 36,040,000; electricity (kw-hr) 1,111,000,000. Production (in 000; metric tons; 1976): cement 123,968; iron ore (60% metal content) 238,200; pig iron 105,600; steel 144,653; aluminum (1975) c. 1,500; copper (1975) c. 1,420; lead (1975) c. 480; zinc (1975) c. 690; magnesite (1975) c. 1,800; manganese ore (metal content; 1975) 2,951; tungsten concentrates (oxide content; 1975) 9.8; gold (troy oz) c. 7,700; silver (troy oz) c. 45,000; sulfuric acid 20,014; caustic soda c. 2,600; plastics and resins c. 3,200; fertilizers (nutrient content; 1975) nitrogenous 8,456, phosphate 4,103, potash 7,944; newsprint (1975) 1,361; other paper (1975) c. 6,900; cotton fabrics (sq m) 6,775,000; woolen fabrics (sq m) 764,000; rayon and acetate fabrics (sq m) 1,627,000; passenger cars (units; 1975) 1,201; commercial vehicles (units; 1975) 765.

TASS/SOVFOTO

A view of Moscow's Red
Square as the Soviet
Union celebrated, on
November 7, the 60th
anniversary of the Bol-
shevik Revolution.

dent and gradualist approach of the Western European comrades by preventing the secretary-general of the Spanish Communist Party, Santiago
Carrillo (*see* BIOGRAPHY), from delivering his
speech of fraternal greetings at 60th anniversary
celebrations of the Bolshevik Revolution in Moscow in November.

Faced with the agitation of the dissidents, the
Soviet authorities tried both repression and persuasion to deal with them. The arrests and harassment of the most vocal protagonists of dissent were
relatively mild when compared with the methods
used to stifle all opposition in Stalin's day. In January *Pravda* published an attack on U.S. journalists;
this was followed by the arrest of George Krimsky,
the Associated Press Moscow correspondent, on
charges of espionage and his expulsion from the
country. The U.S. retaliated by expelling a staff
member of the Soviet news agency, Tass. Yuri Orlov, leading personality of the Helsinki monitoring group in Moscow, was arrested in February.

The authorities continued to combine arrests
with encouraging leading dissidents to emigrate.
For example, in the autumn the dissident Feliks
Serebrov was sentenced for carrying an out-of-date
work pass; the psychologist Ernst Axelrod and the
painter Oscar Rabin were arrested, but Valentin
Turchin, the leader of the Moscow group of
Amnesty International who was arrested in July,
was allowed to emigrate.

There seemed to have been a slight decline in
Jewish emigration, the number of Jews going to
Israel in the first six months of 1977 totaling 3,394,
about 10% less than for the equivalent period in
the previous year. On the other hand, Col. Vladimir Obidin, head of the department concerned
with emigration, stated in January that in the absence of "social" motivation, the would-be emigrants were mainly Jews wishing to be united
with their families and that about 98% of exit requests were being granted. In June another U.S.
journalist, Robert Toth, the Moscow correspondent of the *Los Angeles Times*, was detained and interrogated on suspicion of espionage, but after
some delay he was allowed to leave the Soviet
Union. A young British student of Ukrainian origin, Andrew Klymchuk, was less fortunate; he
was arrested in August while visiting the Ukraine
and might be brought to trial.

Dissent was often linked with violence. On
January 8 a bomb explosion on the Moscow subway killed several people, and the nuclear physicist Andrey Sakharov, one of the leading
personalities among the dissidents, promptly
claimed that the bomb had been planted by the
secret police. In June another bomb went off outside the Sovietskaya Hotel in Moscow; the arrest of
a terrorist was reported soon afterward. A wave of
arson and bomb attacks directed against public
buildings in Georgia, reported in August, led to
calls for stiffer penalties for the destruction of state
property. In September a public riot involving
more than 300 police occurred in the city of
Bryansk, in protest against the seizure by the authorities of a new Baptist prayer house.

The Soviet leaders also worked hard to convince
their public that the dissidents were unrepresenta-
tive, and that the Soviet citizen enjoyed considerable advantages in comparison with the insecurity
and unemployment prevailing in capitalist societies. Thus, when U.S. Pres. Jimmy Carter received
the exiled Soviet dissident Vladimir K. Bukovsky
(*see* BIOGRAPHY) in Washington, D.C., in March,
the Soviet journal *Literaturnaya Gazeta* contrasted
life in the U.S.S.R. with conditions in the U.S.,
infested by "millions of unemployed, racial discrimination, social inequality of women, infringe-
ment of citizens' personal freedom, growth of
crime, etc."

Foreign Affairs. The relationship with the U.S.
obviously underwent a significant change with
the advent of a new administration in Washington
at the beginning of the year. President Carter put
a much greater emphasis on human rights than
had his predecessor, and in the first few months of
his administration the U.S. pressed hard in support of those who called for the full implementation of the Helsinki accords by the Soviet Union.
The Soviet government basically rejected this new
U.S. approach as blatant interference in the internal affairs of the U.S.S.R. In a speech to the Congress of Trade Unions on March 21, Brezhnev
made it clear that "Washington's claim to teach
others how to live cannot be accepted by any sovereign state."

After President Carter's visit to Europe in May
the U.S. tone became less strident, although the
U.S. continued to affirm its commitment to the

cause of human rights. The atmosphere at the Belgrade conference was therefore less acrimonious than had been feared, even though the U.S. delegation pressed its case with vigour and determination. Attitudes toward the chronic crisis in the Middle East reflected this rapprochement between the superpowers, who found common ground in their desire to localize the conflict.

Relationships between the U.S.S.R. and most of the Arab countries, especially Egypt, failed to recover from the setback caused by termination in March 1976 of the 1971 Soviet-Egyptian friendship and cooperation treaty. Egyptian Pres. Anwar as-Sadat's visit to Jerusalem in November was characterized as a "flirtation with Israel," and the U.S.S.R. declined to attend the Cairo preparatory peace talks. Egypt later recalled its ambassador to the Soviet Union.

In Africa Soviet diplomacy appeared to make no progress after the goodwill tour of southern African states by President Podgorny in March. The Soviet Union maintained close relations with Angola, Mozambique, Libya, and Algeria and continued to support the Marxist regime in Ethiopia in its struggle to stem the guerrilla forces in Eritrea and Ogaden. Consequently, the U.S.S.R. withdrew its military support from Somalia, which was actively encouraging the indigenous Somali guerrilla forces in Ogaden. Somalia then joined with Sudan and Egypt in a defensive alliance and sought military supplies in the West. In November Somalia followed the example of the Sudan in May by expelling Soviet civilian and military advisory personnel from its territory. Thus, at the year's end the Soviet Union no longer had a firm grasp on the Horn of Africa and the Red Sea.

The limitation of strategic nuclear arms — the other major issue in Soviet-U.S. relations — appeared to be intractable during the first half of the year. Marshal Ustinov in his statement for Soviet Armed Forces Day in February advised the U.S. against embarking on an arms race, denying that the Soviet Union was trying to achieve strategic superiority. He also stressed, however, that it could match any weapons systems the U.S. might develop. Despite the complications caused by the potential introduction of the cruise missile and the neutron bomb, the U.S. decision to abandon the B-1 bomber was well received in Moscow and toward the end of the year it seemed that another interim agreement on arms limitation might be reached. (*See* Defense: *Special Report.*) A Soviet-British treaty on preventing an accidental outbreak of nuclear war, signed during the visit to Moscow in October by David Owen, the British foreign secretary, was an encouraging pointer in that direction.

Relations with the Chinese, however, did not improve. The Soviet view remained unchanged: there were no irreconcilable differences and the Soviet people had at all times demonstrated a friendly attitude toward the Chinese.

The Economy. Thanks mainly to the favourable 1976 harvest, the economic position of the Soviet Union maintained the levels achieved in previous years without undue difficulty. The constantly increasing involvement of the U.S.S.R.

with the global economic system led to a serious trade deficit with the West, brought about partly by price inflation in the latter. An increase in the cost of travel took place early in the year, and internal fares on Aeroflot, previously the cheapest in the world, went up by 20%. At the same time, the prices of a wide range of luxury goods and of books were raised, while those of a few durable consumer goods went down. N. T. Glushkov, chairman of the State Committee on Prices, went on television to explain that this was "not inflation" but simply the result of higher production and transportation costs caused by the transfer of certain manufacturers to Siberia. He pointed out, with justice, that food remained cheap.

The effect of inflation was much more important in its impact on the foreign trade position of the Soviet Union. The U.S.S.R. was in surplus in its trade with the other countries of the Communist bloc and with the third world, but its deficit, along with that of its Eastern European allies, vis-à-vis the West presented a serious problem. Nevertheless, the Soviet debt position did not deteriorate in 1977 as much as had been feared, thanks mainly to the growing exports of oil and natural gas and to the record harvest of 1976, which finally totaled 223.8 million metric tons of grain. But there was a shortage in the wheat harvest, and in 1977 the Soviet Union expected to have to buy 6 million metric tons of wheat in the U.S.; on the other hand, there was a considerable surplus of barley, which was offered for sale on the world market.

The authorities obviously wanted to repeat the success of the 1976 harvest, and despite poor weather conditions the 1977 winter wheat crop was again a record. The policy of providing incentives for farmers was continued. At the beginning of the year modest housing credits, at low rates of interest, were made available to the rural population. In July *Izvestia* recalled that Brezhnev himself had on several occasions urged that farmers should be encouraged to develop their household plots, the small holdings of land held privately by individual collective farmers to enable them to grow produce for their own use. Obviously, practical results had to be allowed to override ideological considerations, for the household plots, which took up only about 4% of the total arable area, produced a third of the country's meat, milk, vegetables, and eggs, and half of its potato crop.

The results of the 1977 harvest were disappointing, though not disastrous. Only 194 million metric tons of grain were harvested, a decline of 13% from the 1976 record and 9% below target. The crop was still the fourth largest in Soviet history, but the decline in the harvest was significant in relation to the country's needs and expectations (the current five-year plan called for an annual average of 220 million metric tons to 1980).

In the area of energy, the U.S.S.R. had advantages, although some Western experts predicted that an energy shortage would begin to affect the Soviet economy by the mid-1980s, when it could be expected that industrial progress would have raised the current relatively low levels of energy consumption. The U.S.S.R. possessed more than half of the world's proved energy reserves. It exported large quantities of natural gas to West Germany, France, Austria, and Italy as well as to Eastern Europe, and the construction of a new 2,-000-mi pipeline from the Orenburg gas fields in the southern Urals would ultimately double Soviet supplies of natural gas to Eastern Europe. A West German loan was being negotiated by the East European Investments Bank for the Orenburg line. The Soviet Union was prepared to sell energy to the West in exchange for the technology needed to develop its oil and gas deposits; thus, for example, several major U.S. companies were approached in connection with the building of a pipeline from the Tyumen fields to the Soviet submarine fleet's major base at Murmansk, and bids from U.S., West German, French, and Japanese companies were invited for the supply of special gas compression equipment for use in the oil fields.

The critical issue for the nation was the long-term projection of crude oil production in the face of mounting energy consumption. The 1976 production total of 520 million metric tons was yet another record; but in order to meet increased production targets and make good the loss of production due to the exhaustion of oil wells still in use, the Soviet oil industry needed to find an additional output capacity of 450 million tons by 1980. Although offshore drilling had been taking place in the Caspian Sea for decades, the Soviets lacked deep-sea drilling experience. While there was some cooperation with Poland and East Germany in the shallow Baltic, the U.S.S.R. looked to U.S. and Japanese firms for the technology needed to hunt for oil off Sakhalin Island and elsewhere in the Pacific, as well as in the Arctic.

Despite concessions to the miners, including a 30-hour week for workers in "difficult" areas, coal production did not meet its targets in 1976. The long-term solution was seen to lie with nuclear energy. One-fifth of all the electricity-generating capacity to be installed between 1977 and 1980 was to be nuclear, and it was intended that by 1980 the country's nuclear-energy capacity would total 19.4 million kw, equal to that of France or West Germany.

Generally, Soviet manufacturing continued to mark time; the modest targets for 1976 were met, with output up by 4.8% (0.5% in excess of target), real income by 3.7% (on target), and productivity by 3.3% (slightly below target). The increase in productivity was the smallest in 25 years, and the growth rate was low by Soviet standards, especially as steel and coal failed to fulfill their plans. During the first eight months of 1977 there was some slight improvement; overall output was reported to have increased by 5.7% and labour productivity by 4.2%.   (OTTO PICK)

United Arab Emirates

Consisting of Abu Dhabi, Ajman, Dubai, Fujairah, Ras al-Khaimah, Sharjah, and Umm al-Qaiwain, the United Arab Emirates is located on the eastern Arabian Peninsula. Area: 83,600 sq km (32,300 sq mi). Pop. (1975): 656,000, of whom (1968) 68% were Arab, 15% Iranian, and 15%

United Arab Emirates

Indian and Pakistani. Cap.: Abu Dhabi town (pop., 1975, 95,000). Language: Arabic. Religion: Muslim. President in 1977, Sheikh Zaid ibn Sultan an-Nahayan; prime minister, Sheikh Maktum ibn Rashid al-Maktum.

In 1977 Abu Dhabi tried to tighten the structure of the federation. When a new Cabinet was sworn in on January 4, President Sheikh Zaid said it would reflect available talent rather than the interests of each of the emirates. However, a proposal to reduce Abu Dhabi's share of the federal budget from 97 to 75% was opposed by Dubai, Ras al-Khaimah, and Umm al-Qaiwain. The 1977 federal budget totaled 13 billion dirhams—a 200% increase over 1976, largely due to the inclusion of Abu Dhabi's health, education, and information budgets. Defense was allocated $658 million.

An arms agreement was signed with France in April, and a merger of the emirates' armed forces was completed in June. The U.A.E. followed Saudi Arabia's lead in limiting oil price increases. An increase in new banks caused a financial crisis, and failure to limit their numbers led to the resignation of the British president of the U.A.E. Currency Board in June.

Sheikh Zaid visited the two Yemens in March, and various Arab leaders paid visits to Abu Dhabi. At the Afro-Arab summit meeting in Cairo in March, the U.A.E. pledged $137 million to African states. Abu Dhabi's foreign aid amounted to 25% of its revenues. Severe penalties for illegal immigrants and stricter immigration controls were announced.   (PETER MANSFIELD)

United Kingdom

A constitutional monarchy in northwestern Europe and member of the Commonwealth of Nations, the United Kingdom comprises the island of Great Britain (England, Scotland, and Wales) and Northern Ireland, together with many small islands. Area: 244,035 sq km (94,222 sq mi), including 3,041 sq km of inland water but excluding the crown dependencies of the Channel Islands and Isle of Man. Pop. (1976 est.): 55,927,600. Cap. and largest city: London (Greater London pop., 1976 est., 7,028,200). Language: English; some Welsh and Gaelic also are used. Religion: mainly Protes-

United Kingdom

tant with Catholic, Muslim, and Jewish minorities, in that order. Queen, Elizabeth II; prime minister in 1977, James Callaghan.

The Queen's Silver Jubilee. With undiminished attachment to a monarchical constitution, Britain in 1977 marked the 25th anniversary of the accession of Queen Elizabeth II (*see* BIOGRAPHY). It was a Silver Jubilee summer of regal ceremony, royal visits to all parts of the British Isles, and street parties galore in which British subjects were joined by a record number of foreign tourists who made London the most comprehensively cosmopolitan of the world's cities. In addition to attending an estimated 800 local events during the summer months the queen and Prince Philip paid visits to other Commonwealth countries.

In the course of hundreds of speeches the queen took the opportunity to make an occasional political point. With the debate on devolution of power to Scotland and Wales in progress, she told the two houses of Parliament, "I cannot forget that I was crowned queen of the United Kingdom of Great Britain and Northern Ireland. Perhaps this jubilee is a time to remind ourselves of the benefits which union has conferred, at home and in our international dealings, on the inhabitants of all parts of this United Kingdom." In Ottawa she commented warmly on the Canadian achievement of a diverse society with French and British traditions. In Northern Ireland, where her visit was screened by intensive security precautions, she said, "People, everywhere, recognize that violence is senseless and wrong . . . their clear message is that it must stop."

On November 15 a son was born to Princess Anne and her husband, Capt. Mark Phillips. The queen's first grandson, he was also the first royal baby to be born a commoner in more than 500 years. Christened Peter Mark Andrew, he was fifth in the line of succession to the throne. His parents decided that he should not be given a title.

The Economy. Great Britain experienced a great turnabout in the economy in 1977. In the closing months of 1976 a rescue operation had been mounted by the International Monetary Fund (IMF). The exchange rate of sterling had fallen below U.S. $1.60; U.K. currency reserves, standing at around £2,500 million, had touched their lowest level in many years; the spending deficit was put at more than £10,000 million; and as a last ditch defense the Bank of England's minimum lending rate had been hoisted to an unprecedented 15%. In contrast, by the end of 1977 sterling was being held down against upward pressures at about $1.84; currency reserves had risen to a record £11,000 million; the government's borrowing requirement to meet Jubilee expenditure had been cut by one-third; and the minimum lending rate had been lowered in October to 5% to discourage the inflow of foreign money into London (it was raised to a more realistic 7% in November). Significantly, the U.K. was able to take control without a second slice of the available IMF loan.

A year of severe restraint on the wages front brought an estimated 8% decline in spending power. This was the most severe and abrupt drop

in the standard of living, apart from war years, in living memory. Reducing the rate of inflation remained the government's primary economic objective throughout the year. Counterinflation policies were hindered in the first half of the year by increased import prices due to the fall in the sterling exchange rate. This forced the pace of inflation up again, from an annual rate of around 13% in the summer months of 1976 to 15% in December, to more than 18% in the first three months of 1977, and above 20% in April. But this proved to be the turning point.

An inflation rate below 10%, which was the objective for the end of the year, was not reached. Attaining it in the near future would depend on the success of the government in holding down wage increases during the 12 months to mid-1978 to an average of about 10%. Officially, the trade unions had rejected a third successive year of statutory wage restraint, and the government had conceded a return to the principle of free collective bargaining—but with conditions almost as restrictive as statutory restraint. The government set a 10% limit that it was prepared to enforce on the public sector. In the private sector companies that exceeded the 10% limit would be penalized by withdrawal of government contracts. In addition there was to be not less than a 12-month gap between pay increases.

Prime Minister James Callaghan argued the case for holding out against excessive wage claims, making it plain to the Trades Union Congress and to the Labour Party that his government would resign rather than abandon its policy. It was generally conceded that such a move would mean a lost election for Labour, whereas overcoming inflation could well ensure Labour a long term at the helm. Callaghan felt the long-term prospects were good, and opinion polls showed he had at least 80% of the public standing firm behind him. And stand firm his government did, against power workers, police, and a national firemen's strike that dragged on for many weeks.

The government had another reason for enduring what Callaghan himself had said would be a rough winter. The mainspring of the economic recovery was North Sea oil, and only about the middle of 1977 did its effects become strongly felt. With seven fields on stream by midsummer, about half of Britain's oil requirements were being met from the North Sea. It was estimated that this would improve the U.K. balance of payments by £1,400 million in 1977 and by almost twice as much in 1978. From August onward the U.K. ran a substantial balance of trade surplus. This led to a great upsurge in world confidence in sterling that brought money flowing into Britain in embarrassing amounts. In the first nine months the overall balance of payments surplus reached £5,431 million, by far the highest figure ever recorded even for a whole year. The single threat to this recovery was another outbreak of wage inflation, which would make British exports uncompetitive in price.

The chancellor of the Exchequer, Denis Healey, eased the pressure of wage restraint by tax concessions in his main budget in March and in supple-

Scenes from the Silver Jubilee of Britain's Queen Elizabeth II. (Top left) Planting a silver birch; (top right) dressed in regal robes for a procession of the Royal Order of the Garter; (centre left) presenting a bouquet to a one-hundred-year-old subject; (centre right) the Jubilee emblem; (bottom) Britain's greatest ship, the "Queen Elizabeth II," arrives for the Jubilee celebration.

1977

THE QUEEN'S SILVER JUBILEE

mentary mini-budgets in July and October. Income-tax personal allowances and tax-rate thresholds were raised, and the standard rate of income tax was reduced one point to 34%. The Healey budgets also allowed for increased public spending, particularly in construction. Here he was tackling the most intractable of the government's economic problems—unemployment, which was high and proving resistant to conventional treatment by reflation. It crept up in September to 1,-450,000, or 6.1% of the work force, the highest figure since World War II. Within this total the high proportion of young people under age 25, which rose above 40% during the summer, caused special concern.

On December 1 publication of two reports disclosed that the Crown Agents, established in 1833 to raise loans and procure supplies for colonial governments, had sustained losses of £200 million since the early 1970s through financial mismanagement. A public inquiry was established by the government to investigate the matter.

Industry. In a year of stagnant production industrial relations took a turn for the worse. The motor industry was troubled by strikes reflecting conflicts between unions over pay differentials for skilled work, and consequently import car sales captured 50% of the British car market near the end of the year. At the end of September the government approved a loan of £50 million to dispute-ridden British Leyland. Strikes also cost the newspaper industry millions of copies, and some national papers were prevented from publishing for weeks at a time. A regional newspaper in Darlington was stopped for months by a dispute in which the claims of editorial freedom came into conflict with union insistence on a closed shop. In January the Bullock report, an official inquiry into industrial democracy, recommended that worker directors chosen by trade unions have equal representation with management on company boards of directors. The proposal was fiercely resisted by management, and no legislation was introduced.

A dispute over union recognition at Grunwick, a film-processing plant in North London, had been running since August 1976. At the end of 1977 it was still unsettled after attempts by the Association of Professional, Executive, Clerical and Computer Staff to force owner-manager George Ward (see BIOGRAPHY) to recognize union members in his plant had been fought up through the courts to the House of Lords, the ultimate court of appeal. The Grunwick affair had become a symbolic test case for the trade union movement.

Politics. The Labour government's many difficulties were compounded by an insecure majority in Parliament. Although in the opening months of the year it held a clear lead of 32 seats over the Conservatives, the balance was in the hands of 13 Liberals and 28 nationalists of six different political persuasions. Not surprisingly, the devolution bill for Scotland and Wales was the rock on which the government's majority first foundered when on February 22 a motion to impose a timetable on further debate on the bill was defeated by 312–283, and the government found itself obliged to abandon the most important piece of legislation in its program.

A month later the government was confronted with a vote of no confidence that it seemed likely to lose—in which event it would have been obliged to resign. At this time the Conservatives were far ahead of Labour in the opinion polls and would no doubt have won a general election. But there was widespread unease at the prospect of a third election within three years, not least among the Liberal MP's.

The Liberal leader David Steel and Prime Minister Callaghan reached an understanding whereby the Liberals undertook to support the government on certain conditions. Under the terms of the so-called Lib-Lab pact of March 23 it was agreed that the Liberals would work with the government "in pursuit of economic recovery," not joining it but engaging in regular consultation. In legislating for direct elections to the European Parliament, the government also was to recommend a form of proportional representation in the U.K., but this concept was rejected by a free vote of the Commons on December 13 by 319 votes to 222. Though a majority of Labour MP's voted in favour, this brought the entire Lib-Lab pact into question. Although

---

UNITED KINGDOM

Education. (1975–76) Primary, pupils 5,965,702, teachers 249,191; secondary, pupils 4,604,900, teachers 273,385; vocational, pupils 538,242, teachers 78,417; higher, students 301,173, teaching staff 43,245.

Finance. Monetary unit: pound sterling, with (Sept. 19, 1977) a free rate of £0.57 to U.S. $1 (U.S. $1.74 = £1 sterling). Gold, SDR's, and foreign exchange (June 1977) U.S. $11,726,000,000. Budget (1977–78 est.): revenue £37,742 million; expenditure £43,489 million. Gross national product (1976) £122,110 million. Money supply (May 1977) £19,-327 million. Cost of living (1970 = 100; June 1977) 251.

Foreign Trade. (1976) Imports £31,213 million; exports £25,778 million. Import sources: EEC 37% (West Germany 9%, The Netherlands 8%, France 7%); U.S. 10%. Export destinations: EEC 36% (West Germany 7%, France 7%, The Netherlands 6%, Belgium-Luxembourg 5%, Ireland 5%); U.S. 10%. Main exports: nonelectrical machinery 20%; chemicals 12%; motor vehicles 9%; electrical machinery and equipment 8%; diamonds 5%. Tourism (1975): visitors 8,880,000; gross receipts U.S. $2,443,000,000.

Transport and Communications. Roads (1975) c. 368,000 km (including 2,030 km expressways). Motor vehicles in use (1975): passenger 13,950,000; commercial 1,775,000. Railways: (excluding Northern Ireland; 1975) 18,118 km; traffic 36,840,000,000 passenger-km, freight (1976) 20,448,000,000 net ton-km. Air traffic (1976): 30,948,000,000 passenger-km; freight 914,450,000 net ton-km. Shipping (1976): merchant vessels 100 gross tons and over 3,549; gross tonnage 32,923,308. Shipping traffic (1975): goods loaded 51,290,000 metric tons, unloaded 177,220,000 metric tons. Telephones (Dec. 1975) 21,244,000. Radio receivers (Dec. 1974) 42 million. Television licenses (Dec. 1976) 17,995,000.

Agriculture. Production (in 000; metric tons; 1976): wheat 4,773; barley 7,793; oats 806; potatoes c. 5,030; sugar, raw value c. 743; cabbages (1975) 890; cauliflower (1975) c. 327; green peas (1975) c. 800; carrots (1975) c. 506; apples c. 389; dry peas c. 93; tomatoes c. 187; onions c. 213; hen's eggs 795; cow's milk 14,388; butter 79; cheese 221; beef and veal 1,038; mutton and lamb 252; pork 900; wool 31; fish catch 914. Livestock (in 000; June 1976): cattle 14,013; sheep 28,184; pigs 7,932; poultry 116,673.

Industry. Index of production (1970 = 100; 1976) 102. Fuel and power (in 000; metric tons; 1976): coal 123,809; crude oil 12,033; natural gas (cu m) c. 37,-275,000; manufactured gas (cu m) c. 10,300,000; electricity (kw-hr) 276,970,000. Production (in 000; metric tons; 1976): cement 15,781; iron ore (26% metal content) 4,584; pig iron 13,824; crude steel 22,279; petroleum products 90,288; sulfuric acid 3,-272; fertilizers (nutrient content; 1975–76) nitrogenous 1,055, phosphate 464, potash 34; cotton fabrics (m) 374,000; woolen fabrics (sq m) 143,000; rayon and acetate fabrics (m) 493,000; passenger cars (units) 1,334; commercial vehicles (units) 371. Merchant vessels launched (100 gross tons and over; 1976) 1,347,000 gross tons. New dwelling units completed (1976) 325,000.

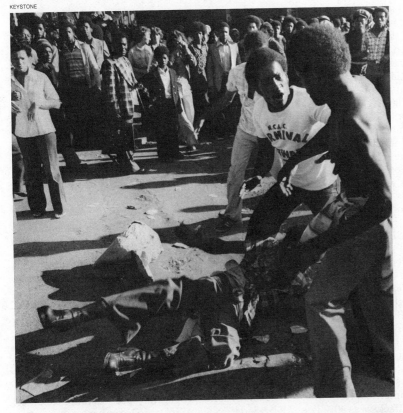

KEYSTONE

An annual festival of the West Indian community of London turned into a riot in August when youths began clashing with police and each other during the Notting Hill carnival.

the agreement was renewed in July and Steel secured the support of the Liberal Party assembly for the pact in September, by-election results and opinion polls indicated that the Liberals were losing voter support. Steel claimed that Liberals could take credit for the improvement of the economy through their influence with Labour ministers and by their rejection of confrontation politics, but many Liberals objected to a pact that kept a Labour government in office.

Early in the year Labour suffered humiliating defeats at by-elections and in local government elections. In April they lost a supposedly rock-solid seat in the mining constituency of Ashfield with a swing of 20.9% to the Conservatives, and in March the Birmingham seat of Stechford was lost with a swing of 17.6%. In the county council elections in May Labour was swept out of power by the Conservatives in Greater London and in the metropolitan counties of Greater Manchester, Merseyside, West Midlands, and West Yorkshire, and was left in control of only three nonmetropolitan counties in England and Wales.

The Conservative Party under the leadership of Margaret Thatcher endured a restless year, with disagreement over economic and industrial policy between free-market monetarists and critics of closed shop trade unionism on one wing and more moderate reformist Conservatives on the other. A party policy document called *The Right Approach to the Economy* published in October took a monetarist line on strict control of the money supply and government expenditure and lower taxation. While rejecting the idea of confrontation with the trade unions or imposing changes on the system of collective bargaining, it said the party would resist any direct political challenge by organized labour. It affirmed the Conservative Party's stand against the closed shop but conceded the right to negotiate a closed shop subject to certain conditions. At the annual Conservative conference Thatcher said that in a conflict with a union determined to bring down the government the issue would be put to a referendum.

The National Front, an extreme right-wing, neofascist fringe party, attracted more attention than votes by a number of provocative marches that led to violent clashes with fringe parties of the extreme left. In one at Lewisham in southeast London in August, more than 100 people were injured. In working-class areas the National Front exploited racist prejudice in elections, and in some places attracted enough support to take third place behind Labour and Conservatives.

Foreign Affairs. The death of Anthony Crosland (*see* OBITUARIES) on February 19 led to the appointment of David Owen (*see* BIOGRAPHY) to succeed him as secretary for foreign and Commonwealth affairs. At 38 the youngest member of the Cabinet, Owen concentrated his attention from April onward on framing a program for peaceful transfer of power in Rhodesia from white rule to the Zimbabwe people by a negotiated settlement. With the backing of the U.S. and after discussions with the heads of neighbouring "front-line" African states, the U.K. presented its package on September 1. (*See* RHODESIA.) Though it had been patiently prepared, the package encountered obstruction by both Rhodesian Prime Minister Ian Smith and some African leaders, and the necessary preliminary cease-fire proved hard to secure.

Britain's relations with the European Economic

Community (EEC) were expected to improve with the U.K. occupying the presidency of the Council of Ministers (by rotation) in the first half of the year, and with Roy Jenkins, an ex-Cabinet minister, taking over as president of the European Commission. Nevertheless, British insistence on putting the national interest first caused irritation and strain within the EEC. Callaghan in particular adopted an aggressively nationalist stance, epitomized in his letter in September to the Labour Party secretary in which he underlined "dissatisfaction felt in Britain about the effect of membership" while rejecting any idea of withdrawal from the EEC. The government later went ahead with a bill for direct elections to the European Parliament, but probably too late for the 1978 election required by the Community.

David Owen quickly stamped his own personal style on British foreign policy, not only by a mix of youthful charm and professionalism but also by his commitment to principle. In particular he joined with U.S. Pres. Jimmy Carter in backing the cause of human rights. Callaghan also played a leading role in the conduct of British foreign policy, establishing close working relations with many heads of government.

Northern Ireland. Although terrorist violence continued in Northern Ireland, it was on a diminishing scale. The secretary of state for Northern Ireland, Roy Mason, told Parliament on December 8 that the number of shooting attacks was 40% less than in 1976, and the number of bombing attacks 60% less. Up to that date in 1977, 67 civilians had lost their lives, compared with 238 in the same period a year earlier. The terrorists, Mason said, were being squeezed out of society by the security forces and by increased rejection by the community. The British government planned to reduce the number of regular troops in Northern Ireland in 1978, but there would be no amnesty for terrorists.

Direct rule by the Westminster government was renewed for another 12 months in June. In August Mason announced a £950 million program to develop industry in Northern Ireland and to attract international companies.

The Nobel Prize for Peace held over from 1976 was awarded to the two founders of the Northern Ireland Peace Movement, Mairead Corrigan and Betty Williams. In spite of terrorist intimidation, they had worked to bring Protestant and Catholic communities together in what they called the Community of the Peace People, which was to be based upon grass-roots community politics. (*See* NOBEL PRIZES.) (HARFORD THOMAS)

See also Commonwealth of Nations; Dependent States; Ireland.

United Nations

Calling 1977 a "year of growing anxiety for the international community," Secretary-General Kurt Waldheim released to United Nations members on September 8 his annual report on the work of the organization. In it he said that he feared "a major international crisis in the not too distant future" unless Israel and the Arab states preserved

a spirit of moderation and realism and resumed negotiating at Geneva; he described the last stages of decolonization in Africa as the "most difficult" and "fraught with great and increasing dangers"; and he deplored the "hardening of positions" over Cyprus and "apparent failure" to carry out previous agreements aimed at settling differences between Greek and Turkish communities there. The political stakes in all three situations were high, Waldheim added, and the dangers of failure "increasingly ominous." If progress toward peaceful settlements did not emerge by the end of the year, he concluded that "the outlook for 1978 will be a serious and unsettled one." In fact, by the end of the year, important developments occurred in all three situations.

Middle East. UN, U.S., and Soviet efforts to bring the Middle Eastern states to the conference table at Geneva made little headway, but that failure was overshadowed by the dramatic visit to Israel by Egyptian Pres. Anwar as-Sadat on the weekend of November 19. Although the visit was largely symbolic, the symbolism was powerful indeed and generated forces that seemed to move Israel and Egypt closer than ever before to a permanent settlement of their 30-year-old conflict. At the UN, Waldheim described the visit as "an important development which could influence further efforts towards peace" in the area. The UN was an observer at the preparatory peace conference called by Sadat in Cairo in late December.

Until the Sadat visit, Middle Eastern prospects were far less happy. In July Israel announced that it had "legalized" three existing settlements on the West Bank of the Jordan River and in August that it had authorized three new ones. On October 28 the UN General Assembly, by a vote of 131–1 (Israel), with 7 abstentions, including the U.S., denounced these settlements and called on Israel to stop immediately any action that would change the legal status, geographic nature, or demographic composition of occupied territories and to comply strictly with the Geneva Convention on the Protection of Civilians in Time of War, a treaty that Israel insisted it was not violating.

In early November a special committee (Senegal, Sri Lanka, and Yugoslavia) reported on what it called a "continuing deterioration" of human rights in Israeli-occupied Arab territories, thus reiterating charges made in February by the UN Human Rights Commission in Geneva. The committee urged the international community to "assume its responsibilities" to end the Israeli occupation. It condemned Israeli policies of annexation and settlement; alleged that Israel had denied the "right of return" to hundreds of thousands of persons and was responsible for "alarming" prison conditions; and charged that Israeli interrogators had abused prisoners. Israel, which had not allowed the group to enter the country, denied all allegations.

In October the UN Relief and Works Agency (UNRWA) submitted to the secretary-general two reports on refugees from Palestine. One dealt with persons displaced after the 1967 war, whom the 31st Assembly had asked Israel to allow to return to their homes. Israel replied in September that it

had taken significant steps to facilitate reunions of the refugees with their families— UNRWA reported that 9,000 displaced persons had returned since 1967—but that it could not allow all of them to return because certain Arab governments would use the opportunity to infiltrate terrorists into Israel, and because the Palestine Liberation Organization (PLO) was committed to destroying Israel. The second report concerned refugees displaced in the Gaza Strip in 1971. Israel told Waldheim that security in the Strip was greatly improved and that new housing projects had enabled refugees to move out of camps there. UNRWA observed, however, that of the 2,554 families affected by demolitions in 1971, only 247 had been provided with accommodations.

Southern Africa. Acting under Chapter VII of the UN Charter, dealing with threats to the peace, breaches of the peace, and acts of aggression, the Security Council on November 4 imposed a mandatory arms embargo against South Africa. The unanimous decision capped two weeks of council debate set off by South Africa's action in banning antiapartheid groups, arresting antiapartheid leaders, and closing antiapartheid newspapers. The embargo applied to weapons and other military and paramilitary equipment and forbade nations to cooperate with South Africa in the manufacturing or developing of nuclear weapons. South Africa characterized the vote as unacceptable interference in its internal affairs and predicted that it would incite further violence. Waldheim said he hoped that South Africa would recognize how grave the council's decision was and would begin immediately to restore to all its people "fundamental human rights" without which peace was impossible.

At about the same time, the General Assembly expressed its indignation over South African policies and adopted its own resolutions calling on governments to close down enterprises in South Africa owned by their nationals or by corporations under their jurisdiction. The assembly condemned relations between the North Atlantic Treaty Organization and other countries with "racist regimes in southern Africa" and urged nations that had not yet done so to adhere to international trea-

ties outlawing apartheid and seeking an end to all forms of racial discrimination.

On August 22 Waldheim opened a world conference for action against apartheid in Lagos, Nigeria, which 100 nations attended. At the final meeting (August 26), the delegates adopted a declaration that called "the liberation of southern Africa . . . from colonial and racist rule" the final step in emancipating Africa from "centuries of domination and humiliation."

South Africa's policies in Namibia also were subjects of the General Assembly's attention. South Africa, which administered the territory (as South West Africa) under a mandate from the League of Nations, had refused to grant Namibia independence despite repeated calls from the UN to do so. Namibia was the subject of eight resolutions in 1977, all adopted in early November. In one, adopted 117–0 with 24 abstentions, the assembly again asked South Africa to open talks under UN auspices with the South West Africa People's Organization (SWAPO) to discuss the "modalities" for transferring power to the people of Namibia. The assembly also declared South Africa liable for reparations to Namibia for damage caused by its "illegal occupation," and rejected South Africa's decision during the summer to administer Walvis Bay in Namibia as part of its Cape Province. The assembly supported the armed struggle of the Namibians, led by SWAPO, to achieve freedom and independence in a united Namibia and urged the UN and member states to intensify support of Namibian independence.

In regard to another troubled area of southern Africa, Rhodesia, the Security Council on June 30 unanimously condemned the "illicit racist minority regime" there for committing acts of aggression against Mozambique and called those acts and other attacks and threats it said had been made against Zambia and Botswana "a serious aggravation of the situation." It asked all UN members to assist Mozambique and dispatched a mission there in July to assess the country's needs. Mozambique was the site (May 16–21) of a conference, sponsored by the General Assembly, to support the peoples of Zimbabwe (Rhodesia) and Namibia.

On September 29 the Security Council, by a vote

of 13–0 (the U.S.S.R. abstaining and China not participating), approved a draft resolution submitted by the United Kingdom that asked the secretary-general to appoint a UN representative for Rhodesia. Britain asked for the representative as a first step toward stopping the guerrilla fighting in Rhodesia and not as an endorsement of a U.S.-backed British plan calling ultimately for the UN to place a peacekeeping force there to help transfer power from the current regime to a new black majority government. On October 4, Waldheim appointed to the post Lieut. Gen. Prem Chand of India, who had had extensive peacekeeping experience in the Congo and in Cyprus. On November 24, Rhodesian Prime Minister Ian Smith announced that he was prepared to accept the idea of universal suffrage, a precondition that black African leaders had set as the price of negotiations to end the fighting.

As for other parts of Africa, Waldheim was concerned in March about an invasion of Zaire from Angola, which brought both Moroccan and French assistance to Zaire. On April 14, the Security Council condemned armed aggression against Benin that had taken place on January 16 and which, a council inquiry committee had concluded, had been mounted from neighbouring Gabon by troops trained in Morocco; Gabon denied this charge. On September 30, the secretary-general expressed concern about growing Ethiopian-Somali tensions and urged both parties to work toward a cease-fire and to settle their dispute peacefully.

Cyprus. In late August the ambassador from Cyprus to the UN charged that Turkey was moving to "colonize" the new town of Famagusta, thus aggravating an "intolerable situation" arising from Turkey's "unhindered violations" of UN resolutions and "crimes against the people of Cyprus involving expulsion of the indigenous inhabitants and systematic implantation of alien populations massively transported from Turkey." On August 31 the Cypriot foreign minister told the Security Council that prospects for peace in Cyprus would be dealt a "mortal blow" if Turkey was allowed to proceed with its "colonization." The council, without taking a vote, approved on September 15 a resolution expressing concern about developments in Cyprus and asking the parties to refrain from acting unilaterally so as to affect adversely prospects for solving their problems justly and peacefully. It also asked representatives of the Greek and Turkish communities on the island to resume negotiations as soon as possible. Meanwhile, the UN Force in Cyprus continued to operate with voluntary contributions from member nations but was reported to be running a deficit in mid-June of $48 million.

Other Matters. The 32nd session of the General Assembly opened on September 20 and elected as its president Lazar Mojsov, deputy foreign minister of Yugoslavia. On opening day UN membership rose to 149 with the admission by acclamation of Djibouti, formerly French Somaliland (which became independent on June 27 and was recommended unanimously by the Security Council on July 7), and of Vietnam (vetoed for membership by the U.S. in 1976 but recommended by consen-

sus of the Security Council on July 20). Mojsov welcomed both new members, commended the aid that the UN had given to Djibouti in achieving its independence, and referred to Vietnam as a "courageous and martyred country" deserving help in reconstruction after 30 years of war.

U.S. Pres. Jimmy Carter addressed the General Assembly twice during the year. The first occasion was at an informal session on March 17 specially convened to hear him pledge U.S. efforts to maintain peace, to reduce the arms race, to help build a better and more cooperative economic system, and "to work with potential adversaries as well as our close friends" to advance human rights. In his second address, on October 4, Carter praised both Mojsov and Waldheim, spoke of the need to curb nuclear weapons and tests, pledged again to limit U.S. arms exports, supported British efforts to bring about majority rule in Rhodesia and UN efforts on behalf of Namibia, urged peace in the Middle East, and cited the draft Panama Canal treaties as an example of U.S. interest in settling disputes peacefully. He declared that the U.S. would not employ nuclear weapons except after an attack on itself or its allies. He also urged all nations to work "to fulfill mankind's aspirations for human development and human freedom," and, in a ceremony at the UN on October 5, signed the UN Covenants on Civil and Political and on Economic, Social, and Cultural Rights—documents completed in 1966, which entered into force in 1976. Despite strong support for the UN in his speeches, Carter gave notice on November 1 that the U.S. would withdraw from the International Labour Organization a few days later.

On November 3 the assembly, without formal vote, called on all nations to take stronger measures against airplane hijacking. These included ratification of the Tokyo, Hague, and Montreal conventions on air security; taking stricter precautions at airports; and adopting other measures to avoid exposing flight crews and passengers to extortion. (RICHARD N. SWIFT)

[552.B.2]

United States

The United States of America is a federal republic composed of 50 states, 49 of which are in North America and one of which consists of the Hawaiian Islands. Area: 9,363,123 sq km (3,615,122 sq mi), including 202,711 sq km of inland water but excluding the 156,192 sq km of the Great Lakes that lie within U.S. boundaries. Pop. (1977 est.): 216,817,000, including 87% white and 11.5% Negro. Language: English. Religion (1974 est.): Protestant 72.5 million; Roman Catholic 48.7 million; Jewish 6 million; Orthodox 3.7 million. Cap.: Washington, D.C. (pop., 1976 est., 702,000). Largest city: New York (pop., 1976 est., 7,453,600). Presidents in 1977, Gerald Rudolph Ford and, from January 20, Jimmy Carter.

In an atmosphere of informality and goodwill, Jimmy Carter (*see* BIOGRAPHY) was sworn in on Jan. 20, 1977, as the 39th president of the United States. He had "no new dream to set forth today," he said in his inaugural address, but rather urged "a fresh faith in the old dream." The U.S. government, he added, must be "competent and compassionate" and "our commitment to human rights must be absolute, our laws fair, our natural beauty preserved; the powerful must not persecute the weak and human dignity must be enhanced."

After the inaugural ceremony, Carter eschewed the presidential limousine and, with his family, walked the mile and a half down Pennsylvania Avenue from the Capitol to the White House. This demonstration of the new president's "common touch" elicited much favourable comment, and Carter further burnished his image as a "man of the people" through innovative use of the broadcast media in the weeks following his inauguration. He addressed the nation in a televised "fireside chat," in which he was shown wearing a sweater; he appeared at a town meeting in Clinton, Mass.; and, in a nationwide radio broadcast, he talked with callers who telephoned the White House from points around the country. All these efforts to establish intimate contact with the people helped to buoy the president's standing in public opinion surveys during the early months of his administration.

As the months passed, however, Carter's popularity began to sag. Blacks, union members, and city dwellers—groups instrumental in his narrow election victory—complained that he was neglecting their needs. Washington political commentators asserted that the president seemed unwilling to delegate authority, often appeared irresolute, and was awkward in his dealings with Congress.

In a year-end interview with James Reston of the *New York Times*, Carter acknowledged that he had been surprised by the complexities of foreign and domestic affairs and disappointed by the opposition to many of his programs. Nevertheless, he expressed confidence that he had established a solid foundation for progress at home and abroad. "This country has been through such an ordeal in the last five or 10 years," Carter told Reston, "that

it is still in a healing stage—Vietnam, CIA, Watergate. It really shook the American people and their confidence in government. I don't think there will be a complete restoration of their confidence until proof is not only complete but extended over a period of time. . . . I think we just have got to go through a long trial period in the minds of the American people before they accept the fact they can trust the American government again."

Foreign Affairs. The "human rights" theme of Carter's inaugural address soon came to be a key element of the administration's foreign policy. Outlining the premises of his foreign policy in a commencement address at the University of Notre Dame on May 22, Carter said, "We can no longer separate the traditional issues of war and peace from the new global questions of justice, equity and human rights." This did not mean "that we conduct our foreign policy by rigid moral maxims." The President understood "the limits of moral suasion." "I have no illusion that changes will come easily or soon," he said. "But I also believe that it is a mistake to undervalue the power of words and the ideas that words embody." (*See* Feature Article: *Human Rights—The U.S. Initiative.*)

The human rights campaign complicated U.S. relations with a number of countries, none more so than South Africa, with its policy of apartheid or racial separation. After meeting with South African Prime Minister B. J. Vorster in Vienna, May 18–20, U.S. Vice-Pres. Walter F. Mondale (*see* Biography) told reporters that no progress had been made in resolving "fundamental and profound disagreement" over apartheid. He had warned Vorster not to "rely on any illusions that the U.S. will in the end intervene to save South Africa," and he indicated that Washington was considering diplomatic action if South Africa continued to deny equal rights to its black majority.

Andrew Young (*see* Biography), the U.S. ambassador to the UN and chief spokesman for the administration's Africa policy, visited South Africa May 21–22 at the invitation of Harry Oppenheimer, a leading South African businessman

United States

Jimmy Carter was sworn in on January 20 by Chief Justice Warren E. Burger as the 39th president of the United States. (Far left) Former president Gerald R. Ford and Sen. Hubert H. Humphrey (wearing hat) looked on.

698

United States

and a supporter of racial reform. Young told a group of 200 South African business leaders that "you have no real alternative" to sharing power with blacks, Coloureds (persons of mixed race), and Asians. "If one believes in the free market system then one must include blacks. . . . If they are not included they have no choice but to look for another system." In later talks with white university students and with both black and white community leaders at a U.S. government office in Johannesburg, Young suggested that blacks use economic boycotts to effect changes in racial policy, as U.S. blacks had done in the 1950s and '60s.

But U.S. pressure on South Africa had no discernible effect, and relations took a turn for the worse following the death of Steven Biko (*see* OBITUARIES), a South African black activist leader and poet, while he was in police detention. Washington reacted sharply to the subsequent South African crackdown on suspected dissidents and to the outcome of an inquest into Biko's death, which found that no person or group was responsible, despite considerable evidence that Biko had been physically abused. The U.S. voted for a UN embargo on arms sales to South Africa but refused to support a proposal for a UN economic embargo.

Possibly the most controversial foreign policy initiative of the Carter administration in 1977 was the signing of two treaties governing the future of the Panama Canal. Carter and Brig. Gen. Omar Torrijos Herrera, Panama's chief of government, signed the accords at a ceremony in Washington on September 7, as leaders of other Western Hemisphere nations looked on. The treaties, which required ratification by the U.S. Senate, would give Panama control over the canal at the end of 1999 and would guarantee the neutrality of the waterway thereafter. (*See* PANAMA.)

Speaking at the signing ceremony, Carter stressed the treaties' "fairness," the fact that they guaranteed the canal's neutrality, and their importance to improved U.S. relations with Latin America. The new canal arrangement "opens a new chapter in our relations with all nations of this hemisphere," he said. "This agreement is a symbol for the world of the mutual respect and cooperation among all our nations." He pointed out that the initiative for a new canal agreement had been "bipartisan"; it had been supported by two Democratic presidents (Lyndon Johnson and Carter himself) and two Republicans (Richard Nixon and Gerald Ford), and Ford, two former secretaries of state in Republican administrations, Henry Kissinger and William Rogers, and Johnson's widow, Lady Bird, were all present at the signing ceremony. Support for the treaties was also voiced by some prominent conservatives, including syndicated columnist William F. Buckley, Jr., and actor John Wayne.

Nevertheless, the outlook for ratification of the treaties was clouded. In mid-August Senators Orrin G. Hatch (Rep., Utah), Strom Thurmond (Rep., S.C.), and Jesse Helms (Rep., N.C.) traveled to Panama to tell U.S. residents of the Canal Zone and Panamanian officials that the treaties were doomed. Public opinion was reported to be running against the treaties, and the senators also had

the support of prominent opponents of the accords, including the Veterans of Foreign Wars, the American Conservative Union (ACU), and Citizens for the Republic, a political group organized by Ronald Reagan, the former governor of California. A newspaper advertisement placed by the ACU proclaimed: "There is no Panama Canal! There is an American Canal at Panama. Don't let President Carter give it away!"

Carter made his first trip to Europe as president in May to attend a two-day "economic summit" meeting with leaders of Britain, Canada, France, Italy, Japan, and West Germany. In a communiqué issued at the end of the conference, the participants pledged to continue policies of moderate economic growth in order to "create jobs while continuing to reduce inflation." The communiqué also rejected protectionist trade policies and promised to "give a new impetus" to the long-stalled Tokyo round of tariff negotiations being conducted under the auspices of the General Agreement on Tariffs and Trade. During the meeting the seven leaders discussed Carter's stand on human rights but took no position on the issue. West German Chancellor Helmut Schmidt had sharply criticized Carter's outspoken support for Soviet dissidents on the grounds that it might provoke the Soviets to adopt even harsher repressive measures.

The human rights issue did in fact strain U.S.-Soviet relations in the early weeks of the Carter administration. In a statement issued on January 27, the U.S. State Department warned Moscow against trying to silence Andrey D. Sakharov, a prominent physicist and outspoken critic of political repression—the first time the U.S. had publicly supported a Soviet dissident. Expressing admiration for Sakharov, the statement went on to say that "Any attempts by the Soviet authorities to intimidate Mr. Sakharov will not silence legitimate criticism in the Soviet Union and will conflict with accepted international standards in the field of human rights."

Subsequently, Carter assured Anatoly F. Dobrynin, the Soviet ambassador to the U.S., that "We are not attacking the Soviet Union, but we are expressing our commitment on human rights." This did not placate Soviet leader Leonid I. Brezhnev, however. In an address before the Congress of Trade Unions in Moscow on March 21, he denounced "direct attempts by official American bodies to interfere in the internal affairs of the Soviet Union" and warned: "A normal development of relations on such a basis is, of course, unthinkable." Referring to the forthcoming visit of U.S. Secretary of State Cyrus Vance (*see* BIOGRAPHY) to the U.S.S.R., he remarked: "We will see what he brings with him." He complained of "stagnation" in U.S.-Soviet relations since the 1976 U.S. presidential election, though he expressed a belief that they would "eventually run a satisfactory course."

What Vance brought with him to Moscow were two proposals for concluding a new strategic arms limitation talks (SALT) agreement to replace the one due to expire in October, but they were rejected out of hand by the Soviets. Speaking at a news conference in Moscow on March 30, after the con-

He was unjustly accused of financial manipulations, Budget Director Bert Lance told a Senate committee in testimony in September. Lance claimed unfair coverage by the media.

clusion of his talks with Soviet leaders, Vance said, "The Soviets . . . did not find either [American proposal] acceptable. They proposed nothing new on their side." Both sides did agree, however, to resume the SALT negotiations in Geneva in May, and in a dinner speech at Des Moines, Ia., on October 21, Carter predicted that an arms agreement with the Soviets would be consummated within "a few weeks." (See DEFENSE: *Special Report.*)

The U.S. and the Soviet Union did combine their efforts to reconvene the Geneva Middle East peace conference, which had recessed after a brief session in December 1973. In a surprise diplomatic initiative, the two countries, as co-chairmen of the conference, issued a joint declaration on October 1 suggesting that the conference guarantee "the legitimate rights of the Palestinian people" and establish "normal peaceful relations" in the region. In its discussion of the Palestinian question, the statement neither mentioned the Palestine Liberation Organization by name nor specified what was meant by Palestinian "rights." The statement also called for: "insuring the security of borders between Israel and the neighbouring Arab states"; "withdrawal of Israeli armed forces from territories occupied in the October 1967 conflict"; participation at Geneva of "the representatives of all the parties involved in the conflict, including the Palestinians"; and Soviet-U.S. willingness to participate in "international guarantees" of secure borders in the region.

The Israeli government rejected the U.S.-Soviet statement as "unacceptable," and the document was also denounced in the U.S. by influential members of Congress, labour leaders, and leaders of the American Jewish community. But the statement was quickly forgotten when Egyptian Pres. Anwar as-Sadat accepted an invitation from Prime Minister Menahem Begin of Israel to come to Jerusalem to discuss a settlement of the Arab-Israeli dispute and to address the Knesset. After some initial hesitation, Carter hailed Sadat's visit as "a great occasion," and the U.S. sent a delegation of observers to the preliminary peace talks convened

by Sadat in Cairo in December. (See MIDDLE EASTERN AFFAIRS.)

On December 29 Carter began his first major overseas trip as president, going first to Poland and then to Iran on the 31st. The planned itinerary included India, Saudi Arabia, France, and Brussels. An earlier, more extensive tour had been canceled so Carter could remain in Washington during a debate on his energy bill.

Domestic Affairs. In its first session, the 95th Congress pursued one of the busiest legislative agendas in recent history. Carter and his new administration sent proposals to Capitol Hill on issues ranging from airbags and aliens to welfare and water projects, until it became conventional wisdom in Washington that the president was trying to accomplish too much too soon. Taking note of the complaints, Carter later promised to slow the flood of legislative proposals.

Prompted largely by the 1976 scandal involving Rep. Wayne Hays and a mistress he kept on his official payroll, both the House and the Senate approved new codes of ethics that placed limits on a member's outside earnings and required more detailed financial statements from members and staff aides. Generally unpopular among members, the reforms were adopted in large measure to quiet public objections to a $12,900 pay raise congressmen received in February. In October, with the pay raise no longer a live issue, the House rejected a more stringent package of rules governing members' conduct. The Senate, meanwhile, voted to reorganize its committee structure. Leon Jaworski, who had been Watergate special prosecutor, was named to head a congressional investigation of the "Koreagate" affair. (See KOREA.)

Congress gave Carter authority, similar to that granted previous presidents, to reorganize the executive branch. It also approved Carter's plan for a single Department of Energy incorporating several formerly scattered agencies. Former defense secretary James R. Schlesinger (see BIOGRAPHY) was named to head the new department. At the height of the coldest winter in the nation's history,

Congress gave Carter authority to order transfers of natural gas to regions facing shortages. But Congress balked at the president's request that it stop funding of a fast breeder nuclear reactor at Clinch River, Tenn. Carter, who opposed the technology as potentially dangerous, vetoed legislation authorizing the funds. By December, however, Congress was considering another bill to appropriate the money.

Carter's energy plan, a package of bills that was the centrepiece of his legislative program, encountered rough going. The House approved the package virtually intact, thanks to the strict timetables and procedural rules laid down by Speaker Thomas P. O'Neill, Jr. (Dem., Mass.). It went along with the president's proposals to continue price controls on natural gas, impose heavy taxes on crude oil and fuels used by industry, and rebate energy-tax revenues to consumers. The Senate — after a filibuster and counterfilibuster that kept the senators at work through all-night sessions — voted to deregulate the price of newly discovered natural gas, and it ignored the energy taxes. When Congress adjourned in December, a House-Senate conference committee was still at work trying to reconcile the many differences between the House and Senate versions of the bills. (See ENERGY.)

Two bills strongly supported by organized labour failed to win approval. One would have permitted common-site picketing, in effect liberalizing permissible strikers' tactics in the construction industry, and the other would have required a certain percentage of imported oil to be carried by U.S. tankers. Congress did pass a new minimum wage bill, raising the hourly level in

The antihomosexual campaign of singer Anita Bryant stirred angry passions on both sides throughout the year. Here demonstrators protested Bryant's concert appearance outside Municipal Auditorium in Kansas City, Missouri, in July.

UPI COMPIX

stages to $3.35 over a four-year period. Both houses passed legislation raising the minimum mandatory retirement age to 70 years, but final action awaited conference committee agreement on exemptions.

In the field of social welfare, Congress revised the food-stamp program to eliminate the controversial requirement that all recipients purchase their stamps. It also agreed to stiff new taxes to shore up the financially shaky Social Security system and rejected Carter's plan to finance the system from general revenues. (See SOCIAL AND WELFARE SERVICES.) House and Senate committees started work, but did not get far, on Carter's $30.7 billion plan to overhaul federal welfare programs. The most emotional issue of the session — use of Medicaid funds to finance abortions — led to a five-month deadlock that held up appropriations for the Departments of Labor and of Health, Education, and Welfare. The year was almost over before the House and Senate agreed to prohibit Medicaid funding except for women whose life or health was endangered and for victims of incest or rape that had been "promptly reported" to a law enforcement or public health agency.

Environmental legislation approved in 1977 included a measure extending the deadline for automobile manufacturers to reduce emissions that cause air pollution. Congress also approved limits on strip-mining operations, and Carter signed the bill, which had been vetoed twice by President Ford. Reacting to Carter's sharp criticism of pork-barrel projects, Congress eliminated or cut funding for nine water development schemes. The 1972 Water Pollution Control Act was extended in legislation that encompassed numerous compromises between environmentalists and industry.

Congress approved a $110 billion Defense Department appropriation, $4 billion less than Carter had requested. Still unsettled was the fate of the B-1 bomber, a supersonic plane sought by the Air Force to replace its aging fleet of B-52s. Carter announced on June 30 that he had decided against production of the B-1; instead, he said, the U.S. should modernize its airborne nuclear deterrent by deploying cruise missiles. But congressional supporters of the B-1 still were trying to salvage some funds for it at year's end. Both houses voted to lift the Byrd Amendment, which had permitted the U.S. to buy chrome from Rhodesia despite UN economic sanctions against that country.

Two important appointments hung fire during most of the year. After an extensive search, Carter named federal judge Frank Johnson as FBI director, but he was forced to withdraw by ill health. A long period of suspense ended on December 28, when Carter announced that G. William Miller, chairman of Textron, Inc., would replace the controversial Arthur Burns as chairman of the Federal Reserve System's Board of Governors.

Only scattered state and local elections were held in 1977. In a dramatic come-from-behind victory, Democrat Brendan Byrne won reelection on November 8 as governor of New Jersey over Republican state senator Raymond H. Bateman. Meanwhile, Republican John Dalton beat Democrat Henry E. Howell, Jr., to become governor of

Virginia. The national significance of the two races was unclear: Carter had campaigned in New Jersey for the winner and in Virginia for the loser. In all, 38 major cities elected mayors November 8. Edward I. Koch (*see* BIOGRAPHY) was elected mayor of New York and pledged to come to grips with the city's widely publicized financial and social problems. Dennis J. Kucinich, 31, became the youngest mayor of a major U.S. city (Cleveland), and Coleman A. Young was reelected in the only major mayoral race between two black candidates (Detroit). Earlier in the year, Tom Bradley was reelected mayor of Los Angeles, and Michael Bilandic was elected mayor of Chicago, succeeding the late Richard Daley. Richmond, Va., and New Orleans, La., elected their first black mayors.

For the women's movement in the U.S., 1977 was a year of both pride and frustration. More than 2,000 women gathered in Houston, Texas, November 18–21 for the National Women's Conference, which was held by congressional mandate, funded by the federal government, and organized by the National Commission on the Observance of International Women's Year. The climax of the meeting was the adoption of a platform of national action to bring about equality for women. The only point on a 25-part prepared agenda that failed to win approval was a proposal for a Cabinet-level women's department in the federal government. In the closing minutes of the conference, about 300 delegates who described themselves as pro-life and pro-family walked off the convention floor singing "God Bless America." They were led by Joan Gubbins, a state senator from Indiana, who opposed the Equal Rights Amendment, legalized abortion, and lesbian rights, all of which received conference backing.

The incident dramatized the fact that Americans as a whole remained deeply divided over the role of women in society. More than 48% of U.S. women aged 20 to 64 worked outside the home, yet a nationwide survey conducted in 1976 by Yankelovich, Skelly and White found that the overwhelming majority of parents—including three-quarters of the working mothers interviewed—believed that women with small children should not work unless the money was really needed. Nearly 70% of the parents questioned said that children were better off when their mothers did not work. According to an April 1977 Harris survey, between 1970 and 1977 the proportion of Americans favouring "efforts to strengthen and change women's status in society today" grew from 42 to 64%, while support for passage of the Equal Rights Amendment to the Constitution fell from 65% in 1976 to 56% in 1977.

The ERA remained in limbo. Victory seemed to be in sight when Indiana became the 35th state to ratify it on January 18. Final ratification required the approval of only three additional state legislatures, and ERA lobbyists were confident of success. Then followed a string of defeats—in Missouri, Nevada, North Carolina, Virginia, and Florida. Sponsors in Oklahoma returned the measure to committee rather than face the certainty of a losing vote, and ERA was bottled up or defeated in committee in Arkansas, Georgia, and Mississippi. Ac-

cordingly, Rep. Elizabeth Holtzman (Dem., N.Y.) introduced legislation in Congress that would extend the deadline for ratification from March 1979 to 1986. Phyllis Schlafly (*see* BIOGRAPHY), a leader of the anti-ERA forces, denounced the extension effort as "an act of desperation" and vowed to fight it through lobbying and, if necessary, in court.

The resignation on September 21 of Thomas B. ("Bert") Lance (*see* BIOGRAPHY) as director of the Office of Management and Budget was a major personal and political embarrassment to Carter, who had campaigned on a promise to bring probity to government. Lance was one of Carter's closest aides and confidants, a relationship dating back to Carter's term as governor of Georgia. The resignation, which Carter accepted "with the greatest sense of regret and sorrow," came in the wake of a continuing controversy over Lance's personal financial dealings.

The allegations against Lance were complex and difficult to comprehend in their entirety. *Time* magazine's May 23 issue contained the first accounting of his heavy personal debts, and as the weeks went on more articles appeared in the *New York Times*, the *Washington Post*, and *Newsweek* magazine. At issue were certain circumstances in the budget director's earlier career as a Georgia banker: (1) an enforcement agreement between the Calhoun (Ga.) First National Bank (which Lance headed) and the U.S. comptroller of the currency had been rescinded a day before Lance's nomination as budget director became known; (2) Lance had paid off two New York bank loans, possibly using the same collateral, two or three days before presenting his net worth statement to the Senate Governmental Affairs Committee; (3) when Lance ran unsuccessfully to succeed Carter as governor of Georgia, his campaign committee operated on an overdraft basis from the Calhoun bank; (4) Lance and his family continued to draw overdrafts in 1974 and 1975, although Lance had promised to stop the practice in a 1973 letter to the regional administrator of the comptroller's office.

Supporters were jubilant and opposition forces glum as the Indiana Senate voted in January to ratify the Equal Rights Amendment to the U.S. constitution. Indiana became the 35th state to ratify the amendment.

702

United States

Antiabortion demonstrators rallied on the grounds of the Capitol before marching to the White House in January.

These and other allegations were examined by the Senate Governmental Affairs Committee during televised hearings in mid-September. On the first day of the hearings Lance presented a lengthy and vigorous defense of his conduct. The committee, on the other hand, appeared bickering, partisan, and unsure of itself. The hearings themselves were a reminder of the committee's failure to investigate Lance thoroughly when his nomination was first considered. But by September the publicity had destroyed Lance's effectiveness in office, and he had no choice except to resign.

On July 13–14, power failure occurred throughout the five boroughs of New York City and in suburban Westchester County, leaving some nine million persons without electricity for between 4½ and 25 hours. The cause of the blackout appeared to have been a series of lightning bolts that struck two of Consolidated Edison Co.'s major 345,000-v transmission lines, automatically shutting down the utility's two largest generating facilities. During the darkness and into the next day there was rampant looting, vandalism, and other criminal activity, leading to the arrest of 3,200 persons. Damage was particularly severe in poor black and Hispanic neighbourhoods.

The U.S. economy generally was sluggish throughout 1977, with unemployment holding steady at about 7% of the work force and the stock market in a prolonged slump. Of particular concern was the mounting trade deficit. As recently as 1975 the U.S. had recorded a trade surplus of $11 billion, but through the first ten months of 1977, U.S. trade was in deficit by $22.4 billion. The November deficit of $2.1 billion marked the 18th consecutive month in which the value of U.S. imports exceeded that of exports. (*See* ECONOMY, WORLD.)

Much of the huge deficit was attributable to the country's increasing dependence on high-priced imported oil products. European monetary experts blamed the trade deficit and Congress' failure to complete action on Carter's energy program for the continuing weakness of the dollar against other major currencies, especially the West German mark and the Japanese yen. U.S. trade officials were pressing Japan to reduce its huge trade surplus vis-à-vis the U.S., which was expected to run as high as $7 billion for the year. Tokyo was asked to voluntarily reduce its exports to the U.S. and to provide greater access to Japanese markets for U.S. products. Meanwhile, there were increasing calls for more protectionist measures, especially from the hard-hit steel industry and from manufacturers of television sets.　　(RICHARD L. WORSNOP)

See also Dependent States.

UNITED STATES

Education. (1976–77) Primary, pupils 25,046,264, teachers 1,167,008; secondary and vocational, pupils 19,441,373, teachers 1,020,051; higher (including teacher training colleges), students (1976) 10,-087,000, teaching staff (1974–75) c. 633,000.

Finance. Monetary unit: U.S. dollar, with (Sept. 19, 1977) a free rate of U.S. $1.74 to £1 sterling. Gold, SDR's, and foreign exchange (June 1977) $13,-850,000,000. Federal budget (1977–78 est.): revenue $401.6 billion; expenditure $459.4 billion. Gross national product (1976) $1,706,500,000,000. Money supply (June 1977) $312.5 billion. Cost of living: (1970 = 100; June 1977) 156.

Foreign Trade. (1976) Imports $129,565,000,000; exports (excluding military aid exports of $190 million) $114,807,000,000. Import sources: Canada 21%; Japan 13%; West Germany 5%; Saudi Arabia 5%. Export destinations: Canada 21%; Japan 9%; West Germany 5%. Main exports: nonelectrical machinery 19%; motor vehicles 10%; cereals 9% (corn 5%); chemicals 9%; electrical machinery and equipment 8%; aircraft 5%. Tourism (1975): visitors 15,-698,000; gross receipts U.S. $4,875,000,000.

Transport and Communications. Roads (1974) 6,139,633 km (including 64,062 km expressways). Motor vehicles in use (1975): passenger 106,712,500; commercial (including buses) 24,837,000. Railways (1975): 331,311 km; traffic (class I only) 15,715,-000,000 passenger km, freight 1,101,870,000,000 net ton-km. Air traffic (1976): 288,020,000,000 passenger-km (including domestic services 240,020,-000,000 passenger-km); freight 9,083,770,000 net ton-km (including domestic services 5,929,200,000 net ton-km). Inland waterways freight traffic (1974) 518,000,000,000 ton-km (including 157,000,000,000 ton-km on Great Lakes system and 246,000,000,000 ton-km on Mississippi River system). Shipping (1976): merchant vessels 100 gross tons and over 4,616; gross tonnage 14,908,445. Ships entered (including Great Lakes international service; 1975) vessels totaling 254,346,000 net registered tons; goods loaded (1976) 258,267,000 metric tons, unloaded 448,220,000 metric tons. Telephones (Jan. 1976) 149,012,000. Radio receivers (Dec. 1974) 401.6 million. Television receivers (Dec. 1974) 121.1 million.

Agriculture. Production (in 000; metric tons; 1976): corn 157,893; wheat 58,444; barley 8,215; oats 8,164; rye 423; rice 5,308; sorghum 18,382; sugar, raw value c. 6,536; potatoes 16,035; sweet potatoes (1975) 639; soybeans 34,425; dry beans 781; cabbages (1975) 1,330; lettuce (1975) 2,372; peanuts 1,-694; onions c. 1,456; tomatoes c. 8,856; apples c. 2,826; oranges 9,506; grapefruit 2,585; peaches (1975) 1,379; grapes 3,649; sunflower seed 336; linseed 187; tobacco 961; cotton, lint 2,298; butter 435; cheese 1,790; hen's eggs 3,844; beef and veal 12,200; pork 5,653; timber (cu m; 1975) 295,802; fish catch (1975) 2,799. Livestock (in 000; Jan. 1976): cattle 127,976; sheep 13,346; pigs 49,602; horses (1975) c. 8,956; chickens 379,192.

Industry. Index of production (1970 = 100; 1976) 122; mining 104; manufacturing 123; electricity, gas, and water 118; construction 93. Unemployment (1976) 7.7%. Fuel and power (in 000; metric tons; 1976): coal 609,500; lignite 22,780; crude oil 401,-594; natural gas (cu m) 559,000,000; manufactured gas (cu m) 25,760,000; electricity (kw-hr) 2,117,624,-000. Production (in 000; metric tons; 1976): iron ore (55–60% metal content) 80,539; pig iron (1975) 74,-515; crude steel 116,311; cement (shipments) 61,613; newsprint 2,846; other paper (1975) 41,555; petroleum products (1975) 601,209; sulfuric acid 29,-954; caustic soda 9,214; plastics and resins 9,260; synthetic rubber 2,313; fertilizers (including Puerto Rico; nutrient content; 1975–76) nitrogenous 9,262; phosphate 6,655, potash 2,099; passenger cars (units) 8,498; commercial vehicles (units) 2,978. Merchant vessels launched (100 gross tons and over; 1976) 1,047,000 gross tons. New dwelling units started (1976) 1,549,000.

THE SUNBELT SURGE

by Niles M. Hansen

For more than half a century the centre of population in the United States has been shifting west and south. In recent years sharply increased streams of migrants out of some of the nation's colder regions have been moving to the Sunbelt, the tier of 15 states in the southern third of the country plus southern California. Between 1970 and mid-1976 the population of the Sunbelt rose by 7,265,000 persons, or 64% of the total national increase. A massive influx of migrants into Florida added 22% to its population between 1970 and 1976. Even more significant has been the diffusion of growth due to migration throughout the South and West during the present decade. Except for Florida, the South had experienced net out-migration prior to 1970, but net in-migration since then has matched that in Florida. Nevertheless, in-migration is not the major cause of the South's recent growth. The region has a relatively high birthrate, and a decline in its out-migration rate has resulted in increased population retention.

The publicity given to recent growth in the Sunbelt has tended to obscure the fact of rapid growth in other areas. For example, between 1970 and 1975 the rate of population increase in the 13 Western states was greater than that in the South, and north-ern California grew more rapidly than Sunbelt California. Moreover, there has been a remarkable revival of nonmetropolitan growth throughout the U.S.

Even within the Sunbelt growth is not a universal phenomenon. Some nonmetropolitan areas with high proportions of blacks continue to stagnate, and some former "boomtown" metropolitan areas that grew as the defense and aerospace industries flourished are now experiencing out-migration.

Despite these qualifications, the rapid growth of the Sunbelt and the relative decline of the Northeast and North Central regions are likely to continue. Already this pattern of change has given rise to new regional alliances, such as the Coalition of Northeast Governors, the Northeast-Midwest Economic Advancement Coalition, and the Southern Growth Policies Board. Although these groups have tended to refrain from casting migration and economic issues in extreme terms of "regional conflict" and "sectionalism," the associated publicity has aroused sentiments in those directions. Thus, in recent years, migration has taken on considerable political as well as demographic and economic importance.

Accessibility and Climate. The recent relative rise of the Sunbelt has taken place during a period largely characterized by national economic stagnation and recession, but the factors underlying the region's expansion are likely to work in its favour even when the national business situation improves. Improvements in transportation and communications networks have served to integrate the South more closely into the nation as a whole. The completion of the Interstate Highway System, which was relatively delayed in the South, the extension of jet airplane service, and the universal presence of na-

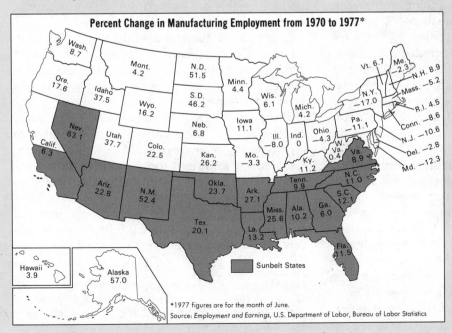

Percent Change in Manufacturing Employment from 1970 to 1977*

Wash. 8.7
Ore. 17.6
Mont. 4.2
Idaho 37.5
N.D. 51.5
Minn. 4.4
Wyo. 16.2
S.D. 46.2
Wis. 6.1
Mich. 4.2
Vt. 6.7
Me. -2.3
N.H. 8.9
N.Y. -17.0
Mass. -5.2
R.I. 4.5
Conn. -8.6
N.J. -10.6
Del. -2.8
Md. -12.3
Nev. 63.1
Utah 37.7
Colo. 22.5
Neb. 6.8
Iowa 11.1
Ill. -8.0
Ind. 0
Ohio -4.3
Pa. -11.1
W. Va. 0.4
Va. 8.9
Calif. 6.3
Ariz. 22.8
N.M. 52.4
Kan. 26.2
Mo. -3.3
Ky. 11.2
Tenn. 9.9
N.C. 11.0
S.C. 12.1
Okla. 23.7
Ark. 27.1
Tex. 20.1
La. 13.2
Miss. 25.6
Ala. 10.2
Ga. 6.0
Fla. 11.5
Hawaii 3.9
Alaska 57.0

■ Sunbelt States

*1977 figures are for the month of June.
Source: *Employment and Earnings*, U.S. Department of Labor, Bureau of Labor Statistics

tional television are cases in point. Air conditioning has overcome the reluctance of many people to put up with the hot Southern summer. On balance, the Southern climate is now an attractive force, as witnessed by the large influx of retired persons. Even in Florida and Arizona, however, retirees account for less than a quarter of the in-migration.

The growth of the Sunbelt appears to be the result of a mixture of economic and noneconomic factors. Recent studies indicate that there is no simple cause-and-effect relationship between average income levels and population growth in Sunbelt communities, though the presence of retirees is a complicating factor. Economists also have found that the relationship between migration and employment is complex. Employment opportunities attract migrants, but it can also be shown that in-migration often creates local jobs. The situation is analogous to that of the chicken and the egg. In any event, it is clear that many people have moved to the Sunbelt or have chosen to remain there because of considerations of climate and life-styles. It is equally clear that the Sunbelt has attributes that are attractive to businessmen.

Economic Advantages. As already indicated, the Sunbelt has benefited from greater access to the rest of the nation. In addition, the region's growth has been self-reinforcing because it has created larger internal markets. Businessmen also have been attracted to the South by the presence of a large pool of workers who have a reputation for hard work and a reluctance to join labour unions, and by wage levels that have been comparatively low. The relatively rapid growth of manufacturing activities in the South has been taking place for more than two decades. For example, manufacturing employment in the South grew at an annual rate of 4% between 1960 and 1970, compared with only 1.1% in the rest of the country. The absolute increase in the South was 1,490,000 jobs, compared with 1,410,000 elsewhere. Since 1970 manufacturing employment growth in the Sunbelt (excluding Nevada) has risen by only 434,000, but the comparable national figure fell by 393,000, with declines of 769,000 in the Northeast and 185,000 in the North Central states.

The postwar industrialization of the Sunbelt—and especially the South—was initially based on low-wage, slow-growth industries, but there has been an upgrading over time of manpower qualifications, types of industry, and incomes. Although manufacturing growth prospects continue to be brighter in the Sunbelt than in the rest of the nation, future regional employment gains will no doubt come in those sectors where they have been greatest in recent years, that is, in services, trade, and state and local government.

Federal Spending. The most controversial issue surrounding the rise of the Sunbelt has been the regional distribution of federal government spending. Some critics have argued that the federal government unfairly subsidizes the Sunbelt at the expense of the older industrial regions of the North. In fact, comparisons of federal tax receipts and expenditures by region do indicate a moderate tilt in favour of the South. Virtually all of this advantage, however, comes from spending for goods and services rather than from grants-in-aid to state and local governments or from transfer payments (the largest category of federal outlays, which includes Social Security, Medicare, unemployment benefits, and the like). Transfer payments are made to individuals on the basis of personal claims and may safely be excluded from the regionalism debate. Since 1970 per capita grant-in-aid receipts in the Sunbelt states have fallen steadily in relation to those in the North, and formula changes adopted in the past two years have accelerated this shift.

The federal spending that definitely has benefited the Sunbelt has been generated by the cost advantages enjoyed by the South and West, such as clear skies for missile testing, economies from the agglomeration of subcontractors, nearness to military installations, and lower private-sector wages. Like the private sector, the federal government has attempted to get the best product for the least cost. The alternative would be to compensate regions with cost disadvantages, which in itself would promote regional confrontation. It has also been maintained that federal subsidies for new capital investment have encouraged the premature scrapping of older facilities (including housing) and that on balance this has harmed the relative economic efficiency of mature industrial regions.

Despite the arguments over the largely unintended regional consequences of various federal policies and programs, the Sunbelt, like other regions, cannot rely on the federal government to solve its problems at the expense of the rest of the nation. The challenge to the region is to complete its industrial modernization; to deal with the massive problem of rural poverty; to develop its energy and agricultural resources; to resolve its social problems under conditions of rapid population growth; and to avoid the environmental degradation that marked the urbanization of the North. This will require a sense of purpose and close collaboration between the private sector and government at all levels.

Niles M. Hansen, a professor of economics at the University of Texas, is the author of Public Policy and Regional Economic Development *and* Human Settlement Systems.

UNITED STATES STATISTICAL SUPPLEMENT
DEVELOPMENTS IN THE STATES IN 1977

Measures to counteract the growth of expensive governmental services were introduced in state legislatures throughout the nation during 1977, with nearly half of the states adopting formal plans to terminate within a set time period agencies that had outlived their usefulness. Concern over finances helped keep state tax hikes down as well.

Faced with failure of the federal government to enact a comprehensive energy plan, many states adopted their own conservation measures during one of the most severe winters of the century. States were also involved in action to undo other perceived failures of the federal government, concentrating on such areas as abortion, equal rights for women, and legalization of the drug laetrile.

It was a bad year for official corruption on the state level, with two House speakers and a sitting governor stripped of office after conviction for felonies involving personal ethics. And exposure of organized rings of child pornographers led to a spate of new legislation outlawing abuse of minors by publishers and procurers. Forty-nine states (all except Kentucky) held regular legislative sessions, and 17 staged special lawmaking meetings during the year.

Party Strengths. Although Republicans managed modest gains, Democrats retained control of three legislatures elected in 1977, in Kentucky, New Jersey, and Virginia. For 1978, Democrats would thus continue to control both houses of 35 state legislatures while Republicans dominated in only 4. All states were solidly Democratic except Colorado, Idaho, South Dakota, and Wyoming (where Republicans formed the majority in both houses); Arizona, Indiana, Kansas, Maine, New York, Utah, and Vermont (where each party controlled one chamber); Montana, New Hampshire, and North Dakota (where one chamber was tied); and Nebraska (which has a nonpartisan, unicameral legislature).

In the only two gubernatorial elections held during the year, Democrats retained power in New Jersey and Republicans kept office in Virginia. That left the lineup among governors for 1978 identical to 1977: 37 Democrats, 12 Republicans, and one independent.

A survey of the nation's 7,600 state legislators indicated 22% were attorneys, down from 26% in 1966. Incidence of lawyer-lawmakers ranged from 2% in Delaware and New Hampshire to 57% in Virginia. Eight percent of the legislators were women and 4% were retired, both increases over the past ten years.

Government Structures and Powers. Concern over the growth of governmental bureaucracy provoked a stampede of "sunset" legislation during the year. As pioneered by Colorado in 1976, the laws typically provide for automatic termination of government agencies and bureaus every few years unless their continuation can be justified to a legislative committee. By the end of 1977, some version of sunset had

been enacted in 23 additional states: Alaska, Alabama, Florida, Louisiana, Arkansas, Georgia, Oklahoma, Indiana, Montana, New Mexico, South Dakota, Utah, Connecticut, Hawaii, Kentucky, Maine, Nebraska, New Hampshire, North Carolina, Oregon, Rhode Island, Tennessee, and Texas. Governors of Iowa and Washington vetoed similar legislature-approved bills.

In line with the trend toward cost-cutting and efficiency, governors throughout the nation ordered many money- and time-saving measures for state government, including hiring and construction freezes, layoffs and firings, and paperwork reduction reviews. Montana and Connecticut enacted thorough overhauls of executive branch structure, while Kansas, Kentucky, and Wisconsin reorganized their judicial systems.

Voters in Kentucky and New York turned thumbs down on ballot proposals for state constitutional conventions. Measures designed to improve voter turnout were rejected in two states. A postcard registration system was defeated by Washington electors in November, and Ohio voters canceled an election-day registration plan already in limited operation. North Carolina voters approved an amendment allowing a second four-year term for the state governor; incumbent Democrat James Hunt was the immediate beneficiary. Only seven states continued to restrict the governor to a single term in office.

Tennessee and West Virginia markedly expanded civil service protection afforded state workers. Alaska selected a unique architectural plan for its new capital, to be built in a wilderness area in the Matanuska-Susitna Valley 70 mi N of Anchorage; the design emphasized man-made lakes and transportation by bus, boat, snowmobile, and ski rather than by automobile. Florida officials moved into a new capitol building during the year but were unable to decide on the fate of the old structure, built in 1845.

Governmental Relations. Interaction between state capitals and the federal government continued at a high level during 1977, but some observers detected a resurgence of federalism — in this case, an assertion of powers by state officials in the face of growing authority from Washington — at work in several areas. State officials were active in pushing for constitutional amendments on abortion and women's rights (*see* below), and by the year's end 19 state legislatures had called on Congress to enact strict rules prohibiting deficit spending by the federal government.

As usual, there were conflicts of varying seriousness between states. The Idaho attorney general threatened to sue the state of Washington for "rain-rustling" if cloud-seeding programs were instituted by Washington to relieve drought conditions. After tempers cooled, Colorado, Nevada, Utah, and Washington went ahead with planned cloud-seeding. The Massachusetts House of

Representatives in June reorganized itself from 240 to 160 members; after losing their only representative to the House, residents of Nantucket and Martha's Vineyard threatened to secede from the state. Gov. Ella Grasso said that Connecticut would welcome the disenfranchised citizens, noting that Connecticut has a long history of harbouring disaffected former residents of Massachusetts.

Finances and Taxes. As a nationwide economic recovery continued into its third year, thereby increasing revenue collections by states, legislative action on taxes during 1977 was exceptionally light. A survey by the Tax Foundation revealed that only 16 states raised the rate of one or more of their major levies, and higher excise taxes on cigarettes, gasoline, and alcoholic beverages accounted for half of the $476 million additional annual revenue from revised rates. A large number of states again reported surpluses of revenue over expenditures, making the year an especially tranquil one at state treasuries.

Personal income tax rates were raised by Nebraska and Louisiana; a planned reduction in Michigan was canceled in order to finance a new budget and economic stabilization fund. Legislators in Kansas and Minnesota raised income-tax rates for high-income taxpayers but lowered them for lower-income citizens. New York also provided for early repeal of a 2.5% surtax and other minor relief for personal income taxpayers.

Four states increased corporate income tax rates: Delaware, Louisiana, New Hampshire, and Nebraska, which had been the only state to do so in 1976. New York extended a sizable corporate tax surcharge for an extra year. Utah reduced its corporate and bank tax, and Oregon, Missouri, and Indiana granted liberalized tax credits to businesses investing in disadvantaged areas.

Maryland and Nebraska increased their sales taxes, and Oklahoma boosted its use tax. Washington, Tennessee, and Rhode Island extended sales tax increases previously scheduled to expire during the year. At least 12 states removed some purchases from sales tax applicability, while Wisconsin added to its sales tax base by including computer services.

Easily hidden excise tax boosts continued to be the most popular method of raising additional revenue. Florida, Delaware, South Carolina, Montana, North Dakota, Nebraska, New Hampshire, and Washington hiked motor fuel taxes. A temporary gas tax increase in Hawaii was made permanent. Oregon and Tennessee imposed new taxes on wines. Florida, Indiana, Kansas, Mississippi, Montana, Nebraska, Oregon, and Virginia raised rates on all alcoholic beverages. Cigarette taxes were increased in Colorado, Florida, Indiana, and South Carolina.

Continued concern over energy problems prompted 20 state legislatures to encourage conservation through tax relief, usually by providing incentives for use of solar energy systems. New severance taxes (taxes on the taking and use of natural resources) were imposed in Colorado, Alabama, South Dakota, North Dakota, and Montana; some existing severance levies were increased in Florida, Minnesota, Oregon, and South Dakota.

Figures accumulated in 1977 showed that state revenue from all sources totaled $185.2 billion during the 1976 fiscal year, an increase of 19.8% from the preceding 12 months. General revenue (excluding state liquor and state insurance trust revenue) was $152.1 billion, up 13%. Total state expenditures rose 16.5% to $182 billion, creating a surplus of $3.2 billion for the year. General expenditures, not including outlays of the liquor stores and insurance trust systems, amounted to $153.7 billion, up 11.1% for the year. Of general revenue, some 58.7% came from state taxes and licenses; 11.9% from charges and miscellaneous revenue, including educational tuition; and 29.4% from intergovernmental revenue (mostly from the federal government).

The largest state outlay was $59.6 billion for education, of which $19.7 billion went to state colleges and universities and $34.1 billion to local public schools. Other major outlays were $29.6 billion for public welfare, $18.1 billion for highways, and $11.1 billion for health and hospitals.

Ethics. Maryland Gov. Marvin Mandel (see BIOGRAPHY) was convicted of corrupting his office for personal profit by a federal jury in Baltimore on August 23. He was the first incumbent governor to be found guilty of a federal crime in more than 40 years. The jury deliberated a record 13 days following a ten-week trial before finding that Mandel had accepted $350,000 in gifts from five codefendants while using the governorship to enrich their businesses. On October 7, Mandel was sentenced to four years in prison, but he remained free indefinitely while appealing the verdict. He had earlier turned over duties of office to Lieut. Gov. Blair Lee III in order to prepare for the trial. Mandel's predecessor as governor was Spiro Agnew, who had been forced to resign as vice-president of the U.S. in 1973 following revelation of a kickback scheme during his gubernatorial term.

Two state House speakers were also forced from office after corruption convictions. Pennsylvania Democrat Herbert Fineman resigned after being convicted of blocking an inquiry into admissions procedures at state medical schools. He was sentenced to two years in prison and fined $5,000. Richard Rabbitt of Missouri, also a Democrat, was sentenced to seven years and fined $18,000 after conviction for extortion and mail fraud. He was charged with taking kickbacks from an architectural firm doing state business and with accepting money from an automobile dealers' association to influence legislation.

Massachusetts state senators Joseph DiCarlo, a Democrat, and Ronald MacKenzie, a Republican, were sentenced to a year in prison after conviction for shaking down a New York consulting firm for $40,000. MacKenzie resigned his office, but DiCarlo refused and was expelled by the Senate on April 4. E. L. Boteler, Jr., a former Mississippi highway director, was convicted of embezzling $100,000 in state funds.

Although most states had approved stricter ethics codes for public officials in the aftermath of Watergate, additional action was taken during 1977. The governors of Minnesota, New York, and North Carolina promulgated new ethics codes for executive employees, including income-disclosure requirements, and the Ohio and Indiana Senates and the Massachusetts House set forth similar measures for their membership. A survey by the National Conference of State Legislatures revealed that by the year's end, 27 states had set up independent ethics or election commissions; 34 had limited campaign spending; all 50 had adopted open meetings laws; and all states except North Dakota required disclosure of campaign contributions and spending by candidates.

Education. States continued to wrestle with attempts to reduce disparities in spending between rich and poor public school districts. After a California Supreme Court decision in 1971 declared unequal spending to violate the state constitution's equal protection clause, 26 states adopted financing plans to increase aid to less wealthy districts, including Tennessee and South Carolina in 1977. Connecticut's Supreme Court became the third (after California and New Jersey) to order abolition of unequal financing as unconstitutional.

But a reaction also developed. Voters in Maine repealed a statewide property tax measure used to equalize funding among districts, leaving future spending plans in doubt. In other court action, California and Virginia joined eight other states in declaring that handicapped children have a right to equal public education with nonhandicapped students.

Health and Welfare. Seven states—Arkansas, Idaho, New Mexico, North Carolina, Nevada, Oregon, and Texas—followed California's 1976 lead and approved "right to die" bills during the year. The legislation typically allows sane patients under certain conditions to refuse the aid of artificial life-sustaining devices.

Maryland became the first state to enact legislative controls over research into recombinant DNA (deoxyribonucleic acid), which was criticized as dangerous and environmentally unsound. The California and New York legislatures also considered DNA regulation, and the New Jersey attorney general ruled that such research was subject to existing state legal strictures.

Nine more states—Alaska, Florida, Idaho, Indiana, Iowa, Montana, New York, Ohio, and Pennsylvania—adopted the uniform child custody jurisdiction act, designed to reduce disputes over snatching of children across state lines by estranged parents. By the year's end 20 had endorsed the act. As laws mandating fixed retirement fell out of vogue, California, Maine, and Vermont were among states outlawing compulsory retirement without cause.

Two federal initiatives failed to generate enthusiasm among states they were designed to aid. The most far-reaching involved a plan for federal takeover of many welfare costs; under the proposal, the federal government would assume 90% of the cost of basic welfare services and every state would be guaranteed at least 10% savings. The other initiative proposed limiting annual increases in hospital costs to 9%. But some states, including Connecticut, Maryland, Massachusetts, New Jersey, New York, and Washington, had already adopted effective plans to curtail hospital cost boosts even more drastically.

Abortion. A major change in direction by the U.S. Supreme Court fueled a long-standing controversy over availability and funding of abortion operations in the various states. On June 20, the high court provided an important modification to its 1973 decision declaring most state antiabortion laws unconstitutional; the new ruling held that states need not provide public funding to poor women unable to pay for such operations themselves. By the year's end, only 15 states (Alaska, California, Colorado, Florida, Hawaii, Idaho, Iowa, Maryland, Massachusetts, Michigan, Oregon, Pennsylvania, Washington, West Virginia, and Wisconsin) plus the District of Columbia still funded elective abortions.

"Right to life" forces continued to press for a U.S. constitutional convention to overturn the Supreme Court's 1973 ruling altogether. During the year, legislatures in 20 states entertained resolutions urging the constitutional convention be convened, and Arkansas, Massachusetts, New Jersey, Rhode Island, South Dakota, and Utah joined Indiana, Louisiana, and Missouri in endorsing the measure. Such a convention is mandatory when two-thirds of the states, or 34, call for it, and the American Civil Liberties Union formally adopted a resolution opposing the move as its top national priority for 1978.

Drugs. Debate over availability of the drug laetrile raged in nearly 30 state legislatures, with backers of the substance succeeding in making the sale (and occasionally the manufacture) legal in 13 states during the year. The federal Food and Drug Administration, citing absence of conclusive scientific evidence about its efficacy in the treatment of cancer, refused to sanction sale of the drug nationwide, but states were free to take action on their own. Alaska, Arizona, Delaware, Florida, Illinois, Indiana, Louisiana, New Hampshire, Nevada, Oklahoma, Oregon, Texas, and Washington responded by legalizing laetrile within their borders.

The trend to reduce penalties markedly for possession of small amounts of marijuana continued to make progress during the year, with Mississippi and New York decriminalizing the offense; by the end of 1977 nine states had removed criminal penalties for possession, typically substituting a small fine for first offenders. A similar bill was approved in the District of Columbia but was vetoed by the Washington mayor. There was one setback, however; a South Dakota decriminalization measure, scheduled to become effective April 1, was repealed by a new legislature, and jail terms were reimposed for marijuana possession.

Two surveys encouraged decriminalization advocates. One, by the National Governors' Conference, reported that use of marijuana had not increased substantially in states that had adopted decriminalization measures. The other survey, by the California Office of Narcotics and Drug Abuse, concluded that the state's marijuana decriminalization measure had resulted in a 74% savings by courts and law enforcement agencies in antidrug expenditures.

Law and Justice. Concern over exploitation of minors by pornographers prompted a spate of new state laws during 1977 that set stiff financial and prison penalties for offenders. Arizona, California, Connecticut, Delaware, Illinois, Michigan, Missouri, New York, New Hampshire, North Carolina, North Dakota, Ohio, Pennsylvania, Rhode Island, South Carolina, Tennessee, and Wisconsin were among states approving new anti-smut measures involving children.

Only one convict, multiple murderer Gary Gilmore in Utah, was executed during the year under terms of a 1976 U.S. Supreme Court decision permitting resumption of capital punishment following a ten-year hiatus. Gilmore, who did not contest his death sentence, was shot by a firing squad at the Utah state prison on January 17, but reviews and legal appeals prevented further executions among the nearly 400 death row inmates in other state prisons.

Oklahoma and Texas became the first states to provide for execution by injection of lethal chemicals; sponsors of the new laws said the process would be more humane than electrocution, traditionally employed in a majority of states. Nine state legislatures—California, Illinois, Maryland, Missouri, New York, South Carolina, Tennessee, Virginia, and Wyoming—enacted new capital punishment laws during the year. Although governors of California, Maryland, New York, and Tennessee vetoed the legislation, lawmakers overrode that veto in California and Tennessee, bringing to 35 the number of states with death penalty laws.

Washington voters approved an anti-smut referendum that effectively banned all adult movies and bookstores. Civil libertarians labeled the measure "outright censorship" and promised a court challenge to its constitutionality. During the year, New Hampshire moved to permit cameras, tape recorders, and broadcast equipment in courtrooms, joining six other states (Alabama, Colorado, Florida, Georgia, Washington, and Nevada) in experimenting with greater media access to criminal justice proceedings.

A perceived failure in the concept of rehabilitation for imprisoned convicts led several states to experiment with stiffer or less flexible sentences, thereby reducing the importance of the parole board. During the year, Illinois joined California, Indiana, and Maine in abolishing the indeterminate sentence, substituting instead a legislatively set fixed prison term without chance of parole. Illinois and Oregon were among states establishing mandatory minimum jail time standards upon conviction of certain crimes, eliminating the chance of probation. However, a study by a federal committee indicated that such laws do not work; in examining New York's tough 1973 drug law that required a stiff jail term for anyone convicted of trafficking, the committee determined that the measure had reduced neither drug use nor crime.

Gambling. The trend toward legalization of state-controlled wagering continued during 1977. Vermont became the 14th state to organize a lottery; Delaware joined four other states in permitting jai alai betting; and Indiana overrode a gubernatorial veto to establish pari-mutuel betting on horse races (though a lower court judge declared the move violated the state constitution). New Jersey completed preparations for the first casino-style gambling in the U.S. outside of Nevada; the casinos were to be limited to Atlantic City and would begin operation early in 1978. By the year's end, only five states—Hawaii, Mississippi, Missouri, Texas, and Utah—allowed no gambling within their borders.

Although state-run wagering was highly praised as a relatively painless method of raising government revenue, a study of gambling operations funded by the federal Law Enforcement Assistance Administration labeled the government operations as a regressive form of revenue collection, an inefficient use of state resources, and a bad bet for gamblers themselves. Noting that illegal bookies return up to 95% of their intake to bettors while state lotteries return only 40–45%, Cornell University professor G. Robert Blakey concluded: "Apart from the question of legality or morality, no one but a fool would gamble with state-run operations."

Environment. California, Maine, and Minnesota followed Oregon's lead and banned aerosol cans using fluorocarbons in future years; federal agencies proposed a nationwide ban, but no action on that proposal was taken during the year. Vermont prohibited sale of detergents with significant phosphate content. Ohio voters, heeding advice from hunters, defeated a constitutional amendment that would have barred the use of leg-hold traps for snaring wild animals.

New York and Massachusetts joined New Jersey in experimenting with government purchase of farmers' land development rights in order to preserve open space in areas threatened by urbanization. Federal courts ordered New York and New Jersey authorities to permit the Anglo-French Concorde supersonic transport, opposed by environmentalists, to land at New York's Kennedy Airport. Regular flights were initiated in November; the Concorde had been using Dulles Airport, near Washington, D.C., for more than a year.

Energy. More than a dozen states were declared major disaster or emergency areas during winter weather conditions that in some areas were the most severe in the 20th century. The winter, characterized by cold and excessive snow in the East and drought in the West, prompted state governors to take a variety of actions to conserve fuel, maintain services, and relieve persons thrown out of work by the weather.

Authorities in Alaska, New Jersey, and Tennessee established special advisory committees to set state energy policies. Louisiana officials approved the nation's first offshore oil port, a $1 billion facility to be constructed starting in 1978. Supertankers, which must currently offload their cargo onto smaller ships, were scheduled to be depositing 1.4 million bbl of oil daily at the port by 1980 and 3.4 million bbl by 1989.

Oregon voters turned down a $439 million non-nuclear energy development program for the state; in 1976, the same electorate rejected a referendum prohibiting nuclear power plant construction. Texas authorized land condemnation for a Colorado-Texas coal slurry. A report by the U.S. secretary of transportation accused most states of doing a poor job in enforcing the 55 mph speed limit. Virginia compiled the best record, with 70% of highway travelers obeying the law; Wyoming, Connecticut, Missouri, Maine, and Texas had the worst, with well over 50% of their drivers ignoring the limit.

Equal Rights. Controversy over the proposed 27th Amendment to the U.S. Constitution, which would prohibit discrimination by sex, heated up during 1977, with proponents seeking an extension of the deadline for state ratification of the measure. During the year, Indiana became the 35th state to ratify the amendment, the first state to endorse ERA since North Dakota in 1975. But Idaho joined Nebraska and Tennessee in attempting to rescind earlier ratification, and the outlook for approval of 38 states by the March 22, 1979, deadline appeared bleak at the year's end. Ten state legislatures buried endorsement bills during the year.

Feminist supporters initiated a boycott of states failing to pass the measure, aiming particularly at convention centres in Illinois, Florida, Georgia, Louisiana, Missouri, Nevada, and Arizona. A U.S. Department of Justice opinion suggested that Congress could extend the 1979 deadline by a mere majority vote; opponents claimed that a two-thirds vote was necessary. The Justice report also maintained that states are forbidden to rescind ratification after once approving it.

California, Connecticut, Missouri, New Jersey, and New York enacted new anti-redlining measures, designed to make mortgage loans available in mixed or minority neighbourhoods. A new federal law prohibiting businesses from cooperating with the Arab boycott of firms supporting Israel preempted state antiboycott laws previously passed by Florida, New York, California, New Jersey, Minnesota, Massachusetts, Maryland, Ohio, Illinois, and Washington.

Prisons. Federal courts continued to find constitutional violations in the operation of many state prisons. During 1977, U.S. judges ordered drastic reductions in the inmate population at Delaware and Oklahoma prisons and a complete shutdown of existing facilities in Rhode Island. Virginia and Florida penal authorities were ordered to supply psychiatric care to mentally disturbed prisoners, and the U.S. Supreme Court ruled that all state prisons must have adequate law libraries for inmate use.

A survey by *Corrections* magazine revealed that 40 states were maintaining overcrowded prisons, 9 of them by more than 1,000 beds, and that 19 states were involved in litigation citing overcrowding. During the year, 283,433 inmates were imprisoned on a typical day, the magazine reported, in prisons with a total rated capacity of 262,768. Faced with legislation fixing mandatory minimum prison sentences for certain crimes, at least a dozen states were planning major correctional construction programs at year's end.

Consumer Protection. State attorneys general at a national meeting negotiated a $40 million settlement with the General Motors Corp. in December to repay consumers who received Chevrolet engines in other GM model automobiles. Twenty-seven states had filed suit against the nation's largest auto manufacturer after it was discovered that a total of 128,000 Buicks, Pontiacs, and Oldsmobiles had been equipped with similar Chevrolet power plants. The settlement guaranteed each purchaser a $200 rebate and a special three-year warranty on the engine.

State laws restricting advertising by attorneys and druggists were overturned by the U.S. Supreme Court, but observers noticed little immediate effect in the form of lower prices or competition benefiting consumers. Courts in Kentucky, Michigan, and New Jersey declared those states' prohibitions of price advertising on eyeglasses to be illegal, and the Federal Trade Commission announced a proposed regulation that would ban such restrictive laws nationwide. During 1977, Oregon became the 12th state to require unit pricing for food items.   (DAVID C. BECKWITH) 707

AREA AND POPULATION

Area and Population of the States

State	AREA in sq mi Total	Inland water[1]	POPULATION (000) July 1, 1970	July 1, 1976[2]	Percent change 1970–76
Alabama	51,609	901	3,451	3,665	6.2
Alaska	586,412	19,980	305	382	25.2
Arizona	113,909	492	1,792	2,270	26.7
Arkansas	53,104	1,159	1,926	2,109	9.5
California	158,693	2,332	19,994	21,520	7.6
Colorado	104,247	481	2,225	2,583	16.1
Connecticut	5,009	147	3,039	3,117	2.6
Delaware	2,057	75	550	582	5.8
Dist. of Columbia	67	6	753	702	−6.8
Florida	58,560	4,470	6,845	8,421	23.0
Georgia	58,876	803	4,602	4,970	8.0
Hawaii	6,450	25	774	887	14.6
Idaho	83,557	880	717	831	15.9
Illinois	56,400	652	11,137	11,229	0.8
Indiana	36,291	194	5,208	5,302	1.8
Iowa	56,290	349	2,830	2,870	1.4
Kansas	82,264	477	2,248	2,310	2.8
Kentucky	40,395	745	3,224	3,428	6.3
Louisiana	48,523	3,593	3,644	3,841	5.4
Maine	33,215	2,295	995	1,070	7.5
Maryland	10,577	686	3,937	4,144	5.2
Massachusetts	8,257	431	5,699	5,809	1.9
Michigan	58,216	1,399	8,901	9,104	2.3
Minnesota	84,068	4,779	3,822	3,965	3.7
Mississippi	47,716	420	2,216	2,354	6.2
Missouri	69,686	691	4,693	4,778	1.8
Montana	147,138	1,551	697	753	8.0
Nebraska	77,227	744	1,490	1,553	4.2
Nevada	110,540	651	493	610	23.7
New Hampshire	9,304	277	742	822	10.8
New Jersey	7,836	315	7,195	7,336	2.0
New Mexico	121,666	254	1,018	1,168	14.7
New York	49,576	1,745	18,260	18,084	−1.0
North Carolina	52,586	3,788	5,091	5,469	7.4
North Dakota	70,665	1,392	618	643	4.0
Ohio	41,222	247	10,688	10,690	—
Oklahoma	69,919	1,137	2,572	2,766	7.5
Oregon	96,981	797	2,102	2,329	10.8
Pennsylvania	45,333	367	11,817	11,862	0.4
Rhode Island	1,214	165	951	927	−2.5
South Carolina	31,055	830	2,596	2,848	9.7
South Dakota	77,047	1,092	666	686	3.0
Tennessee	42,244	916	3,932	4,214	7.2
Texas	267,338	5,204	11,254	12,487	11.0
Utah	84,916	2,820	1,069	1,228	14.9
Vermont	9,609	342	447	476	6.5
Virginia	40,817	1,037	4,653	5,032	8.1
Washington	68,192	1,622	3,414	3,612	5.8
West Virginia	24,181	111	1,746	1,821	4.3
Wisconsin	56,154	1,690	4,433	4,609	4.0
Wyoming	97,914	711	334	390	16.8
TOTAL U.S.	3,615,122	78,267	203,805	214,659[3]	5.3

[1] Excludes the Great Lakes and coastal waters.
[2] Preliminary.
[3] State figures do not add to total given because of rounding.
Source: U.S. Department of Commerce, Bureau of the Census, *Current Population Reports.*

Largest Metropolitan Areas[1]

Name	Population 1970 census	1976 estimate	Percent change 1970–76	Land area in sq mi	Density per sq mi 1976
New York-Newark-Jersey City SCSA	17,033,367	16,839,800	−1.1	5,072	3,320
New York City	9,973,716	9,618,300	−3.7	1,384	6,950
Nassau-Suffolk	2,555,868	2,675,600	4.7	1,218	2,197
Newark	2,057,468	2,060,500	0.1	1,008	2,044
Bridgeport[2]	792,814	801,500	1.1	627	1,278
Jersey City	607,839	597,800	−1.7	47	12,719
New Brunswick-Perth Amboy	583,813	603,900	3.4	312	1,936
Long Branch-Asbury Park	461,849	482,200	4.4	476	1,013
Los Angeles-Long Beach-Anaheim SCSA	9,980,859[3]	10,468,000	4.9	34,007	308
Los Angeles-Long Beach	7,041,980	7,004,400	−0.5	4,069	1,721
Anaheim-Santa Ana-Garden Grove	1,421,233	1,755,600	23.5	782	2,245
Riverside-San Bernardino-Ontario	1,139,149[3]	1,255,500	10.2	27,293	46
Oxnard-Simi Valley-Ventura	378,497	452,500	19.5	1,863	243
Chicago-Gary SCSA	7,610,634[3]	7,650,400	0.5	4,657	1,643
Chicago	6,977,267[3]	7,006,400	0.4	3,719	1,884
Gary-Hammond-East Chicago	633,367	644,000	1.7	938	687
Philadelphia-Wilmington-Trenton SCSA	5,627,719	5,728,600	1.8	4,946	1,158
Philadelphia	4,824,110	4,891,800	1.4	3,553	1,377
Wilmington	499,493	520,200	4.1	1,165	447
Trenton	304,116	316,600	4.1	228	1,389
San Francisco-Oakland-San Jose SCSA	4,425,691[3]	4,642,100	4.9	5,390	861
San Francisco-Oakland	3,109,249[3]	3,158,900	1.6	2,480	1,274
San Jose	1,065,313	1,198,900	12.5	1,300	922
Vallejo-Fairfield-Napa	251,129	284,300	13.2	1,610	177
Detroit-Ann Arbor SCSA	4,669,154	4,638,000	−0.7	4,627	1,002
Detroit	4,435,051	4,389,900	−1.0	3,916	1,121
Ann Arbor	234,102	248,100	6.0	711	349
Boston-Lawrence-Lowell SCSA[2]	3,848,593	3,924,600	2.0	3,114	1,260
Washington, D.C.	2,909,353	3,070,900	5.6	2,812	1,092
Cleveland-Akron-Lorain SCSA	2,999,811	2,893,600	−3.5	2,917	992
Cleveland	2,063,729	1,960,200	−5.0	1,519	1,290
Akron	679,239	667,000	−1.8	903	739
Lorain-Elyria	256,843	266,400	3.7	495	538
Houston-Galveston SCSA	2,169,128	2,680,500	23.6	7,193	373
Houston	1,999,316	2,508,100	25.4	6,794	369
Galveston-Texas City	169,812	172,400	1.5	399	432
Dallas-Fort Worth	2,378,353	2,609,300	9.7	8,360	312
St. Louis	2,410,492	2,372,900	−1.6	4,935	481
Miami-Fort Lauderdale SCSA	1,887,892	2,334,200[4]	23.6	3,261	716
Miami	1,267,792	1,449,300[4]	14.3	2,042	710
Fort Lauderdale-Hollywood	620,100	884,900[4]	42.7	1,219	726
Pittsburgh	2,401,362	2,306,300	−4.0	3,049	756
Baltimore	2,071,016	2,152,400	3.9	2,259	953
Minneapolis-St. Paul	1,965,391	2,033,400	3.5	4,647	438
Seattle-Tacoma SCSA	1,836,949	1,842,200	0.1	5,902	312
Seattle-Everett	1,424,605	1,421,700	−0.2	4,226	336
Tacoma	412,344	420,500	2.0	1,676	251
Atlanta	1,595,517	1,840,800	15.4	4,326	426
San Diego	1,357,854	1,623,400	19.6	4,261	381
Cincinnati-Hamilton SCSA	1,613,414	1,608,300	−0.3	2,620	614
Cincinnati	1,387,207	1,362,300	−1.8	2,149	634
Hamilton-Middletown	226,207	246,000	8.7	471	522
Milwaukee-Racine SCSA	1,574,722	1,583,000	0.5	1,793	883
Milwaukee	1,403,884	1,407,300	0.2	1,456	967
Racine	170,838	175,700	2.8	337	521
Denver-Boulder	1,239,545[3]	1,442,500	16.4	4,651	310
Tampa-St. Petersburg	1,088,549	1,409,500[4]	29.5	2,045	689
Buffalo	1,349,211	1,320,900	−2.1	1,590	831
Kansas City	1,273,926	1,310,900	2.9	3,341	392
Phoenix	971,228	1,243,200	28.0	9,155	136

[1] Standard Metropolitan Statistical Area, SMSA, unless otherwise indicated; SCSA is a Standard Consolidated Statistical Area, which may be comprised of SMSA's.   [2] New England County Metropolitan Area.   [3] Revised.   [4] State-generated data that may not agree with published federal census reports.   Sources: U.S. Dept. of Commerce, Bureau of the Census, *Current Population Reports*; U.S. Dept. of Justice, FBI, *Uniform Crime Reports for the United States, 1976.*

Population Change

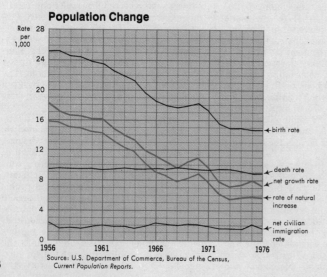

Rate per 1,000 — birth rate, death rate, net growth rate, rate of natural increase, net civilian immigration rate

Source: U.S. Department of Commerce, Bureau of the Census, *Current Population Reports.*

Marriage and Divorce Rates

Rate per 1,000 population — marriage rate, divorce rate*

*Includes annulments.

Source: U.S. Department of Health, Education, and Welfare, Public Health Service, *Monthly Vital Statistics Report.*

Church Membership

Religious body	Total clergy	Inclusive membership
Adventists, Seventh-day	3,207	509,792
Baptist bodies		
American Baptist Association	4,070	1,071,000
American Baptist Churches in the U.S.A.	8,566	1,593,574
Baptist General Conference	959	117,973
Baptist Missionary Association of America	2,700	216,471
Conservative Baptist Association of America	...	300,000
Free Will Baptists	4,191	229,498
General Baptists (General Association of)	1,125	70,000
National Baptist Convention of America	28,574	2,668,799
National Baptist Convention, U.S.A., Inc.	27,500	5,500,000
Nat. Bap. Evang. Life and Soul Saving Assembly	137	57,734
National Primitive Baptist Convention, Inc.	636	250,000
Primitive Baptists	...	72,000
Progressive National Baptist Convention, Inc.	863	521,692
Regular Baptist Churches, General Assn. of	...	240,000
Southern Baptist Convention	55,100	12,917,992
United Free Will Baptist Church	784	100,000
Brethren (German Baptists): Church of the Brethren	1,897	178,157
Buddhist Churches of America	60	60,000
Christian and Missionary Alliance	1,276	150,492
Christian Church (Disciples of Christ)	6,793	1,278,734
Christian Churches and Churches of Christ	5,055	1,040,856
Christian Congregation	1,131	79,230
Church of God (Anderson, Ind.)	2,951	170,285
Church of the Nazarene	7,286	448,658
Churches of Christ	12,800	2,500,000
Community Churches, National Council of	210	125,000
Congregational Christian Churches, Natl. Assn. of	512	90,000
Eastern Churches		
American Carpatho-Russian Orth. Greek Catholic Ch.	68	100,000
Antiochian Orthodox Christian Archdiocese of N. Am.	132	152,000
Armenian Apostolic Church of America	34	125,000
Armenian Church of America, Diocese of the (Including Diocese of California)	67	372,000
Bulgarian Eastern Orthodox Church	11	86,000
Greek Orthodox Archdiocese of N. and S. America	655	1,950,000
Orthodox Church in America	498	1,000,000
Russian Orth. Ch. in the U.S.A., Patriarchal Parishes of	60	51,500
Russian Orthodox Church Outside Russia	168	50,000
Serbian Eastern Orth. Ch. for the U.S.A. and Canada	64	65,000
Syrian Orthodox Church of Antioch	14	50,000
Ukrainian Orthodox Church in the U.S.A.	131	87,745
Episcopal Church	12,240	2,882,064
Evangelical Covenant Church of America	717	73,458
Evangelical Free Church of America	...	70,490
Friends United Meeting	639	65,585
Independent Fundamental Churches of America	1,252	87,582

Religious body	Total clergy	Inclusive membership
Jehovah's Witnesses	none	577,362
Jewish congregations	6,400	6,115,000
Latter Day Saints		
Church of Jesus Christ of Latter-day Saints	19,269	2,391,892
Reorganized Church of Jesus Christ of L.D.S.	15,701	185,839
Lutherans		
American Lutheran Church	6,625	2,402,261
Evangelical Lutheran Churches, Association of	377	95,186
Lutheran Church in America	7,695	2,974,749
Lutheran Church—Missouri Synod	7,414	2,757,271
Wisconsin Evangelical Lutheran Synod	1,155	399,114
Mennonite Church	2,441	96,092
Methodists		
African Methodist Episcopal Church	7,089	1,166,301
African Methodist Episcopal Zion Church	6,873	1,024,974
Christian Methodist Episcopal Church	2,259	466,718
Free Methodist Church of North America	1,591	68,180
United Methodist Church	35,488	9,861,028
Moravian Church in America	219	54,053
North American Old Roman Catholic Church	115	60,124
Pentecostals		
Apostolic Overcoming Holy Church of God	350	75,000
Assemblies of God	13,684	1,302,318
Church of God	2,737	75,890
Church of God (Cleveland, Tenn.)	8,786	365,124
Church of God in Christ	6,000	425,000
Church of God in Christ, International	1,502	501,000
Church of God of Prophecy	5,679	65,801
International Church of the Foursquare Gospel	2,690	89,215
Pentecostal Church of God of America, Inc.	1,900	135,000
Pentecostal Holiness Church, Inc.	1,878	74,108
United Pentecostal Church, International	5,970	405,000
Polish National Catholic Church of America	141	282,411
Presbyterians		
Cumberland Presbyterian Church	712	92,995
Presbyterian Church in America	457	68,993
Presbyterian Church in the U.S.	5,156	887,664
United Presbyterian Church in the U.S.A.	13,772	2,607,321
Reformed bodies		
Christian Reformed Church in North America	810	211,061
Reformed Church in America	1,415	350,734
Roman Catholic Church	58,713	46,325,752
Salvation Army	5,095	380,618
Triumph the Church and Kingdom of God in Christ	1,375	54,307
Unitarian Universalist Association	881	184,522
United Church of Christ	9,607	1,801,241
Wesleyan Church	2,436	96,337

Table includes churches reporting a membership of 50,000 or more and represents the latest information available.
Source: National Council of Churches, *Yearbook of American and Canadian Churches*, 1978.

(CONSTANT H. JACQUET)

THE ECONOMY

Gross National Product and National Income

in billions of dollars

Item	1965[1]	1970[1]	1976	1977[2]
GROSS NATIONAL PRODUCT	688.1	982.4	1,706.5	1,869.9
By type of expenditure				
Personal comsumption expenditures	430.2	618.8	1,094.0	1,194.0
Durable goods	62.8	84.9	158.9	178.6
Nondurable goods	188.6	264.7	442.7	474.4
Services	178.7	269.1	492.3	541.1
Gross private domestic investment	112.0	140.8	243.3	294.9
Fixed investment	102.5	137.0	230.0	273.2
Changes in business inventories	9.5	3.8	13.3	21.7
Net exports of goods and services	7.6	3.9	7.8	−9.7
Exports	39.5	62.5	162.9	178.1
Imports	32.0	58.5	155.1	187.7
Government purchases of goods and services	138.4	218.9	361.4	390.6
Federal	67.3	95.6	130.1	143.6
State and local	71.1	123.2	231.2	247.0
By major type of product				
Goods output	336.6	456.2	764.2	827.1
Durable goods	133.6	170.8	303.4	341.0
Nondurable goods	203.1	285.4	460.9	486.1
Services	272.7	424.6	782.0	855.3
Structures	78.8	101.6	160.2	187.5
NATIONAL INCOME	566.0	798.4	1,364.1	1,505.7
By type of income				
Compensation of employees	396.5	609.2	1,036.3	1,144.7
Proprietors' income	56.7	65.1	88.0	97.0
Rental income of persons	17.1	18.6	23.3	24.9
Corporate profits	77.1	67.9	128.1	140.2
Net interest	18.5	37.5	88.4	98.9
By industry division[3]				
Agriculture, forestry, and fisheries	20.4	24.5	40.8	44.2
Mining and construction	35.9	51.6	87.1	99.5
Manufacturing	170.4	215.4	365.0	410.8
Nondurable goods	65.4	88.1	146.9	159.4
Durable goods	105.0	127.3	218.1	251.4
Transportation	23.1	30.3	50.6	55.5
Communications and public utilities	22.9	32.5	56.8	61.9
Wholesale and retail trade	84.7	122.2	220.7	241.8
Finance, insurance, and real estate	64.0	92.6	160.8	177.8
Services	64.1	103.3	188.2	207.9
Government and government enterprises	75.4	127.4	214.9	227.9
Other	4.7	4.6	14.4	18.4

[1] Revised.   [2] Second quarter, seasonally adjusted at annual rates.
[3] Without capital consumption adjustment.
Source: U.S. Department of Commerce, Bureau of Economic Analysis, *Survey of Current Business.*

Personal Income Per Capita

State	1950	1960[1]	1970[1]	1976[2]
Alabama	$ 880	$1,519	$2,948	$ 5,105
Alaska	2,384	2,809	4,644	10,178
Arizona	1,330	2,012	3,665	5,817
Arkansas	825	1,390	2,878	5,073
California	1,852	2,706	4,493	7,164
Colorado	1,487	2,252	3,855	6,503
Connecticut	1,875	2,838	4,917	7,373
Delaware	2,132	2,785	4,524	7,290
District of Columbia	2,221	2,983	5,079	8,648
Florida	1,281	1,947	3,738	6,108
Georgia	1,034	1,651	3,354	5,571
Hawaii	1,386	2,368	4,623	6,969
Idaho	1,295	1,850	3,290	5,726
Illinois	1,825	2,646	4,507	7,432
Indiana	1,512	2,178	3,772	6,257
Iowa	1,485	1,983	3,751	6,439
Kansas	1,443	2,160	3,853	6,495
Kentucky	981	1,586	3,112	5,423
Louisiana	1,120	1,668	3,090	5,386
Maine	1,186	1,862	3,302	5,385
Maryland	1,602	2,341	4,309	7,036
Massachusetts	1,633	2,461	4,340	6,585
Michigan	1,701	2,357	4,180	6,994
Minnesota	1,410	2,075	3,859	6,153
Mississippi	755	1,222	2,626	4,575
Missouri	1,431	2,112	3,781	6,005
Montana	1,622	2,035	3,500	5,600
Nebraska	1,490	2,110	3,789	6,240
Nevada	2,018	2,799	4,563	7,337
New Hampshire	1,323	2,135	3,737	5,973
New Jersey	1,834	2,727	4,701	7,269
New Mexico	1,177	1,843	3,077	5,213
New York	1,873	2,740	4,712	7,100
North Carolina	1,037	1,590	3,252	5,409
North Dakota	1,263	1,704	3,086	5,400
Ohio	1,620	2,345	4,020	6,432
Oklahoma	1,143	1,876	3,387	5,657
Oregon	1,620	2,220	3,719	6,331
Pennsylvania	1,541	2,269	3,971	6,466
Rhode Island	1,605	2,217	3,959	6,498
South Carolina	893	1,397	2,990	5,126
South Dakota	1,242	1,784	3,123	4,796
Tennessee	994	1,576	3,119	5,432
Texas	1,349	1,936	3,606	6,243
Utah	1,309	1,979	3,227	5,482
Vermont	1,121	1,847	3,468	5,480
Virginia	1,228	1,864	3,712	6,276
Washington	1,674	2,360	4,053	6,772
West Virginia	1,065	1,621	3,061	5,394
Wisconsin	1,477	2,188	3,812	6,293
Wyoming	1,668	2,247	3,815	6,723
United States	1,496	2,222	3,966	6,441

[1] Revised.   [2] Preliminary.
Source: U.S. Department of Commerce, Bureau of Economic Analysis, *Survey of Current Business.*

Average Employee Earnings

September figures

Industry	HOURLY 1976	HOURLY 1977[1]	WEEKLY 1976	WEEKLY 1977[1]
MANUFACTURING				
Durable goods				
Ordnance and accessories	$5.85	$6.38	$235.17	$259.03
Lumber and wood products	4.87	5.20	195.77	209.56
Furniture and fixtures	4.05	4.39	156.33	174.28
Stone, clay, and glass Products	5.43	5.87	224.80	243.02
Primary metal industries	6.95	7.70	283.56	318.01
Fabricated metal products	5.54	5.95	226.59	245.74
Nonelectrical machinery	5.86	6.33	240.26	265.86
Electrical equipment and supplies	5.02	5.46	200.80	221.13
Transportation equipment	6.67	7.27	276.81	308.98
Instruments and related products	4.93	5.28	198.19	214.37
Nondurable goods				
Food and kindred products	5.02	5.42	205.32	217.88
Tobacco manufactures	4.65	5.35	175.77	210.79
Textile mill products	3.78	4.08	148.93	165.65
Apparel and related products	3.49	3.68	122.85	130.27
Paper and allied products	5.58	6.06	237.71	260.58
Printing and publishing	5.79	6.20	218.86	237.46
Chemicals and allied products	6.04	6.52	253.68	271.88
Petroleum and coal products	7.22	7.77	309.02	337.22
Rubber and plastics products	4.85	5.18	198.37	212.38
Leather and leather products	3.48	3.67	126.32	136.89
NONMANUFACTURING				
Metal mining	6.98	7.45	293.16	303.96
Coal mining	8.07	8.63	337.33	391.80
Oil and gas extraction	5.87	6.32	266.50	291.35
Contract construction	7.81	8.20	287.41	304.22
Local and suburban transportation	5.54	6.03	220.49	238.79
Electric, gas, and sanitary services	6.69	7.16	278.30	295.71
Wholesale trade	5.26	5.64	204.61	219.40
Retail trade	3.61	3.88	115.88	122.61
Hotels, tourist courts, and motels[2]	3.06	3.29	96.39	101.99

[1] Preliminary. [2] Excludes tips. Source: U.S. Dept. of Labor, Bureau of Labor Statistics, *Employment and Earnings.*

Unemployment Trends

quarterly averages, seasonally adjusted

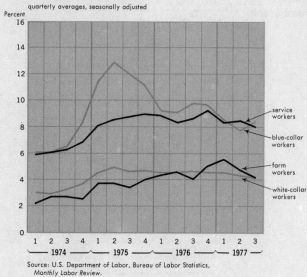

Source: U.S. Department of Labor, Bureau of Labor Statistics, *Monthly Labor Review.*

Value of Agricultural Products, with Fisheries, 1976

in thousands of dollars

State	Corn (grain)	Hay	Soybeans	Wheat	Tobacco	Cotton (lint)	Potatoes	Cattle, calves	Hogs, pigs	Sheep, lambs	Milk[1]	Eggs[2]	Chickens[2]	FISHERIES
Alabama	123,380	45,305	194,712	10,969	1,210	113,232	21,931	244,699	101,641	38	75,770	151,058	7,726	34,370
Alaska	...	...	...	...	...	...	...	241	107	3	2,888	570	43	227,208
Arizona	4,116	107,545	...	127,073	...	274,901	9,290	233,606	16,697	8,288	90,934	6,090	134	...
Arkansas	6,552	55,225	517,104	73,379	...	227,635	...	220,287	53,725	60	74,778	200,703	13,627	3,850[4]
California	89,320	558,996	...	216,916	...	867,113	109,780	652,330	20,510	27,288	1,097,310	399,154	6,150	185,647
Colorado	143,520	156,177	...	119,975	...	...	28,533	602,243	47,955	41,064	90,514	23,567	739	...
Connecticut	...	12,180	...	...	34,107	...	2,223	6,456	1,121	140	68,006	58,584	1,652	2,525
Delaware	44,774	2,928	27,737	3,418	...	...	5,603	2,264	8,631	42	13,598	7,641	452	1,788
Florida	78,624	23,485	44,785	1,980	34,645	2,659	41,931	184,007	25,242	52	246,429	120,244	3,973	88,316
Georgia	328,104	56,175	143,585	10,873	136,755	62,496	...	137,301	180,026	29	137,365	305,641	11,360	12,375
Hawaii	...	...	...	...	...	...	...	18,403	7,447	...	22,274	11,808	207	7,486
Idaho	5,546	201,648	...	170,800	...	...	247,008	228,486	9,121	20,251	141,259	8,928	278	34
Illinois	3,001,992	172,125	1,669,248	220,058	...	0	1,642	371,033	1,009,649	4,046	233,657	64,032	1,582	860
Indiana	1,593,900	116,100	714,384	172,800	19,912	...	6,140	250,350	654,346	3,362	224,246	123,674	4,997	90
Iowa	2,696,625	406,080	1,399,387	8,925	...	...	1,772	1,049,744	1,926,679	11,367	372,448	75,199	2,739	836
Kansas	391,115	235,820	88,879	932,250	...	...	...	904,545	273,733	5,100	137,480	21,244	1,221	10
Kentucky	325,992	131,472	185,725	29,667	566,303	217	...	301,174	145,960	1,132	227,100	24,435	1,345	919[4]
Louisiana	15,973	34,790	358,280	3,812	218	169,697	878	153,038	20,273	128	120,659	36,011	1,992	136,971
Maine	...	25,547	...	...	...	...	101,528	7,009	1,206	328	68,807	103,224	4,689	53,813
Maryland	140,459	35,929	45,956	16,256	31,366	...	1,515	34,953	26,733	429	159,236	18,893	1,036	31,303
Massachusetts	...	17,136	...	...	10,708	...	3,168	6,565	7,699	217	67,215	26,557	1,462	97,605
Michigan	318,263	127,925	79,923	101,574	...	...	35,379	169,495	113,148	3,536	455,070	57,539	2,764	4,145
Minnesota	792,960	406,433	434,427	390,536	...	...	35,243	490,682	504,966	8,274	804,717	83,358	1,231	1,249
Mississippi	21,423	49,720	468,325	16,443	...	336,905	817	203,033	42,157	61	89,131	98,413	7,442	22,006
Missouri	417,240	244,902	558,600	163,350	6,518	47,362	...	696,100	487,574	3,880	278,476	54,870	5,156	149
Montana	2,021	188,744	...	434,819	...	...	8,127	315,793	24,043	9,653	26,161	8,751	198	...
Nebraska	1,183,580	329,721	136,990	254,880	...	...	6,114	1,006,330	449,540	5,707	128,219	25,857	506	19
Nevada	...	64,791	...	3,081	...	...	12,981	58,345	1,189	3,501	17,077	226	2	...
New Hampshire	...	12,376	...	...	...	...	546	4,175	1,392	165	36,348	15,167	1,052	1,083
New Jersey	21,500	19,817	15,667	6,584	...	...	8,872	10,338	7,651	150	57,498	29,638	1,094	34,546
New Mexico	22,176	58,212	...	19,954	...	31,128	2,232	239,266	18,655	7,063	45,603	14,625	336	...
New York	98,498	278,304	1,814	16,038	...	...	57,231	92,755	14,996	1,356	1,015,180	93,565	4,110	32,403
North Carolina	360,960	30,528	157,273	20,880	996,908	23,688	12,501	65,564	289,234	161	178,095	154,106	14,751	27,465
North Dakota	17,280	179,820	12,407	832,730	...	...	44,044	299,365	41,887	5,520	75,431	3,800	271	45
Ohio	910,616	194,022	631,800	194,700	26,676	...	12,176	246,390	291,322	11,114	446,698	85,607	3,728	2,208
Oklahoma	20,316	183,345	33,264	446,040	...	60,492	...	691,376	47,318	1,823	109,759	23,282	922	201[4]
Oregon	2,723	154,240	...	171,941	...	...	80,753	156,888	15,314	10,252	104,651	24,960	459	48,727
Pennsylvania	248,400	237,875	7,673	29,295	13,413	...	31,416	150,104	85,165	2,567	793,490	149,242	13,101	263
Rhode Island	...	1,314	...	...	...	...	3,910	392	852	50	6,642	3,846	207	20,410
South Carolina	112,056	24,380	144,585	11,238	171,780	45,727	...	53,199	66,233	13	59,884	65,169	2,452	14,070
South Dakota	89,280	167,560	30,176	119,160	...	...	858	623,441	240,492	27,908	131,835	20,889	863	277
Tennessee	146,861	75,645	255,150	37,805	151,502	69,876	3,437	262,139	161,971	283	189,930	45,332	1,381	1,768[4]
Texas	450,000	260,445	54,132	325,710	...	1,015,680	21,394	1,677,536	120,685	45,244	353,732	130,814	4,748	127,574
Utah	3,443	97,370	...	16,623	...	...	3,869	81,242	7,008	13,004	90,182	11,792	190	...
Vermont	...	59,345	...	...	...	...	871	17,715	1,179	184	221,850	6,704	185	...
Virginia	119,187	76,101	53,849	23,424	164,874	173	16,724	108,790	76,712	4,618	187,618	46,542	3,014	43,091
Washington	12,705	164,521	...	417,745	...	...	139,500	147,822	10,879	1,925	244,014	47,435	1,213	80,942
West Virginia	13,420	43,628	...	1,344	3,497	...	1,556	33,017	9,389	2,829	34,608	12,440	617	3
Wisconsin	363,188	560,694	21,569	9,066	13,424	...	53,795	293,470	205,560	2,261	1,859,114	49,258	2,740	4,050
Wyoming	3,719	105,678	...	17,231	...	...	5,528	184,838	4,373	17,649	11,357	1,334	30	...
TOTAL U.S.	14,741,807	6,792,119	8,487,406	6,201,342	2,383,816	3,349,572	1,182,816	13,988,334	7,879,385	314,112	11,724,343	3,151,818	142,167	1,352,700

[1] Farm value. [2] Gross income, Dec. 1, 1975–Nov. 30, 1976. [3] Decrease in inventory and death loss of sheep resulted in deficit in number of pounds produced. [4] Estimate.

Sources: U.S. Department of Agriculture, Statistical Reporting Service, Crop Reporting Board, *Crop Values, Meat Animals, Milk, Poultry*; U.S. Department of Commerce, National Oceanic and Atmospheric Administration, National Marine Fisheries Service, *Fisheries of the United States, 1976.*

Principal Manufactures, 1975

monetary figures in millions of dollars

Industry	Employees (000)	Cost of labour [1]	Cost of materials	Value of shipments	Value added by mfg.
Food and kindred products	1,527	$15,891	$123,954	$172,510	$48,142
Meat products	308	3,163	36,656	43,831	7,170
Dairy products	170	1,822	17,831	22,801	4,946
Preserved fruits and vegetables	223	1,920	10,836	16,754	5,975
Grain mill products	114	1,331	14,979	20,685	5,661
Beverages	205	2,444	12,300	20,603	8,258
Tobacco products	66	655	4,396	8,113	3,722
Textile mill products	838	6,418	18,917	31,274	12,110
Apparel and other textile products	1,212	7,689	15,960	31,084	13,381
Lumber and wood products	592	5,269	14,653	25,194	10,456
Furniture and fixtures	398	3,323	5,985	12,421	6,311
Paper and allied products	590	6,984	23,819	41,743	17,927
Printing and publishing	1,073	11,675	13,562	38,135	24,504
Chemicals and allied products	848	11,304	45,142	89,848	45,116
Industrial chemicals	247	3,630	16,348	30,821	14,792
Plastics materials and synthetics	151	1,997	8,695	14,349	5,506
Drugs	151	2,058	3,254	11,242	8,044
Soap, cleaners, and toilet goods	110	1,299	5,695	12,885	7,125
Paints, allied products	60	737	2,994	5,141	2,126
Agricultural chemicals	52	649	4,886	9,184	4,562
Petroleum and coal products	141	2,144	59,099	68,969	10,090
Rubber, misc. plastics products	587	5,945	13,688	27,316	13,674
Leather and leather products	240	1,652	3,117	6,333	3,187
Stone, clay, and glass products	592	6,403	12,339	27,595	15,338
Primary metal industries	1,091	15,015	52,155	81,315	30,554
Blast furnace, basic steel products	534	8,129	27,745	42,732	15,931
Iron, steel foundries	220	2,714	3,938	8,824	4,941
Primary nonferrous metals	58	844	5,787	7,995	2,435
Nonferrous drawing and rolling	162	2,008	10,603	15,010	4,610
Nonferrous foundries	76	813	1,355	2,796	1,435
Fabricated metal products	1,420	16,359	34,528	68,824	34,096
Ordnance and accessories	83	1,006	1,252	2,907	1,657

Industry	Employees (000)	Cost of labour [1]	Cost of materials	Value of shipments	Value added by mfg.
Machinery, except electrical	1,979	$24,702	$44,821	$96,400	$51,471
Engines and turbines	122	1,685	4,190	7,647	3,449
Farm and garden machinery	150	1,877	5,543	9,909	4,382
Construction and related mach.	321	4,209	9,902	19,014	9,510
Metalworking machinery	295	3,715	3,907	10,920	6,945
Special industry machinery	200	2,407	3,999	8,932	4,896
General industrial machinery	291	3,578	5,757	13,149	7,466
Service industry machines	158	1,800	4,434	8,646	3,962
Office, computing machines	226	3,046	4,869	11,568	6,477
Electric and electronic equipment	1,521	17,392	28,690	64,198	34,804
Electric distributing equip.	105	1,153	1,892	4,448	2,486
Electrical industrial apparatus	185	2,032	3,244	7,515	4,213
Household appliances	144	1,483	4,213	7,923	3,588
Electric lighting, wiring equip.	145	1,452	2,693	6,141	3,389
Radio, TV receiving equipment	87	861	3,054	5,158	1,969
Communication equipment	434	5,714	6,998	17,373	10,288
Electronic components, access.	301	3,342	3,958	10,024	5,933
Transportation equipment	1,604	22,770	68,591	113,218	45,155
Motor vehicles and equipment	698	9,847	48,170	69,575	21,182
Aircraft and parts	437	6,591	9,952	22,110	12,872
Ship, boat building, repairing	204	2,316	3,371	6,966	3,568
Railroad equipment	60	798	2,625	4,222	1,566
Guided missiles, space vehicles	147	2,616	2,449	7,035	4,747
Instruments and related products	502	5,854	7,755	22,072	14,116
Measuring, controlling devices	163	1,905	1,851	5,493	3,568
Medical instruments and supplies	111	1,127	1,690	4,336	2,631
Photographic equipment and supplies	100	1,441	2,443	7,627	5,172
Miscellaneous manufacturing industries	395	3,500	6,742	14,647	7,696
All establishments, including administrative and auxiliary	18,345	209,958	597,912	1,041,211	441,850

[1] Payroll only.   Source: U.S. Department of Commerce, *Annual Survey of Manufactures 1975.*

Business Activity

Category of activity	WHOLESALING				RETAILING				SERVICES			
	1960	1965	1970	1974	1960	1965	1970	1974	1960	1965	1970	1974
Number of businesses (in 000)												
Sole proprietorships	306	265	274	337	1,548	1,554	1,689	1,802	1,966	2,208	2,507	2,944
Active partnerships	41	32	30	28	238	202	170	167	159	169	176	191
Active corporations	117	147	166	216	217	288	351	388	121	188	281	391
Business receipts (in $000,000)												
Sole proprietorships	17,061	17,934	21,556	33,762	65,439	77,760	89,315	106,538	23,256	29,789	40,869	51,340
Active partnerships	12,712	10,879	11,325	15,985	24,787	23,244	23,546	27,567	9,281	12,442	18,791	27,231
Active corporations	130,637	171,414	234,885	477,339	125,787	183,925	274,808	410,518	22,106	36,547	66,460	109,643
Net profit (less loss; in $000,000)												
Sole proprietorships	1,305	1,483	1,806	2,942	3,869	5,019	5,767	6,884	8,060	11,008	15,063	17,171
Active partnerships	587	548	557	958	1,612	1,654	1,603	1,874	3,056	4,402	6,189	7,050
Active corporations	2,130	3,288	4,441	15,778	2,225	4,052	5,217	6,221	849	1,505	1,199	2,500

Data refer to accounting periods ending between July 1 of year shown and June 30 of following year.
Source: U.S. Department of the Treasury, Internal Revenue Service, *Statistics of Income: Business Income Tax Returns* and *Corporation Income Tax Returns.*

Retail Sales

in millions of dollars

Kind of business	1960	1965	1970	1976
Durable goods stores [1]	70,560	94,186	114,288	214,169
Automotive group	39,579	56,884	64,966	125,625
Passenger car, other automotive dealers	37,038	53,484	59,388	115,631
Tire, battery, accessory dealers	2,541	3,400	5,578	9,994
Furniture and appliance group	10,591	13,352	17,778	28,963
Furniture, home furnishings stores	...	...	10,483	17,053
Household appliance, TV, radio stores	...	...	6,073	9,200
Building materials, hardware, farm equipment group	11,222	12,388	20,494	38,778
Lumberyards, building materials dealers	8,567	9,731	11,995	21,946
Hardware stores	2,655	2,657	3,351	6,222
Nondurable goods stores [1]	148,969	189,942	261,239	437,715
Apparel group	13,631	15,765	19,810	28,612
Men's, boys' wear stores	2,644	...	4,630	6,325
Women's apparel, accessory stores	5,295	...	7,582	11,123
Family clothing stores	...	...	3,360	5,082
Shoe stores	2,437	...	3,501	4,373
Drug and proprietary stores	7,538	9,186	13,352	19,704
Eating and drinking places	16,146	20,201	29,689	52,290
Food group	54,023	64,016	86,114	140,984
Grocery stores	48,610	...	79,756	131,133
Meat and fish markets	...	...	2,244	3,242
Bakeries	...	...	1,303	1,648
Gasoline service stations	17,588	20,611	27,994	47,731
General merchandise group	...	42,299	61,320	104,168
Department stores and dry goods general merchandise stores	...	...	45,000	81,918
Variety stores	...	...	6,959	8,259
Mail-order houses (department store merchandise)	...	...	3,853	6,584
Liquor stores	4,893	5,674	7,980	11,411
TOTAL	219,529	284,128	375,527	651,884

[1] Includes some kinds of business not shown separately.
Source: U.S. Department of Commerce, Bureau of the Census, *Monthly Retail Trade,*
Bureau of Economic Analysis, *1975 Business Statistics.*

Sales of Merchant Wholesalers

in millions of dollars

Kind of business	1960	1965	1970	1976
Durable goods [1]	56,803	82,861	111,970	210,864
Motor vehicles, automotive equipment	7,883	12,140	19,482	38,784
Electrical goods	8,660	12,681	16,667	28,861
Furniture, home furnishings	2,910	3,777	5,199	7,698
Hardware, plumbing, heating equipment	6,422	8,413	10,858	19,340
Lumber, construction supplies	6,680	9,765	10,863	20,129
Machinery, equipment, supplies	14,287	20,561	27,638	56,379
Metals, metalwork (except scrap)	5,708	9,162	13,647	26,798
Scrap, waste materials	3,296	4,789	6,040	9,642
Nondurable goods [1]	80,477	104,470	135,029	271,685
Groceries and related products	27,661	38,068	53,411	93,899
Beer, wine, distilled alcoholic beverages	7,424	9,464	13,332	21,615
Drugs, chemicals, allied products	5,370	7,180	9,135	16,824
Tobacco, tobacco products	4,164	5,014	6,232	8,724
Dry goods, apparel	6,675	8,804	10,577	17,295
Paper, paper products	4,153	5,612	7,679	13,147
Farm products	11,683	13,711	13,987	45,169
Other nondurable goods	13,346	16,966	22,632	55,012
TOTAL	137,281	187,331	246,999	482,549

[1] Includes some kinds of business not shown separately.
Source: U.S. Dept. of Commerce, Bureau of the Census, *Monthly Wholesale Trade.*

Commercial Banks[1]

December 31, 1976

State	Number of banks	Total assets or liabilities $000,000	SELECTED ASSETS ($000,000) Loans[2]	Investments	Reserves, cash, and bank balances	SELECTED LIABILITIES ($000,000) Deposits Total	Demand	Time	Capital accounts
Ala.	303	11,873	9,685	3,438	1,230	10,170	3,958	4,165	937
Alaska	12	1,593	1,217	394	226	1,374	680	312	123
Ariz.	16	7,539	6,066	1,598	761	6,734	2,390	2,471	488
Ark.	257	7,586	5,971	2,044	926	6,612	2,690	2,452	597
Calif.	210	108,705	78,488	20,352	13,950	88,902	32,126	29,620	6,920
Colo.	281	9,675	7,429	1,980	1,347	8,317	3,633	2,345	732
Conn.	71	8,991	6,745	1,949	1,277	7,614	3,530	1,781	669
Del.	17	2,770	2,368	1,248	197	2,269	875	862	186
D.C.	16	4,551	3,496	1,207	575	3,885	2,058	729	406
Fla.	753	30,500	23,484	10,283	3,749	26,752	10,843	7,695	2,459
Ga.	441	15,964	11,537	2,859	2,145	12,891	6,133	4,834	1,398
Hawaii	8	3,245	2,647	848	324	2,893	1,117	844	231
Idaho	24	3,303	2,739	740	390	2,950	1,049	1,135	217
Ill.	1,225	78,647	64,059	22,184	7,492	61,685	21,699	25,119	5,849
Ind.	406	23,084	18,528	7,277	2,070	19,580	6,626	8,659	1,660
Iowa	652	14,606	12,078	4,320	1,493	13,035	4,250	5,457	1,122
Kan.	615	11,127	8,867	3,213	1,191	9,748	3,796	3,994	932
Ky.	342	12,290	9,506	3,217	1,312	10,614	4,570	4,095	979
La.	254	15,369	11,438	4,278	1,965	13,106	5,435	5,094	1,164
Maine	43	2,451	2,056	600	212	2,157	751	549	193
Md.	113	11,204	8,870	2,453	1,140	9,473	3,776	2,146	845
Mass.	143	18,789	13,804	4,215	2,532	14,778	7,322	3,192	1,493
Mich.	359	36,914	29,773	9,766	4,203	31,756	9,159	10,744	2,798
Minn.	750	19,619	15,944	5,276	2,056	16,210	5,587	6,560	1,495
Miss.	183	7,260	5,681	1,967	915	6,404	2,558	3,048	563
Mo.	706	23,132	17,149	6,466	3,177	19,012	8,328	6,513	1,767
Mont.	155	3,569	2,981	952	348	3,203	1,076	1,376	264
Neb.	450	7,702	6,201	1,858	948	6,718	2,751	2,862	624
Nev.	8	2,372	1,970	749	258	2,143	868	699	179
N.H.	77	2,110	1,758	445	212	1,881	564	457	173
N.J.	195	26,808	21,788	8,416	2,811	23,464	8,337	6,589	2,001
N.M.	82	3,699	2,893	947	436	3,320	1,256	1,436	273
N.Y.	230	170,496	115,748	25,220	32,868	127,303	68,318	41,282	14,556
N.C.	91	15,867	12,318	4,071	1,818	13,086	5,394	4,157	1,276
N.D.	169	3,136	2,718	945	259	2,824	962	1,280	253
Ohio	489	40,070	31,417	12,104	4,372	33,296	11,933	10,300	3,375
Okla.	469	13,290	10,144	3,694	1,843	11,536	4,656	4,854	1,049
Ore.	46	8,300	6,145	1,786	1,019	6,776	2,692	2,070	610
Pa.	386	58,817	47,593	15,047	5,633	46,869	15,570	17,863	4,578
R.I.	14	4,229	3,441	768	350	3,441	905	964	295
S.C.	90	5,108	4,068	1,438	622	4,427	2,364	1,167	443
S.D.	156	3,559	3,031	1,076	339	3,229	961	1,618	272
Tenn.	346	16,422	12,561	3,884	2,050	14,249	5,146	6,042	1,219
Texas	1,357	63,381	45,825	16,079	9,672	52,999	24,443	20,605	4,720
Utah	66	4,294	3,407	954	562	3,802	1,433	1,393	297
Vt.	29	1,638	1,442	376	109	1,486	370	416	124
Va.	283	16,991	13,728	4,230	1,760	14,855	5,304	5,410	1,315
Wash.	84	12,993	9,479	2,190	1,723	10,613	4,227	3,518	857
W.Va.	222	7,253	5,860	2,501	607	6,195	1,959	2,155	606
Wis.	625	19,022	15,409	5,064	1,847	16,486	5,189	6,227	1,399
Wyo.	78	2,099	1,732	587	255	1,878	664	793	163
TOTAL	14,397	1,004,020	763,283	239,557	129,578	825,002	332,283	289,949	77,168

[1] Detail may not add to total given due to rounding; excludes noninsured banks.
[2] Includes investment securities, trading account securities, federal funds sold, and securities purchased under agreements to resell.
Source: Federal Deposit Insurance Corporation, *Assets and Liabilities—Commercial and Mutual Savings Banks—December 31, 1976, 1976 Report of Income.*

Life Insurance, 1976

Number of policies in 000s; value in $000,000

State	Total Number of policies	Value	Ordinary Number of policies	Value	Group Number of certificates	Value	Industrial Number of policies	Value	Credit[1] Number of policies	Value
Ala.	11,766	$37,236	1,762	$17,784	1,520	$14,051	6,758	$2,554	1,726	$2,847
Alaska	541	4,393	112	1,837	297	2,328	12	3	120	225
Ariz.	4,308	24,546	1,591	14,434	1,227	8,111	169	96	1,321	1,905
Ark.	2,517	15,745	878	8,528	601	5,668	533	291	505	1,258
Calif.	29,167	225,579	10,199	112,145	10,863	102,670	2,180	1,435	5,925	9,329
Colo.	4,278	30,514	1,649	16,976	1,313	11,567	250	178	1,066	1,793
Conn.	5,443	41,195	2,334	20,144	1,732	19,420	328	225	1,049	1,406
Del.	1,421	9,252	483	3,789	385	4,834	247	156	306	473
D.C.	2,452	13,952	440	3,717	981	9,314	286	509		635
Fla.	15,101	80,263	4,820	44,909	3,134	28,071	3,843	2,551	3,304	4,732
Ga.	12,410	56,795	2,952	28,099	2,213	21,968	4,550	2,886	2,695	3,842
Hawaii	1,557	13,197	555	7,121	666	5,467	6	3	330	606
Idaho	1,255	7,644	482	4,252	448	2,754	28	13	297	625
Ill.	22,187	141,896	9,066	72,756	5,968	61,283	3,360	2,081	3,793	5,776
Ind.	9,998	58,774	3,911	30,093	2,456	24,246	1,715	1,016	1,916	3,419
Iowa	4,828	32,616	2,442	18,589	1,280	11,984	259	134	847	1,909
Kan.	4,279	25,778	1,859	15,494	1,142	8,442	361	193	917	1,649
Ky.	6,371	29,911	2,088	14,968	1,171	11,849	1,786	967	1,326	2,127
La.	8,985	38,225	1,842	18,826	1,574	14,569	3,853	2,232	1,716	2,598
Maine	1,784	9,391	689	5,070	567	3,595	91	56	437	670
Md.	7,899	46,497	2,738	23,998	1,714	19,292	1,853	1,034	1,594	2,173
Mass.	9,125	61,339	3,935	30,718	2,450	27,923	884	530	1,856	2,168
Mich.	16,233	111,844	5,417	43,323	5,440	61,538	2,041	1,218	3,335	5,765
Minn.	6,059	44,421	2,392	21,283	2,134	20,954	274	148	1,259	2,036
Miss.	3,480	17,482	826	8,722	786	6,659	774	488	1,094	1,613
Mo.	8,673	52,356	3,484	26,282	2,313	22,846	1,347	771	1,529	2,457
Mont.	1,013	6,642	404	3,946	306	2,139	26	11	277	546
Neb.	2,727	18,203	1,338	11,102	665	6,035	136	73	588	993
Nev.	1,150	7,712	241	2,888	412	3,768	16	8	481	1,048
N.H.	1,290	8,289	615	4,888	292	2,881	98	60	285	460
N.J.	11,778	94,637	5,465	47,524	3,044	43,235	1,464	1,083	1,805	2,795
N.M.	1,707	10,472	553	5,161	524	4,470	91	50	539	791
N.Y.	26,938	201,092	11,318	96,686	7,610	94,039	2,092	1,374	5,918	8,993
N.C.	11,804	52,525	3,367	27,056	2,163	19,815	3,742	2,144	2,532	3,510
N.D.	884	6,417	412	3,770	258	2,065	5	3	209	579
Ohio	19,906	124,026	7,918	63,489	4,844	52,025	3,481	2,138	3,663	6,374
Okla.	4,182	27,026	1,598	14,165	1,073	10,684	441	258	1,070	1,919
Ore.	3,088	22,273	1,139	11,069	1,136	9,843	99	48	714	1,313
Pa.	24,143	132,071	9,756	67,011	5,195	55,251	4,793	2,772	4,399	7,037
R.I.	1,851	10,281	779	5,853	551	3,867	197	115	324	446
S.C.	7,372	26,842	2,174	13,732	1,266	9,679	2,619	1,537	1,313	1,894
S.D.	918	6,400	504	4,156	210	1,787	5	2	199	455
Tenn.	8,934	43,512	2,289	20,696	2,093	18,083	2,683	1,597	1,869	3,136
Texas	21,686	135,069	7,488	71,296	5,800	53,558	3,239	2,056	5,159	8,159
Utah	1,979	11,751	659	6,213	769	4,594	96	40	455	904
Vt.	784	4,600	357	2,649	187	1,633	57	34	183	284
Va.	10,301	58,626	3,148	27,323	2,292	27,122	2,631	1,478	2,230	2,703
Wash.	4,876	36,291	1,794	18,152	1,867	16,528	189	88	1,026	1,523
W.Va.	3,191	15,681	936	6,805	687	7,119	616	376	952	1,381
Wis.	7,267	47,887	3,295	26,022	2,356	19,540	490	281	1,126	2,044
Wyo.	545	3,897	233	2,163	163	1,484	7	4	142	246
TOTAL U.S.	382,431	$2,343,063	136,726	$1,177,672	100,138	$1,002,647	67,337	$39,175	78,230	$123,569

[1] Life insurance on loans of ten years' or less duration.
Source: Institute of Life Insurance, *Life Insurance Fact Book '77.*

Savings and Loan Associations

Dec. 31, 1976[1]

State	Number of assns.	Total assets ($000,000)	Per capita assets
Alabama	60	$3,207	$875
Alaska	4	240	629
Arizona	16	3,837	1,690
Arkansas	71	2,737	1,298
California	164	69,142	3,213
Colorado	46	5,650	2,188
Connecticut	36	3,156	1,013
Delaware	19	222	381
District of Columbia	16	3,992	5,686
Florida	122	28,764	3,416
Georgia	99	7,389	1,487
Guam	2	37	307
Hawaii	11	2,029	2,287
Idaho	11	702	845
Illinois	413	29,200	2,600
Indiana	166	7,376	1,391
Iowa	78	4,858	1,693
Kansas	86	4,881	2,113
Kentucky	108	3,991	1,164
Louisiana	112	5,167	1,345
Maine	21	480	448
Maryland	206	7,282	1,757
Massachusetts	166	6,694	1,152
Michigan	66	11,366	1,248
Minnesota	66	7,164	1,807
Mississippi	74	1,970	837
Missouri	118	10,391	2,175
Montana	14	694	922
Nebraska	44	3,395	2,186
Nevada	7	1,189	1,950
New Hampshire	17	776	944
New Jersey	232	15,418	2,102
New Mexico	35	1,414	1,211
New York	137	21,047	1,164
North Carolina	180	7,815	1,429
North Dakota	11	1,439	2,238
Ohio	413	26,917	2,518
Oklahoma	57	3,593	1,299
Oregon	28	4,304	1,848
Pennsylvania	432	16,994	1,433
Puerto Rico	12	1,180	369
Rhode Island	6	597	644
South Carolina	73	4,159	1,460
South Dakota	19	689	1,005
Tennessee	95	4,745	1,126
Texas	320	20,025	1,604
Utah	13	2,230	1,816
Vermont	7	185	388
Virginia	76	5,631	1,119
Washington	48	5,977	1,655
West Virginia	36	995	546
Wisconsin	120	8,465	1,837
Wyoming	14	500	1,283
TOTAL U.S.	4,858	$391,999	$1,798

[1] Preliminary. Components do not add to totals because of differences in reporting dates and accounting systems.
Source: U.S. League of Savings Associations, *Savings and Loan Fact Book '77.*

GOVERNMENT AND POLITICS

The National Executive

December 9, 1977

Department, bureau, or office	Executive official and official title
PRESIDENT OF THE UNITED STATES	Jimmy Carter
Vice-President	Walter F. Mondale
EXECUTIVE OFFICE OF THE PRESIDENT	
Assistant to the President	Zbigniew Brzezinski
	Hamilton Jordan
	James R. Schlesinger
Press Secretary to the President	Joseph L. Powell
Counsel to the President	Robert J. Lipshutz
Special Assistant to the President	Joseph W. Aragon
Office of Management and Budget	James T. McIntyre, Jr., director (acting)
Council of Economic Advisers	Charles L. Schultze, chairman
National Security Council	[1]
Central Intelligence Agency	Adm. Stansfield Turner, director
Domestic Council	Stuart E. Eizenstat, executive director
Office of the Special Representative for Trade Negotiations	Robert S. Strauss, special representative
Council on Environmental Quality	Charles H. Warren, chairman
Office of Telecommunications Policy	William J. Thaler, director (acting)
Council on International Economic Policy	Gus W. Weiss, Jr., executive director (acting)
Council on Wage and Price Stability	Robert W. Crandall, director (acting)
Office of Drug Abuse Policy	Peter G. Bourne, M.D., director
Office of Science and Technology Policy	Frank Press, director
DEPARTMENT OF STATE	Cyrus R. Vance, secretary
	Warren M. Christopher, deputy secretary
Political Affairs	Philip C. Habib, undersecretary
Economic Affairs	Richard N. Cooper, undersecretary
Security Assistance	Lucy Wilson Benson, undersecretary
Management	Benjamin H. Read, deputy undersecretary
Ambassador at Large	Ellsworth Bunker
	Elliot L. Richardson
	Arthur J. Goldberg
Counselor of the Department	Matthew Nimetz
Agency for International Development	John J. Gilligan, administrator
Permanent Mission to the Organization of American States	Gale W. McGee, permanent representative
Sinai Support Mission	C. William Kontos, director
Mission to the United Nations	Andrew J. Young, representative
African Affairs	Richard M. Moose, asst. secretary
European Affairs	George S. Vest, asst. secretary
East Asian and Pacific Affairs	Richard C. Holbrooke, asst. secretary
Inter-American Affairs	Terence A. Todman, asst. secretary
Near Eastern and South Asian Affairs	Alfred L. Atherton, Jr., asst. secretary
International Organization Affairs	Charles W. Maynes, asst. secretary
DEPARTMENT OF THE TREASURY	W. Michael Blumenthal, secretary
	Robert Carswell, deputy secretary
Monetary Affairs	Anthony M. Solomon, undersecretary
Comptroller of the Currency	John G. Heimann, comptroller
Bur. of Government Financial Operations	Dario A. Pagliai, commissioner
U.S. Customs Service	Vernon D. Acree, commissioner
Bureau of Engraving and Printing	James A. Conlon, director
Bureau of the Mint	Stella B. Hackel, director
Bureau of the Public Debt	H. J. Hintgen, commissioner
Internal Revenue Service	Jerome Kurtz, commissioner
Office of the Treasurer	Azie Taylor Morton, treasurer
Savings Bond Division	Azie Taylor Morton, national director
U.S. Secret Service	H. Stuart Knight, director
Bureau of Alcohol, Tobacco and Firearms	Rex D. Davis, director
Federal Law Enforcement Training Center	Arthur F. Brandstatter, director
DEPARTMENT OF DEFENSE	Harold Brown, secretary
	Charles W. Duncan, Jr., deputy secretary
Joint Chiefs of Staff	Gen. George S. Brown, USAF, chairman
Chief of Staff, Army	Gen. Bernard W. Rogers, USA
Chief of Naval Operations	Adm. James L. Holloway III, USN
Chief of Staff, Air Force	Gen. David C. Jones, USAF
Commandant of the Marine Corps	Gen. Louis H. Wilson, USMC
Department of the Army	Clifford L. Alexander, Jr., secretary
Department of the Navy	W. Graham Claytor, Jr., secretary
Department of the Air Force	John Stetson, secretary
DEPARTMENT OF JUSTICE	Griffin B. Bell
Attorney General	
Solicitor General	Wade H. McCree, Jr.
Community Relations Service	Gilbert G. Pompa, director (acting)
Law Enforcement Assistance Admin.	James Gregg, administrator (acting)
Antitrust Division	Donald I. Baker, asst. attorney general
Civil Division	Barbara A. Babcock, asst. attorney general
Civil Rights Division	Drew S. Days III, asst. attorney general
Criminal Division	Benjamin R. Civiletti, asst. attorney general
Land and Natural Resources Division	Peter R. Taft, asst. attorney general
Tax Division	Myron C. Baum, asst. attorney general (acting)
Office of Management and Finance	Kevin D. Rooney, asst. attorney general (acting)
Federal Bureau of Investigation	Clarence M. Kelley, director
Bureau of Prisons	Norman A. Carlson, director
Immigration and Naturalization Service	Leonard F. Chapman, Jr., commissioner
Drug Enforcement Administration	Peter B. Bensinger, administrator
U.S. Marshals Service	William E. Hall, Jr., director
DEPARTMENT OF THE INTERIOR	Cecil D. Andrus, secretary
	James A. Joseph, undersecretary
Fish and Wildlife and Parks	Robert L. Herbst, asst. secretary
National Park Service	William J. Whalen, director

Department, bureau, or office	Executive official and official title
Fish and Wildlife Service	Lynn A. Greenwalt, director
Bureau of Outdoor Recreation	Chris T. Delaporte, director
Energy and Minerals	Joan Davenport, asst. secretary
Office of Minerals Policy and Research Analysis	Hermann Enzer, director
Geological Survey	Vincent E. McKelvey, director
Bureau of Mines	John D. Morgan, director (acting)
Land and Water Resources	Guy R. Martin, asst. secretary
Bureau of Land Management	Curt Berklund, director
Bureau of Reclamation	R. Keith Higginson, commissioner
Bureau of Indian Affairs	Forrest J. Gerard, assistant secretary
DEPARTMENT OF AGRICULTURE	Bob Bergland, secretary
	John C. White, deputy secretary
Rural Development	Alex P. Mercure, asst. secretary
Rural Electrification Administration	David A. Hamil, administrator
Farmers Home Administration	Gordon Cavanaugh, administrator
Marketing Services	Vacancy (asst. secretary)
Agricultural Marketing Service	Barbara L. Schlei, administrator
International Affairs and Commodity Programs	Dale E. Hathaway, asst. secretary
Commodity Credit Corporation	Dale E. Hathaway, president
Conservation, Research, and Education	Malcolm R. Cutler, asst. secretary
Forest Service	John R. McGuire, chief
Soil Conservation Service	Ronello M. Davis, administrator
Agricultural Economics	Howard W. Hjort, director
Statistical Reporting Service	William E. Kibler, administrator
Food and Consumer Services	Carol Tucker Foreman, asst. secretary
DEPARTMENT OF COMMERCE	Juanita M. Kreps, secretary
	Sidney L. Harman, undersecretary
Domestic and International Business	Frank Weil, asst. secretary
Chief Economist	Courtney M. Slater
Bureau of the Census	Manuel D. Plotkin, director
Bureau of Economic Analysis	George Jaszi, director
Science and Technology	Jordan Baruch, asst. secretary
Office of Environmental Affairs	Sidney R. Galler, deputy asst. secretary
National Bureau of Standards	Ernest Ambler, director (acting)
Patent and Trademark Office	C. Marshall Dann, commissioner
Maritime Affairs	Robert J. Blackwell, asst. secretary
Tourism	Fabian Chavez, Jr., asst. secretary
National Oceanic and Atmospheric Administration	Robert M. White, administrator
DEPARTMENT OF LABOR	F. Ray Marshall, secretary
	Robert J. Brown, undersecretary
Administration and Management	Fred G. Clark, asst. secretary
Employment and Training	Ernest G. Green, asst. secretary
Labor-Management Relations	Francis X. Burkhardt, asst. secretary
Employment Standards	Donald E. Elisburg, asst. secretary
Occupational Safety and Health	Eula Bingham, asst. secretary
Labor Statistics	Julius Shiskin, commissioner
DEPARTMENT OF HEALTH, EDUCATION, AND WELFARE	Joseph A. Califano, Jr., secretary
	Hale Champion, undersecretary
Office of Human Development	Arabella Martinez, asst. secretary
Education Division	Mary Berry, asst. secretary
Office of Education	Ernest L. Boyer, commissioner
National Institute of Education	Emerson J. Elliott, director (acting)
Public Health Service	Julius B. Richmond, M.D., asst. secretary
Food and Drug Administration	Donald Kennedy, commissioner
National Institutes of Health	Donald S. Fredrickson, director
Health Resources Administration	Harold Margulies, M.D., deputy administrator
Health Services Administration	George I. Lythcott, M.D., administrator
Center for Disease Control	William H. Foege, M.D., director
Alcohol, Drug Abuse, and Mental Health Administration	Francis N. Waldrop, M.D., deputy administrator
Health Care Financing Administration	Don I. Wortman, administrator (acting)
Social Security Administration	James B. Cardwell, commissioner
Office of Child Support Enforcement	James B. Cardwell, director
DEPARTMENT OF HOUSING AND URBAN DEVELOPMENT	Patricia Roberts Harris, secretary
	Jay Janis, undersecretary
Community Planning and Development	Robert C. Embry, asst. secretary
Federal Housing Commissioner	Lawrence P. Simons
Fair Housing and Equal Opportunity	Chester C. McGuire, Jr., asst. secretary
Policy Development and Research	Donna E. Shalala, asst. secretary
DEPARTMENT OF TRANSPORTATION	Brock Adams, secretary
	Alan A. Butchman, deputy secretary
United States Coast Guard	Adm. Owen W. Siler, USCG, commandant
Federal Aviation Administration	Langhorne M. Bond, administrator
Federal Highway Administration	William M. Cox, administrator
National Highway Traffic Safety Administration	Joan B. Claybrook, administrator
Federal Railroad Administration	John M. Sullivan, administrator
Urban Mass Transportation	Charles F. Bingman, administrator (acting)
St. Lawrence Seaway Development Corp.	David W. Oberlin, administrator
Materials Transportation Bureau	James T. Curtis, Jr., director
DEPARTMENT OF ENERGY	James R. Schlesinger, secretary
	John F. O'Leary, deputy secretary
	Dale D. Myers, undersecretary
Federal Energy Regulatory Commission	Charles B. Curtis, chairman
General Counsel	Eric J. Fygi, general counsel (acting)
Executive Secretariat	Raymond L. Walters

[1] Council comprised of the President of the United States and certain other members.

Senate
January 1978

House of Representatives
membership at the opening of the second session of the 95th Congress in January 1978

Supreme Court

[1]Died Jan. 13, 1978. [2]Died Jan. 12, 1978. [3]Resigned Dec. 31, 1977.

The Federal Administrative Budget

in millions of dollars; fiscal years ending Sept. 30 (1976, June 30)

Source and function	1976	1977 estimate	1978 estimate
BUDGET RECEIPTS	$300,000	$354,000	$393,000
Individual income taxes	131,600	153,100	171,200
Corporation income taxes	41,400	56,600	58,900
Excise taxes	17,000	17,900	18,500
Social insurance taxes and contributions	92,700	108,900	126,100
Estate and gift taxes	5,200	5,900	5,800
Customs duties	4,100	4,700	5,300
Miscellaneous receipts	8,000	6,900	7,200
BUDGET EXPENDITURES	366,500	411,200	440,000
National defense	90,000	100,100	112,300
Department of Defense military functions	88,000	98,000	109,500
Military assistance	500	200	600
Atomic energy defense activities	1,600	800	2,200
Defense-related activities	−100	−100	[1]
International affairs	5,100	7,100	7,300
Conduct of foreign affairs	700	1,000	1,100
Foreign economic and financial assistance	3,600	5,100	5,200
Foreign information and exchange activities	400	400	400
International financial programs	800	1,200	1,100
General science, space, and technology	4,400	4,400	4,700
Agriculture	2,500	2,900	2,300
Farm income stabilization	1,600	1,800	1,200
Agricultural research and services	900	1,100	1,100
Natural resources, environment, and energy	11,300	17,100	19,700
Water resources and power	3,600	4,800	4,900
Conservation and land management	1,200	1,500	1,400
Recreational resources	900	1,200	1,400
Pollution control and abatement	3,100	5,200	5,900
Energy	2,400	4,100	6,100
Other natural resources	900	1,000	1,100
Commerce and transportation	17,200	16,100	19,300
Mortgage credit and thrift insurance	1,200	−2,100	200
Payment to the Postal Service	1,700	2,300	1,500
Other advancement and regulation	900	1,000	1,100
Air transportation	2,600	2,800	3,200
Water transportation	1,600	1,900	2,000
Ground transportation	9,300	10,100	11,300
Other transportation	100	100	100
Community and regional development	5,300	7,700	7,900
Community development	3,500	4,900	5,100
Area and regional development	1,300	2,200	2,300
Disaster relief and insurance	500	600	500
Education, training, employment, and social services	$18,200	$21,100	$19,400
Elementary, secondary, and vocational education	4,700	5,200	5,500
Higher education	2,700	3,400	2,900
Research and general education aids	800	1,100	1,200
Training and employment	6,300	6,800	5,300
Social Services	3,500	4,100	4,000
Health	33,400	39,300	43,200
Health care services	28,700	34,500	26,000
Health research and education	3,100	2,800	2,600
Prevention and control of health problems	1,000	1,100	900
Health planning and construction	800	900	1,300
General health financial assistance	—	—	12,300
Income security	127,400	138,100	143,900
General retirement and disability insurance	77,200	88,100	95,700
Federal employee retirement and disability	8,200	9,700	11,100
Unemployment insurance	19,500	16,400	13,900
Public assistance and other income supplements	22,600	24,000	23,200
Veterans benefits and services	18,400	18,400	18,300
Income security for veterans	8,400	9,100	9,200
Veterans education, training, and rehabilitation	5,500	4,100	3,300
Hospital and medical care for veterans	4,000	4,900	5,100
Other veterans benefits and services	600	600	600
Law enforcement and justice	3,300	3,700	3,800
Federal law enforcement and prosecution	1,900	2,100	2,200
Federal judicial activities	300	400	400
Federal correctional and rehabilitative activities	200	300	300
Law enforcement assistance	900	900	800
General government	2,900	3,700	3,900
Legislative functions	700	900	900
Central fiscal operations	1,800	2,000	2,100
General property and records management	100	300	400
Other general government	500	500	500
Revenue sharing and general purpose fiscal assistance	7,100	8,900	8,100
Interest	34,600	38,000	39,700
Allowances for contingencies, civilian agency pay raises	—	—	2,700
Undistributed offsetting receipts	−14,700	−15,400	−16,400
Employer share, employee retirement	−4,200	−4,600	−4,700
Interest received by trust funds	−7,800	−8,200	−8,700
Rents and royalties on the Outer Continental Shelf	−2,700	−2,600	−3,100

[1] Less than $50,000,000. Source: Executive Office of the President, Office of Management and Budget, *The United States Budget in Brief: Fiscal Year 1978.*

State Government Revenue, Expenditure, and Debt

1976 in thousands of dollars

State	GENERAL REVENUE						GENERAL EXPENDITURE					DEBT		
	Total	State taxes			Intergov-ernmental	Charges & misc.	Total	Education	Highways	Public welfare	Hospi-tals	Total	Issued 1976[1]	Retired 1976[1]
		Total	General sales	Individual income										
Ala.	2,343,266	1,243,258	397,022	224,597	788,859	311,149	2,394,888	1,157,452	345,552	320,002	156,630	979,022	122,350	46,348
Alaska	1,042,880	598,806	—	146,254	281,184	162,890	957,387	318,777	169,329	48,689	11,867	827,846	135,653	21,250
Ariz.	1,559,015	1,017,705	435,504	162,869	356,036	185,274	1,601,190	789,024	248,110	87,189	70,245	91,821	4,600	2,249
Ark.	1,321,379	725,063	240,256	147,688	479,112	117,204	1,334,640	542,608	261,171	216,782	58,961	129,659	12,842	4,454
Calif.	17,684,854	10,761,179	3,742,936	2,957,788	5,374,425	1,549,250	17,062,759	6,401,702	1,159,458	4,490,436	474,739	6,465,717	300,260	304,898
Colo.	1,870,802	964,444	303,705	320,379	582,460	323,898	1,810,630	858,362	244,866	302,227	95,182	126,214	1,050	3,198
Conn.	2,009,383	1,263,832	542,898	50,489	482,699	262,852	2,003,395	633,831	190,582	394,450	137,985	3,068,950	454,650	165,605
Del.	597,677	358,581	—	141,487	126,200	112,896	629,216	291,153	70,943	69,720	22,392	737,502	180,078	40,830
Fla.	4,404,857	2,935,507	1,254,086	—	1,057,697	411,653	4,484,812	1,970,805	612,861	434,298	190,627	1,739,834	213,595	54,491
Ga.	2,923,103	1,676,007	619,375	413,188	976,534	270,562	2,857,552	1,229,076	384,188	480,784	166,516	1,289,771	203,170	68,399
Hawaii	1,105,529	639,198	309,596	184,915	303,188	163,143	1,222,569	426,743	103,544	168,081	67,821	1,304,493	295,000	49,603
Idaho	599,359	328,803	88,873	98,824	198,493	72,063	622,494	231,531	116,809	70,870	12,646	39,443	923	1,073
Ill.	7,627,067	4,782,921	1,674,488	1,216,557	2,133,917	710,229	7,934,310	2,925,262	1,141,875	2,011,648	373,843	3;356,892	738,957	106,790
Ind.	3,117,312	1,915,551	902,589	405,432	735,670	466,091	3,096,367	1,346,430	498,165	360,634	148,161	599,654	32,410	33,668
Iowa	1,989,590	1,199,507	351,872	388,212	543,564	246,519	2,076,253	899,930	409,060	315,624	110,285	125,870	3,270	4,610
Kan.	1,459,443	853,936	300,365	193,730	408,861	196,646	1,441,458	613,004	240,303	245,187	97,895	408,101	124,520	22,735
Ky.	2,447,532	1,403,735	409,193	292,546	742,466	301,331	2,355,861	961,590	420,943	404,545	71,396	1,996,558	97,500	44,349
La.	3,092,100	1,655,576	421,278	117,641	828,092	608,432	3,088,351	1,157,774	554,963	404,847	193,120	1,457,976	287,440	50,845
Maine	891,325	530,565	151,336	52,190	262,740	98,020	867,699	380,663	94,489	154,253	26,199	535,347	102,105	27,922
Md.	3,169,262	1,959,804	419,397	790,364	790,537	418,921	3,447,523	1,265,155	416,374	531,375	184,836	2,517,334	537,605	124,866
Mass.	4,580,975	2,727,594	347,863	1,216,149	1,419,922	433,459	4,436,549	1,262,293	342,698	1,292,557	238,070	4,960,606	1,297,351	177,874
Mich.	6,581,172	3,769,464	1,069,975	1,130,689	1,974,197	837,511	6,819,143	2,533,344	738,891	1,891,588	312,606	1,882,527	312,908	100,072
Minn.	3,580,367	2,218,888	426,541	849,520	945,405	416,074	3,481,150	1,674,331	381,065	548,896	148,969	1,019,908	136,095	49,576
Miss.	1,593,180	874,172	424,838	105,410	544,777	174,231	1,643,157	689,456	301,010	204,321	73,427	774,505	189,515	29,221
Mo.	2,409,566	1,443,799	532,284	338,843	751,515	214,252	2,400,649	976,951	424,329	423,873	143,454	336,697	87,828	28,588
Mont.	595,017	277,745	—	97,520	237,420	79,852	579,434	221,353	123,798	58,210	26,465	85,055	7,400	3,584
Neb.	931,060	489,419	165,665	105,736	307,902	133,739	903,548	311,811	166,232	121,269	57,919	64,051	—	4,622
Nev.	481,996	293,921	100,336	—	141,240	46,835	470,885	193,895	77,726	45,892	8,918	53,163	4,785	3,426
N.H.	416,411	183,778	—	6,175	153,401	79,232	488,389	138,307	93,251	74,724	32,742	303,795	70,964	14,654
N.J.	4,116,910	2,292,438	836,157	101,200	1,212,831	611,641	4,509,870	1,360,452	357,456	1,059,494	220,963	4,013,414	235,010	88,368
N.M.	1,118,997	575,071	243,181	58,191	295,460	248,466	990,343	467,911	147,669	94,335	48,770	186,768	46,925	13,735
N.Y.	17,253,780	9,780,069	2,148,915	3,948,808	5,655,110	1,818,601	17,719,231	5,342,842	781,458	4,225,508	1,216,670	20,451,198	4,340,117	396,571
N.C.	3,361,552	2,059,951	465,862	604,793	918,254	383,347	3,718,894	1,832,273	503,915	388,831	225,247	709,221	199,895	40,955
N.D.	601,290	287,376	110,238	58,776	162,959	150,955	537,055	218,121	99,589	47,519	19,804	70,081	9,665	2,892
Ohio	5,628,234	3,310,704	1,028,253	511,636	1,560,756	756,774	5,886,607	2,305,773	696,111	1,109,689	333,785	3,029,677	480,447	137,191
Okla.	1,864,403	1,000,218	181,862	200,998	548,972	315,213	1,767,550	755,344	257,312	334,276	108,386	947,997	10,803	22,331
Ore.	1,765,225	825,805	—	472,147	617,564	321,856	1,782,499	612,900	272,607	305,365	74,888	2,001,580	368,450	43,654
Pa.	8,029,960	5,127,043	1,395,486	1,062,210	2,248,962	653,955	8,696,719	3,137,195	1,150,328	1,981,653	520,446	5,888,110	763,985	179,892
R.I.	747,171	388,739	111,328	93,192	236,420	122,012	762,317	242,791	40,320	201,728	57,826	508,691	57,241	26,195
S.C.	1,906,935	1,042,485	372,608	244,532	573,991	290,459	2,033,467	847,421	210,707	202,128	120,913	1,045,189	159,607	46,126
S.D.	456,777	192,140	92,756	—	181,585	83,052	470,359	152,559	102,273	67,324	20,660	91,767	25,356	1,242
Tenn.	2,300,555	1,273,215	556,702	22,131	784,746	242,594	2,433,396	1,013,013	473,386	365,102	132,662	950,969	216,107	35,272
Texas	7,283,743	4,214,273	1,484,050	—	1,981,247	1,088,223	6,830,937	3,577,219	753,557	1,058,110	444,742	2,081,822	210,405	75,017
Utah	945,206	474,572	195,910	140,562	340,792	129,842	950,058	492,351	133,574	97,462	37,290	152,292	70,000	6,696
Vt.	443,822	205,293	28,032	58,923	173,868	64,661	445,138	147,017	57,378	86,042	14,038	421,172	19,500	58,664
Va.	3,182,346	1,822,343	385,668	614,575	855,843	504,160	3,149,793	1,319,893	569,650	425,065	221,228	710,951	93,115	39,422
Wash.	2,958,917	1,848,055	996,127	—	768,623	342,239	2,852,148	1,434,040	301,074	418,754	80,685	1,227,331	89,681	53,386
W.Va.	1,459,898	828,790	401,832	140,106	486,876	144,232	1,449,550	507,183	380,790	170,989	54,958	1,174,605	164,066	50,159
Wis.	3,837,564	2,421,077	584,907	959,923	1,005,574	410,913	3,776,642	1,339,480	327,148	769,693	142,711	1,362,143	349,540	58,239
Wyo.	428,896	193,102	80,581	—	177,973	57,821	415,021	121,560	151,580	21,253	10,886	75,335	420	2,370
TOTAL	152,117,660	89,255,517	27,332,726	21,447,895	44,716,919	18,145,224	153,689,852	59,629,951	18,100,467	29,633,291	7,821,474	84,378,624	13,865,159	2,968,177

Fiscal year ending June 30, 1976, except Alabama, September 30; New York, March 31; and Texas, August 31. [1] Long term only.
Source: U.S. Department of Commerce, Bureau of the Census, *State Government Finances in 1976.*

EDUCATION

Public Elementary and Secondary Schools

Fall 1976 estimates

State	ENROLLMENT		INSTRUCTIONAL STAFF				TEACHERS' AVERAGE ANNUAL SALARIES		STUDENT-TEACHER RATIO		Expenditure per pupil
	Elementary	Secondary	Total¹	Principals and supervisors	Teachers, elementary	Teachers, secondary	Elementary	Secondary	Elementary	Secondary	
Alabama	380,102	372,388	39,364	2,105	18,350	18,909	$10,495	$10,704	20.7	19.7	$1,109
Alaska	51,590	39,600	5,163	347	2,385	2,090	20,985	21,123	21.6	18.9	2,780
Arizona	344,737	158,080	26,492	887	16,697	6,785	12,540	13,970	20.6	23.3	1,356
Arkansas	240,004	220,589	24,301	1,243	10,477	11,350	9,528	9,923	22.9	19.4	1,056
California	2,638,000	1,778,000	207,300	9,700	111,300	76,300	16,000	17,400	23.7	23.3	1,571
Colorado	300,750	269,250	33,550	1,500	14,210	14,790	12,625	13,100	21.2	18.2	1,468
Connecticut	430,540	204,900	39,735	2,185	16,900	18,450	13,465	13,827	25.5	11.1	1,770
Delaware	60,754	61,546	7,114	379	2,530	3,702	12,949	13,290	24.0	16.6	1,731
District of Columbia	69,330	56,688	7,398	503	3,351	2,706	...	...	20.7	20.9	1,893
Florida	777,982	760,257	86,259	4,049	37,472	36,033	10,638	10,990	20.8	21.1	1,364
Georgia	672,816	422,326	55,864	2,307	33,907	19,650	11,215	11,646	19.8	21.5	1,076
Hawaii	91,400	85,200	9,311	618	4,400	3,500	15,969	15,969	20.8	24.3	1,196
Idaho	103,368	96,637	10,498	574	4,570	4,813	10,778	11,179	22.6	20.1	...
Illinois	1,338,716	881,819	126,250	7,850	57,000	53,500	14,199	15,551	23.5	16.5	1,733
Indiana	569,717	592,351	62,459	4,270	27,836	27,353	12,231	12,881	20.5	21.7	1,236
Iowa	315,291	289,142	39,034	1,389	15,899	17,400	11,226	12,715	19.8	16.6	1,550
Kansas	237,940	200,260	28,533	1,375	13,597	11,920	11,081	12,716	17.5	16.8	1,458
Kentucky	430,280	263,720	36,195	1,925	19,960	12,340	10,700	11,450	21.6	21.4	1,019
Louisiana	507,450	338,800	44,835	2,243	23,936	18,656	10,083	10,663	21.2	18.2	1,031
Maine	169,371	72,845	12,928	1,052	6,890	4,856	10,340	11,270	24.6	15.0	1,254
Maryland	441,251	420,392	49,680	3,265	21,014	22,583	14,448	14,932	21.0	18.6	1,714
Massachusetts	605,000	564,000	75,100	4,700	30,900	34,500	12,150	12,360	19.6	16.3	1,650
Michigan	1,060,000	1,021,900	103,200	6,958	44,852	43,960	17,374	15,905	23.6	23.2	...
Minnesota	419,327	451,550	50,185	2,125	20,435	24,325	12,830	14,045	20.5	18.6	1,564
Mississippi	282,245	227,600	27,411	1,734	13,550	10,785	9,205	9,641	20.8	21.1	1,087
Missouri	630,956	319,186	55,555	3,298	24,757	23,806	11,352	11,817	25.5	13.4	...
Montana	114,175	57,275	10,220	535	5,300	3,860	11,240	11,984	21.5	14.8	1,644
Nebraska	116,927	146,256	20,175	972	8,727	8,950	10,641	11,690	19.1	16.3	1,457
Nevada	73,000	69,000	6,917	400	3,034	2,977	13,394	13,555	24.1	23.2	1,309
New Hampshire	105,035	70,461	10,808	584	4,467	5,157	10,105	10,800	23.5	13.7	1,180
New Jersey	890,400	536,600	96,900	7,000	47,605	32,595	14,286	14,813	18.7	16.5	1,910
New Mexico	143,888	140,838	14,705	1,105	6,505	6,530	12,000	12,064	22.1	21.6	1,275
New York	1,706,000	1,672,997	195,340	13,590	82,240	89,340	16,800	17,400	20.7	18.7	2,096
North Carolina	832,410	370,919	61,971	3,541	38,101	17,805	11,688	12,713	21.8	20.8	1,137
North Dakota	59,076	70,030	8,203	335	4,450	3,048	9,695	12,077	13.3	23.0	1,343
Ohio	1,340,080	912,155	122,220	6,900	54,000	52,120	12,190	12,800	24.8	17.5	1,305
Oklahoma	318,000	278,000	33,370	1,820	15,200	15,000	10,240	10,720	20.9	18.5	1,197
Oregon	274,000	204,514	28,570	1,950	12,955	10,620	13,250	13,840	21.2	19.3	1,488
Pennsylvania	1,095,500	1,100,000	129,300	5,400	56,800	58,700	13,450	13,750	19.3	18.7	1,729
Rhode Island	100,858	74,242	10,410	540	5,000	4,060	13,080	14,182	20.2	18.3	1,421
South Carolina	389,244	244,458	33,753	2,314	17,736	11,706	10,122	10,801	21.9	20.9	1,049
South Dakota	97,296	50,784	9,342	475	5,323	2,941	10,040	10,270	18.3	17.3	1,215
Tennessee	540,083	342,059	45,020	2,175	24,400	15,735	10,883	11,487	22.1	21.7	1,083
Texas	1,521,993	1,300,761	161,300	8,300	75,800	66,600	11,364	11,744	20.1	19.5	1,075
Utah	168,428	146,043	14,400	800	6,560	6,328	11,991	12,418	25.7	23.1	1,168
Vermont	62,574	41,692	7,215	800	3,155	2,890	10,324	11,006	19.8	14.4	1,390
Virginia	680,069	420,654	65,216	4,474	35,370	25,372	11,450	12,586	19.2	16.6	1,298
Washington	395,749	384,981	39,900	3,060	17,179	16,511	14,521	15,334	23.0	23.3	1,583
West Virginia	233,880	170,586	22,779	1,594	10,934	9,339	11,149	11,781	21.4	18.3	1,127
Wisconsin	521,379	423,958	52,818	2,430	26,300	24,088	12,605	13,373	19.8	17.6	1,697
Wyoming	47,503	43,084	6,039	395	2,692	2,717	12,457	13,082	17.6	15.9	1,640
TOTAL U.S.	25,046,264	19,441,373	2,470,605	140,070	1,167,008	1,020,051	$12,993	$13,662	21.5	19.1	$1,464

Kindergartens included in elementary schools; junior high schools, in secondary schools.
¹ Includes librarians, guidance and psychological personnel, and related educational workers.
Source: National Education Association, Research Division, *Estimates of School Statistics, 1976–77* (Copyright 1977. All rights reserved. Used by permission).

Universities and Colleges

state statistics

State	NUMBER OF INSTITUTIONS 1976–1977		Enrollment¹,² fall, 1976	EARNED DEGREES CONFERRED 1974–1975			State	NUMBER OF INSTITUTIONS 1976–1977		Enrollment¹,² fall, 1976	EARNED DEGREES CONFERRED 1974–1975		
	Total	Public		Bachelor's and first professional	Master's except first professional	Doctor's		Total	Public		Bachelor's and first professional	Master's except first professional	Doctor's
Alabama	56	36	152,000	15,074	5,180	196	Montana	12	9	31,000	3,783	613	81
Alaska	9	7	14,000	610	243	10	Nebraska	29	16	69,000	9,097	1,517	229
Arizona	22	17	145,000	9,278	3,866	413	Nevada	6	5	22,000	1,428	443	15
Arkansas	29	16	64,000	7,225	1,437	105	New Hampshire	24	10	39,000	5,080	721	62
California	252	134	1,458,000	88,662	27,584	3,628	New Jersey	65	31	275,000	26,396	8,163	718
Colorado	39	27	135,000	14,746	3,940	701	New Mexico	17	14	52,000	4,889	1,362	143
Connecticut	46	22	151,000	14,198	5,863	584	New York	287	84	1,028,000	88,023	38,681	3,451
Delaware	10	6	31,000	2,776	485	76	North Carolina	116	73	194,000	24,496	4,480	825
District of Columbia	19	3	87,000	8,908	5,070	568	North Dakota	15	11	28,000	3,674	466	67
Florida	73	37	307,000	27,500	7,258	1,141	Ohio	131	61	382,000	48,401	11,918	1,565
Georgia	67	35	172,000	17,889	7,360	548	Oklahoma	44	29	137,000	14,230	3,850	498
Hawaii	11	8	39,000	3,876	1,298	97	Oregon	43	21	116,000	10,867	3,132	465
Idaho	9	6	37,000	2,880	599	65	Pennsylvania	179	62	446,000	58,814	14,515	1,771
Illinois	149	61	500,000	48,078	16,611	2,131	Rhode Island	12	3	64,000	6,537	1,787	204
Indiana	64	23	207,000	25,683	10,046	1,300	South Carolina	56	32	126,000	11,337	3,116	162
Iowa	61	22	111,000	14,827	2,377	551	South Dakota	17	7	30,000	4,233	695	46
Kansas	52	29	120,000	12,761	3,046	448	Tennessee	67	23	176,000	18,835	4,690	578
Kentucky	38	9	118,000	13,135	4,517	251	Texas	146	92	571,000	53,432	13,803	1,541
Louisiana	31	20	154,000	17,195	4,326	386	Utah	14	9	77,000	9,497	2,293	455
Maine	25	10	39,000	4,759	736	26	Vermont	23	6	29,000	3,850	1,146	41
Maryland	52	30	182,000	17,179	5,015	649	Virginia	73	39	229,000	20,084	4,661	479
Massachusetts	119	33	370,000	39,651	13,887	2,018	Washington	48	33	180,000	17,733	3,616	539
Michigan	94	45	430,000	38,888	14,887	1,635	West Virginia	28	17	73,000	8,639	1,969	110
Minnesota	65	30	183,000	19,496	2,918	540	Wisconsin	58	30	186,000	22,589	5,386	917
Mississippi	45	27	91,000	9,937	2,850	255	Wyoming	8	8	16,000	1,367	352	78
Missouri	83	28	214,000	23,306	6,700	704	TOTAL U.S.	3,038	1,446	10,087,000	975,828	291,474	34,066

Excludes service academies.   ¹ Excludes non–degree-credit students.   ² Estimated.
Source: U.S. Department of Health, Education, and Welfare, National Center for Education Statistics, *Digest of Education Statistics, Education Directory,* and *Earned Degrees Conferred.*

Universities and Colleges, 1976–77[1]

Selected four-year schools

Institution	Location	Year founded	Total students[2]	Total faculty[3]	Bound library volumes
ALABAMA					
Alabama A. & M. U.	Normal	1875	4,613	298	255,600
Alabama State U.	Montgomery	1874	3,600	179	145,000
Auburn U.	Auburn	1856	17,523	1,028	925,000
Birmingham-Southern	Birmingham	1856	1,200	85	118,900
Jacksonville State U.	Jacksonville	1883	6,200	275	227,000
Troy State U.	Troy	1887	10,136	326	266,000
Tuskegee Institute	Tuskegee Institute	1881	3,590	316	225,000
U. of Alabama	University	1831	15,852	877	1,088,500
U. of South Alabama	Mobile	1963	6,957	338	200,000
ALASKA					
U. of Alaska	Fairbanks	1917	3,401	350	303,500
ARIZONA					
Arizona State U.	Tempe	1885	33,366	1,478	1,285,700
Northern Arizona U.	Flagstaff	1899	12,100	210	658,700
U. of Arizona	Tucson	1885	30,146	1,828	1,900,000
ARKANSAS					
Arkansas State U.	State University	1909	7,303	337	287,200
U. of Arkansas	Fayetteville	1871	11,184	736	737,300
U. of A. at Little Rock	Little Rock	1927	9,238	389	277,000
U. of Central Arkansas	Conway	1907	5,355	261	212,500
CALIFORNIA					
California Inst. of Tech.	Pasadena	1891	1,500	280	312,000
Cal. Polytech. State U.	San Luis Obispo	1901	15,000[4]	885[4]	430,000
Cal. State, Dominguez Hills	Dominguez Hills	1960	6,700	400	200,000
Cal. State, Sonoma	Rohnert Park	1960	6,004	474	210,300
Cal. State Polytech. U.	Pomona	1938	12,651	640	302,400
Cal. State U., Chico	Chico	1887	12,816	624	444,700
Cal. State U., Fresno	Fresno	1911	15,526	742	500,000
Cal. State U., Fullerton	Fullerton	1957	20,984	740	412,800
Cal. State U., Hayward	Hayward	1957	11,461	581	461,400
Cal. State U., Long Beach	Long Beach	1949	31,157	1,677	655,200
Cal. State U., Los Angeles	Los Angeles	1947	24,985	1,350	700,000
Cal. State U., Northridge	Northridge	1958	26,981	1,515	600,000
Cal. State U., Sacramento	Sacramento	1947	19,929	874[4]	602,000
Golden Gate U.	San Francisco	1901	9,125	647	216,000
Humboldt State U.	Arcata	1913	7,824[4]	459[4]	235,000
Loyola Marymount U.	Los Angeles	1911	5,250	311	316,000
Occidental	Los Angeles	1887	1,750	124	301,000
San Francisco State U.	San Francisco	1899	22,983	1,300	488,100
San Jose State U.	San Jose	1857	27,283	1,570	700,000
Stanford U.	Stanford	1885	12,469	1,327	3,982,000
U. of C., Berkeley	Berkeley	1868	29,112	1,494	4,917,300
U. of C., Davis	Davis	1905	16,849	996	1,381,800
U. of C., Irvine	Irvine	1960	9,037	478	782,800
U. of C., Los Angeles	Los Angeles	1919	31,734	1,776	3,908,100
U. of C., Riverside	Riverside	1868	4,855	330	878,600
U. of C., San Diego	La Jolla	1912	9,376	585	1,224,800
U. of C., Santa Barbara	Santa Barbara	1944	14,135	659	1,235,500
U. of C., Santa Cruz	Santa Cruz	1965	5,910	312	541,400
U. of the Pacific	Stockton	1851	6,050	402	301,900
U. of San Francisco	San Francisco	1855	6,392	229	441,700
U. of Santa Clara	Santa Clara	1851	7,295	357	315,000
U. of Southern California	Los Angeles	1880	24,478	4,577	1,750,000
COLORADO					
Colorado	Colorado Springs	1874	1,927	195	276,500
Colorado School of Mines	Golden	1874	2,584	225	158,000
Colorado State U.	Fort Collins	1870	17,426	1,100[4]	1,000,000
Metropolitan State	Denver	1963	14,000	395	370,000
U. S. Air Force Academy	USAF Academy	1954	4,400	550	450,000
U. of Colorado	Boulder	1876	33,000	1,800	1,525,800
U. of Denver	Denver	1864	7,825	461[4]	1,500,000
U. of Northern Colorado	Greeley	1889	10,965	665	471,200
U. of Southern Colorado	Pueblo	1933	5,166	285	181,200
CONNECTICUT					
Central Connecticut State	New Britain	1849	12,546	621	288,700
Southern Connecticut State	New Haven	1893	12,567	541	500,000
Trinity	Hartford	1823	2,114	169	583,100
U. S. Coast Guard Acad.	New London	1876	996	120	110,000
U. of Bridgeport	Bridgeport	1927	7,150	391	295,400
U. of Connecticut	Storrs	1881	25,118	1,133	1,325,000
U. of Hartford	West Hartford	1877	8,984	554	260,000
Wesleyan U.	Middletown	1831	2,646	277	750,000
Western Connecticut State	Danbury	1903	5,414	260	118,600
Yale U.	New Haven	1701	9,000	1,500	6,500,000
DELAWARE					
Delaware State	Dover	1891	2,128	128[4]	128,400
U. of Delaware	Newark	1833	18,511	1,166	945,000
DISTRICT OF COLUMBIA					
American U.	Washington	1893	12,994	846	390,300
Catholic U. of America	Washington	1887	7,800	593	900,000
George Washington U.	Washington	1821	22,120	2,573	710,900
Georgetown U.	Washington	1789	11,043	1,284	868,300
Howard U.	Washington	1867	10,018	1,941	887,400
FLORIDA					
Florida A. & M. U.	Tallahassee	1887	5,472	398	273,800
Florida State U.	Tallahassee	1857	21,604	1,060	1,097,400
Florida Tech. U.	Orlando	1963	9,504	336[4]	231,400
Rollins	Winter Park	1885	3,874	170	176,000
U. of Florida	Gainesville	1853	27,838	2,600	1,850,000
U. of Miami	Coral Gables	1925	18,034	1,388	1,178,200
U. of South Florida	Tampa	1960	22,000	1,200	500,000
GEORGIA					
Atlanta U.	Atlanta	1865	1,117	164	300,000
Augusta	Augusta	1925	3,883	177	192,600
Emory U.	Atlanta	1836	7,334	989	1,400,000
Georgia	Milledgeville	1889	3,510	171	130,000
Georgia Inst. of Tech.	Atlanta	1885	8,050	860	800,000
Georgia Southern	Statesboro	1906	6,114	304	380,600
Georgia State U.	Atlanta	1913	21,000	975	546,900
Mercer U.	Macon	1833	1,853	131	180,000
Morehouse[5]	Atlanta	1867	1,425[4]	104	350,000
Oglethorpe U.	Atlanta	1835	1,135	52	100,000
Spelman[6]	Atlanta	1881	1,155	100	38,600
U. of Georgia	Athens	1785	16,711	2,210	1,522,700
HAWAII					
Brigham Young U.-Hawaii	Laie	1955	1,580	85	105,000
U. of Hawaii	Honolulu	1907	21,160	1,403	1,435,000
IDAHO					
Boise State U.	Boise	1932	9,996	503[4]	214,200
Idaho State U.	Pocatello	1901	9,967	385	350,000
U. of Idaho	Moscow	1889	8,158	490	481,000
ILLINOIS					
Augustana	Rock Island	1860	2,335	142	200,600
Bradley U.	Peoria	1897	5,008	350	300,000
Chicago State U.	Chicago	1869	6,880	411	225,900
Concordia Teachers	River Forest	1864	1,118	103	120,300
De Paul U.	Chicago	1898	10,000	532	390,000
Eastern Illinois U.	Charleston	1895	9,384	512	358,000
Illinois Inst. of Tech.	Chicago	1892	6,325	665	1,338,000
Illinois State U.	Normal	1857	19,040	1,175	707,800
Knox	Galesburg	1837	1,001	92	170,000
Lake Forest	Lake Forest	1857	1,080	91	160,000
Loyola U. of Chicago	Chicago	1870	14,917	1,754	654,000
Northeastern Ill. State U.	Chicago	1869	10,148	350	253,300
Northern Illinois U.	De Kalb	1895	21,690	1,184	824,300
Northwestern U.	Evanston	1851	15,000	1,610	3,000,000
Southern Illinois U.	Carbondale	1869	22,537	1,523	1,421,200
SIU at Edwardsville	Edwardsville	1957	12,509	833	683,900
U. of Chicago	Chicago	1891	9,425	1,039	3,886,100
U. of Illinois	Urbana	1867	33,552	2,583	5,075,000
U. of I. at Chicago Circle	Chicago	1965	24,812	2,013	951,300
Western Illinois U.	Macomb	1899	14,285	742	321,200
Wheaton	Wheaton	1860	2,321	185	165,000
INDIANA					
Ball State U.	Muncie	1918	17,139	1,031	730,000
Butler U.	Indianapolis	1855	4,200	250	178,400
De Pauw U.	Greencastle	1837	2,403	180	321,400
Indiana State U.	Terre Haute	1865	12,604	704	700,000
Indiana U.	Bloomington	1820	32,921	1,507	3,242,300
Purdue U.	West Lafayette	1869	30,303	1,019	1,265,200
U. of Evansville	Evansville	1854	4,904	272	243,000
U. of Notre Dame	Notre Dame	1842	8,682	696	1,311,500
Valparaiso U.	Valparaiso	1859	3,700	315	305,200
IOWA					
Coe	Cedar Rapids	1851	1,127	97	105,000
Drake U.	Des Moines	1881	6,802	433	441,900
Grinnell	Grinnell	1846	1,210	129	226,400
Iowa State U.	Ames	1858	21,831	1,624	1,180,900
U. of Iowa	Iowa City	1847	22,512	1,529	1,956,000
U. of Northern Iowa	Cedar Falls	1876	13,368	652	460,900
KANSAS					
Emporia Kansas State	Emporia	1863	6,386	299	550,000
Kansas State U.	Manhattan	1863	19,045	1,426	850,000
U. of Kansas	Lawrence	1866	23,446	1,286	1,800,000
Witchita State U.	Wichita	1895	15,723	852	524,800
KENTUCKY					
Berea	Berea	1855	1,458	139	220,000
Eastern Kentucky U.	Richmond	1906	13,510	644	553,300
Kentucky State U.	Frankfort	1886	2,224	183	150,000
Murray State U.	Murray	1922	8,000	350	315,000
U. of Kentucky	Lexington	1865	20,000	1,875	1,200,000
U. of Louisville	Louisville	1798	16,300	1,136	865,900
Western Kentucky U.	Bowling Green	1907	13,386	580	431,100
LOUISIANA					
Grambling State U.	Grambling	1901	4,500	229	200,000
Louisiana State U.	Baton Rouge	1860	24,880	1,070	1,603,300
Louisiana Tech U.	Ruston	1894	8,914	366	686,700
Northeast Louisiana U.	Monroe	1931	9,098	395	207,300
Northwestern State U.	Natchitoches	1884	6,500	300	200,000
Southern U.	Baton Rouge	1880	9,512	430	265,000
Tulane U.	New Orleans	1834	9,463	910	1,250,000
U. of Southwestern La.	Lafayette	1898	13,318	804	409,000
MAINE					
Bates	Lewiston	1864	1,360	114	250,000
Bowdoin	Brunswick	1794	1,345	121	530,000
Colby	Waterville	1813	1,671	144	330,000
U. of Maine, Farmington	Farmington	1864	1,978	91[4]	72,700
U. of Maine at Orono	Orono	1865	10,688	451[4]	492,500
U. of Maine at Portland-Gorham	Portland	1878	8,025	310	250,000
MARYLAND					
Goucher[6]	Towson	1885	969	122	180,000
Johns Hopkins U.	Baltimore	1876	9,532	1,692	1,975,000
Morgan State U.	Baltimore	1867	6,424	450	174,200
Towson State U.	Baltimore	1866	14,452	719	310,000
U.S. Naval Academy	Annapolis	1845	4,169	546	370,000
U. of Maryland	College Park	1807	34,451	2,255	1,465,100
MASSACHUSETTS					
Amherst	Amherst	1821	1,512	162	517,000
Boston	Chestnut Hill	1863	15,990	809	961,500
Boston U.	Boston	1869	14,245	3,700	1,820,000
Brandeis U.	Waltham	1948	3,642	392	610,000
Clark U.	Worcester	1887	3,118	298	350,000
Harvard U.	Cambridge	1636	18,314	3,326	9,000,000
Holy Cross	Worcester	1843	2,460	190	340,000
Mass. Inst. of Tech.	Cambridge	1861	8,597	1,700	1,500,000
Mt. Holyoke[6]	South Hadley	1837	1,952	194	395,000
Northeastern U.	Boston	1898	39,830	1,982	375,000
Radcliffe[6]	Cambridge	1879	1,948	...	...
Salem State	Salem	1854	11,200	271[4]	165,000
Simmons[6]	Boston	1899	2,695	249	170,000

Universities and Colleges (continued)

Selected four-year schools

Institution	Location	Year founded	Total students[2]	Total faculty[3]	Bound library volumes
Smith	Northampton	1871	2,590	301	850,000
Tufts U.	Medford	1852	6,371	990	492,000
U. of Lowell	Lowell	1895	12,183	839	300,000
U. of Massachusetts	Amherst	1863	24,000	1,400	1,200,000
Wellesley[6]	Wellesley	1870	2,041	261	600,000
Wheaton[6]	Norton	1834	1,189	120	191,400
Williams	Williamstown	1793	1,965	176	461,000
MICHIGAN					
Albion	Albion	1835	1,748	104[4]	210,000
Central Michigan U.	Mt. Pleasant	1892	12,287	749	819,800
Eastern Michigan U.	Ypsilanti	1849	18,500	819	524,000
Ferris State	Big Rapids	1884	9,300	525	238,500
Hope	Holland	1866	2,200	144	173,000
Michigan State U.	East Lansing	1855	41,649	2,600	2,000,000
Michigan Tech U.	Houghton	1885	6,807	468	398,400
Northern Michigan U.	Marquette	1899	8,208	354	266,500
U. of Detroit	Detroit	1877	8,158	514	484,100
U. of Michigan	Ann Arbor	1817	36,843	4,441	4,917,400
Wayne State U.	Detroit	1868	34,818	2,231	1,663,300
Western Michigan U.	Kalamazoo	1903	20,810	1,041	654,300
MINNESOTA					
Carleton	Northfield	1866	1,681	169	261,500
Concordia	Moorhead	1891	2,647	193	223,700
Gustavus Adolphus	St. Peter	1862	2,189	145	156,400
Hamline U.	St. Paul	1854	1,205	105	150,000
Macalester	St. Paul	1874	1,637	154	250,000
Mankato State U.	Mankato	1867	11,655	565	460,000
Moorhead State U.	Moorhead	1885	5,168	318	233,600
St. Catherine[6]	St. Paul	1905	3,109	120	205,500
St. Cloud State U.	St. Cloud	1869	11,525	521	508,700
St. John's U.[5]	Collegeville	1857	1,943	152	272,700
St. Olaf	Northfield	1874	2,947	198[4]	296,400
St. Thomas	St. Paul	1885	3,206	149	190,000
U. of Minnesota	Minneapolis	1851	45,577	3,060[4]	4,000,000
Winona State U.	Winona	1858	4,533	231	172,000
MISSISSIPPI					
Alcorn State U.	Lorman	1871	2,776	128	130,400
Jackson State U.	Jackson	1877	5,960	350	205,900
Mississippi	Clinton	1826	3,002	160	152,000
Mississippi U. for Women	Columbus	1884	3,010	170	211,700
Mississippi State U.	Mississippi State	1878	11,727	690	600,000
U. of Mississippi	University	1848	9,570	484	1,500,000
U. of Southern Mississippi	Hattiesburg	1912	9,500	650[4]	400,000
MISSOURI					
Central Missouri State U.	Warrensburg	1871	9,678	435	315,000
Northeast Missouri State U.	Kirksville	1867	5,488	301	266,100
St. Louis U.	St. Louis	1818	9,375	1,669	970,000
Southeast Missouri State U.	Cape Girardeau	1873	8,400	360	275,000
Southwest Missouri State U.	Springfield	1906	12,565	568	316,000
U. of Missouri-Columbia	Columbia	1839	23,325	3,915	1,836,500
U. of Missouri-Kansas City	Kansas City	1933	10,746	1,108	564,400
U. of Missouri-Rolla	Rolla	1870	4,752	815	248,000
U. of Missouri-St. Louis	St. Louis	1963	11,188	812	381,600
Washington U.	St. Louis	1853	11,265	2,141	1,500,000
MONTANA					
Montana State U.	Bozeman	1893	9,340	411[4]	374,400
U. of Montana	Missoula	1893	8,436	498	550,600
NEBRASKA					
Creighton U.	Omaha	1878	4,979	811	443,500
U. of Nebraska	Lincoln	1869	22,256	1,033	1,318,600
U. of Nebraska at Omaha	Omaha	1908	14,339	725	400,000
NEVADA					
U. of Nevada-Las Vegas	Las Vegas	1951	6,718	539	314,200
U. of Nevada-Reno	Reno	1864	8,465	61	538,500
NEW HAMPSHIRE					
Dartmouth	Hanover	1769	3,960	520[4]	1,000,000
U. of New Hampshire	Durham	1866	11,877	648	732,800
NEW JERSEY					
Glassboro State	Glassboro	1923	13,011	386	307,500
Jersey City State	Jersey City	1927	7,800	458	198,300
Kean Col. of N. J.	Union	1855	13,748	449	195,000
Montclair State	Upper Montclair	1908	14,500	598	320,000
Princeton U.	Princeton	1746	6,070	740	3,000,000
Rider	Lawrenceville	1865	5,500	230	292,000
Rutgers State U.	New Brunswick	1766	39,807	2,237	3,198,500
Seton Hall U.	South Orange	1856	9,902	568	300,000
Stevens Inst. of Tech.	Hoboken	1870	2,200	130	104,200
Trenton State	Trenton	1855	10,819	516	250,000
Upsala	East Orange	1893	1,618	80	135,000
William Patterson	Wayne	1855	12,498	410	256,800
NEW MEXICO					
New Mexico State U.	Las Cruces	1888	11,423	606	510,000
U. of New Mexico	Albuquerque	1889	21,462	864	1,000,000
NEW YORK					
Adelphi U.	Garden City	1896	10,500	545	300,000
Alfred U.	Alfred	1836	2,095	153	203,000
Canisius	Buffalo	1870	4,274	257	208,500
City U. of New York					
Bernard M. Baruch	New York	1919	17,977	1,096	200,000
Brooklyn	Brooklyn	1930	20,812	1,431	739,200
City	New York	1847	16,628	1,000	900,000
Herbert H. Lehman	Bronx	1931	16,279	1,172	286,000
Hunter	New York	1870	26,457	1,685	400,000
Queens	Flushing	1937	30,077	2,007	439,500
Richmond	Staten Island	1965	3,976	262	165,000
York	Jamaica	1966	4,315	275	111,000
Colgate U.	Hamilton	1819	2,500	205	320,000
Columbia U.	New York	1754	13,659	2,280	4,730,500
Barnard[6]	New York	1889	2,124	185	145,000
Teachers	New York	1887	6,107	222	450,000
Cornell U.	Ithaca	1865	16,604	1,514	4,000,000
Elmira	Elmira	1855	2,889	96	129,000
Fordham U.	Bronx	1841	6,501	440	663,000
Hamilton	Clinton	1812	980	92	337,000
Hofstra U.	Hempstead	1935	11,100	560	720,000
Ithaca	Ithaca	1892	4,250	350	247,000
Juilliard School	New York	1905	1,650	200[4]	50,000
Long Island U.	Greenvale	1926	24,400	1,000	488,000
Manhattan[5]	Bronx	1853	4,570	308	200,700
Marymount[5]	Tarrytown	1907	1,006	83	90,000
New School for Soc. Res.	New York	1919	27,000	1,500	175,000
New York U.	New York	1831	40,834	1,900	2,456,000
Niagara U.	Niagara University	1856	4,170	251	200,000
Polytechnic Inst. of N.Y.	Brooklyn	1854	4,606	217	222,000
Pratt Inst.	Brooklyn	1887	4,243	463	215,700
Rensselaer Polytech. Inst.	Troy	1824	5,350	336[4]	234,000
Rochester Inst. of Tech.	Rochester	1829	11,718	947	172,000
St. Bonaventure U.	St. Bonaventure	1856	2,716	154	188,000
St. John's U.	Jamaica	1870	13,754	674	714,000[7]
St. Lawrence U.	Canton	1856	2,231	147[4]	260,000
State U. of N.Y. at Albany	Albany	1844	14,600	840	900,000
SUNY at Buffalo	Buffalo	1846	26,000	1,900	1,678,400
SUNY at Stony Brook	Stony Brook	1957	15,006	643	939,300
State U. Colleges					
Brockport	Brockport	1867	10,730	515	283,800
Buffalo	Buffalo	1867	12,383	560	280,000
Cortland	Cortland	1868	5,693	308	220,000
Fredonia	Fredonia	1867	5,232	279	237,100
Geneseo	Geneseo	1867	5,845	597	289,600
New Paltz	New Paltz	1828	7,543	422	276,900
Oneonta	Oneonta	1889	6,200	425[4]	325,000
Oswego	Oswego	1861	9,143	468	305,400
Plattsburgh	Plattsburgh	1889	5,970	309[4]	266,500
Potsdam	Potsdam	1816	5,045	301	232,900
Syracuse U.	Syracuse	1870	24,468	1,303	1,637,400
U.S. Merchant Marine Acad.	Kings Point	1938	1,069	80	100,000
U.S. Military Academy	West Point	1802	4,417	625	400,000
U. of Rochester	Rochester	1850	8,200	624	1,600,000
Vassar	Poughkeepsie	1861	2,350	211	500,000
Wagner	Staten Island	1883	2,500	209	250,000
Yeshiva U.	New York	1886	3,690	2,493	697,800
NORTH CAROLINA					
Appalachian State U.	Boone	1899	9,969	468	329,000
Catawba	Salisbury	1851	1,103	79	106,000
Davidson	Davidson	1837	1,365	100[4]	225,000
Duke U.	Durham	1838	9,402	804	2,700,000
East Carolina U.	Greenville	1907	11,696	723	522,000
Lenoir Rhyne	Hickory	1891	1,268	104	100,000
N. Carolina A. & T. St. U.	Greensboro	1891	5,345	310	326,000
N. Carolina State U.	Raleigh	1887	17,730	1,073	772,300
U. of N.C. at Chapel Hill	Chapel Hill	1789	20,162	1,928	2,274,200
U. of N.C. at Greensboro	Greensboro	1891	9,964	573	975,000
Wake Forest U.	Winston-Salem	1834	4,619	827	675,200
Western Carolina U.	Cullowhee	1889	6,380	346	230,000
NORTH DAKOTA					
North Dakota State U.	Fargo	1890	6,554[4]	343[4]	315,000
U. of North Dakota	Grand Forks	1883	8,274	460	320,000
OHIO					
Antioch	Yellow Springs	1852	1,486	75	230,000
Bowling Green State U.	Bowling Green	1910	16,054	772	576,600
Case Western Reserve U.	Cleveland	1826	8,000	1,200[4]	1,571,400
Cleveland State U.	Cleveland	1964	16,789	1,075	350,000
Denison U.	Granville	1831	2,211	147	219,500
John Carroll U.	Cleveland	1886	3,600	380	300,000
Kent State U.	Kent	1910	19,353	1,000[4]	1,125,000
Kenyon	Gambier	1824	1,470	119	180,800
Marietta	Marietta	1835	1,472	117	221,400
Miami U.	Oxford	1809	14,752	692	860,900
Oberlin	Oberlin	1833	2,700	226	700,000
Ohio State U.	Columbus	1870	54,640	3,600	2,911,800[7]
Ohio U.	Athens	1804	13,917	774	691,700
U. of Akron	Akron	1870	22,017	620[4]	833,000
U. of Cincinnati	Cincinnati	1819	33,742	2,211	1,193,100
U. of Dayton	Dayton	1850	8,781	342[4]	507,200
U. of Toledo	Toledo	1872	17,498	574[4]	559,800
Wooster	Wooster	1866	1,850	150	200,000
Xavier U.	Cincinnati	1831	6,432	301	165,200
Youngstown State U.	Youngstown	1908	15,898	737	317,800
OKLAHOMA					
Central State U.	Edmond	1890	12,846	476	448,800
Oklahoma State U.	Stillwater	1890	21,930	1,749	1,200,000
U. of Oklahoma	Norman	1890	20,010	1,358	1,881,200
U. of Tulsa	Tulsa	1894	6,362	382	838,000
OREGON					
Lewis and Clark	Portland	1867	3,150	201	157,300
Oregon State U.	Corvallis	1868	16,232	1,638[4]	761,900
Portland State U.	Portland	1946	14,241	556	522,500
Reed	Portland	1909	1,228	104	258,100
U. of Oregon	Eugene	1872	16,762	1,332	1,343,700
PENNSYLVANIA					
Allegheny	Meadville	1815	1,935	125[4]	245,000
Bryn Mawr[6]	Bryn Mawr	1885	1,589	175	451,200
Bucknell U.	Lewisburg	1846	3,250	250	400,000
Carnegie-Mellon U.	Pittsburgh	1900	4,848	415	533,800
Dickinson	Carlisle	1773	1,700	120[4]	278,000
Drexel U.	Philadelphia	1891	9,333	540	350,000
Duquesne U.	Pittsburgh	1878	6,923	487	307,800
Edinboro State	Edinboro	1857	6,755	455	310,500
Franklin and Marshall	Lancaster	1787	2,325	149	240,000
Gettysburg	Gettysburg	1832	1,941	175	231,100
Indiana U. of Pa.	Indiana	1875	11,119	649	393,110
Juniata	Huntingdon	1876	1,173	100	165,000
Lafayette	Easton	1826	2,391	153[4]	334,000
La Salle	Philadelphia	1863	5,900	350	208,000
Lehigh U.	Bethlehem	1865	5,640	374	565,000
Moravian	Bethlehem	1742	1,240	79	141,000
Muhlenberg	Allentown	1848	1,668	118	168,900

Institution	Location	Year founded	Total students[2]	Total faculty[3]	Bound library volumes
Pennsylvania State U.	University Park	1855	60,180	3,070	1,467,600
St. Joseph's	Philadelphia	1851	5,693	289	148,000
Slippery Rock State	Slippery Rock	1889	6,059	386[4]	834,800
Susquehanna U.	Selinsgrove	1858	1,596	201	100,000
Swarthmore	Swarthmore	1864	1,289	163	472,300
Temple U.	Philadelphia	1884	35,600	2,426	1,000,000
U. of Pennsylvania	Philadelphia	1740	20,538	4,722	2,500,000
U. of Pittsburgh	Pittsburgh	1787	29,444	2,516	1,591,400
Ursinus	Collegeville	1869	1,806	77	106,000
Villanova U.	Villanova	1842	7,000	380[4]	450,000
West Chester State	West Chester	1812	9,168	491	330,000
PUERTO RICO					
Inter American U.	San Juan	1912	23,296	1,042	260,000
U. of Puerto Rico	Rio Piedras	1903	26,042	1,476	879,000
RHODE ISLAND					
Brown U.	Providence	1764	6,711	460[4]	1,531,000
Rhode Island	Providence	1854	8,700	364	195,000
U. of Rhode Island	Kingston	1892	10,287	870[4]	650,000
SOUTH CAROLINA					
The Citadel[5]	Charleston	1842	3,328	152	339,000
Clemson U.	Clemson	1889	11,361	850	576,300
Furman U.	Greenville	1826	2,799	175	234,000
U. of South Carolina	Columbia	1801	23,553	1,093[4]	1,147,400
SOUTH DAKOTA					
South Dakota State U.	Brookings	1881	6,412	453[4]	280,000
U. of South Dakota	Vermillion	1882	5,812	550	413,100
TENNESSEE					
Fisk U.	Nashville	1867	1,338	100	181,500
Memphis State U.	Memphis	1909	21,269	896	667,800
Middle Tennessee State U.	Murfreesboro	1911	10,000	600	100,000
Tennessee State U.	Nashville	1909	5,256	300	214,400
Tennessee Tech. U.	Cookeville	1915	7,500	525	315,700
U. of Tennessee	Knoxville	1794	29,711	1,460	1,289,000
Vanderbilt U.	Nashville	1873	7,156	1,015	1,301,600
TEXAS					
Austin	Sherman	1849	1,198	88	164,000
Baylor U.	Waco	1845	9,332	439[4]	787,500
East Texas State U.	Commerce	1889	9,800	620	750,000
Hardin-Simmons U.	Abilene	1891	1,646	122	150,000
Lamar U.	Beaumont	1923	12,800	496	430,000
North Texas State U.	Denton	1890	15,604	1,019	1,034,700
Prairie View A. & M.	Prairie View	1876	5,400	410[4]	195,700
Rice U.	Houston	1891	3,700	445	915,000
Sam Houston State U.	Huntsville	1879	10,593	380	560,000
Southern Methodist U.	Dallas	1911	9,105	460[4]	1,553,100
Southwest Texas State U.	San Marcos	1899	14,670	647	875,000
Stephen F. Austin State U.	Nacogdoches	1923	10,571	442[4]	650,000
Texas A. & I. U.	Kingsville	1925	6,667	267	360,000
Texas A. & M. U.	College Station	1876	28,833	1,600[4]	1,100,000
Texas Christian U.	Fort Worth	1873	6,132	518	860,000
Texas Southern U.	Houston	1947	8,500	427	270,000
Texas Tech. U.	Lubbock	1923	22,528	1,337	1,500,000
U. of Houston	Houston	1927	29,297	1,325	1,090,700
U. of Texas at Arlington	Arlington	1895	16,744	1,075	575,000
U. of Texas at Austin	Austin	1881	41,387	3,863	4,100,000
U. of Texas at El Paso	El Paso	1913	10,550	424	350,000
West Texas State U.	Canyon	1909	6,623	365	231,900
UTAH					
Brigham Young U.	Provo	1875	26,051[4]	1,357	1,300,000
U. of Utah	Salt Lake City	1850	21,671	1,316[4]	1,500,000
Utah State U.	Logan	1888	9,113	462[4]	680,100
Weber State	Ogden	1889	8,818	367	304,200
VERMONT					
Bennington	Bennington	1925	600	75	70,000
Middlebury	Middlebury	1800	1,832	154	325,000
U. of Vermont	Burlington	1791	11,002	1,093	838,300
VIRGINIA					
Madison	Harrisonburg	1908	7,926	468	255,400
Old Dominion U.	Norfolk	1930	15,983	594	393,000
U. of Richmond	Richmond	1830	4,052	312	248,800
U. of Virginia	Charlottesville	1819	15,529	1,321	2,143,200
Virginia Commonwealth U.	Richmond	1838	17,452	2,151	384,300
Virginia Military Inst.[5]	Lexington	1839	1,342	133	249,300
Va. Polytech. Inst. & State U.[5]	Blacksburg	1872	18,477	1,473	800,000
Washington & Lee U.[5]	Lexington	1749	1,698	174	300,000
William & Mary	Williamsburg	1693	4,339	446	1,500,000
WASHINGTON					
Central Washington U.	Ellensburg	1891	6,400	343	285,000
Eastern Washington U.	Cheney	1890	6,837	349	276,300
Gonzaga U.	Spokane	1887	3,101	232	387,900
U. of Washington	Seattle	1861	36,000	3,656[4]	2,188,000
Washington State U.	Pullman	1890	16,693	977	1,300,000
Western Washington U.	Bellingham	1893	9,359	400	350,000
Whitman	Walla Walla	1859	1,055	82[4]	227,600
WEST VIRGINIA					
Bethany	Bethany	1840	993	78	133,000
Marshall U.	Huntington	1837	11,221	500	296,000
West Virginia U.	Morgantown	1867	20,964	1,695	843,600
WISCONSIN					
Beloit	Beloit	1846	1,088	103	230,000
Lawrence U.	Appleton	1847	1,188	133	200,000
Marquette U.	Milwaukee	1881	12,422	765	600,000
St. Norbert	De Pere	1898	1,500	101	116,000
U. of W.-Eau Claire	Eau Claire	1916	10,344	519	316,600
U. of W.-Green Bay	Green Bay	1965	3,641	171	280,000
U. of W.-La Crosse	La Crosse	1909	8,554	651	712,700
U. of W.-Madison	Madison	1848	37,924	2,173	3,200,000
U. of W.-Milwaukee	Milwaukee	1956	24,686	1,648	1,000,000
U. of W.-Oshkosh	Oshkosh	1871	10,000	481[4]	500,000
U. of W.-Platteville	Platteville	1866	4,620	307	176,500
U. of W.-River Falls	River Falls	1874	5,100	230	175,700
U. of W.-Stevens Point	Stevens Point	1894	8,904	500	460,000
U. of W.-Stout	Menomonie	1893	6,071	286[4]	170,000
U. of W.-Superior	Superior	1896	2,418	165	203,000
U. of W.-Whitewater	Whitewater	1868	9,388	539	284,200
WYOMING					
U. of Wyoming	Laramie	1886	8,750	858[4]	650,000

[1] Latest data available; coeducational unless otherwise indicated. [2] Total includes part-time students. [3] Total includes part-time or full-time equivalent faculty.
[4] Total includes full-time equivalent only. [5] Men's school. [6] Women's school. [7] Includes main campus and other regional campuses.

LIVING CONDITIONS

Health Personnel and Facilities

State	Physicians 1977[1]	Dentists 1977	Licensed Practical Nurses 1974	Hospital facilities 1976 Hospitals	Hospital facilities 1976 Beds	Nursing homes 1973 Facilities	Nursing homes 1973 Beds
Alabama	3,951	1,232	10,056	146	25,005	197	14,844
Alaska	366	210	624	25	1,571	8	606
Arizona	4,221	1,104	4,323	80	11,057	88	6,430
Arkansas	2,253	688	6,530	96	13,295	211	17,952
California	47,172	13,369	47,725	631	119,409	4,145	150,956
Colorado	4,871	1,568	5,876	100	14,726	214	16,670
Connecticut	7,113	2,078	7,198	67	19,535	365	23,294
Delaware	908	258	1,165	15	4,567	36	2,213
District of Columbia	3,383	633	2,655	20	10,612	72	3,147
Florida	16,001	3,946	17,130	243	53,365	360	34,956
Georgia	6,383	2,053	13,721	186	30,883	306	25,936
Hawaii	1,567	549	2,189	27	3,883	142	2,726
Idaho	874	418	2,812	52	3,668	64	4,190
Illinois	18,995	5,653	18,564	287	77,312	1,039	80,151
Indiana	6,401	2,156	8,051	139	34,862	495	34,247
Iowa	3,325	1,318	7,100	143	21,721	678	35,152
Kansas	3,221	1,049	4,170	164	18,183	468	22,889
Kentucky	4,320	1,393	6,624	125	19,432	312	18,177
Louisiana	5,266	1,499	9,416	154	24,726	212	17,004
Maine	1,488	468	2,589	54	7,294	341	9,227
Maryland	9,351	2,452	6,814	81	25,103	204	17,755
Massachusetts	14,185	3,933	19,387	190	48,329	945	53,858
Michigan	13,519	4,589	25,419	253	53,223	577	48,567
Minnesota	7,015	2,333	11,477	189	31,385	589	44,661
Mississippi	2,248	716	5,641	111	17,262	143	7,886
Missouri	7,379	2,213	10,809	171	35,139	502	33,644
Montana	915	412	1,907	65	4,397	105	4,759
Nebraska	2,135	901	3,800	108	11,403	251	17,396
Nevada	778	313	1,397	23	3,248	41	1,482
New Hampshire	1,374	438	2,211	33	5,113	130	5,873
New Jersey	13,107	4,464	20,789	144	47,645	549	34,430
New Mexico	1,586	478	2,519	54	6,629	66	3,345
New York	46,614	11,982	45,798	394	151,997	1,083	92,888
North Carolina	7,403	2,041	11,114	159	34,064	838	22,145
North Dakota	725	281	1,741	60	5,740	107	6,631
Ohio	16,201	4,906	29,956	248	70,378	1,163	65,134
Oklahoma	3,223	1,109	7,080	140	17,123	417	29,512
Oregon	4,134	1,600	4,174	87	12,085	312	18,306
Pennsylvania	20,619	5,932	35,578	318	92,565	768	65,963
Rhode Island	1,822	484	2,990	21	7,315	159	6,493
South Carolina	3,304	1,045	5,476	88	17,627	123	8,131
South Dakota	631	295	1,503	70	5,828	160	7,795
Tennessee	6,108	1,874	14,383	154	30,543	244	14,827
Texas	17,309	5,442	42,913	563	77,605	967	80,510
Utah	1,971	776	2,683	38	4,954	120	4,556
Vermont	1,031	265	1,945	21	3,568	101	3,902
Virginia	7,541	2,429	11,260	129	32,217	348	16,732
Washington	6,163	2,511	9,809	129	16,295	382	31,147
West Virginia	2,389	650	4,398	85	15,827	137	4,753
Wisconsin	6,512	2,485	9,322	172	31,146	516	51,960
Wyoming	423	187	648	30	2,656	34	1,896
TOTAL U.S.	369,791	111,178	533,459	7,082	1,433,515	21,834	1,327,704

[1] Non-federal only.   Sources: American Medical Association, *Physician Distribution and Licensure in the U.S., 1976;* American Dental Association, *Distribution of Dentists in the United States by State, Region, District, and County, 1976;* American Nurses' Association, *1974 Inventory of Licensed Practical Nurses;* American Hospital Association, *Hospital Statistics, 1977 Edition;* U.S. Department of Health, Education, and Welfare, Public Health Service.

Crime Rates per 100,000 Population

Metropolitan area	VIOLENT CRIME										PROPERTY CRIME							
	Total		Murder		Rape		Robbery		Assault		Total		Burglary		Larceny		Auto theft	
	1971	1976	1971	1976	1971	1976	1971	1976	1971	1976	1971	1976	1971	1976	1971	1976	1971	1976
Baltimore	929.3	846.6	17.3	11.0	34.2	36.3	497.3	416.9	380.6	382.4	3,248.2	5,453.5	1,414.5	1,453.7	1,193.6	3,492.2	640.2	507.6
Boston	324.9	484.0	4.8	3.8	12.8	20.1	186.4	246.3	120.9	213.7	3,250.7	5,617.8	1,252.9	1,562.0	877.9	2,407.1	1,119.2	**1,648.7**
Chicago	650.1	581.1	13.1	13.4	27.4	24.1	373.6	299.4	236.0	244.2	2,241.3	5,174.9	921.6	1,151.7	669.2	3,331.9	650.5	691.3
Cleveland	493.7	584.6	14.8	15.1	24.8	33.4	319.5	336.2	134.6	199.9	2,716.7	4,576.3	903.6	1,154.2	579.4	2,505.9	**1,233.8**	916.2
Detroit	888.0	960.4	16.3	**18.1**	31.7	44.0	605.3	593.8	234.7	304.6	4,383.2	6,711.9	2,062.2	1,906.4	1,495.7	3,765.5	825.4	1,040.1
Houston	510.6	426.2	**18.1**	16.5	31.9	36.4	264.0	255.1	196.6	118.2	3,008.4	5,482.6	1,555.0	1,703.1	768.7	3,146.6	684.7	632.9
Los Angeles	794.8	951.8	10.7	13.8	**51.3**	**57.9**	348.5	400.9	**384.3**	**479.2**	4,648.8	6,264.6	2,209.0	2,271.3	1,427.2	3,113.3	1,012.6	880.0
Minneapolis	283.8	301.1	3.5	2.9	20.5	27.6	152.3	139.3	107.5	131.3	3,159.2	5,364.5	1,293.9	1,479.2	1,267.3	3,382.9	598.0	502.4
Newark	655.0	568.2	10.4	7.7	23.3	27.7	414.2	306.1	207.1	226.8	3,183.2	5,042.0	1,529.6	1,571.0	972.4	2,856.2	681.3	614.7
New York	**1,134.0**	**1,437.2**	13.6	15.7	22.3	37.2	**790.4**	**915.0**	307.6	467.5	4,173.0	6,415.4	1,820.5	2,263.1	1,400.4	3,057.3	952.1	1,095.0
Philadelphia	418.7	446.2	10.9	10.0	17.7	25.6	241.1	226.6	149.0	183.9	2,130.6	3,781.1	958.9	1,132.3	556.3	2,131.8	615.4	517.1
Pittsburgh	288.5	331.6	4.1	4.8	17.7	21.1	148.4	158.9	118.3	146.7	1,794.1	3,190.2	814.4	896.5	537.8	1,820.8	441.9	473.0
St. Louis	513.6	647.4	12.7	13.1	31.2	38.1	266.1	321.5	203.5	274.6	3,009.4	5,813.5	1,494.7	1,772.4	748.8	3,432.7	765.9	608.4
San Francisco	688.1	802.3	9.4	12.2	39.7	50.4	403.4	420.5	235.6	319.3	**4,826.1**	**7,691.5**	**2,247.6**	**2,458.4**	**1,642.5**	**4,487.1**	936.0	745.9
Washington, D.C.	795.9	620.9	12.3	10.1	36.5	38.3	510.1	367.8	237.1	204.8	3,178.0	5,067.5	1,335.0	1,324.4	1,144.9	3,340.9	698.1	402.2

Boldface: highest rate among listed metropolitan areas.   Source: U.S. Department of Justice, Federal Bureau of Investigation, *Uniform Crime Reports*.

TRANSPORTATION AND TRADE

Transportation

State	Road and street mi [1] 1977	Motor vehicles in 000s, 1976 [2]			Railroad mileage 1976 [3]	Airports 1977	Pipeline mileage 1977 [4]
		Total	Automobiles	Trucks and buses			
Ala.	86,676	2,590	1,962	628	4,534	131	1,660
Alaska	9,930	255	159	96	20	762	193
Ariz.	55,746	1,491	1,080	411	2,036	202	1,355
Ark.	77,451	1,327	887	440	3,522	166	3,071
Calif.	172,841	14,102	11,311	2,791	7,291	804	10,352
Colo.	86,106	1,994	1,490	504	3,384	255	2,396
Conn.	19,044	2,009	1,851	158	634	104	94
Del.	5,244	360	295	65	291	32	3
D.C.	1,101	265	245	20	30	16	[5]
Fla.	98,094	5,603	4,653	950	4,104	391	288
Ga.	102,826	3,263	2,535	728	5,417	262	2,024
Hawaii	3,794	483	410	73	—	51	—
Idaho	57,788	681	428	253	2,631	187	633
Ill.	133,559 [3]	6,542	5,481	1,061	10,555	867	10,914
Ind.	91,662	3,382	2,597	785	6,357	293	4,552
Iowa	112,460	2,157	1,573	584	7,539	250	4,581
Kan.	134,621	1,848	1,257	591	7,524	334	17,152
Ky.	69,706	2,350	1,740	610	3,517	90	2,444
La.	54,814	2,277	1,731	546	3,710	280	9,460
Maine	21,670	680	524	156	1,660	162	353
Md.	26,113	2,508	2,145	363	1,062	135	219
Mass.	32,867	3,192	2,844	348	1,404	141	242
Mich.	118,998	5,723	4,749	974	5,914	421	4,861
Minn.	128,456	2,576	1,977	599	7,294	312	2,841
Miss.	67,708	1,424	1,022	402	3,432	148	3,246
Mo.	117,223	2,924	2,220	704	6,010	358	7,142
Mont.	77,902	620	378	242	4,862	172	3,232
Neb.	96,894	1,218	848	370	5,360	301	3,317
Nev.	50,068	476	355	121	1,573	118	275
N.H.	15,333	504	418	86	751	57	190
N.J.	33,126	4,312	3,882	430	1,679	239	494
N.M.	70,858	863	579	284	2,057	139	6,960
N.Y.	109,419	7,758	6,867	891	5,266	496	1,586
N.C.	91,187	3,837	2,959	878	4,116	251	896
N.D.	106,430	569	338	231	5,060	209	1,773
Ohio	110,620 [6]	7,469	6,546	923	7,677	558	6,524
Okla.	109,606	2,181	1,456	725	4,897	285	20,710
Ore.	108,278	1,678	1,363	315	3,043	286	414
Pa.	116,880	7,979	6,852	1,127	7,888	644	8,097
R.I.	5,537	576	508	68	139	22	17
S.C.	61,294	1,877	1,479	398	3,033	123	668
S.D.	82,426	549	345	204	3,352	131	642
Tenn.	81,567	2,858	2,174	684	3,181	132	739
Texas	257,649	8,674	6,357	2,317	13,273	1,217	65,966
Utah	48,501	881	605	276	1,726	90	1,118
Vt.	13,909 [3]	294	239	55	767	61	177
Va.	63,430	3,398	2,830	568	3,849	240	824
Wash.	84,326	2,666	1,964	702	4,723	334	783
W.Va.	37,244	1,003	759	244	3,460	58	3,511
Wis.	105,520	2,683	2,197	486	5,733	321	926
Wyo.	32,854	358	211	147	1,778	90	7,151
TOTAL	3,857,356	137,287	109,675	27,612	199,115	13,728	227,066

[1] Includes federally controlled roads.   [2] Estimated registration, excluding military. Detail may not add to totals because of rounding.   [3] Preliminary.
[4] Petroleum and products only.   [5] Included with Maryland.   [6] 1976.   Sources: ICC; Dept. of Transportation, FAA, FHWA; Dept. of Energy; Motor Vehicles Manufacturers Assn.

Major Trading Partners, by Value   in millions of dollars

Country	EXPORTS		IMPORTS	
	1971	1976	1971	1976
North America	13,557	32,463	15,719	35,590
Canada	10,365 [1]	24,109	12,692	26,238
Mexico	1,620	4,990	1,262	3,598
South America	3,313	8,601	3,011	7,761
Argentina	391	544	176	308
Brazil	966	2,809	762	1,737
Chile	244	508	91	222
Colombia	378	703	239	655
Peru	258	573	274	379
Venezuela	787	2,628	1,216	3,574
Europe	14,562	35,903	12,881	23,640
Belgium and Luxembourg	1,077	2,991	844	1,119
France	1,373	3,449	1,088	2,509
Germany, West	2,831	5,730	3,650	5,591
Italy	1,314	3,068	1,406	2,530
Netherlands, The	1,786	4,645	534	1,080
Spain	627	2,021	458	914
Sweden	470	1,036	454	918
Switzerland	627	1,173	493	1,025
United Kingdom	2,369	4,799	2,499	4,254
U.S.S.R.	162	2,308	57	220
Asia	9,918	30,541	11,799	39,459
Hong Kong	424	1,115	991	2,413
India	650	1,135	329	708
Indonesia	263	1,036	207	3,004
Iran	482	2,776	136	1,480
Israel	707	1,409	173	423
Japan	4,055	10,144	7,259	15,504
Korea, South	681	2,015	462	2,404
Malaysia	72	536	269	940
Philippines	340	819	496	883
Saudi Arabia	164	2,774	99	5,213
Singapore	315	965	136	695
Taiwan	510	1,635	817	2,989
Oceania	1,168	2,690	895	1,671
Australia	1,004	2,185	619	1,211
Africa	1,631	4,396	1,217	12,547
Algeria	82	487	20	2,209
Nigeria	168	770	130	4,938
South Africa [2]	622	1,360	287	930
Total	44,130 [1]	114,997 [1]	45,563 [1]	120,677 [1]

[1] Includes shipments to or from unidentified countries.   [2] Includes South West Africa.
Source: U.S. Department of Commerce, Domestic and International Business Administration, *Overseas Business Reports*.

Major Commodities Traded, 1976   in millions of dollars

Item	Total [1]	Canada	American Republics	Western Europe	Far East [2]
TOTAL EXPORTS	114,997	24,109 [3]	15,492	32,401	20,358
Agricultural commodities					
Grains and preparations	10,911	143	916	2,997	3,214
Soybeans	3,315	87	76	1,901	882
Cotton, including linters, wastes	1,067	51	6	111	869
Nonagricultural commodities					
Ores and scrap metals	1,284	171	81	636	382
Coal, coke, and briquettes	2,988	760	192	941	1,058
Chemicals	9,958	1,433	2,165	3,528	1,704
Machinery	32,029	6,792	5,460	8,460	4,512
Agricultural machines, tractors, parts	2,930	1,085	525	510	121
Electrical apparatus	9,278	1,555	1,615	2,496	1,968
Transport equipment [4]	16,209	6,745	1,985	2,266	1,197
Civilian aircraft and parts	5,144	166	496	1,496	858
Paper manufactures	1,624	445	342	434	131
Metal manufactures	2,089	666	313	365	186
Iron and steel mill products [5]	1,833	571	427	296	179
Yarn, fabrics, and clothing	1,805	357	379	651	116
Other exports	29,885	5,888	3,150	9,815	5,928
TOTAL IMPORTS	120,677	26,238	13,227	22,784	30,152
Agricultural commodities					
Meat and preparations	1,447	82	327	295	9
Fish	1,855	376	473	339	416
Coffee	2,632	—	1,784	6	136
Sugar	1,154	10	604	5	322
Nonagricultural commodities					
Ores and scrap metal	2,251	991	477	73	50
Petroleum, crude	26,384	2,275	2,197	371	2,568
Petroleum products	5,411	278	1,887	350	240
Chemicals	4,772	1,287	183	2,205	462
Machinery	15,446	2,647	1,111	4,803	6,729
Transport equipment	14,378	6,574	146	3,284	4,327
Automobiles, new	8,928	3,477	[6]	2,548	2,904
Iron and steel mill products	3,809	406	72	1,057	2,232
Nonferrous metals	2,941	1,090	297	679	446
Textiles other than clothing	1,635	32	144	464	884
Other imports	36,562	10,190	3,525	8,853	11,331

[1] Includes areas not shown separately.   [2] Includes Japan, East and South Asia.
[3] Excludes grains and oilseeds transshipped through Canada to unidentified overseas countries.   [4] Excludes parts for tractors.   [5] Excludes pig iron.
[6] Less than $500,000.   Source: U.S. Dept. of Commerce, Domestic and International Business Administration, *Overseas Business Reports*.

Upper Volta

A republic of West Africa, Upper Volta is bordered by Mali, Niger, Benin, Togo, Ghana, and Ivory Coast. Area: 274,200 sq km (105,869 sq mi). Pop. (1975 census): 6,144,000. Cap. and largest city: Ouagadougou (pop., 1975 est., 168,600). Language: French (official). Religion: animist; Muslim and Christian minorities. President and premier in 1977, Gen. Sangoulé Lamizana.

The ban on political parties imposed in May 1974 was lifted in October 1977 and was followed by a constitutional referendum in November; parliamentary and presidential elections were scheduled to take place six months later. On January 14 a ministerial reshuffle suggested the beginnings of change in the military regime. Although all 5 military members of the Cabinet retained their portfolios, 11 new members were introduced who had connections with three of the principal political parties. Nominally illegal, the parties could now play a part in the direction of Upper Volta's affairs.

In spite of this—still very slow—progress toward normalization of political life, Gen. Sangoulé Lamizana appeared to be an isolated figure, while the popularity of former president Maurice Yaméogo, ousted in January 1966, was reviving. New economic difficulties faced the government as a result of floods in August, as well as a drought that necessitated a request in October for immediate aid of 56,000 metric tons of cereals.

(PHILIPPE DECRAENE)

UPPER VOLTA

Education. (1974–75) Primary, pupils 133,660, teachers 2,834; secondary (1973–74), pupils 11,953, teachers 445; vocational, pupils 2,699, teachers 179; teacher training (1973–74), students 362, teachers c. 30; higher, students 756, teaching staff 102.

Finance. Monetary unit: CFA franc, with (Sept. 19, 1977) a par value of CFA Fr 50 to the French franc (free rate of CFA Fr 246.50 = U.S. $1; CFA Fr 429.50 = £1 sterling). Budget (1976 est.) balanced at CFA Fr 21,122,000,000.

Foreign Trade. (1975) Imports CFA Fr 32,390,000,000; exports CFA Fr 9,370,000,000. Import sources (1974): France 40%; Ivory Coast 14%; West Germany 12%; U.S. 9%; Belgium-Luxembourg 5%. Export destinations (1974): France 36%; Ivory Coast 34%; Ghana 7%. Main exports: livestock 36%; hides and skins 18%; cotton 16%; peanuts 15%; karité nuts 7%; sesame seed 6%.

Uruguay

A republic of South America, Uruguay is on the Atlantic Ocean and is bounded by Brazil and Argentina. Area: 176,215 sq km (68,037 sq mi). Pop. (1975 census): 2,764,000, including (1961) white 89%; mestizo 10%. Cap. and largest city: Montevideo (pop., 1975 census, 1,229,700). Language: Spanish. Religion: mainly Roman Catholic. President in 1977, Aparicio Méndez.

Faced by diplomatic pressures from abroad and increasingly open dissidence from labour unions and professional organizations, Pres. Aparicio Méndez formally announced on Aug. 10, 1977, that the military-dominated National Council

---

URUGUAY

Education. (1975) Primary, pupils 355,328, teachers 13,-935; secondary, pupils 143,852, teachers (1969) 9,668; vocational, pupils 38,343, teachers (1973) 3,953; teacher training, students 3,997, teachers (1973) 341; higher, students 33,664, teaching staff 2,545.

Finance. Monetary unit: new peso, with (Sept. 19, 1977) a free commercial rate of 4.97 new pesos to U.S. $1 (8.65 new pesos = £1 sterling). Gold, SDR's, and foreign exchange (May 1977) U.S. $382 million. Budget (1975 actual): revenue 995.2 million new pesos; expenditure 1,333,600,-000 new pesos. Gross domestic product (1975) 8,112,200,-000 new pesos. Cost of living: (Montevideo; 1970 = 100; May 1977) 2,074.

Foreign Trade. (1976) Imports U.S. $598.9 million; exports U.S. $536 million. Import sources (1975): Kuwait 16%; Brazil 13%; U.S. 10%; Argentina 9%; West Germany 8%; U.K. 5%. Export destinations (1975): Brazil 17%; West Germany 11%; Argentina 7%; The Netherlands 7%; U.S. 6%; Italy 5%. Main exports (1975): wool 23%; meat 19%.

Transport and Communications. Roads (1973) 49,634 km. Motor vehicles in use (1974): passenger c. 151,600; commercial (including buses) c. 85,700. Railways: (1976) 2,975 km; traffic (1975) 358 million passenger-km, freight 281 million net ton-km. Air traffic (1976): 83 million passenger-km; freight 170,000 net ton-km. Shipping (1976): merchant vessels 100 gross tons and over 43; gross tonnage 151,255. Telephones (Jan. 1976) 250,000. Radio receivers (Dec. 1974) 1.5 million. Television receivers (Dec. 1974) 350,000.

Agriculture. Production (in 000; metric tons; 1976): wheat 505; corn c. 210; rice 215; potatoes (1975) 121; sweet potatoes (1975) c. 79; sorghum c. 118; sugar, raw value (1975) 115; linseed 62; sunflower seed c. 90; apples c. 36; peaches (1975) c. 40; oranges c. 41; wine c. 101; wool 34; beef and veal c. 375. Livestock (in 000; May 1976): sheep c. 16,000; pigs c. 450; cattle c. 11,500; horses (1975) c. 410; chickens (1975) c. 7,300.

Industry. Production (in 000; metric tons; 1975): crude steel 16; cement 632; petroleum products 1,786; electricity (kw-hr) c. 2,596,000.

Upper Volta

Uruguay

---

would transfer power to an elected civilian government by 1981. The press showed more independence despite censorship controls, and there was criticism of the almost 40% reduction in real incomes as well as of a law that subordinated the traditionally independent judiciary to the executive branch. Reports that a number of army officers were court-martialed for political reasons and navy officers forced into retirement indicated dissidence within the usually tightly knit military circles. In February U.S. Secretary of State Cyrus Vance named Uruguay as one of the countries that would receive reduced foreign aid because of human rights violations. Uruguay promptly declared it would refuse all U.S. aid, but relations with the U.S. improved following announcement of the coming return to civilian rule.

Unshaken from its basic economic strategy of liberalizing business, the regime continued successfully to seek bilateral trading arrangements with Brazil and Argentina (including the joint construction of major hydroelectric dams). The goal was to reduce protective import barriers and divert resources to long-term infrastructural projects while maintaining intact the large farming estates and the existing land tenure system. As a result consumption remained low and investment rose, though less than had been predicted. Manufacturing showed mixed results, while agriculture failed to sustain the increase registered in 1976. Overall economic growth in 1977 was expected to be just under the 2.7% increase (in real terms) of 1976.

(PAUL DOWBOR)

Universities:
see Education

Urban Mass Transit:
see Transportation

U.S.S.R.:
see Union of Soviet Socialist Republics

Vatican City

Venezuela

A 30-ton bronze sculpture by Pericle Fazzini depicting the resurrection of Christ as if after atomic destruction on Earth was unveiled on September 28 at Vatican City by Pope Paul VI (in white robe).

Vatican City State

This independent sovereignty is surrounded by but is not part of Rome. As a state with territorial limits, it is properly distinguished from the Holy See, which constitutes the worldwide administrative and legislative body for the Roman Catholic Church. The area of Vatican City is 44 ha (108.8 ac). Pop. (1976 est.): 700. As sovereign pontiff, Paul VI is the chief of state. Vatican City is administered by a pontifical commission of five cardinals, of which the secretary of state, Jean Cardinal Villot, is president.

In June 1977 Pope Paul named Giovanni Benelli a cardinal and appointed him archbishop of Florence and future president of the Italian episcopal conference. Msgr Giuseppe Caprio was named to replace him as head of the Secretariat of State. Other new cardinals were Joseph Ratzinger, new archbishop of Munich (West Germany); Bernardin Gantin, former archbishop of Cotonou (Benin) and pro-president of the Pontifical Commission "Justice and Peace"; Luigi Ciappi, the pope's theologian; and Frantisek Tomasek, apostolic administrator of Prague (Czechoslovakia). Luigi Cardinal Traglia, doyen of the College of Cardinals, died in November (*see* OBITUARIES).

Among the pope's visitors were the king and queen of Spain, Spanish Premier Adolfo Suárez, Communist leaders Janos Kadar of Hungary and Edward Gierek of Poland, and West German Chancellor Helmut Schmidt, who later in October thanked Paul VI warmly for his offer to take the place of the hostages in a Lufthansa airliner hijacked to Mogadishu, Somalia.

(MAX BERGERRE)

See also Religion.

Venezuela

A republic of northern South America, Venezuela is bounded by Colombia, Brazil, Guyana, and the Caribbean Sea. Area: 899,180 sq km (347,175 sq mi). Pop. (1977 est.): 12,736,700, including mestizo 69%; white 20%; Negro 9%; Indian 2%. Cap. and largest city: Caracas (metro. area pop., 1977 est., 2,664,000). Language: Spanish. Religion: predominantly Roman Catholic. President in 1977, Carlos Andrés Pérez.

The major political parties became increasingly preoccupied in 1977 with preparations for the April 1978 presidential election, and seven candidacies were announced. Among these, the governing Acción Democrática Party nominated its secretary-general, Luis Piñerúa Ordaz; Luis Herrera Campins was nominated by the Social Christian Party (COPEI), the main opposition group; and television personality Renny Ottolina announced his intention to stand as an independent on an anti-establishment-party platform.

In January 1977 Pres. Carlos Andrés Pérez reshuffled the Cabinet and created seven new ministries. The transport section was removed from the Ministry of Public Works and merged with the Ministry of Communications. On July 15 the Cabinet was changed again and new appointments were made in the ministries of Foreign Affairs, Finance, Agriculture, and Defense.

Production of petroleum was held down to prevent depletion of stocks. The official target was 2.2 million bbl a day, but during the year output was increased slightly to an average of 2,270,000 bbl in order to meet demand. In the first half of 1977 the state oil company, Petróleos de Venezuela (Petrovén), recorded net profits of 3,980,000,000 bolivares, compared with 3,570,000,000 bolivares in all of 1976, largely as a result of higher prices. Petrovén announced that it was to assume overall responsibility for exploration and production in the Orinoco belt, where reserves were estimated at 700,000,000,000 bbl. Some experimental schemes were started for extraction of the heavy oil there, but no commercial production was yet possible. Petrovén's budget for 1977 was a record U.S. $2,330,000,000, 30% of which was allocated for capital investment. The president of Petrovén announced that over the next few years $1.6 billion would be invested annually to keep the industry efficient and competitive.

The cost of living rose by 8.1% in the first half of the year, and in July President Pérez introduced an anti-inflation package designed to reduce liquidity and curb property speculation. Banks' reserve requirements were raised, more prices were frozen, house selling prices and profits were regulated, and the use of credit cards was restricted. The private sector was strongly opposed to these measures, and in October some modifications were passed to ease banks' liquidity and credit flows.

After a poor agricultural year in 1976, the government was forced to import basic foodstuffs on a large scale. At the end of September international reserves stood at $8,037,000,000, compared with $8,570,000,000 at the end of 1976. The decline was attributed to the high level of imports, government debt repayment, and capital flight following the anti-inflation package in July.

Venezuela continued to suffer from a lack of skilled manpower needed to implement the fifth

VENEZUELA

Education. (1974–75) Primary, pupils 1,990,123, teachers 63,198; secondary, pupils 583,163; vocational, pupils 34,240; teacher training, students 13,807; secondary, vocational, and teacher training, teachers 35,671; higher (1975–76), students 213,542, teaching staff 15,792.

Finance. Monetary unit: bolívar, with (Sept. 19, 1977) a par value of 4.29 bolivares to U.S. \$1 (free rate of 7.48 bolivares = £1 sterling). Gold, SDR's, and foreign exchange (June 1977) U.S. \$7,919,000,000. Budget (1976 est.): revenue 41,927,000,000 bolivares; expenditure 43,888,000,000 bolivares. Gross national product (1975) 112,070,000,000 bolivares. Money supply (April 1977) 30,-005,000,000 bolivares. Cost of living (Caracas; 1970 = 100; May 1977) 151.

Foreign Trade. (1976) Imports (fob) c. 26,040,000,000 bolivares; exports 37,204,000,000 bolivares. Import sources (1975): U.S. 48%; West Germany 8%; Japan 8%; Italy 6%. Export destinations (1975): U.S. 33%; Netherlands Antilles 20%; Canada 13%. Main exports: crude oil 65%; petroleum products 29%.

Transport and Communications. Roads (1974) 65,718 km. Motor vehicles in use (1973): passenger 820,000; commercial 295,000. Railways: (1975) 175 km (construction began in 1976 on a 3,697-km network planned for completion in 1990); traffic (1971) 42 million passenger-km, freight 15 million net ton-km. Air traffic (1976): 2,535,000,-000 passenger-km; freight 76,832,000 net ton-km. Shipping (1976): merchant vessels 100 gross tons and over 165; gross tonnage 543,446. Telephones (Jan. 1976) 650,000. Radio receivers (Dec. 1974) 1,709,000. Television receivers (Dec. 1974) 1.2 million.

Agriculture. Production (in 000; metric tons; 1976): corn c. 532; rice 277; sorghum c. 238; potatoes (1975) c. 152; cassava (1975) 339; sugar, raw value c. 489; sesame seed c. 50; bananas 890; oranges c. 250; coffee c. 50; cocoa c. 18; tobacco c. 15; cotton, lint c. 28; beef and veal c. 250. Livestock (in 000; 1976): cattle 9,404; pigs 1,880; sheep c. 105; goats c. 1,427; horses (1975) 454; asses (1975) c. 531; poultry 29,410.

Industry. Production (in 000; metric tons; 1976): crude oil 119,756; natural gas (cu m; 1975) c. 10,900,000; petroleum products (1975) c. 43,575; iron ore (metal content) 15,425; cement (1975) 3,455; gold (troy oz; 1975) 18; diamonds (metric carats; 1974) 819; electricity (kw-hr; 1975) c. 21,179,000.

development plan (1976–80). This, together with rising absenteeism, contributed to delays in major projects. Contracts awarded during 1977 included the construction of the 675-km Ciudad Guayana–San Juan de los Morros railway, to be carried out by a Canadian-Spanish-Venezuelan consortium, and the final stage of the 12,000-Mw Guri hydroelectric complex in Guayana by a Brazilian-Venezuelan consortium. Bauxite deposits estimated at 500 million tons of ore discovered in Bolívar State could enable Venezuelan aluminum plants to be supplied entirely with local bauxite.

In April President Pérez visited seven countries in the Middle East and discussed oil prices with fellow members of the Organization of Petroleum Exporting Countries (OPEC). The price-setting ministerial meeting of OPEC was held in Caracas on December 20. The president also visited the U.S. in June where he had talks with Pres. Jimmy Carter. In November he traveled to Brazil where he met with Pres. Ernesto Geisel. (SARAH CAMERON)

Veterinary Science

During 1977 the number of colleges of veterinary medicine in the United States that offered the doctor of veterinary medicine degree totaled 22. Student enrollment for the 1976–77 academic year was 6,571, an increase of 297 over the previous year. Women students made up 32.21% of the first-year class and 28.25% of the total enrollment. Because of limited capacity in U.S. colleges, some U.S. citizens sought admission to foreign colleges. However, additional colleges of veterinary medicine in the U.S. were in the planning stage.

A comprehensive animal disease research program was authorized by the U.S. Congress in October. Federal funds were to be allocated to veterinary colleges and state agricultural experiment stations to conduct research on specific problems. The legislation also authorized funds to cover construction and start-up costs for new colleges of veterinary medicine.

Pseudorabies (Aujeszky's disease), a disease of swine, was on the increase in U.S. swine herds during the year. At the year's end there had been no confirmed cases of pseudorabies in man, but the disease can be transmitted to other mammals and birds. A modified live-virus vaccine prevented some losses but did not confer immunity. Further research to develop a more effective vaccine was in progress.

Contagious equine metritis (CEM), a newly discovered venereal disease of horses, was found during the year in France, the U.K., Ireland, and Australia. The U.S. Department of Agriculture banned the import of equine breeding stock from the affected countries. The disease produced serious economic losses in Thoroughbred breeding establishments. It is believed to have first appeared in France in 1975, and the causative agent seemed to be a microaerophilic gram-negative coccobacillus. Research on CEM was under way in the U.S., U.K., and Ireland.

Screwworm infestation of animals in the southwestern U.S. and in Mexico was markedly reduced as a result of the production and release of sterile screwworm flies produced at Mission, Texas, and in the new facilities at Tehuantepec, Mexico. During the first nine months of 1977 Texas had 35 cases, against 20,300 in the same period of 1976. For the first nine months of 1977 in all of the U.S. there were 192 cases, against 20,557 in the same period of 1976.

Psoroptic cattle scabies, a highly contagious parasitic skin disease of cattle, had increased considerably in the U.S. after 1971. It was found principally in Texas, Oklahoma, Colorado, Kansas, Nebraska, California, and New Mexico. Affected herds lose weight, and young stock fail to gain weight normally. Death rates increase in animals as a result of low vitality and inability to withstand inclement weather. Infected herds are treated twice with a permitted pesticide, and exposed herds are also treated.

Hog cholera (swine fever), which threatened to destroy the swine industry in the U.S. at the end of the 19th century, was eliminated, with the last case confirmed in a herd near Cape May, N.J., on Aug. 1, 1976. Because more than a year had elapsed since the last confirmed case, exports of pork were resumed to Great Britain and other countries that had banned such imports to protect the health of their swine herds. (CLARENCE H. PALS)

[353.C]

A VASECTOMY FOR ROVER

by Roger Caras

An insidious form of pollution that has grown up around man's careless use of his resources has been the pet population explosion. In many parts of the United States today there is a considerable overabundance of man's prime companion animals, dogs and cats. These animals are indiscriminate breeders, reproducing without letup as long as they are sexually intact and allowed to make contact, and there are few communities in the U.S. that are not troubled to some degree with the results of this fact. Although no census has been or ever can be taken, some shocking statistics have been revealed.

The city of Los Angeles spends $1,250,000 each year collecting and killing stray dogs and cats. There are between 40,000 and 60,000 dogs running loose in New York City, causing dog bites to be a major health problem, littering the streets, spreading disease to properly controlled pet animals, and facilitating the spread of vermin by ripping open garbage bags and tipping over garbage pails. Contrary to popular belief, cats and dogs do not control the rat and mouse populations but instead cause them to increase by making food available to rodents that might not otherwise be able to thrive.

There may be as many as 500,000 free-running dogs in the state of Georgia. They inflict enormous losses on dairy and beef cattle farms by inciting cattle to run. In beef animals that causes loss of weight and aborted calves, and in dairy cattle it reduces milk production. Free-running dogs that do not have access to livestock turn to wildlife. In some areas of the country more deer are killed by dogs than by any other cause. Ground-nesting birds and small mammals are bedeviled by cats and dogs.

If estimating the number of dogs involved is difficult, trying to determine the number of cats is wholly impossible. Dogs congregate in packs, and their devastation is often witnessed. Cats are silent, usually nocturnal around man, and solitary. Some observers suggest that there may be six cats on the loose for every dog.

The growing interest in second or country homes

for use during part of the year has added to the problem. City dwellers who are not interested in maintaining pets in the city often adopt puppies and kittens from pounds and shelters on their way out to the "summer place." At the end of the summer, though, many of these part-time country people simply drive off and abandon their pets. Thus, many resort communities are the worst victims of the pet population explosion.

Sterilization. Despite ongoing efforts and a good many hopeful but apparently premature announcements, there is still no chemical method of sterilizing cats and dogs, males as well as females, that has the acceptance of veterinarians. Castrating males and spaying females remain, for both cats and dogs, the only universally accepted alternatives to accidental breedings and further population problems. Unfortunately, many pet owners cannot afford the expense, and as a result kittens and puppies continue to proliferate at an alarming rate.

Los Angeles recently instituted a spay and neuter program that places these procedures within the means of any responsible pet owner. In many communities small spay and neuter operations have been established by private humane societies and shelters. These devices and systems help, but none of them has so far been able to make a real dent in what is almost certainly an annually expanding population. Many health officials consider the problem a major health issue.

Human Indifference. At the base of the problem is human indifference. In today's throwaway society many people have come to treat animals almost as they do plastic gewgaws. Pets are kept as long as it is convenient to do so and then are cast away. The desensitizing effect on a child of taking a beloved pet out to a stretch of country road and pushing it out the door cannot be overstressed. To dispose of a pet in this way is an offense in most areas, but it is almost impossible to catch offenders and prove cases against them, and even when all of that time-consuming and costly work has been done any real punishment is unlikely. Judges seldom do more than levy minimum fines and issue a mild rebuke.

There is one final consideration. The health problems and other nuisances created by free-running dogs and cats must ultimately affect the rights of people to own pets at all. Restrictions seem likely to arise. They will be felt by the people who have no moral compunction about animals but no more so by them than by people who spay and alter their pets, obey their community's leash laws, and would no more abandon an animal than they would a human member of their family. As is often the case in environmental problem areas, the good will suffer along with the bad.

Roger Caras is ABC-TV News Correspondent on Animals and CBS-Radio Pets and Wildlife Commentator.

Vietnam

The Socialist Republic of Vietnam is a southeast Asian state bordered in the north by China, in the west by Laos and Cambodia, and in the south and east by the South China Sea. Area: 338,392 sq km (130,654 sq mi). Pop. (1975 est.): 47,840,000. Capital: Hanoi (pop., 1976 est., 1,443,500). Largest city: Ho Chi Minh City (formerly Saigon; pop., 1976 est., 3,460,500). Languages: Vietnamese, French, English. Religion: Buddhist, animist, Confucian, Christian (Roman Catholic), Hoa Hao and Cao Dai religious sects. Secretary of the Communist Party in 1977, Le Duan; president, Ton Duc Thang; premier, Pham Van Dong.

Consolidation was Vietnam's top priority in 1977. The groundwork for the year's activities was laid in December 1976 with the convening of the first congress in 16 years of the ruling Lao Dong Party, now renamed the Communist Party. It confirmed the existing leadership and expanded the Politburo from 11 to 17 members, in part to accommodate leaders from former South Vietnam. Party chief Le Duan's report to the congress spoke of the need to cleanse the ranks of "degenerate and corrupt elements." National Assembly Chairman Truong Chinh explained the rationale of a new constitution for the country now that reunification had been achieved. Premier Pham Van Dong unveiled a 30 billion dong five-year plan (1976–80) aimed at raising living standards "without living above one's means."

As if to drum up support for the action program, Pham Van Dong visited Europe and the Soviet Union in June. Dong's Soviet visit was not announced until he had had a meeting with Soviet leader Leonid Brezhnev, at which they were said

Foreign minister Nguyen Duy Trinh of Vietnam took his seat in the General Assembly of the United Nations when his country was admitted to the UN on September 20.

Vietnam

VIETNAM

Education. (1975–76) Primary, secondary, and vocational, pupils *c.* 10 million, teachers *c.* 275,000; higher, students *c.* 160,00, teaching staff *c.* 10,000.

Finance. Monetary unit: dong, with (Sept. 19, 1977) a free rate of 1.85 dong to U.S. \$1 (3.22 dong = £1 sterling). Budget (1977 est.) balanced at 8,950,000,000 dong.

Foreign Trade. (1975) Imports *c.* U.S. \$1.1 billion; exports U.S. \$450 million. Import sources: China *c.* 23%; U.S.S.R. *c.* 20%; U.S. *c.* 19%; Singapore *c.* 7%; Japan *c.* 7%. Export destinations: U.S.S.R. *c.* 15%; China *c.* 11%; East Germany *c.* 10%; Japan *c.* 9%. Main exports (1974): clothing *c.* 10%; fish *c.* 10%; rubber *c.* 10%; coal *c.* 5%; beverages *c.* 5%.

Transport and Communications. Roads (1976) 172,945 km. Motor vehicles in use (South only; 1974): passenger *c.* 70,000; commercial (including buses) *c.* 100,000. Railways: (1976) 2,047 km; traffic (South only; 1973) 170 million passenger-km, freight 1.3 million net ton-km. Air traffic (South only; 1975): 120 million passenger-km; freight 1 million net ton-km. Navigable waterways (1976) *c.* 5,500 km. Telephones (South only; Dec. 1973) 47,000. Radio receivers (Dec. 1974) 2,550,000. Television receivers (Dec. 1974) 500,000.

Agriculture. Production (in 000; metric tons; 1976): rice *c.* 12,000; sweet potatoes (1975) *c.* 1,220; cassava *c.* 1,200; bananas *c.* 480; tea *c.* 8; coffee *c.* 8; jute *c.* 22; rubber *c.* 22; pork *c.* 410; timber (cu m; 1975) *c.* 18,400; fish catch (1975) *c.* 1,013. Livestock (in 000; 1975): cattle *c.* 1,760; buffalo *c.* 2,300; pigs *c.* 12,500; chickens (1976) *c.* 56,000; ducks *c.* 42,500.

Industry. Production (in 000; metric tons; 1975): coal *c.* 4,250; cement 685; salt 350; electricity (kw-hr) *c.* 2,300,000.

to have discussed "the problems of cooperation." Much more publicity attended the trip to China, also in June, of Vice-Premier and Defense Minister Vo Nguyen Giap at the head of an 18-man military delegation. Observers were intrigued because the visit was preceded by a program of exercises by the Vietnamese Navy. A dispute was known to exist between the two countries over the Paracel and Spratly islands in the South China Sea. In March, China had vowed to "recover" the Spratly Islands, six of which had been occupied by North Vietnamese troops shortly before the fall of the Saigon regime in 1975. Experts debated whether Giap's visit to Peking was intended to settle the dispute or to sound out the Chinese on military assistance. Le Duan paid a brief visit to Peking in November, during which the Chinese Communist Party newspaper published an editorial indirectly warning Vietnam against close Soviet ties.

That postwar Vietnam was not lowering its military guard was clear even without the hint of a military problem with China. There was no evidence of unit demobilization; veterans leaving the Army were replaced by a continuing flow of fresh recruits. An undisclosed number of former South Vietnamese officers and men with technical skills were also absorbed after careful "reeducation." The most senior active general, Van Tien Dung, defined the policy when he called for a stronger and more modern army to build an "all-people, comprehensive, and modern national defense [to protect Vietnam's] sovereignty and territorial integrity, including territorial water from the borders of the mainland to the offshore islands."

The Army had been strengthened by the acquisition of equipment abandoned by U.S. forces in the South. This included 73 F-5 fighters, 150 bombers, more than 700 other aircraft, 940 naval craft,

A portrait of Ho Chi Minh hangs above a patriotic sign near Ho Chi Minh City (formerly Saigon). Barracks at the left house youth brigades working on new canals.

550 tanks, 42,000 trucks, 130,000 tons of ammunition, and huge quantities of miscellaneous ordnance. The number of rifles was estimated at more than 1.6 million. There were persistent fears in Southeast Asia that some of these arms had become available to insurrectionary forces in neighbouring countries. No hard evidence surfaced to support the suspicion, but Hanoi's public posture of hostility to the Association of Southeast Asian Nations in general and Thailand in particular did nothing to remove it.

Ironically, it was Communist Cambodia that turned out to be Vietnam's bête noire during the year. Apparently, Cambodians had moved across the frontier in the Mekong Delta area soon after the fall of Saigon and before the North Vietnamese could establish full control. By midyear intense fighting had reportedly developed in this area, and travelers who visited Ho Chi Minh City in September claimed that two to three Cambodian divisions had been wiped out. Late in the year there were reports of full-scale battles at regimental level, centred in the Parrot's Beak region of Cambodia which juts into southern Vietnam. Each side accused the other of aggression, and on December 31 Cambodia broke diplomatic relations and suspended air travel between the two countries.

Much of Hanoi's efforts during the year was concentrated on rebuilding its war-shattered economy. The Army was used systematically on economic projects, ex-soldiers taking over key posts in an attempt to impart discipline and efficiency. The five-year plan placed maximum emphasis on agriculture, followed by light industry and then heavy industry. Throughout the year the government sought to attract foreign investment and establish trade relationships abroad. An investment code that came into force early in the year offered inducements to foreign private enterprise, international institutions, and even individuals to invest in Vietnamese agriculture, manufacturing, construction, transport, and natural resources. The export drive produced good results: a 34% expansion over 1976 was expected.

In September Vietnam finally became a member of the UN, the U.S. having withdrawn its opposition. But repeated feelers by Hanoi did not bring much-needed U.S. economic assistance any nearer. Vietnam also had to cope with the continuing embarrassment of escaping refugees, who were being picked up on the high seas by passing ships. They turned up at ports all across Asia, often causing prolonged administrative wrangles. Many who put out to sea in ill-fitted boats never made it. Some officials in Thailand estimated that 2,000 desperate refugees had perished at sea. Vietnam officially kept silent on this issue.   (T. J. S. GEORGE)

Water Sports

Motorboating. Two attempts were made to cross the Atlantic by motorboat during 1977, but only one was successful. Allen Cargile, a 46-year-old boatbuilder, left New York on July 16 with 1,248 gal of fuel, a crew of two, and a TV cameraman. After making a 900-mi detour to Newfoundland to disembark the seriously ill cameraman, Cargile maneuvered his 30-ft craft through a fierce mid-ocean storm that whipped up 40-ft waves and battered his boat with 50-mph winds. On August 16, having averaged 6.47 knots during his transoceanic adventure, he brought the "Cargile Cutter" up the Seine River to Paris. Robert Magoon, a veteran ocean racer from Florida, left Spain on July 1 with a three-man crew. His "Citicorp Traveler" had four powerful Mercury outboards capable of propelling the 36-ft Cigarette at 60 mph. Magoon's goal was to break the 82-hr 40-min transatlantic record set by the liner "United States" on its maiden voyage in 1952. High winds put him so far behind schedule and forced such high fuel consumption that Magoon canceled his trip after reaching the Azores.

In unlimited hydroplane racing, 42-year-old Jerry Bangs was killed at the Seattle (Wash.) Seafair Trophy race on August 7 when he was thrown from his erratically weaving boat during the first heat. Mickey Remund captured the 1977 championship with Bernie Little's "Miss Budweiser."

He took the title by winning regattas at Madison, Ind.; Dayton, Ohio; and San Diego, Calif., and by consistently finishing near the top in the other competitions. Veteran Bill Muncey, who was a serious contender in his new cabover "Atlas Van Lines," wound up in second place. He won at Miami, Fla.; Washington, D.C.; Owensboro, Ky.; and Seattle. He also won the Gold Cup at Tri-Cities, Wash., but scored no points in two of the three races during which he broke down. Muncey's Gold Cup victory, however, was his sixth and went into the books as a new record.

Bernie Little won his fourth national title as an owner and with 28 career victories had more wins than any other owner in history. His "Anheuser Busch Natural Light" finished third on the 1977 circuit. Little also entered offshore racing, using the former "American Eagle" with which Tom Gentry won the 1976 world title. This boat, also named "Anheuser Busch Natural Light," fared well in early races, but Joel Halpern finally won the U.S. offshore championship by a narrow margin. On November 13 Betty Cook of California became the first woman ever to win a world title when she defeated top contenders from five continents for the world offshore championship at Key West, Fla. (JAMES E. MARTENHOFF)

Canoeing. During 1977 Olympic-style flat-water canoeing and kayaking received new funding from the American Canoe Association and the U.S. Olympic Committee. The aim was to develop finer competitors for the next Olympic Games. Whitewater canoeing and kayaking, however, grew more rapidly than other forms of the sport. Watercraft constructed of extra-tough Kevlar fibre also made an appearance. During the U.S. national championships, Eric Evans won the men's whitewater kayak slalom for the eighth consecutive year. At the world championships held in Austria, West Germany took home most of the medals, but Chuck Lyda and Marietta Gillman of the U.S. won the mixed class of the canoe slalom event. River running, especially by dory, continued to grow in popularity, as did canoe poling and kayak surfing. Applications for extended wilderness river trips were so numerous that federal agencies had to resort to lotteries in choosing the names of those who would be granted permits. Consequently, only 6% of those seeking to travel down the Colorado River through the Grand Canyon received permits. The public was upset because commercially operated river trips were exempted but were frequently only partially booked. (ERIC LEAPER)

Water Skiing. At the 15th biennial world championships held in September 1977 at Milan, Italy, Mike Hazelwood became England's first world champion in ten years when he won the overall title. The women's crown went to Cindy Todd of Pierson, Fla., who led the U.S. to its 15th consecutive team title. In other events Bob LaPoint of Castro Valley, Calif., won the slalom; Mike Suyderhoud of Redding, Calif., was first in jumping; and Carlos Suárez of Maracay, Venezuela, the defending overall champion, became tricks champion with a new world record of 7,080 points. Cindy Todd also won the women's slalom and Linda Giddens of Eastman, Ga., captured the jumping event. Maria Victoria Carrasco of Caracas, Venezuela, retained her world title in tricks with a new record of 5,570 points.

In the open division of the U.S. national competition, Ricky McCormick of Winter Haven, Fla., and Camille Duvall of Irving, Texas, took the overall titles. McCormick also won the men's tricks and jumping titles, but the slalom title went to Kris LaPoint of Los Banos, Calif. Cathy Marlow of Pinole, Calif., finished first in the slalom, and Pam Folson of Boynton Beach, Fla., won in tricks. Lin-

Bill Muncey of La Mesa, California, hydroplaning's most successful driver, won the Gar Wood Trophy race on the Detroit River in June.

728

Western Samoa

Fast-paced action was exhibited by Bob LaPoint from Castro Valley, California, in winning the slalom event in the world water skiing championships at Milan, Italy, in September.

da Giddens successfully defended her national jumping title. During the Masters Tournament at Callaway Gardens, Ga., the overall titles went to McCormick and Todd, both former champions.

(THOMAS C. HARDMAN)

Surfing. As in previous years, most of the world's finest surfers headed for Hawaii during the winter of 1976–77 to vie for major titles. Defending champion Mark Richards was dethroned by fellow Australian Mark Warren in the Smirnoff world professional surfing championships for the largest purse of the season. In the Duke Kahanamoku Surfing Classic, however, James Jones took top honours ahead of three other Hawaiians. Rory Russell, also of Hawaii, easily captured the Pipeline Masters with three spectacular tube rides. Defending champion Shaun Tomson of South Africa was eliminated in the preliminaries. Many believed that ABC-TV captured some of the finest waves ever filmed for its "Wide World of Sports." The final event, the World Cup, was won by Ian Cairns of Australia. The International Professional Surfing Association made at least $175,000 available for the Grand Prix circuit, a clear indication of its intention to accelerate its promotion of professional surfing. Enthusiasts hoped that funds would be available to construct artificial reefs so natural surfing areas would be less crowded. (JACK FLANAGAN)

Water Polo. The 1977 European championship brought together the top six finishers in the 1976 Olympic Games, and once again the Hungarian team proved it was the best in the world. Yugoslavia finished second after dropping one match 3–4 to Hungary. Italy was third, followed in order by the U.S.S.R., The Netherlands, West Germany, Spain, and Romania. The 1977 Amateur Athletic Union senior men's outdoor nationals took on a new look with the participation of two teams from east of the Rockies. When the tournament reached the semifinals, it looked like a repeat of 1976 with the California teams of Concord, Stanford, Newport, and the Southern California All-Stars fighting for the championship. Gary Figueroa of Newport was named the tournament's most valu-

able player, but in the final his team could not overcome the initial lead built up by defending champion Concord. The SoCal All-Stars were third and Stanford fourth. Art Lambert's Stanford squad, however, won the 1976 National Collegiate Athletic Association championship by edging UCLA 13–12. Chris Dorst of Stanford blocked three penalty shots and was named most valuable player. In the battle for third place, the University of California at Santa Barbara took an early 5–0 lead over the University of California at Irvine, but lost 7–8 in overtime. (WILLIAM ENSIGN FRADY)

Western Samoa

A constitutional monarchy and member of the Commonwealth of Nations, Western Samoa is an island group in the South Pacific Ocean, about 2,600 km E of New Zealand and 3,500 km S of Hawaii. Area: 2,784 sq km (1,075 sq mi), with two major islands, Savai'i (1,714 sq km) and Upolu (1,128 sq km), and seven smaller islands. Pop. (1977 est.): 152,000. Cap. and largest city: Apia (pop., 1976 census, 32,100). Language: Samoan and English. Religion (1971): Congregational 51%, Roman Catholic 22%, Methodist 16%, others 11%. Head of state (*O le Ao o le Malo*) in 1977, Malietoa Tanumafili II; prime minister, Tupuola Taisi Tufuga Efi.

WESTERN SAMOA

Education. (1976) Primary, pupils 40,490, teachers 1,322; secondary, pupils 8,258, teachers 376; vocational, pupils 284, teachers 57; teacher training, students 411, teachers 20; higher (1975), students 249, teaching staff 9.

Finance and Trade. Monetary unit: tala, with (Sept. 19, 1977) a free rate of 0.60 tala to U.S. $1 (1.04 tala = £1 sterling). Budget (1976 est.): revenue 16,255,000 tala; expenditure 16,321,000 tala. Foreign trade (1976): imports 23,627,000 tala; exports 5,447,000 tala. Import sources: New Zealand 28%; Australia 20%; Japan 15%; U.S. 8%; Fiji 7%; Singapore 5%. Export destinations: New Zealand 36%; West Germany 35%; Japan 8%; The Netherlands 6%; American Samoa 5%. Main exports: cocoa 41%; copra 35%.

Western Samoa

Queen Elizabeth II's Silver Jubilee tour of the South Pacific began in February when the queen and Prince Philip arrived in Western Samoa.

The effects of the continuing decline in prices for copra and cocoa were exacerbated in 1977 by a general drop in agricultural production. The government responded with an attempt to stimulate industrial growth. Invisible earnings, chiefly in the form of remittances from emigrants in New Zealand, were also affected when that country adopted a more restrictive entry policy. Checks on overstayers, repatriations, and, in particular, random police checks on Polynesians in New Zealand had soured relations between the two countries in the latter part of 1976.

Senior police officials were dismissed following the report of a commission of inquiry, released late in 1976. The commission substantiated charges of corruption, inefficiency, brutality, and substandard prisons.

In October 1976 China established an embassy in Apia. The Samoan government, after 15 years of independence, established its own diplomatic representatives in New Zealand. Both moves indicated an increasing tendency for Western Samoa to handle its own foreign relations rather than leaving them to New Zealand under the treaty of friendship. With other members of the South Pacific Forum, Samoa decided in 1977 to declare a 200-mi exclusive economic zone offshore. Apia was to be the headquarters for the new regional shipping line established by the Forum.

(BARRIE MACDONALD)

Winter Sports

The continuing worldwide expansion of winter sports was evidenced by the increasing numbers of nations and individuals actively concerned with contests on snow and ice during 1977. More plentiful means of mechanical ascent provided easier access to suitable snow terrain, and more abundant electrically frozen ice reduced previous climatic limitations.

Skiing. During the year approximately $17 billion was spent in all parts of the world on ski equipment and winter sports vacations, an industry providing about one million jobs, according to an estimate by the Union Bank of Switzerland. The European alpine countries offered 1.5 million beds in winter sports resorts, which had 2,000 aerial cable cars and 8,500 other types of ski lifts. In Switzerland alone, cable cars and ski lifts took in about $150 million during the winter season, a sum equal to half the passenger fares paid on the Swiss Federal Railways.

ALPINE RACING. Ingemar Stenmark, probably the best alpine racer Sweden had produced, retained the men's title in the 11th World Cup series. Klaus Heidegger and Franz Klammer, both from Austria, finished second and third. No one excelled in all events, Klammer proving the outstanding downhiller and Stenmark owing his overall success to convincing supremacy in the slalom and to his second place in the giant slalom. Heini Hemmi of Switzerland won the latter event by a narrow margin over Stenmark.

Lise-Marie Morerod became the first Swiss woman to win the World Cup, holding off the almost legendary Austrian Annemarie Proell-Moser, who was runner-up in a creditable comeback. Proell-Moser had retired the previous season after an unprecedented run of five straight wins. Two more Austrians, Monika Kaserer and Brigitte Totschnig-Habersatter, finished third and fourth, respectively. Morerod was the top scorer in both the slalom and giant slalom, while Totschnig-Habersatter narrowly outpointed Proell-Moser in the downhill.

For the first time since the World Cup began, neither trophy winner earned a single downhill point, and Stenmark did not even compete in a downhill. This prompted some pressure to revise the rules to favour all-arounders rather than specialists and so encourage versatility. The series consisted of 33 men's and 27 women's events spread through four months of meetings in Austria, France, Italy, Japan, Norway, Spain, Sweden, Switzerland, the U.S., West Germany, and Yugoslavia. The concurrently decided Nations' Cup was won for a fifth consecutive year by Austria, which topped both men's and women's standings. Switzerland was runner-up in the overall standings for the third straight year and Italy third.

The fifth European Cup series, contested by racers largely on the fringe of World Cup status, produced first winners for their nations in Peter Popangelov (Bulgaria) and Ursula Konzett (Liechtenstein). The seventh Can-Am Trophy series, at seven North American locations, was won by Raymond Pratte (Canada) and Heidi Preuss (U.S.). Henri Duvillard of France retained the world professional title on the North American circuit, with Josef Odermatt of Switzerland again runner-up and Tyler Palmer of the U.S. third. Duvillard, who won 10 races for a record total of 35 in three seasons, announced his retirement at the end of the season.

NORDIC EVENTS. King Carl XVI Gustaf of Sweden was among a record number of 10,934 starters in the 54th Vasaloppet cross-country race over 85.8 km from Sälen to Mora, Sweden, on March 6. Ivan Garanin was the first Soviet racer to win the event, followed by a Finn, Jorma Kinnunen, and a Swede, Tommy Limby. The informal World Cup series for cross-country events, well supported but still not sealed with an official stamp, was won by Thomas Wassberg of Sweden, with a Finn, Juha Mieto, and another Swede, Thomas Magnusson, second and third. Finland's Ahti Nevada claimed a world record after skiing 280.905 km in 24 hours around a course at Rovaniemi, Fin., on March 30.

Aleksandr Tihonov, of the U.S.S.R. was outstanding in the world biathlon championships, in February at Lillehammer, Norway, winning the

Irina Rodnina and Aleksandr Zaitsev execute a one-handed lift during their free-skating performance in the world figure-skating championships in Tokyo in March. The Soviet couple won their fifth straight pairs title.

UPI COMPIX

10 km, placing third in the 20 km, and taking part in the Soviet relay team victory. Heikki Ikola of Finland won the 20 km.

The world ski-flying championship, with emphasis on distance rather than style, was won by Walter Steiner of Switzerland at Vikersund, Norway, on February 18–20. Runner-up was Toni Innauer, the Austrian world record holder. In an international meeting on March 18 at Planica, Yugos., Bogdan Norcic of the host nation cleared 181 m, 5 m more than the world record, but he fell on landing.

In the 79th Holmenkollen ski festival in Oslo, Norway, on March 11–13, Magnusson took the 50 km and was runner-up in the 15 km behind Mieto. Ulrich Wehling of East Germany won the Nordic combination. Eva Ohlsson of Sweden dominated the women's events, with a victory in the 10 km and second place in the 5 km behind Hilkka Kuntola of Finland. The 90-m jump finale showpiece was won by Aleksey Borovitin of the Soviet Union.

OTHER EVENTS. Professional freestyle, with much of the emphasis on daring acrobatics, continued to profit from its spectacular appeal, advancing more rapidly in North America than elsewhere. The men's World Trophy title was gained by John Eaves of Canada, and the women's was retained by Marion Post of the U.S. Second to Eaves was a fellow Canadian, Greg Athans, with Bob Salerno of the U.S. third. Runner-up to Post was Stephanie Sloan, a Sweden-based Canadian, ahead of Katie Morning of the U.S.

The 31st International Ski Federation congress, the first to be held in the Southern Hemisphere, with a program extending over April 25–30 at Bariloche, Arg., gave formal approval to a cross-country Nordic World Cup biennial series, to begin during the 1978–79 season. The alpine World Cup Commission reverted to its original, less complicated rules whereby future overall winners would be determined by the best three results in each of the standard three disciplines. Amended giant slalom regulations, with fewer gates and greater distances between gates, were calculated to encourage the all-arounder.

The sixth biennial world skibob championships, at Schladming, Austria, on February 21–26, were contested by 43 men and 17 women from nine nations. Alexander Irausek took the men's title for the host country. The new women's champion was Rosalinde Lehner of West Germany.

Ice Skating. A widespread increase in the number of civic-owned indoor ice rinks throughout the world all but ended previous climatic limitations on the sport. Indeed, a large proportion of the world's most active participants had never performed on natural ice.

FIGURE SKATING. The first world ice figure and dance championships to be staged in Asia, in Tokyo on March 1–5, involved 93 skaters from 17 nations. Vladimir Kovalev of the Soviet Union, narrowly beaten the previous year by John Curry, took the men's crown in an event never lacking in drama. Kovalev was pursued closely by Jan Hoffmann, the 1974 winner from East Germany. But neither champion nor runner-up matched the

WIDE WORLD

Sweden's Ingemar Stenmark swoops
around a slalom pole on January 10
at Berchtesgaden, West Germany, on
his way to winning the World Cup.

free skating of Minoru Sano, who, skating last, fittingly ended the first tournament in his own country with a scintillating display that included six triple jumps. He rose from sixth after the figures to third overall, thereby becoming Japan's first medalist in figure skating competition.

Linda Fratianne retained the women's title for the U.S.; the title was undefended by Dorothy Hamill, who, like Britain's Curry, had turned professional. A fall from a triple salchow by Anett Pötzsch, who had led after the figures, perhaps cost the East German girl the title, but she finished a comfortable runner-up, ahead of Dagmar Lurz of West Germany.

The long reign of Aleksandr Zaitsev and Irina Rodnina was extended by their fifth straight pairs victory. The win was a record ninth success for Rodnina, since she had earned four previous wins with Aleksey Ulanov. It was also the 13th successive Soviet victory. The champions' technical proficiency was most notable in their multiple twist lifts, throw axels, and superbly timed double jumps. Their compatriots Aleksandr Vlasov and Irina Vorobieva narrowly held off the promising third-place Randy Gardner and Tai Babilonia of the U.S.

The dance title went to the classically serious and balletic Moscow couple of Andrey Minekov and Irina Moiseyeva. A British resurgence in this event was achieved by Warren Maxwell and Janet Thompson, who took second place in front of another Soviet couple, Gennadi Karponosov and Natalia Linichuk.

The first quadruple twist lift to be performed in an international pairs championship was achieved at the European championships in Helsinki by a Soviet pair, Sergey Shakhrai and his tiny 13-year-old partner, Marina Tcherkasova. Their feat was believed to be possible only because of the abnormal height disparity between the two.

The International Skating Union council, at its 37th congress in Paris on May 23–28, took the unprecedented step of penalizing a nation, as distinct

from individuals, by banning all Soviet judges from the subsequent season's international championships because of a series of judging discrepancies. Another Soviet setback was self-inflicted when Kovalev and Karponosov were both suspended for a year by their national association because of misbehaviour.

Speed Skating. In the men's world ice speed championship, at Heerenveen, Neth., on February 12–13, Eric Heiden became the first U.S. skater to win the overall title since the event began in 1893. Two Norwegians, Jan Egil Storholt and Sten Stensen, the 1974 winner, were second and third. Heiden won the 500 m and Stensen the 10,000 m, but Storholt did not finish first in any of the four races. The 1,500 m went to another Norwegian, Amund Sjobrend, and the 5,000 m to a Dutchman, Hans van Helden.

The women's world speed championship, held the same weekend at Keystone, Colo., produced a Soviet grand slam, Vera Bryndzey, Galina Stepanskaya, and Galina Nikitina finishing in that order. It was the first Soviet women's victory in six years. Bryndzey won the two shorter races, 500 m and 1,000 m, and Stepanskaya the two longer ones, 1,500 m and 3,000 m. The separate world sprint titles for men and women, decided at Alkmaar, Neth., on February 26–27, were won, respectively, by Heiden and Sylvia Burka of Canada.

Four men's world records were broken, all at Medeo, U.S.S.R., during March and April. Evgeny Kulikov, the Soviet sprinter, lowered the 1,000 m to 1 min 15.33 sec. Storholt reduced the 1,500 m to 1 min 55.18 sec, and fellow Norwegian Kay Stenshjemmet clocked the 5,000 m in 6 min 56.90 sec. Another Soviet skater, Viktor Leskin, lowered the 10,000-m mark to 14 min 34.33 sec.

Bobsledding. A new track at Winterberg, West Germany, improvements to another in the same country at Königssee, and considerable renovations to that at Lake Placid, N.Y., made welcome additions to the major facilities for international bobsled racing. Although, for reasons of economy,

WIDE WORLD

Canadian curling team members Art Lobel and Jim Ursel swept vigorously but still lost to a Swedish team (left) in the world curling championships at Karlstad, Sweden, in April.

Königssee and Igls, Austria, continued to use common courses for both bobsledding and luge tobogganing, there were disadvantages in this compromise, and Lake Placid made plans for separate tracks for the 1980 Winter Olympics.

Because of the retirements of several veteran drivers, many newcomers were among participant crews from 15 nations contesting the 44th world championships, at St.-Moritz, Switz., from January 24 to February 6. Meinhard Nehmer, the East German double gold medalist of the previous year's Innsbruck Olympics, again steered a winning sled to retain the four-man title. The successful Swiss two-man bob was driven by Hans Hiltebrand and braked by Heinz Meier. In both events, Swiss and West German crews finished second and third, respectively.

Because unsuitable weather conditions at Sinaia, Rom., caused the European championships to be canceled, greater attention than usual was centred on the Nations' Cup events, for two-man boblets at Königssee on Dec. 27, 1976, to Jan. 1, 1977, and four-man sleds at Igls on January 2–6. Both winning crews were driven by Stefan Gaisreiter of West Germany, the European four-man titleholder.

Tobogganing. Adverse weather conditions hindered the tobogganing season. The 23rd world luge championships, originally scheduled for January at Villard-de-Lans, France, were postponed because of a lack of snow until February 19–20 at Igls. There, Margit Schumann of East Germany achieved a record fifth women's victory. The men's event was won by another East German, Hans Rinn. He and Norbert Hahn retained the two-seater title. In the European luge championships, held at Königssee on February 12–13, the men's and women's titles went to Anton Winkler and Elisabeth Demleitner, both from Austria.

Reto Gansser was the year's outstanding skeleton tobogganist on the Cresta Run at St.-Moritz. (A skeleton toboggan consists of steel runners fastened to a platform chassis with a sliding seat; it is ridden in a headfirst, prone position.) He retained both the major prizes, winning the 68th Grand National, with brother Franco Gansser runner-up and Christian Nater third, and the 54th Cur-

zon Cup ahead of Urs Nater and Poldi Berchtold. All the placed riders were Swiss.

Curling. The 19th world curling championship for the Air Canada Silver Broom was won for a second time by Sweden, the host country, which defeated Canada 8–5 in the final at Karlstad. Sweden had previously held the title in 1973. The winning rink was skipped by Ragnar Kamp and the losing finalist by Jim Ursel. Canada had a tough time disposing of Scotland 8–5 in the semifinals, while Sweden more comfortably defeated the U.S. 5–0. The other six of the ten competing nations were Switzerland, Italy, Norway, France, West Germany, and Denmark. The event, held from March 28 to April 3, was opened by King Carl XVI Gustav of Sweden. Most matches were watched by some 3,000 spectators.

Nine nations contested the European championships, held in West Berlin in December 1976. Switzerland defeated Norway in the men's final, and Sweden beat France in the women's. The third world junior championship was sponsored by Uniroyal in Quebec from February 28 to March 6. Canada, represented by a rink from Prince Edward Island skipped by Bill Jenkins, beat the U.S. in the final. Ten countries competed.

(HOWARD BASS)

See also Ice Hockey.
[452.B.4.g–h]

People's Democratic Republic of Yemen

Wood Products:
see Industrial Review

World Bank:
see Economy, World

Wrestling:
see Combat Sports

Yachting:
see Sailing

Yemen, People's Democratic Republic of

A people's republic in the southern coastal region of the Arabian Peninsula, Yemen (Aden) is bordered by Yemen (San'a'), Saudi Arabia, and Oman. Area: 287,680 sq km (111,074 sq mi). Pop. (1976 est.): 1,749,000. Cap. and largest city: Aden (pop., 1973, 132,500). Language: Arabic. Religion: Muslim. Chairman of the Presidential Council in 1977, Salem Ali Rubayyi; prime minister, Ali Nasir Muhammad Husani.

In 1977 the People's Democratic Republic of Yemen (Aden; South Yemen) improved its relations with both the Yemen Arab Republic (San'a'; North

YEMEN, PEOPLE'S DEMOCRATIC REPUBLIC OF

Education. (1974–75) Primary, pupils 196,466, teachers 6,467; secondary, pupils 38,389, teachers 1,656; vocational, pupils 676, teachers (1973–74) 142; teacher training, students 631, teachers 47; higher, students 934, teaching staff 92.

Finance and Trade. Monetary unit: Yemen dinar, with (Sept. 19, 1977) a par value of 0.345 dinar to U.S. $1 (free rate of 0.60 dinar = £1 sterling). Budget (1975–76 actual): revenue 13,860,000 dinars; expenditure 25,550,000 dinars. Foreign trade (1975): imports 107.8 million dinars; exports 64.7 million dinars. Import sources: U.K. 21%; Japan 8%; China 8%; The Netherlands 5%; Thailand 5%. Export destinations: Canada c. 65%; Australia c. 8%; Angola c. 5%; Yemen (San'a') c. 5%. Main export petroleum products 93%.

Transport. Roads (1975) c. 10,500 km (mainly tracks; including c. 1,400 km with improved surface). Motor vehicles in use (1973): passenger 10,600; commercial (including buses) 7,900. There are no railways. Ships entered (1974) vessels totaling 5,160,000 net registered tons; goods loaded 2,308,000 metric tons, unloaded 3,780,000 metric tons.

Agriculture. Production (in 000; metric tons; 1975): millet and sorghum 61; wheat 12; watermelons 36; dates c. 42; cotton, lint c. 5; fish catch 127. Livestock (in 000; 1975): cattle c. 101; sheep c. 232; goats c. 923; camels c. 40; chickens c. 1,380.

Industry. Production (in 000; metric tons; 1975): petroleum products c. 1,150; salt c. 75; electricity (kw-hr) c. 180,000.

YEMEN ARAB REPUBLIC

Education. (1976–77) Primary, pupils 221,482, teachers (1974–75) 5,773; secondary, pupils 24,873, teachers (1974–75) 835; vocational, pupils 503, teachers (1974–75) 54; teacher training, students 1,650, teachers (1974–75) 130; higher (1974–75), students 952, teaching staff 58.

Finance and Trade. Monetary unit: rial, with (Sept. 19, 1977) a par value of 4.56 rials to U.S. $1 (free rate of 7.95 rials = £1 sterling). Budget (1976–77 est.): revenue 836 million rials; expenditure 1,197,600,000 rials. Foreign trade (1976): imports 1,882,240,000 rials; exports 34,940,000 rials. Import sources: Saudi Arabia 12%; Japan 10%; India 7%; Australia 7%; U.K. 6%; China 6%; The Netherlands 6%. Export destinations: Japan 42%; China 33%; Yemen (Aden) 27%; Italy 18%; Saudi Arabia 16%. Main exports: cotton 33%; hides and skins 20%; coffee 20%.

Agriculture. Production (in 000; metric tons; 1975): barley 220; corn 107; wheat 78; sorghum (1976) c. 1,608; potatoes c. 78; dates 65; coffee c. 5; tobacco c. 5; cotton, lint c. 10. Livestock (in 000; 1975): cattle c. 1,100; sheep c. 3,200; goats c. 7,400; camels c. 120; asses c. 640.

Yemen Arab Republic

Yemen) and Saudi Arabia, while maintaining its close links with the Communist states. Pres. Fidel Castro of Cuba visited Aden on March 10–12 with the reported aim of encouraging a leftist Ethiopia-Somalia-South Yemen alliance. In March, however, following a visit to Aden by Sudanese Pres. Gaafar Nimeiry, Pres. Salem Ali Rubayyi joined the meeting in Ta'izz (North Yemen) of the heads of state of Sudan, Somalia, and the two Yemens, sponsored by Saudi Arabia.

Saudi aid of $50 million for rural electrification and housing in South Yemen was announced. In March the president of the United Arab Emirates visited Aden. Moves toward union with North Yemen made some progress. President Rubayyi visited San'a' in August, but the assassination of the North Yemen head of state on October 11 prevented a return visit. The assassination was denounced by the Aden government as a reactionary plot against union. On May 1 the South Yemen government took over the British Petroleum refinery in Aden. (PETER MANSFIELD)

Yemen Arab Republic

A republic situated in the southwestern coastal region of the Arabian Peninsula, Yemen (San'a') is bounded by Yemen (Aden), Saudi Arabia, and the Red Sea. Area: 200,000 sq km (77,200 sq mi). Pop. (1975): 5,237,900. Cap. and largest city: San'a' (pop., 1975, 134,600). Language: Arabic. Religion: Muslim. Chairman of the Command Council to Oct. 11, 1977, Col. Ibrahim al-Hamdi; head of the Presidential Command Council from October 11, Col. Ahmed al-Ghashmi; premier, Abdel-Aziz Abdel-Ghani.

The assassination of the Yemen Arab Republic (San'a'; North Yemen) head of state, Col. Ibrahim al-Hamdi, on Oct. 11, 1977, jeopardized the coun-

try's stability. He was succeeded by a three-man Presidential Command Council headed by the former chief of staff, Col. Ahmed al-Ghashmi, who pledged to continue Hamdi's policies. Colonel Hamdi's efforts to establish a strong central government and a modernized state controlling the powerful tribal alliances in the north of the country had met considerable resistance. He was attempting to balance the influence of the tribes with that of less conservative urban elements looking for union with the People's Democratic Republic of Yemen (Aden; South Yemen). South Yemen's president visited North Yemen in March, for a summit meeting of Sudan, Somalia, and the two Yemens, and again in August. Colonel Hamdi was about to be the first North Yemeni head of state to visit South Yemen when he was assassinated.

Relations with Saudi Arabia remained close; the North Yemen-Saudi Coordinating Committee met several times, and Saudi aid increased. Economic expansion was stimulated by Saudi and other Arab aid and Yemeni emigrants' remittances, estimated at $500 million a year. (PETER MANSFIELD)

Yugoslavia

A federal socialist republic, Yugoslavia is bordered by Italy, Austria, Hungary, Romania, Bulgaria, Greece, Albania, and the Adriatic Sea. Area: 255,-804 sq km (98,766 sq mi). Pop. (1977 est.): 21,715,-000. Cap. and largest city: Belgrade (pop., 1975 UN est., 870,000). Language: Serbo-Croatian, Slovenian, and Macedonian. Religion (1953): Orthodox 41%; Roman Catholic 32%; Muslim 12%. President of the republic for life and president of the League of Communists in 1977, Marshal Tito (Josip Broz); presidents of the Federal Executive Council (premiers), Dzemal Bijedic to January 18 and, from February 14, Veselin Djuranovic.

The clampdown on political dissidence continued in 1977. In foreign policy, relations with both East and West were cultivated through a series of visits by President Tito and other Yugoslav leaders. Yugoslavia was host to the Conference on Security and Cooperation in Europe, which met from June until December 22 and would reconvene in January 1978.

Yugoslavia

Yiddish Literature:
see Literature

Yugoslavia's first nuclear power station at Krsko, being built by the Westinghouse Electric Corp. of the U.S., neared completion at year's end.

protesting the practice of taking away passports from certain individuals without explanation. On May 6 Vitomir Djilas, a cousin of the former vice-president of Yugoslavia, Milovan Djilas, was sentenced to 2½ years' imprisonment for writing a letter criticizing political conditions in Yugoslavia (though he never actually sent it). A 64-year-old chemist from Sarajevo, Nikola Novakovic, was sentenced to 12 years' imprisonment on August 3 for maintaining contacts with Croat exiles in the West. Branko Mikulic, president of the League of Communists of Bosnia-Hercegovina, announced on October 28 that there would be an amnesty for some of the 500-odd political prisoners in Yugoslavia, coinciding with the national day on November 29, but it would not affect those found guilty of "subversive activities" against the state. In the event over 700 prisoners were either released or had their sentences reduced, including 218 being held for political crimes. Among those freed was the writer Mihajlo Mihajlov, sentenced in 1975 to seven years' imprisonment for spreading hostile propaganda.

President Tito visited Libya in January, but his projected visit to Egypt was canceled because of political unrest in Cairo. On August 16 he embarked on a 24-day tour of the Communist world which took him first to the Soviet Union, then to North Korea, and finally to China, his first visit there. During October 12–21 Tito visited France, Portugal, and Algeria and on his return took a three-week rest on doctors' advice. U.S. Vice-Pres. Walter Mondale visited Yugoslavia in May. The visit was followed by resumption of work on the 632-Mw nuclear power station in Krsko, Slovenia, being built by Westinghouse of the U.S., interrupted because of disagreements with the U.S. over guarantees required from the Yugoslavs about the use of U.S.-supplied nuclear material. Resumption of U.S. arms sales to Yugoslavia was discussed during the visit of U.S. Defense Secretary Harold Brown in October.

Yugoslavia's economic position deteriorated in 1977. The trade deficit in the first eight months of the year reached $3 billion. In October, Berislav Sefer, federal vice-premier in charge of economic

Dzemal Bijedic (*see* OBITUARIES), premier since 1971, was killed in an airplane crash on January 18. On February 14 President Tito appointed as his successor Veselin Djuranovic, president of the Central Committee of the League of Communists of Montenegro. The appointment was approved by the Federal Assembly in Belgrade on March 15. President Tito's 85th birthday was celebrated with great pomp on May 25, but Tito's wife since 1952, Jovanka Broz, disappeared from public life in June against a background of rumours that she had tried to influence senior political and military appointments. In June, Marko Milutinovic, Tito's chief of protocol, was replaced and appointed ambassador to Pakistan, and in October, Milos Sumonja, deputy federal minister of defense, was appointed ambassador to The Netherlands. Both were said to have been close to Jovanka Broz.

On March 16 the Supreme Constitutional Court in Belgrade rejected a petition by 60 intellectuals

YUGOSLAVIA

Education. (1974–75) Primary, pupils 2,866,847, teachers 127,988; secondary, pupils 217,294, teachers 9,887; vocational, pupils 572,869, teachers 11,328; teacher training, students 9,039, teachers 768; higher, students (1975–76) 393,801, teaching staff (1973–74) 19,197.

Finance. Monetary unit: dinar, with (Sept. 19, 1977) a free rate of 18.44 dinars to U.S. $1 (32.12 dinars = £1 sterling). Gold, SDR's, and foreign exchange (June 1977) U.S. $1,828,000,000. Budget (1975 actual): revenue 108,280,000,000 dinars; expenditure 118,410,000,000 dinars. Gross national product (1975) 503 billion dinars. Money supply (Sept. 1976) 185.5 billion dinars. Cost of living (1970 = 100; June 1977) 317.

Foreign Trade. (1976) Imports 134,050,000,000 dinars; exports 88,770,000,000 dinars. Import sources: West Germany 17%; U.S.S.R. 14%; Italy 10%; Iraq 6%; U.S. 5%. Export destinations: U.S.S.R. 23%; Italy 12%; West Germany 9%; U.S. 7%; Czechoslovakia 5%. Main exports: machinery 16%; transport equipment 12%; food 10%; nonferrous

metals 8%; chemicals 7%; timber 5%; clothing 5%; textile yarns and fabrics 5%. Tourism (1975): visitors 5,835,000; gross receipts U.S. $776 million.

Transport and Communications. Roads *c.* 112,000 km. Motor vehicles in use (1975): passenger 1,536,700; commercial 142,500. Railways: (1975) 10,068 km; traffic (1976) 9,884,000,000 passenger-km, freight 21,006,000,000 net ton-km. Air traffic (1976): 2,151,000,000 passenger-km; freight 20,434,000 net ton-km. Shipping (1976): merchant vessels 100 gross tons and over 423; gross tonnage 1,943,750. Telephones (Dec. 1975) 1,301,000. Radio licenses (Dec. 1975) 4,181,000. Television licenses (Dec. 1975) 3,076,000.

Agriculture. Production (in 000; metric tons; 1976): wheat *c.* 5,980; barley 653; oats 320; rye 105; corn *c.* 9,112; potatoes 2,690; sunflower seed 324; sugar, raw value *c.* 560; onions *c.* 225; tomatoes *c.* 358; cabbages (1975) *c.* 699; chillies and peppers (1975) *c.* 341; watermelons (1975) *c.* 469; plums (1975) *c.* 682; apples *c.* 370; wine *c.* 570; tobacco *c.* 80; beef and veal *c.* 360; pork *c.* 304; timber (cu m;

1975) 14,027. Livestock (in 000; Jan. 1976): cattle 5,755; sheep 7,831; pigs 6,536; horses 864; chickens 49,623.

Industry. Fuel and power (in 000; metric tons; 1976): coal 587; lignite 35,694; crude oil 3,880; natural gas (cu m) *c.* 1,700,000; manufactured gas (cu m) *c.* 150,000; electricity (kw-hr) 43,574,000. Production (in 000; metric tons; 1976): cement 7,617; iron ore (35% metal content) 4,256; pig iron 2,121; crude steel 2,698; bauxite 2,032; antimony ore (metal content; 1975) 2.2; chrome ore (oxide content; 1975) 0.6; magnesite (1975) 485; manganese ore (metal content; 1975) 5.4; aluminum 197; copper 136; lead 110; zinc 104; gold (troy oz; 1975) 178; silver (troy oz; 1975) 5,400; petroleum products (1975) 10,068; sulfuric acid 848; cotton yarn 117; wool yarn 44; man-made fibres 82; wood pulp (1975) 595; newsprint 90; other paper (1975) 660. Merchant vessels launched (100 gross tons and over; 1976) 583,000 gross tons.

policy, announced that Yugoslavia would have a $450 million balance of payments deficit at the end of 1977, compared with a $100 million surplus at the end of 1976.

On May 16 Gradimir Tasic, air controller at Zagreb airport, was sentenced to seven years' imprisonment for negligence at the time of the air collision over the airport in September 1976, in which 176 people lost their lives. His seven co-defendants were acquitted. (K. F. CVIIC)

Zaire

A republic of equatorial Africa, Zaire is bounded by the Central African Empire, Sudan, Uganda, Rwanda, Burundi, Tanzania, Zambia, Angola, Congo, and the Atlantic Ocean. Area: 2,344,885 sq km (905,365 sq mi). Pop. (1976 est.): 25,629,000. Cap. and largest city: Kinshasa (pop., 1974, 1,733,-800). Language: French; Bantu dialects. Religion: animist approximately 50%; Christian 43%. President in 1977, Mobutu Sese Seko; prime minister from July 6, Mpinga Kasenga.

On March 8, 1977, a force of Katangese gendarmes, who had taken refuge in Angola after the fall of Moise Tshombe's government in Katanga in 1963, recrossed the border and launched an attack on Shaba (formerly Katanga) Province, threatening the town of Kolwezi, one of the main centres of Zaire's copper-extracting industry. The government of Zaire accused Angola and the U.S.S.R. of supporting the attack and claimed that Cuban troops were involved. Although no evidence of this latter charge was forthcoming, Cuban diplomats were ordered to leave the country, and Pres. Mobutu Sese Seko (see BIOGRAPHY) appealed for an increase in U.S. aid to check what he termed a Communist-inspired attack.

The U.S. responded cautiously with an airlift of medical and certain military supplies, but did not send arms. Mobutu's appeal to France, however, resulted in the supply of transport planes which flew in Moroccan troops. With their aid, the in-

vaders were driven out of the country by the end of May. Angola and a number of other African states, notably Algeria, condemned this foreign intervention. Egypt, however, promised support for Mobutu's government, as did Idi Amin of Uganda, while the presidents of Ivory Coast, Rwanda, and the Sudan applauded the French and Moroccan actions.

The invasion focused attention on Zaire, whose output of copper, cobalt, and uranium was of considerable importance to the Western world. The ineffectiveness of Zaire's troops against a comparatively small invading force showed how precarious was the country's security. More important was the support apparently given to the invaders by the inhabitants of Katanga. Mobutu's government was highly unpopular, as many Zairians thought it was more concerned with obtaining financial benefits for its supporters than with the well-being of the whole country. It was known that a number of formerly prominent Zairians still hoped to bring down the government, but there was a lack of unity among the would-be leaders, and some Western powers feared that Mobutu's overthrow might result in tribal conflict between rival claimants and open the way for Communist intervention.

These fears were strengthened by claims from opponents of Mobutu's government that the invasion had taken place prematurely because of the personal ambition of its leader, and that it had been intended to form part of a more widely coordinated coup. Even among those who wished to support the regime as a unifying force, there were some who felt that Mobutu himself must go. One of the men suggested as a possible replacement, the foreign minister, Nguza Karl-I-Bond, was arrested in August and charged with concealing prior knowledge of the invasion. He was found guilty and sentenced to death but was reprieved by Mobutu and his sentence commuted to life imprisonment. Also sentenced to death were the former chief of staff of Zaire's forces, who had been dismissed as a result of the invasion, and the gover-

Zaire

Pigmy fighting techniques with bows and arrows were demonstrated in April to Zairian soldiers who were fighting against rebels in southern Zaire.

Zambia

nor of Shaba Province, Monguya Mbenge, who had fled to Belgium. Both these men were charged with collaborating with the invaders. Karl-I-Bond's dismissal resulted in a Cabinet reshuffle, and Umba Di Lutete, Zaire's representative at the UN, became the foreign minister in his place. Earlier, in February, Mobutu had dismissed several of his ministers, including Bisengimana Rwema, director of the Political Bureau, a man who had been regarded as one of his closest advisers and a strong critic of Soviet infiltration of Africa.

Conscious of the insecurity of his position, Mobutu launched a new campaign to win the support of the Western powers. In June he visited France to thank Pres. Valéry Giscard d'Estaing for the help he had given, and in July he announced his belief in cooperation between Europe and Africa. To demonstrate his support for democratic government, he replaced the former Executive Council with a new 28-man Executive Council, or Cabinet, including a first state commissioner (prime minister), Mpinga Kasenga, and 13 members of the old council. He also promised parliamentary elections, which were duly held in October. In December the Cabinet resigned (remaining temporarily in office in a caretaker capacity), ostensibly to clear the way for completion of Mobutu's reform program.

A further, strong link between Zaire and the West was the country's enormous debt, estimated at between $2 billion and $3 billion. The possibility that, because of the precarious economic situation, a credit of $250 million might not be forthcoming hung over Zaire early in the year. Stirred, perhaps, by fears aroused by the invasion, and more definitely by an improvement in Zaire's repayment on existing loans, Citibank of New York, which was responsible for organizing the loan, adopted a more optimistic attitude. As of the end of the year, however, the arrangements still had not been successfully completed.

In March 1976 Mobutu had signed an agreement with a West German research organization offering a site in southeastern Zaire for rocket development. The financial benefit to Zaire was considerable, but the agreement aroused strong criticism elsewhere in Africa. The 1973 nationalization of the oil industry had proved less successful than had been hoped, and negotiations were begun with a view to handing 60% of control to foreign companies.   (KENNETH INGHAM)

Zambia

A republic and a member of the Commonwealth of Nations, Zambia is bounded by Tanzania, Malawi, Mozambique, Rhodesia, South West Africa, Angola, and Zaire. Area: 752,614 sq km (290,586 sq mi). Pop. (1977 est.): 5,345,000, about 99% of whom are Africans. Cap. and largest city: Lusaka (pop., 1976 est., 483,000). Language: English and Bantu. Religion: predominantly animist. President in 1977, Kenneth Kaunda; prime ministers, Elijah Mudenda and, from July 20, Mainza Chona.

In 1977 fears of invasion by Rhodesian troops alarmed the country, and Pres. Kenneth Kaunda

ZAIRE

Education. (1973–74) Primary, pupils 3,538,257, teachers (1972–73) 80,481; secondary, pupils 225,606; vocational, pupils 47,579; teacher training, students 62,018; secondary, vocational, and teacher training, teachers 14,483; higher, students 19,294, teaching staff 2,550.

Finance. Monetary unit: zaire, with (Sept. 19, 1977) a free rate of 0.86 zaire to U.S. $1 (1.50 zaire = £1 sterling). Gold, SDR's, and foreign exchange (June 1977) U.S. $92,610,000. Budget (1975 actual): revenue 431.9 million zaires; expenditure 710.5 million zaires. Gross national product (1974) 1,663,800,000 zaires. Money supply (Feb. 1977) 700,230,000 zaires. Cost of living (Kinshasa; 1970 = 100; Dec. 1976) 520.

Foreign Trade. (1976) Imports 546.6 million zaires; exports 747.3 million zaires. Import sources (1975): U.S. *c.* 18%; Belgium-Luxembourg *c.* 15%; West Germany *c.* 13%; Italy *c.* 6%; U.K. *c.* 5%. Export destinations (1975): Belgium-Luxembourg *c.* 38%; Italy *c.* 14%; France *c.* 6%; West Germany *c.* 6%; U.S. *c.* 6%; U.K. *c.* 6%; Japan *c.* 5%. Main exports: copper 42%; coffee 14%; diamonds 6%.

Transport and Communications. Roads (1974) *c.* 145,000 km. Motor vehicles in use (1974): passenger 84,800; commercial (including buses) 76,400. Railways: (1975) 15,245 km; traffic (1973) 447 million passenger-km, freight 3,017,000,000 net ton-km. Air traffic (1976): 691 million passenger-km; freight 66,773,000 net ton-km. Shipping (1976): merchant vessels 100 gross tons and over 32; gross tonnage 107,278. Inland waterways (including Zaire River; 1975) 16,400 km. Telephones (Dec. 1975) 48,000. Radio receivers (Dec. 1974) 2,448,000. Television receivers (Dec. 1974) 7,000.

Agriculture. Production (in 000; metric tons; 1976): rice 210; corn *c.* 410; sweet potatoes (1975) *c.* 294; cassava (1975) 9,172; peanuts 289; dry peas (1975) *c.* 219; palm kernels 70; palm oil *c.* 170; sugar, raw value (1975) *c.* 67; bananas *c.* 76; oranges *c.* 109; coffee *c.* 63; rubber *c.* 42; cotton, lint *c.* 12; timber (cu m; 1975) *c.* 13,690; fish catch (1975) *c.* 125. Livestock (in 000; Dec. 1974): cattle 1,111; sheep *c.* 701; goats *c.* 2,256; pigs 599; poultry *c.* 10,987.

Industry. Production (in 000; metric tons; 1975): coal 90; copper 304; tin 0.6; zinc 66; manganese ore (metal content) 160; gold (troy oz) 103; silver (troy oz) 2,300; diamonds (metric carats) 12,810; petroleum products 564; electricity (kw-hr) *c.* 3,440,000.

ZAMBIA

Education. (1975) Primary, pupils 872,392, teachers 18,096; secondary, pupils 73,049, teachers 3,202; vocational, pupils 5,421, teachers 522; teacher training, students 2,467, teachers 242; higher, students 2,354, teaching staff (1970) 189.

Finance. Monetary unit: kwacha, with (Sept. 19, 1977) a free rate of 0.77 kwacha to U.S. $1 (1.35 kwacha = £1 sterling). Gold, SDR's, and foreign exchange (May 1977) U.S. $110 million. Budget (1976 actual): revenue 456.7 million kwachas; expenditure 664.1 million kwachas. Gross national product (1976) 1,707,000,000 kwachas. Cost of living (1970 = 100; Feb. 1977) 191.

Foreign Trade. (1975) Imports 732,070,000 kwachas; exports 521,050,000 kwachas. Import sources: U.K. 20%; U.S. 12%; Japan 9%; West Germany 7%; South Africa 7%. Export destinations: U.K. 22%; Japan 17%; West Germany 14%; Italy 13%; France 8%. Main export copper 91%.

Transport and Communications. Roads (1972) 34,963 km. Motor vehicles in use (1974): passenger 86,000; commercial (including buses) 62,000. Railways (1976) *c.* 2,200 km (including *c.* 900 km of the 1,870-km Tanzam railway linking Kapiri Mposhi in Zambia with Dar es Salaam in Tanzania). Air traffic (1975): 343 million passenger-km; freight 19.7 million net ton-km. Telephones (Jan. 1976) 77,000. Radio receivers (Dec. 1974) *c.* 100,000. Television receivers (Dec. 1974) 22,000.

Agriculture. Production (in 000; metric tons; 1976): corn *c.* 750; cassava (1975) *c.* 147; millet *c.* 30; sorghum *c.* 46; peanuts *c.* 30; sugar, raw value (1975) *c.* 85; tobacco *c.* 7; cotton, lint *c.* 4. Livestock (in 000; 1975): cattle *c.* 1,797; sheep *c.* 29; goats *c.* 199; pigs *c.* 122; chickens *c.* 8,227.

Industry. Production (in 000; metric tons; 1976): copper 706; coal 789; lead 20; zinc 37; electricity (kw-hr) 7,040,000.

was concerned with the constitutional problems of Rhodesia at the expense of pressing matters at home. Inflation and commodity shortages stirred up discontent, and criticism of the government's socialist policies came from businessmen and civil servants. Three ministers were dismissed for demanding changes in the country's economic and social policies, which, they claimed, were too restrictive. Also, the overwhelming success of a white man, Arthur Piers, over two African opponents in a parliamentary by-election suggested that discontent with the government was widely felt. In July Kaunda replaced his prime minister.

In May the government announced that it intended to investigate the alleged supply of oil to Rhodesia by companies with subsidiaries in South Africa. Later, however, Zambia itself was named by a UN committee as one of 12 countries violating sanctions against Rhodesia. Refugees from the war in Zaire fled into Zambia in April and May.

(KENNETH INGHAM)

Zoos and Botanical Gardens

Zoos. There was some increase in zoo attendance in 1977, despite continuing unfavourable economic conditions. Escalating food costs played a part in bankrupting many smaller establishments, and it was only the more efficient zoos that maintained progress. This point was brought home with the closing of Belle Vue Zoo, Manchester, England, one of the world's oldest zoos. Specialized zoos were increasingly in vogue as visitors no longer expected to see a representative collection of the world's animals.

With improvements in husbandry, animals were living longer in captivity, often exceeding their natural life span by many years. The Evansville (Ind.) Zoo recorded the death of a white-faced capuchin monkey at the age of 47 years 11 months, while a Philippine monkey-eating eagle survived for over 41 years at Rome. Baltimore, Md., had two avian longevity records, 19 years for an Indian blue roller and almost 20 years for a blue whistling thrush. Perhaps the most notable record was at the Philadelphia Zoo, where an orangutan died in 1976 at the age of 56 years and where there was also a 46-year-old gorilla. At Jersey Zoo in the Channel Isles a new longevity record of 15 years was set for the African civet, exceeding the old record by 3 years.

Zoos continued to exchange specimens to form compatible breeding groups, particularly of species declining in the wild state. Frankfurt (West Germany) Zoo sent its Philippine monkey-eating eagle to Los Angeles Zoo to form a potential breeding pair. There were only 6 of these birds in captivity and a maximum of 100 in the wild. Cornell University, Ithaca, N.Y., released 42 captive-bred peregrine falcons into the wild, and some showed signs of forming pairs. Jersey Zoo, which had close links with Mauritius, was setting up breeding groups of several endangered species, including the pink pigeon and the Round Island boa. Thanks

to the work of the World Wildlife Fund, lynx had been reintroduced into Yugoslavia and had bred successfully. British zoos had a long-term program for breeding gorillas; a gorilla born in July 1976 at London Zoo was fathered by a Bristol Zoo male, and Chester Zoo was trying to mate its female with a Bristol male.

Animals considered difficult to breed a few years earlier were now producing regularly. However, a world "first" for the Bateleur eagle was recorded at St. Louis, Mo., and two fairy penguins hand-reared at Melbourne, Australia, were also first-time breedings. Wuppertal, West Germany, had a "first" with barn swallows and Heidelberg, West Germany, with the brown wood owl. Palos Verdes, Calif., had the first killer whale born in captivity, but it died after 15 days. The Slimbridge Wildfowl Trust, England, bred the black-headed duck, previously reared only from eggs taken in the wild. Chester Zoo was the birthplace of the first elephant conceived and born alive (May 8, 1977) in Britain. The baby quickly became a favourite television personality.

At West Berlin the "off-show" carnivore breeding dens were equipped with closed-circuit television. Keepers were thus able to make sure that breeding females were progressing satisfactorily, and members of the public could view what was happening behind the scenes. Among the many conferences held during the year, one of the most important, on "Breeding Endangered Species," was organized by London Zoo and the Fauna Preservation Society and attended by 150 delegates from 22 countries. (G. S. MOTTERSHEAD)

This young bobcat at the Brookfield Zoo near Chicago was "adopted" by Cub Scouts. People who "adopt" pets at the Brookfield Zoo pay for their food, but the animals remain at the zoo.

GARY SETTLE—THE NEW YORK TIMES

People around the world grieved when Victor, a giraffe at Marwell Zoological Park near Winchester, England, died. Victor fell when trying to mate with a female giraffe and was unable to arise.

Botanical Gardens. Steady and continuous development characterized botanical gardens, as existing gardens were extended and new ones established by universities, public authorities, or private enterprise. Throughout the world more than 100 new establishments were being constructed where, despite man's increasing destruction of nature, rare and endangered plants might be conserved while they were still to be found in a natural state. While scientific research had been the main purpose of botanical gardens, conservation—together with public information and education—was becoming an increasingly important objective.

A number of the new gardens opened or being prepared in 1977 were in West Germany. In connection with the 450th anniversary of the Philipps-University in Marburg, the new botanical garden there was opened on June 30 after some ten years' preparation. It had an area of 20 ha and included, besides the order beds and rockery, display and service greenhouses covering, respectively, 1,590 sq m and 3,000 sq m. The total cost was DM 13 million. The University of Düsseldorf's new garden, only about 3 ha in area, featured a 1,000-sq m greenhouse in the form of a Plexiglas geodesic dome, as well as 500 sq m of experimental greenhouses and a 1,100-sq m nursery garden. At Bochum, in the Ruhr University's botanical garden, a large new tropical house was opened in April.

The University of Stuttgart's botanical garden was transferred from the immediate neighbourhood of the Wilhelma Zoological and Botanical Gardens at Bad Cannstadt to Stuttgart-Hohenheim and attached to the botanical garden of Hohenheim University, where it would serve mainly as an experimental garden. At the Munich-Nymphenburg Botanical Garden the big tropical house had been so badly damaged by a storm that it had to be demolished. Subsequently it was rebuilt, and by 1977 it was already well filled with a wide variety of tropical plants. Further restoration of some of the garden's older display houses was planned.

The University of Hamburg planned a "biocentre" in the suburb of Flottbek, in connection with which a 24-ha botanical garden had been under development since 1972. Completely new was the arrangement of order beds in the form of a botanical "family tree" showing the evolution of angiosperms, designed by the Soviet botanist Armen Takhtayan. The extensive regional section and rockery, 4,500 sq m of nursery greenhouses, and ancillary buildings were already completed.

In Switzerland the University of Zürich's new botanical garden, on a ridge along the northern shore of Lake Zürich, was opened in May. This unusually fine garden, publicly financed, featured three Plexiglas cupolas surmounting the greenhouse complex, in which an attractive plant collection was tended with the help of the latest technical equipment.

The department of botany of the University of Durham, England, was building a botanical garden according to the latest principles, mainly for the preservation of threatened vegetation within the region. To this end, extensive natural areas were taken over to provide living material for the necessary seed bank and gene reservoir. Special areas were also devoted to North American woodland plant varieties and plants from Nepal.

S. M. Walters, director of the University Botanic Garden, Cambridge, England, published a trilingual questionnaire in *Gärtnerisch-Botanischen Briefen* directed to all European botanical gardens, asking to what extent they were prepared to cooperate in the conservation of threatened plants within their regions. Positive developments in this direction were reported from botanical gardens in France, The Netherlands, West Germany, Italy, Spain, Australia, South Africa, and Mexico.

(JOHANNES APEL)

[355.C.6]

THE CASE FOR METRICATION

by Louis F. Sokol

With the United States in the process of changing to the use of the metric system as its everyday measurement language, the only question that remains is how can the job be completed at the least cost and with the least disruption to the economy. The debate that had been going on for more than 150 years over whether the United States should adopt the metric system is now only academic.

The change to the use of the metric system, or the International System of Units (SI) as it is officially called, is generally referred to as metrication. It is one of the most misunderstood developments in the United States today. One major reason for this is that the communications media lack sufficient correct information about the reasons and need for the change. As a result, erroneous and often negative information is disseminated to the public, implying that the change now under way can and should be stopped.

Joining the World. At present, every nation in the world either uses the metric system or is in the process of changing to it. In the United States the movement to adopt the SI is being led by the major companies for economic reasons. Increasingly, these companies find that their manufactured products must be based on the SI if they are to be exported. For instance, in 1978 the European Economic Community (EEC) will put into effect a requirement that all documentation and other communications concerning products imported into any EEC nation must use SI metric units. It is expected that other nations will impose similar restrictions. This is the primary reason the U.S. is going metric in the near future.

Most Americans are aware that the United States must increase its exports in order to keep its balance of payments in line. Any action that will help U.S. companies increase their exports of manufactured goods will improve the balance of payments and thus enhance the economic health of the companies and of the country at large.

Thus goods designed for export must be metric.

Louis F. Sokol, a former airline meteorologist, is president of the U.S. Metric Association, Inc., a national nonprofit organization which has been promoting the use of the metric system of measurement in U.S. schools, commerce, and industry for more than 60 years.

But it is wasteful and unrealistic for a nation to continue to work with two different measurement systems. Furthermore, workmen are more efficient when they use the same measurement system at work that they use in their homes and outside environment. It is to the advantage of the United States to complete the change to the use of SI metric units in all sectors of its society as soon as this is economically feasible.

Many of the articles on metrication allude to its allegedly horrendous cost but say nary a word about any benefits to be derived from the change. Experience overseas and with the metrication programs of U.S. companies has shown that costs invariably turn out to be much lower than original estimates indicated. With proper planning and coordination, costs can be kept to a minimum and mainly confined to the areas of education and the acquisition of metric measuring equipment. Furthermore, metrication, since it involves a change, offers an opportunity to review current practices, standards, and product lines with an eye to simplifying or rationalizing many of them, a process that could result in substantial reductions in inventory and overhead costs. Costs are a one-time factor, while benefits will continue for centuries. Metrication can be looked upon as an investment that will pay dividends far into the future.

Metrication has been opposed by some national leaders of the labour movement as well as by some representatives of small business. But experience to date has shown that people who are now using SI metric units on their jobs have had no difficulties; in many cases they have become more proficient at their tasks as a result of the simplicity of measuring and calculating in the SI. Most companies with metrication programs have given their employees the necessary training and have furnished them with the required metric tools. These companies have also assisted their suppliers in adapting to the use of SI metric units.

$10 \times 10 = 100$. A secondary reason the United States is going metric is that the SI is simpler than the English units of our customary system. Most adults have no trouble making simple monetary computations, because U.S. money is decimally based. Likewise, the relationships between multiples and submultiples of metric units are decimally based. Thus it takes less school time to teach children metric units, and the time saved in teaching measurement can be devoted to the study of other subjects. With a little effort, adults can learn the few metric units they need to know for everyday use fairly quickly.

The SI was introduced in 1960 by the 11th General Conference on Weights and Measures (CGPM). The CGPM, which meets every six years, was created by the Metric Convention in 1875. The United States was one of the 17 original signatories to that treaty. The SI contains some of the units of the original metric system developed in France almost 200 years ago along with some newer units added more recently. It consists of seven base units and two supplementary units, from which a host of derived units are formed to meet all the needs of science, commerce, and industry.

The SI is the most complete and efficient set of measurement units that man has been able to devise thus far. It is unique in that there is only one unit for any given physical quantity. For instance, the unit for energy is the joule, regardless of whether the energy is mechanical, chemical, electrical, or nuclear; regardless of whether we call it energy, work, or heat. The same holds true for the unit of power, the watt.

The SI is coherent. This means that derived units do not have multiplying factors in their definitions. This characteristic simplifies scientific and engineering calculations. The SI contains no definitions such as "550 foot-pounds per second equals one horsepower." In the SI one joule per second equals one watt.

The SI is a simple, rational system of units with a set of decimally related prefixes. The prefixes, when added to units, act as numerical multipliers that form multiples or submultiples of the units, thus providing additional units of more convenient size. Take, for example, the SI unit of length, the metre (m), which is about the length of a tall man's stride. When the prefix *milli-*, which has a value of one-thousandth, is added to *metre* it forms a new unit, the millimetre (mm), which is about the thickness of a dime. When the prefix *kilo-*, which means one thousand, is added to *metre* it forms kilometre, which is approximately two-thirds of a mile. In the SI four metric units of length, the kilometre, metre, centimetre, and millimetre, replace 12 English units of length.

While the SI includes units to meet every need, there are only a few that people will have to learn for everyday use. Some metric units are already familiar: the second, minute, and hour for time; the kilowatt for power; the volt for electric potential.

Every person should learn the following four units and three prefixes:

Quantity	Unit	Symbol	Relationship
Length	metre	m	a little longer than a yard
Volume	litre	l or L	a little larger than a quart
Mass (weight)	gram	g	a nickel has a mass of 5 grams
Temperature	degree Celsius	°C	water freezes at 0°C

Prefix	Symbol	Multiplying factor
kilo	k	1,000
centi	c	0.01
milli	m	0.001

Thinking Metric. The secret of learning SI metric units is to think metric and forget about converting back to English units for comparison. This is the approach used in the successful Australian and South African metrication programs. It is being followed in Canada, where the metric changeover in the public sector is well advanced, with all weather reporting and highway signs now on a metric basis. The use of both metric and English units on signs and measuring equipment is not recommended, because the presence of the familiar English units merely serves as a crutch that inhibits learning the new SI metric values. SI metric units should be learned by relating them to familiar activities and measurements, in much the same way that one learns a new spoken language. For instance, with temperature one should remember that water freezes at 0°C, a comfortable room temperature is 22°C, normal human body temperature is 37°C, and water boils at 100°C.

An important point to remember is that the SI is not the old metric system that many Americans learned in school or encountered while traveling in Europe decades ago. The SI has specific rules for the use of unit names and the symbols that represent them. For example, *kilo-* is always pronounced with the accent on the first syllable, whether in kilogram, kilometre, kilowatt, or whatever. Since *kilo-* is a prefix, it cannot be used alone but must always be attached to a unit name. The SI unit of length is spelled "metre," while "meter" refers to an instrument or device.

As the major thrust of metrication takes place, the most important factors are planning and the education of the public. These are the principal tasks of the 17-member U.S. Metric Board, authorized by the Metric Conversion Act of 1975.

Metrication represents progress, and progress can come about only through change. After the changeover to SI metric units is completed and Americans have become accustomed to using them, many will say, "How simple they are—why didn't we do this sooner?"

CONTRIBUTORS

Names of contributors to the Britannica Book of the Year *with the articles written by them.*
The arrangement is alphabetical by last name.

AARSDAL, STENER. Economic and Political Journalist, *Borsen*, Copenhagen.
Denmark

ADAMS, ANDREW M. Free-lance Foreign Correspondent. Author of *Ninja: The Invisible Assassins; Born to Die: The Cherry Blossom Squadrons.*
Combat Sports: *Judo; Karate; Kendo; Sumo*

AGRELLA, JOSEPH C. Turf Editor, *Chicago Sun-Times.* Co-author of *Ten Commandments for Professional Handicapping; American Race Horses.*
Equestrian Sports: *Thoroughbred Racing and Steeplechasing (in part)*

ALLABY, MICHAEL. Free-lance Writer and Lecturer. Author of *The Eco-Activists; Robots Behind the Plow; A Blueprint for Survival; The Home Farm.* Editor of *The Survival Handbook; Dictionary of the Environment.*
Environment *(in part)*

ALLAN, J. A. Lecturer in Geography, School of Oriental and African Studies, University of London.
Libya

ALSTON, REX. Broadcaster and Journalist; retired BBC Commentator. Author of *Taking the Air; Over to Rex Alston; Test Commentary; Watching Cricket.*
Biography *(in part);* **Cricket**

ANDERSON, DAVE. Sports Columnist, *New York Times.* Author of *Countdown to Super Bowl.* Co-author of *Always on the Run.*
Baseball: *Special Report*

ANDERSON, PETER J. Assistant Director, Institute of Polar Studies, Ohio State University, Columbus.
Antarctica

APEL, JOHANNES. Curator, Botanic Garden, University of Hamburg. Author of *Gärtnerisch-Botanische Briefe.*
Zoos and Botanical Gardens: *Botanical Gardens*

ARCHIBALD, JOHN J. Feature Writer and TV Columnist, *St. Louis Post-Dispatch.* Author of *Bowling for Boys and Girls.*
Bowling: *Tenpin Bowling (in part); Duckpins*

ARNOLD, BRUCE. Free-lance Journalist and Writer, Dublin. Parliamentary Correspondent, *Irish Independent.*
Biography *(in part);* **Ireland**

ARRINGTON, LEONARD J. Church Historian, Church of Jesus Christ of Latter-day Saints. Author of *Great Basin Kingdom: An Economic History of the Latter-day Saints; Charles C. Rich: Mormon General and Western Frontiersman; Building the City of God.*
Religion: *Church of Jesus Christ of Latter-day Saints*

AYTON, CYRIL J. Editor, *Motorcycle Sport*, London.
Motor Sports: *Motorcycles*

BABBITT, NATALIE. Writer and Illustrator of Children's Books. Author of *Tuck Everlasting; The Eyes of the Amaryllis.*
Literature: *Special Report*

BALLARD, MARTIN. Director, Book Development Council, London.
Publishing: *Books (in part)*

BARBER, PETER. Editor, *Tobacco*, London.
Industrial Review: *Tobacco*

BARGAD, WARREN. Ratner Professor of Hebrew Literature, Spertus College of Judaica, Chicago. Author of *Hayim Hazaz: Novelist of Ideas; Anthology of Israeli Poetry.*
Literature: *Hebrew*

BASS, HOWARD. Journalist and Broadcaster. Editor, *Winter Sports*, 1948–69. Winter Sports Correspondent, *Daily Telegraph* and *Sunday Telegraph*, London; *The Olympian*, New York City; *Canadian Skater*, Ottawa; *Skate*, London; *Skating*, Boston; *Ski Racing*, Denver; *Sport & Recreation*, London. Author of *The Sense in Sport; This Skating Age; The Magic of Skiing; International Encyclopaedia of Winter Sports; Let's Go Skating.*
Ice Hockey: *European and International;* **Winter Sports**

BATE, JOHN M. Director, Salvation Army International Information Services, London.
Biography *(in part);* **Religion:** *Salvation Army*

BAYLISS, DAVID. Chief Planner (Transportation), Greater London Council. Co-author of *Developing Patterns of Urbanization; Uses of Economics.* Advisory Editor of *Models in Urban and Regional Planning.*
Transportation *(in part)*

BEALL, JOHN V. Business Development Engineer, Fluor Utah, Inc. Author of sections 1 and 34, *Mining Engineering Handbook.* Frequent Contributor to *Mining Engineering.*
Mining and Quarrying *(in part)*

BEATTY, JAMES R. Senior Research Associate, B. F. Goodrich Research and Development Center, Brecksville, Ohio. Co-author of *Concepts in Compounding.*
Industrial Review: *Rubber*

BECKWITH, DAVID C. Correspondent and Writer, *Time* magazine, Washington, D.C.
Law: *Special Report;* **United States Statistical Supplement:** *Developments in the States in 1977*

BERGERRE, MAX. Correspondent ANSA for Vatican Affairs, Rome.
Vatican City State

BICKELHAUPT, DAVID L. Professor of Insurance and Finance, College of Administrative Science, Ohio State University, Columbus. Author of *Transition to Multiple-Line Insurance Companies; General Insurance* (9th ed.).
Industrial Review: *Insurance*

BILEFIELD, LIONEL. Technical Journalist.
Industrial Review: *Paints and Varnishes*

BINSTED, ARTHUR T. E. Chairman, British Bottlers' Institute, London.
Industrial Review: *Alcoholic Beverages (in part)*

BIRON, RODRIGUE. Leader, Union Nationale Party, Quebec National Assembly.
Canada: *Special Report*

BLYTH, ALAN. Music Critic, *Daily Telegraph*, London; Assistant Editor, *Opera*; Broadcaster.
Music: *Introduction; Opera; Symphonic*

BODDY, WILLIAM C. Editor, *Motor Sport.* Full Member, Guild of Motoring Writers. Author of *The History of Brooklands Motor Course; The World's Land Speed Record; Continental Sports Cars; The Bugatti Story; History of Montlhéry.*
Motor Sports: *Grand Prix Racing*

BOLT, PETER H. Secretary, British Committee, World Methodist Council. Author of *A Way of Loving.*
Religion: *Methodist Churches*

BOOTH, JOHN NICHOLLS. Lecturer and Writer; Co-founder, Japan Free Religious Association; Senior Pastor of a number of U.S. churches. Author of *The Quest for Preaching Power; Introducing Unitarian Universalism.*
Religion: *Unitarian Churches*

BORGESE, ELISABETH MANN. Member, Permanent Austrian Mission to the United Nations, and a leading figure in the International Ocean Institute.
Feature Article: *Managing the World's Oceans*

BOSWALL, JEFFERY. Producer of Sound and Television Programs, British Broadcasting Corporation Natural History Unit, Bristol, England.
Life Sciences: *Ornithology*

BOYLE, C. L. Lieutenant Colonel, R.A. (retd.). Chairman, Survival Service Commission, International Union for Conservation of Nature and Natural Resources, 1958–63; Secretary, Fauna Preservation Society, London, 1950–63.
Environment *(in part)*

BRACKMAN, ARNOLD C. Asian Affairs Specialist. Author of *Indonesian Communism: A History; Southeast Asia's Second Front: The Power Struggle in the Malay Archipelago; The Communist Collapse in Indonesia; The Last Emperor.*
Indonesia

BRADSHER, HENRY S. Diplomatic Correspondent, *Washington* (D.C.) *Star*.
Philippines

BRAIDWOOD, ROBERT J. Professor Emeritus of Old World Prehistory, the Oriental Institute, and Professor Emeritus, Department of Anthropology, University of Chicago. Author of *Prehistoric Men* (8th ed.).
Archaeology: *Eastern Hemisphere*

BRAZEE, RUTLAGE J. Senior Seismologist, Environmental Data Service, National Oceanic and Atmospheric Administration, Boulder, Colo.
Earth Sciences: *Geophysics*

BRECHER, KENNETH. Associate Professor of Physics, Massachusetts Institute of Technology.
Astronomy

BRUNO, HAL. Chief Political Correspondent, *Newsweek* magazine.
Biography *(in part)*

BURDIN, JOEL L. Associate Director, American Association of Colleges for Teacher Education. Co-author of *A Reader's Guide to the Comprehensive Models for Preparing Elementary Teachers; Elementary School Curriculum and Instruction*.
Education *(in part)*

BURKE, DONALD P. Executive Editor, *Chemical Week*, New York City.
Industrial Review: *Chemicals*

BURKS, ARDATH W. Special Assistant to the President; Professor of Political Science, Rutgers University, New Brunswick, N.J. Author of *The Government of Japan; East Asia: China, Korea, Japan*.
Japan

BUSS, ROBIN. Lecturer in French, Woolwich College of Further Education, London.
Literature: *French (in part)*

BUTLER, DAVID RICHARD. Information Manager, British Gas Corporation, London.
Energy: *Gas*

BUTLER, FRANK. Sports Editor, *News of the World*, London. Author of *A History of Boxing in Britain*.
Combat Sports: *Boxing*

CALHOUN, DAVID R. Editor, Encyclopædia Britannica, Yearbooks.
Gambling

CAMERON, SARAH. Economist, Lloyds Bank International Ltd., London.
Colombia; Venezuela

CARAS, ROGER. News Correspondent on Animals, ABC-TV; Pets and Wildlife Commentator, CBS Radio.
Veterinary Science: *Special Report*

CASSIDY, VICTOR M. Writer and Editor, currently at work on a biography of Wyndham Lewis.
Biography *(in part)*

CHALMEY, LUCIEN. Honorary Secretary-General, Union Internationale des

Producteurs et Distributeurs d'Énergie Électrique, Paris.
Energy: *Electricity*

CHAPMAN, KENNETH F. Editor, *Philatelic Magazine*; Philatelic Correspondent, *The Times*, London. Author of *Good Stamp Collecting; Commonwealth Stamp Collecting*.
Philately and Numismatics: *Stamps*

CHAPMAN, ROBIN. Senior Economist, Lloyds Bank International Ltd., London.
Cuba; Haiti

CHAPPELL, DUNCAN. Director, Law and Justice Study Center, Battelle Memorial Institute, Seattle, Washington. Co-author of *The Police and the·Public in Australia and New Zealand*. Co-editor of *The Australian Criminal Justice System; Violence and Criminal Justice*.
Crime and Law Enforcement

CHOATE, ROGER NYE. Stockholm Correspondent, *The Times*, London.
Biography *(in part)*; **Sweden**

CHU, HUNG-TI. Expert in Far Eastern Affairs; Former International Civil Servant and University Professor.
China; Taiwan

CLARKE, R. O. Principal Administrator, Social Affairs and Industrial Relations Division, Organization for Economic Cooperation and Development, Paris. Co-author of *Workers' Participation in Management in Britain*.
Industrial Relations

CLEVELAND, WILLIAM A. Geography Editor, *Encyclopædia Britannica* and Britannica Yearbooks.
Mining and Quarrying *(in part)*

CLIFTON, DONALD F. Professor of Metallurgy, University of Idaho.
Materials Sciences: *Metallurgy*

CLOUD, STANLEY W. White House Correspondent, *Time* magazine.
Biography *(in part)*

COGLE, T. C. J. Editor, *Electrical Review*, London.
Industrial Review: *Electrical*

COLLINS, L. J. D. Lecturer in Bulgarian History, University of London.
Cyprus

COPPOCK, CHARLES DENNIS. President, English Lacrosse Union. Author of "Men's Lacrosse" in *The Oxford Companion to Sports and Games*.
Field Hockey and Lacrosse *(in part)*

COSTIN, STANLEY H. British Correspondent, *Herrenjournal International* and *Men's Wear*, Australasia. Council of Management Member, British Men's Fashion Association Ltd. Former President, Men's Fashion Writers International.
Fashion and Dress *(in part)*

CRATER, RUFUS W. Chief Correspondent, *Broadcasting*, Washington, D.C.
Television and Radio *(in part)*

CROSSLAND, NORMAN. Bonn Correspondent, *The Economist*, London.
German Democratic Republic; Germany, Federal Republic of

CVIIC, K. F. Leader Writer and East European Specialist, *The Economist*, London.
Yugoslavia

DAIFUKU, HIROSHI. Chief, Section for Operations and Training, Cultural Heritage Division, UNESCO, Paris.
Historic Preservation

DARBY, ALAN J. H. Publisher and Journalist. Managing Editor, *Sudanow*, Khartoum, Sudan. Khartoum Correspondent, *Financial Times*, London. Director, Alan Darby Publications Ltd., Bromsgrove, England.
Sudan

DAUME, DAPHNE. Editor, Encyclopædia Britannica, Yearbooks.
Biography *(in part)*

DAVID, TUDOR. Managing Editor, *Education*, London.
Education *(in part)*

DAVIS, DONALD A. Editor, *Drug & Cosmetic Industry*, New York City. Contributor to *The Science and Technology of Aerosol Packaging*.
Industrial Review: *Pharmaceuticals*

DAVIS, RUTH M. U.S. Deputy Under Secretary of Defense for Research and Advanced Technology. Former Director, Institute for Computer Sciences and Technology, U.S. National Bureau of Standards.
Computers

d'EÇA, RAUL. Retired from foreign service with U.S. Information Service. Co-author of *Latin American History*.
Brazil

DECRAENE, PHILIPPE. Member of editorial staff, *Le Monde*, Paris. Editor in Chief, *Revue française d'Études politiques africaines*. Author of *Le Panafricanisme; Tableau des Partis Politiques Africains; Lettres de l'Afrique Atlantique*.
Benin; Cameroon; Central African Empire; Chad; Comoro Islands; Congo; Dependent States *(in part)*; **Djibouti; Gabon; Guinea; Ivory Coast; Madagascar; Mali; Mauritania; Niger; Senegal; Togo; Tunisia; Upper Volta**

de la BARRE, KENNETH. Staff Scientist, Arctic Institute of North America, Montreal.
Arctic Regions

DELSON, ERIC. Associate Professor of Anthropology, Lehman College, City University of New York. Research Associate, Vertebrate Paleontology, American Museum of Natural History. Co-author of *A Handbook of Fossil Primates*.
Anthropology

DE PUY, NORMAN R. Pastor and Executive Minister, First Baptist Church of Dearborn, Mich. Author of *The Bible Alive*.
Religion: *Baptist Churches*

DERIAN, PATRICIA M. Coordinator, Office of Human Rights and Humanitarian Affairs, U.S. Department of State.

Feature Article: *Human Rights—The U.S. Initiative*

DIRNBACHER, ELFRIEDE. Austrian Civil Servant.
Austria

DOWBOR, PAUL. Economist, Lloyds Bank International Ltd., London.
Uruguay

DUNICAN, PETER. Chairman, Ove Arup Partnership, London.
Engineering Projects: *Buildings*

EIU. The Economist Intelligence Unit, London.
Economy, World (in part)

ENGELS, JAN R. Editor, *Vooruitgang* (Quarterly of the Belgian Party for Freedom and Progress), Brussels.
Belgium

EVANS, JOSEPH H. President, United Church of Christ, New York City.
Religion: *United Church of Christ*

EWART, W. D. Editor and Director, *Fairplay International Shipping Weekly*, London. Author of *Marine Engines; Atomic Submarines; Hydrofoils and Hovercraft; Building a Ship.* Editor of *World Atlas of Shipping.*
Industrial Review: *Shipbuilding;* **Transportation** (in part)

FABINYI, ANDREW. Director, Longman Cheshire Pty. Ltd., Sydney, Australia.
Publishing: *Books* (in part)

FARR, D. M. L. Professor of History, Carleton University, Ottawa. Co-author of *The Canadian Experience.*
Canada

FENDELL, ROBERT J. Auto Editor, *Science & Mechanics;* Auto Contributor, *Gentlemen's Quarterly.* Author of *The New Era Car Book and Auto Survival Guide.* Co-author of *Encyclopedia of Motor Racing Greats.*
Motor Sports: *U.S. Racing*

FERRIER, R. W. Group Historian, British Petroleum Company Ltd., London.
Energy: *Petroleum*

FIDDICK, PETER. Specialist Writer, *The Guardian*, London.
Biography (in part); **Publishing:** *Introduction; Newspapers* (in part); *Magazines* (in part)

FIELDS, DONALD. Helsinki Correspondent, BBC, *The Guardian*, and *The Sunday Times*, London.
Finland

FIRTH, DAVID. Editor, *The Friend*, London; formerly Editor, *Quaker Monthly*, London.
Religion: *Religious Society of Friends*

FISHER, DAVID. Civil Engineer, Freeman Fox & Partners, London; formerly Executive Editor, *Engineering*, London.
Engineering Projects: *Bridges*

FLANAGAN, JACK. Special Group Travel Newspaper Columnist.
Water Sports: *Surfing*

FOWELL, R. J. Lecturer, Department of Mining Engineering, University of Newcastle upon Tyne, England.
Energy: *Coal*

FRADY, WILLIAM ENSIGN, III. Editor, *Water Polo Scoreboard*, Newport Beach, Calif.
Water Sports: *Water Polo*

FRANCO, JEAN. Chairperson, Department of Spanish and Portuguese, Stanford University. Author of *The Modern Culture of Latin America; An Introduction to Spanish-American Literature; César Vallejo: The Dialectics of Poetry and Silence.*
Literature: *Spanish* (in part)

FRANKLIN, HAROLD. Editor, *English Bridge Quarterly.* Bridge Correspondent, *Yorkshire Post; Yorkshire Evening Post.* Broadcaster. Author of *Best of Bridge on the Air.*
Biography (in part); **Contract Bridge**

FRANZ, FREDERICK W. President, Watch Tower Bible and Tract Society of Pennsylvania.
Religion: *Jehovah's Witnesses*

FRAWLEY, MARGARET-LOUISE. Press Officer, All-England Women's Lacrosse Association.
Field Hockey and Lacrosse (in part)

FRENCH, RICHARD ANTONY. Senior Lecturer in the Geography of the U.S.S.R., University College and School of Slavonic and East European Studies, University of London. Author of *The U.S.S.R. and Eastern Europe.*
Special Preprint: *Novosibirsk*

FRIDOVICH, IRWIN. James B. Duke Professor of Biochemistry, Duke University Medical Center, Durham, N.C. Contributor to *Oxidase and Redox Systems; Molecular Mechanisms of Oxygen Activation.*
Life Sciences: *Molecular Biology* (in part)

FRIEDLY, ROBERT LOUIS. Executive Director, Office of Communication, Christian Church (Disciples of Christ), Indianapolis, Ind.
Religion: *Disciples of Christ*

FROST, DAVID. Rugby Union Correspondent, *The Guardian*, London.
Football: *Rugby*

GADDUM, PETER W. Chairman, H. T. Gaddum and Company Ltd., Silk Merchants, Macclesfield, Cheshire, England. Honorary President, International Silk Association, Lyons. Author of *Silk—How and Where It Is Produced.*
Industrial Review: *Textiles* (in part)

GANADO, ALBERT. Lawyer, Malta.
Malta

GEORGE, T. J. S. Editor, *Asiaweek*, Hong Kong. Author of *Krishna Menon: A Biography; Lee Kuan Yew's Singapore.*
Biography (in part); **Cambodia; Korea; Laos; Southeast Asian Affairs; Thailand; Vietnam**

GJESTER, FAY. Oslo Correspondent, *Financial Times*, London.
Norway

GOLDSMITH, ARTHUR. Editorial Director, *Popular Photography*, New York City. Author of *The Photography Game; The Nude in Photography.* Co-author of *The Eye of Eisenstaedt.*
Photography

GOLOMBEK, HARRY. British Chess Champion, 1947, 1949, and 1955. Chess Correspondent, *The Times* and *Observer*, London. Author of *Penguin Handbook of the Game of Chess; A History of Chess.*
Chess

GOODWIN, R. M. Free-lance Writer, London.
Biography (in part); **Equestrian Sports:** *Thoroughbred Racing and Steeplechasing* (in part)

GOODWIN, ROBERT E. Executive Director, Billiard Congress of America, Chicago. Publisher-Editor of various trade magazines.
Billiard Games

GOULD, DONALD W. Medical Correspondent, *New Statesman*, London.
Health and Disease: *Overview* (in part); *Mental Health* (in part)

GRAHAM, RONALD L. Head, Discrete Mathematics Department, Bell Laboratories, Murray Hill, N.J.
Mathematics: *Special Report*

GREEN, BENNY. Jazz Critic, *Observer*, London; Record Reviewer, British Broadcasting Corporation. Author of *The Reluctant Art; Blame It on My Youth; 58 Minutes to London; Jazz Decade; Drums in My Ears.* Contributor to *Encyclopedia of Jazz.*
Music: *Jazz*

GREENE, FREDERICK D. Professor of Chemistry, Massachusetts Institute of Technology.
Chemistry: *Organic*

GRIFFITHS, A. R. G. Senior Lecturer in History, Flinders University of South Australia. Author of *Contemporary Australia:*
Australia; Australia: *Special Report;* **Biography** (in part); **Nauru; Papua New Guinea**

GROSSBERG, ROBERT H. Executive Director, U.S. Amateur Jai Alai Players Association, Miami, Fla.
Court Games: *Jai Alai*

GROSSMAN, JOEL W. Director, Archaeological Survey Office, Rutgers University, New Brunswick, N.J.
Archaeology: *Western Hemisphere*

GUNDLACH, RICHARD G. Communications Editor, *Electronics* magazine.
Industrial Review: *Telecommunications*

HALE, JOHN. Economist, Lloyds Bank International Ltd., London.
Chile; Latin-American Affairs

HANSEN, NILES MAURICE. Professor of Economics, University of Texas. Author of *Public Policy and Regional Economic Development; Human Settlement Systems.*
United States: *Special Report*

HARDMAN, THOMAS C. Editor and Publisher, *The Water Skier*, American Wa-

ter Ski Association. Co-author of *Let's Go Water Skiing*.
Water Sports: *Water Skiing*

HARRIES, DAVID A. Director, Kinnear Moodie (1973) Ltd., Peterborough, England.
Engineering Projects: *Tunnels*

HASEGAWA, RYUSAKU. Editor, TBS-Britannica Co., Ltd., Tokyo.
Baseball (*in part*)

HAWKLAND, WILLIAM D. Professor of Law, University of Illinois, Urbana-Champaign. Author of *Sale and Bulk Sale Under the Uniform Commercial Code; Cases on Bills and Notes; Transactional Guide of the Uniform Commerical Code; Cases on Sales and Security*.
Law: *Court Decisions*

HAWLEY, H. B. Specialist, Human Nutrition and Food Science, Switzerland.
Food Processing

HEBBLETHWAITE, PETER. Lecturer, Wadham College, Oxford, England. Author of *Bernanos; The Council Fathers and Atheism; Understanding the Synod; The Runaway Church; Christian-Marxist Dialogue and Beyond*.
Religion: *Roman Catholic Church*

HEINDL, L. A. Executive Secretary, U.S. National Committee on Scientific Hydrology, U.S. Geological Survey National Center, Reston, Va. Author of *The Water We Live By*. Co-editor of *Hydrological Maps*.
Earth Sciences: *Hydrology*

HENDERSHOTT, MYRL C. Professor of Oceanography, Scripps Institution of Oceanography, La Jolla, Calif.
Earth Sciences: *Oceanography*

HERMAN, ROBIN CATHY. Sports Reporter, *New York Times*.
Ice Hockey: *North American*

HESS, MARVIN G. Executive Vice-President, National Wrestling Coaches Association, Salt Lake City, Utah.
Combat Sports: *Wrestling*

HOLLANDS, R. L. Hockey Correspondent, *Daily Telegraph*, London. Chairman, Hockey Writers Club; Vice-President, Hockey Association. Co-author of *Hockey*.
Field Hockey and Lacrosse (*in part*)

HOPE, THOMAS W. President, Hope Reports, Inc., Rochester, N.Y. Author of *Hope Reports AV-USA; Hope Reports Education and Media; Hope Reports Perspective*.
Motion Pictures (*in part*)

HORRY, JOHN H. Former Secretary, International Squash Rackets Federation. Contributor to *The Oxford Companion to Sports and Games*.
Racket Games: *Squash Rackets*

HORSBRUGH-PORTER, SIR ANDREW. Former Polo Correspondent, *The Times*, London.
Equestrian Sports: *Polo*

HOTZ, LOUIS. Former Editorial Writer, the *Johannesburg (S.Af.) Star*. Co-author and contributor to *The Jews in South Africa: A History*.
South Africa

HOWKINS, JOHN. Editor, *InterMedia*, International Institute of Communications, London. Author of *Understanding Television*.
Television and Radio (*in part*)

HUNNINGS, NEVILLE MARCH. General Editor, Common Law Reports Ltd., London. Editor of *Common Market Law Reports, European Law Digest*, and *Eurolaw Commercial Intelligence*. Author of *Film Censors and the Law*. Co-editor of *Legal Problems of an Enlarged European Community*.
Law: *International Law*

INGHAM, KENNETH. Professor of History, University of Bristol, England. Author of *Reformers in India; A History of East Africa*.
Angola; Cape Verde; Guinea-Bissau; Kenya; Malawi; Mozambique; Rhodesia; Tanzania; Uganda; Zaire; Zambia

IRF. International Road Federation, Geneva.
Engineering Projects: *Roads*

ISSA. International Social Security Association, Geneva.
Social and Welfare Services (*in part*)

JACQUET, CONSTANT H. Staff Associate for Information Services, Office of Research, Evaluation and Planning, National Council of Churches. Editor of *Yearbook of American and Canadian Churches*.
United States Statistical Supplement: *Church Membership Table*

JARDINE, ADRIAN. Company Director and Public Relations Consultant. Member, Guild of Yachting Writers.
Sailing

JASPERT, W. PINCUS. Technical Editorial Consultant. European Editor, North American Publishing Company, Philadelphia, Pa. Member, Inter-Comprint Planning Committee; Member, Society of Photographic Engineers and Scientists. Editor of *Encyclopaedia of Type Faces*.
Industrial Review: *Printing*

JOFFÉ, EMIL G. H. Journalist and Writer on North African Affairs.
Algeria; Morocco

JONES, C. M. Editor, *World Bowls; Tennis*. Member, British Society of Sports Psychology; Associate Member, British Association of National Coaches. Author of *Winning Bowls; How to Become a Champion*; numerous books on tennis. Co-author of *Tackle Bowls My Way; Bryant on Bowls*.
Bowling: *Lawn Bowls*

JONES, W. GLYN. Professor of Scandinavian Studies, University of Newcastle upon Tyne, England. Author of *Johannes Jørgensens modne år; Johannes Jørgensen; Denmark; William Heinesen; Føroe og kosmos*.
Literature: *Danish*

JOSEPH, LOU. Manager of Media Relations, Bureau of Public Information, American Dental Association. Author of

A Doctor Discusses Allergy: Facts and Fiction; Natural Childbirth.
Health and Disease: *Dentistry*

KAAN, FREDERIK H. Secretary of the Department of Cooperation and Witness, World Alliance of Reformed Churches (Presbyterian and Congregational), Geneva. Author of *Pilgrim Praise; Break Not the Circle* (hymnals).
Religion: *Presbyterian, Reformed, and Congregational Churches*

KANEDA, TAKEAKI. Asian Director, *Sports Illustrated*. Author of *Intellectual Golf*. Translator of *Square-to-Square Golf in Pictures; Total Golf; Shape Your Swing the Modern Way*.
Biography (*in part*)

KATZ, WILLIAM A. Professor, School of Library Science, State University of New York, Albany. Author of *Magazines for Libraries* (2nd ed. and supplement); *Magazine Selection*.
Publishing: *Magazines* (*in part*)

KEDOURIE, ELIE. Professor of Politics, London School of Economics and Political Science. Fellow, British Academy. Author of *Arabic Political Memoirs; In the Anglo-Arab Labyrinth; Nationalism in Asia and Africa*.
Feature Article: *The New Nationalism: Conflicts and Hopes*

KELLEHER, JOHN A. Editor, *The Dominion*, Wellington, N.Z.
Biography (*in part*); **New Zealand**

KELLMAN, JEROLD L. Executive Editor, Publications International, Ltd. Author of *Presidents of the United States*; Contributor to *The People's Almanac*.
Biography (*in part*)

KENNEDY, RICHARD M. Agricultural Economist, Foreign Demand and Competition Division, Economic Research Service, U.S. Department of Agriculture.
Agriculture and Food Supplies

KERRIGAN, ANTHONY. Visiting Professor, University of Illinois. Editor and Translator of *Selected Works* of Miguel de Unamuno (7 vol.) and of works of Jorge Luis Borges. Author of *At the Front Door of the Atlantic*.
Literature: *Spanish* (*in part*)

KILIAN, MICHAEL D. Columnist, *Chicago Tribune*; News Commentator, WTTW Television and WBBM Radio, Chicago.
Aerial Sports

KILLHEFFER, JOHN V. Associate Editor, *Encyclopædia Britannica*.
Nobel Prizes (*in part*)

KIMCHE, JON. Editor, *Afro-Asian Affairs*, London. Author of *There Could Have Been Peace: The Untold Story of Why We Failed With Palestine and Again with Israel; Seven Fallen Pillars*.
Biography (*in part*); **Israel**

KIND, JOSHUA B. Associate Professor of Art History, Northern Illinois University, De Kalb. Author of *Rouault; Naive Art in Illinois 1830–1976*.
Museums (*in part*)

KIRSCHTEN, J. DICKEN. Staff Correspondent, *National Journal*, Washington, D.C.
Feature Article: *A New Alternative in the Energy Crisis*

KITAGAWA, JOSEPH MITSUO. Professor of History of Religions and Dean of the Divinity School, University of Chicago. Author of *Religions of the East; Religion in Japanese History.*
Religion: *Buddhism*

KLARE, HUGH J. Chairman, Gloucestershire Probation Training Committee, England. Secretary, Howard League for Penal Reform 1950–71. Author of *People in Prison.* Regular Contributor to *Justice of the Peace.*
Prisons and Penology

KNECHT, JEAN. Formerly Assistant Foreign Editor, *Le Monde*, Paris; formerly Permanent Correspondent in Washington and Vice-President of the Association de la Presse Diplomatique Française
France

KOPPER, PHILIP. Free-lance Writer, Washington, D.C.
Biography (*in part*); **Nobel Prizes** (*in part*)

KOUTCHOUMOW, JOSEPH A. Secretary-General, International Publishers Association, Geneva. Author of art and children's books.
Publishing: *Books* (*in part*)

KOVAN, RICHARD W. Deputy Editor, *Nuclear Engineering International*, London.
Industrial Review: *Nuclear Industry*

KWAN-TERRY, JOHN. Senior Lecturer, Department of English Language and Literature, University of Singapore. Editor of *The Teaching of Languages in Institutions of Higher Learning in Southeast Asia.*
Literature: *Chinese*

LAMB, KEVIN M. Sports Writer, *Chicago Daily News.*
Biography (*in part*); **Football:** *U.S. Football; Canadian Football*

LARSON, ROY. Religion Editor, *Chicago Sun-Times.*
Religion: *Introduction*

LEAPER, ERIC. Executive Secretary, American Canoe Association, Denver, Colo.
Water Sports: *Canoeing*

LEGUM, COLIN. Associate Editor, *The Observer*, and Editor, *Africa Contemporary Record*, London. Author of *Must We Lose Africa?; Congo Disaster; Pan-Africanism: A Political Guide; South Africa: Crisis for the West.*
African Affairs; Biography (*in part*)

LEIFER, MICHAEL. Reader in International Relations, London School of Economics and Political Science. Author of *Dilemmas of Statehood in Southeast Asia.*
Malaysia; Singapore

LENNOX-KERR, PETER. European Editor, *Textile World.* Author of *Index to Man-Made Fibres Book.* Editor of *Nonwovens '71*; Publisher of *OE-Report*, New Mills, England.
Industrial Review: *Textiles* (*in part*)

LITTELL, FRANKLIN H. Professor of Religion, Temple University, Philadelphia, Pa. Co-editor of *Weltkirchenlexikon*; Author of *Macmillan Atlas History of Christianity.*
Religion: *World Church Membership*

LOEFFLER, EDWARD J. Technical Director, National Machine Tool Builders' Association, McLean, Va.
Industrial Review: *Machinery and Machine Tools*

LOTERY, FRANÇOISE. Economist, Lloyds Bank International Ltd., London.
Costa Rica; Ecuador; Guatemala; Paraguay

LULING, VIRGINIA R. Social Anthropologist.
Somalia

LUNDE, ANDERS S. Consultant; Adjunct Professor, Department of Biostatistics, University of North Carolina. Author of *Systems of Demographic Measurement: The Single Round Retrospective Interview Survey.*
Demography

MACDONALD, BARRIE. Lecturer in History, Massey University, Palmerston North, N.Z. Author of several articles on the history and politics of Pacific islands.
Dependent States (*in part*); **Fiji; Tonga; Western Samoa**

MacDONALD, M. C. Director, World Economics Ltd., London.
Agriculture and Food Supplies: *grain table;* **Transportation:** *table;* statistical sections of articles on the various countries

MACDONALD, TREVOR J. Manager, International Affairs, British Steel Corporation.
Industrial Review: *Iron and Steel*

MACGREGOR-MORRIS, PAMELA. Equestrian Correspondent, *The Times* and *Horse and Hound*, London. Author of books on equestrian topics.
Equestrian Sports: *Show Jumping*

MALLETT, H. M. F. Editor, *Weekly Wool Chart*, Bradford, England.
Industrial Review: *Textiles* (*in part*)

MANGO, ANDREW. Orientalist and Broadcaster.
Turkey

MANSFIELD, PETER. Former Middle East Correspondent, *Sunday Times*, London. Free-lance Writer on Middle Eastern affairs.
Feature Article: *Petrodollars and Social Change;* **Bahrain; Biography** (*in part*); **Egypt; Iraq; Jordan; Kuwait; Lebanon; Middle Eastern Affairs; Oman; Qatar; Saudi Arabia; Syria; United Arab Emirates; Yemen, People's Democratic Republic of; Yemen Arab Republic**

MARKS, SHULA E. Lecturer in the History of South Africa, School of Oriental and African Studies and Institute of Commonwealth Studies, University of London. Co-editor, *Journal of African History.* Author of *Reluctant Rebellion: The 1906–08 Disturbances in Natal.*
Special Preprint: *Southern Africa, History of*

MARSHALL, J. G. SCOTT. Horticultural Consultant.
Gardening (*in part*)

MARTENHOFF, JAMES E. Boating Editor, *Miami* (Fla.) *Herald.* Author of *Handbook of Skin and Scuba Diving; The Powerboat Handbook.*
Water Sports: *Motorboating*

MARTY, MARTIN E. Professor of the History of Modern Christianity, University of Chicago; Associate Editor, *The Christian Century.*
Religion: *Special Report*

MARYLES, DAISY G. Associate Editor, Bookselling and Marketing, *Publishers Weekly*, New York City.
Publishing: *Books* (*in part*)

MATEJA, JAMES L. Auto Editor and Financial Reporter, *Chicago Tribune.*
Industrial Review: *Automobiles*

MATTHÍASSON, BJÖRN. Economist, European Free Trade Association, Geneva.
Iceland

MAURON, PAUL. Director, International Vine and Wine Office, Paris.
Industrial Review: *Alcoholic Beverages* (*in part*)

MAZIE, DAVID M. Associate of Carl T. Rowan, syndicated columnist. Free-lance Writer.
Social and Welfare Services (*in part*)

MAZZE, EDWARD MARK. Dean and Professor of Marketing, W. Paul Stillman School of Business, Seton Hall University, South Orange, N.J. Author of *Personal Selling: Choice Against Chance; Introduction to Marketing: Readings in the Discipline.*
Consumerism (*in part*); **Industrial Review:** *Advertising*

MELLBLOM, NEIL B. Director, News Bureau, Lutheran Council in the USA, New York City.
Religion: *Lutheran Churches*

MEYENDORFF, JOHN. Professor of Church History and Patristics, St. Vladimir's Orthodox Theological Seminary; Professor of History, Fordham University, New York City. Author of *Christ in Eastern Christian Thought; Byzantine Theology.*
Religion: *The Orthodox Church*

MILES, PETER W. Chairman, Department of Entomology, University of Adelaide, Australia.
Life Sciences: *Entomology*

MILLIKIN, SANDRA. Architectural Historian.
Architecture; Art Exhibitions; Museums (*in part*)

MITCHELL, K. K. Lecturer, Department of Physical Education, University of Leeds, England. Honorary General Secretary, English Basket Ball Association.
Basketball (*in part*)

MODIANO, MARIO. Athens Correspondent, *The Times*, London.
Greece

MODRICH, PAUL LAWRENCE. Assistant Professor of Biochemistry, Duke University Medical Center, Durham, N.C.
Life Sciences: *Molecular Biology* (*in part*)

MONACO, ALBERT M., JR. Executive Director, United States Volleyball Association, San Francisco, Calif.
Court Games: *Volleyball*

MORGAN, HAZEL. Production Assistant (Sleevenotes and Covers), E.M.I. Records Ltd., London
Music: *Popular*

MORRISON, DONALD. Associate Editor, *Time* magazine.
Publishing: *Newspapers* (*in part*)

MORTIMER, MOLLY. Commonwealth Correspondent, *The Spectator*, London. Author of *Trusteeship in Practice; Kenya.*
Botswana; Burundi; Commonwealth of Nations; Dependent States (*in part*)**; Equatorial Guinea; Gambia, The; Ghana; Lesotho; Liberia; Maldives; Mauritius; Nigeria; Rwanda; Seychelles; Sierra Leone; Swaziland**

MOTTERSHEAD, G. S. Director-Secretary, Chester Zoo, Chester, England.
Zoos and Botanical Gardens: *Zoos*

MUCK, TERRY CHARLES. Editor, *Handball* magazine, Skokie, Ill.
Court Games: *Handball*

MULLINS, STEPHANIE. Historian, London.
Biography (*in part*)

NAYLOR, ERNEST. Professor of Marine Biology, University of Liverpool; Director, Marine Biological Laboratory, Port Erin, Isle of Man. Author of *British Marine Isopods.*
Life Sciences: *Marine Biology*

NEILL, JOHN. Technical Manager, Submerged Combustion Ltd. Author of *Climbers' Club Guides; Cwm Silyn and Tremadoc, Snowdon South; Alpine Club Guide: Selected Climbs in the Pennine Alps.*
Mountaineering

NELSON, BERT. Editor, *Track and Field News.* Author of *Little Red Book; The Decathlon Book; Olympic Track and Field.*
Track and Field Sports

NETSCHERT, BRUCE C. Vice-President, National Economic Research Associates, Inc., Washington, D.C. Author of *The Future Supply of Oil and Gas.* Co-author of *Energy in the American Economy: 1850–1975.*
Energy: *World Summary*

NEUSNER, JACOB. University Professor, Brown University, Providence, R.I. Author of *Invitation to the Talmud; A History of the Mishnaic Law of Purities.*
Religion: *Judaism*

NOEL, H. S. Free-lance Journalist; Former Managing Editor, *World Fishing*, London.
Fisheries

NOORDZIJ, GERARD P. Assistant Professor, Department of Political Science, Free University of Amsterdam. Author of *Systeem en beleid.*
Netherlands, The; Surinam

NORMAN, GERALDINE. Saleroom Correspondent, *The Times*, London. Author of *The Sale of Works of Art.*
Art Sales

NOVALES, RONALD R. Professor of Biological Sciences, Northwestern University, Evanston, Ill. Contributor to *Handbook of Physiology; Comparative Animal Physiology.*
Life Sciences: *Zoology Overview*

NOVICK, JULIUS. Associate Professor of Literature, State University of New York at Purchase. Author of *Beyond Broadway: The Quest for Permanent Theatres.*
Theatre (*in part*)

OSBORNE, KEITH. Editor, *Rowing,* 1961–63; Honorary Editor, *British Rowing Almanack,* 1961-   . Author of *Boat Racing in Britain, 1715–1975.*
Rowing

OSTERBIND, CARTER C. Director, Bureau of Economic and Business Research, University of Florida. Editor of *Income in Retirement; Migration, Mobility, and Aging; Social Goals, Social Programs and the Aging.*
Industrial Review: *Building and Construction*

OVSYANNIKOV, ALEKSEY. Editor in Chief, *Knizhnoye Obozreniye,* Moscow.
Literature: *Russian* (*in part*)

PAGE, SHEILA A. B. Research Officer, National Institute of Economic and Social Research, London.
Economy, World (*in part*)

PALMER, JOHN. European Editor, *The Guardian*, London.
European Unity

PALMER, S. B. Senior Lecturer, Department of Applied Physics, University of Hull, England.
Physics

PALS, CLARENCE H. Consultant. Former Executive Vice-President, U.S. National Association of Federal Veterinarians; former Director, Federal Meat Inspection Service, U.S. Department of Agriculture. Former Editor, *The Federal Veterinarian.*
Veterinary Science

PARKER, SANDY. Publisher, *Sandy Parker Reports,* a weekly newsletter of the fur industry.
Industrial Review: *Furs*

PARNELL, COLIN. Consultant. Editor, *Wine and Spirit*, London. Publisher, *Decanter Magazine*, London.
Industrial Review: *Alcoholic Beverages* (*in part*)

PATTERSON, SHEILA. Research Associate, Department of Anthropology, University College, London. Author of *Colour and Culture in South Africa; Dark Strangers; Immigrants in Industry.* Co-editor of *Studies in African Social Anthropology.*
Bahamas, The; Barbados; Dependent States (*in part*)**; Grenada; Guyana; Jamaica; Migration, International; Race Relations; Trinidad and Tobago.**

PAUL, CHARLES ROBERT, JR. Director of Communications, U.S. Olympic Committee, New York City. Author of *The Olympic Games, 1968.*
Gymnastics and Weight Lifting

PENFOLD, ROBIN C. Free-lance Writer specializing in industrial topics. Editor, *Shell Polymers.* Author of *A Journalist's Guide to Plastics.*
Industrial Review: *Plastics*

PERTILE, LINO. Lecturer in Italian, University of Sussex, England.
Literature: *Italian*

PETHERICK, KARIN. Crown Princess Louise Lecturer in Swedish, University College, London.
Literature: *Swedish*

PFEFFER, IRVING. Attorney. President, Dover Insurance Co., Ltd. Author of *The Financing of Small Business; Perspectives on Insurance.*
Stock Exchanges (*in part*)

PICK, OTTO. Professor of International Relations, University of Surrey, Guildford, England. Co-author of *Collective Security.*
Union of Soviet Socialist Republics

PLOTKIN, FREDERICK S. Professor of English Literature and Chairman, Division of Humanities, Stern College, Yeshiva University, New York City. Author of *Milton's Inward Jerusalem; Faith and Reason; Judaism and Tragic Theology.*
Literature: *United States*

POLLITT, BRIAN HARRY. Lecturer, Institute of Latin-American Studies, Glasgow University; Visiting Lecturer, Economics Department, University of Massachusetts, Amherst.
Cuba: *Special Report*

PRASAD, H.Y. SHARADA. Political Journalist, Prime Minister's Secretariat, New Delhi, India.
India

PRICE, FREDERICK C. World News Correspondent for the chemical and oil industries, McGraw-Hill. Formerly Managing Editor, *Chemical Engineering.* Editor of McGraw-Hill's *1972 Report on Business & the Environment.*
Chemistry: *Applied*

RANGER, ROBIN J. Associate Professor, Department of Political Science, St. Francis Xavier University, Antigonish, Nova Scotia. Author of *Arms and Politics* (forthcoming 1978).
Defense; Defense: *Special Report*

RAY, G. F. Senior Research Fellow, National Institute of Economic and Social Research, London; Visiting Professor, University of Surrey, Guildford, England.
Industrial Review: *Introduction*

RECKERT, STEPHEN. Camoens Professor of Portuguese, King's College, University of London. Author of *Do cancioneiro de amigo; Gil Vicente: espíritu y letra.*
Literature: *Portuguese* (*in part*)

REIBSTEIN, JOAN NATALIE. Associate Editor, Wesleyan University Press, Middletown, Conn.
Biography (*in part*)

REICHELDERFER, F. W. Consultant on Atmospheric Sciences; Former Director, Weather Bureau, U.S.Department of Commerce, Washington, D.C.
Earth Sciences: *Meteorology*

REID, J. H. Senior Lecturer in German, University of Nottingham, England. Co-editor of *Renaissance and Modern Studies.* Author of *Heinrich Böll: Withdrawal and Re-emergence.*
Literature: *German*

REYNOLDS, ARTHUR GUY. Former Registrar and Professor of Church History, Emmanuel College, Toronto.
Religion: *United Church of Canada*

ROBINSON, DAVID. Film Critic, *The Times,* London. Author of *Buster Keaton; The Great Funnies—A History of Screen Comedy; A History of World Cinema.*
Motion Pictures (*in part*)

RODERICK, JOHN. Foreign Correspondent in Tokyo, Associated Press. Author of *What You Should Know About China.*
Biography (*in part*)

ROSEVEARE, J. C. A. Partner, Freeman Fox & Partners, London.
Engineering Projects: *Dams*

SAEKI, SHOICHI. Professor of Comparative Literature, University of Tokyo. Author of *In Search of Japanese Ego.*
Literature: *Japanese*

SAINT-AMOUR, ROBERT. Professor, Department of Literary Studies, University of Quebec at Montreal.
Literature: *French*

SANDON, HAROLD. Former Professor of Zoology, University of Khartoum, Sudan. Author of *The Protozoan Fauna of the Soil; The Food of Protozoa; An Illustrated Guide to the Fresh-Water Fishes of the Sudan; Essays on Protozoology.*
Life Sciences: *Introduction*

SARAHETE, YRJÖ. Secretary, Fédération Internationale des Quilleurs, Helsinki.
Bowling: *Tenpin Bowling* (*in part*)

SCHOENFIELD, ALBERT. Publisher, *Swimming World.* Contributor to *The Technique of Water Polo; The History of Swimming; Competitive Swimming as I See It.*
Swimming

SCHÖPFLIN, GEORGE. Lecturer in East European Political Institutions, London School of Economics and School of Slavonic and East European Studies, University of London.
Biography (*in part*); **Czechoslovakia**

SCHULIAN, JOHN. Sports Columnist, *Chicago Daily News.*
Basketball (*in part*)

SCHULMAN, ELIAS. Associate Professor, Queens College, City University of New York. Author of *Israel Tsinberg, His Life and Works; A History of Yiddish Literature in America; Soviet-Yiddish Literature.*
Literature: *Yiddish*

SEARS, ROBERT N. Associate Technical Editor, *The American Rifleman.*
Target Sports (*in part*)

SENTMAN, EVERETT EDGAR. Writer, Editor, and Consultant. President, Sentman Publishing Enterprises, Lake Forest, Ill. Author of *The Encyclopedia: A Key to Effective Teaching.*
Food Processing: *Special Report*

SHACKLEFORD, CAMILLE. Director, International Tourism Consultants.
Industrial Review: *Tourism*

SHARPE, MITCHELL R. Science Writer; Historian, Alabama Space and Rocket Center, Huntsville. Author of *Living in Space: The Environment of the Astronaut; Yuri Gagarin, First Man in Space; "It Is I, Seagull": Valentina Tereshkova, First Woman in Space.*
Space Exploration

SHAW, T. R. Commander, Royal Navy. Member, British Cave Research Assn.
Speleology

SHENK, CLAYTON B. Executive Secretary, U.S. National Archery Association.
Target Sports (*in part*)

SIMPSON, NOEL. Managing Director, Sydney Bloodstock Proprietary Ltd., Sydney, Australia.
Equestrian Sports: *Harness Racing*

SMEDLEY, GLENN B. Member of Board of Governors, American Numismatic Association.
Philately and Numismatics: *Coins*

SMITH, R. W. Dean, Graduate School, University of the Pacific, Stockton, Calif. Editor of *Venture of Islam* by M. G. S. Hodgson.
Religion: *Islam*

SMOGORZEWSKI, K. M. Writer on contemporary history. Founder and Editor, *Free Europe,* London. Author of *The United States and Great Britain; Poland's Access to the Sea.*
Albania; Andorra; Biography (*in part*); **Bulgaria; Hungary; Liechtenstein; Luxembourg; Monaco; Mongolia; Poland; Political Parties; Romania; San Marino**

SNIDER, ARTHUR J. Science Editor, *Chicago Daily News.* Author of *Learning How to Live with Heart Trouble; Learning How to Live with Nervous Tension.*
Health and Disease: *Overview* (*in part*); **Life Sciences:** *Special Report*

SOKOL, LOUIS F. President, U.S. Metric Association.
Feature Article: *The Case for Metrication*

SPELMAN, ROBERT A. Administrative Vice-President, National Association of Furniture Manufacturers, Washington.
Industrial Review: *Furniture*

STACKS, JOHN F. Correspondent, *Time* magazine, Washington, D.C. Author of *Stripping: The Surface Mining of America.*
Biography (*in part*)

STAERK, MELANIE. Member, Swiss Press Association. Former Member, Swiss National Commission for UNESCO.
Switzerland

STEEN, LYNN ARTHUR. Professor of Mathematics, St. Olaf College, Northfield, Minn. Author of *Counterexamples in Topology; Annotated Bibliography of Expository Writing in the Mathematical Sciences.*
Mathematics

STERN, IRWIN. Assistant Professor of Portuguese and Spanish, City College of New York, and Ph.D. Program in Comparative Literature, City University of New York. Author of *Júlio Dinis e o romance português (1860–1870).*
Literature: *Portuguese* (*in part*)

STEVENSON, TOM. Garden Columnist, *Baltimore News American; Washington Post;* Washington Post-Los Angeles Times News Service. Book Editor, *American Horticulturist.* Author of *Pruning Guide for Trees, Shrubs, and Vines; Lawn Guide.*
Gardening (*in part*)

STOKES, J. BUROUGHS. Manager, Committees on Publication, The First Church of Christ, Scientist, Boston.
Religion: *Church of Christ, Scientist*

STOVERUD, TORBJORN. W. P. Ker Senior Lecturer in Norwegian, University College, London.
Literature: *Norwegian*

STRAUSS, MICHAEL. Feature and Sports Writer, *New York Times.* Author of *The New York Times Ski Guide to the United States.*
Combat Sports: *Fencing*

SULLIVAN, H. PATRICK. Professor of Religion, Vassar College, Poughkeepsie, N.Y.
Religion: *Hinduism*

SULLIVAN, WALTER. Science Editor, *New York Times.* Author of *We Are Not Alone; Continents in Motion.*
Earth Sciences: *Special Report*

SWEETINBURGH, THELMA. Paris Fashion Correspondent for the British Wool Textile Industry.
Fashion and Dress (*in part*)

SWIFT, RICHARD N. Professor of Politics, New York University, New York City. Author of *International Law: Current and Classic; World Affairs and the College Curriculum.*
United Nations

SYNAN, VINSON. General Secretary, Pentecostal Holiness Church. Author of *The Holiness-Pentecostal Movement; The Old Time Power.*
Religion: *Pentecostal Churches*

TAISHOFF, SOL J. Editor, *Broadcasting,* Washington, D.C.
Television and Radio (*in part*)

TALLAN, NORMAN N. Chief, Processing and High Temperature Materials Branch, Air Force Materials Laboratory, Wright-Patterson Air Force Base, Dayton, Ohio. Editor of *Electrical Conductivity in Ceramics and Glass.*
Material Sciences: *Ceramics*

TATTERSALL, ARTHUR. Textile Trade Statistician, Manchester, England.
Industrial Review: *Textiles* (*in part*)

TERRY, WALTER, JR. Dance Critic, *Saturday Review* magazine, New York City. Author of *The Dance in America; The Ballet Companion.*
Dance (*in part*)

THOMAS, HARFORD. Retired City and Financial Editor, *The Guardian*, London.
Biography (*in part*); **Economy, World:** *Special Report;* **United Kingdom**

THOMPSON, ANTHONY. European Linguist Research Fellow, CLW, Aberystwyth, Wales. General Secretary, International Federation of Library Associations, 1962–70. Author of *Vocabularium Bibliothecarii; Library Buildings of Britain and Europe.*
Libraries

TINGAY, LANCE. Lawn Tennis Correspondent, the *Daily Telegraph*, London. Author of *100 Years of Wimbledon; Tennis, A Pictorial History.*
Biography (*in part*); **Tennis**

TINKER, JON. Director, Earthscan, a service of the International Institute for Environment and Development.
Feature Article: *Nor Any Drop to Drink*

TRIGG, ROBERT H. Senior Economic Adviser and Manager, Institutional Policy Section, New York Stock Exchange.
Stock Exchanges (*in part*)

TRILLING, OSSIA. Vice-President, International Association of Theatre Critics (1956–77). Co-editor and Contributor, *International Theatre.* Contributor, BBC, the *Financial Times*, London.
Biography (*in part*); **Theatre** (*in part*)

TRUSSELL, TAIT. Administrative Vice-President, American Forest Institute.
Industrial Review: *Wood Products*

TUREEN, THOMAS NORTON. Attorney, Native American Rights Fund.
Race Relations: *Special Report*

TURKEVICH, JOHN. Eugene Higgins Professor Emeritus of Chemistry, Department of Chemistry, Princeton University. Author of *Chemistry in the Soviet Union.*
Chemistry: *Physical and Inorganic*

UNHCR. The Office of the United Nations High Commissioner for Refugees.
Refugees

UNNY, GOVINDAN. Agence France-Presse Special Correspondent for India, Nepal, and Sri Lanka.
Bangladesh; Bhutan; Biography (*in part*); **Burma; Nepal; Sri Lanka**

van den HOVEN, ISOLA. Writer on Consumer Affairs, The Hague, Neth.
Consumerism (*in part*)

VAN DOREN, CHARLES. Vice-President, Editorial, Encyclopædia Britannica.
Education: *Special Report*

van PRAAG, JACK H. National Public Relations Director, U.S. Badminton Assn.
Racket Games: *Badminton*

VERDI, ROBERT WILLIAM. Sportswriter, *Chicago Tribune.*
Baseball (*in part*)

VIANSSON-PONTÉ, PIERRE. Editorial Adviser and Leader Writer, *Le Monde*, Paris. Author of *Les Gaullistes; The King and His Court; Les Politiques.*
Biography (*in part*)

VINT, ARTHUR KINGSLEY. Consultant, International Table Tennis Federation, Sussex, England.
Table Tennis

WADLEY, J. B. Writer and Broadcaster on cycling. Editor of *Guinness Guide to Bicycling.* Author of *Tour de France 1970, 1971, and 1973; Old Roads and New.*
Cycling

WARD, BARBARA. Economist with special interest in the third world. President, International Institute for Environment and Development. Author of *The Home of Man; Spaceship Earth.*
Feature Article: *Toward a New International Economic Order*

WARD-THOMAS, P. A. Golf Correspondent, *The Guardian*, London.
Golf

WEBB, GORDON A. Editor, *Toys International*, London.
Games and Toys

WEBB, HENRY, JR. Retired from U.S. Foreign Service.
El Salvador; Honduras; Nicaragua

WEBB, W. L. Literary Editor, *The Guardian*, London and Manchester.
Literature: *Introduction; United Kingdom; Russian* (*in part*); *Eastern European*

WEBSTER, PETER L. Associate Professor, Department of Botany, University of Massachusetts, Amherst.
Life Sciences: *Botany*

WEEDEN, CYRIL. Assistant Director, Glass Manufacturers' Federation, London.
Industrial Review: *Glass*

WHITTINGHAM, RICHARD. Writer. Author of *Martial Justice: The Last Mass Execution in the United States.*
Prisons and Penology: *Special Report*

WIJNGAARD, BARBARA. Economist, Lloyds Bank International Ltd., London.
Argentina; Mexico; Peru

WILLEY, DAVID DOUGLAS. Rome Correspondent, BBC.
Italy

WILLIAMS, BRIAN. Free-lance Writer, London.
Television and Radio (*in part*)

WILLIAMS, L. F. RUSHBROOK. Fellow of All Souls College, Oxford University, 1914–21; Professor of Modern Indian History, Allahabad, India, 1914–19. Honorary Adviser, *Keesing's Contemporary Archives.* Author of *The State of Pakistan; Kutch in History and Legend.*
Afghanistan; Iran; Pakistan

WILLIAMS, PETER. Editor, *Dance and Dancers*, London. Chairman, Arts Council, Great Britain's Dance Theatre Committee; Chairman, British Council's Drama Advisory Committee.
Biography (*in part*); **Dance** (*in part*)

WILLIAMSON, TREVOR. Chief Sports Subeditor, the *Daily Telegraph*, London.
Football: *Association Football*

WILSON, MICHAEL. Technical Editor, *Flight International*, London.
Industrial Review: *Aerospace*

WITTE, RANDALL E. Editor, *Rodeo Sports News.* News Bureau Director, Professional Rodeo Cowboys Association.
Rodeo

WOOD, CHRISTINA. Free-lance Sportswriter.
Racket Games: *Rackets; Real Tennis*

WOOD, KENNETH H. Editor, *The Advent Review and Sabbath Herald.* Author of *Meditations for Moderns.* Co-author of *His Initials Were F. D. N.*
Religion: *Seventh-day Adventist Church*

WOODS, ELIZABETH. Writer. Author of *The Yellow Volkswagen; Gone.*
Literature: *English* (*in part*)

WOOLLER, MICHAEL. Economist, Lloyds Bank International Ltd., London.
Biography (*in part*); **Bolivia; Portugal; Spain**

WOOLLEY, DAVID. Editor, *Airports International*, London.
Transportation (*in part*)

WORSNOP, RICHARD L. Associate Editor, *Editorial Research Reports*, Washington, D.C.
United States

WRIGHT, ALMON R. Retired Senior Historian, U.S. Department of State.
Panama

WYLLIE, PETER JOHN. Professor of Petrology and Geochemistry, University of Chicago. Author of *The Dynamic Earth; The Way the Earth Works.*
Earth Sciences: *Geology and Geochemistry*

YANG, WINSTON L. Y. Professor of Chinese Studies, Department of Asian Studies, Seton Hall University, South Orange, N.J. Author of *Modern Chinese Fiction; Teng Hsiao-p'ing: A Political Biography* (forthcoming).
Biography (*in part*)

YOUNG, M. NORVEL. Chancellor, Pepperdine University, Malibu, Calif. Author of *Preachers of Today; History of Colleges Connected with Churches of Christ; The Church Is Building.*
Religion: *Churches of Christ*

YOUNG, SUSAN. News Editor, *Church Times*, London.
Religion: *Anglican Communion*

YUFIT, ROBERT I. Director, Suicide Assessment Team, Illinois Masonic Medical Center.
Health and Disease: *Mental Health* (*in part*)

YUNEN, RAFAEL EMILIO. Professor of Dominican History and Dominican Geography, Universidad Católica Madre y Maestra, Santiago de los Caballeros, Dominican Republic.
Dominican Republic

Index

The black type entries are article headings in the *Book of the Year*. These black type article entries do not show page notations because they are to be found in their alphabetical position in the body of the book. They show the dates of the issues of the *Book of the Year* in which the articles appear. For example "Archaeology 78, 77, 76" indicates that the article "Archaeology" is to be found in the 1978, 1977, and 1976 *Book of the Year*.

The light type headings that are indented under black type article headings refer to material elsewhere in the text related to the subject under which they are listed. The light type headings that are not indented refer to information in the text not given a special article. Biographies and obituaries are listed as cross references to the sections "Biography" and "Obituaries" within the article "*People of the Year.*" References to illustrations are preceded by the abbreviation "il."

All headings, whether consisting of a single word or more, are treated for the purpose of alphabetization as single complete headings. Names beginning with "Mc" and "Mac" are alphabetized as "Mac"; "St." is treated as "Saint."